Following in the groundbreaking path of its predecessor, the second edition of the *Social Workers' Desk Reference* provides reliable and highly accessible information about effective services and treatment approaches across the full spectrum of social work practice. Succinct, illuminating chapters written by the field's most respected and experienced scholars and practitioners ensure that it will continue to be the sourcebook for all social workers.

Social work practitioners and agency administrators are increasingly confronted with having to do more with less, and must make decisions and provide services as quickly as possible. The *Social Workers' Desk Reference, Second Edition,* builds on the landmark achievement of the first edition with thorough revisions and over 75 all-new chapters. Its outstanding wealth of well-tested knowledge, presented in a crisp, to-the-point manner, makes it an even more vital resource for time-pressed practitioners. Page after page offers an abundance of up-to-date information and key tools and resources such as practice guidelines, program evaluations, validated assessment scales, and step-by-step treatment plans necessary for success in today's managed-care environment. The growing importance of evidence-based practice in social work is reflected throughout the chapters, as well

(continued on back flap)

SOCIAL WORKERS' DESK REFERENCE

SOCIAL WORKERS' DESK REFERENCE

Second Edition

Albert R. Roberts

Editor-in-Chief

Foreword by

Julia M. Watkins

OXFORD
UNIVERSITY PRESS
2009

Oxford University Press, Inc., publishes works that further
Oxford University's objective of excellence
in research, scholarship, and education.

Oxford   New York
Auckland   Cape Town   Dar es Salaam   Hong Kong   Karachi
Kuala Lumpur   Madrid   Melbourne   Mexico City   Nairobi
New Delhi   Shanghai   Taipei   Toronto

With offices in
Argentina   Austria   Brazil   Chile   Czech Republic   France   Greece
Guatemala   Hungary   Italy   Japan   Poland   Portugal   Singapore
South Korea   Switzerland   Thailand   Turkey   Ukraine   Vietnam

Published by Oxford University Press, Inc.
198 Madison Avenue, New York, New York 10016
www.oup.com

Oxford is a registered trademark of Oxford University Press

The Library of Congress has cataloged the first edition as follows:

Library of Congress Cataloging-in-Publication Data
Social workers' desk reference / edited by Albert R. Roberts and Gilbert J. Greene.
    p. cm.
Includes bibliographical references and index.

1. Social service—Handbooks, manuals, etc. I. Roberts, Albert R. II. Greene, Gilbert J.
2. Mental disorders—treatment 3. Social workers—United States—clinical
HV40 .F663 2002
361.3'2—dc21

ISBN: 978-0-19-536937-3   2001021714

9 8 7 6 5 4 3 2

Printed in the United States of America
on acid-free paper

FOREWORD

The extraordinary success of the *Social Worker's Desk Reference*, edited by Albert R. Roberts and Gilbert J. Greene, as well as the enormity of contextual change and scientific advancement since its publication in 2001, speaks to the need for this much-anticipated second edition. The first edition was a major contribution to the profession of social work. Its breadth, purposeful focus on social work interventions, conciseness, readability, and overall usability have made it a favorite of social work practitioners, educators, and students as well as other professionals who form the core of interdisciplinary practice and research.

The *Social Worker's Desk Reference*, second edition, is a well calibrated and thoughtfully inclusive enhancement of the first edition. Its 171 chapters continue with utmost attention to detail the first edition's mission of disseminating straightforward and appropriately nuanced texts written by the foremost experts in the social work profession to capture the complexity of social work practice. It brings to the users the most recent conceptual knowledge and empirical evidence to aid their understanding of social work practice and to guide social work interventions in a vast array of settings from the individual clinical level to community-based empowerment and advocacy.

The articles in total focus on the compelling practice issues of the early twenty-first century. Social work today is driven by a long list of changes: the greater complexity and speed of global human interaction, the struggle of populations for scarce resources of food and energy, worldwide political and economic transactions, rapid advances in the social and behavioral sciences, the far-reaching effects of new discoveries in human biology and neuroscience, and technological advances in the diagnosis and treatment of disease. The enormity of these advances is compounded, and not always

positively, by our sometimes underdeveloped organizational structures and our need for an ever increasing level of knowledge and organizational sophistication as we meet the challenges of this century.

The *Social Worker's Desk Reference* is a fundamental tool that offers innumerable benefits to the profession of social work as we address the old and seemingly intractable, as well as the new and immensely complex issues of our day.

This edition of the *Social Worker's Desk Reference,* is not only a major contribution to the field, it also represents the vision and scholarly dedication of its editor-in-chief, the late Albert R. Roberts. Those of us who have had the honor and the privilege to know and work with him welcome this, his final work, as a tribute to his long-standing energy and vibrancy, his integrity, and his extraordinary commitment to social work. There are few among us for whom we have such respect and admiration. In many ways the publication of this book is a bittersweet acceptance of reality and stands as a monument to the courage and vision of Roberts.

With an acquaintance that spanned more than 25 years, Roberts and I shared many thoughtful conversations and some academic frustrations. We enjoyed sporadic communication about many professional issues until I worked abroad from 1993–2003. On my return to the United States, Al was on the phone, asking for an update and for my input on a publications matter. I was more than happy to hear once again from my friend and note with him the many changes in social work education and the need for the profession to focus on the expansion of the social work knowledge base. At the same time, we acknowledged the imperative of discovering new mechanisms or fostering existing technology transfer for greater and more facile and timely access to that ever-expanding knowledge base. Certainly, the *Social Worker's Desk Reference* is one of those mechanisms.

For the social work profession, Al's death leaves a gaping hole in our reality. His achievements, however, will speak to and for the profession for years to come. Each time the *Social Worker's Desk Reference* is taken off a shelf and opened, we will be reminded of Al and his compelling and fastidious attention to detail and substance. In what may have been Al's last e-mail, written on June 13, 2008, he wrote about another matter we had been discussing and said, "I did my best." Looking back to that message, it was certainly prophetic and actually characterized everything that Al did and his approach to his work and life. Al, you will be missed. Thank you for this volume and your contributions.

Julia M. Watkins, PhD
Executive Director, Council on Social Work
  Education
August 1, 2008
Alexandria, Virginia

ACKNOWLEDGMENTS

For the second edition of the *Social Workers' Desk Reference*, I selected an esteemed group of Associate Editors who were directly responsible for the content of their sections. They decided on the scope and content of the new chapters, and they supervised the revisions of the chapters in their sections that appeared in the first edition of the SWDR. I am grateful to all of the Associate Editors for their willingness to take on this important responsibility and for their dedication to producing sections of the highest quallity: Paula Allen-Meares, José B. Ashford, Rowena Fong, Cynthia Franklin, William R. Nugent, Lisa Rapp-Paglicci, Phyllis Solomon, Bruce A. Thyer, and Vikki L. Vandiver. I would also like to thank honorary Associate Editors James R. Zabora and Kenneth R. Yeager, who worked tirelessly as the volume took shape and whose sound advice is reflected throughout these pages.

The List of Contributors provides the name and affiliation of every contributor. I thank each of them for preparing a chapter that so effectively and concisely explains the practice issues that are critically important to the social work profession.

My deepest appreciation goes to Joan Bossert, Vice President and Publisher at Oxford University Press, who became my friend 10 years ago when we started the first of many discussions that culminated in the first edition of the *Social Workers' Desk Reference*. Her wise advice and valuable insights were instrumental in bringing the first edition of the *Social Workers' Desk Reference*, as well as this second edition, to fruition. The dedication of the staff at Oxford has been phenomenal. Mallory Jensen, Maura Roessner, Jennifer Bossert, and Sue Utter-Wilson (of Bytheway Publishing) were devoted to the successful completion of the second edition of the SWDR, working long hours to ensure that it would be launched on time, despite unforessen difficulties.

The second edition of the SWDR would never have been possible without the state-of-the-art medical treatment provided by my friend and oncologist, Stephen Schreibman, M.D., who exemplifies excellence in the practice of medicine. My wife, Beverly Schenkman Roberts, has been the love of my life for 37 years; she was my sounding board and partner for this and every other scholarly project I have undertaken.

Albert R. Roberts, Ph.D.
Rutgers University, Piscataway, New Jersey
June, 2008

CONTENTS

Foreword   v
JULIA M. WATKINS

Acknowledgments   vii

Contributors   xix

PART I: INTRODUCTION AND OVERVIEW

1 The Synergy and Generativity of Social Work Practice   3
ANITA LIGHTBURN

PART II: ROLES, FUNCTIONS, AND TYPICAL DAILY SCHEDULE OF SOCIAL WORKERS IN DIFFERENT PRACTICE SETTINGS

2 The Social Worker in a Behavioral Health Care Setting   11
CYNTHIA FRANKLIN
CHRISTINE LAGANA-RIORDAN

3 The Addiction Treatment Specialist   20
KENNETH R. YEAGER
DARYL SHORTER

4 The Social Worker in an Outpatient Child and Adolescent Unit   33
LISA RAPP-PAGLICCI

5 The Social Worker in a School Setting   39
MICHAEL S. KELLY

6 The Social Worker as Family Counselor in a Nonprofit Community-Based Agency   45
JACK NOWICKI
LESHAWN ARBUCKLE

7 The Essential Elements of Private Practice Social Work   53
RAYMOND D. FOX

8 Community-Based Mental Health with Children and Families   61
SUSAN C. AYERS
BORJA ALVAREZ DE TOLEDO

9 Social Work Practice in Home-Based Services with Children and Their Families   70
MARTHA MORRISON DORE
CHARLENE ZUFFANTE

10 The Oncology Social Worker in a Medical Setting: Traditional versus Innovative Roles   77
JAMES R. ZABORA

11 The Social Worker in a Police Department   85
KAREN S. KNOX
ALBERT R. ROBERTS

12 The Social Worker in a Domestic Violence Shelter   95
DIANE L. GREEN
BRANDY MACALUSO

13 The Social Worker in Emergency Service Settings   102
TED BOBER
CHERYL REGEHR

PART III: SOCIAL WORK VALUES, ETHICS, AND LICENSING STANDARDS

14   Ethical Issues in Social Work   115
     FREDERIC G. REAMER

15   Risk Management in Social Work   121
     FREDERIC G. REAMER

16   Avoiding Malpractice Lawsuits by
     Following Standards of Care
     Guidelines and Preventing Suicide:
     A Guide for Mental Health
     Professionals   128
     ALBERT R. ROBERTS
     IANNA MONFERRARI
     KENNETH R. YEAGER

17   Social Work Licensing Examinations
     in the United States and Canada:
     Development and
     Administration   136
     DONNA DEANGELIS

18   Social Work Regulation and
     Licensing   148
     ANDREW T. MARKS
     KAREN S. KNOX

19   On Being an Accountable Profession:
     The Code of Ethics, Oversight by Boards
     of Directors, and Whistle-Blowers as a
     Last Resort   156
     SHELDON R. GELMAN

20   The Impaired Social Work
     Professional   163
     FREDERIC G. REAMER

21   How Social Workers Can Do More
     Good Than Harm: Critical Thinking,
     Evidence-Based Clinical Reasoning,
     and Avoiding Fallacies   168
     LEONARD GIBBS

22   Optimizing the Use of Patient
     Safety Standards, Procedures, and
     Measures   174
     KENNETH R. YEAGER
     ALBERT R. ROBERTS
     RADU SAVEANU

23   The Role and Regulations for
     Technology in Social Work
     Practice and E-Therapy: Social
     Work 2.0   186
     JONATHAN B. SINGER

24   Quality Standards and Quality
     Assurance in Health Settings   194
     KENNETH R. YEAGER
     TINA R. LATIMER

PART IV: THEORETICAL FOUNDATIONS AND TREATMENT APPROACHES IN CLINICAL SOCIAL WORK

25   Front Line Crisis Intervention   207
     YVONNE M. EATON
     ALBERT R. ROBERTS

26   Fundamentals of Brief Treatment   215
     JAN LIGON

27   Common Factors in Therapy   220
     JAMES W. DRISKO

28   Task-Centered Practice   226
     ANNE E. FORTUNE
     WILLIAM J. REID
     DEBORAH P. REYOME

29   The Life Model   231
     ALEX GITTERMAN

30   Client-Centered Theory and
     Therapy   235
     WILLIAM S. ROWE
     ALICIA J. STINSON

31   Cognitive-Behavioral Therapy   242
     M. ELIZABETH VONK
     THERESA J. EARLY

32   Psychosocial Therapy   248
     FRANCIS J. TURNER

33   Solution-Focused Therapy   253
     PETER DEJONG

34   Comparative Theories   259
     WILLIAM BORDEN

35   Logotherapy   264
     DAVID GUTTMANN

36   Narrative Therapy   273
     PATRICIA KELLEY

37   Feminist Issues and Practices in
     Social Work   277
     MARY BRICKER-JENKINS
     F. ELLEN NETTING

38   Acceptance and Commitment
     Therapy   283
     KELLY G. WILSON
     EMILY K. SANDOZ
     REGAN M. SLATER

39   A Behavioral Approach to Social Work
     Treatment   288
     DENISE E. BRONSON

40   Using Social Constructivism in Social
     Work Practice   294
     MO YEE LEE
     GILBERT J. GREENE

41   Gestalt Therapy   300
     WILLIAM P. PANNING

42   Object Relations Psychology   305
     WILLIAM BORDEN

43   Using Self-Psychology in Clinical
     Social Work   311
     JERROLD R. BRANDELL

44   How Clinicians Can Effectively Use
     Assessment Tools to Evidence Medical
     Necessity and throughout the Treatment
     Process   317
     KEVIN CORCORAN
     JILL BOYER-QUICK

PART V: ASSESSMENT IN SOCIAL WORK
PRACTICE: KNOWLEDGE AND SKILLS

45   Using the *Diagnostic and Statistical
     Manual of Mental Disorders*, Fourth
     Edition, Text Revision   325
     JANET B. W. WILLIAMS

46   Guidelines for the *Diagnostic and
     Statistical Manual (DSM-IV-TR)*
     Multiaxial System Diagnosis   334
     CARLTON E. MUNSON

47   Clinical Assessment of Bipolar
     Disorder: Balancing Strengths and
     Diagnosis   343
     ELIZABETH C. POMEROY
     DIANE L. GREEN

48   Developing Client-Focused
     Measures   351
     CATHY KING PIKE

49   Brief Screening Instruments   358
     STEVEN L. MCMURTRY
     SUSAN J. ROSE
     RON A. CISLER

50   Person-in-Environment System   371
     JAMES M. KARLS
     MAURA E. O'KEEFE

51   Guidelines for Conducting a Biopsycho-
     social Assessment   376
     SONIA G. AUSTRIAN

52   Guidelines for Selecting and Using
     Assessment Tools with Children   381
     CRAIG WINSTON LECROY
     SCOTT KIYOSHI OKAMOTO

53   Assessment Protocols and Rapid
     Assessment Instruments with Troubled
     Adolescents   385
     DAVID W. SPRINGER
     STEPHEN J. TRIPODI

54   Using Standardized Tests and Instru-
     ments in Family Assessments   390
     JACQUELINE CORCORAN

55   Understanding a Diagnosis: What it Does
     and Does Not Tell You   394
     WILLIAM R. NUGENT

56   Guidelines and Uses of Rapid
     Assessment Instruments in Managed
     Care Settings   400
     LAURA M. HOPSON
     JOHN S. WODARSKI

PART VI: WORKING WITH COUPLES AND FAMILIES

57 Using Genograms to Map Family Patterns   409
    MONICA MCGOLDRICK

58 A Family Resilience Framework   423
    FROMA WALSH

59 Treatment Planning with Families: An Evidence-Based Approach   429
    CATHELEEN JORDAN
    CYNTHIA FRANKLIN

60 Effective Couple and Family Treatment   433
    CYNTHIA FRANKLIN
    CATHELEEN JORDAN
    LAURA M. HOPSON

61 Structural Family Therapy   442
    HARRY J. APONTE

62 Bowen Family Systems Therapy   447
    DANIEL V. PAPERO

63 It Takes One to Tango   452
    MICHELE WEINER-DAVIS

64 Parenting with Love and Limits   457
    SCOTT P. SELLS

65 Integrative Behavioral Couple Therapy   467
    KATHERINE J. WILLIAMS
    FELICIA DE LA GARZA-MERCER
    ANDREW CHRISTENSEN

66 Psychoeducation   474
    JOSEPH WALSH

67 Guidelines for Couple Therapy with Survivors of Childhood Trauma   478
    KATHRYN KARUSAITIS BASHAM

68 Multifamily Groups with Obsessive-Compulsive Disorder   483
    BARBARA VAN NOPPEN

69 Working with Families of Persons with Severe Mental Illness   491
    TINA BOGART MARSHALL
    PHYLLIS SOLOMON

PART VII: DEVELOPING AND IMPLEMENTING TREATMENT PLANS WITH SPECIFIC GROUPS AND DISORDERS

70 Guidelines for Establishing Effective Treatment Goals and Treatment Plans with Axis I Disorders: Sample Treatment Plan for Generalized Anxiety Disorder   497
    VIKKI L. VANDIVER
    KEVIN CORCORAN

71 Using Evidence-Based Practice and Expert Consensus in Mental Health Settings: Step-by-Step Guidelines for Schizophrenia   505
    VIKKI L. VANDIVER

72 Developing Therapeutic Contracts with Clients   514
    JULIET CASSUTO ROTHMAN

73 Developing Goals   521
    CHARLES D. GARVIN

74 Treatment Planning with Adolescents: ADHD Case Applications   526
    DAVID W. SPRINGER
    KIMBERLY BENDER

75 Eating Disorders and Treatment Planning   531
    NINA ROVINELLI HELLER

76 Panic Disorders and Agoraphobia   538
    GORDON MACNEIL

77 Treatment Plans for Clients with Social Phobia   545
    BRUCE A. THYER
    MONICA PIGNOTTI

78 Depression: Integration of Psycho-
dynamic and Cognitive-Behavioral
Practices 552
NINA ROVINELLI HELLER
TERRY B. NORTHCUT

79 The Assessment and Treatment of Post-
Traumatic Stress Disorder 558
M. ELIZABETH VONK

80 Guidelines for Clinical Social Work
with Clients with Dissociative
Disorders 564
LINA HARTOCOLLIS

PART VIII: GUIDELINES FOR SPECIFIC
TECHNIQUES

81 Developing Successful Therapeutic
Relationships 573
LAWRENCE SHULMAN

82 Using Metaphor with Clients 578
STEPHEN R. LANKTON

83 Cognitive Restructuring
Techniques 588
DONALD K. GRANVOLD

84 Using the Miracle Question and Scaling
Technique in Clinical Practice 594
MO YEE LEE

85 Using Evidence-Based Hypnosis 600
WILLIAM R. NUGENT

86 Kundalini Yoga Meditation Techniques
for the Treatment of Obsessive-
Compulsive and OC Spectrum
Disorders 606
DAVID S. SHANNAHOFF-KHALSA

87 Storytelling and the Use of Metaphor
with OCD 613
ALLEN H. WEG

88 Best Practices in Parenting
Techniques 619
CAROLYN HILARSKI

89 Terminating with Clients 627
ANNE E. FORTUNE

90 Bereavement and Grief Therapy 632
ELIZABETH C. POMEROY
RENÉE BRADFORD GARCIA
DIANE L. GREEN

PART IX: GUIDELINES FOR SPECIFIC
INTERVENTIONS

91 Transtheoretical Model Guidelines for
Families with Child Abuse and
Neglect 641
JANICE M. PROCHASKA
JAMES O. PROCHASKA

92 Play Therapy with Children in
Crisis 647
NANCY BOYD-WEBB

93 Child Therapy and Social Skills 652
CRAIG WINSTON LECROY

94 Recognizing Indicators of Child
Maltreatment 659
JUDITH S. RYCUS
RONALD C. HUGHES

95 Guidelines for Social Skills Training
for Persons with Mental
Illness 666
SUSAN GINGERICH

96 Delinquency Prevention and an
Evidence-Based Social Work Interven-
tion: Families and Schools Together
(FAST) 671
LYNN MCDONALD

97 Group Process and Group Work
Techniques 679
PAUL H. EPHROSS AND
GEOFFREY L. GREIF

98 Psychopharmacology and Social
Work 686
KIA J. BENTLEY
JOSEPH WALSH

99   Guidelines for Chemical Abuse and
     Dependency Screening, Diagnosis, and
     Treatment   691
     DIANA M. DINITTO
     C. AARON MCNEECE

100 Trauma-Informed Services   698
     MAGGIE BENNINGTON-DAVIS

101 Supported Employment
     Approaches   704
     MARINA KUKLA
     GARY R. BOND

102 Working with and Strengthening
     Social Networks   710
     ELIZABETH M. TRACY

103 Eye Movement Desensitization and
     Reprocessing with Trauma
     Clients   714
     ALLEN RUBIN

104 Enacting the Educator Role: Principles
     for Practice   720
     KIMBERLY STROM-GOTTFRIED

105 Critical Incident Stress
     Management: Integrated Crisis
     Intervention and Disaster Mental
     Health   726
     GEORGE S. EVERLY JR.
     ALAN M. LANGLIEB

106 Divorce Therapy: The Application
     of Cognitive-Behavioral and
     Constructivist Treatment
     Methods   732
     DONALD K. GRANVOLD

107 Social Work Practice with Sexual
     Issues   737
     PAUL H. EPHROSS
     JOAN C. WEISS

108 Interventions with Borderline
     Personality Disorder   742
     JONATHAN B. SINGER

PART X: CASE MANAGEMENT GUIDELINES

109 An Overview of Case
     Management   751
     JACK ROTHMAN

110 Clinical Case Management   755
     JOSEPH WALSH

111 Case Management Policies and
     Programs with the Developmentally
     Disabled   759
     ELIZABETH LIGHTFOOT

112 Case Management and Child
     Welfare   765
     JANNAH H. MATHER
     GRAFTON H. HULL JR.

113 Case Management in Psychosocial
     Rehabilitation   770
     DAVID P. MOXLEY

114 A Strengths Approach to Case
     Management with Clients with
     Psychiatric Disabilities   778
     CHARLES A. RAPP

115 Case Management with Substance-
     Abusing Clients   784
     W. PATRICK SULLIVAN

116 Social Work Case Management in
     Medical Settings   790
     CANDYCE S. BERGER

117 Case Management with Older
     Adults   796
     CAROL D. AUSTIN
     ROBERT W. MCCLELLAND

118 HIV/AIDS Case Management   801
     BRIAN GIDDENS
     LANA SUE I. KA'OPUA
     EVELYN P. TOMASZEWSKI

119 The Consumer–Provider Relationship
     within Case Management   807
     VICTORIA STANHOPE
     PHYLLIS SOLOMON

PART XI: SOCIAL WORK FIELDS OF
PRACTICE

120   Current and Future Directions of Social
       Work Practice with Children and
       Adolescents   815
       LISA RAPP-PAGLICCI
       ALISON SALLOUM

121   Current and Future Directions of
       Social Work in Adult Mental Health
       Settings   820
       VIKKI L. VANDIVER

122   Development of a Proactive Model of
       Health Care versus a Reactive System
       of Referrals   826
       JAMES R. ZABORA

123   Overview of Alcohol and Drug
       Dependence: Assessment and
       Treatment   833
       KENNETH R. YEAGER

124   Evidence-Based Practice in Older
       Adults with Mental Health Disorders:
       Geriatric Mental Health   843
       ZVI D. GELLIS

PART XII: COMMUNITY PRACTICE

125   An Integrated Practice Model for
       Family Centers   855
       ANITA LIGHTBURN
       CHRIS WARREN-ADAMSON

126   International Perspectives on Social
       Work Practice   863
       KAREN M. SOWERS
       WILLIAM S. ROWE

127   Guidelines for Assertive Community
       Treatment Teams   869
       MARY ANN TEST

128   Community Organizing Principles and
       Practice Guidelines   872
       TERRY MIZRAHI

129   Community Practice Model for the
       Twenty-First Century   882
       MARIE OVERBY WEIL
       DOROTHY N. GAMBLE

130   Legislative Advocacy to Empower
       Oppressed and Vulnerable
       Groups   893
       MICHAEL REISCH

131   Principles and Practice Guidelines for
       Social Action   901
       JACQUELINE B. MONDROS

132   Community Partnerships for
       School-Based Services: Action
       Principles   907
       DENNIS L. POOLE

133   Building Community Capacity in the
       U.S. Air Force: The Community Readi-
       ness Consultant Model   912
       GARY L. BOWEN
       JAMES A. MARTIN
       BRENDA J. LISTON
       JOHN P. NELSON

134   Fathering Programs and Community
       Services   918
       JAY FAGAN

PART XIII: WORKING WITH VULNERABLE
POPULATIONS AND PERSONS AT RISK

135   Overview of Working with Vulnerable
       Populations and Persons at Risk   925
       ROWENA FONG

136   The Legacy of Racism for Social
       Work Practice Today and What Do
       about It   928
       JOSHUA MILLER
       ANN MARIE GARRAN

137   Social Work with Lesbian, Gay, Bisexual,
       and Transgendered Clients   934
       MARY BOES
       KATHERINE VAN WORMER

138   Clinical Social Work with Older
       Adults   939
       VIRGINIA E. RICHARDSON

139   Effective Practice with Refugees and
       Immigrants   944
       MIRIAM POTOCKY-TRIPODI

140   Social Work Practice with Native
       Americans   949
       TERESA A. EVANS-CAMPBELL

141   Social Work Practice with Asian and
       Pacific Islander Americans   954
       HALAEVALU F. OFAHENGAUE VAKALAHI
       ROWENA FONG

142   Social Work Practice with
       Latinos   959
       ILZE A. EARNER
       GENOVEVA GARCIA

143   Social Work Practice with African
       Americans   963
       SADYE M. L. LOGAN

144   The Culturagram   969
       ELAINE P. CONGRESS

PART XIV: SCHOOL SOCIAL WORK

145   Overview of Current and
       Future Practices in School Social
       Work   979
       PAULA ALLEN-MEARES

146   Evidence-Based Violence Prevention
       Programs and Best Implementation
       Practices   985
       RON AVI ASTOR
       RAMI BENBENISHTY
       ROXANA MARACHI
       RONALD O. PITNER

147   Promising Interventions for
       Students Who Have Co-Occurring
       Disorders   1003
       STEPHEN J. TRIPODI
       JOHNNY S. KIM
       KIMBERLY BENDER

148   Effective Interventions for Students
       with Conduct Disorder   1011
       DAVID W. SPRINGER
       COURTNEY J. LYNCH

149   Solution-Focused Brief Therapy
       Interventions for Students at Risk to
       Drop Out   1020
       CYNTHIA FRANKLIN
       JOHNNY S. KIM
       MICHAEL S. KELLY

150   Case Management Interventions with
       Immigrant and Refugee Students and
       Families   1031
       ROWENA FONG
       MARILYN ARMOUR
       NOËL BUSCH-ARMENDARIZ
       LAURIE COOK HEFFRON

151   Treating Children and Adolescents with
       ADHD in the Schools   1038
       STEVEN W. EVANS
       JOANNA M. SADLER
       CHRISTINE E. BRADY

152   Working with Culturally/Racially
       Diverse Students to Improve Connec-
       tion to School and Academic
       Performance   1045
       DAPHNA OYSERMAN

PART XV: FORENSIC SOCIAL WORK

153   Overview of Forensic Social Work:
       Broad and Narrow Definitions   1055
       JOSÉ B. ASHFORD

154   Forensic Social Work and Expert
       Witness Testimony in Child
       Welfare   1060
       CARLTON E. MUNSON

155   An Interest-Based Approach to Child
       Protection Mediation   1071
       ALLAN EDWARD BARSKY

156   Mediation and Conflict
       Resolution   1077
       JOHN ALLEN LEMMON

157   Children Exposed to Domestic
      Violence: Assessment and Treatment
      Protocols   1082
          PETER LEHMANN
          CATHERINE A. SIMMONS

158   Risk Assessment Guidelines for
      Dually Diagnosed Offenders and
      Civil Patients   1091
          JOSÉ B. ASHFORD
          ALBERT R. ROBERTS

159   Step-by-Step Guidelines for Assessing
      Sexual Predators   1098
          GRAHAM GLANCY
          CHERYL REGEHR

160   Elder Abuse   1106
          PATRICIA BROWNELL
          CATHERINE T. GIBLIN

PART XVI: EVIDENCE-BASED PRACTICE

161   Evidence-Based Practice, Science, and
      Social Work: An Overview   1115
          BRUCE A. THYER

162   Developing Well-Structured Questions
      for Evidence-Informed Practice   1120
          EILEEN GAMBRILL
          LEONARD GIBBS

163   Locating Credible Studies for
      Evidence-Based Practice   1127
          ALLEN RUBIN
          DANIELLE PARRISH

164   Critically Appraising Studies for
      Evidence-Based Practice   1137
          DENISE E. BRONSON

165   Randomized Controlled Trials and
      Evidence-Based Practice   1142
          PAUL MONTGOMERY
          EVAN MAYO-WILSON

166   Meta-Analysis and Evidence-Based
      Practice   1149
          JACQUELINE CORCORAN
          JULIA H. LITTELL

167   Systematic Reviews and Evidence-
      Based Practice   1152
          JULIA H. LITTELL
          JACQUELINE CORCORAN

168   Practice Guidelines and Evidence-Based
      Practice   1157
          MATTHEW O. HOWARD
          BRIAN E. PERRON
          MICHAEL G. VAUGHN

169   Integrating Information from
      Diverse Sources in Evidence-Based
      Practice   1163
          EILEEN GAMBRILL

170   Evidence-Based Practice in Social Work
      Education   1169
          ARON SHLONSKY

171   N = 1 Experiments and Their Role in
      Evidence-Based Practice   1176
          BRUCE A. THYER
          LAURA L. MYERS

Glossary   1183

Chapter Credits   1213

Author Index   1215

Subject Index   1239

CONTRIBUTORS

EDITOR-IN-CHIEF

The late ALBERT R. ROBERTS, Ph.D., D.A.C.F.E., was Professor of Social Work and Criminal Justice, and Director of Faculty and Curriculum Development in the Faculty of Arts and Sciences at Rutgers, the State University of New Jersey in Piscataway. He was a college professor for 35 years. Dr. Roberts received an M.A. degree in Sociology from the Graduate Faculty of Long Island University in 1967, and a doctorate in social work from the School of Social Work and Community Planning at the University of Maryland in Baltimore in 1978. Dr. Roberts was the founding Editor-in-Chief of the Brief Treatment and Crisis Intervention journal and the Victims and Offenders journal. He was a member of The Board of Scientific and Professional Advisors and a Board-Certified Expert in Traumatic Stress for The American Academy of Experts in Traumatic Stress, and a Diplomate of the American College of Forensic Examiners. Dr. Roberts authored, co-authored, or edited approximately 250 scholarly publications, including numerous peer-reviewed journal articles and book chapters, and 38 books. A few of his books were the Handbook of Domestic Violence Intervention Strategies (Oxford University Press, 2002), Crisis Intervention Handbook: Assessment, Treatment and Research, 3rd edition (Oxford University Press 2005), Juvenile Justice Sourcebook (Oxford University Press, 2004), Evidence-Based Practice Manual: Research and Outcome Measures in Health and Human Services (co-edited with Kenneth R. Yeager, Oxford University Press, 2004), and Ending Intimate Abuse (co-authored with Beverly Schenkman Roberts, Oxford University Press, 2005). Dr. Roberts was also the editor of three book series: the Springer Series on Social Work, the Springer Series on Family Violence and the Greenwood/Praeger Series on Social and Psychological Issues. Dr. Roberts was the recipient of many awards for his teaching and his scholarly publications.

Prior to his death in the summer of 2008, Dr. Roberts was in the midst of many projects, including his courses on Crisis Intervention, Domestic Violence, Introduction to Criminal Justice, Research Methods, Program Evaluation, Victimology and Victim Assistance, and Juvenile Justice at Rutgers University; training crisis intervention workers, crisis counselors, and clinical supervisors in crisis assessment and crisis intervention strategies; and training police officers and administrators in domestic violence policies and crisis intervention. He was a lifetime member of the Academy of Criminal Justice Sciences (ACJS), a fellow of the American Orthopsychiatric Association, a member of the Council on Social Work Education and the National Association of Social Workers (NASW) since 1974, and was listed in Who's Who in America from 1992 forward.

SECTION EDITORS

PAULA ALLEN-MEARES, PhD, is the Chancellor of the University of Illinois at Chicago. Previously she served as the Dean, Norma Radin Collegiate Professor of Social Work, and Professor of Education at the University of Michigan. Her research interests include the tasks and functions of social workers employed in educational settings; psychopathology in children, adolescents, and families; adolescent sexuality; premature parenthood; and various aspects of social work practice.

JOSÉ B. ASHFORD, MSW, PhD, LCSW is a Professor and Associate Director of the School of Social Work at Arizona State University. He is also the Director of the Office of Forensic Social Work and an Affiliate Professor in the Schools of Criminology and Criminal Justice and Justice and Social Inquiry. Dr. Ashford has published widely on forensic matters, including a co-edited book recognized as one of the most influential books on management of violence risk in the forensic literature.

ROWENA FONG is the Ruby Lee Piester Centennial Professor in Services to Children and Families at The University of Texas at Austin. Her scholarship and research focus on immigrant and refugee children and families, child welfare, and culturally competent practice. She has over 100 publications, including co-authored books on *Culturally Competent Practice with Immigrant and Refugee Children and Families* and *Culturally Competent Practice: Skills, Interventions, and Evaluations.*

CYNTHIA FRANKLIN, PhD, is Professor and Stiernberg/Spencer Family Professor in Mental Health at The University of Texas at Austin School of Social Work, where she is Coordinator of the clinical concentration. Dr. Franklin has published widely on topics such as dropout prevention, clinical assessment, the effectiveness of solution-focused therapy in school settings, and adolescent pregnancy prevention. She served as the past Editor-in-Chief of The National Association of Social Workers' journal Children in Schools.

WILLIAM R. NUGENT, Ph.D., is Professor and Director of the Doctoral Program at the University of Tennessee-Knoxville. He has published widely on research design and methods as well as the development of measurement tools. His research interests are primarily in measurement and assessment, and he has recently been investigating measurement issues in meta-analysis. He has also published research on applications of restorative justice.

LISA RAPP-PAGLICCI PhD, MSW is currently an Associate Professor and Associate Director of the School of Social Work at the University of South Florida. Her research interests include: juvenile crime and violence, at-risk children and adolescents, and prevention.

PHYLLIS SOLOMON, PhD is a Professor in the School of Social Policy & Practice and Professor of So-

cial Work in School of Medicine at the University of Pennsylvania. Dr. Solomon has conducted numerous federally-funded randomized clinical trials for adults with severe mental illness and their families. She reviews research grants for U.S. federal agencies, private foundations, and Canadian organizations. She also co-edited another book, *The Research Process in the Human Services: Behind the Scenes.*

BRUCE A. THYER, PhD, LCSW, is Professor and former Dean with the College of Social Work at Florida State University. Dr. Thyer has authored over 225 articles in refereed journals, over 60 book chapters and produced over 23 books. He is the Founding and current Editor of the bi-monthly peer reviewed journal Research on Social Work Practice, produced by Sage Publications.

VIKKI L. VANDIVER, DrPH, is a Professor of Social Work at Portland State University and Clinical Associate Professor in the Department of Psychiatry at the Oregon Health and Science University's School of Medicine. She also serves as Vice Chair of the Board of Directors for Cascadia Behavioral Healthcare, Inc. a not-for-profit, community-based behavioral healthcare group, and was on the Traumatic Brain Injury Study Committee at the National Academy of Sciences' Institute of Medicine. Her research and teaching interests are in mental health, traumatic brain injury and health promotion.

LIST OF CONTRIBUTORS

Paula Allen-Meares, PhD
Chancellor
University of Illinois at Chicago
Chicago, IL

Borja Alvarez de Toledo, MEd
Director, Family Services Operations
The Guidance Center, Inc.
Cambridge, MA

Harry J. Aponte, MSW, PhD (hc)
Clinical Associate Professor
Programs in Couple and Family
   Therapy
College of Nursing and Health
   Professions
Drexel University
Philadelphia, PA

LeShawn Arbuckle, LCSW
Program Services Coordinator
LifeWorks Youth Shelter
Austin, TX

Marilyn Armour, PhD
Associate Professor
School of Social Work
University of Texas at Austin
Austin, Texas

José B. Ashford, MSW, PhD, LCSW
Professor and Associate Director
School of Social Work
Director of the Office of Forensic Social Work
Affiliate Professor in the Schools of
  Criminology and Criminal Justice and
  Justice and Social Inquiry
Arizona State University
Tempe, AZ

Ron Avi Astor, PhD
Professor
Schools of Social Work and Education
University of Southern California
Los Angeles, CA

Carol D. Austin, MSW, PhD
Professor
Faculty of Social Work
University of Calgary
Calgary, Alberta, Canada

Sonia G. Austrian, DSW
Associate Professor of Public Health and
  Public Health in Psychiatry
Weill Medical College
Cornell University
New York, NY

Susan C. Ayers, LICSW
Executive Director
The Guidance Center, Inc.
Cambridge, MA

Allan Edward Barsky, JD, MSW, PhD
Professor
School of Social Work
Florida Atlantic University
Boca Raton, FL
Member of NASW National Ethics Committee

Kathryn Karusaitas Basham, PhD
Professor
School for Social Work
Smith College
Northampton, MA

Rami Benbenishty, PhD
Gordon Brown Professor of
  Social Work
School of Social Work and
  Social Welfare
Hebrew University of Jerusalem
Jerusalem, Israel

Kimberly Bender, PhD
Assistant Professor
School of Social Work
University of Denver
Denver, CO

Maggie Bennington-Davis, MD
Chief Clinical and Medical Officer
Cascadia Behavioral Healthcare, Inc.
Portland, OR

Kia J. Bentley, PhD
Professor and Associate Dean for Strategic
  Initiatives
Director of PhD Program
School of Social Work
Virginia Commonwealth
  University
Richmond, VA

Candyce S. Berger, PhD
Associate Professor
College of Arts and Sciences
University of Texas at El Paso
El Paso, TX

Ted Bober, MSW, RSW
Program Director
Certificate Program in Crisis
  Management for Workplace Trauma
  and Disasters
Factor-Inwentash Faculty of
  Social Work
University of Toronto
Toronto, Ontario, Canada

Mary Boes, MSW, MPH, PhD
Director, Undergraduate Program
Associate Professor
Department of Social Work
University of Northern Iowa

Gary R. Bond
Chancellor's Professor
Department of Psychology
Indiana University-Purdue University
  Indianapolis
Indianapolis, IN

William Borden, PhD
Senior Lecturer
School of Social Administration
University of Chicago
Chicago, IL

Gary L. Bowen, PhD
Kenan Distinguished Professor
School of Social Work
University of North Carolina
Chapel Hill, NC

Nancy Boyd-Webb, DSW
Distinguished Professor of Social Work
James R. Dumpson Chair in Child Welfare
    Studies
Graduate School of Social Service
Fordham University
Tarrytown, NY

Jill Boyer-Quick, MS
System Application Analyst
Oregon Health Sciences University
Portland, OR

Christine E. Brady
Graduate Student
Department of Psychology
James Madison University
Harrisonburg, VA

Jerrold R. Brandell, PhD, BCD
Distinguished Professor
Chairperson, Graduate Concentration in
    Interpersonal Practice
School of Social Work
Wayne State University
Detroit, MI

Mary Bricker-Jenkins, PhD
Professor Emerita
School of Social Work
Temple University
Philadelphia, PA

Denise E. Bronson, PhD
Associate Professor
College of Social Work
Ohio State University
Columbus, OH

Patricia Brownell, PhD, LMSW
Associate Professor
Graduate School of Social Service
Fordham University
New York, NY

Noël Busch-Armendariz, PhD
Associate Professor
School of Social Work
University of Texas
Austin, Texas

Andrew Christensen, PhD
Professor
Department of Psychology
University of California
Los Angeles, CA

Ron A. Cisler, PhD
Associate Professor
College of Health Sciences
University of Wisconsin
Milwaukee, WI

Elaine P. Congress, BA, MAT, MS, MA, DSW
Professor
Graduate School of Social Service
Fordham University
New York, NY

Jacqueline Corcoran, PhD
Associate Professor
School of Social Work
Northern Virginia Branch
Virginia Commonwealth University
Alexandria, VA

Kevin Corcoran, PhD, JD
Professor
Graduate School of Social Work
Portland State University
Portland, OR

Donna DeAngelis, MSW
Executive Director
Association of Social Work Boards
Culpeper, VA

Peter DeJong, PhD
Professor of Social Work
Department of Sociology and
    Social Work
Calvin College
Grand Rapids, MI

Diana M. DiNitto, PhD
Cullen Trust Centennial Professor
    in Alcohol Studies and Education
Distinguished Teaching Professor
School of Social Work
University of Texas
Austin, TX

Martha Morrison Dore, PhD
Associate Research Professor
Harvard University Medical School
Cambridge, MA
Vice President for Research and Evaluation,
    The Guidance Center, Inc.

James W. Drisko, PhD
Professor and Co-Director of the Doctoral
    Program
School for Social Work
Smith College
Northampton, MA

Theresa J. Early, PhD
Associate Professor and Doctoral
    Program Director
College of Social Work
The Ohio State University
Columbus, OH

Ilze A. Earner, PhD
Assistant Professor
School of Social Work
Hunter College
City University of New York
New York, NY

Yvonne M. Eaton, MSW
Clinical Social Worker
Director of Crisis Services
Community Mental Health Services
Erie, PA

Paul H. Ephross, PhD
Professor
School of Social Work
University of Maryland at Baltimore
Baltimore, MD

Steven W. Evans, PhD
Professor of Graduate Psychology
Alvin V. Baird Jr., Centennial Chair in
    Psychology
James Madison University
Harrisonburg, VA

Teresa A. Evans-Campbell, PhD, MSW
Associate Professor
Director, Center for Indigenous Health and
    Child Welfare Research
University of Washington
Seattle, WA

George S. Everly, Jr., PhD, ABPP
Associate Professor of Psychiatry
The Johns Hopkins University School
    of Medicine
Faculty, Center for Public Health Preparedness
The Johns Hopkins Bloomberg School
    of Public Health
Professor of Psychology
Loyola College in Maryland

Jay Fagan, DSW
Associate Professor of Social Work
School of Social Administration
Temple University
Philadelphia, PA

Rowena Fong, EdD, MSW, BA
Ruby Lee Piester Centennial Professor
    in Services to Children and Families
School of Social Work
University of Texas at Austin
Austin, TX

Anne E. (Ricky) Fortune, PhD
Professor
School of Social Welfare
University at Albany
State University of New York
Albany, NY

Raymond D. Fox, PhD
Professor
Graduate School of Social Service
Fordham University
New York, NY

Cynthia Franklin, PhD
Stiernberg/Spencer Family Professor
    in Mental Health
Coordinator of the Clinical Concentration
    for the Masters Program
School of Social Work
University of Texas at Austin
Austin, TX

Eileen Gambrill, PhD
Professor
School of Social Welfare
University of California
Berkeley, CA

Genoveva Garcia, MSW
Psychotherapist and Assistant to Clinical Director
Metropolitan Center for Mental Health
New York, NY

Renée Bradford Garcia, MSW
Private Practice
Round Rock, TX

Charles D. Garvin, PhD
Professor Emeritus of Social Work
School of Social Work
The University of Michigan
Ann Arbor, MI

Ann Marie Garran, PhD, MSW
Senior Clinical Supervisor
Hunter College Employee Assistance
    Program
New York, NY
Adjunct Professor
School for Social Work
Smith College
Northampton, MA

Felicia de la Garza-Mercer
Graduate Student
Department of Psychology
University of California
Los Angeles, CA

Zvi D. Gellis, PhD
Director, Center for Mental
    Health & Aging
School of Social Policy & Practice
University of Pennsylvania
Philadelphia, PA

Sheldon R. Gelman, PhD
Dean and Professor
Wurzweiler School of Social Work
Yeshiva University
New York, NY

Catherine T. Giblin, LCSW
Director, Assigned Counsel Project & Social
    Work Education Initiative
New York City Department for
    the Aging
New York, NY

Leonard Gibbs, PhD†
Professor
School of Social Work
University of Wisconsin
Eau Claire, WI

Brian Giddens, LICSW, ACSW
Associate Director of Social Work and
    Care Coordination
University of Washington Medical Center
Clinical Associate Professor
School of Social Work
University of Washington
Seattle, WA
Immediate Past President, NASW-WA Chapter
Past President, Society for Social Work
    Leadership in Health Care, WA Chapter

Susan Gingerich, MSW
Independent Trainer and Consultant
Philadelphia, PA

Alex Gitterman, MSW, EdD
Director of PhD Program and Professor
School of Social Work
University of Connecticut
West Hartford, CT

Graham Glancy, MB, ChB, FRCP Psch
Assistant Professor
Faculty of Psychiatry
University of Toronto
Toronto, Ontario, Canada

Donald K. Granvold, PhD
Professor
School of Social Work
University of Texas at Arlington
Arlington, TX

Diane L. Green, PhD
Associate Professor of Social Work
Florida Atlantic University – Jupiter Campus
Jupiter, FL

Gilbert J. Greene, PhD
Professor
College of Social Work
The Ohio State University
Columbus, OH

Geoffrey L. Greif, PhD
Professor
School of Social Work
University of Maryland
Baltimore, MD

David Guttmann
Professor and Dean Emeritus
School of Social Work
University of Haifa
Haifa, Israel

---

† Deceased

Lina Hartocollis, PhD
Associate Dean
Director, Clinical Doctorate in Social Work
    Program
School of Social Policy & Practice
University of Pennsylvania
Philadelphia, PA

Laurie Cook Heffron, MSW
Research Associate
Center for Social Work Research
School of Social Work
University of Texas at Austin
Austin, TX

Nina Rovinelli Heller, PhD
Associate Professor
School of Social Work
University of Connecticut
West Hartford, CT

Carolyn Hilarski, PhD, LCSW, ACSW
Associate Professor
Department of Social Work
Buffalo State College
State University of New York
Buffalo, NY

Laura M. Hopson, PhD
Assistant Professor
School of Social Welfare
State University of New York
Albany, NY

Matthew O. Howard, PhD
Professor
School of Social Work
University of North Carolina
Chapel Hill, NC

Ronald C. Hughes, PhD
Director
North American Resource Center for
    Child Welfare
Institute for Human Services
Columbus, OH
Editor-in-Chief, *APSAC Advisor*

Grafton H. Hull, Jr., EdD
Director, BSW Program
College of Social Work
University of Utah
Salt Lake City, UT

Catheleen Jordan, PhD
Professor of Social Work
School of Social Work
University of Texas at Arlington
Arlington, TX

Lana Sue I. Ka'opua, PhD, DCSW, LSW
Associate Professor and Head of Health
    Concentration
School of Social Work and Cancer Research
    Center of HI
University of Hawai'i, Manoa Campus
Director, Ka Lei Mana'olana Breast Health Project
Honolulu, HI
Co-Editor-in-Chief, *Social Work Journal
    of Indigenous Matters*

James M. Karls, PhD, LCSW
Clinical Associate Professor
University of Southern California
School of Social Work
Los Angeles, CA

Patricia Kelley, PhD
Professor Emerita
School of Social Work
The University of Iowa
Iowa City, IA

Michael S. Kelly, PhD, LCSW
Assistant Professor
School of Social Work
Loyola University
Chicago, IL
Coordinator of Research and Outreach, Loyola
    Family and Schools Partnership Program

Johnny S. Kim, PhD
Assistant Professor
School of Social Welfare
University of Kansas
Lawrence, KS

Karen S. Knox, PhD
Associate Professor
School of Social Work
Texas State University
San Marcos, TX

Marina Kukla
Graduate Student
Department of Psychology
Indiana University-Purdue University
    Indianapolis
Indianapolis, IN

Christine Lagana-Riordan, LCSWC.
Doctoral Student
School of Social Work
University of Texas
Austin, TX

Alan M. Langlieb, MD, MPH, MBA
Director, Workplace Psychiatry
The Johns Hopkins Hospital
Baltimore, MD

Stephen R. Lankton, MSW, DAHB
Executive Director
Phoenix Institute of Ericksonian Therapy
Phoenix, AZ
Editor-in-Chief, *American Journal
  of Clinical Hypnosis*
American Hypnosis Board
  for Clinical Social Work

Tina R. Latimer, RN
Director, Quality and Operational Improvement
The Ohio State University Medical Center
Columbus, OH

Craig Winston LeCroy, PhD
Professor
School of Social Work
Arizona State University, Tucson Component
Tucson, AZ

Mo Yee Lee, PhD
Professor
College of Social Work
The Ohio State University
Columbus, OH
Editor, *Journal of Ethnic & Cultural
  Diversity in Social Work*

Peter Lehmann, PhD, LCSW
Associate Professor
Co-Director, Community Service Center
School of Social Work
University of Texas at Arlington
Arlington, TX

John Allen Lemmon, PhD
Professor
School of Social Work
San Francisco State University
San Francisco, CA

Anita Lightburn, MSS, EdD
Professor of Social Work
Graduate School of Social Work
Fordham University
New York, NY

Elizabeth Lightfoot, PhD
Associate Professor
School of Social Work
University of Minnesota, Twin Cities
St. Paul, MN

Jan Ligon, PhD
Associate Professor
School of Social Work
Georgia State University
Atlanta, GA

Brenda J. Liston
Chief, Community Support, Airman and
  Family Readiness Policy
United States Air Force
Washington, DC

Julia H. Littell, PhD
Professor
Graduate School of Social Work and
  Social Research
Bryn Mawr College
Bryn Mawr, PA

Sadye M. L. Logan, DSW
DeQuincey Newman Professor
Director of the Newman Institute for Peace
  and Justice
College of Social Work
University of South Carolina
Columbia, SC

Courtney J. Lynch, PhD
Assistant Professor
Department of Social Work
University of North Carolina at Charlotte
Charlotte, NC

Brandy Macaluso, BSW
Crime Victim Practitioner
Coalition for Independent Living
Options, Inc.
West Palm Beach, FL

Gordon MacNeil, PhD
Associate Professor
School of Social Work
The University of Alabama
Tuscaloosa, AL

Roxana Marachi, PhD
Assistant Professor
Department of Elementary Education
Lurie College of Education
San José State University
San José, CA

Andrew T. Marks, LMSW
Lecturer
School of Social Work
Texas State University- San Marcos
San Marcos, TX

Tina Bogart Marshall, PhD
Consultant and Part-time Professor
School of Social Work
University of Maryland Baltimore County
  at Shady Grove
Rockville, MD

James A. Martin, PhD, BCD
Associate Professor
Graduate School of Social Work and Social
  Research
Bryn Mawr College
Bryn Mawr, PA
Colonel, U.S. Army (Retired)

Jannah H. Mather, PhD
Dean and Professor
College of Social Work
University of Utah
Salt Lake City, UT

Evan Mayo-Wilson, MGA, MSc
Department Lecturer
Centre for Evidence-Based Intervention
University of Oxford
Oxford, England, United Kingdom

Robert W. McClelland, PhD
Professor
Faculty of Social Work
University of Calgary
Calgary, Alberta, Canada

Lynn McDonald, PhD
Reader in Social Work
Deputy Director, Social Work Division
School of Health Sciences and
  Social Care
Brunel University
London, England, United Kingdom

Monica McGoldrick, MSW, PhD (hc)
Director, Family Institute of New
Jersey
Highland Park, NJ
Adjunct Associate Professor of Clinical
  Psychiatry
Robert Wood Johnson Medical
School
University of Medicine and Dentistry
Piscataway, NJ

Steven L. McMurtry, PhD
Professor
Helen Bader School of Social Welfare
University of Wisconsin
Milwaukee, WI

C. Aaron McNeece, PhD
Dean and Walter W. Hudson Professor
  of Social Work
College of Social Work
Florida State University
Tallahassee, FL

Joshua Miller, PhD, MSW
Professor and Chair of Policy Sequence
School for Social Work
Smith College
Northampton, MA

Terry Mizrahi, PhD
Professor and Chair, Community
  Organization & Planning
School of Social Work
Hunter College
City University of New York
New York, NY

Jacqueline B. Mondros, DSW
Professor and Dean
School of Social Work
Hunter College
City University of New York
New York, NY

Ianna Monferrari, BA
Graduate Student
Rutgers University
New Brunswick, NJ

Paul Montgomery, DPhil
Reader in Psycho-Social Intervention
Centre for Evidence-Based Intervention
University of Oxford
Oxford, England, United Kingdom

David P. Moxley, PhD
Oklahoma Health Care Authority Professor
Professor of Social Work
School of Social Work
University of Oklahoma
Norman, OK

Carlton E. Munson, PhD
Professor
School of Social Work
University of Maryland
Baltimore, MD

Laura L. Myers, MSW, PhD
Department of Social Work
Florida A & M University
Tallahassee, FL

John P. Nelson, PhD
Research Scientist
Family Translational Research Group
Stony Brook University
State University of New York
Stony Brook, NY

F. Ellen Netting, PhD
Professor and Samuel S. Wurtzel
    Endowed Chair
School of Social Work
Virginia Commonwealth University
Richmond, VA

Barbara van Noppen, MSW
Clinical Social Worker
Angel Wellness Center
Providence, RI

Terry B. Northcut, PhD, LCSW
Associate Professor
Director of the Doctoral Program
School of Social Work
Loyola University of Chicago
Chicago, IL

Jack Nowicki, LCSW
Program Development Specialist
Texas Network of Youth Services
Instructor
University of Texas School of
    Social Work
Austin, TX

William R. Nugent, PhD
Associate Professor
College of Social Work
University of Tennessee
Knoxville, TN

Scott Kiyoshi Okamoto, PhD
Associate Professor
Social Work Program
Hawai'i Pacific University
Honolulu, HI

Maura E. O'Keefe, PhD, LCSW
Associate Professor
California State University, Sacramento
Division of Social Work
Sacramento, CA

Daphna Oyserman, PhD
Edwin J. Thomas Collegiate Professor
School of Social Work
Professor, Department of
    Psychology
Research Professor, Institute for
    Social Research
University of Michigan
Ann Arbor, MI

William P. Panning, MSW
Private Practice and Guest Lecturer
College of Social Work
The Ohio State University
Columbus, OH

Daniel V. Papero, PhD
Private Practice
Director of Clinical Services
Georgetown Family Center
Washington, DC

Danielle Parrish, MSW
Doctoral Candidate
School of Social Work
University of Texas at Austin
Austin, TX

Brian E. Perron, PhD
School of Social Work
University of Michigan
Ann Arbor, MI

Monica Pignotti, MSW
Doctoral Program
College of Social Work
Florida State University
Tallahassee, FL

Cathy King Pike, PhD
Professor
School of Social Work
Indiana University
Indianapolis, IN

Ronald O. Pitner, PhD
Independent Research
    Consultant
North Brunswick, NJ

Elizabeth C. Pomeroy, PhD
Professor
School of Social Work
University of Texas
Austin, TX

Dennis L. Poole, PhD
Dean and Professor
College of Social Work
University of South Carolina
Columbia, SC

Miriam Potocky-Tripodi, PhD
Professor
School of Social Work
Florida International University
Miami, FL

James O. Prochaska, PhD
Professor and Director
Cancer Research Center and
    Department of Psychology
University of Rhode Island
Kingston, RI

Janice M. Prochaska, PhD
C.E.O. and Social Work Consultant
Pro-Change Behavior Systems
Kingston, RI

Charles A. Rapp, PhD, MSW
Professor
School of Social Welfare
University of Kansas
Lawrence, KS

Lisa Rapp-Paglicci, PhD, MSW
Associate Professor and Associate Director
School of Social Work
University of South Florida
Tampa, FL

Frederic G. Reamer, PhD
Professor
School of Social Work
Rhode Island College
Providence, RI

Cheryl Regehr, PhD
Dean, Factor-Inwentash Faculty of Social Work
Professor, Faculty of Social Work and Faculty
    of Law
Sandra Rotman Chair
University of Toronto
Toronto, Ontario, Canada

William J. Reid, DSW[†]
Distinguished Professor and Chair, PhD
Program
School of Social Work
State University of New York
Albany, NY

Michael Reisch, PhD, LMSW
Daniel Thursz Distinguished Professor of
    Social Justice
School of Social Work
University of Maryland
Baltimore, MD

Deborah P. Reyome, MSW
Center for Human Services Research
Albany, NY

Virginia E. Richardson, PhD
Professor
College of Social Work
The Ohio State University
Columbus, OH

Albert R. Roberts, PhD[†]
Professor of Criminal Justice and Social Work
School of Arts and Sciences
Rutgers University
Livingston Campus
Piscataway, N.J.

Susan J. Rose, PhD
Associate Professor
Helen Bader School of Social Welfare
University of Wisconsin
Milwaukee, WI

Jack Rothman, PhD
Professor Emeritus
School of Public Affairs
University of California – Los Angeles
Los Angeles, CA

Juliet Cassuto Rothman, PhD, LCSW
Lecturer in Social Welfare and Public Health
University of California – Berkeley
Berkeley, CA

William S. Rowe, DSW
Professor and Director
School of Social Work
University of South Florida
Tampa, FL

Allen Rubin, PhD
Professor
School of Social Work
University of Texas
Austin, TX

[†] Deceased

Judith S. Rycus, PhD, MSW
Program Director
North American Resource Center for
    Child Welfare
Institute for Human Services
Columbus, OH

Joanna M. Sadler
Graduate Student
Department of Psychology
James Madison University
Harrisonburg, VA

Alison Salloum, PhD
Assistant Professor
School of Social Work
University of South Florida
Tampa, FL

Emily K. Sandoz
Graduate Student
Department of Psychology
University of Mississippi
Oxford, MS

Radu Saveanu, MD
Associate Professor of Clinical Psychiatry
Chairman, Department of Psychiatry
Executive Director, Harding Hospital
The Ohio State University
Columbus, OH

Scott P. Sells, PhD
Chief Executive Director
Parenting with Love and Limits
Savannah, GA

David S. Shannahoff-Khalsa
President, The Khalsa Foundation for
    Medical Science
Director, The Research Group for Mind-Body
    Dynamics
Institute for Nonlinear Science
University of California, San Diego
La Jolla, CA

Aron Shlonsky, PhD
Associate Professor
Faculty of Social Work
University of Toronto
Toronto, Ontario, Canada

Daryl Shorter, MD
Addiction Psychiatry Fellow
School of Medicine
New York University
New York, NY

Lawrence Shulman, EdD, MSW
Professor
School of Social Work
State University of New York at Buffalo
Buffalo, NY

Catherine A. Simmons, PhD
Assistant Professor
College of Social Work
University of Tennessee
Knoxville, TN

Jonathan B. Singer, LCSW
Instructor
Social Administration
Temple University
Philadelphia, PA
Host and Founder of The Social
    Work Podcast

Regan M. Slater
Graduate Student
Department of Psychology
University of Mississippi
Oxford, MS

Phyllis Solomon, PhD
Professor
School of Social Policy & Practice
University of Pennsylvania
Philadelphia, PA

Karen M. Sowers, PhD
Dean and Professor
College of Social Work
The University of Tennessee
Knoxville, TN
Co-Editor, Best Practices in Mental Health:
    An International Journal

David W. Springer, PhD
Associate Dean for Academic Affairs
University Distinguished Teaching Professor
School of Social Work
The University of Texas
Austin, TX

Victoria Stanhope, PhD
Assistant Professor
Silver School of Social Work
New York University
New York, NY

Alicia J. Stinson, MSW
School of Social Work
University of South Florida
Tampa, FL

Kimberly Strom-Gottfried, MSW, PhD
Smith P. Theimann Jr. Distinguished Professor
    of Ethics and Professional Practice
School of Social Work
University of North Carolina
Chapel Hill, NC

W. Patrick Sullivan, PhD
Professor
School of Social Work
Indiana University
Indianapolis, IN

Mary Ann Test, PhD
Professor Emerita
School of Social Work
University of Wisconsin-Madison
Madison, WI

Bruce A. Thyer, PhD
Professor
College of Social Work
Florida State University
Tallahassee, FL
Editor, Research on Social Work Practice

Evelyn P. Tomaszewski, MSW
Project Director and Senior Policy Advisor
Practice, Human Rights, and International
    Affairs
National Association of Social Workers
Washington, DC

Elizabeth M. Tracy, PhD
Professor and Doctoral Program Chair
Mandel School of Applied Social Sciences
Case Western Reserve University
Cleveland, OH

Stephen J. Tripodi, PhD
Assistant Professor
College of Social Work
Florida State University
Tallahassee, FL

Francis J. Turner, DSW
Professor and Dean Emeritus
Wilfred Laurier University
Waterloo, Ontario, Canada

Halaevalu F. Ofahengaue Vakalahi, MSW,
    MEd, BS, PhD
Associate Professor of Social Work
Director, MSW Program
George Mason University
Arlington, VA

Vikki L. Vandiver, MSW, DrPH
Professor
School of Social Work
Portland State University
Clinical Associate Professor of
    Psychiatry
School of Medicine
Oregon Health and Science University
Portland, OR

Katherine van Wormer, MSW, PhD
Professor
School of Social Work
University of Northern Iowa
Cedar Falls, IA

Michael G. Vaughn, PhD
School of Social Work
University of Pittsburgh
Pittsburgh, PA

M. Elizabeth Vonk, MSW, PhD
Associate Professor
School of Social Work
University of Georgia
Athens, GA

Froma Walsh, PhD
Mose and Sylvia Firestone Professor
    Emerita
School of Social Service Administration
University of Chicago
Chicago, IL

Joseph Walsh, PhD
Professor
School of Social Work
Virginia Commonwealth University
Richmond, VA

Chris Warren-Adamson, MPhil
Senior Lecturer
School of Social Sciences
University of Southampton
Southampton, England,
    United Kingdom

Allen H. Weg, EdD
Director and Founder
Stress and Anxiety Services of New
    Jersey, PA
Co-Founder and Vice President
New Jersey Affiliate of the Obsessive
    Compulsive Foundation
East Brunswick, NJ

Marie Overby Weil, DSW
Berg-Beach Distinguished Professor of
   Community Practice
School of Social Work
University of North Carolina
Chapel Hill, NC

Michele Weiner-Davis, MSW
Director, The Divorce Busting Center
Founder of Divorcebusting.com
Boulder, CO

Joan C. Weiss, MSW
Executive Director
Justice Research and Statistics Association
   Institute
Private Practice
Rockville, MD

Janet B. W. Williams, DSW
Vice-President of Clinical Development
MedAvante, Inc.
Hamilton, NJ

Katherine J. Williams
Graduate Student
Department of Psychology
University of California – Los Angeles
Los Angeles, CA

Kelly G. Wilson, PhD, BJ
Associate Professor of Psychology
University of Mississippi
Department of Psychology
Oxford, MS

John S. Wodarski, PhD
Professor
College of Social Work
University of Tennessee
Knoxville, TN

Kenneth R. Yeager, PhD
Associate Professor of Psychiatry
Director of Quality Assurance
Department of Psychiatry
Ohio State University Medical School
Columbus, OH

James R. Zabora, ScD
Dean and Professor
National Catholic School of Social Service
Catholic University of America
Washington, DC

Charlene Zuffante, LICSW
Director of Wraparound Services
The Guidance Center, Inc.
Somerville, MA

PART I
Introduction and Overview

1 The Synergy and Generativity of Social Work Practice

Anita Lightburn

The rich store of knowledge in this reference takes many forms, and they all help guide practice in the complex world of social work practice. With over 170 chapters, *The Social Worker's Desk Reference*, second edition, is a testament to the social work profession's commitments to challenging and compelling fields of practice. A unique compendium of intellectual and social capital guided by the vision of Albert Roberts and his associate editors, this volume brings together a pluralism of ideology, theory, and practice. It speaks to our complex understanding of the human condition, the ongoing potential of development, the importance of relationships, family and community, and the hope for healing and recovery.

The expanded second edition of this extensive reference guide inspires confidence that social workers are as much about promoting important values, such as social justice and human rights, as they are about effective practice to meet clients' needs. This volume is built on over a century of social work theory and practice. The breadth of concerns and methods of helping represented here honors the accomplishments of a field that has grown dramatically from a charitable enterprise to a helping profession developed both as an art and science of practice, imbued with values and applied in the art of relational practice. The comments in this introductory chapter are offered as a way of reflecting on the synergy at work through collaboration and integration of practice theory and method and the generativity that is social work's hallmark and maturity, where we continue to move forward to meet the challenges of this time in history, with a spirit to both innovate and work with our traditions providing for the well-being of those who follow.

In the seven years since the first edition of this volume, the profession has paid vigorous attention to developing evidence-based practice with a call for careful implementation studies to translate evidence for practice in diverse settings, open to learning from clients. As we work to close the acknowledged gap between the time research is reported and its implementation in the community, we have brought to light the complexity in realizing this goal (Schoenwald & Hoagwood, 2001). The culture of practice is changing, more is being asked of practitioners, with less financial support to do the work that is envisioned and that should be done. At the same time, interdisciplinary collaboration has increased, integration of theory and practice methods continue to bring together complementary and essential approaches, and service integration is being demonstrated in different practice arenas (Bouis et al., 2007; Brouselle, Lamothe, Mercier, & Perreault, 2007; Humphreys, Regan, River, & Thiara, 2005). Where community is an important resource for development and recovery, we are again seeing innovations that use our knowledge and skills in creative ways, stepping outside traditional practice forms to weave help into the fabric of life as it is lived, whether this is in schools, day care settings for our youngest and older citizens, or on the streets, where youth need to be engaged as contributors to their communities (Durlak et al., 2007; Frazier, Cappela, & Atkins, 2007; Lightburn & Sessions, 2006).

Our understanding of the complexity of client problems grows, as illustrated in the field of developmental science, expanding our understanding of human development and communities' capacity for change (Gilgun, 2005; Saleebey, 2006). We live in exciting times, where our concern for supporting parents and developing communities that care are as much a part of a national mental health agenda as responding to the needs of our diverse population and working to decrease disparities in service provision. Our long-held belief that context matters has actively become a part of how we think about help and practice, and we stretch to consider new paradigms, such as complex theory, where this is fundamental (Hudson, 2000). There is a hopeful emphasis on transformation and change across service sectors even though siloed services exist side by side in communities and agencies. So that, for example, early child services are not well linked to mental health services, child welfare, or substance abuse programs, even though a family with young children requires an integrated approach when parents struggle with traumatic histories and substance abuse that make it difficult to protect and nurture their children. Isolated ideas and theories in similar ways can impede collaboration and service integration. The challenges, though considerable, are being seriously taken on by those who believe we need to develop systems of care that include working with consumers as partners in the complex work required, for example, in reducing child abuse and neglect, domestic violence, and adolescent substance abuse and delinquency and responding to the serious mental health needs of children and adolescents (Epstein, Kutash, & Duchnowski, 2005; Woolston, Adnopoz, & Berkowitz, 2007).

A year after the first edition of *The Social Worker's Desk Reference* was published, a far-sighted report, *Transforming Mental Health Care in America* (New Freedom Commission on Mental Health, 2003) highlighted the seriousness of mental illness across the world, describing the failure of mental health services in the United States. Commissioners who wrote this report set out a mandate to transform mental health practice. Some of the key areas for change included focusing on recovery, reducing stigma, increasing access to services in communities where people live, providing services for the very young, integrating preventive programs into schools, working on the serious problem of suicide, reducing service disparities for minority populations, build-

ing systems of care, providing culturally competent services, and translating research into practice. This important agenda has been the focus of federal initiatives, state policy, and program developments and local agency concern across our country. The U.S. Substance Abuse and Mental Health Association (SAMHSA) has increasingly taken an important role in knowledge dissemination, making available evidence-based programs to support practice decisions, providing technical assistance, and supporting research to further the development of services in each of these areas.

THE STRENGTH OF MULTIPLE PERSPECTIVES

As much as we benefit from the strength of multiple perspectives in meeting the complex needs of the most vulnerable populations, the realities of limited resources remains a serious problem. The tradition of the social work profession as advocates will remain vital to our generativity, as we need to persistently advocate for necessary services with a vision of the options available to ensure humane care. This is a time for fortifying commitment by using multiple perspectives of what is possible and increasing social workers' ability to defend programs and practice on the basis of relevant evidence and a moral imperative to provide interventions that are known to be helpful.

As the structure of service delivery changes, social workers can influence both structure and practice. Examples include the following.

- Working in primary-care settings supported by managed care organizations with carved-out services.
- Promoting community-based approaches to support those with chronic mental illness that depend on partnerships with families and the community.
- Use of systems of care that work to integrate services and maintain children and adolescents who have serious emotional and behavioral problems in their own community.
- Supporting children's development in school programs to mitigate the effects of exposure to violence at home and in the community.
- Developing early intervention programs in day care settings and family support programs that put into practice insights from

the publication *From Neurons to Neighborhoods* (Shonkoff & Phillips, 2000), ensuring the social emotional development for our children.

- Advancing family-centered practice that supports the family caring for a member with mental or physical illness.
- Integrating mental health knowledge and practice into child welfare and criminal justice.
- Investing in prevention and promoting capacity building to enlarge community, individual, and family resources to deal with substance abuse.
- Providing intergenerational programs that meet the needs of older citizens and the very young.

As we work to bring about these service delivery innovations, we need to draw on the resources of this volume and work with the organizations taking on the challenge of organizing advances in practice, such as the National Trauma Consortium. In an environment where many clinicians experience service constraints, time is limited, and workers are increasingly discouraged by bureaucratic requirements, it is important not to sacrifice theory and knowledge because there is not enough time to think through and work out applications. Professional practice requires the responsible use of up-to-date information. For example, even though there has been encouraging signs of increased knowledge, as in our continued study of trauma and its treatment, trauma-informed practice still needs to be developed in most clinics and community-based service settings, such as schools, and early childhood and family centers. Crisis and suicide assessment should similarly be in common use. Integrated theoretical approaches as seen in chapters on the psychodynamic and cognitive-behavioral approaches to depression provide bridges in thinking that will increase practice effectiveness. Current psychopharmacology information also needs to be available across settings.

Case management, basic to quality services in managed care, is enriched by a clinical focus to better meet the complex needs of those with mental illness, HIV/AIDS, cancer, and other chronic illnesses. Clinical models of case management are also beneficial for older adults, substance abusers, and children in protective services. The challenge of working with and strengthening social networks expands resources for care

taking, which is so basic in meeting the needs of isolated parents, children, victims of domestic violence, the mentally ill, and those with disabilities.

Practice skill, fortified with current knowledge, is indispensable for accountable, ethical practice. As we seek to translate the ever-expanding contributions from new fields, such as neuroscience, we need to be curious consumers and pioneers in the application of new understanding of how the brain changes and develops (Doidge, 2007; Gilgun, 2005). Biopsychosocial education needs to be integrated as a fundamental part of programmatic and practice models in a wide range of settings where the public health model promotes prevention for health and mental health (Volland, Berkman, Stein, & Vaghy, 1999). In programs where early intervention models focus on supporting at-risk children and families, the educational role of social workers is combined with clinical and developmental approaches to strengthen resilience. This volume makes such information available for practitioners, students, and program planners.

Other significant signs of our generativity include our renewed concern with oppression and deprivation with our commitment to social justice as purpose and priority for programs and multicultural practice competencies, essential for twenty-first-century service provision. Principles and guidelines to facilitate collaboration with families, in community partnerships, and in multidisciplinary teams chart the direction for mental health care and school-based services (Claiborne & Lawson, 2005). Strengthening resilience in families, models of psychosocial rehabilitation, and attention to the educational role of social workers expand the traditional intervention paradigms and point to the future.

As a national concern, community development, advocacy, and social action increasingly take on more importance in building neighborhoods to deal with the effects of poverty and violence. Developing capacity and opportunities within communities for empowerment to expand the ability for citizens to meet their own needs has been and will continue to be a focus of both federal and foundation initiatives. Coalition building and organizing is fundamental to community practice at a time when public and private agencies need to join with communities to develop resources and influence policy and programs. The varied approaches to capacity building in community practice speak to a growing awareness of the importance of community in its many forms, including faith-based services to meet critical needs of our vulnerable citizens and to support and create opportunities for all community members (Cnaan, Broodie, & Yancey, 2005). The resurgence of community practice is encouraging, because it is a foundation for all social work practice and is based on a revitalized and dynamic systems perspective.

Creative prevention programs for young people shift attention to what is possible when investments are made in supporting development (Durlak et al., 2007; Frazier et al., 2007). Community-based clinical practitioners who are flexible and responsive are providing services in new partnerships with parents, teachers and administrators, community members, paraprofessionals, and volunteers that increase the capacity of the community to support mental health. Early intervention programs, home-based family services, family support, full-service schools and school-based services, and youth programs on the streets and in community centers are some of the examples of preventive and interventional approaches (Lightburn & Sessions, 2006). Practitioners in these community-based programs understand and work with principles of community development and collaborative and interprofessional practice, as much as with group work methods, psychoeducation, family systems work, and individual therapy.

It is within our power to influence decisions about who we care for and help and the degree to which we encourage and participate in collaboration with colleagues in other disciplines. The evidence-based practice model, which emphasizes the technology of practice as advocated by a number of authors, is one way to be accountable. It is also encouraging that social workers are developing the skills of program evaluation and research. Inquiry is vital, and evaluation makes it possible to represent what happens as a result of therapeutic or helping relationships. Rarely, however, does outcome evaluation represent the full story or the dynamics that are essential to understanding both the problem and the help given. This is equally true for programs as it is for practice. The well-known case of marginal results in major outcome studies points to the continued challenge of developing evaluative methods that are more sensitive and valid, include the consumer's voice, and also represent the complex influence of ecosystems on outcomes (Miller, Crabtree, McDaniel, and Stange, 1998; Weiss, 1998). Social workers should have

key roles in program evaluations because we bring an intimate understanding of service delivery and the importance of context in influencing outcomes.

Autonomous practice depends on accessibility to knowledge that informs decisions and promotes accountability. Practitioners can be overwhelmed by the task of evaluating and choosing the most appropriate approaches for working with an individual, family, or group. Accordingly, the authors in this desk reference have provided synthesized state-of-the-art information with step-by-step guides to support practitioners and direct them to key resources. In Part II, a unique introduction to social work practice with sketches of social workers' everyday tasks provides a dynamic perspective of the profession in action from behavioral health and outpatient mental health to schools, clients' homes, police departments, and traumatic stress and emergency settings. Each setting has distinctive requirements and challenges to which the parts of this volume speaks. Part III frames the values of the profession from ethical concerns to licensing standards and serious concerns about legal considerations. Theoretical foundations and treatment approaches include distinctive social work contributions in Parts IV and VI, with crisis intervention, task-centered practice, and the life model to a social worker's perspective on traditional as well as current therapeutic approaches from cognitive-behavioral theory, solution-focused practice, critical family theories, to narrative and social constructivist social work practice, comparative theories, and psychoeducation. Parts V through IX provide indispensable attention to theory in practice and the processes of practice, elaborating on diagnostic assessment methods such as *DSM-IV-TR* and rapid assessment instruments, implementing treatment plans for specific populations, and guidelines for specific interventions and techniques. The complete range of interventions are included, such as the genogram, couples therapy, structural family therapy, and Bowen family systems therapy, psychopharmacology, trauma-informed care, substance abuse treatment, and supported employment approaches for persons with mental illness. Substantive areas of practice are represented from work with children through play therapy, developing social skills, developing competencies in response to child maltreatment to storytelling and metaphor with obsessive-compulsive disorder to bereavement and grief therapy.

Case management, an important social work role and method is described in different settings in Part X, including health and mental health, child welfare, and work with older adults followed by an overview of social work fields of practice in Part XI. This important desk reference, authored by leaders in the field, offers an overview and analysis pointing to the future opportunities for practitioners to shape how services will be provided. Part XII introduces the expanding field of community practice from examples of innovative community-based clinical practice, legislative advocacy, and assertive communities to the nuts and bolts of traditional and evolving methods of community practice, including advocacy and empowerment, social action, community school partnerships, and community capacity building.

Practitioners will find support for working with vulnerable populations at risk in Part XII and the guides needed for best practices in school settings, the integration for social work and the law, practice evaluation, and use of evidence-based practice in Parts XIV, XV, and XVI. Selections in these parts are relevant for practitioners in the field and those studying for the profession, introducing ways to think about evidence, guidelines for implementation, and participation as investigators. In all, the authors of these substantive contributions provide a valuable resource for practitioners who are pressed by limited time and lack support from supervisors or colleagues. The content enables practitioners to advance practice knowledge through critically sifting and testing the approaches that best fit with clients' needs and capabilities.

CONCLUSION

The dramatic changes in health and mental health care create renewed urgency for social workers to reexamine knowledge and theory for practice. In all its parts, this desk reference is a robust introduction to the growing breadth and depth that characterize the many fields of social work practice that embrace diversity and strive to meet the needs of twenty-first-century people and their communities. Noted authors, practitioners, and educators present a range of progressive developments in theory, practice methods, assessment protocols, treatment plans, interventions, and evaluation studies that make an essential contribution to the advancement of practice. This volume is an extraordinary testament to the substance and commitments of the social work profession. It is the most comprehensive and practical source of current information for social work practitioners and leadership in the development of more effective human services. This volume also reflects the synergy in social work practice, where the total is more than the sum of the parts, as we work to integrate best-practice methods and theories for innovative and effective solutions in collaboration with clients, natural helpers, and other human service providers.

The *Social Workers' Desk Reference*, second edition, is substantive evidence of the generativity of the social work profession as we work with the complexity of clients' lives, problems, capacities, and evolving possibilities. This well-honed, prodigious work will be a critical support to social workers as we reaffirm what is relevant and define what needs to be known to practice in new contexts and transform how we work in traditional settings. Albert Roberts has brought together collaborators from diverse fields of social work practice to support the needs of social workers who practice in a wide host of settings. In this regard, the new edition of the *Social Workers' Desk Reference* will be an indispensable, highly practical, and sturdy companion for the generative work ahead.

References

Bouis, S., Reif, S., Whetten, K., Scovil, J., Murray, A., & Swartz, M. (2007). An integrated, multidimensional treatment model for individuals living with HIV, mental illness, and substance abuse. *Health and Social Work, 32*(4), 268–278.

Brouselle, A., Lamothe, L., Mercier, C., & Perreault, M. (2007). Beyond the limitations of best practices: How logic analysis helped reinterpret dual diagnosis guidelines. *Evaluation and Program Planning, 30*(1), 94–104.

Clairborne, N., & Lawson, H. (2005). An intervention framework for collaboration. *Families in Society, 86*(1), 93–103.

Cnaan, R., Broodie, C., & Yancey, G. (2005). Rise up and build cities: Faith-based community organizing. In M. Weil (Ed.), *The handbook of community practice* (pp. 372–386). Thousand Oaks, CA: Sage.

Doidge, N. (Ed). (2007). *The brain that changes itself.* New York: Viking.

Durlak, J., Taylor, R., Kawashima, K., Pachan, M., Du-Pre, E., Celio, C., et al. (2007). Effects of positive youth development programs on school, family and community systems. *American Journal of Community Psychology, 39,* 269–286.

Epstein, M., Kutash, K., & Duchnowski, A. (2005). *Outcomes for children and youth with emotional and behavioral disorders and their families*, 2nd ed. Austin, TX: Pro-Ed.

Frazier, S., Cappela, E., & Atkins, M. (2007). Linking mental health and after school systems for children in urban poverty: Preventing problems, promoting possibilities. *Administration and Policy in Mental Health, 34*(4), 389–400.

Gilgun, J. (2005). Evidence-based practice, descriptive research and the resilience-schema-gender-brain functioning (RSGB). *Assessment. British Journal of Social Work, 35*, 834–862.

Hudson, C. (2000). At the edge of chaos: A new paradigm for social work? *Journal of Social Work Education, 36*(2), 215–230.

Humphreys, C., Regan, L., River, D., & Thiara, R. (2005). Domestic violence and substance use: Tackling complexity. *British Journal of Social Work, 35*(8), 1303–1320.

Lightburn, A., & Sessions, P. (Eds.). (2006). *The handbook of community-based clinical practice*. New York: Oxford University Press.

Miller, W., Crabtree, B., McDaniel, R., & Stange, K. (1998). Understanding change in primary care practice using complexity theory. *Journal of Family Practice, 46*(5), 369–377.

New Freedom Commission on Mental Health. (2003). *Achieving the promise: Transforming mental health care in America. Final report*. DHHS Pub. No. SMA-03-3832. Rockville, MD. Executive summary from http://www.mentalhealthcommission.gov/reports/Finalreport/downloads/ExecSummary.pdf.

Saleebey, D. (2006). A paradigm shift in developmental perspectives: The self in context. In Lightburn, A., & Sesssion, P. (Eds), *The handbook of community-based clinical practice* (pp. 46–62). New York: Oxford University Press.

Schoenwald, S. K., & Hoagwood, K. (2001). Effectiveness, transportability, and dissemination of interventions: What matters when? *Psychiatric Services, 52*(9), 1190–1197.

Shonkoff, J. P., & Phillips, D. A. (2000). *From neurons to neighborhoods: The science of early childhood development*. Washington, DC: National Academies Press.

Volland, P. J. Berkman, B., Stein, G., & Vaghy, A. (1999). *Social work education for practice in health care report*. New York: New York Academy of Medicine Health.

Weiss, C. (1998). *Evaluation*. Saddle River, NJ: Prentice Hall.

Woolston, J., Adnopoz, J., & Berkowitz, S. (2007). *IICAPS: A home-based psychiatric treatment for children and adolescents*. New Haven, CT: Yale University Press.

PART II

Roles, Functions, and Typical Daily Schedule of Social Workers in Different Practice Settings

2

The Social Worker in a Behavioral Health Care Setting

Cynthia Franklin & Christine Lagana-Riordan

The following description is of a typical day in the life of a clinical social worker employed by an outpatient mental health clinic that receives a combination of Medicaid, HMO dollars, and private, managed care contracts.

8:30 A.M.	Arrives at the office, drinks a cup of coffee, and spends the next hour completing HMO paperwork to bill for client sessions from last week.
10 A.M.	Staffing and clinical supervision meeting. Meeting mostly spent on administrative issues concerned with getting more people signed up for Medicaid and how to work in an interagency collaboration with multiproblem families.
11 A.M.	45-minute session for suicidal adolescent who was just released from the hospital (crisis intervention and cognitive therapy).
11:45–11:52 A.M.	Telephone call screening and assisting client with sign-up for Children's Health Insurance Program (CHIP).
11:52 A.M.	45-minute phone call to HMO. Advocates for additional sessions for suicidal adolescent client.
12:37 P.M.	Lunch. Eats sandwich while making phone calls and doing paperwork.
1:15–2:05 P.M.	50-minute session with a 24-year-old divorced mother with four small children—major depression and suicidal thinking. Develops no-harm contract and, with client's permission, contacts her 60-year-old grandmother to help with children and to watch and support the client. Invites grandmother to next session.
2:15 P.M.	45-minute session with couple experiencing marital distress (behavioral therapy, role-play, and homework assignment).
3–3:30 P.M.	Leaves clinic to drive to local high school to attend Admission, Review, and Dismissal (ARD) meeting .
3:30–4 P.M.	Attends routine ARD meeting for special education student with mental disorder (reports on student progress, advocates for student rights).

4–5 P.M.	Conducts bullying prevention group with eight first-year students.	6:20 P.M.	Has dinner with children.
		7:20 P.M.	Goes to present information about the mental health clinic services to local PTA group at school.
5–5:30 P.M.	Does paperwork for school and supports parents who are concerned about their child.	8:45 P.M.	Returns home from PTA meeting.
5:30 P.M.	Leaves school.	9 P.M.	Helps children get to bed.
5:50 P.M.	Picks up children.	10:30 P.M.	Lights out!

Managed care is a mental health system based on cost containment and predicated on the values of efficiency and effectiveness of services. Managed care organizations (MCOs) are no longer exclusive employers for private practitioners. These organizations encompass all private and public practices in mental health, substance abuse, disability services, and other human services. A recent U.S. Substance Abuse and Mental Health Association (SAMHSA) 2000 Tracking Report (Lewin Group, 2001) stated that 42 states had managed behavioral health care programs, and an additional 6 states had recently terminated their programs (Coleman et al., 2005). In addition, the number of health plans contracting with managed behavioral health care organizations rose from 58 percent in 1999 to 72 percent in 2003 (Frank & Garfield, 2007).

Although states have chosen to implement managed behavioral health care in a variety of ways, there are many similarities in how these programs are impacting services to clients (Coleman et al., 2005). Drawing on literature and our personal knowledge of the field, this chapter summarizes recent changes in social work practice created by managed behavioral health care, highlights some of the challenges encountered in the current practice of managed care, and summarizes the competencies needed to develop successful social work practices within this type of practice setting. Two case examples illustrate how clinical social work is conducted within a managed behavioral health care environment.

RECENT CHANGES IN SOCIAL WORK AND MANAGED BEHAVIORAL HEALTH CARE

The advent of managed care has brought many changes in psychotherapy and private practice.

Several distinctions that social workers have drawn in the past no longer apply. For example, there are few differences between private and public work. As private, for-profit practices receive the publicly funded Medicaid contracts and public agencies move to capture the private business contracts, the clients and services provided become similar. There is little distinction made among psychotherapy, counseling, and direct practice. In practice communities, the term *psychotherapy* no longer exclusively implies the psychodynamic understanding of long-term or intrapsychic change. Psychotherapy may refer to diverse interventions. For instance, because insurance companies are more likely to approve short-term interventions, many psychotherapy practices are made up primarily of patients requiring briefer, multimodal interventions intermingled with case management services. Consequently, social workers are using diverse evidence-based methods that have empirical support and can promote changes in a short amount of time, such as a variety of briefer therapies and crisis intervention approaches (Sulman, Savage, & Way, 2001). For detailed information and applications of effective crisis intervention approaches, see Chapter 25. Several examples of briefer therapies with empirical support are also covered throughout this desk reference.

A day at the office in managed care practice can include a variety of activities, including seeing clients in therapy sessions, working with the community on referrals, and dealing with case management issues, as well as providing some telephone counseling and consultations. In addition, social workers may negotiate with MCOs concerning treatment authorization and payment claims. It is not uncommon for practitioners to set aside one day a week for the increasing amount of paperwork and insurance claims.

In recent years, accountability for services and outcomes and the use of evidence-based practices have moved to the forefront of importance in managed behavioral health care. In fact, managed care and evidence-based practice appear to be parallel processes in a movement to develop more accountable and cost effective mental health services (Bolen & Hall, 2007). This practice trend has had an impact on the ways social workers practice and has raised concerns about whether efficiency of care is being given too much attention at the expense of quality of care. Most managed health care organizations, however, hold social workers accountable for certain quality indicators, such as receiving appropriate training, operating within the confines of that training, and achieving positive client outcomes. When these expectations are not met, social workers risk the loss of their contracts or termination of their services (Furman, 2003). Therefore, accurate and detailed documentation has become even more important. For example, with short-term treatment as the norm, many social workers in mental health care settings now treat larger caseloads of clients. With larger caseloads, it is tempting to focus less on documentation and more on direct practice. Social workers within managed behavioral health care systems, however, not only must comply in their daily practices with certain standards of care but must document all client contacts. It is also necessary to show data that document the importance of social work services so that managed care companies will not replace those services with other mental health professionals or services that are able to show more impressive client outcomes (Sulman et al., 2001). In addition, many MCOs are beginning to require that mental health services be evidence-based and that clients show improvement while receiving those services (Coleman et al., 2005).

CASE EXAMPLES

Following are two case examples from the practice of a social worker who works in a managed care environment. Both cases illustrate many of the skills required of social workers practicing in this context, including being up to date on diagnostic systems, developing treatment plans, measuring effectiveness, implementing evidence-based practice, and promoting the efficacy of social work treatment versus other types of treatment. The first example is a mother and son who were ap-proved for five treatment sessions of solution-focused brief therapy. The second example is a female client who was approved for 16 sessions of cognitive-behavioral therapy for the treatment of comorbid anxiety and depression and to avoid repeated inpatient hospitalization.

Case 1: Michael and Carrie

Michael was a 14-year-old male client who was demonstrating behavioral disturbances at home and school. He had recently started skipping classes, staying out until 2 a.m. without permission, and argued frequently with his mother, Carrie, refusing to follow her directions. This behavior had been going on for the past two months and had worsened over the previous three weeks following a disagreement over visiting his father, who lived in another state. Michael wanted to spend the summer with his father, but Carrie did not want him to go for such an extended stay because his father traveled in his job and she believed Michael would not be safe in that environment. Michael said she was "being overprotective." Carrie brought him in for counseling after he came home late one evening with a black eye and refused to tell her what happened. She said she believed he had been in a fight with a local bully and had been ashamed to come home. After an initial and brief mental health assessment, the social worker ascertained that neither Michael nor Carrie displayed symptoms of any specific mental health disorder. Neither was substance abuse involved in Michael's current behavioral disturbances. Carrie was having difficulty setting appropriate limits on his behavior. The current problems seemed to be relational in nature and a diagnosis of parent and child relationship problem was given. Both agreed to participate in solution-focused brief therapy to try to improve their relationship and address the current problems of following parenting directions and accepting limits on behavior.

During the five sessions, the clients were able to focus on one another's strengths, identify what would need to be different for their relationship to improve, and begin taking small steps toward that improvement. Carrie realized that her son always received good grades, and she felt confident about the quality of his friends. Michael realized that he was lucky to have a mother who worried about him because many of his friends did not have the same type of support. After three sessions, both clients reported improvement in their relationship and in Michael's behaviors. They created a plan that required Michael attend class every day and report his after-school and evening whereabouts to his mother. In exchange, Carrie agreed to give Michael more freedom in these areas and compliment his accomplishments at school and home on a more regular basis. After five sessions, the clients felt comfortable terminating services and stated that their plan was working successfully. The social worker also referred them to additional community resources focused on parenting skills and teen empowerment.

This is an ideal case for working in the managed behavioral health care environment because the clients required only brief treatment to alleviate some of their problems. However, not all cases are as straightforward, and many require more complex and time-consuming interventions. More complex cases may not be able to be resolved in the number of sessions provided by the managed behavioral health care organization. To help these clients, clinical social workers become involved in negotiations between the client and the managed behavioral health care organization. Figure 2.1 illustrates this type of complex process, and Case 2 provides an example of how a practitioner might work with a client and the managed behavioral health care organization on behalf of the client.

Case 2: Natasha

Natasha was a 37-year-old female client who had a long history of psychiatric inpatient hospitalizations for comorbid anxiety and depression. Her most recent hospitalization had been 3 months earlier, and she had yet to seek follow-up or outpatient treatment. After reporting increased levels of the anxiety, related physical symptoms (jaw clenching and hand wringing), and suicidal ideation that typically preceded an inpatient stay to her primary care physician, Natasha was referred to the social worker's office. After an initial assessment and review of the past files that Natasha brought to the visit with her, the social worker confirmed her diagnoses of generalized anxiety disorder and major depressive disorder. During the first session, the social worker helped Natasha create a safety plan, contracted with her for safety, and called her designated "safety person" to alert her to Natasha's current problems. After the first session, the social worker called Natasha's HMO to request approval to treat her with cognitive-behavioral therapy and anxiety techniques that had been successful for her in the past. The social worker prepared and suggested a goal-oriented, evidence-based treatment plan to address her needs and assess her progress. Although the social worker requested 20 sessions, the HMO initially suggested that 7 sessions would be the maximum approved. Given the HMO's response, the social worker advocated for the client, explaining her hospitalization history, her current symptoms, and the likelihood that she would require further hospitalization in the near future without intensive, consistent, and ongoing outpatient treatment. The social worker stressed the cost-effectiveness of social work services and his own history of success treating these mental health disorders. The HMO eventually approved Natasha for 16 sessions.

After 16 sessions, she had made adequate progress, as evidenced by improvement on two scales that had been administered on a biweekly basis. Her symptoms of depression moved from the severe range to the minimal range on the Beck Depression Inventory II, and her symptoms of anxiety moved out of the clinical range on the Beck Anxiety Inventory. However, she had not mastered independent coping skills to manage all of her symptoms. Although the HMO denied the request for an additional six sessions, the social worker continued to see Natasha on a weekly basis for a reduced out-of-pocket fee that was only slightly higher than the copayment she had been paying. After 22 weeks of treatment, Natasha had significantly reduced symptoms, no suicidal ideation, and a range of coping skills that she found effective, and she had met all the goals on her treatment plan. At a 6-month follow-up visit, Natasha was still doing well and had avoided rehospitalization.

CHALLENGES TO SOCIAL WORK PRACTICE WITH MCOs

The social work profession provides clinicians with the knowledge and skills needed to practice in managed care. The literature, for example, is replete with examples of how social workers may negotiate the difficult work situations created by MCOs, such as lower fees, fewer sessions for clients, insurmountable paperwork, repeat billings, and outright denial of treatment. Other concerns include a decrease in client self-determination regarding type and length of treatment and confidentiality issues because MCOs are not bound by the same ethical guidelines as social workers. There is guidance in the literature concerning the ethical conflicts faced by social workers working

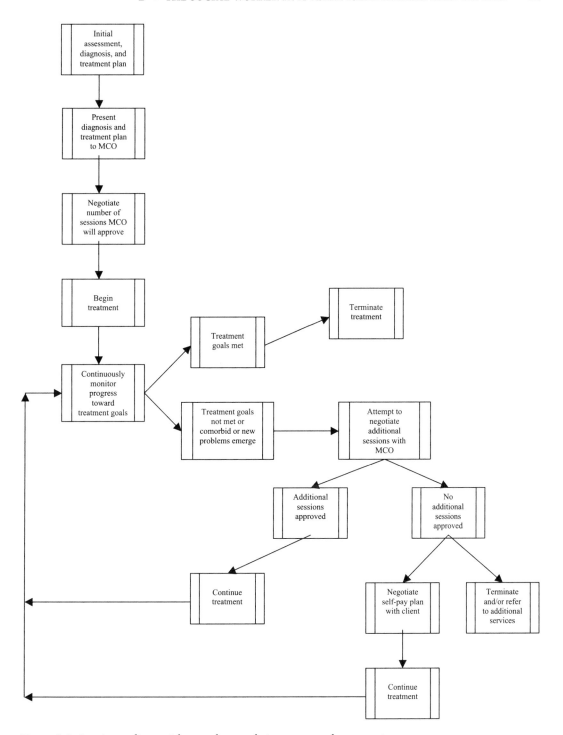

Figure 2.1 Serving a client with complex needs in a managed care environment.

for MCOs and the various responses to ethical dilemmas (e.g., Furman, 2003). For example, when social worker and client agree that it is in the best interest of the client to have additional sessions (even though the managed care company will not pay for more treatment), many social workers choose to see clients for reduced fees or on payment plans instead of terminating treatment. Others advocate directly with the MCOs to have other sessions approved.

Clinical social workers are ready to take on the challenges of work in managed care, but there are concerns about the incompatibility of the business, for-profit model of managed care and the social work helping model. There is general recognition in the literature on the philosophical differences among the for-profit, nonprofit, and charity perspectives of client services. What these differences mean in terms of clinical practice and responses from the social work profession, however, are not agreed on. Some authors focus on social action and on overturning the big business approach to human care, whereas others advocate strategic actions within the current system. Still others see some positive aspects that practices within managed care have introduced, such as more accountability.

Practitioners who work with policies and express philosophical misgivings about accepting the newer privatized systems of health care often focus on macro interventions. The National Association of Social Workers (NASW), for example, filed an antitrust lawsuit and has worked on legislation to force MCOs to offer more consumer rights and ensure quality services (e.g., a patient's bill of rights). Unfortunately, a recent Supreme Court decision (Aetna Health Inc. v. Davila, 2004) thwarted individuals' efforts to overturn some of the intrusive and ineffective features of MCO policies. The court ruled that the patient bill of rights passed by many states was all but invalidated by overarching federal policy. The decision stated that clients are only entitled to compensation for benefits that are denied in error, not for damages caused by wrongful decisions by the HMO (Kopels & Manselle, 2006). In social work practice, for example, clients can be awarded the monetary difference between the number of sessions that the HMO approved and paid for and the number actually needed, but they cannot be compensated for the harmful impact of receiving too little treatment.

TAKING ADVANTAGE OF OUR PROFESSION'S ADVANTAGES

Social work practitioners do not think often enough about their advantages as a professional group. Yet it is a professional mind-set that helps practitioners establish successful practices with MCOs. MCOs prefer generalist practitioners who are skilled in brief cognitive-behavioral and interpersonal therapies (see Chapter 31 on cognitive-behavioral therapy). It is increasingly important for social workers to carve out key roles for themselves when working in the competitive environment that is common of MCOs. Social workers need to show that they provide unique services and can be used at various stages of the treatment process, including assessment, crisis intervention, mental health treatment, posttreatment planning, and as a source of referrals (Sulman et al., 2001).

Therapy within managed behavioral health care is more strengths-oriented and can be highly structured and goal-oriented. The purpose of every session should be to achieve a tangible objective and move clients quickly to achieve overall treatment goals (Teplow, 1997). The brief, goal-oriented nature of these roles is not new to us in social work. In many respects, this type of treatment mirrors our past practices in task-centered casework and problem-solving focused interventions. (See Chapter 28 on the task-centered model and Chapter 149 on brief therapy.)

Clinical social workers have the clinical competencies and preparation to work in managed care, so they simply need to acknowledge this fact and build on their strengths. Past authors have recognized that social workers are prepared and capable of competent work in managed care settings (e.g., Chambliss, Pinto, & McGuigan, 1997). Social work training, for example, provides perspectives on serving dual clients, such as the individual and the organization. Practitioners also feel comfortable combining the roles of case manager, therapist, and other clinical functions. Social workers are prepared for work in interagency collaborations and know how to operate within a network of services. Clinical social workers easily adopt roles such as liaison and advocate, for example, in complex cases when insurance companies deny benefits. In addition, social workers have the relational skills to educate clients about MCO processes, including the right to a second opinion or to appeal a denial of benefits, and can train clients to more effectively voice their complaints to MCOs (Kopels & Manselle, 2006).

Clinical social workers are more cost-effective than many other practitioners, and in the climate of managed care, this gives social workers an advantage. The educational system for social work has focused on practice training and a master's degree can be seen as the advanced credential. At one time, the social work approach to education might have been viewed as a disadvantage, making social workers inferior to those with more years of preparation. In the present context, however, social work's educational philosophy is its strength, giving a natural advantage over professions such as psychology, which require a doctorate. Social workers can communicate with MCOs to demonstrate the cost-effectiveness of outpatient social work treatment compared to inpatient treatment, which often requires use of an expensive multidisciplinary team.

Social workers have a history of working in large bureaucracies and know what it is like to face demands from higher management, shrinking budgets, and funding cuts. They know various policies and program information. By being familiar with the documentation required by federal programs, social workers can meet the demands of paperwork and client eligibility. Although many health practitioners despise these bureaucratic work settings, social workers are somewhat prepared for work in MCOs and are ready to step into a business role.

DEVELOPING EFFECTIVE COMPETENCIES FOR SUCCESSFUL PRACTICE

To better prepare for current-day practice, clinical social workers should develop or improve the following competencies.

Be Ready for the Challenges of Competition and Leadership

Social workers, psychologists, marriage and family therapists, and other mental health professionals perform similar and overlapping jobs, leading to increased competition for clients. MCOs prefer to hire master's-level social workers and psychologists who earn similar salaries. Doctoral-level psychologists frequently are not offered more money for their services and may be hired to do the same work as social workers. Psychological testing is not routinely performed because it is not cost-effective. Social workers and other counselors know how to administer brief, rapid assessment measures and may be as competent in these practices as psychologists are (Franklin, 2001). This means that clinical social workers have to work in interprofessional environments where diverse professionals share clients and compete with one another to offer similar skills. Readiness means a willingness to assume leadership and focus on individual strengths and competencies so as to stand out as a well-equipped practitioner. Being a leader in a multidisciplinary

therapy industry requires clinical social workers to use networking skills to be well connected in the community. This means, for example, attending numerous networking lunches and dinner meetings and doing a lot of volunteer work. The social worker must also stay current on briefs and topic publications in the field, including those describing the most advanced treatments and cutting-edge policy issues. This means, for example, subscribing to publications and attending professional meetings beyond licensing requirements. The social worker must also demonstrate excellent marketing skills, including learning how to discuss one's accomplishments with individual professionals, community groups, and managed care companies. To stand out as a professional, the individual social worker needs a portfolio including, for example, a professional brochure, an online slide or a multimedia presentation, a Web page, and a one-page summary showing overall success with client groups. Social workers must also set aside time to attend meetings and give talks about cases and successful clinical approaches with clients. Last, the social worker must present him- or herself as an expert in one or more areas of practice. This means, for example, having a practice specialty that he or she feels comfortable talking about to others and writing up a few case studies that show remarkable results in that specialty.

Finding a Niche in the Practice Environment

Every state and community is deficient in some areas of service and has other areas where it is difficult to get enough practitioners to serve difficult clients. Most communities or managed care companies have this information. Some communities, for example, need more practitioners with expertise in working with small children or with clients diagnosed with both mental disorders and developmental disabilities. Clinical social workers should target those areas and develop effective practices and directly market themselves as experts in these areas.

Invest in Your Career

The old adage "It takes money to make money" must be observed. To be effective, clinicians must receive training in one or more empirically supported treatments, such as cognitive-behavioral therapy for borderline personality disorders, cognitive-behavioral or interpersonal therapies for depression, or behavioral or emotion-focused marital therapies for conflicted couples. Obtain copies of treatment manuals and recordings of empirically supported therapies. Invest in training from top therapists in the country who have developed empirically supported treatments, and pay for additional supervision of cases. Consider working with a group of colleagues to offset the expense of this training. Once trained in empirically supported treatments, clinical social workers will have several clinical competencies and new practice skills to offer clients and MCOs. Practitioners must consider this type of evidence-based training as a lifelong learning endeavor and this desk reference as a tool in their armament to stay current in the latest practices.

Be Up to Date on Nosological Systems

Be up to date on such systems as the *DSM-IV-TR* (2000) in assessment and diagnosis, and make sure you know the best practices available for different disorders. (See *DSM-IV-TR*, pp. 1–37, for information on classification and diagnosis.) Emphasis on empirically supported treatments has led to a plethora of reviews on the efficacy and effectiveness of social work and mental health practices to identify those that are considered evidence-based (e.g., Goodheart, Kazdin, & Sternberg, 2006; O'Hare, 2005). There is much debate in the field of social work surrounding the definition of evidence-based practice and how they can be taught in schools of social work and used by practitioners. The use of treatment manuals in social work, for example, is currently being debated, as well as issues of whether evidence-based practices are appropriate for diverse clients or those who have dual diagnoses. However, regardless of how practitioners feel about treatment manuals or what constitutes effective practices, there is a larger, more politically powerful force shaping clinical practices. MCOs require treatment manuals, standards of care, treatment guidelines, quality of care perspectives, and so on. For this reason, it is prudent for clinical social workers to learn the correct protocols, standards of care, and empirically supported treatments for *DSM-IV-TR* diagnosis and to follow the development of the *DSM-V*, which is projected to be released around 2012. This current reference further includes an excellent new section (Part XVI) on evidence-based practice that provides reviews of current issues for practice.

Develop Your Expertise in Writing Goal-Oriented Treatment Plans

Most social workers realize the importance of goal-oriented treatment plans. Practice in managed care has made it even more important for clinicians to be proficient at developing specific treatment plans and having measurable goals and improvement indicators. This volume includes numerous ways to measure outcomes in practice, including an excellent appendix of measurement instruments. See Roberts and Yeager (2004) for other research on outcome measures in the health and human services.

Measure Your Own Effectiveness and Present This Information to MCOs

There are three factors usually associated with determining effectiveness in managed care: (1) proof of program efficiency (few sessions, cost savings, least restrictive interventions, nonrepeat customers, etc.), (2) evidence of patient satisfaction (e.g., surveys, customer satisfaction forms), and (3) satisfactory clinical outcomes (e.g., change scores on clinical instruments, numbers of goals met, follow-ups, etc.). Measuring outcomes requires a data management and documentation system that can produce outcome-oriented reports. Springer & Franklin (2003) discuss and illustrate a set of outcome-based, quality assurance tools that are being used to improve outcomes in managed behavioral health care. These new systems are also being used to train clinicians, measure outcomes, and implement some evidence-based practices in community-based systems. Quality assurance and outcome measurement systems, for example, have been used in the United States and Europe to study the effectiveness of managed care services and to benchmark client outcomes within managed behavioral health care (Hermann, Chan, Zazzali, & Lerner, 2006).

Data from clinical outcome measures are also being used as decision tools and for marketing purposes, as well as for research or practice evaluation. For this reason, practitioners within managed care produce reports that show how effective their practices are with certain clients. For example, clinicians may show that 90 percent of their clients referred for major depressive disorder substantially improved on the Beck Depression Inventory II and were terminated within eight to ten sessions. It may also show that these clients rated the services as very good on a patient satisfaction form and that only 5 percent of them have required any other services. There are outstanding chapters in this reference on how to use rapid assessment instruments, assessment scales, and outcome measures.

Deliver Your Practice through the Use of Technologies

Some of the most necessary skills for working in managed behavioral health care are computer and technology skills, including phone counseling, multimedia, and the Internet. One of the key skills is knowing how to set up a Web page, for example. Other skills include how to converse with clients via the Internet and phone counseling. One practitioner, for example, spends her day on the phone with clients, doing assessments and making referrals to appropriate therapists. Another company requires practitioners to conduct initial substance abuse screenings over the phone or Internet. Some therapists book meeting times over the Internet and conduct therapy sessions in online chat rooms. For further practical information on technology and the latest social work Web sites, see Chapter 23.

Do Not Underestimate the Importance of the Basics

Specialized skills for managing particular diseases or disorders, brief therapy and group therapy, and population-based prevention and psychoeducational skills are needed for effective work in MCOs and evidence-based practice (Bolen & Hall, 2007; Franklin & Hopson, 2007). Groups are a cost-effective means of offering treatment. Expertise in leading therapeutic groups and conducting psychoeducational programs are basic skills that serve clinicians well in managed care. For further information on patient education, see Chapters 93 and 95 on social skills training, and see Chapter 68 on multifamily groups. Clinicians should gather and learn effective curriculums for such areas as smoking prevention, weight loss, stress management, anger management, and parent training. Prevention programs that save health care costs may be sold to MCOs as a way of decreasing the cost of mental health and health care.

FUTURE IMPLICATIONS FOR PRACTICE

Managed care is a mental health system based on cost containment and predicated on the values of efficiency and effectiveness of services. This type of system of services parallels practices within the evidence-based practice movement. The number of health plans contracting with managed behavioral health care organizations rose from 58 percent in 1999 to 72 percent in 2003 (Frank & Garfield, 2007). This chapter summarized some of the challenges encountered in the current practice of managed behavioral health care and the competencies needed to develop successful social work practices within this type of practice setting. Two case examples illustrated how clinical social work is conducted within a managed care environment. Social work practitioners have excellent practice skills that can help them excel in these settings, as well as the client advocacy skills needed to assist in the daily negotiations with MCOs over sessions and payments so clients can get the services they need. The future of clinical practice within manage care is uncertain, but every indication is that accountability and cost containment will continue within the health care arena for years to come. Social workers need to stay tuned to the evolving requirements of managed behavioral health care organizations and the ever-changing landscape of mental health/health care policies and financing within the United States.

WEB SITES

Behavioral Healthcare Resource Program at UNC School of Social Work. http://www.bhrp.sowo.unc.edu.
National Committee for Quality Assurance Report Card for Managed Behavioral Healthcare Organizations. http://www.hprc.ncqa.org/mbho.
SAMHSA National Health Information Center, Principles for Systems of Managed Care. http://www.mentalhealth.samhsa.gov/publications/allpubs/MC96-61/default.asp.

References

Aetna Health Inc. v. Davila, 124 S. Ct. 2488 (2004).
Bolen, R. M., & Hall, J. C. (2007). Managed care and evidence-based practice: The untold story. *Journal of Social Work Education, 43*(3), 463–480.
Chambliss, C., Pinto, D., & McGuigan, J. (1997). Reactions to managed care among psychologists and social workers. *Psychological Reports, 80*, 147–154.
Coleman, M., Schnapp, W., Hurwitz, D., Hedberg, S., Cabral, L., Laszlo, A., et al. (2005). Overview of publicly funded managed behavioral health care. *Administration and Policy in Mental Health, 32*, 321–340.

Frank, R. G., & Garfield, R. L. (2007). Managed behavioral health care carve-outs: Past performances and future prospects. *Annual Review of Public Health, 28*, 303–320.

Franklin, C. (2001). Coming to terms with the business of direct practice social work, *Research on Social Work Practice, 11*(2), 235–244.

Franklin, C., & Hopson, L. (2007). Facilitating the use of evidenced-based practices in community organizations. *Journal of Social Work Education, 43*(3), 377–404.

Furman, R. (2003). Frameworks for understanding value discrepancies and ethical dilemmas in managed mental health for social work in the United States. *International Social Work, 46*, 37–52.

Goodheart, C. D., Kazdin, A. E., & Sternberg, R. J. (Eds.). (2006). *Evidence-based psychotherapy: Where practice and research meet.* Washington, DC: American Psychological Association.

Hermann, R. C., Chan, J. A., Zazzali, J. L., & Lerner, D. (2006). Aligning measurement-based quality improvement with implementation of evidence-based practices. Administration and Policy in Mental Health and Mental Health Services Research. Retrieved June 15, 2006, from http://www.springerlink.com/content/k8q67j704vl85370.

Kopels, S., & Manselle, T. (2006) The Supreme Court's pre-emptive strike against patients' rights to sue their HMOs. *Social Work in Health Care, 43*, 1–14.

The Lewin Group. (2001). SAMHSA Tracking system: 2000 state profile on public sector managed behavioral health care. Falls Church, VA: Lewin Group.

O'Hare, T. (2005). *Evidence-based practices for social workers: An interdisciplinary approach.* Chicago: Lyceum Books.

Roberts, A. R., & Yeager, K. R. (2004). *Evidence-based practice manual.* New York: Oxford University Press.

Springer, D. W., & Franklin, C. (2003). Standardized assessment measures and computer assisted assessment technologies. In C. Jordan & C. Franklin (Eds.), *Clinical assessment for social workers: Quantitative and qualitative methods* (pp. 97–138). Chicago: Lyceum Press.

Sulman, J., Savage, D., & Way, S. (2001). Retooling social work practice for high volume, short stay. *Social Work in Health Care, 34*, 315–332.

Teplow, D. A. (1997). Continuing education in the managed care era. In J. M. Schuster, M. R. Lovell, & A. M. Trachta (Eds.), *Training behavioral health care professionals: Higher learning in the era of managed care* (pp. 139–167). San Francisco: Jossey-Bass.

3   The Addiction Treatment Specialist

Kenneth R. Yeager & Daryl Shorter

7:30 A.M.	Arrive at the office, check voicemail and e-mail messages. Keeping in touch with patients, their families, and other professionals is essential in facilitating good care via good communication skills. Today, there are messages from family members of a new patient and several insurance companies seeking information for utilization review.	8 A.M.	Rounds with all staff, setting the tone for the day. When addressing substance abuse and dependence, a group approach assists with building a common awareness of the progression of addictions symptoms both within and between groups of people and drugs of choice. Additionally, this approach creates a common basis for understanding the day's tasks for both staff and patients.

9 A.M.   Facilitate group therapy. Today's group focuses on how active defense structures function as barriers to the group members developing a realistic view of the progression of their illness. A common misperception is that addicted individuals are dishonest; this is not the case. In today's group, Bob is only as honest as his active defense structures permit.

10:30 A.M.   Document session. Once the session is complete, the next task is to document the session in each record. Bob's record will be updated to include the work completed examining his drinking and how his peers' feedback led to him challenging his perceptions and strengthening his level of self-diagnosis.

11 A.M.   Individual assessment, individual counseling session. One common feature to the day is meeting with new arrivals and completing initial assessments. Today is no exception; the assessment of a new patient begins by compiling information gathered in group rounds and combining this with information from the patient's spouse that has been left on voicemail.

12 noon.   Telephone consultation, communication with collateral contacts. As the new patient assessment continues, you return the telephone call made by the spouse of the new admission (Tom). Now that the appropriate release of information is complete, information regarding the case can be shared. Active listening, reassuring, and providing education are all part of the ongoing treatment process.

1 P.M.   Treatment planning. Now that the initial assessment is complete and most of the pieces of the puzzle are in order, a treatment plan for Tom is developed. This plan will serve as a roadmap outlining Tom's care, who will be assisting, and who is responsible for each step along the way.

2 P.M.   Provide medication education to the patient population. Current best practice supports the use of medications specifically to support the recovery process. The physician is responsible for providing feedback related to the medication, and the social worker is responsible for education on the appropriate use of all medication in early recovery. Additionally, it is important to provide education on the role of medication in the overall recovery process, emphasizing the significance of active involvement in all aspects of recovery.

3 P.M.   Perform utilization review processes. In working with Tom and Bob, you have been participating in a work agreement between the treatment facility and the patients' insurance company. Therefore, as the social worker you are required to provide updates on progress in and barriers to the treatment process to the insurance company and review the ongoing plan for care. This process is referred to as utilization review.

4 P.M.   Team meeting, critical communication between staff. As the day comes to a close and second shift arrives, the team meets to review the work of the day. You relate the progress made by Bob in the group and share information gathered from Tom and his wife, describing as clear a picture as possible related to this case. The team is updated on treatment plan development and updates for both Bob and Tom, and discussions related to potential length of stay and

	discharge planning begins. Clear, concise communication is critical because the average length of stay on the detoxification unit is 3.5 days.
5 P.M.	Wrap up, review messages, e-mail, and document outstanding issues. At the end of the day, there is time for a last review of messages, tasks to be completed, e-mail, and last-minute documentation to ensure seamless care of the patient. You are tired, but confident the work of the day has been completed.
5:30 P.M.	Commute home, dinner with family. While driving home, thoughts drift to reflections on

the day's activities. You think, "not exactly banker's hours," but then again, you're not a banker. You are a social worker working in addiction. This is the path you have chosen, and truth be told, you could not be happier doing any other type of work. The reward for social work practice in the field of addictions is intangible. The reward is the ability to reassure a family member, seeing the smile on an addicts' faces when they realize they can work a program of recovery and be clean and in knowing the children of the patients have a brighter future. In reality, it is not about the pay. It is about playing a role in making peoples lives a little better.

THE DAY BEGINS

The day begins early—7:30 A.M. You arrive at the unit and settle in for the day. Usually this begins by checking the messages from the night before. Messages tend to go something like this: "Mr. G. came into the emergency department last evening seeking oxycodone for pain. He was assessed and was determined to have no physical symptoms. A referral was made, but he declined treatment."

The next message is from the wife of a new admission, someone you have not met. You listen to this side of the story, take notes, and hope to be able to compare this against the history you will gather from the patient later in the day. There are also several messages form managed care entities that did not return your calls from the previous day, some requesting updates, others requesting discharge plans.

Once the voicemail messages are done, e-mail is next. There are several from a variety of committees—one for the development of new detoxification protocols, others from peers and other professionals in the community.

GROUP ROUNDS

Group rounds are designed to provide maximum interaction between patients and the treatment

team, which consists of physicians, nurses, social workers, and occupational and recreational therapists. Rounds is where the team sets the tone and plan for the day. Each case is reviewed with the entire community present, and patients are important participants in the discussion. Case review can range from just a check-in to teaching opportunities and discussion of difficult aspects of recovery. Patients also have the opportunity to track the progress others have made. New arrivals have the chance to hear from those who entered the unit 3.5 days ago and are nearing discharge. In all, group rounds serves as the platform for patient and treatment team interaction. If a patient has health insurance, medical necessity must be documented for the patient to remain in a detoxification level of care. It is important to note significant medical symptoms, like an increase in blood pressure and pulse, or the presence of acute withdrawal symptoms, such as tremors. Additionally, the social worker will need to assess and document the presence or absence of comorbid psychiatric or medical concerns. Current evidence suggests that 50 percent of persons seeking addiction treatment suffer from a concurrent psychiatric diagnosis. Approximately 35 percent will require treatment for comorbid medical disorders directly related to alcohol or drug use. Most insurers expect documentation to include the plan for care, estimated length of stay, evidence of family involvement, presence of psychosocial stressors, and the plan to address these stressors. Documentation must also include a coherent plan that addresses each of the identified barriers to recovery and the clinician's recommendations for future care.

APPROACHES TO ADDICTION TREATMENT

The Group Therapy Approach

Patients who seek addiction treatment come from diverse backgrounds. There is no way to predict what type of individual will develop alcohol, cocaine, cannabis, or sedative hypnotic dependence. Despite this diversity, there are important similarities that can be identified and capitalized on within the group process. Groups function as a social microcosm in which participants can develop a clear understanding of their personalities and how addiction has led to distortions in perceptions that now present barriers to recovery (Yalom & Leszcz, 2005).

Groups provide an arena for experimentation and learning for persons in early recovery. They also offer the opportunity for members to give and receive feedback. This interchange of information is the foundation for self-examination, reflection, and consideration of both strengths and weaknesses. More important, it is the venue in which individuals begin the process of redefining who they are, what is important to them, and how they have maintained or strayed from their personal value system.

As individuals discuss their addiction, other group members are encouraged to identify pathological defense structures. An interesting concept of addiction defense structures is that they only fool the individual using them. Other persons within the group can see right through the rationalization, minimization, and externalization. Group members can help an individual struggling with addiction to effectively identify and confront the defense structure. For example, within a group setting Bob states, "Look, I've been drinking for 20 years, and my drinking hasn't hurt anyone. There have been countless nights when I've had a few beers after work, and nobody has been hurt." This statement opens the door for other group members to ask important questions of the true impact of 20 years of drinking. For example, questions may examine the impact on the patient's family: "So, Bob, when you were having these beers after work, did you make it to your kids' school activities? Were you home in time for dinner? Did you have dinner with your family? How did you get home? Did you drive? How many beers did you have before you got behind the wheel?"

The questions provide the opportunity for self-observation. Through feedback provided by the group members, Bob is able to examine the impact of his behavior on others and how the members of the group are viewing his statement. The process of therapeutic self-examination begins to take shape for both Bob and the group members. Bob becomes aware of how others feel about his rationalizations and begins to think about his rationalizations in a different way.

This awareness can sometimes be painful, and the individual will become defensive or shut down. At this point, a skilled group leader will gently nudge Bob to think about what he heard in the group. The more Bob thinks, the more real the experience becomes. Eventually, he begins to question his own distorted thinking. This opens the door to the concept of personal responsibility (Yeager, 1999, 2002).

In any form of therapy, and especially group therapy for addictions, the concept of self-responsibility is pivotal. The assumption of self-responsibility functions as the linchpin of addiction treatment. Without it, there would be little growth and little chance for recovery. Results vary depending on an individual's level of motivation for change (Dearing, Barrick, Dermen, & Walitzer, 2005).

Once the process of change begins, it takes on a life of its own. Changing perceptions lead to changes in behavior. This process of change is apparent to members of the group, who are motivated by the changes observed in others. The process that began with one individual begins to spread through the group. Additionally, individuals in the patient's life outside of the group begin to sense the change. As change progresses, the individual takes increasing levels of risk, challenging previously held misconceptions related to self-defeating behaviors (Connors et al., 2000).

Group therapy has the potential to elicit change in a manner that otherwise may take years to accomplish. Individuals with addiction issues are able to examine their lives through a complex process of self-examination, exploration, and individual commitment to change (see Fig. 3.1). Effective group work lays the foundation for personal growth independent of formalized treatment or therapy sessions.

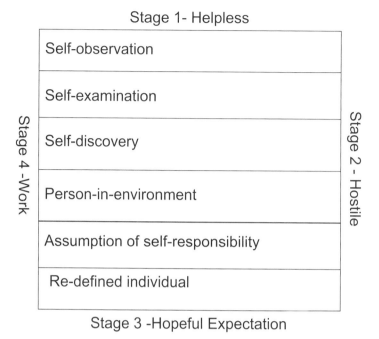

Figure 3.1 As patients progress through stages of self-examination, there is an identifiable progression from hopelessness to hostility, hopeful expectation, and finally work. Each group progression is driven by individual and peer experiences of observation, examination, discovery, assumption of self-responsibility, and redefinition.

Individual Therapy Assessment: Treatment and Discharge Planning

A comprehensive initial assessment is the key to successful addictions treatment outcomes. An accurate assessment requires time and excellent listening skills. By taking the time to hear the patient's perception of her or his illness, the therapist builds the database and establishes rapport. Good assessment skills can streamline the treatment process and assist the therapist in the task of linking the patient to the most effective level and type of treatment. It is important to notice patient cues of what will and will not work for their recovery. For example, sending an individual who has symptoms of social anxiety to Alcoholics Anonymous is not an effective treatment plan (Boardman, Catley, Grobe, Little, & Ahluwalia, 2006; Moyers & Martin, 2006).

Though treatment should be personalized, that is not to say that tried-and-true components of addictions treatment are not viable. Solution-focused approaches, motivational enhancement therapy, groups, and psychoeducational approaches all have a significant role in the process (Miller,

Benefield, & Tonigain, 1993; Miller & Mount, 2001; Miller & Rollnick, 1991). The effective clinician will work to find just the right combination for the individual. Essential components of addictions assessment include:

- Patient health, social, emotional, behavioral, and emotional history.
- Onset, history, and pattern of alcohol and drug use. Prior treatment and response to it (what worked and what did not work).
- Family history of substance use and abuse and mental and physical illness.
- Assessment of potential for self-harm or of harm by others, for example, domestic violence, sexual or physical abuse.
- Presence of prior trauma.
- Educational background, level of education accomplished, educational needs, cognitive barriers to learning.
- Spiritual history, previous coping strategies, effectiveness of coping strategies, presence or absence of social support, current perception of stressors.

- Legal history, employment history, military history.
- Diet, exercise, recreational activities.

When conducting individual addictions therapy, nothing is more important than the establishment of the therapeutic alliance (White, Gazewood, & Mounsey, 2007). Current evidence suggests the relationship between the therapist and the patient is an important factor contributing to patient retention and treatment completion (Meier, Barrowclough & Conmall, 2005; Welch, 2005). The most effective addictions therapists have certain personal characteristics that include (but are not limited to) the following.

Attentiveness. Being open as well as attentive to the conversation, expressions and unstated needs of the individual, despite the potential for distraction throughout the session. The effective therapist is able to rephrase and return information to the patient in a manner that moves the session forward by provoking thought on the part of the individual and is a key component of being available to the patient.

Role model. Most patients report they are looking for cues of how they are expected to act based on the actions of their therapist. Therefore, one of the best ways to teach new behaviors is by modeling desired behavior. Modeling actions such as openness, seriousness, acceptance, and willingness to change through interaction are all important functions of serving as a role model.

Genuineness. Demonstration of a sincere interest in the well-being of others is essential to establishing rapport and moving the patient through the therapeutic process. This includes demonstrating respect for the dignity and worth of the individual, establishing a trusting relationship with the patient, demonstrating competency in assessing the individual's situation, and providing suitable guidance in therapy.

Inquiring. The effective counselor comes from a need-to-know perspective. He or she is naturally inquisitive and interested in a variety of aspects of the individual's life. As the patient's story begins to unfold, the counselor wants to know more. Effective questions are thoughtful and are used to tie previously unlinked aspects of the patient's life together. Well-timed questions lead to examining one's life or experiences from a different perspective. Most important, asking the patient about the different aspects of his or her life keeps him or her involved in the therapeutic process and serves as an indicator of interest in the case.

Critical thinking. Critical thinking is the pathway that the effective counselor uses to provide potential links or explanations to situations, behaviors, or symptoms that the individual has been unable to identify on his or her own or is unable or unwilling to examine without some encouragement. It is not always necessary for the clinician to provide an interpretation of the issue; rather, the clinician can suggest that the individual think of how certain concepts may be tied together and how the compounded impact of several behaviors can lead to problematic situations.

Reflective thought processes. The reflective thought process is a part of attentiveness and listening skills. The reflective thought process is the ability to relate back to the patient what he or she has communicated in a manner that provides the opportunity to verify or clarify what was communicated. The effective counselor also adds statements that will lead the patient to the next logical step in the treatment process. For example, the client may state, "I always seem to make similar mistakes around certain life situations." The therapist may reflect, "It sounds to me as if you find yourself reaching the limit of your coping skills when you reach a certain point in your life. Do you recognize any patterns or common themes that come to mind?"

Summarizing. Summarizing builds on the reflective thought process. It is the art of collecting bits of knowledge within the therapy session and putting them together in a logical order. The summary statement can be used as a springboard for examination of previously less understood processes that may present as barriers to optimal functioning for the individual. Summarizing is the natural conclusion to assessment.

Communication and writing skills. In today's fast-paced world of professional practice, it is not enough for the social worker to connect with and assist the patient through treatment and into the recovery process. The effective social worker faces the task of communicating with an unprecedented number of persons involved in the care of a single patient. Communication with collateral information sources, including but not limited to families, employers, employee assistance programs, other health care professionals, social service agencies, managed care entities and the patient, is critical to the care of the individual. Notes in the medical record must be clear, concise, and to the point. The information in a medical record often provides the clues necessary to link previous care to current and future care. With consideration given to limited time to assess the patient's history, brief and concise notes that accurately paint a picture for other care providers is essential (Yeager, 1999).

DOCUMENTATION

Whether electronic or handwritten, the progress note is a legal document of sequential or chronological narratives outlining the patient's care and response to treatment interventions. It is the record of how the treatment plan was initiated and carried out. This documentation serves as a record of significant clinical events, as well as a record of individual response to therapeutic interventions. The progress note should provide the reader with not only individualized interventions but also a rationale for the intervention in the form of a description of the decision-making process.

When determining the best course of action for any intervention, it is helpful to document the treatment rationale. Additionally, the record should be reflective of the patient response to the intervention, including feedback from the patient as to its effectiveness. It is important that the progress note reflect the give-and-take process of therapeutic intervention in addictions treatment (Joint Commission on Accreditation of Healthcare Organizations, 1997).

When correctly completed, the progress note provides the record of patient response when revision of the care plan is considered. At this point, the progress note should provide all necessary information to aid in revision of the treatment plan.

TREATMENT PLANNING

The term *treatment planning* implies that the social worker will establish a plan, blueprint, or process of care that will serve as the framework to implement various strategies to improve the person's well-being. A treatment plan is a documented plan of action developed in conjunction with the patient and other professionals as necessary. The plan should be the hub of the patient's medical record. Overall, the purpose of the record is to facilitate communication, provide a method of accountability for professionals, support the practice of all professionals interacting with the patient, and improve the quality of practice (Kagle, 2002). The purpose of a treatment plan is to provide clear direction for the course of treatment and assist the individual patient in navigating the care process. To provide such direction, each treatment plan should include goals, objectives, and staff interventions.

Treatment goals are broad statements that describe desirable behavioral changes, are supportive of recovery, and are reflective of the optimal outcome for treatment efforts. Goals are reflective of both the strengths and problems identified in the assessment process and provide a logical and specific relation to the treatment being sought.

Whereas goals are reflective of the overall desired outcome, objectives contained within the treatment plan are statements of targeted, observable, and measurable changes to support recovery efforts. Treatment objectives are specific actions for the patient to take to resolve barriers to recovery. Objectives can be targeted to eliminate or significantly reduce maladaptive behaviors or to bolster strengths inherent in the individual to support recovery efforts (Joint Commission on Accreditation of Healthcare Organizations, 1997; White et al., 2007).

Treatment plans also include staff interventions. Staff interventions are clinical processes and procedures specifically designed to move the patient toward stated treatment goals and objectives. Interventions can range from medication treatments to homework assignments given to the patient. The intervention portion of the treatment should be reflective of the interdisciplinary team, and notes should signify not only the type and frequency of interventions but also the name and discipline of the staff member responsible for completion of the task. Through the use of staff interventions, the treatment plan becomes a contract between the patient and caregivers, outlining specific processes and responsibilities for care. The plan should follow a logical progression from assessment to intervention to staff reassessment and progress naturally to discharge planning (Joint Commission on Accreditation of Healthcare Organizations, 1997; White et al., 2007).

Like any other blueprint or process of care, the treatment plan is a framework susceptible to frequent revision. The revisions are reflective of changes in the individual's life and response to treatment. An effective treatment plan reflects the patient's situation at a certain point in time and is revised regularly so as to have the greatest impact on improving the patient's conditions (Ducharme, Hello, Roman, Knudsen, & Johnson, 2007; McLellan et al., 1998, 1994). The plan will require revision when objectives are met or the circumstances surrounding a patient change.

An effective addictions treatment plan should meet the following qualifications(see Fig. 3.2).

- Is the plan reasonable?
- Will the plan facilitate the desired behavioral change?

- Is the plan attainable? The last thing an individual in early recovery needs is to be set up to fail by a plan that reaches beyond his or her ability.
- Are the goals clearly stated and free from ambiguity so the patient, family members, and other staff can understand them?
- Is the plan measurable?
- Does the plan clearly outline the who, what, when, and where of the plan?
- Is the plan sustainable? That is, does the plan support the patient's need for the level and length of care being provided?

UTILIZATION REVIEW PROCESS

Utilization review describes processes related to communication with managed care entities and

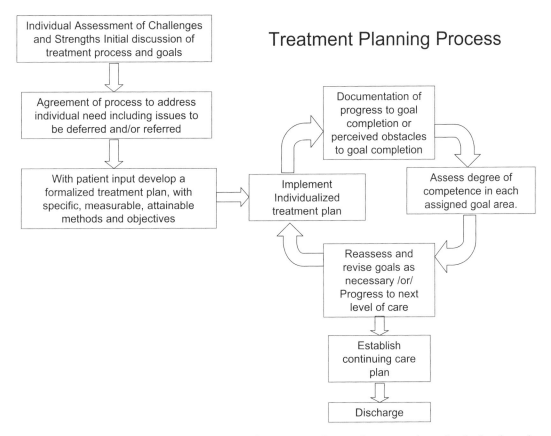

Figure 3.2 Treatment planning is a blueprint for progress designed to meet the individualized needs of the patient as he or she progresses through addiction treatment. The treatment plan begins with the assesment process. The establishment of quantifiable processes and goals are established and agreed on with input from the patient, his or her family, and all members of the treatment plan. The treatment plan is then inplemented, assessed, revised, and again implemented until agreed-on goals are completed.

other payer sources. This process is a cost-control method used by some insurers and employers to evaluate health care on the basis of appropriateness, necessity, and quality. For hospital review, it can include preadmission certification, concurrent review with discharge planning, and retrospective review. The role of social work in utilization review has expanded since the late 1980s, requiring social workers to answer questions such as: "Does the patient require hospitalization?" and "Is the admission one of medical necessity?" That is, can the individual be managed on an outpatient basis or does the individual present with evidence of acute withdrawal syndrome, requiring inpatient hospitalization to manage the severity of illness? Such discussions between payers and providers are necessary to manage both physical and financial aspects of care. The individual's care is tracked as he or she progresses through treatment. Utilization review ensures agreement of patient progress toward completion of established treatment plans and compliance to care and provides the mechanism for reimbursement of services rendered (Cheng, 2007; Sullivan, Sykora, Schneiderman, et al., 1989).

Coordination of care is the key ingredient to success in addiction treatment. Because drug use is considered a chosen behavior, society holds people responsible for recovery efforts. Addiction patients must show that they take responsibility for their recovery for a payer to agree to pay for ongoing care. The care provider is the conduit for information related to patient progress. Inpatient addiction treatment is limited to medically necessary treatment in a 24-hour staffed facility to ensure the individual is safe when with-drawing from the drug of choice. Outpatient levels of care utilization review surround discussion of challenges within the care environment, identification of risk and protective factors, development of social and coping skills, establishing social support networks, and examining and addressing relapse traps and triggers.

Most cases are either dollar- or time-limited, for example, number of sessions per year. The amount of treatment covered by any payer varies greatly. The responsibility of the social worker is to establish a plan for care that functions within the parameters established by the payer and the treatment facility. Consideration of all risk and protective factors combined with individual progress toward the stated treatment plan becomes the basis for decision making for the social worker and the patient. The social worker will use the utilization review process to report on and justify levels of care to establish agreed-on need for ongoing resources to be provided by the payer.

EMERGING MEDICAL MANAGEMENT OPTIONS IN ALCOHOLISM

Supporting treatment requires safe medical detoxification combined with addressing potential relapse pathways. Current literature suggests that there are three major pathways associated with relapse processes that should be considered once abstinence has been established. The first pathway is exposure to the drug (Monti, Rohsenow, & Hutchison, 2000). The second pathway is exposure to conditioning, such as certain people, places, and things (McBride, Le, & Noronha, 2002; Yeager, 2002). The third pathway is exposure to nonspecific stress (Koob, 2000).

From a medical standpoint, the treatment of an alcohol-dependent patient begins with assessment of the withdrawal syndrome and its severity. It is clinically helpful to measure objective signs of withdrawal (i.e., nausea, vomiting, tremor, sweating, hallucinations) by using an assessment tool such as the Clinical Institute Withdrawal Assessment for Alcohol Scale Revised (CIWA-Ar) (Sullivan et al., 1989). The CIWA-Ar provides a score for the severity of alcohol withdrawal, ranging from mild to moderate to severe. Assigning patients to one of these categories based on symptom score helps clinicians determine the need for medication and monitor the course of the alcohol withdrawal syndrome. Subsequently, safe and appropriate amounts of medication can be given to the patient to ease discomfort as well as prevent symptoms of complicated withdrawal, such as delirium tremens or seizures. Generally, benzodiazepines are the medications used in the treatment of the acute alcohol withdrawal syndrome.

Once the patient is safely through detoxification, a discussion of pharmacological therapy for the treatment of alcohol dependence can occur. Generally, there are two types of medications that may be helpful; if taken regularly, they help the patient avoid consuming alcohol and help decrease cravings for alcohol. It is important to note, however, that use of pharmacotherapy for alcohol dependence should occur within the context of psychotherapeutic or behavioral interventions (i.e., Alcoholics Anonymous twelve-step support groups, cognitive-behavioral therapy, relapse prevention training).

Aversive Agents

Disulfiram (trade name Antabuse) works by inhibiting the breakdown of one of alcohol's metabolites, acetaldehyde. The resulting build-up of acetaldehyde causes the development of an unpleasant reaction characterized by nausea, vomiting, headache, facial flushing, sweating, shortness of breath, vertigo, and blurred vision. The reaction is almost immediate, occurring after the ingestion of as little as one drink, and may last up to 30 minutes (Sadock & Sadock, 2004).

There is some evidence regarding the effectiveness of disulfiram in the treatment of alcohol dependence. Disulfiram appears to reduce the number of drinking episodes in alcohol-dependent subjects and may act as a psychological deterrent to drinking. However, there is minimal evidence to suggest that use of disulfiram increases long-term abstinence from alcohol. Additionally, patients struggle with adherence to disulfiram treatment, raising questions about its practicality (Suh, Pettinati, Kampman, & O'Brien, 2006). There are limited data on disulfiram implants or the impact of health care practitioner–supervised administration of disulfiram to patients.

Ultimately, when evaluating patients for the use of disulfiram as a deterrent to alcohol abuse, it is important to consider which persons are likely to be compliant with its use. It may be helpful to propose supervised administration and observed ingestion of the medication, if possible. Because of disulfiram's potential for hepatic damage, it is important to monitor for liver toxicity. Contraindications for disulfiram use include ischemic heart disease and pregnancy. Drug interactions include anticoagulants, phenytoin, and isoniazid. Interactions with alcohol in food and over-the-counter products should be discussed in detail with the patient prior to administration of the medication.

Pharmacotherapy for Alcohol Dependence

Early evidence suggested that acamprosate (trade name Campral) increases abstinence and reduces drinking episodes. This medication works by inhibiting glutamate overactivity. Glutamate is an excitatory neurotransmitter in the central nervous system, and acamprosate reduces its release from the presynaptic nerve terminal. Also, acamprosate causes a reduction in the number of N-methyl-D-aspartate receptors, which are believed to be sensitive to the effects of alcohol postsynaptically. There is some evidence to suggest that these combined effects lead to decreases in alcohol craving and potentially decreases in relapse. The strongest evidence for this phenomenon exists in studies of recently detoxified alcoholics.

Although acamprosate demonstrated early evidence of efficacy in the treatment of alcohol dependence, its clinical utility has been called into question more recently. The Combined Pharmacotherapies and Behavioral Interventions (COMBINE) study, a large, multicenter, randomized controlled trial, found that acamprosate was no different from placebo in reducing risk of heavy drinking (Anton et al., 2006). Thus, there is a need for further study into the effectiveness of acamprosate in the treatment of alcohol use disorders so that its role in treatment can be better elucidated.

There is good evidence that naltrexone (trade name ReVia) can be used to reduce heavy drinking, episodes of drinking, and potential for relapse in short-term trials (lasting less than 12 weeks). Naltrexone is an opioid receptor antagonist, reducing or eliminating the subjective high associated with consumption of alcohol or opioids by blocking the opioid receptor. Furthermore, it is thought that naltrexone helps curb cravings associated with alcohol withdrawal (Sadock & Sadock, 2004). Some evidence suggests that naltrexone can contribute to greater levels of abstinence and reduced craving. Supporting the evidence of naltrexone's efficacy, the COMBINE study found that the drug increased total number of days abstinent from alcohol and decreased risk of heavy drinking (Anton et al., 2006).

The optimal duration of prescribed use of naltrexone remains unknown at this time. Although the drug has a favorable side effect profile, it should be noted that nausea and central nervous system symptoms (i.e., headache, low energy, insomnia, anxiety) may occur. Additionally, it is important to be aware that naltrexone can cause reversible elevations in serum hepatic enzyme concentrations at higher doses. Thus, naltrexone carries an FDA black box warning against use of the medication at dosages above the recommended 50 mg/day. Also, before prescribing naltrexone, it is important to screen for opiate abuse and use caution in those receiving opiate analgesia, because administration of this medicine in these populations could precipitate opioid withdrawal (Anton & Swift, 2003).

THE ROLE OF THE SOCIAL WORKER IN THE ADDICTION TREATMENT TEAM

The social worker is a critical member of the treatment team whose role is to interface with patients and their families, health care professionals (i.e., physicians and nursing staff), and payer sources (see Fig. 3.3).

Working with Patients

- Build therapeutic alliance by establishing rapport through empathetic listening.
- Help patients address ambivalence regarding substance use by discussing motivating factors for change.
- Identify triggers for relapse.
- Provide support in developing behaviors that promote abstinence from substances and/or harm reduction. Discuss behaviors related to reducing risk of HIV/AIDS and hepatitis transmission (i.e., safer sex practices and needle exchange).

Working with Families

- Serve as liaison between patients, families/support networks, and the treatment team.
- Provide information regarding the treatment plan to concerned family members and friends.
- Obtain collateral information to confirm psychiatric, medical, and substance use history given by the patient.

Working with Health Care Professionals

- Assess patients for presence of substance use disorders and co-occurring psychiatric disorders. (Knowledge of *DSM-IV-TR* criteria for substance abuse and dependence as well as mood, anxiety, psychotic, and personality disorders is critical.)
- Assist in the creation of the biopsychosocial formulation, focusing on assessment of risk factors that predispose patients to the development of mental illness and substance use disorders as well as those that contribute to the current episode.
- Help tailor biopsychosocial treatment plans to address both static and dynamic risk factors. If one particular factor (e.g., homelessness) seems to perpetuate the substance use

disorder by exposing the patient to undue stress, then it should be addressed in the treatment plan (e.g., linkage with housing services).
- Speak/meet with outpatient treatment providers (case managers, assertive community treatment team members).
- Interface with community agencies and resources to ensure safe return to community or rehabilitation facilities (i.e., discharge planning).

Working with Payer Sources

- Provide information to Medicare/Medicaid and other payer sources regarding treatment and plan of care.
- Verify patient's benefits status and advocate on their behalf for appropriate receipt of services.

SUMMARY

Social work in the field of addiction treatment is one that offers both a challenging and a rewarding career. Social workers in addiction treatment are required to master a complex skill set, including critical thinking and analytical skills, assessment and treatment planning skills, and individual, family, and group work skills. Most rewarding are the relationships established with patients and co-workers. Social workers practicing within the addiction field have unique opportunities to contribute to individual success, team approaches to individual care, and the interaction among managed care, utilization review, and financial groups responsible for managing shrinking resources.

The challenges are great; every day new evidence emerges related to the treatment of addiction. Efforts on the part of the social worker to remain current with evidence-based approaches are commendable. There are additional challenges of stigma, social and economic barriers to care, social injustice, and poverty to be addressed. On the other hand, rewards of seeing individuals progress into recovery, families reunited, employment saved, and legal issues resolved provide immeasurable rewards. The input of all team members, working in concert with the patient will provide the most efficacious outcome. Social work has a long tradition in working with the addicted and

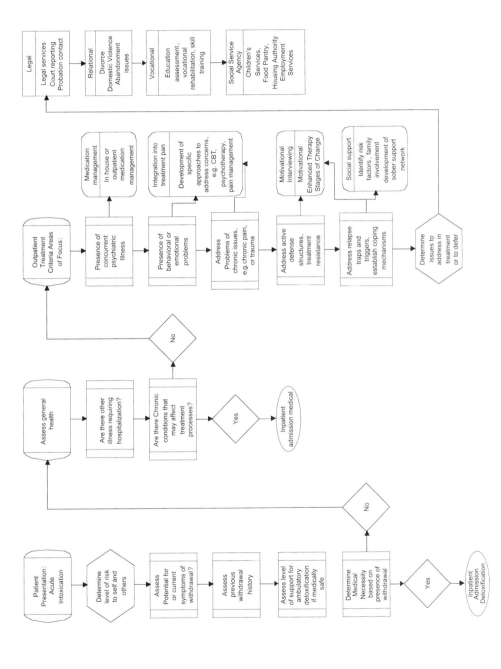

Figure 3.3 Algorithm of social worker responsibilities and activities associated with the addiction treatment process.

their families. It is our hope to provide not only current information but inspiration to lead new and seasoned social workers to experience the rewards of addiction social work.

WEB SITES

Advancing Effective Alcohol and Drug Policy, Prevention, and Treatment. http://www .jointogether.org.

Erowid: Documenting the complex relationships between humans and psychoactives. http:// www.erowid.org. (This site is included for the information provided related to the various drug groups. The authors do not endorse this Web page's promotion of drug use.)

National Institute on Alcohol Abuse and Alcoholism. http://www.niaaa.nih.gov.

National Institute on Drug Abuse. http://www .nida.nih.gov.

U.S. Substance Abuse and Mental Health Services Administration. http://www.samsha.nih.gov.

References

Anton, R. F., & Swift, R. (2003). Current pharmacotherapies of alcoholism: a U.S. perspective. *The American Journal on Addictions, 12*(Suppl 1), S53–S68.

Anton, R.F., O'Malley, S.S., Ciraulo, D.A., Cisler, R. A., Couper, D., Donovan, D.M., et al., COMBINE Study Research Group. (2006). Combined pharmacotherapies and behavioral interventions for alcohol dependence: The COMBINE study: A randomized controlled trial. *Journal of the American Medical Association, 295*(17), 2003–2017.

Boardman, T., Catley, D., Grobe, J. E., Little, T. D., & Ahluwalia, J. S. (2006). Using motivational interviewing with smokers: Do therapist behaviors relate to engagement and therapeutic alliance? *Journal of Substance Abuse Treatment, 31*(4), 329–339.

Cheng, M. (2007). New approaches for creating the therapeutic alliance: Solution-focused interviewing, motivational interviewing, and the medication interest model. *Psychiatric Clinics of North America, 30*(2), 157–166.

Connors, G., DiClemente, C., Dermen, K., Kadden, R., Carroll, K., & Frone, M. (2000). Predicting the therapeutic alliance in alcoholism treatment. *Journal of Studies on Alcohol, 61*(1), 139–149.

Dearing, R. L., Barrick, C., Dermen, K. H., & Walitzer, K. S. (2005). Indicators of client engagement. *Psychology of Addictive Behaviors, 19*(1), 71–78.

Ducharme, L. J., Hello, H. L., Roman, P. M., Knudsen, H. K., & Johnson, J. A. (2007). Service delivery in substance abuse treatment: Reexamining "comprehensive" care. *Journal of Behavioral Health Services & Research, 34*(2), 121–136.

Joint Comission on Accreditation of Healthcare Organizations. (1997). *A Practical Guide to Clinical Documentation in Behavioral Health Care.* Oakbrook Terrace, IL: JCAHO, pp. 19–23.

Kagle, J. D. (2002). Record keeping. In A. R. Roberts & G. J. Greene (Eds.), *Social workers' desk reference* (pp, 27–34). New York: Oxford University Press.

Koob, G. (2000). Animal models of craving for ethanol. *Addiction, 95*(Suppl 2), S73–S81.

McBride, W., Le, A., & Noronha, A. (2002). Central nervous system mechanisms in alcohol relapse. *Alcoholism: Clinical & Experimental Research, 26*(2), 280–286.

McLellan, A. T., Alterman A. I., Metzger, D. S., Grissom G. R., Woody G. E., Luborsky L., et al. (1994). Similarity of outcome predictors across opiate, cocaine and alcohol treatments: Role to treatment services. *Journal of Consuling and Clinical Psychology, 62*, 1141–1158.

McLellan, A. T., Hagan, T. A., Levine, M., Gould, F., Meyers, K., Bengivengo, M., et al. (1998). Supplemental social services improve outcomes in public addiction treatment. *Addiction, 93*(10), 1489–1499.

Meier, P. S., Barrowclough, C., & Conmall, M.C. (2005). The role of the therapeutic alliance in the treatment of substance misuse: a critical review of the literature. *Addiction, 100*(3), 304–316.

Miller, W. R., Benefield, R., & Tonigan, J. (1993). Enhancing motivation for change in problem drinking: A controlled comparison of two therapist styles. *Journal of Consulting and Clinical Psychology, 61*(3), 455–461.

Miller, W. R., & Mount, K. (2001). A small study of training in motivational interviewing: Does one workshop change clinician and client behavior? *Behavioural and Cognitive Psychotherapy, 29*, 457–471.

Miller, W. R., & Rollnick, S. (1991). *Motivational interviewing: Preparing people to change addictive behavior.* New York: Guilford Press.

Monti, P., Rohsenow, D., & Hutchison, K. (2000). Toward bridging the gap between biological, psychobiological and psychosocial models of alcohol craving. *Addiction, 95*(Suppl 2), S229–S236.

Moyers, T., & Martin, T. (2006). Therapist influence on client language during motivational interviewing sessions. *Journal of Substance Abuse Treatment, 30*(3), 245–251.

Sadock, B., & Sadock, V. (2004). *Kaplan and Sadock's comprehensive textbook of psychiatry,* 8th ed. Philadelphia: Lippincott Williams & Wilkins.

Suh, J.J., Pettinati, H.M., Kampman, K.M., & O'Brien, C.P. (2006). The status of disulfiram: A half of a century later. *Journal of Clinical Psychopharmacology, 26*(3), 290–302.

Sullivan, J.T., Sykora, K., Schneiderman, J., et al. (1989). Assessment of alcohol withdrawal: The revised clinical institute withdrawal assessment for alcohol scale (CIWA-Ar). *British Journal of Addiction, 84,* 1353–1357.

Welch, M. (2005). Pivotal moments in the therapeutic relationship. *International Journal of Mental Health Nursing, 14*(3), 161–165.

White, L. L., Gazewood, J. D., & Mounsey, A. L. (2007). Teaching students behavior change skills: Description and assessment of a new motivational interviewing curriculum. *Medical Teacher, 29*(4), 142–159.

Yalom, I., & Leszcz, M. (2005) *The theory and practice of group psychotherapy.* Cambridge, MA: Perseus Books, pp. 117–141.

Yeager, K. R. (1999). *Common characteristics of effective substance dependence counselors: A qualitative study.* Dissertation Abstracts.

Yeager, K. R. (2002). Crisis intervention with mentally ill chemical abusers: Application of brief solution-focused therapy and strengths perspective. *Brief Treatment Crisis Intervention, 2,* 197–216.

4 The Social Worker in an Outpatient Child and Adolescent Unit

Lisa Rapp-Paglicci

SCHEDULE OF A TYPICAL DAY

9:30 A.M.	Finish progress notes from day before and make calls.	2:30 P.M.	Facilitate children's group of sexual abuse victims.
10 A.M.	Individual session with 12-year-old with PTSD.	3:30 P.M.	Write progress notes, call a caseworker, make referrals.
11 A.M.	New client intake—8-year-old and family, possible ADHD.	4 P.M.	Individual and family session with depressed 16-year-old.
12:30 P.M.	Lunch at desk while writing notes and making calls.	5 P.M.	Provide clinical supervision to a new social worker.
1 P.M.	Leave for court.	5:30 P.M.	Facilitate parents' group—learning effective parenting skills.
1:30 P.M.	Testify in court regarding a child's disclosure of sexual abuse.		
2:15 P.M.	Return to office.	7 P.M.	Leave for the day—go to the gym (self-care is essential).

CASE EXAMPLES

The following two case studies are examples of common cases that may present at an outpatient mental health agency for children and adolescents. The first case is a young male with a mild adjustment disorder, and the second is a more serious case of a young female with major depression. The second case also illustrates a typical treatment plan.

Case 1

Jeremy is a 10-year-old white male who presents at the mental health outpatient agency with his mother. Jeremy has been displaying disruptive behavior for the past 2 months at home and school. He refuses to follow directions, speaks rudely to his mother, often fails to complete his homework, and has been receiving low grades in school. His parents have been going through a bitter divorce, and Jeremy spends his time split equally between both parents.

The social worker meets with Jeremy's parents alone at the second session, during which she focuses on the boy's needs and the development of a joint behavior modification plan. The plan includes consistent family rules regarding his behavior, attitude, and school work. The plan also builds on protective and resilience factors present in Jeremy's case. Additionally, it incorporates rules for the parents regarding talking about their spouse in a negative manner (in front of Jeremy) and spending quality time with Jeremy. During the week, the social worker identifies a group for divorced children at Jeremy's school and advocates for his admittance to the weekly group.

During the next family session, Jeremy expresses his frustration with living with two parents, and all decide that he will stay with his mother Monday through Friday and father during the weekends. Jeremy reports that he has earned enough points on his behavior plan for a special movie night with his dad. He has attended two group sessions at school.

In the last family session, the family reported that the disruptive behaviors have ceased. All are satisfied with the living arrangements and negative comments between the parents (in front of Jeremy) have stopped. On last report from Jeremy's teacher, his grades have returned to their normal range. Jeremy will continue with the group at school and has made a new friend there. His mom has decided to attend a group for divorced adults at a nearby community center so that she can better handle the divorce.

Case 2

Tasha is a 16-year-old Latina female who presents with depressed affect. She has lost weight, feels hopeless, and frequently isolates herself in her room. These symptoms have persisted for the past 6 months. Tasha has stopped socializing with friends and has little interest in school or outside activities. She denies suicidal ideation. Her depression began soon after her father lost his job, forcing the family to move to another neighborhood and school. Her boyfriend broke up with her around the same time. There is a history of depression in the family, including a maternal grandmother and an aunt who committed suicide after years of depression. Tasha's parents are very worried about their daughter.

After a thorough assessment of the family, the social worker asks Tasha to complete the Children's Depression Inventory (CDI) to measure her depression. The brief, 27-item inventory is useful for assessing depression in children 6–17 years of age. Tasha scores in the moderate range. She and her family agree to a referral to a child psychiatrist to assess the need for medication, and the family agrees to get her a physical from the family doctor to rule out any other physical problems.

At the next appointment, Tasha's parents state the doctor found her in good health and the psychiatrist has prescribed antidepressants. In addition, Tasha has agreed to work with the social worker using cognitive-behavioral therapy. This intervention was chosen based on the evidence of its effectiveness for depression with adolescents. During this session and the next two, Tasha learns to identify, challenge, and change her negative thoughts and irrational beliefs.

Over the next two sessions, Tasha learns communication and problem-solving skills. Her parents meet with the practitioner separately to understand depression and its symptoms in adolescents. Her father reports that he has secured a new job.

In the next session, Tasha and the practitioner begin talking about termination, and she completes the CDI again. She scores in the mild range. She has begun to renew her interest in school and friends.

During the last session, all the skills Tasha has learned are summarized and her parents join the session to hear about these skills, her last score on the CDI, and to discuss the call that they will receive from the practitioner next month to check on her progress. Her medication is also discussed. Termination is completed. A summary of her treatment plan follows.

Goals	Objectives	Interventions
1. Tasha's depression will be reduced	1. Identify and change negative thoughts and irrational beliefs within 6 weeks 2. Increase communication skills within 6 weeks 3. Increase problem-solving skills within 6 weeks	1. Use cognitive-behavioral therapy 2. Refer to psychiatrist for medication evaluation 3. Teach communication and problem-solving skills
2. Tasha and her family will learn about depression and medication	1. Increase understanding of depression (symptoms, prognosis, etc.) within 6 weeks	1. Provide Tasha and her family with info about depression 2. Provide Tasha and her family with Web sites for reading pertinent info 3. Psychiatrist will provide info regarding Tasha's medications

BRIEF HISTORY AND INTRODUCTION

Mental health outpatient services for children and youth originated in the late 1890s in response to growing concerns about juvenile delinquency and the adult criminal justice system. At the time, judges and reformers felt that adult prisons were inappropriate and unhelpful to juveniles. Most viewed juvenile delinquency and children's emotional problems as a result of problematic parenting and community problems like poverty, immigration, and overcrowding as opposed to a deficit inherent to the child (Pumariega, Winters, & Huffine, 2003). Juvenile courts were established along with child mental health clinics, and in the 1920s these spread and flourished across the United States. Unfortunately, a report from the Joint Commission on Children's Mental Health in 1969 documented the evolution of fragmented and inadequate services for children and noted the increased use of hospitals and residential programs that were miles away from the child's family and community (Winters & Pumariega, 2006). This led to a radical reform in service delivery and supported the principle of integrated service delivery known as "systems of care." The systems of care model focuses on keeping children in the least restrictive environment, close to their home and family, while providing services that work together for the most comprehensive service delivery possible (Silva, Bath, Beer, Minami, & Engel, 2007). Currently, the systems of care model

is used unevenly across the United States. Though this is the standard protocol now in many communities, other community services' remain unsynchronized and fragmented.

Today, child and adolescent outpatient mental health agencies struggle to survive in a competitive social services environment and provide imperative services for children and their families. They contend with managed care constraints; lack of funding; frequent staff turnover; staff quality issues; rapid information growth in the areas of assessment, treatment, and medications; and changes in technology. This, along with trying to serve the close to one in ten children and adolescents who present with mental health disorders, poses quite a challenge (Walsh & Holton, in press).

CURRENT PRACTICE DEMANDS

Clinical Skills

Currently, practitioners serve large caseloads of children and adolescents who evince multifarious problems. They are expected to stay up to date on an expansive number of mental health conditions as well as their assessment, diagnosis, treatment, medications, and referral sources. In addition, practitioners also need to have knowledge of developmental stages of the life span and the clinical skills to work with individuals, families, and groups for both youth and adults. They need to be able to work with crises and in genuinely stressful environments. Practitioners also need to know how to use instruments or rapid assessment scales and how to evaluate their practice. Rapid assessment instruments are quick and easy-to-use standardized measures that can facilitate work with clients. Many of these scales can be located in *Measures for Clinical Practice and Research*, volumes 1 and 2 (Fischer & Corcoran, 2007). These volumes provide numerous scales that cover a wide range of problems and mental health disorders for children, adolescents, adults, and families.

In addition, practitioners are required to have a good understanding of the legal system (juvenile and adult) and have the skills to testify as a mandated reporter or expert witness. To keep their clinical skills up to date, practitioners must go to many trainings as well as stay abreast of the research available.

Other Skills

Besides clinical skills, practitioners need to have other skills to assist within the organization. At present, practitioners need to assist with funding for their agency. Medicaid pays for only some consumers and pays very little; the same goes for private insurance. Therefore, agencies are required to secure their own funding through grants and donors. In doing so, practitioners need to think of their agency as the client and advocate for it. They need to use leadership skills to manage resources and staff, advocate for their agency politically, and try to impact legislation. In addition, practitioners must stay current in the latest technological advances for gleaning and reporting information.

RECENT CHANGES TO SOCIAL WORK PRACTICES

Over the past few years, social work practice in the area of children's outpatient mental health has rapidly evolved. Evidence-based treatment has become more common and has been driven by funders who demand its use. This change in treatment has, like a domino effect, changed assessment protocols, treatment plans, and documentation. For example, assessment must include standardized measures before and after treatment, so that clear evidence of improvement is present. Treatment plans must include clear, objective, measur-

able goals within a timeframe and documentation regarding the achievement of those goals must be clear and specific.

The focus on evidence-based treatment is certainly a positive outcome for clients, because it suggests that the likelihood of receiving ineffective treatment has decreased. However, a negative outcome from this change is the persistent focus on brief treatment, often despite the seriousness of clients' presenting problems. Many funders allow only six sessions with adults and about eight to ten with children. This poses a problem for many clients who present with complex, chronic problems.

Another change that should be noted is the demand for those with a master's in social work (MSW) as leaders and supervisors of agencies. There is a need for MSWs to go into positions of administration and management of agencies, yet many have received no formal training in organizational leadership, management skills, or fiscal responsibilities. However, this is an important change to note. Practitioners rarely stay practitioners during their careers. Schools of social work should look to helping practitioners further develop and hone their clinical skills, so that they can develop into leaders and directors of agencies.

CHALLENGES TO PRACTICING SOCIAL WORK

There are many challenges to practicing social work in the child and adolescent mental health outpatient setting. Like most settings, pay is insufficient and caseloads are high, resulting in many practitioners becoming burned out and leaving the profession.

In addition, many agencies that are referral sources for the mental health outpatient agency have long waiting lists. This makes the referral process difficult at best, and often results in fragmented services for youth and families, which were discussed at the beginning of this chapter. Without a fluid system to assist youth and their families, complex problems are not resolved, and clients return as fast as they are terminated.

The hectic pace in which new treatments and developments in clinical practice occur also poses difficulties in staying current. Unless practitioners spend their off-time reading articles and books and attending trainings, it is close to impossible to stay well versed in modern practice.

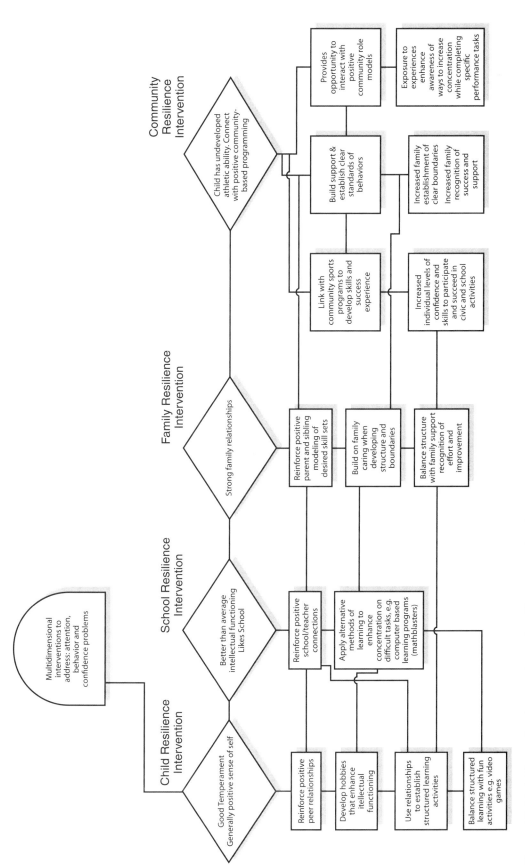

Figure 4.1 Multidimensional protective and resilience care planning.

HOW SOCIAL WORKERS ARE UNIQUELY PREPARED TO MEET THE CHALLENGES

Social workers, unlike other professionals, are uniquely capable of meeting the challenges in this setting because of their specialized training and unique perspective. Social work students are trained to view the world through a person-in-environment lens. In this new landscape, where agencies must be advocated for and practitioners must think like businesspeople, a wide lens is essential. It provides an understanding of the political, legal, and fiscal environment in which agencies function. In short, social workers think and see in systems, and this orientation and philosophy are essential.

This unique view, combined with the clinical skills social workers are taught, makes for a powerful combination. Clinical skills are needed for a variety of practice situations and for the wide variety of clients seen at the outpatient setting. Today, social workers combine protective factors with traditional intervention factors to establish, foster, and grow foundational coping skills that promote resilience. Many clinical programs are establishing working interactions with collateral agencies to expand the agencies role beyond that of traditional treatment approaches combining preventive, and resilience strategies. Preventive interventions are designed to intervene before the emergence of a mental illness or to prevent relapse, disability, or the consequences of emerging mental illness. Multidimensional interventions supportive of resilience enhance the individual capacity to cope with, manage, and transform experiences of adversity into positive life experiences (see Fig. 4.1). Working with family members, community organizations, schools, medical professionals, and the child's innate coping skills and strengths, social workers can optimize environmental factors to support clinical work.

Clinical skills are also needed for working with teams of other professionals, networking with multiple agencies, and for legislative, political, and fiscal advocacy for the agency. In addition, the grant writing skills, which social workers learn, are essential for obtaining grants and funding.

DEVELOPING EFFECTIVE COMPETENCIES FOR SUCCESSFUL PRACTICE: HOW TO BETTER PREPARE FOR CURRENT-DAY PRACTICE IN THIS ARENA

Practitioners today are expected to have more knowledge and more skills than ever before. Most schools of social work appear to be doing an adequate job of preparing students for the profession, however, there are areas which can be improved. Documentation and treatment plans require clear, concise writing with measurable goals. Therefore, schools of social work need to better prepare their students for these tasks by focusing on their writing skills and ability to formulate objective goals for clients. Schools of social work should also focus on defining and understanding what evidence-based practice is and how to use evidence-supported treatment in clinical work. There are many definitions of evidence-based practice. No matter which one is used, the main objective is for students to be able to follow the process to find and implement evidence supported treatment in their agencies. Likewise, students need to be more comfortable with finding standardized measures or rapid assessment instruments for use in their practice and to assist with the evaluation of their practice.

Schools of social work also need to prepare students to be effective business leaders who are able to market and advocate for their agency, understand the fiscal functioning of the agency, and train and manage agency staff. These skills, in addition to leadership skills are essential for the new era of child and adolescent outpatient mental health.

WEB SITES

The American Academy of Pediatrics offers the latest information about health and mental health for infants, children, and adolescents. http://www.aap.org.

The Campbell Collaboration provides systematic review of interventions for a variety of mental health disorders. http://www.campbellcollaboration.org.

The National Institutes of Mental Health offers the latest statistics, treatment, medications, and research regarding mental health in adolescents. http://www.nimh.nih.gov/health/topics/child-and-adolescent-mental-health/index.shtml.

SAMHSA's National Mental Health Information Center provides the latest information on mental health programs, treatment, prevention, and research regarding mental health issues. http: //mentalhealth.samhsa.gov.

The Yale University Child Study Center provides cross-cultural aspects of mental health and training in international child mental health. http://info.med.yale.edu/chldstdy/icmh.

References

Fischer, J., & Corcoran, K. (2007). *Measures for clinical practice and research,* vols. 1 and 2. New York: Oxford University Press.

Pumariega, A. J., Winters, N. C., & Huffine, C. (2003). The evolution of systems of care for children's mental health: Forty years of community child and adolescent psychiatry. *Community Mental Health Journal, 39*(5), 399–425.

Silva, R., Bath, E., Beer, D., Minami, H., & Engel, L.

(2007). Administrative issues in child psychiatry. *Psychiatric Quarterly, 78,* 199–210.

Walsh, J., & Holton, V. (in press). Case management. In W. Rowe & L. Rapp-Paglicci (Eds.), *Comprehensive handbook of social work and social welfare,* vol. 3. New York: Wiley.

Winters, N. C., & Pumariega, A. J. (2006). Practice parameter on child and adolescent mental health care in community systems of care. *Journal of American Academy of Child and Adolescent Psychiatry, 46*(2), 284–299.

5   The Social Worker in a School Setting

Michael S. Kelly

School social work is a subspecialty within social work. School social workers have a 100-year history of delivering services to students and acting as a link between home, community, and school. In high schools, social workers are often active at multiple levels of the school client system. This chapter uses several case examples to show how school social workers can be effective in addressing issues that impact the social and emotional health of individual students and the larger school community.

Following is a typical work day for a school social worker (Kathy) working in a large suburban high school located outside of a Midwestern city.

7:30 A.M.	Kathy arrives at school, looks over paperwork and her schedule for the day, responds to e-mails from teachers and parents, and gathers materials for the social-emotional learning (SEL) program she's doing with the health teacher during fifth and sixth periods.	8 A.M.	Attends an annual review for a student receiving social work services through their individualized education plan (IEP) as part of the school's special education program. At this meeting, it is agreed that social work services will continue for the student into the next

calendar year to address the student's behavior problems.

8:45 A.M.   (second period of the school day) Attends a pupil personnel services (PPS) meeting that is discussing students with behavioral/emotional concerns as well as larger-scale school issues as part of the school's positive behavior support program (known as PBS). Along with other team members (school psychologist, school nurse, police liaison officer, dean, assistant principals), she makes suggestions for potential interventions with students and offers ideas about next steps for the PPS team's antibullying initiative.

10:15 A.M.   (fourth period) Plans to eat an early lunch at her desk but shares her time with a student who has come in to talk about boyfriend problems. The boyfriend is a member of a gang and is refusing to return to school after having dropped out last year. Kathy gives her client a card with her number and the number of the boyfriend's former guidance counselor and advises the student to encourage him to consider returning. She reminds her client that she knows her boyfriend well and would also be willing to meet with both of them together if he's willing. They discuss the importance of his avoiding any more confrontations with rival gang members, and the two make a safety plan in the event that the client is feeling unsafe in social situations with her boyfriend. Another student waits outside her office to talk as well. When she welcomes him in after sending the other student back to lunch, he tells her that he has been using the antianxiety workbook Kathy recommended, and he is finding

that it's working. The two make an appointment for him to come in next week at lunch to continue working on his anxiety problems.

11 A.M.   (fifth and sixth periods) Working with one of the teachers in the health department, Kathy teaches a lesson from the Lions Quest "Skills for Action" curriculum on personal responsibility and healthy decision making. The class begins brainstorming ideas for the service learning component of the curriculum, with an eye toward implementing some of their service projects over the upcoming holiday break.

12:30 P.M.   (seventh period) Kathy has a 30-minute regular weekly session with a student who receives social work services as part of his IEP. The student has high-functioning autism, and in the session Kathy returns to helping him make plans to begin applying for jobs in the community over the holiday break. They write a script together as the student says he's worried that his job interviews won't go well unless the managers interviewing him really understand him. After sending the student back to class, Kathy checks her voicemail and returns a call to a parent who wants to know if there's still room in the Families and Schools Together (FAST) group starting that night. She calls back and assures her that there's still room and confirms the time and meeting room for the group.

1:15 P.M.   (eighth period) As Kathy is working on her Medicaid billing paperwork for the clients she sees at school, she is paged to the assistant principal's office for an emergency session with the assistant principal and two students. The two students were shouting at each other in the hall, and a teacher broke up the argument before it got physical. Kathy knows both students well, because both of them are in her caseload. The assistant principal reminds the two students that they are in danger of getting suspended if their argument continues, and then turns the meeting over to Kathy, who tries to mediate the dispute. The students shake hands at the end of the meeting and head back to class. Kathy and the assistant principal agree that the dispute seems to be resolved for now, but they also agree to monitor the situation closely for future flare-ups.

2 P.M.   (ninth period) This is the weekly time for a classroom group Kathy leads with the teacher in the educable mentally handicapped classroom. The lesson today is based on a modified version of the "Learning for Life" curriculum, which emphasizes vocational training, personal safety, and character education in weekly modules. The teacher ends the session with an impromptu presentation of a birthday card from the class to Kathy (her birthday is that weekend).

2:45 P.M.   School day ends. Back in her office, Kathy makes some calls to therapists and probation officers who work with students on her caseload, updating them on the students' progress. She also returns a call to a community agency interested in doing a substance abuse prevention assembly in conjunction with the school and the town's police department. She gives the agency program coordinator more information on the school's needs, and the two agree to meet with the police lieutenant

sometime next week. Before she can gather her things to head home, a teacher knocks on her door and asks for consultation on a student that has grown withdrawn and depressed.

3:45 P.M.   Before heading home for some family time of her own, Kathy stops by the high school's after-school mentoring program and checks in with the mentoring coordinator to make sure that two students she recently referred to the program have continued to attend. She meets the students and their mentors and gives the mentors her cards, and asks them to contact her if they have any concerns or questions.

4:45 P.M.   Arrives home, visits with her own children (ages 14 and 16), and together they make dinner. Kathy's spouse arrives a little later and the four eat dinner together, trading stories about the day.

6 P.M.   Returns to school to prepare the room for that night's FAST parent group session. She and her coleader for the FAST program (a former parent in the school and a past graduate of the FAST program) review the night's agenda and plan for upcoming sessions.

6:30 P.M.   FAST group begins, with a good turnout of 20 parents.

8:30 P.M.   FAST group ends, with several parent participants staying afterward to talk to Kathy and the parent coleader about their concerns for their children.

9:30 P.M.   Comes home, does dishes with 16-year-old and spouse, and reviews the day.

10:30 P.M.   Lights out, another busy day tomorrow!

INTRODUCTION

Thanks in part to the increased emphasis on providing specialized educational services to students with special needs (highlighted by passage of the landmark legislation Public Law 94-142 [Education of All Handicapped Children Act, 1975]), today there are school social workers in most states providing direct services to students, parents, and teachers.

As the stakes have risen in the past 20 years, with increased concern over such issues as school violence and academic performance for all students through the tougher accountability measures under the No Child Left Behind Act (NCLB) of 2001, school-based intervention research is showing that schools are safer and perform better when the social/emotional climate is enhanced for all students, parents, and staff, not just the neediest students (Astor, Benbenishty, & Marachi, 2003; Durlak & Weissberg, 2007; Erickson, Mattaini, & McGuire, 2004).

Describing what most high school social workers do is complicated by the fragmented and context-driven descriptions of what actually constitutes a school social worker. In a recent survey of state education associations, only 20 states required a master's of social work degree for certification as a school social worker, only 11 require a certification exam, and 19 require no specific degree to do school social work activities in a school (Altschuler, 2006). Most school social workers nationwide seem to be fashioning their work role out of their own skill sets, their specific practice contexts, and whatever local and state laws empower them to do.

Moreover, unlike many other social work positions, school social workers are often supervised by an administrator who is not a social worker (Kelly, 2008). School social workers have to be mindful of personnel expectations and norms more akin to teacher training than social worker training. Additionally, in many states students are identified as needing social work services through the special education IEPs, so a lot of school social workers' workload is already defined for them: they are expected to be the front-line practitioners with some of the most complicated family and adolescent mental health issues that a high school community has.

School social work, as practiced in a high school setting, requires the following skill sets.

1. Strong communication skills, reflected in the ability to speak in public settings and staff meetings as well as in more intimate clinical settings.
2. Knowledge of normal adolescent development and strength-based approaches to help students with their problems.
3. Pragmatic and problem-focused approaches to designing interventions in the school, because many problems in the high school environment are multifaceted and may require the application of interventions at multiple levels of the client system, for example, individual, classroom, and family.
4. Solid grounding in the best recent evidence-based practice (EBP).
5. Administrative, writing, and organizational skills to lead meetings, coordinate SEL programs, and write grants to increase school-based services for students and families (Franklin, Harris, & Allen-Meares, 2006; Frey & Dupper, 2005; Kelly, 2008).

SCHOOL SOCIAL WORK CHALLENGES: NCLB, RTI, AND SPECIALIZATION

There are at least three major policy challenges that school social workers in high schools have to navigate.

NCLB

The NCLB legislation was the farthest-reaching piece of federal education legislation arguably since the special educations laws in the 1970s. It established numerous benchmarks for student performance and created accountability mechanisms for schools that were not meeting average yearly progress targets. What is often less understood is how much NCLB focused attention on educators (including school social workers) becoming "highly qualified" to do their jobs in schools (Constable & Alvarez, 2006), with the law specifying that educators needed additional training to demonstrate their competence and proficiency. Additionally, NCLB mentions the need for educators to use scientific, research-based interventions over 100 times (Raines, 2008), clearly making good EBP skills a priority for any school social workers wanting to survive and thrive. Although it is likely that the reauthorization debate in Congress for NCLB in 2008 will modify some of the more controversial aspects of the legislation, the notion that schools and educators should be focused on using research-based interventions to meet measurable goals is unlikely to change.

Response to Intervention (RTI)

In the middle of the upheavals wrought by NCLB, the Individuals with Disabilities Education Act was amended in 2004, and a new provision was added to allow districts to implement their own response to intervention (RTI) program. RTI is intended to be an early intervention approach to help remove barriers to learning for students before they are referred for traditional special education assessment and services. Whereas different RTI programs differ based on individual school district needs, it is clear that the RTI movement has some key general principles, ones that focus on targeting early academic, counseling, and behavioral supports to students based on data-driven instruction, local assessments, and EBPs. Again, having a solid grounding in EBP will be crucial in helping school social workers contribute fully to RTI initiatives under way in their school community.

Specialization

School social work is not yet a fully specialized subspecialty of social work in all areas. Only 31 U.S. states have a certification process for working in a school, and many states don't require master's-level training to work in a school (Altshuler, 2006). Despite the diversity in school social work certification, clearly the national trend will be to move school social workers to more specialized training and degrees, particularly given the mandates of NCLB. Indiana has already implemented a postmaster's statewide certification program that requires school social workers to show through a portfolio assessment that they can implement EBPs in their work (Constable & Alvarez, 2006).

TODAY'S SCHOOL SOCIAL WORK PRACTICE CONTEXT IN HIGH SCHOOLS

One of the persistent issues for school social workers is role confusion. There is still no universal consensus on what school social workers should spend most of their time doing. Some practitioners work predominantly with the neediest in their school, providing direct clinical services to them, much as they would in an outpatient setting. Others act as consultants to the school, helping the whole school implement prevention-based programming to prevent school violence and increase SEL. In some states, school social workers don't focus on either macro- or micro-level interventions but devote their time to implementing specific school-based programs, like antitruancy and gang violence prevention programs in partnership with local community agencies. Still others have characterized their school social work practice in terms of acting as behavioral consultants to schools, helping their schools design effective behavioral interventions through an RTI or PBS process for at-risk students. Though a range of intervention strategies are being evaluated by national researchers, the tendency to view school social work through a clinical lens appears to be growing in the professional literature that documents actual practice (Staudt, Cherry, & Watson, 2005).

In high schools, school social workers are often active at multiple levels of the school client system. Many serve a caseload of students in regular and special education, providing counseling and support via individual and small group treatment. In addition, school social workers design and implement SEL programs that reach a larger number of students, often implementing these programs in health classes, in advisory periods, or by partnering with interested teachers. After-school and evening programming are also a feature of school social worker practice in high schools, as the initial "day in the life" sample schedule demonstrates (Durlak & Weissberg, 2007). School social workers organize and lead after-school programming for parents as well, such as the FAST group. Finally, many school social workers also serve at an administrative or quasi-administrative level, leading special education meetings, PBS teams, and RTI team meetings. The following case example shows how I have tried to create a practice context that is open to parents and responsive to a variety of mental health, academic, and behavioral problems that students have.

Open House Intake

It's a mild September evening, and I am doing an intake at my school lunch table. It is parents night at the high school, and after the obligatory welcome in the school auditorium from the administration, the parents of our students fan out to follow their teenagers' nine-period schedule. They look as harried and anxious navigating the massive building as their children did their first year at the school. Some parents have wisely enlisted their kids as tour guides, and the fierce sullenness that marks so many teenagers is everywhere.

Open house intake is a yearly tradition for me. After going to the first three periods of their teens' classes, the parents of our high school break for refreshments during their child's scheduled lunch time. I set up a table to greet parents and tell them about social work services available at the high school.

Inevitably, new clients emerge. A soft-spoken mother approaches and asks me to see her son: he was just arrested for shoplifting and she thinks having "somebody to talk with" might help. She gives me permission to talk to the boy's probation officer, and I make a note to call a meeting with the student, his probation officer, and his mother. Clad in matching Chicago Bulls jackets, a Mexican American mother and father fret about their 15-year-old daughter's lack of motivation this year at school and wonder what they can do to reach her. We schedule a family session to explore the problem further.

A stocky Italian American father that I worked with two years ago nervously circles the tables where I'm sitting and then stammers out a bombshell: he and his wife are finally separating after many years of fighting about her drinking. The father tells me he worries about his daughter's reaction to the news, and asks if he can use a session in my office to break to news to his daughter. I say yes, and to my surprise, he calls his daughter over. She has been talking on the other side of the lunchroom with two girlfriends and bounces cheerfully over to us. "Jenny, this is the school social worker, Mr. Kelly. He helped your brother Joe a few years ago, and I want us to talk with him later this week." She briefly smiles at me and then stares blankly at her dad and says with the practiced exasperation all 15-year-olds have for their parents, "Duh, Dad, everybody knows Mr. Kelly. My friend Katie and her mom go to see him. Meet later? Cool, whatever. I gotta go—see you, Mr. Kelly."

Jenny's dad turns to me and says, "Thanks for being here." I am a school social worker doing family-based work in a high school, and I love it.

WEB SITES

Families and Schools Together (FAST) project. http://www.wcer.wisc.edu/FAST/index.htm.
National Registry of Evidence-Based Programs and Practices (NREPP), a service of SAMHSA (Substance Abuse and Mental Health Services Administration) (includes an easy-to-use database describing a variety of interventions that school social workers can use that are considered evidence-based). http://www.nrepp.samhsa .gov/index.htm.
"Safe and Sound," an evidence-based guide to SEL programs developed in 2003 by researchers at the Collaborative for Academic, Social, and Emotional Learning at the University of Illinois–Chicago. http://www.casel.org.
School Social Work Association of America (SSWAA), the national advocacy and education organization for school social workers. http://www.sswaa.org.

References

Altschuler, S. (2006). Professional requirements for school social work and other school mental health professions. in C. Franklin, M. Harris, & P. Allen-Meares (Eds.), *School services sourcebook.* New York: Oxford University Press.

Astor, R., Benbenishty, R., & Marachi, R. (2003). Violence in schools. In P. Allen-Meares (Ed.), *Social work wervices in schools.* New York: Allyn & Bacon.

Constable, R., & Alvarez, M. (2006, Summer). Specialization in school social work: The Indiana example. *School Social Work Journal,* 116–132.

Durlak, J. A., & Weissberg, R. P. (2007). The impact of afterschool programs that promote personal social skills. Retrieved from Collaborative for Academic, Social, and Emotional Learning (CASEL) Web site: http://www.casel.org/downloads/ASP-Full.pdf.

Erickson, C. L., Mattaini, M., & McGuire, M. (2004). Constructing nonviolent cultures in schools: The state of the science. *Children & Schools, 26*(2), 102–117.

Franklin, C., Harris, M. B., & Allen-Meares, P. (Eds.). (2006). *The school services sourcebook: A guide for social workers, counselors, and mental health professionals.* Oxford: Oxford University Press.

Frey, A., & Dupper, D. (2005). Towards a 21st century model of school social work practice. *Children & Schools, 27*(1), 33–44.

Kelly, M. S. (2008). *The demands and domains of school social work practice: A guide to working effectively with students, families, and schools.* New York: Oxford University Press.

Raines, J. (2008). *Evidence-based practice in school-based mental health: A primer for school social workers, psychologists, and counselors.* New York: Oxford University Press.

Staudt, M., Cherry, D. J., & Watson, M. (2005). Practice guidelines for school social workers: A modified replication of a prototype. *Children & Schools, 27*(2), 71–81.

The Social Worker as Family Counselor in a Nonprofit Community-Based Agency

6

Jack Nowicki & LeShawn Arbuckle

Following is a typical day in the life of a clinical social worker employed as a family counselor by a nonprofit youth and family crisis intervention program that receives a combination of state early intervention funds, county funds, and fees for service.

12 noon.	Arrive at the office early. Eat lunch while reviewing daily schedule of clients, agency memos, e-mails, phone messages, and other correspondence.		3–3:30 P.M.	Clinical supervision with graduate student intern—review cases for correct form completion for state funding requirements.
12:20 P.M.	Collect today's client records for review before counseling sessions and begin completing billing slips. Phone call from the emergency shelter about a new youth who needs to be seen today.		3:30–4 P.M.	Prepare for evening clients and phone calls.
12:30 P.M.	Call to client about problem with their son's school and brainstorm some ways parent can talk to the school authorities about youth's truancy. Write a brief note in the record.		4–4:50 P.M.	Meet with runaway youth from shelter. His parents have been contacted and they say, "keep him." The 14-year-old says he has had ongoing difficulties at school and with his stepfather and mother; fighting with stepfather who "kicked him out" because he found out about youth failing and skipping school. I explain the family counseling program, and he says he'll meet with his parents if we can get them to come in, but he will not return home. Youth wants to live with an aunt who also lives in his neighborhood. I call parents again to ask them to come in to meet with us, and leave message on their machine.
12:45 P.M.	Look over case records to choose one to present at staff meeting, finish lunch, and call shelter to set a time to see the youth.			
1–3 P.M.	Staff meeting with family counselors, graduate student interns, and supervisors. Agenda: agency announcements, supervisor directives about documentation, progress report on meeting funding requirements, and case presentations for discussion and planning.		4:50–5 P.M.	Process youth session with interns, asking their ideas about what's next for youth.

5–6:15 P.M.   Crisis session with new Hispanic client and daughter who have extreme conflict with each other over daughter's boyfriend (see Case Illustration 1), culminating in the family crisis. Reframe the crisis as a normal part of adolescence and the mother's parenting struggle to protect the daughter. Identify their coping strategies, resources, and develop an initial action plan. Ask when they think we should meet again, and they say next week. Schedule next meeting and record on initial action plan and give them a copy.

6:15–6:50 P.M.   Session three with family: 34-year-old mother two kids; 17-year-old son not in school and 16-year-old daughter referred by the court after arrest for possession of drugs. Give the family a customer satisfaction survey (usually given at the third meeting). Family reports that things are going better—daughter is maintaining requirements of her release from court. We list things daughter and mom are doing to cope with the court situation, list what is better at home, and brainstorm ways girl can spend time away from friends who bring her trouble. Son agrees to take her with him to activities at the local community center, and mother agrees to make time to go out with her. I wonder if there is a way girl can share progress with her probation officer, and we role-play her talking to him. Document progress and new tasks on the action review plan and set another appointment for next week.

7 P.M.   Next client family not here yet. Return to office to make some brief notes on last two clients.

7:10 P.M.   Call the 7 P.M. client family; they forgot the meeting. Catch up by asking about what's better from last week; note that they're not arguing as much. Ask how they were able to do better: They have all been more respectful of each other since our last meeting. Ask when they want to set a time for a meeting and they think next week, but will call the center later.

7:45 P.M.   Supervise graduate students after their second family session with a family. I use solution-oriented supervision skills to process their session. They begin with the things they think they did wrong, and I redirect them to start with what went right, what skills they used effectively, and what they think the clients would say they did well. From this foundation, we move into what they could have done more of or differently, and the interns list some ideas to try out next time and some things to follow up on in their next session.

8 P.M.   Last sessions ending; remaining counselors and interns finishing up with their clients, scheduling next appointments, and doing some quick processing with each other before making any last-minute notes in their case records. (It is a best practice in crisis centers to ensure counselors have an opportunity to briefly process their sessions with peers so they do not take it home with them.)

8:30 P.M.   Make two phone calls before locking up for the night.

Social workers in private practice have a different set of practice demands than those in a nonprofit agency setting. There are differences in procedures for recordkeeping, responsibilities for providing diagnoses (billing insurance companies for payment), and working as part of a team (having a built-in peer support group). Not-withstanding, this chapter describes the work of social workers as family counselors in a community-based youth and family services agency.

In the past few years, family counselors in community-based agency settings have had to adjust to a number of new challenges, including the following:

- Decreased funding with greater need and more time-consuming documentation requirements.
- Working with more severe presenting problems in youth and parents in communities where the mental health services systems have had to curtail services due to funding cuts.
- Hiring qualified social workers who speak the many languages of an increasingly diverse population.
- Working with family systems that are more diverse than the nuclear family of old; including blended families, alternative lifestyle families, and kinship families.
- Fitting family counseling into a family's increasingly full schedules (with parents wanting the youth to "get fixed").
- Incorporating outcome measures and accountability tools in practice that require continual evaluation of practices used, such as solution-focused, brief family counseling, and other approaches that may be viewed by funders as promising interventions but not as having the empirical studies required for probably efficacious or evidence-based ratings.

Advancement in family counseling theory has documented the paradigm shift from first- to second-order cybernetics (Becvar & Becvar, 2006, p. 64), the move toward briefer and briefer counseling, and the proliferation of approaches to "talk therapy" (Duncan, Miller, & Sparks, 2004, p. 7; Janzen, Harris, Jordan, & Franklin, 2006, p. 9). Along with these changes, practitioners have access to computers that can do increasingly sophisticated searches for meta-analyses of what works in therapy. These empirical methods combined with an increased acceptance of qualitative research to expand the evidence base and begin to show evidence of the applicability of brief family therapies that are grounded in social construction theories and strengths-based approaches (Franklin, 1998, p. 58; Kim, 2008).

As Saleebey (2006) suggests, the concepts of focusing on strengths in social work goes all the way back to the Settlement House movement 100 years ago. Social workers have traditionally been client-centered and have a history of advocating for clients within the very societal structures that marginalize them (Saleebey, 2006, p. 21). Social workers see that generally the person is not the problem: it is the relationship the person has with others (including people and institutions) that constructs the problem. Over years of ongoing study and reflection (Nowicki & Bewsey, 1994), our family counselors settled on a client-centered, family systems approach to working with youth and families in crisis. The agency we work in specifically makes use of solution-focused brief therapy and has developed its own solution-focused crisis intervention approach. Solution-focused brief therapy is a strengths-based approach that evolved out of family therapy approaches and social construction theory. It was originally developed by deShazer (1988), Berg (1994), and colleagues at the Brief Family Therapy Center in Milwaukee. deShazer and Berg, both social work practitioners, were interested in researching what works in therapy to help clients change.

The solution-focused approach has been popular in family therapy circles for more than 25 years and is widely applied in community settings with youth and families. Over the past decade, researchers have also begin to study its effectiveness using experimental and quasi-experimental designs and meta-analysis. The research to date demonstrates that solution-focused brief therapy is a promising approach that deserves more research on its effectiveness with youth and families (Franklin & Jordan, 1999; Gingerich & Eissengart, 2000; Kelly, Kim, & Franklin, 2008; Kim, 2008).

CASE ILLUSTRATION

Given that solution-focused crisis intervention is highly language-based, we present a verbatim transcript of several parts of a crisis session, with the attendant physical descriptions. Our crisis session at 5 P.M. began with Ms. Sanchez and her daughter, Isela (not their real names), coming into the office after the mother had completed the intake forms and Isela had not. After a concise explanation of our brief, crisis-oriented services and the basic parameters of confidentiality, the counselor begins by asking, "Has there been any change for the better since you called?" to find out about presession change. With these folks, the response was puzzled looks, so the counselor continued, "What would the two of you like to accomplish today in this meeting?" (looking from mother to daughter and back again). The counselor is simultaneously conducting a crisis assessment (Slaikeu, 1990) and focusing on what the family wants to achieve in the session. They are based on the family's responses to initial questions related to the precipitating event.

Ms. Sanchez: I want Isela to quit seeing her black boyfriend, period! [The counselor looks over at Isela for a contribution, but she says nothing, looking away.]

Counselor: So [looking back at mom], you want Isela to stop seeing her boyfriend . . . is that part of the crisis that brought you here? [Mom goes on to describe the arguing and fighting she has been in with Isela for the last few weeks, and how it has affected her work and her health. The counselor reflects,] You've been fighting for two weeks? That must be awful. And you say it has impacted your work and health. How have you coped with those difficulties?

Ms. Sanchez: Not very well. I'm about to get in trouble at work for taking so much time dealing with Isela, and I get headaches every time we fight. I told Isela that I am not going to take her calls or talk to her when I'm at work. And I'm going to my doctor to get some better headache medications. [The counselor nods and continues, looks over at Isela for a contribution, but she says nothing, looking away.]

Counselor: So, you are taking some steps to take care of yourself . . . that's good. How else are you coping with the boyfriend situation? [This line of questioning continues, and the mother reports having friends she can confide in, while the counselor observes the youth's behavior closely to find an opening for a question that will bring her into the conversation in a way that works for her. The mom is coping fairly well with the crisis, and no one mentions a "push over the chair" episode. After assessing coping strategies, the counselor tries the same tack with the youth.] So, how are you coping with the conflicts with your mom?

Isela: Fine. Just fine . . ." [There is a slight pause, and then she adds tentatively] I didn't know her headaches came back. But it's not my fault she can't get with the present. Just because my boyfriend is black is no reason not to let me see him!

Counselor: So you wish your mom would accept your seeing an African American boy. And, how are *you* coping with the whole thing?

Isela: I text my friends. [Now she looks up and directly at the counselor.]

Counselor: So, you text your friends. Does that help?

Isela: Yes. They understand me and they agree with me about my mom.

Counselor: [Pauses, glances at the mom, and says to the youth,] Good. It's always nice to have friends. Mom uses her friends and you do, too. [To the mom the counselor asks,] Are there ever times when you and Isela are doing better?

Ms. Sanchez: She does great in school. We used to go shopping together before this all started. Basically we get along well . . . until I found out about this boy. . . she needs to get rid of him.

Isela: [Frowns and adds] No mama. I am not dropping him. You don't even know him. Stop living in the past.

Counselor: So Isela, you're not wanting to "drop" the boy, and you think your mom is living in the past? I wonder . . . suppose you went to sleep tonight, and while you were asleep, a miracle happened, and yet you didn't know that because you were asleep. And then, in the morning, you wake up. The miracle has happened. What is the first thing that would tell you a miracle occurred?

Isela: [Tilts her head, smiles slightly, and says slowly]A miracle . . . I guess it would be that my mom would accept me like I am.

Counselor: That's interesting. The miracle would be that your mom would accept you like you are. And how would that impact you, exactly?

Isela: Well, she wouldn't be so interested in my boyfriend would she? She would be interested in me and what I think.

Ms. Sanchez: [looks over at Isela] If you care so much about him, why don't you bring him around?

Isela: Because you'd dis him. I'm afraid of how you'd treat him.

Ms. Sanchez: Have I ever disrespected anyone you brought over? [The counselor is looking back and forth from mom to daughter, following their conversation with each other and hoping that it works into some sort of plan. They go on talking to each other for about 5 minutes and finally the counselor breaks in.]

Counselor: Wow! You all are really great at talking when you listen to each other. I can tell you are really close. I notice that Isela nods her head in agreement a lot during your talking. Ms. Sanchez, I can tell you listen to your daughter for the most part and seem to consider what she thinks. [The counselor continues to give the two compliments that he has noticed in their conversation and completes the compliments with a question to both of them.] What would tell you, Isela, that your mom is more accepting of your choice of boyfriends? Ms. Sanchez, what would tell you that you could trust your daughter to make a good decision related to the boyfriend thing? [The women look at each other, seemingly awaiting each other's reply.]

Ms. Sanchez: I am worried that Isela is going to have major problems if she ends up with a black.

Isela: Mom! I'm not picking him for a husband! He's just a cool guy that I want to get to know better. And I should be able to pick who I want to see.

Ms. Sanchez: I'm not sure. I don't want you dating him until I know more about him, okay? [The daughter again looks away. The counselor waits a few seconds.]

Counselor: On a scale from one to ten, with one being the pits and ten being you're totally okay with the whole thing, where would you put yourself right this minute?

Ms. Sanchez: Right now I'm at a five, I think.

Isela: Where were you when you came in here tonight?

Ms. Sanchez: Probably a two.

Counselor: So, you've already made some progress on the scale. How's that happened, do you think?

Ms. Sanchez: Well, when I got here I was totally against Isela and that boy, but now it doesn't seem like she is that involved with him as I thought. And I do listen to her.

Counselor: And Isela, where would you be on the same scale from being the pits to ten being totally okay with the whole thing?

Isela: With him I'm at a ten. With mom I'm probably at a seven.

Counselor: So, you're at a seven with the conflict with your mom. What's that about?

Isela: Well . . . I think it bothers her more than me.

Ms. Sanchez: She's right . . . of course it doesn't bother her . . .

Counselor: That makes sense doesn't it? Now, what do you each suppose is the smallest thing you could do more of or differently to move your score up the scale just a half a point or so toward being okay with the whole thing? What could you do or say or whatever?"

Ms. Sanchez reflects that more information about this boy would probably move her up the scale, and Isela adds that it might move her up the scale to be part of giving that information to mom. In the end, they agree that Isela will bring the boy by her house after school to meet the mom. The crisis assessment is wrapped into the solution-focused protocol, including exploration of the precipitating event and its impact on the family; possible lethality issues; the family's personal, material, and social resources; and current coping strategies.

DISCUSSION

The ideas brought out during the assessment and the family's coping strategies with the crisis (Slaikeu, 1990)make up the basic plan from the first session. The counselor is also concerned about the fact (never brought up in the session) that the presenting crisis involved some physical altercation and the possibility of safety issues. The counselor also asked scaling questions about the possibility of further physical fighting and added a task to the daughter's plan for avoiding physical fighting. The task was based on an exploration of how she walks away from altercations at school (a coping skill she already has that she will use at home). At the end of the crisis session the family's action plan looks like the following.

Goal: Ms. Sanchez and Isela are getting along better related to Isela's boyfriend.
Task 1: Isela is bringing the boyfriend over after school to meet mom.
Task 2: Isela is walking away when she thinks she might physically attack mom.
Task 3: Isela is continuing to text her friends for support when angry.
Task 4: Ms. Sanchez is checking out the boyfriend when he visits.
Task 5: Ms. Sanchez is continuing to take care of herself by going to the doctor and not talking to Isela while at work.

This plan is quite specific, whereas many times a crisis plan is constructed with only a few coping tasks after the first meeting. Constructing an action plan depends on the flow of the session, the motivation of the clients to take on several tasks, and the phase of crisis impacting the family. The protocol for crisis sessions with youth and families is included in Figure 6.1.

- Explaining: confidentiality, client's rights, informed consent, agency requirements & procedures (scheduling, research/outcome data collection, etc.).
- Framing: definition of counseling (systemic, strengths-based, crisis-oriented); expertise of the family in finding competencies and solutions; and domino effect; as well as effects of crisis (disequilibrium, disorganization, physical symptoms, and vulnerability... plus opportunity for positive change).
- Assessing the Crisis: precipitating event (including associated behaviors, cognitions, and feelings); lethality (clues for danger to self or others); phase of the crisis (restoring equilibrium or resolving the crisis which indicate different foci / goals) (Slaikeu, 1990).
- Identifying Immediate Coping Strategies: re-establishing effective coping (see Glossary) is necessary before crisis resolution (Roberts, 2000), therefore it is high priority with families in crisis.
- Identifying Strengths & Resources: identifying positive steps family and members have already taken to cope with the crisis, re-establish equilibrium, get back to "normal", use their personal, material, and social resources in the current situation.
- Exploring Exceptions: asking about times when the problem doesn't happen, is not apparent, or is less bothersome, connecting these times to activities and behaviors on the part of family members, and wonder how these times could be increased.
- Asking the "Miracle Question": asking the "miracle question" or asking for video descriptions of a future after the crisis (or without the problem) and expanding this description to include all representational systems (auditory, visual, kinesthetic).
- Creating Positive Futures: exploring with the family what they want to achieve in the counseling meetings; their desired outcomes. These outcomes can be mutual, or individual, based on the level of conflict and agreement between family members.
- Scaling: using self-anchored scales to begin to construct a linear map of the path and progress of family members from the "crisis" to their "outcomes" (Franklin, Corcoran, et. al., 1997) (This visual tool can be used therapeutically in many ways).
- Complimenting: counselors take every opportunity to reflect back to the family the strengths, resources, positive values, positive reframes, and compliments that they notice during the meeting. Sometimes counselors take a break before working with the family to construct an Action Plan so they can consider all the information collected, touch base with a colleague, and/or "plan their strengths-based assessment" of and recommendations about the family situation. Primarily the counselor is using this time to frame the crisis as a situation of possibility and opportunity before taking on the task of constructing the plan.
- Developing an Action Plan: reviewing with the family all that has been discussed (coping strategies, the miracle question, their desired outcomes, their scales) and brainstorming some tasks that will begin to move them in the direction of their desired outcomes. For example, from the scaling conversation, a family member might pick as a task the smallest thing they can do to move up their scale by a half a point. A family member might choose to do one thing more often, differently, or less often. Two family members may choose a "contract" such as "Mom is allowing Johnny to watch TV after he shows her his completed homework". Some tasks may be stated in the format of "an experiment to see what happens".
- Setting A Follow-up Meeting: the last thing that the counselor and family decide is if and when to meet to review the plan and discuss what went well and what they want to explore further or change. This decision is left up to the family because it is assumed they are the expert in determining how soon and how often to meet.

Figure 6.1 Protocol for crisis session with family.

Action planning is a collaborative process between the counselor and the family, with the counselor using Walter and Pellar's (1992) criteria for well-defined goals. Goals and tasks that adhere to these criteria are:

- Positively stated ("Isela is bringing the boyfriend over after school to meet mom").
- In a process form (present continuous tense or gerund form; bringing, continuing, walking, going, talking).
- In the here and now (tasks are achievable in the near future, not over several weeks).
- Specific (tasks are specific: "walking away").
- In the person's control (tasks the person can start and maintain by him- or herself).
- In the family's language (using the language of the family).

As our crisis family counselors are constructing action plans with families, they are simultaneously asking themselves several operant questions (Nowicki, 2007). One question we ask ourselves as we are negotiating tasks is, "Is there a 90 percent chance this will actually happen?" If we think the client will not complete the task, we work to negotiate a smaller or easier option that has a higher likelihood of actually happening. The primary objective here is client participation, not task achievement. At the end of the meeting, the counselor and family construct an action plan on a simple form that includes only positive statements so the family can feel comfortable taping it to their refrigerator. When a person (family) is in crisis, they generally are in some level of disorganization (Slaikeu, 1990; Roberts, 2000), and it can be helpful for them to have a written plan for reference at home. Currently the agency is experimenting with using Barry Duncan's Session Rating Scale (Duncan et al., 2004) to measure client satisfaction with the session.

DEVELOPING EFFECTIVE COMPETENCIES FOR SUCCESSFUL FAMILY COUNSELING PRACTICE

Social workers who want to practice in the field of family counseling have some model social work practitioners to emulate and learn from, including Virginia Satir (one of the founders of family counseling), Lynn Segal (brief family therapy), Lynn Hoffman (historian of family therapy), Dorothy Becvar (systems approach), Peggy Papp (Ackerman Family Institute); Froma Walsh (family resilience practice), Harry Aponte (structural family therapy), Insoo Kim Berg and Steve deShazer (founders of solution-focused therapy), Michele Weiner-Davis (divorce-busting), Matthew Selekman (family therapy with adolescents), and David White (narrative therapy originator). Throughout the development of family counseling, social workers have been drawn to the idea of working with the family as a system of interacting and reacting parts that operate based on rules of systems.

When we collaborate with family systems we must listen more closely to their stories (O'Hanlon, 1995), their theories about change, and what *they* think needs to happen to move in the direction of what they want. For some families, this process includes having discussions about their desired outcomes and possible steps they may take. For others, activities, exercises, and more metaphorical tasks may be the road to take. In this age of immediate gratification, some families enjoy participating in experiential activities (Gerstein, 1994, p. 4) and then processing the activities to understand their relationships with each other before formulating changes they can make to work toward their stated outcomes. For other families, family sculpting, shared art projects, or metaphorical homework tasks are helpful. The social worker must have a bag of tricks that includes many different kinds of activities and strategies to use when the situation calls for creativity to assist the family in moving toward their outcome.

It is also important for social workers preparing to work as family counselors (as well as practicing family counselors) to keep abreast of research findings that impact their work with families. Much of the research related to the effectiveness of various family counseling approaches is important, and so is research on what the clients find to be most helpful. This research directs us to become more outcome-informed and client-centered, according to Duncan and colleagues (Duncan et al., 2004). Research on outcome studies in therapy by Asay and Lambert (1999) indicates that 55 percent of the change that clients experience is related to what they, themselves bring to the table (see Chapter 27 on common factors). Therefore, family counselors can focus more on the family's desires and expectations and helping them use their strengths and resources. Using the family's existing but forgotten resources simplifies and expedites movement toward their outcomes. Returning to a behavior you already have in your repertoire is easier than learning a new one. Finally, we must acknowledge family members' struggles and heroism as we find ways to increase their participation in the counseling process. Active client participation is the single most important factor related to success in family counseling (Duncan et al., 2004, p.36). Whatever it takes to encourage and activate family participation is a good strategy to use with every family member.

In this day and age of accountability, social workers who want to work with families must learn and continue to acquaint themselves with the evidence-based literature, including assessment tools, practices, and outcome measures for families and systems work (Janzen et al., 2006). Especially in the world of the nonprofit, community-based agency that must necessarily receive funding from government sources, these funding sources are requiring evidence-based models of intervention (Becvar & Becvar, 2006; Janzen et al., 2006), even though some researchers suggest that the use of randomized clinical trials to establish efficacious practices is questionable (Duncan et al., 2004).

Another important competency involves continually adding to our bag of tricks strategies and resources that can be useful for working with youth and families. This includes a comprehensive list of community resources in a wide array of topic areas, which can be easily created and maintained by using the Internet and a computer.

Along with lists of outside resources, family counselors can also collect and categorize strategies and techniques to use in various situations that arise in family work, as well as activities that can be used with families (experiential exercises, art activities, play therapy exercises). Some family counselors collect ideas and strategies in binders, calling them their cookbooks of counseling. A collection might include skill instructions on reframing, reflective listening, backdoor compliments; activities from adventure-based counseling, new games, and initiatives; instructions for using miracle questions, self-anchored scaling, task selection; sample metaphors; and lists of therapeutic movies.

One of the important aspects of competency development for new and experienced social workers practicing family counseling is continuing education and supervision. All social workers should have an opportunity to work with their supervisors to construct and maintain professional development plans in which they set annual goals and steps for growth. These can be skill-driven or topic-driven. For example, one family counselor's development plans includes learning more about narrative therapy with families and includes using a narrative approach (White & Epston, 1990)

with live supervision and attending a conference or workshop related to narrative therapy. The supervision plan can also include what the person wants to focus on in his or her clinical supervision. Many family counselors request live supervision or the ability to videotape and process family sessions with their supervisor.

WEB SITES

Allyn and Bacon Family Therapy (historical overview and therapist profiles. http://www .abacon .com/famtherapy/index.html.

American Association of Marriage and Family Therapy. http://www.aamft.org.

Bill's Attic (source of free handouts from Bill O'Hanlon). http://www.brieftherapy.com/ attic /attic.htm.

Divorce Busting: Michelle Weiner-Davis (source of free articles about marriage and marriage therapy). http://www.divorcebusting.com.

The Dulwich Centre (gateway to narrative therapy, community work, and psychosocial support). http://www.dulwichcentre.com.au.

Institute for the Study of Therapeutic Change (Source of Free Session & Outcome Rating Scales): available online at http://www .talkingcure.com.

Solution Focused Brief Therapy Association. http: //www.sfbta.org.

St. Luke's Innovative Resources (online resources to support strengths-based family work. http: // www.innovativeresources.org/aboutus.html.

References

Asay, T. P., & Lambert, M. J. (1999). The empirical case for the common factors in therapy: Quantitative findings. In M. A. Hubble, B. L. Duncan, & S. D. Miller (Eds.), *The heart and soul of change: What works in therapy* (pp. 330–56). Washington, DC: American Psychological Association.

Becvar, D., & Becvar, R. (2006). *Family therapy: A systemic integration*, 6th ed. Boston: Allyn & Bacon.

Berg, I. K. (1994). *Family based services: A solution-focused approach.* New York: Norton.

deShazer, S. (1988). *Clues: Investigating solutions in brief therapy.* New York: Norton.

Duncan, B., Miller, S., & Sparks, J. (2004). *The heroic client: A revolutionary way to improve effectiveness through client-directed, outcome-informed therapy.* San Francisco: Jossey-Bass.

Franklin, C. (1998). Distinctions between social constructionism and cognitive constructivism: Practice applications. In C. Franklin & P. Nurius (Eds.),

Constructivism in practice: Methods and challenges (pp. 57–94). Milwaukee, WI: Families International.

Franklin, C., Corcoran, J., Nowicki, J., & Streeter, C. (1997). Using client self-anchored scales to measure outcomes in solution-focused therapy. *Journal of Systemic Therapies, 16,* 246–265.

Franklin, C. & Jordan, C (1999). *Family practice: Brief systems methods for social work.* Pacific Grove, CA: Brooks/Cole.

Gerstein, J. (1994). *Experiential family counseling: A practitioner's guide to orientation materials, warm-ups, family building initiatives, and review exercises.* Dubuque, IA: Kendall/Hunt Publishing.

Gingerich, W. J., & Eisengart, S. (2000). Solution-focused brief therapy: A review of the outcome research. *Family Process, 39,* 477–498.

Janzen, C., Harris, O., Jordan, C., & Franklin, C. (2006). *Family treatment: Evidence-based practice with populations at risk.* Belmont, CA: Brooks Cole.

Kelly, M. S., Kim, J. S., & Franklin, C. (2008). Solution-focused brief therapy in schools: A 360 degree view. New York: Oxford University Press.

Kim, J. S. (2008). Examining the effectiveness of solution-focused brief therapy: A meta-analysis. *Research on Social Work Practice, 18,* 107–116.

Nowicki, J. (2007). *The STAR action plan. A Texas Network of Youth Services training workshop.* Austin, TX: J. Nowicki.

Nowicki, J., & Bewsey, S. (1994). Competency-based programming in a runaway and homeless youth program. *New Designs for Youth Development, 11*(1), 29–32.

O'Hanlon, B. (1995) Psychotherapy's third wave? The promise of narrative. *Human Givens Journal (2)* 4. Retrieved November 16, 2007 from the World Wide Web: http://www.hgi.org.uk/archive/thirdwave2.htm.

Roberts, A. R. (2000). *Crisis intervention handbook: Assessment, treatment, and research,* 2nd ed. New York: Oxford University Press.

Saleebey, D. (2006). *The strengths perspective in social work practice,* 4th ed. New York: Longman.

Slaikeu, K. A. (1990) *Crisis intervention: A handbook for practice and research, 2ⁿᵈ Ed.* Boston: Allyn & Bacon.

Walter, J., & Pellar, J. (1992). *Becoming solution-focused in brief therapy.* New York: Brunner-Mazel.

White, M. & Epston, D. (1990) *Narrative means to therapeutic ends.* New York: W.W. Norton.

7   The Essential Elements of Private Practice Social Work

Raymond D. Fox

As I prepared this chapter, I received unexpected poignant notes from two former clients, one from 15 years ago, the other from 10 years ago. The first one, Mr. R, a musician and composer who struggled with chronic anxiety and panic, with whom I worked over the course of 3 years, made significant advances. He not only came to remarkable terms with his generalized anxiety but finished an orchestral composition, a symphony that had been delayed for 7 years. Conducting it before a large audience at a major concert hall was a multifaceted celebration. In his note to me, Mr. R commented,

I was going through my files and came across a file I've kept of my work with you. . . . I have always held you up as one of the great saints in my life . . . a quiet, steady, support during one of the stormiest and yet creative periods of my life. Your work with me brought me home, back to myself, a place oft threatened, but never lost. I just wanted to let you know, from a long distant past, how deeply grateful I am for you in my life.

The second letter arrived from Ms. L, a clergyperson who focused our work on heady and troublesome questions of identity, confidence, and philosophical quandaries. Over 4 years she came to terms with accepting being gay, with not needing to "have all the answers," with her role as a pioneer minister in a largely male-dominated religion. One portion of her letter read, "wanted to say hello and let you know that I am doing well, and think of you often and that I never have and never will forget the tremendous help and guidance you provided to me throughout several very difficult years in coming to terms with my internal demons and career decisions."

The remarks of Mr. R and Ms. L made me reflect profoundly on my private practice. What made it work? What made it satisfying? Frustrating? Because little appears in the literature to guide social workers in establishing and maintaining a private practice, this chapter provides an overview of pivotal features of starting and sustaining one—professional, entrepreneurial, and ethical—gleaned from my own personal experience.

Ups and downs, rewards and challenges, merits and limitations in private practice emanate from its nature—being at the same time a professional endeavor and a business venture. Private practitioners assume total responsibility for every aspect of practice. This includes such diverse constituents as observing ethical standards, setting hours and fees, obtaining insurance, assessing, and most important, evaluating effectiveness. In my view, social workers are particularly well educated as practitioners but poorly prepared as entrepreneurs.

THE PROFESSIONAL DIMENSION

A practitioner for the past 40 years and a teacher, consultant, and supervisor for 35 years, I have come to appreciate the need for a commonsense and down-to-earth approach to private practice. Theoretical frameworks and research findings provide a scientific basis for practice but little guidance by way of its art and craft. A creative leap is required to bridge abstract theory and concrete reality. Another creative leap is required to straddle the gap between the professional and the business dimensions of private practice.

Personal Aspect

Only when you are alert to who you are and what you are doing are you sufficiently relaxed, clear, and open-minded to establish and maintain a private practice and better understand clients. It is not possible to be tuned into the feelings of others without first being attuned to your own. Your constant challenge is to understand the interplay between your personal and professional roles and responses. Your personality, values, and sensitivity are the very tools that make you an effective therapeutic instrument. Take time to inventory your unique attributes and skills. Your personhood, in other words, is the essential feature in the establishment and maintenance of the therapeutic alliance.

Because you can react only from what is within yourself, you must know yourself so that your capacity for being in relationship is increased, your ability to react consciously is intensified, and you are freer to make deliberate choices about how to respond to clients. Only by knowing yourself are you in a position to make active and creative use of feelings, thoughts, intentions, and motives to optimize the helping process. Only by knowing your assets and shortcomings (in terms of knowledge and skill base) professionally and entrepreneurially are you in a position to reasonably choose to practice privately.

Awareness leads to more disciplined and clearly directed work as reported in numerous studies. In brief, do what you expect clients to do. Take a hard look at yourself. What is your motivation? Being your own boss? Status? Growing professionally? Earning more money? Minimizing bureaucracy? Maximizing autonomy and independence? Selecting your own client population? Being more creative?

Will you specialize in a method? With a population? With a symptom? Are you fully qualified? Licensed? Do you want a full- or part-time practice? How will you hone your skills further? Advance your knowledge? Do you fully appreciate the consequences in terms of the commitment of time, energy, and money involved in such an enterprise?

Creativity and Fluidity

I encourage a fluid and personal approach to differentially and effectively respond to a wide range of clients with a broad array of problems. As an autonomous practitioner, you can enjoy the freedom, within the bounds of accepted ethical and empirical standards, to employ innovative methods for helping clients fathom their lives and gain deeper understanding. I use a variety of distinctive strategies more fully described elsewhere (Fox, 2001). One method, however, that I have found indispensable, particularly when working with trauma survivors, is journal keeping. The following sketch of Joan, who used this approach, serves as an illustration.

Joan experienced extraordinary trauma throughout her life. She was abandoned by her father at age 3, and his infrequent contact with her was sexually abusive. Her mother suffered a paralyzing automobile accident, leaving her disabled and shifting excessive responsibility to Joan and her younger brother. Joan had serious knee problems, which, treated by a family physician, worsened as a result of injections, causing excruciating pain intended to disguise his having sodomized her at age 12. As a result, she underwent a series of major and painful surgeries for her disabled knee. During our contact she oversaw the care of her mother in a nursing home suffering from Alzheimer's disease; her mother died at a critical juncture in Joan's therapy.

Finding it almost impossible to acknowledge her multiple traumas and articulate their emotional impact, Joan painted. Hers was an art journal. An integral facet of her treatment, it contributed significantly her progress. (Indeed, having read *The Artful Journal: A Spiritual Quest* [Carey, Fox, & Penney, 2002] originally led her to contact me.) She attributed, as did I, her steady improvement to my serious attention to her vivid entries. In them she portrayed unspeakable memories and their emotional residue through the medium of watercolors. During our face-to-face contact she struggled (and did so successfully) to translate these artful images into words. The journal served as an intense source of catharsis for her and a source of insight for both of us.

Joan's frightening nightmares dissipated, and her neck problems and migraines ceased. Her alcohol use to self-medicate when feeling "on edge" desisted. This innovative method promoted her healing.

Evidence Base for Practice: Qualitative Methods

Social work literature promoting evidence-based practice (Pollio, 2006; Proctor, 2003; Rosen, 2003)

challenges unexamined and unsystematic clinical interventions. Practitioners are induced to employ empirically validated interventions linked to clients' goals and objectives and evaluate outcome effectiveness.

Self-reflection constitutes one form of evaluation. Almost axiomatic is supervision. Case conferences and consultation are additional types of quality control and evaluation. These approaches rely almost exclusively on subjective assessment and should be part of every practitioner's routine. An array of other means can serve as supplements—practice logs, intensive case studies, and critical incident analysis. All enable one to conceptualize the stages of practice interaction through the exercise of reconsidering and analyzing contact with clients. All enhance the ability to discern efficiency. Especially in urban areas, often having a glut of practitioners, advanced training and specialization provide a welcome additional edge. Process recording is yet another exceptionally effective and efficient method for self-reflection (Fox & Gutheil, 2000).

Process Recording

Condensed and structured process recording, using the outline recommended shortly, enables you to analyze your practice at all stages of interaction—preparation, intervention, and evaluation. It is time devoted as much to thinking and reflecting as to writing.

Not a discursive narrative, but rather a concise and ordered account, it promotes methodical observation, analysis of the link between goals with strategies for change, examination of your part in the helping endeavor, and ultimately, an assessment of outcome. It documents service, identifies needs, forms a basis for intervention planning, and presents a vehicle for tracking progress and sharing information with others. It can be adjusted at varying junctures to emphasize specific purposes you choose.

The following four-part format is both process- and product-oriented. It provides a channel to focus your critical theoretical thinking (process) about your interaction (process) with clients, as it inspires higher levels of abstraction and critical analysis. It is an instrument to crisply and coherently document and evaluate your work (product). A brief sample excerpt from an actual case process recording of Mr. and Mrs. W accompanies each section. It is written in shorthand, which eases preparation and review.

1. *Preparation and purpose.* Prior to client contact, record the rationale for your contact, key thoughts, aims and plans for the contact, and potential obstacles or pitfalls. Include methods to be used, data to be obtained, preliminary assessment formulations, issues for focused attention, and possible resistance be faced. Some guideline questions include "Am I clear about what my direction? What would be the preferred outcome? Do I have sufficient information and resources? What preliminary arrangements need to be made to enhance the exchange?" A selected concise real-life sample follows: "Marital difficulty. Mrs. W comes alone. Totally reluctant to explore relationship. Need clearer light on interaction and husband. Doubts self, husband, me. Preemptively seeks a divorce. Where from here?"

2. *Intervention.* Describe the ebb and flow of the contact, including the verbal and nonverbal activity. Summarize what occurred interpersonally during your client contact, noting the responses and activity of both of you. Compile observations, including unique and unusual factors, cultural variables, and critical analysis. Include direct quotes to individualize and highlight significant elements. Some guideline questions are "How did the contact begin and end? What changed? What decisions were made? What tasks were accomplished?" The recording entry appeared like this: "Mrs. W responded well. More frank. Recommended couple counseling. Mrs. W herself suggested inviting Mr. W to a session. Offer an 8-week open contract to them."

3. *Thoughts and analyses.* Articulate your spoken and unspoken thoughts and reactions to clients and examines your own and clients' functioning. Include consideration of client strengths, capacity, motivation, as well as impressions regarding the nature and quality of the helping endeavor. Assess, refine, and evaluate the climate of the exchange. Pay special attention to the identification of significant patterns and themes that emerge. In brief, critically evaluate the interface of your activity with clients' progress. Important questions include "What did I learn about myself and my knowledge and skill application? What do I need to know more about in terms of the client(s) and ways of interacting? What was particularly difficult for me or the client(s)? If I were to do it over again what would I do differently?" The process read: "Mr. and Mrs. W present. Was impatient, move too quickly—slow down. Both bring crucial past family baggage. Unpacked; introduce genogram next time."

4. *Overall evaluation and next steps.* Specify "use of self," knowledge, and skills used to reach the stated purpose, to tailor the interaction to clients' expressed and special needs. Reflect on and assess how appropriate, realistic, and effective your strategies for intervention were. Some guideline questions are "How effective was the joining of method of intervention to the needs of the client(s)? What interventions were successful? Which ones did not work? Why? Where am I in all this?" Remarks were: "Went quite well. Mr. and Mrs. W intrigued by genogram. Insights for them and me into repeating patterns. Genogram good idea. Stick with it. Highlight present. Interpret and interrupt repetition of prefigured modes."

Evidence Base for Practice: Quantitative Methods

The subjective methods just outlined are further refined when combined with objective forms of evaluation. Just as your treatment strategies need to be tailored to meet the unique needs of individual clients, so should your evaluation methods be selected with care. Observations of a client over time constitute a single-subject or single-system design for evaluation. Such a quantitative design requires that client behaviors or events be specified in measurable terms. Goals provide this reference point against which change can be compared emphasizing (a) specifying target behaviors, (b) identifying a suitable measure, (c) employing it systematically, (d) analyzing observations over time and (e) charting change. Two discrete methods—single-subject/system design and practice outcome inventory—stress establishing clear and quantifiable before and after pictures of interventions.

Charts or graphs help track client progress. These make it possible to individualize evaluation to the unique characteristics, needs, and dilemmas of your clients. They provide ready visual gauges for both you and the client to track change. Decisions can follow as to whether there is significant change in a desired direction meeting the expressed purpose of treatment. Corrective adjustments can then be rationally and realistically taken.

Easy-to-use prepackaged standardized scales are also available to incorporate into your practice. From analysis of the information gleaned over a series of time intervals, you can make reasonable assessments about treatment success, discuss options for continuing or discontinuing treatment based on these results, alter interventions, make a referral, or terminate. When such methods are incorporated directly into treatment, they truly propel clinical work. No attempt is made here to detail either single-subject/system design or practice outcome inventory, which can encompass sophisticated variations or statistical procedures. Rather, the following illustration is offered with an appeal to seriously consider incorporating some structured and standardized form of evaluation into your practice.

Cognitive therapy focuses on correcting clients' negatively distorted thoughts and helping them think more realistically. Already in a depression, Mr. H's sudden loss of employment as a middle manager activated dysfunctional automatic thoughts, such as "never being able to do anything right," accompanied by feelings of dejection and devaluation and a sense of paralysis of never being able to work again. Accepting these skewed thoughts as a foregone conclusion, his depression deepened. After I explained the cognitive approach and we mutually identified goals, Mr. H agreed to use the Beck Depression Inventory (BDI) within sessions and as homework over a 3-month period to meet his need for recognizing progress together with my need to monitor the success of selected interventions. Originally intended to be practitioner-administered, the BDI is consumer-friendly. I therefore encourage clients and selectively others (family, friends, other involved professionals) to complete it along with the client after obtaining instruction and gaining practice in its application. Mr. H completed one copy of the inventory each day. A weekly composite score of his level of depression was calculated by averaging his daily ratings. Mr. H's wife completed the BDI weekly for that same time period. Mr. H. also kept a mood log each day, which he gave me at our scheduled session. Perusing his journal, I arrived at a separate third score, a composite weekly score, by averaging the daily entries. Such a procedure provided three independent comparative measures of his depression level over the 12-week course of treatment. These three separate indices were graphed.

Remarkable correspondence was noted among the separate scores—his own, his wife's, and mine. For the first 9 weeks of treatment Mr. H's level remained severe; nevertheless, it was steadily declining. The tenth and twelfth week marked a sharp decrease in the level of depression. It was evident that Mr. H was recovering and making healthier adaptations in his life. Most important, it vividly demonstrated to him that feelings of despair could be overcome even though he initially believed that "nothing could really help." For me it affirmed that selected cognitive interventions—journalkeeping, homework, maintaining the BDI—had a positive result.

The graph made it immediately evident by charting the three separate indices that Mr. H had made substantial headway over the 12 weeks toward overcoming his depression. Added diagnostic and clinical advantages accrue from using such a visual method for tracking progress. Beyond being a tangible sign for all of progress, it became a catalyst for further intensive discussion about other adjustments Mr. H needed to make in his treatment as well as in his life. These discussions in turn led to identifying supplementary goals for treatment, including the development of strategies for finding employment.

Self-Care

By virtue of being human beings, but more so by virtue of our role as practitioners, we are affected deeply by the suffering and pain of others. Such resonance is exacerbated by our own exposure to the same incomprehensible events that affect our clients. Take time for solitude and reflection. Periodically attend to and take care of yourself. It has been my experience as a practitioner, supervisor, and consultant that private practice can often be a rather solitary and isolating pursuit. It can make you vulnerable to discouragement, even disillusionment.

Repeatedly dealing with others' stress, anguish, and unexpected crises throughout a career can lead to "compassion fatigue," also known as burnout (Fox, 2003). Be sure to involve yourself regularly with sources of professional and personal support, learn to step back and put limits on yourself, and make a commitment to seek out supervision and, when needed, counseling before depletion sets in and compromises your confidence and competence. Consciously endeavor to involve yourself in satisfying experience outside of work. Avoid the tendency to disengage, not only from clients but from peers and from yourself as well. Foster associations with colleagues so as to be affirmed, glean support, and create avenues to share experience.

ENTREPRENEURIAL DIMENSION

General Issues

Practitioners seem ill prepared for the business side of private practice. They rarely receive relevant education in money matters. Many social workers have special difficulty reconciling their backgrounds with a profit motive and sticking to operating procedures based on management principles. Dealing with a host of financial issues—setting fees, collecting fees, dealing with nonpayment, setting policies for missed appointments, maintaining financial records—add to the discomfort level. Issues abound having to do with establishing and supporting an office. Options are many—developing a home office, renting shared space in or separate from a group practice, subletting a workplace. Accompanying these concerns are those focusing on how to furnish, lay out, and maintain the office. Beyond rent, routine ordinary expenses include utilities, phone, computer, and cleaning. In addition, other, more remarkable factors need to be considered. Among them is whether to offer your services as an independent provider, as part of a group practice along with social work or interdisciplinary colleagues, or as a professional corporation. Obtaining insurance of all types—disability, accident, dwelling, and malpractice—absorbs extra attention.

Be cautioned that setting up a practice, as is evident, is complex and multifaceted. It requires hefty investments of time and money. Be prepared and deliberate in moving forward.

Marketing

Marketing is a further major consideration. From my observation, social workers are uncomfortable with identity, image management, and public relations. How do you present yourself? What is your identity—therapist, counselor, social worker? Exposure is central to boosting a practice and requires comfort in self-promotion and marketing. Steady and reliable referral sources are the life blood of practice. Of paramount importance is networking with colleagues, with like-minded practitioners from allied professions, with community organizations. This is time-consuming and costly. Some questions may guide your thinking. Do you offer presentations at a local library, join a speaker's bureau, submit an ad to a local newspaper or the Yellow Pages? Do you place flyers and announcements in churches or with community merchants? Do you develop a Web site? Affiliations of every sort are required to initiate and sustain a private practice. Do you connect with clinics, hospitals, employee assistance programs, hot lines, mental health agencies, day care? Do you offer workshops to groups such as American Association of Retired Persons, the PTA, the Elks, and so on? Do you make the rounds to doctors, chiropractors, physical therapists, and attorneys to acquaint them with your services?

Over and above being recognized and opening a private practice, you need to build arrangements with other experts with whom to consult about special predicaments that inevitably arise. Relationships with experts, those not in the field, are needed to assist in the day-to-day operation of your practice—accountants, attorneys, insurance agents. Will you (and how will you) employ support personnel, for example, receptionists, secretaries, office cleaners? What will your business cards look like and say? How will you cover vacations? All of these points are integral when approaching practice as a commercial operation based on business principles with contractual operations clearly defined and in writing.

Managed Care

A further important factor entails the dominance of managed care with its attendant benefits and liabilities. Although enrollment in such an organization promises a steady source of referrals, often these are promises only. Frequently, financial remuneration is reduced. Issues of privacy, confidentiality, and freedom of choice in selection of intervention strategy accompany being on the roll. All these issues can affect, possibly negatively, your client–practitioner relationship. It has been my experience that practitioners are frequently forced into a position of having to adjust client contact to suit the managed care company's conditions. Negotiating the type and extent of treatment, advocating for clients' best interests, and obtaining reimbursement for your best efforts constitute major predicaments and often spark ethical dilemmas.

As you think about becoming a managed care provider, become intimately familiar with its regulations about capitation, coinsurance, and copayment.

Health maintenance organizations, created by insurance companies, provide a package of services for a premium usually paid by employers. They made serious demands on the practitioner. These mostly involve accountability.

Recordkeeping is fundamental in any manner of practice, and even more especially so in managed care. More important, as an autonomous practitioner you are morally answerable and legally responsible. Documentation of differential diagnosis, medical necessity, treatment plan, explanation of what occurred in contact, under what circumstances and with what results need to be in compliance with requirements of regulatory and fiscal bodies to ensure accuracy and provision of what is defined as appropriate treatment. In your files, be sure to include referral sources, brief history, medication if indicated, dates, and outcomes. Always kept privileged communication in a completely secure area, under lock and key.

It is a mistake to believe that not keeping notes will protect client confidences and avert subpoenas. Do not attempt to out-think or second-guess contractual entities or legal systems. On a different note, if legal action is brought against you, it would be impossible for you without up-to-date records to retrospectively construct a case and thereby mount a defense.

ETHICAL DIMENSION

Basics

Forcefully stated: *vigilantly observe the Code of Ethics.* You can find it on the National Association of Social Workers Web site.

Malpractice

It is possible (but not probable) that you will face a malpractice accusation. It is prudent to keep in mind the following. To be sued for malpractice, there must first be demonstrated proof that a legal duty existed between you and the client, that you violated that duty by failing to conform to professional standards of care, that evidence exists showing you to be negligent in not conforming to an accepted standards of care, and it can be demonstrated that the client has been harmed or injured in some way and that you were the proximate cause of the injury for which damages are sought. Possible infractions include abandonment of service, mismanagement of the relationship, breach of confidentiality, failure to provide appro-

priate treatment, and prevention of harm to third parties. Other causes are failure to consult with a specialist, defamation, violation of civil rights, failure to be available when needed, untimely termination of treatment, and inappropriate bill collecting methods. Malpractice insurance is requisite even though being sued is extremely unlikely especially for social work practitioners.

Fundamentals

Honor your requirement to garner full informed consent from clients. Honor your obligation toward suicidal clients and your duty to warn potential victims of clients who make threats. Acknowledge and follow through with your duty in cases of suspected or tangible child or elder abuse and neglect. Grasp requirements for court testimony and the elements of subpoena. Present danger overrides confidentiality. Protection trumps jeopardy.

Be honest with yourself and with your clients—there are no guarantees, and there are no relationships, including the practitioner–client relationship, that are totally risk-free for either party.

ELEMENTS OF PRIVATE PRACTICE

What works? What should you keep in mind? What are key elements gleaned from my active and deep reflection on 40 years of practice? These interwoven guideposts build upon and enhance each other.

- *Relating.* Research into practice effectiveness across modalities and theories identifies relationship as the foremost ingredient for success and effectiveness.
- *Hearing their stories.* Accompany clients through their life stories. It creates a structure for catharsis of disturbing affects, cleansing of disquieting memories, and discovery of new perspectives.
- *Naming things for what they are.* Avoid euphemisms—name the "un-nameable"—abuse, rape, assault, victimization, and trauma. Honesty grounds practice and propels the process forward.
- *Blending seriousness and fun.* Neither shy away from difficult material nor be too intrusive. Spontaneity, humor, and paradox advance change and simultaneously provide caring and challenge.

- *Educating.* Offer practical information, advice, alternative viewpoints. Teach self-soothing techniques. Counter distorted thinking patterns.
- *Setting goals.* Mutually set goals to give you and clients the impetus to carry on, direction for the future, marks of and satisfaction in accomplishment in moving forward.
- *Being fair.* Establish reasonable fees, consider a sliding scale, accommodate to contingencies in clients' lives, such as unemployment, illness, disability.
- *Believing.* Believe in the purposefulness of practice, in yourself, in clients' strengths leads to meaningful exploration, examination, and recognition of choice.
- *Creating safety.* Meet clients' basic needs for security and affirmation. It fosters their ability to master their lives, face the challenge of self-discovery and triumph of ownership.
- *Taking an active stance.* Concentrate on clients' aspirations and resiliency engaging in active and genuine collaboration toward interrupting dysfunctional patterns and fostering empowerment.
- *Confrontation.* Challenge any discrepancy directly. Even though it is risky, it keeps both of you on track toward advancing true insight.
- *Balancing.* Maintain a dynamic equilibrium between the interdependent features of professional standards of care and entrepreneurial realities.

A FINAL REMARK

Finally, what brings success in private practice is integrity and reputation. Develop referral sources; confer with other professionals from a variety of related disciplines, market your professional attributes, cultivate small business skills, keep abreast of the changing care environment and trends, preserve the nature of your client relationships, obtain medical and psychiatric consultation when relevant, keep accurate records, and document, document, document. To reiterate, success in private practice arises from integrity and reputation.

WEB SITE

National Association of Social Workers, Code of Ethics. http://www.socialworkers.org/pubs/code.

References

Carey, M., Fox, R., & Penney, J. (2002). *The artful journal: A spiritual quest.* New York: Watson/Gupthil.

Fox, R. (2001). *Elements of the helping process: A guide for clinicians,* 2nd ed. Binghamton: Haworth Press.

Fox, R. (2003). Traumaphobia: Confronting personal and professional anxiety. *Psychoanalytic Social Work, 10*(1), 43–55.

Fox, R., & Gutheil, I. (2000). Process recording: A means for conceptualizing and evaluating practice. *Journal of Teaching in Social Work, 20*(1/2), 39–56.

Pollio, D. E. (2006). The art of evidence-based practice. *Research on Social Work Practice,* 16, 224–232.

Proctor, E. K. (2003). Evidence for practice: Challenges, opportunities, and access. *Social Work Research,* 27(4), 195–197.

Rosen, A. (2003). Evidence-based social work practice: Challenges and promise. *Social Work Research,* 27(4), 197–208.

8 Community-Based Mental Health with Children and Families

Susan C. Ayers & Borja Alvarez de Toledo

A DAY IN COMMUNITY-BASED CHILDREN'S MENTAL HEALTH SERVICES

The following schedule is representative of a typical day in the life of a social worker providing outpatient community services to children and families. Tania is a bilingual licensed social worker with more than 10 years experience in working with families in the office, their home, schools, and other community settings.

9 A.M.	Tania arrives at the Kennedy School for a meeting with the vice principal, school counselor, family liaison, and parent for Rashad, an 11-year-old who is exhibiting aggressive behaviors with peers and is not doing his homework or paying attention in class. The school is concerned about what might be going on at home.
10 A.M.	Tania drives Rashad's mother to her house, and they further discuss the school meeting and evaluate the options proposed (possibility of self-contained classroom). Mother reveals that Rashad's father, with whom he is very close, has recently left the family. Tania offers supportive counseling for the family, which mother eagerly accepts.
10:30 A.M.	Tania arrives at the office, checks messages, and attends a multidisciplinary treatment team meeting, where she is presenting a genogram and elaborating a treatment plan for a new case. She greatly enjoys engaging with her colleagues in examining family dynamics and identifying strategies to address a family's presenting concerns. She is struck as usual by how the social workers in the treatment team have a much more contextual understanding of the family–environment interaction than members from the other professional groups represented on the team.
12 noon.	Tania returns phone calls and writes a progress note of the school meeting over lunch in her office.
12:20 P.M.	A social work intern knocks on Tania's door and wants some direction and consultation about a shared case, the Sanchez family. They decide to schedule a treatment planning meeting involving the worker from the public child welfare agency and the attending psychiatrist. They have some concerns about domestic violence in the Sanchez home and decide to also invite the director of the agency's Child Witness to Violence program to the planning meeting.

12:45 P.M.   Tania leaves a voicemail for the child welfare worker on the Sanchez case to update her on concerns and alert her to the planning meeting to be scheduled soon.

12:50 P.M.   Tania makes a phone call to Maria to remind her of their 5:30 P.M. appointment. Maria has a history of not showing up. She wants to engage Tania over the phone about her son's latest behavioral problem, but Tania invites her to share her concerns at their afternoon appointment. Maria agrees to bring her son, Juan, to the session so that all three can work together to understand and address the difficulties between mother and son.

1 P.M.   Individual session with Carmen, a single mother of three children under age 10, who has struggled with post-traumatic stress disorder (PTSD) from a violent marriage since she emigrated from the Dominican Republic. Carmen comes with her 3-year-old, who is able to play by himself for the first 15 minutes of the session. Carmen has been in treatment for more than 4 years following a psychiatric hospitalization and temporary removal of her two oldest children by the public child welfare agency. She has recently met a man at a group for single parents who seems gentle and kind and interested in her and her children. She and Tania talk about Carmen's fears of getting into another violent relationship and discuss how to prevent that from happening.

2 P.M.   Tania's next scheduled client, Billie, is late for her session. While she waits, Tania decides to fill out two insurance reauthorizations to be able to extend treatment for two of her clients.

2:20 P.M.   Reception calls to let Tania know that Billie has arrived. Focus of session with Billie is on helping her write a résumé to start the process of applying for a job. Billie has been on welfare for some time, struggling with bipolar disorder, but seems ready to take a step toward becoming more active and independent again. She expresses anxiety about this process, but feels confident that with Tania's help she will succeed.

3 P.M.   Tania walks downstairs to the reception area with Billie after their session. She goes to the computer lab with the intention of writing some progress notes. She ends up joking and connecting with co-workers while eating some donuts the clinical director brought.

3:30 P.M.   Tania leaves the office to go to the Esposito home. Parking is difficult around their house, especially with the snow that recently fell in their community.

3:55 P.M.   Tania finally finds parking and gets to the Esposito home. Luisa, a 33-year-old from Nicaragua, is raising her 7-year-old and 2-year-old twins almost by herself because her husband works two jobs with very long hours. She has no car and has a hard time getting to the office for appointments, so Tania decided in the early stages of treatment to provide home-based services. Luisa's 7-year-old son, Miguel, has attention deficit hyperactivity disorder (ADHD) and has been very aggressive toward the twins. The children are constantly running around when not fighting, the TV is blasting, and

Tania often wonders how much she is achieving. But Luisa feels isolated and looks forward to the sessions. Today it is apparent that she has been able to incorporate some of Tania's suggestions about behavioral management of Miguel as he proudly shows her his behavior chart, which already has several stars on it. He tells her excitedly that his mom has promised a trip to McDonald's if he gets ten stars that week.

5:10 P.M.   Tania leaves the Esposito home and travels back to the office, wondering if Maria will make it to their 5:30 P.M. appointment.

5:25 P.M.   When Tania arrives at the office, she is pleasantly surprised to see that Maria and Juan are waiting for her. Juan, a big, strapping 14-year-old, has always been a "good boy" according to his mother, but recently he has become defiant of her authority, refusing to respond to her requests to accompany her to church services and to the grocery store. She fears he is hanging around with a bad

group of friends. Maria's husband died when Juan was a baby, and she had depended on her only child for emotional and social support. At first, Juan slouched in his chair, refusing to engage in the discussion with Tania and his mother. However, as he realized that Tania was not going to side with his mother against him and that she was truly interested in hearing his side of things, he became more involved. It was clear that there needed to be a renegotiation of the parent–child relationship because this young man was approaching adulthood. Tania focused the session on exploring with them what each would like from this new relationship. They agreed to meet again the next week to figure out how they could achieve something that would work for them both.

6:30 P.M.   End of session with Maria and Juan. Tania checks messages, leaves a message for the intake coordinator about a new case she just received, and leaves the office close to 7 P.M.

As she begins the drive home, Tania reflects on her day. She reminds herself that for many of the families she works with, change comes in baby steps. She thinks about smiling Miguel and his new behavior chart with the stars and realizes that Luisa has taken a major step toward more effective parenting. She thinks about Billie, who has struggled with her mental illness but is now ready to move out into the workplace once again, with Tania's support. She thinks about Rashad reacting to the loss of his father by acting out in school and is encouraged that his mother was able to reach out for help with this profound change in family dynamics. Even though many of her cases are difficult and complex and the work takes a long time, Tania knows that the steps her clients make bring her great satisfaction as a clinical social worker.

A NEW DIRECTION IN CHILDREN'S MENTAL HEALTH SERVICES

During the 1960s, as the civil rights movement grew in scope to encompass a wide variety of oppressed groups, including people living in closed institutional settings, judicial decisions supported the right of individuals with mental illness to effective treatment in the least restrictive environment possible. The Community Mental Health Centers Act, passed by Congress in 1964, gave legislative impetus to the movement toward community-based care, including the care of children and adolescents. For the next 20 years, mental health professionals, especially social workers, who have historically made up the largest group of these professionals, worked to establish community alternatives to out-of-home care for children with mental health challenges.

In an article published in 1966 on trends in community mental health, the medical director of the American Psychiatric Association, Walter E. Barton, called attention to new definitions of the word *community* in community mental health, now understood to encompass more than just a geographical area. He noted the important dimensions of culture, race, and ethnicity in defining community: "both behavior and interpretation of psychopathology are influenced by sociocultural factors" (Barton, [1966] 2000, p. 613). As will be seen later in this chapter, cultural awareness has become one of the central tenets in community-based practice with children with emotional and behavioral challenges and their families.

Further impetus to development of community-based mental health services for children came in 1984 in the form of a federal initiative sponsored by the National Institute of Mental Health and funded by Congress called the Child and Adolescent Service System Program (CASSP). This initiative provided grants to individual states and localities for development of innovative mental health services for children. The envisioned services would provide a system of care in each state that would range from the least restrictive traditional outpatient services, such as those provided by the child guidance center model, to the most restrictive inpatient and residential forms of care.

The federal CASSP initiative also funded two centers for children's mental health research, at the University of South Florida and the Portland State University School of Social Work, respectively. Work done at these centers has significantly influenced provision of community-based children's mental health services in the following years. The center at Portland State has been particularly involved in research and advocacy around engaging families as partners in treating children with emotional and behavioral disorders, moving the field away from the damaging parent-blaming stance of past years (Friesen & Poertner, 1995). The center at the University of South Florida, in addition to conducting its own research program focused primarily on school-based and wrap-around services, has sponsored a yearly conference on children's mental health research that has brought together academic and community-based researchers from all over the country and greatly facilitated cross-disciplinary fertilization and transmission of evidence-based practices in the field.

PRINCIPLES OF A SYSTEM OF MENTAL HEALTH CARE FOR CHILDREN

The CASSP concept of a system of care in community-based children's mental health services was well articulated by Stroul and Friedman (1986) in their book, *A System of Care for Seriously Emotionally Disturbed Children and Youth*. In it, the authors lay out the principles that guide provision of children's mental health services in a system of care. According to these principles, services must be the following.

1. *Child-centered:* Treatment should be designed to meet the individual needs of the child, rather than fitting the child into an existing service model. Any treatment plan must consider the child's family and community context, provide services that are developmentally appropriate and child-specific, and build on the strengths of the child and family.
2. *Family-focused:* The family is recognized as the primary support system for the child and should participate as a full partner in all stages of treatment planning and implementation. Each family configuration is unique and may include biological, adoptive, and foster parents, siblings, grandparents, other relatives, and other adults who are committed to the child. Development of mental health policy at state and local levels must also include family participation.
3. *Community-based:* Whenever possible, services should be delivered in the child's home community, drawing on formal and informal resources to promote the child's successful participation in community life. Community resources include not only mental health professionals and provider agencies but also social, religious, recreational, and cultural organizations and any other natural community support networks.
4. *Multisystemic:* Treatment is planned in collaboration with all the systems involved in the child's life. Representatives from these systems along with the family collaborate to define outcome goals for the child, develop a treatment plan, develop the necessary resources to implement the plan, provide appropriate support to the child and family, and evaluate progress.
5. *Culturally competent:* As Barton (1966) noted, both behavior and interpretation of

behavior are determined by sociocultural factors. Therefore, it is essential that children's mental health services are provided by individuals who have the skills to recognize and respect the behaviors, ideas, attitudes, values, beliefs, customs, language, rituals, ceremonies, and practices characteristic of a particular group of people. This is especially important when the child and family ascribe to and are influenced by a cultural tradition that is outside society's mainstream.

6. *Least restrictive/least intrusive:* Services should take place in settings that are the least restrictive and intrusive available to meet the needs of the child and family (Stroul & Friedman, 1986).

DEVELOPMENT OF AN AGENCY-BASED CONTINUUM OF CARE

In the 20-plus years since the CASSP initiative first focused on the gap in the continuum of children's mental health services between traditional individual outpatient treatment and inpatient care, the principles articulated by Stroul and Friedman have been slowly incorporated into the design and delivery of community-based services by state and local agencies and service providers across the United States (Burns & Hoagwood, 2002; Pumariega, Winters, & Huffine, 2003). One such agency is the Guidance Center, Inc. (GCI), serving the greater Boston-area communities of Cambridge and Somerville.

GCI got its start in the mid-1950s, founded by a group of local citizens concerned about the lack of community mental health services for children (Ayers & Lyman, 2006). Ten years later, it became part of the public community mental health system, serving as the child ambulatory service for the city of Cambridge. GCI's early administrators believed that all children in the community were the agency's responsibility, whatever problem they might experience. They understood that the earlier the intervention, the better the long-term prognosis and that most children's disorders could be addressed in the context of the family and community without resorting to institutional care (Ayers & Lyman, 2006). Despite this early commitment to family- and community-based forms of care, in the 1970s and early 1980s, GCI increasingly drifted into a traditional outpatient clinic model that saw the child as the focus of treatment and the family as the source of the child's problems rather than as a collaborator in the child's treatment.

In the late 1980s, a change in GCI leadership brought a reawakening of the former vision of family- and community-focused service delivery. The federal CASSP initiative had begun to research and disseminate new ideas about how to partner with families and community providers to better serve children and youth with emotional and behavioral challenges in their own homes and communities (Louie & Katz-Leavy, 1991). New family-based and wrap-around interventions were being created and tested that seemed able to maintain even the most troubled youngsters in community settings (Burns & Hoagwood, 2002). Furthermore, federal legislation had been enacted requiring public school systems to provide educationally appropriate services to all children, regardless of any special needs. No longer was the lack of adequate educational services in the community a reason for placing a child with mental health challenges in residential care.

RISK AND RESILIENCE IN MENTAL HEALTH SERVICES FOR CHILDREN AND FAMILIES

Over the past two decades, research on factors contributing to psychiatric disorders in children has identified a number of factors that place children at higher risk of developing emotional and behavioral disorders (Shonkoff & Phillips, 2000). Some of these are located within the child, such as a genetic or biologic vulnerability or difficult temperament; others are environmental, such as extreme poverty or disrupted psychological attachments in early life. Having a parent with a mental illness or substance abuse disorder and witnessing or being a victim of family violence and abuse are all risk factors for emotional and behavior disorders in children (Shonkoff & Phillips, 2000). The more risk factors present, the greater the likelihood that the child will experience serious mental health challenges.

Research suggests that about a third of families known to the child mental health system are experiencing acute situational stress. This may be a separation or divorce, illness or death of an important family member, loss of employment, or change in lifestyle, such as a move to a new community. A biologically sensitive child may react to stress and instability in the family system with a worrisome decline in psychosocial functioning. These are often families who have functioned adequately in the past and will, with time-limited therapeutic support and guidance, do so again in the future.

Another third of the families who present in the child mental health system are those who are struggling to care for a child with a biologically based disorder, such as ADHD, autism, or bipolar disorder. These are often normally functioning families who are stressed almost to the breaking point by the demands of caring for a child with special psychosocial or developmental needs. Such families respond well to ongoing professional and peer support as well as psychoeducation to help them adequately understand and nurture the child.

The final third of families referred to community-based children's mental health agencies are those with a high number of personal and environmental risk factors that severely impact the functioning of all members of the family system to some degree. One member, a child, may be presented as the identified client, but even a brief exploration will reveal that others in the family are known to a variety of community service systems, such as child welfare, drug and alcohol treatment, adult mental health, homeless and domestic violence shelters, public education, and even the police, juvenile justice, and adult corrections systems. These are the families who need the most help from community agencies and who have traditionally proved to be the most difficult to reach and to treat.

LEARNING FROM VULNERABLE FAMILIES

As clinicians at GCI began to work more closely to develop partnerships with the parents of children referred for mental health services, it became apparent that graduate school training had not adequately prepared them for the clinical and emotional complexity of community-based work. Most families had psychosocial needs extending far beyond those relating to the identified child and the usual fixed responses (clinic-based treatment, foster care, residential treatment). These families required a holistic approach to engage them in services as well as a different mix of services to address their multiple needs (Lyman & de Toledo, 2006). Such families were often (though not always) headed by a single mother whose own social history was one of abuse, neglect, and

abandonment. Shirley was just such a mother. When her children first came to the attention of the GCI clinical leadership, it was because of the problematic classroom behavior of the fourth child, Marcus, age 8, then living in a local foster home. He and three of his siblings were in separate foster homes, each was in treatment at GCI, including in a sibling group. In addition, there was an effort to engage their foster parents to create some unified parenting strategies among them. It was apparent that the many disruptions, separations, and abuse along their way had affected all of the children, but differently depending on their developmental stages and individual resilience. The children visited their mother periodically with no coordination or communication with the schools, therapists, or among the child welfare agency staff. Only the foster parents were in the planning loop.

Despite these efforts, Marcus's behavior problems continued to escalate, raising questions of what the next clinical step should be, with whom, and to what purpose. One of the biggest challenges in community-based mental health practice is determining who the client is. In the case of this family, there was Marcus, his siblings, all of the school personnel involved with the children, the child welfare agency staff associated with various family members, and the mother, Shirley, who was virtually unknown to those with decision-making authority. In community-based practice with vulnerable families like this, it is essential to establish a helping alliance with each family member as well as the collateral stakeholders, all the while maintaining a position of therapeutic neutrality.

In an effort to better help Marcus as well as understand the chaotic history of the family, GCI contacted the state child welfare agency to convene a case consultation meeting. Attending the meeting were several caseworkers and their supervisor, four GCI therapists who were working with the children and their foster parents, and several school personnel, but no representative for Shirley. It quickly became apparent that few of the people in the room knew each other. There was little shared information among the key players and no systemic understanding of Shirley or the family. There were also no shared treatment goals or plan for the reunification and maintenance of this family system. Each agency or organization involved with the family saw only its piece of the puzzle—its area of concern. To top it off, the child welfare agency expressed little faith in the children permanently reuniting with their mother.

What we learned about Shirley was that she had deeply troubled parents, especially her father, an alcoholic who physically abused his wife and eight children. She became pregnant at 16 years of age, desperate to get out of the household. She had no education or job skills and became trapped living with the father of her child. She also suffered from PTSD and severe recurring depression. Her executive functioning was extremely poor, and to get free of the father of her first child, she began brief liaisons with a series of unstable, controlling, and abusive men with whom she continued to have children. She and her children moved through a succession of homeless shelters, battered women's shelters, relatives' homes, and boyfriends' apartments until she made a suicide attempt and was briefly hospitalized. Shirley's six children had multiple out-of-home placements over the years.

From the case consultation meeting, it became apparent that central to the development and implementation of a successful family-centered treatment plan was the transfer of Shirley's treatment to GCI from the local hospital outpatient program so that her family could be seen as a unit, in one place. Working directly with Shirley allowed GCI clinicians to better understand the family's history and current dynamics and to realistically assess her strengths and challenges as head of the family system. It also enhanced work with the child welfare system, whose caseworkers were supervising weekly visits between Shirley and her children. Helping new, untrained child welfare workers and foster parents understand the children's emotional and behavioral acting out in response to these weekly visits not as "bad behavior" but as expressions of their distress at being separated from their mother, enabled them to become more open to exploring alternative strategies for helping the children manage these feelings.

Work with Shirley and other parents with high levels of psychosocial and material need quickly highlighted the necessity of actively reaching out to these families. Most, like Shirley, are profoundly isolated, having been deeply wounded psychologically, first by their families of origin, then by the state systems put in place to help them, then by other people in their relationships as adults. That these families are reluctant to open themselves up to the relationships required in the therapeutic process is evidence of the strength of self-preservation, and it makes the engagement process more difficult and prolonged. They test the patience of outpatient clinicians who often expect clients to appear for an appointment at a scheduled time, which initially these families cannot do.

In response, GCI added the role of outreach worker to its constellation of services to families. The outreach worker partners with the family's therapist, and together they become a therapeutic team. The outreach worker begins the engagement process with the family by visiting with the "resistant" parent in his or her own home, bringing coffee and donuts to set the stage for a process of giving to the parent, both psychologically and materially. The outreach worker offers concrete support with practical matters: making sure food is on the table, helping create a household budget, even getting the children to school. She accompanies the parent to school meetings and encourages the parent to take the lead in discussions with the teacher, rehearsing beforehand the questions to be asked. She teaches parents how to locate community resources that can be accessed over time by the entire family, creating their own safety net, including child care or youth centers, food pantries, bus schedules, English as a second language classes, and libraries with computer access. The "resistance" parents project is based on fear, mistrust, and a profound sense of shame. Part coach and part cheerleader, the outreach worker becomes a friend and mentor to parents, supporting them through the difficult therapeutic process of change.

Therapeutic work with parents like Shirley is also different than normal clinical work with families, which often focuses on teaching new strategies for child management, educating parents about the diagnosis given their child and its treatment, or helping them deal with stressors in their own lives that are interfering with their ability to respond to their child's special needs.

First, therapists who work with these most vulnerable families must, like the outreach worker, engage parents by clearly demonstrating over and over their own commitment to them. Shirley's first therapist, Mary, was a social work intern when she began working with her. Shirley describes Mary thus: "She was spunky, warm . . . like a sister and friend. She brought me my very first birthday cake. . . . I had never got nothing for birthdays or holidays, so I never celebrated anything." That began to change as she let Mary into her life. "She focused on me and the kids. We had no furniture, so somehow she got some chairs so we could sit on them when she came to visit. She made me get out of the house and go for walks. One time when we had no food she took me shopping, and instead of buying just one of everything she bought two" (Ayers & Lyman, 2006, p. 230). She tells of a turning point in their relationship when Mary gave Shirley her home phone number in case of an emergency. "I didn't believe she really gave me her number, so I called and when she answered, I was so shocked that she was telling me the truth, I hung up" (Ayers & Lyman, 2006, p. 230).

Although social workers have long appreciated the essential importance of the client–worker relationship as the basis for therapeutic change, there was a period of time when it was believed that unless the client expressed readiness to take help by presenting him- or herself at the agency at an appointed time, building a therapeutic alliance and working toward change was not possible. Clients like Shirley have educated us that there are many paths toward relationship building and moving toward change. Social workers must draw on the basic professional tenet of starting where the client is, both literally—in their own homes and communities—and figuratively—in their fear and hesitancy to accept a potentially hurtful stranger into their lives.

Families have often experienced violence in their homes and in their lives. As mentioned previously, Shirley herself was abused physically, psychologically, and probably sexually as a child. As a young woman, she formed relationships with men who abused her and her children as well. This awareness led GCI to develop a program called Children with Voices to serve abused women and their children who have witnessed and may also have experienced this abuse. Shirley participated in the Mothers in Action therapeutic group offered as part of this program. She met other women with experiences similar to hers and formed mutually supportive and therapeutic relationships that continued after the group sessions ended. Her teenagers were eligible for the male and female teen self-defense groups that were specifically designed to increase an adolescent's body awareness and self-esteem and provide acceptable alternative strategies for stress management. Mothers with younger children can participate in a mother-child group designed to help them help their children with the emotional and behavioral effects of witnessing or experiencing abuse and to strengthen mother–child attachments that may have been damaged by the manipulations of a violent partner.

Experience with mothers like Shirley, whose difficult personal histories made nurturing their own children a struggle, also highlighted for GCI the importance of intervening early in the lives of vulnerable parents and their children. The agency added an Early Childhood Services division, which includes Healthy Families, a national home visitation program designed to intervene with adolescent first-time parents to ensure healthy birth outcomes and positive infant development to 3 years of age. Healthy Families enables GCI child development specialists to coach teenagers to become capable parents and maintain the relationship up to 3 years if needed. If a program like this had been available to Shirley decades ago, she may have lived an entirely different life rather than becoming involved with child welfare authorities.

The Early Childhood Services division also includes a state-supported program for pregnant and newly parenting women who have been identified by health care providers as high risk for difficulties in parenting because of a constellation of factors that includes poverty, trauma, domestic violence, parent mental illness, or substance abuse. Intervention with these families continues from pregnancy through childbirth and for the first year of the infant's life. At the end of that time, if there is still concern regarding the risks to the child's normative development, the family is referred to GCI's extensive Early Intervention program that treats children up to age 3 and their families. In addition to treating young children for developmental anomalies, GCI's Early Intervention program assesses the child's social and emotional well-being and works with parents to address any infant mental health concerns.

GCI's work with parents like Shirley has highlighted how individuals from even the most damaging early environments have great reservoirs of strength and resilience that can be developed with support and nurturing over time. Today, Shirley works full-time, and of her four youngest children, three have gone on to college and the youngest graduates from high school this year. This realization of strengths has led to development of an agency-wide focus on family support in which parents who have gained or regained a measure of personal well-being can reach out to lend a hand to others who are currently struggling as they have done. Shirley and other parents are active in developing and implementing parent-to-parent groups and other activities in this initiative. Research shows that giving to others can also be a powerful force for individual growth and change.

This continuum of care for families that has grown up in a community-based children's mental health agency in one locale reflects current evidence-based knowledge for practice. Research has demonstrated the impact of early life experiences on the developing brain as well as the effects of trauma throughout the life span on psychological well-being and social functioning (Shonkoff & Phillips, 2000). Individuals who experience such profound trauma, loss, and rejection in childhood may be ill equipped to provide the nurturing and care that their children require without substantial outside support and guidance over an extended period of time. Yet these same early life experiences may inhibit them from seeking out and accepting such support. It is imperative that community-based children's mental health agencies offer the range of developmental, therapeutic, and outreach services that can accommodate the needs of all families whose children struggle with serious emotional and behavioral challenges.

WEB SITES

National Technical Assistance Center for Children's Mental Health at Georgetown University. Offers information on current trainings, technical assistance, and conferences in the area of children's mental health policy and practice. http://www.gucchd .georgetown.edu/ programs/ta_center.

Research and Training Center on Family Support and Children's Mental Health at Portland State University. The site offers information and resources regarding mental health practice with children and their families with a significant focus on family-centered practice. http://www.rtc.pdx.edu.

University of South Florida's Research and Training Center for Children's Mental Health. Contains links and information on empirically based interventions for children and families. This site also offers information on the conference on children's mental health research held annually in Tampa in late February. www.rtckids.fmhi.usf.edu.

References

Ayers, S. C., & Lyman, D. R. (2006). The development of a community-based system of care. In A. Lightburn & P. Sessions (Eds.), *Handbook of community-based clinical practice* (pp. 221–241). New York: Oxford University Press.

Barton, W. E. (1966). Trends in community mental health programs. *Hospital & Community Psychiatry, 17*(4). Reprinted in 2000 in *Psychiatric Services, 51*(5), 611–615.

Burns, B., & Hoagwood, K. (2002). *Community treatment for youth.* New York: Oxford University Press.

Friesen, B. J., & Poertner, J. (1995). *From case management to service coordination for children with emotional, behavioral, or mental disorders: Building on family strengths.* Baltimore, MD: Brookes.

Louie, I. S., & Katz-Leavy, J. (1991). New directions for mental health services for families and children. *Families in Society, 72,* 277–285.

Lyman, D. R., & de Toledo, B. A.(2006). The ecology of intensive community-based intervention. In A. Lightburn & P. Sessions (Eds.), *Handbook of community-based clinical practice* (pp. 379–397). New York: Oxford University Press.

Pumariega, A. J., Winters, N. C., & Huffine, C. (2003). The evolution of systems of care for children's mental health: Forty years of community child and adolescent psychiatry. *Community Mental Health Journal, 39*(5), 399–425.

Shonkoff, J. P., & Phillips, D. A. (Eds.) (2000). *From neurons to neighborhoods: The science of early childhood development.* Washington, DC: National Academies Press.

Stroul, B. A., & Friedman, R. M. (1986). *A system of care for seriously emotionally disturbed children and youth.* Washington, DC: CASSP Technical Assistance Center, Georgetown University Child Development Center.

9 Social Work Practice in Home-Based Services with Children and Their Families

Martha Morrison Dore & Charlene Zuffante

The following reflects a typical day in the life of a social worker delivering home-based services to families and their children.

8:30–9:30 A.M.	Arrive at office. Hunt for a parking space. Check phone messages and return calls to clients, colleagues, and community partners. Find out from a call to the middle school social worker that Robbie McDonald has skipped school two days in a row.
9:30–9:45 A.M.	Head off to Dobson family home for treatment session with Mrs. Dobson, her partner, Ellie, and Carrie Dobson, age 13, who has just returned home from two weeks in residential treatment for a suicide attempt.
9:45–11:30 A.M.	Home-based session with the Dobson family.
11:30–12 noon:	Travel to ML King Elementary School.
12–1 P.M.	Attend individual education plan (IEP) meeting at school for Keisha, age 8, who is experiencing serious attention and behavior problems in second grade. Support Keisha's mother, who is requesting additional testing by an outside evaluator.
1–1:30 P.M.	Travel back to office. Hunt for parking space.
1:30–2 P.M.	Check messages, return more phone calls, set up next day's home visits.

2–3:00 P.M.	Write progress notes in Dobson file documenting morning's treatment session. Write up summary of IEP meeting and document next steps in Harold case file.
3–3:30 P.M.	Travel to el Bassel family home.
3:30–5 P.M.	Accompany Mr. and Mrs. el Bassel, recent Palestinian immigrants, to the housing office to apply for an emergency transfer because their current neighbors are verbally threatening them because they are Muslims from the Middle East. During travel and waiting time, talk with parents regarding their management of their son, age 11, who is having extreme difficulty adjusting to current school placement.
5–5:30 P.M.	Travel back to office. No problem finding parking.
5:30–6 P.M.	Work on additional case documentation needed for reimbursement under state contract.
6–7 P.M.	Assist colleague with a crisis unfolding in one of her home-based cases. Her client has called her to report that her boyfriend has beaten her and is threatening to harm her child unless she

	agrees to move to Tennessee with him. Work phones to obtain help while colleague keeps client talking on phone.		older teens. The parents suspect he is using drugs and alcohol and may be committing burglaries with the group he is hanging out with.
7–7:30 P.M.	Travel to the McDonald family home.	8:30–9 P.M.	Travel to office.
7:30–8:30 P.M.	Treatment session with Mr. and Mrs. McDonald and their four children, including 13-year-old Robbie, who has recently been skipping school to hang out with a group of delinquent	9–10 P.M.	Check phone messages, check on colleague with domestic violence crisis, return phone calls, write progress notes on family therapy session with McDonald family, document next steps with Robbie.

Social work has a long tradition of home-based service delivery, dating back over 100 years to the friendly visitors of the Charity Organization Society. Although much has changed since that time with regard to knowledge for practice with individuals, families, and children in their own homes, these earliest social workers, like present-day practitioners, recognized that engaging with family members in the context of their daily lives greatly enriched their understanding of the forces that influence current functioning and of the strengths and resources that may be engaged to bring about change.

In the first textbook for training aspiring social workers, *Social Diagnosis*, Mary Richmond (1917) presented her arguments in support of working with clients in their own homes:

(a) Its challenge to the case worker at the outset to establish a human relation. . . . (b) Its avoidance of the need of so many questions, some of which are answered unasked by the communicative hostess and by her surroundings. To the quiet observer, the photographs on the wall . . . the household arrangements are all eloquent. And far more revealing than these material items are the apparent relations of the members of the household to one another—the whole atmosphere of the home; (c) Its provision of natural openings for a frank exchange of experiences. (p. 107)

A review of the current literature on home-based practice reveals that not much has changed since Richmond wrote these words. The value of working with clients in their own homes still emphasizes the importance of establishing a working relationship or "helping alliance" and the greater ease with which the therapeutic relationship de-velops when the client is in familiar surroundings (Johnson, Wright, & Ketring, 2002).

Home-based work provides a ready window into the daily lives of clients. Though it may be possible to keep up a pretense that all is well for an hour a week in an outpatient clinic, it is much more difficult to hide evidence of clinical depression or ongoing substance abuse when one's living environment is filthy and in disarray. It is possible for the home-based social worker to quickly understand why a child is failing in school when there is no time or space set aside in a cramped and noisy apartment for homework, where the television blares 18 hours a day, and where no adult takes responsibility for ensuring that homework is done correctly.

The DelBlasio family consisted of Rachel, a 33-year-old mother, and her ten children ranging in age from 3 months to 14 years. The identified patient in the family was 9-year-old Billy, who was sexually molested by a 26-year-old cousin. Billy revealed the molestation to a school nurse, and Child Protective Services (CPS) was notified. The case was referred by CPS to a home-based family treatment program in an effort to strengthen the family's functioning and prevent an out-of-home placement for Billy.

When the home-based social worker, Susan, arrived at the DelBlasio home, she found a mom who was reluctant to become involved in treatment and a living environment that was chaotic at best. Cockroaches scurried across the trash-strewn floor. At the first family session, it was clear that the older two children, both girls, were carrying a great deal of the responsibility for managing the home and younger children and that Rachel suffered from severe depression, unable to get out of bed to get her children off to school most days. The extreme attention-seeking behavior of the younger children with Susan suggested emotional neglect.

Rachel insisted that she could handle the situation with Billy on her own by confronting the perpetrator's mother and not allowing Billy to have any further contact with his cousin. Efforts to help her help Billy with the emotional effects of the abuse were met with stubborn denial. After a few home visits, Billy took matters into his own hands by requesting to meet with Susan alone. He led her into the room that he shared with five of his siblings. The children in that room all slept together on two queen-sized mattresses pushed together on the floor.

Small for his age and very thin, Billy summoned all of his strength to push a large dresser up against the bedroom door to keep out his brothers and sisters who banged at the door repeatedly, begging to come into the room to see what was going on. Billy motioned for Susan to sit on the floor, where cockroaches scurried about. Feeling her commitment to the child was being tested, she joined him in his life at that moment, and the two of them sat together, flicking the bugs away, while Billy talked of his life at home, at school, and of the sexual molestation experience. In a clinic setting, without this opportunity to enter into the child's life as he lived it on a daily basis, it is doubtful whether the social worker could have gained such a full and complete understanding of the client in his situation so quickly.

As Richmond noted in 1917, home-based work also provides an essential opportunity to observe the interactions of those living in the home with one another. Very often, when a child is referred by a school or medical provider to a mental health center for assessment and treatment, only the mother and occasionally a sibling or two accompany the child to the clinic. Yet as family social workers have noted for years, it is nearly impossible to understand the functioning of an individual family member, especially a child, without also understanding the dynamics of family interaction. What better way to observe these dynamics firsthand than by providing home-based services? What better way to find out that a family's life together is totally disrupted by the demands of caring for grandfather who is 87 and has advanced Alzheimer's disease? What better way to find out that mother's paramour is a violent and abusive man who has punched holes in the apartment wall and kicked the family dog when

the children's noisy play awakened him? What better way to discover that the parents of a boy diagnosed with ADHD are uncertain how to manage his frequently disruptive behavior and that their inability to set appropriate limits has allowed the child to rule the roost? Though an outpatient clinician may learn of any of these situations in due course, the home-based practitioner sees the interaction immediately and firsthand and understands implicitly their impact on the family system and on individual family members.

Carlos, a Spanish-speaking social worker in a home-based program, was assigned to a family of Puerto Rican descent, the Rodriguez family, whose 13-year-old son, Jose, had been given the diagnosis of bipolar disorder. The parents were confused about the meaning of this diagnosis and understandably concerned about its implications for their child's future. As Carlos met with Mr. and Mrs. Rodriguez, Jose, his older brother (age 15), and younger brother (age 10) in their own home, a picture began to emerge of loving, well-meaning parents who were frightened by their middle son's frequent rages, which seemed to occur primarily when Jose was asked to carry out a chore, such as cleaning his room or completing his homework. During these rages, which Mr. and Mrs. Rodriguez attributed to his bipolar illness, Jose would appear out of control, throwing things and breaking furnishings. Once, when asked to go to his room when he became enraged, he refused and proceeded to kick the bedroom door in.

In discussing their parenting styles, the mother readily admitted that she was intimidated by Jose when he was enraged and would retreat to her room until the storm was over. The father, who was a very large man, saw his role as deescalating Jose's rages through physical intimidation, although he denied ever using physical force with the boy. Neither parent believed in setting limits with their sons or in having a set structure in the home, such as specific times for homework or family meals. Both felt that this more laissez-faire approach to parenting had worked well with their other two boys and did not understand why Jose could not handle it, again attributing his behavior problems to his illness.

It was quickly apparent from observing the family in their own home that Jose had learned how to use his illness to control his parents to his own benefit. Helping Mr. and Mrs. Rodriguez examine their ineffective parenting style and identify alternative approaches in which they both could participate was a clear focus of the work with this family. In addition, the importance of structure to a vulnerable child like Jose was part of educating the family about bipolar disorder. Setting up a schedule for homework and meal times as well as for completing chores around the house would help Jose anticipate what he needed to do rather than always feeling like "things were coming at him out of the blue," as he expressed in one family session. Trying alternative ways of doing things while receiving the support and encouragement of their home-based worker helped the Rodriguez family, which had many inherent strengths, including their commitment to one another, make positive changes that benefited all members of the family system.

In *Social Diagnosis*, Richmond also noted that home-based practice provides a multitude of opportunities for "frank exchanges." The home environment is replete with "conversation starters" for clinicians who bring aspects of the environment into the therapeutic process (Reiter, 2006). A picture of the mother's parents on the mantel can initiate a discussion of mother's childhood, revealing that her father was a longtime alcoholic who was emotionally unavailable and that her mother compensated for his emotional absence by becoming emotionally enmeshed with her only child. This may help the home-based clinician better understand her client's difficulties in developing healthy intimate partner relationships and her inability to set appropriate limits and expectations for her 11-year-old son. Helping a mother relate her own childhood experiences to her current parenting practices using elements available in the home environment, such as the picture on the mantel, is a strategy available to home-based clinicians that is seldom accessible to practitioners in clinic settings.

Another important advantage of home-based practice is the ability of this approach to service delivery to reach clients who might otherwise be inaccessible to social work clinicians (Boyd-Franklin & Bry, 2000). One of the first home-based programs described in the contemporary social work literature grew out of a study in the 1950s by social workers in St. Paul, Minnesota, who observed that a small number of families created a high proportion of the demands on the child welfare system there. These families demonstrated myriad difficulties, including domestic violence, substance abuse, and mental health problems, as well as child abuse and neglect. Engaging these families in efforts to address their difficulties and make substantial changes in their often chaotic

functioning proved frustrating and futile for the social workers until it was decided to take services to these families in their own homes rather than wait for them to seek and accept therapeutic services on their own. In this way, many of these families were engaged in treatment, and changes in their overall functioning were observed.

The St. Paul Family-Centered Project, as it was called, and others like it that sprang up around the country in the ensuing years focused on families known to the child welfare system in an effort to ensure family stability and improve family functioning to keep children at home and out of foster care. These early home-based programs contributed to the development of what came to be known as family preservation services. Although there were several different models of family preservation services, perhaps the most widely known and used was Homebuilders, developed by two psychologists in Tacoma, Washington, in the early 1970s.

The Homebuilders model is a brief, 6-week intervention that works with families in crisis who are about to lose their children to foster care (Kinney, Haapala, & Booth, 1991). The work is done almost entirely in the family's home or in other community locations, such as schools or work settings. Homebuilders clinicians carry very small caseloads, are available on call 24 hours a day, and spend as much time as necessary working with the family in the home, especially during the first days or weeks of treatment, when the family is in a crisis state. In addition to crisis theory, the model draws heavily on social learning theory to bring about changes in families' functioning.

Evaluations of the Homebuilders model suggested that it was effective in reducing the number of out-of-home placements of children compared with usual child welfare services. Homebuilders participation also shortened the length of foster care placement and facilitated children's return to their families (Schwartz, 1995). During the 1980s and 1990s, variations on the Homebuilders model were adopted throughout the nation by state child welfare agencies as a result of federal legislation providing funding to states to strengthen families and prevent out-of-home placement of children. Home-based services intended to prevent child placement and reunite families when placement had occurred are currently a staple of most state child welfare systems.

Home-based treatment models have been developed to serve families and children involved with the juvenile justice and mental health systems as well as child welfare. Perhaps the best known home-based model for working with delinquent youth and their families is Multisystemic Therapy (MST). MST was developed in the early 1990s by Scott Henggeler and his colleagues at the Medical College of the University of South Carolina to address the externalizing behaviors of conduct-disordered youth (Henggeler, Schoenwald, Borduin, Rowland, & Cunningham, 1998). As the name of the model suggests, the focus of treatment is on the multiple systems involved in delinquent behavior: the youth, the family, peers, and community institutions, such as the school. MST clinicians work primarily with youth and their families in their own homes and, as in the Homebuilders model, they carry low caseloads; they are available 24 hours a day, 7 days a week to their clients; and the service is time-limited (3–5 months). Unlike Homebuilders, but similar to many other home-based intervention models, MST draws heavily for its theoretical base and practice approach on family systems theory and its applications in family therapy (Henggeler et al., 1998).

The growth of the family therapy movement in the 1960s and 1970s gave social workers working with families in their own homes new tools and strategies with which to approach home-based work. Family systems theory, which underpinned the family therapy movement, guided the interpretation of family dynamics. For example, Murray Bowen, one of the preeminent early theoreticians and family therapy practitioners, gave home-based clinicians working with families an intergenerational perspective on family functioning, now captured so eloquently by the intergenerational family genogram, a staple in the armamentarium of the home-based practitioner (McGoldrick, Gerson, & Shellenberger, 1999).

From family therapist Salvador Minuchin, working at the Philadelphia Child Guidance Clinic, came the focus on family structure and its importance in understanding and treating families in which the parents had lost control of their children. Minuchin's structural family therapy approach taught home-based practitioners to observe the family's structure and seek to understand the patterns of alliances and coalitions that color a family's daily life (Lindblad-Goldberg, Dore, & Stern, 1998). For instance, in families with a delinquent son or daughter, clinicians often see adults who have given up on authoritative parenting for a variety of reasons that include their own substance abuse, clinical depression, marital conflict, or simply being overwhelmed by life stressors. Helping the adults in such families address their own difficulties to resume their role as parent is a frequent focus of structural family therapy (Lindblad-Goldberg et al., 1998).

Jay Haley, Chloe Madanes, and other strategic family therapists gave home-based clinicians useful tools like enactments or brief playlets to illuminate a specific sequence of events in the family, such as having the children in the family act out what happens when father gives an order to teenage son that is ignored or what happens when the family goes on an outing together. These dramatizations of incidents in family life highlight commonly occurring negative interactions among family members no other way can bring out. They also give the home-based practitioner substantive material with which to initiate an alternative behavioral sequence to bring about change. If a particular sequence of events in a family customarily ends badly for some or all of the participants, illustrating this with the family and then having them brainstorm and act out an alternative sequence has the potential for meeting the needs of all participants. Rehearsing the sequence in an in-home session makes it more likely that family members will remember and try it out the next time the opportunity arises.

Family therapy, no matter what the theoretical orientation or school of thought, has given home-based practitioners important permission to use themselves creatively to bring about change in a family's problematic ways of functioning. Doing something differently, whether it is interacting in a different way with a partner or child or accessing new community resources together with a parent and observing how the parent interacts with a resource provider in a community setting, differentiates home-based from clinic-based practice. In traditional clinic-based practice, the focus of interaction between the social worker and client is limited to what the client brings into the session, which represents his or her construction of the reality of his or her life. Helping the client construct a more accurate interpretation can take many weeks or months of treatment. Home-based work speeds this process greatly by giving the clinician immediate access to alternative perspectives, which can then be used to help the client experience the situation in a different way.

In addition to home-based interventions with families in the child welfare and juvenile justice systems, this approach has been extended to families in the mental health system. Spurred in the early 1980s by the federal Child and Adolescent

Service System Program initiative, which funded development of new models of community-based children's mental health services, the state of Pennsylvania invested in developing and implementing a model of home-based services that treated children's mental health needs in the context of their families (Lindblad-Goldberg et al., 1998). The Pennsylvania model was based on an ecological and systemic understanding of factors that contributed to serious emotional and behavioral disturbances in children and drew on structural family therapy to inform its intervention. All of the treatment was done in the home and community and was intended to prevent psychiatric hospitalization and long-term residential care.

One of the systems concepts that the Pennsylvania home-based model emphasized is that of circular causality. This concept focuses clinicians' attention on the circular feedback loops of communication and behavior among family members. These highlight repetitive patterns of family interaction that illustrate the structural difficulties the family is experiencing. For example, a mother subtly counteracts every request her husband makes of their son by negating his authority with the child, or two siblings enter into a covert alliance to act out behaviorally to draw a response from their mother, who is overinvolved emotionally with the third child in the family, who suffers from a chronic illness. This way of understanding family functioning moves away from the practice of blaming specific family members for problems in the family and provides the clinician with a point of intervention and change. Circular feedback loops become apparent very quickly when a clinician spends time with the family in the comfort zone of their own home, and opportunities to challenge these customary ways of behaving are readily available.

Other models of home-based treatment for children and families involved with the mental health system have been developed as well. Beginning in the mid-1990s, clinicians at the Yale Child Study Center have developed and tested a manualized model of in-home psychiatric services called IICAPS (Intensive In-home Child and Adolescent Psychiatric Services) (Woolston, Adnopoz, & Berkowitz, 2007). The model provides for home-based assessment and treatment planning as well as brief family therapy, parent education in child behavior management, social skills development for children, and intervention with environmental resources to build support for the child and family in the community. Each phase of the intervention process is well defined and is accompanied by a series of measures of its effectiveness. IICAPS is a team-delivered intervention. Clinicians are expected to spend up to 5 hours per week in the family home, and the model calls for a 6-month treatment length. IICAPS is currently a Medicaid-approved treatment for children with *DSM-IV-R* Axis I and Axis II diagnoses in the state of Connecticut.

Another home-based intervention designed to support children and adolescents with serious emotional disturbances in their own homes and communities is the wrap-around model in which social workers work intensively with families to identify and put in place all of the resources and services needed to maximize the child's psychosocial functioning. In this model, the treatment plan is developed collaboratively by a care planning team that includes social workers from the wrap-around program, one of whom acts as the primary care coordinator, representatives of community resources (such as a school social worker or therapist from the local outpatient mental health clinic), members of the child's current household, and others the family may wish to include, such as grandparents, close friends or neighbors, and representatives of the referring agency, frequently the juvenile court or state child welfare agency. A primary focus of the wrap-around approach is to end the fragmented way services are often provided to children with serious emotional and behavior disturbances and their families.

The wrap-around model emphasizes honoring the family's voice in care planning. Part of the care coordinator's role is to ensure that team meetings are safe and blame-free for all participants. There is also emphasis on ensuring that cultural differences are acknowledged and respected in the treatment process. The care planning team is charged with developing the goals and strategies necessary to achieve the outcomes the family seeks with regard to maintaining the child in the home and community. These goals often include helping parents or other family members address their own problems or issues that impact the family's ability to provide the care needed by the child.

In recent years, as increased attention has been paid to preventing social and emotional difficulties in young children, particularly as they impact a child's capacity to learn in school, home-based programs for at-risk infants and toddlers have sprung up across the United States. Nationally, programs such as Early Head Start and Healthy Families focus on the functioning of the whole family and may rely on social workers specially trained in early child development to engage, assess, and treat vulnerable families in their own homes (Love et al., 2005). A recent national study of Early Head Start found that families and children treated in their own homes, either fully or in combination with center-based treatment, fared significantly better than those who received only center-based care (Love et al., 2005).

As Richmond recognized early in the profession's development, home-based services have historically been a key component of social work practice in a variety of domains. Social workers, with their ecosystemic understanding of human functioning and their trained capacity to interpret person–situation interaction, are ideally suited to be home-based clinicians. Social workers have long appreciated the importance of observing and engaging their clients where they live, in their own homes and community settings. Contemporary home-based programs build on the unique knowledge and skills of social workers developed and refined in over 100 years of home-based practice to help individuals, families, and children achieve their goals and improve their psychosocial functioning.

WEB SITES

Healthy Families. http://www.healthyfamilies america.org.

Homebuilders, http://www.institutefamily.org.

Multisystemic therapy. http://www.mstservices .com.

National Family Preservation Network. http:// www.nfpn.org.

Wrap-around services. http://www.rtc.pdx.edu/nwi.

References

Boyd-Franklin, N., & Bry, B. H. (2000). *Reaching out in family therapy: Home-based, school, and community interventions.* New York: Guilford.

Henggeler, S. W., Schoenwald, S. K., Borduin, C. M., Rowland, M. D., & Cunningham, P. B. (1998). *Multisystemic therapy for antisocial behavior in children and adolescents.* New York: Guilford.

Johnson, L. N., Wright, D. W., & Ketring, S. A. (2002). The therapeutic alliance in home-based family therapy: Is it predictive of outcome? *Journal of Marital and Family Therapy, 28,* 93–102.

Kinney, J., Haapala, D., & Booth, C. (1991). *Keeping families together: The Homebuilders model.* New York: Aldine de Gruyter.

Lindblad-Goldberg, M., Dore, M. M., & Stern, L. (1998). *Creating competence from chaos: A comprehensive guide to home-based services.* New York: Norton.

Love, J. M., Kisker, E. E., Ross, C., Constantine, J., Boller, K., Chazan-Cohen, R., et al. (2005). The effectiveness of Early Head Start for 3-year-old children and their parents: Lessons for policy and programs. *Developmental Psychology, 41*(6), 885–901.

McGoldrick, M., Gerson, R., & Shellenberger, S. (1999). *Genograms: Assessment and intervention,* 2nd ed. New York: Norton.

Richmond, M. E. (1917). *Social diagnosis.* New York: Russell Sage.

Reiter, M. (2006). Utilizing the home environment in home-based family therapy. *Journal of Family Psychotherapy, 11*(3), 27–39.

Schwartz, I. M. (1995). The systemic impact of family preservation services: A case study. In I. M. Schwartz & P. AuClaire (Eds.), *Home-based services for troubled children* (pp. 157–171). Lincoln: University of Nebraska Press.

Woolston, J., Adnopoz, J. A., & Berkowitz, S. (2007). *IICAPS: A home-based psychiatric treatment for children and adolescents.* New Haven, CT: Yale University Press.

10 The Oncology Social Worker in a Medical Setting

Traditional versus Innovative Roles

James. R. Zabora

The Association of Oncology Social Work (AOSW) was founded 25 years ago to provide support and guidance to social workers who were committed to providing a range of services to cancer patients and their families. Initially, many of the early members worked in comprehensive cancer centers as designated by the National Cancer Institute. Although more resources were generally available for psychosocial care in these settings, the difference in resource allocation was not significantly higher than most general social work departments. However, a few comprehensive cancer centers did possess large oncology social work staffs.

A secondary purpose of the AOSW has always been to advocate for increases in resources to meet the complex needs of cancer patients and their families across the entire disease continuum, from diagnosis to treatment and onto rehabilitation and recovery. Over the years, AOSW has striven to develop appropriate tools to enhance the clinical care that organizational members provide. Examples include the Managed Care Kit, two editions of the *Social Work Research Handbook*, standards of practice, and the Cancer Survivor Toolbox.

However, despite significant progress in the development of training and educational programs as well as the development of National Comprehensive Cancer Network's Distress Management Guidelines (NCCN, 2007), psychosocial services for cancer patients and their families vary significantly across the United States. These distress guidelines promote a prospective model of care that seeks to identify high-risk cancer patients to provide appropriate psychosocial interventions early in the disease trajectory. One of the primary explanations in variations in psychosocial care relates to the type of department in which

oncology social workers attempt to practice. Three brief scenarios follow to illustrate a day in the life of an oncology social worker based on three different departmental models—innovative, progressive, and traditional (Zabora, Brintzenhofe-Szoc, Fox, & Lipton, 2006).

THE INNOVATIVE MODEL

The innovative model is somewhat rare in oncology social work because these departments and programs have developed highly comprehensive and sophisticated services for cancer patients and all members of their families. The characteristics of this model include:

- Diversified mission and service.
- Clinical, education, and research emphasis.
- Prospective clinical interventions.
- Multiple revenue sources.
- Evaluation of effectiveness.

Two clear examples of this type of program are Life with Cancer (LWC) within the Inova Health Care System in Fairfax, Virginia. LWC) was founded 20 years ago by Gordon Hay, MSW, who continues as the current director. The second example is the rapidly developing program at the City of Hope in Duarte, California, under the leadership of Matthew Loscalzo, MSW. First, a description of LWC will be presented, followed by an overview of the City of Hope. LWC offers 45 programs and services on an outpatient basis provided by a multidisciplinary staff of social workers, nurses, and counselors. In addition, staff are also available to address psychosocial concerns on the inpatient oncology unit. All services are offered at no cost to cancer patients and their families based on a sizable endowment that has been developed over the years. In addition, a fundraising campaign has resulted in significant funding to construct the LWC Family Center on the grounds of Fairfax Hospital that will house these comprehensive programs. Examples of programs include:

- Young adults with cancer support group.
- Good Grief bereavement program for children and adolescents.
- Writing for wellness.
- Seated Motion: a chair-based exercise program.
- Family caregivers meeting.
- Spirituality quest.
- Meditation.
- Brain tumor support group.
- Reiki therapy.
- Heads Up group for head and neck cancer patients.

In this type of highly innovative model, these types of programs are truly unique. A program such as reiki therapy allows patients to experience this ancient practice by having a certified therapist place his or her hands on different parts of the body to release tension and discomfort. The writing for wellness program falls under a group of services defined as expressive arts. Through art, music, or journaling, patients pursue their own path to express what is going well with their illness as well as their concerns. In the case of LWC, plans have been developed to integrate psychosocial screening into this model of care with an outcomes assessment system. In this model, all patients will complete a series of three brief standardized instruments that measure distress, severity of symptoms, and quality of life. In this way, all new patients can be assessed based on these critical factors and then provided a range of services to address these needs. Participation in programs and services can be tracked, and repeated measures at 3 months, 6 months, and 12 months can then inform staff of immediate as well as long-term benefit to these programs.

At LWC, an oncology social worker may experience the following type of day.

8:30 A.M.	The social worker reviews the schedule for the day, which includes a series of individual brief therapy appointments, an educational session, a support group, a research meeting, and a possible meeting for program leadership.
9 A.M.	First individual therapy session for a newly diagnosed 34-year-old Stage IIA breast cancer patient who is struggling with treatment options and the impact on her husband and three children.
10:30 A.M.	The social worker moves to her metastatic breast cancer group, where the focus will be the recent death of a member of this group.
12 noon.	A brief lunch ensues in LWC's kitchen area to review activities for the upcoming afternoon.
12:30 P.M.	Preparation begins for an individual therapy session.
1 P.M.	Second individual therapy session occurs for a 68-year old male with late stage lung cancer that focuses on end-of-life care.
2:15 P.M.	The social worker heads for the research group meeting.
2:30 P.M.	The research meeting focuses on methods to evaluate the overall effectiveness of LWC as well as a focus on individual programs.
3:30 P.M.	Following the research meeting, the social worker prepared for her final individual therapy session of the day and an educational presentation to breast cancer patients at 5:30 P.M.
4 P.M.	The third individual session of the day occurs with a 58-year-old breast cancer patient with metastatic disease. Despite a less than optimal prognosis, this patient possesses a high level of determination to survive.

| 5:30 P.M. | Following the final individual session of the day, the social worker quickly transitions to an educational presentation to | | women with cancer and their needs related to family caregivers. |
| | | 7 P.M. | The day comes to an end. |

In the second example, the City of Hope is rapidly developing and implementing a comprehensive psychosocial program for cancer patients and their families. The Sheri and Les Biller Patient and Family Resource Center has been established to provide "a place to feel nurtured, revitalized, and protected [as well as] a sanctuary where you can strengthen and fortify yourself for the challenges ahead." Based on significant gifts from local benefactors, the diverse and unique range of services within the resource center include patient navigation, counseling, support groups, education, palliative care, symptom management, health research, nutritional counseling, rehabilitation, financial counseling, spiritual care, complementary and alternative medicine, patient advocacy, creative arts, pet visitation, and volunteer programs (M. J. Loscalzo, personal communication, 2008).

The programs at the City of Hope are based on the predication of the concept of psychosocial screening and early identification of distress among cancer patients. The goal of this initiative is to comply with the National Distress Management Guidelines as developed by the NCCN and to ensure that "no patients fall through the cracks" as they move through the diagnostic and early treatment phases.

Within this model, the delivery of psychosocial care begins with the process of psychosocial screening that attempts to identify patients with greatest levels of distress and problems related to their diagnosis and treatment (Zabora, Loscalzo, & Weber, 2003). In this highly prospective model, patients and family members are engaged early on the disease trajectory to identify patients at higher levels of distress to prevent needless emotional suffering. The screening tool "How Can We Help You and Your Family" is currently being pilot-tested in three outpatient clinics. A touchscreen version of this tool is currently in development and will be implemented as a standard of care for all outpatients at City of Hope. At the second clinic visit, patients will complete this distress screening instrument on computer tablets with touchscreen technology. In this way, patients can be screened rapidly, and members of the multidisciplinary staff can be alerted in real time by e-mail and by a printed report that details the specific distress and problem-related concerns on any given day.

The following series of activities may resemble a day in the life of a social worker at the City of Hope.

8:30 A.M.	The social worker reviews screening results from the previous day. Based on screening results, the social worker needs to attempt to contact four patients to review the results and schedule an appointment, if possible.		the list of patients screened for distress and illness-related problems. Following these contacts, appointments are made to see these patients on their next clinic visit.
9 A.M.	The social worker attempts to contact the first patient. Once contacted, the patient requests that the discussion occur later in the day. A follow-up call is scheduled for 3 P.M.	10 A.M.	The social worker opens her support group for women with gynecological cancers. The topic for discussion for these 12 women is sexuality and intimacy following a diagnosis of cervical, ovarian, or uterine cancer.
9:30 A.M.	The social worker attempts to contact the first two names on	11:30 A.M.	The social worker returns to her office to attempt to contact the third and fourth names on her

	list of patients with high distress. She manages to contact the fourth patient to set an appointment, and she will devote tome later in the day for the final name.
12 noon.	A group of social workers head for the cafeteria for a brief lunch.
12:30 P.M.	The social worker returns to her office to prepare for three brief therapy sessions that are scheduled for this afternoon.
1 P.M.	First brief therapy session focuses on a patient's ongoing difficulty with accessing medical information from the health care team. The social worker employs a problem-solving approach to develop three strategies to address this issue.
2 P.M.	In the second brief therapy session, the social worker meets with a newly diagnosed prostate cancer patient who is struggling to decide about treatment options. Given the low potential for significant adverse reactions related to prostatectomy, the risk

	of these complications creates significant distress for this patient.
3 P.M.	In the third brief therapy session, the social worker meets with a family who is struggling with end-of-life decisions for the patient, who is 68-year-old father with pancreatic cancer. The patient has been a highly successful college professor who is rapidly deteriorating due to advanced disease. The family reaches an understanding of how treatment will proceed that seems acceptable to all family members.
4 P.M.	The social worker quickly moves to a conference room for family caregivers to conduct a session on the stressors experienced during the care of a loved one with cancer.
5:30 P.M.	The social worker enters her office to check messages and return telephone calls.
6:15 P.M.	The day comes to an end.

THE PROGRESSIVE MODEL

Progressive social work departments attempt to move beyond the traditional focus on discharge planning and linkages to community-based resources. Within this model, this type of department strives to generate a higher level of clinical activity in terms of each patient's attempt to adapt to this difficult diagnosis. Most often, to meet this goal, these departments seek additional funding from external resources, such as the American Cancer Society, the Leukemia and Lymphoma So-

ciety of America, and Susan G. Komen for the Cure (breast cancer foundation). Social work staff within these departments may implement general support groups or be based on specific diagnoses, such as breast or prostate cancer. In addition, educational programs may be developed to assist patients with specific symptoms, such as fatigue. Finally, these departments also attempt to evaluate their services; most often this occurs in the form of patient satisfaction surveys. Given this context, an oncology social worker's day follows.

8 A.M.	Walk rounds begin, but the social worker only attends rounds on a Monday, Wednesday, and Friday schedule. On the other two days, the social worker briefly reviews the rounds log to determine	what new information needs to be considered for active care planning. Throughout rounds, this social worker attempts to provide pertinent psychosocial information that may affect

the delivery of care as well as planning for discharge. In four cases, the social worker describes issues related to social support, concerns about the children of a patient, and the patient's expressions related to depression and level of cancer pain. The social worker leaves rounds with these cases to further assess as well as two discharge planning cases.

10 A.M.   The social worker first visits a 25-year-old woman who has been diagnosed with cervical cancer and was admitted following a series of complications related to her outpatient chemotherapy regimen. Her family has provided little support since the time of her diagnosis, and her friends have gradually withdrawn. The social worker and the patient develop a series of strategies to enable the patient to reconnect with both family members and friends.

11:15 A.M.   The social worker moves to another room to begin an assessment related to a pending discharge. The patient is a 62-year-old former steelworker with early stage lung cancer. The patient was admitted after the initial dose of outpatient chemotherapy when he spiked a high fever in clinic and was admitted for assessment of the etiology of the fever. The fever could be related to his recent surgery. The plan for his discharge to home with intravenous antibiotics is formulated.

11:45 A.M.   Following a few phone calls, the social worker enters the room of a 42-year-old newly diagnosed breast cancer patient who was admitted to assess side effects from radiation therapy. Her primary concern related to her two children, ages 12 and

10. Though they realize that she is ill, she has not told them that she has cancer. An open discussion ensues, and the social worker provides a series of Web-based resources that focus on this specific issue. In addition, she vows to acquire additional information that is available through the hospital's patient library.

12:30 P.M.   The social worker leaves the hospital for a brief lunch.

1:10 P.M.   The social worker attempts to interview the second discharge case that was identified on rounds this morning, however, the patient is away from the unit for a CT scan.

1:15 P.M.   The social worker returns to her office to review final preparations for her support group for patients with metastatic breast cancer that will begin at 2 P.M.

2 P.M.   The 90-minute group begins with eight patients in attendance, and the focus of today's session is managing uncertainty given the status of their disease. The social worker presents some strategies.

3:35 P.M.   The social worker returns to see her second discharge case, but the patient is still unavailable.

3:45 P.M.   An urgent admission is under way from the outpatient clinic for a patient who experienced a significant change in mental status during an infusion. The social worker attempts to locate the family member who was present when this occurred.

3:55 P.M.   The social worker finally locates the family member, who is on the phone just outside the inpatient unit. The family member is attempting to contact and inform other members of the family concerning the admission. Once the calls have been completed, the social worker invites the family member to come to her office to review what occurred as well as address her immediate concerns are.

4:20 P.M.   The social worker escorts the family member back to the patient's room, where the patient seems to be resting comfortably. The social worker informs the patient that she will locate the attending physician to arrange a brief conference to review that status of the patient.

4:45 P.M.   The conference begins with the attending physician, the primary nurse, the social worker, and the wife of the patient. Though all results remain inconclusive, the change in mental status appears to be related to an immediate and adverse reaction to the drug that was administered in the outpatient clinic. The medical team is awaiting a time for a scan to rule out more serious possibilities, such as stroke or bleeding within the brain. Following the meeting, the social worker remains with the patient's wife until family members arrive.

5:15 P.M.   Two family members arrive, and the social worker informs the wife that she will see her again tomorrow. The social worker attempts to visit her second discharge case one final time, but the patients remains sedated following a procedure. This case will be the priority for tomorrow morning.

5:35 P.M.   The day comes to an end.

TRADITIONAL MODEL

Traditional social work departments in hospital settings possess a highly focused mission, with their primary focus being the transition from hospital to home or hospital to a community-based facility, such as a nursing home, rehabilitation center, or hospice. In most instances, social work productivity is closely correlated to the length of stay for each patient. On many medical-surgical units, the average length of stay is often only 2 to 4 days. Given this consistent turnover, social work perceives the greatest contribution as managing the constant flow of patients in these various transitions to avoid extended stays, whereby a payer may deny reimbursement to the hospital if the patient was less than acute. In the case of an oncology inpatient unit, patients are admitted for the management of adverse reactions or symptoms related to outpatient chemotherapy or radiotherapy. Here, the length of stay would also be quite brief.

A second characteristic in this model is that this type of department is highly restricted in the structure of its budget. In these departments, the budget has a sole source, that is, the hospital. This factor places a great deal of pressure to only focus on patient flow on the inpatient areas. In addition, the funds within this single source budget are usually modest which further reinforces the focus on discharge planning and patients' transitions. This factor also prevents any significant program development in ambulatory care areas because the only activity may be related to linking patients and their families to community resources, such as transportation and medical equipment.

A third characteristic is that these departments are volume-driven with limited or no evaluation of their services. Data collection is limited and consists primarily of demographics and problem codes. Consequently, these departments struggle to document their level of effectiveness beyond discharge planning and length of stay. This dynamic places these departments at a significant disadvantage given that numerous factors outside the control of social work could contribute to a longer length of stay beyond the acute phase. For example, a change in Medicaid regulations could create discharge delays for patients with lower levels of resources. Though these delays may be unavoidable, administration may perceive social work as being ineffective.

Given these characteristics, oncology social workers would be compelled to focus on the inpatients units while providing limited services in the outpatient clinics. In terms of a day in the life of a social worker, the following flow might occur.

8 A.M.   Patient walk rounds. As part of the multidisciplinary team, walk rounds occur daily to review each patient in terms of the status of their disease, treatment plan for the day, any potential complications, and a target date for discharge. This morning, the oncology social worker receives three referrals with potential discharge dates within three days. These three cases entail discharge to home with multiple needs, a transfer to a nursing home, and an admission to a hospice program.

10:30 A.M.   Following rounds, the social worker visits each of these three patients to assess their understanding of what may be happening later in the week. The first patient is a 48-year-old homemaker who is anxious to go home but is quite apprehensive given the level of care that she will need. Her husband will visit her at the end of the day after he leaves work. The social worker reassures her that the team will develop a plan for her care at home, and she will return at 4:30 P.M. to meet with her husband. The second patient is an 80-year-old widower who is estranged from his adult children and can no longer care for himself alone at home. Although he recognizes his need for skilled nursing home care, he describes this upcoming transition as depressing. The social worker develops a potential list of homes with this patient and they agree to meet again in the morning. In the final case, a 75-year-old woman had been admitted for severe abdominal pain as well as headaches. Scans confirmed significant advanced disease related to her initial lung cancer diagnosis with metastases throughout her abdomen as well as to her brain. Her mood is somber as the discussion begins about the need for hospice care. She had previously been informed of her status by the attending physician. Her husband and two adult children are present, and all of them attempt to convey their care and support. A specific hospice is identified, and the social worker leaves the room to explore the availability of beds in this facility.

12 noon.   The social worker returns to her office to begin to contact the hospice as well as the lists of nursing homes from the second case. These two cases take precedence since she has until 4:30 P.M. to acquire a list of resources for the initial case. First, she has a quick lunch at her desk. At around 12:20 P.M., she contacts the hospice only to learn that no beds will be available for approximately 3 days. This information could create a dilemma if the patient becomes ready for discharge. The primary focus of care for this patient is pain control and her mental status due to the brain metastases. She explores other potential hospices in the area, only to arrive at the same outcomes.

12:50 P.M.   Her attention now turns to the second case, and she contacts five nursing homes. The normal information is exchanged. The first place is unlikely to accept the patient within the next 7 days, but the second one could accept him in 3 days. Just then, the social worker is paged to the outpatient clinic.

1:30 P.M.   The social worker arrives in the clinic to learn that a patient has missed his appointment due to having a fall at home. This clinic visit is deemed critical given the current status of his treatment. After approximately 25 minutes, the social worker secures a private ambulance for the patient to be transported to clinic.

2 P.M.	The social worker returns to the inpatient unit to discuss nursing home options with the second patient. The patient seems reasonably satisfied with the second option. The social worker attempts to open a discussion about his lack of contact with his family, but the patient prefers not to explore these issues.		for taxicabs. After a brief assessment, the social worker informs the patient that a taxi will arrive in 15 minutes to transport him to this home.
		4:15 P.M.	The social worker returns a final time to her office to review all of the information for her upcoming meeting with the patient and her husband.
2:30 P.M.	The social worker returns to the room of the third case, and the family is still there. An open discussion ensues about the availability of hospice and what this actually means. The social worker attempts to lead the family through a course of what will occur with as much support and compassion as possible. The family appropriately begins to express their profound sadness and grief about the pending death of their loved one.	4:30 P.M.	The social worker arrives to meet with the patient and her husband. All of the resources are discussed, along with the level of insurance coverage. Discharge will probably occur within 2 to 3 days, and there does not appear to be any obstacles to the transition to home. At 5 P.M., the social worker is again paged to the outpatient clinic. Apparently, a patient coded during a routine physical examination, and the social worker needs to address the needs of the family.
3:15 P.M.	The social worker returns to her office to begin to prepare for her 4:30 P.M. meeting with her first referral of the day. The patient will need a hospital bed, a walker, a bedside commode, and nutritional support at home. After approximately eight telephone inquiries, these resources could be in place by the time of discharge in 3 days.	5:05 P.M.	The social worker opens a discussion with the family of the patient who apparently coded. Needless to say, the family is quite distressed and is actively seeking an explanation of what happened. The social worker maintains a balance between addressing their emotional response and accessing accurate information from the medical team concerning the status of the patient. After about an hour, the patient is stabilized and transported to the intensive care unit.
3:45 P.M.	Another page comes from the outpatient clinic. The social worker quickly responds to learn that an indigent patient is stranded in the clinic following his appointment. Fortunately, the social work department has a transportation fund	6:05 P.M.	The day comes to an end.

CONCLUSIONS

The role of the oncology social worker varies significantly across clinical practice settings. Though the majority of settings focus on essential and practical services, examples of highly innovative programs demonstrate the creativity of oncology social workers to envision state-of-the-art psycho-social care. At its best, oncology social workers have designed and implemented the most comprehensive programs for cancer patients and their families. Not long ago, the most comprehensive psychosocial program, as defined by Jimmie Holland, one of the founders of the field of psychosocial oncology, was the program at Johns Hopkins in Baltimore, Maryland, that was developed by James

Zabora and Matthew Loscalzo (Zabora, Loscalzo, & Smith, 2000).

WEB SITES

American Psychosocial Oncology Society. http://www.apos-society.org/professionals/meetings-ed/webcasts/webcasts-multidisciplinary.aspx.

Association of Oncology Social Work. http://www.aosw.org/html/prof-standards.php.

City of Hope. http://www.coh.org/BillerCenter/home.htm.

Life with Cancer. http://www.lifewithcancer.org.

National Comprehensive Cancer Network. http://www.nccn.org/professionals/physician_gls/PDF/distress.pdf.

References

National Comprehensive Cancer Network. (2007). *Distress management guidelines.* Retrieved from NCCN Web site, http://www.nccn.org/professionals/physician_gls/PDF/distress.pdf.

Zabora, J., BrintzenhofeSzoc, K., Fox, N., & Lipton, H. (2006, April). *Evidence-based practice: What is possible now?* Paper presented as a preconference institute at the annual meeting of the Society for Social Work Leaders in Health Care, San Diego, CA.

Zabora, J. R., Loscalzo, M. J., & Smith, E. D. (2000) Psychosocial rehabilitation. In M.D. Abeloff et al. (Eds.), *Clinical oncology* (pp. 2845–2865). New York: Churchill Livingstone.

Zabora, J. R., Loscalzo, M. J., & Weber, J. (2003). Managing complications in cancer: Identifying and responding to the patient's perspective. *Seminars in Oncology, 19*(Supp), 1–9.

11 The Social Worker in a Police Department

Karen S. Knox & Albert R. Roberts

Police-based social work requires specialized education and training to work with diverse types of crime and trauma victims, survivors, and family members. This chapter presents a brief history and an overview of the types of programs, theoretical models, and services in police-based social work. Special clinical issues and intervention skills are addressed, as well as evidence-based practice guidelines.

A DAY IN THE LIFE OF A POLICE-BASED SOCIAL WORKER

Friday, 6 P.M.   Arrive at the south substation and check any case referrals requested by the day shift; then follow up on the sexual assault victim from last night's crisis team shift. There's a message from the Sex Crimes Unit that the victim showed up this afternoon to file charges. Good news! She was ambivalent about filing charges because she blamed herself for getting so drunk.

6:20 P.M.   While returning phone calls, a patrol officer arrives with a child and requests assistance. The girl's parents were just arrested on outstanding warrants during a traffic stop, and while he's booking them, I'll call Child Protective Services (CPS) and stay with her. I find out that the father became combative and fought with the officers, and she witnessed the police using a Taser gun on him. Before calling CPS, I attend to basic needs first—does she need to go to the bathroom, want anything to drink or eat? She asks me questions about where her parents are that I answer as best I can. When CPS arrives, I can go check on the parents and try to let her know something then. Right now, she isn't exhibiting any traumatic reactions, but she may later. Hopefully, CPS will find a relative placement and not have to put her in a shelter or foster home. I provide a comfortable place for us to wait, and because there are some games and art supplies at the station, we check out what she would like to do while we wait. Hopefully CPS arrives before our shift starts.

7:05 P.M.   The CPS on-call investigator arrives, and I brief him on what happened. I tell him she may have a delayed reaction to witnessing her father's altercation with the police and to make sure that whomever she is placed with needs to be aware of what happened. I go check in with the officer so I can then let him know CPS is here and see if we can talk to the mother. We find out the aunt lives here, so CPS investigator contacts her to come to the substation. Then I go back and let the daughter know her mother is okay and her aunt is coming to take her to her house for the night. Hopefully, the mother can make bail tomorrow morning. Father was transported to the emergency room after the incident so I can only let her know that the doctors are taking care of him. Maybe when her aunt gets here, they can find out more from the hospital.

7:45 P.M.   The girl's aunt arrives, and the CPS investigator wants to talk with her, so I stay with the daughter. She is glad to see a familiar face and excited to be leaving. She's getting bored and anxious, so I take her with me when I go get our equipment and gear for tonight's shift and check out the Crisis Team car. Children usually enjoy looking at the police cars, especially the sirens and lights. The crisis team cars don't have those—or the guns and other police equipment—but we do have a computer now, which makes it easier to write up our incident reports because we don't have to wait until we get back to the substation at the end of our shift. When we get back, CPS is done with the aunt, and all three are going to her house, now so he can finish his investigation there.

8 P.M.   The crisis team volunteer shows up on time—this is her first official shift. She finished the 40-hour training a month ago and did her required ride-outs with the patrol officers. She's got good professional experience—she's been at the mental health center for 7 years, so she will be helpful with our 1096 calls—those are psychiatric emergencies or cases the police call "emotionally disturbed persons." I hope it's a slow evening so we can talk—the new volunteers are usually nervous the first couple of shifts, not knowing what

to expect. That's one thing I like about this job—you never know what type of call you'll work. Tonight we're assigned to Charlie sector, which is usually busy on the weekends—lots of family violence and assault calls when people start drinking and partying.

8:20 P.M.   I check out our handie-talkies, we head for the car, and I sign-on that we're in-service with dispatch. The new volunteers have to get familiar with the equipment and radio, so I'll have her practice tonight. Even though it's part of the training, it takes awhile to get comfortable talking on the radio and learning the police codes. We head towards Charlie sector, which is the east side of the city. My volunteer probably isn't familiar with this part of town, so will drive around and give her some orientation to the neighborhood until we get a call.

9:45 P.M.   We get our first call—a request by a patrol officer at a family violence incident. The crime scene was secured and the perpetrator arrested by the time we arrive at the home. The 16-year-old daughter's boyfriend assaulted her father in the front yard, and EMS was on the scene treating the father for non–life-threatening injuries.

10:10 P.M.   After checking with the patrol officer, we meet with the mother and daughter, who are on the front porch. The mother is yelling at the daughter, and the daughter is crying as we try to introduce ourselves. First, we need to deescalate the situation, so I ask if we can speak to them separately. The volunteer goes with the daughter into the house to talk. After letting the mother

vent some more, I ask her to take some deep breaths and talk to me about what happened, She calms down and asks what is going to happen next, so I explain the police procedures. She decides to go with her husband to the hospital. Before she leaves, I let her know that one of the victim services counselors with the Family Violence Unit will be contacting her for follow-up services and give her my card so she can call if she needs anything else tonight.

11 P.M.   I talk to my volunteer and she says the daughter is scared of her mother's reactions and what might happen when her parents return from the hospital. We talk to the daughter about her concerns and explore her options. She decides to call her grandparents to come over and stay with her and her brother tonight and help her talk with her mother and father when they return home. We also talk to her 12-year-old brother, who was asleep during the incident, but awoke and was frightened by the police and ambulance being there. We wait until the grandparents arrive and the scene is cleared, then let them know that Victim Services can provide follow-up services for the family and also give them my card before leaving.

Saturday,
12:45 A.M.   We go to the car to start entering our incident report on the computer, and let dispatch know that we are back in service. My volunteer and I talk about the incident and process our reactions—I'm glad her first experience was a relatively easy case. Then we receive a call from dispatch that we are needed at another call. It's going to be another long shift!

INTRODUCTION AND HISTORY

Police-based social work can be very challenging. You could be working with a victim of sexual assault or a family survivor of a homicide victim. Typical types of cases include:

- child abuse,
- suicides,
- family violence,
- robbery,
- traffic fatalities,
- kidnapping,
- stalking, and
- mental health/psychiatric emergencies.

As first responders, police-based social workers also work with victims of disasters, such as floods, fires, and tornados, as well as terrorist attacks and catastrophic incidents, such as bombings and hostage takings. A police-based social worker must have an eclectic knowledge base and specialized training about a variety of theories and interventions to address diverse types of crime and trauma experiences and their specific impacts on victims, survivors, and their loved ones. Some clients might only need some basic information about the criminal justice process, whereas others require immediate crisis intervention. Police-based social work also requires extensive knowledge of community resources and programs for referrals for basic needs, support services, counseling, safety needs, and advocacy in the legal system.

Social workers have a long history of working in law enforcement, beginning in the early 1900s with the establishment of Women's Bureaus in police departments to work with women and children in need of protective services (Roberts, 2007). However, it wasn't until the 1970s when the battered women's and rape crisis movements became active that the social work presence in law enforcement gained momentum. During the 1980s, the crime victims' movement emerged with the realization that many crime victims were being victimized twice—once during the actual crime, and then again by the criminal justice system, which historically was designed to protect the rights of the criminal/defendant, not the victim/survivor. The crime victims' movement resulted in federal legislation and funding to establish victim assistance programs in all states through the federal Law Enforcement Assistance Administration (LEAA) and the Victims of Crime Act of 1984 (Knox & Roberts, 2007).

Between 1984 and 1997, billions of dollars were allocated to aid victims of domestic violence, sexual assault, child abuse, and other violent crimes; in 1994, both the federal Violence Against Women Act and the federal Law Enforcement and Crime Control Act allocated more funding to state and city police departments to develop crisis intervention and domestic violence counseling programs (Roberts & Fisher, 1997). By 1999, there were close to 10,000 victim/witness assistance, victim services, domestic violence, and sexual assault treatment programs nationwide (Brownell & Roberts, 2002).

OVERVIEW OF VICTIM SERVICES PROGRAMS

Victim service programs are located in law enforcement agencies at the federal, state, and local levels. Most programs typically offer a comprehensive range of essential services with the primary objectives of:

- Providing timely crisis intervention to crime victims, family survivors, and witnesses;
- Using a team approach with police officers and prosecutors during the investigation, the victim/witness statements, and the legal/court process;
- Providing referrals for emergency assistance and follow-up services through community and social services agencies; and
- Assistance in completing victim assistance compensation packets.

Victim services programs in law enforcement range from one staff person in smaller, rural jurisdictions to larger programs in urban areas. Services are provided though a variety of modalities, including letters, telephone and e-mail contacts, home visits, on-the-scene response, day services at the police department, court hearings, and even jail consultations for suicide risk and mental health assessments. Basic need services can be met through:

- Emergency assistance funds,
- Basic needs resources (e.g., locksmiths, food coupons for supermarkets),
- Emergency shelter, and
- Transportation services.

Investigative services include:

- Assisting with interviewing witness and victim statements,

- Death notification,
- Hostage negotiation, and
- Training for law enforcement and community providers.

Psychological services are provided through:

- Crisis intervention,
- Short-term counseling, and
- Training of first responders.

Community-level services include being members of emergency response teams for disasters, catastrophic events, school shootings, and terrorist attacks.

THEORETICAL MODELS

The primary theoretical models used by victim services programs are brief, time-limited, action-oriented approaches that focus on immediate needs, not past issues or problems requiring long-term treatment. Results from a national survey conducted by Knox and Roberts (2002) of law enforcement victim services programs (N = 111) indicate that they use the following theoretical models:

- Crisis intervention (68 percent)
- Grief and bereavement therapy (23 percent),
- Brief or time-limited treatment (20 percent),
- Cognitive-behavioral approaches (9 percent),
- Family therapy (9 percent),
- Reality and/or rational-emotive therapy (9 percent),
- Art/play therapy (5 percent),
- Eye-movement desensitization and reprocessing (3 percent).

The major tenets of crisis intervention derived originally from the central ideas of ego psychology (life developmental stages, psychosocial crises, coping skills, and defense mechanisms) and systems theory (homeostasis, disequilibrium, and interdependence). Crisis intervention is time-limited, and the goal is to help the client mobilize needed support, resources, and adaptive coping skills to resolve or minimize the disequilibrium experienced by the precipitating event. Crisis intervention can be as brief as one client contact or may last up to six to eight sessions. Once the client has returned to her or his precrisis level of functioning and homeostasis, any further supportive

or supplemental services are usually referred out to appropriate community agencies and service providers (Knox & Roberts, 2008).

Cognitive-behavioral, reality, and rational-emotive-behavioral therapy are other brief, time-limited models that share many characteristics with crisis intervention. The cognitive-behavioral principle that an individual's perceptions and cognitions affect his or her beliefs, feelings, and behaviors in an interactive way is essential to crisis theory. The critical incident or precipitating event has to be perceived as a crisis by the client, and individuals involved in the same crisis situation may have very different perceptions, feelings, reactions, and coping skills.

EVIDENCED-BASED PRACTICE GUIDELINES

Most of the research on best practices includes studies describing the types of services and interventions provided by law enforcement victim service programs and which services are most requested by police officers and most used by crime victims (Knox & Roberts, 2002; Sims, Yost, & Abbott, 2005; Winkel, Wohlfarth, & Blaauw, 2004). Other research examines the effectiveness of victim services with specialized client populations, such as domestic violence and partner stalking (Corcoran, Stephenson, Perryman, & Allen, 2001; Logan, Walker, Stewart, & Allen, 2006). A meta-analysis by Patterson (2004) examines the empirical evidence supporting the efficacy of social worker-police crisis teams, and the findings are consistent with those of Corcoran et al. (2001), indicating that police officers who used the crisis team approach report it to be both helpful and effective. Stohr (2005) identifies the following best practices for law enforcement victim services programs:

- Identify the multiple needs of clients;
- Focus services on those who need them most;
- Structure programs to fit the most pressing needs;
- Attract, hire, train, and maintain skilled and knowledgeable professionals;
- Involve clients in their own case and service decisions;
- Provide follow-up or after care services; and
- Build in process and outcome evaluations to enhance service delivery.

SPECIAL CLINICAL ISSUES

Crisis intervention requires a high level of activity and skill on the part of the social worker, and the time frame for assessment and contracting must be brief by necessity. People experiencing trauma and crisis need immediate relief and assistance, and the helping process must be adapted to meet those needs as efficiently and effectively as possible. Therefore, the assessment, contracting, and intervention stages may need to be completed and implemented on the very first client contact. Clients in an active state of crisis are more amenable to the helping process and are more likely to accept help, so this can facilitate completion of such tasks within a rapid response time frame.

Specialized knowledge about specific types of crime victims and traumatic incidents is necessary for effective intervention planning. For example, working with victims of family violence requires education and training on the dynamics and cycle of battering and abuse, familiarity with the community agencies providing services to this client population, and knowledge about the legal options available to victims.

Concrete, basic needs services, such as emergency safety, medical needs, food, clothing, and shelter, are the first priority in crisis intervention. Mobilizing needed resources may require more direct activity by the social worker in advocating, networking, and brokering for clients, who may not have the knowledge, skills, or capacity to follow through with referrals and collateral contacts at the time of active crisis.

Because police-based social workers are part of a team approach with law enforcement, it is important to note that clinical work in a host environment has the potential for many ethical dilemmas and conflicts. Police officers are not bound by the same code of ethics as social workers are, and confidentiality and privacy can be compromised during an investigation.

STEP-BY-STEP TREATMENT MODEL AND GOALS

Roberts's Seven-Stage Crisis Intervention Model is useful in police-based social work because it adapts easily to the different types of crises and to different time frames for intervention (Knox & Roberts, 2008). All of these stages can be completed within one contact if necessary, and in many crisis situations, that may be all the time that is available.

Stage 1: Plan and Conduct a Psychosocial and Lethality Assessment

Assessment is ongoing and critical to effective intervention at all stages, and it begins with an assessment of the lethality and safety issues for the client. With victims of rape, family violence, child abuse, or assault, it is important to assess whether the client is in any current danger and consider future safety concerns in treatment planning. With suicidal clients, it is critical to assess the risk for attempts, plans, or means to harm oneself at the current time, as well as any previous history of suicidal ideations or attempts. The goals of this stage are to obtain information to determine whether the client is in imminent danger and identify and assess critical areas of intervention.

The sexual assault call briefly presented earlier in the chapter serves as a case example. When the crisis team arrives at the scene, the police officers have determined that the perpetrator was not at the location, and the crime scene unit is on the way to gather any potential evidence. Rhonda, the victim, is in her bedroom, so the crisis team leader goes to check on her while the volunteer talks to the patrol officers to get information from them. Rhonda appears to be disoriented and confused about what has happened. She has no visible physical injuries, and the police officers have already checked to see if EMS needed to be called, but she told them she didn't have any pain or injuries as far as she could tell. She says that she had been on a date with a man she had met through a Web site, and they had gone to a restaurant for dinner and drinks. All she can recall is being at the front door of her apartment with her date, and then the rest of the night is a blank. She awoke about 2 A.M. on her couch in the living room with her clothes in disarray, and she called 911 at that time. It is now 2:30 in the morning, and she starts crying while she is talking. The crisis team leader allows some silence and time to respect her need for emotional release before talking further.

At present, although there is no imminent danger or harm, it is necessary to talk with her about going to the emergency room for a rape exam, starting with how important it is to make sure that she is okay physically and to gather physical evidence. Rhonda has a lot of questions about the rape exam that the crisis team leader answers. The crisis team leader explains that the medical procedures are done by a specially trained sexual assault nurse examiner, and the crisis team would accompany her to the emergency room and stay with her until after the examination if she wanted. The crisis team also offers to contact a support person to meet us at the hospital if she wants to have a friend or relative there, too. The team leader also has her get a change of clothes because what she is now wearing will be taken as evidence. Rhonda asks if she can go to the bathroom before leaving, and the crisis team leader relates that it would destroy any physical evidence of sexual assault so it would be best if she could wait. Rhonda is also worried that the perpetrator might have her keys or access to her apartment and is fearful that he may return, so the volunteer asks the patrol officers to secure her apartment and check with the manager about changing her locks as soon as possible. It is now 3:10 A.M. and the crisis team transports Rhonda to the hospital.

Stage 2: Make Psychological Contact and Rapidly Establish the Relationship

The main goals of this stage are to establish rapport and a supportive relationship. Crime victims may question their own safety and vulnerability, and trust may be difficult for them to establish at this time. Therefore, active listening and empathetic communication skills are essential to engaging the client. During this stage, clients need support, positive regard, concern, and genuineness.

As the crisis team transports Rhonda to the hospital, she starts going over the details of the night, which is common for crime victims and helps them become more oriented to the time and sequence of events and able to process what happened. It is important to listen and take notes for the incident report and to let Rhonda talk and vent without too much questioning. There will be plenty of time for that when she has to go give a statement to the Sex Crimes Unit tomorrow. Empathetic communication skills are important at this time to help establish the relationship and encourage her to ventilate and express her emotional reactions.

Stage 3: Identify the Major Problems

The police-based social worker should help the client prioritize the most important problems or impacts by identifying them in terms of how they affect the client's current status. The first priority in this stage is meeting the basic needs of emotional and physical health and safety. The focus must clearly be on the present crisis, and any exploration of past problems or issues must be done rapidly and only to aid in intervention planning.

When we arrive at the hospital, the volunteer goes to check in with the ER social worker to see if there is a private room for us to wait until time for the exam. Emergency waiting rooms are often crowded, loud, and disorienting, and it would be better to have a calmer atmosphere for her so as not to increase any anxiety and distress. We are able to contact her best friend, who is on her way to the emergency room, and Rhonda plans on staying with her after the exam, because she doesn't want to go home. She talks with the crisis team about her present concerns regarding the rape exam and what procedures and tests will be done. She also wants to know what she needs to do to give her statement to the investigator from the Sex Crimes Unit, and what the police will do about arresting the suspect. Other problems she wants help with are getting some more clothes and her car and calling her employer to explain about missing work tomorrow. She says she can stay with her friend for a while, and that she doesn't feel safe returning to her apartment yet.

Stage 4: Deal with Feelings and Providing Support

The primary goal is dealing with the emotional impacts of the trauma event through venting, expression, and exploration of the client's emotions about the crisis event and aftermath. The primary technique used is active listening, which involves listening in an accepting and supportive way, in as private and safe a setting as possible. It is critical that the police-based social worker demonstrates empathy and is supportive. Sometimes victims blame themselves, and it is important to help the client acknowledge and accept that being a victim is not one's fault. Validation and reassurance are especially useful in this stage, because survivors may be experiencing confusing and conflicting feelings.

While waiting, Rhonda starts blaming herself for what happened, saying she should have been more cautious about meeting someone she only knew through the Internet and for drinking and then letting her date drive her home. We are supportive and reassure her that she is not responsible for what happened, that the suspect may have drugged her drink because she has such a lack of recall about what happened after they left the restaurant. This is another important part of the medical exam if there is any concern about a drug-assisted sexual assault.

We talk about other support services available at the victim services unit at the police department and with the rape crisis center. They have on-call volunteers who will come to the emergency room, too, but Rhonda says she is comfortable with us being there. We also explain the center's other counseling and support services so that she is informed of what help is available. We let her know that a police-based social worker will be available for counseling, to answer questions, or provide other assistance when she goes to the station to give her statement, and she can contact the crisis team after day-service hours if she wants to talk or needs anything. When Rhonda goes to give her statement, the police-based social worker will also inform her about victim's compensation and how to apply for benefits and make any other needed community referrals.

Stage 5: Generate and Explore Alternatives

The goal is to achieve a precrisis level of functioning through the client's coping skills and support systems. The police-based social worker may need to be more active and directive in this stage if the client has unrealistic expectations or inappropriate coping skills and strategies. Clients are still distressed and in disequilibrium at this stage, and professional expertise and guidance could be necessary to produce positive, realistic alternatives for the client.

Rhonda's friend arrives before she goes for the rape exam, and we fill her in on what has happened so far and the plans for tonight. Rhonda wants her friend to accompany her to the exam room, so we decide to wait until the exam is done to see how she is doing emotionally and if there is anything else we can assist her with tonight. Afterward, we talk to Rhonda to assess her emotional and physical needs and check if there are any medications or further medical procedures that need to be taken care of before leaving the hospital.

Stage 6: Develop and Formulate an Action Plan

It is important for the client to look at both the short-term and long-range impacts in planning intervention. The main goals are to help the client achieve an appropriate level of functioning and maintain adaptive coping skills and resources. It is important to have a manageable treatment plan, so the client can follow through and be successful. Do not overwhelm the client with too many tasks or strategies, which may set the client up for failure. Ongoing assessment and evaluation are essential to determine whether the intervention plan is appropriate and effective in minimizing or resolving the client's identified problems. During this stage, the client should be processing and reintegrating the crisis impacts to achieve homeostasis and equilibrium in his or her life.

Though we have taken care of Rhonda's immediate concerns and needs for tonight, she will need support and referrals for further counseling and advocacy services through the legal and court process. The police-based social worker can provide short-term crisis intervention and counseling services, and the local rape crisis center offers both individual and group counseling services. The center also has a court liaison providing assistance and advocacy if the suspect goes to trial. This can be a critical time for crime victims that triggers memories and reactions from the assault that need to be addressed in follow-up counseling.

Stage 7: Termination and Follow-Up Measures

Termination begins when the client has achieved the goals of the action plan or has been referred for additional services through other treatment providers. This last stage should help determine whether these results have been maintained or if further work remains to be done. Typically, follow-up contacts are by phone and should be done within 4 to 6 weeks after termination.

The victim services program will contact Rhonda about 6 weeks after the case is closed to assess if there are any issues or problems that the police-based social worker can provide. Because the legal system is often a very long process, this is usually when victims may have questions about what is going on with their case or what is happening in the court system, so there is an opportunity to assist with these types of legal issues and concerns. It is also a time to check whether the victim/survivor has followed up with counseling referrals and treatment or is still in emotional and psychological distress, and to assist with providing other referrals or treatment options.

INTERVENTION SKILLS AND COMPETENCIES

Communication Skills

The police-based social worker needs to be attentive to the tone and level of verbal communications to help the client calm down or deescalate from initial trauma reactions. Being observant of the client's physical and facial reactions can provide cues to the client's current emotional state and level of engagement. It is important to remember that delayed reactions or flat affect are common with crime victims and to not assume that these type of reactions mean that the client is not in crisis. Encouraging the client to vent about the precipitating crisis event can assist in problem identification, and some have an overwhelming need to talk about the specifics of the trauma situation. Others may be in shock, denial, or unable to verbalize their needs and feelings, so information may need to be obtained from collateral sources or significant others.

Intervention Skills

Intervention begins at first contact when victims and survivors may be experiencing confusing and conflicting feelings. The social worker needs to be knowledgeable about the grief process, which many victims and family survivors follow when expressing and venting their emotions. First, clients may be in denial about the extent of their emotional reactions and may try to avoid dealing with them in hopes that they will subside. They may be in shock and not be able to access their feelings immediately. However, significant delays in expression and venting of feelings can be harmful to the client in processing and resolving the trauma.

Some clients express anger and rage about the situation and its effects, which can be healthy, as long as it does not escalate out of control. Helping the client calm down or attending to physiological reactions (such as hyperventilation) are important interventions in this situation. Other clients may express their grief and sadness by crying, moaning, or fainting (referred to as "falling out" in some cultures) and need time and space to express their reactions, without pressure to move along too quickly.

Coping Skills

Healthy coping skills are behaviors or strategies that promote adaptive responses and resolution of the crisis by

1. Using support systems, such as people or resources that can be helpful to the client in meeting needs and resolving problems in living as a result of the crisis.
2. Increasing positive and constructive thinking patterns to reduce the client's levels of anxiety and stress.

The police-based social worker can facilitate healthy coping skills by identifying client strengths and resources. Many crisis survivors feel they do not have a lot of choices, and the crisis worker needs to be familiar with both formal and informal community services to provide referrals. For example, working with a battered woman often requires relocation to a safe place for her and the children. The client may not have the personal resources or financial ability to move out of the home, and the crisis worker needs to be informed about possible alternatives, which could include a shelter program, a protective order, or other emergency housing services.

Termination and Follow-Up Skills

It is important to remember that final crisis resolution may take many months or years to achieve (if ever), and certain events, places, or dates could trigger emotional and physical reactions to the previous trauma. For example, a critical time is during court hearings, when crime victims may reexperience old fears, reactions, or thoughts. This is a normal part of the recovery process, and clients should be prepared to have contingency plans or supportive help through these difficult periods.

Self-Care

Self-care and safety concerns are critical in this setting. The police-based social worker needs to be aware of any potential weapons (part of the risk assessment process) and have an exit code word or plan along with police back-up when working cases on the scene. Even in police stations, dangerous situations can arise when suspects try to flee or fight.

The police-based social worker must also be aware of his or her own emotional reactions and level of comfort when working with clients. It is important to attend to self-care needs to avoid burnout and emotional fatigue. Secondary traumatization effects can be experienced by police-based social workers, and critical incident stress management interventions may be necessary for their psychological health.

WEB SITES

Establishing Victim Services within a Law Enforcement Agency: The Austin Experience, by Susan G. Parker. U.S. Department of Justice, Office of Justice Programs, Office for Victims of Crime. http://www.ojp.usdoj.gov/ ovc/publications/bulletins/evs_3_2001/ welcome.html.

National Organization for Victim Assistance, a private, nonprofit organization committed to the recognition and implementation of victim rights and services. http://www .trynova.org.

Office for Victims of Crime, U.S. Department of Justice. Possibly the single best source for information directly relating to victim assistance and the people who work in this field. Their links to victim assistance and compensation programs are very useful. http://www .ojp.usdoj.gov/ovc/welcome.html.

References

Brownell, P., & Roberts, A. R. (2002). A century of social work in criminal justice and correctional settings. *Journal of Offender Rehabilitation, 35,* 1–17.

Corcoran, J., Stephenson, M., Perryman, D., & Allen, S. (2001). Perceptions and utilization of a police-social work crisis intervention approach to domestic violence. *Families in Society: Journal of Contemporary Human Services, 82*(4), 393–398.

Knox, K. S., & Roberts, A. R. (2002). Police social work. In G. Greene & A. R. Roberts (Eds.), *Social workers' desk reference* (pp. 668–672). New York: Oxford University Press.

Knox, K. S., & Roberts, A. R. (2007). Forensic social work in law enforcement and victim service/victim assistance programs: National and local perspectives. In A. R. Roberts & D. W. Springer (Eds.), *Social work in juvenile and criminal justice settings* (pp. 113–123). Springfield, IL: Charles C. Thomas.

Knox, K. S., & Roberts, A. R. (2008). The crisis intervention model. In P. Lehmann & N. Coady (Eds.), *Theoretical perspectives for direct social work practice: A generalist-eclectic approach* (pp. 249–274). New York: Springer.

Logan, T. K., Walker, R., Stewart, C., & Allen, J. (2006). Victim services and justice system representative responses to partner stalking: What do professionals recommend? *Violence and Victims, 21*(1), 49–66.

Patterson, G. (2004). Police-social work crisis teams: Practice and research implications. *Sterss, Ttrauma, and Crisis: An International Journal, 7*(2), 93–104.

Roberts, A. R. (2007). The history and role of social work in law enforcement. In A.R. Roberts & D. W. Springer (Eds.), *Social work in juvenile and criminal justice settings* (pp. 106–112). Springfield, IL: Charles C. Thomas.

Roberts, A. R., & Fisher, P. (1997). Service roles in victim/witness assistance programs. In A. McNeece & A. R. Roberts (Eds.), *Policy and practice in the justice system* (pp. 127–142). Chicago: Nelson-Hall.

Sims, B., Yost, B., & Abbott, C. (2005). Use and nonuse of victim service programs: Implications from a statewide survey of crime victims. *Criminology & Public Policy, 4*(2), 361–384.

Stohr, M. (2005). Victim services programming: If it is efficacious, they will come. *Criminology & Public Policy, 4*(2), 391–397.

Winkel, F. W., Wohlfarth, T., & Blaauw, E. (2004). Police referral to victim services: The predictive and diagnostic value of the RISK10 screening instrument. *Crisis, 25*(3), 118–127.

12 The Social Worker in a Domestic Violence Shelter

Diane L. Green & Brandy Macaluso

Approximately 8.7 million women are battered each year (Roberts, 2007). Intimate partner violence (IPV) resulted in 1,544 deaths in 2004. Of these deaths, 25 percent were males and 75 percent were females (Tjaden & Thoennes, 2000). Research supported by the National Institute of Justice (NIJ) and others has identified some of the causes of and risk factors for intimate partner violence (often called "domestic violence"). IPV has serious physical, psychological, economic, and social consequences.

One in five women killed or severely injured by an intimate partner had no warning: the fatal or life-threatening incident was the first physical violence they had experienced from their partner. A woman's attempt to leave an abuser was the precipitating factor in 45 percent of the murders of women by their intimate partners (Block, 2003). Early parenthood is a risk factor. Women who had children by age 21 were twice as likely to be victims of IPV as women who were not mothers at that age. Men who had fathered children by age 21 were more than three times as likely to be abusers as men who were not fathers at that age (Moffitt & Caspi, 1999). Although alcohol is not the cause of violence against women, a significant relationship exists between male perpetrator problem drinking and violence against intimate female partners. Severe drinking problems increase the risk for lethal and violent victimization of women in intimate partner relationships. More than two-thirds of the offenders who commit or attempt homicide used alcohol, drugs, or both during the incident; less than one-fourth of the victims did (Sharps, Campbell, Campbell, Gary, & Webster, 2003).

Severe poverty and its associated stressors increase the risk for IPV—the lower the household income, the higher the reported IPV rates (Carlson, Worden, van Ryn, &Bachman, 2000). Moreover, researchers found that reductions in benefits from Aid to Families with Dependent Children (AFDC) were associated with an increase in intimate partner homicides (Dugan, Nagin, & Rosenfeld, 2003).

Intimate partner violence is linked with unemployment; one study found that IPV impairs a woman's capacity to find employment (Goodwin, Chandler, & Meisel, 2003). Another study of women who received AFDC benefits found that domestic violence was associated with a general pattern of reduced stability of employment (Meisel, Chandler, & Rienzi, 2003). Women who have experienced serious abuse face overwhelming mental and emotional distress. Almost half of the those reporting serious domestic violence also meet the criteria for major depression; 24 percent suffer from post-traumatic stress disorder and 31 percent from anxiety (Goodwin et al., 2003).

ROLES AND FUNCTIONS OF A DOMESTIC VIOLENCE SOCIAL WORKER

The schedule for a social worker varies by career field chosen. Domestic violence crisis responders work 12-hour shifts on any given day of the week, including all major holidays. Noncrisis responders work from 8 A.M. to 5 P.M. Monday through Friday, excluding all major holidays. Occasionally, noncrisis responders will have to attend outreach events, trainings, or community education forums held over weekends in which flex time is used. The schedules below illustrate a typical day for a domestic violence advocate (crisis and noncrisis responders) and a typical day for a domestic violence shelter worker.

Crisis Responders

7 P.M.	Shift begins. Answering crisis hotline.		injury. Send intake worker to hospital to complete assessment and provide services.
8:30–10:15 P.M.	Several calls for information and referral sources.	6:40 A.M.	Several calls for information and referrals for services after being victimized that night but waited to call.
2 A.M.	Crisis call: woman in distress after victimization. Needs emergency shelter. Send intake worker to meet victim at police department.	6:55 A.M.	Call for information and service referrals for court case taking place that day.
3:20 A.M.	Crisis call: hospital requesting advocate for victim, severe bodily	7 A.M.	Shift ends.

Noncrisis Responders

8 A.M.	Shift begins.	12 noon.	Lunch.
8:30 A.M.	Return all messages, fax referrals, and schedule new intakes and follow-up appointments.	1 P.M.	Court hearing.
		4 P.M.	Follow-up appointment.
10 A.M.	Intake appointment.	5 P.M.	Shift ends.

Shelter Worker

8:30 A.M.	Shift begins at shelter.	2 P.M.	Community meeting for Domestic Violence Fatality Review Team.
8:45 A.M.	Check on current clients.		
9 A.M.	Arrange intake for new client that arrived overnight.	3 P.M.	Work with traumatized child individual session.
9:30 A.M.	Individual clinical session.	4:30 P.M.	Go to corporate office to pick up new client work that came in.
10:30 A.M.	Take client to DCF for appointment.	5:30 P.M.	Go back to shelter and finalize paperwork, set up for next day support group.
12 noon.	Cover hotline while phone staff goes to lunch.	6 P.M.	Run support group.
1 P.M.	Lunch.	7 P.M.	Shift ends.

When working with the strengths and empowerment models to assist people to gain or maintain independence after being a victim of domestic violence, key objectives are to provide them with education, information, and resources to maintain or gain their independence from an abuser and maintain a safe, healthy lifestyle.

There are many demands and challenges with respect to the community served, environment in which they live, and the resources available. Victims are an easily underserved population due to underidentification. Victims sometimes are not aware of services available to assist them.

Currently, there are high demands for social workers in the victim practitioner field. This newly developed field was designed to provide advocates that could assist in the legal process as well as the healing process after a victimization. With domestic violence being one of the most reported crimes in this field, there have been many programs developed to assist victims with emergency and long-term housing, legal representation, safety planning, counseling, support groups, therapy, transportation, and health care. There has also been a program by the attorney general's office called the Crime Victim Compensation Trust Fund. This program covers an array of crime-related costs, including property loss, wage loss, medical expenses, mental health counseling, loss of support, domestic violence relocation monies, funeral/burial expenses, emergency out-of-pocket expenses, and loss of assistive devices like glasses, dentures, and prostheses.

Recent changes in the victim practitioner field include the development and implementation of additional therapy programs specifically targeting children who were raised in abusive environments to prevent the familial cycle of abusive behavior. Additionally, the legal system in Florida has recognized a need for domestic violence advocates and has created the DOVE unit in Palm Beach County. The DOVE unit only works with victims of domestic violence that are victim-witnesses in current state criminal cases at the state attorney's office. These victim-witnesses are assigned an advocate that will call and inform them of court appearances and the defendant's position in the case and provide counseling on what to expect through the legal process, including possible case outcomes.

Challenges in domestic violence victim advocacy are many. The average practitioner will be presented with new challenges for each case. Because no one situation is the same as another, the same can be said of the challenges you may face. In the area of disabilities, there could be accessibility or discrimination issues. If the victims are undocumented, they may be misinformed of their rights or unaware of programming in the area that may assist them. The lesbian/gay/bisexual/transgender community may have preconceived ideas on treatment and discrimination that prevents them from getting help. One of the biggest challenges is accessing domestic violence programs for men. Because women make up the majority of IPV victims, programs were designed after the Violence Against Women Act was passed in 1994. For the first time in 2005, the act included

rhetoric of male victims of domestic violence to receive services. Elder victims are another population that is exceedingly underserved. The basis for this is the cultural differences in the older population coupled with an attitude of not wanting to dedicate time to go through the legal process.

The practice of social work is ever changing, as is the dynamic of people served. As more areas of need are recognized, there are programs made to fulfill those needs. Victims' rights are being widely recognized by lawmakers, especially regarding domestic violence. New and innovative programs are being introduced almost daily. We have two additional domestic violence shelters in Palm Beach County in addition to the two certified shelters already in use. There are more agencies recognizing the need for counseling services to be offered to victims included in standard services at no charge. Presently, the social work profession is integrating nontraditional approaches, such as victimology, criminal justice, and deinstitutionalization. The practice of social work is becoming more full-service in nature. It seems that training and curriculum is being changed and adopted to better equip social workers with the practice demands that are currently needed. This particular profession is unique in nature—you can find social workers in hospitals, courtrooms, housing professions, schools, and law enforcement. Domestic violence competencies include the ability to:

- Recognize and respond to domestic and family violence;
- Manage one's own professional development in responding to domestic and family violence; and
- Provide crisis intervention and support to those who are experiencing domestic and family violence.

The following are competency standards for intervention workers working with women subjected to domestic abuse and violence:

1. Empower the woman through the process of intervention.
   - Inform the client about domestic violence.
   - Assess and raise issues of safety.
   - Explore options.
   - Invite the client to take a position in relation to domestic abuse and violence.
   - Support the client's decision.
2. Contribute to social action on domestic abuse and violence.

- Provide opportunities for women to have a wider voice in relation to domestic abuse and violence.
- Promote prevention of domestic violence as a community issue.
- Reflect on own work practice.

Guiding Principles

- Client safety is a priority.
- Respect victim's choices.
- Don't blame, threaten, or judge victim.
- Believe the victim.
- Provide choices.

Convey Three Things

1. It's not their fault.
2. They are not alone—this happens to many people.
3. There is help available.

Responding to Disclosures of Abuse

- Empathetic understanding.
- Provide choices and referrals.
- Safety planning if necessary.

The best way to prepare for future endeavors with respect to victim assistance is education, training, and knowing your population. Training and education is only as valuable as its use in practice. There is no clear-cut way to prepare for day-to-day caseloads, because each is unique in circumstance and remedy. When working, on-the-job training is the best way to recognize challenges and develop treatment plans accordingly. Following are two case illustrations that are both victims of domestic violence but with vastly different needs assessments.

ILLUSTRATION 1

Stacey G.
24 years old
Children: 2-year-old twin sons and 4-year-old daughter
Presenting problem: Restraining order

Stacey came in needing an injunction for the protection against domestic violence order filed against her husband. She and her husband were married for 6 years. She recalled that 1 year after marriage, her husband became increasingly forceful with sex. He would pin her down and have sexual intercourse with her. Since the birth of their children, this pattern has gotten worse, with him ordering the children out of the room so he could force himself on her. Stacey admitted not knowing that this was a form of sexual assault because they were married. She was given information about marital rape by an anonymous abuse hotline. She called in after her husband ordered the children out of the room and Stacey, knowing what that meant, told the children to stay. He then proceeded to force her to have sex with the children in the room. The social worker assisted Stacey with filling out and filing the restraining order. She was offered counseling for herself and her children, which she scheduled immediately. She was referred for legal representation for the restraining order injunction hearing. She was also interested in using their services for a divorce. The lethality survey proved it to be a highly lethal situation, and a safety plan was designed. Stacey was offered a referral for shelter but declined, stating she was going to stay with family. The information was given to her if an emergency situation developed where she needed shelter and was told about outreach services she may qualify for. The Victim's Compensation Program was explained. Stacey stated she may seek therapy for her children and would file a compensation claim accordingly. Although she never contacted the police during the events in her marriage, she was encouraged to do so in the future.

After the initial meeting, Stacey called back and gave the court date and information to the social worker for the social worker to accompany her. The social worker met her at the courthouse and went into court with her for support. A restraining order against her husband was granted, and he was subsequently served the divorce papers in the same hearing. Her husband was ordered to pay support payments to her for the children with no visitation. The social worker counsels Stacey on what to expect next and reminds her if she wishes to have legal representation to call regarding the divorce proceedings. Stacey agreed.

The next day, Stacey and her children met with the counselor for their assessment and intake appointment. She was able to set up recurring weekly appointments for family counseling. She informed the counselor that she contacted the shelter for outreach services and was referred to another agency that offers play therapy for the children biweekly on a sliding scale. She already scheduled an intake and assessment appointment with the program and planned on filing a victim's compensation claim to cover the expenses of the therapy.

Stacey called a week later to inform the social worker of the meeting with the attorney for the divorce. She had some concerns and asked for accompaniment to the meeting. The social worker met her at the law office and was able to voice some of the victim's concerns that were discussed in the prior phone conversations. After the meeting, Stacey asked if the social worker would help her file the victim's compensation claim. The social worker was able to set up a meeting in the office to go over the paperwork.

Stacey came in with the forms already filled out but did not understand what attachments were needed. The social worker provided the additional forms that needed to be filed with the application and advised her that the bills needed to be provided with the claim for them to send the check.

Stacey contacted the office approximately 2 months after her appointment to inform the social worker she had filed the victim's compensation paperwork. She received an eligibility letter for her and her children and received a check a week later covering the costs. Because the therapy was recurring, she sent in all subsequent bills and was awaiting the checks to cover those. Stacey thanked me for my services and was awaiting a divorce court date so everything would be finalized. Her soon-to-be-ex-husband had not had any contact with her or her children. She stated she would call if any other services were needed. Her case was concluded after 6 months of inactivity and filed.

ILLUSTRATION 2

Annette W.
52 years old
Presenting problem: Needs food.

Annette came in with her presenting problem being a need for food service. After questioning the nature of her needs, it was found that she was living with her son after exacerbation of her physical disability prevented her from working. She currently has no income and is going through the application process for Social Security disability income. While at her son's house, Annette was being denied food and told that if she wanted to eat, she would be responsible for the purchase of her own food. Starving and unable to buy food, she opened a can of her son's food. When her son found out, he was furious. He began cursing and belittling Annette in a threatening manner. After speaking with the social worker, Annette understood that this behavior was a form of intimidation. She was able to identify the domestic abuse after speaking with the victim practitioner at length and being shown the power and control wheel specific for domestic violence victims with disabilities. A lethality survey was given to Annette and showed a low level of lethality. A safety plan was developed based on her situation. She was added to the agency's food delivery program and filed an application with the social worker for food stamps. After 35 days, Annette received her food stamps EBT card in the mail with her approval letter. She called in and was taken off the food delivery program because she was able to sustain her own food supply. She was instructed to call back if she needed assistance in 6 months when she receives her case review and refile.

As people deal with being victimized, workers can identify common reactions. These reactions are normal but may still mean that the victim requires help to deal with being overwhelmed. Additionally, the severity of the victim's reaction needs to be examined to develop ideas of how to best help victims rebuild their lives. Some victims may benefit the most from relatively minor interventions, for example, sharing information. Others with more severe reactions might require more intensive support that might be provided in a peer group. Finally, there are those clients experiencing severe reactions that may require a referral to mental health counseling or even hospitalization. It would not make sense to only give information to someone experiencing severe distress, nor would it make sense to require a person coping well to enter therapy. Table 12.1 describes a proposed model to help workers think about these issues. The key element to understand is that crime victims are a diverse group with diverse needs. This diversity requires workers to adapt to the victim in providing those services that best meet the victim's needs.

Assessment is ongoing and critical to effective intervention at all stages, beginning with an assessment of the lethality and safety issues for

TABLE 12.1 Severity by Service Type: A Proposed Model

Needs Level	Description	Possible Service Options
Low	They are coping well with few symptoms, easily managed through natural coping skills and social support. They may not have experienced a severe crime or may have many ways to cope.	Minimal services: information sharing, provide written material, brochures of available supports, and education about signs of deeper problems. These services would also be useful for those who do not feel they have any problems but are trying to hide their suffering.
Moderate	Experiencing some symptoms and need to expand coping skills or need a place to deal with overwhelming emotions. Generally they cope well but are overwhelmed by being victimized.	Peer-run support groups, paraprofessional and volunteer support. Some professional support may be needed but only on a short-term basis.
High	Experiencing many symptoms and displaying poor coping behaviors. Overwhelmed by being victimized and with few effective supports. Severe trauma may have occurred. Likely evidence of multiple problems and multiple victimizations.	Need for professional treatment. This may include long-term individual or group therapy or even hospitalization to help the person stabilize.

the victim. With victims of family violence, it is important to assess whether the caller is in any current danger and to consider future safety concerns in treatment planning and referral. In addition to determining lethality and the need for emergency intervention, it is crucial to maintain active communication with the client, either by phone or in person, while emergency procedures are being initiated.

To plan and conduct a comprehensive assessment, the crisis counselor needs to evaluate the following issues: (a) the severity of the crisis, (b) the client's current emotional state, (c) immediate psychosocial and safety needs, and (d) level of client's current coping skills and resources. In the initial contact, assessment of the client's past or precrisis level of functioning and coping skills is useful; however, past history should not be a focus of intake or crisis assessment, unless related directly to the immediate victimization or trauma. Table 12.2 identifies components to be considered in the assessment (Roberts, 2007).

The goals of this stage are assessing and identifying critical areas of intervention while also recognizing the duration and severity of violence and acknowledging what has happened (Roberts, 2007).

Social workers, nurses, and counselors should make assessments and treatment plans to help women to permanently leave the battering relationship. The overriding goal of all domestic violence advocates and clinicians is to reduce and stop the pain and suffering, severe and permanent injuries, as well as domestic violence–related homicides. Victims of intimate partner abuse are at increased risk of suffering from physical and mental health problems. To minimize these negative effects, service providers should follow several basic steps. First, a core needs assessment must be conducted. Second, care must be taken not to retraumatize the victim by the criminal justice system or by recounting their story. Third, the psychological, social, and health effects of trauma identified in the needs assessment must be addressed. Fourth, for those in need, evidence-based multisession interventions should be implemented.

TABLE 12.2 Crisis Assessment (Including Lethality Measures)

---

1. First and foremost, patient/client needs to be stabilized.
   - Assess level of consciousness and orientation
   - Rationality
   - Anxiety
   - Agitation
2. Determine if client is in immediate danger.
   - Any guns or rifles in the home; threatened to use it on client
   - Any weapons used in prior battering incidents
   - Any threats with weapons
   - Any threats to kill client
   - Any criminal history of batterer
   - Client needed emergency medical attention
   - Threats or actually killing a pet
   - Threats of suicide by abuser
   - Batterer's fantasies about suicide or homicide
   - Marital rape or forced sex among cohabitants
   - Increased battering during pregnancy
   - Medical problems as result of pregnancy
   - Medical problems as result of rape (e.g., infections, sexually transmitted diseases, HIV infection, unwanted pregnancy, risk to fetus in a pregnant woman)
   - Psychological torture (e.g., degradation, forced drug use, isolation of victim, sleep or food deprivation, threats to family of victim)

WEB SITES

AARDVARC, Abuse, Rape and Domestic Violence Aid and Resource Collection. Provides links to the stalking laws in all 50 states and other information about stalking. http://www.aardvarc.org.

It Happened to Alexa Foundation. Its purpose is to help support rape survivors through the trauma of the criminal trial, in the hopes that more survivors will go through with the prosecution to put these perpetrators behind bars. Established in 2003, the foundation assists rape victims' families with travel expenses during the litigation process and is the only organization of its kind in the United States. http://www.ithappenedtoalexa.org.

Rape, Abuse and Incest National Network. The nation's largest anti–sexual assault organization. RAINN operates the National Sexual Assault Hotline at (800) 656-HOPE and carries out programs to prevent sexual assault, help victim,s and ensure that rapists are brought to justice. http://www.rainn.org.

Office of Violence against Women, a component of the U.S. Department of Justice. Provides federal leadership to reduce violence against women and administer justice for and strengthen services to all victims of domestic violence, dating violence, sexual assault, and stalking. http://www.usdoj.gov/ovw.

Witness Justice. Provides trauma victims and their loved ones with resources that promote physical, psychological, and spiritual healing. The site features access to experts, message boards, and other print and electronic victim resources. http://www.witnessjustice.org/violence/domesticviolence.cfm.

References

Block, C. R. (2003). How can practitioners help an abused woman lower her risk of death? *NIJ Journal, 250,* 4–7.

Carlson, B. E., Worden, A. P. van Ryn, M., & Bachman, R. (2000). *Violence against women: Synthesis of research for service providers.* Final report to the National Institute of Justice. Washington, DC: U. S. Department of Justice, National Institute of Justice.

Dugan, L., Nagin, D. S. & Rosenfeld, R. (2003). Do domestic violence services save lives? *NIJ Journal, 250,* 20–25.

Goodwin, S. N., Chandler, S., & Meisel, J. (2003). *Violence against women: The role of welfare reform.* Final report to the National Institute of Justice.

Meisel, J., Chandler, D., & Rienzi, B. M. (2003). Domestic violence prevalence and Effects on Employment in Two California TANF populations. *Violence Against Women, 9*(10), 1191–1212.

Moffitt, T. E., & Caspi, A. (1999). *Findings about partner Violence from the Dunedin Multidisciplinary Health and Development Study.* Research in Brief. Washington, DC: U.S. Department of Justice, National Institute of Justice.

Roberts, A. R. (Ed.). (2007). *Battered women and their families: Intervention strategies and treatment approaches*, 3rd ed. New York: Springer.

Sharps, P., Campbell, J. C., Campbell, D., Gary, F., & Webster, D. (2003). Risky mix: Drinking, drug use, and homicide. *NIJ Journal, 250*, 8–13.

Tjaden, P., & Thoennes, N. (2000). *Extent, nature, and consequences of intimate partner violence: Findings from the National Violence Against Women Survey*. Washington, DC: Department of Justice. Available from http://www.ojp.usdoj.gov/nij/pubs-sum/181867.htm.

13 The Social Worker in Emergency Service Settings

Ted Bober & Cheryl Regehr

SOCIAL WORK AT AN AIRPORT EMERGENCY: INCIDENT OVERVIEW

An Airbus aircraft is on a flight to large urban city and scheduled to arrive at 6 P.M. local time. There are 280 passengers and 12 crew members on board. Among the other preflight activities, the flight crew members obtained the weather forecast for their arrival, which included the possibility of snowstorms with thunder.

The take-off and flight were uneventful. In preparation for descending, it became known that a landing gear was not fully engaged and locked. The airport was notified, and emergency operations were initiated on site, and according to proto-cols, an additional 30 emergency contacts were made in the surrounding city. With the conditions on the ground cold and snowy, a landing was attempted. The rear landing gear failed in the process of landing and the plane slid sideways off the runway. A wing touched ground and a fire broke out.

All passengers and crew were evacuated safely, though several people suffered minor injuries and a few experienced serious but not life-threatening injuries. The fire was extinguished by airport emergency teams. A few minutes of the landing were videotaped by motorists on the surrounding highways. Within minutes, the video appeared on local news with the information that there were an unknown number of deaths.

5:30 P.M.	The determination to deploy the airport crisis team will normally be made by the airport duty manager, in consultation with the administrative director and/or clinical director based on the details of the incident. It is quickly decided the deployment of the team is appropriate.	5:35 P.M.	The clinical director (a social worker) is contacted and briefed on the unfolding event. The clinical director contacts the on-duty (on-call) crisis team members, who include emergency professionals and social workers. Each team member will be briefed with the available details of the incident.

5:45 P.M.   The contacted team members arrange to meet at a designated site. An initial assessment indicates that there are over 75 family members and friends waiting the arrival of the passengers. Arrangements will be coordinated between the team and the airport emergency manager to have family members and friends taken to a large ballroom at a hotel next to the airport. The room will serve as a family support and information center.

6:15 P.M.   The plane lands as described.

6:30 P.M.   Team members are deployed to the hotel ballroom and assist the airport and airlines in supporting the family and friends. Initially the information regarding injuries is not available, and family members begin to receive cell phone calls and also see news reports indicating there were several deaths. Rumors and incomplete information heighten the tension in the room.

The social worker and emergency team members coordinate practical assistance, such as the provision of water, juice, sandwiches, and blankets. Additional cell phones are arranged with long-distance calling cards so relatives may contact other family members. Team members learn there were no deaths and all nonseriously injured passengers will be taken to nearby hangar to be assessed medically. Plans are made by the airline to inform the families of the incident, the whereabouts of the passengers, and the next steps. The full extent of injuries has not been assessed, so the information feels incomplete for many family members.

On-site triage leads to a few passengers being taken directly to the hospital. The lead team clinician in consultation with the team requests two team members to go to the hangar to assess practical needs of the passengers. The human resource needs of the team are reviewed, and additional standby social workers and emergency professionals are contacted and requested to assist during the phase of reconnection of families and passengers.

6:45 P.M.   The team, in collaboration with the airline's family assistance team, continues to provide practical information and support. Family members and friends are registered in cooperation with the airlines. The administrative director of the team is in the emergency operation center (EOC). The team has a direct link to EOC leadership to exchange information and coordinate resources.

7:15 P.M.   At the hangar, over 250 passengers are triaged based on medical needs. Additionally, the airport and social workers collect information on contacting relatives or making arrangements for transportation and accommodation for some passengers.

Increasing number of passengers are contacting their family members and friends by cell phones and other handheld devices. The contacted family members are relieved, though many others wait anxiously for additional information. The airlines and airport provide brief details of the incident and report that there were no deaths.

7:30 P.M.   Information is received that that two airport firefighters are injured on site and taken to the hospital. According to protocol, the team would initiate steps to establish a rest area for emergency professionals in the event of a protracted recovery period. Given the proximately of the incident to a hangar, the rest area is planned for the ongoing recovery and investigation team.

7:45 P.M.   Social workers and emergency team members continually reevaluate the needs of three groups: the emergency responders, the family and friends, and the passengers. Plans are being established to reunite passengers and families. Practical social emotional support at this stage focuses on information, practical health and nutrition needs, and facilitating contact with other relatives and friends.

8:30 P.M.   Passengers and family members are reunited in a separate, larger meeting room. Several other community agencies, such as the Red Cross, are also present to assist the airline and airport crisis team to support those without access to additional clothing, transportation, or accommodation. Arrangements have been ongoing to reunite family members with passengers taken to the hospital. In this community, all hospitals have emergency-based crisis teams staffed by social workers.

8:30 P.M.–   Team members are available and
1 A.M.   offer support in a nonintrusive manner. A few family members

and passengers experience overt signs of distress and are supported in keeping with evidence-informed psychosocial first aid. Information on practical assistance and health needs are made available verbally and through print material and a Web site.

2 A.M.   All passenger and family members have returned home or to suitable accommodation. The team members review the evening with a focus on current and potential psychosocial needs and the appropriate follow-up. The airlines family support teams will remain in contact with all passengers. Contact with stand-by team members has been ongoing, and next steps are discussed regarding follow-up needs. On-site team members stand down knowing which team members will be taking on follow-up tasks. Key activities and potential needs are documented.

7 A.M.   New team members are rotated into the incident. They are briefed, and plans are made to make courtesy support calls to the responding airport services and professionals in coordination with the airport management. Print material on the role of the crisis team, professional resilience, and incident stress is made available.

Next 48 Hours

Informal support calls are made to airport services. The crisis team includes firefighters from local services, and they make an informal outreach to the airport fire department. In this event, there are no requests for ongoing or more intensive disaster mental health service for airport staff. The airline has its own internal support services and an external health provider. A few passengers contact the crisis team for information and receive telephone support and referral informa-

tion as indicated. Subsequently the team reviews its activities, performance, and implications for training, policy, and protocol revision.

EMERGENCY SERVICES AND SOCIAL WORK

For most of our human history, small group communal efforts were the heart of rescue and protection efforts. With increasing complexity and social organization, we began to develop systems to safeguard ourselves from fires, injury, and crime, and in the last century significant developments occurred in our society to move toward professional systems of emergency personnel and emergency management. Through the ever-present 24/7 media coverage we are consistently reminded how communities and emergency professionals are affected by large-scale dramatic emergencies and disasters, such as Hurricane Katrina, the SARS outbreak, the Indian Ocean tsunami, and the terrorist attacks in New York, London, Spain, and other countries. These events may distract us from appreciating that each day emergency service professionals face routine challenges in their work—motor vehicle accidents, fires, shootings, and medical emergencies. These daily challenges occur in the context of government oversight, the hassles of bureaucracy and office politics, and the increasing scrutiny of the media and public. All of this is unfolding as new and old risks are merging with a changing world to create new versions of hazards, including pandemics and biological or cyberterrorism.

Western societies have worked to improve response to mass emergencies and disasters by developing stronger emergency management programs. In the United States, new standards are evolving from National Fire Protection Association, the Business Continuity Institute, and the Disaster Recovery Institute International. The Federal Emergency Management Agency (FEMA), under the Department of Homeland Security, has developed the first comprehensive National Response Plan and its companion legislation, the National Incident Management System. In Canada, enhanced emergency management was developed through Public Safety and Emergency Preparedness Canada, which was recently renamed Public Safety, and Bill C12, the Emergency Management Act, enacted in 2006. Internationally, the International Standards Organization Technical Committee is developing new standards, currently called Societal Security, to coordinate and strengthen security, emergency management, and continuity practice and processes.

Emergency management programs are now based on an all-hazards approach and include four interconnected parts: prevention/mitigation, preparedness, response and recovery (Gordon, 2002). The first step of an all-hazards approach is to continually identify the natural and human-made hazards that exist or may develop in a community. The work of emergency professional in broad terms is to not only respond to emergencies but also prevent and prepare for emergencies and disasters, minimize the effects of emergencies, and finally respond effectively and promote recovery in the community as quickly as possible after the event.

Emergency personnel are well-trained professionals with the specialized knowledge to deal with a wide range of emergencies and disasters. Nevertheless, there are aspects of emergency response work that may wear down even the most resilient responder or team. The research literature and the popular press have focused a great deal in recent years on critical events that occur in the line of duty for emergency workers and the impact this may have on them as individuals. This research focus generally involves mass casualties, including natural disasters, bus crashes killing children, explosions on a naval ship, airplane crashes, and terrorist attacks. Equally important are the findings from occupational health research showing that persistent workplace stress in an unresponsive, unsupportive organization erodes the well-being of professionals. Without preparation and support, traumatic or persistent stress will eventually lead to wear and tear on one's health and disrupt one's family and work life—even in the most resilient person. The focus of this chapter is a discussion the effects of daily stresses, disasters on the individual family and organizational level, followed by outline of a continuum of supportive actions and interventions and implications for social work practice and education.

A social-ecological framework suggests individuals, the workplace, and emergency event factors combine to influence disaster-related health outcomes. The outcomes may range from normal stress reactions followed by healthy adaptation or problems in work and living (such as family conflicts or loss of productivity or absenteeism) or specific physical health or psychological problems (such as hypertension, heart disease, depression, or post-traumatic stress). Factors leading to individual differences in outcomes include life experiences, such as general health habits and history of trauma and personal loss; organizational factors, including the presence of effective leadership and support for both the technological and human side of emergencies; and emergency events, including adverse, potentially dangerous working conditions and witnessing the serious injury or death of children and colleagues. These factors will be discussed further in the following sections.

DAILY OCCUPATIONAL STRESSES

Disasters of great magnitude do not happen often in the career of emergency professionals; nevertheless, most are exposed to many gruesome and dramatic events. Most paramedics were likely to have been assaulted (almost 70 percent) and feel that they had been in situations where their lives were at risk (56 percent). Over 40 percent of firefighters in Canada report being exposed to violence against others and witnessing multiple casualties, and approximately 30 percent report experiencing the death of a person in their care (Regehr & Bober, 2005). These exposures have the potential to cause emotional and social distress in even the most seasoned responders. Events such as violence against children, dealing with the intense emotions of families, and exposure to multiple gruesome casualties (such as in a disaster) are most likely to lead to more intense reactions or potentially traumatic symptoms. A study of police officers suggested that the death of a partner, the line-of-duty death of another officer, or the suicide of another officer were among the top stressful events on the job. Large-scale events like disasters have additional factors that lead to stress and distress; these are outlined in Table 13.1.

ADDITIONAL WORKPLACE SOURCES OF STRESS

Although critical event exposures do carry risk, the nature of the emergency service workplace contributes additional risk factors for distress. One such factor is shift work, which leads to problems of fatigue, sleep disturbances, and workplace accidents, as well as such health problems as weight gain, cardiovascular problems, and gastrointestinal disturbances. In addition, the work environment is often unpredictable—high-stress emergency tasks frequently occur between long periods of readiness. One police officer described his work as 2 hours of boredom followed by 2 minutes of sheer terror and 3 hours of report writing (Regehr & Bober, 2005). Organizational change and shifting demands and expectations are an additional source of stress. A Swedish study examined the physiological reactions of police inspectors during a time of organizational change. Survey questionnaires and blood samples were collected shortly after the change and continued at specified time intervals until 3 years after. Significantly, cholesterol levels, cortisol, and testosterone were highly

TABLE 13.1 Emergency Event Conditions that May Increase the Level of Stress

- Shift work, long hours, and time pressures in situations where events are uncontrolled, happening quickly, and lives are threatened.
- Making decisions in chaotic situations, at times with incomplete information.
- Emotional demands of situations where people's health is at stake.
- Witnessing mass casualty incidents, including exposure to grotesque situations.
- Interactions with disaster survivors and bereaved family members.
- Adverse work environments, such as cramped or toxic environments or exposure to adverse weather conditions (cold, rain, snow, high winds).
- Intense public scrutiny pressure and high expectations to resolve the crisis.
- Heightened media attention and scrutiny.
- Worry associated with exposure to chemical, biological, radiological, nuclear, or unknown/invisible toxic agents.
- Worry or fear for the safety of one's family.
- Being unprepared for multiagency, multijurisdictional operations.

Source: ATSDR, 2005; Regehr & Bober, 2005.

correlated with worry and workload (Grossi, Theorell, Jusisoo, & Setterlind, 1999).

Although there is considerable evidence that these emergencies have an impact on workers, many research studies suggest that it may be the everyday hassles associated with routine administrative, bureaucratic, and organizational structures encountered by emergency service workers that occasion considerable stress and strain and form the foundation on which critical events are heaped (Liberman et al., 2002). Critical events encountered by those who are already experiencing stress and perceive that they do not have support from their colleagues, managers, or union in good times, and especially in bad times, are more likely to result in traumatic stress reactions than are critical events encountered by individuals at their optimal level of functioning who know they can count on others when they are facing challenges.

Emergency service organizations often have strong attitudes toward the expression of emotion. Cynicism and pessimism is frequently identified within these organizations, and these factors have been found to be related to higher levels of stress and tension in individual workers. Support from management is one of the primary protective factors in reducing stress and post-traumatic stress reactions in emergency responders. It is therefore gratifying to note that workers have also perceived a great deal of support from both their immediate supervisors and management (Regehr, Hill, & Glancy, 2000). One study examining over 1,700 firefighters and 248 paramedics reported that co-worker support had a profound effect on both job satisfaction and work morale, and although the influence of family support was still significant, it had a much smaller influence on these factors (Beaton, Murphy, Pike, & Corneil, 1997). A negative aspect of social support occurs when the group norms lead to a prohibition of expressed emotion and the discouragement to seek help. Seeking help involves social costs, because the seeker appears incompetent, dependent, and inferior to others.

PUBLIC INQUIRIES

When tragic events occur, they rarely end with the tidying of equipment and completion of paperwork. Rather, society has increasingly moved to the process of postmortem inquiries with the goal of identifying errors and avoiding future deaths. Although the goals of public accountability and quality assurance are laudable, these inquiries do not come without cost. There is a profound effect on the emergency workers who testify in the inquiries. Police, firefighters, and paramedics identify experiences of feeling unprotected, attacked, and presumed guilty of incompetence or negligence when testifying at a postmortem review. These feelings are intensified by the media attention, which is often sensational and vilifying, and the subsequent public response of suspicion and blame. They are deepened when workers view the organizational response to be unsupportive. As a consequence, emergency workers report symptoms of intrusion, avoidance, arousal, and self-doubt that begin with the tragic event itself and continue throughout the review process. In the end, several responders are able to identify positive outcomes from the review process, such as new learning, some positive recognition, system change, and especially vindication. Never-

theless, a dominant theme is that of betrayal, anger, and reduced commitment.

THE EFFECTS OF STRESS AND TRAUMA

In summary, when exposed to tragic events, emergency responders will naturally develop some symptoms of stress. Stress in itself can be a positive motivating force, helping professionals be energized and focused on a task. Occasionally these symptoms may reach a level of intensity and continue for a sufficient period of time to be considered problematic and occasionally become post-traumatic stress disorder (PTSD). Although many studies have supported the view that the intensity of the trauma has a bearing on the severity and chronicity of trauma symptoms in rescue workers (Weiss, Marmar, Metzler, & Ronfeldt, 1995), it is becoming increasingly clear that trauma and distress do not have a simple cause-and-effect relationship. A second set of factors relates to the recovery environment, including personal social supports and organizational supports. Studies have shown that social support from spouses, family, and friends was also significantly associated with trauma scores (Regehr et al., 2000). Additionally, the public and media responses to the event also validate or strain professional well-being.

A final set of factors relates to the personal life experiences of the individual responder. Recent reports have highlighted the importance of individual differences in determining the intensity and duration of trauma-related symptoms (Regehr, Hemsworth, & Hill, 2001; Yehuda, 2001). Mediating variables identified by researchers include a history of trauma before the event, previous mental health problems, or a family history of mental health problems (Luce, Firth-Cozens, Midgley, & Burges, 2002). Cognitive appraisal of an event as manageable and within one's coping ability reduces affective arousal, influences a person's expectations of success, and consequently changes his or her behavior (Bryant & Guthrie, 2007). Thus, a sense of optimism shapes a person's reaction to a crisis and subsequently influences the outcome. The sense of control individuals experience over an event (or over their reaction to an event) is important in understanding trauma reactions. A final individual characteristic is the person's ability to develop and sustain interpersonal relationships or relational capacity. This capacity is useful in understanding individual differences in obtaining social support.

When individuals are exposed to events that threaten the life or cause serious injury to themselves or others, and they consequently experience great fear, helplessness or horror, it is not uncommon for this to result in post-traumatic stress reactions. PTSD consists of three clusters of symptoms. *Reexperiencing symptoms* are when memories of the event intrude on the individual through recurring thoughts, distressing dreams, and flashbacks of the event. *Avoidance symptoms* include efforts to avoid thoughts and feelings about the event or avoidance of places that serve as reminders. Some research suggests this cluster can be divided into two subclusters, effortful avoidance and numbing or detachment symptoms. *Arousal symptoms* may include difficulty getting to sleep, irritability and anger, difficulty concentrating, hypervigilance, and exaggerated startle response.

Though there were no significant differences in the scores of police, firefighters, and paramedics, at any given time, 24.6 percent of emergency responders in our studies had high or severe levels of trauma symptoms (Regehr & Bober, 2005). Other studies of police, fire, and ambulance workers confirm that at any time, somewhere between 25 percent and 30 percent report high or severe levels of trauma symptoms. Longer term effects may include a reduced capacity to handle stressful events, depression, substance use, health problems, and the disruption or impairment in functioning in one's work and home life.

THE EFFECTS ON EMERGENCY FAMILIES

Families of responders are also significantly affected by these incidents. One impact is the fact that the exposed worker at times feels disengaged and emotionally distant from family members: "You almost treat your spouse like another call . . . there is a [emotional] deficit there" (Regehr & Bober, 2005). Another issue is generalized anger and irritability, often vented on family. Furthermore, responders describe generalized fears for the safety of family members and a tendency to become overprotective. Researchers have demonstrated how job-related stresses experienced in a variety of working environments can be transmitted to other family members once the individual returns home. In general, findings suggest that job stress dampens the quality of marital interactions and causes the spouse to feel more negatively toward the relationship (Larson & Almeida, 1999).

Another study using physiological measures discovered that on days officers reported higher levels of stress, both the officers and their spouses showed greater levels of autonomic arousal during conversations (Roberts & Levenson, 2001).

Families are often the forgotten victims of workplace stress and trauma. Family members deal with trauma contagion, they are confronted with attitudes and behaviors of the responder emanating from the exposures on the job, and they fear for the safety of their loved one. Organizations need to expand their notion of support to include the families of emergency professionals. Table 13.2 outlines several steps to promoting resiliency in the family.

SUPPORT AND INTERVENTIONS FOR EMERGENCY RESPONDERS

We use the term *continuum of interventions* to reflect the importance of ongoing and uninterrupted interventions, though the intensity of interventions at any one time must be linked to the health and mental health needs of the emergency responder and the members of responding organizations. For our purposes, interventions are the planned actions to promote well-being and resiliency while preventing or reducing the harm from adversity or advancing the recovery from adversity. In our experience, no matter how attractive interventions for individuals or groups may be, they are not likely to be feasible or well implemented unless politically supported and culturally appropriate for a given organization. Second, all organizations have a direct influence on the health and well-being of their employees. The con-

TABLE 13.2 Steps to Promote Family Resiliency

- Work out family routines systems to accommodate shift work.
- Establish decompression routines between work and home.
- Acknowledge your own reactions to events and work to separate them from responses to family situations.
- Plan responses to questions and comments from children, friends, and neighbors.
- Establish a system of supports in both the workplace and personal life.

Source: Regehr & Bober, 2005.

tinuum of interventions can be generally aligned with the phases of emergencies, namely, psychosocial prevention and preparedness training, such as health promotion programs, organizational and leadership development, family education and support, disaster stress education, and peer support programs. The immediate response and recovery phases may include such programs as emergency psychosocial first aid, consultation and liaison, crisis intervention, risk communication, and post-traumatic stress treatments.

PREVENTION AND PREPAREDNESS TRAINING

There is increasing recognition that promoting resilience to stress and increasing resistance to illness begins with healthy lifestyle and to that end, one good example of health promotion program is PHLAME (Promoting Healthy Lifestyles: Alternative Models' Effects). This evidence-based approach is undergoing multiyear studies consisting of firefighters in several research sites. It is a very promising approach in promoting physical activity, healthy eating habits, and weight management in groups of firefighters.

Predisaster education and training preparation is another excellent support program. This form of preparedness accomplishes several objectives: it provides information on stressful and potentially traumatic events, normal reactions, and the recovery process; it reviews and expands on healthy and flexible coping approaches to match stressful demands and promote recovery; it builds social support among co-workers; and it reduces barriers to seeking help, such as isolation, stigma, and embarrassment. Education on the factors that intensify or mitigate the effects of disasters prepares people to be less vulnerable to extreme stress by reducing uncertainty and helping them appraise a situation in a way that supports their sense of competency, confidence, and control. An important component is to train those in leadership positions on how to provide health promoting support to their staff before, during, and after high-stress emergency events.

Peer support teams have formed the core of trauma-related intervention programs for the past several years. Peer support teams have many advantages, including having indigenous knowledge about the issues faced by the individual workers and the culture and politics of the organization. Peer support programs are a means by which to build capacity and sustainability of knowledge and skills in an organization over time. The challenges in establishing these teams are developing clear roles, boundaries, and ethics and ensuring the team member's well-being. All this requires effective team selection, training, support, and accountability. There are good resources for the development, training, and maintenance of peer support and trauma response teams listed in the resources at the end of this chapter.

PSYCHOSOCIAL FIRST AID

One of the useful services and skills offered by mental health staff or peers under the supervision of mental health professionals in the field is psychosocial first aid, described by Raphael (1986) and recently updated with current evidence-based practices through efforts at the National Center for PTSD and the National Child Traumatic Stress Network (Hobfoll et al., 2007; Ruzek et al., 2007). The objectives of psychosocial first aid are to "to establish safety and security, promote connection to social and restorative resources and modulate stress-related reactions and reduce the initial distress caused by traumatic events and foster adaptive short- and long-term coping." Three practical ways to support professional during the rescue and recovery phases are (1) tangible support, such as food, shelter, tools, equipment, and hands-on help; (2) informational support, including regular updates on risk and safety communications; and (3) social-emotional support. Critical Incident Stress Management is a program that incorporates many elements of psychosocial first aid. Though it is popular among emergency services the research findings are mixed about aspects of the program.

An important part of psychosocial aid is the consultation and liaison function that a social worker can offer to organizational leaders, peer support teams, and, during mass emergencies and disasters, the emergency operation command center. Assistance may be provided with the challenge to manage the hours of work, rotation among intense and dangerous work, assessing fatigue factors, and preparing and staffing rest stations—all critical decisions to be made regarding the safety and well-being of the emergency professionals. Part of this role may include risk communication.

Increasing attention is being paid to risk communication to inform and protect emergency professionals and families about work-related hazards because of high-profile events, such as terrorist attacks and pandemics. For instance, at Ground Zero in New York City, there was evidence of health risks at the site that continued to affect emergency responders years later. At the recovery site, some people wore protective gear, some wore simple paper masks, and most wore no protection at all. Addressing the current and future risks is a key step to assuring well-being and reducing worry among professionals and their families. The SARS outbreak situation in Toronto is another example where risk communication was vital. The status continued to change on an hourly basis as information was gathered regarding the nature of the illness, the mechanism of transmission, and its lethality. Many emergency professionals and family members experienced the stresses of quarantine, incomplete information, worry, and social isolation.

POST-TRAUMATIC STRESS TREATMENT

As discussed, most people recover over time from traumatic stress, and yet for a number of reasons related to their individual characteristics and resources, the nature of the event, and the quality of the psychosocial resources following the trauma, the natural recovery process may be disrupted and some may experience PTSD. Treatment, or at least a consultation, is indicated when responders experience persistent difficulties in relationships, changes in work performance or productivity, withdrawal from usually pleasurable activities, continual symptoms of anxiety or depression, or deteriorating health as noted by fatigue, poor sleep, over- or undereating, or persistent aches and pains. A physical health exam is a useful starting point to other psychosocial treatments. Furthermore, demystifying the process of treatment can be of assistance, as movies and television generally have not portrayed the therapy process accurately or usefully.

In the many excellent reviews and meta-analyses of research related to treatment efficacy for traumatized individuals, it is generally acknowledged that only cognitive-behavioral treatment (CBT) methods have been subject to rigorous evaluation with controlled trials (Ehlers & Clark, 2003; Solomon & Johnson, 2002). The use of Internet-based CBT is currently the focus of a number of research studies. This is not, however, to say these are the only treatments that work; there is good evidence for other approaches including eye movement desensitization and reprocessing and pharmacological treatment for trauma sufferers to assist with symptom management.

IMPLICATIONS

There are five potentially positive social work practice, policy, and education implications of the foregoing discussion. First, given the increasing risk of large scale emergencies and disasters, social work education should include enhancing the knowledge base of social workers to understand the dynamics of emergencies and disasters and how to offer the range of preparedness and recovery interventions. The strengths of social work in crisis intervention, group work, and community development are excellent foundation blocks for this education. The academic community can also use theory and research-based skills to contribute to the growing knowledge of trauma, emergencies, and disasters in specialized populations, such as emergency professionals. Third, social workers can offer the practice skills to assess postdisaster level of distress, the risk for PTSD, and traumatic grief at the individual, family, and organizational level. Social workers can be members of an emergency and crisis support team and also provide effective group training and consultation to support the development of teams to support emergency and disaster personnel. Social workers may also apply their group and community development skills to understand broader community needs and vulnerability as means to advocate for policy and practice change. Some disasters, such as Hurricane Katrina, may have long-term and enduring effects of disrupted social economic and emotional health risks that erode the resiliency of the public and emergency professional. As new and old hazards and vulnerabilities evolve, social workers can ready themselves to offer their research and practice skills to provide culturally relevant services to high-risk professional groups, such as emergency professionals, their families, and organizations.

WEB SITES

Agency for Toxic Substances and Disease Registry. *Surviving Field Stress for Emergency Responders Reference Manual* edition 1.0 (2005). http://www.cdc.gov/phtn/webcast/stress-05/ TrainingWorkbookstress-editp1.pdf.

Center for the Study of Traumatic Stress, Uniformed Services University of the Health Sciences, Bethesda, Maryland. Fact sheets. http://www.centerforthestudyoftraumaticstress.org/factsheets.shtml.

The Centers for Disaster and Extreme Event Preparedness. http://www.deep.med.miami.edu

International Society for Traumatic Stress Studies. http://www.istss.org.

National Center for Posttraumatic Stress Disorder, Veterans Administration. http://www.ncptsd.va.gov.

PHLAME program at the Oregon Health and Science University. http://www.ohsu.edu/hpsm/phlame.cfm.

References

Beaton, R., Murphy, S., Pike, K., & Corneil, W. (1997). Social support and network conflict in firefighters and paramedics. *Western Journal of Nursing Research, 19*(3), 297–313.

Bryant, R. A., & Guthrie, R. M. (2007). Maladaptive self-appraisals before trauma exposure predict posttraumatic stress disorder. *Journal of Consulting and Clinical Psychology, 75*(5), 812–815.

Ehlers, A., & Clark, D. (2003). Early psychological interventions for adult survivors of trauma: a review. *Biological Psychiatry, 53,* 817–826.

Gordon, J. G. (2002) *Comprehensive emergency management for local governments: Demystifying emergency planning.* Brookfield, CT: Rothstein Associates.

Grossi, G., Theorell, T., Jusisoo, M., & Setterlind, S. (1999). Psychophysiological correlates of organizational change and threat of unemployment among police inspectors. *Integrative Physiological and Behavioral Science, 34*(1), 30–42.

Hobfoll, S. E., Watson, P., Bell, C. C., Bryant, R. A., Brymer, M. J., & Friedman, M. J., et al. (2007). Five essential elements of immediate and mid-term mass trauma intervention: Empirical evidence. *Psychiatry, 70*(4), 283–315.

Larson, R., & Almeida, D. (1999). Emotional transmission in the daily lives of families: A new paradigm for studying family process. *Journal of Marriage and Family, 61,* 5–20.

Liberman, A., Best, S., Metzler, T., Fagan, J., Weiss, D., & Marmar, C. (2002). Routine occupational stress and psychological distress in police. *Policing: An International Journal of Police Strategies and Management, 25*(2), 421–439.

Luce, A., Firth-Cozens, J., Midgley, S., & Burges, C. (2002) After the Omagh bomb: Post-traumatic stress disorder in health service staff. *Journal of Traumatic Stress, 15*(1), 27–30.

Raphael, B. (1986). *When disaster strikes: A handbook for caring professionals.* London: Unwin Hyman.

Regehr, C., & Bober, T. (2005). *In the line of fire: Trauma in the emergency services.* New York: Oxford University Press.

Regehr, C., Hemsworth, D., & Hill, J. (2001). Individual predictors of traumatic response: A structural equation model. *Canadian Journal of Psychiatry, 46,* 74–79.

Regehr, C., Hill, J., & Glancy, G. (2000). Individual predictors of traumatic reactions in firefighters. *Journal of Nervous and Mental Disorders, 188*(6), 333–339.

Roberts, N., & Levenson, R. (2001). The remains of the workday: Impact of job stress and exhaustion on marital interactions in police couples. *Journal of Marriage and Family, 63,* 1052–1067.

Ruzek, J. I., Brymer, M. J., Jacobs, A. K., Layne, C. M., Vernberg, E. M., & Watson, P. J. (2007). Psychological first aid. *Journal of Mental Health Counseling, 29*(1), 17–49.

Solomon, S., & Johnson, D. (2002). Psychosocial treatment of posttraumatic stress disorder: A practice friendly review of outcome research. *Psychotherapy in Practice, 58*(8), 947–959.

Weiss, D., Marmar, C., Metzler, T., & Ronfeldt, H. (1995). Predicting symptomatic distress in emergency services personnel. *Journal of Consulting and Clinical Psychology, 63,* 361–368.

Yehuda, R. (2001). Biology of posttraumatic stress disorder. *Journal of Clinical Psychiatry, 62*(Suppl. 17), 41–46.

PART III

Social Work Values, Ethics, and Licensing Standards

14   Ethical Issues in Social Work

Frederic G. Reamer

Social workers' understanding of ethical issues has grown dramatically in recent years. This development mirrors the maturation of the broader field of applied and professional ethics (also known as practical ethics), which began in earnest in the mid-1970s. Contemporary social workers have access to far more knowledge about ethics than earlier generations of practitioners. Today's social workers also face a number of unique, unprecedented ethical issues and challenges. To address ethical issues in the profession—questions concerning the nature of practitioners' duties and obligations—social workers must be familiar with a number of key concepts and resources pertaining to ethical dilemmas and ethical decision making.

ETHICAL DILEMMAS

Social workers encounter a wide range of ethical issues. Most such issues in the profession are routine and relatively straightforward. For example, social workers know that ordinarily they must obtain clients' consent before releasing confidential information, respect clients' right to self-determination, and obey the law. Sometimes, however, such common duties conflict with one another; when faced with these ethical dilemmas, social workers must decide which of their conflicting obligations should take precedence (Congress, 1999; Dolgoff, Loewenberg, & Harrington, 2004; Guttmann, 2006; Linzer, 1999; Reamer, 2006a; Rhodes, 1986; Strom-Gottfried, 2007).

Ethical dilemmas in social work take many forms. Some involve direct practice—that is, the delivery of services to individuals, families, couples, and small groups. Others involve community practice, administration, advocacy, social action, social policy, research and evaluation, relationships with colleagues, and professional education (Reamer, 2001a, 2001b, 2006b). The most common involve actual or potential conflicts among social workers' duties involving the following.

Client Confidentiality and Privileged Communication

Social workers must be clear about the nature of their obligation to respect clients' right to confidentiality and exceptions to this obligation. Ethical dilemmas occur when social workers must decide whether to disclose confidential information without client consent or against a client's wishes (Dickson, 1998; Reamer, 2003). This can occur, for example, when a client threatens to seriously harm a third party, seriously injure him- or herself, or abuses or neglects a child or elderly individual. Ethical dilemmas involving privileged communication occur when social workers are asked to disclose confidential information in the context of legal proceedings (for instance, when a client's estranged spouse requests clinical records as part of a child custody dispute).

Client Self-Determination and Professional Paternalism

It is widely accepted among social workers that clients ordinarily have a fundamental right to self-determination. However, ethical dilemmas arise in exceptional circumstances when, in the social workers' professional judgment, clients' actions or potential actions pose a serious, fore-seeable, and imminent risk to themselves or others. In these instances, social workers must decide whether to limit clients' right to self-determination.

Limiting clients' right to self-determination to protect them from self-harm is called *pater-nalism*. Paternalism can occur in several forms, such as withholding information from clients, mis-leading or lying to clients, or coercing clients.

Laws, Policies, and Regulations

Ordinarily, social workers should uphold rele-vant laws, policies, and regulations. Such compli-ance is important to the smooth functioning of human service organizations and the broader so-ciety. Circumstances may arise, however, when ethical obligations conflict with laws, policies, and regulations. In such cases, social workers must take assertive steps to resolve such conflicts, per-haps through consultation, mediation, lobbying, and other forms of advocacy and social action. On occasion, social workers may be faced with difficult decisions of conscience concerning the obligation to comply with what they believe to be unjust laws, policies, and regulations.

Conflicts of Interest and Boundary Issues

Conflicts of interest occur when a social worker's services to or relationship with a client is compro-mised or might be compromised because of deci-sions or actions in relation to another client, a col-league, him- or herself, or some other third party. Many conflicts of interest involve boundary is-sues or dual or multiple relationships. Boundary issues occur when social workers establish and maintain more than one relationship with clients (for example, when a social worker socializes with a client, discloses personal information to clients, or enters into a business partnership with a client). Dual or multiple relationships can occur simultaneously or consecutively (Reamer, 2001a, 2006b).

Some dual and multiple relationships are pa-tently unethical—for example, if a social worker maintains a sexual relationship with a client or borrows money from a client. Other dual and multiple relationships are more ambiguous and require careful analysis and consultation. Exam-ples include social workers in rural communities

who cannot avoid contact with clients in the su-permarket or recreational settings, social work-ers who are invited by clients to attend an im-portant life event, social workers' relationships with former clients, and social workers' unantic-ipated encounters with clients at an Alcoholics Anonymous meeting when both parties are in recovery.

Professional and Personal Values

Social workers sometimes find that their per-sonal values clash with traditional social work values or the official positions of employers or other organizations with which they are affili-ated professionally. This can occur, for example, when they object to their employers' political views or positions on important public policy is-sues, such as reproductive rights or welfare re-form. Social workers may also find that their personal values conflict with those of their cli-ents. This can occur when clients engage in ille-gal activity or behavior that seems immoral. Reconciling these values-related conflicts can be difficult.

Scarce and Limited Resources

Social workers often are responsible for distrib-uting resources, such as administrative funds, shelter beds, client stipends, and office space. In many instances, they struggle to locate and ob-tain sufficient resources and must make difficult decisions about how best to allocate available re-sources. When making these decisions, social workers must choose which allocation criteria to use (for example, whether to distribute resources equally among eligible parties, based on first-come first-served, or based on demonstrated need or affirmative action guidelines).

Managed Care

The advent of and pervasive influence of man-aged care—policies designed to enhance fiscal re-sponsibility and cost containment in health care and human services—have created many difficult ethical dilemmas for social workers (Corcoran & Vandiver, 1996). Strict funding guidelines, reim-bursement policies, and utilization review have forced social workers to make difficult ethical judgments about serving clients whose insurance benefits have run out; providing inadequate services to clients with complex problems; and exposing clients to privacy and confidentiality risks as a result of sharing information with managed care staff.

Whistle-Blowing

There are times when social workers may be obligated to alert people or organizations in positions of authority to colleagues' unethical behavior or impairment (Bullis, 1995; Jayaratne, Croxton, & Mattison, 1997). Decisions about whether to blow the whistle on a colleague are very difficult. Social workers generally understand that their obligation to protect clients and the public from unethical or impaired colleagues may require such action, but they also understand that whistle-blowing can have serious, harmful repercussions for colleagues whose behavior is reported to state licensing boards, the National Association of Social Workers (NASW), or employers. Whistle-blowing can also pose some risk to the individuals who report collegial misconduct or impairment; this is also a relevant consideration. See Chapter 20 on the impaired social work professional, and Chapter 19 on whistle-blowers for more detailed information.

Evaluation and Research

Many social service agencies involve clients in evaluation or research activities (such as clinical research, needs assessments, and program evaluations). Ethical issues can arise when, for example, social work researchers decide whether to withhold potentially valuable services to clients who have been assigned to a control group as opposed to an experimental (intervention) group, whether to disclose confidential information revealed in a research interview that suggests the respondent has harmed a third party, whether to interview a respondent whose capacity to sign an informed consent form is questionable, and whether any form of deception is justifiable in social work evaluation and research (for instance, concealing the true purpose of a study to avoid influencing respondents and contaminating the results). The advent of institutional review boards (IRBs) to protect research participants has helped social workers and others address these difficult questions, although simple answers are not always available.

ETHICAL DECISION MAKING

In the late 1970s, social workers began to explore the ways practitioners make ethical decisions and attempt to resolve ethical dilemmas. This development also occurred in many other professions during this period. Although discussions of ethics and values have taken place since the profession's formal beginning in the late nineteenth century, deliberate, systematic discussion of ethical decision-making strategies is more recent (Reid & Popple, 1992).

Social work, like most professions, has developed protocols to help practitioners make difficult ethical decisions when they encounter ethical dilemmas (Congress, 1999; Dolgoff, Loewenberg, & Harrington, 2004; Reamer, 1990, 2006a; Strom-Gottfried, 2007). Most of these protocols include an outline of steps that practitioners can follow to approach ethical dilemmas systematically, drawing especially on ethical theory; relevant professional literature; codes of ethics; statutes, regulations, public policies, and agency policies; and consultation. For example, one such model entails seven steps (Reamer, 2006a; also see Congress, 1999, and Dolgoff, Loewenberg, & Harrington, 2004):

1. identify the ethical issues, including the social work values and duties that conflict;
2. identify the individuals, groups, and organizations who are likely to be affected by the ethical decision;
3. tentatively identify all possible courses of action and the participants involved in each, along with possible benefits and risks for each;
4. thoroughly examine the reasons in favor of and opposed to each possible course of action, considering relevant ethical theories, principles, and guidelines; codes of ethics and legal principles; social work practice theory and principles; and personal values (including religious, cultural, and ethnic values and political ideology), particularly those that conflict with one's own;
5. consult with colleagues and appropriate experts (such as agency staff, supervisors, agency administrators, ethics scholars, ethics committees, and, if there are pertinent legal issues, attorneys);
6. make the decision and document the decision-making process; and
7. monitor, evaluate, and document the decision.

Some of the elements of this process require specialized knowledge and skill. For example, social workers should be familiar with ethical theories, principles, and guidelines related to professional practice. Most discussions of ethical theory in the profession's literature focus on what are commonly known as theories of normative ethics. Theories of normative ethics are typically divided into two main schools of thought: *deontological* and *teleological* (including *consequentialist* and *utilitarian* theories). Deontological theories (from the Greek *deontos*, "of the obligatory") claim that certain actions are inherently right or wrong as a matter of fundamental principle. From a strict deontological perspective, for example, social workers should always obey the law and regulations, even when they think that violating a law or regulation is in a client's best interest. From this point of view, social workers should always tell the truth and should always keep their promises to their clients, no matter how harmful the consequences may be.

In contrast, teleological (from the Greek *teleios*, "brought to its end or purpose") or consequentialist theories assert that ethical decisions should be based on social workers' assessment of which action will produce the most favorable outcome or consequences. According to the most popular teleological perspective, utilitarianism, ethical choices should be based on thorough assessments of what will produce the greatest good for the greatest number (positive utilitarianism) or the least harm (negative utilitarianism).

More recently, social workers and other professionals have broadened their application of ethical theory to include so-called virtue ethics and the ethics of care. According to virtue ethics, professionals' ethical judgments should be guided by certain core virtues, such as kindness, generosity, courage, integrity, respectfulness, justice, prudence, and compassion (MacIntyre, 1985). The ethics of care, which is related to virtue ethics, was developed mainly by feminist writers (Baier, 1995; Held, 1993, 2007). According to this view, men tend to think in masculine terms, such as justice and autonomy, whereas women think in feminine terms, such as caring. Proponents of the ethics of care argue that professionals should change how they view morality and the virtues, placing more emphasis on virtues exemplified by women, such as taking care of others, patience, the ability to nurture, and self-sacrifice.

These diverse philosophical perspectives are commonly used to analyze ethical dilemmas from different conceptual viewpoints. Thus, a deontologist might argue that social workers should always comply with child abuse and neglect reporting laws—because "the law is the law"—whereas a teleologically oriented practitioner might argue that social workers' compliance with these mandatory reporting laws should be based on their assessment of the likely consequences—that is, whether complying with the law will produce the greatest good or minimize harm to the greatest possible extent. A social worker who embraces virtue theory would be guided by his or her interpretation of the relevance of core virtues, such as compassion for clients, respect for human dignity, and justice.

Social workers and others disagree about the strengths and limitations of these different philosophical perspectives. Nonetheless, there is general agreement that it is helpful for practitioners to examine ethical dilemmas using these different vantage points to identify, grapple with, and critically assess all pertinent dimensions of the ethical dilemmas they encounter.

Social workers also need to be familiar with updated and increasingly sophisticated professional codes of ethics, especially the current NASW *Code of Ethics* (see Reamer, 2006b). This is only the third code in NASW's history and reflects remarkable changes over time in social workers' understanding of and approach to ethical issues.

The first section of the code, the preamble, summarizes the mission and core values of social work. For the first time in NASW's history, the association has adopted and published in the code a formally sanctioned mission statement and an explicit summary of the profession's core values. These help distinguish social work from other helping professions, particularly with respect to social work's enduring commitment to enhancing human well-being and helping meet basic human needs, empowering clients, serving people who are vulnerable and oppressed, addressing individual well-being in a social context, promoting social justice and social change, and strengthening sensitivity to cultural and ethnic diversity.

The second section, "Purpose of the NASW Code of Ethics," provides an overview of the code's main functions, including identifying the core values, summarizing broad ethical principles that reflect these values, and specific ethical standards for the profession, helping social workers identify ethical issues and dilemmas, providing the public with ethical standards it can use to hold the profession accountable, orienting new practitioners, and articulating guidelines that the profession itself can use to enforce ethical standards among its members. This section also highlights resources social workers can use when they face ethical issues and decisions.

The third section, "Ethical Principles," presents six broad principles that inform social work practice, one for each of the six core values cited in the preamble (service, social justice, dignity and worth of the person, importance of human relationships, integrity, and competence).

The final and most detailed section, "Ethical Standards," includes 155 specific ethical standards to guide social workers' conduct and provide a basis for adjudication of ethics complaints filed against social workers. (The code, or portions of it, is also used by many state licensing boards charged with reviewing complaints filed against licensed social workers and by courts of law that oversee litigation involving alleged social worker negligence or misconduct.) The standards are grouped into six categories concerning ethical responsibilities to clients, to colleagues, in practice settings, as professionals, to the profession, and to the broader society. The code addresses many topics and issues that were not mentioned in the NASW's first two codes (1960 and 1979), including limitations of clients' right to self-determination (e.g., when clients threaten harm to themselves or others), confidentiality issues involving use of electronic media to transmit information (such as cellular phones, the Internet, fax machines), storage and disposal of client records, case recording and documentation, sexual contact with former clients, sexual relationships with clients' relatives and close personal acquaintances, counseling of former sexual partners, physical contact with clients, dual and multiple relationships with supervisees, sexual harassment, use of derogatory language, bartering arrangements with clients, cultural competence, labor-management disputes, and evaluation of practice. Although codes of ethics cannot provide simple, unequivocal solutions to all complex ethical dilemmas, they often provide sound conceptual guidance about important issues to consider when making difficult ethical judgments.

In addition to consulting the code, social workers can access professional ethics consultants, institutional ethics committees, and IRBs. Ethics consultation is now very common in health care settings and is increasingly available in other settings. Typically, ethics consultants are formally educated ethicists (usually moral philosophers who have experience working with professionals or professionals who have obtained formal ethics education) who provide advice on specific ethical issues that arise in practice settings. These consultants can help social workers and other staff identify pertinent ethical issues; assess ethical dilemmas; acquaint staff with relevant ethics concepts, literature, and other resources (such as codes of ethics, policies, statutes, regulations); and make difficult ethical choices.

Institutional ethics committees formally emerged in 1976, when the New Jersey Supreme Court ruled that Karen Ann Quinlan's family and physicians should consult an ethics committee in deciding whether to remove her from life-support technology (a number of hospitals have had panels resembling ethics committees since at least the 1920s). Ethics committees often include social workers as members, along with representatives from various disciplines found in health care and human service settings, such as nurses, physicians, clergy, allied health professionals, and administrators. Some committees include a lawyer, although the lawyer might not be an employee of the agency to avoid a conflict of interest.

Most ethics committees focus on providing case consultation in the form of nonbinding advice. These committees make themselves available to agency staff, clients, and sometimes family members for consultation about challenging ethical issues. Many ethics committees also take steps to examine, draft, and critique ethics-related policies that affect agencies and their employees and clients. In addition, these committees may sponsor ethics-related educational events, such as inservice training, symposia, workshops, conferences, and what have become known as "ethics grand rounds" (Reamer, 1998, 1999, 2001c).

Social workers employed in settings that conduct research may be involved in IRBs. IRBs (sometimes known as a research ethics board or committee on the use of human participants in research) became popular in the 1970s as a result of increasing national interest in research and evaluation. All organizations and agencies that receive federal funds for research are required to have an IRB review the ethical aspects of proposals for research involving human participants.

Social workers' understanding of ethical issues has matured greatly. Literature on the subject, professional education, and in-service training have burgeoned. To practice competently, contemporary professionals must have a firm grasp of pertinent issues related to ethical dilemmas and ethical decision making. This knowledge enhances social workers' ability to protect clients and fulfill social work's critically important, values-based mission.

WEB SITES

American Board of Examiners in Clinical Social Work, Code of Ethics. http://www.abecsw .org/about-code-ethics.php.

Association of Social Work Boards, approved ethics continuing education options. https:// www.aswb.org/education/index.php.

Clinical Social Work Association, Code of Ethics. http://associationsites.com/CSWA/collection// Ethcs%20Code%20Locked%2006%2Epdf.

International Federation of Social Workers: Ethics in Social Work, Statement of Principles. http://www.ifsw.org/en/p38000324.html.

National Association of Social Workers Code of Ethics. http://www.socialworkers.org/pubs/ Code/code.asp.

References

Baier, A. (1995). *Moral prejudices: Essays on ethics.* Cambridge, MA: Harvard University Press.

Bullis, R. K. (1995). *Clinical social worker misconduct.* Chicago: Nelson-Hall.

Congress, E. (1999). *Social work values and ethics.* Belmont, CA: Wadsworth.

Corcoran, K., & Vandiver, V. (1996). *Maneuvering the maze of managed care: Skills for mental health professionals.* New York: Free Press.

Dickson, D. T. (1998). *Confidentiality and privacy in social work.* New York: Free Press.

Dolgoff, R., Loewenberg, F., & Harrington, D. (2004). *Ethical decisions for social work practice,* 7th ed. Belmont, CA: Wadsworth.

Guttmann, D. (2006). *Ethics in social work: A context of caring.* Binghamton, NY: Haworth.

Held, V. (1993). *Feminist morality: Transforming culture, society, and politics.* Chicago: University of Chicago Press.

Held, V. (2007). *The ethics of care: Personal, political, global.* New York: Oxford University Press.

Jayaratne, S., Croxton, D., & Mattison, D. (1997). Social work professional standards: An exploratory study. *Social Work, 42*(2), 187–199.

Linzer, N. (1999). *Resolving ethical dilemmas in social work practice.* Boston: Allyn and Bacon.

MacIntyre, A. (1985) *After virtue: A study in moral theory,* 2nd ed. London: Duckworth.

Reamer, F. G. (1990). *Ethical dilemmas in social service,* 2nd ed. New York: Columbia University Press.

Reamer, F. G. (2001a). *Tangled relationships: Managing boundary issues in the human services.* New York: Columbia University Press.

Reamer, F. G. (2001b). *The social work ethics audit: A risk management tool.* Washington, DC: NASW Press.

Reamer, F. G. (2001c). *Ethics education in social work.* Alexandria, VA: Council on Social Work Education.

Reamer, F. G. (2003). *Social work malpractice and liability: Strategies for prevention,* 2nd ed. New York: Columbia University Press.

Reamer, F. G. (2006a). *Social work values and ethics,* 3rd ed. New York: Columbia University Press.

Reamer, F. G. (2006b). *Ethical standards in social work: A review of the NASW Code of Ethics,* 2nd ed. Washington, DC: NASW Press.

Reid, P. N., & Popple, P. R. (Eds.). (1992). *The moral purposes of social work.* Chicago: Nelson-Hall.

Rhodes, M. L. (1986). *Ethical dilemmas in social work practice.* London: Routledge and Kegan Paul.

Strom-Gottfried, K. (2007). *Straight talk about professional ethics.* Chicago: Lyceum.

15 Risk Management in Social Work

Frederic G. Reamer

Contemporary social workers face several possible risks associated with delivery of professional services. Many of these risks, which may lead to ethics complaints or lawsuits filed against social workers, can be prevented.

To protect clients and related third parties and minimize risk, social workers need to be informed about prevailing standards to prevent ethics complaints and ethics-related lawsuits. Ethics complaints—filed with social work licensing boards or with professional organizations, such as the National Association of Social Workers (NASW)—typically allege that social workers violated widely accepted ethical standards in their relationships with clients, colleagues, employers, or other parties. Ethics-related lawsuits typically claim that social workers were negligent, in the strict legal sense, by virtue of their mishandling of some ethics-related phenomenon, such as processing confidential information or informed consent, maintenance of professional boundaries, use of controversial treatment techniques, conflicts of interest, or termination of services (Reamer, 2003, 2006a, 2006b).

THE NATURE OF RISK MANAGEMENT

Social workers expose themselves to risk when they practice in a manner that is inconsistent with prevailing professional standards (Houston-Vega, Nuehring, & Daguio, 1997; Reamer, 2003; Strom-Gottfried, 2000, 2003). Some ethics complaints arise out of mistakes and oversights. Examples include social workers who inadvertently disclose confidential information in a hallway conversation or fail to protect confidential information transmitted via fax or the Internet. Other complaints and lawsuits arise from social workers' deliberate ethical decisions—for example, when social workers disclose confidential information without clients' consent to law enforcement or child protective services officials or terminate services to a noncompliant client. In addition, some complaints and lawsuits are the result of practitioners' ethical misconduct, such as sexual relationships with clients or fraudulent billing for services.

Social workers can be held accountable for negligence and ethical violations in several ways. In addition to filing lawsuits, parties can file ethics complaints with the NASW or with state licensing and regulatory boards. In some instances, social workers are also subject to review by other professional organizations to which they belong, such as the American Board of Examiners in Clinical Social Work, Clinical Social Work Association, and American Association for Marriage and Family Therapy. In exceptional circumstances, criminal charges may be filed (for example, based on allegations of sexual misconduct or fraudulent billing of an insurance company or state funding agency).

Ethics complaints filed against NASW members are processed using a peer review model that includes NASW members and, initially, the National Ethics Committee. If a request for professional review is accepted by the National Ethics Committee, a NASW Chapter Ethics Committee (or the National Ethics Committee in special circumstances) conducts a hearing during which the complainant (the person filing the complaint), the respondent (the person against whom the complaint is filed), and witnesses have an opportunity to testify. After hearing all parties and discussing the testimony, the committee presents a report to elected chapter officers that summarizes its findings and presents recommendations. Recommendations may include sanctions or various forms of corrective action, such as suspension from NASW, mandated supervision or consultation, censure in the form of a letter, or instructions to send the complainant a letter of apology. In some cases, the sanction may be publicized through local and national NASW newsletters or newspapers. NASW also offers mediation in some cases in an effort to avoid formal adjudication, particularly involving matters that do not involve allegations of extreme misconduct. If complainants and respondents agree to mediate the dispute, NASW facilitates the process.

State legislatures also empower social work licensing boards to process ethics complaints filed against social workers who hold a license. Ordinarily these boards appoint a panel of colleagues to review the complaint and, when warranted, conduct a formal investigation and hearing (some state boards include public members in addition to professional colleagues).

Negligence claims or lawsuits filed against social workers typically allege that they engaged in malpractice in that they failed to adhere to specific standards of care. The standard of care is based on what ordinary, reasonable, prudent practitioners with the same or similar training would have done under the same or similar circumstances (Madden, 1998; Woody, 1996). Departures from the profession's standards of care may result from a social worker's acts of commission or acts of omission. Acts of commission can occur as a result of misfeasance (the commission of a proper act in a wrongful or injurious manner or the improper performance of an act that might have been performed lawfully) or malfeasance (the commission of a wrongful or unlawful act). An act of omission, or nonfeasance, occurs when a social work fails to perform certain duties that ought to have been performed.

Lawsuits and liability claims that allege malpractice are civil suits, in contrast to criminal proceedings. Ordinarily, civil suits are based on tort or contract law, with plaintiffs (the party bringing the lawsuit) seeking some sort of compensation for injuries they claim to have incurred as a result of the practitioner's negligence. These injuries may be economic (for example, lost wages or medical expenses), physical (for example, following a sexual relationship between a practitioner and client), or emotional (for example, depression suffered by a client who did not receive competent care from a practitioner).

As in criminal trials, defendants in civil lawsuits are presumed innocent until proven otherwise. In ordinary civil suits, defendants will be found liable for their actions based on the legal standard of preponderance of the evidence, as opposed to the stricter standard of proof beyond a reasonable doubt used in criminal trials. In some civil cases—for example, those involving contract disputes—the court may expect clear and convincing evidence, a standard of proof that is greater than preponderance of the evidence but less than proof beyond a reasonable doubt.

In general, malpractice occurs when evidence exists that (1) at the time of the alleged malpractice a legal duty existed between the social worker and the client; (2) the social worker was derelict in that duty or breached the duty, either by commission or omission; (3) the client suffered some harm or injury; and (4) the harm or injury was directly and proximately caused by the social workers' dereliction or breach of duty.

In some cases, prevailing standards of care are relatively easy to establish through citations of the profession's literature, expert testimony, statutory or regulatory language, or relevant codes of ethics standards. Examples include standards concerning sexual relationships with current clients, disclosing confidential information to protect children who may have been abused or neglected, fraudulent billing, or falsified clinical records. In other cases, however, social workers disagree about standards of care (Austin, Moline, & Williams, 1990; Haas & Malouf, 2005). This may occur in cases involving controversial treatment methods or ambiguous clinical or administrative circumstances (Reamer, 2006a).

KEY RISKS IN SOCIAL WORK

Social workers' prevention efforts should focus on a number of risk areas (Reamer, 2001b, 2006b). These include the following.

Client Rights

Especially since the 1960s, social workers have developed a keen understanding of a wide range of clients' rights, many of which were established by legislation or court ruling. These include rights related to confidentiality and privacy, release of information, informed consent, access to services, use of the least restrictive alternative, refusal of treatment, options for alternative services, access to records, termination of services, and grievance procedures.

Confidentiality, Privileged Communication, and Privacy

Social workers must understand the nature of clients' right to confidentiality and exceptions to these rights. More specifically, social workers should have sound policies and procedures in place related to:

- solicitation of private information from clients;
- disclosure of confidential information to protect clients from self-harm and protect third parties from harm inflicted by clients;
- release of confidential information pertaining to alcohol and substance abuse assessment or treatment;
- disclosure of information about deceased clients;
- release of information to parents and guardians of minor clients;
- sharing of confidential information among participants in family, couples, and group counseling;
- disclosure of confidential information to media representatives, law enforcement officials, protective service agencies, other social service organizations, and collection agencies;
- protection of confidential written and electronic records, information transmitted to other parties through the use of computers, e-mail, fax machines, phones, and other electronic technology;
- transfer or disposal of clients' records;
- protection of client confidentiality in the event of a social worker's death, disability, or employment termination;
- precautions to prevent discussion of confidential information in public or semi-public areas, such as hallways, waiting rooms, elevators, and restaurants;
- disclosure of confidential information to third-party payers;
- disclosure of confidential information to consultants;
- disclosure of confidential information for teaching or training purposes; and
- protection of confidential and privileged information during legal proceedings (e.g., divorce proceedings, custody disputes, paternity cases, criminal trials, and negligence lawsuits).

To protect clients and minimize risk, social workers should discuss with clients and other interested parties the nature of confidentiality and limitations of clients' right to confidentiality (Dickson, 1998; Polowy & Gorenberg, 1997). Depending on the setting, these topics can include

- the importance of confidentiality in the social worker–client relationship (a brief statement of why the social worker treats the subject of confidentiality so seriously);
- laws, ethical standards, and regulations pertaining to confidentiality (relevant federal, state, and local laws and regulations; ethical standards in social work);
- measures the social worker will take to protect clients' confidentiality (storing records in a secure location, limiting colleagues' and outside parties' access to records);
- circumstances in which the social worker would be obligated to disclose confidential information (e.g., to comply with mandatory reporting laws or a court order, to protect a third party from harm or the client from self-injury);
- procedures that will be used to obtain clients' informed consent for the release of confidential information and any exceptions to this (a summary of the purpose and importance of and the steps involved in informed consent);
- the procedures for sharing information with colleagues for consultation, supervision, and coordination of services (a summary of the roles of consultation and supervision, and coordination of services and why confidential information might be shared);
- access that third-party payers (insurers) or employers will have to clients' records (policy for sharing information with managed care organizations, insurance companies, insurance company representatives, utilization review personnel, employers, and staff of employee assistance programs);
- disclosure of confidential information by phone, computer, fax machine, e-mail, and the Internet;
- access to agency facilities and clients by outside parties (e.g., people who come to the agency to attend meetings or participate in a tour); and
- audiotaping and videotaping of clients.

Informed Consent

Informed consent is required in a variety of circumstances, including release of confidential information, program admission, service delivery and treatment, videotaping, and audiotaping (Berg, Appelbaum, Parker, & Lidz, 2001). Although various courts, state legislatures, and agencies have somewhat different interpretations and applications of informed consent standards, there is considerable agreement about the key elements that social workers and agencies should incorporate into consent procedures (for example, that clients should be given specific details about the purposes of the consent, a verbal explanation, information about their rights to refuse consent and withdraw consent, information about alternative treatment options, and an opportunity to ask questions about the consent process).

Service Delivery

Social workers must provide services and represent themselves as competent only within the boundaries of their education, training, license, certification, consultation received, supervised experience, or other relevant professional experience. They should provide services in substantive areas and use practice approaches and techniques that are new to them only after engaging in appropriate study, training, consultation, and supervision from people who are already competent in those practice approaches, interventions, and techniques. Social workers who use practice approaches and interventions for which there are no generally recognized standards should obtain appropriate education, training, consultation, and supervision.

Boundary Issues, Dual Relationships, and Conflicts of Interest

Social workers should establish clear policies, practices, and procedures to ensure proper boundaries related to:

- sexual relationships with current and former clients;
- counseling former sexual partners;
- sexual relationships with clients' relatives or acquaintances;
- sexual relationships with supervisees, trainees, students, and colleagues;
- physical contact with clients;
- friendships with current and former clients;
- encounters with clients in public settings;
- attending clients' social, religious, or life cycle events;
- gifts to and from clients;
- performing favors for clients;
- the delivery of services in clients' homes;
- financial conflicts of interest;
- delivery of services to two or more people who have a relationship with each other (such as couples, family members);
- bartering with clients for goods and services;
- managing relationships in small or rural communities;
- self-disclosure to clients; and
- becoming colleagues with a former client (Reamer, 2001a).

Documentation

Careful documentation and comprehensive records are necessary to assess clients' circumstances; plan and deliver services appropriately; facilitate supervision; provide proper accountability to clients, other service providers, funding agencies, insurers, utilization review staff, and the courts; evaluate services provided; and ensure continuity in the delivery of future services (Kagle, 1995; Reamer, 2005; Wiger, 2005). Thorough documentation also helps ensure quality care if a client's primary social worker becomes unavailable because of illness, incapacitation, vacation, or employment termination. In addition, thorough documentation can help social workers who are named in ethics complaints or lawsuits (for example, when evidence is needed to demonstrate that a social worker obtained a client's informed consent before releasing confidential information, assessed for suicide risk properly, consulted with knowledgeable experts about a client's clinical issues, consulted the NASW *Code of Ethics* to make a difficult ethical decision, or referred a client to other service providers when services were terminated). See Chapter 16 for detailed information on how to prevent suicide and avoid malpractice lawsuits by following standards of care guidelines.

Defamation of Character

Social workers should ensure that their written and oral communications about clients are not defamatory. Libel is the written form of defamation of character; slander is the oral form. Defamation occurs when a social worker says or writes something about a client or another party that is untrue, the social worker knew or should have known that the statement was untrue, and the communication caused some injury to the client or third party (e.g., the client was terminated from a treatment program or lost custody of a child, or a colleague was disciplined by an agency administrator).

Client Records

Social workers should maintain and store records for the number of years required by state statutes or relevant contracts. Practitioners should make special provisions for proper access to their records in the event of their disability, incapacitation, termination of practice, or death. This may include entering into agreements with colleagues who would be willing to assume responsibility for social workers' records if they are unavailable for any reason.

Supervision

In principle, social workers can be named in ethics complaints and lawsuits alleging ethical breaches or negligence by those under their supervision. Social work supervisors should ensure that they meet with supervisees regularly, address appropriate issues (e.g., treatment and intervention plans, case recording, correction of errors in all phases of client contact, dual relationships, protection of third parties), and document the supervision provided.

Consultation and Referral

Social workers should be clear about when consultation with colleagues is appropriate and necessary and the procedures they should use to locate competent consultants. Similarly, social workers have a responsibility to refer clients to colleagues when they do not have the expertise or time to assist clients in need. Practitioners should know when to refer clients to other professionals and how to locate competent colleagues.

Fraud

Social workers should have strict procedures in place to prevent fraud related to, for example, documentation in case records, billing, and employment applications.

Termination of Services

Social workers expose themselves to risk when they terminate services improperly—for example, when a social worker leaves an agency suddenly without adequately referring a vulnerable client to another practitioner, or terminates services to a very vulnerable client who has missed appointments or has not paid an outstanding bill. Practitioners should develop thorough and comprehensive termination protocols to prevent client abandonment.

Practitioner Impairment, Misconduct, and Incompetence

A significant percentage of ethics complaints and negligence claims are filed against social workers who meet the definition of impaired professional (impairment that may be due to factors such as substance abuse, mental illness, extraordinary personal stress, or legal difficulties). Social workers should understand the nature of professional impairment and possible causes, be alert to warning signs, and have procedures in place to prevent, identify, and respond appropriately to impairment in their own lives or colleagues' lives (Reamer, 1992; Strom-Gottfried, 2000, 2003).

In addition, social workers sometimes encounter colleagues who have engaged in ethical misconduct or are incompetent. Examples include social workers who learn that a colleague is falsifying travel expense vouchers or client records or providing services outside his or her areas of expertise.

In some instances, social workers can address these situations satisfactorily by approaching the colleague, raising the concerns, and helping the colleague devise an earnest, constructive, and comprehensive plan to stop the unethical behavior, minimize harm to affected parties, seek appropriate supervision and consultation, and develop any necessary competencies. When these measures fail or are not feasible—perhaps because of the seriousness of the ethical misconduct, impairment, or incompetence—one must consider blowing the whistle on the colleague. Whistleblowing entails taking action through appropriate channels—such as notifying administrators, supervisors, professional organizations, and licensing and regulatory bodies—in an effort to address the problem. Before deciding to blow the whistle, social workers should carefully consider the severity of the harm and misconduct involved; the quality of the evidence of wrongdoing (one should avoid blowing the whistle without clear and convincing evidence); the effect of the decision on colleagues and one's agency; the whistle-blower's motives (that is, whether the whistle-blowing is motivated primarily by a wish for revenge); and the viability of alternative, intermediate courses of action (whether other, less drastic means might address the problem). Social work administrators need to formulate and enforce agency policies and procedures that support and protect staff who disclose impairment, misconduct, and incompetence conscientiously and in good faith. See Chapter 20 on the impaired social work professional for more detailed information on impaired social workers and how to remedy the situation.

Management Practices

Periodically, social work administrators should assess the appropriateness or adequacy of the agency's government licenses; the agency's papers of incorporation and bylaws; the state licenses and current registrations of all professional staff; protocols for emergency action; insurance policies; staff evaluation procedures; and financial management practices (Kurzman, 1995).

IMPLEMENTING A COMPREHENSIVE RISK MANAGEMENT STRATEGY

Social workers can prevent ethics complaints and ethics-related lawsuits by conducting a comprehensive ethics audit (Reamer, 2001b). An ethics audit entails thorough examination of major risks associated with one's practice setting (whether independent or agency-based practice). The audit involves several steps designed to identify ethics-related risks and minimize harm to clients, social workers, and social service agencies:

1. appoint a committee or task force of concerned and informed staff or colleagues;
2. gather the information necessary to assess the level of risk associated with each ethics-related phenomenon (i.e., clients' rights; confidentiality and privacy; informed consent; service delivery; boundary issues and conflicts of interest; documentation; defamation of character; client records; supervision; staff development and training; consultation; client referral; fraud; termination of services; practitioner impairment, misconduct, or

incompetence; management practices) from such sources as agency documents, data gathered from interviews with agency staff, and national accreditation standards;
3. review all available information;
4. determine whether there is no risk, minimal risk, moderate risk, or high risk for each risk area; and
5. prepare an action plan to address each risk area that warrants attention, paying particular attention to the steps required to reduce risk, the resources required, the personnel who will oversee implementation of the action plan, the timetable for completion of the plan, the indicators of progress toward reducing risk, and plans to monitor implementation of the action plan.

In recent years, social workers have paid increased attention to the risk of lawsuits and ethics complaints filed against practitioners and agencies. To minimize these risks, and especially to protect clients, social workers need to understand the nature of professional malpractice and negligence. They also need to be familiar with major risk areas and practical steps they can take to prevent complaints.

WEB SITES

Resources on Risk Management, NASW Assurance Trust. http://www.naswassurance .org/understanding_risk_management/ resources.php.

"Risk Management Practice Pointers," NASW Assurance Trust. http://www.naswassurance .org/understanding_risk_management/ practice_pointers.php.

"Understanding Risk Management," NASW Assurance Trust. http://www.naswassurance .org/understanding_risk_management/.

References

Austin, K. M., Moline, M. E., & Williams, G. T. (1990). *Confronting malpractice: Legal and ethical dilemmas in psychotherapy.* Newbury Park, CA: Sage.

Berg, J. W., Appelbaum, P. S., Parker, L. S., & Lidz, C. W. (2001). *Informed consent: Legal theory and clinical practice,* 2nd ed. New York: Oxford University Press.

Dickson, D. T. (1998). *Confidentiality and privacy in social work: A guide to the law for practitioners and students.* New York: Free Press.

Haas, L. J., & Malouf, J. L. (2005). *Keeping up the good work: A practitioner's guide to mental health ethics*, 4th ed. Sarasota, FL: Professional Resources Press.

Houston-Vega, M. K., Nuehring, E. M., & Daguio, E. R. (1997). *Prudent practice: A guide for managing malpractice risk*. Washington, DC: NASW Press.

Kagle, J. D. (1995). *Social work records*, 2nd ed. Long Grove, IL: Waveland Press.

Kurzman, P. (1995). Professional liability and malpractice. In R. L. Edwards (Ed.-in-Chief), *Encyclopedia of social work*, 19th ed. (vol. 3, pp. 1921–1927). Washington, DC: NASW Press.

Madden, R. (1998). *Legal issues in social work, counseling, and mental health: Guidelines for clinical practice*. Thousand Oaks, CA: Sage.

Polowy, C. I., & Gorenberg, C. (1997). *Office of General Counsel law notes: Client confidentiality and privileged communications*. Washington, DC: NASW Press.

Reamer, F. G. (1992). The impaired social worker. *Social Work, 37*(2), 165–170.

Reamer, F. G. (2001a). *Tangled relationships: Managing boundary issues in the human services*. New York: Columbia University Press.

Reamer, F. G. (2001b). *The social work ethics audit: A risk management tool*. Washington, DC: NASW Press.

Reamer, F. G. (2003). *Social work malpractice and liability: Strategies for prevention*, 2nd ed. New York: Columbia University Press.

Reamer, F. G. (2005). Documentation in social work: Evolving ethical and risk-management standards. *Social Work, 50*(4), 325–334.

Reamer, F. G. (2006a). *Social work values and ethics*, 3rd ed. New York: Columbia University Press.

Reamer, F. G. (2006b). *Ethical standards in social work: A review of the NASW Code of Ethics*, 2nd ed. Washington, DC: NASW Press.

Strom-Gottfried, K. (2000). Ensuring ethical practice: An examination of NASW code violations. *Social Work, 45*(3), 251–261.

Strom-Gottfried, K. (2003). Understanding adjudication: Origins, targets, and outcomes of ethics complaints. *Social Work, 48*(1), 85–94.

Wiger, D. (2005). *The clinical documentation sourcebook: The complete paperwork resource for your mental health practice*. Hoboken, NJ: Wiley.

Woody, R. H. (1996). *Legally safe mental health practice*. Madison, CT: Psychosocial Press.

16 Avoiding Malpractice Lawsuits by Following Standards of Care Guidelines and Preventing Suicide

A Guide for Mental Health Professionals

Albert R. Roberts, Ianna Monferrari, & Kenneth R. Yeager

Every 17 minutes, someone in the United States commits suicide. This equates to 83 suicides every day throughout the year (Roberts & Yeager, 2005). Suicide results in approximately 30,000 reported deaths annually. The loss of a patient to suicide is often a feared outcome among psychiatrists, psychologists, social workers, and crisis counselors, especially because the law assumes that in most situations suicide is preventable. Suicide accounts for many of the largest monetary settlements and judgments as well as a large proportion of malpractice lawsuits filed against mental health clinicians. Yet clinicians often lack sufficient education on the legal aspects of malpractice associated with patient suicide. This article reviews several legal cases in which psychiatrists or social workers failed to protect patients. This includes failure to conduct a comprehensive biopsychosocial and lethality assessment, failure to warn of imminent risk of suicide, or breach of duty to care standards. Each case presentation concludes with recommendations for actions. Next, the chapter identifies common allegations made in suicide malpractice lawsuits. Conditions necessary to meet the criteria for a malpractice suit are laid out.

The article concludes with the authors' guidelines for managing malpractice risk along with a decision-making flow chart designed to reduce a patient's risk of suicide during the treatment process.

Suicide lethality assessment and risk management of suicidal patients are growing concerns of mental health professionals throughout North America. In fact, a patient's suicidal death and the accompanying malpractice liability can have devastating consequences to a mental health professional's career. Regrettably, there is a dearth of courses and training currently being provided by graduate schools (White, 2002). The exception is a few graduate schools of social work that offer a course in crisis intervention and suicide prevention each year (e.g., University of Texas at Austin School of Social Work, Ohio State University College of Social Work). This chapter begins with a review of case examples. It highlights some actions that should be taken, such as conducting an all-inclusive risk assessment. This is followed by a discussion of the key legal issues surrounding malpractice/negligence law suits. The chapter concludes with the introduction of the guidelines to avoid a malpractice/negligence lawsuit.

RISK ASSESSMENT/MANAGEMENT

What exactly is risk assessment for suicide and what is its importance? Risk assessment examines a person's suicide potential and ways to effectively manage such peril (Berman, 2006).

There are many well-known suicide assessment instruments, such as the Beck Hopelessness

Scale, Beck Depression Inventory (BDI), Scale for Suicide Ideation—Worst Point (SSI-W), Lifetime Parasuicidal Count, SADS Person Scale, Linehan Reasons for Living Scale, Suicide Potential Lethality Scale, and others. One might think that assessment of suicidality would be a simple task. This simply is not the case. Douglas Jacobs (APA, 2003) former chair of the American Psychological Association practice guideline on treatment of patients with suicidal behaviors reports that that 50 percent of individuals who complete suicide are in psychiatric treatment at the time—10 percent are inpatients; and 5 percent to 10 percent are post–hospital discharge. Douglas also reports that with regard to an analysis of records of 100 patients who committed suicide in a hospital, 77 percent denied suicidal intent in their last communication with staff.

One possible explanation of the change is the frequent ambivalence expressed by patients. At intake assessment, patients or their family members frequently report suicidal thoughts, threats, and/or gestures. However, because we may have two different or paradoxical thoughts at almost the same time, many patients decide after several hours in a busy hospital emergency room that they would be more comfortable going home and controlling their own decisions, or they want to live for an upcoming family event. For example, a close family member's high school or college graduation may only be 6 months away. Inadequate lethality assessments and other concerns related to patient assessment, reassessment, orientation of staff regarding suicidal risk measures combined with inadequate staffing levels, and infrequent patient observations contribute to inpatient psychiatric patient suicides. Additionally, the Joint Commission on Accreditation of Hospital Organizations reports that there are a significant number of suicides in general hospital settings. Despite all the risk measures, it is necessary to develop a practice guideline for the risk assessment and treatment of patients with suicidal behaviors that combines practice knowledge, experience, and evidence and takes into account patient rights.

Psychiatrists, social workers, and psychologists sometimes lack the training in assessing the degree of suicidality and conducting a lethality assessment. According to the APA (2003) Practice Guideline for patients with suicidal behaviors: "If the patient has developed a suicide plan, it is important to assess its lethality. The lethality of the plan can be ascertained through questions about the method, the patient's knowledge and skill concerning its use, and the absence of intervening persons or protective circumstances" (p. 23).

We build on the APA (2003) guideline, which is not intended to serve as a standard of care. The APA guidelines have been developed by psychiatrists who are highly experienced clinical practitioners, combined with researchers and academicians. The guideline consists of three parts (A, B, and C). Part A addresses assessment, treatment, and risk management recommendations. This includes key recommendations of the guideline and codes each recommendation according to the degree of clinical confidence associated with the recommendations. Additionally, there is a discussion of assessment of the patient, including consideration of factors that may impact suicidal risk. Recommendations are made with regard to psychiatric management and treatment modalities as well as for documentation of care and potential risk management issues. Part B of the guideline outlines background information, for example, natural history, epidemiology, and course, as well as a review of currently available evidence. Part C is dedicated to drawing from the previous sections, summarizing recommendations and outlining areas where additional research is required to advance the data, knowledge, and practice approaches in addressing high-risk behaviors. We support and build on the APA guideline and are not trying to replace it.

The suicide ideation and assessment flowchart in this chapter takes into account several critical warning signs. The following warning signs are adapted from Roberts and Yeager's (2005, pp. 41, 45) chapter in the third edition of the *Crisis Intervention Handbook*:

- family member reports on drastic behavior change in patient (e.g., banging his head against the wall, or barricading himself in his room for an extended period and not coming out for meals or the bathroom);
- family member reports on patient's suicidal statement;
- patient gives away prized possessions;
- patient indicates that he or she has a firearm in the home and exhibits poor judgment;
- patient indicates depression symptoms;
- patient expresses suicide ideation;
- patient has a suicide plan;

- patient is agitated and exhibits imminent danger to self or others;
- psychotic patient exhibits command hallucinations related to harming self or others;
- patient is intoxicated or high on illegal drugs and acting in an impulsive manner.

The goal of this chapter is to address issues related to risk assessment and management measures, while devising ways to instruct mental health professionals that would safeguard them against malpractice suits. The authors chose a unique and innovative approach. We developed specific actions to *do*. How is it unique and innovative? What does it do that the APA guideline does not? The following section answers these two questions by presenting concise summaries of cases from which a list of practical "do's will be derived.

CASE EXAMPLES

Hanging by a Thread

After watching her husband express hallucinations (thought that his testicles were disappearing), sudden major changes in behavior (such as banging his head against the wall, heavy pacing around in underwear(as well as enunciating a suicide threat of wanting to end his life through hanging, a concerned wife takes her husband to the emergency room of a private hospital (Roberts & Jennings, 2005). The patient is soon transferred to the nearest city hospital with a mental health intake unit, and the mental health technician's completed form is faxed ahead of time to the intake unit. This form notes that Mr. Banach was a danger to himself because he mentioned the desire to end his life through hanging. The patient was then examined and interviewed at the city hospital by an attending physician, Dr. Dang, and later interviewed on the phone via a 20-minute translated phone conversation with a social worker, Chester Scott. Within 1 hour, the attending physician and social worker allow the family to take the patient home, stating that he was sexually dysfunctional due to "drinking problem" (Roberts & Jennings, 2005, p. 2), further advising that he should receive follow-up treatment at an outpatient community clinic. Unfortunately, the social worker and physician failed to make a proper diagnosis of psychosis, depression, and high suicide risk and failed to give the

family proper warning of risk of suicide as well as ensure the patient's safety once he left the hospital. The patient hung himself at approximately 2 A.M. a few hours after his midnight discharge from the hospital (Roberts & Jennings, 2005).

The social worker attempted to defend himself by negating his liability due to his position as a social worker, passing it on to the doctor. The court denied this defense, explaining how the social worker and doctor worked as team, having equal share in the responsibility. Both doctor and social worker were found liable (Roberts & Jennings, 2005).

- *Do*: Diagnose properly (adequate assessment—especially suicide). Gain an understanding of client's hopes and plans for the future, levels of depression and anxiety, psychotic and delusional thoughts, and family members' reports of suicidal threats or gestures (Roberts & Jennings, 2005, p. 4).
- Evaluate properly (see Fig. 16.1).
- Be aware of the nine most serious warning signs for suicide (listed earlier in this article).
- Be knowledgeable on the standard of care (provide a translator to inform not only the patient but the family of important information).
- Become aware of your role in the team.
- Take appropriate action to inform the family of patient's status.
- Don't take family's concerns lightly.
- Be suspicious of highly unusual behavior.
- Take higher precautions if patient demonstrates an active suicide plan.

Gaido v. Weiser

A patient with a history of severe depression and anxiety, previously diagnosed as having multiple sclerosis and having attempted suicide, was released from his inpatient treatment and required that he continue psychiatric treatment (*Gaido v. Weiser* [1989]. 115 NJ 310). The appointment to meet with a new doctor was scheduled for 6 days after his release; in the meantime, the patient began demonstrating anxiety symptoms that were similar to what he had experienced in the past, prior to hospitalization, including a very unusual one: excessive drinking. Concerned, the wife called the new doctor (Dr. Weiser) and asked that he see her husband that same day. The doctor refused the wife's request, given that the patient continued taking his medication—even though

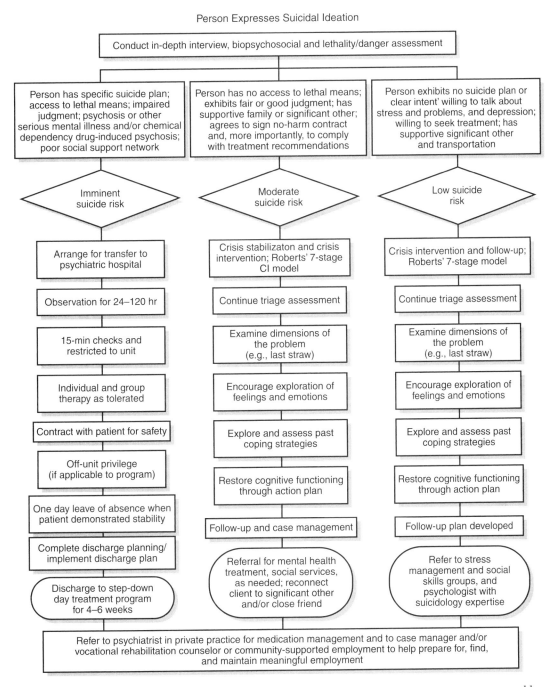

Figure 16.1 Flow chart for assisting suicidal individual. (*Source:* Roberts & Yeager, 2005. Reprinted by permission.)

he did not check what medication had been previously prescribed. The wife continued trying to schedule an earlier appointment; at one point, the doctor agreed to prescribe something (clorazepate) "to take the edge off" (p. 15) while he maintained his position of not being able to see the patient before the scheduled appointment. Patient's body was found on a riverbank, the autopsy found a large amount of water in his stomach, and a 0.23 percent alcohol in his blood. It was concluded that the patient drowned, and the cause of death was "accident." The wife expressed that the doctor did not meet the appropriate standards of care and was negligent in prescribing clorazepate to her husband, "proximately causing decedent's death." The doctor denied "breach[ing] the proper duty of care": "legal obligation imposed on an individual requiring that they exercise a reasonable standard of care while performing any acts that could foreseeably harm others" (APA, 2003). He further stated that if his behavior was found to be negligent, it would not be the "proximate cause"—an event that is legally sufficient to document liability resulting from a legally recognizable injury to be held the cause of that injury (Black, 1999, p. 234) of decedent's death. According to *Black's Law Dictionary*, *negligence* is defined as "an act or omission that is considered in law to result in a consequence so that liability can be imposed on the actor" (Black, 1999, p. 234). The court found the doctor negligent based on the "failure to obtain the patient's hospital records, as well as his failure to ascertain what medication the patient had previously been prescribed" (Baergar, 2001). One would:

• *Do*: Obtain the patient's history (hospital records, medications previously prescribed, current medications, etc.) before making judgments, especially prior to prescribing medication.

Abille v. United States

After being prescribed reserpine—a drug for the control of high blood pressure—the patient began experiencing depressive symptoms (often a side effect of this drug) and suicidal thoughts and decided to admit himself into a hospital. His medical history was taken during intake by a psychiatrist, who noted psychomotor retardation, suicidal ideation, and sleep disturbances (*Abille v. United States* [1980] 482F. Supp. 703).

He later concluded that the patient was suffering from "depressive neurosis," "hypertension," and "reactive depression to reserpine" (p. 2). All patients were given status levels. New patients were usually granted S1 status—the most highly restrictive—only allowing patients to move with an accompanying staff member. Four days after his admission, Abille was allowed to attend mass, shave, and go to mass unattended, granting him S2 status, which was generally given to those that were not thought to be of suicidal risk. He was found dead shortly after he was given a razor for shaving. According to the autopsy report, he took his own life.

Although Dr. Hipolito testified that he changed Abille's status to S2, there was no written record of it. The nurses acted based on the assumption of this presumed change. Thus, the court had to decide if the defendant met the principles of due care in his attempt to safeguard Abille against his own self-injurious behavior. To sustain the burden of proof, in other words, to prove the allegations enunciated by the court (for full list refer to p. 3), three questions were raised:

1. Did Dr. Hipolito in fact change Abille's status?
2. If he did change it, did he exercise due care in doing so?
3. If he failed to exercise due care, was his negligence a proximate cause of Abille's death?

The court found that by allowing the patient to leave the ward by himself, the nurses acted below the standard of care. The court further noted that the psychiatrist's decision to change Abille's level was within the standard of care; however, the way through which he did so was not. There were no notes or any records that could serve as a documentation of his decision making process. Dr. Hipolito was found liable for his failure to "describe accurately and fully in his report of the events and medical orders everything of consequence that he did and which his trained eye observed during the inpatient stay" (p. 8).

• *Do:* Keep an all-inclusive record, from the patient's status to reasons behind choosing a certain decision.
• Avoid making assumptions; make sure there are documented reasons and notes prior to following an order.

Stepakoff v. Kantar

The wife of a patient diagnosed as "manic-depressive psychotic" (*Stepakoff v. Kantar* [1984–1985] 393 Mass. 836; 473 N.I. 2d 1131. No. M—3622) alleged that her husband's psychiatric doctor failed to let her know of his suicidal status and to implement adequate arrangements for her husband's safety.

Experiencing some marital difficulty, the wife went away, letting the patient know that he must be out of the house when she returned, and also informing the doctor of the situation. The doctor tranquilized the wife, stating that her husband should be fine. The psychiatrist was aware of his patient's suicidal tendencies but believed that the patient had strong coping mechanisms; because he had been treating the patient for 15 months, he also thought he had established a close and strong therapeutic relationship with the patient, which would deter him from attempting suicide or from making any major decisions without contacting him first.

The psychiatrist had plans to go on a weekend vacation 2 days after the patient's wife left. He made arrangements for the patient to continue treatment with another psychiatrist while he was away, and agreed to give him a follow-up call every night.

Prior to going on vacation, he had an emergency meeting with the patient, during which he noted a "question of whether he will make it over the weekend" (p. 2). During his statement to the court, the doctor explained this question as not being a suicidal concern, but rather, "Whether he would be able to carry out the activities that he and I outlined, or whether the type of thing that happened to him just preceding his psychiatric admission to Newton-Wellesley [in 1974] would occur . . . it was that type of regression and inability to function that I was questioning" (p. 2).

The court stated how the psychiatrist has a duty to his patient, not to third parties. Thus, the psychiatrist was not found negligent due to the cautious treatment plan he developed in conjunction with the patient, as well as the fact that the patient did not meet the legal criteria to be hospitalized involuntarily at the time.

- *Do*: Be familiar with the legal criteria for involuntary commitment.
- If you need to be absent, make proper arrangements for patient to continue treatment.
- Follow through with plans/stand behind decisions (if you tell the patient you'll call, then do so).
- Document thoughts.
- Reread notes—explain/document certain "incriminating" remarks.

Bates v. Denny

Mr. Bates, a 33-year-old male was brought to the emergency room of a hospital, complaining of pain in his ribs due to falling from a flight of stairs. Several cuts and scratches were found on his wrist during examination, which he explained as being "cat scratches" (*Bates v. Denny* [1990]

No. 89 CA 0401, p. 1). The patient's mother, Irene, was a relative of the emergency room physician and elaborated on her son's psychiatric and hospitalization history, including two recent suicide attempts—overdose on sleeping pills and shooting himself in the abdomen. Concerned that her son was suicidal, she asked for his hospitalization. She further stated that Mr. Bates had stopped taking his medication and expressed a desire to kill himself through use of a gun. However, when questioned, he contested being suicidal and did not agree to being hospitalized.

Dr. Newman performed a mental status evaluation on the patient, and other than noting slurred speech and discontent with family's insistence on hospitalizing him, his behavior was rather normal. The decision to send the patient home was made based on the phone conversation Newman had with the patient's most recent psychiatrist. Also, the patient was not thought to be depressed or psychotic, and the family was to keep close watch, ascertaining that he did not obtain access to a weapon, further stating that involuntarily hospitalizing the patient would perhaps be counterproductive (p. 3). Mr. Bates died the next morning from "a self-inflicted contact gunshot wound to the right temple" (p. 1).

Three psychiatrists provided expert testimony in this case. To summarize arguments that found the psychiatrist negligent were based on the patient's "chronically suicidal" (p. 4) status. During his testimony, one expert stated that because the patient posed a serious threat to himself, the best way to safeguard him was to keep him under a close watch within the safe and highly monitored atmosphere of a hospital. He further stated that if the patient does not demonstrate suicidal ideation, it is up to the mental health professional to make a judgment call as to the truthfulness of the patient's word, perhaps alluding to the doctor's improper judgment.

Arguments against assigning culpability to the psychiatrist were slightly similar, also relying on the elaboration of the patient's "chronically suicidal" status. "A chronically suicidal person is one who has a suicide potential over a long period of time with periods of remission alternating with acutely suicidal states" (p. 4).

Expert testimony as well as the court noted that the patient was in remission state, not acutely suicidal, and did not express any psychotic or suicidal signs, thus it was within the standard of care to allow him to leave. In other words, one cannot maintain a chronically suicidal patient locked up indefinitely. Furthermore, the doctor's actions did not demonstrate a breach in the standard of care due to the fact that the doctor scheduled a follow-up appointment, was aware of the patient's family and clinical history, and also made arrangements to inform the family of the patient's needs. Also, because the patient had a history of being resistant to treatment, involuntarily retaining him would make his treatment worse. Finally, the patient did not demonstrate any of the conditions for involuntary hospitalization—"whether the patient is suicidal, homicidal or gravely disabled" (p. 5)—the rule of the "least restrictive" judgment comes into play. Thus, the psychiatrist was found to have acted within the standard of care.

- *Do*: Obtain patient's clinical and family history.
- Make arrangements for follow-up appointments.
- Be knowledgeable on the necessary conditions for involuntary hospitalization.
- Be aware of the rule of the "least restrictive environment."
- Think decisions through thoroughly.

MALPRACTICE AND NEGLIGENCE

In legal terminology, malpractice is classified as a tort action. *Tort* is a civil wrong committed by one individual (the defendant) that caused some injury to another individual (the plaintiff) (Packman & Harris, 1998).

Negligence is "the failure to exercise the standard of care that a reasonably prudent person would have exercised in the same situation" (Black, 1996, p. 1405). The standard of care is "the degree of care that a reasonable person should exercise", thus differing from situation to situation" (Black, 1996, p. 589). Malpractice is frequently described as "professional negligence," referring to negligence or incompetence on the part of the professional; specifically, "a negligent act committed by a professional that harms another" (Roberts & Jennings, 2005, p. 5). There are two primary areas of focus: an act of commission (i.e., mental health professional doing something that should not have been done) and an act of omission (i.e., mental health professional not taking appropriate action given presenting risk factors) (Roberts & Jennings, 2005, pp. 1–10).

In regard to malpractice suits, the plaintiff must demonstrate that their case against the defendant meets these conditions (action-based elements of proof)

1. Duty of care was owed by the professional to the plaintiff;
2. The professional violated the applicable standard of care—breach of duty;
3. The plaintiff suffered a compensable injury; and
4. Causation, that the plaintiff's injury was caused in fact and proximately caused by the defendant's substandard conduct. (Roberts & Jennings, 2005 pp. 1–10).

In addition to knowing the conditions that must be met in a malpractice suit, it is also important for a practitioner to be familiar with the typical allegations made in a malpractice suit filed in a case of suicide.

The top eight complaint allegations (extracted from the work of Packman et al., 2004) :

- Failure to predict or diagnose the suicide.
- Failure to control, supervise, or restrain.
- Failure to take proper tests and evaluations of the patient to establish suicidal intent.
- Failure to medicate properly.
- Failure to observe the patient continuously (24 hours) or on a frequent enough basis (e.g., every 15 minutes).
- Failure to take an adequate history.
- Inadequate supervision or failure to remove dangerous objects, such as a patient's belt.
- Failure to place the patient in a secure area.

GUIDELINES TO AVOIDING MALPRACTICE/NEGLIGENCE LAW SUITS (FIKKE MODEL)

To obtain a more in-depth understanding of the issues, as well as employ the best precautionary actions against a malpractice/liability suit, the authors' offer the following guidelines.

FIKKE Model of Malpractice Suits

1. *Familiarize* yourself with the common allegations in negligence/malpractice suits.
2. *Implement* an all-inclusive risk assessment strategy (refer to Fig. 16.1).

3. *Know* suicide warning signs, legal terminologies, and their meanings.
4. *Keep* the do's in mind.
5. *Enhance* understanding through case examples.

CONCLUSION

The overriding goal of suicide prevention work is to save lives. The importance of warning signs, lethality assessments, and following standard of care guidelines is critical for this goal. However, even the most competent professional cannot always prevent a patient's suicide attempt, especially in the small number of cases where there are no warning signs. Cases proceed to court only if the suicide was reasonably "foreseeable" and preventable" (Vande Creek & Knapp, 1989). This chapter hopes to increase the knowledge base and skills of social workers treating suicidal persons. The overriding goal being to prevent suicides by providing clinicians with a checklist, decision flowchart, and warning signs for improving assessment and patient management. We identify specific suicide risk practices and familiarize clinicians with the malpractice aspects of their fiduciary duty to protect those under their care.

WEB SITES

American Academy of Psychiatry and the Law. http://www.aapl.org.
American Bar Association. http://www.abanet.org.
American Psychiatric Association, *Patient Safety and Psychiatry*, Recommendations to the Board of Trustees of the American Psychiatric Association, A Task Force Report, Approved by the Board of Trustees, November 2002. http://www.psych.org/MainMenu/PsychiatricPractice/QualityImprovement/PatientSafety_1.aspx.

PsychiatryOnline, American Psychiatric Association Practice Guidelines http://www.psychiatryonline.com/pracGuide/pracGuideTopic_14.aspx.

References

American Psychiatric Association, Work Group on Suicidal Behaviors. (2003). *Practice guideline for the assessment and treatment of patients with suicidal behaviors*. Washington, DC: American Psychiatric Association Press.
Baerger, D. (2001). Risk management with the suicidal patient: Lessons from case law. *Professional Psychology Research and Practice, 32* 4), 356–366.
Berman, A. L. (2006). Risk management with suicidal patients. *Journal of Clinical Psychology, 62*(2), 171–184.
Black, H. C. (1996). *Black's law dictionary*, 7th ed. St. Paul, MN: West Publishing.
Black, H. C. (1999). *Black's law dictionary*, 8th ed. St. Paul, MN: West Publishing.
Packman W., & Harries, E. (1998). Legal issues and risk management in suicidal patients. In B. Bongar, A. Berman, R. Maris, M. Silverman, E. Harris, & W. Packman (Eds.), *Risk management with suicidal patients* (pp. 150–186). New York: Guilford Publications.
Packman, W., Pennuto, T., Bongar, B., & Orthwein, J. (2004). Legal issues of professional negligence in suicide cases. *Behavioral Sciences and the Law, 22,* 697–713.
Roberts, A. R., & Jennings T. (2005). Hanging by a thread: How failure to conduct an adequate lethality assessment resulted in suicide. *Brief Treatment and Crisis Intervention, 5*(1), 1–10.
Roberts, A. R., & Yeager, K. R. (2005). Lethality assessments and crisis intervention with persons presenting with suicidal ideation. In A. R. Roberts (Ed.), *Crisis intervention handbook: Assessment, treatment and research*, 3rd ed. (pp. 35–63). New York: Oxford University Press.
VandeCreek, L., & Young, J. (1989). Malpractice risks with suicidal patients. *Psychotherapy Bulletin, 24*(3), 18–21.
White, T. W. (2002). Improving the reliability of expert testimony in suicide litigation. *Journal of Psychiatry and Law, 32,* 331–353.

17 Social Work Licensing Examinations in the United States and Canada

Development and Administration

Donna DeAngelis

Licensing examinations are a crucial component in nearly every licensed profession in the United States. Social work is no exception: in 2008, every state, the District of Columbia, Puerto Rico, and the U.S. Virgin Islands reported using one or more licensing examinations as a licensure requirement. Two Canadian provinces—Alberta and British Columbia—use the clinical social work licensing examination, and other provinces are considering using one or more of the Association of Social Work Boards (ASWB) examinations. In all of these jurisdictions, a social worker who is otherwise qualified to become licensed may be prevented from obtaining a license if he or she fails the examinations.

In 2007, examinations provided by the ASWB were used in all of the above-mentioned testing jurisdictions except California (which administers state-based written examinations) and Puerto Rico, which administers its own examination in Spanish. The ASWB examinations are the only social work licensing exams with a North American scope and North American passing scores. Over 28,000 tests are administered annually.

The ASWB began as the American Association of State Social Work Boards in 1979 (American Association of State Social Work Boards, 1999). The organization was founded by a group of social work regulators from 12 states; other jurisdictions regulating social work soon joined this core group. One of the first things this newly formed association did was develop national licensing examinations that became available for use in 1983. Since that time, the national social work examination program has increased to use in 49 states, 2 territories, and 2 Canadian provinces. In 1999, the association changed its name to the Association of Social Work Boards to better reflect its new members from Canada.

TESTING FORMAT AND DELIVERY

The ASWB examinations are offered in four categories: bachelors, appropriate for BSWs with 0 to 2 years of experience; masters, for use by MSWs with 0 to 2 years of experience; advanced generalist, for MSWs with two or more years of post-degree experience in nonclinical settings; and clinical, for MSWs with two or more years of post-degree experience in a clinical setting. Details about the various licensure requirements and levels of practice regulated in the United States and Canada, including the examinations required for the various categories of social work licensure, are available at the ASWB Web site in the form of an online comparison guide database.

Each test consists of 170 multiple-choice items, 20 of which are nonscored "pretest" items. Test takers have 4 hours to complete the examination. (Note: Complete content outlines for all ASWB examinations can be found in the ASWB *Candidate Handbook* (2008), the ASWB Practice Analysis Report (2004), on the association's Website, and in other publications.)

The association works with a testing contractor—as of this writing, ACT—that provides psychometric and administration support services. Tests are administered through computers at over 230 testing sites across the United States. (Paper-

and-pencil versions of the tests are administered in Canada.) The computer-based examinations are scored immediately after completion of the test, so that an examinee can get preliminary results on the test day. Results remain preliminary until they are forwarded and accepted by the social work regulatory board. In 2007, national passing percentages for first-time examinees were associate—67.1 percent; bachelors—78.1 percent; masters—73.4 percent; advanced generalist—58.2 percent; clinical—73.9 percent.

TEST CONSTRUCTION: VALIDITY AND RELIABILITY

The ASWB examinations and other professional licensing examinations are called high-stakes examinations because a failing score can prevent an individual from pursuing his or her intended career. This role demands that the examinations be valid and reliable, intertwined concepts that create the basis for a legally defensible examination program.

The primary challenge to a testing program is to find the theoretical line that separates those who are minimally competent from those who are not. Tests could easily be constructed that would separate those with highly advanced knowledge and skills from those without, but they would not be appropriate for use in a licensing system. Legal regulation's focus must remain on making determinations that protect the public from incompetent practice—regulatory bodies cannot restrict licenses to only those practitioners who demonstrate excellence, because excellence and competence are different concepts. In turn, licensing examinations must be able to measure minimum competency and do so consistently—they must, in other words, be *valid* and *reliable*.

Validity

Validity, as it is used in licensing examination programs, refers to the extent to which a test measures what it is supposed to be measuring, and the test's ability to ensure that minimally competent candidates are passing the exam and minimally incompetent candidates are not passing. Validity is accomplished primarily through the way the test is constructed and the method by which passing scores are set. The central component of the ASWB examination program's overall validity rests with the practice analysis process (see following discussion).

Reliability

Basically, reliability refers to the consistency of an examination. A highly reliable test is one that would produce similar scores for each test taker time after time. The reliability of the ASWB examinations is maintained through its test development efforts and the statistical monitoring of individual item (test question) performance.

CONSTRUCTING THE EXAMINATIONS: THE PRACTICE ANALYSIS

The ASWB licensing examinations are constructed according to the guidelines of the American Psychological Association, the Joint Commission on Standards for Educational and Psychological Testing, the American Educational Research Association, and the National Council on Measurement in Education, with psychometric guidance from ACT. The ASWB examinations are based on periodic practice analyses. The practice analysis begins with a survey of social work practice in a wide variety of setting across the United States and Canada—its results shape not only the actual questions that appear on the examinations but the very need for a particular examination at a particular level of practice. From the practice analysis, ASWB finds out what social workers are doing at various levels of practice.

The practice analysis survey lists a series of tasks common to social work and then asks participants to rate how often they perform each task, how critical knowledge of the task is regardless of how often it is performed, and whether the ability to perform this task is a necessary entry-level skill at their particular level of practice. The results give ASWB a highly accurate profile of social work and help the association establish the various categories of examinations offered. The entire analysis is based on standards developed jointly by the American Psychological Association, the American Educational Research Association, and the National Council on Measurement in Education.

The association's first practice analysis was conducted in 1980–1981, with a verification study conducted in 1988. The next practice analysis was completed in 1996, and the most recent analysis was completed in 2003. A new practice analysis is scheduled to begin in 2008.

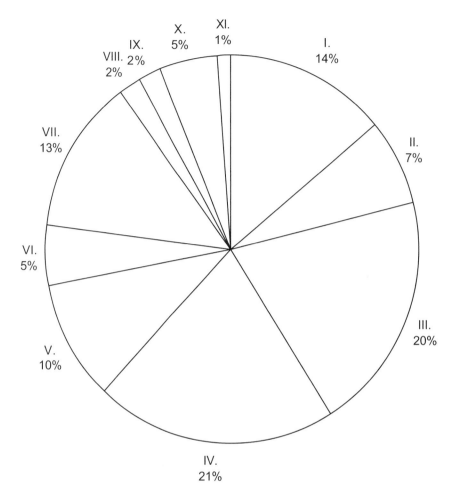

I.   Human Development and Behavior in the Environment
II.   Issues of Diversity
III.   Assessment in Social Work Practice
IV.   Direct and Indirect Practice
V.   Communication
VI.   Professional Relationships
VII.   Professional Values and Ethics
VIII. Supervision in Social Work
IX.   Practice Evaluation and the Utilization of Research
X.   Service Delivery
XI.   Social Work Administration

Figure 17.1 ASWB bachelors examination, content area weights.

After survey results have been compiled and tabulated, subject matter experts sift through the ratings and identify those tasks critical to entry-level practice. Once the most important tasks have been identified, content experts target the knowledge areas that are essential to performing it. Usu-ally, there are several knowledge areas attached to any one task, reflecting the complexity of the social work profession.

With task and knowledge areas defined, content outlines, also called examination blueprints, are created. Essentially, the content outline is the skeletal version of the examination itself, with content heading and subheadings indicating the percentage of items relating to each topic. These content outlines, one for each category of the ASWB examinations, are built on the results of the practice analysis, and guide all item development.

CONTENT OUTLINES: ASWB SOCIAL WORK LICENSURE EXAMINATIONS

Bachelors Examination Content Outline

I. Human Development and Behavior in the Environment (14 percent)
   A. Theoretical approaches to understanding individuals, families, groups, communities, and organizations
   B. Human growth and development
   C. Human behavior in the social environment
   D. Impact of crises and changes
   E. Addictive behaviors
   F. Dynamics of abuse and neglect
II. Issues of Diversity (7 percent)
III. Assessment in Social Work Practice (20 percent)
   A. Social history and collateral data
   B. Use of assessment instruments
   C. Problem identification
   D. Effects of the environment on client system behavior
   E. Assessment of client system's strengths and weaknesses
   F. Assessment of mental and behavioral disorders
   G. Indicators of abuse and neglect
   H. Indicators of danger to self and others
   I. Indicators of crisis
IV. Direct and Indirect Practice (21 percent)
   A. Models of practice
   B. Intervention techniques
   C. Components of the intervention process
   D. Matching intervention with client system needs
   E. Professional use of self
   F. Use of collaborative relationships in social work practice
V. Communication (10 percent)
   A. Communication principles
   B. Communication techniques
VI. Professional Relationships (5 percent)
   A. Relationship concepts
   B. Relationship in practice

VII. Professional Values and Ethics (13 percent)
   A. Responsibility to the client system
   B. Responsibility to the profession
   C. Confidentiality
   D. Self-determination
VIII. Supervision in Social Work (2 percent)
   A. Educational functions of supervision
   B. Administrative functions of supervision
IX. Practice Evaluation and the Utilization of Research (2 percent)
   A. Methods of data collection
   B. Research design and data analysis
X. Service Delivery (5 percent)
   A. Client system rights and entitlements
   B. Implementation of organizational policies and procedures
XI. Social Work Administration (1 percent)
   A. Staffing and human resource management
   B. Social work program management

Masters Examination Content Outline

I. Human Development and Behavior in the Environment (18 percent)
   A. Theories and concepts
   B. Application of knowledge
II. Diversity and Social/Economic Justice (7 percent)
   A. Diversity
   B. Social/economic justice and oppression
III. Assessment, Diagnosis, and Intervention Planning (11 percent)
   A. Biopsychosocial history and collateral data
   B. Assessment methods and techniques
   C. Assessment indicators, components, and characteristics
   D. Indicators of abuse and neglect
   E. Intervention planning
IV. Direct and Indirect Practice (22 percent)
   A. Intervention models and methods
   B. The intervention process
   C. Intervention techniques
   D. Intervention with couples and families
   E. Intervention with groups
   F. Intervention with communities and larger systems
   G. Consultation and interdisciplinary collaboration
V. Communication (7 percent)
   A. Communication principles
   B. Communication techniques

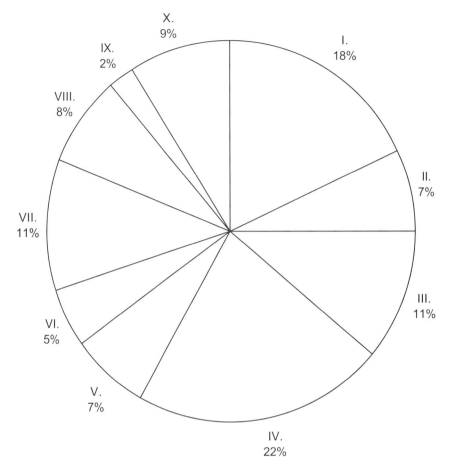

I.   Human Development and Behavior in the Environment
II.   Diversity and Social/Economic Justice
III.   Assessment, Diagnosis, and Intervention Planning
IV.   Direct and Indirect Practice
V.   Communication
VI.   Professional Relationships
VII.   Professional Values and Ethics
VIII.   Supervision, Administration, and Policy
IX.   Practice Evaluation and the Utilization of Research
X.   Service Delivery

Figure 17.2 ASWB masters examination, content area weights.

VI. Professional Relationships (5 percent)
  A. Relationship concepts
  B. Social worker and client roles
  C. Ethical issues within the relationship
VII. Professional Values and Ethics (11 percent)
  A. Professional values
  B. Legal and ethical issues
  C. Confidentiality

VIII. Supervision, Administration, and Policy
  (8 percent)
  A. Supervision and staff development
  B. Human resource management
  C. Finance and administration
IX. Practice Evaluation and the Utilization of
  Research (2 percent)
  A. Data collection

B. Data analysis
C. Utilization of research
X. Service Delivery (9 percent)
   A. Service delivery systems
   B. Obtaining services
   C. Effects of policies and procedures on service delivery

Advanced Generalist Examination Content Outline

I. Human Development and Behavior in the Environment (10 percent)
   A. Theories and models
   B. Human growth and development
   C. Family functioning
II. Issues of Diversity (5 percent)
III. Assessment, Diagnosis, and Intervention Planning (24 percent)
   A. Social history
   B. Use of assessment instruments
   C. Problem identification
   D. Effects of the environment on client behavior
   E. Impact of life stressors on systems
   F. Evaluation of client strengths and weaknesses
   G. Evaluation of mental and behavioral disorders
   H. Abuse and neglect
   I. Indicators of danger to self and others
   J. General assessment issues
   K. Intervention planning
IV. Direct and Indirect Practice (16 percent)
   A. Theories
   B. Methods and processes
   C. Intervention techniques
   D. Intervention with couples and families
   E. Intervention with groups
   F. Intervention with communities
V. Communication (7 percent)
   A. Communication principles
   B. Communication techniques
VI. Relationship Issues (5 percent)
   A. Concepts of social worker–client relationship
   B. Effects of social and psychological factors
VII. Professional Values and Ethics (12 percent)
   A. Values and ethics
   B. Confidentiality
   C. Self-determination

VIII. Supervision and Professional Development (3 percent)
IX. Practice Evaluation and the Utilization of Research (4 percent)
   A. Data collection
   B. Data analysis and utilization
X. Service Delivery (11 percent)
   A. Service delivery systems and processes
   B. Effects of policies, procedures, and legislation
   C. Methods of social work advocacy
   D. Interdisciplinary collaboration
XI. Administration (3 percent)
   A. Management
   B. Human resource management
   C. Financial management

Clinical Examination Content Outline

I. Human Development and Behavior in the Environment (22 percent)
   A. Theories of human development and behavior
   B. Human development in the life cycle
   C. Human behavior
   D. Impact of crises and changes
   E. Family functioning
   F. Addictions
   G. Abuse and neglect
II. Issues of Diversity (6 percent)
   A. Effects of culture, race, and/or ethnicity
   B. Effects of sexual orientation and/or gender
   C. Effects of age and/or disability
III. Diagnosis and Assessment (16 percent)
   A. Assessment
   B. Information gathering
   C. Diagnostic classifications
   D. Indicators of abuse and neglect
   E. Indicators of danger to self and others
IV. Psychotherapy and Clinical Practice (16 percent)
   A. Intervention theories and models
   B. The intervention process
   C. Treatment planning
   D. Intervention techniques
   E. Intervention with couples and families
   F. Intervention with groups
V. Communication (8 percent)
   A. Communication principles
   B. Communication techniques
VI. The Therapeutic Relationship (7 percent)
   A. Relationship theories
   B. Relationship practice

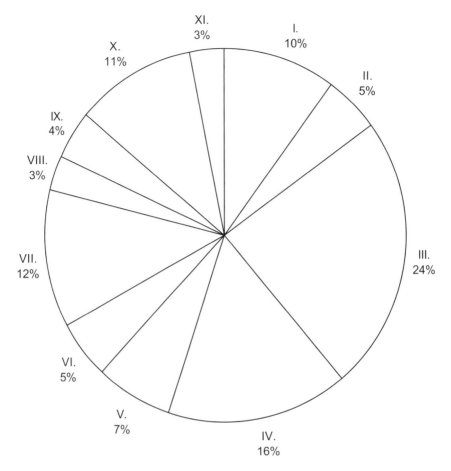

I.   Human Development and Behavior in the Environment
II.   Issues of Diversity
III.   Assessment, Diagnosis, and Intervention Planning
IV.   Direct and Indirect Practice
V.   Communication
VI.   Relationship Issues
VII.   Professional Values and Ethics
VIII.   Supervision and Professional Development
IX.   Practice Evaluation and the Utilization of Research
X.   Service Delivery
XI.   Administration

Figure 17.3 ASWB advanced generalist examination, content area weights.

VII. Professional Values and Ethics (10 percent)
   A. Value issues
   B. Legal and ethical issues
   C. Confidentiality
VIII. Clinical Supervision, Consultation, and
   Staff Development (4 percent)
   A. Social work supervision

   B. Consultation and interdisciplinary
      collaboration
   C. Staff development
IX. Practice Evaluation and the Utilization of
   Research (1 percent)
   A. Evaluation techniques
   B. Utilization of research

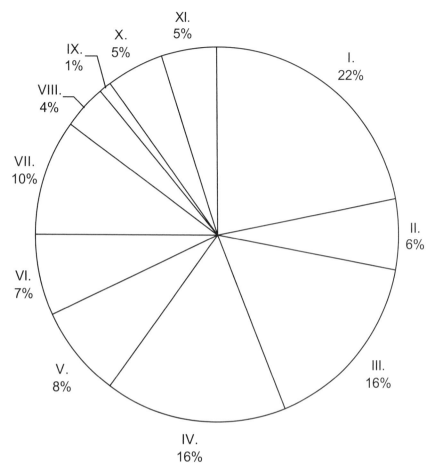

I.   Human Development and Behavior in the Environment
II.   Issues of Diversity
III.   Diagnosis and Assessment
IV.   Psychotherapy and Clinical Practice
V.   Communication
VI.   The Therapeutic Relationship
VII.   Professional Values and Ethics
VIII.   Clinical Supervision, Consultation, and Staff Development
IX.   Practice Evaluation and the Utilization of Research
X.   Service Delivery
XI.   Clinical Practice and Management

Figure 17.4 ASWB clinical examination, content area weights.

X. Service Delivery (5 percent)
    A. Policies and procedures of service delivery
    B. Processes of service delivery
XI. Clinical Practice and Management
    (5 percent)
    A. Advocacy

B. Finance
C. Management and human resource issues

Examinations are created to fit these blueprints, and passing scores (or cut scores) are set using a psychometric process called a modified Angoff method. In this method, social work experts review examination questions on the basis of the abilities of a "minimally competent" practitioner. They then make decisions on the probability that this practitioner will answer correctly. The judgments are averaged, and the averages are used to compute the cut score for the examination as a whole. This score is usually adjusted to reflect the realities of the examinations' use for licensure.

TEST DEVELOPMENT

For each category of examination, ASWB maintains a stockpile of questions, or items, coded to specific content areas. These are written by social work practitioners across the country who have been contracted to write items in various areas of practice. The writers are selected by the association to ensure an accurate representation of practice, ethnic, racial, and geographic diversity and are trained in the fine points of item writing.

Once created and edited, items are presented to the ASWB Examination Committee. This committee is the most important element in the continued health of the examination program, and like the item writing group, it is carefully selected to reflect the diversity of the social work profession. At each of its meetings, the Examination Committee reviews items for possible inclusion on the examinations as pretest items—the audition that every item receives as a nonscored question on an ASWB examination. The committee reviews every new item and must reach consensus before it is pretested on the social work examinations. The committee specifically looks for only one correct answer for each item. If the committee cannot come to consensus, the question is either discarded or changed.

Every item approved for use in the ASWB item pool is coded and statistically tracked, both during its pretest phase and through its use as a scored item. Before any item can be included in the pool of standard scored items, it must perform acceptably as a nonscored pretest item. There are 20 pretest items on every ASWB examination. All pretest items must have several hundred responses before a statistical analysis of its function is meaningful.

The statistical tracking also allows ASWB to attach a difficulty rating to each question. These ratings play an important role in the way the examinations are scored and allow ASWB to create multiple versions of an examination while keeping overall difficulty constant (see section on equating).

To maintain a high level of security, ASWB creates several versions, called *forms*, of each examination, with different combinations of items filling in the required content areas. Examination candidates are tracked and linked to specific forms, so that a failed candidate who retakes the test will never be presented with the same version of an examination.

Equating: Keeping the Difficulty Consistent

When examination forms are created, the individual difficulty levels of the items are accounted for in the passing score for that particular form. Put simply, it is quite possible that any given combination of items will result in a test that is more or less difficult than another form, but this is taken into account when the passing score is set. The passing score adjustments mean that in the end, passing each test requires the same level of ability, even though the questions may vary. The process for accounting for differences in overall difficulty is known as *equating*.

This statistical/psychometric process is essentially invisible to test takers, except to the extent that equating makes it impossible to establish an unchanging number of items that need to be answered correctly to pass every form of each category of an ASWB examination. Candidates taking one form of the examination may have to answer more or fewer questions correctly than candidates taking another form. These variations— typically very slight—are accounted for in the passing score set for each form, so that the overall difficulty of each exam is the same.

ADMINISTRATION POLICIES

The licensing examinations are intended to be measures of social work knowledge, and not tests of reading, deduction, or the values of one culture over another. To guard against overly complex language, all examination items are thoroughly edited for simplicity and straightforward language; jargon is eliminated wherever possible, and readability tests have been conducted on the examinations. The last such test revealed the examinations to function at about the U.S. tenth-grade reading level—more difficult than a national newspaper, but less challenging than the standard social work texts used in most BSW and MSW programs.

Cultural bias is also monitored closely. The association takes steps to guard against this bias by including diverse participants in every phase of examination development and item writing. Furthermore, individual test items are monitored for the presence of differential item functioning (DIF), or the tendency for one subgroup of test takers to answer the item in ways that are disproportionate. When consistent DIF is identified in an item—usually in pretest items that are being tested for possible scored use—the item is returned to the Examination Committee to determine where the problem may lie.

ASWB is also sensitive to the special needs of test takers. Long before the United States adopted the Americans with Disabilities Act, the association was providing accommodations to social workers with disabilities. These accommodations continue today, and range from audiotape and Braille examinations to the provision of readers and sign language interpreters, as well as allowances for extra time in which to complete the examination. Most U.S. jurisdictions also allow the ASWB to make arrangements for test takers whose primary language is something other than English. Typically, these candidates are allowed the use of up to two dictionaries (one of which may be a standard English dictionary) and additional time to complete the test.

TEST REGISTRATION AND ADMINISTRATION

In 2008, all but four states required social workers to apply to the social work regulatory board for licensure before being permitted to register to take the test. Typically, this preapproval process verifies, at a minimum, social work degree earned and, for the independent practice licenses, experience and supervision. Once the regulatory board has reviewed and found requirements for licensure to be in order, it approves the candidate to take the appropriate licensing examination. The candidate contacts ASWB to register for an examination. The candidate must complete a registration form and request any special accommodations at the time of submission and then pay the examination fee by certified check, money order, or credit card. An authorization letter with instructions about how to make a testing appointment and a list of available test centers is sent to the candidate. The candidate follows the instructions for making the appointment and is given a date and time for the test. The appointment is verified, and directions to the test center are sent to the candidate via e-mail.

ASWB and ACT take test security very seriously. Candidates must present their authorization letter and a government-issued photo identification at the test center or they will not be admitted. To make another appointment, the candidates are required to pay another testing fee in its entirety. The candidates are not permitted to bring anything into the testing room, must leave their personal belongings outside of the room, and must sign and denote the time of arrival and departure. Candidates are only permitted to leave the testing room to use the toilet facilities and must sign out and in to do so.

The test is administered at a secure carrel where the view to other computers in the room is blocked. Personnel walk through the testing room periodically and continuously monitor the testing room through a window. Cameras record each testing session, and the tape is kept for a designated amount of time in case there are questions about the testing conditions or test taker behavior.

The appointment time is 4.5 hours—the test-taking time itself is limited to 4 hours, and a half hour is allotted for a tutorial on how to navigate the test on the computer. Candidates must agree to a confidentiality statement on the screen before the test will start; if the candidate does not agree, the test will be terminated and the candidate will forfeit the testing fee. When the candidate indicates that he or she is finished with the test, or when the 4-hour testing time is expired, a ten-question survey about the testing experience will appear for the candidate to complete. After the survey is finished, the computer will provide a score on the screen. A paper score report will also be printed out and given to the candidate.

Because the tests are scored electronically, there is very little probability of a scoring error. When the data from the examinations go back to ACT from the testing center, ACT staff verify that the scores are correct. ASWB does allow candidates to have their examinations hand-scored by ACT for an additional fee. ACT reports candidates' scores weekly to the regulatory board where they are seeking licensure and back to ASWB, where candidates' scores are kept in perpetuity. Candidates may request an official score transfer to another regulatory board at any time for a fee.

CONCLUSION

The licensing examinations developed by ASWB are designed to be used to assist regulatory boards in their legislated mandates to protect the public consumers of social work services. Like professional regulation itself, licensing examinations are not designed to promote or protect a profession. Professions do benefit from valid and reliable examinations to the extent that these tests help verify the abilities of licensees, but the true focus of the ASWB examination program is on measuring social work competency as it relates to protection of the public.

Testing industry guidelines followed by ASWB require the organization to be diligent in the provision of valid, reliable, and fair social work licensing examinations. Developing, monitoring, maintaining, and administering high-stakes licensure examinations is a complex and expensive process that requires ASWB, its board of directors, its staff, and its testing contractor to perform their duties with adherence to social work ethics and psychometric standards.

SAMPLE TEST ITEMS

These are included in ASWB (2008) *Candidate Handbook.*

Bachelors Examination

1. The rapport established between social worker and client is the client's belief that the social worker is:
   A. able to help the client resolve the presenting problem.
   B. understanding and interested in the client's well-being.
   C. like the client in terms of background and social status.
   D. willing to partialize the client's problem into manageable areas.
   Correct answer: B.

2. An explicit agreement between the social worker and client concerning target problems, goals, and strategies of social work intervention and the roles and tasks of the participants is known as a:
   A. contract.
   B. process.
   C. task analysis.
   D. treatment plan.
   Correct answer: A.

Masters Examination

1. A social worker can *best* establish rapport with a client in the first interview by:
   A. understanding the client's view of the problem.
   B. asking only factual information about the problem.
   C. conducting the interview on a first-name basis.
   D. first allowing time for informal, personal conversation.
   Correct answer: A.

2. A client who has completed treatment and resolved the targeted problem is making excessive telephone calls to the social worker. The social worker should:
   A. inform the client that the therapeutic relationship is finished.
   B. refer the client to another social worker in the agency.
   C. limit the number of calls the social worker will accept.
   D. schedule a session to determine any current problems.
   Correct answer: D.

Advanced Generalist Examination

1. A social worker in a family service agency is seeing an adolescent client for the first time. The client was brought by the mother to the agency because the parents suspect the client is abusing drugs. A critical factor for the social worker to recognize in establishing rapport with the adolescent is that the client will:
   A. be unwilling to acknowledge drug abuse to the social worker.
   B. believe the social worker is aligned with the parents.
   C. relate to the social worker only if the client and the social worker are of the same gender.
   D. express feelings of doubt and lack of self-worth.
   Correct answer: B.

2. During the first interview with the social worker, a woman states that she is worried about her teenage daughter. The woman talks

rapidly and intensely about her own history of illness and hospitalizations, her husband's drinking, and problems with her marriage. What is the *best* course of action for the social worker to take?

A. Explore further her husband's drinking.
B. Comment that she seems concerned about many things, and ask her which of these she needs help with.
C. Listen without interruption or comment to relieve her anxiety.
D. Summarize all that she has disclosed at the end of the session.

Correct answer: B.

Clinical Examination

1. A clinical social worker is conducting a first interview with a client who attempts to dominate the interview from the beginning. Among the client's complaints are that his telephone is tapped and his neighborhood is watched by the police. The social worker can *best* establish a beginning level of rapport with the client by:

A. interrupting the client to ask factual questions about his background.
B. asking the client to describe the evidence he has that his telephone is tapped.
C. asking the client about the ways in which the social worker can be helpful with these problems.
D. questioning the client about when he first believed that his house was being watched.

Correct answer: C.

2. In discussing a treatment contract developed with a client, the social worker can *best*

help the client anticipate the course of treatment by:

A. explaining to the client the treatment techniques to be employed.
B. helping the client understand and anticipate obstacles to change.
C. securing the client's commitment to participate fully in all treatment sessions.
D. providing the client with reading material that explains the course of treatment.

Correct answer: B.

WEB SITES

American Board of Examiners in Clinical Social Work Website. http://www.abecsw.org.

Association of Social Work Boards. http://www .aswb.org.

Canadian Association of Social Workers Website. http://www.casw-acts.ca.

National Association of Social Workers (US) Website. http://www.socialworkers.org.

References

American Association of State Social Work Boards. (1999). *Are we there yet? The first 20 years of an association's visionary journey.* Culpeper, VA: AASSWB.

Association of Social Work Boards. (2004). *Analysis of the practice of social work 2003: Final report.* Culpeper, VA: ASWB.

Association of Social Work Boards. (2008). *Candidate handbook ASWB social work licensing examinations.* Culpeper, VA: ASWB.

18 Social Work Regulation and Licensing

Andrew T. Marks & Karen S. Knox

Regulation of social work as a profession serves several purposes in protecting the public, social work practice and services, and the title of social worker. Differences in regulation vary from state to state, ranging from registration and certification to licensure. Each level of regulation has specified minimum competencies based on education, testing, supervision, and experience. Professional development for maintaining regulatory status is mandated through continuing education and training. Current issues impacting regulation and licensing are malpractice, portability, reciprocity, and dual credentialing.

SOCIAL WORK REGULATION AND LICENSING

Social work regulation has been a dynamic, ongoing process of debate and change since the beginnings of the profession in the early 1900s. There are many influences and impacts on social work regulation from political power through appointment to professional boards to financial impacts by third-party reimbursement. Social work regulation protects and enforces the values, ethics, and professional standards of practice and is the primary means of protecting the public and clients of social services through sanctions for professional and regulatory violations. In addition to providing a foundation of who a social worker is and what a social worker can or cannot do in a specific jurisdiction, social work regulation has both supported the acceptance of the profession and continued the quandary of what is social work and who is a social worker.

Protecting the Public

The primary focus of all regulatory bodies, whether voluntary or mandated by government legisla-tion, is protection of the recipients of the professional's service (i.e., consumers), stated most succinctly as "protecting the public." Mandated regulatory bodies are usually created by jurisdiction governance bodies or state legislatures. Their primary goals are to set standards for professional practice, enforce the law, establish rules and regulations that determine minimum qualifications for professional practice, and establish a process to discipline those who do not maintain or continuously meet the established standards. Most regulatory bodies have authority to grant, suspend, and discipline credentials issued by the regulatory body (Biggerstaff, 1995). According to Biggerstaff (1995), social work regulation has four primary purposes:

1. protect the service consumer,
2. protect the profession,
3. protect the individual professional, and
4. aid consumers in the selection of a practitioner in the profession.

Professional regulation through licensing, certification, or registration is a result of the need for government to intervene in activities within the private sector because serious conditions exist in which unqualified practice results in serious threat of harm to public health and safety or economic welfare of the consumer (Biggerstaff, 1995). Additional reasons for social work regulation exist in that the consumer is often unable to correctly evaluate a practitioner's qualifications, and the benefits of credentialing for the consumer clearly prevail over potential harmful effects on the professional (Biggerstaff, 1995).

Another type of social work regulation is through professional organizations and associations that offer voluntary certification as a benefit of membership. Government-sanctioned social worker regulation credentials have proliferated in the

United States since the 1980s, so voluntary credentials have become less utilized by practitioners because many jurisdictions have statutes protecting the practice of a profession with credentialing administered by the jurisdictional governing body. This multitude of required governmental and voluntary professional organizational credentialing is confusing to professionals, not to mention the general public. As a result of the bifurcated credentialing processes, the public has little knowledge or understanding of the difference between mandated or voluntary credentials (Biggerstaff, 1995).

Protecting the Practice of Social Work

At the national level, the Association of Social Work Boards (ASWB) assists the state regulatory boards in carrying out their mandates and is responsible for social worker licensing examination in the United States. The organization developed the Model Social Work Practice Act for state regulatory boards to use to set minimum competency and practice standards for social work practitioners and implement methods for investigating and addressing consumer complaints (ASWB, 2007). The act also includes definitions for social work practice at the bachelors, masters, and clinical levels of social work regulation. The definition of what social work is and what a social worker does is important to the protection of the profession from unqualified practitioners.

Most social worker credentialing bodies require formal education in social work with a degree from an accredited institution of higher education recognized by either the Council on Social Work Education (CSWE) or other formal accreditation body acceptable to the jurisdiction's higher education coordinating agency. Passage of the national social work licensing exam is required in almost all jurisdictions in the United States. Some have additional examination requirements, such as jurisprudence (covering jurisdictional law and rules) and cultural (covering aspects of working with specific populations). Additionally, for some levels of credentialing, qualified supervised experience may be required prior to approval to sit for the exam.

A challenge in protecting the practice of social work is found when boards grant exemptions to the required credentials for government employees or those with extensive employment experience in social services who can be "grandfathered"

in, despite not meeting minimum standards. This can occur when state boards make changes or increase their standards, and it means that someone with a non–social work bachelor's degree could be licensed as a social worker solely because of previous work experience, even though the minimum educational requirement is currently a BSW. Other governmental agencies (such as child protective services and juvenile probation) have exemptions from licensing for employees, but provide services and practices typically requiring licensing in the private or nonprofit sector. An example would be employees at a state youth correctional facility providing sex offender treatment without having social work or sex offender therapist licensure as required by regulatory boards for nongovernment practitioners.

Another challenge in social work regulation is protecting the practice of social work from counseling professionals regulated by other professional boards, educational degrees, and licensing credentials, such as licensed marriage and family therapists (LMFTs), or licensed professional counselors (LPCs). Differentiating social work practice from other helping professions is paramount in defining what social workers can do and what those not regulated as social workers should not do. However, the profession has struggled with this defining activity, because social workers are educated and trained in a variety of different disciplines and therapeutic approaches, so there continues to be a murky definition of professional social work.

Protecting the Title of Social Worker

The protection of the title of social worker and defining who is qualified to engage in social work service are important functions for consumer and professional protection. Defining who a social worker is appears easier than defining what a social worker does, and how that definition is displayed in credentialing can be a source of great confusion. A review of credentialing levels and acronyms for the 50 jurisdictions of the United States, 10 Canadian jurisdictions, the District of Columbia, the Virgin Islands, and Puerto Rico, reveals 42 different titles used to describe social worker credentialing (ASWB, 2007). This multilevel use of acronyms that are often interwoven with various meanings, and levels of education and experience can add a difficult dimension for both consumers and professionals in understanding the social work profession and its regulation.

What is most confusing is that the same acronyms stand for different types or levels of licensing across the jurisdictions. For example:

- LCSW: used for a licensed clinical social worker in Alaska, but is a licensed certified social worker in Alabama. Both licenses require an MSW plus 2 years postgraduate experience and a clinical level examination.
- LMSW: typically used for licensed masters social worker and requires an MSW level of education. However, LGSW (licensed graduate social worker) is used in Alabama, LSW (licensed social worker) is used in Colorado, and ASW (associate clinical social worker) is used in California for MSW-level licensing.
- LBSW: usually indicates a minimum BSW level of education, but some jurisdictions do not have licensing at the bachelor's level, including California, Delaware, Colorado, New York, and Tennessee.
- LSW (licensed social worker) is another common licensing title for undergraduate levels of education, but many states also use LSW to indicate MSW levels. In Arkansas, the LSW indicates a BSW level of education; in Colorado, the LSW indicates a MSW level of education.
- RSW (registered social worker), LICSW (licensed independent clinical social worker), CSW (certified social worker), and SWT (social work technician) are other common titles used across jurisdictions.

Practice Protection versus Title Protection

The development of professional credentials begins with identifying the purpose of the enabling statute. Is the regulation to regulate the practice or the title of the practitioner? If the purpose of professional regulation is to ensure only those individuals specifically educated, trained, and most qualified to engage in practice, then more stringent legislation is required. If the purpose is to ensure that only those meeting the highest standards of education and training are permitted to call themselves social workers but not to prevent those not specifically educated or trained in social work to engage in the practice, then legislation to protect the title is all that is required.

Social workers historically agree that those educated at a master's degree or higher and engaging in independent clinical practice need to be regulated due to the potential risk to consumers by the professional. Most jurisdictions support this philosophy by regulating the independent provision of clinical social work practice and title of clinical social worker. However, the profession remains split on the need for regulation of those at the nonclinical and bachelor's level of practice, as much of this form of social work takes place in the auspices of an agency setting. With more individuals engaging in contract services and independent nonclinical practice, the need to monitor more individuals beyond title protection becomes important.

Registration, Certification, and Licensure

Credentialing is a part of the administrative regulatory function of government in most jurisdictions. Most licensing rules are maintained in the jurisdiction's administrative code. Regulated professionals are afforded due process, and the credential becomes a property right of the individual. The regulatory body issuing the credential may revoke it if the professional commits a violation within the jurisdiction of the regulatory body. Most professional credentialing is divided into three categories—licensing, certification, and registration. At one time, licensing and registration were considered to be government activities.

Licensing is required to participate in specific professions, whereas registration can be voluntary for those who engage in a profession whose title is protected by law. Certification can be voluntary but is not always associated with governing statutes. Certification in practice specializations, such as gerontology or chemical dependency counseling, have been established by various professional associations and organizations. Today, the terms *licensing, certification,* and *registration* are used almost interchangeably among jurisdictions and professions.

Licensing carries with it recognition of acceptance at the professional level and authority to practice in a profession. Licensing usually requires continuing professional education or training to maintain licensure. Certification denotes an individual who meets specific criteria to obtain recognition. In most cases, however, once certified there are no provisions that require maintaining minimum competency, such as mandatory continuing education. Registration symbolizes that one is recognized by a regulatory body as practicing but not necessarily having met specific criteria to engage in the practice of the profession.

A Brief History of Social Work Regulation

Social work as a profession is relatively new to regulation, especially as one of the health care and helping professions. The first attempt at social work regulation dates back to the 1920s in California, and Puerto Rico passed the first credentialing statute for social workers in 1934. California was successful with implementing regulation of social workers by 1945 (Thyer & Biggerstaff, 1989). By 1993, every state and the District of Columbia had some form of social worker regulation (Biggerstaff, 1995).

The first record of a social work organization's action toward legal regulation was in 1947 by the American Association of Social Workers through their delegate assembly (Thyer & Biggerstaff, 1989). The primary purpose for this push for legal regulation was to raise the status of the profession. The National Association of Social Workers (NASW) was created in the mid-1950s with the merger of seven different social work associations and focused on seeking recognition and acceptance for the profession at a legal level in each jurisdiction. During the 1969 delegate assembly, NASW passed a resolution to pursue licensing of social workers in each state. Today NASW continues to serve as the largest organization of social workers in the United States. Although the profession has seen a proliferation of specialty associations representing various practice aspects, such as the Federation of Clinical Social Workers, National Association of Black Social Workers, National Association of Christians in Social Work, Society for Social Work Leadership in Healthcare, and the Latino Social Work Organization, NASW continues to be viewed as the primary association for the profession producing the code of ethics considered to be a standard of conduct for most social work professionals.

Social worker regulators recognized a need for a separate organization to support the burgeoning proliferation of jurisdictional regulation bodies. While the call for regulation began within the professional associations, once implemented, the regulatory bodies and professional associations often found themselves on opposite sides of how best to regulate the social work profession. The American Association of State Social Work Boards (AASSWB) was founded in 1979 as a support mechanism for those jurisdictions with regulatory boards and to assist those considering initiating social worker regulation (ASWB, 2004). AASSWB developed the social work examination program currently in use by jurisdictions for required testing for licensure. In 1999, AASSWB was changed to the Association of Social Work Boards (ASWB) to reflect the growing number of memberships from Canadian jurisdictions (ASWB, 2004).

ROLES AND RESPONSIBILITIES OF THE JURISDICTION REGULATORY BODY

As noted, credentialing is a local (i.e., state) jurisdictional responsibility. The right to issue or remove a credential lies within the enabling statute and structure of the oversight body responsible for implementing and monitoring the regulatory duties. A key question regards how the regulatory body is comprised. Is it primarily comprised of political appointments? Are the appointments derived from both professional (those regulated by the enabling statue) and nonprofessional (those having no connection to the regulated profession)? Or is the regulatory process placed within a bureaucratic agency and duties administered by agency employees with the assistance of technical advisors knowledgeable in the profession or perhaps a formal advisory board? Regardless of the regulatory body composition, the following components will need to be resolved: minimum competency and continuing competency.

Minimum Competency

Education. What will the minimum level of education be for credentialed individuals? This is easier to answer once the body defines whether it is a single tier (licensing at only one level) or multitiered system (credentialing at multiple levels). Credentialing at multiple levels lends itself to defining levels of credentialing by levels of education, for example, that those holding a bachelor's or a masters' degree qualify for specific levels of credentialing. Regulatory bodies also define if the degree must be an accredited degree by a regional or national accrediting body or university accredited by such an accreditation body.

Most schools of social work at universities and colleges in the United States are accredited by the CSWE, and many state jurisdictions specify that degrees in social work must be accredited by CSWE to be eligible for licensure. In Canada, the Canadian Association of Schools of Social Work (CASSW) is the accreditation body. This requirement assists in ensuring public protection by establishing minimum criteria for social work education and granting of social work degrees. A recent challenge in some jurisdictions concerns allowing educational institutions associated with faith-based philosophies to be exempted from CSWE accreditation and their graduates allowed to sit for credentialing.

Testing. The profession of social work benefits by having a nationally accepted examination. Currently, California is the only statewide jurisdiction continuing to use a specific state jurisdictional exam. ASWB contracts with the ACT Center Network to administer and maintain the security of the examination process. Exams are currently offered through ACT exam centers throughout the United States, Puerto Rico, Guam, and the District of Columbia. The local jurisdiction informs candidates which level of examination they qualify to take; although there is some variation, generally the requirements are consistent with the ASWB exam levels. Currently, there are five levels of examination offered by ASWB:

• Associate: social work experience, but education can vary from high school to an undergraduate degree;
• Bachelors: an undergraduate BSW degree from a CSWE-accredited program;
• Masters: a graduate MSW degree from a CSWE-accredited program;
• Clinical: a graduate MSW degree from a CSWE-accredited program, plus 2 years postgraduate clinical experience and approved supervision;
• Advanced generalist: a graduate MSW degree from a CSWE-accredited program, plus 2 years postgraduate experience.

Each exam contains 170 questions, of which 150 are scored, with the additional 20 items being evaluated for use in future versions of the examinations. Candidates taking the exam do not know which are pretest or scored items, and they are encouraged to answer all items to the best of their abilities. The exam questions are simple recall, analysis, and evaluation questions, with the analysis and evaluation questions stemming from a case scenario. The advanced generalist and clinical exams contain more analysis and evaluation questions than the others. The exam is taken

electronically with 4 hours to complete it. There are some jurisdictions that offer the exams in other languages than English, and accommodations are made for persons with disabilities (ASWB, 2007).

Each exam covers the major areas of social work knowledge and skills, and the percentages of the content vary across the different examination levels. For example, the human behavior and the social environment content is 22 percent of the clinical exam but only 10 percent of the advanced generalist exam (Social Work Examination Services, 2005). Practice and assessment content varies in both percentages and types, such as more generalist practice in the bachelors exam and psychotherapy and clinical practice in the clinical exam. Other content is relatively the same across all of the examination levels, such as:

• Communication (7–10 percent),
• Diversity (5–7 percent),
• Values and ethics (10–13 percent),
• Research and practice evaluation (1–4 percent), and
• Professional relationships (5–7 percent). (SWES, 2005)

There are licensing exam workshops sponsored by professional organizations, and social work programs, and Social Work Examination Services has study guides with practice questions that are helpful for preparation and review.

Supervision and experience. Some jurisdictions require a specific amount and type of work experience to be eligible for social worker credentialing. Generally, this is expected at the advanced or clinical levels of practice credentialing or to compensate for deficits in another area of minimum competency, such as formal education. Most jurisdictions define who can supervise the professional experience that is used to seek social worker credentialing. Some jurisdictions require that the supervisor be approved prior to initiating the supervised experience and many require regular updates or reports during the supervised professional experience. Jurisdictions define the amount of supervised experience and how the supervision is to occur (individual or group session).

Additionally, once the professional experience is completed, supervisors must attest to the readiness of the candidate based on the supervised experience. Supervised experience is another method of ensuring the individual possesses the knowledge, skills, and abilities for social worker credentialing. Similar to the internship during the formal social work degree, supervised professional experience provides a hands-on opportunity for regulatory bodies to ensure public health and safety are maintained.

Continued Competency and Continuing Education

Once a professional has successfully achieved the social work credential, most jurisdictions require credentialed individuals to maintain minimum competency, and most hope for increased professional competency through professional experience and additional formal and informal training. Most jurisdictions require credentialed professionals to demonstrate their continued competency through completion of continuing education hours as part of their recredentialing process. These hours may be formally acknowledged by jurisdiction rules (i.e., university or approved continuing education providers) or nationally recognized accrediting body (i.e., ASWB's ACE program).

Traditionally, programs offered for continuing education are for skills that enhance or reaffirm a social worker's professional knowledge, not necessarily specific to those skills necessary for the professional's current employment. Therefore, many continuing education opportunities take place outside the employment setting and at a cost to the employer or professional. Many employers attempt to offer continuing education opportunities for their employees as a benefit of employment. Some offer stipends for conference or workshop attendance if it can be demonstrated that the skills garnered will benefit the credentialed person and the employing agency. Continuing education can be earned through attendance at conferences, workshops, or completion of self-study opportunities. Self-study can be done through reading a professional document and then completing a self-assessment questionnaire or other distance learning opportunities, such as those available online.

Obtaining continuing education credit is one method regulatory boards can verify that a professional is at least continuing to participate in professional learning and training. Whether continuing education equates continuing competency is of great debate among social work professionals, social work educators, and regulatory board members. No specific study demonstrates completely the effectiveness of continuing education

programs (Swankin, LeBuhn, & Morrison, 2006). The only true method to demonstrate minimum competency is for the credentialed individual to sit for reexamination. However, this demonstrates only minimum competency and not true continued competency, as would be expected from a practicing professional. The American Association of Retired Persons states that continuing education programs should include assessment, development of a continuing education plan based on the assessment, and periodic demonstrations of continuing competence by the professional to ensure public health and safety (Swankin et al., 2006). How demonstrations of continuing competency should be implemented is another challenge for social work regulatory boards and professional associations.

CURRENT ISSUES IN SOCIAL WORKER REGULATION AND LICENSING

Portability-Endorsement versus Reciprocity

Reciprocity is defined as when a professional who is licensed in one jurisdiction is automatically licensed in a separate jurisdiction based on the issuance of the original license. Because licensing is a local function, most jurisdictions do not automatically issue a license based on licensure in a different area. Most jurisdictions will provide acceptance of those activities used toward credentialing in a separate jurisdiction, as long as the criteria are as rigorous as those in the new jurisdiction. This process is known as *endorsement*. However, very few jurisdictions have exactly the same criteria for licensure.

A review of the Social Work Laws and Regulations Comparison Database shows jurisdictions vary in the amount of supervised experience, hours of face-to-face supervision, whether the supervision can be in group or individual sessions, the minimum frequency that supervision must occur, and the qualifications of the person providing the supervision that is acceptable for credentialing (ASWB, 2007). To this end, ASWB has created a concept for a model law and encourages all jurisdictions regulating social workers to consider adopting its criteria as a basis for licensure. ASWB has also begun a Social Work Registry to assist credentialed social workers in maintaining documentation related to their licensure, certification, or registration status. This is particularly helpful if a regulated professional has resided in multiple jurisdictions, achieved specialty recognition in one jurisdiction but not another, or has been employed by a federal institution. The goals of the registry are to make verification of information used toward credentialing easier to access, have one place to call for verification of professional credentials held, and have the criteria used to achieve the credentials in one location.

Recent events, such as the tragedy of September 11, 2001, and Hurricanes Katrina and Rita in 2005, have shown the need for greater portability of social workers to perform disaster relief efforts. Additional issues have risen in the field of adoption or custody home studies when the guardian or adoptive family may live in one jurisdiction and the child or children live in a separate one. Whether the professional will be required to be credentialed in the jurisdiction where the matter is handled is not only in the hands of the court but in the authority of the enabling statutes for the regulatory boards. Though some areas grant permission for a credentialed professional to perform in their jurisdiction for a specified period of time without formal efforts to be recognized by the jurisdiction, others do not grant such leniency. As such, professionals who regularly work in multiple jurisdictions must achieve and maintain credentialing in each area they serve professionally. This creates greater confusion to the consumer, especially when credential acronyms are jurisdiction-specific along with the complaint and disciplinary processes. Serving multiple masters, as it were, can also be daunting to the professional, because each jurisdiction may have specific idiosyncratic criteria to its regulatory functions.

Multiple Masters and Dual Credentialing

As market forces drive professionals to find niches to offer greater opportunity for success in providing services, many professionals look to multiple credentials or specialty credentials to boost their marketability. Specialized credentials, certifications, and licenses in play therapy, hypnosis, anger management, mediation, and sex offender therapy are a few examples. One issue is who authorizes and issues the credential. Credentials can be offered by a separate state-governing agency, such as an LPC, an LMFT, or a licensed sex offender treatment provider. Credentials can also be sanctioned by a professional association, such as registered play therapist (RPT) and RPT-supervisor, issued by the Association for Play Therapy.

If under the regulation of two government-sanctioned regulatory boards, professionals may face multiple disciplinary processes that could run into large legal expenses. Additionally, because each process is independent of the other, the timeframe for resolution will be independent as well. It is not uncommon for one regulatory body to issue a sanction and the other to issue a more severe sanction for the same complaint. Practitioners need to provide contact and complaint filing information to each regulatory body for all credentials they hold. Many jurisdictions require professionals to provide signed written statements from consumers regarding the receipt of this information. Also, some boards require their code of conduct be displayed publicly in the professional's primary place of employment that contains information on initiating a disciplinary complaint against a regulated professional.

Although specialty credentials are important for professionals and beneficial for consumers, they can lead to greater confusion for consumers. Additional confusion can occur when the credential offered may be unlawful to display in a professional jurisdiction because the acronym is similar to that of another protected professional title. For example, an RPT (registered play therapy) can also mean registered physical therapist in some jurisdictions. Because the credential offered by the association is not the same as the protected title sanctioned by the government, displaying the credential can lead to legal action against the professional.

Licensing of Social Work Faculty

Thyer and Seidl (2000) debate about whether social work faculty teaching practice courses should be regulated social workers. One argument is that for social work educators to be most effective, they need to be connected to practice, and licensure is one option to ensure that faculty maintain current practice knowledge and technology. However, Seidl argues that there are already adequate academic accountability measures and that requiring licensure does not ensure better teaching of practice by faculty. In his editorial in the *Journal of Social Work Values and Ethics*, Marson (2006) argues that licensing of social work faculty is an ethical issue. Whether it is an ethical issue or an issue of competence, regulation of faculty is an issue of public health and safety. The individual who is most qualified to practice in the profession would therefore be qualified to educate the profession. Just as the profession fought for status and recognition in the beginning of regulation, social work faculty should recognize the importance of qualification to teach beyond that of the doctorate.

CONCLUSION

Regulation and credentialing are important facets of the establishment of an individual's professional identity. Social work as a profession has followed a long historical path toward establishing and maintaining its existence, status, and professional identity as a professional field. Though much progress has been made, there are many issues left to be resolved regarding professional regulation, including the balance of public protection, professional competence and practice, and addressing the need for consistency and continuity on a larger national scale.

WEB SITES

ACT Test Centers Network. http://www.act.org/actcenters/index.html.

Association of Social Work Boards. http://www.aswb.org.

Council on Social Work Education. http://www.cswe.org.

National Association of Social Work. http://www.socialworkers.org.

Social Work Examination Services. http://www.swes.net.

References

Association of Social Work Boards. (2004). *Analysis of the practice of social work: 2003 final report.* Retrieved November 13, 2007, from ASWB Web site: http://www.aswb.org/Practice_analysis_files/ASWBPracticeAnalysis_Final%20Report.pdf.

Association of Social Work Boards. (2007). *Social work laws & regulations comparison database.* Retrieved November 20, 2007, from http://72.167.43.81/cgi-in/LawWebRpts2DLL.dll/EXEC/1/02ig04o0zcpreb107uwbo1ygn72m.

Biggerstaff, M. A. (1995). Licensing, regulation, and certification. In R. L. Edwards & J. G. Hopps (Eds.), *Encyclopedia of social work* (pp. 1616–1624). Washington, DC: NASW Press.

Marson, S. (2006). Editorial comment: Licensing of social work faculty. *Journal of Social Work Values and Ethics, 3*(2). Retrieved November 20, 2007, from www.socialworker.com/jswve/content/view/42/46.

Social Work Examination Services. (2005). *Comprehensive review notes for state social work license examinations.* Brookline, MA: Social Work Examination Services.

Swankin, D., LeBuhn, R. A., & Morrison, R. (2006). *Implementing continuing competency requirements for health care practitioners.* Washington, DC: American Association of Retired Persons. Retrieved November 20, 2007, from http://www.cacenter.org/Implementing%20Continuing%20Competency%20Requirements%20for%20Health%20Care%20Practitioners%20-%202006.pdf.

Thyer, B. A., & Biggerstaff, M. A. (1989). *Professional social work credentialing and legal regulation.* Springfield, IL: Thompson.

Thyer, B. A., & Seidl, F. (2000). Point/counterpoint: Should licensure be required for faculty who teach direct practice courses? *Journal of Social Work Education, 36*(2), 187–201.

On Being an Accountable Profession

19 *The Code of Ethics, Oversight by Boards of Directors, and Whistle-Blowers as a Last Resort*

Sheldon R. Gelman

The issue of accountability has emerged as a major concern in human services, as in most other areas of modern institutional life. The demand for greater accountability has forced those who work in such agencies, as well as those responsible for funding these programs, to look for more appropriate ways to monitor and evaluate program effectiveness and the quality of the services provided by staff. Without the ability to meet accountability demands, the profession of social work and the agencies that employ social workers are placed at risk ethically, legally, and financially. Under the best of circumstances, accountability is a complex concept that is difficult to achieve (Gibelman & Gelman, 2005).

The term *accountability* is rarely defined with any consistency. What is implied covers a range of behaviors and expectations. Barker (2003) defines accountability as: "The state of being answerable to the community, to consumers of a product or service, or to supervisory groups such as a board of directors; an obligation of a profession to reveal clearly what its functions and methods are and to provide assurances to clients that its practitioners meet specific standards of competence" (p. 3). Barker cross-references accountability with quality assurance, which focuses on a monitoring function performed by an agency, as well as an oversight process designed to improve performance.

Terms such as *efficiency* and *effectiveness* are often used in conjunction with accountability and, in this meaning, imply responsibility in the form of an assurance that resources are allocated and services provided in a professional manner, consistent with legal, regulatory, and ethical standards. Such responsibility demands that one be able to explain and demonstrate the relationship between activities or actions and desired or required outcomes. Actions taken and decisions made must be justifiable in terms of clearly stated goals and objectives. Demonstration of outputs, quality, and outcomes have become the hallmarks of accountability for funders (Chait, Ryan, & Taylor, 2004; Demirag, 2004; Ostrower, 2007). Accountability is also the extent to which an organization and its employees are answerable to their constituencies (i.e., the communities they serve, the consumers of services, governing and/or funding bodies, and government) for both processes and outcomes. Accountability to government has taken on new meaning with the passage of the Sarbanes-Oxley Act of 2002 (Public Law no. 107-204), which requires reporting of financial oversight and auditing practices as well as the level of executive compensation. What has become clear is that accountability is synonymous with transparency.

WORKING WITH VULNERABLE POPULATIONS

Clients enter relationships with social service agencies and helping professionals to resolve problems or dilemmas with which they are faced. The nature of the problem may be internal (physical or emotional), external (environmental), or a combination of both. The end result, in any case, is an inability on the part of the client to function satisfactorily in or adapt to the situation or circumstances. At issue is the primacy of the client, a principle rooted in the profession's ethical code (National Association of Social Workers, 1996). Intrinsic to this commitment is the obligation to pursue social change, particularly with and on behalf of vulnerable and oppressed individuals and groups. Two ethical principles are directly applicable:

- Social workers' primary goal is to help people in need and address social problems.
- Social workers challenge social injustice. (NASW, 1996, p. 5)

Social workers are educated and hired to implement these ethical mandates in their practices; they are perceived as possessing expertise in addressing the psychosocial needs of individuals, groups, and communities with attention to social justice and social change. Social workers deal with problems or situations related to oppression, cultural and ethnic diversity, and the promotion of human well-being and can in some way relieve the pain or discomfort they are experiencing (Gelman, 1980). Unfortunately, problems effecting the psychosocial well-being of people have become more complex, and interventions have increasingly become time limited through the dictates of managed care (Gibelman & Gelman, 2005). Social workers are increasingly expected to do "more with less," a paradox that often places them in the position of violating the same ethical codes to which they have committed themselves and which govern accountable professional conduct.

Despite the simultaneous demands and constraints of the practice environment, social workers have a legal, moral, and ethical mandate to their clients, their employing organization, and those who fund services to deliver those services in a professionally responsible and accountable fashion. Failure to act in such a manner has consequences for individual workers and the organizations they represent. These consequences may include loss of privilege, discretionary authority, status, credibility, and even their position.

PUBLIC EXPOSURE OF IMPROPER AND FRAUDULENT PRACTICE

The perceived inability to reconcile the multiple accountability demands in a context of diminished and constrained resources only heightens the legal and ethical risks to which social workers and their employing agencies are susceptible (Kearns, 1996). For example, revelations in both the professional literature and the press have heightened collective awareness of the difficulty in which nonprofit organizations and their employees may find themselves if expectations are not met and risks are not appropriately managed. Examples range from multiple instances of public agencies' failure to prevent children from being abused or to protect the community from mentally ill individuals or sexual predators who harm themselves or others, to glaring examples of organizational wrongdoing perpetrated by administrative officers of such prominent organizations as the following.

- *The United Way of America.* Perhaps the biggest nonprofit story of the 1990s is that of the United Way of America (UWA), a national organization with a $29 million annual budget, and its longtime president, William Aramony. The United Way, a network of 2,100 local organizations, raises more than $3 billion a year for charity. In 1992, in response to concerns expressed by local UWA affiliates, the United Way board of governors set up an independent investigation of the allegations against Aramony. The resulting report concluded that Aramony's "haphazard" management style resulted in a breach of the trust placed in him by the board of governors and the public. Specifically, he was accused of using charitable donations to finance a lavish lifestyle, including support of an expensive condominium, use of a limousine, and trips on the Concorde. Other allegations included his involvement in satellite corporations spun off from the main UWA operation. His salary of $463,000, including fringe benefits, also fueled the fires of public outrage.
- *American Parkinson's Disease Association.* With charismatic leadership, Frank L. Williams oversaw the expansion of the American Parkinson's Disease Association to 90 chapters nationwide. Over a period of 7 years, Williams had quietly embezzled contribution checks worth more than $1 million. He told federal investigators that he stole because his $109,000 a year salary was half that earned by the chief executive officers of comparable charities. According to the organization's president, "at first it had a

terrible impact . . . some people blamed us for it and some still do."(Richardson, 1996, p. 83).

- *Jewish Community Center of Greater Washington.* In 1994, Lester Kaplan, the executive director of the Jewish Community Center of Greater Washington, and three of his aides were accused of embezzling nearly $1 million from the organization. The four were asked to resign in 1994 after an audit by a new accounting firm uncovered massive monetary fraud and deception in the misappropriation of nearly $750,000 over a 9-year period. Another $150,000 was later found to be missing. A year later, during an ongoing criminal investigation, the money was repaid.

- *Bishop Estate.* The trustees of the Bernice Pauahi Bishop Estate, a charitable fund established in 1884 to provide for the education of Hawaiian children, were accused by Hawaii's attorney general of routinely mingling their personal interests with those of the estate. Among the allegations were that trustees covertly diverted $350 million from the principal purpose of the estate, awarded lucrative contracts to their friends and relatives, used estate employees for their own benefit, accepted excessive compensation for their services, spent estate funds to lobby against passage of state and federal legislation aimed at curbing levels of trustee compensation, mismanaged the estate, received kickbacks from real estate transactions, and failed to invest prudently. Four of the trustees were removed in May 1999. The estate paid the Internal Revenue Service $9 million to retain its tax-exempt charitable status. Efforts are being made to have the ousted trustees repay more than $5 million to the estate for legal fees associated with fending off the charges.

- *Goodwill Industries of Santa Clara.* Goodwill Industries of Santa Clara, California, is one of the 187 autonomous local Goodwill affiliates in the United States and Canada. At least seven individuals who were related to alleged mastermind Linda Fay Marcil systematically stole more that $15 million by selling donated clothing and pocketing the proceeds. The systematic looting of proceeds took place over a period of almost 25 years. Money was skimmed from cash registers, and donated clothing was sold by the barrelful to private dealers. One Goodwill official, Carol Marr, committed suicide. More than $400,000 in cash was found in the home and office of Linda Marcil, and more than $1 million in accounts held by Marr.

- *Tuesday's Children.* This charity, which was created to help families who had lost a parent during the 9/11 terrorist attacks failed when its founder, Chris Burke, was found to have improperly diverted more than $300,000 for his own personal use. He was dismissed by the chair of the organization's board of directors after being informed of financial discrepancies by other employees (Barron, 2006).

- *The United Way of New York City.* Former executive director Ralph Dickerson Jr. diverted $227,000 of charitable assets for his personal use in 2002 and 2003 following his resignation and the departure of his personal assistant (Strom, 2006).

- *Gloria Wise Boys and Girls Club.* Two former executives of the New York City organization avoided prison sentences and instead will be fined for their part in the stealing or misallocating of $1.2 million intended for children and the elderly. They faulted the agencies board of directors, who were aware of and approved the expenditures (Williams & Feldman, 2007).

For a comprehensive review of most of these and other cases, see Gibelman & Gelman (2001, 2004); Gibelman, Gelman, & Pollack (1997); Gelman, Gibelman, Pollack, & Schnall (1996).

In all of these instances, better professional training, appropriate oversight and monitoring, and anticipatory action to minimize risks could have prevented the harm that occurred to the agencies, their employees, their various constituencies, and the communities they serve. In other words, somewhere along the line, accountability was forsaken.

The need to minimize risk is both good practice and an organizational imperative, given the rise in the actual and potential number of complaints against human service agencies and their personnel (Gibelman & Gelman, 1999, 2000, 2001, 2004). The need is clear for practical tools that can guide good practice based on legal, ethical, and sound business principles. Areas in which human service organizations are increasingly vulnerable include negligence, breach of duty through acts of omission or commission, conflicts of interest, breaches of confidentiality, inadequate consent, inappropriate or unorthodox treatment, and practicing beyond one's level of training (Antler, 1987; Besharov, 1985; Gelman, 1983, 1995; Joseph, 1989). The range of complaints against human service agencies and practitioners also includes sexual improprieties, incompetence or incorrect treatment, breach of contract, failure to warn, abandonment of clients (certainly an increasingly important issue in a managed care environment), defamation/libel/slander, and exerting undue influence (Gelman, 1988; Roswell, 1988). The potential for unaccountable practice in these areas is made clear by the attention given to each in the NASW Code of Ethics (1996). The imperative to the profession, human service organizations, oversight agencies, and individual practitioners is to take all possible measures to improve and ensure accountability.

SERVICE ACCOUNTABILITY

Use of the following actions and activities by social workers and the organizations they represent can contribute to our becoming a more accountable profession:

- Actively involving clients in service contracting.
- Employing risk management strategies.
- Making evaluation an integral part of practice.
- Enforcing the code of ethics through more aggressive adjudication.
- Engaging in ethics audits.
- Improving the quality of supervision.
- Complying with accreditation standards.
- Providing the training and internal oversight mechanisms necessary to increase the effectiveness of boards of directors.
- Encouraging and sanctioning whistle-blowing as a last resort.

Actively Involving Clients in Service Contracting

The active involvement of clients in their own treatment or service provision is good practice. To ensure that professional knowledge and skill can be effectively utilized, professionals must reassess the basis of their relationship with clients. As a starting point, professionals must recognize the potential power to dominate and coerce those who come to them for help or assistance. They must recognize the destructiveness of uncontrolled discretionary authority, not only because it interferes with the professional–client relationship but also because such behavior will no longer be tolerated by clients.

Clients must be seen as persons, as individuals who are participants in decisions affecting their lives. They must be viewed as and allowed to become choice makers rather than choiceless. The client's autonomy and self-determination must be honored if professionals themselves are to remain autonomous. Today, a number of nonprofit agencies have opened board membership to include former consumers of service or members of their families.

Professionals and clients have contributions to make to the interchange. There must be a mutuality of decision making and role reciprocity. To achieve this mutuality, the rules of the interactional process must be clear, open, and in written contract form. Such involvement allows for reciprocal accountability.

Employing Risk Management Strategies

Risk management is a practice used by many agencies as a response to growing concerns about liability and the difficulty in securing comprehensive and affordable insurance coverage. Risk management involves the ongoing study and assessment of activities and practices that potentially may lead to legal vulnerability (Gibelman & Gelman, 1999).

Risk management is proactive and requires that the organization manages its business in accord with both sound financial practices and applicable laws, regulations, and professional requirements. The business of the organization is conducted in such a way as to reduce risk through evaluation of potential risks that it may assume and implementation of strategic plans to ensure legal, ethical, and professional accountability. Managing risk is a prevention-oriented and ongoing activity to improve the quality of services and prevent negative outcomes (Gelman, in press).

Making Evaluation an Integral Part of Practice

Historically, social service agencies have had a difficult time demonstrating the effectiveness of their interventions. Whereas unsubstantiated claims may have been accepted or unacceptable in the past, today we must demonstrate that specific efforts or activities result in problem resolution or remediation within mandated time frames. We have the knowledge and skill to clearly identify the outcomes of our interventions. We must use and generate data that document what works and what doesn't, in language that is based on our specialized knowledge. Tracking, monitoring, and evaluating case progress and outcomes are an integral component of good practice (Gibelman & Whiting, 1999; Gibelman & Gelman, 2005). Without such proof, we remain unaccountable.

Enforcing the Code of Ethics

The NASW Code of Ethics (1996) details the ethical responsibilities of professional social workers to their clients, employers, colleagues, and the community. Professional ethics are at the core of social work practice. The NASW Code of Ethics serves six purposes.

1. The code identifies core values on which social work's mission is based.
2. The code summarizes broad ethical principles that reflect the profession's core values and establishes a set of specific ethical standards that should be used to guide social work practice.
3. The code is designed to help social workers identify relevant considerations when professional obligations conflict or ethical uncertainties arise.
4. The code provides ethical standards to which the general public can hold the social work profession accountable.
5. The code socializes practitioners new to the field to social work's mission, values, ethical principles, and ethical standards.
6. The code articulates standards that the social work profession itself can use to assess whether social workers have engaged in unethical conduct. NASW has formal procedures to adjudicate ethics complaints against its members. In subscribing to this code, social workers are required to cooperate in its implementation, participate in NASW adjudication proceedings, and abide by any NASW disciplinary rulings or sanctions based on it.

Adherence to the code is essential to accountable practice and minimizes risk to agencies and their employees (for a more detailed discussion, see Chapter 14, 15, and 20).

Engaging in Ethics Audits

Reamer (1998, 1999, 2000) has moved beyond his commentary on the code of ethics to advance the notion of extending the concept of auditing to the subject of professional social work ethics. He proposes that two key knowledge areas form the foundation of an ethics audit:

1. Social workers' familiarity with known ethics-related risks based on empirical data of actual ethics complaints and lawsuits.
2. Current agency procedures for handling ethical issues.

Ethics-related practices can be assessed and assigned to one of four risk categories ranging from no risk to high risk. The level of risk guides the corrective actions that are required. The goal of the exercise is increased accountability. See Chapter 14 for further information.

Improving the Quality of Supervision

Supervision is a tool designed to assist social workers in further developing and refining their skills and professional judgments. Supervision must be provided on a regular and consistent basis by knowledgeable and skilled supervisors who have sufficient time for oversight and a desire to foster the development of their colleagues. The goal is to adhere to established standards of care and to evidence best practices that meet the specific and unique needs of those being served.

Integral to the supervisory process is accurate documentation that details client needs, worker actions, and the basis for the choices and options offered. Records are a critical element in the process of risk management. Today, records must go beyond the documentation of accumulated knowledge and speculation—they are an evolving account of how agencies and workers do their business. Records provide evidence of duties, obligations, and acts of omission or commission (Gelman, 1992). Quality records facilitate the management of risk, reduce potential liability, and contribute to accountable practice.

Complying with Accreditation Standards

Various organizations have developed standards that provide guidance to social service organizations in developing, maintaining, and evaluating their operations and services. Identification with and adherence to standards, whether they involve governance, operations, service requirements, or personnel policies, are essential to the accountability of the profession. Two examples of accrediting bodies that have promulgated standards relevant to social service agencies are the Council of Accreditation Services for Families and Children and the Joint Commission on Accreditation of Health Care Organizations.

Increasing the Effectiveness of Boards of Directors

Philanthropic organizations that are incorporated are required by law to create a board of directors. Agency charters and bylaws in turn specify the responsibilities and obligations of boards and their members. Directors are assigned responsibility for the general direction and control of these organizations. The board is the policy-making body with a legal duty to ensure that the agency's actions are consistent with its goals and objectives. Board members accept this charge without remuneration and act in accord with their civic responsibility (Gelman, in press).

Board members share collective responsibility for the fiscal and programmatic aspects of the organization's performance and the hiring and regular evaluation of the executive director. The board is responsible to funding sources, to the community, to governmental and private regulatory bodies, and to consumers of the agency's services. The board manages the nonprofit corporation, delegating responsibilities appropriately but remaining ultimately accountable for the agency's image and its performance. The board is legally responsible and morally accountable to the agency's various constituencies for its actions or inactions. Thus, "a board which fails in its function of both determining policy and evaluating achievement in support of those policies is negligent in performing its mandated functions" (Gelman, 1983, p. 88).

To ensure the well-being of the organization, the board must act prudently and lead the organization by developing and implementing a viable method for reviewing its performance and evaluating achievements and movement toward goal attainment (Leifer & Glomb, 1992). This involves periodically subjecting itself to external and internal risk analysis. Appropriate board oversight is critical to agency accountability.

Whistle-Blowing as a Last Resort

When all else fails and staff have knowledge of inappropriate or unethical behavior that places clients, co-workers, or the agency at risk, whistle-blowing becomes a tool—a tool that has inherent risks and potentially serious consequences.

The media, often alerted by someone with intimate knowledge of or experience with an organization, play the role of whistle-blower or watchdog. Media accounts not only call attention to faulty or inadequate services or wrongdoing but clearly affect public attitudes toward social services and influence whether an organization will survive (Parenti, 1999). Whistle-blowing is the ultimate step in seeking accountability.

The number of constituencies to whom human service agencies and their employees are accountable has grown exponentially in recent years. Under the best of circumstances, accountability is a complex phenomenon and difficult to achieve. Yet if social work is to remain viable and credible as a profession, it must use every means at its disposal to demonstrate that it is accountable for the process and product of its interventions.

WEB SITES

BoardSource, building effective nonprofit boards. http://www.boardsource.org.
GuideStar. http://www.guidestar.org.
Independent Sector. http://www.independentsector.org/issues/accountability.
OMB Watch. http://www.ombwatch.org.

References

Antler, S. (1987). Professional liability and malpractice. In A. Minahan (Ed.-in-chief), *Encyclopedia of social work*, 18th ed. (pp. 346–351). Silver Spring, MD: NASW Press.
Barker, R. L. (2003). *Social work dictionary*, 4th ed. Washington, DC: NASW Press.
Barron, J. (2006, April 3). 9/11 charity brings failings of man to light. *New York Times*, pp. B1–B2.
Besharov, D. J. (1985). *The vulnerable social worker*. Silver Spring, MD: NASW Press.
Chait, R. P., Ryan, W. P., & Taylor, B. (2004). *Governance as leadership: Reframing the work of nonprofit boards*. San Francisco: Jossey-Bass.
Demirag, I. (2004). Toward better governance and accountability. *Journal of Corporate Citizenship*, 15(Autumn), 19–26.
Gelman, S. R. (1980). Esoterica: A zero sum game in the helping professions. *Social Casework*, 61(1), 48–53.

Gelman, S. R. (1983). The board of directors and agency accountability. *Social Casework, 64*(2), 48–53.

Gelman, S. R. (1988). Roles, responsibilities, and liabilities of agency boards. In M. P. Janicki, M. W. Krauss, & M. Seltzer (Eds.), *Community residences for persons with developmental disabilities: Here to stay* (pp. 57–68). Baltimore, MD: Paul H. Brooks.

Gelman, S. R. (1992). Risk management through client access to case records. *Social Work, 37*(1), 73–79.

Gelman, S. R. (1995). Boards of directors. In R. Edwards (Ed.-in-chief), *Encyclopedia of social work,* 19th ed. (pp. 305–312). Washington, DC: NASW Press.

Gelman, S.R. (In press). Non profit boards: Developing and managing a vital resource. In R. J. Patti (Ed.), *The handbook of social welfare management,* 2nd ed. Thousand Oaks, CA: Sage.

Gelman, S. R., Gibelman, M., Pollack, D., & Schnall, D. J. (1996). Boards of directors on the line: Roles, realities and prospects. *Journal of Jewish Communal Service, 72*(3), 185–194.

Gibelman, M., & Gelman, S. R. (1999). Safeguarding the nonprofit agency: The role of the board of directors in risk management. *Journal of Residential Treatment for Children and Youth, 16*(4), 19–37.

Gibelman, M., & Gelman, S. R. (2001). Very public scandals: Nongovernmental organizations in trouble. *Voluntas: International Journal of Voluntary and Nonprofit Organizations, 12*(1), 49–66.

Gilbelman, M., & Gelman, S. R. (2004). A loss of credibility: Patterns of wrong doing among nongovernmental organization. *Voluntas: International Journal of Voluntary and Nonprofit Organizations, 15*(4), 355–381.

Gibelman, M., & Gelman, S. R. (2005). Ethical consideration in the changing environment of human service organizations. In M. L. Pava & P. Primeaux (Eds.), *Crisis and opportunity in the professions: Research in ethical issues in organizations* (pp. 1–19). Oxford: Elsevier.

Gibelman, M., Gelman, S. R., & Pollack, D. (1997). The credibility of nonprofit boards: A view from the 1990s and beyond. *Administration in Social Work, 21*(2), 21–40.

Gibelman, M., & Whiting, L. (1999). Negotiating and contracting in a managed care environment: Considerations for practitioners. *Health and Social Work, 24*(3), 180–190.

Joseph, M. V. (1989, October 14). At risk: Legal vulnerability and what to do about it. Presentation at the 1989 NASW Annual Conference, San Francisco, CA.

Kearns, K. P. (1996). *Managing for accountability.* San Francisco: Jossey-Bass.

Leifer, J. C., & Glomb, M. B. (1992). *The legal obligations of nonprofit boards: A guidebook for board members.* Washington, DC: National Center for Nonprofit Boards.

National Association of Social Workers. (1996). *Code of ethics.* Washington, DC: NASW Press.

Ostrower, F. (2007). *Nonprofit governance in the United States: Findings on performance and accountability fro the first national representative study.* Washington, DC: Urban Institute.

Parenti, M. (1999). Methods of media manipulation. In R. E. Hierbert (Ed.), *Impact of mass media: Current issues,* 4th ed. (pp. 120–124). New York: Addison Wesley Longman.

Reamer, F. G. (1998). *Ethical standards in social work: A critical review of the NASW Code of Ethics.* Washington, DC: NASW Press.

Reamer, F. G. (1999). *Social work values and ethics,* 2nd ed. New York: Columbia University Press.

Reamer, F. G. (2000). The social work ethics audit: A risk-management strategy. *Social Work, 45*(4), 355–366.

Richardson, L. (1996, July 31). Former charity head ordered to prison. *New York Times,* p. 83.

Roswell, V. A. (1988). Professional liability: Issues for behavior therapists in the 1980s and 1990s. *Behavior Therapist, 11*(8), 163–171.

Strom, S. (2006, April 14). United Way says ex-leader took assets. *New York Times,* p. B5.

Williams, T., & Feldman, C. (2007, March 14). Ex-leaders of Bronx charity avoid prison in fraud case. *New York Times,* p. B4.

20 The Impaired Social Work Professional

Frederic G. Reamer

In recent years, various professions have paid increased attention to the problem of impaired practitioners. Social work's first national acknowledgment of the problem of impaired practitioners was in 1979, when the National Association of Social Workers (NASW) released a public policy statement on alcoholism and alcohol-related problems (NASW, Commission on Employment and Economic Support, 1987). By 1980, a small nationwide support group for chemically dependent practitioners, Social Workers Helping Social Workers, had formed (NASW, 1987). In 1982, NASW established the Occupational Social Work Task Force, which was charged with developing a "consistent professional approach for distressed NASW members" (NASW, 1987, p. 7). In 1984, the NASW delegate assembly issued a resolution on impairment, and in 1987, NASW published the *Impaired Social Worker Program Resource Book*, prepared by the National Commission on Employment and Economic Support, to help practitioners design a program for impaired social workers. In 1996, NASW (1999) completely rewrote its Code of Ethics and included several explicit standards concerning social workers' responsibility to address their own and colleagues' impairment.

Social workers who have direct knowledge of a social work colleague's impairment that is due to personal problems, psychosocial distress, substance abuse, or mental health difficulties and that interferes with practice effectiveness should consult with that colleague when feasible and assist the colleague in taking remedial action. (Standard 2.09[a])
Social workers who believe that a social work colleague's impairment interferes with practice effectiveness and that the colleague has not taken adequate steps to address the impairment should take action through appropriate channels established by employers, agencies, NASW, licensing and regulatory bodies, and other professional organizations. (Standard 2.09[b])

Social workers should not allow their own personal problems, psychosocial distress, legal problems, substance abuse, or mental health difficulties to interfere with their professional judgment and performance or to jeopardize the best interests of people for whom they have a professional responsibility. (Standard 4.05[a])
Social workers whose personal problems, psychosocial distress, legal problems, substance abuse, or mental health difficulties interfere with their professional judgment and performance should immediately seek consultation and take appropriate remedial action by seeking professional help, making adjustments in workload, terminating practice, or taking any other steps necessary to protect clients and others. (Standard 4.05[b])

Organized efforts to address impaired workers have their historical roots in the late 1930s and early 1940s following the emergence of Alcoholics Anonymous and the need during World War II to retain a sound work force (Reamer, 1992). These early occupational alcoholism programs eventually led, in the early 1970s, to the emergence of employee assistance programs (EAPs), designed to address a broad range of problems experienced by workers. In 1972, the Council on Mental Health of the American Medical Association released a statement that physicians have an ethical responsibility to recognize and report impairment among colleagues. In 1976, a group of attorneys recovering from alcoholism started Lawyers Concerned for Lawyers to address chemical dependence in the profession, and in 1980, a group of recovering psychologists inaugurated a similar group, Psychologists Helping Psychologists (Kilburg, Nathan, & Thoreson, 1986; Knutsen, 1977; Laliotis & Grayson, 1985; McCrady, 1989). In 1981, the American Psychological Association held its first open forum on impairment at its annual meeting (Stadler, Willing, Eberhage, & Ward, 1988).

More recently, strategies for dealing with professionals whose work is affected by problems such as substance abuse, mental illness, and emotional stress have become more prevalent and visible. Professional associations and groups of practitioners have convened to examine impairment among colleagues and organize efforts to address the problem (Bissell & Haberman, 1984; Prochaska & Norcross, 1983; Siebert, 2004, 2005). Ironically, however, in contrast to a number of other helping professions, the social work literature contains little discussion of impaired professionals (Bissell, Fewell, & Jones, 1980; Fausel, 1988; Reamer, 2003, 2006; Siebert, 2004, 2005).

EXTENT OF IMPAIRMENT

Both the seriousness of social workers' impairment and the forms it takes vary (Reamer, 1992; Siebert, 2004, 2005). Impairment may involve failure to provide competent care or violation of the profession's ethical standards. It may take such forms as providing flawed or inferior services to a client, sexual involvement with a client, or failure to carry out one's duties as a result of substance abuse or mental illness. Lamb et al. (1987) provided a comprehensive definition of impairment among professionals:

Interference in professional functioning that is reflected in one or more of the following ways: (a) an inability and/or unwillingness to acquire and integrate professional standards into one's repertoire of professional behavior; (b) an inability to acquire professional skills in order to reach an acceptable level of competency; and (c) an inability to control personal stress, psychological dysfunction, and/or excessive emotional reactions that interfere with professional functioning. (p. 598)

Given the distressing absence of empirical data on social workers, it is not possible to estimate the prevalence of impairment within the profession. Therefore, social workers must look primarily to what is known about impairment in professions that are allied with social work, such as psychology and psychiatry. Of course, one cannot infer prevalence rates for social workers on the basis of data from these other professions. However, despite some important differences in their mission, methods, and organizational context, practitioners in these professions offer a number of similar services and face similar forms of occupational stress and strain.

Prevalence studies conducted among psychologists suggest a significant degree of distress within that profession. For example, in a study of 749 psychologists, Guy, Poelstra, and Stark (1989) found that 74.3 percent reported "personal distress" during the previous 3 years, and 36.7 percent of this group believed that their distress decreased the quality of care they provided to clients. Pope, Tabachnick, and Keith-Spiegel (1987) reported that 62.2 percent of the members of division 29 (psychotherapy) of the American Psychological Association admitted to "working when too distressed to be effective" (p. 993). In their survey of 167 licensed psychologists, Wood, Klein, Cross, Lammers, and Elliott (1985) found that nearly one-third (32.3 percent) reported experiencing depression or burnout to an extent that interfered with their work. They also found that a significant portion of their sample reported being aware of colleagues whose work was seriously affected by drug or alcohol use, sexual overtures toward clients, or depression and burnout.

In a prevalence study that included social workers, Deutsch (1985) found that more than half her sample of social workers, psychologists, and master's-level counselors reported significant problems with depression. Nearly four-fifths (82 percent) reported problems with relationships, approximately one-tenth (11 percent) reported substance abuse problems, and 2 percent reported past suicide attempts. In a comprehensive review of a series of empirical studies focused specifically on sexual contact between therapists and clients, Pope (1988) concluded that the aggregate average of reported sexual contact is 8.3 percent by male therapists and 1.7 percent by female therapists. Pope reported that one study (Gechtman & Bouhoutsos, 1985) found that 3.8 percent of male social workers admitted to sexual contact with clients.

CAUSES OF IMPAIRMENT

Several studies reported a variety of forms and sources of impairment among mental health professionals. Guy et al. (1989) and Thoreson, Miller, and Krauskopf (1989) found diverse sources of reported stress in clinicians' lives, including their jobs, the illness or death of relatives, marital or relationship problems, financial problems, midlife crises, personal physical or mental illness, legal problems, and substance abuse. Katsavdakis, Gabbard, and Athey (2004) found that the three most commonly cited problems leading psychiatrists, other physicians, psychologists, and social workers to seek help were suicidal behavior, marital problems, and work-related problems.

Lamb et al. (1987) argued that professional education itself can produce unique forms of stress and impairment, primarily as a result of the close clinical supervision to which students are typically subjected, the disruption in their personal lives often caused by the demands of schoolwork and internships, and the pressures placed on them by academic programs. These authors found that the most common sources of impairment are personality disorders, depression and other emotional problems, marital problems, and physical illness.

This review of research suggests that distress among clinicians generally falls into two categories: environmental stress, which is a function of employment conditions (actual working conditions and the broader culture's lack of support of the human services mission) or professional training, and personal stress, caused by problems with one's marriage, relationships, emotional and physical health, and finances. With respect to psychotherapists in particular, Wood et al. (1985) noted that professionals encounter special problems from the extension of their therapeutic role into the nonwork aspects of their lives (such as relationships with friends and family members), the absence of reciprocity in relationships with clients (therapists are "always giving"), the frequently slow and erratic nature of the therapeutic process, and personal issues that are raised as a result of their work with clients (Kilburg, Kaslow, & VandenBos, 1988; Mahoney, 1997).

RESPONSE TO IMPAIRMENT

Little is known about the extent to which impaired professionals voluntarily seek help for their problems (Olsheski & Leech, 1996). In one of the few empirical studies, Guy et al. (1989) found that 70 percent of the distressed clinical psychologists they surveyed sought some form of therapeutic assistance. Nearly one-fourth (26.6 percent) entered individual psychotherapy, and 10.7 percent entered family therapy. A small portion of this group participated in self-help groups (3.4 percent) or was hospitalized (2.2 percent). Some were placed on medication (4.1 percent). Exactly 10 percent of this group temporarily suspended their professional practice.

These findings contrast with those of Wood et al. (1985), who found that only 55.2 percent of clinicians who reported problems that interfered with their work (substance abuse, sexual overtures toward clients, depression, and burnout) sought help. Approximately two-fifths (42 percent) of all the clinicians surveyed by Wood and colleagues, including impaired and nonimpaired professionals, reported having offered help to impaired colleagues at some time or having referred them to therapists. Only 7.9 percent of the sample indicated that they had reported an impaired colleague to a local regulatory body. Two-fifths (40.2 percent) were aware of instances in which they believed no action was taken to help an impaired colleague.

Several phenomena may explain impaired professionals' reluctance to seek help and the reluctance of their colleagues to confront them about their problems. Until recently, professionals were hesitant to acknowledge impairment within their ranks because they feared how practitioners would react to confrontation and how such confrontation might affect the future relationships of colleagues who must work together (Bernard & Jara, 1986; Coombs, 1997; McCrady, 1989; Wood et al., 1985). Thoreson, Nathan, Skorina, and Kilburg (1983) also argued that impaired professionals sometimes find it difficult to seek help because of their mythological belief in their nearly infinite power and invulnerability. The fact that an increasing number of psychotherapists are involved in private practice exacerbates the problem because of the reduced opportunity for colleagues to observe any unethical or inept practice.

In a valuable study by Deutsch (1985), a diverse group of therapists (including social workers) who admitted to personal problems indicated a variety of reasons for not seeking professional help included the following reasons: they believed that an acceptable therapist was not available, they sought help from family members or friends, they feared exposure and the disclosure of confidential information, they were concerned about the amount of effort required and the cost, they had a spouse who was unwilling to participate in treatment, they failed to admit the seriousness of the problem, they believed they should be able to work their problems out themselves, and they believed that therapy would not help.

In recent years, several organized efforts have been made to identify and address the problems of impaired professionals. There is a growing consensus that a model strategy should include several components (Schoener & Gonsiorek, 1988; Sonnenstuhl, 1989). First, there must be adequate means for identifying impaired practitioners. Professionals must be willing to assume some responsibility for acknowledging impairment among colleagues. Second, a social worker's initial identification and documentation of a colleague's impairment should be followed by speculation about the possible causes and by what Sonnenstuhl (1989) described as "constructive confrontation." Third, once a social worker decides who shall carry out the confrontation, a decision must be made about whether to help the impaired colleague identify ways to seek help voluntarily or to refer the colleague to a supervisor or local regulatory body (such as a NASW ethics committee or a licensing board). Assuming there are sufficient reasons to support a rehabilitation plan, the impaired practitioner's colleague, supervisor, or local regulatory body should make specific recommendations. The possibilities include close supervision, personal psychotherapy, and treatment for substance abuse. In some cases, it may be necessary for a licensing board or ethics committee to impose some type of sanction, such as censure, limitations on the professional's social work practice (for example, concerning clientele that can be served), termination of employment, suspension or expulsion from a professional association, or loss of license.

Unfortunately, relatively little research has been conducted on the effectiveness of efforts to rehabilitate impaired professionals (Fletcher & Ronis, 2005; Sonnenstuhl, 1989; Trice & Beyer, 1984). Moreover, the few published empirical evaluations—which reported mixed results for various treatment programs—focused primarily on impaired physicians (Herrington, Benzer, Jacobson, & Hawkins, 1982; Katsavdakis et al., 2004; Morse, Martin, Swenson, & Niven, 1984; Pearson, 1982; Shore, 1982).

AN AGENDA FOR SOCIAL WORK

For a profession to be truly self-regulating, it cannot rely entirely on the efforts of dissatisfied or abused clients to file complaints about impaired practitioners. The profession must strengthen its efforts to identify impaired practitioners and respond to them in a meaningful way. Social workers, like many other professionals, understandably may be reluctant to confront impaired colleagues. Nonetheless, it is incumbent on the profession

to confront incompetence and unethical behavior and offer humane assistance. Attention should be paid to social workers in solo private practice as well as those who work in group settings, where there may be more opportunity to observe impairment.

Social workers must expand education about the problem of impaired social workers. Relatively few social workers have been trained to identify and confront impairment. The profession's organizations and agencies must sponsor workshops and in-service training on the subject to acquaint social workers with information about the forms that impairment can take, the signs to look for, and ways to confront the problem.

In addition, social workers should develop collegial-assistance programs to assist impaired social workers. Although some cases of impairment must be dealt with through formal adjudication mechanisms (for example, conducted by NASW ethics committees or licensing boards), many cases can be handled primarily by arranging therapeutic or rehabilitative services for distressed practitioners. Impaired social workers should have access to competent service providers who are trained to understand professionals' special concerns and needs. For instance, state chapters of NASW can enter into agreements with local EAPs, to which impaired members can be referred.

Social workers have a keen understanding of human struggle and impairment. The profession has a tradition of addressing the problems of individuals, along with the environmental stresses that surround them. The same tradition must be extended to impaired colleagues.

WEB SITES

Article, "Helping social workers with alcohol and other drug problems. Options for intervening with colleagues." http://www.naswnyc.org/c17.html

Journal of Social Work Values and Ethics. http://www.socialworker.com/jswve/.

Social Work Licensing Laws and Regulations, including ethics guidelines. http://www.datapathdesign.com/ASWB/Laws/Prod/cgi-bin/LawWebRpts2DLL.dll/EXEC/0/19xhre00r17jkw14v2gi81isf2lz.

References

Bernard, J., & Jara, C. (1986). The failure of clinical psychology students to apply understood ethical principles. *Professional Psychology: Research and Practice, 17,* 316–321.

Bissell, L., Fewell, L., & Jones, R. (1980). The alcoholic social worker: A survey. *Social Work in Health Care, 5,* 421–432.

Bissell, L., & Haberman, P. W. (1984). *Alcoholism in the professions.* New York: Oxford University Press.

Coombs, R. H. (1997). *Drug-impaired professionals.* Cambridge, MA: Harvard University Press.

Deutsch, C. (1985). A survey of therapists' personal problems and treatment. *Professional Psychology: Research and Practice, 16,* 305–315.

Fausel, D. F. (1988). Helping the helper heal: Codependency in helping professionals. *Journal of Independent Social Work, 3*(2), 35–45.

Fletcher, C. E., & Ronis, D. L. (2005). Satisfaction of impaired health care professionals with mandatory treatment and monitoring. *Journal of Addictive Diseases, 24*(3), 61–75.

Gechtman, L., & Bouhoutsos, J. (1985). Sexual intimacy between social workers and clients. Paper presented at the annual meeting of the Society for Clinical Social Workers, University City, California.

Guy, J. D., Poelstra, P. L., & Stark, M. (1989). Personal distress and therapeutic effectiveness: National survey of psychologists practicing psychotherapy. *Professional Psychology: Research and Practice, 20,* 48–50.

Herrington, R. E., Benzer, D. G., Jacobson, G. R., & Hawkins, M. K. (1982). Treating substance-use disorders among physicians. *Journal of the American Medical Association, 247,* 2253–2257.

Katsavdakis, K.A., Gabbard, G.O., & Athey, G. I. (2004). Profiles of impaired health professionals. *Bulletin of the Menninger Clinic, 68*(1), 60–72.

Kilburg, R. R., Kaslow, F. W., & VandenBos, G. R. (1988). Professionals in distress. *Hospital and Community Psychiatry, 39,* 723–725.

Kilburg, R. R., Nathan, P. E., & Thoreson, R. W. (Eds.). (1986). *Professionals in distress: Issues, syndromes, and solutions in psychology.* Washington, DC: American Psychological Association.

Knutsen, E. (1977). On the emotional well-being of psychiatrists: Overview and rationale. *American Journal of Psychoanalysis, 37,* 123–129.

Laliotis, D. A., & Grayson, J. H. (1985). Psychologist heal thyself: What is available for the impaired psychologist? *American Psychologist, 40,* 84–96.

Lamb, D. H., Presser, N. R., Pfost, K. S., Baum, M. C., Jackson, V. R., & Jarvis, P. A. (1987). Confronting professional impairment during the internship: Identification, due process, and remediation. *Professional Psychology: Research and Practice, 18,* 597–603.

Mahoney, M. J. (1997). Psychotherapists' personal problems and self-care patterns. *Professional Psychology: Research and Practice, 28*(1), 14–16.

McCrady, B. S. (1989). The distressed or impaired professional: From retribution to rehabilitation. *Journal of Drug Issues, 19,* 337–349.

Morse, R. M., Martin, M. A., Swenson, W. M., & Niven, R. G. (1984). Prognosis for physicians treated for alcoholism and drug dependence. *Journal of the American Medical Association, 251,* 743–746.

National Association of Social Workers, Commission on Employment and Economic Support. (1987). *Impaired social worker program resource book.* Silver Spring, MD: NASW Press.

National Association of Social Workers. (1999). *NASW code of ethics,* rev. ed. Washington, DC: NASW Press.

Olsheski, J., & Leech, L.L. (1996). Programmatic interventions and treatment of impaired professionals. *Journal of Humanistic Education and Development, 34*(3), 128–140.

Pearson, M. M. (1982). Psychiatric treatment of 250 physicians. *Psychiatric Annals, 12,* 194–206.

Pope, K. S. (1988). How clients are harmed by sexual contact with mental health professionals: The syndrome and its prevalence. *Journal of Counseling and Development, 67,* 222–226.

Pope, K. S., Tabachnick, B. G., & Keith-Spiegel, P. (1987). Ethics of practice: The beliefs and behaviors of psychologists as therapists. *American Psychologist, 42,* 993–1006.

Prochaska, J., & Norcross, J. (1983). Psychotherapists' perspectives on treating themselves and their clients for psychic distress. *Professional Psychology: Research and Practice, 14,* 642–655.

Reamer, F. G. (1992). The impaired social worker. *Social Work, 37*(2), 165–170.

Reamer, F. G. (2003). *Social work malpractice and liability: Strategies for prevention,* 2nd ed. New York: Columbia University Press.

Reamer, F. G. (2006). *Ethical standards in social work: A review of the NASW Code of Ethics,* 2nd ed. Washington, DC: NASW Press.

Schoener, G. R., & Gonsiorek, J. (1988). Assessment and development of rehabilitation plans for counselors who have sexually exploited their clients. *Journal of Counseling and Development, 67,* 227–232.

Shore, J. H. (1982). The impaired physician: Four years after probation. *Journal of the American Medical Association, 248,* 3127–3130.

Siebert, D. C. (2004). Depression in North Carolina social workers: Implications for practice and research. *Social Work Research, 28,* 30–40.

Siebert, D. C. (2005). Help seeking and AOD use among social workers: Patterns, barriers, and implications. *Social Work, 50,* 65–75.

Sonnenstuhl, W. J. (1989). Reaching the impaired professional: Applying findings from organizational and occupational research. *Journal of Drug Issues, 19,* 533–539.

Stadler, H. A., Willing, K., Eberhage, M. G., & Ward, W. H. (1988). Impairment: Implications for the counseling profession. *Journal of Counseling and Development, 66*, 258–260.

Thoreson, R. W., Miller, M., & Krauskopf, C. J. (1989). The distressed psychologist: Prevalence and treatment considerations. *Professional Psychology: Research and Practice, 20*, 153–158.

Thoreson, R. W., Nathan, P. E., Skorina, J. K., & Kilburg, R. R. (1983). The alcoholic psychologist: Issues, problems, and implications for the profession. *Professional Psychology: Research and Practice, 14*, 670–684.

Trice, H. M., & Beyer, J. M. (1984). Work related outcomes of the constructive confrontation strategy in a job-based alcoholism program. *Journal of Studies on Alcohol, 45*, 393–404.

Wood, B. J., Klein, S., Cross, H. J., Lammers, C. J., & Elliott, J. K. (1985). Impaired practitioners: Psychologists' opinions about prevalence, and proposals for intervention. *Professional Psychology: Research and Practice, 16*, 843–850.

How Social Workers Can Do More Good Than Harm

21 *Critical Thinking, Evidence-Based Clinical Reasoning, and Avoiding Fallacies*

Leonard Gibbs

AVOIDING HARM

The history of the helping professions provides many vivid examples of dedicated "helpers" (including social workers) who were harming or killing those whom they sought to help (Gibbs, 1991, pp. 1–22). Beyond any doubt, the vast majority of those professionals cared deeply about the children, aged persons, and clients whose troubled lives they sought to aid, but such caring, though vital and necessary, does not provide sufficient basis to ensure success. This chapter outlines three approaches to avoid harming. Each of these approaches challenges established patterns of thinking in social work curricula and practice. Each is essential to avoid harming those who have entrusted their lives to our care. First, one must learn to pose well-built specific questions. How could we possibly avoid harming if we do not question the efficacy of our methods, the accuracy of assessment procedures, and the accuracy of risk assessments? Without posing vital questions in real time as the need arises, we run the risk of consigning our clients to repeated failure and harm. The importance of posing questions and having the dedication to do so seems obvious; Eileen Gambrill and I (Gibbs & Gambrill, 2002) have collected and responded to numerous arguments from academics against evidence-based practice. Second, to avoid harm, we need to think critically and methodologically in elemental and practical ways to avoid common fallacies in reasoning in practice. Such fallacies can blind sound practice judgment and decision making. Finally, we need to measure ability to reason critically about real practice situations to test whether social workers can avoid common errors in clinical reasoning.

EVIDENCE-BASED CLINICAL REASONING

Shelly Stamm will never forget one particular day of her baccalaureate social work fieldwork training. Her fieldwork instructor in child protective services had asked her to go to a local hospital with another social worker to take a shaken baby from his biological parents to a waiting foster home. A scan had identified severe brain damage from multiple strokes; the infant boy was paralyzed on one side of his body. The child would never live a normal life. Shelly had tears in her eyes, as anyone would when she took the baby into her arms. She helped deliver the child to its foster parents and discussed agency services and supports with the foster parents as any professional social worker would; then she did something extremely uncommon for a social work practitioner— she formulated a specific practice question! She asked, "What is the most valid, reliable assessment tool for diagnosing shaken baby syndrome?" (Stamm, 2000). A more specific statement for her question appears in Table 21.1 later.

An electronic search (done on September 1, 2000) of current social work literature in the Social Work Abstracts Database (SWAB) demonstrates why posing a specific, answerable practice question illustrates such unusual thinking. The search revealed no documents for these terms: well-formulated question, well-built question, answerable question, clearly worded question, posing a specific question, and specific question. On September 1, 2000, there were 47 documents in SWAB for the phrase "research question," but none discussed specifically how to pose a well-built clinical question. An updated search in Social Services Abstracts for "research question" done on December 11, 2007, located 82 references, and none of these concerned how to construct a well-built question as a guide to evidence-based practice. A search of Social Services Abstracts for "answerable question," "well-formulated question," "well-built question," "clearly worded question," and "posing a specific question" yielded no results, but three references emerged for "specific question" (none from social work). Apparently, over 7 years' time, almost nothing has been added to the literature in social work regarding how to pose well-built questions. A search that did not follow exactly the same terms discovered one article by Gossett and Weinman (2007) regarding posing a well-built question,

The fact that so little has been written about posing well-built questions in our literature over a 7-year period may reflect the difficulty of learning how to pose such questions. In my file of over 300 effectiveness questions posed by practitioners over the past 19 years for my research methods students, very few are posed specifically enough to meet all criteria for answerability (Gibbs, 1991, p. 114). If we can learn how to pose specific questions from practice, we can find a specific answer. Conversely, if we do not learn how to pose specific questions from practice, we will never find specific answers. As Yogi Berra once said, "You've got to be careful if you don't know where you're going 'cause you might not get there" (Berra, 1998, p. 102).

Well-formulated or well-built questions are clearly enough stated to guide an effective search for their answers in electronic bibliographic databases (Armstrong, 1999; Gibbs, 1991, pp. 165–186; Sackett, Richardson, Rosenberg, & Haynes, 1997, pp. 21–36; Straus, Richardson, Glasziou, & Haynes, 2005, pp. 13–30). Table 21.1 gives examples of five major types of questions from social work practice and four elements of these questions that can help guide an electronic search. All of these questions follow a PICO format, meaning that they specify the patient type, intervention (e.g., assess risk, apply a treatment), comparison (alternate course of action or no action), and outcome (what the worker and client want to accomplish). My book's Web site (http://www.evidence.brookscole.com) can assist in posing well-built questions and also help planning and executing electronic searches for current best evidence.

Learning how to pose well-built questions from practice may have these effects on practice reasoning:

- Social work practitioners who learn to pose well-built questions will be able to avoid harm by questioning whether practice procedures produce harmful effects.
- Social work can move away from an authority-based profession to an evidence-

TABLE 21.1 Four Elements in a Well-Formulated Question

	Client Type and Problem	What You Might Do	Alternate Course of Action	What You Want to Accomplish
	How would I describe a group of clients of similar type? Be specific.	Apply a treatment; act to prevent a problem; measure to assess a problem; survey clients; screen clients to assess risk.	What is the main alternative other than in the box to the immediate left, if any?	Outcome of treatment or prevention? Valid measure? Accurate risk estimation, prevented behavior, accurate estimation of need.
Five Question Types				
Example effectiveness question	If alcoholic adults...	are matched with their most appropriate treatment based on a classification...	or are assigned to treatment based on intake workers' best judgment and treatment availability...	will those matched with treatment have better sobriety?
Example prevention question	If black South African adolescents residing in orphanages at high risk for HIV infection...	are exposed to a peer-led HIV infection program...	or are not exposed to the prevention program...	will the former report fewer risky sexual behaviors?
Example assessment question	If infants referred to a child protective service agency who may have shaken baby syndrome...	are administered some form of shaken baby screening test...	that is compared with a more definitive but expensive CT scan test...	will this screening test have a sufficiently high positive predictive value and interrater reliability to make it practical?
Example description question	If family members of patients with stroke diagnosed with aphasia meet in a hospital support group...	and receive a short client satisfaction questionnaire of all support group participants...		which will the family members list as their areas of greatest and least satisfaction?
Example risk question	If crisis line callers to a battered women shelter...	are administered a risk assessment scale by telephone...	or we rely on practical judgment unaided by a risk assessment scale...	will the risk assessment scale have higher reliability and predictive validity?
Year Question Type: ___ (Insert 4 elements in question section to the right).	(Please fill in.)	(Please fill in.)	(Please fill in.)	(Please fill in.)

Source: This table follows Sackett et al., 1997.

based one (Gambrill, 2000) because we will see the need for answers to specific questions ourselves rather than relying on tradition and authority figures.

- Social work researchers can do qualitative content analyses of practitioners' well-built questions and use them to select research topics of greatest practical significance.

Learning how to pose specific questions from practice constitutes the first, most fundamental, and most essential step in evidence-based practice (EBP). The remaining steps in EBP involve electronically tracking down the best evidence related to the question in bibliographic databases and the Web, critically appraising that evidence, applying the best evidence to make decisions in practice, and finally evaluating the result (Straus et al., 2005).

FIVE TYPES OF PRACTICE QUESTIONS AND FOUR ELEMENTS MAKING THEM WELL BUILT

For the most part, as of this writing, EBP texts come from disciplines outside of social work. Texts that contain the phrase "evidence-based" or "evidence based" in the title include ones in medicine (Geyman, Deyo, & Ramsey, 2000; Greenhalgh, 1997; McKibbon, 1999; Ridsdale, 1998; Sackett et al., 1997; Straus et al., 2005), nursing (Craig & Smyth, 2007), and health care (Dawes et al., 1999). The book by Straus and colleagues might be the one most understandable to persons not in the health sciences. Two examples of EBP texts written by social workers include Rubin (2007) and Gibbs (2003).

EBP has promise for integrating research into social work practice. Studies of social work practitioners demonstrate that those surveyed did not consult research (Rosen, 1994). The scientist practitioner model based on single-subject designs may have proven impractical (Wakefield & Kirk, 1996). Given these problems, EBP might be more effective as a way to integrate research into practice decision making. EBP does not seek to replace clinical judgment; rather, it stands at the juncture between the practitioner's experience, the client's wishes, and the current best evidence. Because evaluating performance marks its final step, EBP does not replace single-subject designs as ways to evaluate practice. Advances in electronic bibliographic databases, the availability of necessary equipment, and the Web's accessibility may make EBP much more practical for social workers than in the past.

AVOIDING PRACTICE FALLACIES

As social workers go about our life-affecting work, they make judgments and decisions that greatly impact others. Social workers weigh suicide risk, they write recommendations regarding probation or incarceration in criminal presentence reports, assess risk for violence, and much more. Consequently, critical thinking by social workers is vitally important to the welfare of clients.

Our thinking must be well reasoned to be worthy of our clients' trust. One way to improve reasoning is to study the ways practice reasoning can go wrong. Common errors in reasoning are "practitioners' fallacies" (Gibbs & Gambrill, 1999, p. 89). Gambrill (1990) wrote the first and most complete guide to practitioners' fallacies for the helping professions (see also, Gambrill, 2005). Here are a few such fallacies (Gibbs & Gambrill, 1999):

- *Relying on case examples*—drawing conclusions about many clients from only one or a few unrepresentative individuals.
- *Relying on testimonials*—claims that a method is effective based on one's own experience.
- *Vagueness*—unspecific descriptions of client problems and related outcomes that make it impossible to determine progress.
- *Assuming soft-hearted therefore soft-headed*—the mistaken belief that one cannot be warm, empathetic, and caring while also being analytical, scientific, and rational in practice. Practitioners' good intentions cannot prevent harm.
- *Relying on newness/tradition*—accepting an assertion about what helps clients because a treatment method is new.
- *Appealing to authority*—assuming that an assertion about clients, including how best to help them, is true based on the status or authority of the person making the argument over a careful examination of the evidence.
- *Anchoring and insufficient adjustment*—the tendency to base estimates of client behavior on an initial piece of information and then not adjusting this estimate in light of new evidence.

These and many other fallacies are defined in Gibbs and Gambrill (1999). We have scant evidence regarding the effects of teaching students to spot practice fallacies. Whyte (1998) did a Solomon four group randomized trial to evaluate ability to spot practice fallacies as taught in a reasoning in practice game. His study, perhaps the most rigorous to evaluate a critical thinking effort in social work, included 136 research methods students in an MSW program. He found statistically significantly positive results.

OPTIMIZING CRITICAL THINKING

What is critical thinking as applied to social work practice? Critical thinking is rigorous, analytical, purposeful, systematic, methodologically sound reasoning that practitioners apply to judging what is true of clients, including determining which methods may help what particular clients. Critical thinkers have a predisposition to pose specific, answerable questions about practice. They know how to find the most logical and evidence-based answers to those questions—avoiding fallacious reasoning. To be truly effective as helping professionals, critical thinkers should be dedicated to clients—whom they genuinely respect and care deeply about. Their dedication should motivate them to be courageous. Critical thinkers should be willing to stand up and fight for principles regarding rational thinking in the helping process. They should do so enthusiastically, because they understand how logical thought can assist them in efforts to help clients.

To optimize critical thinking, we need to define critical thinking and understand it in operational terms. How else will we know if we have effectively implemented it? Measures for critical thinking should, as with other measures, be valid, reliable, easily administered, and easily scored. Efforts to measure critical thinking should avoid a trap that caught the nursing profession: they applied measures developed outside of nursing and, after considerable experience with these measures, discovered the need to devise their own measures specific to nursing practice (Kintgen-Andrews, 1991).

Given my experience in teaching the Research Methods course in social work for 25 years, I believe that the most valid social work measures will provide practice in making decisions that are presented in realistic scenarios, such as those described in the Kintgen-Andrew's (1991) summary

of nursing evidence. Practitioners should be able to exercise critical thinking skills sufficiently to avoid being taken in by human service propaganda. Can practitioners avoid being bamboozled? PRIDE1 tests such ability (Gibbs & Gambrill, 1999, pp. 65–70). Another less valid but more easily administered measure is the Professional Thinking Form (Gibbs & Gambrill, 1999, pp. 75–93). These and other measures will be published in our updated book (Gambrill & Gibbs, in press). I have developed other interactive CD-ROM measures including the Multidisciplinary Interactive Team Thinking Test (MITTT), the Courtroom Interactive Testimony Thinking Test (CITTT), and the Hospital Interactive Team Thinking Test (HITTT). These measures and their evaluations have been published in Gibbs (2003).

In conclusion, caring and compassion are essential but insufficient to avoid harm. Practitioners who pose specific questions about their practice, avoid common errors in practice reasoning, and demonstrate their ability to think rationally about real practice situations are more likely to avoid harming their clients. By doing this, the practitioner fulfills their ethical obligation to enhance clients' well-being to the maximum.

WEB SITES

Coalition for Evidence-Based Policies Website. http://www.evidencebased programs.org.
Evidence-Based Practice for the Helping Professions (book Web site and database). http://www.evidence.brookscole.com.
National Association of Social Workers, Code of Ethics. http://www.socialworkers.org/pubs/code/code.asp.
University of British Columbia Library: Evidence-Based Social Work: http://toby.library.ubc.ca/webpage/webpage.cfm?id=405.

References

Armstrong, E. (1999). The well-built clinical question: The key to finding the best evidence efficiently. *Wisconsin Medical Journal*, 98(2), 25–28.
Berra, Y. (1998). *The Yogi book*. New York: Workman.
Corcoran, J. (2000). *Evidence-based social work practice with families*. New York: Springer.
Craig, J. V., & Smyth, R. (2007). *Evidence-based practice manual for nurses*. Edinburgh: Churchill Livingstone.
Dawes, M., Davies, P., Gray, A., Mant, J., Seers, K., & Snowball, R. (1999). *Evidence-based practice: A*

primer for health care professionals. Edinburgh: Churchill Livingstone.

Gambrill, E. (1990). *Critical thinking in clinical practice: Improving the accuracy of judgments and decisions about clients.* San Francisco: Jossey-Bass.

Gambrill, E. (2000). Evidence-based versus authority-based social work practice. *Families in Society: The Journal of Contemporary Human Services, 80*(4), 341–350.

Gambrill, E. (2005). *Critical thinking in clinical practice: Improving the quality of judgements and decisions,* 2nd ed. Hoboken, NJ: John Wiley & Sons..

Gambrill, E., & Gibbs, L. (In press). *Critical thinking for the helping professions: workbook* 3rd ed. New York: Oxford University Press.

Geyman, J. P., Deyo, R. A., & Ramsey, S. D. (2000). *Evidence-based clinical practice: Concepts and approaches.* Boston: Butterworth Heinemann.

Gibbs, L. E. (1991). *Scientific reasoning for social workers: Bridging the gap between research and practice.* New York: Macmillan.

Gibbs, L. (2003). *Evidence-based practice for the helping professions: A practical guide with integrated multimedia.* Pacific Grove, CA: Brooks-Cole Thomson Learning.

Gibbs, L., & Gambrill, E. (1999). *Critical thinking for social workers: A workbook.* Thousand Oaks, CA: Pine Forge.

Gibbs, L., & Gambrill, E. (2002). Evidence-based practice: Counterarguments to objections. *Research on Social Work Practice, 12*(3), 452–476.

Gossett, M., & Weinman, M. L. (2007). Evidence-based practice and social work: An illustration of the steps involved. *Health & Social Work, 32*(2), 147–150.

Greenhalgh, T. (1997). *How to read a paper: The basics of evidence-based medicine.* London: BMJ.

Kintgen-Andrews, J. (1991). Development of critical thinking and nursing education: Perplexities and insights. *Journal of Nursing Education, 30,* 152–157.

McKibbon, A. (1999). *PDQ evidence-based principles and practice.* Hamilton, UK: B. C. Decker.

Ridsdale, L. (1998). *Evidence-based practice in primary care.* Edinburgh: Churchill-Livingstone.

Rosen, A. (1994). Knowledge use in direct practice. *Social Service Review, 68,* 561–577.

Rubin, A. (2007). *Practitioner's guide to using research for evidence-based practice.* New York: Wiley.

Sackett, D. L., Richardson, W. S., Rosenberg, W., & Haynes, R. B. (1997). *Evidence-based medicine: How to practice and teach EBM.* New York: Churchill Livingstone.

Stamm, S. (2000). *Assessing shaken baby syndrome.* Thesis, University of Wisconsin at Eau Claire.

Straus, S., Richardson, W. S., Glasziou, P., & Haynes, R. B. (2005). *Evidence-based medicine: How to practice and teach EBM,* 3rd ed. Edinburgh: Elsevier Churchill Livingstone.

Wakefield, J. C., & Kirk, S. (1996). Unscientific thinking about scientific practice: Evaluating the scientist-practitioner model. *Social Work Research,* ø(2), 83–94.

Whyte, D. T. (1998). *The effect of an educational unit on the critical thinking skills of social work students.* PhD diss., College of Social Work, University of South Carolina.

22 Optimizing the Use of Patient Safety Standards, Procedures, and Measures

Kenneth R. Yeager, Albert R. Roberts, & Radu Saveanu

There is nothing easy about attempting to provide a safe environment for mentally ill patients who have been recently admitted to an inpatient psychiatric hospital facility. Challenges are literally hidden around every corner. In this chapter, we discuss key concepts of patient safety within behavioral health care facilities with the overriding goal of preventing lethal consequences—patient suicides while under the monitoring of inpatient psychiatric staff. We present a combined quality and risk management approach to the establishment of a culture of safety. This approach encompasses four primary areas. The first is the assessment of patient potential for violence and suicidality. Second is the physical or built environment, focusing on aspects of the physical facility. The third area of focus is dedicated to programmatic approaches to patient safety. The fourth area examines individual patient components that contribute to safety and risk factors.

We first provide an overview of known best practices in providing a safe treatment environment (built or physical environment) for mentally ill patients, focusing on available practice guidelines and evidence-based approaches to patient safety. Our focus then shifts to the patient component in patient safety examining issues within the therapeutic milieu assessment, patient census, patient mix, or the combination of patient diagnosis on a given inpatient unit and staffing patterns. This, combined with patient assessment and the overall program approach to care, forms the facilities safety program. Finally, we review an approach to patient safety combining all outlined aspects into a consolidated approach to patient safety.

SCOPE OF THE PROBLEM

The most significant risk factors for suicide include suffering from a severe mental disorder, such as psychosis or a mood disorder combined with substance abuse, and availability of a lethal method or suicide plan. Retrospective studies of deceased persons, also known as psychological autopsies, have consistently found that over 90 percent of individuals who die from suicide had two or more psychiatric diagnoses documented in their records. However, one of the most hidden mental health problems is inpatient suicides. Approximately 1,500 suicides take place in inpatient hospital units throughout the United States each year, and a third of these take place while the high-risk patient is on 15-minute checks (American Psychiatric Association [APA], 2003).

Several noteworthy studies have been completed on suicide methods and correlates of mentally ill persons who subsequently committed suicide either while in the hospital or within a year of discharge. The majority of the suicides occurred in the community. When comparing hospital to community suicides, the method of suicide seems especially significant. In the community, the most frequent method of suicide was with firearms. In contrast, 62 percent to 75 percent of the hospital-based suicides were from hanging or jumping from high places (Douglas, Ogloff, & Hart, 2003; Joint Commission on Accreditation of Healtcare Organizations [JCAHO], 1998; Kahne, 1968; Roberts, 1973; Shneidman, Farberow, & Leonard, 1962). The implications of this research are that thorough suicide assessments and systematic patient safety protocols in psychiatric hospitals should both be major priorities.

CURRENT CHALLENGES TO PROVIDING INPATIENT PSYCHIATRIC SAFETY

Within the health care industry overall, and certainly in psychiatry, there are great challenges within the concept of "do no harm." In 1999, the Institute of Medicine released its first report on patient safety. This report is considered by many to be the "shot heard around the world" in addressing health care safety. This study, based on extrapolations, projected that 44,000 Americans die each year as the result of medical errors, and the number may be as high as 98,000.

Psychiatry is no stranger to the concept of protecting patients. For years, behavioral health care facilities have provided standards, such as those for windows that do not break and shower rods that do break when sufficient weight is applied. At the time of the Institute of Medicine report, the concept of patient safety seemed familiar to most psychiatric facility administrators and caregivers; most felt comfortable with methods established to provide patient safety. The idea of the need to provide a safe environment for persons with severe mental illness is not new.

The prediction of violence through risk assessments among a population of those who are seriously mentally ill is still being developed. Three forces have led to the attempt to develop better assessment tools to predict risk of violence toward self and others: the deinstitutionalization movement, civil rights and patient rights, and involuntary (civil) commitment proceedings.

Deinstitutionalization, the closing of large and antiquated state mental hospitals, emerged as a way to create a less costly, less restrictive alternative to institutions while emphasizing the need to differentiate between inpatient and outpatient care criteria based on levels of risk (Glancy & Chaimowitz, 2005). The civil rights movement sparked the need for advocacy for persons with mental illness. Numerous civil commitment cases confirmed the need to invoke the professional opinion of psychiatrists or other mental health professionals in the determination of "dangerousness to self or others," which has become the principal determinant for involuntary commitment (Norko & Baranoski, 2005). The increased utilization of voluntary hospitalization for psychiatric patients further heightened the need to clarify criteria for voluntary versus involuntary commitment (Brakel, Parry, & Weiner, 1985; Glancy & Chaimowitz, 2005).

MENTAL ILLNESS AND VIOLENCE

The difficulty in prediction of violence toward self or others stands despite numerous attempts to clarify risk factors within given populations. Many researchers (e.g., Diamond, 1974; Lansing et al., 1997; Roth, 1979; Shah, 1978; Stone, 1975) have attempted to critique the accuracy of prediction of violence within populations of psychiatric patients, with little success. The APA guideline for legislation on the psychiatric hospitalization of adults has stood as the primary source document on this topic. However, despite attempts to increase accuracy of assessing violence toward self or others, efforts have remained largely unsuccessful. The result has been an increased responsibility on the part of psychiatrists to conduct this function, serving as an agent of social control (Bloom, Webster, Hucker, & De Freitas, 2005). This serves as somewhat of a catch-22 for psychiatrists because inability to complete accurate assessments may lead to the tendency to err on the side of institutionalization. But overprediction of harm is a consequence of attempting to predict a low-prevalence situation, which leads to a large number of false positives.

Psychiatrists and social workers continue to struggle to develop more knowledge of factors related to suicide. Accepted predictors of risk are developed from a large number of studies that include various factors, such as specific demographic factors: being male over the age of 45; divorced or widowed; unemployed; experiencing socioeconomic stressors, such as high levels of debt; facing an inability to sustain day-to-day needs; or other psychosocial stressors. Predictors of violence toward self and others typically include the presence of comorbid psychiatric diagnoses, such as depression, alcoholism, drug abuse, schizophrenia, and/or psychotic disorder. Predictors of imminent suicide risk include the presence of suicidal ideation and a specific plan; a history of suicide attempts, based on degree of lethality; and family history of suicide (Link, Andrews, & Cullen, 1992; Link, Stueve, & Phelan, 1998; Morrissey, 2004; Swanson, Holzer, Gangu, & Jono, 1990).

Bush, Fawcett, and Jacobs (2003) indicated three primary problems that limit the usefulness of currently understood correlates of suicide. First is the retrospective nature of previous studies. Most of the early studies compiled data after the suicide. This method has a tendency to skew or distort findings because persons associated with the cases certainly recall interactions that in retrospect seem to indicate the individual's intent to end his or her life. Passing comments, jokes, actions, and phrases are all considered possible signs that were missed. Additionally, this process tends to limit the possibility of rating symptom severity as a predictive correlate for suicide, thus limiting the effectiveness of previous studies.

A second area of concern is the establishment of a predictive timeline with respect to the act of suicide. When reviewing the case in retrospect, individuals may leave out specific relevant indicators or misplace potential correlates within the timeline of the case autopsy. It is possible that persons may overlook certain presuicide behaviors that are indicative of a chronic risk and therefore predictive of the act occurring in the future. Yet other actions and behaviors may be overstated, such as the better understood immediate risks observable within hours, days, or even weeks of the suicide. Therefore, the retrospective study makes it impossible to separate the chronic from the acute correlates for suicide.

Within each of the stated issues are the issues of incompleteness of available data, for observations are based on snapshot recollections from a variety of observers who have knowledge of the suicide (Bush et al., 2003, p. 14). The third identified problematic area is a lack of comparison groups. Without the presence of comparison groups, it is impossible to determine whether a correlate documented within the case was actually associated with the suicide or a clinical feature of an underlying disorder (e.g., depression, schizophrenia, addiction). Thus, it becomes impossible to determine whether patients who are depressed and expressing suicidal ideation have a higher rate of suicide than those who are depressed and denying suicidal ideation (Bush et al., 2003, p. 15).

Bush and colleagues (2003) examined charts for 76 patients who committed suicide while in the hospital or immediately following discharge. For each case, the researchers evaluated the week before suicide, looking for standard risk predictors and using items from the Schedule for Affective Disorders and Schizophrenia (SADS) to determine the presence and severity of symptoms believed to correlate with acute suicide risk.

With regard to standard suicide predictors, only 49 percent of those studied ($n = 37$) had any prior suicide attempt; 39 percent ($n = 30$) were admitted for suicidal ideation, but 78 percent denied suicidal ideation in their last communication with staff regarding potential suicide risk; and 46 percent ($n = 35$) showed no evidence of psychosis. On the schedule ratings, 79 percent ($n = 60$) met criteria for severe or extreme anxiety and/or agitation. The findings indicate that standard risk assessments were of limited value in protecting this group from suicide. The authors of this study concluded that adding severity of anxiety and agitation to current assessment may assist in identification of patients at acute risk for suicide, thus providing effective treatment interventions with the at-risk population.

COMPONENTS OF A CULTURE OF SAFETY

We have developed an equation for patient safety based on the following components:

- patient assessment,
- physical environment,
- program safety,
- patient component.

Patient Assessment

An assessment of potential risk for violence by the National Health Service in the United Kingdom indicates that best-practice discharge should document assessment of risk to harm self or others before release to the community. Furthermore, all parties should agree on any additional risk management strategies and clearly document them in the care or treatment plan (Glancy & Chaimowitz, 2005). Yet as discussed, considerable debate remains regarding the accuracy of such assessment tools. Early instruments tended to rely heavily on historical (static) data, such as the number of prior suicide attempts and deaths or violent assaults on others. This is based on the belief that historical data provide better reliability and stability of trend over time. In diametric contrast is the clinical practice model of risk assessment that relies on snapshots of the dynamic and changing nature of the client case across temporary states of treatment and stabilization. These opposite approaches (clinical prediction versus the use of standardized prediction scales) prompted practitioners to ask which type of risk assessment was a more accurate predictor of both short-term and long-term violence.

According to Mossman (2000), both types of prediction are equal in their abilities to predict violence in the short, medium, and long term. Others have argued that assessment or actuarial tools are more effective, saying that the use of clinical judgment to assess potential risk of violence should be used as an independent adjunct to scaled assessment tools. This debate seems to be mute in that most guides (Violence Risk Appraisal Guide) require clinical judgment as a component of protocol (Glancy & Chaimowitz, 2005).

The Historical Clinical Risk-20 (HCR-20) protocol combines historical data, clinical judgment, and standardized measures in a 20-item scale designed to identify critical factors indicative of risk for violent behavior within the mentally ill population. Ten items consider historical factors; five focus on risk management; and five evaluate current clinical variables, such as impulsivity, negativity, levels of insight, and response to treatment. Risk management factors include treatment compliance, social support, stress factors, and exposure to potentially destabilizing triggers for violence. All of these factors can be observed and rated within the clinical environment, hence supporting clinical work (Douglas, Ogloff, Nicholls, & Grant, 1991; Glancy & Chaimowitz, 2005).

Assessment of Suicidality

Initial and ongoing assessment of suicidality is the foundation for providing safe care within the inpatient psychiatric setting. The APA (2003) has indicated that comprehensive suicide assessment should:

- identify psychiatric signs and symptom;
- assess past suicidal behavior, including intent of self-injurious acts;
- identify family relationships, family history of suicide, mental illness, and dysfunction;
- identify current psychosocial stressors and nature of current crisis;
- identify client strengths and vulnerabilities;
- determine the degree of suicidality (high, medium, low, based on suicide scale);
- determine suicide intent, any plan, and lethality;
- history of suicide attempts or self-harm;
- describe psychosocial situation (score on the Global Assessment of Functioning scale); and

- establish a multiaxial diagnosis (according to APA, 2000).

In 1999, suicidal ideation occurred in an estimated 5.6 percent of the U.S. population, with approximately 0.7 percent of the population attempting suicide. The incidence of completed suicide is much lower. In the general U.S. population, the incidence of suicide is approximately 10.7 for every 100,000 persons, or 0.017 percent of the total population per year (APA, 2003). The rarity of suicide (even within groups of known risk factors) contributes to the impossibility of statistically predicting suicide. To date, no definitive empirical evidence exists to prove the reliability and effectiveness of formal, structured assessment tools used to predict suicide attempts or completions (APA, 2003; Jacobs, 1999; Kanapaux, 2004; Sherer, 2003; Sullivan, Barron, Bezmen, Rivera, & Zapata-Vega, 2005).

According to Malone, Szanto, Corbitt, and Mann (1995), the use of unstructured assessments poses its own risks. Malone and colleagues reported that clinicians failed to document prior suicide attempts among admitted suicide patients nearly 25 percent of the time. Additionally, in 38 percent of discharge patients, clinicians failed to document recent suicidal ideation or planning assessments. Using chart reviews, Bush and colleagues (2003) found inadequate suicide assessments in 78 percent of inpatient completed suicides. Overall, 51 percent lacked documentation of prior suicide attempts; 29 percent were not on suicide precaution protocols; and 28 percent had no current self-harm contracts.

Furthermore, of 50 patients who had documented information on suicidal ideation in their charts, 78 percent had documented denials of such ideation in their last contact with staff. Finally, 79 percent of the patients had documentation in their charts of severe levels of anxiety or agitation within the week prior to the complete suicide. Although there is no clear evidence that a structured clinical assessment tool is effective in preventing a potential inpatient suicide, such an assessment approach is helpful in providing a systematic template for staff in assessing suicidal ideation. A systematic protocol facilitates the use of a common language to communicate concerns about suicide risk and patient safety among staff. The APA guideline for the assessment and treatment of patients with suicide behavior is such a tool (APA, 2003). For a detailed discussion of evidence-based suicide assessment measures, see Roberts and Yeager (2005).

Physical Environment

In considering the safety of psychiatric inpatients, it is important to compile a list of physical safety features within the inpatient facility. It may seem overly simple to indicate a list of features that can improve the safety of an inpatient psychiatric unit. However, patient safety begins with an awareness of features maintained within the facility. The list simply provides a logical place to begin. Direct care staff are frequently not aware of actions taken by the management or hospital administration to ensure patient safety. A review of shifting staffing patterns provides evidence of numerous opportunities for communication to break down among the staff who are responsible for maintaining the safety of the care environment.

The greatest risk within the inpatient psychiatric facility is that of solid-core interior doors. According to the JCAHO (1998), 75 percent of hospital suicides are the result of hanging. Interior doors pose a hanging risk because a sheet or other material can be knotted and used over the door in a manner that will support body weight off the floor.

Case example. Stan (not a real person), a 28-year-old male, was admitted following a fight with his significant other, who reported that Stan "went berserk" throwing chairs, breaking down doors, and screaming that he was going to kill her. She called the police, who came and restrained him. He was transported by emergency medical services to the hospital, where he was admitted. The next morning he was agitated and anxious, but he denied suicidal ideation. Stan was given a provisional diagnosis of depression NOS, R/O (not otherwise specified, rule out) bipolar disorder; he was treated with Depakote (valproate) and Zoloft (sertraline). In the afternoon of the second day of admission, Stan engaged in a shouting match with a peer about what channel the television in the dayroom should be on. He was confronted by staff and quietly led to seclusion for 35 minutes. Following this time, he was able to contract for safety, stating he would not harm himself or others. He remained on close observation (15-minute checks). Stan was quiet for the remainder of the day. He had a good visit with his brother and verbalized futuristic plans. He took his evening medications without argument. Stan slept until 10:30 A.M. On awakening, he spent half an hour in the day area, half an hour getting showered and dressed, and another half an hour at the com-

munity meeting. At 12:20, the unit aid was doing a head count and indicated that Stan was lying on his bed with his eyes open. At approximately 12:30, Stan's roommate entered the room and saw the bathroom door half open. He thought Stan was getting ready for the next group meeting, until he noticed the belt wrapped around the door hinge. The roommate found Stan hanging from the door, feet off the floor, with a belt taut around his neck. He tried to lift Stan but was unable to do so. He ran to the nurses station and informed the staff that Stan was "trying hanging himself." Staff raced to the room and called a code. Stan did not respond to interventions. He was pronounced dead at 12:43 P.M.

The facility's investigation revealed that no one person could be held solely accountable for the event. Observations were completed within the time frame. The facility found evidence that the 15-minute safety checks were done, and the flow sheet was completed. The investigation revealed that the belt had been taken from the closet of another patient, who was not on suicide precautions. Additional findings indicated that staff were provided timely in-service training on the unit's policies and procedures and that they had been adequately trained on the provisions of special observations. Furthermore, the facility had taken steps in the prevention of hanging suicides, which are by far the most frequent form of inpatient suicides. Facilitators had removed potential hanging hazards—such as showerheads, nonbreakaway bars in shower and toilet stalls, ward-robes, and exposed overhead pipes—and they had the approved hinges on the bathroom doors (JCAHO, 1998).

Hanging risks. Hanging risks on interior doors can be minimized by using a single hinge (piano hinge) for the door and by removing the top 6 inches (15.24 cm) from the door; however, this configuration will still provide a pinch point that may support body weight off the floor. Therefore, utilization of curtains, accordion doors, or pocket doors is preferable in the reduction of hanging risks on interior doors (see Figs. 22.1 and 22.2).

Two additional areas of concern to address are attachment points that pose a hanging risk from a sitting or kneeling position and can be used as a twist attachment. The areas of greatest risk are areas where patients are provided privacy for example, support bars (grab bars) in showers and bathrooms. Additionally, plumbing fixtures provide hanging risks. All of these risks can be elim-

Figure 22.1 A knotted sheet can serve as a hanging risk when combined with solid-core hospital doors on inpatient psychiatric units.

Figure 22.2 The combination of a sheet and a solid-core door will support the entire body weight off the ground.

inated by building safety features, such as a stainless steel box around plumbing fixtures and by adding "plates" to grab bars that permit functionality but minimize hanging risk (see Figs. 22.3 and 22.4).

A third level includes twist risks. These would most frequently use lower fixed items, such as sink drains, bed frames, and hard-mounted doorstops. Although these are considered to be slight risks, all aspects of safety and risk should be considered when assessing the relative degree of unit safety. Identifying risks is only the beginning; facilities should consider implementing risk-reduction strategies. As units increase their awareness of safety features, it is quite possible that there will be questions regarding other safety concerns. As these questions arise, there becomes an opportunity to identify and implement risk-reduction strategies.

Identifying Accepted Residual Risk

Once the facility team has completed a thorough and complete assessment of safety features of the environment, it must account for the concept of residual risk. Residual risks are the remaining safety issues that cannot be managed within the systems safety approach implemented within the physical environment. In reality, it is not physically possible to control for all risks present within the treatment environment. Therefore, there needs to be planning inclusive of a staffing pattern that serves as a protective factor to address residual risks that exist naturally within the care environment. For example, patients at risk for self-harm but not severe enough to require one-to-one observations should be monitored every 5 minutes or more frequently to ensure that they cannot use unit-based items to carry out self-harm.

A growing conventional wisdom recognizes that persons considered to be at even moderate risk will complete an act of self-harm within 5 minutes or quicker. When staff are deployed in a manner that optimizes their number within the therapeutic milieu, it is possible to implement ran-

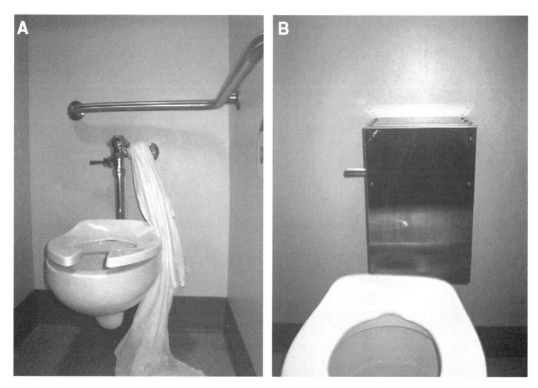

Figure 22.3 Plumbing fixtures pose a hanging risk but can be enclosed to minimize danger.

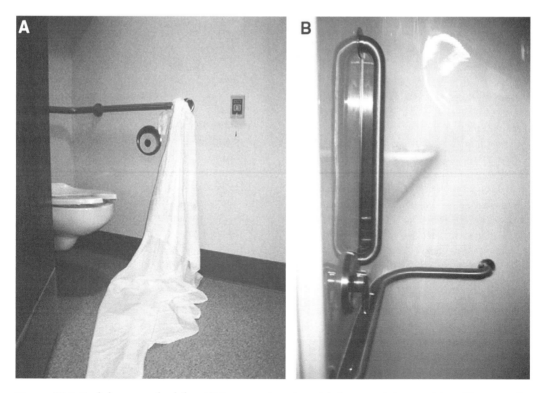

Figure 22.4 Grab bars standard for ADA pose a hanging risk from a sitting position. These can be "plated" to minimize risk.

domized unit sweeps occurring within 5 minutes, using a roving psychiatric tech. Though 15-minute checks remain the standard, for many psychiatric inpatients this measure should not be counted on to maintain safety in the therapeutic milieu.

Potential weapons. This topic brings us to the presence of items that can be used as weapons against staff and other patients. There are increasing numbers of patients seeking admission to psychiatric facilities with forensic histories and backgrounds. For this reason, facilitators conducting a unit safety assessment should consider items that can be used as weapons. For example, wooden drawer units can be pulled out of furniture, splintered, and used to stab. Some hospital beds have cords, which represent a hanging and strangulation risk if used as a weapon. Some beds have mattress stops that can be removed and used as a weapon. Finally, in a search for heavy items, one unit sweep identified front panels that could be removed and used to hit staff or patients with (see Figs. 22.5, 22.6, and 22.7).

Safety rounds. To identify changes occurring over time within the treatment environment, safety rounds should be implemented in psychiatric facilities to identify and reduce risk. Even when using recommended safety devices, facilities must test these and consider potential risk factors for all items introduced into the patient care environment. For example, the specially designed hanger (Fig. 22.8) that will not support body weight could be a risk if a patient were to push a staff

Figure 22.6 Heavy panels, such as those from heating devices, can be used to break windows or as a weapon.

member into this hanger, given its placement on the wall.

Unit members should be aware that although manual beds present less risk owing to fewer wires, there is still a crush factor that must be considered (Fig. 22.9). Figure 22.10 demonstrates the patient's ability to self-harm using the bed as a crush tool. Units should be monitored for items that can be broken down into parts used as weapons; for example, commonly used linen containers can be broken down into several parts as potential weapons (Fig. 22.11).

Finally, items should be considered in combination. In Figure 22.12, the hospital bed has been anchored to the floor to prevent its being used as a barricade; however, when used with the nightstand and chair, barricading the door is possible (Fig. 22.13).

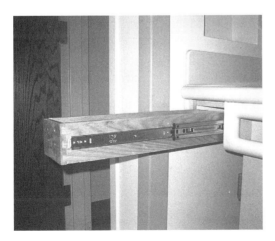

Figure 22.5 Cabinets can be taken apart to make weapons.

Figure 22.7 Some beds have removable headboards, which can be used as weapons.

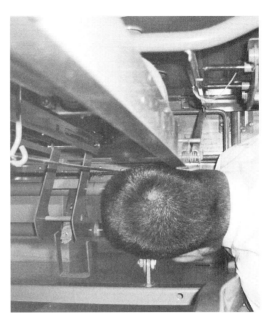

Figure 22.8 Even safety devices can pose a safety risk. Check all items, even those believed to be safe. In this example, safety hooks can cause a puncture wound.

Figure 22.10 Bed frames should be checked to ensure safety stops are in place to minimize crush risk to patients.

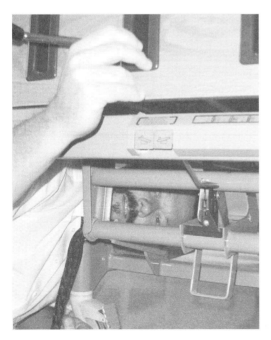

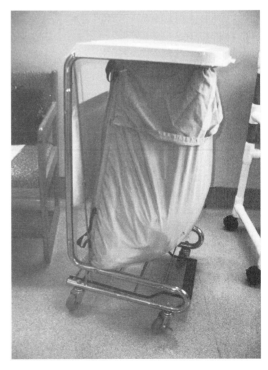

Figure 22.9 Be certain handles have been placed in a manner to minimize patient use to cause injury via crush points.

Figure 22.11 A common linen hamper can be broken down into several potential weapons.

Figure 22.12 Bed is anchored and locked to the floor to prevent barricade situation. This is thought to be a safety feature.

Safety rounds should occur frequently—at least weekly—to set the stage for safety on the unit. Each safety round should be conducted with the intention of testing everything within the treatment environment.

MONITORING THE PHYSICAL ENVIRONMENT

On a daily basis, there are a variety of changes that occur within the treatment environment. Psychiatric staff, nursing staff, and housekeeping may introduce new items into the therapeutic environment daily, and any number of potentially dangerous items can find their way onto a secure unit without staff's considering their potential safety risk. Psychiatric facility staff should at all times maintain an acute awareness of the cleaning solutions being used. Many psychiatric facilities have claimed that they use only nontoxic cleaning agents.

Staff frequently forget the presence of the item within the care environment. Routine safety checks teach staff why it is important to keep track of risk items within the patient care environment. If staff are routinely involved in safety checks, there is a stronger likelihood that they will learn to prevent risk through monitoring the care environment as a matter of routine. Unit safety rounds should increase awareness of potential weapons that are on the unit. Items of risk range from tools that are carried to the unit by maintenance staff, items on cleaning carts, and imple-

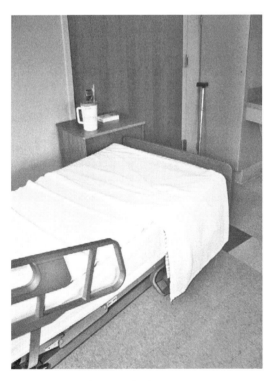

Figure 22.13 The same bed as in Figure 22.12, combined with a nightstand and chair in the room, can be used to create a barricade situation.

ments used by physicians and nursing staff. For example, a stethoscope left in a patient's room can quickly become a mechanism for strangulation of a staff member or another patient. Mop and broom handles can be used as weapons, specifically by a person trained in martial arts. Broken or unsafe furniture, cabinets, and heavy carts used for moving materials from unit to unit all pose safety risks.

ANNUAL SAFETY AUDITS: INCLUDING OUTSIDE PERSPECTIVES

It is a good idea to include a new, different, or fresh set of eyes when examining the physical environment. People frequently become desensitized to their physical working environments. Through the views of outsiders, items considered to be safe can be identified as being unsafe either alone or in conjunction with other items. Historically, interactions between mental health facilities have been limited. As time progresses, facilities are becoming open to sharing both hands-on practice and aggregate data in areas of common concern to improve patient safety. Collaborative interactions and benchmark data to establish quality indicators are all positive steps toward the development of safer patient consumer facilities.

Programmatic Safety: Leadership

In addressing program safety, leadership comprises three primary areas: experience, availability, and understanding the patient safety plan.

Experience. Not only does experience speak to the administration of the facility, it also includes experiences of facility line staff, managers, support staff, and consumer volunteers. True leadership develops an open process and uses information to improve programming that is inclusive of all interactions, thus providing a supportive environment for patients. In such an environment, leadership is not based on developing policy and implementing rules. It is the willingness to examine the reasoning behind rule development and for removal of the rule when doing so is in advocacy of the patient. More important, when leaders see the environment as being interactive with patient/consumer care, safety has the opportunity to become an active ingredient in the therapeutic environment.

Availability. Availability of staff means more than staff-to-patient ratio. It has to do with program development and implementation. Given the opportunity, staff will remain focused on tasks within the nursing station. One of the more innovative programs has moved toward closing nursing stations. In this example, the former areas dedicated to nursing stations have become storage and resource areas. Documentation occurs with wireless laptop computers, with staff consistently circulating in the patient care area, providing greater availability for patients and observation to improve safety.

Understanding the safety plan. Understanding the safety plan is a key element of change. As stated, education about the reasoning behind the safety plan and the staff's involvement in developing the plan is key to the development of effective safety initiatives. Once the safety plan is established, frequent review and critical assessment facilitate keeping it alive in the eyes of the staff and not simply regressing to a policy that exists in the administrator's office.

Critical review of incidents that fall within the scope of the safety plan should include mandatory attendance of the facility's medical director, nursing directors and nursing staff, quality officer, and risk manager. Formal debriefings should explicitly separate facts, feelings, and planning processes to provide successful adaptation of the unit to identified safety issues. Finally, the debriefing should include communication to all staff persons across the continuum of care in a non-blaming or nonpunitive manner.

ALIGNING POLICY, PRACTICE, AND PROCESS

For the purposes of implementation, development of policies without efforts to involve direct care staff may result in communication disconnects that diminish the effectiveness of safety programming, essentially developing an estrangement between knowing and doing. To enhance performance and application of programmatic safety, direct care staff should be involved in all areas of planning. All staff members should feel comfortable interjecting at any stage of the safety program, stating whether a practice is usual. Once the initial safety plan is developed, it should be presented to staff for feedback and potential areas of refinement. The goal is to develop a plan of action that mirrors current practice and refines the practice of staff. In most cases, staff members are eager to improve care. Most are willing to offer potential solutions if they believe their suggestions will be incorporated into the overall plan. The result is a clearly articulated approach to inpatient psychiatric safety programming that incorporates staff input and is thus more likely to be applied as developed.

CONCLUSION

While the debate continues on the utilization of actuarial scaling tools, as opposed to current practice of clinical prediction within the context of clinical practice, the emergence of an increasingly acute population is driving the need to demonstrate better methodologies for assessing, reassessing, and tracking patterns of violence, self-harm, and harm to others in the arena of inpatient psychiatric treatment. As clinical evidence grows, this issue will become a standard-of-care issue. Eventually, risk assessment will be a standard component of clinical psychiatric practice. It is our hope that this chapter gives readers a new perspective with which to view treatment environments, leading to conclusions regarding the safety of the environment that have been previously overlooked. A combined risk management and quality improvement approach provides the ability to identify, define, monitor, and measure risk factors and programmatic deficits.

The goal becomes to build treatment programming in a manner that incorporates best practices of patient safety into not only the program but also the treatment environment. The role of physicians, nurses, social workers, support staff, and facility engineers are becoming clear. What is needed is an interdisciplinary, interactive approach to program safety incorporating the views of consumers and families as knowledge of patient safety continues to grow and evolve into subtle changes that have the potential to determine the fate of patients seeking the safe haven of inpatient psychiatric care.

WEB SITES

Agency for Health Care Research and Quality. http://www.ahrq.gov.
American Psychiatric Association. http://www.psych.org.
Joint Commission. http://www.jointcommission.org.

Joint Commission Patient Safety. http://www.jcipatientsafety.org.

References

American Psychiatric Association. (2000). *Diagnostic and statistical manual of mental disorders,* 4th ed. (text rev.). Washington, DC: APA.

American Psychiatric Association. (2003). Practice guideline for the assessment and treatment of patients with suicidal behaviors. *American Journal of Psychiatry, 160,* 1–50.

Bloom, H., Webster, C., Hucker, S., & De Freitas, K. (2005). The Canadian contribution to violence risk assessment: History and implications for current psychiatric practice. *Canadian Journal of Psychiatry: Revue Canadienne de Psychiatrie, 50*(1), 3–8.

Brakel, S. J., Parry, J., & Weiner, B. A. (1985). *The mentally disabled and the law.* Chicago: American Bar Association.

Bush, K., Fawcett, J., & Jacobs, D. (2003). Clinical correlates of inpatient suicide. *Journal of Clinical Psychiatry, 64,* 14–19.

Diamond, B. (1974). The psychiatric prediction of dangerousness. *University of Pennsylvania Law Review, 123,* 430–452.

Douglas, K., Ogloff, J., & Hart, S. (2003). Evaluation of a model of violence risk assessment among forensic psychiatric patients. *Psychiatric Services), 54*(10), 1372–1379.

Douglas, K. S., Ogloff, R. P., Nicholls, T. L., & Grant, I. (1991). Assessing risk for violence among psychiatric patients: The HCR-20 Risk Assessment Scheme and the Psychopathy Checklist: Screening version. *Journal of Consulting Psychology, 61,* 917–930.

Glancy, G., & Chaimowitz, G. (2005). The clinical use of risk assessment. *Canadian Journal of Psychiatry, 50*(1), 12–17.

Jacobs, D. (1999). Depression screening as an intervention against suicide. *Journal of Clinical Psychiatry, 60*(Suppl 2), 42–45; discussion 51–52, 113–116.

Joint Commission on Accreditation of Healthcare Organizations. (1998, November 6). Inpatient suicide: Recommendations for prevention. *Sentinel Event Alert, 7.*

Kahne, M. (1968). Suicides in mental hospitals: A study of the effects of personnel and patient turn-over. *Journal of Health & Social Behavior, 9*(3), 255–266.

Kanapaux, W. (2004). Guideline to aid treatment of suicidal behavior. *Psychiatric Times, 21*(8), 17–23.

Lansing, A. E., Lyons, J. S., Martens, L. C., O'Mahoney, M. T., Miller, S. I., & Obolsky, A. (1997). The treatment of dangerous patients in managed care—psychiatric hospital utilization and outcome. *General Hospital Psychiatry, 19,* 112–118.

Link, B. G., Andrews, H., & Cullen, F. T. (1992). The violent and illegal behavior of mental patients reconsidered. *American Sociological Review, 57,* 275–292.

Link, B. G., Stueve, A., & Phelan, J. (1998). Psychotic symptoms and violent behaviors: Probing the components of "threat/controloverride" symptoms. *Social Psychiatry and Psychiatric Epidemiology, 33*(Suppl 1), 55–60.

Malone, K. M., Szanto, K., Corbitt, E. M., & Mann, J. J. (1995). Clinical assessment versus research methods in the assessment of suicidal behavior. *American Journal of Psychiatry, 152*(11), 1601.

Morrissey, J. (2004). Patient safety proves elusive. *Modern Healthcare, 34*(44), 6–10.

Mossman, D. (2000). Commentary: Assessing the risk of violence—are "accurate" predictions useful? *Journal of the American Academy of Psychiatry Law, 28,* 272–281.

Norko, M., & Baranoski, M. (2005). The state of contemporary risk assessment research. *Canadian Journal of Psychiatry: Revue Canadienne de Psychiatrie, 50*(1), 18–26.

Roberts, A. R. (1973). Suicide and suicide prevention: An overview. *Public Health Reviews: An International Quarterly, 2*(1), 3–30.

Roberts, A. R., & Yeager, K. (2005). Lethality assessment and crisis intervention with persons presenting with suicidal ideation. In A. R. Roberts (Ed.), *Crisis intervention handbook: Assessment, treatment, and research*, 3rd ed. New York: Oxford University Press.

Roth, L. H. (1979). A commitment law for patients, doctors, and lawyers. *American Journal of Psychiatry, 136,* 1121–1127.

Shah, S., (1978). Dangerousness: A paradigm for exploring some issues in law and psychology. *American Psychology, 33,* 224–238.

Sherer, R. A. (2003). Psychiatrists strive to assure patients' safety. *Psychiatric Times, 20*(6), 23–29.

Shneidman, E., Farberow, N., & Leonard, C. (1962). Suicide—evaluation and treatment of suicidal risk among schizophrenic patients in psychiatric hospitals. *Medical Bulletin/Veterans Administration, 8.*

Stone, A. A. (1975). Comment on Peszke MA—is dangerousness an issue for physicians in emergency commitment? *American Journal of Psychiatry, 132,* 829–831.

Sullivan, A., Barron, C., Bezmen, J., Rivera, J., & Zapata-Vega, M. (2005). The safe treatment of the suicidal patient in an adult inpatient setting: A proactive preventive approach. *Psychiatric Quarterly, 76*(1), 67–83.

Swanson, J. W., Holzer, C. E., Gangu, V. K., & Juno, R. T. Violence and psychiatric disorder in the community: Evidence from the Epidemiologic Hospital Catchment Area surveys. *Hospital Community Psychiatry, 41,* 761–770

23

The Role and Regulations for Technology in Social Work Practice and E-Therapy

Social Work 2.0

Jonathan B. Singer

Social workers have an ethical responsibility to attend to the environmental forces that create, contribute to, and address problems in living (National Association of Social Workers [NASW], 1999). Technologies, such as the Internet, e-mail, cell phones, and Webcams, have significantly changed the way we communicate with each other and interact with our environment. A recent survey found that 80 percent of Americans sought health-related information from the Internet in 2006 (Fox, 2006). As people combine new ways of communicating with new ways of seeking health-related information, there will be a natural evolution toward new ways of providing social work services. Just as the Internet evolved from a collection of static Web pages (Web 1.0) to a virtual community called Web 2.0 (O'Reilly, 2005), the integration of social work with computer and Internet technologies (CIT) creates a new paradigm for social work, which I call *Social Work 2.0*.

The National Association of Social Workers (NASW) and the Association of Social Work Boards (ASWB) recognize technology as a significant environmental force and have published 16 standards for technology in social work, covering clinical practice, administration, advocacy and community organizing, and research (NASW, 2005b). These standards provide a foundation for Social Work 2.0. Although people have been writing about technology and social problems for decades (Gergen, 1991), the integration of computer technology and social work services has been limited by micro factors (e.g., traditional consumers of social work services are the least likely to have access to computer technologies; Fox & Livingston, 2007; Horrigan, 2007) as well as macro factors (e.g., limited funding for current technology and training in possible uses; McCarty & Clancy, 2002). The purpose of this chapter is to review existing literature on technology and social services; identify and define key terms and concepts; and describe uses, benefits, and limitations of technology and social service delivery. My hope is that social workers will see technology as a resource, and engage in the discussion of how Social Work 2.0 can help us better serve traditionally underserved populations.

KEY CONCEPTS

The 13 most important Social Work 2.0 concepts are defined and illustrated in Table 23.1. Some concepts, such as e-therapy and tele-health, have overlapping yet distinct meanings (McCarty & Clancy, 2002). For simplicity, I use the term "e-therapy" when referring to any social work service that is provided using CIT.

USES, BENEFITS, AND LIMITATIONS OF TECHNOLOGY IN SERVICE DELIVERY

The uses, benefits, and limitations of e-therapy in the micro, mezzo, and macro areas of clinical practice, community organizing, and policy issues have been discussed by a number of authors (Banach & Bernat, 2000; Bell, 2007; Fenichel et al., 2002; Kanani & Regehr, 2003; McCarty & Clancy, 2002; McCoyd & Kerson, 2006). The clinical literature is written mostly by psychologists and counselors rather than social workers, reflects clinical wisdom rather than empirical evidence, and addresses such issues as what types of clients access services, what types of services are provided, and what skills and attitudes make for a successful e-therapist (Fenichel et al., 2002). Social workers have contributed extensively to the community organizing and policy literature and have addressed issues such as how to use technology for advocacy of social action (Hick & McNutt, 2002) and how e-therapy services are regulated and reimbursed (Banach & Bernat, 2000; McCarty & Clancy, 2002).

CLINICAL PRACTICE

There are two types of e-therapy: the first is between a client and therapist; the second is self-directed (i.e., without a therapist). The most common e-therapy services are provided by a therapist using delayed communication (asynchronous) like e-mail or discussion boards (Fenichel et al., 2002; Jedlicka & Jennings, 2001), or in real time (synchronously) over chat, text, Webcam, phone, and virtual reality environments like Second Life. Clients can contract with current providers for e-therapy or access e-therapy services through online resources, such as HelpHorizons.com and eTherapistOnline.com, which verify provider credentials and have the infrastructure for accepting payment through credit card and PayPal. Clients register with a user name and password, supply a working e-mail address, and can read descriptions of participating therapists. Once the account has been verified, clients can book sessions through an online calendar and decide which type of e-therapy they would like: e-mail, chat, or phone (either traditional land line or voice over Internet [VoIP]). Billing rates are based on the type of service received. E-mail therapy is billed per e-mail; chat and phone therapies are billed in traditional time blocks or per minute. E-therapy Web sites can provide access to client services, such as discussion boards where people can communicate anonymously with each other, articles on treatment issues, professionally vetted links, and personalized logins where clients can access individualized content such as crisis plans, and client-specific podcasts. Unlike traditional ser-

TABLE 23.1 Definitions and Examples of Technology Terms

Term	Definition	Example of use
Asynchronous communication	Delayed communication; does not occur in real time	Correspondence via letters or e-mail
chat (also known as Instant Messaging, or IMing)	Synchronous Web-based communication	Crisis hotline provides real-time text-based services using a program that loads into a browser, allowing the worker and client to communicate instantly
e-supervision	Supervision using e-mail, chat, phone, or Webcams—anything but traditional face-to-face supervision	Four clinicians from different states dial in to the same tele-supervision group
e-therapy (synonymous with online-, cyber-, e-mail, or chat therapy)	Therapy using technologies, rather than traditional face-to-face services	Client and therapist conduct therapy over e-mail, chat, Webcam, or a virtual world like Second Life
GIS (Geographical Information Systems)	Computer software that allows social workers to map services and identify where service needs exist	Crisis worker at a nationwide crisis hotline locates local referrals for suicidal a client using GIS software
podcast/vodcast	Subscription-based downloadable audio/video files	Client downloads and listens to an audio file created by the therapist on a clinically relevant topic (e.g., relaxation training)
Second Life	An Internet-based virtual world where people can interact with each other and communicate via chat or voice	Services, such as a rape-crisis shelter, are developed and accessed by members of the virtual community
Social Work 2.0	The integration of computer and Internet technologies with traditional social work	Service plans include relevant technology in service provision and goal attainment
synchronous communication	Communication that occurs in real time	Traditional face-to-face social work, such as a therapy session; e-therapy using real time technology (e.g., chat)
tele-health	The use of communication technology to provide services to remote locations	Social worker in a rural area uses the phone for assessment and diagnosis.
VoIP (voice over Internet protocol)	The routing of voice conversations over the Internet	Client uses VoIP to make free phone therapy appointments
Webinar	Internet-based seminar that allows for synchronous communication between people in remote locations and the presenter	Three social workers in different states give an interactive continuing education presentation to social workers from all over the world
Web 2.0	A conception of the Internet as an interactive medium	Consumers and staff co-create the information on an agency Web site using a wiki

vices, e-therapy services can be accessed any-where in the world at any time. Consequently, e-therapists are encouraged to establish boundaries regarding frequency and duration of online communications (Kanani & Regher, 2003).

The second type of e-therapy is self-directed treatment through Web-based modules (Bell, 2007). Self-directed treatments, such as Australia's Mood-GYM, are based on a cognitive-behavioral therapy model and have demonstrated success in reducing symptoms of depression and anxiety (Christensen, Griffiths, & Jorm, 2004). Self-directed treatments have the potential to provide services to thousands of people at minimal costs (Bell, 2007).

E-therapy differs from traditional face-to-face services in a number of important ways. E-therapy reduces structural barriers to treatment, such as transportation and access to providers (McCoyd & Kerson, 2006). For example, people who are homebound (e.g., physical disabilities, agoraphobia, or caregiver constraints) or those who feel stigmatized can access services more easily and anonymously. For example, Fenichel and colleagues (2002) tell of a soldier exploring his sexual orientation who, to protect his military career, chose e-therapy because it promised anonymity. Banach and Bernat (2000) noted that this type of anonymity might attract a type of client previously unwilling to use these services. E-therapy can be anonymous if clients are not required to show proof of identification (such as a credit card or bank account). Some authors have argued that the anonymity of e-therapy reduces power differentials, stigma, and social distance, which results in a more egalitarian and trustworthy relationship and increases the level and quality of self-disclosure (Schopler, Abell, & Galinsky, 1998).

E-therapy is recommended in situations where traditional face-to-face therapy is unavailable, such as in rural areas or with traditionally underserved populations (Emmelkamp, 2005). However, clients in rural areas have less access to broadband (Horrigan, 2007), and Latinos and African Americans are less connected to the Internet than whites are (Fox & Livingston, 2007). Thus clients who might benefit most from Social Work 2.0 are the least likely to have access to the necessary technology. To fulfill social work's historical mission of providing services to disenfranchised and vulnerable populations, we have to advocate for access to technology and consumer-friendly applications of Social Work 2.0.

Some authors have suggested that almost any traditional social work service can be provided online (McCarty & Clancy, 2002). For example, Stofle and Harrington (2002) argue that addiction treatment can be successfully provided over the Internet, and Jedlicka & Jennings (2002) identify the benefits of marital therapy online (e.g., couples have to "fight" over e-mail and therefore have time and space to reflect on what they have said). However, empirical studies have found that for certain diagnoses (e.g., depression, anxiety, phobias), e-therapy is comparable but not better than traditional face-to-face treatments (Bell, 2007; Emmelkamp, 2005; McCarty & Clancy, 2002). A review of studies on the use of computer and video technology for assessment and diagnosis found little or no difference compared to face-to-face services (McCarty & Clancy, 2002). McCarty & Clancy (2002) found that interrater reliability for diagnoses ranged between 0.85 and 0.91 for face-to-face and teleconference diagnoses. Some research suggests that consumers prefer computer-administered to face-to-face assessments because of the shame and stigma associated with revealing certain information, preference of using computer keypads over pen or pencil, or novelty of the computer environment (Sarrazin, Hall, Richards & Carswell, 2002).

E-therapy is commonly conducted using text-based communication such as e-mail or chat. The therapeutic benefits of text-based therapy were first noted by Freud (McCarty & Clancy, 2002) and recently by narrative therapists (White & Epston, 1990). Proponents of online therapy (Banach & Bernat, 2000; Fenichel et al., 2002; Jedlicka & Jennings, 2001; McCoyd & Kerson, 2006) suggested that e-mail or chat therapy, rather than inhibiting therapeutic alliance, increases the clarity and thoughtfulness of communication, as well as emotional expressiveness. This might seem unlikely, considering text-based communication eliminates nonverbal communication and changes in tone of voice. In fact, clients and clinicians are forced to articulate not only thoughts but also nuanced emotions and associated behaviors, resulting in greater reflection and insight into therapeutic conversations. For example, Jedlicka and Jennings (2002) suggested that one benefit of e-mail-based marital therapy is that couples have to fight over e-mail and therefore have time and space to reflect on their communication. Some authors have argued that the text-based environment requires a new set of clinical skills (Fenichel et al., 2002). Fenichel and colleagues (2002) recommend two dozen practical and emotional skills necessary for e-therapists to be effective online communicators, including fast typing, comfort with various computer programs, comfort in a text-only environment, and tolerance for computer glitches.

McCarty and Clancy (2002) suggested that the most important contribution of e-therapy is in revolutionizing recordkeeping. Whereas traditional records (paper or electronic) are essentially a one-sided account of treatment, therapy conducted over e-mail, chat, and even text messaging creates complete record of communication between client and clinician. Even video therapy with Webcams can be stored using new technologies. Clients and clinicians can review past sessions to identify treatment progress and clinicians can use the transcripts in consultation (Murphy & Mitchell, 1998, cited in Kanani & Regehr, 2003).

Critics of e-therapy have identified two significant limitations to anonymous service delivery. The first has to do with consumer protection. Clients are unable to verify the identity or credentials of online therapists (unless they use a service like eTherapist.com or Helpingweb.com), leaving an already vulnerable population open to fraud and abuse. Client confidentiality can be compromised when an attorney subpoenas digital records (e.g., e-mails and text messages) from the Internet service provider, thereby circumventing the traditional safeguard of clinicians being the sole keeper of clinical records. Second, in a crisis situation (either because of a duty to warn, a duty to report, or a need to access local services), it can be impossible for the social worker to verify the client's identity or location. This presents significant liability and ethical challenges. Some authors have suggested that verifying client identity should be a requirement for online therapy, using written contracts and credit card billing to verify clients' identity, address, and that they are of age to consent to service (Fenichel et al., 2002; Jedlicka & Jennings, 2001). However, the long history of phone-based crisis intervention services, and more recently chat-based "hotlines," suggests that face-to-face services are not required, even for life and death situations (Barak, 2007).

A brief example of the oldest and most well-established technology, tele-health (originally called tele-medicine; McCarty & Clancy, 2002), illustrates some of the benefits, challenges, and potentials for technology and social work. Tele-health, the provision of health care over the telephone, and tele-therapy, the provision of therapy over the phone, has enabled social workers to provide services to consumers who are geographically isolated or home-bound. Tele-therapy via cell phones or VoIP programs like Skype can offer the promise of treatment to people who travel for business, such a truck drivers or fishermen, or people who stay at work sites for extended periods of time, such as oil rig crews. Tele-therapy services occur in real time and can include diagnosis, assessment, crisis intervention, short-term or long-term therapy, and follow-up (McCarty & Clancy, 2002). Some authors have suggested that risk assessment screenings be conducted over the phone prior to face-to-face services (King, Engi, & Poulos, 1998). According to the NASW (1999, 2005b), tele-therapy services fall under the guidelines of the NASW Code of Ethics. However, the majority of clinicians who provide tele-therapy are unaware of the relevant legal and ethical standards (Banach & Bernat, 2002; Kanani & Regehr, 2003).

In addition to providing services over the phone, social workers can also receive supervision over the phone (Singer, 2008). Phone supervision has been described as being more focused and satisfying than traditional face-to-face supervision for a number of reasons. (1) Social workers can access content experts regardless of geographic location; (2) it eliminates travel time; (3) those who provide services in their offices can remain in the clinical environment during supervision, increasing connection to the treatment setting and issues related to service provision.

Reimbursement for tele-therapy services is limited to public health insurance. In the past few years, Medicare reimbursement guidelines were updated to recognize individual psychotherapy (CPT codes 90804–90809) over the phone (tele-therapy) as a reimbursable service equivalent to face-to-face services. However, the consumer must be at an authorized Medicare facility to receive the services, limiting the benefit of tele-therapy to reach people who are geographically isolated or home-bound.

COMMUNITY ORGANIZING

For much of the twentieth century, social workers struggled with how vulnerable and marginalized groups were adversely affected by technology (Hick & McNutt, 2002). Social workers fought for child labor laws in the nineteenth century and voting rights for women and minorities in the twentieth century. In the twenty-first century, social workers fight to close the "digital divide." Technology continues to create, contribute to, and address social problems. "Not all technologies will be useful in all social work advocacy situations" (McNutt & Menon, 2008, p. 37). The following are examples of effective uses of technology in community organizing and social work advocacy.

- Geographical Information Systems (GIS) technologies can be used to analyze information about specific geographical regions, such as neighborhoods, ZIP codes, cities, or counties. Advocacy groups can analyze campaign demographics to improve voter participation on key social service issues. GIS can be used by consumer rights advocates to identify areas of need to improve service delivery.
- E-mail lists are a low-cost way of distributing action alerts (e.g., "call your representative now!"). Until the mid-1990s, advocacy groups used the telephone and fax alerts to distribute legislative alerts. This was costly and time-consuming and limited the number of people who could be reached. E-mail has made it possible for small-budget advocacy organizations to turn out numbers that in previous decades were possible only through the largest national organizations (Krause et al., 2002).
- Using technology such as online discussion lists, Web sites, and blogs, issue-oriented and social change Web sites can organize people in one neighborhood or from around the world on a specific issue. For issues such as suicide, which have a relatively low base rate (11 per 100,000) and stigma-related silence, geography and social stigma have made it difficult to organize people to promote change. However, the Internet has made it possible for the friends, family, and loved ones of the nearly 33,000 people annually who die by suicide to come together as a community. For example, the advocacy work of the Suicide Prevention Action Network (SPAN; spanusa.org), was instrumental in helping to pass the $82 million Garrett Lee Smith Memorial Act to fund suicide prevention programs in 36 states and tribes, as well as on college campuses. SPAN used its Web site to send legislative alerts, develop fact sheets for local organizers, publicize media guidelines

for reporting suicides, and raise awareness among politicians.

POLICY ISSUES

As with other professions, such as law, medicine, nursing, and teaching, the licensing and regulation of social work occurs at the state level. Reimbursement for services using federal assistance programs such as Medicaid, Medicare, and State Children's Health Insurance Plans is also organized at the state level. However, e-therapy has no geographical boundaries (Kanani & Regehr, 2003) and this creates a number of important and so far unresolved policy issues (McCarty & Clancy, 2002).

Licensing and Regulation

Current licensure laws do not apply to services provided outside the licensing state. Clients from one state who wish to file a complaint or lawsuit against an e-therapist in another state are in regulatory limbo. When a clinician in Pennsylvania provides services to a client in Texas, the question is, "which state's laws govern?" (McCarty & Clancy, 2002, p. 157). Getting licensed in all 50 states is impractical. Until licensing laws are updated to regulate out-of-state practice, e-therapists should assume that practicing beyond state borders violates their license (Kanani & Regehr, 2003).

Liability and Malpractice

Social workers are increasingly seen as the primary provider of mental health services and consequently are named in more malpractice lawsuits than ever before. The largest provider of malpractice insurance for social workers, NASW Assurance Services, reports that liability coverage is worldwide, unless social workers provide services for which they do not have a license (naswassurance.org). Thus the onus of responsibility lies with social workers to be clear on the limits of state licensure. Case law suggests that a professional relationship can be established by responding to an e-mail.

Confidentiality, Security, and Informed Consent

There is currently no case law that clarifies the confidentiality of e-mails, Webcam images, or text messages. Nor is there precedent for whether e-therapists must maintain a paper chart of electronic communications. E-therapists are encouraged to maintain confidentiality through the use of encryption software and secure storage (Kanani & Regehr, 2003). HIPAA rules addressing confidentiality and securing electronic transmissions apply to e-therapy (Eack & Singer, 2005). Social workers are legally required to obtain informed consent from their clients. McCarty and Clancy (2002) noted that social workers are currently unable to provide evidence of training or competence in e-therapy, nor are they able to provide evidence of the effectiveness of e-therapy. One approach to developing competency in e-therapy is for clinicians to use technology in clinical supervision to both increase their comfort level and to receive consultation on e-therapy issues (Singer, 2008).

Reimbursement

In their review of reimbursement for telemedicine, McCarty and Clancy (2002) noted that ironically, nearly all third-party reimbursement requires face-to-face contact before payment can be provided. Online therapy groups require payment at the time of services and do not bill insurance for services. Although this arrangement is adequate for financially independent consumers, the economically disadvantaged consumers who make up social work's core service recipients will be unable to afford e-therapy. Ideally, social service organizations could develop Social Work 2.0 services, such as text-based technologies like e-mail or chat, tele-health using the phone or VoIP services, or video technologies such as Webcams, to address the needs of clients for whom traditional face-to-face services are inadequate or difficult to access. However, this is unlikely until funding is available.

CONCLUSION

According to the NASW Standards for Clinical Practice (NASW, 2005a), "Clinical social workers shall have access to computer technology and the Internet, as the need to communicate via e-mail and to seek information on the Web for purposes of education, networking, and resources is essential for efficient and productive clinical practice" (p. 21). Over the coming decades, it is likely that some social work services will be entirely computer-based, whereas others will have only minimal integration with technology. As of this writing, a number of empirical studies of online-only treatments are in progress (e.g., Barnes, Harvey, Mitchell, Smith, & Wilhelm, 2007). As today's youth become tomorrow's consumers, their comfort integrating text, voice, and face-to-face communication will present new opportunities to deliver services that maximize the unique strengths of each type of communication. As our clients turn to the Internet with increasing frequency for such information as diagnosis, self-assessment, and medications (Fox, 2006), social workers have an obligation not only to be familiar with technologies and possible uses for service delivery but also to contribute to the information that consumers will find online (Bell, 2007).

WEB SITES

International Society for Mental Health Online. http://www.ismho.org.
Metanoia, portal for e-therapy. http://www.metanoia.org.
MoodGym, online cognitive behavioral therapy to prevent depression. http://www.moodgym.anu.edu.au.
NASW Standards for Technology and Social Work Practice. http://www.socialworkers.org/practice/standards/NASWTechnologyStandards.pdf.
References on Internet-assisted therapy and counseling. http://construct.haifa.ac.il/%7Eazy/refthrp.htm
The Social Work Podcast. http://socialworkpodcast.com.
State profiles of Medicare and Medicaid reimbursement. www.cms.hhs.gov/Telemedicine/03_StateProfiles.asp.

References

Banach, M., & Bernat, F. P. (2000). Liability and the internet: Risks and recommendations for social work practice. *Journal of Technology in Human Services, 17*(2–3), 153–171.

Barak, A (2007). Emotional support and suicide prevention through the internet: A field project report. *Computers in Human Behavior, 23,* 971–984.

Barnes, C., Harvey, R., Mitchell, P., Smith, M., & Wilhelm, K. (2007). Evaluation of an online relapse prevention program for bipolar disorder: An overview of the aims and methodology of a randomized controlled trial. *Disease Management and Health Outcomes, 15,* 215–224.

Bell, V. (2007). Online information, extreme communities and internet therapy: Is the Internet good for our mental health? *Journal of Mental Health, 16*, 445–457.

Christensen, H., Griffiths, K. M., & Jorm, A. F. (2004). Delivering interventions for depression by using the internet: Randomised controlled trial. *British Medical Journal, 328*(7434), 265.

Eack, S. M., & Singer, J. B. (2005). Further considerations about SQL clinic. *Psychiatric Services, 56*(8), 1023–1024.

Emmelkamp, P. M. G. (2005). Technological innovations in clinical assessment and psychotherapy. *Psychotherapy and Psychosomatics, 74*, 336–343.

Fenichel, M., Suler, J., Barak, A., Zelvin, E., Jones, G., Munro, K., et al. (2002). Myths and realities of online clinical work: Observations on the phenomena of online behavior, experience and therapeutic relationships. Retrieved October 12, 2007, from http://users.rider.edu/~suler/psycyber/myths.html.

Fox, S. (2006). Online health search 2006. Pew Internet and American Life Project. Retrieved October 1, 2007, from http://www.pewinternet.org/pdfs/PIP_Online_Health_2006.pdf.

Fox, S., & Livingston, G. (2007). Latinos online. Pew Internet and American Life Project. Retrieved October 1, 2007, from http://www.pewinternet.org/pdfs/Latinos_Online_March_14_2007.pdf.

Gergen, K. (1991). *The saturated self: Dilemmas of identity in contemporary life*. New York: Basic Books.

Hick, S. F., & McNutt, J. G. (2002). *Advocacy, activism, and the Internet: Community organization and social policy*. New York: Lyceum Books.

Horrigan, J. B. (2007). U.S. lags behind: Why it will be hard to close the broadband divide. Pew Internet and American Life Project. Retrieved October 1, 2007, from http://www.pewinternet.org/pdfs/Broadband_Commentary.pdf.

Jedlicka, D., & Jennings, G. (2001). Marital therapy on the internet. *Journal of Technology in Counseling, 2.* Retrieved from http://jtc.colstate.edu/vol2_1/Marital.htm.

Kanani, K., & Regehr, C. (2003). Clinical, ethical, and legal issues in e-therapy. *Families in Society, 84*(2), 155–162.

King, S., Engi, S., & Poulos, S. (1998). Using the Internet to assist family therapy. *British Journal of Guidance & Counseling, 26*(1), 43–52.

Krause, A., Stein, M., Clark, J., Chen, T., Li, J., Dimon, J., et al. (2002). The virtual activist 2.0: A training course. Retrieved November 1, 2007, from http://www.netaction.org/training.

McCarty, D., & Clancy, C. (2002). Telehealth: Implications for social work practice. *Social Work, 47*(2), 153–161.

McCoyd, J. L., & Kerson, T. S. (2006). Conducting intensive interviews using email: A serendipitous comparative opportunity. *Qualitative Social Work: Research and Practice, 5*(3), 389–406.

McNutt, J. G., & Menon, G. M. (2008). The rise of cyberactivism: Implications for the future of advocacy in the human services. *Families in Society, 89*(1), 33–38.

Murphy, L., & Mitchell, D. (1998) When writing helps to heal: E-mail as therapy. *British Journal of Guidance & Counseling, 26*(1), 21–32.

National Association of Social Workers. (1999). *Code of ethics*. Washington, DC: NASW.

National Association of Social Workers. (2005a). *Standards for clinical practice*. Washington, DC: NASW. Available from http://www.socialworkers.org/practice/standards/NASWClinicalSWStandards.pdf.

National Association of Social Workers. (2005b). *Standards for technology and social work practice.* Washington, DC: NASW. Available from http://www.socialworkers.org/practice/standards/NASWTechnologyStandards.pdf.

O'Reilly, T. (2005). What is web 2.0? Design patterns and business models for the next generation of software. Retrieved October 15, 2007, from http://www.oreillynet.com/lpt/a/6228.

Sarrazin, M. S. V., Hall, J. A., Richards, C., & Carswell, C. (2002). A comparison of computer-based versus pencil-and-paper assessment of drug use. *Research on Social Work Practice, 12*(5), 669–683.

Schopler, J. H., Abell, M. D., & Galinsky, M. J. (1988). Technology-based groups: A review and conceptual framework for practice. *Social Work, 43*(3), 254–267.

Singer, J. B. (Host). (2008 January 28). Phone supervision (part I): Interview with Simon Feuerman and Melissa Groman [episode 31]. *Social Work Podcast*. Podcast retrieved April 20, 2008, from http://socialworkpodcast.com/2008/01/phone-supervision-part-i-interview-with.html.

Stofle, G. S., & Harrington, S. (2002). Treating addictions on the internet: Can it be done? A dialogue. *Journal of Social Work Practice in the Addictions, 2*(2), 85–92.

White, M., & Epston, D. (1990). *Narrative means to therapeutic ends*. New York: Norton.

24 Quality Standards and Quality Assurance in Health Settings

Kenneth R. Yeager & Tina R. Latimer

Imagine for a moment that you or a family member has just received a diagnosis associated with a major disease. You have been informed that there will need to be surgery and follow-up care to ensure a full recovery. Immediately, a number of questions come to mind—what type of treatment, what surgical procedure? Who is the best surgeon? What are the risks associated with the procedures, and what is the cost? Today's consumers are driven by quality and cost data. They are used to immediate access to cost and quality in areas of electronics, car dealers, home appliances, and even quick oil change companies. Consumers are demanding similar information related health care quality, cost, and processes.

Initial information related to the status of health care quality came through the Institute of Medicine's (IOM) one-two-punch publications "To Err Is Human" (Kohn et al., 2000) followed by "Crossing the Quality Chasm" (2001). Combined, these publications outlined and quantified in detail medical errors in U.S. hospitals. In response, health care institutions across the United States intensified efforts to measure and improve care provided across a variety of domains. Immediately following release of the IOM reports, quality and operational improvement became the focus of virtually every health and behavioral health professional. Initial, efforts focused on improving patient safety. As time progresses, new wrinkles of accountability have began to emerge (Lukas et al., 2007).

Health care providers now face increasing pressure to publicly report pricing and quality data or face financial consequences through reduced reimbursement rates for entities that choose not to publicly report quality, cost, and patient satisfaction data. Under current Medicare rules, hospitals report quality data related to patient satisfaction and risk-adjusted mortality rates for heart failure. Beginning in 2009, hospitals will be required to report outpatient quality data to receive full reimbursement (Terris & Litaker 2008; Wang, Hyun, Harrison, Shortell, & Fraser, 2006).

Social work as a profession is evolving with new and challenging settings for practice, new roles for social workers, and increasing reliance on the social worker's traditional role of linking multiple disciplines. Social workers are finding that traditional roles are being expanded, and they are now expected to function across systems with a keen focus on specific care plans, outcomes, at-risk populations, and the continuum of care.

Revisions in treatment delivery systems are frequently designed to meet the demands of third-party payers and consumers alike for improvements in the quality of care provided. Today more than ever, quality improvement initiatives need to be clearly documented. Actions taken to improve care should be published and available to payers and consumers of behavioral health care services. Providers and payers are increasingly challenged to provide evidence that the purchaser and patient received a clearly defined value for their time and capital investment.

There is remarkable concern by purchasers, payers, providers, case/care managers, and consumers of health care focusing on reducing expenditures while also maximizing scarce and dwindling resources. Health and behavioral health care providers can meet the call for outcome-driven treatment by using the concepts of continuous quality improvement to answer questions of treatment value and results. Concentrated efforts to ensure the continued viability of organized behavioral health care must have a basis in fact. Documentation of the quality of services and active efforts to improve treatment process are musts if there is to be a guaranteed availability of behavioral health care in the years to come. Social workers are uniquely poised to provide such documentation. More important, if social workers fail to assume this responsibility, there will be other disciplines that will make decisions based on the specific needs of their professional practice (Stulberg, 2008).

This chapter addresses advances in knowledge related to improving the quality of health care, behavioral health care, and agency programs and the emergence of continuous quality improvement (CQI) as the process most frequently accepted by accrediting, regulatory bodies and institutions seeking to improve care (Dowd & Tilson, 1996; Lanza, Lewis, Gregory, & McMillan, 1997). CQI suggests that quality can most effectively be improved by:

- coordinating quality improvement efforts throughout your organization;
- focusing on all key activities of the organization, including direct care staff, management, agency governance, and support services;
- focusing on processes associated with care that impact directly or indirectly on patient/client outcomes, implementing effective performance measures designed to collect reliable data; and
- using accurate data analysis processes and effective presentation models for finalized data.

THE NATURE OF CQI

The shift from the quality assurance programs of the 1980s to the CQI programs of today expanded the focus of quality improvement by fine-tuning the processes, measures, and scope of quality improvement. This has been combined with an approach that builds on strengths of the organization to improve care rather than focusing on deficits. CQI activities include (Joint Commission Comprehensive Accreditation Manual for Hospitals, 1999):

- advancing the scope of assessment and monitoring to include interrelated aspects of services, including governing bodies, management, and support persons, as well as clinical process that affect client patient outcomes; focusing on the processes of services provided rather than on individualized performance.
- gathering feedback from a number of collateral sources, such as cooperating agencies, family members, significant others, support staff, and managed care entities.
- focusing continuing improvement of services provided versus implementing problem-solving processes.

Establish Leadership

Organization leadership should focus on establishing quality improvement responsibilities within the organization, establishing priorities for quality improvement, and ensuring that this approach is carried out. Tasks to be accomplished at this level include answering the following questions.

- What will be monitored?
- How will the study population be chosen?
- What staff will be responsible for completing monitoring?
- What assessment methods will be utilized?
- What issues take priority for assessment?
- How will the organization leadership assist in the monitoring process?
- How will these data be analyzed?
- How will quality-related information be disseminated?

Ongoing roles of the organization's leadership include providing support for quality initiatives, identification of areas of priority, monitoring data that impact each aspect of care, and monitoring services related to patient/client care and effective use of organizational resources in quality improvement activities (Gregoire, Rapp, & Poertner, 1995; Joint Commission, 1999; Osborne & Gaebler, 1992).

Identify Key Functions of the Organization

Most organizations focus on primary or key functions. Key functions may include access to services, recidivism rates, medication use, information management/communications, resource management, and system governance. The focus of quality improvement initiatives always involves understanding and improving the key functions of the organization (Murray & Frenk, 2000).

Organizations can identify key functions by completing an organizational inventory. This inventory should be based on a review of the range of activities associated with patient/client care; sites where care and services are provided; hours of service provided; types of patients served; and a complete range of conditions, circumstances, or diagnoses associated with services provided. The goal is to establish a targeted list of quality improvement activities leading to quality improvement within the organization (Joint Commission, 1999; Murray & Frenk, 2000).

Define the Organization's Scope of Service

Examination of the organization's scope of care and service in combination with key functions of the organization will identify areas of care and service that are important enough to warrant ongoing monitoring. Typically, high-risk and areas of heavy utilization will constitute facets of care prioritized for such monitoring. Some examples include areas of crisis intervention, medication ordering/administration, screening and monitoring of drug sensitivity, admission processes, consultation, responsiveness of staff, accuracy of documentation, and efficacy of discharge planning.

Establish Quality Indicators

Quality indicators are measures that monitor care and services. There are two major types—process indicators and outcome indicators. Process indicators monitor activities provided by the organization that will impact the care provided to a customer. Tools for CQI and effective planning associated with process indicators include brainstorming, flow charting, and cause and effect/fishbone (see Table 24.1). Outcome indicators are the end product of combined processes. These are the short-term and long-term results of services provided by the organization. Quality and improvement tools in measuring outcomes include application of standardized measures for the purpose of scaling, frequency analysis trend analysis, and control charts/analysis (Macleod Clark & Maben, 1999).

Establish Thresholds in CQI

Thresholds are decision points for action and can be predetermined by a single important aspect of care or a developing trend or pattern developing in a service area. Organizational standards, regulatory standards, and benchmarking projects with other providers of similar services are typical sources for establishing CQI thresholds (Meyer, 1999). Whatever the organization decides, the establishment of thresholds are critical trigger points for action within the organization. Thresholds should be carefully balanced to provide proactive responses to areas that have clearly demonstrated a decline in the quality of care.

Collect Data

Potential data sources should be carefully evaluated to ensure the most accurate measure of the quality indicator and the best method of analysis given the staff's skill level with data analysis and statistical processes. Data sources vary depending on the size and specialization of each organization. There are some common sources of data, such as client records, laboratory reports, utilization review findings, admission logs, inquiry calls referral sources, direct observation, and measurement of treatment processes (Berwick, 1996; Hatler, Milton, & Clark, 1999; Joint Commission, 1999). Important questions related to data collection are the following.

- Who will collect the data?
- From what source?
- Will sampling be used? If so, what size is required to be representative of services provided?
- Will data collection be concurrent or retrospective?

TABLE 24.1 Typical Tools Associated with CQI and Plan, Do, Check, Act Processes

Plan	Do	Check	Act
Brainstorming	Flowchart	Check sheet	Brainstorming
C&E fishbone diagram	Frequency analysis	(i.e., patient satisfaction)	Storyboard
Frequency analysis	Check sheets	Flowchart	
Check sheets	Outcome measures		
Control charts	(e.g., depression inventories)		
	Benchmarking		

- Who will organize the data? Will computers be used? How often will the data be analyzed/reported?

Take Action

Following review of data, the quality improvement team should determine the most appropriate and effective actions to take. Team members may implement quality improvement initiatives or forward the results of data collection to organization leadership for consideration and recommendation. Quality improvement actions should be clear and to the point, agreed on by staff and leadership, identified as specific actions, and direct in what persons are responsible for these actions when addressing identified opportunities for improvement.

Provide for Ongoing Evaluation

Ongoing monitoring and evaluation to determine if the actions taken were sufficient to improve services should be implemented. Sustaining improvement is an integral part of CQI. Processes of developing indicators, thresholds, and data analysis processes should be repeated until sustained improvement has been identified.

Disseminate Information

The final step in any continuous quality improvement initiative is the dissemination of knowledge and information. Depending on the size and structure of the organization, reporting on quality initiatives will vary.

Summary

It is important to note that several key points have been emphasized to support quality improvement efforts. They are as follows.

- Incorporate key members of leadership into CQI initiatives.
- Include interrelated governance, management, clinical, and support staff in the quality improvement process.
- Use teams consisting of members familiar with the issues being addressed in quality improvement initiatives.
- Develop CQI initiatives around the natural flow of patient/client services.

- Pay particular attention to customer and supplier relationships, both within and between areas of service.
- Give attention to processes associated with care.
- Continue to evaluate and monitor care processes over extended periods of time in an effort to improve services rather than individualized performance or isolated problem areas.

KEY ATTRIBUTES OF QUALITY IMPROVEMENT MEASURES

Once quality improvement structures and processes have been put in place, consideration must be given to key attributes of quality improvement measures. Key attributes address scientific processes and best practices for providing quality data in an effective, efficient, and sound measurement analysis and reporting processes. They are as follows.

- Use of data derived from significant clinical processes, in accordance with scientifically accepted standards, including risk-adjusted combined with appropriate transparent statistical processes.
- Data comparison is between similar institutions using processes to provide valid hospital quality comparisons.
- All reports of combined providers uses a standardized reporting format to permit comparison within and between provider groups.
  - Statistical processes are clearly described in heading and legend.
  - Data and graphical presentation should not be overcrowded or overstated
  - Percentile rankings should provide reference to actual numbers
  - Nonlinear scaling should be identified as such
  - All symbols beyond commonly accepted should be clearly described.
- Reports contain sufficient detail to permit payers, consumers, and providers to compare performance of specific indicators, procedures, or clinical functions.
- Use of "roll-up" data is limited to identifiable clinical elements that are correlated sufficiently to make the analysis statistically appropriate.

- Quality inferences should be validated by describing sample groups and data sources.
- Service cost data and satisfaction data should be reported separately from ratings based on quality indicators.

PROCESS EXAMPLES FOR CQI

Processes associated with CQI are presented here as a reminder of examples used in the text. Each example is presented to assist in the development of comprehensive, clearly defined, and effective efforts directed at providing care and services within your organization. In addition, a suggested reading list is provided to assist in the development of your organization's individualized continuous quality improvement program.

Brainstorming

A creative process usually applied with teams that facilitates generation of a high volume of ideas in a noncritical, nonjudgmental environment.

Advantages
- Encourages open participation by all members.
- Facilitates team participation, minimizing domination by any single member.
- Permits team members to build on others' ideas while remaining focused on the task at hand.

Structured brainstorming. The task is established and agreed on by all participants. Team members rotate in turns, providing input and ideas. Each idea is then recorded on a board or flip chart. This process continues until each member of the team passes (usually in 10 to 30 minutes). Team members then review the list of ideas to provide additional clarifying feedback or to eliminate any unwanted or duplicated ideas.

Unstructured brainstorming. Essentially the same as structured brainstorming, with the exception that members provide ideas freely without rotation or the requirement to pass. The process is ended when it is clear and agreed on by all participants that new ideas have been exhausted.

Cause and Effect/Fishbone Diagram

This process permits team members to identify and diagram in detail all potential causes to any given condition or area of improvement opportunity. This process is designed to identify root cause(s).

Advantages
- Leads team members to focus on the current reality rather than the history of any given issue, thus minimizing personal interests of team members.
- Facilitates consensus among team members of the root cause of quality improvement opportunities.

The process is as follows.

1. Place the problem statement in a box on the right-hand side of the paper.
2. Identify potential contributing factors, connecting them to the backbone of the fishbone chart.
3. Place identified causes in appropriate category.
4. Ask team members to identify and diagram the flow or sequence of events associated with day-to-day operational procedures/processes.

See Figure 24.1 as an example.

Process Flowchart

The flowchart process is used to graphically depict the actual flow or sequence of events in any process or service provided. The flowchart is an extremely flexible tool that permits team members to examine complex processes to identify potential problem areas and opportunities for improvement.

Advantages
- Graphically depicts the complexity of any given process. Leads to identification of redundancy and streamlining of processes.
- Provides the opportunity to identify ideal flow processes.
- Permits team members to visualize and agree on the steps involved in any given process.
- Can be used as a training aid to understand complex processes.

The process is as follows.

1. Determine the process to be evaluated and boundaries of the process (clearly determine where the process begins and ends).
2. Discuss and agree on the level of detail required to fully understand the process.

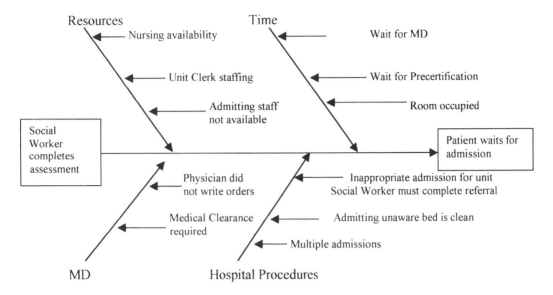

Figure 24.1 Cause and effect fishbone. (*Source:* Ohio State University Medical Center. Reprinted with permission of the Ohio State University Medical Center.)

3. List all major activities, inputs, outputs, and decisions to be made from the beginning to the end of the process.
4. Arrange the steps in the order that they are to be carried out.
5. Draw the process flowchart using the appropriate symbols (see Fig. 24.2).
6. Test the flowchart for completeness by asking, Are the symbols correct? Are the steps in the right order? Is each step correctly connected to the next step? Are the arrows indicating the correct direction?
7. Eliminate any redundancies or unnecessary complexities from the chart.
8. Review the chart with staff who complete the process on a daily basis to verify accuracy. Indicate any changes, additions, or subtractions made by staff and review with team members for approval and incorporation into the flowchart.
9. Finalize the flowchart with periodic review to assure accuracy.

See Figure 24.3 for an example.

Improvement Storyboard

The storyboard is one of many models for making improvements. This model is well suited to continuous quality improvement because it provides, through a repeatable set of steps, a process of actions designed to identify opportunities for improvement (OFIs). The storyboard provides a common language for continuous quality improvement.

Advantages

• Can be used to review information such as process indicators.
• Provides a format for review of customer data.
• Assists in narrowing project focus or to develop project purpose.
• Functions as a springboard in brainstorming activities in performance improvement initiatives.
• Can be used to summarize processes in performance improvement initiatives, including identification of key processes and individuals responsible for completion of the project.

The process is as follows.

1. Teams select the OFI that will be addressed and describe it in detail.
2. Team members define the current reality and processes surrounding the improvement

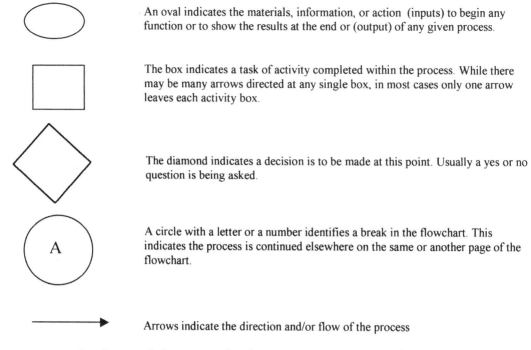

An oval indicates the materials, information, or action (inputs) to begin any function or to show the results at the end or (output) of any given process.

The box indicates a task of activity completed within the process. While there may be many arrows directed at any single box, in most cases only one arrow leaves each activity box.

The diamond indicates a decision is to be made at this point. Usually a yes or no question is being asked.

A circle with a letter or a number identifies a break in the flowchart. This indicates the process is continued elsewhere on the same or another page of the flowchart.

Arrows indicate the direction and/or flow of the process

Figure 24.2 Flowchart symbols. (Reprinted with permission. © 1994 GOAL/QPC.)

opportunity, being cautious to provide as much detail as possible.

3. Members examine all possible root causes of the OFI.

Team members with the input of organizational leadership and direct service providers should work across disciplines to develop a plan for improvement that builds on the strengths of the organization and is inclusive of specific targeted areas for improvement.

Plan

Team members should select the problem/process that will be addressed and describe the improvement opportunity. The current process should be examined to determine all possible causes of flaws currently occurring. Team members should then develop an effective action plan that targets identified process problems.

- *Do.* Team members and all involved staff should work together to implement the solution or change process.
- *Check.* Identified team members and involved staff should review and

evaluate the results of the improvement initiative.

- *Act.* Team members and involved staff should reflect on the processes of the improvement initiative and act on the knowledge gained (Deming, 1986; see Figure 24.4).

Additional Resources

Within the area of CQI, statistics play a remarkable role in measuring progress. This chapter is an overview, and examples of statistical process used in CQI can be found in these sources:

- F. N. Kerlinger, *Foundations of behavioral research* (New York: Holt, Rinehart and Winston, 1986).
- A. Rubin and E. Babbie, *Research methods for social work* (Pacific Grove, CA: Brooks/ Cole, 2001).

As with statistical processes, research and outcome design examples can be found in the following texts:

- K. M. Coughlin, A. Moore, B. Cooper, and D. Beck, *The 1998 behavioral outcomes and*

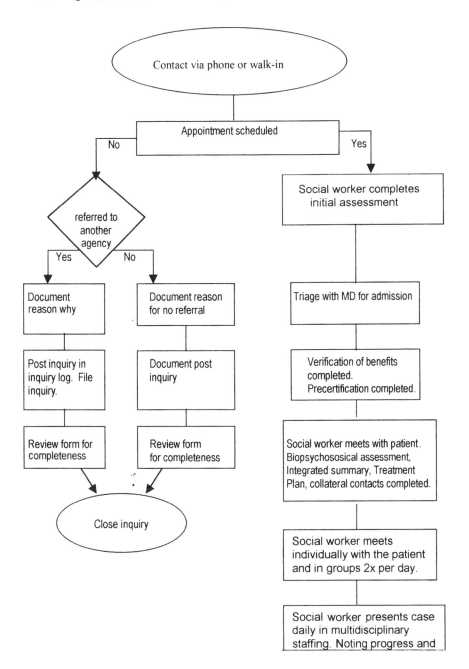

Figure 24.3 Example flowchart intrack process.

guidelines sourcebook (New York: Fulkner & Gray Healthcare Information Center, 1997).

- J. Gunther and F. Hawkins, *Making TQM work: Quality tools for human service organizations* (New York: Springer, 1999).

- D. Neuhauser, E. McEachern, and L. Headrick, *Clinical CQI: A book of readings* (Oakbrook Terrace, IL: Joint Commission on Accreditation of Healthcare Organizations, 1995).

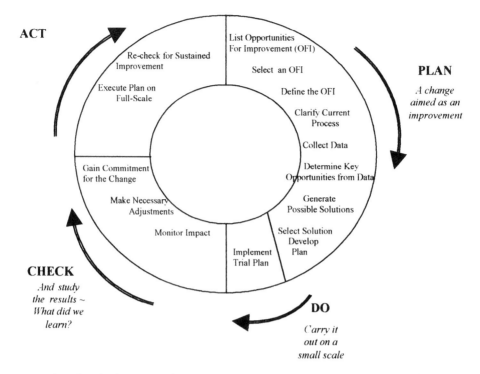

Figure 24.4 Plan, do, check, act, problem-solving/process-improvement model. Based on W. E. Deming's work (1986). (*Source:* Ohio State University Medical Center Leadership Council for Clinical Value Enhancement.)

WEB SITES

Joint Commission on Accreditation of Healthcare Organizations. http://www.jcaho.org.

Joint Commission on Accreditation of Healthcare Organizations publications list. http://www.jcaho.org/Iwapps/online/frntgt_frm.html.

References

Berwick, D. M. (1996). Harvesting knowledge from improvement. *Journal of the American Medical Association, 275*(11), 877.

Deming, W. E. (1986). *Out of crisis.* Cambridge, MA: MIT Press.

Dowd, S. B., & Tilson, E. (1996). The benefits of using CQI/TQM data. *Radiologic Techology, 67*(6), 533.

Gregoire, T., Rapp, C., & Poertner, J. (1995). The new management: Assessing the fit of total quality management and social agencies. In B. Gummer & P. McCallion (Eds.), *Total quality management in the social services: Theory and practice.* Albany, NY: Professional Development Program of Rockefeller College.

Hatler, C., Milton, D., & Clark, C. (1999). Methodological issues in performance improvement in integrated systems. *Journal of Nursing Care Quality, 13*(3), 47.

Institute of Medicine (2001). Crossing the quality chasm: A new health system for the 21st century. Washington, DC: National Academies Press.

Joint Commission Comprehensive Accreditation Manual for Hospitals. (1999). *Standards for behavioral health care: Accreditation policies, standards, and intents.* Oakbrook Terrace, IL: Joint Commission.

Kohn L, Corrigan J, Donaldson M (2000) To Err Is Human: Building a Safer Health System. Washington, DC: Committee on Quality of Health Care in America, Institute of Medicine. National Academy Press. Lanza, M., Lewis, B., Gregory, K., & McMillan, F. J. (1997). The quality function in redesigned organizations. *Journal of Nursing Care Quality, 12*(2), 27.

Lanza, M., Lewis, B., Gregory, K., & McMillan, F. J. (1997). The quality function in redesigned organizations. *Journal of Nursing Care Quality, 12*(2), 27.

Lukas, C., Holmes, S., Cohen, A., Restuccia, J., Cramer, I., Shwartz, M., et al. (2007). Transformational change in health care systems: An organizational model. *Health Care Management Review, 32*(4), 309–320.

Macleod Clark, J., & Maben J. (1999). Health promotion in primary health care nursing: The development of quality indicators. *Health Education Journal, 58*(2), 99.

Meyer, G. (1999). Quality measurement initiatives in the U.S. federal government. Presentation at the Commonwealth Fund.

Murray, C. J. L., & Frenk, J. (2000). A framework for assessing the performance of health systems. *Bulletin of the World Health Organization, 78*(6), 717.

Osborne, D., & Gaebler, T. (1992). *Reinventing government.* Reading, MA: Addison-Wesley.

Stulberg, J. (2008). The physician quality reporting initiative—a gateway to pay for performance: What every health care professional should know. *Quality Management in Health Care, 17*(1), 2–8.

Terris, D., & Litaker, D. (2008). Data quality bias: An underrecognized source of misclassification in pay-for-performance reporting? *Quality Management in Health Care, 17*(1), 19–26.

Wang, M., Hyun, J., Harrison, M., Shortell, S., & Fraser, I. (2006). Redesigning health systems for quality: Lessons from emerging practices. *Joint Commission Journal on Quality and Patient Safety/Joint Commission Resources, 32*(11), 599–611.

PART IV

Theoretical Foundations and Treatment Approaches in Clinical Social Work

25 Front Line Crisis Intervention

Yvonne M. Eaton & Albert R. Roberts

A mother calls asking for someone to take her child away because she can't deal with him anymore; a teenager upset over a recent breakup is contemplating suicide; the wife of a man in a nursing home is hearing voices telling her she needs to end his life, so she cooks a pot of poisoned stew. All of these scenarios are potential crises that social workers may encounter in their work. A crisis can be precipitated by any intensely stressful or traumatic event, as perceived by the client, in which the individual does not have the ego strengths and coping abilities to deal effectively with the presenting problem.

Crisis workers are called on to intervene rapidly with persons in the midst of acute crisis episodes. An acute crisis is not a typical stressor, such as having an argument with one's supervisor at work or getting a parking ticket. Events more likely to precipitate a crisis are traumatic or life-threatening in nature, such as the sudden death of a loved one or the devastation from a tornado or other natural disaster. Several people may experience the same hazardous or traumatic event, but they may not all react by having an acute crisis episode. An individual's ability to mobilize his or her own inner strengths, protective factors, resilience, and positive coping methods are the determinants of whether a traumatic event will escalate into a full-blown crisis state.

Persons experiencing an acute crisis episode initially experience overwhelming feelings of anxiety, agitation, volatility, depressed mood and withdrawal, helplessness, intense fears, night terrors, and/or exhaustion. These reactions culminate in a state of disequilibrium and the inability to cope and make basic rational decisions.

A thorough understanding of crisis theory and crisis intervention are essential for competent social work practice. Social workers should be educated and skilled in handling the full range of acute crises episodes because clients frequently present with difficulties and obstacles to crisis resolution and stabilization without intervention (Knox & Roberts, 2008). Crisis intervention consists of the various techniques used to assist individuals in mobilizing resources and developing plans to overcome the temporary situation. It can provide a challenge, opportunity, and turning point (Roberts, 2005). This chapter provides the practitioner with a theoretical framework, recommended strategies, and crisis intervention skills for effective resolution in all types of settings. Several issues will be addressed to assist the social worker in preparing for timely intervention. The next section begins with two case applications to set the stage for the seven-stage crisis intervention practice model.

THEORETICAL MODEL

Although social workers have been trained in a variety of theoretical models, very little coursework has prepared them with a guide to follow in dealing with crises. Roberts's (1991, 1996, 2000, 2005) seven-stage crisis intervention model provides practitioners with this invaluable framework (Fig. 25.1).

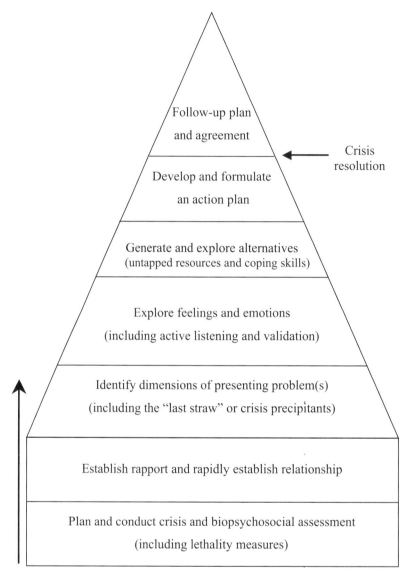

Figure 25.1 Roberts's seven-stage crisis intervention model. (© Albert R. Roberts, 1991. Reprinted by permission of the author.)

Scenario 1

Crisis Services received a call from a mother of a 14-year-old female who had barricaded herself in her bedroom. The mother indicated that she had overheard a phone conversation between the client and her boyfriend that seemed to indicate they had a fight. The mother was concerned about possible suicidal behavior because the client had a history of attempting to overdose after a relationship breakup. Roberts's (2005) seven-stage crisis intervention model was initiated.

Stage 1: Assess lethality. The mother had little information about the current mental status of the client. She indicated that she could hear her daughter crying through the locked and barricaded bedroom door. The mother further indicated that her daughter had proceeded directly to her bedroom after the upsetting phone call, so she felt her daughter did not have any medications to overdose on, but she couldn't be sure. Crisis Services immediately dispatched a worker to the residence.

Stage 2: Establish rapport. Understanding and support were two essential skills used by the crisis worker to establish a working relationship with the client. Immediately requesting her to open her bedroom door would not have been a helpful intervention. Workers need to begin where the client is. Through attentive listening, paraphrasing, and the use of open-ended questions, the worker eventually got the client to agree to let him into her room so they could hear each other better.

Stage 3: Identify problems. Luckily, the client had not yet done anything to harm herself, but she was contemplating suicide. She had a vague plan of overdosing but no available method. The client expressed that her major problem as the breakup with her boyfriend.

Stage 4: Deal with feelings. The worker allowed the client to tell her story about why she was feeling so bad. The worker was able to validate and identify her emotions. They began to explore together more effective ways of coping with her upsetting feelings.

Stage 5: Explore alternatives. Various options were discussed, including inpatient and outpatient mental health services. The client allowed her mother to join the worker and herself during this stage. The mother provided a lot of support and encouragement to the client as well. At this stage, the client indicated that she was feeling better and would not "do anything stupid."

Stage 6: Develop an action plan. The client, mother, and social worker decided on the following action plan:

1. A contract for safety was signed by the client (this is a written agreement in which the client agrees to call Crisis Services for help before she would act on any thought to harm herself or others).
2. A release of information was obtained by the social worker to contact an outpatient provider.
3. An outpatient provider was contacted, and the client received an appointment for the next afternoon.
4. Mother secured all medications per the recommendation of Crisis Services.
5. Both mother and client were given a crisis card with a number to call if any additional concerns or issues arose.

Stage 7: Follow-up. A follow-up phone call was made to the residence the next evening. The mother indicated that the client was in good spirits that day and had attended her first appointment with the therapist. The client told the crisis worker that she was doing great and thought her therapist was "really cool," and she had plans to "go shopping at the mall with friends on Saturday."

Scenario 2

Crisis Services was contacted by the police. A middle-aged woman was found on the railroad tracks with a picture of Jesus in her hand. She was indicating that she heard the voice of God and believed she could stop the train with this picture.

Stage 1: Assess lethality. Although the police had little information and no history about the client, it was a highly lethal situation as the client had responded to command hallucinations that were potentially deadly.

Stage 2: Establish rapport. The social worker attempted to develop a relationship with the client by listening to her perceptions and beliefs. When intervening with a psychotic client, it is essential not to challenge their delusional system nor to play along with it. Challenging the client's fixed beliefs can create a sense of distrust, whereas playing along with delusions or hallucinations could incite violence or mistrust when the worker fails to respond to the perceptions being experienced by the client.

Stage 3: Identify problems. Several problems were identified during the crisis assessment. The client was clearly out of touch with reality, and although not actively suicidal, she was clearly a significant danger to herself. It was also discovered that she had been noncompliant with outpatient services or medications for 3 months.

Stage 4: Deal with feelings. The social worker was able to address the client's feelings of discomfort surrounding her inability to sleep (due to the voices she was hearing). The social worker did not focus on the psychotic thought process. Due to the client's level of psychosis, the social worker was unable to deal with any underlying issues.

Stage 5: Explore alternatives. The client was unable to consider options other than that which she believed God had for her. As a result, the crisis worker had to develop an intervention strategy.

Stage 6: Develop an action plan. The crisis worker, in collaboration with the police, enacted the following plan:

1. The police maintained the safety of the client while the crisis worker pursued the possibility of an involuntary examination warrant.
2. An involuntary commitment was petitioned, and a warrant was issued.
3. The police transported the client to a psychiatric unit.
4. The client was involuntarily committed to the unit.

Stage 7: Follow-up. On a telephone follow-up with the hospital, it was determined that the hospital had started the client on medications and had located family to participate in discharge planning and assist in her care.

THE SEVEN STAGES

Stage 1: Plan and Conduct a Crisis Assessment

This involves a quick assessment of risk and dangerousness, including suicide and homicide/violence risk assessment, need for medical attention, and current drug or alcohol use (Roberts, 2005).

If possible, a medical assessment should include a brief summary of the presenting problem, any medical conditions, current medications (including dosages and last dose), and allergies. This medical information is essential to relay to medical responders attempting to treat problems such as overdoses.

A drug or alcohol assessment should include information about drugs used, amount used, last use, and any withdrawal symptoms the client is experiencing. Any knowledge of PCP ingestion should always precipitate a team crisis response with the police, owing to the likelihood of violent and bizarre behavior.

Stage 2: Rapid Establishment of Rapport and the Therapeutic Relationship

This often occurs simultaneously with stage 1. Conveying respect and acceptance are key steps in this stage. Workers must meet the clients where

they are—for example, if the client begins a conversation talking about his dog, this is where the worker should begin. They must display a non-judgmental attitude as well, ensuring that their personal opinions and values are not apparent or stated (Roberts, 2005). Poise and maintaining a calm and in-control appearance are essential skills in crisis work (Belkin, 1984).

Stage 3: Identify the Issues Pertinent to the Client and Any Precipitants to the Client's Crisis Contact

Use open-ended questions in asking the client to explain and describe the problem and to tell his or her story. This provides the crisis worker with valuable insights into the nature of the presenting problem. It is important for the client to feel that the worker is truly interested and understands him or her; this also helps build rapport and trust. Also helpful during stages 2 and 3 is using the questions of solution-focused therapy (SFT) in identifying the client's strengths and resources, which include discerning their effective past coping skills (Greene, Lee, Trask, & Rheinscheld, 2005; also see Chapter 33). Some of the SFT questions that would be helpful are:

- exception questions (identifying times that the problematic situation is not present or is just a little bit better and what is different about those times compared to the present crisis situation),
- coping questions, and
- questions for identifying past success.

Identifying client strengths and resources should also help in developing rapport and trust, because clients tend to develop comfort more quickly with someone who is not focusing only on their shortcomings—deficits, dysfunction, and failures (Greene et al., 2005).

Stage 4: Deal with Feelings and Emotions by Effectively Using Active Listening Skills

Show the client that you are listening to what he or she is saying by using encouraging statements, such as "uh huh" and "okay." These types of verbal feedback are especially important in telephone intervention. Additional skills include reflection, paraphrasing, and emotion labeling (Bolton, 1984). Reflection involves restating the words,

Suicide risk assessment should include obtaining answers to the following questions:

1. Are you/client having thoughts of self-harm? Yes ( ) No ( ) Unknown ( )
2. Have you/client done anything to intentionally hurt yourself? Yes ( ) No ( )
   If yes, describe _____
3. How long have you/client had thoughts to hurt self? _____
4. How might you/client hurt self? _____
5. Have you/client made any preparations to hurt self? Yes ( ) No ( ) Unknown ( )
   If yes, describe_____
6. Has there been a recent stressful or traumatic event in your life? Yes ( ) No ( )
   If yes, describe _____
7. Do you feel there is hope that things can improve? Yes ( ) No ( )
   If yes, describe _____
8. What keeps you/client from hurting self? _____

Homicide/violence risk assessment should include obtaining answers to the following questions:

1. Are you/client having thoughts to hurt others? Yes ( ) No ( ) Unknown ( )
   If yes, who do you/client think about hurting? _____
2. Have you verbally made any threats to hurt someone else? Yes ( ) No ( )
   If yes, please indicate what you said _____
3. Have you/client hurt anyone already?   Yes ( ) No ( ) Unknown ( )
   If yes, describe what happened _____ Whom did you hurt? _____
   What were the person's physical injuries? _____
4. How long have you/client had thoughts to hurt others? _____
5. How might you/client hurt others? _____
6. Do you have any weapons in your home? Yes ( ) No ( ) Unknown ( )
   If yes, what weapons? _____
7. Have you/client made any preparations to hurt others? Yes ( ) No ( ) Unknown ( )
   If yes, describe _____
8. What keeps you/client from hurting others? _____
9. Did the police ever arrest you? Yes ( ) No ( )
   If yes, please explain what the charges were and the outcome _____

feelings, or ideas of the client; paraphrasing involves restating the meaning of the client's words in the social worker's own language. Emotion labeling involves the worker summarizing the emotions that seem to underlie the client's message—for example, "you sound very angry."

Stage 5: Generate and Explore Alternatives by Identifying the Strengths of the Client as Well as Previous Successful Coping Mechanisms

Ideally, the ability of the worker and the client to work collaboratively during this stage should yield the widest array of potential resources and alternatives. According to Roberts (2005):

The person in crisis is viewed as resourceful, resilient . . . and having untapped resources or latent inner coping skills from which to draw upon. . . . Integrating strengths and solution-focused approaches involves jogging clients' memories so they recall the last time everything seemed to be going well, and they were in a good mood rather than depressed and/ or successfully dealt with a previous crisis in their lives. (p. 19)

Aguilera and Messick (1982) state that the ability of workers to be creative and flexible, adapting ideas to individual situations, is a key skill in effective workers.

Stage 6: Implement the Action Plan

The crisis worker should assist the client in the least restrictive manner, enabling him or her to feel empowered. Important steps in this stage include identifying persons and referral sources to be contacted and providing coping mechanisms (Roberts & Roberts, 2005). Crisis workers at Community Integration Crisis Services in Erie, Pennsylvania, use carbon copy forms to record the plan developed with worker and client. This is a useful mechanism to provide clients with phone numbers and specifics of the plan to follow, and it also provides the necessary documentation for other crisis workers to know what to encourage and reinforce on subsequent contacts with the client (Eaton & Ertl, 2000).

Stage 7: Establish a Follow-Up Plan and Agreement

Crisis workers should follow up with the client after the initial intervention to ensure the crisis has been resolved and to determine the postcrisis status of the client and the situation. This can be accomplished via phone or face-to-face contact. In a team setting, when someone other than the original crisis worker will be conducting follow-ups, a dry erase board can be a good organizational tool. At a glance, all workers can view the list of cases needing follow-up, when follow-up was requested, and items to address during follow-up contact. Of course, documentation in the client's chart would be more detailed and specific.

TRIAGE/SCREENING

According to several of the chapters in Part IV on diagnosis and assessment, the rapid and accurate clinical assessment of clients in crisis and/or trauma are one of the most critical components of intervention. The chapters in the assessment section review different types of diagnostic criteria, brief screening instruments, scales, and tools necessary to measure the severity and magnitude of personal or social dysfunction, mental disorders, and acute crisis states. For detailed information on diagnostic and assessment scales, see the remaining chapters in this part.

A triage/screening form is another useful tool for gathering and recording information about the crisis client's initial contact with the worker. According to Eaton and Ertl (2000), the triage form should include the presenting problem, safety issues (e.g., weapons on the scene and legal history), medical issues, suicide risk, homicide risk, drug and alcohol use, and essential demographic information (name, address, phone number, etc.).

To ensure timely response to all requests for services, Community Integration Crisis Services created an Intervention Priority Scale. This Intervention Priority Scale allows a number from I to IV to be assigned at the time the triage information is obtained, based on clinical criteria. Each number on the scale further corresponds to an outside time limit considered to be safe for response. Examples of priority I include requests for assistance by police/emergency personnel, suicide attempts in progress, suicidal or homicidal individuals with the means currently available, or individuals experiencing command hallucinations of a violent nature. Examples of priority II include individuals who are able to contract for safety or who have reliable supports present, those experiencing hallucinations or delusions, or those who are unable to meet basic needs. Examples of priority III include clients with fleeting suicidal ideation and no feasible plan or with mood disturbance. Priority IVs often include cases in which there is no thought to harm self or others, and there are no psychiatric symptoms present and no other minor situational crises (Eaton & Ertl, 2000).

TELEPHONE CRISIS INTERVENTION

Telephone contact provides the security of anonymity and is frequently the first point of contact for a person in crisis. Additional benefits of phone crisis intervention include convenience, immediate access to assistance, and information and support (Waters & Finn, 1995). The level of responsiveness and quality intervention provided by the telephone crisis worker can make all the difference in determining whether the client will accept further services. Telephone crisis intervention should be available 24 hours per day and staffed by workers specifically trained in crisis techniques. Facilities that provide this level of service should have caller identification on their phone systems and should develop criteria, policies, and procedures for tracing calls as necessary to ensure safety. Telephone crisis centers should have a variety of human resource publications at their disposal to use as reference guides in assisting callers.

MOBILE CRISIS INTERVENTION

Mobile crisis intervention involves individual or team response to the scene of a crisis. The benefits of providing mobile crisis response include increased access to services, additional insights by assessing clients in their natural environments, and quicker intervention (Zealberg, Santos, & Fisher, 1993).

There are two model 24-hour mobile crisis intervention units whose staff provide phone crisis intervention, home visits, mobile transport to hospitals and mental health facilities, crisis intervention for domestic violence victims, and psychiatric emergency services for suicidal adolescents and adults. The first comprehensive program is located in Erie County, Pennsylvania (Eaton & Ertl, 2000), and the second is located in Atlanta, Georgia (Ligon, 2005).

Of primary concern when providing mobile crisis intervention is worker safety. Team response by two trained staff members, partnering with other providers, and use of two-way radios are ways to maximize worker safety. Strong alliances with local police departments should be developed to both support mutual aid to providers and promote the best care for the client (Eaton & Ertl, 2000; Roberts & Roberts, 2000). Membership of police commanders on agency boards, joint training, and letters of commendation are ways to strengthen this collaborative relationship.

Mobile crisis workers should always be attuned to potential dangers. Greenstone and Leviton (1993) suggest adherence to the following safety tips: approach the scene slowly, survey the surrounding area, listen before knocking for any clues/altercations occurring, stand off to the side of doors when knocking, know your entrances and exits, note any objects that could be used as potential weapons, and evaluate verbal and nonverbal behavior of the client as well as other subjects present (Eaton & Ertl, 2000).

WALK-IN CRISIS INTERVENTION

Walk-in crisis intervention allows for greater privacy and control for clients and gives workers access to additional assistance if the situation escalates. Walk-in settings should include low-stimulation office space in which both the client and the crisis worker have equal access to exits. Panic buttons are also recommended with an established procedure for response by the organization if a button is pressed. Greenstone and Leviton (1993) suggest the following for safety in the office: enter elevators only after checking for other passengers, enter rooms after clients, and remove any potential weapons from desks—for example, paperweights, scissors, letter openers.

CRITICAL INCIDENT STRESS MANAGEMENT

Crisis intervention is one of the most demanding and stressful fields in which a social worker may be employed (Moursund, 1998). Crisis workers may be exposed to gruesome and life-threatening events. Eaton and Ertl (2000) indicate that incidents such as completed suicides, dead bodies, and threats and assaults on crisis workers warrant the use of critical incident stress management techniques. Keeping workers safe and ensuring that they can find satisfaction in their work as well as in their personal lives require that they receive support in managing their own stress. Critical incident stress management (CISM) can play an important part in providing that support to workers in crisis intervention programs. It includes a wide variety of techniques and interventions for individuals exposed to life-threatening or traumatic events (Mitchell & Everly, 1993). There are more than 300 crisis response teams using a standardized model of CISM services internationally, as listed by the International Critical Incident Stress Foundation (Everly, Lating, & Mitchell, 2005). The use of CISM techniques allows workers the opportunity to discuss the traumatic event, promotes group cohesion, and educates workers on stress reactions and coping techniques.

CONCLUSION

Social workers are increasingly being expected to treat individuals in a brief, focused manner. Managed care restrictions and concerns of violence are placing pressure on practitioners to be skilled in effectively assessing risks and needs and in providing rapid intervention. Roberts's (1991, 2000, 2005) seven-stage model provides social workers with a framework to follow. The aforementioned skills will assist practitioners in facilitating effective crisis resolution.

Systematic research and crisis intervention outcome studies have made significant progress in identifying best practices. A recent meta-analysis of 36 crisis intervention studies (Roberts & Everly, 2006) indicated that 8 or more hours of intensive in-home crisis intervention over a 1- to 3-month period was consistently found to be highly effective. In addition, multicomponent CISM, also known as group crisis intervention, involving a minimum of three sessions was found to be highly effective in facilitating crisis resolution. The third key finding of the meta-analysis was that crisis intervention is very beneficial but not a panacea, and booster sessions are often necessary several months to a year after completion of the initial crisis intervention program (Roberts & Everly, 2006). In summary, statistical analysis of 36 studies determined that intensive crisis intervention is effective in facilitating crisis resolution and bolstering crisis mastery. More research needs to be planned and carried out to improve crisis assessment, early intervention, and crisis intervention protocols for at-risk individuals and groups in the aftermath of crisis-inducing and trauma-inducing hazardous events.

WEB SITES

The American Academy of Experts in Traumatic Stress. http://www.aaets.org.

The Crisis Intervention Network. http://www.crisisinterventionnetwork.com.

The International Critical Incident Stress Foundation, Inc. http://www.icisf.org.

National Alliance on Mental Illness Crisis Intervention Team, Technical Assistance Resource Center. http://www.nami.org/template.cfm?Section=CIT2.

References

Aguilera, D., & Messick, J. (1982). *Crisis intervention: Theory and methodology,* 4th ed. St. Louis, MO: Mosby.

Belkin, G. (1984). *Introduction to counseling,* 2nd ed. Dubuque, IA: William C. Brown.

Bolton, R. (1984). *People skills.* Englewood Cliffs, NJ: Prentice Hall.

Eaton, Y., & Ertl, B. (2000). The comprehensive crisis intervention model of Community Integration, Inc. Crisis Services. In A. R. Roberts (Ed.), *Crisis intervention handbook: Assessment, treatment, and research,* 2nd ed. (pp. 373–387). New York: Oxford University Press.

Everly, G. S. Jr., Lating, J. M., & Mitchell, J. T. (2005). Innovations in group crisis intervention: Critical incident stress debriefing and critical incident stress management. In A. Roberts (Ed.), *Crisis intervention handbook: Assessment, treatment, and research,* 3rd ed. (pp. 221–245). New York: Oxford University Press.

Greene, G. J., Lee, M., Trask, R., & Rheinscheld, J. (2005). How to work with clients' strengths in crisis intervention: A solution-focused approach. In A. R. Roberts (Ed.), *Crisis intervention handbook: Assessment, treatment, and research,* 3rd ed. (pp. 64–89). New York: Oxford University Press.

Greenstone, J., & Leviton, S. (1993). *Elements of crisis intervention: Crises and how to respond to them.* Pacific Grove, CA: Brooks/Cole.

Knox, K. S., & Roberts, A. R. (2008). The crisis intervention model. In N. Coady & P. Lehmann (Eds.), *Theoretical perspectives for direct social work practice: A generalist-eclectic approach,* 2nd ed. (pp. 249–274). New York: Springer.

Ligon, J. (2005). Mobile crisis units: Frontline community mental health services In A. R. Roberts (Ed.), *Crisis intervention handbook: Assessment, treatment, and research,* 3rd ed. (pp. 602–618). New York: Oxford University Press.

Mitchell, J., & Everly, G. S. Jr. (1993). *Critical incident stress debriefing: An operations manual for the pre-vention of traumatic stress among emergency services and disaster workers.* Ellicott City, MD: Chevron.

Moursund, J. (1998). *The process of counseling and therapy,* 3rd ed. Englewood Cliffs, NJ: Prentice Hall.

Roberts, A. R. (1991.). Conceptualizing crisis theory and the crisis intervention model. In A. Roberts (Ed.), *Contemporary perspectives on crisis intervention and prevention* (pp. 3–17). Englewood Cliffs, NJ: Prentice Hall.

Roberts, A. R. (1996). The epidemiology and definitions of acute crisis in American society. In A. R. Roberts (Ed.), *Crisis management and brief treatment: Theory, technique, and applications* (pp. 16–33). Chicago: Nelson-Hall.

Roberts, A. R. (2000). An overview of crisis theory and crisis intervention. In A. R. Roberts (Ed.), *Crisis intervention handbook: Assessment, treatment, and research,* 2nd ed. (pp. 3–30). New York: Oxford University Press.

Roberts, A. R. (2005). Bridging the past and present to the future of crisis intervention and crisis management. In A. R. Roberts (Ed.), *Crisis intervention handbook: Assessment, treatment, and research,* 3rd ed. (pp. 3–34). New York: Oxford University Press.

Roberts, A. R., & Everly, G. S. Jr. (2006). A meta-analysis of 36 crisis intervention studies. *Brief Treatment and Crisis Intervention: A Journal of Evidence-Based Practice,* 6(1), 10–21.

Roberts, A. R., & Roberts, B. S. (2005). A comprehensive model for crisis intervention with battered women and their children. In A. R. Roberts (Ed.), *Crisis intervention handbook: Assessment, treatment, and research*, 3rd ed. (pp. 441–482). New York: Oxford University Press.

Waters, J. A., & Finn, E. (1995). Handling client crises effectively on the telephone. In A. R. Roberts (Ed.), *Crisis intervention and time-limited cognitive treatment* (pp. 251–289). Thousand Oaks, CA: Sage.

Zealberg, J., Santos, A., & Fisher, R. (1993). Benefits of mobile crisis programs. *Hospital and Community Psychiatry, 44*, 16–17.

26   Fundamentals of Brief Treatment

Jan Ligon

Time and monetary resources can be limited for many social workers. Indeed, managed care models for behavioral health and other social services have radically changed how services are delivered, the amount time allocated, and reimbursement limits for services (Chambliss, 2000; Corcoran & Vandiver, 1996). In addition, limitations in funding for many public and not-for-profit agencies can adversely affect the level of resources, which often results in the need to limit time so as to serve as many clients as possible within the agency's constraints (Goldstein & Noonan, 1999). Finally, brief services are simply the nature of practice and therefore the norm in many settings (schools, hospitals, home health services, and others). Studies cited by Miller, Hubble, and Duncan (1996) note that clients expect for the duration of services to be brief, and the vast majority conclude services in four to eight sessions. Therefore, it is essential for social workers and administrators to be familiar with brief models of practice.

Following an overview of the roots and theory of brief practice, this chapter summarizes the key assumptions, practice components, and approaches to brief social work practice, outcome measures, evidence of effectiveness, limitations, and a case example to illustrate an application of the chapter content.

ROOTS AND THEORY

A time-limited perspective has been dated to the work of psychiatrists with World War II veterans in the mid-1940s (Budman & Gurman, 1988), although more contemporary approaches can be traced to the work of Milton Erickson in the 1950s (de Shazer et al., 1986). Many of the theoretical approaches, assumptions, and techniques of brief work as it is practiced today are grounded in the endeavors of two centers—Mental Research Institute's (MRI) Brief Therapy Center in Palo Alto, California and the Brief Family Therapy Center (BFTC) in Milwaukee, which provided training and resources for 25 years (1982–2007).

MRI began in 1959 and approached working with clients from a theoretical perspective that differed from the more common approaches of that time in several ways.

1. Problems were viewed as normal occurrences in life; this stance was a radical departure

from theories grounded in pathology, deficits, and dysfunction.

2. The purpose of treatment was to make changes, preferably small ones. Insight and meaning, the cornerstone of some treatment, was not the goal of working with clients.

3. The role of the clinician was to be an active and engaged participant who works with what the client brings.

4. The model explicitly limited clients to a maximum of ten sessions based on the assumption that "a time limit on treatment has some positive influence on both therapists and patients" (Weakland, Fisch, Watzlawick, & Bodin, 1974, p. 144).

Unlike MRI, the BFTC approach did not specify a number of sessions, and the focus was on developing solutions to problems (de Shazer et al., 1986). Both MRI and BFTC note the importance of how the therapist views people, their problems, and solutions.

Erickson, a psychiatrist, was an important influence on those involved in the development of brief approaches to treatment. Although he claimed to not have a theoretical basis for his work (O'Hanlon & Weiner-Davis, 1989), two of his terms are fundamental to brief work. The first is *expectancy*; simply stated, this is the social worker's belief that people and situations can change and the lives of people can be better. This concept is deceptively simple; it is one thing to understand the term and another to embrace the concept to the extent that ones practice connotes this sincere belief. Clients pick up on this very quickly, and the effective social worker truly knows that things can be better; it may not happen, but it can. The object is to set the client up for a positive self-fulfilling prophecy. The second term is *utilization*; the work is conducted with what the client brings (O'Hanlon & Weiner-Davis, 1989). In fact, clients brings vast resources with them, including their past successes, survival skills, life wisdom, and stories that are used extensively in brief treatment models (Saleebey, 2005).

CORE PRACTICE SKILLS AND TECHNIQUES

Numerous authors have published detailed accounts of many techniques and strategies that can be employed in brief practice models (Budman & Gurman, 1988; de Shazer et al., 1986; de Shazer & Dolan, 2007; Dewan, Steenbarger, & Greenberg, 2004; Hudson & O'Hanlon, 1991; Miller et al., 1996; O'Hanlon & Weiner-Davis, 1989; Walter & Peller, 2000; Weakland et al., 1974). However, there are five core areas of practice that are common to most approaches: (1) the use of time, (2) the approach to problems and solutions, (3) the use of language, (4) the development and measurement of goals, and (5) the use of a strength's perspective.

Use of Time

Obviously, time is a key concern in brief work, and given that most clients complete fewer than eight sessions, the use of time is actually a very manageable task. It is important to not view time as only that which occurs in the therapy session. Many clients arrive early, and this time can be used to complete not only initial paperwork but also tools that can be helpful in a session, such as rapid assessment instruments to measure problems (Corcoran & Fischer, 2000). Next, clients can be asked about pretreatment change; that is, what has changed since the time the client made the appointment for the first session and the occurrence of the first session? Weiner-Davis found that when asked this "two-third of the clients noticed changes" (de Shazer et al., 1986, p. 215). By inquiring about what is now different and how the client was able to get those pretreatment changes to occur, the social worker can begin to hear information that will help uncover client and family strengths and form solutions for change.

Approach to Problems and Solutions

The therapist's approach to problems is critical. First, it is important to acknowledge and validate clients' problems. If the social worker moves immediately into developing goals and solutions without acknowledging and hearing the clients' problems and issues, the client may not move forward (Hudson & O'Hanlon, 1991). However, to get stuck in a repetitive cycle of only acknowledging the problems will impede forward movement. Next, it is important to ask clients if they have had a similar problem before and to inquire about how they handled it. This information is essential for use in further identifying client strengths, developing goals, and beginning to view potential solutions. Finally, it is important to not get bogged down in the details of the problem but to find out when the problem doesn't happen, which are the times noted as the "exceptions to their problems" (de Shazer & Dolan, 2007, p. 4). This is particularly helpful when working with couples; it is easy to find that an entire session's time has been consumed with accusations about the other partner and pleas for understanding about how it really is in the relationship. The brief therapist cannot afford to lose precious time in this manner, and ultimately it is not helpful to the clients. Therefore, it is important to acknowledge, find the exceptions, and move on (Hudson & O'Hanlon, 1991).

Use of Language

The choice of words in brief treatment is critical; language needs to connote movement, openness, the future, and a feeling that is action-oriented. For example, the early works of MRI (Weakland et al., 1974) noted the importance of discussing *what* is happening or *how* things could be changed. The choice of the word *why*, however, seeks deeper understanding or may imply the need to delve into history; this is not helpful in brief work. O'Hanlon and Weiner-Davis (1989) note that the use of *yet* is helpful; "you haven't found the right job *yet*." Similarly, *when* can keep the dialogue moving forward, which is of key importance in moving toward solutions; "*when* you are working again" implies hope and a future.

Development and Measurement of Goals

At the core of brief work is the development, implementation, and measurement of goals. De Jong and Miller (1995) note that a well-formed goal is one that is important to the client, in the client's language, small, concrete, specific, behavioral, seeks the presence rather than the absence of something, is realistic, worthy, and is a step toward an end (see case example). Clients often do not accomplish goals because they are more of a vision than a goal. For example, "to become independent" or "to live a clean and sober life" are admirable desires for a client, but both are too big. Such goals can be overwhelming and a set-up for failure; both are only attainable through steps leading toward each goal. Therefore, if goals are carefully developed with the client, the likelihood of follow-through is improved, and clients may even do more than the goal once they find

that they are able to experience some initial success. Once measurable goals have been developed, it is important to look at outcomes assessment.

Like all service providers, social workers and agencies are increasingly required to document the outcomes of interventions and programs. Two common methods, self-anchored scales and rapid assessment instruments (RAIs), are helpful and simple ways to quantify outcomes. A self-anchored scale is very easy to develop (see case example) by merely asking the client to rate a problem or situation, one at a time, by scoring it from low to high (1 to 5 or 1 to 10). RAIs for use in assessing a wide range of problems are available from a two-volume sourcebook (Corcoran & Fischer, 2000). Such measures can be repeated at the beginning and end of treatment to establish change from pretest to posttest; measures may also be taken at established increments with the scores plotted to illustrate change over time. RAIs are particularly helpful during the assessment process to determine the severity of such problems as depression, anxiety, or substance use. Some instruments are also available at no cost from the Internet, including the Center for Epidemiologic Studies Depression Scale (CES-D), a long-standing RAI for depression (Radloff, 1977). The Michigan Alcohol Screening Test is a well-established tool for assessing the severity of alcohol problems.

Strengths Perspective

Working from a strengths perspective (Saleebey, 2005) is the antithesis of the approach used by many large human services systems that are based on pathology, dysfunction, symptoms, diseases, and the assignment of diagnoses. Inherent in these approaches, such as the medical model, is an assumption that the service provider is the expert, and the patient is advised what needs to be done by the expert. Social work practice from a strengths perspective recognizes that resources can be tapped in both the social worker and the client, as well as the community. Therefore, the relationship is approached as collaborative and avoids hierarchy; the intent is to empower the client to actively collaborate in the change process. A strengths perspective acknowledges that the client possesses knowledge, abilities, resilience, coping, and problem-solving skills that are there to be employed. Certainly people get stuck, become overwhelmed, or experience events that render them unable to fully make use of their strengths. It is important to identify and amplify strengths so that the client can go back and rediscover what has already worked for him or her in the past. Therefore, the role of the social worker is to facilitate the process, serve as a bridge to the client's own resources, move ahead, and seek solutions.

CASE EXAMPLE

This brief case example is based on an actual client and illustrates some of fundamental techniques reviewed in this chapter. Katie, age 31, called to make an appointment with the employee assistance program (EAP) offered by her company. The service provided three free visits, although additional sessions could be added if needed. During a brief telephone screening, she stated that she had been feeling particularly down about her job and life and thought maybe it would help to talk to a professional because things were not getting better. She was seen for her first appointment 3 days after the initial call.

Katie completed a self-reported instrument for depression (Radloff, 1977) as well as an initial information form in the lobby prior to her appointment. After brief introductions and an overview of the EAP services, Katie discussed that she feels very stuck in her life; she has been in the same job, with a modest salary, for 6 years. She has a high school education and realizes that this has held her back; she wants to move on in her life but finds herself in a rut. The dialogue continues.

Client: It seems lately that I'm not only feeling stuck, but I'm cranky; I cry easier lately.

Worker: You seem to feel trapped, but you want to move on in your life. [Acknowledge] You mentioned feeling down, crying more; how would you rate just how down you've been feeling from 1 to 10 with 1 being really down and 10 feeling on top of the world? [Measurement]

Client: Oh, I think like a 4 lately.

Worker: A 4, and the rating scale you completed for me shows about the same, a moderate level of feeling down. Have you had thoughts of wanting to hurt yourself? [Acknowledgment]

Client: No, never, and I don't drink or do drugs, thank goodness. [Strength]

Worker: That's good to know. Are you taking any medications right now for any reason?

Client: No, I don't take anything, I'm lucky; I'm in good health. And it's not like I'm clueless about my situation; I know that getting a college education would help. I need to do that.

Worker: So I'm hearing that you are a determined woman; you want more. [Validate, strengths] Can you tell me *what* I would *see* you doing *when* you have the college degree? [Language]

Client: Oh that's an easy one; I'd be teaching first grade. That's exactly what I want to do.

Worker: That's great, maybe you've already thought some about the process of getting from here to there. What *will* you do first *when* you begin the process? [Validate, language, goals]

Client: Oh I've thought a lot! I guess it's pretty straightforward—enroll and start classes.

Worker: Do you know which school or program you might pursue?

Client: Oh yes, the college is near my house; I think they have a program, I need to check.

Worker: Would it be possible to pick up some information and bring it next time? [Goals]

Client: Sure, I'll do that. I can stop by after work one day this week. [Goals]

When Katie returned for the next appointment, she had not only brought the catalog but had made an appointment with the admissions counselor for the elementary education program for the next week. This exemplifies the importance of goals that are realistic, small, seek the presence of something (the information), and takes a step toward an end (a college education).

CAVEATS AND CAUTIONS

There are reports that brief therapy has been found to be helpful for many types of problems (Miller, Hubble, & Duncan, 1996) and that clients have been found to be satisfied with only one, two, or three sessions (Ligon, 1996). Brief interventions have been found to be useful in helping children with grief and loss issues (Monroe & Kraus, 2005), for inpatient mental health clients (Durrant, Clark, Tolland, & Wilson, 2007; Lamprecht et al., 2007), for the treatment of substance abuse (Center for Substance Abuse Treatment, 1999), with couples (Davidson & Horvath, 1997), with students ages 11–14 in a school (Newsome, 2005), and with incarcerated adolescents (Tripodi, Springer, & Corcoran, 2007). De Jong (Chapter 33) further summarizes three meta-analyses on solution-focused brief treatment that found small to moderate treatment effects with different populations. However, no single model is universal (Stalker, Levene, & Coady, 1998), and brief therapy is not suitable to all client situations.

Although brief approaches view problems in a different manner than some other methods, they do not excuse the social worker from ethical and competent practice, including the assessment of mental status, medical concerns, and risk for suicide, homicide, child abuse, domestic violence, or other factors.

LOOKING AHEAD

It is common in social work for terms, interventions, and techniques to evolve and change over time. When managed care quickly moved behavioral health services to a time-limited model, the interest in brief techniques escalated. Now the use of this approach is more in the mainstream of methods from which a social worker may choose, depending on the situation. Social workers are likely to continue to operate in environments that are tight on financial and human resources. Therefore, it will be important for them to continue to master the basic skills of brief practice in future years. Used appropriately by qualified and trained social workers, brief therapy models offer an approach that has been found to be helpful to a wide range of clients across many problem areas. Brief social work practice fits well with the profession's values of being with the client, self-determination, empowerment, and respect and dignity for the value and worth of each individual.

WEB SITES

Bill O'Hanlon. Free materials on goal setting. http://www.billohanlon.com.
CSAT/SAMHSA. Free materials on brief substance abuse treatment. http://ncadi.samhsa.gov.
Mental Research Institute, Brief Therapy Center. http://www.mri.org/btc.html.

References

Budman, S. H., & Gurman, A. S. (1988). *Theory and practice of brief therapy.* New York: Guilford.

Center for Substance Abuse Treatment. (1999). *Brief interventions and brief therapies for substance abuse.* DHHS Publication no. (SMA) 99-3353. Washington, DC: Center for Substance Abuse Treatment.

Chambliss, C. H. (2000). *Psychotherapy and managed care.* New York: Allyn & Bacon.

Corcoran, K., & Fischer, J. (2000). *Measures for clinical practice,* 3rd ed. New York: Free Press.

Corcoran, K., & Vandiver, V. (1996). *Maneuvering the maze of managed care: Skills for mental health practitioners.* New York: Free Press.

Davidson, G. N. S., & Horvath, A. O. (1997). Three sessions of brief couples therapy: A clinical trial. *Journal of Family Psychotherapy, 11,* 422–435.

De Jong, P., & Miller, S. D. (1995). How to interview for client strengths. *Social Work, 6,* 729–736.

de Shazer, S., & Dolan, Y. (2007). *More than miracles: The state of the art of solution-focused brief therapy.* New York: Haworth Press.

de Shazer, S., Berg, I. K., Lipchik, E., Nunnally, E., Molnar, A., Gingerich, W., et al. (1986). Brief therapy: Focused solution development. *Family Process, 25,* 207–221.

Dewan, M. J., Steenbarger, B. N., & Greenberg, R. P. (2004). *The art and science of brief psychotherapies.* Washington, DC: American Psychiatric Publishing.

Durrant, C., Clarke, I., Tolland, A., & Wilson, H. (2007). Designing a CBT service for an acute inpatient setting: A pilot study. *Clinical Psychology and Psychotherapy, 14,* 117–125.

Goldstein, E. G., & Noonan, M. (1999). *Short-term treatment and social work practice.* New York: Free Press.

Hudson, P. & O'Hanlon, W. (1991). *Rewriting love stories: Brief marital therapy.* New York: Norton.

Lamprecht, H., Laydon, C., McQuillan, C., Wiseman, S., Williams, L., Gash, A., et al. (2007). Single-session solution-focused therapy and self-harm: A pilot study. *Journal of Psychiatric & Mental Health Nursing, 14,* 601–602.

Ligon, J. (1996). Client satisfaction with brief therapy. *EAP Digest, 16*(5), 30–31.

Miller, S. D., Hubble, M. A., & Duncan, B. (Eds.). (1996). *Handbook of solution-focused brief therapy.* San Francisco: Jossey-Bass.

Monroe, B., & Kraus, F. (Eds.). (2005). *Brief interventions with bereaved children.* New York: Oxford University Press.

Newsome, W. S. (2005). The impact of solution-focused brief therapy with at-risk junior high students. *Children and Schools, 29,* 83–90.

O'Hanlon, W., & Weiner-Davis, M. (1989). *In search of solutions: A new direction in psychotherapy.* New York: Norton.

Radloff, R. S. (1977) CES-D scale: A self-report depression scale for research in the general population. *Applied Psychological Measurement, 1,* 385–401.

Saleebey, D. (2005). *The strengths perspective in social work practice* 4th ed. New York: Allyn & Bacon.

Stalker, C. A., Levene, J. E., & Coady, N. F. (1999). Solution-focused brief therapy—one model fits all? *Families in Society, 80,* 468–477.

Tripodi, S. J., Springer, D. W., & Corcoran, K. (2007). Determinants of substance abuse among incarcerated adolescents: Implications for brief treatment and crisis intervention. *Brief Treatment and Crisis Intervention, 7,* 34–39.

Walter, J. L., & Peller, J. E. (2000). *Recreating brief therapy: Preferences and possibilities.* New York: Norton.

Weakland, J. H., Fisch, R., Watzlawick, P., & Bodin, A. M. (1974). Brief therapy: Focused problem resolution. *Family Process, 13,* 141–168.

27 Common Factors in Therapy

James W. Drisko

The common factors model advances the view that client attributes, clinician attributes, the therapeutic relationship, and expectancies are more important to creating therapeutic change than is the use of specific therapy techniques. Drawing on considerable empirical research, this model augments more simplistic comparisons of psychotherapy and service outcomes and recognizes the complexity of human interactions. Principles derived from the model suggest that attention to a wide variety of factors can enhance psychotherapy and service outcomes. This chapter describes the common factors model, introduces its evidence base, and outlines core principles for clinicians to consider in practice with a wide range of clients.

Common factors refers to a way of thinking about the "active ingredients" that generate change in psychotherapy and social work services. Simply put, the common factors perspective views the client–worker relationship, client factors, social environmental factors, and similarities in worldview between client and social worker as more important to creating change than any specific intervention technique. That is, rather than highlighting specific techniques, like Ellis's ABC technique for tracking irrational beliefs, the common factors approach views the larger interpersonal context (like being able to establish a therapeutic alliance) as most important to generating change. This perspective challenges researchers and scholars to take a broader view of what makes our services effective. This broader view fits well with client interests, the practice wisdom of social workers, and key social work values.

The common factors perspective also fits well with clients' own ideas about change. On a February afternoon, snow had been falling for several hours. I was unsure if I should leave my office—one client had not showed up, and another canceled, but I had one more scheduled. Later, when Mr. B came in to the office, he had a big grin on his face. He said, "I was driving over here and conditions were awful. I was sure you'd have left to go home yourself. Then I got near and even from the street I could see the lights were on. I was really sure you wouldn't be here, but you were! Now I know you care about me." As we talked about his experience, it became clear that my reliability and trustworthiness meant more to him than anything I did as a specific treatment plan. He said he had learned to doubt words spoken by people in authority, and always judged more by actions than words. A few weeks later Mr. B said his girlfriend, who had been negative on his therapy, had also changed her view because of this story. She had begun to be supportive, which made it easier for him to invest in our work together. Our work flourished.

A SCIENTIFIC UNDERSTANDING REQUIRES KNOWLEDGE OF OUTCOMES AND THEIR CAUSES

Both social work practitioners and researchers are concerned with knowing "what works" to help a given client and what aspects of intervention lead to improvement. There are two questions here. First, what is the outcome of intervention, and second, what caused the change? It is important to keep in mind that determining outcomes and identifying the active ingredients that lead to it are both necessary components of a full scientific understanding. Documenting outcomes alone, without knowing what lead to it, is not an adequate scientific understanding of a problem (Drisko, 2000).

Based on compilations of high-quality studies of adults with depression and anxiety problems, there is strong evidence that psychotherapy leads to improvement compared to untreated comparison groups. How much improvement is found? Wampold (2001), synthesizing several studies using meta-analysis, provides a summary statistic called effect size from 0.75 to 0.85 for the impact of these treatments. Effect size statistics range from 0.00 to about 3.0 in value. A 0.75 to 0.85 effect size is characterized as a large impact. According to Rosenthal (1984), it means that the clients completing therapy are better off than 79 percent of people without treatment. This effect size compares favorably to most other medical and social science effect sizes. This research shows that many treatments work to yield improvement on these disorders!

A great deal of recent outcome research focuses on comparing one treatment model or technique to another model on the same disorder. This is useful to determine what treatments are most effective. However, the way in which such research is done tends to emphasize only specific techniques and ignores the impact of the client–clinician relationship and other nontechnique factors that may also influence outcomes. This is because many researchers assume all providers offer sufficient warmth, empathy, and genuineness to clients (e.g., Truax & Carkhuff, 1967). If this is a core condition of psychotherapy, some

say, it does not need to be specified in psychotherapy research because it is always present. On the other hand, to ignore such factors may lead to misleading or incomplete conclusions about what causes change.

As long ago as 1936, Rosenzweig stated that the outcome of different psychotherapies is likely to be about the same. His view was based on the idea that common factors—not specific therapeutic techniques—were indeed the key ingredients of psychotherapeutic success. In the mid-1970s, a research method called meta-analysis was developed. Meta-analysis is a method for combining the results of many studies on the same topic to determine an overall rating of effectiveness, usually an effect size. Since then, several meta-analyses of the outcome of psychotherapy with adults who suffer from depression and anxiety have been completed. Since 1977, few enduring differences across types of psychotherapy have been demonstrated. Even as the technology of meta-analysis has been refined, a common conclusion is that there are no or minimal differences across therapies on these key adults problems (Ahn & Wampold, 2001; Grawe, Caspar, & Ambuhl, 1990; Smith & Glass, 1977; Smith, Glass, & Miller, 1980; Wampold, 2001; Wampold et al., 1997). Furthermore, researchers did not find differences in effect sizes by using a method intended to control for researcher allegiance to particular therapeutic models. Different therapies seem to produce very similar outcomes for these adult disorders.

To be thorough, some meta-analyses of psychotherapy outcomes have reported differences among treatments (see Drisko, 2004; Wampold, 2001). Still the question remains: if psychotherapy works, what factors within it lead to change? Given these findings of no or minimal difference between therapies, perhaps technique is not the main or sole active ingredient leading to change.

COMMON FACTORS IN HEALING

Psychiatrist Jerome Frank studied the characteristics of "healers" in several cultures worldwide. He identified several similarities in their practices despite clear diversity in their belief systems. He concluded that several factors might lead to change in psychotherapy, much as it did in the healing practices of other cultures (Frank, 1971). Based on Frank's work, Lambert (1992) estimated of the percentage of variance attributable to each of the four common factors in psychotherapy.

Lambert (1992) identified four key common factors. These are (1) extratherapeutic factors, (2) the therapeutic relationship, (3) technical factors (specific therapeutic techniques), and (4) expectancy or placebo effects. He estimated that 40 percent of the variance in outcome is due to extratherapeutic factors, 30 percent is due to the therapeutic relationship, 15 percent is due to technical factors, and 15 percent is due to expectancy. This common factors model might explain why meta-analytic research finds no or minimal difference between therapies: extratherapeutic factors and the therapeutic relationship may outweigh the impact of technique and are rarely included in outcome research.

EXPLORING THE COMMON FACTORS

Extratherapeutic Factors: The Client

There are factors in all clients' lives that will support change and others that may limit or impede change. Specific to the client, Lambert and Asay (1984) list:

- level of motivation,
- capacity to trust,
- ability to tolerate affect,
- intelligence
- psychological mindedness, and
- resilience.

These factors combine with the number and severity of challenges the client faces at the same time and the client's ability to identify and stay with a focal problem in the treatment. Outcomes will likely be better where these influences are present and positive; outcomes will probably be worse where they are absent or pose challenges. These findings suggest that pretherapeutic interventions may be helpful or even crucial for some clients to engage and make use of specific therapies.

Prochaska (1999) and others state that readiness to change is another client factor that influences capacity to change. Prochaska suggests that treatment readiness may not be a stable trait but a variable or cyclic phenomenon, so efforts to maximize it may enhance overall effectiveness (or may undermine efforts when treatment readiness is not present). Further, recent work by Castonguay and Beutler (2006) identifying the principles of change behind treatments that have been demonstrated empirically to be effective suggests that very intensive, highly structured intervention from the outset is associated with positive outcomes for people with personality disorders who may prove inconsistent in motivation. To enhance motivation, pretherapeutic interventions may be useful along with attention or involvement with social supports. Motivational interviewing with the client, as well as the client's family and other supports, and working through differences early on are helpful approaches.

Extratherapeutic Factors: The Client's Context

Social workers know that the client's context can play an important role in sustaining involvement in psychotherapy or in undermining this effort (Lambert, 1992). On the other hand, the lack of family and social support—or their absence, or active hostility—can hinder therapeutic change (Drisko, 2004). Similarly, peer and workplace supports can serves as aids, hindrances, or neutral influences to therapy. For many people, spiritual supports and support groups sharing common concerns (such as the therapeutic problem or other issues) can also influence therapy participation and outcome. All this suggests that pretherapeutic or early therapeutic work to engage the support of key people in the client's life will be likely to reduce dropout risk, enhance motivation for change, and limit undermining influences. On a larger scale, neighborhood resources or challenges may ease involvement in therapy or increase the effort required to enter and remain in therapy. It is also clear that the meaning of engaging in psychotherapy, and its very appropriateness as a source of improvement, differs across cultures (e.g., Sue, Zane, & Young, 1994). Thus, the wisdom of seeking therapy and support for the undertaking over time may not be simple or steady for many potential clients. In this case, the following are helpful:

- similarity of race/ethnicity between client and clinician,
- similarity of religious background, or
- acceptance or openness to the client's religious/spiritual views (Castonguay & Beutler, 2006).

Extratherapeutic Factors: The Policy and Agency Context

Though he is not a social worker, Lambert (1992) concentrated on the inner world of the client and did not address the impact of policy and agency factors on the client. I argue that for a client to enter and remain in therapy, several agency factors must be present (Drisko, 2004).

- Clients need to know that services are available.
- Clients need to have trust that the services are likely to help.
- Services must also be accessible—within reasonable geographic proximity, accessible to transportation.
- Services should have no significant barriers for people with disabilities.
- Services also must culturally sensitive to the potential client.
- Services should be user-friendly, even inviting, to people under stress and doubtful of being treated with respect and care.

Contacts prior to meeting the clinician (e.g., the receptionist, agency financial staff) also may aid or hinder engagement in the therapeutic work. Costs should be reasonable, and there should be no undue obstacles in referral procedures and management paperwork. In addition, reimbursement to service agencies must offset the cost of doing business and be sufficient to create supportive working conditions (pay, diversity, supervision, and site) for all staff. Sadly, reimbursement rates for many clinical services are low and may fail to fully meet the actual cost of delivering the service. In turn, insensitive events in the agency may undermine a fragile client's ability to engage with clinical services (Drisko, 2004).

Castonguay and Beutler (2006) also note that clients with a high level of impairment are less likely to benefit from therapy than those with a better level of functioning at pretreatment. In addition, clients diagnosed with a personality disorder are less likely to benefit from treatment than those without a personality disorder. Together, these extratherapeutic factors influence client engagement in services, dropout rates, and overall outcomes. They may account for more of the variance in treatment outcomes than any of the four common factors described by Lambert (1992).

The Therapeutic Relationship

The therapeutic relationship is usually what clinicians label as the *common factor* in psychotherapy (Rosenzweig, 1936). Some believe it is the single most important curative factor (Orlinsky, Grawe, & Parks, 1994). Generally, the psychotherapy literature since the 1950s emphasizes that the caring, warmth, empathy, and acceptance demonstrated by the therapist is vital to therapeutic result. Lambert (1992) noted that relationship factors—as perceived by a given client—are central to a positive and productive therapeutic relationship. In addition, Lambert (1992) and Lambert and Hill (1994) noted that mutual affirmation (which may include accurate and sufficient affective attunement) as well as active encouragement to support affective, cognitive, and behavioral changes, including the taking of risks by the client and clear acknowledgment of change and new mastery, are all elements of the therapeutic relationship. In addition, the importance of recovering from missteps or failures of attunement is noted to be associated with positive outcomes in the practice literature. For all clients, empathy is another vital aspect of the therapeutic relationship. Bachelor (1995) found that the types of empathy (nurturant, insight-oriented, and collaborative) were more apparent and useful at different phases of intervention over time. Key aspects of the therapeutic relationship include:

- affective attunement;
- mutual affirmation, including support for risks and appreciation of positive changes made;
- making efforts to discuss and resolve missteps or failures of attunement;
- goal congruence; and
- use of varying types of empathy over the course of therapy.

The Therapeutic Relationship: Clinician Attributes

Characteristics of the clinician also impact on service outcomes. Castonguay and Beutler (2006) report that:

- clinician effectiveness is increased by demonstration of open-mindedness, flexibility and creativity.

- a secure attachment pattern in the clinician appears to facilitate treatment processes.
- positive impact is likely increased if the clinician is comfortable with emotionally intense relationships and able to tolerate his or her negative feelings toward the client.
- If clinicians are open, informed, and tolerant of various religious views, treatment effects are likely to be enhanced.
- If clients have a preference for religiously oriented therapy, benefit is enhanced if clinicians accommodate this preference.

Consistent with social work's values and ethics, the clinician's openness to differences of many kinds, including religious views and the ability to accommodate and work with religious differences, enhances therapeutic effectiveness.

Technique

Although this chapter addresses common factors rather than specific therapeutic techniques, this does not mean that knowledge of a range of intervention models and the skills to implement them are unimportant. Rather than viewing common factors as a simple contrast to technique, it is optimal to think of a "both/and" relationship. Social workers do need to be knowledgeable, skilled, and well supervised on therapeutic techniques and consistently attentive to the common factors active in intervention.

In defining principles of therapeutic change based on empirically effective treatments, Castonguay and Beutler (2006) report some technique-based findings.

- Therapy is likely enhanced if a strong working alliance is established and maintained.
- Clinicians should attempt to facilitate a high level of collaboration with client during therapy.
- The most effective treatments are those that do not induce client resistance.
- Therapists are likely to resolve alliance ruptures when addressing such ruptures in an empathetic and flexible way.
- Clinicians should not use relational interpretations excessively.
- When relational interpretations are used, they are likely to facilitate improvement if accurate.
- Treatment benefit may be enhanced when interventions are responsive to and consistent with the client's style and level of problem assimilation.

Social workers should bear in mind that training to maximize professional use of self during interventions can be viewed as a set of techniques. Such broad techniques require specific training and close supervision to master effectively. Knowledge and skills in these areas can enhance the effectiveness of interventions.

Expectancy

Offering hope and an expectancy that change is possible can be a powerful aid to generating change. Clients often feel stuck, bruised, or defeated by prior unsuccessful efforts to change. Clients of color or other socially marginalized groups may have suffered from insults and micro-aggressions from people with power over them. Thus, building a positive expectancy that change is possible may be a therapeutic gain in itself, as well as a catalyst for further progress.

Many studies show that placebos can generate useful change. Such studies indicate how important expectancies can be.

One final finding of Castonguay and Beutler (2006) is that clients with high level of impairments respond better when offered long-term intensive treatment than to nonintensive and brief treatment, regardless of treatment model and type of treatment. This provocative finding suggests that people who do not expect to change or who doubt that others will truly work to support their change respond well to intensive and enduring interventions that build hope and demonstrate investment and care from others.

FUTURE PRACTICE APPLICATIONS

The common factors model encourages practitioners and researchers to take a larger, more encompassing view of what leads to change in psychotherapy and social work interventions. Techniques are indeed important but may not the most active ingredients in generating change in human interactions. Both meta-analyses using sophisticated statistical models and principles drawn from analyses of interventions that have been demonstrated to be effective indicate that common factors are important sources of change. In the future, social workers may want to examine more closely how to make use of these factors in their day-to-day practices because attention to common factors will enhance therapeutic outcomes. Practitioners are wise to take a broad view of common factors that may help their clients make and sustain change. Attention to a combination of client, extratherapeutic, relationship, and technique factors may still achieve the best overall results in psychotherapy.

WEB SITES

Counseling resource on "What Works in Therapy." http://counsellingresource.com/books/what-works.

Ingredients of psychotherapy. http://www.psychpage.com/learning/library/counseling/ingredthx.html.

Psychotherapy Integration. http://www.minddisorders.com/Ob-Ps/Psychotherapy-integration.html.

Social work resources. http://www.drisko.net.

References

Ahn, H., & Wampold, B. (2001). Where, oh where, are the specific ingredients? A meta-analysis of component studies in counseling and psychotherapy. *Journal of Consulting and Clinical Psychology, 48*, 251–257.

Bachelor, A. (1995). Clients' perception of the therapeutic alliance: a qualitative analysis. *Journal of Counseling Psychology, 42*(3), 323–337.

Castonguay, L., & Beutler, L. (2006). *Principles of therapeutic change that work.* New York: Oxford University Press.

Drisko, J. (2000). Conceptualizing clinical practice evaluation: Historical trends and current issues. *Smith College Studies in Social Work, 70*, 185–205.

Drisko, J. (2004). Common factors in psychotherapy effectiveness: Meta-analytic findings and their implications for practice and research. *Families in Society 85*(1), 81–90.

Frank, J. D. (1971). Therapeutic factors in psychotherapy. *American Journal of Psychotherapy, 25*, 350–361.

Grawe, K., Caspar, F., & Ambuhl, H. (1990). The Bernese comparative psychotherapy study. *Zeitschrift for Klinische Pscyhologie, 19*, 287–376.

Lambert, M. J. (1992). Implications of outcome research for psychotherapy integration. In J. Norcross & J. Goldstein (Eds.), *Handbook of psychotherapy integration* (pp. 94–129). New York: Basic Books.

Lambert, M. J., & Asay, T. P., (1984). Patient characteristics and their relationship to psychotherapy outcome. In M. Herson, L. Michelson, & A. Bellack (Eds.), *Issues in psychotherapy research* (pp. 313–359). New York: Plenum.

Lambert, M. J., & Hill, C. E. (1994). Assessing psychotherapy outcomes and processes. In: A. E. Bergin & S. L. Garsfield (Eds.), *Handbook of Psychotherapy and Behaviour Change,* (pp. 72–113). New York: John Wiley & Sons.

Orlinsky, D., Grawe, K., & Parks, B. (1994). Process and outcome in psychotherapy—Noch Einmal. In A. Bergin & S. Garfield. (Eds.), *Handbook of psychotherapy and behavior change: An empirical analysis,* 4th ed. (pp. 152–209). New York: Wiley.

Prochaska, J. (1999). How do people change and how can we change to help more people? In M. Hubble, B. Duncan, & S. Miller (Eds.), *The heart and soul of change: What works in therapy* (pp. 227–255). Washington, DC: American Psychological Association.

Rosenthal, R. (1984). *Meta-analytic procedures for social research.* Beverly Hills, CA: Sage.

Rosenzweig, S. (1936). Some implicit common factors in diverse methods of psychotherapy: "At last the Dodo said, 'Everybody has won and all must have prizes.'" *American Journal of Orthopsychiatry, 6,* 412–415.

Smith, M., & Glass, G. V. (1977). Meta-analysis of psychotherapy outcome studies. *American Psychologist, 32,* 752–760.

Smith, M., Glass, G. V., & Miller, T. L. (1980). *The benefits of psycotherapy.* Baltimore: John Hopkins University Press.

Sue, S., Zane, N., & Young, K. (1994). Research on psychotherapy with culturally diverse populations. In A. Bergin & S. Garfield (Eds.), *Handbook of psychotherapy and behavior change: An empirical analysis,* 4th ed. (pp. 783–820). New York: Wiley.

Truax, C. B., & Carkhuff, R. R. (1967). *Toward effective counseling and psychotherapy: Training and practice.* Chicago: Aldine.

Wampold, B. E. (2001). *The great psychotherapy debate: Models, methods and findings.* Mahwah, NJ: Erlbaum.

Wampold, B. E., Mondin, G. W., Moody, M., Stich, F., Benson, K., & Ahn, H. (1997). A meta-analysis of outcome studies comparing bonafide psychotherapies: Empirically 'all must have prizes.' *Psychological Bulletin, 122*(3), pp. 203–215.

28 Task-Centered Practice

Anne E. Fortune, William J. Reid,
& Deborah P. Reyome

The task-centered model is a short-term, problem-solving approach to social work practice (Marsh & Doel, 2005; Reid, 1992, 2000; Reid & Epstein, 1972). The model has variations for work with families and groups (Fortune, 1985), case management (Colvin, Lee, Magnano & Smith, 2008; Naleppa & Reid, 2003), nonvoluntary clients (Rooney, 1992), and generalist practice (Tolson, Reid, & Garvin, 1994). The model has been used worldwide in most types of social work settings (Fortune, McCallion, & Briar-Lawson, in press).

BASIC CHARACTERISTICS AND PRINCIPLES

Focus on Client Problems

Focus of service is on specific problems that clients explicitly acknowledge as being of concern to them.

Problem-Solving Actions (Tasks)

Change is brought about primarily through problem-solving actions (tasks) undertaken by clients outside of the session. The primary function of the treatment session is to lay the groundwork for such actions. In addition, tasks by practitioner and others provide a means of effecting environmental change in the client's interest.

Integrative Stance

The model draws selectively on theories and methods from compatible approaches—for example, problem solving, cognitive-behavioral, cognitive, and family structural. It also provides methods that can be used with other approaches. For example, a core intervention—the task planning and implementation sequence—can be used with any intervention model. The sequence provides structured but flexible guidelines to help clients carry out between-session tasks (homework).

Planned Brevity

Service is generally planned short term by design (6 to 12 weekly sessions within a 4-month period). Extensions beyond these limits are possible.

Collaborative Relationship

Relationships with clients are both caring and collaborative. The practitioner shares assessment information and avoids hidden goals and agendas. Extensive use is made of the client's input in developing intervention strategies not only to devise more effective interventions but also to develop problem-solving abilities.

Empirical Orientation

Preference is given to methods and theories tested and supported by empirical research. Hypotheses and concepts about the client system are grounded in case data. Speculative theorizing about the client's problems and behavior is avoided. Assessment, process, and outcome data are systematically collected. Numerous studies, including eight controlled experiments, have been used to test and improve the model (Fortune, McCallion & Briar-Lawson, in press; Reid, 1997).

OUTLINE OF THE MODEL FOR INDIVIDUALS AND FAMILIES

I. Initial phase (sessions 1–2)
1. Discussion of reasons for referral, especially with nonvoluntary client(s).
2. Exploration and assessment of client-acknowledged target problems.
3. Formation of the service contract, including problems and goals to be addressed, explanation of treatment methods, agreement on durational limits.

4. Development and implementation of initial tasks (see II.3).

II. Middle phase (each session follows the format below)

1. *Problem and task review.* Problems and tasks are reviewed each session to determine progress. The task review provides a record for both the social worker and client as to how the task has gone. This record is also useful in supervision and provides data generally about the kinds of tasks that are effective for particular problems.

2. *Identification and resolution of obstacles to task accomplishment.* If the client has experienced difficulty with the task, internal and external obstacles are reviewed and an effort is made to resolve them. If they cannot be resolved, an alternative task is developed. The practitioner can use whatever interventions may be effective in helping the client overcome the obstacle. For instance, the practitioner may help clients modify distorted perceptions or unrealistic expectations interfering with work on the task. Obstacles involving the external system, such as interactions between a child and school personnel or the malfunctioning of a welfare bureaucracy, may be addressed and a plan for resolving them developed.

3. *Task planning and implementation sequence.*
   - *Task selection.* It is always important to involve the client in task selection through such questions as, "What do you think you might be able to do about this problem?" Or, "Of the things you have tried, what has worked best for you?" Thus, task selection begins with a dialogue in which the client's ideas are elicited. The practitioner tries to build on these ideas and, if needed, suggest others. The practitioner does not assign the task to the client. Practitioners, caregivers, and service providers on case management teams may also take on between-session tasks.
   - *Task agreement.* An agreement between practitioner and client on the client's task may occur after alternative possibilities have been sorted out

and the best selected. Generally an agreement at this point concerns the global nature of the client's proposed action and not the detail, which is developed subsequently. If the client appears to accept the task, agreement may be delayed until planning (see following item) has been completed. In any case, the client's agreement to attempt the task should be explicit.

- *Planning specifics of implementation.* Once a task has been selected, the practitioner and client work on a plan to carry it out. Tasks suggested by practitioners normally need to be customized and fleshed out in collaboration with the client. If the social worker suggests that an alcoholic client participate in a self-help program, an implementation plan might involve determining how such a program might be located, how the client might learn something about it, when he or she would plan to attend the first meeting, and so on. The task plan normally calls for implementation prior to the next session. Regardless of the form of the plan, the practitioner attempts to make sure that it has a high probability of at least some success. It is better to err on the side of having the task be too easy rather than too difficult, because it is important that clients experience success in their work on their problems. Successful performance can create a sense of mastery, which can augment problem-solving efforts. For example, if it seems that the task of attending a self-help meeting would have a low chance of being carried out, the task could be revised to one of locating a group and getting information about it. For the plan to work, it is essential that the client emerge with a clear notion of what he or she is to do. Generally, an effort is made to spell out details of implementation that are appropriate for the task and fit the client's style and circumstances. For some tasks and some clients, a good deal of detail and structure might be called for. For example, if the client is likely to procrastinate about doing the task, it may be important to spell out the time and place where the task will be done. For other tasks and clients, a minimum of structure and detail may make sense. For example, planning may be more general with a task requiring a good deal of on-the-spot improvisation. In any case, the main actions of the task should be clarified, unless they are readily apparent. For example, if the task calls for a mother to show approval if her daughter cleans her room, ways of showing approval and what is meant by cleaning the room should be discussed.

- *Establishing incentives and rationale.* The social worker and client develop a rationale or purpose for carrying out the task if it is not already clear. "What might you gain from doing the task?" would be an appropriate question. The practitioner reinforces the client's perception of realistic benefits or points out positive consequences that the client may not have perceived.

- *Identifying and resolving anticipated obstacles.* An important practitioner function in task planning is to help the client identify potential obstacles to the task and to shape plans so as to avoid or minimize these obstacles. This function is implicitly addressed when the practitioner presses for specificity in the task plan. As details of how the tasks are to be done are brought out, possible obstacles can be identified through "what if?" questions. For example, suppose the task is "Discuss with your partner ways she can help you stay sober." Among the questions the client can be asked is: "What if your partner starts to lecture you?" More generally, the practitioner can ask clients to think of ways that a task might fail. Potential obstacles and ways of resolving them can be discussed. If the obstacles appear too formidable, the task can be modified or another developed. Often the proposed task relates to previous efforts by the clients. Consideration of these efforts and how they may have fallen short can provide another means of identifying potential obstacles. For example, a task under consideration for Mrs. S. is to reward her son with praise

and approval for completing his homework. Previous discussion of the mother–son relationship revealed her difficulties in expressing positive sentiments toward the boy. Her difficulty in doing so might be identified as an obstacle.

- *Guided practice, rehearsal.* The social worker may model possible task behavior or ask clients to rehearse what they are going to say or do. Modeling and rehearsal may be carried out through role-playing, where appropriate. For example, suppose the client's problem is social phobia. The task selected is to "speak up in a class you are attending." The practitioner might take the role of the instructor, and the client could rehearse what he or she might say. The roles could then be reversed, with the worker modeling what the client might say. Guided practice is the performance of the actual (as opposed to simulated) task behavior by the client during the interview; thus, a child may practice reading or a couple may practice communication skills. Guided practice can also be extended to real-life situations—a practitioner might accompany a client with a fear of going to doctors to a medical clinic.

- *Summarizing and recording the task plan.* As a final step, the practitioner and client should go over the plan in summary fashion. In complex tasks, it is often useful to elicit from the client the essentials of the plan. The client is asked to present the plan as he or she sees it. The practitioner can then underscore the essential elements of it or add parts the client has left out. Summarizing the plan gives the practitioner the opportunity to convey to the client the expectation that it will be carried out and that his or her efforts will be reviewed. "So you will try to do _____. We'll see how it worked out next time we meet." Writing tasks down with a copy for the client and another for the practitioner is another useful technique, especially when tasks are complex or when several people are to perform tasks.

4. *Implementation of tasks between sessions.* Clients and (depending on the case) practitioners and others carry out tasks.

III. Terminal phase (final session)

1. Review of target problems and overall problem situation.
2. *Identification of successful problem-solving strategies used by client(s).* Emphasis is on establishing client's success in problem solving and using strategies in similar situations.
3. *Discussion of other ways to maintain client gains.* Maintenance may include "failsafe planning" (what to do if a problem crops up) and self-reinforcement.
4. Discussion of what can be done about remaining problems.
5. *Making decisions about extensions.* Decisions are jointly made by client and practitioner. Extensions are usually time-limited and focused on particular problems or goals. In most cases, a single brief extension will suffice, but in some cases additional ones may be needed. The critical consideration is what can be accomplished by extending service. Often cases that show little progress by the twelfth visit will show no more progress by the twentieth.

WORK WITH GROUPS

In group treatment, small groups—usually from four to eight people—are formed around problems they share in common, such as school failure or issues in caregiving. Members specify problems and undertake tasks related to them, as in individual work. However, in group treatment members assist one another in formulating problems and in work on tasks, including task planning and review. Group members may act as "buddies" between meetings.

Group norms are shaped to encourage task-centered work—for example, expectation that clients will take action and reinforcement of successes. Group processes are used to enhance intervention—for example, reviewing task progress in pairs.

FUTURE

The future of this model suggests that it will continue to grow in applications and research.

CASE ILLUSTRATION: SHARON

Sharon, 50 years old, was recently diagnosed with fibromyalgia. She has a lifetime history of depressive episodes that have not been responsive to medication. Her marriage of 15 years is stable but strained by the past year's health challenges. Her faith has helped her to cope with her health issues, but she is tired and discouraged since the diagnosis of fibromyalgia.

Initial Phase

Sharon described her problem as being very "down" on herself. She is filled with anger over the pain and her body failing her. "I don't like myself. I hate my body. I feel like I need too much. I'm never going to get better. I don't know why God is doing this to me."

She agreed to two target problems: her low self-esteem and coping with the fibromyalgia. She and the practitioner tentatively agreed on three intervention strategies: reversing her negative self-talk, enhancing her support network, and affirming her faith. They contracted to meet for 12 sessions over 3 months.

For an initial task, Sharon suggested building on a motivational healing tape her friends had given her. She liked the testimonials of healing and agreed to create some self-affirmations of her own. She thought of (1) "I love and accept myself just the way that I am," (2) "My body is healing every day in every way," (3) "God is with me and I am at peace." With prompting, she added a phrase about her strengths: "I am kind, compassionate, and understanding." Sharon agreed to repeat one of these ten times each day, beginning when she first woke up.

Middle Phase

At the beginning of the next session (and all sessions after), Sharon reviewed her task: she had repeated the phrases some days, but not others. One issue was remembering to do it, another was her concern that the phrases might be blasphemy, when it was so evident to God that she was unworthy (obstacles). When she did repeat the phrases, she felt a little better for a while. At least, she admitted, they stopped her from "running herself down" as she usually did.

To overcome the obstacles, Sharon suggested writing down the phrases on index cards. On another index card, she wrote down when she should say them: specific times such as waking, eating lunch, and mid-afternoon, and when certain things happened, such as when the pain was so intense she caught herself thinking that God had abandoned her. The practitioner suggested another task: to talk to her pastor about making sense of hard times and God. This task was also intended to strengthen Sharon's support system.

During each session in the middle phase, Sharon and the practitioner reviewed task progress, problem status, and obstacles to task accomplishment. Sharon became adept at using the self-affirmation phrases, adding to them, and substituting them whenever she caught herself thinking something self-defeating. She was relieved when the pastor suggested that God was not vengeful, punishing, or targeting her specifically. She attended several Bible study groups but thought the discussion too trivial, not dealing with real-life issues like her pain. At her physician's suggestion, Sharon began walking, and she enlisted her husband as a companion. He complained with every step, which Sharon found humorous, and both returned from walks cheerful.

Terminal Phase

In the last few sessions, the practitioner reminded Sharon how many sessions remained. She wanted to "continue meeting forever," but did not have further goals to work on. They agreed to end as they had initially contracted.

In the final session, Sharon and the practitioner reviewed the status of the target problems. She felt much better: "Not great, but not down on myself. I can learn to live with the pain, and I know God and others will help me." Sharon walked regularly, mostly with her husband. Her pain levels were more manageable, and this had given her hope. She viewed her husband as a support instead of another obstacle. Her support system was not as strong as the practitioner wished, but Sharon talked occasionally with her pastor and felt God was a support and not condemning her.

Sharon and the practitioner discussed ways for her to continue working on her problems. She planned to carry her index cards and add to her self-affirming phrases. They rehearsed what she would do if she found herself thinking negative thoughts or fearing God's wrath (failsafe

planning). The practitioner reviewed Sharon's considerable problem-solving skills and suggested how to use them if new problems came up. Sharon mused about joining a yoga/stretch class at church for companionship and extra exercise. They discussed how comfortable they are with each other, and how ending their meetings was sad, frightening, and proud of accomplishment all mixed together. At the end, they hugged.

WEB SITE

The Task-Centered Web pages. Contains comprehensive listing of resources for the task-centered model of social work. http://www.task-centered.com.

References

Colvin, J., Lee, M., Magnano, J., & Smith, V.(2008). The Partners in Prevention Program: Further development of the task-centered case management model. *Research on Social Work Practice.* First published on January 7, doi:10.1177/1049731507 310195 .

Fortune, A. E. (Ed.). (1985). *Task-centered practice with families and groups.* New York: Springer.

Fortune, A. E., McCallion, P., & Briar-Lawson, K. (In press). *Advancing practice research in social work for the 21st century.* New York: Columbia University Press.

Marsh, P., & Doel, M. (2005). *The task-centred book.* London: Routledge with Communitycare.

Naleppa, M. J., & Reid, W. J. (2003). *Gerontological social work: A task-centered approach.* New York: Columbia University Press.

Reid, W. J. (1992). *Task strategies: An empirical approach to social work practice.* New York: Columbia University Press.

Reid, W. J. (1997). Research on task-centered practice. *Social Work Research, 21,* 132–137.

Reid, W. J. (2000). *The task planner.* New York: Columbia University Press.

Reid, W. J., & Epstein, L. (1972). *Task-centered casework.* New York: Columbia University Press.

Rooney, R. H. (1992). *Strategies for work with involuntary clients.* New York: Columbia University Press.

Tolson, E. R., Reid, W. J., & Garvin, C. D. (1994). *Generalist practice: A task-centered approach.* New York: Columbia University Press.

29   The Life Model

Alex Gitterman

The development of the Life Model began in 1972 when Professors Carel Germain, Mary Funnye Goldson, and I were asked to reconceptualize the first-year practice courses of a 2-year sequence in social work practice. We set out to develop an integrated social work practice curricula in place of the traditional casework, group work, and community organization methods. We assumed that there were many common concepts and methods in working with people, no matter what size of the system. We deeply believed that services should be based on client needs and preferences rather than the worker's method specialization. In conceptualizing an integrated method, we realized that there were also some distinctive knowledge and skills such as those required to form groups or influence communities, organizations, and legislative processes.

Historically, the profession experienced ideological conflicts between those who emphasized bringing about social change in behalf of social justice, the *cause*, as the primary characteristic of social work, and those who emphasized *function* as the primary characteristic of social work practice, that is, the technologies used by practitioners to bring about individual change (Lee, 1929). Based on our practice and teaching experiences, Germain and I were committed to integrate these traditions. Hence, our second aim was to develop a model that began to build bridges between the treatment and social reform traditions of the profession. Clearly, both cause and function must be hallmarks of practice and education for practice if social work is to be relevant in the new era. Melding cause and function is an essential part of life-modeled practice (Schwartz, 1969, 1971, 1976).

ECOLOGICAL PERSPECTIVE

Ecology, a biological science that examines the relation between living organisms and all the elements of the social and physical environments, provides the theoretical perspective for an integrated practice and the theoretical foundation for the Life Model (Germain, 1981; Germain & Gitterman, 1986b, 1987, 1995, 1996; Gitterman, 1996a; Gitterman & Germain, 1976, 2008). Ecological metaphors offer the theoretical lens for viewing the exchanges between people and their environments. The metaphors include level of fit, adaptation, stress and vulnerability, and resilience. Principles from deep ecology further enhance our understanding that all phenomena are interconnected and interdependent as well as dependent on the cyclical processes of nature. These principles include the interdependence of networks, the self-correcting feedback loops, and the cyclical nature of ecological processes.

Over the life course, people strive to deal with and improve the *level of fit* with their environments. When people feel positively and hopeful about their own capacities and about having their needs fulfilled, and when they view their environmental resources as responsive, they and their immediate environments are likely to achieve a reciprocally sustaining condition of *adaptedness*. Adaptive person–environment exchanges *reciprocally* support and release potentials. Ecological theory perceives "adaptedness" and adaptation as action-oriented and change-oriented processes. Neither concept avoids issues of power, exploitation, and conflict that exist in the world of nature as well as in the social world of human beings. Adaptedness and adaptation are not to be confused with a passive "adjustment" to the status quo (see Germain & Gitterman, 1987; Gould, 1987).

In contrast, when people feel negatively and unhopeful about their own capacities and about having their needs fulfilled, and when they view environmental resources as unresponsive, they and their environments are likely to achieve a poor level of adaptive fit. Stress is the outcome of a perceived imbalance between environmental demand(s) and capability to manage it with available internal and external resources. To relieve the stressful situation, the level of person–environment fit must be improved. This is accomplished by an active change in either people's perceptions and behaviors, in environmental responses, or in the quality of their exchanges.

Many clients who are poor live in oppressive social and physical environments. They are exposed on a daily basis to economic, social and psychological discrimination. In coping with destructive environments, some people steel themselves and mobilize inner strengths and resiliencies—they become survivors rather than victims. Others internalize the oppression and turn it against themselves through self-destructive behaviors, such as substance abuse and unprotected sex. Still others externalize the oppression, strike back, and vent their rage on others less powerful then they through such behaviors as violence, crime, and property destruction. Readily accessible targets often include family members, neighbors, and community residents. These maladaptive person–environment exchanges reciprocally frustrate and damage both human as well as environmental potentials.

In deep ecology, living systems are viewed as networks interacting with other systems of networks—"in intricate pattern of intertwined webs, networks nesting within larger networks" (Capra, 1996, p. 82). These interdependent networks share certain common properties. Their intricate patterns are nonlinear—they go in all directions and develop feedback loops, which allow them to self-regulate by learning from and correcting mistakes. Through the process of self-regulating and self-organizing, new behaviors, patterns, and structures are spontaneously created and the networks' equilibrium constantly evolves. The interdependence of networks and the self-correcting feedback loops allow the living system to adapt to changing conditions and survive disturbances. Thus, interdependence of networks, the self-correcting feedback loops, and the cyclical nature of ecological processes are three basic principles of deep ecology.

SOCIAL WORK PURPOSE AND FUNCTION

The Life Model conceptualizes the purpose of social work as improving the level of fit between people and their environments, especially between people's needs and their environmental resources. This conception of professional purpose is further operationalized through two interrelated professional functions: (1) to help people mobilize and draw on personal and environmental resources to eliminate or at least alleviate life stressors and the associated stress; and (2) to influence social and physical environmental forces to be responsive to people's needs (Germain & Gitterman, 1979, 1980, 1986a, 1996; Gitterman & Germain, 1976, 2008; Gitterman 1996b).

Helping People with Life Stressors

Over the life course, people encounter stressors. These stressors emerge in one or more aspects of living and include difficult life transitions and traumatic life events, environmental pressures, and dysfunctional transactions in collective life (family, group, and community). In life-modeled practice, practitioners and clients assess and intervene in single and multiple life stressors.

Life transitions include stressful developmental transitions, difficult social transitions, and traumatic life events. Developmental transitions, such as adolescence, impose new demands and require new adaptations and coping. Whereas puberty is biological, adolescence is a social construction. The norms related to developmental changes vary across subcultures and dominant society. Developmental transitions are accompanied with competing expectations, changes in family, and peer and social changes in status and roles. People must also deal with the challenges of new experiences and relationships as well as leaving familiar places and relationships. Beginning a new school or job, starting a new relationship, and having a child create new demands and expectation and therefore are often stressful social transitions. Leaving school or job, ending a relationship, and dealing with death and other losses are even more stressful social transitions than new experiences. Traumatic life events, often unexpected and severe, include losses such as the death of a child, loss of a home, rape, and the diagnosis of AIDS and other illnesses. Such events are perceived as overwhelming disasters and lead to intense pain. Biological and social transitions and traumatic events require changes in ways of looking at oneself and the world and have profound impact on interpersonal transactions.

Environmental pressures can arise from the lack of resources and social provisions on the part of some or most social and physical environments. Chronic poverty is the major force responsible for prolonged and cumulative stress.

Violence, insufficient affordable housing, poor schools, and inadequate heath care for children and adults are consequences of economic and social priorities and values. To manage environmental stressors, clients turn to institutions and organization (including social agencies) for assistance. Some provide the required resources. Others are inaccessible and inhospitable to people's needs; withhold needed resources through restrictive policies, regulations, and procedure; and exacerbate rather than ameliorate their stress. Similarly, some social networks (kin, friends, neighbors, co-workers, and acquaintances) provide essential instrumental (goods and services) and expressive (empathy, encouragement) resources. They serve as buffers against life stressors and the stress they generate. Others, however, are destructive, are nonsupportive, or are missing altogether. Similarly, physical settings can be serious life stressors because of deteriorated dwellings (unsafe and insufficient space and lack of required privacy).

Families, groups, and communities also experience the life transitional and environmental stressors already noted. They also experience additional stressors created by their own dysfunctional processes and exploitive and conflicted relationships. Scapegoating and splintering factions are illustrative of dysfunctional processes, which simultaneously weaken individuals as well as the collectivity.

Life transitional, environmental, and interpersonal stressors are interrelated and at the same time distinct. When one is unsuccessfully managed, additional stressors often erupt in other areas of life (the spread phenomenon). Cumulatively, they can overwhelm individual and collective coping capacities, and the individual, group, family, or community/neighborhood may move toward disorganization.

Influencing Social and Physical Environmental Forces

In helping people with life stressors, social workers daily encounter the lack of environmental responsiveness. Thus, the Life Model also includes professional responsibility for influencing environmental forces and bearing witness against social inequities and injustice. This is done by mobilizing community resources to improve community life, influencing unresponsive organizations to develop responsive policies and services, and politically influencing local, state, and federal legislation and regulations to support social justice.

Intervention at the community level is essential to life-modeled practice. The social worker helps mobilize neighborhood and community residents to take action on their own behalf to secure desired formal and informal resources. Helping residents pursue needed resources or services and influence formal and informal structures to be receptive to their efforts are essential interventions to improving the level of fit between people and their environments. The social worker can also help neighborhood and community residents by improving the coordination of existing community resources and increasing their accessibility. When programs and services are unavailable, the social worker may engage his or her agency or a coalition of agencies to develop new programs and services.

Influencing the social worker's own organization to develop new or improve existing services is an essential component of the Life Model's conception of professional function. To be responsive to clients' needs, the social worker must have an active presence in his or her organization. An organizationally isolated worker is not in a position to influence polices, practices, and programs. Similarly, a social worker who does not question organizational structures and processes limits his or her ability to improve agency services. The worker must move beyond prescribed organizational roles in a respectful and skillful manner. The professional task is to simultaneously identify with the organization's mission, the client's needs, and the profession's code of ethics. The Life Model proposes a professional methodology to fulfill this professional function.

The complexities of contemporary practice demand professional involvement in political activity to influence local, state, and federal legislative and regulatory processes. Political acidity includes the simpler form of telephoning and writing letters to policy makers and policy implementers and mobilizing others to do the same. In its more complex form, it includes lobbying, coalition building, testifying, rallying public support, and using the press and other media to influence legislative and regulatory processes (Gitterman & Germain, 2008).

THE HELPING PROCESS

Like life itself, the model of practice is phasic. The helping process is organized into three phases—initial, ongoing, and ending. The phases ebb and flow in response to the interplay of personal and environmental forces. Though not always distinct in actual practice, they are separated to provide practice guidelines. The initial phase presents concepts and methods on the accomplishment of two professional tasks: (1) creating a supportive environment, and (2) developing commonality of purpose. All professional helping and environmental influencing rests clarity of purpose and shared definitions of needs, concerns, goals and respective roles. The shared understanding and initiation of problem-solving activities ushers in the ongoing phase. In this phase, people are helped with their life transitional, environmental, and interpersonal stressors and the major environmental influencing activities are launched. In the ending phase, the worker deals with the feelings aroused by the termination, evaluates what has been accomplished and what remains to be achieved, and develops plans for the future. In community, organizational and legislative activities, the worker evaluates the outcomes and, if effective, attempts to institutionalize the innovation to ensure its permanence.

In the helping process, the professional relationship is characterized by mutuality and reciprocity and is conceived as a partnership. This conception of client and worker roles requires careful attention to variations, required by level of functioning, age, cultural expectations, and lifestyles. If strains evolve between the partners, the social worker invites open and direct communications, reaches for disappointment and anger, and strives to develop greater understanding and mutuality in the relationship.

Social workers must consistently accept and respect each client's (a) race, ethnicity, religion, and spirituality; (b) gender; (c) sexual orientation; (d) age; and (e) particular mental and physical challenges. Such sensitivity requires specialized knowledge about a particular population or person being served by the practitioner and a high level of self-awareness. The combination of specialized knowledge and self-awareness helps ensure a practice that is sensitive to diversity (objective) and difference (subjective) as well as sameness and is responsive to the needs and aspirations of vulnerable and oppressed populations and to the consequences of discrimination. Sensitivity to diversity also requires respect and understanding of people whose characteristics and values may differ from those of the group around them or of the worker. At times, working with people whose backgrounds are similar to us creates its own special challenges (Lum, 2004; Swigonski, 1996).

FUTURE

Life Model practice seeks to elevate the fit between people and their environments. In mediating these transactions, social workers fulfill a dual professional function: helping eliminate (or at least alleviate) life stressors and influencing social and physical environmental forces to be responsive to people's needs. By integrating people's needs for individualized services (function) and environmental reform and social action (cause), the life-modeled social worker is well positioned for the complexities of contemporary conditions and practice dilemmas. Increasingly, our profession will be called on to bear witness against social inequalities and injustices by mobilizing community resources, influencing unresponsive organizations and mobilizing political action, while at the same time providing services that build on individual and collective strengths.

WEB SITES

Alliance for Children and Families. http://www.alliance1.org.
Association for the Advancement of Social Work with Groups. http://www.aaswg.org.
Association for Community Organization and Social Administration. http://www.acosa.org.
Ecology (published by the Ecological Society of America). http://www.esapubs.org/esapubs/journals/ecology.htm.
Global Alliance for a Deep Ecological Social Work. http://www.ecosocialwork.org.

References

Capra, F. (1996). *The web of life*. New York: Anchor Books.
Germain, C. B. (1981). The ecological approach to people environment transactions. *Social Casework, 62*, 323–331.
Germain, C. B., & Gitterman, A. (1979). The Life Model of social work practice. In F. Turner (Ed.), *Social work treatment* (pp. 361–384). New York: Free Press.
Germain, C. B., & Gitterman, A. (1986a). Ecological social work research in the United States. In *Brennpunkta sozialer arbeit* (pp. 60–76). Frankfurt: Diesterweg.
Germain, C. B., & Gitterman, A. (1986b). The Life Model of social work practice revisited. In F. Turner (Ed.), *Social work treatment* (pp. 618–644). New York: Free Press.

Germain, C. B., & Gitterman, A. (1987). Ecological perspective. In A. Minahan (Ed.), *Encyclopedia of social work*, 18th ed. (pp. 488–499). Silver Spring, MD: NASW Press.

Germain, C. B., & Gitterman, A. (1995). Ecological perspective. In R. L. Edwards (Ed.), *Encyclopedia of social work*, 19th ed. (pp. 816–824). Silver Spring, MD: NASW Press.

Germain, C. B., & Gitterman, A. (1996). *The Life Model of social work practice: Advances in theory and practice*, 2nd ed. New York: Columbia University Press.

Gitterman, A. (1996a). Ecological perspective: Response to professor Jerry Wakefield. *Social Service Review*, 70(2), 472–475.

Gitterman, A. (1996b). Advances in the Life Model of social work practice. In F. Turner (Ed.), *Social work treatment: Interlocking theoretical perspectives* (pp. 389–408). New York: Free Press.

Gitterman, A., & Germain, C. B. (1976). Social work practice: A Life Model. *Social Service Review, 50*, 601–610.

Gitterman, A., & Germain, C.B. (2008). *The Life Model of social work practice: Advances in theory and prac*

tice, 3rd ed. New York: Columbia University Press.

Lee, P. R. (1929). Social work as cause and function. In *Social work cause and function: Selected papers of Porter R. Lee* (pp. 3–24). New York: Columbia University Press.

Lum, D. (2004). *Social work practice and people of color: A process-stage approach*, 5th ed. Belmont, CA: Brooks/Cole.

Schwartz, W. (1969). Private troubles and public issues: One social work job or two? In *The social welfare forum* (pp. 22–43). New York: Columbia University Press.

Schwartz, W. (1971). The interactionist approach. In *Encyclopedia of social work*, 17th ed. (pp. 130–191). New York: NASW Press.

Schwartz, W. (1976). Between client and system: The mediating function. In R. Roberts & H. Northen (Eds.), *Theories of social work with groups* (pp. 171–197). New York: Columbia University Press.

Swigonski, M. E. (1996). Challenging privilege through Afrocentric social work practice. *Social Work, 41*(2), 153–161.

30 Client-Centered Theory and Therapy

William S. Rowe & Alicia J. Stinson

Those who seek the help of therapists have often been badly damaged by their experience of life. (Mearns, Lambers, Thorne, & Warner, 2000, p. 90)

WHAT IS CLIENT-CENTERED THEORY AND THERAPY?

Client-centered theory was originated by Carl Rogers more than five decades ago, at a time when the humanistic approach to psychology was evolv-ing and clearly differentiated from the more an-alytical styles of that period. Client-centered the-ory is hypothesized on the belief that all beings have innate means to grow and change beyond their perceived limitations of "self" (e.g., attitude, behavior, and self-concept) toward greater posi-tive personal development when facilitated through consistent and reliable relationships in therapy (Cepeda & Davenport, 2006; Green, 2006; Rog-ers, 1957, 1961; Rowe, 1996; Snodgrass, 2007; Wa-chtel, 2007).

Client-centered therapy is a nondirective approach where the role of the therapist is not to offer direct advice for change or make any other type of suggestion that is usually found in the behavioral therapies but to use self-awareness in relationship to the client, focusing on the here and now of the presenting disparity, and provide a safe environment in which the client is capable of achieving self-actualization. The client-centered therapist shows respect in recognizing that the client is the expert, inherently capable of resolving their challenges in order to live a more complete and satisfying life (Cepeda & Davenport, 2006; Green, 2006).

Client-centered theory and therapy are not based on stages of development or steps of actions to take sequentially with the client; rather, they rely solely on the stance of the therapist to genuinely possess three key humanistic characteristics: empathy, congruency, and unconditional positive regard. Furthermore, these three attitudes are manifested by the therapist and accessed during counseling sessions with the client, who is often experiencing a sense of incongruence, vulnerability, and anxiety. It is essential to the theory of client-centered work that the client perceives and recognizes to some extent these therapeutic attitudes (Bozarth & Brodley, 1991). Table 30.1 offers a more detailed explanation of each of the three elements that are central to the therapist's behavior as client-centered.

In 1957, Carl Rogers hypothesized six conditions as "necessary and sufficient" to promote what he called "constructive personality change" in the individual (p. 241). It is also suggested that as long as the therapist is able to interrelate the three salient qualities discussed earlier (congruence, empathy, and unconditional positive regard), then at a minimum the client will experience positive growth (Snodgrass, 2007; Snyder, 2002). Table 30.2 represents the key principles of client-centered theory.

In addition to Rogers's explanation of the client-centered approach in the helping profession, there

TABLE 30.1 Characteristics of a Client-Centered Therapist

Core Attitude	Required Skill or Behavior of Therapist
Empathy	Sharing the clients' experience from their perspective and understanding it through their frame of reference. This is accomplished through verbal and nonverbal actions. This also includes seeking clarity to the client's experience, not through making an inference or assumption that is inaccurate but, rather, seeking to gain an understanding from the client when we are not certain. Requires truly being present to feeling what the client shares and also experiencing what we as therapists feel in response to the client. Empathetic understanding is not to be confused with simply mirroring or reflecting back to the client what was shared; it is more closely aligned with recognizing what the client is attempting to communicate or struggling with at a deeper level. Communicating this awareness and seeking clarity (e.g., "let me see if I have this correct") assists the client in exploring more deeply their internal process.
Unconditional positive regard (*respect*)	Communicating emotional warmth to clients' needs/issues/statements/problems and notion of self or selves while not providing recommendations, opinions, advice, or solutions. This is referred to as "prizing" the client/individual for who they are as a unique individual. It is necessary to point out that this does not mean the therapist/counselor has to agree or condone the actions/attitudes of the client; likewise, it is not for the therapist to voice personal disagreement with such experiences of the client.
Congruence (*genuineness*)	Demonstrating through (congruent) verbal and nonverbal gestures (e.g., therapist's affect and mood are the same) a deep level of understanding and ability to be honest, genuine, and "whole." This is about being real with the client, not superficial. This does not require diagnosing the client or using terms that are unknown to the client. Truly meet the client where the client is.

TABLE 30.2 Key Principles to Client-Centered Theory

Rogers's Conditions of Client-Centered Theory	Underlying Assumption of Individual	Role of Therapist
Therapeutic *relationship* must exist between client and therapist/counselor	Willing to participate to some extent, capable and competent	Establishes a safe environment for cultivating the relationship; develops the conditions necessary and sufficient for constructive personality change
Client is in a state of *incongruence*	Anxious, vulnerable, distorted sense of real self versus ideal self	Remains integrated in the relationship
Therapist/counselor is *congruent*	Will be able to recognize this through therapist's use of self and will develop trust	Genuine, sincere, authentic; demonstrates a fully integrated presence of self in relationship to client
Therapist experiences *unconditional positive regard* toward the client	Has the capacity to guide, regulate, direct, and control self providing certain conditions exist	Respect, acceptance, warmth, and a non-judgmental attitude
Therapist is *empathetic*	Has rarely experienced this level of understanding, later begins to experience and verbalize unexpressed feelings/emotions	Feels what the client feels, active listening, verbally and nonverbally communicates back to the client in a validating (not evaluating) manner
Communication that the therapist's use of empathy and unconditional positive regard is understood	Experiences self-actualization and happiness; loved and valued by self and others	Maintains commitment to the advancement of love and peace as basic strivings; facilitates and recognizes the client's full growth and potential

have been many others who built on his original hypothesis by expanding its application. One such contributor to this approach is Robert Carkhuff, who elaborated on the three core conditions by adding confrontation, immediacy, and concreteness, also noted as "facilitative conditions deemed essential for effective counseling" (Horan, 1977). In this realm, these qualities or conditions parallel Rogers's core conditions in the following way: concreteness in empathetic understanding is about "being specific"; immediacy with congruence refers to "what goes on between us right now"; and confrontation is seen as useful in "all three of Rogers' conditions" (Brazier, 1996) as "telling it like it is" (Carkhuff, 1971, as cited in Horan, 1977). Carkhuff's emergences in the client-centered approach are often seen as more active and direct than the original precepts and are recognized as qualities that further aid the helping process of the client.

The effectiveness of client-centered therapy is primarily dependent on the relationship between the client and therapist, whereby the therapist is completely aware of him- or herself in relationship to the client and the client is able to communicate unexpressed feelings and emotions that have caused confusion with his or her notion of self. Ultimately, clients are able to experience on their own accord that they are loved and valued, which allows them to realize their fullest potential through self-actualization.

CLIENT-CENTERED PERSPECTIVE AND SOCIAL WORK

The conditions of client-centered theory match the fundamental values and skills of social work. The two have a historically organic relationship based on the shared belief and respect for the individual's worth and dignity, autonomy, self-determination, and ability to improve whatever conditions exist through empowerment of the individual, group, or community. The core skills used by social workers in purposeful relationships include empathy, respect (unconditional positive regard), and authenticity (congruence), which are also noted as the key elements/attitudes to the client centered approach (da Silva, 2005; Hepworth, Rooney, & Larsen, 2001; Rowe, 1996). The following case is presented to illustrate the use of the client-centered approach in social work.

Case Example

Liz, a single female, age 33, sought counseling because of conflicts between her personal needs and those of her family. Liz grew up in a lower to middle-class neighborhood outside of New York City as the older of two daughters to immigrant parents from Europe. Her father, Edward, died suddenly from a heart attack at age 50 when Liz was 15 years old. Her remaining family includes her mother, Rose, age 65; and one younger sister, Angela, age 30. Both reside in New York. Liz lives and works in San Diego, California, where she is an executive marketing manager for a firm that she has been with for over ten years, since graduating from college. She provides financial support to her mother, who is unable to work due to poor health, and occasionally to her sister, who is unable to keep a job due to her substance use (among other problems).

Liz describes her relationship with her sister as strained. The last time they spoke it ended in a "shouting match as usual over Angela taking advantage of their mother, and her continued lack of responsibility with self-care." Liz states that she and her mother have a warm but contentious relationship. She claims that she talks with her mom every day and sends her money monthly for medical and living expenses but is often criticized for being selfish for not doing more to help her sister. Liz says she understands her mother's concerns about Angela and sometimes feels guilty for being resentful of her mother's attitude; however, she doesn't see that it is her problem to take care of her sister any longer. She is also at a point in her life where she wants to meet someone, settle down, and hopefully start a family, but she dismisses the idea as being a "fantasy not reality." Liz describes herself as an overachiever and the only "responsible one" in her family. She has a few close friends with whom she socializes occasionally, but she is adamantly private about her family dynamics and personal situation. Liz arrives at the social workers office feeling depressed, withdrawn. and hopeless about her current and future situation. The following are excerpts from Liz and social worker exploring her feelings about the people she identified as family members in her life.

Liz: [with certainty] I love my mother very much. I take care of her financially . . . and I don't mind. I actually feel like it's my responsibility since she's all alone . . . well, not really alone I suppose. My sister I guess lives with her, but that's a whole other story . . . she's such a loser. [At this point the client has become restless and is looking away and pulling nervously on her sweater.]

Social Worker: I can see you really care about your mom and her well-being. I'm also sensing that maybe you wish your sister were more responsible and involved?

Liz: Yeah . . . that's if she could stop using the drugs and alcohol. I get so angry when she is so neglectful of herself. It hurts my mother so much, but she just doesn't care.

Social Worker: Her lack of care upsets you the most?

Liz: Yes, care for herself and care for others. I almost don't know if I even care anymore about what she does to herself; it's just my mom that I care about. Well that's not totally true . . . I feel guilty saying that. [pauses and starts to become tearful]

Social Worker: [leans forward and offers the client tissues and gently responds] This seems like a really sensitive place for you to be right now.

Here the social worker's use of empathetic skills encourages the client to explore more deeply her feelings of discord around family relations.

Several sessions later, Liz explores her own needs, including the desire for an intimate relationship.

Liz: [hesitantly] I've met this great guy (John) at work and we seem to have a lot in common. I really think I'm beginning to like him and I think he likes me, too.

Social Worker: Tell me more.

Liz: [enthusiastically describes some of her initial conversations with John and her attraction for him, but as she continues to offer more around her feelings she becomes sullen] Well, the truth is it probably won't work anyway. I just keep telling myself that a relationship with him is only a fantasy it will never be a reality for me.

Social Worker: Hmmm. Let me see if I got this right. If you could, you would ideally have a relationship with John. It sounds like you have a special connection with him, and you think he feels it too, yet you believe that this isn't a real possibility?

Liz: [tearfully] Right. I would like that, but I'm so involved with my family's problems. Why would anyone want to sign up for that? It makes me so sad I'll probably just end up alone.

Social Worker: [softly] That makes me sad, too. I wonder if you realize how others see you . . . how I see you. You have such a generous heart and really care deeply about relationships with people you love. These are wonderful qualities for a successful relationship. I wonder how it would feel for you to be that generous with yourself in meeting your own needs.

Again, we see the therapist is using empathetic skills, communicating her feelings of Liz's experience while remaining congruent. The social worker is able to acknowledge Liz's qualities of caring deeply for loved ones and helps her see how this does not have to mean she abandons herself or her own desires. This demonstration helps Liz with accepting that she is lovable, valuable, and capable of having a real relationship and not just the fantasy of one.

Liz returns for her final session after several weeks of continued therapy where she has explored further her desire and need for a real and intimate relationship along with her feelings of responsibility to care for her mother.

Liz: [happily] John and I have been dating now for almost 8 months and it's going really well. I think he could be the one! [smiling] I feel so loved. He's a great guy. Also, I finally convinced my mom to move to California where she will be living with me until we find her a place of her own nearby. I'm so happy about this decision, especially since my sister just moved away and I was worried about [Mom] being alone. This move is really going to allow me to care for my mom in a more involved, sort of hands-on way.

Social Worker: It is such a pleasure to witness how you have grown through your process. It really gives me a great sense of hope. I can see how you have come to appreciate and accept yourself not only as a loving daughter who only wants the best for her mom, but also as a woman who is capable of having a successful relationship and meeting your own needs.

In reviewing this case, we can see that the stance of therapist was to establish a trusting relationship with the client using the three key characteristics of a client-centered approach. Throughout this relationship the social worker shows *unconditional positive regard* for the client by being warm, accepting, and nonjudgmental of the client's presenting conflict; demonstrates *empathy* by being able to communicate an understanding through accurate reflection of the client's feelings; and remains *congruent* even with expressing her own experience of Liz as lovable. Through verbalizing unexpressed emotions, Liz succeeded in reconciling her feelings of despair over the role of caregiver versus her need to be loved and was able to fully realize her potential for happiness and achieve a greater and more fully integrated sense of self.

The Larger Perspective

Social workers can use client-centered practice in a multitude of settings, including family and couples counseling, group therapy, and the larger context of community work (see Table. 30.3). In each of these settings, the therapist uses the three key skills to address each individual or member and his or her unique needs and concerns, ultimately facilitating an ideal scene from the present scene. Also in this framework, the social worker can empower participants by teaching them how to use the client-centered principles with one another to foster the optimum development within their particular system (Barrett-Lennard, 1998; Rowe, 1996; Snyder, 2002).

BRIEF HISTORICAL MILIEU OF ROGERS AND CLIENT-CENTERED THEORY

In 1951, Carl Rogers published the text *Client-Centered Therapy*, which he richly surmises as a book that he believes is "about life, as life vividly reveals itself in the therapeutic process—with its blind power and its tremendous capacity for destruction, but with its overbalancing thrust toward growth, if the opportunity for growth is provided" (Rogers, 1951, p. 5). This last remark reflects his well-known nondirective approach and attitude toward the counseling process.

To attempt to address the complete history of who and what influenced Rogers would not be suitable for this chapter; however, suffice it to say that in his 1961 book, titled *On Becoming a Person* (which is highly recommended reading), he provides the most intimate detail of what he

TABLE 30.3 Client-Centered Principles Within the Micro, Mezzo, and Macro Systems

Family (or Couple)	Group	Community
• Facilitation of children's needs to be fully functioning in the world and in the family • Recognition and encouragement of individuality • Facilitation of open and honest communication • Identification of family goals	• Facilitation of group members to take responsibility for themselves in whatever way is realistically possible • Clarification and solution of problems • Recognition of clients perceived and real self	• Facilitation of community self-perception • Recognition and encouragement of indigenous leadership • Facilitation of the communication among divergent groups • Identification of community goals

Source: Barrett-Lennard, 1988; Rowe, 1996; Snyder, 2002.

coins "some of the psychological highlights of my autobiography, particularly as it seems to relate to my professional life" (p. 5). Rogers was clearly influenced and inspired by a number of social-cultural-contextual factors and beliefs and has been equally reciprocal and influential on the profession of psychotherapy, including social work, over the past 50 years. For example, Hill (2007) acknowledges this influence by citing a recently published report in the *Psychotherapy Networker* (March/April 2007) that "reported that in both 1982 and 2007 Carl Rogers was nominated by a landslide as the most influential psychotherapist in the United States" (p. 260). Apparently, this was the result of a voluntary survey of 2,598 mental health professionals who claim to be "eclectic" in their therapeutic orientations. Additionally, Goldfried (2007) provides that Rogers's infamous 1957 article, "Necessary and Sufficient Conditions for Therapeutic Change" has been "cited in the literature over a thousand times in professional writings originating in 36 countries" (p. 249), positing that this is even "more popular now than it was 20 years ago" (p. 249).

CONCLUSION

If there were a code of conduct for client-centered therapy it might read something like this. Client-centered therapy does not diagnosis, judge, assess, solve, or otherwise profess to know what is "wrong" with the individual. Client-centered therapy focuses on the uniqueness of the individual by respecting, nurturing, loving, and fostering the fragmented aspects of the client's notion of self while the therapist demonstrates and maintains an integrated sense of wholeness.

Client-centered therapy can be viewed as a significant precursor to other effective therapies that are intentionally directive, problem-solving, or behavior-changing in their focus. At a minimum, the client-centered approach is seen as significant in assisting the client to feel understood, loved, and fully integrated through establishing a safe, trusting, and reliable rapport with the therapist. Bohart and Byock (2005) recognize the uniqueness and value of the nondirective client centered approach by asserting that "no matter how many new and effective interventions our field continues to generate, there may always be a place for providing people with a safe space where they can talk to another person who recognizes and tries to understand them primarily as persons and gives them room to think" (p. 209).

Although there are many positive attributes to traditional client-centered therapy, such as autonomy, respect, and dignity for the client, social workers need to remain culturally sensitive and aware of when this approach might not be appropriate or useful. For instance, some clients might come from a culture that highly respects the role of the authoritative figure and would be remarkably uncomfortable to interact in this nonauthoritative environment. Additionally, it is important to gain an understanding of the client's expectations of therapy and their desire for immediate and direct problem solving versus an approach that facilitates and encourages deeper exploration of the self. In these cases, the social worker/counselor is going to serve the individual better by using a different intervention or by referring to a different therapist. One other limitation to consider is that the client-centered approach assumes the client to have an intrinsic motivation to change, and there may be some instances where the individual "may lack motivation to change (e.g., substance abusers, batterers)" as cited in Goldfried (2007, p. 252), and this is obviously going to require the counselor to employ other means to assist the individual in developing this level of motivation.

The client-centered approach is often dismissed as being simple or ambivalent, when in fact it is quite the opposite—it requires the therapist to be highly skilled and evolved not only as a practitioner but also as a fully integrated, self-aware, nonjudgmental, and mature individual capable of understanding and using the core concepts of this modality effectively. Rowe (1996) defends this point well and recognizes the complexity of this approach when he offers that "it is only when (social) workers have had significant experience that they are in a position to rediscover person-centered theory, with its many layers of depth and meaning" (p. 89).

WEB SITES

Association for the Development of the Person-Centered Approach. http://www.adpca.org.

Classics in the History of Psychology, by Christopher D. Green. http://psychclassics .yorku.ca/Rogers/personality.htm.

Institute of Transpersonal Psychology. http://www .itp.edu/about/carl_rogers.cfm.

Person-Centered Counseling. http://www .person-centered-counseling.com/index.htm.

Personality Theories, by Dr. C. George Boeree. http://webspace.ship.edu/cgboer/rogers.html.

References

Barrett-Lennard, G. T. (1998). *Carl Rogers' helping system: Journey and substance.* Thousand Oaks, CA: Sage.

Bohart, A. C., & Byock, G. (2005). Experiencing Carl Rogers from the client's point of view: A vicarious ethnographic investigation. I. extraction and perception of meaning. *Humanistic Psychologist, 33*(3), 187–212.

Bozarth, J. D., & Brodley, B. T. (1991). Actualisation: A functional concept in client-centered therapy. *Handbook of Self-Actualisation, 6*(5), 45–60.

Brazier, D. J. (1996). The post-Rogerian therapy of Robert Carkhuff. Retrieved November 16, 2007, from http://www.amidatrust.com/article_carkhuff .html.

Carkhuff, R. R. (1971). *The development of human resources.* New York: Holt, Rinehart & Winston.

Cepeda, L. M., & Davenport, D. S. (2006). Person-centered therapy and solution-focused brief therapy: an integration of present and future awareness. *Psychotherapy: Theory, Research and Practice, 43*(1), 1–12.

da Silva, R. B. (2005). Person-centered therapy with impoverished, maltreated, and neglected children and adolescents in Brazil. *Journal of Mental Health Counseling.* Retrieved November 8, 2007, from http://www.thefreelibrary.com.

Goldfried, M. R. (2007). What has psychotherapy inherited from Carl Rogers? *Psychotherapy: Theory, Research and Practice, 44*(3), 249–252.

Green, A. (2006). A person-centered approach to palliative care nursing. *Journal of Hospice and Palliative Nursing, 8*(5), 294–301.

Hepworth D. H., Rooney R. H., & Larsen J. A. (Eds.). (2002). *Direct social work practice,* 6th ed. Pacific Grove, CA: Brooks/Cole.

Hill, C. E. (2007). My personal reactions to Rogers (1957): The facilitative but neither necessary nor sufficient conditions of therapeutic personality change. *Psychotherapy: Theory, Research and Practice, 44*(3), 260–264.

Horan, J. J. (1977). Dynamic approaches to decision-making counseling. Counseling for effective decision making. Retrieved November 16, 2007, from http://horan.asu.edu/cfedm/chapter7.php.

Mearns, D., Lambers, E., Thorne, B., & Warner, M. (2000). *Person-centered therapy today: New frontiers in theory and practice.* Thousand Oaks, CA: Sage.

Rogers, C. R. (1957). The necessary and sufficient conditions for therapeutic personality change. *Journal of Counseling Psychology, 21,* 95–103.

Rogers, C. R. (1961). *On becoming a person.* Cambridge, MA: Riverside Press.

Rowe, W. (1996). Client-centered theory: A person-centered approach. In F, J. Turner (Ed.), *Social work treatment,* 4th ed. (pp. 69–93). New York: Free Press.

Snodgrass, J. (2007). From Rogers to Clinebell: Exploring the history of pastoral psychology. *Pastoral Psychology, 55*(4), 513–525.

Snyder, M. (2002). Applications of Carl Rogers' theory and practice to couple and family therapy: A response to Harlene Anderson and David Bott. *Journal of Family Therapy, 24*(3), 317–325.

Watchel, P. L. (2007). Carl Rogers and the larger context of therapeutic thought. *Psychotherapy: Theory, Research and Practice, 44*(3), 279–284.

31 Cognitive-Behavioral Therapy

M. Elizabeth Vonk & Theresa J. Early

Cognitive-behavioral therapy (CBT) is actually a number of related therapies that focus on cognition as the mediator of psychological distress and dysfunction. As the name implies, CBT draws on and combines the theoretical and practical approaches of behavior therapy, dating to the 1950s, and cognitive therapy, dating to the 1960s work of Beck and Ellis (Ledley, Marx, & Heimberg, 2005). Behavior therapy, as developed in the United States from the work of Skinner, redefined various mental illnesses as behavioral problems, hypothesized to have arisen from faulty learning. The greatest progress achieved in behavior therapy came in reducing anxiety disorders and childhood disorders, such as aggressive and oppositional behavior, and in improving the quality of life for people with mental disabilities. Whereas behavior therapy is based on various theories of learning, cognitive therapy is based on the assumption that emotional and behavioral disturbances do not arise directly in response to an experience but from the activation of maladaptive beliefs in response to an experience. Treatment from a cognitive perspective then is directed at identifying and changing maladaptive cognitions, attributions, and beliefs that in turn affect emotional, physiological, and behavioral responses (Ledley, Marx, & Heimberg, 2005).

Before moving ahead to outline the basic concepts and applications of CBT, we present a case study that will be used throughout this chapter to illustrate various aspects of CBT. John, a 38-year-old European American man, sought therapy at his wife's urging. He explained that he has worked for 15 years in the office supply business and recently received a significant promotion to a managerial position. Since receiving the promotion, he has become "extremely worried" that he will fail in his new role. His anxiety is interfering at work where he thinks that he "can't do anything right." He is particularly worried about his performance on various reports that he

is responsible for completing. In spite of his efforts to get it right, minor corrections by his supervisor have been necessary on two occasions. He worries that he will lose his job and become unable to support his family if this continues.

At home, John's anxiety is interfering in his relationship with his wife, who has told him that she is irritated by his absence while he works long hours. She has also complained that when he is home, he is "off in his own world fretting." John wishes his wife would be less critical about his need to work longer hours and spend a lot of time thinking about work. He also worries, however, that he may be "a lousy husband and father"—just like he always feared. He describes a history of anxiety, particularly about work matters, with the current level of anxiety higher than at any previous time. Exploration of early history reveals that John was raised in an intact family in the rural Midwest. He describes his mother as "loving, but always trying to please my father." He describes his father as "mean-spirited and never satisfied with anything, no matter how much I tried." John would like to be less worried and feel better about his relationship with his wife.

BASIC CONCEPTS OF CBT

Three elements of cognition are important when assessing and treating various emotional and behavioral disorders, the first being the actual content of thoughts. We are most aware of the content of automatic thoughts; these are thoughts that come into our minds immediately as life unfolds. More hidden from our awareness are thoughts that are referred to as rules or assumptions; these are thoughts through which we interpret our experiences. For example, John may automatically think, "I can't handle this situation" on receiving critical feedback at work. If he were able to identify a rule related to the situation, it might be "I must be perfect at everything I do."

Specifically, clients' perceptions of themselves, the world, and the future are key variables among emotional and behavioral disorders (Reinecke & Freeman, 2003). Like John, those with anxiety may view themselves as incapable, the world as threatening, and the future as holding great risk of danger. Also considered important for cognitive therapy are meta-cognitions, or thoughts about cognitive processes. For example, John believes that he has a "need to spend a lot of time thinking about work," potentially indicating a belief that it is helpful to worry about the potential threat of losing his job.

The second area of cognitive focus involves core beliefs. Core beliefs are global, durable beliefs about the self and the world that are formed through early life experiences. They are maintained through a process of attending to information that supports the belief while disregarding information that is contrary to it (Beck, 1995). As a child, John experienced intense criticism from his father and seems to have formed a core belief such as "I am totally inadequate." As an adult, he seems to ignore his history of career successes and instead focuses on the few moments in his day in which he has made a mistake or was unsure of himself. At home, he focuses on his wife's current irritation and discounts a 14-year history of marriage that has been "mostly good for both of us."

The third element of cognition involves maladaptive and ingrained styles of processing information, or cognitive distortions. There are many types of distortions (Beck, 1995; MacLaren & Freeman, 2007), a few of which follow, with examples that might be seen in John, who perceives himself as inadequate.

- Catastrophizing: "If my boss criticizes a piece of my work, I will lose my job, be unable to support my family, my wife will leave me, and I will end up homeless."
- Emotional reasoning: "I feel horribly anxious about this report I just completed, so that proves I must have done a terrible job on it."
- Minimization: "I got the employee-of-the-year award purely from luck; it has nothing to do with how well I performed."

Many emotional and behavioral disorders have been characterized by specific cognitive content, schema, and information processing styles (Reinecke & Freeman, 2003). As already mentioned, those with anxiety disorders perceive themselves as inadequate and the world as dangerous and threatening. Regarding information processing, those with anxiety pay greater attention to anxiety-provoking stimuli than they do to neutral stimuli. In panic disorder, the attentional bias is toward bodily sensation, with sufferers more acutely aware of their heart rates than other people. People with social phobia, on the other hand, attend to and make negative evaluations of their own social behavior.

Depression also has been specified in terms of cognitive content and processing styles. Those who are depressed have a negative view of the self, the world, and the future (Beck, 1995). For example, someone who is depressed may think, "I never do anything right; people are never there for me; and moreover, things will never get better." Core beliefs are most often related to perceptions of self-defect, and attention is directed to experiences that focus on loss and failure (Reinecke & Freeman, 2003).

Practitioners of CBT employ understanding of the elements of cognition and their relation to specific disorders, as described previously, in a therapeutic relationship with well-specified roles for both the practitioner and the client. The hallmark of the therapeutic relationship in CBT is collaboration, and roles of both the client and the practitioner are active. The role of the practitioner most closely resembles that of a supportive teacher or guide who holds expertise in cognitive and behavioral therapeutic methods, as well as possesses interpersonal skills (Ledley, Marx, & Heimberg, 2005). The practitioner helps the client learn to identify, examine, and alter maladaptive thoughts and beliefs and increase coping skills. Although the practitioner lends methodological expertise, the client is the source of information and expertise about his or her own idiosyncratic beliefs and assumptions. The client and practitioner thus work together to define goals, set agendas for sessions, and uncover and explore attitudes and beliefs that are significant to the client's well-being. Successful replacement of maladaptive cognitions depends on collaboration between client and practitioner, for the client can provide the most lasting and effective cognitive replacements.

APPLICATIONS OF CBT

The most prominent models of CBT are Beck's cognitive therapy (Beck, 1995), Meichenbaum's cognitive behavior therapy (Meichenbaum, 1994), and Ellis's rational emotive behavior therapy (Ellis, 1996). Although there are differences among them related to, for instance, the therapist's level of direction and confrontation, all of the models share basic elements. All rely on identifying the content of cognitions, including assumptions, beliefs, expectations, self-talk, or attributions. Through various techniques, the cognitions are then examined to determine their current effects on the client's emotions and behavior. Some models also include exploration of the development of the cognitions to promote self-understanding. This is followed with use of techniques that encourage the client to adopt alternative and more adaptive cognitions. The replacement cognitions, in turn, produce positive affective and behavioral changes. Other similarities of the models include the use of behavioral techniques, the time-limited nature of the interventions, and the educative component of treatment.

It is useful to consider the application of CBT in steps. At each step, a great number of specific techniques are available. Only a few are reviewed here due to space limitations.

Assessment

As in many clinical social work assessment processes, cognitive-behavioral assessments may result in a case formulation that includes psychiatric diagnosis; definition of the client's problem in terms of duration, frequency, intensity, and situational circumstances; description of client's strengths; and treatment plan. Cognitive analysis of a client's problem, however, is unique to cognitive-behavioral assessments. Assessment and case formulation includes many of the above-mentioned items, plus a prioritized problem list and working hypothesis that provide a cognitive analysis of the problems (Ledley, Marx, & Heimberg, 2005). Problems are described very briefly and are accompanied by the client's related thoughts, emotions, and behaviors. The working hypothesis, unique to each client, proposes specific thoughts and underlying beliefs that have been precipitated by the client's current experiences. Formulations may also include an examination of the origin of the maladaptive cognitions and information processing style in the client's early life. The working hypothesis is then directly related to treatment planning. As an example, we have created a cognitive conceptualization for John, shown in Figure 31.1.

Teaching the Client the ABC Model

Concurrent with assessment, one of the first tasks of the cognitive-behavioral therapist is to educate the client about the relationship of thoughts, emotions, and behaviors. Leahy (2003) suggests contrasting the client's usual way of describing the relationship of thoughts, emotions, and behaviors with the alternative ABC model. For most people, the usual way to think about it is that an activating event (A) causes an emotional or behavioral consequence (C). For example, John states that because he received criticism on his report (A), he is feeling anxious (C). The ABC model proposes that in actuality, a thought or image representing a belief or attitude (B) intervenes between A and C. Using the same example, following the criticism (A), John may think that he will lose his job (B), resulting in anxiety (C). Clients need to become very familiar with the model through presentation of and practice with personal illustrations.

Teaching the Client to Identify Cognitions

Once the client understands the ABC model, the therapist helps him or her learn to identify thoughts and beliefs. Clients may find that many types of cognitions are relevant for analysis, including those related to expectations, self-efficacy, self-concept, attention, selective memory, attribution, evaluations, self-instruction, hidden directives, and explanatory style (McMullin, 2000). A great variety of useful techniques for the purpose of identifying cognitions are described by McMullin (2000); DeRubeis, Tang, and Beck (2002); and Leahy (2003). The daily thought record is a written method involving a form made up of columns within which clients record activating events (column A), corresponding emotional reactions (column C), and immediate thoughts related to the event (column B). In the case example, John would be taught to identify and record on the form an anxiety-provoking situation from the previous week, such as hearing from his boss that a report needed correction. Next, he would be asked to identify his feelings when the situation occurred. Then he would be prompted to remember what went through his mind at the moment his boss spoke with him. In this instance, he would record his thought, "I can't handle this" in between the situation and the anxious feelings. Another method, the downward arrow technique, is a verbal way to discover the un-

- Prioritized problem list:
  - *worry about work following promotion*
  - *worry about relationship with wife due to work worries*

- The following model, based on and adapted from Beck (1995, p. 18), shows the relationship of John's problematic thoughts, feelings, and behaviors to his situation at work:

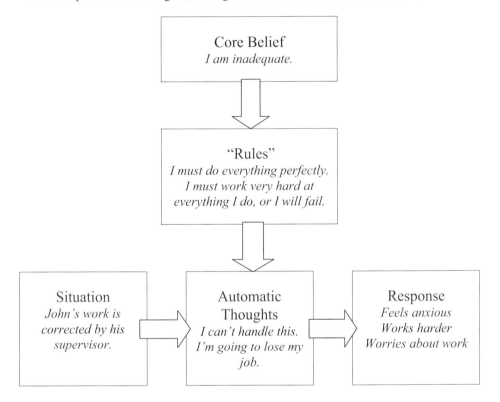

- Based on this model, the working hypothesis is that John has a core belief that he is inadequate. In order to avoid his sense of inadequacy, John operates by "rules" that require him to work very hard and be perfect at everything he does. In addition, he believes that "worrying" helps him to perform better. His promotion has required him to learn new skills which he appears to be learning at a pace that is acceptable to his supervisor. However, the process of receiving corrections activates John's automatic thoughts related to his fear of failure and inability to cope. His preferred cognitive distortions include minimization, catastrophizing, and emotional reasoning. In response to his thoughts, John feels more anxious, works harder, and worries more. The origin of John's core belief and accompanying thoughts, feelings, and behaviors seems to be related to his early childhood experiences that included severe criticism from his father and modeling of anxiety by his mother. He learned early that hypervigilence about potential mistakes, hard work, and perfect performance might help him avoid his father's harsh criticism. Understandably, as a child, he did not have adequate skills to cope with the accompanying anxiety.

- Based on this formulation, treatment interventions will include 1) relaxation and coping skill training; 2) cognitive restructuring of maladaptive thoughts; and 3) cognitive restructuring of the meta-cognition that worrying is helpful.

Figure 31.1 Cognitive formulation for John.

derlying meaning of conscious thoughts through the use of questions such as, "What would it mean to you if the [thought] were true?" Through the use of the downward arrow technique, the client may discover a core belief. John might provide an answer such as, "It would mean I'm incapable." People are generally unaware of their core beliefs that are, nonetheless, very fundamental to the way they feel and behave.

Teaching the Client to Examine and Replace the Maladaptive Cognitions

After identifying thoughts and beliefs, the client is ready to begin examining evidence for and against the cognitions. In addition, the client is encouraged to replace maladaptive cognitions with more realistic or positive ones. Replacement requires frequent repetition and rehearsal of the new cognitions. Again, McMullin (2000), DeRubeis et al. (2001), and Leahy (2003) provide a wealth of information about specific techniques, a few of which are briefly described here.

Many of the techniques are verbal, relying on shifts in language to modify cognitions. In one technique, the client is taught to identify maladaptive thoughts as one of a list of cognitive distortions. Cognitive distortions represent maladaptive thinking styles that commonly occur during highly aroused affective states, making logical thinking difficult. Identification of the use of a distortion allows for the possibility of substituting more rational thinking. Though stopping, a behavioral means to draw attention to the need for substitution, might involve snapping an elastic band. Another technique involves the use of a variety of questions that provide opportunities to evaluate the truth, logic, or function of beliefs (Beck, 1995; Leahy, 2003). Such questions include:

- What is the evidence for and against the belief?
- What are alternative interpretations of the event or situation?
- What are the pros and cons of keeping this belief?

Imagery and visualization are also used to promote cognitive change. For example, clients may be encouraged to visualize coping effectively in difficult situations or visualize an idealized future to provide insight into current goals. McMullin (2000) suggests that imagery techniques are particularly useful to encourage perceptual shifts, whereas language techniques help facilitate change in more specific thoughts and beliefs. A combination of the two types of techniques is often useful.

Other Techniques

Cognitive-behavioral therapists use a wide variety of behavioral techniques, according to the needs of the client. These include relaxation training, assertion training, problem solving, activity scheduling, and desensitization (Beck, 1995; MacLaren & Freeman, 2007). Relaxation training probably would be useful for John.

- Relaxation training involves teaching the client to systematically relax muscles and slow breathing. The client learns to discriminate between tension and relaxation. Through practice, the relaxation response can be easily activated.
- Assertion training provides clients with interpersonal skills that allow for appropriate self-expression. Often these skills are taught and practiced in small groups.
- Problem solving involves teaching the client to solve personal problems through a process of specifying the problem and then devising, selecting, implementing, and evaluating a solution.
- Activity scheduling allows clients to plan for activities that will provide pleasure, socialization, or another identified need during the time between contacts and the practitioner.
- Desensitization provides clients with graduated exposure to anxiety-provoking objects or situations while engaged in behaviors that compete with anxiety, such as relaxation. The exposure may be imaginary or real.

In addition, cognitive-behavioral therapists often assign homework to their clients for the purpose of extending learning beyond the therapy session. Homework assignments vary according to the idiosyncratic needs of the client and generally are designed collaboratively. One common assignment is the use of a form such as the daily thought record.

STRENGTHS OF CBT

Various features of CBT fit well with social work. The collaborative nature of the therapeutic relationship is consistent with the social work value of self-determination. Additionally, the client's active involvement in the change process is consistent with an empowerment approach. CBT's use within an integrative framework that allows for specification of techniques to match individuals' needs is consistent with the ideal of individualizing treatment. More recently, those who have proposed integrative therapy models have examined the role of the client's idiosyncratic meaning in CBT, noting a close kinship with constructive models of therapy (Reinecke & Freeman, 2003).

Many characteristics of CBT lend themselves to the demands of current practice settings. The structure of CBT and the extensive description of its methods in many sources make it an accessible therapy for both novice and experienced practitioners. Because the methods of therapy require initial and ongoing recording of thoughts and behaviors, mechanisms for evaluation are built in, lending support to the use of CBT by clinicians with interest in or need to document the outcomes of their work with clients. Additionally, CBT targets specific problems, thus lending itself to a short-term approach, which is consistent with both the desires of many clients and their third-party payers. Another feature of CBT that is attractive to managed care entities is the well-supported efficacy of the approach, particularly for the treatment of depression and anxiety (Reinecke & Freeman, 2003).

Mounting evidence attests to the versatility of CBT. Specific cognitive-behavioral treatments have been designed for a broad variety of disorders and populations. These include depression, post-traumatic stress disorder, substance misuse, eating disorders, grief and bereavement, children and adolescents, victims of abuse and trauma, aging adults, and families (Reinecke & Freeman, 2003; Ronen & Freeman, 2007).

Future

As we look toward the future, CBT promises to remain vital to the treatment of emotional and behavioral disorders. In fact, it appears that the use of CBT will continue to expand as more is learned about specifying treatments for additional problem areas and populations. At the same time, more treatment providers will apply wide-ranging techniques from CBT into integrative treatment models. Moreover, the versatility of this treatment will enable its continued use in the changing environment of treatment settings. Finally, the fact that CBT has been used successfully across a variety of cultural groups from China to Sweden (Reinecke & Freeman, 2003) shows that it will be able to serve the rapidly changing needs of the increasingly diverse population of people who are served by social workers.

WEB SITES

American Institute for Cognitive Therapy. http://www.cognitivetherapynyc.com/default.asp.
Beck Institute for Cognitive Therapy and Research. http://beckinstitute.org.
National Association of Cognitive Behavioral Therapists. http://www.nacbt.org.

References

Beck, J. S. (1995). *Cognitive therapy.* New York: Guilford.

DeRubeis, R. J., Tang, T. Z., & Beck, A. T. (2001). Cognitive therapy. In K. S. Dobson (Ed.), *Handbook of cognitive-behavioral therapies,* 2nd ed. (pp. 349–392). New York: Guilford.

Ellis, A. (1996). *Better, deeper, and more enduring brief therapy: The rational emotive behavior therapy approach.* New York: Brunner/Mazel.

Leahy, R. L. (2003). *Cognitive therapy techniques: A practitioner's guide.* New York: Guilford.

Ledley, D. R., Marx, B.P., & Heimberg, R. G. (2005). *Making cognitive-behavioral therapy work.* New York: Guilford.

MacLaren, C., & Freeman, A. (2007). Cognitive behavior therapy model and techniques. In T. Ronen & A. Freeman (Eds.), *Cognitive behavior therapy in clinical social work practice* (pp. 25–44). New York: Springer.

McMullin, R. E. (2000). *The new handbook of cognitive therapy techniques.* New York: Norton.

Meichenbaum, D. (1994). *A clinical handbook/practical therapist manual: For assessing and treating adults with post-traumatic stress disorder.* Waterloo, Ontario: Institute Press.

Reinecke, M. A., & Freeman, A. (2003). Cognitive therapy. In A. S. Gurman & S. B. Messer (Eds.), *Essential psychotherapies* (pp. 224–271). New York: Guilford.

Ronen, T., & Freeman, A. (Eds.), (2007). *Cognitive behavior therapy in clinical social work practice.* New York: Springer.

32   Psychosocial Therapy

Francis J. Turner

The term *psychosocial therapy* and its identification with a specific form of therapy holds a long-standing illustrious place in the history of social work. During its ongoing position in the lexicon of the profession, the term has been differentially employed and understood.

It was initially used in a generic sense to stress that an identifying feature of social work therapy consisted of a focus on person and environment. This was seen as a concept that gave social work its own identity among the therapeutic activities of other professions.

Later, as the theoretical base of direct practice developed with the early controversy between the functional and diagnostic schools very much in the foreground, the term *psychosocial* became identified with the diagnostic school. As other theories took their place in the profession's cadre of thought systems, and as we became more comfortable with the acceptability and even importance of a diversity of theories, the psychosocial school was identified as a particular theory in its own right.

Still later, as a more holistic view of treatment attained prominence in the profession, it was strongly recognized that all therapeutic theories, whatever their origin, were based on a person-in-situation perspective when drawn on in social work practice. To reflect this, *psychosocial* became once again a generic term describing the overall orientation of the profession.

More recently, this general use of the term has spread well beyond the borders of social work, and virtually all of the human service professionals move to a broader based view of clients, their problems, and their therapeutic activities. In this way, *psychosocial* is widely used in a generic multidisciplinary manner.

In recent years as a part of this polydiscipline use of the term, there has been a growing usage first in our profession and now by others to add the prefix *bio-* to psychosocial. Thus, bio-psychosocial has become for many the basis on which all help is provided. Adding this further component serves to remind all practitioners that just as it is impossible to separate persons from their social systems, to understand the full gestalt of a client we also need to include an understanding of people's physical condition and overall health.

However, even with this variation in usage and understanding, there is still extant in social work thinking a specific body of concepts, premises, values, and patterns of intervention that together constitute a theory of practice properly titled psychosocial therapy.

Historically, this theory represents the most traditional of social work theories locating its basic origins in the work of Mary Richmond and the stream of therapeutic thought that emerged from her early book *Social Diagnosis*, and the later work, *What Is Social Casework?* These two works are mentioned specifically because this theory has suffered in the sociopolitical history of the profession owing to its strong identification with tradition and the two concepts of diagnosis and casework. That is, there is a sense that because of its origins it is therefore out of date and out of fashion as a distinct theory.

The casework tradition that has served as the basis of psychosocial therapy's origins with its focus principally on treatment of individuals and families was the component of social work most closely identified with first psychoanalytic thinking and other dynamic theories emerging from it, such as ego psychology. However, even with psychosocial therapy's interest in these psychodynamic theories, it was far from a total identification as some would hold. Rather, this approach drew its unique identity from a strong identification with the implications of the "person in situation" concept while adopting and adapting from psychodynamic thinking those concepts and therapeutic strategies that best suited social work. This approach developed while being open to thinking from other sources.

The primary conceptual identification of the psychosocial school was with a method rather than a theory. The method, of course, was casework, a term long a part of the social work lexicon. Casework as it developed as an identifying term for the profession has become a very broad-based methodological concept, far wider than its original therapeutic orientation.

The principal flag bearer of this tradition has been Florence Hollis, whose essential text was *Social Casework: A Psychosocial Therapy* (1963). This work built strongly on the work of earlier casework writers, especially Gordon Hamilton (1951).

The volume originally written by Hollis, then later coauthored by Mary Woods and solely by Woods after Hollis's death, has gone through five editions, the latest one in 1999. All editions have carried the same title. With the recent death of Mary Woods (2007) it will interesting to see if psychosocial therapy continues in the profession with a unique identification or whether it will be viewed more an orientation or viewpoint rather than a distinct theory.

Being identified with casework this orientation to practice viewed itself and was viewed as focusing primarily on work with individuals and secondarily with families. However, as the lines between methods began to open and blur, authors in this tradition began to speak of work with couples, groups, and social systems. Additionally, authors such as Northen (1982) and Turner (1978, 1995, 2005), persons very much in the psychosocial tradition, began to urge a broader base to the system that included work with groups and larger systems.

It would be unfair to suggest that Hollis and Woods limited their perception of practice to individuals, couples, and families. These two leaders of this theory stressed the importance of all methods, but, shaped by the traditions of casework as being more individually client centered, the bulk of their writings and research focused on what Hollis called direct work. As well, because of its close relation to the casework tradition, the psychosocial school of thought is sometimes viewed as being a bit out of fashion as a free-standing theory yet very much in fashion as an important identifying concept for the profession.

A further concept that has created difficulty in the status of psychosocial theory has been its earlier identification with and continued commitment to diagnosis as an important component of treatment. Although once an essential component of practice, for a variety of reasons diagnosis has become an unpopular term in the practice and sociology of the profession for many clinicians.

Hence, it has also has become debated within psychosocial practice.

Diagnosis, for those opposing it, is viewed as placing an overemphasis on pathology; the word *assessment* is preferred. Nevertheless, in practice, the term *diagnosis* does get used but in a manner that highly identifies it with the various *DSM* formulations. It is frequently used in this specific way, rather than viewing diagnosis as an essential component of treatment comprising a much richer and health-oriented viewpoint of the series of judgments or conclusions to which a social work practitioner needs to come based on the range of assessments made about the client and his or her situation.

Nevertheless even with the bits and pieces of historical and sociocultural baggage acquired over the decades, psychosocial therapy is still an important theory in contemporary social work practice and the designation of the theoretical base for many North American practitioners.

A THEORETICAL OVERVIEW

Psychosocial therapy is built on the premise that ethical and effective treatment is an integrated process of assessment, diagnosis, treatment, and evaluation. These processes are not sequential in nature but are ongoing from the first instant with the client until the final closing. A part of these processes includes a formal commitment to a process of evaluation to expand our body of knowledge of evidence-based practice.

The interventive process is multifaceted and built on a paradigm that seeks to establish:

- Who is this client, historically and in the present?
- What are the strengths and limitations?
- What are the existing resources?
- What does this client want?
- What does this client need?
- What can I or someone else do to assist this client in achieving the identified goals?

The interventive process also draws on the total range of theory and technique available from the profession or from others.

In working directly with the client, there are six clusters of technique available to the therapist:

1. To utilize specific components of the relationship.

2. To do specific things with the client.
3. To have the client do specific things within the interview.
4. To have the client do specific things outside of the interview.
5. To do something with the client outside of the interview.
6. To do something for the client outside of the interview.

Case Summary for Psychosocial Theory

Mr. J is a 19-year-old Latino man born in Mexico. He moved to the United States with his family when he was 10. His father died in an industrial accident when he was 12. He is in good physical health and of at least normal intelligence with no evident mental health problems. He has completed high school and is currently working in the kitchen of a fast-food restaurant and living with his mother and two sisters. The family is minimally comfortable financially. He initially presents in a shy, mildly withdrawn manner and once comfortable in a relationship exhibits a quiet pleasant engaging mien.

He was referred to the family agency by his parish priest, to whom he had turned wanting help to better himself socially and economically but was uncertain as to how to go about this.

His male social worker used the first three interviews to help Mr. J develop an open, trusting relationship based on his diagnosis of an early developing mildly strong positive transference, while keeping the content focused on his identified wish to "move ahead." From this basis, the social worker made use of several rapid assessment instruments that focused on identifying areas of interest and skills. From these and material shared in the interviews, it was clear that his identified area of interest was in the management side of the restaurant business, but he was uncertain how to go about it except to talk about looking for a better job.

From here, the social worker engaged Mr. J in some simulated job interviews, at which he did reasonably well with coaching. Next, a contract was established with him that he was to formally apply for two relevant advertised positions before the next interview.

These contacts, although not leading to a job offer, helped Mr. J clarify that a more strategic route to achieve his goals would require further education, the nature and extent of which was

unclear. To assist in this and with the client's agreement, the worker arranged for an interview at the career counseling department of a local community college, and at the client's request the social worker agreed to attend with him.

This interview was very useful; however, it appeared that the client did not have the requisite courses in his high school curriculum and that some make-up work would be required. With the client's permission, the social worker pursued this matter further and established that the fact of the client, being fluently bilingual, could substitute for the missing academic material. Mr. J was accepted into the next class of the college's hotel management program.

Over the next 3 months, the case was kept open on an on-demand basis with a focus on supporting Mr. J in his early adjustment to the program. On a 6-month routine follow-up, it was noted that the client was doing very well in the program and becoming a much more confident and outgoing person.

BASIC CONCEPTS

General

From its earliest days, psychosocial therapy has been an open system strongly committed to the integration of new ideas. Although its roots are in a psychodynamic tradition, it has integrated concepts from most other theories currently driving social work practice. Principal among these are systems theory, existential theory, crisis theory, learning theory, and task and problem-solving theories. This interest in other theories stems partially from an understanding of the role of values in the human condition and the awareness that various theories are built on differing value orientations.

Psychosocial practitioners view practice theories as tools that are differentially used as responding to where and who the client is. Thus, just as this therapy moved from a position that viewed each social worker as having competence in a single modality such as casework or group work, it now deems it essential that practitioners not only be multimethod competent but also multitheoretical in their orientations. Indeed, this openness to new ideas from whatever source has been one of the areas of criticism of this theory, as well as a factor that makes it difficult for some to put firm parameters around it.

Specific

Commitment to knowledge building. Psychosocial therapy is very much an open, changing, dynamic theory that appreciates the expanding base of knowledge reflecting the complexities of clients' lives and the myriad influences that affect them. Thus, there is the responsibility to continuously research and evaluate activities and incorporate new knowledge from whatever its source.

Positive perception of the human potential. Within this system, there is a strong belief in the ability of a person to achieve high levels of satisfying functioning even with the most damaging of early histories. The therapeutic task is to build on a person's strengths and the resources of systems to foster positive growth in individuals and families.

Cognitive and rational along with dynamic. Even though this system is strongly rooted in a psychodynamic tradition, it has welcomed and adopted the insights from the cognitive and rational therapies. Some of the early research, as discussed by Woods, indicated that much of the verbal content of interviews consisted in reflection by the client of material that surfaced in the interviews. All of us use reflective abilities to deal with daily living. Sometimes we do this effectively, whereas at other times this leads to further problems. However the opportunity to reflect with a helping understanding person can lead to more effective functioning.

Power of the helping relationship. Much of the early writing in social work clinical practice focused on the importance and power of the helping relationship and its various characteristics. This type of relationship can and often does contain elements of significant relationships from the client's past that can affect in both positive and negative ways important relationships in the present. Thus, understanding of the reality of transference factors in relationships is still considered an important factor to be kept in mind in understanding the client, although it is much less stressed than in earlier days in this therapy.

Recognition of the unconscious. In psychosocial therapy, the unconscious is still viewed as an important component of personality that influences but does not determine facets of present functioning. Although in day-to-day practice the major part of our work is oriented to the client's current reality, this powerful attribute of one's own personality cannot be ignored.

Importance of history. This theory recognizes that both social workers and clients bring to the present something of our histories. Thus, to fully understand a person we must assess to what extent their present functioning and future aspirations are influenced by their history. This does not mean that, as in earlier days, before we begin our work with a client we take a long and detailed history. It does mean, though, that we are ever on the alert for significant components of earlier history, and when such appear to be important, we pursue it or build on it as it appears necessary. This depends on diagnostic acumen as we seek to assess all components of a client's reality and the significance of each for the present reality with which we are dealing.

Understanding of pathology. Even though this system is optimistic and strength-oriented, it understands that pathology in all its manifestations is a reality. Thus, it is critical that we understand its nature and influence on clients and their families when present. The important aspect of our responsibility to assess pathology is to view it as a continuum. It is rarely a case of yes or no but whether there is any degree of pathology existing that may be of significance to the presenting situation. This requires, of course, a knowledge and understanding of pathology and its many forms and the many factors that go into its development, maintenance, control, and treatment.

Importance of social work diagnosis. Diagnosis is a broad concept with varying content and focus from one profession to another. It is different from assessment, which is also a part of the therapeutic process. In social work, diagnosis is much more complex than the seeking to assign a mental health label. Rather, it is a multifaceted dynamic process in which the practitioner sets out in a formal manner the judgments made about clients and their situations—judgments that serve as the basis for actions to be taken in the conduct of a case, actions for which the social worker takes responsibility.

Focus on everyday living. Stemming from a positive view of human nature and ability to find growth-enhancing ways to address the challenges of day-to-day living, psychosocial therapy understands that many clients can benefit greatly from having these addressed in a therapeutic milieu. For some, dealing with these mundane realities in clients' lives is not seen as the real "meat" of therapy. However, it is often the learning to deal with such life factors that brings considerable relief to clients and leads them to find ways to address other life situations.

The importance of "indirect treatment". The term *indirect treatment* seeks to describe the social worker's interactions with various persons and systems in a client's life to seek to bring about changes that will help the client achieve his or her objective. Unfortunately, this component of therapy is often viewed as less important or less clinical than direct work with clients. Nonetheless, skill in this area can be of great assistance to clients and can help bring about important changes in their lives that would not be achieved in direct work.

Strategic use of time. One of the important resources with which use is made in this approach to therapy is that of time. Rather than seeing time from an administrative perspective only, time can be used therapeutically. Work with a client can be as short as a few minutes to as long as several years of weekly contact. Short-term treatment is not by definition better than long term, nor is the reverse true. The time spent is what the client needs from our diagnostic perspective, not from some external imposition.

Practitioner self-awareness. Not only are clients influenced by their unconscious, so, too, are therapists. Hence, it is important to ensure that responses to clients are as free as possible from distortion or misunderstanding stemming from our own histories. This, of course, is one of the important functions of our professional education.

Supervision and consultation. Although we have moved far beyond the days when training was almost a therapeutic experience for the student, there is still place in our practice for a formal connection with a colleague to ensure objectivity in interactions with clients. Even though many practitioners would not see themselves as psychosocially oriented, today's pattern of student practicum and individual supervision stems from the psychosocial theorists' long-standing emphasis on the need for self-awareness as a critical component of ethical practice and for assistance in achieving it in particular situations.

Minimization of technique. It is interesting to note that as committed as psychosocial theory is to evaluation of our interventions, like the rest of the profession to date, there has been little interest in the discussion of techniques. This phenomenon also exists in other applications to treatment. Yet in a profession committed to building our practice on an ability to evaluate the correlations between the actual things we do with, to, and for clients and the outcome emanating from these, this lacuna in evaluative activities will need to assume greater importance in the days ahead.

CONCLUSION

Psychosocial therapy is an approach to social work practice with a long tradition in the profession. It builds on a broad understanding of individuals, dyads, families, groups, and other societal factors and available resources of each. Its overall goal is to assist people in achieving the highest level of psychosocial functioning through an understanding of their past, present, and future potential.

The theory reflects the century-old commitment of the history of social work. As such, its reputation has suffered in being seen as old-fashioned and out of date. Yet in its ongoing commitment to tested knowledge and innovations, it will continue to stay relevant and stand as the conceptual and operational basis of much of contemporary social work practice.

WEB SITES

Erik Erikson and psychosocial development. http://www.essortment.com/ psychosocialdev_rijk.htm.
GMS Psycho-Social-Medicine. http://www .egms.de/en/journals/psm/index.shtml.
International Journal of Psychosocial Rehabilitation. http://www.psychosocial.com.
Psychosocial Treatments. http://www.nami.org/ Content/ContentGroups/Helpline1/ Psychosocial_Treatments.htm.

References

Hamilton, G. (1951). *Theory and practice of social casework*, rev. ed. New York: Columbia University Press.

Hollis. F. (1963). *Social casework: A psychosocial therapy*, 2nd ed. New York: Random House.

Northen, H. (1982). *Clinical social work*. New York: Columbia University Press.

Turner, F. J. (1978). *Psychosocial therapy*. New York: Free Press.

Turner, F. J. (1995). *Differential diagnosis and treatment in social work*, 4th ed. New York: Free Press.

Turner, F. J. (2005). *Social work diagnosis in contemporary practice*. New York: Oxford University Press.

Woods, M. (1999). *Casework: A psychosocial therapy*, 5th ed. New York: McGraw-Hill.

33 Solution-Focused Therapy

Peter DeJong

The late Steve de Shazer, one of the inventors of solution-focused therapy (SFT), informally referred to it as a way to carry on a useful conversation with clients. The purpose of the conversation is to coconstruct solutions. Practitioners ask the questions that clearly define the approach; clients respond out of their frames of reference. The questions are not-knowing because they put clients into the position of being experts about their own lives. Therapeutic conversations focus on what clients want to be different and how to make those things happen.

HISTORY AND DEVELOPMENT

Although rooted in some respects in the "uncommon" therapy of Milton Erickson and the strategic family therapy of John Weakland and his associates at the Mental Research Institute (Miller, 1997), SFT was largely developed inductively through careful observation of therapy sessions using the one-way mirror at the Brief Family Therapy Center (BFTC) in Milwaukee. In a natural inquiry, de Shazer and his colleagues attempted to set aside past assumptions about client change and pay attention to which clients seemed to be making progress and what the practitioner might be doing that was useful (de Shazer et al., 1986). In this process, they made several discoveries about therapy and invented related techniques that they have continued to refine through ongoing use and observation. It soon became clear that clients who made progress had clearer visions of what they wanted different (goals) and could identify times in their lives when problems were not occurring or were less serious (exceptions). Consequently, more time in therapy sessions, more questioning techniques, and new assumptions about therapy and client change developed around the importance of goal formulation and exception finding.

ASSUMPTIONS

- Clients are competent to coconstruct goals and strategies.
- Clients are the experts about their own lives and the meanings of their experiences. Practitioners should ask about client perceptions and accept them.
- There is not a necessary connection between problem and solution.

- Clients must *do* something differently for change to occur.
- "Only a small change is needed." Once a small step is taken, change often snowballs beyond client and practitioner expectations.
- "If it ain't broke, don't fix it." Practitioner agendas for clients invite client resistance.
- "If it works, don't fix it." When clients can describe how exceptions occur and their contributions to them, suggest they do more of the same.
- "If it doesn't work, do something different." Do not suggest clients do what they say is not useful. (Quoted assumptions from de Shazer, 1985, 1988)

USEFUL QUESTIONS

Goal-Formulation Questions

After brief problem description by a client, practitioners ask the following to begin the coconstruction of goals: When your problem becomes less of a problem, what will be different? What would have to be different by the end of our session for you to say that our time together was not a waste of time? The miracle question is the best known of SFT's goal-formulation questions. It reads: "Suppose while you are sleeping tonight a miracle happens. The miracle is that the problem that has brought you here today is solved— just like that! Only you don't know it because you're sleeping. So when you wake up tomorrow morning, what is the first thing you'll notice that will tell you: 'Wow! Things are really different, a miracle must have happened!'"

The miracle question is an opener for a series of follow-up questions formulated around the client's beginning answer to what will be different when the miracle happens. These follow-ups use who, what, when, and where questions to get details. (Why questions are not asked because they have not proven useful in promoting client change.) For example, to a depressed client who starts out by saying the first difference he will notice is "feeling better," the practitioner continues by asking, "So, when you are feeling better, who will be the first to notice? When might (that person) notice? What will she notice? What else? What will she do when notices you doing that? What will you do then? What will you notice that's different?" And so forth.

Exception-Finding Questions

Exceptions amount to client successes. Identifying them is the best route to discovering and amplifying client strengths and resources. Exceptions related to what clients want are the most useful for building solutions. Examples of exception-finding questions include:

- Are there times when you are even a little bit "less discouraged" (client's words)?
- Are there parts of the miracle which you described to me that are happening already?
- If your friend were here and I were to ask him about whether there are times when you are "less discouraged," what would your friend say?

Once the client identifies an exception, the interviewer follows up with several who, what, when, and where questions for details.

Scaling Questions

Scaling is a useful way to help clients express complex, intuitive observations about past experiences and future possibilities in concrete terms. Clients are asked to scale an observation or possibility from 0 though 10 with the ends of the scale defined by the practitioner.

- On a scale from 0 through 10, where 0 means there is no chance of this miracle happening and 10 means every chance, what are the chances of your miracle actually happening?
- Suppose 0 equals where things were on your problems when you made the appointment to see me, and 10 equals the problem is solved, where are things at today?
- Where 0 equals "no confidence at all" and 10 means "every confidence in the world," how confident are you that you will find a solution to this problem?

Once the client gives a number, the practitioner asks for details about the meaning of that number as well as what will be different when things move up one and more numbers on the scale.

Coping Questions

These are a form of exception questions and are used when clients seem overwhelmed and discouraged beyond the point of trying. Examples include:

- What are you doing to cope—even a little bit—with this situation?
- I'm amazed! With all that has happened to you, I don't know how you make it. How do you do it? How do you get from one minute to the next?
- Ah, so you do it by reminding yourself that your children need you. You must love your children very much! So, how is reminding yourself that your children need you helpful to you?
- Could things be worse? How come they are not?
- Who has been most helpful to you in these struggles?

"What's Better?" Questions

Many other approaches begin second and later sessions of therapy with a review of assigned suggestions or the client's estimate of progress. In SFT, practitioners simply ask another form of an exception-finding question, namely, "What's better?" This procedure is tied to the recognition that solutions are built from exceptions and to observations at BFTC that asking this question most readily elicits successes that occurred since the last session. When given time to think and answer, most clients can identify something better, which the practitioner then invites the client to amplify through additional questions.

SOLUTION-FOCUSED COCONSTRUCTION

The questions used in solution-focused interviews are intended to set up a therapeutic process wherein practitioners listen for and absorb clients' words and meanings (regarding what is important to clients, what they want, and related successes), then formulate and ask the next question by connecting to clients' key words and phrases, continue to listen and absorb as clients again answer from their frames of reference, and once again formulate and ask the next question by similarly connecting. Through this process of listening, absorbing, connecting, and client responding, practitioners and clients together coconstruct new and altered meanings that build toward solutions. Communication researchers Mc Gee, Del Vento, and Bavelas (2005) describe this process as creating new common ground between practitioner and client in which questions that contain embedded assumptions of client competence and expertise set in motion a conversation in which clients participate in discovering and constructing themselves as persons of ability with positive qualities that are in the process of creating a more satisfying life. Here is an example of this conversational process with a client who has just answered the miracle question and is asked about exceptions related to the miracle (from De Jong & Berg, 2008, pp. 15–16).

Therapist: Rosie, I'm impressed. You have a pretty clear picture of how things will be different around your house when things are better. Are there times already, say in the last 2 weeks, which are like the miracle which you have been describing, even a little bit?

Rosie: Well, I'm not sure. Well, about four days ago it was better.

Therapist: Tell me about four days ago. *What was different?*

Rosie: Well, I went to bed about 10 the night before and had a good night of sleep. I had food in the house, because I had gone to the store and to the food pantry on Saturday. I had even set the alarm for 6:30 and got up when it rang. I made breakfast and called the kids. The boys ate and got ready for school and left on time. [remembering] One even got some homework out of his backpack and did it—real quick—before he went to school.

Therapist: [impressed] Rosie, that sounds like a big part of the miracle right there. I'm amazed. How did all that happen?

Rosie: I'm not sure. I guess one thing was I had the food in the house, and I got to bed on time.

Therapist: So, how did you make that happen?

Rosie: Ah, I decided not to see any clients that night, and I read books to my kids for an hour.

Therapist: How did you manage that, reading to four kids? That seems like it would be really tough.

Rosie: No, that doesn't work—reading to four kids at the same time. I have my oldest boy read to one baby, because that's the only way I can get him to practice his reading, and I read to my other boy and baby.

Therapist: Rosie, that seems like a great idea—having him read to the baby. It helps you, and it helps him with his reading. How do you get him to do that?

Rosie: Oh, I let him stay up a half hour later than the others because he helps me. He really likes that.

Later in the conversation, the therapist asks the client to scale how far along to a solution she is.

Therapist: I'd like you to put some things on a scale for me, on a scale from 0 to 10. First, on a scale from 0 through 10, where 0 equals the worst your problems have been and 10 means the problems we have been talking about are solved, where are you *today* on that scale?

Rosie: If you had asked me that question before we started today, I would have said about a 2. But now I think it's more like a 5.

Therapist: Great! Now let me ask you about how *confident* you are that you can have another day in the next week like the one four days ago—the one which was a lot like your miracle picture. On a scale of 0 to 10, where 0 equals no confidence and 10 means you have every confidence, how confident are you that you can make it happen again?

Rosie: Oh, about a 5.

Therapist: Suppose you were at a 6; what would be different?

Rosie: I'd have to be sure that I always had food in the house for breakfast for the kids.

After 30 to 40 minutes of asking questions, the SFT practitioner takes a break for 5 to 10 minutes to reflect, either individually or with a team, about how far the client has come in his or her solution building. The practitioner then formulates a message composed of compliments focusing on the client's achievements and strengths, a bridging statement reflecting the client's goals, and in most cases, a suggestion to observe for or do certain things. All three components are based on the common ground the client and practitioner have coconstructed in the interview. Here is a message based on the case illustration:

Compliments: Rosie, I'm impressed with how much you care about wanting to be a good mom and make a good home for you and your children. I'm also impressed with how clear your miracle picture is about what your home and life will look like after the miracle, and especially that you already are at a five on the way to that miracle.

Bridge: I agree that being a good mom and making a good home is very important right now.

Suggestions: So I suggest that between now and when we meet next, you continue to do the things that got you and your family to a 5 and pay attention for what else you might be doing to get things to a 5 that you are doing but have not noticed yet. Also, since you have an idea of

what will be different when things move up to a 6, be thinking about what it will take to make that happen.

PROTOCOLS

The first session in SFT proceeds from a brief problem description to extended coconstruction of goals to identification of related exceptions and scaling. Later sessions begin with exception finding followed by scaling to measure progress and identify next steps (ongoing goal formulation). Protocols with question prompts are given below (De Jong and Berg, 2008).

First Session

- Problem (How can I help? What tells you that _____ is a problem? What have you tried? Was it helpful?)
- Goal formulation (What do you want different as a result of coming here? Ask the miracle question.)
- Exceptions (Are there times when the problem does not happen or is less serious? When? How does that happen? Times bit like your miracle picture?)
- Scaling
  - Presession change
  - Motivation to work on a solution
  - Confidence of finding a solution
- Break
- Message for client(s)
  - Compliments
  - Bridge
  - Suggestion

Later Sessions

- What's better?
  - Elicit (What's happening that's better?)
  - Amplify (How does that happen? What do you do to make that happen? Is that new for you? Now that you are doing _____, what do you notice different between you and _____ (significant other)? What else is different at your house?)
  - Reinforce/compliment (Not everyone could have said or done _____. So you're the kind of person who is/does/believes _____?)
  - Start again (What else is better?)
- Doing more (What will it take to do _____ again? To do it more often?)

- If nothing is better (How are you coping? How do you make it? How come things aren't even worse?)
- Scaling progress
  - Current level
  - Next level(s) (When you move from ___ (number for current level) to __ (one number up the scale), what will be different? Who will be first to notice? When s/he notices, what will s/he do differently? What would it take to pretend a __ (one number up the scale) has happened?)
  - Termination (How will you know when it's time to stop seeing me? What will be different?)
- Break
- Message for client(s)
  - Compliments
  - Bridge
  - Suggestion

OUTCOMES

The main elements of SFT as we know it today began to appear during the mid- to late 1980s (de Shazer, 1985, 1988). Consequently, outcome studies have been added to the professional literature only in the past 15 to 20 years. Despite its youth, SFT is approaching evidence-based status (Gingerich & Eisengart, 2000; Macdonald, 2007). Macdonald's summary of the research indicates 64 studies of SFT. Six are randomized controlled studies, all showing benefits from SFT with three indicating benefit over existing treatments. Twenty-one are comparison studies with 16 favoring SFT. Effectiveness data are available from more than 2700 cases with a success rate exceeding 60 percent over an average of three to five sessions. Two meta-analyses (Kim, in press; Stams, Dekovic, Buist, & de Vries, 2006) indicate small to moderate effect sizes with equivalent outcomes to other psychotherapies over a lower average number of sessions. Several studies demonstrate that SFT is effective for offenders and other hard-to-treat clients, and socioeconomic status does not affect response to treatment, which is in contrast to all other psychotherapies. SFT is now approved by the U.S. federal government and the states of Washington, Oregon, and Florida. It has also been recognized as a promising practice by the Office of Juvenile Justice. Currently, the European Brief Therapy Association and the Solution Focused Brief Therapy Association are creating treatment manuals of SFT for use in future practice and research.

APPLICATIONS

SFT is not problem-specific. Indeed, preliminary empirical results indicate it is equally effective across a wide range of client problems and a diversity of persons (De Jong & Berg, 2008; Macdonald, 2007). The approach is fast being adopted in a variety of practice settings, is used the same way with voluntary and involuntary clients alike, and is practiced with individuals, couples, families, groups, and organizations (Berg, 1994; Berg & Kelly, 2000; Berg & Miller, 1992; Berg & Shilts, 2005; Berg & Steiner, 2003; De Jong & Berg, 2008; de Shazer & Isebaert, 2003; Jackson & McKergow, 2002; Kelly, Kim, & Franklin, in press; Lee, Sebold, & Uken, 2003; Nelson & Thomas, 2006; Pichot & Dolan, 2003; Sharry, 2001; Walker & Hayashi, 2004; Young & Holdorf, 2002). SFT shows every sign of gathering momentum.

FIT WITH SOCIAL WORK VALUES

Although SFT parts company with the professions' historic use of a problem-solving paradigm, it comports as well or better than problem solving with core professional values, such as respecting human dignity, individualizing service, fostering client vision, building on strengths, and maximizing self-determination (De Jong and Berg, 2008). It does so largely by consistently working within the client's frame of reference and asking questions in ways that always return choice to clients (De Jong & Berg, 2001; de Shazer et al., 2007).

FUTURE IMPLICATIONS

Although clinical observation and theory can never fully be separated, the former has played a greater role in the development of SFT than the latter. Once the techniques were refined, more writing began to appear about the approach's theoretical implications (Berg & De Jong, 1996; de Shazer, 1991, 1994; de Shazer et al., 2007; Miller, 1997). Social constructionism offers the most satisfying account of how clients change through exposure to SFT. Herein, therapeutic solutions are thought to be new or altered meanings. As explained and illustrated earlier, they are coconstructed between client and practitioner through language interaction. The key role for practitioners in this interactive process is always to struggle to formulate the next useful, solution-focused question from the language and meanings contained in the client's last answer. This means that a step-by-step process of questioning and answering questions is important to the change process in SFT. The future of SFT as an effective helping model for social work practice has never been brighter. To advance our knowledge of SFT's unique contribution to helping, it is important for practitioners and researchers to work together so that the model's astute clinical observation and theoretical understandings can be integrated with mechanisms of change research studies that can help us better understand the empowering, interactive change process fostered by SFT.

WEB SITES

Dr. Alasdair Macdonald; summary of outcome research on SFT. http://www.psychsft .freeserve.co.uk.

European Brief Therapy Association. http://www.ebta.nu.

Solution Focused Brief Therapy Association. http://www.sfbta.org.

References

Berg, I. K. (1994). *Family based services: A solution-focused approach.* New York: Norton.

Berg, I. K., & De Jong, P. (1996). Solution-building conversations: Co-constructing a sense of competence with clients. *Families in Society: The Journal of Contemporary Human Services, 77,* 376–391.

Berg, I. K., & Kelly, S. (2000). *Building solutions in child protective services.* New York: Norton.

Berg, I. K., & Miller, S. D. (1992). *Working with the problem drinker: A solution-focused approach.* New York: Norton.

Berg, I.K. & Shilts, L. (2005). Keeping the solutions within the classroom: WOWW approach. *School Counselor,* July/August, 30–35.

Berg, I. K., & Steiner, T. (2003). *Children's solution work.* New York: Norton.

De Jong, P., & Berg, I. K. (2001). Co-constructing co-operation with mandated clients. *Social Work, 46,* 361–374.

De Jong, P., & Berg, I. K. (2008). *Interviewing for solutions,* 3rd ed. Pacific Grove, CA: Thomson Brooks/Cole.

de Shazer, S. (1985). *Keys to solution in brief therapy.* New York: Norton.

de Shazer, S. (1988). *Clues: Investigating solutions in brief therapy.* New York: Norton.

de Shazer, S. (1991). *Putting difference to work.* New York: Norton.

de Shazer, S. (1994). *Words were originally magic.* New York: Norton.

de Shazer, S., Berg, I. K., Lipchik, E., Nunnaly, E., Molnar, A., Gingerich, W., et al. (1986). Brief therapy: Focused solution development. *Family Process, 25,* 207–221.

de Shazer, S., Dolan, Y., Korman, H., Trepper, T., McCollum, E., & Berg, I. K. (2007). *More than miracles: The state of the art of solution-focused brief therapy.* New York: Haworth.

de Shazer, S., & Isebaert, L. (2003). The Bruges model: A solution-focused approach to problem drinking. *Journal of Family Psychotherapy, 14,* 43–53.

Gingerich, W. J., & Eisengart, S. (2000). Solution-focused brief therapy: A review of the outcome research. *Family Process, 39,* 477–498.

Jackson, P. Z., & McKergow, M. (2002). *The solutions focus: The simple way to positive change.* London: Nicholas Brealey.

Kelly, M., Kim, J., & Franklin, C. (In press). *Brief solution-focused therapy in schools: A 360 degree view.* New York: Oxford University Press.

Kim, J. (In press). Examining the effects of solution-focused brief therapy: A meta-analysis using random effects modeling. *Research on Social Work Practice.*

Lee, M. Y., Sebold, J., & Uken, A. (2003). *Solution-focused treatment of domestic violence offenders: Accountability for change.* New York: Oxford University Press.

Macdonald, A. J. (2007). *Solution-focused therapy: Theory, research, and practice.* London: Sage.

McGee, D. R., Del Vento, A., & Bavelas, J. B. (2005). An interactional model of questions as therapeutic interventions. *Journal of Marital and Family Therapy, 31,* 371–384.

Miller, G. (1997). *Becoming miracle workers: Language and meaning in brief therapy.* New York: Aldine de Gruyter.

Nelson, T. S., & Thomas, F. N. (2006). *Handbook of solution-focused brief therapy: Clinical applications.* New York: Haworth.

Pichot, T., & Dolan, Y. M. (2003). *Solution-focused brief therapy: Its effective use in agency settings.* Binghamton, NY: Haworth.

Sharry, J. (2001). *Solution-focused groupwork.* London: Sage.

Stams, G. J., Dekovic, M., Buist, K., & de Vries, L. (2006). Effectiviteit van oplossingsgerichte korte therapie: Een meta-analyse [Efficacy of solution focused brief therapy: A meta-analysis]. *Gedragstherapie, 39,* 81–95.

Walker, L., & Hayashi, L. (2004). Pono Kaulike: A pilot restorative justice program. *Hawaii Bar Journal, 8,* 4–15.

Young, S., & Holdorf, G. (2002). Using solution-focused brief therapy in individual referrals for bullying. *Educational Psychology in Practice, 19,* 271–282.

William Borden

Although most social workers come to characterize their clinical approach as eclectic, there is surprisingly little consideration of the ways practitioners engage differing theoretical perspectives, empirical findings, and technical procedures over the course of psychosocial intervention. This chapter reviews comparative approaches to clinical theory and shows how mastery of the foundational schools of thought strengthens efforts to carry out eclectic, integrative forms of psychosocial intervention. The first part summarizes three lines of inquiry that have shaped integrative approaches to practice, broadly characterized as technical eclecticism, common factors perspectives, and theoretical integration. The second section describes pluralist approaches to clinical theory and outlines core domains of concern in comparative analysis of differing systems. The third part presents a case report and illustrates how a pluralist point of view informs use of differing perspectives over the course of intervention, broadening the range of theoretical concepts, empirical research, and technical procedures applied in the clinical situation.

INTEGRATIVE PERSPECTIVES IN CONTEMPORARY PRACTICE

As a starting point, it is important to acknowledge the growing emphasis on integrative approaches in contemporary psychotherapy and psychosocial intervention. Clinical scholars have increasingly realized the strengths and limits of differing theoretical perspectives over the years, and practitioners have drawn on psychodynamic, cognitive, behavioral, humanistic, and ecological perspectives in fashioning integrative models of practice, seeking to engage a wider range of clients, broaden the scope of intervention, and improve outcomes. Borden (2009) and Wampold (2007) review orienting perspectives and recent developments in integrative conceptions of psychosocial intervention.

Three lines of inquiry have shaped efforts to link theory, empirical data, and technical procedures in integrative conceptions of psychosocial intervention over the last quarter of a century, broadly characterized as technical eclecticism, common factors approaches, and conceptual synthesis or "theoretical integration" (Arkowitz, 1992; Goldfried & Norcross, 1995). The perspectives emphasize differing elements and strategies in their attempts to enlarge the frame of psychosocial intervention and improve therapeutic outcomes.

Technical Eclecticism

According to conceptions of technical eclecticism, practitioners apply procedures pragmatically on the basis of clinical efficacy (Safran & Messer, 1997). The goal is to match specific techniques with circumscribed problems in functioning in light of empirical evidence and clinical expertise. For example, empirical findings and clinical experience support the use of cognitive and behavioral techniques for treatment of a range of problems in functioning associated with post-traumatic stress disorders and borderline personality organization. Procedures are frequently outlined in manuals that guide application in the clinical situation.

The foundation is empirical rather than theoretical, and practitioners assume that therapeutic methods can be applied independently of the theories from which they originate. Technical procedures are drawn from a variety of sources without necessarily endorsing—or even understanding—the supporting conceptual frameworks (Arkowitz, 1992; Goldfried & Norcross, 1995). In this sense, it is the most technically oriented approach to integration. The practitioner could, for example, combine procedures from cognitive, behavioral, experiential, and family systems perspectives in the course of an individual treatment. Representative examples include Arnold Lazarus's multimodal perspective (1992) and Larry Beutler's prescriptive model of intervention, specifying strategies and techniques for treatment of circumscribed problems in functioning (Beutler, 2004).

Common Factors Approaches

In his classic work *Persuasion and Healing*, Jerome Frank explored the ways all forms of psychological healing share common elements, emphasizing the functions of the therapeutic relationship, the healing setting, conceptual schemes that provide plausible explanations of what is the matter and what carries the potential to help, and the core activities of psychosocial intervention that foster change and growth (Frank & Frank, 1991). More than half a century of psychotherapy research has documented the comparable effectiveness of a range of approaches, and there is growing agreement that all of the major systems of psychotherapy—psychodynamic, cognitive, behavioral, humanistic, and ecological—share common elements that account for their relative effectiveness (Wampold, 2007).

The common factors approach is based on the assumption that all therapeutic systems exert their effects largely through the same underlying principles and processes. Clinicians reason that common factors are more important than the specific procedures that distinguish the particular schools of thought and argue that shared elements can serve as the basis for development of more effective approaches to practice.

Accordingly, practitioners focus on the core conditions and basic elements shared by the major schools of thought encompassed in the broader field of psychotherapy. In doing so, they consider client factors, such as motivation and expectations of change; practitioner characteristics, such as warmth, empathetic attunement, and authenticity; the provision of a rationale for problems in functioning and a coherent conceptual framework for interventions; strategic processes, such as experiential learning through interpersonal interaction; interpretive procedures that enlarge understandings of self, relationships, and life experience; and the role of reinforcement, exposure, modeling, and identification in change and growth (Arkowitz, 1992; Borden, 2009; Stricker & Gold, 2003).

Practitioners attempt to identify which elements would appear to be most useful in the treatment of a particular individual on the basis of assessment data and experiential learning in the clinical situation. Some clients, for example, find it useful to explore earlier life events or process their experiences of the helping relationship; others, however, make more effective use of task-centered, action-oriented, educational modes of intervention. Sol Garfield's integrative model of intervention, emphasizing experiential learning, insight, hope, and the sustaining functions of the helping relationship, exemplifies the common factors perspective (Garfield, 2000). Drisko (Chapter 27) covers common factors in more detail.

Theoretical Integration

A third approach emerged out of efforts to develop unifying frameworks that bridge theories of personality, problems in living, and methods of intervention; the aim is conceptual synthesis, beyond a blend of common factors and technical procedures (Goldfried & Norcross, 1995). Whereas the intervention strategies of the integrative system may encompass the procedures used in technical eclecticism, there are crucial differences in the assumptions and conceptualizations that inform decision making and use of particular strategies (Stricker & Gold, 2003). Such frameworks broaden the range of psychological and social phenomena that potentially serve as the focus of treatment and offer varying points of entry. The enlarged conceptual perspective allows clinicians to expand the range of technical procedures used over the course of intervention (Borden, 2009).

By way of example, Paul Wachtel has developed a psychodynamic approach that encompasses behavioral, cognitive, humanistic, systemic, and ecological perspectives, extending his earlier integration of psychoanalytic theory and behavioral concepts (Wachtel, 2008). In the field of social work, Sharon Berlin has developed an integrative cognitive perspective that links neuroscience and cognitive psychology, the major schools of psychotherapy, and framing perspectives in the social work tradition (Berlin, 2002).

THE ROLE OF THEORY IN PRACTICE

The foregoing lines of inquiry deepen our understanding of common factors that operate across the schools of thought and the range of technical strategies employed in eclectic modes of treatment, offering pragmatic frameworks for psychosocial intervention. If clinicians are to carry out integrative forms of practice effectively, however, they must develop an understanding of the foundational theories of the field. In the absence of theoretical knowledge, practitioners do not have conceptual frames of reference to understand the dynamics of change processes or the technical elements they are trying to integrate in eclectic, individualized approaches to intervention. Procedures are deprived of context, and clinicians run the risk of carrying out reductive, mechanized approaches to practice, lacking theoretical rationales for strategies and methods of intervention (Borden, 2009; Gurman & Messer, 2003).

PLURALISM AS COMPARATIVE PERSPECTIVE

Clinical scholars have drawn on philosophical conceptions of pluralism in their efforts to develop frameworks for critical thinking and decision making in comparative approaches to clinical theory (Borden, 2009; Strenger, 1997). Although a review of this work is beyond the scope of the chapter, it is important to identify the defining features of pluralism and its implications for pragmatic use of theoretical concepts, empirical findings, and technical procedures in the clinical situation.

Pluralist points of view emphasize the limits of human understanding and assume that no single framework captures the variousness and complexity of actual experience in the real world. Thinkers and practitioners approach concerns from multiple, independent perspectives, realizing that there are mutually exclusive descriptions of the world and equally valid points of view that inevitably contradict one another. In this respect, pluralist perspectives challenge notions of grand theory, which presume to assert universal truths, and take the more realistic position that theoretical formulations and empirical findings *at best* provide partial, incomplete understandings of experience. William James emphasizes the importance of immediate experience, practical consequences, and implications for action in his conceptions of pluralism and pragmatism (Borden, 2009).

From a pluralist point of view, then, theories serve a range of functions, providing tools for critical thinking and decision making as practitioners carry out their work. Every theoretical system is distinguished by its particular concerns, purposes, methods, strengths, and limits; no single approach—however encompassing it may seem—can possibly meet all needs over the course of intervention.

In spite of the diversity of theoretical perspectives that inform psychosocial intervention, clinical scholars have identified core domains of concern that facilitate efforts to carry out comparative study, encompassing the following areas:

- Historical origins of the theoretical perspective; intellectual traditions, worldviews, and social, cultural, political, and economic conditions that have influenced the development of guiding assumptions and basic concepts; the types of clients, problems in living, and settings that have shaped clinical approaches.
- Conceptions of personality, self, person in context, and development across life course; empirical support for basic propositions; congruence of concepts with core social work values.
- Conceptions of resilience, health, well-being, and the common good.
- Conceptions of vulnerability, problems in living, and psychopathology; extent to which theorists encompass social, cultural, political, or economic contexts of understanding in formulations of vulnerability, need, and problems in functioning.
- Conceptions of psychosocial intervention: core assumptions, change processes, and curative factors; structure and process of intervention; range of application; empirical support for efficacy and effectiveness of approach; implications for emerging models of evidence-based practice (see Gurman & Messer, 2003, for comparative review of classical and contemporary therapeutic systems).

In comparative approaches to theory, practitioners master the foundational schools of thought and engage a range of ideas as they carry out their practice, without committing themselves to any single school or tradition. Pluralist perspectives attempt to foster dialogue across the divergent perspectives that shape contemporary practice, enlarging ways of seeing, understanding, and acting as clinicians work to understand what is the matter and what carries the potential to help. The practitioner enters into different points of view and critically evaluates possible approaches, concepts, and methods in light of the particular circumstances of the clinical situation, assessing choices and potential courses of action as intervention proceeds. The validity of any theoretical concept or method is determined by its *usefulness* in the context of the particular case (Borden, 2009; Strenger, 1997).

Clinical Application

The following case report illustrates the ways in which a pluralist frame of reference guides use of concepts and methods from divergent perspectives over the course of intervention.

The client, age 63, developed diffuse anxiety, signs of depression, and dissociative states 8 months after he was injured in an automobile accident. He had completed a course of rehabilitation in an extended care facility following recovery from life-threatening injuries and had recently returned to his home. He described fluctuating periods of numbing detachment and intrusive recollections of the events surrounding the accident. He reported a growing sense of dread—the feeling that "something bad is about to happen."

The client related a range of symptoms that met diagnostic criteria for post-traumatic stress disorder. Further sources of vulnerability emerged in his developmental history. His mother had died shortly after his birth, and he described ongoing disruptions in caretaking arrangements through childhood and adolescence. He reported ongoing difficulties in establishing relationships in adulthood and described limited contact with extended family or friends; his experience of dependency and isolation following the accident had intensified longings for closeness and connection with others.

Although the focus of intervention centered on problems in functioning precipitated by the traumatic event, the practitioner realized that the client's history of early loss, disruptions in caretaking, and subsequent modes of attachment potentially limited his capacity to establish a collaborative relationship and negotiate the interactive experience of the therapeutic process.

In light of the crucial role of the therapeutic relationship in efforts to sponsor change and growth, the practitioner attended carefully to the development of the working alliance, seeking to create conditions that would sponsor the client's engagement in the therapeutic process. The clinician's warmth, attunement, and responsiveness facilitated the client's experience of acceptance, understanding, and support. The practitioner's use of self and relational provisions were informed by person-centered conceptions of the helping relationship, psychodynamic formulations of the therapeutic alliance and the holding environment, and developmental research on the ways that early loss and disruption in caretaking influence modes of attachment and interpersonal functioning. The cli-

nician reviewed conceptions of post-traumatic stress syndromes with the client to help him understand the nature of his problems in functioning and the core activities of the therapeutic process.

In the first phase of treatment, the client related the course of events following the accident in a detached, impersonal fashion, sometimes speaking in the third person. He showed an absence of emotional responsiveness, consistent with the denial phase of post-traumatic stress reactions, and appeared indifferent as he described events: "I don't know what good it does to talk about any of this. We can't change what has happened. I should be able to get beyond this and live my life." Relational concepts from self psychology and person-centered perspectives guided the clinician's reflection and validation of the client's underlying feelings of fear, helplessness, and hopelessness. The worker's attunement and empathetic processing of his reactions appeared to strengthen the relationship and the holding environment, creating conditions for more active, focused exploration of traumatic events.

The client's experience of numbing detachment fluctuated with periods of diffuse anxiety as he continued to process traumatic states in the middle phase of intervention. The clinician drew on cognitive and behavioral approaches in efforts to help the client manage intrusive recollection of events and disrupt vicious circles of thought, feeling, and behavior that perpetuated problems in functioning. He had come to see the world as a dangerous place, restricting patterns of activity, and viewed people as unsupportive and unreliable, avoiding opportunities to resume contact with extended family and friends in spite of longing for connection.

The clinician used a range of cognitive procedures in efforts to help the client challenge and revise maladaptive schemata ("The world is a dangerous place"), working assumptions ("Nobody really wants to see me"), and automatic thoughts ("I am broken"; "My life is over") that perpetuated his experience of fear, demoralization, and disengagement from activities. The practitioner drew on behavioral methods of exposure in efforts to help the client engage feared aspects of inner experience (memories, images, and thoughts related to the accident) and feared activities in the outer world (interaction with others, activities of everyday life). The client and clinician worked collaboratively to identify tasks that provided occasions to expand patterns of activity and carry out social interaction. Such active modes of intervention provided opportunities for mastery and development of coping strategies and social skills, strengthening the client's morale, self-esteem, and sense of possibility.

The client made considerable progress in efforts to recognize and accept the experience of trauma, manage fluctuations in internal states, and engage relational life. In the final phase of intervention, the clinician drew on humanistic and existential perspectives as the client explored the meaning of the accident and the implications of the event, working to clarify core values and essential concerns that would shape his life plan.

The practitioner's mastery of psychodynamic, cognitive, behavioral, humanistic, and existential perspectives provided the theoretical underpinnings for use of differing concepts, empirical findings, and technical procedures over the course of intervention. Movement from one orientation to another was guided by the nature of specific problems in functioning, the focal concerns of intervention, and the client's capacities to make use of differing strategies. The clinician emphasized the following approaches and procedures in efforts to facilitate change and growth:

1. processing of interactive experience in the therapeutic situation to deepen understanding of modes of attachment and interpersonal behavior;
2. cognitive restructuring;
3. exposure to inner and outer domains of feared experience;
4. development of behavioral skills through modeling and experiential learning; and
5. interpretive procedures to enlarge assumptive world and deepen understanding of self, others, and life experience.

FUTURE APPLICATIONS TO SOCIAL WORK

In the pluralist approach to theory described here, the foundational schools of thought provide contexts of understanding for use of differing concepts, empirical findings, and technical operations over the course of intervention. The clinician

- learns multiple theories, therapeutic languages, and modes of intervention;
- draws on concepts from a variety of perspectives in light of the specifics of the clinical situation; and

- judges the validity of theoretical concepts on the basis of their usefulness in the context of the particular case.

Comparative perspectives make the multiplicity of competing approaches a defining feature of psychosocial intervention. The practitioner aims to establish an ongoing dialogue among representatives of the major schools of thought that sponsors clarification of differing points of view and theoretically informed integration of concepts, empirical findings, and techniques in eclectic, individualized approaches to psychosocial intervention.

WEB SITE

Society for the Exploration of Psychotherapy Integration. http://www.cyberpsych.org/sepi/awards.htm.

References

Arkowitz, H. (1992). Integrative theories of therapy. In D. K. Freedheim (Ed.), *History of psychotherapy: A century of change* (pp. 261–303). Washington, DC: American Psychological Association.

Berlin, S. (2002). *Social work practice: A cognitive-integrative perspective.* New York: Oxford University Press.

Beutler, L. (2004). *Prescriptive psychotherapy.* London: Oxford University Press.

Borden, W. (2009). Taking multiplicity seriously: Pluralism, pragmatism, and integrative perspectives in social work practice. In W. Borden (Ed.) *The play and place of theory in social work.* New York: Columbia University Press.

Frank, J. D., & Frank, J. B. (1991). *Persuasion and healing.* Baltimore, MD: Johns Hopkins University Press.

Garfield, S. L. (2000). Eclecticism and integration: A personal retrospective view. *Journal of Psychotherapy Integration, 10,* 341–356.

Goldfried, M., & Norcross, J. (1995). Integrative and eclectic therapies in historical perspective. In B. Bonger & L. Beutler (Eds.), *Comprehensive textbook of psychotherapy* (pp. 254–273). New York: Oxford University Press.

Gurman, A., & Messer, S. (2003). "Contemporary issues in the theory and practice of psychotherapy: A framework for comparative study, pp. 1–23. In Gurman, A. & Messer, S. (Eds.). (2003). *Essential psychotherapies: Theory and practice,* New York: Guilford Publications, Inc.

Lazarus, A. (2002). The multimodal assessment treatment method. In J. Lebow (Ed.), *Comprehensive handbook of psychotherapy. Vol. 4: Integrative-eclectic* (pp. 241–254). New York: Wiley.

Safran, J., & Messer, S. (1997). Psychotherapy integration: A postmodern critique. *Clinical Psychology: Science and Practice, 4*, 140–152.

Strenger, C. (1997). Hedge hogs, foxes, and critical pluralism: The clinician's yearning for unified conceptions. *Psychoanalysis and Contemporary Thought, 20*(1), 111–145.

Stricker, G., & Gold, J. (2003). Integrative approaches to psychotherapy. In A. Gurman, & S. Messer (Eds.), *Essential psychotherapies* (pp. 317–349). New York: Guilford.

Wachtel, P. L. (2008). *Relational theory and the practice of psychotherapy.* New York: Guilford.

Wampold, B. E. (2007). Psychotherapy: The humanistic (and effective) treatment. *American Psychologist, 62*(8), 857–873.

35   Logotherapy

David Guttmann

Today, some half a billion people in the world are 65 years and older, and their numbers are growing steadily from year to year. Their percentage in the total population of the world will grow even larger during the first half of the present century. It will have a dramatic effect on the well-being of the aged and on the provision of care, services, supports, and benefits for them in terms of quality and quantity. In addition to the unprecedented growth in the numbers of the aged and the "pre-elderly" (age 55+) population, longevity is also increasing. Today it hovers around 80 years in the West and even more in Japan. Women enjoy a longer life span than men on the average. How to make the years in older adulthood meaningful is getting more critical for society and for each aging individual. This chapter presents the theory, underlying philosophy, values, principles, methods, and research on logotherapy as a supplement to the traditional methods of psychotherapy used by social workers working with the aged population.

THE QUESTION ABOUT THE MEANING OF LIFE

The question about the meaning of life raises its head every time life reminds humans of the fact that they will live in this world for only a short time. This question returns and surfaces anew in times of crisis. Each human being who experiences some loss; everyone who becomes disabled due to sickness, accident, or act of terror; each one who loses a beloved person or a cherished ideal that gave purpose and meaning to his or her life; each one who is unwillingly laid off work asks the same questions: Why survive? Why continue to live? Wouldn't it be better to finish life, while I can still do so, instead of continuing to suffer? Does life have any value when I will die in any case?

Doubts about the worthiness of life in this world full of dangers, violence, and aggression, encompass all social classes, not just the poor, downtrodden, unemployed, and sick. Crises can and do happen to all of us, irrespective of social and economic standing. The crisis can center on a wide variety of factors—political, economic, religious, and social—and can paralyze person's soul in whole or in part, depending on the severity that the individual or society attaches to the crisis.

Social workers as helping professionals should remember that the young of today will be the elderly of tomorrow, and they, too, will face questions that press heavily on the present generation of elderly people. What is the meaning of my life? Did I do what was expected of me? Did

I utilize the opportunities life threw in my lap? Did I cope successfully with the changes life brought me? Was I aware that life has an end, that it is temporary, or did I waste the precious time given me?

MEANINGFUL LIVING AS A CENTRAL CHALLENGE IN LIFE

Logotherapy concentrates on the age-old human quest to live a meaningful life. Created by Viktor Emil Frankl, author of the best-selling *Man's Search for Meaning* (1962), *logotherapy* means psychological and spiritual therapy by discovering meaning in life. It combines psychological and existentialist philosophical attitudes to life with a methodology that emphasizes a deep commitment to humanistic values, respect for human dignity and freedom of choice, and the right to choose and form one's life so that it will be meaningful for the individual and for the society in which one lives. This attitude to life is shared by social workers.

Frankl, the founding father of logotherapy, has gone beyond his two illustrious predecessors in psychology, Freud and Adler, who were influential on his development early in his youth as an aspiring physician and psychiatrist. Frankl willingly accepts the debt owed them as originators of theories that have changed the concepts of the human psyche forever. He maintains that the human spirit is the only healthy nucleus found even in the sickest individual. A man can lead a healthy life only when he is in harmony with himself, when he is in good relations with himself, when he is not trying to escape his life task. The human spirit helps one cope with losses that characterize human life mainly in its second half and especially in old age.

Aging constitutes an individual experience that each human being will undergo if he or she is fortunate enough to live a long life. In the industrialized countries of the world, the majority of people enjoy a length of life that was unknown in historical times. Yet despite this great achievement, there are many among the aging population who are not prepared psychologically and spiritually for this period of life and perceive elderly adults negatively—without realizing the value they received from life.

If we could define aging by giving it a number in years, we would do well to begin with the second half of life, at age 50. This number does not necessarily mean that each human being must be old at that age. Human traits are different from one person to next. Yet this number can symbolize a phase in life that is open for new beginnings and to new search for meaningful living. It is more than reasonable to expect that the majority of people would object to voluntarily accept themselves at age 50 as "aged." This objection seems reasonable if aging is perceived as renunciation of life. But if aging is perceived as a period of life in which people can enjoy life in all its richness, then aging could be welcomed and even sought after. Unfortunately, few people think and behave this way. This chapter presents logotherapeutic aims, goals, and methods of intervention that may be helpful to social workers working with the aged along with two cases for illustration.

CASE ONE

Abe, a man in his early sixties, came to me "to treat him of the emptiness that befell on him the past few years." He told me that he was treated by various therapists and methods, including Chinese acupuncture, but aside from the money he spent, he didn't gain a thing. He was still waiting for a turn that would bring an end to his suffering. He asked me suspiciously what method I use in my therapy—psychoanalysis or behavior therapy? I said to Abe, "I use my own method." He seemed perplexed and asked, "You have no other method?" "No," I said. "I try to adapt myself to the special needs of the client. There are many methods in psychotherapy, but you can't help one with methods alone. But if you insist, I tell you that I use logotherapy." I proceeded to briefly tell him about logotherapy, a short-term psychotherapy that concentrates on the importance of discovering meaning in life. I said that in my 30 years of practice I learned to understand the language, the world of concepts, and values of the client, for only that way can one help the client find his or her unique way in life.

"Yes," he said. "I heard something about Frankl. That's okay with me." He seemed relaxed and told me that despite his relatively good physical, social, and economic condition, he felt that something was missing in his life and couldn't find meaning and sense to his existence. He circled the globe twice and had worked as a volunteer in various organizations, yet he could not find peace of mind. Something was missing and was bothering him a great deal. The lack of this "something" was what made Abe's life empty and miserable. He felt that he was living in an "existential vacuum," without a clear purpose and goal. I said to Abe that he could be helped if he would invest hard work and even make some sacrifice for it. "What is it?" he asked. "What you feel is good for you," I said. He was disappointed. "I thought that you would give me something else, perhaps advice." "I don't have such things," I said. "In logotherapy, we don't believe in the concept of 'instant therapy.' There are no short-cuts. Man must work hard on himself to change."

"Logotherapy," I explained to Abe, "is based on choice and responsibility, and these belong first of all to the client. The therapist can only help. He cannot make a decision for the client, for the client is the one who will carry the responsibility for his choices and for his fate. If you want to live a meaningful life now, instead of living in the past, you must make an effort. First you should think about what activity is the most meaningful for you. After you have invested this effort, and made your discovery, then you are free to discuss the ways to achieve your goal." "Do you mean that I have to change my habits; for example to forgo getting up late in the morning and spending hours in a café?" "It depends on you," I said. "You don't have to change a thing if you don't want to. You may stay in your misery and feeling of emptiness." "Good," he said. "I will consider your words. What do I owe you?" "You don't owe me a thing," I said. "You owe only to yourself."

As seen in this case, many elderly people forget the fact that men and women are first of all spiritual beings whose happiness and real wealth is measured in spiritual, emotional, and intellectual gains. The soul is the central factor in the life of each elderly individual, for the soul never ages. Only the body turns elderly and declines, while the soul remains young and continues to develop. True success in life is measured in the spiritual sense, and completeness of life can be attained by wisdom alone. Such success means giving to others—loving, sharing, and finding deeper meaning in everything we do.

One of the advantages of old age is connected to the spiritual freedom one can acquire if one is willing to invest the necessary effort. Spiritual freedom means awareness about responsibility for one's deeds, good and bad. This responsibility is a maxim in logotherapy. It is expressed in the wise use of time and resources for the benefit of society. An elderly person should not become a burden to others. It is important to adopt a healthy lifestyle and refrain from using harmful substances. Today, there are many opportunities for elderly people to remain active, productive, and useful to society long years beyond retirement

The life of a person is a constant struggle between the inner and outer powers of fate. Yet despite the importance of fate, the starting point should be the freedom that exists even in the most severe cases of pathology. This freedom is expressed in the attitude people take toward what is happening to them. A neurotic fatalist prefers to escape by not taking responsibility for his fate, but leaving it up to his "weakness of will." Logotherapy offers ways to cope with the blows of fate. There are four ways offered to the client to change a mentally unhealthy and negative attitude for life to a healthy and positive one. The first includes the notion that to adopt a positive attitude to the blows of fate is a tremendous human achievement. The second involves showing the client something meaningful that is included in the suffering, despite the blow. The need to turn the client's attention from what has been lost to what remains, to what is whole and has not been harmed by fate, is the third way. The final way is adopting a philosophical standpoint or a religious perspective on life that can help the client carry the burden of suffering.

CASE TWO

An illustration to such treatment is the case of a 65-year-old widow who lost her husband after a long battle with cancer. She felt she was useless in the world, and she could have easily fallen into depression and despair. The first phase in the treatment was for her to see that the fate she suffered was not only a disaster but an opportunity to discover new meaning to her life. After this phase was accomplished, the time had come to find the meaning hidden in the suffering. The client was told that suffering without meaning is dangerous and superfluous, and the meaning that she could find in her situation meant seeing life in a different light and understanding that her suffering is not in vain. On the contrary, it could strengthen her spiritually and help her continue living for new goals—instead of the care she gave her husband during his illness. This therapeutic discussion laid the foundation for the next phase in the treatment. Work in that phase concentrated on making an inventory of what remained whole and could serve as basis for her new life—her family, her economic resources, her friends, and her informal support system, and above all her own strong personality. When this client accepted the fact that she had reasons to live, she was able to free herself from her deep mourning.

Whoever has experienced a loss of something that was meaningful in life can relate to the blow of fate that befell him or her as something beyond his or her control. He or she can change attitudes to this event and continue to move forward on the path of life. He or she can find new meaning to existence and be cured mentally.

WHAT IS LOGOTHERAPY?

Logotherapy occupies a special place in psychotherapy. It belongs neither to psychoanalytically oriented schools, behaviorally oriented psychology, religious studies, or personal growth movements. Rather, logotherapy is therapy for the sick, support for the sufferer, education for the confused, and philosophy for the frustrated. Logotherapy includes and deals with the biological, psychological, and spiritual dimensions of a human being. All these come together and are expressed in the functional dimension. Frankl's main goal in creating logotherapy was to make psychotherapy more human. He saw his mission in the world as counteracting any tendencies to reduce human lives to tiny cogs in a large machine.

Frankl built the theory of logotherapy on triangles. Three life events influenced him about the importance of meaning in life (Frankl, 1995). These three events were linked in a symbolic way to the three concepts of meaning in logotherapy: freedom of the will, the will to meaning, and the meaning of life—and to the three worlds of values in which people can discover meaning to their lives. Each of these is briefly presented.

Freedom of the Will

Human beings are blessed with a basic sense of freedom of the will. Freedom of the will is the opposite of fate. Even in Holocaust concentration camps, there was a measure of freedom to choose one's reaction to the conditions in which one had to live. Freedom of the will is not a purpose in itself; it is the pathway to the will to meaning. The basic striving of human beings is to find and fulfill a meaning despite whatever may hinder the fulfillment and satisfaction of basic needs.

The Will to Meaning

Empirical and clinical evidence indicates that homeostatic and psychodynamic models, in which people are seen as motivated entirely by the desire to eliminate or reduce tension, do not capture all there is to a human person (Batthyany & Guttmann, 2006). Whereas psychodynamic (homeostatic) models would tend to predict that once all basic drives and needs are satisfied humans should be in a state of inner harmony and stable mental health, reality seems to tell different stories of people who live in a world of despair, boredom, and frustration. People can be frustrated, even depressed amongst all luxuries. Frankl (1986) maintains that mental health is based on a certain degree of tension between what one is and what one should become. Humans need to strive and struggle for some worthy goal.

PATHWAYS TO MEANING

The "tragic triad"—suffering, guilt, and death—are not strangers to members of a helping profession, such as social work. They are used to dealing with situations in which these ingredients of human existence manifest themselves in various forms and with various forces because no one can escape in life some measure of pain and some feeling of guilt, and no one lives forever. Logotherapy is particularly suited to deal with issues of guilt, suffering, and death. Each of these contain many opportunities for self-transcendence and discovering meaning in life.

Frankl recognized three main pathways to meaning. He called these "worlds of values." The first value, *creativity*, is that of doing a deed. Any achievement or accomplishment may be regarded as proof of the creative deeds that one gives to this world by way of creativity. It does not matter in which area of life, as long as his or her deeds move humanity, society, or family forward. *Experiential values* refer to those one is experiencing through meetings with others, or what one takes from the world "free of charge"—natural beauty, sunset and sunrise, mountains and the sea, flowers and trees, the works of great artists, teachers, writers and poets. Frankl (1986) claims that "the peaks decide the meaningfulness of life, and a single moment can retroactively flood an entire life with meaning" (p. 44). *Attitudinal values* refer to the attitude one takes toward predicaments, such as when one is required to cope with an unalterable fate or an unavoidable suffering. Even if one cannot change the situation or circumstance, one can still choose the attitude toward the condition. Frankl (1986) said, "The way in which he accepts, the way in which he bears his cross, what courage he manifests in suffering, what dignity he displays in doom and disaster, is the measure of his human fulfillment" (p. 44). Meaning can be found in many additional ways: by discovering one's self and uniqueness, choosing an alternative, assuming responsibility, and self-transcendence and/or self-detachment.

Meaning of Life

According to logotherapy, life is unconditionally meaningful, but one has to first differentiate between two definitions of the word meaning: meaning of the moment, and ultimate or supra meaning. A therapist cannot give meaning to a client and should never try to impose it on the client. Meaning must be found and discovered by the client him- or herself.

The meaning of the moment. In each moment, we are requested by life to respond to the meaning offered by some event and realize the potential hidden in that moment. Meaning comes from "getting out of ourselves" toward purposes and goals, toward ideals to achieve and to serve, and toward people to love. When a human being cannot discover, recognize, or accept meaning, he or she finds him- or herself in an "existential vacuum." This vacuum cries out to be filled. Those who cannot fill their lives with some meaning are apt to pay a price in the form of psychiatric symptoms, such as deviations from the social norms commonly accepted in a given culture.

The supra meaning. Frankl was convinced that a religious sense exists in all human beings but he was also aware that not every person can grasp that there is a meaning beyond the physical and psychological world. He used the concept of supra or ultimate meaning to convey that it is not always comprehensible. Supra meaning is not a matter for thought but for belief. We can perceive it only existentially, outside our experience, by faith. Sometimes this sense is buried, and sometimes it is repressed in the human unconscious. Therefore, even someone who is not religious in the broadest sense of this term can find supra meaning to his or her life no less than the believer in God (Guttmann, 1996). Whether one believes in God is a personal matter and a private value. However, for a professional, there is a need to formulate a worldview, a basic perception of this world, which provides a sense of security. Refraining from judging a client's values and attitudes is not sufficient for relieving an elderly client's pain or to comfort him or her in suffering. The effective social worker must make conscious effort to enter the client's value system and use it in a responsible and intelligent way to help with problems whose source is spiritual.

Logotherapeutic Approach to Guilt

In caring for an elderly parent when he or she becomes ill, especially when a parent has to be placed in an institution, one seldom escapes feelings of guilt. Such feelings are heightened when expectations either on the part of the parent or the adult child cannot be met. Guilt may be experienced by the siblings of the caretaker who do not involve themselves to the extent they could in the caretaking functions regarding their aged parents. Feelings of guilt may result from some act committed that was basically wrong or from something that was supposed to be done and was not performed. This is normal guilt in logotherapy. Neurotic guilt is felt by a person without committing any wrongdoing. Neurotic guilt is the intention to do something wrong. For example, when someone secretly wishes the death of an aged and incapacitated parent, and the parent suddenly dies of natural causes, the person wishing the death starts experiencing guilt for having "killed" the parent. Such guilt has no actual cause, yet the guilty person cannot get rid of the feeling by atonement (Sternig, 1984). Existential guilt is different from both actual and neurotic guilt. We feel its effects as confusion, emptiness, restlessness, and meaninglessness in our lives (like in the case of Abe). When we refuse to relate to the world in which we live and negate our responsibility, we feel existential guilt. Logotherapists deal with guilt by helping the client admit it and by trying to change client behavior not only to make amends when it is possible but also to learn from guilt to avoid repeating the behavior that led to the feeling of guilt.

Attitude to Pain and Suffering

Suffering is an integral part of life, like fate and death. Without suffering and death, human life cannot be complete. From birth to death, suffering accompanies every act of growth. Great achievements in life are the results of great suffering. Frankl maintains that suffering would not have a meaning unless it was absolutely necessary. In logotherapy, we differentiate among three types of suffering: that which is associated with an unchangeable fate, that which comes as a result of an emotionally painful experience, and that which arises out of the meaninglessness of one's life. Changing a person's attitude from a preoccupation with suffering and misery to the opportunity to be of service to others and redirecting the mental energy to discover new meaning in life is logotherapy's answer to suffering. Logotherapy perceives unavoidable suffering as an opportunity to demonstrate the human capacity to rise above pain by making use of the "defiant power of the human spirit."

Logotherapy's Approach to Death

Logotherapy's insistence on the unconditional meaningfulness of life, even against the reality of death, is based on Frankl's analysis of the meaning of death for all human beings. Does death takes away the meaning of life? According to logotherapy, the opposite is true. If life was infinite, there would be no need to answer its challenges. Frankl claims that only the potentialities, the questions life asks us, are transitory, whereas our replies remain forever. Nothing is lost in the past. Rather, once something is in the past, it is eternally stored. Nobody can remove it from the past. Human beings are the only creatures on this Earth who are aware of their own death. This discovery should lead us toward the reawakening of responsibility toward life, instead of denying death's existence. This attitude is particularly useful for social workers working with aged people. Instead of a preoccupation with death, one should occupy oneself with living. There are many victims of cancer and other deadly illnesses who do not accept their fate and do not learn to live with their misfortune. These people destroy the little time left them.

Social workers know the importance of support systems for well-being and mental health. Surprisingly, however, hope has not received as much attention. Yet the healing power of hope is a valuable factor for helping professionals. Lack of hope leads to despair. People who are unable to cope with the demands of reality are prone to suicidal behavior. Without a reason to live for someone or something, people may lose interest in life. Enhancing clients' hope and using it to change maladaptive coping behaviors can be achieved by identifying the clients' sources of hope. Identifying the hidden resources of the human spirit, guiding the sufferer toward discovery of meaning in suffering and in death, and redirecting the waning energies of the sick and the aged toward "brave deeds" are roles for social workers and logo-therapists.

PRINCIPLES AND GUIDING VALUES OF LOGOTHERAPY

Logotherapy's philosophy and principles can be viewed as statements of its guiding values. They are the following. Life has meaning, as long as one is conscious, in all circumstances. Humans can find meaning in life even in the most difficult situations. The defiant power of the human spirit is very important for survival, especially in old age. We are not supposed to accept willingly what life brings us. We can revolt against it and turn our defiant power into a weapon of survival. Human beings are three-dimensional—physical, psychological, and spiritual—creatures. People should never be reduced to just one of these dimensions. The therapist who relates only to the psychosocial dimensions diminishes the dignity and self-respect of the human being. The human spirit is the healthy nucleus in each human being. It is free and is not chained to body or soul. Humans can rise above and beyond themselves for the sake of another person in need by virtue of love. We have capacity for self-detachment from constant preoccupation with ourselves by humor and laughter. We live in the present and should look forward to goals we wish to accomplish and should help others lead meaningful lives.

Each person is unique and irreplaceable. Many elderly people should remember that the uniqueness of each person is expressed by his or contribution to the world, by his or her creativity and attitude to life. Meaning is subjective and changes in every situation. We cannot buy meaning, and we cannot transfer it to others. Each has to discover it alone. We are responsible for our choices to respond to the demands of life. Choices are present in every situation. We only have to be aware of them and weigh them according to their meaning for our lives. Spiritual tension is part and parcel of human existence. Humans need spiritual tension to urge them to attain important goals. Discovering meaning in life is not a gift but an achievement. Humans does not know their limitations as long as life does not force them to test these limits. Finally, happiness is a by-product of meaning in life.

LOGOTHERAPEUTIC TECHNIQUES

Logotherapy has several techniques that may be useful for social workers. Frankl's creativity was not limited to the development of the theoretical foundation of logotherapy but has encompassed specific techniques in treating mental disorders and cases of living in existential vacuum. Some of these techniques have become standard features in psychotherapy in general and are used by logotherapists and other practitioners, whereas others are more limited to the former. The main techniques of logotherapy are based on the unique capacity of people to rise above and beyond themselves (self-transcendence) and to distance themselves from preoccupation with their own affairs alone (self-detachment).

Paradoxical Intention as Technique

Briefly stated, paradoxical intention is a wish turned upside down. Clients are guided to wish exactly what they so frantically fear and try to avoid so desperately. What we flee from tends to catch up with us, and the more we fight a fear, the more we become its victims. On the other hand, if we wish to have happen what we fear and support our paradoxical intention with humor, the fear disappears (Lukas, 1986). Anxiety and ironic wish cancel each other out. Frankl (1962) discovered that by turning around the mechanism underlying phobias and obsessions, the vicious circle is cut and the symptom diminishes and finally atrophies.

De-reflection

The second major technique in logotherapy is called de-reflection. This technique is indicated in any disorder or disturbance that stems from excessive self-observation. Hyperreflection and hyperintention can cause widespread psychological problems. Instead of focusing on what is good and meaningful to do in any given situation, the client engages in hyperreflection. This in turn endangers the fulfillment of meaningful tasks. In using this technique, the client is taught how to

ignore the symptom and divert his or her capacities to positive matters.

Two additional techniques in logotherapy are known to social workers. These are modification of attitudes and Socratic dialogue.

Modification of Attitudes

Frankl's "attitudinal values" are perhaps the most important sources for finding meaning in life. This technique is aimed toward relieving distress or despair, widening and strengthening their meaning orientation, helping them discover new potentials, and guiding them to become more mature and responsible adults in their social environment. Many people become sad in their old age because of the losses they experience. Those whose lives are built on one absolute value—be it work, family, love, or success—are particularly prone to danger, for when this value crumbles or fails, they succumb to despair, nervous breakdown, or attempt to run away from life altogether. The best way to protect one's self from falling into despair is to free the value from its absolute measure, so that when it is lost, one may be sad. This sadness may be turned around by modification of attitude to the loss and by redirection of one's thinking and feeling from what was lost to what still can be gained.

An illustration to this type of person is the case of Mr. B, age 68, who spent 40 years of his life as a librarian in a scientific library. When he was told that according to the law he had to retire, he panicked. He claimed that "he would simply die," rather than retire. "My life is empty without my job," he told his therapist. "I don't know what to do, or how I will survive this blow of fate." Logotherapists dealing with such situations rely on Frankl's concept of the defiant power of the human spirit, the ability to counteract blows of fate that can be marshaled to rise up to the task of widening the meaning horizon of a person.

Socratic Dialogue

Socrates's life and teachings serve as an ideal for ethical behavior in the social work profession, and his method of bringing forth the truth and discovering meanings has become the main tool of logotherapeutic work with seekers of help. As seen from the case of Abe, Socratic dialogue in logotherapy is a tool, a technique of self-discovery. It serves many purposes and objectives in work with the aged. It helps one become aware of inner powers that are hidden; it directs one toward finding meaning in life and enables one to review past experiences and envision the future; it provides opportunities for the seeker to reassess the present situation and his or her power and capability to deal with the problem.

Socratic dialogue in logotherapy is used in all the phases of treatment. It helps the client gain distance from the symptoms of his or her malady; leads one toward new attitudes; makes one aware of past successes in overcoming difficulties and enables cooperation between client and therapist in the search for meaning. The following segment of a Socratic dialogue is presented here for illustration from the work of Takashima (1990), a physician who used logotherapy in his medical work. He described a visit with a 50-year-old woman who suffered from depression and anxieties following her daughter's death. This daughter died when she was away on a vacation. Following this tragic event, the woman tried to commit suicide, and when it failed she became depressed. Takashima was requested to help by seeing this patient. The Socratic dialogue that ensued was conducted in the presence of four helping professionals.

Q: If your daughter were alive, who among you would suffer?

A: My daughter.

Q: Do you still love her?

A: Yes, very much.

Q: Would you be willing to suffer instead of her, if she were alive?

A: Of course, I would suffer willingly.

Q: But she has already died and cannot suffer. You can suffer instead of her—if someone has to suffer. Let me give you an example. Suppose that suffering is like water. You are now drowning in the water, and you try to save yourself, despite your feeling that it can't be done, correct?

A: I simply cannot.

Q: But in the water of suffering you can swim instead of drowning?

A: Yes, I think so.

Q: You can even swim nicely.

A: Yes, I will try to do so.

Takashima said that this simple, uneducated woman was able to understand that her suffering had a meaning, and she accepted it. She changed her attitude to suffering from the negative and self-destroying to a positive and constructive one. She cured herself by her wisdom, orientation to meaning, and free decision (Takashima, 1990, pp. 98–100).

EMPIRICAL RESEARCH IN LOGOTHERAPY

When the first issue of the *International Forum for Logotherapy* was published, Frankl expressed his hope that the journal would publish articles based on experimental validation of his intuitive concepts. Empirical research in logotherapy began in earnest with the development of specifically logotherapeutic measuring tools in the 1960s. Constructed from logotherapeutic orientation by Crumbaugh and Henrion (1988), the Purpose in Life test (PIL) is a standardized and validated attitude scale that has been in use by researchers in human behavior, including many social workers. The PIL measures a person's will to meaning and existential vacuum. Failure to find meaning in life may result in a state of emptiness and boredom, and if not relieved it may lead to neurosis. Since its appearance, the research value of the PIL has been demonstrated in hundreds of empirical studies; doctoral dissertations in health, mental health, psychology, social work, and psychiatry; and logotherapy (Batthyany & Guttmann, 2006). This research instrument has been translated into many languages.

The PIL is divided into three parts: part A consists of a 20-item psychometric scale that evokes responses about the degree to which an individual experiences purpose in life. Part B consists of a 13-item "incomplete sentences" scale, and part C contains a biographical paragraph about the participants' life goals, ambitions, hopes, future plans, and motivation in life. Parts B and C are seldom used in clinical work. The PIL is the most frequently used instrument in logotherapy-based research (Batthyany & Guttmann, 2006).

Other research tools much less used in logotherapeutic and in meaning-oriented studies include the Seeking of Noetic Goals test that measures the strength of a subject's motivation to find meaning in life; the Logo test, which measures the subject's inner meaning fulfillment, existential frustration, and "noological illness" (originating in the noological or spiritual dimension of a human being due to lack of meaning in life), and the Meaning in Suffering test (Stark, 1983), which measures the extent to which an individual has found meaning in an unavoidable suffering experience.

SUMMARY

Logotherapy is well suited to social work with the aged. It can help the elderly deal with the crises of old age, especially with the trauma of incurable disease. Elderly people need assistance with the difficulties they face in their struggles for survival, particularly with the need to find meaning in diminishing circumstances. By adopting a logotherapeutic perspective on life, social workers can help the elderly overcome unavoidable suffering by searching for new meanings in their lives.

Logotherapy is not a panacea by itself. It is neither an academic discipline, nor a recognized profession, such as social work. It has only a growing body of theory and research and several more or less commonly accepted methods of intervention. It has no authority over its domain; it cannot grant a university degree. Neither does logotherapy have functional specificity that would set it apart from other mental health occupations. Nevertheless, logotherapy, the pioneering work of Viktor Frankl, could enable social workers to supplement their traditional methods of psychotherapy with techniques to improve effectiveness through clearer understanding of their clients' problems. Social workers could then derive greater personal meaning and satisfaction from their work.

WEB SITE

Viktor Frankl Institut. This is the main Web site for all aspects of logotherapeutic activities. Contains all relevant information about logotherapy, logotherapeutic books, journals, articles, centers, institutions, and awards all over the world. http://www.viktorfrankl.org.

References

Batthyany, A., & Guttmann, D. (2006). *Empirical research in logotherapy and in meaning-oriented existential analysis.* Phoenix: Zeig, Tucker & Thysen.

Crumbaugh, J. C., & Henrion, R. (1988). PIL test: Administration, interpretation, uses, theory and critique. *International Forum for Logotherapy Journal of Search for Meaning, 11,* 76–88.

Frankl, V. E. (1962). *Man's search for meaning: An introduction to logotherapy,* a revised and enlarged edition of *From death camp to existentialism.* New York: Touchstone Books.

Frankl, V. E. (1986). *The doctor and the soul: From psychotherapy to logotherapy,* 2nd ed. New York: Vintage Books.

Frankl, V. E. (1995). *Was ist nicht in meinen Buchern steht lebenserinnerungen* [What is not written in my books]. Munchen: Quintessenz.

Guttmann, D. (1996). *Logotherapy for the helping professional; meaningful social work.* New York: Springer.

Lukas, E. (1986). *Meaning in suffering.* Berkeley: Institute of Logotherapy Press.

Stark, P. L. (1983). Patients' perceptions of the meaning of suffering. *International Forum for Logotherapy Journal of Search for Meaning, 6,* 110–116.

Sternig, P. J. (1984). Finding meaning through existential guilt. *International Forum for Logotherapy Journal of Search for Meaning, 7,* 46–49.

Takashima, H. (1990). *Humanistic psychosomatic medicine.* Tel Aviv: Dvir.

Patricia Kelley

As the twentieth century drew to a close, narrative therapy (NT) became an important trend in clinical social work and family therapy and was part of the postmodern movement that crosses many disciplines, from arts and literature to the social sciences. The postmodern movement is a reaction to modernism, which holds that there are universal laws and truths that can be uncovered through scientific discovery and that all phenomena can be explained if these truths are discovered. Postmodernism challenges the idea of absolute truth and grand theories that explain human behavior.

The narrative approach was developed in the 1980s by Michael White, a social worker/family therapist from south Australia, and David Epston, a social worker/family therapist from New Zealand. It has received worldwide attention since the publication of their book in North America in 1990 (White & Epston, 1990). Although NT began in the family therapy movement, it has also been applied to work at the individual, group, and community levels.

NT developed within the context of the social constructionist and second-order cybernetic movements, which were influencing the field of family therapy in the 1980s. In addition to positioning themselves within the epistemological perspective of social constructionism, White and Epston (1990) drew from the ideas of constructivism, the work of Foucault, and the field of literary criticism. Constructivism focuses on individuals' perceptions and cognitions as shaping their views of reality, whereas social constructionism focuses more on the social and cultural narratives individuals internalize, taking them for granted as constituting "reality." Both views deny objective reality, believing that one's view of reality is constructed out of language use and social interaction. White and Epston incorporate both social constructionism and constructivism in their use of a narrative metaphor in therapeutic work, believing that people create stories of their lives to make sense of all their lived experience. The stories people develop incorporate the dominant social and cultural stories of gender, ethnicity, and power, as well as personal stories coconstructed in interaction with others (family, friends, and professional helpers). These stories constitute the knowledge that people hold about themselves and their worlds. As in postmodern literary criticism, the narrative therapist helps clients "deconstruct" the story lines around which they have organized their lives, assessing the plot, characters, and timeline for meaning, and then look for other "truths" that also exist.

The goal of narrative therapy in social work practice is to help clients first understand the stories around which they have organized their lives and then challenge and broaden them, thus creating new realities. These discoveries can help clients see more alternatives and ways out of an impasse. They can also help clients see more aspects of themselves, including strengths and coping skills they already have, which can be mobilized to fight the effects of the problems they are facing. Conversation is important because language creates our reality; through discourse, reality (including history) is socially constructed (created). NT is more than storytelling, it is story *changing*. The narrative therapist does not deny the harsh realities facing clients, such as poverty, racism, or illness, but the power given to these adverse aspects of their lives and the control the problems have over their lives are challenged.

USING A NARRATIVE APPROACH

NT takes a collaborative approach in working with clients, where clients are experts on their lives, and as the story lines unfold, the client and social worker together discover other realities and join in fighting the effects of the problem. Key concepts of NT are as follows.

- *Externalizing the problem.* In conversation with clients, the problem is externalized, or separated, from the person, whereby the problem (not the person) is the target of change.
- *Problem-saturated stories.* These are the one-dimensional stories clients have about themselves that they have coconstructed in interaction with others and are influenced by social-cultural forces that have restricted them. These stories are examined in session as not the only truth. Clients are challenged to expand their views of self.
- *Mapping the problem's domain.* The effects of the problem over time (past, present, and possible future) and over many domains are examined; in so doing the client can assess what might be done.
- *Unique outcomes.* These are the times clients have not been overcome by the problems that may represent new truths and discoveries about themselves that are often strengths or aspects of the client's story that are not consistent with the problem-saturated dominant story.
- *Spreading the news.* Once clients start experiencing some positive change, they are encouraged to let others know about their successes in fighting the effects of the problems or in not giving in to the problems. This may involve celebrations, certificates, awards, letter writing, or even talking to groups of others facing similar problems.

Using this approach, the social worker does not design an intervention to do something "to" a client. Neither does this clinician assume that a problem or symptom serves a function for the individual (as in psychodynamic approaches) or the family system (as in the family systems approaches), although the problem may have influenced a family's behavior. In fact there are no presumptions about the client.

- Clients are carefully listened to so the therapist can understand their perceptions of the problem and the meanings they ascribe to it.
- Through respectful deconstructive questioning, problems are externalized, and the problem-saturated stories are examined through mapping and questioning.
- In the reconstruction stage, some truths are gently challenged through questioning, and unique outcomes are isolated.

- Therapy is terminated by mutual agreement with plans for spreading the news, often with celebrations or awards.
- NT contains many "wondering" questions to help clients think about and reflect on their interpretations and beliefs about their lived experiences. Through such reflections, they consider other interpretations and other meanings, expanding their view of self. The concept of self is considered fluid and changing.

When possible and practical, narrative therapists like to use "reflecting teams," where members of the team, often trainees, discuss their ideas and questions with each other in front of the family. Their ideas are not considered more true than the families', but as ideas to encourage further self-reflection. At first, one-way mirrors were used for this purpose, with the family and the team changing places to shift who is in front and who is viewing. Now the groups are more likely brought into the room and may consist of significant others or people facing similar situations, as well as the team. The purpose is to encourage further reflection, which may be developed in other ways, too, including letters from therapist between sessions.

Even though the focus is more on meanings than specific behaviors, NT is usually short term, with a few sessions spread over a longer period of time.

The concepts and interventions of NT bear some similarities to solution-focused therapy (SFT) (de Shazer & Berg, 1993) and the strength perspective (Saleebey, 2002) in that they all are empowerment-based approaches aimed at mobilizing clients' strengths and resources. However, these approaches also have some distinct differences.

- The "unique outcomes" of NT are different from SFT's "exceptions" in that they are not asked for but are discovered through careful listening.
- In NT, the discussion of possible futures does not just focus on the hoped for (positive) future but also assesses the potential future if the problem continues to dominate clients' lives.
- Because clients come into the relationship with a problem to solve, ameliorate, or cope with, narrative therapists do not avoid discussing their presenting problems in depth but attend to them as part of the whole story, which is then expanded.

CASE EXAMPLE

Family therapy sessions were held for a mixed family comprising a mother who had married before, her 14-old daughter, Mary Ann, and her second husband, who had never married before. A mutual daughter, aged 7, was not brought to the sessions. The family was concerned that Mary Ann had become rebellious and dropped her previous friends to run with an older boyfriend and his crowd who engaged in dangerous and illegal activities and did not attend school. These activities represented a dramatic shift from her previous good behavior. Her mood had changed to surly and her grades had dropped dramatically.

In sessions, they all discussed perceptions and stories of the situation. Mary Ann discussed how she felt that she was living in a house designed for little girls, with little accommodation for her to grow up and achieve some independence. She also felt that her stepfather did not love her, was mean to her, and favored the younger daughter. The mother discussed how she lived in terror fearing what might happen to Mary Ann if the illegal and dangerous activities continued; she mourned the loss of her close relationship with Mary Ann; and she felt torn between loyalty to husband and daughter. The stepfather discusses feeling left out of the family by the close relationship between the mother and daughter. He admitted being overly strict sometimes as he tried to get into the family. After each member had heard the stories of fears and frustrations of the others, the meanings they made of events shifted. Control and strictness were seen as love and caring, and rebelliousness was perceived as attempts to change and grow.

Adolescence was externalized as a new force entering their lives. They discussed ways to welcome the "new member," making it a positive force instead of a negative one. As the family developed more empathy and understanding for each other and began laughing as they found ways to welcome the new member, compromises were reached, where new independence could be earned by following certain rules. Better judgments equaled new freedoms. Family meetings to agree on the rules were set up and involved the father more. The biological father, 1000 miles away, agreed to support the new rules, demonstrating that all three parents cared enough about Mary Ann to cooperate. Many old truths were deconstructed and new ways to deal with problems emerged.

NARRATIVE THERAPY AND SOCIAL WORK

Narrative therapy is compatible with the traditional social work methods and values of individualizing each client as unique, respecting each client's story, respecting cultural differences, and separating one's own beliefs and values from those of clients through self-understanding and conscious use of self. Social work values are demonstrated through the following methods.

Respectful Listening

By taking a "nonexpert, not knowing" position about the clients' lives, we show respect for their knowledge, and we listen carefully to their ideas. This stance is not the same as neutrality, for some stories are clearly less useful or even harmful (for example, violence) than others, but here the therapist assesses the outcomes and consequences with the client and may challenge the story through deconstruction and by assessing its origins.

Avoidance of Labels

The use of labels and categories for totalizing clients as to who they are is questioned, and through externalization the clients are seen as afflicted with a problem but not constituted of it. For example, a person may be afflicted with a particular medical condition, such as cancer or a serious mental illness, but that affliction is just one part of who they are, not their total being. Thus, a person would not be viewed as a schizophrenic but perhaps as a person suffering from a schizophrenic disorder. Other aspects of the person can be honored and brought forth to fight the effects of the problem, and societal views about the problem can be challenged. In fact, some narrative therapists discard the entire notion of labels, because they objectify people, and such categorizations can serve to oppress persons with certain classifications or labels.

Fostering Empowerment

The political nature of NT, where clients are "liberated" from dominant familial and cultural stories that have restricted them and are urged to take a stand on their own behalf, makes it especially compatible with social work practice.

Emphasis on Social Justice

NT also takes a stand on social justice issues, as best exemplified in the work of New Zealanders Waldegrave, Tamasese, Tuhaka, and Campbell (2003), who developed their own version of NT, called "just therapy" because it focuses on social justice. White has worked on social justice issues and has worked with oppressed communities to challenge the dominant narratives oppressing them. Beginning in 1999, White and others at his Dulwich Family Therapy Training Centre in Adelaide, south Australia, have organized annual international narrative therapy conferences that focus on work with families and communities.

Extension beyond the Office

This bridge between micro and macro practice is useful for social workers and fits in with newer community practice approaches. Narrative therapists work beyond office walls to foster communities of support and empower clients.

Although narrative therapy seems consistent with good social work practice, there are some problems regarding it that have been raised.

1. There is little empirical research supporting NT, partly because postmodernism denies the objectivity that is at the core of empiricism. Epstein (1995) criticizes the postmodern approaches for keeping social work out of the scientific field where it should be placed. Other research approaches, such as qualitative methods and case studies, may address this concern.
2. Minuchin (1998) and Nichols and Schwartz (2006) are concerned that narrative therapists have turned their backs on the defining characteristics of family therapy, not taking family dynamics into account and often not seeing the family as a unit.
3. Kelley (1998) noted that two major trends in clinical practice in the 1990s—postmodernism and managed care—seemed at odds with each other, and that is still true today. Managed care demands *DSM-IV* diagnoses with preapproved treatment plans designed by the clinician and based on empirically proven methods, where as in NT the emphasis is on the therapist and client coconstructing new realities through dialogue rather than conducting problem-solving activities designed by the therapist. Kelley noted, however, that some aspects of narrative therapy, for example, the its short-term nature and cognitive focus, could bridge this seemingly wide gap.

FUTURE PRACTICE APPLICATIONS

The questions regarding narrative therapy have not diminished its impact. As Nichols and Schwartz (2006) have said, narrative therapy is "a perfect expression of the postmodern revolution" (p. 337). The approach that was once considered revolutionary has become more mainstream as evidenced by inclusion in social work texts (Turner, 1996); family therapy texts (Nichols & Schwartz, 2006), books on the subject (Diamond, 2000; Freedman & Combs, 1996; Winslade & Monk, 2000; Zimmerman & Dickerson, 1996), training centers around the world, and journal issues exclusively on NT (*Journal of Brief Therapy*, 2004). White and Epston have continued to develop ideas and publish (Epston, 2004; White, 2000). Furthermore, changes have developed over time as NT broadened its scope to more community and group work (Kelley & Murty, 2003; Vodde & Gallant, 2003), decreasing the distinction between micro and macro practice. The movement demanding more consumer participation in decision making has called for newer methods for social work practice. NT is a product of its time.

WEB SITES

Dulwich Centre. http://www.dulwichcentre.com.au.
Planet Therapy, online mental health learning community. http://www.planet-therapy.com.
Victoria Dickerson (narrative therapy). http://www.victoriadickerson.com.
Yaletown Family Therapy. http://www.therapeuticconversations.com.

References

de Shazer, S.. & Berg, I. K. (1993). Constructing solutions. *Family Therapy Networker, 12,* 42–43.
Diamond, J. (2000). *Narrative means to sober ends: Treating addiction and its aftermath.* New York: Guilford.
Epstein, W. M. (1995). Social work in the university. *Journal of Social Work Education, 31*(2), 281–293.
Epston, D. (2004). Joel: Can you help me train Amber to be a guard dog? *Journal of Brief Therapy, 3*(2), 97–106.
Freedman, J., & Combs, J. (1996). *Narrative therapy: The social construction of preferred realities.* New York: Norton.
Journal of Brief Therapy. (2004). Special issue on narrative therapy, *3*(2).
Kelley, P. (1998). Narrative therapy in a managed care world. *Crisis Intervention, 4*(2/3), 113–123.
Kelley, P., & Murty, S. (2003). Teaching narrative approaches in community practice. *Social Work Review (of New Zealand), 15*(4), 14–20.

Minuchin, S. (1998). Where is the family in narrative family therapy? *Journal of Marital and Family Therapy, 24*, 397–403.

Nichols, M., & Schwartz, R.C. (2006). *Family therapy: Concepts and methods,* 7th ed. Boston: Pearson Educational.

Saleebey, D. (2002). *The strengths perspective in social work practice,* 3rd ed. Boston: Allyn-Bacon.

Turner, F. J. (Ed.). (1996). *Social work treatment,* 4th ed. New York: Free Press.

Vodde, R., & Gallant, J. (2003). Bridging the gap between micro and macro practice: Large scale change and a unified model of narrative-deconstructive practice. *Social Work Review (of New Zealand), 15*(4), 4–13.

Waldegrave, C., Tamasese, K., Tuhaka, F., & Campbell, W. (2003). *Just Therapy—a Journey: A collection of papers from the just therapy team.* Adelaide, New Zealand: Dulwich Centre Publications.

White, M. (2000). *Reflections on narrative practice: Essays and interviews.* Adelaide: Dulwich Centre.

White, M., & Epston, D. (1990). *Narrative means to therapeutic ends.* New York: Norton.

Winslade, J., & Monk, G. (2000). *Narrative mediation: A new approach in conflict resolution.* San Francisco: Jossey-Bass.

Zimmerman, J., & Dickerson, V. (1996). *If problems talked: Adventures in narrative therapy.* New York: Guilford Press.

37 Feminist Issues and Practices in Social Work

Mary Bricker-Jenkins & F. Ellen Netting

Since its emergence in the late 1970s, feminist social work practice has been concerned with women's issues. Most social workers who claim a feminist perspective go well beyond women's issues in their concerns and commitments by focusing on the elimination of all forms of oppression, exploitation, and discrimination; they work for the mobilization of the power of people to create just relations in all spheres of life (Bricker-Jenkins & Lockett, 1995; Figueira-McDonough, 1998). Thus, "feminist practice" is by definition an integration of micro/macro social work practice because it requires a vigilance to context, whether one's primary focus is an individual, group, organization, community, or society (Kemp, 2001).

For numerous reasons, however, there has been a tendency in the past decade for feminist social workers to "roll back" their broad liberatory agenda (Bricker-Jenkins, 2000). Moreover, many feminist approaches to social work have emerged, some of which are in tension with—even paradoxical to—each other. This brief chapter, then, can only hint at the range and complexities of feminist perspectives and applications in social work practice. Several writers (e.g., Saulnier, 1996, 2000; Valentich, 1996) have provided useful summaries of the many feminist theoretical frameworks that influence feminist practitioners, and *Affilia, The Journal of Social Work with Women* has offered peer-reviewed articles representing the range of feminist activity in social work since 1986. There are also analyses of current feminist contradictions and conundrums across practice arenas (Ashcraft & Mumby, 2004; Bricker-Jenkins, 2000). Readers are urged to explore these and other sources with awareness of the risks of generalization, abstraction, and simplification of the complex phenomenon of feminism in social work.

This chapter provides an overview of some components of a feminist conceptual framework, offers a grounded definition of feminist social work practice, explains some major commonalities and differences in approaches among feminist workers, and closes with an assessment of the challenges and future prospects feminist social workers face.

DEFINING FEMINIST PRACTICE(S)

In 1983, Bricker-Jenkins and Hooyman (1986) conducted a small pilot project with the purpose of defining feminist social work practice. The National Association of Social Workers (NASW)–sponsored Feminist Practice Project ensued, and in 1998 the Association for Women in Social Work sponsored a reprise of the project (Bricker-Jenkins, 2000). Both surveys used a small convenience sample and therefore are only suggestive. However, they represent an attempt to ground the definition of feminist practice in the collective experience of diverse practitioners in a range of settings using a variety of modalities and methods. The following discussion of definitions and principles is based primarily on those studies. It covers three overlapping approaches to definition used by different practitioners: as identity, as conceptual framework, and as method. (Elsewhere the terms *ideology*, *ideological framework*, and *metatheory* have been used to label this approach to definition.)

Feminist Practices as Identity

Identifying as a feminist is likely the broadest and most common approach to defining feminist practice, but it is also the most problematic in that "feminist practice is what is done by social workers who say they are feminists." The major problem is obvious: there is no commonly agreed-on definition of *feminist*, and thus it means different things to different people. The major benefits of this approach, however, are that it is inclusive of many perspectives and may generate both critique and creativity in practice. Another benefit is that identity may be the one shared commonality among feminists who vary considerably when it comes to their diverse conceptual frameworks and methods.

Feminist Practices as Conceptual Frameworks

Identifying as a feminist obviously means different things to different people. Because "identifying" is the broadest way of defining feminist practice, feminist identity is similar to a vision around which everyone can rally. But around the specifics that come from fleshing out that vision is where people start to disagree. Basic assump-

tions that undergird conceptualizations vary, and there are multiple conceptual frameworks based on different worldviews that all claim to be feminist.

Saulnier (2000) provides an overview of feminist groups, including liberal, cultural, postmodern, womanist, and radical. Liberal feminist views assume that women should have the same rights as men. Carried to its extreme, this would mean that women should be equally integrated into societal structures. Cultural feminist views perceived women as different from men and often seek parallel structures that are definitively feminist in their cultures. Postmodern views oppose cultural and liberal views because they seek to universalize women's experiences, focusing instead on the plurality of differences, power, and social transformation. Womanist views reflect African American experience and place race (as well as gender) in the forefront of feminist conceptualizations. Radical feminist views assume that without systemic change, everything else is a short-term fix to address sexism. Other writers provide different conceptual categories to corral feminism. The point is that multiple worldviews, composed of basic underlying assumptions, form alternative conceptual frameworks and contribute to the paradoxes faced by persons who identify as feminist but strongly disagree when it comes to thinking about and actually practicing as a feminist social worker (Netting & O'Connor, 2003).

Earlier studies indicate that social workers who label themselves as feminist, despite the considerable differences among them, were distinguishable in attitudes and beliefs from social workers who did not (Katz-Porterfield, 1998; Sandell, 1993). Much effort has gone into attempts to define the conceptual components of feminist frameworks for social work (these are numerous, though sharing much in common, and are amply reviewed in Valentich, 1996); the one presented in Table 37.1 was developed and has been revised by Bricker-Jenkins through in-depth interviews and surveys with feminist practitioners. While it has been used by other researchers of feminist practice, it is by no means uniformly understood or applied. (For fuller discussion and illustrations of the concepts in this framework, see Bricker-Jenkins & Lockett, 1995.)

Even a cursory glance at *Affilia* indicates that a community of practitioners and academics are engaged in revising and reinventing practice from a multitude of feminist perspectives in every imaginable arena. Given the multiplicity of perspec-

TABLE 37.1 A Conceptual Framework for Feminist Practice

Basic philosophy, values, and goals

1. *Collectivism*: The inherent purpose and goal of human existence is self-actualization; however, self-actualization is a *collective* endeavor involving the creation of relationships and conditions that facilitate it.
2. *Politicization*: All practice is inherently political in consequence; feminist practice is explicitly political in intent. Given structural and ideological barriers to self-actualization, practice must address itself explicitly to them.
3. *Pro-woman stance*: Feminist practice is pro-woman but not anti-man; women's diverse histories, conditions, developmental patterns, and strengths are shaped and subjugated under conditions of oppression but can be reshaped through collective work for just relations.

Human behavior and the social environment

4. *Strengths/health*: Because human beings strive in community for safety, health, and self-actualization, it is possible to identify and mobilize individual and collective capacities for healing, growth, and personal/political transformation.
5. *Diversity*: Diversity creates choices for all and thus is a source of strength, growth, and health.
6. *Interdependence*: All things are connected.
7. *Constructivism/constructionism*: "Reality" is an unfolding, multidimensional, politically shaped process. Multiple competing realities coexist in a context of power relations; some are subjugated or silenced.

Practice Methods and Relationships

8. *Personal as political*: Individual and collective pain and problems of living always have a cultural and/or political dimension.
9. *Just relations and structures*: All systems and ideologies of domination, exploitation, and supremacy are inherently violent and inimical to well-being; they can be resisted and replacedin our practice with social forms, processes, and relations that are democratic, reciprocal, synergetic.
10. *Transformation*: Healing, health, and growth are functions of validation, consciousness, and collective transformative action; these, in turn, must be supported and sustained through relationships that preserve and nurture uniqueness, wholeness, and connectedness; the creation of validating environments; and access to resources that meet basic human needs.

Source: Adapted and revised from Bricker-Jenkins, & Lockett, 1995.

tives within that community, any definitions of conceptual frameworks for feminist practice must be fluid, tentative, and evolving and allow for compound—even contradictory—interpretations.

Feminist Practices as Methods

The search for integrative methods for social workers that would incorporate the full range of the social work mission has been advanced but not achieved by feminist practitioners. This is not surprising, given that different conceptual frameworks and their competing assumptions logically lead to different practice methods. Pollio (2000)

suggests that "divisiveness within the voice of feminism is crippling its ability to present a coherent message" (p. 5). Still, the movement slogan "the personal is political" remains a core analytical and methodological tool (Pollio, 2000, p. 7). Table 37.2 is based on a 1998 study that revised a 1983 definition of feminist practice (Bricker-Jenkins, 2000).

An enormous range of direct practice approaches, modalities, methods, and techniques in social work have been revised and adapted by persons who identify as feminist. There are feminists working in the traditions of psychoanalysis, psychodynamics, cognitive-behaviorism, empowerment, and more (Contratto & Rossier, 2005). Feminists have modified techniques from psychodrama, Gestalt psychology, Freirian dialog, narrative analysis, use of symbols and rituals, and conventional problem solving. Beyond adaptation, feminist practitioners have created techniques for gender analysis and power analysis that explore these core realities in women's (and men's) lives.

Saulnier (2000) conducted an exploratory study of a variety of women's groups in San Francisco, asking facilitators to describe connections between the group's methods and feminist or womanist thought. She concludes that using feminist theories (conceptual frameworks) to intentionally guide practice (and operationalize theory) can move toward empowerment and beyond traditional interventions. She provides a chart of feminist groups in which she categorizes methods (processes used) by conceptual framework. For example, a liberal feminist process in one group was psychoeducation, counseling, and 12-step programs; cultural feminist methods included consciousness raising, support, and self-help; postmodern feminist methods were bibliotherapy, education, and support; womanist methods included consciousness raising for women of color and lesbian and bisexual women and community organizing; and radical groups used consciousness raising, support, skill development, and plans of action as methods. Note that some methods overlapped across conceptual frameworks.

Feminist methods in group work practice have been reported by Berwald and Houtstra (2002) in their work with women with disabilities. Seeing traditional casework as pathologizing women's stress borne by lack of resources, two social workers in a rehabilitation setting developed an all-female group designed to raise consciousness, introduce feminist ideas, and enhance networking. Group members often developed materials for the group, were equal participants with the facilitators, provided ongoing feedback, and focused on strengths, empowerment, and change. Berwald and Houtstra evaluated the group experience focusing on improved self-esteem and decreased depression. "Being able to offer a feminist social work group is unique within the context

---

TABLE 37.2 A Definition of Feminist Practice as Integrative Method

In general, feminist practitioners attempting to use an integrative method

- Approach all issues and opportunities presented by social living and social relationships with a view to identifying the power dynamics operating in them and their implications for diverse groups of women;
- Are concerned with the ways in which institutionalized sexism (and usually other oppressive ideologies and behaviors) create problems for all persons and for women in particular;
- Are committed to the development *and use* of specific actions and techniques[a] to create opportunities for and remove structural barriers, both material and ideological, to the fullest possible development of the abilities of individuals and groups; whenever possible, to do so in alliance with those directly affected;
- Identify and build on the strengths and opportunities of individuals, groups, communities, and cultures;
- Are committed to collaborative relationships with people with whom they are working while recognizing and negotiating the differential power inherent in all relationships, including professional ones;
- Tend to view social work practice as a political, liberatory, and transformative practice, that is, as a normatively based and directed effort to enable people to control the conditions of their lives by redefining and moving individual and institutional power in a more egalitarian direction;
- While working to create options for and with people, and while preserving safety, respect, and support for their natural healing and helping processes and the choices they make in relation to their own conditions.

---

[a]For example of preferred techniques, see Bricker-Jenkins, & Lockett, 1995.

Source: Adapted from Bricker-Jenkins, 2000.

of a rehabilitation setting" (Berwald & Houtstra, 2002, p. 82).

There are also feminist methods to work with individuals, families, groups, organizations, and communities. Hyde (2001) lists examples of feminist social movement organizations (FSMOs) that "include peace encampments, lesbian rights networks, economic development and micro lending institutions, cultural centers, displaced homemaker leagues, reproductive rights groups, and credit unions" (p. 47). Hyde's study of FSMOs examines the design and development of organizations promoted as congruent and supportive of feminist principles. Mizrahi (2007) conducted a longitudinal study of a diverse group of 48 women organizers, out of which she developed a framework for feminist organizing. Feminist organizers used methods that included community involvement; emphasized collective problem solving; focused on process as part of the product or goal; used consciousness raising; emphasized consensus, cooperation, collaboration, and coalition building; focused on unity and wholeness, emphasizing collective/shared problem-solving approaches; and used praxis (pp. 40–42).

Feminist methods seek change across the continuum from personal to political and from individual to institutional. The goal is to change not only a condition but also the consciousness and contexts associated with that condition. Feminist methods are intended to generate new consciousness, conditions, and contexts. The process owes much to Freirian method, also used in liberation theology and some forms of popular education. Best conducted in groups and communities, facilitators use problem posing, study, and dialogical methods for consciousness raising and ultimately praxis (action-reflection-action) that transforms both individuals and their worlds.

THE FUTURE FOR FEMINIST PRACTICE

Whether feminist practices will continue to develop within social work depends, in part, on what we expect of them. We can expect continued adaptation of conventional approaches and invention of some "genderized" approaches to healing and helping people survive a marginalizing and often abusive world. Clearly, people who identify themselves as feminists (by whatever definition) will continue to use a feminist stance in their work. Much work is needed to identify the specific features of these definitions and stances,

how they shape individuals' practices, and whether there is indeed any commonality within the "feminist practice as identity" group.

If we hope for more, however, feminist practices may face a number of challenges from inside and out. Reflecting structural changes in the larger economy, shifts in the practice environment hinder the use of many of the hallmarks of feminism such as the use of relational-feminist approaches within which collaborative relationships can be created and maintained (Freedman, 2007). Feminists' challenge to the reification and misuse of categories that label people may be overwhelmed by the near ubiquitous use of the *DSM-IV* as a screen for services, even in the "alternative" services established by feminists for women (and sometimes men) who have been raped, battered, and sexually abused. Structural constraints (such as managed care and short-term therapies) constrict the use of alternative or complementary healing methods and even, in some settings, groups that may become activist. In the face of increasing punishment and state control of people living in poverty, social workers' assigned role has been to prepare women for poverty-level jobs and their children for care by other women being paid poverty-level wages. Finally, in many schools of social work, direct practice has come to mean pathology-oriented, commodified therapy rather than the integration of micro/macro approaches that focus on change. Against these trends, neither social work in general nor feminist practitioners in particular have mobilized as yet. Nevertheless, the "feminist project" continues, perhaps invigorated by a growing awareness that the very harshness of today's economic and political environment provides an opportunity for action toward personal/political transformation.

It is very important to grasp the influence of the conceptual frameworks (theories) that inform practice—the intellectual scaffolding a practitioner uses to construct the particular set of relationships and methods that constitute a practice system. Specifically, the ideological framework of early feminist practice was heavily influenced by variants of a historical-material intellectual tradition. Among other things, this tradition brought notions of shared "truths," objective and institutionalized structures (such as patriarchy or white supremacy) that harmed groups of people (such as women or people of color), and the possibility of personal/political transformation. Practice informed primarily by this tradition will necessarily be activist and partisan. To illustrate, direct practice occurs where personal biographies and social structures intersect; at this place, those working in the historical-materialist tradition will take a stance against certain structures. Thus, practice in this tradition might emphasize forming groups of rape victims to take collective action as survivors against misogyny in a public arena. The meaning of the act of rape to the rapist will likely not be of much concern, at least not initially.

By the late 1980s, postmodern influences were being felt in social work. Many feminist practitioners took a postmodern turn owing to the feminist commitment to diversity, validating multiple truths, amplifying women's voices, and—in general—challenging the cultural mechanisms used to privilege some and subjugate others. Social workers, after all, work with meanings, and the postmodern emphasis on the subjectivity of meanings and fluidity of fact was appealing. Useful tools include narrative therapy, an emphasis on strengths and agency, and examinations of the transactions by which people construct and maintain power in interpersonal relationships and, in general, the ways people construct meaning in their lives emerged in the postmodern era. Thus, to continue the example, a postmodern feminist approach with a woman who had been raped might emphasize the meaning of the act to the individual, might place it in the context of her personal biography, and might use a range of techniques to assist her in creating a new narrative for both. Structural (sociopolitical, cultural, and economic) forces are certainly not ignored in this tradition; they are more likely to be acknowledged, however, than to be dealt with actively as an integral part of the practice.

Conceptual frameworks, built on assumptions of universals, contradict frameworks constructed on subjective, emerging, and changing truths. Therefore, the problem encountered by feminist practitioners is not a diminished commitment but a postmodernist deconstruction of objectivity and grand narrative that has disassembled the intellectual scaffolding used by liberal and radical feminists to do their work. For example, in an evidenced-based practice environment, it is critically important to raise the question of what constitutes evidence. If one's conceptual framework is based on universal truths, then quantitative survey methods designed to collect generalizable data can be used to evaluate one's practice. But if one's conceptual framework is postmodern, then data cannot be generalized, and data collection may require alternative methods that privilege word as well as numeric data (Netting & O'Connor, in press).

It is a given that feminist frameworks and theories, based on differing assumptions and values, conflict with one another. Feminist practitioners, therefore, need to be aware of the conceptual underpinnings that guide their practice. Depending on their assumptions, some methods will be more congruent than others. For example, feminists may agree that change needs to occur, but how they go about making change may be dependent on how they view change. A radical feminist may view collective mobilization of entire communities as necessary to organize for systemic change in societal structures and developing a social movement organization will be the method used. A feminist who believes that one must start with each individual so that they are empowered as persons to make change may begin in an interpretive place in which the meaning of empowerment will be different for each person whose life is touched. Narrative therapy may be the method used. These are very different methods, but both seek to effect change that will ultimately benefit women.

Of critical importance is for feminist social workers to recognize that feminism is diverse, having different standpoints that at times will be diametrically opposed to one another. Living with the paradox of difference is a given, and being able to articulate how one's methods reflect one's conceptual framework is essential. If one's logic does not hold, then critical rethinking one's practice to make it congruent with one's conceptual framework is in order.

WEB SITES

Feminist.com. http://www.feminist.com.
Feminist Majority. http://www.feminist.org.
Feminist Theory Web site. http://cddc.vt.edu/feminism.
National Association of Women. http://www.now.org.
National Women's Studies Association. http://www.nwsa.org.

References

Ashcraft, K. L., & Mumby, D. K. (2004). Rewording gender: *A feminist communicology of organization.* Thousand Oaks, CA: Sage.,

Berward, C., & Houtstra, T. (2002). Joining feminism and social group work practice: A women's disability group. *Social Work with Groups, 25*(4), 71–83.

Bricker-Jenkins, M. (2000). Feminist social work practice: Womanly warrior or damsel in distress? In P. Allen-Meares & C. Garvin (Eds.), *The handbook of social work direct practice*. Thousand Oaks, CA: Sage.

Bricker-Jenkins, M., & Hooyman, N. (Eds.). (1986). *Not for women only: Social work practice for a feminist future*. Silver Spring, MD: NASW Press.

Bricker-Jenkins, M., & Lockett, P. W. (1995). Women: Direct practice. In *Encyclopedia of social work* (pp. 2529–2538). Silver Spring, MD: NASW Press.

Contratto, S., & Rossier, J. (2005). Early trends in feminist therapy and practice. *Women & Therapy, 28* (3/4), 1–11.

Figueira-McDonough, J. (1998). Toward a gender-integrated knowledge in social work. In J. Figueira-McDonough, F. E. Netting, & A. Nichols-Casebolt (Eds.), *The role of gender in practice knowledge: Claiming half the human experience* (pp. 3–40). New York: Garland.

Freedman, S. (2007). Re-examining empathy: A relational-feminist point of view. *Social Work, 52*(3), 251–259.

Hyde, C. (2000). The hybrid nonprofit: An examination of feminist social movement organizations. *Journal of Community Practice, 8*(4), 45–67.

Katz-Porterfield, S. L. (1998). *Feminist social work: An analysis of practice*. PhD dissertation, Barry University, Miami, FL.

Kemp, S. P. (2001). Environment through a gendered lens: From person-in-environment to woman-in-environment. *Affilia, 16*(1), 7–30.

Mizrahi, T. (2007). Women's ways of organizing: Strengths and struggles of women activists over time. *Affilia, 22*(1), 39–55.

Netting, F. E., & O'Connor, M. K. (2003). *Organization practice: A social worker's guide to understanding human services*. Boston: Allyn & Bacon.

Netting, F. E., & O'Connor, M. K. (In press). Recognizing the need for evidenced-based practices in organizational and community settings. *Journal of Evidence-Based Practice*.

Pollio, D. E. (2000). Reconstructing feminist group work. *Social Work with Groups, 23*(2), 3–18.

Sandell, K. S. (1993). *Different voices: Articulating feminist social work*. PhD dissertation, Mandel School of Applied Social Sciences, Case Western Reserve University, Cleveland, OH.

Saulnier, C. F. (1996). *Feminist theories and social work*. New York: Haworth.

Saulnier, C. F. (2000). Incorporating feminist theory into social work practice: Group work examples. *Social Work with Groups, 23*(1), 5–29.

Valentich, M. (1986). Feminism and social work practice. In F. Turner (Ed.), *Social work treatment: Interlocking theoretical frameworks*, 3rd ed. (pp. 564–589). New York: Free Press.

38 Acceptance and Commitment Therapy

Kelly G. Wilson, Emily K. Sandoz, & Regan M. Slater

Acceptance and commitment therapy (ACT) is an emerging approach to the improvement of psychological functioning and shares values and relevance with social work practice (Hayes, Strosahl, & Wilson, 1999). Based in the behavior analytic tradition, ACT focuses on the role of context in maintaining behavior and altering context to promote effective behavior. ACT emphasizes acquiring new behaviors, rather than eliminating symptoms. It carries the underlying assumption that clients, no matter their circumstances or diagnoses, can learn new and more adaptive ways of living.

ACT contains a strong emphasis on the therapeutic relationship (Wilson & Sandoz, in press). Treatment is seen as a collaborative effort between client and therapist aimed at building behavioral patterns that allow for more choices and greater personal freedom. Although ACT has some didactic components, it works predominantly through experiential methods. ACT therapists use techniques that would be familiar to individuals trained in a variety of schools of psychotherapy. ACT emerges from the cognitive-behavioral tradition and thus contains elements common to behavioral treatments, such as exposure and behavioral activation. However, it also contains elements addressing personal meaning, as might be seen in existential treatments, experiential exercises that might be familiar to Gestalt therapists and mindfulness as might be seen in Buddhist psychology.

The primary purpose of ACT is to promote psychological flexibility—the capacity to fully experience and embrace necessary pain to allow for committed, life-affirming action. The following is an overview of six facets of psychological functioning seen as central in ACT (Hayes & Strosahl, 2004).

SIX FACETS OF PSYCHOLOGICAL FLEXIBILITY

- *Self.* Does the client make contact with a transcendent sense of self? Or does the client show an attachment to a relatively narrow sense of self focused on psychological content, such as anxiety, depression, or other difficulties?
- *Being in the present moment.* Does the client bring flexible and focused attention to bear in the present moment, or is functioning dominated by worry, rumination, inattention, and other diversions?
- *Acceptance.* Is the client's behavior dominated by avoidance of difficult thoughts and emotions? Does the client accept difficult psychological content in the service of valued living?
- *Defusion.* Is the client rigidly attached to certain ideas and evaluations of themselves and the world around them? Does the client show the capacity to gently let go of thoughts when letting go would be adaptive?
- *Values.* Does the client have the capacity to move in a valued direction in his or her life? Are values obscured, postponed, or absent? Are values experienced primarily as sources of guilt and shame?
- *Committed action.* Does the client have the capacity to make deliberate acts consistent with their values? Does the client avoid commitment? Does the thought of commitment arouse paralyzing worry and/or rumination?

We use the example of a depressed client to illustrate possible interventions within each of these six facets.

Case Example

Jeff is a 29-year-old returning student in business management. He is currently employed as a waiter at a good restaurant. Although he is good at his job, he aspires to complete his degree and take a job in management. Jeff presents seeking help with his depression associated with his divorce and help "getting control" of his drinking. He describes drinking to intoxication several times each month since his divorce 6 months earlier. Jeff has a 4-year-old daughter from whom he has been estranged since the divorce.

ACT IN PRACTICE

Self

Self work in ACT promotes the broadening of an individual's sense of self beyond particular thoughts, feelings, self-conceptualizations, or other content by which one might define oneself. Often this content is limiting, setting boundaries for what can, should, and will be accomplished. ACT aims to loosen the grip of these limitations by calling to the individual that transcends these contents.

From an ACT perspective, we shape an individual's self every time we ask questions the answer to which begins with "I." With this in mind, we move gently and flexibly in ACT among different aspects of content, and rest on experiences that seem to release the content altogether.

When Jeff presents at the clinic, he is experiencing incredible guilt centered around his failures with the people he loves. His sense of self is focused on these failures. To help him make contact with sense of self beyond his failures, the therapist may ask him to see and express other ways that he experiences himself, beginning with fairly nonthreatening content.

We've talked a lot about the recent mistakes you've made and the things about you that you regret. I wonder if today you could help me get a sense of some other aspects of you. You've mentioned your job, so, to start, if you would just take a minute and close your eyes and see yourself in a moment when you were at work. Maybe you can hear the kitchen's clatter and the murmur of the guests. Just let yourself look around that scene, noticing each detail, and what it is like to be there. [pause] And, now I want you to see yourself being a brother, perhaps you can recall at time playing with your brothers when you were young. Take a moment and linger over that image.

The therapist might repeat this process with other aspects of experience. For example, we might ask him to recall a time when he was sad, bored, joyful, and angry. We might ask him to recall times when he believed things that he no longer believes: "Remember, there was a time you believed in Santa. And then, notice that you don't believe that any more." We might ask the client to picture his body now, when he was a teenager, and when he was school age, lingering over the image of each. Finally, the therapist might find it useful to bring Jeff's attention to bear on his own perspective: "See if you can notice now, that when you were seeing your roles, your emotions, your thoughts, and even your own body at different times, there was a 'you' that was there all those times. Notice that the same you that was there then, is here right now hearing my voice."

Being Present

Present moment work is intended to promote attending in the present in a way that is both flexible and focused. Human attention moves easily from the present moment to a conceptualized past (rumination) or future (worry). When this happens, we are more sensitive to the demands of the conceptualized past and future than to the world around us. Present moment work permeates ACT. In fact, the last exercise would be carried out with the pace and tone of a guided meditation. The content is centered on self, but the exercise is present moment–oriented in process. Being present is a pattern of behavior that can be shaped. To do so, the therapist may speak more slowly, more deliberately, with pauses and coach that pace in the client.

Jeff is very much lost in his conceptualized past. No matter what topic is raised, he reverts to talk about his past failures. His regret and self-loathing are intense, with a quality of rigidity, narrowness, and disconnection. To facilitate Jeff's contact in the present moment with this pain, the therapist might simply guide his pace, volume, and intonation, either by adjusting his own or by instructing it directly.

Jeff, you were just talking about how much you wish you had the chance to do those last few months of your marriage over. I know that this is really important to you, and as you talked, I'm afraid I found myself lost in the words, without getting any sense of your actual experience. I was wondering if you would mind telling me again, this time very slowly, so that I can hear and feel each word as you speak it. Along the way, I will ask you to pause a moment while you and I just breathe that moment in and out. [spoken in a slow and deliberate fashion]

This instruction, or some variation of it, will be presented repeatedly throughout the work any time that Jeff begins to pull from the present and speak in a more inflexible and ruminative manner. It is counterintuitive to go more deeply into ruminative content to disrupt rumination. However, altering delivery style and pausing can increase contact with pain experienced in the present moment, rather than pain remembered and resisted (see Wilson & Sandoz, in press, for discussion of mindfulness interventions in ACT).

Defusion

Defusion in ACT focuses on broadening one's interaction with one's own thoughts about the world. Certain verbal aspects of experience, like evaluations and conclusions, become more real and influential than other aspects of the same experience (e.g., the thoughts, "I had my chance and I failed," or "There is no hope for me"). These thoughts dominate experience and obscure other things going on in the client's life. In ACT, rigid interactions with particular verbal content are referred to as *fusion*.

In the same way that exposure techniques broaden a person's ability to act freely in the presence of external events (heights, small spaces), defusion techniques involve broadening ability to act more freely in the presence of difficult thoughts. In practice, any activity that promotes a flexible interaction with these rigidly held thoughts may promote defusion. Saying a particular thought repeatedly or with atypical intonation, volume, cadence, or quality can impact the client's contact with a troubling evaluation or conclusion (Masuda, Hayes, Sackett, & Twohig, 2004). The slowing of pace described in the previous section on present moment–focused work will also have the effect of defusing the content that is slowed. In ACT, the verbal aspects of the experience are not challenged or refuted logically; rather, a context is created where they can be present without dominating the experience.

Jeff expresses a number of frustrations, disappointments, and evaluations that all end with one resounding conclusion: if his ex-wife, Christy, had loved him more or better, her love might have saved him. The way this conclusion functions in his life, rather than its veracity, is most important in ACT. When this belief is present, Jeff's capacity to make choices that are fruitful is diminished. One commonsense strategy might be to examine the "truth" value of his claim to alter it. Instead, the ACT therapist aims at facilitating a more flexible interaction with his thoughts and feelings about Christy. One method might be to ask Jeff to see through Christy's eyes in a slow, mindful experiential exercise.

I'd like you to imagine that you can see Christy before you. It can be as she looks now, or as you remember her from a time before. Notice her hair, her clothes. Notice her posture and the way she stands. Now take a moment and notice the details of her face, one at a time, starting with her general expression, then moving from her mouth, to her cheeks, to her eyes. And now imagine that you could be drawn into those eyes, as if slowly your awareness could fill her, and you could begin to see the world through her eyes. Notice what it feels like to sit inside of Christy's skin right now. And breathe. And gently rest inside that awareness. When you are ready, I'd like you to open your eyes and come back into the room. And I want you to very slowly and gently tell me what you saw.

From an ACT perspective, any interaction with the conceptualized Christy that is different from his typical resentment will lessen fusion with resentful thoughts. In other words, what is sought is interaction that is different, not blaming or adversarial, with Christy and with thoughts about her. To be clear, the purpose of the exercise is more akin to exposure than to an attempt to gain insight or to correct wrong thinking.

Acceptance

Acceptance work in ACT facilitates full engagement of one's experience from joy to pain, without attempts to change its intensity, frequency, or form. Humans have a unique capacity to respond to the world of inner turmoil as if it were as avoidable as burning building. Unfortunately, the relief that avoidance provides is temporary, and people often find themselves engaged in the same struggle over and over again.

Jeff avoids his feelings of guilt by not returning Christy's concerned phone calls, not pursuing vis-

its with Molly, and continuing to use alcohol, all of which are contrary to the changes he would like to make. The great irony is that he feels bad about not following through with Molly, but in avoiding his guilty feelings, he must also avoid Molly—resulting in even more guilty feelings. The therapist might use metaphor to create a context in which Jeff would be willing to experience hard things.

Jeff, I look at you sitting there and I just see this dark cloud surrounding you. It's like you have all these new places you want your life to go so badly and somehow, everywhere you turn, this cloud is blocking you from even seeing the way. It's got to be terrifying. I see you trying different things—swatting at it, trying to look around it, closing your eyes and ignoring it, or taking a drink and forgetting it, and there you are stuck, and blind, and alone in the same spot. Is that right? Does it seem like that to you? [Jeff indicates yes.] I want to ask you something. Something hard. Not because I want to be cruel but because I want more for you. What if Molly was there with you, just out of arms reach, reaching out and waiting for you to scoop her up? I don't know that it's like this. Maybe not. But if it were, would you be willing to walk into scary, dark places to find her? [Jeff indicates yes.] If the cloud was your own struggle with guilt and sadness, how far would you be willing to go into your own despair, to be able to be a Dad again? What if embracing your own difficulties made it so that you could find your way back to Molly? Would it be worth feeling the way you feel if it let you find your way to Molly?

Values

Rather than a focus on symptom remission, ACT focuses on helping clients develop and enlarge patterns of living that are consistent with what they value. Clients enter therapy very problem-focused. If their problems are chronic, they have often postponed or let go completely of important areas of living. ACT uses semistructured methods to examine ten domains of valued living, including intimate relations, parenting, education, spirituality, recreation, and self-care, among others (Hayes et al., 1999; Wilson & Murrell, 2004). Valued domains are explored in an accepting, open, and mindful way. The ACT therapist attempts with the client to help clarify values, link daily activities to valued domains, and support the client in developing a more varied and flexible approach to living.

In Jeff's case, particular goals might include completion of his education and getting a better job. In exploring these goals, we would examine the link between these particular goals and domains of living that are important to Jeff. For example, his interest in his education might be linked to parenting. Taking a few moments to place proximal goals in the context of deeply held values can add meaning and motivation to the achievement of the proximal goals.

Jeff, I wonder if there is a connection between the things you want to accomplish in your education and parenting. Let's take a moment—first, I would like you to let your eyes go gently closed and as you do, let an image of Molly form. Let yourself see her eyes, her hair, her face, and just let your eyes rest gently on her. [pause] Next, I want you to picture yourself hard at work on your education. Picture yourself in a particular place, perhaps working on an assignment. Let your eyes linger on this image of you studying hard. [pause] And, now, I want you to gently open your eyes and tell me, slowly, gently, what would it mean to you, as a father to Molly, to be that man studying hard.

This question is just the beginning of a series of questions that could build in Jeff the capacity to choose a direction and to see a life that is not centered around problems and limitations.

Commitment

Commitment work in ACT focuses on the process of choosing a particular action that could be part of a valued life. Some people are completely inactive in valued domains. For others, action in these domains is characterized by a choked, rushed quality that is functionally just as avoidant as inaction. Still others experience action in valued domains as a burden.

In ACT, commitment involves choosing a course of action and moving toward a value. Commitment is not a promise to keep to a particular path forever. Finding oneself at odds with one's values is seen as normal in the human condition. From an ACT perspective, commitment is found in the gentle turn back to the valued direction when one finds oneself astray. This is reflected in the way it is trained in treatment. A context is created where action can be chosen for the meaning inherent rather than solely for its immediate outcome, where the size of the movement is less important than the process of moving, where falling away is expected and turning back welcomed.

Jeff deeply values being a father, yet he has remained estranged from his daughter. Horrified by his lack of contact, he moves further away from being the father he wants to be. To help

him experience his capacity to act in service of his value of being a father, the therapist might give him the opportunity to commit to some small action that would orient him toward this goal.

Jeff, I've seen in your eyes the importance of being a father to Molly. Your voice changes when she is present here. I can feel the vitality that being a Dad brings to your life. I was wondering if you'd like to choose one small thing to do that would orient you toward being the Dad. What small thing could you do this very day that would be something a father would do?

Six Interrelated Facets

As is apparent in these suggested interventions, the six facets of functioning that ACT addresses are not independent. Rather, they are wholly interdependent. For example, values work done in a mindful way is likely to have a far greater impact. Likewise, acceptance in the context of deeply held values differs markedly from acceptance for its own sake. Central to all of these interventions is acceptance, openness to experience, and a persistent interest in growing a valued life direction.

CONCLUSION

ACT has been demonstrated in clinical trials to be useful for a wide variety of difficulties, including substance abuse, psychotic disorders, chronic pain and stress, medication-refractory epilepsy, and diabetes management, among others (Hayes, Luoma, Bond, Masuda, & Lillis, 2006). In addition, data suggest that positive outcomes in ACT are mediated by the mechanisms described in the theory (see Hayes et al., 2006). ACT and other acceptance-oriented approaches mark a change in the focus of cognitive-behavioral treatments. Tremendous efforts are being expended to examine empirically this new wave of treatments (Hayes, 2004). In doing so, the cognitive-behavioral tradition promises to bring scientific rigor to the examination areas historically left to less scientifically minded traditions.

WEB SITE

Association for Contextual Behavioral Science (ACBS). The site contains an enormous array of resources, including scheduled workshops, a therapist and trainer registry, as well as downloadable material, including articles, chapters, treatment protocols, assessment materials, and assorted therapist tools. Membership in ACBS is required for downloads, and the membership fee amount is entirely voluntary. http://www.contextualpsychology.org.

References

Hayes, S. C. (2004). Acceptance and commitment therapy, relational frame theory, and the third wave of behavioral and cognitive therapies. *Behavior Therapy, 35,* 639–665.

Hayes, S. C., Luoma, J. B., Bond, F. W., Masuda, A., & Lillis, J. (2006). Acceptance and commitment therapy: Model, processes, and outcomes. *Behaviour Research and Therapy, 44,* 1–25.

Hayes, S. C., & Strosahl, K. D. (2004). *A practical guide to acceptance and commitment therapy.* New York: Springer-Verlag.

Hayes, S. C., Strosahl, K., & Wilson, K. G. (1999). *Acceptance and commitment therapy: An experiential approach to behavior change.* New York: Guilford.

Masuda, A., Hayes, S. C., Sackett, C. F., & Twohig, M. P. (2004). Cognitive defusion and self-relevant negative thoughts: Examining the impact of a ninety year old technique. *Behaviour Research and Therapy, 42,* 477–485.

Wilson, K. G., & Murrell, A. R. (2004). Values work in acceptance and commitment therapy: Setting a course for behavioral treatment. In S. C. Hayes, V. M. Follette, & M. Linehan (Eds.), *Mindfulness and acceptance: Expanding the cognitive-behavioral tradition* (pp. 120–151). New York: Guilford.

Wilson, K. G., & Sandoz, E. K. (In press). Mindfulness, values, and the therapeutic relationship in acceptance and commitment therapy. In S. Hick & T. Bien (Eds.), *Mindfulness and the therapeutic relationship.* New York: Guilford.

39   A Behavioral Approach to Social Work Treatment

Denise E. Bronson

Case Example 1: Sally Adams developed a fear of driving over or under bridges following the 2007 collapse of an interstate highway bridge in Minneapolis. She lives in a city with many bridges, and this phobia has escalated to the point that she is unable to drive without planning long, time-consuming routes to her destination. This has interfered with her ability to get to work on time, and she is in danger of losing her job.

Case Example 2: John and Mary Brown's 4-year-old daughter, Megan, has become unmanageable. Bedtime is especially problematic, and it can take up to 3 hours to get Megan into bed. She pleads with her parents to stay up later, then throws temper tantrums when she is told that she must go to bed. This has started to cause prob-

lems between her parents, who argue over how to handle their daughter.

In both of these cases, interventions based on behavioral principles have been shown to be effective and efficacious in treating phobias and parenting problems. Systematic reviews of the literature indicate that behavioral approaches for treating such cases are supported by the best empirical evidence available (see Web sites listed at end of chapter).

Intervention methods using behavioral principles were first introduced to social work in the 1960s as a result of basic and applied psychological research on learning. Today, behavioral intervention methods are used in a variety of social work settings to effectively address individual issues (e.g., anxiety disorders and phobias, anger management, depression, employment skills, and substance abuse), family concerns (e.g., family violence, parent training, communication, and decision making), and community/social needs (e.g., ecological behavior, seatbelt usage, littering, recycling). Behavioral social work embraces not only the treatment strategies used in each of these areas but also a philosophical and theoretical framework for understanding the reciprocal relationship between people and their environment.

There are several characteristics that distinguish behavioral social work from other treatment approaches.

- Behavioral social work is based on extensive empirical work in basic and applied settings, and ongoing empirical evaluation of service is an integral part of behavioral practice.
- Behavioral interventions are highly individualized and address the unique learning history of each client. An individualized behavioral assessment is therefore extremely important and focuses on identifying the environment in which the problem behavior occurs (antecedents), the behavior itself (response), and what happens afterwards (consequences).
- Principles of learning are applied to understand how behaviors are acquired and maintained. This occurs at all levels— individual, family, group, societal, and cultural.
- Behavioral interventions focus on the presenting problem and strive for outcomes that are clinically and socially meaningful to the client and significant others.
- Maintenance and generalization of changes are not assumed to occur automatically once the desired goals are obtained. Instead, the conditions for ensuring maintenance and generalization are carefully assessed and become an important consideration in developing a successful intervention.

Therapeutic applications of behavioral principles derived from the experimental analysis of behavior and learning first appeared in the mid-1960s in psychology, and by 1967 the first social work book on behavioral methods was published (Thomas, 1967). Subsequently, content on behavior modification was added to the curricula in many social work programs and numerous textbooks and articles by behavioral social workers have

appeared. Behaviorally based methods are some of the most widely used interventions, and accounts of behavior therapy in applied settings have appeared in most social work journals.

KEY CONCEPTS IN BEHAVIORAL SOCIAL WORK

A number of key concepts and technical terms are important in behavioral assessment and intervention. Behaviorists generally classify behavior into two broad categories—respondent behaviors and operant behaviors. *Respondent behaviors* are elicited by stimuli in the environment and involve the autonomic nervous system (i.e., blood pressure, heart rate, rapid breathing, or changes in the glandular system). For example, Sally Adams's fear of bridges in case 1 triggers a number of physiological reactions (rapid heart rate, heightened alertness, sweating, etc.) whenever she approaches a bridge. *Operant behaviors*, on the other hand, are those that "operate" on the environment and are controlled by the environmental consequences that follow. Most overt, observable behaviors fall into this category, including language. For example in case 2, if Megan is praised by a parent for going to bed on time, she is more likely to go to bed on time in the future; conversely, if her parents attend to her temper tantrums, it is likely that the tantrums will increase in frequency or intensity. Furthermore, parents are more likely to use praise in the future if it increases the probability that a child will comply with parental requests. Historically, it was believed that respondent behaviors were controlled by antecedent stimuli and operant behaviors were controlled by consequential stimuli. Although this distinction is still useful, recent research has demonstrated considerable overlap in the processes described by these concepts. In addition, it is clear that genetic and biological factors will set limits on the range and type of respondent and operant behaviors that are possible.

Respondent and operant behaviors are learned in two ways—respondent conditioning and operant conditioning. In *respondent conditioning*, a neutral stimulus (conditioned stimulus, CS) is repeatedly paired with an eliciting stimulus (unconditioned stimulus, UCS). Eventually the neutral stimulus will also elicit a similar response, which is now referred to as the conditioned response (CR). For example, the sudden bright light of a flashbulb (UCS) elicits an eye blink (UCR).

Unfortunately, the camera (CS), through its repeated pairing with the flash (UCS), can also begin to elicit an eye blink (CR), often resulting in family pictures in which the subject's eyes are closed in anticipation of the flash. In Sally Adams's case, repeatedly viewing the images of the interstate bridge collapse elicited emotional reactions that were associated with a previously neutral stimulus (bridges). In this way, phobias are acquired through respondent conditioning when neutral stimuli begin to elicit physiological or fear responses.

Operant conditioning refers to the process of learning in which the future likelihood of the behavior will either increase or decrease depending on the contingencies associated with that behavior. *Contingencies* refer to both the consequences that follow the behavior as well as the antecedents that precede the behavior, indicating the type of consequence that is likely. For example, telling a joke at a party will probably be followed by a friend's laughter. If the same joke is told to the same friend during a lecture, however, the friend might respond with "sshhhh" rather than laughter. In this case, the antecedent conditions associated with a party signal that a positive response (a positive reinforcer) will follow telling a joke, whereas the same behavior in class will receive a negative reaction (a punisher). Our jokester soon learns to discriminate the conditions under which jokes will be reinforced. Similarly, in case 2, it is important to conduct a functional analysis to determine the antecedents (e.g., parental request to go to bed), the behavior (e.g., Megan's temper tantrums), and the consequences that follow Megan's outbursts, which might be increasing the future probability of those tantrums (e.g., parents acquiesce and let her stay up or parental attention).

Behaviorists refer to four types of consequences— positive reinforcers, negative reinforcers, positive punishers, and negative punishers. Any consequence that increases the future probability of the behavior it follows is a *reinforcer*. Positive reinforcers are stimuli that are presented contingent on the occurrence of the behavior (e.g., receiving an allowance for household chores). The termination or removal of an aversive stimulus (negative reinforcement) will also increase the behavior it follows (e.g., putting on a sweater when you feel cold). Conversely, any consequence that decreases the future probability of the behavior it follows is a *punisher*. Positive punishment is the presentation of an aversive stimulus contingent on a behavior (e.g., saying "no" to a child who asks for cookies before dinner), whereas negative punishment is the removal of a reinforcer contingent on a behavior (e.g., turning off the TV when children fight about which program to watch). Reinforcers and punishers are highly individualized and vary according to one's learning history, biological and genetic characteristics, and the setting. The only way to determine which stimuli are reinforcers and punishers is to observe the affect of those stimuli on future behavior.

The schedule of reinforcement is another important concept that refers to the frequency with which a behavior is reinforced. Often when new behaviors are being acquired, they are reinforced after every occurrence; this is called a continuous reinforcement schedule. Usually in the natural environment, however, behaviors are reinforced only intermittently depending on the number of times the behavior is performed (ratio schedules of reinforcement), the amount of time that passes (interval schedules of reinforcement), or the rate of responding (differential reinforcement of high or low rates). Intermittent schedules of reinforcement are most resistant to periods of extinction, when reinforcement that was previously available is withdrawn.

Finally, operant behaviors are often preceded by antecedent stimuli (discriminative stimuli) that cue which behavior will be reinforced in a particular setting. Through a process of discrimination training in which a behavior is consistently reinforced only in the presence of specific stimuli, individuals learn which behaviors are likely to be reinforced in each setting. To illustrate, consider Megan in case 2. When Megan's request to stay up later is made to her mother, permission is usually given; when the request is made to the stepfather, it is usually refused. Megan learns quickly to discriminate those situations (i.e., presence of mother) in which requests to stay up late (behavior) are likely to be reinforced (permission granted) from those situations in which the behavior will not be reinforced.

BEHAVIORAL ASSESSMENT AND INTERVENTION

Assessment in behavioral social work is an extremely important process that is closely linked to decisions about which intervention strategy to use. During assessment (also referred to as a functional analysis), the social worker collects information to determine the antecedents and consequences of the problem behavior, specifies the desired outcomes (the target behavior), and selects the most appropriate therapeutic technique. Clients and significant others are an important part of this process. A summary of the steps used by behavioral social workers during assessment is presented in Table 39.1.

Intervention Strategies

Following the assessment and collection of baseline data, behavioral social workers (1) specify the desired target behavior, antecedents, and consequences; (2) identify a data-collection strategy for monitoring changes in the target behavior; and (3) develop an intervention plan. Maintenance and generalization of changes, once they are obtained, are not assumed to occur naturally, and strate-

gies for ensuring lasting change are included in the intervention planning.

Generally, behavioral interventions can be categorized according to whether the primary activity focuses on modifying the stimulus conditions preceding the behavior, developing the behavior itself, or altering the consequences of the behavior. In many cases, one or more strategies from these three categories are employed simultaneously to address the target problem.

Table 39.2 presents examples of commonly used intervention techniques for modifying stimulus conditions (antecedents). These strategies are used when the assessment shows that the client is able to perform desired behavior but unable to discriminate the appropriate time/place for the behavior or that environmental stimuli elicit problematic emotional states (i.e., phobias).

TABLE 39.1 Steps in Behavioral Assessment

Steps	Activities
1. Identify the problem areas and priorities	• Obtain a list of problem areas from the client(s) using interviews, observation, and standardized assessment questionnaires • Determine priorities for service • Select the problem(s) to be addressed and the desired outcome (target behavior)
2. Specify the target behaviors	• Describe the problem and target behaviors in observable and measurable terms • Determine whether the problem is one of behavioral excesses or behavioral deficits • Determine whether the problem is primarily operant or respondent in nature • Begin collecting pretreatment (baseline) data, if possible, using direct observation, client self-reports on internal states or emotions (using rating scales or standardized questionnaires), and physiological measures

3. Assess the controlling conditions (antecedents and consequences)	• Collect information about the environmental antecedents that precede the problem behavior
	• Collect information about the consequences that immediately follow the problem and target behavior
	• Determine whether the problem is primarily one of:
	  ○ Poor stimulus control (i.e., lack of cues for the appropriate behavior, poor discrimination training, or the presence of stimuli that elicit inappropriate respondent and emotional behaviors
	  ○ Behavioral deficits (i.e., client lacks skills to perform the desired behavior)
	  ○ Inadequate or in appropriate consequences (i.e., client has the necessary skills but reinforcers for the desired behavior are missing, the reinforcers are conflicting or delayed, or the reinforcers consist of inappropriate personal reinforcers that cause harm to others or are culturally disapproved)

TABLE 39.2 Interventions for Modifying Stimulus Conditions

Discrimination training	Procedure in which the desired behavior is reinforced in the presence of appropriate stimuli and not reinforced in the presence of inappropriate stimuli to teach when/where to perform target behavior. Fading can be used to gradually change dimensions of the stimulus to teach difficult discrimination.
Respondent extinction	Process of breaking the connection between the conditioned stimulus (CS) and the unconditioned stimulus (UCS) by repeatedly presenting the CS without the UCS until it no longer elicits the conditioned response (CR).
Systematic desensitization	Method used to treat phobias by gradually exposing client to increasingly anxiety-producing stimuli while engaging in responses incompatible with the anxiety (usually relaxation).

In some cases the assessment indicates that the client has not learned the desired behavior and is therefore unable to perform it. The behavioral social worker will select an intervention designed to teach or train a new behavior. Table 39.3 presents examples of some of the commonly used strategies.

The assessment may indicate that the desired behavior does not occur because the consequences of the behavior are faulty. For example, the environment might not reinforce the desired behavior or could be reinforcing an incompatible, inappropriate behavior. Interventions to modify the consequential contingencies can be grouped into two types of strategies—those that focus on increasing the desired behavior and those that focus on decreasing an undesirable behavior. Frequently, behavioral social workers will be using techniques from both groups simultaneously. Table 39.4 presents examples of both types of strategies designed to alter the consequences following a behavior. The effectiveness of interventions to modify the consequences of a behavior will depend on a number of factors, including the immediacy of the consequence, the salience of the reinforcer or punisher, and the schedule of reinforcement. The behavioral social worker will assess each of these factors and address them in deciding how to intervene.

Areas of Application with Empirical Support

Behavioral assessment and intervention techniques have been used to effectively treat a range of problems from individual to societal concerns. Due primarily to behaviorists' commitment to a scientific approach, a large body of empirical research exists to support the effectiveness of behavioral methods to deal with diverse problems and issues such as obsessive-compulsive disorders, parenting difficulties, treatment compliance problems, sexual dysfunction, drug and alcohol abuse, disruptive classroom behavior, attention deficit hyperactivity disorder, and juvenile offenders. Unfortunately, the majority of current research articles on the clinical applications of behavioral methods are reported in psychological journals, such as *Behavior Therapy*.

TABLE 39.3 Interventions for Developing New Behaviors

Shaping	Teaching a new behavior through gradually reinforcing increasingly complex or precise approximations to the final desired behavior.
Chaining	Procedure used when the final behavior consists of several steps needed to complete the action (e.g., dressing). Chaining can either begin at the beginning or end of the sequence to train each of the stimulus-response sequences needed for the desired behavior.
Modeling	Presenting a live or filmed demonstration of the desired behavior in which the client learns which behaviors are desired and the contingencies under which they occur.

TABLE 39.4 Interventions for Modifying Response Consequences

Increasing desired behavior	*Positive and negative reinforcement*	Presenting a reinforcing stimulus or removing an aversive stimulus, respectively, immediately following the performance of the desired behavior.
	Escape and avoidance conditioning	Similar to negative reinforcement in that an aversive stimulus is removed (escape) or prevented (avoidance) after the occurrence of a response.
Decreasing undesired behavior	*Operant extinction*	Process in which a reinforcer is withheld following an operant response that previously produced that reinforcer.
	Positive and negative punishment	Presenting an aversive stimulus or removing a reinforcer, respectively, immediately following the performance of the undesirable behavior.
	Differential reinforcement	Manipulating the schedule of reinforcement to decrease behavior by reinforcing low rates of responding, zero responding, or incompatible responding.

FUTURE DIRECTIONS

Although behavioral social work has evolved considerably since the introduction of the first textbook in 1967 with the infusion of new, research-based knowledge and interventions, the paucity of articles in social work journals is problematic. Considerable misrepresentation and misunderstanding of the behavioral approach continues and those engaged in behavioral social work generally find it easier to publish their work in non–social work publications. Consequently, social workers are often not aware of recent research and developments in behavioral treatment; unfortunately, this means that social work clients are not benefiting from intervention strategies with proven effectiveness. Greater access to systematic reviews of the research literature in electronic, online databases may make current research more accessible to practitioners in the future.

With the advent of evidence-based practice in social work the future of behavioral social work is very promising. The behavioral approach offers empirically tested, change-focused, client-centered, and environmentally based social work interventions that are highly consistent with the values and objectives of social work practice. Increased efforts to ensure that social workers are knowledgeable and skilled in using behavioral methods will certainly enhance the effectiveness of services and the credibility of the profession.

WEB SITES

American Psychological Association Web site for empirically supported treatments. http://www.apa.org/divisions/div12/cppi.html.
Cambridge Center for Behavioral Studies. http://www.behavior.org.
Campbell Collaboration Web site to find systematic reviews of research on behavioral treatment. http://www.campbellcollaboration.org/index.asp.
Cochrane Collaboration Web site to find systematic reviews of research on behavioral treatment. http://www.cochrane.org.

Reference

Thomas, E. J. (1967). *The Socio-behavioral approach and applications to social work.* New York: Council on Social Work Education.

40 Using Social Constructivism in Social Work Practice

Mo Yee Lee & Gilbert J. Greene

People are "meaning-making creatures" who give meaning to their experiences of the world to make their lives coherent (Rosen & Kuehlwein, 1996). People create their knowledge of the world, their sense of reality, by interacting with the other people, institutions, and organizations within it (Greene, Jensen, & Jones, 1996; Sugiman, Gergen, Wagner, & Yamada, 2007). From this perspective, one's definition of what constitutes reality is socially constructed, a meta-theoretical perspective that has become quite visible in the professional literature of such fields as social work, psychology, counseling, and family therapy in the past 10 to 15 years (Franklin & Nurius, 1998).

This constructivist epistemology tends to hold that there is not a reality existing independently of individual people "out there" in the external world. People cannot objectively observe the world to discover it because the very act of observing changes what is being observed. Consequently, people create reality rather than discover it. Humans actively participate in constructing their knowledge of the world rather than acquire it in a passive, stimulus-response interaction with the environment. In recent years, there has been much literature discussing and applying this constructivist approach to practice (Franklin & Nurius, 1998; Gergen, 2006; Greene, Lee, & Hoffpauir, 2005; Neimeyer, & Mahoney, 1993). The discussion herein of the social construction of reality as applied to social work practice is, in essence, our construction of this literature. There are numerous perspectives on the social construction of reality, and we distill these into three major categories: constructivism, social constructionism, and social constructivism.

According to *constructivism*, there is an objective, external reality, but a person can never experience it directly (Gergen, 1999). A person's sense of reality depends on how the mind constructs knowledge and reality. The structure of the individual human organism and human mind, rather than that of the environment, is the best determinant of the meaning people give to the world as they interact with it (Rosen & Kuehlwein, 1996). In other words, constructivism holds the position that the individual mind is the central mechanism in reality construction; the self is a unified and stable entity regardless of context.

On the other hand, *social constructionism* emphasizes "discourse as the vehicle through which self and world are articulated, and the way in which such discourse functions within social relationships" (Gergen, 1999, p. 60). Reality is constructed through people using language in interactions at all levels of social life. Hence, social constructionism believes social processes are central to reality construction and the self is more fluid and responsive to changes in relationships and contexts (Gergen, 1999).

Social constructivism considers both individual and social factors equally in client change. It holds "that while the mind constructs reality in its relationship to the world, this mental process is significantly informed by influences from social relationships" (Gergen, 1999, p. 60). Consequently, social constructivism takes a both/and position rather than one of either/or. Social constructivism, therefore, is very consistent with the ecological perspective in social work practice (Germain & Gitterman, 1996).

Despite some different views on the social construction of reality, these three perspectives have some common beliefs (Lee & Greene, 1999).

- People are not passive recipients of stimulus-response interaction with their environment but rather actively participate in constructing their knowledge of the world.
- People create rather than discover reality because there is not a completely knowable, objective reality standing outside individuals.

- The very act of observing changes that which is being observed, thus, there is no such thing as an objective observer.
- Integral to the social construction of reality is the use of language in dialogical interaction.

THE CASE OF MICHELLE AND TIM

Michelle (age 35) and Tim (age 38) were Chinese immigrants who came to the United States 2 years ago. They came in for couples therapy because of frequent conflict and fights, which had been disturbing to them. When asked what was their perception of the problems, they identified the stress of adjusting to a new environment, new neighborhood, and new jobs with little social support. The therapist helps the couple notice times that they were not fighting despite being stressed and what was different about those times. At the end of the session, the therapist asked them to think about what would be some good advice that people they trust in their community would give to them.

The couple came in for the next session and reported considerable improvement in their relationship. When asked what was different, Michelle responded that among other things they had tried, she had prepared some special Chinese herbal soup for them to "cool down" their "hot" body systems. She shared that an older couple from their church suggested that they were probably working too hard and did not have a balanced diet. Such a life style contributed to a "hot system" in their bodies, which explained why they were irritable and hot-tempered. That older couple introduced them to a Chinese herbal soup that they suggested might help balance their body systems.

Apparently, Michelle adopted the hot/cold theory to partly explain their marital problems. She also attempted to solve the marital conflict through a balanced diet.

THE CASE OF MARK

Mark was 26 years old and court-ordered to receive treatment after being charged with domestic violence. He was married to Sharon, and they had a 2-year-old son. Sharon also had a 6-year-old daughter from a previous relationship. In the first session, Mark came up with the classic goal of spending more time with his wife, although what he really wanted to do was to get away from her, as he felt she controlled him far too much. Mark was a street kid who grew up in a poor and drug- and crime-ridden neighborhood in a big city on the East Coast. He was raised by his grandmother and had no contact with his parents. Sharon was living on the street with her daughter when Mark met her, and he "rescued" her from the street. Mark just did not get used to be a husband and a father because he still liked, in his own words, to play.

From a social constructivist perspective, the client defines the problem and the solution. Mark is the person who experiences his reality and is at the center of change. Instead of making any assumptions about what might be helpful for him to stop his abusive behavior, the therapist assists Mark in evaluating the effects of potential goal activity. In doing so, Mark begins to identify the contradictions in what he says *should* be helpful as opposed to what he really believes *will* be personally helpful to him. Initially, he thought that spending more time with his family would be the ideal goal. As he evaluates this goal possibility, it becomes evident that it would probably drive him crazy. In fact, spending more time with his wife might lead to even more conflict rather than being a solution. The therapist remained focused and patient with Mark to help him evaluate the relevance of his suggested goal. While doing so, the therapist also reinforced and amplified his motivation to do something different for himself and his family. Mark clarified what he doesn't want to be and began to define who he wants to become. The result was that Mark's commitment to creating positive changes was strengthened as he began to recognize that he deeply cares about his son and stepdaughter and wants to be a good father to his children.

Treatment focuses on helping him carefully evaluate, based on his experience, what is personally meaningful for him. It turns out that he uses "shit-talk" to get out his anger during conflict with Sharon instead of hitting her. However, he realizes that this long-used solution to his physical aggression becomes another problem, and he begins to explore whether he should give up shit-talk and "grow up." He is, however, ambivalent about giving up the behavior. He said, "It's the way we always been, you know. Hit on each other, we're young, you know. Just playing around. All we're doing is horsing around." Mark, however, brought up his childhood experience of witnessing abuse in his family of origin. Instead of focusing on the history of the problem, the therapist uses his childhood experience to reinforce the motivation to be a protective dad. Mark talked about his decision to limit the shit-talk in the bedroom because "kids don't see that stuff. They don't need that. Not the way I grew up. " In the following session, he dramatically states, "I've got to make these changes now, this week, because I do care about my family." In a later session, he shares how he held his wife while she cried after a painful loss. This was difficult and completely new for him. "I wanted to get out of there 'cause I hate that stuff, but I stayed because she needed that. In the past I wouldn't have even looked at her, it would have been her business to get over it." Throughout the final sessions, he is able to clearly define what he is doing as he gives up shit-talk.

GUIDELINES FOR USING SOCIAL CONSTRUCTIVISM IN SOCIAL WORK PRACTICE

Social constructivism is not a separate approach but a meta-framework for thinking about and organizing social work practice. General guidelines have evolved from social constructivism for working with clients in social work practice. These guidelines can be easily integrated with a variety of practice approaches, especially those that have been placed under the constructivist umbrella, such as narrative therapy, solution-focused therapy, language systems therapy, and cognitive constructivism.

Develop a Collaborative Social Worker–Client Relationship

A social constructivist view has significant implications for the social worker–client relationship.

- Because clients are the only "knower" and the "expert" of their individual experiences, realities, and aspirations, their stories, explanations, and narratives are the primary source of valid data to work with in the treatment process. Their stories are no longer data to be filtered through formal treatment theories to help the social worker arrive at a treatment plan.
- Social workers are no longer experts who know the "right" answers to clients' problems. In place of a hierarchical social

worker–client relationship is a more egalitarian and collaborative one.
- The client is the expert on his or her life and determines and actualizes goals for change. The social worker is an expert on constructing a treatment process that focuses on clients finding solutions and desired change.
- Social workers use a collaborative approach to discover expertise and knowledge clients have about themselves and their strengths. Taking such an approach enhances client motivation for accomplishing and achieving treatment goals and positive changes (Lee & Greene, 1999).
- Clients are much more willing to cooperate and collaborate in the treatment process if clinicians assume and treat them as if they have strengths, resources, and expertise.
- The social worker's job is to identify, mobilize, and amplify that part of the client that is motivated to collaborate and change. An approach like this can create a positive self-fulfilling prophecy leading to client collaboration and change.

Focus on and Work toward Client-Defined Goals

From a social constructivist perspective, there are many possible ways of viewing and interpreting a specific phenomenon, and no particular view is more correct, truthful, and real than any others; in other words, multiple realities exist simultaneously. Furthermore, problems and solutions are not objective "realities" but private, local, meaning-making activities of individuals (DeJong & Berg, 2007). A person's orientation to and definition of his or her goals clearly has significant implications for their actions and how they experience life.

- It is very important to discover the client's view of reality rather than trying to get the client to learn the worker's view as informed by expert professional knowledge and formal theories.
- Problem and goal definitions are determined by clients rather than predetermined by expert knowledge reflected in a theoretical perspective. Externally imposed therapeutic goals frequently risk being inappropriate or irrelevant to the needs of clients.

- Clients are more willing to work hard to achieve treatment goals if they define the goals themselves and perceive them as personally meaningful (DeJong & Berg, 2007).

Take a Position of Curiosity

Social workers should be very curious as to how clients view reality, especially because there are equally valid, multiple versions of reality, and clients are the only knowers of their experiences.

- Taking a *position of curiosity* involves the social worker "relinquishing the grasp of professional realities, and remaining curious and open to the client's vocabularies of meaning" (Gergen, 1999, p. 170).
- Social workers show they are truly interested in the client as a unique person when clients experience the worker's curiosity about them and their view of reality. Clients also experience the worker's curiosity as very affirming (Gergen, 1999, p. 159).
- The social worker taking a position of curiosity about the client's view of reality models for clients the importance of and the skills for being curious about their own undiscovered potentials and resources in finding creative solutions to problems.
- The worker demonstrating a position of curiosity in dialoguing with clients also facilitates developing a collaborative relationship with clients.

Take a "Not-Knowing, Nonexpert" Position

Because reality is socially constructed, social workers should not assume they know and understand a client's idiosyncratic assumptions about reality based on professional knowledge.

- The not-knowing position is operating when the social worker has an attitude or belief that she or he "does not have access to privileged information, can never fully understand another person, always needs to be in a state of *being informed* by the other, and always needs to learn more about what has been said or may not have been said" (Anderson, 1997, p. 134).
- Clients are seen as experts on themselves, their problems, solutions, resources, and competencies; they are to teach the worker.
- The social worker needs to be open and curious about the client's views, as well as feel comfortable in not having privileged and presumed knowledge.
- Taking the nonexpert position of not knowing does not mean the worker is passive. If the client asks for an opinion or for information, the worker can provide an honest answer as long as it is presented as one of many possible ideas (DeJong & Berg, 2007).
- The purpose of the work with clients is not giving advice or information in the form of "truth statements," nor is it the primary mechanism for client change.
- People usually do not respond positively to experts in positions of authority; thus, taking a not-knowing/nonexpert position can also facilitate the development and maintenance of a collaborative relationship with clients.

Emphasize and Use the Client's Language

Language is the medium through which personal meaning and understanding are expressed and socially constructed in conversation (de Shazer, 1994). Furthermore, the meaning of things is always contingent on the contexts and the language within which clients describe, categorize, and construct it.

- It is more useful to learn the client's language and concepts and the meanings the client gives to them. According to Duncan, Hubble, Miller, and Coleman (1998), "meeting clients within their idiosyncratic meaning systems and privileging *their* experiences, perceptions, and interpretations, will best serve the therapeutic process" (p. 297). This position is in contrast to expecting clients to learn the professional language/theoretical perspective of social workers.
- By learning the language and meanings unique to a client, the social workers is given important information about the client's explanatory framework (theory) about his or her problem(s) and how to go about finding solutions and making positive changes.
- The social worker does this by using some of the client's key words, phrases, and metaphors. This conveys to clients the importance of their existing ideas, which

further reinforces the client's expertise (Duncan et al., 1998).

- Using the client's language builds on the client's existing strengths and "prevents the client from being trapped in and influenced by a particular theoretical view and increases the chances that any change will generalize outside therapy" (Duncan et al., 1998, p. 302).

Dialogue with Clients in Coconstructing a More Expanded View of Reality

Social workers are in the business of facilitating client change, which is facilitated when social workers use language and dialogue with clients so that clients develop a sense of reality that does not contain their presenting problem(s).

- Social workers should intervene with clients in ways that result in changes in their story (personal narrative), in which they view themselves as worthwhile, competent, and with a greater sense of power and personal agency. When such changes occur, clients have a more expanded view of reality that offers more options and possibilities for living their lives.
- Through language and discourse, social workers discover the client's reality; through language use in dialogue between the worker and client, clients can experience desired changes in their reality. However, in practice the social worker does not and cannot unilaterally cause the client's reality to change.
- A result of this dialogical process is the worker and client *cocreating (coconstructing)* an expanded reality for the client that no longer contains the presenting problem or appreciably lessens its severity.
- For client change to occur, it is necessary for the social worker to introduce *novelty* into the dialogue and the client's narrative as she or he tells their story.
- The dialogical interaction between the worker and client involves a conversation between them which "is a mutual search and exploration through dialogue, a two-way exchange, a criss-crossing of ideas in which new meanings are continually evolving" (Anderson & Goolishian, 1993, p. 27). The worker's intent is to coconstruct (coauthor) a

new narrative with the client while not pushing a new story that the worker prefers.

- The worker is not an expert with a privileged perspective but is an expert in the art of conversation and dialogue (Anderson & Goolishian, 1993).
- Because people tend to be self-organizing and their sense of reality is coconstructed in conversations with others, *instructional interaction*, which occurs in a psychoeducational approach to working with clients, is not likely to be very effective (Efran & Greene, 1996). Therefore, social workers should use *dialogical interaction* with clients in working toward their desired goals and change (Lee & Greene, 1999).
- When suggestions, ideas, and information are given to clients, they are not presented as factual truths about reality but as tentative ideas for discussion.
- Dialogical interaction involves the worker introducing *novelty* to clients and stepping back and assessing how the client responds and adjusts to the novelty (Lee & Greene, 1999).
- Dialogical interaction expands a person's "horizon of understanding" (Gergen, 1999, p. 144) and one's meaning and sense of self are cocreated and changed; this process involves dialogue that is transformative (Gergen, 1999). Dialogues are not just conversations in general but involve "special kinds of relationships in which change, growth, and new understanding are fostered" (Gergen, 1999, p. 148). Because dialogues are inherently powerful in creating and sustaining realities, the preferred dialogues should lead to transformation and change.
- In transformative dialogues, the interactants do not assign blame to anyone, focus on the past, or focus on problems and pathology; rather, they should focus on cooperating with each other instead of conflict, search for solutions and new narratives, and envision a desired future mutually acceptable to them (Gergen, 1999).
- Change is facilitated when the social worker gives primary emphasis to dialogues in which client strengths, resources, and competencies are identified, elaborated, and amplified. That is, the majority of the time dialoging with clients should be spent on discussing their strengths and future goals rather than deficits and the past.

FUTURE PRACTICE APPLICATIONS

The use of the meta-theoretical approach of social constructivism is relatively new in social work practice. Social constructivism provides a useful metaphor for organizing social work practice with clients. Though not a separate practice approach, social constructivism provides several practice guidelines presented and discussed herein that can be integrated with a number of other practice approaches.

Common to these social constructivist inspired practice guidelines are the flowing practice techniques:

- use of open-ended questions in dialoguing with clients.
- defining problems and goals, discovering and amplifying their existing strengths and competencies, and
- questioning and changing assumptions about reality.

Consequently, social workers should become experts on using questions to continue the dialogue until clients change, rather than becoming experts on what clients should do to change their lives.

Our belief is that the practice guidelines presented here are quite consistent with social work values, such as fostering client self-determination, respect for individuals, belief in the inherent worth and dignity of all people, and practicing in ways that are egalitarian and collaborative. In addition, we believe that following these guidelines can enhance the effectiveness of clinical social work practice. A practice approach fits the pragmatic realities of current practice contexts that emphasize managed care and accountability: do what works and discontinue doing what does not work. Such a pragmatic approach is integrally involved in how people socially construct reality.

WEB SITES

Relational Constructionism. http://www.relational-constructionism.org.

Social Construction Theory and Therapeutic Practice. http://www.socialconstruction.org.

Taos Institute. http://www.taosinstitute.net.

References

Anderson, H. (1997). *Conversation, language, and possibilities: A postmodern approach to therapy.* New York: Basic Books.

Anderson, H., & Goolishian, H. (1993). The client is the expert: A not-knowing approach to therapy. In S. McNamee & K. J. Gergen (Eds.), *Therapy as social construction* (pp. 25–39). Newbury Park, CA: Sage.

DeJong, P., & Berg, I. K. (2007). *Interviewing for solutions*, 3rd ed. Pacific Grove: Thomson Brooks/Cole.

de Shazer, S. (1994). *Words were originally magic.* New York: Norton.

Duncan, B. L., Hubble, M. A., Miller, S. D., & Coleman, S. T. (1998). Escaping the lost world of impossibility: Honoring clients' language, motivation, and theories of change. In M. F. Hoyt (Ed.), *The handbook of constructive therapies: Innovative approaches from leading practitioners* (pp. 293–313). San Francisco: Jossey-Bass.

Efran, J., & Greene, M. (1996). Psychotherapeutic theory and practice: contributions from Maturana's structure determinism. In: H. Rosen & K. Kuehlwein (Eds.), *Constructing Realities: Meaning Making Perspectives for Psychotherapists*. San Francisco, CA: Jossey-Bass.

Franklin, C., & Nurius, P. (1998). *Constructivism in practice: Methods and challenges.* Milwaukee, WI: Families International.

Gergen, K. J. (1999). *An invitation to social construction.* Thousand Oaks, CA: Sage.

Gergen, K. J. (2006). *Therapeutic realities: Collaboration, oppression and relational flow.* Chagrin Falls, OH: Taos Institute.

Germain, C. B., & Gitterman, A. (1996). *The life model of social work practice: Advances in theory & practice.* New York: Columbia University Press.

Greene, G. J., Jensen, C., & Jones, D. H. (1996). A constructivist perspective on clinical social work practice with ethnically diverse clients. *Social Work, 41,* 172–180.

Greene, G. J., & Lee, M. Y., & Hoffpauir, S. (2005) The language of empowerment and strengths in clinical social work: A constructivist perspective. *Families in Society, 86,* 267–277.

Lee, M.Y., & Greene, G. J. (1999). A social constructivist framework for integrating cross-cultural issues in teaching clinical social work. *Journal of Social Work Education, 35,* 21–37.

Neimeyer, R. A., & Mahoney, M. J. (1993). *Constructivism in psychotherapy.* Washington, DC: American Psychological Association.

Rosen, H., & Kuehlwein, K. T. (Eds.). (1996). *Constructing realities: Meaning-making perspectives for psychotherapists.* San Francisco: Jossey-Bass.

Sugiman, T., Gergen, K. J., Wagner, W., & Yamada, Y. (2007). *Meaning in action: Constructions, narratives, and representations.* New York: Springer.

William P. Panning

Gestalt is a German word that encompasses several concepts, including wholeness, configuration, and pattern. To those in the field of mental health, it implies a unique form of psychotherapy that holds a holistic view of human nature, focuses on the present moment-to-moment experience to develop awareness, and is more curious about *how* people have come to where they are in life than *why*. Instead of making interpretations, Gestalt therapists work to increase the client's awareness. Gestalt therapy is an existential/phenomenological, experiential approach with a holistic commitment to the intellectual, emotional, physical, and spiritual nature of the client. Therapy focuses on improving contact and awareness in the here and now.

The main emphasis in Gestalt therapy is to not get caught up in talking about what happens in the day-to-day life of the client but to experience as fully as possible what is unfolding in the therapeutic encounter. From this here-and-now vantage point, the therapist can deal directly with what is observable in the client's style. The goals are to:

- work through blocks to contact,
- teach awareness, and
- expand contact boundaries through the help of well-crafted experiments.

The therapist encourages clients to attend to themselves in the emerging process to become who they are authentically rather than trying to be something they are not. With this in mind, there is little interest in "fixing" the person. Furthermore, the therapist believes that he or she does not know what is best for the client nor how the client should think, feel, or behave. Instead, the therapist simply honors the client's lively process and helps clients:

- connect their awareness with their experiences,

- develop good contact skills,
- grow through experiential learning, and
- take responsibility for their thoughts, feelings, and actions.

THE HISTORY OF GESTALT THERAPY

Frederick Perls and his wife, Laura, founded Gestalt therapy in the 1940s. Perls was trained as a psychoanalyst. In 1926, he worked under Professor Kurt Goldstein, who introduced him to the principles of Gestalt psychology and provided him with many of the organizing principles for Gestalt therapy (see Table 41.1). Perls was later influenced by the theory and practices of Wilhelm Reich, who focused on the body in therapy and introduced the concept of character armor. He incorporated Reich's method of present-centered examination into Gestalt by heightening awareness of the client's nonverbal communications and focusing on the client's actions and behaviors. This was practiced by paying careful attention to the stylistic ways the client communicated through gestures, body movement, breathing, musculature, speech, and posture.

THE PRACTICE OF GESTALT THERAPY

Although Gestalt therapy may be briefly introduced in graduate social work programs (Congress, 1996), most instruction is received postgraduate through an intensive 3-year training program taught by seasoned therapists. Mentoring and ongoing supervision from a Gestalt perspective round out the ideal education process. It is not uncommon for dedicated students to also engage in their own therapy to develop self-awareness and enhance their contact skills. Thus, there are as many different ways of practicing Gestalt as there are therapists. Differences arise from the fact that each therapist brings his or her own unique aware-

TABLE 41.1 Basic Principles of Gestalt Therapy

1. Careful attention to the contact experienced during the therapeutic encounter.
2. The development of the experiential "present moment"—the "here and now" of experience, considered to be more reliable than interpretation.
3. Field theory, which states that all phenomena are linked to a part of a larger network of interactions and can be understood only in relation to one another.
4. Figure/ground formation states that what is most important in the moment becomes figural and invites attention, and the unimportant drifts to the background.
5. Identification and exploration of resistances through awareness, exploration, and working through.
6. Identification and working through of introjects, the messages internalized in childhood.
7. The use of the experiment to heighten awareness and promote growth and change.

ness, ability to make healthy contact, and creativity to the process of designing and implementing growth-producing contact and experiments.

Rather than a strict, concrete, step-by-step series of actions, Gestalt therapy is a process that unfolds over time out of the encounter between the client and therapist. This process varies with each client depending on such factors as:

- level of awareness of self and other,
- ability to make contact,
- personal history,
- unique resistances and introjects, and
- diagnostic indicators that determine if the client is neurotic, character disordered, or psychotic.

Much of the actual practice of Gestalt therapy consists of carefully examining the contact that is made in the therapeutic encounter and the resistances that emerge at the contact boundary to protect the person—in the moment—from his or her anxiety.

Contact

In Gestalt therapy, the contact between the therapist and the client (rather than interpretations of thoughts, feelings, or actions) forms the basis for the therapeutic encounter. Contact is the psychological process of engaging with our environment and ourselves. Good contact means to be consciously aware of the present, fully engaged in the experience and nurtured by it. The hallmark of good contact is excitement. When you are in contact with someone, it is an energetically charged experience that you will feel as concern, interest, or curiosity. Poor contact, on the other hand, is indicated by lack of interest, boredom, or fear of being engaged by the experience. Therapeutic contact can be thought of as fully seeing and hearing the client and responding to what the individual says and does. Strengthening contact will ultimately help clients express more clearly what is on their minds, express what they feel, and take ownership of the quality of contact they are making. Ingredients of good contact include:

- clear awareness of the moment,
- clear and direct language that has feeling, and
- responsiveness to the here-and-now experience.

Awareness

The idea of developing awareness of "what is" is a concept originally found in Eastern philosophies, such as Taoism and Zen Buddhism. Perls believed *awareness*, or focusing attention on what is actually happening, was so important that he originally called Gestalt therapy "concentration therapy." From a Gestalt perspective, awareness is an ongoing process of "observing and attending to one's thoughts, feelings, and actions, which include somatic sensations and perceptions, language and movement" (Schilling, 1984, p. 151). Developing awareness involves teaching clients to notice, name, and report on their internal processes, which include thoughts, sensations, gestures, posture, movements, facial expressions, vocal tones, breathing quality, and moment-to-moment resistances. The intention of this focus is to develop insight. With increased awareness, clients discover that their sensations are saying something to them about their present experience. The therapist's task is to help clients learn to listen to what their own sensations are saying. This often begins with teaching clients to notice simple body sensations, which, if attended to, will lead to a feeling. As this process unfolds, clients learn to trust themselves and to increasingly develop self-support.

By developing awareness, clients can expect to:

- understand their internal process by realizing that what is emerging inside them has significance;
- improve their ability to be intimate with others by valuing and reporting their moment-to-moment internal process, as well as their external experience;
- develop an increased understanding of identity by noticing, reporting, and responding to any emotional or physical sensations that lead to feelings or actions; and
- develop their ability to live in the moment, and to expand their contact boundaries.

THE THERAPEUTIC RELATIONSHIP

The therapeutic relationship, which is the process of making contact over time, is the emotional heart and soul of Gestalt therapy and something both the therapist and client can intuitively feel. It is the most powerful means of working through a client's problems and is the medium of growth and change. Only after a relationship is established will clients be willing to explore the more vulnerable areas of their lives. "The client comes into therapy expecting that their needs will meet the same traumatic fate in the hands of the therapist that they were met with in childhood" (Cole, 1994, p. 84). To alter this delusion, the therapist's task is to attend to how the client relates in the present and develop a meaningful, trusting relationship. Therapists must practice good contact, self-awareness, and sensitivity to the emerging contact boundaries of the client. To do this effectively, the therapist must be present-centered and guided by theory that is known so well that it can be forgotten. The focus then becomes the client's humanity.

RESISTANCES

In Gestalt therapy, resistance is accepted as *what is* for clients in their experience of the present moment. Resistances represent *how* clients avoid contact and limit themselves in the present from doing things that would require them to stretch their boundaries and grow. Inasmuch as resistances are essential to the individual's being in the world, they are not something to be broken down. Instead, therapists work to bring them into awareness.

Resistances are identified by observing the client's posture, body movements, expressions, breathing, speech quality, voice tones, and verbal communications. Once resistances are identified and named, clients are taught to report any internal cues that help them track how they experience blocking contact in the present moment. Growing beyond a boundary is subsequently accomplished through experimentation. The five primary resistances are briefly discussed here.

Retroflection

Retroflection is a mechanism by which people hold in what they are afraid to express to others. Energy that is charged and poised for action is turned back on the self. Thus, clients do to themselves what they would like to do to others *or* do to themselves what they would like others to do to them. In both instances, they are turning back on the self what needs to be turned toward the world. The disadvantage of retroflecting is that energy is blocked and not successfully discharged. This can lead to a build-up of anxiety, constant muscle tensions/pain, and physical ailments, such as ulcers, psychosomatic illnesses, and depression.

Common examples of retroflection that can be witnessed in the therapeutic encounter include:

- holding the breath,
- shallow or labored breathing,
- excessive swallowing,
- body tension,
- clenching of the jaw and/or grinding of the teeth,
- biting fingernails,
- shaky and/or monotone voice, and
- stopping midsentence while speaking.

The key to resolving unhealthy retroflection is to help clients get back into their feelings and let go of them appropriately.

Deflection

Deflection is the avoidance of contact and/or awareness by turning aside or pushing something away. The client is taking action but misses the mark by either making no contact or reducing contact. Deflection detracts from genuine contact.

Common examples of deflection include not looking at the person with whom you are attempting to make contact, using verbose/excessive language, vagueness/being abstract or indirect, laughing off important things, and not receiving or taking in what someone is saying.

Projection

Projection is the confusion of self and others that results in attributing to the outside world something that truly belongs to the self. A part of the self or feeling about self is experienced, but not understood or owned as self, and is attributed to another person outside the body. Projection in its unhealthy form is blaming and not taking responsibility for oneself or one's actions. Psychological growth suffers when one is unable to own "unacceptable" parts of the self.

Introjection

Introjection is passively taking in information without discriminating or assimilating. As a result, foreign, undigested information is swallowed without adequate processing or ownership. When a client constantly takes in everything without discrimination and doesn't reject what doesn't fit, it creates an "amorphous" personality.

Confluence

Confluence is the fusion or merging of boundaries through pseudo-agreement to avoid differentiation or separation. This blurring melts the boundary and causes a loss of separate identity. Without well-defined boundaries, it is hard to get to know a person. No contact can develop when there is no clear distinction between where the individual ends and another person begins.

Prolonged confluence deadens the potential for conflict to emerge and to heighten an interaction. Without conflict, interactions become flat and unexciting. This can lead to pathological compliance, codependency, and a submission of one's personal preferences. There is no struggle to develop one's own interests and convictions.

STAGES OF RESISTANCE WORK

The therapist's task is to help the client develop an understanding of the resistance process by explaining what a resistance is, describing how it operates, and identifying how it surfaces in the present moment to block contact. Resistance work involves the following steps.

1. Identifying and witnessing the resistance and noticing how it emerges in the client. This is accomplished through observing nonverbals, attending to how the therapist feels sitting with the client, and listening to the words in which the story is presented.
2. Sensing internal cues to assist clients in developing awareness of and connection to their internal process by noticing the unique sensations they experience.
3. Once clients can feel/sense their resistances, they must begin to report their own process to the therapist. This marks a shift away from the therapist's pointing out the resistances and toward clients taking responsibility for tracking their own processes.
4. Clients are encouraged to move beyond their resistances by experimenting with alternatives that may stretch their contact boundary.

THE GESTALT EXPERIMENT

"A unique quality of Gestalt therapy is its emphasis on modifying a person's behavior in the therapy situation itself. This systematic behavior modification, when it grows out of the experience of the client, is called an experiment" (Zinker, 1977a, p. 123). The experiment is a means of experiential learning that transforms "talking about" a problem into dramatically heightening awareness through creative experimentation. With the support of the therapist, who acts as consultant and coach, clients are given the opportunity to explore their underdeveloped side, try new behaviors, and focus on their verbalizations, fantasies, or physical functioning in the here and now to promote growth and change.

Zinker describes, in *In Search of Good Form* (1977b, p. 194), that an experiment comes out of the encounter and generally involves the following developmental sequence:

- Laying the groundwork.
- Negotiating consent between the therapist and client. Gaining consent is accomplished by asking the client, "Would you like to try something?"

- Grading the work up or down by making the experiment equal the client's readiness, need, and ability. This makes an experiment safe enough to warrant implementation, yet challenging enough to be realistic.
- Surfacing the client's energy and motivation.
- Developing a theme.
- Generating self-support.
- Choosing an experiment, carrying it out, and debriefing the client.

FUTURE APPLICATIONS

Gestalt therapy is more than a mode of treatment. It is a philosophical approach to life that recognizes the importance of awareness and genuine contact to mental health and happiness. Learning the skills of Gestalt therapy helps individuals develop the confidence to move from a self focus out into the world to get their needs met. This is accomplished by honoring "where the client is," respecting the whole person as being more than the sum of independent parts, and acknowledging that a trusting therapeutic relationship is indispensable in fostering growth and change.

Whether working with an individual, couple, family, or group, the practitioner provides good contact that transcends people, diversity, and cultural differences. Gestalt therapy develops a common ground for living, relating, and learning. It is more practice-driven than research-driven. As stated earlier in the chapter, there are as many different ways of practicing Gestalt therapy as

there are therapists. Thus, the future of Gestalt therapy will be a holistic sum total of the practices of its therapists, guided by the basic, client-centered principles of the field.

WEB SITES

Association for the Advancement of Gestalt Therapy. http://www.aagt.org.

Gestalt Institute of Toronto. http://www.gestalt.on.ca.

Gestalt Review. http://www.gestaltreview.com.

Gestalt Therapy Network. http:www.gestalttherapy.net.

Gestalt Therapy Page. http://www.gestalt.org.

Society for Gestalt Theory and Its Applications. http://www.gestalttheory.net.

References

Cole, P. (1994). Resistance to awareness: A Gestalt therapy perspective. *Gestalt Journal, 17*(1), 71–94.

Congress, E. (1996). Gestalt theory and social work treatment. In F. J. Turner (Ed.), *Social work treatment: Interlocking theoretical approaches,* 4th ed. (pp. 341–361). New York: Free Press.

Schilling, L. E. (1984). Gestalt therapy. In *Perspectives on counseling theories* (pp. 148–165). Englewood Cliffs, NJ: Prentice Hall.

Zinker, J. (1977a). *Creative process in Gestalt therapy.* New York: Vantage Books.

Zinker, J. (1977b). *In search of good form: Gestalt therapy with couples and families.* San Francisco: Jossey-Bass.

William Borden

Object relations psychology has emerged as a major paradigm in contemporary psychodynamic thought. Although the perspective encompasses a variety of theoretical systems, thinkers have increasingly come to share fundamental assumptions, core concepts, and essential concerns. This overview traces the development of object relations psychology, introduces basic theoretical formulations and clinical perspectives, and shows how overlapping points of view deepen conceptions of personality development, psychopathology, and therapeutic action in psychosocial intervention. In doing so, it explores the ways relational perspectives enlarge understandings of vulnerability and interpersonal processes in emerging models of evidence-based practice.

Object relations perspectives have increasingly informed efforts to develop realistic and flexible approaches to psychosocial intervention for a range of problems in living, and relational concepts continue to shape development of empirically based methods of psychodynamic psychotherapy (Luborsky & Barnett, 2006). Clinicians have established guidelines for treatment of maladaptive patterns of interpersonal behavior as well as problems in functioning associated with acute stress reactions, post-traumatic stress syndromes, the personality disorders, and other forms of developmental psychopathology (Roth & Fonagy, 2005). In the broader domain of social work practice, object relations perspectives deepen understanding of interactive processes and intervention approaches with couples, families, groups, and organizations (Borden, 2000). Emerging lines of research in neuroscience and developmental psychology promise to strengthen the empirical base of object relations psychology and broaden conceptions of interpersonal behavior, experiential learning, and clinical expertise in reformulations of evidence-based practice perspectives.

DEVELOPMENT OF OBJECT RELATIONS PSYCHOLOGY

Sigmund Freud first introduced the term *object* in the development of his drive psychology, although he linked the construct to notions of instinctual process rather than to concepts of relationship and social interaction; he saw the person as an object through which one achieves instinctual gratification. Although drive psychology served as the central paradigm in psychoanalytic understanding through the early decades of the twentieth century, growing numbers of thinkers challenged Freud's vision of human nature and elaborated alternative perspectives that increasingly emphasized relational concepts and social domains of experience.

The earliest attempts to establish relational points of view encompassed the psychodynamic perspectives of Alfred Adler, C. G. Jung, Otto Rank, and Sandor Ferenczi, originally members of Freud's inner circle. They placed growing emphasis on the role of relationship and social experience in their formulations of personality development, psychopathology, and therapeutic intervention. Adler, for example, envisioned persons as social beings and emphasized concepts of relationship in his therapeutic approach. Jung saw persons as inherently relational and innately social. Rank based his humanistic model of personality on concepts of autonomy, dependency, and relationship, viewing psychology as the science of interpersonal relations. Ferenczi recognized the importance of the early caretaking environment in his conceptions of psychopathology, and he increasingly stressed the curative functions of the therapeutic relationship and interactive process in his reformulations of therapeutic methods. Careful readings of these revisionist thinkers, long neglected in the mainstream literature, show the extent to which they prefigure fundamental object relations concerns.

The widespread experience of separation, loss, and mourning after World War I informed further development of relational perspectives in London during the 1920s. Ian Suttie rejected Freud's drive psychology and proposed that innate needs for love and relationships are the fundamental motivational forces in personality development. He stressed the importance of the social environment in formulations of health and psychopathology and increasingly emphasized the curative functions of relational process in therapeutic intervention.

A second generation of British thinkers, including Melanie Klein, W.R.D. Fairbairn, Donald W. Winnicott, and John Bowlby, began to extend psychoanalytic theory in the 1930s. Working within the Freudian tradition, Klein preserved classical notions of drive and emphasized the internal realm of fantasy in her theoretical system. Over the course of her work, however, she introduced concepts of internal representation (internal objects) and defensive process (splitting, projective identification) that provided crucial points of departure for Fairbairn and Winnicott in their efforts to elaborate relational and social perspectives. In this sense, Klein emerged as a key figure in the transition from drive to relational perspectives.

Fairbairn departed from the classical drive paradigm and introduced models of personality development and psychopathology that led to major reorientations of psychodynamic thought. He theorized that the core tendency in human development is to establish contact and preserve connections with others, and he focused on progressive experiences of dependency in the mother–child relationship. In his model, personality is constituted and structured through ongoing internalization and representation of relational experience. Winnicott emphasized the crucial functions of caretaking figures in personality development, and he saw relational provisions in the "holding environment" of infancy and early childhood as crucial determinants of health and psychopathology. He increasingly focused on domains of self-experience, emphasizing notions of inner coherence, agency, vitality, creativity, play, and personal meaning.

Bowlby argued that the fundamental need to establish contact and connection has adaptive roots in biological survival, and his attachment theory emerged as a major paradigm in empirical study of the mother–child relationship. He proposed that working models of self and others, established in interaction with caretaking figures, guide information processing about relational experience and shape patterns of behavior and adaptation through the life course. More than any other theorist, Bowlby attempted to bridge internal and external domains of experience and describe the processes that lead to establishment of psychic structure and modes of interpersonal functioning.

Three lines of theorizing in America have influenced the development of object relations thought, including the interpersonal tradition of Harry Stack Sullivan and Karen Horney; the self psychology of Heinz Kohut; and the overlapping contributions of Heinz Hartmann, Edith Jacobson, Margaret Mahler, and Otto Kernberg. The last group preserved Freudian concepts of drive, however, and did not embrace the interactive, "two-person" psychology that has become a defining feature of contemporary object relations thought. Greenberg and Mitchell (1983) carried out the first comparative study of object relations theories; for review of subsequent accounts of relational perspectives see Borden (2000).

Object relations concepts have assumed growing importance in neuroscience, cognitive psychology, developmental psychology, experimental psychology, and social psychology. Research on attachment and neurological development documents the crucial functions of relational experience in personality organization and patterns of interpersonal functioning across the course of life (Luborsky & Barnett, 2006; Schore, 2003). Relational perspectives increasingly inform empirical study of infant–caretaker interaction and personality organization, developmental psychopathology, and therapeutic intervention.

THEORETICAL FORMULATIONS AND CORE CONCEPTS

Although the object relations paradigm encompasses divergent lines of inquiry, contemporary theorists increasingly share basic assumptions about the nature of personality development; notions of health, well-being, and the common good; conceptions of vulnerability and psychopathology; and therapeutic elements in psychosocial intervention. The following sections examines core concepts, guiding themes, and fundamental concerns in each of these areas, and considers the implications of object relations perspectives for continued development of evidence-based practice perspectives in clinical social work.

Personality Development

Concepts of motivation emphasize the fundamental need for attachment and relationship throughout the life course. Relational experience shapes the development of mind, personality, or self. The interactive field is the central organizer of psychic structure and function; the core of the person is constituted through ongoing interaction with others in the social environment. Developmental lines of study consider the nature of early caretaking experience, social environments, and emerging capacities for relatedness. According to object relations perspectives, basic prototypes of connection, established in infancy and childhood, are preserved in the form of internalized representations of self and others. Working models of self and others influence subjective states, perceptions of persons, and modes of interpersonal behavior.

Theorists differ in their conceptions of motivational, affective, and cognitive processes believed to mediate the development of personality, and they assume that internalization of interpersonal experience shapes inner representations of self, other, and modes of relating (self in relation to others). Although core representations are derived from interaction in the social environment, they are not memories of events; rather, they are schematic structures formed from the cumulative experience of interpersonal life. Elaboration of schemas is influenced by constitution and temperament, early developmental experience, unconscious fantasy process, and life events. Presumably, ongoing experience generates multiple representation of self, others, and modes of interaction. Investigators theorize that the particular representations guiding perception and behavior at any given moment are determined largely by immediate needs, life circumstances, and social contexts.

Health, Well-Being, and the Common Good

Conceptions of health center on the establishment of basic structures of mind, personality, or self and corresponding capacities for relatedness that influence overall levels of functioning. From this perspective, optimal development leads to a cohesive sense of self, affirming but realistic views and expectations of self and others (inferred self and object representations), and stable and enduring relationships. Theorists stress the role of others in the development of the person and the sustaining functions of relationship, social interaction, and community through the life course. Most thinkers encompass concepts of mastery, coping, adaptation, and self-actualization in formulations of health and fulfillment.

Vulnerability and Psychopathology

Theorists focus on the organization of the self and corresponding modes of interpersonal functioning in their conceptions of vulnerability and psychopathology. Winnicott, Fairbairn, and Kohut emphasize arrests, splits, and deficits in the organization of self-structure. Bowlby describes rigid, anachronistic models of relational experience that shape problematic patterns of attachment and social interaction. Other thinkers, influenced by Klein and Kernberg, center on pathological manifestations of defensive processes, notably splitting and projective identification, associated with the personality disorders. Another group of theorists, drawing on the interpersonal theory of Sullivan and Horney, emphasize constricted patterns of interaction or vicious circles of behavior that perpetuate problems in functioning (Wachtel, 2008).

Thinkers distinguish predisposing, precipitating, and perpetuating factors in formulations of dysfunction. Because the relational field is the primary organizer of psychic structure and function, however, they tend to see early caretaking systems, patterns of interaction, unresponsive social environments, and traumatic events as critical determinants of vulnerability and psychopathology. Although the first generation of theorists centered largely on the nature of the mother–child relationship and critical periods of care in infancy and early childhood, subsequent investigators have broadened perspectives to consider ways contemporary relational experience, life events, and social environments influence problems in living.

Object relations theorists recognize the impact of deprivation and trauma in relational and social domains of experience, just as they realize the organizing and sustaining functions of maladaptive behavior. Following contemporary relational views, most theorists assume that psychopathology is self-perpetuating because it is embedded in more general ways of being and relating that persons have established over the course of development. As Mitchell (1988) explains, there is "a pervasive tendency to preserve the continuity, connections, and familiarity of one's personal, interactional world" (p. 3). Accordingly, however problematic certain behaviors may be, established modes of functioning serve to maintain cohesion and continuity in sense of self, preserve connections with internalized representations of others, and promote safety and security in interpersonal interaction. Clinicians assume that improved interpersonal functioning strengthens self-organization and reduces problems in living associated with all forms of psychopathology.

Psychosocial Assessment and Intervention

Practitioners describe guiding perspectives, core concepts, and basic principles that inform approaches to assessment and treatment. Concepts of therapeutic action emphasize the primary role of the therapeutic relationship in the process of change and the functions of *interpersonal interaction* and *experiential learning* in efforts to deepen self-understanding, strengthen coping capacities, and negotiate problems in living. From this perspective, the clinician provides reparative experiences that modify maladaptive representations of self and others, reorganize patterns of defense, and facilitate more adaptive and fulfilling ways of living. The emphasis on the dynamics of the therapeutic relationship and current patterns of interaction distinguishes object relations perspectives from classical psychoanalytic approaches that focus on childhood conflict and development of insight through interpretive procedures.

Assessment. Object relations perspectives emphasize the following domains of concern in assessment of functioning:

- subjective states, emotions, and moods;
- inner representations of self, others, and modes of relating as inferred from accounts of persons, events, and views of self; and
- capacities for relatedness to others, defensive strategies, and patterns of interpersonal behavior.

The following guidelines serve to focus the assessment process.

- Using a narrative perspective, the clinician encourages clients to relate problems in their own words; the practitioner explores the interpersonal contexts of symptoms or difficulties and presses for concrete detail in accounts of experience.
- The clinician explores the nature of past and current relationships, as well as representative themes and concerns that emerge in discussion of self, interpersonal experience, and life events.
- The clinician observes patterns of interaction during the clinical interview, explores clients' experience of the therapeutic relationship, identifies patterns of defense, monitors evolving transference and counter-transference reactions, and notes potential enactments of dysfunctional behaviors in therapeutic interaction.
- In establishing the focus, the clinician links the presenting problem to representative patterns of interaction that would appear to perpetuate difficulties.

The aims of assessment are to (1) determine general levels of personality organization and interpersonal functioning on the basis of the foregoing criteria, and (2) identify core relational themes, modes of defense, and representative patterns of interaction that precipitate problems in functioning.

Intervention. Object relations theorists recognize the potential influence of common elements believed to facilitate change across the major schools of thought (Frank & Frank, 1991), but they emphasize the role of relational provisions and experiential learning in concepts of therapeutic action. Ongoing interaction between client and clinician facilitates efforts to identify vicious circles of behavior and develop more effective ways of processing information and negotiating interpersonal experience. The therapeutic relationship itself serves as a medium for change, and transference and countertransference states provide crucial sources of experiencing and understanding in efforts to revise internalized representations of self and others, reorganize patterns of defense, develop interpersonal skills, and improve social functioning. Enactments of maladaptive behavior in the therapeutic situation facilitate efforts to clarify problematic modes of interaction and establish more effective ways of negotiating interpersonal situations and life tasks. Theorists view the clinician as a *participant-observer* and stress the reciprocal nature of therapeutic interaction. In doing so, they deepen appreciation of subjective elements and mutuality in the helping process. Over the course of intervention the client internalizes positive aspects of the therapeutic relationship, modifying inner representations of self and others, and establishes more adaptive ways of managing vulnerability and negotiating problems in living. From the perspective of cognitive neuroscience, the core activities of the therapeutic process alter associational networks established over the course of development and facilitate formation of new, adaptive linkages and patterns of behavior (Schore, 2003).

Practitioners working from object relational perspectives emphasize the following principles of intervention.

- The clinician clarifies enactments of maladaptive behavior, exploring defensive functions, and processes transference-countertransference reactions as they occur to help clients recognize and understand problems in living.
- When possible, the clinician links patterns of interpersonal functioning in the therapeutic situation to behavior in past and current relationships.
- The clinician uses descriptive, clarifying, and interpretive statements in efforts to help clients deepen awareness of their own and others' behavior, process subjective experience, better understand reactions to interpersonal events, and alter dysfunctional beliefs and maladaptive forms of behavior.
- The clinician uses problem-solving strategies, task-centered approaches, modeling, and reinforcement in efforts to help clients strengthen coping capacities and interpersonal skills.

CASE REPORT

Assessment

The client, age 28, initiated psychotherapy in a community mental health center after he was suspended from his job. He explained that his manager had placed him on leave because he was "unable to get along with people," and he reported growing feelings of frustration and anger in his interaction with co-workers, characterizing them as "incompetent." Over the course of the interview, the client described ongoing strain and rupture in his dealings with peers and managers, rendering relational life in absolute terms: "people are either with you or against you," he explained. He challenged the social worker's attempts to ex-

plore concerns beyond the workplace, becoming impatient and argumentative and coming to see the session as "useless." He pressured the clinician to "come up with a solution" for his difficulties, showing little capacity to process his experience in the give and take of the interactive process. On the basis of his accounts of relational experience and patterns of interaction during the interview, the practitioner hypothesized that the client used splitting defenses and aggressive behavior as means of managing his experience of vulnerability. The social worker realized that the client's constricted patterns of functioning would potentially limit his capacity to form a collaborative relationship and engage in the therapeutic process.

Intervention

In spite of the foregoing concerns, the client responded to the clinician's *attunement* and *empathetic processing* of concerns and established a working alliance. The conditions of acceptance, understanding, and support facilitated the development of the *holding environment*. The clinician attempted to validate the client's experience, realizing the protective functions of attitudes and behaviors. The client was increasingly able to explore the antecedents and contexts of current problems in functioning. Since childhood, he had been the object of his father's teasing, bullying, and anger. The clinician hypothesized that he had internalized the experience of his father's assaults over the course of development, coming to identify with a representation of his father as hateful, relating to others as his father had interacted with him. Presumably, the representations of self and others encompassed in his working models of interactive experience shaped ways of processing information in interpersonal life and perpetuated aggressive modes of behaviour, precipitating strain, rupture, and loss.

Transference and countertransference states provided points of entry into the dynamics of earlier family life. The client was cold, sarcastic, and bullying in his interactions with the social worker. The ongoing cycle of rupture and repair in the therapeutic relationship served as crucial sources of experiential learning, offering opportunities to process earlier trauma, explore defensive processes, and develop skills in managing his experience of vulnerability, fear, anger, and disappointment. The clinician used interpretive procedures to link past experience with current patterns of behavior in the therapeutic relationship and in the workplace, deepening his understanding of life experience, protective strategies, and ways of relating. The social worker modeled ways of processing subjective experience and problem solving and used explanation as an educational strategy in efforts to help the client understand the nature of his reactions, defenses, and patterns of interaction, helping him disidentify with aggressive aspects of his father. Over time, the client strengthened capacities to regulate emotion, disrupt vicious circles of interaction, limit self-defeating behavior, and negotiate the vicissitudes of interpersonal life in more adaptive and constructive ways.

RELATIONAL PERSPECTIVES AND EVIDENCE-BASED PRACTICE

Relational perspectives promise to strengthen approaches to assessment, case formulation, and treatment planning in emerging conceptions of evidence-based practice. The helping relationship serves as the facilitating medium of intervention, and object relations formulations emphasize the role of interpersonal expertise in efforts to establish the therapeutic alliance; address vulnerabilities and patterns of behavior that potentially compromise engagement, precipitate strain, and limit change; and make flexible use of interactive experience in light of differing capacities, problems in functioning, and the individual, social, and cultural contexts of the client. Converging lines of study document the ways each participant in the relationship influences the process and outcome of intervention, and relational perspectives provide nuanced ways of conceptualizing interactive experience that deepen current formulations of interpersonal behavior in models of evidence-based practice (APA Presidential Task Force on Evidence-Based Practice, 2006; Westen & Bradley, 2005).

FUTURE PRACTICE APPLICATIONS

Overlapping domains of understanding in object relations psychology focus on concepts of self and relationships and continue to reflect fundamental concerns in contemporary culture, social life, and psychosocial intervention. The theoretical systems encompassed in this paradigm shape ways of understanding personality development; health, well-being, and common good; vulnerability and psychopathology; and modes of therapeutic action. As such, object relations theory enlarges our understandings of vulnerability, problems in living, and helping processes as we continue to develop social work theory, research, and practice guidelines.

WEB SITES

International Association for Relational Psychoanalysis and Psychotherapy. http://www.iarpp.org.
Object Relations Theory and Therapy, by Thomas Klee. http://www.objectrelations.org.

References

American Psychological Association Presidential Task Force on Empirical Practice. (2006). Evidence-based practice in psychology. *American Psychologist, 61*(4), 271–285.
Borden, W. (2000). The relational paradigm in contemporary psychoanalysis: Toward a psychodynamically-informed social work perspective. *Social Service Review, 74*(3), 352–379.
Frank, J., & Frank, J. (1991). *Persuasion and healing.* Baltimore, MD: Johns Hopkins University Press.
Greenberg, J., & Mitchell, S. (1983). *Object relations in psychoanalysis.* Cambridge, MA: Harvard University Press.
Luborsky, L., & Barrett, M. (2006). The history and empirical status of key psychoanalytic concepts. *Annual Review of Clinical Psychology, 2*, 1–19.
Mitchell, S. (1988). *Relational concepts in psychoanalysis.* Cambridge, MA: Harvard University Press.
Roth, A., & Fonagy, P. (2005). *What works for whom? A critical review of psychotherapy research,* 2nd ed. New York: Guilford.
Schore, A. (2003). *Affect dysregulation and disorders of the self.* New York: Norton.
Wachtel, P. (2008). *Relational theory and the practice of psychotherapy.* New York: Guilford.
Westen, D., & Bradley, R. (2005). Empirically-supported complexity: Rethinking evidence-based practice in psychotherapy. *Current Directions in Psychological Science, 14*(5), 266–271.

43 Using Self-Psychology in Clinical Social Work

Jerrold R. Brandell

The psychology of the self, which has only recently attained begrudging acceptance among psychoanalysts, has enjoyed an early and enthusiastic reception among dynamically oriented social workers since its introduction as a treatment framework in the late 1970s (e.g., Elson, 1986; Rowe & MacIsaac, 1991).

A relative newcomer among the psychoanalytic psychologies that constitute contemporary psychoanalysis (classical psychoanalysis, ego psychology, object relations theories, and relational psychoanalysis, inter alia), the psychology of the self was introduced by American psychoanalyst Heinz Kohut in a series of essays and books published between 1959 and 1984. Although Kohut originally presented the theoretical and technical innovations of his new psychology within the extant classical drive theory (Greenberg & Mitchell, 1983; Kohut, 1966, 1971), he later expanded and revised his theory (Kohut, 1977, 1984), the end result being a distinctive and fundamentally new psychoanalytic psychology (Brandell, 2004).

The development of self-psychology was, in large measure, guided by Kohut's clinical experiences with analytic clients who seemed unable to benefit from his efforts to use classical formulas in his interpretive work. Despite his assiduous efforts to refine and revise interpretations or alter his timing or the breadth of his interpretive remarks, Kohut found that certain clients failed to improve. He gradually concluded that the problem lay not with technical parameters of his interpretations but with basic theoretical premises of classical psychoanalytic theory. Although these assumptions had proved quite useful in treating the classical neuroses (hysterical, phobic, or obsessive-compulsive), the modal disorders of the late nineteenth and early twentieth centuries, Kohut reasoned that such pathology had gradually been supplanted by other disorders that proved much less amenable to such a theoretical and clinical framework.

The essence of self-psychology may well be captured in its vision of the human condition. The classical or Freudian view of humankind is usually expressed in terms of disturbing wishes and conflicts, an ongoing battle between primordial desire and societal requirements and proscriptions for civilized behavior, ontogenetically recapitulated with each successive generation in an endless cycle. Within such a framework and its oedipal foundation, the development of a capacity to experience guilt, painful as it may be, assumes supreme importance as a basis for the renunciation of instinct. Freud believed that without this ability to renounce instincts, civilized behavior was not possible.

Kohut's vision of the human condition contrasts sharply with that of Freud. He focused much less on primitive desires and the intrapsychic conflicts to which they gave rise, instead focusing on the loss of meaning associated with contemporary life. The dispirited Kohutian man/woman, complaining of chronic ennui or boredom, often described the attainment of long-sought-after rewards or accomplishments as unfulfilling. Or he or she experienced life as a sort of emotional roller coaster, where "exuberant bursts of creative energy alternate with painful feelings of inadequacy," as recognition of individual failures extruded into consciousness. "Relationships, eagerly, even desperately pursued, [are] repeatedly abandoned with an increasing sense of pessimism" at the realization that the fulfillment of one's relational needs is so unlikely (Mitchell & Black, 1995, p. 149).

Kohut attempted to capture the fundamental disparity between the classical psychoanalytic view of human nature and that of self-psychology in his explication of Guilty Man versus Tragic Man. "*Guilty Man* lives within the pleasure principle," attempting "to satisfy his pleasure-seeking drives to lessen the tensions that arise in his erogenous zones" (Kohut, 1977, p. 132). Kohut's archetypal Tragic Man, however—through his failures, uncompleted projects, and unrequited efforts at work and love—illuminates "the essence of fractured, enfeebled, discontinuous human existence" (p. 238). The pathological narcissist's efforts to assuage painful deficiencies, the fragmentation of the psychotic client, and the despair of parents whose children have failed to fulfill parental aspirations and ambitions may all be understood as clinical examples of this perspective, one that is considered unique to the psychology of the self.

BASIC CONCEPTS IN SELF-PSYCHOLOGY

Like its psychoanalytic predecessors (classical theory, ego psychology, and object relations), self-psychology encompasses not only a framework for clinical interventions but also a model for understanding certain aspects of normative human development and developmental deviations, as well as a theory of psychopathology. Though space does not allow a comprehensive examination of each of these, certain terms and concepts from self psychology are common to them all.

Selfobjects

Kohut coined the term *selfobject* to represent a specific kind of object relationship in which the object is experienced as being a part or extension of the subject's self and in which no psychological differentiation occurs. He noted that the control one expects over such selfobjects approximates "the concept of control which a grown-up expects to have over his own body and mind" in contradistinction to the "control which he expects to have over others" (Kohut, 1971, pp. 26–27). Kohut believed that human beings require three distinctly different kinds of selfobject experiences—(1) mirroring, (2) idealizing, and (3) partnering—each of which is, under optimal conditions, made available to the child in an attuned, empathetically resonant interpersonal climate. Mirroring selfobjects "respond to and confirm the child's innate sense of vigor, greatness, and perfection," whereas idealized selfobjects provide the child with the powerful and reassuring presence of caregivers "to whom the child can look up and with whom he can merge as an image of calmness, infallibility, and omnipotence" (Kohut & Wolf, 1978, p. 414). Finally, partnering selfobjects furnish the child with a range of opportunities through which a sense of belonging and of essential alikeness within a community of others may be acquired.

The Tripolar Self

The tripolar self is the name given to that intrapsychic structure associated with the three kinds of selfobject relationships just described, in effect linking each selfobject relationship to a corresponding domain of self experience. Mirroring experiences are associated with an intrapsychic structure known as the *grandiose-exhibitionistic self* and reflect the need for approval, interest, and affirmation; idealizing, with the *idealized parent imago*, reflecting the developmental need for closeness and support from an (omnipotent) idealized other; partnering, with the *alter ego*, and associated with the need for contact with others who are felt to bear an essential likeness to the self. These three poles, in effect, are structures that crystallize in consequence of the various needs of the evolving self "and the responses of those important persons in the environment who function as selfobjects" (Leider, 1996, p. 141).

These three domains are also linked to particular transference configurations that "dramatize and reflect the persistence of archaic selfobject needs" (Leider, 1996, pp. 151–154), revealing injuries to the client's self as well as particular mechanisms used to compensate, defend against, or otherwise conceal deficient self-structure. These three transference configurations (mirror, idealizing, and twinship or alter ego) may exist as pure types, though not infrequently a commingling of selfobject transferences may be observed in a particular client. Both the original, thwarted selfobject needs and the ensuing ruptures are frequently recapitulated in the transference relationship in psychotherapy.

Empathy and Transmuting Internalization

A large part of the appeal self-psychology has held for social work clinicians may revolve around the considerable emphasis it places on the role of empathy, a concept possessing strong cachet in both the clinical social work literature and in the contemporary world of practice. Self-psychology views empathetic processes as having their origin in early infancy and traversing the entire life span, imputing a special significance to traumatic breaches or disruptions in empathic attunement between self and selfobject. Defined as "vicarious introspection" or the feeling of oneself into the experience of another, the capacity of parents and others in the child's selfobject milieu for providing empathetically attuned responses is believed to be critical for healthy development of the self.

Somewhat paradoxically, Kohut also believed that comparatively minor, nontraumatic lapses in parental empathy are equally critical, constituting a sine qua non for healthy development. Such lapses, in a sense, may be thought of as optimally gratifying and optimally frustrating, serving as a catalyst for the child's development of transmuting internalizations. In other words, such breaches or lapses furnish the developing child with just the right amount of frustration to effect the development of a cohesive self-structure. Transmuting internalization is an intrapsychic process whereby a child gradually takes in or internalizes various functions associated with the selfobjects, ranging from self-calming and self-soothing to pride, humor, wisdom, and indefatigability in the pursuit of important goals. Stated somewhat differently, such functions are absorbed and metabolized in a virtually imperceptible process of incremental accretion, ultimately becoming enduring parts of the child's own self-structure, altered by his or her individual imprimatur.

Key elements identified in the sequence of transmuting internalization are, in order: (1) optimal frustration, (2) increased tension, (3) selfobject response, (4) reduced tension, (5) memory trace, and (6) development of internal regulating (self) structures. Self-psychologists view this developmental sequence as analogous, though not identical, to the therapeutic process when one approaches treatment within a self psychological framework.

The Self Types

Self-psychologists believe that the self is best understood within intersecting matrices of developmental level and structural state, and have identified four principal self types:

1. The *virtual self*, an image of the neonate's self originally existing in the parent's mind that evolves in various ways as the parental "selfobjects empathically respond to certain potentialities of the child" (Kohut, 1977, p. 100).
2. The *nuclear self*, a core self emerging in the second year of life, that serves as the basis for the "child's sense of being an independent center of initiative and perception" (Kohut, 1977, p. 177).
3. The *cohesive self*, the essential self-structure of a well-adapted, healthily functioning

individual, whose self-functioning evinces the harmonious "interplay of ambitions, ideals, and talents with the opportunities of everyday reality" (Leider, 1996, p. 143).
4. The *grandiose self*, a normal self-structure during infancy and early childhood developing that comes into existence as a response to the selfobject's attunement with the child's sense of him- or herself as the center of the universe.

Psychopathology in Self-Psychology: Cohesion, Fragmentation, and Disintegration Anxiety

Self-psychologists use the term *cohesion* to refer to a self state characterized by vigorous, synchronous, and integrated psychological functioning. Self-cohesion not only makes the harmonious interplay of ambitions, ideals, and talents possible in the context of everyday life; it also confers a modicum of protection from regressive fragmentation when an individual is faced with adversity or obstacles that prevent the gratification of object or selfobject needs (Leider, 1996). Those who are fragmentation-prone (who, under duress, might develop symptoms such as hypochondriasis, hypomanic excitement, or disturbances in bodily sensation or self-perception) have, by definition, failed to acquire stable, consolidated, and enduring self-structures. Such failures may arise from parental pathology, environmental uncertainties and deficiencies, or a combination of these, though invariably it is the chronic unavailability of parental selfobjects to provide needed functions that is at the root of such disturbances in self-functioning. The developmental basis for various disorders of the self (e.g., narcissistic pathology, borderline conditions, depression, and even psychosis), according to the self-psychologists, is strongly linked to chronically deficient and traumatogenic caregiving environments. Kohut believed that *disintegration anxiety*, defined as the fear of the self breaking up, was the most profound anxiety a human being is capable of experiencing; *disintegration products*, a closely related concept, refers to those symptoms generated by an enfeebled, disharmonious self. Symptoms within this system, as in other psychoanalytic theories of psychopathology, are viewed as manifestations or perhaps signifiers of important dynamic, genetic, and environmental themes. The self-psychological focus on the significance of environmental deficits in shaping pathology, however, contributes to a perspective that may be somewhat unique, even when compared to other psychoanalytic perspectives on pathology.

CLINICAL CASE ILLUSTRATION

Joe, an overweight, 47-year-old, upper-middle-class Italian American Catholic man, originally came for treatment complaining of difficulty in establishing meaningful autonomy from his parents, a "joyless" marriage, and not being able to derive pleasure from his work. Joe and his wife, Lisa, 43, had three children: Don, 22, Lisa's son from an earlier marriage; Robert, 12; and Mike, 7. Joe managed the family business, a small smelting and refining company founded by his father and his uncle some 50 years earlier, that was located in the industrial corridor of a large Northeastern city. Joe's father had been an aggressive and highly successful businessman, although in his personal life he was weak, ineffectual, and unable to lend his son any modicum of real emotional support. Joe had never felt that he could count on his father when the chips were down or in a crisis. At such times, his father was alternately distant or critical and in general seemed largely incapable of any meaningful emotional connection with Joe. He was, moreover, unpredictable; he could "blow" at any moment. Worse yet, Joe believed that his father was contemptuous of him, and had been since childhood.

Relations with his mother were also a source of disappointment and conflict for Joe. From the time he was very young, he found her to be both unreliable and unattuned. She would become very impatient with him when he clung to her at the babysitter's, often leaving him sobbing; throughout his early and middle childhood, she seemed incapable of furnishing him with the emotional safety he required. In fact, he often found himself in the position of placating her or calming her down and generally placing her needs before his in what amounted to a reversal (if not a parody) of the mother–child relationship. Another significant theme in this relationship was Joe's strong sense that his mother was unable to take delight in his appearance. In fact, she shunned him at times, which caused him to feel small, ashamed, and physically repulsive. His struggle to maintain a normal weight, beginning in early childhood, was in some measure due to hereditary factors but was certainly compounded by the fact that food proved a reliable means for alleviating painful affect states and inner emptiness associated with thwarted selfobject needs in both of these relationships.

Though he had never thought of himself as depressed prior to starting treatment, Joe recognized many of his reactions—both at work and at home—as being depressive in nature. Even when he was successful in cementing a lucrative business deal, for example, it wasn't enough to make him happy. He acknowledged that raising his kids, which he believed should be a source of genuine gratification, was instead burdensome and draining. After 6 months of analysis, Joe revealed a recurring fantasy that for him was particularly disturbing and humiliating. In the fantasy, he is traveling alone on a deserted stretch of highway and stops at an isolated rest area. He walks into the men's room and is rather surprised to find another man standing near the rear by the toilet stalls. This man cannot be seen clearly because he is in the shadows. Without hesitating, Joe kneels down in front of the other man, unzips his fly, and begins to perform fellatio. At first, he feels excitement, as the man's penis becomes erect, and then, at the moment of orgasm, a sense of both power and primal satisfaction. This is as far as the fantasy goes. Even though he has had this fantasy for years, he has spoken of it only once before, during a session with his former therapist. At that time, he had expressed concern that it may mean he's gay. Although the therapist tried to reassure him that this seemed very unlikely to her, she "also moved off the topic pretty quickly."

Discussion

Joe suffers from what has been most aptly characterized in self-psychology as a depletion depression. Depletion states and depletion depression, in contrast to the classical syndrome of guilt depression, are born neither from intrapsychic conflict nor from the problems associated with the discharge of aggression implicit in the classical model. Instead, such depression is regarded as a disintegration product, one signaling a structural deficiency that is itself a developmental sequela of early problems in the subject's self/selfobject milieu. In self-psychological terms, Joe failed to attain self-cohesiveness, owing to the unremitting series of traumatic disappointments he had suffered in his relationships with his parents. Indeed, his history was replete with such selfobject failures. Joe's mother, who was chronically overburdened, evinced a marked insensitivity and lack of attunement with her son's emotional needs, further compounded by her own pathological reliance on him as a soothing and calming selfobject. His father, despite his many successes in the business world, had little wisdom to impart to his son and was rarely if ever able to serve as a fount of strength or steadfastness for Joe. Lacking in self-confidence and inner vitality, Joe had gradually come to feel an emptiness that could not be assuaged in his marriage; nor was it alleviated in interaction with his two children, nor even at work in his business relationships. He felt devitalized and impotent, was subject to mercurial fluctuations of mood, and was also markedly sensitive to narcissistic slights. Joe's capacity for the regulation of his self-esteem was minimal, inasmuch as he was highly reliant on the positive valuation of others.

UNIQUE FEATURES OF SELF-PSYCHOLOGY AS A CLINICAL SYSTEM

Although it is no longer possible to speak of self-psychology as a unified theoretical system, there are two hallmarks of any clinical self-psychological approach: (1) the central importance of the therapist's sustained, empathetic immersion in the client's subjective experience; and (2) the concept of selfobjects and selfobject transferences (Mitchell & Black, 1995).

Self-psychologists believe that the therapist's basic attitude of concern and compassionate acceptance and his or her promotion of an ambience of emotional vitality and responsiveness are necessary to bring about the therapeutic remobilization of various archaic selfobject needs, considered a sine qua non for meaningful psychotherapy. This therapeutic stance has often been presented in stark contrast to the "detached, cold, abstemious, surgeonlike demeanor" attributed to Freud and to his rendering of classical psychoanalytic technique (Leider, 1996).

The interpretive process in self-psychology consists of two basic phases: a phase of understanding, superceded by a phase of explanation and interpretation. Both of these phases are deemed essential to the therapeutic process (Kohut, 1984). With the unfolding of the therapeutic process and the establishment of a selfobject transference, the client unconsciously perceives the therapist as fulfilling various selfobject needs. The client's dawning perception that the therapist has somehow failed to satisfy these selfobject needs

(an unavoidable eventuality) leads to fragmentation, archaic affect states, and other sequelae of misattunement. Such therapeutic breaches, however, are not just unavoidable in the view of self-psychology; they are necessary for further psychological growth and structural repair (Leider, 1996).

The phase of understanding commences with the therapist's recognition of the empathetic rupture or breach, which is then conveyed to the client. Such therapeutic communications, accompanied by the therapist's attempt to reconstruct and characterize the events leading to the disruption, serve to reestablish psychological homeostasis (Kohut, 1984). This makes possible explanation, in which the significance of the therapeutic breach is recast in dynamic/genetic terms, permitting the client and therapist to reconstruct "the circumstances of the [client's] childhood in which parental selfobjects" were chronically unavailable, "analogous disruptions occurred, and the self was permanently injured" (Leider, 1996, p. 157).

FUTURE

Self-psychology offers the clinician a dynamic approach to practice applicable to a wide range of presenting problems, one that may be successfully adapted to the diverse clinical populations with whom social workers work. The therapeutic requirements for producing enduring structural changes in the personality cannot always be met within a framework of managed mental health services, and this may be one limitation of a self-psychological approach. However, many of the insights derived from psychoanalytic self-psychology can be readily applied to such modalities as crisis intervention, brief and other time-sensitive treatments, and even supportive therapy. The clinician's capacity for empathetic immersion in the client's subjective experience, a sine qua non of any self-psychological approach to treatment, may not in itself lead to a permanent restructuralization of the self, but its impact at a time of crisis should not be underestimated. Similarly, in parent guidance work, the worker may provide what has been termed "transference parenting" (Chethik, 2000) to a beleaguered parent whose own childhood consisted of an unremitting series of parental selfobject failures. This may have the effect of making the parent somewhat more attuned and responsive to his or her own child's requirements for affirmation, calming and soothing, or partnering.

In its view of normal development and developmental derailments, self-psychology places considerable emphasis on the role of environment in particular, the chronic failures of the selfobject milieux within which individuals develop. As such, it seems especially well suited as a framework for assisting social work clinicians in their continuing efforts both to understand dysfunction and pathology and to provide therapeutic responses to it.

WEB SITES

International Association for Psychoanalytic Self Psychology. http://www.psychologyoftheself.com.
New York Institute for Psychoanalytic Self Psychology. http://www.selfpsychologypsychoanalysis.org.
Self Psychology Page. http://www.selfpsychology.com.
Training and Research Institute for Self Psychology. http://www.trisp.org.

References

Brandell, J. (2004). Psychoanalytic theories of development and dysfunction: Ego psychology, object relations theories, the psychology of the self, and relational psychoanalysis. In J. Brandell (Ed.), *Psychodynamic social work* (pp. 44–69). New York: Columbia University Press.
Chethik, M. (2000). *Techniques of child therapy: Psychodynamic strategies.* New York: Free Press.
Elson, M. (1986). *Self psychology in clinical social work.* New York: Norton.
Greenberg, L., & Mitchell, S. (1983). *Object relations in psychoanalytic theory.* Cambridge, MA: Harvard University Press.
Kohut, H. (1966). Forms and transformations of narcissism. *Journal of the American Psychoanalytic Association, 14,* 243–272.
Kohut, H. (1971). *Analysis of the self: A systematic approach to the treatment of narcissistic personality disorders.* New York: International Universities Press.
Kohut, H. (1977). *The restoration of the self.* New York: International Universities Press.
Kohut, H. (1984). *How does analysis cure?* Chicago: University of Chicago Press.
Kohut, H., & Wolf, E. (1978). The disorders of the self and their treatment: An outline. *International Journal of Psychoanalysis, 59,* 413–425.
Leider, R. (1996). The psychology of the self. In E. Nersessian & R. Kopff Jr. (Eds.), *Textbook of psychoanalysis* (pp. 127–164). Washington, DC: American Psychiatric Association Press.
Mitchell, S., & Black, M. (1995). *Freud and beyond: A history of modern psychoanalytic thought.* New York: Basic Books.
Rowe, C., & MacIsaac, D. (1991). *Empathic attunement: The "technique" of psychoanalytic self psychology.* Northvale, NJ: Jason Aronson.

How Clinicians Can Effectively Use Assessment Tools to Evidence Medical Necessity and throughout the Treatment Process

44

Kevin Corcoran & Jill Boyer-Quick

Clinical social work was once chiefly a three-party system. It was a matter between the patient and the provider, with reimbursement readily paid by insurance companies or governmental agencies. A person became a patient simply by deciding that he or she needed to see a social worker, and together they would decide what the problems and goals were, what the intervention would be, how long it should last, and the costs. Then came managed care at both the private and public levels and everything changed.

Managed care is a four-party system that intervenes between the social worker and patient on behalf of the payer (Corcoran & Vandiver, 1996; Vandiver, 2008). The basic purpose of managed care is to contain costs by controlling wasteful spending. There are many cost-containment procedures in private and public managed care that serve as gatekeepers of what services would be reimbursed, by whom, and for what particular problem. One of the first gatekeeping approaches used in the managed care market was retrospective utilization reviews that evaluated the outcome of treatment and reimbursed according to its success. Because all parties involved were displeased by having provided services only to find that some unknown quality assurance reviewer denied the claim or reduced the reimbursement, retrospective reviews have generally fallen out of favor. Other gatekeeping approaches evaluate the need for service in advance and concurrent with the delivery of services. Gatekeeping prior to service evaluates the eligibility of the request for services and determines, among other things, if the presenting problem is covered by the payment plan, if the presenting problem is distressing or disabling enough to warrant treatment, what the best evidence-based treatment is for specified goals, and how long treatment is to last. Gatekeeping during the treatment evaluates the continuous need for treatment, compliance with the treatment plan, and if additional services are needed. In both circumstances the social worker must demonstrate that clinical services are medically necessary.

As gatekeeping illustrates, social workers now must demonstrate that the client, in fact, warrants treatment. In the past seemingly all interpersonal problems were paid for by either private or public insurance, whereas managed care attempts to control costs by reimbursing only bone fide mental health conditions that result in distress or disability—that is, those medically necessary. Medical necessity in mental health practice is not without limitations. Some practice is necessary but not for medical reasons, such as court-ordered psychiatric evaluations and secured residential services for children and adolescents (Sabin & Daniels, 2000). Behavioral health must use the concept of medical necessity with a broader scope, more in the sense of psychosocial necessity (Sabin & Daniels, 2000) or treatment necessity (Ford, 1998; Vandiver, 2008).

The critical question for the clinical social worker is how to show evidence that the client's condition warrants treatment. There are many ways to demonstrate that a client's presenting problem is a mental health condition and is sufficiently distressing or disabling to require therapy. One method is a psychiatric evaluation that uses a variety of diagnostic tests. Examples of diagnostic tests include the Minnesota Multiphasic Personality Inventory and the Rorschach ink blots. These assessments have a number of limitations for clinical social work (Arkava & Snow, 1978), including that they are costly, lengthy, time-consuming to administer, and frequently require training to interpret. Moreover, because of length, it is not practical to use them over the course of treatment and at follow-up. In contrast, there are a large number of relatively short, self-administered, and easily scored assessment tools available for use by most practitioners (e.g., Fischer and Corcoran, 2007a, 2007b; Nugent, Sieppert, & Hudson, 2001). These assessment tools are frequently called rapid assessment instruments (RAIs; Levitt & Reid, 1981) and generally take only a few minutes to complete. RAIs are useful to evidence medical necessity and when used throughout treatment to monitor client change and goal attainment.

RAIs TO MEASURE TREATMENT NECESSITY

An additional use of RAIs is to provide evidence for the need for treatment. This is based on scores obtained at the intake. Some instruments, such as Hudson's scales (Nugent et al., 2001), can provide this information because they have a cutting score. A cutting score is one that distinguishes those with a clinically significant problem from those without. When using such a measure, if the score is greater or lower than the cutting score, it is persuasive evidence of a need for treatment.

Most psychological measurements do not have cutting scores. In these circumstances, an RAI score may be compared to a norm from either the general population or a clinical sample of patients in treatment. This is known as norm-referenced comparison, and it illustrates the client's problem relative to others with and without that problem. A client's score on an RAI should be different from the general population and similar to those with the same mental health condition. When these observations occur, it is reasonable to conclude that treatment is warranted.

When using RAIs to illustrate the need for treatment, two assessments are recommended: a broadband measure of mental health along with a narrowband measure of the client's specific problem. An excellent broadband instrument is the health survey, which has two short forms (i.e.,

SF-36 and SF-12; Ware, Kosinski, & Keller, 1994). This instrument is particularly useful because it has been evaluated in over 40 countries, is available at no cost, and is accessible from the Internet (www.outcomes-trust.org). The health survey has two composite scores, one measuring physical health and the other measuring mental health. The average score on the SF-36 and SF-12 is about 50 and 35 for the general population and a psychiatric sample, respectively; the standard deviation is 10 for both samples. As the case given later illustrates, Christine's score at the beginning of treatment was 40, and she had a Z-score value of 1.0, reflecting a lower mental health status than about 84 percent of the general population while being similar to the typical psychiatric patient.

One way to precisely show that a client's score is different from the general population and similar to a clinical sample is with a Z-score (Thomlison & Corcoran, 2008). A Z-score is a standardized score that has a mean of zero, a standard deviation of 1, and generally ranges from −3 to +3. A Z-score is determined by subtracting the sample mean from the client score and then dividing that difference by the standard deviation. With a Z-score, a social worker can then compare a client's score with the norm by determining what percent of the sample scored higher or lower than the client—in other words, what percentage have problems more and less severe. This is done by first finding the Z-value in Table 44.1 and then examining the percent above and below the client's score. This information allows the social worker to interpret the client's score relative to the general population and a clinical sample. For example, if a client had a Z-score of 0.1 based on parameters from the general population, then he or she would be just about average and there would be little reason to aver treatment necessity. However, if the norm was from a clinical sample and the Z-score was 0 or so, it is reasonable to assert a need for treatment because the client is similar to the average person who is already in treatment. It is best to calculate a Z-score from the general population and a clinical sample, if the normative data are available. For example, a client with a Z-score of 1 from a general population would be different from 84 percent of the general population, and the social worker could conclude that there is likely a need for treatment. A score of −1 with a clinical sample is more severe than 16.5 percent of those patients in treatment, and it is still likely that treatment is necessary.

The use of Z-scores for determining treatment necessity is relatively easy after a few tries. The proportions above and below the level of the client's score enables the social worker to make rather precise statements of a client's performance compared to clinical and nonclinical samples. These data are persuasive for illustrating treatment necessity. In general, it is difficult to argue that treatment is not needed when the client is different from the general population or similar to a sample of patients already in treatment.

RAIs AND DIFFERENTIAL DIAGNOSIS

A broadband measure, like the SF-36 or SF-12, and a narrowband measure do more than allow the social worker to determine the magnitude or severity of a presenting problem to evidence treatment necessity. RAIs can also greatly facilitate the task of differential diagnosis. For example, whereas the SF-36 produces general scores on health and mental health, it also has more specific items and subscales of symptomatology, such as depression and social functioning; items and subscale scores, then, may very well point the clinician to a more specific differential diagnosis.

Differential diagnosis is essentially distinguishing one particular mental health condition from another. Although a provisional and final diagnosis are codified with the *DSM-IV-TR* (American Psychiatric Association, 2000; see Chapters 45, 46, 47, and others in this volume); the use of

TABLE 44.1 Table of Z-Scores and Proportions

	Proportion of Score				
Z-Score	Lower Than	Higher Than	Z-Score	Lower Than	Higher Than
−3.0	0.13	99.87	0.1	53.98	46.02
−2.9	0.19	99.81	0.2	57.93	42.07
−2.8	0.26	99.74	0.3	61.79	38.21
−2.7	0.35	99.65	0.4	65.54	34.46
−2.6	0.47	99.53	0.5	69.15	30.85
−2.5	0.62	99.38	0.6	72.58	27.42
−2.4	0.82	99.18	0.7	75.80	24.20
−2.3	1.07	99.93	0.8	78.81	21.19
−2.2	1.39	98.61	0.9	81.59	18.41
−2.1	1.79	98.21	1.0	84.13	15.87
−2.0	2.29	97.73	1.1	86.43	13.57
−1.9	2.87	97.13	1.2	88.49	11.51
−1.8	3.59	96.41	1.3	90.32	9.68
−1.7	4.46	95.54	1.4	91.92	8.08
−1.6	5.48	94.52	1.5	93.32	6.68
−1.5	6.68	93.32	1.6	94.52	5.48
−1.4	8.08	91.92	1.7	95.54	4.46
−1.3	9.68	90.32	1.8	96.41	3.59
−1.2	11.51	88.49	1.9	97.13	2.87
−1.1	13.57	86.43	2.0	97.73	2.27
−1.0	15.87	84.13	2.1	98.21	1.79
−0.9	18.41	81.59	2.2	98.61	1.39
−0.8	21.19	78.81	2.3	98.93	1.07
−0.7	24.20	75.80	2.4	99.18	0.82
−0.6	27.42	72.58	2.5	99.38	0.62
−0.5	30.85	69.15	2.6	99.53	0.47
−0.4	34.46	65.54	2.7	99.65	0.35
−0.3	38.21	61.79	2.8	99.74	0.26
−0.2	42.07	57.93	2.9	99.81	0.19
−0.1	46.02	53.98	3.0	99.87	0.13

rapid assessment instruments can help the social worker identify the particular pathology and concomitantly quantify this severity to observe change over the course of treatment and afterward. Moreover, a differential diagnosis is essential if the practitioner is to develop an effective treatment plan. If the client's condition is not differentiated from similar ones, a viable and effective treatment plan is impossible. Under such circumstances of misdiagnosing a mental health condition when benefits of treatment are gleaned, this is likely due to nonspecific factors in treatment, such as a caring relationship, or mostly a matter of chance—dumb luck, if you will.

One of the most critical examples of this is the distinction between the bipolar affective disorders, delusional disorders, schizoaffective disorder, and the schizophrenic disorders. These mental disorders are likely to include abnormality of affect, such as an elevated, expansive, or irritable mood. All might also include disturbed cognition, such as grandiose and persecutory delusions, catatonia, or flight of ideas. Most important, all may evidence psychotic features. The distinctions are subtle but critical: the psychotic symptoms of the mood disorder do not occur in the absence of a prominent mood symptom, whereas psychotic symptoms may be manifested in the others independent of mood symptoms. Similarly, the manic or depressive symptoms may be evident in the schizophrenic disorders but are often not sufficient in duration or magnitude to warrant a diagnosis of one of the mood disorders. In spite of these differences, social workers—like other professionals—are quick to assume that if there are presenting symptoms of psychosis, it is likely a schizophrenia. In fact, however, bipolar disorders are more prevalent than schizophrenia (APA, 2000), which should suggest the likelihood of a mood disorder, or possibly even a stroke, which has a defining feature of disorientation, or being out of touch with reality (i.e., a psychotic feature). As this illustration suggests, an inaccurate differential diagnosis may result in a treatment plan for schizophrenia when the focus of treatment should be for a mood disorder or the immediate admission to the emergency room in the event of a stroke.

In addition to broadband and narrowly tailored RAIs, the ease and accuracy of a differential diagnosis is advanced by using the Appendix A of the *DSM-IV-TR*. Appendix A contains six decision trees for differential diagnosis—namely, disorders due to medical conditions, substance-induced disorder, psychotic disorders, mood disorders, anxiety disorders, and somatoform disorders. The use of these decision trees combined with RAIs, then, enables the social worker to not only observe the magnitude of a client's presenting problem but also isolate his or her mental condition from similar ones. Again, what is paramount here is that if the diagnosis is wrong, so, too, will be the treatment, which will be evident when the social worker monitors client change or attainment of the treatment goals.

RAIs TO MONITOR CLIENT CHANGE AND GOAL ATTAINMENT

Another use of RAIs is to monitor client change and evaluate practice (Fischer & Corcoran, 2007a). They have been used for quite some time by conscientious practitioners for these purposes. RAIs are typically administered before, during, and after treatment to see if the client's problem has changed or goal is obtained. RAIs may be used as a measurement of the treatment goal by establishing an ideal score on the instrument, one that reflects a successful outcome to be reached by the end of therapy. In the example of Christine given later, the goal of treatment was for her score to be about 2 or so, which reflects depression at a nonclinical level or what is typical for the general population.

Measurements before, during, and after treatment compose a simple AB design where scores during the treatment phase (i.e., B) are compared to the scores before treatment begins (i.e., A). This is known as self-referenced comparison. There are three essential elements in this approach to using instruments to monitor the treatment process: (1) a simple research design that reflects the treatment process, such as a treatment period (i.e., B phase) compared to a time of no treatment (i.e., A phase); (2) a systematic means to observe the client, such as an RAI or a broadband measure; and (3) the interpretation of scores by plotting them to see if the client's behavior has been changed. There are, of course, more sophisticated research designs and statistical interpretation of the data (see, e.g., Bloom, Fischer, & Orme, 2006). At minimum, however, the social worker needs to be able to see that change has occurred.

For example, in the case study to follow, Christine enters therapy for depression and scored 8 on the depression subscale of the symptom questionnaire (see Fischer & Corcoran, 2007b). Retrospective baseline data were collected by having her complete the instrument for how she felt "at her worst" and "in general." The instrument is administered repeatedly before 7 of the 12 sessions, and over the course of therapy, scores decrease. At the follow-up Christine's score is 1, reflective of the treatment goal. To compare her performance over the course of treatment, the scores are plotted on a graph for visual analysis of clinically significant change.

Visual analysis clearly requires clinical judgment, as does any statistical analysis. It must be stressed that scores on an assessment tool are simply supplemental information and not a substitute for clinical judgment. By using a simple design and RAIs where scores are understood by visual interpretation, the social worker has added information to evaluate treatment and evidence its effectiveness.

CASE ILLUSTRATION

Admittedly, the use of RAIs to evidence treatment necessity and throughout the treatment process are unfamiliar to many professional social workers. At first, it seems difficult to add this approach to the overburdened demands of practice. The following case illustrates how, with a little practice, it is easy to monitor a client's problem, attainment of a goal, and treatment necessity with RAIs for a client with an accurate differential diagnosis.

Christine is a 32-year-old, college-educated salesperson. For the past year or so, she has been feeling apathetic and is prone to crying spells. She reports she has not been able to sleep well, often waking up several times a night and early in the morning. When she is awake, she does not want to get out of bed. She avoids her family and friends. Christine was referred to a social worker after disclosing to her primary care physician that she had thoughts of suicide. Her managed care organization sent the social worker a number of forms to complete and asked for evidence of medical necessity.

At intake, the social worker thought Christine likely had a mood disorder, and she was given the depression subscale of the symptom questionnaire. By using the decision trees of the *DSM-IV*, the social worker was able to reach a preliminary differential diagnosis of dysthymia because her symptoms were not due to a medical condition and were not physiological effects of substances,

and there had been no evidence of an elevated or expansive mood, which would suggest one of the bipolar disorders. The differential diagnosis must be considered preliminary because at this point in the assessment it is not known if Christine's condition has lasted at least 2 years, a criterion of this form of clinical depression. To help the social worker with this differential diagnosis, Christine was also asked to complete the RAI as representative of when she felt "at her worst" and how she "generally feels." Her scores were 8, 9, and 8, respectively. Aside from showing that Christine's depression is relatively stable, these numbers do not tell the social worker much until interpreted relative to the general population or a clinical sample.

A sample from the general population had a mean depression score of 1.8 with a standard deviation of 2.2. A sample of psychiatric patients had a mean of 10.6 and a standard deviation of 5.9. Christine's depression level of 8 is converted to a Z-score by subtracting the mean and then dividing that difference by the standard deviation. Her Z-score relative to the general population was 2.8. By consulting Table 44.1, it may be argued that Christine is more depressed than 99 percent of the general population. Similarly, her Z-score for the psychiatric population was 0.3, indicating that she is as depressed as 38 percent of those persons already receiving treatment. Based on these scores, it may be concluded that Christine's condition warrants treatment.

Christine and her social worker decide that an appropriate goal of treatment is for her to feel "as happy as the next person." This was operationalized as a score similar to about a third of the general population, a score of approximately 2 or so on this subscale. Christine's progress is monitored by having her complete the subscale measure of depression prior to each therapy session, and her scores are illustrated in Figure 44.1. By graphing the observations, it would appear that Christine has responded favorably to treatment. By the twelfth session, Christine scored a 1 on the depression scale, which reflects her goal; she is now about as depressed as 35 percent of the population, which was also observed at a 1-month follow-up.

SUMMARY

This case illustrates that RAIs are useful to show the need for treatment, determination of a differ-

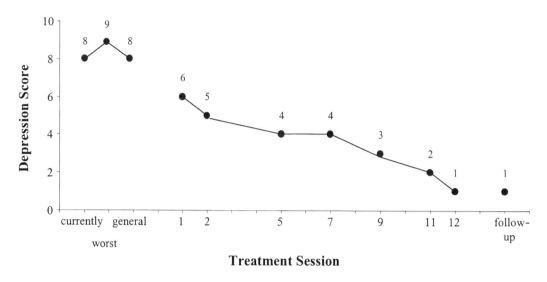

Figure 44.1 Impact of treatment on depression.

ential diagnosis, the monitoring of client progress over the course of clinical intervention, and goal setting. Christine not only decreased the magnitude of her depression over the course of treatment but also met her treatment goal, then and at follow-up. In summary, RAIs serve three functions: (1) as evidence of treatment necessity and in determining an accurate diagnosis; (2) as a tool to monitor client progress; and (3) as an operationalization of a treatment goal. That is, they are useful almost from the beginning and throughout the course of clinical practice. When both broadband measures of mental health problems and narrowband measures of the client's particular problem are used, the social worker has additional tools to evidence that treatment is necessary and, it is hoped, effective.

WEB SITE

Medical Outcomes Trust. http://www.outcome-trust.org.

References

American Psychiatric Association. (2000). *Diagnostic and statistical manual of mental disorders*, 4th ed., re. Washington, DC: APA.

Arkava, M. L., & Snow, M. (1978). *Psychological tests and social work*. Springfield, IL: Thomas.

Bloom, M., Fischer, J., & Orme, J. G. (2006). *Evaluating practice: Guidelines for the accountable professional*. Needham Heights, MA: Allyn & Bacon.

Corcoran, K., & Vandiver, V. L. (1996). *Maneuvering the maze of managed care: Skills for mental health practitioners*. New York: Free Press.

Fischer, J., & Corcoran, K. (2007a). *Measures for clinical practice: A sourcebook. Vol. 2, Adults*. New York: Free Press.

Fischer, J., & Corcoran, K. (2007b). *Measures for clinical practice: A sourcebook. Vol. 1, Couples, families and children*. New York: Free Press.

Ford, W. E. (1998). Medical necessity: Its impact in managed mental health care. *Psychiatric Services, 49*, 183–184.

Levitt, J. L., & Reid, W. J. (1981). Rapid-assessment instruments for practice. *Social Work Research and Abstracts, 17*, 13–19.

Nugent, W. R., Sieppert, J., & Hudson, W. W. (2001). *Practice evaluation for the 21st century*. Pacific Grove, CA: Brooks/Cole.

Sabin, J. E., & Daniels, N. (2000). Public-sector managed behavioral health care: V, Redefining "medical necessity," the Iowa experience. *Psychiatric Services, 51*, 445–459.

Thomlison, B., & Corcoran, K. (2008). *Evidence-based internship: A field manual*. New York: Oxford University Press.

Ware, J. E., Kosinski, M., & Keller, S. D. (1994). *SF-36 physical and mental health summary scales: A user's manual*. Boston, MA: Medical Outcomes Trust. Available from http://www.outcomes-trust.org.

Vandiver, V. (2008). Managed care. In T. Mizrahe & L. Davis (Eds.), *Social work encyclopedia*. New York: Oxford University Press.

PART V

Assessment in Social Work Practice: Knowledge and Skills

45

Using the *Diagnostic and Statistical Manual of Mental Disorders*, Fourth Edition, Text Revision

Janet B. W. Williams

A 39-year-old television reporter, Karen Davis, saw a psychiatrist at her network employee assistance program a few weeks after witnessing the execution of a murderer. For several years, she had been following the story of the inmate as he approached execution. The execution itself was remarkably protracted and gruesome; along with colleagues, she maintained a deathwatch for several hours while various last-minute reprieves were gained and then set aside by judicial bodies, until the final execution took place.

Karen told the psychiatrist, "Once you see someone die, you don't forget what it looks like." She felt that her professional role as an objective recorder was helpful to her initially in that it separated her from her emotional response. She recalled, for example, the sensation of her mouth going dry just at the moment of execution, but this was not accompanied by any emotional response. A feeling of detachment, which she described as "surreal and macabre," persisted for some days after the event. For a week after the execution, she continued to be detached from her feelings and was "in a daze and not like my usual self."

For the past few weeks, since the execution, she has felt unexcited about her work. She was surprised, for example, at her unwillingness to cover a riot, a story about which she normally would have been very enthusiastic. Moreover, she described becoming irritable with angry outbursts at her husband, prompting him to suggest that

they see a marriage counselor. Karen has had trouble staying asleep and often has nightmares. She says that she thinks of the event at least daily, having vivid "snapshot" images of the moment of execution. (This case of acute stress disorder was adapted from "Eyewitness" in the *DSM-IV Case Book*, pp. 35–36.)

This case describes a category that is new to *DSM-IV*: acute stress disorder. It was added to describe acute stress reactions that occur soon after the stressor and last no longer than 4 weeks. Acute stress disorder may predict the later development of post-traumatic stress disorder, so it is important to be able to identify such cases early in their course.

Diagnosis is a critical component of clinical social work education and practice. A diagnostic language allows health professionals to communicate with each other in an efficient and reliable way about the entities with which they deal. To the extent that there is a connection between diagnosis and treatment, an accurate diagnosis guides the clinician to an appropriate treatment choice. Having a consensual diagnostic system has paved the way for the development of practice guidelines (Field & Lohr, 1990; Rosen & Proctor, in press). Diagnostic criteria allow us to identify groups of subjects for research who are more or less homogeneous with respect to diagnosis. If researchers use the same criteria to identify subjects, the results of one treatment study for schizophrenia can be applied to other groups of clients with schizophrenia. (Although there may be differing views about the accuracy of some of the criteria, at least they provide a starting place, from which they can be tested and revised.) Finally, a diagnostic system allows public health statistics to be collected on the prevalence and course of various disorders, so mental health services can be planned.

Few would argue that one of the major advances in mental health in the past two decades was the publication of the *DSM-III* (American Psychiatric Association [APA], 1980). This was followed by the *DSM-III-R* in 1987 (APA, 1987), the *DSM-IV* in 1994 (APA, 1994), and finally the *Diagnostic and Statistical Manual of Mental Disorders*, Fourth Edition, Text Revision (*DSM-IV-TR*) (APA, 2000). Beginning with *DSM-III* and for each successive manual, the revision process involved extensive literature reviews to ensure that all relevant research and clinician experience was taken into account in developing the text and diagnostic criteria, meetings with experts from around the world to achieve consensus about the definitions being proposed, and field trials in which clinicians and researchers applied draft versions of the diagnostic criteria to assess their reliability and validity (American Psychiatric Press, 1994, 1995, 1997; Keller et al., 1995; Rounsaville, Kosten, Williams, & Spitzer, 1987; Spitzer & Forman, 1979; Spitzer, Forman, & Nee, 1979; Spitzer, Williams, Kass, & Davies, 1989). In the *DSM-III* field trials, over 12,000 patients were evaluated by clinicians (including social workers) using drafts of the manual. The development of *DSM-IV* included 12 field trials at more than 70 sites, involving more than 6,000 subjects.

The APA is not expected to publish the next revision of *DSM* (*DSM-V*) before 2008 to 2010. Because this will be more than 15 years after the publication of *DSM-IV*, there was concern that the text in *DSM-IV* would become seriously outdated. Therefore, work was begun on *DSM-IV-TR* about 3 years prior to its publication. Dr. Michael First, editor of the text and criteria of *DSM-IV*, and Dr. Harold Pincus, vice chairperson of the *DSM-IV* Task Force of the APA, began their work by asking experts in the various content areas of *DSM-IV* to review the existing text to determine the need for updating. Committees of experts spent countless hours conducting comprehensive literature reviews in each of the diagnostic areas specified in the *DSM-IV*. *DSM-IV-TR* ensures that the text is up to date; it corrects errors and ambiguities in the *DSM-IV*; and it updates a few of

the diagnostic codes to reflect coding changes in the *ICD-9-CM* (World Health Organization, 1978), the classification of medical conditions mandated by the U.S. government for all health care reporting purposes. The classification of mental disorders and the diagnostic criteria defining them remain the same as in *DSM-IV* with a handful of minor corrections. The final volume serves as a comprehensive textbook of diagnosis, an excellent summary of our state of knowledge in this area. Because of its innovative diagnostic criteria and multiaxial system, the *DSM* manuals have enjoyed widespread international acceptance (Maser, Kaelber, & Weise, 2000).

THE MULTIAXIAL SYSTEM

The *DSM-III* was the first official classification to incorporate a multiaxial system. Although the exact formulation of the axes has evolved with each revision, the basic concepts have remained. Table 45.1 lists the five axes of *DSM-IV-TR*. These are unchanged from *DSM-IV*, except for expanded instructions for making Axis V ratings.

The basic goal of a multiaxial system is to ensure that important areas of clinical information are not overlooked. For example, in an acute care setting such as an emergency room, a clinician might well be able to diagnose a psychotic disorder but might neglect a review of a patient's personality functioning, which is overshadowed by florid psychotic symptoms. Using the multiaxial system, the clinician is directed to assess each of five areas of functioning, including both the psychotic symptoms and the patient's personality functioning. Detailed discussion of how to use the multiaxial system is included in an introductory chapter in *DSM-IV-TR*.

TABLE 45.1 The Multiaxial System of *DSM-IV-TR*

Axis I:	• Clinical disorders • Other conditions that may be a focus of clinical attention
Axis II:	• Personality disorders • Mental retardation
Axis III:	General medical conditions
Axis IV:	Psychosocial and environmental problems
Axis V:	Global assessment of functioning

In the *DSM-IV* multiaxial system, axis II is for recording personality disorders and mental retardation. All other *DSM* disorders are listed on axis I. The reason for listing personality disorders and mental retardation separately on axis II is that their defining features tend to be generally stable over time and of long duration, so there is a greater likelihood that they may be overlooked when the clinician's attention is drawn to the usually more florid axis I conditions. Axis II may also be used to list prominent maladaptive personality features (that do not meet the criteria for a personality disorder) and habitually used defense mechanisms, although neither of these are assigned official code numbers.

Axis I includes all of the mental disorders that are not listed on axis II, as well as the V codes for other conditions that may be a focus of clinical attention. When an individual has more than one axis I or axis II disorder, all should be listed on their respective axes, with the principal diagnosis (or reason for visit) listed first. As many diagnoses as necessary may be listed on axis I and axis II; thus, comorbid mental disorders may be indicated.

Axis III is for listing general medical conditions that are potentially relevant to the understanding or management of the individual's mental disorders. Such conditions are listed in the *ICD-9-CM* outside of the mental disorders (Chapter 5) section. Although social workers are not in the position of diagnosing general medical conditions, they should nonetheless review this important area of functioning. However, when they record the information obtained, they should be careful to indicate the source of the information— for example, "Diabetes diagnosed by Dr. X," or "asthma by report of the client."

It is important to note that general medical conditions can be related to a client's mental functioning in a number of important ways. In some cases, the general medical condition is determined to be the cause of the psychological symptoms, as in the case of hypothyroidism causing depression. A similar relationship may also be expressed by the general medical condition worsening but not being the root cause of the mental disorder. It is by no means easy to tease out such relationships, and this situation may present special challenges to social workers. Whenever a significant general medical condition is suspected, a referral for a medical work-up is indicated. In all cases in which general medical conditions are present, they should be noted on axis III and their related mental disorders listed on axes I and II.

In some cases, a general medical condition is not clearly related to a mental disorder but is important to keep in mind as the clinician manages the client over time. An example might be environmental allergies. When more than one relevant general medical condition is present, all should be noted on axis III. If none are present, the clinician should record "none" on axis III.

Axis IV is for recording psychosocial and environmental problems that may be related to the client's mental disorders. The psychosocial or environmental problems may affect the diagnosis, treatment, or prognosis of the mental disorders. A list of categories of relevant problem areas is provided in *DSM-IV*, with examples of each category (see Table 45.2). Positive stressors (e.g., job promotion) should be listed on axis IV if they are a source of distress or the person has difficulty adapting to the new situation. It is most effective if a clinician notes the category of problems experienced by the client and the specifics of each problem (e.g., housing problem [no heat]).

Finally, axis V (Fig. 45.1) is the 100-point Global Assessment of Functioning (GAF) scale. The clinician must make a summary judgment of the client's overall psychological, social, and occupational functioning. The scale is divided into ten ten-point ranges of functioning. Each range lists degrees of symptom severity and functioning. The clinician determines into which ten-point range the client's symptoms or functioning fall and then assigns a single number within that range to further specify the client's condition. A computer program has been developed to help clinicians assign an appropriate GAF score (First, 1996).

TABLE 45.2 Axis IV: Psychosocial and Environmental Problems

Problems with primary support group
Problems related to the social environment
Educational problems
Occupational problems
Housing problems
Economic problems
Problems with access to health care services
Problems related to interaction with the legal system/crime
Other psychosocial and environmental problems

Consider psychological, social, and occupational functioning on a hypothetical continuum of mental health-illness. Do not include impairment in functioning due to physical (or environmental) limitations

CODE (**Note:** Use intermediate codes when appropriate, e.g., 45, 68, 72).

100   **Superior functioning in a wide range of activities, life's problems never seem to get out of**
I   **hand, is sought out by others because of his many positive qualities. No symptoms.**
91

90   **Absent or minimal symptoms** (e.g., mild anxiety before an exam); **good functioning in all**
I   **areas, interested and involved in a wide range of activities, socially effective, generally**
       satisfied with life, no more than everyday problems or concerns (e.g., an occasional
81   argument with family members).

80   **If symptoms are present, they are transient and expectable reactions to psychosocial**
I   **stressors** (e.g., difficulty concentrating after family argument); **no more than slight impairment**
71   **in social, occupational, or school functioning** (e.g., temporarily falling behind in school work).

70   **Some mild symptoms** (e.g., depressed mood and mild insomnia) **OR some difficulty in social,**
I   **occupational, or school functioning** (e.g., occasional truancy, or theft within the household),
       but generally functioning pretty well, has some meaningful interpersonal relationships.
61

60   **Moderate symptoms** (e.g., flat affect and circumstantial speech, occasional panic attacks) **OR**
I   **moderate difficulty in social, occupational, or school functioning** (e.g., few friends, conflicts
51   with peers or coworkers).

50   **Serious symptoms** (e.g., suicidal ideation, severe obsessional rituals, frequent shoplifting) **OR**
I   **any serious impairment in social, occupational, or school functioning** (e.g., no friends,
41   unable to keep a job).

40   **Some impairment in reality testing or communication** (e.g., speech is at times illogical,
I   obscure, or irrelevant) **OR major impairment in several areas, such as work or school, family**
       relations, judgment, thinking, or mood (e.g., depressed man avoids friends, neglects family,
       and is unable to work; child frequently beats up younger children, is defiant at home, and is failing
31   at school).

30   **Behavior is considerably influenced by delusions or hallucinations OR serious impairment**
I   **in communication or judgment** (e.g.,sometimes incoherent, acts grossly inappropriately,
       suicidal preoccupation) **OR inability to function in almost all areas** (e.g., stays in bed all day;
21   no job, home, or friends).

20   **Some danger of hurting self or others** (e.g., suicide attempts without clear expectation of
I   death, frequently violent, manic excitement) **OR occasionally fails to maintain minimal**
       personal hygiene (e.g., smears feces) **OR gross impairment in communication (e.g., largely**
11   **incoherent or mute).**

10   **Persistent danger of severely hurting self or others** (e.g., recurrent violence) **OR persistent**
I   **inability to maintin minimal personal hygiene OR serious suicidal act with clear expectation**
1   **of death.**

0   Inadequate information.

Figure 45.1 DSM-IV-TR axis V: Global Assessment of Functioning (GAF) scale. (Reprinted by permission of the American Psychiatric Association.)

CATEGORIES OF INFORMATION IN THE
DSM-IV TEXT

The text of *DSM-IV* presents diagnostic information in a systematic format. Text for each disorder is presented for the following areas of information: diagnostic features; subtypes and/ or specifiers; recording procedures; associated features and disorders; specific culture, age, and gender features; prevalence; course; familial pattern; and differential diagnosis. The content of each of these categories of information is described in an introductory chapter in the *DSM-IV* manual.

OVERVIEW OF THE CLASSIFICATION

The *DSM-IV* classification is arranged hierarchically, with 11 major diagnostic classes (see Appendix). Each diagnostic class of mental disorders has at least one "not otherwise specified" (NOS) category. Such a category may be appropriate to assign when there is not enough information to make a more definitive diagnosis; a diagnostic syndrome that is not listed in *DSM-IV* is present (e.g., premenstrual dysphoric disorder); or symptoms of that diagnostic class are definitely present but the clinical features do not fit any of the listed criteria sets.

Two types of categories have been cross-referenced in the *DSM-IV*. Most of the major classes have listed a substance-induced category, even though this category is also listed in the substance-related disorders section. For example, the mood disorder classification lists substance-induced mood disorder, although there are several such categories in the substance-related section. In addition, most of the major classes have a listing for a category due to a general medical condition (e.g., anxiety disorder due to [indicate the general medical condition]). The addition of these two listings to the major classes reminds the clinician to include them in their differential diagnosis of that grouping of mental disorder. In the *DSM-IV* classification, nearly all the major categories that one needs to consider when presented with a client with a prominent mood disturbance are listed together in one area (mood disorders, in this case) in the classification.

The classification itself begins with *disorders usually first diagnosed in infancy, childhood, or adolescence*. This section should be consulted first if one is evaluating an individual under the age of 18. If the appropriate diagnosis is not found here, however, any diagnosis in the manual may be used. For example, major depressive disorder is commonly diagnosed in children, although it is not listed in this first section of the classification. Likewise, for individuals over age 18, the classification outside of this first section should initially be consulted; however, sometimes a diagnosis in this childhood section should be used with an adult (e.g., mental retardation, Tourette's disorder). The most common disorders in the childhood section of the classification are those in the class of attention-deficit and disruptive behavior disorders. This group includes attention deficit hyperactivity disorder (ADHD), conduct disorder, and oppositional disorder.

The next grouping consists of mental disorders that social workers will rarely diagnose: *delirium, dementia,* and *amnestic and other cognitive disorders*. However, social workers will often be involved in the care of persons with these disorders, for example, dementia of the Alzheimer's type.

Clients with *substance-related disorders* will commonly be part of a social worker's practice. In the *DSM-IV* classification, the categories in this class are arranged alphabetically by substance. With each substance group, the disorders known to be caused by that substance are listed. These disorders include the substance use disorders and the substance-induced disorders. The substance use disorders (abuse and dependence) are considered when there is continued maladaptive use of the substance despite significant substance-related problems. Substance abuse includes such symptoms as "recurrent substance use resulting in a failure to fulfill major role obligations at work, school, or home." Substance dependence may include physiological tolerance or withdrawal or other symptoms, such as "a great deal of time is spent in activities necessary to obtain the substance." There are no categories for caffeine or nicotine abuse, and there is no category for dependence on caffeine.

In addition to abuse and dependence, there are categories for each of the substance classes that describe the effects of the substance on the central nervous system. These include intoxication, withdrawal, delirium, persisting dementia, persisting amnestic disorder, psychotic disorder, mood disorder, anxiety disorder, sexual dysfunction, and sleep disorder. It is critical for clinicians to evaluate the possibility of substance use in every client that they see.

Schizophrenia and other psychotic disorders are listed next in the classification. Schizophrenia and schizophreniform disorder share the same diagnostic features but differ in duration of the illness. In the latter, an episode of the disorder lasts between 1 and 6 months; in schizophrenia, the disorder must last 6 months or longer. Schizoaffective disorder involves a period of illness that has symptoms of schizophrenia at the same time as an episode of a mood disorder (either major depressive, manic, or mixed), and during the same period of illness, psychotic symptoms in the absence of a mood episode.

Other categories in this class of disorder include delusional disorder and shared psychotic disorder, both fairly rare, as well as brief psychotic disorder, which covers a period of 1 day to less than 1 month of psychotic symptoms.

Mood disorders may frequently be diagnosed by social workers. They are divided into depressive disorders and bipolar disorders. The former include major depressive disorder and dysthymic disorder, both fairly common. Major depressive disorder occurs in episodes of at least 2 weeks of serious depressive mood or loss of interest or pleasure accompanied by a number of associated symptoms. Dysthymic disorder involves at least 2 years of chronic depressed mood and some additional depressive symptoms. It is not uncommon for these syndromes to occur together. Frequently, a client will complain of dysthymic symptoms for many years and finally seek help when he or she develops a superimposed major depressive disorder. The co-occurrence of these two syndromes is sometimes referred to as double depression. Often, once the major depressive disorder resolves, the dysthymic disorder remains. Major depressive episodes may reappear throughout the individual's life. Bipolar I disorder is characterized by the presence of one or more manic episodes, with or without depressive episodes. In bipolar II disorder, there is one or more major depressive episode and at least one hypomanic episode, but no manic episodes. Manic and hypomanic episodes share similar symptoms, but in manic episodes, by definition, the symptoms cause marked impairment in social or occupational functioning or the need for hospitalization.

Cyclothymic disorder involves a chronic mood disturbance of at least 2 years' duration with periods of hypomanic symptoms and periods of depressive symptoms. The major mood disorders can be further characterized by fifth-digit designations that specify the severity of the disturbance, its features, and its course.

Anxiety disorders are also commonly seen in social work practice, and most social workers should be very familiar with their diagnostic features. Panic disorder can occur with or without agoraphobia. It is characterized by recurrent unexpected panic attacks, which are periods of intense fear or discomfort, accompanied by such symptoms as heart palpitations, sweating, chest pain, nausea, and dizziness. In panic disorder with agoraphobia, there is anxiety about being in places or situations in which help may not be available in the event of a panic attack. Commonly, agoraphobic avoidance develops as the panic attacks recur. In extreme cases, the individual becomes housebound and will not venture out for fear of having a panic attack.

In specific and social phobias, there is marked and persistent fear of a specific object or situation (specific phobia) or a social or performance situation (social phobia). In both disorders, although the person recognizes that the fear is excessive or unreasonable, the object or situation is either avoided or endured with intense anxiety or distress. Furthermore, the avoidance, anticipation, or distress when confronted with the object or situation interferes with the person's functioning or causes marked distress. Specific phobias include the following types: animal, natural environment, blood/injection/injury, and situational. Social phobia may be the generalized type, in which there are fears of almost all social situations. Nongeneralized types include fears of speaking in public or eating in public.

A diagnosis of obsessive-compulsive disorder requires the presence of either obsessions or compulsions, with consequent marked distress or significant interference with functioning. Many cases of this disabling condition have been found to respond to newer treatments available.

Post-traumatic stress disorder requires the development of certain symptoms following exposure to an extremely traumatic stressor. Examples include rape, natural disasters, and military experiences involving death or serious injury. Specific criterion equivalents are provided for applicability to children. This diagnosis requires more than 1 month of symptoms; the similarly defined acute stress disorder would be appropriate for individuals whose symptoms occur within 1 month of the stressor and last less than 1 month.

Finally, in generalized anxiety disorder, there is excessive anxiety and worry most days for at least 6 months. The person finds it difficult to control the worry, and there are a number of associated symptoms, specified in the diagnostic criteria.

Somatoform disorders are frequently seen in medical settings because they are characterized by physical symptoms that suggest a general medical condition but cannot be fully accounted for by it.

In *factitious disorders* there is intentional production or feigning of physical or psychological signs or symptoms to assume the sick role. Fortunately, factitious disorders are fairly rare, but they must be distinguished from malingering, which is not a mental disorder.

The grouping of *dissociative disorders* includes several disorders that are fairly rare, such as dissociative amnesia, dissociative fugue, depersonalization disorder, and one that has gotten more attention in recent years, dissociative identity disorder (called multiple personality disorder in *DSM-III* and *DSM-III-R*). There is tremendous controversy about the validity and prevalence of the latter category.

Sexual dysfunctions in the class of *sexual and gender identity disorders* form the basis of some clinicians' practices. Some of these categories may be quite common, and social workers should be familiar with them. In some cases, referral to a specialist in this area is indicated. Likewise, treatment of paraphilias and gender identity disorders is very specialized.

The class of *eating disorders* includes two disorders that are seen not infrequently by mental health practitioners: anorexia nervosa and bulimia nervosa. Also common is a category whose definition and criteria appear in Appendix B of *DSM-IV-TR*: binge eating disorder. Specialized treatments exist for eating disorders.

Sleep disorders will rarely be diagnosed by social workers. Some of the disorders in this group, however, may be comorbid with other, more common axis I and II disorders, so social workers should be familiar with them. However, when a sleep disorder is suspected, referral to a sleep specialist is indicated for assessment and possible treatment.

Impulse control disorders include disorders in which there is a failure to resist an impulse, drive, or temptation to do something that is harmful to the person or others. This grouping includes kleptomania, pyromania, and pathological gambling.

Adjustment disorders are quite common among children as well as adults. An adjustment disorder should be diagnosed when a person develops maladaptive emotional or behavioral symptoms in response to a recent psychosocial stressor. These symptoms cause either marked distress or significant impairment in functioning. This category is only diagnosed when the symptoms cannot be accounted for by another axis I or II disorder; in this way, adjustment disorder is regarded as a residual category.

Finally, *personality disorders* have been the focus of much research in the past 10 years. The *DSM-IV-TR* lists ten specific personality disorders, and two more are proposed in Appendix B. All of the personality disorders involve long-term patterns of behavior that have been present since adolescence or early adulthood, are pervasive and inflexible, and lead to distress or impairment. It is useful to consider the *DSM-IV-TR* personality disorders in three clusters. Cluster A includes paranoid, schizoid, and schizotypal personality disorders, all of which apply to individuals who appear odd or eccentric. Cluster B includes antisocial, borderline, histrionic, and narcissistic personality disorders, and these categories are often applied to people who appear dramatic, emotional, or erratic. The cluster C categories—avoidant, dependent, and obsessive-compulsive personality disorders—usually apply to individuals who may be anxious or fearful. Many individuals may be diagnosed with more than one personality disorder as well as multiple axis I and II disorders (McGlashan et al., 2000).

ASSESSMENT TOOLS

A number of structured interview guides have been developed to help clinicians and researchers make axis I and II diagnoses, using the specificity of the *DSM* criteria. In addition, versions have been developed for use by lay interviewers and for the assessment of children and adolescents. At this time, the most widely used structured interview guide for *DSM-IV* is the Structured Clinical Interview for *DSM-IV* (SCID; Spitzer, Williams, Gibbon, & First, 1992; Williams et al., 1992) (see Table 45.3). Basically, this guide provides the *DSM-IV* criteria in one column, the questions a clinician would ask to determine the presence or absence of the criteria in a second column, and a scoring format in the third column. By following the SCID, the clinician is guided through a differential diagnosis. A separate version of the SCID, with a somewhat different format, can be used for axis II (SCID-II).

The Diagnostic Interview Schedule (DIS) was developed for trained lay interviewers to facilitate a large-scale epidemiologic survey of mental disorders in the general population (the Epidemiological Catchment Area survey). Version IV of the DIS (DIS-IV) is currently in use. The National Institute of Mental Health sponsored the development of a Diagnostic Interview Schedule for Children (NIMH-DISC), which assesses 34 of the most common psychiatric diagnoses in children and adolescents (Shaffer, Fisher, Lucas, Dulcan, & Schwab-Stone, 2000).

TABLE 45.3 Structured Clinical Interview for *DSM-IV* (SCID): Item Examples for Axis I and Axis II

SCID interview questions (axis I) (from panic disorder)

Have you ever had a panic attack when you *suddenly* felt frightened or anxious or *suddenly* developed a lot of physical symptoms?

If Yes: Have these attacks ever come on completely out of the blue—in situations where you did not expect to be nervous or uncomfortable?

If Unclear: How many of these kinds of attacks have you had? (At least two?)

SCID interview questions (axis II) (from borderline personality disorder)

Have you often become frantic when you thought that someone you really cared about was going to leave you?

What have you done?

(Have you threatened or pleaded with him or her?)

Do your relationships with people you really care about have lots of extreme ups and downs?

Tell me about them.

(Were there times when you thought they were everything you wanted and other times when you thought they were terrible? How many relationships were like this?)

Recurrent unexpected panic attacks (criterion for panic disorder)

1. Frantic efforts to avoid real or imagined abandonment (*Note*: do not include suicidal or self-mutilating behavior covered in item 5).
2. A pattern of unstable and intense interpersonal relationships characterized by alternating between extremes of idealization and devaluation.
3. Either one prolonged relationship or several briefer relationships in which the alternating pattern occurs at least twice.

There has been a proliferation of interview schedules for axis II disorders. For a comprehensive review, please refer to Kaye and Shea (2000).

TEACHING AND LEARNING TOOLS

A number of educational materials have been developed to help people learn to use the *DSM-IV* and teach it to others. The American Psychiatric Press (APPI) has produced several videotapes (Alger, 1995; First, 1994), audiotapes (Frances, 1995), and a number of books (Fauman, 1994; First, Frances, & Pincus, 1995; Frances & Ross, 1996; Frances, First, & Pincus, 1995; Othmer & Othmer, 1994a, 1994b; Spitzer, Gibbon, Skodol, Williams, & First, 1994). In addition, a series of *DSM-IV* sourcebooks documents the clinical and research support for changes in *DSM-IV* (American Psychiatric Press, 1994, 1995, 1997). Computer programs have been developed to help clinicians conduct assessments and record diagnoses (First, Spitzer, Gibbon, & Williams, 1999).

The *DSM-IV* itself also has a number of learning aids. An introductory chapter, "Use of the Manual," describes all of the conventions and abbreviations used. An appendix provides a glossary of technical terms. Other appendixes include an annotated listing of changes in *DSM-IV* (from *DSM-III-R*), an outline for cultural formulation and glossary of culture-bound syndromes, and decision trees for differential diagnosis.

CONCLUSION

A thorough knowledge of our diagnostic system is crucial for social workers because of the universality of *DSM-IV* as a tool for communication among mental health professionals, its contribution to effective evaluation and treatment planning, its usefulness for teaching psychopathology, and its potential as a basis for research. Clinicians working in health and mental health settings should be very familiar with the multiaxial system and the *DSM-IV* diagnostic criteria of the categories with which they deal most often, as well as the differential diagnosis of those disorders so that their clients are ensured accurate assessment. A number of tools, such as the SCID, are available as aids in differential diagnosis.

The provision of diagnostic criteria for each disorder listed in the *DSM*, as well as a multiaxial system for evaluation, has greatly improved the ability to make reliable and valid diagnostic judgments that take the whole person into account. Although significant headway has been made, there is still a long way to go in strengthening the connection between accurate diagnosis and effective treatment for many categories. Likewise, the multiaxial system could be more informative. Social work as a field has had little impact on the development of the *DSM*s, although social workers have much to offer in this regard. It is hoped that future revisions will benefit from the expertise of social work practitioners and researchers.

WEB SITES

American Psychiatric Publishing. http://www .appi.org.

Boston College University Libraries, Social Work–Health and Mental Health. http:// libguides.bs.edu/content.php?pid= 1245&sid=5252.

Diagnostic Interview Schedule. http://epi.wustl .edu/DIS/dishisto.htm.

Multi-Health Systems. http://www.mhs.com.

PsyWeb.com's DSM-IV Guide: http://psyweb .com/Mdisord/DSM_IV/jsp/dsm_iv.jsp.

Structured Clinical Interview for *DSM-IV*. http://www.scid4.org.

The Social Work Podcast feature on DSM Diagnosis for Social Workers. http:// socialworkpodcast.com/2007/01/ dsm-diagnosis-for-social-workers.html.

Acknowledgment

The author gratefully acknowledges the help of Michael B. First.

References

Alger, I. (Ed.). (1995). *DSM-IV: New diagnostic issues*, DSM-IV Sourcebook (vol. 1) (video). Washington, DC: American Psychiatric Press.

American Psychiatric Association. (1980). *Diagnostic and statistical manual of mental disorders*, 3rd ed. Washington, DC: APA.

American Psychiatric Association. (1987). *Diagnostic and statistical manual of mental disorders*, 3rd ed., revised. Washington, DC: APA.

American Psychiatric Association. (1994). *Diagnostic and statistical manual of mental disorders*, 4th ed. Washington, DC: APA.

American Psychiatric Association. (2000). *Diagnostic and statistical manual of mental disorders*, 4th ed., text revision. Washington, DC: APA.

American Psychiatric Press. (1994). *DSM-IV sourcebook*, vol. 1. Washington, DC: APPI.

American Psychiatric Press. (1995). *DSM-IV sourcebook*, vol. 2. Washington, DC: APPI.

American Psychiatric Press. (1997). *DSM-IV sourcebook*, vol. 3. Washington, DC: APPI.

Fauman, M. A. (1994). *Study guide to DSM-IV*. Washington, DC: APPI.

Field, M. J., & Lohr, K. N. (1990). *Clinical practice guidelines : Directions for a new program* (publication Iom, 90-08). Washington, DC: National Academies Press.

First, M. B. (1994). *Busy clinician's guide to DSM-IV* (video). Toronto: Multi-Health Systems.

First, M. B. (1996). *GAF report: Computer-assisted axis V*. Toronto: Multi-Health Systems.

First, M. B., Frances, A., & Pincus, H. A. (1995). *DSM-IV handbook of differential diagnosis*. Washington, DC: APPI.

First, M. B., Spitzer, R. L., Gibbon, M., & Williams, J. B. W. (1999). *Computer-assisted SCID—clinician version* (CAS-CV). Toronto: Multi-Health Systems.

Frances, A. (1995). *DSM-IV audio review*. Washington, DC: APPI.

Frances, A., First, M. B., & Pincus, H. A. (1995). *DSM-IV guidebook*. Washington, DC: American Psychiatric Press.

Kaye, A. L., & Shea, M. T. (2000). Personality disorders, personality traits, and defense mechanisms. In Task Force on the Handbook of Psychiatric Measures, *Handbook of psychiatric measures: A task force report of the American Psychiatric Association* (pp. 713–749). Washington, DC: APA.

Keller, M. B., Klein, D. N., Hirschfeld, R. M., Kocsis, J. H., McCullough, J. P., Miller, I., et al. (1995). Results of the *DSM-IV* mood disorders field trial. *American Journal of Psychiatry*, 152, 843–849.

Maser, J. D., Kaelber, C., & Weise, R. E. (2000). International use and attitudes toward *DSM-III* and *DSM-III-R*: Growing consensus in psychiatric classification. *Acta Psychiatrica Scandinavica*, 102(4), 256–264.

McGlashan, T. H., Grilo, C. M., Skodol, A. E., Gunderson, J. G., Shea, M. T., Morey, L. C., et al. (2000). The collaborative longitudinal personality disorders study: Baseline axis I/II and II/II diagnostic co-occurrence. *Acta Psychiatrica Scandinavica*, 102(4), 256–264.

Othmer, E., & Othmer, S. C. (1994a). *The clinical interview using DSM-IV:* Volume 1: Fundamentals. Washington, DC: APPI.

Othmer, E., & Othmer, S. C. (1994b). The clinical interview using *DSM-IV:* Volume 2: The difficult patient. Washington, DC: APPIs.

Rosen, A., & Proctor, E. (Eds.). (In press). *Developing practice guidelines for social work intervention: Issues, methods, and research agenda*. New York: Columbia University Press.

Rounsaville, B. J., Kosten, T. R., Williams, J. B. W., & Spitzer, R. L. (1987). A field trial of *DSM-III-R* psychoactive substance dependence disorders. *American Journal of Psychiatry, 144,* 351–355.

Shaffer, D., Fisher, P., Lucas, C., Dulcan, M., & Schwab-Stone, M. (2000). NIMH diagnostic interview schedule for children version IV (NIMH DISC-IV): Description, differences from previous versions, and reliability of some common diagnoses. *Journal of the American Academy of Child and Adolescent Psychiatry, 39,* 28–38.

Spitzer, R. L., & Forman, J. B. W. (1979). *DSM-III* field trials: II. Initial experience with the multiaxial system. *American Journal of Psychiatry, 136,* 818–820.

Spitzer, R. L., Forman, J. B. W., & Nee, J. (1979). *DSM-III* field trials: I. Initial interrater diagnostic reliability. *American Journal of Psychiatry, 136,* 815–817.

Spitzer, R. L., Gibbon, M., Skodol, A. E., Williams, J. B. W., & First, M. B. (1994). *DSM-IV casebook.* Washington, DC: APPI.

Spitzer, R. L., Williams, J. B. W., Gibbon, M., & First,

M. B. (1992). The structured clinical interview for *DSM-III-R* (SCID). I: History, rationale and description. *Archives of General Psychiatry, 49,* 624–629.

Spitzer, R. L., Williams, J. B. W., Kass, F., & Davies, M. (1989). National field trial of the DSM-III-R diagnostic criteria for self-defeating personality disorder. *American Journal of Psychiatry, 146,* 1561–1568.

Williams, J. B. W., Gibbon, M., First, M. B., Spitzer, R. L., Davies, M., Borus, J., et al. (1992). The structured clinical interview for *DSM-III-R* (SCID). II: Multi-site test-retest reliability. *Archives of General Psychiatry, 49,* 630–636.

World Health Organization. (1978). *Manual of the international statistical classification of diseases, injuries, and causes of death*, 9th rev., clinical modification. Ann Arbor, MI: Commission on Professional and Hospital Activities.

46

Guidelines for the *Diagnostic and Statistical Manual (DSM-IV-TR)* Multiaxial System Diagnosis

Carlton E. Munson

Social workers have been historically involved with assessment and diagnosis of mental disorders. There has been criticism of social workers' identification with a clinical model of functioning (Caplan, 1995; Kirk & Kutchins, 1992; Kutchins & Kirk, 1997) as well as efforts to devise a more comprehensive model of mental health diagnosis, such as the person-in-environment (PIE)

system developed by the National Association of Social Workers (NASW) (Karls & Wandrei, 1994). The PIE system incorporates the *DSM-IV-TR* classification within its four-factor approach of problems in social functioning, environmental problems, mental health problems, and physical health problems, but it has a number of limitations, including its exclusion of child and adolescent functioning, which is a significant area of social work practice. The limitations of the PIE system and the widespread acceptance of the American Psychiatric Association's (APA) *Diagnostic and Statistical Manual of Mental Disorders*, Fourth Edition, Text Revision (*DSM-IV-TR*) (2000) as the recognized manual for diagnosing mental and emotional disorders establish the APA model as the predominant diagnostic system currently and for the future.

The increased demand for social workers to make formal diagnoses of mental disorders has come from a number of areas including (but not limited to) the following facts.

- Over 48 percent of U.S. citizens will have a significant mental illness in their lifetime (Kessler et al., 1994).
- The *DSM-IV-TR* is a widely read book by professionals as well as laypersons. Many laypeople have knowledge of the *DSM-IV-TR*, which places demand on social workers to have knowledge of the manual (Frances & First, 1998).
- Payers for services require a diagnosis and Global Assessment of Functioning (GAF) score before authorizing or paying for mental health services.
- Public agencies are adopting private payer strategies for service, including the assignment of a diagnosis to each client.
- Nonmedical professionals, such as child welfare workers, probation officers, police, prison staff, school officials, and clergy, are required to serve the mentally ill as mental health services are decreased and the number of psychiatrists declines.

The mandate for social workers to diagnose mental disorders has evolved through licensure laws and judicial review. The legislative sanction has been accompanied by higher standards for diagnosis in the form of increased licensing requirements and more extensive educational content for qualifying to do diagnosis. Though the increased standards have been applied, there is still need for more comprehensive understanding of the role of diagnosis in clinical social work practice because of the increased requirements for social workers to do diagnosis. This chapter provides an overview of how to use the *DSM-IV-TR*, which has been expanding and becoming more complex since the first edition was published in 1952.

THE HERITAGE OF CLASSIFICATION

Learning to make an accurate diagnosis that is documented appropriately is a technical task. The history of classification, on the other hand, is an exciting story of colorful characters and intriguing events. For example, Alois Alzheimer, who is famous for discovering the histological components of a neurological disorder named after him (Alzheimer's disease), worked in Heidelberg, Germany, assisting Emil Kraepelin, the founder of the classification system that is the basis for the *DSM* system. Alzheimer was working to identify the neurology of dementia praecox (precursor of schizophrenia), and his discovery of the disease associated with "senile dementia" was accidental (Berrios, 1996; Berrios & Porter, 1995). In their research, Kraepelin and Alzheimer used a card system to classify patients. This system became the basis for the grouping of disorders Kraepelin devised based on his position that classification should be grounded in a common set of symptoms rather than universal conditions that could be identified and applied to patients (Frances, First, & Pincus, 1995; Shorter, 1997; Thompson, 1987).

It is important to understand the history of classification, not just to be aware of interesting events but also understand that the current classification system is the result of a long history of research that produced a core set of mental disorders that only recently has been expanded. In reviewing the history of classification, it is apparent that little of what is done today with respect to diagnosis, assessment, or treatment is new. The early explanations evolved a core classification of mania, melancholia, and dementia (Shorter, 1997; Stone, 1997). The gradual expansion of this system, with a few diversions, has evolved to over 300 disorders in the *DSM-IV-TR*. There has been an unbroken evolution from the earliest classifications to the present aimed at sorting and consolidating mental disorders. Anyone doing diagnosis and assessment must have basic knowledge of this heritage of classification and the themes that bind historic events. The most common themes are:

- mind and body as separate entities, unified wholes, or interrelated;

- nature versus nurture or heredity versus environment as causes of mental illness;
- limited core of disorders versus many discrete disorders (Stone, 1997);
- categorical (symptom sets) versus process explanations (series of events) of mental illness (Munson, 2001);
- basis for care of the mentally ill as functional status (i.e., mentally ill, mentally retarded, criminal behavior, or poverty);
- family responsibility for mentally ill versus societal responsibility (historically, care was provided by the family and evolved to societal responsibility. The emergence of managed care has returned responsibility to families); and
- causation of disorders and treatments historically as intermingled, resulting in modern emphasis on interrelating diagnosis and treatment.

CURRENT VIEW OF CAUSATION

The evolution of the classification of mental disorders has led to many causal explanations. There was debate about whether to provide reference to causation for each disorder in the *DSM-IV-TR*, and the decision was made to limit descriptions of causation. Only a few disorders in the *DSM-IV-TR* have causation associated with them, such as reactive attachment disorder of infancy or early childhood, mental disorder due to a general medical condition, substance-related disorders, post-traumatic stress disorder, and the adjustment disorders. Post-traumatic stress disorder and the adjustment disorders cannot be diagnosed without the presence of a traumatic event or an identified stressor. Causation is important to developing intervention plans, and a basic orientation to causation is essential to performing diagnosis and implementing and conducting treatment. There is general acceptance that most disorders have multiple causation or multiple factors have to coalesce in order for a disorder to occur.

There are five recognized sources of causation of mental disorders: (1) genetics, (2) biology, (3) substances/alcohol, (4) stress, and (5) physical and psychological assaults (Munson, 2001). The remainder of this chapter provides a summary of how to effectively use the *DSM-IV-TR* to do thorough and accurate diagnosis.

ORGANIZATION OF THE MANUAL

The *DSM-IV-TR* has an organization that must be understood to effectively use the manual. Key sections are described with a brief explanation of the content. This is provided to emphasize the importance of studying these sections in preparation for doing diagnosis.

Contents

Lists all sections of the *DSM-IV-TR*. There are 39 sections listed in the contents, and 18 list categories of disorders that can be assigned a diagnostic code.

Introduction

Explanation of the research focus of the classification system, historical background of the *DSM-IV-TR*, and description of the revision process. Key units in this section are:

1. *Definition of a mental disorder*. Statement of the difference in the criteria for a mental disorder in the *DSM-IV-TR* and the criteria used in the legal system. Any practitioner who works with the legal system should become familiar with this unit.
2. *Ethnic and cultural considerations*. Explanation of diagnostic applications when working with people from diverse cultures. The explanations include variations in clinical presentation of disorders, description of culturally bound syndromes, and an outline for measuring and reporting the impact of culture. The details of these areas are contained in Appendix I of the *DSM-IV-TR*.
3. *Use of* DSM-IV-TR *in treatment planning*. A discussion of diagnosis in relation to treatment. Current practice guidelines for mental health professions require that treatment plans be directly linked to the diagnosis.
4. *Distinction between mental disorder and general medical condition*. Explanation of the distinction between mental disorders and physical disorders, which are referred to as general medical conditions (GMCs); reiterates the view of the APA that there are no absolute distinctions between the mental and the physical.

Use of the Manual

This chapter describes the coding system and types of diagnoses. Key sections of this chapter are as follows.

Coding and reporting. The disorders in the *DSM-IV-TR* have a three- to five-digit code that accompanies the name of the disorder. The number code for each disorder appears to the left of the disorder in the classification section at the beginning of the section that describes each disorder and at the beginning of the description of the criteria sets. The codes also appear in Appendix E, which gives an alphabetical listing of the diagnoses, and in Appendix F, which gives a numerical listing of the diagnoses.

The codes are not sequenced from 1 to 100 and do not appear in sequence in the text of the *DSM-IV-TR*; some disorders have the same number because they are based on the *International Classification of Diseases* (*ICD*) codes, which payers for health and mental health services use to reimburse providers. The *ICD* system consists of physical as well as mental disorders, and the codes range from 1 to 999, with the mental illness codes appearing within that numbering sequence. The *ICD* system was developed by international agreement before the *DSM* classification system was started. Because some *DSM-IV-TR* disorders have the same code, it is important when recording a diagnosis to list both the code and the name of the disorder.

Severity and course specifiers. Specifiers are used to refine subgroupings within a disorder and do not indicate difference in type. There are specifiers that indicate severity of the disorder (e.g., mild, moderate, and severe) and course of the disorder (e.g., in partial remission, in full remission, and prior history). Some disorders require a fifth-digit specifier. When a numeric code is encountered that has an *x* instead of a digit, that means the clinician must supply the digit. For example, the code 296.2x for major depressive disorder, single episode, means the clinician must supply 0 for unspecified severity, 1 for mild, 2 for moderate, 3 for severe without psychotic features, 4 for severe with psychotic features, 5 in partial remission, or 6 in full remission. The *x* is replaced with one of the specifier numbers, and the descriptive term is written to the right of the diagnosis description, for example, 296.21, Major Depressive Dis-

order, Single Episode, Mild. In this example the fifth digit, 1, indicates the mild severity specifier that is written to the right of the description of the disorder.

Other disorders do not have a numeric code indicating the specifiers, but the diagnostician can enter a comma after the text of the disorder and then write the generic specifier. The generic severity and course specifiers are mild, moderate, severe, in partial remission, in full remission, prior history. These specifiers can be added to any disorder that does not have specific specifiers indicated, for example, 308.3 Acute Stress Disorder, Moderate.

Principal Diagnosis

The principal diagnosis is the condition that is the basis for the admission of a person to an inpatient setting or the fundamental reason for the visit of the person to an outpatient setting, and it is the primary focus of clinical attention with respect to treatment. The principal diagnosis is always recorded as the first diagnosis on axis I. If there are multiple axis I diagnoses, the other diagnoses are listed in the order in which they are a focus of clinical attention. If there are axis I and II diagnoses, the principal diagnosis is assumed to be on axis I unless the axis II diagnosis is followed by the phrase "(principal diagnosis)."

Provisional Diagnosis

The specifier *provisional* is used when the diagnostician is reasonably certain the person will meet the full criteria for the disorder but needs more information before the diagnosis can be definitely made. A provisional diagnosis is indicated by writing the phrase "(provisional)" after the diagnosis code and description of the disorder.

Not Otherwise Specified Categories

Each class of disorders has at least one "not otherwise specified" (NOS) category. This category is at the end of the section for the class of disorders and is given when the person has unique features that are in the range of the class but do not precisely fit the category. There are four conditions in which the NOS diagnosis may be the most appropriate designation of the disorder to use.

1. The person conforms to the general
   criteria of the disorder, but the symptoms

do not meet the criteria for a specific disorder.

2. The person does not meet the criteria for any disorder but is in clinically significant distress.
3. There is uncertainty about etiology. This can occur when it is not known if the disorder is due to a GMC, is substance-induced, or is a primary disorder.
4. The diagnostician does not have time to complete data collection, data are inconsistent or contradictory, but the symptoms can be placed within a class of disorders.

Indication of Diagnostic Uncertainty

There are several ways to indicate diagnostic uncertainty within the *DSM-IV-TR*.

1. Use of V codes included in the section of the manual titled "Other Conditions That May Be a Focus of Clinical Attention."
2. Use "799.9 diagnosis or condition deferred on Axis I" or "799.9 diagnosis deferred on Axis II." These codes and labels are used when there is insufficient information to make a diagnosis.
3. Use "300.9 unspecified mental disorder (nonpsychotic)." This code is used when there is a mental disorder present that is not covered in the *DSM-IV-TR*, when no NOS category is appropriate, or when a nonpsychotic disorder is apparent but not enough information is available to diagnose a disorder.
4. The NOS category for a disorder can be used.
5. A diagnosis is given with the "(provisional)" designation.

Criteria for Clinical Significance

The definition of a mental disorder used by the *DSM-IV-TR* requires that the person have clinically significant impairment or distress to be diagnosed. To remind the diagnostician of this, most disorders include a clinical significance criterion stating "causes clinically significant distress or impairment in social, occupational, or other important areas of functioning." This statement establishes a threshold of impaired functioning used in deciding whether a person has a mental disorder. Clinical judgment is crucial in determining clinical

significance. Skill at making good clinical judgments and developing a keen sense of clinical significance comes from experience in evaluating many clients and being familiar with criteria for disorders, as well as from reading practice guidelines and attending continuing education seminars for specific disorders.

Information in the *DSM-IV-TR* Text

The diagnostic classification for each disorder is organized according to a standard set of headings. The following are the headings used (some sections are not used if information is unavailable in that area).

1. *Diagnostic features*. Statement of the diagnostic criteria for the disorder.
2. *Subtypes/specifiers*. Defines and explains subtypes and specifiers if they are used with the disorder.
3. *Recording procedures*. Guidelines for reporting the name of the disorder and for selecting *ICD* diagnostic codes. In some cases, they include instructions for using subtypes/specifiers.
4. *Associated features and disorders*. Usually contains three parts: (a) associated descriptive features and mental disorders; (b) associated laboratory findings; and (c) associated physical examination findings and GMCs.
5. *Specific culture, age, and gender features*. Guidance for taking into consideration cultural, developmental, or gender factors.
6. *Prevalence*. Contains information on occurrence and lifetime prevalence, incidence, and lifetime risk for disorders. Data are reported for different settings when information exists.
7. *Course*. Information on lifetime patterns and usual evolution of the disorder.
8. *Familial pattern*. Describes frequency of the disorder for first-degree biological relatives of the person compared to the general population.
9. *Differential diagnosis*. Identifies how to differentiate the disorder from similar disorders. This section is very important for social workers to understand and use. More sophisticated diagnostic and treatment research mandates that the clinician do accurate differential diagnosis to ensure appropriate treatment.

10. *Diagnostic criteria*. The above sections are followed by a listing of diagnostic criteria for each disorder.

MULTIAXIAL ASSESSMENT

The heart of the *DSM-IV-TR* system is the multiaxial format that uses five levels or areas to constitute a thorough diagnosis. This system recognizes the complexity of diagnosis and the interrelatedness of the factors that are components of diagnosis. The multiaxial system takes into account psychological, physical, internal, external, developmental, and social factors. The five axes that make up the system provide the format for recording individual diagnoses. The axes are:

- axis I clinical disorders,
- other conditions that may be a focus of clinical attention,
- axis II personality disorders,
- mental retardation,
- axis III general medical conditions,
- axis IV psychosocial and environmental problems, and
- axis V global assessment of functioning.

AXIS I CLINICAL DISORDERS AND AXIS II PERSONALITY DISORDERS AND MENTAL RETARDATION

Axes I and II are the key components of the multiaxial system and are used to record the disorders in the classification system. The distinction between the two axes has a historical basis. Axis I is used to record what in the past have been viewed as neuroses and psychoses; axis II is used to record what were referred to as character disorders (Munson, 2001). Neuroses were considered limitations that could impair but not chronically alter almost all areas of functioning and could be effectively relieved with intervention. Character disorders were viewed as long-standing defects ingrained in the developmental process of childhood that caused major, lifelong dysfunction in most aspects of life and were not generally amenable to treatment. Payers historically have reimbursed clinicians for axis I disorders and not axis II disorders, because the former could be changed by intervention and the latter could not be altered, leading to the conclusion

that it was not an efficient use of funds to pay for treatment of intractable disorders (Munson, 2001).

In the current system, Axis I is used to record clinical disorders from the main section of the *DSM-IV-TR* and the section "Other Conditions That May Be a Focus of Clinical Attention." Axis II is used for reporting personality disorders and mental retardation. A separate axis is included for personality disorders and mental retardation to ensure that they are not overlooked because axis I disorders are usually more evident when doing an assessment. Axis II can also be used to record maladaptive personality features and defense mechanisms. The maladaptive defense mechanisms are listed in Appendix B. Recording of personality features and defense mechanisms are recorded without a code.

AXIS III GMCS

Axis III is used to record coexisting physical disorders (GMCs) that may be associated with a mental disorder or may be independent of the mental disorder but related to treatment of the mental disorder. Disorders recorded on axis III are found in the *ICD*. Appendix G of the *DSM-IV-TR* has a summary listing of the medical conditions that can be listed on axis III. The *ICD* code and name of the disorder should be listed in the same format as axis I and II disorders.

Any disorder listed on axis III by a mental health professional who is not a physician should be followed by "as reported by _____." The person who reported the axis III disorder to the diagnostician should be listed. Some examples of how to list the person who reported the axis III disorder are "identified patient," "primary care physician," "mother," "father," "foster mother," or the name of the person reporting the GMC, for example, Axis III: 402.91 Hypertensive heart disease with congestive heart failure *as reported by primary care physician, Dr. John Smith*.

When a mental disorder is believed to be the direct result of a GMC, a "mental disorder due to a general medical condition" should be recorded on axis I, and the GMC should be recorded on axis I and III. Details of this type of diagnosis is explained in the "Mental Disorder Due to a General Medical Condition" section. This diagnosis should be made by a physician or in consultation with a physician. It is usually difficult to distinguish primary mental disorders and mental disorders due to GMCs. The two disorders can be connected through nonphysiological means, or the coexistence of the physical and mental disorders can be coincidental. For example, anxiety disorder symptoms can be precipitated as a psychosocial stressor, rather than resulting directly from the physiological effects of a GMC.

AXIS IV PSYCHOSOCIAL AND ENVIRONMENTAL PROBLEMS

Axis IV is used to report psychosocial and environmental problems (PEPs) that may influence diagnosis, treatment, and prognosis of mental disorders. PEPs are listed in each category and are not assigned a severity score, as was the case in previous editions of the manual.

A PEP can represent a range of events. It can be a negative life event or experience; an environmental difficulty, deficiency, or impediment; a family dysfunction or distress; an interpersonal conflict or stress; absence of social supports; lack of resources; or any other problem that exists in the context of the person's mental disorder. PEPs can also develop as a consequence of the person's mental disorder.

The list of PEPs can be quite long. The diagnostician must make a clinical judgment regarding which PEPs are the most significant in relation to the person's mental disorder. Although all relevant PEPs should be listed, lengthy lists of PEPs should be avoided. If the list gets too long, the practitioner may have to prioritize the PEPs and list only the most significant ones. To control the extent of PEPs listed, only those evident during the year preceding the evaluation are listed. PEPs existing for more than a year can be listed if they continue to contribute to the mental disorder or are a focus of intervention. An example of this would be prior sexual abuse that contributes to a diagnosis of dysthymic disorder and continues to be a focus in the treatment to address the dysthymia.

There are nine categories of PEPs in the *DSM-IV-TR*.

- Problems with primary support group.
- Problems related to the social environment.
- Educational problems.
- Occupational problems.
- Housing problems.
- Economic problems.
- Problems with access to health care services.

- Problems related to interaction with the legal system/crime.
- Other psychosocial and environmental problems.

PEPs should be recorded in very brief phrases, and narrative statements should be avoided. The phrase should include enough detail to convey understanding of the problem in a general sense. For example, instead of "poor academic performance," record "poor grades in science, math, and art." Instead of "loss of job," record "loss of job due to absenteeism."

AXIS V GLOBAL ASSESSMENT OF FUNCTIONING

Axis V provides a scale that gives an estimate of the person's current overall level of functioning. This information can be useful in establishing the degree of impairment, planning treatment, and estimating outcome. The scale ranges from 0 to 100, with 100 representing superior functioning and 1 representing severe impairment and potential to harm self and others. A 0 is entered if inadequate information is available to assign a score. The GAF numeric scale is accompanied by text indicators used in assigning a score. The GAF scale applies only to psychological, social, and occupational functioning. Impairments due to physical or environmental functioning are excluded from the criteria for this scale. The rating assigned to the person should be on the basis of functioning at the time of the evaluation. This is done by listing the time frame in parentheses after recording the score. Multiple ratings at different times can be listed when appropriate, such as when the person has had a psychiatric hospital admission. The admission and discharge GAF scores can be indicative of the course of hospitalization. For example, Axis V: GAF = 55 (at admission), GAF = 70 (at discharge).

SOCIAL AND OCCUPATIONAL FUNCTIONING ASSESSMENT SCALE

In settings where it is appropriate to assess social and occupational functioning, or disability impairment independent of psychological functioning, practitioners can use the Social and Occupational Functioning Assessment Scale (SOFAS), which is included in Appendix B. The SOFAS is a proposed scale that is in the section referred to as "Criteria Sets and Axes Provided for Further

Study," and it can be used to make a social and occupational assessment. The SOFAS scale is based on the same numerical rating scale (0–100) as the GAF but uses slightly different criteria.

GLOBAL ASSESSMENT OF RELATIONAL FUNCTIONING SCALE

A scale for assessing relationship functioning has been included in Appendix B. This scale is titled the Global Assessment of Relational Functioning (GARF) scale. The GARF scale uses the same numerical ratings (0–100) as the GAF with detailed measurement criteria. This scale has special relevance for clinicians who do couples and family assessments and treatment (Yingling, Miller, McDonald, & Galewaler, 1998).

DEFENSIVE FUNCTIONING SCALE

The Defensive Functioning Scale (DFS) is included in Appendix B. Some have argued that this scale is one of the few remaining elements of the manual based on the work of psychoanalytic-oriented theoreticians such as Adolph Meyer (Munson, 2001). Some psychodynamic practitioners believe that the *DSM-IV-TR* lacks useful guidelines for their form of clinical practice (Frances, First, & Pincus, 1995). The DFS is based on defense mechanisms or coping styles that protect the person against anxiety, awareness of danger, or effects of stressors. The defense mechanisms are categorized in groups referred to as defense levels. To use the DFS, the clinician identifies up to seven defense mechanisms in order of prominence that are evident during the evaluation. The DFS is recorded in two parts:

1. Current defenses or coping styles. The clinician records up to seven defenses or coping strategies.
2. Predominant current defense level. The clinician records one of seven designated levels of functioning.

ADDITIONAL CODES

This section lists the codes to use when there is an unspecified mental disorder or no diagnosis is made on axis I or II. The codes listed in this section are:

- 300.9, Unspecified mental disorder (nonpsychotic),

- V71.09, No diagnosis or condition on axis I,
- 799.9, Diagnosis or condition deferred on axis I,
- V71.09, No diagnosis on axis II,
- 799.9, Diagnosis deferred on axis II.

When recording a multiaxial diagnosis, it is confusing to leave an axis blank if no disorder is diagnosed on it. Enter the appropriate V code from this section. If an axis is left blank, anyone reading the multiaxial diagnosis cannot determine whether the clinician forgot to enter the diagnosis or there is no diagnosis on the axis.

RULE OUT

The phrase *rule out* is not used in the *DSM-IV-TR* as it was in previous editions. Rule out has been replaced by *provisional diagnosis*. There are situations in which *rule out* is appropriate when the possibility of a disorder may exist or a disorder can be developing in which the diagnosis-deferred designation would not be used. For example, in the case of a child who has possible symptoms of bipolar disorder and the father has a history of bipolar disorder, *rule out* may be appropriate because bipolar disorder can have genetic links (APA, 2000). The decision to use *diagnosis deferred* or *rule out* is a clinical judgment.

Rule out is no longer used as a multiaxial system term, but there is a conceptual rule-out process that the diagnostician should go through in each case. In most disorders there are rule out–oriented criteria referred to as exclusion criteria. The most common exclusion criteria are related to ruling out substances or GMCs as a cause of the disorder. Other factors or disorders that should be ruled out in the assessment process are malingering or factitious disorder, cultural influences, age-appropriate behaviors, and other conditions that may be a focus of clinical attention, such as physical abuse, sexual abuse, and neglect in children.

TREATMENT PLANNING

Increasingly, practitioners are required to do treatment planning that is clearly stated and based on sound criteria and standardized practice guidelines. Treatment plans are required to be stated in behavioral terms and must be measurable. Goals, problems, and outcomes must be clearly identified. There are expectations that the treatment plan be linked to the diagnosis. This expectation is another reason a person should do a thorough multiaxial diagnosis. Axes I and II relate to the symptoms and behaviors that can be targeted in a treatment plan, and axis IV is critical to PEPs that are basic to treatment planning. The diagnostic criteria should be directly linked to treatment goals and outcome statements. Treatment planning should be a joint effort of the practitioner, the client, and family members (Munson, 2001).

NONAXIAL FORMAT

The *DSM-IV-TR* does not require a multiaxial format for reporting mental disorders. It is recommended that social work mental health professionals use the multiaxial format and do a thorough diagnosis in every case. When practitioners do not follow the *DSM-IV-TR* guidelines for formatting diagnosis, the clinician might be perceived by others as not knowing how to make a diagnosis. In addition, using the multiaxial format can ensure that the diagnostician has not missed any major aspect of the person's functioning.

WEB SITES

BehavNet. http://www.behavenet.com.
Dsmivtr. http://;www.dsmivtr.org.
DSM-V Prelude Project: Research and Outreach. http://www.dsm5.org.
Psychiatry Online. http://www .psychiatryonline.
Psychweb. http://www.Psychweb.com.

References

American Psychiatric Association. (2000). *Diagnostic and statistical manual of mental disorders*, 4th ed., text revision. Washington, DC: APA.

Berrios, G. E. (1996). *The history of mental symptoms: Descriptive psychopathology since the nineteenth century*. Cambridge: Cambridge University Press.

Berrios, G. E., & Porter, R. (1995). *A history of clinical psychiatry: The origin and history of psychiatric disorders*. London: Athlone Press.

Caplan, P. J. (1995). *They say you're crazy: How the world's most powerful psychiatrists decide who's normal*. New York: Addison-Wesley.

Frances, A., & First, M. B. (1998). *Your mental health: A layman's guide to the psychiatrist's bible*. New York: Scribner.

Frances, A., First, M. B., & Pincus, H. A. (1995). *DSM-IV guidebook*. Washington, DC: American Psychiatric Press.

Karls, J. M., & Wandrei, K. E. (1994). *Person-in-environment system: The PIE classification system for social functioning problems*. Washington, DC: National Association of Social Workers Press.

Kessler, R. C., McGonagle, K. A., Zhoa, S., Nelson, C. B., Hughes, M., Eshleman, S., et al. (1994). Lifetime and 12-month prevalence of *DSM-III-R* psychiatric disorders in the United States. *Archives of General Psychiatry, 15*(1), 8–19.

Kirk, S. A., & Kutchins, H. (1992). *The selling of the DSM: The rhetoric of science in psychiatry*. Hawthorne, NY: Aldine de Gruyter.

Kutchins, H., & Kirk, S. A. (1997). *Making us crazy: DSM the psychiatric bible and the creation of mental disorders*. New York: Free Press.

Munson, C. E. (2001). *The mental health diagnostic desk reference: Visual guides and more for learning to use the diagnostic and statistical manual (DSM-IV-TR)*, 2nd ed. New York: Haworth.

Shorter, E. (1997). *A history of psychiatry: From the era of the asylum to the age of Prozac*. New York: Wiley.

Stone, M. H. (1997). *Healing the mind: A history of psychiatry from antiquity to the present*. New York: Norton.

Thompson, C. (Ed.). (1987). *The origins of modern psychiatry*. New York: Wiley.

Yingling, L. C., Miller, W. E., McDonald, A. L., & Galewaler, S. T. (1998). *GARF assessment sourcebook: Using the DSM-IV global assessment of relational functioning*. New York: Brunner/ Mazel.

Clinical Assessment of Bipolar Disorder

Balancing Strengths and Diagnosis

47

Elizabeth C. Pomeroy & Diane L. Green

About 16 percent of the population experiences some type of mood disorder during their lifetime. Females are twice as likely to have a mood disorder. About 5.7 million American adults or about 2.6 percent of the population age 18 and older in any given year, have bipolar disorder (Kessler, Chiu, Demler, & Walters, 2005). Bipolar disorders are equally distributed between males and females. Historically, mood disorders were only diagnosed in adults; however, in recent years, the diagnosis of bipolar disorder in children has been on the rise. Currently, children receive the same diagnosis as adults; therefore, there are no childhood mood disorders listed in the *DSM-IV-TR*. The consensus is that it occurs less often in children than adults, but this difference closes during adolescence. Children tend to show more irritability and emotional swings rather than the classic manic states and are often mistaken as being hyperactive (Kessler et al., 2005).

The disorders discussed in this chapter were previously known as depressive disorders, affective disorders, and sometimes depressive neurosis. Beginning with the *DSM-III*, these problems were categorized under the broad heading of mood disorders, due to the fact they represent a gross deviation in mood. The diagnoses in the Mood Disorders section of the *DSM-IV-TR* (American Psychiatric Association [APA], 2002) are characterized by changes in a person's emotional state that are sufficiently severe to cause significant clinical distress and/or disruption in psychosocial functioning. The term *mood* refers to an internally experienced emotional state that influences an individual's thinking and behavior. A related term, *affect*, refers more specifically to the external demonstration of one's mood or emotions.

This distinction is important because affect and mood may differ; that is, an individual's affect may not be compatible with his or her mood.

This section of the *DSM-IV-TR* is generally organized around four different types of episodes that in turn serve as building blocks for determining specific diagnoses. An episode is a period of time during which a client evidences a particular set of symptoms and as a result, experiences a pronounced alteration in mood and/or a change in social, vocational, and recreational functioning. Specifically, the four episodic states are major depressive, manic, hypomanic, and mixed (APA, 2002).

Two of the most disruptive disorders are bipolar I and bipolar II disorders. *Bipolar disorders* refers to alterations between depression and mania or hypomania. Each is diagnosed based on the number and pattern of episodes the individual has experienced in his or her lifetime. In the coding of each disorder, attention is given to the severity of symptoms and specific characteristics of the most recent episode. The core identifying feature of bipolar disorders is the tendency for manic episodes to alternate with major depressive episodes. Beyond that, bipolar disorders parallel depressive disorders (e.g., a manic episode can occur once or repeatedly). Bipolar I disorder is the alternation of full manic episodes and depressive episodes. The average age of onset is 18 years; however, it can begin in childhood. It tends to be chronic in nature, and unfortunately suicide is a common consequence. In bipolar II disorder, major depressive episodes alternate with hypomanic episodes. The average age of onset is 22 years, and again, it can begin in childhood. Only 10 to 13 percent of cases progress to full bipolar I disorder. This also tends to be chronic in nature (Barlow & Durand, 2004).

The Mood Disorder section in the *DSM-IV-TR* includes a comparatively large number of specifiers, including some that are reflected in the fourth and fifth digits of the numeric coding. Although a listing of the relevant specifiers is included in each disorder's diagnostic criteria, it can be confusing to try to determine which ones apply. Practitioners are encouraged to use the classification listing section to help them determine which set of specifiers is used with each diagnosis. The rapid cycling specifier applies only to bipolar I and II disorders. Rapid cycling pattern is used when a person has at least four manic or depressive episodes within a 12-month period. It should be noted that rapid cycling is a more severe form of bipolar disorder that does not respond well to treatment and appears to be associated with high rates of suicide. Alternative drug treatments (e.g., anticonvulsants, mood stabilizers) are typically used with individuals meeting this specifier criteria.

People experiencing the symptoms of any of the depressive disorders are likely to seek treatment. However, many will approach general medical practitioners rather than those who specialize in treating mental disorders. Seeking medical treatment for a depressive disorder can represent confusion about the problem or reflect the stigma often associated with mental health treatment. Individuals experiencing psychotic symptoms of either depression or mania will likely not seek treatment independently. However, their behavior may result in others arranging involuntary treatment on their behalf.

When assessing someone suspected to have a mood disorder, particular attention should be focused on the person's emotional functioning. Although a thorough history of the presenting problem is required to make a diagnosis, it may be difficult for the client to present detailed and accurate information. People who are severely depressed can be virtually mute, and those experiencing manic mood states may be unable to express themselves coherently. Clearly, the reliability of self-report is very uncertain if someone is experiencing psychotic symptoms. Someone with a history of psychiatric treatment may fear rehospitalization and deliberately minimize symptoms. Consequently, it is often helpful to gather data from collateral sources, such as close friends or relatives, employers, or other professionals to specify both the timing and severity of symptoms.

To assess manic symptoms in adults, two self-report instruments have been shown to have excellent reliability and validity. The Internal State Scale (Bauer, Crits-Cristoph, & Ball, 1991) is a 15-item instrument in which clients indicate the intensity of their mood by marking a line denoting the level of severity of symptoms. The scale has four subscales—well-being, perceived conflict, depression, and activation. Mania is assessed by a well-being score equal to or higher than 125 and activation score equal to or greater than 200. Each item is biphasic. For example, on the items indicating well-being, clients who mark the lower end of the line (scale) are assessed to have depressive symptoms, whereas clients who mark the upper end of the line are assessed to have manic symptoms.

The Self-Report Manic Inventory (Shugar, Schertzer, Toner, & di Gasbarro, 1992) is a 47-item scale that includes statements that clients mark true or false depending on the presence or absence of symptoms during the prior month. The instrument has been validated as a screening tool for the severity of manic symptoms in adults. The scale has a maximum score of 47.

For bipolar clients who are unable to complete a self-report instrument, the Young Mania Rating Scale (Young, Biggs, & Myers, 1978) can be completed by a skilled practitioner. The scale contains 11 items measuring internal mood states and behaviors experienced by the client and reported to the practitioner. Scores may range between 0 and 60.

In some situations, people experiencing more severe mood disorders may constitute a danger to themselves or others. An assessment of suicide risk is of paramount importance in these cases, both at the time of initial contact and on a consistent, ongoing basis throughout treatment. Practitioners must develop skills in this area or use emergency assessment resources that are available in any community (e.g., local community mental health services, emergency rooms).

Across cultures, feelings of weakness or tiredness tend to characterize depression. However, more difficulty is found when comparing subjective feelings that accompany mood disorders. Societies that are more individualistic tend to produce depressive statement using the *I* pronoun, whereas societies that are more integrated focus on *our* statements. However, the prevalence of mood disorders seems to be similar across subcultures, although it occurs more frequently in economically depressed areas. The practitioner should be aware of common variations in the diagnosis and presentation of mood disorders based on diversity. For example, women are roughly twice as likely as men to be diagnosed with a depressive disorder. In the United States, men have been raised to minimize emotional expression regardless of their internal state. On the other hand, women have been taught to use emotional expression as a tool for getting their needs met. Clearly, these gender differences concerning emotional expressiveness can influence the practitioner's perception and diagnosis of the client. Generally, practitioners should be careful to avoid overdiagnosing women with depression, as well as underdiagnosing men.

Similarly, some cultures are more likely to express emotional states in somatic terms. This may be related to a fear that emotions like depression or anxiety will be interpreted as weak or "crazy." Therefore, in some cultures it is more acceptable to complain of a variety of physical symptoms rather than to acknowledge negative moods. For example, complaints of "nerves" or "headaches" may relate to negative moods among Latino clients. In addition, bilingual clients may appear to have more or less symptomatology depending on the language spoken during the interview, as well as the primary language of the practitioner (Malgady & Zayas, 2001). Practitioners should be aware that such variations may occur based on region or family background as well. Generalizations regarding this issue can lead to misunderstanding and misdiagnosis.

SOCIAL SUPPORT

Bipolar I and bipolar II disorders are considered severe mental illnesses. Symptoms associated with these disorders cause serious impairment in the client's social and occupational functioning. Family members and close friends of a person with an affective disorder can feel confused, frustrated, fearful, or angry about the person's dramatic change in mood and inability to cope with daily life events. Families and friends may not understand the problem and why the client can't just snap out of it.

A psychoeducational group for individuals with similar problems may be an additional source of support for the person suffering from a mood disorder. For example, there are support groups for persons suffering from bipolar disorders as well as groups for those affected by depression. These groups provide individuals with a sense of belonging, education concerning the illness, and mutual support. Mental health practitioners conduct some groups; others are organized and run by persons who have previous experience with the disorder (either clients themselves or their family members). With the recent increases in knowledge concerning depression and bipolar moods, there has been a corresponding increase in the numbers of organizations and agencies providing specialized support for individuals with these disorders.

For many people with affective disorders, joining a group may be problematic because of the person's symptoms or because of group availability. Similar constraints may also apply to members of the person's social support system. The Internet contains a wealth of information, including organizations specializing in the support and treatment of persons with mood disorders, online chat rooms and bulletin boards, and current reports and articles related to particular disorders. At the end of this chapter is a list of some useful Internet resources.

Following are two case examples demonstrating a strengths perspective approach.

Case Example 1

Client name: Mary Anne Philips
Age: 30 years old
Ethnicity: African American
Marital status: Married
Children: Danya, age 6

You are a caseworker in the emergency room of a large urban hospital. You work the day shift from 8 A.M. to 5 P.M. Several hours before you came to work, the police brought the client to the emergency room in restraints. The following information was gathered from the police at intake. The police state that Mary Anne Philips, a 30-year-old African American woman, was found dancing half-naked in the middle of a busy intersection in the center of the city at approximately 2 A.M. She appeared to be high on drugs when the police approached her. She told the police that she hadn't taken any drugs and that she was "just high on life." She said she wasn't doing anything wrong, just "having a party." Witnesses stated that Mary Anne had started the evening at a local restaurant and bar. She had been with a couple of gentlemen who seemed to know her. She began telling jokes and buying drinks for everyone at the bar.

At first, she seemed like a person just having fun, but she got louder and rowdier as the night progressed. The two men left, but she stayed at the restaurant, saying loudly, "I'm just getting warmed up here." She sang and danced and finally ended up shoving all the glasses onto the floor and standing on the bar, talking as fast as she could. Customers got irritated, and the bartender asked her to leave. She ignored his request and started singing at the top of her lungs. Finally, the bartender had to force her off the bar and push her out the door. At that point, she began dancing and singing in the street. The bartender told police that she had no more than two drinks throughout the evening. When the police attempted to get Mary Anne out of the road, she became belligerent and began swearing at the officers. They had to take her out of the middle of the intersection by force and handcuff her to get her into the police car. Lab tests indicated no evidence of excessive alcohol or other drugs. The physician on duty had prescribed a sedative, and Mary Anne went to sleep at approximately 5 A.M.

You go to see Mary Anne at 9:30 A.M. She is lying in bed, quietly staring at the ceiling. She seems very subdued in comparison to the description of the previous night. She glances at you as you enter the room but makes no attempt to sit up. You tell her who you are and your reasons for wanting to talk to her. Mary Anne makes no response to your introduction. You ask if she has any relatives you could call for her. She looks over at you and says, "I just want to die. If it weren't for my baby, I'd have been dead a long time ago."

"What's your baby's name?" you ask. "Danya," Mary Anne replies. "I'm such a lousy mother lying here like this. I should be home taking care of her." "Where is Danya now?" you ask.

"She's with my sister. She stayed with my sister last night," Mary Anne responds. "I knew I was racing, so I took her over to my sister's house." "You were racing?" you query.

"Yeah, you know, I start racing sometimes, feeling real good and full of energy like nothing can stop me," Mary Anne says. "But not now; I feel lousy now, like I just want to be left alone to die." "Can you tell me what happened last night?" you ask. "It's like living on a roller coaster," Mary Anne tells you. "One minute you're way up there, and the next minute you're in the blackest hole you can imagine." "And last night, you were way up there?" you query. "Yeah, I was just feeling good and having a good time. It's like you're racing and you can't slow down. Like you're high or something, but I didn't take any drugs. I don't do drugs. This just comes over me sometimes, and I feel like I could take on the world." "Have you ever felt this way before?" you ask. "Oh yeah, up and down, that's how I am," Mary Anne says. "So, sometimes you feel really good and up, and then, sometimes you feel really down. Is that right?" you ask. "Yeah, I'm scared I'm beginning to crash now. It's bad when you come down. It feels real bad," she says. "It lasts for weeks and weeks . . . just down all the time." "How often does this happen, going from one extreme to another?" you ask. "Once a day or once a week or once a month?" "See, for a few weeks I feel great. I can do anything—stay up all night having a good time. I don't sleep or eat or slow down. I just keep on going for a week, maybe two. Then, I begin to crash."

"Do you hear voices or see things when you're feeling high?" you ask. "No, except for my own voice. I can't stop talking either. Gets me into trouble, sometimes," Mary Anne admits.

"What else happens when you're feeling high?" you ask. "I want to party. I can party all night when I'm high. I'm the life of the party," Mary Anne says glumly. "Have you ever gotten in trouble before, like you did last night?" you ask. "Oh yeah," Mary Anne agrees. "I've gotten thrown out of places lots of times, but I usually just move on down the street." "Are you employed?" you ask. "I've tried to keep a job. Just can't seem to stick with it," Mary Anne replies. "How are you feeling right now?" you query. "Feel like hell," she tells you. "This is a rotten way to live, I'm telling you." "How long does the crashing last?" you ask. "Sometimes a few days, sometimes a few weeks," Mary Anne says bleakly. "Describe for me what these down times are like for you," you suggest. "It's like I'm a balloon and someone stuck a needle in me. I'm so sad that nothing looks good. It's hard to get out of bed and face the world. . . . I sleep and sleep and sleep. When I do get up, I'm so tired that it feels like I'm carrying around invisible weights."

"What kinds of things go through your mind when you feel like this?" "I can't think of anything I want to do," Mary Anne tells you. "I can't seem to make myself think anything all the way through. Like making a decision about something no matter how trivial is just impossible. Sometimes, I just wish I were dead." "Are you wishing you would die now?" you ask. "Not yet . . . but it usually does get to that point when I crash." "Have you ever seen a doctor for these changes in your mood?" you ask. "One doctor told me it was just a 'female thing,'" Mary Anne states.

"Maybe it's more than a female thing," you suggest. "Maybe there's some medication that could help even out your moods. Would you be willing to talk to a doctor about how you've been feeling?" you ask. "Okay. I guess it wouldn't hurt," Mary Anne says.

The following are some questions you should consider:

- To what extent do you think Mary Anne may be a danger to herself?
- What other information would be useful in determining her risk?
- What would you like to know about Mary Anne's social support system?
- Are there any steps you would take (given the client's permission) to ensure that her support system stays intact?
- What internal and external strengths do you see in Mary Anne's case?
- What is your initial diagnosis? 296.42 Bipolar Disorder, most recent episode manic, moderate, rapid cycling.

The first three digits for bipolar I disorder are 296. The fourth digit indicates the nature of the current episode, with 4 indicating hypomania or mania (as in this case). The fifth digit would not have been used if the most recent episode were hypomania or unspecified. However, as this case indicates the most recent episode as manic, the fifth digit indicates the severity of the episode; 2 indicates a moderate severity, which is an extreme increase in activity and impairment in judgment. The specifier at the end of the diagnosis of rapid cycling is used because at least four episodes of a mood disturbance was seen in the previous 12 months.

Case Example 2

Client name: Sally Tannerg
Age: 36 years old
Ethnicity: Caucasian
Marital status: Married
Occupation: Homemaker
Children: Three children; currently pregnant with her fourth child

Little information was obtained from a phone call interview with Mrs. Tannerg by the intake worker. She stated that her psychiatrist in Massachusetts had referred her to Dr. Browning in Southfork, Oklahoma, for prescription monitoring. Dr. Browning has referred her to the South-fork Counseling Center to see a therapist. She requested an appointment with a therapist and said only that she had been hospitalized recently in Massachusetts before moving with her family to Oklahoma. She stated that it was very important that she begin therapy immediately but did not want to discuss any details of the problems she has been experiencing lately. The intake worker scheduled her for the first available appointment with you later in the week.

Sally Tannerg is an attractive, 36-year-old woman whose warm and effervescent personality is apparent from the first meeting. You notice that she is several months pregnant. She appears eager to get to your office and asks you how long you have lived in Southfork. You explain to her that you moved to Southfork after completing your master's degree 2 years ago. "When did you move to Southfork?" you ask. Sally wriggles in her chair and enthusiastically begins talking about her husband being relocated to Oklahoma to accept a new position with his company, which develops software for computer companies. She states that she's never lived in the Midwest, having grown up in Boston. She moved to another town in Massachusetts when she got married 10 years ago. "We've been in Southfork for 3 months, and I feel like a fish out of water," Sally tells you. "I've got most of the responsibility for taking care of my three children and as you can see, I'm about to have another one. Bob, my husband, travels 3 or 4 days a week with his job, so I'm stuck at home with my children most of the time . . . not that I'm complaining. Bob has a good job and he has to travel, but it's a lot of work for me, and I haven't made a lot of friends yet. When I lived in Revere, Massachusetts, I had a lot of neighbors who were young mothers like me with kids, and we'd get together and baby-sit for each other and take our children to different activities. It was nice until I got sick."

"What happened when you got sick?" you ask Sally. "Well, I've always been a pretty optimistic, upbeat type person with a lot of energy. Then, suddenly, I had no energy. I was drained. I was so tired I couldn't move and just got completely depressed. I was suicidal and felt hopeless about everything. I thought 'here I am with three little children and I can't get off the couch to take care of them.' I felt like a complete failure as a mother, just completely worthless. I didn't want to do anything except sleep and block out the entire world. I wasn't interested in sex with my husband. I didn't care if I lived or died. It just got so bad that the psychiatrist I was seeing put me in the hospital." Sally slinks down in her chair and sighed deeply.

She takes a deep breath and then begins talking again. "Everything just looked so black. I couldn't imagine feeling any worse . . . and my poor kids. All I could think about was that I would die and they would be motherless. And then I began to feel better. I mean like overnight I felt a whole lot better. I had plenty of energy, and thoughts and ideas just flew through my head and I was on top of the world again. I told the doctor I was just fine and he should let me go home." "How long had you been in the hospital when you began feeling so much better?" you inquire. "About 4 weeks," Sally sighs. "Then I was okay— or so I thought." "So initially, you were really depressed when you went into the hospital, and then you began to feel much better. Were you taking any medication?" you ask. "Well, that's the really scary part about this problem I have. You see, the feeling of being on top of the world didn't last very long. Pretty soon, I was in the depths of despair again, and the medicine wasn't working. So the doctor said I really needed to be on lithium. I didn't want to take anything because by then I knew I was pregnant again. But I was so depressed I didn't know what else to do. I'm so worried about the medicine affecting the baby. The doctor has put me on a low dosage until the baby is born. I'm just keeping my fingers crossed the baby will be okay. Do you think that makes me a bad mother?" "It sounds as if the psychiatrist thinks you really need to be taking lithium right now," you respond. "You're trying to take care of yourself."

"He told me it was absolutely necessary if I wanted to stay out of the hospital," Sally replies. "I never want to go through that experience again. And I'm not sure it's really helping. I have to go get my blood tested every 2 weeks, and I'm not sure I've got enough of the medication in me to do me any good. I have days when I feel like I can function pretty well, and then there are other days when I feel like I'm sliding into a black hole and can't get out of it. It's an awful feeling." "These feelings of depression just started about a year ago? Is that correct?" you inquire. "Yes, I never felt down in the dumps and completely hopeless like I have this year. You know, I remember as a child, my father would have periods of deep depression. He was like Dr. Jekyll and Mr. Hyde. Some days he'd be great to be around and he'd play with us and laugh. Other times, he was really scary. He'd sit in a dark room and stare out the window for hours, and if any of us kids did anything that perturbed him, he'd get so angry that he'd take us behind the house and give us all a spanking. You could never tell what kind of mood he'd be in. I was scared of him my whole childhood. I sure hope I'm not turning into someone like him."

"Did you father ever see a doctor about his moods?" you ask. "No, he thinks only crazy people see psychiatrists. I told Bob not to tell my parents I was in the hospital. They would have disowned me. They are strict, conservative Lutherans, and believe me, they wouldn't ever understand. They'd tell me I'd be okay if I went to church."

It seems to you that Sally identifies with her father's mood swings to some degree, and you decide to get more information about her family of origin. "Tell me what it was like for you growing up in Boston," you say.

Sally sits back in her chair and looks out the window. "Well, it was your typical Lutheran family growing up in the sixties and seventies, I guess. I have five siblings—two older brothers, an older sister, and two younger sisters. My parents were strict and fairly religious. We went to church on Sundays every week without fail. My mother cared for us while my father worked. We were a middle-class family, I guess. We never had a lot of money, but we weren't starving to death either. My parents sent us all to a Lutheran school that cost more than public school but wasn't like a private school. I think I have a real problem with feeling guilty about everything. My father reinforced that feeling of guilt all the time. He was very distant and authoritarian. We got punished a lot as children, and although I don't think I really thought so at the time, it was pretty harsh punishment by today's standards. It seemed like I was always in the way when my father got mad, and I got punished more than my sisters and brothers."

"How do you feel about that time growing up?" you inquire. "I guess I consider it a pretty normal childhood," Sally suggests. "All the kids in the Lutheran school I attended grew up much the same way as I did. I think my mother saved us all from my father's wrath on many occasions. She had a way of diverting his attention away from us when we were in the line of fire." "And what is your relationship like now, with your parents?" you ask. "Since I've been in the hospital, I've discovered I have all this anger toward my father," Sally states. "I've been scared of him my whole life, and I'm tired of feeling that way and I hate how he made me feel. I've never really had any self-esteem and have always felt like I'm cowering in the corner afraid of my own shadow because of what he did to me." "And your mother? How do you get along with her?" you ask. "We get along well. We always have. I think we have a lot in common and she's had to put up with a lot, too," Sally says with a smile.

"Do you feel that the way you were raised has something to do with the depression you've been experiencing, or do you think it's unrelated to your childhood experiences?" you ask. "I don't really know," Sally states. "It's something I want to figure out. The doctor told me some of this could be a neurochemical problem. Sometimes, I feel great and full of energy. In fact, it's hard to slow down. I become really talkative and friendly. It's like everything speeds up. Thoughts run through my head really fast, and I can't even sleep when I feel that good. It's like being high." "How often does that happen?" you ask. "It seems to happen about once a month after I've been really depressed," Sally states. "But it doesn't last as long as the depressed periods." "Do you ever feel that you place yourself in high-risk or dangerous situations when you have a 'high' feeling?" you query.

"No, I don't think so," Sally reflects. "I have some pretty fantastic thoughts, but I don't actually do anything. I've got to think about my children and the one on the way." "Okay, so you feel depressed a lot of the time, and sometimes, about once a month, you feel pretty good and full of energy. How long do you usually have that 'high' feeling?" you ask. "It can last from 3 or 4 days up to a week before I begin sliding downward again," says Sally. "I always hope it will last longer, but it never does." "So, it sounds like one of your goals is to learn how to cope with some of these ups and downs you've been experiencing," you note. Sally says enthusiastically, "Yes, exactly, I need some help with the best way of coping with these moods, especially during this pregnancy." "Would it be all right with you if I talked to the

psychiatrist who is prescribing the medication for you?" you inquire. "I'll need you to sign a consent form." "Absolutely. I'll give you his phone number," Sally asserts. "Would you like to make an appointment on a weekly basis?" you ask.

Sally nods her head vigorously and says, "I'm so glad I've found someone I can talk to who doesn't look at me as if I'm crazy. I definitely want to come once a week to talk to you." "Okay. We'll schedule an appointment for next week," you reply. Sally leaves your office with a little bounce in her step and talks about going to shop for the new baby as you walk her to the reception area.

From this preliminary interview, it would seem that Sally may not have much social support in Southfork.

- How would you go about exploring that issue?
- How important do you think securing local support would be?
- What is your initial diagnosis? 296.89 Bipolar II disorder, depressed, moderate, without full interepisode recovery.

A diagnosis of bipolar II indicates recurrent major depressive episodes with hypomanic episodes. There are no additional digit specifiers because all five digits are used to indicate the diagnosis. However, you should indicate the current or most recent episode (depressed). If and only if the full criteria are currently met for major depressive episode, as in this case, you should specify its current clinical status or features. In this case, "moderate" is indicated. If the full criteria are not currently met for major depressive episode, you would indicate partial remission or full remission. An additional specifier of with rapid cycling was used to indicate that at least four episodes of a mood disturbance existed in the previous 12 months.

CONCLUSION

It is estimated that it takes an average of 5 years from onset of symptoms to reach the correct diagnosis of bipolar disorder (Evans, 2000). As such, bipolar disorder can be difficult to detect partly because bipolar disorder also shares many of the signs and symptoms associated with other psychiatric illnesses such as anxiety disorders and schizophrenia. It is important to keep in mind that a common misperception is that bipolar mood changes are usually quick and drastic. In reality, mood shifts are often quite gradual. An episode—whether depressive or manic—can last for weeks, months, or even years. People with bipolar disorder are not always depressed or manic; they can go for long stretches of time in a normal, balanced mood. The typical person with bipolar disorder has an average of four episodes during the first 10 years of the illness (Keck et al., 2004).

A complete medical history and physical exam should be conducted to rule out other physical conditions. A complete psychiatric history should consider the possibility of other mental disorders. Furthermore, bipolar disorder is characterized by mood swings that tend to cycle. In reviewing a patient's history, previous mood swings (perhaps of less severity or duration) may come to light. A family history of medical and psychiatric concerns should be taken because current research indicates a strong genetic component. Finally, a thorough evaluation of current symptoms should be examined.

WEB SITES

Case history and assessment of a woman suffering from depression. http://www.healthcme .com/dep1/sec1.shtml.

International Foundation for Research and Education on Depression. Provides an overview of depressive disorder and treatment resources http://www.depression.org.

Internet Mental Health, Disorders Page. Provides information on all mood disorders, including overview and treatment issues; contains a link to the surgeon general's Report on Depression in Adolescents and Children. http://www.mentalhealth.com/fr20.html.

Mental Help.net. Contains a variety of information on depression and mania resources, books, and scales. http://www.mentalhelp.net.

References

American Psychiatric Association. (2002). *Diagnostic and Statistical Manual of Mental Disorders,* 4th ed., text revision. Washington, DC: APA.

Barlow, D. H., & Durand, V. M. (2004). *Abnormal psychology: An integrative approach,* 4th ed. Washington, DC: Thomson.

Bauer, M. S., Crits-Cristoph, P., & Ball, W. A. (1991). Independent assessment of manic and depressive symptoms by self-rating. *Archives of General Psychiatry, 48,* 807–812.

Evans, D. L. (2000). Bipolar disorder: Diagnostic challenges and treatment considerations. *Journal of Clinical Psychiatry, 61,* 26–31.

Keck, P. E., Perlis, R. H., Otto, M. W., Carpenter, D., Ross, R., & Docherty, J. P. (2004). *The expert consensus guideline series: Treatment of bipolar disorder 2004. A postgraduate medicine special report.* New York: McGraw-Hill.

Kessler, R. C., Chiu, W. T., Demler, O., & Walters, E. E. (2005). Prevalence, severity, and comorbidity of twelve-month DSM-IV disorders in the National Comorbidity Survey Replication (NCS-R). *Archives of General Psychiatry, 62*(6), 617–627.

Malgady, R. G., & Zayas, L. H. (2001). Cultural and linguistic considerations in psychodiagnosis with Hispanics: The need for an empirically informed process model. *Social Work, 46,* 39–49.

Shugar, G., Schertzer, S., Toner, B. B., & di Gasbarro, J. (1992). Development, use, and factor analysis of a self-report inventory for mania. *Comparative Psychiatry, 33,* 325–331.

Young, R., Biggs, J., & Myers, D. (1978). A rating scale for mania: Reliability, validity and sensitivity. *British Journal of Psychiatry, 133,* 429–435.

Developing Client-Focused Measures

Cathy King Pike

Social workers use client-focused measures to assess the extent of clients' problems, follow their progress over the course of an intervention, and determine when an intervention can be terminated. These measures include a variety of techniques that are developed specifically for a given client and are an inexpensive method of monitoring client progress. Because these measures are based on a client's presenting problems, they sometimes more accurately reflect that client's situation than some standardized measures. A distinct advantage of client-focused measures is that they can be developed using the client's own words and experiences related to presenting problems. A weakness of such measures is that reliability and validity cannot be tested and established. Because of this, the strength of any client-focused measurement depends on the social worker's skill in developing, applying, and using these measures.

This chapter describes how to develop client-focused measures for an example client with generalized anxiety disorder and depression and for her son, who is showing early signs of childhood anxiety. The measures that will be used with the adult client include a client log, client-monitored observation, individualized rating scales, and goal-attainment scales. The measures for the son include behavioral observation, grade reports from school, and an individualized rating scale. Both of these clients' situations are described, followed by the social worker's development of the measures, a discussion of issues related to measurement, and additional tips, plus resources where further information can be obtained.

MS. DAVIDSON AND TREVOR

Ms. Lucinda Davidson is a 29-year-old female who divorced her husband about 8 months ago. The Davidsons have a son, Trevor, who is 7 years old. Ms. Davidson contacted the area mental health agency shortly after she changed jobs at an industrial plant and moved from a clerical assistant to an administrative assistant position. She reported to Jessie, her social worker, that she has been unable to control worrying over a number of things: finances, her child's health and well-being in school, her new job, and household duties. She stated that she is irritable, has difficulty concentrating at work, is unable to participate in social activities, is depressed, and lies awake in bed for long periods at night. Ms. Davidson reported that she has always been a "worrier" and believes her worrying became worse at about the age of 18. She said that her current, constant worry over a number of things became intense after changing jobs. She reported, however, that she is doing well in her new position and likes the additional responsibility. She said that her depression began during her marital separation but has not intensified since then.

In addition, Ms. Davidson mentioned that her son has been having problems related to his performance in school. She stated that he worries a great deal before he is required to take tests and has even experienced nausea and vomiting associated with his anxiety. Ms. Davidson reported that Trevor is very shy and finds interacting with his peers difficult. Because of this, he has no close friends. She fears that Trevor may be experiencing early signs of the sorts of things that have plagued her since the age of 18 and said she wants to try to intervene early with these problems.

Jessie met with Trevor individually to obtain an initial assessment. He readily agreed that he has a "really hard time" with tests and always fears that he will fail, even if he knows "how to do what will be on the test." He also says he would like to be able to talk with people at school more easily and make friends "like all the other kids," but he is afraid to talk with his classmates.

Ms. Davidson and her son will see the staff psychiatrist for medication evaluation, although it is unlikely that Trevor will need pharmacotherapy at this point (Klein, Koplewicz, & Kanner, 1992). Jessie explained and discussed with Ms. Davidson the use of cognitive-behavioral therapy (CBT) as an intervention for her worrying episodes and depression, as well as relaxation and breathing techniques. In fact, Jessie suggested that these same interventions could be used with Trevor. Jessie reported that the primary difference would be that she would need to focus the interventions at Trevor's cognitive developmental level. After meeting with Ms. Davidson and obtaining her agreement, Jessie met with Trevor and Ms. Davidson together. She explained to Trevor that sometimes we hold worries in our minds that make everything we try to do seem more difficult. She explained to Trevor that she wanted to work with him to identify and change the worries that make things difficult to good thoughts about things that currently are a bother to him. Jessie also assured Trevor that she thought she could teach him some "really cool" ways to relax and breathe that would help him when he has to take a test or talk with someone who could become a good friend. Both Ms. Davidson and Trevor agreed to try cognitive-behavioral treatment and relaxation and breathing techniques in conjunction with any medical intervention that may be needed.

Once the interventions were identified and consent was obtained from both clients, the next task was to develop goals and determine what would constitute success in meeting them. Jessie, Ms. Davidson, and Trevor agreed on three goals apiece. These are listed here. By the end of the interventions, Ms. Davidson will:

1. Learn to identify when and about what she worries most frequently and to what extent, be skilled in changing negative thoughts to positive thoughts, and attain a level of comfort for her, as measured through her log and rating scales.
2. Resolve her depression through the use of CBT, as measured by her client log for depression, and through periodic tracking of her secondary symptoms.
3. Increase the social activities for Trevor and herself to at least three per week, with at least one activity they can do together and at least one activity reserved for each to do alone or with peers. Social activities will be measured through client-monitored observation.

By the end of the interventions, Trevor will:

1. Learn skills in and demonstrate management of his test anxiety, as measured by a rating scale and having all grades at least in the passing range.
2. Develop skills in initiating conversations with peers and will participate in at least three conversations per school day with his peers, as measured through behavioral observations.
3. Report at least one session of play with one or more peers per week as part of his social activities.

CLIENT LOGS

First, Jessie needs to learn more detail about Ms. Davidson's worrying episodes to complete her assessment. To accomplish this, Jessie has decided to begin measurement with a client log. Client logs are especially helpful in identifying the circumstances, frequency, and duration of problems. They provide a more detailed picture of the contexts of presenting problems than many clients are able to state verbally during an assessment. In addition, these logs are relatively easy for workers to develop and for clients to complete. Bloom, Fischer, and Orme (2006) presented four different types of client logs: exploratory, interaction, target problem, and evaluation. Exploratory logs help social workers and their clients better understand the nature of presenting problems. Interaction logs are used to identify patterns of communication and interactions between clients and other important people in their lives. Target problem logs are used to identify the antecedents or controlling issues that cause or worsen clients' problems. Evaluation logs contain some type of measurement—for example, behavioral counts or rating scales—to monitor client progress.

Jessie will use a target problem log to identify when Ms. Davidson worries, under what circumstances, and which of her worries seem most frequent and intense. In addition, Jessie will include an evaluation component as part of this target log. To develop the target problem log, Jessie will create a simple form that Ms. Davidson can use to track her worrying episodes. The form will have headings for the type of worry, any event or thought that may have preceded the worry, any thoughts

Ms. Davidson has after she begins worrying, and a rating of the intensity of the worry. Ms. Davidson will keep the log and bring it to her session each week. Examples of the headings for this client's log are:

- worry type;
- event/thought before;
- thoughts after; and
- worry rating.

INDIVIDUALIZED RATING SCALES

Jessie left the last column of the client log for use with an individualized rating scale (IRS) that Ms. Davidson and she will develop to measure the intensity of worry. This will help the client and social worker know how often Ms. Davidson has certain worries and which of these worries seem to be more bothersome to her.

An IRS is a single-item scale that social workers and clients develop together to measure the intensity, frequency, or duration of a specific problem. In this case, Ms. Davidson and Jessie are going to measure the intensity of the worrying episodes. The single-item scale measures only one problem (or construct) along a continuum from low or none to extremely high intensity, frequency, or duration. After identifying the problem and type of scale that they will use, Jessie and Ms. Davidson need to decide on the number of measurement categories used in the scale and the statements used to anchor each number or numbers at equal intervals. These anchors will help Ms. Davidson remember exactly what the numbers on the scale mean and will reduce errors in measurement. In this case, they decided to use a 9-point scale that ranged from 0 to 8. They have anchored every other number with a statement. Each anchored statement should move along equidistant intervals from the previous statement. The unanchored intervals represent a point midway between two anchored statements. Table 48.1 provides an example of the IRS that Ms. Davidson and Jessie developed.

In addition to the client log and IRS for worry, Jessie will develop a client log for Ms. Davidson's depression. When Ms. Davidson feels depressed, she will note events or thoughts preceding her depressed feelings, record her thoughts in response to the depression, and rate her level (intensity) of depression on a second IRS developed for that purpose. As the CBT interventions proceed, Jessie

TABLE 48.1 Level (Intensity) of Worry

8 = Extreme worry with very strong shakiness and feelings of panic, inability to concentrate on work or home duties

7

6 = Worry that intrudes on ability to concentrate, strong amount of nervousness and shakiness, takes at least an hour to resolve

5

4 = Moderate worry, moderate amount of nervousness, and some shakiness lasting no more than 30 minutes

3

2 = Some worry, but it is easily handled and no physical symptoms are present

1

0 = No worry at all

will add another column to each client log. This column will include positive thoughts that Ms. Davidson makes in response to negative cognitions for worry and depression.

Jessie has decided to develop an individualized rating scale for Trevor that will measure his level of anxiety about tests and other graded work in school. To do this, she uses both symbols and words to describe the different levels of anxiety on the chart. Trevor will identify facial expressions that range from no anxiety to extreme anxiety on a scale of 0 to 4 that are anchored with a word or brief expression that he uses as he describes each of these facial expressions. For each day of school, Trevor will carry a sheet of paper that contains ten or more of the rating scales. Each time he has to complete a graded activity, he will fill out the scale with regard to how anxious he feels about the assignment and identify the type and subject of the assignment. Having him complete the scales will help Jessie identify whether there are differences in Trevor's anxiety by type of assignment or subject matter. At each session, Jessie will obtain a total for each day of the previous week and chart these for Trevor to see.

CLIENT-MONITORED OBSERVATION

Jessie decided that a simple type of measurement for Ms. Davidson to complete to measure progress in participation in social events is to have her keep a frequency count of how many social events she and Trevor attend in a week. Social events were collaboratively defined to include any social activity not associated with work hours, including church and any outings in which Ms. Davidson and her son engaged during the week. Each week, both Ms. Davidson and Trevor will complete at least one social activity together and at least one activity separately, either alone or with their respective peers. Ms. Davidson will place the number of social events in which she and Trevor engaged on a line at the bottom of her client log for depression.

GOAL-ATTAINMENT SCALES

A final type of measurement that Jessie will use with Ms. Davidson is a goal-attainment scale (GAS). Jessie decided that she would use this type of scale to measure some of the client's symptoms that were secondary to the primary diagnoses of generalized anxiety disorder and depression. Ms. Davidson had reported that she is irritable, has difficulty concentrating at work, and lies awake in bed at night for long periods of time. Although Jessie wants to know how Ms. Davidson is progressing in these secondary areas, she does not want to burden her client with too many measurement tasks. Because a GAS is used only two to three times during interventions, they are good alternatives for measuring secondary symptoms. In addition, Jessie will keep these scales in the client record to prevent them from forgetting to complete the scales at appropriate intervals.

Goal-attainment scales measure progress at the beginning of the intervention, after several sessions, and either close to or at the end of interventions. Jessie will use three of these scales to assess Ms. Davidson's progress on her secondary symptoms. The scales will measure the client's level of irritation, inability to concentrate at work, and difficulty sleeping. Jessie phrases two of the three symptoms in positive directions. Instead of measuring inability to concentrate and difficulty sleeping, she will measure Ms. Davidson's ability to concentrate and sleep. First, Jessie will need to determine the levels or intensity of each of the symptoms at the beginning of the intervention. Second, Jessie and Ms. Davidson will decide what would constitute some improvement and extensive improvement in each of these areas. Likewise, they will also decide what would constitute some deterioration and extensive deterioration in

each of the three areas. Each of these levels will have a number that ranges from −2 to +2. Third, Jessie and Ms. Davidson will discuss the relative importance of each of the three areas for Ms. Davidson's quality of life. They can do this simply by deciding the level of importance (out of 100 percent) of each of the areas for quality of life. Finally, Jessie will set up a table that describes each scale, contains explanations for each level and the numbered categories, and includes the weight of each scale. To determine Ms. Davidson's level on each scale at different intervals, Jessie will multiply the weight of the scale by the number at that level to obtain a score. Note that at the beginning of the intervention, Ms. Davidson will score a 0 on the three scales because the category for the beginning of the intervention is scored a 0. Table 48.2 provides an example of the GAS used in this case.

BEHAVIORAL OBSERVATION AND GRADE REPORTS

Jessie contacted Trevor's teacher, Mr. Aldridge, and discussed Trevor's progress in school. Although Trevor seems to understand content in class when it is presented, his teacher said that his grades do not reflect his level of knowledge. Because of this, his actual grades are below what his teacher would estimate as his level of academic performance in most areas. In addition, Trevor rarely interacts with the other children in his class, a fact that concerns Mr. Aldridge a great deal. Jessie advised the teacher of her interventions with Trevor and stated that she needs some measures of his academic performance and level of interactions with other children during school. Jessie explained that she would very much appreciate receiving three measures related to Trevor's school performance: (1) a percentage of work completed for homework and other assignments, (2) a report of Trevor's grades for each week in all areas, and (3) a report of the number of times that Trevor interacts with his peers during lunch and recess. Mr. Aldridge agreed to provide these data on a form that Jessie will develop and send to him. His teaching assistant will help by using behavioral observation to document the number of times Trevor engages in conversation with other children at lunch and during recess. They agreed that engagement in conversation would be defined as each time Trevor began or engaged in a verbal interaction.

TABLE 48.2 Goal Attainment Scales for Irritability, Concentration, and Sleep

Levels of Goal Achievement	Irritation Weight: .15	Work Concentration Weight: .45	Sleep Weight: .40
Very high level of improvement since the start of services			
Some improvement since the start of services			
Level at the start of services			
Somewhat worse than at the start of services			
A great deal worse than at the start of services			
+2 = Rarely feel irritated			
+1 = Feel irritated and out of sorts about 25% of the time			
0 = Feel irritated and out of sorts about 50% of the time			
−1 = Feel irritated and out of sorts about 75% of the time			
−2 = Feel irritated and out of sorts almost always			
+2 = Can concentrate at work almost always when needed			
+1 = Can concentrate about 75% of the time at work when needed			
0 = Can concentrate about 50% of the time at work when needed			
−1 = Can concentrate about 25% of the time at work when needed			
0 = Almost always unable to concentrate at work when needed			
+2 = Sleeping on average more than 6 hours per night			
+1 = Sleeping on average about 5–6 hours per night			
0 = Sleeping on average about 4 hours per night			
−1 = Sleeping on average about 2–3 hours per night			
−2 = Sleeping on average less than 2 hours per night			

For now, the length of the interaction will not be documented, only the frequency of the occurrence of the behavior.

DISCUSSION

The measures presented herein are examples of ways that Jessie can measure her clients' progress. However, there are a variety of other methods she could have used to measure progress. For instance, rather than measuring the intensity of worry and depression, she simply could have had Ms. Davidson count the number of times she worried each day and the length of time each day that she felt depressed. The advantage of measuring the intensity of worry is that Jessie could identify how often the client was worried about the issues she mentioned in the assessment and

which of these seemed to bother her more than others. Measuring the intensity of depression also would help Jessie monitor progress in lessening and remedying Ms. Davidson's depression. Another alternative for measuring worrying episodes and depression would have been to develop a GAS for these problems. However, because GASs are used infrequently during interventions, they are less useful to social workers and their clients in tracking ongoing progress toward resolving problems. Another strategy Jessie might have used was to develop an IRS to measure Ms. Davidson's level of enjoyment of social outings. This one-item scale could have been developed to range from no enjoyment at all to extreme enjoyment. Finally, Jessie could have combined CBT and monitoring by having Ms. Davidson count the number of times each day in which she recognized worrying episodes as irrational. There are also a number of other ways that Trevor's test anxiety and lack of interactions with peers could have measured.

At the end of the interventions with Ms. Davidson and Trevor, Jessie will not be able to say for certain that the CBT *caused* Ms. Davidson's or Trevor's improvements. There are two reasons for this. First, Jessie will only be able to see that Ms. Davidson and Trevor have improved beyond where they were at the beginning of the interventions. For ethical reasons, she will not withdraw treatment to determine whether the symptoms return to beginning levels, and this is a requirement of determining causation. Second, the inclusion of any medications would be a confounding factor in determining how well the CBT itself worked for Ms. Davidson. Jessie can monitor the extent that Ms. Davidson improves over the entire course of treatment. Throughout and at the end of the interventions, she can evaluate the extent of improvement for Ms. Davidson since the time of assessment for the combination of CBT and medications. In Ms. Davidson's case, Jessie cannot say which of these treatments resulted in comparatively more improvement. In addition, she cannot claim that the interventions for Trevor *caused* changes in his presenting problems, or which of the interventions that she used affected which of the presenting problems. Although Jessie cannot determine exactly which of the treatments Ms. Davidson and Trevor received was more effective, she can clearly demonstrate improvement through the use of client-focused measures. Because of the ability to measure and document client progress, client-focused measures are powerful tools for treatment evaluation and accountability.

A number of sources provide detailed discussions on measurement in chapters on single-system designs or as complete texts about how to develop client focused measures (Bloom, Fischer, & Orme, 2006; Pike & Meschi, 2004; Rubin & Babbie, 2007; Tripodi, 1994). Some additional tips in developing effective client-focused measurements are listed next.

1. Use more than one measurement for monitoring client progress across major presenting problems. Two or more measures of the same or similar problems may go together visually on a graph as expected, and this provides some evidence of the accuracy of the measures.
2. Use more than one type of client-focused measurement to monitor client progress. These can include a variety of measures—for example, the use of frequency counts and a rating scale.
3. Measures that are as direct as possible tend to be more accurate than indirect measures, which use signs or related behaviors to measure problems. Examples of direct measures are observations of specific behaviors and the use of client logs for particular problems. An example of an indirect measure is a scale of general contentment used to measure job-related anxieties. Although general contentment is related inversely to anxiety, these represent different subjective states and do not provide a clear picture of the problem itself.
4. Clients tend to use more frequently those measures that are easy for them to use and seem relevant to their presenting problems.
5. Client-focused measures are more accurate when the social worker and client state how they will measure and clearly define what is to be measured.
6. Measurement of client progress should be viewed and presented by the social worker as a collaborative effort by both the social worker and the client.
7. Charts are important visual aids in monitoring client progress. These allow clients to see their progress and tend to motivate them to continue work on the problems and measurement tasks. Charts and graphs can be developed using computer programs—e.g., a spreadsheet—or by hand with graph paper.

When a client's behaviors are negative in nature, it is sometimes helpful to have him or her track the positive side of behaviors. Monitoring positive behaviors sometimes increases the occurrence of desirable or positive behaviors.

WEB SITES

Direct Behavioral Observation in School Settings: Bringing Science to Practice (*Cognitive and Behavioral Practice*, 12 [2005], 359–370). This in-depth article reviews the use of behavioral observations in school settings, including information on procedures and providing practical advice for readers. http://www.wjh.harvard.edu/~nock/nocklab/Nock_Kurtz_2005.pdf.

Effects of Cognitive-Behavioral Anxiety Intervention on the School Performance of Students with Emotional or Behavioral Disorders: A Pilot Study. The author conducted a pilot study of the effectiveness of CBT with children with emotional or behavioral disorders. Especially helpful are the details provided with regard to behavioral observation procedures. http://www.waystone.org/proposal/index_assets/product4.pdf.

Individualized Rating Scales. This Web site contains several examples of IRSs that social workers can use with children in schools to assess emotional states and coping. http://askaspecialist.ca.gov/articles/Individualized%20Rating%20Scales.pdf.

Introduction to Single Subject Designs. Information for designing simple single-system designs. Very helpful for those are beginning to learn and use these types of designs for monitoring client progress. http://www.msu.edu/user/sw/ssd/issd01.htm.

A Meta-Analysis of School-Based Social Skills Intervention for Children with Autism Spectrum Disorders (*Remedial and Special Education*, 28(3) [2007], 153–162). This paper provides a meta-analysis (or systematic review) of the results of a number of single system designs for children with autism receiving interventions to improve social skills.

http://www.education.uiowa.edu/reach/documents/AutismandSocialSkills_000.pdf.

Acknowledgment

The author thanks Ms. Margaret Jessie Wilson, an MSW practitioner who works and resides in North Carolina, for her assistance in developing the hypothetical client used in this chapter and her good-natured agreement for the use of her name as the social worker.

References

Bloom, M., Fischer, J., & Orme, J. G. (2006). *Evaluating practice: Guidelines for the accountable professional*, 5th ed. Boston: Allyn & Bacon.

Klein, R. G., Koplewicz, H. S., & Kanner, A. (1992). Imipramine treatment of children with separation anxiety disorder. *Journal of the American Academy of Child and Adolescent Psychiatry*, 31, 21–28.

Pike, C. K., & Meschi, W. A. (2004). The case of Trent revisited: A single-subject research design. In R. F. Rivas & G. H. Hull Jr. (Eds.), *Case studies in generalist practice*, 3rd ed. (pp. 8–13). Belmont, CA: Wadsworth.

Rubin, A., & Babbie, E. (2007). *Research methods for social work*, 5th ed. Belmont, CA: Wadsworth.

Tripodi, T. (1994). *A primer on single-system design for clinical social workers*. Washington, DC: National Association of Social Workers Press.

49 Brief Screening Instruments

Steven L. McMurtry, Susan J. Rose,
& Ron A. Cisler

A child welfare worker provides in-home services to families in which allegations of abuse or neglect were substantiated but risk levels were not great enough to warrant any children's removal for placement in out-of-home care. The worker's job is to assess the needs of the parents or adult caregivers in the home and provide services or make referrals. The problem is that in-home services last only about 3 months, so assessment must be done quickly to allow maximum time for service provision. Also, the social worker's agency is under court supervision following a class action lawsuit, so the worker must show that all assessments are carried out in the most valid way possible. Finally, the range of potential problems affecting caregivers is large, so the worker must be able to screen across areas that range from general mental health to substance use to domestic violence to food insecurity.

A program evaluator in a community mental health center seeks to determine the effectiveness of the center's outpatient services. These consist mostly of case management and short-term individual and group counseling for clients with concerns such as depression, alcohol and drug use, emotional and behavioral problems, and others. Services are typically short-term, lasting from 10 to 90 days. The evaluator has been asked to compare clients' level of functioning on their primary presenting problem before and after intervention. However, as with the previous example, not all subjects have problems in all areas, and each assessment must be valid but brief to prevent the overall measurement package from becoming unmanageably lengthy.

These examples illustrate a dilemma facing many social workers in direct services and service support roles: how to measure client problems and progress accurately but briefly. Similar to practitioners in disciplines such as psychology and psychiatry, social workers increasingly rely on standardized scales. These are measures composed of items and response options that are usually the same for all subjects and are scored in a specific way. The term *standardized* also implies that the measure meets certain psychometric standards and has been tested on enough subjects to provide a basis for evaluating each individual's score.

Standardized scales include broad-spectrum diagnostic tools such as the Minnesota Multiphasic Personality Inventory. It and other early examples tended to be lengthy (100 items or more) and time-intensive (1 hour or longer to administer). Beginning about 1980, more attention was directed toward developing brief measures, called *rapid assessment instruments* (RAIs) (Fischer & Corcoran, 2007). RAIs usually have fewer than 100 items and can be administered in 15 minutes or less. These briefer measures were a better fit with the time available to social workers conducting client assessments, and RAIs such as those in Hudson's (1982) clinical measurement package became widely known. Still, the measurement task facing many social workers is neither diagnosis nor assessment but screening, which involves rapidly scanning many potential problems and identifying those that require further services. For this, the type of measure needed is what we refer to as a *very brief screener* or VBS.

CHARACTERISTICS OF VERY BRIEF SCREENERS

VBSs are defined here as measures of known psychometric accuracy that can indicate the potential presence of clinically meaningful problems in most subjects in 2 minutes or less. Measures containing 200 items or more have sometimes been called screeners, but we consider brevity to be the signal aspect of a VBS. In practice, this means a maximum of about 12 items.

Other characteristics of VBSs are that they are "first warning" rather than full diagnostic instruments, and their use assumes that further testing will occur before a more definitive decision on the presence or absence of a problem can be made. VBSs may take several forms, including that of self-administered questionnaires, interviews by clinicians or others, and observer rating checklists. To make them acceptable to non–help-seeking respondents, VBS items tend to be worded neutrally, and they have been used for purposes as diverse as service referral, needs assessment, epidemiological studies, and measurement of key variables in surveys. Constructs measured by VBSs include both psychological states (e.g., mood, anxiety) and behaviors (substance use, eating disorders). VBSs reviewed here do not include mechanical or other biometric measures, such as blood pressure or body chemistry. Also, due to the volume of instruments available, we restrict the discussion to measures of adult functioning.

CHOOSING A SCREENER

The most important attribute of any assessment tool is its reliability and validity, and the best measures are those for which published results from empirical tests of these qualities are available. Of particular importance are findings regarding known groups techniques that demonstrate each instrument's screening accuracy. The two complementary aspects of this are sensitivity and specificity. *Sensitivity* refers to the ability to assign a positive reading to all those who have the problem (i.e., minimizing false negatives). *Specificity* is a measure's ability to assign a positive reading only to those who have the problem (i.e., minimizing false positives). In a good screener, both sensitivity and specificity are high, but one value can come at the expense of the other. The potential user of the measure must also consider the consequences of misidentification. The presence of false positives risks falsely stigmatizing some individuals, providing services to those who do not need them, and making the intervention appear less useful due to the absence of improve-

ment among false positives. The presence of false negatives means that clients who need help will go unserved; if the problem is serious, this can have dire ramifications for both the clients and others.

A technique called receiver operating characteristics (ROC) curve analysis is often used to assess a measure's ability to find a balance between sensitivity and specificity. Results from the technique are usually reported as area under the curve (AUC). This ranges from 0 to 1 and reflects the ability of the measure to correctly classify respondents as having or not having the attribute in question (e.g., depression, alcohol dependence). Measures in which the AUC is large are those that accurately classify most cases, and AUC values of 0.80 or higher are typically seen as evidence of good measurement performance.

Another factor affecting screening accuracy is the prevalence of a problem in a population. When the target problem affects a relatively small proportion of individuals, even screeners with good specificity can produce unacceptably high ratios of false positives to true positives. For example, suppose 1,000 people are screened for a problem that affects only 2 percent of them, and the screener being used has a specificity of 95 percent. Twenty people (2 percent) can be expected to have the problem, and the measure will correctly identify 19 of those 20 (95 percent). On the other hand, 980 people will not have the problem, but the screener, with an inaccuracy rate of 5 percent, will incorrectly identify 49 of these 980 people as having the problem. The performance of a screener in this regard is usually reported as its *positive predictive value* (PPV), which is obtained by dividing the number of true positives by the combined number of true and false positives. In the example, this would be 19/(19 + 49) = 0.279. Multiplying this result by 100 yields a figure of 27.9 percent, which is the fraction of all cases identified as positives that truly are positives. A related statistic called the negative predictive value (NPV) helps evaluate performance relative to sensitivity. It is computed by substituting true and false negatives for true and false positives in the equation.

SELECTED VERY BRIEF SCREENERS

In this section, we identify VBSs that assess client functioning in six major areas within which social workers may need to screen for client problems—mood, anxiety, eating behaviors, alcohol use, drug use, and general mental health. Our focus is on identifying brief screeners of potential value to both practitioners and those in such roles as evaluation and research. Most of this information is presented in tables that show the name, number of items, and source reference for each measure. If multiple screeners are available in a given category, they are listed within each table based on the frequency of citations of the measure's source article. We tested all measures shown by administering them to at least three undergraduate students, and only those which had an average completion time of 2 minutes or less were included. It is important to note that some brief measures that enjoy considerable popularity in the field are not shown in the tables. This is probably because they did not meet the 2-minute criterion for inclusion, even though their administration times are relatively short.

In the fourth column of each table, a summary of empirical findings regarding the screening accuracy of each measure is provided. This focuses particularly on sensitivity and specificity, plus AUC, PPV, and NPV where available. For the sake of brevity, evidence related to reliability and other types of validity is not reported, except where this is the only type of evidence available and the measure is the only VBS in that category. Prospective users of any measure should always consult its source reference(s) and familiarize themselves with results on all aspects of its validity and reliability before deciding to use it.

The final column in each table provides information such as whether the measure is copyrighted (with those that are not being identified as public domain), whether its items were drawn from other instruments, and general notes about its intended or most appropriate use. It also notes if versions are available in multiple languages.

Table 49.1 identifies VBSs for screening problems related to mood. Among the most common of such problems is depression. Two options for this are the 2- and 9-item versions of the Patient Health Questionnaire (PHQ), which is the self-administered form of the PRIME-MD, an interview measure created for primary care physicians. Both the PHQ-2 and PHQ-9 have good sensitivity and, in particular, good specificity; the PHQ-2 is exceptionally brief. Less well used but able to screen not just for depressed mood but the presence of a depressive disorder is the MOS-8.

As with both versions of the PHQ versions, it has the benefit of being in the public domain. Also shown in Table 49.1 is the Edinburgh Postnatal Depression Scale, which, as its name suggests, seeks to detect postnatal depression. It is sufficiently brief to qualify as a VBS, has good measurement accuracy, and has been widely used in both practice and research. It also has been translated and tested in several languages other than English. Finally, an additional aspect of mood that is often of interest is hopelessness. Though distinct from depression, it may be an additional symptom in cases of major depressive disorder, and findings suggest it can be a marker of suicide risk. One hopelessness measure, the State Hope Scale, qualifies as a VBS. Although patterns of citations suggest it has been used mostly for research, the scale appears to have sufficient measurement accuracy to support other applications.

VBSs shown in Table 49.2 address anxiety-related problems, such as panic, dissociation, and post-traumatic stress. With respect to panic, the Autonomic Nervous System questionnaire was developed to screen patients in primary care settings, where panic symptoms can complicate medical procedures. The Brief Panic Disorder Screen is more oriented toward distinguishing panic from generalized anxiety in outpatients. Both show good sensitivity, which is useful when a low rate of false negatives is needed. A less common but equally serious anxiety-related problem is dissociation, and one available screener is the DES-T, a short version of the Dissociative Experiences Scale. Given the rarity of dissociative disorders, its ability to produce a PPV of 87 percent in a large general population sample is an indication of unusually strong measurement accuracy. Finally, measures of post-traumatic stress are being increasingly used to screen such groups as survivors of individual and large-scale trauma. The Primary Care PTSD Screen has good measurement accuracy (PPV >50 percent) and uses a simple "yes or no" format. Another option, the SPAN, is a shortened version of the well-used Davidson Trauma Scale. It also shows a high PPV, though this was derived from a sample of trauma survivors where base prevalence rates are likely to be high.

Four VBSs designed to screen for the presence of eating disorders are shown in Table 49.3. The most widely cited is the SCOFF questionnaire, named from words in its items such as whether respondents eat until they feel sick. Though developed in Britain, and containing British terms

TABLE 49.1 Mood-Related Problems

Category/Name	Items	Key Reference(s)	Measurement Accuracy	Comments
General depression				
Patient Health Questionnaire (PHQ-9 and PHQ-2)	9	Kroenke, K., Spitzer, R. L., & Williams, J. B. W. (2001). The PHQ-9: Validity of a brief depression severity measure. *Journal of General Internal Medicine, 16,* 606–613. Kroenke, K., Spitzer, R. L., & Williams, J. B. W. (2003). The Patient Health Questionnaire-2: Validity of a two-item depression screener. *Medical Care, 41,* 1284–1292.	Validated on 6000 patients in primary care and obstetric-gynecology clinics. Using a cut-off score of 5, sensitivity for the PHQ-9, was 88% and specificity was 88% against the 20-item General Health Survey. Using a cut-off score of 3 for the PHQ-2, sensitivity was 83% and specificity was 92% against the GHS-20.	Public domain. The PHQ-9 is the depression module of the PRIME-MD, widely used to screen for common mental disorders. The PHQ-2 reduces the length of the measure even further by using only the two necessary *DSM-IV* criteria for depression—the frequency of depressed mood and anhedonia.
MOS 8-item Depression Screener	8	Burnam, M. A., Wells, K. B., Leake, B., & Landsverk, J. (1988). Development of a brief screening instrument for detecting depressive disorders. *Medical Care, 26,* 775–789.	In a sample of 457 medical outpatients, sensitivity ranged from 88% to 100%, specificity ranged from 72% to 77% in relation to clinician judgments. Results indicate a PPV of 11% to 23% and an NPV of 98% to 100%.	Public domain. Developed for use in the National Study of Medical Care Outcomes (MOS). The MOS-8 produces a suggested diagnosis of either major depressive disorder or dysthymia.
Postnatal depression				
Edinburgh Postnatal Depression Scale (EPDS)	10	Cox, J. L., Holden, J. M., & Sagovsky, R. (1987). Detection of postnatal depression: Development of the 10-item Edinburgh Postnatal Depression Scale. *British Journal of Psychiatry, 150,* 782–786.	Tested on 84 women who gave birth in the previous 3 months. Using a cut-off score of 12/13, sensitivity is reported as 86%, and specificity as 78%, with a PPV of 73% when tested against the research diagnostic criteria of major and minor depression. Correlates well with the CPRS-Depression, the SADS, and the *ICD-10* and *DSM-IV*.	Though the EPDS can be used to detect depression in postnatal women, some studies suggest it detects symptoms of anxiety or general distress as well. In other validation studies with prenatal women in non-English-speaking countries, estimates of sensitivity are reported to vary from 65% to 100%, and specificity from 49% to 100%.
Hopelessness				
State Hope Scale	6	Snyder, C. R., Sympson, S. C., Ybasco, F. C., Borders, T. F., Babyak, M. A., et al. (1996). Development and validation of the State Hope Scale. *Journal of Personality and Social Psychology, 70,* 321–335.	Known-groups validity untested. Tested on 168 college students, and correlations of the 2 subscales with the Dispositional Hope Scale are 0.79 and 0.78; with the State Self-Esteem Scale, 0.68 and 0.75, and with the State form of the Positive Affect Scale, 0.65 and 0.55.	Measures temporary hope as opposed to most scales that measure hope as a static trait or disposition. Despite its wide use, no results are available for more diverse populations in age, ethnicity, and socioeconomic status.

TABLE 49.2 Anxiety-Related Problems

Category/Name	Items	Key Reference(s)	Measurement Accuracy	Comments
Panic				
Autonomic Nervous System questionnaire (ANS)	2	Stein, M. B., Roy-Byrne, P. P., McQuaid, J. R., Laffaye, C., Russon, J., McCahill, M. E., et al. (1999). Development of a brief diagnostic screen for panic disorder in primary care. *Psychosomatic Medicine, 61*, 359–364.	Results are from 1476 primary care outpatients in 3 primary care medical clinics. When tested against the Composite International Diagnostic Interview, sensitivity ranged from 94% to 100% and specificity ranged from 25% to 59% with a PPV of 18% to 40% and NPV of 94% to 100%.	Three- and five- item versions report only minimally improved specificity and reduced sensitivity. Responses from a subset of 511 patients were tested against the Beck Anxiety Inventory (using a cut-off of 20), resulting in sensitivity of 67%.
Brief Panic Disorder Screen	4	Apfeldorf, W. J., Shear, M. K., Leon, A. C., & Portera, L. (1994). A brief screen for panic disorder. *Journal of Anxiety Disorders, 8,* 71–78.	Test results are from 143 outpatients. Using a cut-off of 8, sensitivity is reported as 93% and specificity reported as 50% against a diagnosis of primary anxiety on the Structured Clinical Interview for *DSM III-R.*	Distinguishes panic disorder from other more general anxiety disorders. Using a cut-off of 11, sensitivity reported as 78% and specificity as 73%. Internal consistency: α = 0.875.
Dissociation				
Dissociative Experiences Scale–T (DES–T)	8	Waller, N. G., & Ross, C. A. (1997). The prevalence and biometric structure of pathological dissociation in the general population: Taxometric and behavior genetic findings. *Journal of Abnormal Psychology, 106,* 499–510.	Results are from 1055 adults in the general population. Using a cut-off score of 30, sensitivity of 74% and specificity of 100% is reported against the full DES, with a PPV of 87% and NPV of 99%.	A further study of adolescent twins (140 MZ twin pairs and 74 DZ twin pairs) reported 45% of the variance was attributed to "shared environmental influences."

Post-traumatic stress

Primary Care PTSD screen (PC-PTSD)	4	Prins, A., Ouimette, P., & Kimerling, R. (2003). The primary care PTSD screen (PC-PTSD): Development and operating characteristics. *Primary Care Psychiatry, 9*, 9–14.	Tested on 188 male and female primary care patients recruited at VA clinics. Using a cut-off score of 2 yields sensitivity of 91% and specificity of 72% with a PPV of 51% and NPV of 96%.	This is the only PTSD measure that uses a "yes/no" response format. Using a cut-off of 3, for women sensitivity is reported as 70% and specificity 84%; for men, sensitivity is reported as 94% and specificity 92%.
SPAN	4	Melzer- Brody, S., Churchill, E., & Davidson, J. R. T. (1999). Derivation of the SPAN, a brief diagnostic screening test for post-traumatic stress disorder. *Psychiatry Research, 88*, 63–70.	Results are from 243 survivors of various forms of trauma (natural disaster, rape, and combat). Using a cut-off score of 5, sensitivity of 84% was reported, specificity of 91% with a PPV of 89% and a NPV of 91% against the Structured Interview for PTSD.	SPAN corresponds to PTSD diagnosis by structured clinical interview.

TABLE 49.3 Eating Disorders

Category/Name	Items	Key Reference(s)	Measurement Accuracy	Comments
SCOFF Questionnaire	5	Morgan, J. F., Reid, F., & Lacey, J. H. (1999). The SCOFF questionnaire: Assessment of a new screening tool for eating disorders. *British Medical Journal, 319,* 1467–1468. Parker, S. C., Lyons, J., & Bonner, J. (2005). Eating disorders in graduate students: Exploring the SCOFF questionnaire as a simple screening tool. *Journal of American College Health, 54,* 103–107.	Results are available from studies of 214 British subjects (clinical and nonclinical) and 233 subjects (nonclinical). At cut-off of 2 or more, sensitivity ranged from 94.7% to 100%, while specificity ranged from 64% to 93%, using scores form the Eating Disorder Inventory and BITE bulimia measure as criteria.	Public domain. Results from tests of an American version in which some British vernacular was replaced completed on 305 graduate students (see Parker et al.). These show a PPV of 66.7% and NPV of 88.7%.
Eating Disorder Screen for primary care (ESP)	5	Cotton, M. A., Ball, C., & Robinson, P. (2003). Four simple questions can help screen for eating disorders. *Journal of General Internal Medicine, 18,* 53–56.	Validated on 129 university students and 104 primary care patients in Britain. Comparing against results from the Questionnaire for Eating Disorder Diagnoses, sensitivity was 100% and specificity was 71%.	Public domain. A cut-off score of 2 questions answered "yes" is recommended, and sensitivity and specificity values are based on this cut-off.
Eating Disorder Examination–Screening version (EDE-S)	8	Beglin, S. J., & Fairburn, C. G. (1992). Evaluation of a new instrument for the detection of eating disorders in community samples. *Psychiatry Research, 44*(3), 191–201.	Using scores from the full EDE as a criterion, sensitivity for the EDE-S ranged from 0.90–0.94 and specificity ranged from 0.80 to 0.96 across samples. PPV for clinical eating disorder was 0.44, and for bulimia was 0.53.	The validation sample included women aged 16–35 from two community samples receiving care at two general practices in Britain. Cut-off scores used to determine measurement accuracy are not identified in the article.
Eating Disturbance Scale (EDS-5)	5	Rosenvinge, J. H., Perry, J. A., Bjorgum, L., Bergersen, T. D., Silvera, D. H., & Holte, A. (2001). A new instrument measuring disturbed eating patterns in community populations: Development and initial validation of a five-item scale (EDS-5). *European Eating Disorders Review, 9*(2), 123–132.	Tested on two large samples (n = 6313 and 835) of Norwegian teaching and nursing students. Sensitivity of 0.90 and specificity of 0.86 were found relative to a DSM-IV eating disorder diagnosis.	Public domain. A composite score of 16 (1 SD above the mean) is suggested as a clinical cutting score. As yet, no results are available from American samples.

unfamiliar to U.S. respondents, a version using American terms has been produced and tested. Both versions appear to have good accuracy even with nonclinical populations. A second screener, the ESP, was also developed in Britain, again for the purpose of screening primary care patients. Its recommended cut-off score of 2 allows it to minimize false negatives, but the relatively low specificity this produces risks generating high ratios of false positives. Another screener, the EDE-S, comprises eight items winnowed from a larger a set of self-administered questions created from the interview-based Eating Disorders Examination. The EDE-S does not screen for anorexia but has good measurement accuracy in screening for eating disorders in general and for bulimia in par-ticular. Unlike the other three screeners in Table 49.3, the short-form Eating Disturbance Scale (EDS-5) was developed for use with community samples rather than in primary care, but its validation sample included only students, and results are available only from Norwegian subjects. A positive aspect of the eating disorder screeners in Table 49.3 is that three of four (the SCOFF, ESP, and EDS-5) are in the public domain.

Table 49.4 displays six VBSs that screen for alcohol abuse; all are in the public domain. The CAGE is a long-standing and well-used screener for both use and dependence. Results are available from many studies, and these suggest it is highly accurate with some populations but not with others. Users should thus familiarize themselves with this literature before choosing the CAGE. Two alternatives are the AUDIT-C and FAST, which are both subsets of the Alcohol Use Disorders Identification Test (AUDIT). Results from tests of the FAST suggest it has better specificity than the AUDIT-C. However, the FAST is designed for a more specific population (emergency room patients) than the AUDIT-C (primary care patients), and avoiding false positives generally becomes more difficult with broader target populations. The Luebeck Alcohol Dependence and Abuse Screening Test includes items from the CAGE and the Michigan Alcoholism Screening Test. Results suggest it has the best overall accuracy of the four general alcohol abuse screeners shown, and it is widely used in Europe. However, findings from tests of its performance in North American samples are scarce. The final two measures listed, the TWEAK and T-ACE, are designed to detect alcohol use during pregnancy, and both

show reasonable accuracy. However, because both were tested on high-risk subjects, their level of specificity may be problematic in samples with low base prevalence rates.

Table 49.5 list three VBSs available to screen for the abuse of drugs other than alcohol. By far the most frequently cited in the research literature is the DAST-10, a short version of the Drug Abuse Screening Test. It and the RAFFT were designed to detect substance abuse in psychiatric patients, and both have good measurement accuracy when used for that purpose. The Rost Drug Dependence Screener is the only VBS intended for use in general population samples. Results from its initial validation tests suggest it can perform well in that role, but it has been cited infrequently. The final measure shown in Table 49.5 is a set of screening questions for detecting drinking and drug use by mother of young children. It includes alcohol screening questions from the MAST and drug screening questions from the DAST, and its sensitivity is good, but evidence is not available regarding its specificity.

Table 49.6 offers two versatile and often cited screeners for general mental health—the K6 and the MHI-5. These instruments are short, accurate, well validated, easily embedded in questionnaires, and available in the public domain. The K6 has also shown some capacity to screen for serious mental illness in general population samples. Two other measures in the table, the Psychosis Screening Questionnaire and the Cornell Psychiatric Screen, are specifically intended to detect serious mental illnesses, but both have been validated on (and are intended for use with) samples in which the presence of some form of psychiatric problem has already been noted. The final two measures screen, respectively, for borderline personality disorder and the presence of some form of personality disorder, and they, too, were designed for use with psychiatric patients rather than the general population.

The growing availability of VBSs has the potential to dramatically improve the quality of social work assessments. We believe that accurate, versatile, easy-to-use, and no-cost measures, such as the PHQ-2, CAGE, and K6, should become part of the basic measurement toolbox of all direct service professionals in the field. These instruments also have the potential to be similarly valuable in research and evaluation. A further rationale for their use is that they are becoming more common in other disciplines, and knowing

TABLE 49.4 Alcohol Abuse

Category/Name	Items	Key Reference(s)	Measurement Accuracy	Comments
General alcohol abuse				
CAGE	4	Mayfield, D., McLeod, G., & Hall, P. (1974). The CAGE questionnaire: Validation of a new alcoholism instrument. *American Journal of Psychiatry, 131,* 1121–1123. Cherpitel, C. J. (2002). Screening for alcohol problems in the U.S. general population: Comparison of the CAGE, RAPS4, and RAPS4-QF by gender, ethnicity, and service utilization. *Alcoholism: Clinical and Experimental Research, 26,* 1686–1691.	Tested on multiple samples. Sensitivity ranges from 43% to 94%; specificity shows similar ranges. An NIAAA summary says it "may fail to detect low but risky levels of drinking . . . [and] performs less well among women and minority populations."	Public domain. Versions are available in numerous languages. Due to its brevity, the CAGE has become widely used in settings such as primary medical care. Results also suggest it performs well with psychiatric populations.
Alcohol Use Disorders Identification Test (AUDIT-C)	3	Gordon, A. J., Maisto, S., McNeil, M., Kraemer, K. L., Conigliaro, R. L., Kelley, M. E., et al. (2001). Three questions can detect hazardous drinkers. *Journal of Family Practice, 50,* 313–320.	Original sample included 13,438 patients of primary-care physicians. Against a quantity/frequency criterion for problem drinking, the AUDIT-C had a specificity of 68.8%, sensitivity of 94.9%, and AUC of 0.949.	Public domain. Includes the first three questions of the AUDIT, which is one of the most-used measures of problem drinking. The third item of the AUDIT-C, called AUDIT-3, shows some promise as a single-item screener.
Luebeck Alcohol Dependence & Abuse Screening Test (LAST)	7	Rumpf, H.-J., Hapke, U., Hill, A., & John, U. (1997). Development of a screening questionnaire for the general hospital and general practices. *Alcoholism: Clinical and Experimental Research, 21,* 894–898.	Tested on 1167 medical outpatients and inpatients. Against results of psychiatric interviews, sensitivity was 0.82 and specificity was 0.91.	Public domain. Developed by German researchers using two items from the CAGE and five from the Michigan Alcohol Screening Test (MAST).

Test		Validation	Notes
Fast Alcohol Screening Test (FAST)	4	Hodgson, R., Alwyn, T., John, B., Thom, B., & Smith, A. (2002). The FAST alcohol screening test. *Alcohol and Alcoholism, 37,* 61–66.	Subjects in the validation sample were 666 emergency-room patients. Using the full AUDIT as a criterion, and with a cut-off score of 3, sensitivity ranged from 0.91 to 0.97 and specificity from 0.86 to 0.95 across three subgroups.	Public domain. Comprises items 3, 5, 8, and 10 from the AUDIT. Use of item 3 as a stem question is recommended. Results are not available from tests on American samples.

Risk drinking in pregnancy

Test		Validation	Notes
TWEAK	5	Chan, A.W., Pristach, E. A., Welte, J. W., & Russell, M. (1993). Use of the TWEAK test in screening for alcoholism/heavy drinking in three populations. *Alcoholism: Clinical and Experimental Research, 17,* 1188–1192. Russell, M., Martier, S. S., Sokol, R. J., Mudar, P., Bottoms, S., Jacobson, S., et al. (1994). Screening for pregnancy risk-drinking. *Alcoholism: Clinical and Experimental Research, 18,* 1156–1161.	Validation samples included 4473 women visiting a prenatal clinic in Detroit. With a criterion of admitting to drinking at least once during pregnancy and a cut point of 2 or more "yes" answers, AUC was 0.865, sensitivity was 0.78, specificity was 0.84, and PPV was 24%.	Public domain. Three TWEAK items are from the T-ACE and two are from the MAST. The TWEAK performed better than both these measures in screening for risk drinking in the validation sample, but the relatively low PPV means it may return a high rate of false positives in samples with low problem prevalence.
T-ACE	4	Sokol, R. J., Martier, S. S., & Ager, J. W. (1989). The T-ACE questions: Practical and prenatal detection of risk drinking. *American Journal of Obstetrics and Gynecology, 60,* 863–870.	Validated on a sample of 971 pregnant black women at an inner-city clinic. Against a criterion of self-reported risk drinking, sensitivity was 76% and specificity was 79% when using a cut-off score of one affirmative response.	Public domain. Subsequent studies have validated use of the T-ACE for screening expectant fathers and older women. Some results suggest the T-ACE is less accurate than the TWEAK when screening nonblack women.

TABLE 49.5 Substance Abuse

Category/Name	Items	Key Reference(s)	Measurement Accuracy	Comments
General drug abuse				
Drug Abuse Screening Test (DAST-10)	10	Skinner, H. A., & Allen, B. A. (1982). Alcohol dependence syndrome: Measurement and validation. *Journal of Abnormal Psychology, 91*, 199–209.	All available tests that report screening accuracy are from samples of psychiatric patients. These show PPV values ranging from 59% to 74% and NPV values ranging from 90% to 93%.	A cut-off score of 3 is recommended. The measure is copyrighted, but items can be reviewed at http://www .nida.nih.gov/Diagnosis-Treatment/ DAST10.html.
Rost Drug Dependence Screener	3	Rost, K., Burnam, M. A., & Smith, G. R. (1993). Development of screeners for depressive disorders and substance disorder history. *Medical Care, 31*, 189–200.	Tested on a general-population sample of 10,534. Against results from a standardized diagnostic instrument using *DSM-III* criteria, the three-item substance disorder screener showed 91–93% sensitivity and 95–99% specificity across three sites. PPV values ranged from 67–88%, while NPV was 98–99%.	As tested, the measure screened for the presence of any personal history of a diagnosis of drug abuse or dependence. The test sample involved subjects who had utilized outpatient or inpatient health or mental health facilities within the past 6 months.
RAFFT	5	Bastiaens, L., Riccardi, K., & Sakhrani, D. (2002). The RAFFT as a screening tool for adult substance use disorders. *American Journal of Drug and Alcohol Abuse, 28*, 681–691.	Tested on 215 subjects who sought services at a psychiatric emergency and evaluation center. Against results from the Mini-International Neuropsychiatric Interview and a psychiatric evaluation, sensitivity was 83.7%, and sensitivity was 67.4%.	Values for sensitivity and specificity are based on a cut-off scores of three of five RAFFT items being endorsed positively. The CAGE was tested simultaneously with the RAFFT, and it proved superior for detecting alcohol (but not drug) abuse.
Drug/alcohol use in mothers				
Screening Questions for Maternal Drinking and Drug Use	6	Kemper, K. J., Greterman, A., Benett, E., & Babonis, T. R. (1993). Screening mothers of young children for substance abuse. *Journal of Developmental and Behavioral Pediatrics, 14*, 308–312.	Tested on 507 mothers of children age 6 and younger in pediatric clinics. Using a cut-off score of one positive response, items on drug use had 88% sensitivity with respect to the DAST. With the same cut-off score, items on alcohol use had 90% sensitivity compared with the MAST.	Consists of four question from the MAST and two from the DAST. Is designed for screening in pediatric settings as part of a comprehensive psychosocial questionnaire for mothers of young children. The absence of results regarding specificity is problematic, and PPV may be low.

TABLE 49.6 General Mental Health, Serious Mental Illness, and Personality Disorders

Category/Name	Items	Key Reference(s)	Measurement Accuracy	Comments
General mental health				
K6	6	Kessler, R. C., Andrews, G., Colpe, L. J., Hiripi, E., Mroczek, D. K., Normand, S. L. T., et al. (2002). Short screening scales to monitor population prevalences and trends in non-specific psychological distress. *Psychological Medicine, 32,* 959–976. Kessler, R. C., Barker, P. R., Colpe, L. J., Epstein, J. F., Gfroerer, J. C., Hiripi, E., et al. (2003). Screening for serious mental illness in the general population. *Archives of General Psychiatry, 60,* 184–189.	Validated on data from large mail (n > 1,000) and telephone (n > 10,000) surveys. Using Composite International Diagnostic Inventory (CIDI) results as a criterion, AUC was 0.875. Follow-up study of 150 cases showed a sensitivity of 0.36 and specificity of 0.96 in predicting serious mental illness.	Public domain. Two items address depressed mood; one item each addresses motor agitation, fatigue, worthless guilt, and anxiety. Results of follow-up studies suggest it may be useful to screen for serious mental illness as well as general psychological distress. Many translations available.
Mental Health Inventory (MHI-5)	5	Veit, C. T., & Ware, J. E. (1983). The structure of psychological distress and well-being in general populations. *Journal of Consulting and Clinical Psychology, 51,* 730–742. Means-Christensen, A. J., Arnau, R. C., Tonidandel, A. M., Bramson, R., & Meagher, M. W. (2005). An efficient method of identifying major depression and panic disorder in primary care. *Journal of Behavioral Medicine, 28,* 565–572.	In a study of 5,291 adults, showed an AUC of 79.3% when compared against results from the Diagnostic Interview Schedule. In a second study of 246 adult outpatients, testing against results from the PRIME-MD, specificity was 58% and sensitivity was 91% for major depression or panic disorder.	Public domain. Items are a subset of the SF-36. Focuses more than the K6 on screening for affective and anxiety-related aspects of mental health. Correlates well with scores from longer measures, such as the GHQ. Many translations available.
Serious mental illness				
Psychosis Screening Questionnaire (PSQ)	12	Bebbington, P., & Nayani, T. (1995). The Psychosis Screening Questionnaire. *International Journal of Methods in Psychiatric Research, 5,* 11–19.	Against relevant sections of the Schedule for Clinical Assessment in Neuropsychiatry (SCAN), sensitivity = 96.9%; specificity = 95.3%; PPV = 91.2%; NPV = 98.4%	Tested on psychiatric inpatients, outpatients, and presumptive normal medical patients (n = 150) in Britain.

Continued

Cornell Psychiatric Screen	7	Boutin-Foster, C., Ferrando, S. J., & Charlson, M. E. (2003). The Cornell Psychiatric Screen: A brief psychiatric scale for hospitalized medical patients. *Psychosomatics, 44,* 382–387.	AUC for score of 2 is 88% at 90% sensitivity and 87% specificity against clinical diagnosis by a psychiatrist.	Initial tests were on 292 subjects, 45 of whom were identified as needing psychiatric evaluation.

Personality disorders

McLean Screening Instrument for Borderline Personality Disorder (MSI-BPD)	10	Zanarini, M. C., Vujanovic, A. A., Parachini, E. A., Boulanger, J. L., Frankenburg, F. R., & Hennen, J. (2003): A screening measure for BPD: The McLean Screening Instrument for Borderline Personality Disorder (MSI-BPD). *Journal of Personality Disorders, 17,* 568–573.	For cut-off score of 7, sensitivity = 0.87 and specificity = 0.90 for age 30 and younger; 0.03 points higher for each in subjects 25 and younger, using psychiatric diagnosis as criterion.	Based on subset of items from the *DSM-IV* borderline module. Findings are from 200 community volunteers selected for some BPD characteristics and some history of psychiatric treatment.
Standardised Assessment of Personality–Abbreviated Scale (SAPAS)	8	Moran, P., Leese, M., Lee, T., Walters, P., Thornicroft, G., & Mann, A. (2003). Standardised Assessment of Personality–Abbreviated Scale (SAPAS): Preliminary validation of a brief screen for personality disorder. *British Journal of Psychiatry, 183,* 228–232.	Tested on 60 medical outpatients and inpatients sampled on the basis of having some type of psychiatric problem. For score of 3 or more, sensitivity = 0.94, specificity = 0.85, PPD = 0.89 against SCID diagnosis.	Applicable only to populations already receiving psychiatric services. Available results are from subjects in the UK.

when and how to apply, score, and interpret them will allow social workers to work more closely with other professionals and to enhance the effectiveness of their own efforts.

WEB SITES

American Psychological Association Testing and Assessment. http://www.apa.org/science/faq-findtests.html#findinfo.
Buros Institute of Mental Measurement, Test Reviews Online. http://buros.unl.edu/buros/jsp/search.jsp.
Educational Testing Service Testlink. http://www.ets.org/testcoll.

National Institute on Alcohol Abuse and Alcoholism publication. http://pubs.niaaa.nih.gov/publications/Assesing%20Alcohol/index.pdf
World Health Organization publication. http://www.who.int/mental_health/evidence/MH_Promotion_Book.pdf.

References

Fischer, J., & Corcoran, K. (2007). *Measures for clinical practice and research: A sourcebook. Vol. 1: Couples, families, and children.* New York: Oxford University Press.
Hudson, W. W. (1982). *The clinical measurement package: A field manual.* Chicago: Dorsey.

50 Person-in-Environment System

James M. Karls & Maura E. O'Keefe

DEFINITION OF PIE

The person-in-environment (PIE) system, is a system for describing, classifying, and coding the common problems of adult clients served by social workers. Analogous to systems developed for psychiatry, such as the *Diagnostic and Statistical Manual (DSM)* (American Psychiatric Association, 2000) and, for general medicine, the *International Classification of Diseases (ICD-10-CM)* (World Health Organization, 2005), PIE is a system for identifying and recording problems that clients experience in their social functioning in relationships with others and in relation to the community institutions that generally serve to help maintain social functioning.

PIE was created to develop a common language for all social workers in all settings to describe the often complex problems that their clients present. The intention was to clarify the expertise of social workers in the human service field vis-à-vis psychiatrists, psychologists, clergy, and others. PIE attends to the complex biopsychosocial functioning of individuals more thoroughly than other classification systems do, like the *DSM*, and is consistent with the mission and principles of the social work profession that emphasizes social work expertise to assess and remedy "social functioning" problems while simultaneously recognizing problems in the social institutions of society that affect social functioning.

BACKGROUND

PIE operationalizes some of the basic tenets of social work. The primary mission of the social work profession is "to enhance human well-being and help meet the basic human needs of all people, with particular attention to the needs and empowerment of people who are vulnerable, oppressed, and living in poverty environment" (National Association of Social Workers [NASW], 2006, p. 1). The uniqueness of social work among human service professions is its attention to the PIE perspective and its focus on enhancing the social functioning of people. Social workers perform this role by helping people interact more effectively with their environment.

Historically, the social work profession has endeavored to find a unifying perspective that would provide greater cohesiveness to social work practice. Such a perspective would reflect the PIE focus that has become central to the purpose of social work practice. Furthermore, such a perspective would not espouse any particular approach or theory; rather, it would allow for an eclectic approach to case phenomena, and serve to bind together social workers who are all doing different things to carry out the same purpose (Meyer & Mattaini, 1998).

The PIE system was designed with the above in mind. It was initially developed under NASW auspices by a group of social work practitioners and academicians charged with the task of developing a classification system usable in all fields of practice and one that would be user- and client-friendly. After a period of field testing, a book, *Person-in-Environment System* (Karls & Wandrei, 1994a), and instruction manual (Karls & Wandrei, 1994b) were published by NASW. Later, an instructional software program was developed to facilitate recording and analysis of case data (CompuPIE). Social workers around the world have found PIE helpful if not indispensable to their professions. So far, there are translations in Spanish, French, German, Greek, Hebrew, Hungarian, Japanese, Korean, as well as some South African languages.

In 2008, a new version of PIE and its accompanying software were developed that incorporates suggestions and ideas from PIE enthusiasts as to how to improve the system. It also includes a stronger strengths-based emphasis. The mission of PIE, however, remains the same—to provide both practitioner and researcher a tool with which the problems presented by human service clients can be systematically and comprehensively assessed, described, and addressed within an eclectic framework that highlights social work's unique contribution to the human service field.

STRUCTURE OF THE PIE SYSTEM

PIE is a four-factor system. The first two factors form the core description of a client's social functioning. The second pair of factors identify mental and physical health problems using classification systems from other professions. All four are needed to provide a comprehensive picture of a client's problems and strengths.

Factor I identifies and describes the client's problems and strengths in social functioning. The description includes the social role and relationship problems, the type of problems, the severity and duration of the problems, the client's coping ability, and the client's other strengths.

Factor II describes the environmental problems that affect the client's social functioning. It also describes each problem—its severity, duration, and available resources or strengths in the environment that might serve to ameliorate the problem.

Factor III describes the mental health problems the client may be experiencing, including their severity and duration, as well as the client's coping capacities and other strengths.

Factor IV describes the client's physical health problems, their severity and duration, and the client's coping capacities and other strengths.

APPLICATION OF PIE IN PRACTICE

PIE is an assessment tool for use at initial contact, follow ups, and at termination. Use of the PIE system guides the practitioner, facilitating the ordering of the findings of an assessment in a format that allows for clear, focused intervention plans. The practitioner is enabled to conduct an assessment that clarifies the task and role of social work and answer the following questions.

- What are the problems in social functioning presented by this client? What are the client's strengths?
- What problems exist in the social institutions in this community that are affecting the client? What resources/strengths are available?

- What mental health problems are present? What are strengths presented by the client?
- What physical health problems are noted? What are the client strengths in this area?

The PIE system also enables the practitioner to conduct a thorough assessment in a way that is understandable by practitioners in other settings to which the client might be referred. PIE is an instrument not only for recording assessment findings but also for planning, evaluating, and facilitating interventions. It lends itself easily to research, because a numerical code is available to identify problems. Importantly, PIE enables the client to participate more fully in the assessment and intervention plan. Most important, PIE leads to more effective help for the client.

Operationalizing Factor I

The social worker using the PIE system first identifies the Factor I problems presented by the client. Factor I describes the client's social role and relationship functioning and includes six components.

1. A statement of the social role or relationship problems the client is experiencing. In Factor I, there are four major categories of social roles (Familial, Interpersonal, Occupational, and Special Life Situation), and there are 26 specific roles in which problems can be identified.
   a. Familial: Parent, Spouse, Child (Adult), Sibling, and Extended Family
   b. Interpersonal: Lover, Friend, Neighbor, Member, Other
   c. Occupational: Paid Worker, Homemaker, Volunteer, Student, Other
   d. Special Life Situation: Consumer, Caregiver, Inpatient/Client, Outpatient/Client, Probationer /Parolee, Prisoner, Legal Immigrant, Undocumented Immigrant, Refugee Immigrant, Other.

   For example, a marital problem is identified as a Spouse Role Problem; a problem with an employer identified as a Worker (Paid) Role Problem.
2. A descriptor of the kind of problem it is (type). After identifying the social role area in which the client's problem exists, the worker identifies the particular type of social role problem the client is experiencing. Type is used in the PIE system to describe the kind of interactional difficulty that is occurring or

has occurred between the client and another person. Descriptors of the types of problem include the following: (a) Power/Conflict; (b) Ambivalence; (c) Obligation/Responsibility; (d) Dependency; (e) Loss; (f) Isolation; (g) Oppressed; (h) Mixed; and (i) Other. For example, a person losing a spouse by death or divorce is identified as having a Spouse Role, Loss type problem; a parent experiencing problems with a rebellious teenager is identified as having a Parent Role, Power/Conflict type problem.
3. An indication of the severity of the problem on a scale of 1 = lowest severity to 5 = catastrophic.
4. An indication of how long the problem has been present on a scale of 1 = "5 or more years" to 5 = "1 to 4 weeks" (duration).
5. A clinical judgment of the client's ability to cope with the problem on a scale of 1 = outstanding to 6 = inadequate.
6. The social role and relationship strengths of the client.

Operationalizing Factor II

Factor II describes the problems in the client's current environment as it affects his or her social functioning. The environment refers to social institutions, social support networks, and natural helping networks of the client. Factor II includes five components.

1. A statement of the social system type and kind of environmental problems the client is experiencing. In the PIE system, six system types are used. These groupings of social system problems include:
   a. Basic Need System. This encompasses problems in the provision or accessibility of food, shelter, employment, economic resources, and transportation.
   b. Educational and Training System. This includes problems or deficiencies related to education/training institutions and policies.
   c. Judicial and Legal System. This includes problems related to the police and courts.
   d. Health, Safety, and Social Services. This includes problems related to hospitals, clinics, public safety services, and social services.
   e. Voluntary Association System. This includes religious institutions and community support groups.

f. Affectional Support System. This includes the help network most people acquire to varying degrees.

Each type of environmental problem contains 3 to 11 subtypes, which are described and defined and coded in Karls and O'Keefe (2008). For example, a client reporting lack of housing in the community would have the problem described as: Economic, Basic Needs System Problem, shelter, absence of shelter, substandard or inadequate shelter. A client in an unsafe neighborhood: Safety System Problem, violence or crime in the neighborhood.

2. The second component is the severity of each problem on a scale of 1 = lowest severity to 5 = catastrophic.
3. The third component is an indication of how long the problem has been present on a scale of 1 = "5 or more years" to 5 = "1 to 4 weeks" (duration).
4. The fourth component concerns whether the client is having problems in environmental situations because of who he is or her status in society (discrimination). The practitioner thus indicates the social institution in which discrimination is observed and the type of discrimination using the Discrimination Index.
5. The fifth component identifies resources or strengths within the social system that might be used to remedy the client's situation.

Operationalizing Factor III

Factor III lists the mental health problems of the client using the *DSM* axes I and II and its codes. The social worker notes the clinical disorder and the source of the diagnosis, that is, if a professional has made the diagnosis or if it is by client report. The severity of the problem, its duration, and the client's capacity to cope with the condition are noted, as are any other any mental health strengths of the client.

Operationalizing Factor IV

Factor IV lists the physical health problems as diagnosed by a physician or reported by the client. For official diagnoses, the *ICD-10* is used. Similar to Factor III, the social worker notes the severity of the problem, its duration, the client's capacity to cope with the physical health condition, and other any physical heath strengths.

INTERVENTION PLAN

For each of the four factors, the social worker may generate an intervention plan and record (1) goals, (2) recommended interventions, (3) the practitioner or agency that will provide the recommended interventions, and (4) the expected outcome. This step is most frequently completed after all problems have been identified and the practitioner has been able to study the findings on all the PIE factors. Furthermore, for each problem noted, the social worker may prioritize the problem and suggested interventions by ranking the problem as low, medium, or high priority.

CASE EXAMPLE

See Figure 50.1 for a case example.

PIE AS A TEACHING TOOL

PIE has been found to be very useful in helping social work students understand the domain of social work practice as it differentiates areas of expertise from those of other professions. Because a comprehensive and clear assessment is basic to planning and executing interventions, a social work student using PIE learns to conduct client assessments that are clear and understandable. Because the system is essentially atheoretical, it permits teachers to use casework theory or behavior theory they believe best helps in understanding the dynamics of the case.

PIE IN POLICY RESEARCH AND ADMINISTRATION

In addition to data on personal interaction problems, mental health, and physical health, the PIE system can routinely collect information on problems in the community's social policies and institutions. Aggregating these data allows the social policy researcher or the administrator to conduct an ongoing assessment of problems in the community social system and to propose remedies.

Initial Assessment

Client: Brown, Martha   **Assessed By:** M. O'Keefe   **Assess Date:** 9/24/2007

Case History, Dynamics and Comments

Mrs. Brown, a 33-year-old divorced mother of three children, was referred to Family Services by a counselor at her son's school. Her eldest son, Jimmy, age 10, has been getting into fights more frequently at school especially during the past several months. Mrs. Brown reported that her son has been difficult to manage since her divorce two years ago. She reported that he has frequent temper outbursts and bullies younger children and that these behaviors have also been increasing at home during the past several months. Mrs. Brown reported a history of domestic violence in the marriage. She recently learned that her ex husband is planning to remarry and believes that this may be one of the reasons for the increase in her son's behavior problems. Mrs. Brown also expressed concerned about her daughter, age 12, whom she describes as shy and doing poorly academically in school. Client reported that she is feeling overwhelmed and stated, "It is a struggle for me just to get up in the morning."

During the past 3 months Mrs. Brown has been dating a man whom she describes as kind, but added she does not know if she wants to continue this relationship because her son does not like him and this has contributed to arguments between her and her son.

Client's situation is aggravated by financial problems. Since her divorce she has had to move to a smaller apartment in a less desirable and less safe neighborhood. Her ex husband pays only $200/month in child support and he is sporadic in his payments. Also, one month ago due to cutbacks at her place of employment, she now works only 25 hours per week. She has been unable to find additional work and is worried about being able to financially make ends meet.

Mrs. Brown's mood was depressed during the interview. She cried during the session, stating, "Life was just too much for her." She denies any suicidal ideation, stating she would never do that to her children. She is highly motivated and states she "wants help to give her children a better life".

	Recommendation	**Priority**
Factor I: Social Role and Relationship		
Lover Role, Ambivalence Type, Low Severity, 1 - 4 Weeks Duration, Somewhat Inadequate Coping Skills.	Individual therapy	Low
Spouse Role, Mixed Type, Moderate Severity, 1 - 5 Years Duration, Somewhat Inadequate Coping Skills.	Individual therapy Possible group therapy for battered women	Medium
Parent Role, Responsibility Type, Moderate Severity, 1 - 5 Years Duration, Somewhat Inadequate Coping Skills.	1. Individual therapy 2. Conjoint and family therapy 3. Refer son for individual therapy	Medium
Factor II: Environmental Situations		
Economic Resources: Insufficient Resources for Basic Sustenance, Moderate Severity, 1 - 4 Weeks Duration.	Explore community resources	High
Factor III: Mental Health Functioning		
Axis I Diagnosis		
Major Depressive Disorder Single Episode, Moderate Severity, 1 - 4 Weeks Duration, Somewhat Inadequate Coping Skills.	1. Individual Cognitive Behavioral therapy; 2. Psychiatric referral for medication	High
Axis II Diagnosis		
No Diagnosis on Axis II		
Factor IV: Physical Health Conditions		
Frequent headaches Client Report High Severity, 1 - 6 Months Duration, Somewhat Inadequate Coping Skills.	Referral for a neurological workup	High

Strengths and Resources

Factor I: Positive Social Relationships

Parent, Worker Paid.

Factor III: Mental Health Functioning

DSM Axis I Strengths: Notable strengths

Figure 50.1 Case example from CompuPie.

RECORDING AND COMPUTERIZATION

Recording and tabulating the findings of an assessment is often a very difficult and tedious task. A PIE assessment is now made easier with updated CompuPIE software developed to provide a succinct but comprehensive assessment and to print assessment reports (Karls & O'Keefe, 2008).

WEB SITES

CompuPIE. http://www.compupie.org.

National Association of Social Workers. http://www.socialworkers.org.

References

American Psychiatric Association. (2000). *Diagnostic and statistical manual of mental disorders,* 4th ed., text revision. Washington, DC: APA.

Karls, J. M., & O'Keefe, M. (2008). *The PIE manual.* Washington, DC: NASW Press.

Karls, J.M., & Wandrei (1994a). *Person-in-environment system: The PIE classification system for social functioning problems.* Washington, DC: NASW Press.

Karls, J.M., & Wandrei, K.E. (1994b). *The PIE manual.* Washington, DC: NASW Press.

Karls, J.M., & Wandrei (1994). *Person-in-Environment system: The PIE Classification system for social functioning problems.* Washington, DC: NASW Press.

Meyer, C., & Mattaini, M. (1998). The ecosystems perspective: Implication for practice. In M. Mattaini, C. Lower, & C. Meyer (Eds.), *Foundations of social work practice,* 2nd ed. (pp. 3–19). Washington, DC: NASW Press.

National Association of Social Workers. (2006). Code of ethics of the National Association of Social Workers. Washington, DC: Author.

World Health Organization. (2005). *International classification of diseases,* 10th revision, Clinical Modification. Geneva: World Health Organization.

51   Guidelines for Conducting a Biopsychosocial Assessment

Sonia G. Austrian

The assessment process has been a key component of social work practice, beginning with Mary Richmond's book *Social Diagnosis* (1917). Moving from a linear (medical/psychiatric) approach initially designed by Richmond to the broader ecosystems perspective involved a significant change in terminology. In 1979, Meyer (1995), as part of her formulation of the ecosystems perspective, introduced the semantic and, even more important, epistemological change from study, diagnosis, and treatment, where the clinician was viewed as the authority, to exploration, assessment, and intervention, which involved a joint, collaborative effort on the part of the social worker and the client.

The ecosystems perspective is a unifying conceptual construction providing a framework for examining and understanding the complexity of a case at a given point in time while focusing on the interaction and reciprocity of person and environment. *Eco-* refers to the relationship of person to environment, whereas the term *systems*

refers to the interrelatedness, within a systematically defined boundary, of personal and institutional factors impinging on the client. The ecosystems perspective requires rigorous, disciplined assessment, consideration of interrelated phenomena, and results in intervention components based on contextual considerations. The clinician needs to have a broad knowledge base, experience in evaluating interview content, an ability to listen, the presence of a client (with the exception of most mandated clients) who can and wants to participate in the process, as well as an awareness of a range of possible interventions acceptable to client and worker. The clinician may also need to accept that the client may have some problems that are not amenable to intervention.

The ecosystemic framework is not linked to any methodology; it represents the "what is," not the "how to" of a case (Meyer, 1983, 1993). It places primary responsibility for successful case intervention on the complex skill of assessment, which Meyer defines as "the thinking process that seeks out the meaning of case situations, puts the particular case in some order and leads to appropriate interventions. . . . Assessment is the intellectual tool for understanding the client's psychosocial situation, and for determining 'what's the matter'" (1993, p. 2).

The process of assessment consists of five steps (Meyer, 1993, pp. 27–42):

1. exploration,
2. inferential thinking,
3. evaluation,
4. problem definition, and
5. intervention planning.

Whereas steps 1, 4, and 5 involve both client and worker, steps 2 and 3 primarily involve the worker and are based on a knowledge base and experience with similar problems and situations.

EXPLORATION

The step of exploration involves beginning with the presenting request and listening to the client's unique story to acquire and organize case data. It is important to ask "why now?" referring to the client's decision to seek intervention at this time. With the limited number of sessions most clients have under managed care, it is not possible to obtain a full history. Thus, efforts should be made to obtain salient and relevant information related to the presenting problem(s) that will enhance understanding of the context and cause of problems in adaptation and coping. The variables to be addressed will be influenced by the agency setting and mission, as well as the worker's theoretical orientation.

In addition to obtaining information, the social worker must pay attention to the client's appearance, affect, speech, ability to organize data, any apparent contradictions or distortions, and time lines. In addition to being aware of social work's respect for self-determination, the worker, while helping clarify the issues, must be aware of the client's concerns and readiness to share information and be able to focus questions in a way that will allow the client to choose what information to reveal and when. Questions that can be answered yes or no should be avoided, because open-ended questions will yield more data and may identify areas for further exploration.

As exploration continues, it often becomes apparent that the presenting request may not be the presenting problem. The request may be a distortion of the problem or believed by the client to be "safer" to disclose, or presented as a way to enter the system and to get help; it is, of course, an indicator of what the problem may be. The social worker uses a range of knowledge and skills to put together the facts emerging in this phase. Collaboration between client and worker is established as their individual experiences, knowledge, judgment, and thinking complement each other to further identify the problem to be addressed in the intervention. Exploration is an ongoing process with additional data emerging throughout the intervention as the client–worker relationship becomes more trusting and collaborative.

INFERENTIAL THINKING

This is the phase of the assessment process that most reflects the professional social worker's clinical and empirical epidemiological knowledge about the type of problem the client is presenting (Meyer, 1995, p. 267). Here the worker looks at raw data obtained through exploration to determine its meaning. It is an intellectual process that retains the client's individual situation and also moves the case from what has been presented to one that is part of a class of cases. It results in an informed professional opinion about the problem and is the step that most differentiates the professional from the "good friend" when helping the client cope better with problems. Inferential thinking involves combining unique case data with external professional knowledge to arrive at a guide for an intervention plan to best improve the client's mastery and coping. The particular theoretical framework a worker chooses to use is not important; what is essential is the worker's use of a professional knowledge base.

There is always a risk that conclusions reached at this stage of the assessment process may need modification or may be completely inaccurate; therefore, the social worker's statements to a client should be made with some caution. Clients also may not be ready to accept the worker's hypothesis, and it is often helpful to preface a statement with "I may be wrong, but I think that . . ." More often than not, the conclusions of inferential thinking will be proven correct by both client and worker as the intervention proceeds.

In summary, inferential thinking involves reviewing the data obtained through intervention to determine what they mean, whether they are consistent and logical, and whether conclusions are derived from worker intuition and/or direct evidence from the data. The social worker makes decisions about how to use the data on the basis of professional knowledge of similar cases,   classes of cases, theoretical orientation and the type of agency setting, and availability of resources. What emerges is an understanding of "what is the matter" by making significant causal connections.

EVALUATION

This step involves the social worker's assessment of the client's functioning, given the defined problem areas. It includes evaluating the strengths and weaknesses of the person and the environment. A tool that is helpful at this step is an *ego assessment* (Goldstein, 1995, p. 54). As in step 1, the emphasis is on individualizing the client/case. Data obtained from exploration and inferential thinking should result in an understanding of the client's motivation for change, inner resources, resources in the environment, and a realistic assessment of adaptive capabilities.

At this point, it is essential that the worker consider whether areas of ego weakness are related to the presenting problem or are pervasive. For example, does the client have pervasive poor judgment, or is this seen only in one area of functioning, such as in relationships? This information will be helpful in determining an appropriate intervention and realistic goals. Assessment of the environment's changeability is also essential at this point.

PROBLEM DEFINITION

This step moves the assessment process back to the client and social worker. Without mutual agreement about framing the problem, intervention may be seriously hampered. At this point, the presenting request has been modified to the presenting problem by the preceding three steps. Although the client may initially present many problems, what must be agreed on are the problem(s) and the context that will be the focus of attention. In addition, there must be recognition of what is doable given the constraints of the case and the setting. We strive to understand the whole case, yet we act on only a part of it, thus we think globally and act locally.

When the client and worker agree on the problem definition, they proceed to establishing a focus for the intervention. This is especially important because very few cases involve open-ended intervention, and if a focus is not agreed on and adhered to, the intervention can be vague and ineffectual. Information may emerge suggesting another area of concern, and clients can be encouraged to return at a later date for another episode of service to focus on that other problem area. It is also very possible that successfully coping with one problematic area will lead to developing coping skills that will be applicable to other problems.

The mutually agreed on problem definition should always represent the thinking of and be acceptable to both social worker and client. It may vary from the presenting request, and the worker may see a more complex situation, but only with understanding and agreement can the focus of attention be arrived at and a productive intervention planned.

INTERVENTION PLANNING

This final step is based on the four preceding steps. The client and social worker *contract* with respect to modality, time frame, and the need to focus on the defined problem. They also discuss anticipated outcome.

It is essential to good intervention planning that the client and worker have gone through the rigorous, disciplined assessment process. Without supporting evidence, knowledgeable inferential thinking, evaluation, and mutually agreed to problem definition, intervention will be amateurish and fueled by a desire to be helpful, sometimes seen in students or beginning workers. A disciplined professional determines intervention through a carefully constructed assessment framework. This is the science of the process. The art is the social worker's own professionally developed style, area of specialization, empathy, and personality.

In summary, assessment, though grounded in professional knowledge and skill, is an individualized process that demands recognition of the uniqueness of person and situation. It is an ongoing process, with intervention possibly subject to modification as new data emerge. A knowledge of cultural, class, and gender differences and perceptions of problems, emotional or situational, is essential to providing a thorough assessment and good intervention planning. A knowledge of developmental stages, personality theories, and range of family structures can also be important.

ASSESSMENT OUTLINE

Different agencies and fields of practice have their own assessment needs and outlines. The following is a very simple basic outline:

1. demographic data;
2. current and previous agency contacts;
3. medical, psychiatric, substance abuse, and trauma history;
4. brief history of client and significant others, including family history of mental illness;
5. summary of client's current situation;
6. presenting request;
7. presenting problem as defined by client and worker;
8. contract agreed on by client and worker;
9. intervention plan; and
10. intervention goals.

ASSESSMENT TOOLS

There are pictorial tools that can be useful in supplementing the data obtained through the assessment process just described. These tools are used by worker and client together, but time constraints may require that they are given to the clients as homework. Two of the most useful and most commonly used are the eco-map and the genogram. The eco-map, developed by Hartman (1978), is a diagrammatic, interactive, pen-and-pencil picture of the client's relationships to family and the environment. Arrows indicate the directions of involvement, and different kinds of lines indicate the degree of connection. The model is a central circle with connecting surrounding circles. The eco-map presents the current situation, whereas the genogram developed by McGoldrick, Gerson, and Shellenberger (1999) gives a picture of the family relationships over at least three generations. It is useful in helping the worker see how connected the client is with family history, as well as feelings about different members. Information about the family that the person may not have mentioned can be learned pictorially.

Other forms of graphics may be used, some of which are related to fields of practice. As agencies and workers become more familiar with computers, they are beginning to use some of the computer graphics programs that depict the client's relationship to the environment, described in Mattaini (1993)

ASSESSMENT AND CLASSIFICATION

Contemporary clinical social work practice using the ecosystems perspective can be differentiated from the practice of other mental health professionals by its emphasis on assessing the person in environment rather than focusing only on the presenting pathology. Psychosocial assessment is the social work tool for understanding a case and planning intervention.

A tool frequently used in evaluating clients is *DSM-IV-TR* (American Psychiatric Association [APA], 2000). Classification systems such as the *DSM-IV-TR* are descriptive, look for group phenomenon, rely on generalizations highlighting similarities and overlooking differences, are exclusionary, and disregard context. The term *diagnosis* implies an initial effort to narrow case data to fit a diagnostic category, whereas *assessment* recognizes the client's uniqueness and strengths, defines that person's problem within its unique context, and arrives at a personalized intervention. The result of depending on criteria such as *DSM-IV-TR* can be that clients with widely differing life circumstances or experiences could receive the same diagnosis.

The expectation of the use of classification systems was to establish a common language and thus facilitate communication across disciplines, but classification can interfere with a full understanding of a client's problems, which can only be obtained through exploration of aspects not listed in the criteria. In spite of an increased awareness among the general public of the impact of social factors on mental health, the medical model still prevails, especially in this era of managed care, and can result in stereotyping, misdiagnosis, and possible obstruction of intervention.

Knowledge of *DSM-IV-TR* is, however, essential for social workers. It is used to communicate, in a common language, with other mental health providers, as well as with insurance companies who rely on it to determine eligibility for reimbursement. It is useful in organizing observations and the client's history with respect to one aspect of the client's life—the presenting clinical symptoms. However, knowledge of the individual's specific circumstances is essential for an individualized plan. *DSM-IV-TR* is important as an adjunct to assessment and intervention planning. Classifying the client's problems can be useful in directing the line of questioning, as well as indication of the need for medication, especially in this era of managed care where lengthy assessments may not be possible. However, as more social workers are moving away from emphasizing pathology to looking at *recovery* as a focus, Saleebey (2001) has suggested the need for a Diagnostic Strengths Manual or an axis VI, which would identify the strengths of the client and the environment that would assist in promoting recovery.

Although *DSM-IV-TR* and other classification systems will be required to meet requirements for accountability, it is hoped that social workers and social work educators will continue to see that rigorous assessment of person in environment defines our profession. Because a *DSM-IV-TR* diagnosis is increasingly being mandated, the obvious compromise may be making it part of the assessment. As social workers, we must never permit classification systems to let us lose sight of the uniqueness of our clients and their environments. Checklists, used by some managed care plans, will detail symptoms but give little or no understanding of context. Emphasis should be on recognizing that using both classification and assessment are necessary for effective intervention. If the classification system *DSM-IV-TR* and assessment, based on the ecosystem's perspective, are used together to respectfully complement each other, they will clearly be friends, not foes.

WEB SITES

CompuPIE. http://www.compupie.org.

Mental Health Today. How to make your own genogram. http://www.mental-health-today.com/articles/genogram.htm.

Write Enough. http://www.writeenough.org/UK/formats_ecomap.htm.

References

American Psychiatric Association. (2000). *Diagnostic and statistical manual of mental disorders*, 4th ed., Text Revision. Washington, DC: APA.

Goldstein, E. G. (1995). *Ego psychology and social work practice*, 2nd ed. New York. Free Press.

Hartman, A. (1978). Diagrammatic assessment of family relationships. *Social Casework, 59*(10), 465–476.

Mattaini, M. A. (1993) *More than a thousand words: Graphics for clinical practice* Washington, DC: NASW Press.

McGoldrick, M., Gerson, R., & Shellenberger, S. (1999). *Genograms: Assessment and intervention*, 2nd ed. New York: Norton.

Meyer, C. H. (Ed.). (1983). *Clinical social work in an eco-systems perspective*. New York: Columbia University Press.

Meyer, C. H. (1993). *Assessment in social work practice*. New York: Columbia University Press.

Meyer, C. H. (1995). Assessment in social work: Direct practice. In *Encyclopedia of social work*, 19th ed. Washington, DC: NASW Press.

Richmond, M. E. (1917). *Social diagnosis*. New York: Sage.

Saleebey, D. (2001). The diagnostic strengths manual? *Social Work, 46*(2), 183–187.

Guidelines for Selecting and Using Assessment Tools with Children

Craig Winston LeCroy & Scott Kiyoshi Okamoto

Increasing emphasis is being placed on short-term and effective treatment services for children and adolescents (LeCroy, in press). This trend has created a need for practitioners' use of assessment instruments to determine client conditions or problems. In addition to assessment of client conditions or problems, practitioners and program administrators are being required to monitor the outcomes of their work. Therefore, assessment instruments have also been called on to study the effects of practice through the assessment of change over time.

Assessment tools or instruments are just one method for gathering data to make a client assessment. They have become increasingly popular because the current view of the assessment process recognizes the importance of obtaining information from children and adolescents (Smith & Handler, 2006). For a more complete assessment of a child, practitioners need to obtain information directly from children and cannot rely, as in the past, solely on observational assessments, qualitative assessments, and reports from significant others. Table 52.1 lists the various assessment methods that practitioners use in conducting assessments.

One of the critical aspects of conducting a child assessment is that it needs to involve multiple aspects of the child's environment. This is unique to children, because in adult assessment, information is most often based on the adult in question. The child's perspective is important, but others in the child's environment, such as parents, teachers, and peers, can contribute to understanding the nature of the child's situation and behavior. Therefore, children's self-reports must be viewed as one of multiple methods. The most common method to assess children's perceptions of themselves and others are interviews and self-report measures.

Assessment tools include standardized interview schedules, behavior rating scales, and questionnaires. Standardization refers to the use of the same questions, procedures, and scoring of a measure. The same questions are presented in

TABLE 52.1 Examples of Different Types of Assessment Measures

Type of Assessment	Example
Clinical interview	Psychosocial history
Semi-structured interview	Child Assessment Schedule
Behavioral observation	Playground observation of behavior
Role-play test	Behavioral Assertiveness Test for Children
Parent reports	Child Behavior Checklist
Teacher reports	Walker Problem Behavior Identification
Peer assessment	Peer rating of status
Self-reports	Children's Depression Inventory
Client logs	Journal of critical incidents
Nonreactive measure	School records of days absent
Cognitive measure	Preschool Interpersonal Problem Solving Test
Performance measure	Matching Familiar Figures Test

the same way each time the tool is administered. Clients respond to statements indicating a frequency of occurrence of a behavior, or they rate themselves on scaled items in terms of "a little" or "a lot" or "true" and "false" (see Table 52.2 for an example). Assessment tools can summarize a child's condition in a summary score and indicate the degree to which the child experiences a condition. With children, normative data are often available that help practitioners make judgments about the severity of the condition. In addition, such measures typically have reliability and validity established through prior research.

Assessment instruments can be described according to six criteria (Bloom, Fischer, & Orme, 2005): (1) what they measure (i.e., are instruments available to measure all aspects of child functioning?); (2) how well they measure it (i.e., what are the psychometric properties [validity and reliability] of the instrument?); (3) how they are structured (e.g., as true or false statements, on agree/disagree dimensions, or as a series of pictures, such as from happy to sad); (4) how many dimensions they measure (i.e., rapid assessment instruments measure one dimension, but longer questionnaires are multidimensional and have subscales that measure different concepts); (5) from whom they elicit information (e.g., instruments may be self-reports or rating scales that parents or teachers complete); and (6) how much time and other resources are required for their use (i.e., the amount of training needed to administer, score, and interpret the instrument).

TABLE 52.2 Hopelessness Scale for Children

True or false	I want to grow up because I think things will be better.
True or false	I might as well give up because I can't make things better for myself.
True or false	When things are going badly, I know they won't be as bad all the time.
True or false	I can imagine what my life will be like when I'm grown up.
True or false	I have enough time to finish the things I really want to do.
True or false	Some day I will be really good at doing the things I really care about.

Source: Kazdin, 1983.

USES OF ASSESSMENT TOOLS

Assessment tools can serve several different functions, including assessment of a condition or problem, screening for early intervention, assessment of treatment outcomes or effectiveness, assessment of changes throughout treatment, predicting severity of treatment needed by youth, and diagnosis using *DSM* criteria.

Assessment of Condition or Problem

Rapid assessment tools are a useful supplement to traditional assessment techniques (e.g., biopsychosocial history-taking, mental status exams) in assessing the nature and extent of the condition or problem. For example, the Children's Depression Inventory can provide a clinical cutting score, whereby a child is judged to be clinically depressed. Normative data are often available and help in interpreting the results obtained from the measure. The benefit of using assessment tools in the clinical setting is that they provide a seemingly more anonymous context versus a face-to-face interview (King, 1997). This is particularly important for certain populations (e.g., child abuse victims or adolescent sex offenders), where information that is gathered may be perceived by the client as sensitive or embarrassing. Therefore, the combined use of traditional assessment techniques with rapid assessment tools may allow for more in-depth information from the assessment process than reliance on traditional assessment techniques alone.

Screening for Prevention/Early Intervention

Another use for assessment tools is to screen children who are in the early stages of developing behavioral, social, or emotional problems (Merrell, 2007). The importance of early screening is related to the concept of prevention. Through early identification of behavioral, social, or emotional problems, clinicians can help minimize the chances of adverse outcomes associated with child and adolescent psychological disorders and at-risk environmental situations. Screening instruments can be used to predict high risk by offering a score that qualifies for preventive intervention. In general, there is a need for further evaluation when children score one or more standard deviations above a normative mean on an instrument.

Assessment of Treatment

Rapid assessment tools are also useful for assessing changes throughout treatment and for assessing treatment effectiveness. Typically, these tools incorporate a Likert scale format (e.g., "strongly disagree" to "strongly agree," "seldom" to "always") to evaluate the frequency or extent of behavioral, social, or emotional symptoms. The tool can be administered at various points throughout treatment to assess changes throughout treatment, or can be administered pre- and posttreatment to evaluate overall treatment outcome or effectiveness. Examination of individual items in the instrument can also offer useful information for the practitioner. Examples of these types of tools include the Child and Adolescent Functional Assessment Scale (Hodges, Wong, & Latessa, 1998) and the Eyberg Child Behavior Inventory (Robinson, Eyberg, & Ross, 1980).

Diagnosis

Assessment tools can be used to determine the presence of major categorical psychiatric disorders in children (Rutter & Taylor, 2002; Verhulst & Van der Ende, 2002). Typically, these tools are in the form of structured or semistructured interview schedules, where certain responses from the child, adolescent, parent, or teacher will determine the interview questions leading to a specific diagnosis. Examples of these interview schedules include the Diagnostic Interview Schedule for Children and the Anxiety Disorders Interview Schedule for *DSM-IV* (TR): Child Version (see Verhulst & Van der Ende, 2002, for review).

SELECTING ASSESSMENT TOOLS

Practitioners should select assessment tools depending on the particular use they have in mind for the instrument. But how would you choose between different assessment instruments? There are four broad criteria that are important to consider: relevance of the measure to the problem or condition, scientific acceptability, ease of use, and practical considerations.

Relevance is a primary consideration and too often is overlooked by practitioners and program administrators. The most relevant measure is one that can directly assess the impact of the intervention. The goal is to find the most direct measure of the intervention. Often measures are selected that consider a related concept but may not be a direct measure of the treatment. For example, if you are trying to measure changes in a group program designed to increase children's social skills, a measure such as self-esteem is a related concept but not the most direct measure of the program's impact. Instead, a measure such as the Matson Evaluation of Social Skills with Youngsters (Matson, Rotatori, & Helsel, 1983) would be a better choice because it directly measures social skills acquisition. In assessing relevance, keep in mind this primary question (Bloom et al., 2005, p. 209): will it determine whether a target is improving or deteriorating, so that any necessary modifications in the intervention plan can be undertaken?

With regard to scientific acceptability, it is important to use measures that have an acceptable level of reliability and established validity. There are several ways to establish the reliability or internal consistency of the measure, such as Cronbach's α, split-half reliability, odd-even reliability, or test/retest reliability. In general, a reliability of 0.80 is considered good.

Validity is also an important scientific criterion. The standard validity methods include content, construct, concurrent, and predictive validity. By carefully studying the items, practitioners can make a good assessment of the face validity. Do the questions appear to be measuring the concept in a clear and logical manner? Do the authors of the measure report any validity data? One critical aspect of validity that is frequently overlooked is whether the instrument is sensitive to change (i.e., whether the instrument registers the change when it occurs). If you are relying on this instrument to assess treatment progress or as a measure of program outcomes, then previous research demonstrating sensitivity to change is important to assess. Although it is important to seek scientific credibility of the measure, it is also important to note that many measures fall short of documenting good scientific support. Practitioners may need to refer to a standard research text to interpret both the reliability and validity data (see Krysik & Finn, 2006).

Ease of use is an important criterion for real-world use of instruments. For example, part of the popularity of rapid assessment instruments is their ease of use. Instruments should be well designed graphically, have clear directions and clear scoring procedures, and be easy to administer. Related to ease of use are practical considerations. Good assessment tools are easy to find, are easy to obtain in terms of copyright permission (if required), and are not too costly. Some good sources to begin a review of potential instruments include Corcoran & Fischer (1999); McCubbin, Thompson, & McCubbin (1996); Smith & Handler (2006); and Merrell (2007).

SPECIAL CONSIDERATIONS IN USING ASSESSMENT TOOLS WITH CHILDREN

As stated earlier, assessment with children needs to take a multiperson perspective, which is quite different from adult assessment. Children are under the social control of others, and as a consequence, their behavior can be situationally specific. For example, hyperactive behavior in the classroom may not predict overactivity in the home. Indeed, significant others in the child's life are often involved in treatment and hence should be considered in the assessment. Mothers and fathers may not have the same perceptions about a child's behavior problems, and this suggests the need to coordinate multiple sources of information. In fact, sometimes in the assessment process practitioners may discover that they need to design different interventions depending on the situation and perception of the significant other involved. The importance of the child's perspective should not be overlooked. This is particularly true when addressing internalizing as opposed to externalizing disorders. Internal processes such as low self-esteem, subjective feelings of distress, and negative self-statements may be difficult for parents or teachers to identify (LaGreca, 1990). Studies have found that adolescents' reports of depression often go undetected by parents and teachers (Rutter & Taylor, 2002). Therefore, there is a real value in obtaining the child's perspective by using assessment tools.

Children may react to the demand characteristics of the assessment process and may respond in socially desirable ways. To conduct accurate child assessments, practitioners need to limit socially desirable responses. This can be mediated by carefully providing instructions, such as reminding children that there are no right and wrong answers and prompting them to give honest answers.

WEB SITES

Center for HIV Identification, Prevention and Treatment Services. http://chipts.ucla.edu/assessment/ib/main_pages/category2.asp.
New Assessment: Early Childhood Resources, University of New Mexico's Center for Development and Disability. http://newassessment.org/default.cfm.

References

Bloom, M., Fischer, J., & Orme, J. G. (2005). *Evaluating practice: Guidelines for the accountable professional.* Boston: Allyn & Bacon.

Corcoran, K., & Fischer, J. (1999). *Measures for clinical practice: Vol. 1. Couples, families, children,* 3rd ed. New York: Free Press.

Hodges, K., Wong, M. M., & Latessa, M. (1998). Use of the Child and Adolescent Functional Assessment Scale (CAFAS) as an outcome measure in clinical settings. *Journal of Behavioral Health Services & Research, 25,* 325–336.

Kazdin, A. E. (1983). Hopelessness, depression, and suicidal intent among psychiatrically disturbed children. *Journal of Consulting and Clinical Psychology, 51,* 504–510.

King, R. A. (1997). Practice parameters for the psychiatric assessment of children and adolescents. *Journal of the American Academy of Child and Adolescent Psychiatry, 36,* 4–20.

Krysik, J., & Finn, J. (2006). *Research for social work practice with student CD-ROM and ethics primer.* Dubuque, IA: McGraw-Hill.

LaGreca, A. M. (1990). *Through the eyes of the child: Obtaining self reports from children and adolescents.* Boston: Allyn & Bacon.

LeCroy, C. W. (In press). *Handbook of evidence-based child and adolescent treatment manuals.* New York: Oxford University Press.

Matson, J. L., Rotatori, A. F., & Helsel, W. J. (1983). Development of a rating scale to measure social skills in children: The Matson Evaluation of Social Skills with Youngsters (MESSY). *Behavior, Research and Therapy, 21,* 335–340.

McCubbin, H. I., Thompson, A. I., & McCubbin, M. A. (1996). *Family assessment: Resiliency, coping, and adaptation.* Madison: University of Wisconsin Press.

Merrell, K. W. (2007). *Behavioral, social, and emotional assessment of children and adolescents,* 3rd ed. Mahwah, NJ: Erlbaum.

Robinson, E. A., Eyberg, S. M., & Ross, A. W. (1980). The standardization of an inventory of child conduct problem behaviors. *Journal of Clinical Child Psychology, 9,* 22–29.

Smith, S. R., & Handler, L. (2006). *The clinical assessment of children and adolescents: A practitioner's handbook.* New York: Routledge.

Rutter, M., & Taylor, E. (2002). Clinical assessment and diagnostic formulation. In M. Rutter & E. Taylor (Eds.), *Child and adolescent psychiatry,* 4th ed. (pp. 18–32). Malden, MA: Blackwell.

Verhulst, F. C., & Van der Ende, J. (2002). Rating scales. In M. Rutter & E. Taylor (Eds.), *Child and adolescent psychiatry,* 4th ed. (pp. 70–86). Malden, MA: Blackwell.

53

Assessment Protocols and Rapid Assessment Instruments with Troubled Adolescents

David W. Springer & Stephen J. Tripodi

Troubled adolescents present a unique set of challenges and opportunities to the social work practitioner. Though there are clearly similarities between conducting an assessment with adolescents compared with children or adults, there are also distinct differences that warrant special consideration. Adolescents are negotiating specific developmental tasks, such as separating from the family and developing a sexual identity. Anyone who has worked with adolescents will certainly agree that they bring a unique (and often refreshing) perspective to the helping relationship that a competent practitioner integrates into a thorough assessment protocol.

In addition to the importance placed on recognizing the developmental tasks of adolescence during the assessment process, this chapter rests on the assumptions about assessment presented by Jordan and Franklin (1995): "(1) assessment is empirically based, (2) assessment must be made from a systems perspective, (3) measurement is essential, (4) ethical practitioners evaluate their clinical work, and (5) well qualified practitioners are knowledgeable about numerous assessment methods in developing assessments" (p. 3). These assumptions serve as a guide for social workers when determining what type of assessment protocol to implement with adolescents (and their families).

The first of these assumptions, that assessment is empirically based, was addressed in 2005 when the *Journal of Clinical Child and Adolescent Psychology* devoted a special section on developing guidelines for the evidence-based assessment of child and adolescent disorders, where evidence-based assessment (EBA) is "intended to develop, elaborate, and identify the measurement strategies and procedures that have empirical support in their behalf" (Kazdin, 2005, p. 548). In this special issue, Mash and Hunsley (2005) emphasize the great importance of assessment as part of intervention and acknowledge that the development of EBA has not kept up with the increased emphasis on evidenced-based treatment. In fact, there is a significant disconnect between EBA and evidence-based treatment. This is particularly true for youth with comorbid disorders.

COMORBID DISORDERS

The terms *comorbid disorders* and *coexisting disorders* are frequently used interchangeably to describe adolescents who have two or more coexisting diagnoses on axis I or axis II of the *DSM-IV-TR* (American Psychiatric Association, 2000), whereas the term *dual diagnosis* is often reserved to refer to clients with at least one axis I diagnosis and a substance abuse problem. Findings from the National Comorbidity Study indicate that 41 to 65 percent of individuals with substance abuse disorders also meet criteria for a mental disorder, and approximately 43 to 51 percent of those with mental disorders are diagnosed with a substance use disorder (Kessler et al., 2005; Tripodi, Kim, & DiNitto, 2006). Roberts and Corcoran (2005) assert that dually diagnosed adolescents are in fact not a special subpopulation of adolescents but instead the norm. The majority of adolescents seeking services today are thus likely to have substance use problems, mental health diagnoses, as well as myriad social, behavioral, and familial problems (Bender, Springer, & Kim, 2006).

Given the prevalence of coexisting disorders in clinical settings and the seriousness of making false-positive or false-negative diagnoses, it is critical that social work practitioners assess for the presence of comorbid disorders in a deliberate manner rather than making "on-the-spot" diagnoses. A social worker's assessment often helps guide treatment planning. Misdiagnosing an adolescent as not having (or having) a certain set of problems (e.g., mistaking acting out behaviors related to poverty as conduct disorder, confusing symptoms of ADHD with bipolar disorder) can pose serious consequences for the course of treatment (e.g., the wrong medications may be prescribed, adolescents and their families may be turned off to treatment owing to repeated treatment "failures"). Using sound assessment methods can help eliminate such pitfalls.

ASSESSMENT METHODS

There are various methods of assessment available to social work practitioners that can be used with adolescents. These include but are not limited to interviews, self-observation, observation by others, family sculpting, individualized rating scales, rapid assessment instruments, and standardized assessment tools. Though the focus of this chapter is primarily on the use of standardized assessment tools with adolescents, the importance and clinical utility of other available assessment methods, such as conducting a thorough interview, are also underscored.

Interviews

The assessment process typically starts with a face-to-face interview (e.g., psychosocial history) alone with the adolescent so he or she does not feel restricted disclosing information in the presence of his or her family. The family, however, should also be involved for at least part of the interview. The interview serves several purposes, such as an opportunity to establish rapport with the client and allow the client to tell his or her story. Recall that one key assumption of conducting a good assessment is to operate from a systems perspective. Involving the family during part of the interview may help meet this goal, because family members often provide varying perspectives and are often a key factor in an adolescent's life. (It is important to note, however, that the practitioner has to negotiate how to maintain the confidentiality of the adolescent client if also working with the family system.)

Consider the following case for illustration purposes. Roberto, a 14-year-old Hispanic male who has been diagnosed with ADHD and oppositional defiant disorder, is brought into your agency by his parents because he is "failing eleventh-grade Spanish and precalculus, and he won't listen." In addition to obtaining information from Roberto's parents typically covered in a psychosocial history (e.g., medical, developmental, social, and family history), some areas that the social worker may cover with Roberto's parents during an initial interview are as follows:

- Presenting problem and specific precipitating factor (e.g., "Tell me in your own words what prompted you to bring Roberto in for help at this point in time?");
- Attempts to deal with the problem (e.g., "What has your family tried to deal with this problem(s)? What have you tried that has worked?");
- Hopes and expectations (e.g., "What do you hope to get out of coming here for services? If you could change any one thing about how things are at home, what would it be?"); and
- Exceptions to the problem (e.g., "When was the problem not evident in your recent past? What was different then?").

In addition to these areas of inquiry (with variations of the corresponding sample questions), consider some questions that the social worker may ask Roberto individually:

- Peer relationships (e.g., "Tell me about your friends. What do you like to do together?");
- School (e.g., "What are your favorite [and least favorite] classes at school? What about those classes do you like [not like]?");
- Suicide risk (e.g., "When you feel down, do you ever have any thoughts of hurting/ killing yourself? Do you ever wish you were dead? How would you end your life?");
- Substance use (e.g., "What do you drink/use? When was the last time you had a drink/ used? How much did you have? Have you

ever unsuccessfully tried to reduce your substance use?"); and

- Targeted behavior/goal setting (e.g., "If there was any thing that you could change about yourself/your life, what would it be? What do you like most about yourself?").

Of course, the foregoing questions are meant only to illustrate the range of issues that one might address during an interview. A complete psychosocial history needs to be conducted. Information gathered from the face-to-face interview can subsequently be used to inform a more in-depth assessment in targeted areas, which in turn guides treatment planning. Rapid assessment instruments and other standardized assessment protocols may prove useful for this purpose.

Rapid Assessment Instruments and Standardized Assessment Tools

Rapid assessment instruments (RAIs) (Levitt & Reid, 1981) are short-form, pencil-and-paper assessment tools that are used to assess and measure change for a broad spectrum of client problems (Bloom, Fischer, & Orme, 2006; Corcoran & Fischer, 2007; Hudson, 1982). RAIs are used as a method of empirical assessment, are easy to administer and score, are typically completed by the client, and can help monitor client functioning over time. Given the proliferation of RAIs and standardized tools in recent years that measure various areas of adolescent functioning, it can be an overwhelming task to select a tool for use with an individual client. Thus, some guidelines are provided here.

The social worker practitioner needs to take several factors into consideration when choosing an RAI or standardized protocol for use with clients, such as the tool's reliability, validity, clinical utility, directness, availability, and so on (Corcoran & Fischer, 2007). To the extent that an RAI has sound psychometric properties, it helps practitioners measure a client's problem consistently (reliability) and accurately (validity). Using reliable and valid tools becomes increasingly critical as one considers the complexities surrounding assessment with adolescents who (potentially) have comorbid disorders. A brief overview of reliability and validity is provided next; however, the reader is referred to the other sources for a more detailed exposition on these topics (Corcoran & Fischer, 2007; Hudson, 1982; Springer, Abell, & Hudson, 2002; Springer, Abell, & Nugent, 2002).

Reliability. A measurement instrument is reliable to the extent that it consistently yields similar results over repeated and independent administrations. A tool's reliability is represented through reliability coefficients, which range from 0.0 to 1.0. What constitutes a satisfactory level of reliability depends on how a measure is to be used. For use in research studies and scientific work, a reliability coefficient of 0.60 or greater is typically considered acceptable (Hudson, 1982). However, for use in guiding decision making with individual clients, a higher coefficient is needed. Springer, Abell, and Nugent (2002) provide the following guidelines for acceptability of reliability coefficients for use with individual clients:

- <0.70 = Unacceptable,
- $0.70–0.79$ = Undesirable,
- $0.80–0.84$ = Minimally acceptable,
- $0.85–0.89$ = Respectable,
- $0.90–0.95$ = Very good,
- >0.95 = Excellent.

The greater the seriousness of the problem being measured (e.g., suicidal risk), and the graver the risk of making a wrong decision about a client's level of functioning, the higher the standard should be adopted.

Validity. Where reliability represents an instrument's degree of consistency, validity represents how accurately an instrument measures what it is supposed to measure. There are various ways to determine an instrument's validity: content validity (which subsumes face validity), criterion-related validity (concurrent and predictive), and construct validity (convergent and discriminant).

The social worker must make decisions about a measure's validity in relationship to its intended use. In other words, he or she must determine if the measure is valid for that particular client in a particular setting at a given time. A measure may be valid for one client but not for another.

The number of standardized tools developed specifically for use with adolescents has grown considerably in recent years, and it is impossible to review them all here. However, selected standardized tools that may be useful in assessing for comorbid disorders in adolescents are briefly reviewed next. Each tool has sound psychometric properties and can be used to help guide treatment planning and monitor client progress over the course of treatment.

Child and Adolescent Functional Assessment Scale (CAFAS). The CAFAS (Hodges, 2000; Hodges, Xue, & Watring, 2004) is a standardized instrument used to measure the degree of impairment in youth ages 7 to 17. It is a clinician-rated measure, covering eight areas of functioning: school/ work, home, community, behavior toward others, moods/ emotions, self-harmful behavior, substance use, and thinking. In each of these domains, the practitioner chooses behavioral indicators about the youth's functioning. Some sample items are as follows.

- Frequent display of anger toward others; angry outbursts.
- Talks or repeatedly thinks about harming self, killing self, or wanting to die.
- Frequently intoxicated or high (e.g., more than two times a week).
- Frequently fails to comply with reasonable rules and expectations within the home.

The youth's level of functioning in each domain is then scored as severe (score of 30), moderate (score of 20), mild (score of 10), or minimal (score of 0). These scores are graphically depicted on a one-page scoring sheet that provides a profile of the youth's functioning in each area. The CAFAS also contains optional strengths-based and goal-oriented items (e.g., good behavior in classroom; obeys curfew) that are helpful in guiding treatment planning. A computerized software program is available that scores the CAFAS, generates a treatment plan, and produces outcome reports to help practitioners track client progress (Hodges, 2000).

Behavioral and Emotional Rating Scale (BERS). The BERS (Epstein, Mooney, & Ryser, 2004; Epstein & Sharma, 1998) is a 52-item tool that measures functioning in youth ages 11 to 18 across five areas: interpersonal strength, involvement with family, intrapersonal strength, school functioning, and affective strength. Items are scored on a 4-point Likert scale (ranging from "very much like the child" to "not at all like the child"). It can be completed by teachers, parents, and practitioners and is easily scored and recorded on a summary/response form. A key feature that distinguishes the BERS from other standardized tools (e.g., Achenbach's widely used Child Behavior Checklist) is that it is truly based on a strengths perspective (in contrast to a deficit model), and the wording of the items reflects this perspective. Some sample items are as follows.

- Maintains positive family relationships.
- Accepts responsibility for own actions.
- Pays attention in class.
- Identifies own feelings.

The strengths perspective makes this tool particularly appealing to parents, adolescents, and social workers who strive for a helping relationship that centers on client strengths and empowerment.

Adolescent Drug Abuse Diagnosis (ADAD). The ADAD (Friedman & Utada, 1989) is a 150-item semistructured interview instrument that addresses nine areas of functioning: medical, school, employment, social relations, family relations, psychological, legal, alcohol use, and drug use. Severity ratings (on a 10-point scale) are computed for each area to indicate the adolescent's need for treatment in each area.

Additional RAIs. In addition to the standardized tools reviewed here, there are numerous RAIs that can be used with adolescents to measure functioning across various areas, such as risk of running away (e.g., Adolescent Concerns Evaluation), suicidal tendencies (e.g., Multi-Attitude Suicide Tendency Scale), post-traumatic symptoms (e.g., Child and Parent Report of Posttraumatic Symptoms), conduct-problem behaviors (e.g., Eyeberg Child Behavior Checklist), family functioning (e.g., Family Assessment Device, Index of Family Relations), and peer relations (Index of Peer Relations), to name just a few (Corcoran & Fischer, 2007). There are also standardized general behavior rating scales (e.g., Louisville Behavior Checklist, Child Behavior Checklist, Conners Rating Scales) and tools that are useful for measuring the degree of functional impairment (e.g., Children's Global Assessment Scale) (Shaffer, Lucas, & Richters, 1999).

CONCLUSION

The field continues to make progress in developing user-friendly standardized assessment tools with sound psychometric properties that can be used in assessment with adolescents. Although these tools should not take the place of a face-to-face psychosocial history, they should be used to complement the assessment process and track progress in client functioning over the course of treatment. It is important to emphasize that a standardized tool does not take the place of a solid therapeutic helping relationship. A limitation of RAIs is that clients may answer items in a way that presents themselves in a certain light to the social worker. This risk is minimized to the extent that rapport has been established between the social worker and the adolescent and to the extent that the adolescent understands the importance of the assessment process and how it will be used to help him or her make desired changes.

Social workers have an ethical obligation to use empirical assessment protocols and standardized tools whenever possible, rather than relying solely on gut feelings when conducting assessments with adolescents. The potential consequences of misdiagnosing a client, such as Roberto, can be severe. Thus, social worker practitioners are encouraged to make use of available empirically based assessment tools within a systems framework to guide treatment planning, monitor client func-tioning, and evaluate the effectiveness of their interventions.

WEB SITES

Behavioral and Emotional Rating Scale. http://vinst.umdnj.edu/VAID/TestReport.asp?Code=BERS.

Child and Adolescent Functional Assessment Scale. http://www.cafas.com.

Institute of Behavior Research at Texas Christian University. http://www.ibr.tcu.edu.

References

American Psychiatric Association. (2000). *Diagnostic and statistical manual of mental disorders*, 4th ed., text revision. Washington, DC: APA.

Bender, K., Springer, D. W., & Kim, J. S. (2006). Treatment effectiveness with dually diagnosed adolescents: A systematic review. *Brief Treatment and Crisis Intervention*, 6(3), 177–205.

Bloom, M., Fischer, J., & Orme, J. G. (2006). *Evaluating practice: Guidelines for the accountable professional*, 5th ed. Boston, MA: Allyn & Bacon.

Corcoran, K., & Fischer, J. (2007). *Measures for clinical practice: A sourcebook*. Volumes I and II, 4th ed. New York: Free Press.

Epstein, M. H., Mooney, D., & Ryser, G. (2004). Reliability and validity of the behavioral and emotional rating scale (second edition): Youth rating scale. *Research on Social Work Practice, 14*, 358–363.

Epstein, M. H., & Sharma, J. M. (1998). *Behavioral and Emotional Rating Scale: A strength-based approach to assessment. Examiner's manual.* Austin, TX: Pro-ed.

Friedman, A. S., & Utada, A. A. (1989). A method for diagnosing and planning the treatment of adolescent drug abusers (the Adolescent Drug Abuse Diagnosis [ADAD] instrument). *Journal of Drug Education, 19*(4), 285–312.

Hodges, K. (2000). *The Child and Adolescent Functional Assessment Scale self training manual.* Department of Psychology, Eastern Michigan University, Ypsilanti.

Hodges, K., Xue, Y., & Watring, J. (2004). Use of the CFAS to evaluate outcome for youths with severe emotional disturbance served by public mental health. *Journal of Child and Family Studies, 13*, 325–339.

Hudson, W. W. (1982). *The clinical measurement package: A field manual.* Homewood, IL: Dorsey.

Jordan, C., & Franklin, C. (1995). *Clinical assessment for social workers: Quantitative and qualitative methods.* Chicago: Lyceum Books.

Kazdin, A. E. (2005). Evidence-based assessment for children and adolescents: Issues in measurement development and clinical application. *Journal of Clinical Child and Adolescent Psychology, 34*(3), 548–558.

Kessler, R. C., Berglund, P., Demler, O., Jin, R., Merikangas, K. R., & Walters, E. E. (2005). Lifetime prevalence and age-of-onset distributions of DSM-IV disorders in the National Comorbidity Survey replication. *Archives of General Psychiatry, 62*(6), 593–605.

Levitt, J., & Reid, W. (1981). Rapid-assessment instruments for practice. *Social Work Research and Abstracts, 17*(1), 13–19.

Mash, E., & Hunsley, J. (2005). Evidence-based assessment of child and adolescent disorders: Issues and challenges. *Journal of Clinical Child and Adolescent Psychology, 34*(3), 362–379.

Roberts, A., & Corcoran, K. (2005). Adolescents growing up in stressful environments, dual diagnosis, and sources of success. *Brief Treatment and Crisis Intervention, 5*(1), 1–8.

Shaffer, D., Lucas, C. P., & Richters, J. E. (Eds.). (1999). *Diagnostic assessment in child and adolescent psychopathology.* New York: Guilford.

Springer, D. W., Abell, N., & Hudson, W. W. (2002). Creating and validating rapid assessment instruments for practice and research: Part one. *Research on Social Work Practice, 12*, 408–439.

Springer, D. W., Abell, N., & Nugent, W. R. (2002). Creating and validating rapid assessment instruments for practice and research: Part two. *Research on Social Work Practice, 12*, 768–795.

Tripodi, S. J., Kim, J. S., & DiNitto, D. M. (2006). Effective strategies for working with students who have co-occurring disorders. In C. Franklin, M. B. Harris, & P. Allen-Meares (Eds.), *School social work and mental health workers training and resource manual.* London: Oxford University Press.

54

Using Standardized Tests and Instruments in Family Assessments

Jacqueline Corcoran

This chapter discusses the use of standardized self-report measures in work with families. Although it will include traditional family assessment measures, it will also involve instruments germane to common problems families might bring to social work settings. The chapter will involve, first, definitions and descriptions of standardized measures; second, a rationale for using standardized measures in family assessment will be provided. Then, guidelines for selecting inventories will be explored, along with a list of validated measures relevant to social work practice with families. Finally, discussion will center on some of the practical issues that arise when administering measures to family members.

DEFINITIONS AND DESCRIPTIONS

A measure helps determine the existence of certain behaviors, attitudes, feelings, or qualities—and their magnitude—in clients when they come to a social work practitioner for assistance. The first rule for using measures is to employ an already established measure, one that has been standardized, rather than devising and testing a new one. An inventory (the words *measure*, *inventory*, and *instrument* are used interchangeably) is standardized when it has been tested (normed) on a relevant group of people, a process that results in psychometric data—specifically, information about reliability and validity—that has to meet certain acceptable standards. *Reliability* refers to the consistency and the accuracy of the measure, and *validity* involves the extent to which the instrument measures what it purports to measure. For the different methods of determining reliability and validity, please see a social work research text (e.g., Rubin & Babbie, 2008).

Standardization of an instrument also means there are certain procedures for its administration: items are completed in the order they appear, certain items cannot be taken out at the administrator's discretion, nor can only certain items be chosen as items are considered as a set. A certain procedure for scoring the measure has also been developed (Fischer & Corcoran, 2006).

Standardized measures can be completed by the client (self-report); by an important collateral person who can make key observations about the client's behavior, attribute, or attitude (a parent, teacher, or spouse, for example); or by the practitioner using an observational measure. This discussion will concentrate on either client self-report measures or inventories completed by parents of children, because the emphasis here is on family assessment.

RATIONALE FOR USE OF MEASURES

Why should social workers use family assessment measures? After all, they take time away from service delivery, clients may resent filling them out and fail to see their relevance, and they require some effort for the practitioner to find and to figure out how to score. However, the use of instruments in family assessment offer several potential benefits.

- They provide detailed information about feelings—attitudes and qualities, and their magnitude, information that may be difficult to observe overtly (Fischer & Corcoran, 2006).
- They aid in the assessment process, helping the practitioner determine the specific issues to address and to select appropriate services.

- They track client progress to ascertain whether interventions proceed in the needed direction.
- Positive changes may motivate the client to continue to participate in services and to make progress (Fischer & Corcoran, 2006).
- If gathered in sufficient numbers, measures can provide information about the effectiveness of a particular approach or intervention with a group of individuals for an agency, funding source, or dissemination of knowledge to the field.
- They provide evidence to third-party payers for reimbursement or to establish the need for continued services.

SELECTING MEASURES

Selection of measures depends on the purpose for which measurement is targeted (screening, assessment, monitoring progress), the nature of the client's problem, practicality issues, and the psychometric capacities of the instrument (Fischer & Corcoran, 2006). In the purpose of measurement, for example, if the instrument is to assess progress, is it sensitive to clinical change (Johnson et al., 2005)? Issues of practicality include the length of the instrument and the ability of the client to complete it. Fischer and Corcoran (2006) suggest that a scale should take no longer than 10 to 15 minutes to complete. Some measures have both a longer and a shorter version. For instance, the Parenting Stress Index (Abidin, 1995) has a 120-item version and a 36-item version. Other issues of practicality specifically for supervisors and managers include the cost of purchasing measures, the resources involved in training social work staff, the length of time required to score and interpret measures (Johnson et al., 2005), and, if it is necessary to compile the results of multiple scores, the resources involved with finding a usable database system, the construction of a database, data entry, and data analysis.

Psychometric standards for selecting instruments include established validity and reliability. Many agency personnel rely on instruments they have created to assess client functioning and to measure client change. This is ill-advised, despite the prevalence of this practice; without established reliability and validity, "various alternative explanations for the findings (e.g., examiner bias, chance, and effects of maturation) cannot be ruled

out, which seriously restricts the usefulness of findings: (Johnson et al., 2005, p. 7).

Another question related to psychometrics is how similar the client population is on the characteristics of the sample on which the instrument was normed. Many psychological inventories have been normed on undergraduate samples, traditionally from white and middle- to upper-class populations, which may differ in significant ways from high school–educated, low socioeconomic status, and/or minority clients. Although a measure may not necessarily be rejected because it has been normed on a sample dissimilar from the characteristics of a particular client or client group, some care must then be taken on the interpretation of scores.

Several publications have compiled various family assessment instruments. Volume 1 of Fischer and Corcoran (2006) focuses on children, couples, and families. For child and adolescent problems, the interested reader is urged to consult Mash and Barkley (2007), which provides a comprehensive discussion of various self-report instruments, rating scales for teachers and parents, and behavioral observational measures. Corcoran (2000) compiled instruments organized by type of problems for which families may receive services. Corcoran and Walsh (2006) delineate measures that involve child and adolescent DSM-defined diagnoses, and Early and Newsome (2005) discuss measures that emphasize strengths for families. Finally, Johnson et al. (2005) specifically address family assessment in relation to child welfare.

The following section details information on family assessment measures, specifically family functioning, parenting practices, and marital functioning, with demonstrated validity and reliability that have been reviewed by Corcoran (2000).

Family Functioning

Stemming from the field of family therapy and a family systems theoretical approach, three main self-report measures are widely used to assess the family as the unit of attention (Johnson et al., 2005): the McMaster Family Assessment Device, the Family Environment Scale, and the Family Adaptability and Cohesion Evaluation Scale. These instruments are highly correlated with one another and may be used interchangeably (Olson, 2000; Beavers & Hampson as cited in Johnson et al., 2005).

The McMaster Family Assessment Device (FAD) (Epstein, Baldwin, & Bishop, 1983) is a 60-item,

Likert-type self-report measure that assesses over-all health/pathology in a general score, as well as six areas of family functioning: (1) problem solving; (2) communication; (3) roles; (4) affective responsiveness; (5) affective involvement; and (6) behavior control.

The Family Environment Scale (FES) (Moos & Moos, 1981) is a 90-item, true-false questionnaire assessing ten dimensions of family life in three general areas: (1) relationship dimensions, which involve cohesion, expressiveness, and conflict; (2) personal growth dimensions, which involve independence, achievement orientation, intellectual/cultural orientation, moral-religious emphasis, and active-recreational orientation; and (3) system maintenance dimensions, which involve organization and control. There are three different forms of the FES: the real form, which assesses members' perceptions of their families; the ideal form, measuring members' preferred family environments; and the expectations form, which assesses members' expectations about family environments.

The Family Adaptability and Cohesion Evaluation Scales, version IV (FACES IV) (Olson & Gorall, 2003). FACES-IV is a 62-item self-report measure in which members rate their families on two different dimensions: (1) adaptability (ability of a family system to alter structure, roles, and rules in response to situational and developmental stress), and (2) cohesion (emotional bonding). FACES IV also assesses family communication and satisfaction.

Parenting Assessment

Measures of parenting often stem from the field of developmental psychology with the caregiver–child dyad as the unit of analysis (Johnson et al., 2005). We focus on the Child Abuse Potential Inventory and the Parenting Stress Index as prime examples of these types of instruments.

The Child Abuse Potential Inventory (Milner, 1986), a 160-item, self-report survey, includes a 77-item physical child abuse scale with six descriptive factor scales: (1) distress, (2) rigidity, (3) unhappiness, (4) problems with child and self, (5) problems with family, and (6) problems from others. The Child Abuse Potential Inventory can be completed by those with a third-grade reading level.

The Parenting Stress Index (Abidin, 1995) is a 120-item, self-report inventory for parents of children ages 1 month to 12 years. It yields not only a total score of parenting stress but also whether sources of stress may be related to child characteristics (child's adaptability, reinforcing qualities,

demandingness, activity level, mood, and acceptability to the parent) or parental functioning (the parent's sense of competence, isolation, depression, attachment to the child, parent health, perceived restrictions of role, depression, and spousal and social system support). The short form (36 items) has the following subscales: (1) total stress, (2) parental distress, (3) parent–child dysfunctional interaction, and (4) difficult child (Abidin, 1995).

Partner Relational Functioning

Several instruments are designed to assess marital functioning. The Marital Adjustment Test (Locke & Wallace, 1959) is a 15-item self-report assessing the accommodation of partners to each other. The Dyadic Adjustment Scale (Spanier, 1999) is a 32-item self-report inventory measuring marital adjustment with four subscales: (1) dyadic consensus (agreement regarding marital issues), (2) dyadic cohesion (the extent to which partners are involved in joint activities), (3) dyadic satisfaction (overall evaluation of relationship and level of commitment), and (4) affectional expression (the extent of affection and sexual involvement). To measure the frequency of various forms of overt marital hostility (e.g., quarrels, sarcasms, and physical abuse) witnessed by children, use the 20-item O'Leary-Porter Scale (Porter & O'Leary, 1980).

Intimate partner violence can be measured by the Revised Conflict Tactics Scales (Straus, Hamby, Boney-McCoy, & Sugarman, 1996). This 78-item, self-report instrument assesses psychological and physical attacks on a partner, as well as the use of negotiation, in a marital, cohabiting, or dating relationship. The following subscales are included: (1) physical assault, (2) psychological aggression, (3) negotiation, (4) injury, and (5) sexual coercion. The items are asked in the form of questions (what the participant did and what the partner did). They are written at a sixth-grade reading level.

GUIDELINES FOR USING MEASURES

The following are guidelines for the administration of measures:

When Will the Measure Be Completed?

Preferably, before services have begun (so the social worker can assess the impact of intervention)—during intake or at the first contact with the social worker.

Where Will the Measure Be Completed?

A quiet place, free of distractions with a hard writing surface available—a desk or a clipboard—and appropriate writing utensils.

Why Should the Social Worker Be Present if All Family Members are Filling out Measures?

Members might start discussing items among themselves, and the more powerful people in the family might influence others' responses. Children are particularly vulnerable because they often have difficulty reading and understanding items. If parents start reading the measure to the child, children may either respond in a way they think is desirable to the parent, or parents may more actively influence their responses ("You don't feel sad, do you?").

What Procedure Should the Worker Follow in the Administration of Measures?

- Explain the purpose of the measure (see rationale section).
- Read aloud the directions, which includes how the client should respond to items.
- Check the instrument over.
- Score the instrument (in front of the client, if at all possible, so immediate feedback can be provided; Fischer & Corcoran, 2006).
- Repeat the measure at a later date (at a designated time frame, such as every month, at the termination of services, and possibly as a follow-up to services) using similar procedures each time.
- Track scores over time and provide feedback to the client on progress.

What if Clients Seem Unable to Complete Measures?

If individuals are unsure of an answer, they should be encouraged to provide what they think is the best answer. The social worker should avoid interpreting the items or questions.

If a child seems to be struggling to complete an instrument or complains about not being able to understand the items, the practitioner can separate the child from other family members, and the measure can be read aloud to the child.

Adults will not usually volunteer that they cannot read, but if a person seems to be struggling, then the social worker may ask if the client would prefer if items were read aloud with the worker recording responses.

For non–English-speaking clients, the best source of information on the availability of measures written in other languages is the author of the inventory or the publishing house.

If a client complains about difficulties completing a measure, perhaps he or she could agree to come earlier for subsequent sessions so that completion of an instrument can occur in the waiting area and does not interfere with session time. Other alternatives include selecting a measure with fewer items.

What Should the Practitioner Be Checking for When the Instrument Is Completed?

Items left blank, which can be pointed out to the client, so the measure is fully completed.

Bias in terms of social desirability (clients responding in a way that they think pleases the worker, or in a way to suggest that services are either not necessary or should not be terminated) or a response set bias (clients answering items in a particular pattern, e.g., all 4s on a 6-point scale]) (Fischer & Corcoran, 2006). Inquiring about a particular pattern may provide information about the client's level of comprehension of items or the level of cooperation.

CONCLUSION

The use of measurement instruments for assessment and evaluation will, in all likelihood, increase owing to the demands of managed care. The information provided will assist the social worker not only in choosing appropriate measures for use in family assessment but also aid in gaining familiarity with some of the practical matters involved so that the clinical utility of measurement instruments will be maximized.

WEB SITES

Assesments.com. http://www.assessments.com
Child Welfare Information Gateway. Family-centered assessment. http://www.childwelfare .gov/famcentered.
UCLA Subscales of McMaster Family Assessment Device (FAD). http://chipts.ucla.edu/assessment/ IB/List_Scales/McMaster_Family_Assessment .htm.

References

Abidin, R. R. (1995). *Parenting stress index*, 3rd ed. Professional manual. Odessae, FL: Psychological Assessment Resources.

Corcoran, J. (2000). *Evidence-based social work practice with families: A lifespan approach.* New York: Springer.

Corcoran, J., & Walsh, J. (2006). *Clinical assessments and diagnosis in social work practice.* New York, NY: Oxford University Press.

Early, T., & Newsome, S. (2005). Measures for assessment and accountability in practice with families from a strengths perspective. In J. Corcoran, *Building strengths and skills: A collaborative approach to working with clients,* (pp. 359–393). New York: Oxford University Press.

Epstein, N., Baldwin, L., & Bishop, D. (1983). The McMaster family assessment device. *Journal of Marital and Family Therapy, 9,* 171–180.

Fischer, J., & Corcoran, K. (2006). *Measures for clinical practice and research: A sourcebook, Volume 1: Couples, Families, and Children,* 4th ed. New York: Oxford University Press.

Johnson, M., Stone, S., Lou, C., Vu, C., Ling, J., Mizrahi, P., et al. (2005). Family assessment in child welfare services: Instrument comparisons. Retrieved on October 19, 2007, from http://www.bassc.net/html/pdfs/FA_FULL.doc.

Locke, H., & Wallace, K. (1959). Short marital-adjustment and prediction tests: Their reliability and validity. *Marriage and Family Living, 21,* 251–255.

Mash, E. J., & Barkley, R. A. (2007). *Assessment of childhood disorders,* 4th ed. New York: Guilford.

Milner, J. S. (1986). *The child abuse potential inventory: Manual,* 2nd ed. Webster, NC: Psytec.

Moos, R. H., & Moos, B. S. (1981). *Family environment scale manual.* Palo Alto, CA: Consulting Psychologists Press.

Olson, D. H. (2000). Circumplex model of marital and family sysyems. *Journal of Family Therapy, 22,* 144–167.

Olson, D., & Gorrall, D. (2003). Circumplex model of marital and family systems. In F. Walsh (Ed.), *Normal family processes: Growing diversity and complexity,* 3rd ed. (pp. 514–548). New York: Guilford.

Porter, B., & O'Leary, D. (1980). Marital discord and childhood behavior problems. *Journal of Abnormal Child Psychology, 8,* 287–295.

Rubin, A., & Babbie, E. (2008). *Research methods for social work,* 6th ed. Pacific Grove, CA: Brooks/Cole.

Spanier, G. B. (1999). *Dyadic adjustment scale manual.* Toronto: Multi-Healthsystems.

Straus, M., Hamby, S., Boney-McCoy, S., & Sugarman, D. (1996). The revised Conflict Tactics Scales (CTS2). *Journal of Family Issues, 17,* 283–316.

Understanding a Diagnosis

55   *What it Does and Does Not Tell You*

William R. Nugent

Social workers will encounter diagnoses in many fields of practice. Obvious examples are in medical social work, where the practitioner may work with patients diagnosed as having, say, some form of cancer; in mental health, where clients may be diagnosed (by the practitioner or someone else) as having obsessive-compulsive disorder; and less obviously in fields such as child welfare in which a client may be "diagnosed" as having been sexually or physically abused on the basis of some assessment procedure. A diagnosis is a judgment call, an inference, based on the results of some assessment procedure. The assessment procedure can be highly structured and standardized, as in the

Anxiety Disorders Interview Schedule—Revised (Di Nardo, Brown, & Barlow, 1994). Examples of questions asked in this interview are:

- "Have you had times when you have felt a sudden rush of intense fear or anxiety or feeling of impending doom?"
- "In what situation(s) have you had these feelings?"
- "Have you had these feelings come 'from out of the blue,' or while you are at home alone, or in situations where you did not expect them to occur?"

Highly structured and standardized assessment methods can also be found in a medical context, such as in the use of an instrument to measure blood pressure or a testing procedure for detecting the presence of a pathogen. The assessment procedure can also be highly idiosyncratic to the practitioner and highly unstructured, in both assessment methodology and diagnostic criteria, as in free-style interviews (Garb, 1998). The information obtained from the assessment is used to make inferences about whether the client or patient has a particular mental or physical disorder; has experienced a particular event, such as abuse; has engaged in some form of behavior, such as delinquent behavior sub-

sequent to involvement in a juvenile justice program (i.e., has the youth recidivated?); and so forth for other forms of categorical inference.

Frequently, once a diagnosis has been made, the practitioner acts as if this judgment—that the client has a particular medical or psychological condition—is taken to be a given and he or she bases subsequent treatment decisions on this presumption (Garb, 1998). The practitioner acts as if the probability that the client has the disease or disorder, given that he or she has been diagnosed as having it, is a certainty (Garb & Boyle, 2003). The diagnosis is interpreted as indicating that the client "has the disorder." In fact, as you will see in what follows, a diagnosis is a form of probability statement and must be interpreted as such to avoid misdiagnosis and treatment errors leading to iatrogenic outcomes (Gold, 1996; Witztum, Margolin, Bar-On, & Levy, 1995). The issues discussed herein are elaborated in greater detail in Nugent (2004, 2005), and the Web links at the end of this chapter will lead the reader to further information and details.

UNDERSTANDING A DIAGNOSIS

First we review several important concepts. The box in Figure 55.1 shows both reality and the

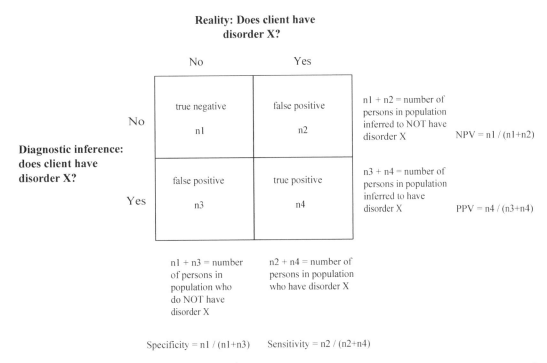

Figure 55.1 Reality/diagnosis box illustrating concepts of sensitivity, specificity, false positives, and false negatives.

outcomes of an inference made by a practitioner, on the basis of assessment results, about whether a client or patient has a particular disorder, what will be generically referred to from hereon as "disorder X." This disorder might be a physical disease, a mental health problem or disorder, an experience of some form of "abuse," or engaging in a particular behavior considered to be problematic, such as some form of delinquent or illegal behavior. The labels above the cells of the box in Figure 55.1 represent reality: a person either has (yes) or does not have (no) disorder X. The labels on the side of the box represent the judgment, or inference, made by a social worker from the results of some assessment procedure about whether or not the person has disorder X: the person has r (yes) or does not have (no) disorder X. The terms within the cells of the box describe the inferences made by the practitioner.

Sensitivity and Specificity

If the person does not have disorder X, and the practitioner infers on the basis of the assessment results that the person does not have the disorder (upper left cell in the box), then this correct inference is referred to as a *true negative*. In this cell, the symbol n1 represents the number of persons in population from which the person comes who do not have disorder X and who are accurately identified as not having the disorder through use of the assessment procedure.

If the person does not have disorder X, but the practitioner infers that the client does have it on the basis of the results from the assessment procedure (lower left cell), then this erroneous inference is referred to as a *false positive*. The symbol n3 in this cell represents the number of persons in the population who do not have disorder X who are erroneously identified as having the disorder on the basis of the assessment procedure.

The proportion of persons in the population who do not have disorder X who are correctly inferred to not have the disorder on the basis of the results of the assessment procedure is referred to as the *specificity* of the assessment procedure. In terms of Figure 55.1, the specificity is given by the fraction n1/(n1 + n3). The proportion of persons in the population who do not have the disorder X but are erroneously inferred to have it is referred to as the *false positive rate* of the assessment procedure. In terms of Figure 55.1, this rate is given by the fraction n3/(n1 + n3).

If the client does have the disorder, and the practitioner infers that the client does indeed have

the disorder on the basis of the results of the assessment procedure (lower right cell), then this correct inference is referred to as a *true positive*. In Figure 55.1, in the lower right cell, the symbol n4 refers to the number of persons in the population who have disorder X who are correctly inferred to have it on the basis of the assessment procedure.

If the person does have disorder X, but the practitioner erroneously infers on the basis of the assessment procedure that the person does not have it (cell in upper right), the erroneous inference is referred to as a *false negative*. The symbol n2 refers to the number of persons in the population who have disorder X but who are erroneously inferred to not have it on the basis of the assessment procedure.

The proportion of persons in the population who have disorder X and are correctly inferred to have the disorder on the basis of the assessment procedure is referred to as the *sensitivity* of the assessment or diagnostic procedure. In Figure 55.1 the sensitivity is given by the ratio n4/(n2 + n4). The proportion of persons in the population who have disorder X who are erroneously inferred to not have the disorder on the basis of the assessment procedure is referred to as the *false negative rate*, which is given by the fraction n2/(n2 + n4).

The sensitivity and specificity can be thought of as characteristics of an assessment or diagnostic procedure that describe how well it works for identifying whether a person has disorder X. Estimates of these values for specific measurement and assessment procedures can be found in the literature, as in Bech, Rasmussen, Olsen, Noerholm, & Abildgaard (2001).

The Positive Predictive Value

The positive predictive value (PPV) of a diagnosis made on the basis of an assessment procedure refers to *the probability that a person who has been diagnosed as having disorder X actually has this disorder*. The PPV of the diagnosis can be thought of as the answer to the question, "I have diagnosed this person as having disorder X using this particular assessment procedure. What is the probability that he or she actually has disorder X?" This probability can be expressed in two ways. The first, as noted, comes from Figure 55.1 and is given by the ratio of true positives divided by the sum of true and false positives; that is, by the fraction n4/(n3 + n4). The second way of expressing the PPV reveals an important characteristic of this index that is hidden in the first: it depends on the prevalence of disorder X in the population of interest. The *prevalence* is the proportion of persons in the population who have disorder X. This second way of expressing the PPV is given in the following formula that makes use of the prevalence of the disorder and the sensitivity and specificity of the assessment procedure.

$$PPV = \frac{prevalence \times sensitivity}{\begin{array}{l}(prevalence \times sensitivity)+ \\ \left[(1-prevalence)\times(1-specificity)\right]\end{array}}.$$

It is critically important to note that the prevalence, or base rate, of the disorder plays a critical role in the PPV. The practitioner cannot make sense of a diagnosis without knowing not only the sensitivity and specificity of an assessment or diagnostic procedure but also the prevalence of the disorder in the population that a client comes from, as has been pointed out by numerous authors (see, for example, Finn, 1982; Gambrill, 1997, 1990).

For example, the prevalence of major depression among adolescents has been estimated to be 0.034 (i.e., 3.4 percent) (Lewinsohn, Hops, Roberts, Seeley, & Andrews, 1993). A recent investigation by Williams, Pignone, Ramirez, and Stellato (2002) synthesized the results of 38 studies, involving 32,000 participants, on the sensitivity and specificity of 16 different measures of depression used to identify persons with major depressive disorder (MDD). The median sensitivity was 0.85, the median specificity was 0.74, and the results suggested that there were no significant differences between any of the instruments. Using these values for the sensitivity and specificity and the MDD prevalence of 0.034, we get a PPV of 0.10 for a diagnosis of MDD based on the results of an assessment using any of these tools. This means that if you diagnosed an adolescent as having MDD using the results from one of these instruments, the probability that the adolescent actually has MDD is only 0.10. The diagnosis is not especially informative because about 90 percent of adolescents diagnosed as having MDD using this assessment approach will be incorrect.

In comparison, in some populations of persons with certain medical conditions, there is evidence that the prevalence of MDD may be relatively high. For example, some research has suggested that the prevalence of MDD among women recently diagnosed with cancer is 0.23 (i.e., 23 percent; Evans et al., 1986). Using this prevalence with the foregoing sensitivity and specificity values, we get a PPV of 0.49 for a diagnosis of MDD. Note that the PPV has increased, given the same sensitivity and specificity, with the higher prevalence rate. Still, in this context the practitioner will know that about 50 percent of the persons diagnosed as having MDD using this assessment approach will not have this disorder.

The Negative Predictive Value

The negative predictive value (NPV) of a diagnosis made on the basis of an assessment procedure refers to *the probability that a person who has been judged as not having disorder X actually does not have this disorder.* The NPV of the diagnosis is the answer to the question, "I have decided, on the basis of results from this assessment procedure, that this person does not have disorder X. What is the probability that he or she actually does not have disorder X?" As with the PPV, this probability can be expressed in two ways. Based on Figure 55.1, it can be expressed as the fraction NPV = n1/(n1 + n2). This way of expressing the NPV hides the role that the prevalence plays in this index. A second way of expressing the NPV is as follows.

$$NPV = \frac{specificity \times (1-prevalence)}{\begin{array}{l}\left[specificity \times (1-prevalence)\right]+ \\ \left[prevalence \times (1-sensitivity)\right]\end{array}}.$$

Note again that the prevalence of the disorder plays a critical role in the NPV. As with the PPV, the practitioner cannot make sense of a judgment that a person does not have a particular disorder or disease on the basis of an assessment method without knowing the prevalence of the disorder in the population that a client comes from, in addition to the sensitivity and specificity of the assessment procedure being used.

For example, taking the sensitivity and specificity values for the measures for detecting MDD and the prevalence estimate of MDD among adolescents, the NPV for a judgment that an adolescent does not have MDD based on the results from one of these instruments would exceed 0.99. The NPV for a judgment that a woman recently diagnosed as having cancer does not have MDD would be slightly lower, about 0.94. In both cases, the NPVs indicate that the judgment that the person does not have MDD is relatively informative. In the first case only about 1 percent of persons determined to not have MDD will in fact have the disorder, whereas in the second about 6 percent will have MDD.

ILLUSTRATIVE *DSM* EXAMPLE

One of the more commonly used diagnostic systems used by social workers is the *Diagnostic and Statistical Manual of Mental Disorders* (DSM) (American Psychiatric Association, 2000). There is a voluminous literature on this system, and no attempt is made here to survey this work on the strengths and limitations of this diagnostic system. The reader is invited to read Chapters 45 and 46 about the *DSM* in this volume.

There is a structured interview protocol, the Diagnostic Interview Schedule (DIS; Robins, Helzer, Croughan, & Ratcliff, 1981), designed to make reliable *DSM* diagnoses. Examples of questions asked as a part of this interview are: "In your entire lifetime, have you ever had an attack of fear or panic when all of a sudden you felt frightened, anxious or uneasy?" and "Have you had an attack like this in the past 12 months?" Recently, Murphy, Monson, Laird, Sobol, and Leighton (2000) conducted research on the DIS and estimated the sensitivity of this interview protocol for detecting MDD to be 0.55 and the specificity to be 0.90. This protocol is believed to lead to more valid and reliable diagnoses than more unstructured interviews (Garb, 1998).

Now assume that the prevalence of MDD among adolescents seeking services is higher than in the general population of adolescents, a plausible presumption. Let's assume for sake of illustration that the prevalence of MDD is actually three times higher among adolescents actually seeking services or being brought in for services by parents or other authority figures, than the prevalence of depression in the general adolescent population. Thus, the prevalence is $3 \times 0.034 = 0.102$, or 10.2 percent. If the DIS is used to diagnose an adolescent as having a MDD, the PPV of this diagnosis is

$$PPV = \frac{.102 \times .55}{(.102 \times .55) + [(1 - .102)(1 - .90)]} = .38.$$

This number can be interpreted as telling us that a given adolescent diagnosed as having MDD using the DIS has a probability of only 0.38 of actually having a MDD. It can also be interpreted as telling us that only 38 percent of the adolescents diagnosed as having a MDD on the basis of the DIS will actually have a MDD.

The NPV of a judgment that an adolescent does not have a MDD on the basis of an interview using the DIS will be

$$NPV = \frac{(1 - .102).90}{[(1 - .102).90] + [.102(1 - 55)]} = .95.$$

Thus, the probability that an adolescent judged as not having a MDD on the basis of the DIS interview, actually does not have a MDD is about 0.95. Only 5 percent of adolescents so judged will actually have a MDD.

WHAT DOES THIS IMPLY ABOUT ASSESSMENT IN SOCIAL WORK PRACTICE?

Practitioners need to recognize that a diagnosis is a form of probability statement as opposed to a finding of fact that a client suffers from some physical or mental disorder. The social worker needs to know the sensitivity and specificity estimates for the assessment procedures they use and the best estimates of the prevalence rates of the various disorders in the populations of persons with whom they work. Without knowing these values, the social worker cannot know the PPVs and NPVs for diagnoses that he or she makes or that have been made by other practitioners, and therefore cannot intelligently interpret what information a diagnosis conveys. This practitioner error has been referred to as the ignoring of base rates (e.g., Gambrill, 1990, 1997; Garb, 1996).

The social worker also needs to appreciate the need for attempting to disconfirm a diagnosis that he or she has made. Typically practitioners endeavor to seek confirmatory evidence, as opposed to disconfirmatory, a form of confirmation bias (Gambrill, 1990, 1997; Garb, 1998). The importance of seeking disconfirmatory evidence can readily be seen using the PPV formula. If we were to assume that the specificity of an assessment procedure was 1.0—a number indicating that the assessment procedure allowed the practitioner to rule out with certainty the presence of a particular *DSM* diagnosis—then regardless of the sensitivity, the PPV of a diagnosis based on the assessment procedure would be

$$PPV = \frac{prevalence \times sensitivity}{(prevalence \times sensitivity) + [(1 - prevalence)(1 - 1)]}$$
$$= \frac{prevalence \times sensitivity}{prevalence \times sensitivity} = 1.$$

$$NPV = \frac{(1-.102).90}{[(1-.102).90]+[.102(1-.55)]} = .95.$$

The PPV will be 1.0, indicating certainty that the client has the disorder that he or she has been diagnosed as having, regardless of the value of the sensitivity. Thus, seeking evidence to disconfirm a diagnostic inference is one of the most important activities a social worker can engage in. The efforts to find disconfirmatory evidence can increase the specificity of the assessment procedure, thereby increasing the PPV of a diagnosis.

If sensitivity and specificity values do not exist for the assessment methods the social worker uses, or prevalence estimates do not exist for the various disorders in the populations with which the practitioner works, then diagnostic methods should not be used. In such a case, the social worker will be operating blindly with respect to what information a diagnosis conveys and will perhaps be tempted to act as if the PPVs and/or NPVs are so high as to demand certain forms of treatment options. In the absence of knowledge of these important pieces of information that are needed to understand what a diagnosis conveys, it would be better to use magnitude estimation forms of assessment and measurement, such as rapid assessment instruments or other forms of standardized scales and interviews (Nugent, 2004, 2005).

WEB SITES

Accuracy of Diagnostic Tests, by Rapid-Diagnostics.org http://www.rapid-diagnostics.org/accuracy.htm.

HIV Testing and Treatment, Hartford University. http://uhavax.hartford.edu/bugl/treat.htm.

Sensitivity and Specificity, from the Medical University of South Carolina. http://www.musc.edu/dc/icrebm/sensitivity.html.

References

American Psychiatric Association. (2000). *Diagnostic and statistical manual of mental disorders,* 4th ed., text revision. Washington, DC: APA.

Bech, P., Rasmussen, N., Olsen, R., Noerholm, V., & Abildgaard, W. (2001). The sensitivity and specificity of the Major Depression Inventory, using the present state examination as the index of diagnostic validity. *Journal of Affective Disorders, 66*(2–3), 159–164.

DiNardo, P. A., Brown, T. A., & Barlow, D. H. (1994). *The anxiety disorders interview schedule for DSM-IV.* Albany, NY: Graywind Publications.

Evans, D., et al. (1986). Depression in women treated for gynecological cancer: Clinical and neuroendocrine assessment. *American Journal of Psychiatry, 143*(4), 447–452.

Finn, S. (1982). Base rates, utilities, and DSM-III: Shortcomings of fixed rule systems of psychodiagnosis. *Journal of Abnormal Psychology, 91*(4), 294–302.

Gambrill, E. (1990). *Critical thinking in clinical practice.* San Francisco: Jossey-Bass.

Gambrill, E. (1997). *Social work practice: A critical thinker's guide.* New York: Oxford University Press.

Garb, H. (1998). *Studying the clinician: Judgement research and psychological assessment.* Washington, DC: APA.

Garb, H., & Boyle, P. (2003). Understanding why some clinicians use pseudo-scientific methods: Findings from research on clinical judgement. In S. O. Lilienfeld, S. J. Lynn, & J. M. Lohr (Eds.), *Science and pseudoscience in clinical psychology* (pp. 17–38). New York: Guilford.

Gold, M. (1996). The risk of misdiagnosing physical illness as depression. In F. Flach (Ed.), *The Hatherleigh guide to managing depression* (pp. 93–112). New York: Hatherleigh.

Lewinsohn, S., Hops, H., Roberts, R., Seely, J., & Andrews, J. (1993). Adolescent psychopathology: I. Prevalence and incidence of depression and other DSM-R disorders in high school students. *Journal of Abnormal Psychology, 102*(1), 133–144.

Murphy, J., Monson, N., Laird, A., Sobol, A., & Leighton, A. (2000). A comparison of diagnostic interviews for depression in the Stirling County study. *Archives of General Psychiatry, 57*(3), 230–236.

Nugent, W. (2004). The role of prevalence rates, sensitivity, and specificity on assessment accuracy: Rolling the dice in social work process. *Journal of Social Service Research, 31*(2), 51–75.

Nugent, W. (2005). The probabilistic nature of diagnosis: Rolling the dice in social work practice. In S. Kirk (Ed.), *Mental disorders in the social environment* (pp. 96–119). New York: Columbia University Press.

Robins, L., Helzer, J., Croughan, J., & Ratcliff, K. (1981). National Institute of Health Diagnostic Interview Schedule: Its history, characteristics, and validity. *Archives of General Psychiatry, 38,* 381–389.

Williams, J., Pignone, M., Ramirez, G., & Stellato, C. (2002). Identifying depression in primary care: A literature synthesis of case-finding instruments. *General Hospital Psychiatry, 24*(4), 225–237.

Witztum, E., Margolin, J., Bar-On, R., & Levy, A. (1995). Stigma, labeling and psychiatric misdiagnosis: Origins and outcomes. *Medicine and Law, 14*(7–8), 659–669.

Guidelines and Uses of Rapid Assessment Instruments in Managed Care Settings

Laura M. Hopson & John S. Wodarski

Managed care organizations (MCOs) require that practitioners provide the most necessary, efficient, and effective services to clients. Increased enrollment in MCOs and their emphasis on accountability has increased the use of rapid assessment instruments (RAIs) among service providers. The need to quickly and accurately assess for multiple presenting concerns, such as co-occurring mental health and substance abuse issues, has also increased the need for using RAIs among social worker practitioners in primary care, mental health, and other community-based settings. In addition, RAIs can help social workers demonstrate the effectiveness of their services through their use in single case designs.

The use of RAIs has grown rapidly with increasing demands for accountability in human services agencies. RAIs are standardized instruments that require little time to complete and score, thereby facilitating assessment and the ongoing evaluation of clinical practice. Fischer and Corcoran (2007) identify over 400 RAIs for use with individuals, couples, and families to assess for a wide array of presenting problems. They also allow social work practitioners to quickly evaluate the effectiveness of their interventions. This chapter discusses the increased use of RAIs due to the influence of managed care and current applications of RAIs for dual diagnosis assessment.

THE INFLUENCE OF MANAGED CARE ON ASSESSMENT

The stringent standards required by MCOs have changed the way services are delivered in human service agencies. It is estimated that 90 percent of insured Americans participate in some form of managed care health plan (Americas Health Insurance Plans [AHIP], 2005). The changes that are being implemented through MCOs come in response to the rising cost of health care in the United States (AHIP, 2005). The managed care system now requires helping professionals (physicians, psychologists, social workers, etc.) to be accountable for the types of service they provide, the type of clientele they serve, and the expense, duration, and outcome of the services provided. Therefore, professionals are required to work accurately, swiftly, empirically, and in a limited amount of time, while delivering more effective and cost efficient services. The standardized requirements of managed care have turned the profession towards creating and using RAIs that are easy to administer, score, and complete without losing validity or reliability (Bloome, Fischer, & Orme, 2006; Steenrod, 2005).

Clinicians report making changes in their assessment practices due to the influence of managed care policies. Projective and time-consuming assessments, such as Rorschach tests and the Wechsler Intelligence Scale, are used less often, whereas standardized brief measures, such as RAIs, are increasingly common (Cashel, 2002; Wood, Garb, Lilienfield, & Nezworski, 2002). In many cases, clinicians must obtain preauthorization from MCOs to be reimbursed for conducting psychological assessment. Even when assessment procedures are authorized, the clinician is often only allowed to bill the MCO for up to 2 hours of assessment procedures. This has discouraged clinicians from conducting traditional comprehensive assessments, which may typically require 4 hours or more (Camara, Nathan, & Puente, 2000;

Turchik, Karpenko, Hammers, & McNamara, 2007). Instead, they are turning to standardized instruments that can be administered quickly. Greater participation in MCOs is associated with increased use of standardized brief assessment instruments among community-based mental health and health service providers (Steenrod, 2005).

RAIs AND PRACTICE EVALUATION

In addition to encouraging the use of brief, standardized assessments, MCOs also require that providers are accountable for achieving treatment goals with clients. They include quality assurance reviews to monitor whether client's needs are being addressed effectively. Service providers are asked to demonstrate that their services are necessary and appropriate for their client population (Bloom et al., 2006). MCOs often require that an external reviewer assess the effectiveness and efficiency of services provided (Bloom et al., 2006).

Practitioners can demonstrate the effectiveness of their interventions to external reviews through the use of RAIs in single case design studies in which they repeatedly evaluate a client's progress toward treatment goals. Practitioners who use these designs work with clients to define specific, measurable treatment goals and measure progress toward these goals with brief, standardized instruments that can be administered on a regular basis, often weekly (Bloom et al., 2006). Because RAIs are reliable, quickly administered, and easily scored, practitioners can feasibly incorporate them into their weekly sessions with clients and monitor changes in scores over time.

SELECTING AN INSTRUMENT

The first step in choosing an instrument is identifying the primary presenting problem that will be measured based on initial assessment interviews. It is also important to consider who will be completing the measurement instrument. Clients often complete RAIs themselves, but there are many situations in which it may be preferable for the social worker or a significant other to complete them. When working with children, for example, parents or teachers will often be completing RAIs (Fischer & Corcoran, 2007).

After determining the appropriate problem area to measure and who will be completing the instrument, the social worker will need to locate an instrument. Fischer and Corcoran (2007) provide a two-volume catalog of RAIs. Several Web sites listed at the end of this chapter are also useful for finding instruments.

In deciding whether an assessment instrument is appropriate for a particular client, social workers should ensure that it has sufficient reliability and validity and has been tested with a population similar to the client in terms of cultural background, ethnicity, socioeconomic status, gender, age, and other demographic characteristics. See Chapter 53 for an overview of reliability and validity as they pertain to RAIs. Standardized measures such as RAIs typically provide scores that indicate the magnitude or intensity of a client's presenting problem (Fischer & Corcoran, 2007). They may indicate a cut-off score that distinguishes scores in the normal range from those in the clinical or problematic range. A detailed description of an RAI, the General Health Questionnaire, is provided next.

The General Health Questionnaire

The General Health Questionnaire (GHQ; Goldberg, 1972) is a measure of nonpsychotic psychological distress. The original version consists of 60 items, and subsequent shorter versions include 30, 28, 20, and 12 items. The 12-item version is widely used because it requires little time to complete and maintains strong psychometric properties (Picardi, Abeni, & Pasquini, 2001). The GHQ-12 can be completed in less than 5 minutes. It is also useful for use when clients require assistance in completing the measure or when clinicians need to read items to clients with limited literacy (Doi & Minowa, 2003).

The GHQ-12 has been found to be an accurate, reliable, and valid measure of psychiatric distress across many different cultural groups and various clinical issues (Doi & Minowa, 2003; Ip & Martin, 2006; Picardi et al., 2001). The instrument has been used in both medical and community settings and has been translated into a number of different languages (Picardi et al., 2001).

Each item on the GHQ-12 has four response categories: less than usual, no more than usual, rather more than usual, or much more than usual. The measure can be scored using a bimodal system in which every item receives a score of 0 for the first two responses or a score of one for the last two responses (0-0-1-1). Using a Likert scoring system, each item receives a score between 0 and 3. Total scores range from 0 to 12 for the bi-modal system and from zero to thirty-six for the Likert system (Montazeri et al., 2003). Higher scores indicate greater psychological distress. The clinical cutoff score is typically 1/2 to 2/3. When using a cut-off score of 2/3, the sensitivity rate has been averaged at approximately 80 percent with a specificity rate of approximately 81 percent (Gureje & Obikoya, 1990; Kapur, Kapur, & Carstairs, 1984; Mari & Williams, 1985). The 1/2 cut-off score has also been used, yielding a 94 percent sensitivity rate, and a 62 percent specificity rate (Van Hemert, Heijer, Vorstenbosch, & Bolk, 1995).

USING RAIs TO ASSESS FOR DUAL DIAGNOSIS

Many instruments exist that are reliable and valid for measuring one aspect of a problem or a particular diagnosis. However, social work practitioners often need to assess for dual diagnoses or co-occurring disorders because many clients may present with multiple presenting problems. Research indicates that substance abuse problems are prevalent among individuals with mental health disorders, for example (Bachman, Drainoni, & Tobias, 2004; Buckley, 2007; Hussey, Drinkard, & Flannery, 2007).

When practitioners do not use accurate, standardized instruments to assess for multiple presenting problems, misdiagnosis is often the result. General practitioners in medical settings often fail to identify mental health conditions such as depression (Van Os, Van den Brink, Van der Meer, & Ormel, 2006). There is some evidence that clients with substance abuse problems are misdiagnosed with mental health conditions such as bipolar disorder (Bhugra & Flick, 2005; Stewart & El-Mallakh, 2007). One small study found that among clients diagnosed with substance abuse and bipolar disorder, less than half had been accurately diagnosed with bipolar disorder (Stewart & El-Mallakh, 2007).

In assessing for dual diagnoses, practitioners need multiple, quick, and accurate assessments to choose a relevant intervention or refer clients to the appropriate helping agent. RAIs can be used to prevent misdiagnosis and ensure that clients are referred to appropriate services. This is also critical when MCOs are involved because quality assurance checks are used to determine that clients are receiving appropriate treatment (Bloom

et al., 2006). Because RAIs are administered so quickly, a clinician can use multiple assessment instruments within a single session. Whereas comprehensive psychological assessments have been known to require up to 4 hours of time, each RAI is likely to require between 10 and 30 minutes to administer. A client who comes to a community health center for a physical concern can be quickly assessed for substance abuse issues that are the primary concern and underlying cause of the physical ailments. Conducting the substance abuse assessment can prevent wasted time and money in addressing the physical concern that is secondary to the substance abuse problem.

RAIs that are effective in identifying substance abuse disorders include the CAGE, Alcohol Beliefs Scale, the Drug Abuse Screening Test, the Substance Abuse Subtle Screening Inventory, and the Michigan Alcoholism Screening Test (Dhalla & Kopec, 2007; Fischer and Corcoran, 2007; Dio & Minowa, 2003; Zeiler, Nemes, Holtz, Landis, & Hoffman, 2002). All of these scales can be administered in primary care, mental health, or substance abuse treatment settings and can yield rapid and accurate assessments. These instruments can be administered with ease, are simply scored, and are supported by empirical evidence as to their validity and reliability. A more detailed description of the CAGE instrument is provided next.

The CAGE Assessment

This RAI is comprised of four questions that relate directly to the effects of the individual's alcohol use. The questions require a "yes" or "no" answer. The CAGE acronym represents the four areas highlighted in the instrument's questions. The questions are as follows:

- Have you ever felt you should *cut* down on your drinking?
- Have people *annoyed* you by criticizing your drinking?
- Have you felt bad or *guilty* about your drinking?
- Have you ever had a drink first thing in the morning to steady your nerves or get rid of a hangover (*eye-opener*)? (Mayfield, McLeod, & Hall, 1974).

Typically, two or more affirmative responses on the CAGE is considered to be an indicator that alcohol abuse is an area of concern for the respondents, although one affirmative response has also been considered to be sufficient (Dhalla & Kopec, 2007). The CAGE scale has been found to be both valid and reliable in primary care as well as in general population surveys (Dhalla & Kopec, 2007). The instrument was found to detect mild and severe cases of alcohol use and dependence (Ross & Tisdall, 1994). In addition, the CAGE scale has demonstrated strong reliability and validity and is comparable to longer scales in terms of psychometric properties (Dhalla & Kopec, 2007).

The CAGE scale is not recommended for all clients. It should not be used with those who have abstained from alcohol usage for 2 years prior to the current assessment, nor with those who are currently receiving or have received treatment for alcohol-related problems. The first group would be immune to detection by the scale, due to its concentration on the past year. The second group would require a more in-depth and specific assessment of their problem beyond the scope of the CAGE scale (Liskow & Campbell, 1995).

To illustrate the use of RAIs to assess for dual diagnosis, consider the following case example. Anna, a 35-year-old Costa Rican woman, is interviewed by a social worker in the intake unit of a community mental health center. In her intake interview, Anna describes feelings of sadness and hopelessness since separating from her husband 7 months ago. She worries that her symptoms have not improved, and she says that she has increasingly used alcohol to cope with feelings of sadness.

Because Anna describes feelings associated with depression and increased alcohol use, the social worker asks her to complete two RAIs: the GHQ-12 and the CAGE. Anna completes the GHQ-12, and her overall score is 25 using the Likert scoring method. This score is above the 2/3 cut-off point, indicating that she is experiencing greater than normal psychological distress. In answering the CAGE questions, Anna agrees that she has felt she should cut down on her drinking and that she has felt guilty about her drinking.

Because Anna's scores indicate that she is experiencing psychological distress and potentially problematic drinking patterns, the social worker assists her in formulating a preliminary treatment goal of reducing symptoms of psychological distress through weekly cognitive-behavioral therapy sessions. The social worker recommends that she complete a more thorough assessment to determine whether she should receive treatment for alcohol abuse or dependence so that she can be referred for additional appropriate services.

ADVANTAGES AND DISADVANTAGES OF RAIs

Efficiency and standardization are the primary advantages of RAIs. They allow for quick identification of attitudes, feelings, and behaviors that may be difficult to observe directly or are socially undesirable. Because they are quick to administer, clinicians can efficiently assess for multiple presenting issues, which can be critical for intervening effectively with clients and connecting them to relevant services. When RAIs are used repeatedly in single case designs, they allow for comparing a client's scores with their previous scores to evaluate progress toward treatment goals. Scores can often be compared with established norms to determine whether a client's scores fall in a normal or problematic range (Fischer & Corcoran, 2007).

RAIs have some important disadvantages as well. Because they have not been validated with every client population, clinicians must be careful that the measure is appropriate. There may be little or no information about the effectiveness of many RAIs with particular cultural groups, clients from different levels of socioeconomic status, or those who come from rural instead of urban areas. RAIs may be sufficient to identify a presenting problem, but additional measures may be needed to provide a more in-depth assessment of the severity or subtle dimensions of the problem. The GAI can identify psychological distress, for example, but additional assessment is needed to determine whether the client is experiencing a chemical imbalance or distorted cognitions or both (Fischer & Corcoran, 2007). A more in-depth assessment may be needed to define an appropriate treatment plan. For these reasons, information obtained from RAIs is most effectively used in conjunction with information obtained during sessions and case consultations with supervisors (Fischer & Corcoran, 2007).

There may be no reliable and valid RAI for assessing some presenting problems. Social work practitioners and researchers may find that there is a need to develop a new RAI to address client needs. Springer, Abell, and Hudson (2002) and Springer, Abell, and Nugent (2007) describe the process of developing and evaluating RAIs to address the lack of appropriate instruments for many client populations and presenting problems. Conceptualizing the design of a new RAI includes defining the construct to be measured, selecting the format of the instrument, writing the items, and submitting the items to experts that can determine whether the items are likely to be appropriate. Validation of the instrument includes determining the types of reliability and validity tests that will be conducted, designing the study to validate the instrument, administering the RAI to a sample, and analyzing the data to evaluate the RAI (Springer et al., 2007). Refer to Springer et al. (2002, 2007) for detailed instructions for carrying out each step of the conceptualization and validation of RAIs.

CONCLUSION

Managed care does have a profound impact on the way that services are delivered by emphasizing time-limited, research-based approaches to assessment and intervention. Although social workers may be more limited in the amount of time they are able to devote to working with a particular client, they can enhance effectiveness by using brief, evidence-based approaches to assessment, such as standardized RAIs. However, evidence-based assessment and intervention techniques cannot replace expertise and experience. RAIs that have been researched extensively may be useless for a client who does not respond well to completing self-report measures. A client's cultural background may influence response to assessment procedures. Clinical judgment will always be critical in determining whether an assessment is appropriate. In evaluating their practice, social workers will need to rely on their expertise in determining whether changes in scores over time represent a meaningful progress toward treatment goals. Although RAIs have limitations, their usage is likely to increase as enrollments in MCOs increase and more providers are required to provide efficient, effective services. By using RAIs in assessment and evaluation of practice, social workers make their services valuable to MCOs and ensure that they are providing necessary and effective services to clients.

WEB SITES

Assessments.com. http://www.assessments.com/default.asp.

National Institute on Alcohol Abuse and Alcoholism. http://pubs.niaaa.nih.gov/publications/Assesing%20Alcohol.

PsychiatrySource.com. http://www.psychiatrysource.com/Assessment_Tools/default.aspx?mid=27.

References

America's Health Insurance Plans. (2005). *Learning center fast facts*. Washington, DC: America's Health Insurance Plans. Retrieved November 26, 2007, from http://www.healthdecisions.org/Learning Center/Facts.aspx.

Bachman, S. S., Drainoni, M. L., & Tobias, C. (2004). Medicaid managed care, substance abuse treatment, and people with disabilities: Review of the literature. *Health and Social Work, 29*(3), 189–196.

Bhugra, D., & Flick, G. R. (2005). Pathways to care for patients with bipolar disorder. *Bipolar Disorders, 7*(3), 236–245.

Bloom, M., Fischer, J., & Orme, J. G. (2006). *Evaluating practice: Guidelines for the accountable professional*. New York: Pearson.

Buckley, P. F. (2007). Dual diagnosis of substance abuse and severe mental illness: The scope of the problem. *Journal of Dual Diagnosis, 3*(2), 59–62.

Camara, W. J., Nathan, J. S., & Puente, A. E. (2000). Psychological test usage: Implications in professional psychology. *Professional Psychology: Research and Practice, 31*(2), 141–154.

Cashel, M. L. (2002). Child and adolescent psychological assessment: Current clinical practices and the impact of managed care. *Professional Psychology: Research and Practice, 33*(5), 446–453.

Dhalla, S., & Kopec, J. (2007). The CAGE questionnaire for alcohol misuse: A review of reliability and validity studies. *Clinical & Investigative Medicine, 30*(1), 33–41.

Doi, Y., & Minowa, M. (2003). Factor structure of the 12 item General Health Questionnaire in the Japanese general adult population. *Psychiatry and Clinical Neurosciences, 57*, 379–383.

Fischer, J., & Corcoran, K. (2007). *Measures for clinical practice and research: A sourcebook two volume set*. New York: Oxford University Press.

Goldberg, D. P. (1972). *The detection of psychiatric illness by questionnaire*. London: Oxford University Press.

Gureje, O., & Obikoya, B. (1990). The GHQ-12 as a screening tool in a primary care setting. *Social Psychiatry and Psychiatric Epidemiology, 25*(5), 276–280.

Hussey, D. L., Drinkard, A. M., & Flannery, D. (2007). Comorbid substance use and mental disorders among offending youth. *Journal of Social Work Practice in the Addictions, 7*(1/2), 117–138.

Ip, W. Y., & Martin, C. R. (2006). Psychometric properties of the 12 item General Health Questionnaire (GHQ-12) in Chinese women during pregnancy and in the postnatal period. *Psychology, Health, and Medicine, 11*(1), 60–69.

Kapur, R. L., Kapur, M., & Carstairs, G. M. (1984). Indian psychiatric survey schedule. *Social Psychiatry, 9*, 71–76.

Liskow, B., & Campbell, J. (1995). Validity of the CAGE questionnaire in screening for alcohol dependence in a walk-in (triage) clinic. *Journal of Studies on Alcohol, 56*(3), 277–281.

Mari, J. J., & Williams, P. (1985). A comparison of the validity of two psychiatric screening questionnaires (GHQ-12 and SRQ-20) in Brazil, using relative operating characteristic (ROC) analysis. *Psychological Medicine, 15*, 651–659.

Mayfield, D., McLeod, G., & Hall, P. (1974). The CAGE questionnaire: Validation of a new alcoholism screening instrument. *American Journal of Psychiatry, 131*, 1121–1123.

Montazeri, A., Mahmood, A. H., Shariati, M., Garmaroudi, G., Ebadi, M., & Abolfazl Fateh, A. (2003). The 12-item General Health Questionnaire (GHQ-12): Translation and validation study of the Iranian version. *Health and Quality of Life Outcomes, 1*, 66.

Picardi, A., Abeni, D., & Pasquini, P. (2001). Assessing psychological distress in patients with skin diseases: Reliability, validity, and factor structure of the GHQ-12. *Journal of the European Academy of Dermatology and Venereology, 15*, 410–417.

Ross, H., & Tisdall, G. (1994). Identification of alcohol disorders at a university mental health center, using the CAGE. *Journal of Alcohol and Drug Education, 39*(3), 119–126.

Springer, D. W., Abell, N., & Hudson, W. W. (2002). Creating and validating rapid assessment instruments for practice and research: Part 1. *Research on Social Work Practice, 12*(3), 408–439.

Springer, D. W., Abell, N., & Nugent, W. R. (2007). Creating and validating rapid assessment instruments for practice and research: Part 2. *Research on Social Work Practice, 12*(6), 768–795.

Steenrod, S. (2005). The relationship between managed care and evidence-based practices in outpatient substance abuse programs. *Best Practice in Mental Health: An International Journal, 1*(1), 31–46.

Stewart, C., & El-Mallakh, R. S. (2007). Is bipolar disorder overdiagnosed among patients with substance abuse? *Bipolar Disorders, 9*(6), 646–648.

Turchik, J. A., Karpenko, V., Hammers, D., & McNamara, J. R. (2007). Practical and ethical assessment issues in rural, impoverished, and managed care settings. *Professional Psychology: Research and Practice, 38*(2), 158–168.

Van Hemert, A. M., Heijer, M. D., Vorstenbosch, M., & Bolk, J. H. (1995). Detecting psychiatric disorders in medical practice using the General Health Questionnaire. Why do cut off scores vary? *Psychological Medicine, 25*(1), 165–170.

Van Os, T. W. D. P., Van den Brink, R. H. S., Van der Meer, K., & Ormel, J. (2006). The care provided by general practitioners for persistent depression. *European Psychiatry, 21*(2), 87–92.

Wood, J. M., Garb, H. N., Lilienfeld, S. O., & Nezworski, M. T. (2002). Clinical assessment. *Annual Review of Psychology, 53*, 519–543.

Yuriko, D., & Masumi, M. (2003). Gender differences in daytime sleepiness among Japanese workers. *Social Science and Medicine, 56*(4), 883–894.

Zeiler, C. A., Nemes, S., Holtz, K. D., Landis, R. D., & Hoffman, J. (2002). Responses to a drug and alcohol problem assessment for primary care by ethnicity. *American Journal of Drug and Alcohol Abuse, 28*(3), 513–524.

PART VI
Working with Couples and Families

57 Using Genograms to Map Family Patterns

Monica McGoldrick

Over the past few decades, genograms have been used increasingly by health care and human service professionals as a practical tool for mapping family patterns (McGoldrick, Gerson, & Petry, 2008). The genogram is a tool in progress. They are becoming a common language for tracking family history and relationships (see Figure 57.1).

Genograms display family information graphically, providing a quick gestalt of complex family patterns; as such, they are a rich source of hypotheses about the evolution of both clinical problems and the family contexts within which problems develop and are generally resolved.

Families are organized within biological, legal, cultural, and emotional structures, as well as according to generation, age, gender, and other factors. Where one fits in the family structure can influence functioning, relational patterns, and the type of family one forms in the next generation. Gender and birth order are key factors shaping sibling relationships and characteristics. When different family configurations are mapped on the genogram, the clinician can hypothesize about possible personality characteristics and relational compatibilities. Cultural issues including ethnicity, race, religion, migration, class, and other socioeconomic factors, as well as a family's time and location in history (Elder, 1977), also influence a family's structural patterns (Carter & McGoldrick, 2005; Congress, 1994; Hardy & Laszloffy, 1995; McGoldrick, 1995, 2001; McGoldrick, Giordano, & Preto, 2005; Walsh, 2003). These factors, too, become part of the genogram map.

Genograms appeal to clinicians because they are tangible and graphic representations of complex family patterns. They allow the clinician to map the family structure clearly and note and update the family picture as it emerges. For a clinical record, the genogram provides an efficient summary, allowing a clinician unfamiliar with a case to quickly grasp a large amount of information about a family and have a view of potential problems. Whereas notes written in a chart or questionnaire tend to become lost in the record, genogram information is immediately recognizable and can be added to and corrected at each clinical visit as more is learned about a family.

Genograms make it easier for clinicians to keep in mind the complexity of a family's context, including family history, patterns, and events that may have ongoing significance for patient care. Just as our spoken language potentiates and organizes our thought processes, genograms, which map relationships and patterns of family functioning and cultural history, help clinicians think systemically about how events and relationships in their clients' lives are related to patterns of health, illness, and resilience.

Gathering genogram information should be an integral part of any comprehensive clinical assessment. There is no quantitative measurement scale by which the clinician can use a genogram in a cookbook fashion to make clinical predictions. Rather, it is a factual as well as interpretive tool, enabling social workers to generate tentative hypotheses for further evaluation in a family assessment. Typically, the genogram is constructed from information gathered during the first session and revised as new information becomes available. Thus, the initial assessment forms the basis for treatment. Of course, we cannot compartmentalize assessment and treatment. Each interaction of the social worker with the family informs the assessment and thus influences the next intervention.

Standard Symbols for Genograms

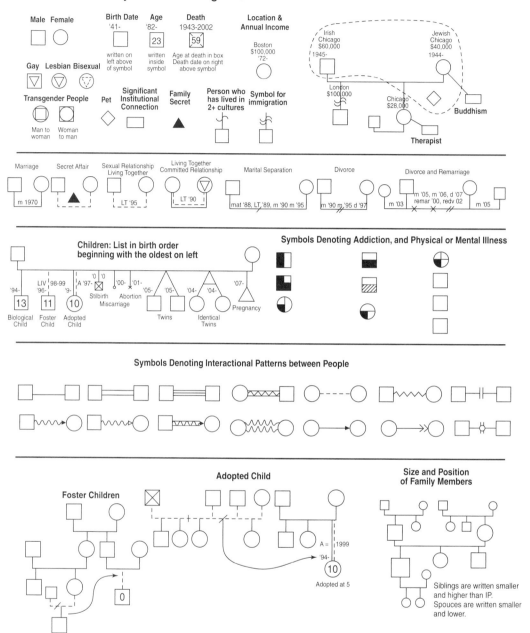

Figure 57.1 Genogram format.

Genograms help social workers get to know their clients; they thus become an important way of engaging with families. Creating a systemic perspective helps track family issues through space and time, and genograms enable an interviewer to reframe, detoxify, and normalize emotion-laden issues. Because the genogram interview provides a ready vehicle for systemic questioning, it begins to orient clients to a systemic perspective as well. The genogram thus helps both the social worker and the client see the larger picture—that is, to view problems in their current and historical context. Structural, relational, and functional information about a family can be viewed on a genogram both horizontally across the family context and vertically through the generations.

Scanning the breadth of the current family context allows the social worker to assess the connectedness of the immediate players in the family drama to each other, as well as the broader system, and evaluate the family's strengths, resilience, and vulnerabilities in relation to the overall situation.

We include on the genogram the nuclear and extended family members, as well as significant nonblood kin who have lived with or played a major role in the family's life. We can also note significant events and problems. Current behavior and problems of family members can be traced from multiple perspectives. The index person (IP, or person with the problem or symptom) may be viewed in the context of various subsystems, such as siblings, triangles, reciprocal relationships, multigenerational patterns, life cycle stages and transitions, as well as in relation to the broader community, social institutions (schools, courts, etc.), and sociocultural context.

By scanning the family system culturally and historically and assessing previous life cycle transitions, the clinician can place present issues in the context of the family's evolutionary patterns. Thus, we include on a genogram cultural and demographic information about at least three generations of family members, as well as nodal and critical events in the family's history, particularly as related to family changes (migration, loss, and the life cycle). When family members are questioned about the present situation in relation to the themes, myths, rules, and emotionally charged issues of previous generations, repetitive patterns often become clear. Genograms "let the calendar speak" by suggesting possible connections between family events over time. Previous patterns of illness and earlier shifts in family relationships brought about through changes in family structure and other critical life changes can easily be noted on the genogram, providing a framework for hypothesizing what may be influencing a current crisis. In conjunction with genograms, we usually include a family chronology, which depicts the family history in order, and often a sociogram or eco-map (Hartman, 1978), which shows how clients are emotionally connected to family and other resources in their lives.

THE FAMILY INFORMATION NET

The process of gathering family information can be thought of as casting out an information net in progressively larger circles to capture relevant information about the family and its broader context. The net spreads out in a number of different directions:

- from the presenting problem to the larger context of the problem;
- from the immediate household to the extended family and broader social systems;
- from the present family situation to a chronology of historical family events;
- from easy, nonthreatening queries to difficult, anxiety-provoking questions; and
- from obvious facts to judgments about functioning and relationships to hypothesized family patterns.

The Presenting Problem and the Immediate Household

In health care situations, genogram information is often recorded as it emerges during medical visits. In family therapy and social service situations, specific problems may be identified, which are the clinician's starting point. At the outset, families are told that some basic background information is needed to fully understand their situation. Such information usually grows naturally out of exploring the presenting problem and its impact on the immediate household. It makes sense to start with the immediate family and the context in which the problem occurs.

- Who lives in the household?
- How is each person related?
- Where do other family members live?

The clinician asks the name, age, gender, and occupation of each person in the household to sketch the immediate family structure. Other revealing information is elicited through inquiring about the problem.

- Which family members know about the problem?
- How does each view it? How has each of them responded?
- Has anyone in the family ever had similar problems?
- What solutions were attempted by whom in those situations?
- When did the problem begin? Who noticed it first? Who is most concerned about the problem? Who the least?
- Were family relationships different before the problem began? What other problems existed?
- Does the family see the problem as having changed? In what ways? For better or for worse?

This is also a good time to inquire about previous efforts to get help for the problem, including previous treatment, therapists, hospitalizations, and the current referring person.

The Current Situation

Next, the clinician spreads the information net into the current family situation. This line of questioning usually follows naturally from questions about the problem and who is involved.

- What has been happening recently in your family?
- Have there been any recent changes in the family (e.g., people coming or leaving, illnesses, job problems)?

It is important to inquire about recent life cycle transitions as well as anticipated changes in the family situation (especially exits and entrances of family members—births, marriages, divorces, deaths, stresses related to health, the law, behavior changes, or the departure of family members).

The Wider Family Context

The clinician looks for an opportunity to explore the wider family context by asking about the extended family and cultural background of all the adults involved. The interviewer might move into this area by saying, "I would now like to ask you something about your background to help make sense of your present problem."

Dealing with a Family's Resistance to Doing a Genogram

When family members react negatively to questions about the extended family or complain that such matters are irrelevant, it often makes sense to redirect the focus to the immediate situation until the connections between the present situation and other family relationships or experiences can be established. An example of such a genogram assessment for a remarried family whose teenage daughter's behavior was the presenting problem has been produced in the videotape *The Legacy of Unresolved Loss* (McGoldrick, 2001). This tape also illustrates how to deal with a family's resistance to revealing genogram information. Gentle persistence over time will usually result in obtaining the information and demonstrating its relevance to the family.

The clinician inquires about each side of the family separately, beginning, for example, with the mother's side: "Let's begin with your mother's family. Your mother was which one of how many children? When and where was she born? Is she alive? If not, when did she die? What was the cause of her death? If alive, where is she now? What does she do? Is she retired? When did this happen? When and how did your mother meet your father? When did they marry? Had she been married before? If so, when? Did she have children by that relationship? Did they separate or divorce or did the spouse die? If so, when was that?" And so on. In a similar fashion, questions are asked about the father. Then the clinician might ask about each parent's family of origin—that is, father, mother, and siblings. The goal is to get information about at least three or four generations, including grandparents, parents, aunts, uncles, siblings, spouses, and children of the IP.

Ethnic and Cultural History

It is essential to learn something about the family's socioeconomic, political, and cultural background to place presenting problems and current relationships in context. When the questioning expands to the extended family, it is a good point to begin exploring issues of ethnicity, because exploring ethnicity and migration history helps establish the cultural context in which the family is operating and offers the therapist an opportunity to validate family attitudes and behaviors determined by such influences (McGoldrick et al., 2005). It is important to learn what the family's cultural traditions are about problems, health care, and healing, and where the current family members stand in relation to those traditional values. It is also important to consider the family's cultural expectations about relationships with health care professionals, since this will set the tone for their clinical responses.

Differences in class background between family members or between family members and the health care professional may create discomfort, which will need to be attended to in the meeting. Questions to ascertain class assumptions pertain not just to the family's current income but also to cultural background, education, and social status within their community. Once the clinician has a clear picture of the ethnic and cultural factors influencing a family (and preferably keeping his or her own biases in check), it is possible to raise delicate questions geared to helping families identify any behaviors that—even if culturally sanctioned in their original context—may be keeping them stuck (see McGoldrick et al., 2005).

The Informal Kinship Network

The information net extends beyond the biological and legal structure of the family to encompass common-law and cohabiting relationships, miscarriages, abortions, stillbirths, foster and adopted children, and anyone else in the informal network of the family who is an important support. Inquiries are made about godparents, teachers, neighbors, friends, parents of friends, clergy, caretakers, doctors, and the like who are or have been important to the functioning of the family; this information is also included on the genogram. In exploring outside supports for the family, the clinician might ask:

- To whom could you turn for financial, emotional, physical, and spiritual help?
- What roles have outsiders played in your family?
- What is your relationship to your community?
- Who outside the family has been important in your life?
- Did you ever have a nanny, caretaker, or babysitter to whom you felt attached? What became of her or him?

- Has anyone else ever lived with your family? When? Where are they now?
- What has been your family's experience with doctors and other helping professionals or agencies?

For particular clients, certain additional questions are appropriate. For example, the following questions would be important in working with gay and lesbian clients (see Burke & Faber, 1997; Green, 2008).

- Who was the first person you told about your sexual orientation?
- To whom on your genogram are you out?
- To whom would you most like to come out?
- Who would be especially easy or difficult to come out to?
- Who is in your social network? (These people should always be added to the genogram.)

Tracking Family Process

Tracking shifts that occurred around births, deaths, and other transitions can lead the clinician to hypotheses about the family's adaptive style. Particularly critical are untimely or traumatic deaths and the deaths of pivotal family members (Walsh & McGoldrick, 2004). We look for specific patterns of adaptation or rigidification following such transitions. Assessment of past adaptive patterns, particularly after losses and other critical transitions, may be crucial in helping a family in the current crisis. A family's past and the relationship family members have to it provide important clues about family rules, expectations, patterns of organization, strengths, resources, and sources of resilience (Walsh, 2006).

The history of specific problems should also be investigated in detail. The focus should be on how family patterns have changed at different periods: before the problem began, at the time of the problem's onset, at the time of first seeking help, and presently. Specific genograms can be done for each of these time periods. Asking how family members see the future of the problem is also informative. Questions may include the following.

- What will happen in the family if the problem continues? If it goes away?
- What does the future look like?
- What changes do family members imagine are possible in the future?

Seeing the family in its historical perspective involves linking past, present, and future and noting the family's flexibility in adapting to changes.

During the mapping on the genogram of the nuclear and extended family, and the gathering of facts about different family members, the clinician also begins to make inquiries and judgments about the functioning, relationships, and roles of each person in the family. This involves going beyond the bare facts to clinical judgment and acumen. Inquiries about these issues can touch sensitive nerves in the family and should be made with care.

Difficult Questions about Individual Functioning

Family members may function well in some areas but not in others, or they may cover up their dysfunction. Often, it takes careful questioning to reveal the true level of functioning. A family member with a severe illness may show remarkable adaptive strengths, and another may show fragility with little apparent stress. Questions about individual functioning may be difficult or painful for family members to answer and must be approached with sensitivity and tact, such as questions about alcohol abuse, chronic unemployment, severe symptomatology, or trauma. The family members should be warned that questions may be difficult, and they should let the clinician know if there is an issue they would rather not discuss. The clinician will need to judge the degree of pressure to apply if the family resists questions that may be essential to dealing with the presenting problem.

Clinicians need to exercise extreme caution about when to ask questions that could put a family member in danger. For example, if violence is suspected, a wife should never be asked about her husband's behavior in his presence, because the question assumes she is free to respond, which may not be the case. It is clinicians' responsibility to be sure their questions do not put a client in jeopardy. The following questions reflect issues of relevance, but not necessarily a format for ascertaining the information, which could require delicate and diplomatic interviewing.

Serious problems
- Has anyone in the family had a serious medical or psychological problem? Been depressed? Had anxieties? Fears? Lost control?
- Has there been physical or sexual abuse?

- Are there any other problems that worry you? When did that problem begin? Did you seek help for it? If so, when? What happened? What is the status of that problem now?

Work
- Have there been any recent job changes?
- Has anyone been unemployed?
- Do you like your work? Do other family members like their work?

Finances
- How much income does each member generate? Does this create any imbalance in family relationships? How does the economic situation compare with that of your relatives?
- Is there any expected inheritance? Are there family members who may need financial help or caretaking?
- Are there any extraordinary expenses? Outstanding debts? What is the level of credit card debt?
- Who controls the money? How are spending decisions made? Are these patterns different from the ways money was handled in the families of origin?

Drugs and alcohol
- Do any family members routinely use medication? What kind and for what?
- Who prescribed it? What is the family's relationship with that physician?
- Do you think any members drink too much or have a drug problem? Has anyone else ever thought so? What drugs? When? What has the family attempted to do about it?
- How does the person's behavior change under the influence of the drug? How does the behavior of others change when a member is drug involved?

Trouble with the law
- Have any family members ever been arrested? For what? When? What was the result? What is that person's legal status now?
- Has anyone ever lost his or her driver's license?

Physical or sexual abuse
- Have you ever felt intimidated in your family? Have you or others ever been hit? Has anyone in your family ever been threatened with being hit? Have you ever threatened anyone else in your family or hit them?

- Have you or any other family members ever been sexually molested or touched inappropriately by a member of your family or someone outside your family? By whom?

SETTING PRIORITIES FOR ORGANIZING GENOGRAM INFORMATION

One of the most difficult aspects of genogram assessment remains setting priorities for inclusion of family information on a genogram. Clinicians cannot follow every lead the interview suggests. Awareness of basic genogram patterns can help the clinician set such priorities. As a rule of thumb, the data are scanned for the following:

- Repetitive symptoms, relationships, or functioning patterns across the family and over the generations. Repeated triangles, coalitions, cut-offs, patterns of conflict, over- and underfunctioning.
- Coincidences of dates—for example, the death of one family member or anniversary of this death occurring at the same time as symptom onset in another, or the age at symptom onset coinciding with the age of problem development in another family member.
- The impact of change and untimely life cycle transitions, particularly changes in functioning or relationships that correspond with critical family life events or untimely life cycle transitions—for example, births, marriages, or deaths that occur "off schedule."

Awareness of possible patterns makes the clinician more sensitive to what is missing. Missing information about important family members, events, or discrepancies in the information offered frequently reflect charged emotional issues in the family. The clinician should take careful note of the connections family members make or fail to make to various events.

A FAMILY SYSTEMS PERSPECTIVE

A family systems perspective views families as inextricably interconnected. Neither people nor their problems or solutions exist in a vacuum. Both are interwoven into broader interactional systems, the most fundamental of which is the family. The family is the primary and, except in rare instances, most powerful system to which we humans belong. In this framework, "family" consists of the entire kinship network of at least three generations, both as it currently exists and as it has evolved through time (Carter & McGoldrick, 2005). Family is, by our definition, those who are tied together through their common biological, legal, cultural, and emotional history and their implied future together. The physical, social, and emotional functioning of family members is profoundly interdependent, with changes in one part of the system reverberating in other parts. In addition, family interactions and relationships tend to be highly reciprocal, patterned, and repetitive. These patterns allow us to make tentative predictions from the genogram.

Coincidences of historical events or concurrent events in different parts of a family are viewed not as random happenings but as occurrences that may be interconnected systemically, though the connections may be hidden from view (McGoldrick, 1995). In addition, key family relationship changes seem more likely to occur at some times than at others. They are especially likely at points of life cycle transition. Symptoms tend to cluster around such transitions in the family life cycle, when family members face the task of reorganizing their relations with one another to go on to the next phase (Carter & McGoldrick, 2005). The symptomatic family may become stuck in time, unable to resolve its impasse by reorganizing and moving on. The history and relationship patterns revealed in a genogram assessment provide important clues about the nature of this impasse—how a symptom may have arisen to preserve or prevent some relationship pattern or to protect some legacy of previous generations.

Families have many different types of relationship patterns. Of particular interest are patterns of relational distance. People may be very close or very distant or somewhere in between. At one extreme are family members who do not speak or are in constant conflict with each other. The family may actually be in danger of cutting off entirely. At the other extreme are families who seem almost stuck together in "emotional fusion." Family members in fused or poorly differentiated relationships are vulnerable to dysfunction, which tends to occur when the level of stress or anxiety exceeds the system's capacity to deal with it. The more closed the boundaries of a system become, the more immune it is to input from the environment, and consequently, the more rigid the family patterns become. In other words, family members in a closed, fused system react automatically to one another and are practically impervious to events outside the system that require adaptation to changing conditions. Fusion may involve either positive or negative relationships—that is, family members may feel very good about each other or experience almost nothing but hostility and conflict. In either case, there is an overly dependent bond that ties the family together. With genograms, clinicians can map family boundaries and indicate which subsystems are fused and thus likely to be closed to new input about changing conditions.

As Bowen (1978) pointed out, two-person relationships tend to be unstable, tending under stress to draw in a third person, stabilizing their relationship by forming a coalition of two in relation to the third. The basic unit of an emotional system thus tends to be the triangle. Genograms can help us identify key triangles in a family system, see how triangular patterns repeat from one generation to the next, and design strategies for changing them (Fogarty, 1973; Guerin, Fogarty, Fay, & Kautto, 1996).

The members of a family tend to fit together as a functional whole. That is, the behaviors of different family members tend to be complementary or reciprocal. This does not mean that family members have equal power to influence relationships, as is obvious from the power differentials between men and women, between parents and children, between the elderly and younger family members, and between family members who belong to different cultures, classes, or races (McGoldrick & Hardy, 2008). What it does mean is that belonging to a system opens people to reciprocal influences and involves them in each other's behavior in inextricable ways. This leads us to expect a certain interdependent fit or balance in families, involving give and take, action and reaction. Thus, a lack (e.g., irresponsibility) in one part of the family may be complemented by a surplus (over-responsibility) in another part. The genogram helps the clinician pinpoint the contrasts and idiosyncrasies in families that indicate this type of complementarity or reciprocal balance.

Clearly, a genogram is limited in how much information it can display at any time. Computer programs (allow clinicians to examine the genogram with multiple levels of detail and explore different aspects one at a time: illness, cultural patterns, education and job history, couple relationships,

and so on. Clinicians gather a great deal more important information on people's lives than can ever appear on genograms. The genogram is just one part of an ongoing clinical investigation and must be integrated into the total family assessment.

MAPPING THE GENOGRAMS OF THOSE WHO GROW UP IN MULTIPLE SETTINGS

Many children grow up in multiple settings because their parents divorce, die, remarry, migrate, or have other special circumstances that require the child to live for a while or even permanently in a different setting. Yet we often fail to keep track of important information about whom children have lived with as they grow up—biological, legal, foster, adoptive, or informal kin relationships. Genograms can greatly facilitate tracking children in multiple living arrangements or foster placements, where the many different family constellations a child lives in are otherwise extremely hard to keep in mind. Indeed, genograms are an exceptionally useful tool to track children's experiences through the life cycle, taking into account the multiple family and other institutional contexts to which they have belonged (Carter & McGoldrick, 2005). The more clearly the clinician tracks the actuality of this history, however complex, the better able he or she is to validate the child's actual experience and multiple forms of belonging. Such a map can begin to make order out of the sometimes chaotic or sudden placement changes a child must go through because of illness, trauma, or other loss. It can also help validate for a child the realities of his or her birth and life connections that vary from traditional norms.

More children than we realize are raised in a number of different households or shift residences many times to foster homes or to various relatives or friends. It is useful for the genogram to show as much of the information as possible on transitions and relationships in children's lives. Although many situations are very complicated, creativity and a commitment to validate all of a child's connections facilitate the clinician's efforts to track and map the family and kin connections. Sometimes the only feasible way to clarify where children were raised is to take chronological notes on each child in a family and then transform them into a series of genograms that show family context. Especially when children have experienced many losses and changes, a complete genogram both validates the losses and offers a rich picture of all the people to whom they have belonged. It can be an important clinical tool to help put children in context.

Adoption

Couple adoption and single-parent adoption can be indicated as in Figure 57.2.

This genogram shows the family of Mia Farrow, who had biological children (including twin sons, Matthew and Sasha) and interracially adopted daughters (Soon-Yi, Lark, and Daisy) with her second husband, André Previn. She then adopted another interracial child (Moses) and one who was American born (Dylan/Eliza) during her relationship with Woody Allen, after which they had a biological child together (Satchel, now called Ronan), and finally she adopted more children on her own. If at all possible, we indicate the cultural background, because it is an important part of anyone's history. By looking at this map of the children of Mia Farrow, one may develop hypotheses about the position of different children. Soon-Yi, for example, came to the family as the oldest of three adopted Asian daughters two years after her younger Asian sister, Lark Song, and one year after her youngest Asian sister, Daisy. Not only were the two younger sisters "older" in their experience with the family, but they were both Vietnamese, whereas Soon-Yi was from Korea. So Soon-Yi's position as outsider among the three adopted Asian sisters may have been built in by the timing and her cultural difference from them. Of course, to more completely track the history of each child in this family, we would want to do genograms for each of the children, showing their biological parents and siblings and whom they lived with at every age growing up, as well as a more complete map of their caregivers and support systems. Friends and mentors, for example, may be important to show on a genogram, especially where children have experienced significant losses.

Where living situations are complicated, a line can be drawn to encircle the households. This is especially important in multinuclear families, where children spend time in different households.

When the "functional" family is different from the biological or legal family, as when children are raised by a grandparent or in an informal adoptive family, it is useful to create a separate genogram to show the functional structure (see Watts-Jones, 1997). Where children have lived as part of several families—biological, foster, and adoptive—separate genograms may help depict the child's multiple families over time.

We can also indicate on a genogram (see Figure 57.3) a lesbian couple with a child born to one of them and adopted by the other. The very small square indicated as the biological parent of Meg is a sperm donor. The grandparents and previous spouses of Fran and Martha are also indicated on the genogram. Burke and Faber (1997) have suggested using a "gendergrid" to help depict the liaisons, long-term bonds, communities, and social networks of lesbian couples. They suggest differentiating three levels of relationship: historical influences, key emotional and social relationships, and primary intimate relationships for the index individual or couple.

Foster Care

We need to acknowledge the relevance of specific foster family history for children who have lived in foster care. Fernando Colon-Lopez grew up in several foster homes after the loss of his mother. As an adult, he has put much effort into exploring his own genogram (1973, 2006, 2008) and helping others think contextually about child placement and foster care as a valid and important aspect of a child's history, which should be attended to as any other experience (Colon, 1978). He has made it clear how important the genogram of the foster family is for the child through the life cycle. He has ongoing connections with the biological grandchildren of his third foster mother. They shared holidays and frequent visits with their grandmother, his foster mother. They have much in common through this shared history, a history that is so often not acknowledged in our foster care system and in society at large, which underemphasizes family ties in its stress on individuality and self-determination.

Colon grew up mostly in foster homes from earliest infancy. The map of all his living situations, including three foster homes, an orphanage, his family of origin, and his family of procreation, is offered in Figure 57.4.

To better understand the sibling patterns with his brothers in the foster home where he spent most of his growing-up years, we might want to show the changing family constellations separately, as in Figure 57.5.

The genogram in Figure 47.5 makes evident the multiple losses that Colon and his foster family had throughout his childhood, but it also indicates their resilience and resourcefulness in being able

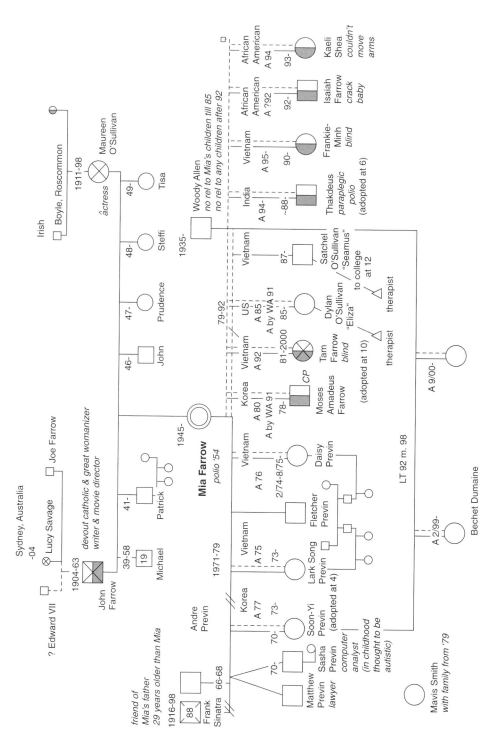

Figure 57.2 Genogram 2: Mia Farrow's children, biological and adopted.

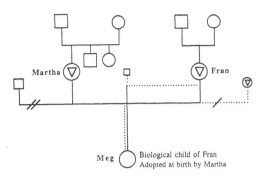

Meg   Biological child of Fran
       Adopted at birth by Martha

Figure 57.3 Genogram 3: Lesbian family.

to deal with these losses, as well as with new re-lationships almost each year. As is evident, Co-lon had experience in virtually every sibling con-stellation during his childhood years, a factor that probably increased his flexibility in dealing with relationships. He was the youngest of three, the oldest of three, the middle of three, the older of two, and the younger of two, but rarely an only child, although, as the one child who remained with the family for his entire childhood, his po-sition there was special. At the same time, the three brothers who stayed for long periods of time (4 years each) not surprisingly had more significance for him, especially because they were all close to Colon in age. Less evident from the ages alone was the extremely special relationship that Colon and his foster mother had with his brother Johnny, who lived in the family for only 4 months but to whom they became very attached. In caring for this severely retarded brother, Co-lon remembers clearly how hard Johnny had tried to learn to say Fernando's name and how he and his mother cried when they had to let Johnny go.

Although the foster care system at that time operated on the principle that children were never to have contact with the previous family once they moved to a new home, his foster mother did not believe in cutting off the past that way and made great efforts to reverse the process. In the early days of placement, one of Fernando Co-lon's foster brothers, Kenneth, was especially de-pressed. Kenneth was one of five brothers, ain spite of the regulations, their foster mother asked Kenneth where the brothers were and took him to see them, after which he began to adjust to his new situation. The foster mother showed great courage to challenge the cutting-off process pro-moted by our social service system.

Colon remains connected to his foster mother's grandchildren, in addition to his close, current con-nections with family members on both sides of his biological family. Whether the relationship is good or bad, beneficial or injurious, it is not to be dis-missed. Organizing family data on genograms has enabled people to put the many fragments of their lives together into a meaningful whole.

Benefits of Open Adoption Policies

Genograms are equally important for children in adoptive care. Luckily, the policy of closed adop-tion is increasingly shifting to a policy of open adoption. After the adoption, both the biological family and the adoptive family are involved in selecting each other for placement of the child and stay connected to each other through the grow-ing years of the child and beyond. This paradigm, which is becoming more widespread in the United States, has eliminated the harmful effects of se-crecy and is a process with integrity that enables all parties to be considered in a humane way. State laws still vary widely, however, in how open or closed the adoption process may be. By using the information from genograms, child care workers can help adoptive children create scrapbooks about their lives with information, photos, and stories about both the biological and adoptive families. In this way the child is truly shared and doubly enriched by having connections with two family systems, rather than one pitted against the "failed" other.

The accepted practice of severing family ties—be they biological, adopted, foster, or blended—is, in our view, extremely detrimental and disre-spectful. It has often led to clinicians being drawn into replacing other relationships in a person's natural system. Such cut-offs may leave practi-tioners depressed, bereft, and weakened, having a "hole" in our hearts. A cut-off of one person tends to potentiate cut-offs of other family mem-bers and the loss of other potentially enriching relationships. It weakens the entire fabric of the family. Social workers' use of genograms can help counter this tendency by making clear the enor-mity of the losses and validating the rich possi-bilities for connection and meaning.

Genograms can also be used for children who have been reared in orphanages, as the touching memoir of John Folwarski (2008) illustrates. Fol-warski figures that he had approximately 3,000 siblings—that is, 3,000 other children in one gen-eration shared the same home (St. Hedwig's Or-phanage in Chicago), the same food, the same holiday rituals, and the same foster parents and

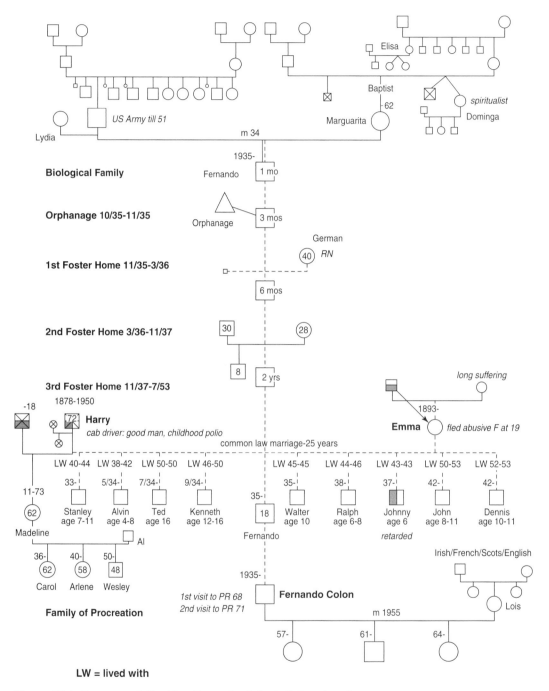

Figure 57.4 Genogram 4: Tracking Fernando Colon's living situations.

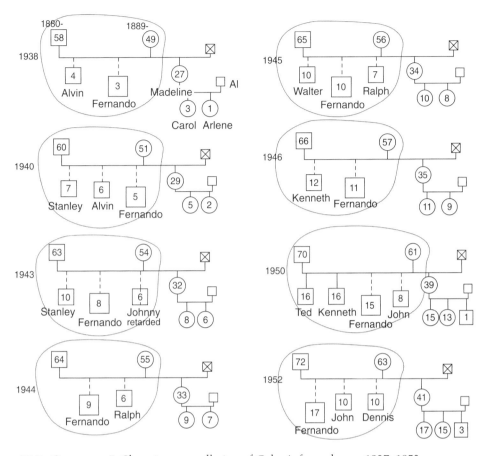

Figure 57.5 Genogram 5: Changing constellation of Colon's foster home, 1937–1953.

grandparents, the nuns and priests who ran the home.

Figure 57.6 shows Folwarski's genogram for the family as he experienced it during the years he grew up (1937–1950). As adults, many of his "siblings" have come together to share memories, reconnecting after many years with teacher/mothers, and have strengthened their sense of family. Indeed, Folwarski describes the experience of creating and looking at his genogram, which had a powerful meaning in validating his history.

CONCLUSION

The physical genogram, which is a highly condensed map of a rich and complex family, can provide an awesome lesson for anyone unable to see beyond the cut-offs that may occur in a family (McGoldrick et al., 2008). We believe that no relationship is to be disregarded or discounted. All our relationships inform the wholeness of who we are and where we come from and, more important, can help us make constructive, conscious choices about who we will be in the future.

One of the most powerful aspects of genograms is the way they can steer people to the rich, ongoing possibilities of complex kin relationships, which are sources of connection and life support. It is not just a shared history that matters but the spiritual power of our survival and our current connections that strengthen us and can enrich our future.

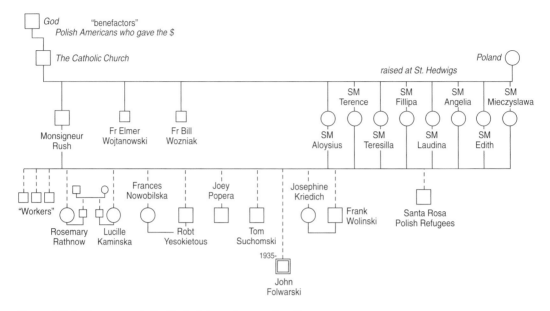

Figure 57.6 Genogram 6: St. Hedwig's orphanage family.

WEB SITES

GenoPro, genealogy software. http://www
.genopro.com

Multicultural Family Institute. http://www
.multiculturalfamily.org.

References

Bowen, M. (1978). *Family therapy in clinical practice.*
New York: Aronson.

Burke, J. L., & Faber, P. (1997). A genogrid for couples.
Journal of Gay and Lesbian Social Services, 7(1),
13–22.

Carter, B., & McGoldrick, M. (2005). *The expanded family life cycle: Individual, family, and social perspectives,* 3rd ed. Boston: Allyn & Bacon.

Colon, F. (1973). In search of one's past: An identity
trip. *Family Process,* 12(4), 429–438.

Colon, F. (1978). Family ties and child placement. *Family
Process,* 17, 289–312.

Colon, F. (2008). The discovery of my multicultural
identity. In M. McGoldrick & K. V. Hardy (Eds.),
*Revisioning family therapy: Culture, race, and gen-
der in clinical practice,* 2nd ed. New York: Guilford.

Colon-Lopez, F. (2006). *Finding my face: The memoir
of a Puerto Rican American.* Victoria, BC: Trafford.

Congress, E. P. (1994, November). The use of culturagrams to assess and empower culturally diverse
families. *Families in Society,* 531–540.

Elder, G. H. Jr. (1977). Family history and the life course.
Journal of Family History, 22, 279–304.

Fogarty, T. (1973). *Triangles. The family.* New Rochelle,
NY: Center for Family Learning.

Folwarski, J. (2008). No longer an orphan in history. In
M. McGoldrick (Ed.), *Revisioning family therapy,*
2nd ed. New York: Guilford.

Green, R. (2008). Gay and Lesbian Couples: Successful
Coping with Minority Stress. In McGoldrick, M. &
Hardy, K. V. (Eds.). *Revisioning Family Therapy:
Race, Culture and Gender in Clinical Practice,*
(2nd ed.) New York: Guilford Press.

Guerin, P., Fogarty, T. F., Fay, L. F., & Kautto, J. G. (1996).
Working with relationship triangles. New York:
Guilford.

Hardy, K. V., & Laszloffy, T. A. (1995). The cultural genogram: Key to training culturally competent family therapists. *Journal of Marital and Family Therapy,* 21(3), 227–237.

Hartman, A. (1978, October). Diagrammatic assessment of family relationships. *Social Casework,*
465–476.

McGoldrick, M. (1995). *You can go home again: Reconnecting with your family.* New York: Norton.

McGoldrick, M. (2001). *The legacy of unresolved loss.*
DVD, available at www.psychotherapy.net.

McGoldrick, M., Gerson, R., & Petry, S. (2008). *Genograms: Assessment and intervention,* 3rd ed. New
York: Norton.

McGoldrick, M., Giordano, J., & Garcia-Preto, N. (2005).
Ethnicity and family therapy, 3rd ed. New York:
Guilford.

McGoldrick, M., & Hardy, K. V. (Eds.). (2008). *Revisioning family therapy: Culture, class, race, and
gender,* 2nd ed. New York: Guilford.

Walsh, F. (2003). *Spiritual resources in family therapy*. New York: Guilford.

Walsh, F. (2006). *Strengthening family resilience*, 2nd ed. New York: Guilford.

Walsh, F., & McGoldrick, M. (2004). *Living beyond loss: Death and the family*, 2nd ed. New York: Guilford.

Watts-Jones, D. (1997). Toward an African American genogram. *Family Process*, 36(4), 373–383.

58   A Family Resilience Framework

Froma Walsh

Over the past two decades, the field of family therapy has refocused attention from family deficits to family strengths. The therapeutic relationship has become more collaborative and empowering of client potential, recognizing that successful interventions depend more on tapping into family resources than on therapist techniques. Assessment and intervention are redirected from how problems are caused to how they can be solved, identifying and amplifying existing and potential competencies. Therapist and clients work together to find new possibilities in a problem-saturated situation and overcome roadblocks to change and growth. This positive, future-oriented direction shifts the emphasis from what went wrong to what can be done for optimal functioning and well-being.

A family resilience approach builds on these developments to strengthen family abilities to overcome adversity. A basic premise guiding this approach is that serious life crises and persistent adversity have an impact on the whole family, and in turn, key family processes influence the recovery and resilience of all members, their relationships, and the family unit. Fostering the family's ability to master its immediate crisis situation also increases its capacity to meet future challenges. Thus, the family is strengthened as problems are resolved, and each intervention is also a preventive measure.

THE CONCEPT OF FAMILY RESILIENCE: CRISIS AND CHALLENGE

Resilience—the ability to withstand and rebound from adversity—has become an important concept in mental health theory and research. Although some are shattered by traumatic experience, others rise above it, able to live and love well. Countering the deterministic assumption that early life trauma damaged lives, studies found that the same adversity may result in different outcomes. For instance, most abused children did not become abusive parents (Kaufman & Ziegler, 1987). What makes the difference?

Early studies focused on individual traits for hardiness, reflecting the dominant cultural ethos of the "rugged individual." Resilience was viewed as inborn or acquired on one's own, as "the invulnerable child" seen as impervious to stress owing to inner fortitude or character armor (Luthar & Ziegler, 1991). An interactive perspective emerged, recognizing that the impact of initial risk conditions or traumatic events may be outweighed by mediating environmental influences that foster resilience. Major studies of resilient children and adults noted the crucial influence of significant relationships, with models and mentors—such as coaches or teachers—who supported them, believed in their potential, and encouraged them to make the best of their lives (Garmezy, 1991; Rutter, 1987; Werner, 1993). However, the skewed clinical focus on family pathology blinded many to the kinship resources that could be found and strengthened, even in troubled families.

A family resilience orientation fundamentally alters that traditional deficit-based lens, shifting the perspective from viewing families as *damaged* to seeing them as *challenged*. Rather than rescuing so-called survivors from dysfunctional families, this approach affirms the family's reparative potential, based on the conviction that both individual and relational healing and growth can be forged out of adversity.

The concept of family resilience has valuable potential as a framework for intervention, prevention, research, and social policy aimed at supporting and strengthening the family. Although some families are shattered by crisis or persistent stresses, others surmount their challenges and emerge stronger and more resourceful. For instance, the death of a child poses a heightened risk for parental divorce, yet couples' relationships are strengthened when they pull together and support each other in dealing with their tragedy. The concept of resilience extends beyond coping and adaptation to recognize the enhanced strengths and growth that can be forged out of adversity.

A family resilience practice approach aims to identify and build key relational processes, with the conviction that both individual and family recovery are best forged through collaborative efforts in the face of adversity. A crisis also becomes an opportunity for reappraisal of life priorities and investment in meaningful relationships and pursuits. The approach is grounded in family systems theory, combining ecological and developmental perspectives to view the family as an open system that functions in relation to its broader sociocultural context and evolves over the multigenerational life cycle.

ECOLOGICAL PERSPECTIVE: STRESS-DIATHESIS MODEL

A biopsychosocial orientation, shared by all family systems approaches, views problem situations and their solutions as involving multiple recursive influences of individuals, families, larger systems, and sociocultural variables. A family resilience approach is grounded in a *stress-diathesis* model, which views most problems as resulting

from an interaction of individual—and family—vulnerability with the impact of stressful life experiences and social contexts.

- Problems may be primarily biologically based, as in serious mental illness, or largely influenced by sociocultural variables.
- Family distress may result from unsuccessful attempts to cope with an overwhelming situation.
- Symptoms may be generated by a crisis event within the family or by a pile-up of stresses that may trigger another crisis.
- Family distress may be fueled by a catastrophic event, such as a major disaster (Walsh, 2007), or by ongoing external stressors, such as persistent conditions associated with poverty, racism, heterosexism, or other forms of discrimination (Green, 2004; Walsh, 2006).

DEVELOPMENTAL PERSPECTIVE: FAMILY COPING, ADAPTATION, AND RESILIENCE

A family resilience approach attends to adaptational processes over time, from ongoing interactions to family life cycle passage and multigenerational influences. Life crises and persistent stresses have an impact on the functioning of a family system, with ripple effects to all members and their relationships. Family processes in response are crucial for coping and adaptation (McCubbin, McCubbin, McCubbin, & Futrell, 1998; McCubbin, McCubbin, Thompson, & Fromer, 1998); one family may be disabled whereas another rallies in response to similar life challenges. How a family confronts and manages a disruptive or threatening experience, buffers stress, effectively reorganizes, and reinvests in life pursuits influences adaptation for all members.

As one example, the presumption that divorce inevitably damages children fails to take into account the multiple variables in risk and resilience over time that make a difference in children's adaptation, including the predivorce climate, postdivorce parental conflict or cut-off, and financial strains (Hetherington & Kelly, 2002). Research that identifies family processes distinguishing those who do well from those who fare poorly can inform therapeutic and mediation efforts for optimal postdivorce child and family adaptation.

In resilience-oriented practice, family functioning is assessed in the context of the multigenerational system moving forward over time.

- A genogram and family time line (McGoldrick, Gerson, & Petry, 2008) are used to schematize relationship information and track system patterns to guide intervention planning.
- It is crucial to note linkages between the timing of symptoms and recent or impending stress events that have disrupted or threatened the family, such as a son's drop in school grades following his father's job loss.
- Frequently symptoms coincide with stressful developmental transitions. Each poses particular challenges, as new developmental priorities emerge, boundaries shift, and roles and relationships are redefined. Families must deal with both predictable, normative stresses, such as becoming parents, and unpredictable, disruptive events, such as the untimely death of a young parent or birth of a child with disabilities.
- Families adapt best when they are able to balance intergenerational continuity and change and maintain links between their past, present, and future.
- Family history and patterns of relation and functioning transmitted across the generations influence response to adversity and future expectations, hopes, dreams, and catastrophic fears.
- The convergence of developmental and multigenerational strains affects family coping ability. Strains increase exponentially when current stressors reactivate vulnerable issues from the past, for example, unresolved conflicts and losses, particularly when similar challenges are confronted (Carter & McGoldrick, 1999).
- It's crucial to inquire about models and sources of resilience in the face of past adversity that might be drawn on or inspire new coping strategies in the current situation.

ADVANTAGES OF A FAMILY RESILIENCE FRAMEWORK

Assessment of healthy family functioning is fraught with dilemmas. Recent postmodern perspectives have heightened awareness that views of family normality, pathology, and health are socially constructed (Walsh, 1993). Clinicians and researchers bring their own assumptive maps into every evaluation and intervention, embedded in cultural norms, professional orientations, and personal experience.

Moreover, the very concept of the family has been undergoing redefinition with the social and economic transformations of recent decades. Changing gender roles and a multiplicity of family arrangements have broadened the spectrum of normal families (Coontz, 1997; Walsh, 2003b). Over the life cycle, children and their parents are likely to move in and out of varied and complex family constellations, each transition posing new adaptational challenges. Yet the persistent myth that one family form is essential for healthy child development—the idealized 1950s norm of the intact nuclear family, headed by a breadwinner father and supported by a homemaker mother—has pathologized others. In fact, family diversity has been common throughout history and across cultures, and a growing body of research reveals that well-functioning families and healthy children can be found in a variety of family arrangements (Walsh, 2003b). What matters more than family form are family *processes* involving the quality of caring, committed relationships.

Research on healthy family functioning over the past two decades has provided empirical grounding to identify and facilitate key processes in intervention with distressed families (Walsh, 2003b). However, most research has been based on studies of white, middle-class, intact families who are not under stress. Family distress and differences from the norm are too often assumed to be pathological. Furthermore, family typologies tend to be static and acontextual, not attending to a family's social or developmental influences and emerging challenges over time.

A family resilience framework offers several advantages.

- By definition, it focuses on strengths under stress.
- It is assumed that no single model fits all family situations. Functioning is assessed in context: relative to each family's values, structure, resources, and life challenges.
- Processes for optimal functioning and the well-being of members will vary over time, as challenges unfold and families evolve across the life cycle.

- This approach to practice is grounded in a deep conviction in the potential for family repair, recovery, and growth out of adversity.

KEY PROCESSES IN FAMILY RESILIENCE

The Walsh Family Resilience Framework identifies nine key processes for resilience, as outlined in Table 58.1. It is informed by three decades of research in the social sciences and clinical field on resilience and well-functioning family systems, The framework synthesizes findings within three domains of family functioning: family belief systems, organizational patterns, and communication processes (Walsh, 2003a, 2006).

- Family belief systems support resilience when they help members (1) make meaning of crisis situations; (2) sustain a hopeful, positive outlook; and (3) draw on transcendent or spiritual values and purpose, most often through spiritual faith, practices, and community (Walsh, 2008).
- In family organization, resilience is fostered by (1) flexible yet stable structure, with strong leadership; (2) connectedness for mutual support; and (3) kin, social, and community resources.
- Communication processes facilitate resilience through (1) information clarity, (2) open expression of feelings and empathetic response, and (3) collaborative problem solving and proactive approach to future challenges.

APPLICATIONS OF FAMILY RESILIENCE APPROACHES

Family resilience–oriented practice uses principles and techniques common among strengths-based approaches but attends more centrally to links between presenting symptoms and family stressors, focusing on family coping and adaptational strategies. Interventions are directed to strengthen relational bonds and tap resources to reduce vulnerability and master family challenges. The family resilience framework is designed to guide assessment, interventions, and prevention to identify and strengthen key processes that foster recovery and growth.

Offering a collaborative, nonpathologizing approach, a family resilience framework has useful application in a range of adverse situations:

- healing from crisis, trauma, and loss;
- navigating disruptive transitions;
- mastering multistress challenges of chronic conditions (e.g., illness, poverty); and
- "bouncing forward" to adapt to changing life conditions.

Specific program applications to date (Walsh, 2002, 2006) include:

- family and community trauma and disaster recovery (Walsh, 2007);
- families facing end-of-life challenges and complicated loss;
- serious mental and physical illnesses, disabilities (Rolland, 1994);
- separation, divorce, and stepfamily reorganization;
- job loss, reemployment: family strains; mobilizing resources;
- family–school partnerships for success of at-risk youth;
- refugee families: resilience-oriented multifamily groups; and
- multiple, long-term recovery challenges in war-torn regions (e.g., Kosovo).

Efforts to foster family resilience benefit all family members, not only those currently presenting symptoms. A systemic assessment may lead to multisystemic approaches depending on the relevance of various system levels to risk reduction, problem resolution, and individual/family well-being. Putting an ecological view into practice, interventions often involve collaboration and change in the community with workplace, school, health care, and other larger systems.

Resilience-oriented family interventions can be adapted to a variety of formats.

- Family consultations, brief intervention, or more intensive family therapy may combine individual and conjoint sessions, including members affected by stressors and those who can contribute to resilience.
- Psychoeducational multifamily groups provide social support and practical information, offering concrete guidelines for stress reduction, crisis management, problem solving, and optimal functioning as families navigate through stressful periods and face future challenges.
- Brief, cost-effective periodic "modules" can be timed around critical transitions or emerging challenges in long-term adaptation,

TABLE 58.1 Key Processes in Family Resilience

Belief Systems

Making meaning of adversity
- View resilience as relationally based
- Normalize, contextualize distress; depathologize, decrease stigma, shame
- Sense of coherence: crisis as meaningful, comprehensible, manageable challenge
- Appraise adverse situation; options; future expectations, fears

Positive outlook
- Hope, optimistic bias; confidence in overcoming barriers
- Encouragement; affirm and build strengths and potential
- Active initiative and perseverance (can-do spirit)
- Master the possible; accept what can't be changed; live with uncertainty

Transcendence and spirituality
- Larger Values, purpose
- Spirituality: faith, rituals and practices, congregational support
- Inspiration: new possibilities, dreams; creative expression; social action
- Transformation: learning, change, and growth from adversity

Organizational Patterns

Flexibility
- Rebound, reorganize to adapt to new challenges
- Regain stability: continuity, dependability, predictability to counter disruption
- Strong authoritative leadership: nurture, guide, protect
- Varied family forms: cooperative parenting/caregiving teams
- Couple/co-parent relationship: mutual respect; equal partners

Connectedness
- Mutual support, collaboration, and commitment
- Respect individual needs, differences, and boundaries
- Reconnection, reconciliation of wounded relationships

Social and economic resources
- Mobilize kin, social and community networks; models and mentors
- Financial security; work/family balance; institutional supports

Communication/Problem Solving

Clarity
- Clear, consistent messages (words, deeds)
- Clarify ambiguous information; truth seeking/truth speaking

Open emotional expression
- Share range of feelings; mutual empathy; tolerate differences
- Responsibility for own feelings, behavior; avoid blaming
- Pleasurable interactions, respite; humor

Collaborative problem solving
- Creative brainstorming; resourcefulness
- Shared decision making; negotiation, fairness, reciprocity
- Focus on goals, concrete steps: build on success; learn from failure
- Proactive stance: prevent crises; prepare for future challenges

for example, a chronic illness, divorce processes, or disaster recovery.

CONCLUSION

Family research and practice must be rebalanced from a focus on how families fail to how they can succeed if the field is to move beyond the rhetoric of promoting family strengths to advance useful practice approaches for distressed families to thrive. Both quantitative and qualitative research contributions are required. The field also needs to address emerging family challenges, from workplace and health care restructuring to caregiving and end-of-life dilemmas with the aging of societies (Walsh, 1999).

This research-informed family resilience framework can be valuable in guiding clinical practice by assessing family functioning on key system variables as they fit each family's values, structure, resources, and challenges and then targeting interventions to foster family strengths as presenting problems are addressed. This collaborative strength-promoting approach involves a crucial shift in emphasis from family damage to family challenges. With the tremendous social and economic upheavals of recent decades and widespread concern about the breakdown of the family, useful conceptual models, such as this framework, are needed more than ever to guide efforts to strengthen family resilience.

WEB SITES

Chicago Center for Family Health. http://www.ccfhchicago.org.

Resilience Research Centre. http://www.resilienceproject.org.

References

Carter, B., & McGoldrick, M. (Eds.). (1999). *The expanded family life cycle: Individual, family, and social perspectives,* 3rd ed. Needham Hill, MA: Allyn & Bacon.

Coontz, S. (1997). *The way we really are: Coming to terms with America's changing families.* New York: Basic Books.

Garmezy, N. (1991). Resiliency and vulnerability to adverse developmental outcomes associated with poverty. *American Behavioral Scientist, 34,* 416–430.

Green, R.-J. (2004). Risk and resilience in lesbian and gay couples. *Journal of Family Psychology, 18*(2), 290–292.

Hetherington, E. M., & Kelly, J. (2002). *For better or for worse: Divorce reconsidered.* New York: Norton.

Kaufman, J., & Ziegler, E. (1987). Do abused children become abusive parents? *American Journal of Orthopsychiatry, 57,* 186–192.

Luthar, S. S., & Ziegler, E. (1991). Vulnerability and competence: A review of research on resilience in childhood. *American Journal of Orthopsychiatry, 61,* 6–22.

McCubbin, H., McCubbin, M., McCubbin, A., & Futrell, J. (Eds.). (1998). *Resiliency in ethnic minority families. Vol. 2. African-American families.* Thousand Oaks: Sage.

McCubbin, H., McCubbin, M., Thompson, E., & Fromer, J. (Eds.). (1998). *Resiliency in ethnic minority families. Vol. 1. Native and immigrant families.* Thousand Oaks: Sage.

McGoldrick, M., Gerson, R., & Petry, S . (2008). *Genograms: Assessment and intervention,* 3rd ed. New York: Norton.

Rolland, J. S. (1994). *Families, illness, and disability: An integrative treatment model.* New York: Basic Books.

Rutter, M. (1987). Psychosocial resilience and protective mechanisms. *American Journal of Orthopsychiatry, 57,* 316–331.

Walsh, F. (1993). Conceptualization of normal family processes. In F. Walsh (Ed.). *Normal family processes* (2nd ed), (pp. 1–25). New York: Guilford.

Walsh, F. (1999). Families in later life: Challenge and opportunities. In B. Carter & M. McGoldrick (Eds.), *The expanded family life cycle.* Needham Heights, MA: Allyn & Bacon.

Walsh, F. (2002). A family resilience framework: Innovative practice applications. *Family Relations, 51*(2), 130–137.

Walsh, F. (2003a). Family resilience: A framework for clinical practice. *Family Process, 42*(1), 1–18.

Walsh, F. (Ed.). (2003b). *Normal family processes: Growing diversity and complexity,* 3rd ed. New York: Guilford Press.

Walsh, F. (2006). *Strengthening family resilience,* 2nd ed. New York: Guilford.

Walsh, F. (2007). Traumatic loss and major disasters: Strengthening family and community resilience. *Family Process, 46,* 207–227.

Walsh, F. (Ed.). (2008). *Spiritual resources in family therapy,* 2nd ed. New York: Guilford.

Werner, E. E. (1993). Risk, resilience, and recovery: Perspectives from the Kauai longitudinal study. *Development and Psychopathology, 5,* 503–515.

Treatment Planning with Families
An Evidence-Based Approach

Catheleen Jordan & Cynthia Franklin

Social workers and other health professionals must document treatment planning to receive third-party payments. Treatment planning is a formalized process of individualizing and operationalizing clients' treatment goals and specifying measurable outcomes to chart therapeutic progress (Jongsma & Dattilio, 2000). Social workers treating families have unique issues in treatment planning, such as specifying goals agreeable to all family members. This chapter describes treatment planning with families, identifies the steps of treatment planning, and summarizes resources for family social workers.

TREATMENT PLANNING WITH FAMILIES

Managed care has encouraged the move toward formalized family treatment planning and the trend toward efficacious, brief family therapy interventions. Systematic treatment planning involves defining measurable goals, objectives, and outcomes as well as evidence-based treatments known to be effective with specific client problems and populations. The treatment plan (see Fig. 59.1 for an example) is a therapeutic guide that helps focus treatment. It is a written contract that may be signed by the client and social worker; it may be modified as the family's goals change. Also, if a treatment team is providing services to the family, the treatment plan specifies which provider is responsible for each specified intervention.

Special challenges in treatment planning with families include selecting problems, goals, and outcomes that are meaningful to all family members. For instance, the parents may desire their child to become more compliant; the child, on the other hand, may desire an end to constant parental nagging! Additionally, problem-focused treatment planning is sometimes at odds with a social work strengths-based approach.

STEPS OF TREATMENT PLANNING WITH FAMILIES

Treatment planning requires the social worker to think through the therapeutic process from assessment to intervention and evaluation. Today's focus on brief, manualized interventions is perfect for this type of planned approach because it requires the problem to be measured. Standardized measures are paper and pencil instruments, completed by the client and/or social worker that provide a score indicating the extent or severity of a client problem. For example, a couple may complete the Hudson Index of Marital Satisfaction; each receives a score indicating the level of satisfaction with the marriage. A score more than 25 indicates a clinically significant problem. Data are collected repeatedly over the course of treatment and graphed so that progress may be tracked. Thus, measurement is used to assess, track, graph, and evaluate client progress over the course of treatment. The following six steps of treatment planning were identified by Jongsma (2004).

Step 1: Problem Selection

Problem selection in family treatment requires the social worker to assess client problems and then prioritize them in a way meaningful to the family. Jordan and Franklin (in press) recommend a problem selection and specification process guided by a person in environment perspective. Problem assessment moves from a global, systems view to an operationalized view of specific problems. For example, a global assessment technique, such as an eco-map, is used to obtain a global view of the family in the context of their important environmental systems. From the map, the social worker is able to conclude that problems stem from an acting out adolescent, for

Problem: Adolescent behavior problems

Definitions: Aggressive conduct that threatens physical harm to family
members

Goals: Eliminate adolescent aggressive behavior

Objectives: **Interventions:**

1.   Family members learn   1. Teach the family the skills of recognizing
        anger management   one's escalating anger, taking a timeout
        techniques   to cool down, acknowledging one's
                                        contribution to the aggressive situation,
                                        negotiating a solution.

2.   Parents and adolescent   2. Teach the parents to negotiate a contract
        establish a behavioral contract   with the adolescent that specifies
                                        rules/expectations, consequences,
                                        and rewards

Diagnosis: 312.8 Conduct Disorder, Adolescent-Onset Type

Figure 59.1 Treatment plan example.

example. With this knowledge, data specific to a particular problem or behavior (e.g. anger, satisfaction) may be collected via standardized measures. In Figure 59.1, the treatment plan example, the problem is adolescent behavior problems. We further specify the meaning of the problem in step 2, the problem definition.

Step 2: Problem Definition

After the problem(s) is selected, it must be defined. The *DSM-IV* is the most agreed on way of categorizing or defining problems, but is not always the most meaningful to family social workers, especially considering the controversy around lack of interreliability of categories. As mentioned before, standardized measures have gained popularity in social work and may be used to quantify client problems. Examples of problems that may be measured in this way include family relationship and satisfaction, marital satisfaction, sexual abuse and family violence, dual career relationship, child and parent relationships, and so

forth. Individual problems such as depression, self-esteem, or anxiety, which may be a part of a family's problem, can also be easily measured using standardized instruments.

Other ways of measuring problems include counting discrete behaviors (e.g., number of family arguments or number of child tantrums) or developing goal-attainment or self-anchored scales. Goal-attainment scales, developed by the social worker, are used to identify outcomes and to operationalize categories indicating successive approximations toward 100 percent goal completion. Numbers are assigned to each category with minus signs indicating lack of progress or deterioration. A typical scale range is from –2 to +2. Self-anchored scales are also developed by the social worker in conjunction with the family. The targeted behavior, for example family satisfaction, is rated from 1 to 5. A rating of 1 may stand for "the most satisfied" and 5 "the least satisfied" that the family can imagine. Anchors, indicating specific family behaviors, are then matched with each numerical ranking. For instance, the family may describe a category 1 ranking, the "most satisfied," as a time when they are having dinner together as a family, engaged in pleasant conversation with no fighting, and so on.

In addition to a focus on problems, the value of a strengths-based approach encourages social workers to measure and intervene by building on client strengths (e.g., number of positive family communications or family outings). These positive behavioral objectives may be incorporated into the treatment plan. In the treatment plan example, Figure 59.1, the problem is defined as aggressive conduct that threatens physical harm to family members. We might determine the problem by the use of counting the discrete number of angry outbursts on the part of the adolescent, or we might find a standardized instrument that measures aggressive behavior or anger. We then develop a goal statement in step 3.

Step 3: Goal Development

One goal statement for each problem specified is recommended by Jongsma (2004). The goal statement is a broadly stated description of what successful outcome is expected. Goals are not necessarily operationalized in measurable terms, as are objectives. Instead, they may be broad statements of the overall anticipated positive outcome. In the sample treatment plan (Fig. 59.1), the goal is to eliminate adolescent aggressive behavior. We could specify additional goals, such as increasing positive family communication or improving parenting skills. Goals may be long-term expectations. We further operationalized the goal by specifying objectives in step 4.

Step 4: Objective Construction

Objectives are the measurable steps that must occur for the goals to be met. Each goal should have at least two objectives; they are operationalized in measurable terms and are the short-term steps necessary to achieve the goal. In the sample plan (Fig. 59.1), the social worker may measure the objective of "family members learn anger management techniques" by having each person role-play the skills that are being taught. Or family members might log their experiences with using each technique in their home setting. The objective is measurable. Jongsma (2004) recommends that target dates be assigned to each objective to focus treatment sessions and ensure brief treatment and problem resolution. As families progress

through treatment, they may add additional objectives. The next step moves the treatment plan from defining and operationalizing problems to specifying the intervention.

Step 5: Intervention Creation

Interventions, the clinicians' tools for treating the problem, should be matched with each objective. Interventions are selected according to the social worker's theoretical and clinical orientation; however, the trend in family social work is toward brief, evidence-based methods that have proven efficacy for specific families or family problems. Another trend in treatment is toward manualized interventions and treatment planners that provide guidelines to the social worker as to how to proceed with specific problems. Also, the greater the operationalization of the treatment, the greater the confidence level of the social worker in attributing positive changes to the intervention. In Figure 59.1, two cognitive-behavioral interventions have been specified. Finally, the treatment concludes with a *DSM* diagnosis.

Step 6: Diagnosis Determination

Treatment planning assumes that an appropriate diagnosis will be determined, based on the overall client family picture. As mentioned before, the diagnostic approach has not been favored by many social workers, due not only to the low interrater reliability associated with differential diagnosis (Jongsma, 2004) but also to social worker's value of strengths-based treatment. Nevertheless, third-party payers in managed care settings require a *DSM* diagnosis. Social workers face the reality of needing to know the characteristics of *DSM* criteria as part of a complete assessment picture. A complete assessment is important to *DSM* diagnosis, because appropriate diagnosis is based on evaluation of clients total biopsychosocial presentation (Jongsma, 2004). In Figure 59.1, the diagnosis is 312.8 Conduct Disorder, Adolescent-Onset Type.

TREATMENT PLANNING RESOURCES FOR FAMILY SOCIAL WORKERS

Jongsma (2004) emphasizes the importance of developing an individualized treatment plan for each client family, based on their own uniqueness. Following are references helpful to the social worker proceeding through each step of the treatment plan.

Problem Selection and Definition

Jordan and Franklin (in press) provide a framework for assessment that teaches the social work practitioner to move from a global, person-in-environment family picture to a more specific, measurable focus on target problems and strengths. Specific standardized instruments for measuring child and family problems are presented by Corcoran and Fischer (2000). Bloom, Fischer, and Orme (2005) discuss a variety of ways available to measure problems, including goal-attainment scaling and behavioral measurement mentioned earlier. Prewritten definitions of common family problems, in behaviorally specific language with problem definition statements, are available from Jongsma and Dattilio (2000).

Goal and Objective Development

Jongsma (2004) discusses goal and objective setting for general practice and for family practice (Jongsma & Dattilio, 2000). Social work research-practitioners, Bloom et al. (2005) discuss goal and objective setting from a single subject design perspective. Their text describes not only how to measure problems but how to set up a system for tracking therapeutic progress.

Intervention Construction and Differential Diagnosis

Lambert (2004) reviews the efficacy of clinical interventions, including child, family, and marital therapy. Several texts written by social workers review methods available for treating families and children (Collins, Jordan, & Coleman, in press; Franklin & Jordan, 1999; Janzen, Harris, Jordan, & Franklin, 2006). Additionally, Reid's (2000) text provides a step-by-step guide for the practitioner in intervention task planning, including tasks for family social workers.

Bloom and colleagues (2005) include software called Singwin, a computerized data analysis program for the ideographic data provided by single case analysis.

Future Applications for Treatment Plans

Treatment plans help ensure a positive future for client families. It helps us set goals and objectives for clients that are measurable and offered in a brief and timely manner. It requires that we specify what we will do in our way of helping. It provides a structure for an evidence-based approach to treatment, which is strongly encouraged and in some cases mandated. Finally, treatment planning requires that we document what we do to ensure accountability to our clients, that we track their progress through the treatment process and ensure that we are working with them to offer the best possible social work treatment that works for them.

WEB SITES

NIDA/SAMHSA Blending Initiative. http://www.nida.nih.gov/blending/asi.html.

S.M.A.R.T. Treatment Planning. http://www.samhsa.gov/SAMHSA_news/VolumeXIV_5/article2.htm.

Spasticity definition. http://www.mdvu.org/library/disease/spasticity/spa_msa_c12.html.

Treatment Planner Software Modules. http://www.4ulr.com/products/counseling/client_groups.html.

References

Bloom, M., Fischer, J., & Orme, J. (2005). *Evaluating practice: Guidelines for the accountable professional*, 5th ed. Needham Heights, MA: Allyn & Bacon.

Collins, D., Jordan, C., & Coleman, H. (In press). *An introduction to family social work*, 3rd ed. Belmont, CA: Cengage.

Corcoran, K., & Fischer, J. (2000). *Measures for clinical practice*, 3rd ed., 2 vols. New York: Free Press.

Franklin, C., & Jordan, C. (1999). *Family practice: Brief systems methods for social work*. Belmont, CA: Cengage.

Janzen, C., Harris, O., Jordan, C., & Franklin, C. (2006). *Family treatment: Evidence based practice with populations at risk*. 4th ed. Belmont, CA: Cengage.

Jongsma, A. E. Jr. (2004). Psychotherapy treatment plan writing. In G. P. Koocher, J. C. Norcross, S. S. Hill III (Eds.), *Psychologist's desk reference*, 2nd ed. New York: Oxford University Press.

Jongsma, A. E. Jr., & Dattilio, J. F. M. (2000). *The family therapy treatment planner*. New York: Wiley.

Jordan, C., & Franklin, C. (In press). *Clinical assessment for social workers: Qualitative and quantitative methods*, 3rd ed. Chicago: Lyceum Books.

Lambert, M. (2004). *Bergin and Garfield's handbook of psychotherapy and behavior change*, 5th ed. New York: Wiley.

Reid, W. J. (2000). *The task planner: An intervention resource for human service professionals*. New York: Columbia University Press.

60 Effective Couple and Family Treatment

Cynthia Franklin, Catheleen Jordan,
& Laura M. Hopson

Over the past 40 years, family therapy has developed into one of the most popular forms of therapy. Research on the practice of family therapy is supported by several disciplines, including social work, psychology, family science, and marriage and family therapy. As a result of this interdisciplinary participation, a number of effective therapeutic methods have developed. This chapter offers a summary of current practices that are being followed. It also summarizes some of the best practices based on current empirical research studies.

CURRENT PRACTICES

Family therapy models are grounded in systems theory and view individual problems in relationship to other family members and significant others in the social environment. The models engage family members in changing dysfunctional family and relationship patterns. Some current practices are summarized here.

In implementing family interventions, practitioners define the family system as those individuals involved with the presenting problem or who could be a resource in developing a solution. In addition to intervening with family members and significant people involved with the problem, therapists may intervene with individuals alone when appropriate. For example, a family therapist might work with an individual client, a live-in couple, a foster family, a social services agency representative, or a teacher. The phrase "problem-determined system" is sometimes used to describe this means of defining the system in which to work.

Family therapists employ an ecological systems perspective by expanding their relationship emphasis beyond the nuclear and extended family to include other societal systems and cultural issues that impact individuals and families. For example, a family's relationship with a social service delivery system, race, gender, and socioeconomic status have become important issues to consider when formulating therapeutic strategies.

In recent years, researchers and practitioners have expanded systems theories and integrated them with other theories for understanding how families function, such as neuroscience, developmental theories, and biological theories. This has resulted in changes in the way that family therapist practice.

- *Families are no longer held responsible for causing severe and persistent mental disorders in family members.* The etiologies of serious and persistent mental disorders are now viewed from a biopsychosocial–spiritual framework and are often assessed from the perspective of stress-diathesis model, which recognizes the role of biology in the development of mental disorders and does not blame the family interactions for these problems. Newer, family-based psychoeducation treatments are offered to family members to help educate them about mental illness and provide social support and the resources that they need to manage and care for mentally ill family members.

- *The division between the medical model and family approaches therefore has diminished.* Older family models have become more flexible by including work with medical professionals and diverse systems of care when helping clients. Family therapists use diverse treatments, such as medication, cognitive-behavioral therapy, or other empirically supported treatments relevant to the presenting problems of individuals as well as family systems.

- *There is an increase in popularity of family approaches that rejects the notions of systems theory.* Postmodern approaches, narrative therapy, and solution-focused brief therapy have become popular alternatives for the practice of family therapy. These newer approaches developed out of family systems theories and in reaction to traditional systems models and have become popular forms of couples and family practice.

Practicing therapists often use a combination of family techniques from different models rather than adhering to one particular approach. Integrationism, technical eclecticism, and the use of common factors are the preferred ways that most practitioners work. A great deal of attention has also been given to effectiveness of common factors in marital and family practice (Sprenkle & Blow, 2004). Multicomponent treatment programs, which emphasize the integration of more than one approach, are increasingly used with client populations. Family researchers, for example, are combining strategies across models to design empirically based treatments for hard-to-serve clients, such as serious juvenile offenders and substance-abusing youths (Henggeler, 1999; Sells, 2000, in press; Szapocznik, Hervis, & Schwartz, 2003).

Feminist, postmodern, and multicultural perspectives are at the forefront of discussions about family models and have redefined our understanding of family systems as follows.

- Feminist viewpoints emphasize the unequal power relations between men and women and how these larger societal issues impact family life and problem solving.
- Postmodern viewpoints emphasize the constructed nature of reality and the need for collaborative relationships between client and therapist. Postmodern family therapists examine how client problems and beliefs are socially constructed, the need to empower marginalized clients, the political nature of therapy, and a need for social justice.
- Multicultural perspectives emphasize the importance of race and culture in therapeutic work.

Multicultural, postmodern, and solution-focused practices also emphasize nonpathological approaches to clients. Family therapists are challenged to be sensitive to issues of diversity, culture, and gender and to recognize clients' strengths. Each therapist is expected to develop responsive interventions that take into account social justice issues.

Family therapists have generally worked with clients using practice methods that focus on changing behavioral and communication patterns, cognitive beliefs, and social context as their major means of helping. In recent years, however, family therapists are emphasizing the importance of attachment processes and emotional states. The use of acceptance strategies, for example, is one of the major means of helping families resolve their differences. Therapies that use emotion-focused techniques have offered effective results for distressed couples and those that have post-traumatic stress disorder (Basham & Miehls, 2004; Christensen & Jacobson, 2000, Johnson, 2002; Wood, Crane, Schaalje, & Law, 2005). Research has also shown that a positive ratio of positive to negative emotions is important for promoting marital satisfaction and healthy family relationships, whereas couples who criticize, show contempt, and stonewall their partners are the most distressed and the most likely to divorce (Gottman, 1998).

Acceptance is believed to be as important in family intervention as directed behavioral change strategies, such as skills training and contracting. Acceptance strategies emphasize the reframing of hard emotions, such as anger, into soft emotions, such as sadness. Discussions about behavioral patterns learned in one's family of origin help couples gain insight, empathy, and acceptance of each other's behavior. Studies have shown that behavioral couples therapies that use acceptance techniques like integrative couples therapy increases the effectiveness of traditional behavioral couples therapies and prolong benefits for these couples after therapy ends, preventing relapse (Christensen, Atkins, Yi, Baucom, & George, 2006; Jacobson & Christensen, 1996).

There is increased optimism over the effectiveness of family therapy approaches and concerns about improving the evidence-based status of family therapy interventions. In the past 10 to 15 years, family therapy researchers and other advocates of these methods have given attention to documenting the brief nature of family therapy and its efficacy with client populations. Meta-analyses demonstrate that marital and family therapies result in positive outcomes for clients (Shadish et al., 1993; Shadish & Baldwin, 2003). Stanton and Shadish (1997), in a meta-analysis of drug abuse outcome studies, found that family interventions are favorable to individual or peer group approaches and have higher retention rates. Among juvenile delinquents, family interventions reduce the risk of rearrest (Woolfenden, Williams, & Peat, 2005).

Recent studies also show that family therapy reduces client utilization of the health care system (Law & Crane, 2000). Most family therapy models currently qualify as effective and brief forms of therapy (Franklin & Jordan, 1999).

EFFECTIVE APPROACHES

Several recent reviews of effective marital and family therapy approaches have been written for practitioners (e.g., Corcoran, 2000; Fraser, Nelson & Rivard, 1997; Hoagwood, 2005; Hogue & Liddle, 1999; Johnson & Lebow, 2000; Lebow, 2000; Pinsof & Wynne, 1995, 2000; Shadish & Baldwin, 2003; Thompson, Pomeroy, & Gober, 2005). Social workers may consult these authors for more comprehensive reviews of marital and family therapy process and outcome studies. This chapter summarizes some of the major conclusions from these reviews about what models work best. It is also important to note that there are varying degrees of disagreement about the effectiveness of therapies depending on what evidentiary criteria are used to examine the studies. The summary provided here is in no way comprehensive of the findings at large or the critical analysis that may exist on any particular perspective.

Results from meta-analyses suggest that it is difficult to distinguish between different models of family therapy when comparing their overall effectiveness against one another (Shadish et al., 1993; Shadish & Baldwin, 2003). All models are more effective than not receiving any therapy at all and show similar statistical effect sizes, indicating that differing approaches have similar results. Across models, characteristics of the therapeutic relationship are important factors moderating the effectiveness of family interventions. A recent meta-analysis indicates that therapeutic relationship variables are good predictors of family therapy outcomes (Karver, Hadelsman, Fields, & Bickman, 2006).

Even so, certain models of family therapy present better outcome research, and evidence has accumulated suggesting that these therapies have clinical efficacy with certain client populations. At the present time, behavioral, cognitive-behavioral, functional, psychoeducational, multisystemic, and structural models of family therapy present the best evidence for their effectiveness. Each one of these approaches also has well-developed clinical protocols, procedures, and treatment manuals to help therapists learn how to do the interventions.

Another efficacious intervention that has been receiving more and more research is the emotion-focused therapy for couples. Research studies on emotion-focused therapy are rapidly progressing, and there is evidence for its effectiveness with distressed couples, including those who experience trauma (Denton, Burleson, Clark, Rodriguez, & Hobbs, 2000; Paivio & Nieuwenhuis, 2001). A recent meta-analysis indicates that emotion-focused therapy may be more effective than behavioral models for treatment of marital distress (Wood, Crane, Schaalje, & Law, 2005).

Strategic family therapy approaches are supported by a number of studies demonstrating promising outcomes in the areas of substance abuse and behavioral disordered youths (Szapocznik & Williams, 2000). Evidence for the strategic model often combines strategic methods with structural family therapy techniques. Some strategic models integrate solution-focused techniques, such as the Parenting with Love and Limits (PLL) approach developed by Scott Sells (Sells, 1998). This approach was developed by a social worker and reports success at being transported and successfully used by social agencies. Participation in PLL is also associated with reduced substance use, aggressive behavior, and depression among adolescents (Sells, Smith, & Rodman, 2006).

Solution-focused brief therapy (SFBT) is another popular strengths-based, family therapy approach that can be applied to individuals or families and is making progress investigating effectiveness. In the past 10 years, several experimental and quasi-experimental studies have accumulated on SFBT showing that it is a promising model with a wide range of problems (Gingerich & Eisengart, 2000; Kim, 2008; Kim & Franklin, 2007; Newsome, 2004). DeJong (see Chapter 33) discusses the fact that three recent meta-analysis have been completed on SFBT, and the results suggest that it is a promising intervention that deserves further research. Interestingly, most of the more rigorous research studies on SFBT have recently appeared. For example, Kim & Franklin (2007) conducted a systematic review of studies of SFBT in schools and discovered that one experimental design study, six quasi-experimental design studies, and one single-case design study on SFBT had been published since 2000. Most of these studies have arrived within the past 2–3 years. The effect sizes calculated by the authors and reported in the individual studies also show SFBT to be a promising intervention for work with children and families within school settings, with most studies having medium and some large effect sizes.

CHOOSING THE BEST OF THE BEST FAMILY INTERVENTIONS FOR YOUR CLIENTS

Behavioral family therapies provide some of the best outcome studies suggesting their effectiveness. Behavioral interventions work with childhood behavioral disorders and autism. Behavioral couple therapies are among the most well researched and effective treatments for distressed couples (Johnson & Lebow, 2000; Shadish & Baldwin, 2005). Behavioral couples therapy has been shown to be especially effective in ameliorating depressive symptoms (Shadish & Baldwin, 2005). Integrated behavioral family therapy integrates family systems theory and cognitive-behavioral therapy and demonstrates positive outcomes with substance-abusing youth (Thompson et al., 2005; Waldron, Slesnick, & Brody, 2001).

Functional family therapy, which integrates systems theory and behavioral methods into its own unique relationship therapy, works with juvenile offenders and their families. There is also evidence to show that functional family therapy reduces arrests in younger siblings (Alexander et al., 1998). Skills training approaches based on behavioral therapies also work in prevention of substance use and antisocial behaviors.

Psychoeducation and multifamily group interventions that provide education and social support are the treatment of choice when working with severe and persistent mental illness, such as schizophrenia and bipolar disorder. Research demonstrates that participation in psychoeducation is associated with increased social supports and improved ability to manage social conflicts, for example (Magliano, Fiorillo, Malangone, De-Rosa, & Maj, 2007).

Structural family therapy interventions work with Hispanic youths who abuse substances, and evidence also exists that structural approaches can be effectively used to engage hard-to reach families in treatment (Paz Pruitt, 2007). There is also some evidence that structural family therapy methods may work with eating disorders (Fishman, 2006). In addition, concepts from structural family therapy serve as the foundation for other evidence-based family therapy approaches (Schinke, Brounstein, & Gardner, 2002).

Brief Strategic Family Therapy (BSFT) integrates concepts from systemic, structural, and strategic models in addressing issues of delinquency, substance abuse, and family relationship problems. The model has been evaluated repeatedly over the course of 25 years and effectively restance abuse while improving family functioning (Szapocznik et al., 2003).

Multisystemic therapy (MST), which uses ecological approaches, intensive family preservation, and structural family therapy, has demonstrated positive outcomes with hard-to-reach juvenile delinquents and substance abusers (Henggeler, 1999; Randall & Cunningham, 2003). This approach also offers sophisticated protocols for engaging hard-to-reach clients and manuals for maintaining the treatment adherence of therapists. This model has been able to demonstrate, for example, that 98 percent of randomly assigned clients remain in treatment; this is a high adherence rate for such a high-risk population (Henggeler, 1999).

Recent controversy about the effectiveness of MST illustrates the challenges of identifying evidence-based interventions. MST is widely accepted as evidence-based by federal funding organizations and practice settings (Franklin & Hopson, 2007). Yet a recent thorough review conducted by the Nordic Campbell Center of the Campbell Collaboration concludes that the intervention is not consistently more effective than alternative treatments (Littell, Popa, & Forsythe, 2005). Over time, new research may call into question the effectiveness of other approaches or provide more evidence for some of the promising programs that are not currently considered to be evidence-based.

Common Characteristics of Effective Approaches

Many evidence-based family approaches share common characteristics or core components. Parent management training is one of the primary components of effective treatment programs, for example (Kazdin & Whitley, 2003). Effective interventions typically include educational components and opportunities to practice new skills, such as communication and problem-solving skills. Practitioners model new behaviors and provide feedback to family members on their ability to implement the behaviors. Intervening on multiple ecological levels is also important, and many effective approaches intervene with family members, school staff, and providers in the community (Schinke et al., 2002).

EXAMPLE OF ONE EFFECTIVE FAMILY THERAPY APPROACH

BSFT

BSFT was developed by Jose Szapocznik at the Center for Family Studies. The model has been used in the context of prevention, early intervention, and intervention for families with children between the ages of 8 and 17 to address issues of delinquency and substance abuse. BSFT is provided in 8 to 24 sessions, depending on the severity of the presenting problems. Sessions may be conducted in office, home, or community settings based on the needs of the family. The model aims to improve outcomes for youth by improving the family environment. Box 60.1 presents a case example presented from the series *Therapy Manuals for Drug Addiction*, published by the National Institute of Drug Abuse (Szapocznick et al., 2003).

Box 60.1 Case Study for BSFT: The Guerrero Family.

CLINICAL PRESENTATION

The Guerrero family consists of a mother, a father, and 11- and 14-year-old sons. They were referred to the clinic by the 14-year-old's school counselor after he was caught smoking marijuana in the school bathroom. The counselor visited the home and found the youngest son and the mother eating dinner. The identified patient and the father were not there. The mother immediately began to list excuses why her oldest son was not home when he should have been. She had trouble accepting what the school counselor had done and insisted that the teacher who had reported him "has it out for my son." Toward the end of the counselor's first visit, the father came home. He ignored his wife and younger son and went directly to the kitchen. On finding no food ready for him, he shouted over his shoulder at his wife, asking her why she had not made him dinner. When the father was asked to join the session, he declined, saying that his wife was in charge of discipline and that she was not doing a good job at it. The 14-year-old did not come home during the counselor's visit.

ESTABLISHING THE THERAPEUTIC SYSTEM

When the counselor first arrived at the Guerrero home, he began to join with the mother. He sat at the dinner table with the mother and the younger son and validated the mother as she complained about the father's disengagement and the oldest son's out-of-control behavior. The younger son chimed in periodically about his brother's sour attitude, and the counselor empathized with his grievances. Although the counselor's initial attempts to join with the father were unsuccessful, the counselor later adopted a more focused approach. When he spoke to the father, the counselor emphasized that his participation was needed to keep his son from getting into more serious trouble. The counselor also assured the father that participating in therapy could help reduce his wife's nagging about his disengagement from the family.

Joining with the drug-abusing son was somewhat more difficult. He resisted the counselor's first few attempts to join with him over the phone and was absent from the home during the counselor's first few visits. Finally, the counselor approached the adolescent at the park after he and his father had had a major fight. The counselor assured the youth that being in BSFT could help ensure that that type of fight would not happen again.

DIAGNOSIS

When the counselor met with the whole family, the mother began to tell him about her son's problems. The counselor asked the mother to tell her son about her concerns. As the counselor encouraged the family members to speak with each other, he also observed the patterns of interaction along the following BSFT diagnostic dimensions.

Organization. A strong alliance exists between the mother and her 14-year-old (problem) son; the father is uninvolved. The children communicate with the father mostly through the mother. The mother and the father do not share much time as a couple. The mother is responsible for child-rearing nearly all the time. The mother and father ally occasionally, but only regarding unimportant issues, such as what to eat for dinner.

Resonance. The mother indicates what her 14-year-old son prefers to eat, and the mother and her 14-year-old son laugh together, both signs of enmeshment. The father is frequently "too busy" to participate in family activities, a sign of disengagement. Complaints of family members about other family members during the interview are highly specific, a sign of adaptive functioning along this dimension.

Developmental stage. The children are not allowed to play outdoors at night. The mother uses her 14-year-old son as her confidante, complaining to him that his father comes home late.

Life context. The father has a demanding job, while the mother finishes her work early and is home by 3 P.M. The family lives in a high-crime neighborhood; drug dealing gangs recruit in the area. The mother and father are not involved in arranging or supervising activities for their adolescent son and his peers. The 14-year-old son is associating with antisocial youth in the neighborhood.

Identified patient. The father comes home late and does not help with chores at home. His 14-year-old son is rebellious, refuses to do chores, and has conduct problems at home and in school. He also comes home late, often very excited and irritable. He stays up much of the night listening to music, then sleeps deep into the day. The 11-year-old son is a model child.

Conflict resolution. Conflicts are diffused through angry blaming and recriminations.

GENERAL DISCUSSION OF THE DIAGNOSIS

In the Guerrero family, the parents have assigned themselves separate role responsibilities. The mother is fully responsible for all child-rearing, and the father's responsibility in this area is very limited. Because there appears to be an unspoken agreement between the parents to be distant from each other, it can be assumed that they prefer their separate role responsibilities for their own reasons. This is maladaptive behavior in terms of child-rearing issues because the father and mother do not cooperate in parenting functions. Rather, it may appear that the mother and the troubled son are the ones allied, with the father off on the side. If one looks a little deeper, it would not be surprising to find that the same patterns of interaction occur around content areas other than child-rearing. In fact, these kinds of interactive patterns or structures are almost always found to reoccur in most aspects of family life. If they occur around one content, they are almost invariably occurring around most (if not all) contents. The lack of a strong parental alliance with regard to child-rearing issues undermines the family's ability to chart an effective and successful course of action. This is particularly troublesome when there are forces external to the family that influence the adolescent's development of behavior problems. These forces include the adolescent's peer group and the behavioral expectations that exist or to which the youth is exposed outside the home. These ecological forces provide training and opportunity for a full rebellion on the part of the adolescent.

A BSFT intervention will target changing the interactional patterns preventing the family from successfully charting the youth's path away from antisocial peer groups and externalizing behaviors. This intervention involves restoring parental leadership capabilities by first creating a parental leadership alliance. In resonance, it becomes clear that because the father is outside of the mother–child alliance, he is less concerned about what goes on within that alliance. Because he stays out, he is emotionally distant (disengaged) from both his wife and his son. In contrast to this, the mother and her 14-year-old son are much closer emotionally and psychologically; thus, they are likely to be enmeshed. Whether one defines the mother as enmeshed with the son or the mother and son as disengaged from the father, it is obvious that there is a difference in the psychological and emotional distance that exists between father and mother and father and son on the one hand and mother and son on the other.

On the dimension of developmental stage, it appears that the 14-year-old boy may be burdened with emotional responsibilities that are more appropriately assigned to a spouse, such as being the mother's confidante. The other child is not allowed out after dark. This seems appropriate given the dangerousness of the neighborhood.

In this family, the identified patient is sometimes the troubled son and sometimes the isolated father. Although the negativity the mother and the 14-year-old show toward the father functions to keep him out of the family, both the mother and father blame their current problems on their oldest son. If he were not rebellious, their separate role arrangement would work quite well for each of them. Unfortunately, conflicts between the mother and the father are not being resolved because their attempts to address their differences of opinion degenerate into blaming wars.

PLANNING TREATMENT BASED ON DIAGNOSIS

Understanding the dimensions that describe family interactions goes a long way toward helping the BSFT counselor define what he or she must do as a counselor: diagnose the problem in terms of specific dimensions of family interactions and then implement strategies to correct problems along these dimensions. Often some dimensions are more problematic than others and need to be the greater focus of the intervention. The counselor diagnosed the oldest son's drug abuse problem in terms of ineffective behavior control resulting from the following.

- Organization: absence of a parental subsystem that works together. Mother and father need to be assigned collaborative tasks that will bring them together.
- Organization: improper alliances. Boundaries must be strengthened between mother and 14-year-old son.
- Resonance: maladaptive boundaries in which one parent is too close (enmeshed) to the problem child, and a second parent is too far (disengaged) from the spouse and that same child.
- Boundaries need to be shifted so that the parents are closer to one another emotionally and interactionally, the children are more "in tune" with each other, and a healthy separation exists between the parents and the children.

- Developmental stage: developmental stage may be inappropriate in that the enmeshed child is burdened and confused by a spousal role (confidante to mom's unhappiness with dad). The counselor should encourage the mother and father to serve as each other's support system.
- Identified patient: enmeshed child is identified by the family as its major problem. The counselor needs to shift the family's attention to help family members understand that the whole system, rather than only the adolescent, is part of the problem. Also, family members need to eliminate negative attitudes and enabling behaviors they display toward the adolescent patient to "free" him to act in a socially appropriate manner.
- Life context: 14-year-old identified patient is involved with a deviant peer group. The mother, father, and patient should negotiate rules and consequences for the adolescent's misbehavior, and boundaries between the family and the outside world need to be strengthened. Additionally, the parents may need to be more involved with the parents of their son's peers to make it easier to more effectively supervise their adolescent's activities.
- Conflict resolution: family may have certain conflicts repeatedly occur and never get resolved because each time differences emerge, they (sometimes) are avoided or (most often) diffused through blaming wars. The counselor should refocus the interaction on the problem each time family members attempt to avoid the issue or change the subject so that the conflict may be negotiated and resolved.

PRODUCING CHANGE

Having diagnosed the problem in terms of these dimensions, the counselor was able to target interventions directly at the problematic interactions within these dimensions. One of the BSFT counselor's first moves was to help the disengaged father get closer to his estranged 14-year-old son. At the same time, the counselor initiated a dialogue between the parents about this youth to try to establish an alliance between the parents around the content of their mutual concern for their son. The next step was help the parents negotiate rules for the youth that once implemented, would bring his out-of-control behavior under control. As these changes were being negotiated, the family displayed frequent conflict avoidance and diffusion. When the family attempted to diffuse or avoid the conflict, the counselor would intervene and return

the topic of conversation to the original conflict. In the process, the family acquired new conflict-resolution skills. The parents were able to agree on rules and consequences for the identified patient's behavior; these were discussed and, where appropriate, negotiated between the parents and the son. Ultimately, the parents were able to set consistent limits, and the adolescent's behavior improved.

FUTURE PRACTICE APPLICATIONS

This chapter summarized recent developments in family therapy practice and research. There is consistent support for the effectiveness of marital and family therapies, although there may be limited evidence supporting the efficacy of particular models. Behavioral, structural, and strategic family approaches appear to have considerable experimental and clinical support for their effectiveness. They also have a long history of applications within the field. Newer models like emotion-focused couples therapy and integrative couples therapy are also building a solid empirical base for their effectiveness. Other promising models, such as SFBT, are developing their experimental research base. Family therapy has come a long way in developing an understanding of the common factors shared by all effective approaches. Evidence-based approaches to family treatment share core components that work.

In reviewing the current state of the evidence, it is important to note research that questions the effectiveness of approaches that are already considered to be evidence-based by experts in the field, such as the recent controversies around multisystemic therapy. As we move into the future, it will be important for social workers to continuously appraise the changing evidence and to stay abreast of new developments in the field.

WEB SITES

American Association for Marriage and Family Therapy. http://www.aamft.org.
Campbell Collaboration. http://www.campbellcollaboration.org.
Cochrane Collaboration. http://www.cochrane.org.
Savannah Family Institute. http://www.difficult.net.

Solution Focused Brief Therapy Association. http://www.sfbta.org.

References

Alexander, J., Barton, C., Gordon, D., Grotpeter, J., Hansson, K., Harrison, R., et al. (1998). *Functional family therapy: Blueprints for violence prevention, book three.* Blueprints for Violence Prevention Series (D. S. Elliott, Series Ed.). Boulder, CO: Center for the Study and Prevention of Violence, Institute of Behavioral Science, University of Colorado.
Basham, K., & Miehls, D. (2004). *Transforming the legacy: Couple therapy with survivors of childhood trauma.* New York: Columbia University Press.
Christensen, A., Atkins, D. C., Yi, J., Baucom, D. H., & George, W. H. (2006). Couple and individual adjustment for two years following a randomized clinical trial comparing Traditional versus Integrative Behavioral Couple Therapy. *Journal of Consulting and Clinical Psychology,74,* 1180–1191.
Christensen, A., & Jacobson, N. (2000). *Reconcilable differences.* New York: Guilford.
Corcoran, J. (2000). *Evidence-based social work practice with families: A lifespan approach.* New York: Springer.
Denton, W. H., Burleson, B. R., Clark, T. E., Rodriguez, C. P., & Hobbs, B. V. (2000). A randomized trail of emotion-focused therapy for couples in a training clinic. *Journal of Marital and Family Therapy, 26*(1), 65–78.
Fishman, H. C. (2006). Juvenile anorexia nervosa: A family therapist's natural niche. *Journal of Marital and Family Therapy, 32*(4), 505–514.
Franklin, C., & Hopson L. M. (2007). Facilitating the use of evidence-based practices in community organizations. *The Journal of Social Work Education, 43*(3), 377–404.
Franklin, C., & Jordan, C. (1999). *Family practice: Brief systems methods for social work.* Pacific Grove, CA: Brooks/Cole.
Fraser, M. W., Nelson, K. E., & Rivard, J. C. (1997). Effectiveness of family preservation services. *Social Work Research, 21,* 138–153.

Gingerich, W. J., & Eisengart, S. (2000). Solution-focused brief therapy: A review of outcome research. *Family Process, 39*, 477–498.

Gottman, J. M. (1999). *The marriage clinic.* New York: Guilford.

Henggeler, S. W. (1999). Multisystemic therapy: An overview of clinical procedures, outcomes, and policy implications. *Child Psychology and Psychiatry Review, 4*, 2–10.

Hoagwood, K. E. (2005). Family-based services in children's mental health: A research review and synthesis. *Journal of Child Psychology and Psychiatry, 46*(7), 690–713.

Hogue, A., & Liddle, H. A. (1999). Family-based preventive intervention: An approach to preventing substance abuse and antisocial behavior. *American Journal of Orthopsychiatry, 69*, 278–290.

Jacobson, N. S., & Christensen, A. (1996). *Integrative couple therapy.* New York: Norton.

Johnson, S. M. (2002). Marital problems. In D.H. Sprenkle (Ed.), *Effectiveness research in marriage and family therapy* (pp. 163–190). Alexandria, VA: American Association for Marriage and Family Therapy.

Johnson, S. M., & Lebow, J. (2000). The coming of age of couple therapy: A decade review. *Journal of Marital and Family Therapy, 26*, 23–38.

Karver, M. S., Handelsman, J. B., Fields, S., & Bickman, L. (2006). Meta-analysis of therapeutic relationship variables in youth and family therapy. *Clinical Psychology Review, 26*(1), 50–65.

Kazdin, A. E., & Whitley, M. K. (2003). Treatment of parental stress to enhance therapeutic change among children referred for aggressive and antisocial behavior. *Journal of Consulting and Clinical Psychology, 71*, 504–515.

Kim, J. S. (2008). Examining the effectiveness of solution-focused brief therapy: A meta-analysis. *Research on Social Work Practice, 18*, 107–116.

Kim, J. S., & Franklin, C. (2007). Solution-focused brief therapy in schools: A review of the literature. Manuscript under review.

Law, D. D., & Crane, D. S. (2000). The influence of marital and family therapy on health care utilization in a health-maintenance organization. *Journal of Marital and Family Therapy, 26*, 281–291.

Lebow, J. (2000). What does the research tell us about couple and family therapies? *Psychotherapy in Practice, 56*, 1083–1094.

Littell, J., Popa, J. H., & Forsythe, B. (2005). Multi-systemic therapy for social, emotional, and behavioral problems in youth aged 10–17. *Campbell Collaboration Review, 2*. Retrieved November 10, 2006, from http://www.campbellcollaboration.org/docpdf/Mst_Littell_Review.pdf.

Magliano, L., Fiorillo, A., Malangone, C., De-Rosa, C., & Maj, M. (2006). Patient functioning and family burden in a controlled, real-world trial of family psychoeducation for schizophrenia. *Psychiatric Services, 57*(12),1784–1791.

Newsome, S. (2004). Solution-focused brief therapy (SFBT) group work with at-risk junior high school students: Enhancing the bottom-line. *Research on Social Work Practice, 14*, 336–343.

Paivio, S. C. & Nieuwenhuis, J. A. (2001). Efficacy of emotionally focused therapy for adult survivors of child abuse: A preliminary study. *Journal of Traumatic Stress, 14*, 115–134.

Paz Pruitt, I. T. (2007). Family treatment approaches for depression in adolescent males. *American Journal of Family Therapy, 35*(1), 69–81.

Pinsof, W. M., & Wynne, L. C. (1995). The efficacy of marital and family therapy: An empirical overview, conclusions, and recommendations. *Journal of Marital and Family Therapy, 21*, 585–613.

Pinsof, W. M., & Wynne, L. (2000). Toward progress research: Closing the gap between family therapy practice and research. *Journal of Marital and Family Therapy, 26*, 1–8.

Randall, J. & Cunningham, P. B. (2003). Multisystemic therapy: A treatment for violent substance-abusing and substance-dependent juvenile offenders. *Addictive Behaviors, 28*(9), 1731–1739.

Schinke, S., Brounstein, P., & Gardner, S. (2002). *Science-based prevention programs and principles.* Rockville, MD: U.S. Department of Health and Human Services.

Sells, S. P. (1998). *Treating the tough adolescent: A family-based, step by step guide.* New York: Guilford.

Sells, S. P. (2000). *Parenting your out-of-control teenager.* New York: St. Martin's.

Sells, S. P. (In press). *Undercurrent therapy for impossible cases.* New York: Guilford.

Sells, S. P., Smith, T. E., & Rodman, J. (2006). Reducing substance abuse through Parenting with Love and Limits. *Journal of Child and Adolescent Substance Abuse, 15*, 105–115.

Shadish, W. R., & Baldwin, S. A. (2003). Meta-analysis of MFT interventions. *Journal of Marital and Family Therapy, 29*(4), 547–570.

Shadish, W. R., & Baldwin, S. A. (2005). Effects of behavioral marital therapy: A meta-analysis of randomized controlled trials. *Journal of Consulting and Clinical Psychology, 73*(1), 6–14.

Shadish, R., Montgomery, L. M., Wilson, P., Wilson, M. R., Bright, I., & Okwumabua, T. (1993). Effects of family and marital psychotherapies: A meta-analysis. *Journal of Consulting and Clinical Psychology, 61*, 992–1002.

Sprenkle, D. H., & Blow, A. J. (2004). Common factors and our sacred models. *Journal of Marital and Family Therapy, 30*(2), 113–129.

Stanton, M. D., & Shadish, W. R. (1997). Outcome, attrition, and family-couples treatment for drug abuse: A meta-analysis and review of the controlled, comparative studies. *Psychological Bulletin, 122*(2), 170–191.

Szapocznik, J., Hervis, O., & Schwartz, S. (2003). *Therapy manuals for drug addiction: Brief strategic family therapy for adolescent drug abuse.* Bethesda, MD: U.S. Department of Health and Human Services.

Szapocznik, J., & Williams, R.A. (2000). Brief strategic family therapy: Twenty-five years of interplay among theory, research and practice in adolescent behavior problems and drug abuse. *Clinical Child and Family Psychology Review, 3*(2), 117–134.

Thompson, S. J., Pomeroy, E. C., & Gober, K. (2005). Family-based treatment models targeting substance use and high-risk behaviors among adolescents: A review. *The Journal of Evidence-Based Social Work, 2*(1/2), 207–233.

Waldron, H. B., Slesnik, N., Brody, J. L., Tuner, C. W., & Peterson, T. R. (2001). Treatment outcomes for adolescent substance abuse at 4- and 7-month assessments. *Journal of Consulting and Clinical Psychology, 69,* 802–813.

Wood, N., Crane, D., Schaalje, G., & Law, D. (2005). What works for whom: A meta-analytic review of marital and couples therapy in reference to marital distress. *American Journal of Family Therapy, 33*(4), 273–287.

Woolfenden, S. R., Williams, K., & Peat, J. K. (2005). Family and parenting interventions for conduct disorder and delinquency: A meta-analysis of randomised controlled trials. *Archives of Disease in Childhood, 86,* 251–256.

61   Structural Family Therapy

Harry J. Aponte

Structural family therapy (SFT) addresses client objectives in the context of the current organization of client relationships vis-à-vis the issues being addressed. It is a systems-based model with one of its primary organizing principles that "changes in a family structure contribute to changes in the behavior and the inner psychic processes of the members of that system" (Minuchin, 1974, p. 9).

SFT has the unique legacy of having been born to meet the needs of poor inner-city youth and their families (Minuchin, Montalvo, Guerney, Rosman, & Schumer, 1967). Its approach speaks directly to how clients experience life more than to conceptual abstractions about their struggles. It achieves quick, palpable results. Lessons learned from poor, underorganized families (Aponte, 1994b, pp. 3–31) who had been structurally undermined by psychological and social stressors are relevant to all families from the general population. SFT is focused on concrete issues, located in the present, mediated through the client's experience in session, based on reorganizing the structure of relationships, built on client strengths, aimed at palpable outcome, and characterized by active therapist involvement. What follows is a brief commentary of the seven basic principles of structural family therapy.

FOCUS ON CONCRETE ISSUES

SFT looks for the urgent issue that has the family's attention and intensity of concern (Aponte, 1998). The therapist attends to the concrete manifestation of the issue, that is, how it is being lived and experienced by the client. The underlying assumption is that the "pain" at the core of the problem-laden experience carries within it the individual, family, and social dynamics that are generating the issue. Moreover, inside the pain-filled experience of the issue lies the goad to prod the efforts needed for change. It follows that the living pain-filled experience confronts people with the challenge to make problem-solving choices. These choices carry within them the worldview, ideals, and moral imperatives that frame people's drive to change. Structural therapists are looking for what motivates clients to action because they intend to build on momentum generated by the concrete manifestation of the client's experience of the issue.

LOCATED IN THE PRESENT

Structural family therapy views the past as "manifest in the present and . . . available to change by interventions that change the present" (Minuchin, 1974, p. 14). The client issue contains the focal point of today's concern, the dynamics currently generating the distress, and traces of the family's history that explain the whys and hows of the problem's birth. By working through the present, the therapist connects with not only today's urgency for relief but also the forces concurrently generating the problem. The turbulence of the present provides the therapist with the most immediate and reliable access to the forces from the past being played out in today's drama. The therapist aims to affect the memories, perceptions, and psychological residue of the past as they play out yesterday's story in today's struggle. The therapist's interventions relate to the present experience of the client with the full force of its impact on the client's life today. The therapy itself is treated as another context in which the issues are now alive and compelling attention.

MEDIATED THROUGH THE CLIENT'S EXPERIENCE IN SESSION

The principal field of intervention for SFT is the family's enactment of their issue in the session (Minuchin & Fishman, 1981, pp. 78–97; Aponte & VanDeusen, 1981, p. 329). The structural therapist looks beyond the verbal account of what has happened at home to how family members interact with each other now as they attempt to articulate the issue and work for a solution within the session itself (Aponte, 1990). That enactment is both the immediate material for assessment and an opportunity for intervention to change attitudes and behaviors.

The client experience embraces all the systems that are directly involved in the issue, whether the source of the problem or potential resources for the solution. The structure of relationships has classically referred to family but can also reflect the internal psychological structure of in-

volved individuals or the relationships of clients with community institutions (Aponte, 1994b, pp. 58–97). The structural therapist relates to the internal emotional experience of the client in session to family members' interactions or to transactions of the clients with school or other community representatives. The structural therapist homes in on the point of convergence of these actors in the field of action to assess and to intervene.

BASED ON REORGANIZING THE STRUCTURE OF RELATIONSHIPS

The structural family therapist pays special attention to the structure of family relationships in relation to the focal issue. There are three basic structural dimensions to all relationships (Aponte & VanDeusen, 1981, pp. 312–313).

1. *Boundaries*. What defines who is in or out of a family relationship vis-à-vis the focal issue, as well as what their roles are in this interaction.
2. *Alignment*. Who is with or against the other in the transactions generating the problem.
3. *Power*. What the relative influence is of the participants in the interactions that make the problem.

A client's focal issue is connected to a characteristic pattern of family interaction that bears changing if the problem is to be solved at its source. This transactional structure is the underlying skeleton of the dynamics that generate the problem. In some circumstances, the pathological structure undergirds a conflict, whereas in others, the faulty structure is inadequate to resolve the client's issue. That is, some problems are the result of conflicting feelings and needs, and others are the consequence of weakly organized relationships, or of a combination of both conflicting and inadequate organization. Structural therapists relate to both the content and the underlying structure of issues the client presents.

Structural therapy was originally known for targeting the faulty structure of poor underorganized families (Aponte, 1994b, pp. 13–31). These underorganized structures were seen as lacking the constancy, coherence, and flexibility to meet life's challenges. In working to help these families solve their problems, structural therapists deepened their appreciation of how all social functioning rests on strong and adaptable structures. With time, SFT gained a reputation for working effectively with emotionally troubled individuals and highly conflicted relationships of more organized families and couples (Aponte & DiCesare, 2000; Minuchin, Rosman, & Baker, 1978).

BUILT ON CLIENT STRENGTHS

SFT centers the therapeutic process on the resources and power of clients to grow and change—the strengths within themselves, their families, and communities (Aponte, 1999). It works through a "search for strength" (Minuchin & Colapinto, 1980). The structural therapist actively engages with the family to impede old, pathological transactional patterns (Aponte & VanDeusen, 1981, pp. 335–336) while working with the family's strengths to build new, positive patterns of interaction. The therapist aims for the family to experience these functional interactions in session as members work on the solutions to their problems. The therapist connects to aspects of the issue that are accessible for making a positive change, however small. The therapist may frame a painful circumstance in terms of the good that clients can draw from the challenge. Clients' spirituality often offers a positive rationale for drawing good out of bad (Aponte, 2002). Structural therapists ultimately formulate the goals of their interventions, even when the immediate objective may be to impede a dysfunctional interaction, in terms of what clients can do to achieve positive change. Every intervention of the therapist has woven into it how to support and mobilize the client's motivation and ability to make positive changes.

AIMED AT PALPABLE OUTCOMES

In much the same way that the structural therapist looks to work through the concrete manifestation of the focal issue, the therapist looks for positive therapeutic outcomes to be represented in changes the client can experience. Because SFT builds experience on experience, positive change builds on positive change. The ultimate outcome of the therapy rests on positive experiences of change, session by session. These palpable goals are evident in the immediate objectives of in-session interventions with enactments and the assignment of home-based tasks. The palpable experience of change gives body to the intended goals of the intervention. The experiential emphasis is a way of looking for intensity that will mobilize motiva-

tion and energy to drive change and to reach deeply within the persons involved. The change that is actively experienced in session is more likely to be lived outside the therapy. The goal is to have clients make these changes their own as they come to know their struggles in new, hopeful levels of experience over which they have exercised their freedom and power to choose to change.

CHARACTERIZED BY ACTIVE THERAPIST INVOLVEMENT

Structural therapists actively engage in the present with family members as clients enact their struggle in the session.

- The initial effort of the therapist is to strategically *join* (Minuchin, 1974, pp. 133–137) the family interaction "in a carefully planned way" (Minuchin, 1974, p. 91). The initial joining action is to gain trust. Subsequently, connecting to the family's interaction becomes a strategic intervention to alter their dysfunctional patterns of interaction.
- Where the structures of these dysfunctional relationships are more resistant to change, therapists may intensify a conflict within a family by drawing attention to their areas of disagreement. Surfacing the pathological dynamics in a live enactment bares them to better assessment and more effective interventions.
- Therapists may seek to block a pathological interaction among family members, making it difficult for them to use the old, sick pattern to deal with the current issue. Structural therapists characteristically use any of a variety of techniques (Minuchin & Fishman, 1981) to affect the family's power balance, transactional alignments, and systemic boundaries.
- Whether or not the therapist needs to begin by disrupting old, dysfunctional interactions, in all cases the therapist will look to support new, more functional transactional patterns. The therapist may verbally affirm the new patterns or actively engage with clients in ways that support the new behaviors and attitudes in the family's in-session enactments.
- In this active engagement with clients, therapists intentionally use their person (Aponte, 1992) to strategically affect the dynamics and structure of family

interactional patterns. To achieve the therapeutic mastery of self, they must have (1) a profound knowledge and awareness of their personal selves, (2) an ability to be connected to their inner personal experience in session, and (3) the discipline to use their person as strategically intended (Aponte, 1994a).

- Once family members have experienced something of their ability to do things differently, structural therapists often assign home tasks meant to embody the new change. The therapy is complete when the family is able to meet its challenges without the intervention of the therapist.

THE FUTURE OF SFT

SFT was created to meet the needs of families whose inner structure was seriously undermined by devastating social stress. This work has contributed a deeper insight into the basic nature of structure in family systems and reparative structural interventions that generate organizational changes in families. The underlying assumption is that change in patterns of relating affect the complexion and quality of emotional interchanges among family members, which in turn impact the psyche of the individuals in the family system. As the social ills of American society spread beyond the inner city to the general population, the need to attend to the foundational structure of families in all levels of society has become apparent. Other models of therapy could well consider using the insights SFT offers to understanding and working with family structure.

New developments in SFT are the added dimension of values and spirituality. The original model spoke of structure in relation to function in human systems. Over time it became apparent, particularly in today's values-fragmented society, that this original formulation needed to be amended to address structure in relation to function *within* the values framework of the system (Aponte, 1994b, pp. 168–185). Because SFT is one of today's more active therapies, therapists using the model inescapably communicate values about life philosophy, morals, and even religious practice. Now, as never before, there is a need for therapists to understand the values inherent in their therapeutic models and the values they personally bring to the work they do. Therapists' spiritual biases will influence what they consider healthy and pathological attitudes and behaviors. Their

worldviews will affect the formulation of goals—that is, what is desirable for any particular therapeutic endeavor. Their spiritual views will help determine the interventions they believe appropriate to people's circumstances. Whether and how therapists use the spiritual resources of clients, their inner faith or religious communities, will have much to do with their own belief systems. SFT needs to incorporate into its theory and practice greater consideration of the spiritual aspects of the human experience.

Bringing the spiritual dimension of life into SFT's framework will mean making it an integral part of training therapists, included within the technical and particularly the personal components of training. The latter will be the greater challenge because focus on the use of self in SFT was a later development in the evolution of the model. Minuchin's perspective has been to "expand" the "therapist's [personal] style" thereby adding to the clinician's "repertoire" (Minuchin, Lee, & Simon, 2006). Aponte's model for the personal aspect of training calls for enhancing the therapist's ability to purposefully direct the use of self through self-knowledge and the ability to consciously access emotions, memories, and personal reactions at the moment of active engagement with clients (Aponte, 1992; Aponte & Winter, 2000). SFT will need to enlarge on its approaches to training in the use of self within the model if it is to include the spiritual with the emotional in a systematic person-training of therapists.

CONCLUSION

SFT is an active, focused approach to therapy that pays special attention to structure within family systems and does so within the client's experience. It pursues specific outcomes to present-day issues while addressing the underlying human relationships and their personal structure in the context of culture, ethnicity, and spirituality—all that gives meaning to their life. Therapists actively engage with clients around the practical experience of their struggles and strategically join them in finding new ways of thinking about and acting on their issues. SFT looks for practical outcomes along with deep-seated changes in the underlying structures that generate and maintain the difficulties people face in life. Because of the active and involved nature of the work, the structural training of therapists draws particular attention to the fuller and more precise strategic use of self. The basic insights of the structural model about the nature of structure within systems and the use of self to influence those structures are concepts that are suitable to other models of today's active therapies. In a social and economic environment in which there is greater emphasis on outcome that is also enduring, SFT has much to offer.

WEB SITES

Books by Harry Aponte. http://www.amazon.ca.
CMTI Press (videos). http://www.cmtipress
.com/videos.htm.
Journal of Family Therapy. www.blackwell-
synergy.com/doi/abs/10.1111/1467-6427
.00067.
Teaching tapes by Harry Aponte. http://www
.goldentriadfilms.com/films/aponte.htm.

References

Aponte, H. J. (1990). *Tres madres: Structural family therapy with an Anglo/Hispanic family.* (videotape). Kansas City, MO: Golden Triad Films.

Aponte, H. J. (1992). Training the person of the therapist in structural family therapy. *Journal of Marital and Family Therapy, 18*(3), 269–281.

Aponte, H. J. (1994a). How personal can training get? *Journal of Marital and Family Therapy, 20*(1), 3–15.

Aponte, H. J. (1994b). *Bread and spirit: Therapy with the new poor.* New York: Norton.

Aponte, H. J. (1998). *Family therapy with the experts: Structural therapy with Harry Aponte.* (videotape). New York: Allyn & Bacon.

Aponte, H. J. (1999). The stresses of poverty and the comfort of spirituality. In F. Walsh (Ed.), *Spiritual resources in family therapy* (pp. 76–89). New York: Guilford.

Aponte, H. J. (2002). Spiritually sensitive psychotherapy. In F. Kaslow (Series Ed.) & R. F. Massey & S. D. Massey (Vol. Eds.), *Comprehensive handbook of psychotherapy: Vol. 3. Interpersonal/humanistic/existential* (pp. 279–302). New York: Wiley.

Aponte, H. J., & DiCesare, E. J. (2000). Structural theory. In F. M. Dattilio & L. Bevilacqua (Eds.), *Comparative treatment of couples problems* (pp. 45–57). New York: Springer.

Aponte, H. J., & VanDeusen, J. M. (1981). Structural family therapy. In A. S. Gurman & D. P. Kniskern (Eds.), *Handbook of family therapy* (pp. 310–360). New York: Brunner/Mazel.

Aponte, H. J., & Winter, J. E. (2000). The person and practice of the therapist. In M. Baldwin (Ed.), *The use of self in therapy,* 2nd ed. (pp. 127–165). New York: Haworth Press.

Minuchin, S. (1974). *Families and family therapy.* Cambridge, MA: Harvard University Press.

Minuchin, S., & Colapinto, J. (Eds.). (1980). *Taming monsters* (videotape). Philadelphia Child Guidance Clinic.

Minuchin, S., & Fishman, H. C. (1981). *Family therapy techniques.* Cambridge, MA: Harvard University Press.

Minuchin, S., Lee, W.-Y., & Simon, G. M. (2006). *Mastering family therapy; Journeys of growth and transformation,* 2nd ed. Hoboken, NJ: Wiley.

Minuchin, S., Montalvo, B., Guerney, B. Jr., Rosman, B., & Schumer, F. (1967). *Families of the slums.* New York: Basic Books.

Minuchin, S., Rosman, B., & Baker, L. (1978). *Psychosomatic families.* Cambridge, MA: Harvard University Press.

62 Bowen Family Systems Therapy

Daniel V. Papero

The Bowen theory consists of eight formal concepts and a central variable (Bowen, 1978). One concept, the *scale of differentiation of self*, forms the core of the theory, and the remaining seven concepts describe different aspects of family functioning. The variable—anxiety—acts as a kind of pressure on the family system, waxing and waning in intensity. Bowen's observations led him to conclude that the family is a system of interdependent people, that individual behavior cannot be understood adequately without including the relationship system in which individual lives and changing degrees of anxiety greatly affect the condition of that system. A highly anxious system behaves predictably differently from a less anxious one. Under the pressure of increased anxiety, various sorts of relationship patterns or series of interactions can be observed, and these patterns tend to repeat whenever the family system is again under pressure.

The concept of the scale of differentiation of self describes individual variation, specifically in the arena of self-regulation and self-determination within the family system and the other important relationship systems of a person's life (Bowen, 1978; Kerr & Bowen, 1988; Papero, 1990). In practical terms, a person's degree or level of differentiation of self can be seen as a degree of resiliency or capacity to function well under the pressure of stress and tension. Bowen hypothesized that a well-differentiated person approached the situations of life with good integration between emotion and cognition and with clearly thought-out values and principles that guide decisions and behavior. Each (emotion and cognition) influences the other, neither dominates, and the person can use each in adapting to changing situations. In a less well-differentiated person, under pressure, emotion dominates cognition and behavior becomes more instinctive and automatic. The well-differentiated person

can participate fully in relationships but does not depend completely on relationships to maintain emotional stability. In this sense, the individual is capable of self-regulation when important relationships are disturbed or unavailable.

Bowen observed that a change in one part of a family led to compensatory changes in other parts of the family. His observations led him to the realization that the family system could be influenced by the actions of an individual family member, particularly if that person occupied an important position in the system and when that individual could

- see and understand better his or her own emotional sensitivity and reactivity;
- become more thoughtful about his or her behavior and what he or she was trying to accomplish, using knowledge of how the family system operated;
- use thinking and knowledge to modify emotional reactivity and his or her own behavior in important relationships; and
- stay in meaningful contact with other members of the system; the entire system could change or shift its functioning.

When the system could change, the behavior and functioning of family members changed as well. The clinical process involved in such an effort is so different from more conventional psychotherapy that Bowen referred to the process as *coaching*.

The coaching process draws heavily on the coach's understanding of family systems theory. It assumes the clinician (1) has direct and ongoing experience in the challenge of working on differentiation of self in his or her own family, and (2) understands and can reasonably operationalize the disciplines of self-regulation, emotional neutrality, maintenance of viable contact, self-definition, and the research attitude that families have found useful in their own efforts to manage their challenges and dilemmas.

The family members involved in the coaching effort:

- regulate the endeavor,
- set the pace,
- identify and engage the challenges, and
- monitor and evaluate the outcomes.

In his personal conversations, Bowen often referred to the process as "a do-it-yourself therapy—almost!" The coach functions as a supervisor of and consultant to the endeavor.

Bowen discovered that clinicians learned most about family systems in their efforts to improve functioning in their own families (Bowen, 1978), and effort with one's own family became a central element in the training of clinicians; it remains so today. In essence, clinicians learning to use the Bowen theory in their clinical efforts work on their own degree of differentiation of self, the central idea in the theory. In the clinician's own family, he or she learns about family systems and the pressures that come to bear on anyone attempting to shift his or her functioning. The clinician learns firsthand about emotional reactivity and its role in the relationship sequences or patterns that are the nature of family interaction.

In the course of his research project on schizophrenia at the National Institute of Mental Health (NIMH), Bowen observed that the families appeared to function more calmly, thoughtfully, and stably after time spent with a researcher than after time spent with a therapist. The researcher could remain more objective than the therapist and direct inquiry toward facts of family functioning. The researcher did not experience the pressure to help the family that the therapists did. The researcher could more easily remain emotionally neutral in the reactive processes of the family. He or she could see all sides to the situation and could avoid taking sides in the dilemma fairly easily. This objectivity and neutrality appeared to bring out the best in the families.

These observations led Bowen to suggest that the clinician could be most helpful to the family when he or she could:

- maintain an attitude and perspective of research and emotional neutrality,
- ask about family facts,

- see the emotional give-and-take among family members without becoming distracted by the content of the family story or taking sides,
- see and comment on both the serious and the humorous sides of the family dilemma, and
- maintain a climate or atmosphere during the clinical session that allowed each participant to work toward becoming his or her most mature self emotionally in interaction with the others.

The clinical process begins with a history of family functioning across at least three generations. In general, the clinician gathers information on each person, living and dead, who has been part of the family. The information collected includes:

- date of birth (and of death, where applicable),
- health history;
- educational history;
- occupational history;
- social history for each person;
- the nature of relationships in the family, currently and historically;
- dates of marriages, divorces, job changes, and changes in residence; and
- the frequency and nature of contact the informants maintain with the broader family.

As the information is gathered, it is entered on a family diagram, a visual representation of the family system (see Papero, 1990, 2000). The process of developing the family diagram helps the clinician (1) identify events that have contributed to the present configuration of the family; (2) note particularly important relationships, including those that display great tension and emotional reactivity; and (3) identify the particular kinds of relationship patterns that characterize the interactions of the family.

The diagram serves as a map or chart guiding the efforts of the clinician and the family. Additionally, informants often find the process interesting and useful, spurring their own efforts to learn more about their families.

The clinical process focuses on two goals: decreasing anxiety and increasing functional differentiation of self. Often, these goals go hand in hand. The effort to decrease anxiety requires that the individual learn to modulate intense emotion by using his or her cognitive or intellectual processes. Cognition comes into play as the individual learns to observe self and others, learning to recognize anxiety in its myriad forms and in his or her efforts to engage in a discipline of self-regulation. Alongside the effort toward self-regulation, the individual works to observe the predictable patterns of the family relationship system that emerge and disappear in response to tension and anxiety in the system. The person also endeavors to define clearly his or her own sets of beliefs and values about the nature of living and about his or her own direction in it. These form the basis, along with knowledge of the system and self-regulation, for the person's effort to define his or her own positions to the important others in the relationship system and to maintain that position as the system responds with pressure to change back.

One of the common relationship processes the people observe, *triangling*, occurs as a two-person relationship becomes tense and anxious. As the discomfort in the pair rises, at some point the tolerance for discomfort is passed, and one makes a move to a significant third person, in effect telling a story about the other partner. Primarily a process of anxiety transfer, triangling alters the sensitivities, cognitive processing, and ultimately behavior of all involved. Triangles change configurations with tension. When the relationship network is fairly calm, the triangling process may be largely invisible. Under moderate tension, the triangle consists of a close twosome and an outsider, who tends to feel excluded and uncomfortable. That outsider responds in a series of well-known moves to gain closeness with one of the two and leave someone else in the outside position (Bowen, 1978; Kerr & Bowen, 1988). However, when tension develops in the close twosome, the outsider is in the more comfortable position, and either of the twosome engages in a series of maneuvers to gain the outside position for oneself and leave the other two in the tense positions.

One classic methodology derived from Bowen theory involves the effort with the two most responsible family members, often spouses. The clinician has four main tasks in using this methodology (Bowen, 1978):

- defining and clarifying the relationship between the two family members,
- keeping self neutral in the family emotional system,
- teaching the functioning of emotional systems, and

- demonstrating differentiation by taking well-thought-out positions for self during the course of the clinical effort.

A basic principle, based on Bowen's observations, underlies the approach: "the emotional problem between two people will resolve automatically if they remain in contact with a third person who can remain free of the emotional field between them, *while actively relating to each*" (Bowen, 1978, p. 251).

A second classic methodology involves the effort with one family member. Here the person works toward enhancing his or her own differentiation within a relationship system, usually the family. According to Bowen (1978), the person essentially strives to:

- gain some control of his or her own emotional reactivity,
- visit the family as often as possible,
- develop the ability to be an objective observer of the family (Bowen, 1978), and
- develop person-to-person relationships in the broad family.

Generally, the family member learns to establish and maintain relationships in which two people can talk to one another about each other, without discussing others (triangling) or talking about impersonal things. The clinician, while fulfilling the four tasks just mentioned, serves as a consultant and supervisor to the effort.

Many people using Bowen theory in their efforts to improve their own functioning additionally work on structured processes of self-regulation. Many have found biofeedback (both classic and neurofeedback) beneficial. Sometimes with the aid of the technology, people discover their own sensitivity to others and the impact that sensitivity has on their functioning and well-being. Some also engage in formal processes of relaxation training and meditation. The use of these adjunctive methodologies depends on the inclinations and motivation of those involved.

The family members involved in the clinical effort begin to use their families as laboratories for their own learning and development.

- They work on managing themselves in the very relationships that have helped shape their identity and in contact with the people to whom they are most sensitive and connected.

- The focus is on the actual relationships of a person's life, with corresponding decreased focus on the therapeutic relationship to the clinician.
- Change occurs in the effort to manage oneself differently in actual relationships, and the importance of the clinical hour decreases.
- The time with the clinician becomes time for reflection, review of efforts made, and planning for future endeavors.

As he or she gains knowledge about self and the family, the person begins in small, microscopic steps to define him- or herself to the family system. This process usually requires that the person (1) think through his or her own view about particular family issues, (2) represent that view in the family context, and (3) remain in viable contact with other family members during their reaction to this statement of position.

In the process, the individual becomes a leader of the family in the sense that his or her functioning begins to affect the entire system in positive ways. Bowen described the process as follows:

Operationally, ideal family treatment begins when one can find a family leader with the courage to define self, who is as invested in the welfare of the family as in self, who is neither angry nor dogmatic, whose energy goes to changing self rather than telling others what they should do, who can know and respect the multiple opinions of others, who can modify self in response to the strengths of the group, and who is not influenced by the irresponsible opinions of others. When one family member moves toward differentiation, the family symptoms disappear. A family leader is beyond the popular notion of power. A responsible family leader automatically generates mature leadership qualities in other family members who are to follow. (Kerr & Bowen, 1988, pp. 342–343)

The following examples are composites of actual situations encountered. Many elements of the descriptions have been changed to protect the confidentiality of the families.

Example 1

Emily, a bright, 7-year-old in first grade, suddenly developed discipline problems in school toward the end of the year. Her behavior had been outstanding, but now she spent several days a week in the principal's office. Previously a pleasant and gentle child, Emily had become surly and aggressive toward other children. Her mother sought clinical assistance.

Utilizing the Bowen theory to guide his efforts, the clinician made the decision to meet with Emily's mother and avoid a direct focus on the behavior of the child. The mother was willing to follow this plan. The clinician constructed Emily's family diagram. Her father and mother had been divorced for several years, and her father had moved to another state the summer before. Emily's paternal grandparents had maintained contact with her, but the arrival of a new grandchild and a serious health situation had resulted in them being less available. Her maternal grandmother had had surgery early in the winter and was recovering more slowly than anticipated. Her maternal great-grandmother had required nursing home care early in the winter, and Emily's grandfather was in charge of managing her care. Emily's maternal aunt and her husband had experienced a reversal in business and were involved in legal processes that caused family members to worry about their future. Finally, tension between Emily's mother and her partner had become very intense and difficult in the week preceding Emily's change of behavior.

The clinical hypothesis posited that Emily's behavioral problems emerged in a family environment of prolonged tension following the changes of the preceding few months. The family met each challenge well, but the cost was reflected in the gradual build-up of tension and anxiety. The immediate trigger for Emily's behavioral change lay in the surge of anxiety between her mother and her partner. The immediate treatment goal would involve reducing anxiety, and the longer range goal would involve the mother's increased use of relationship resources in the family and an effort to address the problem with her partner more directly, working to contain the anxiety to that relationship.

Emily's mother quickly understood and accepted the clinical hypothesis that her child's behavior was linked to the changes in the family and to the surge in tension with her partner. With the clinician, she developed a plan that included increased contact with important family members, a direct nonconfrontational approach with the involved school personnel, and the development of a plan for her efforts toward her partner. She used family relationships to assist her with her thinking about the situation and began a focused effort to address the problem with her partner. Emily's grandparents and to some degree her father increased their contact with Emily, and the mother engaged the school personnel—the teacher and principal—thoughtfully and directly in a calm manner focused on solving problems. Emily's school problems rapidly abated, and her teacher reported that she seemed much happier. She finished the school year well and moved happily into her summer activities. Emily's mother continued the effort to address the difficulties with her partner directly, an ongoing and challenging process.

Example 2

Jim Wilson, a 52-year-old physician's assistant, sought consultation around his reported intense anxiety about finances, recurring episodes of deep depression, a sense of being ill-equipped to function in the world, and deep anger toward his father. He reported at times feeling he would be better off dead but did not see himself as actively suicidal. Mr. Wilson was well regarded in his professional life, working in a clinical setting that assisted low-income people. He was interested in using the Bowen theory to look at his situation; previous therapy had been somewhat useful but had not alleviated the recurring problems.

In the initial meetings, the clinician collected a three-generation history of the family. Mr. Wilson was the oldest of two children; he reported that his younger sister had also struggled with life, perhaps even more than he had, and currently lived in another state in a troubled relationship with a man alleged to be alcoholic. He reported great reactivity to his sister, often being critical of her and avoiding contact with her. Their mother had died of a lingering degenerative illness when both siblings were young adults. In the aftermath of his mother's death, his father had remarried. Mr. Wilson reported that he "lost his father" when he remarried. He meant that his father put his new wife ahead of his children in all matters. He also reported that his father had refused to help him financially, although he was a wealthy man and could easily have done so. Mr. Wilson was divorced from his wife; their two sons were now young adults. He reported that he remained angry and bitter with his ex-wife and avoided contact with her. She had married the man with whom she had had an affair. He resented the time their children spent with her.

The clinical hypothesis posited that Mr. Wilson's complaints reflected a condition of chronic anxiety in the family system marked by distant rela-

tionships and high degrees of emotional reactivity among family members. Mr. Wilson himself was relatively isolated emotionally from important other family members. The plan followed the points noted:

- gain some control of his emotional reactivity,
- visit the family as often as possible,
- develop the ability to be an objective observer of the family (Bowen, 1978), and
- develop person-to-person relationships in the broad family.

Mr. Wilson thought the hypothesis made sense and agreed to begin an effort in his family to make progress on the four areas noted. He agreed to meet with the clinician once a month for consultation on his project. He began by addressing a health concern he had been avoiding, receiving medical assistance and a good outcome. He began to observe himself in the situations of his life and recognize his thought patterns and reactivity that seemed to underlie his anxiety and depression. He noted his own tendency to see himself as helpless and to be what he called "whiny" about his life. He also noted the degree to which he blamed others for his situation and began an effort to expand his perspective, decrease his complaining, and accept more responsibility for his own difficulties in life. He began an effort to be in more direct contact with his father and his wife to represent himself more clearly and carefully to them. His symptoms of depression were the first to disappear, and they did not return in any strength. After some time he was able to approach his father directly, requesting information about a trust fund established as part of his father's estate. His father initially balked but then arranged for Mr. Wilson to speak directly to the managers of the trust. The information received helped allay Mr. Wilson's financial anxieties. He was subsequently able to arrange a loan from the trust that allowed him to move forward on a significant relocation project to be nearer to his children and achieve a long-term goal. He reported that the intensity of his anxiety decreased significantly. He could still experience episodes of acute anxiety, but the more chronic, constant anxiety seemed to have disappeared. He noted as well that his anger and bitterness toward his ex-wife abated greatly, and he was able to be in her presence at family gatherings with much decreased reactivity to her. He no longer tended to talk about her to their children and actually found he wished her well. Mr. Wilson continues his efforts, now with less frequent consultation.

In the case of Emily, the behavioral problem in the child was directly related to a recent series of events in the family and was resolved fairly quickly. In the case of Mr. Wilson, the problems reflected a long and slow build-up over many years and required a slower, persistent approach to attain resolution.

In recent years, the Bowen theory has received increasing attention from people working in corporations and organizations, as well as those who consult with them. The theory and its knowledge base offer insight and practical assistance to those who must work, manage, and lead in the increasingly stressful climate of the modern organization. Although organizations should never be mistaken for families, a number of the concepts transfer cleanly to the world of organizations. Topics like the role of differentiation of self in leadership, triangling and its influence on the workplace, the predictable responses in relationships as tension increases, and the impact of anxiety on the individual and the relationship network can now be found on the agenda of training groups in management and leadership. People in leadership positions report that applications derived from Bowen theory, especially concerning differentiation of self, self-regulation, and self-

management under pressure, are useful to them in their efforts to lead effectively.

WEB SITES

Bowen Center. http://www.thebowencenter.org.
Kansas City Center for Family and Organizational Systems. http://www.kcfamilysystems.com.
Living Systems Counselling. http://www.livingsystems.ca.
Prairie Center. http://www.theprairiecenter.com.
Programs in Bowen Theory. http://www.programsinbowentheory.org.
Southern California Training in Bowen Family Systems Theory. http://www.sctbt.homestead.com.

References

Bowen, M. (1978). *Family therapy in clinical practice.* New York: Aronson.
Kerr, M. E., & Bowen, M. (1988). *Family evaluation.* New York: Norton.
Papero, D. V. (1990). *Bowen family systems theory.* Needham Heights, MA: Allyn & Bacon.
Papero, D. V. (2000). Bowen systems theory. In F. M. Dattilio & L. J. Bevilacqua (Eds.), *Comparative treatments for relationship dysfunction.* New York: Springer.

63   It Takes One to Tango

Michele Weiner-Davis

Who says you need both partners to do couples therapy?

In our first session, Lynn, a sullen-looking 27-year-old, had plenty to complain about. Her husband, Jeff, had been extremely critical of late and seemed emotionally distant from both Lynn and their 18-month-old son, Jason. Lynn felt that Jeff

spent too much time with friends after work and on the weekends; when he was home, he constantly picked on her. With little help around the house, no assistance on the parenting front, and virtually no affection from Jeff, Lynn felt desperately unhappy.

Lynn longed for things to be the way they had once been. "We were better friends back then," she recalled. "We spent a lot of time together and it really didn't matter what we were doing, as long as we were together." I asked, "Lynn, when your relationship was more loving, how was Jeff different?" Without hesitation, she replied, "He was thoughtful and very sensitive to my needs. He had a great sense of humor and was lots of fun to be with."

"And how were you different, Lynn?" I asked. "I was a much happier person back then, no doubt about it," she said.

"When you were a happier person, how were you different with Jeff?"

Lynn admitted that because she was so unhappy, she was "crabbier" than she had been in the past. "I guess I used to be a lot nicer to him." She offered a long list of endearing acts of kindness, like putting love notes in Jeff's lunches or calling him at work to let him know that she was thinking of him. She often used to initiate lovemaking, something she never did anymore. After thinking about the "old Lynn," she wistfully admitted that she liked herself more back then and disliked the angry, resentful person she had become much of the time.

As Lynn described the problems in her marriage, the circular nature of her interactions with Jeff became apparent. Were her crabbiness and standoffishness due to his long absences from home or his criticisms of her, or were Jeff's absences and critical tone due to Lynn's moodiness and withdrawal from him? Knowing that the correct answer was probably both, I suggested an escape route from their marital merry-go-round. "Starting tonight, no matter what you're thinking or feeling about Jeff, act like the old Lynn. Do the things you used to do when you liked yourself more, and watch Jeff very closely to see how he responds."

When she returned for our next appointment 2 weeks later, Lynn was eager to tell me about her experiment. Right after our session, he had come home in a grouchy mood and made a critical comment during dinner. Instead of getting angry and defensive, Lynn simply agreed. She said that Jeff actually looked up at her in amazement, and the rest of the meal went without incident. In fact, Jeff discussed a situation at work that had been troubling him, something he hadn't done in months. When Lynn offered her opinion, he seemed unusually receptive. Lynn felt encouraged.

Later that week, Lynn realized that they hadn't spent time alone for months and reminded herself that she used to be a social coordinator of sorts in their marriage, and that Jeff seemed to appreciate this quality in her. So, despite the fact that she wasn't completely certain of how things would turn out, she arranged for a babysitter and made dinner reservations at one of Jeff's favorite restaurants. Their evening went extremely well, and when they got home, they stayed up late talking.

In the days that followed, Jeff seemed more relaxed and less critical of Lynn. Nevertheless, the time between sessions was not without its rough spots. On a couple of occasions when Jeff made inflammatory comments, Lynn responded in kind, and the tension between them escalated. Although she felt discouraged when this happened, she was beginning to understand how her actions during these tension-filled times impacted Jeff—when she allowed her buttons to get pushed, their unpleasant interactions became even more unpleasant. She also recognized that no matter what Jeff did or said, no matter how his comments or actions made her feel, she was still in control of how she responded. She felt empowered by this realization, and in tense situations asked herself, "What's my goal here? What do I want to have happen?" and then quickly assessed whether what she was about to do would achieve those ends.

I asked Lynn to rate how well things were going in her relationship on a 1 to 10 scale, with 10 being great and 1 being the pits. She replied, "Four weeks ago I would have told you 2. In these last two weeks, I'd have to say 7." Then I asked, "Where on the scale would you need to be to feel satisfied?" She said 8 or 9. So I asked, "What would be one or two things that could happen in your relationship that would bring you up to an 8?" She said, "He would have to say, 'I love you' again and we'd have to make love." I urged her to keep being the "old Lynn" and take note of Jeff's reactions. We scheduled a third meeting and she left.

Two weeks later, a very happy Lynn greeted me. "Well, it happened. We made love and right after we were done, he turned to me and said, 'Lynn, I really love you.' It felt great because he hasn't said that in a long time. I can't believe he's changed so much so quickly." Lynn described quite a few things she had done to maintain the changes and divert unnecessary arguments in the last few weeks. As she spoke, I felt confident that she understood the "magic" behind the "new Jeff." To help her plan for future challenges, I said, "You will undoubtedly hit bumps in the road in the future. If things between you and Jeff start to go downhill, what will you do to get back on track?" With a huge smile on her face, Lynn replied, "I'd remember everything we talked about here—that I got things on track all by myself the first time, and that I can do that again." Her look of confidence was striking. That was the last I saw of her.

From my perspective, there is nothing remarkable about this case. I helped Lynn figure out what she needed to do differently to spark a change in Jeff and in their relationship, and assumed that a positive change in Jeff would be so reinforcing that it would be the beginning of a solution avalanche. It was systems theory 101—"a change in one part of the system leads to changes in other parts of the system." Yet when I discuss Lynn's case and others like it in the workshops I give on solution-oriented therapy, working with one partner to elicit relationship change isn't as mainstream a practice as I once believed. Many therapists question whether Lynn's reports of change were real. Some worry whether, because Jeff hadn't participated in therapy, the changes will stick. Others argue that the burden for relationship change should not have been left solely on Lynn's shoulders. The most burning question turns out to be the most basic—how is it possible to do couples therapy with just one partner?

This question stems from the fact that many therapists define the type of therapy they practice by taking a head count: if one person is present, they're practicing individual therapy; if two or more people are present, it's couples or family therapy. I believe this is misguided—the key to determining which brand of therapy is in use at any given point lies in the therapist's orientation and focus, not the number of people occupying space in the room.

Individual therapy and couples therapy are based on very different premises and require completely different clinical skills:

- Individual therapists delve into intrapsychic processes. They help clients gain insight into themselves, their family of origin, and how these childhood experiences have impacted on their present behavior, attitudes, and feelings. It is the individual therapist's belief that insight is the vehicle for change—that is, once clients understand why they do what they do, they will then be able to change.
- Couples/family therapists, on the other hand, are focused on the observable connections between people in the here and now. They're interested in patterns of interaction—what

people say and do with one another. According to this theoretical orientation, change is brought about not by going inward but by changing observable interactions among people.

Another reason some therapists cannot fathom couples therapy with individuals is that they are trained to believe that relationship problems are best resolved by helping people identify, process, and express their feelings to each other. With this perspective as a starting point, it is easy to see why one would be skeptical about the possibilities for positive relationship change when only one partner is present. Teaching active listening skills to just one person in the relationship is like listening to the sound of one hand clapping.

But couples therapy with individuals is based on different premises. Although good communication skills go a long way toward creating healthy relationships, talking things out isn't the only (nor necessarily the best) way to resolve recurring problems. Though we are affected by what our partners say to us, we are also greatly affected by what they do. For instance, although Lynn had tried for months to convince Jeff to be more loving toward her, nothing she said ever made a difference. When she stopped talking and started changing her actions, Jeff became more responsive.

There might be a familiar ring to Jeff's tuning out Lynn's words but not her actions. During the past few years, we've learned a lot about gender differences. In particular, we've become aware that women in general are more verbal than men, who tend to favor action over words. Women tell me, "I talk until I'm blue in the face" or "I've told him a million times." Instead of teaching them new and better ways to express themselves, I encourage them to say less and do more. Because women are much more likely to come in to therapy solo, teaching action-oriented techniques should be tops on therapists' lists of things to do.

The fact that action-oriented techniques may work better with women under certain circumstances is no consolation to therapists who feel that couples therapy with women is a bad idea because it places all the burden of improving relationships on women's shoulders. Why should women have to dream up ways of approaching men? Why can't men take responsibility for finding more creative ways of reaching women? This position, in my opinion, stems from a lack of understanding of the systemic laws governing change. Change is like a chain reaction. She tips over the first domino, then he changes. When a woman who is dissatisfied in her relationship decides to change her method of getting through to her partner, she isn't doing all the work. Assuming responsibility for creating positive change in life isn't working harder, it's working smarter.

Despite my emphasis on the merits of this approach with women, it's important to point out that I practice couples therapy with men with similar results. Even when the marriage teeters dangerously on the brink of divorce, there is much therapists can do when the man is willing to change. For example, consider the following case.

Ben's wife had asked him to leave the house a week before she filed for divorce. When he scheduled an appointment, he had moved out and was desperately unhappy. He didn't want their 20-year marriage to end, and he wanted to know if there was anything he could do to make her change her mind.

I asked Ben, "If your wife were here now, what would she say you've been doing recently in regard to your marriage?" He said, "She would tell you that I've been pressuring her all the time and that she can't stand it anymore. I've been calling her several times every day and begging her to change her mind. I've been reminding her about all the good times we've shared and have sent her flowers four times. I leave Hallmark cards for her around the house." I asked if this was working, and he said, "No, I've been making things worse."

I explained to Ben that relationships are like seesaws—the more one person does of something, the less the other person does of it. "If you do all the longing for your marriage, it allows her to focus only on the bad points. If you are the emotional one, it gives her room to be cold and withdrawing. So, if you want her to stop pulling away from you, you're going to have to stop pushing her."

I asked him, "What could you do or say that would make Lois sit up and take notice?" Ben responded, "I guess I should stop calling her every day. I should stop saying 'I love you,' because I know it only makes her mad. I should stop asking her if she's changed her mind." I told Ben that he was on the right track and wondered what else he could think of to turn things around. He said, "I'm always so depressed around her. I guess that's not too attractive. If I were more upbeat, and even somewhat enthusiastic about anything in my life, she would really be shocked. That would be noticeable instantly."

I sent Ben home with the following instructions. "Start experimenting by changing how you act when you are in Lois's presence. Do all the things you discussed here today. When you do, one of two things might happen. The first is nothing. When you change, it might not make a difference at all. That's a real possibility. Or she might be intrigued by your changes and start to show some interest in being with you. But I'm warning you, if you get overly enthusiastic and try to get her to move along quickly, she will definitely back off. You must move slowly. Don't discuss the future of your marriage at all for now. And don't move back home until the issues that separated you have been worked out."

Ben was lucky. When he gave Lois some breathing room, she did show interest in revitalizing their relationship. It was a slow process and required a lot of support to keep Ben from becoming impatient. In the end, without Lois ever coming in for therapy, they resolved some long-standing issues, and he returned home. As far as I know, they are still living happily ever after.

TREATMENT PROCESS

My couples work with individuals can be broken down into three simple steps.

First, I help clients figure out what they really want from their partners by establishing clear, concrete goals that always remain in our peripheral vision. I urge clients to talk about what their partners will be doing differently when the relationship is more satisfying. I help clients picture a new, more positive relationship by asking questions such as, "When you start to feel closer and more connected to your husband, what will he be doing differently?" and "If I were a fly on the wall, what would I see the two of you doing differently when your relationship improves?" I emphasize observable actions rather than subjective feelings, to help clients develop clearer signposts for change.

The second item of business is to help my clients become "solution detectives." I want people to view their relationships as a trial-and-error process: when there's a problem, they do something to solve it. They should watch closely for the results. If what they do is working, they should keep doing it. If not, they should switch gears. Although simple in theory, this is not so easy in practice. People get glued to their favorite problem-solving strategies, believing that whatever they're doing to improve their relationships is the right thing. In fact, they think miserable results often signal the need to crank the particular strategy up a notch—that is, do it one more time, with feeling.

Once we establish goals, the third step is to investigate what my clients have done in the past to accomplish these goals. I want to access what's worked and what hasn't. A trademark of the solution-focused therapy approach is to ask clients about problem-free times or periods that are the exceptions. For example, I might say to a client, "I know you've been fighting a lot lately, but there must be times when you get along better. What's different about the times the two of you are more at peace with each other? What does he do differently then? What do you do differently then?" We begin to weed through the frustration and anger provoked by the problems in their relationships and discover what can be learned from the times they get along well. As clients identify what's different about the times things go well, the solution comes into view. My clients can then begin to do what works the moment they leave my office.

Although analyzing the good times is uplifting and informative, I also want to know what hasn't been working. To help clients ascertain dead-end strategies, I ask, "If your partner were here now and you weren't, and I asked, 'In regard to this issue, what does she do that drives you nuts?' what would he say?" I show them how their actions, no matter how effective they should have been in theory, have in reality caused their partners to dig in their heels even further. In other words, I train clients to pay attention to "what is" as opposed to "how things should be." Once we identify what would constitute a new and different approach to the ongoing problem, I send clients home to experiment.

In contrast to therapists who question the value of doing couples therapy with individuals, this approach is often my method of choice for a variety of reasons.

I find I can empower people by showing them that they no longer have to play the waiting game of "I'll change if you change first." Instead, they find themselves back in the driver's seat of their own lives. This is no small feat, given the helplessness and hopelessness people feel when their partners present impenetrable walls.

Working with only one partner allows me to both join with and confront that person in ways that wouldn't be possible if the other partner were present. For example, I can let my client know how well I understand what he or she is feeling about the relationship or about the other partner. It allows me to connect with the person without alienating the partner. On the other hand, because I'm perceived as an ally, I am at liberty to be bolder, more challenging and, at times, less balanced than would be the case if the other partner were present.

Working with only one partner can avoid the unfortunate "ping-pong effect" in therapy, whereby one partner escalates a point of view, triggering the other partner to do the same and so on, until they are completely polarized. It has been my experience that when seen alone, many people are quite willing to take a closer look at their partners' points of view, because they don't feel coerced or that they're losing face. Once they put themselves into their partners' shoes, they're usually more conciliatory.

Does It Work?

Working with one partner is not successful all the time, even in less challenging situations. This method is not a therapeutic panacea. There are times when one person changes and the other doesn't notice or, worse yet, doesn't care. Sometimes the relationship changes are not in the desired direction or of the hoped for magnitude. Occasionally, your client won't stop blaming his or her partner long enough to switch gears. Nothing works all the time. When my clients and I are not getting positive results, we try something else. Working with one partner is only a good strategy if it works. Couples therapy may be an effective approach, but it does not work all the time, either. See Chapters 33, 59, 60, for reviews for literature of research studies on effective marital and family therapies.

FUTURE PRACTICE APPLICATIONS

In the spirit of sharing what has worked for me, I encourage skeptics to do a few things.

First stop telling clients, "Unless he/she joins us, therapy won't work" or "If your husband isn't willing to come in, it means he's not committed to working on your relationship." Some people who are totally committed to their partners wouldn't dream of stepping into a therapist's office. (My own husband of 20-plus years happens to be one of them.) Ascribing negative intent to those who prefer to steer clear of therapy is unfair, often incorrect, and almost always hurtful to those who wish their partners would share their enthusiasm about the benefits of therapy. They end up blaming their partners even more intensely.

Second, make a commitment to temporarily suspend judgment about the viability of working with individuals on relationship issues. Therapists who agree to work with individuals whose partners won't come in but see it as a second-rate approach worry me. We clinicians communicate our presuppositions about people and how they change when we do our work. If we begin therapy with a "this is better than nothing" attitude, we undoubtedly broadcast a pessimistic message about the possibilities for change.

Third, the next time you hear, "My partner won't come in," try viewing the situation as an opportunity rather than a relationship death sentence. Act as if you expect your work with your client to be successful. The results might be surprising! A change in you might just be a powerful catalyst for change in your clients.

WEB SITES

Divorce Busting, Michelle Weiner Davis. http://www.divorcebusting.com.
Network of Social Construction Therapies. http://socialconstruction.talkspot.com.
Solution Focused Brief Therapy Association. http://sfbta.org.

Suggested Readings

O'Hanlon, W., & Weiner-Davis, M. (1988). *In search of solutions: A new direction in psychotherapy*. New York: Norton.
Weiner-Davis, M. (1992). *Divorce busting: A step-by-step approach to making your marriage loving again*. New York: Simon & Schuster.
Weiner-Davis, M. (1996). *Change your life and everyone in it*. New York: Simon & Schuster.
Weiner-Davis, M. (1999). *Getting through to the man you love*. New York: St. Martin's.
Weiner-Davis, M. (2001). *The divorce remedy*. New York: Simon & Schuster.

64 Parenting with Love and Limits

Scott P. Sells

Engaging parents of adolescents with severe behavior problems is challenging for even the most skilled practitioner. The challenge is made more difficult when one tries to engage parents in a parenting education group or family therapy session. In addition, even though parenting groups are widespread, there is question about both their effectiveness and transportability. Transportability is ease of which the average practitioner can take the concepts of a model and integrate them into the real world with real clients. In response to these problems, a model program called Parenting with Love and Limits (PLL) was developed after a 4-year process research study. It is the first program of its kind to combine a parenting education group with family therapy into one complete package over a brief 6- to 8-week period. The model also blends the stages of readiness research to "start where the client is" on the change process to break through parental resistance as well as a manualized program to enhance transportability.

SCOPE OF THE PROBLEM

Increasingly, researchers reveal that adolescents are at risk of developing and maintaining delinquent behaviors when they are exposed to ineffective parenting behaviors, such as poor supervision (Patterson, 2002), rejection (Weisz, 1997), harsh and inconsistent discipline (Conger & Simons, 1997), and poor parenting techniques (Loeber & Farrington, 1998). According to Williams and Chang (2000), "Juveniles will return to future delinquent acts if their parents *remain unchanged* in the areas of consistent limit setting, rebuilding emotional attachments, and improved communication" (p. 159; emphasis added)

In response to these findings, parenting groups have been used to provide parents with new skills to reduce aggressive, antisocial, and delinquent behavior among children and adolescents (e.g., DeGarmo, Patterson, & Forgatch, 2004). However, researchers have found three main problems with this approach.

First, parents may learn a new skill in a parenting group but have no one to show them how to use it through role plays in a family therapy format (see Forgatch, Bullock, & Patterson, 2004). Therefore, parents may learn a new skill in a group only to see it fail when it is delivered improperly for the first time at home. As a result, their motivation to continue treatment plummets.

Second, even though parenting groups are widespread, there are questions about their effectiveness (Rowe & Liddle, 2003). Not surprisingly, parents are not motivated to engage and to continue in group treatment with delinquent teenagers. Parents typically state that their adolescents are solely responsible for their own difficulties and resent coming to parenting groups as a consequence of their adolescent's involvement in the juvenile justice system.

Third, there is a lack of transportability. *Transportability* means the ease of which the average practitioner can take the ideas and concepts of any therapy model and integrate them into the real world with clients (Franklin & Hopson, 2007). A primary complaint from practitioners is that the detailed procedures needed to go from point A to point B are not operationalized. In other words, many therapy models contain generalized concepts but lack a step-by-step roadmap. As a result, moving evidence-based therapies out of the research settings and into the real world of frontline practitioners has been bumpy at best.

HOW ARE THESE GAPS ADDRESSED?

To address these gaps, PLL was developed from a research study (Sells, 1998, 2000; Sells, Smith, & Rodman, 2006). It is the first evidence-based program of its kind to (1) combine both group and family therapy together over a 6- to 7-week period; (2) use the Stages of Readiness Scale as an overlay (see Prochaska, DiClemente, & Norcross, 1992) to break parental resistance; and (3) present a step-by-step roadmap with manuals so that the average practitioner can easily transport the concepts into real-world practice. An overview of each of these core pieces are presented along with two case studies to move the reader through each of the core steps within the PLL model.

Gap 1: PLL Combines Both Group and Family Therapy "Coaching" Together

The grid shown in Table 64.1 illustrates how the PLL model combines both group and family therapy together over a brief 6- to 7-week period. Each group class is custom designed to fill in missing core parenting skills common to adolescent's ages 10 to 17 diagnosed with oppositional defiant or conduct disorder with comorbidity problems such as substance abuse, ADHD, or depression.

Two group facilitators lead a small group of parents and their teenagers (no more than four to six families with no more than 12 people total in the group) in six classes, each 2 hours long. Two co-facilitators are needed because breakout groups were used. Parents and teens met together collectively as a group during the first hour and break into separate groups during the second hour. The coaching piece will use a model called "undercurrents" (see Sells, in press) based on a structural-strategic family therapy paradigm to show parents how to use the newly acquired skills from group.

For example, during week 3, both parents and teens learn the tools necessary to put together their first loophole-free contract with rewards and consequences within a psychoeducation group format. Before the next parenting class, both parents and teens meet individually in family therapy coaching to custom-build their own contract and practice these new skills through role-plays.

These individual family therapy meetings are called "coaching" because unlike traditional talk therapy, the practitioner combines strategic directives with role-plays and the technique of enact-

TABLE 64.1 Parenting with Love and Limits program

Week	PLL Group		PLL Individual Coaching
Week #1	Group 1: Venting and the six reasons why your teen misbehaves?		No coaching first week
Week #2	Group 2: Button pushing	+ →	Coaching 1: Deciding on the problem to fix fast
Week #3	Group 3: Contracting	+ →	Coaching 2: Writing a loophole-free contract
Week #4	Group 4: Putting the contract together as a group	+ →	Coaching 3: Present typed contract to teenager
Week #5	Group 5: Creative consequences (to stop disrespect, school problems, drug use, violence, not doing chores, running away, etc.)	+ →	Coaching 4: See if contract worked or tweak contract so it will work better
Week #6	Group 6: Restoring lost nurturance		(If needed) Coaching #5: To address other problems—Build new contract
Week #7	No group		(If needed) Coaching 6: Present new contract to teenager

Source: For more information on the PLL curriculum please go to http://www.gopll.com.

ments to practice newly acquired skills such as contracting, button pushing, or restoring lost nurturance. In this way, each group provides a new core skill specific to adolescents with oppositional defiant or conduct disorders, and the coaching provides the practice and application before skill implementation in the home.

As common sense as this delivery system sounds (group and coaching together), it is almost never done in mental health. Traditionally, group and individual or family therapies are on separate planets. If both modalities are provided, they do not synchronize together into a continuum of care to capitalize on the strengths of both.

For example, group therapy, if done well, gives overwhelmed and burned-out parents the feeling that they are not alone, as well as a sense of hope. With more single parents, this modality is essential. Resistant and angry parents are also much more willing to listen to the suggestions of other parents "in the trenches." Therefore, when the elements of group cohesion are in place, parents are much more likely to be open to the education and application of new parenting skills. Below is a typical quote from a parent and teenager who graduated from the PLL group. It represents the potential strengths of using a group format for this population.

Class showed us that we were not alone and there are families with many more problems (bad behavior, bad attitudes, drug use, etc.) that we don't have to deal with. This class will help us to avoid those problems. The other parents have been helpful in pointing out ways to get through to Caitlin and how to positively encourage her to do what she needs to—i.e. attend school, helping with chores, etc. It gave us some ideas as to what we can use as tools and how much better rewards work. I think that having a contract in place will help when school starts. This class, I hope, will also help with our son in motivating him. (Martha C.)

In addition, family therapy, if done well, roots out underlying issues that will prevent newly acquired skills from being implemented (i.e., marital conflict, parent substance abuse, etc.) and uses roleplays to show parents how to properly deliver the new skills. A quote from a PLL graduate of both group and coaching provides insight into the overall treatment process:

I needed the group and the coaching. I didn't realize how many buttons Kai knew how to push or how

I took it so personal. The group showed me the tool of "exit and wait" or how to leave our arguing before I blew up but you showed me in coaching what to do and how to do it. We even practiced it with Kai in the room. Without these practice meetings I know I would have lost it and gone right back when she stressed me out. (Sabreen S.)

PLL was developed to capitalize on the unique strengths of both group and family therapy together as one synchronized package. The research results to date have been encouraging with recidivism rates dropping to a range of 25 to 35 percent versus control groups of 50 percent or higher. This research has led PLL to be designated as an exemplary and model program by the Office of Juvenile Justice Delinquency and Prevention (OJJDP).

Gap 2: Breaking Parent Resistance through PLL and the Readiness Scale

Another challenge was breaking through parental resistance. Increasingly, research finding revealed that parents of oppositional or conduct disorders will not attend parenting groups unless court ordered (see Cormack & Carr, 2000). Even with a court order, drop-out rates for parents are exceedingly high. To combat this problem, we looked at the research by Prochaska et al. (1992) for answers. Prochaska and colleagues discovered that a key reason for client resistance was due to a lack of adherence by practitioners within six stages of readiness to change, shown in Table 64.2.

Unfortunately, it was discovered that most practitioners do not "start where the client is," but instead attempted to move a parent directly from precontemplation to action, bypassing contemplation and/or preparation altogether. As a result, the parent would predictably fail in the action stage and, according to Prochaska, "recycle" back into precontemplation with even a greater degree of resistance than before.

In response to this research, PLL used the stages of readiness scale as a theoretical overlay within the program's development. For example, the first three groups (venting, button pushing, and the top five reasons to build an ironclad contract) were specifically designed to move the parent and adolescent into the contemplative stage of readiness.

The curriculum contained a high dosage of nonthreatening experiential role plays and video clips to get the parent or adolescent to experience a cognitive shift by saying something like

TABLE 64.2 Stages of Change

Contemplation	Precontemplation	Preparation
▸ Acknowledge problem and their part in it	▸ Do not see that they are part of problem/solution	▸ Contracting and troubleshooting
▸ Not ready for change yet	▸ Feel situation is hopeless	▸ Need final reassurances
▸ Stalling — "analysis paralysis"	▸ No intention of changing	▸ Dry run role-plays
▸ Wait for magic sign	▸ Want others to change	▸ Make final adjustments
	▸ Others see problem they cannot	
	▸ Minimize or rationalize	

Maintenance	Action	Termination
▸ Consolidate gains	▸ Person or family tries to change or stop problem	▸ Anticipatory guidance
▸ Relapse prevention—troubleshooting	▸ Person or family tries to change environment	▸ Letting go of "old self"
▸ Potential to recycle is initially high	▸ Overlooks possible relapses	▸ Backup plan
▸ Communicate that relapse is normal	▸ If relapse or change fails recycles back to one of three earlier stages	▸ When to use tune-ups
▸ Goal: Spread moments of relapse further apart		▸ Line up support systems and secure a cotherapist

"I never thought about it (button-pushing, contracting) this way before." Once in contemplation, the last three groups (building a contract together, creative consequences, and restoring nurturance) were specifically designed to move them into a stage of preparation by increasing their desire and need for coaching.

Case Example

Fifteen-year-old Galvin was diagnosed with a conduct disorder and symptoms of extreme disrespect, destroying property in the home, and chronic truancy. During the first group, it was apparent that Galvin's single-parent mother, Kelly, was firmly entrenched within the precontemplative stage of readiness. She sat in the back of the room with her arms crossed and repeatedly stated that she did not see that her son had a problem. Galvin's probation office previously informed Michelle (the group leader and coach) that Kelly had never lasted more than two therapy sessions before she dropped out. Galvin's probation officer also described her as angry, burned out, and in extreme denial as to her role in helping her son misbehave.

It was not until the breakout session in the second hour of the first group that Kelly's icy veneer began to melt. A key moment came when Michelle asked the following question to Kelly and the other parents, "When I get to know you better, what qualities will I come to admire about you as a parent?" The question stunned Kelly and the other parents because they had come expecting to be judged or told what to do (action).

Instead, the therapist was asking them to focus on strengths. Kelly's defenses were lowered further when Michelle asked for a show of hands from the other parents as to who thought Kelly was a good parent. Everyone raised their hands. At the end of the first group, the parents said they would return because they felt supported and not so alone. Kelly and many of the other parents were still stuck in precontemplation, but the walls around them were slowly weakening.

Another watershed moment occurred during the second group on button pushing. Kelly and Galvin both admitted that they pushed each other's buttons and had fun putting their top buttons on sticky notes and sticking them all over their body. Galvin picked the buttons that his mom "lectured" and "nagged," and Kelly wrote down that Galvin used "swearing" and "mumbled under his breath." Kelly began to move into contemplation when she saw another parent and her son role-play their last argument in front of the group and playfully pushed each other's buttons. Kelly liked it when another parent held up flashcards that showed the mother dropping in age as she lost control of her emotions and took her son's button pushing so personally. Kelly later said that she could see herself in the mother's shoes.

Kelly and the other parents were shocked that the group leader never openly discussed their teenagers' charges or insinuated on any level that they had to change. Instead, Michelle playfully provided new tools each week through video examples and fun role-plays.

The defining moment came during the fourth class when Kelly watched a parent struggle to put together their first typewritten and loophole-free contract around disrespect. As this mother struggled, Kelly was moved to tears as she watched the other parents in the outer circle move in to support and offer suggestions. For the first time, Kelly began to see how easily a teenager can exploit loopholes and how helpful it was to have both rewards and punishments. Most important, she began to see Galvin not as a "bad kid" but as one who was extremely skillful in finding loopholes to get what he wanted. After this group, Kelly told Michelle that she would attend coaching.

Things really started to move in a positive direction when Kelly connected with another single mother in the group. Kelly was alone and isolated, but this ended when the other mother joined her in several of her coaching sessions for support. Galvin was stunned. For the first time in his life, Kelly became assertive but fair by using rewards instead of empty threats and punishments. During coaching, Michelle also used extensive role-plays (Galvin was in the waiting room) to practice the delivery of the button-buster techniques she learned in group. After two coaching sessions, Kelly felt "battle ready" and delivered the contract to Galvin. He "got worse before he got better," but Kelly stood firm with the support of her friend from group. After 3 weeks, the extreme disrespect, destroying property, and chronic truancy ended.

This case study is a good example of how the stages of readiness scale is effectively used as an overlay to break through parental resistance by using the strengths of both group and family therapy to complement one another. Kelly's rapid movement from precontemplation to contemplation and preparation to action is typical in the PLL model. In sum, here are the steps that made this rapid movement possible.

- *Strengths building in the first group through venting*. During the first group, both parents and teenagers break out into their own respective groups during the second hour. During this time, both parents and teenagers are allowed to vent why they are upset (parents are asked, "What is your worst nightmare with your teenager?" Teenagers are asked, "Who gets on your nerves and why?"). After these questions, the group leader subtly shifts the discussion toward parent and teenager strengths, which not only disarms them but also begins to break down their precontemplative walls. For Kelly, this happened when she realized that she was not alone and felt the other parents support.

- *Experiential exercises and nonthreatening skill building*. For both Kelly and Galvin, the inner/outer circle role-plays were playful and nonthreatening. In addition, they helped Kelly see for the first time her role in helping Galvin misbehave. It was not because she was a bad mother but because she lacked core skills such as anti–button pushing strategies and the ability to troubleshoot or plug up loopholes. Kelly saw these deficits not through the practitioner but through other parent struggles in real time. In turn, this "a ha!" moment rapidly moved Kelly into the contemplative stage of readiness.

- *Village support and coaching*. When Kelly began group, she was alone and had no support and no village. By the time group ended, she had a village and someone who would help her in coaching. This was a turning point and gave her the strength she needed to hold the line with Galvin. In addition, the coaching segment was invaluable to restore her confidence and change her delivery from empty threats to consistent discipline. Kelly also learned how to praise Galvin and "catch him doing something right" through rewards. This combination of love and limits was new and could not have happened without the support of the village and extensive role plays.

Gap 3: PLL Uses a Step-by-Step Roadmap to Increase Transportability

The processes or essential concepts that lead to change and increase transportability are rarely researched. As Kazdin (2003) noted,

Much of the adolescent outcome research reflects empiricism at its best and its worst, namely, repeated demonstrations that various treatments produce change and are better than no treatment. Very little in the way of theory guides therapy research and hypotheses about mechanisms of change. The net effect is that we really do not understand very much about therapy, why and how it achieves change, for whom it is and is not effective and why, and how to optimize therapeutic change. (p. 1)

Therefore, there was a need to answer the question "How does it work?" before using outcome studies to show whether it worked. In response to this challenge, we conducted a 4-year process research study with 83 difficult adolescents and their families (Sells, 1998). These results identified the key mechanisms of change that included such strategies as contracting and the restoration of lost nurturance between parent and child. From this study, a manualized group therapy leader's guide (Sells, 2003), DVDs and videotapes, and a coaching survival kit with a seven-step model were created. In turn, these manuals greatly increased transportability for the frontline practitioner.

The seven-step model in Figure 64.1 illustrates an overview of where group therapy ends and family therapy coaching begins using undercurrent therapy. To implement the micro-steps for the group, the therapist uses the group therapy leader's guide along with the DVDs and parent and teen workbooks. The DVD videos are 3- to 5-minutes sound bites of parent and teen actors who demonstrate each of the major skill sets, such as the top six strategies to restore lost nurturance or the top four strategies to write an ironclad contract.

To implement the coaching piece of the PLL model, a Parent Survival Kit (Sells, 2004) is used that is interactive and also uses video clips to help parents and adolescents implement each of the skills they learned in group. For a detailed discussion of each coaching step, please review *Undercurrent Therapy for Impossible Cases* (Sells, in press).

COACHING SESSION 1

Looking at the seven-step model, the first coaching session includes step 2, top symptoms revealed, and step 3, setting the terms of therapy. Immediately after the second parenting group, the practitioner, who is also the group leader, schedules the first coaching session. During the second group, parents and their teenagers are given specific tools

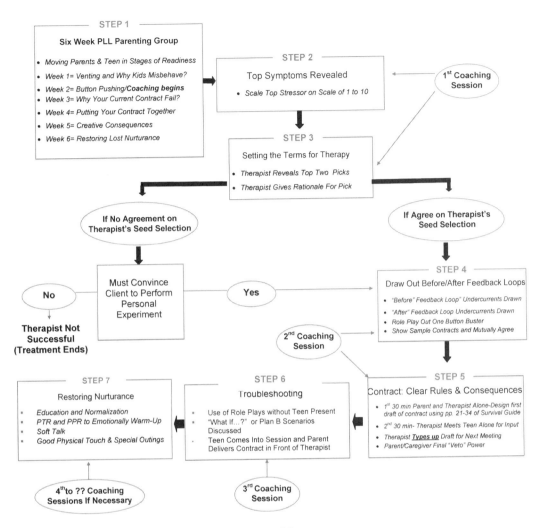

Figure 64.1 PLL seven-step group and coaching model.

to stop button pushing during conflict and confrontation, but they lack a concrete plan of rules and consequences surrounding the problem behavior. The family also has multiple stressors or problem symptoms and they are unsure of which symptom to focus on first and why.

Steps 2 and 3 fill in this important gap by providing practitioners with a specific and transportable micro-step called a stress chart. Using this tool, the practitioner helps the family locate the top stressors that the each family member is experiencing in relation to the adolescent with the behavioral problem. For example, the therapist will ask, "What are the top three stressors that you are experiencing with your teenager?" To accomplish this goal, the therapist draws out the stress chart on a flip chart with a scale of 0 percent

to 100 percent, with 0 percent meaning no stress and 100 percent meaning nonstop stress. For example, 17-year-old Jeremy and his family were asked to reveal their top three stressors on the stress chart, shown in Box 64.1.

Once the stress chart is completed, the practitioner quickly moves into step 3, setting the terms for therapy, or choosing which stressor (symptom) should be tackled first and gives the family supporting rationale. As Figure 64.1 illustrates, if the practitioner agrees with the families symptom (stressor) suggestion, one can proceed to step 4, draw out before and after feedback loops, in the next coaching session with little to no resistance or fanfare. In Jeremy's example, the symptom would be "disrespect" (won't listen), chores, or homework.

BOX 64.1 Stress Chart.

Mother's Top Three Stressors That Cause Her 70%					Dad's Top Three Stressors That Cause His 95%					
#1 *"My husband and I disagree on what to do"*					#1 *"He won't listen"*					
#2 *"Wont'd do chores or homework"*					#2 *"Won't talk about his feeling"*					
#3 *"Looks sad all the time"*					#3 *My wife and I disagree on what to do!*					
					Both Uncles	Krista	Jeremy		David	
					X	X	X		X	
0%	10%	20%	30%	40%	50%	60%	70%	80%	90%	100%

Uncles Top Three Stressors That Cause Their 50%	Jeremy's Top Three Stressors
#1 *The stress they see on David and Krista*	#1 *Yelling with his Aunt and Uncle*
#2 *Jeremy's stubborn refusal*	#2 *Won't Give Me My Freedom*
#3 *No accountability because he is depressed*	#3 *Upset with school, with everything*

However, if the practitioner's selection disagrees with even one of the key decision makers (the parents) it is highly likely that the battle for structure (see Whitaker & Keith, 1981) will be in full gear. This battle occurs any time the practitioner and family disagree on the terms of therapy or goals on which symptom to address first or not at all. When the battle for structure occurs, the practitioner and family reach a proverbial fork in the road. The practitioner can either (1) use persuasion tactics to change the families mind and proceed to step 4, or (2) convince the family to perform a personal experiment to see if the practitioner is right and then proceed onto step 4.

COACHING SESSION 2

The second coaching session includes step 4, before and after feedback loops, and step 5, a contract of clear rules and consequences. This coaching session should take place immediately after the third parenting group. During the third parenting group, the parents and teenager are taught the six main reasons why they need a loophole-free contract and begin to convert the stressor or symptom they produced in the first coaching session into a concrete and written rule. However, the parents lack the insight as to how they help their teenager misbehave (i.e., inconsistent discipline, empty threats, lack of nurturance, etc.) and do not yet possess the tools necessary to put together ironclad rewards or consequences.

The second coaching session fills this important gap in two ways. First, at the onset of the second coaching session, the practitioner takes the top one or two symptoms agreed on at the conclusion of the first coaching meeting and draws them out as "before" feedback loops to visually illustrate for the family where they consistently get stuck. For example, in Jeremy's family, a blown-up re-creation of the "before" feedback loop is shown in Box 64.2.

After the before feedback loop was presented, the family could clearly see how the father's lack of soft talk and empty threats are helping Jeremy gain the upper hand. Once this insight takes place, the practitioner is ready to draw out for the family the "after" feedback loop or what can happen in the future once they use the contracting skills they leaned in the third parenting group.

Once the after feedback loop is presented, the family can see how a well-written contract will

BOX 64.2 Feedback Loop.

#1 "He won't listen" (David's answer from the stress chart)	**"Before" Feedback Loop**
• When I ask him to do his chores, he refuses • When I ask him to do his homework, he ignores me	#4: Walks away with smile on face in victory #2: No do it yourself! (loud voice) David **Jeremy** #1: Get your room cleaned up! (loud voice) #3: You will be grounded for a month! (empty threat)

clarify everyone's roles and provide a roadmap on how to custom-fit the skills learned in group ("exit and wait" button buster). In addition, clear rules and consequences (the contract) would help alter the parent–child power struggle.

Once the feedback loops are completed, the second half of the coaching session consists of writing a first draft of the contract with both parent and teenager input. The contract is a direct spin-off of the after feedback loop, which in turn is directly connected to the symptom or stressor chosen by the practitioner and family within the first coaching session. For example, in Jeremy's family the symptom chosen to work on first was not completing chores. The chore contract, which was a direct reflection of the after feedback loop, is shown in Box 64.3.

As the contract illustrates, roles are clarified and the skills learned in group are illustrated in the feedback loop and custom-fit in coaching for the particular family. Adolescents love to see that that parent also has a contract of what they are agreeing to do.

COACHING SESSION 3 OR 4
OR MORE IF NEEDED

The third coaching session includes step 6, troubleshooting. This coaching session should take place immediately after the fourth parenting group. During the fourth parenting group, one parent goes into the inner circle with the group leader to demonstrate for the rest of the parents in the outer circle how to put together an entire ironclad complete with rewards and consequences. There are also some role-plays to practice the delivery of the contract and "what if?" scenarios or trouble-

shooting. This inner/outer circle piece is done to help the parents appreciate the skill and level of difficulty that contracting involves and move them into the preparation stage of readiness for the third coaching session.

During the third coaching session, the teenager is asked to wait outside in the waiting room while the practitioner and parent meticulously go through the contract to discover loopholes. This process is called troubleshooting. For example, in Jeremy's contract, the practitioner might present the contract and challenge the parents with this "what if" scenario: "What will you do if Jeremy follows you when you try to 'exit and wait?'" The parent and practitioner must then come up with a plan B beforehand and think two steps ahead.

Finally, the practitioner conducts extensive role-plays with the parent by playing the part of the teenager and trying to push their buttons as they attempt to deliver the contract. When parents are ready, the teenager is asked to come back into the room and receive the contract.

The fourth coaching session and additional sessions thereafter are optional and would take place after the fifth and sixth groups based on these three reasons: (1) if the family has severe deficits in restoring nurturance, additional sessions are recommended; (2) if there are other symptoms that need additional contracting, and (3) if the family needs to tweak the existing contract or needs further troubleshooting.

FUTURE PRACTICE APPLICATIONS

This chapter began by outlining the three major gaps in treating resistant parents of adolescents with severe behavioral problems. In sum, these

BOX 64.3 Chore List for Jeremy.

- Take out trash by 6:30 A.M. and then again @ 8:15 P.M.

- Clean room (make bed, all stuff [books/toys/trash/dirty dishes] off floor, and book bag ready for next day) by 5 P.M. Mom or dad give you 15 minutes to fix room if not perfectly clean after 5 P.M.

- Laundry and vacuum his room every Saturday by 6:30 P.M.

Daily Reward = 50 cents @ 5:30 P.M. Can earn up to $3.50 if do all chores for 7 days.

Bonus Rewards

7 straight days = Extra $1.50.

Consequence = No 50 cents that day + no computer or phone that rest of that day +

the next day.

Dad and Mom's Exit and Wait Strategy

Mom or Dad will use the anti–button pushing strategy of exit and wait if Jeremy is (a) not doing what he is told or a prearranged chore, (b) talking back or yelling, (c) with this statement:

"Jeremy we love you but you are not doing your chore. I am going to leave for 3 minutes. If I come back and you are not doing what I asked, the contract that we signed together will be enforced. I know you want to make the right decision because I looking forward to giving you your reward tonight. Good-bye" [immediately exit].

gaps consist of parenting groups that do not synchronize family therapy, an inability to engage resistant parents, and a lack of transportability. Parenting with Love and Limits (PLL) is a 6- to 7-week parenting/family therapy (coaching) model designed with the strengths of both modalities and research that supports its transportability and effective outcomes with adolescents.

A case study illustrated the effectiveness of using Prochaska's research on the stages of readiness scale to break through parental resistance. As this chapter illustrates, PLL offers a step-by-step way of coaching parents and produces high levels of transportability in practice providing practitioners with new tools for helping adolescents and their parents.

WEB SITES

Office of Juvenile Justice Delinquency and Prevention (OJJDP). http://ojjdp.ncjrs.org.

Parenting with Love and Limits. http://www.gopll.com.
Why Try. http://www.whytry.org.

References

Conger, R. D., & Simons, S. L. (1997). Life-course contingencies in the development of adolescent antisocial behavior: A matching law approach. In T. P. Thornberry (Ed.), *Development theories of crime and delinquency: Advances in criminological theory*, (vol. 7, pp. 55–99). New Brunswick, NJ: Transaction.

Cormack, C., & Carr, A. (2000). Drug abuse. In A. Carr (Ed.), *What works with children and adolescents? A critical review of psychological interventions with children, adolescents and their families*. Florence, KY: Taylor & Francis/Routledge.

DeGarmo, D. S., Patterson, G. R., & Forgatch, M. S. (2004). How do outcomes in a specified parent training intervention maintain over time? *Prevention Science, 5*(2), 73–79.

Forgatch, M. S., Bullock, B. M., & Patterson, G. R. (2004). From theory to practice: increasing effective parenting through role plays. The Oregon model of parent management training. In H. Steiner (Ed.), *Handbook of mental health interventions in children and adolescents* (pp. 782–814). San Francisco: Jossey-Bass.

Franklin, C., & Hopson, L. (2007). Facilitating the use of evidence-based practices in community-based organizations. *Journal of Social Work Education, 43*(4), 377–404.

Kazdin, A. E. (2003). *Research design in clinical psychology,* 4th ed. Boston: Allyn & Bacon.

Loeber, R., & Farrington, D. P. (1998). *Serious and violent juvenile offenders,* Thousand Oaks, CA: Sage.

Patterson, G. R. (2002). Etiology and treatment of child and adolescent antisocial behavior. *Behavior Analyst Today, 3*(2), 133–145.

Prochaska, J. O., DiClemente, C. C., & Norcross, J. C. (1992). In search of how people change: Applications to addictive behaviors. *American Psychologist, 47*(9), 1102–1114.

Rowe, C. L., & Liddle, H. A. (2003). Substance abuse in adolescents. *Journal of Marital and Family Therapy, 29*(1), 97–120.

Sells, S. P. (1998). *Treating the tough adolescent: A step-by-step, family-based guide.* New York: Guilford.

Sells, S. P. (2000). *Parenting your out-of-control teenager.* New York: St. Martin's.

Sells, S. P. (2003). *Parenting with Love and Limits leader's guide.* Savannah: Kennikel.

Sells, S. P. (2004). *Parenting with Love and Limits survival kit.* Savannah: Kennikel.

Sells, S. P. (In press). *Undercurrent therapy for impossible case.* New York: Guilford.

Sells, S. P., Smith, T. E., & Rodman, J. (2006). Reducing substance abuse through Parenting with Love and Limits. *Journal of Child and Adolescent Substance Abuse, 15,* 105–115.

Weisz, J. R. (1997). Effects of interventions for children and adolescent psychological dysfunction. In S. S. Luthar, J. A. Burack, D. Cicchetti, & J. R. Weisz, (Eds.), *Developmental psychopathology: Perspectives on adjustment, risk, and disorder* (pp. 3–22). New York: Cambridge University Press.

Whitaker, C., & Keith, D. (1981). Symbolic-experiential family therapy. In A. S. Gurman & D. P. Kniskern (Eds.), *Handbook of family therapy* (pp. 187–225). New York: Brunner/Mazel.

Williams, R. J., & Chang, S. Y. (2000). A comprehensive and comparative review of adolescent substance abuse treatment outcome. *Clinical Psychology: Science and Practice, 7,* 138–166.

65 Integrative Behavioral Couple Therapy

Katherine J. Williams, Felicia De la Garza-Mercer, & Andrew Christensen

Integrative behavioral couple therapy (IBCT; Jacobson & Christensen, 1998) was developed as a treatment for couples that either did not respond to existing behavioral couple therapies or relapsed soon after termination. This chapter introduces the assessment, case formulation, and interventions common to IBCT through both case illustration and treatment description. Efficacy data in support of IBCT are also presented.

CASE ILLUSTRATION

Julia and Josh, an attractive married couple in their mid-thirties, presented for treatment in a local clinic. They had been in a relationship for 8 years and married for 4 years. They had two young children, a 2.5-year-old son and a 1-year-old daughter. Julia and Josh were in the dissatisfied range of relationship functioning, and reported arguments up to twice a day surrounding the amount of time Julia spent at work (and thus away from home). The couple reported that their arguments had increased since their daughter was born; Josh said he thought Julia did not give the family enough time, and Julia was upset with Josh's tendency to express his concern with criticism and anger. Both partners worried they could not overcome the difficulties they were currently facing. Julia and Josh requested therapy after an argument resulted in Julia spending the night at a hotel.

IBCT

IBCT, developed by Andrew Christensen and the late Neil S. Jacobson (Jacobson & Christensen, 1998), seeks to target a wider range of couples than traditional behavioral couple therapy (TBCT; Jacobson & Margolin, 1979). IBCT combines change techniques from existing couple therapies with interventions aimed at increasing emotional acceptance.

Assessment

In IBCT, couples typically participate in three assessment sessions as well as a feedback session. Ideally, the therapist first has a joint session with both partners of the couple. The purpose of this session is to learn about the presenting concerns and history of the relationship, orient the couple to IBCT, determine whether the couple is appropriate for IBCT, and help the couple decide whether IBCT is "the right fit" for them. Couples are also introduced to Reconcilable Differences (Christensen & Jacobson, 2000), a text written for couples participating in IBCT.

In learning about the current problems the couple is facing, the social worker, acting in a role as couples therapist, focuses on emotional reactions (e.g., Josh's sadness and anger related to Julia working so much) more than specific behaviors (i.e., Julia working a lot), and on the general pattern that is often played out in their negative interactions (e.g., Josh's criticism and Julia's defensiveness). The therapist then facilitates a discussion of the history of the relationship, asking about how the couple met, how their relationship developed, and how their current problems came about. The social worker seeks to learn about positive aspects of their relationship and the areas where the couple has particular strengths, in addition to the current problems facing them in their relationship.

At the end of the first assessment session, the IBCT therapist may give partners objective measures to provide information about important areas of the relationship. The most common areas assessed with these measures are relationship quality (e.g., the Dyadic Adjustment Scale; Spanier, 1976), aggressive conflict (e.g., Conflict Tactics Scale; Straus, Hamby, Boney-McCoy, & Sugarman, 1996), and target behaviors (e.g., the Frequency and Acceptability of Partner Behavior Inventory; Doss & Christensen, 2006). Regardless of the method of assessment, it is critical that therapists evaluate couples for intimate partner violence prior to beginning treatment; IBCT therapists do not treat couples whose problems include moderate to severe levels of violence (see Jacobson & Christensen, 1998). For those levels of violence, the therapist should recommend treatment that focuses on the domestic violence rather than on the relational distress.

The second and third assessment sessions are individual sessions with each partner. They typically begin with a confidentiality caveat that the social worker does not withhold information discussed in the individual sessions in joint sessions unless the partner explicitly asks the therapist. In the event that a partner reveals private information to the social worker that is relevant to the couple's relationship (e.g., an ongoing affair), the social worker stresses the importance of working together to share that information with the partner or to quickly resolve the issue (e.g., end the affair). IBCT therapists do not continue therapy if a partner discloses infidelity to the therapist and is unwilling to stop the affair or reveal it to the partner. Social workers should follow these principles when practicing this therapy.

The goal of each session is to gain better knowledge of the current relationship problems and of each individual's personal history, with an eye toward the vulnerabilities that each partner brings to the relationship. Often, the social worker begins by focusing on material that came up in the joint session as well as inquiring about particular items endorsed on the questionnaires. In the discussion of the current relationship problems, the therapist attends to the emotional and behavioral reactions of each partner and the typical interaction pattern that the couple enacts around issues in the relationship. In the discussion of an individual's personal history, the therapist learns about the partner's relationships with close family members and the overall atmosphere in the partner's home during childhood. For example, in the session with Julia, the therapist learned that her single mother struggled to support Julia and her siblings, sometimes feeding the children the same meal for dinner every day of the week. Julia reported that as a result, she often worries about money and not being able to support her children. Josh was the oldest child in his family and was given, in his view, an unfair burden of child care throughout his youth. Now he fears he is thrown into a similar position in his marriage—lots of home responsibility and little individual attention for him.

Another important part of the individual session is to evaluate the level of violence in the relationship and each partner's level of commitment. Therapists trained in IBCT explicitly ask about domestic violence, commitment, and extradyadic affairs, sometimes by focusing on relevant questionnaire items the client may have endorsed. Neither Julia nor Josh reported any violence or affairs; both reported a high level of commitment to their relationship.

Feedback

In the feedback session, the social worker presents her case formulation based on the joint and individual sessions. The formulation is the foundation on which the course of IBCT treatment is built; it is presented as a framework for the couple to understand their problems based on both individual vulnerabilities and differences between the partners. The formulation consists of the couple's relational themes, their individual vulnerabilities related to the themes, and the dysfunctional patterns of interaction (polarization process) that the partners act out around these themes.

Relational themes are the broad issues that divide the partners. In Julia and Josh's relationship, those themes were financial security and household responsibility. Individual vulnerabilities provide emotional fuel to these issues, making them difficult to resolve rationally. For example, Julia's history of financial difficulties made work and money a major anxiety for her; Josh's history of caretaking made child care a sensitive issue for him. The polarization process is the destructive interaction pattern that the partners play out around issues related to their themes. As the term suggests, partners' attempts to change one another often serve to increase the conflict and distance between them, even when often the purpose of trying to change one another is to facilitate intimacy or closeness. The result of this polarization process is a *mutual trap*. For example, the conflict that ensues from Josh's frequent criticism of

Julia for working late makes her feel insecure about the future of their relationship. Her insecurity that the relationship may serve to deepen Julia's fear that she will be unable to provide her family with necessary financial support, and she increases the time she spends at work. The more time she spends at work, the less time Josh has to criticize her, which reinforces her spending time away from home. Josh criticizes Julia to right the child care imbalance between them, but he finds the imbalance increasing rather than decreasing. Thus, Julia and Josh find themselves in a vicious circle of interaction, a mutual trap.

During the feedback session, the social worker presents her treatment plan. Although both change techniques and acceptance strategies are used in IBCT, a typical course of treatment begins with acceptance strategies. Sometimes treatment begins with change techniques, but only if both partners seem motivated to change and are in agreement about the specific changes they would like in their relationship. In the example case, the therapist decided that Julia's avoidance and Josh's emotional reactance regarding her work made the couple ideal for beginning treatment with acceptance work rather than change techniques. It was clear to the therapist that Josh and Julia did not understand one another around this issue.

Beginning with the first treatment session (following the feedback session), and in most subsequent treatment sessions, the social worker focuses on emotionally salient incidents and issues related to the formulation. She pays attention to the emotions of the partners within the session and often finds that examples relevant to the formulation unfold in the session. For instance, when Julia and Josh began to argue about Julia's work in a therapy session, the therapist intervened.

JOSH: If you cared about our family, you would at least make it home in time for dinner.

JULIA: [crying, looking down] I do care, Josh. I just have a lot of responsibilities at work.

THERAPIST: I'd like you two to step back for one second and look at what is happening here. Josh, it seems that you are feeling quite hurt right now, and Julia that you feel pretty put on the spot.

EMOTIONAL ACCEPTANCE TECHNIQUES

Social workers trained in IBCT often begin treatment with acceptance interventions to help partners understand and adapt to each other's behavior. IBCT therapists do this through three acceptance techniques: *empathic joining*, *unified detachment*, and *tolerance building*.

In facilitating empathic joining, the therapists works to reformulate relationship discord in terms of differences between rather than faults within partners and in terms of understandable reactions to such differences, thus allowing partners to empathize with one another's experience. The therapist also focuses on eliciting more vulnerable disclosures of "soft emotions" (e.g., sadness, fear) rather than "hard emotions" (e.g., anger, blame) from partners by suggesting soft emotions as a potential basis of behavior. In the previous example, the therapist suggested that Josh was feeling hurt when he expressed the harder emotion of anger.

Social workers using IBCT techniques help the partners discuss problems with unified detachment, that is, to help partners take a nonjudgmental stance and describe relationship problems in behavioral terms rather than with blame and other intense emotions. The optimal result of this strategy is to change the problem from a "you" or a "her" to an "it" that the partners can join around. Often, IBCT therapists give a couple's interaction pattern a name, which serves to further distance the partners from the difficult emotions of (and often bring humor to) the pattern. Emotional distance allows partners to better understand the behaviors and reactions of one another.

IBCT therapists also use tolerance building to help partners cope with the other's unwelcome but nondestructive behavior. If one partner is not willing or initially resistant to change, then working with the other partner to face and ultimately tolerate the other's behavior is likely the only way for them to maintain a happy, harmonious relationship. When one partner begins to demonstrate some acceptance of the specific behavior, the other partner's appreciation of this tolerance may lead to increased closeness (and sometimes even change of the behavior).

An IBCT therapist uses a number of strategies to build tolerance: positive reemphasis, highlighting the complementary of partners' differences, preparing couples for backsliding, and faking bad behavior. Using positive reemphasis while still validating the negative qualities of such behavior, an IBCT therapist points out the positive functions of behaviors thought by one partner to be solely negative. For example, Josh and Julia's therapist highlighted how the combination of Julia's dedication and Josh's flexibility allows them to function as a couple and take care of their children better than if both partners were similar in that respect; thus pointing out the way Julia and Josh actually complement one another.

Regardless of whether the change is one partner's behavior or the other's understanding of it, there are times when couples lapse into their typical patterns of interaction. Because they have most likely frequently engaged in this pattern when they enter therapy, these lapses are expected and common. Thus, IBCT therapists help partners plan responses to such lapses prior to the occurrence, helping them tolerate lapses if they do happen. Additionally, the therapist encourages each partner to consider alternative means of support (e.g., from friends) and ways of self-soothing (e.g., taking a warm bath, listening to enjoyable music) when in difficult times. When individuals learn to care more for themselves, they may put less pressure on their partners to meet their emotional needs and be less susceptible to perceptions that their partners are at fault for needs not being met.

Rather than working to increase the amount of time Julia spends at home, the therapist involved the couple in a discussion of what time at work means to Julia by discussing the thoughts and feelings that she has around work. Additionally, she invited Josh to talk about his emotional reactions to the time Julia spends at work and what that meant to him. This discussion facilitated empathic joining in that it allowed Julia to better understand the impact of her actions on Josh, and Josh to better understand Julia's reasons for spending so much time at work. In this case, Josh was surprised to find that his wife worried their family would end up in a similar financial situation to that of her family when she was growing up. Thus, her desire to work to help support the family had nothing to do with not wanting to spend time with Josh.

Ideally, such conversations help modify the emotional reaction of one partner to the other's behavior. The conversations Josh and Julia had in therapy helped Josh see that Julia's long hours at work were fueled by her anxiety about money, which allowed him to offer support to his wife, rather than criticizing her for not spending adequate time at home. Julia began to seek support and connection from Josh when she was anxious about their finances, and they worked to establish a savings account with a "prudent reserve" only to be used for emergencies. As sometimes is the case, this focus on acceptance actually created a paradoxical effect: Julia began to work less once she felt less pressure and more understanding from Josh, and they worked together to reduce the anxiety underlying Julia's late nights.

CHANGE TECHNIQUES

Often, as in the case of Julia and Josh, acceptance techniques bring about adequate, spontaneous change in behavior and perception, and traditional change techniques are not necessary. However, as needed, IBCT uses three direct behavior change techniques in treatment: behavior exchange, communication training, and problem-solving training. Typically, these interventions and the rules underlying them are adapted maximally to the needs and peculiarities of the couple,

Behavior Exchange

In behavior exchange, the therapist seeks to increase positive behaviors in the relationship by first identifying those behaviors, then instigating those behaviors, and finally debriefing the occurrence of those behaviors. In a typical treatment scenario, the couple is first asked to identify positive behaviors that each could engage in that would increase the other person's relationship satisfaction. This may be a homework assignment that the couple is asked to bring to their next session. Then the therapist asks the couple to increase the daily frequency of one or more behaviors on their list, with the only guideline being that partners not tell one another which behaviors they will enact. Finally, the therapist debriefs the couple on giving and receiving positive behaviors. In these discussions, partners may provide one another with feedback about specific behaviors so that the couple has a better idea of which behaviors truly do increase perceived satisfaction.

Communication Training

Couples are taught speaker and listener skills in communication training (CT), with the aim being to help partners become more effective communicators with one another. The partners first practice the skills in sessions with corrective feedback and direction from the therapist, and then are encouraged and sometimes given assignments to practice the skills at home. Speaker effectiveness skills include focusing on the self (i.e., using

"I" statements), expressing emotional reactions, and highlighting specific behaviors of their partner that lead to emotional reactions (e.g., "I feel hurt when you stay late at work and forget to call to let me know"). Listener effectiveness skills include paraphrasing and reflecting what one's partner says. This ensures that partners understand one another without misinterpretation common to distressed couples.

Problem-Solving Training

It is expected that there will be times when, regardless of how effectively partners communicate about an issue, they have a hard time reaching a solution. Thus, couples are also taught ways of problem solving that keep them from entering into the mutual trap of dysfunctional problem discussion. As with CT, the therapist first works with the couple during therapy sessions to use problem-solving skills and then recommends that they practice at home to find solutions to problems.

Couples are taught three sets of skills in problem-solving training: problem definition, problem solution, and structuring skills. They first learn how to define problems in terms of specific behavior and the environment in which it occurs. IBCT therapists often ask that partners disclose emotional reactions to also work toward emotional acceptance. Finally, each partner defines his or her role in the problem.

Next, partners learn problem solution skills. The first step in problem solution is brainstorming—the couple is asked to come up with all possible solutions, whether realistic or unrealistic. They then delete unrealistic solutions from the list until they are left with possible solutions to the problem. Partners then agree on a solution, write down and sometimes sign the agreement, and discuss things that might get in the way of instituting the solution. The couple is instructed to post the agreement where both partners will be aware of it, and the therapist checks in with the couple about the agreement for several sessions. If necessary, the agreement may be renegotiated.

The final skills couples are taught are structuring skills. Couples are encouraged to structure their problem-solving interactions so that they set aside a specific time and place to discuss the problem, ideally outside of the immediate problem situation. During their discussion, they are instructed to use skills from CT as well as problem-solving skills and to avoid negative verbal and nonverbal behavior.

OTHER IBCT THERAPIST GUIDELINES

Social workers trained in IBCT seek to remain flexible throughout the intervention techniques. They tailor interventions to the specific areas of deficiency of the couple and sometimes use failed change techniques as indication that relying more on acceptance interventions may be beneficial for the couple. Therapists should attend to in-session interactions and help facilitate in-session repair between partners when necessary. IBCT therapists remain nonjudgmental and accepting of partners and the outcome of the relationship. The goal of IBCT is to help partners have a different type of interaction around difficult issues and allow them to make the most informed decisions for the two individuals within the relationship.

EFFICACY OF IBCT

One of IBCT's strengths, alongside its clinical value, is its empirically demonstrated efficacy. In a preliminary clinical trial, 21 distressed couples were randomly assigned to either IBCT or TBCT (Jacobson, Christensen, Prince, Cordova, & Eldridge, 2000). TBCT is the most widely used and investigated couple therapy, and it was viewed as an appropriate comparison group to IBCT. Findings indicated that IBCT couples more frequently engaged in empathic joining and unified detachment behaviors than TBCT couples, and that IBCT engendered an equivalent, and occasionally greater, amount of change in couple behavior as TBCT. These outcomes suggested that IBCT's dual focus on emotional acceptance and behavioral change may accordingly promote both acceptance-related spontaneous change and therapist-guided, purposeful behavioral change, thus potentially producing couple change in a more efficient manner.

Using a subsample from the same clinical trial (Jacobson et al., 2000) as part of a small pilot study, 12 distressed married couples were randomly assigned to either IBCT or TBCT and were seen for 20–25 sessions at a low-cost fee (Cordova, Jacobson, & Christensen, 1998). Audiotape recordings from their treatment sessions demonstrated that the two treatments had distinct effects on couple communication, whereby IBCT-treated couples had more frequent "soft" emotional expression and less frequent dysfunctional problem solving and "hard" emotional expression. Due to the study's small sample size and low power, however, these results indicated only trends toward significant differences between treatments.

In the largest randomized clinical trial of couple therapy (Christensen et al., 2006) 134 severely and chronically distressed married couples were randomly assigned to either IBCT or TBCT and provided with approximately 26 sessions with trained therapists. Both treatments produced comparable rates of couple improvement and change by the end of treatment, and the two therapies' trajectories of change were distinct over time. TBCT couples improved more rapidly at the onset of treatment than did IBCT couples but also plateaued more quickly than IBCT couples. In contrast, IBCT couples made steadier change throughout the course of therapy, suggesting that although IBCT's tendency to immediately focus on central issues, rather than overt behavioral change, may not produce an instantaneous burst of improvement, it may foster an important environment of emotional acceptance and safety that permits continual, stable change. Simply put, in the case of IBCT, it is possible that slow and steady may indeed win the race.

Results from a growth curve analysis of the aforementioned data further demonstrate significant differences between IBCT's and TBCT's mechanisms of change (Doss, Thum, Sevier, Atkins, & Christensen, 2005). For example, it appeared that whereas TBCT engendered more frequent and positive behavior during the first half of treatment than did IBCT, couples' behavior relapses later on in treatment had a more detrimental impact on relationship satisfaction in TBCT than in IBCT. IBCT facilitated greater acceptance of target behaviors throughout the course of the clinical trial than did TBCT, especially within the second half of therapy, and it is likely that these treatment differences were due to IBCT's continual focus on both behavioral and emotional acceptance.

In the 2-year follow-up, Christensen, Atkins, Yi, Baucom, & George (2006) found that both treatments demonstrated a "hockey stick" pattern of change, such that couple satisfaction dropped immediately following therapy termination and then increased for the majority of follow-up. However, the point at which couples tended to switch from a decreasing to an increasing rate of satisfaction occurred earlier in IBCT-treated couples than in TBCT couples. Furthermore, IBCT couples who stayed together tended to report better and more stable outcomes than their TBCT counterparts who remained together.

In addition to these primary studies, other research has explored IBCT's applicability to specific couple-related issues. For example, IBCT has been explored as a possibly favorable treatment for couples in which one or both partners experience chronic pain (e.g., Leonard, Cano, & Johansen, 2006), such that enhanced emotional acceptance of pain may lead to actual decreases in pain severity and pain-related anxiety.

IBCT may also be an efficacious treatment for couples experiencing infidelity. Analysis of the aforementioned randomized clinical trial data demonstrated that although infidelity couples were more distressed than noninfidelity couples at the onset of treatment, they improved at more rapid rate than their noninfidelity couple counterparts (Atkins, Eldridge, Baucom, & Christensen, 2005). Indeed, the majority of infidelity couples (66 percent) had either improved or recovered by termination and was comparable to the number of improved and recovered noninfidelity couples (65 percent).

CONCLUSION

This chapter describes IBCT, a couple therapy that focuses on emotional acceptance as well as behavioral change. A case illustration provides an example of an IBCT case that evidenced change through acceptance techniques and also described behavior change techniques commonly used with couples in IBCT. The studies mentioned suggest that IBCT is an efficacious treatment for relational distress, as well as specific couple issues (e.g., infidelity, chronic pain) and that its focus on emotional acceptance may function to allow couples to achieve more long-lasting gains than TBCT.

WEB SITES

Integrative Behavioral Couple Therapy. http://ibct.psych.ucla.edu/home.htm.
Christensen Research Lab. http://christensenresearch.psych.ucla.edu.

References

Atkins, D. C., Eldridge, K., Baucom, D. H., & Christensen, A. (2005). Infidelity and behavioral couple therapy: Optimism in the face of betrayal. *Journal of Consulting and Clinical Psychology, 73,* 144–150.

Christensen, A., Atkins, D. C., Yi, J., Baucom, D. H., & George, W. H. (2006). Couple and individual adjustment for two years following a randomized clinical trial comparing Traditional versus Integrative Behavioral Couple Therapy. *Journal of Consulting and Clinical Psychology, 74,* 1180–1191.

Christensen, A., & Jacobson, N. (2000). *Reconcilable differences.* New York: Guilford.

Cordova, J. V., Jacobson, N. S., & Christensen, A. (1998). Acceptance versus change interventions in behavioral couple therapy: Impact on couples' in-session communication. *Journal of Marriage & Family Counseling, 24,* 437–455.

Doss, B. D., & Christensen, A. (2006). Acceptance in romantic relationships: The frequency and acceptability of partner behavior inventory. *Psychological Assessment, 18,* 289–302.

Doss, B. D., Thum, Y. M., Sevier, M., Atkins, D. C., & Christensen, A. (2005). Improving relationships: Mechanisms of change in couple therapy. *Journal of Consulting and Clinical Psychology, 73*(4), 624–635.

Jacobson, N. S., & Christensen, A. (1998). *Acceptance and change in couple therapy: A therapist's guide to transforming relationships.* New York: Norton.

Jacobson, N. S., Christensen, A., Prince, S. E., Cordova, J., & Eldridge, K. (2000). Integrative Behavioral Couple Therapy: An acceptance-based, promising new treatment for couple discord. *Journal of Consulting and Clinical Psychology, 68*(2), 351–355.

Jacobson, N. S., & Margolin, G. (1979). *Marital therapy: Strategies based on social learning and behavior exchange principles.* New York: Brunner/Mazel.

Leonard, M. T., Cano, A., & Johansen, A. B. (2006). Chronic pain in a couples context: A review and integration of theoretical models and empirical evidence. *Journal of Pain, 7*(6), 377–390.

Spanier, G. (1976). Measuring dyadic adjustment: New scales for assessing the quality of marriage and similar dyads. *Journal of Marriage and the Family, 38*(1), 15–28.

Straus, M. A., Hamby, S. L., Boney-McCoy, S., & Sugarman, D. B. (1996). The revised Conflict Tactics Scales (CTS2): Development and preliminary psychometric data. *Journal of Family Issues, 18*(3), 283–316.

66   Psychoeducation

Joseph Walsh

Social workers may conduct family interventions with traditional family therapies or through psychoeducation. Family therapists, using systems perspectives that are germane to social work practice, practice from an assumption that all members of a family unit influence each other's functioning through reciprocal influence. Psychoeducation, on the other hand, emerged from a medical model of mental illness and assumes that interventions may be appropriate for focus on only one impaired family member. This chapter demonstrates how the two perspectives can be combined to resolve family challenges.

Psychoeducation describes a range of individual, family, and group interventions, usually led by human service professionals, that are focused on educating participants about a significant challenge in living and helping them develop adequate social support and coping skills in managing the challenge (Griffiths, 2006). Psychoeducation can be a standalone intervention, but it is often used as one method among several for helping clients and families with a particular problem in living. Other methods may include individual counseling, case management, and family therapy.

The distinctiveness of psychoeducation is its didactic/educational approach, with a nonhierarchical relationship between the client and practitioner and an acknowledgment of the family's expertise in the topic area. The major purpose of psychoeducation is to facilitate a sense of cognitive mastery in the client and family (Hayes & Gantt, 1992). To do so, psychoeducation relies on learning theory (how people acquire, make sense of, and use new information), cognitive psychology (challenging maladaptive thinking processes and suggesting alternative ways of thinking), dynamic psychology (emotional aspects of motivation, purpose, fears, hopes, and perceptions of the self), and developmental psychology (maturational processes and stages of illness and adjustment for both clients and family members) (Constas & Sternberg, 2006).

Family therapy can be defined as interventions in which all members of a nuclear or extended family, rather than any one member, are considered together as a psychosocial system in need of change (Nichols & Schwartz, 2007). Family therapists propose that psychological problems are best explained in terms of circular events that focus on the mutually influential and interpersonal contexts in which problems develop.

Some family therapies include only a portion of an identified family because of the members' differential availability or commitment to the process. In every case, the focus of family therapy is on interpersonal relationships rather than individual processes. Therapy is intended to alter the structure or nature of relationships among family members. Other chapters in this section describe and illustrate common approaches to family therapy, such as the Bowen, structural, and strategic approaches.

CONTRASTING PSYCHOEDUCATION AND FAMILY THERAPY

The philosophy of psychoeducation does not necessarily value family therapy as practiced from different therapeutic models. Some approaches may combine methods, but for the most part, psychoeducation focuses on the general "health" of a family as it works to understand and help one member with an illness or disorder. The illness is unrelated to major systems issues. Psychoeducational programs have become common for families that include a member with schizophrenia, bipolar disorder, and major depression, and they have proliferated among other types of client populations, as will be described later. Psychoeducation developed at a time when many professionals, working from a family systems perspective, tended to label parents as pathogenic in facilitating the development or persistence of schizophrenia in one member. More recently, research on family expressed emotion (EE), measured by ratings of family member hostility toward the ill relative, emotional overinvolvement with the relative, and frequency counts of critical and positive comments about the client (Chambless, Bryan, Aiken, Steketee, & Hooley, 1999), has been attacked as further blaming families for a member's psychosis (Mohr, Lafuze, & Mohr, 2000). As a research measure. EE provides a means for determining the kinds of family environments that put the person with schizophrenia at risk of or protected from symptom relapses.

Family therapists, though not blaming families for the creation or sustenance of a disorder in one member, assert that the presence of problem behavior in one member has effects on the entire system, and the system can be helped to make shared adjustments in the nature of their interactions so that the entire family can function with maximum effectiveness (Nichols & Schwartz, 2007). Psychoeducational programs are clearly not conducive to family therapy when they are provided only for the member who is experiencing the problem. Other programs that tend not to focus on family systems issues include those based on a medical illness of one member. Psychoeducation programs that seem more appropriate to systems interventions include those dedicated to clients with severe mental disorders, attention-deficit hyperactivity disorder, mood disorders, eating disorders, bipolar disorder, schizophrenia, or depression (Griffiths, 2006).

PROGRAM EXAMPLES

An example of nonsystemic psychoeducational family intervention is a multiple family group for persons with bipolar disorder (Brennan, 1995). This is a 14-week program, including six to nine clients and 15–30 family members that meets weekly for 2 hours and is led by two or three professionals, including social workers. The primarily didactic program attends to the two goals of educating members about bipolar disorder and its treatment and enabling members to achieve a measure of control over the symptoms. The program addresses the following topics in sequence:

- Introductions
- What is bipolar illness?
- Medications and other interventions
- Meetings with the patient and family alone to talk about issues related to family burden
- Recognizing and preventing relapse

- Understanding the mental health system
- Problem-solving presentations by guest professionals with role-play demonstrations (the "guests" are optional)
- Client and families are seen alone again, to formulate questions for a planned psychiatrist visit the following week (optional)
- Understanding suicide
- Presentation of a PBS documentary on bipolar disorder (such a formal presentation is also considered optional)
- Presentation on medications by a guest psychiatrist
- Review of intervention guidelines for clients and families (two sessions)
- Program evaluation and summary

The program evaluations indicate universal approval of the program, even though members admitted initial skepticism. Members report that the content on bipolar disorder was important to learning how to manage the course of the illness. They further valued the knowledge that they were not alone with the problem and were relieved to be able to talk about their challenges with supportive others. No long-term data on the impact of the program are available, however.

William McFarlane (2002) and his associates have developed a Multifamily Therapy Group Intervention (MFT) that includes family members and their impaired relatives. This intervention includes family therapy components consistent with family emotional systems theory, structural family theory, and strategic family theory because it attends to emotional, structural, and communications aspects of family life. The intervention targets each family's social networks, cognitive deficits, continuity of care, stress levels, stigma, quality of life, burden, and expressed emotion. The groups are long-term (1 or more years in length), which requires a major commitment from participants. The four major activities of the therapist include joining with the clients and families, conducting an educational workshop, preventing relapse though problem-solving processes, and promoting social and vocational rehabilitation within the group.

The intervention is further organized into four steps: self-triangulation, group interpretation, and interfamily management.

Self-triangulation. The leader is quite directive and becomes the central part of the triangle between family members. She initially focuses on individual families to link their specific problems with appropriate family management guidelines. The leader elicits family interaction patterns and takes the initiative in defining problems in specific, behavioral terms. She is directive in helping the family identify problems and problem-solving sequences. The leader facilitates systems interactions by blocking interruptions of one member by another and controls any extreme displays of affect that can impair problem exploration and resolution.

Group interpretation. The leader works to engage the families with one another, pointing out their similarities and unique contributions to the whole group process. With these commonalities she sets and takes responsibility for processing family interaction themes. Unlike the position taken by some family therapists, she also encourages intragroup social conversation, as this is seen as an important means of developing ties and enabling later discussion of substantive issues.

Cross-family linkages. The leader uses her relationship with family members to promote relationships across family boundaries. When one family introduces a problem for discussion, the leader turns to other families to make this problem relevant to their situations and then facilitates group discussion of solutions.

Interfamily management. The leader attempts to enhance and reinforce interfamily contacts and thereby promotes the process of natural support group development. In this process, families help each other develop appropriate roles, responsibilities, and consequences.

MFT outcome studies have shown that the programs are successful in expanding the client and family's social network (a variable that is associated with lower client relapse rates and fewer hospitalizations) (McFarlane, 2002). Clients and families become more open, cooperative, and appropriately involved across family boundaries. Harmful intrafamily interactions also diminish.

The Unity Multifamily Therapy Group (UMFTG) for treating eating disorders (Tantillo, 2006) is based on assumptions consistent with several family systems approaches. It is similar to structural family therapy because it assumes that negative relational patterns can exist in a family with a member who has an eating disorder. It is also consistent with strategic family therapy, because the eating disorder is presented as something that exists outside the family but creates a tension that obstructs normal development for all members. The group is run by a single therapist as a close-ended, eight-session group with up to six to eight

families in an outpatient setting. Group members are often from the client's nuclear family, family of origin, or partnership, but they may also be others who make up the client's social network.

In UMFTG, families (including the client member) examine the impact of their relationships on the eating disorder and the impact of the eating disorder on their relationships. The goals of the program are to help the family by:

• increasing the quality of family life by decreasing stress, stigma, burden, and disconnections incurred by the disorder;
• enhancing a sense of perceived mutuality with regard to the eating disorder symptoms; and
• promoting relapse prevention.

Within UMFTG, eating disorders are conceptualized as "diseases of disconnection" because family interactions serve to disconnect clients from their genuine internal experience and from other members, and foster the displacement of conflicts and unacceptable feelings onto their bodies. The disorder distorts cognition and convinces clients to stay connected to it as a means of avoiding feelings or resolving conflicts. The disorder also disconnects clients from family members through its ability to exhaust and disempower loved ones. Families worry that whatever they do or say may worsen symptoms. Clients usually feel guilt and shame about the burden of the disorder incurred by the family and often protect them from their authentic feelings and needs. The UMFTG works to identify the sources of disconnection within the family and helps participants learn how to embrace difference and work through disconnection toward authentic connection with the self and others.

This program approach is based on the fact that eating disorders occur predominantly in women and the subsequent role of disconnection in the etiology and maintenance of eating disorders. The gender-informed approach to treatment facilitates psychological change and growth through its family systems interventions. Similar to other multiple-family group approaches, UMFTG involves the development of a therapeutic social network in which there is a combined focus on strategies to improve communication, coping, problem solving, and managing the disorder. However, it moves beyond scientific problem solving toward an emphasis on promoting mutual relationships in recovery.

Outcome studies for the UMFTG have thus far been limited to the experiences of the author and her associates. They report that families are successful in honoring differences with a stronger commitment to one another, and that participants build new relationships in recovery that minimize the impact of the eating disorder. The author calls for randomized studies to further examine the effects of the program.

The importance of family systems theory in psychoeducation has become more evident as the modality is used across many countries and cultures (Sue, 2006). For example, in working with families from China, leaders need to be attuned to structural family characteristics in that culture, including power, roles, and authority. This has also been noted in working with Latino families, with special attention given to the cultural roles of family cohesion and spirituality. The nature of psychoeducation (information giving, personal disclosure, mutual problem solving) must be consistent with traditions in the participants' culture. The stage of the participant's experience with the problem needs to be considered with regard to their readiness and ability to accept certain types of information about a problem.

CONCLUSION

Perspectives on family intervention have evolved over the past 50 years. Systems approaches were most commonly used by family practitioners from the 1950s through the late 1970s. Psychoeducational interventions took ascendancy in the 1980s because of the prevailing biological perspectives on mental illness and emotional disorders. In the past 10 years, a more holistic awareness has evolved that family systems can experience extreme dysfunction as a result of one member's problematic behavioral or health situation. Psychoeducation has become integrated with family therapy toward the goals of developing and strengthening family structures and also changing patterns of emotional interaction.

WEB SITES

Bowen Center for the Study of the Family, Georgetown Family Center. The mission of the center is to promote the development of Bowen family systems theory into a science of human behavior and assist individuals and families in solving major problems through understanding and improving human relationships. The center carries out its mission through training programs, conferences, research, clinical services, and publications. http://www.thebowencenter .org/index.html.

Intensive structural therapy. This site, operated by Dr. Charles Fishman, informs professionals and families about intensive structural therapy, a psychotherapy model based on Minuchin's structural family theory (Minuchin, Lee, & Simon, 1996), which is effective in dealing with eating disorders and the treatment of troubled adolescents. http:// www.intensivestructuraltherapy.com.

PsychoEducational Counseling Services. This company offers a number of psychoeducational programs in small groups to assist individuals and their families understand and cope with emotional and behavioral challenges in relation to anger management, divorce, addiction, death and grief, family violence, parenting, interpersonal skills, behavioral health, building values, positive thinking, positive self-esteem, and teen relationships. http://www.psychoeducation .com.

Substance Abuse and Mental Health Services Administration, U.S. Department of Health and Human Services. *Evidence-Based Practices: Shaping Mental Health Services toward Recovery. Family Psychoeducation.* This site includes detailed research and organizational information for persons who are interested in developing psychoeducational programs for persons with mental illness and their families. http://mentalhealth.samhsa .gov/cmhs/communitysupport/toolkits/ family.

References

Brennan, J. W. (1995). A short-term psychoeducational multiple-family group for bipolar patients and their families. *Social Work, 40*(6), 737–743.

Chambless, D. L., Bryan, A. D., Aiken, L. S., Steketee, G., & Hooley, J. M. (1999). The structure of expressed emotion: A three-construct representation. *Psychological Assessment, 11*(1), 67–76.

Constas, M. A., & Sternberg, R. J. (2006). *Translating theory and research into educational practice: Developments in content domains, large-scale reform, and intellectual capacity.* Mahwah, NJ: Erlbaum.

Griffiths, C. A. (2006). The theories, mechanisms, benefits, and practical delivery of psychosocial educational interventions for people with mental health disorders. *International Journal of psychosocial Rehabilitation, 11*(1), 21–28.

Hayes, R., & Gantt, A. (1992). Patient psychoeducation: The therapeutic use of knowledge for the mentally ill. *Social Work in Health Care, 17*(1), 53–67.

McFarlane, W. R. (2002). *Multifamily groups in the treatment of severe psychiatric disorders.* New York: Guilford.

Minuchin, S., Lee, W., & Simon, G. M. (1996). *Mastering family therapy: Journeys of growth and transformation.* New York: Wiley.

Mohr, W. K., Lafuze, J. E., & Mohr, B. D. (2000). Opening caregiver minds: National Alliance for the Mentally Ill (NAMI) Provider Education Program. *Archives of Psychiatric Nursing, 14*(5), 235–243.

Nichols, M. P., & Schwartz, R. C. (2007). *The essentials of family therapy,* 3rd ed. Boston: Allyn & Bacon.

Sue, D. W. (2006). *Multicultural social work practice.* Hoboken, NJ: Wiley.

Tantillo, M. (2006). A relational approach to eating disorders multifamily therapy group: Moving from difference and disconnection to mutual connection. *Families, Systems, and Health, 24*(1), 82–102.

67 Guidelines for Couple Therapy with Survivors of Childhood Trauma

Kathryn Karusaitis Basham

Two decades ago, when the sociopolitical climate shifted in the United States, a strong influence of feminism reshaped the direction of psychotherapy modalities attuned to survivors of childhood trauma. Affirming the reality of physical, sexual, and emotional abuses of children provided strength to the voices of many adult trauma survivors who suffered the harsh effects of this ill treatment. Although most psychotherapy approaches with this population had previously focused on individual and group interventions, attention has subsequently been paid to developing couple and family approaches for adult survivors of childhood trauma. Psychodynamic theories, in particular object relations theory, provided a general conceptual frame for early couple therapy models (Scharff & Scharff, 1991). Efforts to help couples with improved communication and problem-solving skills were bolstered by a range of cognitive-behavioral couple therapy methods (Basham, 1999).

In more recent years, leading research in attachment theory set the stage for attachment-based models of couple therapy, specifically for trauma survivors. Johnson (2002) has assumed leadership in this arena with an empirically validated practice model that focuses on affect regulation, mentalization, and restoring or developing a secure attachment between partners. Contemporary couple therapy models rest on a firm yet flexible foundation of a synthesis of social and psychological theory models that is useful in grounding couple therapy practice (Basham, 1999, 2007; Basham & Miehls, 2004). Rather than relying exclusively and narrowly on only one theoretical stance, current models aim toward synthesizing multiple social and theoretical perspectives to respond to a wide range of presenting issues.

GUIDELINES FOR COUPLE THERAPY PRACTICE

The following general guidelines highlight central principles that undergird the basic scaffolding for couple therapy practice with trauma survivors.

Relationship and reconnection are central features because traumatic events often rupture an individual's experience of safety, secure attachment, and trust in other people. As a result, a clinician needs to gradually and thoughtfully engage a traumatized couple in a workable therapeutic alliance to reestablish more secure attachments.

Empowerment and locus of control help forge a workable therapeutic alliance with a single- or dual-trauma couple (i.e., one or both partners survived childhood abuse). Because traumatic events often overwhelm child, adolescent, and adult victims with a sense of powerlessness and helplessness, they need to regain a sense of mastery and internal locus of control in their day-to-day lives. As a result, a clinician needs to facilitate a traumatized couple's decision making and renewed experience of agency, without imposing disempowering management.

Resilience fortifies those individuals who have navigated the assaults of traumatic events during childhood, including physical, sexual, and/or emotional abuses. Constitutional "hardiness," social supports, proactive coping styles, and abundant socioeconomic resources serve as important protective factors in mitigating long-term negative mental health and health outcomes. To reduce negativity and undue pathologizing of human responses to horrific events, we need to focus on a couple's strengths and areas of resilience. On the other hand, we must not ignore the deep pain and suffering endured by some adult trauma survivors who wrestle with an acute stress response, post-traumatic stress syndrome (PTSD), complex PTSD, panic disorder, or depression. Because offending adults inflicted abusive treatment toward these clients when they were children, we should clearly not blame these trauma survivors for subsequently developing serious mental health problems.

The "victim–victimizer–bystander" relationship pattern is a central dynamic that occurs both on an intrapersonal and interpersonal basis for trauma survivors. Having experienced victimization in childhood, an adult trauma survivor approaches new relationships with anticipation that other individuals may demonstrate helpless, victim-like ways, an aggressive victimizing manner, or detachment. Many survivors of childhood trauma have also internalized this relationship template, and they view themselves and others within this framework. When this conflictual trauma scenario is unconscious, aspects of the internalized pattern are projected through the process of projective identification.

For example, a dual-trauma couple who presented with relational conflicts around yelling, intense arguments, and inadequate problem solving also struggled with daunting individual trauma-related issues. Jesse, age 48, and Maria, age 45, both survivors of childhood physical abuse, engaged regularly in the destructive forces of a victim–victimizer–bystander relationship scenario. Jesse behaved in a controlling and victimizing manner, alternating with an overly zealous rescuing role where he orchestrated what Maria ate and what clothing she wore. In response, Maria experienced herself as a victim of Jesse's aggression without seeing her own hostility expressed in her verbal harangues.

Synthesis, rather than an integration, of social and psychological theory models allows for pulling together discrete and at times contradictory theoretical constructs into a unified entity to inform our assessments and craft treatment plans. Integrative models often suffer from the untenable objective of aiming to merge diverse theoretical constructs that are often incompatible. Metaphor is helpful in describing this synthesis. If you visualize staring through a crystal at a distant object, you may see differences in the texture and color of the object depending on what part of the glass you are looking through. Similarly, the fabric of a theoretical synthesis shifts color and shape over time during the course of different phases of couple therapy.

In a similar fashion, a case-specific practice model changes the synthesis of theoretical models depending on the unique features and needs assessed for each couple. As a result, the assessment and therapy process sustains a dynamic and reflexive flow of theory models that advance to the foreground while other theoretical models recede.

Although a range of psychological and social theories are available in the knowledge base of a clinician at any given moment, data forthcoming from the couple related to their concerns determine which constellation of theoretical lenses advance to the foreground. Because a relationship base provides the foundation for a couple therapy practice model, we may turn to the lens of object relations or attachment theory to inform how early childhood experiences shaped ways of relating in adult life. Feminist and racial identity development theories help us understand the sociocultural and family context. Intergenerational family theory aims to explore patterns, worldviews, and rituals that may have perpetuated or thwarted the cross-generational transmission of trauma-related effects. A narrative family perspective may illuminate the multiple and unique meanings of a trauma narrative. In recent years, the groundswell of cutting-edge research in trauma and attachment theories further informs our understanding of the neurophysiological effects of traumatic exposure as well as disruptions to attachment. Holding the tension of multiple, often contradictory theoretical perspectives while seeing the broader view requires flexibility in perception, understanding, and action from the clinician.

Cultural responsiveness involves ongoing attunement to issues of diversity throughout the couple therapy. Race, ethnicity, religion, sexual identity, gender, age, disability, and socioeconomic status influence the ways a child experiences traumatic events and how he or she copes in the aftermath of trauma throughout his or her life. A culturally responsive stance moves beyond the accruing of specialized knowledge and skills inherent in a culturally competent practice. Instead, the clinician engages with the couple in a reflexive exchange of ideas that mutually influences their shared understanding of how these various diversity themes shape their presenting issues, their worldviews, and the clinical encounter.

Self-reflection presumes that a clinician explores, on an ongoing basis, the full range of emotional and cognitive responses in practice with traumatized couples. In a psychodynamic conceptual framework, countertransference phenomena involve a complex nexus of personal reactions, a more "objective" response based on projective identification processes, and cultural responses to clients.

Flexibility of the clinician supports flexibility in designing a couple therapy plan with a traumatized couple. Although certain manualized treatment protocols are useful in helping couples work on developing communication and conflict resolution skills, these clients also benefit from establishing a reparative therapeutic relationship that facilitates rebuilding of attachment and connec-

tions. Many traumatized couples comment on how disempowering and objectifying a "cookie-cutter" approach feels to them as they yearn to talk about their unique experiences in navigating painful emotional terrain.

PHASE-ORIENTED COUPLE THERAPY MODEL

A phase-oriented couple therapy model specifically attuned for survivors of childhood trauma relies on a thorough biopsychosocial assessment that reviews a full range of institutional/sociocultural, interactional, and individual/intrapersonal factors (Basham & Miehls, 2004). It includes three therapy phases: phase I, safety, stabilization, and establishment of a context for change; phase II, reflection on the trauma narrative; and phase III, consolidation of new perspectives, attitudes, and behaviors.

The clinician needs to consider cultural congruence, relational capacities, and the dimension of time while crafting a treatment plan with goals that guide choices of clinical interventions. In keeping with a metaphoric image of a therapeutic venture as a sailing journey, a thorough assessment serves both as a compass for directing the work and as a stabilizing anchor. In contrast to sequential, essential stage models, a phase-oriented couple therapy treatment model assumes that various issues may be revisited at different periods throughout the work. During the early sessions of couple therapy, the clinician needs to assess the strengths and vulnerabilities for the couple and each partner in these various institutional, interpersonal, and intrapersonal arenas. The following outline may be used as an assessment guide.

BIOPSYCHOSOCIAL ASSESSMENT

Institutional/Sociocultural

1. Clinician attitudes and responses (countertransference and secondary trauma)
2. Extended family and social support
3. Service delivery context (social policies, finances, political contexts)
4. Previous and current mental health treatment
5. Diversity (race, ethnicity, religion, socioeconomic status, disability, gender, sexual identity)

Interpersonal

1. Victim–victimizer–bystander relationship dynamic
2. Power and control struggles
3. Distancing and distrust
4. Boundary issues
5. Communication patterns

Individual/Intrapersonal

1. Individual cognitive, affective, and behavioral functioning
   - Areas of resilience and complex trauma symptomatology: fears (nightmares, flashbacks, intrusive thoughts); ego fragmentation (dissociation, identity distortion); affective changes and affect regulation/addictions and compulsive behaviors/antisocial behavior; reenactment; suicidality/somatization (insomnia, hypervigilance, numbness versus hyperarousal, startle response, bodily complaints)
2. Intrapersonal
   - Internalized victim–victimizer–bystander dynamic
   - Attachment style

Although as clinicians we continually assess a couple's presenting issues and their progress throughout treatment, a focus can typically be established after several sessions. Areas of strength and vulnerability in these different arenas of a couple's life set the stage for the crafting of a couple therapy plan. For example, Jesse and Maria benefited from an approach that addressed the multiplicity of their problems and helped coordinate their care. Not only was attention paid to interrupting the destructive force of their victim–victimizer–bystander relationship scenario, each partner set individual goals related to strengthening self-care and safety related to their trauma-related symptoms. For example, Jesse set a goal to reestablish his abstinence from alcohol, renew his connections with his sponsor, manage his unstable diabetes, and balance his erratic affect. Maria set goals to address her self-harming suicidal behavior and seek psychopharmological relief from depression. In phase I of couple therapy, we often see goals that improve relational patterns (i.e., minimizing the power conflicts and achieving greater mutuality, improving direct communication, and managing intense affect during conflict resolution).

In addition, self-differentiating goals are also addressed to promote healing and growth both interpersonally and intrapersonally.

Phase I tasks in couple therapy are relevant for all traumatized couples. These objectives aim to ensure (1) a basic sense of physical and psychosocial safety, (2) stabilization of trauma-related symptoms and management of crises, (3) strengthening of self-care and self-differentiation, and (4) establishing a context for growth through developing communication and conflict resolution skills among other new learning.

During this phase of work the following themes are explored in depth:

- Safety.
- Self-care (physical health and mental health; sleep, nutrition, and exercise; substance use and abuse; biobehavioral strategies for stress reduction and self soothing).
- Support systems (e.g., religion/spirituality, family, and community).
- Communication skills.
- Assessment of partnership status (continuation, static, dissolution, growth).

After a couple has accomplished all aspects of phase I goals, they are typically ready to move along to phase II tasks, which involve reflection on the trauma narrative. Given recent controversy in the mental health field related to the dubious benefit of uncovering traumatic memories, I assert that most couples benefit from a reflective sharing of their traumatic experiences, on a cognitive or titrated affective level, without full affective reexperiencing of early traumatic memories.

Work involves reflecting on the trauma-related effects in the present, recognizing and changing the victim–victimizer–bystander dynamic and healing relationships with extended family and family of origin in the here and now. Much grieving about losses of childhood innocence and actual losses of real relationships surface at this time. Traumategenic family environments often rob everyone of ordinary transitional rituals that both celebrate wonderful accomplishments as well as grieve losses through death or divorce. For example, after Maria and John completed phase I tasks, they shared their sorrow with exploring the roots of family violence. As they traced the histories of emigration and poverty for both sets of families of origin, each partner was able to understand the desperate ways of coping with adversity that was passed along intergenerationally. After many shared tears, they talked about interrupting their pattern of emotional violence and shifted away from victimizing each other and themselves. In summary, therapy tasks at this phase include:

- exploration of the meaning of traumatic experiences and building of empathy;
- exploration of the intergenerational legacy of the victim–victimizer–bystander dynamic;
- mourning losses and grieving; and
- Creation of new healing and transition rituals.

Phase III tasks focus primarily on a consolidation of the family of origin work started in phase II, along with additional strengthening of family and community relationships. Couples often experience less shame and isolation as they move more actively into discussions of their intimate sexual partnerships. Parenting often improves as partners listen better and learn to set firm yet benign boundaries. Finally, couples no longer define themselves through the identity of victim or survivor. Instead, they view themselves as thriving with their new approaches to life. The following themes are often addressed as couples consolidate their gains.

- Remediation of trauma-related symptomatology
- Increased empathy and resilience
- More equitable power relationships
- Enhanced sexual and intimate relationship
- Strengthened capacities for self-differentiation and secure attachment
- More effective parenting
- Coherence in complex social identities (e.g., race, ethnicity, gender, sexual identity, age, disability, religion, socioeconomic status)
- Shift in social consciousness

PREPARING FOR FUTURE WORK WITH COUPLES

Because couple therapy with survivors of childhood trauma challenges even the most resilient clinician, recognizing common therapeutic mis-

steps can ease some of difficulty. Clinicians might avoid (1) moving too quickly into a discussion of trauma narratives without completing phase I tasks of safety and self-care; (2) privileging uncovering of traumatic memories that often leads to overwhelming a couple; and (3) ignoring the inevitable countertransference enactments that provide excellent opportunities to understand the couple's inner struggles and facilitate their growth. In contrast, when clinicians recognize the benefit of a fluid, dynamic phase-oriented approach that titrates emotional intensity, they will be better able to manage their countertransference enactments and heal any relational therapeutic ruptures. Even so, it is challenging work. Couples therapy has its rewarding moments. When couples experience a sense of growth and accomplishment, they often describe a transformation of pain and loss into a renewed sense of hope in their relationship.

WEB SITES

American Association of Marriage and Family Therapy (AAMFT). http://www.aamft.org.
International Society for Traumatic Stress Studies (ISTSS). http://www.istss.org.
National Center for PTSD. http://www.ncptsd.va.gov.
Ottawa Couple and Family Therapy Institute. http://www.ocfi.ca.

References

Basham, K. (1999). A synthesis of theory in couple therapy: No longer an unlikely coupling. In T. Northcut & N. Heller (Eds.), *Enhancing psychodynamic therapy with cognitive-behavioral techniques* (pp. 135–157). Northvale, NJ: Aronson.

Basham, K. (2008). Homecoming as safe haven or the new front: Attachment and detachment in military couples. *Clinical Social Work Journal Special Issue, 36*(1), 83–96.

Basham, K., & Miehls, D. (2004). *Transforming the legacy: Couple therapy with survivors of childhood trauma.* New York: Columbia University Press.

Johnson, S. M. (2002). *Emotionally focused couple therapy with trauma survivors: Strengthening attachment bonds.* New York: Guilford.

Scharff, D., & Scharff, J. (1991). *Object relations couple therapy.* Northvale, NJ: Aronson.

68 Multifamily Groups with Obsessive-Compulsive Disorder

Barbara Van Noppen

This multifamily behavioral treatment (MFBT) for obsessive-compulsive disorder (OCD) is specifically designed to both educate and provide direct behavioral intervention to family members in collaboration with the patient. It mimics an individual behavioral treatment program; however, the role the family members (significant support persons) can play in therapy is examined using a group format that includes five to seven families with the OCD patient.

The major goals of the MFBT program are to:

1. Establish a therapeutic alliance with the patient and family, providing a supportive therapy context to facilitate behavioral and cognitive change.
2. Provide psychoeducation on OCD and exposure and response prevention.
3. Develop and implement a behavioral treatment plan for patients to improve their level of functioning, decrease the severity of OCD symptoms, and reduce family involvement in OCD behaviors.
4. Change the family patterns of communication to reduce hostile criticism, overinvolved attitudes, and excessive accommodation; improve family problem solving; and increase positive support. Families learn how to devise and implement family behavioral contracting independent of a therapist.
5. Promote feelings of empowerment, altruism, and empathy while decreasing feelings of isolation, stigma, shame, confusion, and impotence through the group process.
6. Teach OCD patients to use self-instruction through exposure and response-prevention homework assignments.
7. Improve long-term outcome by providing OCD patients and their relatives with education to enhance insight into OCD and with behavioral strategies to manage reoccurrence of symptoms. In addition, group modeling offers patients a normative context to refer to when challenging irrational thoughts and unreasonable behaviors long after the formal group ends.

Clinicians who use this guide are presumed to have experience in behavior therapy for OCD as well as a basic knowledge of and some experience in group and family treatment. For clinicians not familiar with behavior treatment for OCD, recommended reading includes Steketee (1999) and Hyman and Pedrick (1999). For a review of expressed emotion implications for OCD family treatment, see Steketee, Van Noppen, Lam, and Shapiro (1998). For a full description of the clinical application of MFBT, see Van Noppen (1992). It is also recommended that the practitioner be familiar with self-help books about OCD. Also, because this treatment guide is based on theoretical foundations used to develop psychoeducational groups for schizophrenia, it is recommended that the clinician be familiar with Anderson, Reiss, and Hogarty (1986) and McFarlane (1983).

This treatment guide is meant to instruct clinicians on the development and implementation of MFBT for OCD; it is not a substitute for clinical training and ongoing supervision. The MFBT differs considerably from traditional family therapy in that the clinician takes a very active role in providing information, facilitating problem solving, participating in direct and imaginal exposure, making suggestions directly to families, and assigning homework exercises. This may not be customary for dynamically trained clinicians. For MFBT to be effective, the clinician should be clear about and comfortable with the role described. This MFBT is written for adult patients (18 years and older); it can be adapted to be suitable for adolescents and children.

FEATURES AND PROCEDURES OF MFBT

Features

MFBT treats five to seven families (no more than 16 total participants is recommended), including patient and identified significant others who are in considerable daily contact with the patient; "family" can include homosexual as well as heterosexual couples, stepparents, second-degree family members, and so on.

Co-leaders are optimal; at least one of the leaders should have an advanced degree in social work, psychology, or certified counseling and experience in clinical work with individuals, families, and groups and proficiency in cognitive-behavioral therapy with experience in OCD populations.

The sessions are 2 hours long and typically meet in the late afternoon or early evening. The time-limited nature of this treatment program is used to motivate patients.

Procedure

Each patient and family has a pretreatment screening by phone with the therapist(s) to determine appropriateness for the group and readiness for treatment; following this, an intake session is scheduled.

At the intake session, pretreatment forms are completed, symptom severity and family response styles are determined, goals of the group and behavioral therapy principles are discussed, and pretreatment concerns and questions are addressed.

The weekly treatment sessions are:

1. Introductions, ground rules, education about OCD, reading of self-help material.
2. Definition of behavior therapy (exposure and response prevention), in vivo exposure and response prevention, plus homework and self-monitoring.
3. Family responses to OCD and family guidelines; neurobiology of OCD and medications.
4. Behavioral contracting among family members and communication skills training, homework discussion with family group feedback, and problem solving.
5–11. Continued exposure and response prevention (ERP) and family behavioral contracting in vivo and homework assignments.
12. Final weekly treatment session, termination issues, and planning for monthly booster sessions.

Maintenance of gains and relapse prevention are supported in six monthly sessions.

TREATMENT PROCEDURES

Following is a manual for an 18-session MFBT and one 90-minute intake gathering session conducted with each OCD patient and family members.

Information Gathering and Pregroup Screening (90 minutes)

1. Take a general biopsychosocial history and collect information about OC symptoms for treatment planning (20 minutes). Use the Yale-Brown Obsessive-Compulsive Checklist and YBOCS to indicate primary obsessions and major compulsions and symptom severity. Scales can be found in most professional books on OCD diagnosis and treatment (see References).
2. Discuss onset of OCD and efforts to cope (10 minutes).
3. Collect detailed information about OC symptoms; develop hierarchy (15 minutes). Begin exposure hierarchy, as in individual behavior therapy, by collecting information about triggers of obsession and compulsions, situations and objects avoided, intrusive thoughts, and ritualistic patterns of behavior:
4. Teach the patient and family how to rate anxiety according to the subjective units of distress scale (SUDS) and estimate at which treatment session the trigger will be introduced. Record all information on an exposure hierarchy form. The more detailed, the better. See hierarchies in Table 68.1 and use references for more examples. These are two sample hierarchies for a patient who has

TABLE 68.1

Situation	Discomfort (1–100)	Treatment Session
Hierarchy 1: Fears of contamination—cancer from brother and cigarettes		
Holding unopened cigarette pack	45	1
Touching mug brother used	50	1
Touching doorknobs at home	55	2
Holding opened cigarette pack	55	2
Holding "clean" ashtray	60	3
Holding clothes worn by brother	70	4
Touching "dirty" clothes (basement)	85	5
Touching cigarette filter	90	6
Stepping barefoot on a cigarette	95	7
Hierarchy 2: Fear of contamination—cancer from "chemical" contact		
Touching microwaved food	30	1
Pumping gasoline	35	1
Touching sand in sandbox	35	1
Touching artificial sweetener	40	2
Holding batteries	40	2
Touching sand at beach	65	5
Eating food items "scanned" at checkout	75	6
Drinking diet soda	85	7
Eating chicken	100	8

fears of contracting cancer from items associated with a sibling, contact with cigarettes, "chemicals," and certain food.

5. Describe ERP (10 minutes). Give a treatment rationale including the following points:
   - *Exposure* refers to gradual and direct confrontation of situations that provoke obsessive fears. It is designed to break the association between the sensations of anxiety and the objects, situations, or thoughts that produce it through the gradual reduction or habituation of fear. Use the patient's own experiences as examples (e.g., "every time you touch anything associated with body fluids you feel anxious, distressed, or contaminated").
   - *Response prevention* is designed to break the association between ritualistic behavior and the reduction of anxiety or distress. Because compulsions (specify them) lead to less distress temporarily, they are reinforced. Treatment breaks the automatic bond between the feelings of discomfort/anxiety (specify the obsession) and rituals.

6. Description of MFBT program and review of overall goals (5 minutes).
7. Determine the degree of family accommodation and response styles (20 minutes). Administer the family accommodation scale (FAS; Calvocoressi et al., 1999).
8. Homework assignment (5 minutes). Discuss the first homework assignment to read Steketee and White (1990), chapters 1 through 4. Give suggested reading list.
9. Wrap up (5 minutes). Address concern and questions.

Session 1: Building Cohesion and Trust: "We're Not Alone!" Psychoeducational Phase: "What Is OCD?" (2 hours)

1. Welcome (5 minutes). The group leaders introduce themselves and ask each member to introduce him- or herself. Then the group leaders outline the agenda for all 12 sessions, giving dates and times for each.
2. Administrative issues (15 minutes). Review scheduling of sessions, cancellation policy,

group guidelines about confidentiality, and therapist availability.

3. Goals (10 minutes). Each group member is asked to respond to the question, "What do you hope to get out of this group?" Encourage participants to be specific about behavioral change.

4. Definition of OCD (1 hour). Review chapters 1 to 4 in Steketee and White (1990), biological and learned bases of OCD. Distribute YBOCS symptom checklist (self-rated version). Go over each example provided with group members volunteering to read. Encourage disclosure by asking for examples from patients' or family members' experiences. Introduce concepts of exposure and response prevention.

5. Homework (30 minutes). Go-round: each patient chooses a behavioral task challenge to practice daily for homework. Distribute self-rating exposure homework form and explain how to use. If there is time in the session, ask for a patient to volunteer to demonstrate ERP and rate SUD as a group. The homework for every patient for the first week is to practice his or her chosen ERP task and complete homework form. Read Steketee and White (1990) chapters 5 to 10.

Session 2: Psychoeducational Phase: "How Do You Treat OCD?"

1. Check-in (10 minutes). Review the previous group session. The check-in should begin each group.

2. Go-round (10 minutes). Each patient reports on homework completed during the week, including SUDs. If the homework is inadequately completed or reported, discuss problems identified by the patient and family. Encourage group feedback and troubleshoot to define obstacles.

3. Overview of behavior therapy (30 minutes). Define in vivo and imaginal exposure and give examples. A brief description of exposure in vivo may be: "This entails actual direct contact with an object or situation that evokes obsessions. For example, a person afraid of stabbing loved ones might stand in the kitchen before meal times holding knives or scissors near others." A brief description of imaginal exposure may be: "Sometimes people cannot actually

put themselves into their feared situation, such as stabbing one's child. A mental visualization of this situation in detail will evoke fears of harming one's child that will offer exposure practice. Writing a scripted imagery to be read daily, or put onto a tape and listened to, is a way of going about this." Provide a brief description of imaginal exposure for those patients for whom it is relevant (patients whose anxiety focuses on feared consequences that are not fully triggered by in vivo exposure or for whom in vivo exposure is difficult to execute. One possibility is a mental visualization of forgetting to check the stove and coming home to fire engines and a burning house. Another possibility is making a loop tape of a brief description or phrase (i.e., "I will kill my child") or a few words ("kill," "child-killer") that are avoided, dreaded, or evoke aggressive obsessions.

Include a few statements about tolerating initial high anxiety that will decrease over time with repeated, systematic use of exposure and response prevention (habituation). Stress that response prevention must accompany exposure, whether imagined or in vivo. Following are instructions and examples of the sequences of in vivo and imaginal exposure for a patient with contamination fears, and response prevention.

• *In vivo exposure.* The patient, Steve, felt contaminated by feces, urine, sweat, and contact with others. He feared contracting a debilitating disease. The following hierarchy was constructed for Steve: feces, 100 SUDs; urine, 90 SUDs; toilet seats in public bathrooms, 80 SUDs; sweat, 75 SUDs; newspapers, 60 SUDs; doorknobs, 50 SUDs. During in vivo exposure treatment, the following sequence was pursued.

Session 1—Steve walked with the therapist through the building touching doorknobs, especially those of the public restrooms, holding each for several minutes.

Session 2—Steve held newspapers left behind by people in the waiting room.

Session 3—Steve held newspapers and doorknobs. Contact with sweat was introduced by having him place one hand under his arm and the other in his shoe.

Session 4—Exposure began with newspapers and sweat. Toilet seats were added by having the patient sit next to the toilet and place his hands on the seat.

Session 5—Exposure began with contact with sweat and toilet seats. Urine was then introduced by having Steve hold a paper towel dampened in his own urine.

Session 6—Exposure included urine, toilet seats, and sweat with the addition of a piece of toilet paper lightly soiled with his own fecal material.

Sessions 7–12—Daily exposure to feces, urine, and sweat. Homework focused on the objects used during that day's treatment session. Periodic contact with lesser contaminants was continued throughout.

- *Imaginal exposure.* First conduct in the present tense with the therapist describing images in second person ("you see" or "you are going"). When asked what he or she feels or sees or thinks in the image, the patient should respond in the first person ("I'm sitting on _____"). Imaginal scenes should be followed by in vivo exposure to objects or situations related to that scene and provoke similar levels of discomfort. The patient creates a script of a similar scene and records it to listen to for imaginal exposure homework.
- *Response prevention.* Remind participants of the specific instructions for response prevention on the first day of treatment, as well as periodically during treatment. Give a copy of the rules to each patient and his or her family, modeling the instructions after this example for washers.
  Washers: During the response prevention period, patients are not permitted to use water on their body—that is, no hand washing, no rinsing, no wet towels, washcloths, wet wipes, or antibacterial gels except as allowed by the therapist. The use of creams and other toiletry articles (bath powder, deodorant, etc.) is permitted except where use of these items reduces contamination. Water can be drunk or used to brush teeth, with care not to get it on "contaminated" body parts. Supervised showers are permitted every day for target

time, including hair washing. Ritualistic washing of specific areas of the body (e.g., genitals, hair) is prohibited. Exceptions may be made for unusual circumstances—for example, medical conditions necessitating cleansing, food preparation after bathroom use. In these cases, patients may wash briefly (20–30 seconds) and then recontaminate as soon as possible. If prevention of washing forces contamination to items very high on the hierarchy, patients may wash briefly and immediately recontaminate with the items currently being exposed in treatment.

At home, relatives are instructed to be available to the patient should she or he have difficulty controlling a strong urge to wash. If the patient reports such concerns, family members are asked to remain with the patient until the urge decreases to a manageable level. Family members may attempt to stop such violations through firm verbal insistence, but no physical force should be used, and arguments should be avoided. Faucets can be turned off by relatives if the patient gives prior consent to such a plan. Showers can be timed by family, with no direct observation of showering behavior.

- *Review hierarchy* forms as a group and add any additional triggers for exposure. Arrange all designated items hierarchically according to anxiety evoked. The most disturbing item should be presented by session 9 or three-fourths of the way through treatment. Final sessions should include repetitions of earlier ones with minor variations, focusing on those situations that provoke the most discomfort.

4. Homework go-round. ERP (60 minutes). Each patient chooses a behavioral homework task. Use feedback and support from group members to develop the optimal homework assignment. As each patient selects his or her homework, the group leader should try to translate the task in to a form that can be rehearsed in the group—the therapists, patients, and family members who are willing participate in the ERP in vivo while others observe. For example,

- For *harming obsessions* with reassurance seeking and checking, the group leader and patients dampen their hands or touch light switches; other group members follow by touching the same switch. No reassurance seeking or checking is allowed. Level of anxiety is discussed and rated. This is repeated several times to model the homework assignment and to begin the process of habituation. Another exposure challenge is to pass a pair of scissors around the group, point first.
- For *contamination obsessions* with washing and/or passive avoidance, fear of being responsible for something bad happening and checking, hoarding, ordering and arranging, and other obsessions and compulsions, devise in vivo ERP accordingly.

5. Family role (10 minutes). Instruct family members to offer support and encouragement for patient's completion of ERP homework. No major changes to be made without prior negotiation.

Session 3: Psychoeducation: Family Responses to OCD and Family Guidelines: "What Should We Do?"

1. Check-in (10 minutes).
2. Go-round (10 minutes).
3. Psychoeducational lecture on neurobiology of OCD (15 minutes). A videotaped discussion on the neurobiological underpinnings of OCD is viewed in the group if no psychiatrist is able to be present.
4. ERP (60 minutes). In the group, each patient selects exposure items with SUDs level of approximately 50 to 60; continue with in vivo ERP.
5. Family guidelines (15 minutes). Distribute *Learning to Live with OCD* (Van Noppen, Pato, & Rasmussen, 1997) and read as a group. Identify and label family response styles as they emerge in discussion (accommodating, antagonistic, split, oscillating). Encourage discussion.
6. Homework (10 minutes). Each patient reassesses behavioral homework task with family guidelines in mind and adds another challenge.

Session 4: Intensive Treatment Phase: Managing the Symptoms: "Out with Doubt!"

1. Check-in and go-round (20 minutes). Proceed as previously described.
2. Explain family behavioral contracting (20 minutes).
   - One at a time, each family identifies problem areas. How does OCD impose on others? Do family members participate in rituals? Is there a lot of hostile criticism directed toward the patient by family? Do family members take over the patient's tasks and responsibilities? The problems need to be defined in clear, specific behavioral terms.
   - Guide the family to focus on one problem area at a time and define it.
   - Using feedback from the group, family members explore behavioral response options and the possible consequences of each.
   - With ERP in mind, family members select the best response options.
   - The leaders facilitate a negotiation process between family members.
   - When possible, the family rehearses the behavioral contract, during the treatment session in vivo, thereby beginning to implement a new solution.
   - The outcome of the contract is evaluated as a group, adding suggestions based on observations of the family's ability to carry out the plan.
   - If necessary, the family negotiates modifications to the contract. All exposure homework and outcomes of contracts are recorded for homework.

   As described, the group leaders actively guide one family at a time through the process of negotiating a behavioral contract. The leaders suggest the use of ERP in vivo whenever applicable. Begin family behavioral contracting with a clear, somewhat simple situation to provide a rudimentary experience. Get to each family before adjourning and remind families to renegotiate if they find that the contract is too stringent.
3. Homework (10 minutes). Each patient selects individual exposure homework and each family commits to behavioral contact

homework, tracked on appropriate self-monitoring forms.

Session 5: Behavioral Family Treatment Phase: "We Can Make a Difference!"

1. Check-in and go-round (30 minutes).
2. Behavioral contracting (80 minutes). Each family practices behavioral contracting in vivo. ERP with therapist and participant modeling should be used extensively. Each family is allotted 10 to 15 minutes.
3. Homework (10 minutes). Patients and relatives record individual ERP homework and family contracts.

Sessions 6–11: "Practice! Practice! Practice!" and "We Can Take Charge!"

The group leaders follow the same format already described for the remaining weekly sessions. Progressively, patients are increasingly responsible for devising the in vivo ERP task challenges and family contracts, an expectation cultivated by the leaders.

Session 12: Exposure, Contracting, and Termination: "We Have Tools to Do This on Our Own!" (Last Weekly Multifamily Session)

1. Check-in (30 minutes).
2. Go-round (45 minutes). Each family modifies or adds to existing contracts. Group members devise in vivo ERP tasks. Each family presents the ERP plan for the next month.
3. Dealing with termination (25 minutes). Remind the group of the self-instructional nature of behavioral treatment. Review the steps that were taught: create hierarchy, assess distress levels, select exposure situation (either internal or external trigger), devise ERP challenge, record this on a form, and practice it repeatedly for long periods of time until anxiety decreases.
   • Initial anxiety will increase while using ERP.
   • Habituation takes time and practice.
   • Long-term gains are made through perseverance and commitment to treatment.
   • Encourage patients to refer to self-help workbooks.

• Leaders are available to patients between monthly sessions.
4. Complete clinician-rated YBOCS in the group (15 minutes).
5. Discuss monthly check-in sessions (5 minutes). Schedule dates and describe this as a trial period to develop confidence for independent individual ERP and family behavioral contracting.

Sessions 13–18: Monthly Check-In Sessions: "We Have the Tools to Beat OCD" (2 Hours)

The main purpose of these six sessions is to assist patients and their families in the transition from the leader-directed behavioral treatment to the self-instruction form of therapy. Check-in sessions ensure maintenance of treatment gains in the vulnerable time period directly following the weekly 12 sessions. They also provide motivation.

Each session begins in typical fashion with the check-in and go-round, but no in vivo exposure takes place. Patients and family members report on homework tasks, contracts, successes, pitfalls, and general life events that may be influencing the OCD or interfering with behavioral therapy. Leaders are more passive, facilitating the group process and answering questions that require clinical clarification. Clinician-rated YBOCS are collected at each session for pre- and posttreatment comparisons.

At the last monthly session, issues related to treatment termination are acknowledged, and referrals are made for continued behavior therapy or medication if necessary. The FAS for each family in the group is completed. A posttreatment YBOCS under 16 is optimal.

CONCLUSION

MFBT offers several advantages over standard individual behavioral treatment. It is cost-effective by allowing for the simultaneous treatment of five to seven patients and their family members with one or two therapists in 2 hours a week, compared to the same six or seven families treated individually requiring 10 to 14 hours of therapist time per week. This is a savings of up to 12 hours of therapist time per week.

As typically practiced, individual behavioral treatment offers little structured psychoeducation, support, or guidance for the family who has to cope with the symptoms and demands imposed by OCD. The MFBT can be modified to conduct family behavioral treatment with one patient and family members. In this age of managed care and short-term treatments, it makes sense to mobilize natural supports like family systems. Once families understand OCD symptoms and are taught behavioral strategies, they can participate effectively in ERP with the OCD patient. This treatment offers a marked decrease in both cost for treatment and therapist time, as well as the possibility of improving long-term outcome.

WEB SITES

Anxiety Disorders Association of America. http://www.adaa.org.

Medicine Plus (National Library of Medicine and National Institure of Health – OCD. http://www.nlm.nih.gov/medlineplus/obsessivecompulsivedisorder.html.

National Institute of Mental Health Obsessive-Compulsive Disorder. http://www.nimh.nih.gov/health/topics/obsessive-compulsive-disorder-ocd/index.html.

Obsessive Compulsive Foundation (OCF). http://www.ocfoundation.org.

References

Anderson, C., Reiss, D., & Hogarty, G. (1986). *Schizophrenia and the family*. New York: Guilford.

Calvocoressi, L., Mazure, C., Kasl, S., Skolnick, J., Fisk, D., Vegso, S., et al. (1999). Family accommodation of obsessive-compulsive symptoms: Instrument development and assessment of family behavior. *Journal of Nervous and Mental Disease*, 187(10), 636–642.

Hyman, B., & Pedrick, C. (1999). *The OCD workbook*. Oakland, CA: New Harbinger.

McFarlane, W. R. (1983). *Family therapy in schizophrenia*. New York: Guilford.

Steketee, G. (1999). *Overcoming OCD: A behavioral and cognitive protocol for the treatment of OCD*. Oakland, CA: New Harbinger.

Steketee, G., Van Noppen, B., Lam, J., & Shapiro, L. (1998). Expressed emotion in families and the treatment of OCD. *In Session: Psychotherapy in Practice*, 4(3), 73–91.

Steketee, G., & White, K. (1990). *When once is not enough*. Oakland, CA: New Harbinger.

Van Noppen, B. (1992). Multifamily behavioral treatment (MFBT) for OCD. *Crisis Intervention*, 5(1–2), 3–24.

Van Noppen, B., Pato, M., & Rasmussen, S. (1997). *Learning to live with OCD*. New Haven, CT: Obsessive Compulsive Foundation.

69 Working with Families of Persons with Severe Mental Illness

Tina Bogart Marshall & Phyllis Solomon

Practice guidelines for the treatment of severe mental illness recommend involving and engaging families in a collaborative treatment process (American Psychiatric Association [APA], 2006). These recommendations are based on substantial evidence that partnering with families improves client outcomes (Dixon et al., 2001).

WHY COLLABORATE WITH FAMILIES?

Due to the chronic nature of severe mental illnesses, community supports and support networks are integral components in the treatment process. Support networks are crucial for persons with severe mental illness (consumers), because the symptoms of mental illness include confusion, isolation, withdrawal, and other cognitive deficits that often make it difficult for consumers to recognize when they are becoming ill and to reach out for help (Chen & Greenberg, 2004).

It is often presumed that the hardship brought by mental illness leaves many individuals with little or no family contact. For this reason, families are frequently overlooked as potential members of the consumers' support network. However, research indicates that more than 60 percent of consumers live with their families (National Institute of Mental Health [NIMH], 1991), and 77 percent or more have some ongoing contact with family members (Lehman & Steinwachs, 1998). Moreover, families are often the first to recognize warning signs and symptoms of relapse (Herz, 1985).

Over the past 30 years, numerous studies have found that family psychoeducation interventions reduce relapse and rehospitalization for persons with severe mental illness and improved family well-being (McFarlane et al., 2003). Although these interventions differ in their format, duration, and locus of service delivery, they all use a strengths-based approach, view families as resilient, therapeutic agents, and provide

- information about mental illness,
- emotional support,
- problem-solving skills, and
- crisis intervention, based on the notion of collaborating with family members in the treatment of their ill relative.

Furthermore, family psychoeducation is based on the notion of collaborating with family members in the treatment of their ill relative (Dixon et al., 2001; McFarlane et al., 2003).

Partnering with families not only is associated with improved client and family outcomes but also holds benefits for social workers. Social workers gain a better understanding of the client's behavior, symptoms, and level of coping with their illness (Solomon et al., 2002). By working collaboratively with consumers and families, social workers can develop the most effective treatment plan. The following case study demonstrates how social workers can collaborate with clients and their family members to actively pursue clients' personal recovery goals.

CASE STUDY

Annie is a 39-year-old woman with schizophrenia. The symptoms of her illness respond fairly well to medication. Although she has been able to live alone in an apartment for the past 12 years, Annie receives significant support from community providers. She lives an isolated life. Outside of her contact with the mental health center, she has few friends or hobbies.

The social worker at the mental health center talks with Annie about building a social support network. She lets Annie know that many people who receive services at the mental health center find it very helpful to involve a family member or close friend in their mental health treatment. She asks Annie if there is someone she would like to invite to their next session.

Annie tells her that she has a sister who visits regularly. Together, they call the sister and invite her to the next session. During the session, the social worker tells the sister that Annie is interested in building up a circle of supportive family and friends and would like her help. They ask the sister if she is willing to participate in Annie's sessions over the next few weeks, and they can discuss together the types of interests that Annie has had in the past and activities that she may want to get involved with again. Annie's sister agrees.

Over the next 3 weeks, the social worker meets with Annie and her sister. She learns that Annie's sister was very involved with the National Alliance on Mental Illness (NAMI) when Annie first became ill and has a good understanding of her illness. Annie wishes that her brother understood her better and that she could have more contact with him. Annie's sister offers to speak with him and encourage him to attend NAMI support groups with her. The social worker also discovers from the sister that Annie is very artistic. In her early twenties, she won an award for a sketch that she drew. The sister agrees to help Annie find an art class in the community. Annie is hesitant about going by herself, and her sister agrees to take her there.

Six months later, Annie is taking a community art class. She has met several new friends and considers participating in an art exhibition. Her brother calls her regularly and occasionally takes her out to lunch. Annie remains in close contact with her sister, who occasionally joins her for a session.

COMPETENCIES NEEDED TO COLLABORATE WITH FAMILIES

Competencies for working with families of people with severe mental illness have been developed by an expert panel of practitioners, families, consumers and researchers (Coursey, Curtis, & Marsh, 2000). Competencies include:

- understanding the family experience,
- engaging the family in treatment and rehabilitation,
- addressing the needs of families, and

- being knowledgeable about appropriate community resources for meeting family needs.

The expert panel found that for social workers to be responsive to families does not necessarily mean that formal training in a specific intervention is needed. Social workers who are unable to implement a formalized intervention may still participate in some activities to address family needs. Specific attitudes, knowledge, and skills that are needed for social workers to collaborate with families of persons with severe mental illness are outlined next (Mannion, 2000).

Attitudes

1. *Self-examination.* Attitudes in working with families are shaped by mental health providers' training and learning experiences. It is critical for social workers to examine their own feelings and attitudes regarding working with families.
2. *Examination of organizational climate.* Social workers should assess the overall attitude expressed within their agency toward working with families. Negative attitudes toward families may be expressed overtly by administrators, supervisors, or direct service providers and lead to interdisciplinary conflict in treatment teams. Social workers may also perceive a negative organizational climate through a lack of policies and procedures for working with families, a lack of training, or disincentives, such as inappropriate reimbursement mechanisms.

Knowledge

1. *Awareness of the family experience.* Social workers need to understand the normal emotional cycles that families experience as they cope and adapt to having a family member with mental illness.
2. *Knowledge of mental illness.* It is important for social workers to not only accumulate a breadth of knowledge about mental illness but also be able to convey basic knowledge to families in a way that they can comprehend and retain. Social workers should be aware that knowledge is a coping aid for families. Social workers, therefore, need to be knowledgeable about the free educational resources that are available to families, such as those produced by NAMI, Mental Health

America, and the National Alliance for Research on Schizophrenia and Depression, so that social workers can make appropriate referrals.

3. *Knowledge of family interventions.* Social workers should be aware of the benefits of family interventions for providers, consumers, and families. They should be knowledgeable about distinctions between different types of family interventions, such as psychoeducation models, family education, family support, and family consultation. Social workers should also know of interventions offered in their geographical area.

4. *Knowledge of coping and illness management skills.* Social workers should be aware of basic do's and don'ts when addressing family members questions and offering advice. Knowledge of some basic coping and illness management strategies is essential.

5. *Knowledge of the mental health system.* It is critical for social workers to understand not only the services within their own agency but also specific information about services and resources throughout the mental health system. Any printed information that may be shared is helpful to families. Contact your state mental health department or state or local affiliate of NAMI for access to this type of information.

6. *Cultural competency.* Social workers need knowledge of differences in the attribution of mental illness and issues around stigma specific to different cultural/ethnic groups. It is important for social workers to be aware of the acceptability and effectiveness of treatment and services for families from different backgrounds (Solomon, 1998). Social workers should be aware of culturally/ethnically diverse community resources and support systems.

Skills

1. *Discussing family involvement with clients.* Social workers should acquire skills for introducing clients to the benefits of collaboration, working with clients to designate a family member, and discussing with clients their choices in the type of involvement that the family member may have in the treatment process. Social workers should be skilled in eliciting input from clients on an ongoing basis to maintain trust within the therapeutic relationship. Social workers also need to acquire the skills necessary to enhance the collaborative nature of family involvement.

2. *Empathy and support.* It is important for social workers to acknowledge the strengths of consumers and families. In response to coping with their relatives' mental illness and the associated stigma, many families isolate themselves and may question their emotional responses. Identifying the feelings that family members experience as common and natural is an essential component of developing a collaborative relationship with families. Skills in supporting and empathizing with families allow social workers to listen to families' experiences and share their understanding of the normal cycle of coping and adaptation.

3. *Mediation and advocacy.* Skills in mediation allow social workers to assist families with unresolved conflict that they may be experiencing at home or within the mental health system. Social workers may use advocacy skills to intervene on behalf of families or improve the organizational climate within the agency. For example, social workers who encounter confidentiality policies as a barrier to sharing information with families may consider adapting model policies and consent procedures developed by the authors (Marshall & Solomon, 2003).

4. *Teaching and training.* Skills in transferring knowledge about mental illness, mental health treatment, coping, and illness management skills are critical to the work of social workers with families. It is crucial that the information offered is relevant and useful. It is also important that the material is conveyed in a way that maximizes comprehension and retention of the essential points.

5. *Problem solving.* Social workers should acquire skills that assist families in defining problems, generating possible solutions, and deciding on appropriate strategies. Social workers may use problem-solving skills to assist families in defining and addressing a specific issue as it arises. Social workers may also offer to train families to use problem-solving techniques on their own.

6. *Referral.* Referring families to appropriate community resources is a skill that can complement what social workers offer to families to assist them in meeting their needs.

Successful referrals require a high degree of familiarity with the resource. Family members should be prepared as to what they should expect, how to best access the resource, and how the resource will address their specific need(s).

FUTURE

The best practice recommendations for partnering with families are based on research evidence that family psychoeducation improves client outcomes. Although the research indicates that no one specific intervention is more effective than another, the core components of effective interventions are based on the provider–consumer–family collaboration. To achieve these outcomes, social workers must improve their skills for introducing the concept of collaboration to clients and increase their competencies for working with families.

The most recent research concludes that one intervention will not meet the needs of all family members and consumers. It is important to offer a variety of interventions and tailor services to consumers and families to their individual needs (Drapalski et al., in press). Advances over the next 5 to 10 years may allow practitioners to quickly assess the needs of consumers and family members and better target the types of interventions that will be most effective for them.

WEB SITES

National Alliance on Mental Illness (NAMI). http://www.nami.org.

Mental Health America (MHA). http://www.nmha.org.

National Alliance for Research on Schizophrenia and Depression (NARSAD). http://www.narsad.org.

References

American Psychiatric Association. (2006). *Practice guidelines for the treatment of psychiatric disorders. Compendium 2006.* Arlington, VA: APA.

Chen, F., & Greenberg, J. (2004). A positive aspect of caregiving: The influence of social support on caregiving gains for family members of relatives with schizophrenia. *Community Mental Health Journal, 40,* 423–435.

Coursey, R., Curtis, L., & Marsh, D. (2000). Competencies for direct service staff members who work with adults with severe mental illness: Specific knowledge, activities, skills, bibliography. *Psychiatric Rehabilitation Journal, 23,* 8–92.

Dixon, L., McFarlane, W., Lefley, H., et al. (2001). Evidence-based practices for services to families of people with psychiatric disabilities. *Psychiatric Services, 52*(7), 903–910.

Drapalski, A., Marshall, T., Seybolt, D., et al. (In press). The unmet needs of families of adults with mental illness and preferences regarding family services. *Psychiatric Services.*

Herz, M. (1985). Prodromal symptoms and prevention of relapse in schizophrenia. *Journal of Clinical Psychiatry, 46,* 22–25.

Lehman, A., & Steinwachs, D. (1998). Patterns of usual care for schizophrenia: initial results from the schizophrenia patient outcomes research team (PORT) client survey. *Schizophrenia Bulletin, 24*(1), 11–32.

Mannion, E. (2000). *Training manual for the implementation of family education in the adult mental health system of Berks County, PA.* Philadelphia: University of Pennsylvania Center for Mental Health Policy and Services Research.

Marshall, T., & Solomon, P. (2003). Professionals' responsibilities in releasing information to families of adults with mental illness. *Psychiatric Services, 54*(12), 1622–1628.

McFarlane, W., Dixon, L., Lukens, E., et al. (2003). Family psychoeducation and schizophrenia: a review of the literature. *Journal of Marital and Family Therapy, 29*(2), 223–245.

National Institute of Mental Health. (1991). *Caring for people with severe mental disorders: A national plan of research to improve services.* Washington DC: NIMH.

Solomon, P. (1998). The cultural context of interventions for family members with a seriously mentally ill relative. In H.P . Lefley (Ed.), *Families coping with mental illness: The cultural context* (pp. 5–16). San Francisco: Jossey-Bass.

Solomon, P., Marshall, T., Mannion, E., et al. (2002). Social workers as consumer and family consultants. In K. Bentley (Ed.), *Social work practice in mental health* (pp. 230–253). Pacific Grove, CA: Brooks/Cole.

PART VII

Developing and Implementing Treatment Plans with Specific Groups and Disorders

70

Guidelines for Establishing Effective Treatment Goals and Treatment Plans with Axis I Disorders

Sample Treatment Plan for Generalized Anxiety Disorder

Vikki L. Vandiver & Kevin Corcoran

We shouldn't deny the verdict (diagnosis/assessment) but defy the sentence (prognosis/outcome).
—Norman Cousins, *Head First: The Biology of Hope*

This chapter reviews the principles and procedures of goal setting and treatment planning for axis I disorders. Axis I of the *Diagnostic and Statistical Manual, DSM-IV-TR* edition (American Psychiatric Association, 2000), is for reporting clinical disorders, excluding the personality disorders and mental retardation. This means axis I includes 44 diagnoses in 16 categories, a number of medical-psychological conditions, and other conditions that might be the focus of clinical attention. Regardless of the breadth or differences in disorders, the establishment of treatment goals and the development of a treatment plan are predicated on a thorough assessment, diagnosis, and understanding of the client's presenting problem. In fact, the process is sequential, starting with the biopsychosocial-cultural assessment and accurate diagnosis, which in turn, facilitate establishing treatment goals and determine the treatment plans.

BIOPSYCHOSOCIAL-CULTURAL ASSESSMENT

The biopsychosocial-cultural model is based on two premises: (1) client problems are multicausal

and reflect their attempt to cope with stressors given existing vulnerabilities, environment, and resources; and (2) treatment approaches need to be multimodal, flexible, and tailored to the clients' needs and expectations rather than with a single treatment modality.

The first step in establishing treatment goals and an effective treatment plan is to conduct a clinical interview using the biopsychosocial-cultural model of assessment. Generally speaking, a mental health interview revolves around three discrete areas: (1) the dynamic interplay of biology and psychology, (2) social and cultural factors on the client's present mental health status, and (3) past mental health history. The *biological* system deals with the anatomical, structural, and molecular substrates of disease and the effects on clients' biological functioning. The *psychological* explores the effects of psychodynamic factors, developmental impasses or distorted object relations, motivation, and personality on the experience or reaction to illness. The *sociocultural* system examines cultural and environmental stressors, vulnerabilities, resources, and familial influences on the expression and experience of coping with illness. (Kaplan & Sadock, 1998; Sperry, Gudeman,

Blackwell, & Faulkner, 1992). These three areas are discussed accordingly.

Beginning with the bio of the biopsychosocial-cultural section of the interview, the social worker gathers information on current health status (e.g., hypertension) and past health history (e.g., diabetes) or injuries (e.g., brain injury). Additional information includes current medication use (e.g., both allopathic and homeopathic), and health and lifestyle behaviors (e.g., exercise, nutrition, sleep patterns, substance use). A familial health history would also be obtained. Screening tools would include sleep charts and health measures (see Chapter 44; McDowell & Newell, 1996). Additionally, genograms are very useful tools to track family health history (e.g., cancer) and certain genetic disorders (e.g., schizophrenia, substance abuse, mood disorders) and to assess family patterns that may maintain the problem or facilitate the obtainment of treatment goals. Additional information on genograms is found in Chapter 57. Genograms facilitate understanding of the social networks as part of the actual treatment plan and illustrate how assessment and problem-identification tools are used in the entire treatment process. Additional information on social networks is found in Chapter 102, this volume.

Once the social worker has obtained health information, she or he should explore the psychological status of the client. This information would include a broad range of topics, including appearance and behavior, speech and language, thought process and content, mood and affect, and cognitive functioning (including orientation, concentration, memory, insight, and general intelligence). A critical area is the determination of suicidal or homicidal risk and possible need for an immediate referral. Common screening tools are self-reports (e.g., see Chapter 49) and mental status exam. In particular, the mental status represents an attempt to objectively describe the behaviors, thoughts, feelings, and perceptions of the client during the interview (Shea, 1988).

A final section of the biopsychosocial-cultural assessment interview includes information on the sociocultural experiences of the client. Broadly speaking, the social worker gathers information on cultural background (e.g., ethnicity, language, assimilation, acculturation, and spiritual beliefs), environmental connections (e.g., community ties, living conditions, neighborhood, economic status, and availability of food and shelter), and social relations (e.g., familial, friends, employers, strangers, and experiences with racism or discrimination).

Useful assessment tools are eco-maps, which, like genograms, facilitate an understanding of how the social environment maintains the problems and may aid or impede the goal attainment.

ACCURATE DIAGNOSIS

The second step in establishing treatment goals and treatment plans is to accurately diagnose the mental health condition. One of the most useful aspects of the biopsychosocial-cultural assessment is that the model pushes the social worker to consider various perspectives that aid in formulating a diagnostic picture. Toward this end, it is customary to use the *DSM-IV-TR* (APA, 2000) for this purpose.

The conventional approach to formulating a diagnosis begins with developing a client profile using axes I through V of the *DSM*. Briefly, axis I refers to clinical disorders or other conditions that may be the focus of clinical attention—that is, V codes. Axis II is used to record personality disorders and mental retardation. Axis III is used for general medical conditions. Axis IV refers to psychosocial and environmental problems that exacerbate the disorder. Axis V refers to global assessment of functioning, which is determined for the client's current state and highest level of functioning over the past year.

Overall, axes I through V reflect a holistic perspective of the client and permit the worker to use the full benefit of knowledge that the biopsychosocial-cultural model avails. This chapter focuses on goals and treatment planning for axis I, but social workers should use all five axes. As Table 70.1 illustrates, axis I has three categories of diagnoses: clinical disorders, psychological and medical conditions, and V codes; the latter two constitute "other conditions that may be the focus of clinical attention." *Clinical disorders* generally refer to mental health conditions that result in distress or disability that is greater than expected from circumstances of living. Axis I clinical disorders include 15 different diagnostic categories.

In addition to a diagnosis of a clinical disorder, the social worker should consider the 30 different diagnostic options under the category of "other conditions that may be the focus of clinical attention." Sometimes these categories are used when the medical condition is confounding the psychiatric diagnosis or no mental disorder is present and the client is coping with multiple stressors.

TABLE 70.1 Three Categories for AXIS I Disorders

AXIS I Diagnoses	Other Conditions That May Be Focus of Clinical Attention	
Clinical Disorders	Psychological and Medical	V Codes

• Disorders usually first diagnosed in infancy, childhood, or adolescence (excluding mental retardation, which is diagnosed on Axis II)
• Delirium, Dementia, and Amnestic and Other Cognitive Disorders
• Mental Disorders Due to a General Medical Condition
• Substance-Related Disorders
• Schizophrenia and Other Psychotic Disorders
• Mood Disorders
• Anxiety Disorders
• Somatoform Disorders
• Factitious Disorders
• Dissociative Disorders
• Sexual and Gender Identity Disorders
• Eating Disorders
• Sleep Disorders
• Impulse-Control Disorders Not Elsewhere Classified
• Adjustment Disorders
• Other Conditions That May Be the Focus of Clinical Attention
	Psychological Factors Affecting Medical Condition
	• (316) —mental disorders
	    —psychological symptoms
	    —personality traits or coping style
	    —maladaptive health behaviors
	    —stress-related physiological response
	    —other/unspecified psychological factors
	
	Medication-Induced Movement Disorders
	• (331.1) Neuroleptic-Induced Parkinsonism
	• (333.92) Neuroleptic Malignant Syndrome
	• (333.7) Neuroleptic-Induced Acute Dystonia
	• (333.99) Neuroleptic-Induced Tardive Dyskinesia
	• (333.1) Medication-Induced Postural Tremor
	• (333.90) Medication-Induced Movement Disorder NOS
	
	Other Medication-Induced Disorders
	• (995.2) Adverse Effects of Medication NOS
		Relational Problems
		• (V61.9) Relational problem related to a mental disorder or general medical condition
		• (V61.20) Parent-Child Relational Problem
		• (V61.1) Partner Relational Problem
		• (V61.8) Sibling Relational Problem
		• (V62.81) Relational Problem NOS
		
		Problems Related to Abuse or Neglect
		Note: For CHILDREN, specify code 995.5 if focus is on victim; otherwise code refers to perpetrator
		• (V61.21) Physical Abuse of Child
		• (V61.21) Sexual Abuse of Child
		• (V61.21) Neglect of Child
		
		Note: For ADULTS, specify code 995.81 if focus is on victim; otherwise code refers to perpetrator
		• (V61.1) Physical Abuse of Adult
		• (V61.1) Sexual Abuse of Adult
		
		Additional Conditions That May Be the Focus of Clinical Attention
		• (V15.81) Noncompliance with treatment
		• (V65.2) Malingering
		• (V71.01) Adult Antisocial Behavior
		• (V71.02) Child/Adolescent Antisocial Behavior
		• (780.9) Age-Related Cognitive Decline
		• (V62.82) Bereavement
		• (V62.3) Academic Problem
		• (V62.2) Occupational Problem
		• (313.82) Identity Problem
		• (V62.89) Religious or Spiritual Problem
		• (V62.4) Acculturation Problem
		• (V62.89) Phase of Life Problem

As in any biopsychosocial-cultural assessment, the social worker is balancing information regarding the psychological and medical status of the client. When assessing for these areas, the social worker will need to explore psychological factors that affect the medical condition (e.g., major depressive disorder delaying recovery from myocardial infarction). Similarly, medication-induced movement disorders and other medication-induced disorders are important assessment considerations because of their significance in the management of medication (e.g., anxiety disorder versus neuroleptic malignant syndrome).

V codes represent conditions not attributable to a mental disorder that have nonetheless become a focus of therapeutic intervention. Examples include:

- relational problems (e.g., partner relational problem),
- problems related to abuse or neglect (e.g., physical abuse of child), and
- additional conditions (e.g., noncompliance with treatment).

The reader is referred to the *DSM* manual for a thorough review of the criteria for these categories.

The social worker could use the "other conditions" category when:

1. the problem is the focus of diagnosis and treatment and the individual has no mental disorder (e.g., V61.1, partner relational problem in which neither partner has a mental disorder);
2. the individual has a mental disorder, but it is unrelated to the problem (e.g., V61.20, when one partner has a phobia in which case both can be coded); and
3. the individual has a mental disorder that is related to the problem, but the problem is sufficiently severe to warrant independent clinical attention (e.g., V61.9, an individual with chronic schizophrenia in remission may present with marital distress).

ESTABLISHING TREATMENT GOALS

Once the assessment is completed and a diagnosis determined, the social worker and client are ready to develop treatment goals. We suggest five guidelines to establishing treatment goals. Goals should: (1) emerge from the assessment and diagnosis; (2) have maximum client participation; (3) be stated in positive terms; (4) be feasible, realistic, and within the resources of the client; and (5) be well defined, observable, and measurable.

Treatment goals should emerge from the assessment and diagnosis of the client's problem. There should be a nexus between the assessment/diagnosis and goals. For example, if the assessment and diagnosis suggest that the client is experiencing sleep deprivation secondary to an anxiety disorder, the treatment goals (both short- and long-term) would focus on stabilizing sleep patterns while decreasing anxiety and its symptoms.

The establishment of a treatment goal must include the active participation of the client. A goal cannot be ascribed to the client. Clients who actively participate in establishing the treatment goal are more motivated to comply with the treatment plan. Active participation includes homework assigned and completed outside the clinical setting. Treatments that include homework assignments tend to enhance client compliance and facilitate generalizing the changing behavior to other environments.

Treatment goals should be stated in positive terms, if possible. For example, it is more motivating for a client to increase the frequency and intensity of pleasant events than to stop being depressed. Similarly, a substance abuser would not simply want to quit using drugs but to increase the duration between use and the number of days clean and sober. A positively stated goal has the inherent benefit of enhancing compliance with the treatment plan and encouraging clients to participate in what they want and value.

A treatment goal must be feasible for the client to accomplish. If the goal is vague or overly ambitious, the outcome will likely be failure. Instead of improved social functioning, the client could experience a lack of success, disappointment, and erosion in confidence (Wood, 1978). Though the goal must not be too ambitious, it must also be challenging and realistic. Specific and challenging goals are more likely attained than those that are vague and easy. Social workers must also examine what resources the client has to achieve the agreed-on goals. For example, does the client have the bus fare or day care help to attend the scheduled therapy group?

Finally, the treatment goal must be observable. The client, the social worker, or relevant others should be able to observe the change. One convenient way to observe goals is with assessment instruments that help formulate the assessment and diagnosis.

Additionally, many of the mental disorders classified on axis I are rated for severity with the assessment recorded as the fifth digit of the *DSM* code. This is known as fifth-digit coding. Severity is defined as 1 (mild), 2 (moderate), 3 (severe but without psychotic features), and 4 (severe and with psychotic features). An ostensible goal of any intervention is to decrease the severity of the client's distress with the objective of changing some behavior. By assessing the severity before, during, and after treatment, the fifth-digit code provides a broadband assessment of treatment effectiveness.

Well-defined, observable, and measurable treatment goals provide a number of advantages, including reducing disagreements between the client and clinician, providing direction for the treatment plan (which prevents waste of time and resources), and serving as a measure of an effective outcome (Hepworth, Larsen, & Rooney, 1997; also see Chapter 73). A well-defined operational definition of the treatment goal is a necessary condition of an effective treatment plan. Moreover, it is much easier to develop a treatment plan that is likely to be effective when the treatment goal itself is well defined, explicit, and observable.

ELEMENTS OF AN EFFECTIVE TREATMENT PLAN

Once the goals are determined, the final step is to develop a treatment plan. A treatment plan is often described to clients as a roadmap whose destination is determined through mutual collaboration. Effective treatment plans have the following characteristics: (1) they provide specificity, (2) they are guided by industry standards of treatment, and (3) they evidence mutuality.

An effective treatment plan will have specificity. *Specificity* refers to an intervention plan with well-defined components organized in meaningful sequence. In other words, the intervention outlines a set of procedures that delineates what will occur both inside and outside the treatment setting. Sperry and colleagues (1992) identify six factors that need to be specified in treatment planning: setting (e.g., crisis, outpatient, inpatient, and day hospital), format of intervention (e.g., individual, group, medication group, marital/family, combined treatment), duration (short-term with termination date), frequency of contact (e.g., 1 week,

2 months, 1 month, other), treatment strategy (e.g., behavioral, cognitive, supportive/reality, interpersonal), and somatic treatment (e.g., antidepressant, neuroleptic, anxiolytic).

The social worker will want to include measures for monitoring the intervention effects. An integral component of an effective treatment plan is a systematic method to monitor client change and evaluate treatment effectiveness. Thus, the treatment plan should delineate what instruments will be used to monitor the client's condition and treatment process. These observations should be systematically integrated into the intervention as regular feedback and as a reinforcement for progress. This added degree of specificity helps ensure that the client and social worker accurately implement the agreed-on treatment plan.

As these factors suggest, there is more to the treatment plan than just the therapeutic procedures. Even so, this is often the area of greatest concern to the social worker. It is the part of the treatment plan that tells the worker and client what to do to implement an intervention. The task is facilitated by standards of treatment that include the use of treatment manuals and practice guidelines. Manuals are typically step-by-step/session-by-session delineations of a specific treatment protocol. Treatment protocols are found in LeCroy's step-by-step protocol (Chapter 93) for children's social skill development, and van Noppen's step-by-step and session-by-session group multifamily treatment for obsessive-compulsive disorder (Chapter 68). A practice guideline, in contrast, is a condition of treatment that appears to have sufficient empirical support to suggest it should likely be included in practice by the reasonable and prudent provider. Currently there are many published guidelines for practice with a number of mental health disorders. Several of these are available in a compendium from the American Psychiatric Association or Medscapes's Web site on the Internet, and newly developed ones are routinely published in the *American Journal of Psychiatry.*

The final characteristic of an effective treatment plan is *mutuality*. By this, we mean a meeting of minds between the client and the social worker about the entire enterprise of practice. The treatment plan should reflect this as an explicit contract between the client and the social worker. This contract should show the mutuality of the professional relationship and enumerate who will do what, to what extent, under what conditions, by when, and for what purpose or goal.

Overall, social workers need to remember that there is considerable variability between different disorders (e.g., schizophrenia compared to dysthymia), symptom expression (e.g., remission versus active), and functioning (e.g., serious impairment versus moderate difficulty). There is also considerable variability for what treatment is used for different persons with the same diagnosis. For example, a person with dysthymia may need a cognitive intervention with skill training, whereas another may need medication and a compliance program that includes family members. The right intervention correctly implemented for the wrong problem is likely to be ineffective, which underscores the importance of monitoring client change for assessment throughout the course of treatment.

One example of how to apply the right interventions toward a multiproblem situation is illustrated in Table 70.2. This treatment plan describes the sequential elements of the treatment process discussed in this chapter. These elements begin with the assessment model (e.g., biopsychosocial-cultural), applying the screening tools (rapid assessment instruments), formulating a diagnosis, establishing treatment goals (e.g., short- and long-term), and concluding with formulating the treatment plan (e.g., setting, format, duration, frequency, strategy, and somatic treatment).

USING THE STRENGTHS PERSPECTIVE IN ESTABLISHING GOALS AND TREATMENT PLANNING

As discussed elsewhere by Cowger, Rapp, and Sullivan, the strengths perspective focuses on the client's abilities in the assessment and emphasizes the discovery of resources within the client and his or her environment. In our view, the strengths-based perspective has considerable value when applied to the establishment of goals and treatment planning for individuals with axis I disorders. In general, a goal must be attainable by the client, and the easiest way to do so is by using and building on the client's strengths. The process involves mutual collaboration between the provider and the client to develop goals that frame the idea of developing new expectations, constructing new opportunities for the individual and his or her family, and discovering new resources within him- or herself and the environment (Saleebey, 1997). Regardless of the diagnosis, establishing treatment goals using the strengths perspective involves finding the resources within the client, their environment, and relationships and linking these strengths to the treatment plan.

A strengths-based perspective is integrated into the treatment plan by helping clients remember how they have been successful in the past (e.g., what steps they have used), affirming previous success and abilities (e.g., coping skills), and determining what skills, behaviors, motivations, and aspirations can be applied to bring the desired change. Together, client and provider search the environment for forces that enhance life chances while supporting client self-determination and personal responsibility (Saleebey, 1997). In summary, the strengths-based model is useful when applied to the particular goals and treatment approach to attain these goals. Goal-attainment plans that make use of a client's strengths capture a natural nexus that enhances the likelihood of treatment success.

CONCLUSIONS

The establishment of treatment goals and treatment plans is an integral part of a process that begins with assessment and diagnosis. Those goals and treatment plans enhance the likelihood that clients will change. This objective is facilitated by following five guidelines.

1. Treatment goals and treatment plans require a thorough biopsychosocial-cultural assessment and accurate diagnosis of the problem.
2. The treatment goals must be specified in observable terms at the beginning of treatment.
3. The intervention is determined by the goals and should have specific criteria for accomplishing the goals.
4. The intervention should be planned and include a well-explicated delineation of what will occur and when over the course of treatment.
5. The treatment goals and treatment plan should form the explicit contracts for helping clients change and should be implemented according to mutually agreed-upon parameters of the plan.

These guidelines form a rough sequence of the treatment process and help the social worker effectively and efficiently assist clients.

TABLE 70.2 (*Sample*) Treatment Plan

Client Name: Ralph C. *Age:* 45

Reason for Seeking Treatment: Mr. C. is a single, white male who is employed as a bus driver. He states that his employer told him to "get help or don't come back." Mr. C reports insomnia ("only sleeps 2–3 hours a night") and feeling anxious about losing his job despite good work performance reviews. He recently has been complaining to coworkers about his sleep deprivation and fear of wrecking the bus due to nodding off at the wheel. He states that his work has become his life now and that he has virtually abandoned his friends, leisure reading, and church-associated activities. He feels that he is in a vicious cycle of all work and no play and can't seem to shake it off. He does not drink or use drugs and has recently quit his health club so he could concentrate on his work-related responsibilities.

History of Past Treatment: Mr. C has not received any mental health treatment in the past. No remarkable medical history. Receives annual physical and reports no complications.

Assessment Model		Screening Tools	Treatment Goals		Treatment Plan
			Short-Term	Long-Term	(Setting, format, duration, frequency, strategy, and somatic tx)
BIO	→	Sleep chart Genogram	1. Stabilize sleep routine	1. Maintain routine sleep cycle	1. Outpatient setting, individual tx. sessions for 8 weeks using sleep activity diary; evaluate for Sinequan; evaluate for sleep apnea
PSY	→	Mental Status Clinical Anxiety Scale	2. Decrease anxiety	2. Maintain employing stress reduction techniques	2. Outpatient, individual tx for 8 sessions using cog-behavior
SOC	→	Ecomap	3. Increase social contacts outside of work	3. Maintain recreation/leisure schedule	3. Refer to community events calendar and health club; friendship skill building
CULTURAL	→	Ecomap	4. Encourage return to church social activities	4. Increase exposure to new spiritual/social groups	4. Refer to community calendar and provide bibliography

Continued

TABLE 70.2 (*Sample*) Treatment Plan (*continued*)

DIAGNOSIS

AXIS I: 300.02 Generalized Anxiety Disorder (Primary focus of treatment)

           V62.2 Occupational Problem secondary to anxiety disorder

           R/O 307.42 Primary Insomnia

AXIS II: V71.09 No diagnosis on Axis II

AXIS III: None but evaluate for sleep apnea

AXIS IV: Occupational Problem—discord with workers

AXIS V: GAF: 60 (moderate; difficulty at work)

WEB SITES

Dr. David Barlow's adult anxiety center. http://www.bu.edu/anxiety/adult.html.

National Institute of Mental Health. http://www.nimh.nih.gov/health/publications/anxiety-disorders.

Surgeon General. http://www.surgeongeneral.gov/library/mentalhealth/chapter4.

References

American Psychiatric Association. (2000). *Diagnostic and statistical manual of mental disorders*, 4th ed., text revision. Washington, DC: APA.

Hepworth, D., Larsen, J., & Rooney, R. (1997). *Direct social work practice: Theory and skills*, 5th ed. Pacific Grove, CA: Brooks/Cole.

Kaplan, H., & Sadock, B. (1998). *Synopsis of psychiatry*, 8th ed. Baltimore: Williams & Wilkins.

Mcdowell, I., & Newell, C. (1996). *Measuring health: A guide to rating scales and questionnaires*, 2nd ed. New York: Oxford University Press.

Saleebey, D. (1997). *The strengths perspective in social work practice*, 2nd ed. New York: Longman.

Shea, S. (1988). *Psychiatric interviewing: The art of understanding*. Philadelphia: Saunders.

Sperry, L., Gudeman, J., Blackwell, B., & Faulkner, L. (1992). *Psychiatric case formulations*. Washington, DC: authors.

Wood, K. M. (1978). Casework effectiveness: A new look at the research evidence. *Social Work, 23*, 437–459.

71

Using Evidence-Based Practice and Expert Consensus in Mental Health Settings

Step-by-Step Guidelines for Schizophrenia

Vikki L. Vandiver

Today's mental health systems are being impacted by a number of significant aspects of managed care, including prospective payment schemes, capitation, expanding client caseloads, and the demand for clinical approaches that are evidence-based. Increasingly, these same systems demand greater accountability from clinical social workers. Managed mental health care organizations want to know what clinicians are doing (treatment plan), why (assessment and diagnosis), and the effectiveness the treatment intervention (outcomes and evaluation). Evidence-based practice is one attempt to answer these questions. This chapter provides an overview of evidence-based practice, discusses two key approaches in its application (i.e., practice guidelines and expert consensus guidelines), delineates steps for using them in a mental health setting, and concludes with a summary set of guidelines.

Additionally, a case study is provided that illustrates the seven steps for applying evidence-based practice guidelines. Through the case illustration, the reader can see how practice guidelines and expert consensus guidelines are integrated into the clinical assessment and diagnosis process, problem identification, goal planning, intervention development, and development of measurable outcomes followed by evaluation measures.

WHAT IS EVIDENCE-BASED PRACTICE?

Evidence-based practice (EBP) refers to the process of using a variety of databases (e.g., research reports and systematic case studies) to guide interventions that foster meaningful client change. However, there are a variety of lenses through which to observe and apply EBP. Let's review five general definitions.

- *Process.* As a process, EBP attempts to use systematic procedures and blend current best practice, client preferences (when possible), and clinical expertise, resulting in services that are both individualized and empirically sound (Shlonsky & Gibbs, 2004, p. 137).
- *Intervention.* As an intervention, EBP is the use of treatments for which there is sufficiently persuasive evidence to support their effectiveness in attaining the desired outcomes (Rosen & Proctor, 2002, p. 745).
- *Strategy.* As a strategy, EBP is a way for clinicians and clients to select from the corpus of available evidence the most useful information to apply to a particular client who has sought services (Thomlison & Corcoran, 2008).
- *Empirical.* As an empirically driven approach, EBP in behavioral health refers to the use of clinical interventions for a specific problem that has been (1) evaluated by well-designed clinical research studies, (2) published in peer-reviewed journals, and (3) consistently found to be effective or efficacious on consensus review (Rosenthal, 2006, p. 68).
- *Integrative.* As an integrative process, EBP is the blending of best researched evidence and clinical expertise with patient values (Institute of Medicine [IOM], 2001, p. 47)

As one can see, the term *evidence-based practice* is a broad based concept with multiple layers of definitions. What is common across all of these definitions is that evidence is ranked on a continuum from more rigorous, like systematic reviews derived from randomized controlled trials, to less rigorous, like expert consensus guidelines, derived from national panels of interdisciplinary experts. Systematic reviews can be located through two key sites: Cochrane Library and the Campbell Collaboration. Expert consensus guidelines are available through a number of sources, one of which is psychiatric guidelines. Clinicians must be clear about what level of evidence they are using to support a particular intervention.

EBP is based on two principles: the principle of assessment-driven intervention and the principle of the right to informed and effective treatment.

- Principle of assessment-driven intervention. When a mental health intervention is derived from the EBP literature, treatment effectiveness is likely to be enhanced. For the clinician, there is one overriding principle that directs this process: assessment drives intervention. EBP methods are only as good as what they are designed to do. The best evidence for a particular problem will be of questionable value if the problem has been incorrectly framed or the diagnosis incorrect (Rosenthal, 2006). This is why it is so critical to spend quality and quantity time in the front end of the assessment phase doing a thorough diagnostic review.
- Principle of the right to informed and effective treatment. This is a core principle in many of the helping professions. In other words, consumers and family members have a right to information about effective treatments. Moreover, in clinical areas where EBP exists, they also have a right to access effective treatment (Thyer, 2007), even though there is no established legal right to effectiveness (Corcoran, 1998). The EBP principle of informed consent is founded on the notion that clinical approaches must be based on empirical evidence, applied appropriately to the client and situation, and evaluated for effectiveness. This information must be disseminated to clients. Admittedly, all this may not happen routinely, but that does not mean that it should not happen (Vandiver, in press).

There are two key goals for EBP in mental health. The first is to increase the empirical basis and effectiveness of clinical practice by helping clinicians and client select the most accurate, valid information derived from the best available methods. The second is to help clients realize their own strengths to diminish or alleviate symptoms or state of being that causes discomfort, distress, or difficulty in functioning; this is accomplished through the acquisition of behavioral change strategies (Dziegielweski & Roberts, 2004).

LIMITATIONS

Despite the broad-based application and compatibility with social work values, EBP approaches have not always been accepted in mental health settings. Three chief reasons are organizational availability, clinician reluctance, and client/consumer concern. Some organizations do not have a formal mechanism for obtaining and disseminating newly published practice guidelines. Howard and Jensen (1999a) point out that, ironically, far more energy has gone into developing guidelines than in activities designed to increase their use. Similarly, Gates (1995) notes that the literature shows that "simply developing and distributing guidelines does not change clinicians' practice" (p. 71). Clinicians, on the other hand, claim that when manuals are available, the research reports are difficult to read, have differing levels of face validity, are not appropriate for their respective field of practice, or simply are not needed (Howard & Jensen, 1999a). Unfortunately, research bears this out. Rosen, Proctor, Morrow-Howell, and Staudt (1995) report that less than 1 percent of the practice decisions made by social workers were based on empirical findings. Other data revealed that clinicians seldom read research material, do not systematically evaluate the effectiveness of services provided, and do not express an appreciation of the value of research to practice (Rosen et al., 1995). Some argue that the use of EBP must begin in undergraduate and graduate education and field education in particular (Thomlison & Corcoran, 2008). But as Richey and Roffman (1997) caution, "even implementing empirically supported approaches does not result in superior outcomes for participants" (p. 312).

The situation fares no better from the client's perspective. Research by consumers suggests that the recommendations offered through EBP approaches, particularly practice guidelines, do not reflect the more contemporary issues for clients in mental health settings (e.g., the move toward recovery, empowerment, communication, and advocacy skills; Campbell, 1997).

Despite these obstacles, managed care is increasingly requiring social workers in mental health settings to demonstrate the use of efficacious treatment and positive outcomes. Because social workers are the predominant profession employed to provide community-based mental health services (Mowbray, Collins, & Bybee, 1999), practice guidelines can actually benefit practitioners and are a promising approach to increase the empirical basis and effectiveness of their social work practice (Howard & Jensen, 1999b).

PRACTICE GUIDELINES AND EXPERT CONSENSUS GUIDELINES

There are two core approaches to operationalizing EBP in mental health settings: (1) use of practice guidelines, and (2) use of expert consensus guidelines. Although there are a number of practice guidelines in the health and mental health fields (e.g., up to 20,000 guidelines in the medical field alone), this chapter reviews only those related to mental health—specifically those generated out of psychiatric practice.

In the best of all worlds, EBP should be an amalgam of research findings (i.e., practice guidelines; Howard & Jensen, 1999b) and expert consensus (i.e., expert consensus guidelines). One way to differentiate the two approaches is to think of practice guidelines as more quantitative and expert consensus as more qualitative, yet both build on empirical findings. Practice guidelines weigh their clinical recommendations according to the veracity of the supporting evidence. Where empirical evidence is absent, expert consensus plays a greater role in guideline construction. To illustrate the contrast, Table 71.1 displays an example of the table of contents for practice guidelines and expert consensus guidelines for the treatment of schizophrenia.

Practice Guidelines

"Practice guidelines" refers to a set of systematically compiled and organized statements and recommendations for clinical care based on research findings and the consensus of experienced clinicians with expertise in a given practice area (Howard & Jensen, 1999a; Rosen & Proctor, 2002). Terms associated with practice guidelines are *practice protocols, standards, algorithms, options, parameters, pathways,* and *preferred practice patterns.* The goal of practice guidelines is to enable practitioners to find, select, and use interventions that are most effective and appropriate for a given client, situation, and desired outcome.

Practice guidelines for mental health were developed through a rigorous process of expert panel members working to reach agreement about treatment recommendations after reviewing the scientific literature for treatment efficacy. For example, practice guidelines in psychiatry reviewed the following literature sources to develop their recommendations: randomized clinical trials (e.g., random assignment with treatment and control groups), clinical trials (e.g., prospective intervention study), cohort or longitudinal study (e.g., subjects are studied over time without any specific intervention), case-control study (e.g., subjects are identified and information pursued retrospectively), secondary data analysis (e.g., meta-analysis or decision analysis), and literature review (e.g., qualitative studies, case reports, and textbooks; APA, 2006).

TABLE 71.1 Example of Table of Contents for Evidence-Based Practice Guidelines for Schizophrenia

Practice Guidelines for the Treatment of Schizophrenia	The Expert Consensus Guideline Series: Treatment of Schizophrenia

Statement of Intent
Introduction
Development Process
  I. Executive Summary of Recommendations
    A. Coding system
    B. General considerations
  II. Disease Definition, Natural History, and Epidemiology
    A. Clinical features
    B. Natural history and course
    C. Epidemiology
  III. Treatment Principles and Alternatives
    A. General issues
    B. Psychiatric management
    C. Pharmacologic treatments
    D. Electroconvulsive therapy
    E. Specific psychosocial interventions
    F. Other social and community interventions
    G. Treatment settings
  IV. Formulation and Implementation of a Treatment Plan
    A. Acute phase
    B. Stabilization phase
    C. Stable phase
    D. Special issues in caring for patients with treatment-refractory illness
  V. Clinical and Environmental Features Influencing Treatment
    A. Psychiatric features
    B. Demographic and psychosocial variables
    C. Concurrent general medical conditions
  VI. Research Directions
	The Expert Consensus Panels for Schizophrenia
	Introduction
	How to Use the Guidelines
	
	Guidelines
	  I. Strategies for Selecting Medications
	    Guideline 1: Initial treatment for an acute episode
	    Guideline 2: A patient with an inadequate response to initial treatment
	    Guideline 3: Strategies to reduce substance abuse and medication noncompliance
	    Guideline 4: Selecting medications for specific complicating problems
	    Guideline 5: Selecting medications to avoid side effects
	    Guideline 6: The maintenance phase
	    Guideline 7: Prescribing advice
	    Guideline 8: Tips of switching antipsychotics
	  II. Strategies for Selecting Services
	    Guideline 9: Providing inpatient and transitional services
	    Guideline 10: Selecting outpatient services
	    Guideline 11: Working with the family
	    Guideline 12: Essentials of psychosocial evaluation and planning
	  III. Assessment Issues
	    Guideline 13: Diagnostic, evaluation, and differential diagnosis
	    Guideline 14: Medical Evaluation
	  IV. Policy Issues
	    Guideline 15: Financing and organizing care
	    Guideline 16: Cost-effectiveness
	    Guideline 17: Matching care to patient needs
	    Guideline 18: Important community-based services
	    Guideline 19: Measuring outcomes
	
	Survey Results
	Expert Survey Results and Guideline References
	Medication Survey Results
	Psychosocial Survey Results
	A Guide for Patients and Families

Source: APA, 2006.

A number of limitations are associated with the use of practice guidelines. Criticisms have been that they are too lengthy, cumbersome to read, and impractical in content and design. Additionally, they may stifle other therapeutic approaches less amenable to research paradigms and have the potential to be employed in a clinically restrictive way by contemporary care (cost) managers (Kirk, 1999).

On the other hand, the advantages of using practice guidelines is that the clinician only has to cull through one cumbersome document rather than many different journals to obtain the data on the most efficacious treatment identified at the time of publication. Some examples of practice guidelines used in mental health settings are for treatment of schizophrenia, nicotine dependence, substance use disorders, HIV/AIDS, bipolar disorders, panic disorders, acute stress disorder and post-traumatic stress disorder, borderline personality disorder, major depressive disorders, and eating disorders and suicidal behaviors. These are published in the *American Psychiatric Association Practice Guidelines for the Treatment of Psychiatric Disorders* (APA, 2006).

Expert Consensus Guidelines

Expert consensus guidelines (ECGs) are derived from a broad-based survey of expert opinion and consist of a compilation of practical treatment recommendations for the treatment of major mental disorders (McEvoy, Scheifler, & Frances, 1999). Terms associated with this approach include *expert consultation*, *treatment manuals*, and *protocols*. The goal of ECGs is to provide an additional range of clinical and psychosocial information that otherwise may have been excluded from the review of controlled research studies, such as was used to develop the practice guidelines.

An example of the approach to EBP is the ECGs for the treatment of schizophrenia (McEvoy et al., 1999). These guidelines are based on survey responses of 304 experts in the field of medicine, psychosocial rehabilitation, psychology, public policy analysts, academics, family advocacy groups, state mental health commissioners, and medical directors. The entire survey and rating scores are listed in the guidelines. The guidelines were developed by building on existing knowledge in the field and were conceived with the knowledge that many controlled research studies do not address the wide range of clinical issues that occur in clinical practice. The guidelines are based on a synthesis of the opinions of a large group of experts

and can be viewed as an expert consultation, much like social workers would do at a treatment team client staffing.

Like practice guidelines, the ECG approach to EBP also has its limitations. These include recognizing that recommendations are not empirically derived, are based on groups of clients (e.g., diagnostic groups with a presenting problem—schizophrenia, first episode), are intended to apply to the *average* client in each group, and offer no consideration for cultural differences (McEvoy et al., 1999; Steketee, 1999).

On the other hand, ECGs have several advantages. They provide explicit recommendations, are user-friendly in layout and design, provide an educational source to families, offer primary and secondary recommendations more than the generic recommendations of practice guidelines, and provide a Web page that enables professionals nationwide to have access to similar education, training, and information (Reamer, 2001). The ECGs are published as a series through the *Journal of Clinical Psychiatry* and Expert Knowledge Systems. To date, the ECGs that are available include treatment of schizophrenia, attention deficit hyperactivity disorder, bipolar disorder, dementia, depression in older adults, depression in women, obsessive-compulsive disorder, optimal pharmacologic treatment of psychotic disorders, post-traumatic stress disorder, psychiatric and behavioral problems in mental retardation, and using antipsychotic agents in older adults.

STEPS FOR USING PRACTICE GUIDELINES IN A MENTAL HEALTH SETTING

Typically, mental health settings will serve individuals who have a diagnosis of mental disorder and, when possible, family members. As a result, clinicians will need to integrate perspectives of many relevant stakeholders as they apply EBP approaches in their clinical work. There are seven steps that the clinician can use to apply evidence-based practice using practice guidelines. They are (1) conduct a biopsychosocial assessment, (2) arrive at a diagnosis and select diagnostic specific guidelines, (3) identify problem(s), (4) develop goals or planned target of change, (5) develop intervention plan, (6) establish outcome measures, and (7) evaluation. Though these steps should look familiar to most clinicians, what sets the process apart is the reliance on practice guidelines for direction and guidance. These steps are also displayed in Figure 71.1. Each step is discussed next.

Step 1: Conduct a biopsychosocial assessment.
The first step in establishing treatment goals and interventions is to conduct a clinical interview using the biopsychosocial-cultural model of assessment. The assessment will explore health, psychological status, social/occupational, and sociocultural issues. See Chapter 51 for an overview of a biopsychosocial-cultural assessment.

Step 2: Provide a diagnosis and select appropriate practice guideline. Once the assessment is complete, the clinician can provide a diagnosis. The conventional approach to formulating a diagnosis begins with developing a client profile using the categories of axes I through V of the *DSM-IV-TR* (APA, 2000). See Chapter 45 for detailed information on the use of the *DSM-IV-TR*. It is important to complete all five axes to provide a holistic perspective of the client. Once the diagnosis is made, the

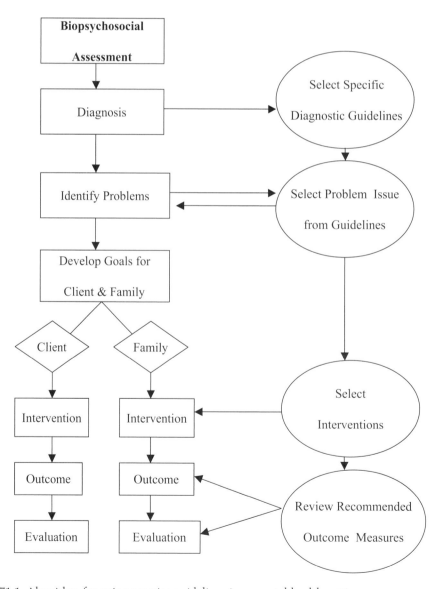

Figure 71.1 Algorithm for using practice guidelines in a mental health setting.

clinician has two options: obtain diagnostic specific guidelines or, if formal guidelines are not available, pursue the self-directed steps outlined elsewhere in this volume. Examples of diagnostic specific guidelines are APA (2006) and McEvoy et al. (1999). See Table 71.1 for a detail of the contents of these guidelines.

Step 3: Use practice guidelines to identify problems. The goal here is to specify the problem(s), including severity and duration, and track the change in those problems throughout the course of treatment. See Chapter 59 for information on treatment planning with families. The idea is to locate your client's problem or your question about treatment in the practice guidelines table of contents (see Table 71.1) and compare your assessment with the guideline recommendations.

Step 4: Develop goals or planned target of change. At this stage, the clinician will work with both client and family to identify goals or targets of change. If possible, it is important to include family members in the process of treatment planning and goal development because treatment of schizophrenia often focuses on outcomes for family members as well as the identified client. Therefore, goals in therapy may go beyond improvement in just client functioning and include improvement in family functioning (Corcoran, 2000). See Chapter 73 for information on developing behaviorally stated treatment goals and Chapter 59 on strategies for change for children and families.

Step 5: Use practice guidelines to develop the intervention plan. Once the client and family have agreed on primary goals, the clinician uses the practice guidelines to develop interventions. For example, if a client presented with first-time complaints of "hearing voices," the expert consensus guidelines recommend "newer atypical antipsychotics for first episode clients with predominantly positive symptoms" (McEvoy et al., 1999, p. 12). When the focus is on the family, the same guidelines recommend family and patient education, because family members may not yet understand that patient's behaviors are a result of the illness. Specific guidelines for families, "A Guide for Patients and Families," are available in McEvoy et al. (1999).

Step 6: Use practice guidelines to establish outcome measures. Rosen and Proctor (2002) define "outcomes" as any condition that an intervention is intended to affect or change. Specifically, the ECG for schizophrenia (guideline 19) lists the following outcome measures as most appropriate in evaluating quality of care: functional status (e.g., ability to relate to peers and family), perception of quality of life (e.g., satisfaction with living and social supports), benefits of care (e.g., positive effects of medication), problems with care (e.g., drug side effects), safety (e.g., contact with legal system), and client and family satisfaction with mental health services (McEvoy et al., 1999). Many of the same indicators are useful for measuring change with family members.

Step 7: Evaluation. Although practice guidelines per se do not address the evaluation component, sound EBP principles suggest that clinicians assess intervention effectiveness through an evaluation component. The type of evaluation recommended here is straightforward and involves baseline, intervention, and follow-up data using self-anchored rating scales or short-item self-report measures (Fischer & Corcoran, 2007). By using research measures, clinicians can monitor progress of the interventions and provide feedback to themselves, client, and family. See Chapter 53 for examples of rapid assessment instruments. Based on the indication of progress, you adapt, modify, or change the approach to facilitate change. The following case example illustrates these seven steps.

CASE EXAMPLE

Bill G. is a 23-year-old white male who is employed as a computer programmer. He was referred to a mental health clinic by his primary physician. The physician had noted that in the past 9 months, Bill had become increasingly delusional (e.g., he believes co-workers "are the children of Satan"), exhibiting odd behaviors at his job at a software company (e.g., hiding documents because "Satan's children would use them to destroy the world") and was progressively becoming more withdrawn from friends and social activities. Although these behaviors have been going on for nearly a year and are quite distressing to the family, Bill on the other hand, does not think there is a problem. At intake, Bill described a rather chaotic, stressful work environment, punctuated by concerns about the personnel department being the "seat of hell and the CEO as the devil incarnate." After completing a full biopsychosocial-cultural history, his axis I diagnosis was 295.30 Schizophrenia, paranoid type, continuous (provisional) with good prognostic features. In an effort to capture Bill's difficulty with work and his family, two additional V codes were added to his diagnostic profile. These were V62.2, Occupational Problem, and V61.9, Relational Problem Related to a Mental Disorder (e.g., family distress).

Once the diagnosis was made, the clinician turned to the *Practice Guidelines for the Treatment of Schizophrenia* (APA, 2006) and the "Expert Consensus Guideline Series: Treatment of Schizophrenia" (McEvoy et al., 1999) as a guide in problem identification. See Table 71.1 for a detail of the contents of these guidelines. Bill's problems are summarized as exhibiting positive symptoms (e.g., delusions), occupational problems, and family distress. The target of change or goals as identified by Bill and his family are to eliminate the "confused thinking" (e.g., positive symptoms), (re)evaluate the work situation, and educate the family and patient on the illness. To address these goals for clients having a first episode, both practice guidelines recommend the following interventions: medication (e.g., using newer atypical antipsychotics) and symptom monitoring performed by physician and case manager; assistance with obtaining medication; collaborative decision making with client, family, and clinician regarding work situation; and patient and family education. Education is imperative because family members may not yet understand that Bill's behaviors are a result of the illness. With regard to outcomes, the ECGs consider client functioning (e.g., client's ability to relate to peers and family and vocational and daily living skills) to be the most important measure of successful treatment of people with early signs of schizophrenia. In Bill's case, the desired outcomes related to client functioning were a reduction of positive symptoms and a decrease in work-related stress. A positive outcome for Bill's family would be increased understanding of the disease process of schizophrenia and skills for coping with family stress. With regard to evaluation, a useful resource for evaluating the remission of Bill's symptoms is the Scale for the Assessment of Positive Symptoms, a 35-item instrument designed to ascertain the positive symptoms of psychopathology (e.g., hallucinations, delusions, bizarreness, and formal thought disorder). Another useful measure to use with Bill and his family members is the Family Assessment Device, a 60-item questionnaire designed to evaluate family functioning. These measures are found in Fischer and Corcoran (2007). Additionally, an excellent resource for applying EBP models to individuals with schizophrenia and their family members is found in Corcoran (2000). In this text, she reviews 13 studies on multifamily interventions with schizophrenia and 24 studies on single-family interventions with schizophrenia.

All in all, these seven steps could take 1 to 3 months to complete, but as with any treatment for mental disorders, the clinical work is never really finished. As most clients and family members will testify, mental illness is a process, not an event—its pattern is unpredictable and its consequences unknown. Consequently, clients relapse, families and clients need continuous support, booster sessions are required, and clinicians continue to be educators and health promoters as they assist clients and families in dealing with this puzzling disorder. However, when clinicians use EBP approaches, which incorporate these steps, the client and family can be confident that the most sound clinical approaches are being used in the treatment of this disorder. In Bill's case, early intervention and a focused treatment approach derived from the use of practice guidelines fostered a good prognosis. He later became a successful CEO of his own computer software company located in the Pacific northwest. He takes his medicine regularly.

CONCLUSION

As suggested, EBP provides promise for more effective interventions by clinicians. Practice guidelines and ECGs, however, are of little value if they are not available or not valued by clinicians and clients. There are three levels of strategies that mental health settings can employ to promote the availability and use of EBP approaches. On an organizational level, mental health administrators need to ensure that practice guideline manuals are accessible to all staff and that training in the use and application of guidelines are frequent and are a part of the agency culture of continuing education.

On a clinical level, mental health clinicians can work with agency administrators, managed care organizations, and client groups to develop internal treatment recommendations, outcomes, and evaluation standards (i.e., like the process for developing ECGs) that are deemed relevant to their client populations. These internally developed strategies could then be paired with existing empirically based and expert consensus derived practice guidelines for maximum treatment options. This also requires training of clinicians to think not only in EBP models but also in the emerging recovery and empowerment models. Additionally, clinicians can work with their colleagues in supervision and supportive consultation to assure that their practices conform to existing practice guidelines. This approach has the added benefit of informing clinicians as to whether they are doing a good job of using the guidelines. For a review of other suggestions for developing clinicians' skills, see Chapter 2 on developing effective practice competencies in managed behavioral health care.

On the client level, the time has come for research and treatment manuals to incorporate the preferences of another "expert"—namely, the client-consumer. The growing emphasis in mental health on consumer values, community care, and broadened measurements of outcomes has had major significance for the way quality and performance are measured (Torrey & Wyzik, 2000; Mowbray et al., 1999). As consumers grow more sophisticated in their research and program evaluation skills, and the recovery movement gains momentum, practice guidelines will need to incorporate client-consumer perspectives on what constitutes components of preferred care. Just as we have family guidelines, the next step will be to have consumer guidelines.

In the meantime, there are four summary guidelines that can be highlighted from this discussion: (1) let the assessment be the guide to selecting the appropriate diagnosis, practice guideline, and intervention; (2) use both practice guidelines and ECGs as a guide to developing specific interventions; (3) for those clinical cases where no existing formal practice guidelines are available (e.g., schizoaffective diagnosis), the social worker can use a self-directed approach to data gathering; and (4) practice guidelines are never a substitute, only a supplement for sound clinical judgment.

WEB SITES

Campbell Collaboration; specializes in systematic reviews; see *Social Welfare*. http://www.campbellcollaboration.org.

Cochrane Library; specializes in systematic reviews. http://www.cochranlibrary.org.

National Registry of Evidence-based Programs and Practices; specializes in database of evidence-based interventions related to mental health and substance abuse. http://www.nrepp.samhsa.gov.

National Institute of Mental Health; specializes in evidence-based or best practices. http://www.nimh.gov.

Psychiatric Guidelines; specializes in ECGs. http://www.psychguides.com.

References

American Psychiatric Association. (2000). *The diagnostic and statistical manual,* 4th ed., text revision. Washington, DC: APA.

American Psychiatric Association. (2006). American Psychiatric Association practice guidelines for the treatment of psychiatric disorders, compendium 2006. Arlington, VA: American Psychiatric Publishing.

Campbell, J. (1997). How consumers/survivors are evaluating the quality of psychiatric care. *Evaluation Review, 21*(3), 357–363.

Corcoran, J. (2000). *Evidence-based social work practice with families.* New York: Springer.

Corcoran, K. (1998). Clients without a cause: Is there a legal right to effective treatment? *Research on Social Work Practice, 8,* 589–596.

Dziegielweski, S., & Roberts, A. (2004). Health care evidence-based practice: A product of political and cultural times. In A. Roberts & K. Yeager (Eds.), *Evidence-based practice manual: Research and outcome measures in health and human services* (pp. 200–205). New York: Oxford University Press.

Fischer, J., & Corcoran, K. (2007). *Measures for clinical practice. Volume 2: Adults,* 4th ed. New York: Free Press.

Gates, P. (1995). Think globally, act locally: An approach to implementation of clinical practice guidelines. *Journal of Quality Improvement, 21,* 71–85.

Howard, M., & Jensen, J. (1999a). Clinical practice guidelines: Should social work develop them? *Research on Social Work Practice, 9,* 283–301.

Howard, M., & Jensen, J. (1999b). Barriers to development, utilization, and evaluation of social work practice guidelines: Toward an action plan for social work. *Research on Social Work Practice, 9,* 347–364.

Institute of Medicine. (2001). *Crossing the quality chasm: A new health system for the 21st century.* Washington, DC: National Academies Press.

Kirk, S. (1999). Good intentions are not enough: Practice guidelines for social work. *Research on Social Work Practice, 9*(3), 302–310.

McEvoy, J., Scheifler, P., & Frances, A. (1999). The expert consensus guideline series: Treatment of schizophrenia. *Journal of Clinical Psychiatry, 60*(suppl. 11), 1–80.

Mowbray, C., Collins, M., & Bybee, D. (1999). Supported education for individuals with psychiatric disabilities: Long-term outcomes from an experimental study. *Social Work Research, 23*(2), 89–100.

Reamer, F. (2001). Ethics and managed care policy. In N. W. Veeder & W. Peebles-Wilkins (Eds.), *Managed care services: Policy, programs, and research.* New York: Oxford University Press.

Richey, C., & Roffman, R. (1997). On the sidelines of guidelines: Further thought on the fit between clinical guidelines and social work practice. *Research on Social Work Practice, 9*(3), 311–321.

Rosen, A., & Proctor, E. (2002). Standards for evidence-based social work practice: The role of replicable and appropriate interventions, outcomes and practice guidelines. In A. Roberts & G. Greene (Eds.), *Social workers' desk reference* (pp. 743–747. New York: Oxford University Press).

Rosen, A., Proctor, E., Morrow-Howell, N., & Staudt, M. (1995). Rationales for practice decisions: Variations in knowledge use by decision task and social work service. *Research on Social Work Practice, 5*, 501–523.

Rosenthal, R. (2006). Overview of evidence-based practice. In A. Roberts & K. Yeager (Eds.), *Foundations of evidence-based social work practice* (pp. 67–80). New York: Oxford University Press.

Shlonsky, A., & Gibbs, L. (2004). Will the real evidence-based practice please stand up? Teaching the process of evidence-based practice to the helping professions. *Brief Treatment and Crisis Intervention, 4*, 137–153.

Steketee, G. (1999). Yes, but cautiously. *Research on Social Work Practice, 9*(3), 343–346.

Thomlison, B., & Corcoran, K. (2008). *The evidence-based internship: A field manual.* New York: Oxford University Press.

Thyer, B. (2007). Evidence-based social work: An overview. In B. Thyer & J. Wodarski (Eds.), *Social work in mental health: An evidence-based approach.* New York: Wiley.

Torrey, W., & Wyzik, P. (2000). The recovery vision as a service improvement guide for community mental health center providers. *Community Mental Health Journal, 36*(2), 209–216.

Vandiver, V. (In press). *Integrating health promotion and mental health.* New York: Oxford University Press.

72 Developing Therapeutic Contracts with Clients

Juliet Cassuto Rothman

Therapeutic contracts are an essential element in working with clients. They provide a framework for focusing and goal setting, clarify roles and expectations, set time frames, and are helpful in evaluating progress and reviewing expectations. A contract is a voluntary joint effort between social workers and clients and provides a source of accountability in evaluating the efficacy of programs and services. Contracts have a specific form, which includes an overarching goal; a set of objectives that are both measurable and time-specific; specific interventions, which include tasks for both clients and workers; and a method of evaluation to determine the accomplishment of objectives. Contracts can be adapted to meet the needs of clients of all ages, cultural milieus, abilities, and concerns in both social work and host settings.

Contracts are agreements between parties that define and describe the nature of the relationship between them, including the responsibilities of each and the penalties that may accrue should one or more of the parties fail to keep the terms of the agreement. To be valid, contracts must be entered into freely by all parties. They may be formal or informal, verbal or written, or simply understood by all parties.

Contracting in social work has a long and not uncontroversial history. However, modern social work practice, with its focus on accountability, has made contracting an integral part of the therapeutic process. Social workers have several contractual relationships as professionals that precede those with specific clients. Contracts with employers, with programs and funding sources, with insurance companies, with the social work profession, and with society as a whole direct, define, and often limit the therapeutic contract. As one of the essential components of the social work processes, therapeutic contracting is most commonly used in work with individuals, children, couples, families, and therapeutic groups.

Contracting with clients supports the profession's values and mission. Through the contract, worker and client make a commitment to each other and to the goals of their work. Contracting empowers clients, focuses on client strengths and resources, and supports informed consent and self-determination. Alcabes and Jones (1985) state that prior to contracting, clients are not "clients" but "applicants," and the contracting process itself socializes "applicants" into their new role of "clients." Thus, the contract becomes the concrete symbol of the mutual commitment of client and worker to addressing and ameliorating the client's problem. Contracts are also powerful relationship-building tools in and of themselves. The contracting process encourages a search for common language, common goals, common objectives, and common commitment to improving the life of the client. The process of contracting continues throughout the time that the client is receiving service, although the specific kind and content of the contract may vary (Hepworth, Rooney, & Larsen, 1997).

A TYPOLOGY OF CLIENT CONTRACTS

Three very different kinds of contracts are used in social service settings, generally in the following order, from broadest to most specific.

The Service Contract, or Service Agreement

Clients generally enter into *service contracts* at the point of contact. Service contracts commonly include (1) the agency's mission, (2) a description of the agency's programs and services, (3) time frames for the provision of services, (4) fees for service or arrangements for reimbursement, (5) policies on confidentiality, (6) right of access to files, (7) releases for video- and tape-recording, and (8) release of information forms (Rothman, 1998). Service contracts are between a client and an agency. They are *not* between a client and a specific worker. The client has come to the agency for service, and the initial relationship is defined in this way. Workers in private practice may create service contracts for their practice by including many of the subjects just noted in a general policy statement for new clients. The worker is responsible for ascertaining that the client has understood the terms of the contract prior to initiating service. It is recommended that worker and client review the provisions of the service contract early in the relationship, so that the worker may clarify any parts that are unclear to the client. Where a client has no or limited familiarity with the English language, it is essential that arrangements be made to provide the service contract information in the client's language. Accommodations for clients with disabilities also need to ensure accessibility of service contract provisions. Clients who are minors may need to have contracts signed by parents or guardians to access certain kinds of services.

The Initial Contract

Initial contracts, developed with or immediately following the service contracts, simply state that worker and client agree that they will explore together whether the worker and the setting can assist the client to meet his or her goals. The process includes gathering, sharing, and assessing information; defining the needs and concerns; developing potential desired outcomes; and exploring whether the agency can provide the needed resources. This is often called the initial assessment period. Initial contracts include time frames that are often defined by the setting, the funding source, or the program. This phase of the work can generally be completed in three interviews if the time frame for the entire process is about 12 to 15 weeks. Because involuntary and mandated clients often do not willingly seek service, motivational and relationship-building processes may require additional time, because it is essential that clients understand that they have a choice about entering into treatment and options about goals and objectives.

Unlike service contracts, initial contracts are often quite informal. However, it is recommended that the worker carefully document all of the terms and conditions of the initial contract, including time frame, in the client's record. If possible, the client may sign or initial the entry to indicate awareness of this plan.

Suggested items to include in an initial contract include (1) meeting times, number of meetings, and location; (2) a review of confidentiality guidelines; (3) an assurance that client is stable and safe, and an agreement about any immediate actions that must be taken; (4) a determination of who will be contacted for information gathering, by whom, and why; (5) a clarification of the reason the client is seeking help at this time in the client's own words; (6) and a discussion of any known policies, guidelines, or rules that may directly impact the client (Rothman, 1998).

When the time of the initial contract is completed, client and worker together define areas of concern, select a focus for their work together, agree on an overarching goal, and begin the process of creating the therapeutic contract. During this initial period, "belief bonding"—the process through which client and worker come together—has occurred; this is a necessary precondition to the development of a successful and viable therapeutic contract (Bisman, 1994). "Belief bonding" occurs when a social worker's competence has been established, worker and client have agreed that change is possible, and the client has been seen as worthy of their joint efforts in effecting the change that both believe can occur (Bisman, 1994).

The Therapeutic Contract

The therapeutic contract builds directly on the service and initial contracts. These provide the general guidelines, information, and resources necessary to develop a therapeutic plan. Therapeutic contracts are the blueprints for the change process that will occur. They are generally formal, written, and signed by both worker and clients; however, variations should be considered if they are appropriate to specific client needs.

In selecting an appropriate theoretical framework for the therapeutic contract, workers may engage clients in the process of selection, use a personally preferred framework, or use the one preferred by the agency. Choice of framework will guide goal setting, as well as the development of objectives and interventions, and should be an integral part of the process of contracting. Although cognitive-behavioral tasks and interventions may be easier to develop owing to the format of the contract, any theoretical framework appropriate to social work will adapt well to the contracting process.

It is also essential that therapeutic contracts be culturally sensitive and support the values and belief system of the client. Contracts developed without such sensitivity can cause additional stress to the client and be a major barrier to long-term success. This requires sensitivity and self-awareness on the part of the social worker and agency policies that support and respect the clients cultural milieu and worldview. It is the responsibility of the social worker to learn about the client's culture and cultural experiences—an excellent source of this information is the client. Ethnographic interviewing may be very helpful in understanding the client's culture and his or her relationship to culture. This may be a part of the initial relationship-building and assessment process, and goals, objectives, and interventions should reflect the client's cultural experiences and concerns.

THE DEVELOPMENT OF THE THERAPEUTIC CONTRACT

Therapeutic contracts have four distinct parts: (1) an overarching goal; (2) several objectives; (3) interventions, treatments, or tasks that will fulfill the objectives; and (4) a mechanism for review and evaluation of the contract. It is important to use language that is clear and comfortable for the client in writing the contract; professional jargon should be carefully avoided.

Contracts themselves should be separate from the main body of recording and progress notes. A clear and simple format is best. The form provided in Figure 72.1 can be adapted as needed to reflect both the client's language and concerns and the agency's context of services and programs. Suggestions are offered for forms of intervention; these can be used as appropriate to the objective.

To illustrate the development and functioning of therapeutic contracts, we will consider Peter, a client with a history of mental illness, who is about to be discharged from a recent hospitalization. Peter has difficulty in maintaining his medical regimen, has no known family support, is fearful and untrusting of social workers, and wants to return to the community. He has been referred to a community mental health agency. We shall follow Peter through the phases of contract development, assessment, and evaluation.

Name: _____

Overarching Goal: _____

Date	Objective	Interventions	Date	Evaluation
	(For each objective)	(For each intervention) (Client, worker, client and worker, other entity) will do _____ (what).		Comment about objective and interventions
	#1 _____ (Action) in _____ (Time Frame) as evidenced by _____ (measurement)	#1. _____ #2. _____ #3. _____ #4. _____ (Numbers will vary by what needs to be done)		#1 _____
		(Continue to list objectives and interventions)		

Client Signature: _____   Worker Signature _____   Date _____

Figure 72.1 Action in time frame.

Step 1: Goals

The overarching goal is generally broad and inclusive, such as "return to community" or, later, "remain in community setting." There should be only one overarching goal; more would diffuse the focus of the work, and the goal selected should be broad enough to encompass many possible objectives.

Step 2: Objectives

Each objective must include three related parts: (1) an action statement, (2) a time frame, and (3) a method for measuring success or failure. The form "*Action* in *Time Frame* as evidenced by *Measurement*" can be used. Other wording may be substituted as desired commensurate with client needs and preferences.

Additionally, the following guidelines will assist the client and worker with this task.

- Objectives should always be reflective of the client's desires.
- Objectives should be reasonably few in number; too many objectives can be overwhelming or can diffuse the client's energy such that nothing is achieved. Too few objectives can severely limit options for action. Three or four is generally a good number to develop.
- Objectives should be reasonably simple, specific, and written using the client's own words.
- Objectives should be measurable and reasonable to achieve in a specified time frame. Time frames can vary for each objective within the contract. However, they should be designed so that the contract is reviewed at least every 3 months to maintain continuity and evaluate progress.
- Objectives should be ordered in time. If one is necessary before another can be achieved, it should be placed first.
- Objectives should be ordered by priority. If a client is strongly motivated toward one objective, or one is more urgent than another, place the more vital one first.
- Objectives should be achievable with reasonable effort. Success will inspire and motivate clients, whereas objectives that require major life changes and complex or difficult actions will be discouraging, will not be achieved, and will reinforce a client's sense of failure and low self-esteem (Rothman, 1998).

Possible objectives for assisting Peter to return to community setting might include:

1. *Assess housing resources in the community* (action) as evidenced by *the development of a list of possible housing* (measurement) in *1 week* (time frame).
2. *Arrange follow-up medical care in the community* (action) as evidenced by *a written agreement with a community health clinic* (measurement) in *2 weeks* (time frame).
3. *Attend one community support group meeting* (action) as evidenced by *support group sign-in sheet* (measurement) in *2 weeks* (time frame).

Step 3: Interventions

Interventions are developed to support *each* objective. They are the *who* and the *what* of the contract. The *who* is generally the worker or the client, but it may be another person or group—a parent, a sibling, and so on. The *what* describes what the person will do. Interventions often use the form *who* will do *what*.

Possible interventions for Peter's second objective might include the following.

- *Worker* (who) will *locate health clinics* (what) in the community that can serve Peter.
- *Worker and Peter* (who) will *review list and select a health clinic* (what).
- *Worker* (who) will *arrange appointment* (what) for Peter at health clinic.
- *Peter* (who) will *request his medical history* (what) from the hospital.
- *Peter* (who) will *take medical history to the clinic* (what) at the appointed time.

Because the therapeutic contract is a joint enterprise, it is vital that both worker and client have responsibilities in the interventions defined. If all of the defined tasks are for the client, the worker–client alliance will be minimized. However, it is not necessary that there be an equal number of tasks for each.

It is also important to consider the client's cultural context in the development of intervention strategies particularly. Strategies should support empowerment, maintenance of culture, and the unique personhood of the client. Cultural resources should be explored and considered when appropriate. It is essential to recognize, however, that cultural attitudes and beliefs may not always support client objectives. In Peter's case, it is important to recognize that it may not be appropriate to involve cultural resources if Peter does not identify with the culture, chooses to separate from his cultural group, or if his culture's understanding and beliefs about mental illness would not support his overarching goal.

Goals, objectives, and interventions together form the therapeutic contract. The remaining piece is the evaluation or assessment, which is completed when the contract is reviewed on completion of the time frames or achievement of an objective, and is presented below.

THE THERAPEUTIC CONTRACT AS A DYNAMIC, EVOLVING SYSTEM

The therapeutic contract is an ongoing assessment tool in the therapeutic process. Each objective has several possible outcomes: (1) it is achieved, (2) it is not achieved, (3) it is partially achieved, or (4) it is unachievable for various reasons.

Achieved Objectives

When an objective is achieved, it should be noted on the contract in the "evaluation" column with the date of the review. It is best if the objective and interventions are not removed, because achievement can serve as a positive reinforcement for the client. Crossing out, highlighting, or writing "achieved" across the objective allows it to remain as a testimony of the client's effort and success. A completed objective is an opportunity for the development of a new one. The new objective can build on the old or develop a new line of action in addressing the client's problem. If more than one objective is achieved, several new ones may be added during a review. New objectives should support the overarching goal that was defined when the original contract was developed.

Objectives Not Achieved

Objectives may not be achieved owing to problems in each of the three sections of the objective statement, development of the tasks and interventions, or external factors. Careful examination and exploration by worker and client can locate and possibly correct the objective so that it may be achieved in another form. If, after review, it is found that the objective cannot be met, it should be discarded and replaced.

Problems with objective statement

- *Problems with the action.* Actions that are not possible due to physical, psychological, emotional, or social barriers will not support the success of an objective. For example, Peter's stated goal is to return to the community. An objective that states "Arrange placement with brother in Miami" when Peter lives in Phoenix does not address the client's stated wishes and desires and thus cannot be successful. An objective that states "Locate a bed in a group home for Peter" will not be met if there are no group homes in the area being considered.

- *Problems with the time frame.* Time frames must be reasonable and appropriate to the difficulty and complexity of the objective. Setting time frames that are too short will frustrate client and worker alike and cause the objective to fail. Time frames that are too long can result in loss of motivation, interest, or impetus.

  "Locate housing in the community for Peter in 3 days" may be setting too short a time frame, whereas "3 months" might be too long for this task. The worker must use knowledge of the community, the client, and resources to develop a time frame that permits achievement of the objective.

  If objectives are not met owing to time frame difficulties, worker and client may reassess and extend the time frame. Time frames should not be extended more than one time. If the problem persists, the objective should be reformulated or rephrased.

- *Problems with the measurement criteria.* There are times when the measurement criteria may measure something, but not necessarily the success of the objective. Peter needs monitoring of his medication regimen. This activity has been addressed as the objective "Compliance with medication regimen as noted by worker for 1 month." The action and the time frame, are appropriate but how will the worker "measure" Peter's compliance without testing or medical monitoring?

"Locate housing in the community as evidenced by placement of Peter in community setting" has similar problems in measurement. Housing may be "located," but Peter may refuse to go, or the hospital may decide he is not ready for release, or there may be a waiting list in the housing complex. "Locate" means something quite different than "placement."

• *Problems with interventions, methods, or tasks.* Objectives may not be achieved if the interventions selected to achieve them are not adequate or are not related to the objective. For example, the objective "Develop a plan for Peter to return to the community in 1 week" cannot be achieved through the task of "Exploring activities available in institution," or even by "Contacting sister in Alaska," as much as that sister might be a support to the client.

The objective "Visit a halfway house with the social worker in 2 weeks" cannot be achieved with an intervention plan that sets up visits to day treatment centers rather than halfway houses. If these are to be included in planning, the objective must be rewritten to bring it in line with the intervention.

Partially Achieved Objectives

An objective that is partially achieved may have one of the previously noted problems. It may be possible to rewrite or rephrase the objective and extend the time frame, thus enabling another opportunity for meeting it.

Unachievable Objectives

Sometimes the objectives chosen may be unachievable owing to any number of factors: limitations in an agency's program; restrictions grounded in policy; changes in the problem, the client's life, or support network; or the refusal of the client to work on the objective. These objectives should be changed as soon as the worker becomes aware of the problem.

CONCLUSION

Therapeutic contracts often serve several functions simultaneously. They support self-determination, informed consent, and empowerment and focus the worker and client on specific tasks, treatments, and objectives. Therapeutic contracts are excellent resources for assessment and measurement of progress and also serve to provide an objective measure of performance for agencies, funding sources, clients, and social workers themselves. As limited time frames and the exigencies of managed care impact client–worker relationships, the therapeutic contract serves as a grounding and a rationale to support and enhance professional social work practice. Built on the foundation created in the work of the service contract and the initial contract, the therapeutic contract is an excellent tool to encourage workers and clients to explore avenues for effecting and enabling change within the client system.

WEB SITE

NASW Standards for Social Work Practice: Child Welfare. http://www .socialworkers.org/practice/standards/ NASWChildWelfareStandards0905.pdf

References

Alcabes, A., & Jones, J. A. (1985). Structural determinants of "clienthood." *Social Work, 30*(1), 49–53.
Bisman, C. (1994). *Social work practice: Theory and principles.* Pacific Grove, CA: Brooks/Cole.
Hepworth, D., Rooney, R., & Larsen, J. A. (1997). *Direct social work practice: Theory and skills.* Pacific Grove, CA: Brooks/Cole.
Rothman, J. (1998). *Contracting in clinical social work.* Chicago: Nelson Hall.

73 Developing Goals

Charles D. Garvin

This chapter defines the concept of goals and the rationale for their use in social work practice. Different types of goals are identified as well as guidelines for establishing them. The chapter concludes with a discussion of the ways that cultural and social circumstances should be taken into consideration in this process.

The development and clarification of clients' goals are necessary steps in bringing about individual as well as environmental changes. According to Hepworth, Rooney, Rooney, Strom-Gottfried, and Larson (2006, p. 314), "Goals specify what clients wish to accomplish." The authors add, "Inherent in goals are desired changes in clients' life situations that correspond to wants and needs identified when problems were explored and assessed." For example, one client's long-range goal was "to be employed as a social worker." That client's short-term goals were to enroll in a school of social work, pass the courses, and complete the other requirements of the school. A barrier to attaining these goals was the client's lack of money. This led to another goal of obtaining money from the client's parents to pay for tuition.

A process that precedes goal setting is that of assessment. The assessment process is related to goals as the assessment provides the practitioner and the client with answers to the following questions. (1) What levels of goal attainment are possible given the resources and limitations present in the clients and their situations? (2) What changes must be sought in clients and their situations to attain specified goals? These changes are specified in terms of short-term goals that must be attained before long-term goals are worked on. Blythe and Reithoffer (2000) recommend instruments that can be used to assess clients in ways that link closely to goal determination.

An example of this was work with John W., who had recently been discharged from a hospital following major heart surgery. A social worker helped him develop a discharge plan that would enable him to return to an active role in the community. This work began with an assessment that included John's previous level of functioning, the level of functioning he could be expected to attain, and the likely length of the recovery process. From this assessment, the social worker and John jointly developed several goals. One of these was to complete a physical therapy program. Barriers to this completion were identified, such as lack of transportation, and the social worker helped John develop means of overcoming these barriers. The physical therapist helped John develop additional goals, one of which was to regain enough strength to enable him to resume his previous employment as a computer repair person.

RATIONALE FOR THE USE OF GOALS IN PRACTICE

According to Hepworth et al. (2006, 316), there are a number of reasons for seeking an agreement between client and practitioner with respect to goals. The agreement:

- ensures that social workers and clients are in agreement, where possible, about outcomes, to be achieved;
- provides direction, focus, and continuity to the helping process and prevents wandering;
- facilitates the development and selection of appropriate strategies and interventions;
- assists social workers and clients in monitoring their progress; and
- serves as outcome criteria in evaluating the effectiveness of specific interventions and of the helping process.

It has also been demonstrated that when clients and workers have not defined goals for their work together, clients are likely to leave treatment prematurely (Meyer, 2001).

GOALS AND PRACTICE PHASE

Goals should be determined during the first phase of practice, when the practitioner is becoming engaged with the client and assessing strengths and resources. As clients develop relationships with the practitioner, they will be more likely to disclose their problems and work toward solving them. As they achieve an agreement with the practitioner on problems, goals, and solutions, they are more likely to have positive feelings toward the practitioner and the work they do together.

Movement beyond this first phase into a work phase cannot occur until an initial relationship has been established, problems identified, goals specified, and an initial work plan created. The amount of time this takes will vary depending on the nature of the problem, the strengths of the client, the skills of the practitioner, the resources that are available, and the presence or absence of conflict between clients and practitioners about these issues. When the agency imposes time limits, this will also be a factor in determining the goals that are chosen and the means that are selected to achieve them.

Goal issues may also arise during subsequent treatment phases. For example, clients may wish to change their treatment goals (1) when they attain them and may continue treatment to work on additional goals, (2) when their situation changes, or (3) when goal attainment does not take place.

TYPES OF GOALS

The practitioner should recognize that there are different types of goals that require somewhat different kinds of interventions in order for the client to attain them. These include the following.

Discrete versus Continuous Goals

Discrete goals are those in which a single outcome is sought, such as admission to a school. Continuous goals are those in which the client or another entity enacts the behavior that constitutes the goal on a number of occasions, such as a parent who disciplines a child by offering rewards instead of punishments.

Goals Related to Different Types of Systems

Goals may relate to outcomes for an individual, a dyad, a small group (including the family), an organization, or even a larger system. The larger the system, the greater the number of people who may have to be involved in not only setting the goal but also working for its attainment.

Goals Related to Different Kinds of Behaviors

Goals may relate to affects, cognitions, or instrumental behaviors or combinations of these. An example of this is a client who experienced anxiety attacks when he spoke in class. One goal was that he no longer experience the anxiety (affect goal); another was that he speak in class (instrumental behavior goal); a third was that he no longer label making a mistake in what he said in class as proving that he was stupid (cognitive goal).

Individual versus Reciprocal or Interpersonal Goals

A goal may relate to the behavior of the client acting alone. An example of this is a client whose goal was to report on time to work every day. The goal, however, may be reciprocal. An example of this was a family meeting with a family therapist. The parents agreed to take their entire family on a outing when the children had all completed their household chores every day for a week.

SELECTION OF GOALS

There are a number of criteria the practitioner should consider in helping clients select their treatment goals. The first of these, as should be obvious from the foregoing discussion, is that the goal, if attained, should reduce or eliminate the problem(s) for which the client has sought help. The client should also have an emotional investment in attaining the goals. If the client or the practitioner is working toward a goal that is not known to the other, the process will be seriously flawed because communication is likely to be confusing to each party, and tensions between them will emerge as a result.

A special problem in negotiating goals is posed by involuntary clients—those who are required, by a court or other system with power, to keep appointments with the practitioner because the system will impose sanctions for nonparticipation in treatment. Hepworth et al. (2006, pp. 317–318) and De Jong and Berg (2001) suggest several approaches for goal setting with such clients. One of these is to look for a common ground between client and system.

GUIDELINES FOR ESTABLISHING GOALS

The goals agreed to by the practitioner and the client should meet a set of criteria and become part of either a verbal or a written contract. These criteria are as follows.

- Goals should be explicit. This means that a specific behavior or circumstance should be indicated. The situation in which the behavior is to occur as well as its frequency or intensity should be described. When workers and clients are vague in specifying goals, this can lead to a lack of focus in their work together (Ribner & Knei-Paz, 2002).
- The attainment of the goal should be measurable. The measures may be either qualitative or quantitative.
- The goal should always be stated in terms of client (not practitioner) behavior. Some practitioners begin goal statements with such phrases as "help the client," which is what we assume the worker will do.
- The goal should be chosen with due regard of client and practitioner to feasibility. This depends on opportunities available in the environment, the attitudes and abilities of significant others, and social, political, and economic conditions. We recommend that the client be given the benefit of the doubt on this issue.
- Legality should be a major issue in selecting a goal. Practitioners should not help clients work to attain illegal or immoral goals. This is not as easy to implement in some situations, such as a terminally ill client who wishes help to commit suicide when offering such help is illegal. Fortunately, the National Association of Social Workers and other professional associations are developing guidelines to help practitioners determine what to do in such situations. At times, the goal is counter to the practitioner's ethics but not those of the profession or society.
- The goal should be one in which the skills and knowledge of the practitioner are adequate to help the client attain the goal.
- The practitioner should consider the consequences for others of contracting with the client to work toward the stated goals. We believe that professional ethics require that the worker not collude with the client to harm others.
- Goals should be stated in positive terms. An example of this is the goal of acquiring ways of appropriately disciplining a child rather than refraining from inflicting inappropriate punishment on the child. We find that working toward positive goals is more likely to occur than the opposite, and this emphasis on client growth enhances self-esteem and a sense of accomplishment.

The steps in establishing goals are the following (Hepworth et al., 2006, pp. 316–317).

Step 1: Identify and Prioritize Problems

The practitioner should ask clients to indicate the problem(s) they hope to solve as a result of coming for treatment. Many clients will state the problem in terms of the behavior of another person, such as, "My son won't go to school" or "My husband criticizes me too much." We have no objection to problems stated in this way. If the worker rejects such statements, many clients will refuse to continue because they will conclude that the worker has no regard for their views. There will be time enough as goals are developed to help the clients to include their own actions in the definition of the situation.

Problem statements in family treatment may take on a different form than in one-to-one treatment. They are likely to involve relationships and interactions, such as a husband and wife who stated that they cannot resolve arguments, agree on how resources are to be spent, or engage in satisfying sexual interactions. It will be useful later in treatment if the family or couple can state the problem in ways that are not solely focused on one family member (the so-called identified patient), but this is not absolutely necessary and may, in some situations, be an impossible demand.

In groups, the first members to define their problems will serve as models for others who find this task more difficult. If the group has been composed of individuals with similar problems, this stage of the process may not be difficult because members may already have decided on the problems they will work on in the group as part of an individual interview held before the group begins.

Examples of problems and related goals

Problem: Parent states problem is the destructive behavior of an adolescent child.

Goals: Learn techniques for negotiating limits with child when child violates a rule set by parent in ways that are satisfying to both parties; learn to state expectations of child's behavior in specific terms that indicate what is expected rather than what is unacceptable.

Problem: Client is failing college courses.

Goals: Organize a schedule for completion of assignments that is realistic in terms of work and recreation; negotiate with biology instructor a date to complete work that is realistic for student and acceptable to instructor.

Step 2: Determine Client's Readiness to Set Goals

Hepworth et al. (2006, p. 326) recommend that when the practitioner believes it is time to work on goals, she or he should determine whether the client agrees that she or he is ready for this process. At times, the client will assert that additional information should be considered before goals are set; at other times, the client will indicate a readiness to proceed.

Step 3: Provide a Rationale for Goals

The practitioner should examine the reasons for goals. Important ideas that should be conveyed here are the weight placed on client self-determination and the relationship of setting goals to determining whether the treatment is effective. The client should be helped to understand that goals represent changes the client would like to see in relationship to the problem if the treatment is successful.

Step 4: Identify and Choose Goals

As indicated earlier, the client is asked what she or he would like to see changed if treatment is successful in ameliorating the problem. At times, especially when the client has limitations owing to age or disability, the social worker may suggest some goals from which the client is invited to make a choice. These choices should be explained and illustrated so that as much input from the client as possible is obtained.

Step 5: Explicate the Goals

There are several components of a well-formulated goal statement, one stated so specifically that its attainment is measurable. Garvin and Seabury

(1997, p. 155) indicate the characteristics of such statements:

- performance (what the learner is to be able to do),
- conditions (important conditions under which the performance is expected to occur), and
- criterion (the quality or level of performance that will be considered acceptable).

These characteristics can be used whether the goal is in terms of the client's own behavior or the behavior of a person or system other than the client. An example of a goal for a client's own behavior is: "Joan, when faced with a derogatory statement from her employer (Sally) with which she does not agree, will calmly indicate her disagreement to the employer." The criterion for the quality of the performance is that the employer will acknowledge that she has heard and understood Joan's views.

Step 6: Determining Feasibility, Benefits, and Risks

The practitioner should avoid encouraging the client to spend a great deal of time and effort trying to achieve a goal that is not feasible when this could have been determined in advance. Hepworth et al. (2006, p. 329) suggest that the practitioner determine feasibility by asking the clients what obstacles they anticipate might block them in achieving their goals. Anticipating obstacles, of course, does not mean the clients should forgo striving to attain the goal, because all goal-attainment activities will come up against obstacles. Rather, are these obstacles so severe that no reasonable amount of effort will overcome them?

Step 7: Determining Goal Priorities

When the client's goals derive from several different problems, the priority attached to each problem will determine the priority of the goal.

These steps for goal setting are summarized in Figure 73.1.

SPECIAL POPULATIONS

The practitioner should take into consideration the cultural and social circumstances of different populations when seeking to determine goals with

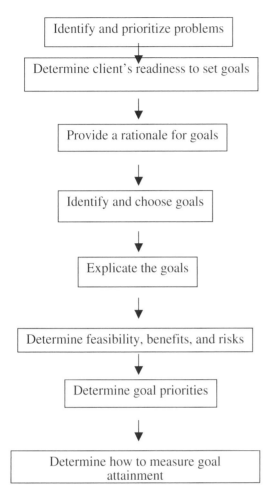

Figure 73.1 Steps in establishing goals.

1. How does the client feel about creating long-term objectives as compared to having objectives that are very short range? That is, does the person give much value to a future orientation as compared to one oriented to the present?
2. How does the individual feel about personal goals as compared to goals oriented to the welfare of one's family, community, or other reference group? Some individuals see it as much more important to work for the betterment of these systems and as almost inconceivable to put one's own welfare ahead of the group.
3. What aspects of living are regarded as the most and least important? Some cultures see family outcomes as the most important; for others, occupational outcomes are the most important; others see educational outcomes as the most important; and still others stress the kind of person the individual is or is becoming as of the highest value. These kinds of beliefs have a strong impact on the goals that the individual will be strongly motivated to attain.

CONCLUSION

The chapter began with a definition of the term *goals*. Goals may refer to ultimate, intermediate, and instrumental outcomes, and these terms were also defined. Goals are chosen in relationship to an assessment of clients and their circumstances, and the connection between goals and assessment data was stressed.

Practice principles for the creation of goal statements were presented. These differ depending on such issues as whether the client is voluntary or involuntary. An important principle is that the goals should relate to the presenting problem, and consequently, the process of problem specification was also described. Finally, this chapter discussed goal issues that arise with different populations, such as those related to gender and ethnicity.

Goal setting is likely to be regarded as even more important in the future than it is now. This will be because of emphases on attaining desired outcomes as a justification for providing managed care services, linking interventions to goals, and empowering clients to select the goals that are appropriate for their cultures and personal lifestyles.

members of these populations. The types of populations considered here are ethnic and cultural groups, age groups, and groups with limited capacities to select goals.

The ethnicity and culture of the client will have an impact on the goals the client will consider. We do not believe, however, in approaching this topic with such generalizations as "Native Americans will favor goal X" because of the variation within groups related to degree of assimilation, specific life experience, and so forth. Nevertheless, we believe that the cultural experiences a person has had will help determine his or her values and aspirations, which in turn will help determine his or her goals. The practitioner should bear in mind, consequently, questions such as the following that may help him or her discuss goals in ways compatible with the client's beliefs.

WEB SITES

Evidence Based Mental Health. http://ebmh
.bmj.com.
Journal of Social Work Research and Evaluation.
http://www.springerpub.com/journals/social_
work_research.html.

References

Blythe, B., & Reithoffer, A. (2000). Assessment and measurement issues in direct practice in social work.
In P. Allen-Meares & C. Garvin (Eds.), *The handbook of social work direct practice* (pp. 551–564).
Thousand Oaks, CA: Sage.

De Jong, P., & Berg, I. K. (2001). Co-constructing cooperation with mandated clients. *Social Work*, 46(4),
361–374.
Garvin, C. D., & Seabury, B. A. (1997). *Interpersonal
practice in social work: Promoting competence and
social justice*, 2nd ed. Boston: Allyn & Bacon.
Hepworth, D. H., Rooney, R. H., Rooney, G. D., Strom-
Gottfried, K., & Larson, J. A. (2006). *Direct social
work practice: Theory and skills*, 7th ed. Belmont,
CA: Thomson, Brooks/Cole.
Meyer, W. (2001). Why don't they come back: A clinical
perspective on the no-show client. *Clinical Social
Work*, 29(4), 325–339.
Ribner, D. S., & Knei-Paz, C. (2002). Client's view of a
successful helping relationship. *Social Work*, 47(4),
379–387.

74 Treatment Planning with Adolescents
ADHD Case Applications

David W. Springer & Kimberly Bender

Treatment plans and treatment goals are established collaboratively between the social worker
and the adolescent and help focus their work together. Goals specify what the adolescent wants
to work on in treatment, and the treatment plan
serves as a game plan for how these goals will be
obtained. Treatment goals and treatment plans are
a critical component of effective social work practice; without them, both social workers and clients run the risk of aimlessly "stumbling around
in the dark" until they happen across a "problem" that needs to be addressed. As consumers
of care, we expect our primary care physicians to
deliver services with some sense of purpose, direction, and expertise. We should expect no less
from social workers and the care they provide.

To this end, treatment plans serve as very useful
tools. This chapter provides guidelines for establishing treatment goals and plans with adolescent clients.

TREATMENT GOALS

The first step in establishing treatment goals with
any client is to conduct a thorough assessment.
This entails allowing the client to tell his or her
story, conducting a psychosocial history, and using standardized assessment tools and rapid assessment instruments as needed. Clients may also
need to be referred for medical and/or psychological testing. Following a thorough assessment,

the social worker and client work together to establish goals for the client. In this sense, goals link the assessment and treatment process.

The following guidelines are helpful in establishing treatment goals. The goals should be (1) clearly defined and measurable, (2) feasible and realistic, (3) set collaboratively by the social worker and the client, (4) stem directly from the assessment process, and (5) stated in positive terms, focusing on client growth. Treatment goals help direct the social worker and the client toward "cognitive, emotional, behavioral, and situational actions" (Cournoyer, 2005, p. 322).

Treatment goals need to be defined clearly and stated in such a way that progress toward the goals can be measured. If goals are stated too ambiguously, clients may become discouraged or feel as if the goals are out of reach. For example, compare the ambiguous goal of "improve school performance" with the more concrete goal of "complete at least 90 percent of homework assignments over the next 2 weeks." The latter goal is more likely to be meaningful and obtainable to the client.

This leads to the second element of establishing treatment goals, which is that they must be feasible and realistic. "Improving school performance" is not only vague, it may not be feasible or realistic because it potentially covers so much ground. Additionally, little discussion between the social worker and the adolescent is needed to create vague goals. By contrast, concrete goals require a serious dialogue to take place so that conceptual ideas about client functioning can be "wrestled to the ground" in clear, day-to-day terms.

To the extent that adolescent clients participate in this discussion, the more likely it is that they will feel a sense of ownership over the established goals, which in turn means that they are more likely to follow through with the treatment plan. Clients (especially adolescents) will experience less buy-in to the treatment process if goals are imposed on them by a social worker or parent. Thus, goal setting needs to be a truly collaborative process among the social worker, adolescent, and his or her parents (when appropriate).

Treatment goals need to stem directly from the assessment process. The assessment should be thorough, empirically based, and grounded in a systems perspective. This minimizes the likelihood that the worker is creating treatment goals based solely on gut feeling or an on-the-spot diagnosis.

Finally, treatment goals need to be stated in positive terms. In other words, the goal should state what the client *will* do rather than what the

client *will not* do. For example, a client will be more motivated and goal directed by a goal that states "attend the entire school day every day for the next 2 weeks" in comparison to a goal that states "stop skipping school."

TREATMENT PLANS

Treatment plans are the next logical step after goals have been formulated, and in practice these two steps often go hand in hand. Treatment plans reflect what specific and concrete steps or interventions are going to be implemented to help the adolescent client obtain his or her goals.

The process of establishing a treatment plan should be collaborative between the adolescent (and his or her family) and social worker. As a natural extension of the movement started under the Child and Adolescent Service System Program initiated in 1984 by the National Institute of Mental Health, many communities across the states have recently received federal funding through the Substance Abuse and Mental Health Services Administration, Center for Mental Health Services to implement a community-based, wraparound approach to service delivery within a system of care (Rosenblatt, 1998). A major emphasis of this approach is providing individualized, client-centered services for youth with serious emotional disturbance and multiple mental health needs. One pragmatic way this is accomplished is to actively involve the youth and his or her family in the development of a treatment plan, recognizing the client as an expert on his or her own life.

The client is an expert on his or her own life, and the social worker can (and should) lend expertise regarding what treatment approaches or interventions are most effective for a given problem. For example, if medication management or cognitive-behavioral therapy has been demonstrated to be effective for a given problem or disorder, the social worker has a responsibility to share this information with the adolescent and his or her family to provide guidance as they develop the treatment plan.

Case Illustration: Steven

Steven is a 15-year-old white male who has been referred to the school social worker by his teacher because "he won't sit still and he doesn't follow instructions." The teacher also complains that Steven has a very short attention span, often gets into trouble in class for blurting out answers, and is easily distracted. Though not previously referred for services, Steven has been having trouble with impulsivity and inattention since starting elementary school. He has no history of past mental health treatment, no remarkable medical history, and denies any substance use.

A thorough assessment would need to be conducted. For example, this might entail the following: interviews with Steven, his family, and his teachers; psychological testing; direct observations of his behaviors in natural settings; and use of standardized assessment instruments (e.g., the Conners Parent Rating Scale Revised [Conners, 1997]). Following this assessment process, suppose it is determined that Steven meets the following diagnostic criteria:

Axis I: 314.01 ADHD, combined type
Axis II: V71.09 No diagnosis on axis II
Axis III: None
Axis IV: Educational problems (poor school performance, discord with teachers); problems with primary support group (discord with parents)
Axis V: GAF = 65 (current)

Furthermore, suppose that specific behavioral problem areas are identified. These areas of concern would be listed and treatment goals (both short- and long-term) would be established with corresponding interventions.

A sample treatment plan for Steven is provided in Table 74.1. Notice that the treatment plan includes both short- and long-term goals and specifies who is responsible for what task. Some treatment plans may also include target dates that reflect when a specific goal is to be reviewed to determine whether it has been accomplished or needs to be revised. The sample treatment plan for Steven is intended to serve as a template. It is important to note that different goals or interventions could have been included or emphasized depending on how problem areas were identified and prioritized by Steven, his family, and/or the social worker. A treatment plan needs to be tailored to the individual and unique needs of the client.

Readers are cautioned against taking a cookie-cutter approach to establishing treatment plans. Suppose that Steven also presented with behavioral problems associated with oppositional defiant disorder, that he was at risk of running away from home, or that he and his parents wanted to enroll him in a different school. These areas of concern would also need to be addressed in the

treatment plan, with corresponding goals and interventions. Obviously, the treatment plan above does not reflect the complexities of treating an adolescent with ADHD. Readers interested in a more detailed exposition on how to treat adolescents with ADHD are referred elsewhere (see Barkley, 2000; Ervin, DuPaul, Kerm, & Friman, 1998; Evans et al., 2006; Pelham, Fabiano, & Massetti, 2005; Raggi & Chronis, 2006; Robin, 1998; U.S. Department of Education, 2006).

One additional note about the case illustration is warranted. The vignette focuses on an adolescent with a diagnosis of ADHD for a reason. ADHD is one of the most common axis I diagnoses encountered by practitioners working with youth; however, other common disorders encountered by practitioners working with adolescents in clinical settings may include disruptive behavior disorders (oppositional defiant disorder and conduct disorder), major depressive disorder, and substance abuse (see American Psychiatric Association [APA], 2000; Christner, Stewart, & Freeman, 2007; Dishion & Kavanagh, 2003).

CONCLUSION

Adolescents are in a unique developmental phase of life where the struggle for autonomy and individuation are amplified. Add to this potentially tumultuous process a *DSM-IV-TR* (APA, 2000) axis I diagnosis or a serious emotional disturbance, and these young people become even more vulnerable to life's ups and downs. Social workers have an ethical responsibility to work closely with the adolescent (and his or her family) to develop a treatment plan that is sensitive to the cultural and other unique needs of the client, grounded in a biopsychosocial perspective and empirically based practice, and measurable. Most important, the adolescent must have input into the development of the treatment plan in a meaningful way to maximize the likelihood that he or she is invested in the treatment process and will sustain lasting change over time.

WEB SITES

Children and Adults with ADHD, national support group association. http://www.chadd.org.
National Institute of Mental Health: Child and Adolescent Mental Health.

TABLE 74.1 Sample Treatment Plan for Steven

Areas of Concern	Short-Term Goals	Long-Term Goals	Treatment Plan
1. Difficulty paying attention 2. Has trouble listening 3. Has trouble organizing 4. Often avoids activities that require sustained mental effort 5. Loses things often 6. Easily distracted 7. Often fidgets or squirms 8. Often leaves seat during class 9. Has difficulty playing quietly 10. Talks excessively 11. Blurts out answers to questions 12. Conflict with parents	1. Steven will begin to take prescribed medication as directed by physician. 2. Steven will begin to increase his on-task behavior, as evidenced by completing 90% of homework assignments. 3. Steven's parents and teachers will create and begin to use a system to monitor homework. 4. Steven will demonstrate improved impulse control, as evidenced by earning 3 points a day in every class (for staying in seat, waiting his turn to talk). 5. Steven's teachers will set up a reward (point) system to reinforce positive behavior and discourage negative behavior. 6. Steven's parents will set firm and consistent limits, using natural rewards and consequences. 7. Steven's teachers will work with him to create a classroom setting that reduces distractions. 8. Steven and parents will improve communication and establish a behavioral contract.	1. Steven will take prescribed medication on a regular basis. 2. Steven will engage in on-task behavior on a regular basis, as evidenced by completing 100% of homework assignments. 3. Steven's parents and teachers will consistently monitor homework. 4. Steven will demonstrate improved impulse control, as evidenced by earning 5 points a day in every class (for staying in seat, waiting his turn to talk). 5. Steven's teachers will maintain a reward (point) system to further reinforce positive behavior and discourage negative behavior. 6. Steven's parents will set firm and consistent limits, using natural rewards and consequences. 7. Steven's teachers will help to maintain a classroom setting that reduces distractions. 8. Steven and parents will maintain improved communication and will modify behavioral contract as needed to aid in parental limit setting and establishing clear rules.	1. Social worker will refer Steven to psychiatrist for medication management and will consult with psychiatrist regularly. 2. Steven, social worker, his parents, and teachers will meet to set up a system to monitor his homework, set up a point system in the classroom (to reinforce positive behaviors), and enhance the classroom setting (to reduce distractions). 3. Steven's parents will attend an 8-week parenting class to learn ways to set limits and boundaries, and use natural rewards and consequences. 4. Steven will learn to use self-monitoring skills (e.g., internal self-talk) to control impulsive behavior at home and in school. 5. Steven and parents will attend weekly family therapy sessions with social worker to clarify rules, enhance communication, establish a behavioral contract, and learn about ADHD.

http://www.nimh.nih.gov/health/topics/child-and-adolescent-mental-health/index.shtml.

References

American Psychiatric Association. (2000). *Diagnostic and statistical manual of mental disorders*, 4th ed., text revision. Washington, DC: APA.

Barkley, R. A. (2000). Commentary on the Multimodal Treatment Study of Children with ADHD. *Journal of Abnormal child Psychology. 28*(6), 595–599.

Christner, R. W., Stewart, J. L., & Freeman, A. (Eds.). *Handbook of cognitive-behavior group therapy with children and adolescents: specific settings and presenting problems*. New York: Routledge.

Conners, C. K. (1997). *Conners Parent Rating Scale—revised.* North Tonowanda, NY: Multi-Health Systems.

Cournoyer, B. R. (2005). *The social work skills workbook.* Belmont, CA: Thomson Brooks/Cole.

Dishion, T. J. & Kavanagh, K. (2003). *Intervening in adolescent problem behavior: A family-centered approach.* New York: Guilford.

Ervin, R. A., DuPaul, G. J., Kern, L., & Friman, P. C. (1998). Classroom-based functional and adjunctive assessments: Proactive approaches to intervention selection for adolescents with attention-deficit hyperactivity disorder. *Journal of Applied Behavioral Analysis, 31*(1), 65–78.

Evans, S. W., Timmins, B., Sibley, M., White, L. C., Zewelanji, N. S., & Schultz, B. (2006). Developing coordinated, multimodal, school-based treatment for young adolescents with ADHD. *Education and Treatment of Children, 29*(2), 359–378.

Pelham, W. E., Fabiano, G. A., & Massetti, G. M. (2005). Evidence-based assessment of attention deficit hyperactivity disorder in children and adolescents. *Journal of Clinical Child and Adolescent Psychology, 34*(3), 449–476.

Raggi, V. L., & Chronis, A. M. (2006). Interventions to address the academic impairment of children and adolescents with ADHD. *Clinical Child and Family Psychology Review, 9*(2), 85–111.

Robin, A. L. (1998). *ADHD in adolescents: Diagnosis and treatment.* New York: Guilford.

Rosenblatt, A. (1998). Assessing the child and family outcomes of systems of care for youth with serious emotional disturbance. In M. H. Epstein, K. Kutash, & A. Duchnowski (Eds.), *Outcomes for children and youth with behavioral and emotional disorders and their families: Programs and evaluation best practice* (pp. 329–362). Austin, TX: PRO-ED.

U.S. Department of Education, Office of Special Education and Rehabilitative Services, Office of Special Education Programs. (2006). *Identifying and treating attention deficit hyperactivity disorder: A resource for school and home.* Washington, DC: U.S. Department of Education.

Eating Disorders and Treatment Planning

Nina Rovinelli Heller

Eating disorders, once defined as anorexia nervosa, in fact include a range of serious disorders, including bulimia nervosa, binge eating, and obesity. Furthermore, although once believed to be a disorder of affluent white, Western, young women, eating disorders are now increasingly seen in both genders, in all ages, and in every ethnic and racial group. The development, course, and treatment of all the eating disorders requires a biopsychosocial treatment and intervention perspective. This chapter reviews pertinent literature regarding the nature of treatment disorders and guidelines for assessment and intervention.

I found I became very obsessed with my weight, eating of food. I was so obsessed that nothing else—I couldn't think about nothing else. I didn't think about the other things that were really going on with me. Being able to feel some of the things that are painful to me has been really helpful in getting rid of that need to keep everything in control and keep everything together—like you have to be put together and ok . . . as soon as I feel that things in my life are a little out of control, somebody's . . . upsetting me . . . instead of thinking that I become, oh, my God, I'm fat and ugly and I need to do something about my weight. (Young adult woman with bulimia; Heller, 1990)

Social workers in a wide range of settings are in front-line positions to identify, treat and prevent eating disorders, including bulimia, anorexia, and obesity-related issues. Social work theories, with their focus on the interaction of individual and the environment, are particularly relevant to the understanding of both the etiology and the treatment interventions of eating disorders. This problem of habituated, health- and life-threatening, deviated eating behaviors is an ideal example of the biopsychosocial configuration in what is seen as a psychiatric and social problem and increasingly as a public health problem. It also strengthens the view that psychiatric problems are, in part, socially constructed. It is no wonder that eating disorders that behaviorally center on the restricting, rejecting, overindulging, or purging of food have risen substantially in the latter half of the twentieth century, typically in developed countries where food is generally plentiful. Likewise, because eating disorders have until fairly recently been associated almost exclusively with young women, researchers have raised questions about the impact of changing gender roles in the development of eating disorders. Finally, with significant impact, are cultural ideals that increasingly favor model-thin female bodies and media that have focused on diet and exercise as a means of self-control and success (Fallon, Katzman, & Wooley, 1996).

According to the *Diagnostic and Statistical Manual* fourth edition, text revision (APA, 2000), anorexia nervosa and bulimia (as well as the lesser known category, Eating Disorder, Not otherwise specified) have been the primary focus of attention in the spectrum of disordered eating. Since 2007, increased attention has been focused on obesity, especially childhood obesity, as a public health epidemic requiring intervention on micro and macro levels. Obesity, according to the *DSM-IV-TR*, is considered a medical diagnosis, coded on axis III. Increasingly, social workers are identifying social, cultural, lifestyle, and psychological issues related to what is undoubtedly the most common eating disorder. Certainly, efforts over the next decade will focus on prevention and intervention, and social workers will be at the forefront of dealing with the myriad psychosocial issues related to both early and chronic obesity. In fact, the foregoing quotation, from a study of people with bulimia, could easily pertain to the person with chronic obesity or binge eating disorder. Though anorexia and bulimia nervosa were once considered to be distinct syndromes, we now know that they exist on a continuum; the same may well be so for those with obesity.

Newsweek named 1981 "the year of the binge-purge syndrome". A year earlier, bulimia was first included as a diagnostic entity in the *DSM*. Since that time, the literature on bulimia has burgeoned, taking its place with the literature regarding the then-better-known anorexia nervosa, which had been reported fairly regularly since the 1940s. "Bulimia, literally ox-hunger, is the name given to an eating disorder which is characterized by recurrent episodes of binge-eating large amounts of high-calorie foods and purging through the use of self-induced vomiting, laxative use or diet pills" (Heller, 1990). Bulimics are often of normal weight but cycle rapidly between restricting food intake, binging, and purging. Onset of illness is typically in adolescence and early adulthood and frequently begins as a social ritual with peers. The large majority of these "experimenting" adolescents do not continue, but a small number go on to develop a secret and ongoing illness. People with bulimia share with their counterparts who have anorexia a distorted body image and issues around self-regulation (regarding food and feelings), but they tend not to "be able" to consistently restrict their food intake to the point of starvation and its secondary effects. Bulimia does carry with it physical risks, and it is not unusual for people with bulimia to have significant electrolyte imbalances and serious dental problems in the form of enamel erosion secondary to gastric reflux in repeated vomiting. In serious cases electrolyte imbalances can result in seizures and mild neuropathies.

Both bulimia and anorexia nervosa appeared to be "new diseases," but reports of anorexics are related in the literature as much as 100 years earlier. In fact, there is some belief that the ascetic religious women of the Middle Ages would meet today's standards for anorexia nervosa. Today, anorexia nervosa is characterized by distorted body image, low weight, severe food restriction, and excessive exercise and is seen in 0.5 to 1 percent of adolescent girls (Sadock & Sadock, 2007). These symptoms can and often do result in malnutrition, starvation, cessation of menses, cardiac problems, osteoporosis, and not infrequently death.

NOT JUST "THE WHITE WOMAN'S DISEASE"

Eating disorders have been considered a disease of young affluent women, and indeed, early anecdotal studies have supported that generalization. However, at least one recent review of research conducted between the early 1970s and the early 1990s indicated that the relationship between anorexia nervosa and high socioeconomic status is unfounded (Gard & Freeman, 1996). These authors also found that bulimia is widespread among those in low socioeconomic groups. Typically, prevention and clinical intervention efforts have been focused on women, whereas in fact increasing numbers of men are being identified as having an eating disorder. Carlat, Camargo, and Herzog (1997) reported on 135 male eating disorder patients and found that although they shared most characteristics with their female counterparts, self-identified homosexuals and bisexuals were more highly represented in those with eating disorders, particularly in bulimia. In fact, of this group, 42 percent of the bulimics identified as homosexual or bisexual, and of the anorexic patients, 58 percent were identified as asexual. Previously, eating disorders in the United States have been identified primarily in Caucasians; more recently, they have been reported among blacks, Latinos, and Asians (Laws & Golding, 1996). Treatment interventions, particularly for people of color, will need to take into account the differential cultural meanings of body image, shape, and weight, as well as the meaning that food and meals play in a culture.

Researchers (Striegel-Moore & Dohm, 2003), in a comparison of white and black women, found that they while they had similar reports of binge eating, the latter group were more likely to have recurrent binge eating. African American and Latino girls whose cultures have historically not valued the "pencil-thin" ideal of the white American culture may be receiving mixed messages about the shapes, sizes, and contours of their bodies. This is an area where further research is greatly needed. First and foremost, social workers must realize that the incidence of eating disorders is increasing in women of color, and we must develop means of understanding how the manifestation is like and not like the "white girl's" eating disorder.

EATING DISORDERS AND COMORBIDITY

Eating disorders have a high comorbidity rate, particularly with the depressive spectrum disorders. Anorexia nervosa is associated with depression in 65 percent of cases, with social phobia at 34 percent and with obsessive-compulsive disorder in 26 percent of cases (Sadock and Sadock,

2007). Noting the overlap of symptoms of eating disorders and depression, Mayer and Walsh (1998) reviewed clinical studies of the efficacy of the selective serotonin reuptake inhibitors (SSRIs) and found mixed reviews. There is some evidence (Schatzberg, 2000), however, that certain SSRIs have independent actions on psychiatric symptoms other than depression. For example, the U.S. Federal Drug Administration has approved the use of fluoxetine (trade name Prozac) for treatment of bulimia nervosa, regardless of a concomitant diagnosis of depression. Kaye, Gendall, and Strober (1998) report that "serotonergic modulating antidepressants suppress symptoms of bulimia, independently of their antidepressant side effects" (p. 825). They go on to note that symptom remission is not effected in severe anorexics, but once normal weight is restored, the SSRIs appear to be effective in preventing relapse. This suggest both that "a disturbance of serotonin activity may create a vulnerability for the expression of a cluster of symptoms that are common to both anorexia and bulimia and that nutritional factors may affect SSRI responses in depression . . . and other conditions" (p. 825).

A small pilot study (Mendlewicz, 1999) suggested that bulimics who are poor responders to SSRI therapy may be those who have cluster B personality disorders, characterized by high levels of impulsivity. In a small sample, Sokol, Gray, Goldstein, & Kaye (1999) found that these subjects responded well to the use of methylphenidate, a drug commonly used to treat attention deficit hyperactivity disorder. Noting possible risks, however, the researchers recommend further research investigation, rather than clinical treatment with methylphenidate at this time.

Obsessive-compulsive behaviors and anxiety are also common in people with eating disorders, particularly anorexia. Compulsive stealing, less common but prevalent, is often not discovered early on in treatment. Sexual adjustment is often delayed, and these patients are often described as asexual. People with bulimia are likely to have mood disorders and problems with impulse control. Many have been sexually abused and suffer dissociative symptoms. Alcohol use is also high in this group, as are a range of self-destructive behaviors including suicidal gestures and self-mutilation (Heller, 1990). Recent research reveals both similarities and differences between clients with bulimia nervosa and body dysmorphic disorder (Gupta & Johnson, 2000).

Recent studies of treatment effectiveness for the range of eating disorders has yielded mixed results. In a systematic review of randomized controlled trials for binge eating disorders, the authors found moderate positive results for medication and behavioral interventions, whereas self-help and other interventions were weak (Brownley, Berkman, Sedway, Lohr, & Bulik, 2007). They also found that treatment-related harms were strong and other factors associated with efficacy of treatment were weak. Individual and group cognitive-behavioral therapy (CBT) was effective up to 4 months posttreatment but did not lead to weight loss. A similar systematic review of studies regarding efficacy of treatment of anorexia nervosa demonstrated that CBT can be effective in relapse prevention, but only in adults after weight restoration. Overall, evidence for treatment of anorexia was weak (Bulik, Berkman, Brownley, Sedway, & Lohr, 2007). Shapiro et al. (2007) found in yet another systematic review of the outcome literature that bulimia nervosa treatment yielded variable results. Clearly, the evidence for treatment efficacy for all eating disorders is weak. Practitioners are encouraged to continue to follow the current literature and emerging research in this area.

These relatively new findings support the recommendation that we become familiar with the complexities of differential diagnosis and consider the wide range or treatment options for people with eating disorders, including psychopharmacological interventions. It is necessary for the clinical social worker to be aware of these research and clinical developments in psychopharmacology and to refer clients as necessary to qualified medical practitioners.

GUIDELINES FOR ASSESSING AND TREATING EATING DISORDERS

Social work intervention can and should occur in a variety of settings and with a three-pronged approach that includes prevention, identification, and treatment. It is critical that any of these interventions reflect an understanding of the sociocultural influences that contribute to and maintain eating disorder symptoms.

Prevention

- Social workers should be familiar with the client groups at risk for developing eating disorders and design and implement psycho-educational efforts appropriate to the age and gender of those groups.

- Prevention programs should ideally take place in "natural" settings, such as schools in athletic departments and health classes and recreation centers.
- Social action can take the form of targeting businesses and advertisements that perpetuate the image of an "ideal" body image for both girls and boys.
- Parent education focused on healthy both healthy eating strategies and the importance of physical activity.

Identification

- Social workers should assume that clients may not readily self-disclose their eating disordered behaviors, which are often associated with secrecy and shame. Hence, disclosure may not occur until the disease has significantly impaired the client's medical status or social and psychological functioning. Social workers should adjust their history taking and style accordingly.
- Data on comorbidity are important in developing the means of identifying people with eating disorders. To identify them in clinical settings, any mental health assessment should include questions about eating behaviors. The clinician is cautioned that in many cases the data will not emerge in a first session but should be raised nonetheless.
- People with histories of sexual abuse, alcohol abuse, and family histories of affective illness or eating disorder should be considered at risk.
- New clinicians should be reminded that normal body weight does not preclude the existence of an eating disorder; in fact, most clients with bulimia are within normal weight ranges.
- Any client who reports or is suspected of an eating disorder should also be referred to a physician, preferably one with expertise in the area, for a full physical examination and laboratory work. Particularly with critically ill anorexics, clear, irrefutable evidence of the impact of starvation on one's physical body may be helpful in minimizing denial of the problem.
- Significant denial and minimization of the problem following disclosure often results in resistance to treatment. Because many people with eating disorders experience difficulties in the area of control and autonomy, establishing joint treatment goals is critical and often arduous.
- A complete psychological, social, and medical history is critical. In the case of young clients, the involvement of family as a collateral source of information is useful.
- Pay particular attention to eating disorders in nonwhite populations who have been significantly understudied, underresearched, and undertreated, in spite of the growing clinical awareness of incidence in people of color.

See Table 75.1 for list of eating disorder assessment measures.

Treatment

- For those clients whose medical status is not seriously undermined and whose functioning is largely intact, an outpatient model of treatment, similar to that described for inpatients, is in order.

TABLE 75.1 Eating Disorder Measures

Name	Type of Measure	Focus
Eating Disorders Inventory (EDI). Garner, Olmstead, & Polivy (1983)	64 item, self report instrument. Children's version available.	Behaviors and attitudes for onset and course of bulimia and anorexia nervosa.
Bulimia Test-Revised (BULIT-R). Smith and Thelen, (1984).	36 item self-report measure	Binge-eating, eating attitudes when not in binge episode.
Eating Disorder Examination (EDE). Cooper & Fairburn. (1987)	Semi-structured interview for comprehensive assessment. Children's Version available.	Anorexia and bulimia, including extreme behavioral methods of weight control.

- In extreme cases, hospitalization may be necessary, and force-feeding for those in a state of severe starvation may follow. Inpatient treatment will include a behavioral protocol, cognitive restructuring, group therapy, nutrition counseling (although many people with eating disorders are nutritional experts themselves), individual treatment, and family interventions.
- Social workers who are working with clients with coexisting substance abuse problems must evaluate the severity of both sets of symptoms and prioritize initial treatment goals. A client who is actively using drugs and alcohol is unlikely to be able to fully participate in a treatment program designed to eliminate symptoms of an eating disorder. Here, too, it would be important to clarify the phenomenological and temporal relationships between the eating disorder behaviors and the substance using behaviors. For example, if a client reports that a feeling of aloneness typically precedes a binge eating episode, it is important to know if his or her feelings of aloneness are intensified by substance use.
- Though many treatment programs are designed as a protocol or as "manualized" interventions, it is critical to recognize that although many people with eating disorders share certain characteristics, there may well be idiosyncratic historical influences and factors that can either promote or impede the chances of treatment success. In other words, it is critical to understand the meaning and function of the particular behaviors to a particular client to find syntonic, effective ways of intervening.
- An understanding of the meaning of the behaviors (restricting, purging, or overeating) and the phenomenology of the symptom development can yield important insights as to the relative importance of this behavior to the client.
- The social worker's understanding of the relative rigidity or flexibility, ambivalence, or secondary gain related to the client's symptoms can be enormously helpful in understanding how best to work with a particular client, regardless of the setting.
- Consider family evaluation and treatment to address both contributing and maintaining factors of symptoms and to identify family strengths.

- Because of the high comorbidity rates in both anorexia and bulimia, a good diagnostic evaluation is critical and may need to take place periodically throughout treatment. For example, it is not unlikely that once eating-related symptoms remit, the client will experience significant depressive symptoms. As with those who have coexisting depressive disorders, clients may also benefit from a trial of a SSRIs.
- Social workers must make frequent use of emerging theoretical and empirical knowledge about incidence and treatment efficacy.

PRACTICE EXAMPLE

Ann was a 16-year-old high school junior when she referred herself to treatment for an eating disorder. For the prior 3 months she had been binging and vomiting on a daily basis. The vomiting was as frequent as four times a day. She became concerned about this and told her health teacher, requesting help in arranging a physical exam and for therapy. Medical findings were negative. Her mother accompanied her on the first interview with the social worker. Ann's height at that time was 5'4", her weight 138 pounds, her highest ever; she desired a weight of 115 or 120 pounds. She was quite athletic in team sports but complained, "I can't seem to make myself exercise." She was and always had been an honor student.

Ann moved to this rural town from a cosmopolitan area 6 months earlier with her mother. An older sister lived nearby. The mother made the decision to move during the school year, giving Ann 1 week's notice. She didn't remember any particular feelings about the move at the time, although she reported having had a large group of lifelong friends in her hometown.

The client's parents divorced when she was 9 years old. Since that time, she had sporadic contact with her father, a businessman, age 57, and she does most of the initiating. He was a recovering alcoholic who continued to use marijuana around the family. Her mother, age 55, began working at low-level clerical positions following the divorce. She presented as meek, mild, and quite dependent. She expressed concern about her daughter's health and stated that she "feels guilty, but I'm not sure why." The mother was slightly overweight, and Ann said she could not "bear to watch her eat . . . it's awful, she just stuffs things in her mouth, I can't stand it."

Ann is the youngest of eight children in an Irish Catholic family. She described her five sisters as "ditzy" and was very clear about wanting a career and not to "ever get too wrapped up" in men. She stated she gets furious at girlfriends who do this. She described her brothers as low achievers in the conventional sense who have poor relationships with their father. Ann's mother had been hospitalized for 12 weeks when the patient was 4 years old for depression, where she received electroconvulsive therapy and tricyclic antidepressants with reportedly good effects. Ann was cared for during this time by her oldest sister who, like her mother, had a younger daughter.

During the first 6 months in her new school, Ann had become active in school activities and made several girlfriends, but she did not feel close to them. She dated several boys, but reported that once she begins to want to spend more time with them, she breaks off the relationship. She related reasonably well to the interviewer, with appropriate affect. There was probably denial of the extent of her sadness, and she expressed significant concern about the welfare of her mother when she leaves home to go to college. However, she was clear that "I don't want to be doing this thing anymore [binging and vomiting]."

Unlike many clients with eating disorders, Ann was self-referred and at least consciously motivated to change her eating behaviors. Her therapist used a combination of CBT and psychodynamic theory to guide the treatment. A food log helped clarify the relationship between the client's feelings, thoughts, and external events and her binging and purging behaviors. This made it possible to being to explore some of the underlying effect while working to build cognitive-behavioral skills aimed at reducing those behaviors. Adjunctive meetings with the client and her mother, and separately with father, allowed Ann to voice some of her concerns about the past and future. Dynamic issues, such as her negative identification with her mother's eating habits and her fears about her own sexuality, were identified and later explored fully. She denied any incidence of sexual abuse, and admitted she felt "uncomfortable" around certain male relatives.

Ann had many of the typical symptoms of bulimia. She also had a positive family history for substance use and mood disorder. Her symptoms began following an unprocessed precipitous move away from her hometown. The symptoms intensified in relation to her social concerns and her significant developmental concern about the well-being of her mother once she was to leave home. Factors in Ann's favor included her self-referral, the recent onset of symptoms, her lack of associated medical problems, and her ability to quickly learn to process feelings associated with the symptom development. She successfully left home for college following a year of outpatient treatment. Follow-up several years later revealed that she had one brief relapse in the first semester of her freshman year, which she curtailed by returning to her use of the food log.

CONCLUSION

Unlike Ann, many people with eating disorders, particularly in the early stages, do not present for treatment. Hence, nonclinical settings, such as schools and colleges, can develop psychoeducational programs for students and can also train resident advisers, deans, and peer counselors to identify risk factors and behaviors. Social workers, with expertise in the areas of community systems, and clinical work, are well poised to develop both prevention and screening programs in these settings. Education in such diverse settings as athletic teams and clubs, dance companies, and exercise clubs may also be useful. Because eating disorder "thinking" is appearing in younger adolescents and children, educational efforts should be focused there as well, before problems manifest into symptoms. Researchers and clinicians both must identify the specific needs of women of color, for whom eating disorders are becoming more common and who may have both similar and dissimilar pathways and courses of illness, requiring targeted treatment interventions.

WEB SITE

National Eating Disorders Association. http://www.nationaleatingdisorders.org.

References

American Psychiatric Association. (2000). *Diagnostic and statistical manual of mental disorders,* 4th ed., text revision. Washington, DC: APA.

Brownley, K. A., Berkman, N. D., Sedway, J. A., Lohr, K. N., & Bulik, C. M. (2007). Binge eating disorder treatment: A systematic review of randomized controlled trials. *International Journal of Eating Disorders, 40*(4), 337–348.

Bulik, C. M., Berkman, N. D., Brownley, K. A., Sedway, J. A., & Lohr, K. N. (2007). Anorexia nervosa treatment: A systematic review of randomized controlled trials. *International Journal of Eating Disorders, 40*(4), 349–362.

Carlat, D. J., Camargo, C. A., & Herzog, D. B. (1997). Eating disorders in males: A report on 135 patients. *American Journal of Psychiatry, 154*(8), 1127–1133.

Cooper, Z., & Fairburn, C. (1987). The Eating Disorder Examination: A semi-structured interview for the assessment of the specific psychopathology of eating disorders. *International Journal of Eating Disorders, 20*(1), 43–50. Retrieved from http://www.cdc.gov/nccdphp/dnpa/obesity/index.htm.

Fallon, P., Katzman, M., & Wooley, S. (Eds.). (1996). *Feminist perspectives on eating disorders.* New York: Guilford.

Gard, M. C., & Freeman, C. (1996). The dismantling of a myth: A review of eating disorders and socioeconomic status. *International Journal of Eating Disorders, 20*(1), 1–12.

Garner, D., Olmsted, M., & Polivy, J. (1983). Development and validation of a multidimensional Eating disorder inventory for anorexia and bulimia. *International Journal of Eating Disorders, 2*(1), 15–34.

Gupta, M. A., & Johnson, A. M. (2000). Non-weight related body image concerns among female eating disorders patients and nonclinical controls: Some preliminary observations. *International Journal of Eating Disorders, 27*(3), 304–309.

Heller, N. R. (1990). *Object relations and symptom choice in bulimics and self-mutilators.* Unpublished doctoral dissertation, Smith College, Northampton, MA.

Kaye, W., Gendall, K., & Strober, M. (1998). Serotonin neuronal function and selective serotonin reuptake inhibitor in anorexia and bulimia nervosa. *Biological Psychiatry, 44*(9), 825–838.

Laws, A., & Golding, J. (1996). Sexual assault history and eating disorder symptoms among White, Hispanic, and African-American women and men. *American Journal of Public Health, 86*(4), 579–583.

Mayer, L. E., & Walsh, B. T. (1998). The use of selective serotonin reuptake inhibitors in eating disorders. *Journal of Clinical Psychiatry, 59,* 15.

Mendlewicz, J. (1999). Predicting response: Serotonin reuptake inhibition. *International Clinical Psychopharmocology, 14,* 1.

Sadock, B. J., & Sadock, V. A. (2007). *Kaplan and Sadock's synopsis of psychiatry: Behavioral sciences/clinical psychiatric,* 10th ed. Baltimore: Williams and Wilkins.

Schatzberg, A. F. (2000). New indications for antidepressants. *Journal of Clinical Psychiatry, 61*(11), 9–17.

Shapiro, J. R., Berkman, N. D., Brownley, K. A., Sedway, J. S., Lohr, K. N., & Bulik, C. M. (2007). Bulimia nervosa treatment: A systematic review of randomized controlled trials. *International Journal of Eating Disorders, 40*(4), 321–336.

Smith, M., & Thelen, M. (1984). Development and validation of a test for bulimia. *Journal of Consulting Clinical Psychology, 52*(5), 863–872.

Sokol, M. S., Gray, N. S., Goldstein, A., & Kaye, W. H. (1999). Methylphenidate treatment for bulimia nervosa associated with a cluster B personality disorder. *International Journal of Eating Disorders, 2* (2), 233–237.

Striegel-Moore, R., & Dohm, F. (2003). Eating disorders in white and black women. *American Journal of Psychiatry, 160*(7), 357–368.

Gordon MacNeil

Panic disorders afflict about 4 percent of the population; about half of those so diagnosed also experience agoraphobia. Panic disorder is characterized by panic attacks and the pernicious fear of additional attacks. Two interventions have shown effectiveness in the acute phase of panic disorder with or without agoraphobia: cognitive-behavioral therapy alone and in combination with medications. In the long run, cognitive-behavioral therapy is the preferred intervention. Cognitive restructuring techniques are recommended to address panic attacks, and the behavioral technique of exposure is recommended for agoraphobia symptoms.

DESCRIPTION OF THE DISORDER

To meet the *DSM-IV-TR* criteria for panic disorder, one must experience recurrent unexpected panic attacks and for at least a month (1) persistent concern about having more attacks, (2) worry about the consequences of the attacks or implications of the attacks, and/or (3) a significant change in behavior as a result of the attacks (American Psychiatric Association [APA], 2000). The attacks must not be due to a medical condition, nor are they better explained by some other disorder, such as social phobia, post-traumatic stress disorder, or a specific phobia. For many, panic disorders are largely related to the person's fear of body sensations; in fact, panic disorder is sometimes referred to as a "fear of one's body" or a "fear of emotions." These individuals become alarmed at the presence of specific physical sensations that they associate with the onset of a panic attack. Because these attacks exacerbate over time, the anticipation of an attack can itself manifest panic. Avoidance responses frequently result in agoraphobia. *Panic attacks* are discrete periods of intense discomfort or fear that include at least four symptoms from the following list.

- Palpitations, rapid heartbeat, pounding heart
- Sweating
- Trembling or shaking
- Sensations of shortness of breath or smothering
- Sensation of choking
- Chest pain or discomfort
- Nausea or abdominal distress
- Feeling dizzy, light-headed, faint
- Derealization or depersonalization
- Fear of losing control or going crazy
- Fear of dying
- Numbness or tingling sensations
- Chills or hot flashes (APA, 2000)

In the case of panic disorder, these symptoms are not initially cued; they do not tend to occur in specific settings or situations. Indeed, the unpredictable nature of their appearance and the dread of their anticipation are hallmarks of panic disorder.

Agoraphobia is defined as an anxiety about being in situations in which escape is difficult or embarrassing or in which help would be unavailable should a panic attack occur (APA, 2000). These fears often relate to being in situations in which one is unable to "get back" to comfortable, secure surroundings.

Panic disorder is a common condition, as is agoraphobia. Approximately 2 percent of the population experiences panic disorder without agoraphobia, 1.5 percent experience panic disorder with agoraphobia, and 5 percent experience agoraphobia without panic disorder (Eaton, Kessler, Wittchen, & Magee, 1994). Women are twice as likely to be diagnosed with panic disorder. It is not unusual for persons to progress from panic disorder without agoraphobia to panic disorder with agoraphobia, as the latter may actually be the result of a dysfunctional coping response to panic disorder alone. The typical age of onset for these disorders is the early to mid-twenties.

CASE ILLUSTRATION

Richard Summerall is a 30-year-old white male. He is trained as a mechanic and has operated his own garage for 4 years. For the past 2 years he has been a used car salesman. Mr. Summerall relates that his panic symptoms started 9 years ago on his first night in the military. That evening, he woke up feeling very hot, short of breath, and panicky. Since then, he has experienced these symptoms rarely, but in the past 3 months he has experienced them more frequently and intensely. He also reports having diarrhea, nausea, shortness of breath, sweating, a fear that he is going crazy, trembling, and shaking. He describes a fear of elevators, car washes, business group meetings, and other places where he feels enclosed. He reports that the most extreme attack occurred 2 nights ago and that he spends considerable time worrying that these attacks will happen again.

Assessment

To establish the presence of panic disorder as well as agoraphobia, the social worker needs to determine the specific nature of the client's symptoms as well as possible triggers for them and the client's responses to these symptoms, with specific attention to avoidance behaviors. The use an informal interview format to gather this information is common, but increasingly clinicians are employing established measures to assess the level of symptomatology exhibited by clients presenting with concerns about panic attacks. The Panic Disorder Severity Scale–Self Report (PDSS-SR; Houck, Speigel, Shear, Rucci, & Stat, 2002) is useful in identifying the frequency of panic attacks, the degree of distress resulting from them, and anticipatory anxiety related to them. The Mobility Inventory for Agoraphobia (Chambless, Caputo, Bright, & Gallagher, 1984) is well accepted as a measure of phobia avoidance. Structured clinical interviews provide a more comprehensive battery of questions that assess the extent to which the individual experiences panic attacks and help rule out other disorders. Two well-established, well-tested instruments for these interviews are the Structured Clinical Interview for the *DSM* axis I disorders (SCID; First, Gibbon, Spitzer, & Williams, 1997) and the Anxiety Disorders Interview Schedule–Revised (ADIS-R; DiNardo & Barlow, 1985). The ADIS-R is particularly useful because it includes a checklist of specific symptoms

as well as items about client thoughts concerning panic attacks, items about avoidance behaviors, and items focusing on functional impairment resulting from panic attacks.

Treatment

A number of reviews of literature and meta-analyses on the treatment of panic disorder and agoraphobia have been conducted recently (see Furukawa, Watanabe, & Churchill, 2007; Himle, Fischer, & Lokers, 2007; Roth & Fonagy, 2005). Although there are some differences in their conclusions, there is general consensus in recommending a treatment protocol that combines medications and psychotherapy; cognitive-behavioral therapy alone appears to be about as effective as the combined model in many instances. Cognitive-behavioral therapy is the most effective psychotherapy choice, with cognitive restructuring being most useful for addressing panic attacks and exposure techniques being preferred for addressing the avoidance behaviors of agoraphobia. Tricyclic antidepressant medications and selective serotonin reuptake inhibitors are the medications of choice in treating panic disorder and agoraphobia. Of note, psychotherapy seems to have more sustainable effect than the use of medications over greater periods of time (Roth & Fonagy, 2005).

TREATMENT PROGRAM

The remainder of this chapter presents a specific treatment program for addressing panic disorders and agoraphobia (see Fig. 76.1). This treatment program consists of two foci; intrapersonal and interpersonal aspects of the panic disorder. There is no specific protocol for the interpersonal foci associated with this treatment program, but it is an integral part of the program nonetheless. For instance, I am careful to include social environment functioning in my assessment of the individual—both strengths and difficulties. Interpersonal problems in which the individual feels trapped or out of control can precipitate panic attacks and panic disorders. I have found that enlisting the help of supportive significant others can add to the prospects of success for this treatment program, especially with the in vivo component.

The intrapersonal aspect has three components: (1) education about the nature of anxiety disorders and panic disorders specifically; (2) cognitive

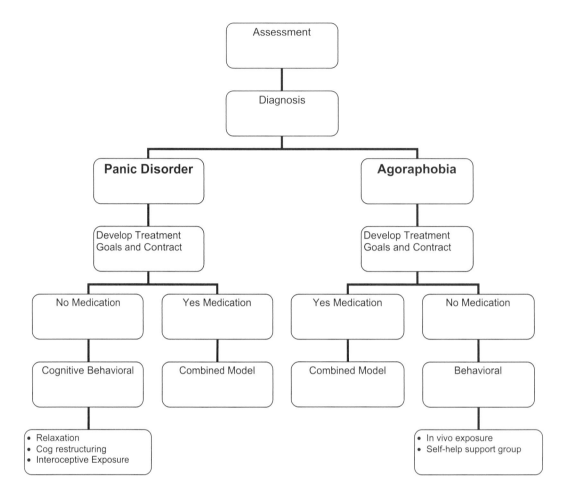

Note that Panic Disorder is typically addressed prior to Agoraphobia when both are present.

Figure 76.1 Algorithm for treatment planning for panic disorder and Agoraphobia.

therapy, including work on the identification of physiological indications of panic, relaxation training; and (3) exposure of some form. A sample treatment plan accompanies the presentation of this program (see Table 76.1).

In general, once the client is educated about the disorder(s), I use interoceptive exposure techniques to address the panic disorder, followed by in vivo exposure techniques to address the agoraphobia. In instances where the consumer is not able to come to the office due to agoraphobia, I try to use phone or e-mail consultation as means of beginning the process.

Clinicians who use this treatment program are presumed to have knowledge of cognitive-

behavioral therapy. This presentation is meant to instruct clinicians on the implementation of the program, but it is not a substitute for clinical training and ongoing supervision.

PROCEDURES

Following are the procedures I use in the intrapersonal foci of this treatment program in sequential order, along with information describing the rationale for the interventions. Although most motivated clients will experience satisfying results within ten sessions, there is tremendous variation in how long it takes people to address the

TABLE 76.1 Sample Treatment Plan for Panic Disorder with Agoraphobia

Assessment Model	Measurement Tools	Short-Term Goals	Long-Term Goals	Treatment Plans
Bio	Medical examination			
Psycho	*DSM-IV-TR* Panic Disorder Severity Scale- Self Report The Body Sensations Questionnaire Mobility Inventory for Agoraphobia	a. Identify sources of anxiety and fears b. decrease panic attacks and agoraphobic responses c. improve coping skills d. improve feelings of control	Maintain treatment progress, employing a. cognitive restructuring b. breathing retraining techniques c. support groups/self-help	Outpatient setting, individual therapy sessions using a. psychoeducation b. cognitive restructuring c. interoceptive exposure d. In vivo exposure
Social	Eco-map	Increase positive social exchanges with family and friends, particularly outside the home	Maintain gains of short term; increase recreational activity outside the home	a. Include family/friends in psychoeducation sessions of indiv. tx. b. Refer to church and community events calendars
Cultural	Eco-map	Encourage involvement in social activities	Increase exposure to new social groups	Refer to community events calendars

psychological demons of panic and agoraphobia. Initial sessions take longer than those at the end of the process, and sessions that require exposure techniques require that the client provoke, endure, and reduce their anxiety within the session. Therefore, this protocol is not presented session by session, as the introduction of new material to the client is flexible and contingent on his or her understanding and (where indicated) mastery of the content up to that point.

Assessment

I screen the client and conduct an assessment, which first includes a referral to a physician to rule out medical causes. Following this, I complete a basic psychosocial assessment. I am careful to explore cultural elements that may contribute to or influence the client's situation and experience. I also pay particular attention to the following aspects of the presenting problem: presentation, pattern, predisposition, perpetuants, and readiness for treatment. I usually use either PDSS-SR (Houck et al., 2002) or the ADIS-R (DiNardo & Barlow, 1985) to obtain this information. If the client does not appear to be ready to actively engage in change-making behaviors, I focus on motivation and support until he or she is ready to begin this program.

With regard to Mr. Summerall, I identify no fewer than six symptoms of panic attacks, and it is clear that he is concerned about the prospect of experiencing more of them. He meets the diagnostic criteria for panic disorder. He also appears to meet the criteria for agoraphobia, as he is fearful of being in situations from which he cannot escape. I would probe to determine if there are specific circumstances associated with his attacks; their frequency, duration, and intensity; and how he responds to them, both with regard to his psychological and physiological responses as well as what he has tried to do to counter the panic attacks. I also would want to determine to what extent they impair his functioning. Finally, although the attacks clearly are disturbing to Mr. Summerall, I would try to determine his readiness to act to change his situation. Many people present with debilitating symptoms but are actually unwilling to "courageously leap off of the ledge" and act differently.

Psychoeducation

I provide the client with information about panic disorders and agoraphobia. I also discuss the goals of the program and ask if the client would like me to provide similar information to family members or friends. I emphasize that I expect members of the client's social support network to know about our work and that the help of others is an important supplement to the work we do in session.

Cognitive Restructuring

The client and I determine initial levels of symptom severity. Although I usually simply ask the client to talk about symptom severity, the information resulting from the instruments used in the assessment is useful as well. In Mr. Summerall's case, the symptoms seem to be serious, but not extreme. That is, they are distressing to him but do not curtail his completing tasks. His is not incapacitated and friends and family have not noticed his symptoms to date.

We identify the client's common responses to anxiety. This includes what he or she has tried as interventions for panic and anxiety and to what extent these have helped. Thus far, Mr. Summerall has been able to escape situations in which he experiences attacks around others. He has tried to control his breathing by taking deep breaths, he has used alcohol on occasion to distract himself from his hypervigilance to body sensations, and he has tried to increase his physical exercise to "wear myself out so that I don't have energy to freak out." We establish that his best efforts have not any appreciable effect on his attacks; they continue to happen and without provocation.

The client and I work on the first of two factors included in the cognitive restructuring intervention: misappraisals of body sensations as being threatening. This process has three parts. First, I provide information about the rationale for the intervention, then we identify misappraisals, and finally we challenge these misappraisals.

I mention that panic disorders are largely related to the client's fear of body sensations. Because panic attacks can present at any time, learning to identify initial indications and how to reduce the physiological manifestations of panic is an important element in the treatment of panic disorder.

Mr. Summerall and I discuss his awareness of his breathing in general and when he becomes anxious. He confides that he is not aware of the former and distressed by the later. I point out that his becoming aware of his breathing as we speak seems to be distressing to him, and he agrees. (This is a common response among this clinical population.) This provides me with an opportunity to begin talking about misappraisals of body sensations and the common experience of tricking oneself into thinking that something is "wrong" simply by becoming aware of "normal" body functions and sensations. Even if one's breathing is rapid, or one is sweating, there may be good reasons for these physiological responses; they don't necessarily denote an attack. We use this idea as we move forward in challenging his misappraisals.

The client and I go through a process of challenging misappraisals of body sensations. First, we create a list of the specific thoughts that he or she has about his or her situation during panic attacks. After we have created a list of these thoughts, I challenge the main items on it one by one, largely by questioning what other interpretations of the body's "signals" might be possible and if these might in fact be likely. (Readers will find specific techniques for this in Barlow & Craske, 2006.) This must be done in a gentle manner that is not patronizing, humiliating, or condescending to the client. Remember, the goal of this part of the treatment program is to empower the client to challenge self-talk related to his or her body sensations (a truly challenging task), so frequent positive reinforcement is warranted. Also, the worker must remember that the intent here is to evoke the "misappraisals" and challenge them *as they are occurring*—in the present tense. I emphasize the use of "I am" statements rather than "I would be" statements in this task.

I always begin my work with the client on anticipatory anxiety at the beginning of a session. Following general catching up and making sure that the client appears to be calm, I make the following comment: "Right now you seem to be pretty calm and relaxed." Once this is verified, I comment that he or she seems "quite safe right here, right now." Again, I wait until this is verified. I ask the client to repeat this phrase a few times, becoming comfortable with it. This statement becomes an anchor that clients use to assess the voracity of their sensations of panic.

Working in consort with the "right here, right now" anchor, I start to educate the client about breathing retraining as a response to anxious feelings. Detailed instructions for this are found elsewhere (see Barlow & Craske, 2006), so I only state here that it is important that the client complete the exercise of *experiencing* relaxed diaphragmatic breathing in the office; talking about it is insufficient. I cannot stress enough the importance of establishing the sensations of calm and a relaxed state; it this state the client must be able to access to succeed in later steps in the treatment process.

It is well worth the time and effort necessary to solidly establish this anchor.

Interoceptive Exposure Treatment

Interoceptive exposure requires that the client be systematically exposed to bodily sensations in a therapeutic context so that he or she can learn at an emotional level not to fear these sensations. This differs from the misappraisals of body sensations in that rather than focusing on *cognitions*, it is a conscious effort to have the client evoke, endure, and reduce the *sensations* of panic in the office. Thus, sessions must be sufficiently long to allow the client to fully provoke and reduce feelings of panic.

The client and I develop a short list of hierarchically ordered body sensations associated with panic attacks. I have the client recall the last panic attack and tell me about the lowest-ordered body sensation and how he or she experienced it at that time. The client usually begins to demonstrate symptoms related to the body sensation at this point. I point this out to him or her, noting that he or she is indeed acting anxious. (Sometimes invoking the memory of a panic attack does not generate the symptoms of panic in the present. In these cases, I have the client do exercises such as breathing through a straw or intentionally hyperventilating to produce the symptoms.)

Once the client reports being anxious (or demonstrates overt signs of anxiety), I guide him or her in the breathing retraining exercise. I am careful to reinforce positive responses during this exercise. We repeat this exercise (up to three times) for this initial body sensation in the office. The client's ability to invoke the panic is often lessened by the end of the third iteration.

I use at least one follow-up session to reinforce gains made in the initial interoceptive session. After we have discussed what happened in the initial interoceptive session, I have the client repeat the process him- or herself. Assuming that he or she is successful in reducing anxiety, I comment that "right here, right now," the client seems safe and calm. This anchor is reinforced as we begin the process of addressing additional body sensations associated with panic. Following the second interoceptive session, I encourage the client to continue the exercise at home. If possible, a supportive family member should be enlisted as a helper in this exercise. (It is common for clients to report that after proceeding through three or four body sensations, they are no longer able to provoke them. In these instances it is possible to use the paradoxical injunction of "prescribing the symptom." When they think they might be on the verge of an attack, I encourage them to "request" it . . . "bring in on, then!" It is interesting that this sometimes provides a useful strategy for clients facing these sensations rather than avoiding them.)

In Vivo Exposure

In vivo exposure treatment is used when the client experiences agoraphobia. It requires that clients engage in exposure practices by which they systematically venture into the situations they have been avoiding. Unlike panic disorders, agoraphobia is related to physical locations, and thus exposure to situations or places is warranted. A similar process to that previously described for interoceptive exposure is used (establishing a hierarchy of anxiety-provoking situations, exposing the client to these sequentially while assisting him or her in confronting and overcoming the anxious feelings). It is worth noting that the sequence presented here typically allows the client to conduct this component of treatment without the worker's direct assistance, sometimes with the aid of written or audio-taped journals. (This is one of the reasons I address the panic disorder prior to addressing the agoraphobia.) In vivo exposure administered by the client is comparable to that administered by the worker. Furthermore, including significant others or spouses in treatment as coaches has beneficial effects for clients.

Although this program has been helpful to many people, it will not be successful with all clients. In this situation, the reader is encouraged to use one of the additional ways of healing, including meditation, exercise, herbal treatments, spiritual support, and self-help groups. With regard to the last item of the list, the Anxiety Disorders Association of America and the National Alliance on Mental Illness are particularly noteworthy, and their Web sites are provided in the reference section.

WEB SITES

Anxiety Busters. http://www.anxietybusters.com.
Anxiety Disorders Association of America. http://www.adaa.org.
Anxiety Disorders.com. http://www.anxieties .com.
Anxiety and Panic Attacks. http://www .anxietypanic.com.
National Alliance on Mental Illness. http:// www.nami.org

References

American Psychiatric Association. (2000). *Diagnostic and statistical manual of mental disorders*, 4th ed., text revision. Washington, DC: APA.

Barlow, D. H., & Craske, M. G. (2006). *Mastery of your anxiety and panic*, 4th ed. New York: Oxford University Press.

Chambless, D. L., Caputo, G. C., Bright, P., & Gallagher, R. (1984). Assessment of fear in agoraphobics: The Body Sensations Questionnaire and the Agoraphobic Cognitions Questionnaire. *Journal of Consulting and Clinical Psychology*, 52, 1090–1097.

DiNardo, P. A., & Barlow, D. H. (1988). *Anxiety Disorders Interview Schedule–Revised*. Albany, NY: Phobia and Anxiety Disorders Clinic, State University of New York.

Eaton, W. W., Kessler, R. C., Wittchen, H. U., & Magee, W. J. (1994). Panic and panic disorder in the United States. *American Journal of Psychiatry*, 151, 413–420.

First, M. B., Gibbon, M., Spitzer, R. L., & Williams, J. B. W. (1997). *Structured clinical interview for DSM-IV axis I disorders SCID I: clinician version, administration booklet*. Washington, DC: American Psychiatric Press.

Furukawa, T.A., Watanabe, N., & Churchill, R. (2007). Combined psychotherapy plus antidepressants for panic disorder with or without agoraphobia. *Cochrane Database of Systematic Reviews*, 1, CD004364. DOI: 0.1002/14651858.CD004364.pub2.

Himle, J. A., Fischer, D. J., & Lokers, L. M. (2007). Panic disorder and agoraphobia. In B. A. Thyer & J. Woodarski (Eds.), *Social work in mental health: An evidence-based approach* (pp. 331–349). Hoboken, NJ: Wiley.

Houck, P. R., Speigel, D. A., Shear, M. K., Rucci, P., & Stat, D. (2002). Reliability of the self-report version of the Panic Disorder Severity Scale. *Depression and Anxiety*, 15, 183–185.

Roth, A., & Fonagy, P. (2005). Anxiety disorders I: Specific phobia, social phobia, generalized anxiety disorder, and panic disorder with and without agoraphobia. In A. Roth & P. Fonagy (Eds.), *What works for whom? A critical review of psychotherapy research*, 2nd ed. (pp. 150–197). New York: Guilford.

Treatment Plans for Clients with Social Phobia

Bruce A. Thyer & Monica Pignotti

The condition known as social phobia (also called social anxiety disorder) is usually amenable to effective treatment through the social worker providing a variety of behavioral therapies centering on social skills building combined with graduated exposure to real-life anxiety-evoking situations. Properly conducted therapy usually produces marked improvements, and in some cases complete cures, that are well maintained. Acceptance and commitment therapy is also emerging as an effective intervention for clients experiencing marked social fears.

Contemporary social workers helping clients who experience significant problems with social phobia are in a very fortunate position indeed. The diagnostic conceptualizations of clinical anxiety have been considerably refined over the last three iterations of the *Diagnostic and Statistical Manual of Mental Disorders* (*DSM*; American Psychiatric Association, 2000), and the newer nomenclature is closer to truth about how clients experience pathological anxiety than the system described in previous editions. Clinicians are also fortunate in that considerable effectiveness and efficacy research involving very sophisticated randomized controlled clinical trials have demonstrated that selected psychosocial treatments are genuinely helpful in ameliorating social phobia, a condition that, if left untreated, is typically chronic and unremitting, causing significant distress and impaired functioning. There are relatively few psychosocial problems facing social workers wherein the outcomes are so potentially favorable. Given this positive state of affairs, it is incumbent on social work practitioners who wish to practice both ethically and accountably to become familiar with evidence-based methods of assessment and intervention found to be useful for socially anxious clients. This chapter will focus on diagnosis, assessment, evidence-based interventions, and treatment goals and planning for clients with social phobia.

CASE EXAMPLE

Fred W. (an actual client with social phobia treated by Thyer), is a self-referred 56-year-old male auto worker from Detroit whose presenting complaint is of extreme apprehension, fears of fainting, marked tremor, and agitation, which are reliably evoked whenever he was in situations involving face-to-face interactions with someone else. This was impairing his ability to work and had greatly restricted his social life. He could not stand in lines with people or participate in the sacrament of communion at the Catholic church he belonged to. The problem was absent in the sole presence of his wife and children. When seated or able to lean against a wall or table, Fred could talk comfortably with anyone. If he had to stand unsupported while listening or talking, he would begin to tremble, perspire, and experience great anxiety. He dated the onset of this problem to an episode some 30 years earlier when he was in the military and was verbally abused by an officer in front of his fellow soldiers. He was unable to respond to the officer's angry tirade, which should have been directed against another soldier, not Fred. The problem has been continuous since that time without any remissions. The assessment and treatment plan for Fred that was carried out is described in Table 77.1.

DIAGNOSTIC CRITERIA AND PREVALENCE OF SOCIAL PHOBIA

The term *social phobia* is often used interchangeably with the term social anxiety disorder (SAD). Many clinical researchers and consumer advocacy organizations are encouraging the use of *SAD* because it promotes recognition of the problem as a serious, treatable condition rather than something to be stoically endured (Liebowitz, Heimberg, Travers, & Stein, 2000). Nevertheless, in the present

TABLE 77.1 Treatment Plan Worksheet for an Actual Client with Social Phobia

| | | Assessment | |
Assessment Domain	Assessment Method	Assessment Goals	Findings
Biological	Client interview	Eliminate possible role of biological factors as causing client's problems	Onset and course consistent with psychosocial etiology Extreme situational specificity of problem. Ruled out organic causes Client not taking any drugs
Diagnostic	*DSM*-based clinical interview *DSM*-based decision tree Rapid assessment instruments	Ascertain that client met *DSM* diagnostic criteria for SP	Client met *DSM* criteria for SP, and no other disorder
Familial	Interview with wife Interview with client (separately and together)	Investigate impact of client's problem on marital/family life	
Specification of situations where client experiences social anxiety	Client interview	Development of a rank-ordered list of social situations producing anxiety	Situations mentioned by client included standing in public waiting lines, church communion, and face-to-face interactions

Treatment Planning

Domain	Intervention Plan	Conduct and Results
Observable behavior (avoidance of unsupported face-to-face contact; observable tremor; seeking physical support)	Graduated real-life exposure; repeated exposure therapy sessions alone. Allow symptoms to develop while remaining standing in front of therapist without support. Find out if behaviors subside and discomfort lessens. Move to more intense and real-life situations outside private office.	Three 60–90-minute sessions in the office eliminated visible tremor and perspiration. Client became very comfortable standing in front of therapist. Subsequent sessions undertaken in large, empty auditorium. Moved to similar sessions involving long lines of people at movie theaters and fast-food restaurants. Therapist modeled and client subsequently imitated an obvious and deliberate tremor while standing in public waiting lines. Client self-conducted exposure exercises in between weekly sessions with, at church and work. Treatment involved eight sessions with therapist, resulting in virtual elimination of problem. Three-year follow-up by phone found continuous absence of presenting problem and greatly enhanced functioning at work and social life.
Cognitive (thoughts of acting in an embarrassing manner; catastrophic thinking: "My boss will see me shaking and fire me!")	Think-aloud during exposure sessions, recognize unrealistic nature of fears, voice more realistic coping responses.	Distressing and catastrophic thoughts gradually reduced after experiencing elimination of tremor, sweating, and support seeking.
Affective (severe anxiety when facing others unsupported; anticipatory anxiety about facing future situations)	Consciously control breathing during exposure sessions, rehearse coping responses in imagination and in real life.	Anxious feelings gradually eliminated during the course of treatment.

chapter, we use the term *social phobia* (SP) so that we can specifically discuss the disorder in relation to the *DSM-IV-TR* (APA, 2000) criteria.

The *DSM-IV-TR* lists 12 distinct anxiety disorders that may apply to children and adults seeking help and who present with the prominent features of anxiety, fear, avoidance, or increased arousal. The diagnostic criteria for SP first appeared in the third edition of the *DSM*, were revised somewhat in *DSM-III-R*, again in the *DSM-IV*, and in the latest text revision, *DSM-IV-TR* (APA, 2000). At present, social phobia is defined by the following diagnostic criteria:

1. A marked and persistent fear of one or more social or performance situations in which the individual is exposed to unfamiliar people or to possible scrutiny by others. The individual fears that he or she will act in a way (or show anxiety symptoms) that will be humiliating or embarrassing.
2. Exposure to the feared social situation almost invariably provokes anxiety.
3. The person recognizes that the fear is excessive or unreasonable.
4. The feared social or performance situations are avoided or else endured with intense anxiety or distress.
5. The avoidance, anxious anticipation, or distress in the feared social or performance situation(s) interferes significantly with the person's normal routine, occupational (academic) functioning, or social activities or relationships, or there is marked distress about having the phobia (APA, 2000, p. 456).

The *DSM* definition further states that these problems cannot be attributed to either substance abuse, a medical condition, or another mental disorder (e.g., panic disorder), and must, in individuals under age 18, have lasted at least 6 months. There is only one specifier for SP, *generalized*, that applies if the fears include most social situations, as opposed to being more circumscribed (e.g., public speaking).

SP is the fourth most common psychiatric disorder in the United States with a lifetime prevalence of approximately 12 percent, exceeded only by major depression, specific phobia, and alcohol dependence (Kessler et al., 2005). The mean age of onset is during the teenage years (Thyer, Parrish, Curtis, Nesse, & Cameron, 1985), although some research has shown a bimodal distribution, with the onset for some individuals occurring ear-

lier in childhood who may have the more generalized form of SP (Stein, Chavira, & Jang, 2001). Alcohol abuse can be a consequence of individuals with social phobia drinking to self-medicate symptoms (Thyer et al., 1986), and a careful assessment of possible alcohol and drug abuse is advisable in its own right. SP has also been shown to be highly comorbid with major depressive disorder and appears to have a negative impact on its course and outcome (Zimmerman & Chelminski, 2003).

FURTHER ASSESSMENT OF SP

Arriving at a *DSM* diagnosis of SP is only a part of a comprehensive social work assessment, which should involve an array of quantitative and qualitative methods of appraisal—the clinical interview; structured client self-reports (e.g., narrative diaries, logs of out-of-home social/public activities); rapid assessment instruments; structured clinical interviews centered around anxiety disorders; medical check-ups to rule out organic causes, including the possible role of medication effects and drug interactions; and possibly interviews with other family members.

There are highly specific rapid assessment instruments and rating scales developed for assessing aspects of SP and related client functioning, and a partial listing of the more recommended tools that can be found in Table 77.2. Pretreatment assessment should involve using one or more of these reliable and valid outcome measures, ideally encompassing a rapid assessment instrument, as well as direct measures of behavior, perhaps systematically recorded by the client or a significant other. Some measures may be administered daily or weekly. Other, more global outcome indicators, such as a quality-of-life scale, a measure of family functioning, or a measure of overall health, could be administered simple pre- and posttreatment.

A functional analysis of the environmental and internal (e.g., troubling thoughts) antecedents to and the consequences to follow behaviors associated with SP (overt actions, feelings, and thoughts) may be highly relevant. Mattaini (1990) provides a recommended review of the importance of such functional analyses as a part of social work assessment.

Once it has been determined that clients meet the *DSM-IV-TR* criteria, it is essential to carefully isolate the parameters or boundaries of their

TABLE 77.2 Recommended Assessment Tools for Social Phobia

- Social Phobia Scale (SPS; measures fear of scrutiny)

- Social Interaction Anxiety Scale (SAIS; measures fear of interpersonal interaction) (*note*: the SPS and SAIS are often used together)

- Social Avoidance and Distress Scale

- Social Anxiety Scale for Children

- Social Phobia and Anxiety Inventory for Children

- Social Phobia Endstate Functioning Index

- Liebowitz Social Anxiety Scale

- Simulated Social Interaction Test

anxiety-evoking stimuli, because various types of social phobia can be quite diverse. A well-established way of accomplishing this is for client and social worker to construct a rank-ordered list of specific social situations that lead to anxiety for the client (Heimberg, 2002). Such a list can then be incorporated into a treatment plan that will be described later in the chapter.

EVIDENCE-BASED RESEARCH AND PRACTICE KNOWLEDGE

Consistent with the recommendations to be found in the surgeon general's report on mental illness (Stacher, 1999), social workers should become competent in providing contemporary evidence-based psychosocial treatments for anxiety disorders. A large body of research exists in support of effective psychosocial interventions for SP, based on various combinations of behavioral and cognitive behavioral approaches (see Heimberg, 2002; Rodebaugh, Holaway, & Heimberg, 2004, for full reviews). Components of these interventions include exposure to feared stimuli, social skills training, relaxation training, and cognitive restructuring and have been successfully conducted in both group and individual therapy settings.

The most important component of the treatment is exposure, the element that all successful interventions for SP have in common. The first step of the process is for the social worker and client to put together a rank-ordered list, from least to most frightening, of social situations that produce anxiety (Heimberg, 2002). Exposure can be accomplished by imagining fearful scenes, usually narrated by the therapist (imaginal exposure); role playing with the therapist or others who resemble people the client fears; or by direct exposure to the feared situation (in vivo exposure). The client agrees to remain in the anxiety-evoking situation with the therapist's support until the anxiety considerably diminishes. Imaginal rehearsal and prolonged exposure in fantasy can be conducted in situations where in vivo exposure is not possible (e.g., an upcoming once-in-a-lifetime solo performance by a musician at Carnegie Hall), although in vivo exposure is usually preferable when possible due to the fact that imaginal exposure is considerably removed from the real thing and considerably less effective at either inducing anxiety or helping the client develop genuinely effective coping and performance skills in real life. Exposure can be carried out in individual or group therapy settings, and clients are usually given exposure exercises as homework, to carry out on their own between sessions.

Social skills training (SST) is based on the premise that a lack of social skills, such as poor eye contact or poor conversation skills, can result in a negative reaction from others, thus causing unpleasant and punishing social interactions with others that provoke anxiety. Even though there is still some debate as to whether all clients need SST (Rodebaugh et al., 2004), this approach has been shown to be effective as both a standalone intervention and in conjunction with exposure-based approaches. A controlled clinical trial conducted (Herbert et al., 2005) that compared cognitive-behavioral group therapy (CBGT) alone with CBGT and SST combined, showed significantly greater gains for the CBGT and SST combination. Moreover, the effect sizes were reported to be the largest found to date for an SP intervention, which means that the results were highly clinically significant and robust.

Relaxation training can be used in conjunction with exposure therapy, although relaxation training alone has not been shown to be helpful and has sometimes been used as a control condition in studies (Rodebaugh et al., 2004). The most commonly used form of relaxation training is progressive muscle relaxation, which is employed in a process called applied relaxation and has been shown to be effective for SP when clients are trained in it and then use it while confronting feared situations (Öst, 1987). Systematic reviews and meta-analyses of the research on SP have shown medium to large effect sizes, indicating clinically significant results for exposure therapy with or without the relaxation component (Rodebaugh et al., 2004).

Even though these highly effective treatments for SP exist, there are clients, especially some with the generalized subtype of SP, who are not helped by such treatments and others who achieve only partial symptom reduction (see Herbert et al., 2005, for a review) and thus, the search for ways to improve existing interventions and conduct research on innovative treatments continues. When using any innovative treatment, it is crucial to provide full informed consent to the client on the state of the evidence and to try the interventions with the most empirical support first. One approach that is being well researched is acceptance and commitment therapy (ACT; Hayes, Strosahl, & Wilson, 1999). ACT is based on behavior therapy, with the addition of mindfulness and acceptance components. Pilot studies have shown promising results when the ACT model is incorporated into exposure therapy for SP (Dalrymple & Herbert, 2007; Ossman, Wilson, Storaasli, & McNeill, 2006). ACT is based on the idea that the primary reason people suffer from psychological disorders is not due to negative emotions per se but to the struggle to control and avoid experiencing such emotions. Unlike many conventional therapies, the explicit goal of ACT is not to eliminate negative emotions or reduce symptoms (although the pilot studies show that this can often occur), but rather to assist the client in giving up struggling against emotions and thus promote a nondefensive acceptance (not mere tolerance) of emotions, including anxiety. The identification of client values and helping the client take committed value-directed action is also an important element of ACT. ACT has also been shown to increase a person's willingness to engage in exposure-based procedures (Hayes, Luoma, Bond, Masuda, & Lillis, 2006) .

TREATMENT GOALS

- Ideally, the goal mutually arrived at with the client with SP seeking assistance is the complete alleviation of pathological anxiety—in other words, a cure.
- More realistically, especially for clients with generalized SP, the goal would be more

enhanced functioning and some relief of symptoms, not necessarily a complete remission of the difficulty. Incorporation of ACT principles may be helpful for such clients.
- Enhanced quality of life, improved relationship and family functioning, more effective vocational functioning, and increased ability to function in other areas of life of value to the client (e.g., hobbies, recreation, social activities, volunteer work).

These constructs are all amenable to reliable and valid qualitative and quantitative measurement (using some of the assessment protocols already described) before, during, and at the completion of treatment, and sometimes thereafter. Such data should be routinely gathered and shared with clients (and perhaps their family members) as appropriate. Graphing relevant data and including these in client records is also a recommended practice.

TREATMENT PLANNING

A representative assessment treatment plan taken from one of the authors' (Thyer) clinical work with socially phobic individuals was presented in Table 77.1.

Social phobia also lends itself very well to social group work treatment, which has been shown to be quite effective (Heimberg, 2002). Former and current social phobics can themselves be very useful as lay therapists (Ross, 1980). Additionally, it has been shown to be helpful, especially for clients with the generalized form of SP, to assess for the need for social skills training, because, as previously noted, this was shown to enhance the effects of exposure therapy (Herbert et al., 2005). For public speaking anxiety, a very friendly and supportive organization called Toastmasters International, devoted to helping individuals improve public speaking and leadership skills, can be very helpful. The Toastmasters program is, in effect, a lay-developed program of graduated exposure therapy sessions. Other helpful resources for addressing SP can be found in Table 77.2.

WEB SITES

Anxiety Disorders Association of America (ADAA). http://www.adaa.org.

The Anxiety Panic Internet Resource (TAPIR). http://www.algy.com/anxiety.

Toastmasters International. http://www.toastmasters.org.

References

American Psychiatric Association. (2000). *Diagnostic and statistical manual of mental disorders,* 4th ed., text revision. Washington, DC: APA.

Dalrymple, K. L., & Herbert, J. D. (2007). Acceptance and commitment therapy for generalized social anxiety disorder: A pilot study. *Behavior Modification, 31,* 543–568.

Hayes, S. C., Luoma, J. B., Bond, F. W., Masuda, A., & Lillis, J. (2006). Acceptance and commitment therapy: Model, processes, and outcomes. *Behaviour Research and Therapy, 44,* 1–25.

Hayes, S. C., Strosahl, K. D., & Wilson, K. G. (1999). *Acceptance and commitment therapy: An experiential approach to behavior change.* New York: Guilford.

Heimberg, R. G. (2002). Cognitive-behavioral therapy for social anxiety disorder: Current status and future directions. *Biological Psychiatry, 51,* 101–108.

Herbert, J. D., Gaudiano, B. A., Rheingold, A. A., Myers, V. H., Dalrymple, K., & Nolan, E. M. (2005). Social skills training augments the effectiveness of cognitive behavioral group therapy for social anxiety disorder. *Behavior Therapy, 36,* 125–138.

Kessler, R. C., Berglund, P., Demler, O., Jin, R., Merikangas, R., & Walters, E. E. (2005). Lifetime prevalence and age-of-onset distributions of DSM-IV disorders in the National Comorbidity Survey Replication. *Archives of General Psychiatry, 62,* 593–602.

Liebowitz, M. R., Heimberg, R. G., Travers, J., & Stein, M. B. (2000). Social phobia or social anxiety disorder: What's in a name? *Archives of General Psychiatry, 57,* 191–192.

Mattaini, M. A. (1990). Contextual behavior analysis in the assessment process. *Families in Society, 71,* 236–245.

Ossman, W. A., Wilson, K. G., Storaasli, R. D., & McNeill, J. W. (2006). A preliminary investigation in the use of acceptance and commitment therapy in group treatment for social phobia. *International Journal of Psychology and Psychological Therapy, 6,* 397–416.

Öst, L. G. (1987). Applied relaxation: Description of a coping technique and review of controlled studies. *Behaviour Research and Therapy, 25,* 397–409.

Rodebaugh, T. L., Holaway, R. M., & Heimberg, R. G. (2004). The treatment of social anxiety disorder. *Clinical Psychology Review, 24,* 883–908.

Ross, J. (1980). The use of former phobics in the treatment of phobias. *American Journal of Psychiatry, 137,* 715–717.

Stacher, D. (1999). *Mental health: A report from the surgeon general—1999.* Washington, DC: Office of the Surgeon General, SAMSHA.

Stein, M. B., Chavira, D. A., & Jang, K. L. (2001). Bringing up bashful baby: Developmental pathways to social phobia. *Psychiatric Clinics of North America, 24,* 661–676.

Thyer, B. A., Parrish, R. T., Curtis, G. C., Nesse, R. M., & Cameron, O. G. (1985). Ages of onset of *DSM III* anxiety disorders. *Comprehensive Psychiatry, 26,* 113–122.

Thyer, B. A., Parrish, R. T., Himle, J., Cameron, O. G., Curtis, G. C., & Nesse, R. M. (1986). Alcohol abuse among clinically anxious patients. *Behaviour Research and Therapy, 24,* 357–359.

Zimmerman, M., & Chelminski, I. (2003). Clinician recognition of anxiety disorders in depressed outpatients. *Journal of Psychiatric Research, 37,* 325–333.

Depression

78 Integration of Psychodynamic and Cognitive-Behavioral Practices

Nina Rovinelli Heller & Terry B. Northcut

Depression, as we know in the twenty-first century, is a common and debilitating condition, affecting individuals, families, and societies across the globe. Lifetime precedent rates are estimated at 20 to 25 percent for the full unipolar depression spectrum, and consequently, the impact on quality of life in all aspects of functioning is tremendous. In the United States, depressive disorders affect 14.8 million adults, or approximately 6.7 percent of the population (Kessler, Chiu, Demler, & Walters, 2005) and is the leading cause of disability for those aged 15 to 44 (World Health Organization, 2004). Just as troubling, prevalence of depression in children and adolescents and young adults has been rising at alarming rates (Gallagher, 2005; Lee, 2005), and depression among the elderly is greater than previously known (Hegel, Stanley, & Areán, 2002; Kennedy, 2000; King, & Markus, 2000; McInnis-Dittrich, 2002). In addition, different types of depression require differential assessment and evaluation of research results for the variety of clinical syndromes along the depression continuum (Reinecke, & Davison, 2002).

THEORETICAL APPROACHES TO THE TREATMENT OF DEPRESSION

Clinical social workers in a wide variety of practice settings work with clients who have both diagnosed and undiagnosed depressive disorders. The identification of people with depression has increased over the past decade, as has the range of available treatment options. With a strong legacy of employing a biopsychosocial perspective, social workers are well positioned to accommodate the growing bodies of knowledge from biological/genetic, psychological, and sociological theo-

ries and evidence-based practices. Social workers in public and private settings are often on the front lines of work with individuals and families and are in positions in which they can pay attention to prevention, identification, and treatment of depressive disorders.

With the advent of second- and third-generation antidepressant medications, biological interventions have become common, whereas half a century ago, psychotherapy alone was the treatment of choice. At that time, psychodynamic or psychoanalytic theory and technique recognized depressive disorders as largely psychological in nature. This reflected the tremendous legacy of Freudian psychology, (which, interestingly enough, originated in Freud's interest in neurobiological processes), viewing depression as "anger toward inward"—in other words, in largely psychodynamic terms. Other psychodynamically oriented theorists have posited that depression is related to mourning, to ambivalence regarding a lost object, to narcissistic injury, or to abandonment fears. Since the late 1970s, cognitive theory (Beck, 1979, 1987; Beck, 1995; Reinecke, & Davison, 2002, among others) has been highly influential in the treatment and research of many psychiatric disorders, most notably depression. Cognitive theory posits that the negative affects experienced in depression are a result of cognitive distortions and faulty thinking processes. The prescribed intervention, then, is the identification and modification of those distortions through psychotherapy.

PSYCHOTHERAPY OR MEDICATION?

Different theoretical schools have historically tried to lay claim to superiority over others in terms of treatment success. This is has been made possible in part by the increased availability of research funding, particularly the National Institute of Mental Health, for psychotherapy evaluation studies. Simultaneously, there has been a shift in the social work field toward identifying evidence-based practices. Psychotherapy evaluation studies are labor-intensive and require sophisticated designs and data analysis (Abbass, 2002). Cognitive therapy, which lends itself well to research studies because of its clearly identified assessment and intervention strategies, has led the way in terms of psychotherapy research. Numerous studies suggest that cognitive therapy is at least as effective as antidepressant medication (Zeiss, 1997). Still others have found that the combination of cognitive therapy and medication therapy is superior (Reinecke & Davison, 2002). Treatment effectiveness studies of psychodynamic interventions have been slower to develop, but Fonagy, Roth, and Higgins (2005) have published an exhaustive review of evidence-based psychodynamic treatment

Social workers look to theory, "practice wisdom," and research to guide our practice. On the basis of all three components, we do have some general guidelines for the assessment of depression. Assuredly, any client who is demonstrating vegetative signs of depression (significant changes in sleep, appetite, weight, libido, or psychomotor retardation or agitation) should be considered for referral to a medication evaluation. Likewise, clients who are suicidal or engaging in self-destructive behaviors in addition to depressed mood, distorted thinking, and feelings of hopelessness or helplessness could possibly benefit from medical intervention. Most of these clients will also benefit from psychotherapy (Areán & Cook, 2002; De Maat, Dekker, Schoevers, & DeJonghe, 2006; Finn, 2000; Reinecke & Davison, 2002). In addition, biopsychosocial assessment can be enhanced with the use of depression measures.

INTEGRATING THEORETICAL PERSPECTIVES

We favor an integrative approach to psychotherapy with depressed clients, specifically one that uses a psychodynamic perspective and integrates specific cognitive techniques. The reasons for this bias toward an integrative approach lie in our understanding that modern psychodynamic theory inherently captures the complexity of the subjective experience of the individual, whereas cognitive theory offers very clear, sometimes prescriptive

techniques aimed at increasing problem-solving skills and changing faulty thinking. The combination of the two approaches offers the opportunity to successfully intervene on both affective and cognitive levels while doing so in a way that includes the idiosyncratic historical, social, and cultural experiences of the client. Strengths of psychodynamic theory as they pertain to the treatment of depression include (1) an understanding of the power of unconscious processes; (2) the awareness of the impact of interpersonal loss on feeling states; (3) the importance of early developmental influences; and (4) the power of the therapeutic relationship, specifically in regard to transference and countertransference phenomenon.

Psychodynamic theory, then, pays particular attention to the feelings or affects of the client, considering these as a central focus for change. Hence, psychodynamic techniques include exploration of feeling states and their etiologies, particularly in the interpersonal realm. Exploration of the past, specifically in terms of its influence in the present, is often central to the therapeutic work, particularly in crisis, or reactive depression (Reinecke & Davison, 2002). Finally, the therapist actively uses the treatment relationship to explore issues such as loss, sadness, and anger. Interpretation of both conscious and unconscious material is central in the work.

Traditionally, cognitive theory has been characterized by (1) a here-and-now orientation; (2) a belief that thoughts affect or determine feeling states; (3) a belief that people who are depressed demonstrate a certain set of cognitive distortions (such as negative thinking, dichotomous thinking, catastrophizing, overgeneralization, selective abstraction, magnification, and minimization. More recently, cognitive theorists who lean more toward the constructivist position than to their behavioral origins see cognitive schemas and attributions that are particular to the depressed client, as they have idiosyncratic meaning. These schemas and attributions are sets of beliefs and assumptions about meaning and causation (e.g., arbitrary influence, personalization) that may have early origins and have been confirmed by subsequent life experiences. In both the early and the more recent cognitive therapies, the therapist directs his or her attention to the identification and correction of faulty cognitions that reinforce the client's depressive stance. Techniques such as problem solving, cognitive restructuring, thought blocking, and Socratic questioning can be very helpful in the changing of depressive cognitions that color the client's view of him- or herself, others, and the world. Through the use of these techniques, combined with in vivo and homework assignments, the client is able to identify, confront, and correct the cognitive distortions that are common to that feeling state.

A client who is depressed is in subjective distress. Both psychodynamic therapists and those who hold a cognitive-constructivist perspective value the importance of the client's narrative of his or her own experience. One depressed client is not like another, although they may share certain characteristics, as noted. For example, one client's sense of lethargy or helplessness may have very different origins, meanings, and manifestations than another's. The psychodynamic therapist is interested in both the conscious and unconscious determinants of this as well as those factors that maintain such feeling states. How-

ever, as many of us have witnessed, insight alone is often not sufficient and sometimes not even necessary to effect therapeutic change. In these instances, the addition of cognitive techniques may be enormously helpful in terms of systematically addressing the cognitive beliefs and distortions that may interfere with the client's "feeling better."

CONSIDERATIONS IN ASSESSMENT AND TREATMENT PLANNING WITH DIVERSE POPULATIONS

Table 78.1 outlines the critical areas for attention, assessment, and intervention with *all* clients, and particular note should be made regarding the need for culturally sensitive and knowledgeable assess-

TABLE 78.1 Guidelines for Assessment and Treatment Planning

- Evaluate carefully for safety risks, including passive and active suicidal behaviors and impulsivity. Consult recent research regarding suicide risk as associated with demographic variables, such as prior attempts, formulation of a plan, and age group.

- Create an empathetic connection with the client.

- Refer for both medical evaluation to rule out depression due to a general medical condition (*DSM-IV-TR*).

- Evaluate for substance abuse and differential diagnosis.

- Refer for evaluation for antidepressant medication, particularly in the presence of vegetative signs of depression.

- Administer a standardized depression scale, e.g., Beck Depression Inventory.

- Evaluate and utilize family and social supports.

- Assess socioeconomic issues and be familiar with relevant research literature.

- Consider developmental and cohort factors and the related research.

- Assess and refer to existing literature regarding incidence and manifestation of depression in certain demographic groups, such as gender, race/ethnicity, sexual orientation, and differential abilities.

- Evaluate affective, cognitive, and behavioral manifestations of depression.

- Encourage clients to verbalize their own understanding and hypotheses about their current depression.

- Be aware of both conscious and unconscious elements of the depression.

- Make judicious use of both insight-oriented exploration and cognitive-behavioral strategies, designed to restore optimum levels of functioning.

- Identify and explore distorted cognitions.

ment with people from diverse backgrounds. For diverse populations, the following areas merit particular attention.

- Consider differences in the presentation of symptoms and the cultural meaning of those symptoms (e.g., somatic complaints).
- Consider possible assumptions and beliefs about mental health providers and mental health treatment within the client(s) cultural system. (e.g., social workers are part of the majority culture, won't understand, etc.).
- Consider different ways of describing depressive symptoms related to cultural differences and/ or geographical differences (e.g., "nerves").
- Consider the possible stigma associated with seeking mental health services from within or outside the client(s) system (e.g., shaming to family, "only for crazy people," etc.) (Boyd-Franklin & Lockwood, 1999; Falicov, 1999, among others).

CASE ILLUSTRATION

The Client's Story

These guidelines are illustrated in the work with a client who enters treatment following a referral from his primary physician. "The doctor just sent me over here, I don't really know why," begins Stan's introduction to the first meeting." Stan is 75 years old and describes symptoms of anhedonia, loss of appetite, weight loss, reduced activity, and withdrawal from previously enjoyed social interactions with friends and family. When the therapist explores the medical history that brought Stan to the doctor, he indicates it was a routine check-up following a heart attack 3 years ago. Currently, Stan is on some heart medications but doesn't report any other health problems other than a weight loss of 10 pounds over 6 months. Stan's work history indicates that he is retired from 35 years with the postal service. "My knees aren't what they used to be, but I can still do what needs doing." He had joined the postal service after serving in the navy during the Korean War. Stan had joined the navy at 18 years old to "do his part." In terms of family and social support networks, Stan has three grown children, two boys, and one girl. Two children have moved away, "living their own lives." One son lives in town with three children of his own. Stan used to see the grandchildren often because he volunteered for baby-sitting or school activities. Now

that the kids are getting close to teenage years, Stan reports not enjoying being around them as much, "they're too noisy or always plugged into those headphones." Stan's wife seems to be "always busy," running from classes to committee meetings, to church services, and so on. According to Stan, she has lost patience with him and no longer asks him to join her when she goes places. They belong to a local Polish Catholic church, where they've been members for over 20 years. Stan has served in various capacities in the church through the years, but has lost interest in even attending over the past 6 months. His daily habits include watching television with his dog, which drives his wife "nuts," he says. "There's really nothing good on, just a bunch of reality TV shows. She's always yelling at me to get out of the house and do something." Socially, Stan used to meet some of the guys down at the neighborhood coffee shop, but "they're getting too fancy these days, with all of the fancy drinks, some of the guys don't like that and moved to a shop farther away." Stan felt it just wasn't worth the effort to him anymore to meet at the new location. When questioned, he denies any passive or active thoughts about suicide and presents no history of erratic or impulsive behavior. Stan's mood is "depressed," showing very little enthusiasm or affect as he discusses his life situation, however, cognitively he is quite sharp with clear short-term and long-term memory capabilities intact. Stan's take on his problems is that, "I've lived longer than my dad—he worked until he was 70 and then dropped dead of a heart attack while he was on the job. He was a hard worker—built houses, put roofs on, painted houses. That's the way it should be— you work until you die."

Case Formulation and Intervention

Stan is facing the developmental challenges of older adulthood, which in his case, include (1) adaptation to retirement; (2) changing role as father and grandfather (children have grown; two have moved away, grandchildren are more involved in their own age-appropriate adolescent interests, wife has increased her activities outside the home, perhaps in response to his depression); (3) changing social network of "coffee buddies"; and (4) his increased sense of vulnerability and mortality related to his heart attack 3 years earlier. Further complicating this generally normative process is Stan's report of depression over the past 6 months, which include vegetative signs of depression such as 10-pound weight loss, anhedonia, loss of appetite, reduced activity and withdrawal from social activities. The social worker appropriately contacts the client's physician to rule out depression as secondary to heart disease and medication and to evaluate for antidepressant medication. Additionally, the social worker could administer either the Beck Depression Inventory (1961) or the Geriatric Depression Scale (Yesavage et al., 1983), both measures with acceptable psychometrics. Depending on the results of this multidimensional assessment, Stan may well be a candidate for combination treatment of antidepressants and psychotherapy.

Stan's presentation with depression suggests both current and historical dimensions. First, like many other older adults of his generational cohort, he may have difficulty believing that his depressive symptoms are attributable to anything other than laziness, weakness, or self-pity. Cognitive strategies could be used to explore his thoughts about his lack of energy, conflict with his wife, and social withdrawal. Additionally, such cognitive beliefs could prevent him from being willing to consider antidepressant treatment and must be fully explored in this context as well. His statement in reference to his father and himself, "that's the way it should be—you work until you die," can be explored for both cognitive assumptions about his depression and his sense of self related to retirement. The cognitive-constructivist therapist might also explore his beliefs about his changing role and expectations related to his family.

Stan has lived 5 years longer than his father and survived a heart attack as well. The psychodynamically oriented social worker might explore any sense of survivor guilt and identification with his father that may unconsciously be affecting his current sense of himself, his vitality, and his mortality.

The social worker, aware of the research that older white men have the highest rate of completed suicide, will also be vigilant about suicidal thinking and plans throughout treatment. Because newer antidepressants sometimes affect an increase in energy before an increase in mood, Stan, like other men his age, could be at an elevated risk in the time period before a medication has had full effect.

Conclusion

We believe that a combination of theoretically informed approaches holds great benefit for a client like Stan. A cognitive-behavioral and psychodynamic integrative approach, embedded in a tra-

ditional social work biopsychosocial perspective provides the opportunity to address both cognition and affect, within a present and historical frame, with the acknowledgment of both conscious and unconscious phenomenon. In this way, we can really meet Stan "where the client is."

Historically, social work theory and practice have been integrative. Particularly in our current practice arena, which demands brief but effective and hence efficient treatment interventions, the integration of cognitive-behavioral and psychodynamic theory is useful. This synthesis draws on the best of both traditions in the attempt to capture the complexity of the human experience, particularly as it manifest in the very common condition of depression. The conscious and deliberate use of perspectives and techniques from both theories allows swift and systematic interventions while not sacrificing the value of the contextual and historical influences that impinge on the healthy functioning and experience of our clients. Furthermore, the increased attempts to understand the complicated processes of both depression and its treatment via research efforts in the areas of differential theoretical approaches and neurobiology hold great promise to the social worker. It becomes a professional responsibility to seek out the most recent research findings, in addition to the knowledge of theory and employment of social work practice skills. The conscious and deliberate use of perspectives and techniques from both theories allows swift and systematic interventions while preserving the value of the contextual and historical influences that impinge on the healthy functioning and experience of our clients.

WEB SITE

National Institute of Mental Health, information on depression. http://www.nimh.nih .gov/health/topics/depression/index.shtml.

References

Abbass, A. (2002). Short-term dynamic psychotherapies in the treatment of major depression. *Canadian Journal of Psychiatry, 47*(2), 193.

Areán, P. A., & Cook, B. (2002). Psychotherapy and combined psychotherapy/pharmacotherapy for late life depression. *Biological Psychiatry, 52*(3), 293–303.

Beck, A. (1961). Beck depression inventory. Philadelphia: Center for Cognitive Therapy.

Beck, A. (1979). *Cognitive therapy of depression*. New York: Guilford.

Beck, A. (1987). *Manual for the revised Beck depression inventory*. San Antonio, TX: Psychological Corporation.

Beck, J. (1995). *Cognitive therapy: Basics and beyond*. New York: Guilford.

Boyd-Franklin, N., & Lockwood, T. W. (1999). Spirituality and religion: Implications for psychotherapy with African American clients and families. In F. Walsh (Ed.), *Spiritual resources in family therapy*. New York: Guilford.

De Maat, S., Dekker, J., Schoevers, R., & DeJonghe, F. (2006). Relative efficacy of psychotherapy and pharmacotherapy in the treatment of depression: A meta-analysis. *Psychotherapy Research, 16*(5), 562–572.

Falicov, C. J. (1999). Religion and spiritual folk traditions in immigrant families. In F. Walsh (Ed.), *Spiritual resources in family therapy*. New York: Guilford.

Finn, C. A. (2000). Treatment of adolescent depression: A review of intervention approaches. *International Journal of Adolescence and Youth, 84*, 253–269.

Fonagy, P., Roth, A., & Higgins, A. (2005) Psychodynamic psychotherapy: Evidence based practice and clinical wisdom. *Bulletin of the Menninger Clinic, 69*(1), 1–59.

Gallagher, R. (2005). Evidence-based psychotherapies for depressed adolescents: A review and clinical guidelines. *Primary Psychiatry, 12*(9), 33–39.

Hegel, M., Stanley, M., & Areán, P. E. (2002). Minor depression and "subthreshold" anxiety symptoms in older adults: Psychosocial therapies and special considerations. *Generations, 26*(1), 44–49.

Kennedy, G. (2000). *Geriatric mental health care: A treatment guide for health professionals*. New York: Guilford.

Kessler, R. C., Chiu, W. T., Demler, O., & Walters, E. E. (2005). Prevalence, severity and comorbidity of twelve-month DSM-IV disorders in the National Comorbidity Survey Replication (NCS-R). *Archives of General Psychiatry, 62*(6), 617–627.

King, D., & Markus, H. (2000). Mood disorders in older adults. In S. K. Whitbourne (Ed.), *Psychopathology in later adulthood* (pp. 141–171). New York: Wiley.

Lee, C. L. (2005). Evidenced-based treatment of depression in the college population. *Journal of College Student Psychotherapy, 20*(1), 23–31.

McInnis-Dittrich, K. (2002). *Social work with elders: A biopsychosocial approach*. New York: Allyn & Bacon.

Reinecke, M. A., & Davison, M. R. (2002). *Comparative treatments of depression*. New York: Springer.

World Health Organization. (2004). *The World Health Report 2004: Changing History, Annex Table 3: Burdens of disease in Dalys by cause, sex, and mortality stratum in WHO regions, estimates for 2002*. Geneva: WHO.

Yesavage, J., Brink, T., Rose., T., Lum, O., Huang, V., Adey, M., et al. (1983). Development and validation of a geriatric depression screening scale: a preliminary report. *Journal of Psychiatry Research, 17*, 37–49.

Zeiss, A. M. (1997). Treatment of late life depression: A response to the NIH Consensus Conference. *Behavior Therapy, 28*(1), 3–21.

79 The Assessment and Treatment of Post-Traumatic Stress Disorder

M. Elizabeth Vonk

Traumatic events occur all over the world. They may be due to natural disaster, such as earthquake or flood; crime-related, such as rape or assault; or war-related, such as combat exposure or torture. Recent estimates indicate that a majority of the adult population in the United States will experience some type of traumatic event during their lifetime. The most common type of exposure for men is war-related, whereas for women, it is rape or assault. This chapter provides an overview of responses to trauma, particularly in relation to the development of post-traumatic stress disorder (PTSD). In addition, effective assessment and treatment methods for PTSD are discussed along with an accompanying case illustration.

People who are exposed to a traumatic event, including those who help with recovery efforts, perceive that their own or others' physical integrity is threatened and often react with horror, fear, or helplessness. Any number of a variety of symptoms may be expected following traumatic events (NCPTSD, 2004):

- *Emotional.* Reactions are generally very intense and may include fear, anxiety, anger, guilt, depression, and numbing. Many may feel overwhelmed by the intensity of their emotions.
- *Cognitive.* Reactions include difficulty concentrating and intrusive thoughts. In addition, survivors must struggle to make sense of an experience that contradicts formerly held assumptions regarding sense of control, safety, trust in self and others, personal power, self-esteem, and intimacy (McCann & Pearlman, 1990).
- *Somatic.* Reactions may include sleep disturbance, nightmares, eating difficulties, and a variety of bodily complaints.

- *Interpersonal.* Reactions include disruptions in intimate and familial relationships, vocational impairment, and generalized social withdrawal.

Although symptomatic responses to trauma are normal, 7 to 8 percent of people in the United States will develop PTSD during their lifetime (Keane, Marshall, & Taft, 2006). Many factors are related to the development of PTSD following a traumatic event, including demographics, the nature of the traumatic event, and pre- and post-trauma characteristics (Keane, Marshall, & Taft, 2006; NCPTSD, 2004). People of all ages develop PTSD, and it appears that children and the elderly are particularly susceptible. In addition, women appear to develop PTSD at a significantly higher rate than men. Life-threatening or extremely intense traumatic events, a history of childhood abuse or psychiatric disorder, and elevated levels of life stress are additional risk factors for the development of PTSD. Conversely, the availability of social support following traumatic events appears to decrease psychopathology.

The current *DSM-IV-TR* definition of PTSD includes six criteria (American Psychiatric Association, 2000):

- Criterion A. The person must be confronted by a traumatic experience involving threat of death, serious injury, or loss of physical integrity to which the person's subjective response is marked by fear, helplessness, or horror.
- Criterion B. The person must have at least one symptom of persistently reexperiencing the traumatic event, including intrusive images or thoughts, dreams about the event, a sense that the event is recurring, intense

distress when reminded of the event, or physiological reactivity to event-related cues.

- Criterion C. The person must have a minimum of three symptoms of avoidance and numbing, including avoidance of thoughts, feelings, or talk about the event; avoidance of activities, places, or people that are reminders of the event; inability to remember parts of the experience; decreased participation in important activities; sense of detachment from others; inability to experience a full range of emotions; or a restricted sense of the future.
- Criterion D. The person must have a minimum of two symptoms of increased arousal, including sleep difficulties, irritability, trouble concentrating, heightened startle response, or hypervigilance.
- Criterion E. The person must have the required array of symptoms for more than 1 month.
- Criterion F. The person must be experiencing impaired functioning at school or work or in relationships.

In addition, the *DSM-IV-TR* definition includes three specifiers: (1) acute, if symptoms have been present for less than 3 months; (2) chronic, if symptoms have been present for 3 months or more; and (3) delayed onset, if symptoms begin at least 6 months after the stressor.

CASE STUDY

Before moving ahead to describe assessment of and intervention for PTSD, I present a case study that will be used throughout this chapter to illustrate various aspects of therapeutic work with people who have PTSD.

Ben, a 26-year-old European American graduate student, sought therapy at a university counseling center following a motor vehicle accident that occurred 4 months earlier. Ben was a passenger in the car and sustained minor injuries. The driver, a close friend, was fatally injured. Ben remembers very little about the accident, has not talked to his fiancée or parents about what happened, and has "buried himself" in school work, hoping to keep his mind away from thoughts of it. He reports feeling numb about his friend's death, stating, "I haven't cried about it at all, even at his funeral." He wonders why he lived through it and

thinks that he "should have done something" to keep his friend from dying. He is also worried about how he has changed since the accident, thinking that he should be "over it." Formerly a confident driver, Ben now feels "jumpy." He used to think of himself as "mellow," whereas he now feels irritable and impatient with his friends' "constant joking around" and his fiancée's "trivial worries" about their wedding plans. What bothers him most and prompted his visit to the counseling center are increasingly disturbing nightmares that disrupt his sleep and flashbacks that interfere with his concentration during the day. Ben wants to return to his former high level of functioning so he can complete his dissertation and enjoy relationships with his fiancée and friends. He reported no previous trauma and no medical complications.

ASSESSMENT OF PTSD

The diagnosis of PTSD is generally made within the context of a complete biopsychosocial assessment. The assessment and diagnosis are based on in-depth clinical interview and utilization of standardized instruments.

The clinical interview allows the interviewer to explore the traumatic event and its aftermath in the context of the client's life. Such interviewing can be challenging, requiring the interviewer to maintain a focus on the trauma and associated memories, thoughts, and feelings; avoid victim blaming; actively listen to frightening or horrifying stories; and tolerate expressions of strong emotion.

In general, the clinical interview should include the client's story about the traumatic event and aftermath; current cognitive, emotional, somatic, and interpersonal difficulties related to the event; pretrauma level of functioning; and ways the person has coped with the event. In addition, the client's family history, previous traumatic or abusive experiences, current living situation, availability of support, and expectations of therapy should be explored. Consideration must also be given to the client's cultural background to gain greater understanding of the context and meaning of the trauma from the client's perspective (Nader, Dubrow, & Stamm, 1999). Finally, the interviewer must be alert to signs and symptoms of other difficulties that often co-occur with PTSD, such as suicidal or homicidal ideation; problems in family functioning; and mood, substance use, and personality disorders (NCPTSD, 2004).

The diagnostic interview may be enhanced with the additional use of one or more standardized assessment tools. Structured interviews provide opportunity for in-depth exploration, including detection of potential co-occurring mental disorders. Self-report measures may be valuable for assessing change in symptomatology over the course of treatment. Detailed information about the following and other structured interviews and self-report measures may be found on the assessment page of the NCPTSD Web site.

Structured Interviews

- The Clinician Administered PTSD Scale (CAPS): assesses PTSD symptoms and impact on functioning related to single or multiple traumas.
- The Structured Interview for PTSD (SI-PTSD): assesses PTSD symptoms and behavioral and survivor guilt.

Self-Report Measures

- Screen for Post-traumatic Stress Symptoms (SPTSS): assesses PTSD symptoms unrelated to specific trauma; used as a preliminary screen for presence of PTSD.
- Post-traumatic Diagnostic Scale (PDS): assesses severity and duration of PTSD symptoms and impact on functioning related to single trauma.

Treatment Goals and Objectives

Treatment goals and objectives follow directly from thorough assessment and are always individualized to particular clients. The following types of goals, however, are frequently included in effective interventions for PTSD.

- Increasing knowledge about and "normalizing" responses to trauma and PTSD.
- Strengthening coping skills and social support systems.
- Reducing guilt and eliminating self-blame.
- Reducing symptoms.
- Increasing functioning in social roles, such as at work and in the family.
- Integrating the trauma into the client's life experience.

Case Study: Assessment and Treatment Goals

Ben's assessment included a thorough unstructured clinical interview, completion of the SI-PTSD, and completion of the self-report PDS. Through this process, the social worker at the counseling center determined that Ben's signs and symptoms met the *DSM-IV* criteria for PTSD. Ben experienced a traumatic car accident in which a close friend lost his life; he felt that his own life was threatened (criteria A). Since the trauma, Ben has been reexperiencing symptoms, including nightmares and intrusive thoughts and images (criteria B). He has had symptoms of avoidance, including feelings of numbness, avoiding thoughts of the accident, and inability to remember details of the accident (criteria C). He also has increased arousal symptoms of irritability and hypervigilance while driving (criteria D). His symptoms have been present since the accident occurred 4 months ago (criteria E), and they have been negatively affecting his dissertation writing and interpersonal relationships with his friends and fiancée (criteria F).

In addition to making the diagnosis, the social worker noted that Ben functioned quite well prior to the accident, had experienced no previous abuse or traumas, and had a good support system that included family and friends. Although Ben did not appear to have a co-occurring mental disorder, his customary coping resources appeared to be overwhelmed; he had developed maladaptive cognitions related to survivor's guilt and gender-related expectations of himself, and his attempts to avoid processing the experience were impeding his recovery.

Ben's treatment goals and objectives were defined collaboratively with the social worker. By working together, the following mutually defined and objectives were established:

- Increase Ben's knowledge about trauma and PTSD
  - Ben will understand "normal" emotional, cognitive, somatic, and interpersonal responses to trauma.
  - Ben will educate his fiancée about trauma and PTSD.
- Increase Ben's ability to actively manage his anxiety at work and in social settings.
  - Ben will increase his ability to concentrate at work.
  - Ben will increase his enjoyment in social settings.

- Decrease the frequency of Ben's nightmares and intrusive thoughts of the accident.
- Increase Ben's ability to tolerate exposure to thoughts and feelings that are reminders of the accident.
  - Ben will be able to describe the accident to the social worker.
  - Ben will be able to describe his experience, its aftermath, and ongoing progress toward recovery with his fiancée and father.
- Modify Ben's beliefs about the accident that are associated with disturbing emotions.
  - Ben will modify his belief that he is somehow to blame for his friend's death.
  - Ben will identify and modify other disturbing thoughts about himself, others, and the world in relation to the accident.

Ben and the social worker agreed to work toward these goals with weekly meetings for a period of 3 months, after which they would reassess to see what additional work might be needed.

TREATMENT OF PTSD

A variety of interventions, both pharmacological and psychosocial, have been tested and found effective in the treatment of PTSD. The strongest evidence has been found for the use of exposure, cognitive, and anxiety management therapies (Keane, Marshall, & Taft, 2006; NCPTSD, 2004). Many of the interventions have been used successfully with both individuals and groups. Each intervention is described separately, and it is important to remember that most practitioners combine a variety of interventions when treating a client with PTSD. Because the range of symptomatology is so great, the particular combination of interventions must be based on the individual needs of each client. More detailed guidance on implementation and individualization of effective interventions for PTSD can be found in Taylor (2006).

Pharmacological Treatments

In general, psychotropic drugs are used to provide relief from specific symptoms, such as anxiety or depression, enabling the trauma survivor to make better use of concurrent psychosocial therapy. Based on an extensive review of empirical research, the Veterans Administration Practice Guidelines for PTSD (NCPTSD, 2004) describe the classes of drugs that have been used to treat PTSD, discuss evidence of effectiveness, and examine both benefits and risks of using particular drugs. Among others, these drugs include antidepressants (tricyclics, monoamine oxidase inhibitors, and selective serotonin reuptake inhibitors [SSRIs]), anxiolytics (benzodiazepines, buspirone), and sleep aids. Without question, the strongest evidence of effectiveness has been found to support the use of SSRIs. Despite the positive effect of SSRIs on PTSD-related symptomatology, treatment of PTSD through the use of pharmacology alone has not proven to be as effective as various psychosocial treatments (Keane, Marshall, & Taft, 2006).

Exposure Therapy

Exposure therapy is a behavioral intervention that involves activation of the traumatic memory through the use of associated imaginal or in vivo cues. It is used to decrease avoidance, intrusive thoughts, flashbacks, trauma-related fears, and panic attacks. The exposure must be of significant duration to allow the client's anxiety level to substantially subside in the presence of the feared but harmless cue. Because the idea of confronting or reliving the traumatic event is frightening, survivors need to have a clear rationale and understanding of how exposure therapies work to be informed participants in the intervention. In addition, the development and maintenance of a trusting therapeutic relationship seems to be essential for successful completion of exposure therapies. A description of exposure therapy designed for use with car accident survivors is described by Blanchard and Hickling (1997).

Cognitive Therapy

The goal of cognitive therapy is to learn to identify and eliminate specific thoughts that are causing negative emotional reactions and behaviors. This is achieved by challenging the thoughts through a process of logical examination of their veracity or functionality, followed by replacement of those that are dysfunctional with more reasonable ones. Dysfunctional beliefs following traumatic events vary, but several themes are common, including overgeneralizations about danger in the world and one's personal vulnerability, unrealistic self-blame and guilt about the event, loss of meaning for one's life, and broken trust in others and self. Foa and Rothbaum (1998) describe cognitive restructuring for use in the treatment of PTSD subsequent to rape.

Anxiety Management

A variety of behavioral and anxiety management interventions have been used to help people with PTSD cope with and manage emotions. One such anxiety management program, stress inoculation training (SIT), was originally developed by Meichenbaum (1997) to treat a variety of anxiety disorders, including PTSD. SIT aims to help clients manage and reduce anxiety through the development of skills such as relaxation and breathing techniques, cognitive restructuring, guided self-dialogue, thought stopping, and role-playing. The treatment takes place in three phases. First, the client is educated about responses to trauma and PTSD. Next, the coping skills are taught to and rehearsed by the client. Finally, the newly developed skills are applied through graduated exposure to stressful cues and memories associated with the traumatic event.

Eye Movement Desensitization and Reprocessing (EMDR)

EMDR combines aspects of cognitive and imaginal exposure techniques with guided eye movements in a specified protocol (Shapiro, 2001). Although many studies have supported the effectiveness of EMDR for the treatment of PTSD, some skepticism about the intervention remains. Specifically, the theoretical foundation and the necessity of eye movements in the treatment have been questioned (Keane, Marshall, & Taft, 2006; NCPTSD, 2004).

Post-Traumatic Growth

Calhoun and Tedeschi (1999) call attention to the potential for growth following traumatic experiences. Without minimizing the negative psychological consequences following trauma for many survivors, these authors examine the ability of some to experience significant personal growth following traumatic experiences. They review literature that identifies several areas of growth, including strengthened interpersonal relationships, changed self-perception that includes both increased vulnerability and strength, and changed philosophy of life that includes a shift in priorities and greater appreciation of life. In addition, the authors address facilitation of posttraumatic growth.

Case Study: Interventions and Evaluation

Having decided on treatment goals and preferred interventions, Ben indicated that he would like to start with exposure therapy to decrease his nightmares and flashbacks. Secondarily, he hoped to be able to share some of his experience with his fiancée, "to help her understand what I've been through." Knowing that the success of exposure relies on a strong therapeutic relationship, the social worker spent time preparing Ben for the intervention. Imaginal exposure was used initially, and was soon followed by in vivo exposure, in which Ben was asked to drive on the street where the accident took place.

During the course of the exposure intervention, the social worker began to identify Ben's distressing beliefs about the accident, his friend's death, safety, and self-blame. A maladaptive cognitive theme emerged in that Ben had come to believe he was to blame for the accident, in part because he asked his friend to wait for him before leaving the apartment, placing their car in harm's way. After teaching Ben the basics of cognitive therapy, the social worker and Ben began to work toward modifying his self-blaming and other dysfunctional beliefs related to the accident.

In addition to exposure and cognitive therapies, the social worker taught Ben a number of anxiety-management skills, including relaxation training and controlled breathing techniques. With encouragement from the social worker, Ben also was able to enlist his fiancée and another close friend for increased support.

At the end of 3 months, Ben was pleased with his progress in several areas. His intrusive and avoidance symptoms had decreased, he was engaging in less self-blame, and he was once again enjoying his relationship with his fiancée. However, he was still experiencing more difficulty with concentration than he would like. The social worker reviewed options, including continuing with cognitive therapy, adding more focus on anxiety-management skills, or augmenting treatment with medication. Ben preferred to continue with cognitive therapy and learn more anxiety-management techniques. As he continued to make progress with his goals, the social worker increased the time between sessions. During the last session, Ben reported that he felt ready to stop treatment. He went on to describe his current thoughts and beliefs about surviving a deadly car crash. Like many survivors of trauma, he was able to acknowledge personal growth along with the difficulties (Calhoun & Tedeschi, 1999). Although he still experienced sadness, moments of anxiety, and anger about the accident and loss of his friend, Ben believed that he had found strengths in himself that he was unaware of before the ac-

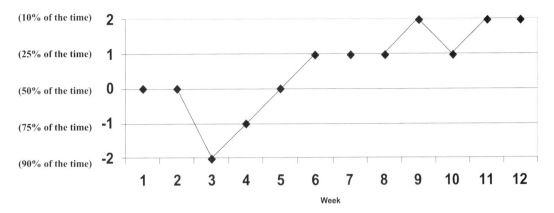

Figure 79.1 GAS self-report for occurrence of nightmares each week.

cident. He also had discovered the value of asking for and receiving support from his close friends.

Throughout treatment, the social worker monitored Ben's progress, relying both on the client's report and on clinical judgment. In addition, however, she used two quantitative methods. First, she made use of goal-attainment scaling (GAS) (Vonk, Tripodi, & Epstein, 2006). GAS is a useful tool for monitoring progress because the scales can be tailored to the individual's goals, are easy to administer, can be administered repeatedly, and can be weighted according to the relative importance of each of the goals. A 5-point goal attainment scale was developed for each of the goals, and at the start of each session Ben to rated his progress on each of them. The use of the GAS method is illustrated in Figure 79.1, showing Ben's progress on the goal of decreasing the frequency of his nightmares. Finally, the PDS, administered at the outset of treatment, was readministered at the close of treatment, at which time Ben no longer met the criteria for the diagnosis of PTSD.

Ben's assessment and treatment story provide an example of how empirically supported methods can be used for effective assessment and treatment of PTSD. Unfortunately, not all clients have PTSD uncomplicated by previous traumas, co-occurring substance use or mental disorders, or support system deficits. In spite of complications, social workers will be best able to provide assistance to people with PTSD through the use of assessment and treatment methods for which effectiveness has been empirically supported.

WEB SITES

International Society for Traumatic Stress Studies-Resources for Clinicians. http://www.istss.org/resources/clinicians.cfm.

National Center for Posttraumatic Stress Disorder. http://www.ncptsd.va.gov/ncmain/index.jsp.

National Institute of Mental Health, PTSD. http://www.nimh.nih.gov/health/topics/post-traumatic-stress-disorder-ptsd/index.shtml; assessment page, http://www.ncptsd.va.gov/ncmain/assessment.

References

American Psychiatric Association. (2000). *Diagnostic and statistical manual of mental disorders*, 4th ed., text revision. Washington, DC: APA.

Blanchard, E. G., & Hickling, E. J. (1997). *After the crash: Assessment and treatment of motor vehicle accident survivors*. Washington, DC: APA.

Calhoun, L. G., & Tedeschi, R. G. (1999). *Facilitating posttraumatic growth*. Mahwah, NJ: Erlbaum.

Foa, E. B., & Rothbaum, B. O. (1998). *Treating the trauma of rape*. New York: Guilford.

Keane, T. M., Marshall, A. D., & Taft, C. T. (2006). Posttraumatic stress disorder: Etiology, epidemiology, and treatment outcome. *Annual Review of Clinical Psychology*, 2, 161–197.

McCann, I. L., & Pearlman, L. A. (1990). *Psychological trauma and the adult survivor.* New York: Brunner/Mazel.

Meichenbaum, D. (1997). *Treating posttraumatic stress disorder: A handbook and practice manual for therapy.* Chichester, UK: Wiley.

Nader, K., Dubrow, N., & Stamm, B. H. (Eds.). (1999). *Honoring differences: Cultural issues in the treatment of trauma and loss.* New York: Brunner/Mazel.

NCPTSD. (2004). *Clinical practice guideline for the management of post-traumatic stress.* Retrieved from http://www.ncptsd.va.gov/ncmain/ncdocs/nc_prod/VAPracticeGuidelines1_2004.pdf.

Shapiro, F. (2001). *Eye movement desensitization and reprocessing: Basic principles, protocols, and procedures,* 2nd ed. New York: Guilford.

Taylor, S. (2006). *A clinician's guide to PTSD: A cognitive behavioral approach.* New York: Guilford.

Vonk, M. E., Tripodi, T., & Epstein, I. (2006). *Research techniques for clinical social workers.* New York: Columbia University Press.

80   Guidelines for Clinical Social Work with Clients with Dissociative Disorders

Lina Hartocollis

Dissociation has been a subject of heated debate since the dawn of modern psychiatry. It continues to generate controversy, and mental health professionals disagree about what it is, its causes, and how to treat it most effectively. Fueling the debate are concerns about the conceptual clarity and validity of dissociation and the disorders associated with it.

DISSOCIATION AND THE DISSOCIATIVE DISORDERS

Dissociation refers to a loosely connected assortment of psychopathological and normative phenomena that involve changes in consciousness or awareness and affect one's ability to access thoughts, feelings, perceptions, and/or memories. The range of dissociative experiences described in the clinical literature is expansive, including distortions in the perception of time (e.g., flashbacks); distortions in self-experience (e.g., depersonalization); distortions in the perception of reality (derealization); amnesia and fugue states; problems with attention; deadening of feeling (also known as emotional numbing); states of confusion; sensory distortions (e.g., tunnel vision); pain tolerance; and movement problems such as paralysis, epileptic-like fits, and tremors in the absence of any neurological or other organic cause. Culture-bound experiences of dissociation include spirit possession and trance states that occur in the context of religious and healing traditions.

Often described as occurring on a continuum, dissociative experiences may be normal or pathological. On the normal end, we engage in a form of dissociation when we daydream, becoming lost in our thoughts and disconnected or dissociated from what is going on around us. Another example of normative dissociation is so-called highway hypnosis, when we drive our car as if on auto-pilot, arriving at our destination and having little or no recall about how we got there. At the other end of the continuum are dissociative experiences that interfere with a person's ability to function normally and cause significant distress and disruption in the sufferer's life.

The *DSM-IV-TR* (American Psychiatric Association [APA], 2000) catalogs five types of dissociative disorders:

- *dissociative fugue*, characterized by sudden, unplanned travel to a place away from the person's usual surroundings, along with confusion about one's identity and inability to remember the past, and sometimes the adoption of a new personal identity;
- *dissociative amnesia*, in which the person suddenly loses the ability to remember important personal information, usually following a traumatic experience;
- *depersonalization disorder*, characterized by feelings of being disconnected from one's mental processes or body, in the absence of psychotic symptoms;
- *dissociative identity disorder*, a condition that is marked by a subjectively experienced fragmenting of the person's sense of identity; and
- *dissociative disorder not otherwise specified.*

Although etiology has not been clearly established for the dissociative disorders, these bizarre and often dramatic conditions are thought to occur as a reaction to certain types of stress or trauma. Examples of physiological or organic stress that may lead to dissociation include brain injury and neurological conditions, such as epilepsy. Dissociative phenomena such as amnesia and depersonalization may occur as a result of sleep deprivation, panic reactions, schizophrenia, and other psychiatric disorders. Psychological or physical threats or assaults that overwhelm the person's coping ability may also lead to dissociative responses. In such cases, dissociation is thought to serve as a defense mechanism that protects the person from intolerable experiences, feelings, or memories. For example, a victim of childhood sexual abuse may describe floating above her body and watching the abuse from a distance.

The trauma–dissociation model has increasingly been used to explain a widening range of psychiatric disorders. Diagnoses and symptom pictures that were once considered to be variations of Freud's classic syndrome "hysteria"—such as dissociative conditions, somatization disorder, borderline personality disorder, and post-traumatic stress disorder (PTSD)—are now conceptualized as having in common the mechanism of dissociation, as well as sharing an etiology that includes childhood trauma.

Eating disorders have also been linked to childhood trauma and dissociation.

Although trauma has been implicated in the development of dissociative disorders, the *DSM* considers the dissociative disorders separately from PTSD, which is listed as an anxiety disorder. According to the *DSM*, dissociative states are rare in people diagnosed with PTSD. At the same time, acute stress disorder, also an anxiety disorder, is characterized by a host of dissociative symptoms (subjective sense of numbing, detachment, or absence of emotional responsiveness; reduction in awareness of surroundings; derealization; depersonalization; or dissociative amnesia). Although it is not yet a *DSM* diagnosis, the phrase "complex post-traumatic stress" has recently been coined to describe the cumulative effects of stressful or traumatic experiences that contribute to a host of psychological difficulties (Chu, 2007; van der Kolk, Roth, Pelcovitz, Sunday, & Spinazzola, 2005).

Few specific treatment protocols have been developed for dissociative fugue, dissociative amnesia, and depersonalization disorder. These conditions are often resolved when the underlying physical or psychiatric disorder is treated or when there is a change in the precipitating situation or problem.

The remainder of this chapter focuses on what is perhaps the most baffling, challenging to treat, and controversial of the dissociative disorders: dissociative identity disorder (DID).

DISSOCIATIVE IDENTITY DISORDER

DID, previously known as multiple personality disorder, is a condition that is thought to develop post-traumatically, most often in persons with a history of severe childhood sexual and physical abuse. Individuals with DID have difficulty maintaining a unified sense of self. They experience themselves as possessing more than one personality state or identity, each with its own thoughts, feelings, behavior patterns, likes, dislikes, history, and other characteristics.

Once thought to be a rare and exotic condition, DID has gained public attention and clinical recognition over the past 25 years, and reports of its incidence have grown. Widely varying explanations for this increase have been suggested, from identification of previously misdiagnosed cases, on one hand, to suggestion, hysterical epidemic, and fad on the other. In any event, it is likely that various overlapping cultural trends helped shape both current constructions of DID and the controversy surrounding it. Prominent among these are heightened public and clinical awareness of child abuse and a shift toward theories of psychopathology that emphasize trauma and dissociation over other explanatory processes. Popularized accounts of multiple personality, such as *The Three Faces of Eve* and *Sybil*, also undoubtedly exerted influence, serving as "prototypical illness narratives" that help shape clinicians' and clients' constructions of the disorder (Hartocollis, 1998).

According to the *DSM-IV-TR*, DID is characterized by the existence of two or more distinct identities or personality states that intermittently take control of an individual's behavior, along with an inability to remember important personal information that is not the result of ordinary forgetfulness. DID is generally diagnosed in adults, less frequently in adolescents and children. With respect to both adults and children, females are much more likely to be diagnosed with DID than males.

Personality states can be male or female and sometimes take animal forms. They are often of different reported ages, sex, or race; they dress differently, hold different values and beliefs, and often have different memories. The changes in appearance and behavior between the different personality states can be dramatic, including differences in vocabulary, handwriting, and other personal characteristics. The relationship between personality states is complex and varied; they can be friendly or antagonistic to one another. The change from one personality state to another is called "switching." Switching from one personality state to another is usually sudden and often a response to psychosocial stressors.

A history of childhood trauma, usually sexual abuse, is thought to be present in most cases of DID. According to the trauma–dissociation model of DID, the child who is constitutionally predisposed defends against overwhelming traumatic experiences by splitting off or dissociating the memories of such experiences from consciousness. The dissociated memories then become part of an alter personality state, held apart from awareness by an amnesic barrier. This protects the individual from remembering the abuse except through periodic, fragmentary reexperiencing of the trauma by the personality states in whom the memories reside.

Recent theory and research has suggested that developmental and bonding failures in early childhood may contribute to the development of dissociative disorders (International Society for the Study of Dissociation [ISSD], 2005; Liotti, 1999). Drawing from attachment theory, this model posits that infants and very young children with frightening and inconsistent caregivers may develop a "disorganized attachment style." This leaves the child especially vulnerable to traumatic experiences that further erode and disorganize the already fragile sense of self and identity. An understanding of the impact of early bonding and developmental insults provides a useful frame when assessing and treating persons diagnosed with DID.

ASSESSMENT AND TREATMENT PLANNING FOR DID

DID has been described as a covert disorder because afflicted individuals often try to hide their distress and multiplicity from others, and sometimes even from themselves, fearing that they will be disbelieved or labeled as crazy. This can make the condition difficult to diagnose.

A number of measurement instruments that detect the presence of dissociation and dissociative symptomatology can be used to aid the assessment process. The Trauma Symptom Inventory dissociation scale (TSI) rates 100 dissociative symptoms according to frequency on a 4-point scale (Briere, 1995). The Dissociative Experiences Scale (DES) is a self-report measure that taps a variety of disturbances in identity, memory, awareness, and other mental processes that are thought to be indicators of dissociation (Carlson & Putnam, 1993). The Dissociative Disorders Interview Schedule (DDIS) (*DSM-IV* version) is a structured interview based on the *DSM-IV* diagnosis for dissociative disorder. It may be administered in 30 to 45 minutes (Ross, 1997).

The following clinical clues to the existence of DID have been suggested: memory distortion and lapses, including fugue (e.g., reports of "lost time"); depersonalization; hearing voices experienced as coming from within the head or self; a history of unsuccessful psychiatric treatments; a history of severe and persistent emotional and/or physical childhood trauma; flashbacks of traumatic memories; identity confusion and identity alteration (ISSD, 2005)

Persons with DID may experience symptoms that overlap with those of mood disorders, substance disorders, sexual disorders, or sleep disorders.

They also often exhibit symptoms of PTSD, such as flashbacks, nightmares, and startle responses. Diagnosis and assessment may be further complicated by clients' susceptibility to suggestion and questions about the validity and reliability of their reports of childhood abuse.

Although there is apparently an association between childhood trauma and adult DID, no clear linear or causal relationship has been established between the two. Moreover, human memory is subject to error and distortion, and persons with dissociative disorders may be especially suggestible. Hence, it is important to proceed with caution when attempting to uncover memories of child abuse.

CASE EXAMPLE

Twenty-one-year-old Carrie has been suffering from depression, episodes of confusion, and lapses of memory, along with a host of other troubling symptoms. Although she currently works as a retail store manager, she has been in and out of hospitals since adolescence, gathering a list of diagnoses such as schizophrenia, borderline personality disorder, and bipolar disorder along the way, but never responding successfully to treatment (see Fig. 80.1).

During early sessions in an outpatient therapy clinic, Carrie describes a painful history of binge eating, self-mutilation (cutting her arms and legs with a razor blade), alcohol abuse, and relationship difficulties. Although at first reticent and mistrustful toward me, she slowly begins to open up. Carrie reveals that she has always been "absentminded," for example, discovering clothes in her closet that she doesn't remember buying. She describes other bizarre episodes of lost time, such as waking up one morning with a new haircut she does not remember getting. She also alludes to having been sexually molested as a child by her father, a physician, although she is very guarded when I ask questions about her childhood, and I do not press her, focusing instead on establishing a trusting therapeutic alliance.

About 6 months into our work together, I attend training on DID and am struck by the similarities between the symptoms I hear described and those that Carrie has exhibited. I wonder if she might be a "multiple." After reading all of the professional literature I can get my hands on about the disorder, my suspicions grow.

Several weeks later, Carrie arrives at my office with a large stuffed white rabbit. Instead of sitting in the chair as usual, she drops to the floor, hugging the stuffed animal and rocking back and forth. When I ask how old she is, Carrie gingerly raises five fingers.

Carrie and I continued to meet for weekly sessions over the course of the next 4 years. Our work focused on using the safety of the therapeutic relationship to help Carrie repair her seriously impaired ability to trust others, process her overwhelming feelings and memories, and gradually integrate her fragmented sense of self.

The therapy ended when Carrie's employer transferred her to another city. Though still prone to dissociate when under stress, Carrie's inner and outer worlds were much less chaotic than when we started our work together. She no longer engaged in self-mutilation (cutting), reported fewer episodes of lost time, and described feeling as if she were "almost whole." She had also recently begun a romantic relationship with a man who she described as a "male version of her shrink but more fun."

TREATMENT GOALS

- Stabilize and reduce symptoms of anxiety, depression, and lack of impulse control.
- Increase self-awareness, self-control, and mastery over emotions.
- Decrease reliance on dissociative defense mechanisms; develop more adaptive coping mechanisms.
- Develop unified sense of self.
- Develop capacity for safe, healthy relationships.

Although there is no empirical evidence to support the claim that any particular approach is most effective in the treatment of DID, the following expert consensus guidelines have been established for working with such clients (Chu, 2007; ISSD, 2005; Lioti, Mollon, & Miti, 2005):

- establish a strong therapeutic alliance without extending treatment boundaries;
- pace the therapy, taking care not to attempt to dismantle dissociative and other defenses too quickly (use of a "staged" treatment approach);
- focus on dissociation and other post-traumatic defensive processes, rather than on the more florid DID symptoms (e.g., personality states); and

Client: Carrie A.; Age: 27

Presenting Problem: Ms. A. is a single white female, who works as a retail store manager. An overweight but attractive and personable young woman, Ms. A. describes a host of troubling behaviors and symptoms since adolescence. In addition to self-mutilation (cutting of arms and legs) and binge eating, Ms. A. also reports sleep difficulties and recurrent nightmares, depressed mood and other depressive symptoms, and generalized anxiety. Other symptoms include lapses of memory or what she called "lost time"—apparent fugue states during which she loses conscious awareness of time and place. She also describes current relationship problems and a history of victimization (current abuse in relationship with boyfriend and past childhood sexual abuse).

History of Past Treatment: Ms. A. sought outpatient psychotherapy once during adolescence and once in her early twenties. Both courses of therapy lasted only several sessions before she abruptly left the treatment. She was hospitalized twice, once after a suicide attempt and once for a major depressive episode.

Treatment Goals

Assessment Model→	Screening Tools→	Short-Term→	Long-Term→	Treatment Plan
BIO→	Genogram	1. Establish trust and set boundaries in therapeutic relationship.	1. Develop capacity for secure, safe attachments.	1. Outpatient tx sessions, long-term, psychodynamic/ cognitive-behavioral.
PSY→	Mental Status Beck Depression Inventory DES Scale*	2. Stabilization and symptom reduction.	2. Increase self-awareness, and self-control.	2. Evaluate for adjunct meds to treat depressive and anxiety symptoms.
SOC→	TSI Scale**	3. Learn to anticipate intense feelings and reactions.	3. Develop "self capacities" (e.g., self-control, self-soothing).	3. Possible adjunctive group therapy.
	Ecomap	4. Gain understanding of purpose of dissociative defenses.	4. Decrease reliance on dissociative defenses; develop more adaptive coping skills.	
			5. Process traumatic memories.	
			6. Establish unified sense of self.	
CULTURE→	Culturegram (rule-out culture-bound syndromes)		7. Develop capacity for secure, healthy attachments.	

*DES: Dissociative Experiences Scale
**TSI: Trauma Symptom Inventory Dissociation Scale

DIAGNOSIS

AXIS I:	300.14 Dissociative Identity Disorder (Primary focus of treatment)
	300.4 Dysthymic Disorder, Early Onset
AXIS II:	V71.09 No diagnosis
AXIS III:	None
AXIS IV:	V62.81 NOS Relational Problems
AXIS IV	GAF: 50

Figure 80.1 Case study of Carrie.

- process trauma but refrain from making recovery of repressed memories the focus of the treatment.

Most DID treatment protocols recommend a staged approach that begins with alliance building and establishing safety inside and out of the therapy, then moves to processing the trauma and beginning integration of the person's sense of identity, and ends with work on self-care and relational skill-building (Chu, 2007; ISSD, 2005; Liotti et al., 2005).

The process of establishing rapport and building a therapeutic alliance should take into account that persons with DID, such as Carrie, often struggle with issues of privacy, trust, control, boundaries and safety. At the outset of the assessment and treatment planning process, it is important to help prepare the client as much as possible for what to expect, and to provide reassurance that he or she may refuse to answer any questions without worrying about ruining the assessment or upsetting the social worker. It is also useful to ask about other assessment and treatment experiences—both positive and negative—and to inquire about what the client hopes to gain from the assessment, for example, "What would you like to better understand about yourself?"

Persons with DID are often unaware of their feelings until they reach overwhelming levels and hence may react to anxiety-producing assessment and treatment strategies by abruptly shifting from little or no affective reaction to dramatic outbursts. In their treatment guidelines for DID, the ISSD recommends "a therapist who is engaged and who actively structures the treatment by anticipating difficulties and by having a clear plan to help the patient through the stages of treatment" (2005, p. 71). For example, during the assessment process, the social worker should help the client learn to anticipate and modulate his or her reactions by asking how the client shows distress and how he or she can be helped to calm down when anxious or afraid.

Along with efforts to calm and stabilize the client, early stage treatment should focus on the management of safety issues. Persons with DID often have chaotic lives, engage in behaviors that put themselves or others at risk (e.g., promiscuity and engaging in unsafe sex, involvement in abusive intimate relationships, as either victim or perpetrator). They also engage in self-destructive behaviors (self-mutilation, substance abuse, eating disorders) and are at high risk for suicide. It has been suggested that such risky and self-destructive behaviors represent a reenactment of traumatic experiences. The social worker can help reduce the client's shame and secrecy by explaining the behaviors as understandable reactions to trauma while actively working to minimize them and keep the client safe.

Safety management should include (1) education about why safety is necessary for successful treatment; (2) safety contracting (including negotiating with particular personality states that are violent or self-destructive; (3) strategies to help the client correct cognitive distortions that fuel unsafe behavior (cognitive-behavioral techniques); (4) crisis management and self-soothing techniques, such as meditation, self-hypnosis; (5) medications, when indicated; (6) treatment plans or referral to specialized programs to deal with eating disorders and substance abuse issues; (7) inpatient hospitalization if the client is in imminent danger of doing serious harm to self or others (ISSD, 2005, p. 93).

Once safety and symptom stabilization have been reasonably established, the second phase of treatment may commence, focusing on processing traumatic memories and beginning to integrate the personality. Because DID is generally viewed as a condition that occurs post-traumatically in people who were abused as children, most treatment approaches include efforts to process or "metabolize" the trauma. However, the question of how much to focus the treatment on recovery of childhood memories of abuse and metabolizing the trauma is controversial, and my preference is to focus on dissociative processes and their defensive functions, rather than on the trauma per se.

Specialized techniques, such as hypnosis and the "mapping" of alter personalities, have been developed for working with DID, but most experts recommend that clinicians follow general best practices of psychotherapy and mental health management (Chu, 2007; ISSD, 2005). So as not to overwhelm or disorganize the client, any probing about sketchy memories and details of traumatic experiences should be approached carefully and with the client's express permission.

In my view, it is preferable to take a neutral position with regard to the reality of any memories of abuse, never denying the reality of the abuse but emphasizing that it is the *meaning* and current impact of these memories on the client that should be the focus of the treatment. In general, the meaning and particular manifestation of symptoms and experiences may differ widely from client to client and should not be eclipsed by the therapist's insistence on adhering to a one-size-fits-all diagnosis, explanatory theory, or treatment approach.

A common therapeutic pitfall in work with clients who have been diagnosed with DID occurs when the therapist becomes overly fascinated with the client's condition, especially the more florid symptomatology of distinct personality states. This can lead to a secondary gain situation in which the therapist's attention reinforces, rather than helps alleviate, the client's maladaptive behaviors and symptoms. Furthermore, overemphasis on the different personality states or alters may lead the therapist to lose sight of important interpersonal dynamics and events that occur within the context of the therapeutic relationship. The valuable opportunity may then be missed of helping the client understand his or her particular ways of relating to the therapist, the origins of these characteristic interpersonal patterns, and how dissociative defense mechanisms such as an alternate personality may be replaced by more adaptive coping behaviors. The ultimate goal in the middle phase of therapy is to achieve a sense of personality integration.

The final phase of DID therapy should focus on consolidating and maintaining treatment gains by focusing on post-therapy self-care strategies (e.g., coaching to help client deal with everyday problems) and relational skill building.

In summary, treatment for DID should provide a holding environment and boundaried corrective emotional experience through which the client can safely process traumatic memories, improve identity integration, and develop healthy coping and relational skills. Although controlled outcome studies are lacking, anecdotal clinical evidence suggests that treatment success with clients suffering from DID is more likely when the therapist follows the general practice guidelines laid out here.

WEB SITES

International Society for the Study of Dissociation. http://www.issd.org.

SAMHSA National Center for Trauma Informed Care. http://mentalhealth.samhsa.gov.

Sidran Institute (Traumatic Stress Education and Advocacy). http://www.sidran.org.

References

American Psychiatric Association. (2000). *Diagnostic and statistical manual of mental disorders,* 4th ed., text revision. Washington, DC: APA.

Briere, J. (1995). *Trauma symptom inventory (TSI).* Odessa, FL: Psychological Assessment Resources.

Carlson, E. B., & Putnam, F. W. (1993). An update on the dissociative experiences scale. *Dissociation,* 6, 16–27.

Chu, J. A. (2007). Treatment of traumatic dissociation. In E. Vermetten, M. J. Dorahy, & D. Spiegel (Eds.), *Traumatic dissociation* (pp. 333–352). Washington, DC: American Psychiatric Publishing.

Hartocollis, L. (1998). The making of multiple personality disorder: A social constructionist view. *Clinical Social Work Journal, 26*(2), 159–176.

International Society for the Study of Dissociation. (2005). Guidelines for treating dissociative identity disorder in adults. *Journal of Trauma and Dissociation, 6*(4), 69–149.

Liotti, G. (1999). Disorganized attachment as a model for the understanding of dissociative psychopathology. In J. Solomon & C. George (Eds.), *Attachment disorganization* (pp. 291–317). New York: Guilford.

Liotti, G., Mollon, P., & Miti, G. (2005). Dissociative disorders. In G. O. Gabbard, J. S. Beck, & J. Holmes (Eds.), *Oxford textbook of psychotherapy* (pp. 203–211). Oxford: Oxford University Press.

Ross, C. A. (1997*). Dissociative identity disorder.* New York: Wile.

van der Kolk, B. A., Roth, S., Pelcovitz, D., Sunday, S., & Spinazzola, J. (2005). Disorders of extreme stress: The empirical foundation of a complex adaptation to trauma. *Journal of Traumatic Stress, 18,* 389–399.

PART VIII
Guidelines for Specific Techniques

81

Developing Successful Therapeutic Relationships

Lawrence Shulman

A middle-aged mother of three comes to a family counseling agency for help dealing with her young children. She has just started a difficult separation from her husband of 20 years. Her main concern is how to deal with her children, who are upset and have been acting out since their father moved out. She tells the agency intake worker that she wants help with dealing with her own feelings of failure in her marriage, supporting her clearly upset children, and starting a new life. At the first interview with her 25-year-old, recently graduated MSW social worker, she notices the worker does not have a wedding ring and asks, "Do you have any children?" The worker responds, "We are here to talk about you, not me." For the balance of the interview, the client appears distracted and uncomfortable, providing minimal responses to the worker's effort to obtain a social history. The worker's notes at the end of the session describe the client as "depressed and resistant."

In this vignette, by putting ourselves in the shoes of the client, we can see that she may really be asking, "Since you don't have children, can you understand my situation and can you help me?" Both of these are reasonable questions in the mind of this client in a first interview. Because of the taboo against directness in relation to authority, the concerns may be raised in an indirect manner. The young worker, feeling defensive, responded in a way that closed off this line of discussion. The client's resistance may be a reaction to the worker's defensiveness.

If the engagement phase is handled well by the social worker, it can increase the possibility of establishing an effective working relationship with the client. The working relationship, also referred to as the therapeutic alliance, is the medium through which the worker influences the client and the outcomes of practice. Elements of the working relationship have been defined in this author's research as rapport ("I get along with my worker"), trust ("I can tell my worker anything on my mind; I can risk my mistakes and failures as well as my successes"), and caring ("My worker cares as much about me as she cares about my children") (Shulman, 1978, 2009).

Clients often bring a number of unstated questions to the first session. "Who is this social worker and what kind of person will he or she turn out to be?" "Can I trust this worker?" "What will our work be about and what will be doing together?" "Can this worker understand and help me or will he or she be judgmental?" In those situations with more than one person present, such as couple, family, group, and community work, there are also concerns about the others in the session.

When these relationship issues are added to what might be ambivalence about seeking and accepting help or accepting that a problem exists, one can easily understand the complexities associated with beginnings. This phase of work requires that the client make a first decision to engage in the process. Whereas a skillful worker can influence that decision, she or he cannot make it for the client. The skills identified in the remainder of this chapter are those that increase the possibility that the client will take that first step. This chapter also identifies the skills that can encourage the client to make the second decision, which is associated with making the transition from the beginning or engagement phase to the middle or work phase. At this point the commitment to work on difficult and often painful tasks is completed. The dynamics and skills that are important in the ending and transition phase of work are beyond the scope of this chapter.

The focus of this article is on core skills or constant elements, which can apply to all forms of practice, and it is important to recognize that the helping relationship is also affected by variant elements. For example, the nature of the problem or the setting of practice can have an important influence. Working in a high school dealing with violence prevention might look somewhat different from working in a hospital with persons with AIDS.

Variations introduced by age (practice with children, teens, adults, and the elderly) may affect how the worker begins and the development of the relationship. Other factors, such as gender, race, ethnicity, sexual orientation, disability, and so on, can all impact how the client perceives the offer of help.

For example, Elze (2006) describes how a school social worker can be GLBT (gay, lesbian, bisexual, and transgendered) sensitive in practice. This is a crucial stage of development for intervention, during which students attempt to come to grips with their sexual orientation and the larger heterosexual population begins to develop its attitudes toward difference. Elze suggests that the social worker needs to demonstrate that he or she is an "askable" person in response to all students using such strategies as employing gender-neutral language when exploring youth's dating interests, sexual behaviors, and so on.

Strategies appropriate for one population may be quite ineffective with another. Working interethnically (for example, a white worker with a person of color) as well as working intraethnically (for example, a Hispanic worker with a Hispanic client) may modify the dynamics and the strategies employed. Practice with voluntary, involuntary, or semi-voluntary clients may also look quite different. For example, a first session of a voluntary parenting group requires a different strategy than one with an involuntary group of men who have been convicted of driving while intoxicated. Finally, practice may be influenced by the worker's theoretical orientation and underlying assumptions.

In spite of the many variations on the theme, the notion of understanding practice against the backdrop of time—the preliminary, beginning, middle, and ending/transition phases of work—and the skills identified in the balance of this article, are proposed as core elements in all of the

variations described. Schwartz (1961) described the importance of these phases of work, adding a preliminary phase to beginnings, middles, and endings/transitions phases first identified in social work by Taft (1942, 1949). He suggested that because clients often raise many of their questions and concerns in an indirect manner, workers needed to prepare to hear the client's indirect cues by developing a preliminary empathy. The skills of the preliminary phase include the following:

- *Tuning in.* An exercise in which the worker develops a tentative, preliminary empathy with the client's feelings and concerns. The worker must also tune in to his or her own emotional state at the start of the relationship because it will impact on the worker's moment-by-moment responses to the client.
- *Responding directly to indirect cues.* The skill of preparing to articulate a client's thoughts and feelings in response to indirect communications in the first session or sessions.

A common illustration of the importance of these two skills was the vignette that began this chapter. The recently divorced mother of three children asks her 25-year-old, unmarried, recent graduate of a school of social work the question: "Do you have children?" Unless the worker has tuned in both to her own feelings of inadequacy because she does not have a child and the real feelings of the mother, it is not uncommon for the worker to respond defensively, "We are here to talk about you, not me!" This response misses what might be the underlying questions: "Can you understand my situation? Will you be able to help me? Will you judge me harshly? Can I trust you?"

A more direct response to the indirect cue might be as follows: "I'm not married, and I don't have any children. Why do you ask? Are you concerned I may not understand what it is like for you? I'm worried about that as well. For me to help, I need to understand. For me to understand, you will have to tell me." In addition to illustrating the power of tuning in and responding directly, this example also illustrates a number of skills identified later in this chapter in the section dealing with the middle or work phase. These skills were found in this author's research to be associated with the development of a positive working relationship when used in the beginning phase of practice (Shulman, 2009). The importance of expression of genuine empathy in developing a positive relationship was supported by Truax (1966) and more recently in the work of Hakansson and Montgomery (2003).

It's important to note that there is a certain individual artistry to practice and that the exact words used by workers may differ while the intent and impact of the skill will be the same. It is also important to emphasize that the worker's empathic responses must be genuine and not a phrase that has been learned and is recited without feelings. Clients know when a worker is simply reflecting their words and not experiencing their feelings. Expressions such as "I hear you saying . . ." with no real affect attached can be experience by clients as artificial empathy.

Another crucial element of the beginning phase, which takes place during the first session(s), is the development of a contract or working agreement between the worker and the client. This contract helps establish a structure that creates the freedom for the work to proceed. A number of first session skills are described next. It is important to note the following.

- A contract may not be fully developed in the first session, and this working agreement can change over time.
- The client must feel an investment in the work or the sessions will constitute an "illusion of work" in which conversations take place but nothing real happens.
- The worker's must make clear the purpose and her or his role in nonjargonized terms to which the client can connect.

The specific contracting skills are as follows (Shulman, 2009).

1. *Clarifying purpose.* The skill of making a brief opening statement, without jargon, which helps clarify the purpose of the session. This skill should be used when initiating a service (for example, a first group meeting) or responding to a client's request for service (for example, "If you can let me know what brought you in today we can see how I might be able to help.").
2. *Clarifying role.* The skill of describing in a brief, nonjargonized manner, the kind of help the social worker can provide. For example, "No, I can't give you the right answer for dealing with your husband. However, I can help you examine how you deal with him now, your feelings about the relationship, how you see yourself now and in the future. Perhaps if we work on this together I can help you find the answer that is right for you."
3. *Reaching for feedback.* The skill of encouraging clients to explain their perceptions of the problem and the areas in which they wish to receive help.
4. *Clarifying mutual expectations.* Developing an agreement on what the client may expect of the worker as well as defining the client's obligations (for example, regular attendance at group sessions; notification if a client must miss an interview).
5. *Discussing authority issues.* Dealing with any issues, raised directly or indirectly, that concern the authority of the worker (for example, the mandated nature of the service; the limits of confidentiality defined by the worker's responsibility as a mandated reporter; the client's stereotypes of authority figures or past experiences with social workers).

Though contracting is always initiated in the first sessions, it is not unusual to have to recontract as the work develops. The client may not have fully understood the implications of the contract. It is not unusual for clients to begin with near problems, which are real to the client but not at the core of the work. As the work proceeds, the client begins to understand his or her issues more clearly and is better able to articulate them. The client may have been in what has been called the precontemplation stage (DiClemente, Prochaska, Fairhurst, & Velicer, 1991). For example, a client in substance abuse counseling may not have accepted that they have a problem with alcohol. Thus, for a number of reasons, contracting remains fluid over time.

As the work continues, the client moves to the crucial transition stage from the beginning to the middle or work phase. This was refereed to earlier as making the second decision. Careful analysis of these transition sessions will reveal that clients may continue to use indirect forms of communication. The client may be embarrassed to raise a difficult issue. Some examples include taboo areas, such as sex, dependency, or death. The client may not be consciously aware of the existence of the problem. The skills that follow are designed to assist clients in telling their stories and telling it with feelings. These skills also assist the client in examining his or her cognitions or thought patterns related to the client's self-perception or perception of the problem or of others. An underlying assumption is that how one feels, affects how one thinks, which affects how one acts, which in turn affects how one feels, and so on. It is the feeling, thinking, and doing connection that is explored in the middle phase of practice.

The following skills can be helpful in this transition phase (Shulman, 2009).

1. *Sessional tuning in.* The skill of developing a tentative, preliminary empathy for issues that may emerge at the start of a specific session (for example, the impact of a traumatic event in a client's life; issues left over from the previous session; the client's potential reactions to information the worker must share; a traumatic community event such as the terrorist attacks on September 11, 2001).

2. *Sessional contracting.* A collection of skills designed to determine the issues or concerns facing clients at a particular session. These may include remaining tentative at the start of the session while listening for indirect cues, asking a client what is on her or his mind, raising previously agreed-on issues directly with the client and checking to see if they are still relevant, checking in with group members at the start of a session.

3. *Elaborating skills.* The skills required for helping clients to tell their story (e.g., listening, containment, questioning, reaching inside of silences).

4. *Empathic skills.* The skills that address the emotional content of the client's experiences (e.g., reaching for feelings, acknowledging feelings, articulating the client's feelings).

5. *Sharing worker's feelings.* The skill of spontaneously sharing appropriate worker affects, which is in response to the productions of the clients. Boundaries need to be respected so that the sharing of worker affect is professional and responsive to the needs of the clients. Issues of countertransference, client stereotyping, inappropriate worker frustration, and so on need to be considered and closely monitored.

6. *Making a demand for work.* A facilitative confrontation in which the worker asks a client to engage in the work agreed on in the contracting stage. Specific skills can include confronting denial, reaching inside of a silence, directly raising a taboo issue, challenging the illusion of work, and so on.

7. *Providing data.* The skill of providing relevant, unavailable information the client needs to deal with the task at hand. Data can include facts, values, beliefs, and so on. Data should be provided in a manner leaving it open to challenge.

8. *Sessional endings and transitions.* The skills involved in bringing a session to a close. These skills may include summarizing, evaluating progress, and discussion of transition issues (e.g., the client's next step, role-play of anticipated future conversations based on the work of the session).

It is not uncommon for a client to disclose a powerful issue at the very end of the session. This has been called in the literature "doorknob therapy," with the image of the client dropping a bombshell with his or her hand on the office doorknob as he or she is about to leave the last session. Even after a good working relationship has been established, a client may be embarrassed to raise issues or concerns in taboo areas.

For example, a female college student may only hint at a difficult time at a party the previous weekend. She may talk at the beginning of a session about being concerned that she drank too much. This could be described as a first offering. The worker responding to the apparent issue of concern over drinking starts to explore the question of substance use in the student's life. As the interview proceeds, the student drops hints of how rowdy the party became and her increasing feelings of concern. This could be considered the second offering. Once again, the worker may begin to respond to issues of safety in a situation where alcohol is being consumed. Almost at the end of the session, the doorknob bombshell emerges, and the student describes having passed out, perhaps being drugged, and waking up in a bedroom in a state of undress and with evidence that she had been raped.

In a serious situation such as this one, the social worker may have to extend the session or arrange a later appointment that same day to deal with the powerful issue which has just emerged. When the issue is addressed, it would be important for the worker to also explore why it was so difficult to raise the incident directly in the beginning of the session. As the client discusses her feelings—which may include shame, self-blame, and so on—which made it difficult to discuss the sexual assault she is actually beginning the discussion of the assault itself.

With this last example, we complete the discussion of the engagement phase of practice and the transition to the middle phase. For a more complete discussion of each phase of practice, see Shulman (2009). The dynamics and skills of the middle (work) phase of practice and the ending and transition phase are discussed in detail, as are the skills for developing a positive working relationship with other professionals and organizations.

WEB SITES

"Beyond the Therapeutic Alliance: Keeping the Drug-Dependent Individual in Treatment," National Institute of Drug Abuse. http://www.nida.nih.gov/pdf/ monographs/monograph165/download165 .html.

"Therapeutic Alliance: A Review of Sampling Strategies Reported in Marital and Family Therapy Studies," Sage Journals Online. http://tfj.sagepub.com/cgi/content/abstract/ 15/3/207.

"Therapeutic Alliance, Focus, and Formulation: Thinking Beyond the Traditional Therapy Orientations," Pyschotherapy.net. http:// www.psychotherapy.net/article/Therapeutic_ Alliance.

References

DiClemente, C. C., Prochaska, J. O., Fairhurst, S. K., & Velicer, W. F. (1991). The process of smoking cessation: An analysis of precontemplation, contemplation, and preparation stages of change. *Journal of Consulting and Clinical Psychology, 59,* 191–204.

Elze, D. (2006). Working with gay, lesbian, bisexual and transgender students. In C. Franklin, M. B. Harris, & P. Allen-Meares (Eds.), *The school services sourcebook: A guide for school-based professionals* (pp. 861–870). New York: Oxford University Press.

Hakansson, J., & Montgomery, H. (2003). Empathy as an interpersonal phenomenon. *Journal of Social and Personal Relationships, 20,* 267–284.

Schwartz, W. (1961). "The Social Worker in the Group." In *New Perspectives on Services to Groups: Theory, Organization, Practice.* New York: National Association of Social Workers.

Shulman, L. (1978). A study of practice skill. *Social Work, 23,* 274–281.

Shulman, L. (2009). *The skills of helping individuals, families, groups, and communities,* 6th ed. Belmont, CA: Wadsworth Brooks/Cole.

Taft, J. (1942). The relational function to process in social case work. In V. P. Robinson (Ed.), *Training for skill in social casework.* Philadelphia: University of Pennsylvania Press.

Taft, J. (1949). Time as the medium of the helping process. *Jewish Social Service Quarterly, 26,* 230–243.

Truax, C. B. (1966). Therapist empathy, warmth, genuineness and patient personality change in group psychotherapy: A comparison between interaction unit measures, time sample measures, and patient perception measures. *Journal of Clinical Psychology, 71,* 1–9.

Stephen R. Lankton

The use of therapeutic stories or metaphors was originally introduced by the early work of Milton Erickson (Erickson & Rossi, 1979). Erickson was generally considered a master at communicating in ways that reduced resistance and motivated his clients to think and act when other therapists had failed. The use of therapeutic metaphor has become recognized as a powerful and potentially effective method of therapeutic intervention (Battino, 2002; Burns, 2001, 2007; Gordon, 1978; Lankton, 1979/2003; Lankton & Lankton, 1986, 1989). This chapter illustrates the use of simple and complex metaphors in treatment and outlines why they work. It highlights the important parameters and bullet points for successfully creating and using therapeutic stories in therapy and in hypnosis. Finally, it includes contraindications for the use of metaphor in therapy.

There has been a growing and continued interest in the use of therapeutic metaphors among social workers whether they are engaged in brief or long-term therapy or the delivery of outpatient or inpatient treatment. Therapeutic metaphor belongs to that group of therapeutic interventions referred to as *indirection*. The definition of metaphor as used in therapy refers to a complex story that holds the user's attention and provides an alternate framework through which clients can entertain novel experience. In using metaphor, the therapist can accomplish the following.

- make or illustrate an important therapeutic point to the client;
- suggest solutions (even threatening ones) not previously considered by the client;
- seed ideas to which the therapist can later return and elaborate;
- decrease the conscious resistance of the client to experiential and cognitive changes;
- reframe or redefine a problem for the client so that the problem is placed in a different context of importance with a different meaning (Zeig, 1980); and

- retrieve and associate experiences including emotions, thoughts, perceptions, and behaviors.

CASE EXAMPLES OF SIMPLE METAPHOR

Client is a 28-year-old woman who recently broke up with her boyfriend of 3 years. The two of them had purchased a home together, and since he moved out, she is afraid to leave the house for fear that he will not pay the bills and she will be stuck with bad credit as a result. The young man is trying to obtain a loan so he can take over the entire mortgage in his name alone. Each time a loan application is applied for or almost approved and then fails to result in him signing a new note, she has mood swings.

Clearly, the client is excited about the possibility of completely ending all relations with him. But she finds herself oscillating between excitement and depression when her hopes of being free of this financial connection fails. This mood shift was interfering with her ability to perform at work, which is why she sought therapy. Of course, she is fully aware of this simple dynamic. However, her insight alone is not helping her reduce her mood swings.

The metaphoric intervention was designed to help her retrieve experiences of various states of self-control that one learns to endure throughout childhood. The following is an excerpt from the metaphor told to this patient.

I want you to close your eyes and just be more comfortable for a minute. It is not necessary that you go into the hypnotic trance, but rather, I'd like you just to be relaxed so you can think about and remember a few things that might occur to you while I speak. You know every child who's ever anticipated a birthday has something in common. When Sally was 4 years old she distinctly remembers that the ornaments on her Christmas tree were large and shiny. She was fascinated as much by the tinsel and the decorations on the tree as she was by the ribbons, paper, and boxes below it. For 6 days preceding Christmas morning, she was unable to sleep as normal. She would wander downstairs after everyone else had gone to bed, and she would shake the boxes and wonder what kind of presents they contained.

One night the mother happened to hear her shuffling the boxes and awoke. Knowing how hard it might be for young girl to contain her excitement when something wonderful was about to happen, the mother made Sally some warm milk and gave her two cookies. As she ate, her mother explained to Sally, as parents often do, that Santa Claus would not be able to come if he found her to be awake at night. She told her, "You need to learn to calm down . . . and to sleep."

Hearing the news about Santa Claus was, of course, not enough to make Sally fall asleep easily that night. She tried different ways of thinking to help propel her into sleep. She tried thinking about the smell of her sheets, taking a nap with her dog, and the comforting, warm feeling she got when her mother gave her milk. Dwelling on any one of those memories would be enough to make anybody become sleepy and calm.

Surprisingly this began working for Sally. She didn't do it very well at 4 years old—she did much better at 5 and 6. But by the time she was 7 years old she had learned to contain her excitement quite well. Even though she was very eager for Christmas to come, she was able to put it out of her mind sufficiently to appear to be a grown-up little girl.

By the time she was 9, she become quite proficient at being happy and having pleasant anticipation but not being so excited that it disrupted her. Somewhere along the way, the mind learns a method of disconnecting itself from disruptive impulses. Children usually take pride in their ability to control their impulsive experiences. You go to bed knowing that you are excited about opening presents in the morning but you put that excitement into quiet pleasant thoughts. Little girls don't usually know that they *are* learning or how to say that they're putting their excitement into pleasant quiet thoughts. But the unconscious can do that anyway. If somebody says to Sally, "Remember that experience, remember that now," that feeling comes. The unconscious knows how to bring that feeling forward. As that quiet feeling of excitement fills the mind, there come even more experiences that are similar and that are brought forward developing a pleasant anticipation that's not disturbing and not distressing.

This short and simple intervention illustrates some of the value of using therapeutic stories in several ways:

- metaphors retrieved experiential resources that are difficult to label and name;

- metaphors provided an altered framework so the client used her own experiences to understand the story ;
- metaphors allow the client to retrieve an experience she did not believe she could retrieve;
- metaphors eliminate the potential resistance that would arise from the client feeling that she could not be calm; and
- it helps the client understand a developmental sequence that suggested a change in her impatience.

Immediately following the telling of that brief story, the client was asked to recall that and other feelings similar in her own life—a direct request for the client to remember those feelings. The client's ability to carry out that direct request had been greatly enhanced by the telling of the story. She was able to remember times in her own life when she contained her mood and excitement. Those experiences were then used in a therapy to help or obtain the goal of keeping her mood stable in the context of waiting for her ex-boyfriend to get the loan.

Let's look at a more complicated goal-directed metaphor used to retrieve the emotion of anger. The client is a 34-year-old male. He was doing his clinical residency in the state of Texas, but he dropped out and moved to Arizona. His depression is complicated by or even creates a further problem of reduced motivation. Being so poorly motivated, he doesn't return to school, he doesn't complete his residency, he doesn't apply for jobs, and he becomes very self-effacing. Broadcasting this attitude in many ways to others, he finds himself taken advantage of by others. He recently lost $4,000 to a stranger whom he thought he was helping as a friend. Instead of being outwardly angry, he is angry at himself. In this situation, the use of direct communication about his feelings would be pointless. He would deny any anger and, were he to feel any anger, he would state that it is inappropriate for him to show it—he was not entitled to do so. In the second session, he was asked to go into trance after he related the incident of being swindled. The following metaphor is a portion of that trance session.

Pete worked as a dishwasher and was a classical guitar player. He had studied with Breem and Segovia and was a genuinely sensitive and accomplished musician. For a while he drove a 1992 Mazda that had a bumper sticker reading "Handel with care, classical guitar player inside."

When he came home from work one day, he found the door unlocked. He was temporarily surprised and angry at himself for not locking it. Fumbling for his keys, he fell into the door and hardly gave a second thought as to why he hadn't locked it. But looking around saw the room was a mess. He was struggling to have understanding of his thoughts.

When he saw the room in disarray, he thought how messy he was not to clean the room better. It says something about you when you keep your room in a mess. But then he saw shirts out on the couch, and the situation changed. It occurred to Pete that he hadn't put his shirts on the couch, he wouldn't have pulled them all out—he must have been robbed.

Now for anyone who knew Pete, they would agree that there was one thing that came through loud and clear about him and that was his dependency on that guitar. He loved it. He would fall asleep with it. He had slept with it once or twice and was teased by his friends. He would spend hours a day dealing with it rather than another person. In fact, he got so good he could substitute his guitar instead of going out on a date. Maybe it was like Linus and his blanket—you know how fretful Linus gets if someone has taken his blanket. It doesn't begin to compare with the feelings Pete was about to have when he realized he was being robbed. At first he thought he *had been* robbed and then he realized he *was being* robbed. He heard noise in the back room, and the apartment should have been empty.

You know how your mind can change when you're in an auto accident, for example. You can remember every incident of that 10-second auto crash as though it had happened over a period of 20 minutes. You remember every change of posture, every movement of a pedestrian, every inch that the cars began to approach each other, everything you did to fasten a seatbelt or close a glove compartment or move something off your lap. It must have been that sense of heightened remembering Pete was having, because he could explain every minute detail that went on that day from that moment.

It must have happened in a few seconds, but it seemed like half an hour. The next thing he realized was a feelings in his legs and he felt his feet carry him across the threshold, hand on doorknob, shoulders relaxed on ribcage, which seemed odd to him. He could feel the blood flow through his arms and the adrenaline. But he felt somehow removed from it in a way that was surprising. He felt the momentum of his body open the door in a very aggressive fashion. But he didn't have any thoughts about it except that he hadn't felt that way so easily and he didn't think it would have been so easy, and yet it seemed to be easier than he would have thought.

In great detail, he explained how he was running into the bedroom where his guitar was and what he was yelling. He heard words pouring out of his mouth that he didn't usually say. Then he saw the man jump out the window with his guitar in hand. Then Pete dived out the window. His realizing he was doing something one doesn't normally do. Your conscious mind can be an observer of an event that your body is doing. Everyone has had the experience of yelling automatically when someone steps on your toe. You don't really realize what you are saying until you hear what you said.

Before that moment had passed, he had both his tennis shoes on the grass outside his bedroom window and was racing across the parking lot. He felt weightless as his feet carried him across the grass. He was surprised to realize you can have a feeling that seems alien to you but have it comfortably when you might have thought you couldn't. He thought feelings had to be heavy, especially this one.

Moving more rapidly than the man who was running, he caught up to the man, who dropped the guitar, and it hit the ground with a *bong*. The strings began resonating. They did so for a good 20 seconds, and before they stopped, he remembered deciding he was going to keep track of how long they resonated because it was something that he always did automatically. Finally, he grabbed the thief by the shoulders and pushed him up against the back of that 1992 Mazda, and bent him over somewhat backward against the back of the trunk.

I don't know where you first feel your sense of muscular power when you do something like that. Maybe you feel your feet firmly on the ground. Maybe you feel a little taller than usual. Maybe you recognize that your breathing is easy and more rapid than usual and your skin is warm. Pete stood there, pulled his fist back, and held it chin level to himself and heard himself saying, "I'm going to clobber you, you son of a bitch." These were words he had never heard come out of his mouth before.

He was about to hit the man, but then turned him around and, pinning his arms behind his back, wrestled him to the ground and held him there. There was a commotion. There was still a ringing in the background. Those guitar strings were still resonating from the topple and bong they had received.

Other people now responded to the brawl. It caught the attention of a passing patrol car, and soon the police descended on the thief. As Pete walked away from the episode, he realized the guitar strings had still been faintly resonating while he held the man on the ground. He knew he could depend on the base notes resonating for about 17 seconds. The entire incident had taken just over 20 seconds from when he went out the back window to having wrestled the man to the ground.

Heart pounding, shoulders and sternum held high, jaw set firmly, feeling the blood pulsing through his neck, Pete would have expected that feeling that way would have been far more uncomfortable. He never thought of himself in any other way than "classical guitar player, handle with care." It's a learning. Your unconscious knows a good deal of experience and can put it together no matter what your conscious mind thinks. Pete memorized that experience of anger, the impulse, the understanding that the unconscious intent is to have that impulse and use it for your needs—and memorize the recognition of not going beyond the bounds of reason, even when you had the chance and it would have been justifiable.

Following the experiences he retrieved listening to this story, it was relatively easy to assist him in thinking through how he could be angry at others and nurture himself. Naturally, the therapy for each of these individuals involved many more aspects of change. This excerpt is meant only to illustrate how therapeutic metaphors is used in non-hypnotic therapy and in hypnosis. As in the previous story, the metaphor allowed the therapist to elicit difficult emotional material without resistance by providing an alternate framework into which the client could project experiences he commonly avoided in his own life.

THE AMBIGUOUS ASPECT OF METAPHOR

Unlike directive and manipulative interventions that, through direct command or connotation, tell clients how to perceive, think, feel, or behave, techniques of indirection allow clients to project their own meaning into what they hear. This in turn allows the therapeutic material to be fit to their personal situation. Because clients must fit their life into the story being told, there is a high degree of relevance and potentially deep meaning. If clients are instructed by therapists to conduct themselves in a certain manner, or say certain sentences in, for instance, directive couples therapy, the response from clients is compliance. This means that the learning has come from outside. However, when clients have determined for themselves a relevant meaning to an otherwise ambiguous story from a therapist, they act on perceptions, behaviors, and feelings that truly belong to them and are a part of them.

Let's examine this ambiguous element more closely. The degree of ambiguity in a therapeutic story can be regulated by the teller so that the story is more or less vague to the listener. Regardless of the degree of vagueness, listeners create their own relevant meaning to understand the story. This accounts for the personalized nature

of the understanding and the lack of mere compliance by listeners. However, as the degree of vagueness increases, there is an exponential increase in the number of possible meanings that listeners can give to the story. It is assumed that listeners sorting through several possibilities at what has been determined to be 30 items per second (Erickson & Rossi, 1979, p. 18) become increasingly absorbed in weighing the best fit for these possible meanings.

This ongoing process of weighing meaning has a number of therapeutic benefits.

- There is an increase in participation by listeners.
- There is a heightened valuation in any meaning by listeners because the meaning has come from with their own experience.
- There is a depotentiation of normal limitations or rigid ego controls as the listener seek a "best fit."
- There is an increase in the duration of time given to examining possible meanings.

This last element, in fact, accounts for a therapeutic effect on clients long after the therapy sessions have ended. Indeed, for a highly meaningful and yet extremely vague metaphoric story, clients reported that they continued to turn it over in their mind for years and do so for events that even years later parallel the original therapeutic learning incident. For this reason, the use of metaphor can be summarized as follows.

- It increases the relevance of therapy for clients and involves clients more highly in their own change process.
- It expands the usual limiting experience that has led to a stabilization of the presenting problem or dynamic and brought the person to therapy.
- It offers an engaging element of ambiguity that may continue to alert listeners to their therapeutic learnings for years after a therapy session.
- It offers a wide range of potentially correct responses within the therapeutic limits.

USES OF METAPHORIC STORIES

As listeners become increasingly engaged or absorbed in a story, there is a reduction in defensive mechanisms that customarily constrain the listener to sets of common experience. That is, listening to a story that symbolizes tenderness can lead a person who normally does not shed tears or weep to do so. The definition mentions that clients can entertain novel experiences. The concept of a novel experience may need slight elaboration. It pertains to experiences that are commonly excluded from the experiential set of the listener. While listening to an absorbing story, clients may, with relative ease, temporarily experience one or several specific experiences that, if therapeutically managed, can assist the listener in creating personal change. The assistance in creating personal change comes about as clients re-examine perceptions or cognitions, emotions, or potential behaviors in light of a recognition that these new experiences, perceptions, or cognitions once thought to be alien actually can be a part of their own personality and experience. In general, it could be said that the usefulness of metaphor in therapy comes into play at any point in therapy where it is advisable or useful for clients to recognize that experiential resources lie within themselves rather than having to introject them from an outside authority.

Metaphor is especially useful when brief forms of therapy, such as solution-focused therapy, hypnotherapy, family or couples therapy, or grief therapy, are the therapeutic modality of choice. Nevertheless, an additional aspect of the ambiguous nature of metaphor suggests that the use of therapeutic metaphor can have great value in long-term therapies, as well.

REDUCTION OF RESISTANCE

Because metaphor offers listeners the ability to apply a wide range or spectrum of potential understandings to what the therapist has said, there is a corresponding reduction in listener resistance. Any therapeutic modality that finds clients to be resistive, possibly due to the nature of the modality itself, will be able to take advantage of metaphoric stories, providing those stories are constructed and shared in a manner that employs the necessary components of therapeutic metaphor.

THE NECESSARY COMPONENTS OF THERAPEUTIC METAPHOR

To be effective, therapeutic metaphor must be perceived and be relevant. It also must engage

listeners and retrieve experience. There are a number of ways these requirements can be fostered in the therapeutic process. There should be a consideration of the relationship of the story to the sensory system primarily used by the listener to process data, material that is taken out of sequence to create dramatic engagement or enchantment, and the retrieval and use of experience that is therapeutically relevant.

The Perception and Relevance of the Metaphor

The most important feature regarding relevance of a metaphor or any experience is that it resonates with either clients' current state or clients' anticipated future state. The metaphor should be constructed to hold the attention of clients' conscious minds. This applies to the vast majority of metaphors that therapists will construct and use. Therapists should consider that clients' understandings or representations of problems are likely to be characterized by them in a preferred sensory system. That is, some clients will relate their problem with the majority of their sensory-specific verbs in a preferred representational system: visual, auditory, or kinesthetic (Lankton, 2003). This can be ascertained by listening to clients' presentations of their problems. When such a preference is discovered, it is imperative that therapists attempt to communicate with clients in their preferred manner of thinking and representing. When receiving metaphor, the conscious minds of clients will be engaged and consider stories more relevant when this connection is honored. Erickson referred to this as speaking the clients experiential language. However, certain portions of a metaphoric story may be strategically represented in a lesser used system for certain purposes. For instance, certain experiences may be more easily retrieved by therapeutic efforts aimed at the lesser used representational systems.

Consider a client who thinks with a predominantly visual set of mental tools. Relating a story that encourages him to see a father and son hugging will have a moving effect of joy or sadness on his conscious mind if he did not receive that type of attention. Hearing the words spoken (his secondarily used sensory system is auditory) by the father in the story saying "Come here and let me hug you, son. I love you and I'm proud of you" may evoke more quickly an emotion of tenderness, joy, or sadness. The difference is due to the fact that the client's understanding of his life is primarily a visual story in his mind that he can easily navigate. Seeing the images created in the telling of the story, it would be easy for him to quickly compare the ideas to his life and think about it. However, thinking with auditory imagery is not as easy for him, and the experience attached to the imagery used by the therapist is, in fact, the experience he retrieves with less resistance. Purposeful regulation of this aspect of a story is a matter of training and experience on the part of therapist.

Metaphors that Are Parallel to the Problem

There are two major categories of metaphor: those that are parallel to the client's problem and those that are parallel to the anticipated goal. Stories that are parallel to the client's current state or problem are far easier to construct and were the first type of metaphors noticed in the process of attempting to simulate the therapeutic work of experts such as Erickson (Gordon, 1978; Lankton, 1979/2003).

The basic idea of the metaphoric stories that are parallel to the problem can be summarized in the understanding of the term *isomorphism*. Metaphors that are isomorphic have the body of their content in a one-to-one correspondence with the experience (that is, the problem state) of the client. A simple way of understanding this is that for every major person, relationship, and activity in the client's problem, there is a corresponding person, relationship, and action in the story told to the client. Again, the degree of distance or vagueness between the elements in the metaphor and the elements in the client's life will reg-

ulate the degree of ambiguity that's introduced and therefore determine how likely it is that the client will make the connection between this story and his or her life.

For example, consider the following variation of isomorphic metaphor that matches the problem. A husband seeks affection from a wife, who ignores him unless blaming him for a fault. The pattern then unfolds as the husband withdraws into depression and the wife becomes angry with him. Table 82.1 lists the situation's components as related by the client, and the columns show the elements of two different stories that could be told. They illustrate two varying degrees of ambiguity.

It should be obvious that despite the similar isomorphic relationship between parts of the story and the problem, the more ambiguous references may not be an apparent match in the mind of the listener. The solution to the dilemma is not shown in the table, only the components that match the problem. However, the sketching of part (or all) of the solution would be the next step for the therapist.

There are two important considerations for the use of isomorphic metaphors. First, it must outline the context or heighten the client's awareness for the problem situation in which the solution will be fitted. Second, isomorphic metaphors need to have resolution that provides some metaphoric solution. In this second aspect of isomorphic metaphors is where beginning therapists may encounter difficulty. There are a few major ways for isomorphic metaphors to be terminated so that they provide a therapeutic conclusion for the problem they have highlighted. The most elegant manner involves the continued and often creative behavior

TABLE 82.1 Isomorphic Construction

Situation	Less Ambiguous	More Ambiguous
husband	lovebird	electric drill
(husband) asks	chirps	(drill) freezes up
needs affection	needs touching	needs oil
wife	girl	mechanic
(wife) ignores	(girl) locks up bird	throws down
(wife) blames faults	(girl) shouts at bird	worries it will burn
(wife) defensive	(girl) recalls messes	brags of skill
(husband) withdraws	(bird) chews cage	(drill) overheats
(husband) depression	(bird) gets ill	(drill) emits smoke
(wife) angry	(girl) sells bird	throws it out

of the protagonist, through whose behavior a solution would be illustrated. A second, less practical method is for the therapist to introduce direct instructions that represent words spoken to the protagonist. This latter example is often called embedded commands or embedded quotes. In this case, the only experience created for the client is that of a verbal idea.

This second option fails to meet the criteria of retrieving experience for a client and often fails to meet the ambiguity element that prevents resistance in the client. However, it is a very practical method for therapists to deliver clear guidelines, instructions, or directives to a client in a fashion that reduces confrontation and thereby allows a client to save face.

The third and least elegant method to create a goal in an isomorphic metaphor is to introduce a break in the normal flow of the protagonist's behavior owing to some unexpected element, such as the protagonist going to therapy, having a dream, or having some sudden sort of epiphany. Although this device within a story will allow the speaker to jump to a solution set, it does so at the expense of the logical flow of the metaphoric content. Even so, it provides an opportunity for experiences to be retrieved that will help alter perception, behavior, emotion, or attitude.

Goal-Directed Metaphors

The second major category of metaphor comprises those that are constructed to become parallel to the goal rather than parallel to the problem (Lankton, 2004; Lankton & Lankton, 1986, 1989;). It is essential to follow a basic protocol to address specific goals of changes in attitude, emotion, and behavior. The content of the metaphors must be ordered so that the metaphor retrieves specific goals for the listener. These protocols can be streamlined or maximized to facilitate if not ensure that the listener's experience will be one of cognitive alteration, emotional alteration, or behavioral sensitizing. To illustrate this, the three self-explanatory protocols for emotion, attitude, and behavior metaphors are listed (Lankton, 2004; Lankton & Lankton, 1986, 1989) here.

A. Affect and emotion protocol
  1. Establish a relationship between the protagonist and a person, place, or thing that involves emotion or affect (e.g., tenderness, anxiety, mastery, confusion, love, longing, etc.).

  2. Detail *movement* in the relationship (e.g., moving with, moving toward, moving away, chasing, consistently pursuing, orbiting, etc.).
  3. Focus on some of the physiological changes that coincide with the protagonist's emotion (be sure to overlap with the client's facial behavior).
B. Attitude change protocol
  1. Describe a protagonist's behavior or perception so it exemplifies the maladaptive attitude. Bias this belief to appear positive or desirable.
  2. Describe another protagonist's behavior or perception so it exemplifies the *adaptive* attitude (the goal). Bias this belief to appear negative or undesirable.
  3. Reveal the *unexpected* outcome achieved by both protagonists that resulted from the beliefs they held and their related actions. Be sure the payoff received by the second protagonist is of value to the client.
C. Behavior change protocol
  1. Illustrate the protagonist's observable behavior similar to the desired behavior to be acquired by the client. There is no need to mention motives. List about six specific observable behaviors.
  2. Detail the protagonist's internal attention or nonobservable behavior that shows the protagonist to be congruent with his or her observable behavior.
  3. Change the setting within the story so as to provide an opportunity for repeating all the behavioral descriptions several (three) times.

Dramatic Aspects of Metaphor

A client's conscious attention can be held by the addition of dramatic devices in the storyline of the metaphor. By holding the client's conscious attention the therapist ensures that the metaphor can become a vehicle for carrying the interventions that retrieve desired experiences. My definition for the construction of dramatic devices in any oral or rhetoric tradition can be seen as a matter of presenting knowledge or information out of sequence. Information that is in a linear, temporal sequence is simply a documentary. However, when various delivery devices, such as tonal inflection, are used to stress certain words as if their meaning is deeper than what is denoted, there is an indication that more than just documentary information is being offered. Furthermore, the hints that are provided by tonal stress in a simple, linear presentation of facts cause the listener to seek that connoted meaning by anticipating what is to come in the story or reevaluating what has been heard so far. However, the actual tactics of creating dramatic hold within a story are more dynamic than simply stressing connoted information.

Looking at Table 82.2, it can be seen that in the course of a storyline, there will be information known to the protagonist (or characters in the story) and information known to the listener (that is, the client). If information known to the protagonist is not known to the listener, mystery arises. For example, in a story, there may be a letter read, a phone call, or a conversation in a secluded location between protagonists. The information shared in that exchange can be illustrated as having great importance. However, that information can be withheld from listeners as a secret or private event. Although it has great meaning to the characters of the story, listeners will not know how the protagonists' behavior has been affected by the information that was concealed from them. As a result, listeners are in a position to try to deduce by anticipation, think back to the character development, or somehow gain a degree of certainty about how the information may affect the outcome of the story.

The element of mystery seems to create a primarily cognitive hold on the listener. It can happen numerous times in a story, and it can also be created by means other than dialogues between the characters in the story. An analysis will reveal that the characters have been shown to be privy to some information not known to the listener. In the case of a therapeutic story, the listener is the client.

Table 82.2 further illustrates that information known to the client or listener but not known to the protagonists or characters in the story creates the situation of suspense. The hold of suspense

is a much more visceral or emotional hold of attention by comparison to mystery. This is often easily created by the storyteller through foreshadowing. In many well-known works of literature, the author gives a glimpse ahead as to how the story is to be framed. This occurs, for instance, when the story begins with comments about how the story will be ended. It is the same in cinema. The motion picture *Gandhi* begins with the assassination of the protagonist. Here we see the archetypal footprint of suspense by means of taking information out of sequence and foreshadowing the later ending of the man's life. However, in cinema, there are more dramatic devices that can be used, such as sirens and flashing lights or the well-known rhythmic percussion in the movie *Jaws*. In a literary or spoken story, material taken out of sequence that reveals flaws or outcomes about the protagonists to the listener will increase the experience of suspense.

Finally, the drama construction table shows that when neither the listener/client nor the protagonist/character have information about an upcoming event, the result will be surprise, shock, or humor when the event occurs. So a sudden death in a story that was not foreshadowed for the listener or expected by the characters will be a surprise. When surprise or shock occurs in a story, listeners search facts they have already heard in the story to put the incident in perspective or examine whether certain information had already existed to predict the surprise. They will also begin to test various anticipated hypotheses to try to predict how the story will turn out.

With any of these dramatic methods the effect is to capture attention and engage listeners in the story by means of encouraging them to make sense of it. The visceral or cognitive energy used to sort through past and anticipated futures in a story is the result of the use of drama. The drama does not need to be award-winning and especially creative. It simply needs to be present in the story to help listeners become more consciously absorbed as they make room to entertain the novel experience created.

Enchantment

As mentioned, one of the devices for understanding the effect of metaphor is the aspect of ambiguity. In addition to drama, ambiguity is one of the major mechanisms that binds the listener to the story. There are few words available for explaining this interpersonal aspect of the phenomenon of

TABLE 82.2 Creating Drama

Type of Drama	Client	Protagonist(s)
Suspense	Knows info	Does not know
Mystery	Does not know	Knows info
Surprise/ shock/humor	Does not know	Does not know

ambiguity. Perhaps one of the best terms to refer to it is *enchantment.* Enchantment can be defined as holding spellbound by or as if by irresistible force, words, or charms and to pique a pleasant mental excitement. This last aspect of creating a pleasant mental excitement is of greatest interest to the therapist constructing a therapeutic metaphor.

Creating dramatic hold in a relevant story with a certain degree of various meanings available maximizes both interest and usefulness of the story for the client. It was mentioned earlier that the degree of ambiguity can be regulated by means of increasing or decreasing vagueness about the connection between events in the client's life or experiences that will be goals for the client and the elements in the story. That is, the elements in the story can be increasingly mundane or increasingly symbolic and abstract in their denoted content. A degree of skill and practice is necessary to develop the ability to maximize the therapeutic impact and regulate this ambiguity with clients. It requires that therapists continue to have a high degree of observation regarding the impact the story is having on the listener. Beyond the regulation of controlled ambiguity within the metaphor, there are other devices that create or regulate the experience of enchantment. These include tonal delivery and word selection, which create a degree of pathos and highly charged meaning for the listener.

INDICATIONS AND CONTRAINDICATIONS

Contraindications for using metaphor fall in two categories. One has to do with the experience level of the therapist, and the other concerns the type and severity of the problem of the client. A therapist who has little skill in the use of indirection techniques and limited clinical skill must consider using metaphoric stories with a greatly limited range of clients, problem severity, and diagnostic categories. The beginning therapist can only comfortably use metaphoric stories for individuals who would be considered vocal and intellectual; mildly neurotic, anxious, depressed; and with problems that are not urgent. With such clients, there is more ability to assess impact and ethically evaluate the efficacy of the technique.

Therapists with a greater degree of clinical experience and experience with the use of indirection and ambiguous interventions will find that it is possible to successfully and ethically employ metaphoric stories with a far greater range of individuals, problem categories, and diagnostic types.

Contraindication for diagnostic types includes individuals who are actively psychotic and those who are moderately to severely borderline. This also includes any neurotic individuals who have extreme difficulties with boundary-related issues. The reason for this concern lies in the fact that such individuals can and will apply multiple meanings to the ambiguity of the metaphor. When the client has demonstrated difficulty retaining cognitive meaning in real-life situations, the use of any technique that exacerbates a concrete intervention is contraindicated. Similarly, the boundary problem finds its difficulty in those individuals who come to believe that the therapist can read their thoughts by the fact that they have projected meaning into a metaphoric story and failed to realize that it is *their* projected meaning, instead thinking that it is a previously known meaning that the therapist has somehow been able to divine from an extraordinary means or from an extraordinary rapport with them.

These extremes do not occur for individuals who do not have boundary or cognitive problems. However, a third category of contraindication includes those who have a great deal of difficulty establishing rapport and trust. For these persons, regardless of their diagnostic category or presenting problem, the credibility of the therapist is continually questioned and evaluated. Using metaphoric stories relies on clients investigating what was said for possible relevant meanings and surrendering a degree of habitual reality testing. As clients become caught up in the relevance, drama, and enchantment of the story, individuals who maintain an analytical distance, while doubting the therapist, are liable to take the ambiguity as a sign that the therapist is not competent to some degree. Again, the clinical experience of the therapist may reduce the number of individuals for whom this type of contraindication is relevant. Therapists with considerable clinical experience are usually skilled at carefully judging the manner in which they need to approach clients to engage them in the change process. The execution of this type of therapeutic judgment can be referred to as the controlled elaboration of ambiguity.

USING METAPHORS WITHIN THE THERAPY PROCESS

Using metaphoric stories need not be constrained to individuals in hypnotic trance. Metaphoric stories can be used at any point in the therapeutic process providing the goal is to retrieve perceptual, attitudinal, emotional, or behavioral changes. Some of the common uses of metaphors even in the early stages of the therapy process are:

- to illustrate a way of using therapy to change problems and arrive at a therapeutic contract;
- to help clients relax;
- to focus clients' thoughts to the situations that have led them to the office; and
- to normalize their situation and helping them articulating their problems.

All of these goals and more at the early stages of therapeutic contact can be not only accomplished with metaphoric stories but possibly accomplished more efficiently. The reason for this is that the degree of choice the listener has in making sense of a metaphoric story reduces the resistance that can come from otherwise attempting to be specific with direct communications of statements and questions about how a client is to think, feel, or behave.

During the change process itself, metaphoric stories can enhance any aspect of therapy where increased mental involvement is indicated and where specific experiences brought into the foreground can enhance therapeutic movement. These times are more numerous than can be mentioned; the more experience the therapist has, the more such moments will be apparent.

CONCLUSION

Using therapeutic metaphor throughout the therapy process can enhance therapeutic movement by retrieving the desired experiences clients need for therapeutic movement. Metaphoric stories need to be constructed in a manner that is relevant to the client, holds their attention, and facilitates the retrieval of experience that is helpful to the therapy process. The degree of ambiguity should be carefully regulated by observing the client's responses to the spoken words.

Therapists must continually observe clients during the delivery of each metaphor. The aim of observation is for the therapist to recognize the degree of relevance the story has for the listener gauging the degree of internal absorption and search and facial expressions, head nods, changes in breathing, and other ideomotor behavior that the client displays. It is also for the therapist to gauge the degree of achievement that clients

accomplish in retrieving desired experiences from the same indicators. Finally, the aim of observation is to gather ongoing diagnostic information as it pertains to the manner in which the client responds to various words and actions denoted and connoted within the story.

Because the activity of delivering and receiving the metaphor is an individual matter, research on the level of resource retrieval and specific resources that a particular metaphoric story may bring is problematic. Clients will respond in a unique way, depending on their needs, background, motivation, and the therapist's skill in observing and delivering metaphor. Outcomes that are achieved by the use of metaphoric stories are truly cocreated. That is, they are a blend of factors of the client's history and motivation coupled with the therapist's ability to provide compelling delivery and meaningful content, as well as therapeutically useful protocol.

Finally, it should be remembered that the listener's achievement of meaning fluctuates with the degree of ambiguity and apparent relevance of the story. Therefore, stories should have some immediate impact on the listener that is useful within the therapeutic sessions. However, some degree of impact can be expected from certain stories days or even years later due to the client's capability to seek useful meanings and project them into the ambiguity provided by a relevant story.

WEB SITES

American Society of Clinical Hypnosis. http://www.asch.net.
Lankton and Associates. http://www.lankton.com.
Milton H. Erickson Foundation. http://www.erickson-foundation.org.

References

Battino, R. (2002). *Metaphoria: Metaphor and guided metaphor for psychotherapy and healing*. New York: Crown.
Burns, G. (2001). *101 Healing stories: Using metaphors in therapy*. New York: Wiley.
Burns, G. (2007). *Healing with stories: Your casebook collection for using therapeutic metaphors*. New York: Wiley.
Erickson, M., & Rossi, E. (1979). *Hypnotherapy: An exploratory casebook*. New York: Irvington.
Gordon, D. (1978). *Therapeutic metaphors: Helping others through the looking glass*. Cupertino, CA: Meta Publication.

Lankton, C., & Lankton, S. (1989). *Tales of enchantment: An anthology of goal directed metaphors
for adults and children in therapy.* New York:
Brunner/Mazel.

Lankton, S. (1979/2003). *Practical magic: A translation of basic neuro-linguistic programming into
clinical psychotherapy.* New York: Crown.

Lankton, S. (2004). *Assembling Ericksonian therapy:*

The collected papers of Stephen Lankton. Phoenix, AZ: Zeig, Tucker, Theisen.

Lankton, S., & Lankton, C. (1986). *Enchantment and
intervention in family therapy: Training in Ericksonian approaches.* New York: Brunner/Mazel.

Zeig, J. (Ed. with commentary). (1980). *A teaching seminar with Milton H. Erickson.* New York: Brunner/
Mazel.

83   Cognitive Restructuring Techniques

Donald K. Granvold

Cognitive restructuring is a term that may be used in a generic sense to represent cognitive change irrespective of the psychotherapeutic modality being employed. Hence, insight gained through psychoanalytic psychotherapy may be considered cognitive restructuring inasmuch as a cognitive change has occurred. In this chapter, cognitive restructuring will be considered from a *cognitive-behavioral therapy* (CBT) and *construc-tivist* perspective.

From a CBT and constructivist orientation, human functioning is conceptualized as the product of the reciprocal interaction of cognition, behavior, emotion, personal factors (emotion, motivation, physiology, and physical phenomena) and social environmental influences. The idea that cognition causes emotion is a common misunderstanding of CBT. To clarify, cognition is regarded as highly influential and first in order of importance, rather than directly causal. Beck and colleagues elucidate this point in addressing cognition in the treatment of depression.

The primacy hypothesis reflects the importance we place on cognition by stating that negative cognition and the biased information processing of negative self-referent information can directly influence other behavioral, motivational, affective, and somatic symptoms of depression. Our position on the primacy of cognition, though not to be misconstrued as a statement of causal priority, may be a unique feature of the cognitive model (Clark, Beck, & Alford, 1999, p. 157).

CBT therapists consistently target cognitive functioning for change although not to the exclusion of other components of human functioning.

SOCRATIC DIALOGUE

Cognitive restructuring is the term used for a variety of procedures focused on the modification of cognitions and cognitive processing. Many approaches to cognitive restructuring use the Socratic method to guide the client in the identification, exploration, modification, and elaboration of cognitions. Other approaches use imagery, guided discovery, and in vivo behavioral procedures to "test out" and modify beliefs.

The goal of cognitive restructuring is to guide the client in the exposure of cognitions influencing untoward, unappealing, discomforting, or dysfunctional outcomes and modify them through further exploration, disputation, or elaboration. Clients are guided in the use of logic or evidence to examine and modify their exaggerated, distorted, or ill-founded beliefs. The first task is to elicit the thoughts, cognitive processing errors, or images contributing to the client's unhappiness or distress. Wells (1997) recommends a Socratic sequence combining general questions with more specific probe questions. Probe questions are useful in gaining clarification and greater detail. The use of reflection and expressions of empathy and affirmation may promote relationship development and client awareness that the therapist clearly understands. The following dialogue illustrates early intervention with a client experiencing high anxiety.

T: What did you feel in the situation? [general question]

C: I felt scared and couldn't stop shaking.

T: When you felt *scared* and *shaky* [reflection] what thoughts went through your mind?

C: I don't know. I just felt awful.

T: Did you think anything bad could happen when you felt like that? [probe]

C: Yes. I thought I looked stupid.

T: What do you mean by stupid? [probe]

C: I thought everyone would notice and think I was an alcoholic or something (Wells, 1997, p. 53).

Cognitive restructuring is incomplete if the process is stopped at mere identification of operative cognitions. After gaining an understanding of the client's thinking and associated emotional responses, the focus shifts to modification efforts. The following is a list of questions for use in modifying thoughts.

- Where is the evidence?
- Is there any evidence to the contrary?
- How strongly do you believe that?
- Could you see yourself . . . with more positive views of self . . . having more trust in your partner's dedication to you . . . having greater purpose in life?
- What is the worst that could happen?
- Could you look at it another way?
- What other meanings can you identify?
- What are the consequences of looking at it this way?

- How do you feel when you think _____?
- Would it be possible to _____?
- What images or sensations do you experience when you think _____?
- What other thoughts flow from that thought (image)?
- Given your current understanding of the impact that our meanings have on the way we think, feel, and are motivated to act, what is your best advice to yourself?
- What if?

Socratic dialogue uses questions like the foregoing to probe for the logic or evidence supporting the client's thinking and explore the consequences of the belief or beliefs. As beliefs fail to demonstrate validity or viability, cognitive restructuring proceeds with the generation of alternative meanings and their consequences (Beck, 1995; Granvold, 1994).

THERAPIST MODELING

It is important that the therapist model desirable cognitive processing in the questions asked. For example, "How did that make you feel?" promotes external locus of control thinking. Such thinking places the power over one's well-being with other people or with one's life circumstances. This violates the cognitive therapy principle that, with a few exceptions, each of us is responsible for our feelings and ultimately our mental health. The question can be rephrased easily as, "How did you feel when . . . ?" Another therapist trap easily avoided is the use of expressions in which information processing errors are evident. For example, to avoid modeling dichotomous thinking the therapist can ask such questions as, "What factors influenced your decision to divorce?" and "When you got angry in traffic, what thoughts were going through your mind?"

CASE EXAMPLE

The following is an illustration of cognitive restructuring with a client who is going through a contentious divorce. By temporary court order, her husband has been given managing conservatorship of their children. Her relationship with her children has been troubled largely due to past episodes of depression and a demanding work schedule. Following the recent separation, she has felt extremely depressed and hopeless, along with feelings of hurt, sadness, loss, and anger. She admits to suicidal ideation but has no plan to do so, nor can she see herself actually committing suicide. Through Socratic dialogue, a web of strong beliefs have been identified that undermine her emotional well-being and promote negative views of self. In the following excerpt, one of the most powerful beliefs from this matrix of meanings is identified and explored for change. The probing is focused on uncovering evidence to support or negate her belief.

Client: I have moved out of the house into an apartment. I've lost everything. I don't have my house. My husband doesn't love me. I don't have my kids anymore. I've lost my children [crying].

Therapist: You have experienced a lot of loss with the separation, and I feel badly that you are going through this. You just said that you have lost your children. Could you tell me more about that thought?

C: I don't see them each night when I come home from work. I've lost them. I'm not a mother anymore.

T: When you think the thought, "I've lost my children," how do you feel?

C: I feel empty and sad . . . and hurt.

T: So the thought, "I've lost my children" promotes some pretty unpleasant feelings.

C: Yes [softly crying].

T: You may recall our past discussions about the role our thoughts tend to play in our feelings. You have expressed the thought that you have lost your children. As evidence to support this thought, you indicated that you don't see them each evening as you did prior to the separation. Let's explore this statement. Have you seen them at all since you moved out 3 weeks ago?

C: Oh yes, I see them one or two nights a week and on Saturday or Sunday, sometimes both days.

T: So despite not seeing them daily, you do spend time with them several times a week.

C: Yes, that's right.

T: Although it is not the same as when you were living in the same household with them, are you their mother when you are spending time with them?

C: Well yes I am, but it doesn't feel the same.

T: In what ways does it feel different?

C: I guess it's different because I know that I am going to my apartment alone, without them.

T: Would you conclude from our discussion that although it isn't the same, you haven't actually lost your children?

C: Yea, I guess that's more accurate.

T: So you're still their mother, and you are continuing to be actively involved in their lives. Earlier you said that you feel sad, empty, and hurt in relation to the thought that you've lost your children. Would you conclude that shifting your thought from, "I've lost my children" to "It isn't the same" is really a more accurate statement of your situation?

C: Yes it is, I guess.

T: You have reported feeling sad, empty, and hurt in relation to the thought that you've lost your children. Though it would be unrealistic to expect these feelings to go away completely, can you detect feeling any *less* sad, empty, and hurt as you think, "parenting isn't the same," rather than "I've lost my children?"

C: It's really hard to tell, but I suppose I don't feel as bad.

T: Perhaps you will be able to detect greater change in your feelings over time. Each time you think, "I've lost my children," would you be willing to answer that thought with, "No, I haven't lost my children, it (parenting) just isn't the same?"

C: Yes, I'll try it.

The therapist guided the client in revising a powerful statement presumably influential in promoting strong feelings. The client realized that the evidence contradicted the meaning she attached to the postseparation change in parenting. She arrived at an alternative meaning that was more consistent with her recent experience as a parent. She also considered the connection between her thoughts and feelings. Based on the awareness that effective cognitive restructuring requires repetition, the client was asked to repeat the reframing whenever the faulty thought occurred. This practice was reviewed at several subsequent sessions. As noted earlier, the thought addressed in this excerpt is one of a web of beliefs contributing to her current views about her children, herself, and her emotional state. She also believed that her children no longer cared for her (e.g., "They never call me"; "They could care less whether I call them or not"; "When we are together, it's all about them"). These and other beliefs were similarly isolated for cognitive restructuring with the focus on the identification of supportive evidence and evidence to the contrary.

USE OF SCALING TO ASSESS CHANGE

Cognitive restructuring may not produce a complete change in the client's beliefs. Thoughts and beliefs determined to strongly contribute to distress, disturbance, self-downing, and unrest may remain active following cognitive restructuring efforts. It is more realistic to expect a reduction in the strength of the view, rather than complete eradication of the belief. To evaluate the effectiveness of the specific cognitive restructuring effort, the therapist may ask the client to rate the current strength of the belief under scrutiny.

T: How much do you believe that your husband is trying to take everything from you?

C: About 50 percent, I guess.

T: How have you managed to drop from 95 to 50 percent?

C: I looked over the proposed property settlement and I can see that he's trying to be fair in that area. I can't let go of the idea completely though, because he's the one with the children [i.e., custody].

T: And now how angry do you feel toward him?

C: Oh, I'm still pretty upset. I guess about a 60 [percent].

T: I see. Although you're still upset, you are making meaningful change in your views and feelings.

COGNITIVE ELABORATION

Many cognitive restructuring efforts are designed to reframe the cognition under consideration, to replace one thought with another. In some circumstances, it may be undesirable to replace a thought or even to directly attempt to reduce its strength even though it may stimulate unappealing responses and mood states. Furthermore, a client may be unwilling to abandon a given thought. Cognitive elaboration (Granvold, 2008) is an alternative approach to cognitive restructuring in which the focus is on the generation of alternative thoughts, views, or meaning constructions without the expectation that the original view be abandoned. This approach is particularly useful with clients who are grieving the death of a loved one.

In the illustration that follows, Blake is struggling with the death of his 28-year-old son, James, who was killed a year earlier in a one-car accident. The accident occurred while James was returning from a hunting trip that Blake had originally planned to make with him. James was drunk at the time of the accident. Blake believes that he is responsible for James's death, that had he been with him on the trip, the accident would not have happened. After exploring the belief that "I am responsible for my son's death" and identifying the associated emotional consequences (depression, loss, pain, helplessness, regret) the focus shifted to cognitive elaboration.

T: Since focusing specifically on blaming yourself for James's death appears to result in other problems, suppose you expand your thoughts about James's death in addition to "It's my fault." What other thoughts do you have about James's life or his premature death?

C: Well, not to be too hard on the kid, but he did have a drinking problem, and, ultimately, I guess that you could say he was responsible for the accident that took his life. He was drunk!

T: Yes, I agree with you that James was responsible for his drinking and the accident. It is somewhat a question of when does a parent quit protecting his child. Blake, can you function with both of these beliefs, "It's my fault" and "James was responsible for his drinking"?

C: Even though they seem contradictory, I think I can.

T: So, it is possible to maintain multiple views or beliefs about a situation.

C: Yes, I think it is.

In this and subsequent sessions, several other meanings were elaborated in relation to James's death (and life) including (1) James's death will have been a waste if I don't do something in his name that could have a positive impact on the problem of drinking and driving in our society (Blake became actively involved in MADD); (2) I need to be very involved with James's son as James's "representative"; (3) James would want me to get past my intense grief and once again enjoy life (a belief generated through a role reversal exercise); and (4) I can still love James strongly and grieve less.

Challenging Blake's initial belief that his son's death is his fault would have been, I believe, less effective than allowing it to stand as one of many meanings in a matrix of constructs surrounding the loss. The generation of multiple meanings through the process of cognitive elaboration dilutes the strength of a given belief and produces a range of consequences. The position of constructivists is that the client will likely realize greater viability among the various constructs generated.

GUIDED IMAGERY

Guided imagery is a viable alternative approach to cognitive restructuring. An early approach to the use of imagery was developed by Maultsby (1975) in the form of rational emotive imagery (REI). Other CBT leaders have also employed the use of imagery as a cognitive restructuring method (Beck & Emery, 1985; Beck & Weishaar, 2008; Ellis, 1977). Several imagery techniques have been advanced for use in the process of cognitive restructuring by these and other clinicians. Edwards (1989) notes that "the main techniques for obtaining an image from which to begin are the visualization of a life event or theme, the reinstatement of a dream or daytime image, and feeling focusing" (p. 286). Images, dreams, and fantasies may be drawn from the client's history or current imagination. Alternatively, the therapist may generate content for use in guided imagery. Though not imperative, it may be helpful to teach the client progressive relaxation for use in conducting guided imagery. In the illustration that follows, guided imagery is used with a Vietnam veteran suffering from nightmares about a specific combat experience in which two of his men were killed. The client feels responsible for their deaths and believes he should have acted to save them. He is a decorated veteran known for his leadership in combat situations. When he awakens from these recurrent nightmares about combat over 40 years ago, he feels extreme sadness and intense self-reproach. On these occasions he acts cold and distant toward his wife and his employees.

T: You said that when you think back on the fire fight in Vietnam in which two of your men were killed, you feel responsible, that you should have acted to save them.

C: That's right. I have vivid dreams about them being torn apart by bullets.

T: Close your eyes. Imagine that you did little to prepare your men for combat and that you are out on patrol. The patrol is attacked, and your men go down beside you. You and your remaining men fight off the enemy and the shooting ends. As you attend to the casualties, how are you feeling?

C: First, I would never act this way. But I'll go along with this thinking. . . . I feel angry with myself, a lot of self-loathing . . . and ashamed for being so irresponsible.

T: So when you think of yourself as failing to prepare your men for combat and casualties result, you feel angry with yourself, self-loathing, and shame. Now this time, imagine that you have prepared your men extremely well for combat. By your instruction, they have become highly skilled soldiers, but you recognize that war is war. Each man knows that he may die in battle. You enter the fire fight as before, and men are lost. The patrol is attacked, and your men go down beside you. You and your remaining men fight off the enemy and the shooting ends. As you attend to the casualties, how are you feeling?

C: I feel pretty empty inside over the loss of these men, but I don't feel as upset with myself. I did what I could do . . . but war is war, as you just said.

In this example, the client was asked to consider himself performing his responsibilities unconscionably by failing to prepare his men for battle (a legitimate basis for accepting responsibility for casualties of war). After identifying the associated feelings, he imagined the same combat scene with the awareness that he *had* prepared his men well for battle. This process resulted in a reduction in the degree to which he felt upset and reinforced the thought, "war is war." The latter thought is one that the client had expressed in an earlier session. The client was a strong candidate for the use of imagery inasmuch as he was experiencing powerful imagery (both nightmares and daydreams) outside therapy sessions.

BEHAVIORAL EXPERIMENTS

Behavioral experiments may be used to identify and modify beliefs, assumptions, and expectations. The client and therapist collaboratively develop a plan for the client to "test out" the veracity or viability of his or her views. In the behavioral experiment, the client may "predict an outcome based on personal automatic thoughts, carry out the agreed-upon behavior, and then evaluate the evidence in light of the new experience" (Beck & Weishaar, 2008, p. 286). Ellis introduced his famous "shame attacking" exercises early in the development of REI in which clients exposed themselves to negative attention, typically with little or no actual disconcerting consequences. Several iterations of the experiment often resulted in cognitive and emotive change.

Behavioral experiments may be enacted in vivo or take place in the therapist's office as role-plays. In some cases, the simple gathering of information may suffice (Beck, 1995). The following are illustrations of clients' evaluation of their beliefs in actual life experiences. A client experiencing social phobia tested the hypothesis that "no one will speak to me" at singles' Sunday school class. By attending the class, she disproved the hypothesis and actually experienced a warm reception by many. Another client saw himself as extremely unappealing and consequently no one would be willing to go out with him on a date. He further believed that if he *was* successful, he would not find the woman desirable. We agreed that this experiment might take several iterations. He went online and made contact with several people. After developing ongoing correspondence with several women, he began arranging dates. His first few efforts actually supported his original hypothesis. On the fourth outing, however, he met a woman whom he found to be highly attractive. They dated for a time. Although their relationship was not sustained, he modified his self-view as a consequence of this experience.

Through behavioral experimentation, clients modify their views as actual life experiences provide evidence that contradicts their conceptualizations. Some clients may approach behavioral experimentation with marked skepticism and strong beliefs that they are "right" in their conceptualizations. For those clients, a review of their personal life experience may be persuasive. Attempt to identify prior life experiences in which anticipation failed to match realized experience (e.g., aerobics classes are for athletic people only). These experiences may serve as useful points of reference in dispelling client reluctance and in developing openness to behavioral experiments.

CONCLUSION

Humans are no strangers to the process of cognitive restructuring in some form. We develop and modify beliefs automatically as part of life span development. We are also, however, creatures of habit. Stored and accessible beliefs operate rather inflexibly, and cognitive processing patterns become routine. When modification of these phenomena is indicated, cognitive restructuring procedures like those presented in this chapter provide a methodology for effective change. Clinicians en-

gaged in cognitive restructuring efforts are invited and encouraged to draw on their creativity individually and collaboratively with their clients in developing efficacious cognitive restructuring strategies.

WEB SITES

Academy of Cognitive Therapy. http://www.academyofct.org.

Association for Behavioral and Cognitive Therapies. http://www.aabt.org.

Constructivist Psychology Network. http://www.constructivistpsych.org.

European Personal Construct Association. http://www.epca-net.org.

REBT Network. http://www.rebtnetwork.org.

References

Beck, A. T., & Emery, G. (1985). *Anxiety disorders and phobias: A cognitive perspective.* New York: Basic Books.

Beck, A. T., & Weishaar, M. E. (2008). Cognitive therapy. In R. J. Corsini & D. Wedding (Eds.), *Current psychotherapies,* 8th ed. (pp. 263–294). Belmont, CA: Thomson.

Beck, J. S. (1995). *Cognitive therapy: Basics and beyond.* New York: Guilford.

Clark, D. A., Beck, A. T., & Alford, B. A. (1999). *Scientific foundations of cognitive theory and therapy of depression.* New York: Wiley.

Edwards, D. J. A. (1989). Cognitive restructuring through guided imagery: Lessons from gestalt therapy. In A. Freeman, K. M. Simon, L. E. Beutler, & H. Arkowitz (Eds.), *Comprehensive handbook of cognitive therapy* (pp. 283–297). New York: Plenum.

Ellis, A. (1977). The rational-emotive approach to sex therapy. In A. Ellis & R. Greiger (Eds.), *Handbook of rational-emotive therapy* (pp. 198–215). New York: Springer.

Granvold, D. K. (1994). Concepts and methods of cognitive treatment. In D. K. Granvold (Ed.), *Cognitive and behavioral treatment: Methods and applications* (pp. 3–31). Pacific Grove, CA: Brooks/Cole.

Granvold, D. K. (2008). Constructivist theory and practice. In N. Coady & P. Lehmann (Eds.), *Theoretical perspectives for direct social work practice: A generalist-eclectic approach,* 2nd ed. (pp. 401–427). New York: Springer.

Maultsby, M. C. (1975). *Help yourself to happiness.* New York: Institute for Rational Living.

Wells, A. (1997). *Cognitive therapy of anxiety disorders: A practice manual and conceptualization guide.* New York: Wiley.

84 Using the Miracle Question and Scaling Technique in Clinical Practice

Mo Yee Lee

The miracle question and the scaling question are integral parts of solution-focused brief therapy, which is originally developed at the Brief Family Therapy Center at Milwaukee by Steve De Shazer, Insoo Kim Berg, and their associates. Solution-focused brief therapy begins as atheoretical, and the focus is on finding "what works in therapy" (Berg, 1994). Building on a strengths perspective and using a time-limited approach, solution-focused brief therapy postulates that positive and long-lasting change can occur in a relatively brief period of time by focusing on "solution talk" instead of "problem talk" (De Shazer, 1985; Nelson & Thomas, 2007). Different from the more traditional approaches, such an approach uses the language and symbols of solution and strengths as opposed to the language of deficits and blame. Treatment focuses on identifying exceptions and solution behaviors, which are then amplified, supported, and reinforced through a systematic solution-building process (Lee, Sebold, & Uken, 2003).

The miracle question and scaling question in many ways synthesize the treatment orientation and practice characteristics of solution-focused brief therapy. Its conversational- and solution-based characteristics are intimately related to three definitive assumptions and practice principles of solution-focused brief therapy.

1. The power of language in creating and sustaining reality. Solution-focused therapy views language as the medium through which personal meaning and understanding are expressed and socially constructed in conversation (De Shazer, 1994). Because "what is noticed becomes reality and what is not noticed does not exist" (Lee et al., 2003, p. 32), there is a conscious effort for the therapist to help the client stay focused on visioning a desirable future and finding small steps to actualize the solution-oriented future. Pathology or problem talk sustains a problem reality through self-fulfilling prophecies and distracts attention from developing solutions (Miller, 1997).

2. A focus on solutions, strengths, and health. Solution-focused brief therapy assumes that clients have the resources and *have the answer*. The focus is on what clients can do versus what clients cannot do. One basic assumption of a systems perspective is that change is constant. No matter how severe is the problem, there must be some exceptions to the problem patterns. These exceptions serve as clues to a solution and represent clients' "unnoticed" strengths and resources (De Shazer, 1985). Consequently, the task for the therapist is to assist clients in noticing, amplifying, sustaining, and reinforcing these exceptions regardless of how small or infrequent they may be. Once clients are engaged in nonproblem behavior, they are on the way to a solution-building process (DeJong & Berg, 2007).

3. Solutions as clients' constructions. Solutions are not objective "realities" but are private, local, meaning-making activities by an individual (Miller, 1997). The importance of and the meaning attached to a goal or solution is individually constructed in a collaborative process. Solution-focused therapy honors clients as the "knower" of their experiences and "creators" of solutions, they define the goals for their treatment and remains the main instigator of change (Berg, 1994).

EVALUATIVE QUESTIONS: CREATING SEARCHES AND PROVIDING FEEDBACK

Influenced by these assumptions and practice principles, the primary purpose of solution-focused interventions is to engage the client in a therapeutic conversation that is conducive to a solution-building process. In this conversation, the clinician invites the client to be the "expert" by listening and exploring the meaning of the client perception of his or her situation. People need useful feedback in the process of change (Lee, Uken, & Sebold, 2007). The therapist can directly provide feedback via listening, affirming, restating, and expanding responses (Lee et al., 2003). Instead of directly providing feedback to clients, evaluative questions serve to initiate a self-feedback process within the client. Such questions ask clients to self-evaluate their situations in terms of their doing, thinking, and feeling. The therapist abstains from making any interpretation of clients' situation or suggesting any ideas; he or she just asks good questions that help clients evaluate different aspects of their unique life situations. Questions are perceived as better ways to create open space for clients to think about and self-evaluate their situation and solutions. Evaluative questions operate from the stance of curiosity and convey the message that we believe *clients* have the answers.

The therapist uses solution-oriented questions, including miracle questions and scaling questions, to assist clients in constructing a reality that does not contain the problem. These questioning techniques are developed by De Shazer, Berg, and colleagues to fully make use of the resources and potential of clients (DeJong & Berg, 2007; De Shazer, 1985).

THE MIRACLE QUESTION

The development of the miracle question was inspired by the work of Milton Erickson (the "crystal ball" technique) (De Shazer, 1985). According to Berg (1994), the miracle question invites clients to create a vision of their future without the presenting problem. A major challenge encountered by most clients in social work treatment is that they know when they have a problem but not when the problem has been successfully addressed. When this happens, clients may be in treatment for a long time because there are no clear indicators of health and wellness. Helping clients develop a clear vision of their future without the problem becomes crucial in successful treatment because it establishes indicators of change and helps gauge clients' progress toward a self-defined desirable future (Berg, 1994; DeJong & Berg, 2007; Lee et al., 2007). When defining a future without a problem becomes a major focus of treatment, accountability for changing one's behavior can be effectively achieved. Defining the desirable future also shifts the focus of attention from what cannot be done to what can be accomplished; it moves clients away from blaming others or themselves and holds them accountable for developing a better, different future.

The miracle question is intended to accomplish the following therapeutic impact.

1. It allows clients to distance themselves from the problem-saturated stories so that they can be more playful in creating a beneficial vision of their future.
2. It facilitates clients to develop a clear vision about a desirable future as "what is noticed becomes reality and what is not noticed does not exist" (Lee et al., 2003, p. 32).
3. Because the focus of the miracle question is for clients to identify small, observable, and concrete changes that are indicative of a desirable future without problem, it establishes indicators of changes and progress that helps clients gauge success and progress.
4. It increases clients' awareness of their choices and offers them an opportunity to play an active role in their treatment (Lee et al., 2007).
5. The question allows clients to be hopeful about their lives, which can be different from their current problem situation.
6. Empowering clients to self-determine what is a desirable future for them. "It creates a personal possible self, which is not modeled after someone else's ideas of what his life should be like" (Berg, 1994, p. 97).

A frequently used version of the miracle question is the following:

Suppose that after our meeting today, you go home, do your things and go to bed. While you are sleeping, a miracle happens and the problem that brought you here is suddenly solved, like magic. The problem is gone. Because you were sleeping, you don't know that a miracle happened, but when you wake up tomorrow morning, you will be different. How will you know a miracle has happened? What will be the first small sign that tells you that the problem is resolved? (Berg & Miller, 1992, p. 359)

Note that the focus is on small signs of change. It is important to help clients describe in great details their solution picture and how it is different from their current behaviors, feelings, and thinking. The more detailed and refined the description, the clearer the indicators of change that will increase the likelihood for the client to actualize their solution picture because "what is noticed become reality." The miracle question only initiates the process for clients to envision a desirable future. It is helpful for the therapist to follow up the miracle question with other solution-focused questions that helps expand the solution picture.

- "Who will be the first person to notice the change? What will they be noticing about you that will tell them that you are different? How will your spouse, you child (any significant others) know that something is different?" (Relationship question)
- "When are there times in your life when you have already been doing this?" (Exception question)

The essence of miracle question is to allow the client to envision a future without problems. As such, social work professionals can be creative in coming up with other versions of future-oriented questions. This can be helpful especially with clients from other cultures or religions who might have their own culture-based interpretation of miracles. Some variations can be:

- "If I run into you a year later and by that time you have already solved the problem that brought you in today, how will I know that you are different? How will you be like then?"
- "If I were to videotape you in a good day, how will you be doing/feeling/thinking differently?"
- "Five years down the road, what do you want yourself to be like?"

Another version is the dream question that reinforces clients' sense of personal agency and therefore is consistent with the goal of empowering clients (Greene, Lee, Mentzer, Pinnell, & Niles, 1998).

Suppose that tonight while you are sleeping you have a dream and in this dream you discover the answers and resources you need to solve the problem that you are concerned about right now. When you wake up tomorrow you may or may not remember your dream but you do notice you are different. As you go about starting your day, what will tell you that you discovered or developed the skills and resources necessary to solve your problem? What will be the first small sign to tell you that you solved your problem?

SCALING QUESTIONS

Scaling questions ask clients to rank their situation and/or goal on a 1–10 scale (Berg, 1994). Usually, 1 represents the worst scenario that could possibly be and 10 is the most desirable outcome. People need feedback in the process of change. Therefore, for change to happen, clients need to be able to self-evaluate their progress and make adjustment accordingly. Scaling questions provide a simple tool for clients to quantify and evaluate their situation and progress so that they establish a clear indicator of progress for themselves (DeJong & Berg, 2007). More important, this is a self-anchored scale with no objective criteria. The constructivist characteristic of the scaling question honors clients as the knowers and the center of the change process. Scaling can be used to help clients rate their perception of progress, motivation for change, confidence to engage in solution-focused behaviors, and so on. Scaling questions are also helpful in assisting clients in establishing small steps and indicators of change in their solution-building process. Some common examples of scaling questions are:

1. Problem severity or progress: "On a 1–10 scale with 1 being the worst the problem could possibly be and 10 as the most desirable outcome, how would you put yourself on the scale? What would be some small steps that you can take to move from a 4 to a 5?"
2. Motivation: "On a 1–10 scale with 1 being you have no motivation to work on the problem and 10 being you would do whatever to change the situation, how would you (or your spouse, your boss, your child, etc.) put yourself on the scale? How would your wife (or other significant others) rank your motivation to change on a 1 to 10 scale?"
3. Confidence: "On a 1–10 scale with 1 being you have no confidence that you can work on the goal and 10 being you have complete confidence that you will continue to work on the goal, how would you put yourself on the

scale? On a scale of 1 to 10, how confident are you that you could actually do that? On a scale of 1 to 10, how confident are you that this will be helpful?"

CASE EXAMPLE: LINDA

Linda was a 47-year-old woman who suffered chronic back pain after a car accident. The pain also affected her mobility. She was living alone. The therapist uses the miracle question to help her envision a more hopeful future.

SWR: Suppose that after our meeting today, you go home, do your things, and go to bed. While you are sleeping, a miracle happens and the problem that brought you here is suddenly solved, like magic. The problem is gone. Because you were sleeping, you don't know that a miracle happened, but when you wake up tomorrow morning, you will be different. How will you know a miracle has happened? What will be the first small sign that tells you that the problem is resolved?

Linda: I won't be so cranky, like an immovable mountain.

SWR: Instead of being cranky, what do you see yourself to be like?

Linda: Be a little more upbeat, cheerful, and perky. Get my mind off of it and focus on areas not on the mountain of pain.

SWR: So you want to distract yourself from the mountain of pain and do something different?

Linda: So when I am around people they are not affected by it and they are dragged down by it.

SWR: Let's say you woke up tomorrow after this miracle happened, what would be the first small thing that you would do and you are not doing it now?

Linda: I don't know. [Pause] Maybe instead of lying in bed staring at the wall, I would get up and open the curtain and turn on my computer, open a book, talk to the cat, anything beside lying in bed and staring at the wall.

SWR: That is what you do now, lie in bed and stare at the wall?

Linda: Yeah.

SWR: When this miracle happens, you would get out of bed, open the curtain, talk to the cat. What else would you do?

Linda: Turn on the computer and get out of bed and do something.

SWR: Do something?

Linda: Maybe sweep, dust, or mop.

SWR: Anything else?

Linda: Go outside and sit in the sunshine.

SWR: Who in your home would notice the change? Is there somebody else living in your home?

Linda: No, just my cat.

SWR: So what your cat would notice different about you that you are not doing now?

Linda: I would be up and maybe play with her.

SWR: So who else would notice the change beside your cat?

Linda: My neighbors, friends.

SWR: What would they notice?

Linda: A more positive outlook.

SWR: How would they notice?

Linda: I would respond to them, not giving the dirty looks when it is not their fault. I would run over. I sort of give them a dirty look. It is a major hurdle for me.

SWR: Who would be most affected by this change?

Linda: I suppose that would help other people as well as me.

SWR: How so?

Linda: You know it would help me because I don't want to be a big drag and that way I won't be dragging people down and it won't be dragging me down because everyone around me is all bummed out, "Oh you poor thing" and all this, and I don't want that. I want to get over it. I want to get over it, I want to get over the top of the mountain and go on from here not just hang around the base all the time.

SWR: Tomorrow, meaning the following morning or next morning, you can do this. On a 1 to 10 scale, 10 being doable that you can do this, and 1 being no chance at all, where would you think you are? [Scaling question regarding feasibility of the change efforts]

Linda: I am at a 6 right now.

SWR: So you are saying getting out of bed in the morning, opening the curtains, turning on the computer, and talking to cat is quite doable because you are at a 6?

Linda: It is doable. I can do that.

SWR: Using the same scale, 10 being you are motivated to do this because it would improve your life, and 1 being you are wishy-washy about it.

Where would you put yourself on the scale? [Scaling question regarding motivation of change]

Linda: I would say an 8 as I don't want to be cranky anymore.

CASE EXAMPLE: ELISE

Elise was a 45-year-old Caucasian single mother with three children from 10 to 16 years old. Her husband passed away a year ago, and she felt extremely overwhelmed trying to take care of her children. She became depressed and attempted to commit suicide by overdosing on sleeping pills. She requested that her children be placed in foster homes while she tried to work things out for herself. She received treatment as part of her case plan to reunite with her children. While thinking what might be a helpful goal for her to work on, Elise pondered and struggled. At first, she mentioned developing a better relationship with her children as something she would like to see happen. However, she also felt overwhelmed as a single mother without the support of her husband. The therapist encouraged her to think about what would be personally meaningful and helpful to her at this time. Elise said that she would like to be more productive, although she did not have a clear idea of what a productive life look like.

Elise: I don't know. I guess I would feel a little different. Maybe just be more productive.

SWR: In what way?

Elise: I am not sure. . . . I am raising three kids and my husband passed away a year ago, and I am doing nothing myself.

SWR: So life is not cool.

Elise: Yes, not whole lot to do, so . . .

SWR: So what would you do different to be more productive?

Elise: I don't know, but I could be more productive than I am right now, I am reading and doing the seven steps right now. That is about it.

SWR: Do you feel being more productive by reading the seven steps and maybe, as you've just said, taking walks? [Important for the client to evaluate whether she has been more productive]

Elise: I am thinking about when the kids come home, my relationship with them is going to be more productive. I have to feel like change a little bit. [Client is still somewhat unclear about what she can do to get her to be more productive]

SWR: Let me ask you a this, you wake up tomorrow morning, you do this and whatever it is to make you more productive. At the end of the day you look at yourself and say, "Man, I am doing well, I really to do it now for myself." What do you think that might be? [This is an different version of the miracle question that helps Elise be more playful about visioning a future when she is more productive.]

Elise: Going through the seven steps, change my ideas and personality more to be a single woman.

SWR: How will people notice that you stand as a single woman, and they know that you are different and how will they know that?

Elise: The way I am acting.

SWR: What will tell them you changed your attitude and you are different from before?

Elise: Oh, gosh, my weight.

SWR: So your weight will be different. I am curious, maybe just in your head, pretend that between now and the next week, your weight has changed. What will be different for you in your daily life that you will be doing and you are not doing right now?

Elise: If my weight changed, I will not watch the same TV shows, and I don't want to read the same book and I don't eat the same junk food.

SWR: You are making big changes in your daily life . . .

Elise: You are right, but this is something that I do want to change.

SWR: What would be the first things that you can possibly do to make this happen?

Elise: I've already walking every day. Maybe I can walk longer and don't watch the 8 o'clock show.

SWR: Anything else?

Elise: Don't go to the snack aisle when doing my grocery shopping. That'll probably do it.

SWR: So what will you get from the store instead?

Elise: Maybe more fresh food, like veggies and fish.

SWR: What do you want to see happen when you take walks and eat more fresh food?

Elise: I'll feel having more control and be more productive in my life, not just lying around like a couch potato and doing nothing.

SWR: So how confidant are you on a 1 to 10 scale that you will be able to talk a longer walk and eat more fresh food between now and next time we get together? [Scaling question regarding confidence about change]

Elise: Well, I do want to change but you know the temptation. [pause] Maybe a 3.

SWR: So what are some small things that you can do to move it from a 3 to a 4? [Using scaling question to establish small steps for Elise to feel more confident]

Elise: That's not easy. Maybe talking to my sister so she can remind me once in a while.

SWR: So maybe taking it to the next step, and next week you just pretend the next step to this change is going through and watching and seeing what you do differently as a result. I will be very interested to hear what you say next time to me about how just going through that next step, what things you do make you different and more productive. Is that possible?

Elise: Oh, yes.

SWR: Just pay attention to "If I like my life to be better, what small things I can do to make it happen?"

GUIDELINES FOR USING MIRACLE QUESTION AND SCALING QUESTION IN SOCIAL WORK PRACTICE

- Use miracle questions to assist clients develop a clear vision of a future without problem.
- Use scaling questions to scale confidence, ability, motivation with respect to clients' change efforts.
- Use scaling questions to establish small steps for further change.
- Be patient: Clients do not have the solution in their mind when they seek treatment, and it is the responsibility of the therapist to create a safe space for them to slowly "paint" their solution picture
- Go for details: assist clients in moving beyond vague descriptions of the desirable future and instead describe them in terms of small, observable, specific, or behavioral steps.
- Reinforce clients motivation: help clients carefully evaluate what may be personally meaningful and useful for them.
- Respectful of client's personal choice and ownership.
- Compliment and acknowledge client's desire for change.

- Help clients evaluate feasibility of the solution picture.
- Focus on small steps that can make clients' life better.
- Help clients develop clear indicators of change so they can recognize successes.

CONCLUSION

The purpose of the miracle and scaling questions are to help clients establish indicators of wellness and gauge progress toward a desirable future. These self-evaluative questions represent a specific type of conversation in which the therapist talks "with" the client (instead of talking to the client) to co-develop new meanings and new realities through a dialogue of "solutions" (De Shazer, 1994; Lee et al., 2003). The challenge for social work practitioners is to collaboratively work with clients so that they can find a future that they feel comfortable as well as good about their choices. The therapist cautiously refrains from providing/suggesting any predetermined solutions or desirable future. The therapist is responsible for creating a therapeutic dialogical context in which clients experience a solution-building process that is initiated from within and grounded in clients' personal construction of the solution reality and cultural strengths (Lee, 2003). The therapeutic process is collaborative and egalitarian, and the client's self-determination is fully respected (DeJong & Berg, 2007). The ultimate goal of miracle and scaling questions, therefore, is consistent with the goal of empowerment that focuses on increasing client's personal and interpersonal power so that they can take relevant and culturally appropriate action to improve their situation (Gutierrez, De-Lois, & GlenMaye, 1995).

WEB SITES

SFT-L, Solution-Focused Therapy online mailing list. SFT-L@listserv.icors.org.
Solution Focused Brief Therapy Association. http://www.sfbta.org.

References

Berg, I. K. (1994). *Family based services: A solution-focused approach.* New York: Norton.
Berg, I. K., & Miller, S. (1992). *Working with the problem drinker: A solution-focused approach.* New York: Norton.

DeJong, P., & Berg, I. K. (2007). *Interviewing for solutions,* 3rd ed. Pacific Grove, CA: Thomson Brooks/Cole.

De Shazer, S. (1985). *Keys to solutions in brief therapy.* New York: Norton.

De Shazer, S. (1994). *Words were originally magic.* New York: Norton.

Greene, G. J., Lee, M. Y., Mentzer, R., Pinnell, S., & Niles, D. (1998). Miracles, dreams, and empowerment: A brief practice note. *Families in Society, 79,* 395–399.

Gutierrez, L. M., DeLois, K. A., & GlenMaye, L. (1995). Understanding empowerment practice: Building on practitioner-based knowledge. *Families in Society, 76,* 534–542.

Lee, M. Y. (2003). A solution-focused approach to cross-cultural clinical social work practice: Utilizing cultural strengths, *Families in Society, 84,* 385–395.

Lee, M. Y., Sebold, J., & Uken, A. (2003). *Solution-focused treatment with domestic violence offenders: Accountability for change.* New York: Oxford University Press.

Lee, M. Y., Uken. A., & Sebold, J. (2007). Role of self-determined goals in predicting recidivism in domestic violence offenders. *Research on Social Work Practice, 17,* 30–41.

Miller, G. (1997). *Becoming miracle workers, Language and meaning in brief therapy.* New York: Aldine de Gruyter.

Nelson, T., & Thomas, F. (Ed) (2007). *Clinical applications of solution focused brief therapy.* New York: Haworth.

85   Using Evidence-Based Hypnosis

William R. Nugent

Hypnosis is best thought of as an approach to intervention or as an intervention model as opposed to a causal-developmental model (Fischer, 1978).[1] Hypnosis could therefore be used as an intervention by social workers approaching their practice from pretty much any theoretical perspective. There are numerous theories of hypnosis (see, for example, Fromm, 1979). Rather than focusing on theories of hypnosis, I intend here to give the reader an introduction to Milton Erickson and Ernest Rossi's utilization model of hypnotherapy (Erickson & Rossi, 1979). Erickson and Rossi (1979) viewed hypnotherapy as a three-stage process: (1) a period of *preparation*; (2) the *activation and utilization* of the client's life experiences and cognitive and affective skills during a period of therapeutic trance; and (3) a *ratification* of therapeutic changes that take place. I briefly review literature on one of the most promising areas for using hypnosis—the management and control of acute and chronic pain.

PREPARATION

In this stage, the social worker first establishes a therapeutic relationship with the client. The social worker can use any of a number of communication methods to help establish this rapport (see Hepworth, Rooney, & Larsen, 1996). In Erickson and Rossi's (1979) model, the rapport that the social worker and client create together can serve as part of a therapeutic frame of reference within which the client's therapeutic responses develop.

In prehypnosis interviews with the client, the social worker obtains information about the client's problems as well as the client's life experiences and learnings. As much as possible is learned about the client's personal history, problems, recreational preferences, field of work, interpersonal skills, mental skills, psychodynamics, temperament, and so on. This information can suggest aspects of the client's life experiences, abilities, and cognitive schema that can be framed (in both the social worker's thinking as well as the client's) as resources that can be used in changing the client's problems. This is an important notion in Erickson and Rossi's (1979) model: any part of a client's repertory of life experiences and skills, including his or her problems, can be used as a part of problem resolution.

For example, suppose that a client presents with physical problems. The social worker learns during assessment that the client enjoys music, finds listening to music very relaxing, and is able to tune out all other sensory awareness (including physical sensations) while listening to music. The client's enjoyment of music and his relaxation and dissociation responses while listening to it could be viewed as important client resources and can be used by the social worker in at least two ways:

1. listening to imagined music could be used as a vehicle to trance induction (see, for example, Erickson & Rossi, 1979, case 5); and
2. the relaxation and loss of awareness of physical sensations that the client experiences while listening to music could be accessed during therapeutic trance and, in a sense, moved out of the context of listening to music and placed into contexts in which the client experiences pain.

Similarly, suppose that the client expresses the strong belief that he is unable to experience hypnotic trance. The social worker might use the client's thoughts expressing this doubt as the actual vehicle for trance induction (see, for example, Erickson, 1959). This aspect of Erickson and Rossi's (1979) model is clearly consistent with the profession's focus on client strengths and in a very real sense views a client's problems as one source of his strengths.

Another important element of the preparation phase is the creation of a *therapeutic frame of reference*. The social worker purposely frames the client's involvement with the social worker and the hypnotherapy to be used into a therapeutic context and works to instill in the client an *expec-*

tancy of change. The social worker might tell the client anecdotes about others with similar problems who experienced positive change as a result of hypnotherapeutic intervention. Erickson and Rossi (1979) argue that expectations of therapeutic change may lead to a suspension of the client's learned limitations that contribute to problems. This creation of an expectancy of change is a part of the therapeutic frame of reference the social worker purposely cultivates. The suspension of disbelief and the high expectation of positive change has been associated with many spontaneous changes thought to be the result of so-called placebo effects (Coe, 1980; Erickson & Rossi, 1979, 1981). In fact, the purposive cultivation of placebo effects can be considered to be an important part of Erickson and Rossi's (1979) model.

THERAPEUTIC TRANCE

Erickson and Rossi (1979) define therapeutic trance as a "period during which the limitations of one's usual frames of reference and beliefs are temporarily altered so one can be receptive to other patterns of association and modes of mental functioning that are conducive to problem-solving" (p. 3). The trance state is viewed as a state in which the client is receptive to new frames of reference and to creative solutions to problems. Erickson and Rossi (1979) conceptualize the dynamics of trance induction and hypnotic suggestion as a five-stage process: the fixation of attention, the disruption of normal "mental sets" and belief systems, the initiation of unconscious search processes, the activation of unconscious processes, and spontaneous hypnotic response.

Fixation of Attention

Fixating a client's attention has been the classical approach to initiating trance. Traditionally, the "hypnotist" would have the person focus his or her gaze on a watch or some other external object. An even more effective focus of attention is the client's own body sensations and internal cognitive and affective experience. Encouraging the client to focus on physical sensations (such as comfort), ongoing cognitive experience (such as her stream of internal dialogue), or internal imagery (such as consciously created visual or auditory images) leads the client's attention inward even more effectively than a focus on some external object.

Erickson and Rossi (1979) differentiate between formal and informal trances. In a *formal trance* the social worker would request the client to focus his attention inward. A progressive relaxation exercise is one means of having the client focus attention inward, in this case to the differing sensations of tension and relaxation. This process is labeled a formal induction in that the social worker interrupts ongoing interactions with the client to request that the client focus on inner aspects of the ongoing experience for the purposes of initiating a therapeutic trance.

In contrast, an *informal trance* occurs when the social worker uses a story or anecdote that serves to hold the client's attention. Confusion and boredom are also useful trance-induction mechanisms (Erickson & Rossi, 1989). Erickson and Rossi (1979) refer to the inner absorption experienced by clients in response to engaging stories, confusion, boredom, and the like as the "common everyday trance." A common everyday trance is defined as those periods during everyday life in which a person becomes so absorbed with some internal experience that they momentarily lose awareness of the external world. This can be used in the utilization model as effectively as can a formal trance for therapeutic purposes.

Regardless of whether a formal or informal trance is to be induced, according to Erickson and Rossi, the most effective means of fixating attention is to accurately acknowledge the client's current ongoing experience. Correctly recognizing and acknowledging the current experience fixates the client's attention and creates a receptivity to therapeutic suggestions.

Disrupting Habitual Frameworks and Belief Systems

In the utilization model, the most useful psychological effect of fixating the client's attention is that it tends to disrupt—or to use a computer analogy, to "take off-line"—the client's normal mental sets and frames of reference for organizing experience. During this brief interruption, latent patterns of association and sensory-perceptual functioning can be experienced. These latent patterns of experience may manifest themselves in a manner that has been described as hypnotic trance. The disruption of clients' normal modes of functioning means that learned limitations are suspended, and they become more open to new means of experiencing and learning. This openness to new experiences and alternative solutions to problems

is the essence of therapeutic trance (Erickson & Rossi, 1979). The purpose of therapeutic trance, formal or informal, is to enable clients to find within themselves new frames of reference that allow them to find solutions to their problems.

Initiation of Unconscious Search Processes

In the Erickson and Rossi (1979) model, the fixation of attention and disruption of normal mental frames of reference initiate an unconscious search, involving unconscious mental processes, for new frames of reference and solutions to problems. The initiation and activation of these unconscious processes embody a creative period in which clients can go through a needed reorganization of their experience. In their model, Erickson and Rossi identify a number of "indirect forms of suggestion," specific verbal and nonverbal communication forms, that presumably activate unconscious search processes. The social worker would use these forms of verbal and nonverbal communication to initiate clients' unconscious search processes in an effort to stimulate them to make needed changes and find solutions to their problems. The indirect forms of suggestion have been discussed in detail by Erickson and Rossi (1989).

Activation of Unconscious Processes and Hypnotic Response

The natural outcome of the unconscious search processes initiated by the fixation of attention, the disruption of normal frames of reference, and the use of the indirect forms of suggestion are the hypnotic responses experienced by the client. In the utilization model, the hypnotic response occurs automatically and autonomously, without the client's conscious, voluntary involvement. When this response occurs, a client may express surprise at what has happened. Erickson and Rossi (1979) note that such surprise can be taken as an indication of the genuine, autonomous nature of the response.

RATIFICATION OF THERAPEUTIC CHANGE

The third stage of Erickson and Rossi's utilization model of hypnotherapy involves the ratification of therapeutic change. In this stage, the social worker will help clients recognize and acknowledge changes they have experienced during trance. Erickson and Rossi (1979) see this stage of the process as being both the most subtle and most important. The social worker helps facilitate client recognition of trance experiences after trance has occurred. This is done so that the client's old negative frames of reference and attitudes do not function to disrupt and prohibit the experience of therapeutic responses resulting from the unconscious search processes that were activated during trance.

An Illustrative Example

Suppose that you have a client who is suffering from pain associated with some medical condition that has not responded to medication, and he or she is seeking your help with the pain. You also know that your client has been trained in progressive relaxation and has developed considerable skill in self-relaxation through this method. This skill can be used as a vehicle for trance induction.

People have numerous common everyday experiences that can be tapped for pain control. One is the common experience of selectively paying attention to parts of our body. Simply put, we tune out parts of our body all the time. For example, until you read the next couple of lines you will most probably be unaware of the feeling of your shoes on your feet (unless maybe you are reading this while barefoot). As soon as you read the previous sentence you became aware of the feeling of your shoes on your feet, but you will soon forget to notice that physical sensation. Another experience most people have had is the sensation of numbness in a hand, or an arm, that results from lying on it the wrong way. A similar sensation most of us have had is the feeling of numbness that results from a numbing shot during a visit to the dentist. Erickson and Rossi maintain that these experiences are "learnings" that are unconsciously remembered and can be accessed through therapeutic trance and used for pain relief. A session of therapeutic trance induction aimed at pain relief might go something as follows. In the following narrative, **bold** words signify forms of indirect suggestion discussed by Erickson and Rossi (1979, 1989). The *italic* words are those spoken with an altered tone of voice and slightly slower cadence than the nonitalicized words are spoken.

First you would focus your client's attention inward by having him or her use skills of self-relaxation. You would talk to your client in a soft voice tone, suggesting that he focus all his attention on the various sensations of relaxation.

Now continue to focus on those feelings of relaxation, without knowing how much more comfortable you can become. And as you continue to breathe in [spoken as client begins to breathe in] . . . and out [spoken as client begins to exhale] . . . continue to focus on the *relaxation* . . . while your unconscious mind listens . . . there is no need for you to listen consciously . . . your unconscious mind can listen carefully as you focus all your attention on the relaxation and more and more comfortable with each breath you take. And certain thoughts may come in to your mind . . . as your unconscious mind focuses on the many experiences you have had, be more and more comfortable as you breathe in [spoken as client begins to breathe in] . . . and out [spoken as client begins to exhale].

You would continue in this manner until you notice that your client is breathing in a slow, diaphragmatic manner, is completely still, is nonresponsive to external stimuli (such as a lack of a startle response), shows a retarded swallow response, and his facial features take on a smooth and relaxed appearance. When you note these indicators of trance (see Erickson & Rossi, 1979), you might then continue.

And as you continue to breathe in [spoken as client begins to breathe in] . . . and out [spoken as client begins to exhale] . . . your unconscious mind can comfortably remember how easy it is to forget . . . people have the experience of losing awareness of parts of their body. I had a friend once who lived in an apartment with a noisy air conditioner. The air conditioner made a loud noise whenever it was on . . . and my friend thought that he would never be able to rest comfortably with the air conditioner making that awful sound. After living in the apartment for a week . . . he realized one day that he had not heard the sound the whole day . . . even though the air conditioner had been on. He had gotten used to the sound and had tuned it out. He had forgotten to pay attention to it. We all have the ability to tune in and tune out. A person can tune out things. People forget to be aware of the feeling of their shoes on their feet every day. You can tune in only comfortable feelings . . . and tune everything else out . . . just like my friend tuned out the obnoxious sound of the air conditioner . . . you can tune out anything obnoxious thing. And your unconscious can remember how you can forget to be aware of . . . as you continue to relax . . . and without knowing it . . . your unconscious can remember the feeling of numbness that you felt at the dentist's office . . .

or that you can feel when your arm goes to sleep. And as soon as your unconscious knows that you will tune in . . . and tune out . . . each and every day . . . in such a way . . . that you feel only the fullness of comfort each and every day . . . in a manner fully meeting your needs as a person . . . then your unconscious mind can have you awaken spontaneously . . . so you can continue as you are . . . breathing in [spoken as client begins to breathe in] . . . and out [spoken as client begins to exhale] . . . with those awarenesses . . . continuing to relaxation even deeper.

You would continue with the relaxation suggestions until your client spontaneously awakens. The spontaneous awakening can be interpreted as a hypnotic response to the suggestion underscored, what Erickson and Rossi (1979) refer to as an implied directive. This is a signal that the client's unconscious mind has found a way for him or her to "feel only the fullness of comfort each and every day," which by implication means that the client will not experience pain as in the past. You would then help your client recognize the experiences of trance, such as feelings of comfort, the reorienting response after the client awakens, spontaneous experiences such as having lost the sound of your voice during the trance, and the spontaneous amnesia for some or all of trance events. Erickson and Rossi (1979) give examples and illustrations of this process of ratification of trance and change.

CONCLUSION

The use of hypnosis is a complex procedure, one that requires appropriate training and experience. The material in this short chapter does not come anywhere close to adequately covering this intervention process, though it does give a brief overview and a brief illustration of the process. I urge interested readers to go to the references cited for further information. You might also want to contact the Milton H. Erickson Foundation, or the American Society of Clinical Hypnosis for further information on training in hypnosis.

You should also consult the research literature on the types of problems that hypnosis should (and should not) be used for. Nugent (1996) briefly goes over some of this literature. Two research reviews that you might start with are those by Bowers and LeBaron (1986) and Wodden and Anderton (1982). The reader might also want to look

at some of the clinical research I have done on Ericksonian hypnotherapy (Nugent, 1990, 1993).

One of the areas with the most evidence supporting the effectiveness of hypnosis as an intervention is in pain management. Numerous studies suggest that hypnosis can help reduce both acute and chronic pain (Askay, Patterson, Jensen, & Sharer, 2007; Hammond, 2007; King, Nash, Spiegel, & Jobson, 2001; Patterson, 2004). A recent systematic review (Richardson, Smith, McCall, & Pilkington, 2006) led to the conclusion that hypnosis is effective for pain management and control. Furthermore, a recent meta-analysis suggested that hypnosis may lead to medium to large effect sizes when used for pain management (Montgomery, DuHamel, & Redd, 2000). Social workers in clinical and medical settings may want to investigate how hypnosis might be used with their clients, children and adult, who are experiencing acute or chronic pain or are preparing to undergo painful medical procedures.

Some have expressed concerns that hypnosis might be used to manipulate or harm clients—for example, by forcing them to engage in criminal behavior. Research has suggested that this cannot happen. Erickson himself explicitly tested this possibility and found that people could not be hypnotized into doing things that they did not want to or that were against their moral and ethical codes (Erickson, 1939; see also Orne, 1962; Coe, Kobayashi, & Howard, 1973). There have also been concerns expressed that hypnosis may have harmful side effects. The one area in which there is evidence that clients might be harmed from hypnotic interventions is in its use as an aid to memory retrieval (see, for example, Kihlstrom & Barnhardt, 1993; Smith, 1983). Before any social worker attempts to use hypnosis as an intervention, he or she should, first of all, be adequately trained and familiar with the research literature on the types of problems for which hypnosis can be effective, those for which it is ineffective, and those for which it might actually bring about harm. These two conditions need to be met for the ethical use of hypnosis as an intervention method.

WEB SITES

American Society of Clinical Hypnosis. http://www.asch.net.
Milton H. Erickson Foundation. http://www.erickson-foundation.org.

Note

1. I have just a few pages to describe the complex intervention approach that is hypnosis. This does not allow me to cover this treatment method in anywhere near the detail the subject requires. The reader may want to supplement the material in this chapter by reading Nugent (1996). There, I give numerous other references that the interested reader can use to gain a deeper understanding of hypnosis.

References

Askay, S., Patterson, D., Jensen, M., & Sharer, S. (2007). A randomized controlled trial of hypnosis for burn wound care. *Rehabilitation Psychology, 52*(3), 247–253.

Bowers, K., & LeBaron, S. (1986). Hypnosis and hypnotizability: Implications for clinical intervention. *Hospital and Community Psychiatry, 37,* 457–467.

Coe, W. (1980). Expectations, hypnosis, and suggestion in behavior change. In F. Kanfer & A. Goldstein (Eds.), *Helping people change: A textbook of methods* (pp. 423–469). New York: Pergamon Press.

Coe, W., Kobayashi, K., & Howard, M. (1973). Experimental and ethical problems in evaluating the influence of hypnosis in antisocial conduct. *Journal of Abnormal Psychology, 82,* 476–482.

Erickson, M. (1939). An experimental investigation of the possible antisocial use of hypnosis. *Psychiatry, 2,* 391–414.

Erickson, M. (1959). Further clinical techniques of hypnosis: Utilization techniques. *American Journal of Clinical Hypnosis, 2,* 3–21.

Erickson, M., & Rossi, E. (1979). *Hypnotherapy: An exploratory casebook.* New York: Irvington.

Erickson, M., & Rossi, E. (1981). *Experiencing hypnosis: Therapeutic approaches to altered states.* New York: Irvington.

Erickson, M., & Rossi, E. (1989). The indirect forms of suggestion. In E. Rossi (Ed.), *The nature of hypnosis and suggestion: The collected papers of Milton H. Erickson on hypnosis* (vol. 1, pp. 452–477). New York: Irvington.

Fischer, J. (1978). *Effective casework practice: An eclectic approach.* New York: McGraw-Hill.

Fromm, E. (1979). The nature of hypnosis and other altered states of consciousness: An ego-psychological theory. In E. Fromm & R. Shor (Eds.), *Hypnosis: Developments in research and new perspectives,* 2nd ed. (pp. 81–104). New York: Aldine.

Hammond, C. (2007). Review of the efficacy of clinical hypnosis with headaches and migraines. *Journal of Clinical and Experimental Hypnosis, 55*(2), 207–219.

Hepworth, D., Rooney, R., & Larsen, J. (1996). *Direct social work practice: Theory and skills,* 5th ed. Belmont, CA: Wadsworth.

Kihlstrom, J., & Barnhardt, T. (1993). The self-regulation of memory: For better and for worse, with and without hypnosis. In D. Wegnerand & J. Pennebaker (Eds.), *Handbook of mental control* (pp. 88–125). Englewood Cliffs, NJ: Prentice Hall.

King, B., Nash, M., Spiegel, D., & Jobson, K. (2001). Hypnosis as an intervention in pain management. *International Journal of Psychiatry in Clinical Practice, 5*(2), 97–101.

Montgomery, G., DuHamel, K., & Redd, W. (2000). A meta-analysis of hypnotically induced analgesia: How effective is hypnosis? *International Journal of Clinical and Experimental Hypnosis, 48*(2), 138–153.

Nugent, W. (1990). An experimental and qualitative evaluation of an Ericksonian hypnotic intervention for family relationship problems. *Ericksonian Monographs, 7,* 51–68.

Nugent, W. (1993). A series of single case design clinical evaluations of an Ericksonian hypnotic intervention used with clinical anxiety. *Journal of Social Service Research, 17,* 41–69.

Nugent, W. (1996). The use of hypnosis in social work practice. In F. J. Turner (Ed.), *Social work treatment: Interlocking theoretical approaches,* 4th ed. New York: Free Press.

Orne, M. T. (1962). Anti-social behavior and hypnosis. In G. H. Estabrooks (Ed.), *Hypnosis: Current problems.* New York: Harper & Row.

Patterson, D. (2004). Treating pain with hypnosis. *Current Directions in Psychological Science, 13*(6), 252–255.

Richardson, J., Smith, J., McCall, G., & Pilkington, K. (2006). Hypnosis for procedure related pain and distress in pediatric cancer patients: A systematic review of effectiveness and methodology related to hypnotic interventions. *Journal of Pain and Symptom Management, 31*(1), 70–84.

Smith, M. (1983). Hypnotic memory enhancement of witnesses: Does it work? *Psychological Bulletin, 94,* 387–407.

Wodden, T., & Anderton, C. (1982). The clinical use of hypnosis. *Psychological Bulletin, 91,* 215–243.

Kundalini Yoga Meditation Techniques for the Treatment of Obsessive-Compulsive and OC Spectrum Disorders

David S. Shannahoff-Khalsa

Kundalini yoga (KY) meditation techniques have been tested for treating obsessive-compulsive disorder (OCD) in two clinical trials. An 11-part protocol has been tested in an uncontrolled trial and also later compared to a different meditation protocol using a randomized matched-groups trial design. In addition to the description of the long-term group benefits, the immediate benefits are presented here in a patient's own words for a single case history of a young woman with OCD, body dysmorphic disorder (BDD), and social anxiety disorder. This multipart protocol is described in complete detail and includes a meditation technique specific for OCD and other techniques specific for anxiety, turning negative thoughts into positive thoughts, meeting mental challenges, managing fears, and anger.

OCD is one of the most disabling of the anxiety disorders and is likened to a "waking nightmare" (Rapoport, 1990). OCD has a lifelong prognosis and is the fourth most common psychiatric disorder following phobias, substance abuse, and the major depressive disorders; it is twice as common as schizophrenia and panic disorder, and it often begins during childhood or adolescence with a lifetime prevalence rate of 2.5 to 5.0 percent (Rasmussen & Eisen, 1990). OCD is among the top ten causes of disability (Murray & Lopez, 1996) and has proven to be refractory to traditional psychodynamic psychotherapy or psychoanalysis (Koran, Hanna, Hollander, Nestadt, & Simpson, 2007). This waking nightmare is commonly considered to be one of the most recalcitrant psychiatric disorders.

Conventional treatment modalities (psychopharmacologic and cognitive-behavioral therapy [CBT] in the form of exposure and response prevention) lack as remedies for quick relief and usu-ally require weeks or months to obtain any symptomatic relief if they can be tolerated, and if they benefit the patient. Improvement with medication requires continuous use, and the majority of patients experience unpleasant drug-induced side effects. Some patients also show regression after an initial success. Four multicenter placebo-controlled trials of clomipramine, fluoxetine, fluvoxamine, and sertraline found Yale-Brown Obsessive Compulsive Scale (Y-BOCS) improvements of 39 percent, 27 percent, 20 percent, and 26 percent for the best dose comparisons, respectively (Greist, Jefferson, Kobak, Katzelnick, & Serlin, 1995). In addition, as many as 40–60 percent of OCD patients remain clinically unchanged after an adequate trial of medication (McDougle, Goodman, Leckman, & Price, 1993). A recent meta-analysis to compare exposure and response prevention to the selective serotonin reuptake inhibitors concluded that behavior therapy "was comparable to the serotonin reuptake inhibitors" (Kobak, Greist, Jefferson, Katzelnick, & Henk, 1998).

This chapter describes the use of an 11-part OCD-specific KY meditation protocol as an effective treatment for rapid relief and as a therapy for a long-lasting reduction or elimination of symptoms. This protocol was previously published in complete detail (Shannahoff-Khalsa, 1997, 2003, 2006). Two year-long trials have tested the efficacy of this protocol. The first trial was an open, uncontrolled pilot (Shannahoff-Khalsa & Beckett, 1996), and the second was a randomized controlled trial (Shannahoff-Khalsa, Ray, Levine, Gallen, Schwartz, & Sidorowich, 1999). The first trial was conducted in an attempt to test a technique that was claimed by yogis to be specific for the treatment of OCD (Shannahoff-Khalsa, 1991). The second trial was conducted to include a group employing two very different meditation techniques for approximately equal time to the KY protocol, in part to control for the expectations of meditation per se and for the effects of personal attention by a therapist in a group setting.

THE PILOT STUDY: AN OPEN UNCONTROLLED TRIAL

Five of eight patients completed a 12-month trial, and the group showed a mean Y-BOCS improvement of 55.6 percent going from a total mean score of 19.8 at baseline to 8.8 at 12 months. The Symptom Checklist-90-Revised Obsessive Compulsive scale (SCL-90-R OC) and Global Severity scale (SCL-90-R GSI) showed mean improvements of 53.3 percent and 52.7 percent, respectively, for the five completers. These five were all previously stabilized with fluoxetine (20–40 mg) for more than 3 months prior to the start of the study. Of the five, three were completely free of medication for at least 5 months prior to the end of the trial, and the other two were reduced by 50 percent. A year later, four of the five subjects had been off medication for periods between 9 and 19 months with lasting improvements. The three dropouts at the 3-month mark were all unmedicated, and their Y-BOCS totals went from a mean of 23.3 to 19.6. One dropped out due to late-stage pregnancy, another to fibromyalgia, and the third to work-related scheduling commitments.

A RANDOMIZED BLINDED CONTROLLED MATCHED TRIAL

Two groups were matched for sex, age, Y-BOCS severity, medication status and were blinded to the comparison protocol. Patients were told that two different meditation protocols would be compared and the trial would run 12 months unless one protocol proved to be more efficacious, and then groups would merge and the new patients would get 12 months with the more efficacious protocol (Shannahoff-Khalsa et al., 1999). At baseline, group 1 (Y-BOCS = 22.75) consisted of 11 adults and 1 adolescent, and group 2 (Y-BOCS = 22.80) consisted of 10 adults. Group 1 employed the KY meditation protocol, and group 2 employed the relaxation response (Benson, 1975) plus the mindfulness meditation technique (Kabat-Zinn,

1990), each for 30 minutes to compare time with the KY protocol. Six psychological rating scales were employed at baseline and 3-month time points: Y-BOCS, SCL-90-R OC and SCL-90-R GSI, Profile of Mood States (POMS, total mood disorder score), Perceived Stress Scale (PSS), and Purpose-in-Life test (PIL).

Seven adults in each group completed 3 months of therapy. Group 1 demonstrated greater and statistically significant improvements on the Y-BOCS, SCL-90-R OC and GSI, and POMS and nonsignificant but greater improvements on the PSS and PIL scales. An intent-to-treat analysis (Y-BOCS) for the baseline and 3-month tests showed that only group 1 improved. Within-group statistics showed that group 1 significantly improved on all six scales, but group 2 had no improvements. At 3 months, group 1 improved 38.4 percent with a Y-BOCS score of 24.6 going to 15.1 (change score of 9.4), and group 2 went from 20.6 to 17.7 (change score of 2.9), a 13.9 percent improvement. For those initially in group 2 who entered KY treatment, their Y-BOCS scores improved 44 percent for their first 3 months of KY therapy. Both groups were merged for an additional year using the KY protocol. When comparing the 0-month baseline (N = 11) for all of those who completed 15 months (N = 11), the improvements were 70.1 percent (Y-BOCS), 58.8 percent (SCL-90-R OC), 60.6 percent (SCL-90-R GSI), 70.1 percent (POMS), 48.3 percent (PSS), and 19.7 percent (PIL), and all changes were statistically significant at $p \leq 0.003$ (analysis of variance). The 0-month baseline Y-BOCS score (N = 11) was 22.1, and the final score at 15 months was 6.6 (N = 11). For these 11 patients, the Y-BOCS totals included three 0 scores, one 1, two 5s, one 6, and an 11, 14, 15, and 16. Six of the 12 medicated patients to enter completed the study. Three of these six were free of medication for a minimum of 6 months prior to study end. The others reduced. The 70 percent mean group Y-BOCS improvement is an unusually high percentage rate for clinical change when compared to other treatment modalities. Seven of these 11 patients have achieved what may be described as a subclinical state for the disorder, and the three 0 scores and one 1 score indicates a state of remission. In this trial, five of the patients started therapy with trichotillomania, and their progress with this OC spectrum disorder seemed to improve in a parallel fashion to their other symptoms. In fact, it appears that all symptoms, regardless of subgroupings, seem to improve at an equal rate over time.

THE EFFECTS OF BRIEF TREATMENT

The following quote is a personal commentary about the immediate effects of treatment by a female (age 20) after using this KY protocol. Her OCD symptoms began at age 10, and her BDD and social anxiety started at age 17. Her OCD symptoms included only obsessions—the fear of harming others. She was convinced that if she called a relative or friend on their cell phones, she would cause a car accident or something horrific. The fear she felt was paralyzing. Her most prevalent OCD fear came in the form of not saying the correct thing in any situation, something that left her "constantly fearful and in check of her own thoughts and words." Her BDD involved rituals—looking in a mirror, sometimes for several hours a day. She had the fear that her right eye and right side of her face were distorted. Prior to KY therapy, she attempted insight-oriented psychotherapy with several therapists for about 1 year. After seeing me the first time and not following through with KY, she again saw a therapist while away at her university. Prior to seeing me the second time, she started using fluoxetine for about 6 weeks, and the side effects became too severe to tolerate. She was switched to paroxetine for 3 weeks, and again the side effects were too severe. In my experience, her short-term response to KY as described next is typical.

I first began my work with David Shannahoff-Khalsa and the KY practice during spring break of the year 2001. The break was taken from the university I was currently attending, where I am now still enrolled as an undergraduate student. I consulted David for various reasons; the main (and most difficult) ones being anxiety (in general social situations), stress (in the competitive nature of the academics at college), and BDD. I had also been previously diagnosed 3 years before with OCD and depression, both of which I was still struggling with. The very first session that I had with David altered my experience of anxiety, so much that the rushing of thoughts that seemed so constantly harrowing before had dissipated to a state of calm and relaxation. In addition to this, the BDD I was experiencing totally disappeared for the remainder of the day. And, finally, the OCD disappeared completely, and the results again lasted for the remainder of the day. Despite the immediate advantages, though, within a week, vacation had ended and I returned to my dorm room at college, complete with roommate, and my practice suffered. I rarely found the opportunity to continue with what David had taught me, and the anxiety became a major problem in my life again. The BDD flourished, consuming nearly 2 hours per day in front of the

mirror. This was extremely difficult to manage, particularly in light of the fact that my homework often took a back seat to my obsessions. After this period, and another painful year following that (this time with four other roommates, and no practice of KY), I finally decided in the summer of 2002 to return to David, this time with the knowledge and certainty that I would dedicate myself to improving my state of mind. Before seeing David at this time, my life had completely fallen apart. At my university, I had decided to consult a psychologist through a program at the university, and she had suggested that I try medication. Following that advice, I consulted a psychiatrist who prescribed fluoxetine for me at 20 mg a day. Even under the influence of the drug for many weeks, I was so completely anxious and depressed simultaneously, that I began to harm myself, by self-mutilating my arm. First I started with the ends of cigarettes, and then, with a razor, cutting so deep on two places on my arm that they required stitches. I also had a severely diminished interest in eating to the point that I would actually avoid two meals per day. I started losing weight, and my mother began to question whether I was also becoming anorexic. It was at this point that my doctor was suggesting hospitalization to my parents that I went back to see David. On the first meeting, everything became manageable again. At this time, I also gave up use of the medication. The yoga put me in a state of balance and gave me peace of mind immediately. I was able to quit cigarettes, and discontinue the self-mutilation as I worked at focusing on my breath and the exercises. I also started to have a normal appetite again. This all happened within a week of meeting with David and continuing the practice. The most beneficial aspect of the experience, however, was the immediate release from anxiety, depression, and OCD that I received upon the first meeting with him again. The continuation of the practice led to a greater state of peace and general strength that has continued up to this day.

By the time she wrote this commentary, she had seen me a total of four times during the month of August. In the previous year, I saw her twice in a 1-week period during her spring break. The comments of this woman for brief treatment are characteristic of almost all those who employ this protocol. The more intense the sessions, the more the immediate benefit to the patient. Some describe the feelings as getting "high" or "intoxicating." Though initially patients may not believe that KY is going to be helpful, their unique positive short-term effects give them the experience to believe that this therapy can either significantly reduce or completely eliminate their obsessions and compulsions for the long run if they develop the self-discipline. Experience shows that different patients require different amounts of practice to gain long-term benefits. However, those that develop a daily or near-daily practice always achieve the most significant benefits.

KUNDALINI YOGA MEDITATION TECHNIQUES

All of the techniques in this protocol can be performed while sitting in a chair. These techniques are from KY as taught by Yogi Bhajan. The protocol for OCD includes eight primary techniques (1–8) to be used on a daily basis and three additional techniques (9–11) to be used at personal discretion. The entire protocol is available on video (see the Internet Yogi).

1. To Induce a Meditative State, "Tuning In"

Sit with a straight spine and with the feet flat on the floor if sitting in a chair. Put the hands together at the chest in prayer pose—the palms are pressed together with 10–15 pounds of pressure between them. The area where the sides of the thumbs touch rests on the sternum with the thumbs pointing up (along the sternum), and the fingers are together and point up and out at a 60-degree angle to the ground. The eyes are closed and focused at the "third eye" (imagine a sun rising on the horizon or the equivalent of the point between the eyebrows at the origin of the nose). A mantra is chanted out loud in a one-and-a-half-breath cycle. Inhale first through the nose and chant "Ong Namo" with an equal emphasis on the *Ong* and the *Namo*. Then immediately follow with a half-breath inhalation through the mouth and chant "Guru Dev Namo" with approximately equal emphasis on each word. The practitioner should focus on the experience of the vibrations that these sounds create on the upper palate and throughout the cranium, while letting the mind be carried by the sound into a new and pleasant mental space. This should be repeated a minimum of three times and was employed in therapy for about 10–12 times. This technique helps create a meditative state of mind and is an essential precursor to the other techniques.

2. Spine Flexing for Vitality

This technique can be practiced either while sitting in a chair or on the floor in a cross-legged position. If you are in a chair, hold the knees with both hands for support and leverage. If you are sitting cross-legged, grasp the ankles in front with both hands. Begin by pulling the chest up and forward, inhaling deeply at the same time. Then exhale as you relax the spine down into a slouching position. Keep the head up straight without allowing it to move much with the flexing action of the spine. This will help prevent a whip action of the cervical vertebrae. All breathing should only be through the nose for both the inhale and exhale. The eyes are closed as if you were looking at a central point on the horizon, the third eye, otherwise described as the notch region on the nose exactly midway between the eyes. The mental focus is kept on the sound of the breath while listening to the fluid movement of the inhalation and exhalation. Begin the technique slowly while loosening up the spine. Eventually, a very rapid movement can be achieved with practice, reaching a rate of one to two times per second for the entire movement. A few minutes are sufficient in the beginning. Later, there is no time limit. Food should be avoided just prior to this exercise. If an unpleasant feeling of light-headedness develops, stop momentarily and then continue. Be careful and flex the spine slowly in the beginning. Relax for 1–2 minutes when finished.

3. Shoulder Shrugs for Vitality

While keeping the spine straight, rest the hands on the knees if sitting in a cross-legged position or with hands on the thighs if on a chair. Inhale and raise the shoulders up toward the ears, then exhale, letting them down. All breathing is through the nose only. Eyes should be kept closed and focused at the third eye. Mentally listen to the sound of the inhalation and exhalation. Continue this action rapidly, building to three times per second for a maximum time of 2 minutes. This technique should not be practiced by individuals who have ADHD.

4. Meditation Technique for Insanity: Reducing Anxiety, Stress, and Mental Tension

Sit and maintain a straight spine. Relax the arms and the hands in the lap. Focus the eyes on the tip of the nose. You cannot see the end, just the sides, which appear blurred while focusing on the tip. Open the mouth as wide as possible, slightly stressing the temporal-mandibular joint; touch the tongue tip to the upper palate where it is hard and smooth in the center. Breathe continuously through the nose only, while making the respiration slow and deep. Let the mental focus be on the sound of the breath; listen to the sound of the inhale and exhale. Maintain this pattern for at least 3–5 minutes with a maximum of 8 minutes on the first trial. With practice, it can be built up to 31 minutes maximum. This technique was originally taught as a meditation for insanity and to curb a restless mind, bringing stillness and mental quietude.

5. Technique for Reducing Anxiety, Stress, and Mental Tension

Sit and maintain a straight spine. The hands are in front of the chest at heart level. The left hand is 2 inches from the chest and the right is about 2 inches behind the left (4 inches from the chest), the left fingers point to the right. The right palm faces the back of the left hand with fingers pointing to the left. The thumbs of both hands point up straight but are not pulled back tightly. The thumbs are in a relaxed upward posture. The eyes are open and focused on the tip of the nose. The breathing pattern is through the nose only. Inhale, then keep the breath in as long as possible, then exhale and keep the breath out as long as possible without creating undue discomfort at any stage. When finished, inhale, maintaining the eye and hand posture and then tense every muscle in the body for about 10 seconds, exhale, and repeat twice. Build the capacity for this technique to a maximum time of 15 minutes. Avoid this exercise if you have high blood pressure or are pregnant. This technique was taught for relaxing the mind due to emotional stress and mental tension, and the following technique was taught to be a complement to its practice.

6. Technique for Reducing Anxiety, Stress, and Mental Tension

Sit as in exercise 5. Eyes are open and focused on the tip of the nose during the entire exercise. Attempt to pull the nose down toward the upper lip by actually pulling the upper lip down over the upper front teeth, using the muscles of the upper lip. The mouth is left open during this exercise with the constant tension on the upper lip. There are three steps to this exercise. Step one: start with the hands and arms up at 45–60 degrees, inhale deeply, tightly clench the fists, and pull them down toward the abdomen. Step two: keep the breath in, eyes focused, and lip pulled and, maintaining tension in the fists, bring the shoulders up toward the ears, tensing the shoulders as they go up. Step three: exhale and relax (but keep the lip pulled down and the eyes at the tip of nose). Repeat the entire exercise six times. Avoid this exercise if you have high blood pressure or are pregnant. This short exercise is claimed to be so effective that it if is done correctly it can relieve the most tense person.

7. Technique for Managing Fears

Sit with a straight spine. Close the eyes. Place the left hand with the four fingertips and thumb grouped and pressed very lightly into the navel point. Place the right hand with the four fingers pointing left above the third eye point (on the forehead, just above the root of the nose) as if feeling your temperature. Play the tape of *Chattra Chakra Varti* (Ancient Healing Ways, Espanola, New Mexico) for 3 minutes while assessing your fears and consciously relating to the mental experience of your fears. No other music will work with this technique, which is claimed to help manage acute states of fear or help eliminate fearful images and negative emotions that have developed due to fearful experiences. The effect is that the negative emotions related to specific events (fears) are replaced with positive emotions, thereby slowly creating a new and different mental association with the original stimulus. This technique is analogous to the practice of exposure and response prevention.

8. Technique for OC Disorders (OCDB)

Sit with a straight spine in a comfortable position, either with the legs crossed while sitting on the floor or in a straight back chair with both feet flat on the floor. Close the eyes. Use the right thumb tip to block the end of the right nostril, with the other fingers point up straight. Allow the arm to relax (the elbow should not be sticking up and out to the side, creating unnecessary tension). A secure plug can also be used for the right nostril. Inhale very slowly and deeply through the left nostril, hold in long, exhale out slowly and completely through the same nostril only (left), hold out long. The mental focus should be on the sound of the breath. Continue this pattern with a maximum time of 31 minutes for each sitting. Initially, begin with a comfortable rate and time, but where the effort presents a fair challenge for each phase of the breath. Holding the breath in or out long varies from person to person. The ideal time per complete breath cycle is 1 minute, where each section of the cycle lasts exactly 15 seconds. This rate of respiration can be achieved within 5–6 months for the full 31 minutes with daily or near-daily discipline. Yogic experiments (Yogi Bhajan, personal communication) claim that 90 days of 31 minutes per day using the perfected rate of one breath/minute with the four 15 seconds/phase will completely eliminate all OC disorders.

9. Meeting Mental Challenges: The "Victory Breath"

This technique can be used at any time. It does not require the practitioner to be sitting. It can be employed while driving a car, while in a conversation, or while taking a test, and so on. Tuning in using technique 1 is not required. The eyes can be open or closed depending on the situation. Take a deep breath through the nose and hold this breath over 3–4 seconds, and during the hold phase only mentally hear the three separate sounds of "vic" "tor" "y," then exhale. Mentally creating the three sounds should take 3–4 seconds, not longer and not less. Hear the sounds separately and do not run them together, but only use 3–4 seconds. The entire time of each repetition should be about 8–10 seconds. It can be employed multiple times until the patient achieves the desired relief. When employed in the therapy sessions, it was usually practiced for 3–5 minutes with the eyes closed and while sitting with a straight spine to maximize the effects. This technique is very helpful as a thought-stopping technique for a patient on the go. There is no time limit to its practice. It can be used to help reduce obsessive thoughts and resist the urge to perform compulsive rituals. Most patients found this to be a very useful technique and great tool for an active day. It can be used at any time a person feels mentally challenged.

10. Chant to Turn Negative Thoughts into Positive Thoughts

This technique should be employed while sitting with a straight spine and with the eyes closed in a peaceful environment. The mantra "Ek Ong Kar Sat Gurprasad Sat Gurprasad Ek Ong Kar" is repeated a minimum of five times and can be practiced from 5 to 11 minutes while chanting it through rapidly with up to five repetitions per breath. Even-

tually, one no longer thinks about the order of the sounds, they come automatically. The mental focus should be on the vibration created against the upper palate and throughout the cranium. If performed correctly, a very peaceful, bright, elevated, and "healed" state of mind is achieved, especially when the practitioner reaches the 11-minute time with five repetitions per breath.

11. Technique for Anger

Sit with a straight spine and close the eyes. Simply chant out loud, "Jeeo, Jeeo, Jeeo, Jeeo" continuously and rapidly for 11 minutes without stopping (pronounced like the names for the letters G and O). During continuous chanting you do not stop to take long breaths, but continue with just enough short breaths to keep the sound going. Eleven minutes is the minimum and maximum time for this technique. This technique is useful even for a red-hot angry mind, and the effects can last up to 3 days, depending on the severity of the anger. Practicing twice a day or more is acceptable for the most severe states.

COMMENTARY ON THE PRACTICE OF TECHNIQUES

The therapeutic focus here should be on perfecting the OCDB using the four 15-second phases per min for the full 31 minutes for 90 consecutive days to eliminate all OC symptoms. However, the obvious question is, "Does the patient have to achieve the full 90 days of perfection or be able to breathe at one breath per minute to become completely free of OCD symptoms?" The answer is no. However, all of those who did become free of all OCD symptoms had a daily or near daily practice for much of the trial. Most patients learned to do the OCDB for 31 minutes, and this can usually be achieved within 3–6 months when only meeting once a week for therapy, when some daily practice is included. However, this does not mean that all patients perfected the OCDB using the one breath per minute rate in 3–6 months. In the second trial, only one patient perfected the OCDB at one breath per minute, and several others came very close to perfection. After the age of 50, the OCDB becomes more difficult, due to an aging nervous system. However, one woman in the second trial was 62 years of age at entry with a baseline Y-BOCS total score of 19 (hoarding and arranging obsessions and rituals). Within

2 weeks she was practicing the whole routine on a near-daily basis and achieved a 0 total score at 6 months, even though she was not able to do the OCDB at one breath per minute. She could only perform the four separate phases at 5 seconds per phase. Patients differ in their symptom severity, general health, vitality, flexibility, and their decision to commit to practice, all of which affect success rates. These techniques can be taught at any age, regardless of medication status. Discipline plays a key role in outcomes. Many patients work hard enough to become completely free of symptoms. However, a significant percentage of patients only work hard enough to reduce their symptoms to a level they can easily tolerate. A patient can learn on his or her first effort to quickly eliminate symptoms that may disappear for several hours. At this point, the patient can develop new hope and lead a much less stressful life. They no longer feel as trapped and hopeless. They know they have a way out of their nightmare. It is also true that most patients will find out how long they can go without practicing. Different multipart disorder-specific KY protocols have also been published for acute stress disorder; major depressive disorder; bipolar disorders; addictive, impulse control, and eating disorders; chronic fatigue syndrome; ADHD and comorbid disorders; and PTSD (Shannahoff-Khalsa, 2006).

WEB SITES

Ancient Healing Ways—Natural, Organic and Spiritual Products. http://www.a-healing.com.
International Kundalini Yoga Teachers Association. http://www.kundaliniyoga.com.
Internet Yogi. http://www.theinternetyogi.com.
Spirit Voyage Music. http://www.spiritvoyage.com.
White Tantric Yoga and Meditation. http://www.whitetantricyoga.com.

Acknowledgment

The Baumgartel-DeBeer Family Fund supported the preparation of this chapter.

References

Benson, H. (1975). *The relaxation response.* New York: Morrow.
Greist, J. H., Jefferson, J. W., Kobak, K. A., Katzelnick, D. J., & Serlin, R. C. (1995). Efficacy and tolerability of serotonin transport inhibitors in obsessive-compulsive disorder. A meta-analysis. *Archives of General Psychiatry, 52*(1), 53–60.
Kabat-Zinn, J. (1990). *Full catastrophe living: Using the wisdom of your body and mind to face stress, pain, and illness.* New York: Delacorte.
Kobak, K. A., Greist, J. H., Jefferson, J. W., Katzelnick, D. J., & Henk, H. J. (1998). Behavioral versus pharmacological treatments of obsessive compulsive disorder: A meta-analysis. *Psychopharmacology (Berlin), 136*(3), 205–216.
Koran, L. M., Hanna, G. L., Hollander, E., Nestadt, G., & Simpson, H. B. (2007). Practice guideline for the treatment of patients with obsessive-compulsive disorder. *American Journal of Psychiatry, 164* (7 suppl), 5–53.
McDougle, C. J., Goodman, W. K., Leckman, J. F., & Price, L. H. (1993). The psychopharmacology of obsessive compulsive disorder. Implications for treatment and pathogenesis. *Psychiatric Clinics of North America, 16*(4), 749–766.
Murray, C. J. L., & Lopez, A. D. (1996). *The global burden of disease: A comprehensive assessment of mortality and disability.* Cambridge MA.: Harvard University Press.
Rapoport, J. L. (1990). The waking nightmare: An overview of obsessive compulsive disorder. *Journal of Clinical Psychiatry, 51*(suppl), 25–28.
Rasmussen, S., & Eisen, J. (1990). *Epidemiology and clinical features of obsessive compulsive disorder.* St. Louis, MO: Mosby.
Shannahoff-Khalsa, D. S. (1991). *Stress technology medicine, a new paradigm for stress and considerations for self-regulation.* New York: Marcel Dekker.
Shannahoff-Khalsa, D. S. (1997). Yogic techniques are effective in the treatment of obsessive compulsive disorders. In E. Hollander & D. Stein (Eds.), *Obsessive-compulsive disorders: Diagnosis, etiology, and treatment* (pp. 283–329). New York: Marcel Dekker.
Shannahoff-Khalsa, D. S. (2003). Kundalini yoga meditation techniques in the treatment of obsessive compulsive and OC spectrum disorders. *Brief Treatment and Crisis Intervention, 3*(3), 369–382.
Shannahoff-Khalsa, D. S. (2006). *Kundalini yoga meditation: Techniques specific for psychiatric disorders, couples therapy, and personal growth.* New York: Norton.
Shannahoff-Khalsa, D. S., & Beckett, L. R. (1996). Clinical case report: Efficacy of yogic techniques in the treatment of obsessive compulsive disorders. *International Journal of Neuroscience, 85* (1–2), 1–17.
Shannahoff-Khalsa, D. S., Ray, L., Levine, S., Gallen, C., Schwartz, B., & Sidorowich, J. (1999). Randomized controlled trial of yogic meditation techniques for patients with obsessive compulsive disorders. *CNS Spectrums: International Journal of Neuropsychiatric Medicine, 4*(12), 34–46.

87 Storytelling and the Use of Metaphor with OCD

Allen H. Weg

Obsessive-compulsive disorder (OCD) is classified by the *DSM-IV-TR* as one of the anxiety disorders. It is characterized by the presence of obsessions, or intrusive ego-dystonic thoughts, images, or impulses, resulting in the experience of anxiety. Obsessions are almost always followed by compulsions (sometimes called rituals), which are thoughts or behaviors that are volitionally carried out by the OCD sufferer and are designed to neutralize the experienced anxiety in some way, providing a temporary sense of relief.

The specific symptoms themselves can vary widely among different clients, even within the same client over time. Typically, obsessions create the experience of uncertainty, and a sense that if one does not resolve this state of doubt quickly by employing a compulsion, something awful will happen. This dreaded consequence may be experienced as a clear and specific catastrophic scenario, as a vague apprehension, or as anticipation of a never-ending state of emotional and/or physiological discomfort.

Most commonly, obsessions take the form of fears that something has become dirty or "contaminated"; that the person has, will get, or will spread a disease or illness; or that the person has hurt someone, whether having hit someone with his car, or insulted or injured a person in some other way. Other common obsessions include the fear that something was left undone or something was left behind, that something is not in its proper place or position, or that it somehow is in need of reorganizing. Additional obsessions concern thoughts that something was not done in just the right way; that the person will lose some kind of self-control, resulting in behavior that is dangerous, illegal, immoral, or embarrassing; or that certain thoughts or behaviors, usually specific words, numbers, colors, or actions, are unlucky in some way.

These feelings result in compulsive rituals designed to remove or lessen the state of doubt or somehow change a state of affairs and avoid the imagined consequences presented by the obsessional thoughts. Compulsions typically present as repeated or ritualized washing, cleaning, or checking behaviors, but can be the repetition of any thought or action, sometimes with specific delineated rules (such as repeating a certain number of times, in a certain order, or doing something while thinking of another particular thing), or may be more vague, requiring repetition until it "just feels right." Often, attempts are made to avoid OCD triggers, which can severely limit a person's ability to function freely, ranging from mild or moderate disruption to a complete loss of functionality.

The foregoing is in no way an exhaustive review of possible OCD symptom pictures. There are compulsive hoarders who fear throwing out anything lest it be found to have some value or purpose in the future. There are persons with religious obsessions, a symptom referred to as scrupulosity, which results in compulsive praying or apologizing. The variation of symptom pictures are endless, and the theme is always the same— an intrusive state of uncertainty, resulting in a rise in anxiety, and a purposeful attempt to neutralize that anxiety through some ritualistic, often repetitive thought or behavior.

Persons with OCD are usually very aware of the nonsensical nature of their symptoms, and they often feel embarrassed and are secretive about them. They see their own behaviors and thought processes as being bizarre or weird and often use those terms in their reports. They do not enjoy doing their compulsions, rather they dread them, but at the same time they feel unable to control their own behavior.

TREATMENT OF OCD WITH CBT

Many articles, papers, and books have been written about the treatment of OCD. Most, if not the vast majority, espouse the application of cognitive-behavioral therapy (CBT) as the therapeutic approach of choice. At the heart of this treatment is the behavioral intervention of exposure and response prevention (ERP) (Foa & Wilson, 2001).

Rather than continuing the strategy of engaging in compulsions or avoidance behaviors, a new strategy is introduced. In ERP, clients are instructed to stop engaging in their compulsive behaviors in response to their obsessions. They are instead encouraged to give themselves some time, with the expectation that over the course of time their anxiety levels will decrease on their own without needing to engage in any compulsive rituals. This process is called *habituation* or *desensitization*, and it is explained to clients that with repeated experiences they will learn to fully trust that they do not need to engage in compulsive rituals to neutralize their obsessive-driven anxiety. Ultimately they will find that they react with lower levels or even no anxiety at all in response to their obsessions.

In ERP, not only are compulsive behaviors discouraged, but approaching or creating those very situations that trigger the urge to engage in compulsive behaviors is *encouraged*. So the very stimuli that were previously avoided by the client—whether things, people, places, situations, activities, or thoughts—are now the stimuli that the client is encouraged to approach. Once this is done, the behaviors that the client used to engage in to give him- or herself relief from anxiety and a sense of control over the illness are now strongly *discouraged*. This treatment protocol is extremely challenging to implement successfully, but there are many aspects of it that are designed to increase treatment compliance and ultimate success. Behaviorally, there are two overriding strategies to accomplish this.

First, there is the idea of creating a hierarchy of exposure, whereby the client, in a collaborative effort with the therapist, determines a ranking of different obsession-triggering stimuli from the least to the most difficult. Once completed, exposure is done first to those items low on the list, generating less intense anxiety for the client, and allowing him or her to see through his or her own experience how desensitization takes place and how those things that at first exposure created significant discomfort no longer do so, even without the employment of compulsions. Once successfully negotiated, the client then moves further up the hierarchy, employing ERP to progressively greater challenges.

A second behavioral strategy involves flexibility in the employment of the response prevention part of the treatment. Here, rather than having the client completely refrain from engaging in any aspect of compulsive behavior, he or she contracts to make at first small and then greater changes in his or her compulsions. These changes may take many forms, and a common one is delaying engagement in the compulsive behavior. A client will expose him- or herself to an obsession-triggering stimulus, say, a contaminated object, and then wait a while before washing his or her hands, lengthening the waiting time with succeeding exposure trials. Another strategy is to have the client change the order of more complicated behavioral compulsions or leave out certain parts. By "loosening up" the foundation of these rituals, the client is ultimately better able to abandon them altogether.

There are also cognitive strategies designed to help with treatment compliance and successful application of ERP, and they include Socratic dialogue, such as, "Well, your anxiety levels dropped significantly with repeated exposures to *that* contaminated object, so what do you think will happen if we do repeated exposures with *this* new object which is triggering your anxiety?"

Finally, education of both the client and significant others about the nature of OCD and its treatment, establishing a trusting rapport with all of those involved in the treatment process, and being a good coach by providing encouragement and congratulations as the client negotiates the hierarchy is essential for success.

INCORPORATING STORYTELLING AND METAPHOR USE IN TREATMENT

In spite of all the foregoing, the greatest challenge in the treatment of OCD remains for the therapist to help the clients who have it and the people who live with them to fully understand the nature of the disorder and its treatment as a prelude to the successful implementation of ERP. Clients and family members often come into treatment completely perplexed by these OCD symptoms. Yet as strange as the symptoms are, they don't hold a candle to the treatment. The CBT of OCD involves some of the most bizarre and outrageous interventions that you are ever likely to encounter in a therapist's office. Most OCD clients are very surprised or even stunned when it is explained to them what they need to do to help make themselves better. They sometimes think the therapist is crazier than they feel. ERP is counterintuitive—you are asked to do exactly the opposite of what you are naturally inclined to do. Something beyond telling is required. Explanations don't seem sufficient when one is being instructed to think and behave in a way that seems contradictory to one's goals. It is often hard to "think outside the box," to think nonlinearly.

In my work with OCD clients over the years, I have found that the most effective way for me to share my understanding of their disorder and introduce them to the unexpected treatment strategies was not to talk to them about OCD at all. Instead, I found myself talking about completely unrelated things, such as memories from my personal life or shared experiences from the mass media and the like, to make a certain point or to get the concept behind an OCD symptom or a treatment intervention. These stories grew in number and expanded from those that addressed only the OCD symptom picture and the CBT application of ERP principles. Additional stories were added over the years and addressed such issues as trust in treatment; anthropomorphizing the OCD as a living, breathing enemy; and the concept of taking an aggressive stance toward the experience of fear (Weg, 2007).

The use of storytelling engages clients to become a more direct part of the therapeutic process wherein they attribute the meanings, conclusions, and lessons of the stories they hear as coming from themselves as opposed to receiving specific instruction and direction from a therapist. This lowers resistance on the part of the client and thus increases the likelihood that the client will accept and incorporate the changes in thinking or behavior that are implied in the story and required for movement in recovery (White & Epston, 1990).

However, the need for ambiguity in the presentation of these stories to accomplish this is not as emphasized here as in previous writings on therapeutic metaphor (Lankton, 2002). Here, the stories are more specific in the message that is being communicated, and a direct link between this message and how it may be applied to some aspect of OCD is often specifically reviewed. Still, because it is not presented as a directive but as a natural conclusion of the narrative, it does not illicit the kinds of resistances that are often triggered by direct suggestions from an external source (e.g., therapist instruction). Many of these stories have no instructions or recommendations, explicit or implicit, embedded within them at all. They are mere vehicles to illustrate and communicate more fully the phenomenological experience of having OCD, and its emotional, social, and behavioral sequelae. In this way, they function in part the way that motivational interviewing does, wherein losses and drawbacks of continuing with the status quo and not making any changes in one's life is reviewed with the client, but no direct suggestions that the client *should therefore* employ these changes is made (Miller & Rollnick, 2002).

OCD CASE PRESENTATIONS WITH APPLICATION OF STORYTELLING

Case 1: Mark

Mark is 12-year-old male seventh-grader who lives with his parents and one younger sibling. His OCD consists of needing to repeat behaviors of all kinds, usually three times. Whenever he walks through a doorway into a room, he has to double back and reenter the room, and then do it once again for a total of three times to feel comfortable. He feels compelled to do the same for sitting down in a chair, turning any electrical device on or off, and a wide myriad of other daily activities, including, at times, verbalizations (e.g., "I love you, I love you, I love you. . . . Good night, good night, good night"). This creates stress within the family and makes Mark feel depressed and frustrated, especially when he is rushed, where he will often feel that he did not do the three times correctly and will then have to repeat the action an additional three times.

CBT treatment for Mark consisted of explaining ERP to him and to his parents, and to begin to introduce the idea of challenging his compulsive repetitive behaviors. Mark initially balked at the idea, feeling that he had too many things that he would need to challenge, and many of the things on his repetitive behaviors list were just too difficult to challenge at all. The clinical intervention at this point was to introduce the concept of an exposure hierarchy, and the story "Flossing," reproduced here, was told to Mark to help illustrate this concept.

I went regularly to my family dentist while I was growing up in Queens, New York. Every 6 months I went to visit him for my checkup, he would say to me, "Allen, you really need to be flossing more often." He would give me a little scare talk about gum disease and send me out of the office with one of those little round tin things with some sample floss in it. I'd get really motivated, make a commitment to myself that I was going to get serious about flossing, and off I'd go, home to floss.

I'd start flossing that first night, but you know, flossing is not so easy if you haven't been doing it much. There's a lot of hand-eye coordination involved. You need to really know your proper angles to get that floss where you want it, and some of the spaces between your teeth can be really tight. And I found that somehow my elbows would get in the way.

I would struggle considerably with this first flossing attempt and found that it would take me something like 30 minutes to just do one quadrant of my mouth. I'd feel spastic and clumsy, stupid and frustrated, and I'd inevitably end up saying to myself, "The heck with this. I don't have time for this!" And I wouldn't floss again until the next time I saw him, 6 months later, at which time the story repeats itself. This went on for years.

Eventually, I went away to college, moved to New Jersey, and found a new dentist. On my first visit with him, he gave me the same "You need to be flossing more" speech. I told him the same story that I just shared with you, admitting that in all likelihood, I would ultimately not follow through with the flossing regime he was recommending. His response was a little bit surprising. He told me, "Allen, this is what I want you to do. Here's the floss. I want you to go home. Floss for 60 seconds, then stop. Even if you only do one tooth, stop after 60 seconds. The next day, start with the same tooth, and do 60 seconds again. That's all."

"Gee," I figured, "I could do *that*!" No big deal, piece of cake. So, that night, I flossed for 60 seconds. The next day I flossed for 60 seconds again, and what ended up happening was that I got a little better at it. Within a couple of days I could do several teeth in 60 seconds. In a couple of more days, 60 seconds allowed me to do about a quarter of my mouth.

Around that time it dawned on me that I had probably developed enough skill to be able to do my whole mouth in under 4 minutes. "Well, I can do *4 minutes!*" I said to myself. And so I did 4 minutes. Soon I was doing it in under 2 minutes. That was 25 years ago, and I haven't stopped flossing yet. And I have great teeth, thank you very much.

What this approach allowed me to do, what resulted in breaking my previous pattern of behavior and jump over that wall of resistance and avoidance, was the acceptance that I didn't have to do "the whole thing," at least not at first. I just had to do this little tiny piece. Sixty seconds. That's where I start. Like the ancient Chinese proverb, a journey of a thousand miles begins with one step.

Debriefing. At this point, I would ask Mark if he would like to approach changing his repeating hab-

its the same way as I changed my flossing habit, one small step at a time. As is usually the case, he asked first how this would be applied to his situation. We discussed the idea of postponing, or waiting for a certain amount of time, say, 10 seconds, after walking through the doorway once, before going back and repeating it two more times. He could then lengthen that time over different trials. Via desensitization and habituation, we would expect that after postponing for a long enough period, he would be able to resist going back to finish the ritual altogether. We also discussed the idea of walking through the doorway three times, but changing which foot went first into the room, as he always required starting with the right foot. In this way we would challenge the rituals in very small ways and only do the least difficult ones first, and work our way up to the more difficult ones—just like flossing teeth for just 60 seconds.

Case 2: Marianne

Marianne is a 36-year-old middle school secretary who lives alone in her own apartment. She has been plagued since mid-adolescence with a severe fear of AIDS. Marianne is a bright and informed woman and clearly understands that blood to blood or sexual contact are the only ways that AIDS can be spread. Yet she will obsess about having been infected if she finds herself in any circumstance where she comes in close proximity with a man who is very thin and "looks like" he may be gay. Whenever this happens, she feels like her clothes have become contaminated, and she usually strips and showers as soon as entering her apartment. In time, her car became contaminated from the clothes, and so she either needed to thoroughly clean the interior of the car, or change and wash her clothes every time she used the car, even if she hadn't seen a gay-looking man that day.

There were small mounds of clothes that had not yet been decontaminated throughout her apartment, and many other items had somehow gotten contaminated because she thought they might have had contact with the clothing. Her avoidant behavior in general led to her living a life that was extremely isolated, and she was moderately depressed as a result of her condition.

Therapy involved her challenging her OCD directly by touching those items that were least contaminated in her mind, spreading the contamination all over her body, and spending longer periods of time without washing. Although the obsessions of getting AIDS remained for very long periods of time after exposure ("How do I know, even months after exposure," she would say, "that I didn't contract AIDS that day but just haven't found out yet?"), her *anxiety* about getting the disease from that exposure decreased rapidly, and her freedom to touch the items she had exposed herself to remained constant. Yet each time she was faced with her next exposure challenge, she would agonize over whether to do it, and if *this* time she might actually get infected. Rather than focusing on probabilities and rational arguments, we focused instead on whether she should *trust* this experience of fear. It is here that I reviewed with her the "Peanuts story," as told here.

We are all familiar with it. It usually is displayed prominently on the first page of the Sunday funnies. Charles Shultz's comic strip, lovingly titled *Peanuts*. If you have followed the comic over the years, or have seen some of the TV holiday specials, you may recall some of the main recurring themes in the *Peanuts* world. There is the little red-headed girl that Charlie Brown worships from afar, the unrequited love that Lucy experiences toward the pianist, Schroeder, and Linus's annual Halloween evening in the pumpkin patch, where he waits, year after year, for the arrival of the Great Pumpkin, never failing to get disappointed. There is Snoopy's fantasy of being the Red Baron, Charlie Brown standing on the pitcher's mound in the pouring rain, outraged that the other kids have left the field, Lucy's psychiatrist office, and Linus's affection for his ever-present blanket.

For now let us focus on one of the smaller Peanuts dynamics—Lucy, Charlie Brown, and the football. The scenario typically runs like this: Lucy asks if she can hold the football edge up on the ground, so Charlie Brown can take a running start and kick the ball out from under her hand, sending it flying across the football field. Charlie Brown refuses, claiming that each time Lucy offers to do this favor for him, she whisks the ball away at the last second, just as he is about to strike it with his foot, causing him to fly skyward and end up flat on his back.

With the sincerity of an angel and the persuasiveness of a lawyer, Lucy somehow convinces Charlie Brown, that, finally this time, she will indeed hold the football in place, allowing him to make contact with it. He caves in and agrees, she holds it, he runs for it, and, as she has done a million times before, she removes the ball at the last second and Charlie Brown ends up lying face up on the ground. The last box in the comic strip usually has Lucy making some flippant remark, such as, "You are just too gullible, Charlie Brown."

We read these comic installments time after time, hoping against hope that Charlie Brown will use his common sense and not believe Lucy's promises, but to no avail. He always does, and she always follows through by removing the football at the last second. We might ask ourselves, "Why does he keep falling for the same trick? Why does he believe her if she consistently dupes him? Hasn't he heard of that old expression, 'Fool me once shame on you, fool me twice, shame on me?'"

Debriefing. The truth is, sometimes it's hard to question a persuasive argument; as one with OCD would know yourself. People with OCD are a lot like Charlie Brown. They believe someone who cannot be trusted. They believe someone who always lies to them. They believe their OCD. At a certain level, OCD talks to the person afflicted with it. It gives orders, threatens, persuades, and intimidates. It does not just throw out the question, "What if you get AIDS?" It follows up with statements like, "Even if you take the test and come up negative for AIDS, I will make you worry that maybe you have it anyway, and I'll make your life so miserable that you won't be able function forever and you won't be able to handle it!"

The OCD sufferer gives in. She gives in because she believes the OCD threats. More than any other, that last threat, the threat that she will become overwhelmed with emotional discomfort for an infinite amount of time and won't be able to "take it," is the one that gets the person to cave in. People with OCD find it incredibly difficult to not trust this feeling, even when they have successfully challenged the OCD many times before and it was clearly demonstrated that they did in fact get over that initial spike of anxiety, that they did for the most part recover, that they were able to move on with their lives, even though they fought back and did not engage in the compulsive reaction. I say "for the most part" because sometimes the lingering doubt or concern can last for a very long time, but I am quick to point out that in those long-term lingering stages of doubt, the person's functioning is usually not really impacted, as was the case with Marianne.

People with OCD often have in their own personal experience and memories that prove that the OCD lies. They know that they have not engaged in the ritualistic response to an obsession and have been able to withstand the resulting discomfort, and, with the passing of time, they have been able to let go of that particular obsession, at least to the point that they could function. Yet for whatever reason, when a new challenge arises, they doubt themselves and their ability to tolerate the discomfort. They believe those OCD lies about what will happen if they don't engage in the tempting ritual.

It is like Charlie Brown experiencing over and over again Lucy's promise, the breaking of that promise, and the resulting humiliation. Yet once again, he chooses to respond to her promise as if the past did not exist. He does not learn from his experience. He concludes that *this* time it *will* be different. Of course, in reality there is nothing to differentiate this particular instance from all the others in the past, and Lucy pulls the football away at the last moment.

So it is with OCD. It is believed when it shouldn't be trusted. It is submitted to when it should be challenged, when it *can* be challenged. Fortunately, life is not like a comic strip. People can successfully face their fears. It is a matter of knowing where to place your trust. The trust should be placed in oneself, in one's own memory of successful challenges to the OCD, in the ability to withstand, persevere, and ultimately overcome whatever emotional torture OCD causes. Remembering that this discomfort is often short-lived and is always ultimately quite manageable is an important ingredient in the battle plan against OCD. It is important to remember that after successfully challenging the OCD and not giving in to the compulsive behavior, one can look back afterward and feel empowered, strengthened, and renewed in hope and anticipation for triumphs yet to come.

It's that wonderful feeling of confidence and self-fulfillment that one gets after doing well on that most difficult school exam, getting that applause at the close of the piano recital, or watching that football take off after striking it at just the right angle with your foot and finding your heart racing with exhilaration as you find yourself scoring the field goal.

CONCLUSIONS

The treatment issues and their corresponding stories reviewed here were chosen as illustrations of storytelling in OCD treatment because they represent relatively common issues for clients (i.e., feeling overwhelmed by the task and using hier-archal exposure, and repeatedly avoiding the next challenge due to overwhelming fear and learning to not trust that fear). There are, however, many other more subtle, bizarre, and idiosyncratic OCD presentations in which storytelling can be particularly effective. The more isolated and confused a client is about his or her disorder or its treatment, the more storytelling can help lighten the intensity of the initial phases of assessment and treatment development. Storytelling is a very user-friendly approach to dealing with the topic of fear, and it provides endless opportunities for the therapist to be creative and appropriately self-disclosing. At the same time they serve to guide the client through the therapeutic process while developing rapport. Finally, because they are visual representations of therapeutic concepts and interventions, for many clients they are more easily recalled, even long after formal treatment has ended, better ensuring the maintenance of treatment gains and faster recovery from any future relapse.

WEB SITES

Motivational Interviewing. http://www .motivationalinterview.org/clinical/whatismi .html.
Obsessive Compulsive Foundation. http:// www.OCFoundation.org.
OCD Online. http://www.OCDonline.com.

References

Foa, E., & Wilson, R. (2001) *Stop obsessing! How to overcome your obsessions and compulsions,* rev. ed. New York: Bantam.

Lankton, S. (2002). Using metaphor with clients. In A. R. Roberts & G. J. Greene (Eds.), *Social worker's desk reference* (pp. 385–391). New York: Oxford University Press.

Miller, W. R., & Rollnick, S. (2002). *Motivational interviewing: Preparing people for change.* New York: Guilford.

Weg, A. H. (2007). *Flying into the darkness: Stories and metaphors exploring the world of OCD.* Manuscript submitted for publication.

White, M., & Epston, D. (1990). *Narrative means to therapeutic ends.* New York: Norton.

Best Practices in Parenting Techniques

Carolyn Hilarski

Parenting success is related to parenting competence (Silver, Heneghan, Bauman, & Stein, 2006). "Okay, but what is competent parenting? What must I actually *do* to be an effective and skillful parent?" To answer these questions, the following discussion takes an ecological approach and define parenting as interactions with a child in a milieu that embodies respect, safety, and genuineness, while attending to the child's temperament and level of attachment. Using these parameters, this chapter describes the current empirical understanding of successful parenting methods that attempt to modify both caregiver and child nonhelpful behaviors, with the intent of increasing homeostasis in families where imbalance lives. The outcome of this caregiving paradigm is associated with child academic success (Reynolds & Ou, 2004), moral development, emotional regulation (e.g., less anxious or depressed), safe behaviors (e.g., child will be more likely to wear a seatbelt or helmet), and social proficiency (Davidov & Grusec, 2006), leading to a reasonable conclusion that competent parenting practices are essential for optimal child outcomes.

PARENT EDUCATION

Parent training appears to be quite effective and available in a plethora of instructional styles and program components (Long, 2007). The key benefits are that caregivers are exposed to a variety of helpful parent–child interactive techniques based on the normal parameters of child development. Educating caregivers about typical child development can be helpful in reducing punitive disciplining methods. Understanding the cognitive and emotional abilities of the child can help the parent reframe behaviors that previously might have been perceived as, for example, spiteful. In the final analysis, parenting practices are most often

influenced by perceptions regarding the caregiver–child interactions.

The timing of parent education is critical. It is suggested to be particularly beneficial for caregivers of younger children for several reasons. First, the child's undesirable behaviors tend to be less ingrained. Second, parental interventions are usually more effective because preschoolers tend to lack strong peer influences. Third, a younger child is generally more accepting of changes in behavioral consequences. Finally, young children, even aggressive ones, tend to continue to show affection with their caregivers.

Classes structured in a group format offer parents the added benefit of socialization, while sharing frustrations and childrearing strategies, in addition to increasing supportive networks. However, parenting programs taken as a whole are inclined to focus on discipline and behavioral strategies to help parents modify youth behavior[1], and, though successful, the process tends to overlook the caregiver–child relationship influenced by the child's temperament and type of attachment. In families where children have consistent behavioral issues, the caregiver–child relationship may be stressed on some level and discipline techniques alone may not modify the circumstance (Davidov & Grusec, 2006).

TEMPERAMENT

Caregivers will often describe their infants as either *easy* (e.g., generally cheerful, adaptable, or unproblematic), *difficult* (e.g., often irritable, emotional, and/or highly resistance to change), or *slow to warm* (e.g., denoting a relatively inactive or indifferent child who may show moderate resistance to new situations). These descriptors appear to remain relatively stable, with some moderation owing to the goodness or poorness of fit between the child and his or her environment (Sigelman & Rider, 2006). Families often need help understanding that temperament can influence the child's level of attachment with the primary caregiver, which can then impact parent disciplining methods (Stovall-McClough & Dozier, 2004). The following case illustrates this development.

Michael

Both his preschool teachers and parents report that Michael, a healthy Caucasian 4.5-year-old male, is disruptive and antagonistic toward other children at school and in his neighborhood. Michael's parents, Ron and Gail, are expecting a new baby and are fearful of how Michael will respond to such a colossal change in their family system. Michael's mother relates that he does not handle change optimistically and will often engage in sullen or tantrum-type behaviors when faced with novel situations. Moreover, they are worried that school peers and teachers will label him a bully or troublemaker.

According to his mom, "Michael was born irritating people around him." While describing the delivery, Gail recounted, "Once I woke from the anesthesia, I was so excited that my child was born. I asked to see my baby. The nurse replied, 'My gosh, can't you hear him? He's been screaming since he entered the world.'" She went on to say, "Michael is indeed a puzzle and very different from my husband and me. Because I don't understand why he insists on fighting or stubbornly disobeying,[2] I sometimes find it difficult to sit and play with him and occasionally use a harsh tone, which makes me feel guilty."

Children with warm, dependent relations in early life are more likely to comply with parental directives. Indeed, the effectiveness of the child's socialization attempts (e.g., aggressive or nonaggressive peer interactions) are associated with the parent–child relationship and a caregivers' style of interaction that is *responsive* (e.g., taking the child's perspective[3]), *supportive* (e.g., praising and showing affection), *attentive* (e.g., listening and encouraging conversation), *guiding* (e.g., providing information), and *receptive* (e.g., inviting emotional expression) (Grusec & Ungerer, 2003). These parenting practices may provide an environment where the child might develop emotional coping and regulation strategies associated with higher self-esteem and positive life outcomes. Keeping this information in mind, consider about the following case.

Chevaun

Sixteen-year-old Chevaun is a junior in high school. She lives in a modest home with her mother (Mary, a seamstress) and stepfather (George, a factory worker). Her mother remarried when Chevaun was 7, shortly after ending a stormy and abusive marriage with Chevaun's father.

Several years ago, according to her mom, "Chevaun changed from a brooding and difficult child to a more cheerful young woman." During this time she asked her parents if she could date. She was given permission, however, with many restrictions on where, when, and with whom she could spend her time. She accepted her parent's rules until about 6 months ago. Since then, her relationship with her parents is reportedly "almost unbearable. She consistently violates her curfew and arrives home smelling like alcohol or worse, drunk. Her grades are suffering and she did not make the cheerleading squad this year."

Chevaun and her stepfather allegedly rarely speak, and the tension is obvious when they occupy the same space. During a recent home visit, Chevaun seemed quite agitated and asserted that "he blames me for everything. He says that I'm the reason the family is so upset. That just isn't true! I know he hates me because I'm not his daughter and I won't obey him anymore. He is so mean. That is why I sometimes drink and don't want to come home"

PARENTING STYLE

Parenting styles are categorized as authoritative, authoritarian, and permissive. These classifications are based on three dimensions: parental control and demands, parental warmth and nurturance, and clarity of parental communication. Both authoritarian and authoritative caregiver styles apply high levels of control in addition to demanding much from their children. However, the authoritarian style often does not include warmth, responsiveness, and age-appropriate levels of control, demanding compliance with no excuses (Baumrind, 1967). In contrast, caregivers with an authoritative style of parenting tend to have close emotional relationships with their children, make reasonable age-appropriate demands that they enforce, explain reasons for their actions, and request and listen to their child's points of view. Childhood exposure to authoritative parenting is linked to the child's perceived competence (Steinberg & Blatt-Eisengart,

2006). Yet parenting practices, born from the caregiver's style, remain an interactive process and may be strongly influenced by the child's temperament (Miller-Lewis et al., 2006).

Michael Revisited

Michael's mother went on to say, "Michael is very high-maintenance! Ron and I have tried everything to make him listen and behave. We just do not know how to handle his outbursts. Sometimes I get so frustrated that I spank him to settle him down.[4]"

During a home visit, Michael was observed interacting with a cousin who was spending the day there. He consistently taunted the child, hitting him with a plastic bat, pushing, and taking toys and even his lunch. Michael's mother ignored the behavior for some time, then asked Michael to "stop being so rowdy." He did not comply. After a few more minutes, his mother spanked him with her hand on his bottom and sent him to his room. He reappeared after a few minutes, playing quietly, then began the hitting behavior again.

The literature suggests that parents may alter their disciplining practices in response to the perceived characteristics of their children (Lindsey, Caldera, & Colwell, 2005).[5] Indeed, it seems reasonable that parents might experience a certain level of stress when rearing children described as difficult and/or different, and these parents might change their parenting strategies (e.g., corporal punishment) in the face of such circumstances. However, corporal punishment, for example, does not teach children self-control (e.g., delayed gratification or compliance for social rewards). Rather, young children may obey out of fear and older children may choose to act out (e.g., delinquent behavior) or in (e.g., depression). Furthermore, this particular disciplining method does not generalize to other undesired behaviors. An alternative option might be redirecting the young child to a more satisfactory activity. For example, if finger painting on the dining room table is not allowed, offer the child a large paper bag to paint on.

In the meantime, Michael's parents are in need of help to reduce their distress about their family's future. The following plan was developed as a negotiable strategy for work with family members.

Treatment Plan for Michael and His Family

Presenting issue: Michael's aggressive behaviors (e.g., hitting, pushing, and taking toys).

Long-term goals: Decrease Michael's aggressive behaviors by 50 percent (4 weeks).
Short-term objectives:

1. Parents and teachers will develop a systematic plan for discipline (Long, 2007)
   1A. Intervention: Parents will agree to read, at a minimum, one section from each of the following parenting education resources specifically focusing on strategies for positive discipline:[6] STEP Program, Love and Logic Program, and Parent Talk.
   1B. Intervention: Parents will agree to practice,[7] one time per day, the following suggested strategies from the parenting resources: controlled choices, directing behavior, describe, and I statements (see Fig. 88.1) (record progress of parental practiced behavior as number of Michael's desired behaviors presented each day; see Knapp, 2005, p. 66.).
   1C. Intervention: Parents and teachers will agree to develop a discipline plan (for home and school) that includes firm limits, reasonable consequences for undesired behavior, and positive reinforcement (encouragement) for desired behavior[8] (Huebner & Mancini, 2003) and record progress[9] (number of desired behaviors in a day).
2. Promote bonding in the classroom and at home (Lee, 2006).
   2A. Intervention: Parents and child will determine a time of day that they will engage in "together" time (any work or play that includes interaction and no distractions, e.g., sharing family stories or looking at family photos, singing, reading, or coloring in the family life book) (Leckman et al., 2004) and record progress (number of Michael's desired behaviors presented each day) (Knapp, 2005).
   2B. Intervention: Teacher and parents will agree to develop a plan that will enhance Michael's bonding in the classroom that may include the teacher and co-teachers engaging in daily chats or greetings, reciprocal smiles, or interactive tasks with Michael and record the outcome (number of desired behaviors in a day) (Huebner & Mancini, 2003; Hunter, 1998).

Controlled Choices
Helpful: 'Would you prefer to take a walk or read a book this morning?

Not helpful: What shall we do this morning?

I-Statements:
'I feel sad when I am hit with the plastic bat because it hurts'

Directing Behavior
Not Helpful: 'Stop being so rowdy'

Helpful: 'Those who can follow the rules may play with the plastic bat'

Describe:
Describe the undesired behavior:
'When you hit your cousin with the bat,'

Describe the resulting feeling:
'I feel sad that your cousin is crying'

Describe desired behavior:
'Please do not hit anyone with the plastic bat'

Helpful:
Parents set enforceable limits without anger

Figure 88.1 Controlled choices.

Chevaun Revisited

Chevaun's stepfather believes that grounding her for 6 weeks is a good way to get her attention

and keep her from drinking, becoming pregnant, or hanging with the wrong crowd.[10] He openly admits to hitting her when she is verbally disrespectful to either him or her mother adding that he "has no use for her anymore because she is so hateful to everyone in the family" (see Fig. 88.2).

Chevaun's mother is distraught with the continuous fighting between her husband and only child. On the other hand, she is worried that her daughter "will come to no good end." She disclosed that she often feels guilty that her daughter was involved in the violence of her first marriage, which is now being repeated. She reports feeling powerless to solve the problem.

Frequently, youths with family issues are drawn to peers with similar environments. There seems to be an unspoken understanding. Moreover, academic failure or underachievement, teen pregnancy, substance use, delinquency, and suicide are not mutually exclusive factors. These variables have a synergy often found within and in the environments of troubled teens. Mary and George's differing parenting styles, George's hostility toward Chevaun, and Mary's depressive withdrawal leave Chevaun in an environment that is unsupportive and nonnurturing (see Fig. 88.2). Indeed, she expressed this perception when describing her family's interactions. The following treatment plan was constructed for negotiable work with this family.

Treatment Plan for Chevaun and Her Family

Presenting issue: Chevaun is breaking family/social rules and parents are reporting both overprotective and harsh parenting practices.
Long-term goals: Parents will successfully use positive disciplining methods on a daily basis resulting in a 50 percent decrease in Chevaun's family/social rule noncompliance (8 weeks).
Short-term objectives:

1. Parents will learn positive parenting practices to increase perceived family homeostasis and bonding.
   1A. Intervention: Parents will read the following books: *Your Defiant Teen* (Barkley & Robin, 2008); *Parenting Teens with Love and Logic* (Cline & Fay, 2006), and *Parent Talk* (Moorman, 1998) in addition to journaling and sharing thoughts and feelings regarding the new information with family members or

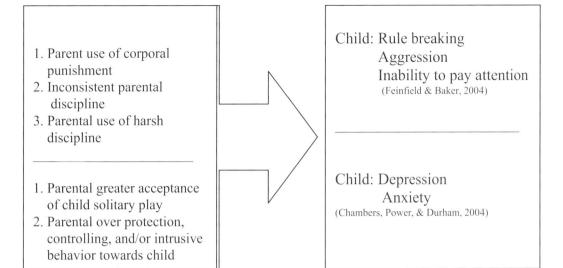

Figure 88.2 Parenting outcomes.

counselor/educational group if involved in that resource.

2. Parents and child will practice various behaviors meant to enable the development of child and parent self-responsibility (see Figs. 88.2, 88.3, and 88.4), increasing the likelihood of family member bonding and family homeostasis and record thoughts and feelings (Best, 2006).

2A. Parents will initiate a daily *family time* (Eaker & Walters, 2002) (e.g., 30 minutes) where the family will talk, share a task (e.g., keep a family journal), play together, plan future together times, share thoughts and feelings with no distractions (e.g., phone calls or television), and journal thoughts and feelings regarding the new structure to share with family members or counselor/ educational group.

2B. Intervention: Parents will offer the child an attainable task and allow the child to complete the undertaking without interference, allowing natural consequences to be the learning opportunity (Cline & Fay, 2006; McMahon, 2003). Family members will review the outcome during family time and, if deemed unsuccessful, offer the opportunity again. All family members will journal their thoughts and feelings about this process and share them with

each other or a counselor or educational group.

2C. Intervention: All family members will perform the rewind game (Knapp, 2005, p. 229) to practice thinking about new ways to solve a problem or behave in response to a circumstance and share results, thoughts, and feelings during family time or with an educational group or counselor.

2D. Intervention: Parents will learn the value of supportive statements, such as "I know you can accomplish this task" (Nelsen & Lott, 2000) and the empowering techniques of listening, power messages, choices, consequences, and permission (Cline & Fay, 2006) and journal thoughts and feelings about using this new behavior to share with family members or counselor/educational group.

2E. Intervention: Both parents and child will work together to form a plan for correcting undesired child behavior. All family members will work through the personal problem-solving activity (Knapp, 2005, p. 211) and share their results during family time or in an educational group or with a counselor.

2F. Intervention: Parents will learn about the reciprocal nature of parent and child interactions (e.g., how their response to their child's behavior may reinforce

Helpful Parenting Behaviors	Consequences	Parent Education
Listen to your child.	Shows respect and caring	Mindfulness: here and now presence that is non-judgmental http://www.sagepub.com/upm-data/15640_E5.pdf thinking skills
Comfort your child	Children are more likely to feel cared for by a parent who is interested in their emotional responses. Increases positive mental representations and attachment (Nelson & Panksepp, 1998)	Mindfulness: understand the thoughts and motives of your child: "What urges my child to behave in this way? C:\Documents and Settings\hilarsc\Desktop\Desk Ref Chapter\CICC - Confident Parenting Description.htm
Provide structure	Children feel safe knowing there is order to their lives	Structures provide necessary limits, yet, need to be flexible (Popkin, 2007)
Use praise	Your words of praise for the smallest accomplishments bolster the child's self-esteem	Praise, Criticism, and Self Esteem Helpful comments: "I need your help"; "Let's negotiate"; "I need a time-out" (Parent Talk) (Moorman, 1998)
Specify desired behavior Communicate	Children feel comfortable knowing the parents' consistent expectations	Community Education Program (COPE) Designed for use with parents of children ages 3-8 years http://www.fsatoronto.com/programs/counselling/parenting.html http://www.sagepub.comupm-data/15637_E2.pdf 1. Parents learn give helpful directions, to praise when desired behaviors are presented, and to use timeout for undesired behaviors 2. Parents learn to give reasons for requests and describe the consequences for non-compliance Red Light (undesired behavior) and Green Light (desired behavior) (Moorman, 1998) Parent states circumstance and child decides what to do (Moorman, 1998)
Be consistent	Inconsistent responses to a child's behavior leave the child confused and cautious regarding how to behavior	Establish house rules and boundaries along with consequences (Hieneman, Childs, & Sergay, 2006) Proactive parenting: *anticipate* an event or interaction and pre-select behavior consistent with family rules (bring toys or snacks to divert the child's attention; Brainstorm positive responses to the child when feeling angry or frustrated)
Spend play, shared work, and/or reading time with your child	• These behaviors encourage caregiver/child attachment. • Play is the principal method by which young children learn and develop. • Sharing chores helps the child to feel needed and embraced in the family system. • Parent/child reading can calm the child and promote bonding.	PCIT (Parent Child Interaction Therapy) http://pcit.phhp.ufl.edu/ Play Techniques Designed for use with parents of children age 2-5 (Hembree-Kigin & McNeil, 1995) C:\Documents and Settings\hilarsc\Desktop\Desk Ref Chapter\MedlinePlus Parenting.htm
Show affection	Sensitive and nurturing interactions and touch increases oxytocin levels in caregiver and child, which influences attachment and temperament of child	Intimacy and Feeling (Parent Talk) (see, Moorman, 1998) Use such phrases as, "I love you"; "I see that …", "I am sorry"; "No" Unhelpful phrases: "I was teasing"; "Act your age"; "What I say goes"

Figure 88.3 Helpful parenting.

undesired child behaviors) by reading step 4 of Barkley and Robin (2008) and journal thoughts and feelings and share these with each other during family time or an educational group or counselor.

CONCLUSION

Parenting can be both a stressful and joyous undertaking that is significantly influenced by parent/ child perceptions, goodness of fit, and interactions (Kendler, 1996). Parenting practices have outcomes (see Figs. 88.2 and 88.3). The professional's job is to enable frustrated parents to find their own understanding of how to help themselves and their child discover mutually satisfying interactions that strengthen and sustain family homeostasis. All family members must be involved and willing to take responsibility for their contributions to the family dynamics in addition to being open to change. Moreover, schools and com-

1. Children are offered choices of potential desired behaviors in a tone that is sensitive and calm
2. Consequences for an undesired behavior may be postponed and contemplated with empathy
3. Parents do not need to own the problem
4. It is the child's responsibility to learn that consequences arise from behaviors and he/she has the ability to ponder possible alternative behaviors for future use (Cline & Fay, 2006)

Figure 88.4 Helpful thinking and behaving for parents.

munities also have a stake in the health and success of future generations. Evidence-based responsible and collective caregiving is a significant factor in that outcome.

WEB SITES

Love and Logic Program. http://www .loveandlogic.com.
Parent Talk. http://www.chickmoorman.com/ PTsystem.html.
STEP Program. http://www.lifematters.com/ step.asp.

Notes

1. Low-income parents tend to prefer behaviorally based education (Wood & Baker, 1999).
2. This is a sign of low reflective functioning or a parent who is unable to empathize (see Slade, 2005).
3. "What makes Michael behave in this way? How do I respond when he behaves like this?" (maternal state of mind and reflective functioning are associated with child caregiver attachment) (Atkinson et al., 2005).
4. Parental stress related to perceived ineffective parenting abilities is associated with the use of corporal punishment.
5. For example, "Michael is a disobedient and high-maintenance child."
6. Preferably within the first week of seeking advice or counseling.
7. Parents will have documented a behavior baseline of at least 3 days (Knapp, 2005).

8. Replacing noncompliance with compliance and cooperation, exercise IXA (Knapp, 2005, pp. 109–110).
9. Behavior baseline documented, exercise VB (Knapp, 2005, pp. 65–66).
10. Grounding is a time-out for teens and not as effective as other parenting methods (see Barkley & Robin, 2008).

References

Atkinson, L., Goldberg, S., Raval, V., Pederson, D., Benoit, D., Moran, G., et al. (2005). On the relation between maternal state of mind and sensitivity in the prediction of infant attachment security. *Developmental Psychology, 41*(1), 42–53.

Barkley, R. A., & Robin, L. (2008). *Your defiant teen: 10 steps to resolve conflict and rebuild your relationship.* New York: Guilford.

Baumrind, D. (1967). Child care practices anteceding three patterns of preschool behavior. *Genetic Psychology Monograph, 75,* 43–88.

Best, A. L. (2006). Freedom, constraint, and family responsibility: Teens and parents collaboratively negotiate around the car, class, gender, and culture. *Journal of Family Issues, 27*(1), 55–84.

Chambers, J. A., Power, K. G., & Durham, R. C. (2004). Parental styles and long-term outcome following treatment for anxiety disorders. *Clinical Psychology and Psychotherapy, 11,* 187–198.

Cline, F., & Fay, J. (2006). *Parenting teens with love and logic: Preparing adolescents for responsible adulthood.* Colorado Springs, CO: NavPress.

Davidov, M., & Grusec, J. E. (2006). Untangling the links of parental responsiveness to distress and warmth to child outcomes. *Child Development, 77*(1), 44–58.

Eaker, D. G., & Walters, L. H. (2002). Adolescent satisfaction in family rituals and psychosocial development: A developmental systems theory perspective. *Journal of Family Psychology, 16*(4), 406–414.

Feinfield, K. A., & Baker, B. L. (2004). Empirical support for a treatment program for families of young children with externalizing problems. *Journal of Clinical Child and Adolescent Psychology, 33*(1), 182–195.

Grusec, J. E., & Ungerer, J. (2003). Effective socialization as a problem solving and the role of parenting cognitions. In L. Kuczynski (Ed.), *Handbook of dynamics in parent-child relations* (pp. 211–228). Thousand Oaks, CA: Sage.

Hembree-Kigin, T. L., & McNeil, C. B. (1995). *Parent-child interaction therapy*. New York: Plenum.

Hieneman, M., Childs, K., & Sergay, J. (2006). *Parenting with positive behavior support: A practical guide to resolving your child's difficult behavior*. Baltimore, MD: Paul H. Brooks.

Huebner, A. J., & Mancini, J. A. (2003). Shaping structured out-of-school time use among youth: The effects of self, family, and friend systems. *Journal of Youth and Adolescence, 32*(6), 453–463.

Hunter, L. (1998). *The effects of school practices and experiences on the bonding of at-risk students to the school*. Ann Arbor, MI: ProQuest Information & Learning.

Kendler, K. S. (1996). Parenting: a genetic-epidemiologic perspective. *American Journal of Psychiatry, 153*(1), 11–20.

Knapp, S. E. (2005). *Parenting skills homework planner*. Hoboken, NJ: Wiley.

Leckman, J. F., Feldman, R., Swain, J. E., Eicher, V., Thompson, N., & Mayes, L. C. (2004). Primary parental preoccupation: Circuits, genes, and crucial role of the environment. *Journal of Neural Transmission, 111*, 753–771.

Lee, T. Y. (2006). Bonding as a positive youth development construct: Conceptual bases and implications for curriculum development. *International Journal of Adolescent Medicine and Health, 18*(3), 483–492.

Lindsey, E., Caldera, Y., & Colwell, M. (2005). Correlates of coparenting during infancy. *Family Relations, 54*, 346–359.

Long, N. (2007). Learning from experience: shifting from clinical parent training to broader parent education. *Clinical Child Psychology and Psychiatry, 12*(3), 385–392.

McMahon, T. (2003). *Teen tips: A practical survival guide for parents with kids 11–19*. New York: Simon and Schuster.

Miller-Lewis, L. R., Baghurst, P. A., Sawyer, M. G., Prior, M. R., Clark, J. J., Arney, F. M., et al. (2006). Early childhood externalising behaviour problems: child, parenting, and family-related predictors over time. *Journal of Abnormal Child Psychology, 34*(6), 891–906.

Moorman, C. (1998). *Parent talk*. New York: Fireside.

Nelson, E. E., & Panksepp, J. (1998). Brain substrates of infant-mother attachment: Contributions of opioids, oxytocin, and norepinephrine. *Neuroscience Biobehavioral Review, 22*(3), 437–452.

Nelsen, J., & Lott, L. (2000). *Positive discipline for teenagers: Empowering your teens and yourself*. Roseville, CA: Prima.

Popkin, M. H. (2007). *Taming the spirited child: Strategies for parenting challenging children*. New York: Fireside, Simon & Schuster.

Reynolds, A. J., & Ou, S. (2004). Alterable predictors of child well-being in the Chicago longitudinal study. *Children and Youth Services Review, 26*, 1–14.

Sigelman, C. K., & Rider, E. A. (2006). *Life-span human development*, 5th ed. Belmont, CA: Wadsworth.

Silver, E. J., Heneghan, A. M., Bauman, L. J., & Stein, R. E. (2006). The relationship of depressive symptoms to parenting competence and social support in inner-city mothers of young children. *Maternal Child Health Journal, 10*(1), 105–112.

Slade, A. (2005). Parental reflective functioning: An introduction. *Attachment and Human Development, 7*(3), 269–281.

Steinberg, L., & Blatt-Eisengart, I. (2006). Patterns of competence and adjustment among adolescents from authoritative, indulgent, and neglectful homes: A replication in a sample of serious juvenile offenders. *Journal of Research on Adolescents, 16*, 47–58.

Stovall-McClough, K. C., & Dozier, M. (2004). Forming attachments in foster care: infant attachment behaviors during the first 2 months of placement. *Developmental Psychopathology, 16*(2), 253–271.

Wood, W. D., & Baker, J. A. (1999). Preferences for parent education programs among low socioeconomic status, culturally diverse parents. *Psychology in the Schools, 36*(3), 239–247.

Anne E. Fortune

All social work service ends eventually. Preparation for ending and interventions during the termination phase affect the benefits clients get from treatment, how long their gains last, and how well they handle the emotional and practical reactions to ending. The termination phase deserves at least as much care and attention as the assessment and intervention phases.

REASONS FOR ENDING SERVICE

The reasons for ending influence participants' expectations, reactions, and appropriate interventions during the termination phase. Common situations for ending social work service include the following.

Ending Planned, Time-Limited Contacts

In time-limited service, participants know how long their contact will last and use that sense of time to frame their work, maintain focus, and motivate participants. Because of the short duration and the knowledge of ending, decisions about when and how to terminate are usually easier than in open-ended service, and less preparation is needed.

Ending Open-Ended Service by Mutual Agreement

If there are no time limits, ending ideally occurs when the client and social worker agree that service is no longer desirable. Most social workers use eclectic indicators of success to determine when to end. These criteria include:

- meeting goals set by the client or practitioner;
- improved behavior and intrapsychic functioning for the client;
- the client expressing readiness to terminate;
- in family treatment, changes in the relationship among family members (such as

improved interaction and communication) and changes in a family's relation to others (such as more appropriate family boundaries or better relations with others); and
- lack of success. Unless the goal is maintaining functioning in a chronic condition, ethical considerations demand that treatment end (1) if there is little improvement and little reasonable expectation of improvement, or (2) if further gains are not worth the time and energy required.

Once a decision is made to end, some time must be spent preparing for ending, often in a formal termination phase that includes new interventions designed to deal with maintaining gains.

Unanticipated Endings with Time to Prepare for Termination

As many as 40 percent to 60 percent of open-ended cases end partly or wholly because of unexpected situational factors. Unanticipated reasons for ending include:

- the social worker leaves an agency or becomes ill;
- a student ends his or her social work internship;
- there are changes in the client's schedule;
- parents remove children from treatment; or
- there are agency constraints, such as excessive caseloads.

In unanticipated endings, progress is rarely optimal. The client and social worker may need to deal with disappointment or anger, and they should plan how the client may continue progress.

Ending in Managed Care

Managed care organizations require administrative review and approval of service that extends beyond an initial time limit. Most social work providers consequently plan time-limited treatment and are reluctant to request extensions. They may be less involved in management of termination and less willing to request extensions because of discouragement at managed care. The uncertainty about outcome when an extension is requested complicates termination, because there may be dashed hopes, anger, and an inability to use the positive effects of time limits. However, recent studies show that extension denials are rare. Whenever possible under managed care, the formal interventions of the termination phase should be conducted, especially after a denied extension.

Transfer to Another Service Provider

The client may transfer elsewhere when service is cut off—for example, if the social worker leaves the agency, more appropriate service is available elsewhere, or the client and worker do not get along. Termination of the relationship between the first social worker and the client is similar to other situations, with the social worker also facilitating the linkage with the new social worker.

Client Drop-Out

Clients may decide to end by dropping out without informing the social worker. Although dropping out is often viewed as a treatment failure, as many as two-thirds of dropouts report considerable progress. However, clients who drop out miss the opportunity to assess the treatment process and solidify gains through planned maintenance interventions.

CLIENT REACTIONS TO TERMINATION

Although much literature describes termination as a gloomy process of mourning, most clients have more positive reactions than negative feelings. The ending of service usually means accomplishments as well as losses and a new beginning and independence for the client. A wide range of reactions is "normal" with individual expressions and cultural variations in what emotions are appropriate and how they may be expressed. There are common reactions during the termination phase.

- Clients naturally evaluate their progress and goal attainment, summarize their work in treatment, and review the treatment process itself.

- In intrapsychic and existential treatments, the focus shifts to concurrent and future outside activities, with clients expressing a growing sense of autonomy.
- Clients are proud of their accomplishments, excited at ending, and satisfied.
- Clients express some ambivalence about ending, including sadness, a wish to continue the relationship, and ambivalence about whether progress is sufficient.
- Clients may reexperience previous losses or recreate earlier treatment experiences, often as part of integrating therapeutic growth.

Less commonly, some clients experience negative reactions that must be handled separately from normal termination reactions. These negative reactions include:

- in successful long-term treatment, a process of mourning the loss of an intense relationship, with stages of denial, anger and loss, depression, and finally acceptance;
- strong anger or bitterness;
- separation anxiety;
- regression to previous inappropriate behaviors or acting out; and
- extreme negative emotions like depression, feeling "destroyed," or loss of self-esteem.

Factors Affecting Reactions to Termination

Several factors affect clients' reactions to termination. The factors and their effect on client reactions include the following.

Reason for termination

- When service ends unexpectedly, reactions are more negative: more anger, mourning, mood disturbances, and a sense of unfinished business.
- When the ending is mutually agreed on, there is more pride and excitement.
- Dropouts are less satisfied than those who end by agreement.

Outcome

- The more successful the outcome, the more positive clients' reactions.
- The more successful the outcome, the more temporary anxiety and a greater distancing

from the therapeutic relationship as clients prepare for the end.

Preparation for ending

- Early preparation (including setting time limits at the beginning) has important benefits: (1) introduction of affective content can be managed to allow therapeutic processing; (2) clients have time to work through their reactions; and (3) clients are less likely to act out during termination.
- Systematic preparation, even when done late, encourages positive reactions and appropriate transitions.
- Informing the client of an unplanned termination late in treatment without enough time to discuss ending is most destructive, often undermining gains and eliciting angry feelings of betrayal.

Previous loss

- Clients with unresolved loss may go through mourning reactions as they re-create the previous experience.
- Other clients with previous losses are better able to handle termination, with less depression and more positive reactions.

Length of treatment

- In long-term treatment, longer treatment is associated with greater turmoil and mood disturbance.
- In short-term treatment, the number of sessions is *not* related to reactions.

Other factors may affect reactions to termination, but the evidence is mixed or studies are lacking; these factors include the quality of the relationship, type of service, treatment modality (group, family, individual), and cohesion in groups.

SOCIAL WORKER REACTIONS TO TERMINATION

Social workers, too, experience a range of emotions at ending with each client. Typical reactions are less intense mirrors of client reactions. They include pride in the client's accomplishments and in one's own therapeutic skill, ambivalence, sadness, a sense of overview of the treatment process, with occasional doubt, disappointment, and guilt about the limits of one's helping ability. Social workers must be aware of their own reactions for several reasons.

- Social workers' reactions affect their ability to recognize when to end or how to intervene— for example, they may enjoy a client or be reluctant to admit they are not helpful.
- Countertransference (attributing one's own feelings to the client) may lead to inappropriate interventions.
- Because clients take their cues from social workers, verbal and nonverbal messages about ending affect client progress, reactions, and ability to terminate well.
- Termination is an important opportunity to assess the treatment process and skill and to reconfirm commitment to helping others.

INTERVENTIONS FOR THE TERMINATION PHASE

Termination interventions should be an integral part of treatment planning. They are different from change interventions in earlier phases of treatment, although they require the same relationship, planning, and implementation skills. The termination interventions are designed to help the client (1) assess progress and the treatment process, (2) generalize gains to other settings and situations, (3) develop skills and strategies to maintain gains, (4) make the transition to no service or to another service, and (5) deal with emotional reactions to ending.

Assessing Progress and Process

A primary task during termination is assessing the status of goals and client problems. Purposes of the progress review, which should be similar in detail to the initial assessment, are to:

- provide data to confirm (or disconfirm) a tentative decision to terminate;
- permit a realistic assessment of progress and help solidify the client's learning during treatment;
- increase the client's sense of mastery and ability to cope, which are important to continued functioning; and
- give information that serves as the basis for other termination interventions—for

example, client strengths for future problem-solving efforts.

The client and social worker also review the treatment process, emphasizing the problem-resolution steps and skills the client can use in the future. By giving an overview of the course of treatment, the review helps bring closure.

Generalizing Gains

Unless deliberate efforts are made to broaden gains, the client's use of new skills may be limited to circumscribed areas—for example, improved communication at work but not with family members. To extend clients' gains to other areas, clients may:

• learn general principles about dealing with problems—for example, problem-solving skills, anger management, or family communication;
• transfer skills from treatment session to their natural environments through homework assignments or tasks—for example, trying out interpersonal skills learned in group treatment at work with colleagues; and
• transfer systematically skills from one situation to another—for example, using social skills in new situations or with different people.

Maintaining Gains

Another concern is how long clients' gains last after treatment ends. Interventions that help maintain gains include:

• increasing the client's sense of mastery through realistic praise and highlighting the client's role in creating and maintaining change;
• teaching general principles that underlie coping and change;
• ensuring that newly learned skills are appropriate for the client's normal environment;
• "fail-safe planning" (Fishman & Lubetkin, 1980) or how to deal with future difficulties, such as handling potential conflict around a child's report card.
• making sure that supports for new skills are available in the client's environment, such as:

1. Bringing the client's support system directly into treatment—for example,

inviting a spouse to termination sessions to discuss maintenance, or including a schoolchild's friends in treatment designed as a "club."
2. Creating a new network through involvement in existing organizations, such as Alcoholics Anonymous, church group, or social interest group (bridge, ballroom dancing, hunting, etc.).
3. Teaching the client how to elicit support from significant others.
4. Conducting follow-up booster sessions that include maintenance interventions, such as reinforcing what the client is doing well, reviewing principles, discussing coping strategies, and planning for the future.

Making the Transition

If the client is not prepared to function without treatment, all the gains can be lost quickly. To ease the transition, the social worker must ensure that any overdependence is reduced and the client is ready to function on his or her own (or with a different service). Interventions that help accomplish the transition out of treatment include, within the content of treatment sessions, a systematic shift in time focus from past activities through present functioning and then a future orientation—for example, from childhood trauma to current handling of emotional triggers to means of responding in the future. Another intervention is attention to outside treatment activities and supports through:

• discussing events in the client's life;
• maintenance and generalization activities such as homework assignments and fail-safe planning; and
• activities that take place away from the normal meeting room, such as a trip to a park for youngsters.

Last, in groups, interventions include reducing cohesion by decreasing the cooperation and interaction in group activities—for example, boys playing table tennis (an individual game) instead of soccer (a teamwork activity), or adults developing homework assignments in pairs rather than in the full group.

When the client is transferring to service elsewhere, additional interventions smooth the transition to the new agency or social worker.

• Linking clients to referral agencies by providing thorough information about contacting the agencies, making an appointment for the clients, or accompanying the clients to the agencies.

- Ensuring that new providers are prepared for the clients by consulting with the providers, explaining expectations, and sharing information (with clients' permission).
- Following up with clients and new providers after their initial meetings to ensure that the connections are made.
- To minimize client feelings of rejection, discussing openly the reasons for termination/transfer and exploring the clients' feelings and expectations of the new service.

Dealing with Clients' Emotional Reactions to Ending

Expressing feelings is an important part of the ending phase. Acknowledging the emotions makes them acceptable, validates the client's experience, and provides models for handling both affect and termination. Interventions to elicit reactions and build on them for therapeutic purposes include the following.

- Helping the client talk about his or her feelings by
  1. exploring expressions of ambivalence (as well as other expressions of emotion).
  2. modeling self-disclosure by introducing the social worker's own reactions (this also helps shift the therapeutic relationship to greater collegiality).
  3. describing in words the emotions a client seems to express nonverbally, such as angry gestures, evading discussion, or hesitant pride.
- Once the client expresses emotion, building on the reactions for other treatment or termination interventions. For example,
  1. using positive feelings (such as pride) in accomplishment to reinforce the client's sense of mastery.
  2. labeling ambivalence and sadness as normal, healthy expressions of ending.
  3. handling strong negative reactions as intensive grief reactions that can be resolved through stages of mourning.
- Introducing activities designed to bring out client reactions and provide opportunity for other termination interventions. For example:

1. an individualized coloring book that includes highlights of a child's treatment. This "memory book" (Elbow, 1987) allows review of treatment process and helps solidify gains (assessing progress and process) and provides a memento for the child (a ritual marker).
2. in an educational group, a "toast" to each person about what members learned from them reinforces learning and a sense of mastery, and celebrates ending.

- Introducing termination rituals. Such rituals help clients deal with conflicting emotions, give a sense of specialness and make connections between past and future. Appropriate rituals include:
  1. culturally defined good-bye markers like hugging and shaking hands.
  2. complex exchanges of mementos with special meaning, such as photographs, certificates of completion, or gifts that convey the essence of a person.
  3. elaborate events, such as graduation ceremonies. Such celebrations may also serve other purposes, including demonstrating individual accomplishments and reviewing the treatment experience—for example in a group to increase self-esteem, a potluck (covered dish) supper with each person contributing his or her ethnic specialty.

SUMMARY

Termination is as important to ethical social work practice as engagement, assessment, and treatment planning. Whatever the reason for ending, early preparation for termination and careful interventions during the termination phase help the client maintain gains and deal with the practical and emotional reactions to ending.

References

Elbow, M. (1987). The memory book: Facilitating terminations with children. *Social Casework, 68,* 180–183.

Fishman, S. F., & Lubetkin, B. S. (1980). Maintenance and generalization of individual behavior therapy programs: Clinical observations. In P. Karoly & J. J. Steffen (Eds.), *Improving the long-term effects of psychotherapy: Models of durable outcome.* New York: Gardner.

Bereavement and Grief Therapy

Elizabeth C. Pomeroy, Renée Bradford
Garcia, & Diane L. Green

Loss is a universal experience that everyone encounters at one time or another during their lives. Loss from the death of a loved one can be especially devastating. Grief resulting from this kind of loss causes significant disruption in a person's functioning both internally (physically and emotionally) and externally (socially and occupationally). Historically, mental health practitioners have received little in-depth training related to grief and loss interventions. In addition, there have been only a few theories of grief and loss that have been postulated by experts in the field. However, as the topic of grief and loss is gaining wider acceptance and more visibility, there is a need for an understanding of the grief process that considers the individual within the context of the environments in which he or she functions, rather than just examining the intrapsychic experience of the individual.

Early conceptualizations of the process of grief and loss formed the initial knowledge base of an unexplored area of human experience and helped us understand the problematic symptoms and damaging consequences of grief. They validated that grief is a negative, painful, and disruptive experience for the mourner. Practitioners often misinterpret these models as being grounded in a problem-oriented perspective and consequently often view a person experiencing grief as someone suffering from an illness that must be cured. As a result, the practitioner may deemphasize the mourner's strengths and resiliencies that can be brought to bear on their unique experience of loss. The strengths-based framework of grief assists practitioners in building on the inherent strengths of the individual while they navigate the grieving process. It encourages mourners to use their positive coping abilities and environmental resources. Furthermore, the strengths-based approach to grief is grounded in the view that grief in response to the death of a loved one

is a natural, normal, and potentially health-producing process that aids the individual in adjusting to the absence of the loved one.

THE STRENGTHS-BASED FRAMEWORK FOR GRIEF

The strengths perspective of social work practice developed by Saleebey (2006) and Rapp (1998) views every client as having assets and resources that enhance his or her ability to cope with life events. These assets and resources can be categorized into individual strengths and environmental strengths. Individual strengths include aspirations, competencies, and confidence (Rapp, 1998). Aspirations include goals, dreams, hopes for the future, ambitions, and positive motivation to achieve and grow. Competencies are manifested by one's unique ability to use talents, skills, and intellect. *Confidence* refers to a person's positive self-regard and his or her belief and tenacity in achieving goals. A person with confidence feels valuable and worthy of positive life events. Strengths are present in every individual. Some people appear to be able to capitalize on their strengths more than others. This phenomenon may be due to a combination of biological, psychological, and social factors. Environmental strengths include resources, social relations, and opportunities. Resources include financial support, access to services, access to information, and other tangible assets. Social relations encompass friends, family, co-workers, neighbors, and others with whom one has interactions. Opportunities refer to the gaps in one's life that are waiting to be filled. They represent positive events that can potentially change one's life. In addition, a person maintains specific niches in life, that is, habitation, job, friends, and leisure activities. According to Rapp (1998), "The quality of the niches for any individual is a function of that person's aspirations, competencies, confidence, and the environmental resources, opportunities, and people available to the person" (p. 42). Together, a person's individual and environmental strengths influence one's sense of well-being, empowerment, and life satisfaction (Rapp, 1998).

For clients who are grieving, the strengths perspective is a particularly salient framework. It builds on previous theories of grief with the addition of a lens that emphasizes the health-producing aspects that are intrinsic to the mourner as well as the process of grief. Focusing on client strengths rather than deficits provides the practitioner with a valuable tool that can aid in assessment and intervention. It effectively highlights aspects of the person and their environment that can be used and enhanced to assist in the grieving process and promote positive growth. The basic tenets of the strengths-based framework of grief are as follows.

1. Grief in response to the death of a loved one is a natural, expectable, and potentially health-producing process that aids the person in adjusting to the absence of the loved one.
2. The symptoms, emotions, and behaviors associated with expected grief reactions represent a process of healthy adaptation and are not inherently pathological.
3. Mourners benefit by knowing that life-enhancing grief reactions are productive and beneficial. Life-enhancing grief reactions are those responses that facilitate healing within the mourner.
4. All persons have individual and environmental strengths that can assist them as they experience grief. The mourner benefits from the reinforcement of those strengths and the encouragement to consciously employ them during the grief process.
5. Environmental conditions can either help or hinder the mourner's ability to adapt to the loss and enhance the person's life.
6. Many symptoms of grief, although they may be uncomfortable and are commonly regarded as negative symptoms, are healthy coping mechanisms in that they facilitate the process of separation, adaptation to change, and integration of the loss.
7. Life-enhancing grief reactions to loss enable accommodation and adaptation to occur. They facilitate the process of psychological separation from the deceased.
8. Life-enhancing grief symptoms should not be discouraged. Rather, they should be allowed expression while being carefully monitored so that they remain helpful to the mourner's process of adaptation.
9. Grief may be considered life-depleting when the symptoms it produces significantly weaken the mourner's aspirations, competencies, and confidence. Life-depleting grief reactions are those responses and circumstances that act as impediments to the expected grieving process and interfere with the mourner's ability to live a fulfilling life.
10. Life-depleting grief reactions thwart the process of adaptation and lead to entropy.
11. Life-enhancing and life-depleting grief reactions exist on a continuum of intensity.
12. The experience of grief evolves over a person's lifetime and is experienced with varying levels of conscious awareness.

STRENGTHS-BASED, EXPECTED GRIEF ASSESSMENT AND INTERVENTIONS WITH INDIVIDUAL CLIENTS

Intervening with bereaved clients from the strengths-based framework of grief involves several skills that originate from a comprehensive understanding of the strengths-based model. The practitioner adheres to the basic tenets of the model while working with the unique situation that the client brings to counseling. Initially, the practitioner allows for the client to present his or her story of the loss and the experience with his or her grief. This story may unfold over many sessions and may be retold from different perspectives. However, the initial presentation of the loss provides the practitioner with information and insights into the client's present experience. Concurrently, the practitioner listens for information that will complete a preliminary assessment of the client's internal and external strengths, resources, and social supports. Some of the skills that the practitioner uses throughout grief counseling include active and empathetic listening, nonjudgmental acceptance of intense emotions, normalizing and educating the client about the grief process, assisting the client with coping skills and resources, and helping the client develop life-enhancing strategies to reengage fully in life. Finally, the practitioner will assist the client in using his or her experience as fuel for personal growth.

According to the strengths-based framework of grief, the term *expected* grief describes the predictable grief experience that reflects the healthy process of separation from the deceased individual. Although it can take on a wide variety of forms, this type of grief is what the practitioner would expect to see with someone who has lost a loved one. Expected grief leads to health-producing growth. The term *complex* grief describes a grief process that is encumbered with internal and/or external complications that interfere with the health-producing growth process of expected grief. If complex grief is not addressed appropriately, it can lead to life-depleting responses.

GROUP INTERVENTIONS FOR ADULTS WITH EXPECTED GRIEF

In addition to individual counseling, group counseling has been used as a primary vehicle for working with the bereaved (Cook & Dworkin, 1992; Rando, 1984; Worden, 1991). Psychoeducational group interventions have been shown to be effective with caregivers of chronically/terminally ill populations such as Alzheimer's, oncological, and dialysis patients (Biegel, Sales, & Schulz, 1991). In addition, psychoeducational groups related to grief and loss have proven to improve well-being and grief resolution, increase social support, and decrease the risk of psychopathology related to unresolved grief issues (Pomeroy & Holleran, 2002). The power of group support and shared, mutual concerns can ameliorate the loneliness and isolation associated with loss. The potential benefit of being with others who share a common experience with grief is tremendous. Group support can effectively minimize the feelings of grief described by Stephen Levine when he writes, "We come to trust ourselves less, we cannot 'feel' the world around us as we once did, so we experience ourselves as 'a bit unplugged'" (Levine, 2005, p. 4).

A STRENGTHS-BASED, PSYCHOEDUCATIONAL GRIEF GROUP

The authors have found that bereavement groups combining the strengths-based framework with a psychoeducational format can greatly enhance a mourner's feelings of competency in relation to managing grief. The term *psychoeducational* refers to the fact that both information and emotional support are provided and enhanced by one another to alleviate some of the painful symptoms associated with grief. It allows for participants to understand the process of grief in a context that includes not only themselves but others. On receiving factual information, group participants are able to dispel some of the myths and unrealistic expectations associated with the grieving process. In addition, the mutual sharing of common experiences creates a community from which each participant can draw strength. Both these dynamics assist in developing the mourners' internal and external resources that are necessary for the healing process to progress. Not only are psychoeducational groups effective, they are also economically feasible for clients who can't afford individual counseling as well as for agencies with limited resources. The following paragraphs outline a psychoeducational group design that uses the strengths-based framework of grief.

THE STRENGTHS-BASED PSYCHOEDUCATIONAL GROUP DESIGN

Group Goals

The goals for this group are to provide individuals with a safe and structured environment in which to adjust to the absence of the loved one. This is accomplished by facilitating an understanding of the life-enhancing aspects of grief, processing the mourner's adaptation to the loss, promoting awareness about life-depleting grief reactions, and enhancing the mourner's coping skills and resources to engage in a life separate from the loved one. These goals underlie the content of the group sessions.

Group Structure

Careful consideration should be made when deciding if a grief group should have an open-ended or closed-ended structure. Open-ended groups allow for new participants to join at any time during the process, whereas closed-ended groups limit membership to participants who commit to a specific number of sessions. Although open-ended groups can potentially accommodate a greater number of participants and provide individuals with immediate assistance, the constant flux in membership can prohibit group cohesion, trust, and advanced development (Toseland & Rivas, 2001). When dealing with a highly emotional issue like grief, it can be difficult for members of open-ended groups to progress beyond the storytelling stage of the loss. Closed-ended groups provide a secure environment in which trusting relationships between members can develop, thereby, encouraging more intimate self-disclosure. On the other hand, these groups are limited to a small number of participants and may not be cost-effective for agencies with limited resources. In addition, if some participants drop out of the group, it may become too small to provide members with a meaningful experience (Toseland & Rivas, 2001).

Time-limited psychoeducational groups based on the strengths-based framework of grief have been found to be practical and productive because of the structured discussion topics, the life-enhancing coping strategies that are encouraged between group sessions, and the trusting relationships that develop between members (Pomeroy, Rubin & Walker, 1995). Although the first two sessions focus on the participants' losses, subsequent sessions guide the participants in the strengths-based coping model outlined earlier. The strengths-based grief group is 6 to 8 weeks in length. This type of structured group is compatible with agencies that specialize in end-of-life care, such as hospice or community outpatient clinics. The facilitator of this type of group also serves as a conduit between participants and community resources.

Group Participants

In addition to designing the group structure, it is important that potential members be screened for appropriateness. Membership should be composed of individuals who have lost a loved one due to death, understand the purpose of the group, understand that active participation includes thoughtful listening as well as discussion, and be able to commit to attending every session. Some individuals are better served by individual counseling rather than group counseling. Bereaved persons whose loss is very recent (0 to 4 weeks) may initially benefit more from the focused attention of an individual therapist. This may also be true for individuals with untreated and severe mental illness, individuals who have many life stresses in addition to the loss, people who are unable or unwilling to share group time with others, or individuals with complex grief.

Group Content

The content of a grief group will be somewhat dependent on the composition of the group members. For example, if the group is composed of all female participants who have lost their mothers, the discussions may highlight mother–daughter relationship issues. On the other hand, if the group is composed of parents who have lost a child, discussions may focus on the need for communication between the surviving parents. However, regardless of the specific issues that the members bring to the group, there is certain content that is covered in all groups using the strengths-based psychoeducational approach. Topics include adjustment to the loss, navigating transitions, family concerns, using community resources, and engaging in outside activities.

A STRENGTHS-BASED, COMPLEX GRIEF GROUP INTERVENTION

Group intervention can also be effective for mourners experiencing a complex grief reaction. They can benefit by having a community of people with whom they can share their grief and by being around others who are also grieving. It is particularly useful for mourners with complex grief reactions to be in groups with others who had loved ones that died in a similar manner. Interventions for these types of groups are highly specific to the population of survivors. The unique issues related to particular types of death can be explored in depth, and problems related to the mode of death can be shared and managed. For example, survivors of suicide groups provide support to people who have experienced suicide in their families. Group members may grapple with the anger they feel toward their loved ones as well as guilt they may carry from their inability to prevent the death. Specialized groups such as these also provide a buffer from the stigma associated with the loss and the lack of social support mourners typically receive in their communities. These groups can also provide information and education about topics of particular concern to the group members. Parents of Murdered Children, for example, has support groups that use the psychoeducational approach to helping family members deal with law enforcement and the judicial system in addition to their grief.

In using the strengths-based framework, the authors have found that complex grief reactions can be addressed in a group setting after the mourner has had some individual counseling or has had time to process the trauma associated with the death. Many mourners with complex grief issues can make the best use of group interventions after some time has passed after the death. This time period may range from 2 to 12 months.

Assistance by way of individual counseling may be recommended prior to participation in a group. Potential members for these types of groups should undergo an individual assessment prior to entering the group to determine their readiness for group participation. In some cases, their needs would be better served in individual counseling. Some mourners benefit from being in individual and group counseling simultaneously. Assessment for group participation should consider the degree of trauma and level of crisis, as well as the person's overall mental health status.

GRIEF GROUP INTERVENTIONS WITH CHILDREN AND ADOLESCENTS

As with adults, group intervention with children and teens can be beneficial to youth who are grieving. One particular advantage of group counseling is that the group provides a place for bereaved youth to find relief from the feeling of being different from their peers because of their loss. Group intervention may take many forms, including family counseling, counseling that involves groups of families, groups that are offered in the community, groups that are hosted in schools, and camps that assist youth with their grief in an outdoor setting. Important components of group intervention with children and teens include sharing the story of the loss, educating and normalizing grief responses, expressing feelings associated with grief, identifying life-enhancing coping mechanisms, addressing feelings of guilt associated with the loss, and memorializing the deceased.

GROUP INTERVENTIONS WITH GRIEVING OLDER ADULTS

As with other populations, support groups for bereaved older adults can provide needed social support and outside activities for persons who might be vulnerable to intense loneliness and isolation. For example, one community has developed an organization that specifically focuses on the need of older widows and widowers for social interaction. The group sponsors monthly events, for which they provide transportation, to engage older people in social activities and opportunities to interact with other widows and widowers. Some of the group's events offer participants opportunities to memorialize their deceased spouse. This organization has grown considerably over the past

decade and is well attended by older community members. In addition, groups that focus primarily on the issues of bereavement often attract older people who are experiencing either expected or complex grief.

GRIEF AND PERSONS WITH SPECIAL CIRCUMSTANCES

Although there are many commonalities among bereaved persons regardless of the type of loss they have experienced, there are also some deaths that are unique in the way they impact the mourner and the healing process. Counselors require specialized knowledge and understanding to be most effective with these types of mourners. For example, the grief experience for persons with disabilities, immigrant populations, divorced families, veterans of war, gay/lesbian/bisexual/transgender populations, mourners of perinatal loss, and victims of crime and domestic abuse are groups that require specialized knowledge and unique interventions. It would be impossible to detail the unique dynamics of all the various kinds of losses found in our vastly diverse society. In some cases, there are books devoted exclusively to the specific circumstances surrounding a particular type of loss. In other cases, there is a dearth of information about a particular life circumstance that a client may present.

The strengths-based framework for grief is particularly germane to populations with special circumstances. Many persons within these groups have developed a reservoir of resiliencies due to their encounters with adversity and discrimination. Because their special circumstances often involve additional stigma and ostracism from society, it is even more important that practitioners identify life-enhancing strategies for assisting them through the grief process. In addition, practitioners will want to help client's develop and access environmental assets.

PRACTICE IMPLICATIONS FOR THE PROFESSIONAL

Working with bereaved individuals is a powerful and moving experience. Although practitioners often describe grief counseling as meaningful, rewarding and profound, there are also moments when it may be experienced as draining, depressing, unsettling, and frustrating. Despite adherence to professional boundaries between client and counselor, the act of being emotionally present for someone who is mourning a loved one touches the practitioner personally as well. In part, this may be because most practitioners have had personal experience with the death of a loved one and can relate to the experiences of their clients. Additionally, the work of grief counseling involves regular and intimate contact with the prevalence, probability, and impact of death, a reality that society encourages us to ignore. Awareness of how the counseling process affects the practitioner is essential to competent and ethical practice with grieving clients.

Self-awareness, quality professional social work supervision, flexibility, and an ability to cope with ambiguity are all necessary components of being a professional grief counselor. Understanding, implementing, and upholding the National Association of Social Workers Code of Ethics is essential for social workers involved with grieving individuals, groups, and families. Finally, social workers practicing in this area benefit from using positive self-care methods, including professional and personal support when needed. Developing an expertise in grief and loss is a rewarding and worthwhile endeavor because social workers in all areas of practice will have clients coping with these emotions throughout their careers.

WEB SITES

Children's Grief and Loss Issues. http://www.childrensgrief.net.

Coping with Grief and Loss: Guide to Grieving and Bereavement. http://www.helpguide.org/mental/grief_loss.htm.

Gift from Within, a nonprofit organization dedicated to those who suffer post-traumatic stress disorder. http://www.giftfromwithin.org.

Grief and Loss Resource Centre. http://www.rockies.net/~spirit/grief/grief.html.

References

Biegel, D. E., Sales, E., & Schulz, R. (1991). *Family caregiving in chronic illness: Alzheimer's disease, cancer, heart disease, mental illness and stroke.* Newbury Park, CA: Sage.

Cook, A. S., & Dworkin, D. S. (1992). *Helping the bereaved: Therapeutic interventions for children, adolescents, and adults.* New York: Basic Books.

Levine, S. (2005). *Unattended sorrow.* New York: Rodale.

Pomeroy, E. C., & Holleran, L. (2002). Tuesdays with fellow travelers: A psychoeducational HIV/AIDS-related bereavement group. *Journal of HIV/AIDS in Social Services, 1,* 61–77.

Pomeroy, E. C., Rubin, A., & Walker, R. J. (1995). The effectiveness of a psychoeducational task-centered group intervention for family members of persons with AIDS: An evaluation. *Journal of Social Work Research, 19,* 142–152.

Rando, T. A. (1984). *Grief, dying, and death: Clinical interventions for caregivers.* Champaign, IL: Research Press.

Rapp, C. A. (1998). *The strengths model: Case management with people suffering from severe and persistent mental illness.* New York: Oxford University Press.

Saleebey, D. (2006). *The strengths perspective in social work practice,* 4th ed. Boston: Pearson Education.

Toseland, R. W., & Rivas, R. F. (2001). *Group work practice,* 4th ed. Needham Heights, MA: Allyn & Bacon.

Worden, J. W. (1991). *Grief counseling and grief therapy: A handbook for the mental health practitioner.* New York: Springer.

PART IX
Guidelines for Specific Interventions

91 Transtheoretical Model Guidelines for Families with Child Abuse and Neglect

Janice M. Prochaska & James O. Prochaska

It would be a mistake to assume that child abuse investigators and caseworkers ignore the issue of change. However, without a reliable and valid means of assessing behavior change, caseworkers often use compliance with case plans as a proxy or indicator of change. Thus, parents who attend parenting classes or go to counseling are seen as changing—even if these same parents continue to deny abuse and neglect. Compliance with a court-ordered program of services or classes is not the same as psychological readiness to change or actual behavior change.

The transtheoretical model of behavior change offers a more reliable, valid, and complex assessment of change than a simple recording of compliance. The model assumes that changing behavior is a dynamic process and that one progresses through a series of stages in trying to modify behavior—precontemplation, contemplation, preparation, action, and maintenance. Thirty years of research on a variety of behaviors have identified interventions that work best in each stage to facilitate change (Noar, Benac, & Harris, 2007).

DEFINITIONS OF STAGES

Each of the five stages represents a period of time, as well as a set of tasks needed for movement to the next stage. Although the time an individual spends in each stage may vary, the tasks to be accomplished are assumed to be invariant.

Precontemplation is the stage at which there is no intention to change behavior in the foreseeable future. Most individuals in this stage are unaware or underaware of their problems. Family, friends, or neighbors, however, are often well aware that the precontemplators have problems. When precontemplators present for help, they often do so because of pressure from others. Usually they feel coerced into changing by a spouse who threatens to leave, children who threaten to disown them, or courts that threaten to punish them.

In studies employing the discrete categorization measurement of stages of change, individuals are asked if they are seriously intending to change the problem behavior in the near future, typically within the next 6 months. If not, they are classified as precontemplators. Even precontemplators can wish to change, but this is quite different from intending or seriously considering change. Items that are used to identify precontemplation on a continuous stage of change measure include, "I have done nothing wrong and resent child welfare getting involved in my life" or "I guess I have faults, but there's nothing that I really need to change." Resistance to recognizing or modifying a problem are the hallmarks of precontemplation.

Contemplation is the stage in which people are aware that a problem exists and are seriously thinking about overcoming it but have not yet made a commitment to take action. People can remain stuck in the contemplation stage for long periods. Contemplators struggle with their positive evaluations of their dysfunctional behavior and the amount of effort, energy, and loss it will cost to overcome it. On discrete measures, individuals who state that they are seriously considering changing in the next 6 months are classified as contemplators. On a continuous measure, these individuals would be endorsing such items as "I have a problem and I really think I should work on it" and "I've started to think I haven't been caring for my kids as well as I can." Serious consideration of problem resolution is the central element of contemplation.

Preparation is the stage that combines intention and behavioral criteria. Individuals in this stage are intending to take action in the next month and have unsuccessfully taken action in the past year. As a group, individuals who are prepared for action report some small behavioral and cognitive changes, such as "I have questions for my caseworker about taking care of my kids" and "If I don't change, I will never be the kind of parent my children need." Although they have made some reductions in their problem behaviors, people in the preparation stage have not yet reached a criterion for effective action, such as not hitting their children or regularly providing supervision and appropriate food and shelter.

Action is the stage in which individuals modify their behavior, experiences, and/or environment to overcome their problems. Action involves the most overt behavioral changes and requires considerable commitment of time and energy. Individuals are classified in the action stage if they have successfully altered the dysfunctional behavior for a period from 1 day to 6 months. On a continuous measure, individuals in the action stage endorse statements like "I am really working hard to change" and "I am doing things about the problem that got me involved with child welfare." Modification of the target behavior to an acceptable criterion and significant overt efforts to change are the hallmarks of action.

Maintenance is the stage in which people work to prevent relapse and consolidate the gains attained during action. For abusive behaviors, this stage extends from 6 months to an indeterminate period past the initial action. For some behaviors, maintenance can be considered to last a lifetime. Being able to refrain from abusive behavior and being able to consistently engage in a new positive behavior for more than 6 months are the criteria for considering someone to be in the maintenance stage. On the continuous measure, representative maintenance items are "I may need a boost right now to help me maintain the changes I've already made" and "I sometimes feel nervous that when child welfare is out of my life, I will fall back on old behavior." Stabilizing behavior change and preventing relapse are the hallmarks of maintenance.

Spiral Pattern

As is now well known, most people taking action to modify chronic dysfunctional behavior do not successfully maintain their gains on their first attempt. Relapse is the rule rather than the exception across virtually all chronic behavioral disorders. Accordingly, change is not a linear progression through the stages. Most clients actually move through the stages of change in a spiral pattern. People can progress from contemplation to preparation to action to maintenance, but most regress to an earlier stage. Some relapsers feel like failures—embarrassed, ashamed, and guilty. These individuals become demoralized and resist thinking about behavior change. As a result, they return to the precontemplation stage and can remain there for extended periods of time.

PRESCRIPTIVE GUIDELINES

Assess the Client's Stage of Change

Probably the most obvious and direct implication for risk assessment is the need to assess the stage of a client's readiness for change and to tailor interventions accordingly. Stages of change can be ascertained by asking the client a simple series of questions to identify his or her stage, for example, "Do you think behavior X is a problem for you now?" (if yes, then contemplation, preparation, or action stage; if no, then maintenance or precontemplation stage) and "When do you intend to change behavior X?" (if "someday" or "not soon," then contemplation stage; if "in the next month," then preparation; if "now," then the action stage).

Beware of Treating All Clients as though They are in Action

Professionals frequently design excellent action-oriented treatment and self-help programs but then are disappointed when only a small percentage of people attend or when large numbers drop out of the program after coming once or twice. The vast majority of clients are *not* in the action stage. Aggregating across studies and populations, we estimate that 10–15 percent are prepared for action, approximately 30–40 percent are in the contemplation stage, and 50–60 percent are in the precontemplation stage. Thus, professionals who approach clients only with action-oriented programs are likely to underserve or misserve the majority of their target population.

Assist clients in Moving One Stage at a Time

If clients progress from one stage to the next during the first month of treatment, they can double their chances of taking effective action in the next 6 months. Treatment programs designed to help people progress just one stage in a month can increase the chances of participants taking action on their own in the near future.

Recognize that Clients in the Preparation Stage Are far More Likely to Achieve Better and Quicker Outcomes

The amount of progress clients make during treatment tends to be a function of their pretreatment stage of change. This has direct implications for assessing risk and selecting and prioritizing treatment goals.

Anticipate Recycling

Most clients will recycle several times through the stages before achieving long-term maintenance. Accordingly, intervention programs and personnel expecting people to progress linearly through the stages are likely to produce discouraging results. Be prepared to include relapse prevention and recycling strategies in treatment, anticipate the probability of recycling, and try to minimize caseworker guilt and client shame over recycling.

Conceptualize Change Mechanisms as Processes, Not as Specific Techniques

Literally hundreds of specific psychotherapeutic techniques have been advanced; however, a small and finite set of change processes or strategies underlie these multitudinous techniques.

Change processes are covert and overt activities that individuals engage in when they attempt to modify problem behaviors. Each process is a broad category encompassing multiple techniques, methods, and interventions traditionally associated with disparate theoretical orientations. Consciousness raising, for example, is the most frequently used process across systems of psychotherapy. But different systems apply this process with very different techniques, including observations, classifications, interpretations, confrontations, feedback, information, and education. Change processes can be used within treatment sessions, between treatment sessions, or without treatment sessions.

Although there are 400-plus ostensibly different psychotherapies, we have been able to identify only 12 different processes of change based on principal components analysis. Table 91.1 presents the ten processes receiving the most theoretical and empirical support in our work, along with their definitions and representative examples of specific interventions.

STAGES OF CHANGE

Do the right things (processes) at the right time (stages). Thirty years of research in behavioral medicine, self-change, and psychotherapy converge in showing that different processes of change are differentially effective in certain stages of change. In general terms, change processes traditionally associated with the experiential, cognitive, and psychoanalytic persuasions are most useful during the earlier precontemplation and contemplation stages. Change processes traditionally associated with the existential and behavioral traditions, by contrast, are most useful during action and maintenance.

In the transtheoretical model, particular change processes are optimally applied at each stage of change. During the precontemplation stage, individuals use the change processes significantly less than people do in any of the other stages. Precontemplators process less information about their problems, devote less time and energy to reevaluating themselves, and experience fewer emotional reactions to the negative aspects of their problems. In treatment, these are the most resistant or the least active clients.

Individuals in the contemplation stage are most open to consciousness-raising techniques, such as observations, confrontations, and interpretations, and are much more likely to use bibliotherapy and other educational techniques. Contemplators are also open to emotional arousal, which raises emotions and leads to a lowering of negative affect if the person changes. As individuals become more conscious of themselves and the nature of their problems, they are more likely to reevaluate their values, problems, and themselves both affectively and cognitively. Both movement from precontemplation to contemplation and movement

TABLE 91.1 Titles, Definitions, and Representative Interventions of Ten Processes of Change

Process	Definition: Interventions
1. Consciousness raising	Increasing information about self and problem: observations; confrontations; interpretations; bibliotherapy
2. Self-reevaluation	Assessing how one feels and thinks about oneself with respect to a problem: imagery; corrective emotional experience
3. Dramatic relief	Experiencing and expressing feelings about one's problems and solutions: psychodrama; grieving losses; role-playing
4. Social liberation	Increasing alternatives for nonproblem behaviors available in society: advocating for rights of repressed; empowering; policy interventions
5. Environmental reevaluation	Realizing the impact of changing or not changing troubled behavior on other people: family value clarification
6. Self-liberation	Choosing and commitment to act and belief in ability to change: decision-making therapy; New Year's resolutions; commitment-enhancing techniques
7. Counterconditioning	Substituting alternatives for problem-related behaviors: relaxation, anger management; assertion; positive self-statements
8. Stimulus control	Avoiding or countering stimuli that elicit problem behaviors: restructuring one's environment (e.g., removing alcohol); avoiding high-risk cues, fading techniques
9. Reinforcement management	Rewarding oneself or being rewarded by others for making changes: contingency contracts; overt and covert reinforcement; self-reward
10. Helping relationships	Seeking and using social support to encourage or help with behavior change: support groups; Parents Anonymous

Source: Adapted from Prochaska, DiClemente, & Norcross, 1992.

through the contemplation stage entails increased use of cognitive, affective, and evaluative processes of change. Some of these changes continue during the preparation stage. In addition, individuals in preparation begin to take small steps toward action and make commitments to bigger steps.

During the action stage, people are putting into practice self-liberation or commitment. They increasingly believe that they have the autonomy to change their lives in key ways. Successful action also entails effective use of behavioral processes, such as counterconditioning (substituting healthier alternatives) and stimulus control, to modify the conditional stimuli that frequently prompt relapse. Reinforcement management, especially self-reinforcement, also comes into frequent use here.

Just as preparation for action was essential for success, so is preparation for maintenance. Successful maintenance builds on each of the processes that came before. Specific preparation for

maintenance entails an assessment of the conditions under which a person would be likely to relapse and development of alternative responses for coping with such conditions without resorting to self-defeating defenses and pathological responses. Continuing to apply counterconditioning, stimulus control, reinforcement management, and helping relationships is most effective when based on the conviction that maintaining change supports a sense of self that is highly valued by oneself and significant others. Table 91.2 lists appropriate interventions for workers based on the processes for each stage.

MORE ABOUT PRECONTEMPLATORS

Most parents in abusive situations experience themselves as being coerced into receiving help. They do not see themselves as in need of change,

TABLE 91.2 Interventions for the Five Stages of Change

Precontemplation	Contemplation	Preparation	Action	Maintenance
Increase awareness about the problem	Reevaluate how things are done	Encourage a commitment	Substitute new ways for old ways	Monitor
				Enforce rules
Move people emotionally	Think about what kind of family one wants to have	Generate a plan	Reinforce verbally	Reinforce
		Build self-efficacy		Give support
Discuss benefits of changing			Reward quickly	Provide feedback
	Look at what will happen if change doesn't occur	Encourage looking at parenting models	Give support	
				Know triggers
Encourage looking at consequences of what is happening now		Set action goals		Follow up and follow through
	Bring cons of changing down		Restructure environment	
Point out discrepancies between ideal and real self as a parent	Examine what restraints are stopping changes		Change family rules	

probably want to change others, and tend to intensely defend their behavior. Precontemplators can remain trapped in this stage without help from others. Often, a first step of the caseworker is to enable the parent to be conscious of the self-defeating defenses that get in the way of looking at change. Becoming conscious of their defenses and how they operate can help clients gain a measure of control over them. Does the precontemplator make the least of things (denial and minimization); have excuses (rationalization); turn outward (projection and displacement); or turn inward (internalization-depression). Once precontemplators are aware of how they defend themselves when they feel threatened, they can work at getting control over their defenses rather than having the defenses control them.

Environmental forces can also help a precontemplator to become unstuck. A child welfare investigation, an arrest, or a school official calling can demonstrate that the environment no longer supports their lifestyle. The precontemplator can progress if they can identify with the environmental forces urging them to change. What not

to do as a worker is to push precontemplators to immediate action, nag them, give up on them, or enable them (avoid discussions and confrontations, or make excuses).

HELP FOR CHRONIC CONTEMPLATORS

Contemplators can see changing as too difficult to decide to take the first step or get sidetracked and become discouraged and disappointed in their efforts. They may also be ambivalent and say to themselves, "When in doubt, don't change." Chronic contemplators substitute thinking for acting. Conflicts and problems hang suspended, decisions are never finalized, and action is avoided. Contemplators need help with seeing the benefits of changing ("I will get to keep my kids," "My kids will benefit," or "I will feel better about myself") and help with reducing the cons ("It's hard to do all that child welfare wants," "I will miss getting high," or "Doing things differently will create problems between me and my partner"). Contemplators using self-reevaluation can begin to imagine how

TABLE 91.3 Two Dimensions of Risk Assessment for Child Abuse and Neglect

Stage of Change	Severity of Risk		
	High	Medium	Low
Precontemplation	No reunification High likelihood of terminating parental rights		Parent education classes Project Early Start
Contemplation		Comprehensive Emergency Services	
Preparation		Parent aide Mother for mother Volunteer support	Family preservation
Action	Family preservation only with close monitoring		Family preservation
Maintenance			Reunification recommended

Source: Adapted from Gelles, 1996.

life would be substantially improved if they were free from their problem behavior.

RISK AND STAGES OF CHANGE

Gelles (1996) combines the dimensions of stages of change and degree of risk and lays out appropriate programs to offer abusive parents by risk and stage of change (Table 91.3). According to Gelles, intensive family preservation programs are most appropriate for families who fit the lower right cell—those where the level of risk is low and the stages of change is action. Family preservation could be used with close monitoring for higher risk families but only those who are in preparation or in action. Family preservation is clearly inappropriate for high-risk families who are in precontemplation and contemplation.

RECENT CHALLENGES AND SUCCESSES

Recently Littell and Girvin (2004) and Corden and Somerton (2004) reviewed and criticized the transtheoretical model in the context of the validity of the stage model and its use in the assessment of parenting. Both articles suggest that the transtheoretical model's practical applications are severely limited in the child welfare field and question such a transfer.

In both reviews, the authors challenged the use of stage of change (a single construct) as a measure but did not address the application of the entire model (including all 15 constructs) to interventions. There is growing evidence that the transtheoretical model can effectively and successfully be applied to adoption readiness, bullying prevention, and partner abuse treatment—all areas related to child welfare.

Prochaska et al. (2005) found that the transtheoretical model helped conceptualize and assess emotional readiness to be an adoptive parent and paved the way for future efforts to develop an intervention that guides professionals in their work with prospective parents. Evers, Prochaska, Van Marter, Johnson, and Prochaska (in press) found that a computer-based individualized and interactive transtheoretical model intervention for bullying prevention in schools, given at three time points over one semester, led to significant reductions in bullying, passive bystander, and victim events. In the middle schools, approximately 22 percent of the treatment group progressed to action or maintenance (always acting with respect) compared to 5 percent of the control group. In the high schools, approximately 29 percent progressed to action or maintenance compared to 10 percent of the control group.

Levesque (2007) developed a multimedia computer expert system program for domestic violence offenders as an adjunct to traditional mandated treatment. In a randomized clinical trial, the transtheoretical intervention group was significantly more likely to be in the action stage (54 percent versus 24 percent) for using healthy strategies to stay violence-free. These studies strongly suggest the application of the transtheoretical model to reduce abusive relationships.

WEB SITES

Cancer Prevention Research Center (home of the transtheoretical model). http://www.uri.edu/research/cprc.

National Clearinghouse on Child Abuse and Neglect (NCCANCH). http://www.nccanch.acf.hhs.gov.

Pro-Change Behavior Systems. http://www.prochange.com. See http://www.prochange.com/domesticviolencedemo for Journey to Change, a family violence program.

References

Corden, J., & Somerton, J. (2004). The trans-theoretical model of change: A reliable blueprint for assessment in work with children and families? *British Journal of Social Work, 34,* 1025–1044.

Evers, K. E., Prochaska, J. O., Van Marter, D. F., Johnson, J. L., & Prochaska, J. M. (In press). Transtheoretical based bullying prevention effectiveness trials in middle schools and high schools. *Educational Research.*

Gelles, R. J. (1996). *The book of David.* New York: Basic Books.

Levesque, D. A. (2007). Expert system intervention for domestic violence offenders. Final report to NIMH (grant no. R44MH62858).

Littell, J. H., & Girvin, H. (2004). Ready or not: Uses of the stage of change model in child welfare. *Child Welfare, 83,* 341–366.

Noar, S. M., Benac, C. N., & Harris, M. S. (2007). Does tailoring matter? Meta-analytic review of tailored print health behavior change interventions. *Psychological Bulletin.*

Prochaska, J. M., Paiva, A. L., Padula, J. A., Prochaska, J. O., Montgomery, J. E., Hageman, C., et al. (2005). Assessing emotional readiness for adoption using the transtheoretical model. *Children and Youth Services Review, 27,* 135–152.

Prochaska, J. O., DiClemente, C. C., & Norcross, J. C. (1992). In search of how people change: Application to addictive behaviors. *American Psychologist, 47,* 1102–1114.

92 Play Therapy with Children in Crisis

Nancy Boyd-Webb

Many adults would like to think that children are like the three monkeys who see no evil, hear no evil, and do no evil. Unfortunately, the very opposite is true of most children, who pick up cues and take notice whenever trouble is brewing, whether or not the adults in their lives tell them about what is occurring. When children are not given logical and true explanations of what has happened, they often create fantasies in their imaginations that may far exceed the magnitude and impact of the actual crisis event. Because we live in a world in which violence, terror, and danger are everyday occurrences in families, schools, and communities, no one of any age is immune to the possibility of exposure and subsequent stress and anxiety related to perceived threats about personal safety.

This chapter focuses on a method of helping children who have become anxious and symptomatic following either a traumatic or crisis event that they experienced personally or about which they heard in the media or through other types of exposure. The chapter defines and discusses crisis intervention play therapy and indicates the types of situations in which it has been found to be helpful. Two brief case vignettes are included, and guidelines for use of this clinical intervention are outlined. This method emphasizes timely intervention to reduce anxiety and problematic behaviors soon after the event to avert the subsequent development of symptoms such as post-traumatic stress disorder.

CRISIS INTERVENTION PLAY THERAPY

Play therapy is the treatment of choice in working with children because it encourages them to communicate through child-friendly play rather than with words. *Play therapy* refers to a helping interaction between a trained adult therapist and a child that seeks to relieve the child's emotional distress through deliberate use of the symbolic communication of play. The assumption is that when children understand that the therapist's role is to help, they will express and work through their emotional conflicts within the metaphor of play. Just as adults talk out their worries, children express their fears and anxieties by playing them out. The play therapist not only helps bring about relief of the presenting symptoms (important as this may be to parents and child) but also works toward removal of impediments to the child's continuing development, so that the prospects for the child's future growth are enhanced (Crenshaw, 2006; Webb, 2007;). The primary purpose of play therapy is to help troubled children express and obtain relief from their conflicts and anxieties symbolically through play in the context of a therapeutic relationship.

Some of the specific elements inherent in play that make it valuable in therapy have been identified as its communication power, its abreaction power (permitting the review of past stress and the associated negative emotions), and its rapport-building power (Reddy, Files-Hall, & Schaefer, 2005). Each child's situation is unique, therefore, the therapy with individual children will have a different emphasis, depending on the specific assessment of the child's problem situation and the child's particular reactions.

Definition of Crisis Intervention Play Therapy

Crisis intervention play therapy is a form of play therapy that aims to help children who have become anxious and symptomatic following a crisis (or traumatic) experience. It uses the broad range of play therapy methods for the purpose of relieving the child's reactions of fear and helplessness. This approach is usually short-term and directive. It relies on the safety of the therapeutic relationship to permit the child to deal with stressful memories, either symbolically or directly, using play materials. Crisis intervention play therapy is especially recommended for single-event and recent traumas. Numerous anecdotal reports attest to the treatment effectiveness of this form of play therapy in helping traumatized children (Brohl, 1996; Shelby, 1997; Webb, 2003, 2004, 2007). When the child has experienced multiple or chronic traumas, a more extended treatment approach may be needed.

Directive versus Nondirective Play Therapy

Often children (and adults) do not want to remember their frightening crisis experiences. Avoidance is typical following a crisis or traumatic event (American Psychiatric Association [APA], 2000), and the child's reluctance to review anxiety-evoking memories presents a challenge to the therapist, who knows that pushing worries away does not cause them to disappear. In fact, the prevailing practice wisdom recommends that for traumatic experiences to be resolved, some form of retrospective review is usually necessary. With directive, crisis/trauma-focused play therapy, a child can gradually process anxious feelings and learn methods to put them in the past so that they no longer hold center stage in the child's present emotional life. Crisis intervention play therapy consists of a mixture of cognitive-behavioral, supportive, and psychodynamic approaches. A primary goal is to help the child achieve an understanding that the crisis situation was in the past and is no longer a current source of threat.

CASE EXAMPLE: TAMMY

The dual play therapy goals of symptom relief and removing obstacles to the child's future development are illustrated in the case of Tammy, a 4-year-old child with severe separation anxiety that kept her from being able to remain in her preschool program. The therapist helped the child by playing out a fantasy story using a ladybug, a bumblebee, and spider puppets in which the "mother" ladybug left her "children" in the care of the bumblebee and spider "mothers" and their little insect "children." The successful outcome in this case occurred because the child identified with the little child ladybugs, and she felt protected by the two insect mothers. Another important factor was that the mother ladybug always returned to her children after leaving them for a period of time. The play scenario repeated the mother's leaving and returning and thus served to desensitize the child to separation experiences.

The crisis event that had precipitated Tammy's anxiety was her mother's successive attempts to get pregnant, causing her parents' sudden departure in the middle of the night to go to the hospital for insemination procedures at the time of ovulation. When Tammy woke up in the morning and found her parents absent, she would become very upset, even though her grandmother was present. Furthermore, when her mother learned several weeks later that she was *not* pregnant, she would break down and cry in front of Tammy, who then became quite anxious about her mother's well-being and reluctant to leave her side.

In play therapy sessions, the story-play with the puppets calmed the child's fears about her mother's seeming abandonment (because the mother puppets always came back). Despite her mother's belief that Tammy was unaware of the pregnancy attempts, she changed her mind when her daughter commented to her after a play session that "the mother spider puppet could lay hundreds and hundreds of eggs!" This statement convinced the mother that Tammy was in fact aware of her infertility problem. After the puppet play, Tammy became able to tolerate being separated from her mother, because she realized that her own parents would not abandon her and that her mother's crying was not within her ability to control. The play therapist also advised the mother to avoid crying openly in Tammy's presence in the future.

The case illustrates both symptom alleviation and enhancement of a child's coping abilities through the use of play therapy and parent counseling. The play therapy helped this girl externalize her fears onto the puppets and also portray her anticipated positive mood at a future time when she would no longer feel afraid. (A full discussion of this case appears in Webb, 2003).

As demonstrated in this case, the therapy of play therapy involves far more than simply playing with a child. Through the interactions with the therapist, the child experiences acceptance, cathartic relief, reduction of troublesome affects, redirection of impulses, and a "corrective emotional experience." In the safety of the holding environment of the playroom, the child can express his or her feelings in fantasy and then eventually move to a state of mastery, which subsequently carries over to the child's everyday life. It is important to emphasize that it is not play per se that produces anxiety relief for the child. Rather, it is play in the context of the therapeutic relationship that provides the critical healing factor (Landreth, 2002). One play therapist commented that "traumatized children need to be heard in the presence of another who is not afraid . . . they need someone to accept their suffering in its cruel entirety" (Shelby, 1997, p. 149).

THE ASSESSMENT PROCESS

It is essential for the social worker who is doing play therapy to take a history focused on the child's reactions to the crisis/traumatic event. Although an extensive psychosocial history may not be feasible because of the pressure of time, the worker needs to have a general sense of how the child was functioning prior to the crisis/trauma, as well as a description of the child's current symptomatic behaviors and how this is interfering with his/her current life.

There are three parts to any assessment of a symptomatic child. I refer to this as the tripartite assessment (Webb, 2007). The specific groups of factors in each part are:

- factors related to the individual child,
- factors related to the support system, and
- factors related to the nature of the traumatic or crisis event.

Space does not permit full discussion of this here, and readers who wish more detailed information about using this assessment tool should consult Webb (2004, 2007).

The first set of data relates to the nature of the child's precrisis adjustment; the second part refers to the nature of the surrounding environment; and the third set of data relates to the nature of the crisis/traumatic event. The play therapist must obtain pertinent information from the parents and other sources regarding these matters to establish appropriate treatment goals. In Tammy's case, the therapist met with the mother once to obtain the background history, including the mother's unsuccessful attempts to become pregnant and Tammy's increasing difficulty remaining and participating in her preschool program.

SETTING GOALS

The focus of treatment following a crisis or trauma is to return the child to his or her precrisis adjustment. Sometimes the child actually becomes emotionally stronger after a crisis because he or she now identifies herself as a survivor. Often, the play therapist tells the young child that she intends to help him or her with any troubles or worries and then invites the child to relate specific concerns either verbally or in play. The treatment goals flow directly from the assessment. In Tammy's case, the child's worry was that something bad might happen to her mother while she was at preschool, and therefore a primary goal was for the mother to assure her child that she was fine and that her sadness would not last forever. An additional goal was to acknowledge that Tammy (in the form of the ladybug child) had the right to be with her friends and have fun without worrying about mother's return.

CASE EXAMPLE: ANNA

This case illustrates the value of timely play therapy intervention following a traumatic event. Anna, age 5, became preoccupied and jumpy in school following a fire that caused a middle-of-the night evacuation from her apartment. She was waking every night, and during the day when at home she always wanted to be in her mother's presence. Although Anna, her parents, and her brother had been safely relocated to a new apartment, the child was disconsolate because she had lost her beloved stuffed bunny with which she slept every night. Her mother did not comprehend the degree of her daughter's loss and the child's need to mourn this.

In play therapy over four sessions with the mother and child together, the therapist encouraged Anna to re-create her traumatic experience in drawing and in play with blocks and toy furniture. Because the therapist acknowledged the loss in her mother's presence, Anna's pain was validated and the mother's awareness was awakened the. After the sessions, the child's symptoms of anxiety and accompanying school inattention resolved. A complete discussion of this case, together with examples of the child's drawings appears in Webb (2003).

Specific Play Therapy Interventions

The play therapy with Anna consisted of several drawings and block play activities in which the child re-created the traumatic event and revealed her ongoing fears of the possibility of a fire in her new apartment. When invited to draw a picture of her old apartment during the fire, Anna inserted a drawing of her bunny in the corner of the paper. This picture was quite distorted, and as she drew it, Anna kept talking about how much she missed her bunny. The play therapist suggested that Anna dictate a letter to her bunny stating her feelings. The therapist wrote the child's message on the drawing and suggested that she add the words, "I love you and good-bye." This activity seemed to have great meaning for Anna. Her mother reported in the next session that Anna had stopped her nighttime waking and was behaving more appropriately in school.

Treatment Goals

As previously stated, the focus of treatment following a crisis or trauma is to return the child to his or her precrisis adjustment. The ultimate goal of crisis intervention play therapy is for the child to gain some feeling of mastery over the crisis event or traumatic experience through the realization that it will no longer continue to impact his or her life. This appeared to happen in Anna's case, and she was able to return to her usual routine after having said her farewells to her beloved bunny and received acknowledgment from the therapist and her mother about her loss.

Specific Intervention Techniques

Play therapy methods cover a range of activities including the use of the following:

- art techniques (including drawing, painting, use of clay and play doughs);
- doll play (using bendable family dolls, doll furniture, army dolls, rescue personnel, fantasy figures such as witches and fairies, stuffed animals, and dinosaurs);

- puppet play (with a variety of friendly and wild animals; family puppets; and worker puppets in the form of both hand puppets and finger puppets. Provision of several adult puppets and child puppets of the same species encourages displacement of family dynamics onto the toys);
- storytelling (sometimes the therapist initiates this by beginning a story and asking the child to complete it);
- sandplay (this involves making scenes in a sandbox, using a variety of miniature toys); and
- board games (may be either specifically therapeutic games or regular games that the therapist selects because of themes that resemble the child's experience).

The assumption in the use of these materials is that the child identifies with the toy and projects and displaces his or her own feelings onto the play figures. Cohen, Mannarino, and Deblinger (2006) emphasize the importance not only of the stressful/traumatic play reenactment but also the need for mental reworking or cognitive restructuring of a trauma event. This entails a verbal review that brings about a changed outlook regarding the experience that occurs through repeated guided interactions in which the therapist directs the child to imagine and describe a different desired outcome to the stressful event. Some specific methods in this cognitive approach might include the use of calming and relaxation techniques, guided imagery, psychoeducation, positive self-talk, and instruction that the child should rely on parents and other competent adults in dangerous situations.

Research has not been able to give definitive conclusions about whether directive or nondirective approaches bring more favorable results in therapy with symptomatic children following crisis or traumatic events. Shelby and Felix (2005) comment that throughout the history of child trauma therapy, there has been debate about how best to intervene. In view of the lack of agreement (and lack of conclusive empirical research findings), it seems understandable that few child therapists currently rely on a *purely* directive or nondirective treatment approach. Hopefully, future research will lend light on this important topic; until then, methods that combine both directive and nondirective treatment will continue to be used to relieve children's distress following crisis or traumatic experiences.

GUIDELINES FOR CRISIS INTERVENTION PLAY THERAPY

This following guidelines should be followed in providing this type of treatment.

- Obtain specialized training and participate in ongoing supervision.
- Establish a supportive therapeutic relationship with the child.
- Teach the child some relaxation methods to help keep anxiety in check.
- Provide toys or drawing materials to assist the child in re-creating the traumatic event.
- Move at the child's pace; do not attempt too much in one session.
- Emphasize the child's strength as a survivor.
- Repeat that the traumatic experience was in the *past*.
- Point out that the child is safe in the present

CONCLUSION

Social workers who plan to do crisis intervention play therapy should be well grounded in play therapy, trauma therapy, and grief counseling. All should seek ways to obtain ongoing support and supervision for themselves to avoid what has been called vicarious traumatization. This refers to the personal reactions of therapists who become traumatized themselves in the course of their work with trauma survivors.

We know how to help traumatized children. It is most gratifying to observe a child's reduction of symptoms and return to precrisis functioning. This work, though very challenging, is also very rewarding and well worth the struggle to help children overcome and cast out the demons of fear that develop after crisis and traumatic experiences.

WEB SITES

Constructive Playthings. http://www.ustoy .com.
Fordham University Graduate School of Social Service, Post-Master's Certificate. http:// www.fordham.edu/gss/tarrytown/nbw.
Play Therapy Training Institute. http://www .ptti.org.
Self-Esteem Shop. http://www.selfesteemshop .com.

University of North Texas Center for Play
Therapy. http://www.coe.unt.edu/cpt
or http://www.centerforplaytherapy
.org.

References

American Psychiatric Association. (2000). *Diagnostic and statistical manual of mental disorders*, 4th ed., text revision. Washington, DC: APA.

Brohl, K. (1996). *Working with traumatized children. A handbook for healing*. Washington, DC: Child Welfare League of America.

Cohen, J. A., Mannarino, A. P., & Deblinger, E. (2006). *Treating trauma and traumatic grief in children and adolescents*. New York: Guilford.

Crenshaw, D. (2006). Neuroscience and trauma treatments. Implications for creative arts. In L. Carey (Ed.), *Expressive and creative arts methods for trauma survivors* (pp. 21–38). London: Kingsley.

Landreth, G. (2002). *Play therapy. The art of the relationship*, 2nd ed. Muncie, IN: Accelerated Development.

Reddy, L., Files-Hall, T., & Schaefer, C. (2005). *Announcing empirically based play interventions for children*. Washington, DC: American Psychological Association.

Shelby, J. S. (1997). Rubble, disruption, and tears: Helping young survivors of natural disaster. In H. G. Kaduson, D. Congelosi, & C. E. Schaefer (Eds.), *The playing cure. Individualized play therapy for specific childhood problems* (pp. 143–169). Northvale, NJ: Aronson.

Shelby, J. S., & Felix, E. D. (2005). Posttraumatic play therapy. The need for an integrated model of directive and nondirective approaches. In L. A. Reddy, T. M. Files-Hall, & C. E. Schaefer (Eds.). *Empirically-based interventions for children* (pp. 79–103). Washington, DC: APA.

Webb, N. B. (2003). (Ed.). *Social work practice with children*, 2nd rev. ed. New York: Guilford.

Webb, N. B. (2004). (Ed.). *Mass trauma and violence. Helping families and children cope*. New York: Guilford.

Webb, N. B. (2007). (Ed.). *Play therapy with children in crisis. Individual, family, and group treatment*, 3rd rev. ed. New York: Guilford.

93   Child Therapy and Social Skills

Craig Winston LeCroy

An increasing emphasis is being placed on a social competence model for understanding, preventing, and remediating the problems experienced by children. This conceptualization asserts that problem behavior in children can be understood in terms of them not having acquired skills appropriate to meet situational demands. Children may fail to develop appropriate social skills for many reasons; however, a deficit in skills can lead to problems in successful adaptation to life tasks.

An important part of the socialization of children can be facilitated by offering social skills training. Social skills therapy or classes teach prosocial skills that substitute for problem behaviors, such as being aggressive or withdrawn. Interpersonal skills can be taught to enhance communication with peers, parents, and authority figures. Stress management and coping skills can be taught to help prevent future problems. Numerous opportunities exist for the implementation of various skills-based programs that can help facilitate the successful socialization of children.

Research strongly suggests that social competence is essential for healthy normal development (Ashford, LeCroy, & Lortie, 2006). Through a child's interactions with peers, many of life's necessary behaviors are acquired. For example, children learn sexual socialization, control of aggression, expression of emotion, and caring in friendship through interaction with peers. When children fail to acquire such social skills, they are beset by problems, such as inappropriate expression of anger, friendship difficulties, and inability to resist peer pressure. This understanding has led to the present focus on changing children's interpersonal behavior with peers. Because many of a child's problem behaviors develop in a social context, teaching social skills is one of the most promising approaches in remediating children's social difficulties.

DEFINING AND CONCEPTUALIZING SOCIAL SKILLS

Social skills can be defined as a complex set of skills that facilitate the successful interactions between peers, parents, teachers, and other adults. The "social" refers to interactions between people; the "skills" refers to making appropriate discriminations—that is, deciding what would be the most effective response and using the verbal and nonverbal behaviors that facilitate interaction (LeCroy, in press).

Social skills training uses two key elements in addressing social adaptation of children—knowledge and skilled performance. To respond appropriately to situational demands, a child must have knowledge of appropriate interpersonal behavior. However, that knowledge must be translated into skilled performance or social skills. Social skills training programs or therapy uses methods to enhance a child's knowledge of social situations and enhance effective performance in those situations. An additional consideration is to plan for generalization so that any new skills learned are translated into different environments, such as playgrounds, schools, and neighborhoods.

The conceptualization of social skills as training suggests that problem behaviors can be viewed as remediable deficits in a child's response repertoire (King & Kirschenbaum, 1992). This focuses on building prosocial responses or skills, as opposed to an emphasis on the elimination of excessive antisocial responses. In this manner, social skills training is a strengths-based approach to helping. Children learn new options to problem situations. Learning how to respond effectively to new situations produces more positive consequences than past behaviors used in similar situations. This model focuses on the teaching of skills and competencies for day-to-day living rather than on the understanding and elimination of defects. It is an optimistic view of children and is implemented in an educative-remedial framework.

DEVELOPING PROGRAM OR THERAPY GOALS AND SELECTING SKILLS

Social skills training can be conducted as a program of skills using a group format or as a treatment plan for an individual child. The first step in the development of a successful program is to identify the goals of the program based on the needs of the target population or individual. What specific skills does the child need to learn? For example, a program goal for withdrawn children is to be able to initiate positive social interactions. Once the goals of the program are clearly defined, the next step is to select the specific skills that need to be learned.

For example, a 5-year-old boy is referred to a child therapy clinic. The teacher reported his behavior as "mean" and "sadistic," explained that he had no friends, and saw him as uncooperative. His mother reported numerous fights he had engaged in, described him as being uncooperative, and complained about the use of swearing and noncompliance when directed to do things. To develop a social skills training therapy program for him, we will need to determine what constitutes the opposite of these negative behavior patterns. For example, he would benefit from learning the following types of skills: how to get along with others without fighting, frustration tolerance, and compliance. Learning how to translate problems into skills is an essential part of providing a skills-based model of treatment. Table 93.1 presents examples of how problems can be conceptualized as skills that need to be learned.

After the skills are selected for the treatment, the practitioner then selects a method to promote the acquisition of the skills. For example, common methods might include behavior modification via modeling, role-play practice and reinforcement, use of supportive empathy, dramatic play, and storytelling. Also, group methods using behavioral rehearsal are popular methods for teaching social skills.

The process of social skills training requires continual attention to refining each skill that is to be taught. After identifying the broad social skills, it is important to divide each into its component

TABLE 93.1 Translating Problems into Skills

Problem	Skills
Withdrawn, moody, and irritable	Being aware of one's feelings
	Getting pleasure from interaction with others
	Controlling one's mood
	Doing more
Impulsive behavior, "acting out"	Complying with demands
	Concentrating, maintaining attention
	Following through, showing persistence
	Delaying gratification
Anxious, dependent behavior, separation difficulties	Relaxing, putting one's body at ease
	Separating from others
	Accepting disapproval of others
	Handling rejection
Feeling unloved, showing no outside enjoyment in life, bored	Getting pleasure from loving acts toward others
	Getting pleasure from exploration
	Anticipating pleasure and fun from activities
	Celebrating one's accomplishments and successes
	Accepting compliments from others
	Getting pleasure from positive attention
Substance abuse	Identifying problem situations
	Using effective refusal skills
	Making friends with nonusing peers
	General problem solving for risky situations

parts so that they can be more easily learned. For example, LeCroy (in press) breaks down the skill "beginning a conversation" into the following six component parts.

1. Look the person in the eye and demonstrate appropriate body language.
2. Greet the person, saying one's own name.
3. Ask an open-ended question about the person. Listen attentively for the response.
4. Make a statement to follow up on the person's response.
5. Ask another open-ended question about the person. Listen attentively to the response.
6. Make another statement about the conversation.

A classic social skills training study by Oden and Asher (1977) sought to improve the social skills and peer relationships of third- and fourth-grade children who were identified as not well liked by their peers. The program taught the fol-lowing four skills: participation, cooperation, communication, and validation/support. The intervention consisted of a 5-week program whereby each skill was (1) described verbally, (2) explained with examples, (3) practiced using behavior rehearsal, and (4) refined through feedback, coaching, and review of progress. The results of the study found that the children increased their social skills and had improved more significantly than a group of elementary schoolchildren who did not partici-pate in the program. Particularly impressive was the finding that the children showed gains in how their classmates rated them on play and peer acceptance at a 1-year follow-up.

Social skills training is often used as an addition to other forms of treatment, for example, as one component of treatment of children with attention deficit disorder and Asperger syndrome or as a supplement to parent management training (see e.g., Hinshaw, Buhrmester, & Heller, 1989; Kazdin, Siegel, & Bass, 1992; Lochman, Barry, & Pardini, 2003). It is often considered the treatment of choice for children with emotional and behavioral disorders (Bloomquist, 2006; Dunn, 2005; Gresham, Cook, & Crews, 2004; Michelson, Sugai, & Kazdin, 2007).

GUIDELINES FOR USING SOCIAL SKILLS TRAINING METHODS

After program goals are defined and skills are selected, there are various methods that can be used for teaching social skills. These methods of influence are the ways the learning of such skills is promoted. There are three main methods of influence used in social skills training: skills-based play therapy, group-based social skills treatment, and behavior modification. Many variations exist within these three main methods, for example, using reinforcement of selected skills during spontaneous play therapy sessions, eliciting stories from the child and using them to reinforce selected skills, conducting spontaneous mutual dramatic play that focuses on selected skills, using conversation and fantasies as a means of rehearsal and reinforcement of skills, and playing games designed to teach social skills (LeCroy, Craig, & Archer, 2001). For this chapter, two of the main methods are described: skills-based play therapy and group-based social skills treatment.

Skills-Based Play Therapy

Although play therapy is often associated with more dynamic approaches to treatment, it can be an excellent method for teaching social skills. However, rather than focusing on the catharsis of feelings in play therapy, the emphasis is on learning new skills to address problematic situations and feelings. In skills-based play therapy, this is accomplished by using scripted modeling plays, reading stories that model skills, encouraging selected skills from the child's spontaneous play, and designing plays and stories that are specific to the child's needs.

A primary method is the use of dramatic play where the practitioner models the skills the child needs to learn by manipulating play material. It is important to provide multiple opportunities to practice skillful patterns of behavior. This is accomplished by conducting modeling plays that allow the child to experience the skill being demonstrated vicariously through the play.

When conducting plays or designing stories (as described next), practitioners should follow

the basic principles established in modeling theory. Strayhorn (1988) summarizes the principles concisely.

1. Use multiple characters to provide exposure to multiple models.
2. Have a role model experience reinforcing consequences of his or her action.
3. Design a character that is seen as desirable and appropriate to the cultural context.
4. Use a coping model whereby the character struggles some but then overcomes those initial difficulties.
5. Use characters that engage in self-talk, demonstrating good coping skills.

In this way, skills-based play therapy is very goal directed—play can be linked directly to the skills needed to be learned by the child. For example, a sample modeling play like the following might be performed for the child.

Sample Modeling Play

This play is designed for a child who is having difficulty sharing and ends up fighting with other children over what to do. The social worker would need to set the play scene; this example uses two boys and how they share when one boy comes over to the other boy's house. A wind-up toy is used as the object that the boys will share. Prior to conducting this play, make sure the child has seen the toy so he or she is not preoccupied with learning about it. Materials needed include two boy action figures and one wind-up toy. The social worker begins by focusing the child's attention on the play, "I'm going to put on a play; you watch and then after I'm done you can play with these toys."

Parent: I'm glad you could come over to play! I have something you two might like to play with.

Robert: What is it?

Skyler: Yea, Mom, what did you get?

Parent: It's a Godzilla gorilla that spits fire when you wind it up!

Robert: Wow, let me see.

Skyler: I want to wind it up, let me wind it up. I know, Robert, would you like to take turns?

Robert: Okay, you can do it first, but then I get to do it right after.

Parent: Great sharing, Skyler. I like how you worked out a good way to share with Robert.

Skyler: Thanks, Mom. Robert was really nice to let me play with it first. Look! I'm winding it up, look at the fire! [Sparks come out of its mouth.]

Robert: Wow, that is really cool.

Skyler: Okay, now it is your turn, Robert.

Robert: Thanks, Skyler. I'll wind it up again. Look, fire is coming out everywhere. Okay, it's your turn again, Skyler.

Skyler: Thank you. [Takes the toy and begins winding it up again.]

Parent [Reenters the room] You two are doing a great job sharing and playing together. Can I get you a snack?

When conducting plays like this one, the practitioner should have play material to enact the different scenes—for example, action figures (a dad, mom, and several children), a house, a play yard, play equipment, a school bus, and miniature toy items like food, TVs, and computers. The play is conducted with great animation; figures are picked up when talking and used in a puppetlike fashion. Different characters have different voices, and the action sequence is fast, matching the attention span of the particular child. After conducting a modeling play, many children will immediately imitate the play, rehearsing the skills that the practitioner is trying to teach the child.

Storytelling. modeling skills through reading An additional method for teaching children social skills is the careful design or selection of stories that model the desired skills. Young children are drawn to storytelling, and stories can be used to demonstrate and model skills they need to learn.

For example, if a target skill is anger management, a story can be constructed where the main character gets frustrated but does not get angry. Another character can provide reinforcement and support: "You just walked away and did not get angry—that's a great skill." If the target skill is friendship abilities, the story might enact a scene in which the target child joins the play of others; for example, "Hi guys, looks like a great soccer game. I'd like to play, too." This character also says to himself, "I'm glad I asked to play soccer with those guys; it's a lot more fun."

The process of using skills-based storytelling can take several venues. First, stories can be told or read to children in play therapy sessions. This provides good variation to the additional methods that should be used in individual sessions. Stories can also be given to parents to read to the child.

The goal should be many repeated exposures of the stories—children like familiar stories, and each repetition provides increased vicarious learning of desired skills.

Group-Based Social Skills Treatment

Social skills training is often conducted in a group format, which provides support and a reinforcing context for learning new responses and appropriate behaviors in a variety of social situations. The group is a natural context for social skills training because of the peer interactions that take place as the members work together. Additionally, the group allows for extensive use of modeling and feedback that are critical components of successful skills training.

The following seven basic steps delineate the process that group leaders can follow when teaching social skills training (based on LeCroy, in press). These guidelines were developed for social skills groups with middle school students. Table 93.2 presents these steps and outlines the process for teaching social skills. For each step, there is a request for group member involvement. This is because it is critical that group leaders involve the participants actively in the skill training. Also, this keeps the group interesting and fun for the group members.

1. *Present the social skill being taught.* The first step for the group leader is to present the skill. The leader solicits an explanation of the skill; for example, "Can anyone tell me what it means to resist peer pressure?" After group members have answered this question, the leader emphasizes the rationale for using the skill. For example, "You would use this skill when you're in a situation where you don't want to do something that your friends want you to do, and you should be able to say no in a way that helps your friends to be able to accept your refusal." The leader then requests additional reasons for learning the skill.

2. *Discuss the social skills.* The leader presents the specific skill steps that constitute the social skill. For example, the skill steps for resisting peer pressure are good nonverbal communication (includes eye contact, posture, voice volume), saying no early in the interaction, suggesting an alternative activity, and leaving the situation if there is continued pressure. Leaders then ask group members to share examples of when they used the skill or examples of when they could have used the skill but did not.

TABLE 93.2 A Summary of the Steps in Teaching Social Skills Training

1. Present the social skills being taught
   A. Solicit an explanation of the skill
   B. Get group members to provide rationales for the skill
2. Discuss the social skill
   A. List the skill steps
   B. Get group members to give examples of using the skill
3. Present a problem situation and model the skill
   A. Evaluate the performance
   B. Get group members to discuss the model
4. Set the stage for role-playing the skill
   A. Select the group members for role-playing
   B. Get group members to observe the role-play
5. Group members rehearse the skill
   A. Provide coaching if necessary
   B. Get group members to provide feedback on verbal and nonverbal elements
6. Practice using complex skill situations
   A. Teach accessory skills, e.g., problem solving
   B. Get group members to discuss situations and provide feedback
7. Train for generalization and maintenance
   A. Encourage practice of skills outside the group
   B. Get group members to bring in their problem situations

3. *Present a problem situation and model the skill.* The leader presents a problem situation. For example, the following is a problem situation for resisting peer pressure. After seeing a movie, your friends suggest that you go with them to the mall. It's 10:45 and you are supposed to be home by 11. It's important that you get home by 11 or you won't be able to go out next weekend.

The group leader chooses members to role-play this situation and then models the skills. Group members evaluate the model's performance. Did the model follow all the skill steps? Was his or her performance successful? The group leader may choose another group member to model if the leader believes they already have the requisite skills. Another alternative is to present to the group videotaped models. This has the advantage of following the recommendation by researchers that the models be similar to the trainee in age, sex, and social characteristics.

4. *Set the stage for role-playing the skill.* For this step, the group leader needs to construct the social circumstances for the role-play. Leaders select group members for the role-play and give them their parts to play. The leader reviews with the players how to act out their role. Group members not in the role-play observe the process. It is sometimes helpful if they are given specific instructions for their observations. For example, one member may observe the use of nonverbal skills, and another may be instructed to observe when no is said in the interaction.

5. *Group members rehearse the skill.* Rehearsal or guided practice of the skill is an important part of effective social skills training. Group leaders and group members provide instructions or coaching before and during the role play and provide praise and feedback for improvement. Following a role-play rehearsal, the leader will usually give instructions for improvement, model the suggested improvements, or coach the person to incorporate the feedback in the subsequent role play. Often, the performing group members will practice the skills in the situation several times to refine their skills and incorporate feedback offered by the group. The role-plays continue until the trainee's behavior becomes more similar to that of the model. It is important that "overlearning" takes place, so the group leader should encourage many examples of effective skill demonstration followed by praise. Group members should be taught how to give effective feedback before the rehearsals. Throughout the teaching process, the group leader can model desired responses. For example, after a role-play, the leader can respond first and model feedback that starts with a positive statement.

6. *Practice using complex skill situations.* The last phase deals with more difficult and complex skill situations. Complex situations can be developed by extending the interactions and roles in the problem situations. Most social skills groups also incorporate the teaching of problem-solving abilities. Problem solving is a general approach to helping young people gather information about a problematic situation, generate a large number of potential solutions, evaluate the consequences of various solutions, and outline plans for the implementation of a particular solution. Group leaders can identify appropriate problem situations

and lead members through the steps. The problem-solving training is important because it prepares young people to make adjustments as needed in a given situation. It is a general skill with large-scale application. For a more complete discussion on the use of problem-solving approaches, see Elias and Clabby (1992).

7. *Train for generalization and maintenance.* The success of the social skills program depends on the extent to which the skills young people learn transfer to their day-to-day lives. Practitioners must always be planning for ways to maximize the generalization of skills learned and promote their continued use after training. There are several principles that help facilitate the generalization and maintenance of skills. The first is the use of overlearning. The more overlearning that takes place in the treatment, the greater likelihood of later transfer of skills. Therefore, it is important that group leaders insist on mastery of the skills. Another important principle of generalization is to vary the stimuli as skills are learned. To accomplish this, practitioners can use a variety of models, problem situations, role-play actors, and trainers. The different styles and behaviors of the people used produces a broader context in which to apply the skills learned. Perhaps most important is to require that young people use the skills in their real-life settings. Group leaders should assign and monitor homework to encourage transfer of learning. This may include the use of written contracts to do certain tasks outside of the group. Group members should be asked to bring examples of problem situations where the social skills can be applied. Finally, practitioners should attempt to develop external support for the skills learned. One approach to this is to set up a buddy system where group members work together to perform the skills learned outside the group.

CONCLUSION

As social workers work toward the goal of enhancing the socialization process of children, methods for promoting social competence, such as social skills training, have much to offer. Social workers can make an important contribution to children, families, and schools through preventive and remedial approaches like those described in this chapter. As we have seen, children's social behavior is a critical aspect of successful adaptation in society. Social skills training provides a clear methodology for providing remedial and preventive services to

children. This direct approach to working with children has been applied in numerous problem areas and with many behavior problems. It is straightforward in application and has been adapted so that social workers, teachers, and peer helpers have successfully applied the methodology. It can be applied in individual, group, or classroom settings. Research supports the efficacy of social skills training; it is perhaps the most promising new treatment model developed for working with children and adolescents.

WEB SITES

Association for Behavioral and Cognitive Therapies. http://www.aabt.org.
Family Village Social Skills. http://www.familyvillage.wisc.edu/general/social-skills.html.
Web Site Directory: Teaching Social Skills. http://www.cccoe.net/social/directory3.htm.

References

Ashford, J. B., LeCroy, C. W., & Lortie, K. (2006). *Human behavior in the social environment: A multidimensional perspective.* Belmont, CA: Wadsworth.

Bloomquist, M. (2006). *Skills training for children with behavior problems, revised edition: A parent and practitioners guidebook.* New York: Guilford.

Dunn, M. A. (2005). *S.O.S. social skills in our schools: A social skills program for children with pervasive developmental disorder, including high functioning autism and Asperger syndrome, and their typical peers.* Shawnee Mission, KS: Autism Asperger.

Elias, M. J., & Clabby, J. F. (1992). *Building social problem-solving skills.* San Francisco: Jossey-Bass.

Gresham, F. M., Cook, C. R., & Crews, S. D. (2004). Social skills training for children and youth with emotional and behavioral disorders: Validity considerations for future directions. *Behavior Disorders, 30,* 32–46.

Hinshaw, S. P., Buhrmester, D., & Heller, T. (1989). Anger control in response to verbal provocation: Effects of stimulant medication for boys with ADHD. *Journal of Abnormal Child Psychology, 17,* 393–407.

Kazdin, A. E., Siegel, T. C., & Bass, D. (1992). Cognitive problem-solving skills training and parent management training in the treatment of antisocial behavior in children. *Journal of Consulting and Clinical Psychology, 60,* 733–747.

King, C. A., & Kirschenbaum, D. S. (1992). *Helping young children develop social skills.* Pacific Grove, CA: Brooks/Cole.

LeCroy, C. W. (In press). Social skills training. In C. LeCroy (Ed.), *Handbook of evidence-based child and adolescent treatment manuals*, 2nd ed. New York: Oxford University Press.

LeCroy, C. W., & Archer, J. (2001). Teaching social skills: A board game approach. In C. Schaefer & S. E. Reid (Eds.), *Game play: Therapeutic use of childhood games.* New York: Wiley.

Lochman, J. E., Barry, T. D., & Pardini, D. A. (2003). Anger control training for aggressive youth. In A. E. Kazdin & J. R. Weisz (Eds.), *Evidence-based*

psychotherapies for children and adolescents. New York: Guilford.

Michelson, L., Sugai, D. P., & Kazdin, A. E. (2007). *Social skills assessment and training with children: An empirically based handbook.* New York: Springer.

Oden, S. L., & Asher, S. R. (1977). Coaching low accepted children in social skills: A follow-up sociometric assessment. *Child Development, 48,* 496–506.

Strayhorn, J. (1988). *The competent child.* New York: Guilford.

94 Recognizing Indicators of Child Maltreatment

Judith S. Rycus & Ronald C. Hughes

All children have an absolute right to a safe, permanent, stable home that provides basic levels of nurturance and care and is free from abuse, neglect, and exploitation. This overarching child welfare value is derived from the foundational values of the social work profession—freedom, justice, human dignity, and beneficence. It reflects the social, moral, and legal responsibility of all social workers to identify children who have been abused or neglected or who are at risk of maltreatment, to report suspected child maltreatment to child protective services authorities, and to help ensure children's safety without compromising either permanence or their well-being.

To achieve these ends, social workers must be versed in the dynamics and indicators of child maltreatment and must be able to advocate on behalf of these children and their families. This chapter helps social work professionals accurately recognize the physical, emotional, and behavioral indicators of abuse and neglect; promote early identification and reporting of maltreated and at-risk children; and support provision of the most appropriate services.

PHYSICAL ABUSE

Physical abuse refers to the nonaccidental infliction of serious physical injury or harm to a child by a parent or caregiver. Physical abuse is manifested by bruises, bone fractures, burns, and injuries to the brain, internal organs, or genitals. Injuries from physical abuse can result in permanent physical damage; scarring; developmental disabilities such as mental retardation, epilepsy, and cerebral palsy; and emotional harm. Severe physical abuse can also lead to death, particularly in infants and young children.

To accurately identify physical abuse, it is essential to differentiate these injuries from typical accidental injuries of childhood. The following general criteria are used to determine whether a child's injuries are potentially the result of abuse:

- the location of the injury on the child's body;
- the shape and appearance of the marks or other injuries;
- the presence of multiple injuries in different stages of healing, suggesting repeated injury;

- the history of how the injury was incurred, and the logical probability of the caregiver's explanation, considering the child's age and level of development.

Certain types of injuries to children are almost always inflicted and should be considered highly suspicious of abuse. However, abusive acts may not always result in observable injuries. When physical injuries are absent or equivocal, certain behavioral and emotional indicators in children and their caregivers can help identify the presence or risk of child abuse. The following are indicators of physical abuse.

Bruises

Bruises are the most obvious signs of physical abuse. However, children often become bruised by running, tripping, or falling during normal play. These normal bruises generally occur on bony prominences, such as knees, shins, elbows, forearms, chin, and forehead, and they are typically circular in shape with a nondescript pattern. ByIn contrast, bruises on soft body parts, such as the cheek, earlobe, upper lip, neck, the fleshy part of the arm, and relatively protected body parts (such as the buttocks, abdominal wall, and the genitals) are uncommon except as the result of abuse.

Many bruises are the result of excessive corporal punishment. Bruising on the buttocks, back of the thighs, and upper and lower back often result from a spanking or whipping where a child is hit with sufficient force to break blood vessels. Linear bruises of 1–2 inches in width are typically caused by a strap or belt; the shape of the eyelets or belt buckle may at times be visible within the bruise. Loop marks on the skin are caused by hitting with a doubled-over electrical cord, rope, fan belt, or coat hanger. Punishment with a blunt instrument often results in a bruise or welt that resembles the shape of the instrument used to inflict the wound. Bruises with bizarre or geometric shapes are almost always inflicted.

Bruises or cuts to a child's neck are often inflicted—accidental injury to the neck is rare. Bruises can result from being choked or strangled by a human hand, a dog collar, or cord. Using rope to bind a child can leave burns, abrasions, or blisters on the skin. Rope burns from corner to corner of a child's mouth may result from gagging a screaming child. Tying a child to a heavy object for restraint can also leave rope burns, tie marks, or cuts on the feet, ankles, and wrists.

Forcefully grabbing or squeezing a child's chin or face creates pressure bruises on the skin that resemble fingertips, fingers, an entire hand, or pinch marks. Slapping or cupping the cheek or pulling on a child's earlobe can also create pinpoint bleeding to the face or head. Any bruise to the face and head should be considered a potentially serious injury, because blows to the head or face can cause brain injury.

Bruises on the inside or outside of an infant or toddler's upper lip, or a tear on the floor of the mouth are often caused by jamming a bottle or pacifier into the child's mouth. Bruises to the mouth cannot be self-inflicted until a child can sit independently and fall forward, cutting their inner lips on their teeth.

Biting a child causes distinctive marks characterized by paired, crescent-shaped bruises with individual teeth marks. Measuring the distance between the canine teeth can determine whether the bite was made by a child or an adult.

Bruises and other injuries to the genitals and inner thigh are almost always inflicted, usually in response to toileting mishaps or during sexual abuse. Two small, opposing crescent-shaped bruises on the penis may represent a pinch mark caused by fingernails. A deep groove on the penis can occur from repeatedly tying it with a string, often to prevent wetting. Adult teeth marks on the genitals suggest sexual abuse. Penetrating injuries of the genitals in children are rarely accidental.

Multiple scars or bruises on different body parts, particularly in various stages of healing, are hallmarks of physical abuse, as they suggest repeated maltreatment rather than an isolated accidental injury. The approximate age of a bruise can be determined by its color, which changes as the bruise heals.

Burns

Several types of burns are characteristic of inflicted injury. Cigarette burns are the most common inflicted burn. They are circular in shape, punched out, consistent in size, and may range from blisters to deep sores, depending on the length of time the cigarette was in contact with the skin. Burns from match tips or incense are similar in appearance but smaller in size. Burns to children's hands may be punishment for thumb sucking. These burns must be differentiated from impetigo, a skin condition caused by a bacteria that causes sores of variable size that crust, ooze, and increase in number over time.

Dry contact burns result from forcibly holding a child against a heating device, such as an iron, heating grate, or radiator; holding a child's hands against a hot stove burner or hot plate; or touching a child's skin with a heated metal object, such as a knife, key, or curling iron. These burns often reflect the pattern of the object that made them. Burns on the backs of the hands are suggestive of abuse. Because children reflexively move away from burn sources after accidental contact, many severe burns are the result of having been forcibly held against a hot object.

Dunking or immersion burns are usually caused by forcibly submerging a child in scalding water. These burns are almost always forms of punishment, often for bed wetting or resistance to toilet training. Typical immersion burns include stocking or glove burns (feet and ankles, or hands and wrists), doughnut burns (burned buttocks and genitals, from being submerged in a jacknife position), and burns to the buttocks and backs of the legs (from being forced to sit in hot water). Scald burns to the buttocks and genitals can be very serious. Inflicted hot water burns typically have very regular and uniform lines of demarcation and a characteristic absence of splash marks. A medical condition called scalded skin syndrome may look like hot water burns but is caused by a *Staphylococcus* bacteria.

Other Inflicted Injuries

Head injuries, skull fractures, a blood clot on the surface of the brain (subdural hematoma) and brain trauma can result from blows to the head caused by dropping, throwing, beating, or hitting a child against a wall or door, or from violent shaking (shaken baby syndrome). Complex or multiple fractures increase the likelihood of inflicted injury. Head injuries of this severity almost never result from falls within a home. These more serious assaults can result in mental retardation, blindness, cerebral palsy, seizures, and death. Serious head injuries cannot generally be identified from a visual inspection of the child. Symptoms typically include chronic irritability or vomiting, diminished consciousness, difficulty breathing, convulsions, or seizures, particularly with a history of trauma to the head.

Many physically abused children have X-ray evidence of bone injuries, often of multiple fractures in various stages of healing. Certain types of broken bone injuries are highly suggestive of child abuse, including fractures caused by forcibly twisting or wrenching a child's limbs (spiral and bucket-handle fractures) or from violent squeezing. Unusual fracture sites, such as shoulder blade, rib, sternum, or collar bone, are also highly suspicious, particularly in infants and young children.

Internal injuries are the second most common cause of death in physically abused children, commonly affecting the liver, spleen, small or large intestine, kidneys, or the pancreas. These generally result from blows or kicks to the abdomen or back. Though bruises may at times overlie internal injuries, in over half the cases of internal injuries there are no visible bruises or marks on the outer abdominal wall. When children present with symptoms of projectile vomiting, abdominal pain, pale grey skin that is cool and clammy to the touch, weak and rapid heartbeat, shallow breathing, eyes staring and dilated, or unconsciousness, serious internal injury should be suspected. Unfortunately, intra-abdominal injuries may not be noticed until several days after their occurrence.

BEHAVIORAL AND EMOTIONAL INDICATORS OF ABUSE

When clear evidence of abusive injury is lacking, behavioral and emotional indicators combined with a history suggestive of maltreatment are used to help identify potential abuse. Very young abused children may be remote, withdrawn, compliant, detached, and unresponsive to engagement and may have ambivalent attachments. They may exhibit signs of stress and anxiety through physical illness and regressive behavior or may exhibit a type of hypervigilence or "frozen watchfulness" in which they are alert to surroundings but remain emotionally withdrawn. They may be timid and easily frightened, ducking, cringing, or flinching in the presence of the parent, or they may be very eager to please, crave affection, and show indiscriminate attachment.

School-age and older abused children may develop aggressive or hyperactive behaviors, be unable to concentrate, or show other indications of depression or anxiety. Some children demonstrate fear of their parents—others are overly eager to please and may themselves assume a caregiving role to meet a parent's needs. Abused children typically have difficulty relating to peers and may be manipulative and aggressive or withdrawn and distant. Indicators of abuse in youth may include lying or stealing, fighting, angry outbursts, aggression, abuse of alcohol or drugs, truancy, emotional and social withdrawal, or reported psychological symptoms of anxiety, depression, or dissociative episodes characterized by feeling "far away, outside of events."

NEGLECT

Neglect can be defined as the failure of parents or caregivers to meet their children's physical, nutritional, safety, medical, and emotional needs, thereby placing these children at high risk of serious injury, illness, developmental delay, or death. Severe neglect, such as chronic malnutrition in an infant or the lack of medical care for a serious illness, can be life-threatening, and more children die from severe neglect than die from physical abuse. In most instances, neglect consists of chronic patterns of substandard or deficient parenting, which do not normally place children at imminent risk of serious harm. However the long-term effects of chronic neglect can cause serious and often permanent damage. Neglected children include the following.

- Children who are abandoned by their parents or left with other caregivers, often strangers, for extended periods of time without parental contact or support. This must be differentiated from children who are cared for by relatives with the parent's agreement.
- Children who are malnourished and dehydrated as a result of improper or infrequent feeding, including the severe malnutrition and grossly impaired physical development associated with failure to thrive. Malnutrition in infants and young children can lead to mental retardation or other brain damage and death. In older children, symptoms of malnutrition may not be as pronounced, but the effects of long-term malnutrition can be just as serious. These children are recognizable by their poor weight gain for height and age, thin extremities, a sallow or pale, pasty appearance, and in young children, a protruding abdomen.
- Children who are ill or injured and do not receive necessary medical care. Failure to provide necessary medical care can exacerbate the process of diseases. It is important to determine if parents suspected of medical neglect understand medical instructions and

have the capacity and means to carry them out.
- Children who live in unsanitary or dangerous physical environments characterized by excessive filth, exposed garbage, rotting food, animal and/or human excrement, broken glass, sharp exposed edges on furniture and other objects, exposed electrical wires, flaking lead-based paint, rats or other vermin in the living environment, and unprotected areas from which children could fall and be injured.
- Children not yet old enough to care for themselves who are left unattended or who are supervised by caregivers who are not competent or willing to meet their needs, placing them at high risk of serious harm.
- Children who are inadequately clothed for the weather, placing them at increased risk of illness or injury.
- Children who lack basic physical care and hygiene. Though a dirty child is not necessarily a child at risk, a chronic lack of physical care can increase the risk of disease or illness. Examples are ulcerative diaper rash from unchanged diapers, and localized or systemic bacterial infections from untreated skin abrasions or other injuries.
- Children who are exposed to the effects of drugs or alcohol, including those who have a positive toxicology at birth, infants who experience drug withdrawal symptoms, or children who are injured from exposure to methamphetamine or chemicals used in its manufacture.
- In some communities, failure to send a child to school is considered educational neglect.

The more obvious physical indicators of serious neglect, including malnutrition, serious illness, or injury, are often easy to identify. Neglected children are often small in stature, underweight, appear to always be hungry, and may beg for, hoard, or gorge on food. They may be unwashed and dirty with offensive body odor, uncombed hair, or unchanged diapers. Neglected children may be chronically tired or drowsy and may regularly fall asleep in school. They may have chronic respiratory ailments or infected and untreated cuts, lacerations, and abrasions. They may be found wandering outdoors, improperly clothed and unsupervised, or may have been left alone at home for long periods of time. Children who are medically neglected may be very, even critically ill and may not be receiving necessary medical care. However, in spite of these visible conditions, the typical indicators of chronic neglect may be more subtle and are exhibited behaviorally and emotionally.

A primary indicator of neglect in children is pervasive developmental delay in physical, cognitive, social, and emotional development. Neglected children often function at developmental levels that are typical of much younger children. Neglected infants may be delayed in mastering fine and gross motor tasks, such as grasping, sitting, self-feeding, crawling, standing, and walking. Neglected childrlen are often described as unresponsive, placid, apathetic, dull, lacking in curiosity, and uninterested in their surroundings; their language development and school performance are often delayed. They may have insecure or ambivalent attachments to adults and may not approach other people or exhibit normal interest in interpersonal interactions. Some may self-stimulate and attempt to comfort themselves rather than turning to adults for help. They may be immature, dependent, and lacking in autonomy and initiative. Many are awkward in peer relationships, may not play, or may play half-heartedly. They may be emotionally withdrawn, apathetic, and depressed or anxious, aggressive, and exhibiting a variety of behavior problems, often as a result of not having limits set on their behavior from adult caregivers.

Because indicators of neglect may not be easy to identify, many cases of chronic neglect go undetected. Conversely, well-meaning social workers may apply a label of *neglect* to less-than-optimal parenting that although not always in a child's best interests, does not place the children at high risk of serious harm. Differences in values, norms, and community standards of acceptable child-rearing, as well as a failure to understand cultural differences in child-rearing, may confound a determination of neglect, particularly when a child is not at imminent risk of serious harm.

Although some neglected children are in grave danger, in most instances neglect consist of long-term patterns of deficient or substandard care in which negative outcomes on child development and well-being accumulate and are exacerbated over a period of time. Whether and how to intervene in such cases is a difficult decision, particularly when families do not want services. However, early identification and preventive services to such families can often reduce risk and promote healthier child development.

SEXUAL ABUSE

Sexual abuse is the involvement of a child by an adult or an older youth in sexual activities committed for the sexual stimulation of the abuser. Sexual abuse can be intrafamilial (the perpetrator is an adult family member known to the child); extrafamilial (the perpetrator is an adult who is neither a biological nor psychological family member, but is usually known to the child); sexual abuse by strangers; exposure to the sexual activity of others and sexually explicit materials; and sexual exploitation, which includes using children as sexual commodities, such as child prostitution, trafficking, and child pornography. Child sexual abuse perpetrators typically use force or intimidation of a child victim to maintain secrecy, and thus many cases of sexual abuse are never reported. Physical evidence is not often present, and in many cases, a child's disclosure is the only indicator of the abuse.

Sexually abusive acts include a wide variety of behaviors on a continuum from subtle exploitation to vaginal or anal penetration. In many cases, the abusive activities progress in scope and severity along this continuum, often as part of a lengthy process of grooming by the abuser. These behaviors include nudity and disrobing by the adult; openly observing a child undressing, bathing, or toileting, for the purpose of the adult's sexual stimulation; exposing the adult's genitals to a child; prolonged and provocative kissing; fondling the child's genitals and directing the child to fondle the adult's genitals; masturbation by the adult while the child observes or directing the child to masturbate; oral–genital contact by both child and adult to each other's genitals; rubbing the pubic area or genitals against the child's genital or rectal area, inner thighs, or buttocks; penetration of the rectum and vagina by fingers or objects; and penile penetration of the anus or vagina.

The most common physical indicators of sexual abuse in children are physical injury to the genitals or rectal area, including cuts, lacerations, bite marks, stretched rectum or vagina, fissures in the rectum, or swelling and redness of genital tissue. The presence of sexually transmitted diseases in children under the age of 12, such as herpes on the genitals, gonorrhea, syphilis, veneral warts, or chlamydia, are also highly suggestive of abuse, as are stains, blood, or semen on the child's underwear, clothing, or body. Unexplained pregnancy in a child without a history of consensual sexual activity should be evaluated for abuse. Some sexually abused children, especially primary school–age children, develop bladder or urinary tract infections with blood and pus in the urine and high frequency of urination, or they may have painful bowel movements or retention of feces. In boys who have experienced anal penetration, lack of bowel control and fecal impaction are common.

At times, physical indicators alone may strongly suggest that sexual abuse has occurred. However, in most cases there will be no physical indicators, particularly if the abuse consisted of kissing, fondling, genital exposure, or observation by the child of adult sexual activity. Moreover, even if there were injuries, they may have healed by the time the abuse is disclosed and the child receives a medical examination. Therefore, supporting data, including interview evidence and correlated behavioral or emotional symptoms, is critical in substantiating sexual abuse.

Many children and adolescents who have been sexually abused exhibit characteristic emotional and behavioral indicators. However, many of these indicators are prevalent in children who have not been sexually abused but are otherwise in crisis, emotionally disturbed, or have been physically abused or neglected. The presence of these indicators cannot, therefore, be considered sufficient evidence to assume that sexual abuse has occurred. Likewise, the absence of such indicators does not necessarily confirm the absence of sexual abuse, since many sexually abused children exhibit few of the indicators typically associated with sexual victimization (Corwin, 1988).

The following factors, particularly when seen in combination with physical indicators of sexual abuse or disclosure by the child, could strengthen the suspicion of sexual abuse.

- Fears and phobias (of the dark, school, going out, going home, being left alone), generalized or free-floating anxiety.
- Age-inappropriate intimate knowledge of sexual facts and activities.
- Aggressive behaviors, tantrums, behavioral acting out, running away from home, fighting.
- Withdrawal from social relationships, secrecy, isolation, and a prevailing lack of trust in relationships.
- Developmentally regressive behaviors in young children, such as enuresis (urinary soiling) or encopresis (fecal soiling); thumb sucking, baby talk, head banging, rocking, and excessively clinging behaviors.
- Disturbances in eating or sleeping, gastrointestinal disturbances, and other somatic complaints.
- Generalized irritability, excessive crying, excessive activity, or an inability to concentrate.
- In older children and adolescents, generalized anger directed toward oneself or others, such as running away, stealing, lying, self-mutilation and self-inflicted injuries, inflicting harm on animals or other people; drug use; suicidal gestures; unexplainable rages.
- Generalized symptoms of anxiety and depression; cries easily, is withdrawn, general lack of interest in others or in surroundings; easily agitated, fearful, and excessively watchful.
- Inappropriate and sexualized behavior toward adults of the opposite sex, generally by female children toward adult men. This should not be confused with the normal, developmentally unsophisticated, immature solicitous behavior of some preschool girls toward teenage boys and men.
- Sexual acting out in preadolescent and adolescent children, including promiscuity and prostitution.
- Excessive (in excess of what is typical and appropriate based on the child's age) and/or public masturbation.
- Enticing, coercing, manipulating, or forcing other children into sexual activities (should be differentiated from normal peer exploration of sexuality, including "doctor" games of mutual disrobing, and other age-appropriate sexual experimentation).
- Creating and playing out sexual scenarios with toys or dolls.
- Adolescent fear of sex (beyond normal adolescent ambivalence).
- Wearing extra layers of clothing, clothing that is excessive for the weather, or large, baggy clothing, in what is believed to be an attempt to hide or protect the body.

Many sexually abused children never disclose the abuse. When sexual abuse victims do disclose, the disclosure may be intentional, whereby a child victim makes a conscious and purposeful decision to tell someone about the abuse, usually to obtain help and protection or to relieve feelings of anger, guilt, fear, or anxiety. By contrast, abuse may be discovered by others because of physical injuries or other evidence of the child's involvement in sexual activity, or through spontaneous utterances during play, at bath or toileting time, or when talking to themselves. All types of disclosure should be taken very seriously and referred to competent child welfare experts for further assessment and investigation.

EMOTIONAL ABUSE

Emotional abuse includes such parental acts as extreme and frequent belittling or verbal denigration of a child, capricious and unpredictable parental responses, or chronic parental indifference. Emotional abuse can be associated with physical abuse or neglect or may be a separate psychological phenomenon. The dynamics of emotional abuse can be extremely complicated and destructive.

Emotional abuse can prevent children from developing into emotionally mature adults. Yet in individual cases it is very difficult to assess the extent of emotional harm or precisely predict the pathology likely to result from emotional abuse. It is particularly hard to identify risk criteria with respect to emotional abuse that have enough validity to warrant agency intervention and family disruption. Therefore, emotional harm that occurs without concurrent physical abuse or neglect is often beyond the legal and practical scope of child protective intervention. However, professionals must recognize when emotional abuse increases the risk of harm to an abused or neglected child, and intervention strategies should be included in case plans to address the child's and the family's emotional needs.

REPORTING SUSPICION OF CHILD MALTREATMENT

Social workers have ethical and legal responsibility to be vigilant in identifying indicators of abuse and neglect in children and in reporting suspicions of child maltreatment to child protection professionals for further assessment and, where indicated, protective intervention. The operative word, however, is *suspicion*. It is not necessary for social workers to determine definitively that a child has in fact been maltreated before reporting. However, reporting all instances of substandard child-rearing are neither helpful nor constructive to families or child protection agencies. By becoming knowledgeable about the various forms of child maltreatment and their common indicators, social workers can help identify and refer those families in most need of protective services, thereby helping prevent serious and permanent harm to children.

CONCLUSION

Child protective services may be the most difficult field of practice within the social work profession. Balancing the rights of children to safety, permanence, and stability with parental rights to make family decisions is a fundamental responsibility of child protective services social workers. This chapter is meant to be an introduction to some of the basic dynamics and indicators of child maltreatment. Advanced education and training are essential for professional social workers who have responsibility to investigate, identify, and/or treat families and children in situations of child maltreatment.

WEB SITES

Child Welfare Information Gateway. http://www.childwelfare.gov.

Cincinnati Children's (Hospital), Child Abuse Identification Toolkit for Professionals. http://www.cincinnatichildrens.org/svc/alpha/c/child-abuse/tools/default.htm.

Field Guide to Child Welfare. http://www.childwelfarefieldguide.com.

"Mandatory Report of Child Abuse and Neglect." http://www.smith-lawfirm.com/mandatory_reporting.htm.

National Information Services Corporation: Product Fact Sheet on Child Abuse, Child Welfare and Adoption. http://www.nisc.com/factsheets/qcan.asp.

Reference

Corwin, D. (1988). *Early diagnosis of child sexual abuse: Diminishing the lasting effects.* Thousand Oaks, CA: Sage Publications.

Additional Resource

Giardino, A.P. & Alexander, R. (2005). *Child maltreatment: A clinical guide and photographic reference, 3rd Edition.* St. Louis: GW Medical Publishing.

95 Guidelines for Social Skills Training for Persons with Mental Illness

Susan Gingerich

Social skills training is an intervention designed to help people improve their communication skills, express their emotions, and increase their effectiveness in social situations. It is a structured method that directly teaches one skill at a time and emphasizes practice, modeling, role-playing, and feedback. Social skills sessions are followed up with home assignments to practice the skill in the real world. Unlike interventions that focus on discussing social difficulties and the possible reasons behind them or simply provide opportunities to socialize, social skills training employs a problem-solving and hands-on approach, where clients identify the skills they want to improve, learn the component steps, and then repeatedly practice the skills with others to gradually increase their effectiveness.

Social skills training has many applications (Gioia-Hasick & Brekke, 2001), and is especially helpful for individuals diagnosed with mental illnesses, who often experience a heightened need for strengthening their social skills. Interventions that include a social skills component have been shown to be effective with people with a wide range of mental illnesses, including schizophrenia (Kopelowicz, Liberman, and Zarate, 2006; Kurtz & Mueser, in press), depression (Donahoe, Aciemo, Hersen, & Van Hassalt, 1995), borderline personality (Linehan, 1993), and bipolar disorder (Miklowitz & Goldstein, 1997). In addition, social skills training has been used to help persons with mental illness reduce substance abuse (Bellack, Bennett, & Gearon, 2007), address physical health issues (Pratt, Bartels, Mueser, & Forester, in press), and reduce the risk of being infected with or spreading infectious diseases (Kalichman, Sikkema, Kelly, & Bulto, 1996). Social skills training has been recommended as an evidence-based practice in guidelines for the treatment of schizophrenia (Lehman et al., 2003), and elements of social skills

training are an important component of two of the evidence-based practices identified by the Substance Abuse and Mental Health Services Administration (SAMHSA): family psychoeducation (Murray-Swank & Dixon, 2005) and illness management and recovery (Gingerich & Mueser, 2005).

This chapter describes the basics of conducting social skills training groups and offers suggestions for tailoring groups to meet the needs of the individual members.

IDENTIFYING PERSONAL GOALS

People are most interested in participating in programs they see as helping them achieve personally meaningful goals. Therefore, before initiating social skills training, it is important for clinicians to meet with individuals to explore and identify their personal goals and consider how skills training might help them achieve those goals. Examples of common goals that people set and pursue in skills training groups include the following:

- making friends,
- developing leisure activities,
- getting a job,
- keeping a job,
- dealing with angry feelings,
- reducing (or stopping) drug and alcohol use,
- being a better parent,
- improving family relationships, and
- getting a boyfriend or girlfriend.

After establishing personal goals, it is much easier for the clinician to design a social skills group that will be useful to achieving those goals and develop role-plays and home assignments that are relevant to the group members.

SELECTING CURRICULUM FOR SKILLS TRAINING

Two widely used approaches to social skills training for persons with mental illness have been developed by Robert Liberman and colleagues and Alan Bellack and colleagues. Liberman's skills training curriculum consists of a series of social skills training modules, referred to as the Social and Independent Living Skills (SILS) program (Liberman, 2007). Each module contains a leader's manual, participants' workbooks, standardized homework assignments, knowledge questionnaires, and a videotape of role-plays demonstrating the skills. SILS modules cover the following skill areas: conversation, friendship and intimacy, medication self-management, leisure for recreation, workplace fundamentals, substance abuse management, symptom self-management, community reentry, and involving families. The primary advantage of the SILS program is that the curriculum and training methods are highly specified and the video materials provide a way to standardize role-plays.

Bellack and his colleagues (Bellack, Mueser, Gingerich, & Agresta, 2004) took a different approach by developing a curriculum for a broad range of interpersonal situations. Sixty-two different skills were developed and grouped into the following nine categories:

- basic skills,
- conversation,
- assertiveness,
- conflict management,
- communal living,
- friendship and dating,
- health maintenance,
- vocational/work, and
- coping skills for drug and alcohol use.

Each category consists of several related skills, each broken down into small steps. By referring to the categories of skills, group leaders can plan the curriculum of a group with similar social skill needs. For example, if a group of clients express concern about their ability to handle conflict, the skills included under the category of conflict management" might be useful:

- compromise and negotiation,
- leaving stressful situations,
- disagreeing with another's opinion without arguing,
- responding to untrue accusations, and
- making apologies.

Group leaders can also design a curriculum by choosing skills from different categories. For example, if a group of clients express an interest in doing activities with other people during their leisure time, the leader might develop the following menu of skills:

- starting a conversation,
- finding common interests with others,
- asking for information,
- making requests,
- compromise and negotiation, and
- problem solving.

The primary advantage to the Bellack approach is that the curriculum is flexible and can be organized in a variety of different ways.

BREAKING DOWN SKILLS INTO STEPS

Social skills are best learned when they are broken down into three or four manageable steps. The following are examples of two skills broken down into steps.

Expressing Positive Feelings

- Look at the person.
- Tell the person what he or she did that pleased you; be specific.
- Use a pleasant tone of voice.

Making a Request

- Look at the person.
- Say exactly what you would like the person to do.
- Tell the person how it would make you feel if he or she did what you are asking.
- In making your request, use phrases like "I would really appreciate it if you would _____." "I would like you to _____." "It's important to me that you help me with _____."

CONDUCTING A SOCIAL SKILLS TRAINING GROUP

Social skills training groups usually consist of four to eight members and are scheduled for 60- to 90-minute sessions. Because more frequent training sessions lead to better skills acquisition, it is preferable to conduct two or three sessions per week, with a minimum of once a week. Depending on the setting and the needs of the clients, groups may be time-limited (e.g., a few weeks to several months) or open-ended. Although it is preferable to have two leaders for social skills training groups, it is possible for a single leader to conduct the group.

Skills training sessions are structured and follow a step-by-step format. However, within the structured format there is ample room for the group leader's individual style, sense of humor, and creativity. In fact, clients often report that they enjoy social skills groups because the skills and role-plays are varied and the sessions are lively. The steps of conducting a social skills group are as follows.

1. *Establish a rationale* for learning the skill. Ask group members, "How do you think this skill would be helpful to you? What are the kinds of situations where you could use this skill?"

2. *Present the steps of the skill* by writing them on a whiteboard or flipchart or by distributing handouts of the steps written in a large, bold typeface. Ask one of the group members to read the steps of the skill aloud. For each step, ask group members, "Why is this step important? How would this step help someone communicate more effectively?"

3. *Model the skill* by demonstrating how you would use the steps in a common situation. Tell the group members, "I'm going to show you an example of how I might use this skill. I would like you to watch me to see if I follow the steps." After your role-play, elicit specific feedback by asking "Did I follow step 1?" "Was I able to follow step 2?", and so on.

4. *Ask a group member to practice the skill* in a role-play. When group members are first learning the skill, it is most effective to ask them to practice the skill as it was modeled by the leader. After they have had more practice, it is often preferable to ask the group members to suggest the content of the role-play, saying, "What is a recent example of when you used this skill—or when you wished you had used this skill?" You can ask group members to role-play by saying something like, "I would like each person to have a chance to practice. Tamika, I would appreciate it if you would go first. The rest of the group will watch and give you some

feedback about how you used the steps. We will always start with positive feedback." For some skills, such as giving compliments, the role-play can be set up between two group members. For skills that might be stressful, such as expressing upset feelings, the role-play is best directed to the group leader.

5. *Ask for positive feedback* from the group members. Ask the members a general question, such as, "What did you like about the way Tamika practiced that skill?" and follow it up with questions about each step, such as "Did Tamika follow step 1?"

6. *Ask for corrective feedback* from group members, encouraging suggestions for improvement rather than criticism. Ask questions such as, "Was there anything that Tamika could have done that would have made her role-play even better?" It is usually preferable to limit suggestions to one or two.

7. *Ask the group member to repeat the role-play* using the corrective feedback (that is, implementing one of the suggestions given in step 6). The second role-play can be requested by saying something like, "I would appreciate it if you would practice this skill one more time. I'd like you to do what you did before, only this time try to look at the person a little more."

8. *Ask for additional positive and corrective feedback*, starting with the positive. Ask, "How was Tamika's role-play this time? Was she able to look at the person? Did that make her request more effective?"

9. *Give everyone a chance to role-play* and receive feedback. Give each group member an opportunity to do a second (or third) role-play to use one of the suggestions provided.

10. *Develop a home assignment* for group members to practice the skill outside the session. Writing the assignment on a sheet of paper, note card, or sticky note will help group members to remember their plan for putting the skill into action. Develop assignments collaboratively be asking group members what they think would be a good way to practice the skill, and helping them decide when and where they will do their practicing. The assignments will be reviewed at the beginning of the next session.

Although the ten steps listed here may appear daunting, most group leaders and members report that with a little practice the steps are easy to remember because of their logical progression.

CASE EXAMPLE

Mr. Lennox is a 24-year-old man who was diagnosed with schizophrenia ay the age of 19. He has had two brief hospitalizations and has responded well to clozapine. At the community mental health center, he tells his counselor, Ms. Ames, that he is pleased with his studio apartment and enjoys his part-time job stocking shelves in a supermarket. However, he speaks very little to his co-workers and spends most of his leisure time watching television alone in his apartment. Ms. Ames notes that he wears sunglasses to his meetings with her and looks down at the floor as he speaks. He does not generate conversation and responds to questions with very brief answers. "I wish I had friends," he reports to Ms. Ames. "I guess I just don't know how to talk to people." Mr. Lennox agrees to join a social skills training group that Ms. Ames is starting that will focus on friendship skills. The group is scheduled to meet for 24 sessions (twice a week for 12 weeks) and will cover six friendship skills.

Because several people in the group have low self-esteem, Ms. Ames decides to teach giving compliments as the first skill to build confidence. During the first two sessions, Mr. Lennox wears his sunglasses (which he continues to do until much later into the group), places his chair outside the circle, and asks to "pass" on doing role-plays. He listens to the other group members doing their role-plays, however, and is able to give brief responses when asked for feedback. During the third session, Ms. Ames asks him to receive a compliment as part of Mr. Jones's role-play. Mr. Jones compliments Mr. Lennox on his T-shirt, which bears the logo of a local sports team. Mr. Lennox looks up briefly and smiles when listening to this compliment. At the fourth session, he agrees to pull his chair into the circle; at the fifth session he agrees to practice the skill of starting a conversation with Mr. Jones. He looks down at the floor and asks Mr. Jones if he likes sports. The group gives him positive feedback about being specific and using a sincere tone. They also let him know that he was not looking at Mr. Jones when he spoke. During his second role-play, he looks up for 3 to 5 seconds and receives praise for improving his performance of the skill.

Mr. Lennox participates in role-plays at a similar level for the next three sessions. At the ninth session, he is able to look at the person for 30 seconds, for which he receives positive feedback. At the twelfth session, he is able to take off his sunglasses for one role-play and looks at the person to whom he is speaking for 30 seconds before putting them back on. The group members give specific positive feedback about the improvement of making eye contact without sunglasses. During the next 12 sessions, Mr. Lennox gradually builds up to leaving off his sunglasses for 75 percent of the time during group sessions and makes eye contact during role-plays for at least 1 minute. During the final session, he practices the skill of finding common interests by speaking in an animated way to another group member about his interest in art, especially paintings. Another group member spontaneously responds, saying that she is also interested in paintings, and they briefly discuss a favorite artist.

By the end of the group, Mr. Lennox has made significant progress in being able to look at people without his sunglasses, making eye contact for longer periods, and generating conversation. On the job, he reports feeling more comfortable talking to co-workers and that people are acting more friendly toward him. He has asked to join another social skills group, focusing on more advanced conversation skills.

TAILORING SOCIAL SKILLS TRAINING

Individuals with mental illness differ greatly, and social skills training groups need to be tailored to reflect those differences. As noted earlier in this chapter, it is important to work collaboratively with the client to identify personally meaningful goals and make sure that the social skills group includes skills that will help him or her achieve those goals. If clients find the groups interesting and relevant to their personal goals, they are much more likely to attend the group, participate actively, and benefit from the skills taught.

During group sessions, the leader can tailor role-plays to make them more relevant to the members' individual goals. For example, if the skill being taught is making requests, the leader might suggest a role-play of "asking someone for a date" to the group member whose goal is to get a girlfriend, whereas he or she might suggest the role-play of "asking a sales clerk to help find the correct size" to the group member whose goal is to shop independently. Home assignments can also be tailored to relate to individual goals. If a group member has the goal of speaking up more at work, she might choose to ask her supervisor for a small change in her schedule as a home assignment for making requests.

For some clients, tailoring might include working with them in individual or couples or family sessions. For example, if a client has severe social anxiety, it might be helpful to begin work on starting conversations in one-to-one sessions before attempting it in a group. If a client primarily has difficulties communicating with his or her partner, it might be more effective to work on skills with the client and the partner. Family sessions using social skills techniques can be helpful for strengthening the communication and problem-solving skills of families coping with the mental illness of one of their members.

CONCLUSION

Although skills training requires structure and repeated practice, it also allows clinicians to use creativity in developing curriculum, role-plays, and home assignments. Perhaps most important, skills training affords clinicians the pleasure of helping clients attain skills that contribute directly to achieving personally meaningful goals and improving their quality of life. The ability to design and conduct social skills training groups is a vital asset for clinicians assisting people with mental illness who are of different ages, diagnoses, and stages of recovery.

WEB SITES

Associated Content, Techniques for Improving Social Skills; a commercial site directed at the general population. It contains a description of common social skills problems that could help normalize difficulties with social situations, such as meeting new people, attending a party, making small talk, public speaking, and expressing empathy. It also includes some strategies for dealing with these situations. Most of the strategies are compatible with social skills training techniques, with the exception of "self-hypnosis." http://www.associatedcontent.com/article/3570/techniques_for_improving_social_skills.html.

Campus Blues, Social Skills; directed to a college population at risk for depression, this site provides a useful general description of common social skills difficulties and techniques used to address them. http://www.campusblues.com/studentoflife_6.asp.

Social Skills Training; includes a good general description of social skills training, including its purpose, techniques, and content. http://www.minddisorders.com/Py-Z/Social-skills-training.html.

Substance Abuse and Mental Health Services Administration (SAMHSA); includes information resources kits for five evidenced-based practices for severe mental illnesses, including illness management and recovery. The information resource kit for illness management and recovery contains a workbook for clinicians and supervisors, which includes educational handouts on nine topics, sometimes referred to as modules. Handout no. 4 is "Building Social Support," which involves developing social skills for meeting new people and getting closer to people one already knows. At the Web address listed here, click on "Workbook for Clinicians and Supervisors" and search for Handout no. 4 and the practitioners' guidelines for it. http://mentalhealth.samhsa.gov/cmhs/communitysupport/toolkits/illness.

References

Bellack, A., Bennett, M., & Gearon, J. (2007). *Behavioral treatment for substance abuse in people with serious and persistent mental illness: A handbook for mental health professionals.* New York: Routledge.

Bellack, A., Mueser, K., Gingerich, S., & Agresta, J. (2004). *Social skills training for schizophrenia: A step-by-step guide,* 2nd ed. New York: Guilford.

Donahoe, B., Aciemo, R., Hersen, M., & Van Hassalt, V. (1995). Social skills training for depressed, visually impaired older adults. A treatment manual. *Behavior Modification, 19*(4), 379–424.

Gingerich, S., & Mueser, K. (2005). Illness management and recovery. In R. Drake, M. Merrens, & D. Lynde (Eds.), *Evidence-based mental health practice: A textbook.* New York: Norton.

Gioia-Hasick, D., & Brekke, J. S. (2001). Social workers as skills trainers. In K. Bentley (Ed.), *Social work practice in mental health: Contemporary roles, tasks, and techniques.* Pacific Grove, CA: Wadsworth-Brookes/Cole.

Kalichman, S., Sikkema, K., Kelly, J., & Bulto, M. (1996). Use of a brief behavioral skills intervention to prevent HIV infection among chronically mentally ill adults. *Psychiatric Services, 46,* 275–280.

Kopelowicz, A., Liberman, R. P., & Zarate, R. (2006). Recent advances in social skills training for schizophrenia. *Schizophrenia Bulletin, 32,* 12–23.

Kurtz, M., & Mueser, K. (In press). A meta-analysis of controlled research on social skills training for schizophrenia. *Journal of Consulting and Clinical Psychology.*

Lehman, A., Buchanan, R., Dickerson, F., Dixon, L., Goldberg, R., Green-Paden, L., Kreyenbuhl, J. (2003). Evidence-based treatment for Schizophrenia. *Psychiatric Clinics of North America, 26*(4), 939–954.

Liberman, R. P. (2007). Dissemination and adoption of social skills training: Social validation of an evidence-based treatment for the mentally disabled. *Journal of Mental Health, 16*(5), 595–623.

Linehan, M. (1993). *Skills training manual for treating borderline personality disorder.* New York: Guilford.

Miklowitz, D., & Goldstein, M. (1997). *Bipolar disorder: A family-focused treatment approach.* New York: Guilford.

Murray-Swank, A., & Dixon, L. (2005). Evidence-based practices for families of individuals with severe mental illness. In R. Drake, M. Merrens, & D. Lynde (Eds.), *Evidence-based mental health practice: A textbook.* New York: Norton.

Pratt, S., Bartels, S., Mueser, K., & Forester, B. (In press). Helping older people experience success (HOPES): An integrated model of psychosocial rehabilitation and health care management for older adults with serious mental illness. *American Journal of Psychiatric Rehabilitation.*

Delinquency Prevention and an Evidence-Based Social Work Intervention

96

Families and Schools Together (FAST)

Lynn McDonald

Most interventions on the lists of evidence-based programs were not created or evaluated by social workers. Why is that? Obtaining federal research grants to conduct rigorous evaluations is part of what is required for an intervention to become identified as evidence based, and social work interventions are often not included on the lists. The programs were generally not developed by social work practitioners in the field. Often, such programs apply cognitive-behavioral psychology with single dimensions, linear thinking, and primarily behavioral approaches. Often, they test a social skills training program presented by trained teachers in a classroom, without considering the influence of stress and oppression. Often, they test a mentoring program that brings a college student for 6 brief months into an at-risk youth's life. Although these simple interventions can more easily be tested and shown to be effective, they are not systemic, complex, or comprehensive. Social workers may not see these interventions as useful, because the interventions do not consider a child within a context, including the child's experiences of change and stress over time, intense family relationships and unique family structure, impoverished neighborhoods with severe underemployment, the violent community and high rates of incarceration, a minority identity in a society with institutionalized racism, and the many structural, political, and legal obstacles to normal child development.

Although these factors are difficult to influence and evaluate, they are the realities of any child's life, and an evidence-based model must address them to have a sustained impact on a child's functioning and to interest a social worker. Social workers balance multiple risk factors every day; they determine how to protect or build protective factors for a child. Contextually based prevention that is responsive to cultural differences and systemic issues, is the exception on the current lists of evidence-based practices. This chapter presents an after-school, multifamily group, community development approach that was developed, facilitated, refined, and tested by social workers in partnership with parents. After it was tested in randomized controlled trials set in poor and distressed communities, it was included on several lists of evidence-based practices. Several critiques of these program lists are highlighted.

AFTER-SCHOOL, MULTIFAMILY GROUPS FOR PREVENTION

Multifamily groups have historically been used in psychiatric settings for family education and residential homes for juvenile delinquents, as well as in hospitals as family support for people suffering from chronic illnesses. Typically, evaluations have been positive and report the unanticipated results that social relationships often develop between and among the participating families. Here the strategy of multifamily groups in after-school settings is deliberately used to build relationships among and across families of same-aged children attending the same community school to reduce stress and social isolation. These groups apply traditional skills of social work, including community organizing, group work, family systems work, and parent-led child therapy, into a manualized, 8-week structured group process to build protective factors for children, which in turn reduce delinquency, drug abuse, and school failure.

There are three stages in this group intervention. (McDonald, Billingham, Conrad, Morgan, & Payton, 1997; McDonald & Frey, 1999; McDonald & Sayger, 1998).

Outreach

The collaborative team, with parents, school staff, and social workers as partners, makes outreach home visits to all families of the designated target group of children, for example, all kindergarteners in a school serving a community that has high numbers of incarcerated youth or gang members. The partners invite each family to participate with other families of children in the same school in an after-school event. A peer parent from the school calls and visits the parents at their homes, perhaps repeatedly, to build a relationship sufficient for the parent to come to one group session.

Weekly Multifamily Group Meetings

Eight to ten families participate in each hub; several hubs can run at the same time. These groups are held after school. Each family sits for 1 hour at a family table, and parents lead family communication games and also share a meal. Two and a half hours of positive activities are facilitated by the trained team, and there are no lectures. Instead, during each of the 8 weeks, the team coaches the parents to lead fun, interactive, family activities, including taking turns to listen and talk and repeated embedded compliance requests. Parents learn to make clear requests and reinforce compliance. They practice playing responsively with their child in one-to-one time each week with supportive coaching by the team; they are also asked to practice responsive play at home daily. Over the 8 weeks of 1 hour of parent self-help group time, parents develop trusting relationships with one another and begin to help each other out side of the group meetings. A graduation ceremony is planned by parents for celebration of the first stage of program completion.

Monthly, Parent-Led, Multifamily Group Meetings

Parent graduates of the weekly meetings are supported to become leaders as they direct their own monthly multifamily groups to maintain relationships. They have locally determined community goals. The size of the monthly groups gradually grows as they integrate the graduates of each new 8-week cycle. The ongoing groups maintain the gains of social support and stronger families, and they represent social capital.

MULTIFAMILY GROUPS CAN EXPRESS SOCIAL WORK VALUES

The structure and processes of the multifamily groups express social work values:

- strengthen preexisting structures of family, school, and community outside the marketplace;

- offer groups to support the enhancement of respectful relationships at local community levels, across the social ecology of the child, family, and school;
- include consumer/parents on a team, who plan and deliver services in partnership with professionals from the school and community agencies;
- require that the team that plans and facilitates the groups be culturally representative of the participants in race, class, religion, language, and cultural heritage: "nothing about us, without us";
- ensure that there is active peer outreach to low-income, stressed, isolated, and marginalized families, which traditional approaches often do not reach;
- engage the most important person in the child's life—the caretaking parent and other close family members—into respectful partnership in the prevention process, using respectful, reciprocal strategies;
- offer weekly group opportunities for families with children the same age, attending the same school, to meet repeatedly, over time, to make social connections, friendships, and thereby build social capital in their communities; and
- shift power with supporting small groups of adults to find their own voices; once the small groups are cohesive and empowered, shift the power from shared governance into a self-governed model for monthly meetings to achieve community goals.

MULTIFAMILY GROUPS CAN APPLY THEORY AND RESEARCH

Theory can guide social work group practice. To increase child well-being, social workers can partner with parents to build protective factors to reduce risk factors. Social work researchers Fagan, Van Horn, Hawkins & Arthur (2007) suggests that a pile-up effect of more than five risk factors correlates with increased risk of delinquency. They studied middle school youth and examined risks as they related to delinquent outcomes. Their studies showed that there was a threshold effect: five or more risk factors dramatically increased the likelihood of delinquency, drug abuse, school dropout, and mental health problems. However, recent studies showed that the absence of even one protective factor was the critical factor, rather than the pile-up of risk factors. Just one or two protective

factors are shown to be able to overcome the effects of multiple risk factors. Unfortunately, few youth with more than five risk factors have even one protective factor. Hawkins and Catalano urge social workers to develop strategies to build protective factors for at-risk youth. After-school multifamily groups may be able to systematically building protective factors in hundreds of families at a time as a community development strategy to prevent delinquency, drug use, school dropout, and mental health problems.

In after-school, multifamily groups one can apply the social ecology theory of child development (Bronfenbrenner, 1979) by engaging children, families, extended families, school, and the neighborhood in positive ways to build layers of micro and macro connections. The groups can also apply family stress theory (Boss, 2002; Hill, 1958) by increasing protective factors for all families against the stresses of modern life. Family stress theory suggests that all families are at risk for crises based on their experiences of multiple stresses outside of their control, unless they have active social connections and the ability to perceive their circumstances in positive ways. By bringing families together for positive activities, social supports and the positive perceptions get reinforced.

Family activities can also be organized to enact family systems theory. They can be organized around the principles of structural family therapy (e.g., reinforcing the hierarchy of the executive subsystem) and functional family therapy (promoting fairness and turn taking communication in families) and communications family therapy (giving each family member the opportunity to say in their own family unit what they are thinking and what they are feeling, while sitting at a family table in the well-lit, safe space of a public school). Parents can be coached and supported to lead the family activities by team members. Informal group processes can be organized to strengthen (1) boundaries around family units, (2) parent–child bonds, (3) parent-to-parent connections, and (4) parent support groups. Published experimental studies from psychiatry, psychology, and sociology can guide the specified processes used in activities for whole family units, parent–child dyads, adult dyads, and adult or youth peer groups. With repetition, these exchanges and interactive opportunities can build long-term informal social support networks and stronger reciprocal personal relationships, that is, "social capital" (Putnam, 2000),across networks of families, schools and community levels.

Family Communication Patterns Can Be Changed in Groups

Research can guide multifamily group practices. Consider Alexander and Parsons's (1973, 1982) classic studies, in which family-based research determined that training families of delinquents in specific communication patterns reduced recidivism rates in the juvenile court system by half. Randomly assigned court-involved adolescents were treated with functional family therapy or no unusual treatment. The risk of a second court-involved offense within 18 months was halved by the family intervention in comparison with the control group.

This research can be applied in multifamily groups by coaching the parents to lead the family communication exercises, which provide the foundation for conflict resolution. The after-school public setting usually blocks familiar conflicted family sequences; instead, each person gets an opportunity each week to be listened to with a fair turn, as the parents asks for each person's perspective. Parents practice helping the family take turns at speaking within family units and making positive inquiries about each other's turns in a family drawing game. These research results can be applied in family table–based activities. By having the parent lead the family communication activity, the parental authority is respected and rehearsed within the family unit time (Minuchin, 1979).

Social Supports for Parents Can Reduce Stress and Child Neglect

The classic research study of Wahler (1983) can be used to justify working in groups with parents at risk for child abuse and neglect. His studies researched the effectiveness of behavioral parent training with single mothers who had been referred to child welfare for child abuse and neglect of their children. In a 6-month follow-up after parent training, he determined that their gains in parenting skills were not maintained if the mothers were socially isolated. Calling them "insular" mothers, he concluded that without an informal support network, parent training was ineffective. Multifamily groups can address these research findings by doing outreach and engagement, to build informal social support networks with small groups of parents who have in common children of the same age attending the same school. In this way, the stress and social isolation

of parent is reduced, which in turn reduces their risk for abusing or neglecting their child.

Another classic in-home direct observation study by Belle (1980) can also guide social work practices. She reported that low-income, depressed mothers showed interactive patterns with their children in predictable ways: they neglected them when they were preoccupied with their depressed mood, and then they were emotionally abusive when the children tried to engage their mothers. However, this was not always the case. If the mother had daily contact with one supportive adult, Belle observed that the negative cycles did not occur. Even just 15 minutes a day of talking with another adult reduced the child neglect.

This research can be applied by structuring daily and weekly time for one-to-one talk time between parents. Each week in the multifamily groups, parents can be invited to meet in dyads for 15 minutes to talk and listen to daily hassles in "buddy" relationships. After just 8 weeks of repeated dyadic encounters, 86 percent of parents reported that they made new friends, whom they continued to see for years. If a family only attended once, twice, or fewer than six times, this did not happen. A minimum number of encounters were needed. New friendships required six weekly encounters to become strong enough to maintain themselves across the shift to monthly meetings and casual encounters in the community.

Parent–Child Bond Can Be Built in Groups

Longitudinal studies and cross-sectional research can also inform social work practice. For example, significant predictors of resilience were reported by Werner and Smith (1992), based on their 30-year longitudinal study of over 600 children born in Hawaii. They found that robust relationships with one's parent or another adult in the community were the most potent protective factors for reducing bad outcomes. Relationships with significant others who really cared distinguished resilient youth from those with poor outcomes, given the same risk-laden communities. In another kind of research, a cross-sectional study discovered the same type of results: the protective factors that most protected youth from risk factors (Resnick et al., 1997) were identified in a study based on interviews of a randomized sampling of 10,000 U.S. youths across social classes. Three factors reduced the negative youth outcomes: positive connections with the parents, positive feelings about school, and no access to guns (for violence). Intimate relationships to which you could turn to discuss stress were critical in helping youth avoid violence, delinquency, substance abuse, and school dropout.

Multifamily groups can be structured to support the strengthening of one-on-one caretaking parent–child relationships by structuring time at each meeting to foster dyadic relationships and positive communication between parent and child. Government-funded research by Kogan (1978) and Webster-Stratton (1991) supports the impact of just 15 minutes of one-to-one responsive parent time during free play. Responsive behaviors by the parent can be coached within the group structure by trained team members who help the parents block directiveness and criticism. Instead, parents are coached by trained teams to practice following the child's lead and initiative within free play.

MEASURING OUTCOMES

Family Engagement and Retention Rates

After school, multifamily groups seem to be unusually successful at engaging and retaining involvement of families who come once. In contrast, families who come to one visit at an outpatient child mental health clinics drop out at a rate of 40–60 percent after the first visit. For Families and Schools Together (FAST), 20 percent dropout rates are reported across over 900 after-school implementations in seven countries. If parents attend once, 80 percent usually complete the 8-week program and participate in the graduation. Of these, 80 percent will return at least once to monthly meetings; 60 percent will return frequently; 10 percent will become parent leaders. Because these programs are voluntary, people only come if they want to do so. Families who are socially marginalized and are generally expected to never attend social functions often return to FAST groups in rural, inner-city, and suburban settings. These retention rates have held constant over hundreds of cycles in hundreds of communities over 19 years.

Quality Assurance of Core Components and Promotion of Local Adaptations

New collaborative teams are trained in the multifamily group processes. Teams receive manuals and learn about the theories and the research base of the intervention, as well as the core components of the evidence-based model and the importance of local adaptation by practitioners and service users. Sites become certified through the FAST National Training and Evaluation Center (a nonprofit) in Madison, Wisconsin. Each new site is visited up to five times by a certified FAST trainer, who trains the local teams to adapt the group processes to fit the community. Trainers come to directly observe three of eight group sessions, discuss the adaptations, and maintain the program integrity. This intensive attention to quality control and clinical supervision results in good outcomes and builds capacity in the multifamily group processes. Each site is required to conduct pre- and postevaluations using standardized measures with established validity and reliability of the child's mental health functioning at home by a parent and at schools by a teacher regarding the child's behaviors in the classroom; parents also report on parent involvement in the school, family conflict levels, and social capital. The results are shared in a written report with each local community within 6 weeks of receiving the completed pre and post forms.

Over time, the expected amount of change in the child's mental health has been established across hundreds of sites as between 20 and 25 percent after only 8 weeks. The replication outcome evaluation data are compared to the norms of the instruments, as well as the norms for FAST programs nationally. In a study of FAST cycles in 53 schools in 13 states, teachers reported statistically significant improvements in conduct disorder (correlated with delinquency), attention span problems (correlated with school failure), and anxiety or withdrawal (correlated with substance abuse; McDonald & Frey, 1999) on the Revised Behavior Problem Checklist by Quay Peterson.

Randomized Controlled Trials: Federally Funded Research

Rigorous research studies have been completed on the social worker–developed, community development, multifamily group strategy described here. The Administration of Child and Youth Families, and the National Institute of Drug Abuse, of the Department of Health and Social Services, the Office of Special Education and Rehabilitation Services, and the Office of Educational Research Institute of the Department of Education each funded randomized controlled trials with large sample sizes and 1- to 2-year follow-up. These four studies were conducted in inner-city schools in New Orleans (nine) and Milwaukee (ten), in three schools serving children living on Native American reservations, and in schools in Madison (nine), a medium-sized city in Wisconsin. Preliminary results suggest that there were positive differences for FAST children versus control group children, using Achenbach's Child Behavior Checklist (CBCL) and the Social Skills Rating Scale (SSRS) by Gresham and Elliot. Externalizing scores as rated 1 year later by parents (ABT draft final report) and as rated by teachers in another study (OERI draft final report) are statistically significantly lower for FAST versus controls. These results suggest that there are systemic changes causing improved child functioning 1 year after FAST on behaviors correlated with delinquency.

Evaluation methodology. Four randomized controlled trials (RCTs) of the FAST program have been completed. All four studies used widely recognized outcome measures of child behavior, with established reliability and validity—the SSRS and the CBCL, which include subscales for social skills, aggression, and academic performance.

The first RCT (Layzer, Goodson, Bernstein & Price, 2001) involved 400 low-income African American children identified as at risk by teachers. These youths were randomly assigned to a FAST treatment group or a control group. Among the families who participated, 77 percent participated in at least one session, 78 percent attended at least five sessions, and the overall completion rate was 60 percent. The evaluation measured the outcome ratings of the children by parents and teachers 1 year after the intervention, using hierarchical linear modeling and an intention-to-treat (ITT) model.

The second RCT (Kratchowill, McDonald, Levin, Bear-Tibbetts, & Demaray, 2004) used universal recruitment of 100 Native American children in kindergarten through second grade from three reservation schools in a generally low-income, rural area. All children were matched into 50 pairs based on five variables: age, gender, grade, tribe, and teacher assessment of high versus low classroom aggression on the CBCL. The matched pairs were then randomly assigned to FAST treatment or control groups. Among the families who participated, 100 percent participated in at least one session, and 80 percent returned for at least five sessions. Pretest–posttest and 1-year follow-up data were collected and analyzed with an ITT model.

The third RCT (McDonald et al., 2006) involved ten urban elementary schools that were randomly assigned to either the FAST treatment group or a comparison condition called FAME (Family Education). A universal treatment strategy was used in which all families with children in the treatment or comparison condition classrooms were recruited for the study. The study included a 2-year follow-up. This study concentrated on a subsample of 130 Latino families (80 assigned to FAST and 50 assigned to FAME) who agreed to participate in the research and with 2-year follow-up teacher data. Among those who agreed to join the study, 89 percent participated in at least one session, 78 percent participated in at least five sessions, and the overall completion rate was 69 percent.

The fourth RCT (Kratchowill, Levin, McDonald, Scalia & Coover, 2006) involved 134 children identified as having behavioral problems from kindergarten through second grade in an ethnically diverse school district that served at-risk, low-income communities. All children were matched into pairs based on five variables: age, gender, grade, race, and teacher assessment of high versus low classroom aggression on the CBCL. The matched pairs were then randomly assigned to FAST treatment or control groups (67 matched pairs). Among families who participated, 100 percent participated in at least one session, and 90 percent returned for at least five sessions. Pretest–posttest and 1-year follow-up data were collected and analyzed with an ITT model.

Evaluation outcomes. The results of the first RCT showed that 1 year after the intervention, children in the FAST treatment group showed significantly more positive scores in social skills (SSRS) than control group children, as rated by parents, and significantly lower scores than children in the control group on the CBCL subscale for externalizing (aggressive) behaviors, as reported by parents. Children in the FAST treatment group also were given higher social skills ratings than the control group from teachers blind to the experimental condition, though the difference was not significant. Parent involvement and volunteering were also significantly higher among FAST parents than control group parents after 1 year.

The results of the second RCT showed statistically significant differences at 1-year follow-up on the CBCL and SSRS. FAST participants were favored over control group participants in assessments by teachers blind to experimental condition regarding classroom behavior and academic performance, and parents indicated that FAST youths were much less withdrawn than were the control youths.

The results of the third RCT showed that Latino children in the FAST treatment group were given statistically higher ratings of academic competence and social skills and statistically lower scores on aggression than children in the FAME control condition.

Finally, the results of the fourth RCT showed no significant differences in the ratings of FAST and control group children on standardized measures by teachers blind to experimental condition. However, parents of children in the FAST group rated their children significantly lower on the CBCL than parents in the control condition. In addition, school district data on the use of special education services showed that children who participated in FAST received one-fourteenth the number of special education services received by children in the control group.

A 4-year follow-up study on 251 families graduated from FAST, funded by the Center for Substance Abuse Prevention (CSAP), Substance Abuse and Mental Health Services Administration (SAMHSA), showed statistically significant increases in the following areas (McDonald et al., 1997; McDonald & Sayger, 1998):

- improvement on parent reports of conduct disorders, attention problems, and anxiety for the elementary children;
- improvements on parent reports of attention problems, anxiety or withdrawal, and psychotic behavior in the middle-school children;
- increases in positive behaviors in the classroom, according to teacher reports;
- increased family cohesion and reduced family conflict;
- increased parent involvement in children's schooling;
- monthly multifamily groups run by parents attended by 62 percent of the graduated families more than twice a year; 23 percent never attend again; and
- increased community involvement by 91 percent of parents; 86 percent reported that they had made new friends at FAST.

LISTS OF EVIDENCE-BASED PROGRAMS

Developed in the community in 1988 by a social worker, FAST was identified as a model program in the list of 34 family-strengthening programs published by Office of Juvenile Justice and Delinquency Prevention in 1994 and 2000, as a solid B-level program. In 2006, the Office of Juvenile Justice and Delinquency Prevention reviewed FAST

again, based on the new RCTs, and upgraded its listed status to exemplary (which is the top-level, i.e., an A-rated program). In 2002, CSAP rated FAST at the top level as a model program (1 of 65 model SAMHSA programs, out of over 1,000 reviewed). In 2006, the Harvard School of Education published a report about the 13 SAMHSA model programs family strengthening programs (including FAST), in which it compared the 13 models and derived recommended best practices. FAST was commended by Harvard for its strong retention rates among low-income, socially marginalized families. In 2007, the Center for Mental Health Services (CMHS, SAMHSA) submitted a report to Congress on evidence-based programs to promote child mental health; 12 evidence-based models were in this report, including FAST.

POSSIBLE LIMITATIONS OF EVIDENCE-BASED LISTS

A current trend in public policy is to demand outcomes from practitioners and require demonstrable effectiveness from agency administrators. This trend is crossing over many arenas in which social workers deliver services, including public, private, and nonprofit. The good news is that tax dollars are gradually becoming focused onto human services approaches that have evidence demonstrating that they work to enhance lives. This is a good development for children, families, and communities who have needs and no voice.

However, cautions exist about the process of developing these short lists. The emphasis on testing the outcomes with RCTs may not be balanced by other factors relevant to the effective replication of evidence-based models. Some questions to include in the generating of the list of family strengthening programs are as follows.

- Do they address complexities of social problems affecting children—for example, systemic issues, access to resources, family structures, racism, poverty, social capital versus social isolation?
- Do they build ongoing positive relationships of natural support systems for and with the youth, and do they build protective factors that will be sustained over time, or do they increase dependency on professionals in short-term relationships?
- Do the developers specify the core components versus the components one can adapt locally? Is there room for creative

adaptations that help the local fit and facilitate the local ownership in replicating evidence-based models?

• Do they respect the input of the local consumers and practitioners who replicate the model and provide a structure for incorporating the feedback of the local replicator in revising and perhaps improving the program?

• Do they have a quality assurance structure for evaluating each new pilot, to determine whether the impact and desired level of outcome is being achieved?

Researchers and policy makers may be raising expectations with promises to community practitioners about effectiveness of evidence-based programs. However, these lists have biases that may compromise the effectiveness of the program replications at a local level. The biases are toward programs that are:

• simple rather than systemic, complex and comprehensive; simple programs are more easily tested in classic experimental designs in university settings;

• developed within university settings, with funding for conducting strong research; to fully examine candidate models with experimental designs, expensive data collection, and sophisticated statistical analyses;

• not developed by social work practitioners, or even codeveloped by community-based practitioners working with clinical researchers to determine their impact;

• seeing parents as the passive recipient of prevention services—that is, to be taught or fixed. Respectful partnerships with parents to address prevention issues of their own children are rare;

• static and not responsive to feedback from consumers, improved adaptations by practitioners in the field, or of relevant new research; and

• not widely replicated in diverse settings, have not engaged low-income diverse parents and therefore have not passed the test of being acceptable and effective in hundreds of replications in varying communities.

WEB SITES

CMHS, child mental health prevention programs. http://familiesandschools.org/media/cmhs-report-to-congress.pdf.

FAST National Training and Evaluation Center. http://www.familiesandschools.org.

Harvard School of Education, family strengthening programs. http://families-andschools.org/media/harvard-lessons-family-best-practice-research-paper.pdf.

OJJDP delinquency prevention programs. http://www.dsgonline.com/mpg2.5/TitleV_MPG_Table_Ind_Rec.asp?ID=459

SAMHSA substance abuse prevention programs. http://www.modelprograms.samhsa.gov/pdfs/model/FAST.pdf.

References

Alexander, J. F., & Parsons, B. V. (1973). Short-term behavioral intervention with delinquent families: Impact on family process and recidivism. *Journal of Abnormal Psychology, 81*(3), 29–35.

Alexander, J. F., & Parsons, B. V. (1982). *Functional family therapy*. Monterey, CA: Brooks/Cole.

Belle, D. (1980). *Low-income depressed mothers: Parent intervention*. Cambridge, MA: Harvard University Press.

Boss, P. (2002). *Family stress management: A contextual approach*. Thousand Oaks, CA: Sage Publications.

Bronfenbrenner, U. (1979). *The ecology of human development: Experiments by nature and design*. Cambridge, MA: Harvard University Press.

Fagon, A. A., Van Horn, M. L., Hawkins, J. D., & Arthur, M. W. (2007). Using community and family risk and protective factors for community based prevention planning. *Journal of Community Psychology, 35*(4), 535–555.

Hill, R. (1958). Social stresses on the family: Generic features of families under stress. *Social Casework, 39*, 139–158.

Kogan, K. L. (1978). Help-seeking mothers and their children. *Child Psychology and Human Development, 8*(4), 204–218.

Kratchowill, T. R., Levin, J. R., McDonald, L., Scalia, P. A., & Coover, G. (2006). Families and Schools Together: A randomized controlled trial of multifamily support groups for children at risk. Manuscript submitted.

Kratchowill, T. R., McDonald, L., Levin, J. R., Bear-Tibbetts, H. Y. & Demaray, M. K. (2004). Families and Schools Together: An experimental analysis of a parent-mediated multifamily group program for American Indian children. *Journal of School Psychology, 42*, 359–383.

Layzer, J. I., Goodson, B. D., Bernstein, L., & and Price, C. (2001). *National evaluation of family support programs: Volume B. Research studies: Final report*. Prepared by ABT Associates. Washington, DC: U.S. Department of Health and Human Services, Administration for Children, Youth, and Families.

McDonald, L., Billingham, S., Conrad, T., Morgan, A., & Payton, E. (1997). Integrating strategies from mental health and community development: The FAST program. *Families in Society, 78*(2), 140–155.

McDonald, L., & Frey, H. (1999). Families and Schools Together: Building relationships. *Juvenile Justice Bulletin*, NCJ 17423, 1–20.

McDonald, L., & Sayger, T. (1998). Impact of a family and school based prevention program on protective factors for high risk youth: Issues in evaluation. *Drugs and Society, 12*, 61–86.

McDonald, L., Moberg, D. P., Brown, R. Rodriguez-Espiricueta, I., Flores, N. I., Burke, M. P., et al. (2006). Afterschool multifamily groups: A randomized controlled trial involving low-income, urban, Latino children. *Children and Schools, 28*(1), 25–34.

Minuchin, S. (1979). *Families and family therapy.* Cambridge, MA: Harvard University Press.

Putnam, R. (2000). *Bowling alone.* Cambridge, MA: Harvard University Press.

Resnick, M. D., Bearman, P. S., Blum, R. W., Bauman, K. E., Harris, K. M., Jones, J., et al. (1997). Protecting adolescents from harm: Findings from the National Longitudinal Study on Adolescent Health. *Journal of the American Medical Association, 278*(10), 823–832.

Wahler, R. G. (1983). Predicators of treatment outcome in parent training: Mother insularity and socioeconomic disadvantage. *Behavioral Assessment, 5*, 301–333.

Webster-Stratton, C. (1991). Coping with conduct-problem children: Parents gaining knowledge and control. *Journal of Clinical Child Psychology, 20*, 413–427.

Werner, E. E., & Smith, R. S. (1992). *Overcoming the odds: High-risk children from birth to adulthood.* Ithaca, NY: Cornell University Press.

97 Group Process and Group Work Techniques

Paul H. Ephross & Geoffrey L. Greif

This overview of group work techniques discusses the importance of placing them within a context that is culturally appropriate and provides clarity as to the group's membership, structure, and length. Techniques also must be considered within the context of the stage of the group and the worker's self-awareness. No list is complete, and the authors encourage the creative use of technique development to meet the needs of group members when evidence-based practices are not available.

CASE ILLUSTRATIONS

In the first case, the River City Consolidated School District has become aware of the fact that a large proportion of disciplinary problems affecting its middle schools (sixth through eighth grades), some involving behaviors verging on and some actually constituting criminal behavior, involving a small minority of students. Teachers estimate that 80–85 percent of the behaviors are committed by 5–20 percent of the children. A program has been undertaken whereby 3 days a week, two social workers with extensive experience working with preadolescents and young adolescents will meet to have lunch and for the period after lunch for group treatment aimed at preventing such antisocial behaviors.

Permission is being asked of the parents of the boys and girls who have been exhibiting antisocial behaviors, first at a series of meetings called for this purpose, and then through home visits and individual discussions with parents. Teachers in the sixth and seventh grades have been asked to nominate children whose parents should be invited to the meetings for purposes of understanding the program and giving permission to their children to participate. The two social workers who will work with the groups met for the first time a few days before the first scheduled meeting with the parents to plan the program together.

The second case, a short-term support group, is in stark contrast to the first case study in its format, goals, and its level of complexity. This group began when parents called the School of Social Work at the University of Maryland following a television reporter's story on the second author's work with grandparents in a Baltimore city public school. The grandparents who called were seeking a group where they would have an opportunity to discuss the trials and tribulations of raising their grandchildren without the active parenting support of their own children, the grandchildren's parents. Due to the demand, a support group based at the School of Social Work was quickly initiated. An MSW student served as a co-leader and screened the members on the telephone. Seven grandparents attended.

The structure of the group and treatment goals were straightforward. It was to be a 4-week group meeting for 90 minutes every other week during the day when the grandchildren were in school. The purpose was to allow the members to:

1. share their experiences in an atmosphere where they could find support;
2. gain insight into their parenting styles and issues they might be confronting;
3. get specific ideas about how the middle generation, their children, could be involved in parenting; and
4. learn about developmental issues.

Shulman (2009), along with others, has written about the benefits of such groups. He includes mutual aid, "all in the same boat" phenomenon, and information sharing among the benefits that members accrue from similar experiences. This was a typical, voluntary parenting group with highly motivated members. The leaders experienced a halo effect because they were, in the eyes of the members, television personalities. The members actively seeking us out and this halo effect allowed us to build a connection with the group members quickly, thus accelerating the beginning stage.

The first group began by the leaders showing the TV clip that resulted in the group's instigation. After we asked the members what they hoped to get from the group and restating the purpose and the ground rules (which included having to report any instances of child abuse to protective services), we asked the members to talk about their situations. At the group's conclusion, we asked them to suggest topics for the next three groups. These included discussing how the members own parenting influences how they (grand)parent, disciplining, involving their own children in parenting the grandchildren, and finding time for themselves when they expected to have retired from parenting responsibilities at this point in their life.

The concluding fourth session centered on the last topic, finding time for themselves, and evaluating the success of the group. Mr. M., who attend group with his wife, stated in his evaluation that "learning that I am not the only one with these problems has been helpful. The group has also given me something to do with my time." Barbara added, "I never realized that the way I was raised affects the way I am raising my grandchild." One of the members was absent but sent in the message that she wished the group could continue and that she had enjoyed it and how nice everyone had been.

The techniques used in this group are common in support groups and included support, reflective listening, programming (showing the television show), probing, cognitive restructuring, allowing for catharsis, sharing of information, insight, education, and in one case, referral for further services.

The phrase "social work with groups" and its synonym, "social group work," have various associations (for us positive) among both social workers and consumers. Many of these associations are pleasant, and stem from the origins of group work method in voluntary agencies, using theoretical bases that stress voluntarism, people helping each other, and the power of the democratic method in facilitating growth in individuals, the development of community, and not only toleration but celebration of historical and cultural differences among people. For others, it brings to mind a tradition of using activities, of which verbal interaction is only one, that have educational and group development benefits as well as educational to therapeutic effects for group members.

Northen and Kurland identified "the dynamic forces that have been most frequently identified as applicable to the practice of social work with groups" as mutual support, cohesiveness, quality of relationships, universality, a sense of hope, altruism, acquisition of knowledge and skills, catharsis, reality testing, and group control (Northen & Kurland, 2001, pp. 25–26). They go on to identify "criteria for selection of a group modality" according to the purpose of service. The three general purposes they identified are "enhancement of relationships," the development and extension of social competence, and coping with stress. They also specify the usefulness of group services for "indirect services," including staff training, collaboration, planning, and social action, which they characterize as aimed at providing knowledge and skills essential for the development of groups and using the "generic values, knowledge, and skills of social work, adapting them to the needs of particular members and to varied group situations."

In addition to the extensive work by Northen and Kurland, there is an abundance of professional literature on work with groups. Two books with which the present authors are involved exhibit this variety. One is our own *Group Work with Populations at Risk* (Greif & Ephross, 2005) and the second is *Groups that Work: Structure and Process* (Ephross & Vassil, 2005)(see also Gitterman & Shulman, 1994; Shulman, 2009). Because of such textual availability, the focus of this chapter is on delineating the specific skills that are part of the group work method and some combination of which constitute the armamentarium of a skilled social worker with groups.

One preliminary caution may be appropriate. There are no techniques or skills that are unique to social work with groups. Many of those employed in social work with groups are also used by teachers, researchers, section chiefs, and other kinds of administrators. What distinguishes social work with groups is not the techniques employed but the purposes for which they are used.

With this in mind, every chain of activities and all participation in the processes of groups by social workers may be viewed as a miniature piece of research. A social worker does or does not speak up in a group, communicates nonverbally, participates or not, makes a suggestion, defends it or doesn't, depending on an assessment formulation of which the worker may or may not be fully aware. From this point of view, every action or nonaction of a worker in a group may be viewed as a piece of research in miniature. Whether the worker's participation helps the group achieve its desired result constitutes the data gathered by "the experiment." If the outcome is that desired, the worker's intervention in the group's process has reached its goal and was functional or helpful. If not, negative findings are found, and the worker, alone or with a colleague, will act differently than had it succeeded. As group members become aware of the purposefulness of a worker's behavior, as they "catch on," so to speak, they will still respond, or not. The group's reaction constitutes a focused, though miniature, piece of research. What makes the worker's intervention effective or not is not whether his or her intervention was unique but whether it was effective in helping the group move on, grow, learn, or develop skills.

Because there is no lack of lists and types of activities and philosophical stances for a social worker with a group, this chapter maintains clear foci: what work should/does/ought a social worker perform with a group, and how does the worker know whether the activity or intervention undertaken was a success? How does a worker act both consciously and in a disciplined fashion on one hand and in a genuine and pleasant fashion, on the other?

We are not able to cover all possible techniques, ways of intervening, and activities that one or a pair of workers may undertake with a group. One or the other of the activities, tasks, or activity media we suggest may in turn suggest a related cluster of activities to each reader.

Two preliminary thoughts deserve mention before we launch into what we have described. One does not have to be an expert in a particular activity or skill to be able to use it with a group. In fact, it has been our observation that expertise and the kind of self-knowledge and self-consciousness that often accompany expertise is often a drawback when using the activity as a program activity, or activity medium with a group. Artists are rather noted for a lack of patience brought about by a focus on technical excellence. This focus may be useful for an artist but is useless for a group worker seeking to help establish a bridge for cooperative problem solving within a group.

Athletes playing competitive sports do and should aim to win. Social workers are much more likely to introduce games for reasons other than winning or scoring the most points. Boating instructors seek to teach proper form, leading to winning in a competitive event. These may well not be the aims of a worker, who views a boat as an ideal place for intimate communication because it suggests both privacy and intimacy. One unifying principle for a social worker's own group participation is conscious use of self. One should be able to answer the questions, without guilt and in a serious fashion, "How do you propose to behave and why? How will you know if you have reached or failed to reach your objective?" "Biography is always important" can serve as an organizing principle as well as naturalness tempered by discipline. A worker in a group needs to accept him- or herself as well as the legitimacy of each group member and the group as a whole. A basic principle is to be able to accept, in-depth, each group member and the entire group, at the same time that one need not accept—in fact, one may strongly disapprove—of the behavior of one or more group members, or the group as a whole.

For example, in the second case at the beginning of this discussion, the leaders may not agree with the grandparents in how they are parenting their grandchildren or treating their children. Yet this does not diminish the legitimacy of the group work itself, and the attempts by the workers to forge supportive connections with the members and between the members.

In the first case illustration, it is proposed that the groups meet in a classroom during school hours. Schools are disciplined places with regard to noise, often have policies regarding strong language, and take minute-by-minute schedules seriously. Social workers with groups often expect and allow a high volume of noise, including profanity, and may not strictly adhere to starting and stopping times. In short, the cultures of group service and public (or private) schools often differ in important ways. Groups need to be helped to understand "the contract" under which they will be guests in someone else's building and subject to the house rules.

SKILLS OF SOCIAL WORK WITH GROUPS

The approach taken in the remainder of this chapter is to focus on the skills required of a social worker with and in groups. Social workers not only work with groups in clinical practice but also require well-developed skills to work in groups that may be administrative, educational, supervisory, or some combination of the three. The listing of skills draws on five major sources in the group work literature, namely, the works by Shulman (2009), Northen and Kurland (2001), Brown (1991), Ephross and Vassil (2005), and Greif and Ephross (2005). Additional sources of the techniques listed are the many decades of practice with groups and teaching of group work in social work education on the part of the authors.

Despite its length, the list is still incomplete, and we invite the reader to add to it, noting skills that are unique to a particular worker or particularly suited for work with a particular population. We refer to "the worker" in the singular, though we believe that some groups and situations justify or require more than one worker.

Some of the skills require no explanation; others have drawn comments or brief explanations from us. We hope that readers will maintain their own lists as an extension of ours and a reflection of their experiences in practice. Two skills are overarching, and the management of these processes influences the life history of groups powerfully. They are, first, influencing and interpreting decisions regarding membership in a group— whether membership is open and subject to change over time or closed for the duration of the group— and the time frame within which the group will exist. Is this group to be highly focused on a particular topic and scheduled to meet within a defined period, such as the 4 weeks in the second case example? Or are these questions subject to the group's influence or decision as the members proceed to take on responsibility for the group's life, program, purpose, and relationship to the organization which brought it into being (potentially illustrated in the first case example)? Sometimes a group's life span is related to life stages of the group's members. Termination with many adolescents' groups is a function of educational stages. For example, a group may come to the end of its span with its members' high school graduation or the end of the school year. A group therapy experience in a prison may conclude with the discharge of a group of prisoners or the end of their period of probation. For the sake of clarity, we may refer to these skills as

1. Management of group formation and relationship to sponsoring organization.
2. Structural contracting and installation of normative standards for membership in the group.

To these basic skills, we add the following.

3. Cultural awareness and sensitivity, reinforced with strong conviction about the importance of ethno/racial identification and its legitimacy.
4. Discussion and agreement on both short and longer-term group goals. In the instances of groups whose members are severely limited by their condition, members' participation

may be equally limited. For other groups, members participate actively in discussion and agreement.

5. The worker's ability to teach, tutor, and point various group members or the group as a whole to learning experiences that may go beyond the confines of the group itself.

Brown (1991) listed 11 skills that relate particularly to groups that sit, discuss, and educate each other and themselves. These skills that workers need, often with the participation of members, are:

6. Giving information, advice, or suggestion, in other words, directing.
7. Seeking information about individuals, the group, significant others, or agency policies and procedures which affect the group.
8. Accepting and reassuring, showing interest.
9. Encouraging the expression of thoughts and feelings.
10. Involving the individuals or group in activity or discussion. Note that these last two skills summarize an enormous range of talent and influences in a very few words. They refer to the "guts" of a great deal of group work and to the skills and behaviors of group members as well as group workers. They involve relationships in depth within the group and between the group and the outside world. "Activity" can encompass the entire range of artistic, athletic, educational, and social activity in which groups can engage.

Brown moves next to techniques by means of which a worker encourages and nurtures insight, maturation, self-exploration, and growth on the part of members.

11. Exploring with the individual or group the meaning of individual or group behavior, as well as life experiences.
12. Reflecting individual or group behavior.
13. Reframing an issue or problem.
14. Partializing and prioritizing an issue or problem.
15. Clarifying or interpreting individual or group behavior, as well as life experiences.
16. Confronting an individual or a group (Brown, 1991, p. 113).

Of course, no one person is skilled in all of these as well as the many techniques that follow. What is desirable is a balance between what a worker (or team of workers) can do on their own, their knowledge of available resources on the part of other members of a staff, and the abilities and skills of group members themselves. Other examples are as follows.

17. Programming and program planning using developmentally and culturally relevant media. This can refer specifically to timing as an intervention also as groups develop at different speeds based on the culture of the group members. Because of this, overly intrusive questioning, for example, may not be appropriate too early in the group.
18. Planning and providing leadership for recreational activities in general.
19. Directing the use of art techniques, such as drawing, cartooning, and crafts techniques, such as plastic arts, weaving, and many others.
20. Reinforcing and/or questioning parental behaviors.
21. Connecting current feelings to past behaviors or experiences.
22. Developing insight at age-appropriate and culturally appropriate levels.
23. Developing, eliciting, and reinforcing insight.
24. Teaching focusing on the here and now, including use of the group as a microcosm.
25. Teaching relaxation techniques.
26. Teaching the importance of "I" messages.
27. Teaching and demonstrating conflict-resolution techniques.
28. Normalizing feelings. This looms large in many groups with developmental goals, including not only children and adolescents but hospital patients with war wounds, victims of various forms of abuse and neglect, and many other populations. Groups are ideal places for the learning of tolerance and management of personal differences.
30. Modeling empathetic and constructive confrontation.
31. Worker self-disclosure and modeling limits to self-disclosure. Self-disclosure is always occurring, in what the worker both chooses to comment on and chooses to not comment on, as well as in what he or she is wearing, finds humorous or serious, and how he or she presents him- or herself. For example, merely introducing oneself as a student or as a licensed worker with a BSW or MSW conveys the worker's view of the importance of education and professionalism.

32. Intervening in the community on behalf of the client group.
33. Responding immediately when appropriate to group, community, and national happenings.
34. Using music to connect with the group culture.
35. Establishing boundaries as appropriate.
36. Teaching and using the skill of contracting.
37. Role-playing as a skill and as a conflict-resolution technique.
38. Videotaping and playing back. This is an underused technique with enormous therapeutic and skill-building potential, particularly for groups and communities in which membership splits are linked to conflict and misunderstandings.
39. Pregroup and postgroup interviewing. The pregroup screening and the postgroup interview to learn about outcomes are marvelous opportunities to use techniques that presage or reinforce group learning;
40. Building and reinforcing self-esteem and competence.
41. Using specifically refined and evidence-based group work packages, such as Critical Incident Stress Debriefing or solution-focused debriefing.
42. Understanding and seeking to influence the community context. This applies to a variety of groups in diverse settings. One should particularly be aware of the potential of these activities for residents of closed communities, such as correctional institutions, long-term hospitals, and the like. It also applies to populations who experience their day-to-day existence as containing levels of exclusion and exploitation that do not fit with the expectations of members of a democratic and diverse society.
43. Representing and being supportive of the social justice aspirations and bases of the social work profession. This applies not only to direct practice—implementing the 52 foregoing principles in direct work with groups—but also being aware of the meanings of what takes place inside and outside the group for its symbolic content and learning potential.
44. Being aware throughout the group's processes of professional ethics, represented by the Code of Ethics of the National Association of Social Workers specifically and by commonly accepted principles of professional ethics in general. This means implementing professional discipline, in part by structuring one's life so that personal

needs are met outside of professional practice. It also requires a personal commitment to a career-long process of learning to upgrade one's skills, ask reputable professional sources for guidance with highly emotionally loaded situations, and in extreme situations, refusing to violate professional ethics despite whatever excuses specific situations may provide.

45. Group work techniques, led by the processes of disciplined, purposeful, and conscious use of self, also apply to working groups. By this, we mean groups that exist not primarily to bring about change in their membership but rather those that have been formed to lead to the production of a tangible product outside the experiences of the members. This product may be a document, such as a budget or a goals statement, one or more positions on public issues, a research proposal, the opening of a new service or a new department of an existing service, or raising funds and other resources to meet community needs (Ephross & Vassil, 2005).

In our opinion, disciplined, goal-directed participation in working groups resembles similar participation by a social worker in a treatment or developmental group more than it differs from it. It is often observed that administrative and leadership accomplishment demands a highly developed—though differently applied—ability to form accurate judgments that have much in common with forming similarly accurate clinical judgments of people, groups, and processes.

Lists of techniques cannot include everything. We encourage workers to creatively develop their own theory-driven approaches when evidence-based as well as wisdom-driven techniques are not available to meet the idiosyncratic needs of a specific group member or group.

STAGES OF GROUP DEVELOPMENT

For some 50 years now, it has been generally agreed that groups in their lives go through direct phases or stages, all other things being equal. Milestones in this conceptualization for social workers have come with the publication of Tuckman (1965) and Tuckman and Jensen's (1977) amplification. In social work with groups, the first widely accepted schema of stages of group development was done by Garland, Jones, and Kolodny (1965).

In our view, all of these formulations relate to a focus by groups, generally in a sequential fashion, on issues that an earlier theorist (Schutz, 1956) had aptly called the interpersonal underworld. Tuckman and Jensen's (1977) formulation added to the earlier formulation of forming, storming, norming, and performing, a final stage of adjourning or termination. This is congruent with the stage model of Garland et al. (1965), which had identified the stages of group development as pre-affiliation, power and control, intimacy, differentiation, and termination. In more recent years, Schiller (1995) has suggested that women's groups go through a somewhat different series of stages, in which the interpersonal bond issues come earlier in the group's history than is traditionally the case in men's groups. Regardless of the stage or phase, we note that the stage of the group has an enormous impact on the use of techniques. For example, asking for insight before support has been given or using icebreaking skills in the tenth meeting that are best suited for a first session would be inappropriate and a misread of the group's developmental stage. Space does not allow a detailed discussion of the phases of group development here, but there are clear implications of each of the stage models for foci of group attention and therefore foci of social worker attention as well.

THE SOCIOLOGY OF GROUP WORK KNOWLEDGE AND SKILL

Social work is only one of the helping professions that uses the therapeutic, socialization, and learning potential of group processes to achieve socially desirable goals. Other professions that employ skills compatible with group work skills in social work include physicians (especially those concerned with mental health), nurses, public health workers, members of the clergy of all religions, psychologists, educators, researchers, administrators, and sociologists concerned with small groups, to say nothing of teachers, researchers, and administrators who carry responsibility for producing social workers and other professionals skilled in guiding group processes. These professions share terminology with social workers and use their own. The translations from one's profession's jargon to another are relatively easy, because the realities of group process and the ways to influence group process are virtually identical.

Some skills in translation of vocabularies are involved in working with other professions, but this translation is both valuable and often necessary, especially in institutional settings, where the employment of a staff of varied background has become increasingly common. It is not clear, as of this writing, whether the traditional category of group worker will survive as a subspecies in social work or social work education. What is clear is that the skills, values, processes, and goals associated with group work are essential parts of social work and allied professions and disciplines.

WEB SITES

American Association of Retired Persons, a great source for grandparent support groups. http://www.aarp.org.
Cochrane Collaboration, evidence-based practice with parenting and adolescent groups. http://www.cochrane.org.

References

Brown, L. N. (1991). *Groups for growth and change.* New York: Longman.
Ephross, P. H., & Vassil. T. V. (2005). *Groups that work: Structure and process,* 2nd ed. New York: Columbia University Press.
Garland, J. A., Jones, H. E., & Koladny, R. L. (1965/1973). A model for stages of development in social work groups. In S. Bernstein (Ed.), *Explorations in group work* (pp. 17–72). Boston, MA: Boston University School of Social Work, ibid., Milford House.
Gitterman, A., & Shulman, L. (Eds.). (1994). *Mutual aid groups, vulnerable populations and the life cycle,* 2nd ed. New York: Columbia University Press.
Greif, G. L., & Ephross, P. H. (Eds.). (2005). *Group work with populations at risk,* 2nd ed. New York: Oxford University Press.
Northen, H., & Kurland, R. (2001). *Social work with groups,* 3rd ed. New York: Columbia University Press.
Schiller, L. Y. (1995). Stages of development in women's groups: A relational model. In R. Kurland & R. Salmon (Eds.), *Group work practice in a troubled society: Problems and opportunities* (pp. 117–138). New York: Haworth.
Schutz, W. C. (1956). *The interpersonal underworld.* Palo Alto, CA: Science and Behavior Books.
Shulman, L. (2009). *The skills of helping individuals, families, groups and communities,* 6th ed. Belmont, CA: Cengage Learning.
Tuckman, B. W. (1965). Developmental sequence in small groups. *Psychological Bulletin, 61,* 384–399.
Tuckman, B. W., & Jensen, M. A. C. (1977). Stages of small group development revisited. *Groups and Organizational Studies, 2*(1), 419–427.

Psychopharmacology and Social Work

Kia J. Bentley & Joseph Walsh

Psychotropic medications are increasingly used at health and mental health agencies to treat clients who have a variety of mental, emotional, and behavioral disorders. Social workers, the largest number of professionals in outpatient mental health settings and who have the most extensive face-to-face interactions with clients, are increasingly called on to be a resource for clients with respect to issues related to medication use. For these reasons, in addition to their commitment to a client-centered value system, social workers have developed five roles for use in their practices. This chapter outlines the current state of the profession with regard to psychopharmacology and further identifies complex issues that will emerge for social workers in the near future.

Case example: Rebecca was a 40-year old divorced attorney with no children, living alone, with schizoaffective disorder, characterized by delusions of persecution and agitated behavior. While representing her law firm overseas, she confronted associates about their inappropriate "spying" on her and threatened lawsuits in retaliation. She was hospitalized against her will by her parents and sister. Although she took medication and quickly stabilized in the hospital, she remained angry and paranoid and refused to take medication as an outpatient, threatening to sue the social worker if he tried to convince her to do otherwise. The family was concerned about additional acting out on Rebecca's part, which could ruin her already damaged legal career.

The introduction of chlorpromazine (trade name Thorazine) in the 1950s is most often associated with stimulating the modern era in psychopharmacology; today psychiatric medications are routinely used in mental health and health settings. Social workers have always had roles in the monitoring of clients' medications, but these roles have expanded dramatically in the past 30 years with the increased use of medications for persons with a variety of disorders and the large number of social workers functioning as primary service providers in those settings.

The explosion of brain research in the past decades and the renewed emphasis on etiological models of mental illness emphasizing genetics and neurotransmission have had a defining influence on pharmacological research and development. Psychiatric medications, similar to other medical interventions, are generally considered to be about 70 percent effective for consumers. Listed here are the five classes of medications with some examples of each, although it must be emphasized that there is much overlap among categories in their use.

1. *Antipsychotics.* Conventional medications include fluphenazine (Prolixin), haloperidol (Haldol), and thioridazine (Mellaril). Atypical medications include risperidone (Risperdal), olanzapine (Zyprexa), aripiprazole (Abilify), and Ziprasidone (Geodon).
2. *Antidepressants.* Three different types of antidepressant medications include the monoamine oxidase inhibitors like phenelzine (Nardil) and tranylcypromine (Parnate); cyclic drugs, such as amiltriptyline (Elavil), nortriptyline (Pamelor), doxepin (Sinequan), and imipramine (Tofranil); and the selective serotonin reuptake inhibitors (SSRIs), including fluoxetine (Prozac), citaprolam (Celexa), paroxetine (Paxil), sertraline (Zoloft), and fluvoxamine (Luvox). Other antidepressants include bupropion (Wellbutrin) and duloxetine (Cymbalta).
3. *Mood stabilizers.* Lithium has been the most widely prescribed medication for the treatment of bipolar disorder, and anticonvulsant drugs including valproate (Depakote), lamotrigine (Lamictal), and others have emerged since the late 1970s as alternatives.
4. *Antianxiety medications.* Benzodiazepines are the largest category of antianxiety drugs, including diazepam (Valium), alprazolam (Xanax), and triazolam (Halcion), but these drugs are not used as much now due to their abuse potential. Increasingly, SSRIs are

effectively used to treat the anxiety disorders. Buspirone (BuSpar) represents another type of antianxiety drug.

5. *Stimulants*. The stimulants and other medications for attention difficulties include amphetamine (Adderall), atomoxetine (Straterra), pemoline (Cylert), and methylphenidate (Ritalin, Concerta).

TOWARD RESPONSIVENESS AND COLLABORATION

Almost all social workers work at least occasionally with clients who use psychotropic medications as part of their intervention plans. In many service settings, social workers assess mental status and inquire about psychiatric medication use as a part of a client's biopsychosocial assessment. However, social workers have recently begun to elaborate a more complete range of professional roles with regard to psychiatric medication. They are more frequently expected by clients and other professionals to possess sound knowledge of medications and their consequences for clients' lives, not just to complement the physician's role but because they bring important insights, techniques, and a special appreciation of client self-determination. Contemporary practice requires the social worker to strive for two related goals with respect to psychiatric medication:

Goal 1: Be an Effective Collaborator with Clients, Families, and Prescribing Physicians

To do this well, social workers should subscribe to the following philosophical practice principles.

- Embrace a client-centered "partnership" perspective around the range of medication-related dilemmas and issues that emerge in practice. This suggests working toward a nonthreatening alliance, a demystification of the helping process, and a mutual sharing of respective expertise.
- Maintain a balanced perspective about psychiatric medication in the face of admittedly complex issues related to human rights and professional roles, and the costs and benefits of medication use.
- Work toward the successful integration of psychosocial interventions and psychopharmacology and recognize the intrinsic power of combined treatments.

- Work toward interdisciplinary relationships characterized by equality, flexibility, decreased professional control, mutual understanding, and shared goals and also appreciate the challenges that emerge in managing parallel treatment.
- Appreciate both the strengths and the limits of clients and their families. Interventions should center on clients and families' unique strengths and aspirations and away from symptoms or weaknesses. Barriers to progress, such as a lack of skills or inadequate resources, must be appreciated.

Goal 2: Be a Meaningful Resource to Participants around Medication-Related Issues and Dilemmas

Social workers can do this by engaging in a range of general activities.

- Being a valuable source of whatever information, support, or "supplies" are called for in reaching specific "wants" and goals of clients with respect to their medication.
- Focusing first on assessing and clarifying medication-related issues, which can occur on psychological, social, strategic, practical, and informational levels.
- Being creative in applying skills and techniques drawn from evidence-based practice theories and models to medication-related issues, and emphasizing the use of both individual and environmental supports and resources.
- Encouraging the client and family to share their own experiences and emotions about medication use, provide input to the helping process, generate and weigh options, negotiate, and offer feedback as decisions are made.

ROLES AND COMPETENCIES IN MEDICATION MANAGEMENT

Six specific and often overlapping contemporary roles for social workers with relevance for psychopharmacotherapy include the following.

The Consultant

The social worker takes an active role while maintaining a nonadversarial position with the provider. The social worker performs preliminary screenings to determine clients' possible need for medication, makes referrals to physicians, assists in information sharing and decision making, and consults with clients and providers as needed. The social worker prepares clients for active participation in the psychiatric assessment. Related responsibilities might include articulating the rationale for the referral, addressing the client's attitude toward psychiatrists, discussing the client's expectations and fears about medications, assessing the client's ability to pay for medication, and addressing issues of adherence. The worker monitors the client's subjective experience as well, particularly the meaning and impact of the referral to the client.

The Counselor

The social worker helps clients articulate goals, see options, weigh alternatives, plan and practice tasks, and take action to solve problems and reach personal goals related to psychiatric medication. Counseling can also involve giving accurate information about medication and offering advice. The counselor recognizes the importance of empathy, especially around the client experience of side effects or impatience with therapeutic effect. Toward this end, listening to the life stories of clients, including how medication, positive and adverse effects, and self-definitions of mental illness or emotional distress are intertwined.

The Advocate

Social workers perform two essential tasks that relate to their ethical mandate to advocate for clients: (1) advocating directly for clients and families, and (2) empowering and facilitating clients to advocate for themselves. Examples of advocacy in psychopharmacotherapy include trying to increase client access to the newest types of medication, obtaining free medication from a drug company when needed, discussing potential overmedication with physicians, challenging a hospital's termination of a clinical trial, or appealing an insurance company that declines coverage of a psychiatric drug. Advocacy is linked with client and family rights, particularly regarding access to quality treatment.

The Monitor

The social worker helps the client keep track of both positive and negative effects of medication so that prompt physician action may be summoned when indicated. This requires that social workers have an understanding of basic pharmacokinetics (effects of the body on a drug) and pharmacodynamics (effects of a drug on the body). In addition, monitoring adverse psychological effects involve watching for any changes in the client's self-image and identity that emerge as a result of using medications. For example, clients may come to view themselves as "sick" people or become overly dependent on medication as a solution to perceived problems. Adverse social effects include any potentially negative consequences that go beyond the individual to consider how medication affects one's employment and standing with certain social institutions. Finally, social workers can be creative in using existing measures or devising systematic procedures to evaluate each medication's effectiveness and a client's response over time.

The Educator

The social worker performs as a teacher and coach for clients, families, and perhaps other providers regarding issues including drug actions, benefits, risks, common side effects, dosing regimens, routes of administration, withdrawal, toxicity, and adherence. In addition, social workers teach and practice the steps in problem solving, and in collaboration with nurses, pharmacists, and others they offer practical suggestions to help clients take medication appropriately. Teaching clients skills in assertiveness and negotiation can help them maximize their relationships to the prescribing physicians.

The Researcher

Using case reports, single case designs, or more elaborate designs, the social worker documents how medications impact the lives of clients and families, how medications interact with other interventions, and how interdisciplinary relationships can be best coordinated.

Figure 98.1 summarizes the social worker's application of the six roles described here, followed by a clinical illustration.

ILLUSTRATION OF THE SOCIAL WORKER'S ROLES

In the case of Rebecca, described at the beginning of the chapter, the social worker learned during

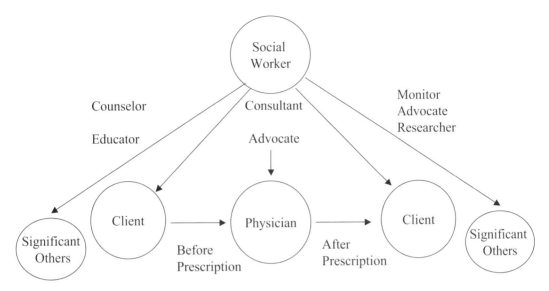

Figure 98.1 Roles of the social worker.

his assessment that the client perceived medication use as evidence that she was "crazy," and taking it would have a devastating effect on her self-image as an independent woman succeeding in a primarily male profession. Furthermore, Rebecca felt that the medication represented efforts of others to control her mind and sabotage her important legal advocacy work. Clearly, the idea of medications had strong, negative meanings to her self-image. Rather than refer her directly to a physician, the social worker spent several weeks getting to know the client, validating her successes and empathizing with her trials, and not pushing her use of medications (counselor role). The client gradually developed trust in the worker, and agreed to a trial of minimal-dose medications that would serve to "help me relax and deal with the stress of my persecution." The social worker met with the physician before Rebecca's first session to let him know of her history and her attitudes about medication (consultant). He also arranged for her to receive free medications for 3 months from the agency's funding pool, even though she did not strictly qualify for it (advocacy). The client admitted that with her level of ambivalence, she would not take medications if she had to pay for them. With the social worker's encouragement, the physician also validated Rebecca's concerns about the medications and agreed to be available, though the social worker, should her ambivalence become more pronounced (monitor). With the social worker's patient intervention, Rebecca eventually accepted

the medication and benefited from it. The social worker continued to emphasize the medication's role in helping her remain calm (educator), and the client took it regularly. He also maintained contact with the client's family, with Rebecca's permission, to inform them of the effects and possible limitations of the medication (educator).

FUTURE DIRECTIONS

Issues of importance to the fields of psychopharmacology and social work practice in the coming years include:

- the appearance of new drug treatments, perhaps with a more precise spectrum of producing drugs without unwanted side effects;
- creative new delivery routes, like brain implants, skin patches, or under-the-tongue medications;
- new information about the differential physical and psychological effects of medications on people of different ages, genders, races, and ethnicities;
- findings about the placebo effect and the additive or interactive effects of combining psychosocial interventions;
- the popularity of herbs, vitamins, and holistic alternatives;
- expanding prescription privileges among nonphysician mental health care providers;

- increased public scrutiny and criticisms of psychiatric medications, clinical drug trials, drug companies, advertising agencies; and
- new models of health care financing that will influence drug availability and use.

Ideal practices for social workers with regard to psychopharmacology will always feature a collaborative helping environment in which the work is comfortably paced but action-oriented, and relationships are characterized by honesty, genuineness, and warmth. There is and should be more attention paid to the ethical dimensions of medication management, such as avoiding subtle coercion of clients, respecting client's decisions not to take medication, being vocal about concerns related to over- or undermedication, and long waiting lists for medication evaluation. Finally, social workers should maintain a critical perspective on medication use in society, but also an appreciation of the power of integrated treatment to improve the quality of lives of people with mental illness and emotional distress.

WEB SITES

Dr. Bob's Psychopharmacology Tips. A unique site that allows you to search for tips (edited by Dr. Robert Hsiung) on psychopharmaceutical use from physician postings. Though not scientific, this site allows you to see direct opinions from prescribers on their experiences with psychopharmaceuticals. http://www.dr-bob.org/tips.

International Center for the Study of Psychiatry and Psychology. Peter Breggin's site, author of numerous books critical of psychiatry and medications. Find information on the dangers of drugs, book lists, reports, excerpts. http://www.icspp.org.

Medicine Net. Run by a network of doctors who want to provide up-to-date comprehensive health info to the public. http://www.medicinenet.com/medications/article.htm.

Mental Health Info Source. Home of community medical education and publishers of Psychiatric Times, with links to news, ask the experts, classifieds, professional directory, conference announcements, and information on disorders and treatment. http://www.mhsource.com.

Mental Health Net. A comprehensive site linking to information on disorders and treatments, professional resources, and journals. Sponsored by CMHC systems. http://www.mentalhelp.net.

National Alliance for the Mentally Ill (NAMI); a national advocacy group with a strong consumer and family member perspective, focusing on serious mental illnesses. http://www.nami.org.

National Institute of Mental Health (NIMH). Public information on specific disorders, diagnosis, and treatment with a section on research activities. http://www.nimh.nih.gov.

National Mental Health Association. Access to fact sheets, pamphlets, merchandise, and position statements on wide a variety of mental health topics, including disorders, medications, and suicide. http://www.nmha.org/index.cfm.

National Mental Health Information Center. Run by the federal government's Center for Mental Health Services. http://www.mentalhealth.org.

Physicians' Desk Reference. For more than 50 years, doctors have relied on the PDR for up-to-date, accurate drug information. The information on this site is written in lay terms and is based on the FDA-approved drug information found in the PDR. http://www.pdrhealth.net.

What You Should Know about Psychiatry and Psychiatric Drugs. Recent classic and popular books (and descriptions of them) that addresses the use and misuse of psychiatric drugs in society. Focus tends to be on those works critical of psychiatry and the pharmaceutical industry. http://www.outlookcities.com/psych.

Related Readings

Bentley, K. J., & Collins, K. S. (2007). Psychopharmacological treatment for child and adolescent mental disorders. In C. Franklin, M. B. Harris, & P. Allen-Meares (Eds.), *The school services sourcebook: A guide for social workers, counselors, and mental health professionals.* New York: Oxford University Press.

Bentley, K. J., & Walsh, J. (1998). Advances in psychopharmacology and psychosocial aspects of medication management: A review for social workers. In J. B W. Williams & K. Ell (Eds.), *Recent advances in mental health research: Implications for social workers* (pp. 309–342). Silver Spring, MD: NASW.

Bentley, K. J., & Walsh, J. (2006). *The social worker and psychotropic medication: Toward effective collaboration with mental health clients, families and providers.* Belmont, CA: Wadsworth.

Bentley, K. J., Walsh, J., & Farmer, R. (2005a). Roles and activities of clinical social workers in psychopharmacotherapy: Results of a national survey. *Social Work, 50*(4), 295–303.

Bentley, K. J., Walsh, J., & Farmer, R. (2005b). Referring clients for psychiatric medication: Best practices for social workers. *Best Practices in Mental Health, 1*(1), 59–71.

Bradley, S. (2003). The psychology of the psychopharmacology triangle: The client, the clinicians and the medication. *Social Work in Mental Health, 1*(4).

Cohen, D. (1988). Social work and psychotropic drug treatments. *Social Service Review, 62,* 576–599.

Cohen, D. (2002). Research on the drug treatment of schizophrenia: A critical appraisal and implications for social work education. *Journal of Social Work Education, 38,* 217–239.

Floersch, J. (2003). The subjective experience of youth psychotropic drug treatment. *Social Work in Mental Health, 1*(4).

Walsh, J., Farmer, R., Taylor, M. F., & Bentley, K. J. (2003). Ethical dilemmas of practicing social workers around psychiatric medication: Results of a national study. *Social Work in Mental Health, 1*(4), 91–105.

99 Guidelines for Chemical Abuse and Dependency Screening, Diagnosis, and Treatment

Diana M. DiNitto & C. Aaron McNeece

According to the National Comorbidity Survey Replication, approximately 15 percent of English-speaking residents of the United States have met the criteria for alcohol or drug abuse or dependence during their lifetime (Kessler et al., 2005). Given the incidence of these problems, social workers need knowledge of alcohol and other drug disorders.

The major categories of drugs of dependence and/or abuse are (1) central nervous system (CNS) depressants, such as alcohol, barbiturates, methaqualone, benzodiazepines, and inhalants; (2) CNS stimulants, such as cocaine and amphetamines; (3) opioids or narcotics, such as heroin, morphine, and codeine; (4) hallucinogens, such as LSD, PCP, psilocybin, mescaline, and peyote; (5) cannabis or marijuana; (6) anabolic steroids used to build muscles and improve appearance; and (7) various over-the-counter drugs used to treat insomnia, coughs, colds, and other maladies, including some herbal preparations and dietary supplements intended to increase energy, sexual performance, appearance, or provide other effects. The National Institute on Drug Abuse (NIDA, 2007) and the Drug Enforcement Administration (2005) are useful sources of information on drugs of abuse.

The causes of alcohol and drug problems are widely debated, and there is growing evidence that genetic and brain chemistry factors are involved (Wilcox & Erickson, 2005). There is also evidence that social and environmental factors influence substance abuse and dependence (McNeece & DiNitto, 2005).

SCREENING

Many instruments that are quickly and easily scored are available for social workers in health and social service settings to use in screening individuals for alcohol and drug problems. Social workers may use self-administered instruments (i.e., clients answer questions using pen and paper or on a computer) or instruments the social worker administers by asking the client questions. Among the brief screening instruments most commonly used with adults are the

- CAGE (the four-item CAGE is among the briefest of all the instruments),
- Michigan Alcoholism Screening Test (MAST),
- Drug Abuse Screening Test (DAST),
- Alcohol Use Disorders Identification Test (AUDIT) (available in many languages), and
- Substance Abuse Subtle Screening Inventory (SASSI).

Some screening instruments have been developed specifically for use with adolescents, such as the Problem Oriented Screening Instrument for Teens and the adolescent version of the SASSI, or with older adults, such as the MAST-Geriatric (MAST-G). The T-ACE and the TWEAK were developed for use in screening for risk drinking during pregnancy. Many of the aforementioned instruments, as well as other instruments for screening, diagnosis, assessment, treatment planning, and measuring outcomes, can be found in Allen and Wilson (2003), along with descriptive information, psychometric information, and information on copyright and sources for obtaining the instruments. Winters (1999) is another source of information on screening with adolescents. Though some instruments have undergone psychometric testing with members of various racial and ethnic groups, the field lacks instruments developed for particular racial and ethnic groups. Regarding tools sensitive to other populations, the Drug and Alcohol Assessment for the Deaf was recently developed and tested in American Sign Language (available through the Gulf Coast Addiction Technology Transfer Center).

Selection of screening devices should be based on the setting in which they are used, including the clientele served (e.g., reading level). Screening is best done (Skinner, 1984) when the:

- client is free of alcohol and other drugs and is mentally stable,
- individual doing the screening builds rapport with the client,

- client knows that corroborating information will be used, and
- client is assured of confidentiality.

In many cases, drug courts, probation or parole officers, or child protective service agencies refer clients to qualified professionals expressly to determine the existence of a substance abuse or dependence problem and the need for intervention. Though these clients may be under duress, they often consent to release of information (i.e., waive confidentiality and allow the information to be released) to the referring agency.

DIAGNOSIS

Screening is generally the first step in the assessment process, but it does not substitute for a diagnostic evaluation made by a qualified clinician. The *DSM-IV-TR* (American Psychiatric Association, 2000), used extensively in the United States, contains diagnostic criteria for substance use disorders. The *DSM-IV-TR* describes three major sets of problems or diagnoses that can result from substance use.

- *Substance-induced disorders*, which include the problems posed by intoxication and withdrawal.
- *Substance-induced mental disorders*, which include a number of problems if they result from substance use, such as psychotic, mood, and anxiety disorders. In crisis situations, it can be difficult to distinguish whether these states were induced by alcohol, other drugs, or mental illness. In addition, a substantial number of people have both mental and substance use disorders (Kessler, Chiu, Demler, Merikangas, & Walters, 2005).
- *Substance use disorders* (abuse and dependence).

The *DSM-IV-TR* defines both substance abuse and dependence as "a maladaptive pattern of substance use leading to clinically significant impairment or distress" (American Psychiatric Association, 2000, pp. 197 & 199). A diagnosis of substance abuse requires that at least one of four criteria have been met within a 12-month period, and the individual must never have met criteria for a diagnosis of substance dependence on this class of drug. Abuse criteria include substance use–

related problems, such as recurrently failing to fulfill important responsibilities, using in hazardous situations, and encountering legal, social, and interpersonal problems.

A diagnosis of substance dependence requires that at least three of seven criteria have been met within a 12-month period. Dependence criteria include tolerance, withdrawal, using greater amounts than intended, unsuccessful attempts to control use, spending substantial time getting alcohol or other drugs and recovering from use, curtailing work or other important activities, and continued use despite problems. This diagnosis does not require that physical dependence be present. Although abuse often precedes dependence, abuse may occur without the development of dependence; therefore, the two diagnoses are distinct. Interview guides such as the Composite International Diagnostic Interview (CIDI) are available to make diagnoses of substance use disorders based on *DSM-IV-TR* criteria (see Allen & Wilson, 2003, for information on the CIDI and other diagnostic tools). Clinicians are more confident in their diagnoses of substance use disorders when they have multiple sources of information on which to rely, such as a diagnostic interview, laboratory tests, and information from collateral sources (e.g., family members, other professionals, and client records).

ASSESSMENT

The most widely used standardized instrument for conducting assessments of adults with substance use disorders is probably the Addiction Severity Index (ASI) (this and other assessment tools are described in Allen & Wilson, 2003). The ASI contains seven domains: medical, employment, alcohol, drug, legal, family/social, and psychiatric, which provide substantial social history information. This type of multidimensional assessment is consistent with social workers' biopsychosocial perspective. The ASI also provides three types of scores (composite scores based on answers to several questions, interviewer-rated severity scores, and client-rated severity scores) that indicate the extent of the clients' problems in each of the seven domains.

Social workers are generally well versed in taking social histories. Because most do not work in chemical dependency treatment programs but encounter clients with these problems, McNeece and DiNitto (2005) provide information and a guide for taking clients' social history in cases where information on alcohol and drug problems is needed. This book is also a basic text on chemical dependency for social workers and other helping professionals and contains information on treatment and populations such as women, adolescents, older adults, racial and ethnic groups, those with mental and physical disabilities, and gay, lesbian, bisexual, and transgender persons. The social history guide addresses ten areas: education, employment, military history (if applicable), medical history, drinking and drug use, psychological or psychiatric history, legal involvement (if applicable), family history, relationships with significant others, and reasons the individual is seeking help. As in screening and diagnosis, assessment can be facilitated when multiple sources of information are available. Chapter 51 in this volume also provides step-by-step guidelines for conducting a biopsychosocial assessment.

TREATMENT PLANNING

Once the nature of the client's substance abuse or dependence and related problems is understood, treatment planning may begin. The American Society of Addiction Medicine (ASAM) (Mee-Lee, Shulman, Fishman, Gastfriend, & Griffiths, 2001) publishes an extensive guide for treatment planning in the chemical dependency field. The placement criteria are in the form of a two-dimensional crosswalk. One dimension of the adult admission crosswalk contains ten components of service that form a continuum or levels of care. They include (1) early intervention, (2) opioid maintenance therapy (when there is physical dependence on opiates), (3) outpatient treatment, (4) intensive outpatient, (5) partial hospitalization, (6) clinically managed low-intensity residential services, (7) clinically managed medium-intensity residential treatment, (8) clinically managed high-intensity residential services, (9) medically monitored intensive inpatient treatment, and (10) medically managed intensive inpatient treatment. The level of treatment recommended is suggested by the second dimension, which contains six factors: (1) intoxication and withdrawal potential (which may indicate the need for some form of ambulatory or inpatient detoxification); (2) other biomedical conditions and complications (suggesting the need for medical care); (3) emotional, behavioral, and cognitive conditions and complications (indicating whether psychiatric or other problems make in-patient care necessary); (4) readiness to change; (5) relapse and continued use or continued problem potential; and (6) the individual's recovery environment (each of which also suggests the intensity of services needed for sustaining remission). The crosswalk makes it clear that treatment selection should be based on the individual client's needs.

A client's readiness for change, and the services needed based on this level of readiness, is often assessed using the transtheoretical model (TTM) of change (Prochaska, DiClemente, & Norcross, 1992). The TTM is also an approach to delineating the stages an individual goes through in changing a behavior like alcohol or drug abuse or dependence. This change process has been conceptualized in five stages (Prochaska et al., 1992):

1. precontemplation (individual is unaware a problem exists),
2. contemplation (individual develops an awareness of problem and starts to think about making changes),
3. preparation (individual intends to make changes soon),
4. action (individual successfully changes his or her situation), and
5. maintenance (individual makes continued changes to avoid relapse).

The stages do not necessarily progress in a linear fashion, and people may relapse and return to some earlier stage in the change process, necessitating a change in treatment or service approaches that will help them move forward.

EVIDENCE-BASED TREATMENT

As the ASAM crosswalk indicates, many modalities are used in treating alcohol and other drug problems. Among the residential services that clients may need are therapeutic communities and halfway houses, which vary in their level of client supervision and monitoring and in the length of stay allowed. In this era of managed care, treatment is becoming briefer, and long stays in intensive inpatient treatment programs are rare. Most clients receive outpatient services.

The literature often discusses treatment for alcohol problems separately from treatment for other drug problems even though these problems often co-occur. Historically, approaches for address-

ing alcohol problems and other drug problems developed separately. In addition, the federal government's National Institute on Alcohol Abuse and Alcoholism (NIAAA) and NIDA, which fund treatment studies, remain separate entities under the National Institutes of Health.

NIDA (1999) describes principles of effective drug addiction treatment.

• No single treatment is appropriate for all individuals.
• Treatment needs to be readily available.
• Effective treatment attends to multiple needs of the individual.
• An individual's treatment and service plan must be assessed continually and modified as necessary.
• Remaining in treatment for an adequate period of time is critical.
• Counseling and other behavioral therapies are critical.
• Medications are an important element of treatment for many.
• Addicted or drug-abusing individuals with coexisting mental disorders should have both disorders treated in an integrated way.
• Medical detoxification is only the first stage of treatment and by itself does little to change long-term drug use.
• Treatment does not need to be voluntary to be effective.
• Possible drug use during treatment must be monitored continuously.
• Treatment programs should provide assessment for infectious diseases and counseling to change risk behaviors.
• Recovery from drug addiction can be a long-term process and frequently requires multiple treatment episodes.

Many approaches have been used to treat alcohol or other drug problems, though evidence-based practices that social workers use usually have a cognitive and/or behavioral basis. Some of the scientifically based approaches to drug addiction treatment for adults that have been identified with NIDA research support are relapse prevention, matrix model, supportive-expressive psychotherapy, individualized drug counseling, and motivational enhancement therapy (MET) (NIDA, 1999). These approaches are often used as components in various treatment modalities (e.g., outpatient and inpatient treatment). Only brief descriptions can be provided here (see NIDA, 1999, for references on these approaches).

In relapse prevention, clients explore the pros and cons of drug use, identify situations that promote use, and learn strategies to avoid or cope with these situations. Relapse prevention is critical because treatment is generally short-term, and clients must develop strategies that will serve them in sustaining recovery.

In the matrix model, the therapist functions as teacher and coach; the treatment incorporates elements of other approaches, such as family education and therapy, relapse prevention, use of mutual-help groups, and urine testing. Supportive-expressive psychotherapy is a time-limited approach that helps clients discuss problematic feelings and behaviors and learn expressive techniques to address interpersonal relationships and other issues without resorting to drug use. Individualized drug counseling targets abstinence or reducing drug use and the multiple problems the client may be experiencing, often through referrals; in addition to achieving short-term behavioral goals there is a focus on longer-term coping strategies and relapse prevention.

MET, based on the principles of motivational interviewing (Miller & Rollnick, 2002), is a client-centered treatment that is usually short-term and focuses on helping clients resolve ambivalence about changing (stopping drug use). MET therapists review objective assessment information about the client's problem in a nonjudgmental way and promote self-efficacy by expressing confidence in the client's ability to change. Though the MET therapist gives advice, the focus is on helping clients come to their own decisions about making change rather than outlining a step-by-step recovery process for the client.

For adolescents, one approach NIDA identifies is behavioral therapy, which includes modeling appropriate behavior, rehearsal and homework, urine tests, and praise and rewards for progress with the goal of developing stimulus, urge, and social control. Another is outpatient multidimensional family therapy, which includes parallel sessions for the individual and family members, incorporates all systems of influence (individual, family, peers, and community), and builds the adolescent's coping and social skills.

The Mesa Grande project is an effort to evaluate the evidence on clinical trials of treatments for alcohol use disorders (Miller & Wilbourne, 2002). Despite some methodological limitations, the project identifies treatments supported by empirical evidence. Among the treatments that generally show benefit that social workers can deliver are brief interventions (generally one or two sessions used to address risk drinking or alcohol abuse rather than dependence; the providers gives advice on how to reduce drinking and often employs other techniques such as reading materials), MET (as described in evidence-based approaches for people with drug problems), and behavioral approaches that focus on enhancing the client's skills and promoting self-efficacy. Behavioral approaches include social skills training, community reinforcement approach, behavioral marital therapy (each of these approaches involve the client's social support network), and behavior contracting and self-monitoring of drinking behavior. Other approaches with demonstrated effectiveness that social workers use are case management, client-centered counseling, and cognitive therapy. Notable themes among efficacious treatments appear to be a focus on building clients' skills and self-efficacy, increasing motivation, and inclusion of significant others (Miller & Wilbourne, 2002). (See the Web site of the University of New Mexico Center on Alcoholism, Substance Abuse, and Addictions for information on studies on these and other approaches included in the Mesa Grande project.)

Although evidence supports the inclusion of significant others in promoting and sustaining recovery, treatment programs often pay insufficient attention to doing so, perhaps due to funding constraints. Assisting families is a strong suit of social workers. Family members need education and counseling to help them cope, whether or not the individual with the substance use disorder desires help.

Another evidence-based approach to the treatment of substance dependence is medication use, generally as an adjunct to psychosocial treatment. Few medications have been approved for use in the long-term treatment of chemical dependency. Methadone maintenance treatment for use with opiate addicts is an exception. Other medications have been tested for use in treating opioid dependence, such as buprenorphine, which was approved for treating opioid dependence in 2002. Despite the reluctance to use medications in treating chemical dependency for fear that one drug is being substituted for another, many more medications are being tested. Some of them, such as naltrexone for use in treating opioid and alcohol dependence and acamprosate for treating alcohol dependence, are not addictive and are used to reduce cravings or euphoric drug effects rather than as drug replacement therapy. Disulfiram (trade name Antabuse), which makes the patient ill if he or she ingests alcohol, has long been used in treating alcohol dependence. The Mesa Grande project includes clinical trials of medications used to treat alcoholism. Social workers need to keep abreast of pharmacotherapeutic developments to refer clients who might realize better outcomes with use of these medications.

MUTUAL-HELP RESOURCES

The first 12-step program founded was Alcoholics Anonymous (AA). Similar groups developed to help people with other drug problems, such as Narcotics Anonymous (NA) and Cocaine Anonymous. These programs are considered spiritual programs, though agnostics and atheists have recovered in them. These programs offer a wealth of literature through their national offices and Web sites, including information directed to professionals.

Other mutual-help programs are Secular Organizations for Sobriety/Save Our Selves (SOS), an alternative to the spiritual programs, and Women for Sobriety (WFS), dedicated to empowerment and other aspects of women's recovery. Another approach is Rational Recovery (RR), which does not rely on group meetings.

The 12-step program for family members and friends of alcoholics is Al-Anon and for families and friends of addicts is Nar-Anon. Groups for children and adolescents are Alatot and Alateen (contact information is the same as for Al-Anon). Other groups for family members have emerged such as adult children of alcoholics groups.

Professionals often make referrals to mutual-help groups, but they may not have attended meetings. Groups such as AA and NA have "open" meetings to help interested individuals learn about them. These groups are usually listed in local phone directories and can be contacted for information on attending meetings. The groups are often different than what visitors (and new members) imagine they will be and are a necessary part of the education that professionals need to discuss with their clients. Although some clients do not find the mutual-help approach useful, they may be the primary recovery resource for other clients. When used in conjunction with professional treatment, mutual-help groups are considered an especially good source of aftercare.

OUTCOME MEASURES

Measuring individual client outcomes in clinical practice is often done informally, but there are tools in the substance abuse and dependency treatment field that can be used to assist with this task. Many of them are found in Allen and Columbus (2003) along with tools for measuring agency- or program-level outcomes. For example, the ASI has a follow-up version that can be used to measure client outcomes following treatment, and the Drinker Inventory of Consequences (DrInC) can also be used in treatment planning and in evaluating treatment outcomes. Several chapters in this volume focus on measuring and evaluating outcomes in health and mental health settings.

WEB SITES

AA World Services. http://www.alcoholics-anonymous.org.

Al-Anon Family Group Headquarters. http://www.al-anonfamilygroups.org.

Alcohol, Tobacco, and Other Drug section of the National Association of Social Workers, with benefits such as a newsletter and continuing education. http://www.naswdc.org/sections/default.asp.

Nar-Anon Family Group Headquarters. http://www.nar-anon.org/index.html.

Narcotics Anonymous World Services. http://www.na.org.

National Institute on Alcohol Abuse and Alcoholism. http://www.niaaa.nih.gov.

National Institute on Drug Abuse. http://www.nida.nih.gov.

Rational Recovery Systems. http://www.rational.org.

Save Our Selves. http://www.sossobriety.org.

Substance Abuse and Mental Health Services Administration (SAMHSA). Includes the Center for Substance Abuse Prevention (CSAP) and the Center for Substance Treatment (CSAT). CSAT's Treatment Improvement Protocols, Technical Assistance Publications, and Treatment Improvement Exchange are geared to meet practitioners' needs. The National Clearinghouse on Alcohol and Drug Information is also a service of SAMHSA. http://www.samhas.gov.

University of New Mexico Center on Alcoholism, Substance Abuse, and Addictions, Mesas Grande project. http://casaa.unm.edu.

Women For Sobriety. http://www.womenforsobriety.org.

References

Allen, J. P., & Columbus, M. (2003). *Assessing alcohol problems: A guide for clinicians and researchers.* Collingdale, PA: Diane Publishing.

Allen, J. P., & Wilson, V. B. (Eds.). (2003). *Assessing alcohol problems: A guide for clinicians and researchers*, 2nd ed. Bethesda, MD: National Institute on Alcohol Abuse and Alcoholism. Retrieved September 30, 2007, from http://pubs.niaaa.nih.gov/publications/Assesing%20Alcohol/index.htm.

American Psychiatric Association. (2000). *Diagnostic and statistical manual of mental disorders*, 4th ed., text revision. Washington, DC: APA.

Drug Enforcement Administration. (2005). *Drugs of abuse, 2005 edition.* Washington, DC: U.S. Department of Justice. Retrieved September 19, 2007, from http://www.usdoj.gov/dea/pubs/abuse/index.htm.

Kessler, R. C., Berglund, P., Demler, O., Jin, R. Merikangas, K. R., & Walters, E. E. (2005). Lifetime prevalence and age-of-onset distributions of *DSM-IV* disorders in the National Comorbidity Survey Replication. *Archives of General Psychiatry*, 62(6), 593–602.

Kessler, R. C., Chiu, W. T., Demler, O., Merikangas, K. R., & Walters, E. E. (2005). Prevalence, severity, and comorbidity of 12-month *DSM-IV* disorders in the National Comorbidity Survey Replication. *Archives of General Psychiatry*, 62(6), 617–627.

McNeece, C. A., & DiNitto, D. M. (2005). *Chemical dependency: A systems approach*, 3rd ed. Boston: Allyn & Bacon.

Mee-Lee, D., Shulman, G., Fishman, M., Gastfriend, D., & Griffiths, J. H. (2001). *ASAM patient placement criteria for the treatment of substance-related disorders*, 2nd ed. rev. Chevy Chase, MD: American Society of Addiction Medicine.

Miller, W. R., & Rollnick, S. (2002). *Motivational interviewing: Preparing people for change*, 2nd ed. New York: Guilford.

Miller, W. R., Wilbourne, P. L. (2002). Mesa Grande: A methodological analysis of clinical trials of treatment for alcohol use disorders. *Addiction*, 97(3), 265–277.

National Institute on Drug Abuse. (2007, February 21). Drugs of abuse information. Retrieved September 19, 2007, from http://www.nida.nih.gov/drugpages.html.

Prochaska, J. O., DiClemente, C. C., & Norcross, J. C. (1992). In search of how people change: Applications to addictive behaviors. *American Psychologist*, 47, 1102–1114.

Skinner, H. A. (1984). Assessing alcohol use by patients in treatment. In R. G. Smart, H. D. Cappell, & F. B. Glaser et al. (Eds.). *Research advances in alcohol and drug problems*, vol. 8 (pp. 183–207). New York: Plenum Press.

Wilcox, R. E., & Erickson, C. K. (2005). The brain biology of drug abuse and addiction. In C. A. McNeece & D. M. DiNitto (Eds.), *Chemical dependency: A systems approach*, 3rd ed. (pp. 42–60). Boston: Allyn & Bacon.

Winters, K. C. (1999). Screening and assessing adolescents for substance use disorders, Treatment Improvement Protocol (TIP) series 31. Rockville, MD: Center for Substance Abuse Treatment.

Maggie Bennington-Davis

Many excellent treatments exist for people with psychiatric and substance abuse disorders. Less attention is paid to understanding the impact of the environment in which these treatments are delivered. This chapter describes trauma-informed services—that is, understanding the complex impact of exposure to trauma and violence and how the environments in which we subsequently interact can either facilitate healing or hamper it.

VIGNETTE

Dustin, age 29, has just finished a psychiatric hospitalization, initiated because of increasing violence at his apartment, delusions, and paranoia. He used drugs in the past. He's been in lots of bar fights. He's been diagnosed with various labels: schizophrenia because of his hypervigilance and fear, mania because of his restless agitation and irritability, and attention deficit hyperactivity disorder because of his apparent inattention.

His father, often intoxicated, used to regularly beat up both Dustin and Dustin's mother. His father left the family when Dustin was 12; his mom, who had three other younger children too, eventually gave Dustin to an aunt to try to deal with. He was in juvenile detention from ages 15 to 17. Since then, he has worked at odd jobs and been in small amounts of legal trouble.

Dustin had a rough hospitalization. He made sure that others in the hospital understood they needed to leave him alone. Although he saw someone else get restrained by the hospital's security force, he never was. He was ready, though, if anyone tried to put their hands on him; he knew he could take care of himself.

He fought sleep in the hospital. He was afraid that if he slept, he would be assaulted. He hated having staff members open his door to check on him—he inevitably startled vigorously.

Women don't bother him much, but he feels very competitive around other men—especially young men or big men. He was likely to yell if someone got too close to him.

He hates listening to music and doesn't like to be near where a TV or radio is on. He wants to have his senses as sharp as possible.

He wasn't eating well—he had heartburn a lot. Mealtimes were hard for him. He was hungry on the one hand, but then experienced discomfort after eating. He didn't tell anyone about this, because he didn't want to seem weak.

After being discharged, Dustin attended day hospital four times per week as part of a transition plan to get him back into his own apartment. He felt much safer in this unlocked program, where he was allowed to keep his own belongings and where he had several choices about which classes and activities he wanted to be in and about when he could come and go. His heartburn was successfully treated. He learned relaxation skills that helped him sleep. He gradually formed trusting relationships with other clients who admired and liked him, as well as with several day hospital staff members who noticed and appreciated his sharp observational skills. He trained as a peer advocate for people entering the locked hospital unit, and eventually joined a task force, making recommendations for improving the participation of patients in their own treatment.

TRAUMA-INFORMED SERVICES

Description and History

Trauma-informed care, according to the National Association of State Mental Health Program Directors (NASMHPD), is "mental health treatment that is directed with a thorough understanding of the profound neurological, biological, psychological, and social effects of trauma and violence on an individual and with an appreciation for the high incidence of traumatic experiences among people who receive mental health services" (Huckshorn, 2005).

Over the past decade, increasing attention has been directed toward the role of exposure to trauma and violence in the developing brain. Study of post-traumatic stress disorder (PTSD) in adults who were profoundly affected by war experiences was joined by the study of children who were affected by exposure to neglect and abuse. Even more recently, these bodies of literature were augmented by the increasingly compelling notion that most people served in public sector mental health programs have a history of trauma.

Trauma is the experience of helplessness in the context of overwhelming force (Hermann, 1992). Such events include a close personal encounter with violence or threats to life or bodily integrity and include rape, assault, severe neglect, starvation, physical abuse, and psychological torture. The hallmark of traumatic experience is "intense fear, helplessness, loss of control, and threat of annihilation" (Andreason, 1995). Essentially, when children fear for their own lives or for the lives of someone they love, they experience trauma (Bloom, 1999).

Prevalence

Nearly a decade ago, a study was published in the *Journal of Traumatic Stress* showing that 94 percent of people using services in an urban mental health center had a history of trauma (Switzer et al., 1999). Many other settings have discovered similar statistics. Ninety percent of public mental health clients have been exposed to trauma (Goodman, Roseberg, Mueser, & Drake, 1997; Mueser et al., 1998). More than 80 percent of adults in psychiatric hospitals and diagnosed with a major mental illness have experienced physical and/or sexual abuse; most of these people experienced the abuse as children (NASMHPD/NTAC, 2004). Two-thirds of people in treatment for substance abuse report childhood abuse or neglect (Center for Substance Abuse Treatment, 2000). All of this is in the context of an epidemic of child abuse and neglect in the United States. In 2004, the National Child Abuse and Neglect Data System logged 3 million official reports of child abuse or neglect. Ten million American children are thought to be exposed to domestic violence annually.

Research Results

What are the consequences of this exposure? The Adverse Childhood Experiences (ACE) study reported that in a white, middle-class sample of 18,000 adults, two-thirds of them had been exposed to at least one ACE, and a majority of those

had been exposed to more than one. They furthermore found a linear correlation between ACE exposure and poor health conditions/health risk behaviors (Felitti et al., 1998). In fact, ACEs are positively correlated with the top ten reasons for death. One-third of children who are abused will have some clear psychological problems as a result (Perry & Szalavitz, 2006).

Mental health providers tend to think of PTSD as a stand-alone entity but are less likely to recognize that those with schizophrenia or bipolar disorder in public mental health systems are also likely to manifest the neurobiological aftermath of traumatic experience (Murphy & Bennington-Davis, 2005). The neurobiological consequences of childhood exposure to trauma and violence are much broader than our traditional notion of PTSD. Traumatic stress is the single most important contributor to later psychiatric morbidity and mortality (Sharfstein, 2006).

Consequence of Childhood Exposure to Trauma

Traumatic experience has the potential for impact on the entire person, including the way people think, learn, remember, think about self, feel about others, and the way sense is made of the world (Bloom, 1997). Although the specific manifestation of trauma in any given individual seeking mental health and addiction treatment varies due to many factors (age of exposure, amount and frequency of exposure, protective factors, coping resources, etc.), when psychological harm does result, it is because the normal stress response has been overwhelmed, making it more reactive and less adaptive (Stien & Kendall, 2004). The person begins to behave as if always in danger, and there tend to be basic features in common. Hyperarousal, intrusive thoughts (reexperiencing), and constriction (disconnectivity or disassociation)

Exposure to traumatic situations results in graded reactions including:

- Hypervigilance
- Disregard of non-relevant information
- Increased heart rate and muscle tone
- Decreased impulse control
- Tendency to aggression and/or
- Dissociation

Perry, B. 2006

(Hermann, 1992). Hyperarousal, or hypervigilance, is the constant scanning of the environment, searching for the next threat, with a low threshold to interpret stimuli as threatening. Others may perceive this behavior as a deficit in attention or as paranoia. Activities that are not pertinent to life or death—such as learning math or writing the alphabet—are disregarded. Others may perceive this as poor attention and concentration, opposition or defiance, or even a learning disability. Increased muscle tone and heart rate are a result of abnormally high levels of catecholamines (Perry & Szalavitz, 2006). Others may perceive this as hyperactivity, poor impulse control, and aggression.

Traumatic exposure also often results in the development of an emotional coping style geared for managing overwhelming feelings as opposed to matching one's emotional response to daily, more routine and mundane situations (van der Kolk, 1997). Others perceive this as chronic overreaction or explosiveness. Dissociation is a primitive neurobiological response to overwhelming odds, where fight/flight is unlikely to be successful and the best defense is to become still, disconnected, and develop psychological distance from whatever uncontrollable horror is occurring (Perry & Szalavitz, 2006). The brain produces endogenous opioids that dull pain and produce a sort of surreal calm. Others perceive this as being zoned out, spaced out, uncaring, trance-like, or even defiance. Most trauma survivors have some combination of these experiences.

Trauma-Informed Services

There are emerging treatments for PTSD. For example, trauma-focused cognitive-behavioral therapy (Cohen, Mannarino, & Knudsen, 2005) is recognized as an evidence-based treatment. Parent–child interaction therapy reduces episodes of reabuse in families (Sharfstein, 2006). Emotional regulation, cognitive processing, and meaning-making skills are individual therapeutic elements of the trauma systems approach (Saxe, Ellis, & Kaplow, 2007). Clonidine, selective serotonin reuptake inhibitors, and other medications calm the stress response of the agitated brain (Perry & Szalavitz, 2006; Saxe et al., 2007). Specific trauma treatments such as these, however, are separate and different from trauma-*informed* services.

A trauma system includes the traumatized person, and the difficulty he or she has in regulating emotion, with the social environment or system of care (including providers) that is not able to help

the person regulate these emotional states (Saxe et al., 2007). A trauma-informed system (and provider) creates environments in which people are more apt to keep themselves regulated—and therefore more able to take advantage of treatments.

Trauma-informed services, then, are created and operated with the assumption in mind that a majority of people served have a history of exposure to trauma and violence and acknowledge and understand the impact of that history. Trauma-informed systems, organizations, programs, and services have an understanding of the vulnerabilities or triggers of trauma survivors that traditional service delivery approaches may exacerbate, so these services and programs can be more supportive and avoid retraumatization (see http://mentalhealth.samhsa.gov/nctic/trauma.asp).

Key components of trauma informed service systems include:

- integrating an understanding of trauma, substance abuse, and mental illness throughout the program;
- reviewing service policies and procedures to ensure prevention of retraumatization;
- involving consumers in designing and evaluating services;
- seeing trauma as an experience that can shape survivors' sense of self and others;
- creating a collaborative relationship between providers and consumer, and placing priority on consumer safety, choice, and control; and
- focusing on empowerment and emphasizing strengths (Brown & Gonzales, 2004).

The fundamental first stage of recovery from trauma is reestablishing a sense of safety (van der Kolk, 2007). In her seminal work, Creating Sanctuary: Toward the Creation of Sane Societies, Sandra Bloom (1997) describes safe environments that promote healing and defines safety as including not just physical safety but also psychological, social, and moral safety. She goes on to define psychological safety as the ability to be safe with oneself, social safety as the ability to be safe in groups, and moral safety as maintaining a value system that does not contradict itself (Bloom, 1997). Trauma-sensitive care seeks to provide this comprehensive application of safety—protection from violence to and from others and oneself. A trauma-informed treatment environment has, as its essence, this fundamental safety.

There are several approaches to developing a trauma-informed environment, beginning with the education of staff, physicians, families, and the people we serve regarding the role of trauma in our lives and in our neurobiology. The culture of a trauma-informed treatment environment is respect, service, safety, and participation.

A trauma-informed environment seeks to insist on the person's involvement in as many aspects of the therapeutic experience as possible. Trauma-sensitive services take into account that the key elements of traumatic experience are powerlessness and disconnection from others. Environments that are coercive or use social isolation and shame as means of control repeat those experiences. Environments that emphasize group membership, partnership, and integration in decision making offer the hope that the person is not, after all, alone.

Emotional dysregulation is a predictable sequel to childhood exposure to trauma (Perry & Szalavitz, 2007). Various factors can set off this dysregulation, which may appear as withdrawal and detachment or anger and aggression. These factors are sometimes referred to as triggers (NETI, 2004). Triggers are events, behaviors, language, and other environmental or emotional stimuli that cause a person's fight/flight/freeze reaction to recur as if the original trauma is occurring all over again. Although any given person has his or her own unique triggers, because of the generalization of stimuli that occurs over time, many triggers are common and predictable. Consider two broad arenas of environment: physical and social. We are quick to pick up on cues of physical environments that signal danger or safety. Broken windows, graffiti with violent messages, dark passages, certain smells, no escape routes, slamming doors, and clanging locks—these tend to put us on alert and are often triggers for people who have a history of trauma and violence. Social environments are also full of either triggers or reassurances. Angry voices, profanity, disrespectful interactions (among staff, or between staff and clients, or among clients), rigidity, and coercion—these are common triggers for many people (including providers).

Psychiatric inpatient settings often include experiences that are antithetical to trauma sensitivity and full of triggers. Many acute and state hospital units involuntarily hospitalize people and are rife with locked doors and glassed-in nursing stations. The physical environment is often hardened to the extent of bars on windows, plastic furniture bolted to the floor, and steel toilets. On admission, some inpatient units require people to disrobe and submit to bodily searches. Schedules are often highly regimented with undesirable consequences for failure to attend groups, meals, and medication times. Some units use a system of earning and losing privileges as behavioral incentives. Treatment planning, case discussions, and family meetings are sometimes held without the patient's attendance, participation, or consent. These sorts of coercion—both overt and covert—cause further trauma and alienation from treaters and treatment systems (Najavits, 2003).

Seclusion and restraint occur in many inpatient and residential settings. Administration of involuntary medications may occur even within view of others. These experiences, likely meant, in the minds of well-meaning staff, to preserve safety are among the most traumatizing and re-

---

Signals of Physical Danger:

- Broken, torn, or damaged furniture
- Bad odors
- No exit
- Bars on windows
- Dark corners and hallways
- Warning signs

Signals of Physical Safety:

- Clean, well-lighted rooms
- Pictures and plants
- Comfortable furniture
- Accessible phones

Signals of Social Danger:

- Angry voices
- Profanity
- Rules without context
- Consequences and punishment
- Public use of shame and humiliation
- Secrecy

Signals of Social Safety:

- Pleasant interactions
- Welcoming people
- Smiles and comforting tone
- Inclusiveness & participation
- Sense of belonging
- Choices

traumatizing elements in mental health services. The cascade of events that lead to and follow seclusion, restraint, and emergency involuntary medication administration reenact loss of emotional and physical control and the experience of punishment and helplessness. In the heat of the reenactment, the person's fight/flight/freeze reactions are in full play, leaving the likelihood of high-level cognitive reasoning, bargaining, and thoughtful planning nearly zero. Trauma-informed services seek to provide environments where these interventions are never necessary—not just that they do not occur. The solution is not to have uncontrolled violence and chaos but to create the kind of atmosphere that does not trigger the fight/flight/freeze response in the first place.

Concretely, there are many strategies to increase awareness of traumatic exposure, increase a sense of community membership, remind people of safety, and set a tone of respect. The starting point is to understand each person's story of exposure to trauma and violence. Gathering a trauma history addresses the experiences of past or current violence and abuse, and is especially attuned to the experience of retraumatization in the context of treatment, such as restraint and seclusion or coercive treatment. The key element here, though, is *listening*. Julie Johnstone, psychologist and consumer, says this, in her doctoral thesis, about listening: "Being listened to and understood is a transformational experience, and that on its own can create a shift in a person's wellbeing. The commitment to a person, to listen and understand their experience, I think holds the potential to completely transform people's experi-

ences of acute psychiatric services, themselves, and the mental health system. (Johnstone, 2002).

Psychoeducation, including what is known about the neurobiology of trauma for both clients and their families, is a key element for recovery. Personal safety plans (Bloom, 1997), which build on the understanding of a trauma history, insight regarding likely triggers in the treatment environment, and strategies for self-control and calming, are important tools for both staff and clients.

The trauma systems therapy approach suggests paying close attention to minimizing the sorts of stimuli that trigger people, which in turn offers maximal opportunity for the person to use high-level cognitive skills which lead to better outcomes for the person. Saxe and colleagues call this the "cognitive wedge" between stimulus and response (Saxe et al., 2007).

Community meeting in residential and inpatient settings creates a regular opportunity for people (staff and clients) to discuss their mutual experience of their shared experience and its feeling of safety (or lack thereof), and what each member of the community can do to contribute to and enhance the feeling of safety. Such a meeting is the lynchpin for developing a sense of community membership (belonging), which in turn forms the basis of agreeing on the social norms that set a tone of social, emotional, and physical safety (Bloom, 1997).

Debriefing scary, violent, and disrespectful events in a group setting involving both clients and staff is an important method of keeping information transparent. All people, staff and clients, even when not directly involved in seclusion, restraint, or other emergencies, are acutely aware when such an event occurs. This awareness heightens the need for vigilance and is a trigger for fear and anxiety. When such events are not discussed openly, people create their own explanations and often develop the fear that bad things happen randomly and may happen to them, too. An open discussion regarding how these events upset all people in the community is the first, essential step to reestablishing a sense of safety (Murphy * Bennington-Davis, 2005).

Staff-to-staff interactions (in addition to staff-to-client interactions) that are collegial, kind, and friendly set a tone of respect. People who are served in mental health settings are acutely aware of others and intuit a feeling of safety—or lack of it—from how those others behave and interact with each other as well as with clients (Murphy & Bennington-Davis, 2005). A trauma-informed setting understands the value of unfailing kindness and courtesy among all

---

Becoming Trauma Sensitive

- Create a culture of respect for both clients and staff
- Listen to peoples' stories
- Psychoeducation for clients and families
- Development of personal safety plan
  - Triggers
  - Reactions
  - Strategies for remaining in control
- Community meeting for both clients and staff
  - Establish social norms
  - Brainstorm strategies for safety
- Debriefing bad events with community members
- Involve clients in all aspects of planning and decision-making

present, including receptionists, therapists, physicians, administrators, and janitors.

Vocabulary and language reflect and drive values and ideas. Words and tone reveal deep-seated beliefs and assumptions. Medicine has a vocabulary all its own, and mental health treatment has developed a unique lingo as well. "Behavioral plan," "privileges," and "noncompliance" are a few examples of patronizing and judgmental vocabulary. As providers become trauma-sensitive, they must find new ways to communicate that do not alienate those they serve and indicate social and moral danger.

Consistent and authentic client involvement—leadership—in treatment planning is a key element of the client maintaining choice and control. Health care generally has a history of sometimes mistakenly protecting people from their own information. Mental health treatment, especially in involuntary settings and often with multidisciplinary and multisystem team members, has had a tendency to set goals and decide on treatment approaches in the absence of the client and family. This practice foolishly leaves out the most important team member's perspective and expertise, and it also recapitulates the experience of marginalization, coercion, helplessness, and neglect.

FUTURE DIRECTIONS

Trauma sensitivity is also applicable to system-level planning. State, county, and agency policy makers and designers often conduct planning and implementation of services and delivery systems without including those they are seeking to serve. This marginalization repeats clients' experience of powerlessness. Sophisticated trauma-informed systems include consumers at every level of discussion, planning, resource allocation, policy making, and implementation of service type.

Mental health and addiction treatment services have much to offer. Science and technology have provided new hope for healing. The neurobiology of trauma and exposure to violence are understood a little more each day. The neurobiology of kindness is an important next step.

Essentially, treatments that are available in public mental health will only become truly effective within the context of the correct treatment *environments*. Those environments involve physical surroundings, but more important, they are made up of human relationships, interactions, and attitudes.

When treatment environments put those we seek to serve on alert, when interactions and interventions reenact earlier experiences of help-lessness, danger, fear, neglect, and marginalization, then we must do better. We can do better. Becoming trauma-informed is the application of science to art: taking what we *know* and using it to provide the right container for how we *do*.

WEB SITES

Anna Institute. http://www.annafoundation.org.
International Society for Traumatic Stress Studies. http://www.istss.org.
National Association of State Mental Health Program Directors. http://www.nasmhpd.org.
National Center for Trauma-Informed Care. http://mentalhealth.samhsa.gov/nctic.
Sanctuary Model. http://www.sanctuaryweb.com.

References

Andreason, N. (1995). Posttraumatic stress disorder. In B. J. Sadock & H. I. Kaplan (Eds.), *Comprehensive textbook of psychiatry*, 4th ed. Baltimore: Williams & Wilkins.

Bloom, S. (1997). *Creating sanctuary: Toward the evolution of sane societies*. New York: Routledge.

Bloom, S. (1999). Trauma theory abbreviated. *Final Action Plan: A Coordinated Community-Based Response to Family Violence*. Attorney General of Pennsylvania's Family Violence Task Force.

Brown, V., & Gonzales, G. (2004). Implementing a trauma-informed residential treatment program. Presented at Dare to Act conference, Ohio, December.

Center for Substance Abuse Treatment. (2000). *Substance abuse treatment for persons with child abuse and neglect issues*. Treatment Improvement Protocol Series, no. 36. DHHS Publication no. (SMA) 00-3357. Washington, DC: U.S. Government Printing Office.

Cohen, J. A., Mannarino, A. P., & Knudsen, K. (2005). Treating sexually abused children: One year follow-up of a randomized controlled trial. *Child Abuse and Neglect, 29*, 135–145.

Felitti, V., Anda, R., Nordenberg, D., Williamson, D., Spitz, A., Edwards, V., et al. (1998). Relationship of childhood abuse and household dysfunction to many of the leading causes of death in adults: The Adverse Childhood Experiences (ACE) study. *American Journal of Preventive Medicine, 14*(4), 245–258.

Goodman, L., Roseberg, S., Mueser, K., & Drake, R. (1997). Physical and sexual assault history in women with serious mental illness: Prevalence, correlates, treatment, and future research directions. *Schizophrenia Bulletin, 23*, 685–696.

Hermann, J. (1992). *Trauma and recovery*. New York: Basic Books.

Huckshorn, K. A. (2005). *Six core strategies to reduce the use of seclusion and restraint planning tool*.

Alexandria, VA: National Association of State Mental Health Program Directors.

Johnstone, J. (2002). Voice, identity, and coercion: The consumer/survivor movement in acute public psychiatric services. Ph.D. thesis, Department of History and Philosophy of Science, University of Melbourne.

Mueser, K., Goodman, L., Trumbetta, S., Rosenberg,S., Osher, F., Vidaver, R., et al. (1998). Trauma and posttraumatic stress disorder in severe mental illness. *Journal of Consulting and Clinical Psychology, 66,* 493–499.

Murphy, T. & Bennington-Davis, M. (2005). *Restraint and seclusion: The model for elimination of use in healthcare.* Massachusetts: HCPro.

Najavits, L. (2003). Seeking safety. Retrieved January 17, 2003 from http://www.seekingsafety.org/3-02%20arts/training%20in%20SS-s.pdf.

NASMHPD/NTAC. (2004). *The damaging consequences of violence and trauma: Facts, discussion points, and recommendations for the behavioral health system.* Washington DC: U.S. Department of Health and Human Services.

Perry, B. & Szalavitz, M. (2006). *The boy who was raised as a dog.* New York: Basic Books.

Saxe, G., Ellis, B., & Kaplow, J. (2007). *Collaborative treatment of traumatized children and teens: the trauma systems therapy approach.* New York: Guilford.

Sharfstein, S. (2006). *Report of the APA Task Force on the biopsychosocial consequences of childhood violence.* Washington, DC: APA.

Stien, P. & Kendall, J. (2004). *Psychological trauma and the developing brain.* Binghamton, NY: Haworth.

Switzer, G., Dew, M., Thompson, K., Goycoolea, J., Derricott, J., & Mullins, S. (1999). Posttraumatic stress disorder and service utilization among urban mental health center clients. *Journal of Traumatic Stress, 12*(1), 25–39.

Van der Kolk, B. (1997). The psychobiology of posttraumatic stress disorder. *Journal of Clinical Psychiatry, 58*(9), 16–24.

101   Supported Employment Approaches

Marina Kukla & Gary R. Bond

Supported employment is an individualized psychiatric rehabilitation approach designed to help people with severe mental illness obtain and maintain competitive employment. Based on the place-train model in the development disabilities field, supported employment was adapted to psychiatric rehabilitation in the early 1980s. It is an evidence-based practice with its principles supported by research. It uses a rapid job search approach; ongoing support is provided by a service provider throughout a client's tenure at a job; mental health services are integrated with employment services. Randomized controlled trials have consistently found that supported employment is more effective than other vocational approaches in helping people with severe mental illness achieve competitive employment. Clients enrolled in supported employment get jobs faster and earn more from employment than do those receiving other types of vocational services. Future research should focus on financing and organization of supported employment services, job development strategies, and ways to increase job tenure of clients.

CASE EXAMPLE OF A SUPPORTED EMPLOYMENT CLIENT

Joe was a 48-year old Caucasian man with schizoaffective disorder. He had a disheveled appearance and spoke in a monotone voice with flat affect. He had been in and out of hospitals over the past

20 years because of psychiatric difficulties and had finally become stable on his medication regimen, but he still experienced daily symptoms of auditory hallucinations and panic attacks. Joe had the goal of returning to work, but he had low confidence because he had not held a stable job in the past 10 years, instead working odd jobs with little success. Soon after Joe told his mental health treatment team about his vocational goals, the employment specialist on the team began working with him to determine what type of job placement he desired. Together the employment specialist and Joe developed a résumé for him, and quickly he began getting interviews at auto repair shops, an area in which he had received formal job training prior to becoming ill. After two interviews, Joe was hired by a nearby service station. The employment specialist worked with the service station manager and arranged a suitable schedule and work environment for him. Occasionally thereafter, the employment specialist would work with Joe and his co-workers to solve interpersonal problems and conflicts that arose. Joe was successful in his job and remained employed at the same shop for over 5 years.

Several factors lead to Joe's success in employment in addition to his hard work on the job. First, the teamwork between Joe and his employment specialist in identifying his preferences and needs in regard to competitive employment was the initial step in securing a successful placement. Second, the job development or the job search matching Joe's preferences performed by the employment specialist was also very important. Third, the work by the employment specialist when Joe first obtained the job was crucial to creating a suitable work environment, training him on job tasks as necessary, and addressing the potential concerns of Joe and his co-workers/supervisors in the supported employment process. Finally, visits by his employment specialist (follow-along support) was critical to effectively addressing problems (i.e., conflicts with co-workers) and significant changes (i.e., a new job supervisor) as they arose and helping Joe maintain his employment in the long term.

DEFINITION AND HISTORY OF SUPPORTED EMPLOYMENT

Definition/Description

Supported employment refers to rehabilitation services that assist clients with severe mental illness obtain and maintain competitive employment in the community through an individualized approach that emphasizes rapid job search and de-emphasizes a stepwise approach of intermediate employment prior to placement in a competitive job. It helps compensate for the challenges presented by mental illness, such as psychotic symptoms, cognitive dysfunction, and a lack of social skills that make obtaining and maintaining employment more difficult. Supported employment services are especially crucial given the finding that the majority of people with severe mental illness want to work, yet most are unemployed (Corrigan, Mueser, Bond, Drake, & Solomon, 2008). Most supported employment programs are found in community mental health centers, which provide mental health counseling, medication management, case management, housing assistance, and other services.

History

Community-based psychiatric rehabilitation services began in the mid-1950s. This era included the deinstitutionalization movement, in which large numbers of people with severe mental illness moved out of inpatient hospitals and into the community. One of the earliest forms of community-based psychiatric rehabilitation was the clubhouse, where people with severe mental illness could go during the day and socialize. Clubhouses fostered the idea that an individual could work and should have an opportunity to work, if they so desired, even if they had spent many years in the hospital and suffered from debilitating psychiatric symptoms. The desire to participate in meaningful, productive activity ultimately led to the need for specific employment services for this population (Becker & Drake, 2003).

The earliest formulation of supported employment was the place-train approach first used in the developmental disabilities field (Wehman & Moon, 1988). The place-train approach assumed that rapid placement into a competitive job in the community with appropriate training and support thereafter would lead to better outcomes for people with even severe disabilities than the traditional train-place approach requiring clients to receive preemployment training prior to placement. Preemployment training was ineffective because of the lack of generalizability of job skills training and the unrealistic nature of the training situation (clients know that it is not the real world).

Given the shortcomings of the train-place approach, the principles of Wehman and Moon's (1988) more successful place-train approach began to be adopted by the mental health field in the late 1980s. The most widely studied, used, and standardized supported employment approach for people with severe mental illness is the individualized placement and support (IPS) model (Becker & Drake, 2003).

RESEARCH BASED PRINCIPLES OF THE IPS MODEL OF SUPPORTED EMPLOYMENT

The IPS model is an evidence-based vocational model. It uses the following research-based principles (Bond, 1998, 2004):

- Zero exclusion: IPS programs serve anyone with severe mental illness who professes an interest in working, regardless of symptoms, work history, lack of skills, strange appearance, or any of the myriad of reasons often given for excluding people from vocational services.
- Goal of competitive employment only. Employment specialists do not place clients in noncompetitive jobs, such as work crews or sheltered workshop positions in which jobs are reserved for those with severe mental illness.
- Rapid job search: The job search begins as soon as the client enters an IPS program. There is no prevocational training or formal vocational assessment (e.g., assessment of job readiness).
- Focus on client choice and preferences: Client job preferences, needs, and abilities, are given paramount importance in identifying jobs during the search as well as in determining what kinds of help will be provided. For example, if the clients prefers not to disclose his or her psychiatric disability to the employer, the supported employment team accommodates this preference.
- Ongoing, informal assessment: Based on direct observation and conversations with clients and employers, the employment specialist continuously assesses the fit between the client preferences and capabilities and the environmental demands. Other life circumstances, including housing and family situations, are also considered. Vocational assessment is an ongoing process

and is not limited to a formal assessment of job skills.
- Time-unlimited, individualized follow-along support. Ongoing follow-along support provided by the employment specialist may include a variety of interventions, including assisting clients in mastering job duties, training of co-workers and supervisors to be more effective in interacting with the client, and suggesting modifications in the work environment to accommodate client's needs.
- Benefits counseling: IPS programs provide clients with personalized information regarding the consequences of employment earnings on their Social Security and Medicaid payments.
- Integration of employment services and mental health treatment: Staff from IPS programs work closely with mental treatment teams and attend treatment team meetings. Ideal integration of supported employment services and mental health treatment is characterized by employment specialists providing mental health information to mental health clinicians and mental health clinicians providing vocational information to employment specialists. For example, in the case of, his employment specialist provides information to mental health clinicians about new symptoms Joe experiences on the job or medication side effects that affect his ability to work. Mental health clinicians (i.e., case managers) provide information to Joe's employment specialist about other aspects of his life, such as changes in his residential status or transportation that could affect Joe's vocational status.

Other important components of the IPS model include small caseloads for employment specialists. In addition, employment specialists only provide employment services and do not have responsibilities for nonvocational services, such as crisis intervention, housing, or other case management tasks.

STEPS IN THE IPS SUPPORTED EMPLOYMENT PROCESS

The following is a step-by-step description of the IPS supported employment process. Although the steps may vary somewhat in temporal sequence and nature dependent on the individual circumstances of each client, this represents the rudimentary process for a typical client.

1. The client expresses a desire to work competitively to a mental health team or the client comes into the community mental health center seeking out help with employment.
2. An employment specialist begins to work with the client, identifying important factors, including the client's preferences, needs, and individual circumstances (i.e., transportation) regarding employment. If the client is receiving Social Security disability benefits, the implications for working are considered, both prior to the job search and after a specific job offer is made.
3. Although not a requirement for enrollment in supported employment, supported employment programs often receive funding from the state or federal vocational rehabilitation system. Consequently, employment specialists typically work closely with this agency on behalf of their clients, initiating contact before the client obtains a job.
4. Within a month's time, the employment specialist begins the job development process and searches for a suitable job for the client.
5. When the client obtains the job, the employment specialist works with the supervisor and co-workers to work out a suitable work environment for the client. The employment specialist also trains the client on job tasks if necessary and whether the client chooses to disclosure his or her disability to the employer.
6. The employment specialist makes routine visits to the client at the job site and intervenes when issues and problems arise throughout the client's tenure at the job. In many instances, the employment specialist is in regular contact with the client's supervisor. Employment specialists also meet often with clients outside the work place. The job support plan is individualized.
7. If employment ends or the client desires a new job placement, the employment specialist works with the client to find another job matching his or her job preferences and needs.

RESEARCH FINDINGS AND OUTCOMES

Vocational Outcomes

Research has found the supported employment is superior to other employment approaches in terms of objective employment outcomes, such as rates of competitive employment (Bond, 2004) and greater earnings from employment (Gold et al., 2006).

Studies of day rehabilitation programs that have converted to supported employment programs have found that they have been able to do so successfully, with improved competitive employment outcomes for clients (Becker et al., 2001). Eleven randomized controlled trials have compared the IPS model of supported employment with various other approaches, finding a significant advantage in competitive employment rates for IPS, as seen in Figure 101.1. These studies have also found that clients receiving supported employment services obtain their first competitive jobs faster compared with clients receiving services in alternative approaches. Specifically, the average number of days to first job for IPS clients is 143 versus 234 days for control clients (Bond, Drake, & Becker, in press).

Nonvocational Outcomes

Participation in a supported employment program does not itself lead to improved nonvocational outcomes. However, clients obtaining competitive employment as a result of receiving supported employment realize other benefits, including improved self-esteem, better symptom control, and higher quality of life (Bond, 2004). The studies suggesting the positive impact of competitive employment on nonvocational outcomes have been correlational (Corrigan et al., 2008). Furthermore, despite clinician fears that working would be too stressful for their clients, studies have found that supported employment is not detrimental to the mental health of clients, as studies of day treatment programs that have converted to supported employment found no adverse outcomes (Becker, Smith, Tanzman, Drake, & Tremblay, 2001).

METHODS FOR THE ASSESSMENT OF OUTCOMES AND EFFICACY

Supported employment studies have typically used objective indicators of competitive employment, such as rates of obtaining employment, time to

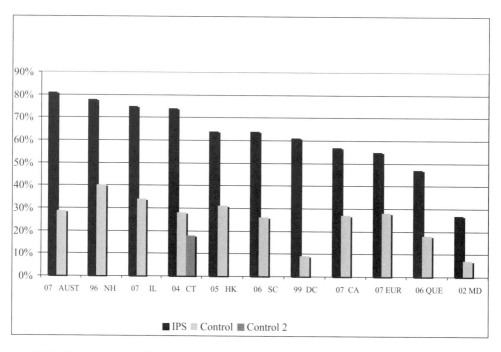

Figure 101.1 Competitive employment rates in 11 randomized controlled trials: individual placement and support.

first job, job tenure, and hours worked per week. Nonvocational outcomes, such as psychiatric symptoms and quality of life, have also been measured (Bond, 2004). Eleven studies of supported employment have used most rigorous research designs, with careful training of clinicians and monitoring of implementation (efficacy methods), and also included real-world settings, service providers, and clients from heterogeneous backgrounds (effectiveness methods) (Bond et al., in press).

Other studies have also been conducted in a multitude of settings, including urban and rural areas, and in countries outside the United States with differing labor conditions (e.g., Australia, Canada, Hong Kong, and several European countries). In the aforementioned studies, assessing fidelity, that is, adherence to the IPS program model, was deemed crucial. Thus, a specific IPS fidelity scale was developed and validated (Bond, Becker, Drake, & Vogler, 1997). Assessing IPS fidelity and making adjustments to practice is also important given findings that better fidelity to the model leads to better employment outcomes for clients (Becker, Smith, Tanzman, Drake, & Tremblay, 2001).

IMPLEMENTATION ISSUES

As already noted, systematically assessing and monitoring supported employment fidelity is a crucial implementation strategy. Several other components of effective implementation that relate closely to fidelity include the following (Bond, McHugo, Becker, Rapp, & Whitley, in press; Corrigan et al., 2008).

- Discontinuing non–evidence-based vocational services (e.g., sheltered workshops, train-place vocational approaches).
- Improving the integration of employment services with clinical and mental health services, via supervisor leadership.
- Changing relevant organizational and structural tasks to be compatible with the supported employment model. These may include such things as changing billing processes and procedures, training staff, endorsing the supported employment philosophy organization-wide, and changing documentation in client records.

- Implementing supported employment programs at exemplary sites that can be models and opportunities for training for later sites.
- Obtaining support and consensus from all stakeholders (i.e., clients, family members, state authorities, practitioners, and administrators).

In addition, studies have found that supported employment may be implemented successfully and is widely generalizable and applicable across community settings (rural and urban) and across various ethnic and minority groups (including African Americans, Hispanic Americans, and Asian Americans), among both young and older adults, and with clients with co-occurring substance use (Corrigan et al., 2008).

PROVIDER COMPETENCIES

Whereas several provider competencies of employment specialists exist that are necessary for successful supported employment services, little research has been conducted in this area. However, some of the most important provider competencies that should be emphasized in practice include:

- hopeful attitudes and the belief that clients with severe mental illness *can* work (Gowdy, Carlson, & Rapp, 2003);
- the ability to form a good "working alliance" or relationship with the client;
- job development skills, or the ability to locate and secure numerous and diverse jobs matching client preferences and needs;
- skills encompassed within each specific phase of employment services (e.g., appropriate ongoing job support to the client) (Drake, Bond, & Rapp, 2006).
- employment specialist motivation and interest in the field of supported employment; and
- employment specialists focus on working in the community in all phases of employment services, rather than in the agency office.

Importantly, these are skills and behaviors that can be taught. The research suggests that appropriate supervision, feedback, and leadership provided to the employment specialist by team leaders and other supervisory-level staff make a difference.

FUTURE RESEARCH DIRECTIONS

Several areas of future research are needed in the supported employment arena, given the paucity of research conducted thus far and the need for improvement of supported employment services in various areas to result in improved client outcomes. Such areas include the following (Drake & Bond, in press):

- provider competencies,
- ways to increase job tenure of clients,
- understanding the overall costs of supported employment and better ways to finance and organize supported employment services,
- better job development strategies,
- ways to enhance career trajectories of supported employment clients, and
- effective ways to address lack of motivation to work.

WEB SITES

Dartmouth Supported Employment Center. http://dms.dartmouth.edu/prc/employment.
Employment Intervention Demonstration Program (Center on Mental Health Services Research and Policy, University of Illinois at Chicago). http://www.psych.uic.edu/eidp.
Evidence-Based Practices: Shaping Mental Health Services Toward Recovery: Supported Employment (SAMHSA). http://mentalhealth samhsa.gov/cmhs/communitysupport/toolkits/employment.
Worksupport.com (Virginia Commonwealth University). http://www.worksupport.com.

References

Becker, D. R., Bond, G. R., McCarthy, D., Thompson, D., Xie, H., McHugo, G. J., et al. (2001). Converting day treatment centers to supported employment programs in Rhode Island. *Psychiatric Services, 52,* 351–357.
Becker, D. R., & Drake, R. E. (2003). *A working life for people with severe mental illness.* New York: Oxford University Press.
Becker, D. R., Smith, J., Tanzman, B., Drake, R. E., & Tremblay, T. (2001). Fidelity of supported employment programs and employment outcomes. *Psychiatric Services, 52,* 834–836.
Bond, G. R. (1998). Principles of the individual placement and support model: Empirical support. *Psychiatric Rehabilitation Journal, 22*(1), 11–23.

Bond, G. R. (2004). Supported employment: Evidence for an evidence-based practice. *Psychiatric Rehabilitation Journal, 27,* 345–359.

Bond, G. R., Becker, D. R., Drake, R. E., & Vogler, K. M. (1997). A fidelity scale for the individual placement and support model of supported employment. *Rehabilitation Counseling Bulletin, 40,* 265–284.

Bond, G. R., Drake, R. E., & Becker, D. R. (In press). An update on randomized controlled trials of evidence-based supported employment. *Psychiatric Rehabilitation Journal.*

Bond, G. R., McHugo, G. J., Becker, D. R., Rapp, C. A., & Whitley, R. (In press). Fidelity of supported employment: Lessons learned from the National EBP Project. *Psychiatric Rehabilitation Journal.*

Corrigan, P. W., Mueser, K. T., Bond, G. R., Drake, R. E., & Solomon, P. (2008). *Principles and practice of psychiatric rehabilitation: An empirical approach.* New York: Guilford.

Drake, R. E., & Bond, G. R. (In press). Future directions for supported employment. *Psychiatric Rehabilitation Journal.*

Drake, R. E., Bond, G. R., & Rapp, C. A. (2006). Explaining the variance within supported employment programs: Comment on "What Predicts Supported Employment Outcomes?" *Community Mental Health Journal, 42,* 315–318.

Gold, P. B., Meisler, N., Santos, A. B., Carnemolla, M. A., Williams, O. H., & Kelleher, J. (2006). Randomized trial of supported employment integrated with assertive community treatment for rural adults with severe mental illness. *Schizophrenia Bulletin, 32,* 378–395.

Gowdy, E. A., Carlson, L. S., & Rapp, C. A. (2003). Practices differentiating high-performing from low-performing supported employment programs. *Psychiatric Rehabilitation Journal, 26,* 232–239.

Wehman, P., & Moon, M. S. (Eds.). (1988). *Vocational rehabilitation and supported employment.* Baltimore: Paul Brookes.

102   Working with and Strengthening Social Networks

Elizabeth M. Tracy

The role of supportive relationships is central to the mission of social work and its practice. Assessing and working with social support systems are considered requisite skills for social work practice, as the following case examples illustrate.

• A teenage mother receives home visits and attends a parent support group to build a supportive social network as she transitions into the role of parent.

• A man who has completed a substance abuse treatment program attends Alcoholics Anonymous and works with his sponsor and case manager to build a social network supportive of sobriety.

• Family members participate in a psychoeducational support group so that they get the support and help needed to cope with a family member with a mental disorder.

Social support refers to the actions that others perform when they render assistance. There are several different types of social support, such as:

• emotional support—having someone listen to your feelings, comfort you, or offer encouragement;

• informational support—having someone teach you something, give you information or advice, or help you make a major decision; and

- concrete support—having someone help in tangible ways, loaning you something, giving you information, helping with a chore, or taking you on an errand.

Social support can take place within naturally occurring helping networks of family, friends, neighbors, and peers, or in groups and organizations that have been specifically created or contrived for this purpose. Formal support includes services delivered by paid human service professionals. Informal support, which is the focus here, can be delivered by kinship networks, volunteers, or local community groups.

People with access to social support resources are in better physical and mental health and are better able to adapt to and cope with life changes. Thompson (1995) has identified several key functions of social support that may reduce or protect against the negative effects of stressful events:

- emotional sustenance and a sense that you are not alone;
- counseling advice and guidance in dealing with challenging life events;
- access to information, services, material resources, and tangible assistance;
- skills acquisition and training; and
- social monitoring and social control of behavior.

Social networks are the primary mechanism through which support functions are made available. The term *social network* refers to a set of individuals and the ties among them. The study of whole networks examines the pattern of relations within a group bounded by geography or some characteristic, such as all the clients in a treatment program. A personal social network focus examines the relations surrounding a focal person, such as an individual client or family. A personal social network approach to assessment and intervention considers the behavior of individuals in the context of the people with whom they directly interact.

Personal social networks consist of several dimensions. Compositional network qualities include:

- size—the total number of people in the network;
- relationships of network members—friends, family, professionals;
- frequency of contact—how often people in the network interact with one another;

- duration—how long people in the network have known one another; and
- reciprocity—the amount of give and take.

Structural network qualities include such features as:

- density—the percent of ties that exist in a network out of all possible;
- components—network members who are connected to one another directly or indirectly;
- multiplexity—the extent to which network relationships serve more than one function or provide more than one type of support; and
- centrality measures—measures of network activity and information flow.

Sometimes composition and structure can be combined, such as identifying whether the most structurally central person is supportive of the client's recovery.

The terms *social network* and *social support* do not necessarily refer to the same concept. People may be surrounded by large social networks but may not feel supported or perceive support from others. They may also not be receiving the types and amount of support that they need. A social support network refers to the set of people who do provide various forms of social support for one another.

Likewise, not all social ties are supportive because interpersonal relationships may be sources of support as well as stress (Lincoln, 2000). Patterns of negative social networks may be evident. For example, social network members may be overly critical or demanding of one another, or members may reinforce or encourage harmful or antisocial behavior, such as drug abuse or gang violence. Social networks may also fail to support efforts to change behaviors or maintain changes in behavior, such as a parent changing from punishment approaches to more positive forms of child management.

Finally, several related concepts are important to note. Enacted support refers to the actual utilization of support resources. Perceived support refers to the extent to which an individual feels that his or her support needs are or would be fulfilled. Network orientation refers to beliefs, attitudes, or expectations concerning the usefulness of network members in helping cope with a problem. Some people may have adequate social networks but may not make use of or access use of their network in times of need owing to a negative network orientation. Another barrier to use of one's social network may be inadequate social skills in requesting help, developing network relationships, and maintaining supportive social ties over time

SOCIAL SUPPORT ASSESSMENT GUIDELINES

Given the complexity of social support, a necessary first task is to complete an accurate assessment of social network resources and the functional qualities of social network relationships. The following questions serve as guidelines for social support assessment.

1. Who is in the network, how are they related to the client, and who could be potential members?
2. What are the strengths and capabilities of the social network? Among the strengths that need to be examined are the number of supportive relationships, variety of supportive relationships, types of support available (emotional, concrete, and informational), and reciprocity among helping relationships.
3. What are the gaps in social support needs? Is there a lack of fit between the types of support network members are willing or capable of providing and the types of support the client needs or desires?
4. What relationships in the network are based on mutual exchange? Does reciprocity seem to be an issue for the client? Is the client always giving to others and thereby experiencing stress and drain? Or does the client appear to be a drain on the network, with the result that network members are stressed and overburdened?
5. What network members are identified as responsive to requests for help, effective in their helping, accessible, and dependable? Do sufficient numbers of network members meet these conditions?
6. What network members are critical of the client in a negative or demanding way? Is the client surrounded by a network that is perceived as negative, nonsupportive, and/or stress-producing?
7. What obstacles or barriers to using social network resources exist? Does the client lack supportive resources or skills in accessing

them? Are network members unable to provide more assistance owing to lack of skills or knowledge, or have they provided support in the past and are now unwilling or unable to continue to do so? Overwhelming family stressors, such as homelessness or substance use, may be present that interfere with the provision of support (Kemp, Whittaker, & Tracy, 1997).

INTERVENTION STRATEGIES

Social network interventions are typically directed toward either structural changes in the social network itself or functional changes in social network relationships. Structural interventions aim to create a new network or supplement one that already exists. Some examples of structural changes include:

• increasing or decreasing the size of the network, as in increasing the number of friends;
• changing the composition of the social network, as in introducing a new cluster or reestablishing network relationships which have been lost; and
• increasing or decreasing the frequency of contact with particular social network members—for example, highly negative network members.

Functional interventions seek to improve or enhance the quality and nature of relationships within a network. This might include increasing or mobilizing various types of support (e.g., concrete emotional or informational support, as in respite care services for a family) or teaching network members new skills for interaction. Some examples of skill-enhancing interventions to facilitate more social support include:

• developing or increasing skills in making friends;
• decreasing negative beliefs about self (if this is a barrier to developing/maintaining supportive relationships), increasing positive self-statements, and increasing the ability to identify personal strengths;
• developing strategies for handling criticism from others;
• increasing assertive skills (if this is a barrier to developing or maintaining supportive relationships);

- increasing communication skills (if this is a barrier to developing or maintaining supportive relationships); and
- teaching reciprocity skills (if this is a barrier to developing or maintaining supportive relationships) to ask for help (Kemp et al., 1997).

The overriding purpose of the social network intervention should be kept in mind. Changes in social support may be desired for a variety of reasons: first, to support maintenance and generalization of treatment efforts, as in building social networks supportive of change (Tracy & Biegel, 2006); second, to serve as a protective factor, as in increasing supportive bonds for children at risk of juvenile delinquency or substance abuse (MacNeil, Stewart, & Kaufman, 2000); and third, to provide a coping mechanism, as in social support provision due to a crisis or life transition (Cameron, 2000).

Examples of Social Network Intervention Strategies

- Network facilitation through network meetings—for example, family group conferencing (Crampton, 2007).
- Additional network clusters, through referral to formal or informal organizations.
- Additional individual network members through a social networking intervention (Biegel, Tracy & Corvo, 1994).
- Peer support programs and mutual aid or self-help groups (Moore, 2005).
- Natural helper intervention (Gaudin, 1993).
- Social and communication skills training (Richey, 1994).
- Extended family support and psychoeducational approaches—for example, teaching family members how to deal with psychiatric symptoms (Mueser, Noordsy, Drake, Fox, & Barlow, 2003).

See Kemp et al. (1997) for further descriptions of these and other intervention strategies.

IMPLEMENTING FOR SUCCESS

A network intervention is not a panacea. Many clients still require professionally delivered services, with social network interventions as a supplement. There are a number of implementation issues to consider.

- Pay close attention to the type of support desired or needed by the client (e.g., informational or emotional) and match the intervention to that need.
- Ensure that *reciprocal* relationships are established.
- Focus on quality of network relationships, not just size of network.
- Recognize that not all networks are supportive and attend to negative or stress-producing network relationships; intervene to enhance these relationships.
- Monitor the effect of interventions on network members to ensure that the network is not overburdened.
- Attend to perceived as well as enacted support.
- Teach skills needed to elicit and maintain supportive relationships, both to the client and network members, as skill deficits may contribute to lack of support.
- Recognize that advocacy may be needed to build supportive resources at the community level.

Social support interventions are challenging to evaluate owing to their complexity. It may be difficult to see immediate results of network interventions. People may perceive supportive interventions differently depending on the timing and source of support. In spite of the limitations of our current knowledge, social support interventions hold promise, and the skills of assessing and mobilizing support are important for every practitioner to acquire.

WEB SITES

American Self-Help Group Clearinghouse. http://www.selfhelpgroups.org.
National Self Help Clearinghouse. http://www.selfhelpweb.org.
National Mental Health Consumers' Self-Help Clearinghouse. http://www.mhselfhelp.org.
Post Partum Support International. http://www.postpartum.net/support-map.html.

References

Biegel, D., Tracy, E. M., & Corvo, K. N. (1994). Strengthening social networks: Intervention strategies for mental health case managers. *Health and Social Work, 19*(3), 207–216.

Cameron, G. (2000). Parent mutual aid organizations in child welfare demonstration project: A report of outcomes. *Children and Youth Services Review, 22*(6), 421–440.

Crampton, D. (2007). Research review: Family group decision making: A promising practice in need of more programme theory and research. *Child & Family Social Work, 12*(2), 202–209.

Gaudin, J. M. (1993). *Child neglect: A guide for intervention.* Washington, DC: Health and Human Services, National Center on Child Abuse and Neglect (NCCAN).

Kemp, S., Whittaker, J. K., & Tracy, E. M. (1997). *Person-environment practice: The social ecology of interpersonal helping.* New York: Aldine de Gruyter.

Lincoln, K. D. (2000). Social support, negative social interactions, and psychological well-being. *Social Service Review, June*, 232–252.

MacNeil, G., Stewart, J. C., & Kaufman, A. V. (2000). Social support as a potential moderator of adolescent delinquent behaviors. *Child and Adolescent Social Work Journal, 17*(5), 361–379.

Moore, B. (2005). Empirically supported family and peer interventions for dual disorders. *Research on Social Work Practice, 15*, 231–245.

Mueser, K. T., Noordsy, D. L., Drake, R. E., Fox, L., & Barlow, D. H. (2003). *Integrated treatment for dual disorders: A guide to effective practice.* New York: Guilford.

Richey, C. A. (1994). Social support skill training. In D. K. Granvold (Ed.), *Cognitive and behavioral treatment: Methods and applications* (pp. 299–338). Belmont, CA: Brooks/Cole.

Thompson, R. A. (1995). *Preventing child maltreatment through social support.* Thousand Oaks, CA: Sage.

Tracy, E., & Biegel, D. (2006). Social networks and dual disorders: A literature review and implications for practice and future research. *Journal of Dual Diagnosis, 2*(2), 59–88.

Eye Movement Desensitization and Reprocessing with Trauma Clients

103

Allen Rubin

Eye movement desensitization and reprocessing (EMDR) was developed in 1987 as a procedure for alleviating stress-related symptoms connected to traumatic memories. Its founder described it as "an interactive, intrapsychic, cognitive, behavioral, body-oriented therapy" that aims "to rapidly metabolize the dysfunctional residue from the past and transform it into something useful" (Shapiro, 1995, pp. 52–53). As its name implies, the EMDR procedure attempts to desensitize clients to distressing memories, feelings, and cognitions and enhance the replacement of negative cognitions with positive ones. Thus, for example, if a woman who has been sexually assaulted is experiencing post-traumatic stress disorder (PTSD) symptoms connected to the assault and blames herself for the assault, the practitioner employing EMDR will try to alleviate the PTSD symptoms, reduce the distress brought on by the memory, and help the woman stop blaming herself.

The EMDR procedure is implemented in the context of an ongoing therapeutic relationship, after a therapeutic alliance is established with the client. It is intended to be used by experienced psychotherapists, in conjunction with other clinical approaches they employ, only after they have received formal EMDR training. Also, therapists are advised to apply EMDR only to target problems that they already are competent to treat. Not all clients are considered appropriate for EMDR treatment. In particular, EMDR may be contraindicated for clients who have dissociative disorders or psychoses, who are experiencing ongoing abuse, and who are chronic cocaine users. Some clients with the foregoing problems, however, are considered appropriate for EMDR treatment in certain situations, assuming the clinician has had special training to use EMDR with clients experiencing these problems. Clinicians interested in employing the EMDR procedure can learn more about contraindications for the procedure when they obtain the training.

Although EMDR incorporates various cognitive-behavioral techniques, its most distinguishing feature is the use of dual attention stimulation. Eye movements usually comprise the dual attention stimulation. Other forms of stimulation include alternating right and left hand taps or alternating sounds in the right and left ear for clients with vision problems or who have difficulty thinking about stressful material while concentrating on tracking the therapist's rapidly moving fingers with their eyes. Some critics consider EMDR to be nothing more than traditional cognitive-behavioral therapy with an added component of dual attention stimulation (Rosen, 1999). Others, however, claim that what distinguishes EMDR is not just the dual attention stimulation but a unique and systematic treatment sequence that incorporates virtually every intervention component thought to be effective in treatment of trauma.

A full description of the EMDR protocol and its theoretical rationale can be found in a text written by Shapiro & Forrest (1997). The method is described as an information-processing therapy that alleviates traumatic memories by integrating them with more positive and adaptive information. It consists of eight phases, with a specific protocol for each phase.

In the first phase, a thorough client history is obtained, and from that a treatment plan is developed. The clinical evaluation during this phase should be comprehensive, and should include a determination of whether there are indications that the client is likely to benefit from EMDR treatment as well as any contraindications for the use of EMDR with the client. A key issue in considering whether a client is likely to benefit is

the assumption underlying EMDR that sometimes current symptoms can be traced to unresolved memories and resolving these "source memories" can alleviate the symptoms. Though this assumption may be fairly obvious regarding PTSD, it is commonly made in EMDR literature and training in regard to other problems, as well.

In the second phase, the client is prepared for the EMDR procedure. Preparation includes building a therapeutic relationship, educating the client about the procedure and possible negative reactions to it, addressing client fears and safety issues, and discussing client goals and expectations regarding treatment. During this phase, the clinician also determines which form of dual attention stimulation would be most comfortable for the client and appears to have the best prospects for efficacy.

In the third phase, an assessment is conducted to determine what target issue and what components thereof are to be addressed. Target components include the presenting problem, the memory associated with the presenting problem, a mental image of that memory, identification of a negative self-statement associated with the memory, identification of a positive self-statement with which to replace the negative one, the emotions associated with the memory, and any physical sensations the client notices when picturing the traumatic memory. During this phase, the client focuses on a mental picture of the traumatic memory, identifies the undesired self-statement about the image, identifies a positive self-statement that they would like to replace the undesired one, reports unpleasant emotional sensations connected with the image, notes where in the body the emotional unpleasantness is felt, and provides a subjective rating of the severity of the distress they feel and how true their preferred self-statement seems to them. That is, the client holds the mental image of the memory while simultaneously thinking of the desired positive self-statement and is then asked to rate how true the desired self-statement feels on a scale from 1 to 7. The client is also asked to think of the emotions evoked in the here and now by the image and the negative self-statement and to rate on a scale from 0 to 10 how disturbing the emotions currently feel when holding the image and negative self-statement in mind. Depending on the level of these two ratings, the therapist may decide to proceed to the next phase or stay in phase three and seek to identify alternative issues or components that are more problematic.

In the fourth phase, the desensitization process is implemented. The client is asked to hold all of the identified target components in mind while the therapist induces the eye movements or an alternate form of dual attention stimulation. The emphasis during this phase is on relying on the dual attention stimulation, not talk therapy, to achieve the desensitization.

If eye movements comprise the dual attention stimulation, the client is asked to visualize the distressful scene and keep in mind the identified cognitions and feelings while visually tracking the therapist's fingers moving rapidly and rhythmically (about 18 inches in front of their face) back and forth, up and down, or diagonally. The speed is about two back-and-forth movements per second. The direction and number of movements varies on an individual basis.

The average duration of each set of dual attention stimulation is approximately 25 seconds. After each set, clients discuss what thoughts, feelings, or images came up during the set, and then report changes in the degree of distress they felt. If not much changed, the therapist likely will repeat one or more sets of stimulation, targeting the same stressful memory, feelings, and cognitions. If new material comes up, the next set(s) will target that new material. This process will then be repeated throughout the treatment session, with each successive set of dual attention stimulation typically targeting the new material that comes up each time. The aim is to reach a point when the client's level of disturbance rating drops considerably (ideally to a level of 0 or 1 on the 10-point scale). Additional sessions can be used as needed to deal with the same or other sources of distress.

In the fifth phase, which commences after successful desensitization in phase 4, additional sets of dual attention stimulation are used to install the desired cognition (i.e., a positive self-statement). The positive cognition is considered to have been successfully installed when the client rates how true the desired self-statement feels as a 6 or 7 on the 7-point validity of cognition scale.

In the sixth phase, a body scan is conducted to see whether any residual material from the target issue remains unresolved. If unresolved material is identified, then phases four and five are applied as needed to that material. The seventh phase involves closure, in which the clinician employs relaxation techniques (such as guided imagery) to alleviate any lingering distress experienced by the client. The need for additional desensitization sessions may be identified during this phase, and clients are asked to maintain a log of any distressing emotions or cognitions they experience between sessions. The eighth phase involves client reevaluation of whether the targeted trauma has been successfully resolved and whether they experience the need for further processing of it.

Each EMDR session involves a varying number of sets. The number and length of the sessions required to achieve meaningful change vary from client to client. Some studies have reported clinically meaningful and stable changes with as few as one to three sessions (Shapiro, 1996a,b). Ninety minutes is the recommended session length for adults and adolescents. Most of the time is taken up by discussion before and after each set. The actual cumulative amount of time the eyes are moving (or other forms of dual attention stimulation are occurring) will be several minutes.

The foregoing protocol applies primarily to adult clients or adolescents. Many children, however, have neither the attention span nor the cognitive capacity to handle the adult procedure. Child therapists using EMDR, therefore, may be advised to improvise quite a bit with each case and deviate from the adult procedure in creative ways (Greenwald, 1999). For example, the EMDR procedure may have to be done very quickly—perhaps in just a few minutes—amid a play therapy session or some other modality not devoted exclusively to EMDR. Fewer sets are used, and there are fewer eye movements per set. Commonly, the sequence of the stages of the adult protocol may be modified for children. For example, the clinician may begin dual attention stimulation regarding a positive thought, saving negative material for a later date. Also, the therapist may choose not to go back to old memories; instead, the focus may be on thoughts impeding present functioning.

Another important difference is that the therapist begins the EMDR process by asking the child to focus on positive images and cognitions and then installs those positive images and cognitions via dual attention stimulation, saving the distressful images and cognitions for later in the process. Greenwald (1994) has recommended various additional improvisations when working with certain types of children. These include, but are not limited to, children who need to be motivated for treatment, cannot tolerate the slow pace of the adult protocol, are unwilling to communicate about the targeted source of distress, are oppositional, have attention deficit hyperactivity disorders, or have been abused. It would be incorrect, however, to conclude that it is all right to be unsystematic in using EMDR with children. To the contrary, the improvisations one uses with children are thought to require "a lot of extra care and planning to ensure that the treatment is really as thorough as it needs to be (Greenwald, personal communication)

Despite having received a great deal of rigorous outcome research supporting its effectiveness in treating adults with noncombat, single-trauma PTSD, EMDR is viewed by many as controversial. One reason is that its proponents have touted it as being effective not only with trauma and fear-based disorders but also with virtually every area of psychopathology—areas in which there is much less supportive research. Another reason is the extreme claims that have been made about it by its proponents, such as by suggesting that only one session is needed to resolve trauma symptoms or by calling it a "breakthrough" therapy (Shapiro & Forrest, 1997). Some have portrayed EMDR as a pseudo-scientific movement that promotes an intervention that merely tacks an unnecessary treatment gimmick (dual attention stimulation) onto imaginal exposure techniques (Olatunji, Parker, & Lohr, 2005–2006). Its detractors have also criticized the fact that its development was not based in theory, and the attempts to connect it to theory have been speculative and changing over the years, including—among others—such notions as stimulating a part of the brain where traumatic memories remain frozen and unprocessed or helping the rational hemisphere of the brain gain access to and process traumatic memories that are stuck in the opposite hemisphere. The same detractors have argued that EMDR proponents keep changing the criteria used for judging the fidelity of EMDR treatment with each outcome study that produces findings that its proponents dislike (Rubin, 2003, 2004).

As noted previously, however, a large number of well-controlled outcome studies and some meta-analyses have supported the effectiveness of EMDR in treating adults with noncombat, single-trauma PTSD (Bisson et al., 2007; Davidson & Parker, 2001; Seidler & Wagner, 2006; Van Etten & Taylor, 1998). In light of that support, Division 12 (Clinical Psychology) of the American Psychological Association deemed EMDR one of three empirically validated treatment approaches that are probably efficacious in treating PTSD (Chambless et al., 1998). The other two were exposure therapy and stress inoculation therapy. In 1999, EMDR was designated in the treatment guidelines of the International Society for Traumatic Stress Studies

as an effective treatment for PTSD (Chemtob, Tolin, van der Kolk, & Pitman, 1999).

There is less research evidence supporting the effectiveness of EMDR in alleviating the trauma symptoms of children. The early evidence supporting the effectiveness of the technique in treating traumatized children was based primarily on several quasi-experiments and other studies with relatively weak controls for various threats to internal validity (Rubin, 2003). Three experimental studies raised questions about the effectiveness of EMDR in treating children whose symptoms were not clearly trauma-based. Two of these experiments compared the efficacy of EMDR with that of in vivo exposure in the treatment of spider-phobic children. One found positive effects for EMDR, particularly on self-report measures, but also found that in vivo exposure had superior effects in reducing avoidance behaviors (Muris, Merckelbach, Holdrinet, & Sijsenaar (1998). It concluded that in vivo exposure is the treatment of choice for this type of phobia, and EMDR adds nothing of value to it. In the other experiment, in vivo exposure produced significant improvement on behavioral as well as self-reported outcome measures, whereas EMDR produced significant improvement only on self-reported spider fear. Also, providing EMDR before in vivo exposure did not enhance the effectiveness of the in vivo exposure treatment (Muris, Merckelbach, van Haaften, & Mayer, 1997).

One randomized experiment (Rubin et al., 2001) raised doubts about the effectiveness of EMDR when treating children whose emotional and behavioral problems are not connected in a narrow fashion to a specific trauma or whose very young ages or clinical problems require improvisational deviations from the standard EMDR protocol. Two experiments, however, supported the efficacy of EMDR in treating PTSD symptoms among children whose symptoms are connected to specific traumas. For example, Chemtob, Nakashima, & Carlson (2002) found that EMDR alleviated PTSD symptoms of elementary school children (aged 6 to 12) who had experienced a hurricane. Jeffres (2004) found that up to five 60-minute sessions of EMDR alleviated PTSD symptoms among children (ages 8–12) who had suffered one or more traumas.

In addition to the need for more evidence regarding the effectiveness of EMDR with children, questions remain unanswered regarding its effectiveness with other target populations and problems. The evidence is mixed, for example, regarding its effectiveness in treating combat PTSD among military veterans (Rubin, 2003). Likewise, there is a shortage of evidence supporting its effectiveness in treating victims of multiple traumas experiencing complex PTSD (Rubin, 2003). Also needed is more evidence to support the claims of some that EMDR is effective in treating a wider range of problems, including less circumscribed ones that may not be caused by trauma, such as self-esteem issues, agoraphobia, dissociative identity disorder, somatic disorders, smoking cessation, chronic depression, obsessive-compulsive disorder, and eating disorders (Rubin, 2003; Shapiro, 1995).

Perhaps the most controversial unanswered questions pertain to whether the dual attention stimulation component of EMDR is really necessary and whether there is a difference in effectiveness between EMDR and exposure therapy. Some randomized experiments have offered limited support to the notion that the distinctive dual attention stimulation component enhances the effects of EMDR and that EMDR is more effective than exposure therapy (Maxfield, Lake, & Hyer, 2004). Some other experiments reached the opposite conclusions and questioned whether the beneficial effects of EMDR can be attributed exclusively to the its imaginal exposure aspects (Olatunji et al., 2005–2006; Rothbaum, Astin, & Marsteller, 2005). Likewise, most of the meta-analytical studies on the effectiveness of EMDR have found that it is no more effective than exposure therapy (Bisson et al., 2007; Davidson & Parker, 2001; Seidler & Wagner, 2006).

The debate as to the necessity of the dual attention stimulation component of EMDR pertains to the need for a more persuasive theoretical explanation as to why and how that component makes a difference. Barker and Hawes (1999) posit a tentative explanation based on the brain imaging studies of van der Kolk and associates. A traumatic experience can impede the brain's ability to process and integrate information and memories connected to the trauma. Reminders of the trauma may trigger intense emotions, vivid images of traumatic details, and physical sensations that occurred during the trauma. Individuals with and without PTSD have differences in brain activity, the size of their hippocampus, and the amount of right versus left hemisphere activity. These differences make individuals with PTSD more susceptible to having their emotional system dominate their cognitive system in processing information, which in turn may make them more susceptible to hyperarousal, dissociation, and difficulties in stimulus discrimination. The dual attention stimulation component of EMDR conceivably activates neurological mechanisms in the brain that enable one's cognitive system to process and integrate information connected to the trauma that had been previously neurologically frozen.

Two brain imaging studies (van der Kolk, 1997; van der Kolk, Burbridge, & Suzuki, 1997) provided tentative evidence supporting this notion. After EMDR treatment six traumatized individuals had brain changes associated with improvements in distinguishing past threats from present experiences and learning from new information rather than remaining focused on the past. Thus, conceivably, dual attention stimulation triggers changes in neuronal activity in the brain. This, however, is not the only plausible hypothesis. Another is that the simultaneous attention to the dual attention stimulation and the traumatic material produces a relaxation response that deconditions the negative associations with the traumatic memory and thus desensitizes the individual (Barker & Hawes, 1999). These are not the only attempts to date to develop a theoretical foundation for EMDR, and others are likely to be forthcoming.

Regardless of the theoretical explanation, there appears to be ample empirical evidence supporting the efficacy of EMDR in treating PTSD symptoms among traumatized adult clients. There is less conclusive evidence supporting its efficacy with children. Although this review has focused on EMDR, its author is aware of substantial empirical support for the effectiveness of trauma-focused cognitive behavioral therapy (TF-CBT) with children (Cohen, Mannarino, & Deblinger, 2006; Cohen, Berliner, & March, 2000). Consequently, clinicians treating traumatized children are advised also to consider TF-CBT as a possible alternative to EMDR.

Additional research will be required to explain why EMDR works. More studies are needed regarding its efficacy in treating a wider range of problems less narrowly connected with PTSD symptoms resulting from a specific trauma, the debate as to whether the dual attention stimulation is really necessary, and the comparative effectiveness of EMDR versus exposure therapy. While awaiting those studies, clinicians treating traumatized adults can be encouraged to use either EMDR or exposure therapy, depending on whether they have been trained in either, can refer to another clinician who has been so trained, and in light of their clinical judgment regarding the unique circumstances and preferences of their clients.

WEB SITES

EMDR bibliography from 1989 through 2005. http://www.trauma-pages.com/s/emdr-refs.php.

EMDR International Association. http://www.emdria.org.

EMDR Network. http://www.emdrnetwork.org.

"EMDR: Taking a Closer Look." http://www.sciam.com/article.cfm?id=emdr-taking-a-closer-look.

"EMDR Treatment: Less Than Meets the Eye?" http://www.quackwatch.com/01QuackeryRelatedTopics/emdr.html.

References

Barker, S. B., & Hawes, E. C. (1999). Eye movement desensitization and reprocessing in individual psychology. *Journal of Individual Psychology, 55* (2), 146–161.

Bisson, J. I., Ehlers, A., Matthews, R., Pilling, S., Richards, D. A., Turner, F., et al. (2007). Psychological treatments for chronic post-traumatic stress disorder: Systematic review and meta-analysis. *British Journal of Psychiatry, 190,* 2, 97–104.

Chambless, D. L., Baker, M. J., Baucom, D. H., Beutler, L. E., Calhoun, K. S., Crits-Christoph, P., et al. (1998). Update on empirically validated therapies, II. *Clinical Psychologist, 51,* 3–16.

Chemtob, C. M., Nakashima, J., & Carlson, J. G. (2002). Brief treatment for elementary school children with disaster-related posttraumatic stress disorder: A field study. *Journal of Clinical Psychology, 58,* 99–112.

Chemtob, C. M., Tolin, D., Van der Kolk, B., & Pitman, R. (1999). Treatment guidelines for EMDR. In *ISTSS PTSD Treatment Guidelines.* International Society for Traumatic Stress Studies.

Cohen, J. A., Berliner, L., & March, J. S. (2000). Treatment of children and adolescents. In E. B. Foa, T. M. Keane, & M. J. Friedman (Eds.), *Effective treatments for PTSD: Practice guidelines from the International Society for Traumatic Stress Studies* (pp. 330–332). New York: Guilford.

Cohen, J. A., Mannarino, A. P., & Deblinger, E. (2006). *Treating trauma and traumatic grief in children and adolescents.* New York: Guilford.

Davidson, P. R., & Parker, K. C. H. (2001). Eye movement desensitization and reprocessing (EMDR): A meta-analysis. *Journal of Consulting and Clinical Psychology, 69,* 305–316.

Greenwld, R. (1994). Eye movement desensitization and reprocessing (EMDR): An overview. *Journal of Contemporary Psychotherapy, 24*(1), 15–34.

Greenwald, R. (1999). *Eye movement desensitization and reprocessing (EMDR) in child and adolescent psychotherapy.* Northvale, NJ: Aronson.

Jeffres, M. J. (2004). The efficacy of EMDR with traumatized children. *Dissertation Abstracts International: B: The Sciences and Engineering, 64*(8-B), 4042.

Maxfield, L., Lake, K., & Hyer, L. (2004). Some answers to unanswered questions about the empirical support for EMDR in the treatment of PTSD. *Traumatology, 10*(2), 73–88.

Muris, P., Merckelbach, H., Holdrinet, I., & Sijsenaar, M. (1998). Treating phobic children: Effects of EMDR versus exposure. *Journal of Consulting and Clinical Psychology, 66,* 193–198.

Muris, P., Merckelbach, H., van Haaften, H., & Mayer, B. (1997). Eye movement desensitization and reprocessing versus exposure in vivo: A single-session crossover study of spider-phobic children. *British Journal of Psychiatry, 171,* 82–86.

Olatunji, B. O., Parker, L. M., & Lohr, J. M. (2005–2006). Pseudoscience in contemporary psychology. *Scientific Review of Mental Health Practice, 4*(2), 19–31.

Rosen, G. (1999). Treatment fidelity and research on eye movement desensitization and reprocessing (EMDR). *Journal of Anxiety Disorders, 13,* 173–184.

Rothbaum, B. O., Astin, M. C., & Marsteller, F. (2005). Prolonged exposure versus eye movement desensitization and reprocessing (EMDR) for PTSD rape victims. *Journal of Traumatic Stress, 18*(6), 607–616.

Rubin, A. (2003). Unanswered questions about the empirical support for EMDR in the treatment of PTSD. *Traumatology, 9,* 4–30.

Rubin, A. (2004). Fallacies and deflections in debating the empirical support for EMDR in the treatment of PTSD: A reply to Maxfield, Lake, and Hyer. *Traumatology, 10*(2), 91–105.

Rubin, A., et al. (2001). The effectiveness of EMDR in a child guidance center. *Research on Social Work Practice, 11*(4), 435–457.

Seidler, G. H., & Wagner, F. E. (2006) Comparing the efficacy of *EMDR* and trauma-focused cognitive-behavioral therapy in the treatment of PTSD: A meta-analytic study. *Psychological Medicine, 36*(11), 1515–1522.

Shapiro, F. (1995). *Eye movement desensitization and reprocessing: Basic principles, protocols, and procedures.* New York: Guilford.

Shapiro, F. (1996a). Eye movement desensitization and reprocessing (EMDR): Evaluation of controlled PTSD research. *Journal of Behavior Therapy and Experimental Psychiatry, 27,* 209–218.

Shapiro, F. (1996b). Errors of context and review of eye movement desensitization and reprocessing research. *Journal of Behavior Therapy and Experimental Psychiatry, 27,* 313–317.

Shapiro, F., & Forrest M. S. (1997). *EMDR: The breakthrough therapy for overcoming anxiety, stress, and trauma.* New York: Basic Books.

van der Kolk, B. A. (1997). The psychobiology of post-traumatic stress disorder. *Journal of Clinical Psychiatry, 58*(suppl 9), 12–24.

van der Kolk, B. A., Burbridge, J. A., & Suzuki, J. (1997). The psychobiology of traumatic memory: Clinical implications of neuroimaging studies. In R. Yehuda & A. C. McFarlane (Eds.), *Annals of the New York Academy of Sciences (vol. 821): Psychobiology of posttraumatic stress disorder* (pp. 99–113). New York: New York Academy of Sciences,.

Van Etten, M., & Taylor, S. (1998). Comparative efficacy of treatments for post-traumatic stress disorder: A meta-analysis. *Clinical Psychology and Psychotherapy, 5,* 126–145.

104   Enacting the Educator Role
Principles for Practice

Kimberly Strom-Gottfried

In kindergartens and elementary schools around the world, the Making Choices curriculum is employed to help children learn problem-solving and employ communication skills to more successfully interact with both peers and adults. Making Choices uses a manualized set of activities and lessons focusing on the social, emotional, and cognitive competencies necessary to build relationships and work collaboratively with others. The program is grounded in a theoretical perspective that links childhood aggression to deficient information processing skills and social-emotional maladjustment. As a result, the lessons focus on accurately discerning others' messages and intentions and selecting and performing strategies for appropriate responses. Research suggests that Making Choices is effective in promoting social competence and reducing both overt and social aggression.

SAS is an analytical software company with over 10,000 employees worldwide, 43,000 corporate customers, and $1.9 billion in revenue. Social workers employed in its work-life unit are responsible for creating and delivering programs to assist employees with goals for wellness, adult and child care responsibilities, and financial security. Successful work-life programming is essential for employee recruitment and retention and has led to consistent recognition of SAS as one of *Fortune* magazine's "100 Best Companies to Work for in America." Educational activities by work-life staff include seminars on budgeting and credit, parenting teens, adoptees, young adults and children with special needs, and navigating Medicaid, Medicare, and Social Security for elderly parents. Classes may arise from the expressed needs of individual clients, from surveys of the workforce, or from environmental scanning on emerging issues in work-life balance.

Many social work settings and interventions require that the worker act as an educator. In this role, social workers may lead educational groups, train volunteers, provide professional or community education workshops, or teach new skills as part of their interventions with clients. Often, however, practitioners may not consider their activities as teaching and therefore may overlook valuable frameworks to assist in their practice. To encourage systematic attention to this role, this chapter summarizes the key elements of an education framework. It is intended to help social workers in a variety of settings to think about the educational aspects of their practice and to more effectively use teaching interventions.

Effective educational practice relies on six essential components:

1. the development of clear and appropriate objectives,
2. an understanding of the learners' needs and abilities,
3. an atmosphere that is conducive to learning,
4. knowledge of the material to be conveyed,
5. the skill to select and use teaching methods appropriately, and
6. the ability to evaluate one's performance and the learners' acquisition of educational outcomes.

Whether one is teaching parenting skills to an individual teenager, conducting a psychoeducational group for mental health consumers, or presenting a course on suicide intervention to a group of volunteers, these steps comprise the necessary components of an effective educational program. Steps 1–6 are ongoing but typically begin well before the worker and learners come together. Step 6 should take place throughout the duration of educational contact, and be done retrospectively as well.

DEVELOPING CLEAR AND APPROPRIATE OBJECTIVES

"No wind is favorable if you don't know your destination." This quote, attributed to Seneca, aptly addresses the first step in any form of social work intervention. Workers must be clear about their purpose in using an intervention or technique, the goals they hope to accomplish, or the intended outcomes their clients expect. Specific to educational interventions, the worker should have some sense of what the learners need or what skills, knowledge, or attitudes they hope the learners will have as a result of the intervention. Because a program's marketing, participant recruitment, location, topic selection, teaching methods, and evaluation all flow from its purpose, it is imperative that the goals be clearly articulated and appropriate for the needs of the end users.

Goals are sometimes an outgrowth of existing work with a client or group. For example, it may be apparent that clients diagnosed with HIV, irritable bowel syndrome, or other conditions can benefit from education about the course and management of their diseases from developing strategies to manage daily activities and relationships

in light of the illness. At other times, educational programs are developed independently, after which participants choose (or are chosen) to participate. The development of Web-based continuing education to meet the needs of professionals desiring continuing education credits in ethics would be one such example.

Planning becomes more complex when a need or service gap is believed to exist but has not yet been documented. In this case, needs assessment strategies should be used to determine the type and nature of the educational need. Needs may be determined through formal surveys or other data sources, interviews with service providers from social work and other disciplines, and from interviews or focus groups with potential consumers or representative groups.

Learning objectives fall into three categories: those geared to achieving knowledge or understanding, achieving skills or abilities, or achieving insight or attitudinal change. Within a given content area, interventions may have one focus ("Learn about diabetes and the diet plan to manage the disease"—a knowledge goal) or several ("Learn about the diabetes diet plan and be able to plan meals that fit in the plan"—knowledge and skills goals). Clarity about the type of learning expected is especially important when workers select their teaching methods, because certain teaching strategies are better suited to some educational goals than others. For example, skill building is better done through simulations or role-plays than a strictly lecture-based teaching format; experiential exercises can effectively lead to understanding and self-examination.

Clear objectives are also important when marketing an educational program. The dangers of advertising a program with an ambiguous purpose include drawing participants with too diverse a range of abilities or interests or discouraging appropriate people from enrolling at all because they cannot determine if the program is for them. Finally, particularly in programs where participants and teachers are evaluated on the outcomes they have achieved, goals must be clearly specified to adequately assess attainment.

UNDERSTANDING LEARNERS' NEEDS AND ABILITIES

Determining the need for and the purpose of an educational endeavor requires consideration of the prospective learners. Actually developing the educational intervention requires taking this understanding a step further and examining the particular life space of the learners, including their abilities, knowledge, attitudes, and what motivation or reluctance they may possess with regard to the content. It involves "tuning in" to the "feelings and concerns that the client may bring to the helping encounter" (Shulman, 1992, p. 56). It may also involve understanding ethnocultural, developmental, and other issues and the way that teaching dynamics are affected by differences among teachers and learners. An accurate understanding of learners will facilitate the selection and sequencing of content and the training methods used. Inadequate tuning in may lead to learners' resentment and resistance, may affect enrollment and attendance, and may lead to the selection of material that is variously rudimentary, irrelevant, or too complex.

A number of teaching principles are predicated on "knowing the learner" both as an aggregate group and as individuals. These include understanding sources of intrinsic and extrinsic motivation, making the material relevant and meaningful for each individual, building on the learner's existing knowledge, sequencing material from the familiar to the unfamiliar, identifying learning styles, and expressing appropriate confidence in the learner's abilities (Kadushin, 1985). The ability to individualize learning makes it more potent, as does forging a relationship in which the participant feels known and valued. Both require actively anticipating and understanding the individual as learner.

DEVELOPING A LEARNING-CONDUCIVE ATMOSPHERE

This component of teaching refers to both the physical environment and the emotional environment in which learning is to take place. Clearly, all learning opportunities carry with them the risk of mistakes or failure. As Kadushin has noted regarding educational supervision, "We learn best when we can devote most of our energies in the learning situation to learning. Energy needed to defend against rejection, anxiety, guilt, shame, fear of failure, attacks on autonomy or uncertain expectations, is energy deflected from learning" (1985, p. 149).

In keeping with this admonition, educators should inform learners about the purposes, processes, and structures for the learning activity. Learners must know what will be expected from

them and what they can expect from the teacher. The teacher should acknowledge and support the learner's risk taking in pursuit of change and establish a climate of trust and safety. When teaching in a group format, guidelines should be established and articulated that will yield a supportive environment for all involved, and the leader should be aware of any dynamics that are impinging on an individual's participation. Some class members may pose challenges to the safety and efficacy of the learning environment. Hostile, monopolizing, inattentive, unprepared or fawning participants may alienate both the instructor and the fellow class members. It is up to the leader to determine the basis for the problematic behaviors and craft an effective response. Some problems arise from poorly specified expectations or norms, and thus the resolutions may be structural in nature. Problems that arise from behavioral, psychological, or interpersonal issues will likely require an individualized intervention. As with other challenges arising in social work practice, supervision and consultation are essential to assist the worker in managing his or her personal responses to the difficulty and the difficulty itself.

The physical climate is also important for effective learning, though generally it is less in the leader's control. Ideally, the facilities should be well suited for the purposes and characteristics of the learners. The literature on group work is relevant here as we consider, for example, the needs of a group of adults in a didactic presentation as compared to those of teenagers in an experiential learning program. The very setting of the educational program should be determined with the purpose and audience in mind. The location, accessibility, safety, parking, available hours, and "reputation" or message carried by the site will influence learner attendance. Keeping the nature of the training and trainees in mind, attention must also be paid to room size, temperature, arrangement, the use of tables or chairs without tables, other furnishings, and the availability of audiovisual equipment, restrooms, and refreshments. Creating the appropriate levels of physical and emotional comfort for learners is a planning task and an ongoing management responsibility for the educator.

KNOWLEDGE OF CONTENT

Implied in accepting the role of educator is the notion that one has some knowledge that can be taught to or shared with another. Yet a stumbling block for many would-be educators is the fear that they don't have a sufficient command of the material to put themselves forth as instructors. This section addresses how much knowledge of content is needed, what sources can be used to enhance or supplement the instructor's knowledge, and how the fear of not knowing enough can be overcome.

How much knowledge is required depends on the needs of the learners and the purposes and structure of the educational program. A single fact about normative child development may be sufficient to inform a client in an intervention around parenting, but a good deal more knowledge will be required if providing an adult education course on the subject. As noted earlier, clarity about the goals of the educational program will be a vital guide. As educators begin to tune in to the program and learners, they get a sense of the depth and breadth of information needed. Reviewing curricula for similar programs or discussing ideas with colleagues and clients will help further identify content needs even prior to the training. These steps often remind facilitators that they know more than they think they do. Where further knowledge of content is needed, presenters can supplement their knowledge through traditional sources, such as texts and journals, interviewing subject experts, or viewing videos and films. In the classroom, presenters can augment the content they have to offer by using educational media, handouts, bibliographies, videos, or outside speakers.

Despite these steps, educators often feel vulnerable about their command of the course content. Such feelings may stem from the mistaken impression that the teacher must be "the sage on the stage" rather than "the guide on the side." This misconception not only places an unrealistic burden on the worker but can deprive all participants of the richness that comes from shared responsibility for learning. Sometimes referred to as student-centered learning, this model encourages the instructor to set the stage and provide the foundation through which all class members can contribute and learn from one another. This approach is consonant with theories of adult education, mutuality, and empowerment-based practice. Even if instructors cannot wholly use such a model, they must address the fear of not knowing. Learners do not expect that instructors will have all the answers, and in fact, will have a greater respect for those who are able to say, "I don't know, I'll check and get back to you" or "I hadn't heard about that. What do you know?" Similarly, the ability to catch and acknowledge mistakes conveys important messages about the

authenticity of the instructor and the acceptability of errors. Conversely, the need to be right or know it all often sets up an adversarial learning environment, in which genuine learning is sacrificed for gamesmanship and defensiveness.

Though there is no definitive answer to "how much content is enough?" there are multiple strategies for adjusting content in the event of over- or underestimation. When planning a program, instructors should anticipate the amount of time they will devote to certain material and think about how they might be able to cut or add as necessary. In multisession groups, instructors can retool between sessions as content needs become apparent. Discussions, experiential exercises, and case studies can be used to take content to a deeper level of application if presenters move through their material more quickly than anticipated. If too much material has been planned, instructors can reexamine the objectives and eliminate less crucial information or outside work or reading can supplement in-class time. In addition, the dilemma can be shared with learners, and their input used to prioritize the content to address with limited time.

SELECTING AND USING TEACHING TECHNIQUES

Many people teach the way they have been taught. Unfortunately, many have been taught in ways that stifle learner involvement, enthusiasm, and critical thinking. Having sat through mind-numbing lectures, tangential discussions, and fun but pointless exercises, they may believe that these are the only available means of conveying information. In fact, there exists an array of teaching approaches; the challenge is not only in finding them, but in selecting them to appropriately meet the needs of the learners and the objectives of the intervention.

Certain structures and teaching techniques are particularly well suited for different teaching goals (Knowles, 1975; Strom-Gottfried, 2006).

Lectures:

- Convey complex material.
- Highlight important facts and concepts.
- Create a cognitive map for future applications.

Exercises, demonstrations, role-plays, and simulations:

- Icebreakers.
- Build group cohesion.

- Foster skill acquisition and rehearsal.
- Generate empathy.
- Model techniques and concepts.
- Facilitate problem solving.

Cases, discussions, and debates:

- Develop insight.
- Foster new perspectives.
- Apply concepts.

Web-based and other instructional technologies:

- Convey complex material.
- Allow self-paced and self-timed learning, review, and repetition.
- Convenient.
- Content, assignments, and discussions can be archived for sharing or future use.

Each teaching method has its own promises and pitfalls. Suggestions for effectively using instructional strategies include (Christiansen, Garvin, & Sweet, 1991; Davis, 2001; Kadel & Keehner, 1994; McKeachie & Svinicki, 2005; Royse, 2001) the following.
    Lectures:

- Limit length or break up with discussions, examples, question and answer sessions, or activities.
- Vary vocal intonations, facial expressions, gestures, and movement about the room.
- Initiate with a compelling question or scenario to be addressed by the lecture content.
- Don't read the lecture, but do read the audience.
- Provide scaffolding for content in outline form through handouts or slide presentations.

Exercises, demonstrations, role-plays, and simulations:

- Link to learning goals or course material.
- Choose judiciously.
- Clearly explain the objectives and directions.
- Be alert to emotional reactions among participants.
- Prompt skill development with modeling, videotaped examples, or discussion of strategies for effective practice.
- Demonstrate support for risk and enthusiasm for the exercise.

- Debrief to identify strengths, weaknesses, and links to learning objectives.

Cases, discussions, and debates:

- Create a supportive, caring, and respectful atmosphere.
- Develop clear learning points.
- Establish ground rules for discussions.
- Allow time for participants to think before responding.
- Encourage or structure alternative perspectives.
- Summarize key outcomes.

Web-based and other instructional technologies:

- Carefully sequence educational modules.
- Make sure materials and directions are clear, thorough, and accurate.
- Design should be visually compelling and user-friendly.
- Anticipate technological glitches.
- Incorporate varied teaching strategies, including real-time meetings, discussion boards, video clips, question and answer sessions, and other interactive opportunities.

When selecting strategies to support various learning objectives, educators must also keep in mind their learners' capacities, the size of their group, and the amount of time they have for instruction. Such variables will affect the mix of teaching strategies employed, the time needed to carry them out, the learners' ability to benefit from the technique, the facilities needed, and the sequencing of material.

EVALUATING TEACHING PERFORMANCE AND LEARNERS' ACQUISITIONS

Most evaluations address two questions: "Were the learning objectives achieved?" and "How effective was the instructor in helping them to be met?" Both elements of evaluation are important. Evaluating satisfaction without having some measure of the benefit of the content is referred to as "popularity polling" (Davis & McCallon, 1974, p. 275). Evaluating attainment without determining what was effective and what wasn't in terms of delivery does not help the instructor generalize the effort to future situations. A variety of measures can be used for each form of evaluation; to some extent, the measure chosen depends on how the information gleaned will be used. If the information will be quantified, for example, to give the learner a grade or to rate the instructor, precise numerical measures will be called for. For other purposes, less precise measures are adequate and sometimes preferable. For example, in measuring what people learned in a social skills training program, observed change or self-reported change may be adequate, whereas a CPR training program would require more definitive measures of competency.

Used alone or in combination with quantifiable ratings, open-ended questions or narrative evaluations can provide feedback with valuable depth and context. For example, the instructor may find that the structure or timing of an exercise was ineffective, not the exercise itself, or the learner may get feedback about particular areas of strength within a specific content area.

In addition to the form of evaluation, timing is another consideration. In general, periodic formal or informal check-in types of evaluation will help both learners and educators reassess their progress toward achieving the objectives and re-prioritize material or alter teaching strategies accordingly. Methods for this include brief self-reports at the end of a session about insights and information achieved or "minute cards" where participants provide written feedback on the meeting.

Effective and ethical instruction arises from the conscientious use of various forms of evaluation to inform practice. In addition to using incremental and cumulative verbal and written feedback from participants, social workers can use peer observers, coaching, and videotaped sessions to continually improve and refine teaching performance.

CONCLUSION

Teaching is an integral part of social work practice, done in a variety of settings with a range of populations. This chapter offers guidance for the creation and delivery of educational interventions and provides resources for further study. It encourages the examination of social work activities from an education framework, advocating that as this function is better defined, models can be further developed, teaching challenges exam-ined, and the necessary knowledge and skills for effective practice specified.

WEB SITES

Association for the Advancement of Social Work with Groups. http://www.aaswg.org.
How Teachers Learn New Technologies. http://www.staffdevelop.org.
International Association of Facilitators. http://www.iaf-world.org/i4a/pages/index.cfm?pageid=3498.
International Association for the Study of Cooperation in Education. http://www.iasce.net.
Making Choices. http://ssw.unc.edu/jif/makingchoices/index.htm.
Teaching Professor. http://www.magnapubs.com/issues/magnapubs_tp.
Tribes, a New Way of Learning and Being Together. http://www.tribes.com.

References

Christensen, C. R., Garvin, D. A., & Sweet, A. (1991). *Education for judgment: The artistry of discussion leadership.* Boston, MA: Harvard Business School.
Davis, B. G. (2001). *Tools for teaching.* San Francisco: Jossey-Bass.
Davis, L. N., & McCallon, E. (1974). *Planning, conducting, and evaluating workshops.* Austin, TX: Learning Concepts.
Kadel, S., & Keehner, J. A. (1994). *Collaborative learning: A sourcebook for higher education.* Pennsylvania: National Center on Postsecondary Teaching, Learning, and Assessment.
Kadushin, A. (1985). *Supervision in social work.* New York: Columbia University Press.
Knowles, M. S. (1975). *Self-directed learning.* New York: Association Press.
McKeachie, W., & Svinicki, M. (2005). *Teaching tips: Strategies, research, and theory for college and university teachers.* Boston: Houghton Mifflin.
Royse, D. (2001). *Teaching tips for college and university instructors.* Needham Heights, MA: Allyn & Bacon.
Shulman, L. (1992). *The skills of helping: Individuals, families, and groups.* Itasca, IL: F. E. Peacock.
Strom-Gottfried, K. J. (2006) Managing human resources. In R. L. Edwards & J. A. Yankey (Eds.), *Effectively managing nonprofit organizations.* (pp. 141–178). Washington, DC: NASW Press.

Critical Incident Stress Management

105 *Integrated Crisis Intervention and Disaster Mental Health*

George S. Everly Jr. & Alan M. Langlieb

The field of crisis intervention grew largely out of military conflicts. Salmon (1919) made a significant contribution to the literature via his recollections and analyses of psychiatric emergencies during World War I. Salmon observed that the English and French medical corps had success in treating the various battlefield neuroses by moving their psychiatric facilities to more forward positions; as a result of these changes, he observed a dramatic increase in the return-to-duty rates achieved by the end of the war. His observations ultimately led to the development of the modern field of psychological crisis intervention and its newer clinical specialty, disaster mental health, having been born in 1992.

In this chapter we discuss the state-of-the-art formulations in crisis intervention and disaster mental health and discuss a strategic approach referred to as critical incident stress management (CISM). CISM is the most widely used crisis and disaster mental health intervention system in the world, having recently been adopted by the United Nations for use with its personnel. CISM is also one of the most misunderstood of the psychosocial interventions, commonly being confused with critical incident stress debriefing (CISD), a small group crisis intervention designed to be used with rescue and recovery as well as military personnel. This chapter provides a brief introduction to the nature and foundations of CISM.

CRISIS INTERVENTION

Crisis intervention has proven an effective front-line intervention to assist the victims of a critical incident who have a psychological crisis (see Everly & Mitchell, 2008, for a comprehensive review of

relevant research). Crisis intervention is defined as a short-term helping process designed to assist in the reduction of acute psychological distress. It is a distinct clinical skill apart from the traditional practices of counseling and psychotherapy. As a result, the effective practice of crisis intervention requires specialized clinical training, as research has clearly demonstrated (Everly & Mitchell, 2008; Stapleton, Lating, Kirkhart, & Everly, 2006).

The clinical goals of crisis intervention are to first stabilize and then reduce the symptoms of distress. The ultimate end result is to restore the individual to adaptive independent function, or if that is not possible, facilitate the individual's access to a higher level of care (Artiss, 1963; Everly & Mitchell, 1999).

The hallmarks that differentiate this type of first intervention from counseling and psychotherapy are threefold and are also known as the acronym PIE. The intervention needs to have: *proximity, immediacy,* and *expectancy.* With respect to proximity, the services should be provided whenever needed. For immediacy, the intervention needs to be as close to the emergence of adverse reactions as possible. Finally, expectancy means that the focus of the intervention will be on the disequilibrium as a result of the current critical incident, not curing preexisting psychiatric syndromes.

Major historical milestones in the development of this field are listed in Table 105.1.

CISM

Prior to the 1990s, crisis intervention was applied in a piecemeal approach. It was later recognized that to be most effective, crisis intervention and disaster mental health services needed to be mul-

TABLE 105.1 Historical Milestones in Crisis Intervention and Disaster Mental Health

- World War I — the first empirical evidence that early intervention reduces chronic psychiatric morbidity
- World War II — the processes of proximity, immediacy, and expectancy identified as important "active ingredients" in effective emergency psychological care
- 1944 — Lindemann's observations of grief reactions to the Coconut Grove fire begins "modem era" of crisis intervention
- 1963/64 — Caplan's three tiers of preventive psychiatry delineated and implemented within the newly created community mental health system (primary, secondary, tertiary prevention)
- 1980 — formal nosological recognition of post-traumatic stress disorder (PTSD) in *DSM-III* "legitimates" crisis and traumatic events as threats to long-term mental health
- 1982 — Air Florida 90 disaster in Washington, DC, prompts reexamination of psychological support for emergency response personnel; first mass disaster use of the group crisis intervention CISD, which as originally formulated in 1974 by Mitchell (1983)
- 1986 — "violence in the workplace" era begins with death of 13 postal workers on the job
- 1989 — International Critical Incident Stress Foundation (ICISF) formalizes an international network of over 350 crisis response teams trained in a standardized and comprehensive crisis intervention model referred to as CISM; ICISF gains United Nations affiliation in 1997
- 1980s — National Organization for Victims Assistance (NOVA) provides crisis intervention and psychosocial support for crime victims and extends services to disaster victims
- 1992 — American Red Cross initiates formal training for the establishment of a nationwide disaster mental health capability; Hurricane Andrew tests new mental health function
- 1993 — Social Development Office (Amiri Diwan), ICISF, Kuwait University, implements a nationwide crisis intervention system for postwar Kuwait; the first such national postwar psychological reconstruction program of its kind
- 1995 — Bombing of the federal building in Oklahoma City underscores need for crisis services for rescue personnel, as well as civilians
- 1996 — TWA 800 mass air disaster emphasizes the need for emergency mental health services for families of the victims of traumas and disasters
- 1996 — OSHA 3148-1996 recommends comprehensive violence/crisis intervention in social service and health care settings
- Late 1990s — Salvation Army initiates emotional and spiritual care for disaster victims
- April 1999 — 14 students, including 2 shooters, are killed at Columbine High School in Littleton, Colorado
- 2001 — Terrorist attacks at the Pentagon and World Trade Center reveal unique challenges of mass disasters in dense urban settings and those associated with mass terrorism
- 2003-2007 — war in Afghanistan and Iraq challenges military to develop new crisis interventions (combat stress control)
- August 2005 — Hurricane Katrina becomes one of the deadliest and the most costly natural disasters in American history; a putative failure in leadership leads to delayed and inadequate disaster response
- On April 16, 2007, the deadliest shooting in U.S. history occurred at Virginia Polytechnic Institute and State University. Thirty-three students and faculty members, including the shooter, were killed and at least 21 others were injured.
- 2007 — The United Nations sets an international standard for crisis intervention and disaster mental health as it adopts an integrated multicomponent critical incident stress management approach as the overarching intervention system for the psychosocial support of its own field personnel

ticomponent and integrated in a continuum of care. CISM was developed in response to that need. CISM has become the most widely used integrated system of its kind in the world, especially now that is has been adopted for use by the United Nations. As mentioned earlier, CISM is often confused with CISD. CISD is a small group crisis intervention originally designed for homogeneous groups of emergency services and military personnel. CISD may be included as one element of the overarching CISM strategic system, but should not be confused with that system.

As defined by Everly and Mitchell (1999, 2008), CISM represents an integrated and comprehensive multicomponent approach to the provision of crisis intervention and disaster mental health services.

The CISM formulation is actually broader and more comprehensive in scope than the historical applications of crisis intervention and is more consistent with Caplan's (1964) comprehensive formulations of preventive psychiatry. Specifically, CISM embodies:

1. primary prevention (i.e., the identification and mitigation of pathogenic stressors);
2. secondary prevention (i.e., the identification and mitigation of acute distress and dysfunctional symptom patterns); and
3. tertiary prevention (i.e., follow-up mental health treatment and rehabilitation services).

Thus, the specific goals of the CISM program are to reduce the

1. duration,
2. severity of, or
3. impairment from traumatic stress arising from crisis situations.

The second goal is to facilitate advanced follow-up mental health interventions when necessary.

In the final analysis, the ultimate goal of CISM is the mitigation of acute, disabling psychological discord and the rapid restoration of adaptive functioning in the wake of a critical (crisis) incident. Thus, CISM represents an amalgam of specific crisis and disaster-related interventions. CISM is the embodiment of the psychological continuum of care.

COMPONENTS OF CISM

Long gone are the days when a small group discussion or a telephone hotline was the only disaster mental health intervention available. Relevant sources agree that crisis and disaster mental health services should be multicomponent and highly integrated. CISM is an integrated multicomponent system's approach, with strategic planning and operational applications. Though there is no single model of a CISM program, there is a common agreement on the general components of such program (see Table 105.2). A comprehensive CISM program needs to be multifaceted and span the entire temporal spectrum of a crisis or disaster.

CISM interventions focus on precrisis phase training through acute crisis phase programs and postcrisis programs. In addition, CISM can be applied to individuals, small groups, large groups, families, organizations, and entire communities, even nations, as in the case of postwar Kuwait. The CISM elements are listed in Table 105.2.

Detailed descriptions of these interventions are beyond the scope of this chapter; nevertheless the components are listed here for purposes of overview and example.

As can be seen from Table 105.2, the key components of a CISM program are:

1. precrisis preparation with the goal of setting appropriate expectancies and response practices prior to an event;
2. surveillance and assessment to determine the need as well as the best method to meet the needs of the victims;
3. strategic planning;
4. individual crisis intervention, face-to-face or via phone, Internet, and so on;
5. large-scale demobilization procedures as well as large-group crisis management briefings after a mass disaster or community crisis and the like;
6. small group discussions (also known as defusings, critical incident stress debriefings, and briefing);
7. family crisis intervention procedures;
8. organizational development interventions;
9. pastoral crisis interventions, and
10. procedures for referrals for additional psychological assessments (Flannery and Everly, 2000).

According to Watson and Shalev (2005),

Early intervention in mass traumatic events should be embedded within a multidisciplinary, multi-tiered disaster mental health system. Early interventions should be utilized in a culturally sensitive manner, related to the local formulation of problems and ways of coping, and applied flexibly, in ways that match needs and situational context and take into account the ongoing stressors, reactions, and resources. (p. 123)

TABLE 105.2 Multicomponent Elements of CISM

Intervention	Timing	Target Group	Potential Goals
I. Pre-event planning/ preparation	Pre-event	Anticipated target/victim population	Anticipatory guidance, foster resistance, resilience
II. Surveillance & assessment	Pre-intervention	Those directly & indirectly exposed	Determination of need for intervention
III. Strategic planning	Pre-event and during event	Anticipated exposed and victim populations	Improve overall crisis response
IV. Individual crisis intervention (including "psychological first aid")	As needed	Individuals as needed	Assessment, screening, education, normalization, reduction of acute distress, triage, and facilitation of continued support
V. Large group crisis intervention			
A. Demobilization	Shift disengagement, end of deployment	Emergency personnel	Decompression, ease transition, screening, triage, education, and meet basic needs
B. Respite center	Ongoing, large-scale events	Emergency personnel, large groups	Respite, refreshment, screening, triage, and support
C. Crisis management briefing (CMB) and large group "psychological first aid"	As needed	Heterogeneous large groups	Inform, control rumors, increase cohesion
VI. Small group crisis intervention			
A. Small group crisis management briefing (sCMB).	Ongoing and postevent; may be repea ted as needed	Small groups seeking information/ resources	Information, control rumors, reduce acute distress, increase cohesion, facilitate resilience, screening and triage
B. Defusing (and small group "psychological first aid")	Ongoing events and postevents ($\leq$12 hours)	Small homogeneous groups	Stabilization, ventilation, reduce acute distress, screening, information, increase cohesion, and facilitate resilience
C. CISD; PEGS	Postevent; ~ 1–10 days for acute incidents, ~3–4 weeks distress, facilitate resilience, postdisaster recovery phase	Small homogeneous groups with equal trauma exposure (e.g., workgroups, emergency services, military)	Increase cohesion, ventilation, information, normalization, reduce acute screening and triage; follow-up essential

Continued

TABLE 105.2 Multicomponent Elements of CISM (*continued*)

Intervention	Timing	Target Group	Potential Goals
VII. Family crisis intervention	Pre-event; as needed	Families	Wide range of interventions (e.g., pre-event preparation, individual crisis intervention, sCMB, PEGS, or other group processes)
VIII. Organizational/community intervention.	As needed	Organizations/communities affected by trauma or disaster response	Improve organizational, community preparedness; leadership consultation
IX. Pastoral crisis intervention	As needed	Individuals, small groups, large groups, congregations, and communities who desire faithbased presencecrisis intervention	Faithbased support
X. Followup; referral; facilitating access to continued care	As needed	Intervention recipients and exposed individuals	Ensure continuity of care

CISM is the manifestation of those recommendations.

EVOLVING GOALS

Setting appropriate goals for psychological crisis intervention and disaster mental health must be predicated on a realistic understanding of what interventions are capable of achieving. However, as crisis intervention formulations were being developed, some believed that early psychological disaster response might exert a preventive effect so as to block the development of post-traumatic stress disorder (PTSD) and other psychiatric reactions, such as major depression. Yet research has not convincingly demonstrated such a global preventive effect (Arendt & Elklit, 2001).

Researchers in this field have instead focused on examining multiple outcomes following disasters and terrorism for various types of interventions. Some researchers noted, "interventions that foster return of function, even though they may not directly prevent psychiatric illness, may be of importance" (Ursano, Norwood, Fullerton, Holloway, & Hall, 2003, p. 336). Deahl et al. (2000) similarly argued that expectations for early psychological intervention should not be focused solely on PTSD. They noted that early psychological intervention may positively affect other aspects of post-traumatic illness that typically go unmeasured. They cite in support of such a conclusion their own randomized controlled trial of early intervention that found a reduction of post-traumatic alcohol use in soldiers returning from a peacekeeping mission in Eastern Europe (Deahl et al., 2000).

Thus, it is important to remember that psychological intervention is not psychotherapy and it is not intended to be a substitute for psychotherapy. Deahl and colleagues (2000) argued that early psychological intervention research is contaminated with the assumption that the outcome goals (and thereby the expectations) for early psychological intervention are commonly confused with the same outcome goals for "treatment." Thus, the prevention/eradication of PTSD or depression may be an inappropriate expectation of psychological crisis intervention.

RESEARCH FINDINGS

Everly and Mitchell (2008) have compiled a comprehensive amalgam of research findings relevant to crisis intervention, disaster mental health, and CISM. Everly et al. (2006) reviewed crisis intervention systems at the workplace, whereas Stapleton et al. (2006) reviewed acute psychological interventions in health care settings. Finally Boscarino, Adams, & Figley (2005) examined the effects of CISM post–mass terrorist attacks. The findings support the notion that early and acute psychological interventions can be effective reducing acute psychological distress.

CONCLUSION

In this chapter, we traced the historical roots of crisis intervention and disaster mental health. After a brief review, we set out to provide an overview of CISM and disaster mental health. We examined CISM as a strategic delivery platform for providing integrated and comprehensive multicomponent psychological/ behavioral services in the wake of critical incidents both large and small.

WEB SITES

American Academy of Experts in Traumatic Stress. www.crisisinfo.org
International Critical Incident Stress Foundation. http://www.icisf.org
International Society for Traumatic Stress Studies. http://www.istss.com.

References

Arendt, M., & Elklit, A. (2001). Effectiveness of psychological debriefing. *Acta Psychiatrica Scandinavica, 104*(6), 423–437.

Artiss, K. (1963). Human behavior under stress: From combat to social psychiatry. *Military Medicine, 128,* 1011–1015.

Boscarino, J. A., Adams, R. E., & Figley, C. R. (2005). A prospective cohort study of the effectiveness of employer-sponsored crisis interventions after a major disaster. *International Journal of Emergency Mental Health, 7,* 9–22.

Caplan, G. (1964). *Principles of preventive psychiatry.* New York: Basic Books.

Deahl, M., Srinivasan, M., Jones, N., Thomas, J., Neblett, C., & Jolly, A. (2000). Preventing psychological trauma in soldiers. The role of operational stress training and psychological debriefing. *British Journal of Medical Psychology, 73,* 77–85.

Everly, G. S. Jr., & Mitchell, J. T. (1999). *Critical incident stress management.* Ellicott City, MD: Chevron.

Everly, G. S. Jr., & Mitchell, J. T. (2008). *Integrative crisis intervention and disaster mental health.* Ellicott City, MD: Chevron.

Everly, G. S. Jr., Sherman, M. F., Stapleton, A., Barnett, D. J., Hiremath, G., & Links, J. (2006). Workplace crisis intervention: A systematic review of effect sizes. *Journal of Workplace Behavioral Health, 21,* 153–170.

Flannery, R., & Everly, G. (2000). Crisis intervention: A review. *International Journal of Emergency Mental Health, 2*(2), 119–125.

Salmon, T. S. (1919). War neuroses and their lesson. *New York Medical Journal, 108,* 993–994.

Stapleton, A. B., Lating, J., Kirkhart, M., & Everly, G. S. Jr. (2006). Effects of medical crisis intervention on anxiety, depression, and posttraumatic stress symp-toms: A meta-analysis. *Psychiatric Quarterly, 77*(3), 231–238.

Ursano, R. J., Norwood, A. E., Fullerton, C. S., Holloway, H. C., & Hall, M. (2003). Terrorism with weapons of mass destruction: Chemical, biological, nuclear, radiological, and explosive agents. In R. J. Ursano & A. E. Norwood (Eds.), *Trauma and disaster: Responses and management* (pp. 125–154). Washington, DC: American Psychiatric Publishing.

Watson, P., & Shalev, A. (2005). Assessment and treatment of adult acute responses to traumatic stress following mass traumatic events. *CNS Spectrum,* 123–131.

Divorce Therapy

106 *The Application of Cognitive-Behavioral and Constructivist Treatment Methods*

Donald K. Granvold

This chapter addresses the challenges character-istic of the divorce process. Therapeutic goals for each stage are delineated, and examples of the application of cognitive-behavioral and constructivist treatment strategies are given.

Divorce is one of the most distressing transi-tions one can undergo. Whether the decision is unilateral or shared, or one is the initiator or the one being left, the process is painful and disruptive. The change following divorce is pervasive, ex-tending across many domains of the individual's life. For most, coming apart carries with it ex-treme emotional consequences. Divorce is simulta-neously an ending punctuated by loss, estrangement, and detachment and a new beginning character-ized by fear of the unknown; challenging novel roles, responsibilities, and behaviors; and promising future possibilities. Client treatment goals can be expected to fluctuate. The desire for a sense of closure regarding the past may prompt a focus on the estranged or ex-mate and the associated fam-ily and social networks. Alternatively, the focus may be on the development of novel or expanded selves to meet current and evolving demands and possibilities (Granvold, in press).

STAGES OF THE DIVORCE PROCESS

The divorce process can be conceptualized as being composed of three overlapping stages: (1) decision making, (2) transition, and (3) postdivorce recov-ery (Granvold, 2000a, 2000b, in press). Each of these stages poses unique challenges to the indi-vidual and each is replete with crisis potential.

Decision Making

I believe that therapists are challenged most greatly in helping individuals/couples with the decision to divorce. Specific methodologies are least well developed in this area. Typically, one or both partners continue their marriage in a state of high dissatisfaction and protracted indecision before ultimately arriving at a decision to divorce. The state of indecision is stressful in itself, characterized by high levels of frustration, anxiety, uncertainty, fear, worry, insecurity, distrust (particularly for the mate who is more greatly committed), hurt, resentment, depression, hopelessness and impending doom, and feelings of disempowerment. There is often erosion in feelings of love, intimacy, sexual desire, and sexual satisfaction. Individuals who are emotionally fragile, highly dependent on the mate, and/or lack self-esteem often experience situation-specific crises as the couple moves toward a final decision. This individual, typically more committed and less likely to decide to leave the relationship, is far more vulnerable to crisis responses.

The following are examples of therapeutic goals during the decision making stage:

- specify factors eroding the relationship;
- optimize relationship functioning (specify and implement strategic change);
- promote frustration tolerance for indecision (i.e., combat low frustration tolerance);
- limit impulsive decision making;
- carefully determine and weigh the factors of satisfaction and dissatisfaction;
- clarify values and life goals related to coupling;
- clearly identify perceived advantages and disadvantages of divorce relative to remaining married;
- consider structured marital separation to interrupt maladaptive patterns of interaction, reevaluate the relationship from an altered perspective, and move more gradually to singlehood (a treatment of choice only for select couples) (Granvold, 1983).

The gravity of the decision on the lives of the couple, their children, extended family, and friends effect great pressure on the decision maker(s). There is typically intense and protracted pain in both the decision maker and the rejected partner. It is noteworthy that divorce appears to be far more likely the consequence of a loss of intimate connectedness than the result of intense conflict (Stanley, 2001). The absence of overt signs of disagreement and dissatisfaction may be confusing to both partners and those close to the couple, particularly offspring.

Transition

Once a decision to divorce is made, the couple enters the transition phase of the divorce process. For many, divorce is largely a consequence of an erosion of love, a shift from feeling "in love" to simply "caring." Despite this shift, interpersonal attachment tends to persist. There is a sense of comfort in the relationship and in the shared physical environment. Dissolving the relationship and physically separating may well have a concomitant profound sense of loss even for those who are no longer in love and who *want* the divorce.

Physical separation and the initiation of legal action are characteristically periods of extreme stress (Wang & Amato, 2000). Clients should be carefully evaluated for their ways of dealing with stress in the event they are putting themselves or others at risk or alternatively, are experiencing significant maladjustment. Of further concern are those who have endured violence in marriage. Separation has been found to instigate additional assaults by abusive partners and first-time violence in previously nonabusive mates. The following are examples of therapeutic goals during the transition phase:

- assess and treat suicidality and homicidal ideation and planning;
- assess death wishes (passive suicide);
- assess and develop strategies for postseparation domestic violence;
- assess alcohol use and prescription and illicit drug use;
- complete strengths and resiliency assessment;
- strategize informing children, family, and friends regarding the divorce;
- promote the expression of loss (emotionally, cognitively, behaviorally);
- develop adaptive strategies for stress management during transition (for example, limit alcohol/drug use, check excessive investment in work, deep muscle relaxation, healthy exercise);
- facilitate effective relationships with children, family, and friends;
- address effecting legal action to dissolve the marriage contract;
- address child custody and parallel parenting issues;
- promote a collaborative property settlement agreement.

The transition phase also requires attention to the specifics of the division of property, physical relocation, child custody, and child support—all of which stimulate emotional reactions. These considerations pose remarkable opportunities for conflict, divorce decision doubt, uncertainty regarding the future, and intense feelings of loss.

Postdivorce Recovery

Postdivorce recovery, as identified earlier, involves pervasive change. In addition to dealing with losses of a physical and emotional nature, the individual is challenged with redefining self and revisioning his or her life. Now it is necessary to establish a monadic identity, independent of the self that evolved and was forged through years of intimate connectedness with the ex-mate. The path of life that had been relatively established and known no longer fits the novel territory in which one now travels. The transition process to postdivorce recovery is replete with pervasive change. Among the changes being experienced are new role relationships with children (for example, single parenting), workmates, extended family, and friends. The development of friendship and intimate relationships as well as participation in network groups (for example, church, interest groups, support groups) have been found to be positively associated with postdivorce adjustment (Krumrei, Coit, Martin, Fogo, & Mahoney, 2007). Although a positive association exists between social support and postdivorce adjustment, the quality of these relationships promotes or undermines well-being (Krumrei et al., 2007).

The clinical and research findings on the effects of divorce are inconsistent. Some experience positive change in the form of relief, a renewed sense of freedom, joy, enhanced self-esteem, increased happiness, greater life satisfaction, greater sense of responsibility, and renewal, whereas others experience such untoward consequences as extreme loss, hurt, depression, social isolation, unhappiness, financial problems, increased risk of health problems, single parenting challenges, reduced life satisfaction, and diminished self-esteem (Baum, Rahav, & Sharon, 2005; Sakraida, 2005). Vulnerability to greater postdivorce maladjustment appears to reside with older versus younger women (Sakraida, 2005), noninitiators of divorce, and those lacking social support (Krumrei et al., 2007). Furthermore, divorce is likely to exacerbate the emotional instability of those with a predivorce history of mental health problems. A substantial number of divorced individuals fall into this category, given the predisposition of poorly adjusted people to divorce.

Literature on the effects of divorce has predominantly reflected a deficit model, emphasizing the negative psychological, social, and health consequences to adults and children. Recent studies have given greater attention to positive short- and long-term consequences in which the divorce process is viewed as potentially a personal development opportunity (Hilton & Kopera-Frye, 2004).

Common maladaptive coping strategies involve the excessive use of alcohol and drugs (prescribed and illicit), oversleep, overexercise, and overinvestment of time and energy in work. Though grieving is a necessary, adaptive process and is unique from person to person, it may become debilitating to those who allow it to become all-consuming.

The following are examples of therapeutic goals during postdivorce recovery:

- delineate and dedicate efforts to the evolution of "possible selves" consistent with the revisioning of one's life;
- establish a quality relationship with children as a single parent (attend to their emotional needs and their need for structure in the reconstituted family);
- develop an effective parallel parenting relationship with the ex-spouse;
- gain closure on the marriage (grieve and seek to emotionally accept the marriage as over);
- promote efficacy expectations regarding present and future life satisfaction;
- generate rejuvenation goals across various categories of life (career, education, hobbies, interests, relationships, lifestyle, geographic and environmental circumstances);
- seek intimate connectedness with others through clear delineation of partner/relationship qualities, active pursuit, deliberate relationship evaluation, and proactive decision making to terminate or maintain the relationship(s) (Krumrei et al., 2007; Wang & Amato, 2000);
- develop and rejuvenate sexuality; and
- activate a lifestyle in which physical health and exercise are priorities.

INTERVENTION

The proposed treatment model incorporates behavioral methods, orthodox cognitive treatment methods, and constructivist conceptualizations and methods (Granvold, 2000a, 2000b, 2008, in press). The unifying factor is the view that cognitive functioning plays a central role in the human condition and human change. Although cognitive functioning plays a crucial role in the development and regulation of human behavior, it is recognized that behavioral activation strategies used in combination with cognitive change represent the most powerful and resilient forms of intervention.

There is remarkable empirical support for the application of cognitive-behavioral treatments (CBTs) to an array of psychological disorders (De-Rubeis & Crits-Christoph, 1998). Many empirically supported psychotherapy treatments (ESTs) richly use cognitive and behavioral intervention procedures in various forms and combinations. Divorced clients can be expected to present with problems and concerns suitable for treatment with methods proven to be efficacious. As noted earlier, there are many psychological consequences of divorce. Among the most typical are depression, anxiety and panic disorders, anger control, post-traumatic stress disorder (particularly relevant for survivors of domestic violence), obsessive-compulsive disorder, alcohol abuse and dependence, and substance abuse and dependence. CBT has been applied successfully in treating each of these problems. CBT interventions continue to be scrutinized and evaluated through extensive ongoing empirical research.

Postmodern conceptualizations of divorce provide an alternative (albeit in many ways compatible) perspective on the process of coming apart and transitioning to single life. Divorce is viewed as necessarily disruptive to the self system with a concomitant array of emotional consequences. A primary treatment goal is the generation of multiple meanings of specific events in the process of divorcing and adjusting to singlehood. Emotional expressions are evoked and processed through an array of cognitive and behavioral methods. Attention is given to the client's redefinition of self and the modification and expansion of intimate and social relationships. Emphasis is placed on the client's strengths and the positive change possibilities inherent in this major life transition (Granvold, 2008, in press).

The constructivist aspects of the intervention are represented in the following enumeration.

1. Conceptualize divorce as a self-system perturbation.
2. Seek to access self-schemata activated by the divorce process with the objective of modifying core ordering processes through construct elaboration.
3. Explore primary attachment relationships as they relate to views of self and the world, including the attachment relationship with the ex-spouse.
4. Promote a view of self as a multifaceted and ever-changing system of identity meanings, rather than a singular, fixed self.
5. Promote emotional expressiveness through guided discovery, imagery, imaginary dialogues (empty chair technique), and therapeutic rituals.
6. Use personal narratives and journaling as change mediums.
7. Accentuate client strengths, personal and social resources, creativity, coping capacities, and resiliency.
8. Collaborate with the client in constructing change mediums, models, and techniques with which the therapist has an expertise and that fit the client.

Although the therapist has expertise regarding both the process of divorce and human change processes, a nonauthoritarian role is assumed in relation to the client. The intervention is strategically the co-construction of the client and therapist. See Chapter 40 for detailed information on constructivist theory and practice.

CLINICAL EXAMPLES

The following are exemplars covering each stage of divorce.

Decision Making

Penny and Jason presented for therapy undecided whether to divorce or remain married. As part of the intervention, the couple used journaling to clarify their expectations of a mate and marriage. They traced their relationship from its inception and noted the evolution of their partner and marriage expectations. In therapy sessions, the couple were guided in the use of their journaling to make specific comparisons of their expectations with their "experience" of the relationship. The process helped them realize that although their marriage had closely aligned with early expectations, they had evolved divergently and no longer found the relationship satisfactorily viable. They reported feeling as if they had made a collaborative decision to divorce, and they shifted their focus to the emotional and practical requirements of coming apart.

Transition

The divorce decision was imposed on Marla by her husband, Mark. Although the relationship was amicable, Marla had been having extreme difficulty with the transition. She drank several glasses of wine each night, had withdrawn from family and friends, and had discontinued her aerobics workout routine that she had done for years. The couple was childless. Having effectively coped with the loss of her father (with whom she was close) 5 years ago, Marla was prompted to compare and contrast her ways of coping with the two losses, her father and Mark. She identified differences in the losses, specifically noting that Mark had been there for her during her grief over her father's death. She concluded, however, that she could implement some of the same coping strategies at this time. She decided to limit her drinking to one glass per night, do something "social" at least one occasion per week, and resume a 4-days-per-week workout regimen. Therapist actions included Socratic questioning, gentle encouragement, and strong verbal support for her plans.

Postdivorce Recovery

Greg presented for therapy a year after his divorce was legally final. His primary goal was to let go of the relationship with his ex-wife, Laurie, and to "feel" divorced. After several sessions, it was apparent that Greg was emotionally ready to let go. An implosion strategy was discussed and planned in the session (Granvold, 1994). The following Saturday, he dedicated 8 hours to grieving the loss of his relationship with Laurie. He looked at pictures and memorabilia, played their music, ate Chinese food in the middle of the bed as they had done many times, smelled a pillow laced with her perfume, and freely cried with no goal to stop the crying. In 3 to 4 hours, the tears dried up. Although it was an emotionally painful experience, at the following session Greg reported a greater sense of closure, as if an emotional connectedness had been purged, a connectedness that could no longer be.

CONCLUSION

Although much has been written about divorce, there is a paucity of information focused on treatment. This gap in the treatment literature

is particularly alarming given the relatively high divorce rate and the emotional trauma associated with coming apart. This chapter has provided treatment guidelines and a limited view of the application of CBT and constructivist methods to treat clients during divorce decision making and beyond.

WEB SITES

Academy of Cognitive Therapy. http://www .academyofct.org.

American Association for Marriage and Family Therapy. http://www.aamft.org.

Association for Behavioral and Cognitive Therapies. http://www.aabt.org.

Constructivist Psychology Network. http:// www.constructivistpsych.org.

European Personal Construct Association. http://www.epca-net.org.

References

Baum, N., Rahav, G., & Sharon, D. (2005). Changes in the self-concepts of divorced women. *Journal of Divorce and Remarriage, 43*(1/2), 47–67.

DeRubeis, R. J., & Crits-Christoph, P. (1998). Empirically supported individual and group psychological treatments for adult mental disorders. *Journal of Consulting and Clinical Psychology, 66*(1), 37–52.

Granvold, D. K. (1983). Structured separation for marital treatment and decision-making. *Journal of Marital and Family Therapy, 9,* 403–412.

Granvold, D. K. (1994). *Cognitive behavioral divorce therapy.* Belmont, CA: Thomson Brooks/Cole Publishing Co.

Granvold, D. K. (2000a). Divorce. In F. M. Dattilio & A. Freeman (Eds.), *Cognitive-behavioral strategies in crisis intervention,* 2nd ed. (pp. 362–384). New York: Guilford.

Granvold, D. K. (2000b). The crisis of divorce: Cognitive-behavioral and constructivist assessment and treatment. In A. R. Roberts (Ed.), *Crisis intervention handbook: Assessment, treatment, and research,* 2nd ed. (pp. 307–336). New York: Oxford University Press.

Granvold, D. K. (2008). Constructivist theory and practice. In N. Coady & P. Lehmann (Eds.), *Theoretical perspectives for direct social work practice: A generalist-eclectic approach,* 2nd ed. (pp. 401–427). New York: Springer.

Granvold, D. K. (In press). Constructivist treatment of divorce. In J. D. Raskin & S. K. Bridges (Eds.), *Studies in meaning 3: Constructivist therapy in the "real" world.* New York: Pace University Press.

Hilton, J. M., & Kopera-Frye, K. (2004). Patterns of psychological adjustment among divorced custo-

dial parents. *Journal of Divorce & Remarriage,*
41(3/4), 1–30.

Krumrei, E., Coit, C., Martin, S., Fogo, W., & Mahoney,
A. (2007). Post-divorce adjustment and social re-
lationships: A meta-analytic review. *Journal of
Divorce and Remarriage, 46*(3/4), 145–166.

Sakraida, T. (2005). Common themes in the divorce
transition experience of midlife women. *Journal
of Divorce and Remarriage, 43*(1/2), 69–88.

Stanley, S. (2001, January). Helping couples fight for
their marriages: Research on the prediction and
prevention of marital failure. Paper presented at
the Annual Conference of the Texas Association
for Marriage and Family Therapy, Dallas.

Wang, H., & Amato, P. R. (2000). Predictors of divorce adjustment: Stressors, resources, and definitions. *Journal of Marriage and the Family, 62,*
655–669.

107 Social Work Practice with Sexual Issues

Paul H. Ephross & Joan C. Weiss

Ms. J. is a 77-year-old woman, widowed for 6 years. Despite some chronic health problems, she is an active member of the city senior center, housed in a building three blocks from her home. Her apartment is in a deteriorated building, with rats and roaches a constant concern. When her grad-uate social work intern excitedly told her that she had found an apartment in a brand-new building for seniors on the other side of town, with its own senior center, Ms. J. refused even to visit the building. "It's too far away, and I'd miss my friends," was all she would say.

Lon is a 16-year-old high school junior. His family immigrated from Asia when he was 7. Al-ways a good student, his grades declined sharply in the past year. He loves sports and made the last spot on the varsity basketball team this year. When his coach found him moping in the school cafeteria and asked what was wrong, Lon blurted out that he is thinking of suicide because he's been involved in something so terrible that he can't tell anybody about it.

Many problems that people bring to social work-ers have sexual components.

- A sexual issue may be the presenting problem, cause or result of the presenting problem, or an underlying problem.

- Sexual needs and behaviors may be exploitive, and a client may be the exploiter, the victim, or both.
- Sexual behaviors may lead to sexually transmitted diseases, of which AIDS is the most frightening and the most publicized.
- Unrequited sexual needs, loneliness, and feelings of alienation are often interrelated.

Sex can be described as the great land of se-crets—often secrets that discredit a person's pub-lic persona. Sexual issues are intertwined with a great deal of human misery. Sexuality is also in-tertwined with much human happiness, but per-sons are unlikely to seek a social worker's help to alleviate that.

Contemporary American society is ambivalent about sex and the varieties of sexual orientations and sexual expressions. Virtually all students of human development have noted the mixed mes-sages that most Americans receive as children and adolescents and throughout their lives. These in-clude an overemphasis on the importance of phys-ical and sexual attractiveness and resultant popu-larity, combined with a high level of sexual shame and pervasive sex-negative (erotophobic) attitudes. Another example of ambivalence, now lessening but still present, is a socially constructed dimorphic conceptualization of sexual desire (Levine, 1998). In the past, sexual activity was viewed as something that men are expected to seek aggressively and women to resist until they are overcome. This dimorphic view has been used as an excuse for a great deal of sexual and other domestic violence and causes many misunderstandings between partners in intimate relationships (Foley, 2005).

However, there are many signs of changes in social norms and attitudes. A belief in a "right to sexual satisfaction" has emerged. Sexual harassment, especially in the workplace, has been clearly defined as undesirable and illegal. Older adults' expectations of sexual expression are changing (Newman & Newman, 2006). Norms and attitudes toward homosexuality, bisexuality, and other sexual expressions are in the midst of a period of rapid social and institutional change. Violence directed against members of sexual minorities coexists with slow but steady progress toward legitimating same-sex unions. Heterosexual single women and gay and lesbian adults seek to become parents through pregnancy or adoption.

Social workers should remember that there is dissensus among and within many ethnic, religious, racial, and cultural groups as to the nature of sexual morality, sex role definitions, and the parts to be played by parents, teachers, and others in relation to children, adolescents, and adults (Cox & Ephross, 1998). The discovery and rediscovery of the sexual abuse of children, date rape, domestic violence, and sexual exploitation by members of the clergy, teachers, and health professionals (including social workers) have had great impact. Research indicating that many sex offenses are not reported has led to greater sensitivity and improved training of law enforcement personnel, prosecutors, judges, and health professionals, though much remains to be done. It is incumbent on social workers to be familiar with their state's statutes requiring reporting of child sexual abuse and boundary violations on the part of health professionals.

INTERVIEWING ABOUT SEXUAL MATTERS

Communicating about sex can be difficult for social workers as well as for clients. People talk about sex using a variety of nonstandard or obscene vocabularies. To interview clients about sexual matters effectively, clinicians need to do the following:

- avoid words and expressions whose meanings may be obscure and find a common, culturally acceptable vocabulary with clients, so that sexual matters can be discussed without undue embarrassment.
- be conscious of their own assumptions and biases, which may affect communication and preclude effective treatment. These factors include but are by no means limited to differences in identity and background between professional and client. Group service formats may be useful in bridging gaps.
- become comfortable with asking questions about others' sexual experiences and willing to listen to authentic answers.
- avoid having their own experiences, values, or beliefs interfere with their ability to communicate with clients about sexual matters, all of which are, by their nature, subject to carrying emotional overtones.

A clinician's level of comfort with sexual communication affects clients powerfully. Some skilled interviewers use an explanatory preface before asking sexual questions to reduce the tension that these questions may cause. For example, one may say, "Now I'm going to ask you some questions about where sex has been and is in your life. It's important that I understand some of your experiences. Please let me know if any of my questions are unclear, or if you want me to explain them." A sexual history, which may take two to four sessions and requires knowledge of sexual life stages, is useful in both learning about the client's sexual experiences and establishing a therapeutic relationship.

The social work intern who was working with Ms. J. in example was working with a client older than her grandmother. It never occurred to her to ask whether Ms. J. has "someone special" in her life. In fact, she does. He is 82 and walks with some difficulty. Ms. J. believes that moving to a distant neighborhood will end their relationship. Why didn't she say so? Probably because women of Ms. J.'s birth cohort were brought up not to discuss intimate matters with much younger women, particularly strangers, especially one of a different race or ethnic background. Answers to questions about sex and relationships may come only in response to skilled and purposeful questions, and then only when a foundation of trust has been created.

Care must be taken regarding confidentiality. Statutory requirements that child abuse, including sexual abuse, be reported and court decisions that a therapist has a duty to warn if harm is intended against someone serve to limit confidentiality, so a blanket promise of confidentiality is not truthful. Early in a professional relationship, one may not be getting truthful answers about as emotionally charged a subject as sex, and a note to review these questions once some trust has developed is in order. Gentle humor, active listening, and a low level of tension in communication are helpful. Shocking clients or being shocked by them is rarely helpful, nor are unjustified personal revelations by the clinician. Sensitivity to age and sex norms is important, and so is an understanding in some depth of cultural and generational differences. Questions that elicit both information and trust are preferable to statements.

In the second example, Lon had engaged in a homosexual encounter with a classmate. He felt both desire and ambivalence about what he had done. He is in an anxiety state. He worries a great deal that he may be gay. He is terrified that his classmates and his teammates on the basketball team will find out what happened and will tease and reject him. Of most concern is his fear of bringing shame to his family through his behaviors. To be of help, the social worker needs to be willing to probe for sexual issues and has to be comfortable about homosexual feelings and what they may or may not mean in an adolescent.

DIAGNOSTIC ASSESSMENT CONSIDERATIONS

The *DSM-IV-TR* (American Psychological Association, 2000) divides sexual and gender-identity disorders into sexual dysfunctions, paraphilias, and gender identity disorders. Specifiers should be used to characterize (1) all primary sexual dysfunctions— lifelong type or acquired type and as generalized type or situational type; and (2) etiological type— due to psychological factors or combined factors. Sexual disorders may be due to a general medical condition (to be specified) or substance-induced (to be specified) or not otherwise specified. Substance-induced sexual dysfunctions, like other sexual dysfunctions, may affect one or more stages of the sexual response cycle—desire, arousal, or orgasm— or may cause pain in sexual activity.

Paraphilias include exhibitionism, fetishism, frotteurism, pedophilia, sexual sadism, transvestic fetishism, and voyeurism, as well as paraphilia not otherwise specified. Several of these have sub-types. Pedophilia, for example, may be specified as sexually attracted to males, to females, or to both and as exclusive type (sexually attracted only to children) or nonexclusive type. Gender identity disorders may appear in children, adolescents, or adults, whereas sexually mature individuals with such a disorder or a sexual disorder may be attracted to males, females, both, or neither. Either a gender identity disorder or a sexual disorder may be described as not otherwise specified. The general rules for the *DSM-IV-TR*'s five-axis diagnostic system apply to all of this chapter's disorders, as do the steps of certainty and the order in which diagnoses are listed.

In assessing the normality or pathology or a client's sexual experience and current expression, it is vital that the clinician understand the client's community, identity, religious beliefs, and social class, as well as specific family situation and living arrangements. *Normal* is a word with many meanings, as is *pathological*. Mental retardation or physical handicap, many illnesses, and lack of attractiveness do not preclude sexual interest or behaviors. Clients who have recovered from cardiac incidents often unrealistically fear a recurrence brought on by sexual activity.

Sexual disorders are often presented and experienced as vaguely defined physical symptoms in various somatic locations or as mental conditions seemingly unrelated to sexual issues or problems. Examples include frequent abdominal distress, mild to moderate pain in the lower back, or a general dysthymia for which there does not appear to be a recognizable stimulus. Conversely, sexual activity and function can be adversely affected by various physical and mental illnesses. Those that cause chronic pain or neurological deterioration, limit mobility, involve lack of contact with reality, or directly affect the organs and systems involved in sexual activities and sexual function are particularly destructive. Other illnesses, conditions, and treatments, such as medication and surgery, can affect sexual desire (libido) and function through their effects on the self-concept of the person and belief in his or her attractiveness (or lack thereof). For example, clinicians should explore the impact of depression and other conditions on the libido and sexual responses and behaviors of clients.

As noted, sexual dysfunctions can be related to ingested substances. These include both prescription and over-the-counter medications, illicit drugs, and in some instances drugs prescribed for other purposes. Whole classes of drugs have, or are believed to have, effects on sexual responses. Writing of the effects of aging on sexual function, Leiblum and Segraves (2000) list 27 medications that are "possible causes of ejaculatory disorders," 27 "drugs associated with decreased libido," and 22 "drugs associated with ejaculatory difficulties" without claiming that any of these lists is exhaustive (pp. 440–442). Some over-the-counter medicines can have adverse sexual side effects that are easily remedied. One example is antihistamines, which dry the mucous membranes and can cause pain on penetration. It should also be noted that Bartlik and Goldberg (2000) identify 34 "potential sex-positive medications for women" (p. 102).

THE IMPORTANCE OF A MEDICAL EXAMINATION

Because it is now clear that a sizable proportion of cases of sexual dysfunction are due either to general medical causes or to both medical and psychological causes, it is imperative that physical causes be considered, identified, or ruled out. Therefore, a medical examination (including appropriate laboratory tests) should be a standard procedure for anyone suffering sexual dysfunction. Referral to a physician who is knowledgeable and skilled in dealing with such patients should include, with the written permission of the client, the reasons for the referral and a request for written feedback of the results of the physical examination and the tests performed.

Where there are definitive findings, a meeting of social worker, client(s), and physician may be useful and may help facilitate understanding on the part of all involved.

TREATMENT OF SEXUAL PROBLEMS

There is an important place for psychosocially based sex therapy approaches, whether or not medical or surgical treatments are also employed. Relationship issues are always important in sexual dysfunction and rarely solved by pharmacology or surgery alone. Where a client has a partner, the partner is always affected, in one way or another, by the sexual problem. If a client does not have a partner, or is unwilling to include the partner in the treatment process, or if the partner is unwilling to participate, the therapy process must be modified to accommodate the particular circumstances.

A well-established view of the stages of treatment of sexual disorder is the acronym PLISSIT (Annon, 1976). In this formulation,

- *P* stands for *permission*, that is, permission to discuss sexual matters, feelings, and experiences.
- *LI* is *limited information*, imparted by the social worker or counselor.
- *SS* stands for *specific suggestions* for the individual or couple who are clients.
- *IT* is *intensive therapy*.

There are several formats of sex therapy. Many involve working with couples with assignments between therapeutic sessions. Some involve intensive, "vertical" use of time, such as several hours per day for a short period of time; others employ "horizontal" time use, such as once a week for several months. Group approaches often have advantages: social workers without post–master's education in sexuality and sex therapy should not attempt intensive therapy without close supervision or as members of a team. MSW-level social workers not only can but have an ethical obligation to give permission, provide limited information, and furnish specific suggestions where careful assessment indicates a need. Consultation with a trained sex therapist (or sex education, depending on the nature of the problem) is often helpful.

MEN'S ISSUES

A great deal of publicity has accompanied the recent development of drugs for the treatment of erectile dysfunction in men. The mass response to the availability of drugs to treat this dysfunction makes clear how concerned millions of American men (and presumably many of their partners) are about this problem. One recent drug to become available, sildenafil (trade name Viagra), has been heavily publicized. Millions of men use sildenafil, and the drug is not inexpensive. Rosen (2000) summarized current research on this drug: it is safe, except for cardiovascular patients who are taking nitrates. It is partially or fully effective in a majority of (but certainly not all) men. Before sildenafil, the drug of maximum interest was a synthetic prostaglandin (alprostadil; trade name MUSE), injected intracavernosally directly into the penis. Later, the same drug became available in pellet form for insertion into the urethra. Other treatments available include the vacuum constriction device, commonly known as the pump, which seeks to produce an erection by surrounding the penis with a vacuum, obtaining an erection, and then maintaining it with the help of an elastic constriction band at the base of the penis. For cases of severe, treatment-refractory erectile dysfunction, both permanently semi-rigid and inflatable penile prostheses are available for surgical insertion. As with all of these treatments, complex psychological, interpersonal, and medical issues surround the use of prostheses, though the results have certainly been evaluated positively by some patients.

WOMEN'S ISSUES

Though much progress has been made in understanding the nature of human sexual responses, social workers need to guard against gaps in their own knowledge and assumptions they have acquired in the process of their own socialization. One example relates to the nature of female sexual response. It is now clear that orgasm can be brought about in women as a result of various forms of stimulation, some more important for some women than for others. No one has yet arrived at a scientific basis for the diversity of women's experiences of orgasm and how to bring it about, nor a reason why anyone should care about these differences. For example, some fully orgasmic women, including many capable of multiple orgasms, do or do not require or enjoy vaginal penetration; do or do not require clitoral stimulation by a partner, a vibrator, or other means in addition to or instead of penis-in-vagina intercourse; do or do not enjoy orgasms as a result of oral or manual stimulation. Though some couples may occasionally enjoy simultaneous (or almost) orgasm, there is no reason to consider this to be superior or inferior to any other timing that is agreeable to the couple involved. The androcentric myth that female orgasms are a man's responsibility is a cultural construct now, one hopes, increasingly consigned to the trash heap of misguided sexual assumptions. An orgasm is an orgasm is an orgasm, regardless of how it is brought about and who one's partner is, or even if one has a partner.

In addition to concerns about and problems with being orgasmic, other common problems for which women seek help include vaginismus (painful spasms of perineal muscles surrounding the outer third of the vagina), dyspareunia (genital pain), and hypoactive sexual desire disorder. Conditions may be universal and lifelong, situational and temporary, or related to specific emotional or physiological changes, such as menopause. These problems are amenable to a variety of treatments, including cognitive-behavioral therapy, the use of dilators, desensitization techniques, and other behavioral approaches, as well as medications, when indicated.

Part of the responsibility of any clinician working with people with sexual issues is to be an educator. All honest educators occasionally respond with a truthful "I don't know" but "I'll find out" or "Let's find out together."

AN ETHICAL PERSPECTIVE

Counseling and treating clients around sexual issues requires self-awareness and a clear sense of boundaries on the part of a social worker. Some boundary issues are clear.

A sexual relationship of any kind between a social worker and a clinical client, present or past, is clearly forbidden, both by the NASW Code of Ethics (1999) and by broader definitions of professional ethics. One should also anticipate that dealing with sexual content will raise feelings and perceptions that will resonate within the social worker's own consciousness. Transference issues, such as the client "falling in love" with the worker, and countertransference issues, such as the worker's fantasy that he or she can solve a client's problem through an intimate relationship, are pitfalls to be concerned about. They exist, of course, in all clinical social work situations but perhaps may occur more often or in greater depth when sexual problems are at issue.

There are several ways of dealing with possible distortions. One is to seek consultation from a respected colleague as needed. Another is to recognize that part of one's professional responsibility is to have a life, that is, to take responsibility for meeting one's own needs outside of the professional framework. Many sexual problems can be treated successfully in individual, couple, and group formats. Successful outcomes are dependent not only on the client's motivation but also on the worker's willingness to engage in discussion of, knowledge about, and skill in recognizing and treating sexual problems.

WEB SITES

American Psychological Association.
 http://www.apa.org/topics/topicsbehavior.

html and http://www.apa.org/pi/lgbc/
guidelines.html.

National Institute on Aging. http://www
.niapublications.org/agepages/sexuality.asp.

Sexuality Information and Education Council
of the United States (SIECUS). http://
www.sexscience.org.

Society for the Scientific Study of Sexuality
(SSSS). http://www.sexscience.org/
publications/index.php.

University of California at Santa Barbara Sex-
Info. http://www.soc.ucsb.edu/
sexinfo.

References

American Psychiatric Association. (2000). *Diagnostic
and statistical manual,* 4th ed., text revision. Washington, DC: APA.

Annon, J. (1976). *The behavioral treatment of sexual
problems: Brief therapy.* New York: Harper & Row.

Bartlik, B., & Goldberg, J. (2000). Female sexual arousal disorder. In S. Leiblum, & R. Rosen (Eds.), *Principles and
practice of sex therapy,* 3rd ed. New York: Guilford.

Cox, C. B., & Ephross, P. H. (1998) *Ethnicity and social
work practice.* New York: Oxford University Press.

Foley, S. (2005). *Sex and love for grown-ups.* New York:
Sterling.

Leiblum, S., & Segraves, R. (2000). Sex therapy with aging adults. In S. Leiblum & R. Rosen (Eds.), *Principles
and practice of sex therapy,* 3rd ed. (pp. 423–448).
New York: Guilford.

Levine, S. B. (1998) *Sexuality in mid-life.* New York:
Plenum Press.

National Association of Social Workers. (1999). *Code
of ethics.* Washington, DC: NASW Press.

Newman, B., & Newman, P. R. (2006) *Development
through life,* 9th ed. Belmont, CA: Wadsworth.

Rosen, R. (2000). Medical and psychological interventions for erectile dysfunction: Toward a compound
treatment approach. In S. Leiblum & R. Rosen
(Eds.), *Principles and practice of sex therapy,* 3rd
ed. (pp. 276–304). New York: Guilford.

108   Interventions with Borderline Personality Disorder

Jonathan B. Singer

Borderline personality disorder (BPD) is one of
10 personality disorders in the *DSM-IV-TR*
(American Psychiatric Association [APA], 2000).
Personality disorders are characterized by inflexible and maladaptive personality traits that cause
significant functional impairment of subjective
distress in social, occupational, or other areas of
functioning (APA, 2000). BPD is one of three
personality disorders (along with histrionic and
narcissistic personality disorders) that are characterized by dramatic, emotional, or erratic individuals. The essential feature of BPD is "a pervasive
pattern of instability of interpersonal relation-

ships, self-image, and affects, and marked impulsivity that begins by early adulthood and is present in a variety of contexts" (APA, 2000, p. 706).
BPD is a severely disabling condition that has one
of the highest suicide rates and higher mental
health utilization than any other disorder (Mc-
Clough & Clarkin, 2004). The challenges posed
by BPD and the professional lore that has grown
up around the disorder has resulted in it being
perceived by professionals and the public as the
most difficult and problematic of all disorders to
assess and treat (Aviram, Brodsky, & Stanley, 2006).
BPD is also the most researched and best under-

stood of all axis II diagnoses (McClough & Clarkin, 2004). This chapter presents an overview of empirically validated and promising approaches to the assessment and treatment of BPD.

ASSESSMENT OF BPD

According to the *DSM-IV-TR* (APA, 2000), prevalence rates for BPD are 1 percent to 2.5 percent in the general population, 10 percent in outpatient settings, and between 20 percent and 50 percent in inpatient settings. Diagnosis of BPD is complicated by the challenges of distinguishing it from other diagnoses, such as bipolar disorder or post-traumatic stress disorder (PTSD); the frequency of cooccurrence with other axis I and axis II diagnoses; and the impact of negative emotional responses that clinicians have to the label of BPD (Aviram et al., 2006; Mayo, 2006; Presley, 2005).

There is no standard assessment protocol for BPD, and most assessments are associated with the chosen treatment approach. However, there are a few issues that should be addressed in all assessments. Because problems associated with BPD are inherently social, assessment should establish how interpersonal instability manifests in interpersonal behaviors and affects relationship quality (McClough & Clarkin, 2004). Assessments should also establish which types of symptoms result in the most significant impairment or distress: cognitive symptomatology, affect dysregulation, or lack of impulse control (Oldham, 2004). Possible assessment questions could include "How do you deal with conflict? Who can you rely on for support? Tell me about a long-term friend whom you feel is 'in your corner.' What do you do when someone makes you mad? Describe to me your ideal relationship."

TREATMENT OF CLIENTS WITH BPD

Until the 1990s, few if any treatments demonstrated effectiveness in reducing core symptoms of BPD. Since then, a number of treatments have demonstrated success in addressing specific features of BPD. Three treatments, dialectical behavior therapy (DBT; Linehan, 1993a, 1993b), mentalization-based treatment (MBT; Bateman & Fonagy, 2001; Fonagy & Bateman, 2007) and cognitive-behavioral therapy (CBT; Davidson, Norrie, et al., 2006; Davidson, Tyrer, et al., 2006), have demonstrated

better outcomes than treatment-as-usual (TAU) in randomized controlled trials (RCTs). One randomized trial compared the effects of a CBT and a psychodynamic treatment (Giesen-Bloo et al., 2006). The following is a brief review of empirically validated and promising treatments for BPD.

Dialectical Behavior Therapy

Marsha Linehan and colleagues originally developed DBT as a treatment for women who engage in self-harming behaviors, but they found that a significant number of their clients met criteria for BPD (Linehan, 1993a). Although DBT is the treatment for BPD with the most empirical support, its efficacy has been demonstrated primarily for women with BPD who self-harm (Feigenbaum, 2007). There is emerging empirical support for the use of DBT with adolescents with BPD, comorbid substance use disorders and BPD, binge eaters, depressed elderly patients, and even families of people with BPD (Chapman, 2006; Hoffman, Fruzzetti, & Buteau, 2007; Hoffman et al., 2005; Rathus & Miller, 2002). In response to criticism that existing research on DBT simply reflects the benefits of having small caseloads, targeted supervision, and a controlled environment, Linehan and colleagues tested DBT against six expert treatments in a community setting (Linehan et al., 2006). The authors reported that compared to the expert treatment condition, clients receiving DBT reported fewer and less severe suicide attempts, used crisis services less, had fewer psychiatric hospitalizations, and had fewer dropouts than the expert treatments.

DBT is a combination of CBT and Zen mindfulness training (Linehan, 1993b). Unique features of DBT include (1) interventions based on mindfulness and acceptance (e.g., finding a balance between emotion and rationality, known as "wise mind"); (2) emphasis on the dialectic (i.e., reality is comprised of ever-changing opposing forces); (3) focus on emotions and the biopsychosocial model (i.e., BPD is understood to be a dysfunction of the emotional regulation system which is part of a biopsychosocial system); and (4) addressing five specific processes of therapy (Chapman, 2006). The five processes and their corresponding treatment modalities are (1) motivating the client to change and rehearsing cognitive and behavioral skills that help clients regulate their emotions in 1-hour weekly individual therapy; (2) enhancing behavioral skills: mindfulness, interpersonal skills, regulation of emotions, and distress tolerance in 2-hour weekly skills training groups; (3) ensuring the generalization of these skills to activities of daily living using as-needed phone consultations with outpatient treatment or milieu therapy for inpatient programs; (4) enhancing therapist capabilities and motivations in 1-hour weekly DBT consultation team meeting; and (5) structuring the treatment environment to support client and therapist capabilities (Linehan, 1993b). DBT is a highly structured treatment, and clinicians might wonder if anything less than strict adherence to the model will be effective in treating people with BPD. A recent study reported success in using a modified version of DBT in uncontrolled environment and incorporating the skills training group with non-DBT individual therapy (Harley, Baity, Blais, & Jacobo, 2007).

Mentalization-Based Treatment

Peter Fonagy and Anthony Bateman developed MBT as a day hospitalization treatment for people diagnosed with BPD (Fonagy & Bateman, 2007). In the only evaluation of the model, MBT demonstrated significant and enduring changes in mood states and interpersonal functioning (Bateman & Fonagy, 1999, 2001). Increased benefits of MBT were reported at 3-month follow-up, and significant difference between the experimental and control groups were reported at a 5-year follow-up (Fonagy & Bateman, 2007). The developers noted that although MBT resulted in no cost savings during the evaluation, improved functioning resulted in considerable after treatment cost savings.

BPD has its origins in psychoanalytic and psychodynamic theory (McClough & Clarkin, 2004). However, there are only a few psychodynamic treatments with any empirical support (Korner, Gerull, Meares, & Stevenson, 2006). MBT is a psychodynamic developmental model for understanding BPD in which mentalizing is the key to treatment. According to Fonagy and Bateman (2007), "Mentalization is the capacity to make sense of self and of others in terms of subjective states and mental processes" (p. 83). The model assumes that people with BPD cannot understand the thoughts and feelings associated with the behaviors of self and others because (1) their own infant mental states were not understood by their caregivers, and (2) as a result, they never developed emotional regulation skills. MBT targets three higher order social cognitive functions that are important in attachment contexts: "affect repre-

sentation and regulation; attentional control, also with strong links to the regulation of affect; and finally mentalization, a system for interpersonal understanding within the attachment context" (Fonagy & Bateman, 2007, p. 84). The challenge for the clinician is to help the client develop emotional regulation without stimulating the attachment system. One way MBT achieves this by eschewing the role of insight and affective exploration in therapy. The developers contend that therapists can do harm to clients who have significant difficulty regulating emotion and who have poor conceptions of self and others by insisting on using traditional insight-oriented psychodynamic treatment.

CBT for BPD

A recent RCT compared TAU with TAU plus CBT (Davidson, Norrie et al., 2006; Davidson, Tyrer et al., 2006). The treatment was based on cognitive-behavioral principles and therefore the interventions focused on the patient's beliefs and behavior that impair social and adaptive functioning. The study results suggested that all participants showed reductions in suicidal ideation, and hospitalization. The TAU + CBT group also showed reductions in dysfunctional beliefs, state anxiety, and distress caused by psychiatric symptom.

Schema-Focused Therapy versus Transference-Focused Psychotherapy

A recent study compared a cognitive-based treatment (schema-focused therapy; SFT) and a psychodynamic treatment (transference-focused psychotherapy; TFP) in a 3-year randomized trial of 82 men and women with BPD (Giesen-Bloo et al., 2006). Giesen-Bloo and colleagues noted that whereas empirically validated treatments such as DBT, CBT, and MBT target specific symptoms, such as self-harm behavior or interpersonal functioning, both SFT and TFP were developed to restructure clients' personalities. Results of the study indicated that participants from both treatments improved significantly on all *DSM-IV* BPD criteria, all effects were apparent after the first year, and there was significant improvement in the quality of life for the majority of participants.

Promising Treatments

With the exception of the treatments in the study by Geisen-Bloo and colleagues, no single pharmacological or psychosocial treatment has demonstrated efficacy in addressing all aspects of BPD. However, there are a number of treatments that hold promise for addressing specific symptoms, populations, or for specific treatment settings (listed in alphabetical order):

- *EMDR.* Brown and Shapiro (2006) presented a case study of treating BPD using eye movement desensitization and reprocessing (EMDR), a recognized trauma therapy. This individual treatment holds promise in addressing trauma issues for people with BPD using a treatment that has some empirical support in other populations.
- *Intermittent-continuous eclectic therapy (ICE).* ICE is a group approach developed in Chile. Menchaca, Perez, and Peralta (2007) described a 1-year pilot study of men and women ages 15 to 40 in an outpatient setting. The authors reported improvement in self-aggression and general symptoms. ICE is one of the few group treatments for BPD. Group treatment holds promise as a cost effective treatment (Marziali, 2002).
- *Interpersonal group psychotherapy (IGP).* IGP is a group approach developed by Marziali and Munroe-Blum (1994, cited in Marziali, 2002). The developers compared 30 sessions of IPG with open-ended, long-term, individual psychoanalytic psychotherapy. Results indicated at posttreatment and at 1-year follow-up, participants in both the experimental and the comparison treatments made gains.
- *Interpersonal psychotherapy (IPT-BDP).* Research is currently being conducted on a version of IPT modified for people with BDP (IPT-BPD; Markowitz, Bleiberg, Pessin, & Skodol, 2007). IPT is an empirically supported individual treatment for people with moderate to severe depression that focuses on the bidirectional influence of interpersonal problems and depressive symptoms. IPT-BDP targets the interpersonal instability and depressed affect commonly encountered in people with BDP (Markowitz, Skodol, & Bleiberg, 2006). An RCT is currently under way.
- *Pharmacotherapy.* Despite recent advances in addressing core symptoms of mood, anxiety, and childhood disorders, pharmacotherapy is not recommended in the treatment of BPD. Treatment guidelines recommend the use of medications to address temporary psychosis and other discrete symptoms (Oldham, 2004), but the evidence to support the use of medications alone, or in combination with psychotherapy is equivocal (Paris, 2005; Paton & Okocha, 2005)
- *STEPPS (Systems Training for Emotional Predictability and Problem Solving)* (Blum, Pfohl, St. John, Monahan, & Black, 2002; Van Wel et al., 2006). STEPPS is a group treatment based on Minuchin's structural family therapy model. Two pilot studies suggest treatment efficacy. RCTs are currently under way (Van Wel et al., 2006).
- *Supportive therapy.* Aviram, Hellerstein, Gerson, and Stanley (2004) used supportive individual therapy with an outpatient population with BPD who engaged in self-harming behaviors. The authors suggested that the approach appeared to be efficacious in engaging people with BPD and minimizing the frequency and intensity of self-harming behavior. However, because this was an open and uncontrolled trial, its findings must be interpreted with caution.

IMPLICATIONS FOR THE FUTURE

There is cause for hope among clinicians and clients that effective treatment of BPD is possible. Recent empirical findings have challenged the long-held belief that BPD is treatment-resistant and follows a chronic disease model (Fonagy & Bateman, 2006; Zanarini, Frankenburg, Hennen, & Silk, 2003). Most treatments reviewed in this chapter conceptualize the root cause of BPD differently, have different targets for change, and thus propose different treatments. However, meta-analyses of BPD treatments suggest there are similar outcomes across therapies (Livesley, 2007). Given the heterogeneity of client characteristics for people with BPD and the variety of approaches used by clinicians in the field (Sharp et al., 2005), the best practices approach to treating BPD is likely to be an integration of treatments rather than a single evidence-based treatment. Livesley (2007) proposed an integrated model for treating BPD, one that is based on three common treatment factors: "(i) A structured approach with a clearly defined treatment model, an explicit treatment frame and contract, and careful adherence to the model; (ii) General change strategies based on the relationship component of the common factors; and (iii) Generic aspects of the specific interventions used by various therapies" (p. 133). Integrated approaches are recommended because of noted limitations of any one treatment, and as a way of increasing treatment allegiance by clinicians with different treatment frameworks. The combination of treatment technique and treatment allegiance has been shown to account for 38 percent of treatment outcome (Wampold, 2001). The best treatments will help clients express emotions without causing harm to self or others, establish fulfilling and stable relationships, and develop a sense of personal mastery.

WEB SITES

Behavioral Tech, Dialectical Behavior Therapy. http://www.behavioraltech.com.

National Institute for Mental Health, Borderline Personality Disorder. http://www.nimh .nih.gov/health/publications/borderline-personality-disorder.shtml.

J. B. Singer, Dialectical behavior therapy, interview with Sabrina Heller. http:// socialworkpodcast.com/2007/10/dialectical-behavior-therapy-interview.html.

References

American Psychiatric Association. (2000). *Diagnostic and statistical manual of mental disorders*, 4th ed., text revision. Washington, DC: APA.

Aviram, R. B., Brodsky, B. S., & Stanley, B. (2006). Borderline personality disorder, stigma, and treatment implications. *Harvard Review of Psychiatry, 14*(5), 249–256.

Aviram, R. B., Hellerstein, D. J., Gerson, J., & Stanley, B. (2004). Adapting supportive psychotherapy for individuals with borderline personality disorder who self-injure or attempt suicide. *Journal of Psychiatric Practice, 10*(3), 145–155.

Bateman, A. W., & Fonagy, P. (1999). The effectiveness of partial hospitalization in the treatment of borderline personality disorder—a randomised controlled trial. *American Journal of Psychiatry, 156,* 1563–1569.

Bateman, A. W., & Fonagy, P. (2001). Treatment of borderline personality disorder with psychoanalytically oriented partial hospitalization: An 18-month follow-up. *American Journal of Psychiatry, 158,* 36–42.

Blum, N., Pfohl, B., St. John, D., Monahan, P., & Black, D. W. (2002). STEPPS: A cognitive-behavioral systems-based group treatment for outpatients with borderline personality disorder—a preliminary report. *Comprehensive Psychiatry, 43*(4), 301–310.

Brown, S., & Shapiro, F. (2006). EMDR in the treatment of borderline personality disorder. *Clinical Case Studies, 5*(5), 403–420.

Chapman, A. L. (2006). Dialectical behavior therapy: Current indications and unique elements. *Psychiatry, 3*(9), 62–68.

Davidson, K., Norrie, J., Tyrer, P., Gumley, A., Tata, P., Murray, H., et al. (2006). The effectiveness of cognitive behavior therapy for borderline personality disorder: Results from the borderline personality disorder study of cognitive therapy (BOSCOT) trial. *Journal of Personality Disorders, 20*(5), 450–465.

Davidson, K., Tyrer, P., Gumley, A., Tata, P., Norrie, J., Palmer, S., et al. (2006). A randomized controlled trial of cognitive behavior therapy for borderline personality disorder: Rationale for trial, method, and description of sample. *Journal of Personality Disorders, 20*(5), 431–449.

Feigenbaum, J. (2007). Dialectical behaviour therapy: An increasing evidence base. *Journal of Mental Health, 16*(1), 51–68.

Fonagy, P., & Bateman, A. W. (2006). Progress in the treatment of borderline personality disorder. *British Journal of Psychiatry, 188*(1), 1–3.

Fonagy, P., & Bateman, A. W. (2007). Mentalizing and borderline personality disorder. *Journal of Mental Health, 16*(1), 83–101.

Giesen-Bloo, J., van Dyck, R., Spinhoven, P., van Tilburg, W., Dirksen, C., van Asselt, T., et al. (2006). Outpatient psychotherapy for borderline personality disorder: Randomized trial of schema-focused therapy vs transference-focused psychotherapy. *Archives of General Psychiatry, 63*(6), 649–658.

Harley, R. M., Baity, M. R., Blais, M. A., & Jacobo, M. C. (2007). Use of dialectical behavior therapy skills training for borderline personality disorder in a naturalistic setting. *Psychotherapy Research, 17*(3), 362–370.

Hoffman, P. D., Fruzzetti, A. E., & Buteau, E. (2007). Understanding and engaging families: An education, skills and support program for relatives impacted by borderline personality disorder. *Journal of Mental Health, 16*(1), 69–82.

Hoffman, P. D., Fruzzetti, A. E., Buteau, E., Neiditch, E. R., Penney, D., Bruce, M. L., et al. (2005). Family connections: A program for relatives of persons with borderline personality disorder. *Family Process, 44*(2), 217–225.

Korner, A., Gerull, F., Meares, R., & Stevenson, J. (2006). Borderline personality disorder treated with the conversational model: A replication study. *Comprehensive Psychiatry, 47*(5), 406–411.

Linehan, M. M. (1993a). *Cognitive-behavioral treatment of borderline personality disorder.* New York: Guilford.

Linehan, M. M. (1993b). *Skills training manual for treating borderline personality disorder.* New York: Guilford.

Linehan, M. M., Comtois, K. A., Murray, A. M., Brown, M. Z., Gallop, R. J., Heard, H. L., et al. (2006). Two-year randomized controlled trial and follow-up of dialectical behavior therapy vs therapy by experts for suicidal behaviors and borderline personality disorder. *Archives of General Psychiatry, 63*(7), 757–766.

Livesley, W. J. (2007). An integrated approach to the treatment of personality disorder. *Journal of Mental Health, 16*(1), 131–148.

Markowitz, J. C., Bleiberg, K., Pessin, H., & Skodol, A. E. (2007). Adapting interpersonal psychotherapy for borderline personality disorder. *Journal of Mental Health, 16*(1), 103–116.

Markowitz, J. C., Skodol, A. E., & Bleiberg, K. (2006). Interpersonal psychotherapy for borderline personality disorder: Possible mechanisms of change. *Journal of Clinical Psychology, 62*(4), 431–444.

Marziali, E. (2002). Borderline personality disorder. In A. R. Roberts & G. J. Green (Eds.), *Social workers' desk reference* (pp. 360–363). New York: Oxford University Press.

Mayo, K. (2006). *Diagnosing borderline personality disorder: The effect of therapists' negative emotional reactions on diagnostic judgments.* Dissertation, Indiana State University.

McClough, J. F., & Clarkin, J. F. (2004). Personality disorders. In M. Hersen (Ed.), *Psychological assessment in clinical practice: A pragmatic guide* (pp. 117–145). New York: Brunner-Routledge.

Menchaca, A., Perez, O., & Peralta, A. (2007). Intermittent-continuous eclectic therapy: A group approach for borderline personality disorder. *Journal of Psychiatric Practice, 13*(4), 281–284.

Oldham, J. M. (2004). Borderline personality disorder: The treatment dilemma. *Journal of Psychiatric Practice, 10*(3), 204–206.

Paris, J. (2005). Recent advances in the treatment of borderline personality disorder. *Canadian Journal of Psychiatry/La Revue canadienne de psychiatrie, 50*(8), 435–441.

Paton, C., & Okocha, C. (2005). Pharmacological treatment of borderline personality disorder. *Journal of Psychiatric Intensive Care, 1*(2), 105–116.

Presley, A. S. (2005). *A critical literature review on the assessment and diagnosis of posttraumatic stress disorder.* Dissertation, Alliant International University, San Diego, CA.

Rathus, J. H., & Miller, A. L. (2002). Dialectical behavior therapy adapted for suicidal adolescents. *Suicide and Life Threatening Behaviors, 32,* 146–157.

Sharp, I. R., Henriques, G. R., Chapman, J. E., Jeglic, E. L., Brown, G. K., & Beck, A. T. (2005). Strategies used in the treatment of borderline personality disorder: A survey of practicing psychologists. *Journal of Contemporary Psychotherapy, 35*(4), 359–368.

Van Wel, B., Kockmann, I., Blum, N., Pfohl, B., Black, D., & Heesterman, W. (2006). STEPPS group treatment for borderline personality disorder in the Netherlands. *Annals of Clinical Psychiatry, 18*(1), 63–67.

Wampold, B. (2001). *The great psychotherapy debate.* New York: Erlbaum.

Zanarini, M. C., Frankenburg, F. R., Hennen, J., & Silk, K. R. (2003). The longitudinal course of borderline psychopathology: 6-year prospective follow-up of the phenomenology of borderline personality disorder. *American Journal of Psychiatry, 160,* 274–283.

PART X
Case Management Guidelines

An Overview of Case Management

Jack Rothman

Case management is a service for highly vulnerable client populations to ensure that they receive the help they need within the fragmented American service delivery system. Frankel and Gelman (2004) state that a key goal of this practice is service access and coordination, which entails community-based assistance that enables chronically impeded persons to live their lives in a natural environment, rather than in an encapsulated institutional one. These vulnerable clients, including persons with persistent mental illness, frail elderly, dependent children, and physical handicaps, have wide-ranging needs requiring continuing care over time. Case management, to meet its aims with such individuals, combines aspects of individual practice and community practice. (For policy dimensions see Gursansky, Harvey, & Kennedy, 2003.)

This presentation focuses on the functions of case management. A model of the practice is offered in Figure 109.1, incorporating 15 functions, and the process of their implementation is discussed. The model was derived from research in a mental health setting and an extensive review of research in multiple settings (Rothman, 1992; Rothman & Sager, 1998). For other case management models, see Cesta and Tahan (2003). The functions specified here are not strictly separate and discrete. Often they flow into one another and overlap. We begin by describing the sequential functions from top to bottom in the center of Figure 109.1. We then move to the left-hand and then the right-hand intermittent set of functions.

SEQUENTIAL FUNCTIONS

1. *Access to the agency*. Clients can come into the organization through referrals of various

kinds. The other access mode is that of outreach, in which the agency extends into the community to both search for and encourage otherwise inaccessible clients, such as the homeless or frail elderly, to enter its service system. The practitioner participates in the access function. but administration ordinarily directs it.

2. *Intake*. Intake includes identifying the client's problem and situation. Also, the practitioner seeks to determine if there is an appropriate agency–client match. Eligibility is examined, and the financial situation is appraised. The client is given information about agency

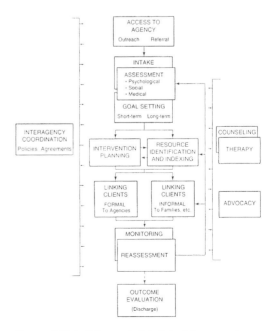

Figure 109.1 Schematic Model of Intervention

services, requirements, and limitations. Some preliminary intervention planning may begin. Intake often is a rather formal process involving the gathering of designated information, filling out standard administrative forms, and giving routine instructions.

3. *Assessment (psychological, social, medical).* Assessment further examines the problem to understand its causes and dynamics. The level of the client's social, psychological, and physical functioning is clarified. For highly vulnerable clients, needs are typically broad and assessment must be inclusive. There is traditional case history development and also use of outside informants from several disciplines, as well as the family and previous agencies that saw the client. Because client empowerment is a major goal, clients are encouraged to participate to their maximum potential in assessment and every other phase of the process. There should be a careful assessment of the family in terms of its potential benefit to the client and its capability to cope with a long-term client.

4. *Goal setting.* Establishing service goals builds on assessment. Most case managers attempt to obtain clients' perceptions of areas needing improvement and to include clients' personal objectives in their own construction of professional objectives. Typically, short- and long-term goals are formulated—for example, acute stress and immediate housing needs versus enhanced self-esteem and occupational aims. It is important to have a realistic outlook on limitations of severely vulnerable clients. A maintenance program to allow the client to function in the community or reduce hospital recidivism may be a sufficient goal in many situations. Expectations have to be realistic, in addition, to sustain staff morale and avoid burnout. With a service goal established, there are two alternatives, step 5 or 6, for the next function in the sequence.

5. *Intervention planning.* The notion of intervention planning encompasses both treatment planning, in the sense of the direct provision of counseling and therapy, and service planning, involving the linking of clients to informal and formal external supports for more practical assistance. Intervention service planning usually involves methods of achieving both short-

and long-term goals. Planning is heavily tied to resource identification and linkage, and these work hand in hand. In developing a plan, many case managers consider the barriers that may be encountered on both the client and the system level and begin to consider contingency plans to cope with these. Clients should be involved to the greatest extent possible in intervention planning (and earlier stages), because they often are able to accurately identify their own needs, thus contributing to more effective service outcomes.

6. *Resource identification and indexing.* This function entails obtaining information on relevant service resources and organizing the data for easy access. A number of means are available for such resource identification: telephone contacts with agencies, attending meetings where agency representatives are present, informal networking, setting up a personal resource file, and using an office resource file or directory. Practitioners should be aware of possible inaccurate or out-of-date information owing to frequent changes in policies and programs. The next step is to link clients to formal and informal support.

7. *Formal linkage to agencies and programs.* Formal linkage functions include such activities as clarifying the service need, careful matching of clients to agencies, initial telephone contact, orienting the client, preparing papers, and visiting agencies. More effective linkage is active and facilitative, with the practitioner often serving as a traveling companion. The practitioner needs to give both concrete and emotional support to facilitate a productive connection. Linkage requires the use of organizational skills (whom to contact, at what level) and community-oriented skills (knowledge of what new services are developing, what legislative policies are applicable, what funding is available) to optimize service connections. Preparing the client for the experience includes such things as providing detailed information, anticipating difficulties, role-playing appropriate client behavior, giving emotional support, and accompanying the client on the first visit.

8. *Informal linkage to families and social networks.* This entails drawing on a range of natural helping networks. Family members can be important, but must be assessed first

to determine whether they have the potential to be helpful and can sustain the burden. The practitioner has to structure time to provide the necessary orientation, training, and consultation for natural helpers to carry out the informal support roles. These linkages also extend to friends, neighbors, and community groups. Cultural considerations should be emphasized, because different groups have available or favor different options. Two overlapping functions follow.

9. *Monitoring.* Systematic contact with agency service providers and informal supports is at the heart of monitoring. Its purpose is to appraise the suitability of provisions made to sustain the client in the community. This can be accomplished through telephoning the contacts, visiting and phoning clients, or having the support individuals or client phone the practitioner. It requires a definite and substantive allotment of time, as crisis situations will arise. The case manager should anticipate dealing with these, necessitating some degree of flexibility in working hours.

10. *Reassessment.* Given a long-term continuing care outlook in many case management situations, recurrent appraisal of the situation is a necessity and may be required at established intervals by agency rules. Each initial client assessment will require a reassessment in time. These can be formal or informal, periodic or ongoing, and at various intervals of frequency. The client should ordinarily participate in the reassessment. A number of factors hinder reassessment: ill-defined goals make assessment difficult; sometimes clients withhold information, or their progress is irregular and uncertain; collateral agencies occasionally fail to provide information; work pressures and time constraints may interfere. Reassessment often leads to looping back in the sequence to a new linkage, different intervention plan, or revised goals.

11. *Outcome evaluation (for termination).* Evaluation differs from reassessment in that it carries the sense of termination or discharge. It ordinarily occurs when clients are ready to operate in a fully independent way without further service, based on the professional judgment of the practitioner. Because most long-term vulnerable clients are in a continuing-care mode that requires ongoing professional attention, such a final outcome evaluation may be rare. For this reason, a broken line has been used in the diagram, signifying that even middle-range termination may not occur (for example, with orphans or the severely disabled).

INTERMITTENT FUNCTIONS

1. *Interagency coordination.* The interagency coordination function deals with the establishment of relationships among agencies to facilitate the linkage function, either through formal policies or by informal agreements between organizations. Formal policies are typically arranged at the highest hierarchical levels and informal arrangements by direct service professionals. These interorganizational understandings relate to service patterns, type and number of clients, and financial payments.

2. *Counseling.* Counseling involves information and advice giving—for example, cuing clients on how to deal with fellow clients in a residential facility. Supportive encouragement of the client is also emphasized, such as pointing out strengths and reinforcing efforts at self-direction. This is typically not highly intrapsychic (as is traditional therapy) and involves "here and now" problem solving, reality testing, imparting socialization skills, and giving practical help in such areas as housing, finances, parenting, and employment. Effective counseling includes such things as teaching basic living skills, using role-playing, and modeling desirable behavior. Because counseling is ordinarily short-term, it can be offered recurrently and at various points in the process.

3. *Therapy.* One should distinguish between long-term therapy, which focuses on deep-seated personality problems, and short-term therapy, which is concerned with immediate problems in living, such as a conflict with a roommate. Most therapy provided by case managers is short-term. Even in mental health settings, therapy should have a present-time emphasis and help clients cope with day-to-day living situations, as the severity of their condition affords them only a limited capacity for basic personality change. Extensive therapy is pursued through

referral to an appropriate source. With severely vulnerable populations, counseling and therapy overlap functionally, and it is difficult to make sharp distinctions between them.

4. *Advocacy*. Advocacy is another intermittent function. It might be needed early in the sequence (exerting pressure on a landlord on an emergency basis to allow a client back into his apartment so that reflective assessment may begin) or may take place later, perhaps at the time of linkage, where an external community agency is inappropriately refusing to provide a service. Advocacy involves an affirmative and assertive approach to assisting a client to receive services or amenities that are being unfairly withheld. The advocate assists the client to move through bureaucratic blocks to obtain benefits.

The model focuses on the functions of case managers in providing care to individual clients. However, case managers also work in the community and with organizations to promote benefits for clients collectively. These broader macro tasks include community education, developing support and self-help groups, and contributing to community change efforts that foster client well-being. A competent case manager will acquire skills in each of these areas to optimize the implementation of practice.

USING THE DIAGRAM

The diagram can be viewed as a roadmap to practice. A map tells the traveler how to get from one point to another, often in unfamiliar territory. The diagram also does this, from the point of seeing clients for the first time, to nesting them securely in supportive situations and allowing for the highest possible quality of life in a natural setting.

Like a roadmap, the diagram does not detail the sharp curves, jarring bumps, and cloudbursts along the way. Still, a road map is a useful tool of travel management within its limitations, just as the diagram can give direction for case management. Through its flexible features of feedback loops and overlapping functions, the diagram does allow for special and individualized conditions that arise. Thus, the sequence is approximate and suggestive rather than a precise, lockstep progression. The diagram helps make practice more systematic and consistent because the professional does

not need to determine fundamental steps in the process for each case.

Focusing strictly on practice leaves open broader inquiries about feasibility. Will the role be adequately funded? Will it be backed up administratively in agencies? Will it be given political and moral support in the community? Are professionals able and willing to carry out the required functions?

Alternative models of case management include, among others: the therapist case manager formulation, in which therapy is a substantial function; the strengths model, in which inherent client capacities are stressed; the supportive care model, which bases the service in a neighborhood and involves natural helpers as the main vehicle of intervention; the psychosocial rehabilitation center approach, using a residential facility with saturated services that include vocational training; the paraprofessional format, emphasizing community referral activities; and the family-as-case-manager service concept. As yet, none of the variations has won predominant professional acceptance or has been found empirically to be superior to others.

RESEARCH ON CASE MANAGEMENT

A review of research on case management reveals diverse findings (Rothman & Sager, 1998). Provision of case management services has frequently been found to be associated with improved quality of life. Studies have demonstrated the positive effects of case management on the ability of the client to remain in a natural community setting without requiring a return to an institutional site. Case management service tends to enhance quality of life and reduce reinstitutionalization. Several studies show simultaneous attainment of these outcomes.

Case management programs have demonstrated positive effects in specific areas of human service: keeping families together, improving school attendance of pregnant teenagers, improving attendance and academic performance, helping pregnant and parenting female drug abusers, and aiding substance abusing offenders.

In regard to cost-effectiveness, medically related case management has generally been associated with cost savings per case, a potential increase in hospital-generated revenues, more rapid discharge, and an increased turnover in cases (Cohen & Cesta, 2005).

Although there is a body of evidence indicating the efficacy of case management, a smaller subset of studies notes a lack of association between case management and positive client outcomes, signaling a need for caution in practice and a call for further research evidence. Toward this end, evidence-based practice is advocated to promote research and evaluation (Lishman, 2007). A related trend is the increasing use of electronic technologies, by which practitioners and agencies communicate with one another and clients obtain online information (Mullahy & Jensen, 2004). This also promotes the advancement of the case management paradigm through enhanced documentation, monitoring, assessment, and accountability.

WEB SITES

American Case Management Association. http://www.acmaweb.org.
Case Management Resource Guide. http://www.cmrg.com.
New York City Managed Care Community As-sistance Program. http://www.nycmccapl.org.

References

Cesta, T. G., & Tahan, H. A. (2003). *The case manager's survival guide: Winning strategies for clinical practice*. St. Louis: Mosby.

Cohen, E. L., & Cesta, T. G. (Eds.). (2005). *Nursing case management: From essentials to advanced practice applications*, 4th ed. St. Louis: Mosby.

Frankel, A. J., & Gelman, S. R. (2004). *Case management: An introduction to concepts and skills*, 2nd ed. Chicago: Lyceum.

Gursansky, D., Harvey, J., & Kennedy, R. (2003). *Case management: Policy, practice, and professional business*. New York: Columbia University Press.

Lishman, J. (Ed.). (2007). *Handbook for practice learning in social work and social change: Knowledge and theory*, 2nd ed. London: Jessica Kingsley.

Mullahy, C. M., & Jensen, D. K. (2004). *The case manager's handbook*, 3rd ed. Boston: Jones & Bartlett.

Rothman, J. (1992). *Guidelines for case management: Putting research to professional use*. Itasca, IL: F. E. Peacock.

Rothman, J., & Sager, J. S. (1998). *Case management: Integrating individual and community practice*. Boston: Allyn & Bacon.

110   Clinical Case Management

Joseph Walsh

Clinical case management is an approach to human service delivery that integrates elements of clinical social work and traditional case management practices. It is used primarily with clients having serious mental illnesses, such as schizophrenia, major depression, bipolar disorder, personality disorders, and substance use disorders. The range of client needs within this population includes social relationships, housing, income support, medical care, job training, recreation, life skills development, counseling, and medication. Interventions are usually provided in mental health agencies.

Clinical social work practice can be defined as the application of social work theory and methods to the treatment and prevention of psychosocial dysfunction, disability, or impairment, including emotional and mental disorders, in individuals, families, and groups. It is based on an application of human development theories within a psychosocial context (NASW, 1989). Case management is an approach to service delivery that focuses on the development of growth-enhancing environmental supports, using resources that are spread across agency systems (Surber, 1994). Case managers work independently or as members of teams, and their traditional activities include assessment, planning, linking, monitoring, and advocacy.

Clinical case management is characterized by a clear understanding of the relationships among the biological, psychological, social, and environmental factors that influence the course of development and severity of a person's mental illness (Wong, 2006). Clinical case managers generally use a biopsychosocial stress-vulnerability model to understand the interplay of these forces. In clinical case management, the social worker combines the sensitivity and interpersonal skill of the psychotherapist with the creativity and action orientation of the environmental architect (Surber, 1994). The practice gives priority to the quality of the relationship between the client and social worker as a prerequisite for the client's personal growth. Those who support clinical case management argue that substituting nonclinicians for appropriately skilled clinicians often leaves consumers in need of interventions with staff who are ill equipped to meet their needs (Essock, Covell, & Drake, 2006). Furthermore, due to the inherent problems with role confusion and authority in traditional case management, the client is best served if the worker is encouraged to function as the primary therapeutic resource. Walsh (2000a) has elaborated a series of clinical case management intervention techniques that draw from psychodynamic, cognitive, behavioral, and social support theories.

Clinical case management includes the following 13 activities within four areas of focus (Kanter, 1996):

- initial phase—engagement, assessment, and planning.
- environmental focus—linking with community resources, consulting with families and caregivers, maintaining and expanding social networks, collaboration with physicians and hospitals, and advocacy.

- client focus—intermittent individual psychotherapy, independent living skills development, and client psychoeducation.
- client-environment focus—crisis intervention and monitoring.

Clinical case management may be implemented within several program models. For example, Floersch (2002) differentiates five models of case management supported by federal, state, and private research monies, including psychiatric rehabilitation, broker, assertive case management, recovery, and strengths. Clinical case management can be practiced in all but the broker model.

TASKS AND ACTIVITIES

Harris and Bergman (1988) have summarized the therapeutic tasks of clinical case management practice as follows:

- forging a relationship, or making a positive connection with a client. This may unfold in a variety of ways depending on a particular client's characteristics, and may range from high levels of interaction to the maintenance of interpersonal formality and distance.
- modeling healthy behaviors to facilitate a client's movement from a position of dependency to one of greater self-direction. When this is successful, the client comes to understand that he or she has unique needs, goals, and skills, and that focused actions can influence the course of events.
- altering the client's physical environment through processes of creation, facilitation, and adjustment.

THE WORKER–CLIENT RELATIONSHIP

The literature review by Sexton and Whiston (1994) supports the worker–client relationship as providing a context for positive outcomes in all clinical situations. This alliance consists of a positive emotional bond between the parties, mutual comfort, and a shared understanding of goals and tasks. It develops over time in unpredictable ways from the expectations, beliefs, and knowledge that each person brings to the relationship. These authors found that the quality of the working alliance, represented by a mutual sense of collaboration, is more predictive of positive outcomes in therapy than any other variable.

The clinical case management relationship is the sustaining link between the client with mental illness and the external world. It provides an environment of safety for the client. Within that context, the client can:

- experience structure as an antidote to disorganization,
- appreciate the significance of internal and external limits as a guard against poor impulse control,
- learn that help is available for most problems,
- improve reality testing,
- experience cognitive and experiential learning, and
- enhance self-esteem through success experiences.

In short, the relationship provides a context in which the full range of medical, rehabilitative, educational, social, and spiritual interventions can be effectively implemented.

Walsh (2000b) asserts that the social worker's management of relationship boundaries in clinical case management is a more complex process than in other forms of intervention. Boundaries include the spoken and unspoken rules that case managers and clients observe about the physical and emotional limits of their relationship. Special boundary challenges in clinical case management include:

- the possibility of dual relationships with the client or his or her significant others (for example, serving as a client's payee),
- unwelcome or inappropriate intrusions into the client's home environment,
- unclear assumptions about self-disclosure for both parties,
- the social worker's use of coercion in the relationship, and
- managing issues of reciprocity (including material transactions and also a client's frequent desire to be the social worker's friend).

CLINICAL SKILLS

In addition to relationship-building skills, the clinical skills needed for long-term work with clients having mental illness include the ability to (Harris & Bergman, 1988; Kanter, 1996, 1995):

- make ongoing judgments about the intensity of one's involvement with a client,
- assess and recognize a client's fluctuating competence and changing needs,
- titrate support so as to maximize a client's capacity for self-directed behavior,
- differentiate the biological and psychological aspects of mental illness,
- help family members cope with their troubled relative,
- appreciate the effects of social factors on a client's sense of competence,
- understand how clients both shape and internalize their environments,
- appreciate a client's conscious and unconscious motives for behavior,
- develop a longitudinal view of the client's strengths, limitations, and symptoms.

Many community-based program developers are reluctant to support clinical case management because of concerns that social workers may focus on psychotherapy in lieu of the full range of case management interventions. Neugeboren (1996) suggests that environmentally focused practice (advocacy and monitoring) requires "sociopolitical" skills, in contrast to "socioemotional" skills required for relationship development, assessment, and planning. This perspective underscores the need for ongoing professional development in all areas of clinical case management practice.

OUTCOME RESEARCH

At times, researchers have attempted to compare case management models with regard to effectiveness. It is difficult, however, to isolate particular models because of intervening variables that confound the relationship between program philosophy and actual practices. A recent literature review by Marshall, Gray, Lockwood, and Green (1998) concluded that although the broker model of case management ensures that more people remain in contact with psychiatric services, it does not produce clinically significant improvement in mental state, social functioning, quality of life, or any other clinical or social variables. A meta-analysis of 44 mental health case management programs provided over a 20-year period, however, indicated that both assertive case management and clinical case management were effective with regard to measures of family burden, family service satisfaction, and cost of care (Ziguras & Stuart, 2000). The two approaches were also equally effective in reducing symptoms, increasing client contact with services, reducing dropout rates, improving social functioning, and increasing client satisfaction. Another recent study also found that clients of clinical case managers made comparable gains to those receiving assertive community treatment (Essock et al., 2006). In a 10-year review of a large care program in the united Kingdom, it was observed that the introduction of clinical case management was associated with an increasing focus on clients with the more severe mental disorders (Cornwall, Gorman, Carlisle, & Pope, 2001).

One gap in the research is that individual case manager effects (rather than program effects) on client outcomes have rarely been examined. In one such study of a nationally known community support program, strong support was found for the differential effectiveness of case managers (Ryan, Sherman, & Judd, 1994). Additional research of this type could more clearly evaluate the practice of clinical case management. Single-subject designs would also be useful in this regard.

CONCLUSION

Two national consensus panels, sponsored by the Center for Mental Health Services and the Center for Health Care Strategies, have identified 11 core competencies for the effective treatment of persons with serious mental illnesses, including the clinical tasks of developing a therapeutic relationship, conducting reliable symptom assessment and diagnoses, and integrating psychosocial and psychopharmacological treatments (Liberman, 2005). Among the issues to consider in developing the therapeutic aspects of clinical case management are worker roles, authority, status, training, caseload, and supervision. These may be addressed in the following ways.

- Program developers should acknowledge that case managers provide therapeutic interventions and direct their recruitment and supervision policies accordingly.
- Because they are the focal point of the client's intervention milieu, clinical case managers must be given authority to assume overall case responsibility.
- Administrators must develop career paths for clinical case managers so that turnover based on low status and pay is not so endemic.

- Caseload size should be controlled so that clinical case managers can realistically attend to the needs of their clients. Caseloads of approximately 20 to 30 clients per worker appear to facilitate effective intervention.

Supporting clinical case management will provide another positive consequence for clients—reduced stigmatization. Among the benefits of acknowledging the therapeutic nature of case manager-client relationships is the implied belief that all persons are capable of psychological growth.

WEB SITES

Community Mental Health journal. http://worldcat.org/wcpa/ow/d40b43ec5414d6c9.html.

Information for Practice: news and new scholarship from around the world; includes articles for social workers about a variety of mental health services and interventions, including case management.http://www.nyu.edu/socialwork/ip.

NASW Standards for Social Work Case Management. http://www.socialworkers.org/practice/standards/sw_case_mgmt.asp.

Psychiatric Services. http://worldcat.org/oclc/29993591&referer=brief_results.

U.S. Department of Health and Human Services, Substance Abuse and Mental Health Services Administration, National Mental Health Information Center, Center for Mental Health Services. http://mentalhealth.samhsa.gov.

References

Cornwall, P., Gorman, B., Carlisle, J., & Pope, M. (2001). Ten years in the life of a community mental health team: The impact of the care programme approach in the UK. *Journal of Mental Health, 10*(4), 441–447.

Essock, S. M., Covell, N. H., & Drake, R. E. (2006). Clinical case management, case management, and ACT: Reply. *Psychiatric Services, 57*(4), 579.

Essock, S. M., Mueser, K. T., Drake, R. E., Covell, N. H., McHugo, G. J., Frisman, L. K., et al. (2006). Comparison of ACT and standard case management for delivering integrated treatment for co-occurring disorders. *Psychiatric Services, 57*(2), 185–196.

Floersch, J. (2002). *Meds, money, and manners: The case management of severe mental illness.* New York: Columbia University Press.

Harris, M., & Bergman, H. C. (1988). Clinical case management for the chronically mentally ill: A conceptual analysis. In M. Harris, & L. Bachrach (Eds.), Clinical case management (pp. 5–13). *New Directions for Mental Health Services, 40.* San Francisco: Jossey-Bass.

Kanter, J. (Ed.). (1995). *Clinical issues in case management.* San Francisco: Jossey-Bass.

Kanter, J. (1996). Case management with longterm patients. In S. M. Soreff (Ed.), *Handbook for the treatment of the seriously mentally ill* (pp. 259–275). Seattle, WA: Hogrefe & Huber.

Liberman, R. P. (2005). Drug and psychosocial curricula for psychiatry residents for treatment of schizophrenia: Part II. *Psychiatric Services, 56*(1), 28–30.

Marshall, M., Gray, A., Lockwood, A., & Green, R. (1998). Case management for people with severe mental disorders. *Cochrane Database of Systematic Reviews, 2,* art. no. CD000050 (DOI: 10.1002).

National Association of Social Workers (NASW). (1989). *NASW standards for the practice of clinical social work.* Silver Spring, MD: NASW Press.

Neugeboren, B. (1996). *Environmental practice in the human services.* New York: Haworth.

Ryan, C. S., Sherman, P. S., & Judd, C. M. (1994). Accounting for case manager effects in the evaluation of mental health services. *Journal of Consulting and Clinical Psychology, 62*(5), 965–974.

Sexton, T. L., & Whiston, S. C. (1994). The status of the counseling relationship: An empirical review, theoretical implications, and research directions. *Counseling Psychologist, 22*(1), 6–78.

Surber, R. W. (Ed.) (1994). *Clinical case management: A guide to comprehensive treatment of serious mental illness.* Thousand Oaks, CA: Sage.

Walsh, J. (2000a). *Clinical case management with persons having mental illness: A relationship-based perspective.* Pacific Grove, CA: Wadsworth-Brooks/Cole.

Walsh, J. (2000b). Recognizing and managing boundary issues in case management. *Journal of Case Management, 9*(2), 79–85.

Wong, D. F. K. (2006). *Clinical case management for people with mental illness: A biopsychosocial vulnerability-stress model.* New York: Haworth.

Ziguras, S. J., & Stuart, G. W. (2000). A meta-analysis of the effectiveness of mental health case management over 20 years. *Psychiatric Services, 51*(11), 1410–1421.

111

Case Management Policies and Programs with the Developmentally Disabled

Elizabeth Lightfoot

Social workers are integrally involved in providing services and supports for people with intellectual and developmental disabilities. One of the primary roles of social workers in the lives of people with such disabilities has been as a case manager, often providing case management services or service coordination through a state or county agency, or more recently through independent social service agencies or even as independent contractors. This chapter provides an overview of intellectual and developmental disabilities, the history of social work case management in relation to people with intellectual and developmental disabilities, and a synopsis of case management activities. Furthermore, this chapter discusses some limitations of social work case management practice and some possible future directions of case management with people with intellectual and developmental disabilities.

INTELLECTUAL AND DEVELOPMENTAL DISABILITIES

Intellectual and developmental disabilities are a diverse group of impairments that impact a person's mental and/or physical functioning. In the United States, a developmental disability is federally defined in the Developmental Disabilities Assistance and Bill of Rights Act of 2000 as a severe, chronic disability of an individual 5 years of age or older that is caused by a mental or physical impairment that begins before a person is age 22, and results in substantial limitations in three or more areas of major life activity, including self-care, language, learning, mobility, self-direction, independent living, and economic self-sufficiency, which necessitates ongoing planning and services coordination. People with many types of diagnoses can fall under this definition, including those with cerebral palsy, autism, hearing impairments, visual impairments, learning disabilities, and intellectual disabilities. Intellectual disabilities are one of the most common types of developmental disabilities. they are defined as being "characterized by significant limitations both in intellectual functioning and in adaptive behavior as expressed in conceptual, social, and practical adaptive skills" (American Association on Intellectual and Developmental Disabilities, 2002). The phrase "intellectual disability" is the new favorable term in the United States, most of Europe, and Australia favor "mental retardation," and many of the largest advocacy and professional organizations in the United States are adopting the phrase "intellectual and developmental disabilities" for their agencies as a more respectful term, such as the American Association on Intellectual and Developmental Disabilities (AAIDD; formerly the American Association on Mental Retardation) (AAIDD, 2007).

Currently, about 1.5 percent of the United States population has an intellectual or developmental disability—about 4.5 million people (Department of Health and Human Services, 2005). The number of people with intellectual or developmental disabilities increased over the twentieth century, as the life expectancy of people with most types of developmental disabilities has increased. In the early twentieth century, virtually no one with intellectual or developmental disabilities lived until age 60. There are now about 650,000 people with developmental disabilities over age 60 in the United States, and this number is expected to double by 2030 to approximately 1.2 million (Heller, Janicki, Hammel, & Factor, 2002). This growing population of people with developmental disabilities, especially older people, will need more supports in accessing services and supports (Lightfoot, 2006).

In the early to mid-twentieth century, people with intellectual and developmental disabilities in the United States were routinely institutionalized, often living in large institutions from birth until death. In these institutions, most people had little access to health care, education, or social activities and had no opportunities to make choices or decisions about any aspect of their lives. In the mid-twentieth century, when disability advocates began condemning the deplorable conditions of these institutions, they began closing in favor of community integration for people with disabilities. People with intellectual and developmental disabilities began living in community settings, receiving support to help with work, school, social activities, and other activities of daily living.

CASE MANAGEMENT AND PEOPLE WITH INTELLECTUAL AND DEVELOPMENTAL DISABILITIES

A new model of community-based services for people with intellectual and developmental disabilities emerged, with social workers playing a key role. People with intellectual and developmental disabilities would no longer be receiving services from one large agency—the institution—and instead would receive services from a variety of systems, such as the education system, the housing system, the health care system, and the vocational rehabilitation system. The concept of case management, originally developed as a social service model for the antipoverty programs in 1960s (Spitalnik, 2000), was adopted in the field of intellectual and developmental disabilities in the 1970s for managing the variety of services that people would access for receiving supports. The Developmental Disabilities Assistance and Bill of Rights Act of 1978 formalized this service model by including it as part of the definition of developmental disabilities, stating that a person fits the definition of developmental disability if he or she needs "special interdisciplinary or generic care, treatment or other services" that are "individually planned and coordinated."

Since case management in this population began in the 1970s, social workers were the professionals charged with providing these case management services. The general social work case management functions of assessment, planning, service linkage, and brokering as described by the National Association of Social Workers in 1980 were the same tasks that social work case managers did when working with people with disabilities (Spitalnik, 2000). Social work case management for people with intellectual and developmental disabilities quickly became a standard service coordination position in most public social service agencies and became a common social work role within state and county government or a service contracted by the government with a private provider agency. The hope for social work case management was that managers would be able to assess the needs of people with intellectual and developmental disabilities appropriately and link them with suitable services, thus facilitating community-based living. However, some have argued that the practice of case management has become standard because the social support system that has emerged is so fragmented that it is impossible to receive services without this service (Soafer, Kreling, & Carmel, 2000).

Whereas case management for people with intellectual and developmental disabilities is generally similar to case management for other groups, there are some unique considerations. First, people with intellectual and developmental disabilities have varying levels of communication skills. Skilled case managers learn how to ascertain the needs and desires of people with these disabilities regardless of their cognitive or communication abilities, but there is always the danger that clients will not be consulted in the management of their own services. Second, the majority of people with developmental disabilities have family and/ or friends that are concerned about whether they are receiving appropriate services. Case management thus involves identifying and including such significant persons in the planning for services, while at the same time being careful not to let the wishes of the family override those of the individual. One model popular for including broader participation in arranging services for people with intellectual and developmental disabilities is person-

centered planning (Abery & McBride, 1998). Third, case management with children and adults with intellectual and developmental disabilities often involves lifelong planning. Most adults with intellectual and developmental disabilities live with relatives (Braddock, 1999), and there is a grave concern by many relatives about the future of their adult children when they are no longer able to care for them. Thus, social work case management with people with intellectual and developmental disabilities necessitates a focus on lifelong planning. Finally, although social work case management with people with intellectual and developmental disabilities necessitates a broad knowledge of supports specific to disability services, it also requires a knowledge of generic community-based supports. As best practices for supporting persons with developmental disabilities are to provide services in community settings, case management involves coordinating a combination of disability and generic supports and services. Although social work case management is still a standard service for people with developmental disabilities, it has changed over the past several decades in relation to new policy developments.

Medicaid Waivers and Case Management

The advent of the Medicaid waiver programs further solidified the role of case management within the lives of people with developmental disabilities, but also inextricably changed case management. The Medicaid Home and Community Based Waiver, which originally passed in 1981, 10 years after the Medicaid program was first approved, authorized states to use Medicaid funds to pay for home and community-based services for older people or those with disabilities who would have otherwise received services in an institution (Duckett & Guy, 2000). These waiver funds could be used to pay for supports that help people live in community-based settings. One of the supports funded by the Medicaid waiver is case management services, so waiver funds are now used to pay for social work case management as a direct service. As the various Medicaid waiver programs are now the number one source of funding for community living for people with disabilities, with roughly 1.4 people with disabilities using one of the Medicaid waivers to support their living in community settings (Harrington & Kitchener, 2003), case management is now entrenched in service provision to people with disabilities.

Consumer-Directed Services and Case Management

In the fields of disabilities and aging, there has been growth in consumer-controlled and consumer-directed services over the past several decades, which has greatly impacted the nature of case management services. The concept of consumer-directed services comes directly from the independent living movement of the United States (Doty, 2000), which arose in part as a reaction to the dependency role that people with disabilities had to assume to receive services and supports. The concept of a professional social worker being in charge of assessing and determining services goes against the concept of independence and consumer choice, which are the backbones of the United States disability movement. Consumer-directed services are an alternative to services that are determined by a professional or an agency, which often are based on the needs of the agency, rather than the individual (Benjamin, 2001). Under a consumer-directed model of service delivery, the consumer of services (often known as the client in social work case management) has more control over what types of services are provided, who the service providers are, and when the services are provided. They may even be able to hire a family member to provide personal care services, rather than receive services from a paraprofessional working for an agency.

There are many variations of consumer-directed models in the United States and Europe, ranging in how much control the consumer has in managing their own services, and the types of services that can be purchased. In some programs, consumers are able to control their own services, under the guidance of a case manager who determines eligibility. These types of consumer-directed programs are now available in many states under the Medicaid waiver or other state programs (Benjamin, 2001). There are other consumer-directed models currently being tested in which the consumers are given a budget, and they are able to purchase the services that they determine are needed (Mahoney, Simone, & Simon-Rusinowitz, 2000). Under this model, case management can be a service that is purchased, but people may opt to manage their own services without a professional case manager. Under consumer-directed services, case management also is not necessarily provided by a public agency, and case management services can be purchased from a provider agency or even an independent contractor. As the state Medicaid programs have expanded the consumer-directed options, the nature

of case management is changing in working with people with intellectual and developmental disabilities, and it is sometimes viewed more as a direct service than an administrative function.

LIMITATIONS OF CASE MANAGEMENT

Many professionals, advocates, and consumers involved in the developmental disabilities field have been dissatisfied with case management services for a variety of reasons. Most of the concerns relate to systems issues, rather than the individual social workers, who are often very committed to providing excellent services. Whereas the concept of case management originally arose as a solution to complex and disjointed services, there are some inherent contradictions to case management that have led to some disenchantment by both social workers and consumers. As the disability service system has grown, it has become vastly complex. There are now many more people in need of services then funds to provide such services. Thus, most case managers have extremely high case loads and are unable to use their social work practice skills in serving these individuals, much less have contact with people on their caseload the required number of times. Social work case managers often are unable to do comprehensive assessments, be involved in individual advocacy on behalf of people they serve, or support individuals with disabilities in advocating for themselves. Furthermore, as the system has grown, it has also grown increasingly inflexible. A social work case manager often has to worry about "filling open slots" in a program, rather than finding a program that would best serve the individual needs of a person. Case managers are frequently not in a position to be involved in systems advocacy because of their role within the agency and the high demands on their time.

The social work case manager is thus placed in a position in which they have two competing demands—helping people with disabilities receive the most appropriate supports and services so that they can be fully included in the community, while at the same time serving a gatekeeping function to preserve the limited resources of the system. Indeed, these two competing tasks are described in the NASW's current Standards for Social Work Case Management (NASW, 1992). Yet in the disability system, many believe that the needs of the large, inflexible, underfunded system has tipped case management toward working for systems preservation before the needs of people with disabilities (AAIDD & ARC, 2002). Because of limited budgets and long waiting lists, case management has often become synonymous with gatekeeping in the disability advocacy movement, with the ultimate administrative function of rationing services. Thus, case management has acquired a negative connotation by many of the consumers of these services. The advent of more widespread consumer-directed services, in which case management becomes more of a service broker rather than an agency gatekeeper role, may help alleviate this underlying tension.

Some people within the disability advocacy movement have had some other concerns with the case management service system for philosophical or social justice reasons. Many have reacted negatively to the medical model paradigm that underlies the case management model. Using the word *case* to refer to an individual comes directly from the medical profession, and many professionals use *case* as shorthand to refer to people on their case loads. Indeed, social work case managers do often refer to people as "cases" rather than people. Thus, it is not uncommon for people within the disability movement to have T-shirts or buttons that read "I'm not a case and I don't want to be managed." Though the terminology surrounding case management may seem benign to professionals, it can be powerful to people receiving services who may reject the notion of needing a professional to manage their lives, reject the notion that they need to adopt a dependent role to receive services, and object to the language used to describe the coordination of their services.

FUTURE OF SOCIAL WORK CASE MANAGEMENT WITH PEOPLE WITH INTELLECTUAL AND DEVELOPMENTAL DISABILITIES

Though social work case management has played a pivotal role in services for people with intellectual and developmental disabilities for the past quarter of a century, the nature of case management will likely shift in the upcoming years. With the rise of consumer-directed options, case management may become viewed again as a direct service, rather than an agency gatekeeping role. Furthermore, the two major intellectual and developmental disabilities organizations in the United States, the ARC and the AAIDD, are now using the phrase "service coordination" to refer to what was historically social work case management housed within

state or local government. Service coordination is considered a more respectful and accurate term for the tasks that have been performed by social work case managers. In a joint position statement, the AAIDD and the ARC (2002) have outlined six major tasks of service coordinators, which they envision as independent coordinators of services. They assert that service coordinators must (1) follow the needs of individuals when designing, coordinating, and monitoring supports and services; (2) develop formal supports based on the needs of an individual, rather than choosing a service because of availability, and develop informal, natural supports for people; (3) represent and advocate for the interests of the individual and family; (4) help individuals and families coordinate their own services if they desire; (5) be unaffiliated with service providers or government agencies; and 6) provide information on service gaps to enable the system to become more responsive (AAIDD & the ARC, 2002). They believe that these service coordinators should be fully funded and have a manageable number of people whose services they coordinate and ideally work independently from organizations that either provide services or fund services. The service coordinators that the ARC and the AAIDD envision are more similar to professional social work case managers, perhaps as envisioned in the 1970s, than to gatekeepers. Though the Medicaid waiver program has allowed for the development of some independent service coordinators similar to this model, the current state and county case management system has a long way to go before it resembles this service coordination model for most people.

In the meantime, it is important that social work case managers follow the needs and desires of individuals with disabilities as much as possible when working with these clients, which would necessitate excellent skills in communicating with people with disabilities, a willingness to conduct individual- and systems-level advocacy, a familiarity with disability history and philosophy, knowledge of both generic and disability specific resources, and a commitment to consumer choice. Unfortunately, most schools of social work include limited content on people with intellectual and developmental disabilities within their curriculum (DePoy & Miller, 1996), and thus few social workers have training in working with people with disabilities or knowledge of the disability movement when initially entering these case management positions. The more the field of social work can connect with the disability field and the disability advocacy movement, the better able social work case managers are to navigate their difficult position of coordinating services for people with disabilities within a limited resource environment.

WEB SITES

Administration on Developmental Disabilities, Department of Health and Human Services. The federal agency that oversees the Developmental Disabilities Assistance and Bill of Rights Act of 2000. http://www.acf.hhs.gov/programs/add.

American Association on Intellectual and Developmental Disabilities. The largest organization for professionals serving people with intellectual and developmental disabilities, this organization also publishes two major journals on intellectual and developmental disabilities and convenes a large annual conference. http://www.aaidd.org.

The ARC, formerly the Association for Retarded Citizens, is the nation's largest community-based agency of and for people with intellectual and developmental disabilities. http://www.thearc.org.

References

Abery, B., & McBride, M. (1998). Look and understand before you leap. *Impact, 11,* 2–3.

American Association on Intellectual and Developmental Disabilities. (2002). Definition of mental retardation. Retrieved December 17, 2007, from http://www.aaidd.org/Policies/faq_mental_retardation.shtml.

American Association on Intellectual and Developmental Disabilities. (2007). Results of the name change. Retrieved December 17, 2007, from http://www.aaidd.org/About_AAMR/name.shtml.

American Association on Intellectual and Developmental Disabilities & the ARC. (2002). AAIDD/ARC position statement: Service coordination. Retrieved December 17, 2007, from http://www.aaidd.org/Policies/pos_service.shtml.

Benjamin, A. E. (2001). Consumer-directed services at home: A new model for persons with disabilities. *Health Affairs, 20*(6), 80–95.

Braddock, D. (1999). Aging and developmental disabilities: Demographic and policy issues affecting American families. *Mental Retardation, 37*(2), 155–161.

Depoy, E., & Miller, M. (1996). Preparation of social workers for serving individuals with developmental disabilities: A brief report. *Mental Retardation, 34*(1), 54–57.

Department of Health and Human Services. (2005). Administration on Developmental Disabilities fact sheet. Retrieved December 17, 2007, from http://www.acf.hhs.gov/programs/add/Factsheet.html.

Doty, P. (2000). The federal role in the move toward consumer direction. *Generations (Fall),* 22–27.

Duckett, M., & Guy, M. (2000). Home and community-based services waivers. *Health Care Financing Review, 63,* 123–125.

Harrington, C., & Kitchener, M. (2003). *Medicaid long-term care: Changes, innovations, and cost containment.* San Francisco: University of California, San Francisco. Retrieved February 17, 2006, from http://www.ncsl.org/programs/health/harrington/sld001.htm.

Heller, T., Janicki, M., Hammel, J., & Factor, A. (2002). *Promoting healthy aging, family support and age-friendly communities for persons aging with developmental disabilities:* Report of the 2001 Invitational Research Symposium on Aging with Developmental Disabilities. Chicago: Rehabilitation Research and Training Center on Aging with Developmental Disabilities, Department of Disability and Human Development, University of Illinois at Chicago.

Lightfoot, E. (2006). Social work practice with older adults with developmental disabilities. In B. Berkman & S. D'Ambruoso (Eds.), *Oxford handbook of social work in aging.* New York: Oxford University Press.

Mahoney, M., Simone, K., & Simon-Rusinowitz, L. (2000). Early lessons from the cash and counseling demonstration and evaluation. *Demonstration and Evaluation, 23*(3), 41–46.

National Association of Social Workers. (1992). NASW standards for social work case management. Retrieved December 17, 2007, from http://www.socialworkers.org/practice/standards/sw_case_mgmt.asp.

Soafer, S., Kreling, B., & Carmel, M. (2000). *Coordination of care for persons with disabilities enrolled in Medicaid managed care: A conceptual framework to guide the development of measures.* Washington, DC: U.S. Department of Health and Human Services.

Spitalnik, D. (2000) Training case managers: Moving to a support approach. *IMPACT: Feature Issue on Support Coordination and Self-Determination for Persons with Developmental Disabilities, 12*(4).

Case Management and Child Welfare

Jannah H. Mather & Grafton H. Hull Jr.

Case management, a process by which complex situations are managed by social workers, plays a major role in child welfare services today. Glissen and Green estimate that "some 3 million children receive child welfare and juvenile justice case management each year" (2006a, p. 488). In the field of social work, case management has grown from a vague definition regarding the organization of services for clients to the development of different models of practice incorporating specific theories, skills, and values. These elements are in turn dependent on the situation or field of practice in which social workers find themselves

Rothman (1992) notes that case management in the child welfare service area began as a response to increased disorganization of families, growing numbers of divorces, and mounting abuse situations. These conditions created an environment in which children and families were in need of increased aid, and few programs could organize their services around these growing numbers. Case management was designed to counter "long-term problematic client conditions, and a community service system that was uncoordinated, ever shifting, and increasingly restrictive" (Rothman, 1992, p. 3). The consequences of these conditions produced a new service concept, one that Rothman says had two central functions: (1) providing individualized counseling services, and (2) linking clients to services and supports in both the formal and informal contexts of the client's life.

In many ways, case management as just defined offered a generalized approach to intervening with clients in child welfare situations. In this definition, the child welfare case manager was expected to work with both the individual and relevant environmental conditions. The belief that case management could produce different results by structuring these processes in a standardized manner had considerable impact on child welfare programs. Child welfare workers could relate intimately with the concept of poorly operating community service systems as described by Rothman (1992). However, the question in case management that was most important to child welfare workers was, "How effective are case management models for chronic and complex client systems?" The evidence to date has been mixed. On the one hand, Burns, Phillips, and Wagner (2004) found that case managers frequently failed to recognize serious mental health needs of the children they served. Too often, children ended up in out-of-home placements that might have been prevented had case managers adequately screened children for mental health concerns. On the other hand, Glissen and Green (2006a) studied the experience of over 1200 children needing specialized case management services. Their findings suggest that when the mental health needs of children are carefully assessed by their case managers and those services are provided, a substantial reduction in out-of-home placements occurs. Another study by the same authors noted that the organizational culture in which the case managers practiced had a major impact on how well these individuals performed their jobs (Glissen & Green, 2006b). Blair and Taylor (2006) found that case management services were crucial to and wanted by kinship caregivers of children placed outside the home. Johnson and Wagner (2005) found that providing case managers with a structured decision-making tool significantly increased reunification and permanency planning of children in Michigan's foster care system.

Child welfare workers see case management as a strong response to the horrendous issues surrounding foster care. As an essential component of permanency planning, case managers perform tasks and functions involved in negotiating and coordinating services, referring clients to agencies, using community services, managing visitations, and assisting families and children with the development of support services (Pecora, Whittaker, Maluccio, & Plotnick, 1992). As part of permanency planning, as well as other specific areas of service for families and children, case management is an integral component of child welfare practice. Specialized models of case management in child welfare have developed primarily as a response to multiproblematic families who were using many different, uncoordinated services, accompanied by a lack of follow-up regarding service outcomes. The focus of these initial models produced a planned method for following a family and child through the maze of services offered and accounting for the resources used. As the role of case management has become more important in child welfare, it has highlighted the need for a knowledge and skill base that reflected the specialized components of child welfare.

KNOWLEDGE AND SKILLS NEEDED IN CHILD WELFARE CASE MANAGEMENT

To produce models of case management practice appropriate to child welfare, delineation of a knowledge and skill base related to child welfare has been offered by several different authors (Mather, Lager, & Harris, 2007; Sallee & LeVine, 1999). The following areas have been seen as consistently relevant.

1. *Human development.* Knowledge of children, adults, families, agencies, and institutions. An ability to understand and apply interviewing skills, data collection assessment, planning, intervention, referral, evaluation, termination, and recording. Knowledge of and competence to work with culturally diverse children and families through a value system that is open and reflective.
2. *Child welfare practice.* Basic knowledge of the mission of child welfare services and child welfare policies and practices. Understanding of outcome data regarding the application of agency, state, and federal policies on families and children.
3. *Agency functioning.* Knowledge of administrative and structural issues affecting the operation of the child welfare agency and the employees who work within that agency. Understanding how agency functioning affects the family and child and the infrastructure needed to create change.
4. *Interdisciplinary understanding and collaboration with professionals from multiple disciplines.* Understanding and recognition of the importance of multiple disciplines in the delivery of services.

Knowledge of how to access services from a diversity of disciplines to ensure positive case outcomes. Knowledge of medical and mental health issues, educational aspects, and judicial rules and laws. The understanding of how to integrate multiple disciplines into the case management process for the child and family.
5. *Holistic practice perspective.* Recognizing that the services for the client must be addressed through a holistic view of the person or family. This perspective takes into account the health, mental health, educational, and spiritual aspects of the person within the environment. Much of the knowledge and skill needed in case management is incorporated into the basic education of all social workers. These include social work roles, purposes, values, and ethics. Mather et al. (2007) note that case managers in child welfare must:

- engage all systems and individuals to be involved in a mutual and positive manner,
- establish quickly the roles of the differing systems within case management,
- work together toward a mutual treatment plan,
- contract for responsibilities in the process and case,
- meet on a regular basis to review goals and outcomes,
- agree with all systems involved on time for termination, and
- always evaluate the case management process as well as the outcome.

Vourlekis and Greene (1992) added to the knowledge base in case management and produced a definition of processes for the social worker. They noted the following characteristics:

- a trusting and enabling worker–client relationship,
- a focus of understanding the person in the environment,
- provision of a continuum of care to clients with complex multiple problems,
- intervening to ameliorate the emotional problems causing a loss of function,
- using the skills of brokering and advocacy in service delivery,
- targeting clients who require a range of community-based and long-term services,
- providing services in the least restrictive environment,

- using assessment of the client's functioning capacity and support network, and
- affirming the social work values of self-determination, dignity, and mutual responsibility.

Though these perspectives provide an understanding of the knowledge and skill base, as well as the processes that a child welfare worker must employ to do good case management practice, the issue of the underlying goals of system management of the case cannot be overlooked.

DIVERGENT PARADIGMS

Different underlying goals in case management appear to be related to the field of practice in which it is used (child welfare, disabilities, aging, etc.). The knowledge (or lack thereof) of these goals often drives the outcome of the case management model. These goals can be part of one or both of two demanding paradigms from which case management developed. Moxley (1996) notes that case management can be either "systems-driven" or "consumer-driven" (pp. 15–20). *Systems-driven case management* is in direct response to the call for efficiency and accountability in social welfare practice, whereas *consumer-driven case management* focuses on providing the best organized practice for clients in complex and chronic situations. From these different paradigms come a variety of case management models that resemble one another in small ways but can never really be conceptualized in a broader, more standardized perspective of practice.

The relationship of this discussion to child welfare becomes important when the emphasis in case management models is not based on both underlying paradigms but rather on one or the other. In the public child welfare system, a focus that looks only at efficiency and accountability is not necessarily helpful to the family and child, whereas a model of case management that focuses only on client needs ignores the realities of the system and will not survive within this setting. The differences in these underlying goals can be seen in the identification of steps applied in case management. Steps in case management, such as (1) problem identification, (2) formulation of goals and objectives, (3) contracting an agreement, (4) implementation and monitoring, and (5) case closure, reflect more of a systems-driven approach to case management. Steps such as (1) outreach, referral, client identification, and engagement; (2) a bio-

psychosocial assessment of the client; (3) the development of a service plan; (4) implementation of the service plan; (5) coordination and monitoring of service delivery; and (6) advocacy on behalf of the family and child denote more of a consumer-driven base of practice. Although neither of these definitions of a model of case management practice appears to be based on specific underlying paradigms, the terminology can be seen as very reflective of the major focus that developed them. In child welfare, the lack of a specific model of practice that incorporates both paradigms will not provide the best services needed, nor will it reflect the best model of practice for case management.

NEW MODELS OF CHILD WELFARE CASE MANAGEMENT

The following three models of case management practice provide examples of how a solid knowledge and skill base along with a focus on both system-driven and consumer-driven paradigms can produce effective models.

Community-Based Case Management

Community-based case management is a model of practice that has proven effective within the child welfare setting when the issues being addressed involve many different community systems and agencies. For example, Cohon and Cooper (1999) describe a community-based case management program called KSN (kinship support network), that focuses on supportive services for kinship caregivers. The primary principle behind community-based case management is the involvement of all community partners in the client's well-being. In the KSN, caregivers are provided more supportive services than is the case when the caregiver and case manager work alone. The increase in services occurs through the involvement of the entire community.

Community models were first identified during the early 1970s as part of a reform supported by the National Institute of Mental Health for the support of persons with severe mental illness living in the community. This model was later expanded to be more inclusive of other populations in need. The community model has always included case management, but more clearly began to be defined as a model of its own when case management began to establish its own practices and designs.

There is general agreement among authors and practitioners that the responsibilities of case management in the community model include the assessment of client needs, referral to services, assurance by case managers that clients have access to services, service coordination analysis of whether these services are meeting client goals, and the continuing provision and accountability of the services within the community.

Strength-Based Case Management

Strength-based case management (East, 1999) is another model that provides a perspective of both the system and consumer-driven paradigms. In strengths-based case management the underlying premise for child welfare workers is that the family and child have the skills and talents to make changes in their lives. This model provides an opportunity for families to focus on their strengths rather than their deficits. A project focused on providing services to grandparents raising their grandchildren found that when case management services focused on the grandparents' strengths and natural skills, the services were more readily utilized and fostered a sense of independence and self-assurance.

Strengths-based case management is strongly linked to the strength-based or empowering approach of social work practice. In this model, clients or client systems are empowered to make changes in their own lives through their own goals and decisions. In this model of case management control of the situation is placed in the client's hands. A study by Coffey (1999) found that in those case management situations where mental health clients had more control over their situation, both treatment participation and satisfaction with services increased. Huebner, Jones, Miller, Customer, and Critchfield (2006) found similar positive outcomes when this model was used. While many child welfare clients have little control over their involvement with services, the greater opportunity for choice given to them, the more likely they will involve themselves in services and have positive outcomes.

Integrated Case Management

Integrated case management involves the participation of differing professions in providing services to a client through the organization of those services around the client's needs, rather than those

of professionals. Cigno and Gore (1999) provide an example of an integrated case management approach in their study of a multiagency children's center. This center provided the opportunity for each family and child to receive services from different agencies and professions within the same facility. The results of the study indicate that clients who aid in the management of their own services, work closely with different agencies and professionals, and have a more holistic approach given to their case feel more positive about the results.

Hubberstey (2001, p. 96) found similar outcomes looking at integrated case management services in her study of the Canadian child welfare system. She concludes:

- "When the focus is on the well-being of the child, parents can learn to set aside their own disagreements with each other or with their "worker" in order to achieve something positive for their child(ren);
- Clients appreciate the more holistic approach that emphasizes their strengths and capacities, not just their problems and deficits;
- By working together, parents and practitioners can develop more appreciation for what each other has to offer and for each others' roles;
- Through their ongoing participation, parents acquire new skills, such as problem-solving, anger management and priority setting, that they can apply to other areas of their lives;
- When everyone has a written copy of the service/care plan, there is a greater likelihood of successful implementation of the service/care plan;
- Allocation of resources is more realistic and better suited to client needs."

In a related study, Christensen and Todahl (1999) found case management used by different disciplines in "relapse prevention" for multiple cyclical reluctant clients. The study identified how case management and planning could be used by a group of different professionals to target specific behaviors and reduce relapse for individual clients. In child welfare services, case management provides a model of care for not only the child and family but also for different professionals who work in the service continuum.

RECOMMENDATIONS

The material that has been developed related to case management suggests that the model must be chosen for its specificity to the situation, the population, the goals of the service, and the practice-based evidence that it can produce both effective processes and outcomes. In child welfare services, a model must be definitive as to its knowledge and skill base. Beyond this, it then becomes important to study and understand which models are most effective and with which populations. The three models presented herein all have merits for child welfare practice and yet appear to have decided differences according to their focus. As the evidence base for case management services with different populations increases, it will be possible to identify those practice approaches showing the greatest promise. Social workers will increasingly consult resources (such as the Campbell Collaborative) to identify effective interventions with specific client populations.. This will be critical to social workers committed to interventions most likely to produce positive outcomes. At the same time, there will be increased attention to models and applications drawn from international research as we learn that our similarities outweigh our differences.

WEB SITES

American Case Management Association. http://www.acmaweb.org.

Campbell Collaborative. http://www.campbell-collaboration.org/SWCG/titles.asp.

Child Welfare League of America. http://www.cwla.org.

NASW Standards for Case Management. http://www.socialworkers.org/practice/standards/sw_case_mgmt.asp#intro.

References

Blair, K. D., & Taylor, E. B. (2006). Examining the lives and needs of child-only recipient kinship caregivers: Heroes stepping up to help children. *Journal of Family Social Work, 10*(1), 1–24.

Burns, B. J., Phillips, S. D., & Wagner, H. R. (2004). Mental health needs and access to mental health services by youths involved with child welfare: A national survey. *Journal of the American Academy of Child and Adolescent Psychiatry, 43*, 960–970.

Christensen, D. N., & Todahl, J. L. (1999). Solution-based casework: Case planning to reduce risk. *Journal of Family Social Work, 3*(4), 3–24.

Cigno, K., & Gore, J. (1999). A seamless service: Meeting the needs of children with disabilities through a multi-agency approach. *Child and Family Social Work, 4*, 325–335.

Coffey, D. S. (1999). *The exploration of affiliation and control in the client-case manager relationship in intensive case management.* PhD diss., Bryn Mawr College.

Cohon, J. D., & Cooper, B. A. (1999). Kinship support network: Edgewood's program model and client characteristics. *Children and Youth Services Review, 21*(4), 311–333.

East, J. F. (1999). Hidden barriers to success for women in welfare reform. *Families in Society, 80*(3), 295–304.

Glissen, C., & Green, P. (2006a). The role of speciality mental health care in predicting child welfare and juvenile justice out-of-home placements. *Research on Social Work Practice, 16*(5), 480–490.

Glissen, C., & Green, P. (2006b). The effects of organizational culture and climate on the access to mental health care in child welfare and juvenile justice systems. *Administration and Policy in Mental Health, 33*(4), 433–448.

Hubberstey, C. (2001). Client involvement as a key element of integrated case management. *Child and Youth Care Forum, 30*(2), 83–97.

Huebner, R. A., Jones, B. L., Miller, V. P., Customer, M., & Critchfield, B. (2006). Comprehensive family services and customer satisfaction outcomes. *Child Welfare, 85*(4), 691–714.

Johnson, K., & Wagner, D. (2005). Evaluation of Michigan's foster care case management system. *Research on Social Work Practice, 15*(5), 372–380.

Mather, J. H., Lager, P. B., & Harris, N. (2007). *Child welfare.* Pacific Grove, CA: Brooks/Cole.

Moxley, D. P. (1996). *Case management by design: Reflections on principles and practices.* Chicago: Nelson-Hall.

Pecora, P., Whittaker, J., Maluccio, A., Barth, R., & Plotnick, R. (1992). *The child welfare challenge: Policy, practice and research.* New York: Walter de Gruyter.

Rothman, J. (1992). *Guidelines for case management.* Itasca, IL: Peacock.

Sallee, A. L., & LeVine, E. S. (1999). *Child welfare: Clinical theory and practice.* Dubuque, IA: Eddie Bowers.

Vourlekis, B. S., & Greene, R. R. (1992). *Social work case management.* New York: A. de Gruyter.

Case Management in Psychosocial Rehabilitation

David P. Moxley

Although case management emerged in human services as a generalist approach to serving people experiencing a multiplicity of needs and life issues, its diffusion was shaped by the search for service continuity across multiple fields of practice. Originally, case management was seen as a means to rectify systems-level problems, such as service integration, plaguing community-based and institutional forms of human service. Brokering forms of case management, for example, sought the creation of bundles or packages of services for consumers whose needs influenced by medical, physical, and psychosocial issues and characterized by complexity and long duration required different types of care and support. Brokering, coordination, and other systems approaches to case management proved to be limited because they often were too general in their focus, failed to specify appropriate recipient populations or intended beneficiaries in rigorous ways, did not specify strategy and methods, and failed to align organizational resources with the role requirements that case management demanded.

Insight into case management effectiveness, largely derived from systematic evaluation of various approaches, indicated that good case management incorporated a specific purpose and set of goals, made explicit the target population that could benefit, and specified relevant methods based on its purpose and the issues potential recipients faced in their daily lives. In addition, good case management aligns requisite resources case managers need to effect meaningful changes in the lives of recipients with purpose and aims of service.

DISTINCTIVENESS OF CASE MANAGEMENT IN PSYCHOSOCIAL REHABILITATION

Case management in psychosocial rehabilitation recognizes the importance of such context and input factors consonant with good service delivery. The distinctiveness of case management is found in the consumer-centered nature of the field of psychosocial rehabilitation in which the management of illness has yielded increasingly to the facilitation of recovery. The concept of recovery envisions recipients becoming more engaged in the achievement of outcomes that bring them life satisfaction while learning to actively manage the psychological, behavioral, physical, and social consequences of psychiatric disability (Anthony, Cohen, Farkas, & Gagne, 2002). Good case management in psychosocial rehabilitation recognizes how psychiatric disability creates numerous barriers to effective functioning, and it also recognizes that recipients likely value life outcomes common to all human beings, including good health, employment, education, reliable and adequate income, and decent housing.

The focus of case management in psychosocial rehabilitation on the fulfillment of such common human needs infuses this approach with practicality combined with recognition of how serious mental illness can frustrate recipients' pursuit and realization of these aims. Case management in psychosocial rehabilitation emphasizes the (1) fulfillment of positive human needs (the psychosocial aspect) manifested in helping people plan actively for a lifestyle and situation they find satisfying, and (2) modification of environments, particularly barriers that frustrate the pursuit and realization of life satisfaction (the rehabilitative aspect; Anthony et al., 2002). Consumer-centeredness is salient when case managers help recipients identify and frame a central outcome with the realization of what they will find satisfying. The ensuing process of planning helps recipients understand their own process of recovery, identify barriers to the achievement of the outcomes they value, and plan to overcome barriers through personal and environmental change. Joining these two aspects within case management literally integrates the psycho-social and the rehabilitative. Such joining moves case management in psychosocial rehabilitation away from an exclusive preoccupation with illness and functioning to incorporate human aspirations and positive psychology as important advanced organizers of practice.

PRECURSORS

The evolution of case management in psychiatric rehabilitation parallels the growth and development of case management in the broader field of human services. One form of case management emerged within the community mental health movement as a means of integrating a range of center-based services, but this approach placed more emphasis on getting people services rather than achieving outcomes that recipients found practical and desirable, including a decent standard of living and a good quality of life. Although coordination of services was seen as important within this approach, management of medication and symptoms of those individuals labeled as seriously mentally ill was a central aspect that makes this approach within the community mental health movement an extension of community psychiatric care.

The failure of the community mental health movement to fully address the demands of deinstitutionalization in the 1970s and the needs of those individuals coping with the most serious and complex forms of psychiatric disability ushered in another form of case management. Influenced by the service integration movement of the 1970s and early 1980s, case management was seen as a way of achieving within local service systems single points of entry, unified needs assessments, and unified client pathways—tactics thought useful in the facilitation of the movement of people through complex community-based systems of care. This form of case management, characteristic of community support systems for people with serious mental illness, sought the integration of medical, social, psychosocial, and behavioral domains. Unlike the community mental health model, this approach extended its reach beyond services offered by various human service agencies to incorporate resources embedded informally in social and community networks charging case management with the challenging responsibility of incorporating all forms of community support into assessment, planning, and action. The National

Institute of Mental Health Community Support Model (NIMH, 1980) gave case management a central and expansive role in systems of care without augmenting professional standing of case managers, the resources they had available to serve a population facing a broad spectrum of serious issues and unmet needs, or the infrastructure to service individuals adequately. The intent of case management within community support systems was to extend practical assistance into the daily lives of people experiencing deinstitutionalization through outreach, home-based services, and the provision of community-based follow-along services. Integration was seen as a principal virtue of this kind of case management, manifesting unification of direct assistance, resources to support daily living, skill development opportunities, and social support.

However, the management of the actual illness and related disability found in symptoms and deficits in self-care served as principal aim: case management sought to respond to the immediate community living needs of people and combat recidivism particularly the revolving-door syndrome in which recipients oscillated between periodic short-term hospital stays and residence in community situations. Nonetheless, as a result of the community support model, case management today is an essential component of local systems that now integrate medical care, social services, mutual support among consumers, rights protection and advocacy, rehabilitation, housing, and employment support.

As deinstitutionalization progressed in the ensuing decade of the 1980s, other forms of case management took root including team-based approaches found in assertive community treatment. An increasing number of state and local service systems adopted this approach, which emerged in the 1970s as a significant innovation in care, and clinical case management, a form of practice that reasserted the importance of a diagnostic perspective, psychotherapeutic interactions, and clinical management in service planning and delivery omitted from community-based forms of case management.

With all of these variants of case management, practitioners tended to view recipients as impaired individuals who needed to accept the limitations their illnesses created. While case managers encouraged the involvement of recipients in joint planning of services and supports, the principal focus of care was on recipient self-acceptance of illness and management of both the primary aspects of the illness and their psychological, behavioral, and medical consequences, placing case management within a paradigm in which medical response was dominant. Case management reflects this paradigm when it focuses mainly on medication and symptom management or relief, a form of service that persists today. The variant of case management found in assertive community treatment offers intensive hands-on services to foster successful community living among people who would otherwise engage in high levels of utilization of potentially expensive care whether inpatient, restrictive, or crisis-oriented. Still within such a variant team-based management of the trajectory and consequences of the illness prioritizes medical aspects of psychiatric disability.

CASE MANAGEMENT IN PSYCHOSOCIAL REHABILITATION

Case management in psychosocial rehabilitation legitimates the medical trajectory and consequences of serious mental illness, but this kind of management seeks to identify, organize, and implement broad-based supports that address and fulfill not only people's immediate and concrete needs for community living but also their needs for growth and development, imbuing it with the qualities of positive psychology, including humanization, hope, and optimism. Case management in psychosocial rehabilitation sought to offset the frequent dehumanization of people coping with psychiatric disabilities. Conversely, it sought to humanize the rehabilitation experience by forming strong partnerships between service providers and recipients, collaborating to advance the quality of life of people coping with the causes and consequences of psychiatric disability. Discerning the strengths of individuals, both internal and external, is a central quality of case management in psychosocial rehabilitation (Rapp & Gocha, 2006).

Rehabilitation case management emerged during a time of rehabilitation pessimism in community psychiatry and was relatively unrecognized during the 1960s through the early 1980s, only to emerge later as a best practice. Case management based on psychosocial rehabilitation principles and practices introduced a new teleology into the care of those with serious mental illness, one asserting hope and optimism for the progress they could realize. Previous generations of case management required professionals to specify what a person needed and should receive through the process of service brokering, an approach that proved largely ineffective. Case management based on psychosocial rehabilitation frames human needs from the perspective of the person, not the illness. It asks fundamental questions like, "What direction do people coping with psychiatric disability want to take in their lives? What outcomes do they value? What opportunities do they want and, as a consequence, what supports do they see as important in order to take advantage of the opportunities they value? What barriers do they feel that they must overcome to achieve what they want for themselves? How satisfied are they with the supports they obtain and what these supports produce in terms of practical changes in the lived experience?"

Such questions are not alien to social work given the profession's commitment to self-determination and empowerment as central values of practice. The questions themselves underscore the importance of relationship and its role in helping recipient and practitioner form an alliance useful in the achievement of recipient identified aims (Brun & Rapp, 2001). The questions themselves suggest an assumption that case management is a catalyst for helping recipients find their voice and articulate their desires in the face of the tremendous personal demands and challenges of serious mental illness. The questions link directly to humanistic and phenomenological dimensions of social work: while a person is struggling with mental illness, the struggle must be understood as an expression of someone traveling a unique and distinctive life journey. The transformational impact of serious mental illness in which a person will not likely return to their premorbid state needs to be understood in terms of how the experience of mental illness can influence life direction and the individual's goal set.

Thus, the correspondence between social work values and case management in psychosocial rehabilitation is strong, as both are founded in a respect for individualization and personalization of the process of care and support and operationalized through a process of humanization. The idea of humanization indicates that the person coping with serious mental illness is still a person who possesses interests, desires, and aims. Case management in psychosocial rehabilitation therefore amplifies the importance of these strivings and the case manager's recognition of the potential for a person's growth and development is a central idea of practice.

ADVANCED ORGANIZERS

Producing the distinctiveness of case management in psychosocial rehabilitation are those advanced concepts that help organize the manner in which practice is undertaken in the field of psychiatric disability. Particularly important are those advanced organizers involving consumer-centered values, narrative and the lived experience, and positive psychology.

Consumer-Centered Values

The idea that people coping with psychiatric disabilities should influence (if not direct) the rehabilitation process as much as possible was introduced in the 1970s and 1980s by a growing consumer and ex-patient movement (Moxley & Mowbray, 1997). Psychosocial rehabilitation was responsive to these consumer-based values by introducing practices legitimating consumer-professional collaboration, self-help alternatives, and mutual support opportunities (Mowbray, Moxley, Jasper, & Howell, 1997). Influenced by an emergent consumer movement, psychosocial rehabilitation sought to make the person (as opposed to the illness) central, not ancillary, within the process of service and support, particularly in making key decisions about care. Rather than requiring the person coping with serious mental illness to be a passive recipient of service, this form of case management required the individual to be an active participant with ownership over the process and outcomes of rehabilitation. Case management in psychosocial rehabilitation values assertiveness from recipients and seeks to empower them as decision makers even in the face of the pervasive challenges serious mental illness can create.

The active involvement of recipients is a legacy of psychosocial rehabilitation and within the process of case management involvement itself is beneficial because recipients make informed choices about their present and future circumstances using their own values and desires. The act of framing life goals based on humanism, optimism, and hope for the future using practical solution-focused practice makes this form of case management distinctive given psychosocial rehabilitation's emphasis on person-centered rather than service-centered aims.

Over the course of two decades, the 1970s, and the 1980s, psychosocial rehabilitation expanded to incorporate a range of supports, including professional services, peer support, and consumer-operated rehabilitation and community living options. The 1990s witnessed the emergence of the support model as a best practice (Carling, 1995), a model prioritizing concrete assistance to help people choose and achieve practical outcomes in areas like housing, employment, education, recreation, and social involvement. A recipient's subjective sense of quality of life as a principal outcome of case management became increasingly salient within psychosocial rehabilitation. To facilitate this outcome, the recovery-based practitioner in psychosocial rehabilitation makes use of environmental specificity in which well-desired supports are positioned to strengthen functioning of a person who learns to perform a specific role in a given environment, such as someone who is learning a job in an employment setting or performing as a student in an educational setting.

Narrative and the Lived Experience

Given the importance of person-centered values within psychosocial rehabilitation, narrative forms of practice figure into case management in important ways. Diagnostic interviewing focuses on symptom identification and clarification and situational considerations of how a person functions given the influence of the label assigned by a psychiatric professional. A narrative approach, however, involves deep listening and the amplification of the person's story with the professional discerning during the story telling process those experiences, situations, strengths, assets, and challenges identified as important (Washington & Moxley, 2008). The narrative itself, replete with central themes that can come to define the direction and strategy of case management, gives the ensuing management plan a personalized profile. People coping with psychiatric disability, for example, whose onset of mental illness was in late adolescence or young adulthood may come to amplify how their educational and vocational aims were frustrated or derailed. "Getting back on track" and "investigating educational or vocational training opportunities" may become salient in the story-telling that engages the psychosocial rehabilitation professional and recipient in discerning direction.

A traditional practitioner, one more tied to the medical paradigm, may think (or even say), "this direction isn't possible. He needs to back off and lower his expectations." A psychosocial rehabilitation professional will likely continue the dialogue, finally reaching a point where a miracle question is asked: "What will go well with your health to help you get back on track with the education you seek?" The achievement of health can become an enabling outcome of a higher level outcome—the pursuit of education. In this example, narrative drives the process and is legitimate within the person-centered paradigm of psychosocial rehabilitation.

Two types of narrative can emerge during the dialogue between recipient and practitioner (Washington & Moxley, 2007). One is the "narrative of plight," in which the recipient frames what isn't and what hasn't gone well over the life course. The narrative of plight may express itself as a form of grieving or mourning—opportunities lost, frustration, and setbacks maybe prominent. Another type is the "narrative of efficacy," in which the recipient reveals strengths, assets, enabling conditions, and opportunities, particularly ones that are on the horizon. These narratives may conflict or even contradict one another and they may compete for ascendance within the dialogue. However, careful listening (by both practitioner and recipient) can reveal a structure within which action can be taken, consistent with the rehabilitation framework. Barriers are appreciated in relationship to an outcome that the person seeks, and strengths and assets (including other people who can assist) are seen as enabling conditions of a desired outcome. Within the narrative of efficacy, strengths can be discerned, and even within the narrative of plight, both practitioner and recipient can appreciate strengths (e.g., tolerating setbacks, coping with stress, getting back on track).

A narrative strategy highlights the humanistic posture of psychosocial rehabilitation found in the personalization of the recipient, who is seen as striving, purposeful, and goal-oriented. The narrative reflects the lived experience: "Here is how I have lived with serious mental illness. Here is how I have changed, suffered, triumphed, endured and my experience has made me distinctive as an individual." The appreciation of the recipient's lived experience can certainly reframe how assessment is undertaken, emphasizing phenomenology in service to the creation of an idiographic profile of the individual's assets, strengths, capacities, and abilities. Successful case management can help recipients produce new narratives, ones populated with new opportunities, new capacities (e.g., good health), valued achievements, and the realization of desired outcomes. The new narrative may hold a special position for the case management professional whose own narrative

of efficacy (found in helping the recipient achieve valued outcomes) is intertwined with the recipient's given the collaborative features of case management in psychosocial rehabilitation.

POSITIVE PSYCHOLOGY

Increasingly psychology, social sciences, and the health and human services are balancing concepts of deficit, disease, disorder, and impairment with those that are positive in their orientation to human development (Lopez, Snyder, & Rasmussen, 2003). Positive psychology is emphasizing research and findings on the influence of such ideas and qualities like faith and spirituality, social capital, virtues like endurance and courage, optimism, well-being, and hope ascend within helping frameworks. These ideas and the research they have fostered suggest that people confronting life-threatening and life-challenging situations may exhibit signs of stress and strain, but they can also exhibit virtues that strengthen their resolve and coping (Wright & Lopez, 2002). A person who experiences numerous setbacks in health may muster cognitive and emotional strategies, helping them reframe the possibility of success in a given situation by modifying adaptive approaches and augmenting coping. Recognizing that people experiencing adversity bring to bear hardiness and resilience is central to positive psychology.

Such a positive psychology is well rooted in psychosocial rehabilitation, so case management recognizes that constructs like hope (anticipation of a positive future) and optimism (an immediate attitude that frames current circumstances in a positive way) figure into the process of support in important ways. Narratives of efficacy suggest optimism and hope in the pursuit of certain opportunities across the life span (such as valuing education and the work ethic) and the ensuing case management plan can play off optimism and hope.

"Okay," says the case manager, "you have been ill but you are very hopeful. What drives your hope?"

"I just know that I can handle college if I can change my living situation and wade into school slowly," the client replies.

"You sound so hopeful. What will help you get ready?"

"Maybe I can visit a community college and talk with counselors. Can you come with me?" the recipient asks.

"Certainly, let's schedule it."

This brief dialogue shows how hope and optimism can link to action. This recipient is getting ready for a new undertaking, and the social worker senses this immediately. Acting on this readiness moves the recipient a little closer to the valued outcome. The case manager as ally is part of the system of optimism and hope that has formed indicative of the collaborative framework of psychosocial rehabilitation.

Paradigm

The paradigm formed by the intersection of the advanced organizers of consumer-centered values, narrative, and positive psychology produces an interesting model of case management practice in psychosocial rehabilitation. The model emerging from this paradigm is as follows.

VALUE ASSIGNED TO THE RECIPIENT'S PERSPECTIVE → NARRATIVE AS A TOOL TO HIGHLIGHT DESIRE AND DIRECTION → NARRATIVE TO IDENTIFY STRENGTHS/ASSETS, ISSUES, BARRIERS → PERSON-CENTERED PLAN → COLLABORATIVE ACTION TO ACHIEVE PERSON-CENTERED OUTCOMES

RECOVERY-BASED CASE MANAGEMENT

As psychosocial rehabilitation continued to evolve during the decade of the 1990s, Anthony (1994) suggested that recovery could become the principal aim of the field, a perspective that has increasingly expanded in scope and research (Davidson, Harding, & Spaniol, 2005). The idea that recovery was possible infused a new idealism about the possibilities for the rehabilitative support of people coping with serious mental illness. Recovery-based psychosocial rehabilitation establishes a framework for the practice of a new form of case management, one founded on the best consumer-centered traditions of the field. Recovery within the context of psychosocial rehabilitation does not mean the person's return to a premorbid state, a view more suggestive of a medical than a rehabilitation model. Many people coping with psychiatric disability would say that their experience was so distressful and challenging that a "return" to the lives they led prior to the onset of their illnesses was not possible or even desired. Many people who label themselves as "survivors" (to emphasize that they literally outlived horrific experiences and mistreatment) are mindful of how their identities were substantially altered by their negative personal experiences, ones induced by inappropriate or iatrogenic service responses, and stigmatizing social reaction.

Recovery requires people coping with serious mental illness to contemplate and answer two questions that appear on face contradictory: How do I live with the illness and its consequences? How do I live without the illness? In answering the first question, people must address how they will respond to stress, symptoms, grief and loss, anger about injustice and deprivation, and the management of morale and positive outlook. In answering the second question, people will address setting a life direction, identifying new roles they want for themselves, obtaining enabling resources, and achieving a lifestyle that brings personal satisfaction and fulfillment.

Psychiatric disability can encapsulate individuals in networks that reinforce their identities as ill individuals and leave few (if any) other options for them to develop identities based on other conceptions of self. Helping people discover how to manage their situations while they learn how to emerge out of the illness, leave it behind, and reformulate their identities based on new lifestyle choices they find satisfying forms the essence of recovery. Although practitioners may think of recovery as a discrete outcome, for many survivors it is a process requiring a personal practice of a "lived experience" involving health promotion and the pursuit of personal meaning. A person's practice of recovery can demand vigilant self-management, self-help, and mutual support. It can require sanctuary, as well as opportunities to witness mistreatment or inadequate support and to provide support to others (Paynter, 1997).

Recovery can involve the creation of new identities based on personal transformation in which people overcome the psychological, behavioral, biological, and social consequences of illness and disability (Moxley & Washington, 2001). Social workers practicing recovery-based case management in psychosocial rehabilitation are mindful of the need to help clients focus on what recovery means for them. These practitioners refrain from defining recovery for recipients since they understand that people must come to learn what recovery means in the context of their own lived experience. The personal process of defining recovery, exploring the outcomes and consequences of recovery, and practicing recovery can help individuals make decisions about how to reduce the centrality of serious mental illness in their lives. Overcoming the illness through the achievement of new roles and lifestyles that bring personal satisfaction, even though a person may need to learn to live with particular symptoms, gives recovery-based case management a transcendent quality (Washington & Moxley, 2001). To paraphrase Victor Frankl (2000), people learn to transcend their situations when they understand the meaning and direction their lives can take.

ASSUMPTIONS AND PROCESS OF RECOVERY-BASED CASE MANAGEMENT

Principal implications of a recovery orientation to case management are as follows.

1. Recovery-based case management values a nondirective approach in which practitioners collaborate with recipients to discover what recovery means to them and actualize supports that contribute to their realization of recovery.
2. The practice of recovery helps people dealing with serious mental illness gain control over each aspect of the case management service process. A basic assumption of this form of case management is that individuals coping with psychiatric disability often lose control of the service process as professionals come to dominate their lives as principal decision makers. Most people coping with serious mental illness use this control responsibly and typically select outcomes they find most personally relevant and pragmatic given their aims and desires. When freely chosen and realized by the client, these outcomes can produce personal fulfillment that in turn contributes to satisfaction as the person defines it. In choosing what outcomes to pursue, people are selecting how to invest their creative energies, giving recovery-based practice an existential flavor.
3. To establish a rehabilitation direction, a case manager who engages in a recovery assessment may work with an individual to answer an important existential question, one that the social, psychological, and biological experience of mental illness can undermine: "How will I direct my creative energies to find fulfillment in my life?" A recovery-based case management plan can help

individuals identify the supports, experiences, and opportunities that will help them illuminate answers to this important question. Recovery-based case management will also help people address another important question: "What help do I need to develop and direct my creative energies?"
4. These two existential questions were never central to other forms of case management because they assumed that the illness would be chronic and pervasive, and as a consequence, people needed only adequate or appropriate medical and social services. For recovery-based case managers, however, helping people find answers to these questions is crucial to the growth and development of recipients.
5. Recovery-based case management assumes an active consumer—that people coping with serious mental illness can and will reflect on what they experience, evaluate their experience, and make decisions to change the process, products, and outcomes of rehabilitative support. So recovery-based case managers collaborate with the people they serve as active decision makers who want to stake out and achieve directions in which they find substantive importance.
6. Recovery-based case managers assume communities are repositories of a great number and variety of supports. In collaboration with the people they serve, case managers discover the ones that recipients find most relevant to the fulfillment of their aims.

CONCLUSION: AN EYE TO THE FUTURE

Shaping case management in psychosocial rehabilitation will be forces emanating from how the field frames the paradigm of serious mental illness, organizes service provision, and responds to the politics of health care coverage. The achievement of parity between health and mental health services will likely bring the care of serious mental illness into primary health care centers and clinics in which family practice physicians and other generalists are increasingly involved in medical management. New pharmaceutical and diagnostic approaches will likely equip such practitioners with more powerful tools for the management of the primary symptoms of serious mental illness.

Networks of care linking medical clinics to psychosocial rehabilitation options will place physicians in central referral roles and innovations in medical education will make these practitioners more mindful of the benefits inherent in combining medical care, social services, and psychosocial rehabilitation options. Parity itself will legitimate the provision of case management services that are outcome-focused and health-oriented in their aims. The further integration of serious mental illness into a neomedical model, one that emphasizes community-based care, health promotion, prevention, and cost-effectiveness (achieved by reducing relapse) can further legitimate a recovery framework within medical care and psychosocial rehabilitation, particularly as positive psychology becomes more dominant within models of care.

Enhanced medical care can assist recipients in considering the next steps in their wellness including a consideration of how best to advance their life satisfaction and quality of life. Feeling better physically and mentally can help recipients invest newfound energy in planning their living situations and acting on their hopes and dreams. Here psychosocial rehabilitation can play an important role. Its distinctiveness and expertise lie in helping recipients move forward through the articulation of plans that recipients find relevant and meaningful. Thus, the future of case management in psychosocial rehabilitation is synergetic within a framework of positive psychology and strengths-based practice. Though it can stand alone, it is probably most potent when combined with other care approaches that incorporate a similar worldview.

WEB SITES

Boston University Center for Psychiatric Rehabilitation. http://www.bu.edu/cpr.

New York Center for Rehabilitation and Recovery. http://www.coalitionny.org/ccrr.

National Mental Health Consumers Self Help Clearing House. http://www.mhselfhelp.org.

National Alliance for the Mentally Ill. http://www.nami.org.

University of Chicago Center for Psychiatric Rehabilitation. http://www.ucpsychrehab.org.

References

Anthony, W. A. (1994). Recovery from mental illness: The guiding vision of the mental health system in the 1990s. In International Association of Psychosocial Rehabilitation Services, *An introduction to psychiatric rehabilitation* (pp. 556–567). Columbia, MD: IAPSRS.

Anthony, W., Cohen, M., Farkas, M., & Gagne, C. (2002). *Psychiatric rehabilitation*, 2nd ed. Boston: Boston University Center for Psychiatric Rehabilitation.

Brun, C., & Rapp, R. (2001). Strengths-based case management: Individuals' perspectives on strengths and the case manager relationship. *Social Work, 46*(3), 278.

Carling, P. J. (1995). *Return to community: Building support systems for people with psychiatric disabilities.* New York: Guilford.

Davidson, L., Harding, C., & Spaniol, L. (2005). *Recovery from severe mental illnesses: Research evidence and implications for practice, volume 1.* Boston: Boston University Center for Psychiatric Rehabilitation.

Frankl, V. (2000). *Man's search for meaning.* New York: Beacon.

Lopez, S., Snyder, C., & Rasmussen, H. (2003). Striking a vital balance: Developing a complementary focus on human weakness and strength through positive psychological assessment. In S. J. Lopez & C. R. Snyder (Eds.), *Positive psychological assessment: A handbook of models and measures* (pp. 3–20). Washington, DC: APA.

Mowbray, C., Moxley, D., Jasper, C., & Howell, L. (Eds.). (1997). *Consumers as providers in psychiatric rehabilitation.* Columbia, MD: IAPSRS.

Moxley, D., & Mowbray, C. (1997). Consumers as providers: Forces and factors legitimizing role innovation in psychiatric rehabilitation. In C. Mowbray, D. Moxley, C. Jasper, & L. Howell (Eds.), *Consumers as providers in psychiatric rehabilitation* (pp. 155–164). Columbia, MD: IAPSRS.

Moxley, D., & Washington, O. (2001). Strengths-based recovery practice in chemical dependency: A transpersonal perspective. *Families in Society, 82,* 251–262.

National Institute of Mental Health. (1980). *Guidelines for community support programs.* Washington, DC: NIMH.

Paynter, N. (1997). Shining reflections: Alive, growing, and building recovery. In C. Mowbray, D. Moxley, C. Jasper, & L. Howell (Eds.), *Consumers as providers in psychiatric rehabilitation* (pp. 2–34). Columbia, MD: IAPSRS.

Rapp, C. A., & Gocha, R. J. (2006). *The strengths model: Case management with people with psychiatric disabilities.* New York: Oxford University Press.

Washington, O. G. M., & Moxley, D. P. (2001). The use of prayer in group work with African American women recovering from chemical dependency. *Families in Society*, 82, 49–59.

Washington, O.G.M., & Moxley, D. P. (2007). "I have three strikes against me": Narratives of plight and efficacy among older African American homeless women and their implications for engaged inquiry. Submitted for publication.

Washington, O.G.M., & Moxley, D. P. (2008). Telling my story: From narrative to exhibit in illuminat-

ing the lived experience of homelessness among older African American women. *Journal of Health Psychology*, 13(2), 154–165.

Wright, B., & Lopez, S. (2002). Widening the diagnostic focus: A case for including human strengths and environmental resources. In C. R. Snyder & S. J. Lopez (Eds.), *Handbook of positive psychology* (pp. 26–44). New York: Oxford University Press.

A Strengths Approach to Case Management with Clients with Psychiatric Disabilities

114

Charles A. Rapp

The strengths model represents a paradigm shift in mental health. The dominant deficit-problem medical model, which has continued for over a century, has been found wanting. The lives of people with severe mental illness continue to be marked by poverty, loneliness, limited opportunities for achievement, pain, and suffering. In contrast, the strengths model is based on the following six principles.

1. The focus is on individual strengths rather than pathology.
2. The community is viewed as an oasis of resources.
3. Interventions are based on client self-determination.
4. The case manager–client relationship is primary and essential.
5. Aggressive outreach is the preferred mode of intervention.
6. People suffering from major mental illness can continue to learn, grow, and change.

Fifteen years of research on the model consistently finds reductions in the use of psychiatric hospitalization, increase in independence of daily living, vocational achievement, social supports, and health. One study found reductions in symptomatology and family burden (Macias, Kinney, Farley, Jackson, & Vos, 1994). A recent study compared consumers receiving assertive community treatment and strengths model case management. No statistically significant differences were found between groups except in reduced symptomatology, which favored the consumers receiving strengths model services (Barry, Zeber, et al., 2003).

ENGAGEMENT AND RELATIONSHIP

The purpose of engagement and relationship is to create a trusting and reciprocal relationship between the case manager and client as a basis for working together. The relationship should be purposeful, reciprocal, friendly, trusting, and empowering. Methods include:

- *Establishing core conditions.* The foundation for the client–case manager relationship is empathy, genuineness, and unconditional positive regard.
- *Mirroring.* People develop their identities and perceptions of the world in large part based on the accumulative feedback they receive. Case managers act as mirrors that are highly sensitive to the abilities, talents, and achievement of clients.
- *Contextualizing.* People who are oppressed have a high degree of self-blame, low self-worth, and lack of confidence. Case managers help clients become aware of the societal context for this situation (e.g., poverty, discrimination) and see others in parallel predicaments.
- *Self-disclosure.* Different from most professional canons, the strengths model encourages *purposeful* self-disclosure. Self-disclosure is a normal component of most relationships. Purposeful self-disclosure can help establish community, bonds of trust, and understanding; validate the normalcy of consumer feelings and concerns; provide examples of how situations can be alternatively handled; and demonstrate effective ways of expressing both positive and negative emotions.
- *Accompaniment.* Most people are scared or anxious when confronting a new task or situation. For people with severe mental illness, that fear and lack of confidence are often acute and immobilizing. Accompaniment refers to the case manager going with the client while the client does a task. Just the presence of a trusted person can often provide the emotional support and boost courage for the client.
- *Reinforcement and celebration.* Most satisfying relationships involve regular (if not frequent) exchange of reinforcing comments. Praise is often warranted for even the smallest achievements.

STRENGTHS ASSESSMENT

The purpose of the strengths assessment is to collect information on personal and environmental strengths as a basis for developing a personal plan. The strengths assessment amplifies the well part of individuals and their environmental connections by identifying clients' assets. These assets are organized into six life domains:

1. *Daily living situation.* Includes the client's residence and specific features like roommates, furnishings, location, condition, access to resources such as food store, laundry, and so on.
2. *Financial.* Focuses on the sources and amount of income, debts and loans, financial and possession assets (e.g., car, home), sources of emergency funds.
3. *Vocational/educational.* Pertains to employment and its features, formal and informal educational activities, specialized training, credentials, and so on.
4. *Social and spiritual supports.* Includes family, friends, co-workers, neighbors, and the nature of the relationships, as well as the role of spiritual beliefs and formal religion.
5. *Health.* Involves the status and resources relevant to physical and dental illness and health promotion (diet, exercise), as well as the mental illness (medications, doctor, side effects, awareness of early warning signs of symptom exacerbation).
6. *Leisure/recreational.* Focuses on the sources and circumstance of enjoyment and fun—the where, what, who of their leisure time.

Each individual's behavior is influenced by the confluence of his or her own personal history, the present social context, and his or her visions of what he or she would like to achieve. Each life domain is therefore divided into three temporal categories: current status, desires and aspirations, and history.

The strengths assessment should be done in a conversational style. It should never resemble a one-sided interrogation. It should take place in a client's natural environment (e.g., apartment, café, park), not in a mental health facility. The gathering of strengths-oriented information begins at the first contact with the client and continues to occur throughout the service.

PERSONAL PLANNING

The purpose of personal planning is to create a mutual agenda for work between the client and case manager focused on achieving the goals the client has set. Goal setting is the centerpiece. Goals are inherent to hope and indispensable precursors to achievement. First-person accounts of recovery place having a purpose squarely in the center of that process. "The beneficial effect of goal setting on task performance is one of the most robust and replicable findings in the psychological literature" (Locke, Shaw, Saari, & Latham, 1981, p. 145).

Personal planning is not something one does apart from normal activities; rather, it is woven into the daily routine with clients: referring to them, writing new goals, discussing them with clients. The Recovery Goal Worksheet (RGW) has been designed to facilitate this process. The following practices are supported by much social science research.

- The RGW (e.g., goals, tasks, resources, etc.) should be derived from information contained in the strengths assessment.
- The first step is to identify the client's "passion statement." This is the desire that the client views as most important at that time.
- The RGW should be created by the client, including setting of goals, steps to reaching the goals, strategies to be used, delegation of responsibility, and establishing time lines. The case manager's job is to help a client do so.
- Each client goal is to be broken into concrete, specific, and discrete short-term goals or tasks with a high probability for achievement.
- Each task or goal should be stated positively (e.g., "Harriet will work until 5:30" rather than "Harriet will not leave work early").
- One of the case manager's jobs is to help the client generate alternative pathways and resources that can be used to attain the goals.
- Each task should contain a designation of who is responsible for completing the task and by what date it will be done.

RESOURCE ACQUISITION

The purpose of resource acquisition is to acquire the environmental resources desired by clients to achieve their goals, ensure their rights, and increase their assets. Mental health is a sense of achievement, a sense of belonging, a sense of self-worth, a sense of choices, and the power to choose.

An individual's mental health, in this sense, is inseparable from the community. Though the community is not the source of mental illness, it is the source of mental health. The community is rich with opportunities, resources, and people. Therefore, a primary task of the strengths model case manager is to break down the walls separating clients from the community, to replace segregation with true community integration.

The principal task of resource acquisition should be to emphasize normal or naturally occurring resources, not mental health services, because community integration can occur only apart from mental health and segregated services. The assumption, which has been largely confirmed in our experience, is that in any given population there are a sufficient number of caring and potentially helpful people available to assist and support clients. The identification and use of community strengths and assets are as critical as the identification and use of individual strengths.

The strengths model eschews the use of the transition model where clients are asked to complete certain prerequisites prior to receiving (earning) the opportunity. For example, a person who wants to live in his or her own apartment may have to first demonstrate "success" in a group home, halfway house, or supervised apartment. In contrast, the strengths-model approach would have the client and case manager (1) set a goal and choose among the alternative settings and resources, (2) get access to the desired resources, and (3) make adjustments and provide the necessary supports to maintain the desired resources.

Much of a case manager's time is devoted to maintaining the resource. For example, to maintain a client who has returned to school by enrolling in a college course, frequently used strategies would include:

1. constructing reasonable accommodations (e.g., test-taking procedures, hours of work, etc.),
2. pairing the client with a travel companion (e.g., another student, co-worker, neighbor),
3. celebrations for achievements,
4. easy access to the case manager by client and setting (give them a business card),
5. arranging for supplements (e.g., tutor, job coach, cleaning service),
6. brokering the use of supportive services e.g., community college disability service office, academic counselors, transportation services, clubs), and

7. ongoing education and consultation to the key actors in the setting.

THE PERFECT NICHE

In many situations, the case manager is called on to help a resource setting adjust or accommodate in some way. There are times, however, when adjustments are not needed by the setting or the client or are very minor. This occurs when the case manager can find the "perfect niche" where the requirements and needs of the setting are perfectly matched with the desires, talents, and idiosyncrasies of the client. The following situation vividly depicts the perfect niche.

Harry, a 30-year-old man, grew up in rural Kansas. Within a 9-month period, both his parents died. Harry, with the help of his aunt and uncle who owned the contiguous ranch, continued to operate a large farming operation. After a while, the relatives began noticing that Harry was "forgetting" to fulfill responsibilities or doing them wrong and was increasingly not eating, bathing, and so on. They reported that he was increasingly "talking strange." A visit to the mental health center led to a diagnosis of schizophrenia and admittance to the state psychiatric hospital.

On discharge, Harry was placed in a group home with services provided by the local mental health center. Although not disruptive, Harry failed to meet the group home's hygiene and cleaning requirements, did not attend mental health center services, and resisted taking his medication. It was reported that he would pack his bags every night, stand on the porch, and announce his leaving, although he never left. Over the next 2 years, Harry's stay at the group home was punctuated with three readmissions to the state hospital.

Harry was referred to a social worker trained in the strengths model. Although Harry was largely uncommunicative, the case manager slowly began to appreciate his knowledge and skill in farming. The social worker took seriously his expression of interest in farming and began working with him to find a place where he could use his skills.

They located a ranch on the edge of town where the owner was happy to accept Harry as a volunteer. Harry and the owner became friends, and Harry soon established himself as a dependable and reliable worker. After a few months, Harry recovered his truck, which was being held by his conservator, renewed his driver's license, and began to drive to the farm daily. To the delight of the community support staff, Harry began to communicate, and there was a marked improvement in his personal hygiene. At the time of case termination, the owner of the ranch and Harry were discussing the possibility of paid employment.

Why is this the perfect niche?

1. The case manager did not ask Harry or the rancher to change anything. Harry's desires and skills were a perfect match for the setting's demands and needs.
2. Harry's so-called deficits (e.g., noncommunication, poor hygiene) were irrelevant to the setting. In fact, the rancher did not talk any more than Harry.
3. Both parties—the client and the key actor—benefited.
4. The "natural" resource cost only a little case management time.

That his communication and hygiene improved was never targeted by the case manager. Yet this radiating impact is a consistent finding of strengths-model practice where success in one area seemingly leads to sometimes dramatic success in other areas.

Locating perfect niches should be a primary goal of all strengths-model case managers. When successful, these niches tend to be stable, produce high levels of client satisfaction and achievement, contribute to the community, and offer gains in other areas. Because case managers do not have to change or "fix" the client and the resource, they are also inexpensive in terms of case manager time and auxiliary mental health services.

THE FUTURE

The strengths model of case management and other strengths-based interventions (e.g., individual placement and support model of supported employment, solution-focused therapy, etc.) continue to grow in popularity in the United States and internationally. Because recovery and evidence-based practices are the two dominant movements in adult mental health, the strengths model is particularly well positioned for further adoption.

A variety of tools have been developed to support dissemination and adoption. First, a fidelity scale has been developed to assess the degree to which implementation of strengths model case management adheres to the practice standards. Table 114.1 contains a partial list of items. Second, a variety of tools and methods have been designed for supervisors to foster high-fidelity implementation (Rapp & Goscha, 2006). Third, a Web site and a Strengths Institute devoted to strengths-based practices has been established by the University of Kansas School of Social Welfare as a repository of relevant information.

WEB SITES

Office of Mental Health and Training, School of Social Welfare, University of Kansas, Lawrence, Kansas. http://www.socwel.ku .edu/mentalhealth.

Strengths Institute, School of Social Welfare, University of Kansas, Lawrence, Kansas. http://www.socwel.ku.edu/ strengths.

TABLE 114.1 Sample of Strengths-Based Case Management Fidelity Scale Items

1. Strengths assessment (SA)
   - The SA is regularly updated.
   - Client interests and/or aspirations are identified in some detail and with specificity.
   - Consumer language is used, e.g., "I want more friends" rather than "increase socialization skills."
   - Talents and/or skills are listed on SA in some detail and specificity.
   - Environmental strengths are listed on the SA in some detail and specificity.
   - SA is used to help clients develop treatment plan goals.
2. The recovery goal worksheet (personal plan) is integrated into CM practice
   - Agency uses the recovery goal worksheet as a stand-alone tool for helping clients achieve goals.
   - Goals on the recovery worksheet should use the client's own language and reflect something they are passionate about.
   - Long-term goal on the recovery goal worksheet is broken down into smaller, measurable steps.
   - Specific and varying target dates are set for each step on the recovery goal worksheet.
   - Goal worksheets are updated during nearly every contact with the client.
3. Naturally occurring resources
   - Case managers make use of more naturally occurring resources than formal mental health resources.
     - During the past 3 months, what percentage of goals worked on did the case manager specifically help the client access a naturally occurring resource to help achieve this goal?
4. Hope-inducing behaviors
   - Case managers exhibit hope-inducing behaviors when interacting with people receiving services or other staff.
   - Case managers exhibit hope-inducing behaviors in the following areas:
     - Interactions at group supervision
     - Interactions with clients in the field
     - Language in progress notes
     - Response to interview questions
   - Supervisor exhibits hope-inducing behavior in the following areas:
     - Interactions at group supervision
     - Interactions with staff and clients during field mentoring
     - Responses to interview questions
   - People receiving services state that case managers exhibit hope-inducing behaviors.
5. Community contact
   - The majority of consumer contact occurs in the community.
6. Caseload ratios
   - Case managers have low caseload ratios (this varies depending on intensity of caseload, but no more than 20:1).

TABLE 114.1 Sample of Strengths-Based Case Management Fidelity Scale Items

7. Supervision

- Supervisor spends at least 2 hours per week providing a quality review of tools related to the strengths model of case management (i.e., strengths assessments and recovery goal worksheets) and integration of these tools into actual practice.
- Supervisor spends at least 2 hours a week giving case managers specific feedback on skills/tools related to the strengths model of case management.
- Supervisor spends at least 2 hours per week providing field mentoring for case managers.

8. Strengths-based group supervision

- The group supervision focuses on discussion of client situations rather than administrative tasks.
- Strengths assessment are distributed to each team member for all client presentations.
- The case manager clearly states what he or she wants help with from the group during the presentation.
- The case manager clearly states what the client's goal(s) are.
- The team asks constructive questions based on the strengths assessment.
- The team brainstorms constructive suggestions related to the strengths assessment to help the client achieve the goal or help the CM engage with person to develop goal. An average of ten suggestions is generated per review.
- A clear plan/strategy is stated for each presentation. The CM states the next steps.

References

Barry, K. L., Zeber, J. E., et al. (2003). Effect of strengths model versus assertive community treatment model on participant outcomes and utilization: two-year follow-up. *Psychiatric Rehabilitation Journal, 26*(3), 268–277.

Locke, E., Shaw, K., Saari, L., & Latham, G. (1981). Goal setting and task performance: 1969–1980. *Psychological Bulletin, 90*(1), 125–152.

Macias, C., Kinney, R., Farley, O. W., Jackson, R., & Vos, B. (1994). The role of case management within a community support system: Partnership with psychosocial rehabilitation. *Community Mental Health Journal, 30*(4), 323–339.

Rapp, C. A., & Goscha, R. J. (2006). *The strengths model: Case management with people suffering with psychiatric disabilities*. New York: Oxford University Press.

115 Case Management with Substance-Abusing Clients

W. Patrick Sullivan

Among the host of social ills that confront American society, many would agree that alcohol and drug abuse and the problems associated with the use and procurement of substances are of prime concern. Alcohol and drug abuse is devastating to individuals and families and constitutes a major social problem. Mark, Levit, Vandivort-Warren, Coffey, and Buck (2007) estimate that 9.4 percent of the U.S. population suffers from a substance abuse disorder. As a result, the price tag for treatment alone reached $20.7 billion in 2003. When direct and indirect costs are considered, the fiscal impact of substance abuse is staggering. Indeed, over a decade ago the total costs of substance abuse, which include crime, lost productivity, mortality, and other similar variables, was projected to exceed $275 billion (SAMHSA, 1998).

These figures have important implications for all Americans, in part owing to the impact of substance abuse on health care service delivery systems, the workplace, the criminal justice system, and the day-to-day lives of ordinary citizens. Given these issues, it is not surprising that the value and effectiveness of treatment services are under constant scrutiny. For example, Barber (1994), expressing the sentiments of many, suggests that "by any set of performance indicators, it is hard to resist the conclusion that our current treatment methods are not working" (p. 521). Though many can debate Barber's bold statement, and even combat it with some facts and figures and personal stories, then, as now, the viability of treatment services is routinely questioned. For this reason alone, the search for innovative methods to improve performance is warranted.

Regardless of where one falls on the debate over treatment effectiveness, most would concede that providing care is not an exact science, and the likelihood that one must repeat treatment is high. Generally, this is explained as endemic to the condition, as many view alcohol and drug abuse as a chronic relapsing condition. Success, it follows, comes only after years of hard lessons, the confrontation of the individual by self and others, and the use of specialized treatment and supportive programs. It is readily acknowledged that substance abuse also results in a life marked by chaos. Thus, unstable relationships, poor work performance, criminal involvement, and other maladies in social life are pervasive in the life of the afflicted.

With concerns about escalating health care costs, and within a social context that appears to value punishment over treatment, there is real pressure to demonstrate the effectiveness of substance-abuse treatment while holding costs steady. Such times, though often disquieting, are also prime moments to examine the assumptions that underpin treatment services and to experiment with new methods to achieve desired results.

THE ROLE OF CASE MANAGEMENT IN ALCOHOL AND DRUG TREATMENT

Case management, once a novel addition to the array of traditional alcohol and drug programs, has become a standard service offering in comprehensive treatment systems (Benshoff & Janikowski, 2000; R. Rapp, 1997; Siegal & Rapp, 1996; Sullivan, Wolk, & Hartman, 1992; Vanderplasschen, Rapp, Wolf, & Broekaert, 2004). Many definitions of case management abound, and accordingly a range of services fall under this rubric, including case coordination, titration of care, and fiscal oversight. Here, case management is described as a direct service function that involves skill in assessment, counseling, teaching, modeling, and advocacy that aims to enhance the social functioning of clients. This service, it is argued, can amplify traditional treatment services by impacting those facets of consumers' lives that account for much human misery—and the lion's share of total costs incurred.

It is easy and perhaps appropriate to view problems in living faced by consumers as the social sequela of the addiction process. From this perspective, treatment that addresses the abuse behavior also attacks the root cause of the serious life problems experienced by clients. Certainly, case management can be conceptualized as an important ancillary service within this framework. However, the rise of case management in drug and alcohol treatment is consistent with efforts to develop more comprehensive service programs that address all aspects of a client's life (Evenson, Binner, Cho, Schicht, & Topolski, 1998; Humphreys & Tucker, 2002; Institute of Medicine, 1990; McLellan, Weinstein, Shen, Kendig, & Levine 2005).

The growing popularity of case management in alcohol and drug treatment also signals the adoption of a different view of addiction and, hence, a new approach to treatment. Vanderplasschen and associates (2004) argues that case management became a viable service as substance abuse problems became "increasingly recognized as multifaceted, chronic and relapsing conditions that required a comprehensive and continuous approach" (p. 913). Barber (1994) presents the possibility that the very essence of addiction may reflect extra-individual forces or at least the commonsense notion of person–environment interaction. Thus, Barber (1994) notes, "some of the phenomena covered by the term 'drug addiction' are best understood at aggregate levels. This is to say that the 'glue' holding an individual to his or her behavior could be just as much a property of the social situation as of the individual" (p. 529). From this frame of reference, social factors can be implicated in the development and maintenance of an addiction and also marshaled to abet the process of recovery.

There are many models of case management, including the broker model, clinical case management, and various forms of assertive outreach. Each of these models has been used in substance abuse treatment. Noel (2006) argues that the "purpose of a case management program determines the focus of case management activities" (p. 312). Nevertheless, among those approaches available, the strengths-model has emerged as a popular choice in alcohol and drug programs (Rapp, 2006; Rapp & Goscha, 2006; Sullivan, 1996; Sullivan et al., 1992). This model, with roots in child welfare and mental health services, is predicated on the principle that behavior is partly influenced by the resources available to people (C. Rapp, 1998; Rapp & Goscha, 2006). Using the strengths approach, the notion of resources is broadly construed, targeting the availability of supportive friends, family, recreation activities, stable residence, and meaningful activities, including work and education. The ability of case managers, working alongside consumers to secure these resources, is posited to improve the effectiveness of treatment. Indeed, a review of outcome research indicates that factors associated with social stability improve the resilience of the treatment effect (Sullivan et al., 1992). Barber (1994) also observes that "the best predictors of treatment success are all social factors" (p. 529).

Unquestionably these observations can be criticized on a number of fronts, particularly given the inability of such research to ascertain the direction of causality. Certainly we would expect people who are clean and sober to perform better socially. Nonetheless, it still stands that case management services geared to address the problems in living faced by consumers, regardless of the nature of the association, can be an important addition to the traditional array of service offerings.

THE PRACTICE OF CASE MANAGEMENT

The practice of strengths-based case management follows the common template that guides most interventions in human services. The difference in strengths-based case management is reflected in the points of emphasis, the nature of the professional-consumer relationship, and the locus of care.

Assessment

Most treatment episodes begin with the completion of an initial assessment, and traditional substance abuse programs are no different. Standard assessment procedures gauge such factors as types of substances abused, the frequency of use, and other measures that ascertain physical and emotional dependence. In case management practice, assessment is seen as an ongoing activity that focuses squarely on consumer functioning, both past and present, in key life domains, including work, leisure time, health, finances, relationships, and living arrangements; specific assessment instruments have been designed for this purpose (Rapp & Goscha, 2006).

Given the impress of substance use, it presents little challenge to decipher the presence of difficulties and uncover the litany of failures that have marked the life of many consumers. The task, however, from the strengths model is decidedly different. Here the purpose is to also expose areas of success, both past and present, and support or rekindle interests that the consumer may still hold. The professional must look behind the malady and dysfunction to see areas of health and strength, for these are the building blocks for the work to follow.

Goal and Case Planning

The process of strengths discovery allows one to view the client as a unique individual, not simply a typical drug abuser or an alcoholic. The assessment process should reveal the whole person, one that holds specific life goals, dreams, and aspirations. With the strengths assessment as a guide, the work phase begins, but with one controversial proviso: the consumer is viewed as the director of the process.

A vexing problem in substance abuse treatment is that for recovery to begin, individuals must suspend activities that while problematic, ordered their day, provided some purpose, and offered a level of gratification. Furthermore, common treatment programs, though perhaps well grounded, are rarely based on consumer choice. In the strengths model, consumers identify the goals important to them; consistent with the functions of case management, these goals are tied to the key life domains addressed in the assessment process.

The process described here is rarely linear. Consumers often fail to follow through or suggest overall goals that may be beyond their current capacity. Skilled case managers are adept at helping clients break even the largest and, perhaps in the minds of others, the most unrealistic goals into a series of manageable, measurable, and documented steps. This process provides a model for addressing life problems in a proactive, organized, and incremental fashion—and learning this skill alone can help consumers avoid relapse when life demands overwhelm them.

Resource Acquisition

If success and recovery are functions of the resources available to people, then it follows that a key function of case management, in conjunction with consumers, is to identify and secure the resources needed to realize case goals.

The development of case goals, and ultimately the resources that are targeted in the care plan, should flow logically from the strengths assessment. This phase of helping requires a measure of creativity and "out-of-the-box thinking." Often professional views of resources are restricted to those specialty services and providers that constitute the human service network. Case managers operating from the strengths model view the community as an unlimited source of resources for consumers preferring to access those supports and services used by all citizens.

Aggressive Outreach

The ability of case mangers to be successful in the art of resource acquisition and helping consumers realize their goals pivots on aggressive outreach. Aggressive outreach serves a plethora of functions that improve treatment programs. Creative case planning requires managers who are keenly aware of the formal and informal resources a community offers, and this is best learned while "on the street." These case mangers can develop relationships with employers, landlords, recreation directors, and other gatekeepers to those nontraditional resources vital to true recovery.

There are other advantages to outreach work that extends the reach of traditional programming. The ability of a case manager to observe consumers in real-world settings provides insights on what life is like in their natural environment. For example, case managers can uncover problems that consumers have heretofore masked, such as illiteracy, while simultaneously providing a glimpse of the strengths individuals possess. By remaining in constant contact with consumers, the case manager can detect signs of impending difficulties and the possibility of relapse.

The natural environment is also the most appropriate site for the consumer to try the skills learned in treatment settings, be it the will to resist contact with troublesome actors or tangible items, like learning to ride the bus or hold a job.

IMPACT OF CASE MANAGEMENT

As case management has grown in popularity in substance abuse treatment, there has been more interest in assessing the efficacy of this service. One pioneer in this area is the Wright State University School of Medicine. Their initial work underscored the important role of case management in improving treatment retention (R. Rapp, 1997). A decade later, this has remained the most robust finding in case management services for those facing addiction (McLellan, et al., 2005; Morgenstern, Bianchard, McCrady, McVeigh, & Morgan, 2006; Soson & Durkin, 2007; Vanderplasschen, et al. 2004; Vanderplasschen, Rapp, Wolf, & Broekaert 2007). The importance of this outcome cannot be minimized because retention has emerged as one of the key variables in overall treatment success in a host of settings and programs and a key mediating variable in a wide array of important client goals from abstinence to employment (Hartmann, Wolk, & Sullivan, 1993; Rapp, 2006; Vanderplasschen et al., 2007).

This ability to engage and retain individuals in treatment is a particularly powerful outcome given that case managers appear to have success with some of the most difficult to treat clients. Soson and Durkin (2007) note that case managers seem to engage homeless clients by offering them a chance to access nonconventional services that they perceive to be potentially useful. McLellan and associates (2005) report that case managers helped revolving-door clients to remain in or access rehabilitation services and ultimately reduce their chronic use of expensive services like detoxification. Coviello, Zanis, Wesnoski, and Alterman (2006) studied the use of case management in methadone treatment and report that case managers helped reengage program dropouts. Likewise, case managers were identified as useful in helping substance abusing women on public assistance to enter and remain in treatment (Morgenstern et al., 2006). Finally, Noel (2006) observes, that when executed as designed, case management can help retain adolescents in treatment, in part because the service focuses on the whole person.

A consistent finding in studies of strengths-based case management in mental health settings has been the success of the goal planning method. The results derived from this method, as demonstrated in a host of settings and with a variety of clientele, are admirable, with goal attainment rates consistently around 7 percent or higher across life domains (C. Rapp, 1998; Rapp & Goscha, 2006). This positive outcome appears to hold in alcohol and drug treatment (R. Rapp, 1997, 2006).

For example, in an early study, R. Rapp (1997) found consumer goal completion rates ranged from 58 percent in leisure time to 77 percent in living arrangements. This level of success has been consistently reported across a wide array of strengths-based case management initiatives for many years (Rapp & Goscha, 2006). These results suggest that case management services make an important contribution to the *process* of recovery.

CHALLENGES AND CONTROVERSIES

Though the rationale for including case management under the umbrella of alcohol and drug treatment may be evident, the introduction and implementation of the model faces a number of stern challenges. For many years, the disease model of alcohol and drug abuse has shaped our understanding of this problem and the treatment designed to help. Case management practice can be viewed as at odds with the disease model, both conceptually and in practice. Much of the work of case managers, particularly resource acquisition and relapse prevention, can be viewed by disease model adherents as professional enabling (Sullivan, Hartmann, Dillon, & Wolk, 1994). From this standpoint, the case manager protects clients from the consequences of their actions, thus delaying, not expediting, recovery. These differing viewpoints can dramatically impact how case management services are accepted and implemented. It is not uncommon for staff in treatment programs to have experienced addiction personally and to have benefited from classic treatment methods. In contrast, case management positions may be filled by those holding college degrees but without direct experience with substance abuse. Consequently, when case management services are introduced to a traditional treatment agency, a clash of cultures may ensue. For case management services to be effectively introduced in many settings requires strong leadership, particularly at the middle management level.

It also remains difficult to untangle the respective contribution of particular models of case management on client outcomes apart from the potential power of the basic case management relationship. In fact, successful execution of the role may mimic what has been referred to in therapy circles as the *real relationship* (Angel & Mahoney, 2007; Gelso et al., 2005). Case managers work alongside consumers in day-to-day situations and on basic life problems. They are there when clients succeed and fail. Case managers serve as advocates, coaches, cheerleaders, and the person who points out how alcohol and drug use impedes progress toward cherished goals in real time and in real-life settings. This aspect alone makes this a powerful relationship. Clearly, case managers become key persons in the life of those struggling with recovery, and first-person accounts affirm this (Brun & Rapp, 2001). Boundaries are still important and must always be monitored carefully.

It is also obvious that by virtue of the addiction process and/or the necessities of survival, denial and deceit are interpersonal issues confronted by professional helpers on a regular basis. In classic treatment, confrontation is used to counter these issues when they arise. However, case management practice is predicated on professional-client relationships marked by partnership and trust. Can this apparent dilemma be resolved? Some argue that the success of strengths-based practice in addiction treatment is inextricably tied to the capability of case managers to forge a mentoring relationship with consumers that is characterized by genuineness and warmth (see Brun and Rapp, 2001; Rapp & Goscha, 2006).

Although case management has been used effectively in a wide range of practice settings, there are specific concerns germane to addiction programs. Many clients in treatment have extensive criminal backgrounds and a history of failed treatments. Taking advocacy roles in such areas as employment and housing, for example, comes with some risk. Key issues to consider are the selection of clients for case management and the timing of services. To date there appears to be no prevailing model to suggest which consumers can benefit from case management or for whom it is contraindicated (Rapp, 1998; Sullivan & Maloney, 1992). Another unanswered question centers on the initiation of case management. Should case managers be assigned at the onset of the treatment experience, or should the consumer be deemed to be in a period of relative stability and sobriety?

The most important issue to be resolved is the future of case management in alcohol and drug treatment. With a resurgence of managed care in behavioral health, all aspects of the service system will be placed under the microscope. If case management can retain people in treatment and prove to be cost-effective, then chances for survival are enhanced. However, one large question continues to loom over the field. Is case management effective? Although there is some

evidence that case management improves client outcomes in addiction services, the results are, at best, modest. The role of case management in improved employment outcomes and legal involvement is certainly encouraging. It also appears that through active outreach, case managers can maintain constant contact with clients, resulting in fewer individuals falling through the cracks and providing a mechanism to detect when relapse and other social difficulties are near.

Still, it is dangerous to oversell the power of case management in alcohol and drug treatment. Vanderplasschen et al. (2004), drawing from an extensive review of outcome studies, argue that "case management for substance use disorders is no panacea, but it positively affects the delivery of services that can help stabilize or improve an individual's complex situation" (p. 920). Therefore, case management is best conceptualized as an important aspect of a well-integrated and organized system of care—not as a standalone service. In many ways, the introduction of case management is consistent with the evolution of drug and alcohol treatment. If substance abuse represents a long-term and relapsing condition, an acute model is inappropriate. Therefore, the true impact of this method may be assessed only in the long run and within the context of the system in which it is embedded (Saleh, Vaughn, Fuortes, Uden-Holmen, & Hall, 2006). To date, longitudinal studies that measure the impact of case management in addiction service are rare. Future research must explore the effectiveness of case management against other standard offerings in addiction programming, as well as the independent contribution the service makes.

WEB SITES

Alcohol Policy Information Service. http://www.alcoholpolicy.niaaa.nih.gov.

National Clearinghouse for Drug and Alcohol Information. http://ncadi.samhsa.gov.

National Institute of Alcohol Abuse and Alcoholism. http://www.niaaa.nih.gov.

National Institute on Drug Abuse. http://www.nida.nih.gov.

National Institutes of Health. http://www.nih.gov.

Substance Abuse and Mental Health Services Administration. http://www.samhsa.gov.

References

Angel, B., & Mahoney, C. (2007). Reconceptualizing the case management relationship in intensive treatment: A study of staff perceptions and experiences. *Administration Policy in Mental Health and Mental Health Services Research, 34,* 172–188.

Barber, J. (1994). Alcohol addiction: Private trouble or social issue? *Social Service Review, 68*(4), 521–535.

Benshoff, J., & Janikowski, T. (2000). *The rehabilitation model of substance abuse counseling.* Stamford, CT: Brooks/Cole.

Brun, C., & Rapp, C. A. (2001). Strengths-based case management: Individuals' perspectives on strengths and the case manager relationship. *Social Work, 46*(3), 278–288.

Coviello, D., Zanis, D., Wesnoski, S., & Alterman, A. (2006). The effectiveness of outreach case management in re-enrolling discharged methadone patients. *Drug and Alcohol Dependence, 85,* 56–65.

Evenson, R., Binner, P., Cho, D., Schicht, W., & Topolski, J. (1998). An outcome study of Missouri's CSTAR alcohol and drug abuse programs. *Journal of Substance Abuse Treatment, 15*(2), 143–150.

Gelso, C., Kelley, F., Fuertes, J., Marmarosh, C., Holmes, S., Costa, C., et al. (2005). Measuring the real relationship in psychotherapy: Initial validation of the therapist form. *Journal of Counseling Psychology, 52*(4), 640–649.

Hartmann, D., Wolk, J., & Sullivan, W. P. (1993). Inpatient and outpatient outcomes in Missouri's alcohol and drug treatment programs. *Journal of Health and Social Policy, 5*(2), 67–76.

Humphreys, K., & Tucker, J. (2002). Toward more responsive and effective intervention systems for alcohol-related problems. *Addiction, 97,* 126–132.

Institute of Medicine. (1990). *Broadening the base of treatment for alcohol problems.* Washington, DC: National Academies Press.

Mark, T., Levit, K., Vandivert-Warren, R., Coffey, R., & Buck, J. (2007). Trends in spending for substance abuse treatment, 1986–2003. *Health Affairs, 26*(4), 1118–1128.

McLellan, A.T., Weinstein, R., Shen, Q., Kendig, C., & Levine, M. (2005). Improving continuity of care in a public addiction system with clinical case management. *American Journal on Addictions, 14,* 426–440.

Morgenstern, J., Bianchard, K., McCrady, B., McVeigh, K., & Morgan, T. (2006). Effectiveness of intensive case management for substance-dependent women receiving Temporary Assistance for Needy Families. *American Journal of Public Health, 96*(11), 2016–2023.

Noel, P. (2006). The impact of therapeutic case management on participation in adolescent substance abuse treatment. *American Journal of Substance Abuse Treatment, 32,* 111–327.

Rapp, C. A. (1998). *The strengths model.* New York: Oxford University Press.

Rapp, C. A., & Goscha, R. (2006). *The strengths model.* New York: Oxford University Press.

Rapp, R. (1998). The strengths perspective and persons with substance abuse problems. In D. Saleebey (Ed.), *The strengths perspective in social work practice,* 2nd ed. (pp. 77–96). New York: Longman.

Rapp, R. (2006). Strengths-based case management: Enhancing treatment for persons with substance abuse problems. In D. Saleebey (Ed.), *The strengths perspective in social work practice,* 4th ed. Boston: Pearson Education.

Saleh, S., Vaughn, T., Fuortes, S., Uden-Holmen, T., & Hall, J. (2006). Cost-effectiveness of case management in substance abuse treatment. *Research on Social Work Practice, 16*(1), 38–47.

SAMHSA (1998). *National household survey on drug abuse: Population estimates 1997.* SAMHAS Office of Applied Studies. HHS pub. no. (SMA) 98-3250. Rockville, MD: SAMHSA.

Siegal, H., & Rapp, R. (Eds.). (1996). *Case management and substance abuse treatment.* New York: Springer.

Soson, M., & Durkin, E. (2007). Perceptions about services and dropout from a substance abuse case management program. *Journal of Community Psychology, 35*(5), 583–602.

Sullivan, W. P. (1996). Beyond the twenty-eighth day: Case management in alcohol and drug treatment. In C. Austin & R. McClelland (Eds.), *Perspectives on case management practice* (pp. 125–144). Milwaukee: Families International.

Sullivan, W. P., Hartmann, D., Dillon, D., & Wolk, J. (1994). Implementing case management in alcohol and drug treatment. *Families in Society, 75,* 67–73.

Sullivan, W. P., & Maloney, P. (1992). Substance abuse and mental illness: Social work practice with dual diagnosis clients. *Arete, 17*(2), 1–15.

Sullivan, W. P., Wolk, J., & Hartmann, D. (1992). Case management in alcohol and drug treatment: Improving client outcomes. *Families in Society, 73,* 195–203.

Vanderplasschen, W., Rapp, R., Wolf, J., & Broekaert, E. (2004). The development and implementation of case management in North America and Europe. *Psychiatric Services, 55*(8), 913–922.

Vanderplasschen, W., Rapp, R., Wolf, J., & Broekaert, E. (2007). Effectiveness of different models of case management for substance-abusing populations. *Journal of Psychoactive Drug, 39*(1), 81–95.

Social Work Case Management in Medical Settings

Candyce S. Berger

There is no standardized definition of case management, nor one accepted approach (NASW, 1992). Many health care professionals claim dominion over case management, including social work. Social work's involvement in case management can be traced to the turn of the twentieth century to the social casework approach. Social casework processes parallel the steps described in case management process: assessment, diagnosis, intervention, and follow-up. Social work case management is rooted in the problem-solving process and incorporates systems and/or ecological theories that balance personal and environmental determinants in understanding illness and health. Social work leaders in health care have emphasized the importance of this biopsychosocial approach in working with patients, dating back to Ida Cannon at the turn of the twentieth century. Cannon emphasized the need to reach out into the community to link hospital and community-based care in a holistic approach to health care delivery. Though the term "case management" may not have appeared in these early writings, the descriptions of services included similar terms, such as screening for high risk, assessment, intervention, brokerage, linkages, evaluation, and follow-up (Berger, 1996). Several factors contributed to the rapid growth of case management in health care settings.

1. *Health care inflation.* As the costs of health care exceeded the ability of individual, organizational, and governmental payers to keep pace with its growth, people began looking for a way to contain costs. Case management was quickly embraced as an effective approach to cut costs, and recent studies have shown improved efficiency and effectiveness (Bierman, Dunlop, Brady, Dubin, & Brann, 2006; Dorr, Wilcox, McConnell, Burns, & Brunker, 2007; Felt-Lisk & Mays, 2002; Laramee, Levinsky,

Sargent, Ross, & Callas, 2003; Riegel et al., 2002; Sweeney, Halpert, & Waranoff, 2007; Vourlekis, Ell, & Padget, 2005).

2. *Legislative initiatives.* Legislation soon followed that extended the breadth of case management services. For example, the Health Maintenance Act of 1973 encouraged comprehensive health services over the continuum of care, including preventive, acute, chronic, and terminal care services. Case management became a primary vehicle to facilitate integration of services. Passage of the Omnibus Budget Reconciliation Act in 1981 and the subsequent Consolidated Omnibus Budget Reconciliation Act in 1985 encouraged the expansion of case management services to the Medicaid population.

3. *Employer benefits.* Employers quickly followed by incorporating case management programs into their health benefits plans. It expanded the role and visibility of case management, particularly in the medical claims arena, with a priority for cost containment.

4. *Chronicity as a leading health problem.* A new set of challenges emerged as chronic illness became a major focus in health care delivery. Rather than the controlled environment of an acute, inpatient unit, health care delivery moved to the community. This move required intensive coordination of service delivery across multiple venues of care (e.g., medications, physician office visits, long-term care, wraparound services). Case management offered an approach that was capable of coordinating multiple systems of care to enhance quality while reducing fragmentation and costs. It is estimated that 125 million people live with chronic conditions (Dorr et al., 2007), which can lead to overutilization of health care services,

increasing costs, and poor health outcomes if their disease is badly managed. One of the biggest challenges to the management of chronic disease is patient adherence to medical recommendations (Felt-Lisk & Mays, 2002; Laramee et al., 2003; NASW, 2007; Vourlekis & Ell, 2007). The World Health Organization (2003 in Vourlekis & Ell, 2007) estimates that 50 percent of the population worldwide adheres to medical recommendations. Case management strategies are increasingly used to address management of patient care, particularly in the area of adherence, because of the perceived positive influence on efficiency and effectiveness. Over the past decade, evidence-based studies have provided increasing data to substantiate these claims.

5. *Prevention.* As rising health care costs associated with acute care placed greater emphasis on prevention as a more cost-effective approach, case management was used to coordinate and monitor patient compliance with prevention strategies.

DEFINING CASE MANAGEMENT

Case management is recognized as integral to health care delivery but remains a source of heated debate. This debate centers not so much on the efficacy of the approach but on its purpose, structure, and professional domain. The debate can often be traced to a lack of agreement as to the definition of case management. Five models of case management are commonly applied in the health care environment (Rose, 1992; Berger, 1996). These models include the following.

1. *Primary care case management.* The primary care physician is responsible for coordinating the care for all of the patients assigned to him or her, mostly associated with health maintenance organizations. This typically involves medical management of disease rather than all aspects of health care need. It is characterized by having one physician responsible for overseeing all of the patient's heath care interventions and synthesizing the medical information (e.g., laboratory, specialist consultations, radiology) to reduce fragmentation and duplication of care. Most health maintenance organizations use this approach by requiring authorization from the primary care physician for all health care services provided and holding him or her fiscally responsible for coordination of services (e.g., capitation).

2. *Medical case management.* This approach focuses on a select group of patients in which severe illnesses and/or injuries require intensive coordination and monitoring of services. The approach requires a good understanding of medications, medical information (e.g., medical diagnosis and interpreting laboratory data), and medical equipment and supplies. The goal is to prevent medical crisis or deterioration of health. Nurses typically are the case managers, though social workers may also fill these roles, particularly with mental health.

3. *Social case management.* This approach emphasizes coordination and monitoring of nonmedical aspects of the patient's environment that impinges on his or her ability to maximize health care services (e.g., social and economic factors that interfere with a patient's ability to follow medical requirements). Nonacute, community-based patients (e.g., frail elderly, chronically mentally ill) typically fall into this category. Social workers and nurses are the primary providers of this approach to case management services.

4. *Medical-social case management.* Medical and social case management are integrated to provide a more holistic approach to managing health care delivery. This is premised on an ecological approach in which medical, social, economic, and cultural factors are synthesized to frame the case management process. It is this model of case management in which the greatest conflict over professional domain occurs, with nurses and social workers often competing for dominance. Team approaches are increasingly being used to maximize opportunities rather than compete for turf.

5. *Benefit case management.* This approach focuses exclusively on the health care benefits, emphasizing the most appropriate use of health care resources. It often combines the dual focus of ensuring appropriate use of benefits (e.g., utilization review) and making benefits more flexible to achieve cost-effective services. It is used primarily within the insurance industry, though hospitals have

incorporated aspects of this model. For example, a hospital may pay to have a ramp built in a patient's home (a service that may not be covered by one's insurance) to discharge the patient earlier. Also, many of the care management protocols used in inpatient settings are premised on effective and timely utilization of resources.

The various models presented here may differ, but they all share a common approach that relies on the sequencing of activities to ensure efficiency and effectiveness in the delivery of health care services. The steps involved in the case management process have been described in many fields of practice, including health care. Although different terms may be employed, they share a common set of generic steps that emanates from a problem-solving approach to intervention (Applebaum & Austin, 1990; Berger, 1996; Dorr et al., 2007; Felt-Lisk & Mays, 2002; Kane, 1992; Kirton, 1999; Laramee et al., 2003; NASW, 2007; Sangalang, Barth, & Painter, 2006; Sweeney et al., 2007; Vourlekis et al., 2005). These steps include:

1. *Case finding.* Potential recipients of case management services are identified through a standardized process using formalized screening criteria. Identification can be based on the type, nature, or extent of an individual's illness/disease (i.e., catastrophic, terminal, chronic, preventive) or the anticipated costs of care (Kane, 1992).
2. *Assessment.* Once identified, recipients of case management services receive an evaluation that can range from a comprehensive, biopsychosocial evaluation to a more focused evaluation of a specific aspect of care (e.g., pattern of resource utilization or eligibility determination). The case management model employed (e.g., social-medical versus benefits case management) and the time perspective (e.g., relevance of information drawn from an individual's past, present, and future situation) will define the scope of the assessment. Care must be taken during the assessment process to ensure the adequacy and reliability of information, because subsequent steps in the case management process are based in the interpretation of these data.
3. *Intervention.* The intervention stage can also span a wide range, varying in scope and intensity. Interventions can be as simple as flexing one's benefits package or providing information and referral to a comprehensive set of interventions that might include several or all of the following services: information and referral, coordination of service delivery through linkages, brokerage of client services, advocacy, provision of concrete services (e.g., arranging transportation), and therapeutic counseling. This last intervention is still a source of much debate as to whether a case manager should also serve as the client's therapist. Careful review and consideration should be given before agreeing to provide this type of care. Regardless of the mix of interventions, each is linked to a measurable outcome or goal, mutually defined by the case manager and the client.
4. *Monitoring.* This set of activities focuses on reviewing the process of case management to ensure appropriateness and timeliness of intervention, and patient compliance. Regardless of how thorough the plan of intervention, problems can occur. An effective case manager regularly reviews the process of care to identify "breakdowns" in the plan. The data are used to alter the intervention plan to promote more effective and efficient care. With the increasing reliance on computerized data systems (e.g., electronic patient records, computerized information systems), monitoring activities can be more thorough and timely. However, sole reliance on these sources of information may give a skewed picture. The case manager cannot underestimate the importance of direct contact with the client to get a thorough understanding of not only *what* has occurred but also *why* (i.e., what factors may be contributing to the problem).
5. *Evaluation.* As with any intervention, a practitioner evaluates the impact of his or her work. Evaluation combines a focus on both the process (e.g., number of contacts, types of services provided) and outcome (e.g., goal achievement, health indices) of case management. Outcomes measures might also include population-based indices, such as changes in health status, quality of life, or financial impact. If clear goals and objectives for the interventions have been identified in step 3, evaluation becomes an easier task.

The steps in case management have been presented as if they represent a linear process. It is important to emphasize that this is a dynamic process; movement can go forward or backward and steps may occur simultaneously, particularly when there are multiple problems being addressed.

CONTEXTUAL FACTORS RELATED TO CASE MANAGEMENT IN HEALTH CARE

Developing and implementing case management in health care is neither a simple nor easy task. There are many factors that shape the practice to create a mosaic of models, providers, and services. This complexity often creates challenges and conflicts that plague its use. The chapter concludes with a set of factors to be considered when developing or implementing a case management program (Berger, 1996).

1. *Case management goals.* What is the primary purpose or focus of the case management program? This will often define the appropriate model of case management (e.g., medical, social, or benefits case management), which professional(s) is most likely to fulfill the role of case manager, and the size of the case manager's caseload.
2. *Location of case management services.* Where will case management be provided? Is it located in the hospital, in the community, or spanning both locations of care? Hospital-based services more often use the medical case management model and typically employ nurses or teams of social workers and nurses as case managers. The phrase "care management" is often used to describe this inpatient approach. Utilization review can be structured as a benefit or medical model and is also prevalent on inpatient units. Community approaches tend to use more of a social or medical-social approach, though "benefits case management" is also evident. Providers are typically nurses, social workers, or case management teams that may consist of nurses, social workers, and other health care providers, and/or consumers. Benefits case management may or may not employ practitioners from health disciplines. Thompson (1998) suggests that community approaches may require interactive case management that uses street-based, hands-on

interventions rather than having the client come to the worker's office. Creating teams that include public health professionals is an excellent option for achieving this level of case management, particularly when spanning inpatient and outpatient arenas. Several studies have validated the positive impact of community-based case management on patient, organization, and system outcomes (Bierman et al., 2006; Dorr et al., 2007; Felt-Lisk & Mays, 2002; Laramee et al., 2003; Riegel et al., 2002; Sweeney et al., 2007; Vourlekis et al., 2005).

3. *Auspices of the program.* Is the case management program internal to the service delivery system (e.g., a hospital has a case management program for its patients) or external to the system of care (e.g., a payer implements a case management program that crosses organizational boundaries)? Internal and external programs are inversely related in terms of their advantages and disadvantages. For example, although internal programs can have greater potential influence based on their formal and informal relationship with key decision makers and providers, they may lack the objectivity and autonomy that are characteristic of external programs when choosing interventions and services for the patient. Several studies have shown the importance of the need for the case manager to be closely related to health care and/or demonstrating expertise in the disease(s) being managed (Laramee et al. 2003; Vourlekis & Ell, 2007).

4. *Who the client is.* While having the illusion of an easy question, the waters become quite murky when one recognizes that health is embedded in an economic, political, and social constellation of players. The "patient" would seem the immediate response and clearly the priority according to NASW standards for case management (2007), whereas the real client may be the hospital, the payer, or society. This becomes a source of major confusion and potential conflict. For example, what happens when an organizational goal and a client goal conflict? Case managers must clarify who is the primary customer of the services and examine the various contextual factors that define the client's goals and objectives. For example, when working with women, the client may be

more than the individual woman; the "client" often encompasses the family system, and a broader base of need will shape the goals and objectives. A distinguishing characteristic of social work case management is the emphasis on advocacy as a primary role.

5. *Professional training of case managers.* Who is the case manager? Should it be a nurse, a social worker, a physician, or some other provider? Some case management programs have employed indigenous providers to be individual case managers or to serve as members of the case management team (Felton et al., 1995). Previous consumers of care are often in a position to enhance outreach services, as well as provide insights into the assessment of client needs. Issues also emerge regarding functional training in case management (e.g., certificate programs) and the credentialing of case managers through state and national programs. Several accrediting bodies for case managers now exist. The American Case Management Association offers credentialing exclusively to social workers and nurses. Professional domain may be less of an issue if one begins with an understanding of the model of case management to be employed. The development of a case management team is an effective alternative to a single-discipline practice, particularly when social and environmental determinants are significant to a patient's health (e.g., social-medical model). These teams have been used with both inpatient (e.g., care maps and utilization review) and community-based approaches (e.g., prenatal care, AIDS).

6. *Caseload.* Goals, intensity of services, duration of contact, and sophistication of the service delivery network will influence caseload size. If management of benefits is the sole objective of case management, caseloads can be extremely large (e.g., one case manager per 10,000 clients). Comprehensive case management may use caseloads that are smaller, and the size will vary according to the intensity of services provided (e.g., one per 20 clients for intensive case management; one per 100 cases where clients are more capable of mobilizing resources independently).

7. *The breadth of the service delivery system.* Case managers typically have a broad definition of the service delivery system (e.g., hospital, outpatient, community agencies, churches). They should also have a good understanding of cultural determinants of health and health behavior, including awareness of different customs and health care practices. Competency in culturally sensitive practice may lead one to incorporate nontraditional providers into the network of care, such as spiritual healers, herbalists, and other complementary and alternative treatment providers.

8. *Power and influence of the case manager.* If the case manager does not have the authority or institutional influence to change the environmental factors that inhibit the delivery of health care services, case management will ultimately fail to achieve significant improvements for the patient. Authority will be influenced by such factors as ownership of the case management program (e.g., insurance companies, agencies, government), auspices (e.g., internal or external), and professional discipline of the case manager. This can determine whether the authority exists to change rules or regulations that present barriers to care.

9. *Ethical challenges.* There is not sufficient space to allow a thorough discussion of the ethical issues that will influence case management practice. Issues of confidentiality, client autonomy, and justice will each surface in a health care delivery system that relies more heavily on health care networks, computer technology, and cost-containment goals (Berger, 1996). Practitioners will need to continuously monitor their practice for ethical dilemmas and draw on the assistance of institutional and/or professional ethical committees to help guide their practice.

FUTURE ISSUES AND DIRECTIONS

As we look to the future, several issues or mandates emerge that are relevant to social work practice and education.

1. *Advances in information and communication technology.* NASW (2007) establishes

face-to-face contact as the standard of care. However, studies have substantiated positive outcomes with the use of telephonic interventions for community-based case management (Laramee et al., 2003; Riegel et al., 2002). The use of computerized technology for patient monitoring is gaining attention in the health care field. For example, computers are set up in the patient's home that are linked to the provider or case manager's office. Regularly scheduled reports (such as symptoms and home testing of blood pressure and glucose levels) are made, triggering provider interventions, as needed. Though research on this new technology is still evolving, it is garnering significant attention from providers, health care administrators, and payers. Use of e-mail, interactive discussions, and discussion boards become effective tools for communication of information. Social workers will need to develop proficiency in these new technologies to enhance case management processes

2. *Evidence-based practice (EBP)*. The development and implementation of health care interventions, including case management, have increasingly relied on evidence-based studies. The EBP literature on case management is rapidly increasing, but predominantly from the field of nursing. To validate social work's role within the case management domain, evidence-based studies are essential. The work of Vourlekis and Ell (2007) provides an excellent example. They have developed a best practices approach to case management based on five key elements: integration of services, culturally competent case managers, individualized services, multisystem interventions, and quality improvement. This approach is theoretically grounded and the elements are evidence based.

Case management in health care settings is a complex and dynamic intervention. Effective implementation will rely on a thorough understanding of the purpose, goals, and contextual factors that shape its practice. Attention should be given to advances in communication technological to facilitate case management processes, as well as evidence-based research to demonstrate practice efficiency and effectiveness.

WEB SITES

American Case Management Association. http://www.acmaweb.org.
Case Management Association of America. http://www.cmsa.org.
NASW Standards for Social Work Case Management. http://www.socialworkers.org/practice/standards/sw_case_mgmt.asp#intro.

References

Applebaum, R., & Austin, C. (1990). *Long-term care case management: Design and evaluation.* New York: Springer.

Berger, C. S. (1996). Case management in health care. In C. Austin & R. W. McClelland (Eds.), *Perspective on case management practice* (pp. 145–174). Milwaukee, WI: Families International.

Bierman, J., Dunlop, A. L., Brady, C., Dubin, C., & Brann, A. (2006). Promising practices in preconception care for women at risk for poor health and pregnancy outcomes. *Maternal Child Health Journal, 10*(suppl 7): 21–28.

Dorr, D. A., Wilcox, A., McConnell, K. J., Burns, L, & Brunker, C. P. (2007). Productivity enhancement for primary care providers using multicondition care management. *American Journal of Managed Care*, 22–28.

Felt-Lisk, S., & Mays, G. P. (2002). Back to the drawing board: New directions in health plans' care management strategies. *Health Affairs, 21*(5), 210–217.

Felton, C. J., Stastny, P., Shern, D. L., Blanch, A., Donahue, S. A., Knight, E., & Brown, C. (1995). Consumers as peer specialists on intensive case management teams: Impact on clinical outcomes. *Psychiatric Services, 46*, 1037–1044.

Kane, R. (1992). Case management in health care settings. In S. Rose (Ed.), *Case management and social work* (pp. 170–203). New York: Longman.

Kirton, C. (1999). Primary care and case management of persons with HIV/AIDS. *Nursing Clinics of North America, 34*, 71–94.

Laramee, A. S., Levinsky, S. K., Sargent, J., Ross, R., & Callas, P. (2003). Case management in a heterogeneous congestive heart failure population. *Archives of Internal Medicine, 163*, 809–817.

NASW Standards for Social Work Case Management. (June 1992). Prepared by the Case Management Standards Work Group.

Riegel, B., Carlson, B., Kopp, Z., LePetri, B., Glaser, D., & Unger, A. (2002). Effect of standardized nurse case-management telephone intervention on resource use in patients with chronic heart failure. *Archives of Internal Medicine, 162*, 705–712.

Rose, S. (Ed.). (1992). *Case management and social work*. New York: Longman.

Sangalang, B. B., Barth, R. P., & Painter, J. S. (2006). First-birth outcomes and timing of second births: A statewide case management program for ad-oles-cent mothers. *Health & Social Work, 31*(1), 54–63.

Sweeney, L., Halpert, A., & Waranoff, J. (2007). Patient-centered management of complex patients can reduce costs without shortening life. *American Journal of Managed Care*, 84–89.

Thompson, B. (1998). Case management in AIDS service sellings. In D. M. Aronstein & B. J. Thompson (Eds.), *HIV and social work a practitiones's guide* (pp. 75–87). New York: Haworth.

Vourlekis, B., & Ell, K. (2007). Best practice case man-agement for improved medical adherence. *Social Work in Health Care, 44*(3), 161–177.

Vourlekis, B., Ell, K., & Padgett, D. (2005). Evidence-based assessment in case management to improve abnormal cancer screen follow-up. *Health & Social Work, 30*(1), 98–106.

117 Case Management with Older Adults

Carol D. Austin & Robert W. McClelland

Although widely used, the term *case management* remains unclear and confusing, sometimes describing benefit management, management of an acute event, community-based interventions, or other types of client management across the continuum of care. In some programs, the case management function has been called care man-agement, care coordination, or care planning. Cli-ents and caregivers have expressed the view that they "are not cases and do not want to be man-aged." At the most general level, case manage-ment can be defined as a coordinating function designed to link clients with various services based on assessed need. There is a need for coordina-tion of care because caregivers and chronically ill older persons may require services from several providers.

The National Association of Social Workers (1992) promulgated standards for social work case management, defining it as "a method of provid-ing services whereby a professional social worker assesses the needs of the client and the client's family, when appropriate, and arranges, coordi-nates, monitors, evaluates, and advocates for a pack-age of multiple services to meet the specific client's complex needs. . . . Social work case management is both micro and macro in nature; intervention oc-curs at both the client and system level" (p. 5).

HISTORY

Case management is now common in programs serving older adults, whether publicly or privat-ely funded. The current state of home- and com-munity-based services is the product of a public policy development process. Case management was mandated in federal legislation authorizing the Home and Community-based Waiver (Omnibus Budget Reconciliation Act of 1981, Public Law no. 97-35, Section 2176).

Case management is central to this program-matic and policy direction for two reasons. It is widely agreed that the delivery system is highly fragmented. Furthermore, individuals meeting el-igibility criteria for home- and community-based services have complex care needs, requiring sys-tematic and comprehensive assessment and an individualized care plan. Case management is a response to the complexity of client circumstances and the problematic state of the delivery system. The case manager attends to individual client's needs and is identified as the agent to overcome the fragmented delivery system, coordinating the complex web of programs, services, and agencies.

The fact that case management remains a central part of programs designed to care for frail elderly in the community is demonstrated by a recent international comparative study. Johri, Beland, and Bergman (2003) reviewed seven international experiments in integrated care in the United Kingdom, United States, Italy, and Canada (Beland et al., 2006; Bernabei et al., 1998; Challis, Weiner, Darton, Hughes, & Stewart, 2001). This study identified common features of an effective integrated system of care: a single point of entry, case management, geriatric assessment, a multidisciplinary team, and use of financial incentives to promote downward substitution.

COMPONENTS OF CASE MANAGEMENT PRACTICE

The goal for case managers is to help clients negotiate the fragmented delivery system while attending to fiscal constraints. Although operationalized in various ways, case management has a common set of core components that includes (1) outreach, (2) screening, (3) comprehensive assessment, (4) care planning, (5) service arrangement, (6) monitoring, and (7) reassessment (Applebaum & Austin, 1990).

1. *Outreach activities*. These are designed to identify persons likely to qualify for and have a need for health and social support services, as well as case management.
2. *Screening* is a preliminary assessment of the client's circumstances and resources to determine presumptive eligibility. Potential clients are screened by means of standardized procedures to determine whether their status and situation meet the program's target population definition.
3. *Comprehensive assessment*. This is a systematic and standardized process for collecting detailed information about a person's physical, mental, and psychological functioning and informal support system that facilitates the identification of the person's strengths and care needs. Typically,

comprehensive assessment focuses on physical health, mental functioning, ability to perform activities of daily living, social supports, physical environment, and financial resources. Many programs have adopted rigorous standardized multidimensional instruments (Gallo, Reichel, & Anderson, 1995).

4. *Care planning*. Information collected during the assessment process is used to develop a plan of care. Care planning requires clinical judgment, creativity, sensitivity, and knowledge of community resources. Case managers consider the willingness and availability of informal caregivers to provide care, attempting to establish a balance between formal and informal services. Clients and caregivers participate in developing the care plan. The care plan specifies services, providers, frequency of delivery, and costs. Care planning is a key resource allocation process and a critical case management function.
5. *Service arrangement*. This involves contacting formal and informal providers to arrange services specified in the care plan. Case managers often must negotiate with providers for services when making referrals to other agencies. When they have the authority to purchase services on their clients' behalf, case managers order services directly from providers. Case managers systemically monitor changes in clients' situations and alter care plans to meet clients' needs.
6. *Ongoing monitoring*. This, combined with timely modification of care plans, helps ensure that program expenditures reflect current client needs and are not based on outdated assessment data.
7. *Reassessment*. This process involves determining whether changes in the client's situation have occurred since the last assessment and also helps in evaluating progress toward accomplishing outcomes specified in the care plan.

THE CHANGING CONTEXT

Practitioners will note a basic flaw in the community-based long-term care programs: the absence of health care services. Case managers could only develop care plans and coordinate covered community-based and in-home services. Clearly, this approach did not adequately address the health care needs of older adults. Older adults needing case management are often identified and assessed in the health care system. Though chronic illness generates the greatest health care costs, medical management programs continue to focus primarily on managing acute events. Medicare beneficiaries in need of case management fall into two groups: (1) individuals recently discharged from the hospital who have difficulty leaving home to receive needed services, and (2) individuals receiving Medicare home health services. Because older adults are major utilizers of health care services, it is necessary to develop delivery systems that integrate services across the continuum of care, with particular attention to involving primary care physicians.

The Program of All-Inclusive Care of the Elderly (PACE) and the Social Health Care Maintenance Organization (S/HMO) completely integrate services and financing for both acute and long-term care services. Both programs incorporate a capitated payment for each participant, blending Medicare and Medicaid funds. This funding method introduces strong incentives for providers to establish cost-containment mechanisms and carefully monitor participant service utilization patterns. Cost containment is a significant responsibility for case managers in managed care settings where providers assume financial risk.

The way Medicare reimburses postacute providers will affect care management. In a cost-based reimbursement system, case managers provide assessment and coordination and can act as a check on excessive use and disorganized service delivery. In a prospective payment system (Medicare risk in HMOs), case managers facilitate beneficiary access to covered services by (1) documenting care needs, (2) ensuring appropriate communication of medical orders to providers, and (3) making referrals for non-Medicare services.

The practice of case management is also affected by the movement toward consumer direction. Although the best practice of case management requires meaningful inclusion of clients and caregivers in care plan development, it is essentially a professionally controlled process. The cash and counseling demonstration, implemented in Arkansas, New Jersey, New York, and Florida, tested a model that significantly enhanced consumer direction by allowing some clients (in the cash allowance group) to make personal choices about how to spend Medicaid funds to meet their personal assistance needs. Other clients received traditional agency-delivered services, including traditional case management. Clients in the case allowance group worked with a counselor to develop a personal assistance care spending plan and were provided with financial management and counseling services (Dale, Brown, Phillips, Schore, & Carlson, 2003; Mahoney, Simon-Rusinowitz, Loughlin, Desmons, & Squillace, et al., 2004). Consumer-directed service options are now common in state Medicaid programs. This means that eligible clients can now manage their own cases, including hiring and supervision of personal care workers.

The policy context for case management has further shifted as a result of the Supreme Count's decision in *Olmstead v. L.C.* (527 U.S. 581, 1999), invoking the "integration mandate" of the Americans with Disabilities Act, which requires public agencies to provide services in the most integrated setting appropriate to the needs of qualified individuals. The court held that states cannot make institutional placement a condition for receiving publicly funded health care and that such requirements constitute illegal discrimination. Olmstead required states to further expand their home and community based services, potentially affecting the care of large numbers of institutionalized and community residing older adults (Fishman, Valdeck, Palermo, & Davis, 2003).

EVIDENCE BASE

Is case management effective? The answer is neither direct nor simple. Evaluation is an inherently political activity, with multiple stakeholders, each potentially looking for different kinds of evidence that demonstrate effectiveness from their perspective. Some stakeholders may have an economic perspective, focused on cost related analyses (cost-effectiveness, cost-benefit, cost-utility, cost-containment), while others may have a managerial orientation, emphasizing standards, regulations, efficiency, and planning. Evaluations of case management have primarily focused on substitution (cost avoidance through substitution of less expensive services for more expensive ones) and efficacy (improved outcomes for clients; i.e., quality of life).

Evaluations of case management effectiveness must be contextualized. Evaluation requires that the intervention is thoroughly specified. Although "definitions of case management abound . . . they do not have enough descriptive power to differentiate between case management programs" (Summers, 2000, p. 90). Summers identified a framework that provides descriptors for case management program evaluations. There are both structural and process elements. The structural elements include the program's purpose and its philosophical approach, whether an individual or team approach is used, whether the case manager has budget holding responsibility, staff/client ratio in the program, the extent to which case management is a specialized service, the program's target population, its funding sources, and status of the case manager. The process elements include the degree of direct care or brokerage, intensity of the intervention, focus on health and/or social needs, degree of client participation, location of client contact, level of intervention (individual, network, or system), and level of cultural competency of case managers. Evaluations that attend to these contextual issues are better able to generate comparable information.

Is there a relationship between client characteristics and the amount of case management time they receive? Is there a dose-response relationship, between the amount of case management time provided and outcomes of interest? Answers to these evaluative questions are program-specific and demonstrate that contextual complexities make it difficult to compare evaluative studies. For example, in one program the average caseload size was 28, and intensive case management was defined as more than 1 hour a week. Clients receiving intensive case management in this program resisted services and were characterized by their frequent, persistent interactions with case managers and providers as well as their physical frailty, dependency, and volatility (Boyle & Sudbury, 2000). In another program, average caseload size was 90 to -100. Here, intensive case management was defined as the provision of 6.5 hours of case management over a 4-month period, or 1.6 hours per month. Clients receiving intensive case management in this program were more likely to have dementia or mental illness, exhibit problematic behaviors, have unstable informal caregiving, have multiple problems, require involvement from adult protective services, or are new cases (Diwan, Ivy, Merino, & Brower, 2001). Intensity of contact between clients and case managers is mediated by programmatic and organizational variables and not determined by client characteristics alone.

How consumer-focused is the evaluation of case management? To what extent are consumers involved in determining what constitutes effectiveness and success in the provision of case management (Summers, 2000)? What do clients find meaningful? To answer these questions, it is necessary to go beyond standard efforts to measure client satisfaction and quality of life. To capture lived experience, it is necessary to take the time to talk with clients, ask open-ended questions, and carefully listen to responses. "There is a notable absence of information about how chronically ill elders and their informal caregivers understand and evaluate current care systems or the degree to which current care systems equitably address the self-care, informal caregiving and psychosocial challenges that elders consider most important" (Capitman, 2001, p. 14).

Recent qualitative research uncovered important insights provided by clients who are enrolled in programs that integrate medical and community support services for older adults (Capitman, 2001; Leutz, Capitman, & Greene, 2001). This research illuminates the multidimensional nature of satisfaction and quality of life by putting a human face on the experience. In the absence of such studies, we lose the voices of clients themselves, what they value, and what has meaning (Moxley, 1997).

PRACTICE CONSIDERATIONS

Case managers provide both client- and system-level interventions (NASW, 1992). Can case managers act as client advocates and system agents simultaneously? Although case managers may operate from a client-centered approach, they will also be responsible for monitoring and controlling service utilization. As case managers assume greater fiscal accountability, there is greater potential for care plan decision making to be influenced by financial pressures. Case managers' independence has two aspects: (1) clinical, and (2) financial.

There has been a continuing debate regarding the extent to which case management should be separated from the direct provision of services. Case managers who are not independent from the hospital, home health agency, nursing home, or community-based service provider may have a conflict of interest that affects their capacity to develop care plans that fully reflect the clients' interests. In health care, perhaps more clearly than in other settings, questions arise about whether quality and cost-containment goals can be reconciled. Inevitably case managers will confront challenging ethical issues (Wetle, 1992).

LOOKING AHEAD

In the future, case management will be a significant feature in the provision of health and social services to older adults in acute, subacute, and chronic care settings, whether in institutional settings, the community, or the home. Wherever case managers are employed across the continuum of care, it will continue to be necessary to examine four basic issues: (1) the scope of case management practice, (2) case managers' fiscal authority, (3) their independence, and (4) quality assurance. These fundamental issues apply to case management at any point on the continuum of care and directly reflect the specific programmatic context within which case management is provided. In the future, as in the past, the scope of services case managers are responsible for, their independence and authority will vary considerably. Consumer direction will be a significant feature in case-managed programs, reflecting the changing locus of control between case managers and clients, families, and caregivers. Legislative and judicial mandates, like the *Olmstead* decision, may further redefine target populations and further strain already scarce case management and service resources.

As long as delivery systems remain seriously fragmented, a situation that does not appear likely to change in the near future, it will be necessary to make efforts to enhance continuity of care, manage transitions, coordinate services, and advocate on behalf of clients. The evidence base for case management will remain mixed, as it has been in the past. Due to the variation in practice, we will continue to be challenged to design comparative evaluations of various approaches to case management. As a result, it will be difficult to state definitively that one approach to case management is more effective than another. Nevertheless, it appears that case management has enough pragmatic value that it is likely to become even more pervasive.

WEB SITES

Case Management Resource Guide. http://www .cmrg.com.

Cash and Counseling. http://www .cashandcounseling.org.

National Association of Professional Geriatric Case Managers. http://www.caremanager .org.

National Conference of State Legislatures, States' Response to the *Olmstead* Decision: A Work in Progress. http://www .ncsl.org.

Olmstead Decision, Center for an Accessible Society. http://www.accessiblesociety.org.

References

Applebaum, R., & Austin, C. (1990). *Long term care case management: Design and evaluation.* New York: Springer.

Beland, F., Bergman, H., Lebel, P., Dallaire, L., Fletcher, J., Tousignant, P., et al. (2006). Integrated services for frail elders (SIPA): A trial of a model for Canada. *Canadian Journal on Aging, 25*(1), 25–42.

Bernabei, R., Landi, F., Gambassi, G., Sgadari, A., Zuccala, G., Mor, V., et al. (1998). Randomized trail of impact of model of integrated care and case management for older people living in the community. *British Medical Journal, 316,* 1348–1351.

Boyle, N., & Sudbury, B. (2000). Client circumstances which contribute to high use of case management time: An exploratory study. *Australian Journal of Case Management, 2*(2), 4–7.

Capitman, J. (2001). *Effective coordination of medical and supportive services.* New York: Visiting Nurse Service of New York.

Challis, D., Weiner, K., Darton, R., Hughes, J., & Stewart, K. (2001). Emerging patterns of care management: Arrangements for older people in England. *Social Policy and Administration, 35*(6), 672–687.

Dale, S., Brown, R., Phillips, B., Schore, J., & Carlson, B. (2003). The effects of cash and counseling on personal care services and Medicaid costs in Arkansas. *Data Watch, 19*(November).

Diwan, S., Ivy, C., Merino, D., & Brower, T. (2001). Assessing need for intensive case management in long-term care. *Gerontologist, 41*(5), 680–686.

Fishman, E., Vladeck, B., Palermo, A., & Davis, M. (2003). *The Olmstead decision and long term care in California: Lessons on services, access and costs from Colorado, Washington and Wisconsin.* Sacramento, CA: California Healthcare Foundation.

Gallo, J., Reichel, W., & Anderson, L. (1995). *Handbook of geriatric assessment,* 2nd ed.. Gaithersburg, MD: Aspen.

Johri, M., Beland, F., & Bergman, H. (2003). International experiments in integrated care for the elderly: A synthesis of the evidence. *International Journal of Geriatric Psychiatry, 18*(3), 222–235.

Leutz, W., Capitman, J., & Greene, C. (2001). Adequate community care: Qualitative findings on service use in the Social HMO. *Journal of Aging and Social Policy, 12*(1), 15–30.

Mahoney, K., Simon-Rusinowitz, L., Loughlin, D., Desmons, S., & Squillace, M. (2004). Determining personal care consumers' preferences for consumer-directed cash and counseling option: Survey of results from Arkansas, Florida, New Jersey and New York elders and adults with disabilities. *Health Services Research, 39*(3), 643–664.

Moxley, D. (1997). *Case management by design: Reflections on principles and practices.* Chicago: Nelson Hall.

National Association of Social Workers. (1992). *NASW standards for social work case management.* Washington, DC: NASW Press.

Summers, M. (2000). Facilitating comparisons between evaluations of case management programs. *Journal of Case Management, 13*(3), 86–92.

Wetle, T. (1992). A taxonomy of ethical issues in case management of the frail older person. *Journal of Case Management, 1,* 71–75.

118   HIV/AIDS Case Management

Brian Giddens, Lana Sue I. Ka'opua, & Evelyn P. Tomaszewski

Case management (CM) has been an effective means for assisting persons with HIV/AIDS since the 1980s. In the early years of the HIV epidemic, CM programs were developed in urban epicenters to meet the growing medical and psychosocial needs of persons infected by HIV. As HIV disproportionately impacted already disenfranchised populations, case managers and other service providers quickly found that they were dealing with a disease condition imbued with significant social stigma and discrimination (Brennan, 1996). Thus, there was a need to broker, coordinate, and monitor services that included legal resources, housing, mental health, substance use treatment, financial and insurance resources, medical services, in-home assistance, and other practical and social support needs.

Since that time, the context of HIV/AIDS, as well as the medical treatment for it, has changed significantly in two distinct ways. Whereas in the early years of the disease HIV was seen as a terminal illness, new treatments have changed the disease to that of a chronic illness for many (though not all) affected persons. Though these treatments help stem progression of the disease and the many opportunistic infections that can occur, treatment regimens require assessment of a person's ability to understand the medical treatment plan, ongoing education about living with a complex chronic illness, and interventions to help ensure adherence.

While the treatment for HIV has changed, so has the medical arena in which those treatments have been provided. The focus on managed care is changing the nature of health care delivery. A majority of states have adopted managed care for their Medicaid recipients with HIV disease (Solomon, Flynn, & Lavetsky, 2005). Regardless of public or private funding, by the 1990s, managed care for chronic illness had become a priority area (Wagner, Austin, & Von Korff, 1996). The models for managing a chronic disease, often labeled disease management, continue to develop to combat the high cost of chronic illnesses such as HIV (Goldstein, 2006). In addition to the shift to managed care, the dynamic nature of the disease requires providers with the knowledge base to manage a multisystem, complex disease that calls for both the expertise of a specialist as well as the skills of a primary care practitioner who can oversee the ongoing treatment plan (Gerbert et al., 2001). In areas that do not have a high occurrence of persons with HIV, this level of expertise may not be readily available (Solomon et al., 2004).

An additional factor in the changing context of HIV/AIDS is the affected populations. HIV can be found in regions and communities throughout the United States, but certain groups are more at risk. According to the Centers for Disease Control and Prevention (CDC, 2007), the largest estimated proportion of HIV/AIDS diagnoses were for (1) men who have sex with men, and (2) adults and adolescents infected through heterosexual contact or sharing injection drug works with someone already HIV positive. In ethnic/racial comparisons, African Americans continue to be disproportionately burdened by HIV incidence (i.e., African Americans comprise 13 percent of the U.S. population, yet account for 49 percent of HIV cases). In comparison to other ethnic/racial groups, African Americans tend to have lower survival rates and higher mortality rates. These disparities are associated with socioeconomic factors, including limited or no access to health care services.

The social work implications are clear. Given the current arenas of HIV epidemiology, treatment, and health care delivery systems, CM services will need to work even more closely with interdisciplinary health care teams and community providers. Assessing for HIV risk, providing education, identifying and accessing available resources, and incorporating risk reduction and adherence counseling into practice will continue to be necessary tasks for case managers.

EVIDENCE BASE FOR HIV CASE MANAGEMENT

The empirical evidence supporting the influence of HIV CM on health, utilization, and cost outcomes serves as an important guide to social work practice, policy advocacy, and social welfare research. However, the extant research in the area of CM is limited by (1) general lack of agreement on the components of a comprehensive CM model, (2) variations in the ways and degree to which case managers link their clientele to services, (3) variation among communities in services available, and (4) methodological challenges to evaluating multiple and interacting factors (e.g., services provided by several agencies) that might potentially influence desired outcomes (e.g., undetectable viral load) (Messeri, Abramson, Aidala, Lee, & Lee, 2002). Thus, in reviewing the research to inform practice, social workers need to consider (1) type(s) of CM services that influence a specific health, utilization, or cost outcome; and (2) segment of the client population most likely to benefit from a particular type of CM service.

The evidence-base for HIV CM suggests the following.

• *Demand for case management will likely increase.* Preliminary findings from a trend analysis of HIV-positive individuals receiving services from Ryan White CARE Act providers suggest that the introduction of combination antiretroviral regimen in 1996 precipitated an increase in service utilization, especially at the point of treatment initiation. The analysis indicates that the demand for CM services will continue to grow, albeit at a more gradual pace (Marconi & Jacobsen, 1999).

• *Case management improves health services utilization.* Longitudinal, self-reported survey data from more than 500 HIV-positive individuals living in New York City indicate that CM and other ancillary services are significantly associated with increasing access to care and client retention in health care systems. Case management services were especially helpful to those with needs related to logistics (e.g., transportation, child care), social environmental factors (e.g., lack of access to housing), individual factors (co-occurring substance use or other mental health diagnoses), and coordination of services (e.g., access to regular source of care). This research also suggests that CM may facilitate entry into a variety of other supportive services that ultimately influence treatment adherence (Messeri et al., 2002).

• *Case management is associated with cost containment.* HIV case management, following the evidence-based practice guidelines of the CDC and the Department of Health and Human Services, was found to improve client adherence to antiretroviral medication regimens and other recommended treatments. During the periods of July 1999–June 2000 and July 2000–June 2001, overall viral load of HIV-positive clients (comorbid conditions and sociodemographic characteristics not specified) was reduced in 35 percent of clientele, and CD-4 count increased among in 46 percent of clientele. These positive health outcomes were shown to significantly reduce the cost of treatments for opportunistic infections and other complications (Specialty Disease Management, 2007).

WHAT IS CASE MANAGEMENT?

CM is a service that links and coordinates assistance from institutions and agencies providing medical, psychosocial, and practical support for individuals in need of such assistance (Support Center for Nonprofit Management & San Francisco Department of Public Health AIDS Office, 1996).

The term CM has been used by several disciplines and institutions to describe coordination activities for clients and patients. *Insurance CM* focuses on utilization of services, with a goal of monitoring and maximizing resources. *Medical CM* may concentrate on achieving improved patient outcomes, based on specific treatment interventions. *Social CM* tends to take a global perspective, emphasizing the psychosocial and spiritual impacts of illness in assessment and treatment planning.

Setting can also differentiate the role of the case manager (Barney & Duran, 1997). Hospital-based programs may allow for a more medically focused style of case coordination, whereas a community-based case manager may be able to work more closely with clients in their home setting, incorporating a more holistic assessment.

For the purposes of this chapter, we will be focusing on an integrated model of HIV/AIDS CM that is interdisciplinary and that incorporates both the medical and social CM perspectives (National Association of Social Workers [NASW], 2002). The integrated model of CM

incorporates the following characteristics into program design:

- population-based screening, triaging the patient to most appropriate level of care;
- emphasizing interdisciplinary management of disease and the factors that are likely to affect treatment and adherence;
- focusing on any need that prevents access to or decreases adherence to treatment;
- advocating for both the patient and the medical system, given the premise that the best care is cost-effective; and
- providing ongoing continuity of care that emphasizes risk reduction and prevention.

ACTIVITIES AND ROLES IN HIV CASE MANAGEMENT

The integrated HIV CM model is guided by the NASW *Standards for Social Work Case Management* (1992) and reflects the ecological view of the profession, commitment to fostering productive relations with other professionals on behalf of the client, and approaches to service delivery that are client-centered, empowerment-based, and culturally responsive. This specific variation of social work CM is unique in several ways. First, HIV CM models recognize that living with the disease poses biopsychosocial and spiritual challenges. The implications of HIV-related stigma are underscored, and at the broadest level of intervention, CM services are optimally delivered in a relationship characterized by acceptance and unconditional positive regard. The social worker providing CM services is often one of the first gatekeepers in the service delivery system, and being a safe, confidential, and respectful contact is emphasized. Second, because crises may occur across the illness spectrum and client needs may vary over time, CM often uses a triage system that prioritizes involvement on crucial points in disease progression. Triaging takes into account various acuity factors, such as basic needs, substance abuse, physical and mental health, and culture or linguistic differences (Thompson, 1998). Third, prevention and risk reduction are components of HIV CM, and the social worker may take on the role of educator/counselor as well as the more generic roles of service broker, advocate, and monitor. The case manager also takes on roles that are linked to the core activities of the initial interview/intake, assessment, and development, implementation, and monitoring of the service plan.

INITIAL INTERVIEW/INTAKE: CASE MANAGER AS SAFE CONTACT, CRISIS COUNSELOR, SERVICE BROKER

The process of HIV CM begins with the initial interview and in many settings is combined with the intake. In the initial interview, the primary goal is to establish a comfortable rapport that facilitates the development of a collaborative working relationship and establishes the social worker as a safe point of contact. In the first encounter, the role of crisis counselor may be important because entry into the service delivery system is often precipitated by crises that require immediate intervention. Information about the scope of services available is integrated into the initial interview.

During the intake, a preliminary assessment of client needs is made with a view toward bridging the gap between service needs and system resources. Client rights, grievance procedures, and responsibilities are reviewed, and informed consent to enroll the client in the service delivery system is obtained. Information necessary to register the client includes confirmation and date of initial AIDS diagnosis or first positive HIV antibody test, health insurance status, HIV disease stage, source of exposure to HIV, CD4 count, homelessness status, active substance use, psychiatric illness, and TB status. Because of the stigmatized nature of HIV, it is vital that social workers explain why information is collected, who will have access to the information, and where records will be maintained.

ASSESSMENT: CASE MANAGER AS CLINICIAN, SERVICE BROKER, LINKER, EDUCATOR

The needs assessment is optimally conducted as a collaborative effort with both case manager and client identifying treatment and service needs, client strengths and natural psychosocial resources, and areas in which service linkage is needed. The assessment is key to establish a baseline profile for initial service referrals, development of the service plan, and criteria for evaluation of service outcomes. Formalized instruments are used to collect information such as basic client data, medical information, living situation, personal history and situation, relationships and social support, health education, psychosocial functioning and mental status, functional status, service needs and issues, and legal issues (Support Center, 1996). Case managers are increasingly taking on two new functions: conducting risk assessments and assessing the ability of the client to adhere to treatment. Assessing HIV transmission risk includes identifying barriers for the client in reducing transmission risk and involves educating clients about HIV transmission and ways to reduce risk. When risk behaviors are identified, these can be addressed through the service plan and monitored within the context of the ongoing CM relationship. The other function of determining capacity for adherence should be done in conjunction with the interdisciplinary team. The role of the case manager is not only to identify and help resolve the psychosocial barriers to adherence but also to advocate for access to new treatments.

Various competencies are required for completion of the comprehensive assessment, including the technical capacity to gather clinical information and the cultural and linguistic competency to collect culturally relevant information. The case manager should work closely with the interdisciplinary team to ensure that client goals are congruent with treatment goals. Key indicators of mental health distress and disorder should be identified and referred for follow-up by a licensed mental health provider.

DEVELOPMENT OF THE SERVICE PLAN: CASE MANAGER AS PLANNER, COLLABORATOR, ADVOCATE

The service plan is central to the CM effort and builds on the information gathered in the assessment. The case manager and client collaborate to make an inventory of problems and issues and to formulate long- and short-term objectives that support the overall goals of health maintenance and independence. Specific planning, guided by realistic objectives, is required to prioritize activities and identify how services will be obtained, monitored, and coordinated among the providing agencies and health care systems. Responsibilities of all parties and a realistic time line should be clearly delineated for accomplishing objectives and relevant activities. When service options are not available to meet identified needs, the case manager may need to consider either advocating for options or designing interim solutions. This is more likely to occur when clients' cultural values or practices are dystonic with that of existing programs, when clients have co-occurring diagnoses, such as substance abuse or a mental disorder, or when clients reside in rural areas with relatively few HIV-specific services. Service plans should be clearly documented in the client's chart along with copies of written correspondence and application forms for entitlement programs, experimental drug protocols, and the like. An abbreviated version of the plan along with contact information may be helpful to offer the client.

IMPLEMENTATION/MONITORING: CASE MANAGER AS BROKER, COORDINATOR, SERVICE MONITOR, COACH

In the implementation phase, the social worker and client take action to accomplish the service plan. Once consent to refer has been obtained, the case manager may employ a number of roles to facilitate the client's receipt of services, including that of broker, monitor, advocate, and coach. As broker, the case manager contacts other providers to pave the way for client referral and may also arrange for ancillary services, such as transportation to appointments. On linkage with services, the case manager maintains regular client contact to monitor that services have been received and rendered in an acceptable way. On occasion the case manager may need to advocate on behalf of the client, thus ensuring that necessary services are received. As coach, the case manager encourages the client to anticipate barriers to access and utilization and, when necessary, works with the client to address these issues. Service plans are usually implemented in increments with careful documentation of client progress, including dates of contact, information on who initiated contact, and any action that resulted from the contact. Obstacles to implementation should be noted, as well as client satisfaction, modifications to the plan, and progress toward specified goals and objectives. Professional social work supervision, peer support, and inter- and intra-agency case conferences are often helpful in addressing implementation difficulties.

CONTINUOUS QUALITY IMPROVEMENT

Ensuring the quality of a CM program, including the evaluation of outcomes, is becoming increasingly important. Not only are funding agencies requiring information on how CM programs meet client needs, but with the field of HIV/AIDS CM changing rapidly, it is imperative that the time spent by staff and administrators is effectively used. Evaluative activities could include assessing client satisfaction with services provided, determining if the affected population in a geographic area is aware of the availability of services, and assessing medical provider satisfaction with CM as a support service.

Besides these traditional evaluation methods, funders are increasingly requiring outcome-based evaluation. Examples of outcome evaluation can include whether CM is helping clients adhere to treatment or whether clients actually engaged with referred services (i.e., tracking not only the number of referrals made to community services but whether the client followed through with the linkage). Quality improvement processes can monitor both the micro and macro level of service provision, ensuring that the needs of the client and the community are met.

CONFIDENTIALITY

The case manager should be clear from the beginning about what information may be shared, under what circumstances it will be shared, and with whom it is shared. The Health Insurance Portability and Accountability Act (HIPAA), as well as specific state and federal privacy regulations, are counters to concerns about managing client records in the digital age; service providers will need to stay current on such regulations. In addition, a commonsense review of agency or institutional processes should be done periodically to ensure that client privacy is maintained.

CULTURAL COMPETENCY

CM services are optimally grounded in the awareness that clients' attitudes and behaviors may vary as associated with race, ethnicity, gender, class, sexual orientation, age, and disability. Cultural competence requires case managers to examine their own cultural values in the context of the helping relationship, actively elicit relevant cultural information, and negotiate understanding and agreement of service needs, care plan, and desired outcomes (Ka'opua, 1998). Referral to culturally compatible services may be important (Barney & Duran, 1997). Culturally competent case management services assume client involvement and ideally reside within a system of cultural and linguistic competence in policies, programs, practice standards, evaluation, and research (NASW, 2000).

CONCLUSION

HIV/AIDS CM will continue to evolve as the social and medical contexts of the disease shift. Accordingly, social workers who provide CM will need to adapt their practices to meet the needs of their CM populations. As CM moved from a primarily social model to one that incorporates funding and medical issues, case managers adapted by gaining knowledge of funding streams and resources. Case managers will also have to learn the language and culture of other disciplines, especially nursing, medicine, and pharmacy. As various forms of CM, managed care and disease management models proliferate from different settings of care and funding, greater coordination will be needed to ensure that redundancies are reduced and that efficiencies are created to maintain more dollars for patient care rather than funding duplicative programs. This will require collaboration among programs and providers. With collaboration comes the need for skills in negotiation, systems thinking, problem solving, and communication. Given that skills such as these are what social workers practice every day, the profession is poised to take a prominent role in the CM field of the future.

WEB SITES

The Body. http://www.thebody.com.
Centers for Disease Control (CDC). http://www.cdc.gov/hiv.
Healthy People/HRSA. http://www.healthypeople.gov/Document/HTML/Volume1/13HIV.htm.
NASW-HIV/AIDS Spectrum Project. http://www.socialworkers.org/practice/hiv_aids/default.asp.
Ryan White. http://hab.hrsa.gov/special projects.htm.

References

Barney, D. D., & Duran, B. E. S. (1997). Case management: Coordination of service delivery for HIV-infected individuals. In M. G. Winiarski (Ed.), *HIV mental health for the 21st century* (pp. 241–255). New York: New York University Press.

Brennan, J. (1996). Comprehensive case management with HIV clients. In C. D. Austin & R. W. McClelland (Eds.), *Case management practice*. Milwaukee, WI: Families International.

Centers for Disease Control and Prevention. (2007). HIV/AIDS in the United States. Retrieved on November 5, 2007 from http://www.cdc.gov/hiv/resources/factsheets/At-A-Glance.htm.

Gerbert, B., Moe, J. C., Saag, M. S., Benson, C. A., et al. (2001). Toward a definition of HIV expertise: A survey of experienced HIV physicians. *AIDS Patient Care and STDs, 15*(6), 321–330.

Goldstein, P. C. (2006). Impact of disease management programs on hospital and community nursing practice. *Nursing Economics, 24*(6), 308–313.

Ka'opua, L. S. (1999) Multicultural competence. In D. M. Aronstein & B. J. Thompson (Eds.), *HIV and social work. A practitioner's guide* (pp. 61–54). New York: Haworth.

Marconi, K. M., & Jacobsen, J. M. (1999). Trends in the use of primary health care and case management among HIV+ individuals. *Association of Health Services Research Meeting, Abstract Book, 16*(160).

Messeri, P. A., Abramson, D. M., Aidala, A. A., Lee, F., & Lee, G. (2002). The impact of ancillary HIV services on engagement in medical care in New York City. *AIDS Care, 14*(suppl 1), S15–S29.

National Association of Social Workers. (1992). *NASW standards for social work case management* [brochure]. Washington, DC: NASW Press.

National Association of Social Workers. (2000). Cultural competence in the social work profession. In *Social work speaks: National Association of Social Workers policy statements 2003–2006* (pp. 71–74). Washington, DC: NASW Press.

National Association of Social Workers. (2002). *NASW HIV/AIDS Spectrum: Mental health training and education of social workers project.* Washington, DC: NASW Press.

Solomon, L., Flynn, C., & Lavetsky, G. (2005). Managed care for AIDS patients: Is bigger better? *Journal of Acquired Immune Deficiency Syndromes, 38*(3), 342–347.

Specialty Disease Management. (2007). *HIV case management.* Retrieved October 4, 2007, from http://www.specialtydisease.com/disease_management.hiv.html.

Support Center for Nonprofit Management & San Francisco Department of Public Health AIDS Office. (1996). *Making the connection: Standards of practice for client-centered HIV case management.* San Francisco: Support Center.

Thompson, B. J. (1998). Case management in AIDS service settings. In D. M. Aronstein & B. J. Thompson (Eds.), *HIV and social work. A practitioner's guide* (pp. 75–87). New York: Haworth.

Wagner, E. H., Austin, B. T., & Von Korff, M. V. (1996). Improving outcomes in chronic illness. *Managed Care Quarterly, 4*(2), 12–25.

119 The Consumer–Provider Relationship within Case Management

Victoria Stanhope & Phyllis Solomon

Case management is the key organizing concept for service delivery for people with psychiatric disabilities. Case management models have differing intensities, ranging from resource coordination once a month to assertive community treatment (ACT), with 24/7 wraparound services. Moreover, models such as intensive case management and ACT have also become the building block for other interventions for this population, such as supported housing, supported employment, and dual diagnosis programs.

Central to case management, whatever the structure, setting, or activity, is the relationship between the case manager and the consumer. Also referred to as the therapeutic alliance or working alliance, the relationship is the vehicle by which the case manager builds trust, understands the consumer, and collaborates with the consumer on service goals. Case management approaches, and ACT in particular, are primarily targeted toward a hard-to-reach population, people who struggle to maintain stability in the community and have tenuous involvement with outpatient services. Therefore, overall engagement and retention in services is often predicated on the ability of the case manager to build and maintain a trusting relationship with the consumer.

THE THERAPEUTIC RELATIONSHIP AND RECOVERY

The therapeutic relationship captures the human processes that are involved in delivering services. Distinct from the structure of the intervention, the process component includes the quality of the social interaction that takes place between the case manager and the consumer—not so much *what* they do but *how* it is done. Although there has been extensive research on the structure of case management models, the actual process of engaging and maintaining consumers in services remains an understudied aspect of case management that may have considerable impact on consumer outcomes.

Increasingly, researchers have been calling for more examination of the process component of case management. The debate over the role of process versus structure in mental health care has been argued for decades, especially within the psychotherapy field. Some psychologists have argued that there is little difference in outcomes across different interventions, and the client–therapist relationship, sometimes referred to as a "common factor," accounts for variations in outcome. A review of a 100 psychotherapy studies found that common factors accounted for 30 percent of therapeutic change, compared with only 15 percent for intervention specific factors (Lambert & Barley, 2001).

More recently, the recovery movement has reaffirmed the importance of the therapeutic alliance by describing how the process of care is as important to recovery as clinical outcomes and that the two are intrinsically connected. Originating from psychiatric rehabilitation and consumer advocacy, the recovery movement challenges the mindset that severe mental illness is chronic and persistent and has brought the consumer perspective into the forefront of service delivery. The following concepts have been identified as central to recovery: hope, meaning, taking an active role, and choice. As a result, care must be individualized and person-centered, placing considerable onus on providers to build collaborative relationships with consumers based on respect and understanding. Providers become facilitators of recovery when they can be supportive, provide information and options, and share in the journey toward self-definition for the consumer. The recovery movement has been embraced by the federal government, and states are now using the tenets of the recovery movement to transform their public mental health service systems (Department of Health and Human Services, 2004).

DEFINING THE THERAPEUTIC RELATIONSHIP

Howgego, Yellowlees, Owen, Meldrum, and Dark (2003) explain the role of relationship in understanding process: "the exploration of the construct of the therapeutic relationship within case management offers an avenue by which interactive process between patients and case managers may be unpacked and analyzed" (p. 170). Traditionally, psychiatric services have not used insight-oriented psychotherapeutic methods, as these interventions were considered to have limited utility for people with severe mental illness, and some even argued that they had detrimental effects. Furthermore, many providers believed that persons with severe mental illness were unable to develop therapeutic relationships. As a result, much of our understanding of the therapeutic relationship has emerged from psychology and psychotherapy.

The terms "therapeutic relationship," "therapeutic alliance," and "working alliance" are all used to connote the relationship between the provider and the client. However, relationship is a broader concept referring to all aspects of the interaction between the provider and client, including provider characteristics and facilitative conditions, as well as the therapeutic alliance. *Facilitative conditions* refer to the extent to which the therapist is empathetic, is warm, and establishes congruence with the client. *Alliance* refers to one specific aspect of the relationship, which is the extent to which the therapist and client form a bond and collaborate together. Bordin's (1979) conceptualized working alliance as having three elements: (1) goals—the agreement on what is to be accomplished; (2) tasks—the acceptance by the provider and the consumer of the responsibilities that form the intervention; and (3) bond—the mutual trust and attachment that develops between the provider and the consumer. This concept of working alliance lends itself well to understanding relationships within case management by incorporating multidisciplinary approaches and diverse tasks beyond psychotherapy.

In the 1980s, the use of innovative rehabilitation strategies precipitated interest in the role of the therapeutic relationship in services for persons with severe mental illness. Despite the findings that insight-oriented psychotherapy was not an effective intervention for this population, consumers stressed the importance of relationship in other services, particularly case management. These authors attributed this importance to the fact that case managers deliver services in vivo, making them a very active presence in all aspects of the consumer's life. The variety of tasks that the case manager performs with the consumer results in them having a more multidimensional role in their consumer's lives than therapists might achieve. Meeting with consumers in their homes and in the community, often spending prolonged amounts of time with their consumers, has the potential to create a unique intensity to the consumer–case manager bond. In addition, clients suffering from schizophrenia, particularly those experiencing homelessness, often report high rates of social isolation and therefore are especially responsive to therapeutic alliances to meet their needs for social contact.

RESEARCH ON CONSUMER–CASE MANAGER RELATIONSHIPS

Although studies on working alliance within case management services have not been extensive, the majority of them have found alliance to be positively correlated with clinical outcomes. One of the first studies examining the impact of alliance on outcomes was by Frank and Gunderson (1990), who followed 142 consumers with schizophrenia and found that alliance predicted improved retention in treatment, medication compliance, symptomatology, and global functioning. Subsequent studies have found increased goal attainment, consumer satisfaction, quality of life, and community living skills resulted from positive alliances (Howgego et al., 2003).

Consumer–case manager relationships are a dynamic phenomenon and their impact on clinical outcomes can vary depending on the treatment stage. The research shows that after 6 months, there is a significant increase in the strength of alliances over baseline, and consumers with poor alliances at this stage are likely to drop out of services within the next 3 months. However, a positive alliance tends to have more impact on outcomes in the early stages on the relationship. One study found that alliance predicted a reduction in symptoms and increased client satisfaction at 6 months but not after 18 months (Klinkenberg, Calsyn, & Morse, 2002). Another factor in how case management relationships evolve over time is the frequency of contacts with the consumer. The research has not been conclusive, with some studies finding few associations between intensity and outcomes and others finding that intensity predicts alliance and satisfaction with services (Klinkenberg et al., 2002).

When studying the working alliance, researchers have found differences in how providers and consumers perceive their bond and the extent to which their perceptions predict clinical outcomes. The psychotherapeutic studies have consistently shown that client ratings of the alliance have greater predictive power than the therapist ratings (Horvath, 2001). In contrast, case management studies have found a stronger correlation between provider perception of alliance and outcome than consumer perception, which suggests either that the case manager perspective on the bond determines consumer progress or that alliance is more linked to consumer progress for the case manager than for the consumer. Often, consumers consider the relationship to be more important than other aspects of services, including provider skill and their own outcomes. Another explanation, more contentious from a consumer-centered perspective, is that consumer judgment of alliance is impeded by psychotic illness. Researchers have concluded that case managers may be able to assess alliance more accurately than therapists because of the in vivo nature of services that allows them to spend more time with the consumer in a variety of settings.

CONSUMER PERSPECTIVES ON THE THERAPEUTIC RELATIONSHIP

Consumers have consistently identified the therapeutic relationship with providers as being the most critical ingredient of case management. More recently, qualitative studies have provided a deeper understanding of the role of the therapeutic relationship in the lives of consumers. In evaluating assertive community treatment, consumers described feeling cared for and a sense of belonging arising from their frequent contact with the team, regardless of whether they were having difficulties. More specifically, clients valued one primary relationship with an ACT team member, and for some it was the only positive helping relationship in their lives. The qualities consumers are searching for in their relationships with providers are finding common ground, feeling known, having someone to talk to, and feeling like "somebody" through the social interaction (Ware, Tugenberg, & Dickey, 2004). Consumers not only express the need for emotional and instrumental support from their case managers but also see their case managers as an important conduit into the social world. By accompanying them on trips to the movies or dinner, case managers fulfill a social role more akin to being a friend or even a family member (Buck & Alexander, 2005).

The apparent merging of provider and friendship roles in consumer–case manager relationships means that the issue of clinical boundaries is particularly pertinent in case management services. Within consumer–case manager relationships, the less controlled context of the relationship means there is greater potential for self-disclosure, reciprocity, and time spent together outside of traditional work hours. As a result, there is often a greater potential for transference issues in case management relationships, although these relationships are not commonly understood as psychotherapeutic. However, all too frequently case managers have little training and supervision on how to negotiate difficult issues related to clinical boundaries. This skill deficit can result in negative consequences for their relationships with their clients.

BARRIERS TO THE THERAPEUTIC RELATIONSHIP

The therapeutic relationship is subject to tensions that exist within all social relationships and also some that arise specifically from the mental health service context. The role of the case managers is to act as the interface between the consumer and a broad array of mental health and social services. As a result, they often have to mediate social control mechanisms embedded in systems of care for people with severe mentally ill. Consumers are forced into treatment by a variety of mandated mechanisms, including inpatient commitment, outpatient commitment, probation and parole, representative payee arrangements, and housing requirements. The presence of these mandates profoundly changes the dynamics of the therapeutic relationship, requiring case managers to negotiate a space between giving therapeutic support and monitoring their consumers' compliance with enforced treatment. Case managers resort to a variety of clinical strategies to persuade, pressure, and coerce reluctant consumers into care. The impact of such strategies on the consumer–case manager relationship varies: coercive strategies may threaten the existing relationship, or the relationship may mitigate feelings of coercion because the consumer trusts the case manager. Often, case managers can exert social influence over the consumer through the relationship and help maintain their engagement in the mental health system. Therefore, although the relationship is a powerful therapeutic tool for case managers, they constantly have to balance being a support for their consumer with minimizing risk to the broader community.

Consumer–case manager relationships are also subject to daily stressors and can be undermined by negative communication. The concept of expressed emotion (EE) is used as an indicator of relationship and focuses more on negative behaviors. EE is measured by criticism, hostility, emotional overinvolvement, and overall quality of relationship. EE was originally developed to examine relationships between family caregivers and persons with severe mental illness, but more recently, it has been applied to consumer-provider relationships (Tattan & Tarrier, 2000). Case managers often have prolonged and intense contact with patients, to a limited extent replicating the stress of family life with mentally ill relatives. A study of 120 case manager–consumer dyads found that 27 percent of the relationships were high EE. Although EE did not predict clinical outcomes, the quality of the relationship did predict positive outcomes, including reduced symptomatology and patient satisfaction. The most important factor appeared to be either the presence or absence of positive attitudes on the part of providers as indicated by the quality of relationship, rather than negative behaviors, such as criticism and hostility. Overall, providers demonstrate fewer negative attitudes than relatives and therefore, the absence of positive attitudes more closely resembles high EE behavior of families (Tattan & Tarrier, 2000).

As with all relationships, the strength of therapeutic alliance is dependent on both the amount of time providers and consumers spend together and the length of time they have known each other. Although case managers have the potential to spend a greater amount of time with the consumers than do therapists, large caseloads and high turnover within the profession often preclude case managers from building relationships with their clients. Clients learn to hold back from relationships with case managers to avoid the inevitable rejection that arises when they leave their positions. The high rates of turnover among case managers is attributed to low salaries and the demands of direct care with consumers who often have poor quality of life, acute psychotic episodes, and difficult behaviors. These constraints, based on how case management services are structured, severely limit the case manager's ability to commit to therapeutic relationships and the consumer's willingness to trust that the case manager will be there for them in the long term.

CONCLUSION

Although the consumer–case manager relationship has not traditionally been considered to be therapeutic, there is a growing recognition that this relationship plays a key role in keeping consumers engaged in services and helping them remain on the path to recovery. As states and localities employ more intense and specialized case management models, such as ACT, they are using clinically trained case managers and allowing them more opportunity to build one-on-one relationships with the consumers. Moreover, the recovery movement has advocated for services that are collaborative and consumer-driven. To deliver such services, case managers will be expected to have the skills to understand the unique qualities of each of their consumers and be able develop goals based on shared decision making and genuine collaboration. They need to know how to support consumers to reach their desired goals. Even more important is the shift in attitudes that is essential for engaging in these behaviors; case managers believing in the capability of consumers to directing their own treatment and achieving their life goals.

WEB SITES

Center for Psychiatric Rehabilitation, Boston University. http://www.bu.edu/cpr.

MacArthur Coercion Study, MacArthur Research Network on Mental Health and the Law, Virginia University. http://www.macarthur.virginia.edu/coercion.html.

National Consensus Statement of Recovery, SAMSHA's National Mental Health Information Center. http://mentalhealth.samhsa.gov/publications/allpubs/sma05-4129.

References

Bordin, E. S. (1979). The generalizability of the psychoanalytic concept of the working alliance. *Psychotherapy: Theory, Research, and Practice, 16,* 252–260.

Buck, P. W., & Alexander, L. B. (2005). Neglected voices: Consumers with serious mental illness speak about intensive case management. *Administration and Policy in Mental Health, 33,* 470–481.

Department of Health and Human Services. (2004). *National consensus statement on mental health recovery.* Rockville, MD: Substance Abuse and Mental Health Services Administration.

Frank, A. F., & Gunderson, J. G. (1990). The role of therapeutic alliance in the treatment of schizophrenia. *Archives of General Psychiatry, 47,* 228–236.

Horvath, A. O. (2001). The alliance. *Psychotherapy, 4,* 365–372.

Howgego, I. M., Yellowlees, P., Owen, C., Meldrum, L., & Dark, F. (2003). The therapeutic alliance: The key to effective patient outcome? A descriptive review of the evidence in community mental health case management. *Australian and New Zealand Journal of Psychiatry, 37,* 169–183.

Klinkenberg, W. D., Calsyn, R. J., & Morse, G. A. (2002). The case manager's view of the helping alliance. *Care Management Journals, 3,* 120–125.

Lambert, M. J., & Barley, D. E. (2001). Research summary on the therapeutic relationship and psychotherapy outcome. *Psychotherapy, 38,* 357–361.

Tattan, T., & Tarrier, N. (2000). The expressed emotion of case managers of the seriously mentally ill: The influence of expressed emotion on clinical outcomes. *Psychological Medicine, 30,* 195–204.

Ware, N. C., Tugenberg, T., & Dickey, B. (2004). Practitioner relationships and quality of care for low-income persons with serious mental illness. *Psychiatric Services, 55,* 555–559.

PART XI
Social Work Fields of Practice

120

Current and Future Directions of Social Work Practice with Children and Adolescents

Lisa Rapp-Paglicci & Alison Salloum

Practice methods with children and adolescents have advanced rapidly over the past few years. Innovative new assessment techniques and instruments and improved interventions require practitioners to know, understand, and read practice research. Clearly, it is difficult for practitioners to master novel assessments and interventions and still have time to critically examine the latest research findings. Therefore, this chapter presents an overview of the current status and future directions of social work assessment and practice with children and adolescents.

ASSESSMENT

Evidence-Based Assessment

Building on the growing field of evidence-based practices, the use of evidence to guide the assessment process is currently evolving. Evidenced-based assessment incorporates the use of evidence and theory to select the aspects, conditions, or domains to be assessed; uses evidence-based assessment tools; and uses the best methods for the assessment processes. An evidence-based assessment can help guide the practitioner and client to choose the best available evidence-based intervention for the assessed condition and to monitor progress throughout the intervention (Hunsley & Mash, 2007).

Accessible and practical evidence-based assessment tools and methods are becoming available for practitioners and clients. These brief and easy-to-use tools, commonly referred to as rapid assessment instruments, are available to assess a child's or family's general functioning and competence relative to specific conditions. Assessment tools and processes are being developed to address situations in various settings and contexts. For example, Glisson, Hemmelgarn, and Post (2002) developed a 48-item general mental health and psychological functioning assessment measure for children (ages 5–18) who are involved with the child welfare or juvenile justice systems. Similarly, Edelson et al. (2007) are developing a 46-item tool to assess children's exposure to domestic violence. In a pilot study, an evidence-based assessment tool was systematically included in the foster care system in Canada to promote resilience and improved outcomes (Kufeldt, McGilligan, Klien, & Rideout, 2006).

These types of evidence-based assessment tools and methods are readily available through various Web sites and books on clinical measures (e.g., Fischer & Corcoran, 2006).

Child-Focused Developmental, Ecological, and Cultural Assessment

An evidence-based assessment with children, adolescents, and their families must include a multidimensional assessment that considers development, ecological context, and cultural influences. These three areas of assessment may be considered the foundation for child-focused assessments. With children, evidence-based assessment often includes assessing caregivers, including multiple informants (such as day care providers or teachers) and sources of data (i.e., observation, school records); understanding the variations and effects of development and culture on the situation; and including a broad-based assessment of competencies and challenges (Achenbach, 2007).

Generally, the younger the child, the more involved the parent or caregiver and significant other adults in the child's daily life will be in the assessment process. With older children, especially adolescents, it is important to engage the youth directly in the assessment process. This may be accomplished by using evidence-based self-report assessment instruments with the child and adolescent. When practitioners conduct the assessment process in a collaborative fashion with the child, the assessment tool can be used to provide education and normalization and elicit specific goals for treatment, as well as highlighting the child's strengths and treatment progress.

Developmental assessments may be used to select the best available treatments for children that take into account the child's developmental status (including emotional, cognitive, biological, social, and behavioral milestones, assets, and delays). As research on evidence-based practices continues, we will learn more about which treatments work best with which populations. More specifically, we will learn how development, gender, culture, and context affect treatment outcomes. Developmentally specific assessment can then be used to suggest developmentally specific treatments to the child and parent or caretaker. For example, recent advances have been made in assessment processes for the mental health needs of infants, toddlers, and young children. With this knowledge, specific prevention and treatment strategies grounded in empirical research for this young population are increasing (for more information about early childhood assessment see the Zero to Three Web page). Similar advances are being made for middle childhood, early adolescence, adolescence, and late adolescence.

The child-in-environment perspective must be considered during the assessment processes. The influences of the relational processes within the child's ecological context may have a significant impact on the child's functioning and growth. Ecological relational processes may include the child's family; school environment and peers; neighborhood and community; recreational opportunities; religious or spiritual membership or rituals; national and international situations; and systems such as foster care, child welfare, and juvenile justice. Though a beginning point for the practitioner is to assess the strengths within the child and child's family (see Early, 2001, for family strengths assessment measures), a more multidimensional assessment is optimal. This encompasses the child's and family's protective or resilience factors and examines the salience of specific and cumulative risks factors (Frazer, Richman, & Galinsky, 1999), including social conditions such as poverty, discrimination, and limited opportunities. A multidimensional assessment can assist the practitioner, child, and family in choosing the most appropriate multimodal and multicontextual interventions.

In addition to developmental and ecological assessment processes, evidence-based assessment must be culturally sensitive. Specific assessment tools are being tested with various cultural groups to establish within group norms. In addition to the use of specific culturally relevant assessment tools, an understanding of the cultural context of the child may lead the practitioner and client to decide on a more culturally congruent evidence-based treatment. A cultural assessment may help the practitioner understand the child and family better and identify cultural resources to include in treatment. Discussing culturally competent practice is beyond the scope of this chapter, and practitioners are encouraged to read the National Association of Social Workers *Standards for Cultural Competence in Social Work Practices* that was developed in 2001 (available on the NASW Web site). Assessments may include areas such as communication patterns, family structure, accepted roles of children, intergenerational conflicts, assimilation of family members, adherence to traditions, spiritual beliefs, values and norms, acceptance of expression of emotions and behaviors, developmental expectations, language preference and proficiency, historical experiences, views of mental health, and help-seeking behaviors.

Client-Centered Process

Evidence-based practitioners value the child and family as a collaborative partner in the assessment process and treatment. Indeed, parents' and children's beliefs, values, and preferences are key factors in successfully implementing evidence-based practice. Program developers and practitioners can ensure that the child, youth, and family members play an active role in the process of assessment, goal planning, treatment choices, and evaluation. During the assessment process, practitioners should assess the client's (child and participating family members) beliefs about credibility (i.e., believable and logical) and effectiveness of the agreed-on intervention or treatment prior to implementation.

Beliefs about credibility of treatment and expectations of improvements may be associated with motivation for and adherence to treatment, which are important factors for effective outcomes (Nock, Ferriter, & Holmberg, 2007).

A collaborative practitioner–client assessment process begins with the initial meeting and continues throughout the intervention to monitor progress and assess outcome and satisfaction. Eliciting feedback from children and families regarding treatment satisfaction and the service delivery process can be empowering for clients. Valuing systematic approaches to hearing from clients about their experiences can lead to improved treatments and delivery of care (Baker, 2007). A collaborative evidence-based assessment may lead to more objective accountability of satisfaction, effectiveness, and improved services for children and families.

Considerations for Child-Focused Evidence-Based Assessment

- Use evidence-based assessment tools and processes to guide client and practitioner in choosing evidence-based practice.
- Conduct a multidimensional assessment that include sources of data, including multiple informants (i.e., parents, caretakers, teachers, and other important child–adult relationships), multiple settings (i.e., home, school, peers), and multiple methods (i.e., rapid assessment instruments, interviews, observations).
- Consider using a broad assessment tool followed by a selected specific condition assessment tool.
- Assess the child's developmental status, including emotional, cognitive, biological, social, and behavioral milestones, assets, and delays and take into account the developmental stage of the child to match appropriate intervention.
- Consider the entire ecological context of child and family.
- Use standardized assessment tools and processes to assess protective factors, competencies, and strengths.
- Use standardized assessment tools or processes to assess risks and emotional, behavioral, and social difficulties.
- Understand the cultural influences on the child, family, and situation and conduct a culturally competent assessment.
- Assess throughout practice to evaluate progress, outcomes, and client satisfaction.

- Practice from a child–family-centered collaborative perspective.
- Assess the child and family's beliefs, values, preferences, and expectations about evidence-based treatment.

TREATMENT

Prevention

Previously, youth began treatment when they had significantly serious disorders or symptoms that significantly impacted their functioning at home, school, or the community. However, research studies have supported what practitioners have observed all along—starting treatment earlier, at the first sign or symptom of difficulty, drastically improves the outcome (Guterman, 2004; Rapp-Paglicci, Dulmus, & Wodarski, 2004). In fact, studies have suggested that preventive interventions delivered before youth exhibit any problems often reduce the severity of disorders or prevent them completely (Fishbein, 2000; Weiz, Sandier, Durlak, & Anton, 2005). This approach is also far more cost-effective than typical interventions, which wait too long and then require more intensive intervention. Thus, prevention programs have been used to intervene early, thereby preventing the disorder completely or lessening its progression. There are many empirically based prevention interventions that are used when youth present no risk factors (universal), exhibit some risk factors (selective), and/or when they evince some symptoms of the problem (indicated). These prevention interventions are now more readily available and used more frequently; however, there is still much work to be done in reframing our thinking to integrate preventive interventions and programs into our current systems. For example, programs need to be given funds for delivering preventive interventions, not just brief interventions after the problems have grown too serious to change.

Evidence-Based Practice and Evidence-Supported Treatment

Many advances have occurred in the development of evidence-based practice (EBP) and evidence-supported treatment (EST) for children and adolescents. Currently, many social problems and disorders of childhood and adolescence have treatments that are evidence supported (Kendall & Beidas, 2007). A significant number include individual, family, and group modalities, and these treatments should be considered first-line intervention options (Nock, Goldman, Wang, and Albano, 2004). The contemporary controversy lies not in *whether* to utilize these practices but *how* to facilitate the implementation from well-controlled research studies to real-world community agencies.

There are many barriers to implementing EBP in agencies. First, practitioners have little time to stay up to date with the rapid expansion of effective treatments. Second, some of the protocols and manuals have prohibitive costs, which individual practitioners and nonprofit agencies cannot afford. Third, the manuals are often too rigid and unrealistic to apply to a real-world agency with real, nonexperimental clients. Additionally, many EBPs do not address comorbid or complex client problems, and finally, some agencies are not supportive of practitioners who wish to take the time and expense to learn and use ESTs.

Despite these barriers, practitioners need to continue to stay abreast of current ESTs and utilize interventions that have been found effective as their first choice. While they wait for further evidence to be produced in underdeveloped areas, they should modify ESTs to fit their unique clientele and monitor their own practice to assess for improvements in clients using older treatment protocols.

Multimodal and Multicontextual Interventions

Research suggests that treatment for youth be multimodal and multicontextual, meaning that interventions should be delivered in various formats for learning and change to occur and that interventions should occur in multiple environments or milieu of the youth. In other words, individual treatment for children alone, without family, school, or community intervention is rarely effective, especially for youth who are having difficulty functioning in various contexts. Likewise, one type of intervention alone, for instance, life skills, is also not empirically supported. Take the following example: a practitioner working with a child experiencing severe difficulty with controlling anger may talk about angry outbursts and their consequences with the child, teach the child anger control skills, role-play/practice the skills, and read a story about a character who learns to control her anger. In addition, the practitioner may use functional family therapy with the child's family to intervene with family difficulties, assist the teacher in developing a behavior modification system for the child at school, and work with the child's soccer coach to help apply the newly learned anger control skills to replace angry outbursts during soccer practice. The comprehensive nature of these interventions will be more likely to produce change than one modality in one context.

Considerations for Child-Focused Evidence-Based Treatment

- Intervene early with evidence-based prevention interventions.
- Stay abreast of ESTs and use with appropriate clients.
- When no known evidence exists for disorders or problems, use older treatment approaches but monitor progress carefully.
- Intervene in multiple contexts (micro, mezzo, and macro).
- Intervene with multiple approaches.

Future Direction for Assessment and Intervention

Understanding the complexities and uniqueness of the child or adolescent by empathetic face-to-face interaction has always been the starting point for the practitioner. Although this will not change, advances in assessment tools and methods will help the practitioner obtain a broader contextual understanding as well as more rapidly ascertain targeted goals. Advances in evidence-based assessment will lead to more research on the influence of development, context, and culture on treatment outcomes and a broader understanding of resilience in childhood. These assessment tools and methods will become standard practices and will be integrated within systems of care for children.

Collaboration with the client will remain central to evidence-based assessment and evidence-based treatment. Once the client and practitioner have collaboratively decided on which evidence-based treatment seems most appropriate, preparation for treatment may be warranted. Studies have begun to show evidence for the effectiveness of orientations to treatment (Broome, Joe, & Simpson, 2001; Czuchry, Sia, & Dansereau, 2006). Treatment readiness or pretreatment sessions assist clients in preparing for the treatment when it is delivered. The sessions are offered prior to the formal treatment and work to engage and motivate the client. The idea began with mandated adults and has found its way into the child and adolescent arena. Treatment readiness sessions seem to be more common with difficult or mandated young clients (adolescent offenders and substance abusers) but may be promising for use with other client populations. They may also show promise for reducing resistance with other interventions and with brief treatments where change is expected to occur quickly. In addition, practitioners may consider using pretreatment sessions prior to family or group treatments.

Developing and implementing evidence-based social work practices for children requires integration and collaboration: the integration of evidence-based assessment and treatment; the integration of social work research and practice; and collaboration with all concerned parties, including children and families, community residents and leaders, practitioners, researchers, child advocates, child systems (i.e., education, child welfare, juvenile justice), and policy makers. Due to the complexities of problems and challenges that children and youth face today, we must advance our learning of the programs or methods that work best for which children, in what settings, at what intensity of delivery, and when the delivery of services are most effective. Barriers to implementation of child-focused evidence-based practices may be overcome by such strategies as Web-based clearinghouses about practices and trainings, easy-to-use manuals that are grounded in real-world practice, and community collaboration to study practice implementation where children, parents, community leaders, practitioners, researchers, and policy makers work together to learn about effective practices.

WEB SITES

Blueprints for Violence Prevention. http://www.colorado.edu/cspv/blueprints.

Campbell Collaboration. http://www.campbellcollaboration.org.

National Center for Childhood Traumatic Stress Network. http://www.nccts.org. See measures review database for assessment tools. http://www.nctsn.org/nccts/nav.do?pid=ctr_tool_searchMeasures.

National Institutes of Health. http://www.nih.gov.

North Carolina Evidence-Based Practice Center (NCEBPC). http://www.ncebpcenter.org.

Substance Abuse and Mental Health Services Administration; see National Registry of Evidence-based Programs and Practices. http://www.samhsa.gov.

Zero to Three. www.zerotothree.org.

References

Achenbach, T. M. (2007). In Peter S. Jensen, Penny Knapp, and David A. Mrazek, Toward a new diagnostic system for child psychopathology: Moving beyond the DSM. *Journal of Child and Family Studies, 16,* 589–591.

Baker, A. J. L. (2007). Client feedback in child welfare programs: Current trends and future directions. *Children and Youth Services Review, 29,* 1189–1200.

Broome, K. M., Joe, G. W., & Simpson, D. D. (2001). Engagement models for adolescents in DATOS-A. *Journal of Adolescence Research, 16*(6), 608–623.

Czuchry, M., Sia, T. L., & Dansereau, D. F. (2006). Improving early engagement and treatment readiness of probationers: Gender differences. *Prison Journal, 86*(1), 56–74.

Early, T. J. (2001). Measures for practice with families from a strengths perspective. *Families in Society, 82*(2), 225–232.

Edelson, J. L., Ellerton, A. L., Seagren, E. A., Kichberg, S. L., Schmidt, S. O., & Ambrose, A. T. (2007). Assessing child exposure to adult domestic violence. *Children & Youth Services Review, 29*(7), 961–971.

Fischer J., & Corcoran, K. (2006). *Measures for clinical practice and research.* Volume 1: *Couples, families, and children,* 4th ed. New York: Oxford University Press.

Fishbein, D. (2000). The importance of neurobiological research to the prevention of psychopathology. *Prevention Science, 1*(2), 89–106.

Frazer, M. W., Richman, J. M., & Galinsky, M. J. (1999). Risk, protection and resilience: Toward a conceptual framework for social work practice. *Social Work Research, 23*(3), 1999.

Glisson, C., Hemmelgarn, A. L., & Post, J. A. (2002). The short form assessment for children: An assessment and outcome measure for child welfare and juvenile justice. *Research on Social Work Practice, 12*(1), 82–106.

Guterman, N. B. (2004). Advancing prevention research on child abuse, youth violence, and domestic violence emerging strategies and issues. *Journal of Interpersonal Violence, 19*(3), 299–321.

Hunsley, J., & Mash, E. J. (2007). Evidence-based assessment. *Annual Review of Clinical Psychology, 3,* 29–51.

Kendall, P. C., & Beidas, R. S. (2007). Smoothing the trail for dissemination of evidence-based practices for youth: Flexibility within fidelity. *Professional Psychology: Research and Practice, 38*(1), 13–20.

Kufeldt, K., McGilligan, L., Klien, R., & Rideout, S. (2006). The looking after children assessment process: Promoting resilient children and resilient workers. *Families in Society, 87*(4), 565–574.

Nock, M. K., Ferriter, C., & Holmberg, E. (2007). Parent's beliefs about treatment credibility and effectiveness: Assessment and relation to subsequent treatment participation. *Journal of Child and Family Studies, 16,* 27–38.

Nock, M. K., Goldman, J. L., Wang, Y., & Albano, A. M. (2004). From science to practice: The flexible use of evidence-based treatments in clinical settings. *Journal of the American Academy of Adolescent Psychiatry, 43*(6), 777–780.

Rapp-Paglicci, L. A., Dulmus, C. N., & Wodarski, J. S. (2004). *Handbook of preventive interventions for children and adolescents.* New York,: Wiley.

121

Current and Future Directions of Social Work in Adult Mental Health Settings

Vikki L. Vandiver

As a field of practice, mental health is a dominant area of employment and service delivery for social work practitioners. Yet many aspects of the mental health field are changing and will continue to change rapidly in the next few years. The past decade has witnessed efforts to bring findings from clinical research on psychosocial interventions into everyday clinical practice (Bruce & Sanderson, 2005).

This chapter reviews the current and future state of social work practice in mental health.

CURRENT STATE OF SOCIAL WORK PRACTICE IN MENTAL HEALTH

Social workers are well represented in a variety of settings that focus on mental health; these settings include community mental health centers, public health departments, behavioral health care agencies, consumer advocacy organizations, inpatient and outpatient units of primary health care settings, residential programs, psychiatric rehabilitation centers, and state departments of health and mental health. Their job titles are as broad as the settings: crisis counselors, diagnosticians, therapists, mediators, educators, skills trainers, case

managers, medication facilitators, consumer and family consultants, collaborators on interagency and interdisciplinary teams, advocates and community organizers, program evaluators and researchers, administrators, and policy analysts (Bentley, 2002).

Bentley and Taylor (2002) discuss key factors that influence the context of contemporary social work practice in mental health. These are scientific and technological, historical, economic, sociopolitical, cultural, legal, and ethical. In the area of scientific and technological advancement, they note that social workers are presently benefiting from an integrative model of practice that incorporates the best research from the neurosciences, including brain functioning and genetics, with the more familiar understanding of environmental stresses and the impact on life events as influencing the development of mental illness. Historical factors, such as deinstitutionalization and costs of community care, have keenly influenced how social workers interface in mental health settings, particularly when one considers the relevance of today's debate about costs shifting care from long-term settings (e.g., institutions) to community-based, short-term treatment programs (e.g., outpatient programs using brief therapy models).

In their role as diagnosticians, social workers regularly deal with economic tensions associated with client access and service provision based on diagnostic specific reimbursement structures that often favor payment for a single psychiatric diagnosis over the more pressing social conditions of poverty and discrimination. Social workers are increasingly called on to broker cultural or sociopolitical differences in which clients from diverse communities and the mental health system may be at odds with one another or when sociopolitical ideology (e.g., insurance lobbyist for pharmaceutical company) clashes with consumer notions of self-determination involving medication-free treatment. Finally, social workers who practice in the mental health field are routinely involved in advocacy roles involving legal challenges to patients rights (e.g., right to refuse medication treatment or right to mental health treatment through parity laws) and ethical dilemmas concerning clients choice and self-determination, even when such determination may prove to be in conflict with community or societal standards (e.g., choice to live homeless or bear arms).

FUTURE DIRECTIONS: ENVISIONING EXCELLENCE

In the previous section, we reviewed several factors that influenced the day-to-day practice of social workers in the mental health field. Let us now turn to future directions in the mental health field. Drake, Merrens, and Lynde (2005) identify six points of excellence that social work practitioners can ensure are a part of future mental health services, practices and policies. These are (1) the role of scientific evidence in developing services, (2) consumer preferences, (3) family and caregiver involvement, (4) clinical expertise, (5) dynamic health and mental health care system, and (6) progressive public policy.

Scientific Evidence

Let us point to two emerging scientific developments in the field of mental health: the dissemination of evidence-based programs and computer technology.

Dissemination of evidence-based programs

In the near future, social workers will be more involved in both research and application of in-terventions that emphasize the biological, psychological, and social underpinnings of specific disorders and their differential response to treatment. Part of this move is influenced by research that has shown that the majority of people seeking mental health treatment are receiving therapeutic approaches of unknown efficacy or of efficacy known to be inferior to evidence-based practice (EBPs) (Addis & Krasnow, 2000). Evidence-based mental health approaches represent an extension of a larger movement in general health care that has a rapidly expanding philosophical, practical, and empirical foundation and is designed to address the gaps in therapeutic approaches. According to the Institute of Medicine (IOM), EBP is the "integration of best research evidence with clinical expertise and patient values" (IOM, 2001, p. 47). This definition serves as a guidepost for the mental health field because it balances the need for comprehensive assessment, clinical judgment, individualized treatment, flexibility, patient preferences, personal choice, and self-determination with sorely needed scientific rigor. However, EBPs, no matter how scientifically derived, will not replace the need for clinical expertise, sensitivity to clients, and family members' needs and wishes.

Though decades of clinical research has led to the development of efficacious psychosocial treatments that have benefited thousands of clients, the movement to identify EBPs has not been without its risks and limitations. Bruce and Sanderson (2005) note that many of the objections to the dissemination of EBPs revolve around the risk of potential misuse by payers and a legal system that may not appreciate the complexities of addressing community mental health needs and the appropriate roles of EBPs in that effort (p. 237). Other risks involving the exclusive use of EBPs may prevent potentially effective, field-developed, or otherwise innovative treatments from being recognized, such as the Canoe Journey, considered by Northwest Native tribal leaders and researchers to be an effective, culturally based, best practice prevention activity. Cruz and Spence (2005) argue that state-mandated EBP have essentially squeezed out the recognition of tribal best practices. One effort to address this risk is the recognition of a growing effort to (1) define and shape best practices using the voice of seasoned practitioners, and (2) collect, evaluate, and disseminate outcome data collected on community-based interventions. Despite the controversy, the movement to research, identify, and disseminate EBPs will continue; social workers, in collaboration with other providers, consumers, and payers of mental health services, will be in a position to influence its course.

Computer technology. One area that is advancing the science base of mental health practice is information technology. As Drake and colleagues (2005) point out, scientific data are more available and accessible to consumers and family members. Increasingly, consumers are able to access information on treatment options (e.g., Web-based practice guidelines), including outcomes and side effects, before they meet with their mental health treatment team to make treatment decisions. Families are able to use the Internet technology to locate support groups in virtually any city in the United States. One of the most nationally recognized support group for families with a Web presence is the National Alliance on Mental Illness (NAMI).

As knowledge of the causes, course, and treatment of mental disorders continue to expand dramatically, so comes the need for better information technology systems. The use of clinical computing methods is one strategy that permits the aggregation of extensive data on routine care, instant availability of risk adjustments for individual consumers, and decision support systems (e.g., algorithms) that facilitate accurate selection of interventions (Drake et al., 2005, p. 472). Bruce and colleagues point out that capturing major domains of client progress, such as symptoms, functioning, or quality of life, in a reliable, valid, relevant, and least burdensome manner is difficult and resource-intensive. Despite these challenges, though, the use of computer-based outcome measurement systems to assess the effects of field-delivered interventions may be one of the few ways of preserving the choice of interventions while tracking client progress that in turn satisfies the demand for accountability to payers (Bruce & Sanderson, 2005). It is anticipated that science and the concurrent use of computer technologies will guide social work practitioners toward mental health interventions that are more preventive in orientation, curative rather than palliative, and target underlying etiological abnormalities rather than just symptoms.

Consumer Preferences

In the future, social workers will be strongly influenced by evolving concepts regarding consumer choice, self-determination, community integration, self-management, cultural competence, self-help, and recovery. It is becoming standard practice for social workers to promote the idea that recovery is possible for anyone suffering from mental health conditions. This practice is seen in such activities as offering a menu of services that clients can choose from, providing holistic care that includes spirituality, and focusing on strengths and resilience, community care options, and activities that promote health and enhance quality of life. The emphasis is on reshaping one's life to accommodate mental health conditions, not being identified by the condition. In particular, the recovery model advances the notion that hope, wellness, and health are desirable goals of treatment and should be a part of every treatment plan. Accordingly, this places a responsibility on social workers to help educate consumers about the risks and benefits of various service and treatment options. Solomon and Stanhope (2006) argue the importance of training social work providers to adopt a consumer-centered approach that reconciles professional values and medical model approaches with consumer-directed choices, preferences, and wellness-oriented outcomes.

Our role is to do better in understanding consumers' awareness of mental illness, effective ways to ensure informed and competent decision making, risk factors for violence, and the use of coercive interventions. Ultimately, more research is needed in the areas of clients' interest, willingness, and ability to fully participate in decision making.

Family or Caregiver Involvement

Increasingly, social workers are being called on to address the needs of family members who care for an ill relative and provide support services for all levels of family members (e.g., parents, siblings, and spouses). One measure of excellence will be a mental health system that has a place for family members to be actively involved with clinical treatment teams. Psychoeducation groups, recognized as an EBP, is one such place where family members or caregivers and clinical teams can come together to collaborate and exchange information in an educational setting. A typical psychoeducation curriculum provides a comprehensive list of proactive activities that family members can use to assist other family members who are in crisis. These activities include listing current medications, tips for recognizing symptoms, and strategies for accessing legal advice and talking with siblings and local health providers.

Clinical Expertise

The future success of mental health services and programs will be dependent on a well-trained workforce. Workforce development is one area that all mental health systems will have to develop to meet the rapidly developing training needs of service providers. Social workers, perhaps more than most disciplines, participate in annual continuing education activities that meet a minimum level of workforce training. However, real workforce development is just that—the entire workforce, which includes all levels of personnel and disciplines (case workers, coaches, skills trainers, therapists, staff, and agency administrators). As discussed earlier, translating evidence-based treatment recommendations into practice requires acceptance and training of practitioners as well as acceptance by clients. Weissman and Sanderson (2002) provide an example of a model for training EBPs applicable across the disciplines. Additionally, there is the need for workforce development initiatives to keep pace with the emerging knowledge base in well-established fields, like psychiatric rehabilitation. One way to do this is to become trained and certified as a psychiatric rehabilitation practitioner with a credential that is recognized across states.

Many educational and attitudinal barriers currently inhibit social workers who work in the mental health field. Many social workers have ambivalence regarding EBPs, recovery orientation, and a shared decision-making process. They make lack the skills and understanding of trauma-informed services needed to participate fully in this directional shift. It can be argued that before trauma-informed services can be instituted, practitioners first need to understand how treatment environments, staff interactions, and interventions can reenact earlier experiences of trauma.

Despite quality social work education, many social workers will still need basic knowledge and training in the skills to deliver evidence-based mental health practices and promote the use of consumer-oriented decision-support systems. This movement is just beginning, as evidenced by initiatives launched by the National Association of Social Workers and the Institute for the Advancement of Social Work Research.

Dynamic Health-Mental Health Care System

Social workers are uniquely positioned to shape the future of mental health services by helping reform the current health and mental health care systems. If one goal of reform is to have a transparent health care system where clients are not segregated by their diagnosis—as in the case of those who present with co-occurring disorders and often have to pick one service provider instead of an integrated system—then social workers can advocate for an integration of service systems. In turn, these systems will need to be run by interdisciplinary team members. Two approaches that reflect this direction are seen in systems integration and principles of therapeutic change.

Systems integration. The move to systems integration is now referred to as vertical systems integration and is the focus of a recently issued report by the National Institutes of Health, Office of Behavioral and Social Sciences Research (2007). This report, titled "The Contributions of Behavioral and Social Sciences Research to Improving the Health of the Nation: A Prospectus for the Future" highlights the need for understanding the interaction of individual vulnerability with human-created environments. Nearly a decade earlier, the IOM report "Promoting Health: Intervention Strategies from Social and Behavioral Research" (2000) issued a similar report summarizing the very best of key social and behavioral research. Their report concluded that the most effective mental health systems need to:

- use multiple approaches (e.g., education, social support, laws, incentives, behavior change programs) and address multiple levels of influence simultaneously (i.e., individuals, families, communities, and nations);
- take account of the special needs of target groups (e.g., women, children, families of children and adults with mental illness);
- take the long view of health and mental health outcomes, as changes often take many years to become established; and
- involve a variety of sectors in our society that have not traditionally been associated with mental health promotion efforts, including law, business, education, social services, and the media (IOM, 2000, p. 6).

Each of these initiatives speaks to the importance of vertical systems integration as a key strategy for mental health system reform. This strategy is familiar for social workers trained to influence reform through systems change. From health care practitioners to policy analysts, most would agree that interventions need to be aimed at improving the health of consumers through activities like health promotion, care planning for health needs, and support with making medical decisions—each of which speaks to the need for vertical systems integration.

Principles of therapeutic change. Another example of the need for a dynamic health and mental health care system can be seen in recent efforts to develop principles of therapeutic change. This effort is in response to provider and agency opposition to the typical lists of EBP treatments that many payer agencies require programs to use. Instead of lists, change principles are identified and are reflective of content and process, such as those related to treatment procedures (specific factors), treatment participants (e.g., the client and therapist), and the therapeutic relationship. This work represents a shift toward recognizing specific and nonspecific factors as intertwined and operating in complex relationships, perhaps differently in different individuals, to produce outcomes (Beutler & Castonguay, 2006).

Ultimately, the future of health and mental health care systems is not simply to establish a new set of evidence-based interventions that outlive their usefulness. Rather the goal is to "produce a dynamic health care system that is capable of continuous self-renewal, in congruence with scientific evidence, in order to provide the most effective services to the widest range of people who need them. Fundamental changes in education, health care funding and accountability will be required to ensure success" (Drake et al., 2005, p. 476). There are several emerging developments in the coming years that will impact health and mental health care systems. These include creative new medication delivery routes like brain implants, skin patches, or under-the-tongue medications; knowledge of differential physical and psychological effects of medications on people of different ages, gender, races, and ethnicities; and new models of health care financing that will influence drug availability and use.

Progressive Public Policy

Social workers are uniquely posed to shape the future of mental health services through policy reform. Most critics argue that evidence supportive of EBPs may show efficacy but is limited concerning utility and, as such, is insufficient to warrant their exclusive use, exclusive funding, and legal penalties for nonuse (Bruce & Sanderson, 2005). No doubt social workers will have ample opportunity to be involved in public mental health policy efforts that promote access and delivery of quality mental health care while at the same time critiquing those policies that promote the wholesale promotion of certain EBP "packages" that have been misused by purchasers or the legal system.

New future directions in which social workers will influence public policy involve the use of research networks to field test current community practices (e.g., between EBPs and treatment as usual) that improve understanding of the relative contributions of each approach. In addition, public payers, such as state divisions of mental health as well as private insurers, are in a position to contribute to this effort if they organize specific projects and seek funding opportunities. Funding and outlets for the results of their efforts are increasing as priorities are shifting toward effectiveness research (Bruce & Sanderson, 2005). For example, future policies must ensure that evidence-based approaches are widely available to persons with co-occurring disorders and that funding programs like Medicaid and Medicare will need to strive to be more integrated rather than the current model of silos, with one possible suggestion being that states lead administrators of addictions and mental health direct integrated offices.

CONCLUSION

As this overview illustrates, social workers currently play a large role in the delivery of current mental health care services and will play an even larger one in shaping the future direction of mental health. Social workers have an opportunity to shape the future of mental health services by ensuring the following points of excellence are a part of any mental health service system: scientifically supported treatment evidence, consumer preference, family and caregiver involvement, clinical expertise through workforce development, dynamic and integrated health and mental health care system, and progressive public policy.

WEB SITES

Campaign for Mental Health Reform. http://www.mhreform.org/policy/ebs.htm.

Institute of Medicine (IOM). http://www.iom.edu.

National Institute of Mental Health. http://www.nimh.gov.

References

Addis, M. E., & Krasnow, A. D. (2000) A national survey of practicing psychologists' attitudes toward psychotherapy treatment manuals. *Journal of Consulting and Clinical Psychology, 68*, 331–339.

Bentley, K. (2002). *Social work practice in mental health: Contemporary roles, tasks, and techniques*. Pacific Grove, CA: Brooks-Cole.

Bentley, K., & Floyd-Taylor, M. (2002). A context and vision for excellence in social work practice in contemporary mental health settings. In K. Bentley (Ed.), *Social work practice in mental health: Contemporary roles, tasks, and techniques* (pp. 1–17). Pacific Grove, CA: Brooks-Cole.

Beutler, L. E., & Castonguay, L. G. (Eds.). (2006). *Empirically supported principles of therapy change*. New York: Oxford University Press.

Bruce, T., & Sanderson, W. (2005). Evidence-based psychosocial practices: Past, present, and future.

In C. Stout & R. Hayes (Eds.), *The evidence-based practice: Methods, models and tools for mental health professionals* (pp. 220–243). Hoboken, NJ: Wiley.

Cruz, C., & Spence, J. (2005). *Oregon tribal evidence-based and cultural best practices*. Statewide report, Office of Addictions and Mental Health Services, Oregon Department of Human Services, Salem.

Drake, R., Merrens, M., & Lynde, D. (2005). The future of evidence-based practices in mental health. In R. Drake, M. Merrens, & D. Lynde (Eds.), *Evidence-based mental health practice* (pp. 471–477). New York: Norton.

Institute of Medicine. (2000). *Promoting health: Intervention strategies from social and behavioral research*. Washington, DC: National Academies Press.

Institute of Medicine. (2001). *Crossing the quality chasm: A new health system for the 21st century*. Washington, DC: National Academies Press.

National Institutes of Health, Office of Behavioral and Social Sciences Research. 2007. *Contributions of behavioral and social sciences research to improving the health of the nation: A prospectus for the future*. Retrieved from http://www.thehillgroup.com/OBSSR_Prospectus.pdf.

Solomon, P., & Stanhope, V. (2006). Recovery: Expanding the vision of evidence-based practice. In A. Roberts & K. Yeager (Eds.), *Foundations of evidence-based social work practice* (pp. 336–348). New York: Oxford University Press.

Weissman, M. M., & Sanderson, W. C. (2002). Problems and promises in modern psychotherapy: The need for increased training in evidence-based treatments. In B. Hamburg (Ed.), *Modern psychiatry: Challenges in educating health professionals to meet new needs* (pp. 132–160). New York: Josiah Macy Foundation.

Development of a Proactive Model of Health Care versus a Reactive System of Referrals

James R. Zabora

Chronic illnesses such as cancer, HIV/AIDS, and renal failure disrupt every aspect of daily living for the afflicted patients as well as their families. Patients' and families' psychological, social, spiritual, and financial resources can be severely challenged due to prolonged treatments, related adverse reactions and complications, and potentially long-term recovery and rehabilitation. This chapter provides a theoretical framework for practical approaches to implement a prospective model of care rather than a reactive system based on staff referrals for social work services. In addition, this chapter serves as a guide to evidence-based social work interventions that can be applied in diverse health care settings.

PSYCHOLOGICAL DISTRESS AMONG THE CHRONICALLY ILL

All of the chronically ill experience varying levels of distress at the time of diagnosis, whereas the literature in psychosocial issues related to cancer is rich and extensive in comparison to other diseases and illnesses. Estimates suggest that more than 10 million Americans live with some form of cancer. Medical costs related to cancer and other chronic illnesses such as cardiovascular disease and diabetes are staggering, but the psychological and social consequences of these chronic illnesses are also great. Despite the publication of distress management guidelines by the National Comprehensive Cancer Network in 1999 (with multiple revisions since that time), availability and access to formalized and structured psychosocial programs for cancer patients, survivors, and families continue to be severely lacking. Frequently, high-quality psychosocial programs tend to be located in National Cancer Institute–designated comprehensive cancer centers, where the overwhelming majority of cancer patients and survivors will not be seen. In reality, nearly 85 percent of all cancer patients do not receive treatment in comprehensive cancer centers but through a range of community-based medical settings and programs. In many instances, this is also true of other chronic illnesses. Critical to social work practice with various chronic illnesses is the development of psychosocial programs and interventions that clearly delineate how patients respond to a diagnosis, as well as the variations that exist in each patient's attempt to adapt to a chronic illness. In addition, models are necessary that apply brief and effective approaches for psychosocial screening to identify high-risk patients and families followed by effective interventions in community settings across the United States (Zabora, Loscalzo, & Smith, 2000).

At the time of diagnosis, a serious and life-threatening condition generates a sense of vulnerability for virtually every patient. Diagnoses such as cancer and AIDS engender fear, produce uncertainty, and create significant demands for any patient. However, in spite of this early trauma, significant evidence indicates that the majority of newly diagnosed patients gradually adapt to this crisis, their diagnosis, and related treatments. Weisman, Worden, and Sobel (1980) described in detail the adaptive process that cancer patients experience. Adaptation begins when patients manage to incorporate the illness into their daily lives and effectively address problems or concerns created by a life-threatening illness. However, studies also indicate that nearly one-third of all cancer patients and survivors experience significantly elevated levels of distress that requires social work interventions. This is true whether the patient is newly diagnosed, in treatment, in remission, or living with a recurrence (Zabora et al, 1997). This fundamental issue requires social workers in health care to reconceptualize how social work services are provided in medical settings.

ADAPTATION AND MANAGEMENT OF A CHRONIC ILLNESS

Based on the early work of a number of researchers, the study of psychological responses to cancer and appropriate interventions has expanded to include time points beyond the initial diagnosis. As patients move through their early reactions, they gain experience as survivors. Survivorship begins on the day of diagnosis as patients begin to redefine all aspects of their lives. Three primary points exist in the psychosocial care of the chronically ill. First, patients experience an "existential plight" (Weisman & Worden, 1976) during the first 3 months following their diagnosis. Though many patients strive to regain a sense of normalcy and control, many still experience intense feelings of distress exacerbated for many by the physical trauma associated with surgery, aggressive therapies, and related adverse reactions and complications. For the most part, patients are forced to acknowledge that their lives will never be the same. Second, if a remission occurs or the disease is under control, patients begin to learn to live with their illness. They incorporate disruptions of daily life into their day-to-day routines. Third, the fear of recurrence or an actual recurrence further complicates the psychosocial course for each patient. Many health care providers assume patients may experience recurrence as the point of highest distress, but this is often not the case. Patients gain critical information and knowledge during the early treatments for their disease. Meanwhile, they have formed supportive relationships with members of the health care team as well as with other patients. Knowledge and support from the team enable patients to anticipate and understand their course of treatment following recurrence and the problems associated with this phase.

Consequently, given these three critical points in time, the first 100 days following diagnosis provides the greatest opportunity to intervene early and integrate effective interventions related to disease management based on the patient's level of distress and through the integration of the family.

Patients who cannot adapt to their clinical circumstances challenge the health care team to respond to a multitude of psychological and social problems. Often, the vulnerability associated with these problems generates significant distress that may not become manifest to the health care team until the patient reaches an observable crisis event. Frequently, referrals to psychosocial providers occur when the patient is severely depressed or anxious, experiencing significant conflicts within the family, or is suicidal (Rainey, Wellisch, & Fawzy, 1983). In addition, studies indicate that physicians and nurses often do not identify patients with elevated levels of anxiety and depression in a timely manner (Newell, Sanson-Fisher, Girgis, & Bonaventura, 2000). On the other hand, screening and early detection of distress and vulnerability can enable health care social workers to provide prospective interventions that are problem-focused and related to disease management that reduce distress, increase quality of life, and enhance medical treatment outcomes.

A THEORETICAL MODEL TO SUPPORT A PROSPECTIVE MODEL OF CARE

Given the issues defined, an appropriate theoretical model must be used to guide the development of approaches and methods to identify chronically ill patients who are at risk to experience significantly elevated levels of distress. Stress model theory (SMT) suggests that any individual must experience a series of cognitive appraisals related to any crisis event or level of distress in their lives (Lazarus, 1991). In other words, before one can act and respond to a crisis such as a new diagnosis to reduce the distress associated with it, the individual must develop a personal meaning of the specific crisis or event. Primary appraisal describes this process as defining what the crisis event means to the person at this point in his or her life. To define the crisis event, people use all of their available resources. SMT postulates that each person possesses a number of internal and external resources. Examples of internal resources include personality, level of optimism, ability to solve problems, and spirituality. Numerous studies have demonstrated the relationships between distress and resources, such as spirituality, problem-solving skills, social support such as the family, and quality of life. Therefore, distress is an appropriate marker for the identification of high-risk patients, if resources are lacking, and problem solving is a critical internal resource to strengthen.

External resources often consist of social supports, such as the family. If social supports are adequate and available, the individual possesses a greater likelihood to define this event in a positive, rather than negative, manner. These internal and external resources not only facilitate the definition of crisis but also promote the development of a secondary appraisal related to effective strategies to respond to any specific crisis event (Lazarus, 1991). Failure to respond to the demands of a crisis event and solve related complex problems may result in significant levels of emotional distress. Emotional distress always causes disruptions in daily functioning. If distress could be detected much earlier, psychosocial interventions could be offered at a more appropriate time in the course of care, such as at the time of diagnosis. If emotional distress is undetected and untreated, "negative appraisals or definitions of the illness" may result, which lead to unhealthy behaviors, a decrease in life satisfaction, and an increase in inappropriate use of health care resources (Allison et al., 1995; Zabora et al., 2000). For example, undetected emotional distress may influence how symptoms are described or may be converted into multiple somatic complaints, such as fatigue and pain, and health care providers may respond by ordering unnecessary evaluations, tests, medications, and treatments.

PSYCHOSOCIAL SCREENING AND EARLY INTERVENTIONS

A serious chronic illness disrupts all components of social integration—family, work, finances, and friendships—as well as the patient's psychological status. Over the extended course of an illness, physical changes and side effects of surgery and therapies create multiple and complex problems and demands for the patient and family. These problems and demands, in conjunction with significant financial assaults, generate a negative synergy, which is often ignored in the care of cancer patients and their families. An integrated model of psychosocial screening and early psychosocial interventions at the time of the initial diagnosis can produce benefit to significant numbers of chronically ill patients and their families.

Much research exists showing a significant association between psychological distress and unsatisfactory quality of life at the time of diagnosis as well as throughout treatment and recovery. For example, it is clear that cancer patients are at risk for the development of psychological symptoms and problems, perhaps to an even greater extent than patients with other medical illnesses. Some of the potential risk factors hypothesized to be involved in the development of cancer patients' distress include social isolation, pessimistic attitudes, loss of control, loss of hope, socioeconomic factors, pain, side effects of cancer treatments, and poor problem-solving skills.

To date, though many investigators have examined the concept of psychosocial screening, little progress has been achieved to demonstrate clinical feasibility, utility, and benefit. Current psychosocial practice is to allow the patient to move through the diagnostic phase into treatment and react to psychological responses as they occur. Psychosocial interventions are frequently offered when the patient reaches a crisis state and is agitated, depressed, or suicidal. Interventions are effective at these acute points, but early identification and intervention may prevent this type of acute or crisis event and contribute to greater adherence to medical treatment regimens, higher patient satisfaction, and enhanced quality of life.

A prerequisite for psychosocial screening is a reliable and valid instrument that is based on the psychological experiences of chronically ill patients (Zabora et al., 1990). Though many standardized measures exist, little work has been undertaken to demonstrate their capability for use within a psychosocial screening program. For 8 years, social work staff of the Johns Hopkins Oncology Center tested methods to implement a high-risk screening program through the use of the Brief Symptom Inventory (BSI). As a result, over 10,000 BSI profiles were amassed in a database with demographic variables. This database is considered by the National Comprehensive Cancer Network to be the largest of its type in the United States. Manipulation of the database enables critical questions to be explored, such as the factors that contribute to the distress level of patients as well as the relationship between distress and the specific cancer diagnosis. Although a screening program existed, it continued to be cumbersome due to the length of the BSI at 53 items. Most patients can complete the BSI in about 10 minutes, and scoring requires computer scanning and redistribution of high-risk cases to the appropriate clinician. A shortened instrument with rapid scoring would expedite this process and link patients to clinicians more quickly. To accomplish this task, a subset of 1,500 cases from the BSI database were subjected to factor analysis in an effort to generate a brief psychological measure of 18 (i.e., the BSI-18) items that can be more easily and efficiently incorporated into routine clinical care in an effort to prospectively identify high-risk patients.

One of the more contentious issues in the field of psychosocial oncology is whether screening for high distress is feasible and beneficial. Although numerous standardized instruments exist for screening, little progress has been made to design and implement prospective psychosocial programs with screening, early interventions, and outcome measures. Despite the fact that in most settings psychosocial resources are limited, social work clinicians and other psychosocial providers continue to struggle with the dilemma of early case identification versus staff referral versus little or no services at all. Early identification with an appropriate intervention enables the health care team to truly offer comprehensive psychosocial care to minimize distress, dysfunction, and suffering. Following interventions, patients' satisfaction with their overall medical care may increase, and in addition, the team may realize potential cost savings in the delivery of care. Furthermore, failure to identify high-risk patients at the point of entry into care may jeopardize the outcomes of cancer therapies. Significant levels of distress may inhibit the patient's ability to fully comprehend complex treatment regimens. As a result, they may not follow medical directives. Finally, undetected and untreated psychological distress may be transformed into somatic complaints, such as fatigue, pain, or sleep disorders. Health care providers may assess the somatic complaint and respond with medications, lab tests, scans, or procedures. Somatic complaints may continue until the true source of the complaint is identified and treated. Brief psychosocial interventions that address significantly elevated levels of anxiety at the initiation of treatment may be far less costly than a series of non–medically appropriate procedures and scans, or an avoidable hospitalization if physical complaints increase in severity. See Figure 122.1 for a description of a prospective model of care with psychosocial screening and early interventions (Zabora, 1998).

APPLICATION OF EVIDENCE-BASED PRACTICE

Given the significant variation in distress that exists from patient to patient, evidence from numerous intervention studies suggest that potentially all chronically ill patients may benefit from some form of social work intervention. For example,

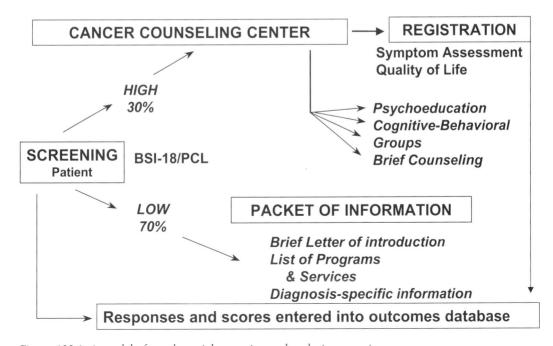

Figure 122.1 A model of psychosocial screening and early intervention.

for patients who experience a lower level of distress, interventions such as psychoeducational programs may provide benefit by providing information and strategies to further enhance their preexisting adaptive capabilities. Furthermore, moderately distressed patients might benefit the most from skill-building groups, where they learn a series of techniques to manage their disease effectively. Finally, patients with the highest level of distress require a mental health approach that might include a combination of brief therapy, family therapy, cognitive-behavioral interventions, or problem solving (Fawzy et al., 1995).

NECESSITY TO INTEGRATE THE FAMILY

The effects of any chronic illness reverberate throughout the family. Families can exhibit significant variation in their ability to adapt and respond to the overall illness experience. A variation in family response exists, and family members can experience increased anxiety and depression, disruptions in social roles, and diminished physical health with an escalation of somatic complaints. A chronic illness such as cancer generates demands that impose severe levels of stress that challenge even the most well-functioning family. These struggles occur as families attempt to serve as the primary source of support for the patient, a buffer against stress, and a facilitator for effective decision making and problem solving (Zabora & Smith, 1991).

When family caregivers are incapacitated by their reactions to a diagnosis and related treatments, the health care team loses a significant resource in the overall care of the patient. Distress in the family undermines decision-making and problem-solving skills. Family members' capacity to be effective caregivers is related to family functioning along the dimensions of adaptability and cohesion. The level of family functioning may simply be inadequate to meet the caregiving expectations of the health care team. Nearly all families experience difficulties and problems if the role of caregiving is prolonged over time. Consequently, an imperative in the care of the chronically ill has emerged to develop effective methods that enhance the problem-solving abilities of family caregivers to resolve difficulties related to the care of the patient outside the hospital.

One approach is COPE, a social problem-solving model that can be taught to patients and family caregivers. COPE has been defined as "the meta-cognitive process by which patients and family members understand the nature of problems in living and direct their coping efforts at altering the difficult nature of the situations themselves, the patients' reactions to them or both." With this conceptual model, problems are defined as specific life circumstances that demand responses for adaptive effective coping responses because of the presence of a variety of obstacles. These obstacles may include ambiguity, uncertainty, conflicting demands, lack of resources, novelty, or all of these (Houts et al., 1996).

CLINICAL CASE EXAMPLE

Mr. Z., a 68-year-old former steel worker, was recently diagnosed with advanced lung cancer at a VA Medical Center. He was initially referred to the Johns Hopkins Oncology Center for confirmation of the diagnosis and exploration of treatment options. Mr. Z. chose to pursue the most aggressive option of a resection of his right lung to remove as much of the tumors as possible. At the time of the surgical consult, Mr. Z. had little to say, and he allowed his wife to ask a number of questions. However, he did state quite clearly that he wished to schedule his surgery as soon as possible. Overall, there was no evidence of acute distress as assessed by the surgeon and the surgical nurse, but it was unclear if Mr. Z. understood the gravity of his diagnosis.

During the registration process, Mr. Z. completed the BSI-18 and the Problem Checklist (PCL). The BSI-18 results indicated a high level of general distress (score = 20), along with elevated levels of depression (score = 10) and anxiety (score = 8). Specifically, he indicated that he was feeling worthless, feeling blue, feeling hopeless, and was experiencing spells of panic and terror. Mr. Z. also indicated that he had concerns about his level of pain (score of 5 on a 10-point Likert scale on the PCL), communication within the family about his illness, and overall financial issues. On receipt of these screening data, the oncology social worker scheduled an appointment with Mr. Z. to develop a treatment plan to address his distress. During this first appointment, the social worker initiated a discussion of the critical need for effective problem solving, a specific cognitive-behavioral intervention for his anxiety, an appointment with family members to facilitate open communication, and an appointment with the center's psychiatrist to assess his level of depression. As a result of this first appointment, Mr. Z. agreed to three family sessions to discuss problem-solving strategies in the context of communication as well as individual sessions to learn progressive muscle relaxation. In addition, the appointment with the psychiatrist was completed, but medication was not indicated at this time.

In essence, rather than allow Mr. Z. to continue struggling with his distress and related concerns, the screening instruments served to identify a number of issues that were amenable to evidence-based interventions. This prospective approach generates the opportunity for social work to assume a leadership role in the management of distress among chronically ill patients and their family members. In addition, health care social workers can employ interventions early, when there is greater likelihood of success, and demonstrate defined outcomes such as increased problem-solving skills, reduced stress, and enhanced quality of life.

FUTURE PERSPECTIVES

Social work in health care faces numerous challenges over the next decade. Whereas a number of social work departments in health care have eliminated, the absolute number of social work positions in health care has remained relatively constant over the past 10 years. Furthermore, in a survey of members of the Society of Social Work Leaders in Health Care, 74 percent of the respondents believe that the status of social work in health care is the same or better than it was 2 years ago, and 70 percent believe that their status is same or better than it was 5 years ago (Zabora, BrintzenhofeSzoc, Fox, & Lipton, 2006). Consequently, social workers in health care need to strive to establish and demonstrate their competence in areas such as psychosocial screening, family care, psychosocial interventions such as problem solving, and demonstration of pertinent outcomes such as quality of life.

If social work is to enhance its position in health care, the profession must address all of the issues discussed in the previous paragraph. Social workers possess the capacity to reverse the current reactive system whereby workers wait for referrals from the health care team to a prospective model where social work assumes the leadership role to implement a system that identifies at-risk patients and families at the time of the original diagnosis. In this way, social work in health care can clearly define a path of identifica-

tion of patients and families that are at a higher level of risk as well as appropriate evidence-based interventions and outcomes. In the past, social work has tended to use outcomes related to discharge planning, such as length of stay, which can vary significantly regardless of social work performance. Payers such as Medicaid in many states can a series of regulations and the impact can dramatically impact on the perception of social work productivity. In other words, a change in regulations can create discharge delays that directly influences how other professions perceive social work performance.

Therefore, social workers in health care must identify critical outcomes to truly demonstrate the benefit of social work interventions. Outcomes such as a decrease in distress, as well as improvements in problem-solving skills and quality of life, would be significant. However, to truly influence the future of social work in health care, an economic outcome is essential. This variable should be related to the changing health care arena where virtually all care is in transition from inpatient to ambulatory care. Rather than a focus on inpatient care, social work needs to turn its attention to the vast number of patients who receive care in ambulatory clinics. Here, social work could conceptualize a relationship between distress and health care utilization, whereby if social work could have a significant impact on the reduction of distress, the savings in dollars to medical settings could be staggering. If distressed patients could be managed more effectively, tests, scans, procedures, and medications could be significantly reduced. In this way, social work could demonstrate a significant economic impact based on specific interventions, such as psychoeducation, brief therapies, cognitive-behavioral interventions, or problem solving. As a result of this sequence of events, social work has demonstrated the capability to identify patients who are at risk, provide the necessary interventions, and confirm the pertinent outcomes such as decreased distress and increased quality of life due to increased problem-solving skills.

WEB SITES

American Psychosocial Oncology Society. http://www.apos-society.org.
Association of Oncology Social Work. http://www.aosw.org.
INOVA Life with Cancer Program, an exemplar of a comprehensive psychosocial program

related to cancer patients and their families. http://www.inova.com/cancer/life_with_cancer_program/index.jsp.

National Comprehensive Cancer Network. http://www. nccn.org.

Society for Social Work Leaders in Health Care. http://www.sswlhc.org.

References

Allison, T. G., Williams, D. E., Miller, T. D., et al. (1995). Medical and economic costs of psychological distress in patients with coronary artery disease. *Mayo Clinic Proceedings, 70,* 734–742.

Fawzy, F. I., Fawzy, N. W., Arndt, L. A., et al. (1995). Critical review of psychosocial interventions in cancer care. *Archives of General Psychiatry, 52,* 100–116.

Houts, P. S., Nezu, A. M., Nezu, C. M., et al. (1996). The prepared family caregiver: A problem-solving approach for family caregiver education. *Patient Education and Counseling, 27,* 63–73.

Lazarus, R. (1991). *Emotion and adaptation.* New York: Oxford University Press.

Newell, S., Sanson-Fisher, R. W., Girgis, A., & Bonaventura, A. (2000). How well do medical oncologists' perceptions reflect their patients' reported physical and psychosocial problems? *Cancer, 83,* 1640–1646.

Rainey, L. C., Wellisch, D. K., & Fawzy, F. I. (1983). Training health professionals in psychosocial aspects of cancer: A continuing education model. *Journal of Psychosocial Oncology, 10,* 103–115.

Weisman, A. D., & Worden, J. W. (1976). The existential plight in cancer: Significance of the first 100 days. *International Journal of Psychiatry in Medicine, 7,* 1–15.

Weisman, A.D., Worden, J.W., & Sobel, H.J. (1980). *Psychosocial screening and intervention with cancer patients: A research report.* Boston: Harvard Medical School and Massachusetts General Hospital.

Zabora, J. R. (1998). Screening procedures for psychosocial distress. In J. C. Holland (Ed.), *Psychooncology* (pp. 653–661). New York: Oxford University Press.

Zabora, J. R., Blanchard, C. G., Smith, E. D., et al. (1997). Prevalence of psychological distress among cancer patients across the disease continuum. *Journal of Psychosocial Oncology, 15,* 73–87.

Zabora, J., BrintzenhofeSzoc, K., Fox, N., & Lipton, H. (2006, April). *Evidence-based Practice: What is possible now?* Paper presented as a pre-conference institute at the annual meeting of the Society for Social Work Leaders in Health Care, San Diego, CA.

Zabora, J. R., Loscalzo, M. J., & Smith, E. D. (2000). Psychosocial rehabilitation. In M. D. Abeloff, et al. (Eds.), *Clinical oncology* (pp. 2845–2865). New York: Churchill-Livingstone.

Zabora, J. R., & Smith, E. D. (1991). Family dysfunction and the cancer patient: Early recognition and intervention. *Oncology, 5,* 31–35.

Zabora, J. R., Smith-Wilson, R., Fetting, J. H., et al. (1990). An efficient method for the psychosocial screening of cancer patients. *Psychosomatics, 3,* 192–197.

123

Overview of Alcohol and Drug Dependence

Assessment and Treatment

Kenneth R. Yeager

Social workers play a key role in the care management of persons struggling with alcohol and drug dependence and abuse. Through case management, social workers complete initial assessments to determine the extent and severity of drug and alcohol consumption and intervene to facilitate acceptance into treatment programming. Whether working in child welfare, schools, hospital, community service, or mental health centers, social workers address the aftermath of alcohol and drug abuse and dependence on a daily basis.

Alcohol and drug abuse is ubiquitous; it is associated with 100,000 deaths annually in the United States. It is the cause of 30 percent of all traffic fatalities. The lifetime prevalence of alcohol and drug dependence is estimated to be 12.5 percent based on a 2002 representative survey of 43,000 U.S. adults. Unfortunately, only 24 percent of the population identified as having a history of alcohol abuse ever receive treatment (Hasin, Stinson, Ogburn, & Grant, 2007; SAMHSA, 2005).

The burden of alcohol dependence in the United States is estimated to be $184.6 billion per year. The break-out of dollars lost is as follows (SAMHSA, 2005):

- Lost earnings due to alcohol related illness: $87.6 billion.
- Lost potential earning due to premature death: $36.5 billion.
- Losses related to auto crashes, fires, and criminal justice: $21.4 billion.
- Medical consequences: $18.8 billion.
- Lost earnings due to criminal activities: $10.1 billion.
- Specialty alcohol services: $7.5 billion.

Drug use in the United States continues to progress. In recent years, methamphetamine/am-phetamine use has grown remarkably. From 1995 to 2005, the percentage of substance abuse treatment admissions for primary abuse of methamphetamine/amphetamine more than doubled from 4 percent to 9 percent. In 2005, about 1.8 million substance abuse treatment admissions were reported to SAMHSA's Treatment Episode Data Set (TEDS). Of these, 169,500 were for primary methamphetamine/amphetamine abuse and 80,000 admissions were for secondary or tertiary methamphetamine/amphetamine abuse.

Other drugs, such as heroin, have demonstrated shifts in methods of use in those seeking treatment for their dependence. According to TEDS, annual admissions for substance abuse treatment for primary heroin abuse increased from 228,000 in 1995 to 254,000 in 2005. The proportion of primary heroin admissions remained steady at about 14 percent to 15 percent of all substance abuse treatment admissions. One interesting change is in the proportion of persons seeking treatment who inhaled heroin. This population increased from 27 percent among the primary heroin admissions in 1995 to 33 percent in 2005. This shift is representative of changes in levels of purity of heroin available today. As the purity level of heroin rises, use of heron through inhalation increases. This shift is reflected in greater heroin use by upper middle-class teens and young adults because inhalation is the preferred method of use for this population.

In the area of analgesics, oxycodone and hydrocodone remain top among sought after pain medications. According to SAMHSA's DAWN report mentions in emergency department visits increased from 4,000 in 1994 to 22,000 mentions in 2002, an increase of 450 percent. This report indicates approximately 29 percent of the oxycodone-related visits involved only oxycodone, 24 percent involved another drug, 29 percent involved two other drugs, and 18 percent involved three or more other drugs.

Additionally, emergency department visits seeking hydrocodone were more than twice as frequent as oxycodone in 1994; they have increased only 170 percent from 9,300 to over 25,000 mentions in 2002. Emergency departments are closely monitoring nonmedical use of analgesics and are using computer networking to track frequent flyers to emergency departments seeking analgesic medication. This population is complicated. Frequently, medical problems exist that require pain management. The difficulty is in determining how much pain medication is required and at what point the individual is abusing the prescription drug. Not all persons seeking analgesics through the emergency department are using analgesics alone. Many use this medication in combination with other mood-altering substances, creating a dangerous combination.

The most frequent substances found in combination with oxycodone and hydrocodone in drug abuse–related emergency department visits were alcohol, benzodiazepines, other opioid pain relievers, and cocaine. Social workers play an important role within emergency departments nationally in assisting other health professionals in the identification, assessment, and referral of prescription drug abusers to appropriate treatment.

It is clear that addressing the physical, social, and emotional consequences of alcohol and drug dependence benefits both the individual and society through the improvement of physical and mental health, productivity, and quality of life (Miller & Swift, 1997; Hoffmann, DeHart, & Fulkerson, 1993).

DIAGNOSIS OF ALCOHOL AND DRUG DEPENDENCE

Substance dependence is defined by the *DSM-IV-TR* as a maladaptive pattern of alcohol and or drug use, leading to clinically significant impairment or distress, as manifested by three or more of the following seven criteria, occurring at any time in the same 12-month period characterized by:

1. tolerance, as defined by either of the following:
2. withdrawal, as defined by either of the following:
3. the substance is taken in larger amounts or over a longer period than was intended.

4. there is a persistent desire or there are unsuccessful efforts to cut down or control use.
5. a great deal of time is spent in activities necessary to obtain, use, or recover from effects of the substance abused.
6. important social, occupational, or recreational activities are given up or reduced because of substance use.
7. substance use is continued despite knowledge of having a persistent or recurrent physical or psychological problem that is likely to have been caused or exacerbated by said substance use.

What Is Substance Dependence?

Dependence is a chronic *progressive and potentially fatal disease*, with genetic, psychosocial, and environmental factors influencing its development and manifestations. It is characterized by continuous or periodic impaired control over drinking, preoccupation with the drug or alcohol and use of drugs or alcohol despite adverse consequences, and distortions in thinking most notably denial.

What Does "Progressive and Fatal" Mean?

"Progressive and fatal" means that the disease persists over time and physical, emotional, and social changes are often cumulative and may progress as drinking continues. Substance dependence causes premature death through overdose; organic complications involving the brain, liver, heart, and many other organs; and contributing to suicide, homicide, motor vehicle crashes, and other traumatic events.

What Does "Primary" Mean?

"Primary" refers to the nature of substance dependence as a disease entity in addition to and separate from other pathophysiologic states which may be associated with it. The term suggests that substance dependence is not a symptom of an underlying disease state.

What Does "Disease" Mean?

A disease is an involuntary disability. It represents the sum of the abnormal phenomena displayed by a group of individuals. These phenomena are associated with a specified common set of characteristics by which these individuals differ from the norm and which places them at a disadvantage.

OVERVIEW OF TREATMENT APPROACHES

Treatment of alcohol and drug dependence includes identification of alcohol and drug abuse and dependence, initiating treatment plans, educating the individual and family about the abuse and dependence, conducting clinically based interventions within group settings, and individual approaches. The interventions include referral to Alcoholics Anonymous, Narcotics Anonymous, or Cocaine Anonymous, employee assistance programs, and couple and family counseling. Early intervention is important because it serves to minimize consequences experienced by the individual abusing illicit substances. Social consequences include legal, marital, employment, and financial problems. Additionally, early intervention minimizes the potential for long-term health and mental health consequences. Later intervention includes referral to detoxification services, health and mental health services, legal intervention, and other services necessary to stabilize the individual (Holder & Blose, 1992; Yeager & Gregoire, 2005).

ASSESSING ALCOHOL AND DRUG DEPENDENCE

There are a variety of current best practices for the diagnosis and management of alcohol and drug addiction. Following is a case study that examines the different ways that alcohol and drug addiction can impact an individual. This case represents different symptoms of dependence as well as different treatment needs.

Working with alcohol- and drug-dependent individuals is challenging and rewarding work that requires both skill and tact. Although resistance and active defense structures are hallmarks of alcohol dependence, resistance is less than one might expect. Williams et al. (2006) reported within a sample of 6400 patients a full 75 percent demonstrated at least minimal levels of willingness to change. When placed within a stages-of-change model, approximately 24 percent presented in the contemplative stage of change and 51 percent demonstrated characteristics of taking action to change drinking patterns.

Social workers serve a unique role in assisting persons with alcohol abuse and dependence issues. Frequently, the task of conducting a complete and thorough assessment of the dependent individual falls to the social worker. Components of a thorough alcohol assessment include, but are not limited to, the following.

Establish the Individual's Perception of the Problem

Begin with the individual's perception of his or her drinking history and the exact nature of the problem. Understanding the individual's perception informs the social worker of where he or she will begin in the treatment process. A willingness to listen openly to the individual's perception of need will also provide an opportunity to begin to gently probe into sensitive areas in a manner that is less intrusive, thus opening channels of communication.

Application of a Disease Frame of Reference

Persons seeking assistance with their drinking frequently feel trapped, guilty, helpless, or hostile. Conducting the initial interview from a disease or illness frame of reference, based in nonjudgmental language minimizes defensiveness while establishing a working relationship. In many cases, individuals are well aware of the need to become active participants in their health care. Just as persons with diabetes or hypertension are responsible for altering their lifestyle to treat their illness, alcohol-dependent persons should be encouraged to assume a greater level of self-responsibility for their treatment.

Construct a Comprehensive Family History

Alcohol and drug dependence has long been determined to have a strong genetic link, therefore, building a family history will begin to normalize the individual's perception of how he or she came to acquire this illness. A good family history should include examination of maternal and paternal drinking patterns and potential alcohol dependence. Examination of lifestyle, community involvement, reputation, marital, legal, employment, spiritual, and educational history will provide important insight into family responses to and perceptions of alcohol and drug dependence.

Establish a Timeline of Alcohol and Drug Use and Amounts Consumed

As the family history unfolds, it provides a natural segue into the individual's experience with alcohol and drug use. Again using a nonjudgmental, inquisitive approach, begin gathering history surrounding childhood perceptions of drinking and drug use, onset of use, type of substances consumed, and under what circumstances. Make a genuine effort to understand the individual's frame of reference surrounding alcohol and drug consumption (especially over-the-counter drugs). When possible, reinforce the person's self-motivational statements and problem recognition while assessing the level of desire to make positive changes in his or her life.

As accurately as possible, begin to piece together daily, weekly, and monthly drinking or drug use patterns. How do weekdays differ from weekends? What happens on payday, holidays, and vacations? Begin to weave together behavioral and consumption patterns. Discuss the meaning of alcohol and drug withdrawal, what it is, what it looks like and the risks associated with it. Based on the individual's pattern of use and potential for withdrawal, a determination can be made regarding the most appropriate level of care. In general, the presence of withdrawal symptoms warrants an inpatient detoxification program. This of course will depend on the drug of use—some drugs require inpatient detoxification and others do not. Those with lesser withdrawal risk are more appropriately treated in an outpatient program.

Always be on the lookout for red-flag responses, such as arrests, domestic disturbances, accidents, and emergency room visits. Also look for comorbidities commonly associated with alcohol and or drug dependence, such as hypertension, diabetes, liver problems, gastrointestinal problems, injuries sustained through accidents, and sleep difficulties.

Examine Social and Emotional Factors

Once the lines of communication are open, the professional can begin the process of examining sensitive areas of the individual's life. While valuing the previously shared family history and perceptions associated with alcohol and drug use,

begin to examine the individuals day-to-day activities to build understanding of social, emotional, and environmental factors associated with alcohol or drug consumption. Seek to understand how the use of mood-altering substances is integrated into the individual's rituals. When and where does he or she drink or use? Whom do they drink or use with, and has this changed over time? If the pattern has changed, question the reason for changes. What are the most common social activities? If there are children, to what extent is the parent involved? How are things in the home? Are family members frequently together, or are there estrangements that exist?

Examine the person's educational, vocational, military, employment, financial legal, spiritual, and recreational history as well as current day-to-day activity patterns. It is important to note that many alcohol or drug abusers replace previously enjoyable activities with drinking or drug use. Question whether substance use has any impact on the social aspects of the individual's life and examine what that impact has been. The assessment process is one of exploration and education, so take time to teach and set boundaries. Avoid the tendency to overexamine areas that present with emotionally charged responses. More often than not, this will lead the assessment away from productive interaction into a dead-end of rationalization, blame, and frustration. Remain positive and avoid demoralizing statements and negative attitudes about alcohol or drug problems and treatment programs.

Summarize and Teach

Use the assessment process to reinforce and direct the individual with summary statements. Summary statements are designed to present the individual with nuggets of information you have summarized. The intent is twofold. First, you are checking to be certain you have heard and understood the person's perception. Second, summarizing statements can be used to tie pieces of information together in a way that leads the individual to insights and conclusions previously not examined. Patients need to understand the impact of substance abuse and dependence. Examination of what has worked for them in the past and what has not worked is an important part of the assessment summary. Frequently, individuals will have stopped drinking for periods of time. Examine what did and didn't work during those time periods. Emphasize that resumption of drinking is not a sign of failure but part of a process.

When possible, family members should be involved in the treatment process. Assessment of potential family involvement should begin with the initial assessment and continue throughout the entire treatment process. Establishment of family support is a strong positive reinforcement for adopting and maintaining new approaches to establishing and maintaining abstinence. Finally, provide information of risks. Family members and patients should understand that alcohol dependence is a chronic, progressive, and potentially fatal disease. It's important to know what they are up against, what role each person has to play, and how support, openness, and self-responsibility can lead to positive changes. Figure 123.1 describes potential approaches to care and integration of social factors to be addressed by social workers when providing comprehensive addition treatment.

THERAPEUTIC APPROACHES

Motivational Enhancement Therapy (MET)

Motivational interviewing (MI) is a counseling technique frequently applied in the treatment of alcohol-dependent or -abusing persons. This approach elicits changes in behavior by helping the individual explore and address ambivalence about change. MET is a nonconfrontational approach that focuses on establishing new and different approaches toward problematic drinking behaviors. Goals of this approach are:

- seek to understand the individual's frame of reference;
- elicit and reinforce the individual's personal motivational statements of problem recognition, desire, intent to change, and confidence in ability to change;
- monitor the individual's readiness to change and maintain a steady and consistent approach to problem resolution; and
- provide support and affirmation of individual choice and potential for self-regulation.

Caroll et al. (2006) conducted a randomized trial of MET motivational interviewing in a community-based substance abuse program setting. Findings from this study indicate that exposure to motivational interviewing demonstrated greater levels of program retention when compared to control groups. However, substance abuse outcomes at 84 days did not differ significantly from controls. Despite this disparity, MI continues to emerge as a best practice in treatment of alcohol abuse and dependence. Current literature indicates that there are more than 160 randomized trials, numer-

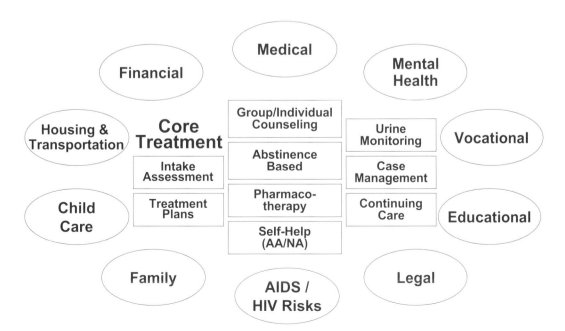

Figure 123.1 Core components of comprehensive services.

ous multisite trials, and recently published meta-analyses of the effectiveness of MI. In these studies, the effectiveness of MI demonstrates wide variability within defined problem areas. In general, positive effects of MI appear early but tend to diminish over time. It is critical to remember that MI effectively captures the individual early in the treatment process, leading to increased participation and potentially increased retention in programming, both of which are key components of successful treatment outcomes.

Cognitive-Behavioral Therapy

Cognitive-behavioral therapy (CBT) is a structured, goal-directed approach designed to help patients learn how thought processes affect their behavior. The social worker helps the individual develop new ways of thinking and behaving through improved cognitive awareness. This leads to an increased ability to adapt to and alter situations within the social environment that present as potential triggers for alcohol consumption.

The evidence for CBT is favorable and indicates it is an effective treatment approach for alcohol dependence and abuse, however, current evidence suggest that CBT is most effective when applied as part of a comprehensive treatment plan (Cutler & Fishbain, 2005).

Solution-Focused Approach

Solution-focused therapy approaches addiction issues from a prospective approach. Rather than examining problems and past behaviors, solution-focused therapy examines current reality, building on the unique strengths and abilities each individual brings to the therapy process. In the treatment of alcohol abuse and dependence solution focused therapy focuses on:

• envisioning the future without alcohol and the problems leading to treatment;
• discovering effective approaches/solutions to present issues;
• encouraging the individual to build on previous successes, plus adding new approaches to methods that have demonstrated success previously;
• directing and facilitating self discovery through self-examination;
• the individual as the expert in developing effective change and solutions rather than the social worker;

• the role of the social worker is to assist in the development of potential solutions; and
• emphasizing the here and now rather than the then and why.

Steve de Shazer and Insoo Kim Berg of the Brief Family Therapy Center in Milwaukee are the originators of this form of therapy.

HOSPITALIZATION AND REFERRAL OPTIONS

There are times that brief intervention is not useful for patients experiencing severe alcohol abuse or alcohol dependence. If the initial assessment suggests severe alcohol dependence, and the individual indicates a willingness to stop drinking, level of care options should be considered. These options consist of the following:

• inpatient detoxification,
• inpatient treatment,
• residential treatment, and
• day treatment or outpatient therapy.

Patients presenting with mild to moderate symptoms of alcohol withdrawal have the potential to be managed within an outpatient treatment setting. Outpatient detoxification has become increasingly popular since the emergence of cost-reduction approaches to substance dependence treatment emerged in the late 1980s and early 1990s.

Patients with more severe withdrawal symptoms and susceptibility to environmental cues are better cared for in inpatient treatment environments that are free of relapse triggers. Many providers placing their patients in an inpatient treatment setting to initiate detoxification and medical stabilization. This is followed by transition into residential or day treatment programs.

The third level of step-down approaches to alcohol dependence involves transition into intensive outpatient treatment, which is comprised of education, group, and individual sessions usually 3 hours in duration occurring three times per week. Following completion of this level of care the individual then transitions into a traditional outpatient treatment. Figure 123.2 presents options for individualized treatment approaches when working with alcohol- and drug-dependent individuals.

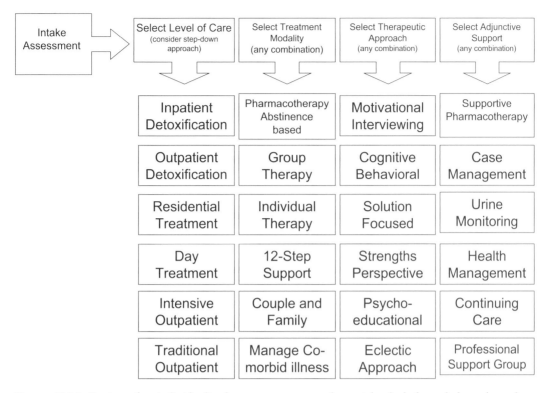

Figure 123.2 Options for individualized treatment approaches with alcohol- and drug-dependent individuals.

CASE EXAMPLE

John G. is a 50-year-old civil engineer who is self-employed and have been extremely successful in development of his business. John has four separate regional offices and travels extensively managing each of them, bidding jobs and interacting with various construction companies on business. Seven months ago, while working, John fell while jumping onto a bulldozer to speak with a friend. He injured two vertebrae (L-4 and L-5) in his lower back in this fall. This injury created severe nerve pain that radiates down his leg and causes limited mobility. John is prescribed an opiate-based pain medication. He has always been a drinker, and he enjoys drinking with business associates. His drink of choice is beer, yet there is no stated history of drug or alcohol abuse in his medical record. Initially, John used the pain meds sparingly, but as time progressed his use of increased. Soon he was taking more than the prescribed amount. On three occasions, his physician increased the strength of his medication. John began to order prescriptions online. He doubled the prescribed dose. He began to miss business appointments

and experienced increased marital stress related to his prescription medication use. Finally, John crashed his company car into a school bus when he apparently fell asleep at the wheel in the middle of the afternoon. At the point of entering treatment, John was facing legal problems related to this accident, financial problems related to lack of attention to his business, marital difficulties as a result of the prescription drug abuse, and an emerging single-episode depressive disorder.

John will benefit from a combined approach of MI and CBT. It is best to begin with motivational interviewing to ensure initial connection with treatment processes. CBT will be appropriate as treatment progresses given John's level of cognitive functioning. This approach can be helpful in assisting him in developing concrete plans to address issues of chronic pain, as well as establishing a plan for returning to work. An initial focus will elicit information and take advantage of change talk revealed in statements such as "I am ready to quit" or "I have to quit to get my life back into order."

Change talk is talk that recognizes a *desire* to change, the *ability* to change, provides *reason* for the change, and describes a *need* to change. Simply remember DARN. However, change does not occur without action or positive steps in the direction of recovery. Action talk requires identification and support of *commitment*; a willingness, intention, determination, or readiness for treatment *activation*; and the willingness and preparedness to take action and actually *taking* positive steps toward recovery, which in John's case requires entering treatment. For action steps, simply remember CAT.

Cognitive-behavioral approaches can be used to frame very specific treatment plans to address underlying issues associated with treatment need and to facilitate continued movement toward established goals. An example of John's treatment goals might look like the following.

Goal 1: John will attend physical therapy at 10 A.M. He will work with Joan to complete 30 minutes of stretching and strengthening exercise during each session.

Goal 2: John will work with Rick (social worker) to address pending legal charges with Mr. Anderson, his attorney. John will complete necessary paperwork to document actions taken to date. This meeting will take place 9 A.M. March 9, in the fifth-floor conference room.

Goal 3: John will write a letter to each of his physicians by noon, March 12, (1) informing them of his entering treatment for substance dependence, (2) specifically describing his program of abstinence, and (3) asking for their assistance in managing his pain without the use of mood-altering substances.

Goal 4: John will continue to build his sober support network by attending three 12-step meetings of his choice on a weekly basis. He will obtain the telephone number of at least one group member per meeting and will make phone contact with at least one person whose number he has collected to discuss the progress he has made in treatment to date.

It is important that treatment goals be specific in nature, measurable, time-limited, and, most important, accomplishable. In this case, John is combining CBT with MI, health care, legal, and social support. In doing so, he is addressing many of the components that brought him to treatment while establishing a firm foundation for ongoing recovery processes. Figure 123.3 outlines multiple options available to care providers when considering treatment and community based support for treatment.

Case autopsy: John was treated initially on the inpatient unit for detoxification and stabilization. He then transitioned into intensive outpatient treatment where he remained under the care of a social worker for a total of 16 sessions. John attended psychoeducational, group, individual, and family sessions while in treatment. He successfully resolved his pending legal issues. The DUI charge was resolved with consequences of probation, 90-day license suspension, and requirement to document ongoing treatment for a 1-year period of time. John returned to his company and now has established 8 years of abstinence.

CONCLUSION

Social workers have a long history of caring for persons with alcohol and drug dependence. Social workers play a key role in the management of persons with alcohol and drug abuse by facilitating acceptance into treatment programming, completion of initial assessments to determine the extent and severity of alcohol consumption or substance abuse, conducting initial therapy sessions designed to optimize engagement in treatment, and establishing realistic, measurable, and specific treatment planning. The role of the social worker in addiction continues to expand and transform to meet the ever increasing needs of those seeking treatment for substance dependence.

Increasingly, this work is being informed by evidence-based approaches to address all aspects of substance abuse and dependence. Today's social worker is facilitating treatment processes not only designed to aid in patient care but to serve as an interface between the patient, a variety of care givers, and a link with critical community based partners in care. Competent skill sets are required to implement complex, multifaceted approaches to care. Traditional social work skills of communication, organization and facilitation, linkage, brokering, and advocating are intertwined with newer skills of monitoring pharmacotherapy, interacting with managed care and other payer sources, performing utilization review, and dealing with an expanding array of therapeutic approaches to address this complex disease. It is our hope that this chapter serves as a foundation on which each social worker will continue to build a knowledge and skill set that is reflective of the need of their individualized treatment setting.

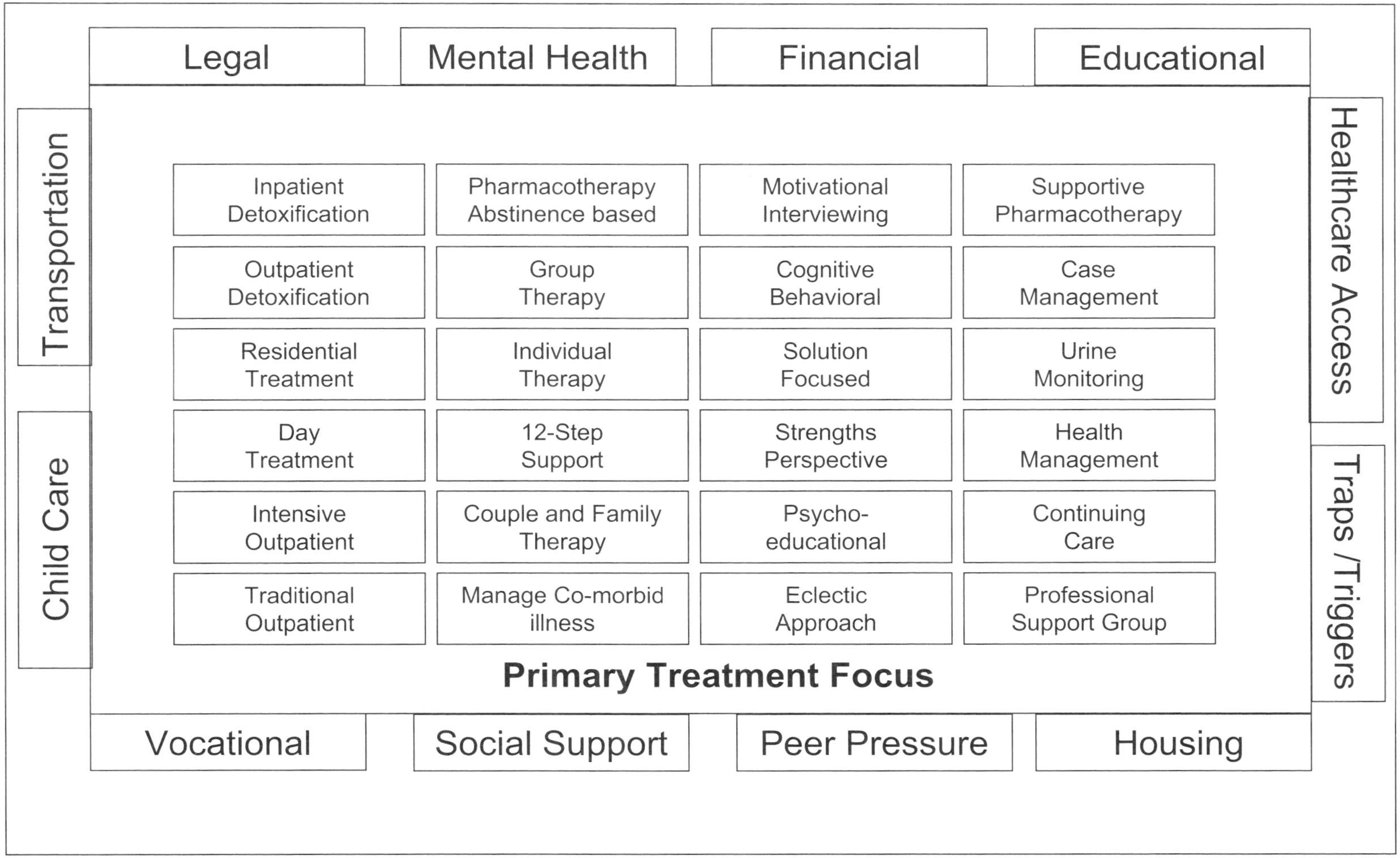

Healthcare Access

Traps /Triggers

Legal Mental Health Financial Educational

Vocational Social Support Peer Pressure Housing

Child Care Transportation

Primary Treatment Focus

Inpatient Detoxification	Pharmacotherapy Abstinence based	Motivational Interviewing	Supportive Pharmacotherapy
Outpatient Detoxification	Group Therapy	Cognitive Behavioral	Case Management
Residential Treatment	Individual Therapy	Solution Focused	Urine Monitoring
Day Treatment	12-Step Support	Strengths Perspective	Health Management
Intensive Outpatient	Couple and Family Therapy	Psycho-educational	Continuing Care
Traditional Outpatient	Manage Co-morbid illness	Eclectic Approach	Professional Support Group

Figure 123.3 Competing social/environmental factors requiring social work intervention.

WEB SITES

Center for Substance Abuse Treatment. http://csat.samhsa.gov.

National Association of Addiction Treatment Providers. http://www.naatp.org.

National Institute on Drug Abuse. http://www.nida.nih.gov.

Substance Abuse and Mental Health Services Administration. http://www.samhsa.gov.

References

Carroll, K. M., Ball, S. A., Nich, C., et al. (2006). Motivational interviewing to improve treatment engagement and outcome in individuals seeking treatment for substance abuse: A multisite effectiveness study. *Drug and Alcohol Dependence, 81*, 301.

Cutler, R. B., & Fishbain, D. A. (2005). Are alcoholism treatments effective? The Project MATCH data. *BMC Public Health, 5*, 75.

Hasin, D. S., Stinson, F. S., Ogburn, E., & Grant, B. F. (2007). Prevalence, correlates, disability, and co-morbidity of DSM-IV alcohol abuse and dependence in the United States: Results from the National Epidemiologic Survey on Alcohol and Related Conditions. *Archives of General Psychiatry, 64*, 830.

Hoffmann, N. G., DeHart, S. S., & Fulkerson, J. A. (1993). Medical care utilization as a function of recovery status following chemical addictions treatment. *Journal of Addictive Disorders, 12*, 97.

Holder, H. D., & Blose, J. O. (1992). The reduction of health care costs associated with alcoholism treatment: A 14-year longitudinal study. *Journal of Studies on Alcohol. 53*, 293.

Miller, N. S., & Swift, R. M. (1997). Primary care medicine and psychiatry: Addictions treatment. *Psychiatric Annals, 27*, 408.

Substance Abuse and Mental Health Services Administration. (2005). *Overview of Findings from the 2004 National Survey on Drug Use and Health* (Office of Applied Studies, NSDUH Series H-27, DHHS Publication no. SMA 05-4061). Rockville, MD: SAMHSA.

Williams, E., Kivlahan, D., Saitz, R., Merrill, J., Achtmeyer, C., McCormick, K., et al. (2006). Readiness to change in primary care patients who screened positive for alcohol misuse. *Annals of Family Medicine, 4*(3), 213–220.

Yeager, K. R., & Gregoire, T. K. (2005). Crisis intervention: Application of brief solution-focused therapy in addictions. In A. R. Roberts (ed.), *Crisis intervention handbook: Assessment, treatment and research*, 3rd ed. (pp. 566–601). New York: Oxford University Press.

124
Evidence-Based Practice in Older Adults with Mental Health Disorders
Geriatric Mental Health

Zvi D. Gellis

The changing demographics of American society have received a great deal of attention in recent years. As the population ages, the overall number of elderly persons with mental disorders, particularly anxiety and mood disorders, will increase. Older adults with mental health problems are likely to have relatively longer life spans in the future due to expected advances in treatments and healthier aging lifestyles. Mental health problems will demand more attention from providers to minimize their effects on disability, the use of health care services, and the quality of life for older adults and caregivers.

This chapter presents evidence-based knowledge on mental disorders in the elderly, focusing on prevalence, comorbidity, consequences, assessment, and evidence-based treatments. The aim is to highlight mental health issues in later life that are pertinent for social work practitioners, researchers, educators, and policy analysts as they confront the challenge of shaping and delivering services to an aging population in the coming decades. If social workers are to respond to the demographic shift, they will need to be knowledgeable in evidence-based treatments for mental health problems in older adults (Gellis & Reid, 2004).

Common mental disorders in late life include anxiety disorders and mood disorders, such as depression. Schizophrenia in late life is less common, but a significant number of persons diagnosed with this serious mental illness as young adults do age. Older adults are seriously underserved by mental health service systems across all care settings. The anticipated large growth in the number of older persons makes the provision of mental health services to this population increasingly important. Combining this growth with an increased rate of emotional disorders magnifies the problem.

Barriers to the provision of care exist at both the individual and system levels. Many older adults are reluctant to seek mental health services due to stigma, denial of problems, access barriers, language barriers, or a lack of culturally appropriate programs. Sometimes older adults do not receive appropriate care when they do seek help due to fragmented mental health services or gaps in services. This is compounded by a critical shortage of professional staff trained in gerontological social work and geriatric mental health field.

DEPRESSION IN LATER LIFE

Depression is a frequent cause of psychological distress and decreased quality of life in older adults (Blazer, 2003; Gellis, 2006). Depression disorders in older adults are relatively prevalent. Inadequate recognition and treatment of these problems at the individual level has important implications for social services, medical, and mental health service use and for the allocation of health care resources. Chronic medical conditions are common in older adults and frequently co-occur with mental disorders, such as depression and anxiety disorders. Mental health problems in later life will demand more attention to minimize their effects on disability and quality of life. Medically ill older adults experience more depressive symptoms, more anxiety, less self-esteem, and lower ability to control many aspects of their lives than people without any disease. Given the effects on daily functioning of depression, anxiety, cognitive decline, and physical illness, understanding mental health problems and efficacious treatments for older adults assumes great importance.

Epidemiology of Depression Disorders

Depression is a serious and prevalent medical illness in older adults. The prevalence estimates of major depression in community elderly samples are low ranging from 1 percent to 4 percent overall, with higher prevalence among women. Prevalence rates for dysthymia are about 2 percent and for minor depression range from 4 to 13 percent with the same pattern of distribution across gender, race, and ethnicity (Blazer, 2002). There are no significant racial or ethnic differences in prevalence rates for depression (Zalaquett & Stens, 2006).

In the medically ill elderly, estimates for major depression range from 10 to 12 percent with an additional 23 percent experiencing significant depressive symptoms (Blazer, 2002). In home health care, estimates of 13.5 percent for major depression and 27.5 percent for clinically significant depressive symptoms were found (Bruce et al., 2002; Gellis, 2006). Rates of clinically significant depressive symptoms among medically ill elderly range from 10 to 43 percent (Gellis, 2006). Depression is twice as prevalent in home health care as in primary care; is persistent and intermittent; and is associated with medical illness, pain, and disability (Lyness, King, Cox, Yoediono, & Caine, 1999). Evidence is clear that late-life depression is one of the most common mental disorders to present in primary care and home health care settings (Gellis, McGinty, Horowitz, Bruce, & Misener, 2007; Lyness et al., 1999).

In long-term care settings, prevalence rates for major depression can range from 12 to 30 percent, and clinically significant depressive symptoms range from 12 to 35 percent (Mojtabai & Olfson, 2004). Depression is underdetected in long-term care facilities and if detected, is inadequately treated (Teresi, Abrams, Holmes, Ramirez, & Eimicke, 2001). The prognosis of depression can often be poor. A meta-analysis of depression outcomes at 24 months estimated that only 33 percent of older patients were well, 33 percent were depressed, and 21 percent had died (Cole, Bellavance, & Mansour, 1999). Depression is also an independent predictor of overall poor treatment compliance and may exacerbate other common chronic medical conditions in older adults.

Suicide in Late Life

In the elderly, suicide is almost twice as frequent as in the general population (Conwell, Duberstein, & Caine, 2002). The elderly account for 20 percent of all suicides, yet they make up only 13 percent of the population (Hoyert, Kung, & Smith, 2005). Some of the most common demographic correlates of suicide are older age, male gender, white race, and unmarried status. Late onset depression is a serious risk factor for suicidal ideation.

In the United States, older white males age 85+ have the highest suicide completion rates (65 per 100,000), exceeding adolescent rates (16.6 per 100,000) (Blazer, 2002). Older men (80+) take their own lives at four to six times the rate of older women (Scocco & DeLeo, 2002). Depression, comorbid anxiety, substance abuse, isolation, loneliness, lack of social supports, and declining physical health are some of the risk factors for suicide among older adults. Retrospective studies identified that greater than 70 percent of older suicide victims have had contact with their primary care provider within months prior to their death (Uncapher, 2000). In these studies, the majority of older patients had late-onset undetected or untreated depressions, likely reflecting high rates of comorbid illness or fears of pain or dependency on others.

Efforts to improve detection and treatment of geriatric depression in health care settings have led to lowered suicide rates (Brown, Bruce, & Pearson, 2001). One recent large multisite randomized trial known as PROSPECT (Prevention of Suicide in Primary Care Elderly: Collaborative Trial) enrolled patients who met criteria for major depression, dysthymic disorder, or minor depression and followed them for a period of 2 years through acute, continuation, and maintenance phases of treatment (Alexopoulos et al., 2005). The experimental intervention was implemented by depression care managers who monitored psychopathology, treatment adherence, response, and side effects at predetermined times. Patients were offered antidepressant medications and/or interpersonal psychotherapy, an evidence-based intervention. The usual care condition included primary care physicians who were notified in writing of the patient's depression diagnosis and informed when the study guidelines indicated suicide risk in individual patients. Physicians received a videotape and printed material on geriatric depression and treatment guidelines. The PROSPECT trial demonstrated that elderly patients receiving a depression care management intervention had less severe depressive symptoms and greater remission rates at 4, 8, and 12 months than patients receiving usual primary care (Bruce et al., 2004).

Comorbidity of Depression in Older Adults

The consequences of depression in later life are potentially serious. Depressive disorders can be persistent, intermittent, and/or recurrent and result in significant physical and psychological comorbidity and functional impairment that negatively influences the course of depression (Lyness et al., 2006). Cole and Dendukuri (2003) completed a systematic review of risk factors for depression in community-dwelling elderly patients that involved a qualitative and quantitative synthesis of the data. They examined 20 studies and identified key risk factors that included female gender, sleep disturbance, disability level, prior history of depression, and bereavement.

Depression with physical illness increases levels of functional disability, use of health services, and health care costs, particularly among older adults (Unützer et al., 1997). It also delays or inhibits physical recovery. Common medical illnesses known to be associated with depression include heart disease, stroke, hypertension, diabetes, cancer, and osteoarthritis. Taken altogether, these findings support the importance of treatment of depression in late life.

EVIDENCE-BASED INTERVENTIONS

Psychosocial Interventions

Psychosocial interventions have been demonstrated to be effective among older adults, particularly those who reject medication due to unpleasant side effects or are coping with low social support or stressful situations (Pinquart & Sorensen, 2001). Evidence-based approaches such as structured cognitive-behavioral therapy (CBT), interpersonal therapy (IPT), and problem-solving therapy (PST) are effective intervention alternatives or adjuncts to medication treatment (de Melo, de Jesus, Bacaltchuk, Verdeli, & Neugebauer, 2005; Gellis et al., 2007).

A recent randomized controlled trial in home care tested the effectiveness of home-delivered PST for depression in the medically ill elderly. Data suggested significant reductions in depression scores over time relative to the usual care condition. Older patients also reported higher quality of life and problem-solving ability compared with usual care patients (Gellis et al., 2007). In another randomized trial, PST was found to decrease symptoms of minor depression in older

home care patients posttreatment and was maintained over a 6-month period (Gellis et al., in press). Elderly participants in the PST group were more satisfied with treatment compared with the control condition.

Brief psychosocial interventions for depression by nonmedical mental health practitioners have demonstrated effectiveness for homebound, frail, medically ill populations (Gellis et al., 2007; Mynors-Wallis, Gath, Davis, Gray, & Barbour, 1997). Adjunct written educational materials for patients and family members have been shown to improve medication adherence and clinical outcomes. Gellis and colleagues (2007) found robust effects in treating geriatric depression using 6 sessions of PST, though other researchers found similar effects using 12 sessions of PST (Gellis & Kenaley, 2008).

The generally recommended treatment of choice for late life depression is a combination of psychotherapy and antidepressant medication. Psychoeducation and watchful waiting are recommended for clinically significant depressive symptoms that last for less than 2 weeks. If symptoms persist, a combined approach of medication and talk therapy is recommended (Blazer, 2002).

Pharmacological Interventions

Antidepressants are widely used for the treatment of moderate to severe depression in older adults. Based on several literature reviews of pharmacologic treatment for geriatric depression, antidepressants are safe and effective treatments for depressed older adults (Salzman et al., 2002). Almost all antidepressant medications are equally effective for treating major depression (Salzman et al., 2002). Antidepressants not only shorten the duration of depressive episodes but decrease the remission rates from depressive disorders. Yet as older adults are prescribed more medications for other medical diseases, the likelihood of self-medication, multiple drug use, drug interactions, and unpleasant side effects increases.

There have been over 30 randomized placebo-controlled clinical trials as well as many comparative trials (Salzman et al., 2002) documenting the efficacy and safety of antidepressant medications (tricyclic antidepressants [TCAs] and selective serotonin reuptake inhibitors [SSRIs]) for older adults with depression. Because SSRIs appear to be as effective as the older TCAs, their use in treatment in late life depression may result in improved outcomes. Due to fewer side effects, SSRIs are frequently the first line of medical treatment (Crystal, Sambamoorthi, Walkup, & Akincigil, 2003).

Minor Depression in Older Adults

Recent attention has been given to minor (also known as subthreshold or subsyndromal) depressive disorders (Koenig, Vandermeer, Chamber, Burr-Crutchfield, & Johnson, 2006). Minor depression is generally defined as the presence of at least two but fewer than five depressive symptoms, including depressed mood or anhedonia during the same 2-week period with no history of major depressive episode or dysthymia but with clinically significant impairment.

Minor depression is a common type of depressive disorder in older adults and is observed in numerous settings more often than major depression (Charney et al., 2003; Lavretsky & Kumar, 2002). Minor depression ranges from 10 to 30 percent in older community-dwelling adults (Hybels & Blazer, 2003) and approximately 5 to 9 percent in primary care. Minor depression has been found to be associated with an increased risk for mortality in older men and has a relatively high prevalence in some ethnic groups. As many as 15 percent of older Latinos, 12 percent of older Asian Americans, and 10 percent of older African Americans meet criteria for minor depression (Arean & Alvarez, 2001).

A recent systematic review of adults and older adults diagnosed with minor depression found remission rates in the range of 46 to 71 percent after 3–6 years (Hermens et al., 2004). Research has been mixed in terms of the evidence on mortality, functional impairment, and prognosis of minor depression in older adults.

CBT, IPT, and PST models appear to be promising treatments for older adults with minor depression. However, the research literature is less clear about these therapies than for major depression due to the dearth of treatment studies, particularly among older adults. One randomized clinical trial reported that a 6-week PST program for minor depression in medically ill elderly patients significantly reduced depressive symptoms and increased personal problem-solving abilities compared with an education control (Gellis et al., in press). Due to the heterogeneity of the few studies on minor depression, results need to be interpreted with caution. One of the next challenges for practitioners and researchers is to develop agreement on the definition of minor depression, its diagnosis, and treatment in older adults.

Depression Screening for Older Adults

Social workers are likely to encounter older adults in many areas of clinical practice. Therefore, it is essential for social workers to recognize geriatric mental health problems and refer or provide treatment. Screening for the detection of depressive disorders involves the use of easily administered inexpensive procedures to identify older adults who may be experiencing psychiatric problems. This is critical because depression, for example, is a treatable mental health disorder with positive outcomes over time. Criteria to justify mental health screening include the following: (1) is the incidence high enough to justify the cost of screening in an agency? (2) Does the problem have a significant effect on the quality of life of the older adult? (3) Is effective treatment available for late-life depression? (4) Are depression screening instruments available that are valid and cost-effective? (5) Are the adverse effects (if any) of depression screening tests acceptable to social workers and older adult clients? It is clear from this review that the prevalence of depression among older adults is frequent enough and causes sufficiently serious health and social consequences to warrant screening. For depression, there are valid cost-effective procedures for screening and effective treatments.

Social workers can play a critical role in increasing the proportion of depressed older adults who obtain treatment. Because comorbidity of depression with health, bereavement, and other social problems is typical in the elderly, social workers are likely to encounter older adults with mental health needs in many community settings (e.g., home health care, community work, social services, home visiting, senior centers, health clinics). If a depressive disorder is suspected, the social worker can screen the older person, using one of several reliable and valid screening tests that are readily available (Center for Epidemiological Studies-Depression Scale, Geriatric Depression Scale, Zung Self-Rating Depression Scale, Beck Depression Inventory, and interview instruments including the Hamilton Rating Scale for Depression and the Cornell Scale for Depression in Dementia).

SPECIAL SETTINGS

Late-Life Depression in Primary Care

Current depression management in primary care is suboptimal, yet depression is prevalent at rates of 5 to 9 percent of the older population. Integration of specialty mental health care within primary care and system of care enhancements, such as collaborative or integrative care, has been found to be effective. A systematic review of 21 studies on collaborative educational and organizational interventions to improve depression management in primary care settings found positive results (Gilbody, Whitty, Grimshaw, & Thomas, 2003). Nonetheless, simple practice guideline documentation and educational strategies were generally ineffective.

Collaborative care approaches are multifaceted intervention packages that involve nurses, social workers, or depression care managers and vary in content and intensity (Swindle et al., 2003). These interventions often aim to increase knowledge about depression through psychoeducation, improve adherence to antidepressant medication, improve physician–patient communication, and decrease depressive symptoms. One of the challenges is in understanding which components are critical determinants of effectiveness in reducing depressive symptoms.

A recent systematic review examined multifaceted depression interventions in primary care (Gellis & Kenaley, 2008). Four studies (Ciechanowski et al., 2004; Doorenbos et al., 2005; Katon et al., 2004; Unützer et al., 2002) employed a multifaceted intervention. The IMPACT intervention included access for up to 12 months to a depression care manager, education, care management, and a choice of either medication support or PST (Unützer et al., 2002). The Pathways case management intervention (Katon et al., 2004) included enhanced education and support combined with antidepressant medication treatment by the primary care physician or a PST intervention delivered in primary care. The PEARLS (Program to Encourage Active, Rewarding Lives for Seniors) intervention included PST, social and physical activation, and recommendations to patients' physicians regarding antidepressant medications (Ciechanowski et al., 2004). Doorenbos and colleagues (2005) administered a multimodal intervention that included problem-solving strategies, self-care management, information and decision making, counseling and support, and communication with primary care providers. All of these studies found that combined use of PST and antidepressant treatment had more favorable depression outcomes compared with PST alone.

Another systematic review found 34 studies of multifaceted collaborative care interventions with outcome data on depressive symptoms and 28 studies on antidepressant medication use (Bower, Gilbody, Fletcher, & Sutton, 2006). Positive effects were found on both antidepressant use and depressive symptom reduction. The studies reviewed found no variables that predicted variation in antidepressant medication use. Nonetheless, several key predictors of depressive symptom outcomes were found, including mental health training background of staff, systematic identification of patients, and continuous depression specialist supervision. This suggests that the depression care manager have expertise and experience in working with depressed patients. Additionally, this is associated with technical expertise, such as knowledge of evidence-based psychosocial treatments and psychotropic medications and the ability to work effectively in collaboration with other health care providers.

Late-Life Depression in Home Health Care

Home care services are essential to maintaining elders with disability in the community and reducing their hospitalization and nursing home use. Yet there is limited knowledge on specific treatments for depressive disorders (Brown, Kaiser, & Gellis, in press; Bruce et al., 2004; Gellis et al., 2007, in press). Compared with the general elderly population, home care recipients are older, more socially isolated, more likely to be women, and have high rates of physical illness and disability and depression. Prevalence rate for major depression is estimated at 13.5 percent in older home care patients (Bruce et al., 2004). These researchers found that depression was highly prevalent, characterized by symptoms and various conditions (functional disability, cognitive impairment, and comorbid vascular disease) associated with poor outcomes.

The older person, treating physician, and health care organizational factors interact to impede the detection and treatment of depression, particularly among older clients. From a biopsychosocial framework, the complexity of depression is reflected by variability in onset, presentation, and course, as well as functional disability, negative life events, and medical comorbidity. The heterogeneity of depression coupled with physical and cognitive impairment, social vulnerabilities, and various medical conditions prevalent in health care makes it more difficult for accurate assessment, diagnosis, and treatment in the elderly population.

Older patients are less likely to voluntarily report affective symptoms of depression. They are more likely to ascribe symptoms of depression to a physical illness. Depressed older adults of various ethnic backgrounds are less likely to use specialty care and more likely to use the general health care system (Unützer et al., 1997).

Leading researchers cite the need for future studies to address critical questions about feasibility, generalizability, and cost of treatment for depressive disorders in home health, use of brief intervention models by nonphysicians, and ways to improve access to care among ethnically diverse and low-income populations (Bruce et al., 2004; Gellis et al., 2007).

Depression in Long-Term Care

In the United States, approximately 5 percent of older adults reside in long-term care (LTC) facilities at any given time. Prevalence rates of depression in LTC vary depending on study definitions and measures used. For elderly patients with major depression, rates range from 6 to 24 percent in nursing homes (Blazer, 2002). Prevalence estimates for minor depression and dysthymia are even higher and range from 30 to 50 percent in the majority of studies; and for subthreshold clinically significant depressive symptoms, the range is 35 to 45 percent (Hyer, Carpenter, Bishmann, & Wu, 2005).

Depression is a frequently comorbid condition with dementia with estimates at 30 percent (Evers et al., 2002). This makes the detection and assessment of depression challenging for the clinician. Many LTC residents present with signs and symptoms that overlap with depression (for example, anhedonia, irritability, flat affect) (Gauthier, 2003). Studies also indicate that depression is a risk factor for dementia (Lichtenberg & Mast, 2003). Therefore, based on consensus practice guidelines, it is recommended to interview caregivers and other reliable informants on behalf of the individual with moderate to severe dementia (American Geriatrics Society & American Association for Geriatric Psychiatry, 2003).

The research literature on interventions for depression in older adults residing in LTC is sparse. Researchers provide preliminary insights into specific psychosocial interventions for depression in LTC (Norris, Molinari, & Ogland-Hand, 2003). Researchers recommend a combined approach to depression treatment, including behavioral interventions and antidepressants. They suggest psychosocial intervention as an initial treatment step and the introduction of medication in more severe forms of depression.

ANXIETY DISORDERS IN LATER LIFE

Research suggests that clinically significant anxiety symptoms affect as many as 20 percent of older adults living in the community. Anxiety disorders are often associated with common age-related medical and chronic conditions, such as asthma, thyroid disease, coronary artery disease, dementia, and sensory loss. Anxiety in later life has been identified as a risk factor for greater disability among older adults in general and has also been associated with less successful recruitment into and outcomes of geriatric rehabilitation services. Researchers and practitioners are beginning to recognize that aging and anxiety are not mutually exclusive—anxiety is as common in the old as in the young, although how and when it appears is distinctly different in older adults. Recognizing an anxiety disorder in an older person poses several challenges. Aging brings with it a higher prevalence of certain medical conditions, realistic concerns about physical problems, and a higher use of prescription medications. As a result, separating a medical condition from physical symptoms of an anxiety disorder is more complicated in the older adult. Diagnosing anxiety in individuals with dementia can be difficult, too: agitation typical of dementia may be difficult to separate from anxiety, impaired memory may be interpreted as a sign of anxiety or dementia, and fears may be excessive or realistic depending on the person's situation.

Epidemiology: Anxiety Disorders

Although anxiety disorders, like most psychiatric conditions, may be less common among older adults than among younger people, epidemiological evidence suggests that anxiety is a major problem in late life. The National Comorbidity Study reported a lifetime prevalence rates of 15.3 percent for *DSM-IV*-diagnosed anxiety disorders in respondents over age 60 (Kessler et al., 2005). Another study of approximately 500 community-dwelling triethnic elders reported prevalence rates of 11.3 percent in blacks, 12.4 percent in Hispanics, and 21.6 percent in non-Hispanic whites age 75 and older (Ostir & Goodwin, 2006).

Phobias and generalized anxiety disorder (GAD) account for most anxiety disorders in late life. Several reviews summarized the prevalence of specific anxiety disorders in older community-based epidemiological samples as follows: phobias, including agoraphobia and social phobia, 0.7–12.0 percent; GAD, 1.2–7.3 percent; obsessive-compulsive disorder, 0.1–1.5 percent; and panic disorder, 0.0–0.3 percent (Alwahhabi, 2003).

The prevalence of subthreshold anxiety, that is, clinically significant anxiety, including symptoms that do not meet criteria for a specific disorder, is common among older adults and may be as high as 20 to 29 percent (Lenze et al., 2005). This includes anxiety symptoms associated with common medical conditions, such as asthma, thyroid disease, coronary artery disease, and dementia, as well as adjustment disorders following significant late-life stressors such as bereavement or caregiving. There is also controversy over whether the prevalence of anxiety has been accurately determined in older adults, because *DSM-IV* criteria may not apply as well, anxiety symptoms may be expressed as somatic features or behavior changes (e.g., aggression, assaultive behaviors), and the clinical presentation of anxiety in late life may be more likely to include depressive symptoms (Beck & Averill, 2004).

Comorbidity and Consequences of Anxiety in Late Life

The high comorbidity of anxiety with medical illness is multidimensional. Anxiety is complex and may be a reaction to a medical illness, may be expressed as somatic symptoms, or may be a side effect of medications. Studies have found an association between anxiety and medical illnesses such as diabetes, coronary heart disease, cancer, chronic obstructive pulmonary disease, and Parkinson's disease (Ostir & Goodwin, 2006). Anxiety in older adults has been found to often co-occur with depression (Beck & Averill, 2004). Approximately 20 percent of older adults with bipolar disorder report lifetime rates of GAD (Goldstein, Hermann, & Shulman, 2006). Furthermore, anxiety symptoms have been found to lead to depressive symptoms (Wetherell, Gatz, & Pederson, 2001).

The consequences of anxiety in late life are potentially serious. Anxiety symptoms and disorders are associated with increased fatigue, greater levels of chronic physical illness, increased dis-ability, lower levels of well-being, worse life satisfaction, and inappropriate use of medical services among older adults (Brenes et al., 2005). In cases of comorbid anxiety and depressive disorders, the likelihood of poor outcomes increases. Comorbid anxiety in late-life depression is associated with poorer treatment response and increased likelihood of dropout (Lenze et al., 2005).

Pharmacological Treatment for Anxiety Disorders

In part because of the tendency for older adults to present to primary care physicians, anxiolytic medications, including benzodiazepines, are the most common treatment for late life anxiety (Lenze et al., 2005). Benzodiazepine users are also more likely than nonusers to experience accidents requiring medical attention, due to increased risk of falls, hip fractures, and automobile accidents (Tamblyn, Abrahamowicz, du Berger, McLeod, & Bartlett, 2005). Older patients taking benzodiazepines are also more likely to develop disabilities in both mobility and activities of daily living (Gray et al., 2006). These medications can also cause tolerance and withdrawal, interactions with other drugs, and toxicity.

Although safer medications, particularly SSRIs, are often used to treat geriatric anxiety, they can cause unpleasant side effects, and some older people prefer not to take them. Furthermore, SSRIs have not completely replaced benzodiazepines as a treatment for anxiety in older people. Safe and effective alternative treatments for anxiety, appealing to an older population, are clearly needed.

Psychosocial Interventions for Anxiety Disorders

The efficacy of evidence-based psychosocial interventions have been tested using randomized trials for geriatric anxiety and reviewed with emerging evidence of support for their use (Ayers, Sorrell, Thorp, & Wetherell, 2007). Several studies have provided some support for the use of relaxation training and CBT for treatment of anxiety (Gorenstein et al., 2005; Mohlman et al., 2003; Stanley et al., 2003). In recent years, CBT has been shown to be superior to waitlist conditions, medication management–only conditions, supportive control conditions (e.g., supportive counseling, minimal contact, discussion group), and usual care (Gorenstein et al., 2005; Mohlman et al., 2003; Stanley et al., 2003).

In summary, mental health problems such as depression and anxiety disorders are associated with increased disability, lower levels of well-being, and increased use of medical services among older adults. Geriatric social work practitioners require specialized skill sets in assessing and managing mental disorders of late life. In examining the scientific evidence, routine screening for mental health problems in older adults is warranted. The implications of not detecting the possibility of mental disorders in the elderly are serious.

WEB SITES

American Psychiatric Association. http://www .apa.org/ppo/issues/olderdepressfact.html.
CSWE Gero-Ed Center Teaching Modules. http://depts.washington.edu/geroctr/ Curriculum3/sub3_1_4TeachingModules.
NIMH Web site on Older Adults and Depression. http://www.nimh.nih.gov/ health/publications/older-adults-depression-and-suicide-facts.shtml.

References

Alexopoulos, G., Katz, I., Bruce, M., Heo, T., Ten Have, T., Raue, P., et al. (2005). Remission in depressed geriatric primary care patients: A report from the PROSPECT study. *American Journal of Psychiatry, 162*(4), 718–724.

Alwahhabi, F. (2003). Anxiety symptoms and generalized anxiety disorder in the elderly: A review. *Harvard Review of Psychiatry, 11*(4), 180–193.

American Geriatrics Society & American Association for Geriatric Psychiatry. (2003). Consensus statement on improving the quality of mental health in U.S. nursing homes: Management of depression and behavioral symptoms associated with dementia. *Journal of the American Geriatric Society, 51,* 1287–1298.

Arean, A., & Alvarez, J. (2001). Prevalence of mental disorder, subsyndromal disorder and service use in older disadvantaged medical patients. *Interpersonal Journal of Psychiatry in Medicine, 31*(1), 9–24.

Ayers, C.., Sorrell, J. T., Thorp, S., & Wetherell, J. (2007). Evidence-based psychological treatments for late-life anxiety. *Psychology and Aging, 22*(1), 8–17.

Beck, J. G., & Averill, P. M. (2004). Older adults. In D. Mennon, R. Heimberg, C. Turk (Eds.), *General-ized anxiety disorder: Advances in research and practice* (pp. 409–433). New York: Guilford.

Blazer, D. (2003). Depression in late life: Review and commentary. *Journal of Gerontology: Medical Sciences, 58A,* 249–265.

Bower, P., Gilbody, S., Fletcher, J., & Sutton, A. (2006). Collaborative care for depression in primary care. *British Journal of Psychiatry, 189,* 484–493.

Brenes, G., Guralnik, J., Williamson, J., Fried, L., Simpson, C., & Simonsick, E. M. (2005). The influence of anxiety on the progression of disability. *Journal of the American Geriatrics Society, 53*(1), 34–39.

Brown, E. L., Kaiser, R. M., & Gellis, Z. D. (in press). Screening and assessment of late life depression in home health care: Issues and challenges. *Annals of Long Term Care: Clinical Care and Aging.*

Brown, G., Bruce, M., & Pearson, J. (2001). High-risk management guidelines for elderly suicidal patients in primary care settings. *International Journal of Geriatric Psychiatry, 16*(6), 593–601.

Bruce, M. L., McAvay, G. J., Raue, P. J., Brown, E. L., Meyers, B. S., Keohane, D. J., et al. (2002). Major depression in elderly home health care patients. *American Journal of Psychiatry, 159,* 1367–1374.

Bruce, M., Ten Have, T., Reynolds, C., Katz, I., Schulberg, H., Mulsant, B., et al. (2004). Reducing suicidal ideation and depressive symptoms in depressed older primary care patients: A randomized controlled trial. *Journal of the American Medical Association, 291*(9), 1081–1091.

Charney, D., Reynolds, C. F., Lewis L., Lebowitz, B. D., Sunderland, T., & Alexopoulos, G. (2003). Depression and bipolar support alliance consensus statement on the unmet needs in diagnosis and treatment of mood disorders in late life. *Archives of General Psychiatry, 60*(7), 664–672.

Ciechanowski, P., Wagner, E., Schmaling, K., Schwartz, S., Williams, B., Diehr, P., et al. (2004). Community-integrated home-based depression treatment in older adults. *Journal of the American Medical Association, 291,* 1569–1577.

Cole, M., Bellavance, F., & Mansour, A. (1999). Prognosis of depression in elderly community and primary care populations: A systematic review and meta-analysis. *American Journal of Psychiatry, 156,* 1182–1189.

Cole, M., & Dendukuri, N. (2003). Risk factors for depression among elderly community subjects: A systematic review and meta-analysis. *American Journal of Psychiatry, 160*(6), 1147–1156.

Conwell, Y., Duberstein, P., & Caine, E. (2002). Risk factors for suicide in later life. *Biological Psychiatry, 52*(3), 193–204.

Crystal, S., Sambamoorthi, U., Walkup, J. T., & Akincigil, A. (2003). Diagnosis and treatment of depression in the elderly Medicare population: Predictors, disparities, and trends. *Journal of the American Geriatrics Society, 51*(12), 1718–1728.

de Melo, M., de Jesus, M., Bacaltchuk, J., Verdeli, H., & Neugebauer, R. (2005). A systematic review of research findings on the efficacy of interpersonal therapy for depressive disorders. *European Archives of Psychiatry and Clinical Neurosciences, 255,* 75–82.

Doorenbos, A., Given, B., Given, C., Verbitsky, N., Cimprich, B., & McCorkle, R. (2005). Reducing symptom limitations: A cognitive behavioral interv-ention randomized trial. *Psycho-Oncology, 14,* 574–584.

Evers, M., Samuels, S., Lantz, M., Khan, K., Brickman, A., & Marin, D. (2002). The prevalence, diagnosis and treatment of depression in dementia patients in chronic care facilities in the last six months of life. *International Journal of Geriatric Psychiatry, 17*(5), 464–472.

Gauthier, S. (2003). Clinical aspects. In A. Juillerat, M. Van Der Linden, & R. Mulligan (Eds.), *The clinical management of early Alzheimer's disease: A handbook* (pp. 21–34). Mahwah, NJ: Erlbaum.

Gellis, Z. D. (2006). Mental health and emotional disorders among older adults. In B. Berkman (Ed.), *Oxford handbook of social work in health and aging* (pp. 282–310). New York: Oxford University Press.

Gellis, Z. D., & Kenaley, B. (2008). Problem solving therapy for depression in adults: A systematic review. *Research on Social Work Practice, 18,* 117–131.

Gellis, Z. D., McGinty, J., Horowitz, A., Bruce, M., & Misener, E. (2007). Problem solving therapy for late life depression in home care elderly: A randomized controlled trial. *American Journal of Geriatric Psychiatry, 15*(11), 968–978.

Gellis, Z. D., McGinty, J., Tierney, L., Burton, J., Jordan, C., Misener, E., et al. (In press). Randomized controlled trial of problem-solving therapy for minor depression in home care. *Research on Social Work Practice.*

Gellis, Z. D., & Reid, W. J. (2004). Strengthening evidence-based practice. *Brief Treatment and Crisis Intervention Journal, 4,* 155–165.

Gilbody, S., Whitty, P., Grimshaw, J., & Thomas, R. (2003). Educational and organizational interventions to improve the management of depression in primary care. *Journal of the American Medical Association, 289*(23), 3145–3151.

Goldstein, B., Herrmann, N., & Shulman, K. (2006). Comorbidity in bipolar disorder among the elderly: Results from an epidemiological community sample. *American Journal of Psychiatry, 163*(2), 319–321.

Gorenstein, E., Kleber, M., Mohlman, J., de Jesus, M., Gorman, J., & Papp, L. (2005). Cognitive-behavioral therapy for management of anxiety and medication taper in older adults. *American Journal of Geriatric Psychiatry, 13*(10), 901–909.

Gray, S. L., LaCroix, A. Z., Hanlon, J. T., Penninx, B. W., Blough, D. K., Leveille, S. G., et al. (2006). Benzodiazepine use and physical disability in community-dwelling older adults. *Journal of the American Geriatrics Society, 54*(2), 224–230.

Hermens, M., van Hout, H., Terluin, B., van der Windt, D., Beekman, A., van Dyck, R., et al. (2004). The prognosis of minor depression in the general population: A systematic review. *General Hospital Psychiatry, 26*(6), 453–462.

Hoyert, D., Kung, H., Smith, B. (2005). Deaths: Preliminary data for 2003. *National Vital Statistics Reports, 53*(15), 1–48.

Hybels, C., & Blazer, D. (2003). Epidemiology of late life mental disorders. *Clinical Geriatric Medicine, 19,* 663–696.

Hyer, L., Carpenter, B., Bishmann, D., & Wu, H. S. (2005). Depression in long-term care. *Clinical Psychology: Science and Practice, 12*(3), 280–299.

Katon, W., Von Korff, M., Lin, E., Simon, G., Ludman, E., Russo, J., et al. (2004). A randomized trial of collaborative care in patients with diabetes and depression. *Archives of General Psychiatry, 61,* 1042–1049.

Kessler, R. C., Berglund, P., Demler, O., Jin, R., Merikangas, K. R., & Walters, E. E. (2005). Lifetime prevalence and age-of-onset distributions of DSM-IV disorders in the national comorbidity survey replication. *Archives of General Psychiatry, 62,* 593–602.

Koenig, H., Vandermeer, J., Chambers, A., Burr-Crutchfield, L., & Johnson, J. (2006). Minor depression and physical outcome trajectories in heart failure and pulmonary disease. *Journal of Nervous and Mental Disease, 194*(3), 209–217.

Lavretsky, H., & Kumar, A. (2002). Clinically significant non-major depression: Old concepts, new insights. *American Journal of Geriatric Psychiatry, 10*(3), 239–255.

Lenze, E., Mulsant, B. H., Mohlman, J., Shear, K., Dew, M. A., Schulz, R., et al. (2005). Generalized anxiety disorder in late life: Lifetime course and comorbidity with major depressive disorder. *American Journal of Geriatric Psychiatry, 13*(1), 77–80.

Lichtenberg, P., & Mast, B. (2003). Psychological and nonpharmacological aspects of depression in dementia. In P. Lichtenberg, D. Murman, & A. Mellow (Eds.), *Handbook of dementia: Psychological, neurological and psychiatric perspectives* (pp. 309–334). Hoboken, NJ: Wiley.

Lyness, J., King, D., Cox, C., Yoediono, Z., & Caine, E. (1999). The importance of subsyndromal depression in older primary care patients: Prevalence and associated functional disability. *Journal of the American Geriatric Society, 47*(6), 647–652.

Mohlman, J., Gorenstein, E., Kleber, M., de Jesus, M., Gorman, J., & Papp, L. (2003). Standard and enhanced cognitive-behavior therapy for late-life generalized anxiety disorder. *American Journal of Geriatric Psychiatry, 11*(1), 24–32.

Mojtabai, R., & Olfson, M. (2004) Major depression in community-dwelling middle-aged and older adults: Prevalence and 2 and 4 year follow-up symptoms. *Psychological Medicine, 34*(4), 623–634.

Mynors-Wallis, L. M., Gath, D., Davies, I., Gray, A., & Barbour, F. (1997). Randomized controlled trial and cost analysis of problem-solving treatment given by community nurses for emotional disorders in primary care. *British Journal of Psychiatry, 170,* 113–119.

Norris, M., Molinari, V., & Ogland-Hand, S. (Eds.). (2003). *Emerging trends in psychological practice in long-term care.* New York: Haworth.

Ostir, G. V., & Goodwin, J. S. (2006). Anxiety in persons 75 and older: Findings from a tri-ethnic population. *Ethnicity and Disease, 16*(1), 22–27.

Pinquart, M., & Sorensen, S. (2001). How effective are psychotherapeutic and other psychosocial interventions with older adults? A meta-analysis. *Journal of Mental Health and Aging, 7*(2), 207–243.

Salzman, C., Wong, E., & Wright, B. C. (2002). Drug and ECT treatment of depression in the elderly, 1996–2001: A literature review. *Biological Psychiatry, 52*(3), 265–284.

Scocco, P., & DeLeo, D. (2002). One year prevalence of death thoughts, suicide ideation and behaviors in the elderly population. *International Journal of Geriatric Psychiatry, 17*(9), 842–846.

Stanley, M. A., Beck, J. G., Novy, D. M., Averill, P. M., Swann, A. C., & Diefenbach, G. J. (2003). Cognitive-behavioral treatment of late-life generalized anxiety disorder. *Journal of Consulting and Clinical Psychology, 71*(2), 309–319.

Swindle, R., Rao, J., Helmy, A., Plue, L., Zhou, X., Eckert, G., et al. (2003). Integrating clinical nurse specialists into the treatment of primary care patients with depression. *International Journal of Psychiatry in Medicine, 33*(1), 17–37.

Tamblyn, R., Abrahamowicz, M., du Berger, R., McLeod, P., & Bartlett, G. (2005). A 5-year prospective assessment of the risk associated with individual benzodiazepines and doses in new elderly users. *Journal of the American Geriatric Society, 53*(2), 233–241.

Teresi, J., Abrams, R., Holmes, D., Ramirez, M., & Eimicke, J. (2001). Prevalence of depression and depression recognition in nursing homes. *Social Psychiatry and Psychiatric Epidemiology, 36*(12), 613–620.

Uncapher, H. (2000). Physicians are less likely to offer depression therapy to older suicidal patients than younger ones. *Geriatrics, 55,* 82.

Unützer, J., Katon, W., Callahan, C., Williams, J., Hunkeler, E., Harpole, L., et al. (2002). Collaborative care management of late-life depression in the primary care setting. *Journal of the American Medical Association, 288,* 2836–2845.

Unützer, J., Patrick, D. L., Simon, G., Grembowski, D., Walker, E., Rutter, C., et al. (1997). Depressive symptoms and the cost of health services in HMO patients age 65 years and older: A 4-year prospective study. *Journal of the American Medical Association, 277,* 1618–1623.

Wetherell, J., Gatz, M., & Pedersen, N. L. (2001). Longitudinal analysis of anxiety and depressive symptoms. *Psychology and Aging, 16*(2), 187–195.

Zalaquett, C., & Stens, A. (2006). Psychosocial treatments for major depression and dysthymia in older adults: A review of the research literature. *Journal of Counseling and Development, 84,* 192–201.

PART XII
Community Practice

125

An Integrated Practice Model for Family Centers

Anita Lightburn & Chris Warren-Adamson

Family centers have developed over the past decades in neighborhoods, community centers, churches, and schools. Many centers are mandated by legislation and reflect wide variation in structure and auspice. With roots in the settlement house movement, grassroots and professional approaches are blended to meet goals of prevention, early intervention, support, and empowerment. Parents who need support find that these friendly neighborhood resources are a place to connect with other parents, and in many instances they discover pathways to deal with serious family concerns, meet educational goals, and cope with mental health problems.

To enable families to stay together and protect their children, community-based family centers have become an important resource for young families when more than traditional child welfare services are needed. Many family centers become a functioning community, and as such they are an important resource for families who come with basic survival needs, who may be victims of violence and abuse, and who often have chaotic life histories with the added burden of living in poverty. These multifaceted family centers are also referred to as family resource centers, child and family centers, or family support centers. Family centers may become a local system of care, where families receive a range of services including access to needed resources, often through colocated services.

COMMUNITY-BASED FAMILY CENTERS

Each family center is shaped by the community in which it is located, participants' cultural traditions

(staff and families), and the unique culture developed within the center itself. The family center community usually includes parents, children, young people, grandparents, friends, an interdisciplinary group of professionals, and natural helpers. Parents describe family centers as their safe haven, where they experience a family-like environment in contrast to the violence in their homes and neighborhoods. At friendly walk-in centers, parents are welcomed to join in programs with others who have been referred or are mandated to attend by protective services because their children are at risk for abuse or neglect. These centers are unique because they frequently manage to integrate child protective work with a host of other therapeutic, educational, and supportive services.

In family centers, parents have an opportunity to be part of a community that works, where they can receive help through a complex array of structured and creative offerings, such as parents' support groups and family play sessions, social action committees, and mentoring opportunities. The family center community is similar to a community of learners where capacity building is a shared goal for staff and participants. Capacity building takes many forms. Examples include staff development, building connections within the family center community, and providing opportunities for parents to take meaningful roles in supporting and running the center's program. This includes both informal and formal help that develops through parents' collaborative relationships with other parents and staff.

Service provision in family centers varies, depending on funding as well as center leadership and the collaboration between professional and local helpers. For example, some centers emphasize group programs over individual counseling, including parenting groups that provide support and use parent training curricula, and skill-building groups focused on such topics as budgeting, nutrition, job hunting skills, and coping with substance-abusing family members. Community building and empowerment practice is central to many centers where informal leadership by parents is promoted, reinforcing parents' strengths and their roles in a host of activities, such as rituals and celebrations that benefit the family center and local community. For staff there is the challenge of meeting parents' personal needs while balancing the needs of the whole community. There is both an art and science to making it all work, with a good measure of humor and excellent management! Family centers are noted for having a unique synergy that contributes significantly to the helping experience and positive outcomes for children, parents, and center staff (Hess, McGowan, & Botsko, 2003; Lightburn & Warren-Adamson, 2006; Tunstill, Aldgate, & Hughes, 2007).

EVIDENCE FOR AN INTEGRATED PRACTICE MODEL

It is valuable to consider lessons learned about what works in family centers, as well as to build a theoretical understanding of how development and change occur in these complex community programs (Warren-Adamson & Lightburn, 2006). A brief highlight of major findings, including case studies and a number of empirical studies, suggests that family centers are an important resource contributing to a range of important outcomes for parents and children. Case studies of family centers across the globe report outcomes of enhanced family stability, parent and child development, and parents' progress in attaining self-sufficiency (Batchelor, Gould, & Wright, 1999; Hess et al., 2003; Lightburn & Kemp, 1994; McMahon & Ward, 2001; Tunstill et al., 2007; Warren-Adamson, 2002). Although more empirical studies are needed, there is evidence that family centers have shown success in providing a continuum of services with good outcomes for fragile families (Comer & Fraser, 1998; McCroskey, 2006). Findings from a national study of 665 family support programs showed that these programs produce positive effects for children's cognitive and social development, parental attitudes, and behavior. Positive outcomes were heightened when an early childhood education component was included, parent groups were provided rather than home visits, peer support opportunities for parents were provided, parent self-development was a program goal, and professional staff were used rather than paraprofessional (Layzer & Goodson, 2001). Research also indicates that collaborative learning in support groups is particularly valuable for parents (Berry, Cash, & Hoge, 1998; Golding, 2000; Ireys, Divet, & Sakawa, 2002).

Practice in family centers requires an understanding of how the family center community contributes to family and child well-being, because these communities can be integral to belonging, identity, and achieving personal goals. We introduce an integrative model of family center practice based on a theory of change developed from cross-national examples of family centers, with support from current research cited, developmental theory, and prevention and developmental science (for elaboration of this practice model, see Lightburn & Warren-Adamson, 2006; Warren-Adamson & Lightburn, 2006).

A WORKING THEORY OF CHANGE

In Figure 125.1, an integrative model of practice based on a working theory of change is proposed as a guide for practice in family centers. To meet the complex needs that bring parents to family centers, it is useful to have a flexible model of practice to respond to the diverse needs and strengths of center participants. This model of practice takes into account the realities for parents as well as the potential for change that a family center supports. This integrative model of practice necessarily includes building the family center community as well as using individual, family, group, and case management methods. In addition, these centers are systems of care; hence, an important aspect of this integrative model of practice includes work that strengthens collaboration and connection with service providers and community resources. Because family centers are often seen as beacons in their communities, there is the added work of influencing and shaping what happens there, such as working to decrease neighborhood violence.

Historically, the absence of a theory of change has been an enduring problem for family center practice, despite the fact that different models of

Resources

- Community-based Family Center Site
- Leadership
- Professional staff (multidisciplinary)
- Non-professional staff
- Funding
- Parent contributors to center services
- Co-located services at the center (education, day care, etc.)
- Community services linked to center

Goals

- Build a family center community
- Meet children and parents' needs for protection
- Nurture development of parents & children
- Support the attachment bonds of children & parents
- Influence child placement
- Help parents meet mental health needs

Objectives

Build a multi-disciplinary staff team
- Mission driven
- Training & supervision
- Team meetings to support flexible roles & collaboration/ coordination for responsive services

Create and maintain culture of care
- Provide belonging & safe haven for families
- Provide protective factors to balance risk for parents and children
- Facilitate & support mutual aid within center

Respond to parent's agendas:
- Personal (for attachment, therapy – individual & family)
- Protective (learning to parent, make decision in best interest of child)
- Social and learning needs, and need to be part of social change in center and neighborhood

Strategies

1) Community building strategies
2) Capacity building through collective learning
3) Comprehensive individualized services
4) Supportive services (facilitating use of co-located or linked community services)
5) Problem solving, crisis intervention, & family group decision making
6) Use of FC* community, drop in, creative outreach with informal services, provide containment & holding
7) Therapeutic services (individual & family)
8) Group services (mutual aid, support, community)
9) Family services: recreation, informal activities
10) Empowerment approaches & education
  - Psychosocial learning
  - Transformative & experiential learning
  - Capacity building

Outcomes

Short-Term
Steps along the way
- Capacity of FC's* culture of care to nurture & protect families
- Parent's engagement; then small steps in achieving personal goals

Long-term
- Child and family safety and well-being
- Child & parent development; Family center community development
- Reduce need for placement; Reunification

Implementation

Figure 125.1 Integrated family center theory of change and implementation guide. (*Source:* Adapted from Warren-Adamson, & Lightburn, 2006). F.C. denotes Family Center.

intervention have been adopted. A theory of change is a working framework that explains the relationships between the family center program components and desired outcomes. The theory of change presented in Figure 125.1, based on knowledge of human behavior, the process of psychosocial development, and ecological systems, helps practitioners and family center leadership understand what interventions will be important and the pathways that staff and participants need to take to work toward their goals. The outcome goal is a community that serves as a dynamic resource for vulnerable families based on an understanding of how preventive services buffer stress and reduce risk so that learning, growth, and healing can occur (Warren-Adamson & Lightburn, 2006). This theory of change for family center practice maps goals and objectives. These are followed by connections to strategies and resources that are essential to support intended outcomes. Implemented in collaboration with stakeholders in a family center, the theory of change can assist program developers, staff, and families focus on what is most important and also help describe personal, program, and family center community steps along the way in the process of development and change.

The theory of change presented describes an integrated family center model. The basic resources, goals, objectives, and strategies of the model, along with anticipated outcomes, are presented.

FAMILY CENTER RESOURCES

The critical resources on which the change process depends are described in the left column of Figure 125.1. A host of resources make it possible to reach family center goals; some of the most indispensable are described. For example, the importance of place is highlighted as one of the key resources for the family center that includes a building, an accommodating place that becomes a tangible connection for families, both in the here and now, and a place to hold in their minds. The family center is a symbol of belonging and community for participants. The center site is as important as a family home, welcoming and familiar, with reminders of staff and friends, achievements experienced, and possibilities that have yet to be explored.

Family center leadership is also a critical resource, one that has the capacity to contain and encourage the range of formal and informal roles, activities, and internal and external interconnections needed to fulfill the center's mission. Leadership is crucial in building the family center community around a mission that can be valued by all. Most centers benefit from a multidisciplinary staff, including social workers with community-building, clinical, and case management skills; family therapists; and early education specialists, who work in tandem with natural helpers and parents in supporting center programs. Parents are essential contributors to the development of the family center community, as they take increasingly active roles in day care programs, working with reading groups, organizing food and clothing donations, and holiday celebrations.

Family centers are funded through state and local sources. Funding challenges are frequent, and maintaining financial support requires the creative involvement of all stakeholders, including advocacy and grant seeking to garner support for center programs (Tunstill et al., 2007; Warren-Adamson & Lightburn, 2006). Special programs are frequently developed through imaginative collaborations with community service providers, including negotiations that result in colocated services. The services that are invited to colocate within the family center are an important resource that responds to parents' needs for education, access to employment programs, including job placement, and specialized services, such as substance abuse programs. Ready access to opportunities for personal development makes it possible for parents to make significant progress toward self-sufficiency (Lightburn & Kemp, 1994). When there are limits to a family center's space for colocating services, good coordination and links with community resources become essential and provide an important role for the family center staff. Equally important are the family center's links to community services cultivated and facilitated by family center staff to meet families' complex needs.

FAMILY CENTER GOALS

Every family center must define goals specific to its purpose and mandate. The goals outlined in the second column of Figure 125.1 represent commonly held goals in family centers. These include (1) building a sense of community, (2) meeting family needs for safety and protection, (3) nurturing psychosocial development of parents and children, (4) supporting family attachment bonds, (5) reducing the need for child placement, and

(6) promoting the mental health and well being of all family members.

Meanings that we have attached to these goals are as follows.

- Community describes both a family center community where all who participate have a role and a culture of care that is a product of this community.
- Meeting protection needs means responsibility to protect children along with the wider notion of safety for parents and the community.
- Nurturance is a complex notion that assumes an actual and symbolic parenting role for the community and parents over time. Nurturance is essential for positive psychosocial development of both parents and children.
- Supporting attachment bonds develops Bowlby and others' idea of the importance of diverse and multiple attachments, such that the center in its complexity can encourage and provide some of these attachments over time (McMahon & Ward, 2001; Warren-Adamson & Lightburn, 2006). At the same time, attachment bonds are recognized as critical to a child's development, and therefore an important goal is to support these bonds between parents and their children
- Influencing placement means that the center's integrated services are focused on working toward achieving the goal of preventing out-of-home placement, and when this is not possible, it means the better management of foster or residential placement through supporting visitation and transition plans to reunite the family; or it can mean negotiating and sustaining kinship care instead of foster care, and so on.
- Helping parents meet mental health needs means promoting well-being as well addressing mental health concerns, such as depression and post-traumatic stress disorder, that impact on parents' ability to nurture their children.

OBJECTIVES WITH STRATEGIES TO GUIDE FAMILY CENTER PRACTICE

In the model for family center practice depicted in Figure 125.1, the center column defines the objectives designed to support achievement of the model's goals and the strategies that will achieve these objectives.

Staff Development

A family center requires investment in building the capacity of a multidisciplinary team. Collaborative practice is essential, supported by a clear mission, supervision, training, and team meetings. Family centers' missions reflect local needs and traditions and are shaped by stakeholders and leadership. For example, the mission of an integrated family center would be to ensure nurturance and protection of children and parents through the center community's culture of care that includes access to needed resources and services. Leadership oversees ongoing investment in the family center staff through capacity building to ensure development of a vital learning organization that helps staff continue to gain knowledge and skill (Brandon, 2006; Hess et al., 2003; McMahon & Ward, 2001).

Creating and Maintaining a Culture of Care

A crucial objective in the family center practice model is the development of a culture of care that makes it possible to meet parents' diverse agendas (their hopes, purpose, and investment in coming to the center). Strategies that create the culture of care include activities that result in containment, protection, mutuality, and support. The culture of a family center, like that of a school, contributes to the psychosocial development of its participants by shaping communication, experience, and identity. A culture of care is evident in the center community's shared values. Formation of a culture of care promotes safety for children, families, and staff. This involves recognizing and attending to risk and abuse as well as educating community members in alternative problem-solving strategies, rather than tolerating or denying dangerous situations.

Mandated supervision of children is part of this culture, wherein the best interests of children are seriously attended to with the support of protective services. At the same time, a clear message is given that the family center will work collaboratively to keep parents and children together. This will be a new experience for most families, who have often failed to work well with service systems that are child-focused, where parents feel blamed and there is limited flexibility in the way services are provided. The family center's culture of care is in significant contrast to the culture of neglect and abuse many families know, where isolation, loneliness, anxiety, and fear rob children and parents of love and nurturance (Warren-Adamson & Lightburn, 2006).

A key to how the family center culture shapes outcomes is found in the use of time. Parents need opportunities to experience relationships that nurture through acceptance and continuity with flexible responses when there are unexpected and repeated crises. For parents, this community becomes a family—the nurturing, accepting family that many have never known. A strong commitment to families communicates understanding when they are not yet able to grasp how their lives can change. This culture of care provides an important holding environment (McMahon & Ward, 2001; Warren-Adamson & Lightburn, 2006). As such, it supports development and growth, using parents' strengths and promoting new abilities, where parents' development is as important as their children's.

The values of family-centered practice and family empowerment are enacted through the cultural norms of the family center community, including through personal helping relationships. Investment in supporting the many facets of the culture of care increases the family center's protective factors that buffer risk and support parents' coping skills. For example, community building is vital where staff work to engender positive norms that hold center life together, such as mutual aid, hope, kindness, and positive expectation. The change process depends on promoting this positive culture that benefits from a learning organization approach that considers the best interests of all.

PARENTS' AGENDAS

The strategies listed in the fourth column in Figure 125.1 build on all that is best, diverse, and challenging in our knowledge about effective interventions and are derived from several traditions of practice: child welfare, therapeutic, and community care, including capacity and community building and advocacy. Effective strategies in implementing family center practice goals and objectives include problem solving, crisis intervention, individual and family therapy, mutual aid groups, parent education, empowerment practice, as well as social action groups and educational opportunities with informal activities.

AN INTEGRATED MODEL OF THE PROCESS OF FAMILY CENTER PRACTICE

An integrated model of the process of family center practice is represented in Figure 125.2. The model integrates four different areas that identity a focus for practice based on a parent's different agendas. This framework responds to the spoken and unspoken, known and yet to be recognized needs, reasons, and hopes that parents bring to the family center. Agenda is the term used to describe family center staff and parent's collaboration to identify a focus for their participation in center programs. Agenda is used instead of contract or treatment plan. It is important to respond to parents' needs and priorities as their personal goals/agenda evolve with their involvement in the center. Practice in family centers is based on collaborative, family-centered principles that recognize parents as active contributors in all outcomes. Parents are contributing members of the community, not cases to be treated and managed.

The parents' agenda as depicted in the model in Figure 125.2 includes the following four domains.

1. *Personal agenda,* reflecting parents' desire to attach and bond with others, be guided and mentored, and gain resources. Personal agendas can be met in a variety of ways, including work with case managers as a means for connecting parents with the range of possible opportunities and services, work with a mentor or guide on steps to self-sufficiency, or work with a therapist to meet interpersonal and mental health needs. Mental health needs are normalized with a focus on building relationships and learning and developing coping skills in a supportive environment.

2. *Protection and problem-solving agenda,* including learning how to protect and nurture one's children and one's self, as well as gain competence in parenting. Many parents have to fulfill mandated requirements to prove they are competent; others want to meet basic needs and find their way out of poverty, domestic violence, or substance abuse. This domain can include learning to solve problems at points of crisis and later

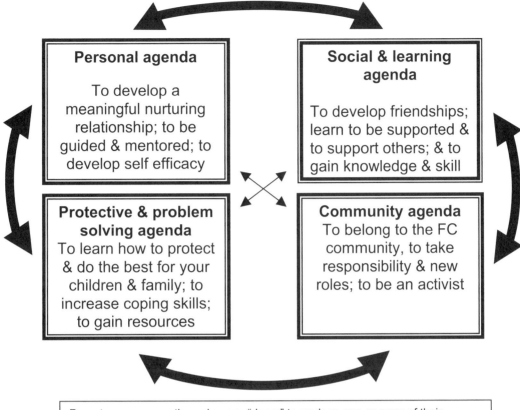

Figure 125.2 Parents' agendas.

develop problem-solving skills to work with family parenting and personal concerns. Of primary importance is the need to establish safety plans that ensures that children are protected and nurtured in their families and communities. This includes recognizing the effects of trauma and understanding the path to recovery, with appropriate parent education opportunities (Whipple & Wilson, 1998) and evidence-based trauma programs that include parents and children (Dass-Brailsford, 2007).

3. *Social and learning agenda,* which includes developing friendships, learning to be supported, and supporting others. The experience of mutual aid and being valued as

a member of the family center community is an essential contributor to parents' development and recovery, as friendships and support are invaluable in raising children in impoverished or dangerous neighborhoods. Parents are usually interested in group programs, as they share many concerns and can mutually benefit from working on issues with each other, such as managing family life, budgeting, and preparing for employment. Parents often need help identifying what they need to learn and how this best can happen.

4. *Community agenda,* which involves learning to belong and take responsibility, including new roles in the family center community,

and to be an activist. Parents' membership as part of the community reinforces their belonging and provides opportunities for them to join with other parents and staff. Experience as an active community member can increase a parent's authority and sense of efficacy because they have a role as a citizen to influence and shape the community culture and to advocate for change.

Comprehensive programs offered in many family centers make it possible to meet multiple social and mental health needs described in the parents' agendas. As Figure 125.2 indicates, parents can be engaged to work on one or more agendas. A parent's progress in meeting goals with one agenda can influence his or her desire to work on other agendas. A parent's work on different agendas would influence the progress made overall, as indicated by the directional arrows in Figure 125.2. The challenge for family center practice is imagining and understanding how to facilitate the working of the whole while also focusing on specifics. For example, integration of comprehensive services that aim to meet requirements of mandated protection includes a focus on development for parent and child. Some parents have been victims of violence, and for them to grow in competence as a parent they need help with their own recovery and healing. Services must be individualized, responding to a parent's main concern, while being aware of challenges and abilities. Service integration happens over time, in response to a parent's needs, priorities, and abilities to engage in the work of the agenda, and is similarly based on the capacity of the family center to provide different forms of help.

WORKING WITH OUTCOMES

The diverse and complimentary avenues for development and change described in the theory of change sets us on the road to identify outcomes that include familiar long-term outcomes—such as well-being, protected children, more intact families, community development, and so on—alongside what we describe as steps on the way. Outcomes as steps on the way have a particular resonance for practitioners and they are twofold. First, there are those small steps that can include parents meeting personal goals, such as small skills in building relationships and exercising personal authority to ensure safety for oneself and one's

children. Second, practitioners in particular contribute to outcomes that define the community of care in developing mutuality, modeling behaviors, and providing containment through parenting behaviors, creative activity, and conviviality. Such outcomes construct a community of care and contribute to change that cannot be fully explained by the traditional names we attach to intervention. The outcomes column should become a valued representation of what is expected and hoped for, as well as a realistic statement of what is possible.

CONCLUSION

This chapter described an integrated practice model for family centers by explaining a step-by-step logical approach to building such a center, illustrating possible pathways for engagement, development, and change. The framework for practice in Figure 125.1 was developed in response to the goals set out in the theory of change. We suggested intervention in centers involves meeting parents' different agendas (see Fig. 125.2), with many helping strategies and a broad tradition of intervention to meet a variety of goals, and something special that, when you put it all together with energy and commitment, results in a culture of care, providing the "glue" for service integration. Family centers are exceptional because they are more than a system of care; they are a special community that makes a difference for families and staff and their larger community.

WEB SITES

Community Family Centers. http://www
    .communityfamilycenters.org/cfc_home
    .html.
Family Center. http://www.thefamilycenterinc
    .org/index.htm.
National Resource for Family-Center Practice
    and Permanency Planning. http://www
    .hunter.cuny.edu/socwork/nrcfcpp.

References

Batchelor, J., Gould, N., & Wright, J. (1999). Family
    centers: A focus for the children in need debate.
    Children and Family Social Work, 4, 197–208.
Berry, M., Cash, S. J., & Hoge, L. A. (1998). Creating
    community through psycho-educational groups

in family preservation work. *Families in Society: The Journal of Contemporary Human Services, 79*, 15–24.

Brandon, M. (2006). Confident workers, confident families: Exploring sensitive outcomes in Family Center work in England. *International Journal of Child and Family Welfare, 9*, 79–91.

Comer, E., & Fraser, M. (1998). Evaluation in six family support programs: Are they effective? *Families in Society, 79*(2), 134–148.

Dass-Brailsford, P. (2007). *A practical approach to trauma*. Los Angeles: Sage.

Golding, K. (2000). Parent management training as an intervention to promote adequate parenting. *Clinical Child Psychology and Psychiatry, 5*(3), 357–371.

Hess, P., McGowan, B., & Botsko, M. (2003). *Nurturing the one, supporting the many*. New York: Columbia University Press.

Ireys, H., Divet, K., & Sakawa, D. (2002). Family support and education. In B. Burns & K. Hoagwood (Eds.), *Community treatment for youth: Evidence-based interventions for severe emotional and behavioral disorders* (pp. 154–176). New York: Oxford University Press.

Layzer, J., & Goodson, B. (2001). *National evaluation of family support programs*. Cambridge, MA: Abt Associates.

Lightburn, A., & Kemp, S. (1994). Family support programmes: Opportunities for community-based practice. *Families in Society: The Journal of Contemporary Human Services, 75*, 16–26.

Lightburn, A., & Warren-Adamson, C. (2006). Evaluating family centers: The importance of sensitive outcomes in cross-national studies. *International Journal of Child and Family Welfare, 9*, 11–26.

McCroskey, J. (2006). Community programs in the US. In C. McAuley, P. Pecora, & W. Rose (Eds.), *Enhancing the well being of children and families through effective interventions* (pp. 313–320). London: Jessica Kingsley.

McMahon, L., & Ward, A. (Eds.). (2001). *Helping families in family centres: Working at therapeutic practice*. London: Jessica Kingsley.

Tunstill, J., Aldgate, J., & Hughes, M. (2007). *Improving children's services networks: Lessons from family centres*. London: Jessica Kingsley.

Warren-Adamson, C. (Ed.). (2002). *Family centres and their international role in social action*. Aldershot, UK: Ashgate.

Warren-Adamson, C., & Lightburn, A. (2006). Developing a community-based model for integrated family centre practice. In A. Lightburn & P. Sessions (Eds.), *The handbook of community-based clinical practice*, New York: Oxford University Press.

Whipple, E., & Wilson, S. (1996). Evaluation of a parent education and support program for families at risk of physical child abuse. *Families in Society: The Journal of Contemporary Human Services*, 227–239.

126 International Perspectives on Social Work Practice

Karen M. Sowers & William S. Rowe

Although our world is becoming easier to navigate, the complexity of social issues and their impact globally demands that social workers respond. International social work practice, a new and exciting area of practice, may hold the key to solutions for a peaceful, thriving, and sustainable environment for future generations. This chapter addresses social work practice in the global arena and provides an understanding of the interconnectedness of social work and social development across the globe. Some examples provide illustrations of ways international social work is making a difference to empower people, communities, and organizations.

Social work practice was primarily developed in response to local needs—most often to serve the powerless and disadvantaged and address issues in managing the developmental challenges of everyday living. As populations expanded and immigration and migration grew, it became clear that the challenges facing people in achieving their individual and collective goals were in many ways more similar than they were different (Sowers & Rowe, 2007).

The increased impact of globalization over the past few decades has highlighted the similarities of social problems. The initial response was a presumption that social work practices in developed countries were the most desirable and effective and needed only simple cultural adjustments to be applied to human and social problems everywhere. However, it became clear that no single location or country has the preferred methods for all, although various countries may have exemplar programs or best practices that can be instructive to others (Sowers & Rowe, 2007).

INTERNATIONAL SOCIAL WORK

The definitions and conceptualizations of social work differ greatly across cultural contexts. Initially, international social work was concerned with comparing social work as it exists in different cultures and countries. The view of the social worker as one who primarily provides individual clinical services originated in Western industrial countries. Most societies, however, have always had a role for individuals who worked to improve conditions for community members. Clinical practice is more characteristic of industrialized countries, and community organizers in Western countries have learned many of their strategies and practices from their peers in developing countries (Rowe, Hanley, Moreno, & Mould, 2000). Although *social work* is the term most commonly used in the United States and other industrialized countries, *social development* or *developmental social welfare* is often used in developing nations.

Over the decades, social work has grown and matured worldwide. Currently an effort is being made to address social work from a global perspective—as one profession practicing in many different countries. This effort is led by two international organizations, the International Federation of Social Workers (IFSW) and the International Association of Schools of Social Work (IASSW). In 2001 the IFSW (n.d. a) and IASSW

(n.d.) jointly agreed on an international definition of social work:

The social work profession promotes social change, problem solving in human relationships and the empowerment and liberation of people to enhance well-being. Utilizing theories of human behavior and social systems, social work intervenes at points where people interact with their environments. Principles of human rights and social justice are fundamental to social work.

INTERNATIONAL SOCIAL WORK PRACTICE

Global social work practice is based on the values of human rights and social justice. The most universal beliefs that characterize social work globally include the principle of social inclusion as core to the alleviation of poverty and the promotion of self-determination and self-sufficiency of disenfranchised and vulnerable people and the inherent value of people and the responsibilities of societies to create conditions in which people can thrive (Morales & Sheafor, 2001).

Social workers interested in or engaged in global social work practice should be familiar with and practice within the international standards and guidelines for social work practice. These include the Global Qualifying Standards for Social Work Practice (IFSW, n.d. a), the International Code of Ethics (IFSW, n.d. b), the IFSW policy statement on human rights (1996), and the Universal Declaration of Human Rights (United Nations, 1994).

Practicing within the Cultural Context

Social and cultural realities can create both challenges and opportunities in global social work practice. Global social work practice requires that social workers become aware of their own values, biases, and beliefs and must value and respect differences as well as understand the dynamics of difference (Sowers-Hoag & Sandau-Beckler, 1996).

For example, in 1986, New Zealand restructured its social welfare department in response to growing criticism that it was too bureaucratic, emphasized individualized casework services, neglected local needs, and failed to respond to cultural needs of specific groups. The new model adopted by New Zealand allowed for joint decision making and resource sharing with communities. The model particularly targeted indigenous communities, using community as provider within the delivery system. Changes in social work practice included the development of culturally sensitive practice with strong links to indigenous communities. The promotion and funding of preventive, community-based services were determined by local communities. (For more information see Barretta-Herman, 1994.)

As can be seen from this example, the most effective approaches to advancing human rights require cultural sensitivity and responsiveness and embrace inclusive strategies that encompass culture and religion and the roles played by local power structures and institutions (United Nations Population Fund, n.d.). Because societies and cultures are increasingly complex and changing, social workers practicing in a global context must be lifelong learners and willing to change, adapt, and use strategies that are relevant and specific to differing situations (Sowers & Rowe, 2007).

Today, poverty, inequality, and human distress are issues to which social workers respond everywhere in the world. Certain social issues, including population aging, immigration and migration, substance abuse, human-made and natural disasters, and health and mental health, transcend nation-states. The following provides some examples of worldwide social problems addressed by social workers.

Substance Abuse and HIV

In many cities around the world HIV disease has reached epidemic proportions. On the basis of global 1992 data, the World Health Organization (n.d. a) estimated that "over 5 million people injected drugs, that between 150,000 and 200,000 drug injectors died every year, and that at least half of those deaths were associated with HIV." Global efforts are needed to support safe behavior among HIV-infected substance abusers and among drug abusers in general. Because of the critical need to support safer behavior, particularly in cities with a high prevalence of HIV, cities, governments, nongovernmental organizations, and other groups are implementing harm reduction programs (Sowers & Rowe, 2007). Harm reduction is defined as "policies and programs which attempt primarily to reduce the adverse health, social and economic consequences of mood altering substances to individual drug users, their families, and their communities" (In-

ternational Harm Reduction Association, n.d.). This new global approach is especially useful in the prevention of HIV/AIDS.

In contrast to a punitive approach to drug abuse, the harm reduction model views addiction as an adaptive response to a wide cross-section of individual and collective variables that may influence behavior. Practitioners using the harm reduction perspective develop interventions that reduce drug-related harm without necessarily promoting abstinence as the only solution. Harm reduction for injecting drug users primarily aims to help them avoid the negative health consequences of drug injecting and improve their health and social status. These approaches recognize that for many drug users total abstinence from harmful substances is not a feasible option in the short term. It focuses on helping users reduce their injection frequency and increase safety. To be effective, harm reduction strategies must be embedded into comprehensive prevention and intervention packages for injecting drug users (World Health Organization, n.d. a). The following are typical components identified by the World Health Organization (n.d. a) that have a significant potential to reduce individual risk behaviors associated with drug injection:

- needle-syringe programming provides drug users with access to clean injection paraphernalia, including needles and syringes, filters, cookers, drug containers, and mixing water. These interventions may also collect used needles and syringes. These programs serve as information points for drug and HIV disease education and provide referral for treatment services. Their ability to break the chain of transmission of HIV and other bloodborne viruses is well established.
- drug substitution treatment involves the medically supervised treatment of individuals with opioid dependency. The primary goal of drug substitution treatment may be abstinence from illicit drug use but many patients are unable to achieve complete abstinence. There is clear evidence that some drug substitution treatments, such as methadone maintenance, can significantly reduce unsafe injection practices of those who are in treatment and at risk of HIV infection.

The application of harm reduction principles to other problematic substances, such as ecstasy, tobacco, and alcohol is a fairly recent event but has shown widespread effectiveness and public acceptance in many places across the globe.

In Argentina, 39 percent of those diagnosed with HIV acquired the virus through IV drug use. Past harm reduction activity efforts had little effect. In response, a specific harm reduction approach with poor populations in Buenos Aires using a community-based outreach approach with specific emphasis on drug users, their sexual partners, and children was developed with the participation of 23 pharmacies. This approach proved successful, reaching 900 drug users with preventive messages in a 3-month period. In location-specific areas, preventive materials were distributed by drug users, former drug users, and local pharmacies (Rossi et al., 2001).

Mental Health

Mental health problems are common to all countries. They are the cause of immense human suffering, disability, social exclusion, and poor quality of life. Across the globe, about one in every four persons going to health services has at least one mental, neurological, or behavioral disorder. Mental and behavioral disorders are estimated to account for 12 percent of the global burden of disease, yet the mental health budgets of the majority of countries constitute less than 1 percent of total health expenditures. Unfortunately, even in countries with well-established mental health services, fewer than half of those individuals needing care make use of available services. This is related both to the stigma attached to individuals with mental health and behavioral disorders and to the inadequacy of the services provided (World Health Organization, 2001).

According to the World Health Organization (n.d. b), good mental health care flows from the following basic principles:

- diagnosis,
- early intervention,
- rational use of treatment techniques,
- continuity of care,
- availability of a wide range of services,
- consumer involvement,
- partnership with families, and
- involvement of the local community.

Integration of mental health treatment into primary health. The prevalence of mental disorders is worldwide, and many persons suffering from mental and behavioral disorders are first seen in primary care settings. This is probably because mental health problems are often associated with physical disease. But because many primary care providers do not have specialized training in mental illness, these disorders are often not detected. A global trend has been the integration of mental health care into basic primary health care by training primary care and general health care staff in the detection and treatment of common mental and behavioral disorders. With appropriate information and training of providers, patients discharged from psychiatric facilities can effectively followed up in primary health care settings. This is a particularly important initiative in countries where community-based mental health services do not exist. In many developing countries, well-trained health care workers have been able to provide treatment effectively and efficiently for persons with mental illnesses. In fact, experiences in some African, Asian, and Latin American countries indicate that adequate training of health care workers in the early recognition and management of mental disorders can reduce institutionalization and improve clients' mental health outcomes (Sowers & Rowe, 2007).

There are an estimated 4 million people with schizophrenia in India. It is estimated that this impacts approximately 25 million family members. Recognizing that outcome of the disorder is strongly influenced by social factors, especially family, the Indian government developed a system of support to people with schizophrenia. According to the World Health Organization (n.d. c) components effecting outcomes included:

- a manual for family intervention produced in local languages.
- training of the local health workers. Training focused on the appropriate identification, management, and referral for mental health problems and how to implement actual interventions.
- brief psychoeducational interventions were provided to 1500 families. Content included information about mental illness, basic training in daily living, problem solving, and communication skills. Pharmacological treatment was provided to patients. Day centers were opened for people with mental disorders.
- nongovernmental organizations were mobilized and actively involved in the project. Emphasis was placed on awareness-raising events and information dissemination about mental health problems and their management.

Natural and Human-Made Disasters

Recent events around the world underscore our lack of preparedness and ability to respond to the aftermath of disasters. Natural and human-made disasters often strike communities with little or no warning. Although social workers have a long history of responding to disaster trauma, few have knowledge or experience in dealing with disasters that have occurred with increased frequency and intensity. As disasters occur more frequently and with greater intensity, disaster response, relief, and recovery efforts have become more complex. To respond in a timely and appropriate manner to the likely psychological distress experienced by trauma survivors, social workers must understand the nature of the problems survivors may experience, the types of help they may need, and the level of preparedness of the health and human service delivery systems in place to respond to those needs (Sowers & Rowe, 2007). The World Health Organization's Department of Mental Health and Substance Dependence (2001) research findings provide lessons learned about responses to catastrophes.

- Intense emotional reactions in the face of these events are expected and normal.
- There is a trajectory of responses over time, most often starting early and subsiding within weeks and months. But for some people, the onset of responses may be delayed. Left unattended, some reactions may become long-term problems and lead to considerable disability.
- Responses are highly individualized, can be quite intense, and sometimes are conflictual.
- The range of feelings expressed may be quite broad.
- There may be temporary disruptions in normal coping mechanisms. Problems with sleep, nightmares, concentration, intrusive thoughts, and preoccupation with reliving the events are not uncommon.

Guidelines for providing help in the aftermath of a catastrophe are provided by the Department of Mental Health and Substance Dependence (n.d.).

- Create opportunities for people to share experiences in supportive groups.
- Provide accurate and practical information, especially concerning the larger recovery efforts.

- Give particular consideration to the needs of special groups, such as children, those who have been most intensely exposed, or those who have a history of previous events.
- Children and adolescents will need the support of their caregivers. Exposure to television, movies, or print matter that offers graphic depictions of the destruction or victims should be limited.
- As many as 30 percent of people who experience the most direct exposure to the events may go on to develop more serious mental health concerns and should be referred for services if they develop persistent problems.

Promising new approaches are focusing on risk reduction from natural disasters. One such innovative approach is the "sustainable livelihoods" model. This approach analyzes the range of vulnerabilities in poor communities and outlines specific assets within the community. Vulnerability and capacity analysis is a valuable new field tool currently being used to assess communities' disaster resilience and mobilize risk reduction (International Federation of Red Cross and Red Crescent Societies, 2002).

CONCLUSION

The increase in the recognition of the importance of international social issues has spurred an increased demand for social workers. As welfare, economic, and foreign policies become ever more globally interdependent, there is a need for global social work practice. Hopefully the future will see a reduced tendency in social work to dichotomize between global and domestic social work issues. The fostering of mutual exchanges of experiences and information between social workers in different societies can only advance our practices. We have much to learn from each other.

WEB SITES

International Association of Schools of Social Work. http://www.iassw-aiets.org.
International Consortium for Social Development. http://www.icsd.org.
International Federation of Social Workers. http://www.ifsw.org.
United Nations. http://www.un.org.

World Health Organization. http://www
.who.int.

References

Baretta-Herman, A. (1994). Revisioning the community as provider: Restructuring New Zealand's social services. *International Social Work, 37*(1), 7–21.

Department of Mental Health and Substance Dependence. (n.d.). *How to address psychosocial reactions to catastrophe.* Retrieved November 30, 2007, from http://www.who.int/child-adolescent-health/Emergencies/Disaster_reactions.htm.

International Association of Schools of Social Work. (n.d.). *An international community of schools and educators in social work: An international definition of social work.* Retrieved November 24, 2007, from http://www.iassw-aiets.org.

International Federation of Red Cross and Red Crescent Societies. (2002). *World disasters report 2002.* Geneva: International Federation.

International Federation of Social Workers. (1996). *International policy on human rights.* Hong Kong: IFSW.

International Federation of Social Workers. (n.d. a). *International Federation of Social Workers definition of social work.* Retrieved November 24, 2007, from www.ifsw.org/Publications/4.6e.pub.html.

International Federation of Social Workers. (n.d. b). *The ethics of social work principles and standards.* Retrieved November 25, 2007, from http://www.ifsw.org/Publications/4.4.pub.html.

International Harm Reduction Association. (n.d.). *What is harm reduction?* Retrieved November 27, 2007, from http://www.ihra.net/index.php?option=articles&Itemid=3&topid=0&Itemid=3.

Morales, A. T., & Sheafor, B. W. (2001). *Social work: A profession of many faces,* 9th ed. Boston: Allyn & Bacon.

Rossi, D., Cymerman, P., Erenu, N., Faraone, S., Goltzman, P., Rojas, E., et al. (2001). Rapid assessment and response in IDUs in Buenos Aires. In *2000 global research network meeting on HIV prevention in drug using populations* (pp. 42–45). Washington, DC: National Institute on Drug Abuse.

Rowe, W., Hanley, J., Moreno, E. R., & Mould, J. (2000). Voices of social work practice: International reflections on the effects of globalization. *Canadian Social Work, 2*(1), 65–86.

Sowers, K. M., & Rowe, W. S. (2007). *Social work practice and social justice: From local to global perspectives.* Belmont, CA: Thomson-Brooks/Cole.

Sowers-Hoag, K. M., & Sandau-Beckler, P. (1996). Educating for cultural competence in the generalist curriculum. *Journal of Multicultural Social Work, 4*(3), 37–56.

United Nations. (1994). *Human rights: A compilation of international instruments,* vols. 1 and 2). New York: United Nations.

United Nations Population Fund. (n.d.). *Culture matters—working with communities and faith-based organizations: Case studies from country programmes.* Retrieved November 25, 2007, from http://www.unfpa.org.

World Health Organization. (2001). *The world health report 2001.* Retrieved November 25, 2007, from http://www.who.int/whr2001/2001/main.

World Health Organization. (n.d. a). *Harm reduction approaches to injecting drug use.* Retrieved November 27, 2007, from http://who.int/hiv/topics/harm/reduction/en.

World Health Organization. (n.d. b). *Mental health.* Retrieved November 23, 2007, from http://www.who.int/mental-health/en.

World Health Organization (n.d. c). *India: Support to people with schizophrenia.* Retrieved November 30, 2007, from http://www.who.int/mental_health/management/en/draft_without_pictures.pdf.

127 Guidelines for Assertive Community Treatment Teams

Mary Ann Test

Assertive community treatment (ACT), also known as a program of assertive community treatment (PACT), is an effective evidence-based service delivery model for providing comprehensive community-based treatment and support to persons with a severe and persistent mental illness. An ACT team serves as a fixed point of responsibility for a designated group of consumers and is available to them 24 hours a day, 7 days a week. The team uses an outreach approach to deliver comprehensive and integrated community treatment, rehabilitation, and support services wherever its clients need them. The majority of services are provided in vivo, that is, in consumers' places of residence, work, recreation, or other community settings.

WHAT KINDS OF CLIENTS DOES AN ACT TEAM SERVE?

ACT is designed to serve consumers with severe and persistent mental illness who are not effectively served by the traditional mental health system or by approaches that provide less intensive support. These persons often suffer such severe symptoms or functional impairments that they need extra assistance in multiple aspects of community living. Indicators include frequent hospital admissions, time in jail or homelessness, a poor quality of life in the community, and dual challenges such as mental illness and substance abuse. The most frequent diagnoses of persons served by an ACT team are schizophrenia, schizoaffective disorder, and severe mood disorders.

WHAT ARE THE VALUES AND GOALS OF ACT?

The ACT approach is based on the belief that all citizens, including those challenged by the most

severe and persistent mental illnesses, have a right to live a decent and satisfying life in the community. The fundamental premise of ACT, now validated by numerous controlled research studies, is that if mental health consumers receive sufficient assistance and support in the community, hospitalization (and homelessness) can be prevented or almost eliminated, and these persons can live freely in the community at a decent and satisfying quality of life. ACT works respectfully and collaboratively with consumers to help them in reaching their own goals in the areas of housing, community tenure, social relationships, work and education, management of symptoms and life stressors, and community integration, empowerment, and recovery. The program's overall goals are to assist consumers to live satisfying, hopeful, and contributing lives in the community.

WHAT IS THE COMPOSITION OF AN ACT TEAM AND HOW MANY CLIENTS DOES IT SERVE?

The ACT team *itself* provides its clients with most needed treatment, rehabilitation, and supportive services, rather than brokering these out to other providers. Hence, an ACT team requires a multidisciplinary staff and a rich staff-to-client ratio (i.e., 1:10). A team of 10 to 12 full time equivalents (FTE) staff serve approximately 100 clients. Staffing requires at least 16 hours of psychiatrist time for every 50 clients; an array of mental health professionals from disciplines such as nursing, social work, rehabilitation counseling, psychology, or occupational therapy; and several bachelor's level or paraprofessional mental health workers. Each team also has at least one peer counselor/peer specialist (i.e., a person with a serious mental illness who is further along in their recovery than the clients being served by the team). ACT staff serve as both specialists and generalists. They work together as a team so that all staff are familiar with and at times work with all of the consumers being served by the team. The result is that there is always someone available who is familiar with and ready to assist each consumer regardless of who is working on a particular day or shift.

WHAT ARE THE UNIQUE FEATURES OF ACT SERVICE DELIVERY?

1. The ACT team itself provides almost all biopsychosocial services to its clients rather than brokering them out. This kind of "one-stop shopping" avoids the creation of a fragmented service system and allows for true integration of treatment, rehabilitation, and supportive services.
2. The team is *mobile* and provides most services in vivo, on the client's territory rather than in an office or agency setting.
3. Services are *highly individualized* and are tailored to address each client's current needs and preferences, rather than the more common practice of slotting clients into a group of existing programs or services.
4. Staff are available to clients 7 days a week, 24 hours a day. Day and evening shifts are staffed in person; during night hours an on-call system is used through which a team member can be easily reached via a beeper.
5. Services are provided in an *ongoing*, rather than time-limited, fashion, so that consumers may receive treatment and supports as long as they need and want them. Every effort is made, however, to assist clients in growing more autonomous.
6. The ACT team maintains an assertive, "can-do" approach and works to adapt the environment and themselves to meet the client's needs rather than requiring the client to adapt to or follow the rules of a treatment program. Consumers are not discharged for noncompliance. Rather, staff regard it as their responsibility to find ways of working with clients that are compatible with their needs and preferences and that will, over time, assist them in gaining a better quality of life.

WHAT SERVICES/INTERVENTIONS DOES AN ACT TEAM PROVIDE?

An ACT team provides intensive, practical, "side by side" assistance in the following areas, based on a collaborative treatment plan developed and regularly updated with the consumer:

A. Assistance in meeting daily living needs:
 1. decent housing (usually apartments in normative settings);
 2. activities of daily living (e.g., grocery shopping, cooking, use of transportation);
 3. adequate financial resources—accessing, budgeting;
 4. physical health and dental care—referral and transportation to.
B. Assistance with personal and psychological well-being, for instance,
 1. frequent supportive and problem-solving contacts;
 2. medications based on collaborative planning and frequent evaluations with the team psychiatrist;
 3. substance abuse treatment;
 4. consumer groups for strategy sharing and support;
 5. long-term 1:1 relationship with a staff member to provide education about the illness, symptom self-management, and support in the process of recovery;
 6. crisis availability—24 hours/day, 7 days/week;
 7. brief hospitalization when needed.
C. Assistance with work, education, social relationships, and recreation, for example,
 1. work rehabilitation available to all; supported employment focus; implemented by ACT team members;
 2. education—for example, assistance with GED; continuing education;
 3. "in community" leisure activities; group support and skill learning; linkages to community groups, including consumer self-help.
D. Support and education to family, significant others, and community members.

HOW OFTEN ARE ACT CLIENTS SEEN?

Frequency of contact is highly individualized, based on client needs and preferences, and varies greatly among clients and within the same client across time. Frequency may range from several contacts a day to one to two contacts per month.

IN WHAT WAY IS ACT EFFECTIVE, AND WHAT IS THE EVIDENCE?

ACT has strong empirical support based on numerous controlled studies (Lehman & Steinwachs, 1998; Marshall & Lockwood, 2005). ACT is consistently recommended in practice guidelines for the treatment of adults with severe mental illness who are at high risk for hospital readmission and who cannot be maintained by more usual community-based care (American Psychiatric Association, 2004). Relative to randomly assigned control clients, clients treated by an ACT team generally demonstrate these outcomes (note that results vary somewhat by study) (Dixon, 2000; Stein & Santos, 1998; Test, 1998):

A. marked reduction in days spent in inpatient settings, with no greater time spent homeless or in jails/prisons (almost all studies);
B. more days in independent living (many studies);
C. less psychiatric symptomatology (many studies);
D. greater client and/or family satisfaction (many studies);
E. more favorable work functioning (a few studies);
F. more favorable social functioning (a few studies).

Several of these studies have assessed the relative economic costs and benefits of ACT versus the comparison (standard care) treatment. Findings suggest that the costs of ACT are either the same or less than standard care. The primary cost of ACT is for the team itself, given its high staff-to-client ratio. These costs are offset by the fact that ACT clients use few other services and incur much reduced inpatient costs. Not surprisingly, the ACT model is most cost-effective when it is used to treat persons who are at high risk for hospitalization (Weisbrod, Test, & Stein, 1980).

WHERE CAN INTERESTED STAFF GET MORE INFORMATION ABOUT THE ACT MODEL AND HOW TO IMPLEMENT IT?

A very detailed "how to do it" manual on ACT has been published by the NAMI Anti Stigma Foundation (Allness & Knoedler, 2003). This manual also contains the national "standards" for what an ACT program is, including what clients the program targets, information about staffing, and details about implementation of the range of services delivered by an ACT team. This manual can be ordered through the NAMI Web site.

WEB SITES

ACTA Association, organization of ACT programs that meets yearly. http://www.actassociation.org.

National Alliance on Mental Illness. http://www.nami.org.

SAMHSA toolkit for developing ACT programs. http://mentalhealth.samhsa.gov/cmhs/communitysupport/toolkits/community.

State of Iowa's standards for their ACT program. http://www.medicine.uiowa.edu/icmh/act.

References

Allness, D. J., & Knoedler, W. H. (2003). *A manual for ACT Startup.* Arlington, VA: NAMI.

American Psychiatric Association. (2004). *Practice guideline for the treatment of patients with schizophrenia,* 2nd ed. Arlington, VA: APA.

Dixon, L. (2000). Assertive community treatment: Twenty-five years of gold. *Psychiatric Services, 51,* 759–765.

Lehman, A. F., & Steinwachs, D. M. (1998). Translating research into practice: The Schizophrenia Patient Outcomes Research Team (PORT) treatment recommendations. *Schizophrenia Bulletin, 24,* 1–10.

Marshall, M., & Lockwood, A. (2005). Assertive community treatment for people with severe mental disorders. Cochrane Schizophrenia group. *Cochrane Database of Systematic Reviews, 2,* 2005.

Stein, L. I., & Santos, A. B. (1998). *Assertive community treatment of persons with severe mental illness.* New York: Norton.

Test, M. A. (1998). Community-based treatment models for adults with severe and persistent mental illnesses. In J. B. W. Williams & K. Ell (Eds.), *Recent advances in mental health research* (pp. 420–436). Washington, DC: NASW Press.

Weisbrod, B. A., Test, M. A., & Stein, L. I. (1980). Alternative to mental hospital treatment: II. Economic benefit-cost analysis. *Archives of General Psychiatry, 37,* 400–405.

128 Community Organizing Principles and Practice Guidelines

Terry Mizrahi

This chapter is based primarily on practice wisdom from my own experiences over 35 years. It is also informed by the literature and by the cumulative field experiences of community organizing and planning students at the Hunter School of Social Work. I address the reader as "you" and assume that you are reading this when you initiate or are being called on to respond to an issue, or address an agency or community need. "You" also includes the group or the other people with whom you are working. The phrase "target of change" is used to mean whichever body (a person, agency, or a system) you are trying to influence. These principles are not laid out in a linear order. Several of them need simultaneous consideration before taking action; others are interactive, so following one may affect your response to another. I provide a list of resources at the end of this chapter that feature community organizing theory and practice.

PRINCIPLE 1: EFFECTIVE ORGANIZING BALANCES PROCESS AND PRODUCT

A key assumption is that there is never sufficient time, staff, and other resources to involve people in making change (the process) and accomplishing a specific goal or task (the product). Both are important, so the question is how to operationalize and balance them. Process means that there must be enough discussion to achieve a consensus to move ahead, and a mechanism to ascertain the intensity as well as breadth of any disagreement. You need enough process to gauge people's interest in and commitment to the task and take into account the needs of the affected group.

Involvement of people creates a sense of investment and can ultimately lead to a sense of ownership of the product. You need time to build trust, and that can be done by working on the task while reflecting periodically on the process: "How we are doing?" "Whom did we lose?" "Whose voice do we need to hear from?"

The solutions to managing time so that you achieve the product without sacrificing the process are to (a) calculate a more complete and realistic timetable; (b) modify expectations if necessary; (c) prioritize what is essential with those involved; and (d) ascertain who else can assist with the project. Organizing means planning for contingencies, allow more time than necessary, follow through, and pay attention to detail. Redundancy reinforces efficiency.

PRINCIPLE 2: PLANNING IS A COMPLEX SOCIOPOLITICAL AND TECHNICAL PROCESS

Planning is not just about data collection, goals, and timelines or who can write a clear, internally consistent proposal. Rather, planning, as a part of organizing is a sociopolitical as well as technical process. Values, power, and resources inform the way you and your constituency define the problem and select the solutions. A value base or ideology includes basic assumptions about why a problem exists, why needs are not being met, why conditions are not optimal, that is, who's to "blame" for the problems identified. Power means understanding that some*body* (with a small or capital B), that is, some individual or group has the ability to make decisions about how resources are allocated and whether to implement the program or change a policy. Resources include creating or redistributing the assets and the means to solve a problem. Hence, the strategies you select for influencing the decision makers to achieve your goal are done within a social-political context.

For example, substance abuse was identified as a national problem in the 1960s when it spread beyond the ghetto to middle-class America; homelessness became a national crisis when the number and type of people living on the streets moved beyond "derelict row" in the 1970s. Mental retardation "came out of the closet" when President John F. Kennedy disclosed that he had a mentally retarded sister in the 1960s. While middle-class parents had been organizing and planning services throughout the 1950s, mental retardation became a national program because the president used his office to create funding opportunities for facilities and programs. Conversely, HIV/AIDS did not become a national priority as soon as many experts believe it should have been because President Ronald Reagan did not publicly address the nation on this issue until 1986.

PRINCIPLE 3: THERE IS NO SUCH THING AS "RATIONAL" AND "IRRATIONAL" FROM THE PERSPECTIVE OF HOW PROBLEMS ARE DEFINED OR RESOURCES ARE ALLOCATED

Many times as part of the process of identifying problems, someone may say that a particular system or structure or policy doesn't make sense; "It's irrational." When someone makes such a statement, it should be reframed by asking that person or group instead: "To whom does it make sense?" "For whom is it functional and working?" "Why hasn't that policy been changed, if it isn't working?" You will usually uncover reasons why conditions or attitudes have remained in place, why a need wasn't met, why people have resisted change, or why a new program wasn't implemented. Usually the case does make sense from the perspective of those who maintain that system.

A new program can be an implied criticism of the existing system. It may mean that a group perceives they will lose power if that program is created. In other words, it's not irrational for groups that may be affected to attempt to maintain the status quo. Understanding this allows you to identify the covert and overt reasons for resisting change and develop strategies to decrease resistance.

It is important to understand that "rationality," when it means utilitarian, is itself an ideology, one that is usually associated with capitalism and pragmatism. Therefore, if the word or concept is invoked, you need to ask if the term "rational" is being used to prevent deliberations, values such as fairness, equality, and justice, or if it is being used to divert or discredit those who have a progressive value base.

It is also important to assert that there is no such thing as value-free planning and organizing. Values and beliefs inform the problem definition and solving process, that is, why, when, and how a problem is defined, which in turn shape the proposed solutions that emanate from that definition.

To take the example of homelessness noted in principle 2, the problem was ignored until a combination of deinstitutionalization of mental hospitals and gentrification of formerly abandoned and neglected neighborhoods resulted in hundreds of thousands of people without a place to live. However, the solutions to homelessness were informed by values and ideology, not on the basis of need alone. Those who perceived it as a housing problem advocated for the right to shelter and housing; those who perceived it as a mental health problem advocated for services; those who perceived it as a civil liberties problem advocated for personal choice and the right to be left alone; and those who perceived it as a criminal justice and morality problem advocated for incarceration, involuntary commitment, forced work, and other social control measures.

These political and ideological arguments about rationality should not obfuscate your need to be logical, systematic, and problem-focused. It is necessary to anticipate the steps, activities, people, and resources needed to produce a coherent plan, implement it, and evaluate it, and also to identify contingencies for situations beyond your control. Analytical skills are a vital part of making systematic change.

PRINCIPLE 4: KNOW AND MAKE YOUR CASE

Needs assessments are a critical part of community organizing and planning practice. It is essential to ask the question: "How do you know there is a problem?" "How do you know there is a need for a particular intervention?" "Who believes there is a problem/need?" "Who is defining the problem/need? Why at this time?" "How serious is the problem/need?" "How pervasive is it?"

As noted in principles 2 and 3, defining the need has an ideological as well as factual component. For example, if it is reported that 30 percent of the students in a particular school or community did not complete high school, the questions posed might include: "Is that a problem?" "For whom is that a problem?" "Why should anyone care?" Answers to those kinds of questions will depend on several factors: whether the norm is to complete high school, whether it is desirable to complete high school, whether that figure has gone up or down in the last several years, how that figure compares to other communities, the alternatives to and consequences of not completing high school, and so on. Remember, the way a problem is defined will determine the proposed solution(s). If you report that 30 percent of the students dropped out of school last year, there is already an implied causation. "Drop out" implies a willful act on the part of the student or neglect on the part of parents or the community. Consider the difference when you say that 30 percent of the students were "pushed out" or "turned out" last year. The latter implies the problem lies with the school system.

Once you define the problem, the next step is to document the problem. Answering questions entail gathering quantitative and qualitative data, sometimes called empirical (objective) and perceptual (subjective) information. The best needs assessments are those that use both; they present statistics as well as humanize the issue. Be prepared to communicate in writing, verbally, and visually. In making your case, use numbers and narration, namely, interviews, case studies, anecdotes.

Next, consider the ways to convey that information to make the strongest, most convincing case. First the various audiences need to be identified. How will you reach the different communities; how do they best receive information? Communicating with the decision makers may be different from communicating with supporters and allies. To reach the public at large, you may need different means and messages than the ones used for reaching clients and constituencies. Will it be in the form of a letter or a report? Who writes and signs it? What does it say? Presentation is as important as the content. *Pithy* and *poignant* are the key words in persuasive communication. Make it brief with emotion! Is there a public or private forum where it should be presented? Who will be there? Who else should be invited or know about the event? What materials should be presented (e.g., fact sheets, photos or videos of the conditions, testimonies of people directly affected, experts and influential people in the field)?

For example, several years ago, a director of a public health clinic helped create additional funding for dentistry for low-income adults. He launched a public awareness campaign showing enlarged photographs of decayed mouths of adults. He took them to many public forums in that community and then to the press. When asked the age and country of the people with this severe dental disease, no one could guess that they were New York City residents 20 to 40 years old. This created public sentiment for increasing coverage of preventive dental care for low-income populations.

PRINCIPLE 5: THE COMMUNITY IS NOT MONOLITHIC

In engaging in a change effort or trying to build the influence of your constituency, the organizer must pay attention to historic tensions, interpersonal conflicts and interorganizational as well as structural inequalities that prevent people from working together. This principle has to do with the way organizations and coalitions manage tensions that come from within.

The auspice and background of the organizer is critical. The relationship between organization that is leading the campaign (whether at a grassroots or coalition level) and the constituency it wishes to reach are the important factors. Is the organization trustworthy? Is there a track record of competency? The organizer is not a free agent. As you begin outreach, the reputation of the organization counts. Are the organization and organizer from the community or from outside? There are benefits and limitations to both. An inside organization has a track record and already has its allies and (most likely) detractors; an outside organization (e.g., a university, a foundation, a corporation) especially if it is mainstream and powerful, may or may not have a positive track record. A person with the same identity as the constituency may be accepted more easily, but an outside person with a different background may bring new ideas, connections, and a fresh perspective and may be able to bridge diverse groups.

If the aim is to build a diverse constituency or coalition, that is multicultural or includes segments of a community that have been excluded, additional thoughtfulness must be brought to the fore. Historic and current differences by class, race, gender, ethnicity, status, or sexual orientation have to be factored in from the beginning. Experience has shown the difficulty to include excluded groups after a process has begun. Consider the groundwork that has to be done on the way to the first meeting. Acknowledge and anticipate heightened sensitivities if new partners from different backgrounds are coming together for the first time, or if groups that distrust each other are returning to a new table.

PRINCIPLE 6: KNOW THE DECISION-MAKING STRUCTURES OF THE TARGET SYSTEM: THE FORMAL (AUTHORITY) AND INFORMAL (INFLUENCE) COMPONENTS. KNOW WHO THE CRITICAL AND FACILITATING ACTORS ARE

The task here is to understand the concept of power; which *body* (person) or *Body* (group, structure) can make the change you want. It is important to analyze the two faces of power—authority and influence. The "critical" actors are the actual legitimate decision makers, those with the sanctioned formal authority to grant the request, make the change, and allocate the resources. The facilitating actors are those who can influence the critical actors because of their relationship to them. Many times, people don't know who has the formal power because it is hidden, or the system is complicated. The best approach is to do a power analysis beforehand. Who are the people and organizations who control the systems you want to influence? For example, the authority in a hospital may be vested in the board of trustees and the medical boards. The department of health, which in most states has the authority to grant or suspend an operating license, has the ultimate power—although they may not readily use it. The authority to evict a tenant rests with a land-lord, but the local or state government may create regulations to curb their absolute power through regulations or the courts.

The formal system of authority is usually found on some version of an organizational chart. These are usually in the form of a diagram that shows the chain of command, that is, who reports to whom in the hierarchy, who controls certain activities, and to whom they are accountable internally. Don't be surprised if the organizational chart is difficult to obtain. Many organizations don't want to reveal the formal authority; they may conceal differences between those designated to make decisions and those who actually make them. Often, groups will be told that the organizational table is in transition.

Knowing someone's formal position can help decide the level of intervention in the system. If someone says they can't make a certain decision, you want to ascertain whether they are being accurate or "buck passing." It is essential to ask, "Who can make the change or grant the request?" The persons you approach inside the system may become a facilitating actor in the process of making change if they reveal their formal or informal relationship to the critical actor(s). There are many instances where organizers were at the wrong door.

There is also a need to know and use the informal structures of influence. Influence is that face of power acquired by people when they do not have the authority to make decisions. Clearly people are able to amass power to make change by virtue of being able to influence the decision-making bodies. There are many ways groups can be powerful when they can't command, "Just do it!" People have power through the positions they hold, their past history of action, longevity in a system, perceived effectiveness and expertise, connections to the decision makers, ability to control a large constituency, persistence, and willingness to take risks.

Organizing power by using strategies of influence is an essential skill set. Organizers use these strategies to bring pressure to bear on the structures of authority to convince them to make the needed changes, fund programs, reallocate resources, and so on. Different tactics will be needed for confronting public/government and private/corporate power. Depending on the issue, many changes can be made at lower levels in both public and private bureaucracies. It is not always necessary to go to the top.

PRINCIPLE 7: ASSUME NOBODY KNOWS ANYTHING, ANYTIME

This principle assumes, for political and strategic purposes, that those in charge are ignorant of the problem or need. Your first step is to define and document the need in a way that gives the decision makers a chance to respond, even if you believe that those in control already have the requisite information on which to act. Once you present the problem and possible solutions, the ball is in their court. If they really did not know the extent or seriousness of the problem, then this is a genuine opportunity to influence and negotiate change by presenting the necessary information and making a cogent argument as discussed in principle 4.

If they already knew about the problem but didn't act, they are more apt to respond when directly presented with the need. You have given them a chance to save face. In the best scenario, they will do something about the issue (i.e., clean up the park, fund a program, pass legislation, allocate staff time for an activity, etc.). In the worst scenario, they will delay or oppose the solution. If they don't respond, your group has greater legitimacy for moving ahead—from presenting additional information to using more intense persuasive and pressure tactics. Document all the steps taken in this process, and keep the relevant people, constituencies, and organizations informed.

PRINCIPLE 8: DO NOT ASSUME THAT THE SYSTEM YOU WANT TO INFLUENCE IS A UNIFIED, MONOLITHIC SYSTEM

Look for internal strains, divisions, and vulnerability. Seek friends and allies from within. Most organizations try to create a culture of unity; at the very least, they attempt to present a unified front to the public. However, that doesn't mean that there is unanimity among staff as to their positions, policies, or programs, especially in large bureaucracies. In analyzing the system you are trying to influence, it is essential to ascertain who on the inside of that system feels similarly about an issue as does your group/constituency? Those inside people can provide important pieces of information, including the identification of the critical and facilitating actors. They know about the organization's policies, procedures, and culture.

Conversely, those insiders may need your group for support, legitimacy, resources, and even pressure to do their job more effectively (see principle 12 if you are on "the inside"). The principle of exchange is pivotal. You provide them with the capacity to be more influential on the inside, and they help your group on the outside.

The expose of the conditions at Willowbrook State Institution for the Mentally Retarded in New York City in the early 1970s provides a case in point. It was the result of several years of professional staff and families trying to convince those in charge to improve the horrendous conditions. Many courageous social workers, resident psychiatrists, and other staff inside the institution clearly worked with advocacy and family groups on the outside by providing necessary information to media and government sources. When investigative reporter Geraldo Rivera turned his cameras on the site, it was because people on the inside obviously blew the whistle. There are also many cases where staff worked behind the scenes to convince the decision makers to improve conditions before the public became aware of the situation.

There is difficulty in exploiting the complexities or tensions with an agency or target system. Although this approach may rally people initially, it may also create difficulty in negotiating later on in the process. It also may prevent those on the inside from cooperating for fear of antagonizing their leaders and managers. The principle is to proceed cautiously and deliberately, allowing time for the people on the inside to persuade others of the need to grant the request or meet the demand as discussed in principle 9.

PRINCIPLE 9: ASSUME GOODWILL AND COMMON CAUSE ON THE PART OF THE WORKERS AND THOSE WHO RUN THE SYSTEM

This may seem to contradict principle 8, but in reality, both tensions have to be managed at the same time—both are truths. Line and support staff, professionals included, are usually loyal to their places of employment. Most people want to do a good job most of the time (based on the Y and human relations theories of management). The reasons for this are many. It may be because of the pride they take in their own work or because they understand the many obstacles impeding major changes. It could be their sense of vulnerability, their fears of being outspoken, or their uneasiness with proposed alternatives. They may have been coopted, or they may have made the system work for them.

Even if you uncover disillusionment, fears, or inertia among certain staff, caution must still be exercised in publicly criticizing the whole agency or system. Staff or clients may agree with the problems being raised; however, they do not automatically want those problems uncovered in public. Time and again, organizers have underestimated the sense of workers' and clients' feelings of hurt or anger at perceived attacks on their system. Even when the outside group attempts to separate or not blame all workers or supervisors equally, there may be resistance to change from those groups.

As noted in principle 6, it is vital to gauge the tacit or active support of at least some people on the inside and identify the extent of their loyalty. This will help you assess whether those in control of the institution/agency have the power to use a "we/they" division to create rifts between those on the outside and those on the inside. For example, when a neighborhood health organization began criticizing a local hospital for inadequate care, the organization's leaders assumed the hospital workers, most of whom were the same background or came from the same neighborhood, would join in their public meetings or issue a statement of support. Private conversations revealed that many staff were angered that no one had asked them their opinions on issues or strategies. A "divide and conquer" strategy ensued, with the hospital director firing the few sympathetic workers who joined with the health organization and promoting a few others who were then coopted. The rest of the staff remained silent. This came as a total surprise to the organization seeking change.

Therefore, your group should attempt to carefully frame the problem in consensus terms, at least initially, so it is not presented or perceived as a "win/lose" scenario (see principle 7). The goal can be stated in ways that recognize that everyone wants to, for example, help children, provide quality health care, have a clean environment, professionalize staff, and so on. Alternatively, the problem could be reframed so that your group conveys its understanding of the difficulties that

the agency/system has in meeting the needs of its clients or constituency. Demonstrate to the staff, the public, the clients, how the agency/system is interfering with or defeating its own goals or mission. Where possible, appeals should be made to self-interest as well as altruism. "It's good for you and good for the community!"

PRINCIPLE 10: ASSUME THE PRINCIPLE OF LEAST CONTEST. ESCALATE THE PROCESS ONLY AS NEEDED

Both to receive credibility and support, your group should not antagonize the targets prematurely or unnecessarily. Intervene just high enough to get job done. Strategies of influence exist on a continuum of social change tactics from consensus to contest. These range from presenting information in persuasive ways, to negotiation and bargaining processes, to offering incentives, to more conflictual tactics including threats (e.g., going to the media), to using social action strategies of mass mobilization, protest, resistance, and disruption.

In general, you should not begin with adversarial and confrontational tactics as per principle 7—give people a chance to change voluntarily. On the other hand, you cannot assume that information alone will be sufficient to produce major change. The strategic question to answer is: "What will it take to have the issue seriously addressed?" A well-thought-out response will determine the process and timing of moving from the least to the most conflictual strategies. The cogent questions are: "How long have you been waiting for change to occur? How long can you wait? What is your group prepared to do next? What is needed to move to the next step? What are the consequences of moving from one stage to next?"

This means that you need to build support for your effort, preferably before and not during a crisis. You don't want to alienate potential allies who are either on the inside or on the outside. You need to build credibility before your group goes above or around someone, exposes someone, and so on. It is essential to have factual information and engage in a democratic decision-making process with your group and its allies so that you cannot easily be isolated or proven wrong.

In intensifying and escalating the pressure on those with the authority, you must pay attention to ethical considerations, such as whether your constituency is informed about the tactics in which they are being asked to engage. If there is a chance of provocation or serious repercussions, participants should have the ability to make an informed choice, to the extent that the risks can be anticipated. Organizers can't promise their constituencies immunity from the consequences of their actions, for example, "Your landlord can't evict you" or "Your boss can't fire you." Even when this is legally correct, a person can still be harmed emotionally, financially, and even physically. Collectively, people need to know the consequences of moving from lawful protest to civil disobedience. This is especially important around tactics that have legal ramifications, for example, events that need police permits, trespassing laws, and so on. The principle should be one of no surprises!

PRINCIPLE 11: THERE WILL ALWAYS BE OPPOSITION TO CHANGE AT SOME LEVEL, BE IT ACTIVE OR PASSIVE RESISTANCE

It is essential to assume that some*body/Body* will be opposed to the change your group wants to make. You may hear such things as "It can't be done," "We've tried it before and it can't work," "We can't afford it," and so on. Always anticipate opposition and obstacles. Therefore, it is important to know the opposing side's arguments by playing out alternative responses to the problem and by testing the waters with the facilitating actors who can influence the decision makers. Analyze who may be opposed to the suggested solutions being offered and why they may be opposed.

Effective organizers will help develop strategies to counter or neutralize opposition where they can, as well as identify those elements in the change process that they or the group cannot control. They will also help identify all the allies and potential sources of support. In doing this, it is essential not to write off your potential allies, even if they have been adversaries on other issues. Short of those intense ideological battles where there is little room for compromise (e.g., abortion rights, affirmative action, etc.), appeals for support can be made to most sectors of society. Arguments may need to be different for different groups. You may appeal to such factors as reputation, pride, and professional expertise to gain or keep people on the side of change.

Sometimes the opposition is not always apparent because the implications of the change may not be visible until the change process is under way. Don't assume that all the opposition is external or conversely that it is being orchestrated from the target of change. Consider that communities are not monolithic. There may be as much division and difference within a community as between "the community" and the target of change (see principle 5). Sometimes the opposition may surface as inertia and inaction rather than visible and articulated differences.

To the extent possible, it is important to have one or more responses to anticipated resistance. For example, one tactic of the opposition is often to ask, "So how would you fix it?" or "What would you do if you were in charge?" Understand that groups engaged in social change are not obligated to come up with solutions. In a democratic society, citizens have the right to raise questions and hold those in charge accountable for outcomes. The latter have the authority, resources, and expertise to run the show. Your group has a right to point out that things aren't working and there must be a better way.

However, you are more likely to be credible and effective if you have thought through the arguments for why the current situation has to change and how it can be changed. If the response to your request is, "We don't have the funds," your group may be able to counter with "We know where you can get them" or "We know from where they can be taken." When the response is, "We can't do that," your group has to ask "Who says?" Ask for the written policies, which may or may not exist.

Another tactic of the opposition is to divide and conquer or discredit a group. This has happened when organized groups left out of the decision-making process began to challenge the authority of those in control. Those in charge may question your credibility and representativeness. Again, any individual or group in a democracy can challenge the government, but also be prepared for repercussions.

Behind closed doors, it is important to identify who your spokespeople will be and what message you want to convey even if you can't always control all the events. Establishing some procedures and protocols in advance is essential. It is always helpful to have some counterexpertise, meaning trustworthy allies and supporters who have the professional knowledge or political experience to challenge the opposition on its own terms.

Your group must come to agreement on the following: Is your group willing to negotiate? What is the bottom line? What happens if they say no? What happens if they say yes? What happens if they ask your group to come up with a proposal or to join a task force? There is no one right or wrong answer, except the principle of anticipating opposition and being prepared for differential outcomes.

PRINCIPLE 12: IF YOU TRY TO MAKE CHANGE FROM THE INSIDE, ASSESS RISKS REALISTICALLY—IDENTIFY AND WEIGH COSTS AGAINST GAINS

You can engage in major change from within your own system or agency, if you strategically assess your role. By being on the inside, you already have a foot in the door. You have the legitimacy to ask for and obtain information; you know who makes decisions and how the system really works, that is, its informal as well as formal structure. You know the history of past efforts to engage in change, and most important, you have some credibility, longevity, and allies within that structure. Working to improve an organization from within is not disloyal. It may be the only ethical course to pursue.

Nevertheless, it is essential to play out for yourself and with your constituents the generic question: "What's the worst that can happen if . . . ?" You have to ascertain the support you have to minimize your isolation or ostracism. There are times when hard choices have to be made as to how far to take a social change project. To determine the type and extent of action to be undertaken, you should consider pragmatic things, such as feasibility of success, and factors such as the seriousness and pervasiveness of the situation. Is there an imperative to act? Is there a sense of urgency? Is the timing right? Is there a window of opportunity?

There will be some risk to every action taken. It is important to anticipate actual or perceived repercussions (as per principle 11) from peers, line or support staff, supervisors, managers, and clients on the inside. Therefore, if a major change that affects a department or the whole agency is needed, or if the required action includes an implied criticism of your agency or system, you must employ principles 7, 8, and 9. Consider that there is a long continuum from doing nothing to getting fired.

The importance of keeping your own house in order cannot be stressed enough. Rarely will you be sanctioned for your organizing activities directly. You are more likely to be called to task for not doing your paid job. Pay attention and don't be caught off-guard. People are reprimanded for not turning in reports on time, leaving early, not following up. To minimize any criticism directed at you for trying to improve a service, change a policy, or have an employee removed from a position, you should take on additional responsibilities. Become an exemplar in your position. Demonstrate your value to your employer and the clients.

If you are working with people on the inside, it is essential neither to overpromise protection nor to underestimate repercussions. Organizers can never assert that nothing untoward will happen to those participating in a change process. On the other hand, it is essential to uncover any perceived fears, even if not grounded in reality, so they can be addressed by you or the group. People are often caught short when they haven't thought through principle 11.

PRINCIPLE 13: NOTE TAKING AND RECORDKEEPING IN GENERAL ARE POLITICAL, NOT CLERICAL FUNCTIONS

If information is power, than obtaining and recording information is a political process. The persons or group in charge of those processes may be the most powerful ones in that organization. Although what and how records are kept should be a group decision, experienced organizers always want to be involved in that process.

Documentation includes taking minutes, corresponding with people, recording actions and inactions, keeping people on track and reminding people of past decisions through letters, memos, e-mail, and written records. Taking minutes is a skill, a value, and a process. It helps gauge and set the tone for the way a group makes decisions as well as what decisions were made. Documents are accountability tools; they help keep processes and outcomes transparent and keep the people involved, focused, and honest. They also provide a historical account, preserving the institutional memory.

Indeed, you can assess the seriousness, effectiveness, and cohesiveness of a group/organization by whether minutes are taken and reviewed and how people are engaged in their production and review. Experience has demonstrated that if there are no minutes of a meeting or group process, chances are nothing will change. Experience has also shown that those in charge (the critical actors) will often resist formal recording of minutes. Those seeking the change must create a paper trail that includes agreements and timetables.

Minutes can be a diagnostic tool to assess an organization's culture, structure and history. When organizations spend an inordinate amount of time refuting minutes, you can infer that they have a lot of distrust and an inability to move ahead. When minutes are pro forma without much attention paid to them, you can infer an organization without much investment or involvement of its participants.

If possible, at least two people should attend all important meetings or be conferenced in. It is important to prepare someone in the group to take notes of strategic meetings, regardless of whether the person in charge agrees to have notes taken. After an event or a meeting, the leader or spokesperson of the group should write a letter or send an e-mail thanking them and stating your understanding of what took place and what was agreed to. Highlight any disagreements and next steps. The same thing applies with strategic phone calls. It should not be surprising that there are memory lapses (intentional or not) and different interpretations with regard to issues addressed, and promises made. Without a record, there will be little or no progress.

PRINCIPLE 14: THE MEDIA ARE UNPREDICTABLE AND APOLITICAL. PROCEED WITH CAUTION

Given the variety of media today—electronic media, blast e-mails and faxes, and the more traditional print media (newspapers, magazines, mainstream and alternative presses), plus TV (network, cable, public), and radio—the organizer needs to know the basic tools and something about these various outlets. For long-term campaigns or for controversial issues, your group may need to retain a media consultant for a fee or on voluntary basis.

As part of an outreach campaign, first identify whom you want to reach and then decide how they are best reached. You need to know how they receive their information. What mass media do they use? What ethnic and community media are there? Do they use the Internet?

Second, identify and cultivate a person in each of those outlets used (*outlet* is a generic term for all the different types of media). Who writes or talks about your topic or issue? Be proactive with them. Call them often. Send them materials about your organization. Invite the outlet to your site and ask them to meet with your constituency. Become their expert on the issue.

Community and ethnic newspapers and radio and even cable TV are more accessible than mainstream media and may be of great value for certain stories. Research has shown that letters to the editor are the second most read section of a newspaper (after sports) and are highly read in magazines as well. It may be difficult to get an article into the *New York Times* or a story on national network TV, but there are hundreds of smaller outlets in your community.

How do you craft a message so that the media will want to publish or cover the issue? How do you convey your story in compelling ways? At this juncture, organizers and most media part ways. Organizers (social workers, human rights and social justice advocates) want to publicize stories that are serious and pervasive. The story you want told probably involves many people who are in that circumstance, for example, who are suffering from what the government or a corporate body is doing—or not doing—to them. The target of change may be providing inadequate or denying services, they may be cutting back on opportunities and pathways, limiting resources, and so on. You usually want to show universality and document the numbers of people affected.

Most media on the contrary want to show just the opposite. They cover the unusual, the bizarre, and the extreme. If there are thousands of people collecting an inadequate amount of public assistance, or if the child welfare system discriminates against parents of color, they will feature the "welfare queen" or the one tragic case of major child abuse. Journalists, regardless of whether they are liberal or conservative, whether the outlet is a tabloid or an intellectual magazine, don't generally portray the usual or typical. They don't cover the good news. They are prone to exaggeration and hyperbole; they like to cover conflicts and dissension. The slant is usually toward the sensational.

Therefore, the organizing principle when the media comes knocking is that you cannot control the outcome. Chances are they won't cover the story the way you want them to. So the decision your group must make is whether to reach out to the media and make every effort to educate them in advance where possible. It helps to provide succinct background material that is a quick read but substantive at the same time.

The media have the same biases as other institutions in our society. They usually reflect rather than lead a community. There are many examples of media coverage that reflect institutional inequalities. They will generally focus on the professional rather than on the client or recipient. They will seek out males more than females; they will gravitate more to the white (or majority) people than the people of color. Therefore, practically speaking, if you want to downplay those disparities and to assure a unified and accurate message, prepare spokespersons in advance. Agree to channel the media to designated people and provide everyone with a few sound bites, should they be asked. If relevant, try to pair professional and indigenous leaders so that new and undervalued (by the media) voices are up front and visible. Learn to handle the pressure and avoid the seduction of instant celebrity.

If the coverage you received portrays the story differently from what you wanted, write a letter to the editor and to the author and publisher or owner of the outlet. Let your own constituency and allies know what you attempted to convey. Don't be disillusioned with the outcome.

CONCLUSION

These principles are meant as guides to action and will apply differentially, depending on the auspices of your agency, the goals identified, the political and economic context of the community, issue, and the system driving the organizing. Organizers cannot control all the variables, but acquiring these competencies along with your commitment to the long haul go a long way. Remember the three H's: humanity, humility, and humor.

WEB SITES

Association for Community Organization and Social Administration. http://www.acosa.com.
Community Organizing Toolbox. http://www.nfg.org/cotb.

Education Center for Community Organizing. http://www.hunter.cuny.edu/socwork/ecco.
On-Line Conference of Community Organizing and Development. http://www.comm-org.wisc.edu.

Resources

Bobo, K., Kendall, J., & Max, S. (2001). *Organizing for social change: Midwest academy manual for activists*, 3rd ed. Santa Ana, CA: Seven Locks Press.

Eichler, M. (2007). *Consensus organizing: Building communities of mutual self interest.* Thousand Oaks, CA: Sage.

Getsos, P., & Minieri, J. (2007). *Tools for radical democracy; how to organize for power in your community.* San Francisco, CA: Jossey-Bass.

Kirst-Ashman, K. K., & Hull, G. H. (2006). *Generalist practice with organizations and communities*, 2nd ed. Belmont, CA: Thomson Brooks/Cole.

Hardcastle, D. A., & Powers, P. R., with Wenocur, S. (2004). *Community practice: Theories and skills for social workers*, 2nd ed. New York: Oxford University Press.

Homan, M. S. (2008). *Promoting community change: Making it happen in the real world*, 4th ed. Belmont, CA: Thomson Brooks/Cole.

McNutt, J. G., & Hick, S. F. (Eds.). (2002). *Advocacy, activism, and the Internet: Community organization and social policy*. Chicago: Lyceum Books.

Netting, F. E., Kettner, P. M., & McMurtry, S. L. (2008). *Social work macro practice*, 4th ed. Boston: A&B/Pearson.

Rivera, F. G., & Ehrlich, J. L. (Eds.). (1998). *Community organizing in a diverse society*, 3rd ed. Boston: Pearson/Allyn & Bacon.

Rothman, J., Erlich, J., & Tropman, J. (Eds.). (2001a). *Strategies of community intervention*, 6th ed. Itasca, IL: F.E. Peacock.

Rothman, J., Erlich, J., & Tropman, J. (Eds.). (2001b). *Tactics and techniques of community intervention*, 4th ed. Belmont, CA: Thomson Brooks/Cole.

Rubin, H. J., & Rubin, I. S. (2007). *Community organizing and development*, 4th ed. Boston: Pearson/Allyn & Bacon.

Sen, R. (2003). *Stir it up: Lessons in community organizing and advocacy*. San Francisco, CA: Jossey-Bass.

Smock, K. (2004). *Democracy in action: Community organizing and urban change*. New York: Columbia University Press.

Staples, L. (2004). *Roots to power: A manual for grassroots organizing*, 2nd ed. Westport, CT: Praeger.

Weil, M. O., & Reisch, M. (Eds.). (2005). *Handbook of community practice*. Thousand Oaks, CA: Sage.

129 Community Practice Model for the Twenty-First Century

Marie Overby Weil & Dorothy N. Gamble

Throughout the history of social work, community practice has been a major method embodying the profession's empowerment tradition and social justice values (NASW, 1996; Simon, 1994). With the complexities of current societies; rapid technological, social, and economic change; and the globalization of trade and communication, community practice at local, regional, national, and international levels is an even more essential element to revitalize democracy in the United States and encourage democratic societies internationally to build and nurture inclusive, supportive, nonracist, and nonsexist communities and institutions. Societies across the world are becoming more multicultural, and globally there are now more internally displaced persons than at any previous time. With these global changes and the realities of both internal and cross-national conflicts, protection of human rights, particularly the rights of women and girls, becomes increasingly critical in efforts to build and maintain socially just communities. Political divides in the early decades of the twenty-first century revolve not only around differing conceptions of national common good but around the different paths to and conceptions of the common good in international and global terms. Building on the long evolution of citizenship and individual liberty, Dahl argues that the third transformation of democracy would ensure self-government, safeguard individual and group rights, protect the vulnerable, strengthen democratic process, and increase citizen knowledge of the political economy to democratize and connect social and economic development and build accountability in our larger institutions (Dahl, 1989). The moral, political, and economic equation for human development requires an understanding of global social and economic interdependence. Vandana Shiva describes the "Declaration of Interdependence," sponsored by the Democracy Collaborative, as growing from the recogni-

tion that "we are earth citizens and have earth identities which are both the particular identity of place, and the global planetary identity. As members of communities, we have multiple community identities. . . . These diverse, multiple identities shape our sense of self and who we are. And these diversities are not inconsistent with our common humanity. Without diversity, we have no humanity" (2005, p. 142). These issues of democratic revitalization and transformation are the central purview of community practice in all its forms; the skills and knowledge for building and rebuilding community are critical for those who work to achieve positive and sustainable development and pluralistic, multicultural societies in a global economy.

Community practice encompasses a broad scope, ranging from grassroots organization and development to human services planning and coordination. It employs multiple methods of empowerment-based interventions to strengthen participation in democratic processes, reform human service systems, and assist groups and communities in advancing their concerns and organizing for social justice. This chapter presents community practice models that are widely identifiable in interventions employed in the early decades of the twenty-first century. They are rooted in traditions evolving from the settlement house movement, the charity organization society movement, the rural development movement, and the organizing and development histories of diverse ethnic and racial groups (Betten & Austin, 1990; Rivera & Erlich, 1998).

MODELS OF COMMUNITY PRACTICE FOR THE TWENTY-FIRST CENTURY

Eight basic models of community practice are described here. They illustrate approaches in wide use in many parts of the world that are expected to persist. Community practice efforts focus primarily on the following general purposes.

Community Practice Purposes

- *Improving the quality of life.* Refers to work responding to basic human needs, such as food and shelter, security, opportunities for education and basic health, freedom from violence, opportunities to organize in free spaces, and participate in goals and decisions that will affect one's life, as well as the lives of one's family and community members. Examples include securing a railroad crossing gate in a rural community, devising strategies to improve education and opportunities for marginalized youth, and even the design and implementation of global strategies for sustainable development.
- *Advocacy.* Involves doing research to determine what structures and behaviors limit people and their communities from reaching their full potential, then following up by working with people who wish to diminish the barriers or expand the opportunities for healthy development by planning purposive change activities. Examples are lobbying for improved services for children with severe emotional or behavioral problems; campaigning for human rights for women, working for rights of GLBT groups, homeless people, and others who are deprived of basic rights; or passing legislation to fund minority group economic development projects through such structures as the Community Reinvestment Act.
- *Human social and economic development.* Involves any improvements in communities that can expand and improve people's livelihoods. Livelihoods are both the paid and unpaid work that people do to either gain income or nurture families and communities. Examples include facilitating the establishment of a local farmers' or artists' cooperative, strengthening the social supports of families and communities through grassroots leadership and teamwork training, organizing for municipalities to pass a living wage law, and even global efforts such as the establishment of the Millennium Development Goals.
- *Service and program planning.* Involves the assessment of needs for a whole community or specific populations and the development of plans, resources, and structures to meet those needs. Services, for example, may be modified, reorganized or relocated to respond to a newly recognized need or an emerging population. New services must be designed, for example, to respond to emerging needs of HIV/AIDS orphans, former child soldiers, homeless adolescents, and people living to be 95 or 100 years of age or older.
- *Service integration.* Involves establishing a range of services and linking them so that a continuum of care is in place for the broad needs of community members. Examples include building the continuum of family support, preservation, and child welfare services; establishing a network of well-connected services for both healthy and frail senior citizens; or providing food, protection, relocation opportunities, and services for new starts for refugees and internally displaced persons from international or national conflicts.
- *Political and social action.* Involves engagement in the political process to change existing policies, establish new progressive legislation, or change policy makers. Activity in political and social action is direct, open, and nonviolent. It requires free spaces in which people can gather, organize, and speak out, especially those who have been excluded from political involvement in the past. Political and social action seeks to foster institutional change for inclusion and equity, and increase participatory democracy and equality of opportunity in local, regional, and international institutions. Organizing for the rights, protection, and welfare of children by the Children's Defense Fund and Amnesty International's efforts to prevent torture and secure release of political prisoners worldwide are examples of political and social action that is not partisan.
- *Social justice.* Involves building toward human equality and opportunity across race, ethnicity, gender, and nationality. Examples are working to insure basic education for girls in all countries, full political participation for women, making reparations to Japanese Americans for internment during World War II, and building the fabric of civil and human rights laws both nationally and globally.

The value base of community practice not only respects the dignity of the individual but also focuses on the interdependence of families and communities and the development of legislative, political, and distributive justice. Community practitioners work with competing views of issues using multiple strategies to solve problems that inevitably arise within and among diverse groups in communities. America's reality as a pluralistic society where communities of color are still struggling for inclusion increases the need for skilled multicultural organizing and development of multicultural human service organizations (Gutierrez, Lewis, Nagda, Wernick, & Shore, 2005). The eight models depicted in Table 129.1 are analyzed in terms of outcome, change targets, constituencies, scope of concern, and primary social work roles through lenses of globalization, human rights, and multiculturalism (Gamble & Weil, 2008). Though the models are described as particular entities in the chart for analytic clarity, elements of the models are often observed in interaction—being mixed or phased as organizations and groups respond to new challenges or shifts in the environment (Rothman, Erlich, & Tropman, 2008).

Neighborhood and Community Organizing

Much of community organizing still depends on the face-to-face opportunities available to people in geographic proximity, such as a neighborhood, rural community, parish, or county. This model of community practice has a focus on activities that will increase the leadership, planning, and organization-building skills of ordinary people to help them develop power at the neighborhood or village level and increase community well-being. It is the bedrock of democratic institutions. When people at the grass roots of society can learn how to organize their efforts, be inclusive in their organization building, engage in democratic decision making, set priorities, access resources, and reach their goals, they have learned basic lessons of democracy. Increasing their capacity to work on basic community problems makes it possible for citizens to change conditions to improve the quality of life for all residents. This model of community practice can be seen in a variety of forms across the globe, in the democracies that have been working at neighborhood organizing for hundreds of years yet still tend to exclude the most vulnerable groups in society, as well as in the newly emerging democracies of Eastern Europe, Africa, Asia, and South America.

Neighborhood and community organizing has the dual focus of building the capacity of individuals to lead and organize while at the same time accomplishing a task that will enhance the quality of life for the geographic area. Elements of this model are found in any setting in which people who live in close proximity come together to create needed change. One example is the Center for Community Action in Lumberton, North Carolina, which combines community learning and action on social, economic, political, multicultural, environmental, intergenerational, spiritual, and moral issues. Others include Project MASH (Make Something Happen) in the Stowe Village Housing Project of Hartford, engaged in community organizing as well as job and service development; COPS of San Antonio, which has a focus on broad-based community development; and CARE (Community and Resource Exchange) of Minneapolis and Hennepin County, Minnesota, established to fight drugs and crime.

Organizing Functional Communities

The essence of this model is its focus on communities of interest—functional communities—rather than geographic. The focus in organizing communities of interest is advocacy for social justice and policy change to promote acceptance and inclusion of the chosen issue. In their efforts toward social justice, functional communities also seek to change general attitudes and behaviors and may develop services for their specific population that have not been adequately addressed in the mainstream service system. Examples are development of service systems for women, evolving from feminist organizing, consisting of rape crisis centers and domestic violence programs, and more recently expanding to deal with women's employment and economic development issues. Functional communities typically engage in community education, as is illustrated in the gay and lesbian community's work to educate others about AIDS and to press for appropriate health care, supportive health policy, and social, economic, and civil rights of people who are HIV-positive.

As functional communities organize, build internal capacity, and conduct research about their issues, members may move from mutual support to become strong advocates and leaders, as have parents of children with severe emotional disturbances in the Alliance for Mentally Ill Children and Adolescents and people working against toxic waste sites.

TABLE 129.1 Models of Community Practice in Twenty-First Century Contexts

Comparative Characteristics	Neighborhood & Community Organizing	Organizing Functional Communities	Social, Economic, & Sustainable Development	Program Development & Community Liaison	Social Planning	Coalitions	Political & Social Action	Movements for Progressive Change
Desired outcome	Develop capacity of members to organize; direct and/or moderate the impact of regional planning and external development	Action for social justice focused on advocacy and on changing behaviors and attitudes; may also provide service	Initiate development plans from a grassroots perspective; prepare citizens to make use of social and economic investments; open livelihood opportunities	Expansion or redirection of agency program to improve community service effectiveness; organize new service	Neighborhood, citywide or regional proposals for action by (a) neighborhood groups; (b) elected body; and/or (c) planning councils	Build a multi-organizational power base large enough to influence program direction and/or draw down resources	Action for social justice focused on changing policies or policy makers	Action for social, economic and environmental justice that provides new paradigms for the healthy development of people and the planet
Systems targeted for change	Municipal/regional government; external developers; local leadership	General public; government institutions	Banks; foundations; external developers; laws that govern wealth creation	Financial donors and volunteers to programs; beneficiaries of agency services	Perspectives of (a) neighborhood planning groups; (b) elected leaders; (c) human services leaders	Elected officials; foundations; government institutions	Voting public; elected officials; inactive/potential participants in public debates and elections	General public; political, social, and economic systems; livelihood opportunities
Primary constituency	Residents of neighborhood, parish, rural community, village	Like-minded people in a community, region, nation, or across the globe	Low-wealth, marginalized, or oppressed population groups in a city or region	Agency board and administrators; community representatives	(a) neighborhood groups; (b) elected leaders; (c) social agencies and interagency organizations	Organizations and citizens that have a stake in the particular issue	Citizens in a particular political jurisdiction	Leaders, citizens, and organizations able to create new visions and social structures

Continued

TABLE 129.1 Models of Community Practice in Twenty-First Century Contexts (*continued*)

Comparative Characteristics	Neighborhood & Community Organizing	Organizing Functional Communities	Social, Economic, & Sustainable Development	Program Development & Community Liaison	Social Planning	Coalitions	Political & Social Action	Movements for Progressive Change
Scope of concern	Quality of life in geographic area; increased ability of grassroots leaders and organizations to improve social, economic, and environmental conditions	Advocacy for particular issue or population (examples: environmental protection; women's participation in decision making)	Income, asset, and social support development; improved basic education and leadership skills; access to capital and "green" livelihoods	Service development for a specific population (examples: children's access to health care; security against domestic violence)	(a) neighborhood-level planning; (b) integration of social, economic, and environmental needs into public planning arena; (c) human services coordination	Specified issue related to social need or concern (examples: concern for access to HIV/AIDS medications; prison reform)	Building the level of participation in political activity; ensuring that elections are fair and not controlled by wealth	Social, economic, and environmental justice within society (examples: basic human needs; basic human rights)
Social work/community practice roles	Organizer Facilitator Educator Coach Trainer Bridge Builder	Organizer Advocate Writer/Speaker Facilitator	Negotiator Bridge builder Promoter Planner, educator Manager Researcher Evaluator	Spokesperson Planner/evaluator Manager/director Proposal writer Trainer Boundary spanner Visionary	Researcher Proposal writer Communicator Planner Manager Evaluator	Mediator Negotiator Spokesperson Organizer Bridge builder Leader	Advocate Organizer Researcher Candidate Leader	Advocate Facilitator Leader

Increase of multicultural societies worldwide ↔ Globalization ↔ Expansion of rights for women & human rights.

Source: Adapted from Gamble, & Well, 2008.

Examples of functional communities include the ARC, which functions in many localities and as a national group to improve services and advocate for the rights of children and adults with developmental disabilities; environmental organizations; and groups such as Amnesty International, which documents human rights violations and seeks protection and justice for political prisoners worldwide through local advocacy groups.

Social, Economic, and Sustainable Development

Providing opportunities for people to increase their social and economic security has been a central focus of social work. To be effective, social and economic development projects must work together within a context of sustainable development. Development efforts are currently framed under four rubrics:

- basic *human development*, the focus of the United Nations Human Development Index, which measures progress using a composite focused on life expectancy at birth, knowledge (based on literacy rate and school enrollment), and adjusted per capita income in purchasing power parity (UNDP, 1999, pp. 159–160);
- *social development*, focused on basic life skills and livelihood education (especially for the poor), promotion of gender equality, and most critically short-term amelioration and long-term eradication of poverty through policy investments in marginalized groups and communities, expanding their capacities, building social capital, and providing programs that can improve well-being and create economic opportunity (Hall & Midgley, 2004);
- *economic development* that invests in meeting human needs and building adequate incomes and assets by employing empowerment strategies to move families and communities out of absolute poverty (Friedmann, 1992); and
- the newer and critical concept, *sustainable development*, described in the 1987 report of the World Commission on Environment and Development as "development that meets the needs of the present without compromising the ability of future generations to meet their own needs" (p. 43). Sustainable development encompasses social

and economic development that restores and protects the natural environment (Estes, 1993; Hart, 1999).

Historically, many community development programs have focused on either economic development or social capacity building. In recent years, there has been a growing focus on integrated development strategies to move people out of poverty through combined human capacity building, popular education, and locally controlled economic development. Some recent programs are targeted to build personal assets. Individual development accounts (IDAs) and individual training accounts (ITAs) are local, statewide, and national programs that match the savings of a low-wealth person who is saving for a training or educational program, the startup of a small business, or the purchase of a home. IDAs and ITAs are seen as individual ladders to help people climb out of poverty (Schreiner et al., 2001). Coupled with other workforce strategies, they may be especially helpful to those people who have been on the poverty borderline for many years. Though individuals need these kinds of programs to be able to develop creative entrepreneurial skills, individual strategies are insufficient without companion programs that focus on broader social and economic barriers to development.

Community development corporations, of which there are thousands across the United States, often combine efforts to change the community by decreasing barriers to economic and social resources (e.g., Bethel New Life). These corporations often combine increasing the availability of resources to broad groups of people in the community (e.g., community reinvestment funds and community development block grants) with individual training to help people take advantage of such resources (e.g., home buyers' clubs and microenterprise loan circles) and with increased social and economic infrastructure (e.g., increasing affordable housing stocks, developing health clinics, day care, and after-school enrichment programs). In this strategy, it is not just the individual who is changing; it is the whole landscape of the community that is changing with visible infrastructure and options for social support and economic advancement.

Program Development and Community Liaison

Community liaison is an integral aspect of program development. The central goal and desired outcome of this model is to design and implement a new or improved service that has been assessed as needed by a community or population. It engages agency staff in planning with community representatives and clients or potential consumers for expansion or redirection of agency programs to improve service effectiveness. The interaction of community and service programs can be strengthened with the involvement of potential consumers and citizens in the needs assessment process, utilization of focus groups, development of advisory bodies, and involvement of potential consumers and community leaders in policy-making boards. As a program is designed and implemented, mechanisms for feedback to and from the community are valuable in keeping new programs on target. Although new services are designed to serve vulnerable populations more effectively, program designers, coordinators, staff, and board members will also gain new perspectives as they are able to develop effective mutual planning strategies with community members.

The scope of concern is service development for a particular population or geographic area and a better partnership between an agency and the communities it serves. In early stages, workers take on roles as planners, proposal writers, spokespersons, or mediators and become facilitators in the interaction process with constituent community groups and external supporters. As a program becomes established, workers often take on roles as managers, monitors, and evaluators to ensure that the program stays on track, meets its goals for service, and remains responsive to the community and changing environment. Increasingly, service and system reform efforts emphasize the ongoing responsibility to be "learning organizations" and to "learn for sustainability" (Senge, Laur, Schley, & Smith, 2006). The intensive work to develop the family preservation and support models of the Children's Bureau of Los Angeles presents one example of this model that stressed development of strong outcome evaluations of new programs (McCroskey & Meezan, 1992).

Social Planning

Social planning can operate at a range of levels: community, agency, coalition, elected body, or governmental bureau, and with a neighborhood, village, city, county, regional, national, or international focus. This method of practice strengthens neighborhoods or larger areas through community renewal combining social and economic development, building housing and community infrastructure, and coordinating social services and community programs. Traditionally, it is known for using rational problem-solving approaches and increasingly incorporates grassroots groups, citizens groups, and a broader range of community voices in participatory planning (Weil, 2005). Current examples include the planning and development in the Dudley Street area of Boston (Medoff & Sklar, 1994), reemergence of local planning councils in Kansas, Florida, and Massachusetts; area agencies on aging; specialized funding federations, such as Women's Way or United Black Fund; community action agencies; community mental health boards; and human resource commissions.

Because planners engage with such a wide variety of individuals and groups, they need excellent communication, facilitation, and management skills, as well as technical skills in research, needs assessments, participatory planning, evaluation, and proposal development. Planners increasingly organize community meetings to gather ideas and educate the public about directions for services and development. They engage community leaders in effective development strategies for fundraising, evaluation, and modification of programs. Significant efforts to open up planning processes, including strong consumer and community participation, are becoming the norm. The Our Children Today and Tomorrow planning project in western North Carolina, for example, engaged parents and children intensively in its 3-year process to plan appropriate and family-friendly services for children.

In a major metropolitan area, the Phoenix Futures Forum offered a broad-based long-range planning and community-building process that involved hundreds of residents during a period of rapid population and economic growth. It focused on outcomes of 21 major new initiatives and eventual involvement of many forum participants on city boards and commissions (Plotz, 1992).

Increasingly, planners are making use of conceptual models that can help them encompass the broad social, natural, and economic resources available to any community setting. For example, the Aspen Institute provides a community planning workbook that incorporates the strengths of planning strategies with economic development, building civic capacity and stewardship of natural and cultural resources. Community groups making use of this kind of guide can find an accessible path to more comprehensive planning, emphasizing more inclusive participation. In addition, the work of Castelloe (1999) creates an integrated model of community change that can guide planners through a theoretical framework incorporating the characteristics and processes that could lead to community improvement and away from community deterioration over time. These kinds of conceptual tools are essential to social planning efforts.

Coalitions

Coalitions make it possible for separate groups to work together for collective social change. As defined by Mizrahi and Rosenthal, a "social change coalition is: a group of diverse organizational representatives who join forces to influence external institutions on one or more issues affecting their constituencies while maintaining their own autonomy" (1993, p. 14). They describe coalitions as having a time-limited life span that is typically filled with dynamic tensions resulting from the simultaneous demands on organizational representatives to remain autonomous while at the same time building a new organization from the compatible interests of the diverse members. Increasingly, some coalitions establish themselves as long-term organizations, such as the Coalition for the Homeless in Los Angeles and the Domestic Violence Coalitions located in many states dedicated to assisting women and ending family violence.

The desired outcome for social-change coalitions is to build multiorganizational power bases large enough to influence social program direction, with the potential to garner resources to respond to the common interests of the coalition. Elected officials are often the systems targeted for change as citizens press for more favorable policies. Government institutions that may have the authority to respond to a particular social concern, but not the readiness to do so, are also the targets of coalitions' advocacy, education, and action strategies.

Coalition building typically requires a major time commitment; for this reason, only organizations that have a stake in the particular issues will engage in longer term involvement. Examples of coalitions found in many communities are those organized for affordable housing, against the increase in teen pregnancy and teen violence, for service programs for the elderly, and for environmentally safe economic development. A coalition of major human service, child advocacy, and professional groups have successfully lobbied for federal support for family-centered, community-based services over the past two decades. This coalition with leadership from the Children's Defense Fund, Child Welfare League, Family Impact Seminar, and NASW, among others, successfully lobbied for implementation of the 1993 Family Support Act (P.L. 103-66). Coalitions for the homeless have been successful in many urban areas in establishing shelters and services, and some are also concerned with development of low-income housing. To stay together, coalitions develop complex exchange relations and find ways to balance their commitment to the issues that hold them together with the individual agendas and perspectives of member organizations (Roberts-DeGennaro & Mizrahi, 2005). Mattessich, Murray-Close, Monsey, and Wilder Research Center (2001) have analyzed 40 studies of collaboration and identified six major domains and related factors that contribute to establishing and maintaining successful collaborations: positive environment, cooperative membership, flexible processes and structures, effective communication, shared purpose, and sufficient resources.

Social workers are likely to be leaders and spokespersons in human service coalitions, using mediation and negotiation skills to balance internal tensions and maintain the coalition's focus. In coalitions of advocacy groups focused on alternative services, such as coalitions against domestic violence, social workers will also have roles that emphasize group and interorganizational facilitation, teaching and coaching, leadership development, conflict negotiation, and skills in organizational relations and planning.

Political and Social Action

This model embodies action for social, political, or economic justice with a focus on changing the agenda of policy makers, changing policies, or changing policy makers. When public agendas and policy directions become so skewed as to cause harm and decrease opportunities for human development, political and social action becomes the means to redress wrongs and put forward a progressive agenda. Social and political action campaigns conduct research and document a problem, select a target and change strategy, generate the power to effect a solution, and use effective communication and direct action to implement promised changes.

Social action seeks progressive change through building powerful local community organizations that can counter the status quo with a visible agenda and a critical mass of people advocating openly for change. Social and political action efforts can change the power relations in a larger community, make people aware of their own power through consciousness raising and group solidarity, and engender personal changes so that people recognize and use their own power more effectively. Collective action can stimulate a sense of community and activate community power.

Political and social action can begin small, as did the exploration of problems at Love Canal, and grow as that effort did to become a national citizens' environmental protection organization. Members of Appalachian communities who had participated in training at the Highlander Center undertook major investigative research to document the toxic waste being dumped illegally in their county, causing the waste dump to be closed (*You Got to Move*, 2008).

Social action organizations may join with other local groups or form coalitions that can apply pressure at national levels. For example, ACORN (Association of Community Organizations for Reform Now) has developed housing and worked with other local and national organizations to end redlining by banks and guide negotiated community reinvestment strategies to provide loans in low-income neighborhoods. In the South, black farmers have been involved in long legislative struggles to rectify discrimination in federal loan procedures, and across the nation many organizations have been involved in "living wage," "school reform," voter registration, and civic participation efforts.

The goal of progressive social and political action is to shift the balance of power so that those who have been excluded in earlier decision-making processes become players in future decisions. This goal is grounded in processes for strengthening participatory democracy and building social justice. The surge of civil society across the globe is a growing phenomenon that is being recognized as an important force by governments, international economic organizations, and multinational corporations (Hawken, 2007; Shiva, 2005). Social workers can help facilitate the development of civil society in newly independent nations as well as older democracies.

Movements for Progressive Change

Progressive social movements have occurred when large groups seek to change harmful social and environmental conditions. Wood and Jackson define social movements as groups "that attempt to produce or prevent radical or reformist types of change" (1982, p. 3). Social movements promote action for social change that provides a new paradigm for the way we respond to a particular population group or social issue. The systems targeted for change are the general public and especially political systems. The abolitionist movement in the United Kingdom is credited with being the earliest mass movement for human rights; to be progressive, movements must support both human rights and social justice. In the United States, the civil rights movement is perhaps the best known and most far-reaching example of a social movement; it created conditions and expectations that fostered civil and social rights work in La Raza, the women's movement, and the later disabilities rights movement (MacNair, Fowler, & Harris, 2000). New paradigms related to these groups emerged with the success of the movements. Both legislation and attitudes have begun to focus more on abilities than disabilities; women increasingly exercise equal rights and move into leadership positions. Although racism and prejudice have not disappeared, Latinos, African Americans, and Native Americans have established civil rights and continue to work toward social and economic equality. In social movements, social work roles are typically those of advocate and facilitator. Social workers, in keeping with the values of the profession, will be allied with social movements that support democracy, individual dignity, the rights of minorities, the needs of the poor, sustainable development, and the broad goals of human development and liberation.

Social movements often occur when protest erupts as the result of intensifying oppression or when great and inequitable changes in the political or social system occur. Localized protests may call attention to widespread oppression; when those protests engender widespread support and mass empathy, a social movement emerges. Piven and Cloward analyzed four different American social movements and conclude that "both the limitations and opportunities for mass protest are shaped by social conditions" (1979, p. 36). There may be only a small window of opportunity for change provided by the temporary relaxation of the social order brought about by widespread social protest. They suggest that the best strategy to achieve sought-for change through social movements is to extend that window of opportunity through organizing and action.

Social movements that maintain momentum can achieve significant change. The election of Nelson Mandela as president of South Africa was the outcome of a social movement and long-term struggle to end the system of apartheid and to establish civil and social rights for black South Africans. The efforts toward human rights in Latin America, Africa, Asia, Eastern Europe, and other parts of the world continue. As a social movement succeeds, the ideals that it has advanced are accepted as new, legitimated political and social norms.

CONCLUSION

The descriptions of these eight models, coupled with the historical and value discussion that places community practice in its social work context, provide some guidance for those working in a wide range of community efforts. One value of examining these models is to realize the multiple roles social workers have to play in facilitating individual, group, organizational, and community development toward democratic institution building. Social workers are called on to be organizers, teachers, coaches, advocates, facilitators, negotiators, mediators, planners, researchers, managers, proposal writers, spokespersons, promoters, and political candidates.

Community practice at all levels is influenced by local, national, and global changes. Citizens the world over are no longer leaving initiatives for social change just to governments and business. Social workers who are knowledgeable and have skills to contribute to this process will coach community members to become change agents in their communities. There will always be a role for social workers in the area of neighborhood and community organizing. The technology exists to communicate across the globe in seconds, but we still do most of our community building in face-to-face groups and organizations. The new communication technologies are particularly helpful for organizing functional communities, and these communities can benefit from social work's knowledge of social action, need and asset assessment, service and program development, and leadership.

There will be a tremendous need for social workers skilled in community social and economic development in the next several decades. As societies recognize the need to incorporate the lessons of sustainable development and human develop-ment into the equations for economic progress, social workers can facilitate the dialogue to help local and regional groups create new paradigms for sustainable development. The work of social planning will focus on developing more humane and inclusive social and economic systems for communities. Communities no longer will accept development that squanders the environment, tramples the vulnerable, and unjustly divides the profits. Application of social work's value and knowledge base, to new theoretical concepts for inclusive comprehensive and participatory work can make a significant contribution to social planning. Program development, community liaison, and service coordination will be the primary foci of organizations' administrators and managers as they seek to involve the consumers of human services as partners in planning and providing human services in all its varieties. Political and social action will always be in the purview of social work as long as one of the strong values of the profession is social justice. The NASW *Code of Ethics* makes it very clear that "social workers should engage in social and political action that seeks to ensure that all people have equal access to the resources, employment, services, and opportunities they require to meet their basic human needs and to develop fully" (1996, p. 27). Because social workers are skilled in the facilitation of groups and organizations, they will be key actors in building the coalitions needed in the coming decades. Though social workers are not typically major leaders of social movements, their skills as advocates and facilitators are critical for preparing groups and organizations to participate in progressive social movements.

In all these models there is a need for high levels of interpersonal, process, task, and technical skills. A particular skill needed by those working in community practice will be for facilitation methods using popular education and participatory planning (Chambers, 1997; Freire, 1970). Community practice workers will need to understand that the work they do is often long and arduous; however, the rewards in contributing to development of a more just and democratic society are enormous.

WEB SITES

Aspen Institute. http://www.aspeninstitute.org.
Bethel New Life. http://www.bethelnewlife.org.
Center for Participatory Change. http://www.cpcwnc.org.

Community Tool Box. http://ctb.ku.edu/en.

Highlander Center. http://www.highlander-center.org.

Praxis. http://www.sp2.upenn.edu/~restes/praxis.html.

UNDP. http://www.undp.org.

Universal Declaration of Human Rights. http://www.un.org/Overview/rights.html.

References

Betten, N., & Austin M. J. (Eds.). (1990). *The roots of community organizing, 1917–1939.* Philadelphia: Temple University Press.

Castelloe, P. (1999). Community change: An integrated model. In P. Castelloe, *Community change and community practice: An organic model of community practice.* PhD diss., School of Social Work, University of North Carolina at Chapel Hill.

Chambers, R. (1997). *Whose reality counts? Putting the last first.* London: Intermediate Technology Publications.

Dahl, Robert. (1989). *Democracy and its critics.* New Haven, CT: Yale University Press.

Estes, R. (1993). Toward sustainable development: From theory to praxis. *Social Development Issues, 15*(3): 1–29.

Friedmann, J. (1992). *Empowerment: The politics of alternative development,* 2nd ed. Oxford: Blackwell.

Freire, P. (1970). *Pedagogy of the oppressed.* New York: Seabury Press.

Gamble, D., & Weil, M. (2008). Community: Practice interventions. In T. Mizrahi & L. Davis (Eds.), *Encyclopedia of social work,* 20th ed. New York: NASW and Oxford University Press.

Gutierrez, L., Lewis, E. A., Nagda, B. A., Wernick, L., & Shore, N. (2005). Multicultural community practice strategies and intergroup empowerment. In M. Weil (Ed.), *The handbook of community practice* (pp. 341–359). Thousand Oaks, CA: Sage.

Hall, A., & Midgley, J. (2004). *Social policy for development.* Thousand Oaks, CA: Sage.

Hart, M. (1999). *Guide to sustainable community indicators,* 2nd ed. North Andover, MA: Hart Environmental Data.

Hawken, P. (2007). *Blessed unrest: How the largest movement in the world came into being and why no one saw it coming.* New York: Viking.

MacNair, R. H., Fowler, L., & Harris, J. (2000). The diversity functions of organizations that confront oppression: The evolution of three social movements. *Journal of Community Practice, 7*(2), 71–88.

Mattessich, P. W., Murray-Close, M., Monsey, B. R., & Wilder Research Center. (2001). *Collaboration: What makes it work,* 2nd ed. St. Paul, MN: Fieldstone Alliance.

McCroskey, J., & Meezan, W. (1992). Social work research in family and children's services. In

J. Brown & M. Weil (Eds.), *Family practice* (pp. 199–213). Washington, DC: Child Welfare League of America.

Medoff, P., & Sklar, H. (l994). *Streets of hope: The rise and fall of an urban neighborhood.* Boston: South End Press.

Mizrahi, T., & Rosenthal, B. (1993). Managing dynamic tensions in social change coalitions. In T. Mizrahi & J. D. Morrison (Eds.), *Community organization and social administration* (pp. 11–40). New York; Haworth Press.

NASW. (1996). *Code of ethics.* Washington DC: NASW Press.

Piven, F. F., & Cloward, R. S. (1979). *Poor people's movements: Why they succeed, how they fail.* New York: Vintage Books.

Plotz, D. A. (1992). *Community problem solving case summaries* (vol. 3). Washington, DC: Program for Community Problem Solving.

Rivera, F. G., & Erlich, J. L. (Eds.). (1998). *Community organizing in a diverse society* 3rd ed. Boston: Allyn & Bacon.

Roberts-DeGennaro, M., & Mizrahi, T. (2005). Human service coalitions. In M. Weil (Ed.), *Handbook of community practice* (pp. 305–318). Thousand Oaks, CA: Sage.

Rothman, J., Erlich, J. L., & Tropman, J. E. (Eds.). (2008). *Strategies of community intervention,* 7th ed. Peosta, IA: Eddie Bower.

Schreiner, M., Sherraden, M., Clancy, M., Johnson, L., Curley, J., Grinstein-Weiss, M., et al. (2001). *Savings and asset accumulation in individual development accounts.* St. Louis, MO: George Warren Brown School of Social Work.

Senge, P., Laur, J., Schley, S., & Smith B. (2006). *Learning for sustainability.* Cambridge, MA: Society for Organizational Learning.

Shiva, V. (2005). *Earth democracy: Justice, sustainability, and peace.* Cambridge, MA: South End Press.

Simon, B. L. (1994). *The empowerment tradition in American social work: A history.* New York: Columbia University Press.

You Got to Move: Stories of Change in the South. (2008). Video produced and directed by Lucy Massie Phenix and Veronica Selver. First Run/Icarus Films.

United Nations Development Program (UNDP). (1999). *Human development report.* New York: Oxford University Press.

United Nations General Assembly. (1987). Report on the world commission on environment and development.

Weil, M. (2005). Social planning with communities. In M. Weil (Ed.), *The handbook of community practice* (pp. 215–243). Thousand Oaks, CA: Sage.

Wood, J. L., & Jackson, M. (1982). *Social movements: Development, participation, and dynamics.* Belmont, CA: Wadsworth.

130 Legislative Advocacy to Empower Oppressed and Vulnerable Groups

Michael Reisch

The concept of advocacy is derived from law. It means to speak up, to plead the case for another, or to champion a cause, often for a group (e.g., children or the severely mentally ill) that cannot speak out on its own behalf. Legislative advocacy refers to activities in the political arena that focus on the promotion of the common welfare or the securing and protection of rights and services of a specific population. By definition, it involves both partisanship and politics—roles that may produce some discomfort among many social workers. Yet there is a long history of legislative advocacy in the social work profession. Many of the most significant advances in social policy, such as Social Security, Medicare, Medicaid, and the development of programs to protect vulnerable populations, were implemented through the legislative advocacy of social workers and their allies (Axinn & Stern, 2008). As a consequence of policy devolution, since the early 1980s the focus of legislative advocacy efforts has shifted to the state and local arenas. The examples cited herein come from such efforts, where social workers often have more opportunity to exercise their skills and their influence.

ELEMENTS OF LEGISLATIVE ADVOCACY

Legislative advocacy incorporates elements of political struggle, negotiation, cooperation, and compromise. More than in other forms of advocacy, however, the need to compromise in the legislative arena often generates ethical conflicts among social workers. Although each ethical dilemma that emerges in the legislative advocacy process must be resolved on its own terms, it is generally useful to keep in mind that legislative advocacy is not an end in itself but often one of several complementary strategies employed to achieve particular policy goals. It must therefore be conceived in terms of how it meets both the short-term and long-term needs of its constituents.

In this context, the major tasks of legislative advocacy can be summarized as follows:

- The application of expertise and technical assistance to the development of legislation or to the monitoring of the budget process in the legislative arena.
- The organization of support for legislators who are willing to take risky leadership positions on an issue of concern to one's organization and its constituents.
- The monitoring of all legislation that is relevant to one's constituents, including all committee votes and party caucuses that influence the course of particular bills.
- The development of ongoing cooperative professional and personal relationships with other legislative advocates and with the staff of legislators and legislative committees. The adoption of term limits by many state legislatures has made this aspect of legislative advocacy more challenging.
- The creation and utilization of media contacts and the use of a media advocacy strategy, including the Internet, to complement work in the legislature itself (Hick & McNutt, 2002).
- The use of the legislative advocacy process to organize, educate, and train constituents (and thereby contribute to their empowerment) through such means as the establishment of phone trees, e-mail lists, Web sites, and advocacy networks; the orchestration of letter writing, fax, e-mail, and phone campaigns; and the maintenance of a visible presence at legislative hearings and other key legislative events.

• The use of the legislative process and complementary media activities to spotlight particular issues, educate the public and one's constituents, arouse popular support, publicize a group's positions and policy alternatives on key legislative issues, inform legislators about the issues, and provide legislators with the opportunity to test public reactions to their positions on new or controversial policy issues (Leighley, 2004).

THE PURPOSES OF LEGISLATIVE ADVOCACY

Legislative advocacy is a means to mobilize people, raise political consciousness, and accentuate the shortcomings of societal institutions and structures, while working to improve the quality of life or expand the rights of specific populations, particularly those who are in a position of power and resource disadvantage. Such efforts require the mobilization of resources and a focus on specific targets to benefit oppressed and vulnerable people. In the case of legislative advocacy, these targets can be divided into three categories: targets of influence, targets of mobilization, and targets of benefits (Schneider & Lester, 2001).

Targets of influence include legislators, stakeholders, executive department heads and key staff, the media, and other influential advocates. The work of Welfare Advocates, a statewide coalition in Maryland, the Michigan League for Human Services, and Philadelphia Citizens for Children and Youth (PCCY)—each of which seeks to influence both legislation and the annual budget process on behalf of its constituents—is an example of this type of advocacy. Targets of mobilization consist of those individuals and groups whose resources and energy are needed to promote a particular legislative agenda. The focus of groups like Coleman Advocates for Children and Youth in San Francisco, Children Now in Oakland (California), and the Los Angeles Roundtable for Children often falls into this category. Targets of benefits usually refer to the constituents on whose behalf the advocacy effort is undertaken, although sometimes the general public may be the intended or potential beneficiaries of legislative advocacy. Efforts in Michigan by the National Association of Social Workers to achieve parity for mental health services are a good illustration of this form of advocacy. The work of grassroots organizations, such as the Kensington Welfare

Rights Organization in Philadelphia and the Michigan Welfare Rights Organization in Detroit are also good illustrations of this type of work. In certain legislative advocacy campaigns, the target of mobilization and the target of benefits overlap considerably.

A key element in the latter type of legislative advocacy is the mobilization of constituents' resources and their focus on a particular policy goal in a legislative setting. In this context, mobilization is the process of increasing the ability of constituents to act collectively by building their loyalty to a common set of objectives and increasing their ability to influence the course of legislation. Successful legislative advocacy, therefore, involves multiple forms of mobilization—defensive, offensive, and preparatory—depending on the availability of resources, the relative power of legislative advocates, and the particular issues at hand (Richan, 2006).

During the past quarter century, most advocacy efforts by social workers and their allies have been defensive in nature. Statewide advocacy coalitions in New York, California, Michigan, Maryland, and Pennsylvania, for example, fought to reduce the impact of federal policies on state provisions for low-income groups. A statewide coalition in Oregon defeated a well-funded antigay ballot initiative. Broad-based coalitions in California defeated ballot propositions that would have eliminated funding for HIV/AIDS services, slashed welfare benefits, or banned the use of demographic data about race and gender to target resources to vulnerable populations. Advocacy organizations in New York and Pennsylvania, working with sympathetic state officials, protected low-income populations, particularly children, from the most severe effects of federal cutbacks. Unfortunately, many of these efforts have not succeeded, as the recent passage of anti–affirmative action and gay marriage initiatives demonstrates.

Even during politically conservative times, however, offensive advocacy is possible (Shaw, 2001). For example, during the peak years of the Reagan presidency, Welfare Advocates in Maryland were able to lobby successfully for increases in Aid to Families with Dependent Children grants that boosted benefits by about 35 percent and, in alliance with other groups, for expanded housing and nutrition services for low-income persons. In the midst of a recession and statewide fiscal crisis during the early 1990s, Coleman Advocates for Children and Youth created the first "children's budget" in San Francisco's history and twice passed an amendment to the city charter guaranteeing funding for children's services. A few years ago, working with a broad-based coalition, Children Now helped pass a comprehensive after-school program for California's children and youth. Today, groups at the national and state levels are engaged in advocacy to expand children's health care, defend Social Security and Medicare, and revise the provisions of the Personal Responsibility and Work Opportunity Reconciliation Act (PRWORA, also known as "welfare reform").

Legislative advocacy can have a variety of purposes beyond the passage or blockage of a particular bill. Often, it is a means to strengthen one's organization or coalition or expand its membership base. By speaking out for welfare recipients at a time when their needs were being ignored in the political arena, Welfare Advocates grew from a small group of Baltimore-based professionals to a statewide coalition with over 250 members. Groups which advocated on behalf of persons with HIV/AIDS, the victims of domestic violence, and homeless persons have experienced similar growth despite the initial lack of public awareness or unpopularity of these issues.

Advocacy can also serve as a vehicle to complement the service delivery objectives of participating organizations. Many of the professionals who joined advocacy campaigns organized by PCCY, Coleman Advocates, Children Now, the Michigan League for Human Services, and the Los Angeles Roundtable for Children participated out of both self-interest and altruistic motives. The legislative or budgetary victories they achieved often provided increased funding for their agencies' programs. Successful advocacy campaigns also increased public awareness of the issues being addressed by service providers and enabled them to raise their community profile and expand community-based fundraising efforts. Even losing efforts can help boost an organization's profile and public awareness of its issues. They can also strengthen interorganizational relationship among potential allies and help build grassroots leadership.

The following discussion lists the variety of purposes that legislative advocacy can serve for social workers.

Legislative advocacy can serve as a means to increase client competence by educating clients to testify before legislative committees or meet with individual legislators. Coleman Advocates has been particularly effective in training the parents of low-income children, through a group called

Parent Advocates for Youth, and youth themselves, through a group called Youth Making a Change, to engage in such activities. Throughout the United States, youth-oriented advocacy organizations are substantially increasing the level of civic participation among youth, particularly those from racial and ethnic minority communities, while addressing issues of specific concern to them (Checkoway & Gutierrez, 2006).

Legislative advocacy can encourage one's organization to be more responsive in assessing the needs of clients and in understanding the conditions of their lives. The increased involvement by local United Way organizations and the work of the Los Angeles Roundtable for Children are good examples of this effect.

Legislative advocacy can facilitate intracommunity or interagency cooperation by requiring participating organizations (e.g., in an advocacy coalition) to channel their efforts through a structured, disciplined, and cooperative process. New York's long-standing Counter Budget organization, a statewide advocacy coalition of providers and advocates, is an excellent illustration of this type of impact. Starting in the 1970s as a small, outspoken group that provided alternatives to the state budget, for many years Counter Budget's work was an anticipated part of the state's annual fiscal process. Its efforts not only put the needs of low-income populations regularly on the agenda of the state legislature, they also strengthened intergroup relationships and diminished competition among agencies for scarce resources. Annual report cards on legislators, such as those produced by Coleman Advocates, or on the state of children, such as those produced by Children Now and the Children's Defense Fund, have had similar consequences.

Legislative advocacy, by the very demands it creates for improved information, extensive public education campaigns, greater political sophistication, and stronger ties with constituents and their communities, can stimulate needed organizational changes. Numerous state chapters of NASW have become more effective and more efficient in their operations as they became more involved in legislative advocacy.

Legislative advocacy can serve as a catalyst for the redistribution of resources and power within an agency, a community, and an advocacy coalition itself. Coleman Advocates' successful Children's Budget Campaign brought in millions of new dollars to children's programs in San Francisco, and the passage of the Children's Amendment it sponsored led to the establishment of a permanent Office of Children, Youth, and Families in the city. This ensured the ongoing influence of advocacy and service organizations in the city's annual budget development process. In fact, the current director of the office, Margaret Brodkin, was the former director of Coleman Advocates and the leader of these two initiatives.

Legislative advocacy, by externalizing client, worker, and agency problems and focusing on a mutually selected target, enables clients and workers to cope more effectively with the stresses in their daily lives and interactions. For decades, welfare rights organizations and advocates for the mentally disabled and their families, such as the National Alliance on Mental Illness, have noted such effects.

THE ROLES OF LEGISLATIVE ADVOCATES

Legislative advocates play multiple roles depending on the needs of their constituents, organizational imperatives, and political circumstances (Jansson, 2003). At times, local advocacy groups like Coleman Advocates and PCCY and national organizations such as the Children's Defense Fund, Children Now, and the National Association of Child Advocates focus on a specific population, such as children in poverty. Alternatively, legislative advocates can play the role of ombudsperson or broker. In the former role, they can help articulate the needs of clients or service providers to policymakers or assist clients and constituents in making their voices heard by organizing community forums and speak-outs, online discussion lists, and discussion sites. As brokers, legislative advocates can work with legislative staff to negotiate compromises in the language of legislation that involves both their constituents and other interested parties. Or, as in the case of Welfare Advocates in Maryland and Coleman Advocates in San Francisco, they can become directly involved in shaping the budget proposals of key government departments. In cases where there is no direct involvement of one's constituents, the expertise of legislative advocates may help in identifying common ground among competing groups. A good illustration of the latter is the work of Children Now in revising FCC regulations to reduce corporate influence on children's programming. The coalition Children Now

helped organize groups from all over the ideological spectrum.

On some occasions, as a favor to a sympathetic legislator, advocates can be catalysts for compromise when they have no direct interest in a piece of legislation. In return, the legislator may agree to sponsor or "carry" a bill promoted by the advocates. This role underscores the importance of developing expertise on a range of substantive issues, as well as the legislative process itself, to increase advocates' visibility and viability in the legislative arena.

STRATEGIES AND TACTICS OF LEGISLATIVE ADVOCACY

Although the overall goal of legislative advocacy is to influence the policy-making process on behalf of clients and constituents, the paths to attain this goal vary considerably depending on the presenting issue, the political climate, and the relative influence of legislative advocates and their allies in a particular context. Often when advocates have little prior experience in legislative work or the issue is relatively new, the major focus of legislative advocacy is to obtain, organize, and present data to illuminate the scope of the problem for which a legislative solution is sought. As advocates acquire a reputation for reliability in their area of expertise, they are often called on to prepare more focused reports or presentations for a legislative committee or a particular legislator who is a potential sponsor of a bill. In such instances, advocates may be asked to conduct research, write or present expert testimony, or help draft the legislation itself. This requires advocates to balance their interest in acquiring visibility with their need to obtain critical political support. It also potentially jeopardizes the role of advocates as forces outside of the political process who speak for the people. Once advocates "win"—that is, play an insider's role in key legislative or fiscal processes, as occurred in San Francisco, Philadelphia, and Maryland—they risk jeopardizing their ability to criticize the actions of governments with which they are now cooperating and the perception of the public, organizational allies, and constituents regarding their integrity and trustworthiness. Weighing the trade-offs of such situations is critical; it requires assessing the trustworthiness of the legislators and administrators involved and the long-term implications of decisions.

For example, the decision whether to testify about a particular piece of legislation involves the consideration of the following factors:

- Whether the advocate (or his or her surrogate) possesses sufficient knowledge of the subject and adequate presenting skills to testify successfully.
- Whether the advocate can provide supporting data—both statistics and case examples—for his or her value-based appeals.
- Whether the highly public act of testifying on this particular issue would be politically useful to the long-term goals of one's constituents. Factors to consider in this regard include the extent of public and political support for an issue, the immediacy of the issue, and the degree to which such testimony would undermine advocates' relationships with key political leaders, organizations, or allies.
- Whether the testimony would add anything new and constructive to political debates. This could include new information (as groups like Welfare Advocates, Children Now, the Michigan League for Human Services, and PCCY often provide legislators), new interpretations of existing information (such as Counter Budget and Coleman Children's Budget Campaign presented), or a new emphasis to existing policy initiatives (such as promoting the needs of women on welfare for child care to become self-sufficient).
- Whether it is important that a particular constituency—through its advocates—take an independent position on a piece of legislation instead of providing background support.

Occasionally, an effective tactic for legislative advocates is the use of electoral campaigns to develop potential support for a specific legislative agenda and expand advocates' visibility within the community. Participation in electoral campaigns can also help expand the political awareness of staff, constituents, and clients and increase advocates' influence around nonlegislative initiatives of importance to their constituents. This influence is particularly critical once a bill promoted by advocates is introduced or a long-term legislative strategy has been initiated. It is important, however, to distinguish between the utility of ballot initiatives (or referenda) and elections focused on candidates.

Although ballot measures have become increasingly popular in an era of frequent political stalemate, electoral campaigns that focus on particular candidates can also be used to promote a policy agenda on behalf of vulnerable populations. Although advocacy organizations must be careful to remain nonpartisan (i.e., not back a particular candidate or party) or risk losing their nonprofit status, they can and often do get involved in educating the electorate about the central issues of a campaign. Coleman Advocates regularly sponsors candidate forums that ask mayoral aspirants to pledge their support for children's issues. It also issues an annual report card, grading local politicians on their efforts on behalf of children. PCCY uses mayoral and legislative elections to host a series of neighborhood events in which candidates are asked to address the needs of children and their families. Statewide groups like Welfare Advocates in Maryland and Children Now in California regularly take advantage of gubernatorial elections to promote particular policy initiatives through ballot propositions. These provide opportunities to pressure candidates to take clear positions for or against a specific measure.

After a bill has been introduced, advocates rarely limit their efforts to the legislative body that is considering the legislation. They often engage in a broad range of public educational activities in cooperation with allies. These include neighborhood-based town meetings, conferences, speakouts, and demonstrations. Increasingly, advocacy organizations are using the Internet to educate the public and stimulate community participation in policy debates. Usually, advocates will adopt an "inside/outside" strategy that combines direct meetings with legislators to lobby for or against a bill with media advocacy and public education campaigns to increase external pressure on the legislators.

Research on successful legislative advocacy (Andrews & Edwards, 2004; Hoefer, 2005) found the following factors to be determinants of success: consistent and continuous involvement of constituents, well-established and varied means of communication, ongoing positive relationships with legislative targets, skills in consensus building and the mobilization of public opinion, and the establishment of credibility on a focused set of issues. Advocates' efforts that reflected the diversity of constituency groups were also more likely to gain recognition for their activities and to obtain access to key decision makers.

BARRIERS TO SUCCESSFUL
LEGISLATIVE ADVOCACY

The obstacles to successful legislative advocacy fall into three broad categories: those that are created by the political-economic environment; those that are inherent in the legislative process; and those that are inherent in advocacy work itself.

The most obvious obstacle to successful legislative advocacy is the presence of a generally unfavorable political environment for social welfare programs, particularly those on behalf of low-power and stigmatized groups (Haynes & Mickelson, 2006). Attempts to influence traditional centers of power, such as legislatures, often encounter overt and covert hostility from opponents and even skepticism from potential allies. This may be expressed through harassment by influential legislators, their staff, or other gatekeepers to the policy-making process. Examples include the failure of staff in Maryland, California, and Pennsylvania to provide advocates with up-to-date schedules of hearings or to provide assistance in drafting a bill. Sometimes, advocates can be distracted by the presence of other "wedge" issues that, because of their urgency, compel advocacy organizations to shift from an offensive to a defensive posture. At other times, a pressing fiscal crisis (such as recently occurred in Michigan) makes it more difficult for advocates to adopt a proactive agenda.

Another environmental obstacle is the difficulty of sustaining a "conflict posture" in a legislative setting. Legislative advocacy is a time-consuming and expensive strategy that can drain the resources and energy even of the strongest individuals and their organizations. Organizations that operate on a shoestring budget and rely primarily on volunteers, such as Welfare Advocates, often have difficulty sustaining their efforts over time. Other groups, like Coleman and PCCY, which are engaged in a wide range of initiatives, sometimes have trouble maintaining a high degree of mobilization among supporters and constituents. Recently, the influence of external funders, particularly foundations, has restricted the activities of advocacy organizations or compelled them to focus on issues which the funder, rather than their constituents, has defined as critical. In such cases, advocates must choose their battles very carefully. The lack of sufficient time to become familiar with the details of the legislative process and cultivate essential personal and institutional relationships is often a serious problem.

A third barrier is the increasing fragmentation of the policy-making process within legislatures as a consequence of the growing specialization of committees, budgets, and proposed legislation. As legislative advocates, social workers may experience frustration over the need to reframe broad issues into the narrow requirements of policy legislation. An additional complication in this regard is the competition among legislative committees for jurisdiction over policy initiatives. Here, the importance of developing and sustaining personal relationships with legislators and particularly their staffs is critical. Unfortunately, the imposition of term limits makes the development of such relationships more difficult. A partial solution to this problem is to make additional efforts to strengthen ties with media contacts, officials in the executive branch of government, and legislative staff, who often have longer tenures than the politicians for whom they work.

A related obstacle within the legislative process itself is the difficulty of identifying the locus of accountability for policy decisions. This contrasts sharply to advocacy efforts outside of the legislative arena where success is often determined by a focus on a clearly defined "enemy." Another inherent problem is the broad range of skills required to succeed in the legislative arena. On one hand, these skills are more political than those to which most social workers are accustomed. On the other hand, they involve more compromise than is customarily used by aggressive advocates in nonlegislative settings. Advocates also experience an ongoing tension between the time and effort involved in expanding the participation of community-based constituents and the pressures of the policy-making process.

Persistent constraints on policy development, usually as the result of legal or constitutional procedures or the politics of the legislative process, constitute a third source of frustration within the legislative arena. Recently, the greatest constraints on effective advocacy have been the limits placed on legislative action by economic conditions, the constitutional requirement of balanced budgets, voter spending initiatives (at the state and local level) that can restrict or target funding in heavily prescribed ways, fiscal cutbacks around domestic programs, and the resource disadvantage social workers experience as legislative advocates in comparison with wealthier groups. Advocacy groups, however, have found solutions to these dilemmas. These include creative framing of the issues (e.g., promoting a Children's Budget or demanding $1/day for low-income families), developing innovative tactics (e.g., Coleman Advocates taking over City Hall with a "baby brigade"), and using legislators' language, such as "self-sufficiency," as the basis for promoting such issues as mental health parity and the needs of welfare recipients for quality child care, job training programs, and transportation subsidies.

GUIDELINES FOR LEGISLATIVE ADVOCACY

In sum, successful legislative advocacy includes the following components.

- Consistent and continual engagement in the legislative process even when the legislative body is not in session. This is particularly important in states where the legislature meets for only a few months (as in Maryland) or not every year (as in Texas). Scheduling briefing meetings with legislators in off months is one way to do this. Often, university faculty who are engaged in community-based policy research can assist advocates in this regard by translating their research into formats that are user-friendly in the advocacy arena. The Bay Area Social Services Consortium in California is a good example of this.
- Ongoing research on the orientation and priorities of the legislators advocates are seeking to influence. The distribution of regular publications to legislators and department heads is an effective means for advocates to make their presence felt. PCCY's *Watching Out for Children in Changing Times*, Welfare Advocates' *Guide to Welfare in Maryland*, Children Now's award-winning publications and Web sites, and the Children Defense Fund's *A Children's Defense Budget* are successful examples of this technique.
- Provision of technical and political information to legislators and their staffs even on those issues that are of indirect concern to advocates (to build trust and credibility that can be tapped during efforts on behalf of difficult or unpopular issues). Participation in legislative briefings on such topics as energy assistance, transportation problems, and economic development issues has helped achieve these objectives. More recently, advocates have presented critical information about the socioeconomic impact of global warming, the effects of the North

American Free Trade Agreement, and the impact of restrictive immigration policies.
- Developing personal as well as political relationships with legislators and their staff. This frequently requires informal contacts at fundraisers, conferences, and workshops.
- Maintaining clarity on the long-term goals of legislative advocacy efforts even as they shift tactical focus. Monthly lunches, annual retreats, or conferences of advocacy groups or coalitions can be particularly helpful in maintaining advocates' focus in a complex, rapidly changing environment. In addition, advocacy organizations can link their Web sites to each other and develop their own online discussion lists and chat rooms.
- Developing sensitivity to the views of legislative opponents as well as allies, particularly legislators who are key committee chairs.
- Recognizing that legislators and their staffs have unexamined and unquestioned prejudices and learning how to confront these prejudices directly without alienating potential supporters. These are best addressed through direct, person-to-person contact and not through public confrontations or Internet-driven correspondence.
- Learning how to take risks despite the overriding ethos of compromise in the legislative arena. The successful efforts of Welfare Advocates, Coleman Advocates, and Counter Budget in bucking the political tide demonstrate how new ideas, even if risky, can catch on and help promote the interests of vulnerable groups.
- Convincing others that one's objectives are socially worthy and not self-serving. This can be accomplished by emphasizing common human values and seeking common ground on which seemingly intractable policy questions can be resolved.
- Supporting efforts of coalition partners on issues that are not directly of concern to one's organization or constituents.
- Framing policy questions in terms that are consistent with the worldviews of legislators and learning when to refrain from legislative advocacy efforts to avoid cultivating resentment among legislators. It is critical for advocates to "change their tune" from time to time so that their message continues to be heard by politicians, the public, and the media, all of which, unfortunately, have short attention spans. It is also important for

advocates to know when the political climate is hostile to their message and to save their resources and energy for another day.

- Acquiring sensitivity to the egos of legislators and the political pressures they are experiencing and shaping advocacy arguments around their political and personal imperatives. This requires advocates to connect issues to the specific needs of each legislator's district or to other issues that the legislator already supports.
- Creating ongoing mechanisms to influence the legislative process, such as action research committees; informal, issue-specific groups of constituents to develop strategies and public information materials; and regular training sessions for constituents and supporters about various aspects of the legislative process such as public speaking and meeting with policy makers.

THE FUTURE OF LEGISLATIVE ADVOCACY

Since the late nineteenth century, legislative advocacy by social workers has transformed the social landscape of the United States and led to improvements in the material well-being of millions of Americans. It has shaped the domestic policy agenda of the nation, altered the balance of power at the state and local level, facilitated the emergence of leaders at the community level, and enhanced the status of the social work profession. Over the past three decades, however, much of that advocacy has been defensive in nature, involving efforts to minimize spending cuts or the elimination of long-standing social protections.

Despite the conservative political and fiscal climate, several recent trends produce guarded optimism about the future of legislative advocacy. A notable development is the growing emphasis on expanding the civic participation of clients and constituents (Checkoway and Gutierrez, 2006; Richan, 2006). Through such collaboration, legislative advocates can identify new issues, reframe old problems in creative ways, and apply new methods of analysis and explanation to contentious topics. A related trend is growing access to the Internet, which has enabled advocates and their constituents to develop increasingly sophisticated databases and communication networks, share ideas and advocacy strategies, and respond

more rapidly and proactively during the policy formation process. Finally, in response to the consequences of economic globalization, legislative advocates have begun to incorporate regional and international perspectives into local advocacy efforts and to build transnational alliances on such diverse issues as poverty, immigration, civil rights for gays and lesbians, trafficking in children and women, and the impact of climate change.

WEB SITES

Alliance for Justice. http://www.afj.org/fai/nonprof.html.

Center on Budget and Policy Priorities, Washington, DC. http://www.cbpp.org.

Children's Defense Fund, Washington, DC. http://www.cdf.org.

Influencing State Policy, Richmond, VA. http://www.statepolicy.org.

Urban Institute, Washington, DC. http://www.ui.org.

References

Andrews, K. T., & Edwards, B. (2004). Advocacy organizations in the U.S. political process. *Annual Review of Sociology, 30,* 479–506.

Axinn, J., & Stern, M. (2008). *Social welfare: A history of the American response to need,* 6th ed. Boston: Allyn & Bacon.

Checkoway, B., & Gutierrez, L. M. (Eds.). (2006). *Young people making community change.* Binghamton, NY: Haworth.

Haynes, K., & Mickelson, J. (2006). *Affecting change: Social work in the political arena,* 6th ed. Boston: Pearson/Allyn & Bacon.

Hick, S. F., & McNutt, J. G. (Eds.). (2002). *Advocacy, activism, and the Internet: Community organization and social policy.* Chicago: Lyceum Books.

Hoefer, R. (2005). Altering state policy: Interest group effectiveness among state-level advocacy groups. *Social Work, 50*(3), 219–227.

Jansson, B. S. (2003). *Becoming an effective policy advocate: From policy practice to social justice,* 4th ed. Pacific Grove, CA: Thomson/Brooks Cole.

Leighley, J. E. (2004). *Mass media and politics: A social science perspective.* Boston: Houghton Mifflin.

Richan, W. C. (2006). *Lobbying for social change,* 3rd ed. New York: Haworth.

Schneider, R. L., & Lester, L. (2001). *Social work advocacy: A new framework for action.* Belmont, CA: Wadsworth/Thomson Learning.

Shaw, R. (2001). *The activist's handbook.* Berkeley, CA: University of California Press.

Principles and Practice Guidelines for Social Action

Jacqueline B. Mondros

"Social action is a collective endeavor to promote a cause or make a progressive change in the face of opposition" (Hardcastle, Wenocur, & Powers, 2004p. 349). Rubin and Rubin (2005) define organizing as a process that links three goals: solving problems that people face individually and collectively; building permanent, democratically controlled organizations that build and sustain capacity for joint problem solving; and empowering people and their communities, thereby increasing their ability to solve their own problems. Similarly, Staples (2004) describes the "dual emphasis on participatory process and successful outcomes" (pp. 6–7). Social action requires a large number of people because individuals lack the power to make the desired change (Checkoway, 1995). The large numbers become a source of power, either because they represent a large voting bloc or, through media coverage, are able to shift public opinion, or they are able to put pressure on those with power to make the desired change. Though achieving the change is critical (Hall, 1999), much of the social action literature emphasizes that participants undergo consciousness raising or empowerment as they seek and achieve change goals (Staples, 2004).

The people who engage in social action share something in common. It may be a shared characteristic (e.g., members of the same racial group or social class, such as the working poor), a common condition (e.g., persons with disabilities), or a common goal (e.g., the passage of gun control legislation). The people may also share common space (e.g., residents of a neighborhood or union members in a workplace). The desired change can be about economic, social, or political conditions, rights, and or processes and can affect a neighborhood, city, state, or nation or have global implications.

Several authors have sought to categorize various types of social action activities (Fisher, 1995; Mondros & Wilson, 1994; Weil & Gamble, 2005). For purposes of this chapter, social change efforts will be categorized broadly into lobbying, mobilizing, and organizing models. Few social action efforts, however, have the luxury of using a single approach. Change at these levels is extraordinarily challenging and engages very powerful opponents. A thorough assessment of the context of the change is necessary to guide the selection of the appropriate social action model.

AUSPICIOUS TIMES

Social psychologists have used historical data to study "auspicious moments for change" or what McAdam, McCarthy, & Zald (1996) call environments that are "protest ready." Three theories for protest predominate: people protest in response to changing economic conditions, that is, either sudden deprivation or improved conditions that result in rising expectations (Morrison, 1978); people protest when they are in a position to form formal and informal organizations that encouraged and made collective action possible (Gamson, 1975; McCarthy & Zald, 1977); and protest occurs when people develop a shared perception of injustice and a sense of shared identity (Gamson, 1992; Mansbridge, 2001; Meyer, Whittier, & Robnett, 2002). These theories help explain why activism among women, labor union members, welfare recipients, African American and Latino groups, environmentalists, students, antiwar protesters, people with disabilities, and the LGBT community is prevalent at some moments and not in others. Some researchers have suggested that a convergence of variables results in protest (Morris & Mueller, 1992; Ryan & Gamson, 2006).

SPECIFYING THE DESIRED CHANGE

All social action is undertaken to effect change. Desired changes can range from sweeping transmogrification to relatively specific and limited. Mobilizing models tend to have far-reaching change goals—for example, antiglobalization campaigns that seek to end unfair labor practices. Mobilizing efforts are often called social movements to signify the societal transformations they envision. Lobbying models tend to have legislative change goals and specify legislative changes—for example, proposals for gun control or single-payer health insurance systems. When the opposition is particularly obdurate, lobbying organizations will posit electoral goals to elect legislators who will vote for the desired change. Organizing models tend to have very specific change goals—for example, to provide public transportation in a rural county or to prevent the building of a new arena using city funds. The feasibility and temporality of a goal is also important; organizing models tend to look for goals that are operational and can be achieved in a relatively brief period of time, whereas lobbying models frame goals around legislative calendars, and mobilizing organizations tend to take the long-term view. The degree to which the problem and solution are specifically defined will, to a large extent, determine the length of time spent on the problem and the model of social action used.

CHANGE ACTIVISTS

The change activists are those who will act in an attempt to make the change. Organizing models insist that those directly affected by the problem are motivated by oppression and self-interest and therefore are the most reliable activists for change and most willing to invest in a protracted and difficult social action campaign. This model emphasizes developing grassroots leaders who direct the social action agenda. Empowerment of these leaders is an important part of the organizing model (Checkoway, 1995; Staples, 2004). Lobbying and mobilizing models generally involve altruistic persons clamoring for change on behalf of others. In these models, the sheer numbers of

supporters make the change possible. In all models, large numbers of persons must be recruited to the cause, and the organizer must figure out how to reach them. In lobbying and mobilizing models, this usually means enlisting people to the cause through the media, leafleting, direct mail campaigns, and advertising for supporters. In organizing models, recruitment tends to take the form of door knocking, house meetings, and soliciting people at schools, churches, local businesses, or at their workplace.

CHANGE TARGETS

The change target refers to the persons or group that must consent for a change to occur. In lobbying models, the change target emerges from the political environment—the legislators who must enact a law, a politician who may be prevailed on to introduce a ballot initiative, or voters who must be convinced to pass a referendum. For many mobilizing organizations, the change target is both more ambitious and ambiguous. For example, the target might be to change the public's opinion on world trade or the behavior of a multinational corporation. In an organizing model, the change target is usually a decision maker or a group of decision makers who have the authority to change the situation. For example, a group of neighborhood residents may target the planning commission to stop plans for a new arena in an already congested inner-city neighborhood.

Whatever the target of the change effort, the organizer will need to consider the most effective means of convincing the target to make change. Consideration of persuasive arguments, the targets' friends and associates, the target's public comments on issues, and how best to get the group's message across will all give clues about how to approach the target most effectively.

RESOURCES FOR CHANGE

Often the decision about the nature of action is based on the resources available for the effort. The most valuable organizational resources are time, staff, and money. When there is little time, few staff, and little money, a splashy public protest may be the most efficient way of broadcasting the organization's message widely. The dramatic display hopes to make the protest appear significant. More money will allow for more publicity over time, and the message can be transmitted to a larger audience using multiple means. Lobbying organizations raise money through donations and memberships so that they may use various media to press for their desired ends. The organizing model places emphasis on acquiring resources to hire staff who will recruit people, intensively prepare leaders, help them devise strategies, and build a powerful organization.

STRATEGY AND TACTICS

Strategy is a question of what action is to be taken to make the desired change. Strategy is based on two ideas: (1) what is most likely to influence decision makers and allies to make the desired change, and (2) what is possible given the time and resources available. Tactics are the actions or events that implement the strategy.

The degree to which the environmental context is favorable for change and the social position of the change actor suggests whether an insider or outsider approach is warranted (Hoefer, 2000). Hoefer writes, "An inside strategy tries to influence policy by 'working through the system' and approaching legislative and executive branch decision makers directly. An outside strategy tries to influence . . . by indirect means, including litigation and protest" (p. 87) Mondros (2005) recommends insider lobbying strategies when the environment is favorable and change agents are high status, and outsider strategies used in mobilizing and organizing models when the environment is unfavorable and the change actors are low status.

Hardina (2000) identifies a range of tactics associated with the strategies of collaboration, persuasion, and contest. Lobbying models tend to use persuasive strategies aimed at influencing the views of voters and legislators. Supporters are asked to write letters, make phone calls and visits to government officials and legislators, and sign petitions in support of the change. Mobilizing organizations tend to use public protest and perhaps civil disobedience to attract the attention of new supporters and the media. Organizing models tend to meet with the decision makers who have been identified as the targets, make demands and negotiate for change, and use the media to make the issue visible and embarrassing to the target. This conflict strategy is aimed at winning an agreement

or "victory" that motivates the leaders toward other change goals. Suppositions about change goals, change activists, targets, resources, and strategies tend to cluster into social action models. Table 131.1 displays the assumptions and associated models.

STEPS TO TAKE IN TAKING SOCIAL ACTION

Because change is often difficult and time and resources may be limited, the organizer is advised to carefully plan any social action effort. The following steps are encouraged to guide the organizer's thinking and actions.

1. The first task of the organizer is to identify a problem that requires a change, most likely by talking to people about the types of obstacles faced by them and their friends, neighbors, co-workers, or clients in their daily lives. A problem that is specific, locally controlled, immediate, and concrete will be more amenable to change than one that is large, abstract, remote, and far-reaching. It is easier to change the way the state reimburses kin for relative foster care than it is to radically alter the entire foster care system. Once the problem is identified, the organizer should begin to postulate a tentative solution to the problem. Again, it is generally advised to partialize a large problem into small, doable changes that would provide some relief, if not solve the problem fully. The small change goal can then be expanded and built on throughout the social action process. A third consideration is the timeliness of the proposal for change. If the organization is proposing a new law, then the legislative calendar will provide a time frame. Organizers are advised to look for "windows of opportunity." For example, organizations can capitalize on media exposure about the issue.

2. The second step is to identify the activists—those who might either be affected by the problem or care about it for sentimental or altruistic reasons. It is important to know something about these people. How many people support the change? Do they know each other? If you can find only 50 people interested in the problem, then your social

TABLE 131.1 Social Action Models Associated with Suppositions about Change

	Lobbying	Mobilizing	Organizing
Change goal	Pass a law or ordinance; elect supporters of legislation	Long-term changes	Small specific changes
Change activists	Large numbers of supporters, most of whom will not be intensively involved at any point in time	Large numbers of supporters, most of whom will not be intensively involved over time	Smaller numbers of committed and self-interested individuals who will be intensively involved over a long time period
Change target	Voters, legislators, and politicians who will pass the law	Public opinion; key decision makers in government and corporations	Person or people directly responsible for solving the problem
Change resources	Money, time, and staff to persuade public and legislators	Little money, little time, few staff	Money for staff and time of committed self-interested participants
Change strategy	Petitions, media, letters, phone calls, visits	Public protest, civil disobedience	Meetings with change targets to apply direct pressure, dramatic events

change effort is likely to be small and local, unless you can build broader support during the campaign. If the activists already know each other, it is easier to bring them together to work on the change. If they don't know each other, they must either develop alliances or work toward change independent of one another. For example, the lobbying strategies of petitions and letter writing can be carried out by independent activists. It is important to know whether the change activists can be counted on to work intensively for the change and how long they can be expected to continue their involvement. Campaigns that require meetings with public officials and negotiations will require more deeply committed activists over a longer period. It is also important to consider other potential allies. The more challenging the change and the more obstinate the opposition, the more people are needed to press for it, so increasing the size of the group of supporters is an important consideration.

Steps 1 and 2 are interchangeable. It can be equally effective to contact people to discover their needs and problems, or begin by identifying the problem and then locating the people who are experiencing or concerned about it.

3. The next step entails talking to people about the problem so that the organizer has a better sense of what is wrong, why it is wrong, and what will improve circumstances. Conversations are often begun individually. As the organizer meets individuals interested in the same problem, he or she may want to bring people together to discuss it. The group serves the function of validating people's experiences, helps them feel less powerless and alone, and develops camaraderie and a reference group for action. This step is particularly important if the people are few in numbers and members of an oppressed and powerless minority who are pursuing a difficult change.

4. As the people begin to talk about their problem, agreement about a change goal must begin. It is critical for people to decide what they believe will solve the problem. The organizer may encourage people to select a goal that is specific, concrete, and feasible.

Smaller scale changes give people a place to begin and builds their confidence for larger changes. However, the goal cannot be insignificant. People will feel exploited by an organizer who tries to convince them that something meaningless is actually significant or that they pursue a partial solution because it is the only one they could reasonably achieve. It is also important to identify a solution that many people can support. No social change effort can afford to divide a constituency.

5. The next step involves learning as much as one can about the problem. How many people experience it? Who are they? What causes the problem? Does the problem involve any discrimination? What solutions to the problem have been tried? What does the law say about this problem? Have other groups tried to attack this problem? What did they do? Who might oppose this change, and who might support it? Why? How could your opponents' views be influenced?

6. Identification of the target of the change is next. Targets are defined early, and others may emerge during the process. If the desired change is large scale and will take a long time to realize, it may be important to first try to influence the attitude of the general public before attempting to confront a target. This is the way much of the antismoking legislation came into being. There may also be lower level decision makers who can be approached for support before the key power holder. Several decision makers may be approached either sequentially or at once. It's important to learn something about the targets. Who are they? What is their history? What are their responsibilities? What views do they hold? If it is a politician, how does he or she vote and what kinds of public stands has he or she taken? Who influences him or her? What trade, fraternal, or religious associations does he or she have? Knowledge of the target can be used in pressuring him or her for change.

7. The next step involves bringing people together to talk about the strategy for the change, that is, what steps the group will take to solve the problem. Is there a legislative calendar that will need to be followed? What will influence the legislators—a petition, a letter writing campaign, visits from constituents? Is there some event or media event that could be used to publicize the change? If so, what kind of public protest will capture attention? What kind of dramatic presentation can be used? Will a meeting with the decision maker be required? If so, what should be included in the meeting, and who will take what roles? What do you want to ask the target to do? What arguments made by whom might get the decision maker's attention? Is there pressure that needs to be brought to bear? It is important to identify several different ways of approaching the target, to develop a repertoire of possibilities to influence the target. In general, tactics escalate from friendly persuasion to open conflict, depending on what is necessary to influence the target. Tactics that irritate, alienate, or repulse potential allies, such as blocking traffic at rush hour, should typically be avoided so as not to lose support.

8. Taking whatever action has been decided on by the group is the next step. It is important that after people take action, the organizer encourage them to reflect on what they have done and feel positive about it. Most people find it hard to take action, so the more people can feel encouraged, empowered, and positive, the more energy and endurance they will have for future work.

9. Because social change seldom occurs easily, the next step is to improve the environment for change. This might involve widening the circle of participants by attracting new activists, bringing media attention to the cause, or trying more confrontational tactics to pursue the target. For example, if a decision maker refuses to meet, protesters may go to his home with picket signs. If the organization has succeeded in its goal on a partialized problem, a related problem might be tackled. Throughout the action phase, people need to discuss where they are in relation to achieving the change goal, and therefore, what they want to do next.

10. When the decision maker finally agrees and the change is realized, be it the passage of a law, a new agreement, or a change in the public's view on an issue, change activists should be helped to celebrate their accomplishment with a party or some recognition ceremony. This celebration reinvigorates the activists for future change efforts.

WEB SITES

Association for Community Organization for Reform Now. www.acorn.org.

Association for Community Organization and Social Administration. http://www.acosa.org.

Center for Community Change. http://www.communitychange.org.

Discover the Networks.org: a guide to the political left. http://www.discoverthenetworks.org.

Information Education. http://www.infed.org/community/b-comorg.htm.

North American Humanist Forum. http://www.newhumanistforum.org.

References

Checkoway, B. (1995). Six strategies of community change. *Community Development Journal, 30*(1), 2–20.

Fisher, R. (1995). Social action community organization: Proliferation, persistence, roots, and prospects. In J. Rothman, J. L. Erlich, & J. E. Tropman with F. M. Cox (Eds.), *Strategies of community organization: Macros practice*, 5th ed. (pp. 327–340). Itasca, IL: F. E. Peacock.

Gamson, W. A. (1975). *The strategy of social protest.* Homewood, IL: Dorsey Press.

Gamson, W. A. (1992). The social psychology of collective action. In A. Morris & C. Mueller (Eds.), *Frontiers in social movement theory* (pp. 53–76). New Haven, CT: Yale University Press.

Hall, M. (1999). *Poor people's social movement organization: The goal is to win.* Westport, CT: Praeger.

Hardcastle, D. A., Wenocur, S., & Powers, P. R. (2004). *Community practice: Theories and skills for social workers.* New York: Oxford University Press.

Hardina, D. (2000). Models and tactics taught in community organization courses. Findings from a survey of practice instructors. *Journal of Community Practice, 7*(1), 5–18.

Hoefer, R. (2000). Human services interest groups in four states: Lessons for effective advocacy. *Journal of Community Practice, 7*(4), 77–94.

Mansbridge, J. (2001). The making of oppositional consciousness. In J. Mansbridge & A. Morris (Eds.), *Oppositional consciousness: The subjective roots of social protest* (pp. 1–19). Chicago: University of Chicago Press.

McAdam, D., McCarthy, J. D., & Zald, M. N. (Eds.). (1996). *Comparative perspectives on social movements: Political opportunities, mobilizing structures, and cultural framings.* Cambridge: Cambridge University Press.

McCarthy, J., & Zald, M. (1977). Resource mobilization and social movements. *American Journal of Sociology, 82,* 1212–1242.

Meyer, D., Whittier, N., & Robnett, B. (Eds.). (2002). *Social movements identity, culture and the state.* New York: Oxford University Press.

Mondros, J. (2005). Political, social, and legislative action. In M. Weil (Ed.), *The handbook of community practice* (pp. 276–286). Thousand Oaks, CA: Sage.

Mondros, J., & Wilson, S. (1994). *Organizing for power and empowerment.* New York: Columbia University Press.

Morris, A., & Mueller, C. (1992). *Frontiers in social movement theory.* New Haven, CT: Yale University Press.

Morrison, D. E. (1978). Some notes toward theory on relative deprivation, social movements, and social change. In L. E. Genevie (Ed.), *Collective behavior and social movements* (pp. 202–209). Itasca, IL: F. E. Peacock.

Rubin, H. J., & Rubin, I. S. (2005). The practice of community organizing. In M. Weil (Ed.), *The handbook of community practice* (pp. 189–203). Thousand Oaks, CA: Sage.

Ryan, C., & Gamson, W. A. (2006). The art of reframing political debates. *Contexts, 5*(1), 13–18.

Staples, L. (2004). *Roots to power: A manual for grassroots organizing*, 2nd ed. Westport, CT: Praeger.

Weil, M. O., & Gamble, D. (2005). Evolution, models, and the changing context of community practice. In M. Weil (Ed.), *The handbook of community practice* (pp. 117–149). Thousand Oaks, CA: Sage.

Community Partnerships for School-Based Services
Action Principles

Dennis L. Poole

A *community partnership* is an alliance between citizens and practitioners to bring about planned change for the public good. *Community* stems from the Latin word *communis*, which implies something shared and public. The term *partnership* derives meaning from its derivative, *partner*. A partner once referred to a piece of timber used to buttress the deck or mast of a wooden sailing ship. This is a fitting analogy to the discussion here. Community partners for school-based services work together to achieve a public good that is above and beyond the reach of any one partner—namely, the safe passage of the community's youth into responsible adulthood.

SAFE PASSAGE OF YOUTH

Most adolescents make the passage to responsible adulthood safely. They enter the labor force, become effective parents, and participate in the mainstream of community life. But an increasing number of teenagers do not make this transition successfully. Harmful environmental conditions and risky behaviors often result in trauma, obesity, substance abuse, delinquency, or school failure, which handicap them as adults.

A powerful consensus has emerged over the past decade that no single community institution is powerful enough to support youth during this critical developmental stage of life. Dryfoos (2000) calls it the safe passage movement. As with all social movements, this one aims to bring about fundamental changes in social relationships between community institutions. A major goal is to replace fragmented, uncoordinated services for youth with integrated, collaborative networks of support.

Advocates of the safe passage movement call on schools and agencies to build *seamless* institutions. A priority concern is delivery of integrative community services in school settings—hence the term *school-based services*.

School-based services cover a variety of types and nomenclatures (Dryfoos, Quinn, & Boukin, 2005). Many of them include the word *center* in their name—for example, youth center, family resource center, school health center, and after-school center—to indicate the central location of multiple support services in a school site. Other school-based services use the words *program* or *clinic* to reflect the delivery of one primary community service, such as a school dental clinic, psychosocial counseling program, school mentoring program, and a case management program. Still others fall under the rubric of full-service community schools, which integrate health, youth development, family, and other community services to support student learning.

COMMUNITY PARTNERSHIPS

The common denominator in virtually all school-based service initiatives is the presence of community partnerships. Powerful alliances between citizens and practitioners are needed to disrupt status quo arrangements between community institutions that serve youth and their families in piecemeal fashion.

School-based services usually do not materialize without such partnerships (Epstein, 2002). Institutional boundaries between schools and agencies are rigid, inflexible, and impenetrable in many communities. Each institution has its own set of rules, regulations, and customs, which prohibit sharing of information, staff, facilities, and financial resources with other community institutions. Fixed institutional boundaries surface in school-based service initiatives when school superintendents, say, deny requests by mental health centers to outpost therapists at school sites; health department directors block efforts by schools to conduct preventive health screenings; and youth center directors insist that after-school services be provided in their own facilities.

Community partnerships have the potential to remove or blur previously fixed institutional boundaries between schools and community agencies. They can minimize interagency competition, reduce fragmentation in service systems, and increase efficient use of community resources (Anderson-Butcher & Ashton, 2004).

ACTION PRINCIPLES

Social workers can play a leadership role in community partnerships for school-based services. Six action principles in the community partnership model are offered in Figure 132.1 to guide them throughout the capacity-building process.

Community Agenda Building

Initiate the process by getting a core group of citizens and practitioners to place the issue on the community agenda. "Agenda building" refers to predecisional processes that lead decision makers to select some issues for deliberation and reject others (Cobb & Elder, 1983). The challenge is to convince them that an issue deserves a prominent position on the community's agenda. An agenda is the list of items that a school board, youth council, city human services commission, or other community decision-making body is willing or able to consider at a given point in time.

To illustrate, let's assume that the issue is school failure. A social worker learns that a fourth of the students at a middle school are being written off as school failures. Standardized test scores are low; school behavioral problems are high; and these students are at imminent risk of being left behind their peers in high school. Let's also assume that the appropriate community decision-making body to address the issue is the city healthy youth commission. The social worker knows that complex social, emotional, and health forces stand in the way of success of at-risk students, and multiple community support services are needed to prevent failure in the middle school.

The social worker's first leadership task is to identify a core group of concerned citizens and professionals that can get the issue placed on the agenda of the city commission. A common flaw at this stage of the process is for practitioners to try to address the issue without citizens. The practitioner must appreciate the key role citizens play in agenda building. Citizens are the central actors in a democracy—and trustees of the public interest (Cooper, 1991). Hence, the social worker's first task is to bring a sense of citizenship to the capacity-building process. This begins by heeding the adage that "an issue is not an issue until three or four leading citizens say it's an issue."

Members of the agenda-building group should represent four types of power. One member should have *political* power. Citizens elected this person to represent their interests on the city council, local school board, county commission, or state legislature. Another member should have *economic* power. Citizens recognize this person as a successful business leader committed to youth services—the board president of the local United Way, for example. Another member should have *moral* power. Citizens respect this person as a longstanding advocate for youth and families. One or two other members of the group should also have *technical* power—a principal, teacher, or agency practitioner with expertise on prevention of school failure.

The social worker should meet with each of these representatives individually, and then as a group, to discuss the issue and develop a strategy to get it placed on the meeting agenda of the city healthy youth commission. Once this is achieved, the social worker helps the group prepare for the meeting. (A citizen delivers the presentation, rather than a professional, who might be perceived as having a personal stake in the outcome.) The main objective of the meeting is for the commission to vote in favor of a motion to establish a community partnership structure to investigate school failure at the middle school, then report back with key findings and strategic recommendations.

Community Partnership Structure

Develop a community partnership structure to involve citizens and practitioners in the capacity-building process. Once the issue achieves agenda status, the next phase is to build a community partnership structure and sustain it throughout

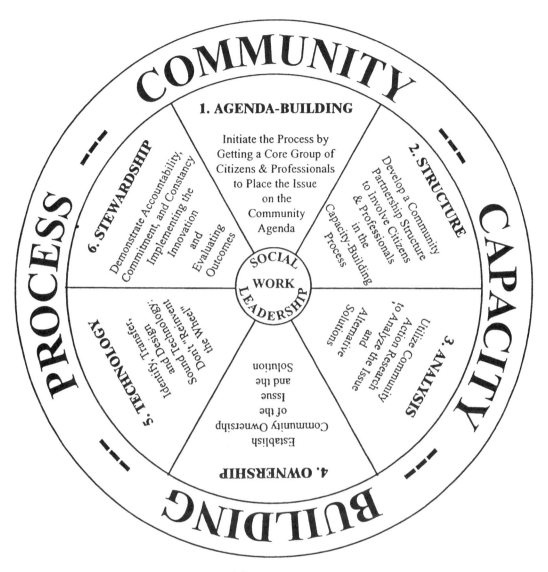

Figure 132.1 Community partnership model.
(*Source:* © Dennis L. Poole, School of Social Work, University of Texas at Austin, 2000.)

the process. This type of structure provides a channel through which responsible citizens can take a leadership role with practitioners in solving pressing community problems. It usually operates under the auspices of a community decision-making body, taking the form of a committee, task force, or advisory council. Citizen-driven and action-oriented, a community partnership structure fosters shared responsibility for local problems, prompts behavioral change in community institutions, and initiates and sustains reform efforts over time (Poole, 1997).

Let's assume that the city healthy youth commission decided to establish a 25-member com-

munity partnership structure called the Youth Safe Passage Committee. The social worker must ensure that the majority of the members appointed to the committee are leading citizens in the community, including the chairperson. The balance of the members should be practitioners from schools and community agencies with resources to address school failure in the middle school. School representatives might include the superintendent, middle school principal, a teacher, guidance counselor, or social worker. Agency representatives might include administrators or staff of the public health department, mental health center, department of human services, or YMCA.

The social worker's knowledge and skills in social group work are essential to the future success of the Youth Safe Passage Committee. The practitioner may need to negotiate an agreement with the director of his or her own agency to provide staff support services to the committee. As in treatment groups, this leadership function is performed by helping a community work group identify goals and objectives, facilitating group action and interaction, maintaining group cohesiveness and member satisfaction, and providing means for group task performance (Ephross & Vassil, 2005). The entire capacity-building process for school-based services is likely to disintegrate if the group maintenance needs of the Youth Safe Passage Committee are not met.

Analysis

Use community action research to analyze the issue and alternative solutions. The analysis phase of the capacity-building process involves community action research. Traditional research will not satisfy the full requirements of this phase. Hiring a consultant to analyze the issue, report findings, and offer recommendations will not suffice. The main objective is for the community to become the research team, not a consultant or a few practitioners (Minkler & Wallerstein, 2003).

As in traditional research, community action research seeks to improve the quality of decision making through careful collection of facts. But greater emphasis is given to participatory strategies than to nonparticipatory strategies. Key informant interviews, public forums, surveys, and focus groups are used to engage divergent community groups and organizations in data collection and analysis. These strategies foster broad-based community participation, increase public awareness of the issue, and identify community partners that must share in the solution.

Accordingly, the leadership role of the social worker is to ensure that each member of Youth Safe Passage Committee participates in the process and shares ownership of the findings and proposed solutions. Tasks include helping committee members reach consensus on the nature, scope, and causes of school failure at the middle school; identify alternative strategies for the community to address the issue; and submit a written report to the city healthy youth commission with recommendations. The social worker may help write the report, but his or her name is not prominently displayed. The authors are the members of the committee that gathered the information, analyzed the findings, and identified solutions penned into the report by staff.

Community Ownership

Establish community ownership of the issue and solution. "Ownership" refers to actions taken by a community decision-making body that demonstrate it owns an issue. Community ownership is established when this body has power to define the issue, determine its causes, and assign responsibility to local institutions to implement a solution. Some community institutions will not want to give up their power to define the issue because it would mean forfeiting their right to control the solution. Others will want to "disown" the issue because they might be asked to share responsibility in solving it (Gusfield, 1981).

In the example of school failure, the main leadership role of the social worker is to shift ownership of the issue from the school system to the community at large. The practitioner must recognize that prevention of failure at the middle school cannot take place without a change in the status quo. The community—via the city healthy youth commission—must demonstrate that it owns the problem and will hold relevant local institutions accountable for their fair share of the solution. At some point in the capacity-building process, a community institution will attempt to renege on prior public commitments to solve the problem or attempt to control the solution. The city human service commission must win this battle for ownership of the issue and solution.

Technology

Identify, transfer, and design sound technology: don't reinvent the wheel. In the technology phase, attention of the social worker shifts to the identification, transfer, and design of a sound technology to implement the strategy adopted by the city healthy youth commission. Frequently, too little attention is devoted to this important phase of the capacity-building process. Organizations that do not have adequate and appropriate staff, facilities, hardware, funding, or intervention techniques usually have great difficulty implementing a new product or service innovation (Poole, Ferguson, & Schwab, 2005).

The social worker must recognize that school failure is not a new issue. Other communities have faced the same issue and devised good technical solutions. The social worker must help the Youth Safe Passage Committee find these solutions, assess their outcomes, determine transferability, and modify the solution to fit the particular needs and specifications of his or her community. Library research, surfing the Internet, phone calls, and site visits help the social worker meet this challenge. Fortunately, ample literature exists on the causes of school failure, and an array of solutions involving diverse practitioners have been tested in school settings (Dryfoos et al., 2005). Roles for social workers in the solutions are rich and varied (Openshaw, 2008).

The practitioner must also help the committee ensure that all relevant community institutions contribute resources—cash or in kind—to implement the plan. Most school-based service innovations require a diversified funding base, reflecting the complexity of interventions needed to prevent school failure. Though a diversified funding base is usually needed to sustain a school-based service innovation over time, small contributions from the Junior League, the United Way, or private donors can be used as seed money. These contributions foster community ownership, provide an opportunity to test the viability of the technology, and give the community time to secure larger, stable sources of funding, chiefly from state or federal agencies.

Stewardship

Demonstrate accountability, commitment, and constancy implementing the innovation and evaluating outcomes. Once the city healthy youth commission endorses the technical plan, and startup funding is secured, the work of the Youth Safe Passage Committee shifts to the stewardship phase of the capacity-building process. *Stewardship* means to hold something in trust for another, beginning with the willingness to be accountable for outcomes to some larger body than ourselves—namely, the community (Block, 1993).

Stewardship is the most difficult phase in the capacity-building process. School-based service innovations never work exactly as planned. Community partners become disgruntled, paperwork gets burdensome, resources grow thin, and early outcomes inevitably fall short of expectations (Payne, Gottfredson, & Gottfredson, 2006; Poole, 1997).

During the stewardship phase, it is easy for community partners to lose sight of the fact that they must fulfill the public trust—they must deliver the public good they promised and be accountable for the results. Self-interest, feelings of defeat, and burnout take a toll on partners in this phase of the process. The social worker must demonstrate courage to withstand criticism, constancy to maintain vigilance, commitment to reach the community goal, honesty to admit shortcomings, creativity to fix problems, and optimism to repel defeat.

This phase is not for the light-hearted. Victory stands faintly at the end of a long, dark tunnel. Reaching it brings great joy, however, and restores public confidence in schools and community agencies. Fortunately, a community partnership has many partners. Each partner can buttress and support the innovation when one partner is weak or behaves irresponsibly. The partnership also makes flight from social responsibility difficult because the community holds the partners accountable for the public trust bestowed on them. Good stewards finds ways to implement an innovation as planned, refine the technology as needed, and produce outcomes that make a difference in the performance of youth in school.

CONCLUSION

Safe passage of youth to responsible adulthood require schools and agencies to provide seamless services in school settings. Community partnerships between citizens and practitioners are needed to disrupt status quo arrangements that serve youth and families in piecemeal fashion. Social workers can take a leadership role in building and sustaining school-based service initiatives by adhering to the six action principles of the community partnership model presented in this chapter.

WEB SITES

Center for Schools and Communities. http://www.center-school.org.
Coalition for Community Schools. http://www.communityschools.org/insideschools.html.
School Social Work Association of America. http://www.sswaa.org.

References

Anderson-Butcher, D. & Ashton, D. (2004). Innovative models of collaboration to save children, youth, families, and communities. *Children and Schools,* *26,* 39–53.

Block, P. (1993). *Stewardship.* San Francisco: Barrett-Koehler.

Cobb, R., & Elder, C. (1983). *Participation in American politics.* Baltimore, MD: John Hopkins University Press.

Cooper, T. (1991). *An ethic of citizenship for public administration.* Englewood Cliffs, NJ: Prentice Hall.

Dryfoos, J. G. (2000). *Safe passage: Making it through adolescence in a risky society.* New York: Oxford University Press.

Dryfoos, J. C., Quinn, L., & Boukin, C. (2005). *Community school in action: Lessons from a decade of practice.* New York: Oxford University Press.

Ephross, P., & Vassil, T. (2005). *Groups that work.* New York: Columbia University Press.

Epstein, J. (2002). *School, family, and community partnerships: Your handbook for action.* California: Corwin Press.

Gusfield, J. (1981). *The culture of public problems.* Chicago: University of Chicago Press.

Openshaw, L. (2008). *Social work in schools.* New York: Guilford.

Minkler, M., & Wallerstein, N. (2003). *Community-based participatory research for health.* San Francisco: Jossey-Bass.

Payne, A., Gottfredson, D., & Gottfredson, G. (2006). School predictions of the intensity of implementation of school-based prevention programs: Results from a national study. *Prevention Science, 7,* 225–237.

Poole, D. L. (1997). The SAFE project: Community-driven partnerships in health, mental health, and education to prevent early school failure. *Health and Social Work, 22,* 282–289.

Poole, D. L., Ferguson, M., & Schwab, A. J. (2005). Managing process innovations in welfare reform technology. *Administration in Social Work, 29,* 101–116.

133

Building Community Capacity in the U.S. Air Force
The Community Readiness Consultant Model

Gary L. Bowen, James A. Martin, Brenda J. Liston, & John P. Nelson

Military bases vary on a number of dimensions, including their operational mission, their corresponding demographic composition, and the characteristics of their host community. Bases also differ in their ability to achieve positive community results—"aggregate, broad-based outcomes that reflect the collective efforts of individuals and families who live within a specified area" (Bowen, Martin, Mancini, & Nelson, 2000, p. 9). Resiliency is one such community result that reflects the aggregate success of community members

and families to manage their personal and family lives in the context of adversity and positive challenge.

The U.S. Air Force (AF) has long provided broad-based programs and services to support adaptation, readiness, and retention. Over the past decade, AF agencies have embraced a new community-based model of service delivery that parallels rapid and profound changes in the size, composition, and stationing of military forces (Bowen, Martin, & Mancini, 1999; Bowen, Martin, & Nelson, 2002). AF community-based practice models focus on promoting interagency collaboration and strengthening the interface between formal and informal networks of social care as a means to promote member and family resiliency (Bowen, Mancini, & Martin, 2002).

Overall, community-based models provide agencies a strategy to address support needs associated with increased operational tempo without commensurate increases in agency budgets. Lessons from the first Gulf War and subsequent large-scale deployments demonstrate the need for and the benefit of agencies working together in more integrative and collaborative ways to address community needs, as well as the importance of agencies partnering with and mobilizing informal support networks on behalf of members and families (Hoshmand & Hoshmand, 2007; Martin, Mancini, Bowen, Mancini, & Orthner, 2004).

Airman and Family Readiness Centers (A&FRCs) are the focal agency for addressing the support needs of AF members and families. These centers (formerly Family Support Centers) operate on every AF base under the worldwide management of the AF Airman and Family Services Division (HQ USAF/A1SP). The A1SP recently revised its concept of operations and staff training programs with the goal of strengthening members and families through enhanced and targeted community-based outreach efforts. A new A&FRC Community Readiness Consultant (CRC) strategy is being implemented across the AF in an effort to expand outreach to units (typically at the squadron level—a unit of typically a few hundred military members) and to the broader base community.

This chapter describes the model of community capacity, which is the cornerstone of this outreach strategy. This model, which embraces members and families within their social context, focuses on the nexus between formal and informal networks of social care as the target of intervention and prevention efforts. We first describe the CRC strategy; we conclude by discussing empirical support for the community capacity model and the need for continued research and evaluation of community practice initiatives that are framed and informed by this model.

THE CRC STRATEGY

The new CRC strategy promotes interagency collaboration, encourages proactive unit leadership in support of members and families, and builds informal community connections for purposes of fostering a sense of community, promoting individual and family adaptation, and ensuring personnel preparedness to successfully perform military duties. This service delivery strategy is strengths-based and results-focused. It contrasts greatly with the more stove-piped, remedial, menu-driven services model that informed A&FRCs operations since the early 1980s.

A key component of the strategy is unit outreach. CRCs assist unit commanders in meeting their leadership responsibilities for the health, welfare, and readiness of unit members. Instead of attempting to fit the needs of unit members and families into preexisting programs and services, CRCs work in partnership with unit leaders to identify and prioritize needs that compromise readiness and retention. CRCs work within the scope of the A&FRC's mission; they are trained to help unit commanders locate and obtain necessary resources that fall outside the organizational boundaries of the A&FRC (Orthner, Bowen, & Mancini, 2003). CRCs capitalize on the availability of formal and informal community resources in planning and implementing responses to priority issues—networking and collaboration are the cornerstones of this community-based approach to practice.

The work of CRCs with units is informed by a six-step process: engagement, assessment, planning, implementation, evaluation, and sustainment (Orthner et al., 2003). The AF has committed significant resources to train CRCs in this model, which is framed and informed by a results management (RM) approach to the design and delivery of services (Orthner & Bowen, 2004). RM focuses agency efforts on clearly defined and anticipated results. A key aspect of the RM approach is to identify community partners who will help achieve the desired results. The aim is to work with leaders to develop a unit service action plan focused on issues where the A&FRC has a defined role. This plan specifies desired results, identifies key partners, indicates services and supports that will be provided to the unit, and specifies everyone's roles, responsibilities, and activities. Importantly, the CRC and unit leaders are co-developers of the plan.

Online assessment tools have been designed to inform, monitor, and evaluate service action plans (Bowen, 2007; Bowen & Martin, 2006). These tools examine respondents' perceptions about sources of informal and formal support in their lives and about their perceived success in adapting to life challenges and meeting AF responsibilities. These tools have features that are consistent with a community capacity approach to practice, and they directly support the work of CRCs. For example, after completing an online inventory, respondents can go to an easy-to interpret, confidential summary profile of their responses. They can also consult and download specific helpful strategies for increasing social connections in their lives, and they can e-mail their unit CRC with questions and comments or request information about available information and supports. CRCs are able to view and download a summary group profile that aggregates the responses across a particular unit, including open-ended respondent comments. An advanced selection tool allows CRCs to generate profiles for specific respondent subgroups. The Web site also has a link for downloading, completing, and managing unit service action plans.

THE COMMUNITY CAPACITY MODEL

The CRC practice strategy aligns with a larger community capacity model that was developed and tested by a team of researchers from the AF and civilian communities (Bowen et al., 2000; Mancini, Bowen, & Martin, 2005). A review of this model demonstrates the heuristic and stimulus value of explanatory models to the development of specific practice strategies. This community capacity model has had program and practice implications not only for A&FRCs but also for other AF agencies, including the Family Advocacy Division, which coordinates the AF's response to child and spouse maltreatment (Bowen et al., 2002; Mancini, Nelson, Bowen, & Martin, 2006).

The community capacity model includes three major components: (1) formal networks, (2) informal networks, and (3) community capacity. From the perspective of the model, variation in the aggregate success of members and families to manage their personal and family lives in the context of adversity and positive challenge (across AF bases, as well as across time for any single base community), is explained by how successfully formal and informal networks of social care operate and interact with one another in the generation of community capacity. Community capacity, which reflects the level of social organization in the community, is hypothesized as the link between community networks and community results. Social care is defined as tangible, informational, and socioemotional support available for military members and their families. The level of social care provided to members and families

through the combined forces of these networks can range from high to low. Each component of the model is elaborated in the following discussion, including a discussion of the hypothesized linkages between these components and between community capacity and individual and family resiliency.

Formal and Informal Networks of Social Care

Three networks of formal and informal social care are identified in the community capacity model: (1) community agencies, (2) unit leaders, and (3) informal community connections. Formal networks, which include base agencies and unit leaders, reflect the military policies and systems of social care that operate as instruments of socialization, support, and social control. Base agencies promote social care by demonstrating a customer and strengths-based orientation in their coordination and delivery of intervention and prevention services to members and families. Unit leaders provide social care by promoting connections between members and families, helping members and families balance work and family demands, and when needed, helping unit members and families access and secure support services. The effectiveness of formal networks of social care depends in part on securing necessary input and participation from community members.

Informal networks, which include informal community connections, are voluntary and less organized. They include personal and collective relationships and group associations, such as unit-based support groups and relationships with extended family members, work associates, neighbors, and families. Mutual exchanges and reciprocal responsibilities constitute the cornerstones of informal network construction. Informal network members promote social care by reaching out to make connections with one another, exchanging information and resources, and when needed, helping one another secure support from community programs and support services—all examples of social capital.

Bowen and Martin (1998) describe these networks as power substations of social care in the community, which have turbines in the form of trust, commitments and obligations, information exchanges, positive regard and mutual respect, and norms of shared responsibility and social control. As compared to formal networks, informal networks play a more active and often a more important role in the day-to-day life of members and families. They typically operate as the first level of social care when members and families need support and assistance.

From the perspective of intervention and prevention planning, an important function of formal networks is to strengthen informal community connections. Formal networks may grow at the expense of informal networks (McKnight, 1997). For example, community agencies may plan and sponsor events for community members that members are capable of planning and sponsoring for themselves. When unit leaders and base agencies perform functions the informal community is capable of providing for itself (i.e., overfunctioning), informal community networks may be diminished. When the system of formal and informal networks is fully operative and complementary in a base community, a protective and resilient web of support surrounds and sustains members and families (Bowen, Orthner, Martin, & Mancini, 2001).

Unit leaders play a particularly important role in the community network—they stand between informal networks on one side and base agencies on the other. In many respects, the unit is synonymous with community in the AF, and the identity of members and families typically derives more from their unit association than from their base or local civilian community residency (Bowen et al., 1999; Bowen & McClure, 1999).

Community Capacity

From the perspective of the model highlighted here, community capacity is the concept that links the operation of formal and informal networks of social care to produce community results. It involves two components assumed to mutually reinforce each other over time. First, community capacity reflects the extent to which base agencies, unit leaders, and community members demonstrate a sense of *shared responsibility* for the general welfare of the community and its members. When network members share responsibility for the general welfare, they invest time and energy in making the community a better place to live, work, and play, and they work together to promote the common good.

In addition to feelings of shared responsibility, base agencies, unit leaders, and community members demonstrate *collective competence* in taking advantage of opportunities for addressing community needs and confronting situations threatening the safety and well-being of commu-

nity members. They pull together in the context of opportunity or adversity to identify community needs and assets, define common goals and objectives, set priorities, develop strategies for collective action, implement actions consistent with agreed-on strategies, and monitor results.

As defined, community capacity represents behaviors and action, rather than the potential for action. When community capacity is high, members and families have access to resources and opportunities to complete duty requirements and mission requirements; develop community identity and pride; meet individual and family needs and goals; participate meaningfully in community life; solve problems and manage conflicts; and affirm and maintain stability and order in personal, family, and work relationships.

Networks and Community Capacity

Community capacity springs from the actions and interactions *within* and *between* base agencies, base and unit leaders, and community members— a social energy that flows from the union between formal and informal community networks. As such, community capacity is distinct from the processes from which it emerges, and the fund of capacity is more than the sum total of actions in formal and informal networks. The *bonding* (within) and *bridging* (between) activities by these formal and informal networks of social care provide the cornerstones for achieving community results associated with member and family resiliency.

Bonding, which Putnam (2000) describes as "sociological superglue" (p. 23), captures the cohesion, trust, and positive regard within groups, such as within informal networks of social care. Putnam describes *bridging* as the "sociological WD-40" (p. 23), or the strength of ties among individuals across groups, such as the working relationships between unit leaders and representatives of base agencies. The ongoing processes of bonding and bridging among members from various segments of the community form a complex union that powers community capacity and provides a means to achieve community results.

Community Capacity and Community Results

Community capacity may have upper and lower threshold effects in its relationship to community results. Above a certain level of community capacity, further increases in capacity may not be associated with the further promotion of community results. On the other hand, once community capacity declines below a certain level, community results may decrease precipitously. This is consistent with Crane's (1991) epidemic model of community effects, in which problems spread like a contagion once a certain level of community vulnerability is reached.

The influence of community capacity may vary over the work and family life course (Bowen, Richman, & Bowen, 2000). AF families may need community capacity to be high in times of peak operational demands, such as during a deployment. The nature and impact of community capacity must be considered in the context of individual time (where individuals are in their own stage of development, including the military/work career), family time (where individuals are in the family life cycle), and historical time (the current context, including the economy and current military conflicts). These three aspects of time can intersect and merge in interesting and challenging ways as members and families move through the life course.

EVIDENCE BASE: IMPLICATIONS FOR RESEARCH AND EVALUATION

The community capacity model served as a template in the AF's development and implementation of the CRC strategy. Although the research literature supports unit leaders as the key leverage points in promoting member and family resiliency (Bowen, 1998; Pittman, Kerpelman, & McFadyen, 2004), the model includes two additional strategy platforms for launching community building efforts: interagency collaboration and informal network development. At present, CRCs influence these community building components largely through unit-based efforts, including their use of other agencies as partners in planning and implementation of service action plans, as well as in their work with unit commanders to mobilize members and families in support of one another. The A&FRC also performs a base-level direct practice role, providing a range of support services, such as financial counseling and education.

Although the CRC strategy awaits formal evaluation, a body of basic research supports this application of the community capacity model. In an investigation with a probability sample of 20,569 married AF members, unit leader support exerted a positive and significant indirect effect on family adaptation through its direct effect on sense of community and informal community support (Bowen, Mancini, Martin, Ware, & Nelson, 2003). In a more recent investigation with 10,102 married active-duty AF members, positive perceptions of community capacity had a strong and direct effect on self-reported symptoms of depression; these perceptions were also a significant mediator of the effects of formal and informal support networks on depression, including agency support, unit leader support, and neighbor support (Bowen, Martin, & Ware, 2004).

In addition to this program of basic research, program research in other areas has provided support for AF interventions that incorporate community-based components. For instance, the AF's suicide prevention program, which incorporates interagency planning and coordination, commander awareness education and training, and peer monitoring, has been associated with a reduced rate of suicide and reductions in other adverse outcomes in an evaluation using a quasi-experimental design (Knox, Litts, Talcott, Feig, & Caine, 2003). Additional research is needed to test linkages between concepts in the community capacity model, as well as evaluate community initiatives consistent with its central linkages to provide an evidence base for community practice in the AF.

WEB SITES

Air Force Crossroads. http://www.afcrossroads.com.

Airman and Family Readiness Flight (A&FRF). http://ask.afpc.randolph.af.mil/famops.

Better Together, an initiative of the Saguaro Seminar: Civic Engagement in America at Harvard University. http://www.bettertogether.org.

Civic Practices Network (CPN). http://www.cpn.org.

Military OneSource. http://www.militaryonesource.com.

References

Bowen, G. L. (1998). Effects of leader support in the work unit on the relationship between work spillover and family adaptation. *Journal of Family and Economic Issues, 19,* 25–52.

Bowen, G. L. (2007). *The personal assets inventory.* Chapel Hill, NC: Bowen & Colleagues. Retrieved

October 20, 2007, from, https://pai.communities-inblue.org.

Bowen, G. L., Mancini, J. A., & Martin, J. A. (2002). Community capacity building in the United States Air Force. *NCFR Report, 47*(1), F10, F13.

Bowen, G. L., Mancini, J. A., Martin, J. A., Ware, W. B., & Nelson, J. P. (2003). An empirical test of a community practice model for promoting family adaptation. *Family Relations, 52*, 33–52.

Bowen, G. L., & Martin, J. A. (1998). Community capacity: A core component of the 21st century military community. *Military Family Issues: The Research Digest, 2*(3), 1–4.

Bowen, G. L., & Martin, J. A. (2006). *The unit assets inventory*. Chapel Hill, NC: Bowen & Colleagues. Retrieved October 20, 2007, from https://uai.communitiesinblue.org.

Bowen, G. L., Martin, J. A., & Mancini, J. A. (1999). *Communities in Blue for the 21st century*. Fairfax, VA: Caliber Associates.

Bowen, G. L., Martin, J. A., Mancini, J. A., & Nelson, J. P. (2000). Community capacity: Antecedents and consequences. *Journal of Community Practice, 8*(2), 1–21.

Bowen, G. L., Martin, J. A., & Nelson, J. P. (2002). A community capacity response to family violence in the United States Air Force. In A. R. Roberts & G. J. Greene (Eds.), *Social workers' desk reference* (pp. 551–556). New York: Oxford University Press.

Bowen, G. L., Martin, J. A., & Ware, W. B. (2004, November). Community capacity and the health of married active duty members. In G. L. Bowen (Chair), *Community capacity and the health of military families*. Symposium conducted at the National Council on Family Relations 66th Annual Conference, Orlando, Florida.

Bowen, G. L., & McClure, P. (1999). Military communities. In P. McClure (Ed.), *Pathways to the future: A review of military family research* (pp. 11–34). Scranton, PA: Marywood University.

Bowen, G. L., Orthner, D. K., Martin, J. A., & Mancini, J. A. (2001). *Building community capacity: A manual for U.S. family support centers*. Chapel Hill, NC: Better Image Printing.

Bowen, G. L., Richman, J. M., & Bowen, N. K. (2000). Families in the context of communities across time. In S. J. Price, P. C. McKenry, & M. J. Murphy (Eds.), *Families across time: A life course perspective* (pp. 117–128). Los Angeles: Roxbury.

Crane, J. (1991). The epidemic theory of ghettos and neighborhood effects on dropping out and teenage childbearing. *American Journal of Sociology, 96*, 1226–1259.

Hoshmand, L. T., & Hoshmand, A. L. (2007). Support for military families. *Journal of Community Psychology, 35*, 171–180.

Knox, K. L., Litts, D. A., Talcott, G. W., Feig, J. C., & Caine, E. D. (2003). Risk of suicide and related adverse outcomes after exposure to a suicide prevention programme in the US Air Force: Cohort study. *British Medical Journal, 327*, 1376–1380.

Mancini, J. A., Bowen, G. L., & Martin, J. A. (2005). Community social organization: A conceptual linchpin in examining families in the context of communities. *Family Relations, 54*, 570–582.

Mancini, J. A., Nelson, J. P., Bowen, G. L., & Martin, J. A. (2006). Preventing intimate partner violence: A community capacity approach. *Journal of Aggression, Maltreatment, and Trauma, 13*(3/4), 203–227.

Martin, J. A., Mancini, D. L., Bowen, G. L. Mancini, J. A., & Orthner, D. (2004, April). *Building strong communities for military families* (NCFR policy brief). Minneapolis, MN: National Council on Family Relations.

McKnight, J. L. (1997). A 21st-century map for healthy communities and families. *Families in Society, 78*, 117–127.

Orthner, D. K., & Bowen, G. L. (2004). Strengthening practice through results management. In A. R. Roberts & K. Yeager (Eds.), *Handbook of practice based research* (pp. 897–904). New York: Oxford University Press.

Orthner, D. K., Bowen, G., & Mancini, D. (2003, December). *The community readiness unit service guide for Air Force Space Command family support centers*. Colorado Springs, CO: U.S. Air Force Space Command Family Matters.

Pittman, J. F., Kerpelman, J. L., & McFadyen, J. M. (2004). Internal and external adaptation in Army families: Lessons from Operations Desert Shield and Desert Storm. *Family Relations, 53*, 249–260.

Putnam, R. D. (2000). *Bowling alone*. New York: Simon & Schuster.

Fathering Programs and Community Services

Jay Fagan

Public concern about fathers and families has persisted since the last writing of this chapter in 2002. Although most children in the United States have fathers who are present in their lives, many children continue to have limited access to their fathers. The limited presence of fathers in the lives of some children is compounded by the fact that today's involved fathers spend significantly more time with their children than their parents did with them. Furthermore, the expectations of what it means to be a "good father" have changed from that of being a breadwinner and playmate to being a breadwinner, playmate, nurturer, and active caregiver. The growing divide between children who have actively involved fathers and children who have uninvolved fathers is not just a matter of the quantity and quality of parenting. Children living in poverty are about twice as likely as children living in higher income families not to have their biological father living in their household.

Although most children, poor and nonpoor, see their nonresident biological fathers on a regular basis, a significant proportion of children have little to no contact with their fathers. For example, 34 percent of children born to unmarried parents did not visit their nonresident fathers in the previous year. The high rate of incarceration among low-income parents has separated many fathers from their children—1.5 million children have a parent (usually a father) in prison, and 3.5 million children have a parent on parole or probation in the United States. The prison population has increased 400 percent during the past 25 years.

This chapter presents an overview of the fathering field, with a specific emphasis on community practice with fathers. The first section of this chapter reviews the policy developments of the past few years and the types of programs that are being developed in communities. The second section presents an overview of three conceptual perspectives that are useful for thinking about community practice with fathers. The third section examines the major practice approaches in use to work with fathers.

COMMUNITY-WIDE AND NATIONAL FATHERHOOD INITIATIVES

Public policy has played a significant role in raising interest in fathers. Early in his administration, President George W. Bush indicated that he was determined to make "committed, responsible fatherhood a national priority." As a result, a number of new programs were started, and several were bolstered during the past several years. In February 2006, Congress passed the Deficit Reduction Act of 2005, which provides up to $50 million for responsible fatherhood programs. Funds can be used to provide activities that promote or sustain marriage, promote responsible parenting, improve the economic status of fathers, or develop national media campaigns to promote responsible fatherhood.

New methods have also been implemented to ensure that noncustodial parents, usually fathers, pay child support. The national child support program (Child Support Enforcement) established a national directory of all newly hired employees for inclusion in state and national directories. This provision speeds direct withholding of child support from wages and helps track obligated parents across state lines. Another recent change has been the integration of child support enforcement requirements into a wide variety of federal programs, such as the food stamp program. For example, a single custodial parent must make efforts to gain child support from the noncustodial parent before becoming eligible for food stamps. These tougher enforcement rules have resulted in a fourfold increase in the receipt of child support by noncustodial parents between 1976 and the end of the 1990s. Children whose fathers pay child support in full are nearly twice as likely to visit their fathers as children whose fathers pay no child support (43 percent versus 79 percent).

At the national level, there has also been growing concern with the lack of effort by child welfare agencies to reach out to fathers of children placed in foster care. Most children in foster care are not living with their fathers at the time they are removed from their homes; once in foster care, these children experience even less contact with their nonresident fathers. Interviews conducted with 1,222 caseworkers in four states found that although most caseworkers know the identities of the fathers of children in care, only 55 percent of the workers had ever contacted the fathers of study children (Office of the Assistant Secretary for Planning and Evaluation, 2006). Data such as these have led to a number of local initiatives to involve fathers in the planning process for children in foster care.

Head Start, the largest federal program of early childhood services, has continued to expand its fatherhood initiative. In 2006, Head Start served a total of 909,000 children nationwide. More than 211,000 Head Start fathers participated in organized regularly scheduled activities designed to involve them in Head Start and Early Head Start programs.

Practice with fathers at the community level has continued to mature as agency staff become more experienced and better trained to work with fathers. Many communities have taken advantage of the expertise and experience of practitioners and planners who have been involved in the fathering field for some time now. Programs such as the National Fatherhood Initiative have developed numerous staff training programs that have been implemented throughout the United States. Communities have developed consortia of fathering programs, pooling their resources as a means of implementing widespread training of staff to work with fathers.

Many new Internet and print materials have been published aimed at improving services for fathers and articulating practice approaches for working with fathers. A widely used tool for social service agencies is the Father Friendly Checkup, a self-assessment instrument used to ascertain the extent to which one's organizational operations encourage father involvement in the activities and programs offered by the organization. Fagan and Palm (2004) published *Fathers and Early Childhood Programs* to assist practitioners working with fathers of young children. Research on programs for fathers has been helpful in showing how programs evolve. McAllister, Wilson, and Burton (2004) conducted in-depth qualitative interviews to study one program's evolution toward father involvement. The authors identified five stages of program maturation. In stage 1, the roles and needs of fathers were sometimes discussed with mothers, but the mother–child dyad was the main focus of the program. In stage 2, the program made efforts to involve fathers, primarily through male-only activities. In stage 3, there was a shift from male-only activities for fathers to including fathers in all aspects of the program, including home visits, family goal planning, and intake. In stage 4, the program staff began to think more holistically about fathers. Staff engaged fathers in relation to their parenting concerns, but they also worked with men around their own personal goals. In stage 5, fathers were viewed as co-parents. Staff also thought more reflectively about the father's relationship to his child, and they encouraged both fathers and mothers to think reflectively about their own relationships to the child.

CONCEPTUAL PERSPECTIVES

There is no single conceptual perspective that has guided thinking about community practice with fathers. Three approaches that have been applied to work with fathers in the recent literature are generative fathering, microstructural theory, and the strengths perspective. The notion of generative fathering draws on Eriksonian theory and the concept of generativity to understand fathering (Hawkins & Dollahite, 1997). Generative fathering refers to fathering that meets the needs of the next generation across time and context. A fundamental premise of this approach is that fathers have a social-psychological need to meet the needs of the next generation. Another critical aspect of generative fathering is that fathering is a developmental process that demands continual efforts to move toward good fathering. This perspective is particularly appropriate for conceptualizing interventions with fathers because it (1) deemphasizes thinking about fathers as deficient and emphasizes their strengths and potential for growth; (2) allows for diversity in parenting styles among fathers from various ethnic, racial, and class backgrounds; and (3) does not set a minimum standard that excludes fathers who may be striving to become good fathers.

The microstructural model suggests that structural conditions in society promote behavior that is normally attributed to a specific gender (Fagan & Palm, 2004). According to this perspective, fathers are always in the process of adapting to structural forces in the environment. Thus, structural conditions may either promote or hinder fathers from fulfilling their responsibilities. Microstructural theory suggests that community programs also may promote or hinder father involvement with children. Accordingly, programs should engage in assertive outreach with fathers and work toward building more father-friendly organizations as a means of encouraging and supporting father participation in the family.

The practice of building on strengths should be a basic principle of work with fathers in community practice. Palm (1997) suggested that practitioners find it easy to identify strengths in men who behave like "good mothers." "The purpose of acknowledging male strengths is not to reinforce male/female stereotypes, but to avoid the tendency to see characteristics of female socialization as the only model for good parenting" (Palm, 1997, p. 178). Examples of fathers' strengths in parenting include playfulness, promoting risk taking, encouraging problem solving, providing a sense of security, and serving as a bridge to the world outside of the family.

COMMUNITY PRACTICE APPROACHES

Practice approaches that are commonly used to work with fathers in the community include support groups, parent education, and father involvement activities. There are generally two types of support groups that are being conducted with fathers—therapeutic and empowerment-based support groups. Franklin and Davis (2001) have used therapeutic support groups to work with African American fathers. The major themes that are promoted in their groups include resisting disengagement from children, using empathy and tenderness to promote resilience, developing a family-oriented masculinity, and developing positive self-views. Franklin and Davis recommend starting therapeutic support groups for African American men from the ongoing community programs (i.e., schools) that men already perceive as useful to them. They also suggest using an integrative psychotherapeutic approach to guide the group process. This therapeutic approach draws from different practice models judged to be effective for fathers' particular presenting issues.

Empowerment-based support groups work best with groups of fathers who have experienced persistent oppression and disenfranchisement. Two such groups are divorced fathers who perceive that their rights as fathers have been violated and African American fathers who have been exposed to constant media images portraying them as uninvolved with their children and not good family men. Fagan and Stevenson (2002) reported on the development and implementation of one empowerment-based support group program for African American Head Start fathers. The goals of the group were to assist the participating fathers in taking control over their own destinies, protecting themselves from internalizing the disempowered male role identity as characterized by society, and dismantling the stereotypical images of African American fathers held by others and by themselves. One of the unique characteristics of this support group was training a small group of fathers to become group leaders. The evaluation of this program showed that fathers in the empowerment-based program reported significantly more positive attitudes about their ability to teach their preschool-age children and significantly higher parenting satisfaction than fathers who watched a series of videotapes on positive parenting (Fagan & Stevenson, 2002). The following case example illustrates the experience of one father in this program.

Mr. Jones spent 2 and a half years in prison for possession and selling illegal drugs. He was determined to "clean up his act" in prison in part because his children's mother abused drugs and was unable to provide consistent care to their two children. The children were removed from the mother's home and placed in foster care while the father was still incarcerated. Mr. Jones was a regular and active participant in a drug and alcohol group while in prison. On his release, he became actively involved with his children and their child welfare caseworker. He intended to obtain custody of the children because the mother was making little progress in her own recovery. Mr. Jones joined the Head Start fathers group, wanting support with parenting two young school-age children. Parenting young children is challenging under the best of circumstances, and it was particularly challenging to Mr. Jones because of his transitory relationship with his children in the past. He also wanted support from the group because of the challenges presented by his caseworker. He felt that his caseworker expected more of him as a father than she would of a mother. In Mr. Jones's experience, the caseworker and those before her were less trusting of a man's ability to be a good parent. Mr. Jones was very open about his perception of discrimination and was able to discuss these matters with his child welfare caseworker. He made good use of the group and was able to obtain custody of the children after an extended period of time.

Father involvement activities are most often implemented in schools, Head Start programs, and recreational centers. For example, the program components of one Head Start father involvement initiative included (1) fathers volunteering in the classroom, (2) weekly Father's Day programs in each Head Start site, (3) father sensitivity training for early childhood staff members, and (5) father–child recreation activities (Fagan & Palm, 2004). The overall goals of father–child activities in early childhood settings are to increase fathers' involvement with their children, improve fathers' positive parenting, and foster children's academic readiness.

Parent education for fathers has been implemented in many community settings. Fagan and Palm (2004) have described some fundamental differences between parent education for mothers and for fathers. First, fathers come to parent education groups seeking a closer relationship with their children, whereas mothers come to parent education groups seeking support from and a connection with other parents. Second, parent educators must be aware that fathers and mothers often have different knowledge bases and skills. Fathers tend to have little experience with providing child care during childhood and youth, whereas mothers often have considerable experience with child care in the early years. Third, fathers and mothers frequently differ in their interactional styles with children and in their expectations for children. Fathers are more likely to engage in physically stimulating play with young children, whereas mothers are more likely to play with toys. Fathers also spend more of their time playing with children. Fifth, there are frequently differences in disciplinary styles between mothers and fathers. Fathers tend to be more controlling and consistent in their discipline, whereas mothers are more ambivalent about control.

Although not typically considered to be a community practice approach, the Internet has become a growing source of parent education for fathers. Grant, Hawkins, and Dollahite (2001) have identified several significant reasons for this new phenomenon. The learning styles of many men are compatible with Internet-based learning opportunities. The Internet provides a private, individualized method of learning. Many men are reluctant to attend parent education workshops or groups. The Internet also offers opportunities to share both concerns and excitement about their work as fathers and therefore it has the potential to reduce fathers' sense of isolation.

CONCLUSION

Public concern about the role of fathers in families has resulted in the development of a vast array of new services for fathers. Since I last wrote this chapter in 2002, I have seen the fathering field continue to expand services in communities and reach more families. There continues to be a lack of rigorous evaluation research on the benefits of these programs, although several recent studies have shown positive but moderate effects of first-time fathers participating in home visitation services (Magill-Evans, Harrison, Benzies, Gierl, & Kimak, 2007).

Fagan and Hawkins (2001) suggested that practitioners should begin to look beyond traditional social services to determine what works best in reaching out to fathers. The basis of this recommendation is evidence from practitioners and researchers suggesting that men's help-seeking behavior is different from that of women's behavior Fathers are more difficult to reach and more cautious about participating in parenting education and support, and they have fewer support systems for positive change. Finally, Fagan and Hawkins (2001) also observed that well-intentioned organizations are frequently not prepared to work with fathers. Many agencies are not prepared for the high level of assertive outreach that must be conducted to involve fathers in their programs. Practitioners will need to attend to the needs of organizations to achieve success at working with fathers.

WEB SITES

Father Friendly Check-up. http://www .fatherhood.org/checkupsocial.asp.
National Fatherhood Initiative. http://www .nfi.org.
National Responsible Fatherhood Clearinghouse. http://www .fatherhood.gov/father/index.cfm.
Promoting Responsible Fatherhood federal resource site. http://fatherhood.hhs.gov.

References

Fagan, J., & Hawkins, A. J. (Eds.). (2001). *Clinical and educational interventions with fathers*. Binghamton, NY: Haworth.

Fagan, J., & Palm, G. (2004). *Fathers and early childhood programs*. Clifton Park, NY: Delmar.

Fagan, J., & Stevenson, H. (2002). An experimental study of an empowerment-based intervention for African American Head Start fathers. *Family Relations, 51*, 191–198.

Franklin, A. J., & Davis, T. III. (2001). Therapeutic support groups for primary intervention for issues of fatherhood with African American men. In J. Fagan & A. J. Hawkins (Eds.), *Clinical and educational interventions with fathers* (pp. 45–66). Binghamton, NY: Haworth.

Grant, T. R., Hawkins, A. J., & Dollahite, D. C. (2001). Web-based education and support for fathers: Remote but promising. In J. Fagan & A. J. Hawkins (Eds.), *Clinical and educational interventions with fathers* (pp. 143–170). Binghamton, NY: Haworth.

Hawkins, A. J., & Dollahite, D. C. (Eds.). (1997). *Generative fathering: Beyond deficit perspectives*. Thousand Oaks, CA: Sage.

Magill-Evans, J., Harrison, M. J., Benzies, K., Gierl, M., & Kimak, C. (2007). Effects of parenting education on first-time fathers' skills in interactions with their infants. *Fathering, 5*, 42–57.

McAllister, C. L., Wilson, P. C., & Burton, J. (2004). From sports fans to nurturers: An Early Head Start Program's evolution toward father involvement. *Fathering, 2*, 31–59.

Office of the Assistant Secretary of Planning and Evaluation. (2006). Child welfare casework with nonresident fathers of children in foster care. Retrieved on October 1, 2007, from http://aspe.hhs.gov/hsp/06/CW-involve-dads/ib.htm.

Palm, G. F. (1997). Promoting generative fathering through parent and family education. In A. J. Hawkins & D. C. Dollahite (Eds.), *Generative fathering: Beyond deficit perspectives* (pp. 167–182). Thousand Oaks, CA: Sage.

PART XIII

Working with Vulnerable Populations and Persons at Risk

135

Overview of Working with Vulnerable Populations and Persons at Risk

Rowena Fong

Although all people are vulnerable, circumstances and situations make some people more vulnerable than others (Fong, 2004; Fong, McRoy, & Hendricks, 2006). Persons of color, whether born in the United States or abroad, aging or older adult persons, and men and women who are gay, lesbian, bisexual, and transgendered (GLBT) experience conflicts to which others in the larger society may not be subjected. These experiences may involve racism, ageism, heterosexism, discrimination, oppression, harassment, hate crimes, rejection, homophobia, ridicule, or unjust misrepresentations.

In this section on vulnerable populations, authors Joshua Miller and Ann Marie Garran (Chapter 136) emphasize that "racism is a process that uses the differences of appearance or culture as a basis for making generalizations about intelligence and trustworthiness to justify systematic acts of subjugation and mistreatment of targeted persons." Social workers working with these vulnerable populations need to be aware of the problems and risk factors imposed on these people and find culturally appropriate interventions and solutions that, as Miller and Garran (2008) advocate, will build a "web of resistance" to dismantle racism and other oppressive attitudes and actions.

The profession of social work acknowledges the vulnerability of these populations and has taken measures to enforce standards and policies to allow for culturally sensitive considerations. For example, the National Association of Social Work (NASW)

Standards for Cultural Competence in Social Work Practice (2001) specifically mandates in standard 3 on cross-cultural knowledge that social workers "shall have and continue to develop specialized knowledge and understanding about the history, traditions, values, family systems, and artistic expressions of major client groups they serve" (p. 1). This requires that social workers take the time to learn about the history and historical trauma, traditions and cultural values, and family systems of African Americans, Latinos and Mexican Americans, Asian and Pacific Islander Americans, and Native Americans as the chapters in this section describe.

In 2006, NASW published *Social Work Speaks: Policy Statements 2006–2009*, which enunciates a commitment to improving policies and practices related to racism; immigrants and refugees; lesbian, gay, and bisexual issues; long-term care; and end-of-life care. The policy statements apply to the vulnerable populations of GLBT persons and older adult individuals. For the aging population, the Council on Social Work Education (CSWE) supports the National Center for Gerontological Social Work Education, which offers a social work curriculum related to the understanding of the needs and appropriate assessments and interventions for this specific group of people. The populations of older adults, GLBT persons, people of color, both native and foreign-born, exemplifies NASW's and CSWE's concerns for diversity issues related to race, gender, age, abilities, and sexual orientation.

People who are targeted because they are different, whether it is because of race, age, gender, sexual orientation, political persuasion, abilities, or socioeconomic class, become vulnerable and feel at risk. The NASW *Code of Ethics* (1999) mandates that all social workers "help meet the basic needs of all people who are vulnerable, oppressed, and living in poverty" (p. 1). Dignity and worth are basic needs of all people. These basic needs can be facilitated by increased culturally competent knowledge and practices, which this section on vulnerable populations will provide.

DIVERSITY AND ETHNIC POPULATIONS

Several authors in this section draw attention to the broad diversity within and between ethnic groups. Sadye Logan, in Chapter 143, makes the consequences of such intragroup variation for her subject population quite plain: "Given the diversity which exists in terms of values, education, income, lifestyles, and perceptions in the African American community, it is extremely challenging, if not impossible, to write a definitive article that captures clinical social work practice with this ethnic group." In Chapter 140 Teresa Evans-Campbell mentions that in the United States "there are over 560 federally recognized tribes, including 223 village groups in Alaska and close to 200 unrecognized tribes." Halaevalu Vakalahi and Rowena Fong, Chapter 141, note that Asians include distinctly different groups from East Asia, South Asia, Southeast Asia, and Pacific Islanders from Polynesia, Micronesia, and Melanesia.

Diversity within ethnic group populations applies to both American-born and foreign-born populations. Miriam Potocky-Tripodi, in Chapter 139, emphasizes the differences in legal statuses in the immigrant and refugee populations. Elaine Congress, in Chapter 144, reports that an estimated "one out of three immigrants are undocumented, while more than half of the immigrants who entered the country [U.S.] since 2000 are undocumented." Describing the Mexican immigrant population in Chapter 142, Ilze Earner and Genevova Garcia report that "Mexican immigrants currently represent the largest ethnic group of Latinos in the United States. Due largely to changes in migration patterns and immigration law, 20 percent of all legal and 67 percent of undocumented immigrants come from Mexico." In summary, this section on vulnerable populations highlights the diversity within the native and foreign-born populations of persons of color.

VULNERABILITY AND RISK FACTORS

Persons of color are joined as numbers of vulnerable populations by GLBT individuals. In Chapter 137, Mary Boes and Katherine van Wormer describe the risk factors for members of the GLBT population: "Few groups are maligned in our society, as are persons who are identified as, or are suspected of, gender nonconformity, or having a same-sex sexual orientation. The most extreme forms of discrimination, including ridicule and violence, are reserved for transgendered persons or those who have the psychological sense of being female when they are psychologically male or vice versa."

Poor psychological and physical well-being are risk factors for older adults leaning toward depression, isolation, and failing health. Author Virginia Richardson writes Chapter 138 about "a 75-year-old single man living in low-income senior housing who became depressed after he stopped driving when his vision deteriorated."

Depression and poor mental health are risk factors for older adults, GLBT clients, persons of color, and other vulnerable populations such as immigrants and refugees. Some authors describe how assessment practices can point toward these risk factors. Congress describes one tool. The Afro-centered genogram referred to in Chapter 143 is another tool. Earner and Garcia's chapter also recommends the genogram.

Vulnerability and risk factors can be mediated by approaching the populations from an empowerment and strengths perspective framework, often used in working with the GLBT and the older adult populations. In working with African Americans, Mexican immigrants, Native Americans, and Asian and Pacific Islander Americans, the chapter authors emphasize the need to use the strengths perspective approach to empower these vulnerable populations. Vakalahi and Fong discuss cultural values as strengths and their role in Asian and Pacific Islander cultures. Fong and Furuto (2001) describe the importance of cultural values in culturally competent social work practice and their role as protective factors in ethnic populations who highly uphold traditional values in their families and communities.

CULTURALLY COMPETENT EVIDENCE-BASED PRACTICE

Evidence-based practice is important in determining the effectiveness of an intervention on a problem area, and some authors mention specific therapies that work well with their vulnerable populations. Logan emphasizes the need to use an Africentric and strengths-based orientation and mentions that there are "emergent and traditional practice approaches" that support such an orientation. They include solution-focused brief therapy, solution-oriented therapy, gender-sensitive therapy, cognitive-behavioral therapy, psychoeducational family therapy, task-centered treatment, structural family therapy, narrative therapy, and crisis treatment. Richardson discusses using cognitive-behavioral and interpersonal therapy with older adults, but cautions that these interventions were "originally developed for younger persons and need to be modified when used with older persons."

The use of narrative therapy is recommended when working with Mexican immigrant families in Chapter 142. Chapter 141 mentions the use of family group conferencing, an emergent evidence-based practice intervention in child protective services, used with the Pacific Islander case example. There is the tendency in working with ethnic American-born and foreign-born populations to determine which evidence-based intervention may apply to the ethnic group, and practitioners need to be cautious to not exclude indigenous interventions that work with ethnic populations and support the strengths perspective of supporting cultural values. Evans-Campbell, in Chapter 140, says,

Increasingly, the field of social work is moving toward the use of evidence-based practice interventions and strategies with diverse populations. Unfortunately, the use of evidence-based interventions with AIAN people is complicated by the lack of intervention research that includes Native clients or examines Native-specific practice models. . . . When working with Native people, social workers might also consider practices that are considered promising in that there is emerging empirical evidence of their success.

There are a growing number of Native-designed programs designated as promising practice models by agencies such as Indian Health Service and SAMHSA.

In conclusion, this section on vulnerable populations includes chapters on social work practice with native-born and foreign-born populations of African Americans, Mexican Americans and immigrants, Asian and Pacific Islander Americans; Native Americans; GLBT clients, older adults, refugees and immigrants; help-seeking pathways to care; culturagrams with culturally diverse immigrant families; and the legacy of racism. The chapters point out the diversity among the ethnic populations, the vulnerability and risk factors, and both evidence-based and culturally competent social work practices.

References

Fong, R. (Ed.). (2004). *Culturally competent practice with immigrant and refugee children and families.* New York: Guilford.

Fong, R., & Furuto, S. (Eds.). (2001). *Culturally competent practice: Skills, interventions, and evaluations.* Boston: Allyn & Bacon.

Fong, R., McRoy, R., & Hendricks, C. (Eds.).(2006). *Intersecting child welfare, substance abuse, and family violence: Culturally competent approaches.* Alexandria, VA: Council on Social Work Education.

Miller, J., & Garran, A. (2008). *Racism in the United States: Implications for the helping profession.* Belmont, CA: Thomson Brooks/Cole.

National Association of Social Work. (1999). *Code of ethics.* Washington, DC: NASW Press.

National Association of Social Work. (2001). *Standards for cultural competence in social work practice.* Washington, DC: NASW Press.

National Association of Social Work. (2006). *Social work speaks: NASW policy statements 2006–2009.* Washington, DC: NASW Press.

The Legacy of Racism for Social Work Practice Today and What to Do about it

Joshua Miller & Ann Marie Garran

The United States has been a nation for over 230 years and is renowned for its democratic tradition. It is also a country that was founded with a "racial contract" (Mills, 1997) that has shaped its culture, laws, institutions, practices, and the relationships between different ethnic and racial groups. Racism is as much a part of the American tradition as democracy is, and it is very much a social factor today. Yet many white citizens, who are consciously against racism, view racism as something that happened in the past with little relevance today. For social workers to practice in accordance with the NASW Code of Ethics, we need to understand how racism shapes lives, constrains opportunity for some, and confers privileges to others based on a social construction of race, and most important, how to confront the racism that exists in society that also lurks inside the psyches of practitioners. The spectrum of racism today ranges from institutional barriers and neglect of those who are the targets of racism, cultural biases, intergroup conflict, and segregation to interpersonal transactions and internalized prejudices and stereotypes (Miller & Garran, 2008). It is manifested in communities, agencies, organizations, social policies, and the relationships and interactions that people have—or because of racism rarely have.

Racism is based on the erroneous notion of race: that there are distinct racial groups and generalizations can be made about these groups based on alleged genetic or cultural differences or deficiencies. The American Anthropological Association [AAA] (1998) has made a statement that based on available scientific evidence of genetic similarities and differences between so-called racial groups, there are no significant distinctions and there is one race, the human race. Of course, there are differences in height, skin color, facial features, and other phys-

ical characteristics, but these are not the differences that justified enslavement of African Americans, genocide of Native Americans, prohibitions against immigration for Chinese Americans, or disenfranchisement of Mexican Americans living in the Southwest, all of which are a part of this nation's heritage. Race has limited value as a biological or genetic construct but has been a useful underpinning for ideologies justifying the domination of one "racial" group by another. Racism is a process that uses the differences of appearance or culture as a basis for making generalizations about intelligence and trustworthiness to justify systematic acts of subjugation and mistreatment of targeted peoples. In fact, the notoriously unreliable, historically shifting notion of race is more a consequence of racism than racism is due to the existence of distinct races. In the end, race is a social construction that determines who wields power and who has social passports of privilege.

In this chapter we discuss why social workers should be concerned about racism and what racism in the United States looks like today. We also discuss institutional racism; more subtle, unconscious forms of racism, such as aversive racism (Dovidio, Gaertner, Kawakami, & Hodson, 2002) and racial microaggressions (Pierce, Carew, Pierce-Gonzalez, & Wills, 1978; Solorzano, Ceja, & Yosso, 2000); internalized stereotypes and racial prejudices; and how this is encapsulated in social identities (Miller & Garran, 2008). We conclude with some ideas about how to talk about race and racism, work with racism in direct practice, confront racism in the community, and how social service organizations can become antiracism organizations. Our purpose is to take an unvarnished look at racism in the United States and the implications of it for social workers. Due to the brevity of this chapter, we particularly emphasize the role of white people and those with white skin privilege in maintaining racism. Although some of what we say might seem a bit jarring and provoke strong emotions, our goal is not to make people angry or feel badly about themselves: we want social workers to eradicate racism, not point fingers at one another or feel immobilized by feelings of guilt or shame.

We need to briefly situate ourselves and define some terms that we will be using. One author (Miller) is a white, Jewish American male, and the other author (Garran) is a Puerto Rican and African American female. We have taught antiracism courses together for 10 years and have coauthored a textbook for human service professionals about antiracism (Miller & Garran, 2008). We use the terms "white" and "people of color" because they are the most common social constructions currently in use that convey who is and who is not targeted by racism. Due to the complexity of racism, we have been reluctant to define it in a way that reduces or overly simplifies its meaning. We agree with Memmi (2000) that racism involves the domination of people who are defined as being members of a racial or ethnic group by another group of people based on alleged differences of genetics, culture, values, and behavior. Racism in our view is manifested as a spectrum, where there are core practices that are common to all forms of it (Miller & Garran, 2008). Figure 136.1 diagrams the range of ways that racism is expressed, all of which have occurred in the United States, many of which are still operating.

WHY IT IS IMPORTANT FOR SOCIAL WORKERS TO CARE ABOUT RACISM

All citizens should care about racism, because it undermines a just society and ultimately compromises everyone, including those with race privilege who often live in fear or are not in touch with their own biases, prejudices, and stereotypes. It is particularly important for social workers to understand how racism works and how to confront it because our very mission is to connect and empower people and work with them to improve their psychosocial functioning, as well as advocating for social policies that further human well-being. Racism divides and alienates people, creates barriers to social participation, limits potential, and inhibits psychosocial growth. Racism engenders feelings of anger, rage, guilt, and shame that can be overwhelming and can lead to health, psychological, social, and behavioral problems.

Social workers are bound by a code of ethics that commits us to work for social justice and to respect and value every individual and their cultural context. This code states that the "primary mission of the social work profession is to enhance human well-being and help meet the basic human needs of all people, with particular attention to the needs and empowerment of people who are vulnerable, oppressed, and living in poverty" (NASW, 1999). Racism is the ultimate in social injustice that clearly values some people and cultures while denigrating others. Racism is a force that prevents social workers from adequately and ethically being able to do their jobs.

A BRIEF HISTORY OF RACISM IN THE UNITED STATES

Almost immediately after the arrival of Europeans in the New World, Europeans from a number of nations—Spain, England, France, and Holland—attempted to subjugate, kill and dislocate the Native American population that was already living here. The more than 600 autonomous societies in the Americas were met with disease, slaughter, and attempts at enslavement by European explorers and settlers (Wilson, 1998). Some estimate that there was a 95 percent death rate of Native Americans within a few generations after European settlement (Stannard, 1992). In the first 90 years of the American republic, *every* treaty with Native Americans was broken by the U.S. government (Wilson, 1998). Native Americans were not granted citizenship until 1924.

From the beginning of settlement by Europeans, there was slavery, which evolved into chattel slavery, lifelong and intergenerational, that became limited to African Americans. Many of the founding fathers of the U.S. were slave owners—George Washington, Thomas Jefferson, James Madison, James Monroe, and Andrew Jackson, who was also known for his brutal treatment of Native Americans. After slavery was abolished following the Civil War, black codes, Jim Crow, violence (including lynching), and other forms of legal and de facto state terror and segregation managed to severely limit political, social, and economic opportunities for African Americans (Miller & Garran, 2008). While European immigrants were being recruited to work in Northern factories after the Industrial

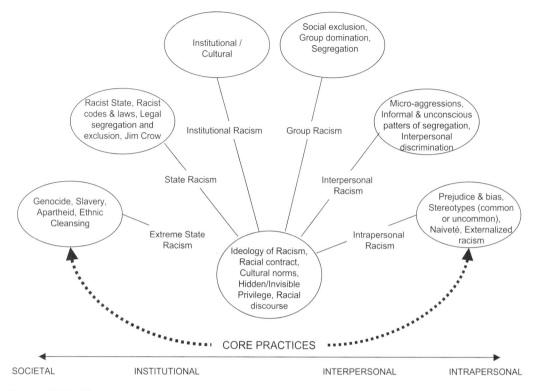

Figure 136.1 The spectrum of racism.

Revolution, African Americans were unable to compete for these jobs due to structural impediments, such as Jim Crow, in the South and racial discrimination in the North (which was not limited to employers and included trade unions). Thus it is important to note that many white people who descend from those immigrants were able to benefit from upward social mobility that depended on their assumption of white privileges at the expense of people of color (Steinberg, 2001).

In the Southwest, Mexicans living in what is now Texas, New Mexico, California, Colorado, and Nevada (which had been part of Mexico prior to the Mexican-American War), lost their land, citizenship, and ability to compete for and hold jobs. In 1882, the Chinese Exclusion Act prohibited immigration to the United States by people from China (at exactly the same time that Europeans were immigrating to the United States), and the Gentleman's Agreement of 1907 prohibited Japanese immigration. Though it was difficult for groups like the Irish, Jews, and Italians when they first arrived in the United States, and there was much discrimination and racial and ethnic stereotyping, they still had advantages unavailable to people of color and as such, within a few generations became "white" (Guglielmo & Salerno, 2003; Ignatiev, 1995; Sacks, 1996; Steinberg, 2001).

It is not possible for social workers to grasp the severe racial inequality that exists today without acknowledging the historical privileges afforded white immigrants and the consistent oppression and exclusion facing people of color.

RACISM IN THE U.S. TODAY

It is no longer acceptable to legally deprive people of their rights, enslave them, or murder them due to their race. Racism in the United States is an ongoing project that has evolved and shifted over the course of time. The fact that the most extreme forms of racism are illegal and considered socially abhorrent does not mean that there may not be regression or that racism is not still a major force in U.S. society today. Since September 11, 2001, the so-called war against terrorism has had echoes of America's racist past—tightening the borders, demonizing certain ethnic groups, suspending legal rights and civil liberties—to name a few worrying trends. But today, the forms of racism of the past are no longer legally or socially acceptable, though there are still many racist incidents that occur.

What is still contested are myriad forms of racism that continue to impede the civil rights and socio-economic progress of people of color. As

Figure 136.1 illustrates, one major form of racism is institutional racism, where many people of color—particularly poor African Americans, Latinos, and Native Americans—face a web of institutional barriers, where they are unable to live in certain neighborhoods, have less access to quality education and health care, face greater exposure to unsafe and unhealthy environments, are more likely to be targeted by law enforcement, are less likely to go to college, are underrepresented politically and overrepresented in prisons, and who consistently have less ability to accumulate wealth and achieve upward mobility (Miller & Garran, 2007, 2008). Another aspect of institutional racism is a public discourse, amplified by the media, which legitimates it. This discourse normalizes white leadership, privilege, and power and promulgates stereotypes about African Americans, Asian Americans, Latino Americans, and other people of color. It is evident in television shows, news broadcasts, magazine advertisements, and the decisions made by the editors of newspapers and other media about what is news and how it will be portrayed (Miller & Garran, 2008). This discourse shaped public opinion about welfare reform, consistently portraying welfare mothers as African Americans, despite the fact that the majority of women on welfare were white (Gillens, 1999).

Figure 136.1 also illustrates intergroup racism, where one racial group has privileges and powers and others are marginalized or considered "minorities." For instance, look at the racial/ethnic staffing pattern of your social service agency. Who are the receptionists and secretaries? Who are the senior managers? Who are the clients, and who are the workers? Who is on the board of directors? What are the norms and culture of the office? What theories of human behavior in the social environment are being used and what cultural biases are embedded in them? These are but a few questions that begin to highlight how "normal" and ubiquitous white privilege is in most social service organizations. As Tim Wise (2003) has put it, whites swim in a sea of racial privilege, which is mostly invisible.

INTERNALIZED AND INTERPERSONAL RACISM

The ubiquitous nature of racism and white privilege shape how people see the world and how they feel about themselves and others. One way to think about this is that people have social identities.

Social identity is how we view ourselves in relation to other people. It encompasses the groups that we see ourselves as being members of and excluded from, as well as the thoughts, feelings, and perceptions that accompany these identifications. Ultimately, social identity is our sense of our self in a social world. There are many dimensions of social identity—such as gender, ethnicity, social and economic class, race, and sexual orientation—and some of these dimensions shift over time while others remain constant. Different aspects of social identity come to light depending on the social context. For example, in a class where the professor is white and most of the students are white, the one or two students of color may be very conscious of their race. Conversely, many white class members do not think about their race at all and are more aware of their class, gender, sexual orientation, or ethnicity (Miller & Garran, 2008).

When social identity is mirrored, reflected, and advantaged by society (e.g., being white, male, heterosexual, middle-class, physically able, etc.) the privileges that accompany the identity are often difficult to discern by the person with benefits from this special status (McIntosh, 1989, 1992; Miller & Garran, 2008; Wise, 2003). Discourses accompany these privileges that whitewash them away, so that effort, hard work, good character, and the right values are explanations for the success of one group (white people) rather than exploitation, segregation, resource hoarding, and unequal opportunity. Thus stereotypes emerge that provide inner templates to match outer social realities and offer cognitive justifications for a socially unequal and unfair world. A white person with values and ideals that are altruistic and egalitarian may harbor stereotypes about people of color that are beneath the radar of consciousness but still manage to shape beliefs and behaviors (Dovidio et al., 2002; Miller & Garran, 2008).

Unexamined stereotypes can lead to "aversive racism" (Dovidio et al., 2002), where a well-intentioned white person is unaware of his or her prejudices and yet acts on these biases. Examples include hiring decisions in agencies or segregated housing patterns in neighborhoods, where a white person did not "choose" to live in a nearly all-white neighborhood yet feels compelled to do so. Aversive racism can contribute to subtle interactions—making or not making eye contact, a forced smile, stumbling over the words "race" or "racism"—that "create a force field of discomfort" (Kaufman, 2001, p. 33). Another way to conceptualize these interactions is to see them as "microaggressions"—

subtle but repeated verbal and nonverbal insults, put-downs, and social incursions that are injurious to people of color but often occur without the conscious awareness of the white person (Miller & Garran, 2007; Pierce et al., 1978; Solorzano et al., 2000). The consequences of microaggressions are a relentless assault on one's social identity, which, aside from being painful and exhausting, can lead to people of color to withdraw from interactions with white people.

ORGANIZATIONAL RACISM

Social service organizations are the nexus between institutional racism and internalized/interpersonal racism. It is nearly impossible for a mainstream social service organization to not have to deal with racism, as they are part of a society permeated with racism and staffed by many people with internalized racism—they mirror the complexity of racism in society at large. Thus racism affects hiring and retention, staffing patterns, policies toward clients, theoretical biases and pathologizing of clients, interpersonal relationships between staff, and organizational power, influence, and decision making (Miller & Garran, 2008). Only through sustained and intentional efforts to become an antiracism organization can social service organizations go beyond token or symbolic measures to challenge racism (Donner & Miller, 2005; Miller & Garran).

DISMANTLING RACISM AND CREATING A WEB OF RESISTANCE

There are no simple measures that will eradicate racism, nor will it happen over a short period of time. The history, ubiquity, and complexity of racism make dismantling it a daunting prospect. Yet we must not let the weight of racism overwhelm us; without hope there is no prospect of changing things. So what can social workers do?

- *Learn about it.* There is no shortcut to learning about racism in all of its forms, including how it is inside of and in between people. Racism evokes strong feelings—pain, anger, sorrow, guilt, shame—and these emotional reactions can lead people to want to challenge it without adequately understanding it. Learning about racism and deciphering its many manifestations is an ongoing project. Learning must take place cognitively through

education as well as emotionally and psychologically through introspection and self-awareness.
- *Working with others.* Racism alienates and isolates people from one another. Social workers are committed as a profession to ending social injustice and are used to working together. The best way to undermine racism is to create multiracial coalitions that pool resources and offer mutual aid and support. Coalitions help to sustain motivation and attention to this issue.
- *Creating anti-racism organizations.* Most social workers practice in agencies, and social service organizations serve clients who have been targeted by racism. Organizations can make antiracism commitments in their mission statements; hire, retain, and empower more staff of color; review practices toward clients as well as the theories that guide such practices; offer antiracism trainings; facilitate intergroup dialogues; and work to become truly multicultural.
- *Creating inclusive communities.* All social workers and clients live somewhere, although often not in the same place. In general, communities offer safety, security, and opportunities for social mobility and increasing economic and social capital; they are also are sites of much institutional racism and can be places that are dangerous and glaringly devoid of the resources and amenities necessary to survive and eventually advance. Social workers can act to create communities where they live and work that are inclusive and where everyone is treated fairly, respectfully and has access to decent education, jobs, and other resources.
- *Being heard.* Social workers must engage in discourses and conversations that are not only among themselves but also with the greater public. The stereotypes and biases embedded in the mass media and culture can be identified, deconstructed, and challenged by social workers who set an example by their professional ethics and offer an alternative vision of a just and nonracist society.
- *Challenging and changing laws, institutions, and practices.* This is a huge task, but it is not insurmountable. We have seen many laws and practices—for example, slavery, Jim Crow, legal segregation, forced internment—

changed over time. There is much more work to do but it can be done if social workers articulate a vision, break things down into manageable pieces, and work in concert with others concerned about racism to dismantle racist policies and promulgate the means to achieve social justice.

Ultimately, all of these actions form a "web of resistance" to racism (Miller & Garran, 2008; Werkmeister Rozas & Miller, in press). Central to all of the activities we have described are core values—seeing clearly, listening and hearing, connecting with others, compassion, and sustained engagement. Racism has been around for a long time and will not be eliminated easily, but the core values of the web of resistance correspond to those articulated by the social work profession. If we can aspire to live up to the vision of our profession, we can all be antiracism activists and allies.

WEB SITES

EdChange Organization. http://www .edchange.org/multicultural/sites/white .html.
ERASE Racism Organization. http://www .eraseracismny.org/html/.
PBS Television's interactive site for the broadcast series on race. http://www.pbs .org/race/000_General/000_00-Home .htm.
Understanding Prejudice. http://www .understandingprejudice.org/.
Voices of Civil Rights. http://www .voicesofcivilrights.org/.

References

American Anthropological Association. (1998). AAA statement on race. *American Anthropologist, 100*(3), 712–713.
Donner, S., & Miller, J. (2005). The road to becoming an anti-racism organization. In A. Lightburn & P. Sessions (Eds.), *Community based clinical practice*. New York: Oxford University Press.
Dovidio, J. F., Gaertner, S. L., Kawakami, K., & Hodson, G. (2002). Why can't we all just get along? Interpersonal biases and interracial distrust. *Cultural Diversity and Ethnic Minority Psychology, 8*(2), 88–102.

Gillens, M. (1999). *Why Americans hate welfare*. Chicago: University of Chicago Press.
Guglielmo, J., & Salerno, S. (2003). (Eds.). *Are Italians white: How race is made in America*. New York: Routledge.
Ignatiev, N. (1995). *How the Irish became white*. New York: Routledge.
Kaufman, C. (2001). A user's guide to white privilege. *Radical Philosophy Review, 4*(1/2), 30–38.
McIntosh, P. (1989). White privilege: Unpacking the invisible knapsack. *Peace and Freedom, July/Aug*, 10–12.
McIntosh, P. (1992). White privilege and male privilege: A personal account of coming to see correspondences through work in women's studies. In M. Anderson & P. H. Collins (Eds.), *Race, class and gender: An anthology* (pp. 70–81). Belmont, CA: Wadsworth.
Memmi, A. (2000). *Racism*. Minneapolis: University of Minnesota Press.
Miller, J., & Garran, A. (2007). The web of institutional racism. *Smith College Studies in Social Work, 77*(1), 33–67.
Miller, J., & Garran, A. (2008). *Racism in the United States: Implications for the helping professions*. Belmont, CA: Thomson Brooks/Cole.
Mills, C. W. (1997). *The racial contract*. Ithaca, NY: Cornell University Press.
National Association of Social Workers. (1999). *National Association of Social Workers code of ethics*. Washington, DC: NASW Press.
Pierce, C., Carew, J., Pierce-Gonzalez, D., & Wills, D. (1978). An experiment in racism: T.V. commercials. In C. Pierce (Ed.), *Television and education* (pp. 62–88). Beverly Hills, CA: Sage.
Sacks, K. B. (1996). How did Jews become white folks? In S. Gregory & R. Sanjek (Eds.), *Race* (pp. 78–102). New Brunswick, NJ: Rutgers University Press.
Solorazano, D., Ceja, M., & Yosso, T. (2000). Critical race theory, racial microaggressions, and campus racial climate: The experiences of African American college students. *Journal of Negro Education, 69*(1/2), 60–73.
Stannard, D. E. (1992). *American holocaust: The conquest of the New World*. New York: Oxford University Press.
Steinberg, S. (2001). *The ethnic myth: Race, ethnicity and class in America*, 3rd ed. Boston: Beacon Press.
Werkmeister Rozas, L., & Miller, J. (In press). Discourses for social justice: The web of racism and the web of resistance. *Journal of Ethnic and Cultural Diversity*.
Wilson, J. (1998). *The earth shall weep: A history of Native America*. New York: Grove.
Wise, T. (2003). Whites swim in racial preference. Znet. Retrieved December 11, 2007, from http://www .zmag.org/content/showarticle.cfm?ItemID=3113.

Social Work with Lesbian, Gay, Bisexual, and Transgendered Clients

Mary Boes & Katherine van Wormer

This chapter summarizes basic knowledge for strengths-based practice with lesbian, gay, bisexual, and transgendered populations. The focus is on typical situations in which this knowledge is required, such as in health care, in a school setting, and in family counseling. Attention is paid to professional issues and the controversy of so-called conversion therapy. Two case studies are provided.

Lesbian, gays, bisexuals, and transgendered persons seek social work services for the same reasons heterosexuals do—out of grief for the loss of a loved one, for depression and other mental conditions, for court-mandated substance-abuse treatment, for relationship issues. Additionally, lesbians, gays, bisexuals, and transgendered persons have unique issues pertaining to their sexual orientation and gender identity, the social stigma of their differentness, rejection by families and friends, the impact of AIDS on the lives of gay men, and coming-out issues for all age groups. Heterosexuals also seek help for matters related to homosexuality—for example, concern over gender-appropriate behavior in a young son, the shock of learning an offspring is gay or lesbian, or the discovery that a spouse is having an affair with someone of the same sex. Nevertheless, in the best tradition of the client-centered approach, social workers should follow the lead of the client in addressing the specific issue that propelled him or her to seek professional help in the first place.

Two key principles attract such persons and their families to seek professional help: the promise of confidentiality and the tradition of nonjudgmental acceptance. Perhaps for these reasons, and owing to a reluctance to talk of these matters to family members, friends, or clergy, gays and lesbians are more likely than heterosexuals to see a therapist (Goldstein & Horowitz, 2003). African Americans seeking assistance related to their sexuality, however, are likely to find few, if any, therapists of color with relevant training.

Few groups are as maligned in our society as those who are identified as or suspected of gender nonconformity or having a same-sex sexual orientation. The most extreme forms of discrimination, including ridicule and violence, are reserved for transgendered persons or those who have the psychological sense of being female when they are physiologically male or vice versa (see van Wormer, 2007).

In recognition of the homophobia (fear of homosexuality) and heterosexism in society, the social work profession strives to prepare practitioners who will promote respect for people of all sexual orientations. According to Carol Tully (personal communication), the three basic forms of homophobia are pervasive—*institutional* homophobia, which is perpetuated by the traditional structures of society; homophobia at the *individual* level, evidenced by insulting jokes and hate crimes; and *internalized* homophobia, which is awkwardness that gays and lesbians, especially teens, feel about themselves.

In its policy statement on lesbian, gay, and bisexual issues, the National Association of Social Workers (NASW) (2006) states its commitment to advancing policies and practices that will improve the status and well-being of all lesbian, gay, and bisexual people.

Similarly, the American Psychological Association (APA) Committee on Lesbian and Gay Concerns endorses positive attitudes toward gays as a group. From the brochure issued by the APA (2007, pp. 1–4) we learn that:

- sexual orientation is most likely the result of a complex interaction of environmental, cognitive, and biological factors;
- sexual orientation exists along a continuum that ranges from exclusive homosexuality to exclusive heterosexuality;

- although persons can choose whether to act on their feelings, psychologists do not consider sexual orientation to be a conscious choice;
- children reared by gay or lesbian parents are psychologically as well adjusted as children reared by heterosexual parents; and
- most pedophiles and child abusers are heterosexual men.

CASE ILLUSTRATIONS

As a small child, Lee was very popular at school and sang in the school and church choirs. When puberty hit, however, he developed an identity crisis related to his sexuality and teasing by other kids who regarded him as a sissy. The bullying escalated to the extent that Lee started missing school; he faced a religious crisis as well.

The school social worker's assessment revealed that Lee was depressed, lonely, and at times suicidal, confused about his gender identity. She met with Lee weekly and referred him to an after-school facilitated group that helped students wrestle with issues related to gender identity. Intervention was planned with classmates who were engaged in bullying.

The Williams had three sons, the youngest, age 7, was extremely feminine, insisting that he was, in fact, a girl and begged to wear dresses. His favorite children's books were stories of mermaids. The child who called himself Rose had been diagnosed by a psychiatrist as suffering from gender dysmorphia.

Mrs. Williams took Rose from psychologist to psychologist, hoping to find help somewhere for her daily struggles with the child who refused to act "normal." Finally, she was referred to a social worker who specialized in gender identity issues. The social worker educated the family about transgendered children and presented an option they had never considered—to let Rose live life as the girl her brain said she really was. Because the transformation was immensely complicated, socially and medically, a plan for long-term counseling and consultation was agreed on.

CONVERSION THERAPY VERSUS THE STRENGTHS APPROACH

Against the backdrop of a growing conservative political and religious climate, gay men and lesbians are sometimes persuaded to seek psychother-apy to change the focus of their sexual attraction. The basic tenets of conversion therapy are:

- homosexuality is a sin, and salvation can come through faith in Jesus Christ;
- psychotherapy can cure a mental disorder (secular therapists);
- the cause of homosexuality is a dominant mother and passive father;
- people can change their sexual identity through treatment; and
- converts who repudiate their former gayness can be role models to gays and lesbians to help them change.

Such claims are repudiated by NASW (2000, 2006) and the APA (2007) as completely invalid and ideologically based.

Because homosexuality is not a mental disorder, treatment to change one's sexual orientation is unwarranted. NASW (2000) has issued a caveat against the resurgence in conversion therapies. Such therapies are viewed by the association as a violation of the social work code of ethics' requirements of competence and commitment to clients' self-determination. False claims by therapists of documented success stories in converting people to heterosexuality can lead to severe emotional damage, whether through the claims or through the treatments, according to NASW.

In sharp contrast to the dictates of "reparative" treatments is the strengths or empowerment perspective as it pertains to gay and lesbian practice. From a strengths perspective, we offer the following guidelines to practice with gays, lesbians, bisexuals, and transgendered persons.

- Seek the positive in terms of people's coping and survival skills, and you will find it.
- Listen to the personal narrative, the telling of one's own story in one's own voice, a story that ultimately may be reframed in light of new awareness of unrealized personal strength.
- Validate the pain where pain exists and reinforce persistent efforts to alleviate the pain (including, if desired, *not* acting on the feelings and/or reducing isolation in multiple ways).
- Help people recover from the specific injuries of oppression, neglect, and domination.
- Don't dictate; collaborate through an agreed-on, mutual discovery of solutions among helpers, families, and support networks. Validation and collaboration are integral steps

in the consciousness-raising process that can lead to healing and empowerment.
- Move from self-actualization to transformation of oppressive structure, from individual strength to higher connectedness.

Also using an empowerment approach, Tully (2000) advocates a client–practitioner relationship built on mutual respect and reciprocity to uplift and empower gays and lesbians effectively in an oppressive, homophobic environment. Tully urges social workers to avoid the assumption of heterosexuality in the creation of a gay-friendly space. Among her recommendations are to:

- avoid standardized face sheets and documents that presume everyone is heterosexual;
- include some lesbian- and gay-friendly magazines or newspapers in the waiting area; and
- train staff to be gay-friendly and nonhomophobic.

SELECTED AREAS OF SOCIAL WORK PRACTICE

In this section, we focus on two areas of social work practice with special relevance to sexual minorities—social work with adolescents and family and couples counseling.

Social Work with Adolescents

Struggling to survive in environments (school, home, church) that are more often than not hostile to their very being, gay and lesbian youth have many intense personal issues to resolve. The message sent by society, including one's own community, is that gender nonconformity and gay or lesbian identity, unlike racial and ethnic identity, is a choice that can and should be concealed (van Wormer, 2007).

Among the most pressing issues concerning adolescent gays and lesbians that we have gleaned from experience and the literature are:

- the turmoil involved in coming out to yourself, discovering who you are and who you are not;
- deciding who to tell, when, and how to tell it;
- rebuilding relationships and grieving rejections when the truth is known;
- developing new and caring support systems;

- protecting oneself from a constant onslaught of attacks of one who is openly out or from the guilt feelings accompanying the secrecy and deception of being in the closet;
- coping with the school's failure to be inclusive of youths struggling with gender issues and ridicule from their peers for being different;
- internalized homophobia (from the larger society);
- problems with alcohol and other drug abuse as a means of self-medication;
- for youths who don't come to terms with who they are or who are rejected by their parents, alcohol and other drug abuse, homelessness, unsafe practices, and suicide are major risks.

Typically, closeted gay youths are referred to treatment for symptoms of their distress, such as anxiety, drug use, and depression; rarely are they asked about their sexual concerns. Typically also, youth who are confused about their sexual identity are falsely reassured, as are their parents, that their confusion is just a passing phase. Such denial is harmful and compounds the risk for suicide (van Wormer, Wells, & Boes, 2000).

The one area of social work practice with the greatest relevance for youth suicide prevention is school social work. School counselors, psychologists, and social workers can counsel high-risk students and bullies to get at the source of their displaced hostility: one exemplary program is found in Toronto, Canada, where approximately 90 school-based social workers work with a wide variety of issues, including those pertaining to sexual orientation and gender identity.

In the state of Massachusetts, thanks to the Safe Schools Initiative signed into law in 1993, about half the high schools have gay-straight alliances. Advisors meet with gay, lesbian, and bisexual questioning students in small groups in which they discuss their sexuality and alcohol and drug use (Massachusetts Department of Education, 2007). In the absence of openly gay and lesbian teacher role models—a serious absence in itself—a community of adult-led gay and pro-gay students to provide peer support is essential.

For effective strengths-based practice, social workers in a school setting can:

- help institute programs in the school to prevent bullying and verbal abuse of students who are deemed different;

- challenge homophobic practices in the school setting;
- in individual counseling sessions seek out stories of personal growth and resilience;
- through empathetic listening and referral to affirming support groups and activist organizations, help open the door to new support systems;
- be careful in prematurely assigning labels to youths such as gay, straight, or bi; help students discover their own identities;
- make sure the school library contains helpful information about homosexuality and homophobia;
- provide teacher workshops on homophobia and school bullying; organize gay/lesbian panels from a nearby college to address the school on a yearly basis; and
- connect with PFLAG (Parents, Families, and Friends of Lesbians and Gays), which has implemented a program across North America to work with parent teacher associations and engage in speaker panels.

Family Counseling

In working with families in therapy for whatever reason, social workers would do well to be alert to instances of sex role rigidity and homophobia, which restrict the emotional and sexual expression of individual members. In addition, virtually all marriage and family counselors will encounter the issue of sexual orientation from time to time as members come in to discuss the crisis that pertains to disclosure or work with lesbian and gay couples on issues unrelated to orientation. In any case, some typical family configurations known to family therapists are lesbian and gay parents with child custody or adoption issues; nongay parents with gay or lesbian children who have come out to them; gay or lesbian families with different ethnic traditions and in-law concerns; and couples experiencing domestic violence or substance abuse.

To be a family headed by a same-sex couple in a heterosexist society is to wrestle with weighty issues at every turn: childbearing or child custody arrangements; when and how to come out to children; and how much to tell people at church, school, work, or in the neighborhood. In other words, how does one walk the fine line between discretion and openness in dealing with the outside world? Issues of extended family acceptance, gender socialization of the children, and internalized homophobia in one or both partners can under-

mine the healthiest same-sex relationships. Forced to shape their own rituals and traditions, these unorthodox families are blazing the trail for themselves and others.

Effective work with lesbian and gay couples requires that workers be familiar with the unique norms of the lesbian and gay community to avoid pathologizing what may be normative behavior for couples in that community. Heterosexual therapists who lack personal experience and comfort in working with lesbians may react in ways that repeat the rejecting experiences with significant others in their lives (Goldstein & Horowitz, 2003).

Helpful guidelines for providing family therapy with gay and lesbian family members are provided by Substance Abuse Mental Health and Services Administration (SAMHSA, 2004) and for work with transgendered populations dealing with issues of HIV/AIDS (SAMHSA, 2000).

For work with elderly lesbian, gay, and transgender couples, see Kimmel, Rose, and David (2006). Topics relevant to older sexual minorities, such as retirement, legal issues, and grandparenting, are discussed.

Religion is an issue that is never far from the surface in the lives of gays and lesbians. A common theme woven through the gay and lesbian narrative is an upbringing in which the church, synagogue, or mosque was a kind of sanctuary from the cruelties of childhood. Ultimately, however, many gays and lesbians feel rejected by the orthodox religions of their childhoods. A therapist who is knowledgeable of biblical passages of love and acceptance can offer solace to the client steeped in a negative interpretation and out-of-context guides. A focus on love, not condemnation, and a grasp of spirituality as love toward oneself and others can offer an invaluable source of strength to sexual minorities and their families who are grappling with these truths. Referrals to gay and lesbian clergy and to gay-friendly churches such as Metropolitan Community Churches, Unitarians, and Quakers or Friends Meetings can be a tremendous boon in helping clients regain the spirituality of their youth (van Wormer et al., 2000).

Finally, to help all family members move from denial and questioning ("what did we do wrong?") to acceptance and even advocacy, they should be encouraged to attend meetings of PFLAG. Scattered all across the United States, PFLAG chapters offer emotional support without criticizing visitors who are not ready to accept the sexual orientation of their loved one. A viewing of the movie *The Truth about Jane*, similarly, would be tremendously helpful to a family member struggling with a partner's or child's coming out.

CONCLUSION

Within the clinical context, through the medium of a caring relationship, the practitioner seeks to boost the lesbian, gay, or bisexual client through the aforementioned steps to strengths-based practice: seek the positive; hear the narrative; acknowledge the pain; collaborate (not dictate); and pave the way for further growth through helping others. What lesbians and all sexual minorities have to overcome along with their practitioners is the long conspiracy of silence that has served to keep generations of people from sharing the truths about their lives and their loves.

Adherence to the social work mission and values demands that the profession and those who represent it take a strong and proactive position on the individual, organizational, and educational levels on gay and lesbian issues. The goal that we in the helping professions are working toward is not mere acceptance or toleration but *celebration* of the strengths of this largely invisible minority, strengths that, at least to some extent, come from living both within society and apart from it. Like members of other groups rendered invisible in a patriarchal and highly puritanical society, gay men and lesbians have unique histories (both individually and as a whole), creative family forms, gender role flexibility, and vast social networks. The gay and lesbian contribution to underground culture as well as mainstream arts—art, music, dance, and literature—has been incalculable. To social work practitioners, the challenge is to discover and reinforce the special insights and resiliencies that have developed out of the uniqueness of lesbian and gay experience.

WEB SITES

Gay, Lesbian, and Straight Education Network (GLSEN). http://www.glsen.org.

Parents, Families, and Friends of Lesbians and Gays (PFLAG). http://www.pflag.org.

Transfamily. http://www.transfamily.org.

References

American Psychological Association. (2007). *Just the facts about sexual orientation and youth.* Committee on Lesbian, Gay and Bisexual Concerns. Washington, DC: Office of Public Communications. Retrieved November 2007 from http://apa.org/pi/lgbc/publications.

Goldstein, E., & Horowitz, L. (2003). *Lesbian identity and contemporary psychotherapy.* Hillsdale, NJ: Analytic Press.

Kimmel, D., Rose, T., & David, S. (2006). *Lesbian, gay, bisexual and transgender aging,* 2nd ed. New York: Columbia University Press.

Massachusetts Department of Education. (2007). Safe schools program for gay and lesbian students. Retrieved November 2007 from www.doe.mass.edu/cnp/safe/ssch.html

National Association of Social Workers. (2000). *Position statement: "Reparative" and "aversion" therapies for lesbians and gay men.* Retrieved November 2007 from http://www.socialworkers.org/diversity/lgb/reparative.

National Association of Social Workers. (2006). *Social work speaks: NASW policy statements 2006–2009.* Retrieved November 2007 from http://www.naswpress.org/publications.

Substance Abuse and Mental Health Services Administration. (2000). *Treatment Improvement Protocol (TIP) 37. Substance abuse treatment for persons with HIV/AIDS.* Retrieved November 2007 from http://www.ncbi.nlm.nih.gov/books.

Substance Abuse and Mental Health Services Administration. (2004). *Treatment Improvement Protocol (TIP) 39. Substance abuse treatment and family therapy.* Retrieved November 2007 from http://www.ncbi.nlm.nih.gov/books.

Tully, C. (2000). *Lesbians, gays, and the empowerment perspective.* New York: Columbia University Press.

van Wormer, K. (2007). *Human behavior and the social environment, micro level: Individuals and families.* New York: Oxford University Press.

van Wormer, K., Wells, J., & Boes, M. (2000). *Social work with lesbians, gays, and bisexuals: A strengths perspective.* Boston: Allyn & Bacon.

Clinical Social Work with Older Adults

Virginia E. Richardson

Social workers who have kept abreast of the most contemporary empirically based interventions for older adults will be in great demand in the twenty-first century as the population ages. Gerontological social workers will need to consider the complexities inherent in older persons' problems by implementing an integrative gerontological practice framework along with specialized therapeutic interventions designed for older persons. Treatments will vary depending on the practice setting, mode of intervention(s), and level of directiveness. Although many interventions that were originally developed for younger persons work equally well with older adults, others, including cognitive-behavioral and interpersonal therapy, require modifications when used with older persons.

Well-trained social workers are needed in adult day centers, home health programs, mental health centers (both inpatient and outpatient), hospitals, retirement communities, senior centers, nursing homes, and assisted living facilities. One in five Americans will be 65 years of age or older by 2050, and almost 40 percent of these older persons will be from diverse ethnic backgrounds. Americans age 85 or more are one of the fastest growing population segments in the world. Social workers' knowledge about community services, commitment to a biopsychosocial perspective, and participation on interdisciplinary teams place them in a unique position to link older adults to supportive services and to counsel those who need help.

Older persons' problems are complex and involve interrelated biological/health, psychological, social, and cultural dimensions. Reactions to medications and certain medical disorders—such as hyperthyroidism, myocardial infarction, strokes, Parkinson's disease, and specific cancers—can precipitate psychiatric conditions, such as anxiety and depression. At the same time, psychiatric conditions can influence physical health. Social influences impact older persons' access to health care, transportation, housing, and support services.

Social workers must take into account the complexities inherent in older persons' problems and consider micro and macro influences, psychological and social events, communalities and variances, and policies and inequalities that affect their lives. Instead of working separately on particular problems, gerontological social workers must intervene concomitantly and simultaneously in multiple areas and at all levels, including affective, cognitive, social, behavioral, and environmental.

An integrative gerontological practice approach that embraces social work's traditional emphasis on biopsychosocial-cultural practice will more effectively address the myriad problems most older persons confront than treatment approaches that focus on only one area. Such an approach synthesizes theories from aging and social work by integrating relevant themes from both. It includes using a life course perspective, recognizing diversity and heterogeneity among older persons, adopting a multi- and interdisciplinary practice approach and attending to power and inequalities among older adults and in their use of services (Richardson & Barusch, 2006). Well-developed therapies work better when they are combined with social and environmental interventions. For example, a social worker might help a recently bereaved older woman by assisting her with her feelings of grief and addressing the financial losses that most widows face during bereavement. Caregivers of older persons with dementia need support groups, respite care, and home health aides, but they also need policies, such as the National Family Caregiver Support Program, that target those who need help with the burdens and stresses of caregiving.

Mr. Frank, a 75-year-old single man living in low-income senior housing, became depressed after he stopped driving when his vision deteriorated. A social worker who was asked to help Mr. Frank with his depression first developed rapport with him by listening to him talk about his loneliness and feelings of frustration about his inability to visit with his friends. After assessing Mr. Frank's health, thoughts, actions, and feelings along with his environmental resources and background characteristics, Mr. Frank and the social worker created a treatment plan to address his problems. The social worker linked Mr. Frank to transportation services that would drive him to his friends' homes, and Mr. Frank agreed to meet with the social worker for 10 sessions, during which they would use a cognitive-behavioral treatment approach modified specifically for older persons to assess and change Mr. Frank's negative thoughts. They agreed that they would reevaluate his progress after these sessions and alter the treatment plan accordingly.

The social worker used an integrative gerontological practice approach with Mr. Frank by intervening on micro and macro levels, that is, by addressing the thought processes that were exacerbating his depression and identifying appropriate community services that could strengthen his support systems and subsequently empower him. The social worker also supplemented the integrative treatment with an age-specific, evidenced-based intervention, that is, cognitive-behavioral treatment designed specifically to treat late life depression (Laidlaw, Thompson, & Gallagher-Thompson, 2004). Problem-specific interventions created from empirically evaluated studies are now available to treat older adults' anxiety reactions, substance abuse problems, complicated grief reactions, and disruptive behaviors associated with dementia. Social workers must know about and learn how to use these interventions if they expect to effectively treat older persons' problems. Social workers typically apply these interventions during listening, assessment, and intervention phases.

THE LISTENING PHASE

The primary purpose of the listening phase is for social workers to develop rapport with older clients and provide them with opportunities to "tell their stories," in their words and from their perspective in a safe, secure, and comfortable context. This is especially important with older persons who distrust formal help. By listening to older persons and allowing them to share their experiences, social workers help these clients reflect on their feelings and find meaning in their lives. This process helps older persons achieve what Erik Erikson (1963) refers to as "integrity," which is "a feeling of wholeness or unity of personality and includes a sense that life has purpose and meaning" (Richardson & Barusch, 2006, p. 66). During the listening phase, social workers strive to accomplish the following goals with their older clients. These goals are to:

• build rapport by validating elderly persons' feelings and concerns;
• help older persons manage, accept, and gain control over feelings;
• identify stressors and precipitating factors contributing to problems;
• encourage older persons to present their problems from their own subjective perspective;
• help older adults find meaning by sharing their experiences, from their viewpoints, and in their words; and
• attend to cohort and cultural influences that affect how older clients approach and respond to treatment (individuals from some ethnic backgrounds may resist talking about their private lives to strangers and consider these issues too personal to disclose to outsiders).

THE ASSESSMENT PHASE

Social workers should assess older clients' functioning in multiple areas, including:

• basic self-care, often referred to as activities of daily living (such as eating, mobility, dressing, bathing, and using the toilet and bladder functioning);
• more complex activities, such as instrumental activities of daily living (including cooking, cleaning, laundry, paying bills and handling finances, and managing health and physical functioning that often require consultations with physicians);
• cognitive functioning (such as short- and long-term memory and orientations to time, place, and person);
• perceptions and feelings (including how older adults manage their emotions and whether they suffer from anxiety, depression, or other psychiatric disorders);
• social resources (e.g., relationships with friends, neighbors, and family members) as

well as environmental resources (including finances, housing, and use of services); and

- cultural and ethnic influences (such as worldviews and levels of acculturation).

In addition to comprehensively assessing older clients, social workers should know how to use age- and problem-specific assessment tools, such as the Geriatric Depression Scale, the Geriatric Depression Scale-Short Form, Geriatric Hopelessness Scale, Geriatric Suicide Ideation Scale, Short Michigan Alcoholism Screening Instrument-Geriatric Version, Inventory for Complicated Grief, and the Revised Memory and Behavior Problems Checklist.

THE INTERVENTION PHASE

Interventions for older persons should be based on their biopsychosocial assessments and tailored to meet their unique circumstances. The nature and severity of their problems, the extent of their personal and social resources, the cultural context, and the setting (e.g., hospital, nursing home, adult day center, or mental health program) all influence treatment strategies, including:

- the type and length of treatment;
- the mode of intervention (e.g., advocacy and individual, family, group, and community interventions);
- the level of directiveness (e.g., nondirective, collaborative, or directive techniques);
- intervention modifications; and
- age- and problem-specific interventions.

The setting often determines the *type and length of treatment*. Hospital social workers frequently use crisis-oriented skills to advocate for older adults' needs and help them and their families manage unexpected illnesses, determine necessary levels of care, and find relevant community resources. Social workers who are in community settings have more time to provide short-term treatment for those who need help with specific problems, such as meals, day treatment, home health care, and—when needed—long-term treatment for depression or anxiety. Because of the demands on their time, social workers in nursing homes usually provide crisis intervention and short-term problem solving. Older persons at risk for mental health problems more often participate in treatment when they receive help at primary

care settings that integrate mental health services at these locations than when they are referred to specialty mental health clinics. Such collaborative efforts between social workers and primary care practitioners are needed to effectively reach older persons at greatest risk for mental health problems (Bartels et al., 2004). These integrated services in primary care settings especially are effective in improving access to and involvement in psychiatric treatment among older African American persons at risk for anxiety and depression (Ayalon, Areán, Linkins, Lynch, & Estes, 2007). Home-based interventions, such as Brief Problem-Solving Therapy in Home Care (PST-HC), are needed when depressed older persons are too frail to leave their homes (Gellis, McGinty, Horowitz, Bruce, & Misene, 2007).

Multiple modes of intervention, such as advocacy and individual treatment, and group and community approaches are usually required when social workers assist older persons. Social workers often use groups for older persons with depression or dementia, especially in nursing homes and retirement communities. They frequently use environmental approaches in specialized care units and in older persons' homes. Advocacy is an essential aspect of clinical social work with older persons who struggle not only with ageism but also with health and economic policies that contribute to high levels of impoverishment among older women, especially those from diverse ethnic backgrounds.

Regardless of the setting, social workers provide older persons and their families with support, information, and problem solving, and they help them resolve disputes, learn more about an aging parent's illness, and help families transfer loved ones to nursing homes and other long-term care facilities. As more multigenerational families emerge and increasing numbers of grandparents raise grandchildren, social workers will be needed to comprehensively assess caregiving families and intervene on multiple levels with these families in various settings, for example, in the community and in hospitals, hospices, and nursing homes. Social workers will need to know specific caregiving assessment tools and skills training to help caregivers manage behavior problems that arise in care recipients; screening tools for evaluating elder abuse; and multicomponent intervention models to educate caregivers and empower care recipients.

The level of directiveness that social workers use with older persons depends on several factors although most social workers will work coopera-tively with older clients and their families. With older persons who have mild problems and strong social and personal resources, social workers can use nondirective approaches by strengthening these clients' resources, using psychoeducational coun-seling approaches, and referring them to self-help groups, such as caregiver and bereavement sup-port groups, which are usually client-directed. A collaborative strategy typically requires more mu-tual work with older clients to identify problems, evaluate potential solutions, and implement changes. For example, in the case of Ms. Smith, a 65-year-old African American woman who sought help for feeling "stressed out" about caring for her father, the social worker used a collaborative ap-proach by helping her:

- identify issues;
- prioritize them;
- consider solutions; and
- evaluate these.

Although Ms. Smith typically eschewed formal ser-vices, she agreed to join a caregiver support group and bring her father to adult day care, where he could socialize with others in a safe environment. She also consented to individual counseling to work on her depression. The social worker empowered Ms. Smith by:

- providing her with information about caregiving;
- linking her to adult day care and a caregiver support group; and
- offering her individual treatment for her depression.

When older clients' problems are severe—for ex-ample, they feel suicidal or have severe reactions to medication—social workers must intervene di-rectly. These clients often need hospitalization.

Many interventions originally designed for younger persons work equally well with older adults, but others require modifications. The most common modifications include supplementing in-terventions with memory and training aids to over-come cognitive, auditory, and visual impairments. Shorter but more frequent sessions effectively pre-vent and counteract older clients' fatigue, and home visits work well with frail older persons who no longer drive. Relaxation techniques that incorpo-rate imaginal exercises often assuage those with arthritis or other physical limitations. When psy-chotropic medications are involved, social workers should coordinate care with physicians and other health professionals and carefully attend to any adverse reactions or other harmful side effects that might arise. Many clinical social workers par-ticipate in geriatric interdisciplinary care teams with other health professionals. All social work-ers who plan to work with elderly persons should acquire training in interdisciplinary teamwork and learn how to conceptualize and implement interdisciplinary assessments and interventions, speak and understand the language and termi-nologies used by professions, and skillfully re-solve conflicts. Interdisciplinary teams benefit older persons by offering more integrative treatment, resulting in fewer problems from interaction ef-fects of different interventions and less redun-dancy in services (Mellor & Lindeman, 1998).

Age- and problem-specific interventions for par-ticular problems, such as anxiety, depression, de-mentia, or substance abuse, have become increas-ingly available to clinical gerontologists. One of the most successful treatments for anxious and for depressed older adults especially when com-bined with medication, is cognitive-behavioral therapy. Laidlaw, Thompson, Dick-Siskin, and Gallagher-Thompson (2003) have outlined several procedural modifications to cognitive-behavioral therapy when practitioners use it with older peo-ple. Social workers should:

- present information slowly and repetitively with older adults who have memory problems;
- tape meetings to allow older clients to hear the meetings again and practice homework assignments between sessions;
- work in interdisciplinary teams that address physiological and health problems along with environmental ones;
- instill hope by sharing with older clients information about the efficacy of treatment for late-life depression; and
- incorporate storytelling and other narrative approaches.

Interpersonal psychotherapy for late-life de-pression is another effective treatment approach for older adults that is problem-focused, collab-orative, and psychoeducational (Hinrichsen & Clougherty, 2006). Depending on the identification of the major problem areas during initial sessions, practitioners typically focus on clients' complicated grief reactions, interpersonal conflicts, role transitions, or interpersonal deficits during intermediate sessions.

Efficacy studies of cognitive behavior therapy and interpersonal psychotherapy are promising especially among the "young old." These approaches might need to be combined with antidepressant medication to effectively treat those 70 years of age or older and prevent relapses (Reynolds et al., 1999, 2006). Frail older adults with limited mobility may benefit more from home-based interventions, such as PST-HC.

Substance abuse by older adults is a neglected area in gerontological social work in part because ageist attitudes, such as the belief that older problem drinkers are intractable to treatment, contribute to the fact that many older adults with drug and alcohol problems remain untreated or are noticed only after their problems become serious enough to warrant hospitalization. These attitudes persist despite studies that have demonstrated that older persons complete and benefit from treatment more often than younger persons (Sartre, Mertens, Areán, & Weisner, 2003).

As social workers help more older adults, they must know how to assess and treat the complex problems these clients typically present in treatment. In contrast to those who remain uninformed of contemporary gerontology interventions, social workers who can apply an integrative gerontological practice framework along with validated age-specific interventions will more likely address the multifaceted problems that older people will evince in this new century.

WEB SITES

American Society on Aging. http://www.asaging.org/index.cfm.

Association for Gerontology Education in Social Work. http://www.agesw.org.

CSWE Gero-Ed Center (The National Center for Gerontological Social Work Education). http://depts.washington.edu/geroctr/index.html.

Gerontological Society of America. http://www.geron.org.

Institute for Geriatric Social Work. http://www.bu.edu/igsw/education/online/index.html.

References

Ayalon, L., Areán, P. A., Linkins, K., Lynch, M., & Estes, C. L. (2007). Integration of mental health services into primary care overcomes ethnic disparities in access to mental health services between black and white elderly. *American Journal of Geriatric Psychiatry, 15,* 906–912.

Bartels, S. J., Coakley, E., Zubritsky, C., Ware, J. H., Miles, K. M., Areán, P. A., et al. (2004) Improving access to geriatric mental health services: A randomized trial comparing treatment engagement with integrated versus enhanced referral care for depression, anxiety, and at-risk alcohol use. *American Journal of Psychiatry, 161,* 1455–1462.

Erikson, E. (1963). *Childhood and society,* 2nd ed. New York: Norton.

Gellis, Z., McGinty, J., Horowitz, A., Bruce, M. L., & Misener, E. (2007). Problem-solving therapy for late-life depression in home care: A randomized field trial. *American Journal of Geriatric Psychiatry, 15,* 968–978.

Hinrichsen, G. A., & Clougherty, K. F. (2006). *Interpersonal psychotherapy for depressed older adults.* Washington, DC: American Psychological Association.

Laidlaw, K., Thompson, L., Dick-Siskin, L., & Gallagher-Thompson, D. (2003). *Cognitive behaviour therapy with older people.* West Sussex, UK: Wiley.

Laidlaw, K., Thompson, L., & Gallagher-Thompson, D. (2004). Comprehensive conceptualization of cognitive behavior therapy for late life depression. *Behavioral and Cognitive Psychotherapy, 32,* 389–399.

Mellor, M. J., & Lindeman, D. (1998). The role of the social worker in interdisciplinary geriatric teams. *Journal of Gerontological Social Work, 30,* 3–7.

Reynolds, C. F. III, Dew, M. A., Pollock, B. G., Mulsant, B. H., Frank, E., Miller, M. D., et al. (2006). Maintenance treatment of major depression in old age. *New England Journal of Medicine, 354,* 1130–1138.

Reynolds, C. F. III, Frank, E., Perel, J. M., Imber, S. D., Cornes, C., Miller, M. D., et al. (1999). Nortriptyline and interpersonal psychotherapy as maintenance therapies for recurrent major depression: A randomized controlled trial in patients older than 59 years. *Journal of the American Medical Association, 281,* 39–45.

Richardson, V. E., & Barusch, A. S. (2006). *Gerontological practice for the twenty-first century: A social work perspective.* New York: Columbia University Press.

Sartre, D. D., Mertens, J. M. Areán, P. A., & Weisner, C. (2003). Contrasting outcomes of older versus middle-aged and younger adult chemical dependency patients in a managed care program. *Journal of Studies on Alcohol, 64,* 520–530.

Effective Practice with Refugees and Immigrants

Miriam Potocky-Tripodi

Social work practice with refugees and immigrants requires understanding of four fundamental elements: (1) the distinction between the two groups; (2) the stages of migration; (3) the role of culture, ethnicity, and minority status; and (4) the importance of evidence-based practice. An understanding of these fundamental elements lays the foundation for effective practice with these populations. This discussion addresses these fundamental elements, using two case examples for illustration. Then, necessary components of effective practice are presented and their practice implications for the two cases considered.

CASE EXAMPLES

Lakshmi, age 37, came to the United States 6 years ago from India as a legal immigrant accompanying her husband, a software engineer who was hired by a U.S.-based multinational corporation. The couple has two sons, ages 10 and 12. Lakshmi does not work outside the home. Both parents are fluent in English, and the family has a comfortable socioeconomic status. Recently, Lakshmi's 75-year-old mother-in-law came from India to live with the family. The mother-in-law requires some assistance from Lakshmi in her activities of daily living. Additionally, some family conflicts have arisen due to the mother-in-law's disapproval of the boys' Americanized behaviors. Lakshmi is also concerned about her own mother, who still lives in India and is in poor health. Lakshmi has recently been experiencing migraine headaches and has sought medical care from her physician.

Fernando, age 30, came to the United States from Cuba 4 months ago. He arrived in Florida following a 3-day boat journey during which he became sunburned and dehydrated and two of his companions drowned. In Cuba, Fernando had been a journalist and had been imprisoned for

1 year for writing an article that was critical of the Cuban government. On arrival in the United States, he was granted refugee status. He now lives with a sister and her family, who had come to the United States previously. He has minimal English ability and is presently employed as a parking valet. He has begun drinking heavily.

FUNDAMENTAL ELEMENTS

Immigrants Versus Refugees

There is a fundamental distinction between immigrants and refugees. Immigrants leave their countries voluntarily in search of better economic opportunities or family reunification, as illustrated in the case of Lakshmi. In contrast, refugees are forced out of their countries because of human rights violations against them, as illustrated by Fernando. Immigrants may be further divided into legal and illegal. Whether a person is a legal or illegal immigrant or a refugee has implications for his or her experiences during the migration process, as will be described shortly.

Stages of Migration

The migration process consists of three major stages: premigration and departure, transit, and resettlement (Drachman, 1992).

Premigration and departure. The premigration stage entails loss of family and friends and loss of a familiar environment. Both Lakshmi and Fernando have experienced these losses. Generally, the losses are greater and the premigration and departure experience is more traumatic for refugees than for immigrants. Because refugees live in politically oppressive conditions or in the midst of war, they may have been subject to discrimination, violence, rape, torture, death of family members, or imprisonment, as in Fernando's case.

Refugees often leave under hurried, chaotic, and dangerous conditions. In many cases, they flee in the midst of armed conflict. They may be victims of violence or may have witnessed violence, rape, torture, or killing. In some cases, refugees leave in mass movements, with hundreds or thousands of people. Because refugees flee under these the chaotic conditions, they usually must leave almost all their possessions behind. Thus, they lose their homes and other assets. Furthermore, refugees do not know when, if ever, they will be able to return to their countries. Thus, leaving behind family and friends is particularly painful because they know they may never see them again. Fernando left Cuba in a boat on short notice, and he fears that if he returned he would be imprisoned again.

In contrast, immigrants typically are able to plan their departure well in advance, and they leave under relatively calm conditions. They do not have to abandon their possessions; they can take some assets, especially money, with them, and they retain ownership of their property. Typically, there are no political barriers to prevent them from returning to their country, so they know they can return, even though it may not be for a long time. Nonetheless, the separation from home and family is painful, as illustrated by Lakshmi, who is likely feeling some guilt about leaving her mother behind.

Not all refugees and immigrants experience all the losses and traumas that can occur during this stage. However, some degree of loss occurs in all cases. The experiences during this stage influence the later stages of the migration process. In particular, these experiences affect people's health and mental health later.

Transit. The transit stage involves the physical move from one country to another. Again, this experience is usually more traumatic for refugees than immigrants. The experience also differs between legal and illegal immigrants. For legal immigrants, the transit usually entails arrival by plane and is typically not traumatic, as in Lakshmi's case. However, for illegal immigrants and refugees, the transit may be dangerous or life-threatening. Immigrants who enter the United States illegally often experience a dangerous transit where they are at the mercy of paid smugglers. Refugees may pass through areas of armed conflict and may be subject to or witness the same atrocities as in the premigration and departure stage. They may undertake a lengthy journey on foot, during which they may face starvation, dehydration, hypothermia, or other physical ailments. Some refugees leave by boat. Often, these boats are in poor condition and overloaded. Sinking, drowning, and illness or deaths due to sun exposure are not uncommon, as in Fernando's case. In many cases, refugees are placed in refugee camps in neighboring countries before they are sent to a permanent home in the United States or another country. These camps usually consist of tent cities. They are often overcrowded and have poor sanitary conditions. Diseases and violence in the camps are not uncommon. Refugees may remain in such camps for years before obtaining permission to enter the United States. Refugees who arrive directly in the United States requesting asylum may be placed in a detention center while their case is decided. In some cases, these individuals have remained in detention for months or years.

Again, not all legal immigrants, refugees, and illegal immigrants have the same transit experiences. Trauma experienced during the transit can affect the person's adaptation in the later stage, resettlement.

Resettlement. Resettlement is the last stage of the migration process. This stage can be seen as lasting throughout people's stay in the new country, which may be the rest of their lives. This is the stage during which social workers in the United States encounter and work with immigrants and refugees such as Lakshmi and Fernando. Issues that arise during this stage include adaptation to the cultural norms of the new country; health and mental health problems; language, education, and employment issues; changing family dynamics; and discrimination, racism, and xenophobia from members of the host society. Many of these challenges are evident in Lakshmi's and Fernando's cases. Again, these issues are usually more difficult to cope with for refugees than for immigrants.

Culture, Ethnicity, and Minority Status

Culture refers to the norms of conduct, beliefs, traditions, values, language, art, skills, and interpersonal relationships within a society (Lum, 2007). For example, Lakshmi's culture places high importance on obligations of adult children to their parents, as reflected in her situation. *Ethnicity* refers to groupings of people based on shared elements such as physical appearance, culture, religion, and history (Devore & Schlesinger, 1999).

Most immigrants and refugees can also be considered *minorities*, meaning that they are disadvantaged and receive unequal treatment in the host society (Devore & Schlesinger, 1999; Lum, 2007). Culture, ethnicity, and minority status affect people's life experiences, including their utilization and response to formal helping systems. For example, Fernando may not actively seek formal help due to the cultural value of machismo in traditional Hispanic cultures.

Evidence-Based Practice

Many interventions have not been specifically evaluated for refugee and immigrant clients. Therefore, social workers must have knowledge of the existing empirical literature and be able to determine what interventions, or modifications of interventions, appear most promising for immigrant or refugee clients based on demonstrated effectiveness for other populations. Social workers then need to adapt existing interventions or programs to make them culturally compatible with the ethnic backgrounds of immigrant or refugee clients. To determine whether these adaptations were successful, social workers need understanding of various evaluation methods.

COMPONENTS OF EFFECTIVE PRACTICE

The foregoing elements provide the foundation for effective practice with refugees and immigrants. Such practice consists of specific sets of attitudes and beliefs, knowledge, and skills. These necessary components are summarized next, based on a synthesis of the literature on culturally competent practice (Potocky-Tripodi, 2002), adapted specifically for refugees and immigrants.

Attitudes and Beliefs for Effective Practice with Refugee and Immigrant Clients

Effective social workers:

- are aware that practice cannot be neutral, value-free, or objective.
- are aware of and sensitive to their own cultural heritage.
- are aware of how their own cultural backgrounds and experiences, attitudes, values, and biases influence psychological processes.

- are aware that their decisions may be ethnocentric.
- are aware of their negative emotional reactions toward refugee and immigrant groups that may prove detrimental to their clients.
- are aware of stereotypes and preconceived notions that they may hold toward refugee and immigrant groups.
- are willing to make purposive changes in their feelings, thoughts, and behaviors toward refugee and immigrant groups.
- value and respect differences that exist between themselves and clients in terms of ethnicity, culture, and beliefs, and are willing to contrast their own beliefs and attitudes with those of their immigrant and refugee clients in a nonjudgmental fashion.
- respect clients' religious and/or spiritual beliefs and values about physical and mental functioning.
- respect indigenous helping practices and respect ethnic community intrinsic help-giving networks.
- value bilingualism and do not view another language as an impediment to practice.
- value the social work profession's commitment to social justice.
- value the importance of evidence-based practice.
- are able to recognize the limits of their competencies and expertise.

Knowledge for Effective Practice with Refugee and Immigrant Clients

Effective social workers are knowledgeable about:

- multiple theories of social science, human behavior, and social work practice.
- their own racial and cultural heritage and how it personally and professionally affects their definitions and biases of normality, abnormality, and the practice process.
- how oppression, racism, discrimination, and stereotyping affect them personally and in their work.
- how their communication style may clash or facilitate the practice process with refugee and immigrant clients and how to anticipate the impact it may have on others.
- demographic characteristics, life experiences, cultural heritage, and historical backgrounds of different refugee and immigrant groups.

- family structures/hierarchies, values, and beliefs of different refugee and immigrant groups.
- the effects of culture, ethnicity, and minority status on personality formation, life choices, manifestation of psychological disorders, help-seeking behavior, and the appropriateness or inappropriateness of practice approaches.
- culture as a source of cohesion, identity, and strength as well as strain and discordance.
- a refugee or immigrant group's adaptive strategies.
- ethnic community characteristics and community resources.
- how a person's behavior is guided by membership in families, groups, organizations, and communities.
- how sociopolitical influences, such as immigration issues, poverty, racism, stereotyping, discrimination, and powerlessness, impact the lives of refugee and immigrant clients and may influence the practice process.
- the cultural characteristics of generic social work practice and how they may clash with the cultural values of different refugee and immigrant groups.
- potential bias in assessment instruments and diagnostic systems.
- institutional barriers that prevent refugees and immigrants from using health, mental health, and social services.
- empirical literature on intervention effectiveness.
- program and practice evaluation methods.

Skills for Effective Practice with Refugee and Immigrant Clients

Effective social workers:

- take responsibility for providing the language requested by the client.
- have a strong ability to develop client mutual respect/acceptance, and regard.
- are able to overcome client feelings suspicion, distrust, or anger.
- use a positive and open communication style.
- use appropriate terms and words, visual clues, tone, facial expressions, and cadence.
- follow culturally appropriate relationship protocols.

- sincerely convey signals of respect congruent with the client's cultural beliefs.
- use appropriate self-disclosure.
- identify the client's problem in terms of wants or needs, levels, and details.
- use ethnographic interviewing skills to help identify the problem.
- assess the problem within the client's total biopsychosocial context.
- help clients determine whether a problem stems from racism or bias in others so that clients do not inappropriately blame themselves.
- assess stressors and strengths relevant to the problem and its resolution.
- use assessment and testing instruments appropriately.
- actively involve their clients in goal-setting and contracting.
- help clients prioritize problems.
- educate their clients about the processes of intervention, such as goals, expectations, legal rights, and the worker's orientation.
- establish culturally acceptable goals and objectives.
- formulate multilevel intervention alternatives.
- identify and use the client's definition of successful coping strategies and problem resolution strategies.
- select culturally appropriate, empirically based interventions.
- formulate explicit contracts.
- enhance or restore a client's psychosocial functioning and seek to redress structural inequities at the societal level.
- tailor intervention strategies to differences in help-seeking patterns, definition of problems, and selection of solutions.
- use a blend of formal and informal helping resources.
- consult with traditional healers or religious and spiritual leaders and practitioners when appropriate.
- explore issues of authority or equality in the therapeutic relationship.
- aim to increase personal, interpersonal, or political power of individuals, families, groups, and communities through empowerment techniques.
- aim to promote a sense of the collective, increase access to resources and to co-developed client–worker solutions.

- exercise institutional intervention skills on behalf of clients to eliminate biases, prejudices, and discriminatory practices.
- monitor intervention implementation and client progress.
- review progress and growth with clients.
- refer clients to other workers or agencies if they believe they are unable to help.
- evaluate problem change and attainment of objectives.
- evaluate intervention effectiveness.
- address the client's and worker's feelings about termination.
- help clients establish goals and tasks for the future.
- connect clients with other community resources.
- establish a follow-up plan.
- evaluate agency effectiveness.
- facilitate maintenance of client change.
- implement follow-up contacts.
- collect client information during follow-up.
- evaluate follow-up data.
- reinstate intervention if necessary.

Case Example Practice Implications

Lakshmi has come to her physician seeking help for migraine headaches. Her doctor may identify stress as a potential contributing factor to the pain. The physician may offer medication and may also refer Lakshmi to a social worker for a stress reduction intervention. Being familiar with the foregoing practice principles, the social worker should recognize the multiple stressors in Lakshmi's life and explore these with her. The client's stress stems from the various experiences in the different stages of her migration process, and from the generational conflicts in her household due to differential acculturation of family members. The social worker may suggest family counseling to address this issue. The worker should also explore whether Lakshmi has a support system outside her family; if not, the worker should connect Lakshmi with other immigrant women from India, who will probably be able to provide mutual support. The worker should also discuss with Lakshmi various alternatives for the care of both her mother-in-law and her own mother, bearing in mind the cultural values relevant to this.

As a recently arrived refugee, Fernando is probably receiving initial resettlement assistance from a government program. Such a program primarily focuses on employment. The social worker should recognize that Fernando is underemployed and may be feeling depressed due to the loss of his occupational status. The worker should help him enroll in English classes and a retraining program that will help him attain a job commensurate with his skills. The worker should also realize that Fernando is likely traumatized by his past imprisonment and by witnessing the drowning of his boat companions. Thus, the worker should explore the possibility of mental health counseling, bearing in mind that Fernando will not be likely to be initially receptive to the idea due to cultural values. The worker should also explore alternate housing for Fernando, as living with his sister and her family may be creating additional stress for all of them.

CONCLUSION

Effective social work practice with refugees and immigrants is based on an understanding of certain fundamental factors, combined with the development of specific attitudes, beliefs, knowledge, and skills. The development of these competencies is a continuous learning process. Social workers should continually evaluate their practice and the policies and procedures within their agencies to determine how they might better serve and be more effective with refugee and immigrant clients.

WEB SITES

Canadian Council for Refugees Best Settlement Practices. http://www.ccrweb.ca/bpfinal.htm.

Diversity Rx. http://www.diversityrx.org.

Grantmakers Concerned with Immigrants and Refugees. http://www.gcir.org.

References

Devore, W., & Schlesinger, E. G. (1999). *Ethnic-sensitive social work practice*, 5th ed. Boston: Allyn & Bacon.

Drachman, D. (1992). A stage-of-migration framework for service to immigrant populations. *Social Work, 37*, 68–72.

Lum, D. (Ed.). (2007). *Culturally competent practice: A framework for understanding diversity and justice issues*, 3rd ed. Belmont, CA: Thomson.

Potocky-Tripodi, M. (2002). *Best practices for social work with refugees and immigrants.* New York: Columbia University Press.

Social Work Practice with Native Americans

Teresa A. Evans-Campbell

After enduring centuries of institutional racism and discriminatory policies, many American Indian and Alaska Native people have high levels of mistrust of social workers and are hesitant to seek assistance from social service agencies. To provide culturally sensitive services to Native families, it is incumbent on social work professionals to learn about the history of social work in Native communities and the use of relevant practice strategies. This chapter presents information on four areas that are central to practice with American Indians and Alaska Natives (AIANs): (1) the cultural context of practice with AIANs, (2) historical trauma and healing in Native communities, (3) evidence-based interventions relevant to social work practice with Natives, and (4) practice competencies for work with Native individuals, families, and communities.

CASE

June is an Oneida woman who recently relocated with her two school-aged children from a large reservation community to a major metropolitan area. June is working full-time at a department store and is enrolled in two college courses. The family lives with her sister, who watches the children after school and in the evenings while June attends class. June has a strong work history and has always done well in school, but she feels unable to concentrate on anything right now. She reports having symptoms of depression and anxiety for the past several months and feels "overwhelmed" with her life. June has usually relied on traditional practitioners to support her wellness, but she feels disconnected from other Natives in the city. Although she misses her family and friends on the reservation, June states that her family home is not a healthy place for her children right now due to her mother's alcoholism and erratic

behavior. In addition, she feels that she needs to be in the city to support her sister, who recently finished a drug treatment program. June reports that she attended Indian boarding school in elementary school and was physically abused there. She came to see you after getting a referral from her primary physician and has never seen a social worker or mental health professional before.

Goals in Assessment Phase

- Assess cultural affiliation and identity, especially in relation to treatment preferences and options.
- Assess length and extent of symptoms related to depression and anxiety.
- Begin exploring possible sources of stress for the client.
- Explore family strengths and coping strategies successfully used in the past.
- Develop a timeline documenting significant life events, historically traumatic community events, ceremonies, and rites of passage in the family. Work with the client to document related individual and familial reactions.
- Create a culturagram to help assess cultural needs related to wellness, social support, and the provision of mental health services.
- Consider how societal oppression and institutionalized racism have impacted the client's life and her community.
- Anticipate spending considerable time building trust.

Treatment Goals

- Intervention strategies that focus on having clients themselves determine goals and objectives (e.g., solution-focused work) may be especially helpful in helping empower Native clients.

- Build on positive coping strategies and develop new strategies to combat stress and anxiety.
- Help identify strengths and resiliencies in the client's family and community history.
- Honor the client's commitment to Native traditional spirituality and support her work with traditional practitioners in addition to or in place of social work interventions.
- Explore relevant treatment resources at tribal or Native agencies in the region.
- Explore cultural and social events that may be of interest.

THE CONTEXT OF PRACTICE WITH NATIVE PEOPLE

Terminology

Numerous terms are used to describe the indigenous people of North America, including Native American, American Indian/Alaska Native, and First Nations. Many Native people instead prefer to identify by their specific tribal affiliation. Although there is no one universally accepted term, most Native people have strong preferences regarding terminology, and it is incumbent on social workers to ask clients which term is preferred. In this chapter, the terms *AIAN* and *Native* are used interchangeably.

Diversity among AIANs

The term *AIAN* encompasses an extremely diverse group of people. In the United States, there are over 560 federally recognized tribes, including 223 village groups in Alaska and close to 200 unrecognized tribes (U.S. Bureau of the Census, 2001). The size of tribal nations is varies widely, ranging from only 2 members (in several California tribes) to over 100,000 members (U.S. Bureau of the Census, 2001). According to the 2000 census, approximately 2.5 million people reported they were AIAN, and another 1.5 million reported that they were multiracial AIAN people. Contrary to common portrayals in the media, more than 60 percent of AIAN people now live in urban settings (U.S. Bureau of the Census, 2001). The urbanization of the Native population has occurred over the past several decades, often as the result of federal policies including tribal termination and relocation. The vast majority of literature on social work practice with AIANs, however, contin-

ues to be based on experiences with reservation-based populations.

Though there are some generally shared norms and values among Native people, each tribal nation is distinct in terms of culture, language, and social customs, and each nation itself encompasses a diverse population of tribal members. At the same time, American Indian families are increasingly multitribal, multicultural, and multiracial, and there is also tremendous variation in the level of acculturation among AIAN people. Though such diversity exists, Natives have endured generations of concerted stereotyping, and non-Natives often carry profound misconceptions about AIAN people and AIAN cultures. Given the great diversity among Native people, social workers must place a strong focus on cultural affiliation and cultural identity in the assessment phase, relying on Native clients to best articulate how they identify culturally (Weaver, 2003).

THE HISTORICAL CONTEXT FOR PRACTICE WITH AAIANS

An understanding of the historical context in which contemporary Native people live is imperative for culturally relevant social work practice. Over successive generations, Native people have endured a series of traumatic assaults that have had profound consequences for families and communities. An extensive body of literature documents these assaults, which have included community massacres, forced relocation, the forced removal of children though Indian boarding school policies, and the prohibition of spiritual and cultural practices (e.g., Stannard, 1992). Although Native peoples have demonstrated enormous resilience in spite of this history, such events have had a toll on the mental health and wellness of Native families. Our ability to understand the full impacts of these traumatic events and develop relevant interventions is constrained by conceptual and empirical limitations within commonly used models of trauma and traumatic response. Standard diagnostic categories capture some trauma-related symptoms experienced by AIANs (e.g., nightmares about traumatic events) but are limited in their ability to explore the effects of multiple, intergenerational traumatic events. Moreover, current models of trauma focus primarily on negative responses to trauma and are only beginning to explore the ways people cope and maintain wellness.

Recently, social workers have begun to view the concept of historical trauma as an important consideration in wellness among historically oppressed communities. Scholarship exploring historical trauma in Native communities draws from the seminal work of Maria Yellow Horse Brave Heart and her colleagues at the Takini Network (Brave Heart 1999a,b, 2000; Brave Heart & DeBruyn, 1998). Historical trauma is conceptualized as a collective complex trauma inflicted on a group of people that share a specific group identity or affiliation—ethnicity, nationality, and religious affiliation. It is the legacy of numerous traumatic events a community experiences over generations and encompasses the psychological and social responses to such events over generations (Brave Heart, 1999a,b, 2000). Brave Heart and her collaborators explored the impacts of a range of historically traumatic events on mental health among the Lakota and documented a collection of common responses that they call "historical trauma response." This response is similar to symptomatology identified among Jewish Holocaust survivors and their descendents and includes rumination over past events and lost ancestors, survivor guilt, feeling numb in response to traumatic events, anger, depression, and intrusive dreams and thoughts (Brave Heart, 1999a,b, 2000; Brave Heart & DeBruyn, 1998). Growing evidence suggests, however, that although some Native people have negative reactions associated with historically traumatic events, they also exhibit many areas of resilience and strength.

In addition to intergenerational losses, contemporary Native communities also suffer from some of the highest rates of lifetime traumatic events, including interpersonal violence (e.g., Tjaden & Thoennes, 2000), child abuse and neglect (Cross, Earle, & Simmons, 2000), poor health and mental health (Walters, Simoni, & Evans-Campbell, 2002), and an ongoing barrage of microaggressions and racist stereotypes. Given both the historical context and the high rate of contemporary stressors faced by Native people, it is not surprising that AIANs have among the highest rates of mental health disorders in the United States (Substance Abuse and Mental Health Services Administration [SAMHSA], 2001).

The Use of Evidence-Based Interventions with Native People

There is clearly a critical need for effective models of practice with Native people. Increasingly, the field of social work is moving toward the use of evidence-based practice interventions and strategies with diverse populations. Unfortunately, the use of evidence-based interventions with AIAN people is complicated by the lack of intervention research that either includes Native clients or examines Native-specific practice models. Instead, practitioners often rely on evidence-based interventions that have shown success with non-Natives and then adapt them for work with Native populations. In some cases, the work to culturally adapt interventions is extensive and involves active participation from Native community members and practitioners. Numerous culturally adapted programs have been empirically tested and have shown success with Native populations (e.g., The American Indian Life Skills Development suicide prevention curriculum, several trauma-related treatment models developed by the Indian Country Child Trauma Center). In other cases, cultural adaptation is only superficial—using Native words or Native images in media materials, for example—and the core strategies used in work remain culturally inconsistent.

When working with Native people, social workers might also consider practices that are considered promising in that there is emerging empirical evidence of their success. There are a growing number of Native-designed programs designated as promising practice models by agencies such as the Indian Health Service and SAMHSA. In addition, many indigenous practice models have strong support in tribal communities but still lack empirical validation. In these cases, taking a broader perspective on what constitutes evidence can be helpful. For example, support for many indigenous healing practices may also come in the form of practice-based evidence, including the historical use of healing strategies, community acceptance, and the integration of a healing strategy into the culture of a community (BigFoot, 2007).

PRACTICE COMPETENCIES

To help provide an empowering context for practice with Native families, a number of indigenous social work practice competencies are outlined. Several of these strategies have been adapted from a set of decolonizing practice competencies presented by Evans-Campbell and Walters (2006). These strategies are not meant to be exhaustive but should be seen as a base to build on in work with families and communities.

Using a Culturally Relevant Framework for Practice

Social work practice with AIAN people requires familiarity with Native norms and values, an understanding of the history of colonization, and an appreciation of the diversity both among and within Native communities. Accordingly, each intervention should be culturally specific and tribally relevant. Thus, social workers should not assume that a program designed for practice with Lakota people will be effective with Yakama tribal members. Interventions must also be aligned with the level of cultural connection (Weaver, 2003) and identity needs of each individual. Though many Native people are closely tied to their communities, others have a more tenuous connection which may influence their choice in services. Moreover, some Native people feel alienated from their tribal culture and experience identity-related mental health issues, including depression, low self-esteem, and anxiety. To help those suffering from feelings of alienation, social workers can connect families with Native cultural and social resources in their area. In many cities, Native organizations run programs specifically targeted to Native people (e.g., talking circles for Native parents and Native youth programs), and nearby tribal communities may offer their services to Native families who are not tribal members.

Enacting a Historically Relevant Framework for Practice

Social workers should have training around the history of colonization in the United States and its impact on Native wellness and family processes. Through the process of exploring cultural narratives and history, practitioners can work with clients to identify traditional ways of addressing trauma as well as cultural strengths that can be built on in practice. It is also essential that workers gain a fundamental understanding how social work has played a role in the institutional racism that Native people have experienced. For many decades discriminatory child welfare policies and practices were perpetrated on Native communities by social workers and public child welfare workers.

Documenting Historically Traumatic Events and Colonial Trauma

Though the lives of Native people are contextualized within a history of colonization and historically traumatic events, many people are not aware of the specific events that have impacted their communities and families. Practitioners can assist clients in learning about their histories by completing genograms, historical narratives, and historical timelines with individuals and families. These charts should document births, death, cultural events, specific historically traumatic events, as well as corresponding responses at the individual and familial level. Through such exercises, family survival strategies, coping patterns, and anniversary reactions to historically traumatic events are made explicit and can be clearly linked to traumatic events.

Focusing on Resilience and Strength

Although all indigenous people share a history of historical trauma and contemporary stress, these experiences do not define Native people. Native families have tremendous histories of strength and intergenerational resiliencies, which should be a core focus of work. Social workers are in a unique position to help illuminate family strengths and identify how these strengths are currently manifested in the family system.

Taking Time to Build Trust

Studies show that Native people have high levels of mistrust around public social services agencies, including Child Protective Service (CPS), mental health agencies, and health care settings (e.g., Evans-Campbell, under review). This may be especially true in the field of child welfare where generations of Native children have been impacted by policies designed to assimilate them or remove them from the care of Native families, including the Indian boarding school movement, the Indian Adoption Act, and the long history of CPS intervention in Native families. Such views are not surprising in light of this history and might even be reframed as a healthy reaction to what was historically a real threat. Accordingly, practitioners should be prepared to spend a significant amount of time building trust, especially in initial sessions with Native people. Intervention models that rely on client-initiated goals and objectives (e.g., motivational interviewing) may be especially helpful in this regard.

Communicating about Historical Trauma

Communication around historically traumatic events is an integral piece of healing. At certain times, responses such as denial or anger may be quite functional, and protective responses to trauma especially while a person is attempting to survive major catastrophic traumas such as boarding school or genocide (Danieli, 1998). However, the maintenance of such responses will undermine individual and family health over time. When individuals are emotionally prepared and ready, social workers can assist in exploring historical losses and making links to current family functioning. An important area of focus may be intergenerational anniversary patterns, which are often unconscious to individuals and families. For example, a Native mother may become anxious or preoccupied with the safety of her children around the anniversary of the time her parents were taken to Indian boarding school.

Supporting Clients in the Use of Traditional Healing Methods

Native clients may also need additional assistance from traditional healers or Native practitioners and social workers should be prepared to help identify appropriate traditional resources. In addition, some communities have lost important cultural tools and rituals that historically addressed loss and grief. Although it would be inappropriate for non-Native workers to attempt to impart cultural knowledge, practitioners can be invaluable as they support community members in reclaiming or relearning traditions and creating new ways to heal.

Endings in Practice with Native People

Termination with Native clients often requires a relatively extended timeframe as well as worker flexibility around commemorating the worker–client relationship. As noted previously, Native clients tend to establish trust with workers slowly and may invest a substantial amount of energy into relationship building. After a lengthy process of building trust, termination may require more time and planning on the part of the worker. The loss of the therapeutic relationship may also trigger feelings related to earlier losses (both lifetime and intergenerational) experienced by the client. Moreover, workers should be flexible about the process of termination and associated rituals. In many AIAN communities, the end of a significant relationship is usually acknowledged and celebrated, and Native clients may wish to commemorate the termination with a traditional practice, event, or gift.

CONCLUSION

In summary, culturally relevant social work practice with Native people will require commitment and creativity. All social workers must increase their understanding of how current life stressors are experienced within the context of historical trauma in Native communities. Workers must also be committed to developing and empirically testing potentially effective treatments for lifetime and historical trauma with Native communities. Finally, and perhaps most important, social work practitioners and scholars should continue to investigate community strengths as well as resilience and healing strategies found effective in Native communities. There is a small but growing literature exploring the strengths and resiliencies that result from survival in the face of historical traumas, and it could be argued that in indigenous communities, historical events have enhanced community ties and underscored the importance of retaining culture and tradition. Social workers must ask themselves how best to build on these strengths to support wellness.

WEB SITES

Indian Country Child Trauma Center, evidence-based practice models. http://www.icctc.org.
Indian Health Service. http://www.ihs.gov.
National Indian Child Welfare Association. http://www.nicwa.org.
Substance Abuse and Mental Health Services, reports related to AIANs. http://www.oas.samhsa.gov/race.htm#Indians.

References

BigFoot, D. (2007). Evidence-based practices in Indian country. Presentation at the Institute for Indigenous Wellness Research, Seattle, WA.

Brave Heart, M. Y. H. (1999a). Gender differences in the historical trauma response among the Lakota. *Journal of Health and Social Policy, 10*(4), 1–21.

Brave Heart, M. Y. H. (1999b). Oyate Ptayela: Rebuilding the Lakota Nation through addressing historical trauma among Lakota parents. *Journal of Human Behavior in the Social Environment,* (1/2). 109–126.

Brave Heart, M. Y. H. (2000). Wakiksuyapi: Carrying the historical trauma of the Lakota. *Tulane Studies in Social Welfare, 21–22,* 245–266.

Brave Heart, M. Y. H., & DeBruyn, L. M. (1998). The American Indian holocaust: Healing historical unresolved grief. *American Indian and Alaska Na-tive Mental Health Research, 8,* 56–78.

Cross, T. A., Earle, K. A., & Simmons, D. (2000). Child abuse and neglect in Indian country: Policy is-sues. *Families in Society: The Journal of Contem-porary Human Services, 81*(1), 49–58.

Danieli, Y. (Ed.). (1998). *International handbook of multigenerational legacies of trauma.* New York: Plenum Press.

Evans-Campbell, T. A. (Under review). Far from home: The legacy of Indian boarding school on mental health and substance use among urban American Indian/Alaska Natives.

Evans-Campbell, T., & Walters, K.L. (2006). Indigenist practice competencies in child welfare practice: A decolonization framework to address family vio-lence and substance abuse among First Nations peoples. In R. Fong, R. McRoy, & C. Ortiz Hen-dricks (Ed.)., *Intersecting child welfare, substance abuse, and family violence: Culturally competent approaches.* Washington, DC: CSWE Press.

Stannard, D. (1992). *American holocaust.* Oxford: Ox-ford University Press.

Substance Abuse and Mental Health Services Admin-istration. Culture, race, and ethnicity—a supple-ment to *Mental Health*: A report of the Surgeon General. Rockville, MD: DHHS, 2001.

Tjaden, P., & Thoennes, N. (2000). *Full report on the prevalence, incidence and consequences of violence against women* (NCJ 183781). Washington, DC: National Institutes of Justice.

U.S. Bureau of the Census. (2001). *2000 census counts of American Indians, Eskimos, Aleuts, and Amer-ican Indian and Alaska Native areas.* Washing-ton, DC: Racial Statistics Branch, Population Division.

Walters, K. L., Simoni, J. M., & Evans-Campbell, T. (2002). Substance use among American Indians and Alaska Natives: Incorporating culture in an "indigenist" stress-coping paradigm. *Public Health Reports, 117*(1), 104–117.

Weaver, H. (2003). Cultural competence with First Na-tions peoples. In D. Lum (Ed.), *Culturally compe-tent practice: A framework for understanding di-verse groups and justice issues.* Pacific Grove, CA: Brooks/Cole.

141 Social Work Practice with Asian and Pacific Islander Americans

Halaevalu F. Ofahengaue Vakalahi & Rowena Fong

The Asian and Pacific Islander population is a diverse group often mistakenly lumped together and insufficiently differentiated. Asian Americans themselves are a varied group composed of doz-ens of nationalities and ethnic groups from East Asia, South Asian, and Southeast Asia. East Asians include individuals from the countries of China, Japan, Korea, and the Philippines. South Asians ar-rive from Pakistan, India, Sri Lanka, Bangladesh, Nepal, and Bhutan. The Southeast Asians come from Burma/Myanmar, Singapore, Thailand, Laos, Cambodia, Vietnam, Indonesia, East Timor, and

Brunei. Most of these nations are, in turn, com-posed of numerous tribal and ethnic groups, such as the Hmong, who emigrated in significant num-bers from Laos to the United States in the after-math of the Vietnam War.

Pacific Islanders include individuals from the South Pacific island groups of Polynesia, Micro-nesia, and Melanesia. Pacific Islanders have histor-ical experiences with colonization, immigration, oppression, marginalization, and discrimination that have led to enormous mistrust of foreign systems. Those who migrate to the United States, in particular, experience the consequences of cultural duality, language barriers, poor health, underemployment, and undereducation as well as oppression, exploitation, discrimination, and disintegration of cultural identity (Yoshihama, 2001). In fact, every new generation of Pacific Islander immigrants encounter discrimination from government entities and Caucasian American communities (Millett & Orosz, 2001). Consequently, according to the U.S. Bureau of the Census (2007), Pacific Islander Americans are one of the most economically, educationally, and politically disadvantaged populations in the United States today.

Though there is great heterogeneity among Asians and Pacific Islanders in terms of social class, educational achievement, and professional occupation, the majority of Asians and Pacific Islanders do experience aspects of racism and discrimination. Despite oppressive encounters, this group possesses cultural strengths that can inform culturally relevant and sensitive practice, policy, education, and research. Examples of these cultural strengths include close family relationships, extended family network, love for children, respect for the elderly, reciprocity and sharing, and communal responsibility (Vakalahi, Godinet, & Fong, 2006). Family is first and the center of all relationships; it is the agent of socialization where honor, respect, nurturing, and collaboration are taught and practiced (Fong & Furuto, 2001). It is a basic cultural belief in most Asian and Pacific Islander groups that a house without children is a house without life. Children are embraced, paid attention to, and seldom left alone when crying. From their earliest years, children are taught to respect the elderly. The good of the whole and interdependency are valued above individual benefits and achievements (Lee, 1997; Mokuau, 1991).

CASE ILLUSTRATIONS

Case 1: The Problem of Cultural Conflict

Seini is a 17-year-old Tongan female, born in Tonga, raised in Hawaii, and living with her parents and brothers in a low-income area in Honolulu. Her family migrated from Tonga when she was 10 years old. Her annual family income is about $20,000, primarily from her father's seasonal employment. The primary language spoken in her home is Tongan. She is a senior in high school but struggles to earn enough credits to graduate on time. Seini is currently working with a probation officer due to her involvement in multiple fights in school,

allegedly associated with gang violence. She has described to her school counselor the struggles of living in dual cultures that demand one thing at home and another in school. She has experienced conflict with Tongan cultural traditions and customs imposed by her family and community, her family's low socioeconomic status, the negative impact of her low-income neighborhood, and peer pressure to be tough.

Seini talks about the overwhelming demands for giving to family, community, and church members, which often result in insufficient funds to meet her family's own needs. She often feels resentful of this cultural practice because she feels that it adds unnecessary pressure on her parents and additional responsibilities on her and her siblings. Seini feels that her Tongan culture is very important, but there have to be limits to the demands and expectations. On the other hand, her parents are intimately involved in community, cultural, and church functions. They live by cultural values of reciprocity, sharing, discipline, respect for parents and the elderly, and taking responsibility for family and extended family. They discipline their children through spanking, scolding, and grounding, which are acceptable in the Tongan culture. Interestingly, Seini accepts such disciplinary methods as appropriate and beneficial for teaching what is wrong and right. Nonetheless, she feels that she does not fit into either her American or Tongan culture. Such acculturative stress is a well-documented contributing factor to deviant behavior.

Consequences of the immigration experience hinder some of the cultural practices that Tongans are accustomed to observing in Tonga. Collectivity and reciprocity are easier to practice in Tonga because families live in close proximity and because of the perspective that it is an honor and a responsibility to care for each other. In the United States, family members live far apart, often by necessity, and lifestyle demands are more complex. The immigration experience also entails language barriers and the responsibility for Seini to translate for her parents in many incidences. When Seini interprets for her parents in the larger society, the parent–child role is reversed. Furthermore, living in a multigeneration home with other immigrant family members brings about additional responsibilities for Seini's parents. Scarce resources are definitely an issue. However, even if one person breaks the low-income cycle, that person is expected to contribute more back to the family, which perpetuates the scarcity of resources.

Despite these risk factors, Seini does have sources of protective factors from which a service provider can draw strength, even if she does not realize it. In relation to the Tongan culture, the practice of reciprocity, sharing, unconditional love for children, parents' wishes for their children to stay in school, Seini's respect for her parents and other family members, and her desire to some-day change her situation of low-income status, negative peer pressure, and gang violence are all sources of protection for Seini.

Case 2: The Intervention of Family Group Conferencing

Kaimana is a 16-year-old part-Hawaiian male who was removed from his home and placed in the custody of Child Protective Services (CPS) for alleged physical and emotional abuse by his step-father. He lived with his stepfather, who is Caucasian, and his mother, who is part Hawaiian, in Waianae farmland. His family had extremely limited material resources and social support systems. His family worked on the farm, earning an annual income of approximately $15,000. Kaimana and his siblings often missed school; their dirty fingernails and uncombed hair made them appear to be physically neglected.

CPS decided that family reunification was the planned outcome, and the intervention of family group conferencing was held. In organizing the conference, individuals involved from the family's side included Kaimana, his parents, his stepfather's sister, his neighbors, and the family social worker from a private agency. Other members of the conference included Kaimana's CPS worker, the CPS supervisor, a mental health specialist, and the conference facilitator, who was from a neutral agency.

Initiating the conference, the facilitator explained the family group conferencing process to all involved parties. Kaimana's parents were given the choice of starting with a prayer or *pule*, as it is called in Hawaiian language, which they refused. In the effort to clarify any misunderstanding and decrease mistrust of the system, social work professionals explained to the family their obligations to uphold the law to report abuse and protect children. They explained that their involvement as professionals was not intended to disrespect the family, and asked for the family's cooperation in working together for Kaimana. The social workers then identified the goal of the family group conference was to reunite Kaimana and his family, ensuring Kaimana's safety, developing specific goals and objectives that were culturally relevant, and identifying resources necessary to meet those goals.

First, the facilitator met with Kaimana's family, and together they developed specific goals and objectives for family reunification and safety and identified resources necessary to meet those goals. Simultaneously, social work professionals met in a separate session with the same tasks. Second, after the individual sessions, both groups came together, and the perspectives of each group were shared. For a period of time, processing, dialogue, negotiations, and explanations took place among the groups to reach a common plan. At the end of the processing session, the common plan consisted of a step-by-step document of tasks, timelines, and each person's responsibility. This document became the contract. For example, Kaimana was required to continue attending therapy for his anger problem and establish a personal safety plan. His stepfather was required to attend anger management courses and continue meeting with the social worker from the private agency to focus on improving communication with his spouse and children and explore the conflict of differing cultural values. The social worker was then required to follow up on the family's progress.

PRACTICE CONSIDERATIONS

In both case examples, in working with Asian and Pacific Islander children and families, cultural values play a major role in the understanding of the conflict of the case, the process of handling the case, and the intervention chosen to apply to the case.

General guidelines for service providers to consider include:

- the historical and cultural experiences with colonization and immigration, and social and economic consequences.
- the within-group diversity and need for bicultural and bilingual skills that respond to cultural duality and population changes.
- the reality of living in the United states, yet being embedded in the culture of origin.
- the need to understand the influence of cultural values, customs, lifestyles, and practices on behavior.
- the need to understand Asian and Pacific Islanders' perspective of shame and stigma associated with seeking mental health services.

- the cultural emphasis on collaboration, collectivity, reciprocity, and interdependency.
- the need to carefully bridge the community with multiple systems of help and interagency collaboration.
- the development of appropriate assessment to treatment options based on consultation with the community to understand cultural taboos and protocols for social and family interactions.
- the effects of living in multigeneration homes and family hierarchy.
- the prominent position of religious and church leaders in the lives of community members.
- the reduction of barriers to service use by advocating for the hire of Asian and Pacific Islander employees or contractors, building workforce capability and capacity, and physical space that reflect respect for diversity.
- the need to develop relevant cultural competency objectives and quality services.

Treatment Plan

- Each step of the individual treatment plan needs to encompass cultural values, beliefs, and practices as well as lifestyles and social realities of Asians and Pacific Islanders.
- Treatment plans need to consider the role of family, ethnic community, religious and church community, when it is appropriate to include their contributions.

Assessment

- Social workers need to conduct a full assessment of the biopsychosocial-spiritual dimensions of the self and relevant systems including the person, family, peers, community/neighborhood, school, and culture.
- Social workers need to ask questions regarding family characteristics and lifestyle, perception about mental health service seeking, relationships in the community and with the church and religious community, time of migration to the United States, and preference for a service provider.
- Social workers need to inquire about the role of the family and the ethnic community as well as the preference for ethnic-related resources. Questions to ask are: "Tell me about your family. Tell me about your community. Are you involved in your church and religious community? When did you migrate to the United States? Do you have any preferences for a particular type of worker to work with you? Is there anyone in the family or community that you would like to involve in our work with you? How connected is your family to your Asian or Pacific Islander culture?"

Treatment Goals

The following are suggested treatment goals.

- Increase overall social functioning in the family, community, and larger society.
- Increase consistent access to available services.
- Reduce family, community, and cultural barriers to continuous physical health and mental health.
- Maintain positive cultural connections.
- Develop capability and capacity to function positively in a dual culture.
- Reduce the impact of acculturative stress.
- Increase problem-solving options and capabilities.
- Develop the skills to increase needed resources.
- Find a balance in meeting individual and collective needs by developing win-win solutions.

Intervention Strategies

Although there are many evidence-based intervention strategies that will work with Asian and Pacific Islander individual and family clients, the following three are grounded in cultural values of community and family sharing and responsibility.

- Outreach is the action of reaching out to family and community members to support and implement interventions.
- *Ho'oponopono* is the Hawaiian process of family problem solving, including prayer, food sharing, and forgiveness of wrongdoings.
- Family group conferencing is an intervention used with biological family members and fictive kin to discuss how the treatment plan will be implemented and followed through by persons committed to the family's preservation.

CONCLUSION

Social work practitioners and service providers, both Asian and Pacific Islander and non–Asian and Pacific Islander, need to be competent with the necessary values and beliefs, knowledge, and skills to provide quality services for Asians and Pacific Islanders. It is recommended that the following practices be used with Asian and Pacific Islander clients:

- Use multiple treatment strategies, including outreach and family conferencing, as necessary.
- Understand Asian and Pacific Islander cultural processes, development, protocols, and taboos.
- Understand the particular Asian or Pacific Islander group involved and their values and beliefs, customs, traditions, and practices.
- Facilitate and work with large and small family and community groups.
- Work as a team member and the flexibility to switch roles when necessary (i.e., active involvement or observer only).
- Experience working within Asian and Pacific Islander communities.
- Be bicultural or of Asian and Pacific Islander ancestry.
- Be bilingual in any of the Asian and Pacific Islander languages.

WEB SITES

Asian and Pacific Island Wellness Center. http://www.apiwellness.org/home.html.

Asian and Pacific Islander American Health Forum. http://www.apiahf.org.

Asian and Pacific Islander Coalition on HIV/AIDS. http://www.apicha.org/apicha/main.html.

Asian and Pacific Islander Institute on Domestic Violence. http://www.apiahf.org/apidvinstitute/default.htm.

Asian Pacific Islander Legal Outreach. http://www.apilegaloutreach.org/index.html.

U.S. Census Bureau. http://www.census.gov/population/www/socdemo/race/api.html.

References

Fong, R., & Furuto, S. (Eds.). (2001). *Culturally competent social work practice: Skills, interventions and evaluation.* Boston: Allyn & Bacon.

Lee, E. (1997). *Working with Asian Americans: Guide for clinicians.* New York: Guilford.

Millett, R., & Orosz, J. J. (2001). Understanding giving patterns in communities of color. *Fund Raising Management, 32*(6), 25–27.

Mokuau, N. (Ed.). (1991). *Handbook of social services for Asian and Pacific Islanders.* New York: Greenwood.

U.S. Census Bureau. (2007). *Facts for features. Asian/Pacific American heritage month.* Retrieved November 22, 2007, from http://www.census.gov/Press-Release/www/releases/archives/facts_for_features_special_editions/009714.html.

Vakalahi, H. O., Godinet, M., & Fong, R. (2006). Pacific Islander Americans: Impact of colonization and immigration. In R. Fong, R. G. McRoy, & C. O. Hendricks (Eds.), *Intersecting child welfare, substance abuse, and family violence.* Washington, DC: Council on Social Work Education Press.

Yoshihama, M. (2001). Immigrants-in-context framework: Understanding the interactive influence of socio-cultural contexts. *Evaluation and Program Planning, 24,* 307–318.

Social Work Practice with Latinos

Ilze A. Earner & Genoveva Garcia

Immigrants from Mexico represent the largest and fastest-growing group of Latinos in the United States. Social work practice with this group entails a clear understanding of the importance of traditional cultural values and norms and of the competing and reciprocal demands of transnational life. These include the dual processes of assimilation and integration as they affect individuals and families in adjusting to life in American society while at the same time maintaining ties to their country of origin. Knowledge of how immigration status affects individual and family life is critical. Case of immigrant family from the Mixteca region illustrates family acculturation issues and parent–child conflict. Effective tools in formulating assessment and treatment goals include stages of migration frameworks, person-in-environment perspectives, the use of cultural liaisons, informal networks of support, spiritual or religious practices from a strengths perspective, and facilitating the development of migration narratives, especially in helping individuals and families understand, analyze, and negotiate transnational life.

Mexican immigrants currently represent the largest ethnic group of Latinos in the United States. Due largely to recent changes in migration patterns and immigration law, 20 percent of all legal and 67 percent of undocumented immigrants come from Mexico (Zuniga, 2004). Traditional geographic sending and receiving areas are also changing; new Mexican-origin populations have sprung up in Georgia, the Carolinas, Pennsylvania, and Rhode Island, driven largely by economic opportunities. In New York City, births to Mexican mothers have increased by 232 percent between 1980 and 1996. The largest sending area from Mexico is the Mixteca region, a distinct cultural and ecological zone that includes the south central states of Guerrero, Oaxaca, and Puebla. Two-thirds of the Mexican population in New York City is from the Mixteca region (Smith, 2006).

Social workers who practice with Latinos must consider a number of factors in the assessment of individuals and families and in formulating treatment goals. Primary among these are gender, generation, length of stay in the United States, primary language spoken, family present in the United States and in Mexico, and immigration status (Segal & Mayadas, 2005) as well as educational, occupational, and class differences (Pine & Drachman, 2005). In addition, social workers must be familiar with and understand the role of immigration law, fear of deportation, and how hostile and discriminatory attitudes impact individuals, families, and communities in accessing educational, economic, and health care systems. The person-in-environment and strengths perspectives (Saleebey, 1997) also allow social workers to identify individual and family resilience, coping mechanisms, identity formation and competence (Germain & Gitterman, 1980).

The case of Fernando and Teresa is instructive and is used to illustrate each of these factors in the development of a family assessment and formulation of treatment goals.

FERNANDO AND TERESA

Fernando G. is a 35-year-old Mexican male living in New York City; he came to the United States 13 years ago, along with his wife, Teresa, 33. Both grew up and previously lived in Puebla, Mexico. Neither Fernando nor Teresa speak English well; their immigration status is undocumented. In Mexico, Fernando completed the fifth grade and worked performing unskilled labor after he left school. Teresa finished the third grade and then stayed at home, helping her mother with house chores. Currently, Fernando works in construction for a small contractor; it is only recently that he obtained this job that has allowed him to be able to provide for his family with a modest but steady income. He works about 13 hours per day, but whenever he has an opportunity, he also volunteers at his local church doing maintenance work and restoring parts of the church. Along with other members of his community, he restored the church basement where he and others gather to practice folkloric dance. Fernando and his wife are both very active in their community and church. Fernando's extended family in New York includes two brothers and sisters-in-law. In Puebla, Fernando's parents remain in the family home. Teresa's father is deceased, and her mother lives in Mexico with two of Teresa's younger sisters, one of whom is disabled.

Fernando and Teresa have three children, Cesar, a 13-year-old boy; Aurora, a 10-year-old girl; and Fernando Jr., a 5-year-old boy. All three children were born in the United States; Teresa migrated across the border when she was pregnant with Cesar. The couple paid a "coyote"' to smuggle them across the border between Texas and Mexico.

Because neither of the parents have legal documents, they have spent the 13 years in New York City invested in working long hours to make money to support themselves, pay off their border crossing debt, as well as send monthly remittances home to their families. The conditions under which both of them have worked have always been extreme: both have been abused by employers, exploited by having to work long hours and being paid less than minimum wage, and receiving no benefits or health insurance. Teresa worked on and off until her youngest child was born; now she devotes her time to care of the family and home.

Fernando and Teresa sought professional help because they were having many problems with Cesar. They began by seeking advice from their priest, using their traditional frame of reference as to whom you would turn to for help; they ended up being connected to a mental health practitioner in a local community-based organization through members of the church where they came for family counseling sessions. During intake, the parents stated that they were worried Cesar was starting to act in a disrespectful manner at home and was hanging around neighborhood kids that they considered to be a bad influence. Cesar speaks mostly English, except with his parents, and presents with an oppositional affect and symptoms of depression. He dresses in baggy pants, wearing them low in hip-hop fashion, and always wears a cap that hides his face. When sternly asked by his father to remove the hat because it "showed bad manners,"

Cesar complied but followed up his father's request by making a face. He has been having trouble at school as well; he is missing classes, doing poorly academically, and has gotten into a number of physical altercations with other students. He was recently suspended for starting a fight on school grounds.

Their oldest son's behavioral problems have created a complex crisis in the family. Parents are often concerned about adolescent behavior and may seek help in trying to identify the developmental, emotional, and psychological factors involved, and for Fernando and Teresa an added issue was that of "cultural betrayal." In this family, as in most Mexican families, hierarchy is very important; being disrespectful toward the father, the man of the house, is a serious personal, familial, and ultimately community offense. Fernando and Teresa feel that Cesar's behavior indicates that not only have they failed at being good parents, they have failed their community because Cesar would not be perceived as a "good man"' to those outside of the family. When asked about the impact of Cesar's behavior, both parents reinforced the family hierarchy but at the same time blamed each other. Fernando stated that because his wife was the one who was taking care of the home, it was clear that she had not educated their son adequately, she had not taught him the appropriate values and norms of behavior expected of a Mexican man. Teresa, though not directly blaming Fernando, acknowledged that he was the man of the house, but because he always had to work, he was not home often enough to enforce discipline.

To deal with Cesar's behavior problems, Fernando and Teresa suggested that the best course of action would be to send Cesar to Mexico to live with his paternal grandparents until his behavior is corrected. They state that they trust the grandparents will be good disciplinarians and turn their son into a good man. They think that in 1 or 2 years under their care, Cesar's problematic behavior would be cured.

ASSESSMENT

Assessment of the family incorporated the following issues:

- family acculturation;
- help-seeking behavior;
- family identity, values, and norms;
- immigration status;

- family strengths and resources;
- migration process;
- intergenerational assimilation; and
- spiritual practice.

The parents have resided in the United States for 13 years; however, because of their undocumented immigration status, they have not integrated into American society. Their status also impacts their ability to trust or engage with "outsiders"—underscoring the importance of engagement and developing a trusting relationship with the family through their church and community, their primary support network. Process of migration frameworks (Drachman, 1992; Sluzki, 1979) are useful both in placing the family within the context of migration based on their personal circumstances and at the same time allowing social workers to identify expectable issues and problems along the immigration trajectory. A major challenge for immigrant parents is how to maintain their cultural values and ethnic identity as their children begin to adopt new values, ways of thinking, and roles to function in American society. Children assimilate more quickly than adults, resulting in culture clashes within the family that can lead to delinquent behaviors, especially gang involvement (Smith, 2001). Whereas many immigrant parents believe that sending their children, especially adolescents back home to learn how to *portarse bien* (behave properly), sometimes these measures have the intended results, other times they only deepen gang involvement (Smith, 2001).

TREATMENT INTERVENTION AND GOALS

Family counseling lasted for 7 months and the following treatment interventions were utilized:

- family genograms,
- migration narratives,
- informal support networks, and
- school-based support services.

The goals of intervention were the following:

- facilitating family adjustment and acculturation,
- improving parent–child communication,
- parenting skills regarding discipline and expectations,

- empowering parents around educational/ school issues, and
- expanding family support networks/ resources.

Family counseling involved the parents and two oldest children, Cesar and Aurora. The primary focus of intervention focused on identity issues related to migration and acculturation, parenting skills around discipline, and Cesar's problems in school. Through the use of genograms, whereby the family drew a visual picture of their transnational family, the parents and children were able to begin talking about their immigration story. Narrative offers a tool to facilitate communication between family members about powerful emotional issues involved with migration, such as sacrifice, motivation, hopes, and fears. It also enables the entire family to share their individual and collective struggles to adjust to their life in U.S. society. Like many immigrant parents, Fernando and Teresa had not talked to their children about what prompted them to leave Mexico, how they got across the border, and what they hoped to accomplish in America for their family's future. Likewise, the parents needed to hear about the stressors affecting their children, including the sense of not belonging in American society, of feeling uprooted and separate from their extended family, and of being perceived as unwanted outsiders. The parents' undocumented immigration status created a climate of constant fear about deportation and of being found out for their children.

The parents were also helped in overcoming their fear and lack of knowledge in working with the school to address Cesar's educational difficulties; by using the network of religious and community support systems to act as interpreters and cultural liaisons, the family was encouraged to meet with Cesar's teachers and guidance counselors; they were also assisted in exploring afterschool and other community-based youth programs for both Cesar and Aurora.

CONCLUSION

The case of Fernando and Teresa, recent undocumented immigrants from Mexico and their three U.S.-born children, illustrate the complex and conflicting issues affecting recent immigrant families and their children. Stages of migration frameworks and knowledge about how immigration status affects family adjustment and functioning are critical to assessment and intervention. Special attention is given to the role that informal support networks, especially religious or spiritual and ethnic communities can play in facilitating a family's ability to access school-based resources for their children and address educational difficulties. Genograms and narrative therapeutic techniques are discussed as they facilitate a focus on family strengths, resources, and resilience and promote communication between parents and children around the struggle to negotiate identity and adjust to life in American society.

WEB SITES

American Humane Association: Migration and Child Welfare National Network. http://www.americanhumane.org/site/PageServer?pagename=pc_initiatives_migration.

Bridging Refugee Youth and Children's Services. http://www.brycs.org.

Immigrant Legal Resource Center. http://www.ilrc.org.

National Council of La Raza. http://www.nclr.org.

References

Drachman, D. (1992). Stages of migration and assessment of immigrant families. *Social Work, 37*(1), 68–72.

Germain, C., & Gitterman, A. (1980). *The life model of social work practice.* New York: Columbia University Press.

Pine, B., & Drachman, D. (2005). Effective social work practice with immigrants and refugee children and their families. *Journal of Child Welfare, 84*(5), 537–562.

Saleebey, D. (1997). *The strengths perspective in social work practice.* New York: Longman.

Segal, U., & Mayadas, N. (2005). Assessment of issues facing immigrant and refugee families. *Journal of Child Welfare, 84*(5), 563–584.

Sluzki, C. (1979). Migration and family conflict. *Family Process, 18,* 373–390.

Smith, R. (2001). Mexicans: Economic, political, and educational problems and prospects. In N. Fonner (Ed.), *New immigrants in New York.* New York: Columbia University Press.

Smith, R. (2006). *Mexican New York: Transnational lives of immigrants.* Berkeley: University of California Press.

Zuniga, M. (2004). Latino children and families. In R. Fong (Ed.), *Culturally competent practice with immigrant and refugee children and families.* New York: Guilford.

143 Social Work Practice with African Americans

Sadye M.L. Logan

AN OVERVIEW AND PROFILE OF THE AFRICAN AMERICAN COMMUNITY

Given the diversity that exists in terms of values, education, income, lifestyles, and perceptions in the African American community, it is extremely challenging (if not impossible) to write a definitive chapter that captures clinical social work practice with this ethnic group. It is therefore important for readers using this information to approach this information with the understanding that this is a generic or holistic conceptualization with applications to a diverse group of people that will require modifications to be effectively applied.

Within this context, it is important to further acknowledge that African Americans constitute one of the largest ethnic groups of color in the United States, with a population numbering 13 percent of the total U.S. population, or 33.8 million people (McKinnon, 2003). The vast majority of ancestors of this amazingly resilient and diverse group of people came to the United States as enslaved Africans and remained in bondage for over 200 years. It is generally believed that the majority, if not all, of the enslaved Africans were taken from the western parts of the African continent (Gutman, 1975). The process of enslavement is believed to have resulted in what is defined today as post-traumatic stress disorder (PTSD) that has produced an intergenerational impact on the emotional health of African Americans (Logan, Denby & Gibson, 2007). This process, which included institutional racism, discrimination, and oppression, has produced a schizophrenic type of existence for the enslaved Africans and their descendents. Although the majority of the Africans remained enslaved, some were able to purchase their freedom and remained free. Others were forced back into slavery; many were fathered by their white owners and looked white; some of those who looked like their white fathers prospered and were in some instances also owners of slaves

(Johnson & Roak, 1984). The majority of the enslaved Africans lived in the Southern parts of the United States, where more than 50 percent of the African American population still reside today (McKinnon, 2003). A significant proportion of this population consists of female-headed household with children under 18 years of age. These female-headed families frequently live below the poverty level (McKinnon, 2003).

Social work practice will most likely occur with those African Americans experiencing the impact of PTSD, poverty, mental illness, and other forms of problems in living. Social work practice with these families and children and adult African American clients will require not only that practitioners be culturally responsive but that an integrated, holistic, ethnically sensitive approach be embraced. Such an approach reflects a strengths-based biopsychosocial-spiritual orientation to helping. Practice experience has shown that a multi-contextual approach, embracing the whole client, is necessary to address the multifaceted concerns most African Americans persons bring to the helping encounter (Boyd-Franklin, 1989; Logan & Freeman, 2004). These multicontextual issues (see Fig. 143.1) serves as a framework for guiding the practice process. The inclusion of an ethnic-sensitive (Devore & Schlesinger, 1996), strengths-based (Saleebey, 2001), spiritually oriented (Logan & Freeman, 2004) perspective expands the traditional biopsychosocial orientation, thereby being more responsive to the needs and experiences of African American clients. The ethnic-sensitive, strengths-based, spirituality-oriented approach is based on the following concepts: African centeredness, spirituality, strengths perspective and empowerment.

- *African-centeredness.* This perspective acknowledges African culture, expression, values, beliefs and instructions. It underscores interconnectedness as a way of being in

THE INDIVIUAL	IMMEDIATE HOUSELHOLD	EXTENDED FAMILY	COMMUNITY AND SOCIAL CONNECTIONS	LARGER SOCIETY
• Age • Gender & sexual orientation • Temperament • Developmental or physical disabilities • Culture, race, ethnicity • Class • Religious, philosophical, spiritual values • Finances • Autonomy skills • Affiliative skills • Power/privilege or powerlessness/ abuse • Education and work • Physical or psychological symptoms • Addictions and behavioral disturbances • Allocation of time • Social participation • Personal dreams	• Type of family structure • Stage of family life cycle • Emotional climate • Boundaries, patterns, and triangles • Communication patterns • Negotiating skills • Decision-making process	• Relationship patterns • Emotional legacies, themes, secret, family myths, taboos • Loss • Socio-economic level and issues • Work patterns • Dysfunctions: addictions, violence, illness, disabilities • Social and community involvement • Ethnicity • Values and/or religion	• Face-to-face links between individual, family, and society • Friends and neighbors • Involvement in children's school and activities • Political action • Recreation or cultural groups	• Social, political, economic issues • Bias based on race, ethnicity • Bias based on class • Bias based on sexual orientation • Bias based on religion • Bias based on disability • Power and privilege of some groups because of hierarchical rules and norms held by religions, social, business or governmental institutions • How does family's place in hierarchy affect relationships and ability to change?

Figure 143.1 Multicontextual framework.
(*Source:* Carter, & McGoldriek, 2005.)

world that suggests wholeness and balance. Ultimately, it affirms a conscious as well as unconscious connection of people of African descent with their past and present.

• *Spirituality.* This orientation is concerned with the belief in the wholeness of what it means to be human, a belief that relates to a person search for a sense of meaning and a morally fulfilling relationship with the world in which they live.

• *Strengths perspective.* This perspective builds on the belief that within every human being exist an inner or inherent energy or life force that is available to guide and support us in living our lives in productive, fulfilling ways.

• *Empowerment*. This perspective serves as a treatment process and a treatment goal. It places emphasis on the clients' abilities and desires to take control of their lives and view themselves positively and competently. Within this broad context empowerment incorporates these themes: a developmental process, a psychological state, and liberation from oppression.

CLINICAL ISSUES

The primary clinical issue for working effectively with African American clients is concerned with the social worker's willingness to embrace a paradigm shift that incorporates the worldviews of African Americans. Worldviews are typically defined as one's perceptions of oneself in relation to other people, nature, objects, and institutions. Scholars on black family life have conceptualized worldviews of African Americans as African-centered and strengths-based (see Fig. 143.2). This perspective is based on the values and ethos of the people of Africa and the people of African descent (Turner, 1996). However, it is important to note that black families and children vary in the extent to which

they exemplify Africentric values, attitudes, beliefs, and characteristics. It has been shown that this information can be useful to practitioners in the assessment and intervention phases of their work.

PRACTICE APPROACHES AND INTERVENTION TECHNIQUES

The search for effective practice approaches and intervention strategies for working with clients of African descent has been ongoing. The first definitive textbook addressing this subject appeared in the late 1980s (Boyd-Franklin, 1989) and the early 1990s. Authors proposed a culturally specific framework or perspective. This perspective expanded the traditional psychosocial perspective and embodied a biopsychosocial spiritual orientation. Emphasis is placed on the cultural and spiritual, which includes cultural identity, cultural explanation of illness and health, natural support systems, worship or faith-based centers and institutions, ethnic community and social organizations, and cultural factors between the client and worker (Lum, 1996). Within this context, an Africentric and strengths-based orientation is proposed. As indicated earlier, this orientation not only includes the history, culture, and worldviews of African American but also pro-

Some' 1998	Hill 1997	Logan and Freeman 2000 Logan 2001 Logan, Freeman and McRoy, 1990	Martin and Martin, 2002	McAdoo, 1997 & 2003	Schiele, 2000
-Rituals of healing -Indigenous technologies -Healthy Community -Spiritual World -Village Community	-Strong Kinship bonds -Strong work orientation -Strong achievement orientation -Strong religious orientation -Adaptability of family roles	-Inner (inherent) strengths -Unity Wholeness -Self healing Empowerment stance -Positive change -Loving and caring -Collectivism -Nurturance -Support -Perseverance	-Religious consciousness tradition -Fraternal orders -Unions -Ethnic -Women clubs -Race consciousness -Extension of extended families -Institution of black helping tradition Pro socialization of children	- Kinship and mutual assistance -Extended family -More than provision of basic needs	-Afro-centricity -Human liberation -Spirituality -Collectivity -Self-knowledge -Inclusiveness -Strong mother-child bond

Figure 143.2 Values, characteristics, attitudes, and beliefs of African Americans. (*Source:* Logan, & Freeman, 2004.)

vides a multidimensional or multilevel framework for practice, assessment, and intervention. Emergent and traditional practice approaches supports this orientation. These include:

- solution-focused brief therapy,
- solution-oriented therapy,
- gender-sensitive therapy,
- cognitive-behavioral therapy,
- psychoeducational family therapy,
- task-centered treatment,
- structural family therapy,
- collaborative language systems approaches,
- narrative therapy,
- empowerment and strengths perspectives, and
- crisis treatment. (Walsh, 2006)

Given the range of practice approaches for working with African American clients, it is important to note that the practice interventions may overlap. It is, therefore, crucial to note that despite the similarities, these strategies may have very different purposes (Walsh, 2006). In addition to the more generic strategies identified in the various practice approaches, the African-centered genogram, the cultural eco-map, cognitive restructuring, culturally relevant readings, and family albums are more specific practice strategies for working with African American clients (Logan & Freeman, 2004).

The treatment plan flows naturally from the assessment process (see Fig. 143.3) and is based on a collaborative partnership (Lipchick, 2002). In this regard, the social worker should (Logan & Freeman, 2004):

1. identify and understand the cultural identity of African American families and their unique history of enslavement and the continuing impact of living in an environment of oppression, racism, and gross inequalities;
2. assume the existence of strengths for the family, search for exceptions, and support the family's strengths through the inclusion of significant others and through affirmations and an emphasis on solutions; and
3. walk and work side by side with client systems as partners.

As the social worker and the African American client work toward a clear definition of presenting concerns, the identification of specific, concrete, achievable treatment goals, and treatment strategies selected from the diverse range of practice approaches may reflect micro, meso, and/or macro levels of interventions. Micro-level interventions include empowerment, crisis, family treatment, solution finding, existentialism, and competitive restructuring. Meso-level interventions involve the expanded family, fictive kin, place of worship, schools, and various community support systems. Macro-level interventions address policy, planning, community organizing, policy, advocacy, and administration.

The treatment plan, based on the identified needs of the client systems and culturally diverse treatment strategies, includes the treatment goals, desired outcome, expected change, and agreement or contracting between all parties involved in the change process. As indicated earlier, assessment and treatment tools may consist of the following.

1. *The cultural eco-map* highlights the family as a unit and focuses on both the immediate or the African American ethnic group environment and larger extended environments beyond the individual or family's environment (Logan & Freeman, 2004). In focusing on these three broad aspects of the map, the social worker maybe guided by questions such as those related to:

   a. the individual or family unit basic needs, food and shelter, preventive health care and good medical resources, satisfactory work experiences, and unit's ability to agree on and fulfill functional roles while meeting individual needs;
   b. the nature and quality of African Americans' ethnic group environment, is the neighborhood safe and reasonably pleasant to live in, quality of family ties, intergenerational issues, and membership in social clubs.; and
   c. the nature and quality of relationship to the broader extended environment with respect to the educational and vocational enrichment, availability and assessment of needed resources, meaningful connections with other ethnic groups, feelings of inclusiveness, and the ability to deal with an oppressive and racist environment.

2. *The African-centered genogram* is based on two major assumptions about family relationships. These assumptions address

Three Broad Areas of Work	Related Tasks:
Assessment Includes:	Individual, group, family and community history Religious/spiritual heritage Migration history Impact of racism and other form s of oppression Economic issues Cultural issues Environmental issues Self-image/ethnic identity issues
Intervention Focuses on:	What the client system wants to see changed or different Empowerment: Individual, family, community Strengths, self help, positive change, and collaborative partnership Advocacy at the community level Schools and social service agencies: Responsiveness to the needs of families and communities Action-oriented strategies
Evaluation includes:	Concrete measurable culturally relevant goals agreed on by the client system African-centered diagnoses (incorporates client's ideas about illness and healing) Ongoing goal and task reviews

Figure 143.3 An African-centered framework.
(*Source:* Logan, & Freeman, 2004.)

kinship, including fictive kinds (those not related by blood or marriage) and functional relationships (Watts-Jones, 1997, p. 377).

a. In African American families, kinship must be regarded and understood as it is constructed by the ethnic or racial group of the particular family.
b. Functional relationships are as important to represent in a genogram as biological relationships. Functional relationships are based on performances and interactions. For example, a biological grandmother may serve a functional role as mother to her grandchild.

Together these culturally sensitive tools serve as useful instruments not only in assessing the strengths and presenting concerns of the African American client but also in providing new insight and information about the family's cultural heritage, cultural, and ethnic identity, intergenerational patterns, and ways of being in the world.

ASSESSMENT AND TREATMENT PLANS

A culturally responsive social worker, in working with African American clients, will seek to understand and apply the African-centered approach to the three phases of process (see Fig. 143.3). In this process, Lum (1996) suggests that the social worker not only reinterprets and reconceptualizes psychosocial factors as socioenvironmental impacts and psycho-individual reactions but also acknowledges cultural strengths that include the cultural and the spiritual. Additionally, the following factors may serve to strengthen the social assessment skills of the social worker (Green, 1995, pp. 80–81).

- A worker should think about clients in terms of group characteristics and group strengths, as well as clinical pathology and agency protocols of problem resolution.
- A worker should examine group strengths as they are understood by community members themselves and should view the client as a potential teacher to the worker as well as the recipient of services.
- A worker should openly use indigenous sources of help, which may mean granting credence to lay practitioners from ethnic communities.
- A worker should have a systematic learning style and a supportive agency environment that recognize culturally distinctive modes of behavior and respond to them appropriately.

EVIDENCE OF PRACTICE EFFECTIVENESS

Evidence of practice is viewed by some as a movement within the social work profession (Walsh, 2006). Vandiver (2002) and others view it as a process using a variety of sources in the professional literature to select interventions that are most likely to promote client change. It is suggested that the evidence-based practitioner should follow a three-tiered approach to selecting interventions to use with clients.

1. The first tier of is based on established practice guidelines or recommendations that are based on research findings.
2. The second tier of guidelines are based on the expert consensus of clinicians with expertise in a certain area of practice.
3. The third tier is based on self-directed practice that is immediately available to the social worker, such as experience, journal reports, and peer and supervisory input.

Despite the intention within the social work profession to use treatment strategies that have been shown to be effective, efforts to identify evidence-based practice models have been controversial (Walsh, 2007). Practice effectiveness with African American clients clusters around the third tier of evidence-based practice. However, research has consistently shown that structural family treatment is more effective than other clinical modalities with African American clients (Santisteban et al., 1997). The client populations have included families with children and adolescents with substance use problems and other behavioral issues and concerns.

Although structural family therapy provides a useful perspective for evidence-based practice with African American clients, a major concern relates to an inherent bias about what constitutes an appropriate family structure. This therapy was based on its founders belief that many multiproblem families lacked strong executive authority and rules. This executive authority was relegated to the paternal figure or the father in the family, who was viewed as the head of the household. This notion was challenged by a feminist critique in the 1980s and continues to be a cautionary point of reference for social workers. Given the increasing diversity in family forms worldwide, it is imperative that social work practitioners not hold specific assumptions about what constitutes family structures prior to a comprehensive assessment process.

CONCLUSION

Effective social work practice with African Americans is based on knowledge and understanding of the history and cultures of the African American people. Recommended practice approaches and strategies incorporate aspects of traditional practice approaches and emergent approaches within an African-centered framework. Emphasis is placed on a collaborative, spiritually oriented empowerment perspective.

WEB SITE

National Alliance on the Mental Illness, Family Guide to Mental Health: What You Need to Know. http://www.nami.org/MAC/familyguide.

References

Boyd-Franklin, N. (1989). *Black families in therapy: A multisystems approach.* New York: Guilford.

Carter, B., & McGoldrick, M. (2005). *The expanded family life cycle: Individual, family and social perspectives*, 3rd ed. Needham Heights, MA: Allyn & Bacon.

Devore, W., & Schlesinger, E. (1996). *Ethnic-sensitive social work practice*, 4th ed. Boston: Allyn & Bacon.

Green, J. W. (1995). *Cultural awareness in the human services: A multiethnic approach,* 2nd ed. Boston: Allyn & Bacon.

Gutman, H. G. (1975). *Slavery and the number game: A critique of times on the cross.* Urbana: University of Illinois Press.

Johnson, M. P., & Roak, J. (1984). *Black masters: A free family of color in the old South.* New York: Norton.

Lipchick, E. (2002). *Beyond technique in solution-focused therapy: Working with emotions and the therapeutic relationship.* New York: Guilford.

Logan, S., Denby, R., & Gibson, P. (2007). *Mental health care in the African American community.* New York: Haworth.

Logan, S., & Freeman, E. (2004). An analysis integration and application of Africentric and strengths approaches to black families and communities. In E. Freeman & S. Logan (Eds.), *Reconceptualizing the strengths and common heritage of black families* (pp. 25–38). Springfield, IL: Charles C. Thomas.

Lum, D. (1996). *Social work practice and people of color: A process-stage approach,* 3rd ed. Pacific Grove, CA: Brooks/Cole.

McKinnon, J. (2003). *The black population in the United States.* March 2002 Current Population Report Series, P 20-541. Washington, DC: U.S. Bureau of the Census.

Saleebey, D. (2001) *The strengths perspective in social work practice,* 3rd ed. Needham Heights, MA: Allyn & Bacon.

Santisteban, D. A., Coatsworth, J. D., Perez-Vidal, A., Mitrani, V., Jean-Gilles, M., & Szapocznik, J. (1997). Brief structural/strategic family therapy with African American and Hispanic high-risk youth. *Journal of Community Psychology, 215*(5), 453–471.

Turner, R. J. (1996). Affirming consciousness: The Africentric perspective. In J. E. Everett, S. S. Chipungu, & B. P. Leashore (Eds.), *Child welfare: An Africentric perspective* (pp. 36–57), New Brunswick, NJ: Rutgers University Press.

Vandiver, V. L. (2002). Step-by-step practice guidelines for using evidence-based practice and expert consensus in mental health settings. In A. R. Roberts & G. J. Greene (Eds.), *Social worker's desk reference* (pp. 731–738). New York: Oxford University Press.

Walsh, J. (2006). *Theories for direct social work practice.* Belmont, CA: Brooks/Cole.

Watts-Jones, D. (1997). Toward an African American genogram. *Family Process, 36*(4), 373–383.

144   The Culturagram

Elaine P. Congress

American society is becoming increasingly diverse, a fact that has been well documented in both professional literature and the media. Immigrants are entering the United States in record numbers; since 2000, 10.3 million immigrants have arrived, the highest number ever recorded in U.S. history within a 8-year period (U.S. Bureau of the Census, 2007). Over 37.9 million immigrants now live in the United States (Camorata, 2007). It is estimated that one out of three immigrants are undocumented, while more than half of the immigrants who entered the country since 2000 are undocumented (U.S. Bureau of the Census, 2007). One in eight U.S. residents are immigrants, and in large metropolitan areas such as New York City, the majority of the population already come from countries in Asia, South and Central America, and the Caribbean (New York City Department of City Planning, 2004).

From our professional beginning in settlement houses, social workers have always sought to advance the well-being of immigrant populations.

The code of ethics stresses the importance of non-discrimination based on race, ethnicity, national origin and will add a clause about immigration status. Furthermore, social workers are advised to practice cultural competent practice (NASW, 1999).

Though there has been growing literature and focus in social work practice and education on cultural competency, professional literature on immigrants, also has increased dramatically in the past decade. A review of social work abstracts for the past 10 years on immigrants in the United States yielded 115 articles, 97 which had been written in the past 5 years. Most have focused on direct practice issues in working with different immigrant populations, including Latino populations (Ardila, 2005), Korean Americans (Rhee, Chang, &Youn, 2003), South Asians around HIV/AIDS (Bhattacharya, 2004), Mexican women (Morgan, 2003), Chinese American elders (Stokes, Thompson, Murphy, Gallagher Thompson, 2001), Korean immigrants (Kim, 2002), post-traumatic stress disorder among Liberian immigrants (Jarbo, 2001), and African immigrants (Kamya, 1997). Only one article identified a more general need for more social work practice, research, and education with immigrants (Feldman, 1998).

The culturagram, a family assessment instrument, grew out of the recognition that families are becoming increasingly culturally diverse and social workers must be able to understand cultural differences between and within families. When attempting to understand culturally diverse families, it is important to assess the family within a cultural context. Considering a family only in terms of a generic cultural identity, however, may lead to overgeneralization and stereotyping (Congress & Kung, 2005). A Puerto Rican family who are American citizens and have lived in the United States for 40 years is very different from an documented Mexican family that emigrated last month. Yet both families are considered Hispanic/Latino. Even within the same ethnic groups, each family has had a different immigration and acculturation experience.

THE CULTURAGRAM

Whereas the eco-map (Hartman & Laird, 1983) and genogram (see Chapter 57) are useful tools in assessing the family, they do not emphasize the important role of culture in understanding the family. The culturagram was developed to help in understanding the role of culture in families

(Congress, 1994, 1997; Congress & Kung, 2005). This tool has been applied to work with people of color (Lum, 1999), battered women (Congress & Brownell, 2007), children (Webb, 2001), older people (Brownell, 1997), families in crisis (Congress, 2000) Mexican families (Congress, 2004a, 2004b), Latino and Asian families (Congress & Kung, 2005), and family development theory (Congress, 2008).

The culturagram represents an attempt to individualize culturally diverse families (Congress & Kung, 2005). Completing a culturagram on a family can help a clinician develop a better understanding of the family. Revised in 2007, the culturagram (see Fig. 144.1) examines the following areas:

- reasons for relocation;
- legal status;
- time in community;
- language spoken at home and in the community;
- health beliefs;
- impact of trauma and crisis events;
- contact with cultural and religious institutions, holidays, food, and clothing;
- oppression, discrimination, bias, and racism;
- values about education and work; and
- values about family—structure, power, myths, and rules.

Reasons for relocating vary among families. Many families come because of economic opportunities in the United States, whereas others relocate because of political and religious discrimination in their country of origin. The main reason families migrate is often because a family member or friend has preceded them. For some families, it is possible to return home again, and they often travel back and forth for holidays and special occasions. Others know they can never go home again. Some families move within the United States, often from a rural to a more urban area.

The legal status of a family may have an effect on both individuals and the family as a whole. If a family is undocumented and fears deportation, members may become secretive and socially isolated. Latency age children and adolescents may be discouraged from developing peer relationships because of the fears of others knowing their immigration secret.

The length of time in the community may differ for individual family members. Usually, family members who have arrived earlier are more

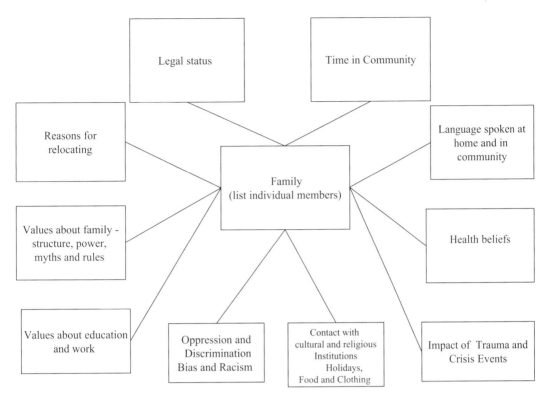

Figure 144.1 Culturagram–2007.

assimilated than other members. A current phenomenon involves mothers first immigrating to the United States and then sending for their children. These circumstances can certainly impact individual and family development. A young infant left in the care of relatives in the homeland may have difficulties developing trust because of the lack of continuity in parenting during this crucial early period. Also, the family with young children that is disrupted when the mother emigrates to America may face challenges in reuniting as a family after a several-year hiatus. Another key factor is that family members are different ages at the time they relocate. Because of attending American schools and developing peer relationships, children are often more quickly assimilated than their parents. This may lead to conflictual role reversals in which children assume a leadership role.

Language is the mechanism by which families communicate with each other. Often families may use their native language at home, but may begin to use English in contacts with the outside community. Sometimes children may prefer English because they see knowledge of this language as most helpful for survival in their newly adopted country. This may lead to conflict in families.

A most literal communication problem may develop when parents speak no English and children speak their native tongue only minimally.

Families from different cultures have varying beliefs about health, disease, and treatment (Congress & Lyons, 1992). Often, health issues impact on culturally diverse families, as for example when the primary wage earner with a serious illness is no longer able to work, a family member has HIV/AIDS, or a child has a chronic health condition such as asthma or diabetes. Also, mental health problems can impact families negatively. Families from different cultures may encounter barriers in accessing medical treatment or may prefer alternative resources for diagnosing and treating physical and mental health conditions (Devore & Schlesinger, 1998). Both legal and undocumented immigrants may lack health insurance and not have financial resources to pay for needed health care (Chang-Muy & Congress, 2008). Many immigrants may use health care methods other than traditional Western European medical care involving diagnosis, pharmacology, x-rays, and surgery (Congress & Lyons, 1992). The social worker who wishes to understand families must study their own unique health care beliefs.

Families can encounter developmental crises as well as "bolts from the blue" crises (Congress, 1996). Developmental crises may occur when a family moves from one life stage to another. Stages in the life cycle for culturally diverse families may be quite different from those for traditional middle-class families. For example, for many culturally diverse families, the "launching children" stage may not occur at all, as single and even married children may continue to live in close proximity to the parents. If separation is forced, this developmental crisis might be especially traumatic.

Families also deal with "bolts from the blue" crises in different ways. A family's reaction to crisis events is often related to its cultural values. For example, a father's accident and subsequent inability to work may be especially traumatic for an immigrant family in which the father providing for the family is an important family value. Whereas rape is certainly traumatic for any family, the rape of a teenage girl may be especially traumatic for a family who values virginity before marriage.

Immigrant individuals and families may have experienced traumatic events in their country of origin or during transit to the United States. Often immigrant families suffer from poverty and discrimination as they try to access needed educational, vocational, and social services. The current policies about undocumented immigrants certainly leads to continual traumatic experiences for immigrant families.

Contact with cultural institutions often provides support to an immigrant family. Family members may use cultural institutions differently. For example, a father may belong to a social club, the mother may attend a church where her native language is spoken, and adolescent children may refuse to participate in either because they wish to become more Americanized. Religion may provide much support to culturally diverse families, and the clinician will want to explore the contact with formal religious institutions.

Each family has particular holidays and special events. Some events mark transitions from one developmental stage to another—for example, a christening, a bar or bat mitzvah, a wedding, or a funeral. It is important for the social worker to learn cultural significance of important holidays for the family, because they are indicative of what families see as major transition points within their family. These holidays are often associated with culture-specific foods or clothing.

Many immigrants have experienced oppression in their native countries, which has led to their departure from their homelands and immigration to the United States. Some immigrants may have been the majority population in their home country and thus never experienced prejudice until their arrival in the United States. Here they may be the victim of discrimination and racism based on language, cultural, and racial differences. The current U.S. policies on undocumented immigrants further serves to separate and discriminate this newcomer population from other Americans. After review of previous versions of the culturagram and feedback about the instrument, this area was recently added as important in understanding the immigrant family experience.

All families have differing values about work and education, and culture is an important influence on such values. Social workers must explore what these values are to understand the family. Economic and social differences between the country of origin and America can affect immigrant families. For example, employment in a low-status position may be very denigrating to a male breadwinner. It may be especially traumatic for an immigrant family when the father cannot find work or only work of a menial nature. Sometimes, there may be a conflict in values. This occurred when an adolescent son was accepted with a full scholarship to a prestigious university miles from home. Though the family had always believed in the importance of education, the parents believed that the family needed to stay together and they did not want to have their only child leave home, even to pursue education.

Another example occurs when American latency-age children often attend large schools far from their communities and begin to develop peer relationships apart from their families. For culturally diverse families that come from backgrounds in which education has been minimal and localized, and even where young children were forced to work and care for younger siblings, the American school system's focus on individual academic achievement and peer relationships may seem strange. Furthermore, immigrant children who bring a history of individual or family oppression may feel very isolated and lonely in their new environments.

Each family has its unique structure, its beliefs about power relationships, myths, and rules. Some of these may be unique to the cultural background of the family. The clinician needs to explore these family characteristics individually and also understand them in the context of the family's cultural background. Culturally diverse families may have differing beliefs about male–female relationships, especially within marriage. Family structure may encounter conflict in American society with its more egalitarian gender relationships. This may result in an increase in domestic violence among culturally diverse families. Also, child-rearing practices especially in regard to discipline may differ in culturally diverse families. This may result in increased reporting to Child Protective Services.

The following vignette illustrates how the culturagram can be used to better understand a family with its unique cultural background.

Statement of Problem

Mrs. Carmen Perez, 35 years old, contacted the Family Service Agency in her community because she was having increasing conflicts with her 14-year-old son, Juan, who had begun to cut school and stay out late at night. The past Christmas holidays had been especially difficult—Juan had disappeared for the whole New Year's weekend. She also reported that she had a 10-year-old daughter Maria who was "an angel." Maria was very quiet, never wanted to go out with friends, and preferred to stay at home helping her with household chores. Mrs. Perez indicated the source of much conflict was that Juan believed he did not have to respect Pablo, as the latter was not his real father. Juan complained that his mother and stepfather were "dumb" because they did not speak English. He felt it was very important to learn English as soon as possible because at school several students had made fun of his accent. He felt his parents did not understand how difficult his school experience was, and he believed that teachers favored lighter-skinned Latinos. Juan had much darker skin than his mother, his stepfather, or his half-sister, Maria.

History

When she was 20, Mrs. Perez had moved to the United States from Puerto Rico with her first husband, Juan Sr., because they were very poor in Puerto Rico and had heard there were better job opportunities here. Juan Sr. had died in an automobile accident on a visit back to Puerto Rico when Juan Jr. was 2. Shortly afterward, she met Pablo, who had come to New York from Mexico to visit a terminally ill relative. After she became pregnant with Maria, they began to live together. Pablo indicated that he was very fearful of re-turning to Mexico, because several people in his village had been killed in political conflicts. Because Pablo was undocumented, he had been able to find only occasional day work. He was embarrassed that Carmen had been forced to apply for food stamps. Carmen was paid only minimum wage as home care worker. She was very close to her mother, who lived with the family. Her mother had taken her to a spiritualist to help her with her family problems before she had come to the neighborhood agency to ask for help. Pablo has no relatives in New York, but he has several friends at the social club in his neighborhood.

Discussion

After completing the culturagram (see Fig. 144.2), the social worker was better able to understand the Perez family, assess their needs, and begin to plan for treatment. For example, she noted that Pablo's undocumented status was a source of continual stress in this family. She referred him to a free legal service that provided help for undocumented people in securing legal status. The social worker also recognized that there had been much conflict within the family because of Juan's behavior. She had concern that Maria might have unrecognized problems. Finally, she was keenly aware of family conflicts between Pablo and Juan. To help the family work out its conflicts, the social worker referred them to a family therapist who was culturally sensitive and had experience with intergenerational conflicts.

FUTURE DIRECTIONS OF MULTICULTURAL PRACTICE

The culturagram has been seen as an essential tool in helping social workers work more effectively with families from many different cultures. Not only does it help the social worker achieve greater understanding of the culture of a family, it can also point the way toward future treatment. The case example demonstrates how the culturagram can be useful in arriving at decisions about treatment planning and intervention.

Current practice looks to evidence that specific interventions are effective. Students and practitioners have used the culturagram in their professional practice with families and reported that it is helpful in engaging families in a nonthreatening way. Culture is seen through a multidimensional lens rather than as a monolithic entity. Initial

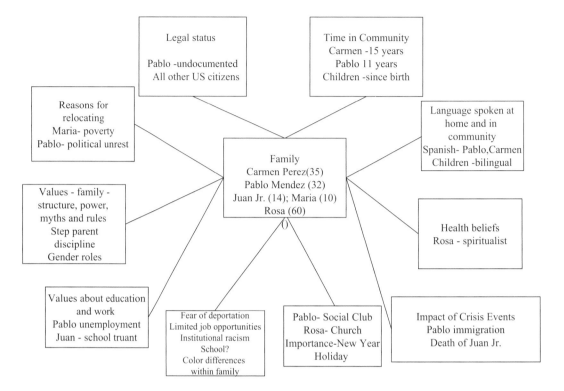

Figure 144.2 Culturagram–2007. Perez family.

evaluation of the culturagram has been positive, and there are further plans to assess its effectiveness in promoting culturally competent practice.

With the increased number of immigrants in the United States, there will be greater demand for culturally competent practice with immigrant clients and families. Social workers will need to study what methods and models are the most effective. The culturagram emerges as a useful method to better understand and plan interventions with immigrant families.

WEB SITES

NASW Standards for Cultural Competence in Social Work Practice. http://www .socialworkers.org/practice/standards/ NASWCulturalStandards.pdf.

National Center for Cultural Competence. http://www11.georgetown.edu/research/ gucchd/nccc/.

Article in "The New Social Worker Online," Culturally Competent Social Work Practice With Latino Clients. http://www .socialworker.com/home/Feature_Articles/

Ethics/Culturally_Competent_Social_Work_ Practice_With_Latino_Clients/.

References

Ardila A. (2005). Spanglish: An anglicized Spanish dialect. *Hispanic Journal of Behavioral Sciences*, 27(1), 60–81.

Bhattacharya G. (2004). Health care seeking for HIV/ AIDS among South Asians in the United States. *Health Social Work*, 29(2).

Brownell, P. (1997). The application of the culturagram in cross-cultural practice with elder abuse victims. *Journal of Elder Abuse and Neglect*, 9(2), 19–33.

Camarota, S. (2007). Immigrants in the United States, 2007: A profile of America's foreign-born population. *Backgrounder* 1–43. Washington, DC: Center for Migration Studies.

Chang-Muy, F., & Congress, E. (2008). Social work with immigrants and refugees: Legal issues, clinical skills, and advocacy. New York: Springer Publishing Company.

Congress, E. (1994). The use of culturagrams to assess and empower culturally diverse families. *Families in Society*, 75, 531–540.

Congress, E. (1996). Family crisis: Life cycle and bolts from the blue: Assessment and treatment. In A. Roberts (Ed.), *Crisis Intervention and brief treat-*

ment: Theory, techniques, and applications (pp. 142–159). Chicago: Nelson-Hall.

Congress, E. (1997) Using the culturagram to assess and empower culturally diverse families. In E. Congress, *Multicultural perspectives in working with families* (pp. 3–16). New York: Springer.

Congress, E. (2000). Crisis intervention with culturally diverse families. In A. Roberts, *Crisis intervention handbook*, 2nd ed. (pp. 431–449). New York: Oxford University Press.

Congress, E (2004a). Crisis intervention and diversity: Emphasis on a Mexican immigrant family's acculturation conflicts. In P. Meyer (Ed.), *Paradigms of clinical social work*, vol. 3, *Emphasis on diversity* (pp 125–144). New York: Brunner-Routledge.

Congress, E. (2004b). Cultural and ethical issues in working with culturally diverse patients and their families: The use of the culturagram to promote cultural competent practice in health care settings. *Social Work in Health Care*, 39(3/4), 249–262.

Congress, E. (2008). Individual and family development theory. In P. Lehman and N. Coady (Eds.), *Theoretical perspectives for direct social work practice: A generalist-eclectic approach*, 2nd ed. (pp. 83–104). New York: Springer.

Congress, E., & Brownell, P. (2007). Application of the culturagram with culturally and ethnically diverse battered women. In A. Roberts (Ed.), *Battered women and their families*. New York: Springer.

Congress, E., & Kung, W. (2005). Using the culturagram to assess and empower culturally diverse families. In E. Congress and M. Gonzalez, *Multicultural perspectives in working with families* (pp. 2–21). New York: Springer Publishing Company.

Congress, E., & Lyons, B. (1992). Ethnic differences in health beliefs: Implications for social workers in health care settings. *Social Work in Health Care*, 17(3), 81–96.

Devore, W., & Schlesinger, E. (1999). *Ethnic-sensitive social work practice*. Boston: Allyn & Bacon.

Feldman R. A. (1998). Catch the wave. *Journal of Social Work Education*, 34(2), 162–164.

Hartman, A., & Laird, J. (1983). *Family oriented treatment*. New York: Free Press.

Jarbo, M. (2001) War experience, PTSD, and sequelae among adult Liberian immigrants who experienced the civil war as children or adolescents. Dissertation, New York University.

Kamya, H. A. (1997). African immigrants in the United States: The challenge for research and practice. *Social Work*, 42(2), 154–165.

Kim, Y. (2002). The role of cognitive control in mediating the effect of stressful circumstances among Korean immigrants. *Health Social Work*, 27(1), 36–46.

Lum, D. (1999). *Social work practice and people of color: A process-stage approach*, 2nd ed. Pacific Grove, CA: Brooks Cole.

Morgan, E. (2003). Against the odds: An exploratory study of Mexican immigrant women with technical education. *Hispanic Journal of Behavioral Sciences*, 25(2), 201–221.

National Association of Social Workers. (1999). *Code of ethics*. Washington, DC: NASW Press.

New York City Department of City Planning, Population Division. (2004). *The newest New Yorkers 2000*. New York: NYC-DCP 04–09.

Rhee, S., Chang, J., & Youn, S. (2003). Korean American pastors' perceptions and attitudes toward child abuse. *Journal of Ethnic Cultural Diversity in Social Work*, 12(1), 27–46.

Stokes, S. C., Thompson, L. W., Murphy, S., & Gallagher Thompson, D. (2002). Screening for depression in immigrant Chinese-American elders: Results of a pilot study. *Journal of Gerontological Social Work*, 36(1/2), 27–44.

U.S. Bureau of Census. (2007). *Current population survey*, 113th ed. Austin, TX: Reference Press.

Webb, N. B. (2001). *Culturally diverse parent–child and family relationships*. (New York: Columbia University Press.

PART XIV
School Social Work

145 Overview of Current and Future Practices in School Social Work

Paula Allen-Meares

The primary purpose of this part is to provide social workers and related school-based professionals with current and diverse empirical data on interventions/approaches that address the needs of various pupil groups. Between 4 million and 6 million students are thought to have serious mental health issues, which, if left untreated, can affect their futures, their lives, and society in general (Rogers, 2003). The U.S. Department of Health and Human Services (2006) states that of the 3 million reports of child abuse or neglect investigated in 2004, more than half occurred with school-aged children. With these sobering statistics, federal requirements for providing remedial learning and services for special needs children such as No Child Left Behind and IDEA, and the mandate that educators (teachers and other school personnel) report suspected abuses, the school setting becomes one of the more likely places for effective services. What is necessary to deliver these services? Where will the future of school-based intervention take us?

In this discussion, we highlight some elements and issues in the future of school social work, a practice field that will be ever more firmly rooted in a growing evidence base. In addition, we add a brief summary of issues specific to the selection of evidence-based interventions, methods of getting school social workers to accept and use evidence-based practices, and why school and communities should create partnerships for mental health services for children and adolescents.

EVIDENCE-BASED: DEFINITIONS

The future of school social work may very well rest on the emerging growth and reliance on evidence-based practices (EBPs), theories, interventions, and treatments. Although there is not currently a consensus about the definition of this concept (Hoagwood, 2003; Rubin & Parrish, 2007), many disciplines use the concept, and various definitions may be found within them. Social work, in particular, has embraced the concept as a way to address the perceived gap between research and practice (Brekke, Ell, & Palinkas, 2007; Gould, 2005; Rubin & Parrish, 2007). In this chapter, we attempt to define *evidence-based* in a manner that can be commonly understood.

Originally adopted from the medical field, EBP in social work refers to the process of implementing and integrating tested research evidence into practice. Mullen (2004) forwards that "evidence-based practice is considered any practice that has been established as effective through scientific research according to some set of explicit criteria" (p. 8). Woody, D'Souza, and Dartman (2006) state that EBP within the social work realm has recently come to mean a movement that embraces several other terms; empirically supported interventions, empirically supported treatments, and evidence-based interventions all fall under the umbrella of EBP. Gilgun (2005) details "four cornerstones" of EBP in social work, which include "1) research and theory; 2) practice wisdom, or what we and other professionals have learned from our clients, which also includes professional values; 3) the person of the practitioner, or our personal assumptions, values, biases, and world views; and 4) what clients bring to practice situations" (p. 52).

In other words, EBP stresses the need for a scientific base in theories and methods *applied* to social work practice. The theoretical must be tested and proven to generate best practices, which ultimately support a sound knowledge base, and to ensure the very same effectiveness and efficiency in service delivery mentioned. Often termed across disciplines as "translational science" (Brekke, Ell, & Palinkas, 2007; Neuhauser, Richardson, Mackenzie, & Minkler, 2007), this theory is firmly ensconced with the idea that evidence cannot exist in a vacuum, and "EBP, by definition, facilitates the very best qualities of social work when a social worker involves clients in a collaborative process to consider available evidence or lack of evidence" (Regehr, Stern, & Shlonsky, 2007). Brekke and colleagues suggest that social work is uniquely situated to play a role in the translational science movement, with schools being an opportune and indeed desired setting for direct applicability of EBP.

It is important to remember that using any evidence-based treatment with children, regardless of its efficacy, will bring with it special challenges due to the fact that children and adolescents are not the same as adults. These differences ("children undergo more rapid psychological, neuronal, and psychological changes over a briefer period than adults," Hoagwood, Burns, Kiser, Ringeisen, & Schoenwald, 2001, p. 1181), must be considered. In addition, practitioners must take into consideration a transactional or person–environment fit in evaluating a child's interactions with family, their educational setting, and their community, as well as how each of those systems interacts with the other (e.g. how the family interacts with the school, how the school fits into its community, etc.) (Bowen, 2007).

THE SCHOOL

Given the fact that children spend a large portion of their time in school (7 hours a day, 5 days a week, 10 months a year), it makes sense that the educational community plays a strategic role in the lives of children and their families. Indeed, the school has historically been a location in which social workers felt they could assist in children's health and welfare. Jessie Taft, an early leader in the functionalist movement, wrote: "The only practical and effective way to increase the mental health of a nation is through its school system. Homes are too inaccessible. The school has the time of the child and the power to do the job" (Taft, 1923, p. 398). More recently, Dr. S. Hyman, then director of the National Institute of Mental Health, spoke to the importance of the school system as the context for the identification and treatment of school children needing mental health treatment (Rees, 1997).

The *Report of the Surgeon General's Conference on Children's Mental Health* (U.S. Department of Health and Human Services, 2000), calls attention to the growing numbers of youth (one in five) suffering needlessly because their emotional, behavioral, and developmental needs are not being met. It strongly suggests that the nation needs to urgently address the emotional, behavioral, and developmental needs of our youth.

Furthermore, this report recognizes that the responsibility for mental health care, in particular, for our youth, is dispersed across numerous settings/organizations: schools, primary care, the juvenile justice system, and child/family welfare systems to name only a few. Even when evidence-based treatments are available for use by providers, use of those treatments, in many instances, remains low.

Unfortunately, families often cannot turn to the community anticipating relief and assistance. Brener, Weist, Adelman, Taylor, and Vernon-Smiley (2007) document the barriers families often face in access varied and dispersed services, such as those provided through community-based organizations, medical centers, and private practice, such as lack of knowing the services are available, lack of funds to pay for such services, lack of transportation to or from the services provider, and stigma.

It is imperative to note, especially when discussing the future of school social work and the populations for which social workers provide services, that cultural barriers may often play a role in the assessment, intervention considerations, and actual provision of social work services in schools. If one of the main foci of social work is improving the fit of the person in the environment, here is one specific instance in which having a comprehensive understanding of the pupil and how he or she behaves in a specific context or as a part of a cultural group is required to determine the most appropriate course of intervention with a child and his or her family and their cultural community.

While ripe for identifying and treating children who exhibit social and mental health needs, the educational system itself is often at the mercy of institutional, local, or federal pressures or demands. As Sipple (2007) states, "The American public educational system is a beleaguered public institution fraught with relentless criticism," adding that "schools are facing ever-challenging and complex educational situations while at the same time an unprecedented inspection and expectation of practice and performance" (pp. 1–2). Services such as special education are underfunded, and state support is either erratic or dwindling depending on the means of each state. Schools have to involve the multiple stakeholders in its governance and decision making, reform and restructure itself to obtain excellence and relevancy, and do all of this while being cost-efficient and effective. In addition, today's educational system has numerous responsibilities on its doorstep: federal, state, and local standards, desegregation, student diversity, underachieving students, and what to do with overachievers. Add to this the expectation that physical, emotional, and behavioral problems will be addressed, and you have an environment that is overwhelmed with multiple agendas and roles. Clearly, the school and its personnel cannot achieve these multiple and important imperatives in isolation of other relevant and interested parties (e.g., community, parents, etc.).

Pertinent professional providers located in the community in collaboration with parents and school personnel will need to become a part of the solution and respond to the mental health and/or health issues that are going undiagnosed among pupils. We envision unusual and innovative collaborations and partnerships between the school and its community network of service providers in the decades ahead. Two emerging solutions include school-based health centers, which provide mental and physical health services, and arrangements for "linked" services—that is services provided via community providers in locations other than school (Brener et al., 2007). Furthermore, knowledge from a cross-section of practices and empirical literatures is needed to arm these professionals with new ways to identify, treat, and prevent mental illness among children and adolescents. "No one discipline has a privileged view of either pathogenesis or treatment of mental disorders" (Rees, 1997, p. 8).

SOME CRITERIA FOR THE SELECTION OF EVIDENCE-BASED INTERVENTION

As reflected in this volume, various interventions have different levels of scientific sophistication or rigor undergirding them. It is important to note that (as already mentioned) in social work, the accepted position on EBP is increasingly one that balances scientific rigor with practice knowledge, clinical judgment, client reaction, common sense, and context. When considering what interventions to

use in a school setting, or a school/community provider collaboration, the following criteria should be taken into consideration (note that this list is not exhaustive).

1. Where does the study fall on the continuum of scientific rigor? Whereas there is an informal hierarchy of accepted rigor (Rosenthal, 2006; Rubin and Parrish, 2007), typically a treatment is considered to be well established if two or more studies find it superior to wait-listed control conditions or one experiment must meet criteria for a well-established treatment or three single case studies must be conducted (Rogers, 2003). Outcome measures must be relevant, and evaluation measurements must be of high quality and meet appropriate psychometric standards. More recent standards have included that rigor include "at least one significant long-term follow-up" (Flay et al., 2005).

2. Was the design of the study effective? Evidence-based treatment should be supported by group design or single-subject experiments (Rogers, 2003).

3. Is the study transportable? One of the challenges of using evidence-based interventions is transportability—that is, will the outcomes of the scientific study that validated this intervention in a laboratory or a clinical setting be consistent when applied in a school setting (Hoagwood et al., 2001)?

4. Is the study generalizable to multiple populations and/or across multiple sites? With few exceptions, "there are no statistical methods for assessing the generalizability of a program's effects" (Flay et al., 2005). Therefore, practitioners should investigate whether the research was conducted with appropriate subgroups with same or similar results.

5. Are there contextual variables required for optimal outcomes? Services to children/ youth are delivered in a variety of unique contexts—schools, child and family agencies, family, correctional systems, and community mental health centers. It is therefore urgent for the practitioner to know the context in which the research on the intervention was conducted (Hoagwood et al., 2001).

6. What were the characteristics of the experimental/treatment group, in terms of important demographics, and problem in functioning? Attention to the fit with the

population that is the target of the intervention is important (Hoagwood et al., 2001). In other words, there should be congruency between the experimental sample and those that are the target of application in practice.

7. Does the intervention consider co-occurring disorders? Often the intervention focuses on one specific disorder and does not adequately take into account the possibility of other disorders that are present, or the heterogeneity of the mental health problems broadly defined within childhood and adolescence (Hoagwood, 2003).

8. Is the intervention age-appropriate and/or developmentally sensitive? For example, an intervention found to be effective with preadolescent youth to reduce depression may well be ineffective for adolescent youths (Hoagwood et al., 2001); similarly, effective treatments used with adults may not affect children in the same manner.

9. Is the intervention culturally sensitive? Was the target group in the experiment/clinical group or single-case design comparable in terms of race/ethnicity, and so on? As the population of the United States continues to become larger and more diverse, this factor will become increasingly important (Rogers, 2003).

IMPLEMENTATION IN PRACTICE SETTING

With the growing focus of evidence-based knowledge to inform practice how do practitioners integrate that which they know, with that which science proves to be effective? Huang, Hepburn, & Espiritu (2003), state that "changing practice is a formidable task that occurs at a painstakingly slow pace, often requiring not only changes in practice behaviors, but restructuring programs and allocating an infusion of upfront resources" (p. 1). How do we make this move to a more effective service delivery?

According to a meta-analysis, several strategies have been used to influence behavioral health care professionals to incorporate EBPs into their professional behaviors (Gira, Kessler, & Poertner, 2004). These include the following.

1. *Dissemination.* One of the most important aspects of getting practitioners to explore and use new approaches and scientific data is simply ensuring that they are exposed to it. A simple way to do this is through dissemination. This approach can range from the publication of guidelines, mass mailings, Web sites, compiled notebooks, and so on.

2. *Continuing education.* Continuing education coursework and seminars are a part of many professions, encouraging practitioners to stay current on methods and literature after obtaining a degree. This approach has been found to be effective in exposing practitioners to evidence-based materials and theory in randomized controlled trials, when small group activities and practice sessions are available to participants.

3. *Knowledge transfer and transformation.* Through education, academic publishing, and presentations, the acceptance and use of evidence-based social work practice as an accepted foundation can be passed on through translation of evidence into practice, in the classroom as well as in training rooms and board rooms (Regehr et al., 2007; Tierney, 2005).

4. *Audit and feedback.* Audit and feedback are snapshots of a practice over a period of time. Experts review a practitioner's interaction with clients and provide documentation regarding the practitioner's use of evidence-based theories and methods. Documentation may also include feedback about the "congruency between practice and best evidence" (Gira et al., 2004, p. 73).

5. *Leadership.* Woody and colleagues (2006) call for first CSWE and subsequently NASW to address their roles in both the teaching and implementation of EBP. NIMH has already taken a stand on the implementation and dissemination of EBP as a foundation for mental health interventions (NIMH, 2000) and has recently issued a call for empirical-based research to inform social work and health care services (NIMH, 2006a, 2006b).

6. *Technology.* Technology may be used in a variety of ways, whether tracking practice statistics, educating patients, or access patient data during consultation (Tierney, 2005). Social workers typically use technology to keep records and collect data, not to choose or document effective treatments, although the potential to plan or choose interventions ripe for the asking by using materials and resources available through resources

available on the Web, via interlibrary loan, and through other technologies.

7. *Mass media campaigns.* Campaigns target the consumer of intervention services, working on the patient's right and ability to ask the right questions, press for different treatments, and basically manage their own care. These campaigns might include TV ads, pamphlets, and so on.

Methods matter. It must be mentioned that written materials have been proven to be less efficacious than "in-person, intensive, and interactive strategies, which could include seminars, telephone supervision, and consultation," and so on (Woody et al., 2006). Similarly, organizational climate, staff attitudes, and characteristics of those adopting EBP will continue to be factors in how EPB information is disseminated and accepted (Glisson et al., 2008).

WHERE DO WE GO FROM HERE?

Social work practitioners, both in and out of school settings, are seeing a definite shift from traditionally accepted practices to the cutting-edge best practices. It is important to remember that whether a practitioner is quick to embrace new and better practices or moves slowly and deliberately toward the future, the ultimate goal of treatment and intervention should be concerned with the health and mental health of the children they are charged with helping.

The importance of evidence in social work and other health and mental health services has been embraced at the highest levels of administration. The 2003 Surgeon General's Report (U.S. DHHS, 2003) identified several key goals crucial to the treatment of children with mental health issues as social work other social sciences move from the tried and true to the tested and approved. They are as follows.

1. The development, dissemination and implementation of best practices derived from a scientific evidence base must continue.
2. Knowledge on a variety of factors, including social and psychological development, must be researched "to design better screening, assessment, and treatment tools, and to develop prevention programs" (p. 5).
3. Research on contexts (e.g., school, family, culture, etc.) must be supported. This research will assist us in identifying opportunities "for promoting mental health services and for providing effective prevention, treatment, and services" (p. 5).
4. Research to develop and test innovative behavioral, pharmacological, and other "mixed" interventions must also be encouraged.
5. Research on proven treatments, practices, and services developed in a lab must be increased, particularly the assessment of their effectiveness in "real-world settings" (p. 5).
6. Similarly, the effectiveness of clinical/community practices must also be studied in context.
7. Development of model programs should be encouraged, particularly those that can be sustained on a community level.
8. Private and public partnerships are key elements in facilitating the dissemination and cross-fertilization of knowledge.
9. The understanding of children's mental health care needs must increase. Additionally, training to assist practitioners to address the various mental issues among children with special health care needs and their families is necessary and urgent.
10. Research on factors that facilitate or impede the implementation of scientifically proven interventions must take place as part of the evaluation process.

KEY POINTS TO REMEMBER

For practitioners, particularly those involved in services for children and adolescents, to successfully take a step toward a future practice undergirded by scientific evidence, the following must be kept in the forefront of their minds.

• EBP is built on a scientific foundation, meaning that it has been tested using specific criteria and proven effective. Implementation of evidence-based theories and practices into real-world application involving client input, clinical knowledge, and practice experience will ensure that social workers and other mental health professionals are using the best practices for the children they serve.
• The use of these evidence-based best practices may be useful in a school setting if additional criteria, such as scientific rigor, are considered.

- School is one area where a large portion of children may be diagnosed and assisted with mental health or other social issues.
- When appropriate to do so, the creation of partnerships with family, community agencies, and other resources will help sustain change.
- Training, further research, and technical support opportunities are needed to increase the likelihood that practitioners will adopt EBPs.

References

Bowen, G. L. (2007). Social organization and schools: A general systems theory perspective. In P. Allen-Meares (Ed.), *Social work services in schools* (pp. 60–79). Boston: Pearson Education.

Brekke, J. S., Ell, K., & Palinkas, L. A. (2007). Translational science at the National Institute of Mental Health: Can social work take its rightful place? *Research on Social Work Practice, 17*, 123–133.

Brener, N. D., Weist, M., Adelman, H., Taylor, L., & Vernon-Smiley, M. (2007). Mental health and social services: Results from the School Health Policies and Programs Study 2006 (Report). *Journal of School Health, 77*(8), 486–499.

Flay, B. R., Biglan, A., Boruch, R. F., Castro, F. G., Gottfredson, D., Kellam, S., et al. (2005). Standards of evidence: Criteria for efficacy, effectiveness and dissemination. *Prevention Science, 6*(3), 151–175.

Gira, E. C., Kessler, M. L., & Poertner, J. (2004). Influencing social workers to use research evidence in practice: Lessons from medicine and the allied health professions. *Research on Social Work Practice, 14*(2), 68–79.

Gilgun, J. F. (2005). The four cornerstones of evidence-based practice in social work. *Research on Social Work Practice, 15*(1), 52–61.

Glisson, C., Landsverk, J., Schoenwald, S., Kelleher, K., Hoagwood, K. E., Mayberg, S., et al. (2008). Assessing the organizational social context (OSC) of mental health services: Implications for research and practice. *Administration and Policy in Mental Health and Mental Health Services Research, 35*, 98–113.

Gould, N. (2005). An inclusive approach to knowledge for mental health social work practice and policy. *British Journal of Social Work, 36*, 109–125.

Hoagwood, K. (2003, Spring/Summer). Evidence-based practice in children's mental health services: What do we know? Why aren't we putting it to use? *Data Matters, 6*, 4–5.

Hoagwood, K., Burns, B. J., Kiser, L., Ringeisen, H., & Schoenwald, S. K. (2001). Evidence-based practice in child and adolescent mental health services. *Psychiatric Services, 52*(9), 1179–1189.

Huang, L. N., Hepburn, M. S., & Espiritu, R. C. (2003, Spring/Summer). To be or not to be . . . evidence-based? *Data Matters, 6*, 1–3.

Mullen, E. J. (2004). Evidence-based social work—theory and practice: Historical and reflective perspective. In E. J. Mullen (Ed.). *Evidence-based practice in a social work context—the United States case* (pp. 1–12). Helsinki: National Research and Development Centre for Welfare and Health (STAKES).

National Institute of Mental Health. (2000). *Report of National Advisory Mental Health Council's Behavioral Science Workgroup, Translating behavioral science into action.* NIH Publication no. 00-4699. Bethesda, MD: NIH.

National Institutes of Health. (2006a). *Research on social work practice and concepts in health* (R03) (no. PA-06-082). Bethesda, MD: Department of Health and Human Services.

National Institutes of Health. (2006b). Research on social work practice and concepts in health (R21) (no. PA-06-083). Bethesda, MD: Department of Health and Human Services.

Neuhauser, L., Richardson, D., Mackenzi, S., & Minkler, M. (2007). Advancing transdisciplinary and translational research practice: Issues and models of doctoral education in public health. *Journal of Research Practice, 3*(2). Retrieved January 31, 2008, from http://jrp.icaap.org/index.php/jrp/article/view/103/97.

Rees, C. (1997, November/December). Ask the doctor: On children and mental illness. *NAMI Advocate, 8*, 10.

Regehr, C., Stern, S., & Shlonsky, A. (2007). Operationalizing evidence-based practice: The development of an institute for evidence-based social work. *Research on Social Work Practice, 17*, 408–416.

Rogers, K. (2003). Evidence-based community-based interventions. In A. J. Pumariega & N. C. Winters (Eds.), *The handbook of child and adolescent systems of care* (pp. 149–170). San Francisco: Jossey-Bass.

Rosenthal, R. (2006). Overview if evidence-based practices. In A. R. Roberts & K. R. Yeager (Eds.), *Foundations of evidence-based social work practice* (pp. 67–80). New York: Oxford University Press.

Rubin, A., & Parrish, D. (2007). Views of evidence-based practice among faculty in master of social work programs: A national survey. *Research on Social Work Practice, 17*, 110–122.

Sipple, J. (2007). Major issues in American schools. In P. Allen-Meares (Ed.), *Social work services in schools* (pp. 1–25). Boston: Pearson Education.

Taft, J. (1923). The relation of the school of mental health of the average child. *Proceedings of the National Conference of Social Work* (p. 398). Chicago: University of Chicago Press.

Tierney, S. (2005). Reframing an evidence-based approach to practice. In A. Bilson (Ed.), *Evidence-based practice in social work.* London: Whiting & Birch.

U.S. Department of Health and Human Services. (2000). *Report of the surgeon general's conference on children's mental health: A national action agenda.* Washington, DC: Department of Health and Human Services.

U.S. Department of Health and Human Services, Administration for Children and Families. (2006). *Child maltreatment 2004.* Washington, DC: U.S. Government Printing Office.

Woody, J. D., D'Souza, H. J., & Dartman, R. (2006). Do master's in social work programs teach empirically supported interventions? A survey of deans and directors. *Research on Social Work Practice, 16,* 469–479.

146

Evidence-Based Violence Prevention Programs and Best Implementation Practices

Ron Avi Astor, Rami Benbenishty, Roxana Marachi, & Ronald O. Pitner

Part XIV responds to the concerns of school social workers and other school professionals, including the growing incidence of violence and conflict in schools. This chapter addresses best practices in predicting, preventing, and coping with school violence and specific situations, such as conflicts between students, conflicts between students and teachers, gang behavior, rape and sexual harassment, bullying, and violent aggressiveness. This chapter provides specific guidance for working with teachers in their management of conflict and behavior in the classroom, for forming alliances between parents and school staff, and for influencing a nonviolent school environment and culture.

GETTING STARTED

Social work as a profession has contributed to the national and international dialogue concerning violence prevention programs in schools (Benbenishty & Astor, 2005). School social workers play an increasingly important role in shaping and implementing policy, interventions, and procedures that make U.S. schools safer.

To use resources to the best advantage and maximize program effectiveness, it is helpful for school mental health professionals to not only know the dynamics and best approaches for assessing and intervening in school violence but also be familiar with available model programs already studied and found to be effective. This chapter reviews several examples of effective violence prevention programs as well as model school safety programs.

One great weakness in establishing evidence-based violence prevention programs is that they are often introduced to schools with a "top-down" approach, ignoring variations in local school contexts (Benbenishty & Astor, 2007; Benbenishty, Astor, & Estrada, 2008). Even model programs that have been demonstrated to be effective in large-scale research studies have a better chance for success at a school if the program matches the needs and values of the community, the school, and the school staff (Astor, Benbenishty, Marachi, & Meyer, 2006). To assist readers in achieving such a match, whether adapting one of the programs introduced in this chapter or using another guide to develop one's own program, we offer monitoring and mapping approaches to guide in developing local data to inform a bottom-up program and in tracking program interventions.

WHAT WE KNOW

Table 146.1 presents examples of the most researched model school safety programs available to schools and practitioners and includes the names of the programs, Web sites where the programs can be explored, program components, outcome measures, and results from studies. We also include a more extensive list of Web sites and resources for each program at the end of the chapter. The programs listed in Table 146.1 have been rated as effective by multiple national organizations. Our designation of effective is a composite of ratings from 11 independent scientific organizations that evaluated the most popular school violence prevention programs. Criteria considered in designating a program as effective include (1) evidence of effectiveness based on rigorous evaluations with experimental or quasi-experimental designs, (2) the clarity of the program's goals and rationale, (3) the fit between the program content and the characteristics of the intended population and setting, (4) the integration of the program into schools' educational mission, (5) the availability of necessary information and guidance for replication in other settings, and (6) the incorporation of posttreatment and follow-up data collection as part of the program. We describe in detail four of the five programs listed in Table 146.1.

BULLYING PREVENTION PROGRAM

The Bullying Prevention Program (BPP) is a comprehensive, multicomponent bullying reduction and prevention program designed for students in grades 1–9. It was developed during the 1970s by Dan Olweus to reduce bully and victim problems in Norwegian schools. Since then, it has been translated into more than 12 languages and successfully established in schools in more than 15 countries. The BPP has been shown to reduce levels of bully and victim incidents by 33 percent to 64 percent (see Table 146.1). (For a current review of bullying as a school problem, see Limber, 2006).

Content

As seen in Table 146.1 under Program Components, the BPP is implemented at three levels of the school environment—the total school, classroom, and the individual student. At the school level, the BPP establishes antibullying policy in the school system. To raise awareness and quantify the prevalence of bullying in the school, administrators distribute an anonymous 29-item student questionnaire to all students. A school conference day about bullying is established to talk about the results of the assessment and discuss interventions. Additionally, schools create a BPP coordination team in which a representative administrator, teacher, counselor, parent, and student come together to lead the program implementation. In the BPP program, the school adopts rules against bullying and explains to students the negative consequences for bullying behavior. All staff receive training to learn about the harmful consequences of bullying, increase supervision in areas on campus that are prone to violence, and provide systematic reinforcement of rules applied to all students.

At the classroom level, students have regular workshops about the harmful consequences of bullying. Students have discussions about bullying and violent behaviors, watch video presentations of bullying situations, write about ways to combat the problem, and engage in role-play. Students are encouraged to increase their knowledge and empathy regarding bullying.

The individual student level involves direct consequences for bullying behaviors. There are focused interventions with those identified as bullies and victims, as well as bystanders. The parents of involved students are given help and support to reinforce nonviolence at home. School mental health workers play an essential role in more serious cases of bullying.

The goal of using interventions through all three levels is to ensure that students are given a consistent, coordinated, and strong message that bullying will not be tolerated. The BPP teaches students that everyone has a responsibility to pre-

TABLE 146.1 Model Violence Prevention Programs and Evaluation Sources

Program (Authors)	Grade	Participants	Program Components	Outcome Measures	Results
Bullying Prevention Program (Olweus, 1993) http://www.clemson.edu/olweus	4th–7th grades	2,500 students in 42 primary and secondary schools in Norway. The program is now international and is being applied in 15 countries. The materials are translated into more than 12 languages.	Core components of the program are implemented at the school level, the class level, and the individual level. • Distribution of anonymous student questionnaire assessing the nature and prevalence of bullying • Development of positive and negative consequences for students' behavior • Establishment of a supervisory system • Reinforcement of schoolwide rules against bullying • Classroom workshops with video and discussions to increase knowledge and empathy • Interventions with perpetrators and victims of bullying • Discussions with parents	Student self-report measures collected at introduction of the program, 4 months after introduction, 1-year follow-up, and 2-year follow-up. • Reports of incidents of bullying and victimization • Scale of general youth antisocial behavior • Assessment of school climate—order and discipline • Measure of social relationships and attitude toward school	The results show a 33%–64% reduction in the levels of bully incidents. The author found a 30%–70% reduction in aggregated peer rating variables. In addition, there was no displacement of bullying to before or after school. There was also a significant reduction in antisocial behavior such as fighting, theft, and truancy. The school climate showed marked improvement, with students reporting an increased satisfaction with school in general, positive social relationships and positive attitude toward schoolwork and school. Rated effective—1, 2, 3, 4, 6, 7, 8, 9

Continued

TABLE 146.1 Model Violence Prevention Programs and Evaluation Sources (*continued*)

Program (Authors)	Grade	Participants	Program Components	Outcome Measures	Results
Child Development Project (Battistich, Schaps, Watson, & Solomon, 1996) http://www.devstu.org	3rd–6th grades	4,500 students in 24 elementary schools from 6 diverse districts throughout the United States.	This is a comprehensive model focused on creating a cooperative and supportive school environment. Classroom components include: • Staff training in cooperative learning • Implementation of a model that fosters cross-grade "buddying" activities • A developmental approach to discipline that fosters self-control • A model to engage students in classroom norm setting and decision making Schoolwide community-building activities are used to promote school bonding and parent involvement activities, such as interactive homework assignments that reinforce the family–school partnership.	Data were collected after 1 year and 2 years of intervention. Teachers were assessed through four 90-minute observations and annual teacher questionnaires. Student assessments were self-report surveys of drug use and delinquent behavior.	Results showed that students experienced a stronger sense of community and more motivation to be helpful, better conflict-resolution skills, greater acceptance of people who are different, higher self-esteem, stronger feelings of social competence, less loneliness in school, and fewer delinquent acts. Statistically significant decreases were found for marijuana use, vehicle theft, and weapons. By the second year of the program, students in schools showed significantly lower rates of skipping school, carrying weapons, and stealing vehicles (p's <0.01). Rated effective—3, 4, 5, 6, 7, 9

| FAST Track- *(Families and Schools Together)* (Conduct Problems Prevention Research Group) *http://www.fasttrackproject.org* | Three cohorts of students. Grades 1-10 (still ongoing) | At-risk kindergartners identified based on combined teacher and parent ratings of behavior (CBCL). Highest 10% recruited for study. N = 445 intervention children N = 446 control group children | *Long-term* program. Weekly enrichment program for high-risk children and their parents. Students placed in "friendship groups" of 5–6 students each. Discussions, modeling stories and films, role-plays. Sessions focused on reviewing and practicing skills in emotional understanding and communication, friendship building, self-control, and social problem solving. Parents meet in groups led by family coordinators to discuss parenting strategies, then 30-minute parent–child cooperative activity time; biweekly home visits. Academic tutoring provided by trained tutors in 30-minute sessions 3X/week | • Externalizing Scale of CBCL, *oppositional, aggressive, and delinquent* behaviors
 • *Parent Daily Report*, degree to which child engaged in aggressive and oppositional behaviors during previous 24 hrs (Given 3x)
 • Child behavior change
 • Teacher assessment of acting out behaviors in school (Teacher Report Form, Achenbach, 1991)
 • Scale from the TOCA-R (Teacher Observation of Classroom Adaptation—Revised)
 • Authority acceptance scale
 • Peer rating of aggressive and hyperactive-disruptive behaviors. | Intervention group had higher scores on emotion recognition, emotion coping, and social problem solving compared to control group. It also had lower rates of aggressive retaliation compared to control group. Direct observation results:
 • Intervention group spent more time in positive peer interaction than did the control group.
 • Intervention group received higher peer social preference scores than control group.
 • Intervention group had higher language arts grades than control group.
 * Rated: Effective – 2, 3, 6, 8, 9, 11 |

Continued

TABLE 146.1 Model Violence Prevention Programs and Evaluation Sources (continued)

Program (Authors)	Grade	Participants	Program Components	Outcome Measures	Results
PATHS curriculum (Component of FAST Track)	1st–5th grades over three cohorts (Results from grade 1 findings only are reviewed here)	198 intervention classrooms 180 control classrooms matched by school size, achievement levels, poverty, and ethnic diversity. 7,560 total students. 845 students were in high-risk intervention or control conditions. (6,715 students non-high-risk children)	Quality of implementation was assessed by observer rating of teacher's • Skill in teaching PATHS concepts • Management of the classroom • Modeling and generalizing PATHS throughout day • Openness to consultation	1. Teachers were interviewed about behavior of each child in class (fall/ spring of first grade) 2. Sociometric assessments (peer nominations made by students) collected to assess: • Peer aggression • Peer hyperactivity/ disruptiveness • Peer social status 3. Quality of classroom atmosphere was assessed by observer ratings assessing the following: • Level of disruption • Ability to handle transitions • Ability to follow rules • Level of cooperation • Use of problem-solving skills	Hierarchical linear modeling (accounting for gender, site, cohort, and intervention) Intervention classrooms had lower ratings of hyperactivity/disruptive behavior, aggression, and more favorable observer ratings of classroom atmosphere. Three cohorts of intervention, so teachers administered curriculum, 1, 2, or 3 times. When teacher experience was included in analyses, teachers who taught more cohorts had higher classroom atmosphere ratings (by neutral observer). Teacher skill in program implementation was also related to positive outcomes. Rated effective—2, 3, 6, 8, 9, 11

- Ability to express feelings
- Ability to stay focused on task
- Criticism *vs.* supportiveness

Evaluating Sources

1. American Youth Policy Forum. See Mendel (2000). Programs are categorized as *Effective* (refer to http://www.aypf.org).
2. Blueprints for Violence Prevention. Programs are divided into *Model and Promising* (refer to http://www.colorado.edu/cspv/blueprints).
3. Center for Mental Health Services, U.S. Department of Health and Human Services, Prevention Research Center for the Promotion of Human Development. Programs are divided into *Effective and Promising* (refer to http://www.prevention.psu.edu).
4. Center for Substance Abuse Prevention, Substance Abuse and Mental Health Services Administration, Department of Health and Human Services, National Registry of Effective Programs. Programs are divided into *Model, Promising, and Effective* (refer to http://www.modelprograms.samhsa.gov).
5. Department of Education, Safe and Drug Free Schools. Programs are divided into *Exemplary and Promising* (refer to http://www.ed.gov/programs/dvpcollege/index.html).
6. Communities that Care. See Posey et al. (2000). Programs are categorized as *Effective* (refer to http://www.channing-bete.com/prevention-programs/communities-that-care/research.php).
7. Sherman et al. (1998). Programs are categorized as *Effective* (refer to http://www.ncjrs.org/works).
8. *Youth Violence: A Report of the Surgeon General.* Programs are divided into *Model and Promising; Level 1—Violence Prevention; Level 2—Risk Prevention* (refer to http://www.surgeongeneral.gov/library/youthviolence).
9. Title V (OJJDP), *Effective and Promising Programs Guide.* Washington, DC: Office of Juvenile Justice and Delinquency Prevention, Office of Justice Programs, U.S. Dept. of Justice. Programs are divided into *Exemplary, Effective, and Promising* (refer to http://www.dsgonline.com).
10. Centers for Disease Control: National Center for Injury Prevention and Control—Division of Violence Prevention. *Best Practices of Youth Violence Prevention: A Sourcebook for Community Action 2002.* Programs are categorized as *Effective* (refer to http://www.cdc.gov/ncipc/dvp/bestpractices.htm).
11. Hamilton Fish Institute on School and Community Violence. Programs are divided into *Effective and Noteworthy* (refer to http://www.hamfish.org/ programs).

vent bullying, either by refusing to support the behavior or by alerting an adult to the problem.

Theoretical Rationale and Conceptual Framework

The BPP is based on a systematic restructuring of the school environment that redirects bullying behavior and provides rewards for more prosocial behavior. The conceptual framework is based on research on the development and modifications of aggressive behavior, as well as positive child-rearing dimensions (Olweus, Limber, & Mihalic, 1999). The goal is to create a school environment that (1) is characterized by adults who are engaged and caring, (2) has firm limits to unacceptable behavior, (3) has consistent responses of no rewards and negative consequences for violent behavior, and (4) has adults who act as authorities and positive role models (Olweus et al., 1999).

Much of the success of the BPP can be attributed to it being a schoolwide program, so that it becomes an integral part of the school environment. Students and adults participate in most of the universal components of the program. Indeed, teachers, parents, and administrators play an important role in the success of the program. School staff and parents are expected to (1) become aware of the extent of the bullying problem in their school through assessments, (2) gain an understanding of the significance and harmful effects of bullying, and (3) take an active role in enforcing rules against bullying behavior (Olweus et al., 1999).

Evaluation

As seen in Table 146.1, the first and most comprehensive evaluation study of this program was conducted with 2,500 students in Norway (also see Olweus et al., 1999). However, since then, this program has been implemented and positively evaluated in many countries (Limber, 2006). Evaluation of this program has consistently demonstrated significant reductions in bully/victim reports across many cultures. General antisocial behaviors, such as vandalism, fighting, theft, and truancy, are reduced. Improvements are also found in classroom culture in that students reported improved order and discipline at school, more positive social relationships, and more positive attitudes toward school and schoolwork.

CHILD DEVELOPMENT PROJECT

The Child Development Project (CDP) is an ecological approach to intervention that collaboratively involves teachers, parents, and students working to influence all aspects of the school community (Developmental Studies Center, 1995). Its main objective is to create a cooperative and supportive school environment for children in grades K–6. Established in 1981, the CDP strives to foster shared commitment to prosocial, democratic values in two specific ways: adult guidance and direct participation by children (Developmental Studies Center, 1995). Throughout this process, children are able to develop a sense that the school community cares for them, and they, in turn, begin to care about the school community.

Teachers are trained to implement most components of the intervention, and ongoing consultation and support are provided by the Developmental Studies Center. Research indicates that schools should make a minimum of a 3-year commitment to the CDP if it is to be effective (Northwest Regional Educational Laboratory, 1998). The CDP has been established in 165 elementary schools, and it has been shown to be effective in both ethnically and socioeconomically diverse settings (Battistich et al., 1996; Battistich, Solomon, Watson, & Schaps, 1997; Northwest Regional Educational Laboratory, 1998; Solomon, Watson, Battistich, Schaps, & Delucchi, 1996).

Theoretical Rationale and Conceptual Framework

CDP's theoretical framework is guided by research on socialization, learning and motivation, and prosocial development (Battistich, Schaps, Watson, Solomon, & Lewis, 2000). Its overall objective is for schools to be transformed into caring and supportive communities in which everyone works collaboratively in the learning process. Such a focus is expected to foster children's intellectual and sociomoral development, self-direction, competence, and belonging (Battistich et al., 2000). Where these qualities are fostered, children become attached to and invested in the school community, which in turn leads them to internalize the school norms. School norms typically promote prosocial activity (e.g., concern for others) and proscribe antisocial activity (e.g., drug use or gang activity). The program is based on the idea that children's internalization of school norms will solidify their commitment to the school's community values.

Content

There are four interrelated goals on which the components of the CDP are based: (1) building warm, stable, supportive relationships; (2) attending to social and ethical dimensions of learning; (3) honoring intrinsic motivations; and (4) teaching in ways that support students' active construction of meaning (Battistich et al., 2000). These goals are interwoven into the five major components of CDP: literature-based reading and language arts, collaborative classroom learning, developmental discipline, parent involvement, and schoolwide activities.

The first three components are all designed for the classroom. The literature-based readings component is most directly focused on teaching for understanding. Thus, the selection of books is designed to help teachers foster a deeper and more empathetic understanding of the readings among the students. The component that involves collaborative learning emphasizes the importance of working with others in a fair and cooperative manner. The final classroom component involves building care and respect for everyone in the classroom community (Northwest Regional Educational Laboratory, 1998). The two other components' foci go beyond the classroom. Parent involvement is designed to develop meaningful conversations between adults and their children; schoolwide activities are focused on allowing participation by all and avoiding hierarchies and competition (Northwest Regional Education Laboratory, 1998).

Implementation

At least 80 percent of the school faculty must support their school's adoption of the CDP for it to be established there. Training is conducted by Developmental Studies Center staff and involves initial consultation and planning to identify needs and goals; a 3-day summer institute to orient teachers on the CDP components and materials; 3 half-day follow-up workshops conducted during the school year; three on-site sessions, each lasting 2.5 days, which include consultation, in-class demonstrations, co-teaching, and planning; and professional development support kits that can be used to train new staff (Developmental Studies Center, 2004).

Evaluation

As seen in Table 146.1, CDP strengthens students' sense of their school as a community, their ethical and social resources (e.g., conflict-resolution skills, social problem-solving skills, commitment to democratic values, concern for others), academic motivation (e.g., liking for school), and abstention from drug use and other problem behaviors (e.g., gang-related activity) (Battistich et al., 1996, 1997, 2000; Northwest Regional Education Laboratory, 1998). Moreover, positive effects were reported 2 years after students left elementary school with regard to those students' conflict-resolution skills, self-esteem, and involvement in extracurricular activity (Developmental Studies Center, 1995).

FAST TRACK

The FAST Track Project is a long-term comprehensive intervention that encompasses multiple facets of children's social contexts. The intervention is comprehensive in that it has both universal (schoolwide) components and targeted components, which attempt to provide focused assistance to children at high risk of antisocial behaviors and their social systems. One of the great strengths of this program is its detailed attention to the intersection of the multiple contexts that contribute to children's developmental outcomes. The FAST Track prevention program aims to improve child competences, parent effectiveness, the school context, and school–home communications with the intention of preventing antisocial behavior across the developmental trajectory.

Theoretical Rational and Conceptual Framework

The developmental theory guiding this intervention addresses the interaction of multiple influences on the development of antisocial behavior. These various elements include socioeconomic factors, family dynamics, peer influences, school factors, and the child's temperament.

Content

There are four FAST Track sites in the United States, with a total of 891 children (and their families) participating (with nearly equal numbers of at-risk children in both intervention and control groups). The initial sample consisted of children identified at risk by a combination of teacher and parent ratings of their behavior. Children in the intervention group were provided with a host of services, including weekly enrichment programs, involvement in "friendship groups," and sessions in which they were taught and had opportunities to practice social skills. The parents of the intervention children were also provided with family coordinators who conducted biweekly home visits in efforts to enhance their parenting behavior management skills, specifically in the areas of praise, time-outs, and self-restraint. Children in the intervention group were also provided with three 30-minute academic tutoring sessions each week.

When the children in the intervention group reached adolescence (grades 6–10), the group-based interventions were deemphasized. However, the intervention retained its curriculum-based parent and youth group meetings to support children in their transition into middle school (grades 5–7). In continuation of the earlier targeted model, individual support was provided for participants and their families to strengthen protective factors and reduce risk factors. The targeted intervention at the adolescent phase focused on academic tutoring, mentoring, home visiting and family problem solving, and supporting positive peer group involvement. To address the multiple contexts in the adolescents' lives, the school tried to establish relations with the community agencies that served the participants.

FAST Track also included an important universal component for children in the first through the fifth grades in the target schools. This school-based intervention consisted of teacher-led curricula called PATHS (Promoting Alternative Thinking Strategies), designed to provide children with strategies in understanding the development of emotional concepts, social understanding, and self-control. Because PATHS has been evaluated separately and shown to have independent positive effects, we present it separately in the next section. Some schools may choose to adopt only sections of the overall program, such as PATHS.

Evaluation

FAST Track is one of the more rigorously evaluated comprehensive violence prevention programs and has become widely known as one of the leading models of an effective approach to prevention of antisocial behaviors in youth. As shown in Table 146.1, evaluation studies of FAST Track have revealed positive outcomes for program participants. In addition to those differences highlighted in the table, the prevention revealed statistically significant improvements in the targeted children's social-cognitive and academic skills, in addition to reductions in their parents' use of harsh discipline. The intervention children also demonstrated considerable behavioral improvements at home, in the classroom, and on the playground during and following their elementary school years. In addition to these behavioral improvements, the intervention children were at a reduced risk of being placed in special education classes than children in the control conditions. The findings generalized across ethnicity, gender, and a host of child and family characteristics.

PATHS

PATHS is the classroom curriculum component of the FAST Track intervention program. We present it separately because PATHS has been adopted and studied independently of FAST Track. PATHS was designed to promote emotional and social competence and to reduce aggression and other behavior problems in children in grades K–5 (Greenberg & Kusché, 2006). PATHS focuses on four domains related to school success: (1) prosocial behavior and friendship skills, (2) emotional understanding and self-control, (3) communication and conflict resolution, and (4) problem-solving skills (Conduct Problems Prevention Research Group, 2002). PATHS provides teachers and counselors with training, lesson modules, and ongoing consultation and support. Additionally, parents receive information and activities to complete with their children.

PATHS can be used with all elementary school–age children, and ideally it should be ongoing, beginning in kindergarten and continuing through fifth grade. It has been field-tested and researched in regular education classroom settings and in settings that serve special needs students, such as the deaf, hearing-impaired, learning disabled, emotionally disturbed, mildly mentally delayed, and gifted (see Greenberg & Kusché, 1998; Greenberg, Kusché, Cook, & Quamma, 1995).

Theoretical Rationale/Conceptual Framework

PATHS is based on five conceptual models (Greenberg, Kusché, & Mihalic, 1998). First, the ABCD (affective-behavioral-cognitive-dynamic) model of development promotes skills that are developmentally appropriate. The second model is an eco-behavioral system orientation that focuses on helping the teacher use these skills to build a healthy classroom atmosphere. The third model involves neurobiology and brain organization for cognitive development. The fourth is psychodynamic education that was derived from developmental psychodynamic theory. Finally, the fifth model includes psychological issues related to emotional awareness or emotional intelligence. These conceptual models come together in this curriculum to provide a comprehensive and developmentally based program that addresses students' cognitive processes, emotions, and behaviors.

Content

The PATHS curriculum (Greenberg et al., 1998) is taught three times a week for a minimum of 20–30 minutes a day. The curriculum contains four units with a total of 119 lessons in each unit. They consist of the following: (1) A "Turtle" unit focusing on classroom behavior, emotional literacy, and self-control; (2) "Feeling and Relationship Unit" focusing on building self-esteem and social competence; (3) a "Problem-Solving Unit" with instruction on the 11-step model of social problem solving and positive peer relations; and (4) a "Supplementary Lessons Unit" containing 30 lessons that delve more in depth into PATHS concepts. The lessons are age-appropriate, and can be seen in Table 146.2; the lessons for third-grade students match developmental stages and cover the conceptual domains of self-control, emotional understanding, self-esteem, peer relations, and problem solving.

The PATHS curriculum includes comprehensive materials, and the Basic PATHS Kit (grades 1–5) includes an instructor's manual, five curriculum manuals, feelings photographs, feelings face cards, two wall charts, and four full-color posters. The Turtle unit (for kindergarten classrooms) includes an instructor's manual, curriculum manual, turtle puppet with pad, turtle stamp, and poster. Teachers receive on-site training and technical assistance to ensure effective implementation of the program.

Evaluation

PATHS was evaluated between 1994 and 2003 in various research studies using randomized control groups and was found to be effective. As seen in Table 146.1, PATHS has been found to be a model or effective program by at least six groups that review violence prevention programs nationwide for effectiveness. An overview of results from all trials reveals a reduction in aggressive behavior, conduct disorder, and violent solutions to social problems. In addition, results found an increase in self-control, vocabulary for emotions, cognitive skills, and ability to tolerate frustration and to effectively use conflict-resolution strategies (http://www.modelprograms.samhsa.gov/pdfs/model/PATHS.pdf). The findings have been consistent across teacher reports, self-reports, and child tests and interviews.

Tools and Practice Examples

In the PATHS curriculum, each unit builds on the preceding units. Table 146.3 consists of an excerpt from supplementary lesson 93 and is intended for third-graders.

The objective of this lesson is to discuss the idea of self-control as an internalized process, and it emphasizes the concept of using thinking to control one's behavior and distinguish between feelings and behaviors. The teacher reads a story about a boy named Thomas who had problems with self-control, was angry, and would get into fights with other children. Throughout the story, students learn the three steps for calming down to gain control of their behavior. The lesson is followed by the teacher drawing a hierarchy of feelings and behaviors on the board and asking questions to encourage classroom discussion.

Students are encouraged to talk about how they felt when they acted without thinking first, and to say whether things got out of control and how they felt about the outcome. This lesson teaches students anger management and problem-solving skills through a developmentally appropriate story that is easy to relate to and gets them talking.

MONITORING AND EVALUATING VIOLENCE PREVENTION PROGRAMS

A review of the school safety literature strongly suggests that model school safety programs should be developed and implemented in a process that ensures their relevance and applicability to each specific site (Astor et al., 2006). These are important assumptions of the programs described in this chapter as well as program interventions described in part XIV:

- fitting a program to a school involves grass-roots participation.

TABLE 146.2 PATHS Lessons for Grade 3

Lesson Topic	Volume & Lesson No.	Conceptual Domains				
		Self-Control	Emotional Understanding	Self-Esteem	Peer Relations	Problem Solving
PATHS Rules	Vol. 1, L 1	X		X	X	X
PATHS kid/Complimenting/Self-esteem	Vol. 1, L 2	X		X	X	X
Anger Intensity	Vol. 1, L 10		X		X	
Anger Management/Control Signals	Vol. 1, L 11–12	X		X	X	X
Fear Intensity/Sad Intensity	Vol. 1, L 15–17		X		X	
Disgusted, Delighted	Vol. 1, L 21		X		X	
Frustrated, Disappointed/Hopeful, Proud/Ashamed, Guilty,	Vol. 2, L 23–32, 37		X		X	
Curious/Interested/Bored, Confused/Worried/Sure,						
Anxious/Calm, Shy/Lonely						
Embarrassed/Humiliated	Vol. 2, L 33–34		X		X	
Intentionality (Accident/Purpose), Manners	Vol. 3, L 38–44		X		X	
Jealous/Content, Greedy/Selfish/Generous, Malicious/Kind,	Vol. 3, 48–56		X		X	
Rejected/Included, Excluded, Forgiving/Resentful						
Informal Problem Solving	Vol. 5, 90–92	X				X
Self-Control and Problem Prevention	Vol. 5, L 93–94	X				X
Friendship	Vol. 5, L 95–97.	X	X	X	X	X
Teasing	Vol. 5, L 98–101	X	X	X	X	X
Apply Problem-Solving Steps	Vol. 4, L 89	X				X

TABLE 146.3 PATHS Learning Self-Control Volume 5, Lesson 93

Introduction	"Today I'm going to tell you a story about a boy who had problems, but he learned a new way to help himself."
Story: "Thomas in Control"	This is a story about a boy who did not like to go to school. Thomas felt very upset about going to school. He wanted to run outside and play with his toys or ride his bike or watch television or play a game. Thomas did not like to sit quietly. It was hard for him to pay attention when the teacher or the other kids were talking in class. Instead, Thomas would tease whoever was sitting beside him, by grabbing their pencils and books, by making faces at them, or by whispering to them. The other kids would get angry at Thomas when he bothered them and would yell at him or would do some of the same things back. Then everyone would get caught and would get into trouble. That's why some of the kids thought that Thomas was troublemaker. Sometimes when they went out to the playground at recess, the other kids would still be mad at Thomas, and they would get into a fight. All of this hate and resentment made Thomas feel very uncomfortable inside. One day when he was feeling his worst, the playground teacher told Thomas that he had to go to the principal's office because he hadn't been following the playground rules. "You know," said the principal in a very calm voice, "you have a very big problem, but I'll share a secret with you. You already have the answer to your problem with you. You carry it with you everywhere you go. It's your ability to think. Whenever you feel upset, when you are angry or frustrated, you can use your mind and think. You can stop, take a long, deep breath, and say the problem and how you feel. When you remind yourself to stop and calm down, it's like taking a rest for a minute. You can rest until you feel calm. That is how you can control yourself. And when you can control yourself, then people will say, 'Thomas has good self-control. He thinks before he does something that will cause problems.'" The principal showed Thomas the three steps for calming down. Then the principal reminded Thomas that the next time he felt upset or angry, he could think about the control signals and could calm himself down. Thomas liked the idea and wanted to try it himself. He wanted to do well in school, he wanted his teacher to like him, and he especially wanted to make friends.
On board	Begin drawing on the chalk board Feelings: comfortable and uncomfortable/ Behavior OK and not OK.
Discussion	Ask students to name the different feelings and behavior that Thomas felt and list them under the appropriate categories. Ask them to discuss the relationships between these feelings and behaviors if they are able to do so. Ask students to name the kinds of things that bug them in the classroom, playground, lunchroom, and so on, and list them in the categories. This will help students become aware of what they do that bothers others. Ask student if using the three steps to calm down would help with any of the things they listed.

Story excerpt reduced for space reasons from Greenberg, & Kusché, 1995; available for review on http://www.channing-bete.com.

- students and teachers in the school need to be empowered to deal with the problem.
- democracy is the core of a good school safety program.
- schools should demonstrate a proactive vision surrounding the violence problem in their school.

Implementing interventions or components of any model program is likely to be slightly different for every school. An eye toward the overall assumptions and flexibility should enable each school to adapt the program or general principles to its unique demographic, philosophical, and organizational needs.

DATA AND PROGRAM EVALUATION

An important element of successful school safety programs is the ongoing and interactive use of data. This perspective proposes that the continuous and ongoing analysis and interpretation of data is an essential part of the intervention process. Data are used to create awareness, mobilize different school constituents, assess the extent of the problem, plan and implement interventions, and conduct evaluations. Information is provided on a continuous basis to different groups in each step of the intervention process. Unfortunately, many U.S. schools purchase evidence-based programs but do not collect any data about their own district or school (Benbenishty & Astor, 2007).

The process of building and implementing school safety programs is continual and cyclical, always changing to respond to new circumstances and emerging needs. Hence, the evaluation of the program's progress becomes a reassessment of the situation, leading to a new cycle of awareness building, planning, modifying, and evaluating. A school's failure to gather site-specific and comparative data could be a significant obstacle in (a) assessing whether that specific school has a violence problem, (b) adapting a school safety program, and (c) evaluating the implementation process and outcomes of the program.

Monitoring and school mapping can help create a "whole-school response" and help the school identify, create, and/or adapt programs to the site. Monitoring is the ongoing process of collecting and using data to shape, fit, match, and evaluate the intervention. The value of monitoring comes from the two levels of information processing involved: description and comparison. The description of basic frequency of certain behaviors may be quite instructive. For example, it is helpful to know how many weapon-related events or sexual assaults occur at a specific school.

Using Comparisons

In general, comparisons enhance the value of information by putting it in context (Benbenishty, Astor, & Zeira, 2003). To adapt a program, it is imperative to ascertain (a) which acts are more problematic than others, (b) which grade levels are victimized more, and (c) how violence levels in a specific school compare over time and for different ethnic, age, and gender groups. For example, if bullying is not a major problem in the school, it does not make sense to adopt an antibullying program. Perhaps bullying is a problem only in one grade level within a large school, whereas other forms of violence are problems in other grades. Though these concerns may sound like common sense, very few schools actually collect systemic information to ascertain the extent of the school safety problem. Currently, many districts and schools across the United States are purchasing expensive violence prevention programs targeting a specific form of violence (e.g., sexual harassment, bullying, weapon use) without data about the extent of the problem in their schools. This creates a chain of difficulties through the implementation process and later in the evaluation of the program. If the problem was never established, it is difficult to know if the program ever worked. Hence, it is important to examine levels of violence over time.

Using Mapping as a Monitoring Tool

Mapping is a qualitative tool that can help monitor and generate the kind of comparisons just discussed. Mapping does not require extensive training and can provide valuable information that helps implement, monitor, and assess the ongoing health of a program. This procedure is designed to involve school constituents by revealing how forms of violence within a school building interact with locations, patterns of the school day, and social organizational variables (e.g., teacher–student relationships, teachers' professional roles, and the school's organizational response to violence; for more detail see Astor & Meyer, 1999; Astor, Meyer, & Behre, 1999; Astor, Meyer, & Pitner, 2001). An important goal of this procedure is to allow students and teachers to convey their personal theories about why specific locations and times in their schools are more dangerous. This process greatly facilitates the implementation and evaluation of the model programs reviewed in the first sections of this chapter.

Step-by-Step Instructions

Mapping, interviews, and interventions. The first step in this assessment procedure is obtaining a map of the school. Ideally, the map should contain all internal school territory, including the areas surrounding the school and playground. In communities where the routes to and from school are dangerous, a simple map of the surrounding neighborhood may be added to the assessment process. The focus groups should begin with the facilitator distributing two sets of identical school maps to each individual.

Map A and B: Two photocopied maps of the school are needed for each student and teacher. One map should be used to determine where students and teachers think the most events involving violence occur. Participants should also be asked to identify the locations (on the maps) of up to three of the most violent events that have occurred within the past academic year. Next to each marked event on the map, participants should be asked to write the following information: (1) the general time frame of the event (e.g., before school, after school, morning period, afternoon period, evening sports event, between classes, etc.), (2) the grade and gender of those involved in the violence, and (3) their knowledge of any organizational response to the event (e.g., someone was sent to principal's office, suspended, sent to peer counselor, done nothing to, etc.). On the second map, members should be asked to circle areas or territories that they perceive to be unsafe or potentially dangerous. This second map provides information about areas within the school that participants avoid or fear even though they may not possess knowledge of a particular event. Figure 146.1 represents an example of a combined school map showing violent events and unsafe places by location, time, gender, and age.

Discussion of violent events and areas. The first part of the group discussion should center on the specific events and the areas marked as unsafe or dangerous on their personal maps. We have asked questions such as "Are there times when those places you've marked on the maps are less safe?" "Is there a particular group of students that is more likely to get hurt there?" and "Why do you think that area has so many incidents?" The overall purpose of the group interviews is to explore why bullying or victimization occurs at those specific times and in those specific spaces. Consequently, the interviews should also focus on gathering information regarding the organizational response to the event (e.g., "What happened to the two students after the event?" or "Did the hall monitors intervene when they saw what happened?"), procedures (e.g., "What happens when the students are sent to the office after a fight?" "Did anyone call the parents of the bully or victim?"), follow-up (e.g., "Do the teachers, hall monitors, and/or administrators follow up on any consequences given to the students?" or "Did anyone check on the welfare of the victim?"), and clarity of procedures (e.g., "Does it matter who stops the bullying?" e.g., a volunteer, security guard, teacher, or principal).

Interviewers should also explore participants' ideas for solutions to the specific violence problems (e.g., "Can you think of ways to avoid bullying or victimization in that place?" or "If you were the principal, what would you do to make that place safer?"). In addition, the interviewer should explore any obstacles that participants foresee with implementation (e.g., "Do you think that type of plan is realistic?" "Has that been tried before? What happened?" or "Do you think that plan would work?"). Such obstacles could range from issues related to roles (e.g., "It's not my job to monitor students during lunch") to discipline policy and issues of personal safety (e.g., "I don't want to intervene because I may get hurt").

In schools that have already started model programs designed to address school violence, specific questions should be asked about the effectiveness of those interventions, why they work or do not work, and what could be done to make the current measures more effective. We recommend that the interviewer ask both subjective questions (e.g., "Do you think the antiviolence program is working? Why do you think it works, or why does it not work?") as well as specific questions related to the reduction of victimization (e.g., "Do you believe the antiviolence program has reduced the number of fights/name calling [or any other type of violence the school is interested in preventing] on the playground? Why or why not?").

Transferring all of the reported events onto one large map of the school enables students and staff to locate specific "hot spots" for violence and dangerous time periods within each individual school (see Fig. 146.1 for an example). The combined data are presented to all school constituents, and they are asked to once again discuss and interpret the maps. Teachers and students use the maps and interviews to suggest ways to improve the settings and what aspects of the program are working or not working. For example, in one school, events were clustered by time, age, gender, and location. In the case of older students (eleventh- and twelfth-graders), events were clustered in the parking lot outside of the auxiliary gym immediately after school, whereas for younger students (ninth- and tenth-graders), events were reported in the lunchroom and hallways during transition periods. For this school, the map suggested that interventions be geared specifically toward older students, directly after school, by the main entrance, and in the school parking lot. Students and teachers agreed that increasing the visible presence of school staff in and around the parking lot for the 20 minutes after school had great potential for

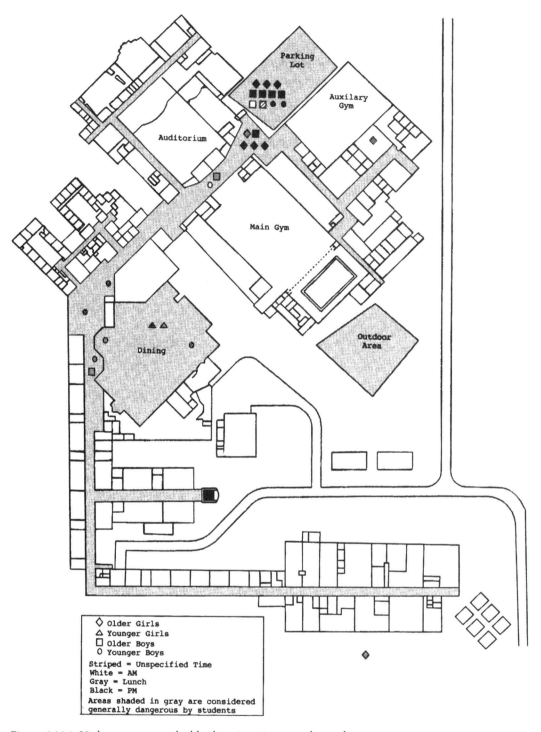

Figure 146.1 Violent events marked by location, time, gender, and age.

reducing the number of violent events. Younger students were experiencing violence mainly before, during, and after lunch, near the cafeteria. Many students expressed feelings of being unsafe between classes in the hallways. This school already had an antibullying program, and it was able to incorporate this specific type of intervention into existing activities designed to stem school violence.

Compiling all the interview suggestions into themes is an important second step in adapting context relevant interventions. Students, teachers, and administrators may have differing viewpoints regarding the organizational response of the school to a violent incident. Relaying the diversity of responses to students, teachers, and administrators can provide an opportunity for reflection and may generate ways to remedy the violence problem in certain situations. When the data are presented to students, teachers, and administrators, they can center their discussions on why those areas are dangerous and what kinds of interventions could make the location safer. Mapping methods provide data-based approaches to gathering information about bullying/victimization in schools. Moreover, they provide site-specific information, which makes it easier for schools to address these problems.

Identifying specific target groups for interventions is another way data can/should be used. A school could use this monitoring system to identify particular problem areas in their school. They could then track progress in reducing violence in these locations over time and by different groups.

In recent years, the Geographical Information Systems (GIS) and Web technology provide many more opportunities for mapping violence-related issues both within schools and in the routes to and from schools. For instance, the Los Angeles Unified School district is experimenting with a Web-based application is used to present students with maps of their school and of its surrounding neighborhood. Students indicate on the map important information, such as places where they hang out, saw violent incidences, or avoid because they fear they would get hurt. These maps are then presented with color codes that highlight information that is important for planning interventions focused on dangerous locations.

KEY POINTS TO REMEMBER

Based on our review of programs, it appears that successful schoolwide intervention programs have the following core underlying implementation characteristics.

- They are comprehensive, intensive, ecological, and require buy-in from school and community.
- They raise the awareness and responsibility of students, teachers, and parents regarding the types of violence in their schools (e.g., sexual harassment, fighting, and weapons use).
- They create clear guidelines and rules for all members of the school community.
- They target the various social systems in the school and clearly communicate to the entire school community what procedures should be followed before, during, and after violent events.
- They focus on getting the school staff, students, and parents involved in the program. They often fit easily into the normal flow and mission of the school setting.
- They use faculty, staff, and parents in the school setting to plan, implement, and sustain the program.
- They increase monitoring and supervision in nonclassroom areas.
- They include ongoing monitoring and mapping, which provide information that schools can use to tailor a program to their specific needs and increase its chance of success.

WEB SITES

Blueprints for Violence Prevention. http://www.colorado.edu/cspv/blueprints.

Bullying Prevention Program. http://www.clemson.edu/olweus.

Center for Disease Control, National Center for Injury Prevention and Control—Division of Violence Prevention. http://www.cdc.gov/ncipc/dvp/bestpractices.htm.

Child Development Project. http://www.devstu.org.

Department of Education, Safe and Drug Free Schools. http://www.ed.gov/about/offices/list/osdfs/index.html?src=mr.

FAST Track. http://www.fasttrackproject.org.

Hamilton Fish Institute on School and Community Violence. http://www.hamfish.org/programs.

Promoting Alternative Thinking Strategies (PATHS). http://www.channingbete.com/positiveyouth/pages/PATHS/PATHS.html.

Substance Abuse and Mental Health Services Administration. http://www.modelprograms.samhsa.gov.

U.S. Department of Health and Human Services, Prevention Research Center for the Promotion of Human Development. http://www.prevention .psu.edu

U.S. Office of Juvenile Justice and Delinquency, Prevention & Title V. http://www.dsgonline .com.

Youth Violence: A Report of the Surgeon General. http://www.surgeongeneral.gov/library/ youthviolence.

References

Achenbach, T. M. (1991). *Manual for teacher's report form and 1991 profile.* Burlington, VT: Department of Psychiatry, University of Vermont.

Astor, R. A., Benbenishty, R., Marachi, R., & Meyer, H. A. (2006). The social context of schools: Monitoring and mapping student victimization in schools. In S. R. Jimerson & M. J. Furlong (Eds.), *Handbook of school violence and school safety: From research to practice* (pp. 221–233). Mahwah, NJ: Erlbaum.

Astor, R. A., & Meyer, H. (1999). Where girls and women won't go: Female students', teachers', and social workers' views of school safety. *Social Work in Education, 21,* 201–219.

Astor, R. A., Meyer, H., & Behre, W. J. (1999). Unowned places and times: Maps and interviews about violence in high schools. *American Educational Research Journal, 36,* 3–42.

Astor, R. A., Meyer, H. A., & Pitner, R. O. (2001). Elementary and middle school students' perceptions of safety: An examination of violence-prone school sub-contexts. *Elementary School Journal, 101,* 511–528.

Battistich, V., Schaps, E., Watson, M., & Solomon, D. (1996). Prevention effects of the child development project: Early findings from an ongoing multi-site demonstration trial. *Journal of Adolescent Research, 11,* 12–35.

Battistich, V., Schaps, E., Watson, M., Solomon, D., & Lewis, C. (2000). Effects of the child development project on students' drug use and other problem behaviors. *Journal of Primary Prevention, 21,* 75–99.

Battistich, V., Solomon, D., Watson, M., & Schaps, E. (1997). Caring school communities. *Educational Psychologist, 32,* 137–151.

Benbenishty, R., & Astor, R. A. (2005). *School violence in context: Culture, neighborhood, family, school, and gender.* New York: Oxford University Press.

Benbenishty, R., & Astor, R. A. (2007). Monitoring indicators of children's victimization in school: Linking national-, regional-, and site-level indicators. *Social Indicators, 84*(3), 333–348.

Benbenishty, R., Astor, A. R., & Estrada, J. N. (2008). School violence assessment: A conceptual framework, instruments, and methods. *Children and Schools, 30*(2), 71–81.

Benbenishty, R., Astor, R. A., & Zeira, A. (2003). Monitoring school violence on the site level: Linking national-, district-, and school-level data over time. *Journal of School Violence, 2*(2), 29–50.

Conduct Problems Prevention Research Group. (2002). The implementation of the Fast Track program: An example of a large-scale prevention science efficacy trial. *Journal of Abnormal Child Psychology, 30,* 1–17.

Developmental Studies Center. (1995). *Child Development Project.* Retrieved May 18, 2004, from http://www.ed.gov/pubs/EPTW/eptw5/eptw5a .html.

Developmental Studies Center. (2004). *Comprehensive program: The Child Development Project.* Retrieved May 27, 2004, from http://www.devstu .org/cdp/imp_prof_devt.html.

Greenberg, M. T., & Kusché, C. A. (1998). Preventive interventions for school-age deaf children: The PATHS curriculum. *Journal of Deaf Studies and Deaf Education, 3*(1), 49–63.

Greenberg, M. T., & Kusché, C. A. (2006). Building social and emotional competence: The PATHS curriculum. In S. R. Jimerson & M. J. Furlong (Eds). *Handbook of school violence and school safety: From research to practice* (pp. 395–412). Mahwah, NJ: Erlbaum.

Greenberg, M. T., Kusché, C. A., Cook, E. T., & Quamma, J. P. (1995). Promoting emotional competence in school-age children: The effects of the PATHS curriculum. *Emotions in developmental psychopathology* [special issue], *Development and Psychopathology, 7*(1), 117–136.

Greenberg, M. T., Kusché, C. A., & Mihalic, S. F. (1998). *Blueprints for violence prevention, Book 10: Promoting alternative thinking strategies (PATHS).* Boulder, CO: Center for the Study and Prevention of Violence.

Limber, S. P. (2006). The Olweus Bullying Prevention Program: An overview of its implementation and research basis. In S. R. Jimerson & M. J. Furlong (Eds). *Handbook of school violence and school safety: From research to practice* (pp. 293–308). Mahwah, NJ: Erlbaum.

Mendel, R. A. (2000). *Less hype, more help: Reducing juvenile crime, what works and what doesn't.* Washington, DC: American Youth Policy Forum.

Northwest Regional Educational Laboratory. (1998). *The catalog of school reform models.* Retrieved May 23, 2004, from http://www.nwrel.org/scpd/ catalog/ModelDetails.asp?ModelID=6.

Olweus, D. (1993). *Bullying at school.* Cambridge, MA: Blackwell.

Olweus, D., Limber, S., & Mihalic, S. F. (1999). *Blueprints for violence prevention, Book 9: Bullying prevention program*. Boulder, CO: Center for the Study and Prevention of Violence.

Posey, R., Wong, S., Catalano, R., Hawkins, D., Dusenbury, L., & Chappell, P. (2000). *Communities That Care prevention strategies: A research guide to what works*.

Sherman, L. W., Gottfredson, D., MacKenzie, D., Eck, J.,

Reuter, P., & Bushway, S. (1998). *Preventing crime: What works, what doesn't, what's promising*. Report to the U.S. Congress, prepared for National Institute of Justice, by Department of Criminology and Criminal Justice, University of Maryland.

Solomon, D., Watson, M., Battistich, V., Schaps, E., & Delucchi, K. (1996). Creating classrooms that students experience as communities. *American Journal of Community Psychology, 24*, 719–748.

147 Promising Interventions for Students Who Have Co-Occuring Disorders

Stephen J. Tripodi, Johnny S. Kim, & Kimberly Bender

Elizabeth, a school social worker at a large urban high school, distributed brochures to teachers explaining the symptoms of co-occurring disorders. After reading about the symptoms, one teacher decided to refer one of her students, Anne, who exhibited signs of depression and substance abuse. After spending a couple of counseling sessions creating a therapeutic alliance and establishing rapport with Anne, Elizabeth set up a meeting with the girl's family to assess their knowledge of the disorders and begin to determine whether they would be an asset in treatment. In assessing the family dynamics during this counseling session, Elizabeth found them to be a resource for Anne because they supported her treatment, yet still understood the importance of firm guidelines, consistent consequences, and positive reinforcement.

After meeting with the entire family, Elizabeth met with Anne alone and asked her to complete the Problem Oriented Screening Instrument for Teenagers (POSIT), which affirmed the suspicion that Anne was abusing substances. Elizabeth continued to meet with Anne individually to create a comfortable place for her to disclose information that she may not want to discuss in front of her parents. To assess the extent of Anne's problems, Elizabeth asked her about the frequency of her drug use, triggers, and current consequences of both disorders before discussing the relationship between her depression and substance use. Elizabeth began to create a treatment plan with Anne and her family, which included individual cognitive problem-solving treatment, family behavior treatment, and group counseling. She further explained to Anne and her family that the substance use disorder and depression would be treated simultaneously.

In a subsequent counseling session with Anne, Elizabeth had her complete the University of Rhode Island Change Assessment Questionnaire (URICA), which is a tool to measure level of motivation to change. The results indicated that Anne lacked motivation to change, so Elizabeth talked to her about the problems the two disorders have caused. Specifically, she was asked to discuss specific and current consequences that she was experiencing as a result of her substance use and mental health problems and how she might want to change them.

As Anne's motivation increased, Elizabeth's techniques changed from persuasion to engagement to active treatment. During treatment, Elizabeth helped Anne enhance her problem-solving abilities. For example, together they anticipated difficult situations for Anne, thought through potential responses, discussed the consequences of each response, and chose reactions that made the most sense in the long run. As treatment progressed and Anne's substance use reduced, Elizabeth implemented relapse prevention techniques, including role-playing high-risk situations, establishing incentives for sobriety, and identifying a supportive mutual help group for Anne to attend after their counseling sessions ended.

Many youth in need of social work services have co-occurring mental and substance use disorders. Findings from the National Comorbidity Survey indicate that 41 to 65 percent of individuals with substance abuse disorders also meet criteria for a mental disorder, and approximately 43 to 51 percent of those with mental disorders are also diagnosed with a substance use disorder (SAMHSA, 2002). Rates of co-occurring disorders are highest during adolescence and young adulthood (Kessler et al., 2005). School professionals providing services to high-risk youth are thus likely to encounter youth with co-occurring disorders.

Adolescents with co-occurring disorders are defined as those who simultaneously have a substance use disorder and a mental disorder. The mental disorders that most commonly co-occur with substance use disorders are conduct disorders (CDs), attention deficit hyperactivity disorders (ADHD), depression, bipolar disorder, and post-traumatic stress disorder (PTSD) (see Table 147.1). As many as 80 percent of adolescents in treatment for substance abuse have CDs, between 20 and 40 percent have ADHD, up to 50 percent have mood disorders, and up to 40 percent have at least one anxiety disorder (Kessler et al., 2005).

Though researchers have begun to study adolescents with co-occurring disorders, development of effective treatment approaches is still in its infancy. Youth with co-occurring disorders often have complex needs that can be costly and time-intensive to treat (Bender, Springer, & Kim, 2006). This can create challenges for developing and empirically testing treatment approaches. Moreover, effective interventions should not only reduce youths' substance use but also improve internal (such as depression and anxiety) and external (such as CD) mental health problems.

A review of controlled studies highlights two treatment approaches—individual cognitive problem-solving and family behavior treatment (Azrin et al., 2001)—that show the most promise in reducing substance use disorders and improving both youths' internalizing and externalizing mental disorders (Bender et al., 2006). Moreover, cognitive-behavioral therapy demonstrates success in reducing substance use and internalizing disorders (Kaminer, Burleson, & Goldberger, 2002). Another treatment, multisystemic therapy, appears to be effective with externalizing disorders (Henggeler, Pickrel, & Brondino, 1999).

This chapter draws from various screening, assessment, and treatment approaches supported by recent research that can help school social workers working with students who have co-occurring disorders. These approaches include educating staff and students on co-occurring disorders, working with students' families, creating a therapeutic alliance, enhancing motivation, preventing relapse, and identifying referral sources.

INCREASING STAFF AND STUDENTS' KNOWLEDGE OF CO-OCCURRING DISORDERS

When school social workers and mental health professionals collaborate with teachers, administrators, and families, they enhance the chances of meeting the needs of students with co-occurring disorders. Often, school staff and administrators know little about this topic, so providing in-service training on identifying symptoms and behaviors typical of co-occurring disorders is an important service. School social workers can also help create awareness about the problem through informational posters, brochures, and class presentations. Students and teachers are frequently aware of other students who are using substances or exhibiting symptoms of co-occurring disorders, but they may not know what to do or how to help.

TABLE 147.1 Description of the Most Common Mental Disorders that Co-Occur with Substance use Disorders in Adolescents

Conduct Disorder	Attention Deficit Hyperactivity Disorder (ADHD)	Major Depressive Disorder	Bipolar Disorder	Post-Traumatic Stress Disorder
Basic rights of others or major age-appropriate societal norms or rules are consistently broken.	Inattention and/or hyperactivity-impulsivity is more persistently frequent and severe than is typical of individuals at a comparable level of development. Some symptoms that cause impairment must have been present before age 7. Some impairment from the symptoms must be present in at least two settings. Clear evidence of interference with developmentally appropriate social, academic, or occupational functioning.	At least 2 weeks marked by either depressed mood or loss of interest or pleasure in nearly all activities. With children and adolescents, the mood may be irritable rather than sad. Must also experience at least four additional symptoms (changes in appetite or weight, sleep, and psychomotor activity; decreased energy; feelings of worthlessness or guilt; difficulty thinking, concentrating, or making decisions; or recurrent thought of death or suicidal ideation, plans, or attempts).	Clinical course is characterized by occurrence of one or more manic episodes or mixed episodes. Episodes of substance-induced mood disorder (due to the direct effects of a medication, other somatic treatments for depression, a drug of abuse, or toxin exposure) or of mood disorder due to a general medical condition do not count toward a diagnosis of bipolar disorder.	Development of characteristic symptoms following exposure to an extreme traumatic stressor involving direct personal experience of an event that involves actual or threatened death or serious injury, or other threat to one's physical integrity; or witnessing an event that involves death, injury, or a threat to the physical integrity of another person; or learning about unexpected or violent death, serious harm, or threat of death or injury experienced by a family member. Characteristic symptoms include persistent reexperiencing of the traumatic event, persistent avoidance of stimuli associated with the trauma and numbing of general responsiveness, and persistent symptoms of increased arousal.

Source: Adapted from American Psychiatric Association, 2000.

It is important to provide information on how teachers and students can refer students who may have co-occurring disorders. School social workers can involve parents by sending informational letters about substance use disorders, mental disorders, co-occurring disorders, ways parents can help their children, and services the counseling department provides. The stigma attached to mental disorders and substance use disorders is substantial and may be compounded when the problems co-occur. Parents may not know how common it is for both types of disorders to occur together or recognize the need to intervene, since such problems may be more than passing stages in child and adolescent development. Figure 147.1—which can be presented and discussed with teachers, families, and students— provides information on the predictors and consequences of co-occurring disorders.

SCREENING AND ASSESSMENT

When co-occurring disorders are suspected, students should be screened to accurately identify those who could benefit from more comprehensive assessment and services. POSIT is a helpful standardized instrument for screening adolescents for co-occurring disorders. Table 147.2 describes the completion time, required reading levels, and the domains measured for POSIT. Researchers

have found POSIT to be a valid instrument, as evidenced by its convergent validity, construct validity, and discriminate validity (Hall, Richardson, & Rembert, 1998). Interested readers should read Hall and colleagues (1998) for the specific bivariate correlation analyses. Furthermore, regarding the test-retest reliability for POSIT, researchers found the substance abuse and mental health components to have favorable alpha scores (> 0.70), indicating that POSIT is a reliable instrument (Knight, Goodman, Pulerwitz, & DuRant, 2001).

Initial screening may indicate the need for a comprehensive assessment. Assessment provides an opportunity to look at the adolescent's life in a holistic manner, and it allows the social worker to develop the necessary rapport to establish a beneficial therapeutic alliance with the adolescent and his or her family. The assessment considers the adolescent's strengths; home and living situation; relationship to the child welfare, mental health, juvenile justice, and school systems; educational history; family history of substance abuse and mental health problems; and medical status.

Parents' or guardians' presence at the assessment interview enables the social worker to obtain an early developmental history and assess family dynamics (Riggs, 2003). The social worker should assess how the family enhances or reduces the potential for success by determining if there is active substance abuse or mental illness in other

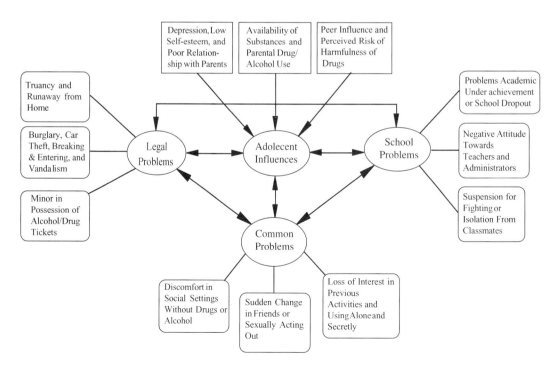

Figure 147.1 Predictors and consequences of adolescents with co-occurring disorders.

TABLE 147.2 Screening Instruments for Adolescents with Co-Occurring Disorders

General Characteristics of the Problem-Oriented Screening Instrument for Teenagers (POSIT)	
Completion time:	30 minutes
Required minimum reading level	5th grade
Domains instruments measure	Substance abuse
	Psychiatric disorders
	Behavior problems
	School adjustment
	Health status
	Peer relations
	Social competency
	Family adjustment
	Leisure/recreation
	Vocational status
	Aggressive behavior/delinquency

Source: Rahdert, 1991.

family members. The social worker should also explore how the family views mental illness and addiction (psychological problem, illness, weak character, or the results of negative peer influences). According to Riggs (2003), guidelines for enhancing screening and assessment include:

- interview the parents or guardians first;
- interview the adolescent separately to elicit information he or she may not feel comfortable disclosing in front of parents;
- be straightforward with the adolescent;
- be empathic, nonjudgmental, and supportive with all;
- ask the adolescent about patterns and frequencies of use for each substance, triggers for using, perceived motivation for using, consequences for using, and treatment goals; and
- supplement information by collecting data from the adolescent's family, available case studies, the school system, and health care providers.

WORKING WITH ADOLESCENTS WHO HAVE CO-OCCURRING DISORDERS

When working with adolescents who have co-occurring disorders, the likelihood of a successful outcome increases when substance use and mental disorders are treated simultaneously—also known as

"integrated treatment." The adolescent needs education to understand both disorders and their interactions (Chatlos, 1994). Education should cover risk factors, precipitating events, and the progression of the problems. To assess the student's understanding of his or her co-occurring disorders, the social worker might ask, "What do you see as the relationship between your substance use disorder and your mental disorder?" The social worker should focus on current instances of negative consequences or outcomes to enable the adolescent to recognize the effect that drug use has had on his or her life (Evans & Sullivan, 2001; Manwani & Weiss, 2003).

A therapeutic alliance between the social worker and the adolescent is critical. Establishing this alliance increases youths' engagement and commitment in the treatment process; without engagement, youth with co-occurring disorders are particularly at risk for dropping out of services and having poor outcomes (Williams & Chang, 2000). Adolescents with co-occurring disorders require a comprehensive and individualized treatment plan that includes individual therapy, group therapy, family involvement, and educational services (Kessler et al., 2005). The social worker should encourage parents to commit to involvement in the treatment plan and family therapy to create a supportive family recovery environment (Chatlos, 1994).

During the first few counseling sessions, the social worker must work with the adolescent to establish goals to eliminate or reduce substance use and begin to address the co-occurring disorders and other issues (Riggs, 2003). Following goal identification, the social worker should create a contract with the adolescent identifying peers with whom he or she should and should not associate (e.g., law-abiding versus non–law-abiding peers), places that should be avoided, specific hours to be home, specific hours for homework, and times for attending self-help groups (Chatlos, 1994). Family members should be encouraged to join community support groups like Al-Anon (for families of alcoholics) or the National Alliance for the Mentally Ill (for families of individuals who have mental illness).

If the adolescent has successfully abstained from substances in the past, the social worker should recognize that accomplishment, state how difficult that must have been, and ask how the client was able to refrain from drugs. As the adolescent maintains increased periods of abstinence, the social worker should help him or her identify areas in which his or her life is improving (Evans & Sullivan, 2001). The social worker should also compliment the adolescent when he or she demonstrates stability and effort, such as participating in therapy, controlling anger, and engaging in healthy activities, and help the adolescent identify areas where improvement in the mental disorder has resulted in change in other areas of life, such as acting out less in the classroom. Positive reinforcement of these and other gains helps adolescents create those conditions more often. Two empirically supported interventions, individual cognitive problem-solving (ICPS) and family behavioral treatment (FBT), are promising in treating youth with co-occurring disorders (Azrin et al., 2001). ICPS helps youth learn cognitive strategies for problem solving and decision making, such as stopping and thinking, defining the problem, identifying potential consequences of each possible response, and making the most reasonable decision. FBT focuses on reducing reinforcers of substance use by involving family and peers in treatment interventions. Interventions aim to control urges and reduce stimulus through developing communication skills and contracting for behavioral change (Azrin et al., 2001).

ENHANCING ADOLESCENTS' MOTIVATION

Adolescents with co-occurring disorders must be motivated to change for interventions to be effective. If the adolescent is not willing to change, the social worker should work on increasing their client's motivation level. URICA is a tool to measure level of motivation to change (Greenstein, Franklin, & McGuffin, 1999). The level of motivation will determine the approaches the social worker employs. Although the method is not yet validated with adolescents who have co-occurring disorders, Evans and Sullivan (2001) have adopted a four-level model of motivation specifically for adolescents with co-occurring disorders that corresponds well with evidence indicating a strong association between treatment retention and positive outcomes. The following are the four levels of the model. (1) Engagement, where providers work to convince clients that treatment has some value (e.g., through films or peer groups). (2) Persuasion, which consists of attempts to convince the client of the need for help (e.g., through values clarification exercises). (3) Active treatment with an emphasis on developing skills and attitudes needed to maintain sobriety and mental health. (4) Relapse prevention to help the adolescent incorporate techniques for sustaining the skills needed to maintain abstinence and mental health (e.g., use of an ongoing mutual-help group).

RELAPSE PREVENTION

Relapse prevention is a vital component of treatment for those with co-occurring disorders. The social worker helps the adolescent identify effective methods to deal with alcohol or drug cravings and ways to recognize and avoid situations that present a high risk of relapse for both types of disorders (Manwani & Weiss, 2003). Role-playing may help decrease the chances of substance use relapse. Role-playing may include situations in which friends or family members overtly or covertly encourage the client to use drugs, how to cope with emotions without using drugs, and how to socialize and have fun while sober. Relapse among adolescents with substance use and mental disorders is highest in situations of negative emotional states, like stress and interpersonal conflict (Roget, Fisher, & Johnson, 1998). Other high-risk situations include urges and temptations (parties where drugs are present), positive emotional states (the desire to celebrate achievements), negative physical states (such as sickness or physical injury), and positive interpersonal contact (interactions with potential dating partners) (Roget et al., 1998).

Before concluding treatment, a relapse prevention plan should be developed to help all the parties involved in the adolescent's treatment. Roget et al. (1998) recommend incorporating the following in relapse prevention plans:

- probation terms (if applicable to the client's legal situation),
- family rules,
- school attendance and grade requirements,
- participation in aftercare (e.g., outpatient therapy group or mutual-help groups),
- agreement to participate in drug testing,
- relapse consequences, and
- compliance incentives (initially, a reward for each week of sobriety).

The social worker should inform families that the overwhelming majority of individuals with substance use disorders relapse at least once and often more than once. Furthermore, professionals should not blame themselves when clients misbehave or relapse. It is important to remember, however, that expecting relapse does not mean accepting relapse. Parents should also continue to implement immediate consequences should relapse occur.

REFERRALS

The *ASAM Patient Placement Criteria for the Treatment of Substance-Related Disorders* (National Institute for Drug Abuse, 1991) is a good tool to consult when considering a referral to outpatient services, intensive outpatient services with partial hospitalization, residential and intensive inpatient services, and medically managed intensive inpatient services. For example, outpatient treatment is appropriate when an adolescent with co-occurring disorders recognizes that he or she has a problem, is not in immediate danger, and has an intact support group.

Inability to remain abstinent or exacerbation of mental illness may necessitate referral to residential treatment. When residential treatment is needed, the social worker should look for a controlled milieu, such as a therapeutic community, that can address both mental and substance use disorders. Treatment centers that use immediate consequences, both positive and negative, and a reduction of privileges for upper-level residents (with longer treatment tenure and positive behavior) when lower-level residents misbehave may increase the likeliness of a successful outcome (Evans & Sullivan, 2001).

CONCLUSION

Treating youth with co-occurring disorders is challenging for a number of reasons. This population requires treatments that are engaging, address multiple problems, and create sustainable

---

TABLE 147.3 Guidelines for Treatment

Ten Preliminary Treatment Guidelines for Dually Diagnosed Adolescents
1. Assessment is multipronged, ongoing, and includes practitioner, parental, and self-monitoring so that treatment is responsive to the changing needs of the client.
2. Treatment strategically enhances engagement and retention.
3. Treatment plans are flexible and allow for client choice and voice.
4. An integrated treatment approach is used to address mental and substance use disorders concurrently.
5. Treatment is developmentally and culturally sensitive to match the unique needs of the client system.
6. Treatment is ecologically grounded and systems oriented and includes those important to the client, such as family members, friends, and school personnel.
7. Treatment taps several domains of the client's functioning to enhance the client's problem-solving and decision-making skills, affect regulation, impulse control, communication skills, and peer and family relations.
8. Treatment is goal-directed, here-and-now focused, and strengths-based.
9. Treatment requires active participation by all members involved, including "homework" assignments.
10. Interventions aim to produce sustainable changes over the course of treatment and beyond to prevent relapse or redirect the client if relapse occurs.

Source: Adapted from Bender, Springer, & Kim, 2006.

change. To provide such services, professionals must help school staff, students, and families overcome the stigma and blame associated with co-occurring disorders. Once adolescents accept help, a number of techniques and strategies have been developed to improve outcomes for this vulnerable group. Preliminary guidelines—derived from treatments shown to be most promising with youth who have co-occurring disorders—can aid school social workers and other professionals seeking to serve this population (Bender et al., 2006) (see Table 147.3). To the greatest extent possible, school professionals should aim to implement services that follow these guidelines. Doing so is likely to benefit students with co-occurring disorders and their families by reducing substance use, improving mental health problems, and ultimately enhancing academic outcomes.

WEB SITES

Bazelon Center for Mental Health Law. http://www.bazelon.org/issues/children/factsheets/co-occuring.htm.

National Alliance for the Mentally Ill. http://www.nami.org/Content/ContentGroups/Illnesses/Dual_Diagnosis_Fact_Sheet.htm.

Substance Abuse and Mental Health Services Administration. http://www.oas.samhsa.gov/2k5/youthMH/youthMH.htm.

References

American Psychiatric Association. (2000). *Diagnostic and statistical manual of mental disorders*, 4th ed., text revision. Washington, DC: American Psychiatric Press.

Azrin, N. H., Donohue, B. Teichner, G. A., Crum, T., Howell, J., & DeCato, L. A. (2001). A controlled evaluation and description of individual-cognitive problem solving and family-behavior therapies in dually-diagnosed conduct-disordered and substance-dependent youth. *Journal of Child & Adolescent Substance Abuse, 11*(1), 1–43.

Bender, K., Springer, D. W., & Kim, J. S. (2006). Treatment effectiveness with dually diagnosed adolescents: A systematic review. *Brief Treatment and Crisis Intervention, 6*(3), 177–205.

Chatlos, J. C. (1994). Dual diagnosis in adolescent populations. In N. S. Miller (Ed.), *Treating coexisting psychiatric and addictive disorders* (pp. 85–110). Center City, MN: Hazelden.

Evans, K., & Sullivan, M. (2001). *Dual diagnosis: Counseling the mentally ill substance abuser*. New York: Guilford.

Greenstein, D. D., Franklin, M. E., & McGuffin, P. (1999). Measuring motivation to change: an examination of the University of Rhode Island change assessment questionnaire (URICA) in an adolescent sample. *Psychotherapy, 36*(1), 47–55.

Hall, J. A., Richardson, B., & Rembert, J. K. (1998). Validation of the POSIT: Comparing drug using and abstaining youth. *Journal of Child and Adolescent Substance Abuse, 8*, 29–61.

Henggeler, S. W., Pickrel, S. G., & Brondino, M. J. (1999). Multisystemic treatment of substance-abusing and -dependent delinquents: Outcomes, treatment, fidelity, and transportability. *Mental Health Services Research, 1*, 171–184.

Kaminer, Y., Burleson, J. A., & Goldberger, R. (2002). Cognitive-behavioral coping skills and pscyhoeducation therapies for adolescent substance abuse. *Journal of Nervous and Mental Disease, 190*, 737–745.

Kessler, R. C., Berglund, P., Demler, O., Jin, R., Merikangas, K. R., & Walters, E. E. (2005). Lifetime prevalence and age-of-onset distributions of DSM-IV disorders in the National Comorbidity Survey replication. *Archive of General Psychiatry, 62*, 593–602.

Knight, J. R., Goodman, E., Pulerwitz, T., & DuRant, R. H. (2001). Reliability of the Problem Oriented Screening Instrument for Teenagers. *Journal of Adolescent Health, 29*, 125–130.

Manwani, S., & Weiss, R. (2003). 5 keys to improve counseling for dual diagnosis patients: An empathic approach can be effective when treating psychiatric patients with substance use disorders. Retrieved August 1, 2004, from http://www.currentpsychiatry.com/2003_09/0903_counseling.asp.

National Institute for Drug Abuse. (1991). *The adolescent assessment/referral systems manual* (DHHS Publication no. [ADM] 91-1735). Rockville, MD: National Institute for Drug Abuse.

Rahdert, E. R. (1991). *The adolescent assessment/referral system manual* (DHHS Publication no. ADM91-1735). Rockville, MD: National Institute on Drug Abuse.

Riggs, P. D. (2003). Treating adolescents for substance abuse and comorbid psychiatric disorders. *Science and Practice Perspectives*, 18–32.

Roget, N. A., Fisher, G. L., & Johnson, M. L. (1998). A protocol for reducing juvenile recidivism through relapse prevention. *Journal of Addiction & Offender Counseling, 19*(1), 33–34.

Substance Abuse and Mental Health Services Administration. (2002). *Evidence-based practices for co-occurring disorders: Interventions for children and adolescents with co-occurring disorders.* Rockville, MD: U.S. Department of Health and Human Services.

Williams, R. J., & Chang, S. Y. (2000). A comprehensive review of adolescent substance abuse treatment outcomes. *Clinical Psychology: Science and Practice, 7*, 138–166.

Effective Interventions for Students with Conduct Disorder

David W. Springer & Courtney J. Lynch

GETTING STARTED

School-aged children and adolescents with externalizing disorders are a challenging, yet rewarding population to help. Many school-based practitioners, teachers, and administrators may be all too familiar with the behaviors associated with a diagnosis of conduct disorder (CD), such as aggressive behavior toward others, using a weapon, fire setting, cruelty to animals or persons, vandalism, lying, truancy, running away, and theft (American Psychiatric Association, 2000). The *DSM-IV-TR* allows for coding a client with one of two subtypes of CD: childhood-onset type (at least one criterion characteristic occurs prior to age 10) and adolescent-onset type (absence of any criteria prior to age 10). A youth must be engaged in a pattern of behavior over an extended period of time (at least 6 months) that consistently violates the rights of others and societal norms.

Part of what makes helping school-aged youth with CD so challenging is the multifaceted nature of their problems. Fortunately, in recent years, significant advances in psychosocial treatments have been made to treat children and adolescents with disruptive behavior disorders. Unfortunately, some states operate with policies that exclude conduct-disordered students from eligibility for services in schools. Nevertheless, in keeping with a recent U.S. surgeon general's report (U.S. Department of Health and Human Services, 2001), this chapter is grounded in the assumption that CD youth can be helped using innovative and research-based interventions. Some of these evidence-based practices (EBPs) are applied to the case example of Alex. For our purposes here, Rosen and Proctor's (2002) definition of EBP has been adopted, whereby "practitioners will select interventions on the basis of their empirically demonstrated links to the desired outcomes" (p. 743).

WHAT WE KNOW

Classroom-based interventions of conduct problems have not received as much attention as interventions for conduct problems in the home (Fonagy & Kurtz, 2002). Little and Hudson (1998) reviewed classroom interventions and concluded that these interventions are diverse, lack empirical support, and are often not consistent with home-based interventions. Nevertheless, there are some general factors that are associated with lower levels of problem behaviors in schools, including strong positive leadership; high pupil expectations; close monitoring of pupils; good opportunities to engage in school life and take on responsibility; well-functioning incentive, reward, and punishment systems; high levels of parental involvement; an academic emphasis; and a focus on learning (Brody, Dorsey, Forehand, & Armistead, 2002; Connell, Dishion, Yasui, & Kavanagh, 2007). All of these factors have an overall positive influence on youth development, learning, and behavior management.

WHAT WE CAN DO

Among the effective interventions for children with conduct problems, two were found to be well established, according to the Division 12 (Clinical Psychology) Task Force on Promotion and Dissemination of Psychological Procedures (Brestan & Eyberg, 1998). One of these is the Incredible Years Parents, Teachers and Children's Training series, developed by Webster-Stratton and based on a trained leader using videotape modeling to trigger group discussion. Randomized control group studies support using the program as a treatment program for parents of children ages 3 to 8 years with conduct problems and as a prevention program for high-risk families (see Reid, Webster-

Stratton, & Baydar, 2004; Webster-Stratton, 1984, 1998). The second well-established approach is parent-training programs based on Patterson and Gullion's (1968) manual *Living with Children* (Alexander & Parsons, 1973; Bernal, Klinnert, & Schultz, 1980; Wiltz & Patterson, 1974). See Table 148.1 for supporting studies. In short, parent management training (PMT) is the only intervention that is considered well established for the treatment of conduct disorder.

Several treatments for children with conduct problems were found to be probably efficacious, according to the same criteria (Brestan & Eyberg, 1998). Probably efficacious treatments for preschool-age children include parent–child interaction therapy, time out plus signal seat treatment, delinquency prevention programs, and parent-training programs. Two treatments meeting the probably efficacious criteria designed for use with school-age children are problem-solving skills training and anger coping therapy. Finally, four treatments for adolescents with conduct problems were found to be probably efficacious: multisystemic therapy, assertiveness training, rational-emotive therapy, and anger control training with stress inoculation. See Table 148.2 for supporting studies.

PARENT MANAGEMENT TRAINING

PMT is a summary term that describes a therapeutic strategy in which parents are trained to use skills for managing their child's problem behavior (Kazdin, 2004), such as effective command giving, setting up reinforcement systems, and using punishment, including taking away privileges and assigning extra chores. Although PMT programs may differ in focus and therapeutic strat-

egies used, they all share the common goal of enhancing parental control over children's behavior (Cavell, 2000; Davis, 2007; DeGarmo, Patterson, & Forgatch, 2004; Nock & Kazdin, 2005; Reid, Webster-Stratton, & Baydar, 2004; Scahill et al., 2006; Webster-Stratton, 1998).

Though PMT approaches are typically used for parents with younger children (Serketich & Dumas, 1996), they have been successfully adapted for parents with adolescents (see Bank, Marlowe, Reid, Patterson, & Weinrott, 1991; Barkley, Edwards, Laneri, Fletcher, & Metevia, 2001; Barkley, Guevremont, Anastopoulos, & Fletcher, 1992). The effectiveness of parent training is well documented and, in many respects, impressive. Still, school practitioners should be aware that studies examining the effectiveness of PMT with adolescents are equivocal, with some suggesting that adolescents respond less well to PMT than their younger counterparts do (Dishion & Patterson, 1992; Kazdin, 2002). In much of the outcome research, PMT has been administered to individual families in clinic settings, while group administration has been facilitated primarily through videotaped materials. PMT has been effective in reducing conduct problems and increasing positive parenting behaviors when implemented on a large scale as part of early school intervention (Head Start) programs (Webster-Stratton, 1998; cited in Kazdin, 2004).

PROBLEM-SOLVING SKILLS TRAINING

Problem-solving skills training (PSST) is a cognitively based intervention that has been used to treat aggressive and antisocial youth (Kazdin, 1994). The problem-solving process involves helping clients

---

TABLE 148.1 Well-Established Treatments and Supporting Studies

Best-Supported (Well Established) Treatments	Supporting Studies
Videotape Modeling Parent Training	Reid, Webster-Stratton, & Hammond (2003); Spaccarelli, Cotler, & Penman (1992); Webster Stratton (1984, 1990, 1994, 1998); Webster-Stratton, Kolpacoff, & Hollinsworth (1988); Webster-Stratton, Reid, & Hammond (2001)
Parent Training Based on Living with Children	Alexander & Parsons (1973); Bernal, Klinnert, & Schultz (1980); Wiltz & Patterson (1974)

TABLE 148.2 Probably Efficacious Treatments and Supporting Studies

Promising (Probably Efficacious) Treatments for Preschool-Aged Children Supporting Studies	
Parent–Child Interaction Therapy	Eyberg, Boggs, & Algina (1995); McNeil, Eyberg, Eisenstadt, Newcomb, & Funderburk (1991); Zangwill (1983)
Time-Out plus Signal Seat Treatment	Hamilton & MacQuiddy (1984)
Delinquency Prevention Program	Tremblay, Pagani-Kurtz, Masse, Vitaro, & Phil (1995); Vitaro & Tremblay (1994)
Parent Training Program for School-Aged Children	Peed, Roberts, & Forehand (1977); Wells & Egan (1988)
For School-Aged Children	Kazdin, Esveldt-Dawson, French, & Unis (1987a, 1987b); Kazdin, Siegel, & Bass (1992)
Problem-Solving Skills Training	
Anger Coping Therapy	Lochman, Burch, Curry, & Lampron (1984); Lochman, Lampron, Gemmer, & Harris (1989)
For Adolescents	
Multisystemic Therapy	Borduin et al. (1995); Henggeler, Melton, & Smith (1992); Henggeler et al. (1986)
Assertiveness Training	Huey & Rank (1984)
Rational-Emotive Therapy	Block (1978)
Anger Control Training with Stress Inoculation	Feindler, Marriott, & Iwata (1984); Schlichter & Horan (1981)

Source: This table was compiled by synthesizing information from Brestan, & Eyberg, 1998.

learn how to produce a variety of potentially effective responses when faced with problem situations (D'Zurilla & Nezu, 2001). Regardless of the specific problem-solving model used, the primary focus is on addressing the thought process to help adolescents address deficiencies and distortions in their approach to interpersonal situations (Kazdin, 1994). A variety of techniques are used, including didactic teaching, practice, modeling, role-playing, feedback, social reinforcement, and therapeutic games (Kronenberger & Meyer, 2001).

The problem-solving approach includes five steps for the practitioner and client to address: (1) defining the problem, (2) brainstorming, (3) evaluating the alternatives, (4) choosing and implementing an alternative, and (5) evaluating the implemented option. Several randomized clinical trials (Type 1 and 2 studies) have demonstrated the effectiveness of PSST with impulsive, aggressive, and CD children and adolescents (see Baer & Nietzel, 1991; Durlak, Fuhrman, & Lampman, 1991; Kazdin, 2000; cited in Kazdin, 2002). Webster-Stratton and colleagues have developed a small-group treatment program that teaches problem solving, anger man-

agement, and social skills for children ages 4 to 8 years, and two randomized control group studies demonstrate the efficacy of this treatment program (Webster-Stratton & Hammond, 1997; Webster-Stratton & Reid, 2003a; Webster-Stratton, Reid, & Hammond, 2001, 2004). Problem-solving training produces significant reductions in conduct symptoms and improvements in prosocial behavior among antisocial youth.

VIDEOTAPE MODELING PARENT PROGRAM

Webster-Stratton's Videotape Modeling Parent Program, part of the Incredible Years training series, was developed to address parent, family, child, and school risk factors related to childhood CDs. The series is a result of Webster-Stratton's own research, which suggested that comprehensive videotape training methods are effective treatments for early onset oppositional defiant disorder/CD. The training series includes the Incredible Years Parent Interventions, the Incredible Years Teacher

Training Intervention, and the Incredible Years Child Training Intervention, each of which relies on performance training methods, including videotape modeling, role-play, practice activities, and live therapist feedback (Webster-Stratton & Reid, 2003b).

The parent component aims to promote competencies and strengthen families by increasing positive parenting skills, teaching positive discipline strategies, improving problem solving, and increasing family supports and collaboration, to name a few. The teacher component of the series aims to promote teacher competencies and strengthen home–school relationships by increasing effective classroom management skills, increasing teachers' use of effective discipline and collaboration with parents, and increasing teachers' abilities in the areas of social skills, anger management, and problem solving. The child component aims to strengthen children's social and play skills, increase effective problem-solving strategies and emotional awareness, boost academic success, reduce defiance and aggression, and increase self-esteem.

Webster-Stratton and Reid (2003b) assert that the most proactive and powerful approach to the problem of escalating aggression in young children is to offer their programs using a school-based prevention/early intervention model designed to strengthen *all* children's social and emotional competence. Their reasons are threefold: (1) offering interventions in schools makes programs more accessible to families and eliminates some of the barriers (i.e., transportation) typically encountered with services offered in traditional mental health settings; (2) offering interventions in schools integrates programs before children's common behavior problems escalate to the point of needing intense clinical intervention; and (3) offering a social and emotional curriculum, such as the Dinosaur School program, to an entire class is less stigmatizing than a "pull-out" group and is more likely to produce sustained effects across settings and time.

TOOLS AND PRACTICE EXAMPLE

Practice Example

Alex is a 12-year-old white male who was recently arrested at school for stealing several items from his teacher, including a cell phone, $200, a watch, a lighter, and some pocket-sized school supplies. At the time of the arrest, Alex was found to be in possession of marijuana. For these offenses, he was placed on probation and ordered to receive mental health counseling for the length of his probation. Alex has always had minor behavior problems, and over the past year his behavior problems have escalated considerably. He lives with his parents and three siblings in a rural farming community. Though it was never confirmed, Alex's parents suspect that he was responsible for setting a small grass fire in a field behind their home last month. Alex frequently returns home from school with items that do not belong to him, and he engages in physical fights on the school bus at least once a week. Witnesses to these altercations report that Alex instigates fights with no apparent provocation. Although he tests above grade level in most subjects and his IQ falls within the normal range, Alex's teachers report that he is in danger of failing the sixth grade because he does not complete class or homework assignments. When his parents gave a blank check to his sibling for a school project, Alex stole the check and attempted to cash it for $50. At home, his siblings complain that Alex steals things from them, bullies them into doing things his way, and breaks their belongings. Last month, he denied carving his initials into the bathroom wall and breaking his bedroom window with a baseball.

Among the various options available for use with Alex and his family, his school social worker chose to use interventions that had a solid evidence base in an effort to maximize the possibility for a successful outcome. As the first active phase of treatment, a thorough assessment is the cornerstone of a solid treatment plan (Springer, 2002). During their initial session, the school social worker conducted a complete biopsychosocial assessment with Alex and his parents, which resulted in the following diagnoses.

Axis I   312.81: Conduct disorder, childhood-onset type, moderate
Axis II   V71.09: No diagnosis
Axis III None
Axis IV   V61.8: Sibling relational problem
          V62.3: Academic problem
          V61.20: Parent–child relational problem
          Involvement with juvenile justice system
Axis V   GAF=45

In light of Alex's diagnosis, his age (12 years), the evidence supporting the use of PMT and PSST as probably efficacious approaches, and the availability of his parents to participate in his treatment, the school social worker chose to use PMT and PSST. Using a combination of these methods together tends to be more effective than using either treatment alone (Kazdin, 2003). Both treatments are manualized and have core sets of themes and skills domains for treatment sessions.

PMT with Alex

One core session of PMT teaches parents to use positive reinforcement to change behavior. Alex's social worker first spent some time training his parents to pinpoint, define, and observe problematic behavior in new ways, focusing on careful inspection of the problems. She then worked with the family to develop a token system to be implemented in their home, which would provide them a structured, consistent way to reinforce Alex's behavior. Rather than creating an exhaustive list of behaviors that would be difficult to track, Alex's parents began with three target behaviors/goals that they believed would be easier to manage and accomplish: respecting others' property and belongings, completing and turning in homework, and riding the school bus without fighting. In reviewing Alex's behavior, his father realized that Alex experienced very few behavior problems when he worked on outdoor projects with him. Spending time outdoors with his father, extra recreation/video game time, and an extra trip to the corner store to spend his money were the main incentives integrated into the token system. The tokens, paired with praise, were contingent on Alex's behavior specific to the targeted behaviors/goals. The social worker spent the bulk of this treatment session modeling and role-playing the implementation of this token system, developing the parents' proficiency in prompting, praising behavior, and delivering consequences.

The social worker reviewed the previous week's events in each subsequent session, reenacting and rehearsing problems or difficulties as needed. The social worker met with Alex's parents to review the purpose and effective use of time out as an intervention. The last time he was in time out, Alex threw a baseball through his bedroom window. They discussed finding a safer time-out area in the house, where Alex could be directly monitored, and removing possibly dangerous items from his bedroom. The social worker cautioned Alex's parents that his behaviors might escalate

as they begin to implement these new interventions. She encouraged them to have back-up plans in the event that their first attempt to intervene did not work. Together, they role-played some possible scenarios and practiced back-up plans, alternating roles to develop proficiency. See Sells (1998) for step-by-step and detailed descriptions on developing creative and proactive interventions with parents who have challenging adolescents.

PSST with Alex

Because the parents were actively participating in his treatment, the first few sessions with Alex were spent not only introducing steps in problem solving but discussing the token system and how consequences (positive or negative) were contingent on his behavior. Alex was initially very confident in his ability but anticipated that his siblings would sabotage his efforts with their constant provocations and false accusations of stealing. Hearing this, the social worker introduced the following self-statements in problem solving to guide Alex's behavior and lead to developing effective solutions (Kazdin, 2003):

1. What am I supposed to do?
2. I have to look at all my possibilities.
3. I'd better concentrate and focus in.
4. I need to make a choice.
5. I did a good job (or) Oh, I made a mistake.

Alex reported that he often fought with his siblings because they provoked him, so the social worker engaged Alex in multiple role-plays, repeatedly practicing how he might respond to perceived provocation. The social worker effusively praised Alex's quick recall of the self-statements and his efforts to use a "stop and think" technique that she modeled and prompted. Additionally, they practiced how to respond to mistakes and failures without exploding at others or destroying property. Alex's parents were instructed to praise and reward his efforts to avoid conflicts and employ the problem-solving steps in everyday situations at home. Subsequent treatment sessions would require Alex to use the steps in increasingly more difficult and clinically relevant real-life situations (Kazdin, 2003).

It is important to note that medication management was not part of Alex's treatment plan. Although there is survey evidence for the significant use of polypharmacy in the treatment of children with CD in the United States, "medication cannot be justified as the first line of treatment for conduct problems. A diagnosis-based approach, which defines primary or comorbid psychiatric disorders associated with aggression, should guide the pharmacological treatment of CD" (Fonagy & Kurtz, 2002, p. 192).

Had Alex been younger (age 4–8 years), the social worker could have selected from the range of interventions available under the Incredible Years Training Series. One of the appealing qualities of this approach is that it has been tailored for work with youth in school settings.

KEY POINTS TO REMEMBER

Some of the key points from this chapter are as follows.

- CD youth in schools can be effectively treated.
- There are two well-established and a range of probably efficacious treatment approaches from which to select when working with CD youth.
- Using a combination of PMT and PSST together tends to be more effective than using either treatment alone (Kazdin, 2003). Both are manualized and have core sets of themes and skills domains for treatment sessions.
- Medication cannot be justified as the first line of treatment for conduct problems.
- One of the well-established approaches, the Incredible Years Training Series, was developed to address parent, family, child, and school risk factors related to childhood CDs.
- The most proactive and powerful approach to the problem of escalating aggression in young children is to offer their programs using a school-based prevention/early intervention model designed to strengthen all children's social and emotional competence.

Despite the promising treatment effects produced by the interventions reviewed here, existing treatments need to be refined and new ones developed. We cannot yet determine the short- and long-term impact of evidence-based treatments on CD youths, and it is sometimes unclear what part of the therapeutic process produces change.

A child's eventual outcome is most likely dependent on the interrelationship among child, parent, teacher, and peer risk factors; accordingly, the most effective interventions should be those that assess these risk factors and determine which programs are needed for a particular family and child (Webster-Stratton & Reid, 2003b).

The focus in this chapter has been geared toward school social workers and other mental health practitioners working with individual students in school settings. We cannot emphasize enough that contextual issues should not be ignored. Equally important in sustaining therapeutic change with CD youth are issues surrounding classroom management and strategies that promote positive behavior through schoolwide interventions. Accordingly, practitioners must work collaboratively with parents, teachers, peers, and school administrators to sustain change across settings. For a detailed exposition on best practice models for schoolwide interventions, the reader is referred to Bloomquist and Schnell (2002), which is an excellent source.

WEB SITE

Incredible Years Parent, Teacher, and Child Programs. http://www.incredibleyears.com.

References

Alexander, J. F., & Parsons, B. V. (1973). Short-term behavioral intervention with delinquents: Impact on family process and recidivism. *Journal of Abnormal Psychology, 81,* 219–225.

American Psychiatric Association. (2000). *Diagnostic and statistical manual of mental disorders,* 4th ed., text revision. Washington, DC: APA.

Baer, R. A., & Nietzel, M. T. (1991). Cognitive and behavioral treatment of impulsivity in children: A meta analytic review of the outcome literature. *Journal of Clinical Child Psychology, 20*(4), 400–412.

Bank, L., Marlowe, J. H., Reid, J. B., Patterson, G. R., & Weinrott, M. R. (1991). A comparative evaluation of parent training interventions for families of chronic delinquents. *Journal of Abnormal Child Psychology, 19,* 15–33.

Barkley, R., Edwards, G., Laneri, M., Fletcher, K., & Metevia, L. (2001). The efficacy of problem-solving communication training alone, behavior management training alone, and their combination for parent-adolescent conflict in teenagers with ADHD and ODD. *Journal of Consulting and Clinical Psychology, 69,* 926–941.

Barkley, R. A., Guevremont, D. C., Anastopoulos, A. D., & Fletcher, K. E. (1992). A comparison of three family therapy programs for treating family conflicts in adolescents with attention-deficit hyperactivity disorder. *Journal of Consulting and Clinical Psychology, 60,* 450–462.

Bernal, M. E., Klinnert, M. D., & Schultz, L. A. (1980). Outcome evaluation of behavioral parent training and client-centered parent counseling for children with conduct problems. *Journal of Applied Behavior Analysis, 13,* 677–691.

Block, J. (1978). Effects of a rational-emotive mental health program on poorly achieving disruptive high school students. *Journal of Counseling Psychology, 25,* 61–65.

Bloomquist, M. L., & Schnell, S. V. (2002). *Helping children with aggression and conduct problems: Best practices for intervention.* New York: Guilford.

Borduin, C. M., Mann, B. J., Cone, L. T., Henggeler, S. W., Fucci, B. R., Blaske, D. M., et al. (1995). Multisystemic treatment of serious juvenile offenders: Long-term prevention of criminality and violence. *Journal of Consulting and Clinical Psychology, 63,* 569–578.

Brestan, E. V., & Eyberg, S. M. (1998). Effective psychosocial treatments of conduct-disordered children and adolescents: 29 years, 82 studies, and 5,272 kids. *Journal of Clinical Child Psychology, 27*(2), 180–189.

Brody, G. H., Dorsey, S., Forehand, R., & Armistead, L. (2002). Unique and protective contributions of parenting and classroom processes to the adjustment of African American children living in single-parent families. *Child Development, 73*(1), 274–286.

Cavell, T. A. (2000). *Working with parents of aggressive children: A practitioner's guide.* Washington, DC: American Psychological Association.

Connell, A. M., Dishion, T. J., Yasui, M., & Kavanagh, K. (2007). An adaptive approach to family intervention: Linking engagement in family-centered intervention to reductions in adolescent problem behavior. *Journal of Consulting and Clinical Psychology, 75*(4), 568–579.

Davis, M. (2007). Parent management training: Treatment for oppositional, aggressive, and antisocial behaviour in children and adolescents. *Behaviour Change, 24*(2), 122–123.

DeGarmo, D. S., Patterson, G. R., & Forgatch, M. S. (2004). How do outcomes in a specified parent training intervention maintain or wane over time? *Prevention Science, 5*(2), 73–89.

Dishion, T. J., & Patterson, G. R. (1992). Age effects in parent training outcomes. *Behavior Therapy, 23,* 719–729.

Durlak, J., Fuhrman, T., & Lampman, C. (1991). Effectiveness of cognitive-behavior therapy for maladapting children: A meta-analysis. *Psychological Bulletin, 110,* 204–214.

D'Zurilla, T., & Nezu, A. (2001). Problem-solving therapies. In K. Dobson & S. Keith (Eds.), *Handbook of cognitive-behavioral therapies,* 2nd ed. (pp. 211–245). New York: Guilford.

Eyberg, S. M., Boggs, S., & Algina, J. (1995). Parent–child interaction therapy: A psychosocial model for the treatment of young children with conduct problem behavior and their families. *Psychopharmacology Bulletin, 110,* 204–214.

Feindler, D. L., Marriott, S. A. A., & Iwata, M. (1984). Group anger control training for junior high school delinquents. *Cognitive Therapy and Research, 8,* 299–311.

Fonagy, P., & Kurtz, A. (2002). Disturbance of conduct. In P. Fonagy, M. Target, D. Cottrell, J. Phillips, & Z. Kurtz (Eds.), *What works for whom? A critical review of treatments for children and adolescents* (pp. 106–192). New York: Guilford.

Hamilton, S. B., & MacQuiddy, S. L. (1984). Self-administered behavioral parent training: Enhancement of treatment efficacy using a time-out signal seat. *Journal of Clinical Child Psychology, 13,* 61–69.

Henggeler, S. W., Melton, G. B., & Smith, L. A. (1992). Family preservation using multisystemic therapy: An effective alternative to incarcerating serious juvenile offenders. *Journal of Consulting and Clinical Psychology, 60,* 953–961.

Henggeler, S. W., Rodick, J. D., Bourdin, C. M., Hanson, C. L., Watson, S. M., & Urey, J. R. (1986). Multisystemic treatment of juvenile offenders: Effects on adolescent behavior and family interaction. *Developmental Psychology, 22,* 132–141.

Huey, W. C., & Rank, R. C. (1984). Effects of counselor and peer-led group assertiveness training on black adolescent aggression. *Journal of Counseling Psychology, 31,* 95–98.

Kazdin, A. E. (1994). Psychotherapy for children and adolescents. In A. E. Bergin & S. L. Garfield (Eds.), *Handbook of psychotherapy and behavior change,* 4th ed. (pp. 543–594). New York: Wiley.

Kazdin, A. E. (2000). *Psychotherapy for children and adolescents: Directions for research and practice.* New York: Oxford University Press.

Kazdin, A. E. (2002). Psychosocial treatments for conduct disorder in children and adolescents. In P. E. Nathan & J. M. Gorman (Eds.), *A guide to treatments that work,* 2nd ed. (pp. 57–85). New York: Oxford University Press.

Kazdin, A. E. (2003). Problem-solving skills training and parent management training for conduct disorder. In A. E. Kazdin & J. R. Weisz (Eds.), *Evidence-based psychotherapies for children and adolescents* (pp. 241–262). New York: Guilford.

Kazdin, A. E. (2004). Psychotherapy for children and adolescents. In M. J. Lambert (Ed.), *Bergin and Garfield's handbook of psychotherapy and behavior change,* 5th ed. (pp. 543–589). New York: Wiley.

Kazdin, A. E., Esveldt-Dawson, K., French, N. H., & Unis, A. S. (1987a). Effect of parent management training and problem-solving skills training combined in the treatment of antisocial child behavior. *Journal of the American Academy of Child and Adolescent Psychiatry, 26,* 416–424.

Kazdin, A. E., Esveldt-Dawson, K., French, N. H., & Unis, A. S. (1987b). Problem-solving skills training and relationship therapy in the treatment of antisocial child behavior. *Journal of Consulting and Clinical Psychology, 55,* 76–85.

Kazdin, A. E., Siegel, T. C., & Bass, D. (1992). Cognitive problem-solving skills training and parent management training in the treatment of antisocial behavior in children. *Journal of Consulting and Clinical Psychology, 60,* 733–747.

Kronenberger, W. S., & Meyer, R. G. (2001). *The child clinician's handbook,* 2nd ed. Needham Heights, MA: Allyn & Bacon.

Little, E., & Hudson, A. (1998). Conduct problems and treatment across home and school: A review of the literature. *Behavior Change, 15,* 213–227.

Lochman, J. E., Burch, P. R., Curry, J. F., & Lampron, L. B. (1984). Treatment and generalization effects of cognitive-behavioral and goal-setting interventions with aggressive boys. *Journal of Consulting and Clinical Psychology, 52,* 915–916.

Lochman, J. E., Lampron, L. B., Gemmer, T. C., & Harris, S. R. (1989). Teacher consultation and cognitive-behavioral interventions with aggressive boys. *Psychology in the Schools, 26,* 179–188.

McNeil, C. B., Eyberg, S., Eisenstadt, T. H., Newcomb, K., & Funderburk, B. W. (1991). Parent-child interaction therapy with behavior problem children: Generalization of treatment effects to the school setting. *Journal of Clinical Child Psychology, 20,* 140–151.

Nock, M. K., & Kazdin, A. E. (2005). Randomized controlled trial of a brief intervention for increasing participation in parent management training. *Journal of Consulting and Clinical Psychology, 73*(5), 872–879.

Patterson, G. R., & Gullion, M. E. (1968). *Living with children: New methods for parents and teachers.* Champaign, IL: Research Press.

Peed, S., Roberts, M., & Forehand, R. (1977). Evaluation of the effectiveness of a standardized parent training program in altering the interaction of mothers and their noncompliant children. *Behavior Modification, 1,* 323–350.

Reid, M. J., Webster-Stratton, C., & Baydar, N. (2004). Halting the development of conduct problems in Head Start children: The effects of parent training. *Journal of Clinical Child and Adolescent Psychology, 33*(2), 279–291.

Reid, M. J., Webster-Stratton, C., & Hammond, M. (2003). Follow-up of children who received the incredible years intervention for oppositional defi-

ant disorder: Maintenance and prediction of 2-year outcome. *Behavior Therapy, 34*(4), 471–491.

Rosen, A., & Proctor, E. K. (2002). Standards for evidence-based social work practice: The role of replicable and appropriate interventions, outcomes, and practice guidelines. In A. R. Roberts & G. J. Greene (Eds.), *Social workers' desk reference* (pp. 743–747). New York: Oxford University Press.

Scahill, L., Sukhodolsky, D. G., Bearss, K., Findley, D., Hamrin, V., Carroll, D. H., et al. (2006). Randomized trial of parent management training in children with tic disorders and disruptive behavior. *Journal of Child Neurology, 21*(8), 650–656.

Schlichter, K. J., & Horan, J. J. (1981). Effects of stress inoculation on the anger and aggression management skills of institutionalized juvenile delinquents. *Cognitive Therapy and Research, 5,* 359–365.

Sells, S. P. (1998). *Treating the tough adolescent: A family-based, step-by-step guide.* New York: Guilford.

Serketich, W. J., & Dumas, J. E. (1996). The effectiveness of behavioral parent training to modify antisocial behavior in children: A meta analysis. *Behavior Therapy, 27,* 171–186.

Spaccarelli, S., Cotler, S., & Penman, D. (1992). Problem-solving skills training as a supplement to behavioral parent training. *Cognitive Therapy and Research, 16,* 1–18.

Springer, D. W. (2002). Assessment protocols and rapid assessment instruments with troubled adolescents. In A. R. Roberts & G. J. Greene (Eds.), *Social workers' desk reference* (pp. 217–221). New York: Oxford University Press.

Tremblay, R. E., Pagani-Kurtz, L., Masse, L. C., Vitaro, F., & Phil, R. (1995). A bimodal preventive intervention for disruptive kindergarten boys: Its impact through mid-adolescence. *Journal of Consulting and Clinical Psychology, 63,* 560–568.

U.S. Department of Health and Human Services. (2001). *Youth violence: A report of the Surgeon General.* Rockville, MD: DHHS.

Vitaro, F., & Tremblay, R. E. (1994). Impact of a prevention program on aggressive children's friendships and social adjustment. *Journal of Abnormal Child Psychology, 22,* 457–475.

Webster-Stratton, C. (1984). Randomized trial of two parent-training programs for families with conduct-disordered children. *Journal of Consulting and Clinical Psychology, 52,* 666–678.

Webster-Stratton, C. (1990). Enhancing the effectiveness of self-administered videotape parent training for families with conduct-problem children. *Journal of Abnormal Child Psychology, 18,* 479–492.

Webster-Stratton, C. (1994). Advancing videotape parent training: A comparison study. *Journal of Consulting and Clinical Psychology, 62,* 583–593.

Webster-Stratton, C. (1998). Preventing conduct problems in Head Start children: Strengthening parenting competencies. *Journal of Consulting and Clinical Psychology, 66*(5), 715–730.

Webster-Stratton, C., & Hammond, M. (1997). Treating children with early-onset conduct problems: A comparison of child and parent training interventions. *Journal of Consulting and Clinical Psychology, 65*(1), 93–109.

Webster-Stratton, C., Kolpacoff, M., & Hollinsworth, T. (1988). Self-administered videotape therapy for families with conduct-problem children: Comparison with two cost effective treatments and a control group. *Journal of Consulting and Clinical Psychology, 56,* 558–566.

Webster-Stratton, C., & Reid, M. J. (2003a). Treating conduct problems and strengthening social emotional competence in young children (ages 4–8 years): The Dina Dinosaur treatment program. *Journal of Emotional and Behavioral Disorders, 11*(3), 130–143.

Webster-Stratton, C., & Reid, M. J. (2003b). The incredible years parents, teachers, and children training series: A multifaceted treatment approach for young children with conduct problems. In A. E. Kazdin & J. R. Weisz (Eds.), *Evidence-based psychotherapies for children and adolescents* (pp. 224–240). New York: Guilford.

Webster-Stratton, C., Reid, M. J., & Hammond, M. (2001). Social skills and problem solving training for children with early-onset conduct problems: Who benefits? *Journal of Child Psychology and Psychiatry, 42*(7), 943–952.

Webster-Stratton, C., Reid, M. J., & Hammond, M. (2004). Treating children with early onset conduct problems: Intervention outcomes for parent, child, and teacher training. *Journal of Clinical Child and Adolescent Psychology, 33*(1), 105–124.

Wells, K. C., & Egan, J. (1988). Social learning and systems family therapy for childhood oppositional disorder: Comparative treatment outcome. *Comprehensive Psychiatry, 29,* 138–146.

Wiltz, N. A., & Patterson, G. R. (1974). An evaluation of parent training procedures designed to alter inappropriate aggressive behavior of boys. *Behavior Therapy, 5,* 215–221.

Zangwill, W. M. (1983). An evaluation of a parent training program. *Child and Family Behavior Therapy, 5,* 1–6.

149 Solution-Focused Brief Therapy Interventions for Students at Risk to Drop Out

Cynthia Franklin, Johnny S. Kim, & Michael S. Kelly

The application of solution-focused-brief therapy (SFBT) with students in school settings has grown over the past 10–12 years. The literature indicates that solution-focused brief therapy has been applied in school settings to a number of problems including student behavioral and emotional issues, academic problems, social skills, and dropout prevention (Berg & Shilts, 2005; Franklin, Biever, Moore, Clemons, & Scamardo, 2001; Franklin & Hopson, in press; Franklin, Streeter, Kim, & Tripodi, 2007, cited in Kim & Franklin, under review; Kral, 1995; Metcalf, 1995; Murphy, 1996; Murphy & Duncan, 2007; Sklare, 1997; Webb, 1999). Because of its brief nature and flexibility in working with diverse problems, SFBT can be a practical intervention approach for school social workers to use (Franklin et al., 2001; Kelly, Kim, & Franklin, 2008; Newsome, 2004). This chapter describes SFBT and its growing research evidence, and further illustrates the steps and techniques involved in implementing this approach.

SOLUTION-FOCUSED BRIEF THERAPY

Solution-Focused Brief Therapy is different in many ways from traditional approaches to treatment. It is a competency-based model, which minimizes emphasis on past failings and problems, and instead focuses on clients' strengths and previous successes. There is a focus on working from the client's understandings of her/his concern/situation and what the client might want different. The basic tenets that inform Solution-Focus Brief Therapy are as follows:

- It is based on solution-building rather than problem-solving.
- The therapeutic focus should be on the client's desired future rather than on past problems or current conflicts.
- Clients are encouraged to increase the frequency of current useful behaviors.
- No problem happens all the time. There are exceptions—that is, times when the problem could have happened but didn't—that can be used by the client and therapist to co-construct solutions.
- Therapists help clients find alternatives to current undesired patterns of behavior, cognition and interaction that are within the clients' repertoire or can be co-constructed by therapists and clients as such.
- Differing from skill-building and behavior therapy interventions, the model assumes that solution behaviors already exist for clients.
- It is asserted that small increments of change lead to large increments of change.
- Clients' solutions are not necessarily *directly* related to any identified problem by either the client or the therapist.
- The conversational skills required of the therapist to invite the client to build solutions are different from those needed to diagnose and treat client problems. (T. Trepper, E. McCollum, H. Korman, W. Gingerich, & C. Franklin. [2007]. *Solution focused therapy treatment manual for working with individuals*. Unpublished manuscript, Research Committee of the Solution Focused Brief Therapy Association, p. 1)

The development of SFBT originated in the early 1980s at the Brief Family Therapy Center in Milwaukee with two social work practitioners, Steve de Shazer and Insoo Kim Berg, and a group of practitioner/researchers who were studying therapies behind a one-way mirror. Some important researchers were involved in the early study of this approach, such as Wally Gingerich, who also did the first systematic review of SFBT research (Gingerich & Eisengart, 2000). Berg and de Shazer wanted to answer the question, "What works in therapy?" These practitioners were interested not only in the change process but also how to help clients change efficiently and effectively. SFBT was influenced by the Mental Research Institute Brief Therapy model and the family systems therapy approaches of the day and had theoretical roots with ecosystems theories. Later, in the 1990s, SFBT became strongly associated with social construction models and social constructivist views within family systems therapies. Readers are referred to other chapters in this volume that review brief therapy, family systems, and constructivist theoretical perspectives and practice approaches in more detail.

SFBT became popular and widely used in mental health practice the 1990s mostly due to the demands for briefer counseling interventions. SFBT has grown exponentially since that time. A recent database search revealed that there are 50 books in print on SFBT, SFBT associations in over 10 countries, and several annual national and international conferences devoted to SFBT (Kelly et al., 2008).

SFBT's Emergence in Schools

Practitioners began to use the SFBT techniques in schools during the 1990s with the first publications and small research studies appearing in print around the mid-1990s (e.g., Kral, 1995; LaFountain & Garner, 1996; Metcalf, 1995; Murphy, 1996; Sklare, 1997). Since that time, the SFBT literature for school practitioners across disciplines has been growing (e.g., Berg & Shilts, 2005; Franklin & Gerlach, 2007; Kelly et al., 2008; Metcalf, 2008; Murphy, 2008; Murphy & Duncan, 2007; Webb, 1999) with increasing reports of SFBT interventions and programs being implemented in schools in both the United States and Europe (Kelly et al., 2008).

School-based interventions may be implemented at different levels of the school's programs and with different groups within the school environ-ment. For example, the techniques of SFBT have been used to:

- help at-risk students in individual, group, and family interventions (Murphy, 2008);
- coach teachers in using solution-building talk (see the WWOW program, Kelly et al., 2008);
- change interactions between parents, teachers, and students, such as parent/teacher meetings (Metcalf, 1995, 2008); and
- change the school culture, such as when an entire school adopts the solution-focused change philosophy and trains all staff (including teachers and principals) in SFBT techniques (Franklin & Streeter, 2003, cited in Kelly et al., 2008).

Franklin and Gerlach (2007) summarize reasons why SFBT may be a good match for public school settings. First, public schools frequently serve high-risk populations, such as homeless teens, immigrants, and teen parents. Many students referred for services in the school may also be considered mandated or involuntary clients, and SFBT is an approach to helping that was developed for the purposes of being effective with at-risk populations. Second, schools often face students with multiple challenges, yet have little time or money for therapy and require very practical solutions to the day-to-day issues that may prevent the educational achievement of a student. SFBT focuses on practical goals using active listening and strengths assessment and facilitates collaboration with others involved in the student's life. Finally, SFBT is very flexible and open to the use of techniques from other therapeutic interventions if they are used thoughtfully to accommodate the student's goals (Franklin & Gerlach, 2007).

THE GROWING EMPIRICAL SUPPORT FOR SFBT IN SCHOOLS

Kim and Franklin (under review) recently reviewed the literature on SFBT in schools. This systematic review only included the most rigorous studies that used experimental designs, with standardized measures, and met criteria for a solution-focused intervention. Table 149.1 summarizes the results of that review.

Table 149.1 indicates that one experimental design study, six quasi-experimental design studies, and one single-case design study on SFBT in

TABLE 149.1 SFBT Studies in Schools

Study	Design	Outcome Measure	Sample Size	Sample Population	Results
Springer, Lynch, Rubin (2000)	Quasi-experimental	Hare Self-Esteem Scale	10	Hispanic Elementary students	SFBT group made significant improvements on the Hare Self-Esteem Scale, whereas the comparison group's scores remained the same. However, no significant differences were found between the SFBT and comparison groups at the end of the study on the self-esteem scale.
Franklin et al. (2001)	Single case	Conners' Teacher Rating Scale	7	Middle school students 10–12 years old	Five of seven (71 percent) improved per teachers report.
Newsome (2004)	Quasi-experimental	Grades; attendance	52	Middle school students	Statistically significant results with SFBT group increasing mean score of 1.58 to a mean score of 1.69 while grades for the comparison group decreased from a mean score of 1.66 to a score of 1.48. No difference on attendance measure.
Corcoran (2006)	Quasi-experimental	Conners' Parent Rating Scale; Feelings, Attitudes, & Behaviors Scale for Children	86	Students aged 5–17	No significant differences between groups with both improving at posttest. This lack of difference may be because the comparison group received treatment as usual, which had many cognitive-behavior therapy components that have been empirically validated.

| Franklin, Moore, & Hopson (2008) | Quasi-experimental | Child Behavior Checklist (CBCL)—Youth Self Report Form—Internalizing, & CBCL Externalizing; Teacher's Report Form—Internalizing & Externalizing Score | 67 | Middle school students | Internalizing & Externalizing score for the Teacher Report Form showed SFBT group declined below clinical level by posttest and remained there at follow-up while comparison group changed little. Internalizing score for the Youth Self Report Form showed no difference between the groups. Externalizing score showed SFBT group dropped below the clinical level and continued to drop at follow-up. |
| Franklin, Streeter, Kim, & Tripodi (2007) | Quasi-experimental | Grades; attendance | 85 | At-risk high school students | SFBT sample had statistically significant higher average proportion of credits earned to credits attempted than the comparison sample. Both groups decreased in the attendance mean per semester; however, the comparison group showed a higher proportion of school days attended to school days for the semester. Authors suggested that the attendance between groups may not be a fair comparison because SFBT group worked on a self-paced curriculum and could decrease their attendance when completed. |

Continued

TABLE 149.1 SFBT Studies in Schools (*continued*)

Study	Design	Outcome Measure	Sample Size	Sample Population	Results
Froeschle, Smith, & Ricard (2007)	Experimental design	American Drug & Alcohol Survey Substance Abuse; Subtle Screening Inventory Adolescent version 2; Knowledge exam on physical symptoms of drug use; Piers-Harris Children's Self-Concept Scale version 2; Home & Community Social Behavior Scales; School Social Behavior Scales 2nd ed.; grade point average	65	8th grade females	Statistically significant differences were found favoring SFBT group on drug use, attitudes toward drugs, knowledge of physical symptoms of drug use, and competent behavior scores as observed by both parents and teachers. No group differences were found on self-esteem, negative behaviors as measured by office referrals, and grade point averages.

Source: From Kelly, Kim, & Franklin, 2008. Adapted with permission of the authors.

schools have been published since 2000. Most of these studies have arrived within the past 2 years, perhaps suggesting that more school researchers are conducting outcome studies on SFBT.

Kim and Franklin's (under review) review indicates that SFBT is a promising and useful approach in working with at-risk students in a school setting. Some of the positive findings from the systematic review are as follows:

- helps students reach goals;
- helps students alleviate their concerns;
- improves academic achievement (e.g., credits earned);
- helps students reduce the intensity of their negative feelings;
- helps students reduce drug use; and
- helps students manage their conduct problems (Franklin et al., 2001; Franklin & Gerlach, 2007; Froeschle, Smith, & Ricard, 2007; Kelly et al., 2008; Newsome, 2004).

There were some mixed results found in the Kim and Franklin (under review) systematic review, but enough positive differences were found favoring SFBT to view it as a promising intervention for school settings. The effect sizes calculated by the authors and reported in the individual studies also show SFBT to be promising, with most studies having medium and some large effect sizes.

SOLUTION-BUILDING HELPING PROCESS AND TECHNIQUES

SFBT is a strengths-based approach that helps school social workers build solutions with their students. The solution-focused helping process, often referred to as solution building, is a purposeful conversation resulting in changes in perceptions and social interactions. The solution-building process or conversation is often contrasted to the problem-solving process. However, Harris and Franklin (2008) have pointed out that it shares values and some similarities with social problem solving and task-centered types of problem solving. The differences, however, are also noteworthy. Approaches to problem solving, for example, focus on the resolution of problems through understanding the problems, enumerating alternatives that can solve the problems, and choosing an alternative. In contrast, solution building changes the way people think about presenting problems and identify future behaviors and tasks that have the potential to accomplish desired goals and outcomes (De Jong & Berg, 2008). SFBT has developed a number of techniques that are used in solution building to guide students in the change process. Box 149.1 defines and illustrates several of the counseling techniques.

SFBT has developed its own structure for social work interviews that is used to guide the change process. The session may be thought of as being a continuous process of elements that are structured in process sequences. De Jong (Chapter 33) defines this structure of the solution-focused interview and the follow-up sessions. Thinking of student interview in this way may help the school social worker guide the client toward a purposeful solution-building conversation and offer a framework for how to apply the various techniques of the solution-focused approach. See Table 149.2 for a quick guide concerning conversations using the SFBT session structure including ways to use various solution-focused techniques in the change process.

An SFBT session structure must be flexible enough to adapt to the individual needs of each student but also structured enough to provide guidance to school social workers about the change process.

CASE STUDY

Franklin, Kim, and Tripodi (2006) suggest that most solution-focused interviews occur during the traditional 50-minute session. In schools, however, these interviews may last for shorter periods of time, 20–30 minutes, for example. Regardless of the time, the structure of SFBT interview may be divided into three parts. The first part usually is spent making small talk with the student to find out a little bit about his or her life. During this first part, the school social worker may be looking to understand the student's interests, motivations, competencies, and belief systems. The following case example provided by Franklin et al. (2006) illustrates the structure of a solution-focused session in schools and several techniques.

Social Worker: Hello, Charles. I understand your teacher, Mrs. Park, sent you here to see me because you're at risk of failing out of school. But I'd like to hear from you the reason you are here to see me and how this can help you? [Allows student to state what the problem is]

Box 149.1 SFBT Techniques for Solution-Focused Schools.

Exception Questions- Questions to explore past experiences in a student's life when the student's problem might reasonably have been expected to occur but somehow did not or was less severe.

- *"When does the problem not occur?"*
- *"What was different about those times when things were better between you and your teacher?"*
- *"Even though this is a very bad time, in my experience, people's lives do not always stay the same. I will bet that there are times when the problem of being sent to the principal's office is not happening, or at least is happening less. Please describe those times. What is different? How did you get that to happen?"*

Relationship Questions- Relationship questions allow the student to discuss their problems from a third person point of view. This sequence of questions makes the problem less threatening and allows the school social worker, counselor or teacher, to assess the student's viewpoints, and the student to practice thinking about the problem from the viewpoint of others.

- *"What would your teacher say about your grades?"*
- *"What would your mother say?"*
- *"If you were to do something that made your teacher very happy, what would that be?"*

Scaling Questions- Scaling questions are a sequence of questions used to determine where students are in terms of achieving their goals. The school social worker has the option to use scaling questions to quantify and measure the intensity of internal thoughts and feelings along with helping the student anchor reality and move forward from their goals (Franklin & Nurius, 1998; Pichot & Dolon, 2003). Many different variations of this technique can be used such as asking for percentages of progress, or using smiling and frowning faces for small children.

- *On a scale from one to ten, with one being the lowest and ten being the highest, where would you rate yourself in terms of reaching your goals that you identified last week?*
- *On a scale from one to ten, with one being that you never go to class and ten being that you have perfect attendance, where would you put yourself on that scale? What would it take to move up two numbers on the scale?*
- *On a scale of 1-10 with one being that you are getting into trouble every day in the class and ten being that you are doing all your school work and not getting into trouble, where would you be on that scale?*

The Miracle Question- The miracle question strengthens the student's goals by allowing them to reconstruct their story, imagining a future without the student's perceived problem (Berg & De Jong, 1996; De Jong & Berg, 2001). Additionally, the school social worker uses the miracle question to help students identify ways that the solution may already be occurring in their life.

Now, I want to ask you a strange question. This is probably a question no one has asked you before. Suppose that while you are sleeping tonight a miracle happens the problem that brought you here is solved. However, because you are sleeping, you don't know that the miracle has happened. So, when you wake up tomorrow morning, what will be the first thing that you notice that is different that will tell you a miracle has happened and the problem which brought you here is solved?

Goal Setting/Goaling- Goal Setting is used as a verb in SFBT, sometimes referred to in the literature as "goaling." Goals are considered the beginning of behavior change, not the end. The school social worker and the student negotiate small, observable goals, set within a brief timeframe, that lead to a new story for the student. A goal should describe what a student is to do instead of the problem behavior. The negotiation of goals should start immediately between the school social worker and student.

Break For Reflection- Taken near the end of the session to help formulate a positive ending to the session.

Compliments And A Set Of Take Away Tasks- Continuous affirmation of the student's strengths and character and suggested behavioral tasks that reinforce client solutions.

You did that?
I am amazed.
How did that make you feel?
I bet your mother was pretty proud of you?
That seemed to work! Do you think you could do that again?

Source: From Franklin, Kim, & Tripodi, 2006.

Student: I don't know. I hate this school and I just want to drop out so that people will leave me alone.

SW: So if I'm understanding you correctly, you're here to see me because you hate the school and a lot of people—your teachers and maybe your parents—have been bugging you about your grades and doing homework?

S: Yeah.

SW: So what sorts of things do you like to do when you're not in school?

S: Ummm, I like to hang out with my friends.

SW: What do you and your friends talk about when you're hanging out?

S: I don't know. We talk about basketball and music and stuff. [social worker will continue to develop rapport and try to find out student's interests and belief systems]

The second part of the session, which takes up the bulk of the time—around 40 minutes in traditional sessions but maybe shorter in school interviews—is spent discussing the problem, looking for exceptions, and formulating goals. One of the key components to SFBT that has been emphasized in this chapter is working with the student to identify the problem, look for times when the problem is absent, look for ways the solution is already occurring, and develop attainable goals to help resolve the problem. This second part is usually initiated with questions like, "How can I help you?" or "What is the reason you have come to see me?" or "How will you know when counseling is no longer necessary?" (Sklare, 1997).

SW: Okay, so how can I help you or what can you get out of our meeting today so that you know it's been worth your time to see me?

S: I want my teachers and my parents to stop bugging me about my grades and doing homework. This school is just a waste of my time, and my classes are stupid.

SW: Is there a class that you didn't think was stupid or a waste of time? [example of looking for exceptions]

S: My English class last year was cool because we got to read some interesting books and have good discussions about them.

SW: What made the books interesting and the discussions good?

S: Well, they were books that I could understand and relate to. My teacher also made the time and effort to explain things to us and made sure we all got a turn to speak our thoughts.

SW: You said you hated this school, but yet you haven't dropped out yet. How have you managed to do that? [allows student to identify possible solutions and possible successes to what they've already been doing]

S: Well, I'm still going to some of my classes, but at this point I just don't care anymore.

SW: Charles, for those classes that you do attend, what would your teacher say about your academic work? [example of relationship question]

S: I guess they might say that I don't pay attention in class, that I don't do my homework, and that I'm not trying.

TABLE 149.2 Structure of SFBT Interviews

	Begin Session →	Exploring Solutions →	Assessing Progress →	Reflection Break →	End Session
Goals of the stage	• Rapport building • Shift focus away from problem talk • Support student	• School social worker and student build solutions together; • Have student take responsibility for own solutions; • Discussion is on possible solutions in concrete behavioral details	• Continue to provide compliments • Create small, attainable, concrete goals • Explore steps to achieving the goals	• Continue supporting student • Reflect on student's strengths and resources • Identify future steps	• Assess whether to schedule another appointment; • Lay groundwork for future sessions.
Questions to ask	*How can I help you?* *What has to happen while talking with me today that will make it worth your time to come?*	*What kinds of things have you done in the past that have worked for you?* *What would be different about the problem in your life?* *When is the problem better? Even a little bit?*	*What would your parents say about your progress?* *Who would be the most surprised if you did well on that test?* *What would your friends say is the biggest change they've noticed in you?*	*I'd like to take a minute to think about what we've discussed. Would that be all right with you?*	*Has this been helpful?* *What has been helpful for you about our meeting?* *Would you like to meet again?*
Keys points to remember and SFBT techniques	• Use student's words and metaphors • Focus on student's definition of the problem	• Use exception questions • Use miracle question to elicit details of student's goals • Focus on strengths	• Elicit incidents of small changes Students have made • Use scaling questions • Use relationship questions	• Formulate 4–5 genuine compliments for student • Formulate tasks towards the solution • Formulate possible homework assignment.	• Client and school social worker both determine whether to meet again

SW: Do you agree with that?

S: I guess, but it's just that the classes are so stupid and boring.

SW: I'd like to ask you an unusual question. It's probably something no one has ever asked you before. Suppose, after we're done and you leave my office, you go to bed tonight and a miracle happens. This miracle solves all the problems that brought you here today but because you were sleeping, you didn't know it occurred. So the next morning you wake up and you sense something is different. What will you notice that is different that lets you know this miracle occurred and your problems are solved? [example of the miracle question]

S: I guess I wouldn't be cutting class and maybe getting better grades.

SW: What will you be doing differently to get better grades?

S: I would probably be better prepared for class.

SW: What does being better prepared for class look like? [continue to probe and elicit more details and examples]

S: I'd pay attention in class and take some notes.
SW: What else will you be doing differently when you're getting better grades?

S: Probably doing my homework and not causing trouble in class with the teacher.

SW: So, what will you being doing instead of causing trouble in class?

S: Listen and sit there and take notes, I guess.
SW: So on a scale from 1 to 10, with 1 being "I'm dropping out of school no matter what" and 10 being "the miracle solved my problems and I'm going to graduate," where would you say you are right now? [example of a scaling question]

S: Three.

SW: What sorts of things prevent you from giving it a 2 or a 1?

S: Well, I know I need to get my high school diploma because I always thought I might go study how to be a med tech at college. I like *CSI* and want to work in forensics.

SW: Wow! You want to study forensics. So, you need to finish school for that. So, what would need to happen for you to be a 4 or a 5?

S: I'd need to start coming to classes and doing my work. [examples of student identifying goals

and solutions. Social worker would continue looking for solutions that are already occurring in Charles's life and collaborate on identifying and setting small, attainable goals]

The final part of the session lasts around 5–10 minutes. It involves giving the student a set of compliments, homework, and determining whether to continue discussing this topic at another time. In school settings, practitioners such as teachers and social workers have separated this last part from the rest of the conversation. The break, for example, might be extended, and the conversation might pick up in different class periods or at a different times of the day (e.g., before and after lunch).

SW: I'd like to take a minute to write down some notes based on what we've talked about. Is there anything else you feel I should know before I take this quick break?

S: No.

SW: [after taking a break] Well Charles, I'd like to compliment you on your commitment to staying in school despite your frustrations. You seem like a bright student and understand the importance of finishing high school. I'd like to meet with you again to continue our work together. Would that be all right with you?

S: Sure.

SW: So for next week, I'd like you to try and notice when things are going a little bit better in your classes and what you're doing differently during those times.

FUTURE APPLICATIONS

SFBT has been used in schools since the 1990s, and promising empirical support is emerging on this approach. SFBT is a practical, brief intervention for school settings and can help school social workers engage and work with students on diverse problem areas. This approach builds on student strengths and competencies and shows respect for each person. SFBT offers conversational, questioning techniques that help school social workers engage students in a solution-building process that helps students discover goals, tasks and behaviors that change future outcomes. The future is what SFBT focuses on, and this future focus is perhaps one of its distinguishing characteristics. When applying SFBT, a school social worker must act as a coach and a facilitator that creates an interpersonal context where the solutions emerge from the student. As the case example illustrated, SFBT offers an interview structure and a set of counseling techniques that help social workers successfully facilitate the solution-building process in schools.

WEB SITES

Garza High School, A Solution-Focused High School. http://www.austinschools.org/garza.

Solution-Focused Brief Therapy Association. http://www.sfbta.org.

References

Berg, I. K., & De Jong, P. (1996). Solution-building conversation: Co-constructing a sense of competence with clients. *Families in Society, 77,* 376–391.

Berg, I. K., & Shilts, L. (2005). *Classroom solutions: Woww approach.* Milwaukee, WI: Brief Family Therapy Center.

Corcoran, J. (2006). A comparison group study of solution-focused therapy versus "treatment-as-usual" for behavior problems in children. *Journal of Social Service Research, 33,* 69–81.

De Jong, P., & Berg, I. K. (2001). Co-constructing co-operation with mandated clients. *Social Work, 46,* 361–381.

De Jong, P., & Berg, I. K. (2008). *Interviewing for solutions,* 3rd ed. Pacific Grove: Brooks/Cole.

Franklin, C., Biever, J., Moore, K., Clemons, D., & Scamardo, M. (2001). The effectiveness of solution-focused therapy with children in a school setting. *Research on Social Work Practice, 11,* 411–434.

Franklin, C., & Gerlach, B. (2007). Solution-focused brief therapy in public school settings. In T. S. Nelson & F. N. Thomas (Eds.), *Handbook of solution-focused therapy: Clinical Applications* (p. 169). New York: Haworth.

Franklin, C., & Hopson, L. (In press). Involuntary clients in public schools: Solution-focused interventions. In R. Rooney (Ed.), *Strategies for work with involuntary clients,* 2nd ed. New York: Columbia University Press.

Franklin, C., Kim, J. S., & Tripodi, S. J. (2006). Solution-focused brief therapy interventions for students at-risk to dropout. In C. Franklin, M. B. Harris, & P. Allen-Meares (pp. 691–704). *The school services sourcebook.* New York: Oxford University Press.

Franklin, C., Moore, K., & Hopson, L. M. (2008). Effectiveness of solution-focused brief therapy in a school setting. *Children and Schools, 30,* 15–26.

Franklin, C., & Nurius, P. (1998). Distinction between social constructionism and cognitive constructivism: Practice applications. In C. Franklin & P. Nurius (Eds.), *Constructivism in practice: Methods and challenges* (pp. 57–94). Milwaukee, WI: Families International.

Franklin, C., & Streeter, C. L. (2003). *Creating solution-focused accountability schools for the 2st century: A training manual for Garza High School.* Austin: University of Texas, Hogg Foundation for Mental Health.

Franklin, C., Streeter, C. L., Kim, J. S., & Tripodi, S. J. (2007). The effectiveness of a solution-focused, public alternative school for dropout prevention and retrieval. *Children and Schools, 29*(3), 133–144. In Kim, J. S., & Franklin, C. (Under review). Solution focused brief therapy in schools: A review of the literature. *Psychotherapy Theory, Research, Practice, and Training.*

Froeschle, J. G., Smith, R. L., & Ricard, R. (2007). The efficacy of a systematic substance abuse program for adolescent females. *Professional School Counseling, 10,* 498–505.

Gingerich, W., & Eisengart, S. (2000). Solution-focused brief therapy: A review of outcome research. *Family Process, 39,* 477–496.

Harris, M.B., & Franklin, C. (2008). *Taking charge: A school-based life skills program for adolescent mothers.* New York: Oxford University Press.

Kelly, M. S., Kim, J. S., & Franklin, C. (2008). *Solution-focused brief therapy in schools: A 360-degree view of the research and practice principles.* New York: Oxford University Press.

Kim, J. S., & Franklin, C. (Under review). Solution-focused brief therapy in schools: A review of the literature. *Psychotherapy Theory, Research, Practice, and Training.*

Kral, R. (1995). *Strategies that work: Techniques for solutions in schools.* Milwaukee, WI: Brief Family Therapy Press.

LaFountain, R. M., & Garner, N. E. (1996). Solution-focused counseling groups: The results are in. *Journal for Specialists in Group Work, 21,* 128–143.

Metcalf, L. (1995). *Counseling toward solutions: A practical solution-focused program for working with students, teachers, and parents.* San Francisco: Jossey-Bass.

Metcalf, L. (2008). *Counseling toward solutions: A practical solution-focused program for working with students, teachers, and parents,* 2nd ed. San Francisco: Jossey-Bass.

Murphy, J. (1996). Solution-focused brief therapy in the school. In S. Miller, M. Hubble, & B. Duncan (Eds.), *Handbook of solution-focused brief therapy* (pp. 184–204). San Francisco: Jossey-Bass.

Murphy, J. J. (2008). *Solution-focused counseling in schools,* 2nd ed. Alexandria, VA: American Counseling Association.

Murphy, J. J., & Duncan, B. L. (2007). *Brief intervention for school problems,* 2nd ed. New York: Guilford.

Newsome, S. (2004). Solution-focused brief therapy (SFBT) groupwork with at-risk junior high school students: Enhancing the bottom-line. *Research on Social Work Practice, 14,* 336–343.

Pichot, T., & Dolan, Y. (2003). *Solution-focused brief therapy: It's effective use in agency settings.* Binghampton, NY: Hawthorne.

Sklare, G. (1997). *Brief counseling that works: A solution-focused approach for school counselors* (pp. 43–64). Thousand Oaks, CA: Corwin Press, Sage.

Springer, D., Lynch, C., & Rubin, A. (2000). Effects of a solution-focused mutual aid group for Hispanic children of incarcerated parents. *Child and Adolescent Social Work Journal, 17,* 431–442.

Webb, W. H. (1999). *Solutioning: Solution-focused interventions for counselors.* Philadelphia: Accelerated Press.

150

Case Management Interventions with Immigrant and Refugee Students and Families

Rowena Fong, Marilyn Armour,
Noël Busch-Armendariz, & Laurie Cook Heffron

Immigrant and refugee children and youth, because they have different migration journeys and statuses that impact their adjustments and acculturation experiences once they arrive in the United States, experience different problems and have common but also distinctive needs. It is important that school social workers become equipped and use case management skills in working with immigrant and refugee students and their families because of the complexities of their problems and the interrelatedness between the students and their families.

The United States has always been a multicultural society, but refugee and immigrant students are increasing in numbers and creating more complexities. Delgado, Jones, and Rohani (2005) report,

Almost 10 percent of all newcomers are under the age of 18 years, compared to the average 28.3 years for U.S. citizens . . . . Since 1990 the number of immigrant families has increased seven times faster than the corresponding number of native-born families. . . . One out of every five youth had one foreign born parent in 1995. (p. 20)

Many immigrant and refugee children and youth have to make adjustments that most students in the United States don't confront. Some foreign-born students overcome language and cultural barriers with apparent ease. Many more, however, endure very stressful transitions to the United States (Fong, 2004a). Difficulties in transition are due to problems that may even include experiences of torture, rape, and abandonment, which carry over into the classroom environments.

School social workers have the challenge of addressing these problems because they interfere with academic learning and performance. In working with immigrant and refugee students, social workers need to manage multiple problems, including those affecting the student personally and those tangential to the students' family because of the interconnectedness between the student and the family. For example, an immigrant or refugee child or youth from a non–English-speaking family is frequently called on to act as interpreter. This role often interferes with the student's school functioning because of missed school days. Thus, the school social worker must address the family's need as it impacts the student's academic functioning. Special skills are required to manage the multiple needs of child and family simultaneously. These skills are often found in using case management as an intervention, an evidence-base practice frequently used in mental health settings with other populations.

Children of immigrant families, according to Suarez-Orozco and Suarez-Orozco (2001), "follow many different pathways; they forge complex and multiply determined identities that resist easy generalizations. Some do extremely well in their new country . . . others struggle to survive" (pp. 1–2). Though most refugee children may initially adjust with few problems, those whose families have experienced torture either in their home countries or their migration journeys are likely to manifest symptoms of post-traumatic stress disorder (PTSD) after resettlement. Although there are stories of valedictorians and National Merit finalists among immigrant and refugee children, these should not obscure the reality of other problems of school dropouts, substance abusers, and unwed teen mothers among the undocumented immigrant and refugee youth populations.

DIFFERENT STATUSES

It is important for school social workers to know the difference between immigrants and refugees and determine which status fits their foreign-born students. Understanding their status can help a social worker to understand the specific stresses with which students may be dealing. Because of the diversity within the two basic groups of immigrants and refugees, each status classification carries specific stressors that are likely to affect academic performance.

Immigrant populations differ from refugees in that they have the option of returning to their home countries, whereas refugees are forced to leave their home countries and settle elsewhere. Thus, an immigrant child or youth with legal documentation has adjustments to make because of struggles with acculturation and usually language

proficiency, but the student and his or her family can go back to the country of origin and resume normal life.

Undocumented immigrant youth, however, have entered the United States with their families without legal documentation. They leave their countries of origin looking for better economic opportunities and living conditions. Most of them encounter some difficulty during transition. Because of their temporary status, fears of exposure and deportation constantly produce anxiety.

Refugees are those children, youth, and families who are forced to leave their countries of origin because they have experienced human rights violations, fear for their lives and safety, and may have experienced torture. Asylum seekers are non-U.S. citizens who "enter the United States either on temporary visas or as undocumented entrants and who request and receive political asylum after arrival" (Foner, 2001, p. 36). For this group, the lengthy period of waiting to find out if they have been granted asylum in the United States causes a lot of stress even when the family is living here. Students frequently pick up on the parents' stressors and bring these anxieties into the school environment.

Unaccompanied refugee minors are another category of newcomers that social workers may find in the school setting. These children have come to the United States with their refugee parents, but the parents have been separated or killed in the process of transit. Legal guardians have to be established for these children, who are temporarily parentless, homeless, and rootless. In the case of some unaccompanied refugee minors, they are legally allowed to stay in the United States, but their parents have been deported.

In both immigrant and refugee populations, school social workers may find another foreign-born group of children and youth who are called the 1.5 generation. This group is between the first and second generation. They were born and raised in their home countries or in refugee camps, but arrived in the United States when they were still young enough to later forget their native tongue and traditional beliefs and customs. Delgado, Jones, and Rohani (2005) write of these children: "Although potentially able to successfully blend the best of both cultures, not all youth experience this as their reality." Describing his experience of the 1.5 generation, Ryu (1992, p. 50) writes of feeling anchored in neither culture. Though bilingual, he is also "bi-illiterate," although bicultural, he also feels "biculturally deprived" (p. 52).

These different statuses inform the school social workers of what kind of difficulties the immigrant and refugee children and youth have endured and are continuing to experience. Dropping out, truancy, language deficiencies, poor social skills, gang involvement, and academic failure may all be indicators of family stressors and difficulties in adjusting to the United States.

EVIDENCE-BASED INTERVENTIONS

Working with multicultural immigrant and refugee children requires both empirically validated and indigenous interventions that encompass both the student's school problems and the family's overall adjustment problems. Though several evidence-based interventions have been used with various ethnic groups of immigrant and refugee children and youth, most focus only on the child or youth and his or her school-related problems. The most commonly used evidence-based interventions are individual and group work with cognitive-behavioral therapy (CBT) as the primary treatment modality.

Congress and Lynn (1994) used group work in public schools to help immigrant children deal with feelings of loss, depression, and alienation. Kataoka et al. (2003) implemented an eight-session CBT group for third- through eighth-grade Latino immigrants suffering from trauma-related depression and PTSD. They found that those students who were in the intervention group had significantly greater improvement in PTSD. Though parents and teachers were eligible to receive support services and psychoeducation, there are no results reported and there is no indication that the child and family were treated simultaneously.

CASE MANAGEMENT SERVICES

An approach that focuses on the students' problems and the families' stressors simultaneously is needed in working with immigrant and refugee children and youth in schools. The usual pattern in the schools is to offer services only to students with services to families done outside of the school. In the case of immigrant and refugee students and families, an alternative model using case management services with a school social worker is important to consider because of the complexity and the interrelatedness of the child and family's problems. Some case management services have been in school-based health clinics where the school social workers coordinate care from outside social services. School social work and school-based mental health services have focused on evidence-based interventions with discussions among school psychologists focusing on the need for "more emphasis on public health, prevention, and improving how schools address youngsters who manifest problems" (Adelman & Taylor, 2002, p. 83).

Used in other disciplines, such as mental health, disability rehabilitation, family welfare, and services with older adults, the case manager has a role in multidisciplinary teams: "a case manager coordinates the team's plan and acts as the liaison between the client, the team, and provider of social services" (Dubois & Miley, 2005, p. 348), and "case management is appropriate when the clients' situation requires multiple services" (Dubois & Miley, 2005, p. 433). "Case management with individual clients has functions including outreach, assessment from multiple social agencies or departments, assessment, case planning, assessing resources, advocacy, monitoring, and evaluation" (Dubois & Miley, 2005, p. 435) and "case management coordinates the social services that children and families receive from multiple social agencies. . . . Multisystem children need services from multiple social agencies or departments" (Rose & Fatout, 2003, p. 158).

School social workers serving immigrant and refugee youth frequently encounter these multisystem students whose problems belong not only to the student but also to the student's family. Often family services must be involved, and the school social worker has to coordinate with them. School social workers need to handle the immigrant or refugee youth and his or her school problems through individualized education plans (IEPs) and team meetings with counselors, teachers, and other school personnel. This coordination of services is accomplished via case management skills. Case management is one of several interventions, including art, play, and narrative therapy, used effectively with immigrant and refugee children and families.

Though case management has been documented as an effective evidence-based practice intervention, its use still needs exploration because the procedure of comparing immigrants to nonimmigrants is very difficult, given the different contexts and special needs of the immigrant population. Case management skills for the school social worker needs to include working with the child, family, ethnic community, and the social service providers.

Case management is the "strategy for coordinating services and ensuring the accountability of service providers" (Dubois & Miley, 2005, p. 239). Case management strategies for clients with multiple needs requires the social worker to "appraise their needs, identify relevant services, develop comprehensive plans, advocate client's rights to services, and monitor the actual delivery of services" (Dubois & Miley, 2005, p. 239).

These five strategies are used as practice guidelines in case management:

- appraise client needs,
- identify relevant services,
- develop comprehensive plans,
- advocate client's rights to services, and
- monitor the actual delivery of services.

Appraising Needs

Appraising the needs of immigrant and refugee children and youth demands that the school social worker approach the assessment process from macro to micro levels of practice. The "Person-in-Family-in Community" model (Fong, 1997) helps school social workers organize their approach and the actual questions to be used with students. The assumption is that immigrant or refugee students are not alone and are part of their community as well as their family; thus, the school social worker must ask questions at the macro societal level and the mezzo family level. To find out what the student needs may also require questions about the students' home country and how those needs would manifest themselves there. See Figure 150.1 for more detailed questions to ask about the child, family, and ethnic community.

Identifying Relevant Services

To identify relevant services for immigrant and refugee students and families Chow (2001) suggests organizational assessment practice principles formulated under a "user profile" and a "service profile" (p. 216). The user profile is done to assess who will be using the services. The user can be a child or family system. The suggested questions to ask are the following.

- Who will be using the services?
- What is their ethnic background?
- What is their immigration history? When did they arrive in the United States?
- What is their family background?
- What is the family structure?
- What is their citizenship status?

Individual	Family	Community
1)What is the birth order of the child?	1)What's the immigration status of the family?	1)Is the family a part of an ethnic community?
2)What is the gender of the child?	2)What languages do the parents speak?	
3)Is the child an interpreter for the family?	3) What were the family routines in the home country?	2) Does the family have supports in the community?
4)What familiar practices does the child miss from the home country?	4) What are the family's strengths?	

Figure 150.1 "Person-in family-in community" model (Fong, 1997).

- What is their socioeconomic background?
- Are there family members who are literate in their language?
- Are there family members literate in English?
- Will they need an interpreter? If so, what dialect?

The service profile is done to assess what kinds of services will be relevant and used by that client population, based on the information received in the user profile. Questions to ask are as follows.

- What services currently exist in the community in working with this ethnic population?
- Do linguistically diverse staff members offer these services (i.e., will the services offer the correct language dialect for the client?)?
- Are the staff members immigrants or refugees themselves?
- Are the agencies offering the range of preresettlement and postresettlement services?
- Are the services easily accessible by public transportation?
- Are the services offered at times when the immigrants or refugees can access them?
- Is the philosophy of the agency's offering of services congruent with societal values stressed in the home countries of the immigrants and refugees?
- Are there barriers (e.g., financial limitations and eligibility requirements) to accessing these services?

Develop Comprehensive Plans

Because the immigrant and refugee student is an integral part of the family system, school social workers may have to not only develop student IEPs but also individualized family service plans (IFSPs). Culturally competent contextual social work practice (Fong, 2004b) is a framework that would guide getting to the cultural uniqueness of the immigrant and refugee student and his or her family. In developing IEPs and IFSPs, this framework emphasizes the "integration of differential legal statuses, transitioning in social environments, and adaptations in human behaviors" (p. 44).

Advocate Clients' Rights to Services

Immigrant and refugee students are a disempowered group with many needs, thus it is important for a school social worker to include in his or her management of the case a strong advocacy tendency toward finding the services and resources to meet these needs.

Monitor the Actual Delivery of Services

Important in this part of the case management skills is to have skills to follow up on the actual implementation of the treatment plans (IEPs and IFSPs) and the delivery of services recommended. To make sure that the treatment plans are followed and the services are actually delivered, the school social worker has to carefully review the plans with an interpreter who speaks the correct language dialect.

CASE EXAMPLE

The A family, consisting of two parents and three sons ages 14, 16, and 19, arrived in the United States in 2003 as political refugees from Eastern Europe. There the family was persecuted due to their ethnic identity and fled their home during the war. After experiencing traumatic incidents of kidnapping and torture, they lived in bombed-out homes before taking refuge in a camp for dislocated persons.

The family has had several difficulties adjusting to the school system in the United States. First, it had been years since the children attended school due to the conflict in their country of origin, and all arrived without documentation of grade level. The oldest son was encouraged to find work, and the other children were placed in grade 9. They were placed in ESL classes, which were primarily in Spanish-English, despite the fact that neither child spoke Spanish or English on arrival.

Class scheduling presented additional problems. For example, the middle son, whose written name resembled a Hispanic name, was placed in Spanish 3. When the school counselor was contacted to discuss this situation, she suggested placing him in a flower arranging course. It was difficult for the counselor to understand why neither scenario would be in the best interest of the student.

Absences and school suspension proved to be obstacles for this family, as they do with many refugee families. Refugees are often away from school for various reasons, such as initial medical check-ups. Likewise, the A family children were often needed as interpreters during food stamp interviews, medical appointments, and immigration and documentation procedures. Not fully understanding the requirement of written parental permission, both students encountered difficulties with unexcused absences. Subsequently, Mrs. A. missed parent–teacher conferences due to miscommunications and the language barrier. One child was also suspended for fighting with another student who insulted Mrs. A. The student explained that in his country of origin, these sorts of verbal attacks are incredibly hostile and provoking. The student did not understand why he was punished for defending his mother.

CASE EXAMPLE APPLICATION

Step One: Appraise the Needs

Because the boys have not been in school for years, accurate grade levels need to be determined. Because they are from Eastern Europe, it is highly unlikely that Spanish would be a language of familiarity or choice. Assessment of reading, writing, listening, and spoken language abilities needs to be done as well as finding an interpreter of the appropriate language background. An assessment of the boys' strengths and interests needs to be done to avoid misplacement into courses neither appropriate nor of interest to the boys. An assessment of the family's immediate needs would help explain the boys' multiple absences. The family does not seem to understand the American school system practices and need case management skills to focus on their needs simultaneously with the needs of the boys in school.

Step Two: Identify Relevant Services

The services of an interpreter speaking the appropriate language dialect are very important because placing the boys in Spanish-speaking classes is not appropriate. The interpreter should work with the school social worker, who will manage assessments for the boys in the areas of language ability, strengths and vocational interests, and appropriate course selections. Once the family's needs are determined, the social worker should contact refugee resettlement agencies to see what services are available, particularly the use of appropriate interpreters.

Step Three: Develop Comprehensive Plans

The school social worker should be developing both IEPs and IFSPs for these refugee students and their family. However, building the relationship and developing trust may take more time because the social worker may not know about

the refugee family's culture, values, and migration experiences. This knowledge should be included in both IEPs and IFSPs. The school social worker should case manage both plans. With regard to extracurricular opportunities, both students have a keen interest in sports, especially basketball, soccer, and swimming. However, their grades have not been adequate to allow participation on school teams. Coaches have tried to recruit them for soccer and basketball and provide incentive to improve their grades, but this has been unsuccessful. An IEP is needed to incorporate their athletic interests as incentives to motivate their interest in learning the English language and passing courses.

Step Four: Advocate Client's Right to Services

School social workers should lobby their principals to develop services for the growing immigrant and refugee student populations. Minimally, every educational institution should have on hand a list of relevant interpreters to be available to the school social workers. By using case management skills, social workers have a better way to know and advocate for the student and his family to get the comprehensive picture of the needs that require attention.

Step Five: Monitor the Actual Delivery of Services

The treatment intervention used with the students and their family consisted mainly of the school social worker's advocacy for the family with the school system, medical and mental health providers, and other refugee social service providers. For example, the social worker educated school personnel about the refugee experience and other barriers faced by the family. Advocacy also involved helping each family member better understand the workings of the various American systems. With regard to case management, the social worker assisted in the coordination of medical and mental appointments, including referrals, transportation, language interpretation, and management of medications. All this was done as a case manager to ensure and monitor the services for these refugee students and their family.

CONCLUSION

Immigrant and refugee children and youth have different migration journeys and statuses, which impact their adjustments and acculturation experiences once they arrive in the United States. Those with no legal or with temporary permanent status (undocumented immigrants, asylum seekers, and unaccompanied refugee minors) have additional stressors of fears of exposure and deportation. Because children and youth bring their problems and anxiety about their families into the classroom, case management is an important intervention for addressing both client systems simultaneously. It is very important that school social workers become equipped and use case management skills in working with immigrants and refugee students and their families because the complexities of their problems and the interrelatedness between the students and their families. In summary, school social workers need to:

- know the different statuses and advocate for the client's rights for culturally competent services,
- understand the importance of migration journeys when assessing client needs,
- work with both the immigrant and refugee student and his or her family when identifying relevant services, and
- become equipped to use case management skills and develop comprehensive IEPs and IFSPs.

WEB SITES

Bridging Refugee Youth and Children Services (BRYCS). http://www. brycs.org.

Center for Applied Linguistics, Cultural Orientation Resource Center. http://www .culturalorientation.net.

Immigration Legal Resource Center. http://www .ilrc.org.

U.S. Committee for Refugees and Immigrants, National Center for Refugee and Immigrant Children. http://www.refugees.org.

References

Adelman, H., & Taylor, L. (2002). School counselors and school reform: New directions. *Professional School Counseling, 5*(4), 83–90.

Chow, J. (2001). Assessment of Asian American/ Pacific Islander organizations and communities. In R. Fong & S. Furuto (Eds.), *Culturally competent practice: Skills, interventions, and evaluations* (pp. 211–224). Boston: Allyn & Bacon.

Congress, P., & Lynn, M. (1994). Group work programs in public schools: Ethical dilemmas and cultural diversity. *Social Work in Education, 61*(2) 107–114.

Delgado, M., Jones, K., & Rohani, M. (2005). *Social work practice with refugee and immigrant youth.* Boston: Allyn & Bacon.

Dubois, B., & Miley, K. (2005). *Social work: The empowering profession,* 5th ed. Boston: Allyn & Bacon.

Foner, N. (Ed.). (2001). *New immigrants in New York.* New York: Columbia University Press.

Fong, R. (1997). Child welfare practice with Chinese families: Assessment issues for immigrants from the People's Republic of China. *Journal of Family Social Work, 2*(7), 33–47.

Fong, R. (Ed.). (2004a). *Culturally competent practice with immigrant and refugee children and families.* New York: Guilford.

Fong, R. (2004b). Contexts and environments for culturally competent practice. In R. Fong (Ed.), *Culturally competent practice with immigrant and refugee children and families* (pp. 44). New York: Guilford.

Kataoka, S., Stein, D., Jaycox, H., Wong, M., Escudero, P., Tu, W., et al. (2003). A school-based mental health program for traumatized Latino immigrant children. *Journal of American Academy of Child and Adolescent Psychiatry, 42*(3), 311–318.

Rose, S., & Fatout, M. (2003). *Social work practice with children and adolescents.* Boston: Allyn & Bacon.

Ryu, C. (1992). 1.5 Generation. In J. Lee (Ed.), *Asian Americans* (pp. 50–54). New York: New Press.

Suarez-Orozco, C., & Suarez-Orozco, M. (2001). *Children of immigration.* Cambridge, MA: Harvard University Press.

151 Treating Children and Adolescents with ADHD in the Schools

Steven W. Evans, Joanna M. Sadler, & Christine E. Brady

Students with attention deficit hyperactivity disorder (ADHD) are some of the most frequently referred students to school mental health professionals. School-based treatments can be the best interventions for helping these students succeed socially, academically, and behaviorally. Descriptions of school-based interventions for children and adolescents with the disorder are included in this chapter. The descriptions and case examples provide important considerations for modifying intervention and assessment approaches based on developmental differences and changes in context between elementary and secondary schools. Intervention plans for both case studies include parent involvement in the assessment and treatment procedures.

ADHD is a chronic condition appearing in 3 percent to 5 percent of school-aged children. The core symptoms of the disorder include problems with inattention, hyperactivity, and impulsivity. Many of the impairments exhibited by children with ADHD manifest at school, including problems completing school assignments, disruptive behavior, breaking school and classroom rules, social problems, and disorganization. Problems with disorganization are often the most obvious, due to cluttered desks, bookbags, binders, and lockers. Although less obvious, disorganization is also evident in poor time management skills, reading and writing difficulties, and poor listening comprehension. In addition, children with ADHD are at greater risk for other problems, including aggression, oppositional behavior, substance use, irresponsible sexual behavior (e.g., sex-

ually transmitted diseases, unwanted pregnancies), school dropout, delinquency, driving violations, and accidents. Social workers in schools have a unique opportunity to intervene with these youth and make a positive difference in their lives. They can observe students in socially demanding situations, such as the cafeteria, transitions between classes, and recess, as well as academically challenging situations in the classrooms. A school social worker who is knowledgeable about the identification and treatment of youth with ADHD can have a large, beneficial impact on a child with the disorder by educating colleagues, working with the child's parents, and coordinating intervention efforts.

ELEMENTARY SCHOOL

There are many characteristics of an elementary school classroom that make it well suited for both the identification and treatment of children with ADHD. Elementary school students typically stay within one or two classrooms for several hours each day, where they encounter both academically and socially challenging situations on a regular basis. School social workers may observe children in these situations in both structured and unstructured activities. The opportunity to regularly observe in these situations allows social workers to gain a thorough understanding of a child's strengths and weaknesses and gauge progress in response to interventions. Taking advantage of these opportunities requires that a school social worker understands the manifestations of the disorder in schools. Some common characteristics of elementary school–aged children with ADHD that can be observed in a classroom are listed below. Not every characteristic is true of all children with the disorder, but they are common of many. Furthermore, these characteristics are not diagnostic criteria for ADHD; rather, they are descriptive of how teachers and other students perceive children with ADHD.

- The materials in the student's desk are very messy, and the child has trouble finding things when asked by the teacher.
- The child is seen by peers as annoying, "hyper," or "weird."
- The teacher reports that working with the child can be exhausting.
- The child may raise his or her hand to participate in class discussions and then forgets what he or she was going to say or makes a statement that is irrelevant or redundant.
- During seatwork time in class, the child is frequently off-task. The student may do things to escape extended seatwork periods, such as sharpen pencils, go to the bathroom, or report not feeling well and ask to go to the nurse.
- The child fails to complete work and give it to the teacher on time.

Interventions for children with ADHD tend to be behavioral, and many involve training parents and teachers to implement the interventions in the classroom or home. Counseling, play therapy, and self-esteem groups are unlikely to be effective with these children. There is also little evidence that social skills training is effective at improving social deficits among these children. Educating parents and teachers about children with the disorder and training them to consistently provide these interventions over time is a critically important role for school social workers who wish to help children with the disorder.

SECONDARY SCHOOL

One of the biggest changes from elementary school to secondary school for children with ADHD is the increased demand to function independently. In secondary schools, students are expected to bring materials to class without prompting, keep track of assignments without monitoring, and complete work independently. Many secondary students with ADHD fail these expectations. Attempts to remedy such problems are considerably more complicated at the secondary level for several reasons. First, the transition to secondary schools typically includes a switch from having one teacher who is with the child all day to the child having a variety of teachers for different subjects. A school social worker attempting to help a child in middle or high school faces the prospect of negotiating with several teachers over a variety of settings. Second, as children with ADHD progress into the upper grades, they encounter many teachers whose training and focus tends to be more content-driven than child-driven when compared to elementary school teachers. The emphasis on content at the secondary level is encouraged by the new testing requirements of the No Child Left Behind Act and related high school graduation requirements.

Third, practitioners in secondary schools appear to rely more heavily on accommodations—as opposed to interventions—compared to practitioners in elementary schools. Accommodations include strategies such as giving students extended time on tests, providing students with class notes, accepting late work without penalty, and other techniques that do more to change the expectations of adults than the competencies of students. Accommodations are frequently used in individualized education plans (IEPs) or 504 plans for students with ADHD, and are recommended on many Web sites and in books written about the topic. Unfortunately, most accommodations are not evidence-based and can be detrimental when they are the primary mode of assistance.

In contrast, interventions are techniques that train students to meet the expectations of teachers through skill acquisition and enhancement. These techniques include teaching organization skills, study skills, and behavior management. From a pedagogical standpoint, interventions are consistent with the goal to train children to be educated and competent adults. Interventions tend to take more work and are less likely to provide immediate relief to distressed parents and teachers than accommodations; however, they are more likely than accommodations to improve the functioning of children with ADHD. Not surprisingly, there is a growing evidence base for many school-based interventions (see recent reviews by Raggi & Chronis, 2006; Wolraich et al., 2005).

CASE ILLUSTRATIONS

The following sections include descriptions of two case illustrations that include some assessment and intervention techniques that may be employed by school social workers. The first involves a student with ADHD in an elementary school, and the second involves a child in a secondary school. Additional information about the interventions described in this section is available in other reviews of treatments (e.g., DuPaul & Stoner, 2003; Evans, White, Sibley & Barlow, 2007).

Elementary School Case

Andrew is a 9-year-old white male who was referred to the school social worker (Rebecca) by his fourth-grade teacher. The teacher's primary complaints were that he did not stay in his seat and he interrupted the classroom environment by speaking at inappropriate times and being the "class clown." The teacher also reported that Andrew infrequently completed his classwork and homework, and when he did turn it in, his work had many careless mistakes. She stated that Andrew had problems interacting with his peers and provided the example that during recess he refused to play by the rules of games that the other children were playing.

Assessment. The first step of the assessment was to identify the questions posed by the teacher's referral. There are many potential questions that could be addressed based on Andrew's referral, including possible eligibility for special education or a 504 plan, determining if he met *DSM-IV* criteria for a disorder, and gathering information that would help guide the selection of interventions. Rebecca elected to focus her assessment on gathering data that will inform the selection of interventions (information about other assessment strategies may be obtained from Pelham, Fabiano, & Massetti, 2005).

The social worker began by interviewing the teacher and Andrew's parents. These interviews were used to gather specific information about the behavior problems, determine what interventions had already been attempted, and gain a sense of the ability of the parents and teacher to consistently implement interventions over time. The teacher reported that she allowed Andrew to use the computers during free time at the end of the day if he demonstrated good behavior in class. She reported that this was not very effective, as

they often disagreed about whether Andrew had a "good" day, and other children complained that they were well behaved but not allowed to use the computer. She noted that after trying this for approximately a week she discontinued it due to the arguments, classmate complaints, and lack of improvement.

When Rebecca interviewed the parents, she learned that they did not have any problems with Andrew. They reported that he came home from school and played video games or "ran around" outside. He did not participate in any clubs, teams, or other organizations. Andrew has an older sister who spends a great deal of time with her friends and is very involved in activities in the community. The siblings spend very little time together, and the parents reported that Andrew had no responsibilities or chores at home. The parents were concerned about his problems at school, but wondered about the teacher's approach because Andrew did not have problems at home, and problems at school in previous years were minor. This led Rebecca to interview teachers who had Andrew in their classes in previous years. These teachers reported that it was difficult to keep Andrew on-task and he had problems getting along with other children. The teacher from the previous year reported that she did not refer Andrew to the child study team because she was able to work with him individually so that he was able to make adequate progress.

After gathering information from the parents and teachers and observing Andrew in various activities, the school social worker concluded that he may meet diagnostic criteria for ADHD, but she focused her feedback to the parents on implications for home- and school-based interventions. She determined that the minimal expectations at home may have led to the lack of apparent problems in that setting. Reports from previous teachers confirmed his current teacher's concerns and were consistent with a general trend toward increasing impairment as children with ADHD get older. She had doubts about the parents' ability to consistently implement interventions at home, but was confident that the teacher could consistently provide some basic behavioral interventions.

Intervention plan. Based on her assessment of Andrew, Rebecca planned three interventions. The first involved providing information about ADHD and other disruptive behavior disorders to the parents. She emphasized the risks associated with children with ADHD and the importance of providing effective interventions. Rebecca encouraged the parents to consult with their physician, but neither recommended nor discouraged medication treatment. The parents were told that there were many interventions that they could initiate whether or not Andrew met diagnostic criteria for ADHD. The second intervention was to encourage the parents to participate in a parent training program that focused on parenting techniques for parents of children with disruptive behavior. Rebecca conducted ten-week parent training groups once or twice each semester depending on demand and encouraged the parents to participate in the next group. During the parent training meetings, the school social worker helped parents establish a daily report card with their children's teachers (detailed information about developing a daily report card is available at the Web site for the Center for Children and Families; see link at end of chapter). In spite of some reservations about whether the parents would consistently implement such an intervention, she felt that participation in this group was a good first step, and if this was not successful, she may work with them individually after the parent training program ended.

The third intervention Rebecca planned for Andrew involved working with his teacher. She met with the teacher and provided information about ADHD, including the chronic nature of the disorder and the need for consistent intervention over time. She explained that many effective interventions may take many weeks of consistent implementation to be effective, and the teachers could expect that Andrew's response over those weeks would be quite variable on a daily basis. The social worker also emphasized the need to provide immediate and clear responses to Andrew's desirable and undesirable behaviors. The teacher's previous intervention provided the reward too long after the behavior, and the contingencies appeared to be unclear to both the student and the teacher. When asked, the teacher chose two behaviors to target initially: task completion and interrupting. Together the teacher and social worker clearly defined these behaviors and established a system of providing immediate feedback to Andrew. The frequency of these behaviors was translated into points that were redeemable for small rewards and privileges twice each day, including just prior to lunch and again prior to the dismissal bell.

In addition to the potential benefit of this point system, Rebecca implemented this intervention because it was something that could easily be integrated into a daily report card if the parents were able to manage this intervention. The points could be reported to parents each day and the parents could provide rewards contingent on the scores on the daily report card. If the parents were not able to implement the daily report card intervention at home, the classroom point system could still provide significant benefit without the parents' collaboration.

Secondary School Case

Lisa is a 15-year-old girl who was referred to the school social worker (Mike) due to poor academic performance, truancy, and defiant behavior. She moved to the school district at the beginning of the school year when she enrolled in the ninth grade. Lisa failed three of her classes during the first grading period and teachers reported that she did not seem to care about school and they could not help her.

Assessment. Mike began his assessment by interviewing Lisa's teachers, and the feedback he received from them was very inconsistent. Some teachers reported that they had no problems with Lisa and she was earning a C or D in their classes. Other teachers reported that she was disruptive, never completed any work, was verbally defiant to the teacher, and was failing their classes. The variability across teachers led Mike to review Lisa's information from her previous school. These records were sparse, but revealed that her grades tended to range from D's to B's. There was no information regarding any behavior problems. A call to the school social worker at Lisa's previous school indicated that teachers believed that Lisa had a poor attitude and could be irritable and inappropriate in class, but this was not considered a serious problem. Lisa's few friends tended to be younger than her, and she functioned on the periphery of the social groups. The previous school social worker remembered that Lisa may have seen a mental health professional in the community, but she was never given details of those services. Lisa had never been referred to the child study team or for an evaluation. The school social worker could not recall any interactions with her parents.

Given the inconsistent teacher reports, Mike went back to talk to the teachers and observe some of their classes. He found that the teachers who reported the most problems with Lisa tended to have traditional classrooms, with moderate to high expectations for their students. The teachers who reported that they had few problems operated more informally than the others, and although the teachers stated that they gave homework, they also gave the students more than enough time during class to complete it. Lisa's work in these classes was not high quality, but she did enough to meet the minimal expectations. She did speak out in these classes, but so did many other students, and traditional classroom rules were not strictly enforced. Mike recognized that the more self-control and independent task completion that was expected of Lisa, the more problems she tended to exhibit.

Mike then contacted Lisa's parents and asked them to meet him at the school to discuss Lisa's progress and transition to the new school. He asked them to bring old school report cards and the results of any previous evaluations that had been completed. Lisa's parents appeared relieved to meet with him and discussed at great lengths their concerns and frustrations. They spoke of choosing their battles and attempting to monitor and influence Lisa's behavior, but reported little success and a lot of worry and concern about the girl's future. They had long ago abandoned efforts to get Lisa to help with chores at home, stating that it was more trouble than it was worth. Lisa had met with a counselor in their previous community for a few months, but they concluded that this had been "a waste of time." The counselor had told them that Lisa had "issues" to resolve, but her problems never showed any sign of improvement. As a result, her parents had concluded that mental health professionals could not help them.

A review of Lisa's report cards revealed that teachers had added comments to her cards since first grade indicating that she had trouble completing work and was disorganized. Early report cards also revealed that she had trouble getting along with other children and was easily distracted. The parents reported that they shared these concerns with Lisa's pediatrician, and he had discussed the possibility of prescribing medication for her. They were not sure what medication was considered, but at that time the parents were opposed to giving her medication for her behavior problems.

Finally, Mike invited Lisa to his office to gather information from her perspective. She reported that she was doing fine both socially and academically. Mike questioned her about some of the teacher reports and low grades. Lisa replied by stating that some teachers do not like her. She acknowledged becoming frustrated with them, but claimed that her statements to the teachers were appropriate in response to the unfair accusations and other mean statements that teachers made to her. Lisa reported having many friends and a happy social life. When asked specifically about the ages of her friends, she did acknowledge that some of her friends were younger than her, but stated that she also had friends in the ninth grade. Mike also asked to look at Lisa's bookbag and binder. The items were very disorganized and old papers, food wrappers, and other items were mixed into her school materials. There was very little information recorded in her assignment notebook, and Lisa stated that she did not use it because she remembers all of her assignments.

Intervention plan. The results of the assessment led Mike to conclude it was likely that Lisa met diagnostic criteria for ADHD. He developed a plan to work directly with her parents, her teachers, and Lisa. He asked Lisa's parents to meet with him again so he could provide them with feedback about his assessment and discuss options for helping Lisa. His goals for this meeting included educating her parents about ADHD, identifying community resources that could help them, offering them the opportunity to work with him to address some school-related problems such as homework, and reviewing and discussing his plans for working with Lisa and her teachers at school. When they met he provided some reading material for the parents (e.g., Zeigler-Dendy & Zeigler, 2003; CHADD fact sheets) and discussed the course of ADHD through childhood and into adolescence. He also shared with them that insight-oriented therapies, like the one they reported was provided to Lisa by the community counselor, are not likely to adequately address the problems associated with ADHD. Mike assured them that there are mental health professionals who understand best practices for these youth, and they may be able to help Lisa. Mike shared information with them that helped the parents become wise consumers. He also encouraged the parents to speak to Lisa's physician if they were interested in medication treatment. Finally, Mike provided the parents with contact information for the local parent support and advocacy group and encouraged them to consider attending a meeting.

After educating the parents about ADHD and treatment options, Mike talked to them about implementing some interventions at home that might help Lisa both academically and with their parent–child relationship. Mike scheduled a standing meeting with the parents for 3 weeks to share information about a homework management plan and basic communication and problem-solving procedures. Additional parent meetings could be scheduled on an as-needed basis. He spoke with them about maintaining consistent communication between the home and school and offered to be the liaison between the parents and teachers.

Finally, Mike shared with the parents his plans for working with Lisa and her teachers. He explained that the majority of Lisa's problems were in classes where the teachers expected students to work independently outside of class, strictly adhere to classroom rules, and had higher expectations regarding behavior. When teachers did not have these expectations, Lisa's irresponsible and disrespectful behaviors were less of a problem. Mike also told the parents about the extreme disorganization that he discovered in Lisa's binder and bookbag and the lack of an effective system for recording assignments. The parents asked about ideas they heard about from other parents, where teachers gave the students longer time on tests, provided them with written notes from the class and a list of the assignments that were due, and did not penalize the students for late assignments. Mike told the parents that these were accommodations that are sometimes used with students with problems similar to Lisa's, but he discouraged the parents from relying on these techniques. He told them that there is no evidence that these techniques improve the behavior or skills of children with ADHD or related problems. It was his experience that these accommodations do make it easier for students to receive improved grades, but only because adults start expecting less from them and not because the students have improved in any way. He even explained how these may be detrimental to Lisa because they remove the responsibility for her to find the means to be successful. He stated that it is unlikely that future employers would make such accommodations, and Lisa needed to learn to adjust to reasonable expectations. He reviewed a series of interventions designed to improve her ability to succeed in regular education settings such as an organization intervention (Evans et al., 2008), daily report card (Evans & Youngstrom, 2006) and other school-based interventions

(see Evans et al., 2007; Wolraich et al. 2005) designed to improve Lisa's ability to meet the expectations of regular education teachers. He told the parents that it may take a few weeks or even months before Lisa showed adequate improvement, and he would provide them with updates about her progress. The parents reported feeling a little overwhelmed with this information, but told Mike that they would read the material, discuss the information that had been shared, and return for their next appointment.

CONCLUSION

School-based social workers are in a position that allows them to have an important impact on the lives of children and adolescents with ADHD. Their training and skills combined with their position within schools provides school social workers with a unique opportunity to participate in the assessment of children with ADHD, as well as coordinate effective home- and school-based interventions. In addition, school social workers can be a very effective liaison to community mental health providers to coordinate care. The case studies in this chapter were intended to provide information and examples of effective strategies to help students with ADHD achieve in school. Of course, there are many child and family characteristics that may enhance or compromise response to these interventions. Findings from a large clinical trial of children with ADHD revealed that comorbid anxiety, prior medication use, poverty, severity of symptoms, and maternal depression moderated outcomes in their study (see Hinshaw, 2007, for complete review). Interestingly, sex of the child and comorbid oppositional defiant disorder or conduct disorder did not significantly alter outcomes.

Many of the common concerns that practitioners experience when working with youth with ADHD were described in the case studies, including the belief by the children that they do not have problems and do not need help, inconsistent reports from teachers about the child's behavior and academic progress, the temptation to rely on accommodations instead of interventions, and the barrier to further care that can result from receiving ineffective interventions. Many additional challenges are inherent in the process of trying to implement interventions such as those described including variability in the willingness of teachers and parents to participate in the process. Clearly, excellent consulting and communication skills are a critical prerequisite to effectively working with these youth in schools. It is by no means an easy task, but it is a necessary one and the benefits afforded to the youth can be life changing.

WEB SITES

Center for Children and Families, daily report card. http://ccf.buffalo.edu/pdf/school_daily_report_card.pdf.

National Resource Center on ADHD. http://www.help4adhd.org.

SchoolMentalHealth.org. http://www.schoolmentalhealth.org.

References

DuPaul, G. J., & Stoner, G. (2003). *ADHD in the schools: Assessment and interventions strategies*, 2nd ed. New York: Guilford.

Evans, S. W., White, L. C., Brady, C., Schultz, B. K., Sibley, M., & Van Eck, K. (2008). *A school-based organization intervention for young adolescents with ADHD: Patterns of responding.* Manuscript submitted for publication.

Evans, S. W., White, L. C., Sibley, M., & Barlow, E. (2007). School-based mental health treatment of children and adolescents with attention-deficit/hyperactivity disorder. In S.W. Evans, M. Weist, & Z. Serpell (Eds.), *Advances in school-based mental health interventions: Best practices and program models* (vol. 2). New York: Civic Research Institute.

Evans, S. W., & Youngstrom, E. (2006). Evidence based assessment of attention-deficit hyperactivity disorder: Measuring outcomes. *Journal of the American Academy of Child and Adolescent Psychiatry, 45*(9), 1132–1137.

Hinshaw, S. P. (2007). Moderators and mediators of treatment outcome for youth with ADHD: Understanding for whom and how interventions work. *Journal of Pediatric Psychology, 32,* 664–675.

Pelham, W. E., Fabiano, G. A., & Massetti, G. M. (2005). Evidence-based assessment of attention deficit hyperactivity disorder in children and adolescents. *Journal of Clinical Child and Adolescent Psychology, 34,* 449–476.

Raggi, V., & Chronis, A. M. (2006). Interventions to address the academic impairment of children and adolescents with ADHD. *Clinical Child and Family Psychology Review, 9,* 85–111.

Wolraich, M. L., Wibbelsman, C. J., Brown, T. E., Evans, S. W., Gotlieb, E. M., Knight, J. R., et al. (2005). Attention deficit hyperactivity disorder in adolescents: A review of the diagnosis, treatment and clinical implications. *Pediatrics, 115*(6), 1734–1746.

Zeigler-Dendy, C. A., & Zeigler, A. (2003). *A bird's-eye view of life with ADD and ADHD: Advice from young survivors.* Cedar Bluff, AL: Cherish the Children.

Working with Culturally/Racially Diverse Students to Improve Connection to School and Academic Performance

Daphna Oyserman

OVERVIEW OF THE PROBLEM

Poor School Performance is Common and Carries Many Risks

Failing in school predicts lower adult income (U.S. Department of Education, 2002) and unemployment (U.S. Department of Education, 1999). Substance use increases risk of school dropout (Zimmerman & Schmeelk-Cone, 2003). Being engaged in school, putting effort into school, and performing well in school reduce risk of early substance use (Bryant and Zimmerman, 2002; Choi, 2007; Zimmerman & Schmeelk-Cone, 2003) and early sexual behavior (Choi, 2007; Ramirez-Valles, Zimmerman, & Juarez, 2002). Minority status, poverty, low parent involvement in school, and other factors increase risk of school underperformance (Oyserman, Brickman, & Rhodes, 2007); only 50 percent of African Americans graduate high school on time (Orfield, Losen, Wald, & Swanson, 2004).

The Role of School Social Work

School-based preventive intervention can help youth link their hopes and dreams for the future to current effort in school. Though much everyday behavior—having a snack after school, watching television, playing on the computer, text-messaging friends—may seem automatic, even mindless, and certainly not purposeful, these choices—to watch another TV show, talk on the phone, or do homework—accumulate into an academic trajectory and link to the sense youth make of their future.

When present action does not feel linked to meaningful future goals, it is easy to be distracted and lose track of goals. School social workers can use brief group-based intervention techniques to make school-focused possible selves more salient. School-to-Jobs (STJ) is an intervention developed and tested with low-income youths, primarily African-Americans and Latinos. STJ uses a culturally sensitive approach. It has significant effects on important outcomes assessed via multiple sources, and results have been replicated. STJ reduces behavior problems and depressive symptoms and improves grades, attendance, school engagement, and effort (Oyserman, Bybee, and Terry, 2006). At 2-year follow-up, large effects were found for change over time in time spent doing homework. Moderate effects were found for change over time in grades, unexcused absences, initiative taking, and disruptiveness. Standardized test scores, available at 1-year follow-up, also improved. Depression (CESD) scores, available at 2-year follow-up, declined. Effects extend and replicate early results documented with an after-school version STJ (Oyserman et al., 2002).

Identity-Based Motivation Theory (IBM)

IBM (Oyserman, 2007) can help guide thinking about preventive intervention in school. IBM is a conceptual model linking identity, future orientation, self-regulation, and positive youth development. IBM proposes that when the future feels far away ("happens later"), adult possible selves (e.g., "I'll be a doctor," "I won't be a junkie," "I'll be a model for my community") may be salient, but proximal possible selves (e.g., "I'll be a good student") won't be salient. This is a problem because proximal possible selves are necessary to focus youth's attention on school. Proximal possible selves are salient when the future feels proximal ("starts now"). When the future feels proximal, youth are more likely to see the present as mattering for their future.

Of course, most children have a sense that risky behavior, like substance use and too early sexual activity, can derail attaining adult possible selves. High hopes about the future are not enough, however. Adult possible selves are unlikely to improve effort and engagement with school unless they are linked with more proximal goals and strategies to attain them. Because school success is critical for adult future success, these proximal goals and strategies direct children's attention to school-focused effort. As children move from elementary to middle school, those lacking proximal goals and strategies are likely to experience academic failure, making abstract goals about adult success no longer possible to attain. As the gap between the concrete reality of school failure and abstract images of future success becomes painfully clear, youth become more vulnerable to substance use. Once faced with school failure, youth may not be able to create alternative successful future images that would enable them to successfully transition to adulthood. Not being able to create an alternative successful future image should also increase the positive pull of substance use and of early initiation of sexual activity.

Preventive Intervention is Needed to Reduce Risk of Initiation and of Declining School Performance

Poor academic achievement, poor attendance, and school failure are sufficiently common as to warrant preventive intervention efforts. Dropout rates are higher in poor, urban neighborhoods than in more affluent communities, and risk is much higher for male (Orfield et al., 2004), low-income (Blair, Blair, & Legazpi, 1999), and African American (Orfield et al., 2004) youths. National on-time graduation rates are 50 percent for African American youth and 43 percent for African American males. Because substance use, initiation of sexual activity, and poor school performance are correlated, an intervention that targets perceived closeness of the future and improves school performance is likely to reduce risk of both sexual activity and initiation of substance use by shifting youth to a more successful developmental trajectory. Without a targeted intervention, low-income youth have fewer strategies to attain their school-focused proximal goals, perhaps because their families lack the social capital to know how to do well in school, the material resources to obtain outside mentoring, or time and resources to be involved in school (Oyserman et al., 2007). Neighborhood characteristics may heighten vulnerability if identity-relevant positive role models are rare and if identity-relevant "anti-models" provide images of failure to attain possible selves without clear guidance as to how to avoid these negative outcomes (Oyserman, Gant, and Ager, 1995).

Aim

Our goal as social workers should be to bolster youth's sense that current effort in school matters and fits important identities. A school-based intervention to bolster the link between current future goals and strategies especially important for low-income youth. Following Oyserman's IBM model, school disengagement and failure are less likely when youth believe that (1) current effort in school matters for their future, (2) current effort in school is congruent with important identities, and (3) current effort in the face of difficulties as an indication that school is really important. Youth with school-focused proximal goals and strategies that are cued in context and perceived as congruent with social identities (e.g., race/ethnicity, gender) and who interpret difficulty in working on the goal as meaning that the goal is important will be less likely to fall behind in school and so less likely to initiate sexual behavior and substance use.

PREVIOUS RESEARCH

Effective Possible Selves

Possible selves are personalized images of goals, both positive (for example, an image of oneself with the A in algebra) and negative (for example, an image oneself having to repeat the eighth grade). A number of studies suggest that possible selves differ in their effectiveness in self-regulation (focusing youth on current action to work on the goal). Self-regulatory effort improves when youth have both positive and negative (or feared) possible selves in the same domain ("balanced" possible selves) (Oyserman & Markus, 1990) and when youth have incorporated detailed strategies into their possible selves ("plausible" possible selves)

(Oyserman, Bybee, Terry, & Hart-Johnson, 2004). When possible selves are balanced, self-regulation is strengthened and becomes more focused because individuals select strategies that both increase the likelihood of becoming like their positive and decrease the likelihood of becoming like their negative possible self (Oyserman & Markus, 1990). When possible selves are more plausible, then predeveloped strategies (e.g., "set my alarm," "go to class even if my friends skip") are more likely to be cued. Indeed youth with plausible school-focused possible selves are able to improve their grades over the course of the school year, whereas those whose school-focused possible selves were less linked with strategies did not succeed in doing so (Oyserman et al., 2004). Though most low-income youth have at least one possible self focused on school, few have school-focused possible selves that include multiple strategies (Oyserman et al., 2007).

Contextual Cuing of Possible Selves

Not only is the potential self-regulatory impact of having a possible self-goal undermined when possible selves are not balanced or plausible, self-regulatory effectiveness is also undermined when social contexts do not cue possible selves. Because information that is cued (chronically or situationally made salient) is likely to be used in judgments and decision making (Higgins, 1996), contextually cued possible selves should influence self-regulatory behavior more than those that are not cued. Although resource-rich contexts, such as a middle-class neighborhood and school, provide models of success and a developed structure to guide the process of attaining school-focused possible selves, this is unlikely to be the case in resource-limited contexts. In middle-class contexts, strategies may be automatically cued—parents, teachers, parents of friends all converge to emphasize homework, persistence in the face of difficulty, tutoring, or staying after school if needed. In low socioeconomic status contexts, strategies are unlikely to be automatically cued because these contexts are less likely to present easily accessible models or to guide success, and youth are more likely to encounter adults who are unemployed, have low academic attainment, and hold nonprofessional jobs (e.g., Roderick, 2003). Given lack of easily accessible models or automatically cued strategies, youth may maintain an abstract commitment to education and express high aspirations without connecting school-focused or feared off-track possible selves to everyday behavior (for qualitative description see Roderick, 2003).

Possible Selves and Inoculation from Overinterpretation of Difficulty

By taking into account how judgment and behavior is influenced by the information that is salient in the moment, social workers can understand two of the central puzzles about outcomes for low-income and minority youth. In the early adolescent years, youth report valuing education and do not report substance use. Yet educational attainments are low and by early adulthood, serious problems with substance use begin to emerge. These puzzling results can be understood by thinking about how these youth are likely to make sense of the future and their possible selves. Working on one's school-focused possible selves is likely to be difficult. To judge what this difficulty means (e.g., Are school-focused and feared off-track possible selves "true" possible selves or do they contradict other important social identities? Is attaining one's school-focused possible selves plausible or not worth the effort?), teens must answer the implied questions: "Why is engaging in this school-focused possible selves so hard for me; is this really the true me?" and "Do we (i.e., members of my group) have possible selves like this?" Likewise, they must judge whether particular behavioral patterns (e.g., asking for help) are likely to work and if they contradict in-group identity (e.g., "Will asking the teacher for help actually help me succeed in school or is it just a 'white' thing to do?"). But if these strategies do not feel like in-group things to do or if difficulty is interpreted as meaning they are not self-relevant, youth will have difficulty engaging in these strategies even if they believe them to be effective.

When imagining possible selves is accompanied by a meta-cognitive experience of difficulty, the feeling of difficulty is likely to be interpreted with the following rule of thumb: "things that are hard to think of are less likely to be true" (Schwarz & Clore, 1996). Students are thus likely to infer that working on the possible self is too hard, that the possible self is not a "true" self that is worth pursuing and investing effort in but a "false" self, one that conflicts with social identities.

Though the experience of meta-cognitive difficulty is generally interpreted as meaning "not true for me," a number of studies have documented that other interpretations are possible (Rothman & Schwarz, 1998). Sports stories abound with reinterpretation of the meaning of experienced difficulty (e.g., "no pain, no gain") and the need to keep trying (e.g., "You miss 100 percent of the shots you don't take"). In the case of attempting to attain school-focused possible selves, although the meta-cognitive experience of difficulty is generally interpreted as "not the true me," the experience of difficulty could be reinterpreted to mean other things. Difficulty can be viewed as a normative part of the process (e.g., "Success is 1 percent inspiration and 99 percent perspiration"). Difficulty can also provide evidence of progress (e.g., "The important things in life are the ones you really have to work for"); if difficulty and failures along the way are viewed as critical to eventual success, then difficulty is evidence of striving.

Successful movement toward positive school-focused possible selves and away from feared school-focused possible selves requires ongoing behavior; it is not enough to complete one homework assignment or stay after class one day. If one's meta-cognitive experience is that working on a possible self is difficult and if this difficulty is interpreted with a naive theory that ease is associated with truth, then difficulties associated with working toward the possible selves will undermine it. Low-income and minority youth are likely to experience at least three sources of difficulty — difficulty bringing to mind school-focused possible selves and linking them to strategies; difficulty sustaining the behavioral self-regulation possible selves strategies entail, and difficulty integrating school-focused possible selves and social identities.

The STJ intervention was developed based on this research base, with a goal of enhancing the self-regulatory impact of the possible selves of high-risk youths. This was to be accomplished by evoking possible selves and strategies to attain them, forge links between possible selves and strategies that are not otherwise automatic, inoculate youth from misinterpreting failure and setbacks in attaining these possible selves, and create a link between social identity and possible selves.

Whereas effects for meta-cognitive experience were not directly tested, ease is typically the basis for meta-cognitive judgment, so trainers took care to ensure that sessions felt easy, so students would not immediately develop a meta-cognitive sense that thinking of the future is hard and therefore "not for me." The intervention was based in school so that strategies articulated in the intervention would be cued in school. Intervention activities were structured to make school-focused possible selves salient, create links between school-focused possible selves and strategies, associate the expe-rience of difficulty with progress toward meaningful goals, and create a space in which school-focused possible selves and social identity are congruent.

Together, these activities were designed to inoculate youth from withdrawing effort to attain positive and avoid negative school-focused and feared off-track possible selves. This change in possible selves was expected to evoke persistent change in long-term self-regulatory behavior. That is, it was expected that behavior relevant to school-focused possible selves (e.g., doing homework) would increase and that behavior undermining school-focused possible selves (e.g., misbehaving in class) would decrease. Over time, sustained self-regulatory behavior should produce better academic outcomes (e.g., GPA) and reduce risk of involvement in behaviors antithetical to engagement with school, such as early initiation of substance use.

Each session focused on developing an aspect of possible selves. Beginning session topics included linking school-focused possible selves to important social identities (e.g., gender or racial-ethnic groups), linking proximal possible selves to more distal adult possible selves, discussing how possible selves are influenced by role models, and linking present action to obtaining possible selves. Later sessions focused on identifying strategies that would help youth obtain their possible selves and coping with difficulty that they might encounter along their paths. Program activities involved individualized activities, such as creating a timeline into one's future, active participation by students, and group work. Once the youth sessions were complete, two final sessions included youth and parents with the goal of providing youth and parents structured activities to talk about possible selves and strategies to attain them.

Evidence of Effects

The after-school test of the intervention followed youth to the end of the academic year and documented significantly reduced risk of being sent out of class, significantly improved attendance and time spent doing homework, as well as change in the youth's possible selves (Oyserman, Terry, & Bybee, 2002). A second randomized clinical trial of the intervention involved an in-school test (Oyserman et al., 2006), wherein significant change was found in grades and attendance by school records, as well as reduction in grade retention. Again effects were mediated by change in youth possible selves. Because success has been replicated in randomized control trials, the program can be called probably efficacious if the highest criteria are both randomized control trials and also testing by multiple researchers.

THUMBNAIL SKETCH OF THE STJ INTERVENTION

Low-income, LGBT youth, and youth of color may find it difficult to create positive and believable possible selves focused on school as a pathway to adulthood unless these possible selves are fostered in a social context that creates local norms highlighting the relevance of academic achievement for being part of one's ethnic, racial, or LGBT identity group. However, relevant research is mostly correlational and necessarily leaves unanswered how to translate findings about correlations between possible selves, school involvement, and racial-ethnic-sexual identity into a framework for change. To address this issue, a brief intervention, outlined here in Tables 152.1 and 152.2, was designed with funding from the National Institutes of Health to engage low-income youth of color in developing clearly articulated possible selves that linked current school involvement with adult futures. The underlying

TABLE 152.1 Detailed Outline: Session 1

- Greet/welcome participants/check names against roster/greet latecomers

- Trainers introduce each other (name, from University of Michigan, trait each has that helps them succeed in work or school)

- Introduce observer/emphasize role to observe trainers to help improve program (not grade students)

- Ask what an *introduction* is: (is a way of saying who you are and what you can contribute)(write def. on newsprint)

- Different goals for introductions (depends on context)

- Ask about skills and abilities for succeeding in school (since this is school to jobs)

- Write tasks and examples on newsprint

- Introduction activity (partners learn of partner skills, introduce) (pass out marbles/ask for questions before task begins/circulate, check for understanding)

- Ask youth to introduce partners/ask for repetition of names

- *Expectation/Concern* task, explain concepts (expectations/concerns) (Use newsprint to write group expectations & concerns)

- Reinforce and repeat four basic themes that will be covered. (setting clear goals for next year and afterward/developing strategies to work on these goals/thinking about a path to the future/working with teachers, parents, and others in the community as resources)

- Elicit *group rules* (write on newsprint)

- State aim of program—use prepared newsprint

- State goal—use prepared newsprint

- Group naming activity: explain activity (give examples, elicit ideas)

- Explain session schedule/provide contact information/write on board

- Review—ask participant to name all names

- Explain task, line up from youngest to oldest without talking (encourage/when completed, ask month of birth)

- Congratulate/reinforce cooperation

Continued

TABLE 152.1 Detailed Outline: Session 1 *(continued)*

- Explain task, stand in circle, cross arms in front, and grab hands of two people across the circle, then without letting go of hands, get them uncrossed so that we are again in a circle
- Trainers are part of the circle/congratulate/reinforce cooperation
- Next session will work on adult images, what will adulthood be like for you?
- Provide snacks
- Pass out session evaluation forms
- Ask for help rearranging the room
- Pick up evaluation forms, make sure attendance form is filled out
- Say goodbyes, rate participant participation

TABLE 152.2 Detailed Outline: Session 2

- Greet participants by name/take attendance
- Say today is session 2, adult images
- Ask for what happened last session (elicit activities/elicit rationale)
- *Adult Images* task—choosing pictures that represent visions of yourself as an adult.
  - Each to pick at least 10 pictures
  - What do they mean for you?
  - When these will be true of you?
  - Afterward all will share
- Make sure instructions are clear
- Have participants begin
- Pass out snacks
- Mingle—check for understanding
- Have everyone rejoin circle
- Sharing adult images task—show pictures and explain to group, while group listens and pays attention to common themes that emerge
- Explain task—each participant to write on newsprint something that they thought was similar about everyone's adult visions
  - Ask for questions
  - Mingle, help individually as needed
- Discuss themes that are there and areas that are missing (jobs, family, friends, community involvement, lifestyle)
- Review concept of *adult domains*—adult images can be about jobs, family, friends, community involvement, lifestyle.
- Explain concept—adult images can be *goals* if they are worked on, we will discuss in coming sessions.

TABLE 152.2 Detailed Outline: Session 2

- Next session will identify role models

- Pass out session evaluation forms

- Pick up evaluation forms and adult images worksheets, make sure attendance is filled out

- Goodbyes

- Rate participation/label newsprint

assumption is that if one could help youth articulate achievement-oriented possible selves in a positive peer-based social context that implicitly framed academic achievement as part of racial-ethnic-sexual identity, one should be able to bolster not only youth's possible selves but also their sense of connection to school and involvement in school more generally. The intervention involves small groups of about 12 students and has been tested as both an after-school and an in-school program for middle school students.

Middle school youth are cognitively able to conceptualize possible selves and are on the brink of the important transition to high school, so they are likely to be beginning to speculate about what the future will hold for them. In terms of risk, as outlined, risk of failing to develop academically focused possible selves is particularly high for low-income youth. These youth face particular difficulties in the adolescent transition due to the combined risk of fewer role models for success and more neighborhood exposure to unemployment, poverty, crime, and other social risk factors.

Parents and community members are included in optional sessions at the end to anchor youth in an adult worldview, provide opportunities to practice skills needed to obtain support from adults, and allow youth to see that their emerging possible selves were supported by parents and community members. Adults are brought in as tools for youth rather than as teachers or authority figures.

WEB SITES

"School Interventions." http://www.ncjrs.gov/html/ojjdp/jjbul9910-1/sch.html.
University of Michigan, Department of Psychology. http://sitemaker.umich.edu/daphna.oyserman.

References

Blair, S. L., Blair, M. C., & Legazpi, M. A. (1999). Racial/ethnic differences in high school students' academic performance: Understanding the interweave of social class and ethnicity in the family context. *Journal of Comparative Family Studies, 30*, 539–555.

Bryant, A. L., & Zimmerman, M. A. (2002). Examining the effects of academic beliefs and behaviors on changes in substance use among urban adolescents. *Journal of Educational Psychology, 94*, 621–637.

Choi, Y. (2007). Academic achievement and problem behaviors among Asian Pacific Islander American adolescents. *Journal of Youth and Adolescence, 36*(4), 403–415.

Higgins, E. T. (1996). The "self digest": Self-knowledge serving self-regulatory functions. *Journal of Personality and Social Psychology, 71*, 1062–1083.

Orfield, G., Losen, D., Wald, J., & Swanson, C. B. (2004). *Losing our future: How minority youth are being left behind by the graduation rate crisis.* Cambridge, MA: Civil Rights Project at Harvard University. http://www.urban.org/UploadedPDF/410936_LosingOurFuture.pdf,

Oyserman, D. (2007). Social identity and self-regulation. In A. Kruglanski & E. T. Higgins (Eds.), *Handbook of social psychology,* 2nd ed. (pp. 432–453). New York: Guilford.

Oyserman, D., Brickman, D., & Rhodes, M. (2007). School success, possible selves and parent school-involvement. *Family Relations, 56*, 279–289.

Oyserman, D., Bybee, D., & Terry, K. (2006). Possible selves and academic outcomes: How and when possible selves impel action. *Journal of Personality and Social Psychology, 91*, 188–204.

Oyserman, D., Bybee, D., Terry, K., & Hart-Johnson, T. (2004). Possible selves as roadmaps. *Journal of Research on Personality, 38*, 130–149.

Oyserman, D., Gant, L., & Ager, J. (1995). A socially contextualized model of African American identity: Possible selves and school persistence. *Journal of Personality and Social Psychology, 69*, 1216–1232.

Oyserman, D., & Markus, H. (1990). Possible selves and delinquency. *Journal of Personality and Social Psychology, 59*, 112–125.

Oyserman, D., Terry, K., & Bybee, D. (2002). A possible selves intervention to enhance school involvement. *Journal of Adolescence, 24,* 313–326.

Ramirez-Valles, J., Zimmerman, M. A., & Juarez, L. (2002). Gender differences of neighborhood and social control processes: A study of the timing of first intercourse among low-achieving, urban, African American youth. *Youth and Society, 33,* 418–441.

Roderick, M. (2003). What's happening to the boys? Early high school experiences and school outcomes among African American male adolescents in Chicago. *Urban Education, 38,* Special Issue: *Education African American Males,* 538–607.

Rothman, A. J., & Schwarz, N. (1998). Constructing perceptions of vulnerability: Personal relevance and the use of experiential information in health judgments. *Personality and Social Psychology Bulletin, 24,* 1053–1064.

Schwarz, N., & Clore, G. L. (1996). Feelings and phenomenal experiences. In E. T. Higgins & A. Kruglanski (Eds.), *Social psychology: Handbook of basic principles* (pp. 433–465). New York: Guilford.

U.S. Department of Education, National Center for Education Statistics. (2002). *The condition of education 2002* (NCES 2002-025). Washington, DC: U.S. Government Printing Office.

U.S. Department of Education, National Center for Education Studies. (1999). *The condition of education 1999* (NCES 99-022). Washington, DC: U.S. Government Printing Office.

Zimmerman, M. A., & Schmeelk-Cone, K. H. (2003). A longitudinal analysis of adolescent substance use and school motivation among African American youth. *Journal of Research on Adolescence, 13,* 185–210.

PART XV
Forensic Social Work

.

Overview of Forensic Social Work
153 *Broad and Narrow Definitions*

José B. Ashford

Social workers have long recognized that the law is an important mechanism for achieving many of its professional aims. Most of the early social workers involved in the establishment of the profession collaborated with lawyers in dealing with many different types of social problems. Harriett Bartlett (1970, p. 19) wrote that the social work profession started in many ways by helping individuals who "fell through the cracks of the medical and legal systems." Indeed many social work pioneers, such as Jane Addams, tested many of their theories about crime and other social problems in the newly formed urban courts of Chicago (Willrich, 2003). In particular, Addams played a key role in the establishment of the juvenile court and the modern municipal court system that replaced the traditional justice of the peace courts of Illinois (Willrich, 2003).

Inasmuch as law and social work interactions were pivotal to the formation of many aspects of social work as a profession, the subspecialty of forensic social work is of much more recent historical origins (Reamer, 2007). Most social work practitioners involved in law and social work interactions never used the term *forensic* to describe the application of their expertise to legal matters until social workers began practicing as members of forensic psychiatric teams. Psychiatric social workers in a number of states were members of clinical teams that were responsible for performing court-ordered evaluations of criminal defendants. Like the psychologists on these teams, social workers carried out their assessment and treat-ment duties on these teams under the supervision of a psychiatrist. This form of medical dominance inhibited the development of forensics as a subspecialty in social work and in psychology for many years (Dix & Poythress, 1981).

CHALLENGES TO THE MEDICAL DOMINANCE OF FORENSIC PRACTICE

Forensics is a term that is derived from the Latin *forensis*, meaning "forum." In Roman times, the forum was the public place where issues were debated before a group of citizens. However, this meaning of forensics changed and began to be restricted to legal questions in courts of law around the seventeenth century. During this time period, the term *forensic* began to be applied to legal questions involving the causes of a person's death. Medical practitioners were the first group of professionals (other than clergy, lawyers, and judges) who were involved in assisting the courts with these forensic issues. That is, physicians were initially called to assist the courts as scientific experts in determining the cause of a person's death. This form of practice led to the development of the field of forensic medicine.

Traditionally, physicians were also the first group of scientific experts called on to identify signs of illness associated with disturbances of a defendant's mind. However, psychiatric and legal historians have written that questions about the mental capabilities of individuals were originally handled by testimony from laypersons who knew the defendant (Gutheil, 2005; Skalevag, 2006). These witnesses would confirm whether the defendant had a "weak mind" from birth or whether they had acquired a derangement of mind that had been observed by individuals who knew the defendant prior to the defendant's involvement in the crime. Priests or other religious authorities were also called to assist the courts in assessing the mental culpability of an offender prior to the nineteenth century. However, they were no longer allowed to make these assessments after assumptions about human nature and illnesses began to be influenced by evolving conceptions of illnesses in the medical sciences (Skalevag, 2006).

After scientific assumptions about mental illnesses entered the legal culture, the courts only allowed professionals with medical training to conduct assessments of criminal forensic issues such as competency-to-stand trial or criminal responsibility (not guilty by reason of insanity, guilty but insane, or diminished criminal responsibility assessments). Some early challenges to this medical expertise were raised by philosophers. For instance, Immanuel Kant (1970) did not believe that the mental condition of an offender fell under the competence of medicine. "According to Kant, questions concerning the mental faculties are psychological so that answers should come from the faculty of philosophy" (Mooij, 1998, p. 340). Psychology here is not the discipline of psychology that had not been established when Kant was writing. Kant assumed that philosophers knew much more about human nature and mental faculties than medical practitioners during his period of history (Mooij, 1998). Nonetheless, most criminal codes deferred to medical professionals for addressing forensic issues involving mental health concerns up until the 1980s.

During the 1970s, psychologists, nurses, and social workers began to challenge psychiatry's claim to ultimate responsibility for treatment of forensic and other patients (Dix & Poythress, 1981). Up to this point in history, practice in most mental health settings was dictated by a 1954 resolution approved by the American Psychiatric Association, the American Medical Association, and the American Psychoanalytic Association. This resolution contended:

The medical profession fully endorses the appropriate utilization of the skills of psychologists, social workers, and other professional personnel in contributing roles in settings directly supervised by physicians. . . . When members of these professions contribute to the diagnosis and treatment of illness, their professional contribution must be coordinated under medical responsibility. (Dix & Poythress, 1981, p. 962)

Although successful campaigns were lunched by social workers and psychologists to achieve independent practice in various areas of mental health, the fight was a bit more difficult for social workers than for psychologists in forensic areas of practice. One presumed drawback for including social workers as independent forensic evaluators was licensure (Dix & Poythress, 1981). When psychologists made their case for inclusion in forensic practice, fewer states licensed social workers than clinical psychologists. However, the licensure problem for social workers has changed dramatically since the initial challenges by psychologists of medical dominance of forensic mental health practice. That is, many states currently license clinical social workers who, as mental health professionals, can diagnosis individuals for the purpose of treating mental disorders. However, this important change in the definition of social work practice did not result in many modifications of criminal codes. Many codes continue to only authorize psychiatrists to conduct competency and insanity assessments. Most criminal statutes still demand either the participation of a physician or limit participation to psychiatrists or psychologists. Although the statutory language does not exclude social workers explicitly from forensic mental health evaluations in many jurisdictions, the language in most states demands the participation of either a psychiatrist or a psychologist.

In making psychology's case for independent forensic practice, Dix and Poythress (1981) made a convincing argument about how expertise for forensic assessments should be determined. Donald Langsley, a former president of the American Psychiatric Association, had questioned the motives behind psychologists, social workers, and other nonmedical professionals seeking independent practice opportunities. Langsley argued that these requests for opportunities to function as independent practitioners should not be motivated by the pursuit of economic gain and financial rewards, but instead by dispassionate examination of education and demonstrated competencies in clinical areas of practice. To this end, Dix and Poythress (1981) wrote a law review article that questioned whether medical education justified medical superiority. In the article, they examined the issue of psychology's demonstrated competence in many areas of civil and criminal forensic mental health matters. Social workers also achieved recognition as forensic experts in some jurisdictions by independently demonstrating their competence in forensic areas of practice.

RECOGNITION OF SOCIAL WORKERS AS EXPERT WITNESSES

Although many social workers on forensic psychiatric teams developed demonstrated expertise as forensic evaluators, there was still a bias in the legal community against treating social workers as expert witnesses for competency to stand trial and insanity issues. For instance, the court in *People v. Parney* (1977, 74 Mich. App. 571, 296 N.W. 2d 568) held that a forensic social worker was not qualified to give expert testimony as to issues of competency to stand trial. However, nonbinding statements in this decision (dicta) pointed out that this holding was not based on the capabilities of any particular social worker but on a court rule that mandated presentation of psychiatric evidence regarding competency. This type of regulatory prohibition that affected the court's assessment of a social worker's expertise is still common in many states. However, there was a landmark decision involving a clinical social worker that challenged psychiatry's dominance in New York in the case of *People v. Gans* (1983, 465 NYS. 2d 147). In this case, the New York court held that a clinical social worker with appropriate training and experience was qualified to testify as an expert witness to a defendant's mental condition and prognosis in competency evaluations.

Today, most states still require that at least one examiner is a psychiatrist, but there is mounting evidence that courts are willing to deem a social worker an expert in making mental health diagnoses in criminal forensic and civil forensic matters by examining the nature and quality of their training and experience (see *Conely v. Commonwealth of Virginia*, 2007, 643 S.E. 2d 131; *America West Airlines v. Tope*, 1996, Court of Appeals of Texas, 935 S.W. 2d 908). In addition, some states now allow statutorily for other experts to perform forensic evaluations in criminal matters besides psychiatrists and psychologists (e.g., Connecticut, Delaware, Iowa, Louisiana, Maine, New Mexico, North Carolina, North Dakota, Nevada, Oklahoma, Tennessee, Texas, Utah, Wisconsin, and Virginia). However, Nevada limits the expertise

of social workers to performing these evaluations in misdemeanor offenses; Virginia limits the scope of social work's expertise as an evaluating expert to cases involving juvenile offenders when psychiatrists and psychologists are not available.

Like psychologists, forensic social workers established an identity in the specialty of forensics by gaining acceptance as experts in performing criminal assessments. However, the specialty is expanding to more general legal issues for a variety of reasons, and now we are seeing definitional differences about how to define this burgeoning area of professional social work practice.

DEFINING FORENSIC SOCIAL WORK

As the public's interest about law has increased, the focus of social workers has also shifted from the application of its expertise from traditional fields of practice to legal issues that require the application of professional social work knowledge to achieving legal ends and purposes in civil and in criminal law contexts. The professional practice of forensic social work within or in consultation with the civil and criminal legal systems has been defined in many different ways. Forensic social work is narrowly defined as professional practice by social workers who are engaged regularly as experts in the provision of evaluation and treatment services for the judicial system to achieve legal ends or purposes. The National Organization of Forensic Social Work (NOFSW) has described on its Web site that the application of social work expertise "goes far beyond clinics and psychiatric hospitals for criminal defendants being evaluated and treated on issues of competency and responsibility. A broader definition includes social work practice which in anyway is related to legal issues and litigation, both criminal and civil." This broader definition includes practice in child welfare, corrections, law enforcement, victim services, and many other areas of practice that do not involve legal questions being litigated in the judicial process.

Today, social workers are using the term *forensic* much more than in the past (Neighbors, Faust, & van Beyer, 2002). However, the education and certification of forensic social workers still has a long way to go. A survey of schools of social work supported by NOFSW and the National Council of Juvenile and Family Court Judges found that only 4.3 percent of the 122 schools surveyed offered classes on forensic social work

(Neighbors et al., 2002). The results also showed that only three schools offered a concentration in this practice area. However, a number of other schools have started concentrations and courses on forensics since the completion of this survey. In addition, there are a few schools of social work that have established postgraduate certifications in forensic social work practice in the past few years.

CURRENT FORENSIC SOCIAL WORK FUNCTIONS

Forensic social workers are applying their professional expertise to a variety of legal questions and issues in the civil and in the criminal justice systems. Some of the roles and functions performed by forensic social workers serving the judiciary and the legal system include the following.

Testifying in litigation
  • Expert witness
  • Fact witness
  • Education witness
Consultation and training
  • Consulting expert to the defense, prosecution, or the judiciary
  • Consultant or liaison to parole boards, public defender offices, police departments, prosecution offices, and specialty treatment courts
  • Consultants to advocacy groups involved with lobbying the courts through the development of amicus briefs
  • Training law enforcement, correctional, and judicial staff
Evaluation, assessment, and report writing
  • Perform court-ordered evaluations of mental capacities, children's interests, parental competencies, capacities to testify, and mitigating factors
  • Assessments of risks, needs, and strengths for child welfare, mental health, correctional, and victim agencies involved with the legal system
  • Perform social and psychosocial investigations
  • Assessments of risk of victimization or dangerousness
  • Treatment and service planning for victims, offenders, and participants in family court and other domestic relation courts.
Treatment, crisis intervention services, and case management oversight

  • Treating civil and criminal forensic patients
  • Treating adult and juvenile offenders
  • Case management of civil and criminal individuals under various forms of court jurisdiction
  • Assessing and treating victims of domestic violence and crime
Alternative dispute resolution
  • Child protective services mediation
  • Family mediation
  • Victim and offender dialogue/mediation
Research and program evaluation
  • Development of risk assessment instruments
  • Scientific investigations of principles of socializing and therapeutic jurisprudence
  • Scientific investigations of court processes and outcomes
  • Evaluating forensic assessment and treatment protocols

Each of these functions and roles require that the forensic social worker is conversant with relevant legal considerations. To be an effective forensic practitioner, the social worker must also understand how their ethical obligations are influenced by participation in litigation and other legally relevant concerns. Some rules of thumb include:

  • offer services only in areas where one has appropriate education, training, and experience;
  • separate therapeutic and supervisory roles from expert witness roles;
  • consultants to legal teams should not serve as expert witnesses in the cases for which they were hired as consulting experts;
  • provide appropriate admonitions of a lack of confidentiality and of privilege in court-ordered evaluations and forensic treatment contexts; and
  • clarify reporting responsibilities and duties.

ORGANIZATION OF THE PART ON FORENSIC SOCIAL WORK

This part of the *Social Workers' Desk Reference* includes chapters written by leading authorities in the field of forensic social work. The authors describe the emerging roles and functions of forensic social workers with an explicit focus on examining the latest assessment protocols, treatment guidelines, treatment planning processes, and evidence-based strategies for providing professional social work services in the civil and the criminal legal systems. The section begins with three chapters that examine legal issues involving forensic social workers who are practicing in ways consistent with narrow or more traditional definitions of forensic social work. These chapters examine different ways that forensic social workers are providing services relevant to litigation issues: step-by-step guidelines for preparing expert witness testimony in child welfare cases (Chapter 154), guidelines and principles for implementing interest based mediation in child protection cases (Chapter 155), and mediation and conflict resolution (Chapter 156).

Another important role performed by forensic social workers in different contexts is assessing risk. Some of the types of risk assessment performed by forensic social workers include:

- risk assessments of mentally ill and substance-abusing offenders for risk of violence and repeat criminality;
- assessments of dangerousness among convicted sex offenders and/or sexual predators;
- domestic violence and child maltreatment risks; and
- assessments of whether individuals petitioned for involuntary hospitalization are a danger to self or others.

In this part, we have several chapters from social work experts that focus on various types of risk assessment with offenders and victims. Chapter 157 focuses on risk assessment in domestic violence and child protective services; Chapter 158 on assessing risk in dually diagnosed offenders and civil patients; and Chapter 159 on guidelines for assessing sexual predators and their risks.

Other chapters in this forensic section focus on forms of forensic social work that specialize in the treatment of nontraditional forensic patients who are victims of crime or abuse. Chapter 157 offers strategies for treating children exposed to domestic violence. This chapter is followed by one dealing with elder abuse (Chapter 160).

CONCLUSION

This part examines the practical tasks confronting social workers in the application of their pro-

fessional knowledge to a variety of old and new roles performed by forensic social workers. This examination shows how forensic social workers are still engaged in the assessment and treatment of forensic psychiatric patients, and that they have also started to extend their expertise to a variety of other legal issues and contexts. Clearly, the face of forensic social work practice has changed significantly since the early days of the profession. The upshot is that practitioners in this specialty area of social work practice need guidelines that can assist them in responding to the evolving standards of law and other distinct challenges encountered by those serving traditional and nontraditional forensic clients. This part of the volume begins with an examination of clinical guides to practice for forensic social workers who are serving as expert and fact witnesses in child welfare disputes.

WEB SITES

Federal Rules of Evidence for Expert Witnesses: Rule 702. http://expertpages.com/federal/federal.htm.

National Council of Juvenile and Family Court Judges. http://www.ncjfcj.org/content/blogcategory/351/416.

National Organization of Forensic Social Work. http://www.nofsw.org.

References

Bartlett, H. (1970). *The common base of social work practice.* New York: NASW Press.

Dix, G. E., & Poythress, N. G. (1981). Propriety of medical dominance of forensic mental health practice: The empirical evidence. *Arizona Law Review, 23,* 961–989.

Gutheil, T. G. (2005). The history of forensic psychiatry. *Journal of the American Academy of Psychiatry and Law, 33,* 259–262.

Kant, I. (1970). Antropologie in pragatischer hinsicht (1978) (Antropology). In Weischedel (Ed.), *Werke* (vol. 4, pp. 260–399). Darmstadt: Wissenshaftliche Buchgesellshaft.

Mooij, A. (1998). Kant on criminal law and psychiatry. *International Journal of Law and Psychiatry, 21,* 335–341.

Neighbors, I. A., Faust, L. G., & van Beyer, K. (2002). Curricula development in forensic social work at the MSW and post-MSW levels. In I. A. Neighbors, A. Chambers, E. Levin, G. Nordman, & C. Tutrone (Eds.), *Social work and the law: Proceedings of the National Organization of Fo-*

rensic Social Work, 2000. (pp. 1–11). New York: Haworth.

Reamer, F. G. (2007). Foreword. In D. W. Springer & A. R. Roberts (Eds.), Handbook of forensic mental health with victims and offenders. New York: Springer.

Skalevag, S. A. (2006). The matter of forensic psychiatry: A historical enquiry. Medical History, 50, 49–68.

Willrich, M. (2003). City of courts: Socializing justice in progressive era of Chicago. New York: Cambridge University Press.

154

Forensic Social Work and Expert Witness Testimony in Child Welfare

Carlton E. Munson

This chapter deals with forensic social work practice in the context of expert witness testimony regarding children and adolescents, but most of the content can be applied to any form of forensic social work. Social workers are increasingly performing forensic child welfare work by providing evaluations of children and families and testifying as experts in relation to court- or attorney-requested assessments as well as testifying as fact witnesses in connection with therapeutic intervention (Gutheil & Applebaum, 2000). Social workers do not generally have training in how to do legal assessments or how to provide effective expert and fact witness testimony. Social work education programs at the baccalaureate, master's, and doctoral level do not provide academic instruction in forensic social work, and there are limited continuing education offerings in this area. A few social work schools have developed forensic specializations, but these do not have a specific focus on child welfare practice. Social work has not been as diligent as psychiatry and psychology in developing forensic specialty professional organizations. The National Orga-

nization of Forensic Social Work (NOFSW) was founded in the 1970s and offers training, conferences, and publications. In 1987, The NOFSW approved a revised and updated forensic social work code of ethics. The size of the NOFSW is small compared to the number of social workers providing forensic services.

ENTERING FORENSIC WORK

Training and Knowledge Needed

Forensic assessments and expert witness testimony require highly specialized training and experience. Before entering expert witness practice, the social worker should receive training in forensics and the roles of expert witnesses. The primary areas that a child welfare expert witness should have training in should include but are not be limited to the following (key resources are cited):

• Child and adolescent development (Berk, 2006; Bukatko, 2007; Newcombe, 1996).

- Child and adolescent psychopathology (Jensen, Knapp, & Mrazek, 2006; Ollendick & Hersen, 1998).
- Adult psychopathology (Kaplan & Sadock, 2007).
- Attachment theory (Cassidy & Shaver, 199; Oppenheim & Goldsmith, 20079; Prior & Glaser, 2006; Solomon & George, 1999).
- Traumatic stress theory (Carlson, 1997; Nader, 2007; Schiraldi, 2000; van der Kolk, McFarlane, & Weisaeth, 2006; Wilson & Keane, 2004; Wolchik & Sandler, 2007).
- Basic developmental neurology (Applegate & Shapiro, 2006; Cozolino, 2006; Harris, 1995; Martin, Volkmar, & Lewis, 2007).
- Basic understanding of psychopharmacology (Brown, Carpenter, & Simerly, 2005; Thompson, 2007).
- Basic understanding of genetics (Klug, Cummings, & Spencer, 2005).
- Basic knowledge of substances and alcohol use/abuse/dependence (American Psychiatric Association [APA], 2000c; Ksir, Hart, & Ray, 2005; Lowinson, Ruiz, Millman, & Langrod, 2005).
- Basic child welfare practice (Crosson-Tower, 2006, 2007; Hobbs, Hanks, & Wynne, 1999; Lutzker, 1998; Myers et al., 2002).
- Ability to administer and interpret standardized measures and instruments (APA, 2000b; Groth-Marnat, 2005; Kaplan & Saccuzzo, 2004).
- Knowledge of forensic specialization practice (Munson, 2007; Springer & Roberts, 2007; Vance, 1997).
- Knowledge of local, state, and federal laws relevant to clinical practice specialization and expertise (Dyer, 1999; Myers, 2006).
- General knowledge of forensic practice (Ackerman, 1999; Albert, 1986; English & Sales, 2005; Gudjonsson & Haward, 1998; Heilbrun, Marczyk, & DeMatteo, 2002; Melton, Petrila, Poythress, & Slobogin, 2007; Saltzman & Furman, 1999)
- Specific knowledge of child and family forensic practice (Benjamin & Gollan, 2003; Myers, 1998; Sparta & Koocher, 2006)
- Specific knowledge of custody evaluation practice standards (Ackerman, 2006; Gould & Martindale, 2007; Stahl, 1994).
- Specific knowledge of how to provide expert and fact witness testimony (Bernstein & Hartsell, 2005; Brodsky, 1991, 1999; Ceci & Hembrooke, 1998; Gutheil & Dattilio, 2008; Tsushima & Anderson, 1996).

Fact and Expert Witnesses

On entering forensic work, the practitioner must understand the difference between expert and fact witnesses. Expert witnesses and fact witnesses are different in most jurisdictions. Fact witnesses are also referred to in some jurisdictions as "treaters." A treater mental health professional can be called to testify to the treatment that has been provided to a person. He or she testifies only to the facts of the treatment and does not offer opinions about factors outside the context of the treatment. If the witness is not testifying as an expert, the testimony is in the form of opinions or inferences limited to those rationally based on perception and helpful in clarifying testimony or determination of a contested issue. Expert testimony is admitted, in the form of an opinion, if the court determines that the testimony will assist the trier of fact (judge or jury) in understanding the evidence or to determine a fact in question. In making that determination, the court establishes (1) whether the witness is qualified as an expert by knowledge, skill, experience, training, or education; (2) the appropriateness of the expert testimony on the particular subject; and (3) whether a sufficient factual basis exists to support the expert testimony. An expert opinion is not necessarily inadmissible because it embraces an ultimate issue to be decided by the trier of fact, but an expert witness testifying with respect to the mental state or condition of a defendant in a criminal case may not state an opinion or inference as to whether the defendant had a mental state or condition constituting an element of the offense because that issue is for the trier of fact to decide. This exception does not apply to an ultimate issue of criminal responsibility. Expert witnesses can give opinions and inform the trier of fact for courts to make the best possible decision in cases. For this reason, judges are granted liberal discretion in allowing expert testimony (Mueller & Kirkpatrick, 1999).

It is recognized that fact or treater witness can be an advocate for the client and therefore would be appropriately biased in favor of the client. An expert witness is not to be an advocate and should be objective and impartial. A treater or fact witness should never be an expert in the same case because of the advocacy and impartiality conflict.

Some attorneys and judges will attempt to have a fact witness also give expert witness testimony; the fact witness should politely decline the invitation and point out the conflict that is created by performing the two roles simultaneously. If the judge insists the fact witness render an expert opinion, the witness should comply with the judge's directive to avoid being charged with contempt of court (Gutheil & Dattilio, 2008). An expert should not become the treater of the same client after providing expert witness testimony for the client because of the future potential for conflict of being a subsequent treater.

Managing Risk

Forensic social work practitioners are at higher risk for lawsuits and regulatory board complaints, and the practitioner should have the maximum professional liability insurance coverage and confirm that the insurance carrier provides coverage for lawsuits and regulatory board complaints. The practitioner should be thoroughly familiar with the National Association of Social Workers (NASW) Code of Ethics (NASW, 1996) and the NOFSW Code of Ethics (NOFSW, 1987). The forensic practitioner should review the state licensing board regulations. Most states do not have specific licensing regulations related to forensic practice, but some have a statutory code of ethics that is used as the criteria for investigation of complaints that is independent of the NASW and NOFSW ethics codes. The forensic practitioner needs to establish what code of ethics applies in a particular state.

Confidentiality

Confidentiality is of increased complexity in forensic work. Mental health professionals have become much more concerned with confidentiality in the past decades because of confusing state and federal mandates about confidentiality. In the legal arena, the concept of confidentiality is replaced with the concept of "privileged communication." In the law, information the client provides to a professional remains the "property" of the client, and the client owns the right to control the information with respect to disclosure as part of the judicial process (Albert, 1986; Saltzman & Furman, 1999). The forensic practitioner must consult with the client about disclosure of information that may find its way in to the legal process, but the concept of confidentiality in the professional sense is an invention of codes of ethics

that apply to any disclosure of client information in any context, not just the judicial process. With confidentiality, the professional owns and controls the information and makes the decision as to whether the information will be released with or without the consent of the client. For example, if child maltreatment has been disclosed by the client or the client threatens to harm a person or property, the professional is compelled to disclose the information to the authorities without client consent.

The best protection in this situation is for the forensic practitioner to have an advance written informed consent that details who will be provided information. The traditional abuse reporting and threats of harm or destruction of property reporting should be included, and the disclosure of information to judges and attorneys should be detailed even if the evaluation is court-ordered. The client should be provided a copy of the consent.

The 20/20 Rule

An expert witness should organize practice based on the 20/20 rule. The rule refers to the formula that the expert practitioner devote at least 20 hours per week to work in the clinical area of practice in which the expert offers testimony. The practitioner also should not receive more than 20 percent of total income from expert witness work. The first part of the formula relates to competency, and the second part to impartiality, objectivity, and bias. Practitioners who earn more than 20 percent of total income from expert witness work are subject to allegations of operating from the "hired gun" principle.

Bias

Bias is a key feature of forensic work. The practitioner should make special efforts in all aspects of forensic work to guard against allegations of bias. Bias is important because the role of the expert is exclusively to provide objective, scientific information that will educate and assist the trier of fact (judge or jury) in rendering a decision in a case. The following general forensic practice standards can be helpful in avoiding allegations of bias and keeping a pledge of objectivity.

• Request that the court appoint you to do the expert witness work. If the court does not appoint you, maintain independence from the attorney who pays your fee.

- Avoid doing work for an attorney who insists on knowing your opinions before hiring you. Understanding lawyer motivations based on personality functioning has been described by Daicoff (2004).
- Always work on a retainer basis. It is not recommended that an expert testify in a case if the services provided have not been prepaid. Some states require that experts work on a retainer basis.
- Do not have any informal or non–case-related contact with any parties to a case. This would include attorneys for the parents and attorneys for children.
- Never render an opinion about a person you have not interviewed or tested.
- Interview all relevant parties to a case before rendering opinions.
- Base opinions on scientific evidence that is cited in the report to the court or is explained in oral testimony.
- Use standardized measures to support clinical observations. For example personality testing to support a diagnosis of Antisocial Personality Disorder (APA, 2000a).
- Submit reports to the court or attorney well in advance of the hearing so all parties can have reasonable time to review the reports before the hearing.
- Never withhold are delay submission of relevant material.

CASE PREPARATION

Preparation for legal system involvement begins the moment the practitioner receives a referral. A thorough and complete record of all activity should be maintained from the time the first contact with a client takes place. The report of an assessment and evaluation is the cornerstone of expert or fact witness testimony. Social workers entering the legal arena to do assessments should be clear about the purpose of the evaluation. In clinical practice with children and adolescents, this can cover a number of areas, including:

- short- and long-term effects of neglect, physical abuse, sexual abuse, and witnessing domestic violence;
- mental injury of a child;
- custody decisions;
- impact of reunification with a parent after a long separation (attachment issues);

- termination of parental rights (TPR);
- mental status and functioning of parents in anticipation of reunification with a child; and
- domestic and international child abduction.

FORENSIC EVALUATIONS

Expert witness testimony does not always involve the expert being directly involved with the parties. In some cases, the expert may only do a records review and testify on the basis of that review or submit an affidavit that documents the expert's qualifications, the results of the review, and the opinions. In other cases, the expert may only serve as rebuttal witness after listening to the testimony of other witnesses. In most cases, the expert will do an evaluation that becomes the basis of the expert testimony. A forensic evaluation is significantly different than a traditional psychotherapeutic assessment, which is used exclusively by the therapist for treatment planning. Forensic evaluations are used by lawyers to make a case based on establishing truth through fact-finding, and mental health professionals use probabilities and ranges of prediction in doing evaluations. The forensic evaluation of children places an additional burden on the forensic evaluator because of the developmental focus, the need for special child-oriented communications skills (Sparta & Koocher, 2006), and the inability of children to make decisions independently. A fundamental rule of any expert report writing is that the reports should only be written at the request of the judge or retaining attorney. In some situations reports are not discoverable, but all reports should be written based on the assumption they would be discoverable (Babitsky & Mangraviti, 2002).

The forensic evaluation should consist of a standard protocol that is routinely used with cases based on the clinician's specialty practice area. The assessment should include contact with all persons who have relevance to the outcome of the case. Clinical interviews should be conducted with pertinent individuals and standardized measures used when appropriate (e.g., to confirm diagnosis of depression or post-traumatic stress disorder, to determine suitability for custody or level of parenting stress). The evaluator should contact collateral sources that may have information relevant to the issues explored in the evaluation (such as child welfare workers, therapists, medical and psychiatric hospitalization reports, police, school counselors, teachers, employers, and probation officers).

Evaluation reports should be clear, concise, and carefully proofed before submission. Various outlines for submission of reports have been devised (Koocher, Norcross, & Hill, 2004; Melton et al., 2007; Nurcombe & Partlett, 1994; Sattler, 1998). The following outline is recommended for child and adolescent reports.

- *Reason for evaluation.* This should be a brief statement of the purpose of the evaluation and the referral source.
- *Procedures.* There should be identification of information sources, persons interviewed, and standardized measures used. A brief statement should be included that describes how suggestive questioning and inducements for participation were avoided (see Ceci & Bruck, 1995).
- *Abuse history.* Identify presence or absence of any individual or family history of neglect, physical abuse, sexual abuse, or domestic violence.
- *Background.* Summarize information relevant to the factors that led to the presenting problem.
- *Family and individual history.* Provide detailed family history data, including information about parents, siblings, education, employment, social functioning, and religious activity.
- *Developmental history.* Include a survey of the mother's use of tobacco, alcohol, substances, and prescription medications during pregnancy. Note if there were any complications during pregnancy or at birth. A review for premature birth, low birth weight, eating/feeding problems during infancy, problems with toilet training, or problems entering school. There should a review of the father's role in the child's development on the relevant factors listed for the mother.
- *Developmental milestones.* Assess and note appropriate developmental milestones of children and adolescents. This can be done with standardized measures or milestone checklists. The most common areas of development are physical, self-help, social, communication, and intellectual (Berk, 2006). Language development can be a crucial indicator of development in combination with maltreatment. Language delays are common

(Amster, 1999) and are so prevalent in the child welfare population that they can be used diagnostically for maltreated children (Munson, 2001a).

- *History of out-of-home placements.* Include as much information as possible about past and current placements. This applies to children and adults.
- *Visitation.* If the child is not in the care of the parents, give a summary of the visitation schedule and note whether visitation is supervised.
- *Criminal justice history.* Give a history of all arrests, convictions for criminal offenses, and civil litigation the child or parent has experienced.
- *Substance/alcohol history.* Provide a history of substance or alcohol use or abuse or dependence by child and parents based on the *DSM-IV-TR* (APA, 2000a) criteria.
- *Medical history.* Report major illnesses, injuries, hospitalizations, and family history of illness for the child and parents. Document date of last physical examination. If the client has not had a physical examination in the past 30 days, this should be noted and the client referred for medical screening to rule out any general medical conditions that could be a source of dysfunction. Children should also be referred for dental, vision, and hearing screenings if there have been no screenings in the last year.
- *Medications.* Note past and current medications, including dosage information. Review for use of herbal medications or culturally bound medications. If the client is taking medication, record the most recent administration prior to the evaluation session.
- *Mental health treatment.* Review past and present inpatient and outpatient mental health treatment. Record diagnoses received and names of therapists, quality of relationship with the therapists, and the outcome of the treatment.
- *School.* For children, report school functioning academically and behaviorally. For adults, report amount of education.
- *Clinical interview.* Record the identified client's mental status, interview behavior and demeanor, speech, language, somatic complaints, perception, cognition, judgment, memory, intellectual functioning, emotions, interpersonal skills, and access to weapons.

- *Standardized measures.* Give descriptions and summaries of standardized measures administered. Interpretation of objective measures should be described in clear, concise language. The interpretation should be focused on the purpose of the evaluation and the recommendations.
- *Diagnosis.* Provide a thorough *DSM-IV-TR* multiaxial diagnosis (see Munson, 2000, 2001a, 2001b).
- *Summary and conclusions.* Give a concise summary of the case and provide an integrated analysis of the significant aspects of the findings. Conclusions should be supported with citations of empirical research and clinical literature that support findings and conclusions. In complex cases, it helps to have subsections of this section. The recommended subheadings are Summary of Facts, Findings, Conclusions and Opinions, and Limitations.
- *Recommendations.* Based on the findings, the diagnosis, the conclusions, and the opinions, the evaluator should make specific recommendations, with justification for each recommendation.

In preparing the written report, it is recommended that the guidelines below be followed.

- Indicate source of statements and use qualifier words when you do not have direct knowledge of a fact. Use phrases, such as "reported by," "reportedly," and "according to."
- Use professional language, such as "appeared to be intoxicated," not "he was drunk"; "Indications are she deliberately made inaccurate statements," not "She lied to me"; "limited intellectual capacity," not "mentally retarded," unless diagnosed through standardized tests.

Use language in reports that is familiar to the courts. This language can be derived from written opinions of appeals courts. Do not attempt to make legal statements, but use brief, legal phrases to express concepts. For example, phrases that can be helpful are:

- best interest of the child,
- general well-being of the child,
- risk to the child,
- safety of the child,
- vulnerability of the child,
- special needs child,
- influences likely to be exerted on the child,
- preference of the child,
- fitness of person seeking custody,
- adaptability of person to the task,
- environment and surroundings child will be reared in,
- potential for maintaining natural family relations,
- opportunities for the future life of the child,
- prior voluntary abandonment or surrender of custody,
- parental rights versus performance of parental duties,
- chronic and enduring mental illness,
- persistent and ongoing problems.

DIAGNOSIS AND EXPERT TESTIMONY

There has been controversy about the legal sanction for clinical social workers to do diagnosis. A series of appellate legal opinions have confirmed the admissibility as evidence diagnosis performed by clinical social workers where there is legislative sanction. The Maryland Court of Appeals, in a case that involved the author, unanimously affirmed the statutory right of licensed clinical social workers to perform diagnosis, testify as expert witnesses, and testify to the ultimate issue (In Re Adoption/Guardianship no. CCJ14746, 360 Md 634, 2000). The opinion of the court and the NASW and others amicus brief (Brief for NASW et al., 1999) filed in this case can be helpful to forensic social workers in other states who have been legally challenged in the right to diagnose.

Diagnosis of mental and emotional disorders is included in most state practice acts and is directly stated in practice acts of 35 states (American Association of State Social Work Boards, 2007). The states that include the word *diagnosis* in their practice acts are Alabama, Alaska, Arizona, Colorado, Connecticut, Delaware, Florida, Idaho, Illinois, Iowa, Kansas, Louisiana, Maine, Maryland, Massachusetts, Minnesota, Mississippi, Missouri, Montana, Nevada, New Hampshire, New Jersey, New Mexico, New York, North Carolina, Ohio, Oklahoma, Oregon, Rhode Island, South Carolina, South Dakota, Texas, Vermont, West Virginia, Wisconsin, Wyoming, and the District of Columbia. All other states, except three, permit diagnosis but use alternate terminology.

BEFORE THE HEARING

Expert testimony occurs after the report has been submitted, and the expert's testimony should be based on the procedures and findings contained in the report. A basic rule to remember is that expert witness testimony is only as good as the attorney who offers the professional as an expert. Experts tend to believe that the entire case depends on their testimony and how well they perform. This is not usually the situation. There are often many witnesses in a case and many factors that influence and determine the outcome. An expert's testimony is to offer findings and opinions in a truthful, fair, and factual manner, which can assist the trier of fact in making a decision, and that should be paramount in expert testimony.

An expert witness should request to meet with the attorney who will be offering the expert to the court. Such a meeting can be helpful in preparing how the expert wants to present testimony and what is to be highlighted. It is important to ask the attorney all questions about the nature of the testimony. The attorney should be provided with written information about your credentials prior to the hearing. If you meet with the attorney, review your written materials, organize them, and highlight key points. Separate from your report, develop an outline of key points you want to testify to, and commit the outline to memory.

AT THE HEARING

The classic advice holds regarding attire and demeanor. Dress professionally, act professionally, and arrive in court early. Bring all materials related to the case. Avoid talking with anyone in the waiting room, courtroom, or hall while waiting to testify. This includes colleagues, attorneys, police, strangers, or the parent or child about whom you are testifying. Do not smile, laugh, or joke with anyone in the presence of the judge or jury before, during, or after testifying. For confidentiality reasons, do not leave a briefcase or hearing materials unattended at any time.

ON THE STAND

Before testifying, request the attorney to qualify you as an expert by reviewing your credentials

for the court. Sometimes attorneys are conscious of the need to proceed rapidly and may do a brief review of your credentials, especially if you have testified in the court in the past. If you are easily and quickly qualified as an expert, it is important to include in your testimony responses that call attention to your qualifications. For example, substantive comments can be prefaced with comments such as, "In my 20 years of work with this population, it is my experience that . . ." or "As part of my training I became familiar with research that supports . . ." Such comments could be crucial if there is an appeal of your testimony.

Procedural qualification of experts focuses on the concepts of knowledge, skill, experience, training, and education because these are the areas identified in the law as basic to being an expert (Mueller & Kirkpatrick, 1999). The process of expert qualification includes review of professional education (degrees and dates received, internships, specialized training, continuing education, honors, awards, licenses, certifications; Tsushima & Anderson, 1996), employment history, number of clients evaluated or treated, research activity, publications, professional paper presentations, and the amount of prior testimony as an expert witness.

The attorney who is challenging your testimony will use the voir dire procedure, which is the opposing attorney's opportunity to test and challenge your credentials and competency to testify, as well as to challenge expert testimony in general (for example, citing research indicating that expert opinions are no more accurate than those of laypersons). There may be attempts to show bias in requesting information about fees received for testimony, or your personal history as a victim of abuse or domestic violence to show you are on a mission, promoting a cause, or engaged in advocacy. Voir dire is a standard legal procedure that should not be viewed as a personal attack, although it may seem to be. This can be the most difficult phase of expert testimony, as attacks on education, training, and experience can be intense (Tsushima & Anderson, 1996). The key is to be calm and answer questions directly and honestly. Never become defensive or argumentative during this stage of testimony, especially when feeling attacked personally or professionally. Consider the following example.

Attorney Question (AQ): It is true that the social work profession is on the lowest tier of therapists, with psychiatrists at the top, psychologists next, and social workers at the bottom, correct?

Expert Answer (EA): No, that is not the situation today. It was like that 40 years ago. Clinical practice with children and adolescents today is quite complex and requires multidisciplinary expertise. All recognized mental health professionals are equal members of the evaluation or treatment team. Social workers have the most historical expertise in child welfare, and we often provide leadership in this area. We provide the majority of the mental health services in the United States and have evolved significant research and expertise in the mental health field.

A general rule of testimony is to avoid anticipating what the judge or the attorneys are dealing with or attempting to elicit. Simply answer the questions on the basis of what you did, the reason you did it, and the opinions you formulated. Ask attorneys to repeat unclear questions. Answer only the questions that are asked, and do not attempt to expand on a previously given answer. Focus on the immediate question you are being asked. It is recommended that you look at the judge when giving opinions, look at the attorney when giving facts, and avoid looking at the client when giving difficult testimony. Always look at the judge when giving answers to questions asked by the judge.

If the opposing attorney asks a question directly from your notes or report he or she received as part of the discovery process, ask for the specific page number of the report and answer on the basis of the content of the report. It is also a good policy to make verbal reference to your report. Use statements such as, "In my report summary section, I indicated . . . " or "My background information section of the report confirms that . . . " and "the results of my testing explained on page 6 of the report indicate . . . " This is an effective way to call the judge's or jury's attention to your findings. Do not read from the report. Testify from memory and request the court to allow you to review your report or supporting documents if a technical question is asked that requires a precise answer, such as actual test scores.

CROSS-EXAMINATION

Cross-examination is always difficult because it is the opposing attorney's second chance to challenge the expert witness. In the voir dire phase of testimony, there is a general challenge to qualifications to testify, and in the cross-examination, there are specific challenges of the validity of the

expert's procedures and conclusions in the specific case. It is important to remain calm and factual and not alter voice level when such challenges are made. Do not let the attorney make you angry or provoke you. This requires a significant amount of self-control. It is important to remember that you are there to provide facts and opinions related to what you do routinely in conducting assessments. Hesitate when you think you should not answer a question to give the attorney who offered you as an expert an opportunity to object.

During cross-examination, refrain from thinking the case outcome hinges on your testimony, and do not attempt to analyze the effect of your testimony while you are testifying. Focus on the accuracy and scientific basis of your testimony.

Try to avoid answering hypothetical questions, such as the following.

AQ: Hypothetically, if my client had a relative who could provide care for this child, could the child adjust to placement under these circumstances?

EA: It depends. It depends on the home study of the relatives, their parenting skills, the child's bond and attachment with the foster parents, and history of contact with the relatives as well as other factors. So it would be difficult for me to answer that question.

During cross-examination, an expert can use questions to expand on previous answers or to make additional points.

Example 1

AQ: My client was evicted from her apartment because she had no job, could not pay her rent, and DSS would not give her assistance, wasn't she?

EA: My notes indicate that she was evicted because she was having loud parties, and the police were called because of substance use. This was consistent with statements she made to me that she had been using cocaine regularly for the past 3 years. I have no record that she ever asked for assistance with her rent.

Example 2

AQ: Then all you can testify to is that there were arguments between my client and the mother? There was no real domestic violence in this relationship, was there?

EA: Recurring shouting and belittling are violent acts. In addition, there is increased risk to the child because the father frequently uses alcohol. He has been apprehended for violence in the community. He denies he abused the mother. Since the mother died when the child was 14 months old, the child may have special needs and have uneasy temperament. All of these facts increase the risk of violence against the child by the father.

Avoid defensiveness when asked questions that can be viewed as attacks on your ethics. It is best to respond with a simple statement of ethical obligations.

AQ: Is it true that you wrote in your report that my client had a history of multiple foster care placements knowing it would harm her in this TPR hearing?

EA: No, my professional ethics code would not allow me to do that. I wrote it because generally accepted practice guidelines for parental rights cases require recording all relevant information regarding this case.

AFTER THE HEARING

After a hearing, the best way to prepare for the next time you will testify is to review your testimony and think of ways you could have testified more effectively. Do not obsess about the effect of your testimony, rather, analyze ways you can improve responses in the future. Write down key questions from your testimony that you may be asked in future cases and review them before you testify again.

CONCLUSION

Serving as an expert is difficult under any circumstances. It is a complex aspect of mental health practice that is increasing. Forensic social work is truly one of the artistic and scientific aspects of practice that requires discipline, skill, and preparation. Providing expert witness testimony is fundamental to the expert role and the following nine key summary principles of fact an expert witness testimony should be used as a concise guide before testifying.

1. Determine if you are a fact or expert witness and do not agree to perform both roles in the same case.

2. Only agree to be an expert witness on a retainer basis and never accept a fee for fact witness testimony.
3. Thoroughly document all activity and organize documents for testimony.
4. Commit to memory your credentials and organize them by education, training, skill, knowledge, and experience.
5. While waiting to testify, remain silent and safeguard your documents.
6. Do not become defensive when challenged and respond in a calm voice using your knowledge as your guide.
7. Only answer questions asked.
8. If necessary, expand on yes/no questions and qualify hypothetical questions.
9. After testifying, reflect on what you said, but do not obsess about the effectiveness of the testimony. *Remember*: Your testimony is only as good as the attorney who sought you to testify.

Note

Content of this chapter pertains to legal issues and offers suggestions for forensic social work professionals participating in legal proceedings. No comments herein should be considered as legal advice. Information in this chapter is generic and may not be applicable to some states and jurisdictions. The reader should consult an attorney for legal advice regarding cases that are relevant to the content of this chapter.

WEB SITE

National Organization of Forensic Social Work. http://www.nofsw.org.

References

Ackerman, M. J. (1999). *Essentials of forensic psychological assessment.* New York: Wiley.
Ackerman, M. J. (2006). *Clinician's guide to custody evaluations.* New York: Wiley.
Albert, R. (1986). *Law and social work practice.* New York: Springer.
American Association of State Social Work Boards. (2007). *Social work laws and board regulations: A comparison guide: Social Work Practice and Related Definitions.* Culpeper, VA: AASSWB.
American Psychiatric Association. (2000a). *Diagnostic and statistical manual of mental disorders,* 4th ed., text revision. Washington, DC: APA.

American Psychiatric Association. (2000b). *Handbook of psychiatric measures*. Washington, DC: APA.

American Psychiatric Association. (2000c). *Practice guidelines for the treatment of psychiatric disorders: Compendium 2000*. Washington, DC: APA.

Amster, B. J. (1999). Speech and language development of young children in the child welfare system. In J. A. Silver, B. J. Amster, & T. Haecher (Eds.), *Young children and foster care* (pp. 117–157). Baltimore: Brookes.

Applegate, J. S., & Shapiro, J. R., (2006). *Neurobiology for clinical social work: Theory and practice*. New York: Norton.

Babitsky, S., & Mangraviti, J. J. (2002). *Writing and defending your expert report: The step-by-step guide with models*. Falmouth, MA: SEAK.

Benjamin, G. A. H., & Gollan, J. K. (2003). *Family evaluations in custody litigation: Reducing risks of ethical interactions and malpractice*. Washington, DC: American Psychological Association.

Berk, L. E. (2006). *Development through the life span*, 4th ed. Boston: Allyn & Bacon.

Bernstein, B. E., & Hartsell, T. L. (2005). *The portable guide to testifying in court for mental health professionals: An A–Z guide to being an effective witness*. New York: Wiley.

Brief for National Association of Social Workers et al. (1999). In Re adoption/guardianship no. CCJ14746. Maryland Court of Appeals (no. 134, September term,).

Brodsky, S. L. (1991). *Testifying in court: Guidelines and maxims for the expert witness*. Washington, DC: American Psychological Association.

Brodsky, S. L. (1999). *The expert witness: More maxims and guidelines for testifying in court*. Washington, DC: American Psychological Association.

Brown, R. T., Carpenter, L. A., & Simerly, E. (2005). *Mental health medications for children: A primer*. New York: Guilford.

Bukatko, D. (2007). *Child and adolescent development: A chronological approach*. Boston: Houghton Mifflin.

Carlson, E. B. (1997). *Trauma assessment: A clinician's guide*. New York: Guilford.

Cassidy, J., & Shaver, P. R. (Eds.). (1999). *Handbook of attachment: Theory, research, and clinical applications*. New York: Guilford.

Ceci, S. J., & Bruck, M. (1995). *Jeopardy in the courtroom: A scientific analysis of children's testimony*. Washington, DC: American Psychological Association.

Ceci, S. J., & Hembrooke, H. (1998). *Expert witnesses in child abuse cases: What can and should be said in court*. Washington, DC: American Psychological Association.

Cozolino, L. (2006). *The neuroscience of human relationships: Attachment and the developing social brain*. New York: Norton.

Crosson-Tower, C. (2006). *Exploring Child welfare: A practice perspective*, 3rd ed. Boston: Pearson.

Crosson-Tower, C. (2007). *Understanding child abuse and neglect*, 7th ed. Boston: Pearson.

Daicoff, S. S. (2004). *Lawyer, know thyself: A psychological analysis of personality strengths and weaknesses*. Washington, DC: American Psychological Association.

Dyer, F. J. (1999). *Psychological consultation in parental rights cases*. New York: Guilford.

English, P. W., & Sales, B. D. (2005). *More than the law: Behavioral and social facts in legal decision making*. Washington, DC: American Psychological Association.

Gould, J. W., & Martindale, D. A. (2007). *The art and science of custody evaluations*. New York: Guilford.

Groth-Marnat, G. (2005). *Psychological testing and assessment*, 12th ed. Boston: Allyn & Bacon.

Gudjonsson, G. H., & Haward, L. R. C. (1998). *Forensic psychology: A guide to practice*. New York: Routledge.

Gutheil, T. G., & Applebaum, P. S. (2000). *Clinical handbook of psychiatry and the law*, 3rd ed. Philadelphia: Lippincott Williams & Wilkins.

Gutheil, T. H., & Dattilio, F. M. (2008). *Practical approaches to forensic mental health testimony*. Philadelphia: Lippincott Williams & Wilkins.

Harris, J. C. (1995). *Developmental neuropsychiatry: Assessment, diagnosis, and treatment of developmental disorders* (vol. 2). New York: Oxford University Press.

Heilbrun, K., Marczyk, G. R., & DeMatteo, D. (2002). *Forensic mental health assessment: A casebook*. New York: Oxford University Press.

Hobbs, C. J., Hanks, H. G. I., & Wynne, J. M. (1999). *Child abuse and neglect: A clinician's handbook*, 2nd ed. London: Churchill Livingstone.

Jensen, P. S., Knapp, P., & Mrazek, D. A. (Eds.). (2006). *Toward a new diagnostic system for child psychopathology: Moving beyond the DSM*. New York: Guilford.

Kaplan, H. I., & Sadock, B. J. (2007). *Synopsis of psychiatry: Behavior science/clinical psychiatry*, 10th ed. Baltimore: Williams & Wilkins.

Kaplan, R. M. & Saccuzzo, D. P. (2004). Psychological testing: Principles, applications, and issues. Emeryville, CA: Wadsworth.

Klug, W. S., Cummings, M. R., & Spencer, C. (2005). *Concepts of genetics*. New York: Benjamin Cummings.

Koocher, G. P., Norcross, J. C., & Hill, S. S. (Eds.). (2004). *Psychologists' desk reference*. New York: Oxford University Press.

Ksir, C. J., Hart, C. L., & Ray, O. S. (2005). *Drugs, society, and human behavior*, 11th ed. New York: McGraw-Hill.

Lowinson, J. H., Ruiz, P., Millman, R. B., & Langrod, J. G. (2005). *Substance abuse: A comprehensive textbook*, 4th ed. Philadelphia: Lippincott Williams & Wilkins.

Lutzker, J. R. (Ed.). (1998). *Handbook of child abuse research and treatment*. New York: Plenum Press.

Martin, A., Volkmar, F. R., & Lewis, M. (Eds.). (2007). *Lewis's child and adolescent psychiatry: A comprehensive textbook*, 4th ed. Philadelphia: Lippincott Williams & Wilkins.

Melton, G. B., Petrila, J., Poythress, N. G., & Slobogin, C. (2007). *Psychological evaluations for the courts: A handbook for mental health professionals and lawyers* 3rd ed. New York: Guilford.

Mueller, C. B., & Kirkpatrick, L. C. (1999). *Federal rules of evidence: With advisory committee notes, legislative history, and cases*. Gaithersburg, NY: Aspen Law and Business.

Munson, C. E. (2000). *The mental health diagnostic desk reference: Visuals, guides, and more for learning to use the Diagnostic and Statistical Manual, DSM-IV-TR*. New York: Haworth.

Munson, C. E. (2001a). *Clinical social work supervision*, 3rd ed. New York: Haworth.

Munson, C. E. (2001b). *The mental health diagnostic desk reference: Visuals, guides, and more for learning to use the Diagnostic and Statistical Manual (DSM-IV-TR)*, 2nd ed. New York: Haworth.

Munson, C. E. (2007). Forensic social work and expert witness testimony. In D. W. Springer & A. R. Roberts (Eds.), *Handbook of forensic mental health with victims and offenders: Assessment, treatment and research* (pp. 67–92). New York: Springer.

Myers, J. E. B. (1998). *Legal issues in child abuse and neglect practice*, 2nd ed. Thousand Oaks, CA: Sage.

Myers, J. E. B. (2006). *Child protection in America: Past, present and future*. New York: Oxford University Press.

Myers, J. E. B., Berliner, L., Briere, J., Hendrix, C. T., Jenny, C., & Reid, T. A. (2002). *The APSAC handbook of child maltreatment*, 2nd ed. Thousand Oaks, CA: Sage.

Nader, K. (2007). *Understanding and assessing trauma in children and adolescents: Measures, methods, and youth in context*. New York: Routledge.

National Association of Social Workers. (1996). *Code of ethics of the National Association of Social Workers*. Washington, DC: NASW Press.

National Organization of Forensic Social Work. (1987). *Code of ethics*. Middletown, CT: National Organization of Forensic Social Work.

Newcombe, N. (1996). *Child development: Change over time*, 8th ed. New York: Harper Collins.

Nurcombe, B., & Partlett, D. F. (1994). *Child mental health and the law*. New York: Free Press.

Ollendick, T. H., & Hersen, M. (Eds.). (1998). *Handbook of child psychopathology*, 3rd ed. New York: Plenum Press.

Oppenheim, D., & Goldsmith, D. F. (Eds.). (2007). *Attachment theory in clinical work with children: Bridging the gap between research and practice*. New York: Guilford.

Prior, V., & Glaser, D. (2006). *Understanding attachment and attachment disorders: Theory, evidence and practice*. Child and Adolescent Mental Heath Series. London: Jessica Kingsley.

Saltzman, A., & Furman, D. M. (1999). *Law in social work practice*. Chicago: Nelson-Hall.

Sattler, J. M. (1998). *Clinical and forensic interviewing of children and families: Guidelines for the mental health, education, pediatric, and child maltreatment fields*. San Diego: Jerome M. Sattler.

Schiraldi, G. R. (2000). *The post-traumatic stress disorder sourcebook: A guide to healing, recovery, and growth*. Los Angeles: Lowell House.

Solomon, J., & George, C. (Eds.). (1999). *Attachment disorganization*. New York: Guilford.

Sparta, S. N., & Koocher, G. P. (Eds.). (2006). *Forensic mental health assessment of children and adolescents*. New York: Oxford University Press.

Springer, D. W., & Roberts, A. R. (2007) *Handbook of forensic mental health with victims and offenders: Assessment, treatment and research*. New York: Springer.

Stahl, P. M. (1994). *Conducting custody evaluations: A comprehensive guide*. Thousand Oaks, CA: Sage.

Thompson, K. (2007). *Medicines for mental health: The ultimate guide to psychiatric medication*, 2nd ed. Charleston, SC: Book Surge.

Tsushima, W. T., & Anderson, R. M. (1996). *Mastering expert testimony: A courtroom handbook for mental health professionals*. Mahwah, NJ: Erlbaum.

Vance, H. B. (Ed.). (1997). *Psychological assessment of children: Best practices for school and clinical settings*, 2nd ed. New York: Wiley.

van der Kolk, B. A., McFarlane, A. C., & Weisaeth, L. (Eds.). (2006). *Traumatic stress: The effects of overwhelming experience on mind, body, and society*. New York: Guilford.

Wilson, J. P., & Keane, T. M. (Ed). (2004). *Assessing psychological trauma and PTSD*. New York: Guilford.

Wolchik, S. A., & Sandler, I. N. (2007). *Handbook of children's coping: Linking theory and intervention*. New York: Plenum Press.

An Interest-Based Approach to Child Protection Mediation

Allan Edward Barsky

The primary purpose of the child protection system is to safeguard minors from abuse and neglect. When child maltreatment allegations are brought to the attention of protective services, child protection workers (CPWs) are mandated to assess whether abuse or neglect has occurred and determine which interventions, if any, are necessary to protect the welfare of the child. Each year, protective services across the United States screen over 2.1 million allegations and substantiate abuse or neglect in over 1.3 million cases (Child Welfare League of America, 2007). Child protection laws require CPWs to use the least intrusive methods required to safeguard children. Accordingly, CPWs strive to offer support and voluntary services in a manner that allows children to remain in the custody and care of their parents. When CPWs are unable to engage families on a voluntary basis, they may petition courts to order family involvement in child welfare services or children's removal from their homes. Protective services remove over 145,000 children from their parents' homes each year, and there are over 500,000 children in out-of-home care at any given point in time (Child Welfare League of America, 2007). Given the magnitude of problems related to child maltreatment, child protection agencies and courts have experimented with alternatives to traditional services and judicial processes. One such alternative is child protection mediation.

Child protection mediation (sometimes called dependency mediation) refers to a collaborative conflict resolution process guided by an impartial third person who facilitates communication between parents, CPWs, and others involved in child protection cases to develop an agreement that satisfies the child's safety and welfare. Child protection mediation developed in Colorado and California in the 1980s before spreading across the United States and Canada (Barsky & Trocmé, 1998; Olson, 2003; Thoennes, 2002). In some pi-

lot projects, mediation was viewed as a way to divert cases from costly court processes to relatively speedy, informal processes that would reduce legal costs for protective services, families, and the state. Mediation has proven its effectiveness as a cost-saving alternative (Gatowski, Dobbin, Litchfield, & Oetjen, 2005), but the nature and extent of savings depends on the model being evaluated. Although the term *child protection mediation* sounds like a specific process, there are many different models, including settlement-focused, interest-based, and transformative. (A related model of mediation is "evaluative mediation," in which the mediator provides parties with an assessment of the likely outcomes of a case if it went to court or arbitration, to encourage parties to settle based on the knowledge of these expected outcomes.)

- "Settlement-focused mediation (SFM)" refers to a task-focused problem-solving process designed to help parties efficiently resolve their immediate disputes. Mediators typically meet with parties and their attorneys for one or two sessions (each lasting 30–90 minutes). They focus on settling legal issues, rather than underlying emotional and relationship issues. In some cases, attorneys do most of the talking for their clients. By keeping cases out of court, SFM saves money, leads to faster disposition of cases (which may promote permanency planning), and avoids the acrimony that often occurs when cases proceed to an adversarial trial (Barsky, 2007; Gatowski et al., 2005).
- "Interest-based mediation (IBM)" refers to a problem-solving process in which the mediator helps parties resolve their underlying concerns, not just the legal issues (see Fig. 155.1). IBM typically requires two to eight sessions. Whereas SFM often results in

compromise solutions (in which both sides concede some of what they want to reach a middle ground), IBM is designed to promote win-win solutions (in which parties use creative approaches to achieve common ground that satisfies everyone's primary concerns). The purported advantages of an interest-based approach include greater satisfaction with the outcomes, increased likelihood of following through on commitments, better relationships between the parties (Fisher, Ury, & Patton, 1997; Folberg, Milne, & Salem, 2004), and earlier termination of protection cases because of greater parental cooperation (Barsky, 2007).

• "Transformative mediation" refers to a process-oriented conflict management process in which the mediator provides an environment that allows the parties to articulate their concerns, hear one another in a more meaningful way, empathize with one another's concerns, and take greater control over how they want to handle their conflict (Bush & Folger, 2005). Transformative mediation does not have a set time limit, though it typically requires 2 to 10 sessions. The success of transformative mediation does not depend on whether the parties resolve conflict or save money. In fact, transformative mediation may improve how parties interact and manage conflict, even if they do not reach agreement.

Although each model has its benefits, this chapter focuses on IBM, given its balance between task and process orientations. IBM helps parties reach agreements and avoid court, while also helping them build better relationships, learn problem-solving skills, and feel greater satisfaction with the outcomes of the process (Olson, 2003). Building better relationships between family members and child protection workers is particularly impor-

tant in child protection cases so the parties can work together on a voluntary basis and for the benefit of the child (Barsky & Trocmé, 1998).

This following section describes child protection situations in which IBM may be appropriate. The balance of this chapter demonstrates IBM skills and strategies by following a case example through the six stages of the IBM process.

WHEN MEDIATION IS APPROPRIATE

Many of the earliest pioneers in child protection mediation came from the field of divorce mediation. Divorce mediators typically suggest screening out cases involving domestic violence, alcohol or drug abuse, or mental illness (Folberg et al., 2004). In the case of domestic violence, how could mediation be safe or fair if the abused spouse lives in fear of the perpetrating spouse? In the case of substance abuse or mental illness, how could a party with diminished capacity negotiate fairly and competently within the mediation process? In child protection cases, the vast majority of cases involve domestic violence, substance abuse, and/or mental illness. Thus, screening out cases with these factors would mean that mediation could rarely be used. When early mediation proponents asked CPWs and administrators if they would be willing to try mediation, they had significant concerns about its safety and fairness. Many were concerned that mediators would pressure CPWs to compromise on children's safety and well-being to reach agreements with parents. In practice, however, the presence of CPWs in the mediation process fosters safety and fairness and distinguishes this process from divorce mediation. Mediators are supposed to remain neutral and impartial throughout the mediation process. They have no decision-making power over the parties. CPWs, however, are mandated to assess for abuse and neglect and take whatever steps are needed to en-

---

• Focus on Interests, Not Positions.
• Invent Options for Mutual Gain.
• Apply Objective Criteria.
• Improve Communication.
• Build a Positive Negotiating Relationship.
• Consider Alternatives. Obtain Commitments (Fisher, Ury, & Patton, 1997).

Figure 155.1 Major tenets of interest-based mediation.

sure the child's welfare. Although mediators encourage CPWs to keep an open mind about different ways of ensuring the child's welfare, they do not encourage CPWs to make compromises on it (e.g., to tolerate a certain degree of abuse or neglect) (Barsky, 1997a).

Given that neglect and abuse are not negotiable, the question remains, what *is* negotiable? The following examples illustrate situations in which mediation may be appropriate.

- Teachers report a student's parents for abusing him by using a strap as a means of corporal punishment. The child's life is not in immediate danger. The parents initially refuse to cooperate with the CPW. During the first court hearing, the judge refers the CPW and parents to mediation to try to establish acceptable forms of punishment for the child's misbehavior.
- Protective services determine that a stepfather has been sexually abusing a 10-year-old girl. They place her in an aunt's care, so her immediate safety is ensured. The CPW and mother agree to try mediation to develop a plan whereby the girl can be returned safely to her mother's care.
- A 13-year-old boy has been living in foster care for 2 years due to physical abuse and neglect related to his parent's alcoholism. He refuses to see his parents for scheduled visits. The parents accuse the foster parents of turning their son against them. The parents, son, and foster parents agree to try mediation to sort through their conflicts. Given the parents' ongoing alcohol problems, the mediator establishes a ground rule that they must be sober when they attend mediation.
- Protective services brought a 3-month-old girl into foster care for "failure to thrive" (growth failure due to undernutrition). Her mother died during labor. Her father was unable to take proper care of his daughter due to depression. The father's depression starts to improve following successful use of psychotherapy and antidepressants. The father does not trust the CPW to be fair with him, so he asks for a mediator to help them negotiate conditions for returning the daughter to his care.
- A court has issued a temporary guardianship order for a young girl whose parents live on the streets. An order for permanent guardianship seems likely, given that the

parents' lives remain unstable and the CPW wants to make permanent plans for the child. The parents and the CPW agree to use mediation to see if they can work out an agreement for voluntary surrender of parental rights, so the parents can participate in choosing adoptive parents under an open adoption process (Maynard, 2005; Thoennes, 2002).

As these scenarios illustrate, mediation can be used in a broad range of situations, including various forms of abuse or neglect. Although one might assume that mediation is appropriate for mild cases and court is required for severe ones, this assumption does not hold true in practice. Parties involved in severe cases may actually have stronger motivation to make things work in mediation because the stakes are so high—particularly for a parent who risks temporary or permanent placement of a child in out-of-home care (Barsky, 1997b).

SIX STAGES OF MEDIATION

The IBM process may be broken down into six stages: intake and preparation, orientation to mediation, issue definition, exploring interests, negotiation and problem solving, and finalizing an agreement. To demonstrate the skills and strategies that mediators use in each stage, consider the following scenario.

Pam has a 16-year-old son, Sandy. One day, Pam discovers a bag of women's clothes in Sandy's closet. When she confronts him, he says he admits that he feels like a woman trapped in a man's body. Pam loses her temper and says that what he is doing goes against God and nature. When Sandy says he plans to dress as a woman in public, Pam throws him out. He moves into a friend's house. The friend's parents call protective services to report Pam for abandoning her child. Chelsey, the CPW assigned to the case, tries to engage Pam, but she refuses to cooperate. She says her son is dead to her. Chelsey's supervisor recommends mediation as a way to engage Pam.

1: Intake and Preparation

Mediators typically receive referrals from the court or from the parties themselves. Although some jurisdictions permit judges to order parties into mediation, most provide mediation on a voluntary basis. The mediator's primary tasks during this stage are to inform the parties about the mediation process, assess their readiness to mediate, and prepare them to participate in a constructive manner. Mediators do not assess how the case should be resolved, because this is the parties' responsibility. Mediators do assess the nature of the conflict and how to improve the way that the parties communicate and negotiate with one another.

In the case example, a private practice mediator named Marsha accepts the referral. During intake, Marsha discovers that Chelsey is a professional social worker who is very familiar with mediation. The first time her supervisor referred her to mediation, she was skeptical because she believed her role was to mediate. She felt like going to mediation was tantamount to admitting she was incompetent. During mediation, she discovered that mediators could engage parties in a manner that was different from CPWs, because they were neutral and had no decision-making power. She learned to trust how mediators could empower parents to make decisions and work collaboratively (Barsky & Trocmé, 1998). Chelsey summarizes what she sees as the key issues in the case and offers to be supportive in any way possible.

Neither Pam nor Sandy know anything about mediation, so Marsha meets with each of them separately to explain the process and assess their readiness to participate. Pam says she does not trust protective services because she thinks they are uncaring and incompetent. Without commenting on protective services, Marsha tries to establish her own caring and competence by demonstrating empathy, unconditional positive regard, genuineness, and knowledge of the mediation process. Marsha explains that one of the purposes of mediation is to promote more effective communication. Pam admits that she was responsible for cutting off all communication with her son and that she feels ambivalent about whether to try making amends. On one hand, she feels embarrassed that her son dresses like a woman, and she wonders what she did to make her son that way. On the other hand, she loves her son—at least the son that she thought she had. Marsha helps Pam save face by noting that mediation will focus on what to do now, not what happened in the past or who is responsible for what. She helps Pam prepare by asking her to prepare two lists: one listing the things she loved about the "old Sandy" and one listing concerns she had about the "new Sandy."

When Marsha meets Sandy, he asks to be addressed as male, even though he self-identifies as transgendered. Marsha asks whether he has any concerns about mediation. Sandy says he does not want to come to mediation if his mother is going to yell or insult him. Marsha discusses how they can use ground rules for communication to make sure that communication is safe and productive. Sandy suggests that mediation may be a waste of time because his mother is too closed-minded. Marsha invites Sandy to talk about the possibility that his relationship with his mother could improve. He responds that the chances are less than 10 percent. They explore the consequences of no improvement versus the consequences of some improvement. Sandy agrees that it is worth trying mediation, even if the chances of improvement are limited. Marsha enhances Sandy's hope without imposing ideas or moving him too quickly. In preparation for the first joint meeting, Marsha offers Sandy reading material on transgenderism and the coming out process. She suggests that this may help him understand his mother's reaction to his coming out, as well as how to explain his situation in language she can hear.

2: Orientation to Mediation

During the first joint session, the mediator provides an opening statement, explaining the mediation process, how it differs from court or therapy, the roles of the parties, what happens if the parties reach an agreement, and what happens if they do not. During the orientation, the mediator asserts control over the communication process while stressing that the parties are responsible for any decisions. The mediator explains his or her role as an impartial third party, who helps clients resolve conflict, but does not impose decisions or take sides.

As Marsha summarizes the agreement-to-mediate form, Pam asks how she is being paid. Marsha explores this concern, discovering that Pam's underlying question is whether Marsha is impartial. Marsha discloses the government department that funds mediation services and empathizes with Pam's concern that both Marsha and Chelsey receive salaries from the government, even though they work for different departments. Marsha invites the parties to let her know if they ever have concerns that she is demonstrating bias, given that her aim is to be neutral and fair to all. By remaining nondefensive and forthright, Marsha enhances Pam's trust.

Marsha invites the parties to set ground rules for a safe and productive conversation. She starts with Sandy, given their discussion about yelling and insults. Sandy suggests a rule that his mother should not raise her voice or say rude things to him. Pam responds defensively, arguing she is not rude and "how dare you speak to your mother like that?" Marsha separates the person from the problem by suggesting that they both seem to be interested in using respectful language. She reframes their concerns into a mutual rule, "Everyone will speak to each other calmly and respectfully." All agree. Chelsey commends Sandy and Pam for reaching their first agreement. They develop other ground rules and review the rest of the agreement to mediate. Marsha invites questions and ensures that they understand the agreement before asking them to sign it. Although Pam and Sandy express doubts about each other's ability to be reasonable, Marsha expresses optimism in each of their abilities to reach an agreement that satisfies everyone's interests.

3: Issue Definition

This stage begins with storytelling, as the mediator asks parties to describe what concerns they would like to resolve in mediation. The mediator permits the parties to vent feelings and review the history of the conflict, demonstrating empathy to build trust and model active listening. The mediator puts appropriate limits on storytelling, refocusing the parties on future-oriented problem solving. As each party describes its concerns, the mediator summarizes key points and highlights the main issues that they bring to mediation. By identifying common concerns and helping the parties articulate their priorities, the mediator helps them reach an agreement on which issues to focus on for the rest of the mediation.

Pam seems to be the most distrustful of the mediation process, so Marsha asks her to be the first to "briefly describe the situation that brought you to mediation and what issues you would like to resolve in mediation." Pam describes the family history, including the challenges of being a single mom and how much she loves Sandy. Marsha paraphrases key points, highlighting the positive relationship Pam had with Sandy. Pam describes the day she discovered Sandy was dressing like a woman. She reflects back her feelings, reframing her shock and disgust into uncertainty and parental concern. Pam invites Sandy to summarize what he heard from his mother. Sandy

responds, "It's all about her . . . what she wants me to be, not what I am or how I should be treated." Pam appeals to Marsha to stop him from being so disrespectful. Marsha reminds everyone of the ground rules. She resumes control over the process by asking Pam what issues she hopes to resolve in mediation. Pam says she wants to talk about how Sandy can be cured of his problem, so everything can be normal again. Marsha generalizes the concerns to offer an issue that all parties feel comfortable discussing, "So you'd like to talk about what could be done to reestablish better relationship between you and your son." Pam agrees, so Marsha writes this issue on the flipchart.

Marsha asks Sandy to discuss his concerns. He describes how he felt abandoned by his mother just when he needed her most. Pam cuts in. Marsha gently reminds her to let Sandy finish, offering her a pen to write down her concerns so she can remember them for later. Sandy goes into a long, detailed discussion of his struggle coming to terms with his transgenderism. Pam asks what transgenderism is. Marsha invites Chelsey to explain. Part of Chelsey's explanation includes professional jargon, so Marsha reframes it into plain language. Marsha then asks Sandy what issues he'd like to resolve. Sandy says he wants to figure out where he is going to live. Marsha lists this issue on the flipchart.

When Marsha asks Chelsey what issues she believes are important to discuss, she says she would like to discuss the possibility of family reunification. If that is not possible, then they need to discuss alternate living arrangements for Sandy. Marsha helps the parties see how they are basically talking about the same issues—the possibility of improving Marsha and Sandy's relationship so Sandy can move home, and where Sandy should live if moving home is not feasible.

4: Exploring Interests

The primary objective of this stage is to help the parties focus on their underlying concerns. The mediator invites parties to look beneath their stated positions and wishes and focus on what really matters to them. By helping the parties focus on their underlying concerns, needs, hopes, and expectations, the mediator helps them disengage from a battle over whose position is right or wrong. When Pam says she's not ready for Sandy to return home, Marsha explores why. Pam says Sandy is obviously sick and needs help, help that she cannot provide. Marsha reframes these concerns, "So you'd like to make sure that Sandy is well and gets the help he needs to be well." Sandy reacts, "I'm not sick. I just need to be allowed to be who I am." Marsha asks if this means he wants to be treated with respect. Sandy nods. Marsha lists Pam's and Sandy's interests, and asks Chelsey if she would like to add any others. Chelsey suggests including shelter, safety, and parental care. Marsha reviews the interests with the parties and incorporates their suggestions to conclude a list of their common and separate interests.

5: Negotiation and Problem Solving

The mediator encourages the parties to problem solve based on their underlying interests. Problem-solving strategies include focusing parties on the future, generating a list of creative options that may satisfy their interests, and helping the parties evaluate options using objective criteria.

When Marsha initiates brainstorming, Pam suggests that Sandy see a shrink. Sandy retorts that Pam should see a shrink. Marsha does not judge. She simply writes their options on the flip-chart and invites them to continue brainstorming. Chelsey suggests other helpful resources, such as PFLAG for Pam and a transgender support group for Sandy. All three parties then brainstorm various living arrangements for Sandy: return home immediately or in a few weeks; remain with friends; go into foster care; or stay with a relative.

Marsha helps the parties establish objective criteria for selecting the best options. They agree that the ideal helping resources are ones that are nonjudgmental, private, expert at dealing with transgender issues, and easily accessible. Marsha then helps them apply these criteria to their options. Although Pam originally thinks PFLAG is just for parents of lesbians and gay men, Chelsey informs her that they also serve parents of transgender or questioning youth. Pam agrees to contact the local PFLAG coordinator for more information, saying she wants to find out how other parents deal with similar issues. Sandy agrees to see a counselor that specializes in transgender issues, stating that he feels more comfortable talking privately to one person rather than a group. Chelsey originally asks Sandy and Pam to sign confidentiality release forms so she can speak with the PFLAG coordinator and counselor. Sandy and Pam stress that privacy is important, so Chelsey agrees to follow-up with Sandy and Pam after

their meetings rather than talk to the others. Marsha congratulates them for agreeing on support services. They go through a similar problem-solving process to determine where Sandy will live, identifying objective criteria and choosing the best options based on these criteria.

6: Finalizing the Agreement

Once the parties reach a tentative agreement, the mediator helps them decide how to finalize it. If a court case has been initiated, the mediator typically provides the agreement to the parties' attorneys to submit it to court for an order on consent of the parties. If no court case has been initiated (as in the case example) the agreement may be formalized as part of the clients' treatment plan with the protection agency (Barsky, 1997a).

Marsha reviews the terms of the agreement with the parties to check for any problems and ensure they are committed to it. They have agreed that Sandy will stay at his grandmother's house on a temporary basis. Chelsey will facilitate referrals to PFLAG for Pam and a transgender counselor for Sandy. Pam ensures that the language of the written agreement is clear, positive, future-focused, and balanced. She includes provisions for follow-up, specifying each party's roles and responsibilities. If the parties have any problems with implementation, they agree to return to mediation to work through these concerns. Marsha concludes the process by reinforcing the progress made by the parties. Even though Sandy is going to live with his grandmother, they have opened communication between Sandy and Pam, and they have developed trust with Chelsey, who will help them work toward permanent living arrangements for Sandy.

When successful, mediation helps CPWs and family members work together in a collaborative fashion, ensuring the child's safety and welfare in the least intrusive means possible.

WEB SITES

British Columbia Ministry of the Attorney General, Child Protection Mediation. http://www.ag.gov.bc.ca/dro/child-protection/index.htm.
London (Canada) Child Protection Mediation Project, Discussion Guide for Communities

Implementing Child Protection Mediation. http://www.ag.gov.bc.ca/dro/child-protection/index.htm.

National Center for State Courts, Mediation: Child Protection Mediation. http://www.ncsconline.org/WC/Publications/KIS_ADRMed_Trends99-00_Pub.pdf.

References

Barsky, A. E. (1997a). Child protection mediation. In E. Kruk (Ed.), *Mediation and conflict resolution in social work and the human services* (pp. 117–139). Belmont, CA: Brooks/Cole.

Barsky, A. E. (1997b). Why parties agree to mediate: The case of child protection. *Family and Conciliation Courts Review, 35*(2), 164–183.

Barsky, A. E. (2007). *Conflict resolution for the helping professions.* Belmont, CA: Brooks/Cole.

Barsky, A. E., & Trocmé, N. (1998). Essential aspects of mediation in child protection cases. *Child and Youth Services Review, 20,* 629–656.

Bush, R. A. B., & Folger, J. P. (2005). *The promise of mediation: The transformative approach to conflict,* 2nd ed. San Francisco: Jossey-Bass.

Child Welfare League of America. (2007). *National data analysis system.* Retrieved October 22, 2007, from http://ndas.cwla.org/data_stats/access.

Fisher, R., Ury, W., & Patton, B. (1997). *Getting to yes: Negotiating agreement without giving in,* 3rd ed. New York: Penguin.

Folberg, J., Milne, A., & Salem, P. (2004). *Divorce and family mediation: Models, techniques, and applications.* New York: Guilford.

Gatowski, S. I., Dobbin, S. A., Litchfield, M., & Oetjen, J. (2005). Mediation in child protection cases: An evaluation of the Washington, DC, Family Court. Retrieved October 22, 2007, from www.ncjfcj.org/images/stories/dept/ppcd/pdf/dc%20mediation%20evaluation%20final.pdf.

Maynard, J. (2005). Permanency mediation: A path to open adoption for children in out-of-home care. *Child Welfare, 84*(4), 50–526.

Olson, K. B. (2003). Lessons learned from a child protection mediation program: If at first you succeed and then you don't. . . . *Family Court Review, 41,* 480–496.

Thoennes, N. (2002). Hamilton County Juvenile Court: Permanent custody mediation. Center for Policy Research. Retrieved October 17, 2007, from http://www.centerforpolicyresearch.org/reports/Hamilton%20County.pdf.

156 Mediation and Conflict Resolution

John Allen Lemmon

Mediation is a role that professionals from business, law, social work, and other disciplines may assume. The neutral and impartial mediator works with disputants to help them reach agreement. If they cannot come to an agreement, the mediator's work is finished. No decision is imposed by the mediator. No evaluation or recommendation is made to a court, because these roles would conflict with encouraging clients to speak openly and honestly, as they would to their psychotherapist or their attorney.

THE CONFLICT RESOLUTION CONTINUUM

Persons with conflicts have choices about resolution. Doing nothing is an option. Avoidance may work. When disputants engage in negotiation, they attempt to reach an agreement. They may converse directly or communicate with the help of an agent who advocates for their client. This agent may be an attorney or social worker, and informal advocates such as family members may become involved. Clergy or psychotherapists may be asked to help clients with whom they have a current professional relationship to advocate when a dispute arises, or they may be approached for this reason. In mediation, the third party involved does not seek an outcome for a particular client. The mediator is concerned that any agreement reached be understood by and is fair to each of the disputants. Ethical codes for mediators have stated the need to be neutral, impartial, and an advocate for weaker or absent parties, such as children or frail elders, a difficult balance. The essence of mediation is that if agreement cannot be reached by the parties, the mediator does not switch roles and become an evaluator. In the event of an impasse, an evaluation that results in recommending which divorced parent should have primary responsibility for a minor child is an essential role, but it must be filled by a different person than the mediator if the parties are to speak freely in mediation. Otherwise, there is a sense of betrayal akin to having the client's attorney, clergy, or therapist testify against them in court. The fact that the judge formally makes the decision does not change the role conflict when mediators cross over to become evaluators who write reports and testify in court.

Crossover is a volatile issue in mediation. For example in California, if no agreement is reached, the mediator is barred by the evidence code from testifying. Nothing in writing may be admitted to a subsequent court proceeding. Are there any exceptions? Yes, in the situation of the custody mediation, courts are permitted to adopt a local rule that allows crossover so that the mediator becomes an evaluator in self-described "recommending" counties. This leads clients to say, "When I was in mediation, my mediator testified against me." Such a role conflict leads to ethical dilemmas for professionals from a number of fields. The confidentiality of mediation has been the cause of cases brought against mediators as well as others in the process.

CASE ILLUSTRATIONS

Can a client sue her attorney if information from a "confidential mediation brief" submitted to the mediator is also submitted without authorization to the apposing party? In *Wimsatt v. Kausch* (152 Cal. App. 4th 137), decided in 2007, the court noted that the California Supreme Court "has clearly

and unequivocally stated that we may not craft exceptions to mediation confidentiality. . . . Courts [in other states] addressing situations akin to the present case have permitted the disclosure of confidential communications made during the course of a mediation." In *Avary v. Bank of America* (Tex. Ct. App. 2002 72 S.W. 3d 779), discovery was permitted when beneficiaries alleged breach of fiduciary duty by an executor in rejecting a higher settlement demand. However, "The stringent result we reach here means that when clients, such as Kausch, participate in mediation they are, in effect, relinquishing all claims for new and independent torts arising from mediation, including legal malpractice causes of actions against their own counsel."

Can a former husband move to correct a spousal support agreement he negotiated in mediation, citing discussions during the process? In California as well as a number of other states, this strict interpretation of mediation confidentiality applies in family disputes as well. In *Eisendrath v. Superior Court* (2003; 109 Cal. App. 4th 351)

A former husband moved to correct a spousal support [called alimony in some states] agreement negotiated in mediation. Noting at the time he negotiated and executed the agreement, he had not been represented by counsel, the former husband argued many of the conversations that occurred before the agreement was signed would demonstrate it do not accurately reflect the parties' understanding. Eisenstadt held the discussions which purportedly inconsistent with the finalized agreement were inadmissible. (cited in *Wimsatt v. Kausch*)

Can minors charged with vandalism in a delinquency petition compel the testimony of the mediator of the victim's prior civil harassment suit? In *Rinaker v. Superior Court* (1998; 62 Cal. App. 4th 155),

two minors were accused of vandalizing a car. The victim's civil harassment suit was resolved in mediation. Thereafter, the two minors were charged in a delinquency proceeding with vandalism. . . . In the delinquency case, the minors sought to compel the civil mediator to testify that in the mediation the victim admitted that he had not seen who had committed the vandalism. The mediator objected, arguing that statements made during mediation were to remain confidential pursuant to Evidence Code section 1119. *Rinaker* noted that section 1119 is applicable in civil and noncriminal proceedings, and that a juvenile delinquency proceeding was considered to be "civil." However, mediation confidentiality had to give way to the constitutional rights of the minors. (cited in *Wimsatt v. Kausch*)

Arbitration also brings a third party to help disputants reach an agreement. However, the arbitrator has the power to impose a binding decision on the parties if they cannot reach an agreement themselves. Arbitration awards are typically final and not subject to appeal, even if the arbitrator does not follow current law. Only in cases where the arbitrator exceeded the scope of what was to be decided or otherwise significantly failed to follow procedures might a judicial review be granted. Arbitration clauses are often written into employment contracts, requiring employees with a dispute to arbitrate rather than file suit in court. Challenges to mandatory arbitration for customers with conflicts have come from consumer groups charging that there may not be a choice in the marketplace or that the notice of changing to mandate arbitration was in fine print on the back of an envelope of a monthly statement. Civil rights groups have stated—and some appellate justices have agreed—that Congress did not intend for allegations of racial or sexual bias to be arbitrated with no recourse to the courts.

Health maintenance organizations requiring arbitration have been criticized by judges for not following their own procedures for a timely process and for having a stable of "the usual suspects" as arbitrators. There is a movement away from arbitration in organizations. One reason is the loss of control by all parties. A single arbitrator taking years to order the break-up of Andersen, the giant accounting and consulting firm, is a cautionary example. Another factor has been a increasing number of sexual harassment cases in the workplace of both *Fortune* 500 companies and small nonprofit organizations. The trend is to offer mediation and permit clients access to the court if that is their choice.

Adjudication is a decision or verdict rendered by a judge or jury. Filing suit is the most formal conflict resolution procedure. Although "going to court" may appear to be the way most conflicts are resolved, over 95 percent of civil cases are settled without a verdict. This means that the parties resorted to another option after starting a lawsuit. Why? Sometimes the parties have had as much justice as they can afford. Litigation is expensive, and if the call from the attorney comes to "refresh the retainer" (a request for more fees),

many disputants decide to settle or muddle through by continuing to agree to disagree. The passage of time may alter a litigant's perception of the need to continue, as one may discovery of the strength of the case while preparing for court.

Sometimes a formal decision by the court is desired by one or all parties. Note that unlike mediation, where all parties must agree to the final terms of any agreement, and even in many instances whether to participate, in adjudication, if one party files suit, any named respondents are subject to the court. Just as many combatants prefer arbitration until they receive an adverse award, lawsuits may reflect unwarranted optimism by at least one party.

Unlike arbitration, an unhappy litigant may seek an appeal. Appeals are not automatically granted in most civil cases. Only a small percentage of cases filed for appeal by one of the parties are selected for review by the typical appellate body. Appeals take years and additional funds. A case could wend its way from a state trial court, to an appellate panel, to that state's Supreme Court, and then to the U.S. Supreme Court. Some cases can be slated for fast track to bypass intermediate courts at the request of the trial court judge or one of the parties. Some cases persist because they have been certified as a class action, acting on behalf of both the named parties and others similarly situated. This is a way to resolve a large number of potential as well as present conflicts.

A conflict resolution continuum must allude to violence or physical aggression, which could be defined as negotiation carried out by other means. From street brawls to international conflicts, aggression is one way, however unsavory, of resolving disputes. To prevent violence, mediation is taught in elementary and secondary schools, and children wearing "Conflict Manager" T-shirts can be found on playgrounds in countries around the world, including those with a history of armed conflict between factions within their own borders. Peace studies programs in universities and groups like the Harvard Program on Negotiation analyze how aggression and negotiation are linked.

BENEFITS OF MEDIATION

The options reviewed, from ignoring or avoiding conflict through mediation, have the advantage of leaving the disputing persons in control of their conflict. No one can impose a settlement on them until they reach the point in the continuum where they involve an arbitrator or judge or resort to violence. A mediator may help the disputants translate their points of view to each other, doing considerable face-saving in the process. The mediator can ask clarifying questions that the parties might not tolerate from one another, because the mediator is new to the dispute. A partial agreement can be reached, with unresolved issues left for another option on the conflict resolution continuum. If no agreement appears likely, the mediator or any of the parties can stop the process, and the entire dispute can be addressed by other procedures on the continuum. Again, unlike arbitration, the parties are free to seek relief from the courts if they are not willing to reach an agreement in mediation.

MEDIATION: FIELD OF PRACTICE OR SKILL-BASED?

For those either seeking a mediator or considering becoming a mediator, a central question is how much the mediator should know about the general area from which the conflict arises. Could a mediator help parents resolve custody issues for their minor children without knowing state law that would apply if the dispute ends up in court? Could that same mediator help organizations resolve workplace conflicts without awareness of relevant federal, state, and local law?

One point of view is that mediation is foremost a set of skills. A good mediator would recognize universal stages in any conflict and apply techniques to move from anger to agreement. The other position is that virtually all disputants are *Bargaining in the Shadow of the Law*, as Mnookin and Kornhauser (1979) reminds us. What would be agreed to in mediation could hinge in great part on what would likely happen in court.

Even established professions hedge this question of general skills versus subject matter expertise. A licensed physician can perform any medical procedure. A licensed attorney can represent a client in court regardless of the nature of the conflict. However, medicine offers voluntary certification—being "board certified"—for certain fields of practice. Similarly, a number of states offer attorneys meeting certain task and experience requirements the opportunity to take a test to become a certified specialist in a field, such as family law or estate planning.

The questions of subject matter expertise and role conflict are important because many media-

tors have a profession of origin, such as law or social work, where they may still be licensed. Are they attorneys or social workers simply acting in a mediative manner? What if a mediator holds both degrees and licenses, and requirements for each license conflict? Such instances involving threats of violence or allegations of abuse are all too common. If a mediator who is not an attorney offers legal advice, does that constitute the unauthorized practice of law? If the mediator is an attorney and provides legal advice to each party, is that a dual representation conflict that violates ethical canons?

Best practice is for the mediator to ask the disputants to sign an agreement to mediate, specifying that only mediation will be provided, even if the mediator holds professional licenses in other fields. This agreement states that if the parties need legal or financial advice, a psychotherapist, or any other professional services, they should seek it elsewhere. Such a document can also serve as a fee agreement, as well as listing relevant state law concerning privileged communication—that nothing said or written in mediation can be introduced into any subsequent court proceeding—and any exceptions. Finally, procedures—again citing any pertinent law—that constitute an agreement, termination, or impasse can be cited.

REGULATING MEDIATION

Ethical codes have been developed by a number of conflict-resolution organizations that provide guidelines for self-regulation by mediators. What is likely in the future? No state licenses mediators yet. Licensing is protection of duties—"You can't do that," unless you meet requirements listed in state law—whereas certification is title protection only—"You can't call yourself that," unless you meet the requirements under state law. One state that certifies mediators, Florida, takes a field of practice approach by certifying separately by category. Mediators who deal with community conflicts, such as barking dogs or blocked driveways, are called county court mediators after taking 20 hours of training and observing, then conducting mediations under observation. Family mediators must hold certain graduate degrees, such as social work, or be licensed as a lawyer, a certified public accountant, or a physician who is certified in psychiatry; meet experience requirements; take a 40-hour training and observe; and then conduct relevant mediations under observation.

Some states have required a generic mediation training of 30 or 40 hours. Others have combined such a course with a 20-hour session dedicated to a particular field of practice. Still other jurisdictions require a basic 30-hour family or 40-hour divorce mediation training to be on a panel to receive mediation referrals. Most of these courses have been provided privately by pioneers in the field, as was the case with law and psychotherapy in their early days. However, an increasing number of certificate programs in conflict resolution and the mediation role are being offered by universities.

NEW APPLICATIONS OF MEDIATION

Family mediation is expanding from custody mediation to financial matters related to divorce. Mediation of conflicts throughout the family life cycle is increasing. Programs offering permanency planning mediation in child welfare as a way to increase open adoptions, mediating with blended families to address issues of instant intimacy and different rituals, and mediation between adult children and their aging parents concerning problems in living are examples. Dependency mediation programs are addressing issues listed in petitions to the juvenile court. Increasingly, federal legislation has a mediation provision. Many disputes that involve the Americans with Disabilities Act have been successfully mediated. The National Association of Social Workers has built mediation into its policies.

Organizations are designing conflict-resolution systems that offer a range of options reviewed here, with mediation as the fastest-growing role. Employee assistance programs often provide mediation, either directly or by referral. The Equal Employment Opportunity Commission has a mediation program. Family business members are asking mediators to help them with succession planning and other tasks when family dynamics conflict with standard business practice.

There is no dearth of disputes in our personal and professional lives. Conflict resolution is a growth industry. Mediating between parties to help them tailor an agreement to their needs can be rewarding. Whether or not mediation evolves into its own profession, the key is to distinguish the mediation role from others.

WEB SITES

American Arbitration Association, http://adr.org.

Mediate.com, http://mediate.com.

National Association of Social Workers. http://www.socialworkers.com.

Program on Negotiation, Harvard Law School. http://www.pon.harvard.edu.

Reference

Mnookin, R., & Kornhauser, L. (1979). Bargaining in the shadow of the law: The case of divorce. *Yale Law Journal, 88*(5), 960–997.

Children Exposed to Domestic Violence

Assessment and Treatment Protocols

157

Peter Lehmann & Catherine A. Simmons

Each year in the United States, approximately 15 million children witness, intervene, and/or cope with the aftermath of domestic violence (McDonald, Jouriles, Ramisetty-Mikler, Caetano, & Green, 2006). Although the immediate concerns of physical and emotional safety dictate intervention strategies, for many, the effect of this exposure continues into adulthood. By focusing on professional knowledge and skill building, this chapter provides social workers with a practice overview that can help guide intervention with this important population. To this end, a brief summary of the impacts that exposure to domestic violence has on children is presented. Then, skill-building constructs are discussed including (1) the signs of safety approach and (2) five principles essential to intervention strategies with this population. It is important to highlight that when working with children exposed to domestic violence, strategies should always be risk-focused (e.g., aimed at reducing risk and/or its impact), protection-focused (e.g., counterbalancing risk by resource building), and process-focused (e.g., building child and family competencies) (Masten & Coatsworth, 1998).

PROFESSIONAL KNOWLEDGE

The body of knowledge explaining the impact that exposure to domestic violence has on children is well developed (e.g., Buckley, Holt, & Whelan, 2007; Cunningham & Baker, 2004; Edleson, Ellerton, & Seagren, 2007; Fantuzzo & Fusco, 2007; Geffner, Jaffe, & Suderman, 2000; Groves McAl-

ister, 2002; Holden, Geffner, & Jouriles, 1998; Jaffe, Wolfe, & Wilson, 1990; Peled, Jaffe, & Edleson, 1995; Roberts, 2007). In summarizing the vast literature, Carlson (2000) noted six primary themes. First, a number of theoretical perspectives endeavor to explain children's diverse behavioral, emotional, and cognitive responses to exposure. Second, children's reactions to exposure include emotional distress, anger, fear, anxiety, and a desire to intervene. Third, children's short-term reactions include externalizing, internalizing, and social problems. Fourth, most children exposed to domestic violence experience long-term adjustment problems. Fifth, a number of mediating factors affect children's responses. Sixth, definitive links exists between exposure to domestic violence and trauma responses (Carlson, 2000).

RESPONSES TO EXPOSURE

To better understand the effects of childhood exposure to domestic violence it is helpful to cluster responses into two categories: (1) typical responses and (2) trauma sequelae. The first of these clusters, typical response, refers to those responses many children exposed to domestic violence report. These typical responses are problematic yet not technically a diagnosable because they are considered normal reactions to abnormal circumstances. From these reactions, three subcategories emerge: (a) immediate concerns, behavioral and emotional; (b) physical functioning; and (c) long-term concerns, behavioral and emotional (Table 157.1).

TABLE 157.1 Typical Responses to Childhood Exposure to Domestic Violence

Immediate Concerns Behavioral and Emotional	Physical Functioning	Long-Term Concerns Behavioral and Emotional
• Internalizing, externalizing, and social competency problems • Cognitive/social functioning • School difficulties • Delinquency-related behavior • Emotional difficulties (e.g., depression, self-blame/guilt)	• Somatic and physical complaints • Developmental delays	• Adult depression and reduced self-esteem • Poor interpersonal skills • Intergenerational repetition of violence • Adult criminal behavior

It is important to note that these responses are directly impacted by mediating and protective factors. Mediating factors (Table 157.2) are those intrinsic and extrinsic aspects that work to either buffer or expand the risk for healthy development when children are exposed to domestic violence. Protective factors are those intrinsic and extrinsic elements that work to provide a buffer that increases the child's resilience. Practically, categorizing responses is useful to identify with immediate clinical presentation as well as predicting long-term concerns. It is important to note that although generalizations can be made, overlaps between the behavioral and emotional factors and traumatic consequences often coexist. Likewise, each child's experience is unique.

The second cluster of responses can be grouped into trauma sequelae. Multiple studies document the presence of post-traumatic stress disorder (PTSD) in children as a consequence of exposure (e.g., Jaffe, Wolfe, Wilson, & Zak, 1986; Kerig, Fedorowicz, Brown & Warren, 1995; Lehmann, 2000; Lehmann, Spence, & Simmons, 2006; Rossman, 1994, 1998; Scheeringa & Zeanah, 1995; Silvern & Kaersvang, 1989). Although findings have consistently documented re-experiencing, avoidance, and arousal symptoms indicative of PTSD, a shift in the literature recently has discussed the applicability of these symptom clusters in diagnosing children. Some have suggested the PTSD nomenclature needs to be broadened (Wolfe & Birt, 1995). Likewise, others have raised a number of diagnostic concerns related to PTSD (e.g., Cook et al., 1995; van der Kolk, 2005). These researchers argue that PTSD diagnostic criteria are not child-sensitive in that children who experience multiple traumatic experiences may display complex disturbances. It is argued that this leads to

mistakenly seeing children with co-morbid symptoms, thus running the risk of losing the complexity of symptom presentation and possibly applying unhelpful treatment conditions. From this it is clear that a broadened view of trauma symptomatology is needed when working with children exposed to domestic violence. In an effort to broaden and deepen the understanding of trauma responses some researchers have proposed a new diagnostic category, the trauma developmental disorder (Fig. 157.1) (National Child Traumatic Stress Network [NCTSN], 2003; van der Kolk, 2005). The trauma developmental disorder is organized around three major issues inherent in children's response to traumatic events. First, emotional and/or behavioral dysregulation typically follows exposure to traumatic events. Second, many children experience stimulus generalization—the notion the violence and hurt will continue unabated. Finally, many children organize their behaviors to avoid the impact of the traumatic event. By identifying these three response patterns, social workers can better understand socioemotional effects of childhood exposure to domestic violence.

Two conclusions are worth noting from the abbreviated literature review. First, continuing research is an ongoing priority. As the empirical field improves, so will the ability to develop a greater understanding of this impacted population. The trauma developmental disorder is one good example. Research has moved into brain development, stress and coping, and intervention (Perry & Szalavitz, 2007; Ziegler, 2002). A new scientific field has opened, providing a greater holistic appreciation of the child. Second, the presence of both factors suggests that children may have clearly identified mental health issues.

TABLE 157.2 Child Exposure: Mediating and Protective Factors

Child Factors	Family Factors	Secondary/Associated Factors
Mediating Factors		
• Age • Type of exposure • Singular vs. multiple exposure • Child exposure to maltreatment • Child exposure to community violence • Child exposure to media violence (e.g., television, videos) • Time since last violent event • Child temperament (e.g., shy, fearful)	• Intensity of maternal exposure to violence/ maternal impairment • Child temperament (e.g., shy, fearful) • Co-occurrence of substance abuse • Single-parent household • Poverty • The importance of a cultural context	• Legal difficulties • Multiple moves, including both home and school • Already existing school- and/or community-related problems • Inappropriate law enforcement
Protective Factors		
• Intelligence • Interpersonal skills • Emotion and problem-focused skills • Temperament • Child's appraisal of events • Child's knowledge of safety	• Positive parental and family support • No history of multiple victimization • Emotional availability of mother • Role of extended family • Community factors • Availability of community safe homes and shelters • Response of community providers • School intervention projects	

INTERVENTION: BUILDING CHILD AND FAMILY SAFETY

As a response to the growing literature on the needs of children exposed to domestic violence, there has been a proliferation of intervention strategies studied, including group therapy (Loosley, Drouillard, Ritchie, & Abercromby, 2006), crisis intervention (Lehmann & Spence, 2007), individual, and/or play therapy (Osofsky, 2004) and family therapy (Brendler, 2006). It should not be surprising then that treatment programs must continue to build healthy family systems between children who have been exposed to domestic violence and their caregivers. Van der Kolk (2005) recommends four standards of intervention: (1) creating predictable and environments for children, (2) enhancing parenting capacity to manage intense affect, (3) helping parents be mindful of the impact of exposure on their children, and (4) helping the child find competencies with less focus on deficits. In addressing these needs, the final section of this chapter summarizes practice-based signs of safety approach. Although initially designed for child protection work, many of the principles of this model may be applicable in assisting children and their families who have experienced domestic violence according to the recommended standards of intervention.

The signs of safety approach (Turnell, 2003, 2007; Turnell & Edwards, 1997, 1999; Turnell, Elliott, & Hogg, 2007; Turnell & Essex, 2007) has

A-Exposure
        Multiple or chronic exposure to one or more forms
        of developmentally adverse interpersonal trauma
        (e.g. exposure to violence and/or various forms of
        maltreatment)

B-Triggered pattern of repeated dysregulation to the presence
of cues. Changes persist and do not return to baseline; not
reduced in intensity by conscious awareness
        Affective
        Somatic (e.g. physiological, motoric)
        Behavioral (e.g.reenactment, cutting)
        Cognitive (e.g. thinking it may happen again,
confusion, dissociation)
        Relational (e.g. clinging, acting out, oppositional)
        Attributional (e.g. self-blame, guilt)

C-Persistently altered attributional expectancies
        Negative self-attribution
        Distrust of caretaker
        Loss of expectancy of protection by caretakers
        Loss of trust in professionals
        Lack of access to social justice/retribution

D-Functional Impairment
        Educational
        Familial
        Peer
        Legal
        Vocational

Figure 157.1 Trauma developmental disorder (NCTSN, 2003; van der Kolk, 2005).

developed as a compassionate, safe, but rigorous child protection risk assessment to deal with difficult cases. Underlying the approach has been a purposeful attempt to find and create more constructive ways at handling difficult cases. In keeping within a safe-from-harm perspective, attempts are made to create a balance between potential danger, the safety/competency, and goals of what the family needs to accomplish so the case could be closed. In this approach, being cognizant of the risk for potential harm is never minimized.

For the purposes of working with children exposed to domestic violence, the signs of safety approach may be seen as an applied intervention. The approach is concrete enough to take into account the varied and complex responses while also being broad enough to build on the recommendations/strategies of van der Kolk (2005) and Masten and Coatsworth (1998). At the heart of the signs of safety approach are two fundamen-tal notions of good practice and intervention: aspiring to partnership and creating conversations of solution building.

Aspiring to Partnership

The core component of the signs of safety approach develops partnerships with children and their caregivers (A. Turnell, 2000, *Aspiring to partnership: The signs of safety approach to child protection*, unpublished document). Partnership is "a notion that promotes participation, cooperation, and collaboration" (p. 8) between the social worker, child, and family. The model views partnerships as one of many skills that may include but are not limited to (a) encouraging the child's participation in defining the issues and treatment planning, (b) providing a safe environment for the expression of feelings, (c) promoting caregiver input that might build on the ability to provide stability/

consistency, and (d) building nets of safety from violence in the home, school, or community. In addition, Turnell and Edwards (1999) have some fundamental therapist tasks that help bring about successful partnerships. In working with exposed children, we support these tasks including (a) being detailed about getting accurate information, (b) being mindful of properly planning with the child and family, (c) being goal-focused on what the child/family wants, (d) recognizing where one is likely to find signs of safety, and (e) working to create small changes with children and families. These partnerships are an important component in forming alliances that inform the therapeutic relationship (Duncan, Miller, & Sparks, 2007; Saleebey, 2006).

Solution Building

A signs of safety approach includes the idea of creating conversations around solutions with children and families. Turnell has adopted a solution-focused brief therapy (SFBT) approach in much of his work. SFBT is a goal-directed and nondeficits approach to practice developed by Insoo Kim Berg, Steve De Shazer, and colleagues at the Brief Therapy Center in Milwaukee, Wisconsin (de Shazer et al., 2007). SFBT works at developing collegial and helpful relationships with clients working with them to recognize their own strengths, exceptions, and solutions to what concerns them. A main component of SFBT helps clients define their goals for change by attending to *solution talk* rather than *problem talk* (de Shazer et al., 2007). SFBT is operationalized by a number of assumptions (Fig. 157.2) that include specific intervention. These interventions include asking about presession changes, goal setting, the miracle question, coping/scaling questions, compliments, session breaks, and end-of-session tasks (de Shazar et al., 2007).

PRACTICE PRINCIPLES

The signs of safety approach consists of five practice principles when meeting with children and families. The principles can overlap with one another and, with the exception of principle 1, do not necessarily need to be followed in sequential order. Specific questions related to each principle are highlighted. Figure 157.3 may be used conjointly and has been adopted from the Signs of Safety Assessment and Planning form (Turnell & Edwards, 1999). The form can be a session template for keeping notes as well as a reference point to the child/family and social worker. Furthermore, we use the "worry" to "good things" form as a collaborative relationship-building tool and as an indicator to child, family, and practitioner that recognizes the worry or "scary" issues and the good or "safe" elements of family life.

Practice Principle 1: Understanding the Position of the Child or Family Member

Understanding the position of each family member helps the social worker appreciate the impact exposure has on the child and/or all family members as they unpack the values, beliefs, and meanings of violence (Turnell & Edwards, 1999). Principle 1 begins to create a context that helps a child make some sense of what happened. The social worker will listen for or notice clinical issues but will also give the child a chance to talk about his or her experiences, how the child feels about what happened, where "dad" may fit into the picture, how this all affects one at school, and so forth (Fig. 157.4). Questions, in effect, ask the how, what, where, or when of past violence that details what is important to the child/family. Thus it becomes possible to begin a therapeutic partnership leading the way to speak about (a) what happened and how we can be safe, (b) the impact on the child and

---

> - *If it isn't broken, don't fix it*
> - *If it works, do more*
> - *If things aren't working do something different*
> - *Small steps can lead to big changes*
> - *The solution is not necessarily related to the problem*
> - *The language of solution development is different from that needed to describe a problem*
> - *Every problem has an exception*, and h)*the future is created and negotiable (de Shazar et al., 2007)*

Figure 157.2 SFBT assumptions.

WORRY
What worries you/
your family

(some items can be in between)

GOOD THINGS
What are good the
happen to you/
your family?

Scaling Worry: If 10 means your worries are the worst and 0 is the opposite, where are you today? _____

Child/Family Goals: What would you like different? (specific, in detail)

What's the first sign of small progress you will see?

Figure 157.3 Worry and good things form. Adopted from Turnell & Edwards (1999), with permission.

family (c) what the child or family would like to see changed.

Practice Principle 2: Discovering Exceptions and Strengths

An important principle is listening for and finding competencies and resources in children and family members. There will be times when a child or adolescent does not experience the problem or when a mother has found a way to soothe her anxious child (Fig. 157.5). An important task for social workers is to individualize the personal resources one hears from listening to what has been helpful or worked. Children and families who ex-

perience violence can be demoralized and hearing about their strengths/exceptions can be another way of building mastery that already exist (Macdonald, 2007; Turnell & Edwards, 1999).

Practice Principle 3: Goal Setting

We argue that successful work depends on knowing where the client (child or family) wants to go, thus goal setting defines the work ahead for a social worker (George, Iveson, & Ratner, 2000). Inquiring about what one wants out of therapy, what the objectives are, or what is the smallest thing one wants to "start on" may be useful (Fig. 157.6). Goal setting with children or their fami-

1. How can we help you?
2. Would you like to tell us what happened?
3. What worries you the most?
4. What is the most important thing you would like to talk about?
5. Are you safe now? How do you make yourself safe?
6. How do you manage your child's behavior?
7. How do you cope with your feelings?
8. What bothers you the most about what happened?
9. How is all this effecting you at school?
10. Would you like to talk with me in the playroom?
11. Can you tell me about what scares you the most?

Figure 157.4 Questions that will help build an understanding of the position of the child and/or family member.

1. When are the times you don't feel this way? When are you the most happy? What's your best day like?
2. What's been one time you could have gotten angry but didn't? What's the most important thing about being a
3. Mother to a child who has witnessed so much violence? What are some of the good things that have
4. happened to you and your family? Tell me about a time you were able to make yourself safe?
5. What are the good things that happen in your family?

Figure 157.5 Questions that will help build a discovery of exceptions and strengths.

lies exposed to domestic violence should be detailed, concrete, specific, ultimately becoming the central focus of work. At the same time, the social worker should have a clinical understanding as to whether goals are doable, within reach, and small enough to be accomplished. In addition, an important therapeutic goal when working with this population is not losing a focus for developing a picture and action plan that can address safety from violence. The worry to good things form (Fig. 157.3) is one example how goals can be charted for present and future reference in sessions.

Practice Principle 4: Scaling Safety and Progress

Scaling is a user-friendly SFBT tool that assesses and rates the position of the child/parent on a particular point of view, behavior, feeling, and so on (Fig. 157.7. Scaling responses from 0 through 10 are subjective, but they provide an evaluation of where one stands, for example, in relation to taking some action and reaching goals (de Shazer et al., 2007). Macdonald (2007) has also characterized scaling as helping clients move from an all-or-nothing position to something more manageable. When asking an adolescent how they are

managing past violence—"so what will you be doing more of when you get to a 5.5 from your current 5 of coping with dad's anger?"—one assumes that whatever one does is a change that could occur at some point soon and that it can happen in a way that matches the stated needs.

Practice Principle 5: Asking about Willingness, Confidence, and Capacity

Solution-focused practice assumes that human change is constant; therefore, social workers are in the position of helping families decide which direction they want to go (C. Iveson, personal communication, November 1, 2007). Consequently, the final principle of willingness, confidence, and capacity are terms developed into questions that have the potential to help one move forward (Fig. 157.8). Carrying out plans of safety, setting new rules for non violence in a family, saying no to drugs or alcohol, or agreeing to speak softly to one's upset child may be hard to accomplish. Again, exposure to violence can create a climate of hopelessness, one of failed change; however, the final principle asks questions that are intended to motivate a child or family and ultimately build belief or hope in small, sustainable ways.

1. What is the main thing you want to accomplish with us?
2. What do you want to be different?
3. What's the first thing you will be doing when you feel safer?
4. What needs to happen that will tell you your child's behavior has improved?
What goal would you think is important to set for yourself when it comes to parenting about those things that worry you?

Figure 157.6 Questions that will help build goal setting.

1. On a scale of 0 to 10 where 10 means you've made peace with your father's violence and 0 is the opposite
2. Where are you today?
   a. If 0 was when you first came in to see us and 10 is where you're satisfied you no longer need therapy, where are you
3. How well do you think you have helped your child cope with what's happened?
4. How confident are you 0-10 of reaching your goal?

Figure 157.7 Questions that will help build on safety and progress.

1. How confident do you feel that you have a good safety plan in place?
2. What skills do you know you have that tells you that you'll be successful making new friends?
3. How confident are you that you'll notice the red flags of dating violence?
4. What makes you so confident that violence will no longer be a part of your life?
5. How might your mom notice you are willing to give this another try?

Figure 157.8 Willingness, confidence, and capacity questions.

CONCLUSION

The population of children exposed to domestic violence represents a very real concern and ongoing social problem. The issues surrounding the impact of exposure are complex, requiring social workers to have an informed understanding of all the dynamics. This chapter focused on a summary of behavioral and traumatic indicators of exposure to violence and a series of interventions that can build safety in the lives of children and their families. To this end, a signs of safety approach building on the themes of partnership and solution building was considered. Five adapted signs of safety principles that can be used with children and their families were presented.

WEB SITES

Family Violence Prevention Fund. http://www.fvpf.org.
Signs of Safety. http://www.signsofsafety.net.
Solution-Focused Brief Therapy Association of America. http://www.sfbta.org.
Trauma Center. http://www.traumacenter.org.

References

Brendler, J. (2006). A model for disrupting cycles of violence in families with young children. In L. Combrinck-Graham (Ed.), *Children in family contexts* (pp. 433–455). New York: Guilford.

Buckley, H., Holt, S., & Whelan, S. (2007). Listen to me! Children's experiences of domestic violence. *Child Abuse Review, 16*, 296–310.

Carlson, B. E. (2000). Children exposed to intimate partner violence: Research findings and implications. *Trauma, Violence, & Abuse, 1*, 321–342.

Cook, A., Spinnazzola, J., Fored, J., Lanktree, C., Blaustein, M., Cloitre, M., et al. (2005). Complex trauma in children and adolescents. *Psychiatric Annals, 35*, 390–398.

Cunningham, A., & Baker, L. (2004). *What about me? Seeking to understand a child's view of violence the family*. London, ON: Centre for Children and Families in the Justice System.

de Shazer., S., Dolan, Y., Korman, H., Trepper, T., McCollum, E., & Berg Insoo, K. (2007). *More than miracles: The state of the art of solution-focused brief therapy*. New York: Haworth.

Duncan, G., Miller, S., D., & Sparks, J. (2007). Common factors and the uncommon heroism of youth. *Psychotherapy in Australia, 13*, 34–43.

Edleson, J. L., Ellerton, A. L., & Seagren, E. A. (2007). Assessing child exposure to adult domestic violence, *Child and Youth Services Review, 29*, 961–971.

Fantuzzo, J. W., & Fusco, R. A. (2007). Children's direct exposure to domestic violence crime: A population-based investigation. *Journal of Family Violence, 22*, 543–552.

Geffner, R. A., Jaffe, P. G., & Sudermann, M. (Eds.). (2000). *Children exposed to domestic violence: Intervention, prevention, and policy development.* New York: Haworth.

George, E., Iveson, C., & Ratner, H. (2000). *Solution focused brief therapy course notes.* London: Brief Therapy Practice.

Groves McAlister, B. (2002). *Children who see too much: Lessons from the child witness to violence project.* Boston, MA: Beacon.

Holden, G. W., Geffner, R., & Jouriles, E. N. (Eds.). (1998). *Children exposed to marital violence: Theory, research and applied issues.* Washington, DC: American Psychological Association.

Jaffe, P. G., Wolfe, D. A., & Wilson, S. (1990). *Children of battered women.* Newbury Park, CA: Sage.

Jaffe, P. G., Wolfe, D. A., Wilson, S., & Zak, L. (1986). Family violence and child adjustment: A comparative analysis of girl's and boy's behavioral symptoms. *American Journal of Psychiatry, 143*, 74–77.

Kerig, P. K., Fedorowicz, A.E., Brown, C.A., & Warren, M. (2000). Assessment and intervention for PTSD in children exposed to violence. In R. A. Geffner, P. G. Jaffe, & M. Sudermann (Eds.), *Children exposed to domestic violence: Current issues in research, intervention, prevention, and policy development* (pp. 161–184). Binghamton, NY: Haworth.

Lehmann, P. (2000). Posttraumatic stress disorder (PTSD) and child witnesses to mother-assault: A critical first review. *Children and Youth Services Review, 22*, 275–306.

Lehmann, P., & Spence, E. (2007). Complex trauma and crisis intervention with children in shelters for battered women. In A. R. Roberts (Ed.), *Battered women and their families: Intervention strategies and treatment programs* (pp. 181–212). New York: Springer.

Lehmann, P., Spence, E., & Simmons, C. (2006). Children exposed to domestic violence. *Family Violence & Sexual Assault Bulletin, 22*, 12–20.

Loosley, S., Drouillard, D., Ritchie, D., & Abercromby, S. (2006). *Groupwork with children exposed to woman abuse: A concurrent group program for children and their mothers.* London, ON: The Children's Aid Society of London & Middlesex.

Macdonald, A. (2007). *Solution-focused therapy: Theory, research, and practice.* Los Angeles: Sage.

Masten, A. S., & Coatsworth, D. (1998). The development of competence in favorable and unfavorable environments. *American Psychologist, 53*, 205–220.

McDonald, R., Jouriles, E. N., Ramisetty-Mikler, S., Caetano, R., & Green, C. E. (2006). Estimating the number of American children living in partner-violent homes. *Journal of Family Psychology, 20*, 128–136.

National Child Traumatic Stress Network (NCTSN). (2003). *Complex trauma in children and adolescents.* Retrieved July 1, 2006, from http://www.nctsnet.org.

Osofsky, J. D. (2004). *Young children and trauma: Intervention and treatment.* New York: Guilford.

Peled, E., Jaffe, P. G., & Edleson, J. L. (Eds.). (1995). *Ending the cycle of violence: Community responses to children of battered women.* Thousand Oaks, CA: Sage.

Perry, B. D., & Szalavitz, M. (2007). *The boy who was raised as a dog: What traumatized children can teach us about loss, love, and healing.* New York: Basic Books.

Roberts, A. R. (Ed.). (2007). *Battered women and their families: Intervention strategies and treatment program.* New York: Springer.

Rossman, B. B. (1994). Children in violent homes: Current diagnostic and treatment considerations. *Family Violence & Sexual Assault Bulletin, 10*, 29–34.

Rossman, B. B. (1998). Descartes's error and posttraumatic stress disorder: Cognition and emotion in children who are exposed to marital violence. In G. W. Holden, R. Geffner, & E. N. Jouriles (Eds.), *Children exposed to marital violence: Theory, research and applied issues* (pp. 223–256). Washington, DC: American Psychological Association.

Saleebey, D. (2006). *The strengths perspective in social work education,* 4th ed. Boston: Pearson.

Scheeringa, M. S., & Zeanah, C. H. (1995). Symptom expression and trauma variables in children under 48 months of age. *Infant Mental Health Journal, 16*, 259–270.

Silvern, L., & Kaersvang, L. (1989). The traumatized children of violent marriages. *Child Welfare, 68*, 421–436.

Turnell, A. (2003, May). Signs of safety. Workshop presented at Salesmanship and Youth Club of Dallas, TX.

Turnell, A. (2007). Thinking and practicing beyond the therapy room: Solution-focused brief therapy, trauma, and child protection. In T. S. Nelson & F. N. Thomas (Eds.), *Handbook of solution-focused brief therapy: Clinical applications* (pp. 295–314). New York: Haworth.

Turnell, A., & Edwards, S. (1997). Aspiring to partnership: The signs of safety approach to child protection. *Child Abuse Review, 6*, 179–190.

Turnell, A., & Edwards, S. (1999). *Signs of safety: A solution and safety oriented approach to child protection work.* New York: Norton.

Turnell, A., Elliott, S., & Hogg, V. (2007). Compassionate, safe and rigorous child protection practice with biological parents of adopted children. *Child Abuse Review, 16*, 108–119.

Turnell, A., & Essex, S. (2007). Working with "denied" child abuse: The resolutions approach. New York: Open University Press.

van der Kolk, B. (2005). Trauma developmental disorder. *Psychiatric Annals*, 401–408.

Wolfe, V. V., & Birt, J. (1995). The psychological sequelae of child sexual abuse. *Advances in Clinical Child Psychology, 17*, 233–263.

Ziegler, D. (2002). *Traumatic experience and the brain.* Phoenix, AZ: Acacia.

158

Risk Assessment Guidelines for Dually Diagnosed Offenders and Civil Patients

José B. Ashford & Albert R. Roberts

The current population of offenders in the United States under correctional supervision is about 7.2 million (Bureau of Justice Statistics, 2008a). This figure includes individuals on probation, in prison, in jails, and on parole. The breakdown of individuals in state and in federal prisons is slightly above 2.2 million (Bureau of Justice Statistics, 2008b). Each year, approximately 780,000 adult offenders reenter the community from federal and state prisons, and about 10 million are released from local jails (Ashford, Sternbach, & Balaam, in press). Researchers estimate that about 80% of the offenders in our prisons have a substance abuse disorder and 16% have a mental disorder (Ashford, Sales, & Reid, 2001; Ashford, Sternbach, & Balaam, in press).

Two-thirds of the offenders reentering the community from correctional facilities are rearrested within 3 years of release. Four out of five of these offenders are placed on some type of postrelease supervision (Ashford, Sternbach, & Balamm, in press). Public offenders under correctional supervision have to be assessed for safety issues prior to their release, including risks of recidivism and risks of violent recidivism. These risk assessments

can differ for persons diagnosed with serious mental disorders because of some of the controversy surrounding the relationships between mental disorders and crime and mental disorders and violence (Ashford, Wong, & Sternbach, 2008; Hodgins & Janson, 2002).

This chapter reviews and examines guidelines for assisting forensic social workers in assessing risk of violence in mentally disordered substance abusing offenders, risk of homicidal behavior in persons being petitioned for involuntary treatment under civil commitment legislation, and risk of criminal recidivism for offenders diagnosed with serious mental disorders.

CASE EXAMPLE

Christine is a social worker employed in an "alternative treatment" program for mentally ill offenders and those with both mental illness and a substance-abuse disorder. This program offers substance-abuse counseling and referrals to mental health, health, and social service providers. She has been asked to assess Fred, an individual who has been repeatedly arrested in the past 6 years for various offenses, including theft, possession of an illegal substance, harassment, and assault. Fred has a long history of involvement with the mental health treatment system as well. In the past 3 years, he has been hospitalized briefly four times, each time being released after only a few days. Fred has failed to keep appointments for treatment at the community mental health center and repeatedly goes off his medication. When he stops taking his medication, he can become loud, agitated, and angry. He uses crack cocaine when he begins to hear voices. Fred lives with his elderly mother, who is frequently the victim of his aggressive behavior. The last time Fred assaulted his mother, she called the police and he was arrested. Now the judge must decide whether to incarcerate Fred or release him to the alternative-to-treatment program in the community. To release Fred to treatment, the judge feels he wants some form of guarantee that Fred will not become violent.

ASSESSING MENTALLY ILL OFFENDERS

Early research on the relationship between mental disorders and crime found no relationship (Ashford et al., 2001). The seminal study by Monahan and Steadman (1984) found that arrest rates for persons with major mental disorders were no higher than for the general population of individuals from comparable social and economic backgrounds (Ashford et al., 2001). Moreover, Monahan and Steadman concluded that the same factors that predict criminal risk in populations of ordinary offenders will predict criminal risk in persons diagnosed with serious mental disorders. However, there is a growing body of evidence that is suggesting that the relationships between mental disorders and crime is much more complex than was previously believed (Ashford, Wong, & Sternbach, 2008; Hodgins & Janson, 2002).

The relationship between mental disorder and dangerousness is also not without controversy. A serious stigma that persons with mental illness face is the issue of dangerousness (Corrigan & Copper, 2005). Members of the public still hold conceptions about mental illness that link mental illness with violence. For instance, the results from a national probability survey showed that 75 percent of the participants in this study viewed people with mental illness as being dangerous

(Link, Phelan, Bresnahan, Stueve, & Pescosolido, 1999). The media has played an unfortunate role in shaping many of these public viewpoints by how it characterizes persons with mental illness who are involved in serious crimes. "It is important for all social workers to be aware that labeling by ultraconservative legislators and sensational journalistic accounts of one or two psychotic subway killers may sell newspapers, but they grossly misrepresent the facts regarding mental illness" (Roberts & Rock, 2002, p. 662).

- Are the mentally ill likely to be violent?
- Are those with a substance abuse problem violent?
- Are those who have both a diagnosable mental illness and a co-occurring substance abuse disorder likely to commit crimes of violence?

Corrigan and Copper (2005) examined existing evidence on the relationship between mental illness and violence. In their examination of this issue, they found that the Treatment Advocacy Center (TAC) and the Health Policies section of the American Enterprise Institute (AEI) falsely concluded that there is a "strong" association between mental illness and violence. The advocates and scholars from these organizations estimated rates of violent homicides among persons with mental illness using inappropriate data that led to false conclusions about the mentally ill. Namely, they used valid evidence to make generalizations about the entire population of persons with mental illness without identifying specific symptoms or disabilities associated with mental illness that are playing a causal role in violence (Corrigan & Copper, 2005). Moreover, the conservative scholars from these organizations mischaracterized the relationship between mental illness and violence as being much stronger than the data actually supports (Corrigan & Copper, 2005).

Persons with mental illness span a spectrum that ranges from individuals who would be violent to individuals who are more likely to be victims of violence. Some recent studies point to persons with serious mental disorders as being at an increase risk for crime (Link & Stueve, 1995) and risk for violence (Ashford, 1989; Hodgins & Janson, 2002). In addition, there is some evidence that supports a link between schizophrenia and a variety of antisocial behavior, including violent crime and homicide (Glancy & Regehr, 1992). However, it is by no means clear that the majority of persons with a mental illness are violent including persons with a diagnosis of schizophrenia (Rice, Harris, & Quinsey, 2002). The results of the multimillion-dollar study of violence risk that was funded by the MacArthur Foundation showed that a diagnosis of schizophrenia and symptoms of psychosis were negatively related to risk of future violence (Rice et al., 2002).

On the other hand, there are certain characteristics of mentally ill offenders that place them at higher risk of committing violent crimes than persons in the general population (Roberts & Rock, 2002). For instance, individuals with co-occurring substance-abuse problems and mental illness are among the highest risk for violent behavior (Swanson, Borum, Swartz, & Monahan, 1996). Moreover, the MacArthur study found that the strongest predictors were scores obtained from the screening version of the Psychopathy Checklist, a diagnosis of antisocial personality disorder, anger as measured by the Novaco Anger Scale, and drug or alcohol abuse (Rice et al., 2002).

Given the high risk for violence in mentally ill offenders, forensic social workers need tools to help them in assessing their risks for violence. They also need tools to aid them in assessing persons for involuntary detention for treatment of their mental disorders. Under existing civil commitment legislation, the issue of dangerousness to others "is now a principal standard for inpatient commitment, outpatient commitment, and commitment to a forensic hospital" (MacArthur Research Network, 2008, p. 2). Because of this standard, forensic social workers have the common duty of performing assessments to determine a mentally ill person's danger to others. Some researchers estimate that from 10 to 17 percent of the persons seen by emergency mental health professionals have homicidal thoughts, and about 5 percent have both suicidal and homicidal risks (Thienhaus & Piasecki, 1998). Individuals presenting with these characteristics have to be assessed for their imminent risk for violence.

VIOLENCE RISK ASSESSMENT

There is a growing literature in mental health about using formalized risk assessment instruments in making judgments about a person's risk for violence (Rice, Harris, & Quincy, 2002; Monahan et al., 2001, for example). This parallels a growing use of standardized screening and assessment tools in general areas of mental health and substance abuse practice. However, most of the existing instruments in mental health and substance abuse are not specifically geared to predicting violent behavior or dangerousness. In addition, no instrument is perfect. In fact, Monahan and colleagues (2001) have demonstrated that actuarial instruments alone are not accurate enough to predict risk of violence and dangerousness. Rather, the best predictor of future risk is the use of data obtained from a reliable and a valid actuarial instrument that is combined with the clinical experience and wisdom of the mental health professional. Namely, the clinician must integrate the results from a standardized instrument with his or her knowledge, experience, and empathetic understanding of persons with a diagnosis of a serious mental illness (Thienhaus & Piasecki, 1998).

Actuarial instruments rely heavily on static factors, such as the age of the offender at first offense, and as a result can be insensitive to changes in individuals because of involvement in treatment or changes in the environment that may have resulted in increased or decreased stress or access to intended victims (see Roberts & Rock, 2002). However, the use of dynamic risk factors in predicting violence is not without controversy. Rice and colleagues (2002) have written that there are no studies that demonstrate that changes in many of our presumed dynamic variables were associated with a parallel change in risk. Without this evidence, Rice and colleagues (2002) do not believe that dynamic factors can be legitimately considered a dynamic risk factor. However, there was one study that produced some evidence that changes in hostility were useful in identifying offenders with a change in their risk for violence (Rice et al., 2002). In other words, some of the best predictors continue to be variables that are static.

- A history of previous violence is widely recognized as one of the best indicators of future violence.
- A history of substance abuse also increases risk for violent behavior.
- A history of a psychopathic personality diagnosis is another strong predictor variable (see Roberts & Rock, 2002).

When these risk factors occur together in the same person, the risk for future violence or dangerousness can be considerably higher.

The MacArthur Violence Risk Assessment Study presents some of the most recent findings on the assessment of violence in persons with mental illness that is based on one of the largest available samples (N = 1,136). The MacArthur study measured 134 risk factors. About half had statistically significant bivariate relationships with violence measured in the community 20 weeks after study participants were discharged from a hospital. Some of the relevant risk factors identified from this study's research include:

- gender,
- prior violence,
- childhood experiences of having been physically abused,
- a co-occurring diagnosis of substance abuse and mental disorder (strongly predictive of violence),
- psychopathy as measured by the Hare Psychopathy checklist,
- a suspicious attitude toward others,
- violent thoughts such as thinking or daydreaming about harming others,
- anger as measured by the Novaco Anger Scale (MacArthur Research Network, 2008).

When the bivariate results in the MacArthur study were combined in a multiple iterative classification tree (ICT), the model showed considerable predictive accuracy for the study's construction sample. This model developed in the MacArthur study has been retested on a new sample of patients who fell within high and low risk classifications for violence established in the construction sample; the results showed some shrinkage, but still had good predictive accuracy (Monahan et al., 2005). The reader is directed to this work for detailed information on risk factors, as well as on issues in risk assessment methodology (MacArthur Research Network, 2008; Monahan et al., 2005).

Risk Factors and Data Needed for Predicting Risk of Violence

The primary step to take in any effort to prevent violence among mentally ill substance abusers is to improve the accuracy and validity of violence risk assessments. "It has been demonstrated that clinician experience alone is not sufficient to accurately assess future violence" (Roberts & Rock, 2002). When clinicians only employ their clinical judgment, they are able to predict violence rates with a level of accuracy that is not much better

than either flipping a coin or using other methods of chance (Loza & Dhaliwal, 2005). The following are the fixed (unchangeable) and the treatable risk factors that have been identified in the literature for enhancing the accuracy of judgments by mental health professionals.

Fixed or static risk factors

- Age at intake—first hospitalization
- Any threats of violence at admission intake
- Any violent episodes during the hospital admission
- Expand one's database to include information about past acts of violence
- Criminal history: prior arrest history and crime seriousness
  - minor offense, for example, vandalism, truancy, malicious mischief
  - moderate offense, for example,, simple assault, shoplifting, larceny
  - major offense, for example, robbery, rape, homicide
- Physically abused as a child
- Sexually abused as a child
- History of mother or father being a drug abuser
- Mother or father having a criminal history
- Death of a parent by suicide
- Death of a parent by homicide
- Diagnosis of a head injury (either with or without loss of consciousness)

Treatable risk factors

- Diagnosis of antisocial personality disorder
- Diagnosis of psychosis, for example, schizophrenia
- Diagnosis of bipolar disorder
- Diagnosis of depression
- Diagnosis of substance abuse, for example, cocaine, heroin, opiates, stimulants, sedatives
- Diagnosis of alcoholism
- Long periods of unemployment
- Suicide attempt(s)
- Violent fantasies
- Level of functioning (adapted from Monahan et al., 2001)

Collection of data on risk factors should include documentation of the nature, duration, and magnitude of all critical incidents. Emphasis should be devoted especially to understanding trauma during childhood, any history of violence, any suicide attempts, and criminal history. One of the limitations of using some structured risk assessment instruments is that the questions are structured with "yes/no" or checklist responses. To avoid the potential problems associated with this form of questioning, practitioners also need to include open-ended questions in their assessment protocol.

SPECIFIC GUIDELINES FOR ASSESSING CIVIL PATIENTS

Most clinicians are more likely to obtain more background information on individuals who are incarcerated in the criminal justice process than on those who are being detained for purposes of civil commitment. Many civil commitment statutes require that an assessment be completed within 72 hours. In addition, the criterion or outcome of the risk assessment in many civil processes has some other important qualitative differences.

In a legal sense, there is an important substantive issue as to whether existing epidemiological information on violence in mental patients is relevant to assessing risk in emergency service context because of the nature of the risk decision. In the emergency context, the practitioner is focusing on responding to the commitment standard of imminent harm, which involves a short-term rather than long-term risk of violence or dangerousness over future months or years (Thienhaus & Piasecki, 1998). Yet most databases used in constructing actuarial instruments for assessing risk of violence rely on base rates of violence that are useful for assessing long-term risks. In addition, the individuals presenting in emergency service contexts are generally in an acute psychiatric crisis, which requires some important qualitative differences in the focus of the forensic social worker's assessment.

Thienhaus and Piasecki (1998) have provided some useful guidelines for practitioners in assessing patients presenting with homicidal ideation in emergency service contexts.

- Your safety should be a priority.
- Evaluate the homicidal threat by examining whether the patient sees alternatives besides violence to concerns expressed on interview about rejection, threat, or humiliation.
- Try to expand one's database about past violence by questioning family about history,

gathering available medical and police records; questioning the patient about intended victims, any ideation involving potential harm, and acquisition of a weapon; and any globally aggressive statements like "I am going to get them."
- Assess contributions of the psychopathology, for example, command hallucinations, delusional beliefs, feelings of being controlled by outside forces, reduction in impulse control, mania, and other relevant diagnostic risk factors.
- Suicidal risk.
- Identify potential deterrents, such as religious beliefs or fear of legal consequences.
- Determine whether the patient will be returning to an unchanged situation in the community, and try to see the situation from the patient's perception.
- Avoid using no-homicide contracts because they can falsely reassure the clinician.
- Request urine or drug screens because intoxicated patients are at higher risk for violence on discharge.
- Get a second opinion.
- Document the rationale for your decision to release an individual to the community.
- Fulfill your Tarasoff duties.

ASSESSING RISK OF RECIDIVISM

The assessment of risk of general recidivism in mentally ill offenders involves different base rate, stakes, and theoretical considerations from assessments of risk of violence in the mentally ill. We are now in our fourth generation of offender assessment of risk in the criminal justice system (Andrews, Bonta, & Wormith, 2006). The first generation relied on unstructured judgments by forensic and correctional professionals on the probability of an offender reengaging in criminal behavior. The second generation included empirically based risk assessment instruments consisting primarily of static risk factors that were not guided by any theories of crime (e.g., Burgess's salient risk factors). By some accounts, the third generation revolutionized thinking about notions of treatment and rehabilitation in the criminal justice system by differentiating between the concepts of risk and needs. This generation of instruments shifted the focus of the classification of offender risk to matching risk to treatment and rehabilitation considerations. The authors of this revolution were Andrews and Bonta (1994), who created the risk, needs, and responsivity (RNR) theory for classifying offenders for treatment.

The RNR theory of offender classification assumes that treatments must be matched "to information derived from underlying concerns or foci of offender classification: offender risk, offender needs, and offender responsivity" (Ashford et al., 2001, p. 3). In the RNR theory, risk refers to nontreatable factors that are associated with the outcome of criminal recidivism. This component of the classification system helps clinicians identify high-risk offenders, but does not help them understand why the person is likely to reoffend. "To this end, Andrews and Bonta (1994) have identified a special category of needs known as criminogenic needs" (Ashford et al., 2001, p. 4). These needs are factors that are dynamic or changeable and have empirical links with criminal outcomes. Last, responsivity is a concept that deals with general and specific forms of treatment responsiveness. General responsivity recognizes the importance of matching offenders to behavioral, social learning, and cognitive-behavioral strategies because these types of interventions have proven to be more effective in working with offender populations. On the other hand, specific responsivity refers to the notion of matching services to specific characteristics of the offender, such as their cognitive abilities, personality, motivation, age, gender, and ethnicity (Andrews et al., 2006).

The literature rooted in RNR theory has identified major, moderate, and minor risk factors associated with offender recidivism. The big four are:

- history of antisocial behavior, for example, early and continuing involvement in a variety of antisocial acts in a variety of situations and contexts;
- antisocial personality patterns;
- antisocial cognition, such as attitudes, values, beliefs, and rationalizations that support participation in antisocial acts; anger, resentment, and defiance; and identification with criminal others; and
- antisocial associates (Andrews et al., 2006).

Additional major risk factors include poor monitoring and supervision by family members or marital partners, instability in school or work, substance abuse, and limited involvement in noncriminal leisure activities (Andrews et al., 2006).

The major risk factors identified by RNR researchers are consistent with social learning, general personality, and social psychological theories of crime. For this reason, some scholars are beginning to conclude that many of the minor predictors, like a diagnosis of a major mental disorder, are best understood by taking into account their association with the big four risk factors that reflect core social learning and other social psychological principles. In keeping with this viewpoint, the fourth generation of risk prediction attempts to improve on fidelity to the principles underlying RNR theory. Some of the instruments that best predict recidivism that include data information system for monitoring and supervising offenders in the community are:

- the Correctional Assessment and Intervention system (CAIS) developed in Wisconsin,
- the Correctional Offender Management Profiling for Alternative Sanction (COMPAS),
- Offender Intake Assessment (OIA) of the Correctional Service of Canada, and
- Level of Service/Case Management Inventory (LS/SMI).

Each of these instruments structures system responses to offender management and treatment based on offender risk of recidivism. There are also instruments that show excellent predictive validity for assessing violent recidivism in mentally disordered offenders: the Hare Psychopathy Checklist, the Violence Risk Appraisal Guide, and the HCR-20.

CONCLUSION

This chapter examined assessments of short-term risk of violence in civil commitment contexts, assessments of violence and criminal recidivism in various practice context involving offenders diagnosed with serious mental disorders, and variations in outcomes and risk assessment factors. In addressing these variations in risk assessment contexts, the chapter also examined important distinctions in the violence prediction and the correctional classification literature concerning dynamic risk factors. Specifically, there are differences in the use of dynamic factors in predicting risk of violence from the use of dynamic risk factors in designing treatment plans for offenders. Moreover, the chapter clarified how the use of static risk factors from actuarial assessment instruments is enhanced by combining results from these instruments with the clinical wisdom and the experience of forensic social workers.

WEB SITES

Assessment and Management of Violence Risk. http://www.violence-risk.com.

Correctional Assessment and Intervention System (CAIS). http://www.Nccd-crc.org/need_main.html.

Correctional Offender Management Profiling for Alternative Sanction (COMPAS). http://dpca.state.ny.us/technology.htm.

References

Andrews, D. A., & Bonta, J. (1994). *The psychology of criminal conduct.* Cincinnati, OH: Anderson

Andrews, D. A., Bonta, J., & Wormith, J. S. (2006). The recent past and near future of risk and/or need assessment. *Crime & Delinquency, 52,* 7–27.

Ashford, J. B. (1989). Offense comparisons between mentally disordered and non-mentally disordered offenders. *Canadian Journal of Criminology, 31,* 35–48.

Ashford, J. B., Sales, B.D., & Reid, W. H. (2001). Introduction. In J. B. Ashford, B. D. Sales, & W. H. Reid (Eds.), *Treating adult and juvenile offenders with special needs* (pp. 3–27). Washington, DC: American Psychological Association.

Ashford, J. B., Sternbach, K. O., & Balaam, M. (In press). Offender reentry and home based interventions. In S. Allen & E. Tracy (Eds.), *Delivering home based services: A social work perspective.* New York: Columbia University Press.

Ashford, J. B., Wong, K. W., & Sternbach, K. O. (2008). Generic correctional programming for mentally ill offenders: A pilot study. *Criminal Justice and Behavior, 35,* 457–473.

Bureau of Justice Statistics. (2008a). Corrections statistics. Retrieved February 10, 2008, from http://www.ojp.usdoj/bjs/correct.htm#programs.

Bureau of Justice Statistics. (2008b). Prison statistics: Summary findings. Retrieved February 8, 2008, from http://www.ojp.usdoj.gov/bjs/prisons.htm.

Corrigan, P. W., & Copper, A. E. (2005). Mental illness and dangerousness: Fact or misperception, and implications for stigma. In P. W. Corrigan (Ed.), *On the Stigma of mental illness: Practical strategies for research and social change.* Washington, DC: American Psychological Association.

Glancy, G., & Regehr, C. (1992). Forensic psychiatric aspects of schizophrenia. *Psychiatric Clinics of North America: Clinical Forensic Psychiatry, 15,* 575–589.

Hodgins, S., & Janson, J. G., (2002). *Criminality and violence among the mentally disordered.* New York: Cambridge University Press.

Link, B. G., Phelan, J. C., Bresnahan, M., Stueve, A., & Pescosolido, B. A. (1999). Public conceptions of mental illness: Labels, causes, dangerousness, and social distance. *American Journal of Public Health, 89,* 1328–1333.

Link, B. G., & Stueve, A. (1995). Evidence bearing on mental illness as a possible cause of violent behavior. *Epidemiologic Review, 17,* 172–181.

Loza, W., & Dhaliwal, G. K. (2005). Predicting violence among forensic correctional populations. *Journal of Interpersonal Violence, 20,* 188–194.

MacArthur Research Network. (2008). The MacArthur violence risk assessment: Executive summary. Retrieved February 10, 2008, from http://www.macarthur.virgnia.edu/risk.html.

Monahan, J., Steadman, H. J. (1984). The impact of state mental hospital deinstutionalization on United States prison populations, 1968–1978. *The Journal of Criminal Law and Criminology (1973–), 75*(2), pp. 474–490.

Monahan, J., Steadman, H. J., Robbins, P. C., Appelbaum, P., Banks, S., Grisson, T., et al. (2005). An actuarial model of violence risk assessment for persons with mental disorders. *Psychiatric Services. 56,* 810–815.

Monahan, J., Steadman, H. J., Silver, E., Appelbaum, P., Mulvey, E., Roth, L., et al. (2001). *Rethinking risk assessment: The MacArthur Study of Mental Disorder and Violence.* New York: Oxford University Press.

Rice, M. E., Harris, G. T., & Quinsey, V. L. (2002). The appraisal of violence risk. *Current Opinion Psychiatry, 15,* 589–593.

Roberts, A. R., & Rock, M. (2002). An overview of forensic social work and risk assessments with the dually diagnosed. In A. R. Roberts & G. J. Green (Eds.), *Social workers' desk reference* (pp. 661–668). New York: Oxford University Press.

Swanson, J., Borum, R., Swartz, M., & Monahan, J. (1996). Psychotic symptoms and disorders and the risk of violent behavior in the community. *Criminal Behaviour and Mental Health, 13,* 1–18.

Thienhaus, O. J., & Piasecki, M. (1998). Assessment of psychiatric patients' risk of violence towards others. *Psychiatric Services, 49,* 1129–1147.

Step-by-Step Guidelines for Assessing Sexual Predators

Graham Glancy & Cheryl Regehr

Over the latter half of the twentieth century, legislators have been designing sentencing laws to reflect prevailing views regarding the rehabilitation of sex offenders. By the end of the twentieth century, the public became increasingly concerned about recidivism rates in sex offenders, culminating in the Washington State Community Protection Act in 1990. This legislation established a new law for the civil commitment of persons found to be in new parlance "sexually violent predators" (State of Washington, 1991). Unlike its predecessors, this law was not linked to sentencing but was intended to civilly commit the offender following completion of a prison term (Glancy, Regehr, & Bradford, 2001; Zonana, 1999). Despite vigorous debate and arguments against the Washington State sexual predator model, similar legislation has been enacted in most states (Zonana, 1999). These laws call for mental health practitioners to assess dangerous sexual offenders and predict the risk of future harm to others.

One in two females and one in three males report being the victim of unwanted sexual acts at some time in their lives (Badgley et al., 1984). Furthermore, in conditions of secrecy, Abel et al. (1987) found that sexual offenders admitted to multiple paraphilic acts for which they were not charged. For instance, 153 nonincestuous pedophiles reported 43,000 acts, suggesting 281 acts per offender. It should be noted that the rate of admitted offenses was highest among "hands-off" offenders, including such offenses as exhibitionism, and lower among offenders who had physical contact with the victims. On the other hand, the reported recidivism rates for sexual offenders are approximately 10–15 percent, which appears very low compared to the approximately 40 percent rate of recidivism reported for all categories of offenders. The apparent contradictions in both victim and offender reports of sexual violence and criminal changes and convictions for sexual crimes, as evidenced by recidivism rates, points to the importance of assessment tools that identify those offenders at highest risk to the public.

This chapter describes the process of a risk assessment for those offenders considered under sexual predator laws. It should be noted at the outset that these assessments must be thorough and completed by someone with expertise in the area for two main reasons. First, these assessments are hotly contested in courts, and second, the outcome of the assessment has profound implications for individual liberty and community safety. Consequently, we recommend the use of multidisciplinary teams wherever possible, in which variously trained professionals contribute their expertise.

The recommended process for sexual predator assessment involves the following:

- clinical interview
- information from collateral sources
- specialized tests
  - psychometric testing
  - sexual preference testing
  - attitude testing
  - actuarial schemes aimed at predicting specific risks

CLINICAL INTERVIEW

While Quinsey, Khanna, and Malcolm (1998) have argued that the clinical interview is unnecessary and unhelpful when actuarial tests are to be used, the prevailing standards in the field suggest that a clinical interview should be performed whenever possible (Boer, 2006; Zonana, 2000). The interview process should be extensive and would ideally include more than one interview, depending on the circumstances. It is certainly possible that the assessor may be denied access to the person being assessed, but efforts at gaining access should be clearly documented. Furthermore, denied access to the patient should be explicitly stated in the conclusions as a cautionary caveat.

At the outset of the interview, the assessor should inform the client of the limits of the confidentiality inherent in the situation. First and foremost, it is imperative that the interviewer is clear in identifying the agency requesting the assessment and the intended nature and purpose of the assessment. It should also be made clear whether a report will be prepared, the form of this report (verbal or written), and to whom the report is being submitted. If the assessment is for legal purposes as opposed to clinical or inherently helpful purposes, this should be stated. Any other limits to confidentiality that may be relevant, such as the duty to warn and protect a third party or child, should also be stated at the outset (Glancy, Regehr & Bryant, 1998). It may be necessary to remind the client of these limits to confidentiality at various stages in the assessment process as various processes, such as a therapeutic alliance may undermine their critical judgment (Regehr & Antle, 1997).

The clinical interview should focus on a full psychosocial history performed in the normal manner. However, there should also be a focus on the sexual offenses to define a pattern of offending, cognitive distortions, and the offense cycle. Other issues such as insight, judgment, and remorse are important. A history of the individual's participation in treatment and what he has learned in treatment can be particularly helpful. The individual should be asked about discharge plans, contingency plans, and future treatment options. Specific tests, some of which are easily administered, may help focus the interview and serve as memory aid contributing to a more comprehensive interview.

CORROBORATING DATA

Corroborating data should be considered essential in the assessment of sexual predators. An interview with family members allows the assessor to compose a picture of the person within the context of his or her family and background. Specific family issues and dynamics may be helpful in understanding the person and would there-

fore be paramount in the design of a treatment plan. Also included in collateral information may be police synopses of the offenses, court transcripts, victim statements, and evidence. Previous records of treatment, counseling, or other contacts with mental health agencies are also helpful. See Table 159.1.

TESTING

Considering the magnitude of the issue under question when assessing sexual predators, test-

TABLE 159.1 Aspects of Assessment for Sexual Predators

Clinical Interview

Limits of confidentiality
Historical factors
Dynamic factors

Corroborating Data

Family
Legal data
Previous treatment records

Testing
Psychometric
MMPI/MCMI
  Neuropsychological
Biomedical
  Neuroimaging
  Endocrine
Sexual preference
  Penile plethysmography
  Visual reaction time
  Polygraphy
Attitude and history
  Clarke Sexual History Test
  Abel & Becker Cognition
  Attitudes toward Women Scale
  Burt Rape Myth Scale
  Michigan Alcoholism Screening Test
Actuarial tests
  RRASOR
  Static 99
  SONAR
  MnSOST
  SVR-20
  Risk Matrix 2000/Sexual
  PCL-R

ing should be as comprehensive as possible. Some of the methods of testing addressed in this chapter require referral to other professionals with specialized training or credentials; other methods are easily administered by social workers.

Psychometric Testing

Most psychometric testing, though not all, requires a registered clinical psychologist. Some of the more general tests, such as the MMPI, can be most helpful in determining the personality profile of the offender. In addition, a neuropsychological screen can assist in identifying neurological contributors (Langevin & Watson, 1996).

Biomedical Testing

A range of biomedical tests may also require referral and may be relevant and indicated in specific cases. This could include electroencephalograms, CT scans, and other imaging studies where it is felt that specific brain pathology may be relevant. Endocrine testing may also be helpful.

Sexual Preference Testing

Sexual preference testing should be considered a specialized field and should only be attempted if one has the requisite qualifications in the area. Three specific measures should be considered.

Penile plethysmography. Initially described by Freund (1979), sexual preference testing or phallometry is the single best indicator of a paraphilia (Langevin & Watson, 1996). It involves the measurement of penile volume or circumference when an individual is confronted with a variety of standardized stimuli. The reported reliability coefficients are as high as 0.87 for the sensitivity of the test and as high as 0.95 for the specificity (Abel et al., 1984). The test can be invalidated by attempts to fake, although such attempts can often be detected. Penile plethysmography is primarily a clinical approach, and caution should be exercised when using this test in the legal context (Zonana, 1999). In many jurisdictions, especially Canada, it is routinely used in clinical and psycholegal assessments of sexual offenders referred to forensic services. In many other jurisdictions, it is used primarily as part of a comprehensive treatment approach (Scott, 1994). This test is particularly valuable in the clinical confrontation of nonadmitters who may subsequently

admit to the offense, thereby facilitating treatment success.

We cannot emphasize strongly enough that phallometrics, like any other approach described in this chapter, should only be considered as one part of a complete assessment. It should be performed by a recognized laboratory, using standardized test materials, an appropriate setting, and a procedure respecting the dignity of the client. Results should be scrutinized for faking, taking into account the client's mental state, age, and any physical illnesses, such as diabetes, that may effect the results of testing.

Visual reaction time. A newer test that holds great promise has now been developed by Abel, Huffman, Warberg and Holland (1998). This test has some advantages over phallometric testing in that it can be administered in an hour, requiring only a laptop computer and does not require the use of naked stimuli material. Although a useful test at this stage, it is debatable whether it has reached the accepted standard for admissibility in court (Krueger, Bradford, & Glancy, 1998); nevertheless it has been ruled admissible in some jurisdictions. Impressive figures of the test's sensitivity and specificity have been reported with some independent replication (Johnson & Listiak, 1999).

Polygraphy. Polygraphy (or the lie detector) is another test that has been used during the assessment and treatment of sex offenders. This again does not meet the standard for admissibility in court but can be used as an adjunctive test (Zonana, 1999).

Attitude and History Measures

Langevin and Watson (1996) and Zonana (1999) outline some specific tests that may be important in the assessment of sex offenders and people with paraphilia, which include the following: Clarke Sexual History Questionnaire-R (Langevin & Paitich, 2005); Abel and Becker Cognition Scale (Abel et al., 1984); Attitudes toward Women Scale (Check, 1988); Burt Rape Myth Acceptance Scale (Burt, 1980); and Michigan Alcohol Screening Test, MAST (Selzer, 1971).

One of the problems of these tests is their transparency. Unlike the more sophisticated tests, such as the MMPI, they do not have specific validity scales and are easily faked. In theory, these tests are very useful, and if you can ensure the honesty of the client, the tests can play a vital role in the design of a treatment plan and also in the prediction of dangerousness. For instance, the Abel Cognition Scale identifies cognitive distortion in sex offenders that can be modified in treatment (Abel et al., 1984). The MAST may identify alcoholism, which can be addressed in treatment and is also an important variable in predictive instruments (Selzer, 1971). The Clarke Sexual History Questionnaire-R (Langevin, & Paitich, 2005) can give an indication of the number and severity of paraphilias present. Obviously, caution needs to be used given the self-report nature of these instruments.

Actuarial Risk Assessment Schemes

In recent years, considerable attention has focussed on the development of actuarial measures to predict risk of future danger. The most popular of these schemes include the VRAG/SORAG, the RRASOR, the Static-99, the SONAR, the SVR-20, the RMS/Sexual, and the MnSOST. Some studies have suggested that actuarial tools may be more accurate than clinical judgment alone (Grove & Meehl, 1996), and as noted previously, some experts suggest that actuarial tests should be used alone without the confusion of clinical judgment (Quinsey et al., 1998). Nevertheless, others have suggested that the assertion that actuarial tests should be used in the absence of a clinical interview is ridiculous and absolutely unsupported by data (Boer, 2006; Zonana, 2000). Actuarial scales are designed following retrospective research for factors associated with recidivism in offender populations. These factors are then combined and weighted, producing a score that is assumed to give an assessment of risk. See Table 159.1 for a comparison of tests.

VRAG/SORAG. The history of actuarial scales for sex offenses starts with the VRAG, which is an actuarial test designed to predict risk for general violence, followed by the development of the SORAG, which focuses more specifically on sexual crimes (Quinsey, Harris, Rice, & Cormier, 1998). These actuarial tests aim to estimate the long-term likelihood that an individual with a history of sexual offenses will commit any act of violence. Information thus far is only published in a book and has not been peer-reviewed in scientific journals. Several criticisms have been levied against these instruments, including broad definitions of violent offenses used by the developers, the use of static factors alone as predictors

(e.g., age at first offense), and sampling strategies that were limited to high-risk offenders in a maximum security hospital who had limited opportunities for recidivism in a natural setting. There have also been ethical concerns about the original leading to their development (Regehr, Edwardh, & Bradford, 2000). Caution should be used when administering these tests.

MnSOST-R. The Minnesota Sex Offender Screening Tool (Revised), MnSOST(R), is a 16-item actuarial scale developed to assess long-term (6-year) risk of sexual recidivism among extrafamilial child molesters and rapists excluding incest offenders (Epperson, Kaul, & Hesselton, 1998). It includes both static and some dynamic factors related to the prediction of sexual recidivism. Reasonably good prediction rates are reported by the developers. The scale was derived from a selected sample of 123 sexual reoffenders, a random sample of 120 nonsexual reoffenders, and a random sample of 144 nonreoffenders. Methodology regarding the development of the measure has been criticized on the basis of sample size and sample selection. The data of the original work are only available as a conference presentation and have not been subjected for peer review.

RRASOR. The RRASOR is a test that was based on the author's comprehensive meta-analysis of predictors of sexual offense recidivism in 61 studies (Hanson & Bussiere, 1998). The RRASOR (Hanson, 1997) was developed to assess the risk for sexual offense recidivism using a limited number of easily scored items that could be used by relatively untrained raters using commonly available information. Testing on the instrument is impressive in that seven highly varied samples from three countries were included. The scale is moderately accurate in predicting sexual recidivism (essentially equal to the VRAG and the MnSOST(R)), but according to the author should not be used in isolation. It should be noted that the measure does not include phallometric testing, which is one of the strongest predictors in Hanson's meta-analysis. This was a deliberate move because the RRASOR was intended for use as a quick checklist that includes only four items: prior sex offenses; age less than 25; having any male victims; and any extrafamilial victims.

Static-99. Hanson has to be given credit for not resting on his laurels and moving forward to help design the Static-99. Collaborating with Thornton

TABLE 159.2 Actuarial Prediction Tests

	Strengths	Limitations
VRAG/SORAG 1998 VRAG—12 items plus the PCL-R SORAG—13 items plus the PCL-R	Moderate ability to predict violence Good for mentally disordered offenders	Requires training for PCL-R, includes any form of minor violence, standardized on small number of high-risk offenders, no dynamic factors
MnSOST(R) 1998 16 items	Some dynamic factors, easy to score	Validation sample too small
RRASOR 1997 4 items	Easy to score, moderate ability to predict sexual violence, well validated	Simplistic, no dynamic factors
Static-99 1999 10 items	Easy to score, moderate ability to predict sexual violence, well validated	No dynamic factors
SONAR 2000 2 items	Considers dynamic factors, may predict short-term and long-term risk of sexual violence	Not yet well tested
SVR-20	Easy to use, dynamic and static factors, good predictive validity	Not empirically derived
Risk Matrix 2000 Sexual	Relatively good predictive validity, easy to score	Not yet well validated
PCL-R 1991 20 items	Recognized psychological test, well validated	Requires training, no dynamic factors

(1997; A 16 year follow-up of 563 sexual offenders released from HM Prison Service in 1979, unpublished data), who produced the SACJ-MIN, the authors considered the possibility that a combination of the two scales would predict better than the original scale (Hanson & Thornton, 2000). The new scale was created by adding together items from RRASOR and the SACJ-MIN. The Static-99 was indeed more accurate than the RRASOR or SACJ-MIN alone in predicting both sex offense recidivism and general violent recidivism. The authors present observed recidivism rates of 5, 10, 15 years and divide scores on the Static-99 into low, medium low, medium high, and high. The authors conclude that the Static-99 showed a moderate predictive accuracy for both sexual recidivism and general recidivism. They note that the Static-99 is intended to be a measure of long-

term risk potential. They also point to the lack of dynamic factors that could be useful in selecting treatment targets, measuring change, and predicting when offenders are likely to recidivate, suggesting some caution is advised.

SONAR. Hanson in his early work, already noted, has always cautioned that actuarial scales should be used as part of an empirically guided clinical approach (Hanson, 2000). For this instrument, Hanson and Harris (1998) organized the dynamic or changeable risk factors into a structured assessment procedure. They considered five so-called stable factors, which included intimacy deficits, negative social influences, attitudes tolerant of sex offending, sexual self-regulation, and general self-regulation with four so-called acute factors, which are substance abuse, negative mood, anger, and victim access. They then tested the validity of the scale using data previously collected from 208 sex offenders who had recidivated sexually while on community supervision. They compared this group with a comparison group of 201 sex offenders who had not recidivated. They found that the scale showed a moderate ability to differentiate between recidivism and nonrecidivism. The scale showed adequate internal consistency and moderate ability to differentiate between recidivism and nonrecidivism. This is a new test that has not been independently validated, but again we must give credit to Hanson who continues to improve on his original instruments and analyses. This test begins to answer some of the criticisms that have been levied against actuarial testing

SVR-20. The SVR-20 is a clinically guided checklist designed to assess risk for sexual violence recidivism in sex offenders. This scheme is a relatively easy to use, straightforward, structured risk assessment guide developed by researchers at Simon Fraser University (Boer, Hart, Kropp, & Webster, 1997). It relies fairly heavily on clinical skills and includes the PCL-R as a major item. It includes dynamic and static factors and lends itself well to issues of managing risk and modifying risk factors. It is highly recommended for the practitioner. It consists of 20 items divided into 3 risk factor domains: sexual offenses, psychosocial adjustment, and future planning. The scoring system allows the user to rate items as not present, somewhat or possibly present, or clearly present. The manual for the instrument suggests that a global professional judgment of low, medium, or high risk of sexual recidivism can be obtained.

De Vogel, de Ruiter, van Beek, and Mead (2004) compared the integrated reliability and the predictive validity of the SVR-20 to the Static-99 in a Dutch sample of treated sex offenders. They found the SVR-20 had fairly good predictive validity (AUC 0.83), significantly better than the Static-99, which had an AUC of 0.66.

Risk Matrix 2000/Sexual. This actuarial risk measure was developed by Thornton (1997), based on the structured anchored clinical judgment scale (SACJ). It is constructed to yield four summary risk categories: low, medium, high, and very high risk. It is considered two-dimensional in that it uses a stepwise approach to scoring. It relies on

the factors in the Hanson and Bussiere (1998) meta-analysis. The measure contains three risk items in step 1 (number of previous sexual experiences, number of criminal appearances, and age) that can be translated into a risk category. In the second step, four factors (any conviction for sexual offense against a male, conviction for sexual offense against a stranger, any conviction for a noncontact sex offense, and never been married) are noted. These are considered aggravating factors, and if present, they raise the risk category. It was validated on two prison samples and gave moderately good predictive accuracy. Subsequently, there have been few cross-validation studies. One study (Craig, Beech, & Browne, 2006) found that this instrument obtained marginal accuracy in predicting sexual reconviction in the sex offender group and was comparable to the Static-99 and the SVR-20. Additionally, the authors found that combining four factors—namely, history of foster care, history of substance abuse, history of employment problems, and history of school maladjustment—increased the accuracy in predicting sexual reconviction.

PCL-R. Psychopathy appears to be a central construct relevant to sex offenders as well as other offender groups, such as juvenile delinquents, adult offenders in general, and mentally disordered offenders. Research from a variety of sources has consistently demonstrated that high psychopathy scores are related to sexual offending (Seto & Lalumière, 2000). The Psychopathy Checklist was developed by Hare (1991) to screen for psychopathy in criminal populations and assess changes in psychopathic symptomatology over time. It is supported by a plethora of evidence describing its interrater reliability and validity. It is a historically based assessment procedure that requires at least a 2- or 3-hour interview with the individual where possible. In addition, corroborative information is generally needed. The PCL should be considered a psychometric test, and it is recognized by psychological associations as such. It is recommended that users take a training course. Such courses are available from time to time in various jurisdictions. Nevertheless, the PCL-R, along with its manual, is a comparatively easy-to-use psychometric test with a very simple scoring system that does not require computer assistance. Given the excellent research to which it has been subjected, it is a useful tool in the assessment of sexually aggressive men.

General Comments Regarding Actuarial Tests

We believe that it was Lord Kelvin who said, "Without measurement there can be no science." Esquirol countered with, "One should never be absolute in practice." Considerable controversy exists about the place of actuarial testing in the assessment of sexual offenders (Norko & Baranoski, 2005; Sreenivasan, Kirkish, Garrick, Wineberger, & Phenixa, 2000; Zonana, 2000). It appears clear that most agree that actuarial tests should only be used in association with other clinical methods of evaluation. It is argued that the use of risk appraisal instruments alone may not meet the standard for admissibility in court and may even be unethical according to some professional associations (Sreenivasan et al., 2000). In fact, in a Florida case, it was concluded that "None of these actuarial instruments seem to include whether the person has been or is being treated, whether he has been or is still incarcerated, is under house arrest or is comatose, although to the unsophisticated one or more of these would seem to bear heavily on future conduct" (In re Valdez, Smith et al., 6th Judicial Circuit, Florida, p. 6).

Although static factors may be easier to score and can often be gleaned from files, it would unfortunate if these were the only criteria for a comprehensive assessment. Additionally, they do not assist the assessor in looking at unique relevant factors in an individual client, such as a person who may have a few past offenses who presents with overwhelming urges to molest in a new situation where a child relative has moved into his house temporarily. It is true to say that the SONAR and the SVR-20 represent a development of previous tools in that it begins to address dynamic factors. We agree with Sreenivasan and colleagues' (2000) conclusions that the responsibility of the clinician is to understand how the individual risk factors are represented in a specific patient. They, like many commentators, have concluded that guided clinical judgment should be the norm.

CONCLUSIONS

We conclude, therefore, that a comprehensive approach to the assessment of a sexual offender requires a combination of as many of the foregoing approaches as are feasible in the circumstances. Every effort should be made to complete a clinical examination and adjunctive testing as described. Only in this way can the known risk factors be applied to an individual in the context of the individual's current state and unique circumstances.

WEB SITES

MnSOST(R). http://www.mosac.mo.gov/Documents/SOrisk-assessment.pdf.

PCL-R. http://www.pearsonassessments.com/tests/hare.htm.

RRASOR. http://ww2.ps-sp.gc.ca/publications/corrections/199704_e.pdf.

Risk Matrix 2000. http://psg275.bham.ac.uk/forensic_centre/External%20Documents/SCORING%20GUIDE%20FOR%20RISK%20MATRIX(ver-Feb%202007).pdf.

SONAR. http://ww2.ps-sp.gc.ca/publications/corrections/200001b_e.asp.

Static-99. http://ww2.ps-sp.gc.ca/publications/corrections/199902_e.pdf.

SVR-20. http://www3.parinc.com/products/product.aspx?Productid=SVR-20.

VRAG/SORAG. http://www.mhcp-research.com/ragpage.htm.

References

Abel, G., Becker, J., Cunningham-Rathner, J., Rouleau, J., Kaplan, M., & Reich, S. (1984). *Treatment of child molesters.* Atlanta, GA.: Emory University School of Medicine.

Abel, G., Becker, J., Mittelman, S., Cunningham-Rathner, J., Rouleau, J., & Murphy, D. (1987). Self-reported sexual crimes of non-incarcerated paraphiliacs. *Journal of Interpersonal Violence, 2,* 3–25.

Abel, G., Huffman, J., Warberg, B., & Holland, C. L. (1998). Visual reaction time and plethysmography as measures of sexual interest in child molesters. *Sexual Abuse: A Journal of Research & Treatment, 10*(2), 81–95

Badgely, R., Allard, H., McCormick, N., Proudhock, P., Fortin, D., Ogilvie, D., et al. (1984). *Sexual offenses against children* (vol. 1). Ottawa: Canadian Government.

Boer, D. (2006). Sexual offender risk assessment strategies: Is there a convergence of opinion yet? *Sex Offender Treatment, 1,* 1–4.

Boer, D., Hart, S., Kropp, P., & Webster C. (1997). *Manual for Sexual Violence Risk–20 (SVR20): Professional guidelines for assessing risk of sexual violence.* Vancouver: British Columbia Institute Against Family Violence.

Burt, M. (1980). Cultural myths and supports for rape. *Journal of Personality and Social Psychology, 38,* 217–230.

Check, J. (1988). Hostility toward women: Some theoretical considerations. In G. Russell (Ed.), *Violence in intimate relationships* (pp. 29–42). Great Neck, NY: PMA.

Craig, L. A., Beech, A., & Browne, K. D. (2006). Cross validation of the Risk Matrix 2000 sexual and violent scales. *Journal of Interpersonal Violence, 21*(5), 612–633.

de Vogel, V., de Ruiter, C., van Beek, D., & Mead, G. (2004). Predictive validity of the SVR 20 and Static-99. *Law and Human Behaviour, 28*(3), 235–251.

Epperson, D., Kaul, J., & Hesselton, D. (1998). *Final report of the development of the Minnesota Sex Offender Screening Tool–Revised.* Presentation at the 17th Annual Research and Treatment Conference of the Association for the Treatment of Sexual Abusers, Vancouver, BC.

Freund, K. (1979). Phallometric diagnosis with nonadmitters. *Behavioural Research and Therapy, 17,* 451–457.

Glancy, G., Regehr, C., & Bradford, J. (2001). Sexual predator laws in Canada. *Journal of the American Academy of Psychiatry and the Law, 29,* 232–237.

Glancy, G., Regehr, C., & Bryant, A. (1998). Confidentiality in crisis: Part I—the duty to inform. *Canadian Journal of Psychiatry, 43,* 1001–1005.

Grove, W., & Meehl, P. (1996). Comparative efficiency of informal (subjective impressionistic) and formal (mechanical, algorithmic) prediction procedures: The clinical statistical controversy. *Psychology, Public Policy and Law, 2,* 293–323.

Hanson, R. (1997). *The development of a brief actuarial risk scale for sexual offense recidivism* (user report). Ottawa: Department of the Solicitor General.

Hanson, R. (2000). *Using research to improve risk assessment for sex offenders.* Presentation to the American Academy of Psychiatry and the Law. Vancouver, BC.

Hanson, R., & Bussiere, M. (1998). Predicting relapse: A meta-analysis of sexual offender recidivism studies. *Journal of Consulting and Clinical Psychology, 66*(2), 348–362.

Hanson, R., & Harris, A. (1998). *Dynamic predictors of sexual recidivism* (user report). Ottawa: Department of the Solicitor General.

Hanson, R., & Thornton D. (2000). Improving risk assessments for sex offenders: A comparison of three actuarial scales. *Law and Human Behaviour, 24,* 119–136.

Hare, R. (1991). *Manual for the revised Psychopathy Checklist.* Toronto: Multihealth Systems.

Johnson, S., & Listiak, A. (1999). The measurement of sexual preference—a preliminary comparison of phallometry and the Abel assessment. *Sex Offender, 3*(26), 1–19.

Krueger, R., Bradford, J., & Glancy, G. (1998). Report from the Committee on Sex Offenders: The Abel assessment for sexual interest—a brief description. *Journal of the American Academy of Psychiatry and the Law, 26*(2), 277–280.

Langevin, R., & Paitich, D. (2005). *The Clarke sexual history questionnaire for males—revised.* Toronto: Multihealth Systems.

Langevin, R., & Watson, R. (1996). Major factors in the assessment of paraphilias and sex offenders. *Journal of Offender Rehabilitation, 23,* 39–70.

Norko, M., & Baranoski, M. (2005). The state of Contemporary Risk Assessment. *Canadian Journal of Psychiatry, 50,* 18–26.

Quinsey, V., Harris, G., Rice, M., & Cormier, C. (1998). *Violent offenders: Appraising and managing risk.* Washington, DC: American Psychological Association.

Quinsey, V., Khanna, A., & Malcolm, P. (1998). A retrospective evaluation of the regional treatment sex offender treatment program. *Journal of Interpersonal Violence, 13,* 621–624.

Regehr, C., & Antle, B. (1997). Coercive influences: Informed consent in court mandated social work practice. *Social Work, 42,* 300–306.

Regehr, C., Edwardh, M., & Bradford, J. (2000). Research ethics with forensic patients. *Canadian Journal of Psychiatry, 45,* 892–898.

Scott, L. (1994). Sex offenders. In A. Roberts (Ed.), *Critical issues in crime and justice* (pp. 61–76). Thousand Oaks, CA: Sage.

Selzer, M. (1971). The Michigan Alcohol Screening Test: The quest for a new diagnostic instrument. *American Journal of Psychiatry, 127,* 1653–1658.

Seto, M., & Lalumière, M. (2000). Psychopathy and sexual aggression. In C. Gatcono (Ed.), *The clinical and forensic assessment of psychopathy: A practitioner's guide* (pp. 330–350). Mahwah, NJ: Erlbaum.

Sreenivasan, H., Kirkish, P., Garrick, T., Wineberger, L., & Phenix, A. (2000). Actuarial risk assessment models: A review of critical issues related to violence and sex offender recidivism assessments. *Journal American Academy of Psychiatry and the Law, 28,* 438–448.

State of Washington. (1991). Sexually violent predators statute, revised code of Washington, chapter 71.07.

Thornton, D. (1997). [A 16 year follow-up of 563 sexual offenders released from HM Prison Service in 1979]. Unpublished data.

Zonana, H. (1999). *Dangerous sex offenders. A task force report of the American Psychiatric Association.* Washington, DC: American Psychiatric Association.

Zonana, H. (2000). Sex offender testimony: Junk science of unethical testimony. *Journal American Academy Psychiatry and the Law, 28,* 386–388.

160 Elder Abuse

Patricia Brownell & Catherine T. Giblin

This chapter provides an overview of elder abuse and neglect, including the scope of this social problem; definitions, profiles, and causative theories of abuse; assessment, detection, and intervention strategies; elder abuse and mistreatment involving special populations; and current and future issues of concern. The role of the social worker is emphasized throughout.

SCOPE OF PROBLEM AND THE ROLE OF THE FORENSIC SOCIAL WORKER

Elder mistreatment came to the fore as a form of family violence in the early 1980s (Tomita, 2006). National efforts to address this social problem included passage of reporting laws, public education, development of intervention strategies and models (notably interdisciplinary and multiagency consultation teams), and criminal prosecution of abuses that rise to the level of a crime as defined by state penal codes (Tomita, 2006).

Mistreatment of older adults takes many forms, including physical, financial, and emotional or psychological abuse (United Nations, 2003). Professionals, including social workers, are on the front lines to detect, assess, and intervene in situations involving mistreatment, as well as develop, implement, and evaluate strategies that reflect empowerment and protective responses. Estimates of prevalence rates vary, ranging from 3.2 percent (Pillemer & Finkelhor, 1988) to 10 percent (U.S. House of Representatives, 1990). A recent national study on elder abuse found an incidence rate of 1.2 percent (Thomas, 2000). Given the hidden nature of domestic violence, this is thought to be greatly underestimated.

Early studies suggested family caregivers, particularly daughters, were most likely perpetrators of abuse because of caregiver stress (Steinmetz, 1988). Later studies suggested that abuser characteristics were more likely than victim characteristics to be predictors of abuse (Brownell, Berman, & Salamone, 1999).

Although most legislation related to elder mistreatment remains at the state level, recently concerted efforts have been made to pass an elder justice act at the federal level. This would provide a definitional framework for elder mistreatment nationally, as well as federal funding for state-based programs (Edwards, 2007). On the international level, the International Network for the Prevention of Elder Abuse (INPEA) is promoting awareness of elder abuse worldwide through initiatives like the World Elder Abuse Awareness Day (INPEA, 2007).

Nationally, the National Center on Elder Abuse and the National Committee for the Prevention of Elder Abuse promote education and research on elder mistreatment. The need for empirically based research on elder abuse prevention and intervention provides an opportunity for social work practitioners and researchers to engage in partnerships with older adult victims and their families to address this gap in knowledge (Chalk & King, 1998; National Research Council, 2003).

Because of the complex nature of elder abuse, the emotional dynamics linking victim and abuser, and the multiple service systems that must be engaged to ensure a successful service plan, social workers are the professionals best equipped to address this social problem. This is because social workers have expertise in practice with families and individuals, experience in working as part of interdisciplinary teams, knowledge of service systems and how to engage them on behalf of clients, and skill in identifying service needs and advocating for new policies and programs.

Social workers also work in many different agency and institutional settings, where they may come into contact with elder abuse and neglect. Forensic social work is a practice specialty that focuses on the legal aspects of interdisciplinary practice and incorporates social work practice in family violence, including elder abuse, the courts, and law enforcement. In elder abuse, forensic social work is operationalized as policies, practice, and social work roles with juvenile and adult offenders and victims of crimes (Roberts & Brownell, 1999).

DEFINITIONS OF ELDER ABUSE AND NEGLECT

The most commonly used definitions of elder abuse and neglect include physical and psychological neglect and abuse and financial abuse (Tomita, 2006). Elder abuse and neglect definitions are categorized according to the behaviors of the abuser, intent of the abuser, and perceptions and to some extent the decisional capacity and health status of the victim. According to Tomita, these can include:

- physical abuse and neglect. The infliction of physical pain or injury, physical coercion (confinement against one's will), sexual abuse, and willful or unintended failure to provide needed food, clothing, and medications.
- psychological abuse and neglect. The infliction of mental anguish, name-calling, threats, and isolating and excluding from activities.
- financial abuse. The illegal or improper exploitation or use of funds or other resources.

Tomita (2006) also identifies undue influence as a syndrome that can occur when care-dependent older adults are exploited by caregivers who use their position of trust as an opportunity for gaining control over the dependent older adult's decision making. In situations of institutional abuse and neglect, extremely dependent older people with unaddressed high care needs may exhibit such symptoms as dehydration, malnutrition, and pressure sores. Finally, violations of rights is an overarching theme in elder abuse: this is defined as the denial of the basic human right to live free of abuse (United Nations, 2003).

THEORIES OF ELDER ABUSE AND NEGLECT

A number of theoretical explanations for elder abuse and neglect have been proposed. A partial listing is presented here.

- Caregiver stress. Abuse may be perpetrated by an overwhelmed or unprepared caregiver.

The caregiver may be a spouse, adult child or other relative, or a formal caregiver who is an employee of a nursing home or home care agency (Anetzberger, 2000).
- Abuser impairment. An abuser may be physically and/or mentally impaired: mental illness, dementia, developmental disability, or substance abuse may be a factor (Ramsey-Klawsnik, 2000).
- Victim impairment. A victim may self-neglect or abuse, refuse all needed services because of lack of insight into need or capacity to care for self, become vulnerable to abuse through choice of companions or lack of self-protection, or present care needs that overwhelm caregivers.
- Aging-out spouse abuse. One spouse or partner may behave abusively toward the other as part of a long-standing pattern of behavior or because of the onset of illness or dementia of one or both (Brandl, 2000).
- Abuser criminality. A victim may be the target of a scheme perpetrated by a stranger or criminal with the intent to defraud or gain from the victim (Brownell et al., 1999; Heisler, 2000).

For the helping professional, an awareness of the older person's lifestyle, care needs, decisional capacity, and immediate and extended family situation is important in the assessment of degree of risk for abuse or neglect to which the older person may be subject.

With the exception of self-abuse and neglect, elder abuse and mistreatment always includes a victim (who must be at least 60 years of age) and an abuser. Elder abuse and mistreatment can be further explained by breaking it down into several categories. These include domestic violence (family maltreatment), institutional abuse, and scams perpetrated against the elderly by strangers who befriend older adults for the purpose of exploiting them, or who use telemarketing or mail schemes for financial exploitation.

ASSESSMENT, DETECTION, AND INTERVENTION STRATEGIES

The helping professional should be alert to the possibility and risk of elder abuse and neglect when serving older adults in social service or health care settings. In addition, he or she should be knowledgeable about assessment criteria and techniques. According to Breckman and Adelman

(1988), in their classic book, *Strategies for Helping Victims of Elder Mistreatment*, a good assessment requires gathering six types of information from the client or patient. These are safety, access, cognitive status, emotional status, health and functional status, and social and financial resources. Two additional categories include patterns of abuse and cultural beliefs, traditions, and immigration history.

Detection: What Are Signs and Symptoms of Elder Abuse and Neglect?

In conducting a preliminary assessment of whether an older adult may be the victim of elder abuse, a social worker should be alert to signs and symptoms that may suggest a problem.

- Physical: bruises, welts, scratches, burns, fractures, lacerations, or punctures; bleeding under scalp or missing patches of hair; unexplained genital infections or venereal disease (sexual abuse).
- Psychological: sleep disturbances, change in eating patterns, unexplained weight changes, depression and crying, paranoid references, low self-esteem, extreme fearfulness, confusion and disorientation, and apathy or agitation.
- Financial: complaints of hunger or lack of food; unexplained inability to pay bills; overinvolvement of family relative in financial affairs of client; refusal of client or caregiver to pay for needed assistance, even though finances appear to be adequate; and unexplained withdrawals from bank account or complaints about being taken to the bank by the client.

Assessment to Determine If Elder Abuse Is a Factor and the Level of Risk to the Victim

The purpose of an assessment of elder abuse and neglect should take into consideration a number of factors. Does the cognitive capacity of the older adult suggest an empowerment or protective strategy? Is the older adult at imminent risk of harm? How can his or her autonomy and self-determination be taken into consideration? How best can his or her needs and capacity be balanced against the needs and capacity of the family or formal caregiving system? A trusting rela-

tionship between a social worker and an older adult who may be victimized by a family abuser as well as a safe place to talk are essential for a good assessment of possible abuse or neglect, if the victim has capacity.

A good assessment includes the following:

- *Safety.* Is the older adult in immediate danger? Does he or she understand the risks and consequences of decisions concerning safety? What steps can be taken to increase his or her safety? Who has access to the older adult's household? Are there family members or friends who can serve in a protective capacity? What is the potential for abusive behavior on the part of family members?
- *Access.* Are there barriers preventing access to the victim in case of danger? Can a trusted family member or friend assist if necessary? Is the older adult victim or suspected victim a candidate for adult protective services or legal advocacy services? Are the older adult or family members seeking to prevent an investigation or assessment of the client's safety?
- *Cognitive status.* Does the victim or suspected victim show evidence of dementia or other impairment (through the use of a mini-mental status exam)? If cognitive impairment is present, is it the result of a reversible health or mental health condition, or is it related to organic causes and irreversible? Is it severe enough to impair decision-making capacity? To what extent does the older adult's impairment render him or her unable to understand the possible risks or consequences of his or her situation? To what extent does his or her impairment render him or her unable to reliably report on potentially abusive circumstances?
- *Mental health status.* Does the older adult appear to be depressed, ashamed, guilty, fearful, or angry? Is he or she reluctant to discuss the possibility of abuse or neglect, in spite of evidence that this may be occurring? Does he or she rationalize or dismiss family tension or conflict? Does the client manifest depression, paranoia, fear, or anxiety? To what extent can this be explained by the disease stage? Does the client show evidence of denial? To what extent is this related to the disease stage? Does the older adult show evidence of post-traumatic stress syndrome (PTSD) as the result of prolonged abuse?

- *Health and functional capacity*. Does the older adult suffer from a medical problem? Does the older person require assistance with activities of daily living, and if so, who provides it? It is important to note whether a caregiver has the ability (emotional, cognitive, intellectual, financial) to provide this care in a responsible way. Could mistreatment cause or exacerbate existing medical conditions? Is the client capable of self-protecting? If care-dependent, is the older adult client property hydrated and nourished?

- *Social and financial resources*. Does the older adult have family members, friends, or formal supports that provide reliable care? Does he or she have sufficient financial resources? Do family members interact with the older adult in a manner consistent with their cultural values? Are there any family members or others with access to the older adult's home who are mentally ill, are substance abusers, or have a history of criminal behavior? Are the designated caregivers for the older adult capable and willing to provide the level of care necessary for his or her well-being?

- *Older adult victim attributes*. Whereas studies on elder abuse and mistreatment present mixed findings on the characteristics of elder abuse victims that predict abuse or mistreatment by others, some attributes have been found to pose a risk or vulnerability for abuse or exploitation. Is the older adult abusive or violent? Does he or she exhibit behaviors such as repeated questioning, extreme clinging, incessant talking, extreme passivity, or constant moving and wandering? Does the older adult have a history of being abused or mistreated? Does the older adult have friends or companions apart from family members? Is he or she a substance abuser? Is the older adult a caregiver for an impaired or dependent family member?

- *Abuser attributes*. Risk assessment studies have identified characteristics of abusers as being more salient than those of victims. Is the available caregiver overwhelmed or clearly not capable of providing adequate care, resulting in passive neglect or unintentional abuse? Is a family member or significant other also a substance abuser, or suffering from untreated mental illness or depression? Is a family member or significant other unemployed or living a lifestyle he or she cannot afford to sustain?

- *Pattern of abuse*. Any assessment of elder abuse, neglect, or maltreatment should include an assessment of the frequency and intensity of the abuse, as well as the intent of the abuser. Also noted should be whether the abuse has increased in frequency and severity over time. Some studies on younger spouse abuse and child abuse suggest that abuse can escalate over time; however, elder abuse may be more chronic and persistent and still have a negative effect on the health and quality of life of the older victim. The intent of the abuser is important to note because this information can help determine the appropriate intervention. For example, abuse perpetrated by a spouse in the secondary stage of Alzheimer's disease would suggest a different intervention strategy than abuse perpetrated by a substance-abusing grandchild. Has abuse intensified or become more frequent over time? Is the perpetrator aware that behavior in question can be categorized as abusive?

- *Cultural beliefs, traditions, and immigration history*. An emergent area of concern is that of the impact of culture and ethnicity on domestic violence. Congress (1997) presents a model assessment form, the culturagram, which can be used by helping professionals to assess a client's cultural beliefs, traditions, and immigration history. This assessment form can be used to assess the risk and impact of elder abuse and maltreatment on a family, based on the family's cultural background and degree of acculturation (Brownell, 1997).

Intervention Strategies: What Are the Most Effective Strategies for Ensuring the Safety and Well-Being of Older Adults at Risk of or Experiencing Abuse or Neglect?

Planning and implementing effective intervention strategies for elder abuse and neglect require effective and multifaceted assessments incorporating the dimensions just outlined. Three main categories of interventions include social services, health and mental health services, and the legal and criminal justice system. Though not mutually exclusive, decisions as to which option to use are dependent on a number of factors. These include the mental and physical characteristics of both victim and abuser, the preference of the victim and the intent of the abuser, and whether the abusive act or acts meet the standard of a crime as defined by state penal codes (Brownell, 1998). Family court interventions for order of protection from abusers who are related in specific ways to the older adult victim and guardianships for impaired victims who lack capacity to protect themselves from harm are example of other protective remedies that social workers may use in interdisciplinary relationships and settings.

It is essential that all phases of the intervention process include environmental as well as client assessments. Categories of interventions include prevention, protection, case management, counseling and treatment, respite and assistance, empowerment (education and training), law enforcement and courts, and living arrangements (which may need to be changed). State and county adult protective service programs may be primary agencies in some states for investigating elder abuse and neglect and developing and implementing intervention plans (Wolf, 2000).

Is the Older Adult at Risk of Abuse or Neglect, But Not Currently Experiencing This Problem?

There are ways that older adults can protect themselves from abuse, maltreatment, and exploitation. Learning to avoid falling victim to scams is important. Refusing to provide housing or resources for substance-abusing or dangerously mentally ill relatives is another. Ensuring that sufficient in-home assistance is available to avoid overstressing available caregivers or ensuring the care of potentially abusive-dependent relatives is also important. Local agencies on aging, as well as county district attorney and state attorney general offices, are good resources for information on protection from elder abuse.

Assessing the cognitive capacity of an older adult at risk of abuse or exploitation is essential. Like adults of any age, older adults have the right to make decisions about their lives that may seem to reflect poor judgment, unless they are suspected of lacking the capacity to make an informed decision or of being unable to understand the consequences of their decisions. Assessments by adult protective service agencies that reveal the need for involuntary intervention are important (Ott, 2000). However, the unimpaired older adult who refuses services may need to be called or kept in touch with until that person is ready

to make changes in his or her life to ensure better protection from harm.

Assisting the Batterer

Domestic violence advocates sometimes resist the option of providing services to the batterer, on the grounds that finite resources should be targeted to the victim. In cases of elder abuse and neglect, however, it may be necessary to assist the abuser to ensure that the victim will accept services. Studies have demonstrated that older victims are often very protective of their abuser if that person is an impaired adult child, grandchild, or spouse/partner (Brownell et al., 1999).

CONCLUSION

Elder abuse is a complex phenomenon, and any actual or suspected case of elder abuse must be assessed before an intervention strategy is formulated and implemented. By remaining alert to the possibility of abuse, however, social workers can improve the safety and well-being of the older clients they serve.

WEB SITES

American Psychological Association, "Elder Abuse and Neglect: In Search of Solutions." http://www.apa.org/pi/aging/eldabuse.html.
Elder Abuse Foundation. http://www.elder-abuse-foundation.com.
Medicine Plus (National Library of Medicine and National Institute of Health), Elder Abuse. http://www.nlm.nih.gov/medlineplus/elderabuse.html.
National Center on Elder Abuse (U.S. Administration on Aging). http://www.ncea.aoa.gov/ncearoot/Main_Site/index.aspx.

References

Anetzberger, G. J. (2000). Caregiving: Primary cause of elder abuse? *Generations, 24*(11), 46–51.
Brandl, B. (2000). Power and control: Understanding domestic violence in later life. *Generations, 24*(11), 39–45.
Breckman, R., & Adelman, R. (1988). *Strategies for helping victims of elder mistreatment*. Newbury, CA: Sage.
Brownell, P. (1997). The application of the culturagram in cross-cultural practice with elder abuse vic-

tims. *Journal of Elder Abuse and Neglect*, 9(2), 19–33.

Brownell, P. (1998). *Family crimes against the elderly: Elder abuse and the criminal justice system*. New York: Garland.

Brownell, P., Berman, J., & Salamone, A. (1999). Mental health and criminal justice issues among perpetrators of elder abuse. *Journal of Elder Abuse and Neglect*, 11(4), 81–94.

Chalk, R., & King, P. A. (1998). *Violence in families: Assessing prevention and treatment programs*. Washington, DC: National Research Council and Institute of Medicine.

Congress, E. P. (1997). Using the culturagram to assess and empower culturally diverse families. In E. P. Congress (Ed.), *Multicultural perspectives in working with families* (pp. 3–16). New York: Springer.

Edwards, M. (2007, July–August). Protecting the vulnerable. *AARP Bulletin*, 18–19.

Heisler, C. J. (2000). Elder abuse and the criminal justice system: New awareness, new responses. *Generations*, 24(11), 52–58.

International Network for the Prevention of Elder Abuse. (2007). *World elder abuse awareness day June 15, 2007: WEAAD 2007 reports from around the world*. Retrieved July 20, 2007, from http:// www.inpea.net.

National Research Council. (2003). Elder mistreatment: Abuse, neglect, and exploitation in an aging America. In R. J. Bonnie & R. R. Wallace (Eds.), *Panel to review risk and prevalence of elder abuse and neglect* (Committee in National Statistics and Committee on Law and Justice, Division of Behavioral and Social Sciences and Education). Washington, DC: National Academies Press.

Ott, J. M. (2000). The role of adult protective services in addressing abuse. *Generations*, 24(11), 33–38.

Pillemer, K., & Finkelhor, D. (1988). The prevalence of elder abuse: A random sample survey. *Gerontologist*, 28, 51–57.

Ramsey-Klawsnik, H. (2000). Elder abuse offenders: A typology. *Generations*, 24(11), 13–16.

Roberts, A. R., & Brownell, P. (1999). A century of forensic social work: Bridging the past to the present. *Social Work*, 44(4), 359–369.

Steinmetz, S. (1988). *Duty bound: Elder abuse and family care*. Newbury Park, CA: Sage.

Thomas, C. (2000). The first national study of elder abuse and neglect: Contrast with results from other studies. *Journal of Elder Abuse and Neglect*, 12(1), 1–14.

Tomita, S. (2006). Mistreated and neglected elders. In B. Berkman & S. D'Ambruoso (Eds.), *Handbook of social work in health and aging* (pp. 219–230). New York: Oxford University Press.

United Nations. (2003). *Political declaration and Madrid international plan of action on ageing*. New York: UN Department of Public Information.

U.S. House of Representatives. (1990). *Elder abuse: A decade of shame and inaction*. Washington, DC: U.S. Government Printing Office, Comm. Pub. no. 101-752.

Wolf, R. S. (2000). Elders as victims of crime, abuse, neglect, and exploitation. In M. B. Rothman, B. D. Dunlop, & P. Entzel (Eds.), *Elders, crime, and the criminal justice system: Myth, perceptions, and reality in the 21st century* (pp. 19–42). New York: Springer.

PART XVI
Evidence-Based Practice

161

Evidence-Based Practice, Science, and Social Work

An Overview

Bruce A. Thyer

The process of evidence-based practice (EBP) was introduced to the social work literature about a decade ago (Gambrill, 1999) and represented the extrapolation of the emerging principles of evidence-based medicine to the purposes of our discipline. EBP is fundamentally quite different from precursor perspectives that addressed the potential of applying scientific methods to social work practice, predecessor movements such as psychoanalytic theory and its variants, behavioral social work (BSW) and its cognitive offshoots, and empirical clinical practice (ECP; Jayaratne & Levy, 1979; Siegel, 1984). BSW and ECP shared the ideas that social workers should select their choice of interventions from those best supported by empirical research, and also the recommendation that when feasible, social workers should evaluate the outcomes of their clinical practice using single-system research designs (SSRDs). The former idea is difficult to criticize, but it does leave out many important considerations, such as whether the clinician is adequately trained to deliver the empirically supported treatment, the availability of resources required to provide the indicated treatment, the ethical appropriateness of the intervention, an assessment of environment considerations and client preferences and values, and other factors that bear on the possibility of delivering scientifically supported interventions. The recommendation concerning the use of SSRDs to evaluate outcomes at the level of the individual case has been written about extensively (Thyer & Thyer, 1992), and even successfully applied to a limited extent, but lacking any external reinforcers to support the

efforts, busy social workers have not really adopted SSRDs on a widespread scale.

The process of inquiry known as EBP has received considerable attention within the field of social work over the past decade (see Roberts & Yeager, 2003, 2006), so much so that this second edition of the *Social Worker's Desk Reference* has an entirely new part devoted to it. There is some confusion as to what is meant by the term EBP, and this initial descriptive entry will help set the stage for understanding the succeeding chapters. Here are a couple of brief definitions from primary resources in the field of evidence-based medicine, definitions from which most extrapolations to other fields, such as social work, are derived:

The conscientious, explicit, and judicious use of current best evidence in making decisions about the care of individual patients. The practice of evidence-based medicine requires integration of individual clinical expertise and patient preferences with the best available external clinical evidence from systematic research. (Guyatt & Rennie, 2002, p. 412)

"Evidence-based medicine (EBM) requires the integration of the best research evidence with our clinical expertise and our patient's unique values and circumstances" (Straus, Richardson, Glasziou, & Haynes, 2005, p. 1). By replacing the medically laden term "patients" with the more encompassing word "clients," the foregoing definitions can be potentially seen to readily apply to all the helping professions, including social work. What is also conspicuous in these definitions is the equal weight given to the core factors of scientific evidence, clinical expertise, patient preferences, and the client's unique values and circumstances. No one factor is implied to be more important that the others—all are important, and each can potentially trump the others. This definitional egalitarianism is important to realize from the outset because some professionals erroneously believe that in EBP research evidence is accorded greater weight that other factors. Straus et al. (2005) go on to operationally define what is meant by "best research evidence," "clinical expertise," "patient values." and "patient circumstances" and describe the five steps that comprise the process of EBP.

- *Step 1:* Convert our need for information about the causes of problems, and for possible interventions, into an answerable question.
- *Step 2:* Track down the best evidence with which to answer that question.
- *Step 3:* Critically appraise that evidence for its validity, impact, and applicability.
- Step 4: Integrate the critical appraisal with our clinical expertise and the client's unique values and circumstances.

- *Step 5:* Evaluate our effectiveness and efficiency in carrying out steps 1–4 and seek ways to improve our practice.

The other entries comprising this part of the *Social Worker's Desk Reference* address each of these five steps. Again, EBP does not privilege scientific research findings above other considerations in making practice decisions, but it does insist that such factors be accorded their due weight. It is worth repeating this principle because a common misconception of EBP is that it gives primacy (if not sole attention) to research findings and ignores other crucial elements of practice decision making.

This valuing of scientific research is not an unfamiliar concept to professional social work and indeed has been a defining characteristic of the formal discipline, something that set it aside from impulsive altruism, the efforts of faith-based social missionaries, or unsystematic secular efforts aimed at helping others. Consider the quotes presented in Table 161.1, selected as representative of the century-long perspective that science and empirical research must be integrated into social services. Indeed, scientific charity and scientific

TABLE 161.1 Illustrative Quotations Documenting the Supposed Close Linkage Between Science and Social Work

- "Charity is a science, the science of social therapeutics, and has laws like all other sciences" (Kellogg, 1880, cited in Germain, 1970, p. 9).
- "Many of the leaders of the conference [the 1884 meeting of the National Conference on Charities] accepted the implications of a scientific approach to social work problems. They acted on the tacit assumption that human ills—sickness, insanity, crime, poverty—could be subjected to the study and methods of treatment . . . . This attitude raised these problems out of the realm of mysticism and into that of a science . . . . As a result of the adoption of this scientific attitude, conference speakers and programs looked forward toward progress . . . . They believed in the future; that it was possible by patient, careful study and experimentation to create a society much better than the one they lived in" (Bruno, 1964, pp. 26–27).
- "To make benevolence scientific is the great problem of the present age" (Toynbee, 1912, p. 74).
- No considerable group of social caseworkers . . . seem to have grasped that the reliability of the evidence on which they base their decisions should be no less rigidly scrutinized than is that of legal evidence by opposing counsel . . . . Thoughts and events are facts. The question whether a thing be fact or not is the question whether or not it can be affirmed with certainty" (Richmond, 1917/1935, pp. 39, 53).
- "The scientific spirit is necessary to social work whether it is a real profession or only a go-between craft . . . . The elements of scientific approach and scientific precision must be back of all social reform . . . . It is almost superfluous to ask why social work should take on the character of science. It is hardly a question of 'may or may not.' Rather, should we say, it is a matter of the categorical must"(Todd, 1920, pp. 66, 75).
- Social work is defined as "All voluntary efforts to extend benefits which are made in response to a need, are concerned with social relationships, and avail themselves of scientific knowledge and methods" (Cheney, 1926, p. 24).

TABLE 161.1 Illustrative Quotations Documenting the Supposed Close Linkage Between Science and Social Work

- "The faculty and students of a professional school of social work should together be engaged in using the great method of experimental research which we are just beginning to discover in our professional educational programme, and which should be as closely knit into the work of a good school of social work as research has been embodied into the programme of a good medical school" (Abbott, 1931, p. 55).
- "The difference between the social work of the present and of all preceding ages is the assumption that human behavior can be understood and is determined by causes that can be explained . . . any scientific approach to behavior supposes that it is not in its nature incomprehensible by sensory perception and inference therefrom" (Bruno, 1936, pp. 192–193).
- "[In German social work] everywhere the belief in science, in learning and in the scientific spirit is in evidence" (Salomon, 1937, p. 33).
- "Employment of scientifically approved and tested techniques will ensure the profession the confidence and respect of clients and the public, for increasingly the social casework process will operate more certainly for known and desired ends in the area of social adjustment" (Strode, 1940, p. 142).
- "The scientific approach to unsolved problems in the only one which contains any hope of learning to deal with the unknown" (Reynolds, 1942, p. 24).
- "Social work must develop its 'own science,' with its 'own field of knowledge,' tested in its own research laboratories" (Eaton, 1956, p. 22).
- "I believe that it is possible to understand scientifically the movement of social and economic forces and to apply our strength in cooperation with them" (Reynolds, 1963/1991, p. 315).
- [a]Every part of the professional foundation curriculum should . . . help bring students to an understanding of and appreciation of the scientific, analytic approach to knowledge-building in practice. The ethical use of scientific inquiry should be emphasized throughout . . . . The content on research should impart scientific methods of building knowledge and of evaluating service delivery in all areas of practice" (CSWE, 1982, pp. 10–11).
- "It is important to provide the most effective treatment available. This entails professionals keeping current on the research on treatment effectiveness for the particular client populations" (Tutty, 1990, p. 13).
- "Social workers should base practice on recognized knowledge, including empirically based knowledge, relevant to social work practice" (NASW, 1996, p. 20).
- "Social work education combines scientific inquiry with the teaching of professional skills to provide effective and ethical social work services . . . . The content prepares students to develop, use, and effectively communicate empirically based knowledge, including evidence-based interventions" (CSWE, 2001, p. 3, 10).

philanthropy were the original names for the social casework movement in the United States (Bremmer, 1956).

The assertions found in Table 161.1 clearly indicate that the principles of EBP are congruent with central core descriptions of social work dating back to the beginnings of our field. There is much to learn and nothing to fear from a careful appraisal the model of EBP. The original phrase "evidence-based medicine" as currently conceived, first appeared in 1992 in an article written by Gordon Guyatt and colleagues (Evidence-Based Medicine Working Group, 1992) and several concurrent developments and issues lead to its widespread acceptance within medicine and then rapidly through the other helping professions. Among these was the recognition that practitioners really needed valid information about the causes of and possible remedies for the problems clients bring. Another was the recognition that books, traditional journals, conferences, and other usual sources of information were comparatively inefficient ways to acquire this information. Another motivational factor was an increasing awareness that as our clinical expertise is enhanced with years of experience, our knowledge about contemporary developments related to assessment and intervention research often declines. Many practitioners simply do not have much discretionary time to track down clinically useful information through traditional but cumbersome methods, such as reading professional journals or attending continuing education workshops. Though these limiting factors were and are operative in the lives of most social workers, other developments in technology and professional infrastructure pointed to some possible solutions. Among these were the increasing usefulness of the Internet as a means of locating valid information rapidly, the creation of the Cochrane and Campbell Collaborations as international and interdisciplinary organizations devoted to crafting comprehensive systematic reviews for answering commonly asked questions related to practice, and the emergence of journals focused on publishing much more clinically relevant research studies (e.g., *Research on Social Work Practice, Evidence-Based Mental Health, Brief Treatment and Crisis Intervention: A Journal of Evidence-Based Practice*). The concatenation of these events and developments set the stage for the emergence of EBP.

There is some concern that EBP is primarily oriented toward clinical practice, but this is a misconception. The Center for Evidence-Based Social Policy is just one of a number of organizations and interest groups interested in applying the principles of EBP to more macro-levels of practice. The empirical literature devoted to EBP and macro-level social work is growing (e.g., Thyer, 2001, in press), so much so that an entire journal, *Evidence and Policy*, deals with this topic. A literature search of various social science research databases using key words such as "evidence-based management" or "evidence-based administration" will also reveal a burgeoning body of literature.

Another misconception is that EBP is somehow a development unique to the United States. In reality, the major authors in the field of evidence-based medicine were British and Canadian; the Cochrane Collaboration is headquartered in England, and the Campbell Collaboration is based in Norway, with local centers located in the United States and Canada. Thyer and Kazi's (2004) book describes EBP-related developments not just in the United States, Canada, and Great Britain but also in Israel, Hong Kong, Finland, South Africa, and Australia. The protocols developed by the Cochrane and Campbell Collaborations for the development of systematic reviews explicitly call for using international teams of experts to ensure that relevant non-English literature is not overlooked. EBP is not scientism, nor is it another example of U.S. hegemony in the realm of social work education and practice. It is the natural fruition and maturation of professional tendencies that have existed in our discipline worldwide since its inception in the late 1880s.

Nor does EBP tell social workers what to do with their clients. It does not develop lists of scientifically approved treatments, nor does it prepare practice guidelines. It does lay out a systematic process whereby the social worker seeking information to help him or her make important practice decisions related to choosing assessment and intervention methods can best formulate useful questions capable of being answered. It provides guidance in locating and critically appraising this information. It helps integrate this research-based data into other critical domains, such as one's clinical skills; the clients values, preferences, and situation; available resources; and professional ethical guides, to then arrive at a decision. It also guides us in evaluating effectiveness in delivering services. EBP helps us find out what we need to know to arrive at practice decisions. What we choose to do remains the prerogative of the individual social worker. It may be that a clinician seeks guidance about possibly effective treatments for someone who is severely depressed. A review of the literature may disclose some interventions shown to generally be quite helpful for depressed persons, such as cognitive-behavioral therapy or interpersonal psychotherapy. But if the client is also intellectually disabled, the social worker may well choose to not to provide one of these empirically supported interventions if it is judged that the client lacks the cognitive abilities to be successfully engaged in these treatments. In such a case, the social worker could still be said to be operating within the EBP framework.

Over 80 years ago, John Dewey (1927, p. 179) said, "Men have got used to an experimental method in physical and technical matters. They are still afraid of it in human concerns." The emergence and adoption of EBP within social work suggests that we are overcoming such fears.

WEB SITES

Brief Treatment and Crisis Intervention: A Journal of Evidence-based Practice. http://brief-treatment.oxfordjournals.org.

Campbell Collaboration. http://www.campbellcollaboration.org.

Cochrane Collaboration. http://www.cochrane.org.

Coalition for Evidence-based Social Policy. http://
   coexgov.securesites.net/index
   .php?keyword=a432fbc34d71c7.
Evidence & Policy. http://www.ingentaconnect
   .com/content/tpp/ep.
Evidence-based Mental Health. http://ebmh
   .bmj.com.
The Evidence-Based Program Database. http://
   alted-mh.org/ebpd/index.htm.
Research on Social Work Practice. http://www
   .sagepub.com/journalsProdDesc.
   nav?prodId=Journal200896.
Social Programs that Work: What Works
   and What Doesn't Work in Social
   Policy: Findings from Well-Designed
   Randomized Controlled Trials. http://www
   .evidencebasedprograms.org.

References

Abbott, E. (1931). *Social welfare and professional ed-
   ucation.* Chicago: University of Chicago Press.
Bremmer, R. H. (1956). Scientific philanthropy: 1873–
   93. *Social Service Review, 30,* 168–173.
Bruno, F. (1936). *The theory of social work.* New
   York: D. C. Health.
Bruno, F. (1964). *Trends in social work: 1874–1956.*
   New York: Columbia University Press.
Cheney, A. (1926). *The nature and scope of social work.*
   New York: D. C. Health.
Council on Social Work Education. (1982). Curricu-
   lum policy for the master's degree and baccalau-
   reate degree programs in social work education.
   Social Work Education Reporter, 30(3), 5–12.
Council on Social Work Education. (2001). *Educational
   policy and accreditation standards.* Alexandria,
   VA: CSWE.
Dewey, J. (1927). *The public and its problems.* Athens,
   OH: Swallow Press.
Eaton, J. W. (1956). Whence and whither social work:
   A sociological perspective. *Social Work, 1*(1),
   11–26.
Evidence-Based Medicine Working Group. (1992).
   Evidence-based medicine: A new approach to teach-
   ing the practice of medicine. *Journal of the Amer-
   ican Medical Association, 268,* 2420–2425.
Gambrill, E. (1999). Evidence-based practice: An alter-
   native to authority-based practice. *Families in So-
   ciety, 80,* 341–350.
Germain, C. (1970). Casework and science: A histori-
   cal encounter. In R. Roberts & R. Nee (Eds.),
   Theories of social casework (pp. 3–32). Chicago:
   University of Chicago Press.

Guyatt, G., & Rennie, D. (Eds.). (2002). *Users' guides
   to the medical literature: Essentials of evidence-
   based clinical practice.* Chicago: American Medi-
   cal Association.
Jayaratne, S., & Levy, R. (1979). *Empirical clinical prac-
   tice.* New York: Columbia University Press.
National Association of Social Workers. (1996). *Code
   of ethics.* Washington, DC: NASW Press.
Reynolds, B. C. (1942). *Learning and teaching in the prac-
   tice of social work.* New York: Farrar & Rinehart.
Reynolds, B. C. (1963/1991). *An uncharted journey.*
   Silver Spring, MD: NASW Press.
Richmond, M. (1917/1935). *Social diagnosis.* New York:
   Sage.
Roberts, A. R., & Yeager, K. R. (Eds.). (2003). *Evidence-
   based practice manual: Research and outcome
   measures in health and human services.* New
   York: Oxford University Press.
Roberts, A. R., & Yeager, K. R. (Eds.). (2006). *Foun-
   dations of evidence-based social work practice.*
   New York: Oxford University Press.
Salomon, A. (1937). *Education for social work.* Zur-
   ich: Verlag fur Recht und Gessellscaft A-G.
Siegel, D. (1984). Defining empirically based practice.
   Social Work, 29, 325–329.
Straus, S. E., Richardson, W. S., Glasziou, P. & Haynes,
   R. B. (2005). *Evidence-based medicine: How to
   practice and teach EBM* (third edition). New York:
   Elsevier.
Strode, H. (1940). *Introduction to social casework.*
   New York: Harper and Brothers.
Thyer, B. A. (2001). Evidence-based approaches to com-
   munity practice. In H. Briggs & K. Corcoran (Eds.),
   *Social work practice: Treating common client prob-
   lems* (pp. 54–65). Chicago: Lyceum.
Thyer, B. A. (In press). Evidence-based macro-practice:
   Addressing the challenges and opportunities for
   social work education. *Journal of Evidence-Based
   Social Work.*
Thyer, B. A., & Kazi, M. A. F. (Eds.). (2004). *Interna-
   tional perspectives on evidence-based practice in
   social work.* London: Venture Press.
Thyer, B. A., & Thyer, K. B. (1992). Single system research designs in social work practice: A bibliography from 1965–1990. *Research on Social Work
   Practice, 2,* 99–116.
Todd, A. J. (1920). *The scientific spirit and social work.*
   New York: Macmillan.
Toynbee, A. (1912). *Lectures on the industrial revolution in eighteenth century England.* London: Long-
   mans, Green.
Tutty, L. (1990). The response of community mental
   health professionals to client's rights: A review
   and suggestions. *Canadian Journal of Community Mental Health, 9,* 1–24.

162 Developing Well-Structured Questions for Evidence-Informed Practice

Eileen Gambrill & Leonard Gibbs

A key step in evidence-based practice (EBP) is translating information needs (knowledge gaps) related to practice and policy decisions into well-structured questions that facilitate a search for related research in relevant databases (e.g., Straus, Richardson, Glasziou, & Haynes, 2005). Reasons include the following.

- Vague questions lead to vague answers; specific questions are needed to gain specific answers to guide decisions.
- It can save time during an electronic search. The better formed the question, the more quickly related literature (or the lack of it) may be revealed.
- If we do not pose clear questions about decisions, we may be less likely to seek and discover helpful research findings and change what we do; we may harm clients or offer clients ineffective methods.
- It is a countermeasure to arrogance that interferes with learning and the integration of practice and research; if we seek answers, we will discover how tentative answers are and how much we do not know.
- It is necessary for self-directed, lifelong learning.

The better formed the question, the greater the efficiency of searching should be. Research in medicine suggests that physicians answer only a small percentage of questions that arise by consulting relevant research sources (e. g., Ely et al., 1999). We have no such information in psychology, psychiatry, or social work. There is a tendency to underestimate the difficulty in carrying out this step.

Background questions concern general knowledge about a problem or situation. This may include knowledge of psychological, biological, or sociological factors related to a concern. Such questions include "a question root (such as who, what, when, where, how, why) with a verb" (Straus et al., 2005, p. 16) as well as some aspect of a condition or item of interest. An example is "What causes hoarding behavior?" Foreground questions concern knowledge to inform decisions. Background knowledge informs foreground knowledge. As Straus et al. (2005) note, as experience in an area increases, need for background knowledge decreases and need for foreground knowledge increases (p. 17).

BEING AWARE OF INFORMATION NEEDS

We are unlikely to search for information if we are not aware of our ignorance. Sources of uncertainty include limitations in current knowledge, lack of familiarity with knowledge available, and difficulties distinguishing personal ignorance and lack of competence and actual limitations of knowledge (Fox, 1959). Being aware of our ignorance as well as our knowledge is key to the process and philosophy of EPB. Information needs may concern the following. (See DUETs listed under Web Sites at end of chapter.)

1. *Description of clients*: how to gather and accurately interpret information concerning client characteristics and circumstances.
2. *Causes*: how to identify causes or risk factors regarding concerns including iatrogenic harms.
3. *Indicators of certain problems*: knowing these and using this knowledge to understand client concerns.
4. *Setting priorities*: when considering possible causes, how to select those that are likely, serious, and responsive to intervention.

5. *Assessment measures*: how to select and interpret assessment measures to understand client concerns based on accuracy, acceptability, safety, expense, and so on.

6. *Prognosis*: how to estimate a client's likely course over time and anticipate likely complications of problems.

7. *Treatment*: how to select services that do more good than harm and that are worth the efforts and costs of using them.

8. *Prevention*: how to reduce the chance of problems by identifying and modifying risk factors and how to identify concerns early by screening.

9. *Experience and meaning*: how to empathize with clients, appreciate the meaning they find in their experiences, and understand how this meaning influences successful outcomes.

10. Self-improvement: how to keep up to date, improve skills, and provide a better, more efficient care system. (Adapted from Straus et al., 2005, p. 20)

No matter who initiates the questions, we consider finding relevant answers as one of the ways we serve our [clients], and to indicate this responsibility we call these questions ours. When we can manage to do so, we find it helpful to negotiate explicitly with our [clients] about which questions should be addressed, in what order, and by when. And, increasingly often we're discovering that [clients] want to work on answering some of these questions with us. (Straus et al., 2005, p. 20).

FOUR-PART QUESTIONS

Straus et al. (2005) suggest posing four-part questions that describe the population of clients (P), the intervention of concern (I), what it may be compared to (including doing nothing) (C), and hoped-for outcomes (O)—PICO questions. (See Table 162.1 for examples of four-part questions.) A well-formed question should meet the following criteria: (1) It concerns a problem of concern to clients. (2) It affects a large number of clients. (3) It is probably answerable by searching for related research findings. Gibbs (2003) refers to well-formed questions as COPES questions. First, they are client-oriented. They are questions clinicians pose in their daily practice that affect clients' welfare. Second, they have practical importance. They concern problems that arise frequently

in practice. For example, child protective service workers must assess risk. Asking questions about what types of clients present the greatest immediate risk for child abuse is critical. Third, COPES (PICO) questions guide an electronic search for related research findings. Fourth, hoped-for outcomes are identified. The process of forming a specific question often begins with a vague general question and then is crafted into a well-structured question. Synonyms can be used to facilitate a search. For example, if abused children are of concern, other terms for this may be "maltreated children, neglected children, mistreated children." Posing well-formed questions is more the exception than the rule in most professional venues. Initial background reading may be valuable in focusing a question to rapidly find relevant research in a major search engine, such as Google.

DIFFERENT KINDS OF PRACTICE/POLICY QUESTIONS

Different kinds of practice/policy questions (about diagnosis, prognosis, harm, effectiveness, prevention, risk, assessment, or description) require different research methods to critically test them. A variety of questions may arise with one client or family. Let's say a social worker is employed in a hospice and counsels grieving parents who have lost a child. General *descriptive* questions include, "What are the experiences of parents who lose a young child?" "How long do these last?" "Do they change over time and if so, how?" Both survey data and qualitative research such as focus groups, in-depth interviews, and participant observation can be used to explore such questions. Research may be available that describes experiences of grieving parents based on a large randomly drawn sample of such parents. A research report may describe the experiences of clients who seek bereavement counseling using in-depth interviews. Questions concerning risk may arise—such as, "In parents who have lost a young child, what is the risk of depression?"—as well as questions about effectiveness. For parents who have lost a young child, is a support group compared to no service more effective in preventing depression? Prevention questions may arise. For parents who have lost a young child, is brief counseling compared to a support group more effective in preventing depression from interfering with care of other children? When selecting key terms to

TABLE 162.1 Examples of Four-Part Questions

Question Type	Client Type and Problem	What You Might Do	Alternate Course of Action	Hoped-for Outcome
	Describe a group of clients of a similar type; be specific	Apply a treatment to prevent a problem; measure to assess a problem; survey clients; screen clients to assess risk	Describe the main alternative	Outcome of intervention or prevention? Valid measure? Accurate risk estimation: Accurate estimation of need?
Effectiveness	Disoriented aged persons who reside in a nursing home	Reality orientation therapy	Compared to validation therapy	Which results in better orientation to time, place, and person?
Prevention	Sexually active high-school students at high risk for pregnancy	Exposure to baby—think-it-over	Compared to didactic material on the proper use of birth control methods	Which group has fewer pregnancies during an academic year and more knowledge of birth control methods?
Assessment	Elderly nursing home residents who may be depressed or have Alzheimer's disease or dementia	Complete a depression screening test	Compared to a short mental examination test	Which measure most efficiently and reliably discriminates between depression and dementia?
Description	Children	Raised with depressed mothers	Compared to mothers who are not depressed	Which group will have the least prevalence of developmental delays?
Prediction/ risk	Preschool children	With antisocial behavior	Compared to children who do not display such behavior	What is the risk of antisocial behavior in adolescence?
Harm	Nonsymptomatic adults	Who participate in depression screening program	Compared with those who do not	Which results in the least harm?
Cost-benefit	Mothers with poor parenting skills whose children have been removed from their care	Purchase service from another agency	Compared to offering parent training in-house	Which is most effective and cost saving?

Note: The format for all questions is based on Straus et al., 2005.

use to search for related research, quality filters relevant to the question type (e.g., effectiveness, risk) are included. For example if the question is an effectiveness one, relevant quality filters include systematic review, meta-analysis, and study synthesis. If the question concerns risk, relevant methodological filters include sensitivity, specificity, and predictive validity.

Effectiveness Questions

Many questions concern the effectiveness of service methods, such as anger management programs. Consider the terrorist attacks of September 11, 2001, at the World Trade Center in New York. Let us say that an agency administrator wants to find out what methods (if any) may be of value in decreasing related stress reactions. The question may be posed as "In people recently exposed to a catastrophic event, would brief psychological debriefing, or nothing, decrease the likelihood of post-traumatic stress disorder?" This is an effectiveness question, and ideally we would discover a systematic, high-quality review or meta-analyses of randomized controlled trials related to our question. We may discover the number needed to treat (NNT)—how many clients would have to receive an intervention for one to be helped. (See Bandolier's user-friendly guide describing how to calculate NNT. http://www.medicine.ox.uk.bandolier/band36/b36.html.) A search of the Cochrane database would reveal psychological debriefing for preventing post-traumatic stress disorder (PTSD) by Rose, Bisson, Churchill, and Wessely (2001). This critical appraisal showed that there was no benefit of debriefing; one study showed a significantly increased risk of PTSD in those receiving debriefing. Thus, the administrator would *not* be inclined to recommend this method because critical tests found it to be either ineffective or harmful.

Prevention Questions

Prevention questions direct attention to the future. These include questions about the effectiveness of early childhood visitation programs in preventing delinquency at later developmental stages. Examples are, "In young children, do early home visitation programs, compared with no service, influence the frequency of delinquency as adolescents?" "For parents who have lost a young child, is bereavement counseling or a support group most valuable in decreasing prolonged dysfunctional grieving?" Here, too, well-designed randomized controlled trials control for more biases than do other kinds of studies.

Prediction (Risk/Prognosis) Questions

Professionals often attempt to estimate risk, for example, of future child maltreatment. A key question here is: "What is the validity of a risk assessment measure? What is the false positive rate (clients incorrectly said to have some condition such as be suicidal), and false negative rate—clients inaccurately said not to have this characteristic (e.g., not be suicidal)? A four-cell contingency table is of value in reviewing the accuracy of such measures. A well-built risk prognosis question is: "In abused or neglected children placed in foster care, will an actuarial risk assessment measure, compared to a consensus-based model, provide the most accurate predictions regarding reabuse when children are returned to their biological parents?"

Assessment Questions

Clinicians use a variety of assessment measures. These measures differ in their reliability (for example, consistency of responses over time) and validity (whether they measure what they purport to measure). The sample used to gather data and provide "norms" on a measure (scores of a certain group of individuals) may be quite different than clients of concern, so these norms may not apply. A well-built assessment question is: "In frail elderly people who appear depressed, is the Beck Depression Inventory or the Pleasant Events Schedule most accurate in detecting depression?"

Description Questions

Professionals also seek descriptive information, such as the experiences of caregivers of frail elderly relatives. A description question is: "In those who care for dying relatives, what challenges arise and how are they handled?" Some description questions call for qualitative research. For example, questions concerning in-depth experiences related to given events, such as loss of an infant or living in a nursing home, call for research methods that can provide such accounts such as in-depth interviews and focus groups. In-depth surveys may yield related information. Other kinds of description questions require descriptive data involving large samples regarding problems and their causes. Survey data may provide information about the percentage of grieving parents who continue to grieve in certain ways with certain consequences over years. It may provide information about the percentage of divorces and other consequences and describe how parents cope with them. Here, too, we should consider the quality of related research.

Questions about Harm

Decisions may have to be made about how many people have to receive some assessment measure or service for one to be harmed. This is known as *number needed to harm* (NNH). Important considerations here include: "How many people would we have to screen to identify one person who could benefit from help?" "How many of these would be harmed by simply taking the test who are not at risk?" Any intervention, including assessment methods, may harm as well as help.

Questions about Cost-Benefit

Limited resources highlight the importance of cost-benefit analyses. What is the cost of offering one service compared to another, and how many people benefit from each service? Criteria for reviewing cost benefit studies can be found in many sources such as Guyatt et al. (2008).

Questions about How to Encourage Lifelong Learning

Integrating practice and research requires lifelong learning. An example of a question here is: "In newly graduated professionals, will a journal club, compared to a 'buddy system' be most effective in maintaining evidence-informed practice skills?"

SELECTING AND SAVING QUESTIONS

Which questions are most important to pose? As Straus et al. (2005) note, there are many more questions than time to answer them. First they suggest selecting questions in relation to the nature of clients' concerns (what is most important to client well-being). Other filters include what is most vital to self-learning needs, what is most feasible to answer in time available, what is most interesting, and what questions are likely to reoccur? Straus et al. (2005) also suggest scheduling—describe what is needed to answer a question. Some questions require immediate answers; others do not. They suggest saving questions as a third strategy, so that answers to recurring questions can be retrieved. They estimate that it takes 15 seconds to record a question. Options they suggest for saving questions include writing questions down on a three- or four-column form (client, intervention, comparison, outcome), dictating into a pocket-sized recorder, or using a PDA (see PICOmaker). Using a structured approach to posing questions helps practitioners pose more specific questions. As Straus et al (2005) note, "Good questions are the backbone of both practicing and teaching [EBP], and [clients] serve as the starting point for both" (Straus, et al., 2005, p. 24).

Questions and answers can be prepared as critically appraised topics (CATs). These consist of brief (one-page) descriptions of a question, search strategy, related research found, critical appraisal of the research, and clinical bottom line (Straus et al., 2005). A CAT summarizes a process that begins with a practice question, proceeds to a well-built question, describes the search strategy used to locate the current best evidence, critically appraises what is found, and makes a recommendation based on what is found. CATs may be prepared for journal club presentations. The Centre for Evidence-Based Medicine Web site provides an outline and criteria for preparing a CAT. Content on this site regarding levels of evidence can be drawn on to rate the quality of evidence specific to different types of practice questions. Critical appraisal worksheets are provided to facilitate evaluation of the quality of evidence. A CATmaker is also included that:

- prompts a clinical question, search strategy and key information about studies found;
- provides online critical appraisal guides for assessing the validity and usefulness of the study;
- automates the calculation of clinically useful measures (and their 95 percent confidence intervals);
- facilitates description of the clinical bottom line;
- creates one-page summaries (CATs) that are easy to store, print, retrieve, and share (as both text and HTML files);
- provides prompts to update CATs; and
- facilitates teaching others how to practice EBP.

COMMON ERRORS

Errors that may occur when posing questions include having more than one question in a question and trying to answer the question before stating it clearly. Gibbs (2003) notes that students often do not draw a distinction between a practice or policy question (useful to guide a search) and a research question (specific to answering a question by collecting data). Leading or loaded questions may be well built, including all elements of a four-part question, but imply that only a particular answer is acceptable, such as, "For persons who may be at risk for suicide, who receive the Brief Psychiatric Rating Scale or Beck Depression Scale, how much higher will the positive predictive value of the former be for predicting suicide?" (What if it is lower?) Confusing a research question with a well-built search question can restrict the chances to find useful evidence. A research question specifies a specific time frame, specific location, and may specify a particular outcome measure, for example, "Among interdisciplinary teams functioning during 2007 at Veterans Administration Hospital Psychiatric Units that apply evidence-based practice methods, or apply conventional teamwork methods, will patients served by the former have lower scores on symptom rating scales?" This question is too specific and will prematurely limit a search; better that the question be posed more generally as follows: "For interdisciplinary, transdisciplinary, or multidisciplinary teams following evidence-based practice procedures or following standard team procedures, will patients of the former fare better?"

Vague questions are so unspecific that they net nothing useful. For example, "What is the most effective treatment for depression?" A better question might be: "For women experiencing depression after giving birth, which psychotropic medications have been used to what effect on symptoms of depression?" Novices may pose different questions compared to experts in an area who are familiar with practice-related research regarding a concern and the complexity of related factors. A lack of assessment knowledge may result in overlooking important individual differences in a client's circumstances or characteristics. For example, posing an effectiveness question before discovering factors that contribute to depression (such as, "In adults who are depressed, is cognitive-behavioral therapy, compared to medication, most effective in decreasing depression?") may overlook the fact that for this client, recent losses in social support are uppermost, which suggests a different question, such as, "In adults who are depressed because of recent losses in social support, is a support group or individual counseling more effective in decreasing depression?"

OBSTACLES

Literature concerning EBP suggests that posing well-structured questions can be difficult. Thus, one obstacle is thinking it is easy and giving up when difficulty occurs. Ely and coauthors (2002) conducted a qualitative study investigating obstacles to answering physicians' questions about patient care with evidence. Participants included 9 academic/generalist doctors, 14 family doctors, and 2 medial librarians. They identified 59 obstacles. Those related to forming clear questions included the following.

- Missing client data requiring unnecessarily broad search for information. Ely and coauthors note that questions that include demographic or clinical information and information about client preferences may help focus the search. They note that the kind of information that would be of value will vary depending on the question and may not be clear until the search is underway.
- Inability to answer specific questions with general resources. A specific question was "What is this rash?" and vague cries for help, "I don't know what to do with this client," cannot be answered by a general resource.
- Uncertainty about the scope of the question and unspoken ancillary questions. For example, it may not be apparent that the original question should be expanded to include many ancillary questions.

Obstacles related to modifying the question include the following.

- Uncertainty about changing specific words in the question.
- Unhelpful modifications resulting from flawed communication.
- The need for modifications apparent only after the search has begun.
- Difficulty modifying questions to fit a four-part question format (client, intervention, comparison, and outcome).
- Trying to solve too many questions at once.
- Trying to answer a question while posing it.

Posing clear questions may be viewed as a threat. Questions are not benign, as illustrated by the fate of Socrates. Staff who pose questions in their agency may create discomfort among other staff, perhaps because they are doing something unfamiliar or because others view such staff as impertinent or disloyal to the agency or profession. Supervisors may not have experience in posing answerable questions and wonder why it is of value; learning to pose well-formed questions has probably not been a part of their education. Other obstacles include lack of training in how to pose well-structured questions, lack of needed tools to follow through on searches, lack of motivation to consider criteria on which decisions are made, and fears that there are more questions than answers.

OPTIONS FOR DECREASING CHALLENGES

Options for addressing challenges include providing repeated guided experience in posing well-structured practice and policy questions during professional education programs and providing effective continuing education opportunities that provide such skills. (See, for example, description of problem-based learning using the process of EBP in Straus et al., 2005.) Learning by doing is emphasized in EBP. The more we use a skill, the more facility we gain with it, if we have access to corrective feedback. Unless we try to perform a certain skill, we cannot determine our competency level. Posing well-structured practice/policy questions may sound easy, but it can be quite difficult. Similarly, searching for related research findings may sound easy until we try to do it and run into obstacles. Well-structured questions related to information needs that frequently arise could be crafted and shared with colleagues in the form of CATs.

WEB SITES

Centre for Evidence-Based Medicine, CATmaker. http://www.cebm.net/index.aspx.
Childwelfare. http://www.childwelfare.com.
Database of Uncertainties about Effects of Treatments (DUETs). http://www.duets.nhs.uk.

Equator Network. http://www.equator-network .com.
Middlesex University, Mental Health CATS. http://www.lr.mdx.ac.uk/hc/chic/CATS/ index.htm.
PICOmaker. http://www.library.ualberta.ca/ pda2one/pico.
University of Alberta library, CAT tutorial. http:// www.library.ualberta.ca/subject/health-sciences/catwalk/index.cfm.
University of Michigan, CAT list. http://www .umich.edu/pediatrics/ebm.
University of North Carolina, CAT list. http:// www.med.unc.edu/medicine/edursrc/!catlist .htm.
University of Western Sydney (Occupational Therapy), CAT list. http://www.otcats .com.

References

Ely, J. W., Osheroff, J. A., Ebell, M. H., Bergus, G. R., Levy, B. T., Chambliss, M. L., et al. (1999). Analysis of questions asked by family doctors regarding patient care. *British Medical Journal, 319,* 358–361.

Ely, J. W., Osheroff, J. A., Ebell, M. H., Chambliss, M. L., Vinson, D. C., Stevermer, J. J., et al. (2002). Obstacles to answering doctors' questions about patient care with evidence: Qualitative study. *British Medical Journal, 324,* 710–718.

Fox, R. C. (1959). *Experiment perilous: Physicians and patients facing the unknown.* Glencoe, IL: Free Press.

Gibbs, L. E. (2003). *Evidence-based practice for the helping professions.* Pacific Grove, CA: Brooks/Cole.

Guyatt, G. H., Rennie, D., Meader, M., & Cook, D. (2008). *Users' guide to the medical literature: A manual for evidence-based clinical practice.* Evidence-Based Medicine Working Group JAMA and Archives. American Medical Association.

Rose, S., Bisson, J., Churchill, R., & Wessely, S. (2001). Psychological debriefing for preventing post traumatic stress disorder (PTSD). *Cochrane Database of Systematic Reviews, 1.*

Straus, S. E., Richardson, W. S., Glasziou, P., & Haynes, R. B. (2005). *Evidence-based medicine: How to practice and teach EBM,* 3rd ed. New York: Churchill Livingston.

Locating Credible Studies for Evidence-Based Practice

Allen Rubin & Danielle Parrish

Evidence-based practice (EBP) is a decision-making process that "requires the integration of the best research evidence with our clinical expertise and our [client's] unique values and circumstances" (Straus, Richardson, Glasziou, & Haynes, 2005, p. 1). This process consists of five steps: (1) converting the need for information into an answerable question; (2) tracking down the best evidence to answer this question; (3) critically appraising this evidence for its validity, impact, and usefulness; (4) integrating this appraisal with our clinical expertise and what we learn about our client's values, expectations, and background; and (5) evaluating our effectiveness in implementing our decision and the prior four steps (Straus et al., 2005). This chapter builds on the first step of the EBP process (question formulation) and describes the second step by proposing five major considerations when locating credible studies for evidence-based practice: (1) asking a well-formulated EBP question, (2) identifying trustworthy and useful evidence resources to answer this question, (3) developing and executing a successful search strategy, and (4) taking stock of the available evidence.

EBP IN SOCIAL WORK: HARNESSING THE INFORMATION REVOLUTION

The EBP process is a unique model of integrating research and practice that relies heavily on the use of technology to access the best available evidence. Gibbs (2007) suggests, "EBP is genuinely a new response to the information revolution and a philosophical interpretation of how to harness this revolution" (p. 146). Whereas prior efforts to disseminate research findings to practitioners were laden with barriers, a handful of trends born out of this revolution have greatly improved the ease with which busy practitioners can more quickly access useful information to inform their practice.

First, the number of empirical studies using true experimental designs has increased steadily within social work and various allied professions, providing a larger pool of information to draw from when making practice decisions (Shlonsky & Gibbs, 2004). Second, a recent survey of National Association of Social Workers (NASW) practitioners reported that 97 percent of social workers have access to the Internet at work, home, or both, thereby allowing for real-time access to Web-based evidence resources (O'Neill, 2003). Third, the widespread access of the helping professionals to the Internet and the EBP movement has led to the sprouting of myriad Web-based resources designed to improve both the access to and dissemination of practice-related research evidence.

Despite these encouraging developments, the success of engaging in the EBP process hinges largely on the ability of practitioners to both easily and quickly locate the *best* available evidence. Because the Web contains a countless number of practice-related resources that vary in their trustworthiness and rigor, practitioners must learn about existing high-quality Web-based resources and develop the skills to critically appraise unfamiliar or new resources as they emerge. Practitioners would also benefit by learning specific search strategies that will enable them to quickly search within these resources to find the most relevant information for answering their practice questions. Without this information and these skills, the search for evidence can be fruitless, time-consuming, and frustrating.

THE IMPORTANCE OF ASKING A WELL-BUILT EBP QUESTION

The success of step 2 of the EBP process is contingent on whether the practitioner has identified a well-formulated EBP question. A well-formulated

EBP question helps (1) focus our limited time to identifying the most pertinent evidence to our client's situation, and (2) identify useful search terms to guide our search for the best available research evidence (Straus et al., 2005). Because the development of a clear and specific EBP question is intricately linked to the quality of the evidence we find and the identification of key search terms, it is necessary to briefly visit this topic.

Straus and colleagues (2005) identify two major categories of EBP questions: background and foreground. Background questions are generally posed when a practitioner has limited experience with a particular practice situation or population and is looking for general background information to inform their practice (e.g., a specific practice problem, diagnosis, comorbidity, risk factors, issues related to cultural sensitivity or competence) (Straus et al., 2005). Although background information can be found in single articles, this information is often well summarized in more recent textbooks. For this reason, this chapter focuses less on background questions and more on how to locate evidence to answer foreground questions.

Foreground questions are asked when the practitioner has more experience with the practice situation and population, and wants to locate information to guide practice decisions or actions (Straus et al., 2005). Specifically, these questions ask about the effectiveness of interventions, programs, or policies for specific practice situations. Key elements of a foreground question include some or all of the following: (1) client characteristics and practice situation (always), (2) intervention (if known in advance), (3) comparison intervention (if relevant), and (4) desired Outcomes (usually). Practitioners who have conducted a good assessment of the practice situation should be able to identify items 1 and 4, it is conceivable that if they are not familiar with all of the effective interventions, programs, or policies, they will not know items 2 or 3 prior to the search.

The most useful EBP questions are posed specifically enough to guide an effective electronic search for the evidence (Gibbs, 2003). This means providing enough descriptive terms within the question to capture the idiosyncratic characteristics of a particular client or target population so that these terms can later be used to search for and locate evidence with the greatest relevance to the client. These terms might include age or age group, gender, ethnicity or race, income, rural/urban, and so on. The practitioner must use his or her judgment to select the terms that are most important with regard to the treatment setting, client, or target population.

IDENTIFYING USEFUL AND TRUSTWORTHY EVIDENCE RESOURCES

Identifying Useful Resources

After composing a well-built EBP question, the next step is to identify which resources would yield the most trustworthy, current best available evidence. Due to the lag time between the publication of research findings and that of textbooks, it is not sufficient to rely on textbooks to provide the *current* best available evidence. It is also not enough to subscribe to one or even a handful of specific journals, as they will only represent a small part of the existing literature to answer an EBP question. For this reason, it is impossible to know if what little *may* be found is the *best* evidence. According to Straus and colleagues (2005), any money that was previously spent on these resources would best be redirected toward purchasing resources (many of which are now Web-based) that provide or synthesize a larger and more recent cross-section of the extant literature.

A Model for Accessing Practitioner-Friendly Resources

Resources that provide the necessary access to high quality practice related research evidence vary greatly in the way they disseminate this information. A model for recognizing the most useful and "evolved" information services for answering practice-related questions has been proposed by Haynes (2007), one of the coauthors of *Evidence-Based Medicine*, and adapted by the authors for use within the social work profession (see Figure 163.1). This model differs from the EBP effectiveness research hierarchy, which is concerned with the kinds of research studies that have a high degree of internal validity, such as systematic reviews, randomized controlled trials, and quasi-experimental designs with a low probability of a selection bias. In contrast, the purpose of this model is to describe the information resources that best disseminate the information generated from these high-quality studies to busy practitioners. According to this model, the most user-friendly options for busy practitioners reside toward the top of the pyramid, as these resources summarize the information generated from the bottom two layers, thus sparing practitioners the time required to comb through the results of original research studies. Haynes (2007) emphasizes, "At each level, the standards for evidence generation, retrieval, selection and analysis should be explicit and at the highest evidence standard possible" (p. 6). Therefore, it is essential that evidence-based practitioners critically appraise information resources at all levels within this model using the skills emphasized in step 3 of the EBP process.

A *summary*, which resides at the top of the pyramid, draws all of the available high-quality evidence from the three layers below to integrate all of the information within a specific practice area into an up-to-date summary (Haynes, 2007). According to Haynes (2007), a summary "integrate[s the] best available evidence . . . to provide *a full range of evidence* [emphasis added] concerning management options for a given . . . problem" (p. 6). A summary then resides at a higher level on this hierarchy than syntheses or systematic reviews because it provides a broader picture of the literature by reporting on all synopses, syntheses, and studies pertaining to a general practice area. For example, a systematic review might report on only one or two interventions for treating a particular disorder, whereas a summary would compile all of the most recent outcome research on all of the known effective treatments for that disorder, with details about varying levels of sup-

port for these disparate interventions in the form of a book or monograph. Although it was mentioned previously that typical textbooks are no longer useful for identifying effective interventions, this type of publication differs in that it should be updated on a regular basis to capture any new emerging research in the area.

One potentially useful summary is *Clinical Evidence*, an online decision support tool that constantly updates and summarizes high-quality evidence (both articles and reviews) on topics within mental health and medicine. Unfortunately, there are not currently any social work resources that both provide a broad summary of high-quality practice research and frequent updating. The primary author of this chapter, however, is in the process of coediting a book series titled *The Clinician's Guide to Evidence-Based Practice* (Rubin & Springer, in press) that will succinctly summarize the state of evidence within broad mental health and substance abuse treatment areas.   addition, this resource will provide in-depth guidelines on how to carry out the interventions identified as having the most rigorous research evidence. If this resource or any similar broad summary of the literature that is not frequently updated is used, a search for recent resources from other parts of the pyramid should be conducted to ensure access to additional research that may have emerged for a particular practice situation.

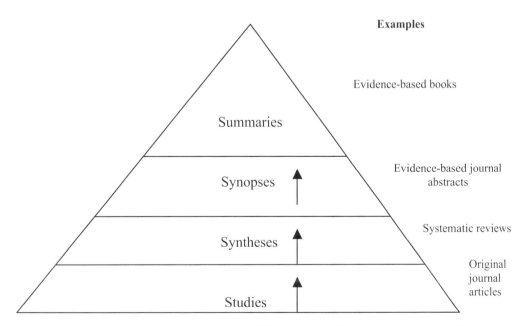

Figure 163.1 Model for recognizing the most useful and "evolved" information services for answering practice related questions. (*Source:* Adapted from Haynes, 2007.)

The second layer is a *synopsis*, or a brief description of an original article or systematic review (Haynes, 2007). Synopses reside second on the pyramid because the brief description saves time for the practitioner, as she does not need to access and read the original source. Reputable synopses should reference the original research summarized, report the results quantitatively, and ideally offer an easy way to access these sources if additional information is needed. Synopses can be found in evidence-based journal abstracts, such as *Evidence-Based Mental Health*. This is a multidisciplinary journal whose authors survey a wide range of international journals with strict criteria to identify high-quality outcome studies that are clinically relevant. They synthesize this information in a short, clinically informative summary. SAMHSA also provides a National Registry of Evidence-Based Programs and Practices, which offers a searchable online registry of mental health and substance abuse interventions and programs. The research supporting these interventions have been reviewed and rated by independent reviewers, and this information is available for practitioners to review.

The third layer is comprised of *syntheses* or systematic reviews (Haynes, 2007). Systematic reviews are "based on a rigorous search for evidence, explicit scientific review of the studies uncovered in the search, and systematic assembly of the evidence to provide as clear a signal about the effects of a[n]. . . intervention as the evidence will allow" (Haynes, 2007, p. 5). Syntheses are the best resource when there is not a current summary to broadly summarize the evidence or a synopsis to succinctly describe the results of individual studies or reviews, or if more in-depth information is needed about the existing evidence. Syntheses are third on the pyramid because they can save busy practitioners time from reading all of the original individual studies that may pertain to a particular practice issue. Syntheses are also often a better source than individual studies for practitioners because the authors of such reviews are likely to have a more complete access to all of the existing literature and an advanced level of expertise in appraising and synthesizing research studies.

Many useful systematic reviews for social work practice are available either on the Cochrane Collaboration or Campbell Collaboration Web sites. Both organizations are nonprofit, independent groups that were created to provide practitioners with up-to-date, accurate practice information. The Cochrane Collaboration primarily provides information for health care professionals, but also has information on topics such as depression, anxiety, schizophrenia, and dementia and cognitive impairment. Access to full-text Cochrane reviews requires a subscription, although abstracts can be read on line free of charge. The Campbell Collaboration offers a searchable database of randomized controlled trials and systematic reviews of social, psychological, education, and criminological research. Online access to both the reviews and abstracts on this site are free of charge. In addition, OVID EBMR offers one-stop shopping for both Cochrane and Campbell reviews and those published in other sources (Haynes, 2007). Finally, systematic reviews can be located through typical databases that also retrieve individual studies, such as PsycINFO, which are available with a subscription or may be accessed through a public or public university library. Many public libraries are now offering free remote access to databases that house full-text articles to the public at large. If these databases cannot be accessed through a local library, or if these databases are insufficient, public university libraries will allow members of the public to access these databases in person (remote access is usually restricted to students and faculty).

Original studies comprise the bottom layer of the pyramid. If sufficient information cannot be accessed from the three layers above this, high-quality single studies that evaluate the outcome of an intervention provide the next best source of information to guide practice. Using evidence from individual studies requires that the practitioner obtain a broad sample of the existing literature, and then critically appraise these studies for both their rigor and practice relevance. SUMSearch was developed to assist evidence-based practitioners in identifying a broad sample of the relevant literature by combining meta-searching and contingency searching to search multiple Internet sites and then collating these findings into one summary page. Other high-quality databases include PsycINFO, PubMed (which includes Medline), Social Services Abstracts, and AgeLine.

PsycINFO is updated on a monthly basis, and indexes and abstracts over 1,700 sources, including international material. There are over 1.8 million individual records dating back to 1887. PubMed provides access to citations in the medical and mental health literature, and is maintained by the U.S. National Institutes of Health (NIH). The Social Service Abstracts contained 137,654 sources dating back to 1979 as of November 2007, and it is updated monthly (averaging 5,500 new sources per year) to provide coverage of current research in the areas of social work and the human services. AgeLine contains detailed summaries of the literature of social gerontology as well as aging-related research from social work and the allied fields. AgeLine contains over 75,000 English-language publication abstracts going back to 1978, and is updated every 2 months with approximately 800 new citations.

Whereas *Social Work Abstracts* has been described as the "primary source of articles on social work and social welfare, as well as on related fields" by NASW Press, recent reviews of this database found that in comparison to others (PsycINFO, Sociological Abstracts, and Medline), it covered a very small number of social work–related journals, was updated much less frequently, had the fewest number of records, and often omitted important papers relevant to social work (Holden, Barker, Covert-Vail, Rosenberg, & Cohen, 2008; Shek, 2008). *Social Work Abstracts* is thus not alone a sufficient database for obtaining a good cross-section of the existing research literature to guide EBP.

If nothing is found in one of the above databases or if there is a need to expand the search, Google Scholar or Google can be used. Google Scholar provides access to a broad array of scholarly literature, while the regular Google search engine searches across a much larger sample of Internet sites beyond scholarly literature. For this reason, it is best to start with Google Scholar to narrow your search to what are more likely to be reputable sources. Both of these sites are best used by using the advanced search option, which will assist the user in better combining key search terms.

Practice Guidelines

In addition to the sources already listed, many organizations have begun to provide *practice guidelines*, or a list of recommended treatments or practice techniques that meet a set of predetermined criteria. This criterion varies based on the source, and so it is important to become familiar with the inclusion and exclusion strategy before using these resources to guide practice decisions. Practice guidelines are distinguished from summaries for several reasons. First, they tend to provide a limited picture of the existing research evidence. Division 12 of the American Psychological Association, for example, limits their list of empirically supported treatments to the criteria listed in Figure 163.2. This list, though useful for identifying interventions that meet this strict level of rigor, does not include effectiveness studies or other interventions with varying levels of support. For this reason, practice guidelines do not provide the broad picture offered by a summary that may enable the practitioner to consider all variations of the best available evidence when trying to match this evidence with the unique characteristics and preferences of the client system.

I. At least two good group design studies, conducted by different investigators, demonstrating efficacy in one or more of the following ways:
   A. Superior to pill or psychological placebo or to another treatment
   B. Equivalent to an already established treatment in studies with adequate statistical power (about 30 per group).

OR

II. A large series of single case design studies demonstrating efficacy. These studies must have:
   A. Used good experimental designs and
   B. Compared the intervention to another treatment as in I.A.

FURTHER CRITERIA FOR BOTH I AND II:

III. Studies must be conducted with treatment manuals.
IV. Characteristics of the client samples must be clearly specified.

Figure 163.2 American Psychological Association definition for empirically validated treatments: well-established treatments.

Second, practice guidelines may not rely solely on the research evidence when identifying the best interventions and may not provide a detailed picture of the research evidence. One example is the American Psychiatric Association's detailed summary of practice guidelines for a variety of DSM IV disorders, which relies on a combination of the research evidence and clinical consensus when constructing these guidelines and does not consistently describe the state of the research evidence in detail for the interventions described. Thus, although practice guidelines can be useful, the evidence-based practitioner would need to consult additional sources to ascertain whether excluded interventions with a disparate level of empirical support might better fit the client's unique characteristics, values, and circumstances or to obtain additional information on the research evidence. Practitioners should also be especially vigilant in appraising these resources for potential bias, as practice guidelines are often developed by work groups whose members may have a vested interest in a certain intervention approach. A number of other practice guideline resources related to social work interventions and programs have been developed, such as the Evidence-Based Program Database, the National Guidelines Clearinghouse, the OJJSP Model Programs Guide, and the California Evidence-Based Clearinghouse for Child Welfare.

IDENTIFYING TRUSTWORTHY EVIDENCE RESOURCES

All evidence resources must be critically appraised for their rigor and relevance to practice. For the upper three layers, the retrieval and selection of evidence and the synthesis or analysis procedure should be made explicit and should reflect the following standards. First, the search and inclusion strategy should not be too narrow or restrictive. The best resources will rely on multiple reputable databases, use a well-defined search strategy, and include both published and unpublished sources as well as dissertation research. Second, the authors should present their process for assessing the quality of selected studies, with particular attention to designs that have unbiased measurement and a high level of internal validity, such as randomized controlled trials and quasi-experimental designs that control for or lack an apparent selection bias. Finally, the resource must be critiqued for a potential bias due to funding or sponsorship, because

bias can greatly influence how individual studies are selected, synthesized, and interpreted. When appraising databases that house individual studies, key criteria include (1) having a substantial number of journals and records related to the topic of interest, and (2) frequent updating of records (at least monthly).

DEVELOPING AND EXECUTING A SUCCESSFUL SEARCH STRATEGY

Many of the resources discussed so far require the use of search terms to locate the information that is specific to answering your EBP question. Although some of these sources vary with regard to their general search infrastructure, most follow similar rules and logic. If you are very unfamiliar with a resource, it may be useful to scan its search guidelines to ensure that you are using the right search strategy or to meet with a librarian or information specialist who is familiar with this resource to obtain additional guidance. This section will first present the most common search strategies that apply to the widest number of databases and online resources, which include Boolean operators, truncation, identification of synonyms, quotation marks, and methodological filters. Following a discussion of these strategies, a brief discussion on how to best initiate the search using these techniques will be presented.

Search Strategies

Boolean operators are connecting words that determine the logic by which two or more terms are searched within an electronic database. The most common Boolean operators are AND, OR, and NOT. The term AND narrows the search by only returning publications that contain both or all of the terms (see Figure 163.3). If searching for "teenagers" AND "pregnancy," the list of articles would be limited to those that contain both of these key words. The term OR as shown in Figure 163.3, expands the search by including all of the publications that include one or both of the search terms. This connector is often used when there are common synonyms for one of the key search terms. For example, a search may require connecting the terms (teenager OR youth OR adolescent) to obtain all of the relevant articles that describe a person between the ages of 12 and 18. Notice that the example terms were placed in parentheses—this is required for the OR connec-

These diagrams represent a search of two key words (represented by each circle) using each kind of Boolean operator in a separate search. The shaded area represents what the search will yield when connected with AND, OR, or NOT.

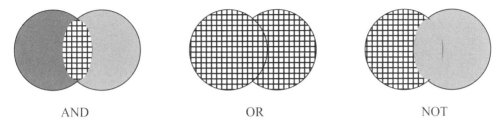

AND   OR   NOT

Figure 163.3   Use of Boolean operators to narrow or expand a search.

tor to work properly. The term NOT is used to narrow the search by excluding information that is irrelevant. It does this by retrieving records that only retrieve the first search term and reject all that include the second search term (see Figure 163.3). For example, if interested in self-harm behavior but not suicide, the search term might include "self-harm behavior" NOT "suicide." Keep in mind, however, that NOT may discard useful as well as less useful references. Using the example, the search will only include publications that include "self-harm behavior," but not any that include both "self-harm behavior" and "suicide," which may have relevance to answering the EBP question.

Truncation is a way to expand the search by including all variations of characters that follow a word stem by using a symbol, most commonly an asterisk (*) or a dollar sign ($). For example, "prevent*" will retrieve prevention, preventing, prevented, or prevents. One truncation symbol typically returns one to five characters following a word stem, whereas a double asterisk (**) returns an unlimited amount of characters. A ques-

tion mark (?) or other form of truncation can also be used to search for variations of characters within a word, for example, "wom?n" would yield both "woman" and "women." To find the correct truncation symbol for a specific database, consult the help section within the database.

Synonyms expand the search by including all possible terms for a particular key word or phrase of interest. Although this can be done using simple brainstorming, it is best to consult the database's thesaurus, if one is available, so that an exhaustive list of the major terms used within that specific database can be generated for the major concept of interest. As mentioned previously, synonyms are connected to one another using the Boolean operator OR, and then this list of terms is linked together with terms of a different concept by the term AND (see Figure 163.4).

Quotation marks limit the search to combinations of words or phrases such as "child welfare." While searching for both terms "child" and "welfare" separately will likely yield many relevant hits in child welfare, it will also return records, for example, that discuss the general welfare of

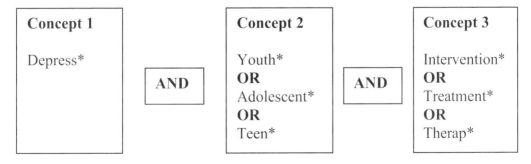

Concept 1		**Concept 2**		**Concept 3**
Depress*	AND	Youth* **OR** Adolescent* **OR** Teen*	AND	Intervention* **OR** Treatment* **OR** Therap*

Figure 163.4   Structuring a search using synonyms and Boolean operators.

children or perhaps public assistance and the effect on children, rather than articles limited just to the child welfare system.

Methodological filters limit the search to the best available research studies specific to answering an EBP question (Gibbs, 2003). Using the terms listed in Figure 163.5, the evidence-based practitioner is able to more quickly locate and limit the search to outcome studies with the most rigorous designs. One way to conduct the search would be to use these terms to drill down through the research hierarchy at each level, starting with the systematic review terms, proceeding to the experimental design terms, and finally to the quasi-experimental design terms (see Figure 163.5). The practitioner would start by combining with the key search terms from the EBP question with the systematic review search terms to first identify any such reviews that have been done for the practice problem. If little or nothing was found, the search could be expanded to include the terms that represent experimental designs and quasi-experimental designs. If nothing is yielded using these terms, the search can be expanded further by combining more general terms such as "outcome" and "study" to search for the lower levels of *best available* evidence, keeping in mind that these sources are very tentative in providing evidence of effectiveness. As shown in Figure 163.5, these terms must be connected by OR to obtain

all possible combinations of these terms. There are additional methodological search terms for background EBP questions related to assessment and diagnosis, description of experience and meaning, and risk/prognosis (Gibbs, 2003; Straus et al., 2005) provided in Gibbs's (2003) book.

Starting the Search

Because searching is an iterative process that often requires several attempted combinations of search terms, there is not one way to begin or carry out this process. When engaging in the evidence-based process, however, key search terms should be extracted from the EBP question to narrow the search to the information most relevant to the client's idiosyncratic characteristics and the issue(s) for which he or she sought help. One way to start the search then would be to extract the most relevant words directly from the question and then create a list of synonyms for each word. Next, this list can be used to create a search term that begins by connecting each word in the list of synonyms by OR and enclosing them within parentheses. Next, each list enclosed within parentheses would be connected by an AND. This search term would be further altered by identifying word stems that need to be truncated, and phrases should be enclosed in quotation marks. The end result is an initial search term that limits the search to the

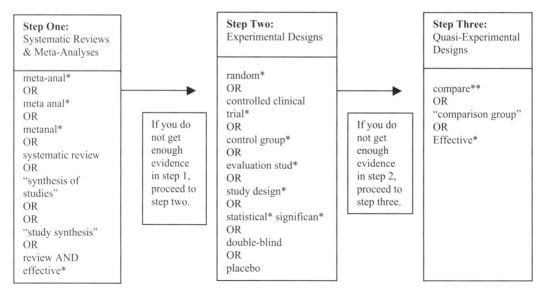

****If looking for a prevention study: AND prevent*

Figure 163.5 Use of methodological search filters to locate research studies for evidence-based practice. Many of these terms were taken or adapted from Gibbs (2003).

specific characteristic of the client system and the presenting problem related to the EBP question, while expanding the search to all possible variations of these search terms in the form of synonyms and word stems. An example search term is shown in the case study.

Taking Stock of the Available Evidence

After entering the first search term, the next step is to take stock of what was returned. Two major considerations are the length of the list and the relevance of the items on the list. The first step should be to examine the titles and abstracts to get a sense of what kinds of studies the search term netted. If the list of results is too long and many items seem irrelevant, AND and NOT can be used to limit the search. If the list is small or nothing has been returned, you can do one of the following: (1) try to identify additional or more accurate synonyms or new search terms; (2) reduce the number of key words used in your search or separate some of your key words by OR instead of AND (it may be that there is research on the presenting problem but not for a client with the same characteristics); or (3) identify a better database or resource to try the search. If this does not work, it may be that there is currently a lack of research evidence for that particular problem and an opportunity to expose this gap for further research. When this happens, it is all the more important to evaluate practice outcomes to ensure that whatever intervention eventually selected works with that client.

CASE STUDY

Angelica is a 35-year-old Hispanic mother of two who recently settled in a new city after leaving her abusive husband and a supportive women's shelter. She has taken the advice of her counselor at the shelter and decided to enter therapy to deal with her post-traumatic stress disorder (PTSD) symptoms. She is currently most interested in dealing with her difficulty sleeping and nightmares. EBP question: "What is the most effective treatment to alleviate an adult Hispanic female's PTSD symptoms?"

The first step is to identify the best information resource to answer this question. Because *Clinical Evidence* offers a summary on PTSD with adults, this reference would be consulted first, as it falls at the top of the hierarchy of practitioner-friendly resources. This source is also reputable and regularly updated. If after reading this resource, additional information was needed to inform a clinical decision, a search of the Cochrane Collaboration using a search term would be conducted. In this case, there was a jump from the *summary* layer to the *syntheses* layer, skipping the *synopsis* layer, because the synopsis layer is not likely to provide any additional in-depth information than the summary, whereas a synthesis or comprehensive systematic review is more likely to do so. Because the EBP question is important for informing the key search terms, practitioner judgment would be used to underline the most important terms within the question for this search, as follows: "What is the most effective *treatment* to alleviate an *adult Hispanic female*'s *PTSD* symptoms (with a specific focus on difficulty sleeping and nightmares)?"

Next, a list of synonyms would be created to ensure that all variations of the words are included in the search. Within the Cochrane Collaboration, the MeSH search option offers a thesaurus. The word "treatment" was synonymous within this database with "therapeutics" and combined with terms "treatment effectiveness," "treatment outcome," and "treatment efficacy." The word "adult" was synonymous with "middle aged." The term "women" was not synonymous with any other words, whereas "Hispanic" was linked to "Hispanic Americans." Finally, the term "PTSD" was selected for the search. Because the Cochrane collaboration library is a collection of systematic reviews and high-quality clinical trials, there is no need to use the methodological search terms to weed out irrelevant publications. The initial search term would be as follows: (treatment* OR therapeutics OR "treatment effectiveness" OR "treatment outcome" OR "treatment efficacy") AND (adult* OR middle aged) AND women AND (Hispanic OR "Hispanic Americans") AND PTSD.

This search term yielded the following two studies:

- Cognitive-behavioural interventions for children who have been sexually abused. G. M. Macdonald, J. P. T. Higgins, P. Ramchandani (2006).
- Behavioural and cognitive behavioural training interventions for assisting foster carers in the management of difficult behaviour. W. Turner, G. M. Macdonald, J. A. Dennis (2007).

Of course, based on the titles, it is obvious that neither of these reviews is relevant to the

EBP question. For this reason, the search will be limited to the following term, taking out ethnicity, which may only be discussed in the body of the review: (treatment* OR therapeutics OR "treatment effectiveness" OR "treatment outcome" OR "treatment efficacy") AND (adult* OR middle aged) AND women AND PTSD. This change expanded the search to 10 reviews, 2 of which included the following:

- Psychological treatment of post-traumatic stress disorder (PTSD). J. Bisson, M. Andrew (2007).
- Pharmacotherapy for prevention of post-traumatic stress disorder. J. C. Ipser, S. Seedat, D. J. Stein (2006).

The review on psychological treatment of PTSD examined the evidence for the following PTSD interventions: trauma-focused cognitive-behavioral therapy/exposure therapy (TFCBT), stress management (SM), other therapies (supportive therapy, nondirective counseling, psychodynamic therapy, and hypnotherapy), group cognitive-behavioral therapy (group CBT), eye movement desensitization and reprocessing (EMDR). The results of this analysis are presented in detail, and the authors of this study concluded the following:

There was evidence individual TFCBT, EMDR, stress management and group TFCBT are effective in the treatment of PTSD. Other non-trauma focused psychological treatments did not reduce PTSD symptoms as significantly. There was some evidence that individual TFCBT and EMDR are superior to stress management in the treatment of PTSD at between 2 and 5 months following treatment, and also that TFCBT, EMDR and stress management were more effective than other therapies. (Bisson & Andrew, 2007)

Because both a summary and systematic review of many of the existing PTSD interventions were accessed from reputable sources, these intervention options and the varying levels of empirical support can be presented to the client as a part of an informed consent process.

WEB SITES

California Evidence-Based Clearinghouse for Child Welfare. http://www.cachildwelfareclearinghouse.org.

Campbell Collaboration. http://www.campbellcollaboration.org/index/html.
Clinical Evidence. http://clinicalevidence.bmj.com/ceweb/conditions/index.jsp.
Cochrane Collaboration. http://www.cochrane.org.
Evidence-Based Mental Health. http://ebmh.bmj.com.
Google Scholar. http://scholar.google.com.
National Guidelines Clearing House. http://guideline.gov.
National Registry of Evidence-Based Programs and Practices http://www.nrepp.samhsa.gov/find.asp.
Office of Juvenile Justice and Delinquency Prevention Model Programs Guide. http://www.dsgonline.com/mpg2.5/mpg_index.htm.
SUMSearch. http://sumsearch.uthscsa.edu.

References

Bisson, J., & Andrew, M. (2007). Psychological treatment of post-traumatic stress disorder (PTSD). *Cochrane Database of Systematic Reviews, 3,* no. CD003388.
Gibbs, L. (2003). *Evidence-based practice for the helping professions: A practical guide with integrated multimedia.* Pacific Grove, CA: Brooks/Cole-Thompson Learning.
Gibbs, L. (2007). Applying research to making life-affecting judgments and decisions. *Research on Social Work Practice, 17,* 143–150.
Haynes, B. (2007). Of studies, syntheses, synopses, summaries and systems: The "5S" evolution of information services for evidence-based health-care decisions. *Evidence Based Nursing, 10,* 6–7.
Holden, G., Barker, K., Covert-Vail, L., Rosenberg, G., & Cohen, S. (2008). Do social workers deserve better? An examination of *Social Work Abstracts. Research on Social Work Practice, 18,* 487–499.
O'Neill, J. V. (2003). Nearly all members linked to the internet. *NASW News, 48*(2), 9.
Rubin, A., & Springer, D. (In press). *The clinician's guide to evidence-based practice.* Hoboken, NJ: Wiley.
Shek, D. T. L. (2008). Comprehensiveness of *Social Work Abstracts* as a database for researchers and practitioners. *Research on Social Work Practice, 18,* 500–506.
Shlonsky, A., & Gibbs, L. (2004). Will the real evidence-based practice please stand up? Teaching the process of evidence-based practice to the helping professions. *Brief Treatment and Crisis Intervention, 4,* 137–153.
Straus, S. E., Richardson, W. S., Glasziou, P., & Haynes, R. B. (2005). *Evidence-based medicine: How to practice and teach EBM,* 3rd ed. Edinburgh: Elsevier Churchill Livingstone.

Critically Appraising Studies for Evidence-Based Practice

Denise E. Bronson

Critically appraising the available research is perhaps the most important step in evidence-based practice and, for many social workers, the most intimidating. Often practitioners do not consider themselves to be experts in research designs or statistical analysis, and they question their ability to assess the quality of the research. Fortunately, the primary purpose of appraising a research report is to determine if the conclusions drawn from the study are valid, credible, and relevant for practice; this assessment does not require a sophisticated knowledge of research or statistical methods. Appraising a study can be done by anyone with a basic understanding of research methods who also possesses (1) the ability to think critically, (2) a willingness to challenge their own biases and practice preferences, and (3) a systematic strategy to ensure that each study is evaluated according to the same criteria. The ultimate goal of a critical appraisal is to determine if there is sufficient trustworthy evidence to suggest that an intervention or treatment program is effective and can be used to address a practice problem.

Thinking critically helps you carefully examine the conclusions that are provided by the authors of a study and evaluate the validity of the research. Merely reading the conclusion or discussion section of an article and accepting the authors' assessment of the research will not be sufficient to guide evidence-based practice; it is not enough to assume that if a study is published in a professional journal then the research and conclusions are trustworthy. This was clearly illustrated in a recent article that examined the conclusions presented in 138 social work outcome studies published in professional journals (Rubin & Parrish, 2007). Rubin and Parrish found that authors often reported causal inferences that were not warranted by the research designs used and misrepresented the evidentiary value of the research. A critical perspective helps you carefully examine

the claims made by researchers and avoid being misled by distorted conclusions in the research reports. It also challenges you to think about other factors that impact the credibility of the research, such as the reasons for undertaking the research, how the research was funded, and who did the research.

Adopting a critical perspective does not end with the appraisal of the research. It is equally important to be aware of any possible biases you bring to the critical appraisal process. Examining your own biases or practice preferences will help you avoid the "I'll-see-it-when-I-believe-it" syndrome (Gilovich, 1993). Those with this syndrome tend to be (1) more likely to identify and remember research that supports their preferences, (2) less likely to search for disconfirming evidence, (3) less critical of research that supports their biases, and (4) highly critical of research that does not (Kahneman, Slovic, & Tversky, 1982). One way to minimize this tendency is to subject all research to the same evaluative criteria using a systematic approach to critically appraising the studies.

The critical appraisal process presented in this chapter focuses on assessing the outcome or effectiveness research in social work. Research serves many different purposes in social work, and not all types of research are conducive to the type of critical appraisal needed to guide evidence-based practice. The strongest evidence to support an intervention's effectiveness will be obtained from a systematic review of experimental studies. When a systematic review is not available, we are forced to rely on single studies while keeping in mind that "a single study often fails to detect, or exclude with certainty . . . difference in the effects of two therapies" (Egger, Smith, & O'Rourke, 2001, p. 11). In recent years, there has been considerable debate on the use of qualitative research in EBP, but no consensus has been reached on how to assess the quality of qualitative research or the role it should play in evidence-based practice. Both the Cochrane and Campbell Collaborations have methods groups working on criteria for assessing the quality of qualitative research and a variety of standards have been proposed (Petticrew & Roberts, 2006; Popay, French, & Mallinson, 2007; Saini, 2007). However, until appraisal guidelines are agreed on for qualitative research, quantitative outcome research will continue to be the foundation for evidence-based practice. It is also the focus of this chapter.

To be useful for evidence-based practice, research must be both valid and credible. A valid study is one that allows us to make causal inferences about the effects of an intervention and allows us to determine whether the intervention is likely to work in other settings. A credible study is one that is trustworthy. That is, the study is characterized by transparency, honest reporting of methods and limitations, and a willingness to consider alternative explanations for the observed outcomes. Validity and credibility go hand in hand, yet it is possible to have a highly valid but not credible study (e.g., research on the benefits of chewing gum sponsored by the chewing gum producers) or one that seems very credible but is not valid. Although there is no such thing as a perfect study, a critical appraisal of a study's validity and credibility allows you to assess "the degree to which a study is affected by bias and whether the degree of bias is large enough to render the study unusable" (Petticrew & Roberts, 2006, p. 131). Critically appraising the available research will allow you to identify the strengths and weakness of the research, help you decide how much faith you can have in the studies, and assist you in deciding whether the research can meaningfully guide your practice decisions.

VALIDITY

One way to assess the quality of a study is to determine if the research is valid. The validity of the research refers to two things: (1) the extent to which the changes observed after introducing an intervention can be attributed to the intervention (internal validity), and (2) the extent to which the results of the research are applicable and relevant for use with other populations or in other settings (external validity) (Campbell & Stanley, 1963). Your ability to assess both types of validity will depend largely on the quality and comprehensiveness of the written report (Egger,

Smith, & Altman, 2001). A good report is thorough and transparent. That is, it provides detailed information about the study design and methods, the subjects and setting, and the service providers so that you can reasonably judge whether the research has good internal and external validity. It honestly acknowledges the limitations of the research and potential biases that may have affected the outcomes of the study.

Internal Validity

A study will have good internal validity if the research design and methods allow you to establish a causal relationship between the treatment and the observed outcomes while eliminating other possible explanations (See Table 164.1). This is sometimes referred to as treatment efficacy in the literature. According to the American Psychological Association (2002), "*treatment efficacy* refers to a valid ascertainment of the effects of a given intervention as compared with an alternative intervention or with no treatment, in a controlled clinical context. The fundamental question in evaluating efficacy is whether a beneficial effect of treatment can be demonstrated scientifically" (p. 1053). The research design will usually dictate the overall rigor of the study and the strength of the conclusions that can be made from the results, but other biases can also detract from the internal validity. The strongest research design for establishing a causal relationship between an intervention and specific outcomes is a randomized control trial (RCT). In this design, participants are randomly assigned to treatment and no-treatment conditions to create comparison groups that are equivalent in all dimensions except for exposure

TABLE 164.1 Assessing the Internal Validity of Research

1. Equivalent comparison groups (preferably created by randomization) were used to test the intervention.
2. The research report addresses the following types of potential biases:
   a. Attrition
   b. Selection
   c. History
   d. Maturation
   e. Response
   f. Observer
   g. Treatment fidelity

to the treatment or intervention. If the group outcomes differ after the intervention is delivered, the differences are attributed to the treatment.

Unfortunately, RCTs are difficult to implement in clinical settings and, as a result, there are few such studies in social work. Some researchers use a variety of strategies to try to create equivalent groups without randomization, but these methods do not remove the possibility of unmeasured systematic errors. These efforts and the use of less rigorous research designs, such as those relying on nonequivalent comparison groups or case studies, will not address many threats to internal validity and make it impossible to fully assess the effectiveness of the intervention. Despite these limitations, research employing less rigorous research designs is still useful in identifying trends, promising treatments, and directions for future RCT research. Petticrew and Roberts (2006) recommend the following if no RCT exists.

1. Look for a very large effect size (i.e., the measure of an intervention's impact) to reduce the possibility of a false positive finding.
2. Give greater credence to research that reports the treatment was ineffective or harmful. Studies with negative findings are less likely to be published so you are less likely to make a false negative decision.
3. Use single-subject (N = 1) research methods to evaluate the intervention when you implement it with clients.
4. Look for another treatment approach for which RCTs are available.

The internal validity of a study can also be influenced by a number of other potentially biasing factors that might lead the researcher to over- or understate the impact of the intervention. The checklist for assessing internal validity lists some of the most common threats to internal validity. Each one offers a possible alternative explanation for any changes observed after the introduction of an intervention. They are:

- *attrition* biases—systematic differences in the types of people who drop out of the research in each group (attrition should be less than 20 percent);
- *selection* bias—differences that exist between groups before the intervention is introduced (needs to be evaluated to establish equivalence even for RCTs);

- *history*—events that occur concurrently with the intervention and could cause the observed outcomes;
- *maturation*—naturally occurring changes over time that might look like a treatment effect;
- *response* bias—subjects or clients are aware of their group assignment and respond in ways that are consistent with their assignment or in ways that are likely to satisfy the researchers;
- *observer* bias—researchers who are aware of the experimental conditions may unintentionally see what they want to see during data collection; and
- *treatment fidelity*—the implementation of the treatment must be monitored to insure that those in the treatment group are receiving the same intervention and that those in the no-treatment group are not receiving the experimental intervention.

A comprehensive research report will discuss how these biases may have influenced the research outcomes and will examine alternative explanations that might account for the observed differences between the treatment and nontreatment groups.

External Validity and Relevance

Assessing the external validity of the research allows you to judge whether the changes attributed to the intervention are likely to occur when the treatment is implemented with other clients, in other settings, and by different therapists (see Table 164.2). The relevance of a study for social work practice and policy depends on the external validity or generalizability of the results. External validity is especially important when deciding if an intervention can be adopted in a practice setting. Unfortunately, there is often a trade-off between internal and external validity. For example, research that takes place in a highly controlled setting may achieve good internal validity, but the generalizability of the findings may be reduced. If given the choice, researchers will usually strive for internal validity over external validity (Campbell & Stanley, 1963). This preference has lead to the proverbial gap between research and practice and underscores the need for assessing the external validity and relevance of research.

TABLE 164.2 Assessing the External Validity and Relevance of the Research

1. The sample used in the study is representative of people for whom the intervention/treatment will be used.

2. The results of the study can reasonable be generalized to:
   • A larger population
   • A smaller population (small group or individual)
   • A group of similar size

3. The study provides detailed information on the following:
   • The subjects of the research
   • The setting in which the treatment was delivered
   • Characteristics of those who provided the intervention

4. The intervention has been replicated with other populations, in other settings, or with other therapists.

5. The intervention can be disseminated (i.e., training materials and manuals exist).

To assess the external validity and relevance of a study, it is important to determine if the subjects, setting, and therapists in the research are similar (representative of) the clients you are serving and the setting in which you are working. Generalizations from research can extend from (1) a small group of subjects to a larger population, (2) a large experimental group to a small group or individual, or (3) one similarly sized group to another (Shadish, Cook, & Campbell, 2002). It is important to consider the type of generalizations that can be made from the research as you appraise its external validity.

Appraising a study's external validity and relevance is largely a matter of judgment. A good research report will describe how subjects were selected for the study and provide detailed information on client demographics, the environment in which services were delivered, and characteristics of the service providers (e.g., training, experience, education, and personal characteristics).

Finally, the generalizability of research findings is more likely if the study has been replicated with other subjects, in other settings, or by other researchers. This requires searching the bibliographic databases for similar studies that evaluate the intervention. The generalizability of the research will also be enhanced by the availability of training materials and manuals to facilitate the dissemination of the intervention. Training materials help ensure that there is treatment fidelity when the intervention is implemented in diverse settings.

CREDIBILITY

The credibility of the research is often overlooked in the appraisal process (Carlson, 1995), and yet the believability and trustworthiness of the study must be considered. If you read an article in the newspaper reporting on the results of research demonstrating the benefits of chewing gum for stress reduction you might question the credibility of the report if the research was paid for by a company that produces chewing gum. Similarly, studies completed by social work researchers who receive funding from an ideologically driven foundation or researchers who gain financially from the success of an intervention they developed should receive extra scrutiny. There are many factors that contribute to the overall credibility of a study. As with the assessment of external validity and relevance, appraising the credibility of research is largely a matter of judgment, and your ability to judge will depend on the completeness and transparency of the report.

Most journal articles provide information on the author's place of employment and the source of funding for the research. This information may provide some insight into any ideological biases or prejudices that could impact the research. The Campbell and Cochrane Collaborations have also called for researchers to provide information on possible conflicts of interest or previous research activities that might influence the conduct or conclusions of the current project. Finally, in a comprehensive and transparent research report, the author will clearly state the purpose for conducting the research and will honestly report the evidentiary status of the research. Taken together (see Table 164.3), information on the researcher's background, the source of funding, and the reports' overall appearance of transparency will help you appraise the believability and credibility of the research as you consider its applicability to practice.

CONCLUSIONS

Critically appraising the available evidence for evidence-based practice involves a basic knowledge

TABLE 164.3 Assessing the Credibility of the Research

1. Detailed information is provided about the researcher, including place of employment, previous research, and potential conflicts of interest.
2. Information is provided about the funding for the research and the funding organization.
3. Information about possible financial gains for the researcher associated with the outcomes of the research are presented.
4. The author has clearly presented the purpose of the research.
5. The research report appears to be transparent and is honest about the evidentiary status of the research.

of research methods, critical thinking, a willingness to challenge your own biases, and a systematic approach to assessing the quality of a study. Although it is not an exact science, carefully examining the validity, relevance, and credibility of a study will reveal the strengths and limitations of the research and enable practitioners to judge the value of the research for clinical practice. These are essential activities for evidence-based practice in social work. Practitioners who routinely apply critical appraisal skills to their reading of the research literature will be prepared to use the best available evidence to guide practice decision making and will usher in a new era that promotes the integration of social work research and practice.

WEB SITES

Evidence for Policy and Practice Information and Co-ordinating Centre. http://eppi.ioe.ac.uk/cms.
National Registry of Evidence-based Programs and Practices, review criteria. http://www.nrepp.samhsa.gov/review-criteria.htm.

Preventing Crime: What Works, What Doesn't, What's Promising (National Institute of Justice). http://www.ncjrs.gov/works.

References

American Psychological Association. (2002). Criteria for evaluating treatment guidelines. *American Psychologist, 57,* 1052–1059.
Campbell, D. T., & Stanley, J. C. (1963). *Experimental and quasi-experimental designs for research.* Chicago: Rand McNally.
Carlson, E. R. (1995). Evaluating the credibility of sources: A missing link in the teaching of critical thinking. *Teaching of Psychology, 22,* 39–41.
Egger, M., Smith, G. D., & Altman, D. G. (Eds.). (2001). *Systematic reviews in health care: Meta-analysis in context.* London: BMJ.
Egger, M., Smith, G. D., & O'Rourke, K. (2001). Rationale, potentials, and promise of systematic reviews. In M. Egger, G. D. Smith, & D. G. Altman (Eds.), *Systematic reviews in health care: Meta-analysis in context* (pp. 3–22) London: BMJ.
Gilovich, T. (1993). *How we know what isn't so: The fallibility of human reason in everyday life.* New York: Free Press.
Kahneman, D., Slovic, P., & Tversky, A. (Eds.). (1982). *Judgement under uncertainty: Heuristics and biases.* Cambridge: Cambridge University Press.
Petticrew, M., & Roberts, H. (2006). *Systematic reviews in the social sciences: A practical guide.* Malden, MA: Blackwell.
Popay, J., French, B., & Mallinson, S. (2007). *Using narrative synthesis guidance in systematic reviews.* Paper presented at the Seventh Annual International Campbell Collaboration Colloquium, May 14–16, London.
Rubin, A., & Parrish, D. (2007). Problematic phrases in the conclusions of published outcome studies: Implications for evidence-based practice. *Research on Social Work Practice, 17,* 334–347.
Saini, M. (2007). *A pilot study of the quality and rigor in qualitative research form.* Paper presented at the Seventh Annual International Campbell Collaboration Colloquium, May 14–16, London.
Shadish, W. R., Cook, T. D., & Campbell, D. T. (2002). *Experimental and quasi-experimental designs for generalized causal inference.* Boston: Houghton Mifflin.

165 Randomized Controlled Trials and Evidence-Based Practice

Paul Montgomery & Evan Mayo-Wilson

Randomized controlled trials (RCTs) are the most useful studies to inform practice. They are most commonly used to determine if interventions are effective. Simply, RCTs include at least two groups, usually an intervention group and a comparison group. Participants typically have an equal chance of being assigned to each group. Clients are normally allocated individually, but trials might assign multiple individuals (e.g., by classroom, nursing home, or drug treatment center). These are called *cluster randomized* trials (Boruch, 2005). Intervention and comparison groups are usually assessed before and after intervention.

RCTs provide:

- top-quality evidence of safety and effectiveness,
- limitation of researcher bias, and
- identification of causes.

This chapter explains the key features of RCTs, how to critique them, and how to use them in practice. To illustrate the main features and benefits of RCTs, it includes two case studies.

CASE STUDIES

Booklets for Children with Sleep Problems

This study was about the sleep problems of children with learning disabilities (mental retardation) conducted in the community by Montgomery, Stores, & Wiggs (2004). These sleep problems are severe, common, and generally considered difficult to treat. It is known that the best form of intervention is behavioral, but scarce resources limit access to these treatments. This study aimed to investigate a brief behavioral treatment of sleep problems by comparing (1) face-to-face delivered treatment versus control and (2) booklet-delivered treatment versus controls. The participants were the parents of 66 severely learning disabled children aged 2–8 years with settling and/or night waking problems. They were randomized, and the behavioral treatments were presented either conventionally face-to-face or by means of a 14-page easy-to-read illustrated booklet. A composite sleep disturbance score was derived from sleep diaries kept by parents.

The study found that both forms of treatment were almost equally effective compared with controls. Two-thirds of children who were taking over 30 minutes to settle five or more times per week and waking at night for over 30 minutes four or more times per week improved on average to having such settling or night waking problems for only a few minutes or only once or twice per week (H = 34.174, df = 2, p < 0.001). These improvements were maintained after 6 months. It was known before the study began that these behavioral interventions are the most effective treatments available. This study assessed their effectiveness when delivered by booklet. The study used waitlist controls so that participants in the comparison group received an intervention after 6 weeks. This is known as a *crossover* design. In conclusion, it found that booklet-delivered behavioral treatments for sleep problems are likely to be as effective as face-to-face treatment for most children in this population.

In this example, the participants, interventions, key outcome measure, and comparison groups were clear and explicit. Social workers dealing with such children now have a cheap, simple intervention to offer parents. They can be sure that the results were unbiased and that both the booklet and face-to-face behavioral treatment are effective.

Cambridge-Somerville Youth Study

The Cambridge-Somerville Youth Study tested an intervention to reduce childhood delinquency (McCord, 1978). It was based on the theories of Richard Clark Cabot, a professor of clinical medicine and social ethics at Harvard University and president of the National Conference in Social Work. Cabot believed that childhood delinquency was related to poor home environments. He thought social workers could act as a positive force in the lives of children. Therefore, he designed an intervention to target at-risk boys under age 12; to avoid stigma, low-risk boys were included as well. Boys were matched in pairs; one in each pair was assigned to the treatment group on the basis of a coin toss. Recruitment began in 1935 and follow-up of 506 participants began in 1942.

Intervention

- Build close relationships and provide assistance to boys and their families.
- Provide counseling and referrals to specialists.
- Provide academic tutoring, participation in sports, and a woodwork shop operated by the study.
- Summer camp.
- Families receive help with problems (e.g., illness and unemployment).

The program lasted until 1945, at which time boys in the intervention group had received about 24 annual visits for more than 5 years. By 1948, some surprising results had emerged. Court records found that more boys in the *treatment* group had been charged with a crime and had been charged with more offenses (264 versus 218). In 1979, when the men were 47 years old, 248 men in the treatment group and 246 men in the control group were located. Most participants in the treatment group said the program had helped them by keeping them out of crime and off the streets. However, these participants were more likely to have been convicted of crimes indexed by the Federal Bureau of Investigation. They were more likely to have been diagnosed as alcoholic, schizophrenic, or manic depressive. They were more likely to have died. Furthermore, participants receiving more of the intervention were more likely to have adverse outcomes.

Several theories may explain why the study had such adverse effects. For example, the inter-vention may have increased unsupervised time with other delinquent children, increasing the chance that children would brag about delinquent behavior and encourage misbehavior. Though a rigorous evaluation showed the intervention had adverse effects, the Cambridge-Somerville Youth Study was a theoretically sound, well-planned intervention. It was led by experts, delivered by skilled practitioners, and carefully implemented. Although the intervention was well received by participants and their families, it clearly caused long-term harm. An RCT to test the effectiveness of this intervention may have prevented further harm to thousands of boys.

KEY FEATURES OF RCTs

Well-performed, large randomized trials are the best evidence of intervention effectiveness (Altman, 1991). They are better than any other study design at demonstrating causal relationships. All RCTs are *prospective,* that is, forward-looking, which is necessary for testing causal hypotheses. For A to cause B, A must happen before B. By following a group over time, RCTs can measure change in an outcome that can be attributed to the independent variable, the intervention.

Unlike studies using quasi-experimental methods (e.g., a one-group before-and-after comparison), RCTs offer a reliable *counterfactual* scenario. That is, the comparison group shows you what would have happened to participants if they had been treated differently. Groups of participants in nonrandomized studies may differ due to *selection bias.* Imagine you want to know if group therapy is helpful for heroin users. You could compare people in a group therapy program with other heroin users, but they would probably differ in several ways. For example, the people in group therapy might be more committed to change.

Randomization is the best way to eliminate differences between groups on known as well as *unknown* variables. Splitting a small group by chance could result in *unbalanced* groups, but as the number of participants increases, randomization is increasingly likely to result in similar groups. To further reduce the likelihood of unbalanced groups, you could randomly assign subgroups (e.g., men and women) separately, thereby controlling a known variable while maintaining the benefits of randomization.

Splitting a study population by chance is the best way to eliminate *confounding variables*—variables other the intervention that may influence the results—and the effects of selection bias. Additionally, randomization makes it difficult to predict which group a person will join if they enroll in the trial. It may not be possible to blind clients and practitioners in social work; however, it is always possible to blind the assessors, the people who analyze the results.

Before they begin enrolling participants, researchers must state who will be included in an RCT. Researchers must specify the *inclusion criteria*, for example, the age and sex of participants and the problems (e.g., insomnia) they must have. Researchers must also specify the *exclusion criteria*, which are reasons a person would not be allowed to participate. For example, a study of Internet-based therapy for depression might exclude participants who are actively suicidal for ethical reasons. Ideally, researchers will select participants like those seen in clinical practice so that the results generalize to real-world settings. In summary, well-designed RCTs will possess the following features:

- prospective,
- minimize selection bias,
- eliminate confounding variables,
- control for known and unknown variables,
- explicit inclusion and exclusion criteria,
- allocation can be concealed, and
- researches and assessors can be blinded.

ARE RANDOMIZED TRIALS ETHICAL?

Many social workers believe that RCTs are unethical because (1) participants in one group may not receive a intervention, and (2) practitioners may not be able to offer what they think is the most effective intervention for a problem. These are valid concerns that apply to many types of research. On the other hand, well-intentioned interventions can have no effect, thereby wasting time and resources. Worse, they can cause harm, as in the Cambridge-Somerville Youth Study. Researchers and practitioners must balance ethical values to determine when RCTs are necessary and appropriate. RCTs may be justified when:

- It is unclear if an intervention has positive effects.
- It is unknown if one intervention works better than another.

- An intervention may cause harm (e.g., through unwanted side effects).
- The costs/benefits of an intervention are unknown.

Though we often have good reasons to think a particular intervention will have positive effects, questions of treatment effectiveness can only be resolved through empirical investigation. If you developed a new intervention, you would start with a theory and design a strategy to achieve positive impacts for your clients. To be thorough, you would consider reasons the intervention might not work, ways it might harm participants, and whether the cost was worth the benefits. Based on your knowledge of the problem, the available resources, and your client's characteristics and preferences, you would make a guess about the outcomes of your treatment. But how would you demonstrate that it worked? How would you know what would have happened if you had acted differently or if the burden on participants was worth the payoffs? Maybe another intervention would have been more efficient, thereby increasing resources to serve other clients.

Researchers refer to this uncertainly as *equipoise*, not knowing if one thing is better than another. Randomized trials are the best way of resolving this uncertainty. They can show if interventions have beneficial effects. Furthermore, RCTs can be designed to overcome many common ethical objections. For example, they can involve multiple treatment arms in which participants in *all* groups receive help. A trial might be designed to compare a new, untested intervention to *treatment-as-usual*, that is, the normal form of care (e.g. a social worker and the client choose an intervention). A wait-list comparison group is a common solution to ethical concerns whereby all participants receive the intervention sooner or later. However, long-term comparisons between groups are impossible once everyone in the study has received the intervention.

Randomized trials should test interventions that match the goals and values of clients. To be ethically justified, they must resolve an important uncertainty about the effectiveness, safety, or relative benefits of an intervention.

UNDERSTANDING RCTs

As with any other study design, some RCTs will be better than others. Although there are many strengths to the method, not all RCTs are of high quality. Before using the results of a trial, you will need to assess its validity and applicability to your situation (Strauss et al., 2005). Interventions being investigated should be described precisely. What use is a trial on an intervention if you don't have enough detail to replicate the intervention as it was conducted? This should include details about how the intervention was delivered (e.g., its frequency and duration). Often, study authors publish manuals of their interventions, and this information may be provided in a separate paper.

Interventions should be delivered in a replicable ways. You may think there is little point in having results from a study that cannot be used in everyday social work. With this in mind, the delivery of the intervention, the resources required, and the role of participants should be considered. Did the investigators check that the intention was delivered properly? Did the clients actively participate? For example, if a trial of cognitive-behavioral therapy showed that it doesn't work for depression, you might ask if all the therapists did the same sort of treatment or if the clients were able to attend all sessions.

The population under study needs to be well described so that the reader knows what sort of clients joined the study and which were excluded. If an intervention worked for people between 18 and 35, would you use it for an 85-year-old client? A precise description of the population is necessary for you to determine whether you can apply its results to your clients. The measures used in the study need to be clear. If meaningful, well-validated instruments are used, then the trial will be all the more useful. Often, objective measures are better than subjective questionnaires. For example, if you wanted to know if an intervention for truant children improved school attendance, you would be interested in the number of days children attended school; you might be less interested, when assessing efficacy, in a trial measuring children's attitudes toward school.

Comparison groups should be realistic. If a new intervention is under study, it may be most useful to compare it to the usual form of care rather than to no intervention. Comparing an intervention to something that your clients would never receive doesn't provide useful information. The method by which study participants are randomized should be described. Even subconsciously, researchers can influence results. Methods of randomization should not be vulnerable to influence by the researcher. To ensure that selection bias does not confound the results of a trial, researchers should assign participants by pulling numbers

from a hat, applying a computerized random number generator or some similar process. Assigning people by other means (e.g., date of birth or alternating assignment) is *not* random and could introduce confounding variables. For instance, if randomization was done by giving participants who attended a social work clinic a particular intervention according to the day of the week, the effect of the intervention might be confused with the impact of different staff with varying levels of skill who work different days of the week. Furthermore, these methods make it difficult to maintain *allocation concealment* because one can predict a participant's assignment before enrolling the participant in the trial. To prevent this, a person unconnected to the trial should control the allocation of participants. For example, a statistician might generate a random number list. After a social worker assesses a potential trial participant, the social worker should call the statistician to find out his group assignment. To prevent bias at later stages, it may be important to blind people involved in the trial.

Finally, there should not be too many outcome measures. If researchers have too many, the chances of finding a positive result by chance will increase. That is to say, at a 5 percent significance level, 1 in 20 measures will be positive as a result of chance alone. For this reason, studies might have only one primary outcome and perhaps two or three secondary measures.

THE ANALYSIS OF RCTs

Figure 165.1 is a flow chart showing how the participants moved through the study by Montgomery, Stores, and Wiggs (2004). Note that all the children randomized at the beginning are included in the final analysis.

This is known as an *intention to treat analysis*. Other types of analyses might be called *completers only*, *per protocol*, or *available case*. The method chosen may influence results considerably. For example, if participants found an intervention unacceptable, they might drop out of a study. An analysis of completers would disguise the fact that the intervention was not acceptable for many participants. Therefore, researchers should account for all people randomized, including those who dropped out of the trial. You may see that researchers "carry forward" data from baseline (i.e., assume that nothing has changed) or assign mean values to missing cases (which may inflate the apparent benefits of an intervention). If a study does

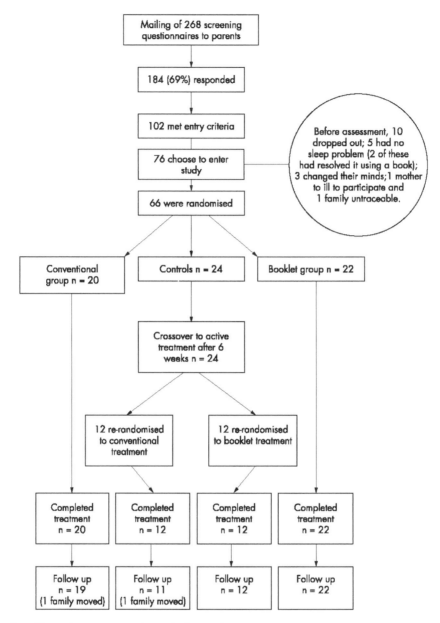

Figure 165.1 Flow of participants through the study.

not account for participants who dropped out, you should consider what impact this could have had on the results.

Statistics

Most RCTs use statistical tests that compare two groups. They may also report some trends and correlations. Some of the more frequently used tests are shown in Table 165.1. It is important to

think whether the researchers used the correct test to be certain of the results. Table 165.1 describes some statistical methods used to analyze RCTs.

HOW TO RECOGNIZE A GOOD RCT

Asking the following questions when considering a randomized trial will help assess its quality.

TABLE 165.1 Frequenty used Statistical Tests

Parametric Test	Nonparametric Test Version	Purpose of Test	Example
Two-sample (unpaired) t test	Mann-Whitney U test	Compares two independent samples drawn from the same population	To compare the group that received the booklet with those who were in the control group
One-sample (paired) t test	Wilcoxon matched pairs test	Compares two sets of observations on a single sample	To compare sleep duration within one group before and after intervention
One-way analysis of variance (F test) using total sum of squares	Kruskall-Wallis analysis of variance by ranks	Effectively, a generalization of the paired t or Wilcoxon matched pairs test where three or more sets of observations are made on a single sample	To compare more than two observations, e.g., booklet versus face-to-face versus control
Two-way analysis of variance	Two-way analysis of variance by ranks	As above, but tests the influence (and interaction) of two different covariates	In the above example, to determine if the results differ in girls versus boys
χ^2 test	Fisher's exact test	Tests the *null hypothesis* that the distribution of a discontinuous variable is the same in two (or more) independent samples	To assess whether the responders to an intervention were from a particular subgroup, e.g., ethnicity
Correlation coefficient (Pearson's r)	Spearman's rank correlation coefficient ($r\sigma$)	Assesses the strength of the straight line association between two continuous variables	To assess whether sleep duration correlates with severity of learning disability

Was the Study Valid?

Think about the similarity of the groups. Was the intervention the only thing that was different? Aside from the intervention, were the two groups treated in the same way? Were outcomes influenced by biased assessment? Was allocation concealed, and were people blinded as required? Did everyone in the intervention group receive the intervention, and did anybody in the comparison group receive the intervention (this is sometimes called *contamination*)? Could missing data and dropout have influenced the results? Were the outcomes, measures, and analyses selected in advance and reported completely? Was the trial registered in advance (e.g., with ClinicalTrials.gov) and if so, did the researchers report results as intended?

What Were the Results?

How large was the effect? Is this *clinically significant* (i.e., would this change be meaningful to one of your clients)? Was it statistically significant, or could it have been the result of chance? Look for statistical tests like standard deviations and confidence intervals. If these are large, which is common in the case of small trials, this may lead you to conclude that individual differences between participants is substantial, in which case the intervention may not be reliable.

Are the Results of This Trial Useful for My Clients?

Consider the degree to which your clients are like those in the trial to assess the *generalizability* of the study. Did the trial include everyone who might benefit from the intervention? Did it exclude people with the characteristics and problems you see in your practice? Was the setting similar to your setting? Could you do this intervention or afford this intervention? Consider if the measures reported are what you are really interested in knowing. Remember RCTs are about groups and their results may not apply directly to your client (this is called the *ecological fallacy*).

CONCLUSION

RCTs are the strongest form of experimental evidence in intervention studies. They should be preferred over other comparison studies because they minimize bias and eliminate confounding factors of all kinds, known and unknown. Ethical concerns can be addressed in a number of ways (Sheldon & MacDonald, 2006). If more RCTs can be performed in social work, the field will have a much stronger evidence base to ensure that effective interventions are delivered without harming clients and that the benefits of this work outweigh its costs.

WEB SITES

ClinicalTrials.gov, National Institutes of Health. http://clinicaltrials.gov.
CONSORT Statement- up to date versions of which are best accessed via. http://www.equator-network.org.
Critical Appraisal Skills Programme, Making Sense of Evidence. http://www.phru.nhs.uk/Doc_Links/rct%20appraisal%20tool.pdf.

References

Altman, D. G. (1991). Randomisation [Editorial]. *British Medical Journal, 302*, 1481–1482.
Boruch, R. F. (Ed.). (2005). Place randomized trials: Special issue. Annals of the American Academy of Political and Social Sciences, 598.
McCord, J. (1978). A thirty-year follow-up of treatment effects. *American Psychologist, 33,* 284–289.
Montgomery, P., Stores, G., & Wiggs, L. (2004). The relative efficacy of two brief treatments for sleep problems in young learning disabled (mentally retarded) children: A randomised controlled trial. *Archives of Disease in Childhood, 89*, 125–130.
Sheldon, B., & MacDonald, G. (2006). *Rethinking social work*. London: Routledge.
Straus, S. E., Richardson, W. S., Glasziou, P., & Haynes, R. B. (2005). *Evidence-based medicine: How to practice and teach EBM*. Edinburgh: Churchill Livingstone.

Meta-Analysis and Evidence-Based Practice

Jacqueline Corcoran & Julia H. Littell

Evidence-based practice (EBP) is defined as the integration of the best available research evidence with clinical expertise and client values to make informed decisions in individual cases. Systematic reviews (see Chapter 167) and meta-analyses can contribute to the evidence base for social work practice and policy by providing thorough and unbiased summaries of empirical research (see Littell, Corcoran, & Pillai, 2008, for an elaboration of points made in this chapter).

Meta-analysis is the quantitative synthesis of data from multiple studies. It uses statistical methods to estimate average effects across studies, identify differences between studies, and suggest possible explanations for those differences.

How does meta-analysis differ from systematic review? A systematic review aims to comprehensively locate and synthesize the research literature that bears on a particular question. If results lend to the synthesis of findings from two or more primary studies, then a systematic review can include meta-analysis, the focus of this chapter.

Meta-analyses offer many advantages over other methods of summarizing results of quantitative studies, including:

- better estimates of population parameters (more accurate representation of phenomena in the population of interest),
- ability to assess multiple outcomes (a separate meta-analysis can be conducted for each relevant outcome domain when data are available),
- systematic accounts for moderators (participant, treatment, or study design characteristics) that influence outcomes, and
- tests and adjustments for biases that can be introduced by small samples and publication processes.

Meta-analyses have disadvantages as well.

- They cannot make up for poor quality in the original studies.
- Combining results across different types of studies, treatments, samples, settings, and/or outcomes is not always appropriate.
- Meta-analysis relies on effect sizes, which are not easily understood by many people.

Many of the disadvantages can be eliminated or minimized through correct applications of meta-analytic procedures. These procedures are explained in more detail in Littell et al. (2008), Lipsey and Wilson (2001), and Petticrew and Roberts (2006).

EFFECT SIZES

The ability to synthesize studies is informed by converting the results of original studies to common metrics, called effect sizes, which are then combined across studies. An *effect size* is a measure of the strength (magnitude) and direction of a relationship between variables. The choice of ES measures is influenced by the purpose and design of a study and the format of the data. Most ES metrics fall into three main categories, related to proportions (univariate proportions or averages can be derived from multiple studies), correlation coefficients (studies that assess relationships between variables without inferring causal directions are likely to report measures of association), and means. Studies that test intervention effects and other kinds of causal inferences typically report differences (e.g., between treated and untreated groups) in terms of proportions or average scores.

The *standardized mean difference* (SMD) is useful when scores are reported in different ways or different scales are used to assess the same construct. The SMD, also known as Cohen's *d* (Cohen, 1988), is the mean difference divided by the pooled standard deviation of the two groups. The SMD is probably the most well-known ES.

For dichotomous data (received a certain screening or not), the most commonly used ES measures are the *odds ratio* (OR) and the *risk ratio* (RR). *Odds* refer to the chance that something will happen compared to the chance that it will not. *Risks* are probabilities.

Although effect size provides a crucial index of the average effect within and across studies, it is not easily understood by many people. Therefore, ESs can be translated into metrics that have meaning for clinicians and policy makers. For example, dichotomous data can easily be converted from risks to percentages. Cohen (1988) also proposed standards for interpreting OR, SMD, and correlation coefficients.

META-ANALYTIC METHODS IN BRIEF

In meta-analysis, ESs from individual studies are presented, along with their confidence intervals, in graphs called Forest plots. The confidence intervals give us a "margin of error" for each ES and tell us whether the ES is statistically significant (if the confidence interval includes the region of no difference, the effect is not significant).

Study ESs are then pooled (averaged) together using weighting procedures that allow more precise ESs, and those from larger studies to make a greater contribution to the overall average than results that are less precise (including results of smaller studies). These procedures are called inverse variance weighting. There are several ways to do this. Some meta-analyses assume that all studies are estimating the same population effect size; others do not make this assumption. The former use "fixed effect" models, the later use "random effects."

Meta-analysts can compute effect sizes for subgroups of interest (e.g., separate effects for girls and for boys) and test to see whether differences between subgroups are significant (using moderator analysis). They can assess the influence of decisions made during the review process (using sensitivity analysis) and can assess and adjust for the influence of publication bias and small sample bias on results.

IMPLICATIONS FOR PRACTITIONERS

Practitioners should be able to locate and understand a publication on meta-analysis because it can summarize a whole body of knowledge on a certain topic of interest. As with systematic reviews, the first places to look for meta-analyses are the online libraries maintained by the nonprofit Cochrane Collaboration and Campbell Collaboration. The Cochrane Collaboration synthesizes results of studies on effects of interventions in health care, and the Campbell Collaboration synthesizes results of research on interventions in the fields of social care (education, social welfare, and crime and justice). Both the Cochrane and the Campbell Collaborations produce systematic reviews and meta-analyses (when there are enough studies) to inform decisions about health and social programs and policies. These are usually the best places to search because their meta-analyses tend to be high quality. However, these databases do not have reviews on every possible topic. Therefore, it may be necessary to search library databases, such as Psychinfo and Medline/Pubmed, running key words related to the topic with "meta-analysis."

The methodology and the statistics of meta-analysis can become quite complex, so the lay reader should probably look to the "plain language summaries" of the Cochrane Collaboration, the synopsis and the abstract of the Campbell Collaboration, and the abstract and discussion sections of articles on meta-analysis. In order to understand some of the essential elements that comprise meta-analysis, we will provide a summary of two meta-analyses that have relevance to practitioners (see Table 166.1).

CONCLUSION

Meta-analysis can be used to synthesize information on many topics that are important for social work practice and social policy. Because meta-analysis is time-consuming and requires trained discipline, it is not likely to be conducted by practitioners or policy makers. However, the information gleaned from meta-analysis can be a tremendous contribution to consumers, practitioners, and policy makers who want to use accurate assessments of current knowledge to inform their choices. Meta-analysis can minimize sampling error and bias in attempts to synthesize the growing body of empirical research relevant to social work. Thus,

TABLE 166.1 Sample Summaries of Meta-Analyses

Author and Purpose	Inclusion Criteria	Sample	Results
Lipsey, Landenberger, & Wilson (2007) To systematically review the effectiveness of CBT treatment with criminal offenders in terms of reoffending. A secondary purpose was to examine moderators that influenced variation in effect size.	Participants: "criminal offenders, either juveniles or adults, treated while on probation, incarcerated, institionalized, or during aftercare/parole" (p. 7) Intervention: Cognitive-behavioral treatment Designs: Randomized or matched nonrandomized group designs that compared CBT to a non-CBT condition Studies: Published and unpublished studies from any country and written in any language Outcome: Criminal offending after treatment Years included: 1965 to 2005	N = 58 studies met inclusion criteria. More adult than juvenile samples; treatment was typically less than 20 weeks; 50% of the studies involved incarcerated participants; predominantly male samples; treatment providers tended to evidence little mental health background and received minimal training.	CBT programs resulted in a 25% decrease in offending recidivism over control conditions. No differences between adult and juveniles in terms of outcomes. Programs that were implemented well and offered critical elements of CBT (anger control and interpersonal problem solving) showed more positive effects. People who are at higher risk to reoffend did better as a result of CBT than low-risk offenders.
Wilson & Lipsey (2006) examined the effectiveness of social information processing programs implemented in the school setting for youth identified with anger and behavior problems. Social information processing programs are a type of cognitive-behavioral treatment.	Participants: School-aged children (kindgergarten through 12th grade) selected for intervention because of behavioral problems or for risk factors associated with behavioral problems (such as high activity) Interventions: Focus on social information processing Designs: Randomized and matched nonrandomized designs with a control group (defined as no-treatment, wait-list, or treatment-as-usual, not another treatment) Studies: Any country, both published and unpublished studies Outcome: Behavior or externalizing problems	N = 47 studies 90% published in United States, mostly male samples, 40% with low SES samples, 45% of studies comprised children 9–11 years, mainly group-based interventions	Participants in social information processing treatment evidenced fewer aggressive/behavioral problems after treatment compared to controls. Moderator analysis: children who were already showing problems did better than those who were at risk for problems, children in special education settings showed less improvement than others; groups were more effective than one-on-one interventions; longer programs and those that were better implemented had better outcomes.

it has an important role in the development of knowledge for human services.

WEB SITES

Campbell Collaboration. http://www.campbellcollaboration.org.

Cochrane Collaboration. http://www.cochrane.org.

Database of Abstracts of Reviews of Effect (DARE). http://www.york.ac.uk/inst/crd/crddatabases.htm.

References

Cohen, J. (1988). *Statistical power analysis for the behavioral sciences* (2nd ed.). Hillsdale, NJ: Lawrence Erlbaum Associates.

Lipsey, M., Landenberger, N., & Wilson, S. J. (2007). Effects of cognitive-behavioral programs for criminal offenders. Campbell Collaboration Library. Retrieved from http://www.campbellcollaboration.org/doc-pdf/lipsey_CBT_finalreview.pdf.

Lipsey, M. W., & Wilson, D. B. (2001). *Practical meta-analysis*. Thousand Oaks, CA: Sage.

Littell, J. H., Corcoran, J., & Pillai, V. (2008). *Systematic reviews and meta-analysis*. New York: Oxford University Press.

Petticrew, M., & Roberts, H. (2006). *Systematic reviews in the social sciences: A practical guide*. Oxford: Blackwell.

Wilson, S. J., & Lipsey, M. W. (2006). School-based social information processing interventions and aggressive behavior for pull out programs (part 2). Retrieved from http://www.campbellcollaboration.org/docpdf/wilson_socinfoprocpull_review.pdf.

167 Systematic Reviews and Evidence-Based Practice

Julia H. Littell & Jacqueline Corcoran

Systematic reviews can contribute to the evidence base for social work practice and policy by providing thorough and unbiased summaries of empirical research. A systematic review aims to comprehensively locate, critically appraise, and synthesize results of empirical research that bears on a particular question. If results lend themselves to a statistical synthesis, then a systematic review can also include meta-analysis (see Chapter 166).

Gibbs (2003) and others have shown practitioners how to find, critically appraise, and use empirical evidence to information practice. "Ideally, practitioners should be able to rely on reviewers to isolate the best evidence for them and to distill it for its essence to guide practice decision-making.

Unfortunately, conventional reviews have fallen far short of such expectations" (Gibbs, 2003, p. 153). Traditional research reviews are often "haphazard" (Petticrew & Roberts, 2006). They tend to rely on convenient samples of published studies and unclear methods of assessment and synthesis; as a result, they are vulnerable to biases of researchers, reviewers, and publication and dissemination processes (Littell, 2008). Unfortunately, many lists of "evidence-based practices" are based on traditional review methods. Because practitioners and policy makers rarely have the time to locate and critically appraise original studies themselves, unbiased reviews of empirical research are needed to provide reliable summaries of evidence for practice and policy.

Systematic reviews are designed to compensate for the weaknesses of traditional reviews of research. Systematic reviews can provide transparent, comprehensive, and unbiased analyses and summaries of available research on a particular topic that is relevant for social work practice and social policy.

The phrase "systematic review" connotes a scientific approach to every step in the review process, combined with the use of specific methods to minimize bias and error. Unfortunately, this term has been used rather loosely in the social work and social science literature. So-called systematic reviews vary in quality and credibility. Therefore, it is important for practitioners to understand what systematic reviews are and how to evaluate them.

In this chapter, we describe the steps in the systematic review process. We consider different types of systematic reviews and provide examples. Finally, we offer suggestions for finding systematic reviews and guidelines for evaluating them.

STEPS IN A SYSTEMATIC REVIEW

Systematic reviews are observational studies that follow the basic steps of the research process. These steps include problem formulation and planning, sampling, data collection, data analysis, interpretation, and presentation of results (Cooper & Hedges, 1994). In a systematic review, previous studies are identified and analyzed. Specific steps in a systematic review are listed next.

1. Problem formulation and planning
   - Develop a set of clearly formulated objectives and specific, answerable research questions or hypotheses.
   - Form a review team with the necessary substantive, methodological, and technical expertise.
   - Create explicit inclusion and exclusion criteria that specify the problems or conditions, populations, interventions, settings, comparisons, outcomes, and study designs that will and will not be included in the review.
   - Develop a written *protocol* that details in advance the procedures and methods to be used.
2. Sampling: Identification and selection of relevant studies
   - In collaboration with information specialists, identify and implement a comprehensive and reproducible strategy to identify all relevant studies. This includes strategies to find unpublished studies.
   - At least two reviewers screen titles and abstracts to identify potentially relevant studies.
   - Retrieve published and unpublished reports on potentially relevant studies.
   - Determine whether each study meets the review's eligibility criteria. Two reviewers judge each study, resolve disagreements (sometimes with a third reviewer), and document their decisions.
3. Data collection
   - Reliably extract data from eligible studies onto standardized forms. Assess inter-rater reliability, resolve disagreements, and document decisions.
4. Data analysis
   - Describe key features of included studies (in a narrative, tables, and/or graphs).
   - Systematically and critically appraise the qualities of included studies.
   - When possible, present study results in effect size metrics, with 95 percent confidence intervals.
   - If a systematic review lends itself to combining quantitative results of two or more primary studies, then it can (and often should) include meta-analysis.
5. Interpretation and presentation of results

Interested readers can find detailed explanations of these steps and the procedures and methods used in systematic review elsewhere (see Cooper & Hedges, 1994; Higgins & Green, 2006; Littell, Corcoran, & Pillai, 2008; Petticrew & Roberts, 2006).

TYPES OF SYSTEMATIC REVIEWS AND EXAMPLES

Any question or topic that can be addressed with empirical research methods can also be the subject of a systematic review of prior studies. To date, most systematic reviews have focused on effects of health care and social interventions. These reviews tend to include randomized controlled trials (RCTs) when those studies are available, because they usually provide the most credible evidence of intervention effects. The Cochrane Collaboration has produced approximately 3,000 systematic reviews of RCTs on effects of health care interventions, including pharmacological, medical, and psychosocial treatments for HIV/AIDS, mental health, substance abuse, and related medical and social problems.

Some systematic reviews include other types of studies, either in addition to or instead of RCTs. This is because other study designs can sometimes provide credible evidence of effects or because the reviewers may be interested in other kinds of questions. Systematic reviews produced by the Campbell Collaboration focus on effects of interventions in social care (education, crime and justice, and social welfare), and they include RCTS as well as other study designs. Topics that have been covered include effects of interventions aimed at preventing teenage pregnancy, welfare-to-work initiatives, cognitive-behavioral therapies for specific conditions, after-school programs, volunteer tutoring programs, drug treatment programs, parent training, and so forth.

Creative synthesis of qualitative data from naturalistic studies has begun, sometimes in combination with systematic reviews of studies of intervention effects. For example, staff of the EPPI Centre in London produced a mixed-methods synthesis that includes a systematic review of RCTs on effects of interventions aimed at improving children's healthy eating habits, along with a "views analysis" (content analysis) of themes that emerged from naturalistic studies of children's views of health and eating (Thomas et al., 2004). This approach provides information about intervention effects and the views of those who are the targets of these interventions.

Systematic reviews have also been used to synthesize observational studies epidemiological data on the incidence and prevalence of various conditions. New methods are being developed to combine results of studies on the diagnostic and prognostic performance of assessment tests. For example, Aron Shlonsky and colleagues at the University of Toronto have embarked on a Campbell review of the predictive validity of instruments that are used to assess the risk of child maltreatment.

Sometimes systematic reviews turn out to be "empty"—that is, reviewers could not find any studies that meet their inclusion criteria. The Cochrane Collaboration published such empty reviews because they provide useful information on current gaps in knowledge. This information has been used to set funding priorities for further research, especially in the United Kingdom.

FINDING SYSTEMATIC REVIEWS

The best systematic reviews can be found in online libraries (or databases) that have been developed and maintained by organizations devoted to the production and dissemination of rigorous, unbiased reviews. These groups provide free access to systematic reviews (or to their abstracts) on the Web. As mentioned, the Cochrane Collaboration produces and disseminates systematic reviews of interventions in health care. The Cochrane Database of Systematic Reviews is available online. The Campbell Collaboration synthesizes results of research on interventions in the fields of social care (education, social welfare, and crime and justice). The Campbell Library is also on the Web. The Centre for Reviews and Dissemination (CRD) at York maintains a large database of systematic reviews on a variety of topics in health and social care. Although the CRD databases include reviews that vary in quality, CRD staff have provided some appraisal of the quality of most of these reviews.

If these sources to not contain reviews on topics of interest, it may be necessary to search regular bibliographic databases, such as Psychinfo and Medline/Pubmed, running key words related to the topic with "systematic review." These sources will produce reviews of varying quality.

The Cochrane Collaboration and other organizations provide useful plain-language summaries of systematic reviews. When such summaries are not available, readers should find useful information in abstract and discussion sections of reports on systematic reviews.

EVALUATING SYSTEMATIC REVIEWS

Systematic reviews can provide practitioners with useful summaries of large (or small) bodies of research. However, some systematic reviews are more thorough and careful than others. Because there are variations in the quality—and credibility—of systematic reviews, practitioners should know how to critically appraise systematic reviews.

Guidelines and standards for systematic reviews have been developed by the Cochrane Collaboration, the Campbell Collaboration, and others. To the extent possible, these guidelines are based on evidence about features of the research and review processes that minimize bias and error. Building on available guidelines and evidence,

Shea and colleagues (2007) developed a checklist for assessing the qualities of systematic reviews (AMSTAR). An adapted version of this checklist is shown in Table 167.1. This includes questions that readers should ask in evaluating the quality of a systematic review.

As shown in Table 167.1, systematic reviews should follow predetermined protocols. They should be based on independent judgments (from multiple raters) on key decisions, such as study eligibility and coding; use comprehensive searches that include efforts to find relevant unpublished studies; identify studies that were included and excluded; describe included studies; assess the scientific quality of included studies and use this assessment in evaluating study results; use appropriate methods for combining results across studies (see Chapter 166); assess the potential effects of publication bias on results; and report funding sources and conflicts of interest.

CONCLUSION

Systematic reviews can provide comprehensive, unbiased summaries of research on many topics that are important for social work practice and social policy. These reviews aim to minimize error and bias and critically appraise the quality of available studies. They are very labor-intensive, but can produce more reliable information than traditional narrative reviews of research. Social work practitioners and policy makers will find the information from systematic reviews useful

TABLE 167.1 Assessing the Quality of Systematic Reviews

1. Was a protocol developed in advance?
The research question and inclusion criteria should be established before the conduct of the review.

2. Was there duplicate study selection and data extraction?
There should be at least two independent data extractors, and a consensus procedure for disagreements should be in place.

3. Was a comprehensive literature search performed?
At least two electronic sources should be searched. The report must include years and databases used. Key words must be stated, and where feasible the search strategy should be provided. All searches should be supplemented by consulting current contents, reviews, textbooks, specialized registers, or experts in the particular field of study, and by reviewing the references in the studies found.

4. Was the status of publication (i.e., gray literature) used as an inclusion criterion?
The authors should state that they searched for reports regardless of their publication type. The authors should state whether they excluded any reports (from the systematic review), based on their publication status, language, etc.

5. Was a list of studies (included and excluded) provided?
A list of included and excluded studies should be provided.

6. Were the characteristics of the included studies provided?
In an aggregated form such as a table, data from the original studies should be provided on the participants, interventions, and outcomes. The ranges of characteristics in all the studies analyzed (e.g., age, race, sex, relevant socioeconomic data, disease status, duration, severity, or other conditions) should be reported.

7. Was the scientific quality of the included studies assessed and documented?
A priori methods of quality assessment should be developed and followed. Multiple questions or items about possible sources and types of bias are preferred to overall quality rating scales.

8. Was the scientific quality of the included studies used appropriately in formulating conclusions?
The results of the methodological rigor and scientific quality should be considered in the analysis and the conclusions of the review and explicitly stated in formulating recommendations.

Continued

TABLE 167.1 Assessing the Quality of Systematic Reviews *(continued)*

9. Were the methods used to combine the findings of studies appropriate?
For the pooled results, a test should be done to ensure the studies were combinable, to assess their homogeneity. If heterogeneity exists, a random effects model should be used and/or the clinical appropriateness of combining should be taken into consideration (i.e., is it sensible to combine?).

10. Was the likelihood of publication bias assessed?
An assessment of publication bias should include a combination of graphical aids (e.g., funnel plot, other available tests) and/or statistical tests.

11. Was the conflict of interest stated?
Potential sources of support should be clearly acknowledged in both the systematic review and the included studies.

Source: Adapted from Shea et al., 2007.

for making decisions about how best to help clients with the resources available.

WEB SITES

Campbell Collaboration. http://www.campbellcollaboration.org.
Centre for Reviews and Dissemination at the University of York. http://www.york.ac.uk/inst/crd/crddatabases.htm.
Cochrane Collaboration. http://www.cochrane.org.
EPPI Centre. http://eppi.ioe.ac.uk/cms.
Guidelines for assessing systematic reviews (AMSTAR, Assessment of Multiple Systematic Reviews). http://www.biomedcentral.com/content/supplementary/1471-2288-7-10-S1.doc.

References

Cooper, H., & Hedges, L. V. (1994). *The handbook of research synthesis.* New York: Sage.
Gibbs, L. E. (2003). *Evidence-based practice for the helping professions: A practical guide with integrated multimedia.* Pacific Grove, CA: Brooks/Cole-Thompson Learning.
Higgins, J. P. T., & Green, S. (Eds.). (2006). *Cochrane handbook for systematic reviews of interventions.* Chichester, UK: Wiley. Retrieved July 11, 2007, from http://www.cochrane.org/resources/handbook.
Littell, J. H. (2008). How do we know what works? The quality of published reviews of evidence-based practices. In D. Lindsey & A. Shlonsky (Eds.), *Child welfare research: Advances for practice and policy* (pp. 66–93). New York: Oxford University Press.
Littell, J. H., Corcoran, J., & Pillai, V. (2008). *Systematic reviews and meta-analysis.* New York: Oxford University Press.
Petticrew, M., & Roberts, H. (2006). *Systematic reviews in the social sciences: A practical guide.* Oxford: Blackwell.
Shea, B. J., Grimshaw, J. M., Wells, G. A., Boers, M., Andersson, N., Hamel, C., et al. (2007). Development of AMSTAR: A measurement tool to assess the methodological quality of systematic reviews. *BMC Medical Research Methodology, 7.* Retrieved from http://www.biomedcentral.com/1471-2288/7/10.
Thomas, J., Harden, A., Oakley, A., Oliver, S., Sutcliffe, K., Rees, R., et al. (2004). Integrating qualitative research with trials in systematic reviews. *British Medical Journal, 328,* 1010–1012.

Practice Guidelines and Evidence-Based Practice

Matthew O. Howard, Brian E. Perron, & Michael G. Vaughn

Guidelines for clinical practice in medicine and allied health professions have proliferated exponentially over the past two decades. A search of the PubMed computerized bibliographic database of the National Library of Medicine conducted on February 1, 2008, using the search delimiter "clinical practice guidelines," identified a total of 11,627 published practice guidelines and an impressively large subset of 598 practice guidelines indexed within the prior year. In the mental health specialty area, the American Psychiatric Association (2006) recently published a 1,600-page compendium of *Guidelines for the Treatment of Psychiatric Disorders*, offering comprehensive care recommendations for diagnosis, assessment, and treatment of 13 prevalent mental health conditions. Clearly, manifest interest in guidelines has soared in medicine and the other health professions in recent years. Factors contributing to the emergence and growth of guideline development activities in the 1980s were described by Howard and Jenson (1999a) and Walker, Howard, Lambert, and Suchinsky (1994).

Although thousands of practice guidelines have been developed for health professionals, lamentably few guidelines have been specifically developed by or for human or social services workers. Nathan (2007) noted that

despite initial efforts more than a decade ago by a task force of the Society of Clinical Psychology (Division 12) to establish a list of empirically validated treatments . . . and subsequent efforts by psychologists and others to identify treatments that meet empirically supported standards . . . the American Psychological Association has not sponsored an effort to develop a set of treatment guidelines for professional psychology practice. As a result, psychologists are left with suboptimal choices: to use the American Psychiatric Association's

guidelines; to use those of other organizations, such as the Veterans Administration; or to use none. (p. 8)

Social workers are similarly disadvantaged by the absence of available professional practice guidelines, although calls for a practice guideline development initiative in social work that date back more than a decade (see special issue on practice guidelines,, *Research on Social Work Practice,* 9 [1999]).

Although practice guidelines can be expensive, time-consuming, and logistically demanding to develop, it is not altogether clear why professional psychology and social work have lagged so conspicuously behind other health professions in developing practice guidelines. However, it is likely that the availability of greater monies, a more pressing demand for accountability, and an abundance of relevant randomized controlled trials from which to construct practice guidelines account for some of the differences across health and social service professions in guideline development activity. Potential barriers to guideline development in social work were delineated by Howard and Jenson (1999b) and by the authors of papers in the special issue of *Research on Social Work Practice* devoted to guidelines just referenced.

DEFINITIONAL ISSUES

A number of definitions of practice guidelines have been proffered, but by far the most influential is the notion that guidelines are "systematically developed statements to assist practitioner and patient decisions about appropriate care for specific clinical circumstances" (Institute of Medicine, 1990, p. 27). Although the origins of the guideline movement in clinical medicine are apparent in the definition of guidelines, there is no obvious reason why practice guidelines could not be developed for application in micro, mezzo, and macro social work practice contexts.

A variety of nuanced terms are broadly synonymous with the concept of practice guidelines, including practice "standards," "options," "parameters," "clinical decision rules," "preferred practice patterns," "clinical pathways," and "algorithms," to name only a few. In general, practice guidelines, options, and parameters allow considerable flexibility in their application, whereas standards, decision rules, pathways, and algorithms are often more prescriptive in nature. Careful attention should be paid to the definitions of guidelines and related constructs employed by the organizations developing them. For example, the American Psychological Association (2005) defined *practice guidelines* relatively broadly as, "recommendations to professionals concerning their conduct and the issues to be considered in particular areas of psychological practice, in contrast to *treatment guidelines*, which provide specific recommendations about clinical interventions to be delivered to clients" (p. 976).

Published guidelines are very heterogeneous in their characteristics. Some are authored by a single individual, others by a small group of self-appointed or nominated experts, and still others by a committee of several hundred clinical and research experts including representatives of pertinent client groups and professional organizations. Guidelines can run from several pages to more than 100 pages in length; offer advice based on "expert consensus" only or graded recommendations carefully tied to a meticulously weighting of the undergirding scientific evidence; and provide practice recommendations ranging from very general to highly specific in nature. Guidelines not only facilitate effective treatment but can also offer useful recommendations for optimal screening, assessment, diagnostic, prognostic, and prevention activities. The significant heterogeneity of extant guidelines, in conjunction with the sheer number of such guidelines, poses potential problems for conscientious guideline users. These issues will be addressed next in reference to guideline quality assessment.

RISKS AND BENEFITS OF GUIDELINES

Practitioners have often greeted guideline development and dissemination efforts with apprehension and even overt hostility. Attitudinal studies indicate that many practitioners believe guidelines will lead to reduced practitioner autonomy, "cookbook," formulaic, or "one-size-fits-all" practice, and a focus on issues (e.g., cost containment) other than those directly having to do with clients' preferences and best interests. Concerns have also been raised about practitioners' potentially increased liability to malpractice actions if nonadherence to guideline recommendations is widely accepted as an affirmative indication of failure to comply with the standard of care in a given practice area.

Countering these claims, guideline proponents contend that guidelines allow for considerable flexibility in their application, can lead to superior client outcomes through more consistent and conscientious application of demonstrably effective interventions, can promote more efficient and equitable utilization of scare health care and social service resources, and can thereby lead to greater credibility for the social work profession. Howard and Jenson (1999a, 1999b) and Howard, McMillen, and Pollio (2003) present highly detailed discussions of putative virtues and limitations of professional practice guidelines.

In recent years, perhaps as a result of increased exposure to practice guidelines, practitioners across a range of health professions other than social work appear to have adopted attitudes more favorable to clinical guidelines. Initial concerns about health care practitioners' potentially heightened susceptibility to malpractice torts following guideline adoption have not generally been born out. In general, guideline development has become widely accepted in the health care professions and has recently been characterized as a growth industry.

GUIDELINE QUALITY

Prominent studies have identified substantial variations in guideline quality (e.g., Shaneyfelt, Mayo-Smith, & Rothwangl, 1999). In consequence, efforts to promote greater adherence to preferred guideline development processes and to provide practitioners with a tool to judge guideline quality have received increasing attention. Particularly notable in this regard is the AGREE instrument developed for the purpose of assessing guideline quality. With regard to guideline scope and purpose, AGREE criteria assess whether the overall objective(s), practice issue(s) addressed, and clients to whom the guideline applies are specifically described. AGREE criteria pertaining to stakeholder involvement require that individuals from all pertinent professional groups and representatives of affected client groups be incorporated into the guideline development process. Furthermore, the group of users for whom the guideline is intended should be explicitly stated, and the guideline itself pilot tested among identified end users.

AGREE criteria also require evidence of systematic literature search methods, use of explicit criteria for including evidence, and well-explicated methods for formulating practice recommendations and comprehensively considering effects, side effects, and possible risks of treatment. Also important, in this vein, are explicit links between supporting evidence and practice recommendations, external review of guidelines prior to publication and dissemination, and a carefully articulated plan for updating the guideline to ensure its currency.

AGREE standards for guideline presentation and publication assess whether practice recommendations are clearly stated, specific in nature, and readily identifiable, and if alternative options for client care are available, they are systematically raised and discussed. Finally, guidelines should address potential organizational impediments to their adoption, cost implications of their application, and key criteria by which their effectiveness can be assessed. Guideline authors should have full editorial independence from the professional, institutional, or governmental body funding development of the guideline.

For additional information regarding an important international effort to promote best practices in guideline development, readers are referred to the GRADE Working Group.

Additional questions to ask about published guidelines have been raised by Greenhalgh (2006) in her book, *How to Read a Paper: The Basics of Evidence-Based Medicine*. These include the following.

- Did the preparation and publication of the guideline involve a significant conflict of interest?
- Is the guideline concerned with the appropriate topic, and does it state clearly the target group it applies to?
- Did the guideline development panel include *both* an expert in the topic area *and* a specialist in the methods of secondary research (e.g., meta-analyst, health economist)?
- Have the subjective judgments of the development panel been made explicit, and are they justified?

- Have all the relevant data been scrutinized and rigorously evaluated?
- Has the evidence been properly synthesized, and are the guideline's conclusions in keeping with the data on which they are based?
- Does the guideline address variations in practice and other controversial areas (e.g., optimum care in response to genuine or perceived underfunding)?
- Is the guideline clinically relevant, comprehensive, and flexible?
- Does the guideline take into account what is acceptable to, affordable for, and practically possible for patients?
- Does the guideline include recommendations for its own dissemination, implementation, and regular review?

In addition to offering useful methods by which published guideline quality might be assessed and thereby increased, various theorists have forwarded criteria by which the appropriateness of the topical focus of proposed guidelines might be evaluated. Generally, it is held that the most useful guidelines address conditions currently characterized by wide and largely unexplained variations in the practice methods used to treat them, that are either costly or risky to treat or both, and where the investment in client care and outcomes is likely to be repaid in increased economic returns and improved client outcomes. Ideally, guideline development efforts should be undertaken in areas where consensus is likely achievable vis-à-vis best practice recommendations and where there is a reasonable probability that guideline recommendations can be successfully implemented. In social work, it is likely that the most effective guidelines will be developed conjointly by academics and practitioners who are working in the settings and with the client populations affected by the guidelines. Proactive consideration of these attributes by groups developing guidelines could increase the utility and quality of the resultant guidelines considerably.

GUIDELINE DISSEMINATION, IMPLEMENTATION, AND ADHERENCE

Experience with practice guidelines over the past decade clearly indicates that merely developing a guideline is no assurance that it will be adequately disseminated or implemented. For example, in recent years, several large surveys of practicing psychologists and physicians revealed that many had not received a copy or summary of current smoking cessation treatment guidelines, were unfamiliar with their content, and did not know whether they were compliant with smoking cessation guideline recommendations or whether the guidelines themselves promoted comparatively more effective smoking cessation intervention outcomes.

A variety of methods have been employed to disseminate practice guidelines, including those approaches referred to as *passive diffusion* methods (e.g., e-mail or direct mailings to members of professional organizations or publication of guidelines in professional journals or newsletters), *active implementation* strategies (e.g., training and reliance on local professional opinion leaders to disseminate guideline information, computerized informatic reminder systems, use of clinical audit and feedback methods, administrative supports, and academic detailing—the latter consisting of outreach visits to professional practitioners designed to promote select practices), and *educational approaches* (e.g., continuing professional education and conference/workshop attendance).

Traditionally, the most widely employed and least effective guideline dissemination approaches have been those of the passive diffusion and educational type. Extensive reviews of the effectiveness of these approaches have concluded that there is weak support for didactic interventions, traditional continuing professional education, and direct mailings; moderate support for clinical audit and feedback methods and use of local peer opinion leaders; and relatively strong empirical support for computerized client care reminder systems, academic detailing, and multimodal and complex guideline dissemination interventions. Consistent conclusions were reached in a review of 41 relevant studies, which found that "evidence indicates that guideline adherence is not high without specific intervention, but that certain interventions (typically multifaceted and resource-intensive ones) improve adherence" (Bauer, 2002, p. 138).

Characteristics other than the manner and method by which they are developed and disseminated can also influence guideline adoption. Qualities of the guidelines themselves (e.g., those that do versus do not require learning new skills, that are consistent versus inconsistent with extant norms and values for practice); attitudes, professional roles, and other personal and professional characteristics of the health care and human service workers who are potential guideline users; attributes of the practice setting including incentives for adoption of and adherence to guidelines and relevant regulatory requirements; and client factors (e.g., personal preferences, race, and socioeconomic status) can also influence the extent to which clinical guidelines are successfully implemented.

Perceived barriers to guideline adoption include perceptions that guidelines will be time-consuming and resource-intensive to develop, discourage practice innovation, promote average rather than exemplary practice, tend not to reflect local practice conditions if developed by national bodies, and rapidly become outdated. Several recent evaluations indicate that use of guidelines as part of a continuous quality improvement program can promote enhanced adherence to guidelines and superior client outcomes.

GUIDELINE EFFECTIVENESS

Two primary questions have been raised with regard to practice guidelines: Are they effective in changing practitioners' behaviors in the intended manner and, given these changes, are clients' outcomes enhanced as a result of greater practitioner adherence to guidelines? One analysis of 59 studies of guideline effectiveness (Grimshaw & Russell, 1993), noted that only 4 of 59 studies failed to report significantly positive effects of guideline implementation on processes of care. Nine of 11 studies included in this evaluation found significantly beneficial effects of guideline implementation on clients' outcomes. Given the notable heterogeneity in the methods by which they are developed, disseminated, and implemented and the many different conditions and client/professional groups for which they have been developed, it is likely that guideline effectiveness will vary considerably. Far greater study is needed of the conditions under which guidelines can be expected to produce the most favorable outcomes possible for clients receiving care for a variety of social problems. See Agency for Healthcare Research and Quality Web site for a review of guideline effectiveness studies.

PRACTICE GUIDELINES AND EVIDENCE-BASED PRACTICE

Clinical practice guidelines were initially identified as a promising means by which evidence-based practice could be promoted in clinical medicine. More recently, Howard, McMillen, and Pollio

(2003) and Howard, Allen-Meares, and Ruffolo (2007) called for widespread training of social work students and faculty in the methods of identifying, accessing, critiquing, modifying, and implementing practice guidelines and associated practice-relevant scholarly products, such as systematic reviews and meta-analyses. Howard et al. (2007) argued that practice guidelines are effective teaching tools for the promotion of evidence-based practice, readily accepted by students and practitioners, and widely applicable in that they do not require every student practitioner or professional social worker to acquire and maintain relatively sophisticated information science and research skills.

Some proponents of evidence-based practice in social work take a less favorable view of guidelines, contending that practice guidelines are time-consuming and expensive to develop, rarely updated, rapidly outdated, and never published in many practice areas and for many client groups in part because the empirical evidence on which they might be based is not available. Proponents of evidence-based practice who are *not* supportive of an emphasis on guideline development and guideline-based practice education in social work, call for students to be trained in the methods of evidence-based practice per se: formulation of important practice questions that lend themselves to computerized bibliographic searching, location of pertinent evidence via identification and appropriate searching of relevant bibliographic databases, critical appraisal of practice-relevant evidence, incorporation of obtained evidence into practice decision making and intervention delivery, and assessment of the effectiveness of implemented evidence-based interventions and modification of treatment practices as needed. Each of these five steps of evidence-based practice requires specific training and skills that all social work students and professional practitioners should learn, these theorists argue, because they provide social workers with the ability to remain current in a wide range of practice areas over the course of their careers.

Presently, it is unclear how acceptable evidence-based practice training is to social work students or professionals and how effectively, and under which conditions, students acquire skills for evidence-based practice most readily. For that matter, it is unclear how receptive students are to guideline-based practice education, although some advocates believe that many will be comparatively more receptive to secondary research products, such as practice guidelines, systematic reviews, meta-analyses,

and empirically supported manualized interventions because these products offer clinically relevant evidence-based practice recommendations but do not require that students read and critique large numbers of primary research studies.

CONCLUSIONS AND FUTURE DIRECTIONS

Practice guidelines have proliferated widely across medicine and allied health professions, and many such guidelines are useful to social workers interested in evidence-based practice. Nonetheless, social work should initiate a guideline development movement, with the intention of developing empirically based practice guidelines in areas of core and unique importance to social work practice. Profession-specific guidelines could do much to promote better practice in social work nationally and would eventually increase the credibility and long-term viability of the social work profession.

It is currently unclear which of the many national social work organizations should sponsor a guideline development movement or whether a consortium of organizations should take on this challenge. Questions also remain about how priority areas should be identified for development of social work practice guidelines and which criteria should be employed to make such determinations.

Incipient efforts to evaluate promising new methods for incorporating clients' perspectives, cost and other economic considerations, and issues relevant to race and gender on guideline development efforts are under way. Additional investigations of these issues in relation to guideline development and effectiveness are needed. Furthermore, agency-related and other organizational and contextual factors are likely critical determinants of the extent to which guidelines are adopted by practitioners, but have received little attention in the social work or general psychosocial literatures pertaining to practice guidelines.

Over the past decade, there are indications that social workers have become significantly more supportive of a profession-wide movement to evidence-based practice, although the best methods for accomplishing this transition are the subject of considerable debate. Some proponents believe that practice guidelines are useful tools to promote evidence-based practice that appeal to students and practitioners because they are specifically focused on practice issues and do not require practitioners to become researchers or sophisticated consumers of research. Conversely, some critics of practice guidelines contend that given the expense and logistical requirements necessary for their development, it is unlikely many guidelines will be developed in social work. Furthermore, these critics argue that guidelines rapidly become outdated and thus, all social work students should be trained in the steps of evidence-based practice enunciated most prominently by Sackett and colleagues (Sackett, Rosenberg, & Gray, 1996). At present, the comparative acceptability, virtues, limitations, and effectiveness of these two competing (but potentially complementary) approaches to the promotion of evidence-based practice in social work remain unknown and the subject of ongoing passionate disagreement.

WEB SITES

Agency for Healthcare Research and Quality. http://www.ahrq.gov/clinic/ptsafety/chap51 .htm
AGREE Collaboration. http://www .agreecollaboration.org.
GRADE Working Group. http://www .gradeworkinggroup.org.
Guidelines International Network. www.g-i-n.net.
National Guideline Clearinghouse. http://www .guideline.gov.

References

American Psychiatric Association. (2006). *Guidelines for the treatment of psychiatric disorders: Compendium 2006.* Washington, DC: American Psychiatric Association Press.

American Psychological Association. (2005). Determination and documentation of the need for practice guidelines. *American Psychologist, 60,* 976–978.

Bauer, M. S. (2002). A review of quantitative studies of adherence to mental health clinical practice guidelines. *Harvard Review of Psychiatry, 10,* 138–153.

Greenhalgh, T. (2006). *How to read a paper: The basics of evidence-based medicine.* Malden, MA: Blackwell.

Grimshaw, J., & Russell, I. I. (1993). Effect of clinical guidelines on medical practice: A systematic review of rigorous evaluations. *Lancet, 342,* 1317–1322.

Howard, M. O., & Allen-Meares, P., & Ruffolo, M. C. (2007). Teaching evidence-based practice: Strategic and pedagogical recommendations for schools of social work. *Research on Social Work Practice, 17,* 561–568.

Howard, M. O., & Jenson, J. M. (1999a). Clinical practice guidelines: Should social work develop them? *Research on Social Work Practice, 9,* 283–301.

Howard, M. O., & Jenson, J. M. (1999b). Barriers to development, utilization and evaluation of social work practice guidelines: Toward an action plan for social work. *Research on Social Work Practice, 9,* 347–364.

Howard, M. O., McMillen, C. J., & Pollio, D. E. (2003). Teaching evidence-based practice: Toward a new paradigm for social work education. *Research on Social Work Practice, 13,* 234–259.

Institute of Medicine. (1990). *Clinical practice guidelines: Directions for a new program.* Washington, DC: National Academies Press.

Nathan, P. E. (2007). Psychiatric practice guidelines: A step forward for psychiatry. *PsycCRITIQUES, 52,* 1–10.

Sackett D. L., Rosenberg, W. C., & Gray, J. A. M. (1996). Evidence-based medicine: What it is and what it isn't. *British Medical Journal, 312,* 71–72.

Shaneyfelt, T. M., Mayo-Smith, M.F., & Rothwangl, J. (1999). Are guidelines following guidelines? *Journal of the American Medical Association, 281,* 1900–1905.

Walker, R. D., Howard, M. O., Lambert, M. D., & Suchinsky, R. (1994). Medical practice guidelines. *Western Journal of Medicine, 161,* 39–44.

169 Integrating Information from Diverse Sources in Evidence-Based Practice

Eileen Gambrill

Evidence-based practice requires the "integration of best research evidence with our clinical expertise and our [client's] unique values and circumstances (Straus, Richardson, Glasziou, & Haynes, 2005, p. 1). Practitioners must decide what particular characteristics of clients and their contexts to attend to and how to weigh them. They have to decide what information to gather and how to do so. Integrating information and making a decision together with the client as to what to do is often burdened with uncertainties, such as the extent to which external research findings apply to a particular client. Here is where cognitive biases such as tendencies to consider only data that confirm initial assumptions thrive. This step requires integrating information concerning external research findings with circumstances and characteristics of the client, including their values and expectations and available resources, and, together with the client, deciding what to do. The time and effort devoted to making a decision should depend on the potential consequences in relation to making a faulty or good decision and what is needed, based on external research findings and prior experience.

Clinical expertise refers to "the ability to use our clinical skills and past experience to rapidly identify each client's unique health state and diagnosis, their individual risks and benefits of potential interventions, and their personal circumstances and expectations" (Straus et al., 2005, p. 1).

Increased expertise is reflected in many ways, but especially in more effective and efficient [assessment] and in the more thoughtful identification and

compassionate use of individual [clients'] predicaments, rights and preferences in making clinical decisions about their care . . . . Without clinical expertise, practice risks becoming tyrannized by external evidence, for even excellent external evidence may be inapplicable to or inappropriate for an individual [client]. Without current best external evidence, practice risks becoming rapidly out of date, to the detriment of [clients]. (Sackett, Richardson, Rosenberg, & Haynes, 1997, p. 2)

Client preferences are considered as well as access to needed resources. Questions include (Glasziou, Del Mar, & Salisbury, 2003) the following: Do research findings apply to my client? That is, is a client similar to clients included in related research? Can I use this practice method in my setting (e.g., are needed resources available?) If not, is there some other access to programs found to be most effective in seeking hoped-for outcomes? What alternatives are available? Will the benefits of service outweigh the harms of service for this client? What does my client think about this method? Is it acceptable to my client? What if I don't find anything? Many application barriers enter at this stage. Gathering information about their frequency and exact nature will be useful in planning how to decrease them. Examples include chaotic work environments, being overwhelmed by problems/issues due to large caseloads, lack of resources, and poor interagency communication and collaboration. Information may be available about certain kinds of clients, but these clients may differ greatly, so findings may not apply. Resources available will limit options.

DO RESEARCH FINDINGS
APPLY TO CLIENTS?

A great deal of practice-related research consists of correlational research (e.g., describing the relationship between certain characteristics of parents and child abuse) and experimental research describing differences among various groups (e.g., experimental and control). In neither case may the findings apply to a particular client. Differences may influence the potential costs and benefits of an intervention to a particular client. Norms on assessment measures may be available, but not for people like your client. (Note, however, that norms should not necessarily be used as a guideline for selecting outcomes for individual clients because outcomes they seek may differ from normative criteria and norms may not be optimal, for example, low rates of positive feedback from teachers to students in classrooms.)

The unique characteristics and circumstances of a client may suggest that a particular method should not be used because negative effects are likely or because such characteristics would render an intervention ineffective if it were applied at a certain time. For example, referring clients to parent-training programs who have a substance abuse problem may not be effective. Thus, there may be other problems that influence the effectiveness of a method. The unique factors associated with a problem such as depression may influence the effectiveness of a given method (e.g., medication, increasing pleasant events, and decreasing negative thoughts). Claims regarding the validity of a practice guideline may not apply to a particular client, agency, or community. Knowledge of behavior, how it is influenced, and what principles of behavior have been found to apply to many individuals may provide helpful guidelines. Questions suggested by Sheldon, Guyatt, and Haines (1998) about whether a particular intervention applies to an individual client are as follows.

1. Is the relative risk reduction that is attributed to the intervention likely to be different in this case because of client characteristics?
2. What is the client's absolute risk of an adverse event without the intervention?
3. Is there some other problem or a contraindication that might reduce the benefit?

4. Are there social or cultural factors that might affect the suitability of a practice or policy or its acceptability?
5. What do the client and the client's family want?

ARE THEY IMPORTANT? THE
"SO-WHAT QUESTION"

If external research findings apply to a client, are they important? Would they make a difference in decisions made? Were all important outcomes considered? Were surrogate outcomes relied on—those that are not of direct practical relevance but assumed to reflect vital outcomes? The term POEMS refers to patient-oriented evidence that matters. Grandage, Slawson, Barnett, and Shaughnessy (2002) suggest the following for judging usefulness:

$$usefulness = (validity \times relevance)/work.$$

HOW DEFINITIVE ARE THE
RESEARCH FINDINGS?

Reviews found may be high-quality systematic reviews or incomplete, unrigorous reviews. In the former, there may be strong evidence not to use a method (e.g., harmful effects have been found) or strong evidence to use one (e.g., critical tests show the effectiveness of a program). Often there will be uncertainty about what is most likely to be effective (See DUETs listed under Web Sites at end of chapter). Different views of the quality of evidence related to programs abound (e.g., see Littell, 2005).

WHAT IF THE EXPERTS DISAGREE?

Although practitioners and clients may often have to depend on the views of experts, such dependence is not without its risk, as illustrated by studies comparing recommendations of clinical experts to what is suggested based on results of carefully controlled research (Antman, Lau, Kupelnick, Mosteller, & Chalmers, 1992). In some situations, we could seek and review the quality of evidence for ourselves. At other times, this may not be possible due to time constraints. Indicators of honesty of experts include (1) accurate description of controversies, including methodological and conceptual problems with preferred positions; (2) accurate description of well-argued disliked views; (3) critical appraisal of both preferred and well-argued alternative views; and (4) inclusion of references regarding claims made so readers can examine these for themselves.

WILL POTENTIAL BENEFITS OUTWEIGH POTENTIAL RISKS AND COSTS?

Every intervention, including assessment measures, have potential risks as well as potential benefits—for example, a false positive or negative result. Will the benefits of an intervention outweigh potential risks and costs? We can estimate this in a number of ways: RRR (relative risk reduction), ARR (absolute risk reduction), and NNT (number needed to treat) (see Bandolier worksheet for calculating NNT). A nomogram can be used to calculate the NNT based on absolute risk in the absence of treatment (Guyatt & Rennie, 2002). How many clients have to receive a harm reduction program to help one person? Is there any information about NNH (the number of individuals who would have to receive a service to harm one person)? ARR should always be given; RRR is highly misleading. Accurately communicating risk to clients is much easier using frequencies rather than probabilities (Gigerenzer, 2002).

HOW CAN PRACTITIONERS HELP CLIENTS TO MAKE DECISIONS?

The lack of correlation between what someone says he or she wants (their preferences) and what he or she does (their actions) is considered such a big issue, with so little related research, that the latest model of evidence-based practice carves out preferences and actions as a separate area to be considered (Haynes, Devereaux, & Guyatt, 2002). For example, although many people say they want to pursue a certain goal, their actions often do not reflect their stated preferences; that is, they don't do anything. In view of tendencies of some clients to match the goals and values of their therapists and other sources of behavioral confirmation in the helping process and the role of subtle influences such as question wording and order on the expression of preferences, a variety of methods of inquiry should be used to discover beliefs and preferences, rather than relying on one method, which may result in inaccurate accounts.

How decisions are framed (in terms of gains or losses) influences decisions; different surface wordings of identical problems influence judgments (framing effects). Gains or losses that are certain are weighed more heavily than those that are uncertain. Clients differ in how risk-averse they are and in the importance given to particular outcomes. Occasions when discovering client preferences is especially important include those in which (1) options have major differences in outcomes or complications; (2) decisions require trade-offs between short- and long-term outcomes; (3) one choice can result in a small chance of a grave outcome; and (4) there are marginal differences in outcomes between options (Kassirer, 1994). Presentation of risks and benefits by professionals is often quite misleading (e.g., see Gigerenzer, 2002). Thus, a key step in helping clients make a decision is for practitioners themselves to be aware of errors they make in estimating risk and presenting options (e.g., framing biases).

Discovering client beliefs and preferences may require involving them in a decision analysis. Decision aids can be used to inform clients about risks and benefits of different options. Such aids can "personalize" information by allowing clients to ask questions important to them. They can highlight vital information often overlooked, such as absolute risk. Benefits include reducing the proportion of clients who are uncertain about what to choose, increasing clients' knowledge of the problem, options, and outcomes, creating realistic expectations, improving the match between choices and a client's values, increasing informed participation in decision making, and increasing adherence to components of an intervention directly linked to success (e.g., see O'Connor et al., 2004; see also Cochrane Decision Aid Register).

CAN THIS METHOD BE IMPLEMENTED EFFECTIVELY IN MY AGENCY?

Can a plan be carried out in a way that maximizes success? Are needed resources available? Do providers have the skills required to carry out plans? Can needed resources be created? There may be vital differences in provider adherence to practice guidelines that decrease the safety and effectiveness of an intervention. Current service patterns may limit options. Barriers to implementation may be so extensive that Straus et al. (2005, p. 170–171) refer to them as "the killer B's:

1. The Burden of Illness (the frequency of a concern may be too low to warrant offering a costly program with high integrity);
2. Beliefs of individual clients and/or communities about the value of services or their outcomes may not be compatible with what is most effective;
3. a Bad Bargain in relation to resources, costs, and outcome; and
4. Barriers such as geographic, organizational, traditional, authoritarian, or behavioral.

Problems may have to be redefined from helping clients attain needed resources to helping them to bear up under the strain of not having them or involving clients with similar concerns in advocacy efforts to acquire better services. Questions Sackett et al. (1997) suggest for deciding whether to implement a guideline include the following (p. 182):

1. What barriers exist to its implementation? Can they be overcome?
2. Can you enlist the collaboration of key colleagues?
3. Can you meet the educational, administrative, and economic conditions that are likely to determine the success or failure of implementing the strategy?
   • Credible synthesis of the evidence by a respected body.
   • Respected, influential local exemplars already implementing the strategy.
   • Consistent information from all relevant sources.
   • Opportunity for individual discussions about the strategy with an authority.
   • User-friendly format for guidelines.
   • Implementable within target group of clinicians (without the need for extensive outside collaboration).
   • Freedom from conflict with economic and administrative incentives and client and community expectations.

ARE ALTERNATIVE OPTIONS AVAILABLE?

Are other options available, perhaps another agency to which a client could be referred? Self-help programs may be available. Here, too, familiarity with practice-related research can facilitate decisions.

WHAT IF CLIENTS' PREFER UNTESTED, INEFFECTIVE, OR HARMFUL METHODS?

The acceptability of plans must be considered. This will influence adherence to important procedural components associated with success. Most interventions used by professionals in the interpersonal helping professions have not been tested; we don't know if they are effective, not effective, or harmful. Untested methods are routinely offered in both health and social care. Methods critically tested and found to be ineffective or harmful should certainly not to be offered. If an effective method is available, the costs and benefits of using this compared to a preferred ineffective method could be described. Untested methods that continue to be preferred and used should be tested to determine whether they do more good than harm.

WHAT IF A SEARCH REVEALS NO RELATED RESEARCH?

A review of research findings related to important practice questions and related information needs may reveal that little or nothing is known. Ethical obligations to involve clients as informed participants and to consider their preferences provide a guide, that is, limitations of research findings should be shared with clients and empirically grounded practice theory as well as client preferences can be used to guide work with clients. Evidence-informed practice involves sharing ignorance and uncertainty as well as knowledge in a context of ongoing support (Katz, 2002).

WHAT IF RELATED RESEARCH IS OF POOR QUALITY?

A search will often reveal that there is uncertainty regarding the effectiveness of a method. The phrase "best practice" is used to describe a hierarchy of evidence (e.g., Straus et al., 2005, p. 169). The phrase "best evidence" could refer to a variety of different kinds of tests that differ greatly in the extent to which claims are critically tested. Available research may be low on this hierarchy in relation to critical tests of a practice or policy (e.g., a case series). However, this may be the best that is available. For example, if there are no randomized controlled trials regarding an effectiveness question, then we move down the list. This is what must be done in the everyday world because most interventions used in psychiatry, psychology, and social work have not been critically tested. Instead of well-designed randomized controlled trials regarding an intervention, only pre/post studies may be available, which are subject to many rival explanations regarding the cause of change. Some guidelines are described as "well-established" if two well-designed randomized controlled trials show positive outcomes. It is less misleading to say that a claim has been critically tested in two well-controlled trials and has passed both tests. This keeps uncertainty in view. Whatever is found is shared with clients and practice theory as well as client preferences must be used to fill in the gaps.

WHAT IF RESEARCH IS AVAILABLE BUT IT HAS NOT BEEN CRITICALLY APPRAISED?

One course of action is to critically appraise this literature. However, the realities of practice may not allow time for this. Perhaps an expert in the area can be contacted. If the question concerns a problem that occurs often, interested others can be involved in critically appraising related research. In the United Kingdom, questions asked by physicians are tracked, and those that occur often guide selection of topics for research and/or systematic review. We could do the same in social work.

BALANCING INDIVIDUAL AND POPULATION PERSPECTIVES

One of the most challenging aspects of practice is considering both individuals and populations. There is only so much money and time. Decisions made about populations often limit options of individuals. Ethical issues regarding the distribution of scarce resources are often overlooked.

COMMON ERRORS

Common errors in integrating information from diverse sources are related to common cognitive biases such as overconfidence, wishful thinking,

influence by redundant information, and confirmation biases. Availability biases such as influence by vivid data are common as are representative biases (influence by associations that may be misleading rather than informative). Eagerness to help clients may encourage unfounded confidence in methods suggested. Lack of reliability and validity of information is often overlooked, resulting in faulty inferences. Jumping to conclusions may result in oversimplification of causes of a client's concerns. Or the opposite may occur, as in suggesting obscure complex causes, none of which provide intervention implications. Lack of evidence may be shared with clients in an unempathetic manner.

ONGOING CHALLENGES AND EVOLVING REMEDIES

Obstacles include both personal and environmental characteristics (see "Can this method be implemented effectively?"). Ongoing challenges include encouraging practitioners to be honest with clients about uncertainties in a supportive manner (Katz, 2002), minimizing common cognitive biases in integrating data, and avoiding influence of inflated claims in the professional literature about "what works" and what accounts for client concerns. Organizational cultures may discourage raising questions regarding services offered and needed tools, such as access to vital databases, may not be available. Biases intrude both on the part of researchers when conducting research and when preparing research reviews (MacCoun, 1998) as well as at the practitioner level when making decisions. Availability biases, such as a preferred practice theory and preconceptions regarding certain kinds of people, as well as representative biases, including stereotypes, may interfere with sound integration of external research findings with client values, expectations, and unique circumstances and characteristics. Many components of EBP are designed to minimize biases such as jumping to conclusions, for example, using "quality filters" when seeking research related to a question. EBP highlights the play of bias and uncertainty in helping clients and attempts to give helpers and clients the knowledge and skills to handle this honesty and constructively. Consider the attention given to training both clients and helpers in critical appraisal skills in reviewing research findings related to practice questions.

We can draw on literature concerning judgment, problem solving and decision making to discover common biases and how to avoid them, including discussion of organizational obstacles and how to address them (Gambrill, 2005). We can take advantage of literature investigating expertise to help practitioners "educate their intuition" (Hogarth, 2001) and take advantage of guidelines described in the critical thinking literature to minimize biases. Helping professionals learn from their experience in ways that improve the accuracy of future decisions is a key priority. This will require arranging corrective feedback that permits the development of "informed intuition" (Hogarth, 2001). One problem arises when someone who does not have this expertise thinks they do and imposes, perhaps by selective attention, an inaccurate view on a situation. They may generalize a decision-making method to a situation in which it is not useful.

Use of handheld computers to guide decisions may be of value in decreasing errors and common biases. Such aids can be used to prompt valuable behaviors, to critique a decision (for example, purchasing services from an agency that does not use evidence-informed practices), to match a client's unique circumstances and characteristics with a certain service program, to suggest unconsidered options, and to interpret different assessment pictures (Guyatt et al., 2008). Use of clinical pathways and handheld computers with built-in decision aids, such as flow charts, are already in use in the health arena, as are decision aids for clients (see earlier discussion). Just as the narratives of clients may help us understand how we can improve services, the narratives of practitioners may help us identify challenges and opportunities to integrating information from diverse sources (Greenhalgh & Hurwitz, 1998).

RELATED ETHICAL DILEMMAS

Ethical issues that arise in integrating data and making decisions illustrate the close connection between ethical and evidentiary issues. These include ethical obligations of practitioners to accurately inform clients regarding the uncertainties involved in making decisions, including the evidentiary status of recommended methods and their risks and benefits together with the risks and benefits of alternative methods. Should clients be informed regarding effective methods that an agency cannot offer? Should practitioners continue to offer methods of unknown effectiveness? Is it ethical to offer an intervention in a diluted form of unknown effectiveness? Should practitioners be well informed regarding how to accurately present risks and benefits? Although the answers may clearly be yes, descriptions of everyday practice reveal a different picture. Yet another ethical issue relates to controversies regarding the relative contributions of the person of the helper, the alliance, and the particular intervention, to outcome. If it is true that the former contributes more than the latter, this should be considered in deciding what to do (see Wampold, 2006).

WEB SITES

Centre for Evidence-Based Medicine. http://www.cebm.net.

Centre for Evidence-Based Medicine, University of Toronto. http://www.cebm.utoronto.ca.

Database of Uncertainties about the Effects of Treatments (DUETs). http://www.duets.nhs.uk.

Skeptic's Dictionary. http://www.skepdic.com.

References

Antman, E. M., Lau, J., Kupelnick, B., Mosteller, F., & Chalmers, T. C. (1992). A comparison of results of meta-analyses of randomized controlled trials and recommendations of clinical experts: Treatments for myocardial infarction. *Journal of the American Medical Association, 268*(2), 240–248.

Gambrill, E. (2005). *Critical thinking in clinical practice: Improving the quality of judgments and decisions,* 2nd ed. New York: Wiley.

Gigerenzer, G. (2002). *Calculated risks: How to know when numbers deceive you.* New York: Simon & Schuster.

Glasziou, P., Del Mar, C., & Salisbury, J. (2003). *Evidence-based medicine workbook.* London: BMJ Books.

Grandage, K. K., Slawson, D. C., Barnett, B. L. Jr., & Shaughnessy, A. F. (2002). When less is more: A practical approach to searching for evidence-based answers. *Journal of the Medical Library Association, 90*(3), 298–304.

Greenhalgh, T., & Hurwitz, B. (1998). *Narrative based medicine: Dialogue and discourse in clinical practice.* London: BMJ Press.

Guyatt, G. H., Rennie, D., Meade, M., & Cook, D. (2008). *Users' guides to the medical literature: A manual for evidence-based clinical practice.* Evidence-Based Medicine Working Group JAMA & Archives. Chicago: American Medical Association.

Haynes, R. B., Devereaux, P. J., & Guyatt, G. H. (2002). Editorial. Clinical expertise in the era of evidence-based medicine and patient choice. *ACP Journal Club, 136*(A11), 1–2.

Hogarth, R. M. (2001). *Educating intuition*. Chicago: University of Chicago Press.

Kassirer, J. P. (1994). Incorporating patient preferences into medical decisions. *New England Journal of Medicine, 330*, 1895–1896.

Katz, J. (2002). *The silent world of doctors and patients*. Baltimore, MD: John Hopkins University Press.

Littell, J. (2005). Lessons from a systematic review of effects of multisystemic therapy. *Children and Youth Services Review, 27*, 445–463.

MacCoun, R. (1998). Biases in the interpretation and use of research results. *Annual Review of Psychology, 49*, 259–287.

O'Connor, A. M., Stacey, D., Entwistle, V., Llewellyn-Thomas, H., Rovner, D., Holmes-Rovner, M., Tait. V., et al. (2004). Decision aids for people facing health treatment or screening decisions. (Cochrane Review). In the Cochrane Library (1). Chichester, UK: John Wiley & Sons.

Sackett, D. L., Richardson, W. S., Rosenberg, W., & Haynes, R. B. (1997). *Evidence-based medicine: How to practice and teach EBM*. New York: Churchill Livingstone.

Sheldon, T. A., Guyatt, G. H., & Haines, A. (1998). Getting research findings into practice: When to act on the evidence. *British Medical Journal, 317*, 139–142.

Straus, D. L., Richardson, W. S., Glasziou, P., & Haynes, R. B. (2005). *Evidence-based medicine: How to practice and teach EBM*, 3rd ed. New York: Churchill Livingstone.

Wampold, B. E. (2006). The psychotherapist. In J. C. Norcross, L. E. Beutler, & R. F. Levant (Eds.), *Evidence-based practices in mental health: Debate and dialogue on the fundamental questions* (pp. 200–207). Washington, DC: American Psychological Association.

170 Evidence-Based Practice in Social Work Education

Aron Shlonsky

The infusion of evidence-based practice (EBP) into social work education has begun in earnest and is still in the initial stages of widespread adoption. This initial stage can be characterized by a growing excitement about the prospect of training students to provide services that are both effective and in line with the core social work value of self-determination. On the other hand, the field is emerging from a long struggle to define EBP and find ways to integrate its philosophy and specific steps into mainstream social work education. This chapter briefly reviews the current state of implementation of EBP in schools of social work, offers suggestions for shaping individual classes, and provides strategies for the infusion of EBP across the social work curriculum.

CASE EXAMPLE

A school of social work in North America is up for accreditation and is considering infusing EBP into their new MSW curriculum. As yet, they are unsure about the extent to which they are willing and able to change the way they have always done things, but there is an acknowledgment that the curriculum is dated and requires substantial revision. There are great methodological (e.g., quantitative versus qualitative) and epistemological (e.g., postmodern/poststructuralist versus postpositivist) divides among full-time faculty, adjunct faculty, field liaisons and instructors, and students. The dean is well respected among her faculty and, like any good social worker, she values diversity of opinion and would like to make the transition to EBP an inclusive process. What steps can she take to successfully formulate a new curriculum based on the philosophies and steps of EBP? How should individual faculty members begin to infuse EBP into their classrooms?

THE ADOPTION OF EBP IN SOCIAL WORK EDUCATION

The surge of interest in EBP across disciplines over the past decade is reflected in the number and content of peer-reviewed journal articles as well as the appearance of the phrase "evidence-based" in journal titles, both new and old (Fig. 170.1). Between 1995 and 2002, the percentage of articles using the phrase "evidence-based" increased exponentially across the disciplines of social work, nursing, medicine, and psychology (Shlonsky & Gibbs, 2004). A number of leading social work journals have recently published special issues on EBP, including *Research on Social Work Practice* (2003 and 2007), *Brief Treatment and Crises Intervention* (2004), and the *Journal of Social Work Education* (2007). Several books have also appeared, most notably Leonard Gibbs's (2003) *Evidence-Based Practice for the Helping Profession*, Rosen and Proctor's (2003) *Developing Practice Guidelines for Social Work Intervention*, and

Roberts and Yeager's (2003) *Evidence-Based Practice Manual*. The two major social work conferences, the Council on Social Work Education's Annual Program Meeting and the Society for Social Work and Research's annual conference, have begun to devote considerable presentation slots to researchers and educators presenting on EBP. As well, the first national (U.S.) conference devoted to teaching EBP was convened by Allen Rubin at the University of Texas at Austin in October 2006. In short, EBP has quickly become the new practice archetype, yet definitional issues have arisen in these early stages of adoption.

In keeping with the other chapters in this part, EBP here is defined as it is in medicine as "the conscientious, explicit and judicious use of current evidence in making decisions about the care of individual patients" (Sackett, Richardson, Rosenberg, & Haynes, 1997, p. 71). Though this ideal is difficult to argue with, there has been a great deal of debate with respect to the definition of evidence and how it is gathered and used (Gibbs & Gambrill, 2002), and this is of great import to social work education because we cannot teach what we cannot define. Specifically, there has been confusion about whether EBP entails simply using an empirically validated treatment for a given client problem, and this basic misunderstanding has been one of the major barriers to implementation. However, the original model is quite explicit. EBP at the indi-

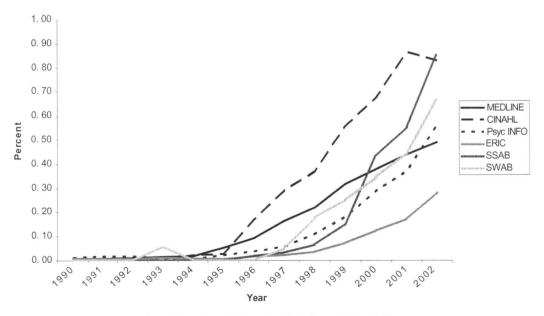

Figure 170.1 Percentage of "evidence-based" hits by discipline: 1990–2002.

vidual, community, and policy levels must include five steps: posing a practice-relevant, answerable question; systematically searching the extant literature; appraising what is found and combining these findings with what is known about client preferences/actions and clinical state/circumstances to help clients make context-sensitive decisions; and evaluating the outcome. The original EBP approach is inclusive of and even relies on both practice guidelines and empirically supported treatments (ESTs), but is not defined by and goes beyond their use.

Various approaches to teaching EBP have been adopted by schools across North America, each fashioning their curriculum differently, and all attempting to move the philosophy and methods to practice. George Warren Brown University in St. Louis was the first school to reshape its entire curriculum to reflect a practice guidelines approach (Howard, McMillen, & Pollio, 2003), including measures to ensure that students are trained in at least one EST (e.g., cognitive-behavioral therapy for depression). The University of Toronto changed its approach to teaching research, opting to teach the steps of EBP and training students to evaluate research rather than training them to conduct research. Oxford University has gone in yet a different direction and, rather than offering a degree in social care, is now offering a degree in evidence-based social intervention. More recently, other schools have begun to reshape their approach to teaching social work. For instance, Columbia University now offers several courses in EBP and has begun to shape its curriculum accordingly, and the University of Tennessee is now in the process of infusing their entire curriculum with EBP. Of course, there are others and an even larger number of individual academics who are integrating EBP into their courses.

TEACHING EBP IN THE CLASSROOM: A GENERAL SET OF GUIDELINES

Creating a Culture of Inquiry

The definition of EBP is best understood when both the guiding philosophy and the model's accompanying set of systematic steps are clearly explained. The philosophy is the starting point and should include reference to the overall model, ethical obligations to provide the most effective services to clients, and the integration of evidence with client values/preferences and clinical state/circumstances should be stressed. Only then

do the five steps of EBP begin to make sense. However, this initial understanding must also be accompanied by critical thinking (see Table 170.1). That is, search and evaluative tools are necessary but insufficient components of EBP. Every step in the process requires healthy doses of curiosity, skepticism, and a passion for finding the best possible knowledge in the service of helping, and these qualities must be brought out and supported in students. Rather than being mechanical or reductionistic, EBP at its core embraces the complexity of experiences, circumstances, and tendencies of each and every client (Shlonsky & Stern, 2007).

In a very real sense, EBP is a way of putting critical thinking into systematic action, and this requires creating an atmosphere that encourages independent, critical thought. Thus, rather than simply teaching the mechanics of EBP, students must learn how to think critically and conceptually about the systematic information they have gathered and consider ways to apply it to important practice and policy decisions. Questioning

---

TABLE 170.1 Teaching EBP in the Classroom

1. Creating a culture of inquiry
   - Critical thinking
   - Socratic questioning
   - Exercises that highlight biases and inconsistencies
   - Exploration of ethical obligations to clients and the profession

2. Learning to live with uncertainty
   - Model uncertainty
   - Provide tools to dispel ignorance

3. Using a problem-based learning (PBL) framework
   - Small group format
   - Clinically integrated approach

4. Anticipating problem areas
   - Provide examples
   - Maintain student interest
   - Model several searches and appraisals
   - Series of small assignments

5. Expressing probabilities
   - NNT
   - Effect size

6. Starting with a single client

7. Build dynamic knowledge over time

the underlying assumptions we make about evidence and about clients is welcome—indeed, it is essential. Socratic questioning, if done in a manner that is not threatening (i.e., curious but demanding speculation), seems to set the tone from the very beginning. Such an approach is interactive and leads by example. Students tend to pick up this approach fairly quickly with each other and the instructor, making for very lively and stimulating discussions. Several exercises and discussions within the Socratic framework can help facilitate this process. These include:

- exercises that highlight perceptions of evidence (e.g., Gibbs & Gambrill, 1999);
- exercises that highlight cognitive and other biases in decision making (e.g., Gambrill, 2006);
- an accounting of social interventions that have been harmful;
- discussion of controversial findings from the literature; and
- communication of the ethical obligation to inform clients of the risks and benefits of a proposed course of action (Gambrill, 2003), which implies that such information has been systematically gathered and is known by the practitioner.

Learning to Live with Uncertainty

Social work students clearly want to be of service to their clients, and this may engender difficulties in the face of the inevitable uncertainty that arises when working with challenging, multiproblem client situations. There is often no single right path to successful assessment and treatment, and this is sometimes difficult for students to accept. An EBP approach does not shy away from such uncertainty. Rather, it embraces the unknown with curiosity and speculation. Thus, it is crucial that instructors model uncertainty and, rather than stopping with "I don't know," finding a way to generate the next level of inquiry. In particular, EBP insists on transparency of research findings and sharing ambiguous or uncertain findings with clients.

Using a Problem-Based Learning (PBL) Framework

Rather than relying solely on lectures, EBP best taught using a clinically integrated approach. PBL, as developed by McMaster University in Canada, uses a small group format (seven or eight stu-

dents) to present cases (these can be clinical, community, or policy oriented) and employs critical dialogue to identify knowledge gaps. In the interim between meetings, students individually use EBP methods to pose questions and find evidence, bringing information back to the group for further discussion and case plan development. Taking students through several examples, from initial assessment through the search and appraisal of evidence and then back to the client or policy question, provides ample opportunities to become more proficient at this process while maintaining student interest. Sometimes this can be accomplished using a combination of videos and written assignments (see, for example, Howard et al., 2003) where students are asked to make decisions that rely on their clinical or policy and evaluative skills. By linking instruction with real and/or realistic clients, students are trained to think critically in an applied way, and this process appears to improve knowledge, skills, attitudes, and behavior when compared to more standard forms of pedagogy in medical school (Coomarasamy & Khan, 2004). Hopefully, such educational success translates into a generation of life-long learners (Gray, 1997; Sackett et al., 1997) who will not be satisfied with knowledge that will soon be obsolete.

Anticipating Problem Areas

Question posing and developing a search strategy are deceptively difficult, especially the first time. Appraising studies can also be a challenge, especially for students who shy away from numbers or who become easily frustrated by the often technical language contained in scientific papers. Much care and attention must be spent at these crucial junctures. If a student has a bad experience with his or her first attempt at the steps of EBP, they lose interest and become dismissive of the entire process. There is nothing more frustrating for a student than to spend hours on a failed search. Some strategies for avoiding this pitfall include:

- providing numerous examples of answerable questions;
- relating questions directly to key practicum concerns or, in special circumstances, unique student interests;
- working individually with students to develop questions, especially focusing on clearly specifying their intervention and outcome terms;

- inviting a librarian or other search expert to demonstrate how to conduct EBP searches. This should include:
  - tours of the various subject-specific databases,
  - developing search terms,
  - use of Boolean operators,
  - use of wildcards, and
  - use of methodological filters by question type (see Gibbs, 2003);
- providing numerous examples of search strategies by question type;
- providing simple methodology appraisal forms and opportunities to practice evaluating study quality;
- encouraging students to first look for systematic reviews at the Campbell and Cochrane Collaborations;
- providing ample opportunity for students to ask for help; and
- segmenting larger assignments into smaller pieces to ensure that students are on target at each stage.

Expressing Probabilities

Students and clients often struggle with understanding and presenting findings from their reviews of the literature in real-world terms. One of the more important tools for translating research findings into readily understandable formulations of risk is number needed to treat (NNT). This tool is basically a reworking of absolute risk reduction (1/ARR) into a format that almost anyone can understand. NNT gives students the number of people that need to be treated to prevent one bad outcome. The other side of NNT, number needed to harm (NNH), can also be a useful tool. For instance, an intervention might have an absolute risk reduction of 0.2 (e.g., 40 percent of the treatment group relapsed and 60 percent of the control group relapsed), translating into an NNT of 5 (1/ARR = 1/0.2). Thus, for every 5 people who receive the treatment, 1 person who would have relapsed will remain healthy. This number takes into account the fact that some people who do not receive the treatment will remain healthy and some people in the treatment group will relapse, a point many people miss when thinking about treatment interventions. Spending considerable class time on this construct in an introductory course is both necessary and helpful. Although students might find such calculations difficult at first, their intuitive understanding of risk and benefit will be enhanced and, once mastered, NNT can be a powerful tool to use with clients. As well, effect size (measure of the magnitude of difference between groups in an intervention study) is an important construct for students to understand so they can fully appreciate the difference between statistical and real world significance (Shlonsky & Stern, 2004).

Starting with a Single Client

Critics of EBP often point out that social workers do not have the time to go through the five steps—such an approach is unrealistic. Although the techniques cited in this chapter and in this part of the volume substantially decrease time spent, as does repeated application, such criticisms do have merit. In all likelihood, it is unreasonable to follow the EBP process for every decision made. However, students can be encouraged to pick one client facing a problem that often occurs in the field placement setting. Over time and many such clients, a knowledge base can be generated that serves a far greater number.

INFUSING EBP ACROSS THE SOCIAL WORK CURRICULUM

EBP is not a single-semester endeavor and should not be presented to students as such. There is far too much information, the process must be practiced to adequate levels of speed and accuracy, and the proper integration of findings with specific clients, programs, and policies is a complex endeavor. Rather, it is a cumulative process that should be woven through all facets of the curriculum. This requires that schools and departments of social work must somehow become as facile as individual practitioners in adopting new approaches as evidence emerges.

Broad Strategies

There are several steps that should be considered when making such a transition (Table 170.2). Most important, the inclusive philosophy of EBP must be stressed. That is, similar to teaching in the classroom, the basic definition and steps of EBP must be clearly understood and conveyed to faculty. In addition, leaders (both internal and external) should be sought out and engaged to facilitate the adoption of innovation (Rogers, 1995). Incorporating the EBP framework into different

TABLE 170.2 Broad Strategies for Infusing EBP Across the Curriculum

1. Have the discussion—make sure you're all on the same page with respect to definitional issues. Identify and begin to deal with misunderstandings and disagreements, epistemological, and otherwise.
2. Identify and marshal internal resources with expertise and/or interest in EBP.
3. Identify external resources. Who can be brought in to objectively lead you through some of this process? An outside resource is sometimes less threatening and may be one way to avoid personal entanglements that are sure to arise.
4. Decide how the EBP framework can be used across curricular areas:
    a. Research
    b. Clinical practice
    c. Policy and management
    d. Community
    e. Social justice and diversity
5. Decide whether and how empirically supported treatments (ESTs) will be taught.
6. Decide how to involve the field.
7. Decide how to maintain curricular focus with adjuncts (especially important in large schools).

curricular areas can also be a challenge, especially areas that are traditionally resistant to empirical approaches. A narrow conceptualization of EBP, perceived or otherwise (e.g., that EBP amounts to using evidence from random clinical trials), may be translated as a thinly veiled attempt at foisting positivism on the entire faculty (Jenson, 2007). This must be avoided. With respect to distinguishing between EST's and EBP, faculty must decide on whether to train students in ESTs and practice guidelines, and which ESTs should be chosen.

Finally, decisions must be made about how to involve the field and maintain curricular focus among adjunct professors. An easy approach to involving practicum partners is to evolve a culture whereby students engage with field instructors and placement agencies to pose and begin answering critical questions of import to the field (Gibbs, 2003). For the field, conferences and trainings in EBP, ESTs and other content areas could help facilitate this process. Mostly, though, the field

will need to begin to see how having students using the steps of EBP can actually benefit their agencies through systematic efforts to uncover current best evidence in relevant practice areas. Still, some agencies will not want to have such light shed on their practices, and students will inevitably encounter placements using interventions or supporting policies that have little or no empirical basis (Howard, McMillen, & Pollio, 2003). This brings the student and classroom yet another opportunity to explore controversy and to strategize about how to facilitate change at the agency or policy level. Adjuncts must also be factored into the equation because they teach a large proportion of the classes. One strategy is to create an adjunct liaison position and coordinate instructional content across subject areas (Springer, 2007). Another strategy is to have full-time faculty members coordinate all sections of each class, ensuring that EBP content is infused courses.

Establishing an Introductory EBP Course

If EBP is to be woven throughout the curriculum, it must begin with the basics. Rather than the standard research class devoted to teaching students how to conduct research (a class where most students will neither learn enough to conduct good research nor develop a desire to try), why not introduce students to the process of EBP? In other words, change the curriculum to include an EBP class that touches on the various elements of research but is more practically geared toward systematically searching, understanding, appraising, and using the literature. The basics taught in this class can then be expanded and reinforced in subsequent core and specialization classes, including the basic tenets of research (e.g., basic study design, reliability, validity). Links to specific case examples in this and subsequent classes can help solidify learning. In this way, basic research methodology becomes a part of social work practice (Shlonsky & Stern, 2007).

Building on Courses and Assignments

Replication is the heart of science, and repetition is the heart of EBP. Repeating the process, using different client or policy questions, is essential to achieve a level of speed and proficiency that will enable students to continue the process on graduation. Moreover, EBP is, at its core, a lifelong learning process (Sackett, Richardson, Rosenberg,

& Haynes, 1997). Not only will the questions change as one practices, the evidence base will continue to grow and, in some cases, will change practice. One way to ease the pain of repetition is to envision classes as building on one another, much like general practice courses (i.e., moving from generalist practice in the first year to more specialized classes in the second). Although the basic EBP approach is unchanging in its methods, skills within the framework can be reinforced and expanded in subsequent classes as students begin to acquire greater practice skills. For instance, the first year of an MSW program can focus on the nuts and bolts of posing an answerable question, searching the literature, and appraising what is found. In the second year, content-specific courses include the process but focus more on integrating current best evidence with client preferences/actions and clinical state/circumstances. As well, the second-year classes include a more nuanced consideration of how other factors (e.g., training, organizational resources, political context) enhance or detract from the adoption of EBP, possibly influencing the process of individual and social change (Regehr, Stern, & Shlonsky, 2007).

Encouraging Single-Subject Design for Evaluation

For clinical interventions, N = 1 studies can be seen as the pinnacle of evaluating personal practice. They are the key to ascertaining whether interventions are working for clients. Advanced research classes would be well served by paying considerable attention to single-subject designs. Advanced clinical practice courses can also play a role in the fifth step of EBP by requiring students to formulate an evaluation plan as part of their coursework.

Developing Community Partnerships

Good community and agency partnerships are essential to the health of any school of social work, and this is no less the case as faculties move to embrace EBP. Key practice questions should drive research, and these are typically generated when practitioners and administrators notice a gap in knowledge. If research is not relevant to practice, its benefits are limited at best. EBP's bottom-up approach (Gibbs, 2003) requires that community and agency partners help drive the research agenda. To this end, community and agency partners should be encouraged to participate in and com-

mit to the development of EBP at the university through ongoing training/continuing education (e.g., ESTs) and capacity building. As well, processes should be developed whereby community and agency partners are encouraged to generate research questions and join with faculty to carry out new investigations.

Avoiding False Claims and Developing a Long-term Vision

EBP is an emerging approach and it will take considerable time, effort, and resources to make it work. EBP is not a quick fix for all that ails social work and the related helping professions. We must be honest about our current limitations, including the lack of evidence in some content areas, the confines of scarce agency resources and time, and the difficulty of integrating evidence with client context. We have a long way to go. Nonetheless, this wholesale shift in philosophy and practice is promising to the extent that clients will become increasingly well informed; are more likely to be offered high-quality, effective services; and will have greater attention paid to their desires and values.

WEB SITES

BEST training on evidence-based practice in social work at Columbia University. http://www.columbia.edu/cu/musher/Website/Website/EBP_OnlineTraining.htm.
Campbell Collaboration. http://campbellcollaboration.org.
Centre for Evidence-based Medicine, University of Toronto. http://www.cebm.utoronto.ca.
Cochrane Collaboration. http://www.cochrane.org.
Council on Social Work Education (CSWE) EBP page. http://www.cswe.org/CSWE/research/resources/Evidence-Based+Practice.
Evidence-Based Practice for the Helping Professions companion Web site for Gibbs (2003). http://www.evidence.brookscole.com.

References

Coomarasamy, A., & Khan, K. S. (2004). What is the evidence the evidence-based practice changes anything? A systematic review. *British Medical Journal, 329,* 1017–1021.

Gambrill, E. (2003). Evidence-based practice: Sea change or the emperor's new clothes? *Journal of Social Work Education, 39,* 3–23.

Gambrill, E. (2006). *Social work practice: A critical thinkers guide,* 2nd ed. New York: Oxford University Press.

Gibbs, L. (2003). *Evidence-based practice for the helping professions: A practical guide with integrated multimedia.* Pacific Grove, CA: Brooks/Cole-Thomson Learning.

Gibbs, L., & Gambrill, E. (1999). *Critical thinking for social workers: Exercises for the helping professions.* Thousand Oaks, CA: Pine Forge Press.

Gibbs, L. E., & Gambrill, E. (2002). Evidence-base practice: Counterarguments to objections. *Research on Social Work Practice, 12,* 452–476.

Gray, J. A. M. (1997). *Evidence-based healthcare: How to make health policy and management decisions.* New York: Churchill Livingstone.

Howard, M. O., McMillen, C., & Pollio, D. E. (2003). Teaching evidence-based practice: Toward a new paradigm for social work education. *Research on Social Work Practice, 13,* 234–259.

Jenson, J. M. (2007). Evidence-based practice and the reform of social work education: A response to Gambrill and Howard and Allen-Meares. *Research on Social Work Practice, 17,* 561–568.

Regehr, C., Stern, S., & Shlonsky, A. (2007). Operationalizing evidence-based practice: The development of an institute for evidence-based social work. *Research on Social Work Practice, 17,* 408–416.

Roberts, A. R., & Yeager, K. R. (Eds.). (2003). *Evidence-based practice manual.* New York: Oxford University Press.

Rogers, E. M. (1995). *Diffusion of innovation,* 4th ed. New York: Free Press.

Rosen, A., & Proctor, E. (Eds.). (2003). *Developing practice guidelines for social work intervention: Issues, methods, and research agenda.* New York: Columbia University Press.

Sackett, D. L., Richardson, W. S., Rosenberg, W., & Haynes, R. B. (1997). *Evidence-based medicine: How to practice and teach EBM.* New York: Churchill Livingstone.

Shlonsky, A., & Gibbs, L. (2004). Will the real evidence-based practice please step forward: Teaching the process of EBP to the helping professions. *Journal of Brief Therapy and Crisis Intervention, 4,* 137–153.

Shlonsky, A., & Stern, S. (2007). Reflections of the teaching of evidence-based practice. *Research on Social Work Practice, 17,* 603–611.

Springer, D. W. (2007). The teaching of evidence-based practice in social work higher education—living by the Charlie Parker dictum: A response to papers by Shlonsky and Stern, and Soydan. *Research on Social Work Practice, 17,* 619–624.

171 N = 1 Experiments and Their Role in Evidence-Based Practice

Bruce A. Thyer & Laura L. Myers

From the inception of evidence-based practice (EBP), authorities in this field have advocated that clinicians consider undertaking a type of experimental study they labeled the N = 1 randomized controlled trials (RCTs). The primary reference book *Evidence-based Medicine: How to Practice and Teach EBM* (Strauss, Richardson, Glasziou, & Haynes, 2005) includes a positive description of this type of design:

The n-of-1 trial applies the principles of rigorous clinical trial methodology to . . . determine the best treatment for an individual patient. It randomizes time, and assigns the patient . . . active therapy or placebo at different times, so that the patient undergoes cycles of experimental and control treatment, resulting in multiple crossovers to help both our patient and us to decide on the best therapy. (Strauss et al., 2005, p. 172)

The experimental logic of the N = 1 RCT can perhaps be best illustrated with an example. A child has been diagnosed with hyperactivity and a physician has prescribed a medication to help calm him down. The parents doubt that drugs will be helpful and are resistant to following this treatment recommendation. However, with the helpful intervention of a social worker, they agree to give it a try for several weeks on an experimental basis. Two identical bottles of pills are prepared, one bottle is labeled A and contains (unknown to the parents or child) the active medicine, whereas bottle B contains similar-looking pills lacking any active ingredient (e.g., a placebo). The social worker arranges for the teacher to rate the child's behavior in school at the end of each day, using a valid behavior rating scale. Flipping a coin, the social worker assigns the child to receive either pill A (heads) or pill B (tails) each day for a 2-week period. The social worker prepares a simple line graph, with behavior ratings scored on the vertical axis, and the days of the week on the horizontal one. The ratings for the days pill A is administered are plotted and connected, and the ratings for pill B are similarly portrayed. If there is no overlap in the two sets of lines, and the ratings during the days the child received the active medication are unambiguously those in which behavior was improved, then clear and compelling evidence of a genuinely experimental nature has demonstrated the superiority of the active drug over placebo.

This type of demonstration has several functions. First, we have empirical proof that the drug is helpful with this individual client, which is, after all, a highly desirable outcome of practicing EBP. Second, the evidence may alleviate the parents' reservations about using medication, and help them decide to continue its use. This example presupposes that the medication has no significant side effects, is not unreasonably expensive, that taking it is not prohibited by the family's religious beliefs, and so on. If the two sets of lines connecting the two different treatment conditions had significant overlap, then the effects of the active drug versus placebo would be less clear. Completely overlapping lines would suggest that the medicine was little better than placebo and need not be used at all. This is also good to know.

Within the field of psychotherapy, this type of design is called the alternating treatments design (ATD; Barlow & Hayes, 1979). In January 2008, we searched the PsycINFO database using "alternating treatments design" as key words appearing in journal abstracts and found over 200 published examples of its use across a wide array of disciplines, including audiology, medicine, education, and psychology. An ADT was used by social worker Steven Wong to help empirically determine how one's immediate environmental situation affected the psychotic-like behavior of person suffering from chronic mental illness (Wong et al., 1987). The client, Tom, was a 37-year-old man with a diagnosis of chronic schizophrenia who was experiencing his fourth hospitalization. Systematic assessments of Tom's psychotic-like mumblings were tape recorded via a wireless microphone attached to his shirt for five sessions of unstructured free time in the hospital day room where he had access to usual recreational materials (e.g., television, stereo, magazines, books, table games, cards, etc.) but was otherwise left alone. The subsequent experimental phase consisted of randomly alternating between two interventions, a 40-minute session in the day room begun by prompting the client to read articles he found interesting from an assortment of novel magazines offered to him, versus spending 40 minutes in the room without any reading prompting or access to novel magazines (identical to the original baseline condition). These two treatments were randomly alternated for 18 consecutive sessions, and the percent of time Tom spent engaged in stereotypic laughter and mumbling, reliably recorded, was the dependent variable (outcome measure). The results are depicted in Figure 171.1. It is very clear that when Tom was given something interesting to do (e.g., reading) his psychotic-like behavior was markedly reduced, relative to having unstructured free time. There is no overlap in the two sets of data, providing compelling evidence that the simple intervention was causally responsible for these behavioral differences. Because a clear causal inference is possible via the intentional manipulation of the intervention and control conditions, this N = 1 randomized controlled trial can be legitimately classified as a true experiment.

Within the field of EBP, such randomized N = 1 trials are held in such high esteem that it has been claimed that these studies provide a *stronger* foundation for making decisions about the care of individuals than does the evidence derived from

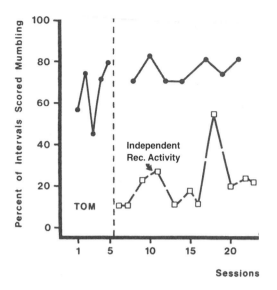

Figure 171.1 Percentage of intervals scored mumbling or solitary laughter in baseline sessions (circles) and in recreation sessions with independent activity (squares). From Wong et al. (1987, p. 80) with permission from the Society for the Experimental Analysis of Behavior.

systematic reviews, meta-analyses, individual RCTs, and other evidentiary sources (see Guyatt et al., 2002, p. 12)! This certainly turns the usual apex of the evidentiary hierarchy on its head! But recall the definition of EBP: "The conscientious, explicit, and judicious use of current best evidence in making decisions about the care of *individual patients*" (Straus et al., 2005, p. 280, emphasis added). What better evidence regarding the appropriateness of a given intervention than a clear and compelling demonstration that it really seems to work with *our client*? Large-scale group studies very rarely make use of true probability samples, a prerequisite for generalizing findings, and in any case probability theory only permits inferences upward from sample to population, not downward from a sample (as in an RCT) to an individual.

CAN N = 1 STUDIES REALLY BE CALLED EXPERIMENTS?

Within the social work research literature, the term "experiment" is almost exclusively reserved for nomothetic studies involving relatively large groups of clients who are randomly assigned to receive an experimental psychosocial intervention, to a no-treatment condition, to treatment-as-usual, or to a placebo-control group. Pretreatment assessments may be used, and posttreatment assessments are essential to make any inferences about possible differential effects of the conditions to which the clients were exposed. Any posttreatment differences may be plausibly ascribed to their assigned condition (e.g., to the active or experimental treatment) as opposed to some rival explanation (e.g., passage of time, regression to the mean, concurrent history, etc.). Such designs have the potential to possess high internal validity in that any conclusions drawn about the relative effects of the experimental conditions can be seen as quite credible, with the random assignment feature controlling for other possibilities. Such designs are called RCTs and can indeed be quite powerful.

However, traditional RCT methodology is often required in social work intervention research only because of the large amount of variance present in our studies. Frequently the independent variable (e.g., treatment) exerts modest effects at best and may be quite labile, readily influenced by client idiosyncrasy or environmental contextual factors. In other words, our interventions are often not robust. Dependent variables (e.g., outcome measures) may lack precision, being subject to various forms of bias, and contain a large amount of noise or unexplained variation as well. These factors essentially *require* the use of sophisticated inferential statistics to separate out the "real" effects of treatment from the noise and also necessitate studies having sufficiently large sample sizes to possess adequate statistical power to accomplish this task. But keep in mind that nomothetic research designs and inferential statistics are just one set of tools to accomplish experimental demonstrations. Extremely powerful treatments do not require such sophisticated controls because their effects are obvious and compelling, swamping the sometimes unwanted variance caused by client and context.

Table 171.1 provides some descriptions of what is meant by the term "experiment" in its broader sense. The crucial factor that distinguishes the true experiment from other forms of research is the deliberate, planned manipulation of an intervention, and the systematic observation of its possible effects. Sample size has no bearing on the validity of this principle. Such an experimental study may involve 1,000 participants, 100, 10, or even only 1. The crucial test is whether clear effects can be observed. If the answer is yes, you have a legitimate demonstration of the value of the treatment, that is, an experiment. If not, one is faced with two possibilities. One is that the treatment simply does not work. The second is that the treatment "works," but its effects are so minimal that they could not be detected with the research design and sample size used.

Studies involving small groups of clients (or even only one client) minimize Type I experimental errors (claims that a real effect is present, when it is really not) but are more liable to Type II errors (claiming that an effect is not present, when it really is). Studies with sizable groups minimize Type II errors (they are less likely to miss small but reliable effects of treatments) and are more liable to make Type I errors (claiming that an effect occurs, when it really does not). The use of p values derived from inferential tests, absent reporting their associated effect sizes, promotes Type I errors in nomothetic research. We learn more about reliable, albeit trivial, effects. Reporting effect sizes

can help reduce this problem. Conversely, N = 1 studies are not very good at detecting small effects of our treatments (that is, are prone to Type II errors), and some researchers consider this a good thing, in that we are less liable to claim positive effects for trivially effective interventions, channeling our energies into pursing treatments with powerful, robust effects. Usually the data from N = 1 studies are graphically depicted and inferences are made on the basis of visual inspection alone. If they cannot be seen by the naked eye, unaided by inferential statistics, then the conservative researcher concludes that any reliable effects are of such small magnitude as to be of little clinical importance. This means that conclusions derived from N = 1 research tend to be more robust, in terms of internal validity because confident conclusions are rare, absent visually compelling evidence, such as that displayed in Figure 171.1.

OTHER FORMS OF EXPERIMENTAL N = 1 DESIGNS

The N-of-1 RCT or ATD is not the only type of within-client research design that can be applied to evaluate the effects of interventions with individual clients. Other selected N = 1 designs may also permit robust conclusions using the same logic applied with the ATD, namely, repeated demonstrations of an effect, following the introduction or removal of a treatment. In the ATD this introduction or removal of a treatment condition is dictated by the toss of a coin. If the outcome measure reliably fluctuates in a manner closely consistent with the manipulation of the treatment, we have

TABLE 171.1 Some Definitions of the Term Experiment

- "A study in which an intervention is deliberately introduced to observe its effects" (Shadish, Cook, & Campbell, 2002, p. 12).
- "One or more independent variables are manipulated to observe their effects on one or more dependent variables" (Shadish et al., 2002, p. 12).
- "The manipulation of one or more independent variables conduced under controlled conditions to test one ore more hypotheses, especially for making inferences of a cause-effect character. Involves the management of one or more dependent variables" (Corsini, 2002, p. 351).
- "Manipulations of subject and/or intervention is the essence of experimental method. . . . The demands of science and of practice have lead to a whole array of experiments. They include experiments designed . . . with the subjects serving as controls for themselves" (Wollins, 1960, p. 255).
- "N of 1 RCT An experiment in which there is only a single participant, designed to determine the effect of an intervention or exposure on that individual" (Guyatt & Rennie, 2002, p. 418).

increasing confidence that these outcome fluctu-ations can be attributed to the treatment itself, or to its removal. The more such demonstrations, the greater the internal validity.

Similar simple logic is the basis for causal in-ference in a type of N = 1 study called the ABAB design. Here, A refers to a period of time when the client received no formal treatment. The time pe-riod could conceivably be hours, days, weeks, or months, depending on the nature of the problem and circumstance surrounding it. During this A or baseline phase, a credible outcome measure is ad-ministered a number of times, and the data are plot-ted on a line graph, with time on the horizontal axis and the outcome measure scaled on the ver-tical axis. Ideally, the first baseline line is long enough to obtain data that are visually stable, for example, not obviously getting better (it is okay if they are getting worse). Then the treatment is introduced, and the outcome measure continues to be assessed. Ideally, one sees an immediate im-provement after the treatment begins during this second, or B, phase. The data continue to be plot-ted and these improvements themselves stabilize. Thus far, one has completed an AB N = 1 study, one that possesses only one apparent demonstra-tion of a functional relationship between in the in-troduction of a treatment and client improvement. Unfortunately, only one such demonstration does not usually qualify a study to be labeled as a true experiment. A number of rival explanations can-not be ruled out with this simple design, for ex-ample, concurrent history, regression, placebo, the problem may have a cyclic nature, and so on. To help rule out such threats, the intervention, B, is withdrawn or removed, and the baseline condi-tion are reinstated (the second A phase). Ideally the client relapses—ideally, that is, from the per-spective of providing an experimental demonstra-tion. If this happens, then we now enjoy two dem-onstrations of an apparent functional relationship between the treatment and the problem—one when the treatment was introduced (the client got bet-ter) and the second when the treatment was re-moved (the client got worse).

The second A phase is then followed by the re-introduction of the treatment for a period of time comprising the second B phase. Ideally, the client improves once again, leaving the social worker with three solid demonstrations of experimental con-trol of outcome by the treatment—twice when the treatment was introduced (the client got better) and once when the treatment was removed (the

client got worse). When graphically depicted, with obvious demarcations in the data between the four phases of the study, this is usually a very convinc-ing demonstration of the effects of treatment. The inferential logic remains the same between the ABAB design and the ATD, repeatedly introduc-ing the treatment or its removal. Strong effects are evident to practitioners, clients, and neutral ob-servers alike. Absent strong effects (for example, in the case of only minor changes in the data, or con-siderable overlap in the range of data between ad-jacent phases), the same conservative principles suggest that one conclude the intervention is not clinically valuable. Again, Type II error is more likely (you will miss minor but reliable effects) and Type I error minimized (you are very unlikely to conclude that a strong effect is present, when it is really not).

The possible permutations of these simple prin-ciples are numerous. A further demonstration may be possible, as in the ABABAB design. One may try to compare the relative efficacy of two inter-ventions, as in the ABAC design. These types of n = 1 designs relying on changes in the data co-incident with the introduction of the treatment and its *removal* are obviously only possible for interventions with short-lived effects. If a treat-ment can be expected to produce a durable improve-ment, then the ABAB design will not be useful, be-cause the relapse anticipated during the second B phase with not be forthcoming. Example of such interventions may include teaching the client a social or intellectual skill, the attainment of per-sonal insight (perhaps via psychotherapy), per-sonal growth or strengthening of psychological resources, the removal of phobic fears or obsessive-compulsive behaviors, or acquiring a cognitive cop-ing skill (e.g., rationale self-talk). Discontinuing such an intervention will not necessarily obliterate any clinical gains made by the client, and thus the ABAB design, or other N = 1 study that de-pends on client relapse occurring following the re-moval of a treatment for causal inferences to be made about the effects of treatment is not usually a suitable N = 1 design in such circumstances.

When one is applying a treatment that is ex-pected to produce not only immediate but also du-rable effects, another form of N = 1 experimen-tal called the multiple baseline (MBL) design may be possible. The MBL also relies on the same logic as other experimental clinical research designs—repeatedly demonstrating that an effect is observed when a treatment is applied. There are various types of MBL designs, and one of the more common is MBL across clients. This design requires that you have two or more clients seeking treatment about the same point in time, with a similar problem, for which you believe a particular treatment is appropriate. Let's use as an example two clients who present for help in overcoming a specific phobia. You begin with a baseline phase for both clients, having searched the literature and located one (or more) credible outcome measures. When each client has stability in their baseline data (the A phase), you begin treatment (say, gradual real-life exposure therapy) for client 1 (transitioning into the B phase) but *not* for client 2 (who remains in the A phase). The internal validity of this design depends on seeing rapid improvements in client 1 but *not* in client 2. Some time passes, client 1 continues to improve, and you then begin treating client 2 with a similar program of exposure therapy (the B phase). Imagine two AB designs stacked atop each other, with the lower one having a longer baseline, but each having stable baseline data, and marked improvement only when treatment begins during the B phase. This approach in effect permits two possible demonstrations of experimental control, each time when the treatment was applied to two different clients. Two demonstrations is much better than one (as in a simple AB design), and three such demonstrations, as in an MBL design across three clients, approaches the internal validity of the ABAB design (which also can yield three demonstrations).

A second form of MBL is called the MBL across settings design, and it may be used to determine the effects of one particular therapy on one problem experienced by one client in different contexts. As an example, suppose a child client displayed hyperactive behavior, in the home, and in the school, and this was posing a significant problem for the child. In the MBL across settings design, baselines would be taken of hyperactive behavior in the two settings, and displayed on two stacked AB-type graphs depicted. When the baseline data are stable in both settings, an intervention (say, a point system to reward in-seat behavior) is initiated in one setting only, say, the school, whereas the baseline condition is maintained in the other setting (the home). Experimentally, one desires to see immediate improvements in the first setting, and stable, problematic conditions continuing in the second one. Then, after some time, the same intervention is applied in the other setting, with, it is hoped, a similar positive effect. This design also

constitutes providing two demonstrations of experimental control, an improvement over only one, and adding a third setting for baselining and intervention enhances internal validity event further.

The third and final form of MBL design is the MBL across problems design, and it may be useful in clinical situations wherein one client presents with two or more problems potentially amenable to treatment by the same intervention. Imagine a child doing poorly in two subjects at school, arithmetic and reading. With the cooperation of the teacher, the social worker gets regular reports of the child's grades in each of these two subjects. These grades are separately baselined, and then an intervention, say, tutoring, is provided in *one* subject, but not in the second, which continues to be baselined. Experimentally, one wishes to see that the first academic subject (for which tutoring was provided) displayed immediate and marked improvements in grades, whereas the second subject remained stable (with poor grades). Then the same intervention, tutoring, is provided to the second subject, which then also immediately displays a sharp improvement in grades. Again, the logic is the same, with two or more demonstrations of an effect—the problem is stable, an intervention is applied, and the problem is significantly improved. The MBL across three or more problems is even more convincing than with only two, and in certain circumstances, for example, clear data, a valid outcome measure, and treatments that can be deliberately introduced, the social worker is capable of providing genuinely experimental results, outcomes so compelling that most doubts are removed as to the effectiveness of the intervention.

In any research design, nomothetic or N = 1, poor results mean that experimental control has not been demonstrated, and internal validity is low. But if powerful effects are exerted by the treatment, these can be compellingly disclosed in N = 1 studies. The ATD is one N = 1 study with the potential to demonstrate internally valid conclusions. N = 1 studies using withdrawal designs, such as the ABAB, or the various forms of MBL designs, are also capable of permitting causal inferences. There is no claim that the experimental N = 1 studies can be applied in every clinical situation, but certainly their versatility permits far greater use than they have heretofore enjoyed as a method of evaluating clinical outcomes in social work practice. And N = 1 designs of lesser internal validity, such as the B, AB, or ABA types (see Thyer & Myers, 2007) are even more readily

TABLE 172.2 Some Indications for Considering N = 1 Experiments in Evidence-Based Practice

- Is there a way to reliably and validly assess the client's problem/condition, e.g., a credible outcome measure is available? (The answer should be yes)
- Can the outcome measure be repeatedly assessed over time? (The answer should be yes)
- Are the effects of social work intervention likely to have a rapid onset? (The answer should be yes)
- Is using an N = 1 design ethically acceptable? (The answer should be yes)
- Is participating in an N = 1 design acceptable to the client? (The answer should be yes)
- Is the intervention feasible? (The answer should be yes)
- Will the effects of intervention likely be durable or permanent? If yes, then a multiple baseline design may be indicated. If not, then a withdrawal or alternating treatments design may be most useful.

applicable in everyday practice. The use of N = 1 studies within social work is not of hypothetical value. A bibliography on the topic (Thyer & Thyer, 1992) prepared 17 years ago found over 200 published examples.

EBP has long advocated that practitioners evaluate the effects of their interventions using experimental N = 1 research designs. Thus far the EBP literature in this regard has given limited attention to one type of N = 1 study, the alternating treatments design. However there is a more diverse array of N = 1 designs that have the potential to yield truly experimental results, and these deserve serious consideration by the social worker seeking to practice within the model known as evidence-based practice. Table 171.2 list some pragmatic indications for considering using an N = 1 study to evaluate outcomes in evidence-based practice.

WEB SITES

Campbell Collaboration. http://www .campbellcollaboration.org.
Center for Evidence-based Medicine. http:// www.cebm.utoronto.ca.
Cochrane Collaboration. http://www.cochrane .org.

References

Barlow, D. H., & Hayes, S. C. (1979). Alternating treatments design: One strategy for comparing the effects of two treatments in a single subject. *Journal of Applied Behavior Analysis, 12,* 199–210.

Corsini, R. J. (2002). *The dictionary of psychology.* New York: Brunner-Routledge.

Guyatt, G., B. Haynes, B., Jaeschke, R., Cook, D., Greenhalgh, T., Meade, M., et al. (2002). Introduction: The philosophy of evidence-based medicine. In G. Guyatt & D. Rennie (Eds.), *Users' guides to the medical literature* (pp. 5–71. Chicago: AMA Press.

Guyatt, G., & Rennie, D. (Eds.). (2002). *Users' guides to the medical literature.* Chicago: AMA Press.

Shadish, W. R., Cook, T. D., & Campbell, D. T. (2002). *Experimental and quasi-experimental designs for generalized causal inference.* New York: Houghton Mifflin.

Strauss, S. E., Richardson, W. S., Glasziou, P., & Haynes, R. B. (2005). *Evidence-based medicine: How to practice and teach EBM.* New York: Elsevier.

Thyer, B. A., & Myers, L. L. (2007). *The social worker's guide to evaluating practice outcomes.* Alexandria, VA: CSWE Press.

Thyer, B. A., & Thyer, K. B. (1992). Single-system research designs used in social work practice: A bibliography from 1965–1990. *Research on Social Work Practice, 2,* 99–116.

Wollins, M. (1960). Measuring the effect of social work intervention. In N. Polansky (Ed.), *Social work research* (pp. 247–272). Chicago: University of Chicago Press.

Wong, S. E., Terranova, M. D., Bowen, L., Zarate, R., Massel, H. K., & Liberman, R. P. (1987). Providing independent recreational activities to reduce stereotypic vocalizations in chronic schizophrenics. *Journal of Applied Behavior Analysis, 20,* 77–81.

GLOSSARY

Compiled by Mallory Jensen

AB design: A single-system research design for comparing client functioning during treatment (i.e., the intervention or B phase) with client functioning before treatment (i.e., the baseline or A phase). The AB design is used to monitor client change and evaluate treatment outcomes.

ABC model: Originally devised by Albert Ellis, this model inserts cognition as a mediating factor between people's experiences and their emotional/behavioral responses to those experiences. *A*ctivating events are followed by *b*eliefs that result in *c*onsequences of emotions and behaviors.

Access to care: The opportunity for consumers to obtain needed services, with attention to such issues as the location of service, hours of operation, and affordable fees.

Accountability: Providing information, in useful form, to others who must make decisions or take action regarding a person, case, situation, agency, or community. A social worker may be accountable to a supervisor, community, clients, the court, a board of directors, the profession, and others. Being accountable means being responsible for providing services in accordance with high standards.

Actuarial risk assessment: An empirically derived estimation of the likelihood of maltreatment recurrence over time; it has consistently demonstrated higher levels of reliability and validity when compared to consensus-based approaches and clinical judgment in estimating the probability of recurrences.

Adaptedness: A favorable person-in-environment fit that supports human growth and well-being, and preserves and enriches the environment.

Adverse effect: The physical, psychological, or social effect of an intervention that is unintentional and unrelated to its desired actions.

Advocacy: To speak up in favor of an issue, to plead the case for another, or to champion a cause, often for individuals and groups that cannot speak out on their own behalf. Types of advocacy include self-advocacy, case advocacy (for an individual client), and class advocacy (on behalf of a group or category of individuals in similar circumstances).

Affordable housing: Housing for which the occupant generally pays no more than 30 percent of gross income for rent.

Age-specific intervention: An intervention based on empirical studies designed specifically to treat older persons' problems.

Aggressive outreach: Direct and intensive services that occur in the consumer's home and natural community.

Alliances/coalitions: In a family or group, relationships formed between two or more individuals that serve a specific function in influencing interpersonal dynamics

Allocation concealment: Disguising group assignment, particularly upcoming assignments, in clinical studies. Without it, even properly developed random allocation sequences can be subverted.

Ambiguity in therapy: Forms of speech, metaphors, imagery, body movements, and so on, that stimulate a search process in the listeners to find their own relevant meanings.

Anger outburst: Extreme display of emotion characterized by irritability, physical or verbal attack, and rage with negativism that is considered maladaptive when it occurs without an immediate catalyst.

Anorexia nervosa: A disorder characterized by self-induced starvation and severe fear of gaining weight and looking fat, resulting in medical symptoms related to starvation.

Antecedent: An environmental event or stimulus that precedes a response. When the antecedent signals that a response is or is not likely to be followed by a reinforcer, it is referred to as a discriminative stimulus.

Anxiety-management technique: Behavioral processes such as progressive relaxation training, guided self-dialogue, and thought stopping, aimed at teaching clients to reduce and cope with debilitating anxiety.

Anxiolytics: A class of drugs that reduce anxiety; also known as minor tranquilizers.

Arbitration: A conflict resolution process conducted by a neutral third party, who can impose a legally binding decision if the disputants cannot agree.

Assertive community treatment (ACT): An evidence-based service delivery model in which the same clinical team, using largely outreach methods, provides comprehensive community-based treatment, rehabilitation, and supportive services to persons with severe and persistent mental illness. This model is also known as PACT, or Program of Assertive Community Treatment.

Assessment: The process of systematically collecting data about a client's functioning and monitoring progress in client functioning on an ongoing basis. In this way, social workers identify and measure specific problem behaviors as well as protective and resilience factors, and to determine whether treatment is necessary. Information is typically gathered from a variety of sources (e.g., individual, family members, case records, observation, rapid assessment tools). Types of assessment include biopsychosocial history taking, multidimensional crisis assessment, symptom checklists, functional analysis, behavioral measurement, and mental status exams.

Asset development: The process of assisting families or individuals in gaining wealth by building capital through home ownership, savings accounts, retirement accounts, and investment portfolios.

Assisted suicide: Hastening one's death, in the face of a life-threatening illness or debilitating condition, with aid from another person. This term is generally used to refer to actions taken by a physician, but the assistance (which is illegal in some states) can also be from other health professionals, friends, or family members.

Attention deficit/hyperactivity disorder (ADHD): A persistent pattern of inattention, hyperactivity, and impulsivity in two or more settings (e.g., school, work, or home). The *DSM-IV-TR* lists three subtypes: combined type, predominantly hyperactive-impulsive type, and predominantly inattentive type (which most closely resembles what was previously termed attention deficit disorder, or ADD).

Authority theme: Issues having to do with to the relationship between the client (individual, family, or group) and the social worker.

Awareness: A growing consciousness and developing internal knowledge of self through thoughts, sensations, feelings, actions, and memories, and an external attentiveness to others and the environment.

Baseline: The assessment phase of practice, when the frequency of a specific behavior, client functioning, or attitudes are measured over time prior to an intervention.

Behavioral experiment: The identification and test of the validity of a client's thoughts through enactments in actual life experience or through role-plays.

Behavioral family therapy: Family therapies that emphasize reinforcing and punishing family relationships with one another and with the social environment. These therapies are action-oriented and focus on learning new skills that modify behavioral functioning and reframe and alter cognitive perceptions.

Behavioral observation: The process of carefully defining an overt activity or event and tracking the frequency, intensity, or duration of its occurrence. Behaviors should be specified in detail so that others can accurately count the same behavior in the same way.

Behavioral social work: A research-based treatment approach founded on learning theory, which holds that much behavior is learned through contingencies of reinforcement and/or punishment. Consequently, problematic behavior can be possibly be unlearned and prosocial behavior can be learned to replace it. Specific, measurable behaviors are the targets for intervention. A behavioral assessment is first done to identify what environmental changes are needed to modify problematic behavior. A treatment plan is then developed for changing the contingencies of reinforcement and/or punishment. The target behavior is measured in a baseline period and then monitored throughout the treatment process once intervention begins.

Best practice: A technique or methodology that, through empirical research, has proven in the past to reliably lead to a desired result.

Biopsychosocial model: An attempt to integrate a vision of a client as a person, in situation, not unlike the social work concept of person–environment fit. This model recognizes that biological factors are necessary but not sufficient for understanding a human person in a social world. Although psychosocial factors such as stress, anxiety, and depression may underpin many conditions, some disorders may be understood to be truly biopsychosocial. There is a known genetic basis to many illnesses, but it is understood that social and environmental triggers must be present to bring about the potential illness. Therefore, this term is applied to phenomena that consist of biological, psychological, and social elements.

Biopsychosocial-cultural assessment: A comprehensive assessment model that ascertains the influence and interplay of biology, psychology, learnings, social environmental, and cultural factors on a client's mental health. It is the basis of the multiaxial diagnostic system of the *DSM*.

Bipolar I: A level of depression characterized by presence of episodes of major depressive disorder and at least one documented manic or mixed episode.

Bipolar II: A level of depression characterized by at least one major depressive episode that is accompanied by at least one hypomanic episode.

Blocking: A worker intervention that prevents the execution of undesirable, unethical, or inappropriate behaviors by the group as a whole or individual members.

Borderline personality disorder: A pervasive pattern of instability of interpersonal relationships, self-image, and affects, along with a marked impulsivity that begins by early adulthood and is present in a variety of contexts. People with BPD have among the highest suicide, attempted suicide, and mental health utilization rates of those with any psychiatric disorder.

Boundaries: The spoken and unspoken rules that case managers and clients observe about the physical and emotional limits of their relationship.

Boundary-spanning role: The part played by agency practitioners who have the capability and responsibility to make connections with other organizations and agencies in the community. This promotes coordination and joint effort on behalf of clients.

Brief treatment: An approach to working with clients that acknowledges up front that there is a time limit to treatment. Models vary and may include specific session limits (for example, up to 12 sessions) or time limits (for example, up to 3 months).

Broker: A case manager who conducts assessment, develops care plans, and makes referrals to provider agencies for services. Brokers cannot authorize or purchase services for their clients.

Bulimia nervosa: A pattern of binge eating combined with attempts to avoid weight gain, such as purging, alternate calorie restriction, laxative use, and/or overexercise.

Bullying: Attacking an individual, often on the basis of a perceived difference or vulnerability; usually associated with school and workplace attacks.

Capacity building: A strengths-based approach to community building that involves preparing and supporting staff, natural helpers, and parents to increasing their skills and knowledge for personal, organizational, professional, and family center development. Critical to capacity building is gaining access to needed resources and services.

Capitation: A method of financing health and mental health programs common in many managed care plans, in which providers agree to offer a specified package of services for a predetermined cost. The payment is most often made on a monthly basis. The provider is responsible for delivering or arranging for the delivery of a designated range of health care services for this predetermined payment, regardless of actual cost of the services. There is concern by social workers that high-risk, high-user, vulnerable populations will be disadvantaged under capitated arrangements.

Caregiver: One who provides services to a client in the home or immediate community environment. This may be a family member, a community member, or a paid provider.

Care planning: A process, including clients and caregivers, that translates information collected during assessment into a plan of care, identifying services to be delivered, formal and informal providers, frequency of service delivery, and cost. Care planning is a resource-allocation process.

Caring: One element of the construct "working relationship;" the client's sense that the worker is concerned about him or her and that the worker wishes to help with those concerns the client believes are important.

Case management: A service that links and coordinates assistance from institutions and agencies providing medical, psychosocial, and concrete support for individuals in need of such assistance. It is the process of social work intervention that helps people organize and use the supports, services, and opportunities that enable them to achieve life outcomes that they value. Additionally, it is a direct practice method that involves skills in assessment, counseling, teaching, and advocacy that aims to improve the social functioning of clients served. In this service concept, clients are provided both individualized counseling and are linked to other needed services and supports.

Case record: A written and authenticated compilation of information that describes and documents the assessment and present, past, and prospective services to the consumer.

CAT (Critically Appraised Topic): A brief (one-page) description of a well-structured question, search strategy, related research found, critical appraisal of what is found, and clinical bottom line.

Catharsis: The emotional relief experienced following the process of revealing one's inner anxieties and conflicts. For adults, this can occur through talking about one's problems; for children, this relief can occur through play containing elements of the conflict and anxiety.

Change activist: Someone who acts in an attempt to make a change on another person or community's behalf and may charge a modest fee (e.g., ministers, priests, spiritualists, and folk healers).

Change strategy: The action taken to pursue a desired change based on (1) what is most likely to influence decision makers and allies to make the desired change, and (2) what is possible given the time and resources available.

Change tactics: The actions or events that implement change strategy.

Change target: The person or group that must consent for a change to occur.

Child abuse and neglect: The physical or mental injury, sexual abuse, negligent treatment, or maltreatment of a person under the age of 18.

Child protection mediation: A conflict resolution process in which an impartial third party assists parents, children, child protection workers, extended family members, foster parents, or others to resolve conflict in cases involving child abuse or neglect (also called "dependency mediation").

Child support: Provision of financial resources by the parent who does not have primary custody of the child to meet the daily needs of the child.

Circular causality: A repetitive pattern of interaction between two or more individuals that results in an undesirable outcome for one or more of those involved. The term may also refer to a systems perspective that focuses on the mutual influences and interpersonal contexts in which problems develop.

Class action suit: A court action filed on behalf of named parties as well as a larger number of persons who are said to be "similarly situated" (in comparable circumstances).

Client-monitored behaviors: Actions, thoughts, or feelings that clients track over time. More easily identifiable behaviors tend to be both recognizable by clients and more accurately reported than those they perform automatically or subconsciously.

Clinical algorithm: Schematic diagrams outlining the decision pathways described in a practice guideline. The diagram is usually formatted in a decision-tree format, with yes/no options presented at each decision point.

Clinical case management: An approach to human service delivery that integrates elements of clinical social work and traditional case management practices. The social worker combines the sensitivity and interpersonal skill of the psychotherapist with the creativity and action orientation of the environmental architect.

Clinical expertise: The integration of current best research evidence, client preferences and actions, and clinical state and circumstances.

Clinical social work: This practice area includes case advocacy, case management, psychotherapy, clinical supervision, teamwork, behavior analysis and therapy, and program development. Therefore, clinical social work practice emphasizes direct work with individuals, families, and small groups, but is not limited to psychotherapeutic models and practices.

Clinical syndrome: A cluster of symptoms and behaviors that are defined as a mental disorder. Clinical syndromes are diagnosed on axis I of the *DSM-IV-TR* system.

Cluster randomized trial: A trial in which groups or areas are assigned a condition at random. May be used when an intervention can only be administered to the group (e.g., a public education campaign), to avoid contamination (e.g., by assigning schools rather than children or classrooms) or to reduce effort and save money.

Coalition: An organization of organizations formed for a common purpose or social agenda, while each maintains its own identity. Coalitions have a series of inherent dynamic tensions that need to be balanced: cooperation and conflict, unity and diversity, mixed loyalties, and accountability and autonomy.

Code of ethics: A formal document ratified by a group or organization containing ethical principles, guidelines, and standards. The most frequently adopted code of ethics for social workers has been approved by NASW, and is called the NASW Code of Ethics.

Cognitive bias: An unconscious tendency to distort one's views in a certain direction.

Cognitive distortion: Attitudes, thoughts, or beliefs that are irrational or illogical.

Cognitive elaboration: The generation of alternative conceptualizations of a given event, phenomenon, or stimulus condition. This process is completed in recognition that multiple meanings exist for all human experience.

Cognitive restructuring: The use of logic and evidence to modify cognitions and cognitive processing. Socratic dialogue, guided imagery, and behavioral experiments are typical approaches associated with the cognitive behavior therapy approach.

Cognitive-behavioral therapy: A treatment model emphasizing the primacy of thoughts and beliefs in influencing feelings and subsequently actions. Interventions include social skills training, problem solving, cognitive restructuring, and communication skills training. Also known as a theoretical approach to treatment that stresses the role of thoughts, beliefs, perceptions, and attitudes on feelings and behavior. Techniques include cognitive restructuring; cognitive coping skills such as problem solving, self-reinforcement, and relaxation; and training in social skills, assertiveness, and communication. Behavioral methods, such as rehearsal, modeling, reinforcement, and coaching, are typically employed for the delivery of content.

Cohesive self: The essential self-structure of a well-adapted, healthily functioning individual whose self-functioning evinces the harmonious interchange of ambitions, ideals, and talents with the events of everyday life.

Common factors perspective: An integrative approach to psychosocial intervention that emphasizes core elements shared by the major systems of psychotherapy rather than specific technical procedures associated with particular schools of thought. Common factors include client characteristics, such as motivation and expectations of change; practitioner characteristics, such as attunement, empathy, and authenticity; provision of rationale for problems in functioning and conceptual framework for intervention; and strategic processes, such as experiential learning, interpretive procedures, modeling, reinforcement, and exposure.

Community-based case management: A model of case management that emphasizes involvement of all community partners in the client's well-being. It benefits from the synergy that occurs when multiple stakeholders work together to deliver client services and has been particularly effective in the child welfare field.

Community-based services: Services that are situated in the home environment of clients and are easily accessible to them. The term is often associated with decentralization of services.

Community capacity. A form of social organization that emanates from the operation and interaction of formal and informal networks of social care in the community that allows community members to demonstrate *shared responsibility* and *collective competence* for addressing community needs and confronting situations that threaten the safety and well-being of the community.

Community organizing: The process of bringing people and groups together to collectively address a need, solve problems, or improve a social condition.

Community partnership: An alliance between citizens and practitioners to bring about planned change for the common good.

Community practice: The generic term for social work intervention at the community level, defined geographically or functionally, including practice in the neighborhood, around a common issue or a shared identity. Its components include community building, organizing, development, and planning.

Community results: Aggregate, broad-based outcomes that reflect the collective efforts of individuals and families who live within a specified area.

Comorbidity: When two or more diseases or conditions that coexist or co-occur.

Compassion fatigue: In social workers and counselors, weariness, loss of confidence, often accompanied by self-doubt and loss of conviction in one's knowledge and methods, resulting from unrelieved and intense interaction with clients and lack of self-support systems.

Computerized practice management: Computer programs that keep track of basic patient information, appointments, insurance authorizations, and billing and payments. They may also include assessment information and progress notes. Most are designed primarily for individual and small group practices.

Conceptual framework: A guiding set of interrelated assumptions, based on one's worldview, that is used to provide direction for practice methods.

Conduct disorder: A *DSM* diagnosis that involves an entrenched pattern of behavior in which a person violates the basic rights of others or where major age-appropriate societal norms or rules are violated. This pattern involves four categories of behaviors: aggressive conduct either causing or threatening harm to people or animals; nonaggressive conduct leading to property loss or damage; deceitfulness or theft; and serious violations of rules. The person demonstrates at least three such behaviors in the past year, with at least one in the past 6 months.

Confidentiality: Involves safeguarding personal information from unwarranted disclosure. Under the NASW Code of Ethics, social workers are expected to maintain confidentiality by collecting only essential information about their clients, revealing clients' confidences only for compelling reasons, and disclosing information to third parties only with proper informed consent from the client or others acting on their behalf.

Congruence: A practitioner's display of genuineness and honesty with the client.

Consensus-based safety assessment: List of factors (some of which may come from research) that are thought by a convened group to be related to the likelihood of immediate harm.

Constituency: The group with whom or about which a social worker organizes. Constituents may include clients, consumers, residents, members, parents, students, service recipients, and patients.

Construct: An active processing or organizing experience in an individual's mind. Personal constructs represent personal or shared meanings.

Construct elaboration: The generation of alternative conceptualizations of a given event, phenomenon, or stimulus condition. This process is completed in recognition that multiple meanings exist for all human experience.

Constructivism: A worldview postulating that there is an objective, external reality but a person can never experience it directly and that the structure of the individual human organism and human mind, rather than that of the environment, is the central mechanism in reality construction.

Consumer-directed services: An approach to service delivery for older people and people with disabilities in which consumers have a degree of decision-making authority about their own services.

Consumer-driven case management: A case management model that emphasizes providing the best organized practice for clients in complex and chronic situations.

Contact boundary: The point where self meets other, distinguishing one person from another. The flexibility of this boundary determines the quality of the contact with the other and ultimately the stretching of all boundaries, which from a Gestalt perspective represents growth.

Contact: The psychological process of engaging with the environment and ourselves. Contact refers to the quality of the way one is in touch with and experiences the world.

Contamination: This occurs when members of the control group in an experiment inadvertently receive the intervention. It may be prevented by sampling natural clusters.

Continuum of care: A wide range of health and social services, provided in the home, community, and institutional settings designed to serve older adults as their needs change over time. It is more than a collection of service components. It is an organized, coherent, and integrated service system.

Contract: An agreement between parties that defines the relationship between them, the responsibilities of each party, and penalties to each should agreements not be met. To be valid, contracts must be entered into freely and without coercion. There are three kinds of contracts used with clients in social work. The *service* contract describes and defines the relationship between the client and the service provider, agency, or program. The *initial* contract develops the tasks of the initial period, which include gathering information, assessment, and problem definition. The *therapeutic* contract defines worker or client objectives in the change process and the tasks, treatments, and interventions that enable their achievement, assigns specific tasks and responsibilities, and develops both a time frame and a system of measurability. The contract is the plan that worker and client will follow in achieving the mutually determined goal.

Contracting process: A worker-initiated effort, usually in the beginning phase of the work, to establish the purpose of the contact, explain the worker's role, gain some sense of the client's issues (feedback), and deal with issues of authority.

Controlled elaboration of ambiguity: Refers to the therapist's responsibility for introducing the sufficient amount of ambiguity during the telling of a therapeutic story to ensure that the client's attention is engaged and resistance is minimal.

Co-occurring services: Where two or more problems exist together (mental illness, domestic violence, substance abuse, developmental disability, etc.), services or programs are provided one after the other (serially), at the same time without information sharing (parallel), at the same with information sharing (coordinated), or at the same time by the same agency (integrated).

Coping question: A form of solution-focused query used when clients seem overwhelmed and discouraged beyond the point of trying. Answers can assist the social worker in moving forward with the client toward solution development.

Core beliefs: Basic beliefs about oneself, others, and the world that are formed early in childhood

and are relatively inaccessible to awareness. Over-generalized, durable beliefs about the self and world may be formed through early life experiences.

Council on Social Work Education (CSWE): Founded in 1952, CSWE is social work's accrediting body for Bachelor's and Master's degree programs in the United States.

Countertransference: Role-responsive complements or counterparts to psychological transference reactions. According to contemporary psychodynamic relational perspectives, the clinician functions as a participant-observer and provides opportunities for creation, recognition, clarification, and revision of maladaptive patterns of interaction.

Crisis assessment: An objective appraisal of a client's perception of present and past situational stressors in terms of personal threat, ability to cope, and barriers to actions, as well as the type of aid needed from the crisis worker.

Coyote: A human smuggler who bring migrants across the border between Mexico and the United States for a fee; often associated with gangs or organized crime rings.

Criminogenic needs: Dynamic risk factors that are empirically linked with recidivism outcomes.

Crisis: A situation that exceeds an individual's coping ability, and leads to severe affective, cognitive, and behavioral malfunctioning. The main cause is an intensely stressful, traumatic, or hazardous event, but two other conditions are also necessary: (1) the individual's perception of the event as the cause of considerable upset and/or disruption; and (2) the individual's inability to resolve the disruption by previously used coping methods. An event or situation that is experienced as distressing and challenging of human adaptive abilities and resources.

Crisis intervention: A therapeutic interaction that seeks to decrease perceived psychological trauma by increasing perceived coping efficacy. It is a timely intervention that focuses on helping mobilize the resources of those differentially affected.

Critical incident stress management (CISM): An integrated, comprehensive, multicomponent crisis intervention system, with interventions for crisis-induced stress symptoms, with efforts beginning in the precrisis phase and lasting through the acute crisis phase into the postcrisis phase.

Critical incident stress: A characteristic set of psychological and physiological reactions or symptoms in response to a stressor event that can overwhelm the person's capacity to psychologically cope with an incident.

Cultural liaisons: Community-based paraprofessionals, often from the same country or culture or who share a religious or spiritual practice, that can act as trusted intermediaries between immigrants and service providers, facilitating access to services and resources.

Culturagram: This family assessment tool attempts to individualize culturally diverse families and make their needs more approachable for social workers who may be from a very different background. The culturagram examines ten different areas, from the client's contact with cultural and religious institutions to the amount of time the client has spent in the community, in order to best make his or her issues accessible to the social worker or other practitioner helping her out:

- Reasons for relocation
- Legal status
- Time in community
- Language spoken at home and in the community
- Health beliefs
- Impact of trauma and crisis events
- Contact with cultural and religious institutions, Holidays, Food and Clothing
- Oppression, Discrimination, Bias and Racism
- Values about education and work
- Values about family –structure, power, myths, and rules

Culturally competent practice: The ability to recognize similarities and differences in culture; when a social worker comprehends the norms of conduct, beliefs, traditions, values, language, art, skills, and interpersonal relationships within a society, and has the ability to help clients from cultures other than those of the social worker.

Cultural trauma: Chronic, repetitive insults inflicted on individuals who are marginalized based on race, disability, sexual identity, or religion.

Culture-bound syndrome: A pattern of unusual behavior that is specific to a culture or subculture. The behavior may or may not be related to a *DSM-IV-TR* diagnostic category.

Culture of care: Provided through norms and values, expressed in communication and action, in ways that shapes the character and function of the family center community and the personal identity of parents and staff.

Debriefing: An organized approach to the management of stress responses, entailing a group meeting using a facilitator who is able to help disclosure of feelings and reactions to a critical incident.

Deconstruction: Unpacking a concept or issue or showing how it is constructed; finding its limits and gaps.

Deconstructive questioning: Questions designed to challenge one's problem-saturated story as the only truth.

Deep structure: A collection of unedited life experiences from which thoughts, behaviors, and language are composed.

Defense structures: Theoretically, unconscious mental processes by addicted persons, including denial, projection, rationalization, and repression, that present as a result of psychological conflict to protect against, loss of self-esteem, or other unacceptable feelings or thoughts.

Defusing: A form of critical incident stress debriefing that may be spontaneous and is usually performed very shortly (within a few hours) after a critical incident.

Deinstitutionalization: Releasing clients from closed institutions, such as state mental hospitals, and providing similar relevant services in a less restrictive environment, preferably a normal residential situation.

Depression: A disturbance of mood marked by inability to enjoy activities and relationships, feelings of hopelessness and worthlessness, problems sleeping and eating, and thoughts of suicide.

Desensitization: Also called *habituation*, this is the process whereby a person experiences decreased levels of anxiety after being exposed to feared stimuli repeatedly and for long periods of time.

Detoxification: The planned withdrawal from use of an addictive substance, usually under professional and/or medical care.

Developmental disability: A severe, chronic disability caused by a mental or physical disabilities beginning before the age of 22 that results in substantial functional limitations in at least three areas of major life activity, including self-care, receptive and expressive language, learning, mobility, self-direction, and capacity for independent living or self-sufficiency.

Diagnosis: A discrete process of determining through observation, examination, and analysis the nature of a client's illness, disorder, or functional problems.

Diagnosis-related groups (DRGs): A diagnosis-based classification system, used under the prospective payment system for Medicare, in which hospitals are reimbursed for inpatient costs on a per discharge basis, regardless of actual length of stay or cost. DRGs may be thought of an early form of managed care and a modified version of capitation. Social worker roles in discharge planning were greatly enhanced under this system, begun in 1982, because of the pressures to discharge Medicare patients earlier than in the past (length of stay reduction).

Diagnostic criteria: Detailed descriptions, called diagnostic criteria, are provided in the *Diagnostic and Statistical Manual of Mental Disorders* for each of the specific mental disorders. These specify the rules for inclusion and exclusion symptoms and other features when making each diagnosis.

Diagnostic and Statistical Manual of Mental Disorders, **Fourth Edition, Text Revision** *(DSM-IV-TR)*: The latest edition of the official manual of mental disorders used in the United States and many other countries, published by the American Psychiatric Association. It provides a listing of all of the officially recognized mental disorders and their code numbers, as well as the diagnostic criteria used to identify each disorder.

Dialectical behavior therapy (DBT): A combination of cognitive-behavioral therapy and Zen mindfulness training that was developed as a treatment for self-harming women with borderline personality disorder.

Disequilibrium: An emotional state that may be characterized by confusing emotions, somatic complaints, and erratic behavior. The severe emotional discomfort experienced by the person in crisis propels him or her toward action that is aimed at reducing the subjective discomfort.

Dissociative disorders: A group of mental disorders characterized by dissociative experiences that often interfere with a person's ability to function normally and cause significant distress and disruption in the sufferer's life, although dissociation may also be a defensive state of consciousness that protects one from traumatic experiences.

Domestic violence: Physical and/or sexual violence (use of physical force) or threat of such violence; or psychological/emotional abuse and/or coercive tactics when there has been prior physical and/or sexual violence, between persons who are or were spouses or nonmarital partners (e.g., boyfriend/girlfriend).

Eco-systems perspective: An understanding that individuals and families influence and are influenced by those in immediate proximity, such as a household, as well as by the surrounding environment of the neighborhood, community, and society.

Educational intervention: The skilled and purposeful application of instructional methods to achieve clinical or programmatic objectives, such as staff development, psychoeducational programs, skill acquisition, health promotion, and public awareness campaigns.

Educational Policy and Accreditation Standards (EPAS): The standards, including curricular content, by which the Council on Social Work Education (CSWE) accredits bachelor's and master's degree social work degree programs in the United States.

Educator role: In social work, providing clients and other learners with the necessary skills and knowledge to effectively carry out their roles. Social workers acting as educators create an environment conducive to learning and provide relevant information in a useful, comprehensible way.

Effect size: A statistic used to measure the degree of difference between two groups on some variable.

Effectiveness study: An outcome study of social work intervention conducted under naturalistic treatment conditions, with real clients and everyday practitioners.

Efficacy study: Highly controlled experimental outcome studies of social work intervention using protocol-based treatments, well-trained and supervised practitioners, and carefully screened clients.

Egalitarian relationship: A relationship based on the assumptions that the client and worker are both resources and share in the power base, assessment, goals, plans, and taking action to make change.

Ego state: The actually experienced reality of one's mental and physical ego at any given moment.

It consists of *parent* (borrowed), *adult* (responsive to present reality), and *child* (genetic and archaic). The ego model is derived from the theoretical model called transactional analysis.

Elaborating: The process of helping the client tell his or her story.

Eligibility: The process of determining whether an individual, family, group, or community meets the specific criteria/qualifications needed to receive services.

Empathic joining: The shift from blame to a nonjudgmental stance and empathy for one's partner.

Empirically Supported Treatment: An approach to service delivery that has been carefully evaluated, typically through multiple randomized clinical research trials in different settings, and found to be effective with the population it is designed to serve.

Employment specialist: A vocational worker or rehabilitation worker who provides employment services to the client; employment specialists work with clients to find jobs (job development) and also provide ongoing follow-along support once the job has been obtained.

Empowerment: A process through which people become strong enough to participate within, share in the control of, and influence events and institutions affecting their lives, and in part necessitates that people gain particular skills, knowledge, and power to influence their lives and the lives of those they care about.

Empowerment practice: A way of engaging in practice that emphasizes overcoming direct and indirect blocks to action on behalf of oneself and others in the personal, interpersonal, and political spheres. This latter requires action in concert with others. Direct power blocks are oppression and various other kinds of external disempowerment; indirect blocks are internalized attitudes of self-doubt, shame, helplessness, and negative self-valuing.

Empowerment-based social work practice: Intervening with client systems in a way that results in them developing a greater sense of power over their life, destiny, and environment, at personal, interpersonal, and contextual (organizational/community) levels.

Enactment: The process through which a family lives out its focal struggle in a therapy session that approximates its experience at home.

End-of-life care: Comprehensive care that addresses the physical and psychosocial needs of persons who have a life-threatening or eventually fatal illness or condition, which can include medical intervention as well as counseling, spiritual support, and other forms of intervention.

Engagement: Also called *joining*, this is the process of a case manager symbolically entering into the life of an individual or family, establishing a reciprocal, trusting emotional connection to support an individual or family in a process of change.

Environmental specificity: The placement of a support in a specific environment so that it offsets a functional limitation of a person and increases his or her ability to function in the environment and perform successfully a specific role.

Equipoise: The mental state of not knowing which intervention would be best for a client. It is the ethical position required to conduct a randomized controlled trial.

E-therapy (synonymous with online, cyber-, e-mail, or chat therapy): The use of modern remote technologies, rather than traditional face-to-face service.

Ethical decision making: The deliberate use of ethics-related concepts and guidelines to address ethical dilemmas and issues.

Ethical dilemma: A situation in social work practice where two or more professional duties or obligations conflict.

Ethics complaint: A complaint filed against a social worker with a licensing board, regulatory body, or professional association alleging violation of ethical standards.

Ethnicity: Groupings of people based on shared elements such as physical appearance, culture, religion, and history.

Evaluation: A process used to determine the effectiveness of a particular program or intervention. Effectiveness data may come from a variety of sources (e.g., rapid assessment tools, observation, case records). The results of an evaluation are used to inform agency and system policies, funding of agencies, and development of programs.

Evidence-based practice: The conscientious, explicit, and judicious use of the current best scientific evidence in making decisions about social work assessment and intervention, also taking into account clinical expertise, client preferences and circumstances, and professional ethics.

Exceptions: Those times in a client's life when the presenting problem is not occurring or is less severe. These exceptional times provide valuable information about what is different when the problem is not actively present, including strengths and coping skills from which to build solutions.

Expectancy: The social worker's confidence and belief in the ability and desire of people to make changes in their lives. When clients sense that the social worker believes that change is possible, they are more likely to begin the process of making changes.

Experiential exercises: These teaching methods emphasize the use of activities to help learners deepen understanding of issues, practice skills, and develop new insights. Examples include role-plays, simulations, skits, icebreaking exercises, and team projects.

Experiment: The deliberate manipulation of one or more independent variables (treatments) conducted under controlled conditions to test hypotheses, especially for making inferences of a cause and effect character.

Expert consensus guidelines (ECGs): Derived from a broad-based survey of expert opinion and consist of a compilation of practical treatment recommendations for the treatment of major biological and mental disorders.

Exposure therapy: A behavioral technique in which a person is gradually exposed in real life to anxiety-provoking stimuli. It is used as a treatment for a variety of anxiety disorders.

Expressed emotion: The quality of communication between people, specifically the presence of hostility, criticism, and emotional overinvolvement. The concept emerged from research on communication between family members and consumers and has more recently been applied to the communication between providers and consumers.

Externalizing problem: 1.) Behavior, disruptive, or conduct problems, problems that have a primarily negative effect on others (e.g., conduct disorder, oppositional defiant disorder, substance abuse, attention deficit and hyperactivity disorder). 2.) In conversation with clients, the problem is externalized, or separated, from the person, whereby the problem and not the person is the target of change.

Extratherapeutic factor: Any aspect of the client's physical, psychological, and social world that influence how services are understood and valued.

These factors are viewed as having the greatest single impact on service outcome.

False memory syndrome: A lay term used to describe memories of events that did not happen. Such memories are confabulated or fabricated, usually, but not exclusively, in the course of therapy aimed at retrieving early childhood memories of abuse.

Family assessment tools: Graphic displays of family issues that can be used to understand, empower, and point toward treatment interventions for the family. Three important family assessment tools are the eco-map that looks at the relationship of the family with the outside environment, the genogram that examines the intergenerational relationships within the family, and the culturagram that looks at specific cultural aspects within diverse families.

Family consultation: The process by which a family member seeks the advice or opinion of a professional (the consultant) and works collaboratively with the consultant for the purpose of clarifying a situation, reaching a decision, solving a problem, or accomplishing an objective.

Family intervention: Models for working with families of persons with severe mental illness, such as psychoeducation, family education, family support, and family consultation, that help families understand and support their ill relatives. Research indicates that providing these interventions to families improves client outcomes.

Family resilience framework: Practice orientation, key processes, and intervention principles to facilitate family resilience in response to crisis, trauma, or loss; disruptive transitions; and chronic, multistress conditions now and in the future.

Family support: An intervention that provides emotional support, empathy, information, and networking for families of persons with severe mental illness.

Family systems therapy: An approach in which in which all members of a nuclear or extended family are conceptualized as a psychosocial system in need of change and individual problems are viewed as symptoms of interactional sequences in the family. Treatment therefore centers on work with the family as a whole, altering the sequences of interactions, and examining the functions that symptoms serve for the system.

Father involvement: The activities of fathers aimed at fostering the health, well-being, and development of one's child. These activities include direct engagement with the child, accessibility to the child, and assuming responsibility for the child.

Feminism: 1.) A way of viewing and being in the world that evolved from an analysis of women's collective experience with patriarchy. For most feminists, while promoting the interests of women and addressing women's issues, feminism necessarily involves a commitment to ending all forms of oppression and exploitation. 2.) A position advocating for the political, social, and economic equality of men and women.

Feminist practice: Can be defined by one's identity as a feminist, by a conceptual framework that is based in strongly held assumptions, or by methods used.

Fidelity: Adherence to the program model, associated with improved outcomes for clients.

Filial therapy: a structured psychoeducational program combining play and family therapy in which parents are trained to be therapeutic change agents for their own children.

First-order change: Change in operation when the attempts to solve the presenting problems are actually maintaining the problem.

Follow-up: A phase of the basic model of single-subject design methodology in which client functioning is measured reliably and validly over time and compared with the intervention phase to determine whether changes observed immediately after an intervention persist.

Forensic social work: Any form of social work practice that is related in some way to legal issues or litigation in the criminal or civil legal systems.

Full-service community schools: Schools with programs that combine into a concerted effort to integrate health, youth development, family, and other community services to support student learning.

Functional analysis: As assessment procedure that describes the functional relationships between antecedents to a behavior, the behavior, and the consequences that follow the behavior.

Gatekeeper: A person that directs or links a person to informal or formal sources of help.

Generalization: The extent to which learning in treatment transfers to an individual's day-to-day life. Practitioners must always be planning for ways to maximize the generalization of skills learned and promote their continued use after training. Principles involved in generalization include overlearning, varying the stimuli used in training, and encouraging the use of skills in real-life settings.

Generalized anxiety disorder: A DSM diagnosis of a subclass of the anxiety disorder where anxiety is experience in most situations.

Generative fathering: Fathering techniques that meet the needs of the next generation across time and context.

Genogram: A family map, usually of at least three generations. It records information about a person's biological, legal, emotional, and spiritual family members and their relationships over at least three generations. Genograms display family information graphically in a way that provides a quick gestalt of complex family patterns; as such, they are a rich source of hypotheses about how clinical problems evolve in the context of the family over time.

Globalization: The worldwide integration of humanity and the compression of both the temporal and spatial dimensions of planetwide human interaction.

Goal: A broad, long-term target for a identified problem or desired change that may or may not be reached while the client is in treatment. In treatment planning, the goal is a broadly stated description of what successful outcome is expected. The *goal* of the social work intervention is broad and inclusive, is culturally sensitive, may be achieved through various means, and remains constant throughout the course of the social worker–client relationship.

Goal-attainment scaling: A method of monitoring client progress by identifying the client's problem level at the point of assessment and stating what would constitute "some" and "extensive" improvement and "some" and "extensive" deterioration in progress with a given problem. Problems then are often weighted by how important it is to improve in any of two to four areas. Measurement with goal-attainment scales is usually completed only a few times over the course of an intervention.

Goal-directed metaphor: A type of metaphor constructed to move characters in a manner likely to retrieve targeted and needed experiences in the client but that do not attempt to match the client's problem in content or body of the story.

Grief therapy: Treatment focused on alleviating dysfunctional traumatic or complicated grief reactions.

Group: A small collection of individuals in which there is interaction around some commonality and that may contain a variety of interactional dynamics, including mutual support, goal attainment, acquisition of knowledge and skills, universalization, catharsis, and instillation of hope.

Guided imagery: Therapeutic use of visual imagery as a means of promoting and effecting cognitive, emotional, and behavioral change. Images may be obtained from life events, dreams and daydreams, and fantasies. Often, relaxation techniques are used in conjunction with the procedure.

Health maintenance organization (HMO): A form of health insurance that only allows clients to visit professionals in a specific network. For behavioral health services, HMOs may offer in-house salaried clinicians or may contract with clinicians who may be salaried, fee-for-service, or capitated. HMOs often have strict rules limiting services and monitor clinician behaviors for compliance.

Hierarchal construction: Behavioral intervention of creating a list of feared stimuli or situations organized from least feared to most feared. The client then uses this hierarchy in exposure therapy, each time moving up the list after having a significant drop in experienced fear at the previous listed item.

HIV/AIDS: HIV (human immunodeficiency virus) is a retrovirus that can cause a breakdown of the body's immune system, leading in many cases to the development of acquired immune deficiency syndrome (AIDS) or related infections or illnesses. AIDS is the name originally given to an array of diseases and malignancies that occur in adults who previously had healthy immune systems. Certain markers (opportunistic infections, cancers, T-cell count) now constitute a diagnosis of AIDS.

Holistic: Describes a practice perspective that takes into account the health, mental health, educational, and spiritual aspects of clients within their environments.

Home-based services: Therapeutic and care management services delivered primarily in the client's home.

Homosexual: A male or female person whose sexual attraction, both physical and affectional, is primarily directed toward persons of the same gender.

Hospital case management: Uses a collaborative process among health care providers to case find, assess, plan, intervene, monitor, and evaluate delivery of health care services for hospital-based patients.

Human rights: Those fundamental entitlements that are considered to be necessary for developing each personality to the fullest. Violations of human rights are any arbitrary and selective actions that interfere with the full exercise of those fundamental entitlements.

Hypervigilance: Constant scanning of the environment, using all senses, for any threats.

Hypnosis: A heightened state of internal concentration that has further characterized by a reduction in processing of external perception. An intervention procedure involving the fixation of attention, disruption of normal modes of cognitive functioning, and initiation of change through use of indirect forms of suggestion.

Ideomotor signs: Behaviors exhibited by clients that are the result of private thoughts, images, and sensations.

Immigrant: A person who voluntarily leaves his or her country of origin expecting to live in the host country legally with the option to return to the country of origin. Immigrants may be legally admitted or reside in the new country illegally (in which case they are referred to as undocumented aliens).

Imminent harm: A situation in which there are predictions of a client's involvement in violence within 24 hours after he or she is seen by the forensic evaluator.

Indirect suggestion: Any number of verbal patterns that are believed to initiate unconscious search processes.

Indirect treatment: Those aspects of a social work intervention that involve persons, resources, and situations of significance in a client's life, the goals of which are to bring about change or benefit to the client.

Individualized education plan (IEP): A written plan developed in schools with interventions and/or accommodations for children who qualify for special education services.

Individualized placement and support model (IPS): An approach to supported employment that has been shown to be an empirically-supported treatment in providing services to people with severe mental illness. IPS features an individualized approach with an emphasis on competitive employment, rapid search for a competitive community job, and the integration of mental health and employment services.

Individualized rating scale: A single-item scale developed to measure a client's level on a problem over time. These scales are usually developed in collaboration with the client and use the client's own words to describe differing levels of a problem. These scales can be used repeatedly.

Informal helper: A layperson in a culture's local community system, such as kinship networks, neighbors, volunteers, and community groups that provide information, advice, emotional, and social support.

Informed consent: Involving clients in making decisions based on competence, knowledge, and choice. Social workers have an ethical obligation to obtain clients' informed consent for services and prior to releasing information. Clients can give informed consent if they are mentally competent; are informed of the risks, benefits, and possible consequences of their choices; and are free to make choices. The client's informed consent for services or for release of information should be documented in the record.

Insider strategy: Attempts to influence policy by working through the system and approaching legislative and executive branch decision makers directly through legislative and political action.

Institutional ethics committee (IEC): An interdisciplinary group of professionals and other parties in a human service organization that provides a forum for discussion of ethical dilemmas and issues.

Institutional review board (IRB): An interdisciplinary group of professionals and other parties in a human service organization responsible for the protection of human subjects involved in research.

Integrative gerontological practice: A treatment model based on a biopsychosocial-cultural framework that incorporates themes from aging and social work, includes a life course perspective, takes into account diversity among older persons, adopts a multi- and interdisciplinary practice approach, and attends to power and inequalities among older adults and in their use of services.

Intellectual disability: A disability characterized by significant limitations in intellectual functioning and adaptive behavior as expressed in conceptual, social, and practical adaptive skills. This is the preferred term in the United States for what was once called "mental retardation," and it has growing international currency.

Intensive case management: Case management services marked by low caseloads with an emphasis on aggressive outreach and in-home and community care.

Interdisciplinary: Implies a group of professionals from different disciplines who jointly bring their particular professional perspectives to bear on solving a problem. This process requires role division based on expertise, communication, interdependence, and coordination.

Interim notes: After a service plan has been developed, the social worker regularly documents changes in the client situation, movement toward achieving goals, and other information in the record. These interim or progress notes serve to inform others who read the record about development of the case over time.

Intermittent explosive disorder: Several discrete episodes of a client's failure to resist aggressive impulses that result in serious assaultive acts or destruction of property whereby the degree of aggressiveness expressed during the episodes is grossly out of proportion to any precipitating psychosocial stressors.

Intention to treat: A method of analysis that treats participants as member of the groups to which they were assigned, regardless of what happened during the study, including participants who did not receive the intervention and those who dropped out.

Interest-based mediation: An approach to conflict resolution in which an impartial third party helps people involved in a conflict by focusing them on their underlying interests and ways of collaborating for their mutual benefit (i.e., to develop creative win-win solutions).

International social work: International professional action by social workers and the capacity in the profession for such action. The four dimensions of international action are internationally related domestic practice and advocacy, professional exchange, international practice, and international policy development and advocacy.

Interpersonal empowerment: Acquisition of knowledge, skills, and assertiveness to participate in matters that impact the control and mastery of one's life.

Intervention: The methods, strategies, tasks, or assignments that a clinician will use to assist the client in achieving the identified goals and objectives. Interventions define the *who* and the *what* that will enable the specific responsibilities and actions to be taken by worker and client during the course of treatment.

Intervention phase: During intervention, when a specified plan is implemented to change client functioning, information is provided about changes in the nature and severity of the client's problem as measured by the same variables employed during baseline, with the results then compared to the baseline results.

Intervention planning: Planning for treatment activity that promotes client problem or symptom reduction or elimination based on a diagnosis and assessment of client problems and/or symptoms.

Introject: An emotionally charged message from parents, siblings, significant others, and institutions that shapes a person's view of the world and feelings about the self.

In vivo service: Service provided at the site where a client uses them in daily living, rather than in a classroom or agency site; for example, when a client is taught to cook on his or her own stove rather than in the kitchen of a day treatment center.

Isomorphism: Refers to any content that corresponds to the client's problem and/or solutions on a one-to-one basis—that is, thing-for-thing and action-for-action.

Least restrictive environment: The provision of mental health services in settings that are the closest to everyday life that an individual with a mental disorder can manage.

Legislative advocacy: The activities in the political arena that focus on the promotion of the common welfare or the securing, expansion, or protection of rights and services of a specific population. It can serve as a means to mobilize people, raise political consciousness, and accentuate the contradictions within society.

Level of fit: Measurement of the degree of compatibility between the perceived needs, capacities, behavioral styles, and goals of people, and the characteristics of the environment in which they live.

Life stressor: Life transitions, traumatic events, environmental and interpersonal pressures that disturb the level of person:environment fit and a prior state of relative adaptedness.

Linking: An intervention in groups in which the worker ties together common elements in the communication pattern of members to assist them in identifying more closely with one another.

Maladaptive belief: A habitual cognition that causes emotional and behavioral distress.

Malpractice: A form of negligence involving a breach of professional duty that causes harm or injury to the client.

Managed care: A formal system of health care delivery and financing that attempts to influence or control access, utilization, costs, and quality of services. This system consists of networks of health care providers, third-party funding sources, and other fiscal intermediaries that provide health and mental health services for those participating in the network. It is primarily sponsored by investor-owned, for-profit organizations referred to as managed care organizations (MCOs). Even Medicare and Medicaid managed care plans tend to be privately owned. Managed care is thus market-driven. There is a large range of types of plans; the most well known is the health maintenance organization (HMO), consisting of a self-contained panel of doctors. A gatekeeping primary care physician controls patient access to all other services (specialists, hospitals, etc.). When managed care is applied to mental health care, it is often referred to as behavioral health.

Manualized treatment: Sequenced and prescribed content and activities to systematize and standardize interventions. Manualized treatments usually use evidence-based practices and facilitate the adoption and evaluation of interventions.

Mediation: A conflict resolution process conducted by an impartial third party, who does not impose a decision or make a recommendation to the court if the disputants cannot reach an agreement.

Medicaid: A jointly funded federal–state health insurance assistance program for people with disabilities, older people, and other people with limited resources. The federal government mandates states to pay for hospital care, home health care, physician services and nursing home care for eligible people, and states can choose to pay for additional services under Medicaid, such as personal assistance services and intermediate care facilities for the mentally retarded. Medicaid is the largest funder of nursing home care and community living costs for people with intellectual and developmental disabilities.

Medicaid waiver: An exception to the usual Medicaid rules, allowing states to use Medicaid funds to provide community-based services to people with disabilities who would otherwise need to be cared for in an institution.

Medical model: A perspective on human behavior that locates the sources of many problems in living within an individual primarily as the result of biological factors, as opposed to cultural or personal background issues.

Mental disorder: A clinically significant, individual functional, behavioral, or psychological syndrome manifested by distress, disability, or risk of harm that is not a culturally accepted reaction to an event. (See the *DSM-IV-TR* for a more detailed definition and explanation.)

Mental health outcome: Any condition that an intervention is intended to affect or change. Common empirically based outcome measures for mental health are functional status, perception of quality of life, benefits of care, problems with care, safety and client/family satisfaction with mental health services.

Mentalization: The capacity to make sense of self and of others in terms of subjective states and mental processes. This concept makes up the core of mentalization-based treatment, an evidence-based psychodynamic therapy for the treatment of borderline personality disorder.

Meta-analysis: A statistical method used to summarize the effects of several studies in a particular area.

Meta-cognitions: Thoughts or beliefs about cognitive processes.

Metaphor: An altered framework of presenting ideas, by means of which clients can entertain novel and potentially therapeutic experiences.

Methodological filter: A search term intended to limit a database search to the best available research studies specific to answering an evidence-based practice question.

Middle (or work) phase: The phase of work in which the client and the worker focus on dealing with issues raised in the beginning phase or with new issues that have emerged since then.

Migration narratives: Personal accounts of migration arising out of the use of regular narrative therapy in order to help immigrants examine, understand, and contextualize the migration process for the purposes of healing.

Minor depression: The presence of at least two but fewer than five depressive symptoms including depressed mood or anhedonia during the same 2-week period with no history of major depressive episode or dysthymia but with clinically significant impairment

Minority: Any member of an ethnic group whose population is a numerical minority in a society; minorities sometimes receives unequal and disadvantageous treatment in the society, but may also be part of a privileged upper class.

Miracle question: A question used in solution-focused therapy in which the client is asked to describe what would be different if there were a miracle and the problem went away. The question is useful in helping the client describe a desired future in which the presenting problem no longer exists or is significantly improved.

Mixed mood disorder: Characterized by the simultaneous presence of symptoms of major depression and mania, with depression being predominant in the presence of increased activity.

Mobilization: The organization and application of constituents' resources toward a particular policy goal in a legislative setting. In this context, mobilization is the process of increasing the ability of constituents to act collectively by building their loyalty to a common set of objectives and increasing their ability to influence the course of legislation. Mobilization can take multiple forms—defensive, offensive, and preparatory—depending on the availability of resources, the relative power of advocates, and the particular issues at hand.

Modeling theory: An explanation derived from social learning theory of how new behaviors are acquired. Modeling can be used in treatment programs through stories, plays, and role-plays. Individuals either watch or experience vicariously the behaviors of the person modeling the behaviors to be learned. This process increases the likelihood that the individual will be able to perform a behavior similar to that modeled in the future.

Monitoring: Keeping abreast of client progress.

Mood stabilizer: A pharmacologic agent such as lithium, valproate, or carbamazepine that may control, delay, or prevent episodes of mania.

Multiaxial system of *DSM-IV*: The multiaxial system of the *DSM-IV* has five axes, each of which guides the clinician to evaluate a domain of information that may help plan treatment and predict outcome. The axes include information about mental disorders, personality disorders and mental retardation, general medical conditions, psychosocial and environmental problems, and global psychosocial functioning.

Multisystemic therapy: An empirically supported intervention approach developed for the treatment of youth in the juvenile justice system. This approach takes an ecological view in that many interlocking systems are seen as involved with individual behavior problems, with treatment targeted at the various systems levels.

Mutual trap: The cycle of interaction that results from partners becoming polarized about an issue following attempts to change one another.

N = 1 experiment: A research design of high internal validity wherein each person serves as his or her own control. Such experiments are characterized by the repeated valid assessment of one or more outcome measures and the repeated introduction or removal of one or more treatments.

Narcissistic personality disorder: One of the personality disorders described in the DSM-IV-TR, distinguished by a stable pattern of grandiosity, sense of entitlement and omnipotence, and fantasies of boundless success and brilliance.

Narrative therapy: A form of therapy based on the assumption that people organize their experience through stories. This approach to therapy stresses the significance of meaning and takes into account the sociocultural context in which people live and the impact this context has on the stories that dominate their lives. Narrative therapy focuses on creating and sustaining therapeutic dialogues in which clients restory their lives in new and more desirable ways that represent more satisfying and empowering interpretations of clients' lives. These new stories can be cocreated with clinicians, who consult with clients to help them find new possibilities. This approach offers practices to enact a strengths perspective, a collaborative working relationship, and an ethic of respect and accountability.

Natural helper: A nonprofessional, such as a family member, relative, friend and neighborhood advocate, or other volunteer, who provides multifaceted support in the family-centered community.

Naturally occurring resource: A nonsegregated resource that is routinely used by the general population of a given area.

Near problem: A legitimate issue raised by clients, early in the relationship, to establish trust before raising more difficult and often threatening issues.

Negative punishment: A process of intervention derived from social learning theory in which a reinforcing stimulus is removed following a behavior to decrease the future frequency of the behavior.

Negotiation: A conflict resolution process in which the disputants attempt to reach an agreement either by communicating directly or through agents.

Neurotransmitter: A chemical substance located near nerve cell synapses that transmit electrical impulses (communication) between nerve cells and along nerve pathways.

Niche: The environmental habitat of people, including the resources they use and the people they associate with. Niches can be entrapping or enabling.

Noetic or spiritual dimension: Contains those unique human capacities that make one a human being, such as the will to meaning, creativity, imagination, humor, faith, love, conscience, being responsible for someone or for some ideal, striving toward goals, and learning from past experiences.

Noticing: A process of intervening to help a client become more aware of the meaning potentials in their life.

Number needed to harm (NNH): Statistically, the number of people that need to receive a service for one to be harmed.

Number needed to treat (NNT): Statistically, the number of people that need to receive a service for one to benefit. It is the inverse of the absolute risk reduction.

Object relations psychology: A major paradigm in psychodynamic thought that encompasses overlapping theories of personality development, psychopathology, and psychosocial intervention. In this paradigm, emphasis is given to the motivational force of attachment and relationship in human development; it views interactive experience as the central organizer of psychic structure and function.

Objective: In treatment planning, the measurable steps that must occur for the change goals to be met in problem solving. The objective is derived from the goal and enables its fulfillment. Objectives define a course of action, a time frame, and a method of measurement to evaluate and assess achievement.

Online social work: Involves the use of telecommunications and information technology to provide social work services over the Internet. See also E-THERAPY.

Operant behavior: Behavior that affects the environment to produce consequences and is, in turn, controlled by those consequences. In general, many overt behaviors (including language) are operant behaviors.

Outcome measurement: The use of observable and measurable standardized indicators of intervention effects based on an intervention plan.

Outcome of service: The result achieved because of interventions, as measured against the treatment objectives specified in the service plan; the consequences of service that can be demonstrated in some objective manner.

Outsider strategy: Attempts to influence by indirect means, including litigation and protest using mobilization and community organization. Contrast with insider strategy.

Overarching goal: The broad and inclusive focus of work with an individual client or group, toward which all of the goals and interventions will be directed. The overarching goal should relate to client needs and concerns, strengths, resources, and client choices, which have been explored during the initial contract/assessment phase of the work.

Palliative care: Care for persons at the end of life that focuses on comfort and support instead of cure for a disease, illness, or condition. One example of palliative care is hospice, a program for persons who are not seeking aggressive medical treatment and have an estimated prognosis for life expectancy of 6 months or less.

Paraphilia: A group of disorders described in the DSM-IV-TR that are characterized by recurrent, intense sexual urges, and fantasies.

Parent training: An approach based on the behavioral principle of operant conditioning in which the consequences of a behavior determine its behavior. Parents are taught to set behaviorally specific goals, positively reinforce prosocial behavior, and

ignore or punish deviant behavior. Modeling is also used.

Parents as partners: A concept that recognizes parents as the primary focus of a child's life and requires that social workers and other mental health clinicians actively collaborate with parents in addressing the mental health needs of their children.

Partializing: An important part of problem solving, in which problems or concerns are broken down into smaller and more manageable units.

Partner abuse intervention program (PAIP): Community based programs designed to interrupt and prevent the recurrence of physical and nonphysical aggression against a currently or formerly intimate partner.

Passion statement: An expression of the goal or desire that is most important to a consumer at that time.

Patriarchy: A structural arrangement that privileges the views, interests, and activities of men over women. Because it is structural by nature, all men benefit from it even when they, as individuals, oppose the arrangement. Men as well as women work to end patriarchy as a system that is inimical to the full development of all persons.

Penile plethysmography: Sexual preference testing, also known as phallometry, that involves the measurement of penile volume or circumference when the individual is confronted with a variety of standardized sex-related stimuli.

Perceived self: How a person sees self and how others see them.

Perfect niche: A setting where the requirements and needs of the setting are perfectly matched with the desires, talents, and idiosyncrasies of the consumer.

Personal empowerment: The attitudes, values, and beliefs about self-efficacy, self-esteem, and having rights.

Personal planning: The process for creating a mutual agenda for work between the client and case manager, focused on achieving the goals that the client has set.

Personality disorder: A pervasive, inflexible, and enduring pattern of traits depicted by a persistent pattern of internal experience and outward behavior that diverges notably from cultural expectations, is pervasive and rigid, begins by adolescence or early adulthood, continues over time, and invariably results in significant distress or dysfunction. Personality disorders are diagnosed on axis II of the *DSM-IV-TR* multiaxial system.

Personality states: These recurrently take control of a schizophrenic person's behavior; each state is characterized by its own thoughts, feelings, behavior patterns, likes, dislikes, history, and other characteristics.

Perturbation: A state of system disequilibrium characterized by disorganization and distress resulting in adaptation and emerging complexity and differentiation.

Pharmacodynamics: The effects of a drug on the human body, including such phenomena as the therapeutic index, potency, dose response, lag time, tolerance, and positive and adverse effects.

Pharmacokinetics: The body's response to the presence of a drug, including absorption, distribution, metabolism, and excretion.

Pharmacotherapy: The treatment of a disease or disorder with drugs.

Phase of practice: Practice occurs in a specific sequence of beginnings, middles, and endings, although activities in each phase may be revisited at a later phase, if necessary. With respect to goals, the beginning phase is the one in which assessment and goal specification occur. The middle phase involves work to attain goals. The ending phase includes an evaluation of goal attainment.

Phenomenological: The focusing on the client's experience as it unfolds moment to moment in the therapeutic encounter.

PICO question: Patient-oriented question consisting of description of the population of patients (P), intervention of concern (I), what it may be compared to (C), and hoped-for outcome (O).

Planned short-term treatment: Social work service that is brief by design, generally fewer than 12 sessions during a 3- to 4-month period. It can be contrasted with open-ended service, which may continue indefinitely or may turn out to be brief if the client drops out or if the purpose of the intervention is accomplished quickly.

Podcast/vodcast: Subscription-based downloadable audio/video files.

Police-based social worker: Practitioners who work in federal, state, and city law enforcement agencies to provide counseling and support services to crime victims, witnesses, and family survivors.

Positive punishment: A process of intervention in which an aversive stimulus is presented following a behavior to decrease the future frequency of the behavior.

Positive reinforcement: A process of intervention in which a stimulus is presented following a behavior to increase the future frequency of the behavior.

Postmodernism: An approach to knowledge that claims there are many productive methods of knowledge development; that truth and reality, especially in social realms, often have multiple meanings; that universal principles discount cultural (and other) diversities; and that all ideas and actions inevitably reflect values.

Practice guideline: A set of systematically compiled and organized statements and recommendations for clinical care usually based on research findings and the consensus of experienced clinicians with expertise in a given practice area regarding efficacy and effectiveness. Practice guidelines are often in the form of treatment protocols that provide social work practitioners with explicit, well-defined procedures and instructions on how to conduct psychosocial interventions for specific client problems/disorders.

Pretreatment change: What is different or what has changed from the time the client made the appointment and to coming for the first session. Clients often begin to make changes even before the first encounter with the social worker and what is different provides valuable information about client strengths and problem-solving abilities.

Prevalence: A statistical term referring to the number of cases in a population that have a particular disease during a given period of time.

Primary care: Managed care has encouraged the central role of the primary care physician in coordinating patients' health needs. The locus of care is shifting from in-patient acute, tertiary, and specialty care to ambulatory and community based care and to physician offices, group practices, and health maintenance organizations.

Problem-based learning (PBL): An instructional style that engages students in course material through the presentation of a problem or question that they must solve together.

Problem-saturated story: One-dimensional, often negative, stories clients have constructed about themselves in interaction with other people and social cultural forces, which have restricted them from seeing their full potential. These stories are usually only one part of the client's experience but have overshadowed other experiences that contain successes, strengths, resources, and competencies.

Problem solving therapy: An empirically-supported psychosocial intervention for depression that focuses on the identification and implementation of adaptive solutions to daily problems.

Problem-specific interventions: Interventions created from rigorous studies that treat specific problems, such as anxiety, depression, or substance abuse problems.

Process measures: Measures of patient care that are concerned with activities specific to the provision of patient care. In essence, process measures focus on "what" has been provided to patients and "how."

Process recording: A form of qualitative evaluation using a condensed and structured outline that fosters reflection and promotes analysis of intervention while providing documentation of progress and assessment of outcome.

Professional negligence: Violation of a professional standard of care, including a breach of professional duty that causes harm or injury and may open the violator to legal action by the clients concerned.

Professional socialization: The process by which members of particular professions are inducted into their profession's values and ethics, language, preferred roles, methods of problem solving, and establishment of priorities.

Protocol: A plan for a study or research review that is developed in advance to specify the methods and procedures that will be used.

Provider-consumer-family collaboration: The engagement and involvement by professionals of families in the often lengthy and complicated treatment process of their relative with severe mental illness.

Psychiatric disability: Cognitive, emotional, behavioral, or personality conditions that can reduce functioning and modify conduct and interpersonal interactions in such a way that a person departs from normative expectations. Psychiatric disability is judged by certain diagnostic categories, duration of the illness or symptoms, and severity of impact on role and interpersonal functioning.

Psychiatric medication: Medications in five classes (antidepressants, mood stabilizers, antianxiety,

antipsychotic, and psychostimulants) used in primary care, psychiatry, and other specialties that are intended to alter mood, thoughts, or behavior.

Psychiatric rehabilitation: An approach to service delivery that focuses on helping people coping with serious mental illness to overcome their psychiatric disabilities through the augmentation of support, the development of skills, the reduction of barriers, and the creation of opportunities to advance their quality of life.

Psychodynamic theory: Those theories of social work practice that put particular stress on the inner life of a client, both as a way of understanding the client's strengths and limitations and, more important, to seek to effect changes that will enable a client to function in a more satisfying, growth-enhancing manner.

Psychoeducation: A model of individual, family, or group intervention focused on educating participants about a significant challenge and helping them develop adequate coping skills for managing the challenge

Psychological flexibility: The capacity to fully experience and embrace necessary pain and to interact flexibly with verbal constructions of the world in order to allow for committed, life-affirming action.

Psychosocial: A concept used in two ways in social work literature. The first way describes a specific theory and practice in social work from the dual orientation of person, understood in psychodynamic terms, and a person's societal roles and systems. It is also used in a more generic sense to identify or describe social work clinical practice from a diverse theoretical base.

Psychosocial rehabilitation: A humanistic approach to the support of people coping with the causes and consequences of serious mental illness in which recipients obtain support to set a direction and outcome they find meaningful. Rehabilitation facilitates the achievement of this direction through personal change and environmental modification.

Quality assurance (QA): A process or set of activities to maintain and improve the level of care provided to patients (also known as quality improvement, QI). These activities may include review, formal measurements, and corrective actions. The QA/QI function is a standard part of health insurance plans and all institutional health care providers. Managed care often demands that providers present QA/QI findings to the sponsoring plans, especially data on the outcome of care. In the era of managed care, it also has become critical for social workers to be able to demonstrate their effectiveness in measurable terms.

Quality of care: A multidimensional construct that includes patient care *structure*, patient care *process*, and patient care *outcomes*.

Question, well-structured: A practice or policy question consisting of three or four parts that starts with a client/problem and includes an intervention, comparison, and outcome, that facilitates an efficient, effective search for related research. Key terms in the question, together with appropriate quality filters, are used to search for related research.

Radiating impact: The prevalent finding that progress or achievement in one client-set goal leads to unplanned achievements in other areas of life.

Randomized controlled trial (RCT): An outcome study of treatment effectiveness using an experimental design. Such designs usually involve pre and post-assessments of client-system functioning and random assignment of clients to treatment and to alternative conditions such as no-treatment, standard care, or placebo treatment.

Rapid assessment instruments (RAIs): RAIs provide a brief standardized format for gathering information about clients. These instruments are scales, checklists, and questionnaires that are relatively brief, often fewer than 50 items, and easy to score and interpret. RAIs have established psychometrics and can reliably ascertain an individual's traits in terms of their frequency, intensity, or duration.

Rapid cycling: Four or more mood episodes a year of either bipolar I or bipolar II.

Recidivism: Recurrence of criminal activity in an offender. "Recidivism rate" refers to the general frequency of reoffense in a particular group of offenders.

Reconstructive questioning: These questions are designed to open semantic space for new realities. Such questions open the client to new ideas and discoveries—different ways of seeing a reality.

Recovered memory: A purported memory of a past traumatic event, believed to have been concealed from consciousness by repression or dissociation, but retrieved or recovered intact at a later point in time

Recovered memory therapy: A controversial form of psychotherapy aimed at retrieving traumatic memories that are believed to be repressed or dissociated. Although there is no one method for this, the techniques used most typically include hypnosis, truth serum, guided imagery, dream interpretation, age regression, free association, journaling, psychodrama, primal scream therapy, reflexology, massage, and other forms of body work to recover body memories.

Recovery: The process of developing individual potential and realizing life goals while surmounting the trauma and difficulties presented by behavioral, emotional, or physical challenges. For persons with a serious mental disorder, recovery involves a process of personal transformation in which the disorder becomes less central in a person's life as he or she achieves outcomes that increasingly bring personal meaning and life satisfaction.

Reflecting team: A team of members who observe an interview and then have a conversation with each other in which they express their reflections, questions, and ideas while the family or person whose experience is being reflected on observes.

Reframing: A second-order change intervention in which the facts of a situation are given a plausible, alternative definition previously not considered by those involved in the problematic situation. Usually, reframing provides an alternative positive meaning to some aspect of the problem or person with the problem that was previously defined negatively. For a positive reframe to be effective, it must be plausible to those in the problematic situation; the success rate is higher when the reframe is presented tentatively.

Refugee: A person who is outside his or her country of nationality and is unable or unwilling to return to that country because of persecution or a well-founded fear of persecution based on the person's race, religion, nationality, membership in a particular social group, or political opinion.

Reliability: A measurement tool that is reliable to the extent that similar results are consistently obtained on repeated and independent administrations of the tool.

Remarried family: This set of relationships is like those in a stepfamily except that at least one partner has been previously married.

Resilience: The ability to withstand and rebound from adversity, with recovery and growth out of crisis events or persistent life challenges.

Resistance: The expression of how people hold themselves back. A resistance signals the approach of an emerging contact boundary.

Resource acquisition: The process for acquiring the environmental resources desired by clients to achieve their goals, ensure their rights, and increase each person's assets.

Respondent behavior: Behavior that is reflexive in nature and elicited by preceding stimuli. Often emotional and physiological reactions are respondent behaviors.

Risk management: Measures designed to prevent negligence lawsuits and ethics complaints.

Role-playing: Setting up an opportunity for someone to practice and rehearse a skill. Usually this involves acting out brief real-life situations, with one person practicing the skill and another person responding to or receiving the skill.

Safe passage movement: An effort to bring about fundamental changes in social relationships between schools and community institutions by replacing fragmented, uncoordinated services for youth with integrated, collaborative networks of support.

Scaling question: A versatile technique employed to measure client progress, motivation, and confidence; scales generally run from 0 through 10 with the poles jointly defined by the practitioner and client. Scaling can also be used to rate a problem, feeling, or situation in terms of severity, frequency, desirability, and so on.

Schemas: "Rules of life" that individuals develop as a result of life experiences. They shape cognitive understanding.

Schema-focused therapy: This approach challenges self-defeating schemas through techniques like imagery and cognitive monitoring so the schemas no longer rule the client's perception of themselves and others.

Screening: Use of observation, records (if available), and standard questions to indicate the likelihood that an individual has a problem or issue other than the one for which he is referred. The screen is used to decide whether an assessment for the problem or issue is warranted. Screening is usually completed in 5 minutes or less.

Script: Attempts to repeat, in derivative form, a transference drama, which, like theatrical scripts, are primal dramas of childhood. It is a life plan based on decisions made in childhood, reinforced by parents, and justified by subsequent events.

Secondary trauma: Anxiety-related problems experienced by caregivers, first responders, and family members related to their interactions with someone who experiences a traumatic event.

Second-order change: A shift that occurs when an intervention introduces novelty to people stuck in the vicious circle of unsuccessfully trying to solve a problem. Because such interventions are not consistent with what the people involved assume about change, they have to accommodate their assumptions to the novelty of the interventions. Such accommodation results in growth and change of the person(s) stuck in the initial vicious circle involving the problem and, it is hoped, resolution of the problem.

Self-actualization: To fully realize and become one's fullest potential.

Self-care: Efforts by distressed people to alleviate symptoms by applying personal consultation and services to alleviate a health or mental health problem.

Self-psychology: A treatment orientation in psychoanalysis that encourages the growth of an integrated and cohesive intrapsychic structure through empathetic attunement and the internalization of particular functions initially proffered by the therapist.

Self-anchored scale: A technique used to request a person to rate a problem or situation using a scale (for example 1= not a problem to 5 = a significant problem) to quantify the degree of severity. For example, "Could you please rate your level of anxiety about taking the test from 1 to 5?" This crudely quantifies the level of the client's test anxiety.

Self-object: Psychologists use the term *self* to describe individuals who perform one of three functions that sustain and promote healthy development of the self: mirroring (responding to and affirming the child's innate sense of vigor, greatness, and perfection); idealizing (those with whom the child can merge as an image of calmness, infallibility, and omnipotence); and partnering (those with whom the child feels an essential affinity).

Self-report measure: A pencil-and-paper instrument completed by the client to assist in the assessment of certain behaviors, attitudes, feelings, or qualities, and their frequency, duration, and/or magnitude.

Selection bias: Systematic differences between group participants that may result from decisions about care, prognosis, client preference, or responsiveness to treatment.

Serious mental illness: A label used to characterize people who possess a major psychiatric diagnosis, substantial deficits in functioning, and an illness of long duration. Characterizes those individuals who are coping with long-term psychiatric concerns and who require high levels of service and support.

Service management: A model of case management in which the case manager can purchase or authorize services for his or her clients. These case managers are financially accountable for the care plans they develop.

Severe and persistent mental illness: A mental illness that results in serious impairment in functioning in daily community living and persists across time or is so frequently recurrent that such disability is long term.

Sexual disorder: A sexual dysfunction, paraphilia, gender identity disorder, or a sexual disorder not otherwise specified. Sexual disorders involve desired sexual objects, sexual response cycle, or arousal cues.

Sexual dysfunction: A problem characterized by a disturbance in the processes involving the sexual response cycle or by pain associated with sexual intercourse.

Sexual history: A history, usually obtained through a face-to-face interview but sometimes from a pencil-and-paper document, that reveals a person's sexual knowledge and experiences at each stage of development up to the present.

Sexual orientation: The commonly accepted, scientific term for the direction of sexual attraction, emotional and/or physical attraction, and its expression.

Sexual predator: A legal term referring to someone who seeks a relationship with another solely for the purposes of sexual assault.

Sexual response cycle: The stages of this cycle are desire, excitement, orgasm, and resolution. Disorders of sexual response may occur at one or more of these stages.

Shared decision making: An interactive collaborative process between the health care provider and the consumer that is used to make mental health decisions, where the provider becomes a consultant to the consumer, helping them by providing information and discussing options.

Signs of safety partnership: An approach to child protection that promotes the participation, cooperation, and collaboration between the social worker, child, and family.

Single-subject design methodology: The procedures employed in implementing a research design for evaluating the effectiveness of practice with one client unit—that is, individual, couple, family, or group.

Skills-based play therapy: An action-oriented treatment approach using scripted modeling plays, stories that model skills, selected skills from the child's spontaneous play, and plays and stories that are specific to the child's needs.

Social action: A collective endeavor to promote a cause or make a progressive change in the face of opposition.

Social constructivism: An epistemological perspective that takes the view that there is not an objective reality standing independently outside the individual knower, and that both individual and social processes are involved in the social construction of reality.

Social diagnosis: The series of judgments about clients and their situations for which the practitioner assumes responsibility made throughout the life of a case, which serve as the basis for intervention.

Social history: A component of the social work record. It includes detailed descriptions of the client and the situation, currently and in the past. The social history involves both a process (collecting information) and a product (the document). It focuses attention on personal, family, social, and environmental issues, and assists the social worker in developing an understanding of the client-situation in context and over time.

Social justice: The concept of a society in which justice is achieved in every aspect of society, rather than merely the administration of law. As there is no objective, known standard of what is *just*, the term can be amorphous and refer to sometimes self-contradictory values of justice. A just society is generally considered one that affords individuals and groups fair treatment and a just share of benefits.

Social justice clinical practice: An approach to clinical practice that attempts to promote the promotion of social justice in all thinking and action. This newly emerging approach critiques existing theories and practices and develops new ones from the point of view of advancing distributive and relational justice.

Social phobia or social anxiety disorder: A persistent fear of one or more social or performance situations in which the individual experiences unfamiliar people or possible scrutiny. The individual fears that he or she will be humiliated or embarrassed by acting in a way or showing anxiety symptoms, and this fear and anxiety interferes with the person's social functioning.

Social planning: The process of defining and documenting a social need (problem analysis), establishing and implementing goals and objectives, and evaluating the effort, effectiveness, and outcomes.

Social skills: These can be defined as a complex set of skills that facilitate the successful interactions between peers, parents, teachers, and other adults. The "social" refers to interactions between people; the "skills" refers to making appropriate discriminations—that is, deciding what would be the most effective response and using the verbal and nonverbal behaviors that facilitate interaction.

Social skills training (SST): A well established form of behavior therapy that involves didactic instruction, role-playing, rehearsal, and reinforced practice of ill-developed social skills. This practice is more effective when conducted in carefully titrated real-life situations, although exposure and practice in imagination may be useful when re-creating real life social situations is not practical.

Social support: Emotional and concrete assistance received from other people. Such assistance involves formal and informal means of aid to clients in the community that allows them to function optimally in a natural setting.

Social work diagnosis: A series of judgments, made by a therapist about the client's person and his or her social systems, that serves as the therapist's basis of interventions and for which he or she is prepared to accept professional responsi-

bility. A social work diagnosis may include a DSM-IV-TR classification.

Sociopolitical empowerment: Participation in the sociopolitical process to affect issues and concerns that impact the control and mastery of one's life.

Socratic dialogue: The dialectic method of exploration using questions and answers to produce conclusions. This questioning procedure is frequently used by cognitive-behavioral therapists in the cognitive restructuring process.

Solution-focused brief therapy (SFBT): A competency-based brief therapy model that respects the client's capacities to solve his or her own problems and charges the therapist with the job of creating a context by which this can happen. This approach focuses on the future and facilitates changes in language and cognition and coaches clients to take active steps toward solution building.

Spirituality: A search for purpose, meaning, and connection between oneself, other people, the universe, and the ultimate reality, which can be experienced within either a religious or a nonreligious framework.

Selective Serotonin Reuptake Inhibitors (SSRIs): A class of antidepressants used to treat anxiety disorders and other conditions. They are said to work by boosting the amount of a neurotransmitter (serotonin) that is linked to mood regulation.

Stages of readiness: The developmental stages (precontemplative, contemplative, preparation, maintenance, and termination) that clients tend to go through when changing their attitudes, beliefs or behaviors. When a practitioner does not match their intervention to the particular stage of readiness that the client is in, resistance to treatment will result.

Stages of change: The temporal dimension that represents when particular changes occur. Stage also represents a continuum of motivational readiness to take and sustain action. Stages of the transtheoretical model include precontemplation, contemplation, preparation, action, and maintenance.

Stages of migration: A time sequence of the process of international migration that consists of premigration and departure, transit, and resettlement. Each stage entails unique psychosocial stressors that may influence health and mental health.

Standard of care: What an ordinary, prudent practitioner with the same or similar training and education would have done under the same or similar circumstances.

Standardized measure: Paper-and-pencil instruments, completed by the client and/or social worker, that provide a score indicating the extent or severity of a client problem or strength. A measure is standardized when it has been tested (normed) on a relevant group of people, the process of which results in psychometric data, specifically, information about reliability and validity. Also, there are certain procedures for administration, scoring, and interpretation.

Stepfamily: This family type is formed of an adult couple and at least one child from a previous relationship of one of the adults who live in the same household.

Strategic family therapy: A present-focused therapy model that emphasizes the understanding of the client's construction of reality and focuses intervention on altering the dysfunctional interactional patterns that are believed to maintain the client's presenting problems.

Strategic therapy: When the clinician goes into each session with a client with a plan for conducting the session and intervening in the client system based on the clinician's hypotheses about what dynamics are involved in maintaining the problem.

Strategy: A plan for action that links problems and solutions and depends on an ongoing assessment of the actions and sentiments of other actors, including one's own constituency, the target, and the general public.

Strengths: An individual's intellectual, physical, and interpersonal skills, capacities, interests, and motivations.

Strengths assessment: Specialized assessment tools and processes that are designed to capture the current and past involvement and success of clients in a wide range of life domains including education, employment, housing, health, and use of leisure time. Information is collected on both personal and environmental strengths as a basis for developing a treatment plan that involves building on and amplifying those strengths.

Strengths-based case management: A case management model in which the underlying premise is that the client or family and child have the skills and talents to make changes in their lives. This model provides an opportunity for clients

or families to focus on their strengths rather than their deficits.

Stress: Internal (physical or emotional) responses to a life stressor that exceeds one's perceived personal and environmental resources to cope with it.

Structural family therapy: A therapy model that defines the family as a system whose structure consists of predictable patterns that govern the family members interactions. The goal of this therapy is change the family structure by reinforcing boundaries and helping parents resume parental authority and appropriate roles.

Structured clinical interview for *DSM-IV* (SCID): A semi-structured interview guide for making *DSM-IV* diagnoses. It provides diagnostic criteria from *DSM-IV*, interview questions for clinicians to determine whether criteria are present, and a place to record ratings.

Structured contextual assessments: Detailed appraisals of individual and family functioning; these are used to develop case plans and treatment goals.

Substance use disorder: A maladaptive pattern of substance use leading to clinically significant impairment or distress.

Substance abuse treatment: State and federally regulated programs for men and women with substance use disorders. Substance abuse treatment may include behavioral therapy, medications, or their combination. Mutual aid groups such as AA are integral to, but outside of substance abuse treatment.

Supervision: An interaction in which a supervisor is assigned or designated to assist and direct the practice of a supervisee through teaching, administration, and helping.

Support: A resource, the use of which helps an individual to function more effectively in a specific environment.

Supported employment: An approach to helping people with mental illnesses find and keep competitive employment within their communities. Supported employment programs are staffed by employment specialists who have frequent meetings with treatment providers to integrate supported employment with mental health services.

Supported housing: An empowerment and integration model that places consumers in independent housing coupled with flexible individualized services to facilitate community integration.

Surface structure: Behavioral and linguistic responses of edited experience used to convey meaning and pursue desired outcomes.

Switching: The change from one purported personality state to another; usually sudden and often a response to psychosocial stressors.

Synapse: In the brain, the tiny space between cell axons and dendrites filled by neurotransmitters ferrying electrical impulses from one cell to another.

Synergy: When all the parts of the center work together to create the "sum is more than the parts" phenomena that is important to positive program and individual outcomes. The synergy within a center develops the collaboration that results in protective factors to buffer risks for parents and children and promotes transformation and change.

Synopsis: A brief description of an original article or systematic review used to support evidence-based practice.

Synthesizing: A worker intervention that connects specific issues, feelings, or patterns a client is reporting or experiencing.

System of care: A range of programs and services for individuals with mental disorders from the most restrictive locked psychiatric units to the least restrictive community-based outpatient settings.

Systematic review: A comprehensive, unbiased, and reproducible review of prior studies that follows a detailed protocol. This involves a clearly formulated research question, explicit inclusion and exclusion criteria, systematic methods to comprehensively identify relevant studies, agreement on key decisions and coding, critical appraisal of the quality of evidence, and analysis and synthesis of data collected from the studies.

Systems-driven case management: A model of case management emphasizing efficient and effective delivery of organizational services. Efficiency is achieved through rationing of services, enhanced coordination of service delivery, using less expensive alternatives, and controlling clients' behavior.

Tactics: Short-term activities undertaken as part of a strategy for change.

Targets of benefits: The constituents on whose behalf advocacy efforts are undertaken. Some-

times the general public is the intended beneficiary of legislative advocacy.

Targets of influence: Those individuals and groups that are the focus of legislative advocacy efforts. They include the legislators (and their staffs), other political stakeholders, executive department heads (and key staff), the media, and other influential opinion makers and advocates.

Task planning and implementation sequence: In the task-centered model, a systematic sequence of practitioner and client activities designed to help clients develop and carry out problem-solving actions or tasks. Activities include task selection and planning, establishing incentives and a rationale for the task, anticipating obstacles, task rehearsal, task agreement, and summarizing and recording the task. The sequence, or elements of it, can be used in any form of intervention that makes use of between-session tasks or homework assignments.

Task-centered: The name of the model developed by William J. Reid and Laura Epstein in the early 1970s, in which intervention is focused on helping clients develop and carry out specific problem-solving actions or tasks. The term may be used more generally to refer to any intervention with this focus.

Technical eclecticism: Integrative approach to psychosocial intervention that emphasizes pragmatic application of technical procedures on basis of clinical efficacy; the aim is to match specific techniques with problems in functioning in light of empirical evidence and clinical expertise; this is the most technically oriented form of integration.

Technique: An observable action or object introduced by the social worker into the treatment process aimed at achieving a particular specific therapeutic outcome. Such action or object is replicable by others, has a level of professional approbation and is understandable from a relevant theoretical perspective.

Theoretical integration: Integrative approach to psychosocial intervention that emphasizes conceptual synthesis rather than blend of common elements or technical procedures; unifying frameworks link theories of personality, problems in living, and methods of intervention; generally regarded as the most challenging integrative strategy.

Therapeutic alliance: The collaborative and affective bond between social worker and client.

Therapeutic change agents: Term used for parents who are supervised by filial therapists to work directly with their own children to effect therapeutic change in them.

Therapeutic relationship: In the common factors model, the client–clinician relationship is one key source or catalyst of change, not simply a taken-for-granted background for the impact of specific therapeutic techniques. Factors that contribute to the relationship are clinician characteristics, the empathy or warmth shown to the client by the clinician, and how the clinician and client collaborate together on treatment goals.

Tolerance building: Reduced sensitivity of a partner to the other partner's unfavorable behavior as a result of exposure to the behavior.

Transaction: A single stimulus and a single response, verbal or nonverbal. It is the unit of social interaction.

Transference: According to psychodynamic theory, the patterns of expectation, established over course of development and life experience, that influence perceptions of other persons, interpretation of events, and modes of interpersonal behavior. In a therapeutic relationship, it occurs when the client responds in a nonaware manner to the therapist as if the therapist were someone of significance from the client's past. When properly understood, this phenomenon can be a source of growth for the client.

Transgender: A person who identifies as a member of a gender other than that of his or her own body.

Transmuting internalization: The developmental process whereby a function formerly performed by another is taken into the self and becomes the enduring, unique psychological structure of that individual, occurring via optimal frustration and optimal gratification, and characterized by incremental accretion and consolidation.

Transnational life: This theoretical perspective explains the growing trend of close ties between migrants and their home countries. It entails practices, relationships, and identities that maintain a close relationship to the country of origin by immigrants and their children and affects acculturation and assimilation.

Transparency: Clarity of goals and outcomes in terms organizational operation. The absence of barriers or obstacles to understanding decision making and responsibility.

Transparency: The therapeutic practice of publicly situating ideas in one's experience so as to clarify what they are based on between the worker and clients; intended to help clients clarify the reasons they have sought assistance. As a product it is a mutual agreement between the worker and the client as to the nature of the problem and the meaning ascribed to the factors influencing the problem.

Transpersonal: A philosophical perspective on human behavior that focuses on human development and potential beyond the development of rationality and autonomous ego to the possibility of self-transcendence and unity with the ultimate reality.

Transportability: The ease of which the average practitioner can take the ideas and concepts of any therapy model and integrate them into the real world with real clients.

Transtheoretical model: A multidimensional approach to change that includes the advanced integration of change processes and principles derived from the leading theories of behavior change.

Trauma: Experience involving actual or threat of death, serious injury, or loss of physical integrity to which the person responds with fear, helplessness, or horror. These experiences involve distressing physical or psychological incidents outside a person's usual range of experience.

Treatment: A process in which a qualified professional practitioner interacts with a client to alleviate symptoms, produce change in behavior, or improve functioning. Also referred to as *intervention*.

Treatment goal: An aim mutually identified by the social worker and client toward which they will work toward during the course of treatment. Goals should be clearly defined, observable, measurable, feasible, and realistic; stated in positive terms; stem directly from the assessment; and set collaboratively by the social worker and the client.

Treatment planning: A formalized process of individualizing and operationalizing clients' treatment goals and specifying measurable outcomes to chart therapeutic progress. A specific plan is mapped out in clear, concise, and measurable terms for the treatment of a client's specific problem and achieving mutually defined treatment goals.

Triangles: The formation of relationships in families and other systems that involves two people functioning in relation to a third, usually reducing tension in the initial dyad. The collusion of the two in relation to the third is the defining characteristic of a triangle. The behavior of one member of a triangle is a function of the behavior of the other two, and behavior is reciprocal.

Tricyclic antidepressants: A class of antidepressants useful with some anxiety disorders. They purportedly work by regulating several neurotransmitters.

Triggers: Events, behaviors, language, and other environmental or emotional stimuli that cause a person's fight/flight/freeze reaction to recur as if the original trauma is occurring.

Tripolar self: According to psychodynamic theory, the mental structure linking particular kinds of self-selfobject relationships with corresponding poles of self experience, consisting of the grandiose-exhibitionistic self, the idealized parent imago, and the alter ego.

Typology: A framework for organizing information into coherent broad categories that contribute to understanding a given phenomenon conceptually.

Undocumented immigrant: A person who comes to live in the host country without legal documentation; this term is preferred rather than "illegal immigrant."

Ultimate reality (ultimate environment): Conceptualizations of the highest level of reality, understood differently by persons of various spiritual belief systems and/or at different levels of spiritual development or consciousness.

Unconscious process: Any cognitive, affective, motor, and other psychophysiological process that operates beyond a person's conscious control.

Unified detachment: Partners' description of problems in interactions in an emotionally detached and nonjudgmental manner.

Unique outcome: In conversation with clients, any time when a narrative therapist notes that a client has not been overcome by his or her problems—or has successfully challenged them. These outcomes may represent new truths about themselves which may be strengths that present new options.

Utilization: Social work practice that uses and values what the client brings, including strengths and inner resources. The social worker accepts not only what the client brings but what is brought is valued and essential to helping the client.

Utilization review: A process in which established criteria are used to evaluate the services provided in terms of cost-effectiveness, necessity, and effective use of resources.

Validation: The social worker's unbiased acknowledgment and confirmation of a client statement or problem. If the social worker does not validate client concerns, he or she may not move forward; if social workers only validate clients they may not move on; the key is to validate and then move on.

Validity: A measurement tool is valid to the extent that it *accurately* captures or measures the construct for which it is intended.

Values: The preferences, beliefs, traditions, practices, and customs considered desirable by a particular group of people.

Victim blaming: Subtle or blatant assignment of blame and responsibility to the victim of a traumatic event.

Victim services: Crisis and short-term counseling services, community referrals, and legal advocacy provided to crime victims, witnesses, and family survivors through law enforcement and the court systems.

Vitamin: An organic substance essential in small amounts for growth and bodily activity and that may be effective in treating some mental and emotional disorders.

Vulnerable clients: People who have sought assistance with a problem or issue whose disabilities and impediments are serious and long term and make it difficult for them meet ordinary personal and social requirements or to fulfill activities of daily living.

Will to meaning: A central human motivational dynamic and reason for human behavior.

Womanism: One form of feminism arising from the African American experience and focusing on the importance of race as well as gender.

Working alliance: This refers to one aspect of the therapeutic relationship—how the consumer and provider collaborate together to achieve treatment goals. The alliance is measured according to the extent to which the consumer and the provider collaborate on setting goals and completing tasks, and the strength of the bond between them.

Z-score: A standardized score that has a mean of zero and a standard deviation of one. A Z-score allows the client's score to be compared relative to another sample. Scores are computed by taking the scale mean from a client raw score and dividing by the standard deviation.

CHAPTER CREDITS

CHAPTER 124

Zvi D. Gellis, "Evidence-Based Practice in Older Adults with Mental Health Disorders: Geriatric Mental Health." This chapter appeared in an earlier version as "Older Adults with Mental and Emotional Problems" in Barbara Berkman (Ed.), *Handbook of Social Work in Health and Aging* (2006).

CHAPTER 145

Paula Allen-Meares, "Overview of Current and Future Practices in School Social Work." This chapter appeared in an earlier version as "Where Do We Go from Here? Mental Health Workers and the Implementation of an Evidence-Based Practice," in Cynthia Franklin, Mary Beth Harris, and Paula Allen-Meares (Eds.), *The School Services Sourcebook: A Guide for School-Based Professionals* (2006).

CHAPTER 146

Ron Avi Astor, Rami Benbenishty, Roxana Marachi, and Ronald O. Pitner, "Evidence-Based Violence Prevention Programs and Best Implementation Practices." This chapter appeared in an earlier version (by Ron Astor, Roxana Marachi, Rami Benbenishty, and Michelle Rosemond) as "Evidence-Based Violence Prevention Programs and Best Implementation Practices," in Cynthia Franklin, Mary Beth Harris, and Paula Allen-Meares (Eds.), *The School Services Sourcebook: A Guide for School-Based Professionals* (2006).

CHAPTER 147

Stephen J. Tripodi, Johnny S. Kim, and Kimberly Bender, "Promising Interventions for Students Who Have Co-Occurring Disorders." This chapter appeared in an earlier version (by Stephen J. Tripodi, Johnny S. Kim, and Diana M. DiNitto) as "Effective Strategies for Working with Students Who Have Co-Occurring Disorders," in Cynthia Franklin, Mary Beth Harris, and Paula Allen-Meares (Eds.), *The School Services Sourcebook: A Guide for School-Based Professionals* (2006).

CHAPTER 148

David W. Springer and Courtney J. Lynch, "Effective Interventions for Students with Conduct Disorder." This chapter appeared in an earlier version as "Effective Interventions for Students with Conduct

Disorder" in Cynthia Franklin, Mary Beth Harris, and Paula Allen-Meares (Eds.), *The School Services Sourcebook: A Guide for School-Based Professionals* (2006).

CHAPTER 149

Cynthia Franklin, Johnny S. Kim, and Michael S. Kelly, "Solution-Focused, Brief Therapy Interventions for Students at Risk to Drop Out." This chapter appeared in an earlier version (by Cynthia Franklin, Johnny S. Kim, and Stephen J. Tripodi) as "Solution-Focused, Brief Therapy Intervention for Students at Risk to Drop Out" in Cynthia Franklin, Mary Beth Harris, and Paula Allen-Meares (Eds.), *The School Services Sourcebook: A Guide for School-Based Professionals* (2006).

CHAPTER 150

Rowena Fong, Marilyn Armour, Noël Busch-Armendariz, and Laurie Cook Heffron, "Case Management Interventions with Immigrant and Refugee Students and Families." This chapter appeared in an earlier version (by Rowena Fong, Marilyn Armour, Noel Busch Armendariz, Laurie Cook Heffron, and Anita McClendon) as "Case Management Intervention with Immigrant and Refugee Students and Families" in Cynthia Franklin, Mary Beth Harris, and Paula Allen-Meares (Eds.), *The School Services Sourcebook: A Guide for School-Based Professionals* (2006).

CHAPTER 151

Steven W. Evans, Joanna M. Sadler, and Christine E. Brady, "Treating Children and Adolescents with ADHD in the Schools." This chapter appeared in an earlier version (by Carey E. Masse, Steven W. Evans, Ruth C. Brown, and Allen B. Grove) as "What Parents and Teachers Should Know: Effective Treatments for Youth with ADHD" in Cynthia Franklin, Mary Beth Harris, and Paula Allen-Meares (Eds.), *The School Services Sourcebook: A Guide for School-Based Professionals* (2006).

CHAPTER 152

Daphna Oyserman, "Working with Culturally/Racially Diverse Students to Improve Connection to School and Academic Performance." This chapter appeared in an earlier version in Cynthia Franklin, Mary Beth Harris, and Paula Allen-Meares (Eds.), *The School Services Sourcebook: A Guide for School-Based Professionals* (2006).

AUTHOR INDEX

Abass, A., 553
Abbott, C., 89
Abbott, E., 1117
Abel, G., 1098, 1100, 1101
Abell, M. D., 189
Abell, N., 387, 403, 404
Abeni, D., 401
Abercromby, S., 1084
Abery, B., 761
Abidin, R. R., 391, 392
Abildgaard, W., 396
Abolfazl Fateh, A., 402
Abrahamowicz, M., 849
Abrams, R., 844
Abramson, D. M., 802
Achenbach, T. M., 816, 989
Achtmeyer, C., 835
Aciemo, R., 666
Ackerman, M. J., 1061
Adams, R. E., 731
Addis, M. E., 821
Adelman, H., 980, 981, 1033
Adelman, R., 1107
Adey, M., 556
Adnopoz, J. A., 4, 75
Ager, J., 1046
Ager, J. W., 367
Agresta, J., 667
Aguilera, D., 211
Ahluwalia, J. S., 24
Ahn, H., 221
Aidala, A. A., 802
Aiken, L. S., 475
Akincigil, A., 846
Albano, A. M., 818
Albert, R., 1062
Alcabes, A., 515
Aldgate, J., 856, 858
Alexander, J., 436
Alexander, J. F., 674, 1012

Alexander, L. B., 809
Alexander, R., 665
Alexopoulos, G., 844, 846
Alford, B. A., 588
Alger, I., 332
Algina, J., 1013
Allard, H., 1098
Allen, B. A., 368
Allen, J., 89
Allen, J. P., 692, 693, 696
Allen, S., 89
Allen-Meares, P., 42, 1161, 1215
Allison, T. G., 828
Allness, D. J., 871
Almeida, D., 108
Alterman, A., 787
Alterman, A. I., 27
Altman, D. G., 1138, 1143
Altschuler, S., 42, 43
Alvarez, J., 846
Alvarez, M., 42, 43
Alwahhabi, , F., 849
Alwyn, T., 367
Amato, P. R., 733, 734
Ambrose, A. T., 815
Ambuhl, H., 221
Amster, B. J., 1064
Anastopoulos, A. D., 1012
Anda, R., 699
Anderson, C., 483
Anderson, H., 297, 298
Anderson, L., 797
Anderson, R. M., 1061, 1066
Anderson-Butcher, D., 908
Andersson, N., 1155, 1156
Anderton, C., 604
Andreason, N., 699
Andrew, M., 1136
Andrews, D. A., 1095, 1096
Andrews, G., 369

Andrews, H., 175
Andrews, J., 397
Andrews, K. T., 897
Anetzberger, G. J ., 1107
Angel, B., 787
Annon, J., 740
Anthony, W., 770
Anthony, W. A., 775
Antle, B., 1099
Antler, S., 159
Antman, E. M., 1164
Anton, B. S., 817
Anton, R. F., 29
Apfeldorf, W. J., 362
Aponte, H. J., 442, 443, 444, 445
Applebaum, P., 1093, 1094
Applebaum, P. S., 124, 1060
Applebaum, R., 792, 797
Applegate, J. S., 1061
Archer, J., 655
Ardila, A., 970
Arean, A., 846
Areán, P. E., 552
Areán, P. A., 553, 941, 943
Arendt, M., 731
Arkava, M. L., 318
Arkowitz, H., 259, 260
Armistead, L., 1011
Armour, M., 1216
Armstrong, E., 169
Arnau, R. C., 369
Arndt, L. A., 830
Arthur, M. W., 673
Artiss, K., 726
Asay, T. P., 51, 222
Ashcraft, K. L., 277
Asher, S. R., 654
Ashford, J. B., 652, 1091, 1092, 1096

Ashton, D., 908
Askay, S., 604
Astin, M. C., 718
Astor, R., 42
Astor, R. A., 985, 986, 995, 998, 1215
Athey, G. I., 164, 166
Atkins, D. C., 434, 472, 473
Atkins, M., 3, 6
Atkinson, L., 625
Austin, B. T., 801
Austin, C., 792, 797
Austin, K. M., 122
Austin, M. J., 882
Averill, P. M., 849, 850
Aviram, R. B., 742, 743, 745
Axinn, J., 893
Ayalon, L., 941
Ayers, C., 849
Ayers, S. C., 65, 68
Azrin, N. H., 100, 1004, 1008

Babbie, E., 200, 356, 390
Babitsky, S., 1063
Babonis, T. R., 368
Babyak, M. A., 361
Bacaltchuck, J., 845
Bachelor, A., 223
Bachman, R., 95
Bachman, S. S., 402
Badgely, R., 1098
Baer, R. A., 1013
Baerger, D., 132
Baghurst, P. A., 621
Baier, A., 118
Baity, M. R., 744
Baker, A. J. L., 817
Baker, B. L., 623
Baker, J. A., 625
Baker, L., 444, 1082
Baker, M. J., 717
Balaam, M., 1091
Baldwin, L., 391
Baldwin, S. A., 434, 435, 436
Ball, C., 364
Ball, S. A., 837
Ball, W. A., 344
Balustein, M., 1083
Banach, M., 187, 189, 190
Bank, L., 1012
Banks, S., 1094
Barak, A., 187, 189, 190
Baranoski, M., 175, 1104
Barber, J., 784, 785
Barbour, F., 845
Baretta-Herman, A., 865
Barkely, R. A., 1012
Barker, K., 1131
Barker, P. R., 369
Barker, R. L., 156
Barker, S. B., 718
Barkley, R., 1012

Barkley, R. A., 391, 528, 622, 624, 625
Barley, D. E., 808
Barlow, D. H., 344, 395, 539, 542, 543, 713, 1177
Barlow, E., 1040
Barnes, C., 192
Barnett, B. L., Jr., 1164
Barnett, D. J., 731
Barney, D. D., 803, 806
Barnhardt, T., 604
Bar-On, R., 395
Barrett, M., 305, 306
Barrett-Lennard, G. T., 239, 240
Barrick, C., 23
Barron, C., 177
Barron, J., 158
Barrowclough, C., 25
Barry, K. L., 778
Barry, T. D., 654
Barsky, A. E., 1071, 1072, 1073, 1074
Bartels, S., 666
Bartels, S. J., 941
Barth, R., 765
Barth, R. P., 792
Bartlett, G., 849
Bartlett, H., 1055
Bartlik, B., 740
Barton, C., 436
Barton, W. E., 64
Barusch, A. S., 939, 940
Basham, K., 434, 478, 480
Bass, D., 654, 1013
Bastiaens, L., 368
Batchelor, J., 856
Bateman, A. W., 743, 744, 745
Bath, E., 35
Batthyany, A., 267, 271
Battino, R., 578
Battistich, V., 988, 992, 993
Baucom, D. H., 434, 472, 473, 717
Bauer, M. S., 344, 1160
Baum, M. C., 164, 165
Baum, N., 734
Bauman, K. E., 674
Bauman, L. J., 619
Baumrind, D., 620
Bavelas, J. B., 255
Baydar, N., 1012
Bearman, P. S., 674
Bearss, K., 1012
Bear-Tibbets, H. Y., 676
Beaton, R., 107
Bebbington, P., 369
Bech, P., 396
Beck, A., 552, 556
Beck, A. T., 244, 246, 588, 592, 745
Beck, D., 200
Beck, J., 552
Beck, J. G., 849, 850
Beck, J. S., 243, 245, 246, 589, 593

Becker, D. R., 705, 706, 707, 708
Becker, J., 1098, 1100, 1101
Beckett, L. R., 606
Becvar, D., 47, 52
Becvar, R., 47, 52
Beech, A., 1103
Beekman, A., 846
Beer, D., 35
Beglin, S. J., 364
Behre, W. J., 998
Beidas, R. S., 817
Beland, F., 797
Belkin, G., 210
Bell, C. C., 109
Bell, V., 187, 189, 192
Bellack, A., 666, 667
Bellavance, F., 844
Belle, D., 674
Benac, C. N., 641
Benbenishty, R., 42, 985, 986, 995, 998, 1215
Bender, K., 386, 1004, 1009, 1215
Benefield, R., 24
Benett, E., 368
Bengivengo, M., 27
Benjamin, A. E., 762
Benjamin, G. A. H., 1061
Bennett, M., 666
Bennington-Davis, M., 699, 702
Benoit, D., 625
Benshoff, J., 784
Benson, C. A., 802
Benson, H., 607
Benson, K., 221
Bentley, K., 820
Bentley, K. J., 690, 691
Benzer, D. G., 166
Benzies, K., 921
Berg, I. K., 47, 215, 216, 253, 255, 256, 257, 274, 296, 297, 522, 594, 595, 596, 599, 1020, 1021, 1025, 1026
Berg, J. W., 124
Berg Insoo, K., 1086
Berger, C. S., 790, 791, 792, 793, 794
Bergersen, T. D., 364
Berglund, P., 385, 548, 691, 848, 1004, 1007
Bergman, H., 797
Bergman, H. C., 756, 757
Bergus, G. R., 1120
Berk, L. E., 1060, 1064
Berkman, B., 5
Berkman, N. D., 533
Berkowitz, S., 4, 75
Berlin, S., 260
Berliner, L., 718
Berman, A. L., 128
Berman, J., 1106, 1107
Bernabei, R., 797
Bernal, M. E., 1012

Bernard, J., 165
Bernat, F. P., 187, 189, 190
Bernstein, B. E., 1061
Bernstein, L., 676
Berra, Y., 169
Berrios, G. E., 335
Berry, M., 856
Berward, C., 280, 281
Berwick, D. M., 196
Besharov, D. J., 159
Best, A. L., 623
Best, S., 106
Betten, N., 882
Beutler, L., 222, 223, 224
Beutler, L. E., 717
Bewsey, S., 47
Beyer, J. M., 166
Bezmen, J., 177
Bhattacharya, G., 970
Bhugara, D., 402
Bianchard, K., 787
Bickman, L., 435
Biegel, D., 713
Biegel, D. E., 634
Bierman, J., 790, 793
Biever, J., 1020, 1022, 1025
BigFoot, D., 951
Biggerstaff, M. A., 148, 149,
    151
Biggs, J., 344
Biglan, A., 981
Billingham, S., 672, 677
Binner, P., 785
Birt, J., 1083
Bishmann, D., 848
Bishop, D., 391
Bisman, C., 516
Bissell, L., 164
Bisson, J., 1123, 1136
Bisson, J. I., 717, 718
Bjorgum, L., 364
Blaauw, E., 89
Black, D., 745
Black, D. W., 745
Black, H. C., 132, 134
Black, M., 311, 315
Blackwell, B., 498
Blair, K. D., 765
Blair, M. C., 1046
Blair, S. L., 1046
Blais, M. A., 744
Blanch, A., 794
Blanchard, C. G., 827
Blanchard, E. G., 561
Blaske, D. M., 1013
Blatt-Eisengart, I., 620
Blazer, D., 843, 844, 845, 846, 848
Bleiberg, K., 745
Block, C. R., 95
Block, J., 1013
Block, P., 911
Bloom, H., 175

Bloom, M., 320, 352, 356, 382,
    383, 387, 400, 401, 402, 432
Bloom, S., 699, 700, 702
Bloomquist, M., 655
Bloomquist, M. L., 1016
Blose, J. O., 835
Blough, D. K., 849
Blow, A. J., 434
Blum, N., 745
Blum, R. W., 674
Blythe, B., 521
Boardman, T., 24
Bober, T., 106, 108
Bobo, K., 881
Bodin, A., 216, 217
Boer, D., 1098, 1101, 1103
Boers, M., 1155, 1156
Boes, M., 936
Boggs, S., 1013
Bohart, A. C., 240
Bolen, R. M., 13, 19
Bolk, J. H., 402
Boller, K., 76
Bolton, R., 210
Bonaventura, A., 827
Bond, F. W., 287, 550
Bond, G. R., 705, 706, 707, 708,
    709
Boney-McCoy, S., 392, 468
Bongar, B., 134
Bonner, J., 364
Bonta, J., 1095, 1096
Booth, C., 73
Borden, W., 259, 260, 261, 305, 306
Borders, T. F., 361
Bordin, E. S., 808
Borduin, C. M., 74, 1013
Boruch, R. F., 981, 1142
Borum, R., 1093
Borus, J., 331
Boscarino, J. A., 731
Boss, P., 673
Botsko, M., 856, 859
Bottoms, S., 367
Bouhoutsos, J., 164
Bouis, S., 3
Boukin, C., 907, 911
Boulanger, J. L., 370
Bourdin, C. M., 1013
Boutin-Foster, C., 370
Bowen, G. L., 912, 913, 914, 915,
    916, 980
Bowen, L., 1177, 1178
Bowen, M., 74, 416, 447, 448, 449,
    450
Bowen, N. K., 916
Bower, P., 847
Bowers, K., 604
Boyd-Franklin, N., 73, 555, 963,
    965
Boyle, N., 799
Bozarth, J. D., 236

Braddock, D., 761
Bradford, J., 1098, 1100, 1101
Bradley, R., 310
Bradley, S., 691
Brady, C., 790, 793, 1043,
    1216
Brakel, S. J., 175
Bramson, R., 369
Brandell, J., 311
Brandl, B., 1107
Brandon, M., 859
Brann, A., 790, 793
Brave Heart, M. Y. H., 951
Brazier, D. J., 237
Breckman, R., 1107
Brekke, J. S., 666, 979, 980
Bremmer, R. H., 1117
Brendler, J., 1084
Brener, N. D., 980, 981
Brenes, G., 849
Brennan, J., 801
Brennan, J. W., 475
Bresnahan, M., 1092
Brestan, E. V., 1011, 1012, 1013
Briar-Lawson, K., 226
Bricker-Jenkins, M, 277, 278, 279,
    280
Brickman, A., 848
Brickman, D., 1045, 1046, 1047
Briere, J., 566
Bright, I., 434, 435
Bright, P., 539
Brink, T., 556
BrintzenhofeSzoc, K., 77, 831
Brodley, B. T., 236
Brodsky, B. S., 742, 743
Brodsky, S. L., 1061
Brody, G. H., 1011
Brody, J. L., 436
Broekaert, E., 784, 785, 787, 788
Brohl, K., 648
Brondino, M. J., 1004
Bronfenbrenner, U., 673
Broodie, C., 6
Broome, K. M., 818
Brounstein, P., 436, 437
Brouselle, A., 3
Brower, T., 799
Brown, C., 794
Brown, C. A., 1083
Brown, E. L., 844, 847
Brown, G., 844
Brown, G. K., 745
Brown, L. N., 682, 683
Brown, M. Z., 743
Brown, R., 676, 798
Brown, R. T., 1061
Brown, S., 745
Brown, T. A., 395
Brown, T. E., 1039, 1043
Brown, V., 700
Browne, K. D., 1103

Brownell, P., 88, 970, 1106, 1107, 1109, 1110
Brownley, K. A., 533
Bruce, M., 844, 845, 847, 848
Bruce, M. L., 743, 844, 941
Bruce, T., 821, 822, 824
Bruck, M., 1064
Brun, C., 772, 788
Brunker, C. P., 790, 792, 793
Bruno, F., 1116, 1117
Brussiere, M., 1101
Bry, B. H., 73
Bryan, A. D., 475
Bryant, A., 1099
Bryant, A. L., 1045
Bryant, R. A., 107, 109
Brymer, M. J., 109
Buchanan, R., 666
Buck, J., 784
Buck, P. W., 809
Buckley, H., 1082
Buckley, P. F., 402
Budman, S. H., 215, 216
Buetler, L., 259, 260
Buetler, L. E., 824
Buhrmester, D., 654
Buist, K., 257
Bukatko, D., 1060
Bulik, C. M., 533
Bullis, R. K., 117
Bullock, B. M., 458
Bulto, M., 666
Burbridge, J. A., 718
Burch, P. R., 1013
Burges, C., 107
Burke, J. L., 413, 417
Burke, M. P., 413
Burleson, B. R., 435
Burleson, J. A., 1004
Burnam, M. A., 361, 368
Burns, B., 65
Burns, B. J., 765, 980, 981, 982
Burns, G., 578
Burns, L., 790, 792, 793
Burr-Crutchfield, L., 846
Burt, M., 1100
Burton, J., 845, 846, 847, 919
Busch-Armendariz, N., 1216
Bush, K., 175, 176, 177
Bush, R. A. B., 1072
Bushway, S., 991
Buteau, E., 743
Bybee, D., 507, 513, 1045, 1047, 1048
Byock, G., 240

Cabral, L., 12, 13
Caine, E., 844, 845
Caine, E. D., 916
Caldera, Y., 621
Calhoun, K. S., 717
Calhoun, L. G., 562

Callahan, C., 847
Callas, P., 790, 791, 792, 793, 795
Calsyn, R. J., 809
Calvocoressi, L., 485
Camara, W. J., 400
Camargo, C. A., 532
Camarota, S., 969
Cameron, G., 713
Cameron, O. G., 548
Campbell, D., 95
Campbell, D. T., 1138, 1139, 1140, 1179
Campbell, J., 403, 507
Campbell, J. C., 95
Campbell, W., 276
Cano, A., 473
Capitman, J., 799
Caplan, G., 727, 728
Caplan, P. J., 334
Cappela, E., 3, 6
Capra, F., 232
Caputo, G. C., 539
Carew, J., 928, 932
Carey, M., 55
Carkhuff, R. R., 221, 237
Carlat, D. J., 532
Carling, P. J., 773
Carlisle, J., 758
Carlson, B., 790, 793, 795, 798
Carlson, B. E., 95, 1061, 1082
Carlson, E. B., 566
Carlson, E. R., 1140
Carlson, J. G., 717
Carlson, L. S., 709
Carmel, M., 761
Carnemolla, M. A., 707
Carpenter, B., 848
Carpenter, D., 350
Carpenter, L. A., 1061
Carr, A., 460
Carroll, D. H., 1012
Carroll, K., 23
Carroll, K. M., 837
Carstairs, G. M., 402
Carswell, C., 189
Carter, B., 409, 415, 416, 425, 964
Cash, S. J., 856
Cashel, M. L., 400
Caspar, F., 221
Caspi, A., 95
Cassidy, J., 1061
Castelloe, P., 889
Castonguay, L., 222, 223, 224
Castonguay, L. G., 824
Castro, F. G., 981
Catalano, R., 991
Catley, D., 24
Cavell, T. A., 1012
Ceci, S. J., 1061, 1064
Ceja, M., 928, 932
Celio, C., 3, 6
Cepeda, L. M., 235, 236

Cesta, T. G., 751, 754
Chaimowitz, G., 175, 176, 177
Chait, R. P., 156
Chalk, R., 1106
Challis, D., 797
Chalmers, T. C., 1164
Chambers, A., 846
Chambers, J. A., 623
Chambers, R., 891
Chambless, D. L., 717
Chambliss, C., 16
Chambliss, C. H., 215
Chambliss, D. L., 475, 539
Chambliss, M. L., 1120, 1125
Chan, A. W., 367
Chan, J. A., 18
Chandler, D., 95
Chang, J., 970
Chang, S. Y., 458, 1007
Chang-Muy, F., 971
Chapman, A. L., 743
Chapman, J. E., 745
Chappel, P., 991
Charlson, M. E., 370
Charney, D., 846
Chatlos, J. C., 1007, 1008
Chavira, D. A., 548
Chazan-Cohen, R., 76
Check, J., 1100
Checkoway, B., 895, 900, 901, 902
Chelminski, I., 548
Chemtob, C. M., 717
Chen, F., 491
Chen, T., 191
Cheney, A., 1116
Cheng, M., 28
Cherpitel, C. J., 366
Cherry, D. J., 43
Chethik, M., 315
Childs, K., 624
Chiu, W. T., 343, 552, 692
Cho, D., 785
Choi, Y., 1045
Chow, J., 1034
Christensen, A., 434, 467, 468, 472, 473
Christensen, C. R., 724
Christensen, D. N., 768
Christensen, H., 189
Christner, R. W., 528
Chronis, A. M., 528, 1039
Chu, J. A., 565, 567, 569
Churchill, E., 363
Churchill, R., 539, 1123
Ciechanowski, P., 847
Cigno, K., 768
Cimprich, B., 847
Ciraulo, D. A., 29
Cisler, R. A., 29
Clabby, J. F., 658
Claiborne, N., 5
Clancy, C., 187, 189, 190, 191, 192

Clancy, M., 887
Clark, C., 196
Clark, D., 110
Clark, D. A., 588
Clark, J., 191
Clark, T. E., 435
Clarke, I., 218
Clarkin, J. F., 742, 743, 744
Clemons, D., 1020, 1022, 1025
Cline, F., 622, 623, 625
Cloitre, M., 1083
Clore, G. L., 1047
Clougherty, K. F., 942
Cloward, R. S., 890
Cnaan, R., 6
Coady, N. F., 219
Coakley, E., 941
Coatsworth, D., 1082, 1085
Coatsworth, J. D., 968
Cobb, R., 908
Coe, W., 601, 604
Coffey, D. S., 768
Coffey, R., 784
Cohen, A., 194
Cohen, D., 691
Cohen, E. L., 754
Cohen, J., 1150
Cohen, J. A., 651, 700, 718
Cohen, M., 770
Cohen, S., 1131
Cohon, J. D., 767
Coit, C., 734
Colapinto, J., 444
Cole, M., 844, 845
Cole, P., 302
Coleman, H., 432
Coleman, M., 12, 13
Coleman, S. T., 297, 298
Collins, D., 432
Collins, K. S., 690
Collins, M., 507, 513
Colon, F., 417
Colon-Lopez, F., 417
Colpe, L. J., 369
Columbus, M., 696
Colvin, J., 226
Colwell, M., 621
Combs, J., 276
Comer, E., 856
Comtois, K. A., 743
Cone, L. T., 1013
Conger, R. D., 458
Congress, E., 115, 117, 300, 970, 971, 972
Congress, E. P., 409, 1109
Congress, P., 1033
Conigliaro, R. L., 366
Conmall, M. C., 25
Connell, A. M., 1011
Conners, C. K., 528
Connors, G., 23
Conrad, T., 672, 677

Constable, R., 42, 43
Constantine, J., 76
Constas, M. A., 474
Contratto, S., 280
Conwell, Y., 844
Cook, A., 1083
Cook, A. S., 634
Cook, B., 553
Cook, C. R., 655
Cook, D., 1178
Cook, E. T., 994, 997
Cook, T. D., 1140, 1179
Coomarasamy, A., 1172
Coombs, R. H., 165
Coontz, S., 425
Cooper, A. E., 1092
Cooper, B., 200
Cooper, B. A., 767
Cooper, H., 1153
Cooper, T., 908
Cooper, Z., 534
Coover, G., 676
Corbitt, E. M., 177
Corcoran, J., 89, 391, 435, 511, 512, 1022, 1149, 1153
Corcoran, K., 36, 50, 116, 215, 216, 217, 218, 317, 318, 320, 358, 384, 385, 387, 388, 390, 391, 393, 400, 401, 402, 403, 432, 506, 507, 511, 512, 815
Corden, J., 646
Cordova, J. V., 472
Cormack, C., 460
Cormier, C., 1101
Corneil, W., 107
Cornes, C., 943
Cornwall, P., 758
Corrigan, J., 194
Corrigan, P. W., 705, 707, 708, 709, 1092
Corsini, R. J., 1179
Corvo, K. N., 713
Costa, C., 787
Cotler, S., 1012
Cotton, M. A., 364
Coughlin, K. M., 200
Couper, D., 29
Cournoyer, B. R., 527
Coursey, R., 492
Covell, N. H., 756, 758
Covert-Vail, L., 1131
Coviello, D., 787
Cox, C., 844, 845
Cox, C. B., 738
Cox, J. L., 361
Cozolino, L., 1061
Crabtree, B., 6
Craig, J. V., 171
Craig, L. A., 1103
Cramer, I., 194
Crampton, D., 713
Crane, D. S., 434, 435

Crane, J., 916
Craske, M. G., 543
Crenshaw, D., 648
Crews, S. D., 655
Critchfield, B., 768
Crits-Cristoph, P., 344, 717, 735
Cross, H. J., 164, 165
Cross, T. A., 951
Crosson-Tower, C., 1061
Croughan, J., 398
Crowin, D., 664
Croxton, D., 117
Crum, T., 1004, 1008
Crumbaugh, J. C., 271
Cruz, C., 821
Crystal, S., 846
Cullen, F. T., 175
Cummings, M. R., 1061
Cunningham, A., 1082
Cunningham, P. B., 74, 436
Cunningham-Rathner, J., 1098, 1100, 1101
Curley, J., 887
Curry, J. F., 1013
Curtis, G. C., 548
Curtis, L., 492
Customer, M., 768
Cutler, R. B., 838
Cymerman, P., 866
Czuchry, M., 818

da Silva, R. B., 238
Daguio, E. R., 121
Dahl, R., 882
Daicoff, S. S., 1063
Dale, S., 798
Dallaire, L., 797
Dalrymple, K. L., 549, 550
Danieli, Y., 951
Daniels, N., 317
Dansereau, D. F., 818
Dark, F., 808, 809
Dartman, R., 979, 982, 983
Darton, R., 797
Dass-Brailsford, P., 861
Dattilio, F. M., 1061, 1062
Dattilio, J. F. M., 429, 432
Davenport, D. S., 235, 236
David, S., 937
Davidov, M., 619
Davidson, G. N. S., 218
Davidson, J. R. T., 363
Davidson, K., 743, 744
Davidson, L., 775
Davidson, P. R., 717, 718
Davies, I., 845
Davies, M., 326, 331
Davies, P., 171
Davis, B. G., 724
Davis, L. N., 724
Davis, M., 798, 1012
Davis, T., III, 920

Davison, M. R., 552, 553
Dawes, M., 171
De Freitas, K., 175
de Jesus, M., 845, 849, 850
De Jong, P., 217, 218, 255, 256,
        257, 296, 297, 522, 1025,
        1026
De Matt, S., 553
de Melo, M., 845
de Ruiter, C., 1103
De Shazer, S., 594, 595, 599
de Shazer, S. , 47, 51, 215, 216,
        217, 253, 254, 257, 274, 297,
        1086
de Toledo, B. A., 66
de Vogel, V., 1103
de Vries, L., 257
Deahl, M., 731
Dearing, R. L., 23
DebBruyn, L. M., 951
Deblinger, E., 651, 718
DeCato, L. A., 1004, 1008
DeGarmo, D. S., 458, 1012
DeHart, S. S., 834
DeJong, P., 594, 595, 596, 599
DeJonghe, F., 553
Dekker, J., 553
Dekovic, M., 257
Del Mar, C., 1163
Del Vento, A., 255
DeLeo, D., 844
Delgado, M., 1031, 1032
DeLois, K. A., 599
Delucchi, K., 992
Demaray, M. K., 676
DeMatteo, D., 1061
Deming, W. E., 200
Demirag, I., 156
Demler, O., 343, 385, 548, 552,
        691, 692, 848, 1004, 1007
Denby, R., 963
Dendukuri, N., 845
Dennis, J. A., 1135
Denton, W. H., 435
Depoy, E., 763
Dermen, K. H., 23
De-Rosa, C., 436
Derricott, J., 699
DeRubeis, R. J., 244, 246, 735
Desmons, S., 798
Deutsch, C., 164, 165
Devereaux, P. J., 1165
Devore, W., 945, 946, 963, 971
Dew, M., 699
Dew, M. A., 849, 943
Dewan, M. J., 216
Dewey, J, 1118
Deyo, R. A., 171
Dhaliwal, G. K., 1094
Dhalla, S., 402, 403
di Gasbarro, J., 344
Di Nardo, P. A., 395

Diamond, B., 175
Diamond, J., 276
DiCesare, E. J., 444
Dickerson, F., 666
Dickerson, V., 276
Dickey, B., 809
Dick-Siskin, L., 942
Dickson, D. T., 115, 123
DiClemente, C., 23
DiClemente, C. C., 458, 460, 575,
        644, 694
Diefenbach, G. J., 849, 850
Diehr, P., 847
Dillon, D., 787
Dimon, J., 191
DiNardo, P. A., 539, 542
DiNitto, D. M., 385, 691, 693
Dirksen, C., 743, 744
Dishion, T. J., 528, 1011, 1012
Divet, K., 856
Diwan, S., 799
Dix, G. E., 1055, 1056
Dixon, L., 491, 666, 871
Dobbin, S. A., 1071
Docherty, J. P., 350
Doel, M., 226
Dohm, F., 532
Doi, Y., 401, 402
Doidge, N., 5
Dolan, Y., 216, 217, 1086
Dolan, Y. M., 257, 1026
Dolgoff, R., 115, 117
Dollahite, D. C., 919, 921
Donahoe, B., 666
Donahue, S. A., 794
Donaldson, M., 194
Donner, S., 932
Donohue, B., 1004, 1008
Donovan, D. M., 29
Doorenboos, A., 847
Dore, M. M., 74, 75
Dorr, D. A., 790, 792, 793
Dorsey, S., 1011
Doss, B. D., 468, 472
Doty, P., 762
Douglas, K., 174
Douglas, K. S., 177
Dovidio, J. F., 928, 931
Dowd, S. B., 195
Dozier, M., 620
Drachman, D., 944, 959, 961
Drainoni, M. L., 402
Drake, R., 699, 821, 822, 824
Drake, R. E., 705, 706, 707, 708,
        709, 713, 756, 758
Drapalski, A., 494
Drinkard, A. M., 402
Drisko, J., 221, 222, 223, 260
Drouillard, C., 1084
Dryfoos, J. G., 907, 911
D'Souza, H. J., 979, 982, 983
du Berger, T., 849

Duberstein, P., 844
Dubin, C., 790, 793
Dubois, B., 1033, 1034
Dubrow, N., 559
Ducharme, L. J., 27
Duchnowski, 4
Duckett, M., 761
Dugan, L., 95
DuHammel, K., 604
Dulcan, M., 331
Dulmus, C. N., 817
Dumas, J. E., 1012
Duncan, B., 47, 51, 52, 215, 216,
        218
Duncan, B. L., 297, 298, 1020,
        1021
Duncan, G., 1086
Dunlop, A. L., 790, 793
Dunn, M. M., 655
DuPaul, G. J., 528, 1040
Dupper, D., 42
DuPre, E., 3, 6
Duran, B. E. S., 803, 806
Durand, V. M., 344
DuRant, R. H., 1006
Durham, R. C., 623
Durkin, E., 787
Durlak, J., 3, 6, 43, 1013
Durlak, J. A., 42, 817
Durrant, C., 218
Dusenbury, L., 991
Dworkin, D. S., 634
Dyer, F. J., 1061
Dziegielweski, S., 506
D'Zurilla, T., 1013

Eack, S. M., 192
Eaker, D. G., 623
Earle, K. A., 951
Early, T., 391
Early, T. H., 816
East, J. F., 768
Eaton, J. W., 1117
Eaton, W. W., 538
Eaton, Y., 212, 213
Ebadi, M., 402
Ebell, M. H., 1120, 1125
Eberhage, M. G., 163
Eck, J., 991
Eckert, G., 847
Edelson, J. L., 815, 1082
Edwardh, M., 1101
Edwards, B., 897
Edwards, D. J. A., 592
Edwards, G., 1012
Edwards, M., 1106
Edwards, S., 1084, 1086, 1087
Edwards, V., 699
Efran, J., 298
Egan, J., 1013
Egger, M., 1137, 1138
Ehlers, A., 110, 717, 718

Ehrlich, J. L., 881
Eicher, V., 621
Eichler, M., 881
Eimicke, J., 844
Eisen, J., 606
Eisengart, S., 257, 435, 1021
Eisenstadt, T. H., 1013
Eissengart, S., 47
Elbow, M., 631
Elder, C., 908
Elder, G. H., Jr., 409
Eldridge, K., 472, 473
Elias, M. J., 658
Elklit, A., 731
Ell, K., 790, 791, 792, 793, 795,
    979, 980
Ellerton, A. L., 815, 1082
Elliott, J. K., 164, 165
Elliott, S., 1084
Ellis, A., 242, 244, 592
Ellis, B., 700, 702
El-Mallakh, R. S., 402
Elson, M., 311
Ely, J. W., 1120, 1125
Elze, D., 574
Emery, G., 592
Emmelkamp, P. M. G., 189
Engel, L., 35
Engi, S., 190
English, P. W., 1061
Entwistle, V., 1165
Ephross, P., 910
Ephross, P. H., 681, 682, 684, 738
Epperson, D., 1101
Epstein, I., 563
Epstein, J., 907
Epstein, J. F., 369
Epstein, L., 226
Epstein, M., 4
Epstein, M. H., 388
Epstein, N., 391
Epstein, W. M., 276
Epston, D., 52, 189, 273, 276, 615
Erenu, N., 866
Erickson, C. K., 691
Erickson, C. L., 42
Erickson, M., 578, 581, 600, 601,
    602, 603, 604
Erikson, E., 940
Erlich, J., 881
Erlich, J. L., 882, 884
Ertl, B., 212, 213
Ervin, R. A., 528
Escudero, P., 1033
Eshleman, S., 335
Espiritu, R. C., 982
Essex, S., 1084
Essock, S. M., 756, 758
Estes, C., 941
Estes, R., 887
Estrada, J. N., 985
Esveldt-Dawson, K., 1013

Evans, D., 397
Evans, D. L., 349
Evans, S. W., 528, 1007, 1008,
    1009, 1040, 1043, 1216
Evans-Campbell, T., 952
Evenson, R., 785
Everly, G. S., Jr., 213, 214, 726,
    728, 731
Evers, K. E., 646
Evers, M., 848
Eyberg, S., 1013
Eyberg, S. M., 383, 1011, 1012, 1013

Faber, P., 413, 417
Fabiano, G. A., 528, 1040
Factor, A., 760
Fagan, J., 106, 919, 920, 921
Fagon, A., 673
Fairburn, C., 534
Fairburn, C. G., 364
Fairhurst, S. K., 575
Falicov, C. J., 555
Fallon, P., 531
Fantuzzo, J. W., 1082
Faranone, S., 866
Farberow, N., 174
Farkas, M., 770
Farley, O. W., 778
Farmer, R., 691
Farrington, D. P., 458
Fatout, M., 1033
Faulkner, L., 498
Fauman, M. A., 332
Fausel, D. F., 164
Faust, L. G., 1057, 1058
Fawcett, J., 175, 176, 177
Fawzy, F. I., 827, 830
Fawzy, N. W., 830
Fay, J., 622, 623, 625
Fay, L. F., 416
Fedorowicz, A. E., 1083
Feig, J. C., 916
Feigenbaum, J., 743
Feindler, D., 1013
Feinfeld, K. A., 623
Feldman, C., 158
Feldman, R., 621
Feldman, R. A., 970
Felitti, V., 699
Felix, E. D., 651
Felt-Lisk, S., 790, 791, 792, 793
Felton, C. J., 794
Fenichel, M., 187, 189, 190
Ferguson, M., 910
Ferrando, S. J., 370
Ferriter, C., 817
Fetting, J. H., 828
Fewell, L., 164
Field, M. J., 325
Fields, S., 435
Figley, C. R., 731
Figueira-McDonough, J., 277

Files-Hall, T., 648
Findley, D., 1012
Finkelhor, D., 1106
Finn, C. A., 553
Finn, E., 212
Finn, J., 383
Finn, S., 397
Fiorillo, A., 436
First, M. B., 326, 327, 331, 332,
    335, 341, 539
Firth-Cozens, J., 107
Fisch, R., 216, 217
Fischer, J., 36, 215, 216, 217, 318,
    320, 352, 356, 358, 382, 383,
    384, 387, 388, 390, 391, 393,
    400, 401, 402, 403, 432, 511,
    512, 600, 815
Fishbain, D. A., 838
Fishbein, D., 817
Fisher, G. L., 1008
Fisher, P., 88, 331
Fisher, R., 213, 901, 1072
Fishman, C., 477
Fishman, E., 798
Fishman, H. C., 436, 443, 444
Fishman, M., 693
Fishman, S. F., 630
Fisk, D., 485
Flannery, D., 402
Flannery, R., 728
Flay, B. R., 981
Fletcher, C. E., 166
Fletcher, J., 797, 847
Fletcher, K., 1012
Fletcher, K. E., 1012
Flick, G. R., 402
Floersch, J., 691, 756
Flores, N. I., 676
Floyd-Taylor, M., 820
Flynn, C., 801, 802
Foa, E., 614
Foa, E. B., 561
Fogarty, T., 416
Fogarty, T. F., 416
Fogo, W., 734
Folberg, J., 1072
Foley, S., 738
Folger, J. P., 1072
Folwarski, J., 419, 421
Fonagy, P., 305, 539, 553, 743, 744,
    745, 1011, 1016
Foner, N., 1032
Fong, R., 925, 926, 955, 1031,
    1034, 1035, 1216
Ford, W. E., 317
Fored, J., 1083
Forehand, R., 1011, 1013
Forester, B., 666
Forgatch, M. S., 458, 1012
Forman, J. B. W., 326
Forrest, M. S., 715, 717
Forsythe, B., 436

Fortin, D., 1098
Fortune, A. E., 226
Fowler, L., 890
Fox, L., 713
Fox, N., 77, 831
Fox, R., 55, 57
Fox, R. C., 1120
Fox, S., 186, 187, 189, 192
Frances, A., 332, 335, 341, 509,
    511, 512
Frank, A. F., 809
Frank, E., 943
Frank, J. B., 260, 308
Frank, J. D., 221, 260, 308
Frank, R. G., 12, 19
Frankel, A. J., 751
Frankenburg, F. R., 370, 745
Frankl, V., 776
Frankl, V. E., 265, 267, 268, 269,
    270
Franklin, A. J., 920
Franklin, C., 17, 18, 19, 42, 47, 50,
    52, 257, 294, 385, 432, 435,
    436, 458, 1020, 1021, 1022,
    1023, 1024, 1025, 1026, 1027,
    1216
Franklin, M. E., 1008
Fraser, I., 194
Fraser, M., 856
Fraser, M. W., 435
Frazer, M. W., 816
Frazier, S., 3, 6
Freedman, J., 276
Freedman, S., 281
Freeman, A., 243, 246, 247, 528
Freeman, C., 532
Freeman, E., 963, 965, 966, 967
Freire, P., 891
French, B., 1138
French, N. H., 1013
Frenk, J., 195, 196
Freund, K., 1100
Frey, A., 42
Frey, H., 672, 675
Fried, L., 849
Friedman, A. S., 388
Friedman, M. J., 109
Friedman, R. M., 64, 65
Friedmann, J., 887
Friesen, B. J., 64
Friman, P. C., 528
Frisman, L. K., 758
Froeschle, J. G., 1024, 1025
Fromer, J., 424
Fromm, E., 600
Frone, M., 23
Fruzzetti, A. E., 743
Fucci, B. R., 1013
Fuertes, J., 787
Fuhrman, T., 1013
Fulkerson, J. A., 834
Fullerton, C. S., 731

Funderburk, B. W., 1013
Fuortes, S., 788
Furman, D. M., 1061, 1062
Furman, R., 13, 15
Furukawa, T. A., 539
Furuto, S., 926, 955
Fusco, R. A., 1082
Futrell, J., 424

Gabbard, G. O., 164, 166
Gaebler, T., 195
Gaertner, S. L., 928, 931
Gagne, C., 770
Galewaler, S. T., 341
Galinsky, M. J., 189, 816
Gallagher, R., 539, 552
Gallagher-Thompson, D., 940, 942,
    970
Gallant, J., 276
Gallen, C., 606
Gallo, J., 797
Gallop, R. J., 743
Gambassi, G., 797
Gamble, D., 884, 886, 901
Gambrill, E., 168, 171, 172, 397,
    398, 1115, 1168, 1170, 1172
Gamson, W. A., 901, 902
Gangu, V. K., 175
Gant, L., 1046
Gantt, A., 474
Garb, H., 395, 398
Garb, H. N., 400
Garcia-Preto, N., 409, 413
Gard, M. C., 532
Gardner, S., 436, 437
Garfield, R. L., 12, 19
Garfield, S. L., 260
Garland, J. A., 684, 685
Garmaroudi, G., 402
Garmezy, N., 424
Garner, D., 534
Garner, N. E., 1021
Garran, A., 925, 928, 929, 931, 932,
    933
Garrick, T., 1104
Garvin, C. D., 226, 524
Garvin, D. A., 724
Gary, F., 95
Gash, A., 218
Gastfriend, D., 693
Gates, P., 507
Gath, D., 845
Gatowski, S. I., 1071
Gatz, M., 849
Gaudiano, B. A., 549, 550
Gaudin, J. M., 713
Gauthier, S., 848
Gazewood, J. D., 25, 26
Gearon, J., 666
Gechtman, L., 164
Geffner, R., 1082
Geffner, R. A., 1082

Gelles, R. J., 646
Gellis, Z., 941
Gellis, Z. D., 843, 844, 845, 846,
    847, 848, 1215
Gelman, S. R., 156, 157, 158, 159,
    160, 161, 751
Gelso, C., 787
Gemmer, T. C., 1013
Gendall, K., 533
George, C., 1061
George, E., 1087
George, W. H., 434, 472
Gerbert, B., 802
Gergen, K., 187
Gergen, K. J., 294, 297, 298
Gerlach, B., 1021, 1025
Germain, C., 959, 1116
Germain, C. B., 231, 232, 233, 294
Gerson, J., 745
Gerson, R., 74, 379, 409, 421, 425
Gerstein, J., 51
Gerull, F., 744
Getsos, P., 881
Geyman, J. P., 171
Gfroerer, J. C., 369
Giardino, A. P., 665
Gibbon, M., 331, 332, 539
Gibbs, L., 114, 171, 172, 506, 1127,
    1128, 1134, 1170, 1174, 1175
Gibbs, L. E., 168, 169, 1121, 1125,
    1152, 1170, 1172
Gibelman, M., 156, 157, 158, 159,
    160
Gibson, P., 963
Gierl, M., 921
Giesen-Bloo, J., 743, 744
Gigerenzer, 1165
Gilbody, S., 847
Gilgun, J., 4, 5
Gilgun, J. F., 979
Gillens, M., 931
Gilovich, T., 1137
Gingerich, S., 666, 667
Gingerich, W., 215, 216, 1020,
    1021
Gingerich, W. J., 47, 253, 257, 435
Gioia-Hasik, D., 666
Giordano, J., 409, 413
Gira, E. C., 982
Girgis, A., 827
Gitterman, A., 231, 232, 233, 294,
    681, 959
Given, B., 847
Given, C., 847
Glancy, G., 107, 175, 176, 177,
    1092, 1098, 1099, 1100
Glaser, D., 790, 793, 795, 1061
Glass, G. V., 221
Glasziou, P., 169, 171, 1115, 1116,
    1120, 1121, 1124, 1127, 1128,
    1134, 1145, 1163, 1166, 1176,
    1177, 1178

GlenMaye, L., 599
Glissen, C., 765
Glisson, C., 815, 983
Glomb, M. B., 161
Gober, K., 435, 436
Gocha, R. J, 772
Godinet, M., 955
Gold, J., 260
Gold, M., 395
Gold, P. B., 707
Goldberg, D. P., 401
Goldberg, J., 740
Goldberg, R., 666
Goldberg, S., 625
Goldberger, R., 1004
Goldfried, M. R., 240, 241, 259, 260
Golding, J., 532
Golding, K., 856
Goldman, J. L., 818
Goldsmith, D. F., 1061
Goldstein, A., 533
Goldstein, B., 849
Goldstein, E. G., 215, 378, 934, 937
Goldstein, M., 666
Goldstein, P. C., 802
Gollan, J. K., 1061
Goltzman, P., 866
Gonsiorek, J., 166
Gonzales, G., 700
Goodheart, C. D., 18
Goodman, E., 1006
Goodman, L., 699
Goodman, W. K., 606
Goodson, B., 856
Goodson, B. D., 676
Goodwin, J. S., 848, 849
Goodwin, S. N., 95
Goolishian, H., 298
Gordon, A. J., 366
Gordon, D., 436, 578, 583
Gordon, J. G., 105
Gore, J., 768
Gorenberg, C., 123
Gorenstein, E., 849, 850
Gorman, B., 758
Gorman, J., 849, 850
Gorrall, D., 392
Goscha, R., 785, 787, 788
Goscha, R. J., 782
Gossett, M., 169
Gotlieb, E. M., 1039, 1043
Gottfredson, D., 911, 981, 991
Gottfredson, G., 911
Gottman, J. M., 434
Gould, F., 27
Gould, J. W., 1061
Gould, N., 856, 979
Gowdy, E. A., 709
Goycoolea, J., 699
Goyle, P., 395
Grandage, K. K., 1164

Grant, B. F., 833
Grant, I., 177
Grant, T. R., 921
Granvold, D. K., 589, 591, 732, 733, 735, 736
Grawe, K., 221, 223
Gray, A., 171, 757, 845
Gray, J. A. M., 1162, 1172
Gray, N. S., 533
Gray, S. L., 849
Grayson, J. H., 163
Green, A., 235, 236
Green, J. W., 968
Green, P., 765
Green, R., 413, 757
Green, R. J., 424
Green, S., 1153
Greenberg, J., 306
Greenberg, L., 311, 491
Greenberg, M. T., 994, 995, 997
Greenberg, R. P., 216
Greene, C., 799
Greene, G. J., 210, 294, 296, 298, 596
Greene, M., 298
Greene, R. R., 766
Greenhalgh, T., 171, 1159, 1168, 1178
Green-Paden, L., 666
Greenstein, D. D., 1008
Greenstone, J., 213
Greenwald, R., 716, 717
Gregoire, T., 195
Gregoire, T. K., 835
Gregory, K., 195
Greif, G. L., 681, 682
Greist, J. H., 606
Grembowski, D., 845, 848
Gresham, F. M., 655
Greterman, A., 368
Griffiths, C. A., 474, 475
Griffiths, J. H., 693
Griffiths, K. M., 189
Grilo, C. M., 331
Grimshaw, J., 847, 1160
Grimshaw, J. M., 1155, 1156
Grinstein-Weiss, M., 887
Grissom, G. R., 27
Grisson, T., 1094
Grivin, H., 646
Grobe, J. E., 24
Grossi, G., 106
Groth-Marnat, G., 1061
Grotpeter, J., 436
Grove, W., 1101
Groves McAllister, B., 1082
Grusec, J. E., 619, 620
Gudeman, J., 497
Gudjonsson, G. H., 1061
Guerin, P., 416
Guerney, B., Jr., 442
Guevremont, D. C., 1012

Guglielmo, J., 930
Guitierrez, L., 884
Gullion, M. E., 1012
Gumley, A., 743, 744
Gunderson, J. G., 331, 809
Gunther, J., 201
Gupta, M. A., 533
Guralnik, J., 849
Gureje, O., 402
Gurman, A., 261
Gurman, A. S., 215, 216
Gursansky, D., 751
Gusfield, J., 910
Guterman, N. B., 817
Gutheil, I., 55
Gutheil, T. G., 1056, 1060, 1061, 1062
Guthrie, R. M., 107
Gutierrez, L. M., 599, 895, 900
Gutman, H. G., 963
Guttmann, D., 115, 267, 268, 271
Guy, J. D., 164, 165
Guy, M., 761
Guyatt, G., 1115, 1117, 1124, 1165, 1178, 1179
Guyatt, G. H., 1164, 1165, 1168

Haapala, D., 73
Haas, L. J., 122
Haberman, P. W., 164
Hagan, T. A., 27
Hageman, C., 644, 646
Haines, A., 1164
Hakansson, J., 575
Hall, A., 887
Hall, J., 788
Hall, J. A., 189, 1006
Hall, J. C., 13, 19
Hall, M., 731, 901
Hall, P., 366, 402
Halpert, A., 790, 792, 793
Hamby, S., 392
Hamby, S. L., 468
Hamel, C., 1155, 1156
Hamilton, G., 249
Hamilton, S. B., 1013
Hammel, J., 760
Hammers, D., 401
Hammond, C., 604
Hammond, M., 1012, 1013
Hamrin, V., 1012
Handelsman, J. B., 435
Handler, L., 381, 384
Hanks, H. G. I., 1061
Hanley, J., 864
Hanlon, J. T., 849
Hanna, G. L., 606
Hanson, C. L., 1013
Hanson, R., 1101, 1102
Hansson, K., 436
Hapke, U., 366
Hardcastle, D. A., 881, 901

Harden, A., 1154
Hardina, D., 903
Harding, C., 775
Hardy, K. V., 409, 416
Hare, R., 1103
Harley, R. M., 744
Harpole, L., 847
Harrington, C., 761
Harrington, D., 115, 117
Harrington, S., 189
Harris, A., 1102
Harris, E., 134
Harris, G., 1101
Harris, G. T., 1093
Harris, J., 890
Harris, J. C., 1061
Harris, K. M., 674
Harris, M. B., 42, 1025
Harris, M. S., 641, 756, 757
Harris, N., 766
Harris, O., 47, 52, 432
Harris, S. R., 1013
Harrison, M., 194
Harrison, M. J., 921
Harrison, R., 436
Hart, C. L., 1061
Hart, M., 887
Hart, S., 174, 1103
Hart-Johnson, T., 1047
Hartman, A., 379, 411, 970
Hartmann, D., 784, 785, 787
Hartocollis, L., 566
Hartsell, T. L., 1061
Harvey, J., 751
Harvey, R., 192
Hasin, D. S., 833
Hatler, C., 196
Haward, L. R. C., 1061
Hawes, E. C., 718
Hawken, P., 890
Hawkins, A. J., 919, 921
Hawkins, D., 991
Hawkins, F., 201
Hawkins, J. D., 673
Hawkins, M. K., 166
Hayashi, L., 257
Hayes, R., 474
Hayes, S. C., 283, 284, 285, 286,
    287, 550, 1177
Haynes, B., 1128, 1129, 1130, 1178
Haynes, K., 898
Haynes, R. B., 169, 171, 1115,
    1116, 1120, 1121, 1124, 1127,
    1128, 1134, 1145, 1163, 1165,
    1166, 1170, 1172, 1175, 1176,
    1177, 1178
Headrick, L., 201
Heard, H. L., 743
Hedberg, S., 12, 13
Hedges, L. V., 1153
Heesterman, W., 745
Heffron, L. C., 1216

Hegel, M., 552
Heijer, M. D., 402
Heilbrun, K., 1061
Heimberg, R. G., 242, 243, 244,
    545, 549, 550
Heisler, C. J., 1107
Held, V., 118
Heller, N. R., 531, 532, 533
Heller, T., 654, 760
Hellerstein, D. J., 745
Hello, H. L., 27
Helmy, A., 847
Helsel, W. J., 383
Helzer, J., 398
Hembree-Kigin, T. L., 624
Hembrooke, H., 1061
Hemmelgarn, A. L., 815
Hemsworth, D., 107
Hendricks, C., 925
Hendrix, C. T., 1061
Heneghan, A. M., 619
Henggeler, S. W., 74, 434, 436,
    1004, 1013
Henk, H. J., 606
Hennen, J., 370, 745
Henrion, R., 271
Henriques, G. R., 745
Heo, T., 844
Hepburn, M. S., 982
Hepworth, D., 501, 515, 600
Hepworth, D. H., 238, 521, 522,
    523, 524
Herbert, J. D., 549, 550
Hermann, J., 699, 700
Hermann, R. C., 18
Hermens, M., 846
Herrington, R. E., 166
Herrmann, N., 849
Hersen, M., 666, 1061
Hervis, O., 434, 436
Herz, M., 491
Herzog, D. B., 532
Hess, P., 856, 859
Hesselton, D., 1101
Hetherington, E. M., 424
Hick, S. F., 187, 190, 881, 893
Hickling, E. J., 561
Hieneman, M., 624
Higgins, A., 553
Higgins, E. T., 1047
Higgins, J. P. T., 1135, 1153
Hill, A., 366
Hill, C. E., 223, 240
Hill, J., 107
Hill, R., 673
Hill, S. S., 1064
Hilton, J. M., 734
Himle, J., 548
Himle, P. R., 539
Hinrichsen, G. A., 942
Hinshaw, S. P., 654, 1043
Hiremath, G., 731

Hiripi, E., 369
Hirschfeld, R. M., 326
Hoagwood, K., 3, 65, 979, 980, 981,
    982
Hoagwood, K. E., 435, 983
Hobbs, B. V., 435
Hobbs, C. J., 1061
Hobfoll, S. E., 109
Hodges, K., 383, 388
Hodgins, S., 1091, 1092
Hodgson, R., 367
Hodson, G., 928, 931
Hoefer, R., 897, 903
Hoffman, J., 402
Hoffman, P. D., 743
Hoffmann, N. G., 834
Hoffpauir, S., 294
Hogarth, R. M., 1168
Hogarty, G., 483
Hoge, L. A., 856
Hogg, V., 1084
Hogue, A., 435
Holaway, R. M., 549
Holden, G., 1131
Holden, G. W., 1082
Holden, J. M., 361
Holder, H. D., 835
Holdorf, G., 257
Holdrinet, I., 717
Holland, C. L., 1100
Hollander, E., 606
Holleran, L., 634
Hollingsworth, T., 1012
Hollis, F., 249
Holloway, H. C., 731
Holmberg, E., 817
Holmes, D., 844
Holmes, S., 194, 787
Holt, S., 1082
Holte, A., 364
Holton, V., 35
Holtz, K. D., 402
Holzer, C. E., 175
Homan, M. S., 881
Homes-Rovner, M., 1165
Hooley, J. M., 475
Hooyman, N., 278
Hops, H., 397
Hopson, L., 19, 458, 1020
Hopson, L. M., 436, 1023
Horan, J. J., 237, 1013
Horowitz, A., 844, 845, 847, 848,
    941
Horowitz, L., 934, 937
Horrigan, J. B., 187, 189
Horvath, A. O., 218, 809
Hoshmand, A. L., 913
Hoshmand, L. T., 913
Houck, P. R., 539, 542
Houston-Vega, M. K., 121
Houstra, T., 280, 281
Houts, P. S., 830

Howard, M., 507, 604
Howard, M. O., 1157, 1158, 1160,
    1161, 1171, 1172, 1174
Howell, J., 1004, 1008
Howell, L., 773
Howgego, I. M., 808, 809
Hoyert, D., 844
Huang, L. N., 982
Huang, V., 556
Hubberstey, C., 768
Hubble, M. A., 215, 216, 218, 297,
    298
Hucker, S., 175
Huckshorn, K. A., 698
Hudson, A., 1011
Hudson, C., 4
Hudson, P., 216, 217
Hudson, W. W., 318, 358, 387, 403,
    404
Huebner, A. J., 621
Huebner, R. A., 768
Huey, W. C., 1013
Huffine, C., 35, 65
Huffman, J., 1100
Hughes, J., 797
Hughes, M., 335, 856, 858
Hull, G. H., 881
Humphreys, C., 3
Humphreys, K., 785
Hunkeler, E., 847
Hunsley, J., 385, 815
Hunter, L., 621
Hurwitz, B., 1168
Hurwitz, D., 12, 13
Hussey, D. L., 402
Hutchison, K., 28
Hybels, C., 846
Hyde, C., 281
Hyer, L., 718, 848
Hyman, B., 483
Hyun, J., 194

Ignatiev, N., 930
Imber, S. D., 943
Ip, W. Y., 401
Ireys, H., 856
Isebaert, L., 257
Isper, J. C., 1136
Iveson, C., 1087
Ivy, C., 799
Iwata, M., 1013

Jackson, M., 890
Jackson, P. Z., 257
Jackson, R., 778
Jackson, V. R., 164, 165
Jacobo, M. C., 744
Jacobs, A. K., 109
Jacobs, D., 175, 176, 177
Jacobsen, J. M., 802
Jacobson, G. R., 166
Jacobson, N., 434

Jacobson, N. S., 434, 467, 468, 472
Jacobson, S., 367
Jaeschke, R., 1178
Jaffe, P. G., 1082, 1083
Jang, K. L., 548
Janicki, M., 760
Janikowski. T., 784
Janson, J. G., 1091, 1092
Jansson, B. S., 896
Janzen, C., 47, 52, 432
Jara, C., 165
Jarbo, M., 970
Jarvis, P. A., 164, 165
Jasper, C., 773
Jayaratne, S., 117, 1115
Jaycox, H., 1033
Jean-Gilles, M., 968
Jedlicka, D., 187, 189, 190
Jefferson, J. W., 606
Jeffres, M. J., 717
Jeglic, E. L., 745
Jennings, G., 187, 189, 190
Jennings, T., 130, 134
Jensen, C., 294
Jensen, D. K., 755
Jensen, J., 507
Jensen, M., 604
Jensen, M. A., 684, 685
Jensen, P. S., 1061
Jenson, J. M., 1157, 1158, 1174
Jin, R., 385, 548, 691, 848, 1004,
    1007
Jobson, K., 604
Joe, G. W., 818
Johansen, A. B., 473
John, B., 367
John, U., 366
Johnson, A. M., 533
Johnson, D., 110
Johnson, J., 846
Johnson, J. A., 27
Johnson, J. L., 646
Johnson, K., 765
Johnson, L., 887
Johnson, L. N., 71
Johnson, M., 391, 392
Johnson, M. L., 1008
Johnson, M. P., 963
Johnson, S., 1100
Johnson, S. M., 434, 435, 436, 478
Johnstone, J., 702
Johri, M., 797
Jolly, A., 731
Jones, B. L., 768
Jones, D. H., 294
Jones, G., 187, 189, 190
Jones, H. E., 684, 685
Jones, J., 674
Jones, J. A., 515
Jones, K., 1031, 1032
Jones, N., 731
Jones, R., 164

Jongsma, A. E., 429, 431, 432
Jordan, C., 47, 52, 385, 432, 435,
    845, 846, 847
Jorm, A. F., 189
Joseph, M. V., 159
Jouriles, E. N., 1082
Juarez, L., 1045
Judd, C. M., 758
Juno, R. T., 175
Jusisoo, M., 106

Kabat-Zinn, J., 607
Kadden, R., 23
Kadel, S., 724
Kadushin, A., 722
Kaelber, C., 326
Kaersvang, L., 1083
Kagle, J. D., 26, 124
Kahn, K., 848
Kahn, K. S., 1172
Kahne, M., 174
Kahneman, D., 1137
Kaiser, R. M., 847
Kalichman, S., 666
Kaminer, Y., 1004
Kampman, K. M., 29
Kamya, H. A., 970
Kanani, K., 187, 189, 190, 191, 192
Kanapaux, W., 177
Kane, R., 792
Kanner, A., 352
Kant, I., 1056
Kanter, J., 756, 757
Ka'opua, L. S., 806
Kaplan, H., 497
Kaplan, H. I., 1061
Kaplan, M., 1100, 1101
Kaplan, R. M., 1061
Kaplow, J., 700, 702
Kapur, M., 402
Kapur, R. L., 402
Karls, J. M., 334, 372, 374, 375
Karpenko, V., 401
Karver, M. S., 435
Kasl, S., 485
Kaslow, F. W., 165
Kass, F., 326
Kassirer, J. P., 1165
Kataoka, S., 1033
Katon, W., 847
Katsavdakis, K. A., 164, 166
Katz, I., 844, 847, 848
Katz, J., 1166, 1167
Katzelnick, D. J., 606
Katz-Leavy, J., 65
Katzman, M., 531
Katz-Porterfield, S. L., 278
Kaufman, A. V., 713
Kaufman, C., 931
Kaufman, J., 423
Kaul, J., 1101
Kautto, J. G., 416

Kavanagh, K., 528, 1011
Kawakami, K., 928, 931
Kawashima, K., 3, 6
Kaye, A. L., 332
Kaye, W., 533
Kaye, W. H., 533
Kazdin, A. E., 18, 382, 385, 436,
    462, 654, 655, 1012, 1013,
    1015, 1016
Kazi, M. A., 1118
Keane, T. M., 558, 561, 562, 1061
Kearns, K. P., 157
Keck, P. E., 350
Keehner, J. A., 724
Keith, D., 464
Keith-Spiegel, P., 164
Kellam, S., 981
Kelleher, J., 707
Kelleher, K., 983
Keller, M. B., 326
Keller, S. D., 318
Kelley, F., 787
Kelley, M. E., 366
Kelley, P., 276
Kelly, J., 424, 666
Kelly, M., 257
Kelly, M. S., 42, 47, 1020, 1021,
    1024, 1025, 1216
Kelly, S., 257
Kemp, S., 856, 858
Kemp, S. P., 277, 712, 713
Kemper, K. J., 368
Kenaley, B., 845, 847
Kendall, J., 699, 881
Kendall, P. C., 817
Kendig, C., 785, 787
Kendler, K. S., 624
Kennedy, G., 552
Kennedy, R., 751
Keohane, D. J., 844
Keonig, H., 846
Kerig, P. K., 1083
Kerlinger, F. N., 200
Kern, L., 528
Kerpelman, J. L., 916
Kerr, M. E., 447, 449, 450
Kerson, T. S., 187, 189
Kessler, M. L., 982
Kessler, P. E., 343
Kessler, R. C., 335, 369, 385, 538,
    548, 552, 691, 692, 848, 1004,
    1007
Ketring, S. A., 71
Kettner, P. M., 881
Khanna, A., 1098, 1101
Kichberg, S. L., 815
Kihlstrom, J., 604
Kilberg, R. R., 163, 165
Kim, J., 257
Kim, J. S., 47, 386, 435, 1004, 1009,
    1020, 1021, 1023, 1024, 1025,
    1027, 1215, 1216

Kim, Y., 970
Kimack, C., 921
Kimerling, R., 363
Kimmel, D., 937
King, B., 604
King, C. A., 653
King, D., 552, 844, 845
King, P. A., 1106
King, R. A., 382
King, S., 190
Kinney, J., 73
Kinney, R., 778
Kintgen-Andrews, J., 172
Kirk, S., 171, 509
Kirk, S. A., 334
Kirkhart, M., 726, 731
Kirkish, P., 1104
Kirkpatrick, L. C., 1061, 1066
Kirschenbaum, D. S., 653
Kirst-Ashman, K. K., 881
Kirton, C., 792
Kiser, L., 980, 981, 982
Kisker, E. E., 76
Kitchener, M., 761
Kivlahan, D., 835
Kleber, M., 849, 850
Klein, D. N., 326
Klein, R., 815
Klein, R. G., 352
Klein, S., 164, 165
Klinkenberg, W. D., 809
Klinnert, M. D., 1012
Klug, W. S., 1061
Knapp, P., 1061
Knapp, S. E., 621, 623, 625
Knei-Paz, C., 523
Knight, E., 794
Knight, J. R., 1006, 1039, 1043
Knoedler, W. H., 871
Knowles, M. S., 723
Knox, K. L., 916
Knox, K. S., 88, 89, 90, 207
Knudsen, H. K., 27
Knudsen, K., 700
Knutsen, E., 163
Kobak, K. A., 606
Kobayashi, K., 604
Kockmann, I., 745
Kocsis, J. H., 326
Kogan, K. L., 675
Kohn, L., 194
Kohut, H., 311, 312, 313, 315
Koladny, R. L., 684, 685
Kolpacoff, M., 1012
Koob, G., 28
Koocher, G. P., 1061, 1063, 1064
Kopec, J., 402, 403
Kopelowicz, A., 666
Kopels, S., 16
Kopera-Frye, K., 734
Koplewicz, H. S., 352
Kopp, Z., 790, 793, 795

Koran, L. M., 606
Korman, H., 257, 1020, 1086
Korner, A., 744
Kornhauser, L., 1080
Kosinski, M., 318
Kosten, T. R., 326
Kraemer, K. L., 366
Kral, R., 1020, 1021
Krasnow, A. D., 821
Kratchowill, T. R., 676
Kraus, F., 218
Krause, A., 191
Krauskopf, C. J., 164
Kreling, B., 761
Kreyenbuhl, J., 666
Kroenke, K., 361
Kronenberger, W. S., 1013
Kropp, P., 1103
Krueger, R., 1100
Krumrei, E., 734
Krysik, J., 383
Ksir, C. J., 1061
Kuehlwien, K. T., 294
Kufeldt, K., 815
Kumar, A., 846
Kung, H., 844
Kung, W., 970
Kupelnick, B., 1164
Kurland, R., 681, 682
Kurtz, A., 1011, 1016
Kurtz, M., 666
Kurzman, P., 126
Kusché, C. A., 994, 995, 997
Kutash, K., 4
Kutchins, H., 334

Lacey, J. H., 364
LaCroix, A. Z., 849
Laffaye, C., 362
LaFountain, R. M., 1021
Lafuze, J. E., 475
Lager, P. B., 766
LaGreca, A. M., 384
Laidlaw, K., 940, 942
Laird, A., 398
Laird, J., 970
Lake, K., 718
Laliotis, D. A., 163
Lalumière, M., 1103
Lam, J., 483
Lamb, D. H., 164, 165
Lambers, E., 235
Lambert, M. D., 1157
Lambert, M. J., 51, 221, 222, 223,
    432, 808
Lammers, C. J., 164, 165
Lamothe, L., 3
Lampman, C., 1013
Lamprecht, H., 218
Lampron, L., 1013
Landenberger, N., 1151
Landi, F., 797

Landis, R. D., 402
Landreth, G., 649
Landsverk, J., 361, 983
Laneri, M., 1012
Langevin, R., 1100, 1101
Langrod, J. G., 1061
Lankton, C., 578, 584
Lankton, S., 578, 582, 583, 584, 615
Lanktree, C., 1083
Lansing, A. E., 175
Lantz, M., 848
Lanza, M., 195
Laramee, A. S., 790, 791, 792, 793, 795
Larsen, J., 501, 600
Larsen, J. A., 238, 515
Larson, J. A., 521, 522, 523, 524
Larson, R., 108
Laszlo, A., 12, 13
Laszloffy, T. A., 409
Latessa, M., 383
Latham, G., 780
Lating, J., 726, 731
Lating, J. M., 213
Lau, J., 1164
Laur, J., 888
Lavetsky, G., 801, 802
Lavretsky, H., 846
Law, D., 434, 435
Law, D. D., 435
Laws, A., 532
Lawson, H., 5
Laydon, C., 218
Layne, C. M., 109
Layzer, J., 856
Layzer, J. I., 676
Lazarus, A., 259
Lazarus, R., 827, 828
Le, A., 28
Leahy, R. L., 244, 246
Leake, B., 361
LeBaron, S., 604
Lebel, P., 797
Lebow, J., 435, 436
Lebowitz, B. D., 846
LeBuhn, R. A., 153
Leckman, J. F., 606, 621
LeCroy, C. W., 381, 652, 653, 654, 655, 656
Ledley, D. R., 242, 243, 244
Lee, C. L., 552
Lee, E., 955
Lee, F., 802
Lee, G., 802
Lee, M., 210, 226
Lee, M. Y., 257, 294, 296, 298, 594, 595, 596, 599
Lee, P. R., 231
Lee, T., 370
Lee, T. Y., 621
Lee, W., 477

Lee, W. Y., 445
Leech, L. L., 165
Leese, M., 370
Lefley, H., 491
Legazpi, M. A., 1046
Lehman, A., 491, 666
Lehman, A. F., 871
Lehmann, P., 1083, 1084
Leiblum, S., 740
Leider, R., 312, 313, 315
Leifer, J. C., 161
Leighley, J. E., 894
Leighton, A., 398
Lenze, E., 849
Leon, A. C., 362
Leonard, C., 174
Leonard, M. T., 473
LePetri, B., 790, 793, 795
Lerner, D., 18
Lester, L., 894
Leszcz, M., 23
Leutz, W., 799
Leveille, S. G., 849
Levene, J. E., 219
Levesque, D. A., 646
Levin, J. R., 676
LeVine, E. S., 766
Levine, M., 27, 785, 787
Levine, S., 606, 634
Levine, S. B., 738
Levinsky, S. K., 790, 791, 792, 793, 795
Levinson, R., 108
Levit, K., 784
Leviton, S., 213
Levitt, J., 387
Levitt, J. L., 318
Levy, A., 395
Levy, B. T., 1120
Levy, R., 1115
Lewinsohn, S., 397
Lewis, B., 195
Lewis, C., 992, 993
Lewis, E. A., 884
Lewis, L., 846
Lewis, M., 1061
Li, J., 191
Liberman, A., 106
Liberman, R. P., 666, 667, 758, 1177, 1178
Lichtenberg, P., 848
Liddle, H. A., 435, 458
Lidz, C. W., 124
Lieblum, S., 740
Liebowitz, M. R., 545
Lightburn, A., 3, 6, 856, 857, 858, 859, 860, 861
Lightfoot, E., 760
Ligon, J., 213, 218
Lilienfeld, S. O., 400
Lillis, J., 287, 550
Limber, S. P., 986, 992

Lin, E., 847
Lincoln, K. D., 711
Lindblad-Goldberg, M., 74, 75
Lindeman, D., 942
Lindsey, E., 621
Linehan, M., 666
Linehan, M. M., 743, 744
Ling, J., 391, 392
Link, B. G., 175, 1092
Linkins, K., 941
Links, J., 731
Linzer, N., 115
Liotti, G., 566, 567, 569
Lipchik, E., 215, 216, 253, 966
Lipsey, M., 1151
Lipsey, M. W., 1149, 1151
Lipton, H., 77, 831
Lishman, J., 755
Liskow, B., 403
Listiak, A., 1100
Litaker, D., 194
Litchfield, M., 1071
Littell, J., 436, 1164
Littell, J. H., 646, 1149, 1152, 1153
Little, E., 1011
Little, T. D., 24
Litts, D. A., 916
Livesley, W. J., 745
Livingston, G., 187, 189
Llewellyn-Thomas, H., 1165
Lochman, J. E., 654, 1013
Locke, E., 780
Locke, J., 392
Lockett, P. W., 277, 278, 279
Lockwood, A., 757, 871
Lockwood, T. W., 555
Loeber, R., 458
Loewenberg, F., 115, 117
Logan, S., 963, 965, 966, 967
Logan, T. K., 89
Lohr, J. M., 717, 718
Lohr, K. N., 325, 533
Long, N., 619, 621
Loosley, S., 1084
Lopez, A. D., 606
Lopez, S., 774
Lortie, K., 652
Loscalzo, M. J., 79, 85, 828
Losen, D., 1045, 1046
Lott, L., 623
Lou, C., 391, 392
Loughlin, D., 798
Louie, I. S., 65
Love, J. M., 76
Lowinson, J. H., 1061
Loza, W., 1094
Lubetkin, B. S., 630
Luborsky, L., 27, 305, 306
Lucas, C., 331
Lucas, C. P., 388
Luce, A., 107
Ludman, E., 847

Lukas, C., 194
Lukas, E., 270
Lukens, E., 491
Lum, D., 234, 945, 946, 965, 967, 970
Lum, O., 556
Luoma, J. B., 287, 550
Luthar, S. S., 423
Lutzker, J. R., 1061
Lyman, D. R., 65, 66, 68
Lynch, C., 1022
Lynch, C. J., 1215
Lynch, M., 941
Lynde, D., 821, 822, 824
Lyness, J., 844, 845
Lynn, M., 1033
Lyons, B., 971
Lyons, J., 364
Lyons, J. S., 175

Maben, J., 196
MacCoun, R., 1167
Macdonald, A., 1087, 1088
Macdonald, A. J., 257
MacDonald, G., 1148
Macias, C., 778
MacIntyre, A., 118
MacIsaac, D., 311
MacKenzie, D., 991
Mackenzie, S., 980
MacLaren, C., 243, 246
Macleod Clark, J., 196
MacNeil, G., 713
MacQuiddy, S. L., 1013
Madden, R., 122
Magee, W. J., 538
Magill-Evans, J., 921
Magliano, L., 436
Magnano, J., 226
Mahmood, A. H., 402
Mahoney, A., 734
Mahoney, C., 787
Mahoney, K., 798
Mahoney, M., 762
Mahoney, M. J., 165, 294
Maisto, S., 366
Maj, M., 436
Malangone, C., 436
Malcolm, P., 1098, 1101
Malgady, R. G., 345
Mallinson, S., 1138
Malone, K. M., 177
Maloney, P., 785, 788
Malouf, J. L., 122
Maluccio, A., 765
Mancini, D. L., 913
Mancini, J. A., 621, 912, 913, 914, 915, 916
Mangraviti, J. J., 1063
Mann, A., 370
Mann, B. J., 1013
Mann, J. J., 177

Mannarino, A. P., 651, 700, 718
Mannion, E., 491, 492
Mansbridge, J., 901
Manselle, T., 16
Mansour, A., 844
Mant, J., 171
Manwani, S., 1007, 1008
Marachi, R., 42, 986, 995, 1215
March, J. S., 718
Marconi, K. M., 802
Marczyk, G. R., 1061
Margolin, G., 468
Margolin, J., 395
Mari, J. J., 402
Marin, D., 848
Mark, T., 784
Markowitz, J. C., 745
Markus, H., 552, 1046, 1047
Marlowe, J. H., 1012
Marmar, C., 106, 107
Marmarosh, C., 787
Marriott, S. A. A., 1013
Marsh, D., 492
Marsh, P., 226
Marshall, A. D., 558, 561, 562
Marshall, M., 757, 871
Marshall, T., 491, 493, 494
Marson, S., 154
Marsteller, F., 718
Martens, L. C., 175
Martier, S. S., 367
Martin, A., 1061
Martin, C. R., 401
Martin, J. A., 912, 913, 914, 915, 916
Martin, M. A., 166
Martin, S., 734
Martin, T., 24
Martindale, D. A., 1061
Marx, B. P., 242, 243, 244
Marziali, E., 745
Maser, J. D., 326
Mash, E., 385
Mash, E. J., 391, 815
Masse, L. C., 1013
Massel, H. K., 1177, 1178
Massetti, G. M., 528, 1040
Mast, B., 848
Masten, A. S., 1082, 1085
Masuda, A., 285, 287, 550
Mather, J. H., 766
Matson, J. L., 383
Mattaini, M., 42, 372, 548
Mattaini, M. A., 379
Mattessich, P. W., 889
Matthews, R., 717, 718
Mattison, D., 117
Maultsby, M. C., 592
Max, S., 881
Maxfield, L., 718
Mayadas, N., 959
Mayberg, S., 983
Mayer, B., 717

Mayer, L. E., 533
Mayes, L. C., 621
Mayfield, D., 366, 402
Maynard, J., 1073
Mayo, K., 743
Mayo-Smith, M. F., 1158
Mays, G. P., 790, 791, 792, 793
Mazure, C., 485
McAdam, D., 901
McAllister, C. L., 919
McAvay, G. J., 844
McBride, M., 761
McBride, W., 28
McCahill, M. E., 362
McCall, G., 604
McCallion, P., 226
McCallon, E., 724
McCann, I. L., 558
McCarthy, J., 901
McCarthy, J. D., 901
McCarty, D., 187, 189, 190, 191, 192, 707
McClough, J. F., 742, 743, 744
McClure, P., 915
McCollum, E., 257, 1020, 1086
McConnell, K. J., 790, 792, 793
McCord, J., 1143
McCorkle, R., 847
McCormick, K., 835
McCormick, N., 1098
McCoyd, J. L., 187, 189
McCrady, B., 787
McCrady, B. S., 163, 165
McCroskey, J., 856, 888
McCubbin, A., 424
McCubbin, H., 424
McCubbin, H. I., 384
McCubbin, M., 424
McCubbin, M. A., 384
McCullough, J. P., 326
McDaniel, R., 6
McDonald, A. L., 341
McDonald, G. M., 1135
McDonald, L., 672, 675, 676, 677
McDonald, R., 1082
McDougle, C. J., 606
McDowell, I., 498
McEachern, E., 201
McEvoy, J., 509, 511, 512
McFadyen, J. M., 916
McFarlane, A. C., 1061
McFarlane, W., 491
McFarlane, W. R., 475, 476, 483
McGee, D. R., 255
McGilligan, L., 815
McGinty, J., 844, 845, 846, 847, 848, 941
McGlashan, T. H., 331
McGoldrick, M., 74, 379, 409, 412, 413, 415, 416, 421, 425, 964
McGonagle, K. A., 335
McGowan, B., 856, 859

McGuffin, P., 1008
McGuigan, J., 16
McGuire, M., 42
McHugo, G. J,, 707, 708, 758
McInnis-Dittrich, K., 552
McIntosh, P., 931
McKeachie, W., 724
McKergow, M., 257
McKibbon, A., 171
McKinnon, J., 963, 965
McKnight, J. L., 915
McLellan, A. T., 27, 785, 787
McLeod, G., 366, 402
McLeod, P., 849
McMahon, L., 856, 859, 860
McMahon, T., 623
McMillan, F. J., 195
McMillen, C., 1171, 1172, 1174
McMillen, C. J., 1158, 1160
McMullin, R. E., 244, 246
McMurtry, S. L., 881
McNair, R. H., 890
McNamara, J. R., 401
McNeece, C. A., 691, 693
McNeil, C. B., 624, 1013
McNeil, M., 366
McNeill, J. W., 550
McNutt, J. G., 187, 190, 191, 881,
    893
McQuaid, J. R., 362
McQuillan, C., 218
McRoy, R., 925
McVeigh, K., 787
Mead, G., 1103
Meade, M., 1178
Means-Christensen, A. J., 369
Meares, R., 744
Mearns, D., 235
Medoff, P., 888
Meehl, P., 1101
Mee-Lee, D., 693
Meezan, W., 888
Meichenbaum, D., 243, 244, 562
Meier, P. S., 25
Meisel, J., 95
Meisler, N., 707
Meldrum, L., 808, 809
Mellor, M. J., 942
Melton, G. B., 1013, 1061, 1064
Melzer-Brody, S., 363
Memmi, A., 929
Menchaca, A., 745
Mendel, R. A., 991
Mendlewicz, J., 533
Menon, G. M., 191
Mentzer, R., 596
Mercier, C., 3
Merckelbach, H., 717
Merikangas, K. R., 385, 691, 692,
    848, 1004, 1007
Merikangas, R., 548

Merino, D., 799
Merrell, K. W., 382, 384
Merrens, M., 821, 822, 824
Merrill, J., 835
Mertens, J. M., 943
Meschi, W. A., 356
Messer, S., 259, 261
Messeri, P. A., 802
Messick, J., 211
Metcalf, L., 1020, 1021
Metevia, L., 1012
Metzger, D. S., 27
Metzler, T., 106, 107
Meusser, K., 699
Meyer, C., 372
Meyer, C. H., 376, 377
Meyer, D., 901
Meyer, G., 196
Meyer, H., 998
Meyer, H. A., 986, 995, 998
Meyer, R. G., 1013
Meyer, W., 521
Meyers, B. S., 844
Meyers, D., 344
Meyers, K., 27
Michelson, L., 655
Mickelson, J., 898
Midgley, J., 887
Midgley, S., 107
Miehls, D., 434, 478, 480
Mihalic, S. F., 992, 994, 995
Miklowitz, D., 666
Miles, K. M., 941
Miley, K., 1033, 1034
Miller, A. L., 743
Miller, G., 253, 257, 594
Miller, I., 326
Miller, J., 925, 928, 929, 931, 932,
    933
Miller, M., 164, 763
Miller, M. D., 943
Miller, N. S., 834
Miller, S., 47, 51, 52, 595
Miller, S. D., 215, 216, 217, 218,
    257, 297, 298, 1086
Miller, S. I., 175
Miller, T. D., 828
Miller, T. L., 221
Miller, V. P., 768
Miller, W. E., 341
Miller, W. R., 6, 24, 605, 695
Miller-Lewis, L. R., 621
Millett, R., 955
Millman, R. B., 1061
Mills, C. W., 928
Milne, A., 1072
Milner, J. S., 392
Milton, D., 196
Minami, H., 35
Minieri, J., 881
Minkler, M., 910, 980
Minowa, M., 401, 402

Minuchin, S., 276, 442, 443, 444,
    445, 477, 674
Misener, E., 844, 845, 846, 847,
    848, 941
Mitchell, D., 190
Mitchell, J., 213
Mitchell, J. T., 213, 726, 727, 728,
    731
Mitchell, P., 192
Mitchell, S., 306, 307, 311, 315
Miti, G., 567, 569
Mitrani, V., 968
Mittelman, S., 1098
Mizrahi, P., 391, 392
Mizrahi, T., 281, 889
Mnookin, R., 1080
Moberg, D. P., 676
Moe, J. C., 802
Moffitt, T. E., 95
Mohlman, J., 849, 850
Mohr, B. D., 475
Mohr, W. K., 475
Mojtabai, R., 844
Mokuhau, N., 955
Molinari, V., 848
Moline, M. E., 122
Mollon, P., 567, 568
Molnar, A., 215, 216, 253
Monahan, J., 1092, 1093, 1094
Monahan, P., 745
Mondin, G. W., 221
Mondros, J., 901, 903
Monk, G., 276
Monroe, B., 218
Monsey, B. R., 889
Monson, N., 398
Montalvo, B., 442
Montazeri, A., 402
Montgomery, G., 604
Montgomery, H., 575
Montgomery, J. E., 644, 646
Montgomery, L. M., 434, 435
Montgomery, P., 1145
Monti, P., 28
Moody, M., 221
Mooij, A., 1056
Moon, M. S., 705, 706
Mooney, D., 388
Moore, A., 200
Moore, B., 713
Moore, K., 1020, 1022, 1023, 1025
Moorman, C., 622, 624
Moos, B. S., 392
Moos, R. H., 392
Mor, V., 797
Morales, A. T., 864
Moran, G., 625
Moran, P., 370
Moreno, E. R., 864
Morey, L. C., 331
Morgan, A., 672, 677
Morgan, E., 970

Morgan, J. F., 364
Morgan, T., 787
Morgenstern, J., 787
Morris, A., 902
Morrison, D. E., 901
Morrison, R., 153
Morrissey, J., 175
Morrow-Howell, N., 507
Morse, G. A., 809
Morse, R. M., 166
Mossman, D., 177
Mosteller, F., 1164
Mould, J., 864
Mounsey, A. L., 25, 26
Mount, K., 24
Moursund, J., 213
Mowbray, C., 507, 513, 773
Moxley, D., 773, 775, 799
Moxley, D. P., 767, 773, 774, 775, 776
Moyers, T., 24
Mrazek, D. A., 1061
Mroczek, D. K., 369
Mudar, P., 367
Mueller, C., 902
Mueller, C. B., 1061, 1066
Mueser, K., 666, 667, 699
Mueser, K. T., 705, 707, 708, 709, 713, 758
Mullahy, C. M., 755
Mullen, E. J., 979
Mullins, S., 699
Mulsant, B., 844, 847, 848
Mulsant, B. H., 849, 943
Mulvey, E., 1093, 1094
Mumby, D. K., 277
Munro, K., 187, 189, 190
Munson, C. E., 336, 339, 341, 342, 1061, 1064, 1065
Murhpy, J., 398
Muris, P., 717
Murphy, D., 1098
Murphy, J., 1020, 1021
Murphy, L., 190
Murphy, S., 970
Murphy, T., 699, 702
Murray, A., 3
Murray, A. M., 743
Murray, C. J. L., 195, 196, 606
Murray, H., 743, 744
Murray, S., 107
Murray-Close, M., 889
Murray-Swank, A., 666
Murrell, A. R., 286
Murty, S., 276
Myers, J. E. B., 1061
Myers, L. L., 1181
Myers, V. H., 549, 550
Mynors-Wallis, L. M., 845

Nader, K., 559, 1061
Nagda, B. A., 884

Nagin, D. S., 95
Najavits, L., 701
Nakashima, J., 717
Naleppa, M. J., 226
Nash, M., 604
Nathan, J. S., 400
Nathan, P. E., 163, 165, 1157
Nayani, T., 369
Neblett, C., 731
Nee, J., 326
Neiditch, E. R., 743
Neighbors, I. A., 1057, 1058
Neimeyer, R. A., 294
Nelson, C. B., 335
Nelson, E. E., 624
Nelson, J., 623
Nelson, J. P., 912, 913, 914, 916
Nelson, K. E., 435
Nelson, T., 594
Nelson, T. S., 257
Nemes, S., 402
Nesse, R. M., 548
Nestadt, G., 606
Netting, F. E., 278, 282, 881
Neugebauer, R., 845
Neugeboren, B., 757
Neuhauser, D., 201
Neuhauser, L., 980
Newcomb, K., 1013
Newcombe, N., 1060
Newell, C., 498
Newell, S., 827
Newman, B., 738
Newman, P. R., 738
Newsome, S., 391, 435, 1020, 1022, 1025
Newsome, W. S., 218
Nezu, A., 1013
Nezu, A. M., 830
Nezu, C. M., 830
Nezworski, M. T., 400
Nich, C., 837
Nicholls, T. L., 177
Nichols, M., 276
Nichols, M. P., 474, 475
Nietzel, M. T., 1013
Nieuwenhuis, J. A., 435
Niles, D., 596
Niven, R. G., 166
Noar, S. M., 641
Nock, M. K., 817, 818, 1012
Noel, P., 785, 787
Noerholm, V., 396
Nolan, E. M., 549, 550
Noonan, M., 215
Noordsy, D. L., 713
Norcross, J., 164, 259, 260
Norcross, J. C., 458, 460, 644, 694, 1064
Nordenberg, D., 699
Norko, M., 175, 1104
Normand, S. L. T., 369

Noronha, A., 28
Norrie, J., 743, 744
Norris, M., 848
Northen, H., 249, 681, 682
Norwood, A. E., 731
Novy, D. M., 849, 850
Nowicki, J., 47, 50, 51
Nuehring, E. M., 121
Nugent, W., 395, 399, 604
Nugent, W. R., 318, 387, 403, 404
Nunnally, E., 215, 216
Nunnaly, E., 253
Nurcombe, B., 1064
Nurius, P., 294, 1026

Oakley, A., 1154
Obikoya, B., 402
Obolsky, A., 175
O'Brien, C. P., 29
O'Connor, A. M., 1165
O'Connor, M. K., 278, 282
Oden, S. L., 654
Oetjen, J., 1071
Ogburn, E., 833
Ogilvie, D., 1098
Ogland-Hand, S., 848
Ogloff, J., 174
Ogloff, R. P., 177
O'Hanlon, B., 51
O'Hanlon, W., 216, 217
O'Hare, T., 18
O'Keefe, M., 374, 375
Okocha, C., 745
Okwumabua, T., 434, 435
Olatunji, B. O., 717, 718
Oldham, J. M., 743, 745
O'Leary, D., 392
Olfson, M., 844
Oliver, S., 1154
Ollendick, T. H., 1061
Olmstead, M., 534
Olsen, R., 396
Olsheski, J., 165
Olson, D., 392
Olson, D. H., 391
Olson, K. B., 1071, 1072
Olweus, D., 987, 992
O'Mahoney, M. T., 175
O'Malley, S. S., 29
O'Neill, J. V., 1127
Openshaw, L., 911
Oppenheim, D., 1061
O'Reilly, T., 187
Orfield, G., 1045, 1046
Orlinsky, D., 223
Orme, J. G., 320, 352, 356, 382, 383, 387, 400, 401, 402, 432
Ormel, J., 402
Orne, M. T., 604
Orosz, J. J., 955
O'Rourke, K., 1137
Orthner, D., 913

Orthner, D. K., 915
Orthwein, J., 134
Osborne, D., 195
Osher, F., 699
Osheroff, J. A., 1120, 1125
Osofsky, J. D., 1084
Ossman, W. A., 550
Öst, L. G., 550
Ostir, G. V., 848, 849
Ostrower, F., 156
Othmer, E., 332
Othmer, S. C., 332
Ott, J. M., 1110
Otto, M. W., 350
Ou, S., 619
Ouimette, P., 363
Owen, C., 808, 809
Oyserman, D., 1045, 1046, 1047, 1048, 1216

Pachan, M., 3, 6
Packman, W., 134
Padgett, D., 790, 792, 793
Padula, J. A., 644, 646
Pagani-Kurtz, L., 1013
Painter, J. S., 792
Paitich, D., 1100, 1101
Paiva, A. L., 644, 646
Paivio, S. C., 435
Palermo, A., 798
Palinkas, L. A., 979, 980
Palm, G., 919, 920, 921
Palmer, S., 743, 744
Panksepp, J., 624
Papero, D. V., 447
Papp, L., 849, 850
Parachini, E. A., 370
Pardini, D. A., 654
Parenti, M., 161
Paris, J., 745
Parker, K. C. H., 717, 718
Parker, L. M., 717, 718
Parker, L. S., 124
Parker, S. C., 364
Parks, B., 223
Parrish, D., 979, 981, 1137
Parrish, R. T., 548
Parry, J., 175
Parsons, B. V., 674, 1012
Partlett, D. F., 1064
Pasquini, P., 401
Pato, M., 488
Paton, C., 745
Patrick, D. L., 845, 848
Patterson, D., 604
Patterson, G., 89
Patterson, G. R., 458, 1012
Patton, B., 1072
Payne, A., 911
Paynter, N., 775
Payton, E., 672, 677
Paz Pruitt, I. T., 436

Pearlman, L. A., 558
Pearson, J., 844
Pearson, M. M., 166
Peat, J. K., 434
Pecora, P., 765
Pedersen, N. L., 849
Pederson, D., 625
Pedrick, C., 483
Peed, S., 1013
Pelcovitz, D., 565
Peled, E., 1082
Pelham, W. E., 528, 1040
Pellar, J., 51
Peller, J. E., 216
Penman, D., 1012
Penney, D., 743
Penney, J., 55
Penninx, B. W., 849
Pennuto, T., 134
Peralta, A., 745
Perel, J. M., 943
Perez, O., 745
Perez-Vidal, A., 968
Perlis, R. H., 350
Perreault, M., 3
Perry, B., 699, 700, 701
Perry, B. D., 1083
Perry, J. A., 364
Perryman, D., 89
Pescosolido, B. A., 1092
Pessin, H., 745
Peterson, T. R., 436
Petrila, J., 1061, 1064
Petry, S., 409, 421, 425
Petticrew, M., 1138, 1139, 1149, 1152, 1153
Pettinati, H. M., 29
Pfohl, B., 745
Pfost, K. S., 164, 165
Phelan, J., 175, 1092
Phenix, A., 1104
Phenix, L. M., 892
Phil, R., 1013
Phillips, B., 798
Phillips, D. A., 5, 65, 69
Phillips, S. D., 765
Piasecki, M., 1093, 1095
Picardi, A., 401
Pichot, T., 257, 1026
Pickrel, S. G., 1004
Pierce, C., 928, 932
Pierce-Gonzalez, D., 928, 932
Pignone, M., 397
Pike, C. K., 356
Pike, K., 107
Pilkington, K., 604
Pillai, V., 1149, 1153
Pillemer, K., 1106
Pilling, S., 717, 718
Pincus, H. A., 332, 335, 341
Pine, B., 959
Pinnell, S., 596

Pinquart, M., 845
Pinsof, W. M., 435
Pinto, D., 16
Pitman, R., 717
Pitner, R. O., 998, 1215
Pittman, J. F., 916
Piven, F. F., 890
Plotnick, R., 765
Plotz, D. A., 888
Plue, L., 847
Poelstra, P. L., 164, 165
Poertner, J., 64, 195, 982
Polivy, J., 534
Pollack, D., 158
Pollio, D. E., 55, 279, 1158, 1160, 1171, 1172, 1174
Pollock, B. G., 943
Polowy, C. I., 123
Pomeroy, E. C., 435, 436, 634, 635
Poole, D. L., 909, 910, 911
Popa, J. H., 436
Popay, J., 1138
Pope, K. S., 164
Pope, M., 758
Popkin, M. H., 624
Popple, P. R., 117
Porter, B., 392
Porter, R., 335
Portera, L., 362
Posey, R., 991
Post, J. A., 815
Potocky-Tripody, M., 946
Poulos, S., 190
Powers, K. G., 623
Powers, P. R., 881, 901
Poythress, N. G., 1055, 1056, 1061, 1064
Pratt, S., 666
Presley, A. S., 743
Presser, N. R., 164, 165
Price, C., 676
Price, L. H., 606
Prince, S. E., 472
Prins, A., 363
Prior, V., 1061
Pristach, E. A., 367
Prochaska, J., 164, 222
Prochaska, J. M., 644, 646
Prochaska, J. O., 458, 460, 575, 644, 646, 694
Proctor, E., 325, 506, 507, 511, 1170
Proctor, E. K., 55, 1011
Proudhock, P., 1098
Puente, A. E., 400
Pulerwitz, T., 1006
Pumariega, A. J., 35, 65
Putnam, F. W., 566
Putnam, R., 673
Putnam, R. D., 915

Quamma. J. P., 994, 997
Quinn, L., 907, 911
Quinsey, V., 1098, 1101
Quinsey, V. L., 1093

Radloff, R. S., 217, 218
Raggi, V., 1039
Raggi, V. L., 528
Rahav, G., 734
Rahdert, E. R., 1007
Raines, J., 42
Rainey, L. C., 827
Ramchandani, P., 1135
Ramirez, G., 397
Ramirez, M., 844
Ramirez-Valles, J., 1045
Ramisetty-Mikler, S., 1082
Ramsey, S. D., 171
Ramsey-Klawsnik, H., 1107
Randall, J., 436
Rando, T. A., 634
Rank, R. C., 1013
Rao, J., 847
Raphael, B., 109
Rapoport, J. L., 606
Rapp, C., 195
Rapp, C. A., 632, 633, 708, 709,
    772, 782, 784, 785, 787, 788
Rapp, R., 772, 784, 785, 787, 788
Rapp-Paglicci, L. A., 817
Rasmussen, H., 774
Rasmussen, N., 396
Rasmussen, S., 488, 606
Ratcliff, K., 398
Rathus, J. H., 743
Ratner, H., 1087
Raue, P., 844
Raue, P. J., 844
Raval, V., 625
Ray, L., 606
Ray, O. S., 1061
Reamer, F., 509
Reamer, F. G., 115, 116, 117, 118,
    119, 121, 122, 124, 125, 160,
    163, 164, 1055
Redd, W., 604
Reddy, L., 648
Rees, C., 980, 981
Rees, R., 1154
Regan, L., 3
Regehr, C., 106, 107, 108, 187, 189,
    190, 191, 192, 980, 982, 1092,
    1098, 1099, 1101, 1175
Reich, S., 1100, 1101
Reichel, W., 797
Reid, F., 364
Reid, J. B., 1012
Reid, M. J., 1011, 1012, 1013,
    1014, 1016
Reid, P. N., 117
Reid, W., 387
Reid, W. H., 1091, 1092, 1096

Reid, W. J., 226, 318, 432, 843
Reif, S., 3
Reinecke, M. A., 243, 247, 552, 553
Reisch, M., 881
Reiss, D., 483
Reiter, M., 73
Reithoffer, A., 521
Rembert, J. K., 1006
Rennie, D., 1115, 1117, 1124,
    1165, 1168, 1179
Resnick, M. D., 674
Restuccia, J., 194
Reuter, P., 991
Reynolds, A. J., 619
Reynolds, B. C., 1117
Reynolds, C., 844, 847, 848
Reynolds, C. F., 846
Reynolds, C. F., III, 943
Rhee, S., 970
Rheingold, A. A., 549, 550
Rheinscheld, J., 210
Rhodes, M., 1045, 1046, 1047
Rhodes, M. L., 115
Ribner, D. S., 523
Ricard, R., 1024, 1025
Riccardi, K., 368
Rice, M., 1101
Rice, M. E., 1093
Richan, W. C., 894, 900
Richards, C., 189
Richards, D. A., 717, 718
Richardson, B., 1006
Richardson, D., 980
Richardson, J., 604
Richardson, L., 158
Richardson, V. E., 939, 940
Richardson, W. S., 169, 171, 1115,
    1116, 1120, 1121, 1124, 1127,
    1128, 1134, 1145, 1163, 1166,
    1170, 1172, 1174, 1176, 1177,
    1178
Richey, C., 507
Richey, C. A., 713
Richman, J. M., 816, 916
Richmond, M., 1116
Richmond, M. E., 71, 72, 73, 76, 376
Richters, J. E., 388
Rideout, S., 815
Rider, E. A., 620
Riegel, B., 790, 793, 795
Rienzi, B. M., 95
Riggs, P. D., 1006, 1007, 1008
Ringeisen, H., 980, 981, 982
Risdale, L., 171
Ritchie, D., 1084
Rivard, J. C., 435
Rivas, R. F., 634, 635
River, D. A., 3
Rivera, F. G., 881, 882
Rivera, J., 177
Roak, J., 963
Robbins, P. C., 1094

Roberts, A., 506
Roberts, A. R., 18, 50, 51, 88, 89,
    90, 95, 100, 128, 129, 130,
    131, 134, 174, 177, 207, 208,
    210, 211, 212, 213, 214, 385,
    1061, 1082, 1092, 1093, 1094,
    1107, 1115, 1170
Roberts, B. S., 212, 213
Roberts, H., 1138, 1139, 1149,
    1152, 1153
Roberts, M., 1013
Roberts, N., 108
Roberts, R., 397
Roberts-Gennaro, M., 889
Robin, A. L., 528
Robin, L., 622, 624, 625
Robins, L., 398
Robinson, E. A., 383
Robinson, P., 364
Robnett, B., 901
Rock, M., 1092, 1093, 1094
Rodebaugh, T. L., 549
Roderick, M., 1047
Rodick, J. D., 1013
Rodman, J., 435, 458
Rodriguez, C. P., 435
Rodriguez-Espiricueta, I., 676
Roffman, R., 507
Rogers, C. R., 235, 236, 237, 239,
    240
Rogers, E. M., 1173
Rogers, K., 979, 981, 982
Roget, N. A., 1008
Rohani, M., 1031, 1032
Rohsenow, D., 28
Rojas, E., 866
Rolland, J. S., 426
Rollnick, S., 24, 605, 695
Roman, P. M., 27
Ronen, T., 246
Ronfeldt, H., 107
Ronis, D. L., 166
Rooney, G. D., 521, 522, 523, 524
Rooney, R., 501, 515, 600
Rooney, R. H., 226, 238, 521, 522,
    523, 524
Rose, S., 791, 1033, 1123
Rose, T., 556, 937
Roseberg, S., 699
Rosehthal, B., 889
Rosen, A., 55, 171, 325, 506, 507,
    511, 1011, 1170
Rosen, G., 715
Rosen, H., 294
Rosen, R., 740
Rosenberg, G., 1131
Rosenberg, S., 699
Rosenberg, W., 169, 170, 171,
    1163, 1166, 1170, 1172, 1174
Rosenberg, W. C., 1162
Rosenblatt, A., 527
Rosenfeld, R., 95

Rosenthal, R., 221, 506, 981
Rosenvinge, J. H., 364
Rosenzweig, S., 221, 223
Rosman, B., 442, 444
Ross, A. W., 383
Ross, C., 76
Ross, C. A., 362, 566
Ross, H., 403
Ross, J., 550
Ross, R., 350, 790, 791, 792, 793, 795
Rossi, D., 866
Rossi, E., 578, 581, 600, 601, 602, 603, 604
Rossier, J., 280
Rossman, B. B., 1083
Rost, K., 368
Roswell, V. A., 159
Rotatori, A. F., 383
Roth, A., 305, 539, 553
Roth, L., 1093, 1094
Roth, L. H., 175
Roth, S., 565
Rothbaum, B. O., 561, 718
Rothman, A. J., 1047
Rothman, J., 516, 751, 754, 765, 881, 884
Rothwangl, J., 1158
Rouleau, J., 1098, 1100, 1101
Rounsaville, B. J., 326
Rovner, D., 1165
Rowe, C., 311
Rowe, C. L., 458
Rowe, W., 235, 238, 240, 241, 864
Rowe, W. S., 864, 865, 866, 967
Rowland, M. D., 74
Roy-Byrne, P. P., 362
Royse, D., 724
Rubin, A., 171, 200, 356, 390, 635, 717, 718, 979, 981, 1022, 1129, 1137
Rubin, H. J., 881, 901
Rubin, I. S., 881, 901
Rucci, P., 539, 542
Ruffolo, M. C., 1161
Ruiz, P., 1061
Rumpf, H. J., 366
Russell, I. I., 1160
Russell, M., 367
Russo, J., 847
Russon, J., 362
Rutter, C., 845, 848
Rutter, M., 383, 384, 424
Ruzek, J. I., 109
Ryan, C., 902
Ryan, C. S., 758
Ryan, W. P., 156
Ryser, G., 388
Ryu,C., 1032

Saag, M. S., 802
Saari, L., 780

Sabin, J. E., 317
Saccuzzo, D. P., 1061
Sackett, C. F., 285
Sackett, D. L., 169, 170, 171, 1162, 1163, 1166, 1170, 1172, 1174
Sacks, K. B., 930
Sadler, J. M., 1216
Sadock, B., 29, 497
Sadock, B. J., 532, 1061
Sadock, V., 29
Sadock, V. A., 532
Safran, J., 259
Sager, J. S., 751, 754
Sagovsky, R., 361
Saini, M., 1138
Saitz, R., 835
Sakawa, D., 856
Sakhrani, D., 368
Sakraida, T., 734
Salamone, A., 1106, 1107
Saleebey, D., 4, 47, 216, 217, 274, 380, 502, 632, 959, 963, 1086
Saleh, S., 788
Salem, P., 1072
Salerno, S., 930
Sales, B. D., 1061, 1091, 1092, 1096
Sales, E., 634
Salisbury, J., 1163
Sallee, A. L., 766
Salmon, T. S., 726
Salomon, A., 1117
Saltzman, A., 1061, 1062
Salzman, C., 845
Sambamoorthi, U., 846
Samuels, S., 848
Sandau-Beckler, P., 864
Sandell, K. S., 278
Sanderson, W., 821, 822, 824
Sanderson, W. C., 823
Sandier, I. N., 817
Sandler, I. N., 1061
Sandoz, E. K., 283, 285
Sangalang, B. B., 792
Sanson-Fisher, R. W., 827
Santisteban, D. A., 968
Santos, A., 213
Santos, A. B., 707, 871
Sargent, J., 790, 791, 792, 793, 795
Sarrazin, M. S. V., 189
Sartre, D. D., 943
Sattler, J. M., 1064
Saulnier, C. F., 277, 278, 280
Savage, D., 12, 13, 16
Saxe, G., 700, 702
Sayger, T., 672, 677
Scahill, L., 1012
Scalia, P. A., 676
Scamardo, M., 1020, 1022, 1025
Schaalje, G., 434, 435
Schaefer, C., 648
Schaps, E., 988, 992, 993
Scharff, D., 478

Scharff, J., 478
Schatzberg, A. F., 533
Scheeringa, M. S., 1083
Scheifler, P., 509, 511, 512
Schertzer, S., 344
Schicht, W., 785
Schiller, L. Y., 685
Schilling, L. E., 301
Schinke, S., 436, 437
Schiraldi, G. R., 1061
Schlesinger, E., 963, 971
Schlesinger, E. G., 945, 946
Schley, S., 888
Schlichter, K. J., 1013
Schmaling, K., 847
Schmeelk-Cone, K. H., 1045
Schmidt, S. O., 815
Schnall, D. J., 158
Schnapp, W., 12, 13
Schneider, R. L., 894
Schneiderman, 28
Schnell, S. V., 1016
Schoener, G. R., 166
Schoenwald, S., 983
Schoenwald, S. K., 3, 74, 980, 981, 982
Schoevers, R., 553
Schopler, J. H., 189
Schore, A., 306
Schore, J., 798
Schreiner, M., 887
Schulberg, H., 844, 847, 848
Schultz, B., 528
Schultz, L. A., 1012
Schulz, B. K., 1043
Schulz, R., 634, 849
Schumer, F., 442
Schutz, W. C., 685
Schwab, A. J., 910
Schwab-Stone, M., 331
Schwartz, B., 606
Schwartz, I. M., 73
Schwartz, N., 1047
Schwartz, R. C., 276, 474, 475
Schwartz, S., 434, 436, 847, 1052
Schwartz, W., 231, 574
Scocco, P., 844
Scott, L., 1100
Scovil, J., 3
Seabury, B. A., 524
Seagraves, R., 740
Seagren, E. A., 815, 1082
Sebold, J., 257, 594, 595, 599
Sedway, J. A., 533
Sedway, J. S., 533
Seedat, S., 1136
Seely, J., 397
Seers, K., 171
Segal, U., 959
Seidl, F., 154
Seidler, G. H., 717, 718
Sells, S. P., 434, 435, 458, 462, 1015

Selver, V., 892
Selzer, M., 1100, 1101
Sen, R., 881
Senge, P., 888
Sergay, J., 624
Serketich, W. J., 1012
Serlin, R. C., 606
Sessions, P., 3, 6
Seto, M., 1103
Setterlind, S., 106
Sevier, M., 472
Sexton, T. L., 756
Seybolt, D., 494
Sgadari, A., 797
Shadish, W. R., 434, 435, 436,
    1140, 1179
Shaffer, D., 331, 388
Shah, S., 175
Shalev, A., 728
Shanahoff-Khalsa, D. S., 606
Shaneyfelt, T. M., 1158
Shapiro, F., 562, 714, 715, 716, 717,
    718, 745
Shapiro, J. R., 533, 1061
Shapiro, L., 483
Sharer, S., 604
Sharfstein, S., 699, 700
Shariati, M., 402
Sharma, J. M., 388
Sharon, D., 734
Sharp, I. R., 745
Sharps, P., 95
Sharry, J., 257
Shaughnessy, A. F., 1164
Shaver, P. R., 1061
Shaw, K., 780
Shaw, R., 894
Shea, B. J., 1155, 1156
Shea, M. T., 331, 332
Shea, S., 498
Sheafor, B. W., 864
Shear, K., 849
Shear, M. K., 362, 539, 542
Shek, D. T. L., 1131
Shelby, J. S., 648, 649, 651
Sheldon, B., 1148
Sheldon, T. A., 1164
Shellenberger, S., 74, 379
Shen, Q., 785, 787
Sherer, R. A., 177
Sherman, L. W., 991
Sherman, M. F., 731
Sherman, P. S., 758
Shern, D. L., 794
Sherraden, M., 887
Shilts, L., 257, 1020, 1021
Shiva, V., 882, 890
Shlonsky, A., 506, 980, 982, 1127,
    1170, 1171, 1173, 1174, 1175
Shneidman, E., 174
Shonkoff, J. P., 5, 65, 69
Shore, J. H., 166

Shore, N., 884
Shortell, S., 194
Shorter, E., 335
Shugar, G., 344
Shulman, G., 693
Shulman, K., 849
Shulman, L., 573, 575, 576, 577,
    680, 681, 722
Shwartz, M., 194
Sia, T. L., 818
Sibley, M., 528, 1040, 1043
Sidorowich, J., 606
Siebert, D. C., 164
Siegal, H., 784
Siegel, D., 1115
Siegel, T. C., 654, 1013
Sieppert, J., 318
Sigelman, C. K., 620
Sijesnaar, M., 717
Sikkema, K., 666
Silk, K. R., 745
Silva, R., 35
Silver, E., 1093, 1094
Silver, E. J., 619
Silvera, D. H., 364
Simerly, E., 1061
Simmons, C., 1083
Simmons, D., 951
Simon, B. L., 882
Simon, G., 845, 848
Simon, G. M., 445, 477
Simone, K., 762
Simoni, J. M., 951
Simon-Rusinowitz, L., 762, 798
Simons, S. L., 458
Simonsick, E. M., 849
Simpson, C., 849
Simpson, D. D., 818
Simpson, H. B., 606
Sims, B., 89
Singer, J. B., 190, 192
Sipple, J., 980
Skalevag, S. A., 1056
Skinner, H. A., 368, 692
Sklar, H., 888
Sklare, G., 1020, 1021, 1027
Skodol, A. E., 331, 332, 745
Skolnick, J., 485
Skorina, J. K., 165
Slade, A., 625
Slaikeu, K. A., 48, 49, 50, 51
Slawson, D. C., 1164
Slesnik, N., 436
Slilvern, L., 1083
Slobogin, C., 1061, 1064
Slovic, P., 1137
Sluzki, C., 961
Smith, A., 367
Smith, B., 844, 888
Smith, E. D., 79, 85, 827, 828, 830
Smith, G. D., 1137, 1138
Smith, G. R., 368

Smith, J., 604
Smith, L. A., 1013
Smith, M., 192, 221, 534, 604, 707,
    708
Smith, R., 959, 961
Smith, R. L., 1024, 1025
Smith, R. S., 674
Smith, S. R., 381, 384
Smith, T. E., 435, 458
Smith, V., 226
Smith-Wilson, R., 828
Smock, K., 881
Smyth, R., 171
Snodgrass, J., 235, 236
Snow, M., 318
Snowball, R., 171
Snyder, C., 774
Snyder, C. R., 361
Snyder, M., 236, 240
Soafer, S., 761
Sobel, H. J., 826
Sobol, A., 398
Sokol, M. S., 533
Sokol, R. J., 367
Solomon, D., 988, 992, 993
Solomon, J., 1061
Solomon, L., 801, 802
Solomon, P., 491, 493, 705, 707,
    708, 709, 822
Solomon, S., 110
Solorazano, D., 928, 932
Somerton, J., 646
Sonnenstuhl, W. J., 166
Sorensen, S., 845
Sorrell, J. T., 849
Soson, M., 787
Sowers, K. M., 864, 865, 866, 967
Sowers-Hoag, K. M., 864
Spaccarelli, S., 1012
Spanier, G., 468
Spanier, G. B., 392
Spaniol, L., 775
Sparks, J., 47, 51, 52, 1086
Sparta, S. N., 1061, 1063
Speigel, D. A., 539, 542
Spence, E., 1083, 1084
Spence, L., 821
Spencer, C., 1061
Sperry, L., 497
Spiegel, D., 604
Spinazzola, J., 565
Spinhoven, P., 743, 744
Spinnazzola, J., 1083
Spitalnik, D., 760, 761
Spitz, A., 699
Spitzer, R. L., 326, 331, 332, 361, 539
Sprenkle, D. H., 434
Springer, D., 1022, 1129
Springer, D. W., 18, 218, 386, 387,
    403, 404, 1004, 1009, 1014,
    1061, 1174, 1215
Squillace, M., 798

Sreenivasan, H., 1104
Srinivasan, M., 731
St. John, D., 745
Stacey, D., 1165
Stacher, D., 549
Stadler, H. A., 163
Stahl, P. M., 1061
Stalker, C. A., 219
Stamm, B. H., 559
Stamm, S., 169
Stams, G. J., 257
Stange, K., 6
Stanhope, V., 822
Stanley, B., 742, 743, 745
Stanley, J. C., 1138, 1139
Stanley, M., 552
Stanley, M. S., 849, 850
Stanley, S., 733
Stannard, D., 950
Stannard, D. E., 929
Stanton, M. D., 434
Staples, L., 881, 901, 902
Stapleton, A., 731
Stapleton, A. B., 726, 731
Stark, M., 164, 165
Stark, P. L., 271
Stastny, P., 794
Stat, D., 539, 542
Staudt, M., 43, 507
Steadman, H. J., 1092, 1093, 1094
Steenbarger, B. N., 216
Steenrod, S., 400, 401
Stein, D., 1033
Stein, D. J., 1136
Stein, G., 5
Stein, L. I., 871
Stein, M., 191
Stein, M. B., 362, 545, 548
Stein, R. E., 619
Steinberg, L., 620
Steinberg, S., 930
Steiner, T., 257
Steinmetz, S., 1106
Steinwachs, D., 491
Steinwachs, D. M., 871
Steketee, G., 475, 483, 485, 486,
    509
Stellato, C., 397
Stens, A., 844
Stephenson, M., 89
Stern, L., 74, 75
Stern, M., 893
Stern, S., 980, 982, 1175
Sternbach, K. O., 1091, 1092
Sternberg, R. J., 18, 474
Sternig, P. J., 268
Sterns, S., 1171, 1173, 1174
Stevenson, H., 920
Stevenson, J., 744
Stevermer, J. J., 1125
Stewart, C., 89, 402
Stewart, J. C., 713

Stewart, J. L., 528
Stewart, K., 797
Stich, F., 221
Stien, P., 699
Stinson, F. S., 833
Stofle, G. S., 189
Stohr, M., 89
Stokes, S. C., 970
Stone, A. A., 175
Stone, M. H., 335, 336
Stone, S., 391, 392
Stoner, G., 1040
Storaasli, R. D., 550
Stores, G., 1145
Stovall-McClough, K. C., 620
Straus, D. L., 1163, 1166
Straus, M., 392
Straus, M. A., 468
Straus, S., 169, 171
Straus, S. E., 1115, 1116, 1120, 1121,
    1124, 1127, 1128, 1134, 1145
Strauss, S. E., 1176, 1177, 1178
Strayhorn, J., 655
Streeter, C., 50
Streeter, C. L., 1020, 1021, 1023
Strenger, C., 261
Stricker, G., 260
Striegel-Moore, R., 532
Strober, M., 533
Strode, H., 1117
Strom, S., 158
Strom-Gottfried, K., 115, 117, 121,
    125, 521, 522, 523, 524, 723
Strosahl, K., 283, 284, 286
Strosahl, K. D., 550
Stroul, B. A., 64, 65
Stuart, G. W., 757
Stueve, A., 175, 1092
Stulberg, J., 195
Suarez-Orozco, C., 1032
Suarez-Orozco, M., 1032
Suchinsky, R., 1157
Sudbury, B., 799
Sudermann, M., 1082
Sue, D. W., 477
Sue, S., 222
Sugai, D. P., 655
Sugarman, D., 392
Sugarman, D. B., 468
Sugiman, T., 294
Suh, J. J., 29
Sukhodolsky, D. G., 1012
Suler, J., 187, 189, 190
Sullivan, A., 177
Sullivan, J. T., 28
Sullivan, M., 1007, 1008, 1009
Sullivan, W. P., 784, 785, 787, 788
Sulman, J., 12, 13, 16
Summers, M., 799
Sunday, S., 565
Sunderland, T., 846
Surber, R. W., 756

Sutcliffe, K., 1154
Sutton, A., 847
Suzuki, J., 718
Svinicki, M., 724
Swain, J. E., 621
Swankin, D., 153
Swann, A. C., 849, 850
Swanson, C. B., 1045, 1046
Swanson, J., 1093
Swanson, J. W., 175
Swartz, M., 3, 1093
Sweeney, L., 790, 792, 793
Sweet, A., 724
Swenson, W. M., 166
Swift, R., 29
Swift, R. M., 834
Swigonski, M. E., 234
Swindle, R., 847
Switzer, G., 699
Sykora, K., 28
Sympson, S. C., 361
Szalavits, M., 699, 700, 701
Szalavitz, M., 1083
Szanto, K., 177
Szapocznik, J., 434, 435, 436, 437,
    968

Tabachnick, B. G., 164
Taft, C. T., 558, 561, 562
Taft, J., 574, 980
Tahan, H. A., 751
Tait, V., 1165
Takashima, H., 271
Talcott, G. W., 916
Tamasese, K., 276
Tamblyn, R., 849
Tang, T. Z., 244, 246
Tantillo, M., 476
Tanzman, B., 707, 708
Tarrier, N., 810
Tata, P., 743, 744
Tattan, T., 810
Taylor, B., 156
Taylor, E..., 383, 384
Taylor, E. B., 765
Taylor, L., 980, 981, 1033
Taylor, M. F., 691
Taylor, R., 3, 6
Taylor, S., 561, 717
Tedeschi, R. G., 562
Teichner, G. A., 1004, 1008
Ten Have, T., 844, 847, 848
Teplow, D. A., 16
Teresi, J., 844
Terluin, B., 846
Terranova, M. D., 1177, 1178
Terris, D., 194
Terry, K., 1045, 1047, 1048
Test, M. A., 871
Thelen, M., 534
Theorell, T., 106
Thiara, R., 3

Thienhaus, O. J., 1093, 1095
Thoennes, N., 95, 951, 1071, 1073
Thom, B., 367
Thomas, C., 1106
Thomas, E. J., 289
Thomas, F., 594
Thomas, F. N., 257
Thomas, J., 731, 1154
Thomas, R., 847
Thomlison, B., 318, 506, 507
Thompson, A. I., 384
Thompson, B., 793
Thompson, B. J., 803
Thompson, C., 335
Thompson, D., 707
Thompson, E., 424
Thompson, K., 699, 1061
Thompson, L., 940, 942
Thompson, L. W., 970
Thompson, N., 621
Thompson, R. A., 711
Thompson, S. J., 435, 436
Thoreson, R. W., 163, 164, 165
Thorne, B., 235
Thornicroft, G., 370
Thornton, D., 1101, 1102, 1103
Thorp, S., 849
Thum, Y. M., 472
Thyer, B., 506
Thyer, B. A., 151, 154, 545, 548,
    550, 1115, 1118, 1181,
    1182
Thyer, K. B., 1115, 1182
Tierney, L., 845, 846, 847
Tierney, S., 982
Tilson, D., 195
Timmins, B., 528
Tisdall, G., 403
Tjaden, P., 95, 951
Tobias, C., 402
Todahl, J. L., 768
Todd, A. J., 1116
Tolin, D., 717
Tolland, A., 218
Tolson, E. R., 226
Tomita, S., 1106, 1107
Toner, B. B., 344
Tonidandel, A. M., 369
Tonigan, J., 24
Topolski, J., 785
Torrey, W., 513
Toseland, R. W., 634, 635
Tousignant, P., 797
Toynbee, A., 1116
Tracy, E., 712
Tracy, E. M., 712, 713
Trask, R., 210
Travers, J., 545
Tremblay, R. E., 1013
Tremblay, T., 707, 708
Trepper, T., 257, 1020, 1086
Trice, H. M., 166

Tripodi, S. J., 218, 385, 1020, 1023,
    1025, 1027, 1215
Tripodi, T., 356, 563
Trochmé, N., 1071, 1072, 1074
Tropman, J., 881
Tropman, J. E., 884
Truax, C. B., 221, 575
Trumbetta, S., 699
Tsushima, W. T., 1061, 1066
Tu, W., 1033
Tucker, J., 785
Tuckman, B. W., 684, 685
Tugenberg, T., 809
Tuhaka, F., 276
Tully, C., 936
Tuner, C. W., 436
Tunstill, J., 856, 858
Turchik, J. A., 401
Turnell, A., 1084, 1085, 1086, 1087
Turner, F., 717, 718
Turner, F. J., 249, 276
Turner, R. J., 965
Turner, W., 1135
Tutty, L., 1117
Tversky, A., 1137
Twohig, M. P., 285
Tyrer, P., 743, 744

Uden-Holmen, T., 788
Uken, A., 257, 594, 595, 599
Uncapher, H., 844
Unger, A., 790, 793, 795
Ungerer, J., 620
Unis, A. S., 1013
Unützer, J., 845, 847, 848
Urey, J. R., 1013
Ursano, R. J., 731
Ury, W., 1072
Utada, A. A., 388

Vaghy, A., 5
Vakalahi, H. O., 955
Valentich, M., 277, 278
van Asselt, T., 743, 744
van Beek, D., 1103
van Beyer, K., 1057, 1058
Van den Brink, R. H. S., 402
Van der Ende, J., 383
Van der Kolk, B., 700, 717
van der Kolk, B., 1083, 1084, 1085
van der Kolk, B. A., 565, 718, 1061
Van der Meer, K., 402
van der Windt, D., 846
van Dyck, R., 743, 744, 846
Van Eck, K., 1043
Van Etten, M., 717
van Haaften, H., 717
Van Hassalt, V., 666
Van Hemert, A. M., 402
Van Horn, M. L., 673
van Hout, H., 846
Van Marter, D. F., 646

Van Noppen, B., 483, 488
Van Os, T. W. D. P., 402
van Ryn, M., 95
van Tilburg, W., 743, 744
Van Wel, B., 745
van Wormer, K., 934, 936
Vance, H. B., 1061
VandenBos, G. R., 165
Vanderplasschen, W., 784, 785,
    787, 788
Vandiver, V., 215, 506
Vandiver, V. L., 116, 317, 968
Vandivort-Warren, R., 784
VanDuesen, J. M, 443, 444
Vassil, T., 910
Vassil, T. V., 681, 682, 684
Vaughn, T., 788
Vegso, S., 485
Veit, C. T., 369
Velicer, W. F., 575
Vendermeer, J., 846
Verbitsky, N., 847
Verdeli, H., 845
Verhulst, F. C., 383
Vernberg, E. M., 109
Vernon-Smiley, M., 980, 981
Vidaver, R., 699
Vinson, D. C., 1125
Vitaro, F., 1013
Vladeck, B., 798
Vodde, R., 276
Volger, K., 708
Volkmar, F. R., 1061
Volland, P. J., 5
Von Korff, M., 847
Von Korff, M. V., 801
Vonk, M. E., 563
Vorstenbosch, M., 402
Vos, B., 778
Vourlekis, B., 790, 791, 792, 793,
    795
Vourlekis, B. S., 766
Vu, C., 391, 392
Vujanovic, A. A., 370

Wachtel, P. L., 260, 307
Wagner, D., 765
Wagner, E., 847
Wagner, E. H., 801
Wagner, F. E., 717, 718
Wagner, H. R., 765
Wagner, W., 294
Wahler, R. G., 674
Wakefiled, J. C., 171
Wald, J., 1045, 1046
Waldegrave, C., 276
Waldron, H. B., 436
Walitzer, K. S., 23
Walker, E., 845, 848
Walker, L., 257
Walker, R., 89
Walker, R. D., 1157

Walker, R. J., 635
Walkup, J. T., 846
Wallace, K., 392
Waller, N. G., 362
Wallerstein, N., 910
Walsh, B. T., 533
Walsh, F., 409, 413, 424, 425, 426, 428
Walsh, J., 35, 391, 690, 691, 756, 757, 966, 968
Walter, J., 51
Walter, J. L., 216
Walters, E. E., 343, 385, 548, 552, 691, 692, 848, 1004, 1007
Walters, K. L., 951
Walters, L. H., 623
Walters, P., 370
Wampold, B., 746
Wampold, B. E., 221, 259, 260, 1168
Wandrei, K. E., 334, 372
Wang, H., 733, 734
Wang, M., 194
Wang, Y., 818
Waranoff, J., 790, 792, 793
Warberg, B., 1100
Ward, A., 856, 859, 860
Ward, W. H., 163
Ware, J. E., 318, 369
Ware, J. H., 941
Ware, N. C., 809
Ware, W. B., 916
Warner, M., 235
Warren, M., 1083
Warren-Adamson, C., 856, 857, 858, 859, 860, 861
Washington, O., 775
Washington, O. G. M., 773, 774, 775, 776
Watanabe, N., 539
Watchel, P. L., 235
Waters, J. A., 212
Watring, J., 388
Watson, M., 43, 988, 992, 993
Watson, P., 109, 728
Watson, P. J., 109
Watson, R., 1100
Watson, S. M., 1013
Watts-Jones, D., 417, 967, 969
Watzlawick, P., 216, 217
Way, S., 12, 13, 16
Weakland, J. H., 216, 217
Weaver, H., 950, 952
Webb, N. B., 648, 649, 650, 970
Webb, W. H., 1020, 1021
Weber, J., 79
Webster, C., 175, 1103
Webster, D., 95
Webster-Stratton, C., 675, 1011, 1012, 1013, 1014, 1016
Weg, A. H., 615
Wehman, P., 705, 706

Weil, M., 884, 886, 888
Weil, M. O., 881, 901
Weiner, B. A., 175
Weiner, K., 797
Weiner-Davis, M., 216, 217
Weinman, M. L., 169
Weinstein, R., 785, 787
Weisaeth, L., 1061
Weisbrod, B. A., 871
Weise, R. E., 326
Weishaar, M. E., 592
Weisman, A. D., 826, 827
Weisner, C., 943
Weiss, C., 6
Weiss, D., 106, 107
Weiss, R., 1007, 1008
Weissberg, R. P., 42, 43
Weissman, M. M., 823
Weist, M., 980, 981
Weisz, J. R., 458, 817
Welch, M., 25
Wellisch, D. K., 827
Wells, A., 589
Wells, G. A., 1155, 1156
Wells, J., 936
Wells, K. B., 361
Wells, K. C., 1013
Welte, J. W., 367
Wenocur, S., 881, 901
Werkmeister Rozas, L., 933
Werner, E. E., 424, 674
Wernick, L., 884
Wesnoski, S., 787
Wessely, S., 1123
Westen, D., 310
Wetherell, J., 849
Wetle, T., 800
Whelan, S., 1082
Whetten, K., 3
Whipple, E., 861
Whiston, S. C., 756
Whitaker, C., 464
White, K., 485, 486
White, L. C., 528, 1040, 1043
White, L. L., 25, 26
White, M., 52, 189, 273, 276, 615
White, T. W., 128
Whiting, L., 160
Whitley, M. K., 436
Whitley, R., 708
Whittaker, J., 765
Whittaker, J. K., 712, 713
Whittier, N., 901
Whitty, P., 847
Whyte, D. T., 172
Wibblesman, C. J., 1039, 1043
Wienrott, M. R., 1012
Wiger, D., 124
Wiggs, L., 1145
Wilbourne, P. L., 695
Wilcox, A., 790, 792, 793
Wilcox, R. E., 691

Wilhelm, K., 192
Williams, B., 847
Williams, D. E., 828
Williams, E., 835
Williams, G. T., 122
Williams, J., 397, 847
Williams, J. B. W., 326, 331, 332, 361, 539
Williams, K., 434
Williams, L., 218
Williams, O. H., 707
Williams, P., 402
Williams, R. A., 435
Williams, R. J., 458, 1007
Williams, T., 158
Williamson, D., 699
Williamson, J., 849
Willing, K., 163
Willrich, M., 1055
Wills, D., 928, 932
Wilson, D. B., 1149
Wilson, H., 218
Wilson, J., 929
Wilson, J. P., 1061
Wilson, K. G., 283, 285, 286, 550
Wilson, M. R., 434
Wilson, P., 434, 435
Wilson, P. C., 919
Wilson, R., 614
Wilson, S., 861, 901, 1082, 1083
Wilson, S. J., 1151
Wilson, V. B., 692, 693
Wiltz, N. A., 1012
Wineberger, L., 1104
Winkel, F. W., 89
Winslade, J., 276
Winter, J. E., 445
Winters, K. C., 692
Winters, N. C., 35, 65
Wise, T., 931
Wiseman, S., 218
Wittchen, H. U., 538
Witztum, E., 395
Wodarski, J. S., 817
Wodden, T., 604
Wohlfarth, T., 89
Wolchik, S. A., 1061
Wolf, E., 312
Wolf, J., 784, 785, 787, 788
Wolf, R. S., 1110
Wolfe, D. A., 1082, 1083
Wolfe, V. V., 1083
Wolk, J., 784, 785, 787
Wollins, M., 1179
Wolraich, M. L., 1039, 1043
Wong, D. F. K., 756
Wong, E., 845
Wong, K. W., 1091, 1092
Wong, M., 1033
Wong, M. M., 383
Wong, S., 991
Wong, S. E., 1177, 1178

Wood, B. J., 164, 165
Wood, J. L., 890
Wood, J. M., 400
Wood, K. M., 500
Wood, N., 434, 435
Wood, W. D., 625
Woods, M., 249
Woody, G. E., 27
Woody, J. D., 979, 982, 983
Woody, R. H., 122
Wooley, S., 531
Woolfenden, S. R., 434
Woolston, J., 4, 75
Worden, A. P., 95
Worden, J. W., 634, 826, 827
Wormith, J. S., 1095, 1096
Wright, B., 774
Wright, B. C., 845
Wright, D. W., 71
Wright, J., 856
Wu, H. S., 848
Wynne, J. M., 1061
Wynne, L. C., 435
Wyzik, P., 513

Xie, H., 707
Xue, Y., 388

Yalom, L., 23
Yamada, Y., 294

Yancey, G., 6
Yasui, M., 1011
Ybasco, F. C., 361
Yeager, K. R., 18, 23, 26, 28, 128, 129, 131, 177, 835, 1115, 1170
Yehuda, R., 107
Yellowlees, P., 808, 809
Yesavage, J., 556
Yi, J., 434, 472
Yingling, L. C., 341
Yoediono, Z., 844, 845
Yoshihama, M., 955
Yosso, T., 928, 932
Yost, B., 89
Youn, S., 970
Young, K., 222
Young, R., 344
Young, S., 257
Youngstrom, E., 1043

Zabora, J. R., 77, 79, 85, 827, 828, 829, 830, 831
Zak, L., 1083
Zalaquett, C., 844
Zald, M. N., 901
Zanarini, M. C., 370, 745
Zane, N., 222
Zangwill, W. M., 1013
Zanis, D., 787

Zapata-Vega, M., 177
Zarate, R., 666, 1177, 1178
Zaya, L. H., 345
Zazzali, J. L., 18
Zealberg, J., 213
Zeanah, C. H., 1083
Zeber, J. E., 778
Zeig, J., 578
Zeigler, A., 1042
Zeigler-Dendy, C. A., 1042
Zeiler, C. A., 402
Zeira, A., 998
Zeiss, A. M., 553
Zelvin, E., 187, 189, 190
Zewelanji, N. S., 528
Zhoa, S., 335
Zhou, X., 847
Ziegler, D., 1083
Ziegler, E., 423
Ziguras, S. J., 757
Zimmerman, J., 276
Zimmerman, M., 548
Zimmerman, M. A., 1045
Zinker, J., 303
Zonana, H., 1098, 1100, 1101, 1104
Zubritsky, C., 941
Zuccala, G., 797
Zuniga, M., 959

SUBJECT INDEX

AA (Alcoholics Anonymous), 24, 28, 116, 163, 696, m
AAIDD (American Association on Intellectual and Developmental Disabilities), 760, 763
AARP (American Association of Retired Persons), 153
AASSWB (American Association of State Social Work Boards), 151
abandonment of clients, 159
ABC model of CBT, 244
Abille v. United States, 132
abuse
    alcohol, 365, 366–7, 691–7
    child, 59, 88, 90, 358, 641–7, 659–65
    domestic, 88
    drug, 368, 691–7, 784–9
    elder, 59, 97, 1106–11
    emotional, 478–9, 665
    intimate partner, 392
    physical, 478–9, 565, 659–65, 699
    sexual, 478–9, 565, 663–5, 699, 738, 1098–104
    See also domestic violence shelter practice; substance abuse
academic performance, 42
acamprosate, 29
acceptance, 284, 286, 434
acceptance and commitment therapy (ACT), 283–8, 550
accessibility issues, 97
accident insurance, 58
accompaniment, 779
accountability
    in managed care practice, 13
    in private practice, 59
    in school-based practice, 42
    service, 159–61
    in social services, 156–9
accreditation standards, complying with, 160–1
ACE (Adverse Childhood Experiences) study, 699
acronyms, credentialing, 149–50
ACT (acceptance and commitment therapy), 283–8, 550

ACT (assertive community treatment), 807, 869–71
action, 642
action alerts via e-mail, 191
action planning, 47–51, 92, 211–12
active client participation, 52
active listening, 91, 210
activists, change, 901
activity scheduling, 246
acts of commission, 158
acts of omission, 122, 158
ACT Test Centers, 136–7
actuarial risk assessment, 1101–4
acute alcohol withdrawal syndrome, 28
acute stress disorder, 325–6, 330, 565
ADA (Americans with Disabilities Act), 798
ADAD (Adolescent Drug Abuse Diagnosis), 388
adaptation, 231, 424
addictions assessment, 24–5
addictions therapists, characteristics of effective, 25–6
addiction treatment practice, 20–33
    approaches to, 23–6
    documentation, 26
    group rounds, 22–3
    medical management options in alcoholism, 28–9
    social worker's role in treatment team, 30–2
    treatment planning, 26–7
    typical daily schedule, 20–2
    utilization review process, 27–8
    Web sites, 32
ADHD (attention deficit/hyperactivity disorder), 66, 1039–44
ADHD treatment planning, 526–30
adjustment, 231
adjustment disorders, 331
Adler, Alfred, 305
Adolescent Concerns Evaluation, 388
adolescent disorders, 329, 385–9
Adolescent Drug Abuse Diagnosis (ADAD), 388

adolescents
   ADHD treatment planning, 526–30
   assessment tools for, 381–4, 385–9
   and cancer
      See also oncology social work in a medical setting
   chemical abuse and dependency screening, 692
   child welfare case management, 765–9
   community-based care for, 63
   conduct-disordered youth, 74, 459, 1011–19
   current and future directions of social work practice,
      815–18
   delinquency, 458, 671–9
   dually diagnosed, 385
   eating disorders, 331, 476–7, 531–7
   Families and Schools Together (FAST), 671–9
   family centers, 855–63
   gay and lesbian issues, 936–7
   grief group interventions with, 636
   interventions for abuse and neglect, 641–7
   and parent education, 619
   PLL (Parenting with Love and Limits), 457–67
   school-based services, 907–12
   suicide prevention, 936
   warp-around model of care for, 75
   See also child and adolescent outpatient practice;
      community-based mental health with children
      and families; domestic violence shelter practice;
      family counselor in nonprofit community-
      based agency; home-based practice with
      children and families;
      school-based practice; school social work
adoption, 417, 419–21
adult mental health, 820–5
Adverse Childhood Experiences (ACE) study, 699
advocacy, 4, 893–900
advocates, domestic violence, 97
Aetna Health Inc. v. Davila, 16
affective disorders, 343
African American fathers, 919
African American Head Start, 919
African-centeredness, 963–4
aged population
   See older adults
AgeLine, 1130
agency funding, 36
aging, 762
   See also older adults
agoraphobia, 330, 538–44
AGREE criteria, 1158
agreements, service, 515, 575
AIAN (American Indians/Alaska Natives), 949–54
AIDS, 737
Air Force, 912–17
Al-Anon, 696
Alaska Natives, 949–54
Alateen, 696
Alatot, 696
alcohol abuse, 691–7
alcohol abuse, VBSs for, 365, 366–7
alcohol dependence treatment, 23, 833–42
   See also addiction treatment practice
Alcoholics Anonymous (AA), 24, 28, 116, 163, 696

alcoholism
   case management for, 784–9
   in practitioners, 163
   See also addiction treatment practice
alcohol use
   CAGE assessment for, 402–3
   during pregnancy, 365, 367–8
Alcohol Use Disorders Identification Test (AUDIT),
   365–6, 692
alcohol withdrawal syndrome, 28
algorithms, 507
alignment, 443
all-hazards approach, 105
alliance, working, 808–9
allocation criteria, 116
alter ego, 312
alternating treatments design (ATD), 1177
alternatives, exploring, 211
Alzheimer's disease, 335
ambiguous circumstances, 122
ambulance workers, 108
American Association for Marriage and Family
   Therapy, 121
American Association of Retired Persons (AARP), 153
American Association of State Social Work Boards
   (AASSWB), 151
American Association on Intellectual and
   Developmental Disabilities (AAIDD), 760, 763
American Bar Association, 135
American Board of Examiners in Clinical Social
   Work, 121
American Cancer Society, 80
American Indians, 949–54
American Parkinson's Disease Association, 157–8
American Psychiatric Association, 135, 185
American Psychological Association, 164
American Psychological Association (APA)
   Committee on Lesbian and Gay Concerns, 934
American Society of Addiction Medicine
   (ASAM), 692
Americans with Disabilities Act (ADA), 798
American West Airlines v. Tope, 1057
amnesia, 564
anger, 93
anger management therapy, 19
anorexia nervosa, 331, 531–7
ANS (Autonomic Nervous System questionnaire),
   360, 362
answerable questions, 169–71
Antabuse, 29
antianxiety mediations, 686–7
antidepressants, 686
antipsychotics, 686
anxiety, disintegration, 313
anxiety disorders, 330, 351–7, 447–52, 497–505, 533,
   606–12, 848–50
   See also panic disorders; social phobia
Anxiety Disorders Interview Schedule, 395, 539
anxiety management, 562
anxiety-related problems, VBSs for, 360, 362–3
AOSW (Association of Oncology Social Work), 77
APA Committee on Lesbian and Gay Concerns, 934

APA Practice Guideline for patients with suicidal behaviors, 129
appraising studies for EBP, 1137–41
approach to problems and solutions, 216–17
Aramony, William, 157
arbitration, 1079
ARC, 762
arousal symptoms, 108
art therapy, 78
ASAM (American Society of Addiction Medicine), 692
Asian and Pacific Islanders, 954–8
assault, sexual, 88, 90–2, 98
assertion training, 246
assertive community treatment (ACT), 807, 869–71
assessment
    addictions, 24–6
    alcohol and drug dependence, 835–7
    in behavioral social work, 290–1
    biopsychosocial, 376–80, 480–2
    bipolar disorder, 343–50
    borderline personality disorder (BPD), 743
    brief screening instruments
        See brief screening instruments
    case management for HIV/AIDS, 804
    case management in medical settings, 792
    chemical abuse and dependency screening, 691
    child and adolescent, 36, 381–4
    child-focused developmental, ecological and cultural, 815–16
    of civil patients, 1095
    client-focused measures, 351–7
    of client's stage of change, 642
    cognitive-behavioral, 244
    and CQI, 195
    crisis, 5, 101, 210
    ego, 378
    elder abuse/neglect, 1108–9
    evidence-based, 815–17
    family, standardized tests and instruments, 390–4
    of functioning, 340
    of generalized anxiety disorder, 497–8
    and goals, 521
    importance of being up to date on, 18
    integrative behavioral couple therapy (IBCT), 468–9
    lethality and safety, 90–1, 98–101
    mania, 344
    panic disorders, 538, 542
    parenting, 392
    physical inpatient environment, 178–9
    play therapy with children in crisis, 649
    in police department-based practice, 92
    protocols and RAIs for troubled adolescents, 385–9
    psychosocial, 90–1, 308–9
    PTSD, 558–64
    rapid, 36, 38
    of risk of recidivism, 1095–6
    severity by service type, 100
    sexual dysfunction, 739
    sexual predators, 1098–104
    social support, 712
    strengths, 779
    substance abuse case management, 785–6
    suicide, 5, 128, 175–7, 211, 344
    tools to evidence medical necessity, 317–22
    of treatment, 383
    using the DSM-IV-TR
        See Diagnostic and Statistical Manual of Mental Disorders
    violence, 175–7
    violence risk, 1093–5
    of withdrawal syndrome, 28
    See also diagnosis; screening
assessment-driven intervention, 506
assessment outline, 379
assessment questions, 1123
assessment tools
    See assessment; diagnosis; screening
Association of Oncology Social Work (AOSW), 77
Association of Social Work Boards (ASWB), 120, 136–7, 144–6, 149, 153–4, 187
ASWB Candidate Handbook, 136
asynchronous communication, 188
ATD (alternating treatments design), 1177
attachment-based models of couple therapy, 478
attachment theory, 478
attention deficit/hyperactivity disorder (ADHD), 66, 1039–44
attentiveness, 25
attitudes, modification of, 270
attitudinal values, 267–8, 270
attrition bias, 1139
AUDIT (Alcohol Use Disorders Identification Test), 365–6, 692
audits, ethics, 160
auspicious moments for change, 901
authoritarian parenting style, 620
authoritative parenting style, 620
autism, 66, 436
automatic thoughts, 242
Autonomic Nervous System questionnaire (ANS), 360, 362
autonomous practice, 6
autopsies, psychological, 174
Avary v. Bank of America, 1078
aversive agents for alcohol dependence, 29
aversive racism, 931–2
avoidance symptoms, 108
avoiding harm, 168–73
awareness, 301–2
axis I disorders, 497–505

background questions, 1128
backsliding, 470
Bates v. Denny, 133–4
Beck Depression Inventory (BDI), 57, 129
Beck Hopelessness Scale, 128–9
Behavioral and Emotional Rating Scale (BERS), 388
behavioral approach to social work, 288–93
behavioral experiments, 592–3
behavioral indicators of abuse, 661–2
behavioral observation, 354–5
behavior disorders in children, risk factors for, 65
behavior exchange, 471

being present, 284, 285
benchmarks, 42
benefit case management, 791–2
benzodiazepine, 28
bereavement and grief therapy, 632–7
BERS (Behavioral and Emotional Rating Scale), 388
BFTC (Brief Family Therapy Center), 47, 215–16, 253, 437–40, 594
bias, in EBP studies, 1139–40
bias, in forensic social work, 1062–3
bill of rights, patient, 16
binge eating disorder, 331, 531–7
biofeedback, 449
biological system, 497–8
biologic vulnerability, 65
biomedical testing, 1100
biopsychosocial assessment, 376–80, 480–2, 497–8
biopsychosocial education, 5
bipolar disorder, 66, 330, 343–50, 474–5
bisexual issues, 97, 934–8
Bishop Estate, 158
blogs, 191
bolts from the blue crises, 972
bombings, 88
bombshell, 576
bonding, 915
borderline personality disorder (BPD), 565, 742–7
boundaries, 116, 124, 443
Bowen Family Systems Therapy, 447–52
Bowlby, John, 306, 307
BPD (borderline personality disorder), 565, 742–7
BPP (bullying prevention program), 986–92
brainstorming, 74, 198
breach of contract, 159
breach of duty, 122, 158
brief family therapies, 47
Brief Family Therapy Center (BFTC), 47, 215–16, 253, 437–40, 594
Brief Panic Disorder Screen, 362
brief screening instruments, 358–71
　　alcohol abuse, 366–7
　　anxiety-related problems, 362–3
　　eating disorders, 364
　　general mental health, serious mental illness, personality disorders, 369–70
　　mood-related problems, 361
　　overview, 358–60, 365
　　substance abuse, 368
　　Web sites, 371
Brief Strategic Family Therapy (BSFT), 436
brief treatment, 215–20
brochure, professional, 17
bruises, 660
BSFT (Brief Strategic Family Therapy), 436
Budman, S. H., 215, 216
bulimia nervosa, 331, 531–7
bullying prevention program (BPP), 986–92
Burke, Chris, 158
burnout, 36, 57–8, 165
burns, 660–1
business considerations of private practice, 58–9

Business Continuity Institute, 105
buttons, pushing, 461

CAFAS (Child and Adolescent Functional Assessment Scale), 388
CAGE screener, 365, 366, 402–3, 692
California Evidence-Based Clearinghouse for Child Welfare, 1132
Cambridge-Sommerville Youth Study, 1143
Campbell Collaboration, 1130, 1140, 1150, 1154
Campral, 29
cancer
　　See oncology social work in a medical setting
Cancer Survivor Toolbox, 77
cannabis dependence treatment, 23
capacity building, 855
career investment, 17–18
caregivers, 358
caseloads
　　in child and adolescent outpatient practice, 36
　　in managed care practice, 13
case management
　　benefit, 791–2
　　child welfare, 765–9
　　clinical, 755–8
　　clinical models of, 5
　　community-based, 767–8
　　consumer-driven, 767
　　consumer-provider relationship within, 807–11
　　for the developmentally disabled, 759–64
　　HIV/AIDS, 801–6
　　integrated, 768
　　in medical settings, 790–6
　　medical-social, 791
　　older adults, 796–801
　　overview, 751–5
　　primary care, 791
　　psychosocial rehabilitation, 770–7
　　recovery-based, 775–6
　　social, 791
　　strengths approach to clients with psychiatric disabilities, 778–83
　　strengths-based, 768
　　substance abusing clients, 784–9
　　systems-driven case management, 767
CASSP (Child and Adolescent Service System Program), 64, 65, 74–5, 527
catastrophic incidents, 88
catastrophizing, 243
causation of mental disorders, 336
cause, 231
cause and effect, 198
CBT (cognitive-behavioral therapy), 28, 57, 242–7, 352, 553–4, 588, 838
CD (conduct disorder), 1011–19
CDP (Child Development Project), 992–3
celebration, 779
cell phones, 186
Center for Epidemiologic Studies Depression Scale (CES-D), 217
Center for Mental Health Services, 527
certification, 42, 150–1

CES-D (Center for Epidemiologic Studies Depression Scale), 217
chaining, 292
challenges
    in child and adolescent outpatient practice, 36–8
    in domestic violence shelter practice, 97–8
    in establishing peer support teams, 109
    for family counselor in nonprofit community-based agency, 47
    in family treatment planning, 429
    in managed care practice, 14–16
    in patient safety, 175
    in school-based practice, 42–3
    in social work regulation, 149
    in substance abuse case management, 787–8
    in transtheoretical model of behavior change, 646–7
change, effecting, 901
character disorders, 339
Charity Organization Society, 71
charts, 56–7
chat room therapy, 19, 187, 188
checklists, 380
chemical abuse and dependency screening, 691–7
chemical dependency, in practitioners, 163
child abuse, 59, 88, 90, 358, 641–7, 659–65
Child Abuse Potential Inventory, 392
Child and Adolescent Functional Assessment Scale (CAFAS), 383, 388
child and adolescent outpatient practice, 33–9
    case examples, 34–5
    challenges in, 36–8
    current practice demands, 35–6
    essential competencies, 38
    introduction and history, 35
    recent changes in, 36
    typical daily schedule, 33
    Web sites, 38
Child and Adolescent Service System Program (CASSP), 64, 65, 74–5, 527
child and family centers, 855–63
Child and Parent Report of Posttraumatic Symptoms, 388
Child Behavior Checklist, 388
child-centered treatment, 64
Child Development Project (CDP), 992–3
child guidance center model, 64
childhood aggression, 720
childhood anxiety, 351–7
childhood disorders, 329
childhood trauma, 565
childhood trauma, adult survivors of, 478–82
child-in-environment perspective, 816
child neglect, 358, 661–3, 674
child protection mediation, 1071–7
child protection social workers (CPWs), 1071
Child Protective Services (CPS), 71
children
    and aggression, 720
    assessment tools for, 381–4
    and cancer
        See oncology social work in a medical setting

child protection mediation, 1071–7
child welfare case management, 765–9
conduct-disordered youth, 74, 459, 1011–19
current/future directions of social work practice with, 815–18
and domestic violence, 1082–91
early parenthood as risk factor for domestic violence, 95
environmental risk factors for, 66
Families and Schools Together (FAST), 671–9
family centers, 855–63
and genograms
    See genograms
grief group interventions with, 636
hopelessness scale for, 382
infancy disorders, 329
interventions for abuse and neglect, 641–7
and parent education, 619
personal risk factors for, 66
play therapy, in crisis, 647–52
PLL (Parenting with Love and Limits), 457–67
recognizing indicators of maltreatment, 659–65
resilience in, 65–6, 423
risk factors for emotional and behavioral disorders in, 65
school-based services, 907–12
social skills training, 652–9
temperament of, 619–20
See also child and adolescent outpatient practice; community-based mental health with children and families; domestic violence shelter practice; family counselor in nonprofit community-based agency; home-based practice with children and families; school-based practice; school social work
Children Now in Oakland, 894, 895, 897, 899
Children's Amendment, 895–6
Children's Defense Fund, 896, 899
Children's Depression Inventory, 382
Children's Global Assessment Scale, 388
child safety, 1084–9
Child Support Enforcement, 918
child welfare, expert testimony in, 1060–70
child welfare case management, 765–9
chronic conditions, 790–1, 826–32
    See also HIV/AIDS
chronic contemplators, 645–6
chronicity, 790–1
circular casualty, 75
CISD (critical incident stress management), 213, 726
CISM (critical incident stress management), 726–32
CIT (computer and internet technologies), 186–93
CITTT (Courtroom Interactive Team Thinking Test), 172
City of Hope, 77, 79–80
civil lawsuits, 121–2
civil patients, 1091–7
civil rights movement, 63, 175
CIWA-Ar (Clinical Institute Withdrawal Assessment for Alcohol Scale Revised), 28
Clarke Sexual History Questionnaire, 1101
classification of mental disorders, history of, 335–6

classification systems, 379–80
clearly worded questions, 169–71
client-centered process, 816–17
client-centered theory and therapy, 235–41
client-defined goals, 296
client-focused measures, 351–7
client logs, 352–3
client-monitored observation, 353–4
client participation, active, 52
client records, 125
   See also recordkeeping
client rights, 122–3
client self-determination, 14
client self-report measures, 390–4
client-therapist relationship, 807–11
clinical case management, 755–8
clinical disorders, 339, 498–9
Clinical Institute Withdrawal Assessment for Alcohol
   Scale Revised (CIWA-Ar), 28
clinical practice guidelines, 1157
clinical reasoning, evidence-based, 169–71
clinical significance, 338
Clinical Social Work Association, 120–1
cluster randomized control trials, 1142
coaching, 447–8, 458, 462–5
coalitions, 889
Cocaine Anonymous, 696
cocaine dependence treatment, 23
Cochrane Collaboration, 1130, 1140, 1150, 1153
Code of Ethics, Clinical Social Work Association, 120
Code of Ethics, NASW, 59, 118–19, 124, 159, 160,
   163, 970
code of ethics, social workers' vs. police, 90
coding and reporting of mental disorders, 337
coexisting disorders
   in adolescents, 385–6
   physical, 339–40
   See also comorbid disorders
cognition, 588
cognitions, 244–6
cognitive-behavioral therapy (CBT), 28, 57, 242–7,
   352, 553–4, 588, 838
cognitive distortions, 243
cognitive elaboration, 591
cognitive mastery, 474
cognitive processing, 700
cognitive psychology, 474
cognitive restructuring, 542–3, 588–93
cognitive therapy, 561
Cohen's *d*, 1150
cohesion, 313
cohesive self, 313
Coleman Advocates for Children and Youth, 894–5,
   896, 897
collaborating with family systems, 51–2
collaborative relationship, 226
colonial trauma, 952
Combined Pharmacotherapies and Behavioral
   Interventions (COMBINE) study, 29
commitment, 287
commitment, involuntary/voluntary, 175
committed action, 284

committees on the use of human participants in
   research, 119
common factors approaches, 260
common factors in therapy, 220–5
common good, 307
communication skills, 25–6, 91
communication training (CT), 471
community, 64
community-based case management, 767–8
community-based family centers, 855–63
community-based mental health with children and
   families, 61–9
   agency-based continuum of care, 65
   case example, 66–9
   new direction in, 63–4
   principles of, 64–5
   risk and resilience in, 65–6
   typical daily schedule, 61–3
   Web sites, 69
community-based treatment, 64
community capacity in the U.S. Air Force, 912–17
community liaison, 887–8
Community Mental Health Centers Act, 63
community organizing, 872–81
community organizing via Internet, 190–1
community partnerships for school based services, 907
community practice, 5–6
   building community capacity in the U.S. Air Force,
     912–17
   community organizing, 872–81
   family centers, 855–63
   fathering programs, 918–22
   guidelines for assertive community treatment
     teams, 869–71
   guidelines for social action, 901–6
   international perspectives, 863–8
   legislative advocacy for oppressed and vulnerable
     groups, 893–900
   model for the twenty-first century, 882–92
   overview, 5–6
   partnerships for school-based services, 907–12
   See also fields of practice; social work practice, roles
     and functions
Community Readiness Consultant (CRC), 913
community resources, 52
comorbid disorders
   in adolescents, 385–6
   medical, 22
   in older adults, 845
   See also coexisting disorders
comorbidity and eating disorders, 532
comparative theories of social work, 259–64
compassion fatigue, 57–8
competencies, essential
   See essential competencies
competent parenting, 619
competition, 17
complaints, 121–2
complex post-traumatic stress, 565
CompuPIE, 372–5
computer and internet technologies (CIT), 186–93
   See also technology

computer graphics programs, 379
computer skills, 19
concern, 91
concreteness, 237
conditioned response (CR), 289
conditioned stimulus (CS), 289
conditioning, escape and avoidance, 293
conduct disorder (CD), 1011–19
conduct-disordered youth, 74, 459, 1011–19
Conely v. Commonwealth of Virginia, 1057
confidentiality, 123, 805
    in e-therapy, 190–2
    ethical issues in, 115, 119
    in forensic social work, 1062
    in human services agencies, 159
    in managed care practice, 14
    during police investigations, 90
    in private practice, 58–9
confirmatory evidence, 398
conflict resolution, 1077–81
conflicts of interest, 116, 124, 158
conflicts of values, 116
confluence, 303
confounding variables, 1144
confrontation, 237, 485
congruence, 236–7
Connors Rating Scales, 388
consent, inadequate, 159
consequentialist theories of ethics, 118
constriction, 699
constructive confrontation, 166
constructivism, 273, 294–9
consultation
    ethics, 116, 119
    in psychosocial therapy, 252
consumer-case manager relationships, 808–11
consumer-centered values, 773
consumer-directed services, 762
consumer-driven case management, 767
consumer protection, 148–9
consumer-provider relationships, 808–11
contact, 301
contamination obsessions, 488
contemplation, 641–2
content of thoughts, 242
contextualizing, 779
contingencies, 290
continued competency, 153
continuing education, 17–18, 36, 52, 153
continuous goals, 522
continuous quality improvement (CQI), 195–7
continuous reinforcement schedule, 290
contracting, 378
contract law, 122
contracts, therapeutic, 514–20, 575
controversial treatment methods, 122
conversation starters, 73
conversion therapy, 935–6
co-occurring disorders, students with, 1003–10
coordination of care, 28
COPES questions, 1121
coping mechanisms, 211

coping questions, 254–5
coping skills, 93, 424
core beliefs, 243–4
core values, 118
Cornell Psychiatric Screen, 365, 370
cost-benefit questions, 1124
cost-control, 28
cost-effectiveness, 16, 19
Council of Accreditation Services for Families and
    Children, 161
Council on Mental Health of the American Medical
    Association, 163
Council on Social Work Education (CSWE), 149
countertransference, 741
couples treatment, 433–42
couple therapy with individuals, 452–7
couple therapy with survivors of childhood trauma,
    478–82
course specifiers, 337
Courtroom Interactive Team Thinking Test
    (CITTT), 172
CPS (Child Protective Services), 71
CPWs (child protection social workers), 1071
CQI (continuous quality improvement), 195–7
CR (conditioned response), 289
CRC (Community Readiness Consultant), 913
creativity
    in home-based child and family practice, 74
    in private practice, 54–5
    as value, 267
credentialing
    See licensing of social workers
credibility, in EBP studies, 1140
Crime Victim Compensation Trust Fund, 97
criminal charges, 121–2
criminal justice, 97
crises, 972
crisis assessment, 5, 101, 210
crisis intervention, 207–14, 726–32
Crisis Intervention Handbook, 129
crisis intervention play therapy, 648–51
crisis resolution, 93
crisis responders, 97
crisis session with family, protocol for, 50
crisis team, 90–2
Critical Incident Stress Management, 109
critical incident stress management (CISM), 213,
    726–32
critical thinking, 25, 171–2, 1137
cross-family linkages, 476
"Crossing the Quality Chasm," 194
crosswalk, ASAM, 692
CS (conditioned stimulus), 289
CT (communication training), 471
cues, indirect, 574
culturagrams, 969–75
cultural aspects of mood disorders, 344–5
cultural competency, 492, 805–6
culturally competent evidence-based practice, 926–7
culturally competent treatment, 64–5
culturally/racially diverse students, 1045–52
cultural responsiveness, 480

cultural sensitivity, 477, 816, 864–5
culture, 995–6
curiosity, 297
cyberterrorism, 105
cyclothymic disorder, 330

dangerousness to self or others, 175–7
DAST (Drug Abuse Screening Test), 365, 368, 692
data collection in CQI, 196–7
data management, 18
Davidson Trauma Scale, 360
DBT (dialectic behavior theory), 743–4
DDIS (Dissociative Disorders Interview
    Schedule), 566
DEA (Drug Enforcement Agency), 691
deadening of feeling, 564
death
    bereavement and grief therapy, 632–7
    logotherapeutic approach to, 269
decision making, ethical, 117–20
deep ecology, 232
defamation of character, 124–5, 159
defense structures, 23
deficient information processing skills, 720
deficit-based lens, 424
deficit-problem medical model, 778
deflection, 302–3
defusion, 284, 285–6
deinstitutionalization, 97, 175
delinquency prevention, 671–9
delinquent teenagers, 458
deontological theories of ethics, 118
Department of Homeland Security, 105
dependency mediation, 1071
depersonalization, 564–5
depression, 5, 243, 343, 351–7, 474, 479, 552–7
depression in older adults, 843–50
depressive disorders, 330, 343
depressive neurosis, 343
deprivation, 5
derealization, 564, 565
de-reflection, 270
dereliction of duty, 122
description questions, 1123–4
desensitization, 246, 614
DES-T, 360, 362
detoxification, 28–9, 838
developmental crises, 972
developmental delay, 663
developmental disabilities, 760
Developmental Disabilities Assistance and Bill of
    Rights Act, 760–1
developmentally disabled, case management for,
    759–64
developmental psychology, 474
diagnosis
    vs. assessment, 249, 251, 379
    being up to date on, 18
    and expert testimony, 1065
    of generalized anxiety disorder, 498–9
    of psychiatric disorders in children, 383
    understanding, 394–9

using the DSM-IV-TR, 325–34, 337–8
    See also assessment; screening
Diagnostic and Statistical Manual of Mental
    Disorders, Fourth Edition (DSM-IV-TR), 325–34
    assessment tools, 331–2
    bipolar disorder, 343–50
    classifications of diagnoses, 238–331
    and family treatment planning, 430–1
    guidelines for using, 335–42
    multiaxial system, 326–8
    overview, 325–6, 379–80, 398
    teaching and learning tools, 331–2
    Web sites, 333
Diagnostic Interview Schedule (DIS), 331, 398
Diagnostic Interview Schedule for Children, 331
diagnostic uncertainty, 338
dialectic behavior theory (DBT), 743–4
dialogical interaction, 298
dialogue, 298–9
Dickerson, Ralph, Jr., 158
DID (dissociative identity disorder), 565–70
differential diagnosis, 319, 338
differential reinforcement, 290, 293
dilemmas, ethical, 115–17
directive play therapy, 648
direct work, 249
DIS (Diagnostic Interview Schedule), 331, 398
disabilities issues, 97
disability insurance, 58
Disaster Recovery Institute International, 105
disaster response, 88, 867
    See also emergency services practice
discharge planning, 26
disconfirmatory evidence, 398
disconnectivity, 699
discrete behaviors, 430
discrete goals, 522
discrimination issues, 97
discrimination training, 290, 292
discriminative stimuli, 290
discussion boards, 187
disease, chronic, 801
disease, defined, 834
disease management, 801
diseases of disconnection, 476–7
disequilibrium, 92
disintegration anxiety, 313
disintegration products, 313
dissociation, 360, 362, 564, 699–700
dissociative amnesia, 565
dissociative disorders, 331, 564–70
Dissociative Disorders Interview Schedule (DDIS), 566
Dissociative Experiences Scale, 360, 362
dissociative fugue, 565
dissociative identity disorder (DID), 565–70
distressed practitioners, 163
Distress Management Guidelines, NCCN, 77
distress screening instruments, 79
disulfiram, 29
diversity
    ethnic, 926
    family, 425

divorce, 424
divorce therapy, 732–7
documentation
    in addiction treatment, 22–3, 26
    in child and adolescent outpatient practice, 38
    of effectiveness, 18
    importance of, 124
    in managed care practice, 13
    in private practice, 59
    and professional impairment, 166
    in the supervisory process, 160
domain, problem's, 274
domestic violence, 88
domestic violence advocacy, 97
domestic violence shelter practice, 95–102
    challenges in, 97–8
    essential competencies, 97–8
    roles and functions of, 95–8
    typical daily schedule, 95–6
    Web sites, 101
donors, 36
doorknob therapy, 576
DOVE units, 97
drama in metaphors, 584–5
dramatic hold, 586
drive psychology, 305–6
drop out, students at risk to, 1020–31
drug abuse, 691–7, 784–9
drug abuse, VBSs for, 368
Drug Abuse Screening Test (DAST), 365, 368, 692
Drug and Alcohol Assessment for the Deaf, 692
drug dependence treatment, 833–42
Drug Enforcement Agency (DEA), 691
drug substitution treatment, 865
DSM-IV-TR
    See Diagnostic and Statistical Manual of Mental
        Disorders
DSM-V, 18
dual credentialing, 154
dual diagnosis, 385–6, 402
dually diagnosed adolescents, 385, 1009
dually diagnosed offenders, 1091–7
dual relationships, 116, 124
dual-trauma couple, 479
duty, dereliction/breach of, 122
dwelling insurance, 58
Dyadic Adjustment Scale, 392
dynamic psychology, 474
dysthymic disorder, 330

EAPs (employee assistance programs), 163
Early Childhood Services of GCI, 68
Early Head Start, 75–6
ease of use, of assessment tools, 383
Eating Disorder Examination - Screening Version
    (EDE-S), 364, 365
eating disorders, 331, 476–7, 531–7, 565
eating disorders, VBSs for, 360, 364, 365
Eating Disorder Screen for primary care (ESP),
    364, 365
Eating Disturbance Scale (EDS-5), 364, 365
EBA (evidence-based assessment), 385, 815–17

EBM (evidence-based medicine), 1115, 1117
EBP (evidence-based practice)
    See evidence-based practice (EBP)
ECGs (expert consensus guidelines), 509
ecological perspective, 231–2, 424
eco-maps, 379, 411, 429, 970
economic development, 887
economic injuries, 122
ecosystems, influence of, 6
ecosystems perspective, 376–80
EDE-S (Eating Disorder Examination - Screening
    Version), 364, 365
Edinburgh Postnatal Depression Scale (EPDS),
    360, 361
EDS-5 (Eating Disturbance Scale), 364, 365
education
    biopsychosocial, 5
    continuing, 17–18, 36, 52, 153
    master's in social work (MSW), 36, 42, 43
    minimum, 151–2
    parent, 619
    predisaster, 109
educational stress, in practitioners, 165
Education of All Handicapped Children Act, 42
educator, social worker as, 720–5
EE (expressed emotion), 474–5
effectiveness
    and accountability, 156
    in managed care practice, 18–19
effectiveness questions, 1123
effect sizes (ES), 1149
efficiency, 156
efficiency of care vs. quality of care, 13
ego assessment, 378
Eisendrath v. Superior Court, 1078
elder abuse/neglect, 59, 97, 1106–11
elderly population
    See older adults
e-mail, 186–7
e-mail action alerts, 191
EMDR (eye movement desensitization and
    reprocessing), 562, 714–20, 745
Emergency Management Act (Canada), 105
emergency management programs, 105
emergency services practice, 102–11
    effects of stress and trauma, 107–8
    effects on families, 108–9
    incident overview, 102–4
    introduction, 104–6
    occupational stress, 106
    positive implications, 110
    post-traumatic stress treatment, 110
    prevention and preparedness training, 109
    psychosocial first aid, 109–10
    public inquiries, 107
    Web sites, 110
    workplace stress, 106–7
emotional abuse, 478–9, 665
emotional acceptance techniques, 469–71
emotional disorders in children, risk factors for, 65
emotional dysregulation, 701
emotional impacts of trauma, 91–2

emotional indicators of abuse, 661–2
emotional injuries, 122
emotional neglect, 72–5
emotional numbing, 564
emotional reasoning, 243
emotional regulation, 700
emotional stress, in practitioners, 164–5
emotion-focused marital therapy, 18, 434–5
emotions, 588
   in crisis intervention, 210
   hard/soft, 470
   and occupational stress, 106–7
   and trauma, 91–3
   See also feelings
empathic joining, 470
empathy, 223, 236–7, 312–13
empirical orientation, 226
employee assistance programs (EAPs), 163
empowerment, 275–6, 479, 965
enacted support, 711
enactments, 74
enchantment, 585–6
ending service with clients, 627–31
endorsement, 153
enslavement, 963
environmental forces, 233
environmental risk factors for children, 66
environmental stress, in practitioners, 165
environmental vulnerability, 65
EPDS (Edinburgh Postnatal Depression Scale), 361
Epidemiological Catchment Area survey, 331
episodic states, 343
equating, 144
equipoise, 1144
erectile dysfunction, 740
Erickson, Milton, 215–16, 253
erotophobic attitudes, 737
ERP (exposure and response prevention), 614
ES (effect sizes), 1149
escape and avoidance conditioning, 293
ESP (Eating Disorder Screen for primary care), 364, 365
essential competencies
   in American Indians/Alaska Natives practice, 950
   in child and adolescent outpatient practice, 38
   in child welfare case management, 765–6
   in clinical case management, 757
   in domestic violence shelter practice, 97–8
   in expert witness testimony in child welfare, 1060–1
   by family counselor in nonprofit community-based agency, 51–2
   in managed care practice, 17–19
   in police department-based practice, 88, 93
   in social work with groups, 682–4
   supported employment approaches to, 709
   in therapeutic relationships, 573–7
   for working with families of people with severe mental illness, 492–4
establishing rapport, 91
e-supervision, 188
eTherapistsOnline, 187

e-therapy, 186–93
ethical decision making, 117–20
ethical dilemmas, 115–17
ethical issues
   and accountability, 156–62
   in case management, 794
   in confidentiality, 115, 119
   in evaluation, 117
   in managed care practice, 14
   in management practices, 126
   in obeying laws, 116, 118
   in obeying policies and regulations, 116
   in private practice, 59
   in research, 117
   in service delivery, 124
   in social work, 115–20
   Web sites, 120
ethics, consequentialist theories of, 118
ethics audits, 160
ethics consultation, 116, 119
ethics of care, 118
ethics-related law suits, 121–2
ethnic diversity, 926
ethnicity, 995–6
evaluation, 6, 92, 159–60
   and CQI, 197
   ethical issues in, 117
   open-ended, 378
evaluation logs, 352
evaluative mediation, 1071
evaluative questions, 595
everyday living, 251–2
evidence-based assessment (EBA), 385, 815–17
evidence-based clinical reasoning, 169–71
evidence-based hypnosis, 600–5
evidence-based medicine (EBM), 1115, 1117
evidence-based practice (EBP)
   and accountability, 6
   and avoiding harm, 168, 171
   in child and adolescent outpatient practice, 38
   children and adolescents, 817–18
   in community-based mental health with children and families, 65
   critically appraising studies for, 1137–41
   debate surrounding, 18
   developing well-structured questions, 1120–6
   integrating research, clinical skills, and client circumstances, 1163–9
   introduction, 3
   locating credible studies for, 1127–36
   in managed care, 13
   meta-analysis, 1149–52
   N = 1 experiments, 1176–82
   and object relations psychology, 310
   in older adults with mental health disorders, 843–52
   overview, 1115–19
   in police department-based practice, 89
   practice guidelines, 1157–62
   qualitative methods in private practice, 55
   quantitative methods in private practice, 56–7
   randomized control trials (RCTs), 1142–8

and schizophrenia, 505–14
in school-based practice, 42–3
school social work, 979–85
in social work education, 1169–75
systematic reviews, 1152–6
Evidence-Based Program Database, 1132
evidence-based treatment, 36, 385, 694–6
evidence-supported treatment, 817–18
examinations
   See licensing examinations
exception-finding questions, 254
exceptions to problems, 217
exclusion criteria, 1144
exit and wait, 460
expectancy, 216, 224
experience, amount required for credentialing, 152–3
experiential learning, 308
experiential values, 267
experimental designs, 47
expert consensus guidelines (ECGs), 509
expert consultation, 509
expert witness, 36, 1057
expert witness testimony in child welfare, 1060–70
exploration, 377
exploratory logs, 352
exploring alternatives, 211
exposure and response prevention (ERP), 614
exposure therapy, 561
exposure treatment, 543–4, 549
expressed emotion (EE), 474–5
externalizing the problem, 274
external validity and relevance, 1139–40
extratherapeutic factors, 222–3
Eyberg Child Behavior Inventory, 383
Eyeberg Child Behavior Checklist, 388
eye movement desensitization and reprocessing
   (EMDR), 110, 562, 714–20, 745

FACES IV (Family Adaptability and Cohesion
   Evaluation Scale), 391–2
facilitative conditions, 808
factious disorders, 330
fact witnesses, 1061–2
faculty, licensing of, 154–5
failure to warn, 159
faith-based services, 5
fallacies, practitioners', 171–2
falling out, 93
false negative, 359, 396–7
false positive, 359, 396–7
falsified clinical records, 122
familial pattern, 338
families
   Bowen Family Systems Therapy, 447–52
   and couples therapy, 433–42
   of emergency responders, 108–9
   and fathers, 918–22
   and genograms
      See genograms
   as partners, 64
   of persons with severe mental illness, 491–4
   psychoeducation of, 474–8

redefinition of, 425, 434
resilience in, 65–6, 423–8
risk factors in, 65–6
structural family therapy, 442–6
treatment planning with, 429–32
underorganized, 442, 443
   See also child and adolescent outpatient practice;
      community-based mental health with children
      and families; domestic violence shelter practice;
      home-based practice with children and
      families; school-based practice
Families and Schools Together (FAST), 40, 671–9
Family Adaptability and Cohesion Evaluation Scale
   (FACES IV), 391–2
family assessment, 390–4
Family Assessment Device, 388
family centers, 855–63
family chronology, 411
family counselor in nonprofit community-based
   agency, 45–53
   action planning, 49–51
   advancement in theory of, 47
   case illustration, 47–9
   challenges in, 47
   essential competencies, 51–2
   typical daily schedule, 45–6
   Web sites, 52
family diagram, 448
family diversity, 425
Family Environment Scale (FES), 391–2
family-focused treatment, 64
family functioning, 391–2
family information net, 411–15
family resilience framework, 423–8
family resiliency, 108
family resource centers, 855–63
family safety, 1084–9
family standardized self-report measures, 390–4
family support centers, 855–63
family systems, collaborating with, 51–2
family systems theory, 477
family systems therapy, 74
family task-centered model, 226–9
family therapy, 433–42, 442–6, 474–5
family therapy movement, 74
family time, 620
family violence, 90
FAST (Families and Schools Together), 40–1, 671–9
Fast Alcohol Screening Test (FAST), 365, 367
FAST Track Project, 993–4
Father Friendly Checkup, 919
fatherhood initiatives, 918
fathering programs, 918–22
fathers, 918–22
Federal Emergency Management Agency (FEMA), 105
Federation of Clinical Social Workers, 151
feedback, 195, 469, 595
feedback loops, 463–5
feelings
   and cognitive therapy, 57, 89
   in crisis intervention, 210
   deadening of, 564

feelings (*Continued*)
  therapist's self-awareness of, 54
  trauma impact on client and, 91–2
  trauma impact on therapist and, 107–8
  See also emotions
FEMA (Federal Emergency Management Agency), 105
female sexual response, 741
feminism, 478
feminist development theory, 480
feminist family treatment models, 434
feminist issues and practices, 177–83
Ferenczi, Sandor, 305
FES (Family Environment Scale), 391–2
fields of practice
  adult mental health, 820–5
  alcohol and drug dependence, 833–42
  children and adolescents, 815–18
  older adults with mental health disorders, 843–52
  proactive vs. reactive health care, 826–32
  See also community practice; social work practice,
    roles and functions
Fikke Model of Malpractice Suits, 134
financial issues of private practice, 58–9
firefighters, 104, 106–8
fires, 88
First Nations, 950
first responders, 88
first warning instruments, 359
fishbone diagram, 198–9
fixation of attention, 601–2
flashbacks, 564
floods, 88
flowcharts, 198–201
fluidity in private practice, 54–5
follow-up, 92, 93, 212
food service needs, 99
foreground questions, 1128
forensic evaluations, 1063–5
forensic social work
  assessing sexual predators, 1098–104
  child protection mediation, 1071–7
  children exposed to domestic violence, 1082–91
  dually diagnosed offenders and civil patients,
    1091–7
  elder abuse/neglect, 1106–11
  expert witness testimony in child welfare, 1060–70
  mediation and conflict resolution, 1077–81
  overview, 1055–60
formal trance, 602
for-profit model of managed care, 16
foster care, 73, 417–19, 765
foundational coping skills, 38
four-part questions, 1121–2
frank exchange, 73
fraud, 122, 125
fraudulent practice, 157–9
freedom of will, 267
Freud, Sigmund, 305–6, 552, 565
front line crisis intervention, 207–14
frozen watchfulness, 661
fugue states, 564
function, 231

functional analysis, 290
functional communities, 884–5
functional family therapy, 436
functioning, assessment of, 340
funding, agency, 36, 38

GAF (Global Assessment of Functioning) scale, 177
Gaido v. Weiser, 130–2
GARF (Global Assessment of Relational Functioning)
  scale, 177, 341
Garrett Lee Smith Memorial Act, 191
GAS (goal-attainment scales), 354–5
gatekeeping, 317
gay/lesbian/bisexual/transgendered (GLBT)
  sensitivity, 97, 574
GCI (Guidance Center, Inc.), 65–9
gender identity disorders, 331, 739
gender nonconformity, 934–8
general depression, VBSs for, 361
General Health Questionnaire (GHQ), 401–2
generalized anxiety disorder, 330, 351–7, 497–505
general medical conditions (GMCs), 339–40
genetic vulnerability, 65
genograms, 74, 379, 409–23, 970
  for children in multiple settings, 416–21
  family information net, 411–15
  family systems perspective, 415–16
  overview, 409–11
  setting priorities for organizing information, 415
  Web sites, 422
genuineness, 25, 91, 236–7
Geographical Information Systems (GIS), 188
Geriatric Depression Scale, 941
Geriatric Hopelessness Scale, 941
geriatric mental health, 843–52
Geriatric Suicide Ideation Scale, 941
gerontological practice, 939
Gestalt experiment, 303–4
Gestalt therapy, 300–4
GHQ (General Health Questionnaire), 401–2
GIS (Geographical Information Systems), 188
GLBT (gay/lesbian/bisexual/transgendered)
  sensitivity, 97, 574
Global Assessment of Functioning (GAF) scale, 177
Global Assessment of Relational Functioning (GARF)
  scale, 341
Gloria Wise Boys and Girls Club, 158
GMCs (general medical conditions), 339–40
goal-attainment scales (GAS), 354–5, 430
goal-directed metaphors, 584
goal-formulated questions, 254
goal-oriented treatment plans, 18
goals, 320–1, 780
  client-defined, 296
  development and clarification of, 521–6
  development and measurement of, 217
  in substance abuse case management, 786
  See also treatment goals
goal setting for axis I disorders, 497–505
Goldstein, Kurt, 300
Goodwill Industries of Santa Clara, 158
GRADE Working Group, 1159

grandiose-exhibitionist self, 312
grandiose self, 313
grants, 36, 38, 42
graphs, 56–7
greatest good, 118
grief group interventions with children and
        adolescents, 636
grief process, 93
grief therapy, 632–7
Ground Zero, New York City, 110
group-based social skills treatment, 656–8
group interpretation, 476
group process, 679–85
group rounds, 22–3
group therapy, 19, 23–4, 229–30
group work techniques, 679–85
Guidance Center, Inc. (GCI), 65–9
guided imagery, 592
Guidelines for the Treatment of Psychiatric
        Disorders, 1157
guilt, logotherapeutic approach to, 268
guilty man, 311

habituation, 614
Haley, Jay, 74
hanging risks, 178–9
hard emotions, 470
hardiness, 423, 479
harm, avoiding, 168–73
harm, questions about, 1124
harming obsessions, 488
harm reduction, 865
Hartmann, Heinz, 306
Hay, Gordon, 77
HCR-20 (Historical Clinical Risk-20) protocol, 177
Head Start, 75–6, 919, 921
health, 307
health care inflation, 790
Health Insurance Portability and Accountability Act
        (HIPPA), 192
Health Maintenance Act, 790
health maintenance organizations (HMOs), 59
Healthy Families, 68, 75–6
healthy families, 425
HelpHorizons, 187
helping process, 233–4, 251
helplessness, 553
highlighting, 470
highway hypnosis, 564
HIPPA (Health Insurance Portability and
        Accountability Act), 192
Historical Clinical Risk-20 (HCR-20) protocol, 177
historical trauma, 952–3
history
    of classification of mental disorders, 335–6
    patient's, 24–5
    psychosocial, 386
HITTT (Hospital Interactive Team Thinking Test), 172
HIV/AIDS, 801–6, 865–6
HMOs (health maintenance organizations), 59
Hoffman, Lynn, 51
holistic approach to treatment, 66

Holland, Jimmie, 84
Home and Community-based Waiver, 796
home-based practice with children and families, 70–6
Homebuilders, 73
homework, 246
homophobia, 934
hopelessness, 360, 361, 553
hopelessness scale for children, 382
horizon of understanding, 298
Horney, Karen, 306
Hospital Interactive Team Thinking Test (HITTT), 172
hospitalization, 838
hostage takings, 88
"How Can We Help You and Your Family," 79
Hudson Index of Marital Satisfaction, 429
Hudson's scales, 318
human development, 887
human-made disasters, 867
human participants in research, 119
human services agencies, 157–9
Hurricane Katrina, 105, 110, 154
Hurricane Rita, 154
hyperarousal, 699–700
hyperventilation, 93
hypervigilence, 661, 699–700
hypnosis, 600–5
hypomania, 343
hysteria, 565

IBCT (integrative behavioral couple therapy), 467–73
IBM (identity-based motivation theory), 1045
IBM (interest-based mediation), 1071–6
ICD (International Classification of Diseases)
        codes, 337
idealized parent imago, 312
idealizing, 312
identity-based motivation theory (IBM), 1045
IEP (individual education plan), 39, 42
IGP (interpersonal group psychotherapy), 745
IICAPS (Intensive In-home Child and Adolescent
        Psychiatric Services), 75
imagery, 246
immediacy, 237
immigrants, 944–8, 1031–7
Impaired Social Worker Program Resource Book, 163
impairment, 125–6
impairment, practitioner, 163–8
impulse control disorders, 331
inadequate consent, 159
inappropriate treatment, 159
inclusion criteria, 1144
incompetence, professional, 125–6, 159
    See also impairment, practitioner
independent living movement, 762
Index of Family Relations, 388
Index of Peer Relations, 388
Indian Ocean tsunami, 105
indirect cues, 574
indirection, 578
indirect treatment, 252
individual education plan (IEP), 39, 42
individual goals, 522

individualized placement and support (IPS), 706
individualized rating scales (IRS), 353
Individuals with Disabilities Education Act, 43
individual therapy, 19, 24–6
individual therapy assessment, 24–6
individual therapy for couples, 452–7
ineffective parenting behaviors, 458
infancy disorders, 329
inferential thinking, 377–8
infidelity, 471
inflation, health care, 790
informal trance, 602
informed consent, 59, 124, 191–2
ingredients of psychotherapy, 225
initial contracts, 515–16
injuries, 661
ink blots, Rorschach, 318
Inova Health Care System, 77
inpatient addiction treatment, 28
inpatient psychiatric safety
    See patient safety and suicide
inpatient suicide
    See patient safety and suicide
inquiring perspective, 25
inquiry, 6
Institute of Medicine (IOM), 194
institutional homophobia, 934
institutional racism, 932
institutional review boards (IRBs), 117, 119
instructional interaction, 298
instruments, assessment
    See assessment
insurance, 58
integrated case management, 768
integrated crisis intervention and disaster mental
    health, 726–32
integrated service delivery, 35
integrative behavioral couple therapy (IBCT), 467–73
integrative perspectives in contemporary practice,
    259–60
integrity, 940
intellectual disabilities, 760–4
Intensive In-home Child and Adolescent Psychiatric
    Services (IICAPS), 75
interaction logs, 352
interest-based mediation (IBM), 1071–6
interfamily management, 476
intergenerational family genogram, 74
intergenerational family theory, 480
intermittent schedules of reinforcement, 290
internal consistency, of assessment tools, 383
internalized homophobia, 934
Internal State Scale, 344
International Classification of Diseases (ICD)
    codes, 337
International Federation of Social Workers: Ethics in
    Social Work, 120
international social work, 863–8
International Standards Organization Technical
    Committee, 105
Internet, 19, 186–93
    See also technology

Internet-based learning, 921
interoceptive exposure treatment, 543–4
interpersonal goals, 522
interpersonal group psychotherapy (IGP), 745
interpersonal interaction, 308
interpersonal psychotherapy (IPT-BDP), 745
interval schedules of reinforcement, 290
intervention, 308–9
intervention, crisis, 207–14
intervention planning, 378
intervention programs, trauma-related, 109
interventions
    in EBT trials, 1142–8
    specific
        See specific interventions
    staff, 26
intervention skills, 93
interviews, 386
intimate partner violence, 392
intrapsychic change, 12
introjection, 303
intrusive thoughts, 699
inventory, 390
Inventory for Complicated Grief, 941
investment in career, 17–18
involuntary commitment, 175
involving clients in service contracting, 159
invulnerable child, 423
IOM (Institute of Medicine), 194
IPS (individualized placement and support), 706
IPT-BDP (interpersonal psychotherapy), 745
IRBs (institutional review boards), 117, 119
IRS (individualized rating scales), 353
isomorphic metaphors, 583
isomorphism, 583
issues identification, 210
"I" statements, 471

Jacobs, Douglas, 129
Jacobson, Edith, 306
Jewish Community Center of Greater
    Washington, 158
Johns Hopkins, 84
Joint Commission, 185
Joint Commission on Accreditation of Health Care
    Organizations, 26, 161
Joint Commission on Children's Mental Health, 35
Joint Commission Patient Safety, 185
journaling therapy, 78
Jung, C. G., 305
juvenile courts, 35
juvenile justice case management, 765–9

K6 screener, 365, 369
Kaplan, Lester, 158
Kensington Welfare Rights Organization, 894
Kernberg, Otto, 306, 307
key attributes of quality improvement measures,
    197–8
key functions of healthcare organizations, 195–6
Klein, Melanie, 306, 307
Kohut, Heinz, 306

Kraepelin, Emil, 335
Kundalini yoga meditation, 606–12

labels, avoidance of, 275
language, client's, 297–8
language, use of, 217
lapses, 470
LAST (Luebeck Alcohol Dependence and Abuse
    Screening Test), 365, 366
Latino Social Work Association, 151
law enforcement
    See police department-based practice
Law Enforcement and Crime Control Act, 88
Law Enforcement Assistance Administration
    (LEAA), 88
laws, ethical issues in obeying, 116, 118
lawsuits, 121–2
Lawyers Concerned for Lawyers, 163
leadership skills
    in child and adolescent outpatient practice, 36, 38
    and CQI, 195
    developing, 17
    in programmatic safety, 184
least harm, 118
least restrictive/least intrusive treatment, 64, 65
legal issues, 59, 97
legal system, understanding of, 36
legislative advocacy for oppressed and vulnerable
    groups, 893–900
lesbian, gay, bisexual and transgendered (LGBT)
    issues, 97, 934–8
lethality and safety assessment, 90–1, 98–101
Leukemia and Lymphoma Society of America, 80
level of fit, 231
liability, 191
liaison, community, 887–8
libel, 124, 159
licensing, out-of-state practice, 191
licensing examinations, 136–47, 152
    administrative policies, 144–5
    content outlines, 139–44
    registration and administration, 145
    sample questions, 146
    test construction: practice analysis, 137–9
    test construction: validity and reliability, 137
    test development, 144
    Web sites, 147
licensing of social workers, 148–55
life-long learning, 18, 1124
    See also continuing education
Life Model, 231–5
life stressors, 232–3
Lifetime Parasuicidal Count, 129
Life with Cancer (LWC), 77–9
Likert scale, 383, 388
limited resources, 116
Linehan Reasons for Living Scale, 129
listening, active, 91, 210
the lived experience, 773–4
lobbying, 116
locus of control, 479
logotherapy, 264–72

long-term change, 12
Los Angeles Roundtable for Children, 894, 895
Loscalzo, Matthew, 77, 85
Louisville Behavior Checklist, 388
Luebeck Alcohol Dependence and Abuse Screening
    Test (LAST), 365, 366
LWC (Life with Cancer), 77–9

Madanes, Chloe, 74
Mahler, Margaret, 306
maintenance, 642
major depression, 474
major depressive disorder (MDD), 330, 397–8
maladaptive cognitions, 246
maladaptive thoughts, 243
male victims of domestic violence, 97
malfeasance, 122
malpractice, 59, 122, 128–35, 191
malpractice insurance, 58
maltreatment of children, indicators of, 659–65
managed care
    ethical dilemmas in, 116–17
    and family treatment planning, 429
    and medical necessity, 317
    models of, 16
    and private practice, 58–9
    terminating with clients, 627–8
    See also managed care practice
Managed Care Kit, 77
managed care organizations (MCOs), 12, 505
managed care practice, 11–20
    and accountability, 157
    advantages of professionalism, 16–17
    case examples, 13–14
    challenges in, 14–16
    essential competencies, 17–19
    future implications, 19
    rapid assessment instruments (RAIs) in, 385–9
    recent changes in, 12–13
    typical daily schedule, 11–12
    Web sites, 19
management practices, ethical, 126
mandated reporter, 36
mania, 343–4
mapping family patterns
    See genograms
mapping the problem's domain, 274
Marcil, Linda Fay, 158
margin of error, 1150
Marital Adjustment Test, 392
marital functioning, 392
marital hostility, 392
marketing skills, 17, 58
Marr, Carol, 158
martial problems, in practitioners, 164–5
MAST (Michigan Alcohol Screening Test), 217,
    365, 692
master's in social work (MSW), 36, 42, 43
MAST screener, 365
maternal drinking and drug use, 368
maturation, in EBP studies, 1139
MBL (multiple baseline) design, 1180

MBT (mentalization-based treatment), 744
McLean Screening Instrument for Borderline
    Personality Disorder (MSI-BPD), 370
McMaster Family Assessment Device, 391–2
MCOs (managed care organizations), 12, 505
    See also managed care practice
MDD (major depressive disorder), 330, 397–8
meaningful living, 265
meaning-making skills, 700
meaning of life (logotherapy), 264–72
meaning of the moment, 268
measure, defined, 390
measures, client-focused
    See client-focused measures
Measures for Clinical Practice and Research, 36
media as whistle-blower, 161
mediation, 116, 1077–81
mediation, child protection, 1071–7
Medicaid, 11–12, 36, 82, 191, 798
Medicaid Home and Community Based Waiver, 761
Medicaid waivers, 761
medical case management, 791
medical management options in alcoholism treatment,
    28–9
medical necessity, 317–22
medical-social case management, 791
Medicare, 191, 194, 798
medication management, 687–8
Medline, 1130
mental health, 820–5
mental health, general, VBSs for, 369–70
mental health, international, 866
Mental Health Inventory (MHI-5), 369
mental health services, failure of in U.S., 3
mental illness, 491–4
    in elderly, 844
    in practitioners, 164–5
    serious, VBSs for, 369–70
    social skills training for persons with, 666–71
    and violence, 175–6
    worldwide, 3
mentalization-based treatment (MBT), 744
mentally ill offenders, 1092–3
Mental Research Institute, 253
Mental Research Institute (MRI) Brief Therapy
    Center, 215–16
mental retardation, 760
Mesa Grande project, 695
MET (motivational enhancement therapy), 24, 694–5,
    837–8
meta-analysis, 47
meta-cognitions, 243
metaphors, 578–88, 613–18
Mexican immigrants, 959
MFBT for OCD, 483–90
MFT (Multifamily Therapy Group Intervention),
    474–5
MHI-5 (Mental Health Inventory), 365, 369
Michigan Alcohol Screening Test (MAST), 217,
    365, 692
Michigan League for Human Services, 894, 895
Michigan Welfare Rights Organization, 894

microaggressions, 931–2
migration, 994
minimization, 243, 252
minimum competency, 151–2
Minnesota Multiphasic Personality Inventory, 318, 358
Minnesota Sex Offender Screening Tool (Revised)
    (MnSOST-R), 1101
minority status, 995–6
Minuchin, Salvador, 74
miracle question, 254, 594–9
mirroring, 312, 779
misconduct, 125–6
misfeasance, 122
MITTT (Multidisciplinary Interactive Team Thinking
    Test), 172
MnSOST-R (Minnesota Sex Offender Screening Tool)
    (Revised), 1101
mobile crisis intervention, 212–13
Mobility Inventory for Agoraphobia, 539
modeling, 292, 589, 655–6
Model Social Work Practice Act, 149
models of managed care, 16
modification of attitudes, 270
mood disorders, 330, 343–50
MoodGYM, 189
mood-related problems, VBSs for, 360, 361
mood stabilizers, 686
MOS 8-item Depression Screener, 361
motivational enhancement therapy (MET), 24, 694–5,
    837–8
MSI-BPD (McLean Screening Instrument for
    Borderline Personality Disorder), 370
MST (Multisystemic Therapy), 74, 436
MSW (master's in social work), 36, 42, 43
Multi-Attitude Suicide Tendency Scale, 388
multiaxial system of the DSM-IV-TR, 326–8, 335–42
multicultural family treatment models, 434
multicultural practice, 5
multidimensional protective and resilience care
    planning, 37–8
Multidisciplinary Interactive Team Thinking Test
    (MITTT), 172
multifamily behavioral treatment (MFBT) for OCD,
    483–90
multi-family groups for prevention of delinquency,
    672–8
multifamily groups with obsessive-compulsive
    disorder, 483–90
Multifamily Therapy Group Intervention (MFT),
    474–5
multimedia presentation, 17, 19
multimodal/multicontextual interventions for
    youth, 818
multiple baseline (MBL) design, 1180
multiple jurisdiction practice, 154
multiple personality disorder, 565–70
multiple relationships, 116
Multisystemic Therapy (MST), 74, 436
multisystemic treatment, 64
music therapy, 78
mutual-help resources, 696
mutuality, 501

N = 1 experiments, 1176–82
NA (Narcotics Anonymous), 696
naltrexone, 29
NAMI (National Alliance on Mental Illness), 492
Nar-Anon, 696
Narcotics Anonymous (NA), 696
narrative, 773–4
narrative of efficacy, 774
narrative of plight, 774
narrative therapy (NT), 273–7
NASW (National Association of Social Workers), 16, 117, 121, 151, 163, 187
NASW Code of Ethics, 59, 118–19, 124, 159, 160, 163
NASW Standards for Clinical Practice, 192
National Alliance on Mental Illness (NAMI), 492
National Association of Black Social Workers, 151
National Association of Child Advocates, 896
National Association of Christians in Social Work, 151
National Association of Forensic Social Work (NOFSW), 1057
National Association of Social Workers (NASW), 16, 117, 121, 151, 163, 187
National Association of social Workers Code of Ethics, 120
National Cancer Institute, 77
National Child Abuse and Neglect Data System, 699
National Comorbidity Study, 385
National Comorbidity Survey Replication, 691
National Comprehensive Cancer Network (NCCN), 77, 79
National Distress Management Guidelines, 79
National Fire Protection Association, 105
National Guidelines Clearinghouse, 1132
National Incident Management System, 105
National Institute of Mental Health, 64, 527
National Institute on Drug Abuse (NIDA), 691
National Response Plan, 105
National Trauma Consortium, 5
natural disasters, 867
NCCN (National Comprehensive Cancer Network), 77, 79
NCLB (No Child Left Behind Act), 42–3
needle-syringe programs, 865
negative predictive value (NPV), 359
negative utilitarianism, 118
neglect
    child, 358, 661–3, 674, 699
    elder, 59, 1106–11
negligence, 121–2, 128–35, 158
negotiation, 14
neighborhood organizing, 884
networking, 17
network orientation, 711
neurofeedback, 449
From Neurons to Neighborhoods, 5, 12
neuroscience, 5
neuroses, 339
neutrality, 448
niche, practice, 17
NIDA (National Institute on Drug Abuse), 691
No Child Left Behind Act (NCLB), 42–3

NOFSW (National Association of Forensic Social Work), 1057
nonaxial format for reporting mental disorders, 342
noncrisis responders, 97
nondirective play therapy, 648
nonexpert position, 297
nonfeasance, 122
nonprofit organizations, accountability of, 157–9
normative dissociation, 564
normative ethics, 118
nosological systems, 18
not-knowing position, 297
"not otherwise specified" diagnosis, 337–8
novelty, 298
NPV (negative predictive value), 359
NT (narrative therapy), 273–7
nuclear self, 313

obesity, 531–7
objective reality, 273
objectives, treatment, 26
objectivity, 448
object relations psychology, 305–10
observer bias, 1139
obsessive-compulsive disorder (OCD), 330, 483–90, 533, 606–12, 613–18
occupational health research, 105
occupational Social Work Task Force, 163
occupational stress, 106
OCD (obsessive-compulsive disorder), 330, 483–90, 533, 606–12, 613–18
odds ratio (OR), 1150
offenders, dually diagnosed, 1091–7
office, establishing and supporting, 58
Office of Children, Youth, and Families, 896
Office of Juvenile Justice Delinquency and Prevention (OJJDP), 460
OFIs (opportunities for improvement), 199
OJJDP (Office of Juvenile Justice Delinquency and Prevention), 460
OJJSP Model Programs Guide, 1132
older adulthood, 264–72
older adults
    case management for, 796–801
    clinical social work with, 939–43
    community based services for, 761–2
    with mental health disorders, 843–52
O'Leary-Porter Scale, 392
Olmstead v. L. C., 798, 800
omission, acts of, 122
Omnibus Budget Reconciliation Act, 790, 796
oncology social work in a medical setting, 77–85
    innovative model, 77–80
    progressive model, 80–2
    traditional model, 82–4
    Web sites, 85
online chat room therapy, 19
online discussion lists, 191
online slide presentation, 17
open adoption, 419–21
open-ended questions, 299, 377
operant behaviors, 289

operant conditioning, 290, 293
opportunities for improvement (OFIs), 199
oppositional defiant disorder, 459
oppressed groups, 893–900
oppression, 5
options, 507
OR (odds ratio), 1150
organizational change, 106
organizational racism, 932
outcome indicators, 196
outcome measurement, 18
out-of-home placement, 73
outpatient addiction treatment, 28
outreach workers, 67

PACE (Program of All-Inclusive Care of the
    Elderly), 798
Pacific Islanders, 954–8
PACT (program of assertive community treatment),
    869–71
pain and suffering, 268–9
pain management, 604
pandemics, 105
panic attacks, 538
panic disorders, 330, 360, 362, 479, 538–44
Panic Disorder Severity Scale - Self Report
    (PDSS-SR), 539
Papp, Peggy, 51
paradoxical intention, 270
paradoxical thoughts, 129
paramedics, 106–8
parameters, 507
paraphilias, 739
parental empathy, 313
parental resistance to therapy, 458
parent-blaming, 64
parent-child bond, 674–5
parent-child interaction therapy, 700
parent education, 619
parenting, 619–26
parenting assessment, 392
parenting education groups, 457–67
Parenting Stress Index, 391, 392
parenting styles, 620
Parenting with Love and Limits (PLL), 435, 457–67
parent management training (PMT), 436–7,
    1012, 1015
Parent Survival Kit, 462
parent training therapy, 19
participant-observer, 308
partnering, 312
partner relational functioning, 392
paternalism, 115–16
pathological defense structures, 23
pathology, 251
PATHS, 994–7
pathways, 507
pathways to meaning, 267–8
patient bill of rights, 16
Patient Health questionnaire (PHQ), 360–1
patient-oriented evidence that matters
    (POEMS), 1164

patient rights, 175
patient safety and suicide, 174–86
    aligning policy, practice and process, 184–5
    challenges in, 175
    components of safety culture, 176–83
    mental illness and violence, 175–6
    monitoring the physical environment, 183–4
    overview, 174–5
    safety audits, 184
    Web sites, 185
pay issues, 36
payment plans, 15
PayPal, 187
PBL (problem-based learning), 1172
PBS (positive behavior support program), 39
PCCY (Philadelphia Citizens for Children and Youth),
    894, 895, 896, 897, 899
PCL-R, 1103
PC-PTSD (Primary Care PTSD Screen), 360, 363
PDS-SR (Panic Disorder Severity Scale - Self
    Report), 539
peer review, 121
peer support teams, 109
Pennsylvania home-based model, 75
People v. Parney, 1057
PEPs (psychosocial and environmental problems), 340
perceived support, 711
Perls, Frederick, 300
Perls, Laura, 300
permissive parenting style, 620
personal distress, in practitioners, 164–5
personality development, 307
personality disorders, 331, 339
personality disorders, VBSs for, 369–70
personal planning, 779
personal risk factors, children, 66
personal social networks, 711
person-centered values, 773
Person Expression Suicidal Ideation, 131
person-in-environment (PIE) system, 334–5, 371–6
person-in-environment lens, 38
persons at risk
    See vulnerable populations and persons at risk
pharmacological treatments for PTSD, 561
pharmacotherapy, 745
pharmacotherapy for alcohol dependence, 29
phase-oriented couple therapy, 480
Philadelphia Child Guidance Clinic, 74
Philadelphia Citizens for Children and Youth (PCCY),
    894, 895, 896, 897, 899
philanthropic organizations, 157–9, 161
PHLAME (Promoting Healthy Lifestyles: Alternative
    Models' Effects), 109
phone counseling, 19
phone supervision, 190
PHQ (Patient Health questionnaire), 360–1, 365
physical abuse, 478–9, 565, 659–65, 699
physical injuries, 122
PICO questions, 169, 1121
PIE (person-in-environment) system, 371–6
Pincus, Harold, 326
planning, intervention, 378

planning, treatment, 26–7, 341–2

plans, payment, 15

playlets, 74

play therapy with children in crisis, 647–52

PLL (Parenting with Love and Limits), 435, 457–67

pluralism, 261–3

PMT (parent management training), 436–7, 1012, 1015

podcasts, 187, 188

POEMS (patient-oriented evidence that matters), 1164

police department-based practice, 85–94
   evidence-based practice guidelines, 89
   intervention skills and competencies, 93
   introduction and history, 88
   special clinical issues, 90
   step-by-step treatment model and goal, 90–3
   theoretical models, 89
   typical daily schedule, 85–7
   Web sites, 94

police officers, 106–8

policies, ethical issues in obeying, 116

political and social action, 889–90

poor parental supervision, 458

portability of credentials, 153–4

portfolio, marketing, 17

Portland State University School of Social Work Research and Training Center on Family Support and Children's Mental Health, 64

POSIT (Problem Oriented Screening Instrument for Teens), 692, 1003

positive behavior support program (PBS), 39

positive predictive value (PPV), 359, 396–9

positive psychology, 774–5

positive reemphasis, 470

positive regard, 91

positive utilitarianism, 118

postmodern family treatment models, 434

postmodernism, 273

postmortem review, 107

postnatal depression, VBSs for, 361

post-traumatic growth, 562

post-traumatic stress disorder (PTSD)
   in African Americans, 963
   assessment and treatment of, 558–64
   in children exposed to domestic violence, 1083
   and couples therapy, 434, 479
   diagnosis/assessment of, 330, 360, 363
   in emergency responders, 107–8
   emerging treatments for, 700
   treating with EMDR, 714–19

post-traumatic stress treatment, 110

power, 443

PPV (positive predictive value), 359, 396–9

practice, social work
   See social work practice, roles and functions

practice guidelines, 507, 509–13

practice niche, 17

practice/policy questions, 1121–2

practice protection, 149, 150

practice protocols, 507

practice skill, 5

practice specialty, 17

practitioner impairment
   See impairment, practitioner

practitioner's fallacies, 171

precontemplation, 575, 641, 644–5

prediction questions, 1123

predictors of violence, 175–6

predisaster education, 109

preferred practice patterns, 507

pregnancy, alcohol use during, 365, 367–8

premigration and departure, 994–5

preparation, 642

preponderance of evidence, 122

present-centered examination, 300

present danger, 59

prevalence, 338, 397–8

prevention and preparedness training, 109

prevention questions, 1123

preventive interventions, 38

PRIDE1, 172

primary care case management, 791

Primary Care PTSD Screen (PC-PTSD), 360, 363

PRIME-MD, 360

principal diagnosis, 337

prioritization, 91

privacy, 123
   See also confidentiality

private insurance, 36

private practice, 53–60
   elements of, 59–60
   entrepreneurial dimension, 58–9
   ethical dimension of, 59
   introduction, 53–4
   professional dimension of, 54–8
   and professional impairment, 165
   Web sites, 60

private vs. public practice, 12

privileged communication, 115, 123

proactive vs. reactive health care, 826–31

problem-based learning (PBL), 1172

problem definition skills, 471

problem identification, 378

Problem Oriented Screening Instrument for Teens (POSIT), 692, 1003

problems and solutions, approach to, 216–17

problem-saturated stories, 274

problem solution skills, 471

problem-solving actions, 226

problem-solving skills training (PSST), 1012–13, 1015–16

problem-solving training, 471

process recording, 55–6

professional brochure, 17

professional development, 52
   See also continuing education

professional protection, 148–9

Professional Thinking Form, 172

professional vs. personal values, 116

program evaluators, 358

Program of All-Inclusive Care of the Elderly (PACE), 798

program of assertive community treatment (PACT), 869–71

progressive change, 890–1
progress notes, 26
projection, 303
Promoting Healthy Lifestyles: Alternative Models'
    Effects (PHLAME), 109
protest ready environments, 901
protocol for crisis session with family, 50
protocols, 509
provisional diagnosis, 337, 341
PSQ (Psychosis Screening Questionnaire), 365, 369
PSST (problem-solving skills training), 1012–13,
    1015–16
psychiatric disabilities, case management of, 778–83
PsychiatryOnline, American Psychiatric Association
    Practice Guidelines, 135
psychodynamic theory, 553
psychoeducation, 474–8, 491, 542, 701
psychoeducational approaches to addictions
    treatment, 24
psychoeducational programs, 19
psychological autopsies, 174
psychological distress among chronically ill, 826–32
psychological system, 497–8
Psychologists Helping Psychologists, 163
psychometric testing, 1100
psychopharmacology, 686–91
psychoses, 339
Psychosis Screening Questionnaire (PSQ), 365, 369
psychosocial and environmental problems (PEPs), 340
psychosocial assessment, 90–1, 308–9
psychosocial first aid, 109–10
psychosocial history, 386
psychosocial oncology
    See oncology social work in a medical setting
psychosocial rehabilitation, 770–7
psychosocial therapy, 248–53
psychotherapy, 12
Psychotherapy Integration, 225
psychotic disorders, 329–30
psychotropic medications, 686–91
PsycINFO, 1130
PTSD (post-traumatic stress disorder)
    See post-traumatic stress disorder (PTSD)
public accountability, 107
public exposure, 157–9
public inquiries, 107
publicity, adverse effects of, 107
public protection, 148–9
Public Safety (Canada), 105
Public Safety and Emergency Preparedness
    Canada, 105
public speaking anxiety, 550
public vs. private practice, 12
PubMed, 1130
punisher, 290
punishment, 293
pushing buttons, 461

quality assurance, 18, 107, 156
    See also quality standards and assurance
quality indicators, 196
quality of care vs. efficiency of care, 13

quality standards and assurance, 194–203
    continuous quality improvement (CQI),
        195–7
    introduction, 194–5
    key attributes of quality improvement measures,
        197–8
    process examples for CQI, 198–202
    Web sites, 202
quasi-experimental designs, 47
questionnaires
    See assessment; brief screening instruments; client-
        focused measures; rapid assessment
        instruments (RAIs)
questions
    open-ended, 299
    in solution-focused therapy, 254–5
    well-formulated, 169–71
    well-structured, 1120–6, 1127–36
Quinlan, Karen Ann, 119

racial identity development theory, 480
RAFFT screener, 368
rage, 93
RAIs (rapid assessment instruments)
    See rapid assessment instruments (RAIs)
randomized control trials (RCTs), 1138–9, 1142–8,
    1153, 1176–82
Rank, Otto, 305
rape, 88, 90–2, 98
rapid assessment instruments (RAIs)
    for adolescents, 385–9
    for children, 382–3
    and differential diagnosis, 319–20
    as essential competency, 36, 38
    in managed care, 400–5
    to measure treatment necessity, 318–19
    to monitor change and goal attainment, 320–1
    and practice evaluation, 401
    qualifying outcomes with, 217
    for social phobia, 548–9
    See also brief screening instruments
rapid cycling pattern, 344
rapport, 91, 210, 573
Rational Recovery (RR), 696
ratio schedules of reinforcement, 290
RCTs (randomized control trials), 1138–9, 1142–8,
    1153, 1176–82
reading, modeling skills through, 656
reality/diagnosis box, 395
reasoning, clinical, evidence-based, 169–71
reassurance, 91
recidivism, 1095–6
reciprocal goals, 522
reciprocity
    among practitioners, 165
    of credentials, 153–4
reconnection, 479
recontracting, 575
recordkeeping, 59, 160, 190
    See also documentation
recovery, 380
recovery-based case management, 775–6

Recovery Goal Worksheet (RGW), 780
recovery movement, 808
recycling through change, 643
reduced fees, 15
reexperiencing symptoms, 108, 699
referral process, 36
reflecting teams, 274
reflective thought process, 25, 251
refugees and immigrants, 944–8, 1031–7
regard, positive, 91, 236–7
regulation
    of out-of-state practice, 191
    of social work, 148–55
regulations, ethical issues in obeying, 116
rehabilitation, psychosocial, 770–7
rehabilitation plans, for practitioners, 166
rehearsing, 74
Reich, Wilhelm, 300
reiki therapy, 78
reimbursement, for telemedicine, 192
reinforcement, 290, 293, 779
reinforcer, 290
relapse, 642
relapse pathways, 28
relapse prevention, 768
relapse prevention training, 28
relational capacity, 107
relationship, 479
relaxation training, 246, 549–50
relevance of assessment tools, 383
reliability of assessment tools, 383, 387, 390–1
research, EBP, XXX
research, ethical issues in, 117
research-based interventions, 42–3
research ethics boards, 119
resettlement, 995
residual risk, inpatient, 179–83
resilience
    in child and adolescent outpatient practice, 38
    and childhood trauma, 479
    in children and families, 65–6
    family, 108
resistances, 302–3
resolution, crisis, 93
resource acquisition, 780–1, 786
resource management, 36
resources
    for change, 901
    for EBP, 1128–32
    scarce/limited, 116
respect, 236–7
respectful listening, 275
respondent behaviors, 289
respondent conditioning, 289
respondent extinction, 292
responders, emergency
    See emergency services practice
response bias, 1139
response prevention, 485
response to intervention (RTI), 43
restraining orders, 98
retroflection, 302

ReVia, 29
review hierarchy, 487
Revised Conflict Tactics Scales, 392
Revised Memory and Behavior Problems
    Checklist, 941
RGW (Recovery Goal Worksheet), 780
Richmond, Mary, 248
rights, client, 122–3
right to informed and effective treatment, 506
Rinaker v. Superior Court, 1078–9
risk, and stages of change, 646
risk assessment, violence/suicide, 175–7
risk communications, 109–10
risk drinking in pregnancy, 365, 367–8, 692
risk factors, children and families, 65–6
risk management, 121–7, 128, 159
Risk Matrix 2000/Sexual, 1103
risk/prognosis questions, 1123
risk ratio (RR), 1150
risks, inpatient safety, 176–85
rituals, 613
Robert's Seven-Stage Crisis Intervention
    Model, 90
role confusion, 43
role model, 25
Rorschach ink blots, 318, 400
Rost Drug Dependency Screener, 365, 368
RR (Rational Recovery), 696
RR (risk ratio), 1150
RRASOR, 1101
RTI (response to intervention), 43
rugged individual, 423
rule out (diagnosis), 341

SAD (social anxiety disorder), 545–51
SADS (Schedule for Affective Disorders and
    Schizophrenia), 176
SADS Person Scale, 129
safe passage movement, 907
safety, child and family, 1084–9
safety audits, 184
same-sex sexual orientation, 934–8
SAMHSA Tracking Report, 12
SAPAS (Standard Assessment of Personality -
    Abbreviated Scale), 370
Sarbanes-Oxley Act, 156
SARS outbreak, 105, 110
SASSI (Substance Abuse Subtle Screening
    Inventory), 692
Satir, Virginia, 51
Scale for Suicide Ideation - Worst Point
    (SSI-W), 129
scale of differentiation of self, 447
scaling, 591
scaling questions, 254, 594–9
scarce resources, 116
Schedule for Affective Disorders and Schizophrenia
    (SADS), 176
schedule of reinforcement, 290
schema-focused therapy (SFT), 744
schizophrenia, 329–30, 474, 505–14
school-based intervention, 42

school-based practice, 39–44
  challenges in, 42–3
  diverse role of social worker in, 43–4
  introduction, 41
  typical daily schedule, 39–41
  Web sites, 44
school-based services, 907–12
school safety programs, 985–1003
school social work
  children and adolescents with ADHD, 1039–44
  culturally/racially diverse students, 1045–52
  immigrants and refugees, 1031–7
  overview, 979–85
  SFBT for students at risk to drop out, 1020–31
  students with conduct disorders, 1011–19
  students with co-occurring disorders, 1003–10
  violence prevention, 985–1003
school social workers
  See school-based practice
schools of social work, 38
School-to-Jobs (STJ), 1045, 1048–9
school violence, 42
scientific acceptability, of assessment tools, 383
SCOFF questionnaire, 364, 365
scope of services, 196
screening, 212, 382, 691
  See also assessment; diagnosis
screening accuracy, 359
screening instruments, brief
  See brief screening instruments
searches, 595
search strategies, EBP, 1132–3
secondary traumatization effects, 93
Second Life, 187, 188
secrets, 737
Secular Organizations for Sobriety/Save Our Selves
  (SOS), 696
security, in e-therapy, 191–2
sedative hypnotic dependence treatment, 23
Segal, Lynn, 51
SEL (social-emotional learning), 39, 43
selection bias, 1139
Selekman, Matthew, 51
self-actualization, 236–7
self-anchored scales, 217, 430
self-awareness, 54
self-care, 57–8, 93
self-cohesion, 313
self-determination, 14, 115–16, 119, 447
self-disclosure, 779
self-examination, 23–4, 492
selfobjects, 312
self-observation, 23
self-psychology, 311–16
self-reflection, 480
self-regulation, 447, 449
self-report instruments, 344
Self-report Manic Inventory, 344
self-report measures, family, 390–4
self-responsibility, 23
self-soothing, 470
self-triangulation, 475–6

self types, 313
self work in ACT, 284–5
sensitivity, of screening instruments, 359, 396
sensory distortions, 564
service agreements, 515
service contracting, involving clients in, 159
service contracts, 515
service coordination, 763
service delivery, ethical issues with, 124
services, faith-based, 5
settlement-focused mediation (SFM), 1071
Settlement House movement, 47
seven-step group and coaching model, 463
severe mental illness, 491–4
severity by service type: a proposed model, 100
severity specifiers, 337
Sex Crimes Unit, 91
sex-negative attitudes, 737
sex offenders, 1098–104
sexual abuse, 478–9, 565, 663–5, 699, 738, 1090–104
sexual assault, 88, 90–2, 98
sexual dysfunctions, 739
sexual identity disorder, 331
sexual improprieties, 159
sexual involvement/relations with clients, 122,
  164–5, 741
sexual issues, 737–42
sexually transmitted diseases (STDs), 663, 737
sexual orientation, 934–8
sexual preference testing, 1100
SF-12, 319
SF-36, 319
SFBT (solution-focused brief therapy), 47, 435, 594–9
SFBT for students at risk to drop out, 1020–31
SFM (settlement-focused mediation), 1071
SFT (schema-focused therapy), 744
SFT (solution-focused therapy), 253–8, 274
SFT (structural family therapy), 442–6
shame attacking, 592
shaping, 292
shelter workers
  See domestic violence shelter practice
Sheri and Les Biller Patient and Family Resource
  Center, 79
shift work, 106
S/HMO (Social Health Care Maintenance
  Organization), 798
Short Michigan Alcoholism Screening
  Instrument, 941
short-term interventions, 12
single parents, 459
single-trauma couples, 479
situational stress, 65–6
skills-based play therapy, 655
skill sets
  See essential competencies
slander, 124, 159
slavery, 963
sleep disorders, 331
SMD (standard mean difference), 1150
smoking prevention therapy, 19
snapshot images, 325

social action, 889–90, 901–6
Social and Occupational Functioning Assessment Scale
    (SOFAS), 340
social anxiety disorder (SAD), 545–51
social case management, 791
Social Casework: A Psychosocial Therapy, 249
social competence, 652–3
social construction theories, 47
social constructivism, 273, 294–9
social development, 887
Social Diagnosis, 71, 73, 248
social-emotional learning (SEL), 39, 43
social functioning problems, 371–6
social group work, 680
Social Health Care Maintenance Organization (S/
    HMO), 798
social identity, 931
socialization of children, 652–9
social justice, 5, 276
social networks, 710–14
social phobia, 330, 545–51
social planning, 888–9
Social Services Abstracts, 169, 1130
social skills training, 549, 666–71
social support, 107, 710–14
social support for bipolar disorders, 345
social work
    in behavioral care setting, 11–20
    introduction and overview, 3–8
    primary mission of, 372
    purpose and function of, 232–3
    schools of, 38
    values of, 257
Social Work 2.0, 188
Social Work Abstracts, 1131
Social Work Abstracts Database (SWAB), 169
social worker
    as educator, 720–5
    as expert witness, 1057
social worker impairment
    See impairment, practitioner
Social Workers Helping Social Workers, 163
social work helping modes of managed care, 16
Social Work Laws and Regulations Comparison
    Database, 153
Social Work Licensing Laws and Regulations, 166
social work practice, roles and functions
    addictions treatment, 20–33
    autonomous, 6
    child and adolescent outpatient, 33–9
    community, 5–6
    community-based with children and families, 61–9
    domestic violence shelter, 95–102
    emergency services, 95–102
    evidence-based, 3, 6
    family counselor in nonprofit community-based
        agency, 45–53
    feminist, 277–83
    fraudulent, 157–9
    gerontological, 939
    home-based, with children and families, 70–6
    managed care, 11–20
    multicultural, 5–6
    multiple jurisdiction, 154
    oncology, in a medical setting, 77–85
    police department-based, 85–94
    private, 53–60
    private vs. public, 12
    resilience-oriented, 423–8
    school-based, 39–44
    social constructivism in, 294–9
    task-centered, 226–30
    technology in, 186–93
    trauma-informed, 5
    See also fields of practice
social work practice, synergy and generativity of, 3–8
Social Work Registry, 153
Social Work Research Handbook, 77
social work resources, 225
social work with groups, 680
Societal Security, 105
Society for Social Work Leadership in Healthcare, 151
sociocultural system, 497–8
sociogram, 411
Socratic dialogue, 270–1, 588–9
SOFAS (Social and Occupational Functioning
    Assessment Scale), 340
soft emotions, 470
solution building, 1025
solution-focused approaches to addictions treatment,
    24, 838
solution-focused brief therapy (SFBT), 47, 435, 594–9,
    1020–31
solution-focused crisis intervention, 47
solution-focused therapy (SFT), 253–8, 274
solution-oriented questions, 595
somatization disorder, 565
somatoform disorders, 330
SONAR, 1102–3
SOS (Secular Organizations for Sobriety/Save Our
    Selves), 696
"so-what" question, 1164
SPAN (PTSD screen), 360, 363
SPAN (Suicide Prevention Action Network), 191
specialty, practice, 17
specific interventions
    borderline personality disorder (BPD), 742–7
    chemical abuse and dependency screening, 691–7
    child therapy and social skills, 652–9
    divorce therapy, 732–7
    eye movement desensitization and reprocessing
        (EMDR), 714–20
    Families and Schools Together (FAST), 671–9
    families with child abuse and neglect, 641–7
    group process and group work techniques,
        679–85
    integrated crisis intervention and disaster mental
        health, 726–32
    play therapy with children in crisis, 647–52
    psychopharmacology, 686–91
    recognizing indicators of child maltreatment,
        659–65
    sexual issues, 737–42
    social networks, 710–14

specific interventions (*Continued*)
    social skills training for persons with mental illness,
        666–71
    social worker as educator, 720–5
    supported employment approaches, 704–10
    trauma-informed services, 698–704
specificity
    of screening instruments, 359
    of treatment plans, 501
specific phobia, 330
specific questions, 169–71
specifiers, severity and course, 337
spiral pattern of change, 642
spirituality, 964
spreading the news, 274
SSI-W (Scale for Suicide Ideation - Worst Point), 129
staff interventions in addiction treatment, 26
stages of change, 643–4
stages of readiness scale, 461
stages of readiness to change, 460–1
Standard Assessment of Personality - Abbreviated
    Scale (SAPAS), 370
standardized assessment tools, 387
standardized measures, 36, 390–4
standardized scales, 57, 358
standard mean difference (SMD), 1150
standards, 507
Standards for Clinical Practice, NASW, 192
Standards for Social Work Case Management, 762
standards of care, 122, 128–35
standards of practice, 77
State Children's Health Insurance Plans, 191
State Hope Scale, 360, 361
states of confusion, 564
Static-99, 1101–2
STDs (sexually transmitted diseases), 663, 737
Stepakoff v. Kantar, 132–3
stewardship, 911
stimulants, 687
STJ (School-to-Jobs), 1045, 1048–9
stories, therapeutic, 578–88
storyboards, 199–200
storytelling, 613–18, 656
St. Paul Family-Centered Project, 73
strategic family therapy approaches, 435
strength-based approaches, 42, 47, 431
strength-based case management, 768
strengths assessment, 779
strengths perspective, 217–18, 964–5
strengths perspective in goals and treatment
    planning, 502
stress
    in crisis intervention, 213
    in ecological perspective, 231
    in emergency services practice, 105–10
    occupational, 106
    situational, 65–6
    workplace, 106–7
stress chart, 463–4
stress-diathesis model, 424
stress management therapy, 19
stressors, life, 232–3

structural family therapy (SFT), 74, 442–6
Structured Clinical Interview, 331, 539
structuring skills, 471
students
    with conduct disorders, 1011–19
    with co-occurring disorders, 1003–10
    culturally/racially diverse students, 1045–52
studies, appraising, for EBP, 1137–41
subjective distress, 554
subpoena, 59
substance abuse
    case management for, 784–9
    in children and adolescents, 1003–10
    and international social work, 865–6
    by older adults, 943
    in practitioners, 164–5
    during pregnancy, 368
    VBSs for, 368
Substance Abuse and Mental Health Services
    Administration, 527
Substance Abuse Subtle Screening Inventory
    (SASSI), 692
substance dependence, defined, 834
substance-induced disorders, 692
substance-related disorders, 329
suicide, 5
    adolescents, 936
    APA Practice Guideline for patients with suicidal
        behaviors, 129
    assessment for, 5, 128, 175–7, 211, 344
    avoiding malpractice lawsuits, 128–35
    and depression, 553
    and mood disorders, 344
    in older adults, 844
    of police officers, 106
    in practitioners, 164–5
    predictors of, 175–6
    risk consultation in jails, 88
    See also patient safety and suicide
Suicide Potential Lethality Scale, 129
Suicide Prevention Action Network (SPAN), 191
suicide risk assessment, 211, 360
Sullivan, Harry Stack, 306
summarizing ability, 25
SUMSearch, 1130
supervision
    amount required for credentialing, 152–3
    and ethics complaints, 125
    by parents, 458
    in psychosocial therapy, 252
    quality of, 160
    via phone, 190
supported employment, 704–10
support groups, 345
supportive relationships, 710–14
support services, 91
support systems, 93
supra meaning, 268
survivors of childhood trauma, 478–82
Susan G. Komen for the Cure, 80
sustainable development, 887
Suttie, Ian, 306

SVR-20, 1103
SWAB (Social Work Abstracts Database), 169
switching, 566
synchronous communication, 188
systematic desensitization, 292
systematic reviews and EBP, 1152–6
systems-driven case management, 767
systems of care model, 35

T-ACE screener, 367
talk therapy, 47
target problem logs, 352
targets, change, 901
task-centered practice, 226–30
tasks, problem solving, 226
teacher, social worker as, 720–5
teachers, licensing of, 154–5
technical eclecticism, 259–60
techniques, therapeutic
    See therapeutic techniques
technology, 19, 36, 186–93, 910–11
TEDS (Treatment Episode Data Set), 833
teenagers
    See adolescents
teenagers, delinquent, 458
tele-health, 187, 188, 190
teleological theories of ethics, 118
telephone crisis intervention, 212
tele-therapy, 190
terminating with clients, 627–31
termination of services, 92, 93, 125, 953
terrorist attacks, 88, 105
tests, licensing
    See licensing examinations
text-based therapy, 189–90
TFP (transference-focused psychotherapy), 744
theoretical integration, 260
theory of change for family centers, 856–7
therapeutic alliance, 808
therapeutic assistance, for practitioners, 165
therapeutic change, 824
therapeutic contracts, 514–20
therapeutic groups, 19
therapeutic relationship, 210, 223–4, 573–7, 807–11
therapeutic stories, 578–88
therapeutic techniques, 224
    bereavement and grief therapy, 632–7
    cognitive restructuring, 588–93
    developing successful therapeutic relationships,
        573–7
    evidence-based hypnosis, 600–5
    kundalini yoga meditation for OCD, 606–12
    metaphors, 578–88
    miracle question and scaling, 594–9
    parenting, 619–26
    storytelling and metaphor with OCD, 613–18
    terminating with clients, 627–31
therapeutic trance, 601–2
therapist modeling, 589
therapy
    acceptance and commitment, 283–8
    anger management, 19
    art, 78
    behavioral intervention, 288–93
    Bowen Family Systems Therapy, 447–52
    brief, 47
    Brief Family Therapy Center (BFTC), 437–40
    Brief Strategic Family Therapy (BSFT), 436
    chat room, 19, 187, 188
    client -centered, 235–41
    cognitive behavior, 28
    common factors in, 220–5
    couple therapy with individuals, 452–7
    divorce, 732–7
    emotion-focused marital, 18, 434–5
    e-therapy, 186–93
    family, 433–42
    family systems, 74
    functional family, 436
    Gestalt, 300–4
    group, 19, 23–4
    individual, 19, 24–6
    journaling, 78
    logotherapy, 264–72
    motivational enhancement, 24
    Multisystemic Therapy (MST), 74
    multisystemic therapy (MST), 436
    music, 78
    obsessive-compulsive disorder, 483–90
    online chat room, 19
    parental resistance to, 458
    parent-child interaction, 700
    parent training, 19
    phase-oriented couple, 480
    psychoeducation, 474–8
    psychosocial, 248–53
    psychotherapy, 12
    reiki, 78
    schema-focused, 744
    self-psychology, 311–16
    smoking prevention, 19
    solution-focused, 253–8
    solution-focused brief therapy (SFBT), 435
    stress management, 19
    structural family, 74, 442–6
    survivors of childhood trauma, 478–82
    talk, 47
    task-centered model, 226–9
    tele-therapy, 190
    text-based, 189–90
    transference-focused, 744
    trauma-focused cognitive behavioral, 700
    weight loss, 19
    See also treatment approaches
thinking, critical, 25, 171–2, 1137
thoughts
    content of, 242
    intrusive, 699
    maladaptive, 243
thresholds in CQI, 196
time, use of, 216
title protection, 149–50
Toastmasters International, 550
"To Err is Human," 194

tolerance building, 470
tort, 122
tracking family history and relationships
    See genograms
tragic man, 311
tragic triad, 267–8
training, importance of, 36
training preparation, 109
trances, 602
transference, 741
transference-focused psychotherapy (TFP), 744
transformative dialogues, 298
transformative mediation, 1072
Transforming Mental Health Care in America, 3
transgendered issues, 97, 934–8
transit, 995
translational science, 980
transmuting internalization, 312–13
transportability, 457, 458, 462
transtheoretical model of behavior change, 641–7
trauma
    colonial, 952
    and dissociative disorders, 565
    historical, 952–3
    and journal keeping, 55
    See also domestic violence shelter practice;
        emergency services practice; forensic social
        work; police department-based practice; post-
        traumatic stress disorder (PTSD)
trauma contagion, 108
trauma developmental disorder, 1083
trauma-dissociation model, 565
trauma-focused cognitive behavioral therapy, 700
trauma-informed practice, 5
trauma-informed services, 698–704
trauma-related intervention programs, 109
Trauma Symptom Inventory dissociation scale
    (TSI), 566
traumatogenic family environments, 481
treaters, 1061
treatment, assessment of, 383
treatment approaches
    brief treatment, 215–20
    crisis intervention, 207–14
treatment-as-usual, 1144
Treatment Episode Data Set (TEDS), 833
treatment fidelity, 1139
treatment goals
    in addiction treatment, 26–7
    in ADHD treatment, 526–7
    development and clarification of, 521–6
    in police department-based practice, 90–3
treatment manuals, 18, 509
treatment objectives, 26
treatment planning, 26–7, 341–2
    ADHD, 526–30
    depression, 552–7
    dissociative disorders, 564–70
    eating disorders, 531–7
    with families, 429–32
    generalized anxiety disorder, 497–505

panic disorders, 538–44
PTSD, 558–64
schizophrenia, 505–14
for social phobia, 545–51
triage, 212
triangling, 449
tripolar self, 312
true negative, 396–7
true positive, 396–7
TSI (Trauma Symptom Inventory dissociation
    scale), 566
Tuesday's Children, 158
tuning in, 574
tunnel vision, 564
TWEAK screener, 365, 367
twelve-step programs, 28, 696
20/20 rule, 1062

UCS (unconditioned stimulus), 289
UMFTG (Unity Multifamily Therapy Group), 476–7
unconditional positive regard, 236–7
unconditioned stimulus (UCS), 289
unconscious, 251
unconscious search, 602
undercurrents model of coaching, 458
underorganized families, 442, 443
undue influence, 159
unified detachment, 470
The United Way of America, 157
The United Way of New York City, 158
Unity Multifamily Therapy Group (UMFTG),
    476–7
University of Rhode Island Change Assessment
    Questionnaire (URICA), 692
University of South Carolina Medical College, 74
University of South Florida Research and Training
    Center for Children's Mental Health, 64
URICA (University of Rhode Island Change
    Assessment Questionnaire), 692
U.S. Air Force, 912–17
use of language, 217
use of time, 216
U.S. Substance Abuse and Mental Health
    Organization (SAMHSA) Tracking Report, 12
utilitarian theories of ethics, 118
utilization, 216
utilization review process, 27–8

validation, 91
validity, of assessment tools, 383, 387–8, 390–1
values
    in ACT, 284, 286–7
    core, 118
    of logotherapy, 269–70
    professional vs. personal, 116
    social work, 257
    worlds of, 267–8
VBSs (very brief screeners)
    See brief screening instruments
vegetative signs of depression, 553
venting, 91, 93

very brief screeners (VBSs)
    See brief screening instruments
victimology, 97
victim practitioner, 97–8
victim services, 88–9
Victims of Crime Act of 1984, 88
victim's rights, 97
victim-victimizer-bystander, 479, 481
victim-witnesses, 97
Videotape Modeling Parent Program, 1013
violence
    and mental illness, 175–6
    predictors of, 175–6
Violence Against Women Act, 88, 97
violence prevention in schools, 985–1003
Violence Risk Appraisal Guide, 177
violence risk assessment, 1093–5
virtual reality environments, 187
virtual self, 313
virtue ethics, 118
visualization, 246
in vivo exposure, 544
vodcasts, 188
VoIP (voice over Internet), 187, 188
voluntary commitment, 175
volunteer work, 17
VRAG/SORAG, 1101
vulnerability, genetic, 65
vulnerable families, 66–9
vulnerable populations and persons at risk, 156–7,
        893–900
    African Americans, 963–9
    American Indians/Alaska Natives, 949–54
    Asian and Pacific Islanders, 954–8
    culturagrams, 969–75
    Latinos, 959–62
    lesbian, gay, bisexual and transgendered, 934–8
    older adults, 939–43
    overview, 925–7
    racism, 928–33
    refugees and immigrants, 944–8

waivers, Medicaid, 761
walk-in crisis intervention, 213
walking nightmare, 606
Walsh, Froma, 51
Walsh Family Resilience Framework, 426
Web 2.0, 188
Webcams, 186–7
webinar, 188
Web pages, 17, 19
Web sites, 276
    acceptance and commitment therapy (ACT), 287
    accountability and ethics, 161
    addiction treatment, 32
    ADHD treatment planning, 528
    adult mental health, 824
    African Americans, 968
    alcohol and drug dependence, 838
    American Indians/Alaska Natives, 953
    Asian and Pacific Islanders, 954–8
    assessing sexual predators, 1104

assessments for troubled adolescents, 389
assessment tools, using to evidence medical
        necessity, 322
assessment tools for children and adolescents, 384
avoiding harm, 172
behavioral approach to social work, 293
bereavement and grief therapy, 637
biopsychosocial assessment, 380
borderline personality disorder (BPD), 746
Bowen Family Systems Therapy, 452
brief screening instruments, 371
brief treatment, 219
building community capacity in the U.S. Air Force,
        915
case management, 755
case management for HIV/AIDS, 806
case management with older adults, 800
chemical abuse and dependency screening, 696
child and adolescent outpatient practice, 38
child protection mediation, 1076–7
children and adolescents, 819
children and adolescents with ADHD, 1039–44
children exposed to domestic violence, 1089
child therapy and social skills, 652–9
child welfare case management, 768
client-centered theory and therapy, 241
client-focused measures, 356–7
clinical case management, 758
clinical social work with older adults, 943
cognitive-behavioral therapy, 247
cognitive restructuring, 593
common factors in therapy, 225
community organizing, 881
community partnerships for school-based
        services, 911
community practice for the twenty-first century,
        891
comparative theories of social work, 263
CompuPIE, 375
consumer-provider relationship within, 808–11
couple and family treatment, 440
couple therapy with individuals, 457
couple therapy with survivors of childhood
        trauma, 481
crisis intervention, 214
critical incident stress management (CISD), 731
culturagrams, 974
culturally/racially diverse students, 1051
depression, 554
developing well-structured questions for EBP, 1126
developmentally disabled, 764
development and clarification of goals, 526
diagnosing mental disorders, 333, 342
diagnosis, understanding, 399
dissociative disorders, 570
divorce therapy, 732–7
domestic violence shelter practice, 101
dually diagnosed offenders and civil patients,
        1095–6
eating disorders, 536
EBP and N = 1 experiments, 1180
EBP and systematic reviews, 1156

EBP in social work education, 1175
EBP: integrating research, clinical skills, and client
    circumstances, 1164
EBP practice guidelines, 1162
elder abuse/neglect, 1110
emergency services practice, 110
and e-therapy, 187, 191
ethical issues, 120
evidence-based hypnosis, 604–5
evidence-based practice (EBP), 1117
expert witness testimony in child welfare, 1068
eye movement desensitization and reprocessing
    (EMDR), 714–19
Families and Schools Together (FAST), 678
families of persons with severe mental illness, 494
family assessment, 394
family centers, 862
family counselor in nonprofit community-based
    agency, 52
family resilience framework, 428
fathering programs, 921
feminist issues and practices, 282
forensic social work, 1059
generalized anxiety disorder, 505
Gestalt therapy, 303–4
guidelines for assertive community treatment
    teams, 871
guidelines for social action, 901
home-based practice with children and families, 76
indicators of child maltreatment, 665
integrative behavioral couple therapy (IBCT), 473
international social work, 867
kundalini yoga meditation for OCD, 612
Latinos, 959–62
legislative advocacy for oppressed and vulnerable
    groups, 900
lesbian, gay, bisexual and transgendered issues, 938
licensing examinations, 147
Life Model, 234
locating credible studies for EBP, 1136, 1140
logotherapy, 272
malpractice, standards of care and preventing
    suicide, 135
managed care practice, 19
mediation and conflict resolution, 1081
and meta-analysis, 1152
metaphors, 587
miracle question and scaling, 599
mood disorders, 350
narrative therapy, 276
object relations psychology, 310
obsessive-compulsive disorder, 490
older adults with mental health disorders, 850
oncology social work in a medical setting, 85
panic disorders, 544
parenting, 625
Parenting with Love and Limits (PLL), 466
patient safety and suicide, 185
play therapy with children in crisis, 651
police department-based practice, 94
practitioner impairment, 166

private practice, 60
proactive vs. reactive health care, 831–2
psychoeducation, 477
psychological distress among chronically ill, 831–2
psychosocial rehabilitation, 775–6
psychosocial therapy, 252
psychotropic medications, 690
PTSD (post-traumatic stress disorder), 562
quality standards and assurance, 202
racism in social work practice, 933
RAIs in managed care setting, 405
randomized control trials (RCTs), 1148
refugees and immigrants, 948
regulation and licensing, 155
risk management, 126
schizophrenia, 513
school-based practice, 44
self-psychology, 316
sexual issues, 741
SFBT for students at risk to drop out, 1030
social constructivism, 299
social networks, 712
social skills training for persons with mental illness,
    666–71
social worker as educator, 720
solution-focused therapy, 258
storytelling and metaphor with OCD, 618
structural family therapy, 446
student immigrants and refugees, 1037
students with conduct disorders, 1015–16
students with co-occurring disorders, 1010
substance abuse case management, 787–8
supported employment approaches, 709
task-centered practice, 230
therapeutic contracts, 520
therapeutic relationships, 577
transtheoretical model of behavior change, 647
trauma-informed services, 701
treatment planning with families, 432
violence prevention in schools, 1001
Wechsler Intelligence Scale, 400
weight loss therapy, 19
Welfare Advocates, 894, 896, 897
well-being, 307
well-formulated questions, 169–71
well-structured questions, 1120–6, 1127–8
WFS (Women for Sobriety), 696
"what if" scenario, 465
What is Social Casework?, 248
"what's better" questions, 255
whistle-blowing, 117, 161
White, David, 51
Williams, Frank. L., 157–8
the will to meaning, 267
Wimsatt v. Kausch, 1078
Winnicott, Donald W., 306, 307
withdrawal syndrome, alcohol, 28
Women for Sobriety (WFS), 696
workplace stress, 106–7
worlds of values, 267–8
worrying, 351–7

wrap-around model of home-based intervention, 75
wrap-around services, 64, 65, 807
writing skills, 25–6

Yale-Brown Obsessive Compulsive Scale
    (Y-BOCS), 606

Young Mania Rating Scale, 344
youth
    See adolescents; children

Zabora, James, 85
Z-score, 318–19

(continued from front flap)

as by the inclusion of an entire section devoted to showing how to use evidence intelligently and efficaciously.

The *Social Workers' Desk Reference, Second Edition,* speaks directly to the daily realities of social workers in private, non-profit, and public settings, whatever their expertise and in all areas of practice: assessment and diagnosis, ethics, risk assessment, program evaluation, and beyond. Case managers, clinical social workers, supervisors, and administrators alike who have come to rely on the previous volume will quickly find its successor just as indispensable.